The Princeton Review

PrincetonReview.com

THE BEST 377 COLLEGES

2013 Edition

By Robert Franek, Laura Braswell, and

The Staff of The Princeton Review

Random House, Inc., New York
2013 Edition

The Princeton Review, Inc.
111 Speen Street, Suite 550
Framingham, MA 01701
E-mail: editorialsupport@review.com

ISBN 978-0-307-94487-0

Senior VP—Publisher: Robert Franek
Editor: Laura Braswell
Production: Deborah A. Silvestrini
Production Editor: Michelle Krapf
Content Director: David Soto
Student Survey Manager: Stephen Koch

Printed in the United States of America on partially recycled paper.

10 9 8 7 6 5 4 3 2 1

2013 Edition

ACKNOWLEDGMENTS

Each year we assemble an awe-inspiringly talented group of colleagues who work together to produce our guidebooks; this year is no exception. Everyone involved in this effort—authors, editors, data collectors, production specialists, and designers—gives so much more than is required to make *The Best 377 Colleges* an exceptional student resource guide. This new edition gives prospective college students what they really want: The most honest, accessible, and pertinent information about the colleges they are considering attending.

My sincere thanks go to the many who contributed to this tremendous project. I know our readers will benefit from our collective efforts to collect the opinions of current students at the outstanding schools we profile. A special thank you goes to our authors, Jen Adams, Andrea Kornstein, Eric San Juan, Amy Weil, Nick Laqualia, Aditi Chakravarty, Jennifer Anne Clark, Jenny Zbrizher, and Ai Hirashiki, for their dedication in poring through tens of thousands of surveys to produce the campus culture narratives of each school profiled. Thanks to Evan Schreier and Lauren Schacher for checking student quotes. Very special thanks goes to Laura Braswell for her editorial commitment and vision. A warm and special thank you goes to our Student Survey Team, Stephen Koch, Courtney Richter, Lyle Friedman, and Steven Aglione, who continue to work in partnership with school administrators and students alike. My continued thanks go to our data collection pro, David Soto, for his successful efforts in collecting and accurately representing the statistical data that appear with each college profile. The enormousness of this project and its deadline constraints could not have been realized without the calm presence of our production partners at Penn Foster: Deborah Silvestrini, Michelle Krapf, Vince Bonavoglia, and Danielle Joyce. Jeff Orr and his team's dedication, focus, and most important, careful eyes, continue to delight and remind me of what a pleasure it is to work on this project each year. Special thanks also go to Jeanne Krier, our Random House publicist, for the dedicated work she continues to do on this book and the overall series since its inception. Jeanne continues to be my trusted colleague, media advisor, and friend. I would also like to make special mention of Tom Russell and Nicole Benhabib, our Random House publishing team, for their continuous investment and faith in our ideas. Last, I thank my TPR Partner Team, Scott Kirkpatrick, Michael Bleyhl, Paul Kanarek, Brian Healy, and Lev Kaye for their confidence in me and my content team and for their commitment to providing students the resources they need to find the right fit school for them. Again, to all who contributed so much to this publication, thank you for your efforts; they do not go unnoticed.

Robert Franek
Senior VP—Publisher
Lead Author—*The Best 377 Colleges*

DOONESBURY By Garry Trudeau

CONTENTS

PART I: INTRODUCTION

Getting into Selective Colleges: A Guide for High School Students

What we've put together in this book is a guide to the nation's 377 most academically outstanding institutions so that you can be informed about the unique opportunities these schools offer and what it's really like to be a student at them. As selective as you'll be about choosing the right college for you, know that many of the colleges we profile will be selective in choosing the students right for them. While some of the schools you'll read about here admit upwards of eighty percent of their applicants, the majority have many more applicants than they have seats to fill, and some admit less than ten percent of the students who apply. That means—depending on which colleges you're pinning your hopes on attending—you are likely going to have to put quite a bit of effort into getting in. High grades in challenging courses are just the beginning!

If you're like most of the two million high school students who apply to college each year, you're probably wondering what college admissions officers are really looking for in an applicant. What exactly does it take to get into college? What can I do to make my application stand out? Once I get accepted, how do I know which college is best for me?

In order to get you started on the road to a successful application, we're going to give you a few goals, suggestions and tips for checkpoints along the way. This brief primer will help you know what you should be doing year by year in high school to prepare yourself for admission to your "best" college.

6 STEPS TO GETTING INTO COLLEGE

Sure, high school is supposed to be fun, but putting some effort into your schoolwork and extracurricular experiences can make applying to your choice colleges a lot less stressful. Though it might sound like boring advice, the following steps are extremely important!

1. Work hard for good grades.
2. Enroll in challenging courses.
3. Spend time preparing for the ACT or SAT and SAT Subject Tests.
4. Polish your writing skills.
5. Establish relationships with teachers and advisors who can write strong letters of recommendation for you.
6. Get involved in some activities, community service, or work experiences that will enable you to show your values, talents, and skills.

NEED MORE HELP?

For more information on how you can make the most of your high school years and turn those experiences into a successful college application, check out our offering of college admissions books at PrincetonReviewBooks.com.

Freshman Year

Getting a good start is the best way to get a strong finish! You don't want to have to play catch-up during your junior and senior years when you're supposed to be focusing on bigger things. During your freshman year, make sure you concentrate on your studies and work hard to earn good grades. Get to know your teachers and ask for their help if you are having trouble in a subject—as well as if you just really enjoy it and want to learn more. They'll most certainly want to help you do your best. If there is an honor roll at your school, make it a goal to get on it. And if your grades are so good that you qualify for membership in the National Honor Society, pat yourself on the back and don't think twice about accepting the invitation to join. Make it a point to meet your guidance counselor so you can begin pinpointing colleges you may be interested in and studying for the courses and admission tests they require. The great thing about freshman year is that you have plenty of time to focus on projects that can make your admissions applications during your senior year look the best they can. Make sure you take hold of that opportunity!

"During your freshman year, make sure you concentrate on your studies and work hard to earn good grades."

Read a Good Book! (or two)

Strong vocabulary and reading skills are essential to doing well on the SAT and ACT (and most tests you'll take for that matter—even math tests require good reading skills!). By cracking open a few good books, you can do some early prep for both tests. Here are some books we love by interesting authors. Not only will you learn some stuff by reading them, but we think you'll love them too!

- *The Curious Incident of the Dog in the Night-Time: A Novel* **by Mark Haddon**
- *A Heartbreaking Work of Staggering Genius* **by Dave Eggers**
- *Life of Pi* **by Yann Martel**
- *Reading Lolita in Tehran* **by Azar Nafisi**
- *White Teeth* **by Zadie Smith**

Another Good Book

For extra practice building your vocabulary, check out our *Word Smart* books. Our flagship *Word Smart* book has more than 1,400 words including our "SAT Hit Parade": words most frequently on the SAT.

Sophomore Year

As a sophomore, you'll need to stay focused on your studies. If you didn't earn strong grades during your freshman year, start doing so this year. Scope out the Advanced Placement courses that are offered at your school. You'll want to sign up for as many AP courses as you can reasonably take, starting in your junior year. In sophomore year, you'll also want to choose one or more extracurriculars that interest you. Admissions officers tell us they look favorably on involvement in student government, student newspaper, community service, and sports. What you don't want to do is overload your schedule with activities just to rack up a long list of extracurriculars. Colleges would much rather see you focus on a few worthwhile extracurriculars than divide your time among a bunch of different activities that you're not passionate about. Your sophomore year is when you'll have an opportunity to take the PSAT. Given every October, the PSAT is a shortened version of the SAT. It is used to predict how well you will do on the SAT, and it determines eligibility for National Merit Scholarships. While your PSAT scores won't count until you retake the test in your junior year, you should approach this as a test run for the real thing, because the real thing is coming, and it's coming fast. Sophomore year will be over before you know it, and you'll soon have to step it up and be running strong in the critical part of the race to reach the application finish line.

"Colleges would much rather see you focus on a few worthwhile extracurriculars than divide your time among a bunch of different activities that you're not passionate about."

What Should You Do This Summer?

Ahhh, summer. The possibilities seem endless. You can get a job, intern, travel, study, volunteer, or do nothing at all. Here are a few ideas to get you started:

- **Go to college:** No, not for real. However, you can participate in summer programs at colleges and universities at home and abroad. Programs can focus on anything from academics (stretch your brain by taking an intensive science or language course) to sports to admissions guidance. This is also a great opportunity to explore college life firsthand, especially if you get to stay in a dorm.
- **Prep for the PSAT, SAT, or ACT:** So maybe it's not quite as adventurous as trekking around Patagonia for the summer (it's also not as expensive!) or as cool as learning to slam dunk at basketball camp, but hey, there's nothing adventurous or cool about being rejected from your top-choice college because of unimpressive test scores. Plus, you'll be ahead of the game if you can return to school with much of your PSAT, SAT, and ACT preparation behind you.
- **Research scholarships:** College is expensive. While you should never rule out a school based on cost, the more scholarship money you can secure beforehand, the more college options you will have. You'll find loads of info on financial aid and scholarships (including a scholarship search tool) on our site, PrincetonReview.com.

Get Help

Admissions officers will want to see that you've earned high grades in challenging classes. The Princeton Review's Cracking the AP Exam series offers test-prep guides to the most popular AP subject tests to help give you a leg up on passing the exams. High AP scores can boost your chances of admission; plus they are used for placement in college courses and for awarding college credit (ka-ching! ka-ching!). We also offer *Cracking the PSAT/NMSQT,* which has two full-length practice tests and tips on how to score your best on the test. And a great vocabulary will help you with both AP classes and the PSAT, so sign up for lots of help on PrincetonReview.com.

Junior Year

Your junior year is going to be exciting and challenging and extremely important in your academic career. You'll start the year off by taking the PSAT in October. High PSAT scores in junior year qualify you for the National Merit Scholarship competition. To become a finalist, you also need great grades and a recommendation from your school. It's critical that your junior-year grades be solid. When colleges look at your transcripts, they put a heavy emphasis on junior-year grades. Decisions are made before admissions officers see your second-semester, senior-year grades and possibly before they see your first-semester, senior-year grades! During your junior year, you'll probably take the SAT or ACT test for the first time. Most colleges require scores from one of these tests for admission and/or scholarship award decisions. Also take time during your junior year to research colleges, and, if possible, visit schools high on your "hopes" list. When researching colleges, you'll want to consider a variety of factors besides whether or not you can get in, including location, school size, majors or programs offered that interest you, and cost and availability of financial aid. It helps to visit schools because it's the best way to learn whether a school may be right for you. If you can schedule an interview with an admissions officer during your visit, it may help him or her discover how right you may be for the school.

ACT or SAT?

Not sure which test to take? First make sure that all the schools to which you're applying accept both tests (nearly all colleges now do so, but it's best to check). Then take the test on which you do better. Visit PrincetonReview.com to take a free assessment test that will help you identify whether the ACT or SAT is better for you. We also have a book on this very subject: *ACT or SAT? Choosing the Right Exam for You.* More and more students are opting to take the ACT in addition to, or instead of, the SAT. No matter which test you end up taking, you should plan to spend three to twelve weeks preparing for the tests.

About the SAT: The SAT is comprised of Math, Critical Reading, and Writing sections. Colleges will see your individual section scores and your composite score, but generally they'll be most concerned with your composite score. Currently, a "Score Choice" policy is in place. It allows students to choose which scores (of a complete SAT test, not of one section of a test) will be sent to colleges. However, some colleges are asking to see all of your test scores, so be sure to check this out on a per-school basis.

About the ACT: The ACT has an English, Reading, Math, and Science section, plus the optional Writing section. (Some schools require the essay, so be sure to ask before you take the test.) You can take the ACT several times and choose which of your scores will be sent to the colleges.

About SAT Subject Tests: Most highly selective colleges also require you to take at least two SAT Subject Tests in addition to the SAT or ACT. If you have SAT Subject Tests to take, plan now. You can't take the SAT and SAT Subject Tests on the same day.

Senior Year

It's finally here! Senior year! It's now time to get serious about pulling everything together on your applications. Deadlines will vary from school to school, and you will have a lot to keep track of, so make checklists of what's due when. If you're not happy with your previous SAT scores, you should take the October SAT. If you still need to take any SAT Subject Tests, now's the time.

When you ask teachers to write recommendations for you, give them everything they need. Tell them your application deadline and include a stamped, addressed envelope, or directions on how to submit the recommendation online, and be sure to send them a thank-you note after you know the recommendation was turned in.

Your essay, on the other hand, is the one part of your application you have total control over. Don't repeat information from other parts of your application. And by all means, proofread! You'll find tips from admissions officers on what they look for (and what peeves them the most) about college applicants' essays in our book, *College Essays That Made a Difference.*

If you have found the school of your dreams and you're happy with your grades and test scores, consider filing an early decision application. Many selective colleges commit more than half of their admissions spots to early decision applicants. To take this route, you must file your application in early November. By mid-December, you'll find out whether you got in—but there's a catch. If you're accepted early decision to a college, you must withdraw all applications to other colleges. This means that your financial aid offer might be hard to negotiate, so be prepared to take what you get. Regardless of which route you decide to take, have a backup plan. Make sure you apply to at least one safety school—one that you feel confident you can get into and afford. Another option is to apply early decision at one school, but apply to other colleges during the regular decision period in the event that you are rejected from the early decision college.

We know how exciting but stressful the final decision can be. If you're having a difficult time choosing between two colleges, try to visit each of them one more time. Can you imagine yourself walking around that campus, building a life in that community, and establishing friendships with those people? Finally, decide and be happy. Don't forget to thank your recommenders and tell them where you'll be going to school. Some of the best times of your life await!

Our Other Helpful Books

The college admissions process is overwhelming, and counselor appointments can be few and far between at some schools. That's why The Princeton Review got more than 200 top college counselors to share their secrets about getting that crucial acceptance letter! *The Portable Guidance Counselor* helps you maximize your college chances with answers to key questions: What should I look for during college visits? How many AP classes should I take? What do college admissions officers really want to see on an application?

Our *K & W Guide to College Programs and Services for Students with Learning Disabilities or Attention Deficit/Hyperactivity Disorder* profiles more than 300 schools and includes advice from specialists in the field of learning disabilities, and strategies to help students identify and successfully apply to the best programs for their needs.

Our *Gay & Lesbian Guide to College Life* ebook addresses challenges that LGBT students face from finding and applying to colleges to dealing with campus life issues. Appendixes provide lists of LGBT scholarships, support networks, advocacy groups, and academic/career resources.

Our *300 Best Professors* book highlights great professors at great schools so you can be more successful in college and after college.

You'll find information about these and our more than 150 guidebooks at PrincetonReviewBooks.com.

Paying for College: Savvy Strategies for Financial Aid

The Princeton Review's *Paying for College Without Going Broke* is the only annually updated guide to financial aid that has detailed, line-by-line strategies for completing the highly complicated FAFSA for the upcoming school year (as well as the CSS/PROFILE form) to one's best advantage. It explains how the financial aid process works and reveals strategies—all legal—for maximizing your eligibility for aid. Authored by Kal Chany, one of the nation's most widely sourced experts on college funding, it also includes annually updated information on education tax breaks, college savings programs, and student and parent loans.

Check out Kal Chany's "26 Tips for Getting Financial Aid . . ." on pages 7–9.

26 Tips for Getting Financial Aid, Scholarships, and Grants and for Paying Less for College

by Kalman A. Chany, author of *Paying for College Without Going Broke*

(Random House/Princeton Review Books)

Getting financial aid

1. Learn how the aid process works. The more and the sooner you know about the process, the better you can take steps to maximize your aid eligibility.
2. Apply for financial aid no matter what your circumstances. Some merit-based aid can only be awarded if the applicant has submitted financial aid application forms.
3. Don't wait until your child is accepted to apply for financial aid. Do it when applying for admission.
4. Complete all the required aid applications. All students seeking aid must submit the FAFSA (Free Application for Federal Student Aid); other forms may also be required. Check with each college to see what's required and when.
5. Get the best scores you can on the SAT or ACT. They are used not only in decisions for admission but also financial aid. If your scores and other stats exceed the school's admission criteria, you are likely to get a better aid package than a marginal applicant.
6. Apply strategically to colleges. Your chances of getting aid will be better at schools that have generous financial aid budgets. (Check the "Best Value Colleges" list and Financial Aid Ratings for schools in this book and on PrincetonReview.com.)
7. Don't rule out any school as too expensive. A generous aid award from a pricey private school can make it less costly than a public school with a lower sticker price.
8. Take advantage of education tax benefits. A dollar saved on taxes is worth the same as a dollar in scholarship aid. Look into Coverdells, education tax credits, and loan deductions.

Scholarships and grants

9. Get your best possible score on the PSAT: It is the National Merit Scholarship Qualifying Test and also used in the selection of students for other scholarships and recognition programs.
10. Check your eligibility for grants and scholarships from your state. Some (but not all) states will allow you to use such funds out of state.

11. Look for scholarships locally. Find out if your employer offers scholarships or tuition assistance plans for employees or family members. Also look into scholarships from your church, community groups, and high school.

12. Look for outside scholarships realistically: they account for less than five percent of aid awarded. Research them at PrincetonReview.com or other free sites. Steer clear of scholarship search firms that charge fees and "promise" scholarships.

Paying for college

13. Start saving early when the student is an infant. Too late? Start now. The more you save, the less you'll have to borrow.

14. Invest wisely. Considering a 529 plan? Compare your own state's plan which may have tax benefits with other states' programs. Get info at savingforcollege.com.

15. If you have to borrow, first pursue federal education loans (Perkins, Stafford, PLUS). Avoid private loans at all costs.

16. Never put tuition on a credit card. The debt is more expensive than ever given recent changes to interest rates and other fees some card issuers are now charging.

17. Try not to take money from a retirement account or 401(k) to pay for college. In addition to likely early distribution penalties and additional income taxes, the higher income will reduce your aid eligibility.

Paying less for college

18. Attend a community college for two years and transfer to a pricier school to complete the degree. Plan ahead: Be sure the college you plan to transfer to will accept the community college credits.

19. Look into "cooperative education" programs. Over 900 colleges allow students to combine college education with a job. It can take longer to complete a degree this way but graduates generally owe less in student loans and have a better chance of getting hired.

20. Take as many AP courses as possible and get high scores on AP exams. Many colleges award course credits for high AP scores. Some students have cut a year off their college tuition this way.

21. Earn college credit via "dual enrollment" programs available at some high schools. These allow students to take college level courses during their senior year.

22. Earn college credits by taking CLEP (College-Level Examination Program) exams. Depending on the college, a qualifying score on any of the thirty-three CLEP exams can earn students three to twelve college credits. (See Princeton Review's *Cracking the CLEP, 5th Edition.*)

23. Stick to your college and your major. Changing colleges can result in lost credits. Aid may be limited/not available for transfer students at some schools. Changing majors can mean paying for extra courses to meet requirements.

24 . Finish college in three years if possible. Take the maximum number of credits every semester, attend summer sessions, and earn credits via online courses. Some colleges offer three-year programs for high-achieving students.

25. Let Uncle Sam pay for your degree. ROTC (Reserve Officer Training Corps) programs available from U.S. Armed Forces branches (except the Coast Guard) offer merit-based scholarships up to full tuition via participating colleges in exchange for military service after you graduate.

26. Better yet: Attend a tuition-free college. Check out the nine institutions in this book on the "Tuition-Free Schools Honor Roll" list on page 53.

Want to Search by Tuition?

We say it over and over: Never rule out applying to a college because of its "sticker" price. Many schools are very generous with their financial aid, and it can cost less to attend an expensive private college than an inexpensive public university. Check out our book of "The Best Value Colleges"; the 2012 edition profiles 150 colleges (75 public and 75 private) we saluted in February 2012 as our recommended "best value" picks in the nation. You'll also find the list in this book on page 54. (Also in that section of the book, check out our list "Great Financial Aid" on page 41: it names the top twenty schools at which students we surveyed were happiest with their financial aid awards.) In this book, in addition to giving you tons of facts and stats about the schools' financial aid offerings and policies (we even have a Financial Aid Rating) in the school profiles, we also offer an index of colleges in this book sorted by tuition. You'll find it on page 822.

There is also an index by location!

Great Schools for 20 of the Most Popular Undergraduate Majors

Worried about having to declare a major on your college application? Relax. Most colleges won't require you to declare a major until the end of your sophomore year, giving you plenty of time to explore your options. However, problems may arise if you are thinking about majoring in a program that limits its enrollment—meaning that if you don't declare that major early on, you might not get into that program at a later date.

On the flip side, some students declare a major on their application because they believe it will boost their chances of gaining admission. This is a slippery slope to climb, however. If you later decide to change your major and it involves switching from one school within the college to another (from the school of arts and sciences to the school of business, for example), it can be tricky.

Never choose a college solely on the perceived prestige of a particular program. College will expose you to new and exciting learning opportunities. To choose a school based on a major before you even know what else is out there would limit you in many ways. (Choosing a school based on program availability is a different story.) You may also want to investigate opportunities to design your own major.

How Did We Compile These Lists?

Each year we collect data from more than a thousand colleges on the subject of—among many other things—undergraduate academic offerings. We ask colleges not only to report which undergraduate majors they offer, but also which of their majors have the highest enrollment and the number of bachelor's degrees each school awarded in these areas. The list below identifies (in alphabetical order) twenty of the forty "most popular" majors that the schools responding to our survey reported to us. We also conduct our own research on college majors. We look at institutional data, and we consult with our in-house college admissions experts as well as our National College Counselor Advisory Panel (whom we list in our index, pages 825–826) for their input on schools offering great programs in these majors. We thank them and all of the guidance counselors, college admissions counselors, and education experts across the country whose recommendations we considered in developing these lists. Of the roughly 3,500 schools across the United States, those on these lists represent only a snapshot of the many offering great programs in these majors. Use our lists as a starting point for further research. Some schools on these lists may not appear in the *Best 377 Colleges* (these are marked with an asterisk*), but you can find profiles of them in our *Complete Book of Colleges, 2013 Edition.*

Great Schools for Accounting Majors

- Alfred University
- Auburn University
- Babson College
- Baylor University
- Birmingham-Southern College
- Boston College
- Boston University
- Brigham Young University (UT)
- Bucknell University
- Calvin College
- Claremont McKenna College
- Clemson University
- College of Charleston
- Cornell University
- DePaul University
- Drexel University
- Duquesne University
- Elon University
- Emory University
- Fordham University
- Georgetown University
- Indiana University—Bloomington
- Iowa State University
- James Madison University
- Lehigh University
- Michigan State University
- New York University
- Northeastern University
- Pennsylvania State University—University Park
- Pepperdine University
- Rider University
- Rochester Institute of Technology
- Seton Hall University
- Suffolk University
- Temple University
- Texas A&M University—College Station
- University of Houston
- University of Illinois at Urbana-Champaign
- University of Michigan—Ann Arbor
- University of Pennsylvania
- University of Southern California
- The University of Texas at Austin

Great Schools for Agriculture Majors

- Angelo State University
- Arizona State University
- Auburn University
- Berea College
- California State University Stanislaus
- Clemson University
- College of the Atlantic
- College of the Ozarks
- Colorado State University
- Cornell University
- Gettysburg College
- Hampshire College
- Iowa State University
- Kansas State University
- Louisiana State University
- Michigan State University
- North Carolina State University
- Pennsylvania State University—University Park
- Prescott College
- Purdue University—West Lafayette
- Texas A&M University—College Station
- Texas Christian University
- Truman State University
- Tuskegee University
- University of Arizona
- University of Arkansas—Fayetteville
- University of California—Davis
- University of Florida
- University of Georgia
- University of Hawaii—Manoa
- University of Idaho
- University of Illinois at Urbana-Champaign
- University of Kentucky
- University of Maine
- University of Maryland—College Park
- University of Massachusetts Amherst
- University of Missouri—Columbia
- University of Nebraska—Lincoln
- University of Tennessee
- University of Vermont
- University of Wisconsin—Madison
- University of Wyoming
- West Virginia University

Great Schools for Biology Majors

- Agnes Scott College
- Albion College
- Austin College
- Baylor University
- Brandeis University
- Carleton College
- Christopher Newport University
- Colby College
- Cornell University
- Drexel University
- Duke University
- Guilford College
- Harvard College
- Haverford College
- Howard University
- Illinois Wesleyan University
- Indiana University—Bloomington
- Johns Hopkins University
- Louisiana State University
- Loyola University—Chicago
- Massachusetts Institute of Technology
- Mount Holyoke College
- The Ohio State University—Columbus
- Ohio University—Athens
- Pomona College
- Reed College
- Rice University
- Swarthmore College
- Temple University
- Texas A&M University—College Station
- University of California—Davis
- The University of Chicago
- University of Dallas
- University of Delaware
- University of Denver
- University of Houston
- University of New Mexico
- University of the Pacific
- Wofford College
- Xavier University of Louisiana

Great Schools for Business/Finance Majors

- Babson College
- Bentley University
- Boston College
- Carnegie Mellon University
- Champlain College
- Christopher Newport University
- City University of New York—Baruch College
- Cornell University
- DePaul University
- Emory University
- Florida State University
- Indiana University—Bloomington
- Iowa State University
- Lehigh University
- Massachusetts Institute of Technology
- Miami University (OH)
- Michigan State University
- New York University
- Northwestern University
- Ohio University—Athens
- Portland State University
- Rice University
- Roanoke College
- Seattle University
- University of California—Berkeley
- University of California—Los Angeles
- The University of Chicago
- University of Florida
- University of Houston
- University of Illinois at Urbana-Champaign
- University of Michigan—Ann Arbor
- University of Pennsylvania
- University of Southern California
- The University of Texas at Austin
- University of Virginia
- Washington University in St. Louis

Great Schools for Communications Majors

- Baylor University
- Boston University
- Bradley University
- City University of New York—Hunter College
- Clemson University
- College of Charleston
- Cornell University
- Denison University
- DePaul University
- Duquesne University
- Eckerd College
- Emerson College
- Fairfield University
- Fordham University
- Gonzaga University
- Gustavus Adolphus College
- Hollins University
- Indiana University—Bloomington
- Iowa State University
- Ithaca College
- James Madison University
- Lake Forest College
- Loyola University—New Orleans
- Michigan State University
- Muhlenberg College
- New York University
- Northwestern University
- Pepperdine University
- Ripon College
- Salisbury University
- Seton Hall University
- St. John's University (NY)
- Stanford University
- Suffolk University
- Syracuse University
- University of California—San Diego
- University of California—Santa Barbara
- University of Iowa
- University of Maryland—College Park
- University of Southern California
- The University of Texas at Austin
- University of Utah

Great Schools for Computer Science/Computer Engineering Majors

- Auburn University
- Boston University
- Bradley University
- Brown University
- California Institute of Technology
- Carnegie Mellon University
- Clemson University
- Drexel University
- Florida State University
- George Mason University
- Georgia Institute of Technology
- Gonzaga University
- Hampton University
- Harvey Mudd College
- Iowa State University
- Johns Hopkins University
- Lehigh University
- Massachusetts Institute of Technology
- Michigan State University
- New Jersey Institute of Technology
- Northeastern University
- Northwestern University
- Princeton University
- Rice University
- Roanoke College
- Rochester Institute of Technology
- Rose-Hulman Institute of Technology
- Seattle University
- Stanford University
- State University of New York at Binghamton
- State University of New York—University at Buffalo
- Texas A&M University—College Station
- United States Air Force Academy
- University of Arizona
- University of California—Berkeley
- University of California—Los Angeles
- University of California—Riverside
- University of Illinois at Urbana-Champaign
- University of Massachusetts Amherst
- University of Michigan—Ann Arbor
- University of Washington

Great Schools for Criminology Majors

- American University
- Auburn University
- North Carolina State University
- The Ohio State University—Columbus
- Ohio University—Athens
- Quinnipiac University
- Suffolk University
- University of Delaware
- University of Denver
- University of Maryland—College Park
- University of Miami
- University of New Hampshire
- University of South Florida
- University of Utah
- Valparaiso University

Great Schools for Education Majors

- Auburn University
- Barnard College
- Bucknell University
- City University of New York—Brooklyn College
- City University of New York—Hunter College
- Colgate University
- The College of William & Mary
- Columbia College (MO)*
- Columbia University
- Cornell College
- Cornell University
- Duquesne University
- Elon University
- Gonzaga University
- Goucher College
- Hillsdale College
- Indiana University—Bloomington
- Loyola Marymount University
- Marquette University*
- McGill University
- Miami University (OH)
- Nazareth College
- New York University
- Northeastern University
- Northwestern University
- The Ohio State University—Columbus
- Simmons College
- Skidmore College
- Smith College
- Trinity University (TX)
- University of Maine
- The University of Montana—Missoula
- Vanderbilt University
- Villanova College
- Wagner College
- Wellesley College
- Xavier University (OH)

Great Schools for Engineering Majors

- California Institute of Technology
- Carnegie Mellon University
- Columbia University
- The Cooper Union for the Advancement of Science and Art
- Cornell University
- Drexel University
- Duke University
- Franklin W. Olin College of Engineering
- Georgia Institute of Technology
- Harvard College
- Harvey Mudd College
- Illinois Institute of Technology
- Johns Hopkins University
- Massachusetts Institute of Technology
- Pennsylvania State University—University Park
- Princeton University
- Purdue University—West Lafayette
- Rose-Hulman Institute of Technology
- Stanford University
- Texas A&M University—College Station
- University of California—Berkeley
- University of California—Los Angeles
- The University of Texas at Austin
- University of Wisconsin—Madison
- Worcester Polytechnic Institute

Schools marked with an asterisk do not appear in the *Best 377 Colleges*.
You can find those school profiles in the *Complete Book of Colleges, 2013 Edition*.

Great Schools for English Literature and Language Majors

- Amherst College
- Auburn University
- Bard College (NY)
- Barnard College
- Bennington College
- Boston College
- Brown University
- City University of New York—Hunter College
- Claremont McKenna College
- Clemson University
- Colby College
- Colgate University
- Columbia University
- Cornell University
- Dartmouth College
- Denison University
- Duke University
- Emory University
- Eugene Lang College The New School for Liberal Arts
- Fordham University
- George Mason University
- Gettysburg College
- Harvard College
- Johns Hopkins University
- Kenyon College
- Pitzer College
- Pomona College
- Princeton University
- Rice University
- Stanford University
- Syracuse University
- Tufts University
- University of California—Berkeley
- The University of Chicago
- University of Michigan—Ann Arbor
- University of Notre Dame
- University of Utah
- Vassar College
- Washington University in St. Louis
- Wellesley College
- Yale University

Great Schools for Environmental Studies Majors

- Allegheny College
- Bates College
- Bowdoin College
- Catawba College
- Colby College
- College of the Atlantic
- Colorado College
- Dickinson College
- Eckerd College
- Emory University
- The Evergreen State College
- Green Mountain College
- Harvard College
- Hobart and William Smith Colleges
- Juniata College
- Middlebury College
- New College of Florida
- Northeastern University
- Occidental College
- Pitzer College
- Pomona College
- Portland State University
- Prescott College
- Sonoma State University
- State University of New York at Binghamton
- University of California—Berkeley
- University of California—Santa Cruz
- University of Colorado—Boulder
- University of Idaho
- The University of Montana—Missoula
- University of New Hampshire
- The University of North Carolina at Asheville
- The University of North Carolina at Chapel Hill
- University of Oregon
- University of Redlands
- University of the Pacific
- University of Vermont
- Warren Wilson College
- Washington College

Check out our free downloadable resource, The Princeton Review's *Guide to 322 Green Colleges* at www.princetonreview.com/green-guide.

Great Schools for History Majors

- Bowdoin College
- Brown University
- Centre College
- Colgate University
- College of the Holy Cross
- Columbia University
- Drew University
- Furman University
- Georgetown University
- Grinnell College
- Hampden-Sydney College
- Harvard College
- Haverford College
- Hillsdale College
- Kenyon College
- Oberlin College
- Princeton University
- Trinity College (CT)
- Tulane University
- University of Virginia
- Wabash College
- Yale University

Great Schools for Health Services Majors

- Bellarmine University
- Boston University
- Clemson University
- The College of Idaho
- College of the Ozarks
- Creighton University
- Drexel University
- Duquesne University
- Gettysburg College
- Gustavus Adolphus College
- Hampton University
- Hendrix College
- Howard University
- Ithaca College
- Johns Hopkins University
- Kalamazoo College
- Marywood University
- Monmouth University (NJ)
- Nazareth College
- Northeastern University
- Ohio University—Athens
- Purdue University—West Lafayette
- Quinnipiac University
- Sacred Heart University
- Saint Anselm College
- Saint Louis University
- Simmons College
- State University of New York—Stony Brook University
- Suffolk University
- Texas A&M University—College Station
- Tulane University
- University of Alabama at Birmingham
- University of Central Florida
- University of Cincinnati
- University of Florida
- University of Houston
- University of Miami
- University of Oklahoma
- University of Utah
- Wagner College
- Washington University in St. Louis
- Westminster College (UT)
- Wheaton College (IL)
- William Jewell College

Great Schools for Journalism Majors

- American University
- Boston University
- Carleton College
- Columbia University
- Emerson College
- Hampton University
- Howard University
- Indiana University—Bloomington
- Loyola University—New Orleans
- Northwestern University
- Ohio University—Athens
- Pennsylvania State University—University Park
- Samford University*
- St. Bonaventure University
- Syracuse University
- Temple University
- University of Florida
- University of Maryland—College Park
- University of Missouri—Columbia
- The University of North Carolina at Chapel Hill
- University of Oregon
- University of Southern California
- The University of Texas at Austin
- University of Wisconsin—Madison

Great Schools for Marketing and Sales Majors

- Babson College
- Baylor University
- Bentley College
- Duquesne University
- Fairfield University
- Hofstra University
- Indiana University—Bloomington
- Iowa State University
- James Madison University
- Miami University (OH)
- Providence College
- Seattle University
- Siena College*
- Syracuse University
- Texas A&M University—College Station
- University of Central Florida
- University of Michigan—Ann Arbor
- University of Mississippi
- University of Pennsylvania
- University of South Florida
- The University of Texas at Austin

Great Schools for Mathematics Majors

- Agnes Scott College
- Bowdoin College
- Bryant University
- Bryn Mawr College
- California Institute of Technology
- Carleton College
- College of the Holy Cross
- The College of Idaho
- Grinnell College
- Hamilton College
- Hampton University
- Harvard College
- Harvey Mudd College
- Haverford College
- Macalester College
- Massachusetts Institute of Technology
- Randolph College
- Reed College
- Rice University
- St. Lawrence University
- St. Olaf College
- State University of New York—University at Albany
- United States Coast Guard Academy
- The University of Chicago
- University of Rochester
- Wabash College

Schools marked with an asterisk do not appear in the *Best 377 Colleges.*
You can find those school profiles in the *Complete Book of Colleges, 2013 Edition.*

Great Schools for Mechanical Engineering Majors

- Bradley University
- California Institute of Technology
- Clarkson University
- Drexel University
- Franklin W. Olin College of Engineering
- Georgia Institute of Technology
- Harvey Mudd College
- Iowa State University
- Lehigh University
- Massachusetts Institute of Technology
- New Jersey Institute of Technology
- North Carolina State University
- Purdue University—West Lafayette
- Rose-Hulman Institute of Technology
- Stanford University
- State University of New York—University at Buffalo
- Stevens Institute of Technology
- United States Military Academy
- University of California—Berkeley
- University of Illinois at Urbana-Champaign
- University of Michigan—Ann Arbor
- Worcester Polytechnic Institute

Great Schools for Nursing Majors

- Angelo State University
- Baylor University
- Bellarmine University
- Calvin College
- The Catholic University of America
- Drexel University
- Duquesne University
- Fairfield University
- Florida Southern College
- Indiana University of Pennsylvania
- Loyola University—Chicago
- Montana Tech of the University of Montana
- Ohio Northern University
- Saint Louis University
- Texas Christian University
- The University of Alabama—Tuscaloosa
- University of Pennsylvania
- University of Wyoming
- Valparaiso University
- Villanova University
- Washington State University
- Xavier University (OH)

Great Schools for Political Science/Government Majors

- American University
- Amherst College
- Bard College (NY)
- Bates College
- Bowdoin College
- Brigham Young University (UT)
- Bryn Mawr College
- Carleton College
- Claremont McKenna College
- College of the Holy Cross
- Columbia University
- Davidson College
- Dickinson College
- Drew University
- Furman University
- George Mason University
- The George Washington University
- Georgetown University
- Gettysburg College
- Gonzaga University
- Harvard College
- Kenyon College
- Macalester College
- Princeton University
- Stanford University
- Swarthmore College
- Syracuse University
- University of Arizona
- University of California—Berkeley
- University of California—Los Angeles
- University of Washington
- Vassar College
- Yale University

Great Schools for Psychology Majors

- Albion College
- Bates College
- Carnegie Mellon University
- Christopher Newport University
- Clark University
- Colorado State University
- Columbia University
- Cornell University
- Dartmouth College
- Duke University
- George Mason University
- Gettysburg College
- Harvard College
- James Madison University
- Lewis & Clark College
- Loyola University—Chicago
- New York University
- Pitzer College
- Portland State University
- Princeton University
- Roanoke College
- Smith College
- Stanford University
- University of California—Davis
- University of California—Los Angeles
- University of California—Riverside
- University of California—Santa Barbara
- University of California—Santa Cruz
- University of Houston
- University of Michigan—Ann Arbor
- University of Southern California
- The University of Texas at Austin
- University of Utah
- Washington University in St. Louis
- Yale University

How and Why We Produce This Book

This Year's Edition

In the twenty years since the first edition of this book, our Best Colleges guide has grown considerably. We've added more than 150 colleges to the guide and deleted several along the way. How we choose the schools for the book, and how we produce it, however, has not changed significantly over the years (with the exception of how we conduct our student survey—more on this follows).

To determine which schools will be in each edition, we don't use mathematical calculations or formulas. Instead we rely on a wide range of input, both quantitative and qualitative. Every year we collect data from nearly 2,000 colleges that we use for our *Complete Book of Colleges,* this book, and our web-based profiles of schools. We visit dozens of colleges and meet with their admissions officers, deans, presidents, and college students. We talk with hundreds of high school counselors, parents, and students. Colleges also submit information to us requesting consideration for inclusion in the book. As a result, we are able to maintain a constantly evolving list of colleges to consider adding to each new edition of the book. Any college we add to the guide, however, must agree to support our efforts to survey its students via our anonymous student survey. (Sometimes a college's administrative protocols will not allow it to participate in our student survey; this has caused some academically outstanding schools to be absent from the guide.) Finally, we work to ensure that our roster of colleges in the book presents a wide representation of institutions by region, character, and type. Here you'll find profiles of public and private schools, Historically Black Colleges and Universities, men's and women's colleges, science- and technology-focused institutions, nontraditional colleges, highly selective schools, and some with virtually open-door admissions policies.

For this year's edition, we added six schools to the guide: Allegheny College, Becker College, City University of New York—City College, University of Hawaii—Manoa, University of Tampa, and Virginia Wesleyan College.

Our ranking lists in this edition are based on our surveys of 122,000 students attending the 377 colleges in the book. We surveyed about 330 students per campus on average, though that number varies depending on the size of the student population. We've surveyed anywhere from twenty-some students at Deep Springs College (100 percent of the all-male student body) to more than 1,000 collegians at such colleges as Drexel University, Clemson University, and the United States Military Academy.

All of the institutions in this guide are academically terrific in our opinion. The 377 schools featured—our picks of the cream of the crop colleges and universities—comprise only the top fifteen percent of all colleges in the nation. Not every college will appeal to every student, but that is the beauty of it. These are all very different schools with many different and wonderful things to offer. We hope you will use this book as a starting point (it will certainly give you a snapshot of what life is like at these schools), but not as the final word on any one school. Check out other resources. Visit as many colleges as you can. Talk to students at those colleges—ask what they love and what bothers them most about their schools. Finally, form your own opinions about the colleges you are considering. At the end of the day, it's what YOU think about the schools that matters most, and that will enable you to answer that all-important question: "Which college is best for me?"

> *"We worked to create a guide that would help people who couldn't always get to the campus nonetheless get in-depth campus feedback to find the schools best for them."*

The History of This Book

When we published the first edition of this book in 1992, there was a void in the world of college guides (hard to believe, but true!). No publication provided college applicants with statistical data from colleges that covered academics, admissions, financial aid, and student demographics along with narrative descriptions of the schools based on comprehensive surveys of students attending them. Of course, academic rankings of colleges had been around for some time. They named the best schools on hierarchical lists, from 1 to 200 and upwards, some in tiers. Their criteria factored in such matters as faculty salaries, alumni giving, and peer reviews (i.e., what college administrators thought of the schools that, in many cases, they competed with for students). But no one was polling students at these terrific colleges about their experiences on campus—both inside and outside the classroom. We created our first Best Colleges guide to address that void. It was born out of one very obvious omission in college guide publishing and two very deep convictions we held then and hold even more strongly today:

- One: The key question for students and parents researching colleges shouldn't be "What college is best, academically?" The thing is, it's not hard to find academically great schools in this country. (There are hundreds of them.) The key question—and one that is truly tough to answer—is "What is the best college for me?"

- Two: We believe the best way for students and parents to know if a school is right—and ultimately best—for them is to visit it. Travel to the campus, get inside a dorm, audit a class, browse the town and—most importantly—talk to students attending the school. In the end it's the school's customers—its students—who are the real experts about the college. Only they can give you the most candid and informed feedback on what life is really like on the campus.

Guided by these convictions, we worked to create a resource that would help people who couldn't always get to the campus nonetheless get in-depth campus feedback to find the schools best for them. We culled an initial list of 250 academically great schools, based on our own college knowledge and input from fifty independent college counselors. We gathered institutional data from those schools and surveyed 30,000 students attending them (about 120 per campus on average). We wrote the school profiles, incorporating school data and extensive quotes from surveyed students, and we compiled for the book more than sixty ranking lists of top twenty schools in various categories based on our surveys of students at the schools.

With support from nearly a million students who've participated in our student surveys over the years, and administrators at nearly 400 colleges, we're pleased to offer what we continue to believe is the most substantive resource you can find to know which of these 377 schools may be best for you.

About Our Student Survey for Our "Best Colleges" Books

Our undergraduate student survey is a mammoth undertaking. In the first few years that we published this book, we formally surveyed students at all of the colleges and universities in the book on an annual basis. By the time we had gone through a few editions, we found that barring some grand upheaval or administrative change on campus, there's little change in student opinion from one year to the next, but that shifts emerge in a third or fourth year (as surveyed students leave or matriculate). With this in mind, we switched to a three-year cycle for formally resurveying each campus. Thus, each year we target about 150 campuses for resurveying. We resurvey colleges more often than that if colleges request it (and we can accommodate the request) or if we believe it is warranted for one reason or another.

In the early years, our surveys were conducted on campuses and on paper, but the launch in the late 1990s of our online survey (http://survey.review.com), has made it possible for students to complete a survey anytime and anywhere. Now all of our student surveys are now completed online.

Online surveys submitted by students outside of a school's normal survey cycle and independent of any solicitation on our part are factored into the subsequent year's rankings and ratings calculations. In that respect, our surveying is a continuous process. All colleges and universities whose students we plan to survey are notified about the survey through our administrative contacts at the schools. We depend upon them for assistance in notifying the student body about the availability of the online survey via e-mail.

The survey has more than eighty questions divided into four sections: "About Yourself," "Your School's Academics/Administration," "Students," and "Life at Your School." We ask about all sorts of things, from "How many out-of-class hours do you spend studying each day?" to "How do you rate your campus food?" Most questions offer students a five-point grid on which to indicate their answer choices (headers may range from "Excellent" to "Awful"). Eight questions offer students the opportunity to expand on their answers with narrative comment. These essay-type responses are the sources of the student quotations that appear in the school profiles. Once the surveys have been completed and responses stored in our database, every college is given a score (similar to a grade point average) for its students' answers to each question. This score enables us to compare students' responses to a particular question from one college to the next. We use these scores as an underlying data point in our calculation of the ratings in the profile sidebars and the ranking lists in the section of the book titled "School Rankings and Lists."

Once we have the student survey information in hand, we write the college profiles. Student quotations in each profile are chosen because they represent the sentiments expressed by the majority of survey respondents from the college; or, they illustrate one side or another of a mixed bag of student opinion, in which case there will also appear a counterpoint within the text. In order to guard against producing a write-up that's off the mark for any particular college, we send our administrative contact at each school a copy of the profile we intend to publish prior to its publication date, with ample opportunity to respond with corrections, comments, and/or outright objections. In every case in which we receive requests for changes, we take careful measures to review the school's suggestions against the student survey data we collected and make appropriate changes when warranted.

HOW THIS BOOK IS ORGANIZED

Each of the colleges and universities in this book has its own two-page profile. To make it easier to find and compare information about the schools, we've used the same profile format for every school. Look at the sample pages below: Each profile has nine major components. First, at the very top of the profile you will see the school's address, telephone, and fax numbers for the admissions office, the telephone number for the financial aid office, and the school's website and/or e-mail address. Second, there are two sidebars (the narrow columns on the outside of each page, which consist mainly of statistics) divided into the categories of Campus Life, Academics, Selectivity, and Financial Facts. Third, there are four headings in the narrative text: Students Say, Admissions, Financial Aid, and From the Admissions Office. Here's what you'll find in each part:

The Sidebars

The sidebars contain various statistics culled from our surveys of students attending the school and from questionnaires that school administrators complete at our request in the fall of each year. Keep in mind that not every category will appear for every school—in some cases the information is not reported or not applicable. We compile the eight ratings—Quality of Life, Fire Safety, Green Rating, Academic, Profs Interesting, Profs Accessible, Admissions Selectivity, and Financial Aid—listed in the sidebars based on the results from our student surveys and/or institutional data we collect from school administrators.

These ratings are on a scale of 60–99. If a 60* (60 with an asterisk) appears as any rating for any school, it means that the school reported so few of the rating's underlying data points by our deadline that we were unable to calculate an accurate rating for it. (These measures are outlined in the ratings explanation below.) Be advised that because the Admissions Selectivity Rating is a factor in the computation that produces the Academic Rating, a school that has 60* (60 with an asterisk) as its Admissions Selectivity Rating will have an Academic Rating that is lower than it should be. Also bear in mind that each rating places each college on a continuum for purposes of comparing colleges within this edition only. Since our ratings computations may change from year to year, it is invalid to compare the ratings in this edition to those that appear in any prior or future edition.

Finally, these ratings are quite different from the ranking lists that appear in Part 2 of the book, "School Rankings and Lists." The ratings are numerical measures that show how a school "sizes up," if you will, on a fixed scale. Our sixty-two ranking lists report the top twenty (or in some cases bottom twenty) schools of the 377 in the book (not of all schools in the nation) in various categories. They are based on our surveys of students at the schools and/or institutional data. We don't rank the schools in the book 1 to 377 hierarchically. Here is what each heading in the sidebar tells you, in order of their appearance:

Quality of Life Rating

On a scale of 60–99, this rating is a measure of how happy students are with their campus experiences outside the classroom. To compile this rating, we weighed several factors, all based on students' answers to questions on our survey. They included the students' assessments of: their overall happiness; the beauty, safety, and location of the campus; comfort of dorms; quality of food; ease of getting around campus and dealing with administrators; friendliness of fellow students; and the interaction of different student types on campus and within the greater community.

"Ratings are quite different from the ranking lists. The ratings are numerical measures that show how a school "sizes up," if you will, on a fixed scale. Our sixty-two ranking lists report the top twenty (or in some cases bottom twenty) schools of the 377 in the book (not of all schools in the nation) in various categories."

Fire Safety Rating

On a scale of 60–99, this rating measures how well prepared a school is to prevent or respond to campus fires, specifically in residence halls. We asked schools several questions about their efforts to ensure fire safety for campus residents. We developed the questions in consultation with the Center for Campus Fire Safety (www.campusfiresafety.org). Each school's responses to eight questions were considered when calculating its Fire Safety Rating. They cover:

1. The percentage of student housing sleeping rooms protected by an automatic fire sprinkler system with a fire sprinkler head located in the individual sleeping rooms.
2. The percentage of student housing sleeping rooms equipped with a smoke detector connected to a supervised fire alarm system.
3. The number of malicious fire alarms that occur in student housing per year.
4. The number of unwanted fire alarms that occur in student housing per year.
5. The banning of certain hazardous items and activities in residence halls, like candles, smoking, halogen lamps, etc.
6. The percentage of student housing fire alarm systems that, if activated, result in a signal being transmitted to a monitored location, where security investigates before notifying the fire department.
7. The percentage of student housing fire alarm systems that, if activated, result in a signal being transmitted immediately to a continuously monitored location, which can then immediately notify the fire department to initiate a response.
8. How often fire safety rules-compliance inspections are conducted each year.

Schools that did not report answers to a sufficient number of questions receive a Fire Safety Rating of 60* (60 with an asterisk). You can also find Fire Safety Ratings for the *Best 377 Colleges* (and several additional schools) in our *Complete Book of Colleges,* 2013 Edition. On page 53 of this book, you'll find a list of the schools with 99 (the highest score) Fire Safety Ratings.

Green Rating

We asked all the schools we collect data from annually to answer a number of questions that evaluate the comprehensive measure of their performance as an environmentally aware and responsible institution. The questions were developed in consultation with ecoAmerica (www.ecoAmerica.org), a research and partnership-based environmental nonprofit that convened an expert committee to design this comprehensive rating system, and cover: 1) whether students have a campus quality of life that is both healthy and sustainable; 2) how well a school is preparing students not only for employment in the clean energy economy of the twenty-first century, but also for citizenship in a world now defined by environmental challenges; and 3) how environmentally responsible a school's policies are. Each school's responses to ten questions were considered when calculating its Green Rating. They cover:

1. The percentage of food expenditures that go toward local, organic, or otherwise environmentally preferable food.
2. Whether the school offers programs including free bus passes, universal access transit passes, bike sharing/renting, car sharing, carpool parking, vanpooling, or guaranteed rides home to encourage alternatives to single-passenger automobile use for students.
3. Whether the school has a formal committee with participation from students that is devoted to advancing sustainability on campus.
4. Whether new buildings are required to be LEED Silver certified or comparable.
5. The schools overall waste diversion rate.
6. Whether the school has an environmental studies major, minor or concentration.
7. Whether the school has an 'environmental literacy' requirement.
8. Whether a school has produced a publicly available greenhouse gas emissions inventory and adopted a climate action plan consistent with eighty percent greenhouse gas reductions by 2050 targets.
9. What percentage of the school's energy consumption, including heating/cooling and electrical, is derived from renewable resources (this definition included 'green tags' but not nuclear or large scale hydro power).
10. Whether the school employs a dedicated full-time (or full-time equivalent) sustainability officer.

Colleges that did not supply answers to a sufficient number of the green campus questions for us to fairly compare them to other colleges receive a Green Rating of 60*. On page 53 of this book and on our website at www.princetonreview.com/green-honor-roll, you'll find a list of the schools with 99 (the highest score) Green Ratings.

Check out our free downloadable resource, The Princeton Review's *Guide to 322 Green Colleges*, at www.princetonreview.com/green-guide.

Type of school
Whether the school is public or private.

Affiliation
Any religious order with which the school is affiliated.

Environment
Whether the campus is located in an urban, suburban, or rural setting.

Total undergrad enrollment
The total number of degree-seeking undergraduates who attend the school.

"% male/female" through "# countries represented"
Demographic information about the full-time undergraduate student body, including male to female ratio, ethnicity, and the number of countries represented by the student body. Also included are the percentages of the student body who are from out of state, attended a public high school, freshmen living on campus, and belong to Greek organizations.

Survey Says . . .
A snapshot of key results of our student survey. This list shows what the students we surveyed felt unusually strongly about, both positively and negatively, at their schools (see the end of this section for a detailed explanation of items on the list).

Academic Rating
On a scale of 60–99, this rating is a measure of how hard students work at the school and how much they get back for their efforts. The rating is based on results from our surveys of students and data we collect from administrators. Factors weighed included how many hours students reported that they study each day outside of class, students' assessments of their professors' teaching abilities and of their accessibility outside the classroom and the quality of students the school attracts as measured by admissions statistics.

% of students returning for sophomore year
The percentage of degree-seeking freshmen returning for sophomore year.

4-year graduation rate
The percentage of degree-seeking undergraduate students graduating in four years or less.

6-year graduation rate
The percentage of degree-seeking undergraduate students graduating within six years.

Calendar
The school's schedule of academic terms. A "semester" schedule has two long terms, usually starting in September and January. A "trimester" schedule has three terms, one usually beginning before Christmas and two after. A "quarterly" schedule has four terms, which go by very quickly: the entire term, including exams, usually lasts only nine or ten weeks. A "4-1-4" schedule is like a semester schedule, but with a month-long term in between the fall and spring semesters. (Similarly, a "4-4-1" has a short term following two longer semesters.) It is always best to call the admissions office for details.

Student/faculty ratio
The ratio of full-time undergraduate instructional faculty members to all undergraduates.

Profs interesting rating

On a scale of 60–99, this rating is based on levels of surveyed students' agreement or disagreement with the statement: "Your instructors are good teachers."

Profs accessible rating

On a scale of 60–99, this rating is based on levels of surveyed students' agreement or disagreement with the statement: "Your instructors are accessible outside the classroom."

Most common regular class size; Most common lab size

The most commonly occurring class size for regular courses and for labs/discussion sections.

Most popular majors

The majors with the highest enrollments at the school.

Admissions Selectivity Rating

On a scale of 60–99, this rating is a measure of how competitive admission is at the school. This rating is determined by several factors, including the class rank of entering freshmen, test scores, and percentage of applicants accepted.

% of applicants accepted

The percentage of applicants to whom the school offered admission.

% of acceptees attending

The percentage of accepted students who eventually enrolled at the school.

accepting a place on wait list

The number of students who decided to take a place on the wait list when offered this option.

admitted from wait list

The percentage of applicants who opted to take a place on the wait list and were subsequently offered admission. These figures will vary tremendously from college to college, and should be a consideration when deciding whether to accept a place on a college's wait list.

of early decision applicants

The number of students who applied under the college's early decision or early action plan.

accepted early decision

The percentage of early decision or early action applicants who were admitted under this plan. By the nature of these plans, the vast majority who are admitted ultimately enroll.

Range SAT Critical Reading, Range SAT Math, Range SAT Writing, Range ACT Composite

The average and the middle fifty percent range of test scores for entering freshmen.

Don't be discouraged from applying to the school of your choice even if your combined SAT scores are 80 or even 120 points below the average, because you may still have a chance of getting in. Remember that many schools value other aspects of your application (e.g., your grades, how good a match you make with the school) more heavily than test scores.

Minimum TOEFL

The minimum test score necessary for entering freshmen who are required to take the TOEFL (Test of English as a Foreign Language). Most schools will require all international students or non-native English speakers to take the TOEFL in order to be considered for admission.

Average HS GPA

The average grade point average of entering freshman. We report this on a scale of 1.0–4.0 (occasionally colleges report averages on a 100 scale, in which case we report those figures). This is one of the key factors in college admissions.

% graduated top 10%, top 25%, top 50% of class

Of those students for whom class rank was reported, the percentage of entering freshmen who ranked in the top tenth, quarter, and half of their high school classes.

Early decision/action deadlines

The deadline for submission of application materials under the early decision or early action plan.

Early decision, early action, priority, and regular admission deadlines

The dates by which all materials must be postmarked (we'd suggest "received in the office") in order to be considered for admission under each particular admissions option/cycle for matriculation in the fall term.

Early decision, early action, priority, and regular admission notification

The dates by which you can expect a decision on your application under each admissions option/cycle.

Nonfall registration

Some schools will allow incoming students to register and begin attending classes at times other than the fall term, which is the traditional beginning of the academic calendar year. Other schools will allow you to register for classes only if you can begin in the fall term. A simple "yes" or "no" in this category indicates the school's policy on nonfall registration.

Applicants also look at

These lists are based on information we receive directly from the colleges. Admissions officers are annually given the opportunity to review and suggest alterations to these lists for their schools, as most schools track as closely as they can other schools to which applicants they accepted applied, and whether the applicants chose their school over the other schools, or vice versa.

Financial Aid Rating

On a scale of 60–99, this rating is a measure of the financial aid the school awards and how satisfied students are with the aid they receive. It is based on school-reported data on financial aid and students' responses to the survey question, "If you receive financial aid, how satisfied are you with your financial aid package?" On page 53 of this book you'll find a list of the schools with 99 (the highest score) Financial Aid Ratings.

Annual in-state tuition

The tuition at the school, or for public colleges, the cost of tuition for a resident of the school's state. Usually much lower than out-of-state tuition for state-supported public schools.

Annual out-of-state tuition

For public colleges, the tuition for a non-resident of the school's state. This entry appears only for public colleges, since tuition at private colleges is generally the same regardless of state of residence.

Required fees

Any additional costs students must pay beyond tuition in order to attend the school. These often include fitness center fees and the like. A few state schools may not officially charge in-state students tuition, but those students are still responsible for hefty fees.

Tuition and fees

In cases when schools do not report separate figures for tuition and required fees, we offer this total of the two.

Comprehensive fee

A few schools report one overall fee that reflects the total cost of tuition, room and board, and required fees. If you'd like to see how this figure breaks down, we recommend contacting the school.

Room and board

Estimated annual room and board costs.

Books and supplies

Estimated annual cost of necessary textbooks and/or supplies.

% needy frosh receiving need-based scholarship or grant aid

The percentage of all degree-seeking freshmen who were determined to have need and received any need-based scholarship or grant.

% needy UG receiving need-based scholarship or grant aid

The percentage of all degree-seeking undergraduates who were determined to have need and received any need-based scholarship or grant.

% needy frosh receiving non-need-based scholarship or grant aid

The percentage of all degree-seeking freshmen, determined to have need, receiving any non-need based scholarship or grant aid.

% needy ugrads receiving non-need-based scholarship or grant aid

The percentage of all degree-seeking undergraduates, determined to have need, receiving any non-need based scholarship or grant aid.

% needy frosh receiving need-based self-help aid

The percentage of all degree-seeking freshmen, determined to have need, who received any need-based self-help aid.

% needy ugrads receiving need-based self-help aid

The percentage of all degree-seeking undergraduates, determined to have need, who received any need-based self-help aid.

% frosh receiving any financial aid

The percentage of all degree-seeking freshmen receiving any financial aid (need-based, merit-based, gift aid).

% UG receiving any financial aid

The percentage of all degree-seeking undergraduates receiving any financial aid (need-based, merit-based, gift aid).

% UG borrow to pay for school

The percentage who borrowed at any time through any loan programs (institutional, state, Federal Perkins, Federal Stafford Subsidized and Unsubsidized, private loans that were certified by your institution, etc., exclude parent loans). Includes both Federal Direct Student Loans and Federal Family Education Loans (prior to the FFEL program ending in June 2010).

% frosh and ugrad need fully met

The percentage of needy degree-seeking students whose needs was fully met (excludes PLUS loans, unsubsidized loans and private alternative loans).

Average % of frosh and ugrad need met

On average, the percentage of need that was met of students who were awarded any need-based aid. Excludes any aid that was awarded in excess of need as well as any resources that were awarded to replace EFC (PLUS loans, unsubsidized loans and private alternative loans).

Avg Indebtedness

The average per-borrower cumulative undergraduate indebtedness of those who borrowed at any time through any loan programs (institutional, state, Federal Perkins, Federal Stafford Subsidized and Unsubsidized, private loans that were certified by your institution, etc.; exclude parent loans).

Nota Bene: The statistical data reported in this book, unless otherwise noted, was collected from the profiled colleges from the fall of 2011 through the spring of 2012. In some cases, we were unable to publish the most recent data because schools did not report the necessary statistics to us in time, despite our repeated outreach efforts. Because the enrollment and financial statistics, as well as application and financial aid deadlines, fluctuate from one year to another, we recommend that you check with the schools to make sure you have the most current information before applying.

Students Say

This section shares the straight-from-the-campus feedback we get from the school's most important customers: The students attending them. It summarizes the opinions of freshman through seniors we've surveyed and it includes direct quotes from scores of them. When appropriate, it also incorporates statistics provided by the schools. The Students Say section is divided into three subsections: Academics, Life, and Student Body. The Academics section describes how hard students work and how satisfied they are with the education they are getting. It also often tells you which programs or academic departments students rated most favorably and how professors interact with students. Student opinion regarding administrative departments also works its way into this section. The Life section describes life outside the classroom and addresses questions ranging from "How comfortable are the dorms?" to "How popular are fraternities and sororities?" In this section, students describe what they do for entertainment both on-campus and off, providing a clear picture of the social environment at their particular school. The Student Body section will give you the lowdown on the types of students the school attracts and how the students view the level of interaction among various groups, including those of different ethnic, socioeconomic, and religious backgrounds.

All quotations in these sections are from students' responses to open-ended questions on our survey. We select quotations based on the accuracy with which they reflect overall student opinion about the school as conveyed in the survey results.

Admissions

This section lets you know which aspects of your application are most important to the admissions officers at the school. It also lists the high school curricular prerequisites for applicants, which standardized tests (if any) are required, and special information about the school's admissions process (e.g., Do minority students and legacies, for example, receive special consideration? Are there any unusual application requirements for applicants to special programs?).

Financial Aid

Here you'll found out what you need to know about the financial aid process at the school, namely what forms you need and what types of merit-based aid and loans are available. Information about need-based aid is contained in the financial aid sidebar. This section includes specific deadline dates for submission of materials as reported by the colleges. We strongly encourage students seeking financial aid to file all forms—federal, state, and institutional—carefully, fully, and on time.

The Inside Word

This section gives you the inside scoop on what it takes to gain admission to the school. It reflects our own insights about each school's admissions process and acceptance trends. (We visit scores of colleges each year and talk with hundreds of admissions officers in order to glean this info.) It also incorporates information from institutional data we collect and our surveys over the years of students at the school.

From the Admissions Office

This section presents the key things the school's admissions office would like you to know about their institution. For schools that did not respond to our invitation to supply text for this space, we excerpted an appropriate passage from the school's catalog, web site, or other admissions literature. For this section, we also invited schools to submit a brief paragraph explaining their admissions policies regarding the SAT (especially the Writing portion of the exam) and the SAT Subject Tests. We are pleased that nearly every school took this opportunity to clarify its policies as we know there has been some student and parent confusion about how these scores are evaluated for admission.

Survey Says

Our Survey Says list, located in the Campus Life sidebar on each school's two-page spread, is based entirely on the results of our student survey. In other words, the items on this list are based on the opinions of the students we surveyed at those schools (not on any quantitative analysis of library size, endowment, etc.). These items reveal popular or unpopular trends on campus for the purpose of providing a snapshot of life on that campus only. The appearance of a Survey Says item in the sidebar does not reflect the popularity of that item relative to its popularity among the student bodies at other schools. To ascertain the relative popularity of certain items/trends on campus, see the appropriate ranking (e.g., for the Survey Says item

"Career Services are Great," see the "Best Career Services" ranking). Some of the terms that appear on the Survey Says list are not entirely self-explanatory; these terms are defined below.

Different types of students interact: We asked students whether students from different class and ethnic backgrounds interacted frequently and easily. When students' collective response is "yes," the heading "Different types of students interact" appears on the list. When the collective student response indicates there are not many interactions between students from different class and ethnic backgrounds, the phrase "Students are cliquish" appears on the list. Note: This topic is not based on demographic data about the student body.

No one cheats: We asked students how prevalent cheating is at their school. If students reported cheating to be rare, the term "No one cheats" shows up on the list.

Students are happy: This category reflects student responses to the question "Overall, how happy are you?"

Students are very religious or Students aren't religious: We asked students how religious students are at their school. Their responses are reflected in this category.

Diverse student types on campus: We asked students whether their student body is made up of a variety of ethnic groups. This category reflects their answers to this question. This heading shows up as "Diversity lacking on campus" or "Diverse student types on campus." It does not reflect any institutional data on this subject.

Students get along with local community: This category reflects student responses to a question concerning how well the student body gets along with residents of the college town or community.

Career services are great: This category reflects student opinion on the quality of career/job placement services on campus.

About Those College Ranking Lists

Finding a college that has terrific academics is easy. There are hundreds of academically great colleges out there. Their campus cultures, student bodies, and school offerings, however, differ widely. Finding the academically great school that is right for you is the tough part. Hence, we compile not one ranking list but sixty-two unique lists, each one reporting the top twenty (or in some cases bottom twenty) schools from our Best Colleges book in a specific category.

None of the lists are based on what we think of the schools (though members of the media, the public, and school administrators mistakenly credit or blame us for the results, saying "According to The Princeton Review, X school is the best in the nation for…" or "The Princeton Review ranks Y school the tenth most…."). In fact, the only thing we say is that all of the 377 colleges in this book are outstanding (hence, the "Best" designation). It's what students think of their schools—how they rate various aspects of their colleges' offerings and what they report to us about their campus experiences—that results in a school's appearance on our ranking lists.

Here you won't find the colleges in the book ranked hierarchically, 1 to 377. We think such lists—particularly those driven by and perpetuating a "best academics" mania—are not useful for the people they are supposed to serve (college applicants). More and more college administrators—including several at schools ranked high on these lists—agree. In fact, the primary reason we developed this book was to give applicants and parents better and broader information that will help them winnow a list of colleges right for them.

About eighty-five percent of the schools in our book end up on one or more of the lists in each edition. The students are the raters—we are simply the folks who compile the ranking lists based on their opinions. To college officials happy about the lists their schools are on, we say don't thank us, we're just the messengers. To college officials unhappy about the lists their schools are on (and unsurprisingly, it is mainly they who say our student survey has no validity whatsoever), we say don't blame us, we're just the messengers.

All of these ranking lists are based entirely on students' answers to questions on our surveys (e.g., our "Best Campus Food" list and inverse list, "Is it Food?" are each based on the single survey question, "How do you rate your campus food?") or students' answers to a combination of survey questions (e.g., our "Party Schools" list and our inverse list, "Stone-Cold Sober Schools" are each based on students' answers to survey questions concerning the use of alcohol and drugs on their campuses, the popularity of the frat/sorority scene on their campuses, and the number of hours they say they study each day outside of class time).

Each list covers one of many aspects of a college's character that can be helpful in deciding if it's the right or wrong place for an individual student. The lists report on a wide range of issues that may be important, either singly or, more likely, in combination. Our ranking lists cover: financial aid, campus facilities and amenities, extracurriculars, town-gown relations, the student body's political leanings, social life, race/class relations, gay-friendly (or not so friendly) atmosphere, career services, athletic facilities, and more.

> *"It's what students think of their schools—how they rate various aspects of their colleges' offerings and what they report to us about their campus experiences—that results in a school's appearance on our ranking lists."*

Our newest addition is one ranking list category: "Students Most Satisfied with Overall Experience."

The ranking list category that media covers the most (though it appears fifty-seventh among the lists in our "School Rankings and Lists" section, and is only referenced briefly in our press materials) is the "Party Schools" list. It's even been the subject of a Doonesbury cartoon (which appears on the frontispiece of this book) as well as a USA TODAY editorial in which the paper commended us for reporting the list, calling it "a public service." Our "Party Schools" list draws a wide range of reaction every year. Some students complain that their college didn't make the list, while others are irate because their college did. One reporter from the *Washington Post* whose alma mater was number one on the list several years back wrote a column in which he argued that the ranking was grossly undeserved: He had recently visited his campus and pronounced the then current student body lame as "partiers" compared to the revelers of his day.

Many incorrectly assume that an institution that shows up on the "Party Schools" list is not an advisable college to attend. We recommend all 377 schools in this book as outstanding institutions at which to earn one's college degree. But just as the schools on our "LGBT-Unfriendly" list may not be ideal campuses for gay students, the schools on our "Party Schools" list may not be ideal for students seeking a campus at which the use of alcohol and drugs and the frat/sorority scene is, well, less exuberant.

On the other hand, no one should make the mistake of assuming that the colleges and universities that don't show up on our "Party Schools" list are in any way insulated from the influences of alcohol and drugs on their campuses. An oft-quoted Harvard University School of Public Health study published in 2000 found that forty-five percent of undergraduates, in general, binge drink (consume five or more alcoholic beverages in one sitting for men, four drinks or more for women).[1] These facts are alarming, as they should be. College administrators face tremendous challenges in creating and enforcing campus alcohol and drug use/abuse policies. Many struggle with problems resulting from the prevalence of bars and liquor stores near their campuses; at some universities that have appeared on our "Party Schools" list there are more than 100 such establishments within a few miles from the campus. "Dry campus" policies often exacerbate the problem, driving drinking off-campus, making it even more dangerous for students.

Despite the claims of some administrators at colleges that have repeatedly made our "Party School" list that our reporting this list promotes drinking on campuses (a group of such administrators receiving funding through the American Medical Association to address their campus alcohol problems made the news several years back with this claim, after which USA TODAY published the editorial praising our ranking as a "public service"), we neither encourage nor discourage students who wish to drink. None of our lists promote behavior: They report on it, plain and simple. What we promote is information.

What we do say to college students—as we have said in this very section of this book for more than 10 years—is this: If you're going to drink, do it safely, smartly, responsibly, and legally. If you're going off campus to drink, don't drive back drunk—get a designated driver. Don't let a peer situation (fraternity rush, etc.) put you in jeopardy—it's simply not worth it. Don't use alcohol or drugs as a badge of your coolness—there's not much of a fine line between someone who's socially engaging and someone who's totally disengaging because he or she has performed a chemical auto-lobotomy. Last, don't simply take responsibility for yourself; remember to keep an eye on your friends, and never leave them passed out and alone.

---

1 Harvard University School of Public Health. "College Student Binge Drinking Rates Remain High Despite Efforts by School Administrations." www.hsph.harvard.edu/news/press-releases/2000-releases/press03142000.html.

Finally, we would like to thank all the college officials, college counselors, advisors, students, and parents, who have made this annual guide possible by supporting us these past twenty years. Our ranking lists have, collectively, been based on surveys of more than 750,000 students whose input has been vital to our publication of this book. We know that it has helped students find great colleges perfect for them, and it has brought to the colleges in our book many outstanding students who otherwise may not have considered attending their institutions.

WE WANT TO HEAR FROM YOU

To all of our readers, we welcome your feedback on how we can continue to improve this guide. We hope you will share with us your comments, questions, and suggestions. Please contact us at editorialsupport@review.com. We welcome it.

To college applicants, we wish you all the best in your college search. And when you get to your campuses and settle in to your college life, come back to us online; participate in our survey for this book at http://survey.review.com. Let your honest comments about your schools guide prospective students who want your help answering the $64,000 question (goodness knows, the sticker price at some schools may be that high or even higher!): "Which is the best college for me?"

PART 2

School Rankings and Lists

We present our 62 "Top 20" ranking lists in eight categories.

Academics/Administration

Quality of Life

Politics

Campus Life

Town Life

Extracurriculars

Social Scene

Under each list heading, we tell you the survey question or assessment that we used to tabulate the list. We tally student responses to several questions on our survey for our lists "Best Classroom Experience," "Best Quality of Life," and the five lists in our Schools by Type rankings (including our "Party Schools" and "Stone-Cold Sober Schools" lists). Be aware that all of our 62 ranking lists are based entirely on our student surveys. They do not reflect our opinions of the schools. They are entirely the result of what students attending these schools tell us about them: It's how students rate their own schools and what they report to us about their campus experiences at them that make our ranking lists so unusual. After all, what better way is there to judge a school than by what its customers—its students—say about it?

ACADEMICS/ADMINISTRATION

Best Classroom Experience

Based on a combination of survey questions concerning teachers, classroom/lab facilities, classes attended, and amount of in-class discussion

1. Swarthmore College
2. Reed College
3. Grinnell College
4. United States Military Academy
5. Whitman College
6. Wellesley College
7. Bennington College
8. St. John's College (MD)
9. University of Richmond
10. Franklin W. Olin College of Engineering
11. Sarah Lawrence College
12. Wabash College
13. Middlebury College
14. Thomas Aquinas College
15. Mount Holyoke College
16. Bard College at Simon's Rock (MA)
17. Beloit College
18. Scripps College
19. Denison University
20. Carleton College

Students Study the Most

How many out-of-class hours do you spend studying each day?

1. California Institute of Technology
2. Franklin W. Olin College of Engineering
3. Reed College
4. Massachusetts Institute of Technology
5. Harvard College
6. Princeton University
7. United States Military Academy
8. The University of Chicago
9. Harvey Mudd College
10. Haverford College
11. Middlebury College
12. Davidson College
13. Marlboro College
14. Carnegie Mellon University
15. Bennington College
16. The Cooper Union for the Advancement of Science and Art
17. Grinnell College
18. Hillsdale College
19. Gettysburg College
20. Bard College at Simon's Rock (MA)

Students Study the Least
How many out-of-class hours do you spend studying each day?

1. The University of Alabama—Tuscaloosa
2. University of North Dakota
3. West Virginia University
4. City University of New York—Baruch College
5. University of Mississippi
6. University of Maryland, College Park
7. Florida State University
8. University of Iowa
9. James Madison University
10. University of Alabama at Birmingham
11. St. John's University (NY)
12. University of South Carolina—Columbia
13. Catawba College
14. Rider University
15. University of New Orleans
16. University of Idaho
17. University of Rhode Island
18. Ohio University—Athens
19. University of Florida
20. University of Maine

Professors Get High Marks
Are your instructors good teachers?

1. Sarah Lawrence College
2. Reed College
3. Wellesley College
4. Hillsdale College
5. Claremont McKenna College
6. Harvey Mudd College
7. Middlebury College
8. Hamilton College
9. Kenyon College
10. Colby College
11. Austin College
12. Millsaps College
13. St. John's College (MD)
14. Bard College at Simon's Rock (MA)
15. Bard College (NY)
16. Swarthmore College
17. Marlboro College
18. Whitman College
19. Franklin W. Olin College of Engineering
20. Carleton College

Professors Get Low Marks
Are your instructors good teachers?

1. Rutgers, The State University of New Jersey—New Brunswick
2. University of Illinois at Urbana-Champaign
3. United States Merchant Marine Academy
4. California Institute of Technology
5. University of North Dakota
6. Indiana University of Pennsylvania
7. New Jersey Institute of Technology
8. University of California—San Diego
9. University of Rhode Island
10. University of Connecticut
11. Iowa State University
12. University of Kentucky
13. Stevens Institute of Technology
14. Georgia Institute of Technology
15. City University of New York—Baruch College
16. University of Minnesota—Twin Cities
17. University of Idaho
18. University of California—Davis
19. Temple University
20. Michigan Technological University

Most Accessible Professors
Are your instructors accessible outside the classroom?

1. United States Military Academy
2. Southern Methodist University
3. United States Coast Guard Academy
4. Claremont McKenna College
5. Davidson College
6. United States Naval Academy
7. Sweet Briar College
8. Hillsdale College
9. University of Puget Sound
10. Wellesley College
11. Pomona College
12. Reed College
13. Skidmore College
14. Wittenberg University
15. St. John's College (MD)
16. Hampden-Sydney College
17. Randolph College
18. United States Air Force Academy
19. Wabash College
20. Whitman College

Least Accessible Professors
Are your instructors accessible outside the classroom?

1. McGill University
2. United States Merchant Marine Academy
3. New Jersey Institute of Technology
4. University of Kentucky
5. Georgia Institute of Technology
6. University of Maine
7. University of South Florida
8. Stevens Institute of Technology
9. St. John's University (NY)
10. Rutgers, The State University of New Jersey—New Brunswick
11. Temple University
12. Sonoma State University

13. Howard University
14. Hampton University
15. University of California—Los Angeles
16. Portland State University
17. University of Illinois at Urbana-Champaign
18. Illinois Institute of Technology
19. Michigan State University
20. State University of New York—Stony Brook University

Class Discussions Encouraged

How much of your overall class time is devoted to discussion as opposed to lectures?

1. Colorado College
2. Champlain College
3. Bennington College
4. Sarah Lawrence College
5. Prescott College
6. St. John's College (NM)
7. St. John's College (MD)
8. Wagner College
9. University of Redlands
10. Bard College at Simon's Rock (MA)
11. Thomas Aquinas College
12. Reed College
13. Marlboro College
14. College of the Atlantic
15. United States Military Academy
16. Grinnell College
17. Rollins College
18. Sweet Briar College
19. Wesleyan College
20. New College of Florida

Most Popular Study Abroad Program

How popular is studying abroad at your school?

1. Elon University
2. Goucher College
3. Dartmouth College
4. Kalamazoo College
5. Austin College
6. American University
7. Marist College
8. Tufts University
9. University of Dallas
10. Georgetown University
11. Eckerd College
12. Indiana University—Bloomington
13. Colby College
14. University of Denver
15. Boston University
16. Pepperdine University
17. Susquehanna University
18. Bentley University
19. Skidmore College
20. Willamette University

Best Health Services

Based on students' assessments of student health services/facilities on campus

1. Pennsylvania State University—University Park
2. University of California—Los Angeles
3. The University of Texas at Austin
4. University of Pittsburgh—Pittsburgh Campus
5. University of Georgia
6. United States Military Academy
7. Villanova University
8. University of Minnesota—Twin Cities
9. California State University—Stanislaus
10. University of California—Davis
11. Whitman College
12. Calvin College
13. North Carolina State University
14. Rice University
15. The College of Wooster
16. Baylor University
17. University of Oregon
18. Georgia Institute of Technology
19. Willamette University
20. Susquehanna University

Best Career Services

Based on students' rating of campus career/job-placement services

1. Northeastern University
2. Pennsylvania State University—University Park
3. Claremont McKenna College
4. University of Richmond
5. Clemson University
6. University of Florida
7. Southern Methodist University
8. Lafayette College
9. Rensselaer Polytechnic Institute
10. American University
11. Barnard College
12. Grove City College
13. Stevens Institute of Technology
14. Tulane University
15. University of Southern California
16. Bentley University
17. Missouri University of Science and Technology
18. Virginia Tech
19. University of Pittsburgh—Pittsburgh Campus
20. University of Texas at Austin

Best College Library

Based on students' assessment of library facilities

1. Harvard College
2. United States Military Academy
3. Columbia University
4. Stanford University
5. Emory University
6. Yale University
7. Hampden-Sydney College
8. The University of Chicago
9. Princeton University
10. Middlebury College
11. Brigham Young University (UT)
12. University of Wisconsin—Madison
13. Cornell University
14. The College of New Jersey
15. West Virginia University
16. University of Virginia
17. Dartmouth College
18. Colgate University
19. University of Michigan—Ann Arbor
20. Loyola Marymount University

This Is a Library?

Based on students' assessment of library facilities

1. Clarkson University
2. Bradley University
3. United States Merchant Marine Academy
4. Tuskegee University
5. University of Dallas
6. Prescott College
7. Howard University
8. College of the Atlantic
9. Duquesne University
10. Bard College at Simon's Rock (MA)
11. Bard College (NY)
12. Seattle University
13. Emerson College
14. Montana Tech of the University of Montana
15. Drexel University
16. Green Mountain College
17. University of Hawaii at Manoa
18. Juniata College
19. Birmingham-Southern College
20. Wells College

Great Financial Aid

Based on students' assessments of how satisfied they are with their financial aid package

1. Princeton University
2. University of Virginia
3. New College of Florida
4. Swarthmore College
5. Yale University
6. Pomona College
7. Claremont McKenna College
8. Columbia University
9. Thomas Aquinas College
10. Vassar College
11. Washington University in St. Louis
12. Stanford University
13. Rice University
14. Cornell College
15. Beloit College
16. Hillsdale College
17. Franklin W. Olin College of Engineering
18. Grinnell College
19. University of Redlands
20. Colgate University

Financial Aid Not So Great

Based on students' assessments of how satisfied they are with their financial aid package

1. New York University
2. Pennsylvania State University—University Park
3. University of Maryland—College Park
4. University of Delaware
5. Quinnipiac University
6. Duquesne University
7. Emerson College
8. Villanova University
9. Spelman College
10. Colorado State University
11. Providence College
12. Grove City College
13. Hofstra University
14. Miami University
15. Sonoma State University
16. University of California—Santa Cruz
17. Elon University
18. DePaul University
19. University of Wisconsin—Madison
20. University of Washington

Best-Run Colleges

Overall, how smoothly is your school run?

1. Elon University
2. Rice University
3. Claremont McKenna College
4. University of Southern California
5. Washington University in St. Louis
6. Pomona College
7. The University of North Carolina at Chapel Hill
8. Stanford University
9. United States Coast Guard Academy
10. Bowdoin College
11. Rose-Hulman Institute of Technology
12. Kansas State University
13. Princeton University
14. Georgia Institute of Technology

15. Clemson University
16. Brigham Young University (UT)
17. Whitman College
18. Wheaton College (IL)
19. Yale University
20. Wofford College

Administrators Get Low Marks

Overall, how smoothly is your school run?

1. New York University
2. United States Merchant Marine Academy
3. Eugene Lang College
4. Wells College
5. Hampshire College
6. Howard University
7. University of New Orleans
8. City University of New York—Baruch College
9. Randolph College
10. New Jersey Institute of Technology
11. Hampton University
12. St. John's University (NY)
13. Tuskegee University
14. University of Hawaii at Manoa
15. Illinois Institute of Technology
16. Catholic University of America
17. State University of New York—Purchase College
18. Manhattanville College
19. University of New Mexico
20. University of Rhode Island

Their Students Love These Colleges

Overall, how satisfied are you with your school?

1. Claremont McKenna College
2. Rice University
3. Virginia Tech
4. Washington University in St. Louis
5. Stanford University
6. Pomona College
7. Pennsylvania State University—University Park
8. Clemson University
9. Middlebury College
10. University of Dayton
11. University of California—Santa Barbara
12. Whitman College
13. Kansas State University
14. Carleton College
15. Dartmouth College
16. Vanderbilt University
17. Yale University
18. Franklin W. Olin College of Engineering
19. Loyola Marymount University
20. Swarthmore College

QUALITY OF LIFE

Happiest Students

Overall, how happy are you?

1. Rice University
2. Bowdoin College
3. University of California—Santa Barbara
4. Clemson University
5. Vanderbilt University
6. Claremont McKenna College
7. Thomas Aquinas College
8. Kansas State University
9. University of Southern California
10. Pomona College
11. Stanford University
12. University of Mississippi
13. Pennsylvania State University—University Park
14. Brown University
15. Southern Methodist University
16. University of Dayton
17. Hamilton College
18. Loyola Marymount University
19. Washington University in St. Louis
20. Occidental College

Least Happy Students

Overall, how happy are you?

1. Montana Tech of the University of Montana
2. Marywood University
3. New Jersey Institute of Technology
4. United States Merchant Marine Academy
5. Indiana University of Pennsylvania
6. United States Naval Academy
7. Clarkson University
8. Illinois Institute of Technology
9. University of Maine
10. City University of New York—Baruch College
11. University of North Dakota
12. University of Hawaii at Manoa
13. Manhattanville College
14. McGill University
15. United States Coast Guard Academy
16. Xavier University of Louisiana
17. Rider University
18. California Institute of Technology
19. Alfred University
20. Suffolk University

Most Beautiful Campus

Based on students' rating of campus beauty

1. Florida Southern College
2. Princeton University
3. Sweet Briar College
4. University of Mississippi

5. Lewis & Clark College
6. Colgate University
7. University of California—Santa Cruz
8. Rollins College
9. Rhodes College
10. Mount Holyoke College
11. Pepperdine University
12. Warren Wilson College
13. Dartmouth College
14. University of Richmond
15. Ohio University—Athens
16. United States Military Academy
17. Quinnipiac University
18. University of Notre Dame
19. Hanover College
20. University of San Diego

Least Beautiful Campus

Based on students' rating of campus beauty

1. Case Western Reserve University
2. Harvey Mudd College
3. New Jersey Institute of Technology
4. Clarkson University
5. University of Dallas
6. University of Tennessee
7. State University of New York—Purchase College
8. Rutgers, The State University of New Jersey—New Brunswick
9. Rochester Institute of Technology
10. Illinois Institute of Technology
11. Xavier University of Louisiana
12. Indiana University of Pennsylvania
13. New York University
14. University of North Dakota
15. Rider University
16. City University of New York—Hunter College
17. Clark University
18. Montana Tech of the University of Montana
19. Temple University
20. Prescott College

Easiest Campus to Get Around

Based on students' assessments of ease of getting around their campus

1. Davidson College
2. Dartmouth College
3. St. John's College (NM)
4. Franklin W. Olin College of Engineering
5. Wabash College
6. St. John's College (MD)
7. Claremont McKenna College
8. Skidmore College
9. Reed College
10. New College of Florida
11. Webb Institute
12. Susquehanna University
13. Rose-Hulman Institute of Technology
14. Macalester College
15. Columbia University
16. Austin College
17. Amherst College
18. The College of Idaho
19. Thomas Aquinas College
20. Rhodes College

Best Campus Food

Based on students' rating of campus food

1. Bowdoin College
2. Virginia Tech
3. University of Massachusetts Amherst
4. James Madison University
5. Washington University in St. Louis
6. Wheaton College (IL)
7. College of the Atlantic
8. Cornell University
9. Bryn Mawr College
10. Saint Anselm College
11. Bates College
12. University of Notre Dame
13. St. Olaf College
14. Purdue University—West Lafayette
15. University of Georgia
16. Scripps College
17. Tufts University
18. Miami University
19. Gettysburg College
20. St. Lawrence University

Is It Food?

Based on students' rating of campus food

1. Fordham University
2. New College of Florida
3. Wells College
4. Hampden-Sydney College
5. Ohio Northern University
6. St. John's College (NM)
7. United States Merchant Marine Academy
8. Catawba College
9. Drew University
10. Hampton University
11. Alfred University
12. Amherst College
13. State University of New York at Albany
14. Flagler College
15. Missouri University of Science and Technology
16. Hiram College
17. Catholic University of America
18. Wesleyan College
19. Denison University
20. Coe College

Best College Dorms

Based on students' rating of dorm comfort

1. Washington University in St. Louis
2. Smith College
3. Loyola University Maryland
4. Franklin W. Olin College of Engineering
5. Bennington College
6. Bowdoin College
7. Scripps College
8. Skidmore College
9. Bryn Mawr College
10. Amherst College
11. Christopher Newport University
12. Northeastern University
13. The George Washington University
14. Pomona College
15. Texas Christian University
16. Dartmouth College
17. Sonoma State University
18. Trinity University
19. Sweet Briar College
20. The University of Chicago

Is That a Dorm?

Based on students' rating of dorm comfort

1. United States Merchant Marine Academy
2. Tuskegee University
3. University of New Mexico
4. United States Coast Guard Academy
5. University of Washington
6. Hampton University
7. College of the Ozarks
8. United States Naval Academy
9. Whittier College
10. Alfred University
11. Cornell College
12. Prescott College
13. State University of New York at Albany
14. Manhattanville College
15. Spelman College
16. Rider University
17. University of Wyoming
18. University of South Florida
19. Duquesne University
20. The University of North Carolina at Greensboro

Best Quality of Life

Based on The Princeton Review's QUALITY OF LIFE RATING (page 24)

1. Bowdoin College
2. Rice University
3. Dartmouth College
4. Kansas State University
5. Claremont McKenna College
6. Virginia Tech
7. Barnard College
8. Agnes Scott College
9. Washington University in St. Louis
10. Franklin W. Olin College of Engineering
11. Smith College
12. Brown University
13. Whitman College
14. Pomona College
15. Vanderbilt University
16. Emory University
17. Wheaton College (IL)
18. Pennsylvania State University—University Park
19. Auburn University
20. Macalester College

POLITICS

Most Conservative Students

Based on students' assessment of their personal political views

1. Texas A&M University—College Station
2. Hillsdale College
3. Thomas Aquinas College
4. Grove City College
5. University of Dallas
6. College of the Ozarks
7. United States Merchant Marine Academy
8. Auburn University
9. United States Naval Academy
10. Hampden-Sydney College
11. Brigham Young University (UT)
12. United States Military Academy
13. Wheaton College (IL)
14. Clemson University
15. United States Coast Guard Academy
16. Baylor University
17. Southern Methodist University
18. United States Air Force Academy
19. Angelo State University
20. Ohio Northern University

Most Liberal Students

Based on students' assessment of their personal political views

1. Bard College (NY)
2. Bennington College
3. Sarah Lawrence College
4. Macalester College
5. Warren Wilson College
6. College of the Atlantic
7. Reed College
8. The Evergreen State College
9. Eugene Lang College
10. Marlboro College
11. Skidmore College

12. Swarthmore College
13. Brandeis University
14. Pitzer College
15. Grinnell College
16. Lewis & Clark College
17. Smith College
18. University of Puget Sound
19. New College of Florida
20. Oberlin College

Most Politically Active Students

How popular are political/activist groups?

1. American University
2. Georgetown University
3. The George Washington University
4. Amherst College
5. New College of Florida
6. University of Southern California
7. Texas A&M University—College Station
8. Warren Wilson College
9. United States Military Academy
10. University of Maryland—College Park
11. Grinnell College
12. University of Notre Dame
13. College of the Atlantic
14. New York University
15. The University of Chicago
16. Hampshire College
17. Bard College (NY)
18. Trinity College (CT)
19. The Ohio State University—Columbus
20. University of Michigan—Ann Arbor

Election? What Election?

How popular are political/activist groups?

1. College of the Ozarks
2. Ohio Northern University
3. Becker College
4. Duke University
5. University of Scranton
6. University of Tampa
7. Stonehill College
8. Salisbury University
9. Indiana University of Pennsylvania
10. Alfred University
11. Wagner College
12. Monmouth University (NJ)
13. City University of New York—Baruch College
14. University of California—Davis
15. Rensselaer Polytechnic Institute
16. Loyola University Maryland
17. Rutgers, The State University of New Jersey—New Brunswick
18. Rose-Hulman Institute of Technology
19. The University of South Dakota
20. Nazareth College

DEMOGRAPHICS

Lots of Race/Class Interaction

Do different types of students (black/white, rich/poor) interact frequently and easily?

1. City University of New York—Hunter College
2. Temple University
3. George Mason University
4. City University of New York—Queens College
5. Babson College
6. University of Alabama at Birmingham
7. Rice University
8. University of Miami
9. Loyola University New Orleans
10. University of Maryland—College Park
11. University of New Mexico
12. Stanford University
13. California State University—Stanislaus
14. Occidental College
15. University of Toronto
16. Illinois Institute of Technology
17. State University of New York—Stony Brook University
18. Agnes Scott College
19. Franklin W. Olin College of Engineering
20. Columbia University

Little Race/Class Interaction

Do different types of students (black/white, rich/poor) interact frequently and easily?

1. Providence College
2. University of Notre Dame
3. Miami University
4. Gettysburg College
5. Quinnipiac University
6. University of New Hampshire
7. Sonoma State University
8. Catholic University of America
9. Villanova University
10. Fairfield University
11. Warren Wilson College
12. Boston College
13. United States Merchant Marine Academy
14. Texas Christian University
15. University of Dallas
16. Grove City College
17. Trinity College (CT)
18. Furman University
19. Rhodes College
20. Chapman University

LGBT-Friendly

Do students, faculty and administrators treat all persons equally, regardless of their sexual orientation and gender identity/expression?

1. Emerson College
2. University of Wisconsin—Madison
3. Stanford University
4. Franklin W. Olin College of Engineering
5. New York University
6. New College of Florida
7. Bennington College
8. Warren Wilson College
9. College of the Atlantic
10. Wellesley College
11. Smith College
12. Whitman College
13. Macalester College
14. Bryn Mawr College
15. Brandeis University
16. Sarah Lawrence College
17. Pitzer College
18. Prescott College
19. Grinnell College
20. Oberlin College

LGBT-Unfriendly

Do students, faculty and administrators treat all persons equally, regardless of their sexual orientation and gender identity/expression?

1. Grove City College
2. Hampden-Sydney College
3. College of the Ozarks
4. Wheaton College (IL)
5. University of Notre Dame
6. Catholic University of America
7. Texas A&M University—College Station
8. Wake Forest University
9. University of Rhode Island
10. Baylor University
11. Calvin College
12. Brigham Young University (UT)
13. Boston College
14. Thomas Aquinas College
15. University of Dallas
16. University of Tennessee
17. Indiana University of Pennsylvania
18. Hillsdale College
19. Pepperdine University
20. University of Wyoming

Most Religious Students

Are students very religious?

1. Brigham Young University (UT)
2. Thomas Aquinas College
3. Wheaton College (IL)
4. Hillsdale College
5. University of Dallas
6. Grove City College
7. College of the Ozarks
8. University of Notre Dame
9. Calvin College
10. Baylor University
11. Pepperdine University
12. Auburn University
13. Texas A&M University—College Station
14. Clemson University
15. Furman University
16. Kansas State University
17. Spelman College
18. United States Naval Academy
19. University of Mississippi
20. Tuskegee University

Least Religious Students

Are students very religious?

1. Reed College
2. Bennington College
3. Bard College (NY)
4. Skidmore College
5. Emerson College
6. Amherst College
7. Lewis & Clark College
8. The Evergreen State College
9. Pomona College
10. Grinnell College
11. Sarah Lawrence College
12. Macalester College
13. Bard College at Simon's Rock (MA)
14. Warren Wilson College
15. Prescott College
16. Marlboro College
17. Vassar College
18. Beloit College
19. Kalamazoo College
20. Pitzer College

TOWN LIFE

College City Gets High Marks

Based on students' assessment of the surrounding city or town

1. Georgetown University (D.C.)
2. Tulane University (LA)
3. The George Washington University (D.C.)
4. Boston University (MA)
5. New York University (NY)
6. Barnard College (NY)
7. American University (D.C.)
8. Columbia University (NY)
9. Stevens Institute of Technology (NJ)
10. University of Michigan—Ann Arbor (MI)
11. The University of North Carolina at Asheville (NC)

12. College of Charleston (SC)
13. City University of New York—Hunter College (NY)
14. DePaul University (IL)
15. University of Vermont (VT)
16. Southern Methodist University (TX)
17. Colorado State University (CO)
18. Suffolk University (MA)
19. University of Wisconsin—Madison (WI)
20. The University of Texas at Austin (TX)

College City Gets Low Marks

Based on students' assessment of the surrounding city or town

1. Tuskegee University (AL)
2. United States Coast Guard Academy (CT)
3. New Jersey Institute of Technology (NJ)
4. Albion College (MI)
5. University of the Pacific (CA)
6. Wabash College (IN)
7. Hofstra University (NY)
8. Wheaton College (MA)
9. Ohio Northern University (OH)
10. Union College (NY)
11. Baylor University (TX)
12. Bates College (ME)
13. Clark University (MA)
14. University of Notre Dame (IN)
15. Hillsdale College (MI)
16. United States Military Academy (NY)
17. Lehigh University (PA)
18. Wittenberg University (OH)
19. Beloit College (WI)
20. College of the Holy Cross (MA)

Town-Gown Relations Are Great

Do students get along well with members of the local community?

1. Clemson University (SC)
2. Kansas State University (KS)
3. Davidson College (NC)
4. Virginia Tech (VA)
5. Rice University (TX)
6. College of the Ozarks (MO)
7. Wheaton College (IL)
8. Saint Michael's College (VT)
9. Washington State University (WA)
10. Franklin W. Olin College of Engineering (MA)
11. University of Mississippi (MS)
12. Agnes Scott College (GA)
13. Auburn University (AL)
14. University of Alabama at Birmingham (AL)
15. Macalester College (MN)
16. North Carolina State University (NC)
17. Brigham Young University (UT)
18. Catawba College (NC)
19. Ripon College (WI)
20. Saint Anselm College (NH)

Town-Gown Relations Are Strained

Do students get along well with members of the local community?

1. Trinity College (CT)
2. Duke University (NC)
3. Lehigh University (PA)
4. University of Notre Dame (IN)
5. Union College (NY)
6. Northwestern University (IL)
7. Sarah Lawrence College (NY)
8. United States Merchant Marine Academy (NY)
9. University of Maryland—College Park (MD)
10. Bates College (ME)
11. Howard University (D.C.)
12. Providence College (RI)
13. New Jersey Institute of Technology (NJ)
14. Fairfield University (CT)
15. Albion College (MI)
16. Hofstra University (NY)
17. Franklin & Marshall College (PA)
18. College of the Holy Cross (MA)
19. The College of Wooster (OH)
20. Bennington College (VT)

EXTRACURRICULARS

Best Athletic Facilities

Based on students' rating of campus athletic facilities

1. United States Military Academy
2. Georgia Institute of Technology
3. West Virginia University
4. University of Maryland—College Park
5. Ohio University—Athens
6. Kenyon College
7. Loyola University Maryland
8. University of Dayton
9. University of Illinois at Urbana-Champaign
10. Southern Methodist University
11. The Ohio State University—Columbus
12. Pennsylvania State University—University Park
13. Rice University
14. Texas Christian University
15. University of South Carolina—Columbia
16. Calvin College
17. University of Richmond
18. Wabash College
19. University of Missouri
20. Bradley University

Students Pack the Stadiums

How popular are intercollegiate sports?

1. University of Notre Dame
2. The University of North Carolina at Chapel Hill
3. University of Florida
4. Florida State University
5. University of Southern California
6. University of Iowa
7. Auburn University
8. West Virginia University
9. University of Michigan—Ann Arbor
10. The Ohio State University—Columbus
11. Pennsylvania State University—University Park
12. University of Mississippi
13. University of Maryland—College Park
14. University of Georgia
15. Clemson University
16. University of Wisconsin—Madison
17. The University of Texas at Austin
18. Virginia Tech
19. University of Oklahoma
20. Villanova University

There's a Game?

How popular are intercollegiate sports?

1. Prescott College
2. College of the Atlantic
3. St. John's College (NM)
4. Bennington College
5. New College of Florida
6. Thomas Aquinas College
7. Marlboro College
8. Champlain College
9. Reed College
10. Franklin W. Olin College of Engineering
11. St. John's College (MD)
12. New York University
13. Bard College at Simon's Rock (MA)
14. University of California—Santa Cruz
15. Sarah Lawrence College
16. Bard College (NY)
17. Harvey Mudd College
18. The Evergreen State College
19. The Cooper Union for the Advancement of Science and Art
20. Emerson College

Everyone Plays Intramural Sports

How popular are intramural sports?

1. Clemson University
2. University of Notre Dame
3. Providence College
4. Grove City College
5. University of Dayton
6. United States Military Academy
7. Pennsylvania State University—University Park
8. Mercer University
9. University of Nebraska—Lincoln
10. Creighton University
11. Florida Southern College
12. Colorado College
13. United States Coast Guard Academy
14. University of Wisconsin—Madison
15. Whitman College
16. University of Florida
17. Wabash College
18. Gonzaga University
19. The University of North Carolina at Chapel Hill
20. Florida State University

Nobody Plays Intramural Sports

How popular are intramural sports?

1. Prescott College
2. New College of Florida
3. College of the Atlantic
4. Sarah Lawrence College
5. The Cooper Union for the Advancement of Science and Art
6. Spelman College
7. Emerson College
8. Reed College
9. Bennington College
10. Barnard College
11. Suffolk University
12. New York University
13. Randolph College
14. Bard College (NY)
15. Bryn Mawr College
16. Xavier University of Louisiana
17. Bard College at Simon's Rock (MA)
18. Marlboro College
19. Manhattanville College
20. Sweet Briar College

Best College Radio Station

How popular is the radio station?

1. Emerson College
2. DePauw University
3. Ithaca College
4. St. Bonaventure University
5. Seton Hall University
6. Hofstra University
7. Westminster College (PA)
8. Brown University
9. University of Puget Sound
10. The Evergreen State College
11. Guilford College
12. Bates College
13. Knox College

14. Sacred Heart University
15. Fordham University
16. University of Kansas
17. Howard University
18. The College of Wooster
19. Skidmore College
20. Chapman University

Best College Newspaper

How do you rate your campus newspaper?

1. Pennsylvania State University—University Park
2. The University of North Carolina at Chapel Hill
3. Yale University
4. Brown University
5. University of Wisconsin—Madison
6. University of Kansas
7. University of Maryland—College Park
8. University of Florida
9. University of California—Santa Barbara
10. University of Georgia
11. Cornell University
12. Colorado State University
13. Syracuse University
14. University of South Carolina—Columbia
15. Tufts University
16. University of Michigan—Ann Arbor
17. Ohio University—Athens
18. North Carolina State University
19. The University of Texas at Austin
20. Northwestern University

Best College Theater

How do you rate college's theater productions?

1. State University of New York—Purchase College
2. Carnegie Mellon University
3. Yale University
4. Wagner College
5. Emerson College
6. Bennington College
7. Drew University
8. Muhlenberg College
9. Ithaca College
10. Indiana University—Bloomington
11. Northwestern University
12. Oberlin College
13. New York University
14. Sarah Lawrence College
15. Bard College (NY)
16. Skidmore College
17. Kenyon College
18. Brown University
19. Elon University
20. Suffolk University

SOCIAL SCENE

Lots of Greek Life

How popular are fraternities/sororities?

1. DePauw University
2. Vanderbilt University
3. University of Illinois at Urbana-Champaign
4. Texas Christian University
5. Bucknell University
6. Miami University
7. Transylvania University
8. Wofford College
9. Gettysburg College
10. University of South Carolina—Columbia
11. Union College (NY)
12. Southern Methodist University
13. Cornell University
14. Syracuse University
15. University of Mississippi
16. University of Nebraska—Lincoln
17. Pennsylvania State University—University Park
18. Florida State University
19. University of Georgia
20. The University of Alabama—Tuscaloosa

Lots of Beer

How widely used is beer?

1. West Virginia University
2. Ohio University—Athens
3. Bucknell University
4. Colgate University
5. University of Florida
6. University of Wisconsin—Madison
7. Pennsylvania State University—University Park
8. University of Illinois at Urbana-Champaign
9. University of Iowa
10. Bates College
11. Florida State University
12. University of Texas at Austin
13. University of Georgia
14. Colby College
15. St. Bonaventure University
16. University of California—Santa Barbara
17. Syracuse University
18. Boston College
19. Eckerd College
20. University of New Hampshire

Got Milk?

How widely used is beer?

1. Brigham Young University (UT)
2. College of the Ozarks
3. Wheaton College (IL)
4. Wesleyan College

5. City University of New York—Brooklyn College
6. Xavier University of Louisiana
7. Spelman College
8. Grove City College
9. City University of New York—City College
10. City University of New York—Queens College
11. City University of New York—Baruch College
12. Howard University
13. University of Houston
14. Calvin College
15. United States Military Academy
16. City University of New York—Hunter College
17. United States Coast Guard Academy
18. California State University—Stanislaus
19. Simmons College
20. United States Air Force Academy

Lots of Hard Liquor

How widely used is hard liquor?

1. Providence College
2. Tulane University
3. St. Bonaventure University
4. University of Georgia
5. Ohio University—Athens
6. University of Iowa
7. University of California—Santa Barbara
8. West Virginia University
9. Syracuse University
10. DePauw University
11. Quinnipiac University
12. University of Wisconsin-Madison
13. Miami University
14. University of Illinois at Urbana-Champaign
15. University of Maryland—College Park
16. University of Texas at Austin
17. University of Florida
18. Bucknell University
19. Louisiana State University—Baton Rouge
20. Pennsylvania State University—University Park

Scotch and Soda, Hold the Scotch

How widely used is hard liquor?

1. Brigham Young University (UT)
2. College of the Ozarks
3. Wheaton College (IL)
4. City University of New York—Brooklyn College
5. Grove City College
6. Wesleyan College
7. City University of New York—City College
8. City University of New York—Queens College
9. City University of New York—Baruch College
10. Thomas Aquinas College
11. Calvin College
12. United States Coast Guard Academy
13. California State University—Stanislaus
14. Xavier University of Louisiana
15. United States Air Force Academy
16. United States Military Academy
17. Pepperdine University
18. Baylor University
19. Spelman College
20. United States Naval Academy

Reefer Madness

How widely used is marijuana?

1. University of Colorado—Boulder
2. University of California—Santa Cruz
3. Eckerd College
4. Skidmore College
5. Green Mountain College
6. The Evergreen State College
7. Warren Wilson College
8. New York University
9. State University of New York—Purchase College
10. University of California—Santa Barbara
11. Bard College (NY)
12. West Virginia University
13. Lewis & Clark College
14. Colorado College
15. University of Vermont
16. Guilford College
17. Ithaca College
18. Sarah Lawrence College
19. Grinnell College
20. Reed College

Don't Inhale

How widely used is marijuana?

1. United States Coast Guard Academy
2. Thomas Aquinas College
3. Brigham Young University (UT)
4. College of the Ozarks
5. United States Naval Academy
6. United States Military Academy
7. Wheaton College (IL)
8. United States Merchant Marine Academy
9. United States Air Force Academy
10. Westminster College (PA)
11. Hillsdale College
12. City University of New York—Brooklyn College
13. Calvin College
14. University of Notre Dame
15. City University of New York—Baruch College

16. City University of New York—City College
17. City University of New York—Queens College
18. Furman University
19. Baylor University
20. University of Dallas

SCHOOLS BY TYPE

Party Schools

Based on a combination of survey questions concerning the use of alcohol and drugs, hours of study each day, and the popularity of the Greek system

1. West Virginia University
2. University of Iowa
3. Ohio University—Athens
4. University of Illinois at Urbana-Champaign
5. University of Georgia
6. University of Florida
7. University of California—Santa Barbara
8. Florida State University
9. Miami University
10. Syracuse University
11. Pennsylvania State University—University Park
12. DePauw University
13. University of Wisconsin—Madison
14. University of Mississippi
15. The University of Texas at Austin
16. University of Maryland—College Park
17. University of South Carolina—Columbia
18. James Madison University
19. University of Maine
20. University of Tennessee

Stone-Cold Sober Schools

Based on a combination of survey questions concerning the use of alcohol and drugs, hours of study each day, and the popularity of the Greek system

1. Brigham Young University (UT)
2. Wheaton College (IL)
3. United States Naval Academy
4. United States Coast Guard Academy
5. Grove City College
6. United States Military Academy
7. City University of New York—Brooklyn College
8. Wesleyan College
9. Wellesley College
10. Calvin College
11. City University of New York—City College
12. City University of New York—Queens College
13. Franklin W. Olin College of Engineering
14. Agnes Scott College
15. Simmons College
16. United States Air Force Academy
17. Pepperdine University
18. Becker College
19. The Cooper Union for the Advancement of Science and Art
20. California State University—Stanislaus

Jock Schools

Based on a combination of survey questions concerning the popularity of intercollegiate sports, intramural sports, and the Greek system

1. Clemson University
2. University of Florida
3. University of Nebraska—Lincoln
4. Pennsylvania State University—University Park
5. The University of North Carolina at Chapel Hill
6. University of Georgia
7. Florida State University
8. University of South Carolina—Columbia
9. University of Maryland—College Park
10. Wabash College
11. The Ohio State University—Columbus
12. University of Kansas
13. Villanova University
14. Kansas State University
15. University of Tennessee
16. Creighton University
17. Syracuse University
18. University of Connecticut
19. United States Military Academy
20. North Carolina State University

Future Rotarians and Daughters of the American Revolution

Based on a combination of survey questions concerning the political persuasion, the use of drugs, the popularity of student government, and the level of acceptance of the gay community on campus

1. Hillsdale College
2. College of the Ozarks
3. Wheaton College (IL)
4. Grove City College
5. Thomas Aquinas College
6. Brigham Young University (UT)
7. United States Naval Academy
8. University of Dallas
9. United States Coast Guard Academy
10. Auburn University
11. United States Military Academy
12. Calvin College

13. Baylor University
14. United States Merchant Marine Academy
15. Clemson University
16. Pepperdine University
17. University of Mississippi
18. Westminster College (PA)
19. Ohio Northern University
20. Wabash College

Birkenstock-Wearing, Tree-Hugging, Clove-Smoking Vegetarians

Based on a combination of survey questions concerning the political persuasion, the use of drugs, the popularity of student government, and the level of acceptance of the gay community on campus

1. Reed College
2. Bennington College
3. Bard College (NY)
4. Sarah Lawrence College
5. Warren Wilson College
6. The Evergreen State College
7. Skidmore College
8. Lewis & Clark College
9. New College of Florida
10. Beloit College
11. Pitzer College
12. Colorado College
13. Wesleyan University
14. Grinnell College
15. State University of New York—Purchase College
16. Bard College at Simon's Rock (MA)
17. The University of North Carolina at Asheville
18. Green Mountain College
19. Marlboro College
20. University of California—Santa Barbara

Deep Springs Honor Roll

Since Deep Springs is a two-year college (and the only one in The Best 377 Colleges), we remove it from our rankings tallies in order to avoid comparing "apples and oranges." Instead we present this list of some ranking categories in which Deep Springs ranks high (or low, as it were) among the best colleges in our book.

Got Milk?
Stone-Cold Sober Schools
Scotch and Soda, Hold the Scotch
Don't Inhale
There's a Game?
Town-Gown Relations Are Great
LGBT-Friendly
Least Religious Students
Most Liberal Students
Most Beautiful Campus
Easiest Campus to Get Around
Best Campus Food
This Is a Library?
Most Accessible Professors

PRINCETON REVIEW'S "FINANCIAL AID RATING," "FIRE SAFETY RATING," AND "GREEN RATING" HONOR ROLLS

We salute theses schools that received a 99 (the highest score) in the tallies for our "Financial Aid," "Fire Safety," and "Green" Ratings—three of eight ratings on some of the school profiles in this book as well as in our *Complete Book of Colleges, 2013 Edition,* and at www.PrincetonReview.com. Our school ratings are numerical scores (Note: They are not ranking lists) that show how a school "sizes up" on a fixed scale. They are comparable to grades and based primarily on institutional data we collect directly from the colleges.

Financial Aid Honor Roll

Schools are listed in alphabetical order. See page 28 for information on how our "Financial Aid Rating" is determined.

Claremont McKenna College
Colgate University
Columbia University
Grinnell College
Pomona College
Princeton University
Swarthmore College
Thomas Aquinas College
Vassar College
Yale University

Fire Safety Honor Roll

Schools are listed in alphabetical order. See page 24 for information on how our "Fire Safety Rating" is determined.

Adelphi University*
Bay Path College*
Bentley University
The Citadel, The Military College of South Carolina*
College of Mount St. Joseph*
The College of Saint Rose*
Dominican University of California*
Duquesne University
Georgian Court University*
Husson University*
Kennesaw State University*
Michigan Technological University
Milwaukee School of Engineering*
The Ohio State University—Newark*
Plymouth State University*
Saint Mary-of-the-Woods College*
Southern Illinois University—Edwardsville*
Suffolk University
University of Minnesota, Morris*
Western Kentucky University*

Schools marked with an asterisk do not appear in the *Best 377 Colleges.* You can find those school profiles in the *Complete Book of Colleges, 2013 Edition.*

Green Honor Roll

Schools are listed in alphabetical order. See page 25 for information on how our "Green Rating" is determined.

American University
Arizona State University
California Institute of Technology
California State University, Chico*
Catawba College
Chatham University*
College of the Atlantic
Columbia University
Georgia Institute of Technology
Goucher College
Green Mountain College
Harvard College
Northeastern University
San Francisco State University*
University of California—Santa Cruz
University of South Carolina—Columbia
University of Washington
University of Wisconsin—Oshkosh*
University of Wisconsin—Stevens Point*
Vanderbilt University
Warren Wilson College

Tuition-Free Schools Honor Roll

The following schools have been excluded from our ranking lists dealing with financial aid:

Berea College
College of the Ozarks
The Cooper Union for the Advancement of Science and Art
United States Air Force Academy
United States Coast Guard Academy
United States Merchant Marine Academy
United States Military Academy
United States Naval Academy
Webb Institute

We commend these schools on their ability to do the seemingly impossible: not charge tuition. While some charge students for room and board and other fees, the overall cost of attendance at these schools is very low, and at some schools: free! (Note: We do not include these schools in our ranking lists dealing with financial aid, since they would have an unfair advantage over schools that charge even a moderate tuition.)

THE PRINCETON REVIEW'S 150 BEST VALUE COLLEGES FOR 2012

The Princeton Review collaborated with USA TODAY to bring you this list of 150 Best Value Colleges in February 2012. We selected the 150 schools—75 private and 75 public—based on 30 factors covering academics, costs, and financial aid. We reported the two lists in alphabetical order and named the top 10 ranking schools in each group. For more information on this project, visit us online at www.PrincetonReview.com/best-value-colleges.aspx. At USA TODAY's site, you can find information about each school with an exclusive analysis in an interactive database and map at www.usatoday.com/news/education/best-value-colleges. For detailed profiles of all these great schools, see our companion book, *The Best Value Colleges: The 150 Best-Buy Schools and What It Takes to Get In.*

Top 75 Private

Agnes Scott College
Amherst College
Barnard College
Bates College
Beloit College
Boston College
Bowdoin College
Brandeis University
Brown University
Bryn Mawr College
Bucknell University
California Institute of Technology (#9)
Carleton College
Centenary College of Louisiana
Centre College
Claremont McKenna College
Colby College
Colgate University
College of the Atlantic
College of the Holy Cross
Colorado College
Columbia University
Cornell College
Cornell University
Dartmouth College
Davidson College
DePauw University
Duke University
Emory University
Franklin W. Olin College of Engineering
Georgetown University
Gettysburg College
Grinnell College
Hamilton College (#10)
Hanover College
Harvard College (#4)
Harvey Mudd College
Haverford College
Hillsdale College
The Johns Hopkins University
Lafayette College
Macalester College
Massachusetts Institute of Technology
Middlebury College
Mount Holyoke College
Northwestern University
Occidental College
Pomona College (#6)
Princeton University (#3)
Randolph College
Reed College
Rice University (#5)
Scripps College
Sewanee—The University of the South
Stanford University
Swarthmore College (#2)
Thomas Aquinas College
The University of Chicago
University of Notre Dame
University of Pennsylvania
University of Redlands
University of Richmond
Vanderbilt University
Vassar College
Wabash College
Wake Forest University
Washington University in St. Louis (#7)
Wellesley College
Wesleyan College
Wesleyan University
Wheaton College (IL)
Whitman College
Williams College (#1)
Wofford College
Yale University (#8)

Top 75 Public

Appalachian State University*
California Polytechnic State University, San Luis Obispo*
California State University—Long Beach*
Christopher Newport University
City University of New York—Brooklyn College
City University of New York—Hunter College
Clemson University
College of Charleston
The College of New Jersey
The College of William and Mary (#6)
The Evergreen State College
Florida State University
Georgia Institute of Technology

Schools marked with an asterisk do not appear in the *Best 377 Colleges*. You can find those school profiles in the *Complete Book of Colleges, 2013 Edition*.

Indiana University—Bloomington
Iowa State University
James Madison University
Kansas State University
Longwood University*
Missouri University of Science and Technology
New College of Florida (#3)
New Mexico Institute of Mining & Technology*
North Carolina State University
The Ohio State University—Columbus
Purdue University—West Lafayette
Southern Utah University*
St. Mary's College of Maryland
State University of New York at Binghamton (#4)
State University of New York at Geneseo
State University of New York at New Paltz*
State University of New York—College of Environmental Science and Forestry*
State University of New York—Oswego*
State University of New York—Stony Brook University
State University of New York—University at Buffalo
Truman State University
University of California—Berkeley
University of California—Davis
University of California—Irvine*
University of California—Los Angeles
University of California—Riverside
University of California—San Diego
University of California—Santa Barbara
University of California—Santa Cruz
University of Central Florida
University of Colorado—Boulder
University of Delaware
University of Florida (#7)
University of Georgia (#8)
University of Houston
University of Illinois at Urbana-Champaign
University of Kansas
University of Mary Washington
University of Maryland, College Park
University of Massachusetts Boston*
University of Michigan—Ann Arbor
University of Minnesota, Crookston*
University of Minnesota—Twin Cities
University of Missouri—Kansas City*
The University of North Carolina at Asheville
The University of North Carolina at Chapel Hill (#1)
University of North Carolina—Wilmington*
University of North Florida*
University of Oklahoma
University of Pittsburgh at Bradford*
University of Pittsburgh—Pittsburgh Campus
University of South Carolina—Columbia
The University of South Dakota
University of Tennessee
University of Tennessee at Martin*
The University of Texas at Austin (#10)
University of Virginia (#2)
University of Washington (#9)
University of Wisconsin—Eau Claire*
University of Wisconsin—Madison (#5)
Utah State University*
Virginia Tech

Top 10 Private Schools

1. Williams College
2. Swarthmore College
3. Princeton University
4. Harvard College
5. Rice University
6. Pomona College
7. Washington University in St. Louis
8. Yale University
9. California Institute of Technology
10. Hamilton College

Top 10 Public Schools

1. The University of North Carolina at Chapel Hill
2. University of Virginia
3. New College of Florida
4. State University of New York at Binghamton
5. University of Wisconsin—Madison
6. The College of William & Mary
7. University of Florida
8. University of Georgia
9. University of Washington
10. The University of Texas at Austin

Schools marked with an asterisk do not appear in the *Best 377 Colleges*. You can find those school profiles in the *Complete Book of Colleges, 2013 Edition*.

PART 3

THE BEST 377 COLLEGES

AGNES SCOTT COLLEGE

141 East College Avenue, Decatur, GA 30030-3770 • Admissions: 404-471-6285 • Fax: 404-471-6414

CAMPUS LIFE

Quality of Life Rating	**99**
Fire Safety Rating	**95**
Green Rating	**93**
Type of school	private
Affiliation	Presbyterian
Environment	metropolis

STUDENTS

Total undergrad enrollment	827
% male/female	0/100
% from out of state	38
% from public high school	71
% frosh live on campus	92
% African American	31
% Asian	3
% Caucasian	40
% Hispanic	7
% international	10
# of countries represented	29

SURVEY SAYS . . .

No one cheats
Lab facilities are great
Students get along with local community
Students love Atlanta/Decatur, GA
Great off-campus food
Dorms are like palaces
Campus feels safe
Frats and sororities are unpopular or nonexistent

ACADEMICS

Academic Rating	**90**
% students returning for sophomore year	84
% students graduating within 4 years	58
% students graduating within 6 years	65
Calendar	semester
Student/faculty ratio	11:1
Profs interesting rating	95
Profs accessible rating	96
Most classes have	10–19 students
Most lab/discussion sessions have	10–19 students

MOST POPULAR MAJORS

English language and literature; history; psychology

APPLICANTS ALSO LOOK AT AND OFTEN PREFER

University of Georgia, Georgia State University

AND SOMETIMES PREFER

Georgia Institute of Technology

AND RARELY PREFER

Mercer University—Macon

STUDENTS SAY "..."

Academics

"Great location. Gorgeous campus. Superb academics." That's how a typical Scottie sums up the argument for Agnes Scott College, a small all-women's school located a stone's throw from Atlanta. "The [school's] mission statement sums it up perfectly," one student writes: "Agnes Scott educates women to think deeply, live honorably, and engage the intellectual and social challenges of their times." Nowhere is this more apparent than in Agnes Scott's Honor Code ("our greatest strength," one student writes), which "is moderated by the student-run Honor Court." The code "has many benefits," including "self-scheduled and unproctored exams," infusing the campus with a sense of mutual trust. It also helps students manage their demanding academic workloads. As one student warns, "Courses are challenging and the...workload is heavy, especially during midterms and exams. Most classes are back-heavy, so if you don't do homework during the semester then finals can become incredibly stressful." A caring and attentive faculty and administration also help. "To say they are committed and available is an understatement," one student tells us. "All the deans and most faculty members know students by name." The consensus among students is that faculty members are all dedicated to their field and to teaching, and they're skilled at both. Finally, the school's "huge endowment" has many here bragging about the school's "amazing financial aid packages," another plus.

Life

Scott is "a quiet campus" where students "are dedicated to their own pursuits, which makes it an environment conducive to being productive and focused, but it's next to Atlanta, so [we're] never at a loss for things to do." Challenging academics mean students "stay on campus and study and get things done during the week. Everyone studies, goes to class, is involved in clubs, and chills out in each others' dorms" from Monday through Thursday. Then, "on the weekends, everyone leaves campus," often to socialize with students from "another college such as Georgia Tech, Emory, Georgia State, or Morehouse." Because of the school's "great location, students are able to easily get off campus and refresh themselves with the city life," although some feel a car "is pretty much a must" to reap full benefits, which include "concerts, clubs, and movies in Atlanta. If you like to shop, you definitely shop in Atlanta. Lenox Square Mall, Atlantic Station, and Perimeter Mall are some of the more popular places to shop." Students also love Atlanta's funky little Five Points neighborhood and even have some favorite hot spots in hometown Decatur, an upscale Atlanta satellite that's home to a variety of coffee shops and eateries.

Student Body

"It's almost impossible to describe a typical student" at Agnes Scott, where "you'll find everyone from preppy, Southern Baptist, Republican, in-state student debutantes to radical, vegan, communist lesbians, and everyone in between." As one student puts it, "We vary from women in pearls and plaid skirts to women in black parachute pants and metal in their noses." "Diversity is definitely one of Agnes Scott's strong points," students here agree. These "ambitious high-achievers" "not only consistently attend classes, but they are also involved in so many things—clubs, student government, taking more than the standard number of classes, work study, etc.—that they barely have time to get everything done. Nearly everyone on campus is concerned about and dedicated to one issue or another, whether it's gender equality, the environment, or refugee women in Atlanta." They're "an intense and passionate bunch" that "fully [expects] to make advances in whatever it is they want to do."

FINANCIAL AID: 404-471-6395 • E-MAIL: ADMISSION@AGNESSCOTT.EDU • WEBSITE: WWW.AGNESSCOTT.EDU

THE PRINCETON REVIEW SAYS

Admissions

Very important factors considered include: Class rank, application essay, academic GPA, recommendation(s), rigor of secondary school record, standardized test scores if submitted, character/personal qualities, talent/ability. *Important factors considered include:* Extracurricular activities, volunteer work, work experience. *Other factors considered include:* Alumni/ae relation, first generation, geographical residence, interview, level of applicant's interest, racial/ethnic status, state residency. ACT with writing component required. TOEFL required of all international applicants. High school diploma is required and GED is accepted. *Academic units recommended:* 4 English, 3 mathematics, 2 science (2 science labs), 2 foreign language, 2 social studies, 2 history.

Financial Aid

Students should submit: FAFSA. Regular filing deadline is May 1. The Princeton Review suggests that all financial aid forms be submitted as soon as possible after January 1. *Need-based scholarships/grants offered:* Federal Pell, SEOG, state scholarships/grants, private scholarships, the school's own gift aid. *Loan aid offered:* Direct Subsidized Stafford, Direct Unsubsidized Stafford, Direct PLUS. Applicants will be notified of awards on a rolling basis beginning March 1. Federal Work-Study Program available. Institutional employment available. Off-campus job opportunities are excellent.

The Inside Word

Agnes Scott waives the application fee for those who apply online; all it will cost you is your time. Take the time to craft a solid application if you want to be considered seriously, as this is a very competitive school where admissions officers give each candidate a very careful look. A strong application that creates a compelling portrait may well overcome moderate shortcomings in high school grades or test scores, especially if bolstered by an enthusiastic interview during a campus visit.

THE SCHOOL SAYS ". . ."

From the Admissions Office

"Who will you become? If you are looking for a liberal arts college that will help you explore, strive, and surpass what you think is your potential, then consider Agnes Scott College. Our students and alumnae say it best:

"'I found the academic program to be extremely challenging at Agnes Scott; but it's not overwhelming—it's easy to go to your teachers and ask for help because they know who you are and take a personal interest.'—Evan Joslin, Class of 2008, Atlanta, Georgia.

"'Agnes Scott College didn't teach me what to think. They taught me how to think,' says Jessica Owens, class of 1998, who majored in biology at ASC, received a master's degree in cancer biology from Stanford and an MBA from Harvard.

"Students find their passions and their voices through guaranteed internships, international study experiences, and collaborative learning in places like the science center, facilities that were designed expressly to facilitate faculty-student research. Your next four years are about you. We invite you to come for a visit and imagine the possibilities for you."

SELECTIVITY	
Admissions Rating	**90**
# of applicants	2,284
% of applicants accepted	46
% of acceptees attending	22
# accepting a place on wait list	29
# admitted from wait list	2

FRESHMAN PROFILE	
Range SAT Critical Reading	525–630
Range SAT Math	500–630
Range SAT Writing	530–630
Range ACT Composite	23–29
Average HS GPA	3.7
% graduated top 10% of class	40
% graduated top 25% of class	72
% graduated top 50% of class	96

DEADLINES	
Early action	
Deadline	11/15
Notification	12/15
Regular	
Priority	3/1
Nonfall registration?	yes

FINANCIAL FACTS	
Financial Aid Rating	**87**
Annual tuition	$31,980
Room and board	$10,150
Required fees	$215
Books and supplies	$1,000
% needy frosh rec. need-based scholarship or grant aid	100
% needy UG rec. need-based scholarship or grant aid	100
% needy frosh rec. non-need-based scholarship or grant aid	23
% needy UG rec. non-need-based scholarship or grant aid	23
% needy frosh rec. need-based self-help aid	90
% needy UG rec. need-based self-help aid	89
% frosh rec. any financial aid	100
% UG rec. any financial aid	99
% UG borrow to pay for school	67
Average cumulative indebtedness	$26,148
% frosh need fully met	23
% ugrads need fully met	24
Average % of frosh need met	87
Average % of ugrad need met	88

ALBION COLLEGE

611 EAST PORTER, ALBION, MI 49224 • ADMISSIONS: 517-629-0321 • FAX: 517-629-0569

CAMPUS LIFE

Quality of Life Rating	**68**
Fire Safety Rating	**72**
Green Rating	**87**
Type of school	private
Affiliation	Methodist
Environment	village

STUDENTS

Total undergrad enrollment	1,495
% male/female	51/49
% from out of state	8
% frosh live on campus	90
# of fraternities	6
# of sororities	6
% African American	4
% Asian	2
% Caucasian	82
% Hispanic	3
% international	4
# of countries represented	23

SURVEY SAYS . . .

No one cheats
Lab facilities are great
Great computer facilities
Students are friendly
Low cost of living
Frats and sororities dominate social scene
Lots of beer drinking

ACADEMICS

Academic Rating	**80**
% students returning for sophomore year	84
% students graduating within 4 years	65
Calendar	semester
Student/faculty ratio	13:1
Profs interesting rating	86
Profs accessible rating	94
Most classes have	10–19 students
Most lab/discussion sessions have	10–19 students

MOST POPULAR MAJORS

biology/biological sciences; economics; psychology

APPLICANTS ALSO LOOK AT AND OFTEN PREFER

University of Michigan—Ann Arbor, Michigan State University, Grand Valley State University

AND SOMETIMES PREFER

Adrian College

AND RARELY PREFER

Calvin College

STUDENTS SAY ". . ."

Academics

Armed with a "great reputation" and a "small-town feeling," Albion College provides undergraduates with a "rigorous but rewarding" academic experience replete with "huge opportunities." Students here truly appreciate that Albion works diligently to foster an environment that "encourages questions [and] thinking" all the while aiming to "provide personal attention to each student." While the college certainly offers a "great liberal arts education," undergrads are especially quick to highlight the strong science, premed, and business programs. Indeed, students like to boast that Albion "has a very high rate of students being accepted into medical school." And business majors point to the Gerstacker Institute for Business and Management, which allows students to "gain real-world experience" and even the potential to walk away with "a job offer." Of course, regardless of discipline or department, Albion undergrads are full of praise for their teachers. As one thrilled student eagerly shares, "The professors care about their students' success and are always there to help." Importantly, they are "very knowledgeable in their material and try to make sure you learn as much as possible." Further, they are "easily approachable," "extremely passionate about their work," and always "available for discussions." As one content undergrad sums up, "I would say that the overall experience has been great, and I couldn't be more pleased with my decision to attend Albion College."

Life

While Albion students are often quite "studious" during the week, once the weekend rolls around they certainly know how to get "crazy [and] exciting." Fortunately, there "is almost always something going on on campus." Indeed, the "Union Board plans lots of free activities, concerts, comedians, etc." Moreover, those interested in the party scene will be delighted to discover that fraternities and sororities are very popular at Albion. As one thrilled undergrad notes, "Greek life is fantastic. It really is the cornerstone of our campus. Every weekend there is a party or something going on at the fraternities. Whether you are into drinking or not, the guys there know how to have a good time." While students bemoan the fact that "there's not much to do in the city of Albion," they do take solace in finding other off campus options. As another satisfied student reveals, "Bigger cities like Jackson and Battle Creek are only a fifteen- or twenty-minute drive away, so if you're looking for a day at a mall, that's always an option. Plus, the college sponsors sending buses and vans to take students to places like Ann Arbor or Lansing. Generally you can find something to do."

Student Body

At first glance, Albion College appears to be "a microcosm of upper-class metro-Detroit and Chicago." Therefore, it's not surprising that a "slightly right-leaning, white, and Greek-loving [student body seems to be] the norm." However, those seeking more diversity should fear not! One student assures us, "I have met anarchists and proud communists. There is a mix, but you have to dig for it." Beyond race and political affiliation, undergrads here find their peers to be "serious about school but also very fun and friendly." Moreover, they are "bright individuals that want to succeed" and certainly people who "value their education." They also seem to have "a million interests," which they vigorously pursue through a number of extracurricular activities and programs. As one socially satisfied undergrad sums up, "I think there is a club or niche here where everyone can find a group of people they fit in with. I truthfully would feel comfortable sitting down at a table with anyone of my classmates in the cafeteria and having lunch with them."

FINANCIAL AID: 517-629-0440 • E-MAIL: ADMISSION@ALBION.EDU • WEBSITE: WWW.ALBION.EDU

THE PRINCETON REVIEW SAYS

Admissions

Very important factors considered include: Application questions, academic GPA, recommendation(s), rigor of secondary school record, standardized test scores, alumni/ae relation, character/personal qualities, extracurricular activities, first generation, geographical residence, level of applicant's interest, state residency, talent/ability, volunteer work, work experience. SAT or ACT required; ACT with or without writing component accepted. TOEFL required of all international applicants. High school diploma is required and GED is accepted. *Academic units required:* 4 English, 3 mathematics, 3 science (2 science labs), 2 foreign language, 3 social studies, 1 history. *Academic units recommended:* 4 mathematics, 4 science, 3 foreign language, 4 social studies.

Financial Aid

Students should submit: FAFSA. Regular filing deadline is March 1. The Princeton Review suggests that all financial aid forms be submitted as soon as possible after January 1. *Need-based scholarships/grants offered:* Federal Pell, SEOG, state scholarships/grants, private scholarships, the school's own gift aid. *Loan aid offered:* Direct Subsidized Stafford, Direct Unsubsidized Stafford, Direct PLUS, Federal Perkins. Applicants will be notified of awards on a rolling basis beginning March 15. Federal Work-Study Program available. Institutional employment available. Highest amount earned per year from on-campus jobs $5,330. Off-campus job opportunities are fair.

The Inside Word

Albion's growing reputation means that earning a coveted acceptance letter is no easy feat. Academic success takes precedence, and applicants should have taken a challenging high school curriculum including a handful of honors and advanced placement courses. Of course, admissions officers are also concerned about maintaining a vibrant community, so careful attention will also be paid to essays and extracurricular activities.

THE SCHOOL SAYS ". . ."

From the Admissions Office

"An Albion education will take you beyond the classroom, beyond our campus, and beyond conventional thinking. It will challenge your mind and open your heart. It will help you discover what you're meant to do with your life. And it will prepare you to live it well. Through the Albion Advantage, you'll get the practical knowledge and the purposeful direction that will fully equip you to succeed. You'll identify your goals through a four-year individualized career plan and build a strong foundation in the liberal arts. You can sharpen your career focus and develop your professional skills through the internships and other real-world experiences offered in these specialized programs: Carl A. Gerstacker Institute for Business and Management, the Gerald R. Ford Institute for Leadership in Public Policy and Service, the Institute for Premedical Professions and Health Sciences, the Center for Sustainability and the Environment, and the Fritz Shurmur Center for Teacher Development. And you can unleash your creativity and curiosity through the multitude of research experiences available in our Foundation for Undergraduate Research, Scholarship, and Creative Activity and Prentiss M. Brown Honors Program.

"Albion students are prepared to make an impact. They go on to the nation's top graduate and professional schools and to leadership roles in the sciences and medicine, business, law, education, the arts, and social services.

"On our residential campus, more than 100 campus organizations cater to a wide range of student interests. Our athletic teams regularly head to NCAA Division III postseason play, and our equestrian team members compete regionally and nationally. Check us out online at www.albion.edu, or visit us in person to learn more about what Albion has to offer."

SELECTIVITY	
Admissions Rating	74
# of applicants	1,637
% of applicants accepted	92
% of acceptees attending	24

FRESHMAN PROFILE	
Range SAT Critical Reading	520–630
Range SAT Math	570–670
Range SAT Writing	510–600
Range ACT Composite	22–28
Minimum paper TOEFL	550
Minimum web-based TOEFL	79
Average HS GPA	3.4
% graduated top 10% of class	16
% graduated top 25% of class	44
% graduated top 50% of class	75

DEADLINES	
Early action	
Deadline	12/1
Notification	10/1
Regular	
Priority	12/1
Deadline	8/1
Nonfall registration?	yes

FINANCIAL FACTS	
Financial Aid Rating	83
Annual tuition	$32,100
Room and board	$9,260
Required fees	$562
Books and supplies	$900
% needy frosh rec. need-based scholarship or grant aid	100
% needy UG rec. need-based scholarship or grant aid	100
% needy frosh rec. non-need-based scholarship or grant aid	85
% needy UG rec. non-need-based scholarship or grant aid	90
% needy frosh rec. need-based self-help aid	82
% needy UG rec. need-based self-help aid	85
% frosh rec. any financial aid	98
% UG rec. any financial aid	99
% UG borrow to pay for school	60
Average cumulative indebtedness	$33,319
% frosh need fully met	19
% ugrads need fully met	20
Average % of frosh need met	88
Average % of ugrad need met	83

ALFRED UNIVERSITY

ALUMNI HALL, ONE SAXON DRIVE, ALFRED, NY 14802-1205 • ADMISSIONS: 607-871-2115 • FAX: 607-871-2198

CAMPUS LIFE

Quality of Life Rating	**67**
Fire Safety Rating	**65**
Green Rating	**68**
Type of school	private
Environment	rural

STUDENTS

Total undergrad enrollment	1,846
% male/female	49/51
% from out of state	23
% frosh live on campus	98
% African American	5
% Asian	2
% Caucasian	68
% Hispanic	3
% international	2
# of countries represented	18

SURVEY SAYS . . .

Students are friendly
Frats and sororities are unpopular or nonexistent
College radio is popular
Lots of beer drinking

ACADEMICS

Academic Rating	**74**
% students returning for sophomore year	71
% students graduating within 4 years	50
% students graduating within 6 years	69
Calendar	semester
Student/faculty ratio	12:1
Profs interesting rating	79
Profs accessible rating	71
Most classes have	10–19 students
Most lab/discussion sessions have	fewer than 10 students

MOST POPULAR MAJORS

business/commerce; ceramic sciences and engineering; fine/studio arts

APPLICANTS ALSO LOOK AT AND OFTEN PREFER

Rochester Institute of Technology, Clarkson University

AND SOMETIMES PREFER

State University of New York—University at Buffalo, Ithaca College

AND RARELY PREFER

Hartwick College

STUDENTS SAY ". . ."

Academics

Alfred University is a small school with an impressive range of world-class majors. The school is known for its "excellent art program," particularly its ceramics and glass majors, as well as for its engineering and psychology programs. While some students at Alfred focus only on their majors, students happily report that there are a "variety of academic opportunities" and that it's "easy to take subjects outside your major." This is appreciated by many, including one art student who likes that Alfred offers "other majors versus a traditional art [school] setting. If I had decided to change majors, Alfred has almost every opportunity." Alfred's "outstanding, talented, dedicated" faculty is one of its biggest draws. An English writing student gushes that professors "bring a level of vibrancy and academic encouragement through enthusiasm to the classroom." "The professors are always pushing you to reach your full potential" and are "always willing to put time into student independent projects." Students also rave about the small classes sizes. "It is the closest to one-on-one teaching you can get," a clinical and counseling psychology major notes, and "The classroom size is perfect for a more personalized education."

Life

Alfred's "beautiful," "small" campus and its "somewhat rural location" are big draws for students looking for a quieter academic experience with a strong "sense of community." Of course, its location means the weather isn't exactly tropical. One student notes that it can feel like "it's basically winter here for about eighty percent of the school year, and it snows constantly." Luckily, "There is always something to do on weekends and week days," for distraction, such as "student club productions…and fundraisers and an excellent selection of movies shown on campus." On top of that, "There are so many clubs and options that you can find something to do," and "Every sports team is supported, and superfans are at every event." "The facilities are amazing," particularly the "great" art buildings and the engineering facilities. Alfred's "strong equestrian program" and barn are also a big draw. Students find some of Alfred's dorms to be "pretty outdated," and there's a bit of grumbling about the "hit-or-miss" and "expensive" dining facilities.

Student Body

Alfred has a "warm" atmosphere, and "You can't go down the street without receiving a smile." Students are "friendly, outgoing, and involved," and many do community service work and are active in one of Alfred's many clubs or organizations. The prominent art school means that there's a large presence of creative types on campus, and the equally prominent engineering school ensures a good mix of personalities. One student notes, "A pretty significant gap between the prevalent, spunky art students and the more reclusive engineers," but another adds that this means students are "well-acquainted with people from a variety of studies and backgrounds and with a variety of interests." Most people believe that "everyone finds their own little niche," but they appreciate that it "definitely does not mean they stay there—you are allowed to float between everything." In fact, "More often than not, you'll see engineers rubbing elbows with philosophy majors and artists chilling with math and chemistry majors."

FINANCIAL AID: 607-871-2159 • E-MAIL: ADMISSIONS@ALFRED.EDU • WEBSITE: WWW.ALFRED.EDU

THE PRINCETON REVIEW SAYS

Admissions

Very important factors considered include: Class rank, recommendation(s), rigor of secondary school record, character/personal qualities, extracurricular activities. *Important factors considered include:* Application essay, standardized test scores, volunteer work, work experience. *Other factors considered include:* Interview. SAT or ACT required; ACT with or without writing component accepted. TOEFL required of all international applicants. High school diploma is required and GED is accepted. *Academic units required:* 4 English, 2 mathematics, 2 science (2 science labs), 2 social studies. *Academic units recommended:* 4 mathematics, 3 science (3 science labs), 3 social studies.

Financial Aid

Students should submit: FAFSA, institution's own financial aid form, state aid form, noncustodial PROFILE, business/farm supplement. Regular filing deadline is March 15. The Princeton Review suggests that all financial aid forms be submitted as soon as possible after January 1. *Need-based scholarships/grants offered:* Federal Pell, SEOG, state scholarships/grants, private scholarships, the school's own gift aid. *Loan aid offered:* Direct Subsidized Stafford, Direct Unsubsidized Stafford, Direct PLUS, Federal Perkins, college/university loans from institutional funds, private alternative loans. Applicants will be notified of awards on a rolling basis beginning February 15. Federal Work-Study Program available. Institutional employment available. Off-campus job opportunities are poor.

The Inside Word

Alfred is a fine university with a solid local reputation. The allure for arts students is obvious—Alfred's programs in the arts are especially well-regarded—and as a result, competition is fiercest among applicants for these programs. A killer portfolio, even more than great grades and standardized test scores, is your most likely ticket in. Competition for the engineering school is also tight. Applicants will need to have thrived in a rigorous high school program.

THE SCHOOL SAYS ". . ."

From the Admissions Office

"The admissions process at Alfred University is the foundation for the personal attention each student can expect during their time at AU. Each applicant is evaluated individually and receives genuine, individual care and consideration.

"The best way to discover all Alfred University has to offer is to come to campus. We truly have something for everyone with more than sixty courses of study, twenty-one NCAA Division III sports and two IHSA sports and over ninety student-run clubs and organizations. You can tour campus; meet current students, faculty, coaches and staff; attend a class; and eat in our dining hall—experience firsthand what life at AU is like.

"Alfred University is a place where students are free to pursue their dreams and interests—all of them—no matter how varied or different. Academics, athletics, co-ops, study abroad, internships, special interests—they're all part of what makes you who you are and who you are going to become."

SELECTIVITY	
Admissions Rating	79
# of applicants	2,825
% of applicants accepted	70
% of acceptees attending	27
# of early decision applicants	34
# accepted early decision	31
FRESHMAN PROFILE	
Range SAT Critical Reading	480–590
Range SAT Math	500–610
Range SAT Writing	470–570
Range ACT Composite	21–26
Minimum paper TOEFL	550
Minimum web-based TOEFL	80
Average HS GPA	3.2
% graduated top 10% of class	20
% graduated top 25% of class	52
% graduated top 50% of class	86
DEADLINES	
Early decision	
Deadline	12/1
Notification	12/15
Regular	
Priority	2/1
Nonfall registration?	yes
FINANCIAL FACTS	
Financial Aid Rating	82
Annual tuition	$25,974
Room and board	$11,498
Required fees	$910
Books and supplies	$1,050
% needy frosh rec. need-based scholarship or grant aid	100
% needy UG rec. need-based scholarship or grant aid	99
% needy frosh rec. non-need-based scholarship or grant aid	54
% needy UG rec. non-need-based scholarship or grant aid	54
% needy frosh rec. need-based self-help aid	87
% needy UG rec. need-based self-help aid	89
% frosh rec. any financial aid	92
% UG rec. any financial aid	90
% UG borrow to pay for school	82
Average cumulative indebtedness	$31,159
% frosh need fully met	18
% ugrads need fully met	16
Average % of frosh need met	87
Average % of ugrad need met	84

ALLEGHENY COLLEGE

ALLEGHENY COLLEGE, MEADVILLE, PA 16335 • ADMISSIONS: 814-332-4351 • FAX: 814-337-0431

CAMPUS LIFE	
Quality of Life Rating	73
Fire Safety Rating	72
Green Rating	89
Type of school	private
Environment	town

STUDENTS	
Total undergrad enrollment	2,094
% male/female	47/53
% from out of state	45
% from public high school	83
% frosh live on campus	99
# of fraternities	6
# of sororities	5
% African American	5
% Asian	3
% Caucasian	84
% Hispanic	5
% international	1
# of countries represented	34

SURVEY SAYS . . .

Students are happy
Great library
Career services are great
Students are friendly
Students are environmentally aware

ACADEMICS	
Academic Rating	91
% students returning for sophomore year	87
% students graduating within 4 years	76
% students graduating within 6 years	80
Calendar	semester
Student/faculty ratio	12:1
Profs interesting rating	89
Profs accessible rating	92
Most classes have	10–19 students
Most lab/discussion sessions have	10–19 students

MOST POPULAR MAJORS

biology/biological sciences; economics; psychology

APPLICANTS ALSO LOOK AT AND OFTEN PREFER

Boston University, Bucknell University, Kenyon College, University of Rochester, Denison University

AND SOMETIMES PREFER

The College of Wooster, Skidmore College, Gettysburg College, Dickinson College

AND RARELY PREFER

Miami University, Pennsylvania State University—University Park, University of Pittsburgh—Pittsburgh Campus, Washington & Jefferson College, Duquesne University

STUDENTS SAY ". . ."

Academics

Tiny Allegheny College in western Pennsylvania is a school "where people exude passion about what they are involved in," and the curriculum is "all about applying your knowledge to your experiences." The school allows students to combine completely unrelated majors and minors (in fact, it requires both), which means students "practically create [their] own education," and a student has "the freedom to dabble in my many areas of interest." "Allegheny students are known for their 'unusual combinations' of interests such as a major in biology and a minor in dance," explains a student. This "unique and valuable educational experience" provided by a school that "truly cares about the learning process" is a boon to students looking to forge any path in life (as well as those who are unsure), and the small population means that there are "many researching opportunities." "Faculty members reach out to students about internship and research opportunities often."

The "amazing," "very passionate" professors "go above and beyond to make sure their students understand the material." Professors are "great about teaching the material to you in a variety of ways until you understand." "I have never once felt dumb or like I couldn't handle something after getting help one on one," says a student. "I love my professors. I consider some of them to be friends, and most of them to be mentors," says another. Professors focus on student contribution "in and out of the classroom," so there are lectures, but students are the main focus. If you would rather have peers look at your work, then "there are plenty of consultants and tutors who are more than willing to help." The "workload is large," and the academics are demanding, but "The school is very understanding of how special and different each student is and tries to help each student excel in their own way."

Life

Attending Allegheny "is a lot of work," but "There is still time to be social and make the best friends of your life." "It can get wild on weekends," but for the most part people "are very studious during the week," and "students care for their grades." With so much leeway in academic studies, it's not surprising that the administration is concerned with "making sure that there is a place for everyone." Student activities are well-organized and plentiful, and the school works just as hard at "promoting [a] statement of community." The school organizes many late night activities: "We always have some type of performer, like comedians, musicians, or magicians." "There is a place for everyone with the different clubs and organizations on campus," says a student. "If you get involved enough, you'll rarely have a boring moment," says a student. The "mutual respect [among] students, faculty, and the administration" feeds into the overall happy satisfaction with life, and "Most students find their area either through work, class, sports, or clubs." Greek life is healthy here, but not overpowering. Some say that food services "are repetitive and not very good"; luckily, the green, scenic campus "has many open spaces," and the school's commitment toward sustainability has always been apparent.

Student Body

Allegheny's strong emphasis on community invites "very diverse" students who are "completely accepting and understanding of everyone's needs, interests, and feelings." Upperclassmen are "really welcoming to freshmen," and "the importance of being unique" is stressed from the get-go. Everyone is fun loving, but "always knows when to stop socializing and get to work." This "mixed bag" all get along well, but "We usually have at least a tiny nerdy side." Cliques aren't that common among this group of 2,100 "liberal, idealistic, and global thinkers," and though students normally find their niche within the first three semesters, they "are always eager to meet new people and do new things." Students say that there "is a lot of support to help minority students fit in."

FINANCIAL AID: 800-835-7780 • E-MAIL: ADMISSIONS@ALLEGHENY.EDU • WEBSITE: WWW.ALLEGHENY.EDU

THE PRINCETON REVIEW SAYS

Admissions

Very important factors considered include: Class rank, academic GPA, rigor of secondary school record. *Important factors considered include:* Recommendation(s), standardized test scores, character/personal qualities, extracurricular activities, interview, level of applicant's interest. *Other factors considered include:* Application essay, alumni/ae relation, first generation, geographical residence, racial/ethnic status, talent/ability, volunteer work, work experience. SAT or ACT required; ACT with writing component recommended. TOEFL required of all international applicants. High school diploma is required and GED is accepted. *Academic units required:* 4 English, 3 mathematics, 3 science, 2 foreign language, 3 social studies, 1 academic elective.

Financial Aid

Students should submit: FAFSA. The Princeton Review suggests that all financial aid forms be submitted as soon as possible after January 1. *Need-based scholarships/grants offered:* Federal Pell, SEOG, state scholarships/grants, private scholarships, the school's own gift aid, Veterans Educational Benefits, Yellow Ribbon Program. *Loan aid offered:* Direct Subsidized Stafford, Direct Unsubsidized Stafford, Direct PLUS, Federal Perkins, private loans from commercial lenders. Applicants will be notified of awards on a rolling basis beginning March 1. Federal Work-Study Program available. Institutional employment available. Highest amount earned per year from on-campus jobs $9,230. Off-campus job opportunities are excellent.

The Inside Word

A whopping seventy-three percent of Allegheny's student body is in the top twenty-five percent of their class. The typical admit here has solid high school grades in a demanding curriculum and above-average standardized test scores. The school's stellar admissions officers are known to take the time to get to know applicants' full profiles and prove to be strong advocates for students during the admissions process.

THE SCHOOL SAYS ". . ."

From the Admissions Office

"Allegheny is the premier college in the country for students with 'Unusual Combinations' of interests and talents. Students develop combinations of majors and minors in areas that may, at first glance, seem unrelated: biology and economics; political science and music; history and psychology. There is an abiding passion for learning and life and shared inquiry that spans individuals as well as areas of study. Building on a combination of academic disciplines and passions, every student completes a comprehensive Senior Project. This significant piece of original scholarly work has a creative, analytical or experimental focus and the experience culminates with an oral defense in front of faculty experts and mentors. The project demonstrates the skills most prized by employers and graduate schools: the ability to complete a major assignment, to work independently, to analyze and synthesize information and to write and speak persuasively. Exploring academic disciplines from multiple perspectives leads students to extraordinary outcomes. Biochemistry majors highlight their skills learned in communication arts to start marketing careers at the Environmental Protection Agency. English majors collaborate with our pre-health advisors and enjoy acceptance rates to graduate and medical schools between 80 and 100 percent—twice the national average. Over and over again, we hear from leaders in business, government, medicine, education and community service that the future belongs to individuals who are innovators, inventors, and big picture thinkers, those who think both analytically and creatively. It is this preparation for the global marketplace that Allegheny is known for providing."

SELECTIVITY

Admissions Rating	**90**
# of applicants	4,770
% of applicants accepted	58
% of acceptees attending	20
# accepting a place on wait list	340
# admitted from wait list	25
# of early decision applicants	122
# accepted early decision	59

FRESHMAN PROFILE

Range SAT Critical Reading	530–660
Range SAT Math	540–640
Range SAT Writing	520–640
Range ACT Composite	23–29
Minimum paper TOEFL	550
Minimum web-based TOEFL	80
Average HS GPA	3.7
% graduated top 10% of class	43
% graduated top 25% of class	73
% graduated top 50% of class	93

DEADLINES

Early decision	
Deadline	11/15
Notification	12/15
Regular	
Deadline	2/15
Notification	4/1
Nonfall registration?	yes

FINANCIAL FACTS

Financial Aid Rating	**87**
Annual tuition	$37,260
Room and board	$9,540
Required fees	$350
Books and supplies	$1,000
% needy frosh rec. need-based scholarship or grant aid	100
% needy UG rec. need-based scholarship or grant aid	100
% needy frosh rec. non-need-based scholarship or grant aid	17
% needy UG rec. non-need-based scholarship or grant aid	15
% needy frosh rec. need-based self-help aid	87
% needy UG rec. need-based self-help aid	88
% frosh rec. any financial aid	99
% UG rec. any financial aid	98
% frosh need fully met	35
% ugrads need fully met	32
Average % of frosh need met	91
Average % of ugrad need met	89

AMERICAN UNIVERSITY

4400 MASSACHUSETTS AVENUE, NORTHWEST, WASHINGTON, D.C. 20016-8001 • ADMISSIONS: 202-885-6000 • FAX: 202-885-1025

CAMPUS LIFE

Quality of Life Rating	**94**
Fire Safety Rating	**75**
Green Rating	**99**
Type of school	private
Affiliation	Methodist
Environment	metropolis

STUDENTS

Total undergrad enrollment	6,793
% male/female	41/59
% from out of state	84
% frosh live on campus	98
# of fraternities	11
# of sororities	12
% African American	5
% Asian	6
% Caucasian	57
% Hispanic	8
% international	7
# of countries represented	128

SURVEY SAYS . . .

Career services are great
Students love Washington, D.C.
Great off-campus food
Low cost of living
Political activism is popular
Students are environmentally aware
Internships are widely available

ACADEMICS

Academic Rating	**86**
% students returning for sophomore year	90
% students graduating within 4 years	74
% students graduating within 6 years	77
Calendar	semester
Student/faculty ratio	12:1
Profs interesting rating	83
Profs accessible rating	81

MOST POPULAR MAJORS

business/commerce; international relations and affairs; mass communication/media studies

APPLICANTS ALSO LOOK AT AND OFTEN PREFER

The George Washington University, Georgetown University, Brown University, Tufts University, Boston College, College of William and Mary, Harvard College, Yale University

AND SOMETIMES PREFER

Boston University, New York University

AND RARELY PREFER

Northeastern University, Fordham University

STUDENTS SAY ". . ."

Academics

American University exploits its Washington, D.C., location—that facilitates a strong faculty, prestigious guest lecturers, and "a wealth of internship opportunities"—to offer "incredibly strong programs" in political science and international relations. "The poli-sci kids are all going to be president one day, and the international studies ones are all going to save the world," a student insists. The school of communication also excels, and the school works hard to accommodate "interdisciplinary majors and the opportunities associated with studying them," which include "taking advantage of the resources of the city. The school values learning out of the classroom as much as learning in the classroom." As you might expect from a school with a strong international relations program, "AU's study abroad program is one of the best." Although AU "does not have the automatically recognizable prestige of nearby Georgetown," that's not necessarily a drawback; on the contrary, "The administration and professors go out of their way to ensure a great academic experience," in part because the school is trying to "climb in the rankings and gain recognition as one of the nation's top universities." However, some concede, "The university could improve programs in other fields, aside from its specialties in international studies, public affairs, business, and communication."

Life

"The greatest strength of AU is the activity level both politically and in the community," students tell us, noting that during the most recent election the campus "was a proxy holy war...Whether it was signs in windows, talk in the class or in the hallways, t-shirts, or canvassing in Metro-accessible Virginia, students on both sides took November 4 religiously." As one student explains, "Let's put it this way: A politician who comes to campus is likely to draw about ninety percent of the student population [and] an AU basketball game, about nine [percent]." Students get involved in the community through "campus outreach by student-run organizations," which many see as "the school's greatest asset." The typical undergrad is "incredibly engaged and active...Students seek internships in every line of work, becoming actively involved in a field of interest before graduation." When it's time to relax, "Washington, D.C., offers limitless opportunities to explore." Many "enjoy partying and hanging out off-campus and on campus (even though AU is a 'dry campus')," but there are also "a lot of people who don't drink and have a very good time just using what D.C. has to offer: museums, restaurants, parks, cinemas, theaters, and shops." As one student sums it up: "The city is the school's greatest resource. You will never run out of things to do in Washington."

Student Body

AU attracts a crowd that "tends to be very ideologically driven." "Liberals run the show," most here agree, although they add that "Plenty of students don't fit this mold, and I've never seen anyone rejected for what they believe." The campus "is very friendly to those with alternative lifestyles (GLBT, vegetarian, green-living, etc.)," but students with more socially conservative inclinations note that "while AU boasts about the many religious groups on campus, there is still a general antipathy toward piety." The perception that some departments outshine others is reflected in the way students perceive each other; one says, "You have the political studies know-it-alls, the international studies student who thinks he is going to save the world, the artsy film/communication students, and the rest [who] are unhappy students who couldn't get into George Washington or Georgetown."

FINANCIAL AID: 202-885-6100 • E-MAIL: ADMISSIONS@AMERICAN.EDU • WEBSITE: WWW.AMERICAN.EDU

THE PRINCETON REVIEW SAYS

Admissions

Very important factors considered include: Academic GPA, rigor of secondary school record, standardized test scores, level of applicant's interest. *Important factors considered include:* Application essay, recommendation(s), extracurricular activities, volunteer work. *Other factors considered include:* Alumni/ae relation, character/personal qualities, first generation, geographical residence, racial/ethnic status, talent/ability, work experience. SAT or ACT required; ACT with writing component required. TOEFL required of all international applicants. High school diploma is required and GED is accepted. *Academic units required:* 4 English, 3 mathematics, 3 science (2 science labs), 2 foreign language, 2 social studies, 3 academic electives. *Academic units recommended:* 4 English, 4 mathematics, 4 science, 3 foreign language, 4 social studies, 4 academic electives.

Financial Aid

Students should submit: FAFSA, institution's own financial aid form. Regular filing deadline is February 15. The Princeton Review suggests that all financial aid forms be submitted as soon as possible after January 1. *Need-based scholarships/grants offered:* Federal Pell, SEOG, state scholarships/grants, private scholarships, the school's own gift aid, *Academic merit scholarships:* Presidential Scholarships, Dean's Scholarships, Leadership Scholarships, Phi Theta Kappa Scholarships (transfers only), Tuition Exchange Scholarships, United Methodist Scholarships, and other private/restricted scholarships are awarded by the Undergraduate Admissions Office. Most scholarships do not require a separate application and are renewable for up to three years if certain criteria are met. *Loan aid offered:* Direct Subsidized Stafford, Direct Unsubsidized Stafford, Direct PLUS, Federal Perkins, college/university loans from institutional funds. Applicants will be notified of awards on or about April 1. Federal Work-Study Program available. Institutional employment available. Off-campus job opportunities are excellent.

The Inside Word

Despite strong competition from other area powerhouses, American sees a strong application pool that allows it to be very selective. Admissions rates have declined significantly in recent years. In addition to asking students to indicate their intended field of study, the university is also interested in clear demonstrations of interest on the part of applicants.

THE SCHOOL SAYS ". . ."

From the Admissions Office

"American University is located in the residential 'Embassy Row' neighborhood of Washington, D.C. Nestled among embassies and ambassadorial residences, AU's campus offers a safe, suburban environment with easy access to Washington's countless cultural destinations via the Metrorail subway system. A global center of government, Washington, D.C., stands unmatched in academics, professional, and cultural resources. AU's faculty includes scholars, journalists, artists, diplomats, authors, and scientists. Combining a liberal arts core curriculum with in-depth professional programs, academics at AU provide the necessary balance between theoretical study and hands-on experience. Our Career Center will work with you to enhance this experience with access to unique internship opportunities available only in Washington. Combine this with our diverse national and international student body and our world-class study abroad program, and AU can open up a world of possibilities."

SELECTIVITY

Admissions Rating	**93**
# of applicants	16,924
% of applicants accepted	43
% of acceptees attending	20
# accepting a place on wait list	1,277
# of early decision applicants	565
# accepted early decision	415

FRESHMAN PROFILE

Range SAT Critical Reading	590–710
Range SAT Math	580–680
Range SAT Writing	580–690
Range ACT Composite	27–31
Minimum paper TOEFL	550
Minimum web-based TOEFL	80
Average HS GPA	3.8
% graduated top 10% of class	49
% graduated top 25% of class	82
% graduated top 50% of class	98

DEADLINES

Early decision	
Deadline	11/15
Notification	12/31
Regular	
Deadline	1/15
Notification	4/1
Nonfall registration?	yes

FINANCIAL FACTS

Financial Aid Rating	**79**
Annual tuition	$38,982
Room and board	$13,920
Required fees	$517
% needy frosh rec. need-based scholarship or grant aid	81
% needy UG rec. need-based scholarship or grant aid	58
% needy frosh rec. non-need-based scholarship or grant aid	38
% needy UG rec. non-need-based scholarship or grant aid	40
% needy frosh rec. need-based self-help aid	94
% needy UG rec. need-based self-help aid	93
% UG borrow to pay for school	44
Average cumulative indebtedness	$27,479
Average % of frosh need met	92
Average % of ugrad need met	80

AMHERST COLLEGE

CAMPUS BOX 2231, AMHERST, MA 01002 • ADMISSIONS: 413-542-2328 • FAX: 413-542-2040

CAMPUS LIFE

Quality of Life Rating	**89**
Fire Safety Rating	**71**
Green Rating	**61**
Type of school	private
Environment	town

STUDENTS

Total undergrad enrollment	490
% male/female	49/51
% from out of state	88
% from public high school	58
% frosh live on campus	100
# of countries represented	24

SURVEY SAYS . . .

No one cheats
School is well run
Dorms are like palaces
Campus feels safe
Low cost of living
Musical organizations are popular

ACADEMICS

Academic Rating	**98**
% students returning for sophomore year	94
% students graduating within 4 years	89
% students graduating within 6 years	94
Calendar	semester
Student/faculty ratio	8:1
Profs interesting rating	92
Profs accessible rating	97
Most classes have	10–19 students
Most lab/discussion sessions have	fewer than 10 students

MOST POPULAR MAJORS

economics; political science and government; psychology

APPLICANTS ALSO LOOK AT AND OFTEN PREFER

Princeton University, Yale University, Harvard College

AND SOMETIMES PREFER

Brown University, Williams College, Stanford University, Dartmouth College

AND RARELY PREFER

Tufts University, Vassar College, University of Virginia

STUDENTS SAY ". . ."

Academics

With just more than 1,700 students, Amherst College "has a strong sense of community born of its small size" that goes hand-in-hand with an atmosphere that "encourages discussion and cooperation." Many here are quick to praise the "fantastic" professors and "supportive" administration. "Professors come here to teach," says one undergrad, "not just to do research." The "enriching" academics are bolstered by the "dedicated" faculty, but slackers be warned: You must be "willing to sit down and read a text forward and backward and firmly grasp it" as "skimming will do you no good." Besides having "easily accessible" professors, some students also appreciate that "registration is done by paper" as "it forces you to talk to your advisor." Another student notes, "I'm amazed at how easy it is to sit down for a casual lunch with anyone in the administration without there having to be a problem that needs to be discussed." Indeed, most here agree, "The support for students is as good as anyone could expect." However, some mention that despite the "administration, staff, and faculty" being "accessible and receptive to student input on every level," the "realities of running a small school in this economic climate mean a lot of suggestions won't be acted upon any time soon." Nevertheless, Amherst's alumni have a solid track record when it comes to obtaining postgraduate degrees—so much so that some think of the college "as prep school for grad school."

Life

While students at Amherst are "focused first and foremost on academics, nearly every student is active and enjoys life outside of the library." "There's a club or organization for every interest" here, and students assure us that if there isn't one that you're interested in, "the school will find the money for it." Students also praise the "awesome" dorms (some say they're "as spacious, well-maintained, and luxurious as many five-star hotels"), for being "designed to facilitate social interaction." Coincidentally, the dorms tend to serve as the school's social hub, particularly since Greek organizations were banned back in 1985. Amherst makes up for the lack of frat houses with "a number of socials put on by student government and I-Club (International Club) that are held throughout the year at bars downtown." And don't worry if you don't have a car since these events "have free buses that transport students to and from the bars." Some bemoan that the town of Amherst is "incredibly small" and doesn't feature much in the way of fun. Others take solace in "the many eateries in town that feature lots of ethnically diverse foods" and "go to sporting events." And since Amherst is part of the Five Colleges consortium, there's "an extended social life to be had," however "not that many people go out of their way to experience it." For those who like liquor with their extracurricular activities, most "drink on campus instead of off campus" thanks to some "huge apartment parties."

Student Body

Traditionally, the student body at Amherst has been known by the "stereotype of the preppy, upper-middle-class, white student," but many here note that the school is "at least as racially diverse as the country and more economically diverse than people think." That's not to say that the college doesn't have "a sizeable preppy population fresh from East Coast boarding schools," but overall students here report, "Diversity—racial, ethnic, geographic, socioeconomic—is more than a buzzword here." The campus is also "a politically and environmentally conscious" place, as well as a "highly athletic one." The school's small size "means that no group is isolated and everyone interacts and more or less gets along." Others, however, aren't as convinced about the student body's unity. "There is definitely a divide in the student body," says one undergrad. "The typical Amherst student is either an extremely quiet, bookish nerd or a lumbering, backward-baseball-cap-wearing jock." That said, the school is filled with "open-minded, intellectually passionate, and socially conscious critical thinkers." As one student puts it, "Most students—even our most drunken athletes and wild party-goers—are concerned about learning and academics."

FINANCIAL AID: 413-542-2296 • E-MAIL: ADMISSION@AMHERST.EDU • WEBSITE: WWW.AMHERST.EDU

THE PRINCETON REVIEW SAYS

Admissions

Very important factors considered include: Application essay, academic GPA, recommendation(s), rigor of secondary school record, standardized test scores, character/personal qualities, extracurricular activities, first generation, talent/ability. *Important factors considered include:* Class rank, alumni/ae relation, volunteer work. *Other factors considered include:* Geographical residence, state residency, work experience. ACT with writing component recommended. TOEFL required of all international applicants. High school diploma or equivalent is not required. *Academic units recommended:* 4 English, 4 mathematics, 3 science (1 science lab), 4 foreign language, 2 social studies, 2 history.

Financial Aid

Students should submit: FAFSA, CSS/Financial Aid PROFILE, noncustodial PROFILE, business/farm supplement. Income documentation submitted through College. The Princeton Review suggests that all financial aid forms be submitted as soon as possible after January 1. *Need-based scholarships/grants offered:* Federal Pell, SEOG, state scholarships/grants, private scholarships, the school's own gift aid. *Loan aid offered:* Direct Subsidized Stafford, Direct Unsubsidized Stafford, Direct PLUS, Federal Perkins, college/university loans from institutional funds. Applicants will be notified of awards on or about April 1. Federal Work-Study Program available. Institutional employment available. Off-campus job opportunities are excellent.

The Inside Word

Membership certainly has its benefits at Amherst College. For the price of entry to this school students also gain entrance to the prestigious Five Colleges consortium, which allows enrolled students to take courses for credit at no additional cost at any of the four participating consortium members (Hampshire College, Mount Holyoke College, Smith College, and the University of Massachusetts—Amherst). And this deal isn't just confined to the classroom: Students can use other schools' libraries, eat meals at the other cafeterias, and participate in extracurricular activities offerred at the other schools. And don't worry about how you'll get there—your bus fare is covered, too.

THE SCHOOL SAYS ". . ."

From the Admissions Office

"Amherst College looks, above all, for men and women of intellectual promise who have demonstrated qualities of mind and character that will enable them to take full advantage of the college's curriculum...Admission decisions aim to select from among the many qualified applicants those possessing the intellectual talent, mental discipline, and imagination that will allow them most fully to benefit from the curriculum and contribute to the life of the college and of society. Whatever the form of academic experience—lecture course, seminar, conference, studio, laboratory, independent study at various levels—intellectual competence and awareness of problems and methods are the goals of the Amherst program, rather than the direct preparation for a profession.

"Applicants must submit scores from the SAT plus two SAT Subject Tests. Students may substitute the ACT with the writing component."

SELECTIVITY

Admissions Rating	**99**
# of applicants	8,110
% of applicants accepted	15
% of acceptees attending	40
# accepting a place on wait list	1,098
# admitted from wait list	3
# of early decision applicants	440
# accepted early decision	118

FRESHMAN PROFILE

Range SAT Critical Reading	670–770
Range SAT Math	670–770
Range SAT Writing	680–770
Range ACT Composite	30–34
Minimum paper TOEFL	600
Minimum web-based TOEFL	100
% graduated top 10% of class	87
% graduated top 25% of class	97
% graduated top 50% of class	100

DEADLINES

Early decision	
Deadline	11/15
Notification	12/15
Regular	
Deadline	1/1
Nonfall registration?	no

FINANCIAL FACTS

Financial Aid Rating	**98**
Books and supplies	$1,000
% needy frosh rec. need-based scholarship or grant aid	128
% needy UG rec. need-based scholarship or grant aid	97
% needy frosh rec. need-based self-help aid	107
% needy UG rec. need-based self-help aid	88
% frosh rec. any financial aid	60
% UG rec. any financial aid	57
% UG borrow to pay for school	42
Average cumulative indebtedness	$12,843
% frosh need fully met	100
% ugrads need fully met	100
Average % of frosh need met	100
Average % of ugrad need met	100

ANGELO STATE UNIVERSITY

ASU STATION #11014, SAN ANGELO, TX 76909-1014 • ADMISSIONS: 325-942-2041 • FAX: 325-942-2078

CAMPUS LIFE

Quality of Life Rating	**78**
Fire Safety Rating	**92**
Green Rating	**69**
Type of school	public
Environment	city

STUDENTS

Total undergrad enrollment	6,105
% male/female	45/55
% from out of state	1
% from public high school	96
# of fraternities	3
# of sororities	2
% African American	7
% Asian	1
% Caucasian	60
% Hispanic	27
% Native American	1
% international	1
# of countries represented	24

SURVEY SAYS . . .

Great computer facilities
Low cost of living
Very little drug use

ACADEMICS

Academic Rating	**67**
% students graduating within 4 years	16
% students graduating within 6 years	31
Calendar	semester
Student/faculty ratio	21:1
Profs interesting rating	79
Profs accessible rating	76
Most classes have	20–29 students
Most lab/discussion sessions have	20–29 students

MOST POPULAR MAJORS

business/commerce; nursing/registered nurse (rn, asn, bsn, msn); psychology

STUDENTS SAY ". . ."

Academics

A formidable player in the Texas Tech University System, Angelo State offers students a "very affordable" education coupled with a "wide range of degree programs." Importantly, a "small-town feel" permeates the campus, and students are quick to assert that "you're not just a number at Angelo." While the university has a handful of great departments, undergrads here are especially quick to highlight the stellar biology, nursing, physical therapy, and music programs. Like many schools, the quality of professors can run the gamut. Fortunately, as one undergrad happily shares, the vast majority are "brilliant, energetic, and inspiring." Indeed, they're "enthusiastic about their subjects" and "genuinely care about their students." And while they "have high success standards, [they] are also willing to do almost anything to help you meet those standards." Another student elaborates, "Angelo State's faculty is very dedicated to their students and to helping us grow. There is never a need to hesitate to ask a question, or to speak with a professor one on one for better understanding." Finally, one extremely content student sums up the Angelo State experience with the confident assertion, "I feel like I am receiving the best education money can buy!"

Life

Undergrads at Angelo State proudly proclaim that their campus is "always alive and buzzing." The university sponsors a number of events that "range from movie marathons to Monopoly, Texas Hold'em, and Call of Duty tournaments." One happy undergrad eagerly adds to the list, "On campus, there are many activities to get involved as for example, intramural sports, video games available in main lobbies at each door, a renovated…gym with new equipment, walking program is perfect. There are also many events on campus sponsored by a student council and they bring comedians, singers, and other fun activities." A fellow student interjects, "The combination of the brand new fitness center with the popular intramural activities has made this a very active campus, where physical education and team sports are very popular." Hometown San Angelo is "relatively small" and "conservative." However, "Plenty of good restaurants" are available along with bowling, shopping, and movies. Lastly, when students are itching to get away, they can easily explore all that Texas has to offer. As one eager undergrad elaborates, "The good news is that we are centrally located. Because we are only about three or four hours from Lubbock, San Antonio, Austin, or the DFW area, most students plan multiple trips to these areas throughout the semester."

Student Body

When asked to describe their peers, the first adjective that leaps out of the mouths of Angelo State students is "friendly." Indeed, the vast majority "seem[s] outgoing and is involved in many different activities around school or in the community." In addition, they're "down-to-earth" and aim to "balance [their] social life with making good grades." As one ecstatic student gushes, "I haven't spoken with a student that has found a place where he/she has not felt welcome." Indeed, we are assured, "To fit in, all you have to do is get involved in something—that way the different networks of friends are available to you and you get to know a lot of people." Finally, it should be noted that the university also has a decent number of returning students, and most report a seamless transition. As one student shares, "Nontraditional students blend in quite well. I have a family and live off campus, but I feel very comfortable in the classroom and interacting with all students and professors."

ANGELO STATE UNIVERSITY

FINANCIAL AID: 325-942-2246 • E-MAIL: ADMISSIONS@ANGELO.EDU • WEBSITE: WWW.ANGELO.EDU

THE PRINCETON REVIEW SAYS

Admissions

Very important factors considered include: Class rank, rigor of secondary school record, standardized test scores. SAT or ACT required; ACT with or without writing component accepted. TOEFL required of all international applicants. High school diploma is required and GED is accepted. *Academic units recommended:* 4 English, 3 mathematics, 3 science, 2 foreign language, 3 social studies, 1 computer science, 1 academic electives.

Financial Aid

Students should submit: FAFSA. The Princeton Review suggests that all financial aid forms be submitted as soon as possible after January 1. *Need-based scholarships/grants offered:* Federal Pell, SEOG, state scholarships/grants, private scholarships, the school's own gift aid, Federal Nursing Scholarships. *Loan aid offered:* Direct Subsidized Stafford, Direct Unsubsidized Stafford, Direct PLUS, Federal Perkins, Federal Nursing, state loans, college/university loans from institutional funds. Applicants will be notified of awards on a rolling basis beginning April 1. Federal Work-Study Program available. Institutional employment available. Off-campus job opportunities are good.

The Inside Word

The admissions criteria for Angelo State are fairly straightforward. Applicants must have successfully completed a rigorous college prep program and, depending on where their class ranking falls, meet specific standardized test requirements. Those who don't meet the minimum requirements might still be admitted on a conditional basis.

THE SCHOOL SAYS ". . ."

From the Admissions Office

"Angelo State University remains an affordable institution with a superb record of sending graduates on to success in business, agribusiness, health care, and education as well as in medical, law, and professional school. ASU maintains strong academic programs in traditional fields, such as physics, biology, mathematics, education, business, agriculture, and nursing, while developing innovative offerings like the computer science department's computer gaming design sequence, ranked by The Princeton Review as one of the top fifty in the nation.

"Because of strong academics and a substantial gift aid program, including the Carr Scholarship Program, which annually awards scholarships totaling approximately $4 million, ASU remains one of the top educational values in Texas. About sixty-seven percent of ASU students receive gift aid, financial support which does not have to be repaid to the university. ASU targets students in the top forty-five percent of their class or with 990–1100 SAT and 21–24 ACT scores for gift aid. Additionally, ASU offers its Blue and Gold Guarantee program for students from low income families.

"Because of its low twenty-one to one student/faculty ratio and individualized instruction, ASU attracts many first-generation students, who benefit from special programs and scholarships. A quarter of the student body is Hispanic, enhancing the university's overall diversity. Comprehensive academic advising and numerous opportunities for international study enhance the college experience on the 268-acre Angelo State campus known for its safety and modern academic, residential and recreational facilities."

SELECTIVITY

Admissions Rating	65
# of applicants	4,527
% of applicants accepted	93
% of acceptees attending	35

FRESHMAN PROFILE

Range SAT Critical Reading	420–530
Range SAT Math	440–550
Range ACT Composite	18–23
Minimum paper TOEFL	550
Minimum web-based TOEFL	79
% graduated top 10% of class	14
% graduated top 25% of class	30
% graduated top 50% of class	75

DEADLINES

Regular Deadline	8/22
Nonfall registration?	yes

FINANCIAL FACTS

Financial Aid Rating	73
Annual in-state tuition	$4,994
Annual out-state tuition	$15,524
Room and board	$8,022
Required fees	$2,499
Books and supplies	$1,500
% needy frosh rec. need-based scholarship or grant aid	90
% needy UG rec. need-based scholarship or grant aid	90
% needy frosh rec. non-need-based scholarship or grant aid	61
% needy UG rec. non-need-based scholarship or grant aid	45
% needy frosh rec. need-based self-help aid	61
% needy UG rec. need-based self-help aid	66
% frosh rec. any financial aid	89
% UG rec. any financial aid	82
% UG borrow to pay for school	59
Average cumulative indebtedness	$21,462
% frosh need fully met	30
% ugrads need fully met	25
Average % of frosh need met	54
Average % of ugrad need met	50

ARIZONA STATE UNIVERSITY

PO BOX 870112, TEMPE, AZ 85287-0112 • ADMISSIONS: 480-965-7788 • FAX: 480-965-3610

CAMPUS LIFE

Quality of Life Rating	**71**
Fire Safety Rating	**84**
Green Rating	**99**
Type of school	public
Environment	metropolis

STUDENTS

Total undergrad enrollment	58,184
% male/female	50/50
% from out of state	23
% from public high school	93
% frosh live on campus	70
# of fraternities	31
# of sororities	23
% African American	5
% Asian	6
% Caucasian	61
% Hispanic	19
% Native American	2
% international	3
# of countries represented	120

SURVEY SAYS . . .

Great computer facilities
Great off-campus food
Everyone loves the Sun Devils
Student publications are popular
Lots of beer drinking
Hard liquor is popular

ACADEMICS

Academic Rating	**70**
% students returning for sophomore year	84
% students graduating within 4 years	33
% students graduating within 6 years	58
Calendar	semester
Student/faculty ratio	24:1
Profs interesting rating	72
Profs accessible rating	72
Most classes have	10–19 students
Most lab/discussion sessions have	20–29 students

MOST POPULAR MAJORS

business, management, marketing, and related majors; biological and biomedical sciences; education; engineering; visual and performing arts

STUDENTS SAY ". . ."

Academics

Arizona State University's "greatest strength is the great depth of its faculty and wealth of opportunities offered to students." Many students say they chose ASU because it "offers a huge range of classes and majors at a reasonable cost for in-state students." Students also say the university provides "the best of both worlds: a large research university and an honors program tailored for individual needs." The Honors College and The Walter Cronkite School of Journalism and Mass Communication stand out as notable programs that offer "targeted education." Despite this, a Russian major points out, "The school still has a reputation for partying, which is not totally undeserved. The student body is not full of future Einsteins." Many ASU students, however, believe you get from the university what you put into it and say, "A large number of students truly care about the education they are receiving." While "for the most part, ASU is home to engaging professors that are genuinely concerned with the success of their students," "the large auditorium classes are an absolute joke."

Life

At ASU, "There is always something happening on campus," and students say, "ASU is all about diversity and open doors; there are a million distinct opportunities to get involved in whatever you're passionate about." Many rave, "Campus life is amazing. There is always something to do, someone to hang out with, or places to be," adding, "The weather is nice enough to sit outside and study a lot." A kinesiology majors says, "The overall culture is very Southern California," but "The west side of campus has more of a Portland feel, which is more individual and artsy. It all depends on where you decide to get plugged in." Despite praise for ASU's dedication to "pursuing new ways to become more sustainable and encouraging 'going green' throughout campus, classrooms, and offices," many students feel, "ASU should concentrate on renovating old buildings, which are falling apart" and gripe about inconsistent air conditioning during the hottest months. Some students complain that ASU needs to "improve in advising and the overall process of changing a major," and some say, "The red tape can be very frustrating, especially as a new student."

Student Body

With an enrollment of more than 50,000 undergraduates, "It's hard to define typical" when it comes to describing the ASU student body. "Due to the huge student population size and plethora of social events and organizations, any student can find a niche and a group of people with similar interests." Some say, "There is a minority of students who work hard and care about their educations surrounded by a majority only concerned with drinking, partying, and getting a better tan." It's also pointed out that "because the party atmosphere is so huge, those students seem to have the largest voice." However, others say, "Even the party kids care about their grades," and the typical student is "laid-back but invested in their future." One political science major jokes, "I would say the hardest part for students fitting in is dealing with the heat." Most agree, "The 'dry campus' rules are *far* from followed, and even for those who don't break those rules, there are places right across the street for students to drink at their leisure," adding, "Tempe is great—if you're in college," and "Tempe has many fun activities both indoors and outdoors, depending on the weather! From hiking to biking, all kinds of sports, going downtown and being around the museums and history, to having a good time hanging out with friends on Mill Avenue."

FINANCIAL AID: 480-965-3355 • E-MAIL: ADMISSIONS@ASU.EDU • WEBSITE: WWW.ASU.EDU

THE PRINCETON REVIEW SAYS

Admissions

Very important factors considered include: Class rank, academic GPA, standardized test scores. *Important factors considered include:* Rigor of secondary school. ACT with or without writing component accepted. TOEFL required of all international applicants. High school diploma is required and GED is accepted. *Academic units required:* 4 English, 4 mathematics, 3 science (3 science labs), 2 foreign language, 1 social studies, 1 history, 1 fine arts.

Financial Aid

Students should submit: FAFSA. The Princeton Review suggests that all financial aid forms be submitted as soon as possible after January 1. *Need-based scholarships/grants offered:* Federal Pell, SEOG, state scholarships/grants, private scholarships, the school's own gift aid, Federal Nursing Scholarships. *Loan aid offered:* Direct Subsidized Stafford, Direct Unsubsidized Stafford, Direct PLUS, Federal Perkins. Federal Work-Study Program available. Institutional employment available. Off-campus job opportunities are good.

The Inside Word

ASU clearly outlines all the requirements for admission on its website. The applications of students who meet all the requirements go under "individual review" and are carefully evaluated by the admissions team. Students interested in Barrett, The Honors College may apply for admission only after submitting an application to ASU.

THE SCHOOL SAYS ". . ."

From the Admissions Office

"ASU is breaking down the walls of the traditional academic experience to increase the impact of education and research in local and global communities. As the New American University, ASU is committed to interdisciplinary connections, academic excellence, and societal impact. We are bold and forward-thinking, and we see challenges as opportunities.

"With 250-plus undergraduate majors, ASU is a learning environment where personal expression is valued as much as research and discovery. ASU champions intellectual and cultural diversity and welcomes students from all fifty states and 120-plus nations. Our distinguished faculty receives prestigious honors including the Nobel Prize and membership in the National Academies. Student achievements include Goldwater, Rhodes, Marshall, and Fulbright scholars.

"ASU has four unique campuses in metropolitan Phoenix. State-of-the-art living and learning facilities are found at ASU's Downtown Phoenix campus. The campus creates strong learning and career connections for 11,500-plus students with media, health care, corporate, and government organizations.

"The Polytechnic campus, located in Mesa, Arizona, is home to 9,000-plus students who are exploring professional and technical programs. Thousands of square feet of new laboratory space make way for project-based learning.

"ASU welcomes 55,000-plus students studying at the historic Tempe campus. The Sun Devils athletic complex, performing arts facilities, and high-tech research space create a dynamic and engaging learning environment.

"At the West campus in northwest Phoenix, ASU offers business, education, and interdisciplinary arts and science programs to 10,000-plus students. The campus's award-winning architecture and lush landscaping are designed to create a close-knit learning community."

SELECTIVITY

Admissions Rating	77
# of applicants	29,722
% of applicants accepted	89
% of acceptees attending	35

FRESHMAN PROFILE

Range SAT Critical Reading	480–610
Range SAT Math	490–630
Range ACT Composite	21–27
Minimum paper TOEFL	500
Minimum web-based TOEFL	61
Average HS GPA	3.4
% graduated top 10% of class	28
% graduated top 25% of class	58
% graduated top 50% of class	84

DEADLINES

Regular	
Priority	2/1
Nonfall registration?	yes

FINANCIAL FACTS

Financial Aid Rating	73
Annual in-state tuition	$9,208
Annual out-state tuition	$21,807
Room and board	$8,953
Required fees	$512
Books and supplies	$1,000
% needy frosh rec. need-based scholarship or grant aid	96
% needy UG rec. need-based scholarship or grant aid	89
% needy frosh rec. non-need-based scholarship or grant aid	16
% needy UG rec. non-need-based scholarship or grant aid	7
% needy frosh rec. need-based self-help aid	56
% needy UG rec. need-based self-help aid	73
% frosh rec. any financial aid	90
% UG rec. any financial aid	80
% UG borrow to pay for school	49
Average cumulative indebtedness	$19,227
% frosh need fully met	25
% ugrads need fully met	16
Average % of frosh need met	70
Average % of ugrad need met	59

AUBURN UNIVERSITY

108 MARY MARTIN HALL, AUBURN, AL 36849-5149 • ADMISSIONS: 334-844-4080 • FAX: 334-844-6436

CAMPUS LIFE

Quality of Life Rating	**96**
Fire Safety Rating	**80**
Green Rating	**85**
Type of school	public
Environment	town

STUDENTS

Total undergrad enrollment	20,436
% male/female	51/49
% from out of state	45
% from public high school	89
% frosh live on campus	67
# of fraternities	27
# of sororities	17
% African American	7
% Asian	2
% Caucasian	86
% Hispanic	3
% Native American	1
% international	1
# of countries represented	81

SURVEY SAYS . . .

Great library
School is well run
Students are friendly
Students get along with local community
Students are happy
Everyone loves the Tigers
Student publications are popular
Student government is popular

ACADEMICS

Academic Rating	**73**
% students returning for sophomore year	89
% students graduating within 4 years	36
% students graduating within 6 years	66
Calendar	semester
Student/faculty ratio	18:1
Profs interesting rating	74
Profs accessible rating	79
Most classes have	20–29 students
Most lab/discussion sessions have	20–29 students

MOST POPULAR MAJORS

business administration and management; mechanical engineering; secondary education and teaching

APPLICANTS ALSO LOOK AT AND SOMETIMES PREFER

University of Florida, University of Georgia, University of Alabama—Tuscaloosa, Clemson University, Georgia Institute of Technology, University of Mississippi, University of Tennessee, Louisiana State University—Baton Rouge

STUDENTS SAY "..."

Academics

Auburn University is a traditional Southern school full of Southern hospitality that provides a surprisingly "family-like atmosphere" for a school of 25,000 and an unsurprising level of school spirit. "Auburn people are proud to be Auburn people," says a student. Such a large student body has the power to enact change, and the school actually listens to the constant desire "to improve academically, to make the campus safer and the facilities better, to improve the aesthetic appeal of the campus, and to address student demands." "Auburn has really accessible faculty and administration that care if the students here succeed." With this constant growth added on top of longstanding tradition, the university is "all about the Auburn family—whether it's football games, student organizations, or academics, we're all in it together!" Along with its generous scholarships, the school's reputable honors program and veterinary and engineering schools are also big draws, but "There's a major for everyone." "I'll be the first one to tell you that Auburn engineers are some of the best you'll ever have the pleasure of working with," says an engineering student. Some professors are "amazing," and "Others are less than that," but students are generally satisfied. "For the most part, my professors have been extremely intelligent people who further my knowledge and are able to increase my interest in subjects I might not have had interest in," says a student. The faculty emphasizes "not the course material, but how to apply what we learn in the classroom to real-life issues and to look beyond just knowing but understanding." Finally, the research at Auburn is "top-notch." Regardless of your area of study, the school provides "many services to help you achieve the goal you are trying to accomplishment."

Life

Auburn is "a big school in a small college town, where the people are friendly and love their football." On this "nice comfortable campus," everyone is "amiable, outgoing, and pleasant," and "There are so many groups and ways to get involved that it's almost ridiculous. If you can think of it, you can find a class or club about it!" As one student lovingly puts it, "Auburn creates a sense of family during the first few months after moving away from your biological family, and it lasts through life." To say "Auburn football is popular" is to make the understatement of the century; "Football is religion at Auburn," and students say, "If you don't like Auburn football at least a little, you might have trouble finding friends to do things with on a Saturday!" UPC at Auburn "provides many events around campus that are free to students for students to have fun," and people often "go to fraternity parties or downtown" from Wednesday to Saturday. The nearby arboretum and Chewacla Park are "nice places to go" for hiking, camping, and outdoor activities.

Student Body

Though the school was once mainly populated by Alabamans, "Auburn is becoming more diverse," and a large percentage are from out-of-state (though still mainly the South), so "it's not hard to fit in...because you meet people that came from areas just like you." There are also a fair number of legacy Tigers here who are carrying on family tradition: "I was born an Auburn Tiger...my doorbell at home plays the Auburn fight song, and I was also grounded for a week in high school for saying 'roll tide' to my father. He said it was disrespectful," says one student. Typical students "tend to look like they are in fraternities or sororities—even if they aren't in them" (though about a third of students are). Most students "have good values and aren't prejudiced toward anyone in particular," and there are so many types of people and groups that "it is practically impossible to not find somewhere you 'fit in.'"

FINANCIAL AID: 334-844-4634 • E-MAIL: ADMISSIONS@AUBURN.EDU • WEBSITE: WWW.AUBURN.EDU

THE PRINCETON REVIEW SAYS

Admissions

Very important factors considered include: Application essay, academic GPA, standardized test scores. *Important factors considered include:* Rigor of secondary school record, alumni/ae relation, character/personal qualities, extracurricular activities, first generation, geographical residence, level of applicant's interest, state residency, talent/ability, volunteer work, work experience. *Other factors considered include:* Recommendation(s). SAT or ACT required; ACT with writing component required. TOEFL required of all international applicants. High school diploma is required and GED is accepted. *Academic units required:* 4 English, 3 mathematics, 2 science (1 science lab), 3 social studies. *Academic units recommended:* 4 English, 3 mathematics, 3 science (2 science labs), 1 foreign language, 4 social studies.

Financial Aid

Students should submit: FAFSA. The Princeton Review suggests that all financial aid forms be submitted as soon as possible after January 1. *Need-based scholarships/grants offered:* Federal Pell, SEOG, state scholarships/grants, private scholarships, the school's own gift aid. *Loan aid offered:* Direct Subsidized Stafford, Direct Unsubsidized Stafford, Direct PLUS, Federal Perkins, Federal Nursing, college/university loans from institutional funds. Applicants will be notified of awards on a rolling basis beginning October 2. Federal Work-Study Program available. Institutional employment available. Highest amount earned per year from on-campus jobs $10,920. Off-campus job opportunities are good.

The Inside Word

Auburn admissions officers have more than 15,000 applications to sort through each year. Applicants meeting certain baseline GPA, curricular, and standardized test score levels are admitted by rule. Applicants who fall far short of these baselines are nearly always rejected, except for those with unique talents and traits that will contribute substantially to campus life. Letters of recommendation, essays, and extracurricular activities are the make-or-break point for borderline candidates. Starting in 2012, applicant's test scores must be submitted directly from the testing agencies.

THE SCHOOL SAYS ". . ."

From the Admissions Office

"Auburn University is a comprehensive land-grant university serving Alabama and the nation. The university is especially charged with the responsibility of enhancing the economic, social, and cultural development of the state through its instruction, research, and extension programs. In all of these programs, the university is committed to the pursuit of excellence. The university assumes an obligation to provide an environment of learning in which the individual and society are enriched by the discovery, preservation, transmission, and application of knowledge; in which students grow intellectually as they study and do research under the guidance of competent faculty, and in which the faculty develop professionally and contribute fully to the intellectual life of the institution, community, and state. This obligation unites Auburn University's continuing commitment to its land-grant traditions and the institution's role as a dynamic and complex, comprehensive university."

SELECTIVITY

Admissions Rating	**88**
# of applicants	18,323
% of applicants accepted	70
% of acceptees attending	33

FRESHMAN PROFILE

Range SAT Critical Reading	550–680
Range SAT Math	570–680
Range SAT Writing	530–650
Range ACT Composite	24–30
Minimum paper TOEFL	550
Minimum web-based TOEFL	79
Average HS GPA	3.8
% graduated top 10% of class	45
% graduated top 25% of class	68
% graduated top 50% of class	91

DEADLINES

Early action	
Deadline	10/1
Notification	10/15
Regular	
Priority	2/1
Deadline	6/1
Notification	2/15
Nonfall registration?	yes

FINANCIAL FACTS

Financial Aid Rating	**68**
Annual in-state tuition	$7,296
Annual out-state tuition	$21,888
Room and board	$9,992
Required fees	$1,402
Books and supplies	$1,100
% needy frosh rec. need-based scholarship or grant aid	87
% needy UG rec. need-based scholarship or grant aid	73
% needy frosh rec. non-need-based scholarship or grant aid	20
% needy UG rec. non-need-based scholarship or grant aid	10
% needy frosh rec. need-based self-help aid	63
% needy UG rec. need-based self-help aid	81
% frosh rec. any financial aid	62
% UG rec. any financial aid	52
% UG borrow to pay for school	47
Average cumulative indebtedness	$24,778
% frosh need fully met	29
% ugrads need fully met	17
Average % of frosh need met	62
Average % of ugrad need met	52

Austin College

900 North Grand Ave, Suite 6N Sherman, TX 75090-4400 • Admissions: 903-813-3000 • Fax: 903-813-3198

CAMPUS LIFE	
Quality of Life Rating	85
Fire Safety Rating	71
Green Rating	81
Type of school	private
Affiliation	Presbyterian
Environment	town

STUDENTS	
Total undergrad enrollment	1,319
% male/female	47/53
% from out of state	11
% from public high school	84
% frosh live on campus	97
# of fraternities	6
# of sororities	6
% African American	4
% Asian	14
% Caucasian	62
% Hispanic	14
# of countries represented	11

SURVEY SAYS . . .

Students are happy
Career services are great
School is well run
No one cheats
Students are friendly
Campus feels safe

ACADEMICS	
Academic Rating	84
% students returning for sophomore year	84
Calendar	semester
Student/faculty ratio	12:1
Profs interesting rating	97
Profs accessible rating	92
Most classes have	10–19 students
Most lab/discussion sessions have	fewer than 10 students

MOST POPULAR MAJORS

biology/biological sciences; business/commerce; psychology

APPLICANTS ALSO LOOK AT AND OFTEN PREFER

Trinity University, Southwestern University

AND SOMETIMES PREFER

Baylor University, Texas A&M University—College Station, Texas Christian University

AND RARELY PREFER

Hendrix College, University of Dallas

STUDENTS SAY ". . ."

Academics

Austin College, a "small school with a huge amount of opportunities," "is about active learning and creating unique experiences for each student" through "unsurpassed opportunities for internships, studying abroad, and a personalized learning experience," students tell us. "A strong premed program" attracts many undergraduates to this campus; psychology, political science, international relations, environmental studies, language programs featuring "the Jordan Family Language House, the language tables in the cafeteria, conversation classes, and incredibly easy access to study abroad," and an education program "where one can get a [master's degree in teaching]" also earn students' accolades. Students are especially enthusiastic about AC's "JanTerm," "where for the month of January students take one intensive course," and "Many students take the opportunity to go abroad or do internships or directed studies of their choice." Best of all, students benefit from "matched tuition when abroad," which means that "all scholarships and loans remain in place for your tuition abroad." Academics entail "a well-rounded and difficult curriculum that really gives students…bang for their buck," combined with "tough classes, hard work, and great people." The end result, undergraduates explain, is "a fun yet academically challenging place that is more home than school."

Life

Campus life at Austin College is pretty much what you would expect at a small school in a small town. Undergraduates "generally chill out at their friend's places" or "house hop, have dinner parties, [or attend] writer's circles, Friday Night Happy Hour, painting circles, garden parties, tea parties, [and other] quaint little things." AC also has "a great Greek community, although it's entirely local" (that is, unaffiliated with national Greek organizations) and an effective campus activities board that "has some kind of event planned for almost every night (bingo, movies, etc.). They also get tickets for midnight showings at Cinemark and free bowling at the local alley." Hometown Sherman contributes "a dollar cinema, which isn't too shabby" and "local bars and restaurants [that] run nightly specials," but otherwise it "is not a very active or exciting town, so you have to try a little harder to enjoy yourself." Students note, "We're only an hour away from Dallas and Denton, and an hour-and-a-half to Fort Worth, so a large city isn't too hard to reach." All in all, things are pretty low key at AC. "In general, a lot of people spend a lot of time on schoolwork and studying, at an on-campus job, at some sort of service organization, or [participating in] an extracurricular," one student sums up.

Student Body

Though small, Austin College is large enough to "host a regular buffet of savant-level geniuses, artistic hippie types, and driven athletes." Undergrads tend to be "very studious" to the point that "everyone here is a bit of a nerd." One student elaborates: "Take every nerd from every high school…and put them all in one place. That's Austin College, and once all the fresh eccentric kids arrive, they reassemble into what a 'normal' school should look like, with jocks, theater groups, musicians, academics, class clowns, homecoming queens, and library workers." They're also "pretty liberal, aware of social issues…and focused on the importance of service to others." Though, in the past, students have noted that there's "not much racial diversity among students due to the size, price, and location of the school." Recent efforts to increase minority representation on campus have been a big success. "Though Presbyterian, Austin College is very religiously diverse, and students of all religions (including the irreligious) are accepted." Most here "are from the Dallas/Fort Worth area."

FINANCIAL AID: 903-813-2900 • E-MAIL: ADMISSION@AUSTINCOLLEGE.EDU • WEBSITE: WWW.AUSTINCOLLEGE.EDU

THE PRINCETON REVIEW SAYS

Admissions

Very important factors considered include: Academic GPA, rigor of secondary school record. *Important factors considered include:* Class rank, application essay, recommendation(s), standardized test scores, character/personal qualities, extracurricular activities, talent/ability. *Other factors considered include:* Alumni/ae relation, first generation, geographical residence, interview, racial/ethnic status, religious affiliation/commitment, state residency, volunteer work, work experience. SAT or ACT required; ACT with writing component required. TOEFL required of all international applicants. High school diploma is required and GED is accepted. *Academic units required:* 4 English, 3 mathematics, 3 science (2 science labs), 2 foreign language, 2 social studies, 1 visual/performing arts, 1 academic elective. *Academic units recommended:* 4 English, 4 mathematics, 4 science (3 science labs), 3 foreign language, 3 social studies, 2 visual/performing arts.

Financial Aid

Students should submit: FAFSA. The Princeton Review suggests that all financial aid forms be submitted as soon as possible after January 1. *Need-based scholarships/grants offered:* Federal Pell, SEOG, state scholarships/grants, private scholarships, the school's own gift aid. *Loan aid offered:* Direct Subsidized Stafford, Direct Unsubsidized Stafford, Direct PLUS, Federal Perkins, state loans, college/university loans from institutional funds, alternative loans through various sources. Applicants will be notified of awards on a rolling basis beginning March 1. Federal Work-Study Program available. Institutional employment available. Highest amount earned per year from on-campus jobs $1,164. Off-campus job opportunities are good.

The Inside Word

The admissions process at Austin College is similar to the process at most competitive, small, private colleges. Rigor of high school curriculum, grades, and standardized test scores are paramount, but admissions officers also dig down into essays, recommendations, and record of extracurricular achievement in search of a more complete portrait of each applicant. A campus visit, including an interview with an admissions officer, is a good way to signal your serious interest in attending AC.

THE SCHOOL SAYS ". . ."

From the Admissions Office

"Few schools the size of Austin College offer a greater emphasis on all things global, highlighted by a nationally recognized study abroad program. Three-quarters of the class of 2009 studied abroad while attending Austin College, and an average seventy percent of students in the past ten years have studied abroad, exploring more than fifty countries on six continents. In fact, Austin College has been ranked number one in the nation four of the past six years by the Institute of International Education for percentage of study abroad participation among liberal arts colleges.

"Study abroad takes many forms at Austin College, including January Term, internship programs, and service opportunities such as the new Global Outreach summer program that has sent students on self-designed international service projects in Costa Rica, Ethiopia, Ghana, Guatemala, India, Kenya, Lebanon, Nigeria, Pakistan, Peru, Russia, South Africa, Thailand, and Vietnam. In 2010 alone, Austin College students once again furthered their educations on nearly every continent, including North America, South America, Europe, Asia, Africa, and Australia. For January Term, students visited twenty-five countries on five continents—all except Australia and Antarctica. Austin College biology professor George Diggs covered the coldest continent with a January sabbatical trip to Antarctica, where his research involved capturing videos of penguins, leopard seals, and humpback whales, as well as photos of animals and a small tuft of grass he found on the Antarctic Peninsula."

SELECTIVITY	
Admissions Rating	85
FRESHMAN PROFILE	
Range SAT Critical Reading	580–680
Range SAT Math	570–680
Range SAT Writing	560–650
Range ACT Composite	24–29
Minimum paper TOEFL	550
DEADLINES	
Early action	
Deadline	1/15
Notification	3/1
Regular	
Priority	1/15
Deadline	5/1
Nonfall registration?	yes
FINANCIAL FACTS	
Financial Aid Rating	98
Annual tuition	$31,110
Room and board	$10,078
Required fees	$160
Books and supplies	$1,200
% needy frosh rec. need-based scholarship or grant aid	100
% needy UG rec. need-based scholarship or grant aid	100
% needy frosh rec. non-need-based scholarship or grant aid	13
% needy UG rec. non-need-based scholarship or grant aid	18
% needy frosh rec. need-based self-help aid	89
% needy UG rec. need-based self-help aid	83
% frosh rec. any financial aid	97
% UG rec. any financial aid	98
% frosh need fully met	100
% ugrads need fully met	100
Average % of frosh need met	100
Average % of ugrad need met	100

BABSON COLLEGE

LUNDER HALL, BABSON PARK, MA 02457 • ADMISSION: 781-239-5522 • FAX: 781-239-4006

CAMPUS LIFE

Quality of Life Rating	**96**
Fire Safety Rating	**83**
Green Rating	**90**
Type of school	private
Environment	village

STUDENTS

Total undergrad enrollment	2,007
% male/female	56/44
% from out of state	57
% from public high school	50
% frosh live on campus	100
# of fraternities	4
# of sororities	3
% African American	4
% Asian	12
% Caucasian	38
% Hispanic	10
% international	27
# of countries represented	72

SURVEY SAYS . . .

Great computer facilities
School is well run
Diverse student types on campus
Campus feels safe
Low cost of living
Internships are widely available

ACADEMICS

Academic Rating	**95**
% students returning for sophomore year	94
% students graduating within 4 years	91
Calendar	4-1-4
Student/faculty ratio	14:1
Profs interesting rating	93
Profs accessible rating	93
Most classes have	30–39 students

MOST POPULAR MAJORS

accounting; entrepreneurial and small business operations, other; finance

STUDENTS SAY ". . ."

Academics

Babson is a school well-suited to the age of specialization. Its business is business; if you're looking for a well-regarded undergraduate degree in business, Babson can serve your needs because the school "offers multiple opportunities for students to gear their own educations" to develop "a complete set of management skills." As one student puts it, "When I took a quick look at the curriculum, I was positive whatever I wanted to study in business could be found" at Babson. The school is best known for its emphasis on entrepreneurship; all freshmen must undertake the school's Foundations in Management and Entrepreneurship immersion course, during which undergrads create their own startups. Those who choose to pursue the field further can jockey for space in E-Tower, a "community of twenty-one highly motivated entrepreneurs chosen to live together" and immerse themselves in all things entrepreneurial (similar housing options are available for students in, among others, finance and green business). Internship opportunities are abundant thanks to the school's reputation and proximity to Boston, providing students "a hands-on experience of how things work in the real world." Professors "want nothing more than to see their students learn and do well. Many…refer to themselves as 'pracademics' because they have had such amazing real-world experience from which they can draw on in the classroom. From executives of Fortune 500 companies to entrepreneurs who own multimillion dollar companies, the knowledge of professors at Babson is only rivaled by their desire to see students do well." Career placement services here "are really strong."

Life

Babson is in the "perfect location," "near Boston but not in it." One student explains: "We are not in the busy city life on a daily basis, but we are able to get into Boston very easily, whether it's driving, taking the T, or the Babson Shuttle that drops you off right in the center of Fanueil Hall." (The shuttle runs only on weekends.) Campus life, once considered sub-par, "is definitely a lot better. [Student government] sponsors and hosts many events throughout the months to keep students entertained and involved," including "Knight Parties, where there are monthly dance parties in one of our large auditoriums" and "spring, winter, and fall weekend, where they have entertainment and bands come to the school. This year we even had Jimmy Fallon come for a comedy concert in the fall—the show was packed; it was standing room only." Students report, "A favorite hangout on a Thursday night is the pub, where there is entertainment and food. Babson [provides] supervised drinking for those of legal drinking age." The school's numerous student-run clubs "are very motivated, providing diverse and educating events" such as mixers and symposia.

Student Body

"It is hard to pinpoint a typical student, as Babson is so diverse," but the common thread is that "we all view business as a primary, shared strand that can link our interests and passions in order to help us make a difference in the world." Babson "is an international college. Outside of our library, there is a flag tree where the flags of different students represented on our campus are flown to show our diversity. We have students from about sixty-seven different countries," and students "learn from each others' differences. It is one of the great pieces of knowledge we are able to pick up at Babson." The "dominant domestic students will be the preppy white boy and girl who treat their designer clothes like aprons," while "international students are mostly of Indian and Hispanic descent who do not refrain from displaying their wealth," all supplemented by "a small population of students that are swimming in personal debt to attend Babson or could never place a foot on the campus if it weren't for their financial aid."

FINANCIAL AID: 781-239-4219 • E-MAIL: UGRADADMISSION@BABSON.EDU • WEBSITE: WWW.BABSON.EDU

THE PRINCETON REVIEW SAYS

Admissions

Very important factors considered include: Application essay, academic GPA, recommendation(s), rigor of secondary school record, standardized test scores, character/personal qualities. *Important factors considered include:* Class rank, extracurricular activities. *Other factors considered include:* Alumni/ae relation, first generation, geographical residence, interview, level of applicant's interest, racial/ethnic status, state residency, talent/ability, volunteer work, work experience. SAT or ACT required; ACT with writing component required. TOEFL required of all international applicants. High school diploma is required and GED is accepted. *Academic units recommended:* 4 English, 4 mathematics, 4 science (3 science labs), 4 foreign language, 2 social studies, 2 history, 1 pre-calculus.

Financial Aid

Students should submit: FAFSA, CSS/Financial Aid PROFILE, noncustodial PROFILE, business/farm supplement. Federal tax returns, W-2s, and Verification Worksheet. Regular filing deadline is February 15. The Princeton Review suggests that all financial aid forms be submitted as soon as possible after January 1. *Need-based scholarships/grants offered:* Federal Pell, SEOG, state scholarships/grants, the school's own gift aid. *Loan aid offered:* Direct Subsidized Stafford, Direct Unsubsidized Stafford, Direct PLUS, Federal Perkins, state loans. Applicants will be notified of awards on or about April 1. Federal Work-Study Program available. Institutional employment available. Highest amount earned per year from on-campus jobs $5,400. Off-campus job opportunities are good.

The Inside Word

Babson's national profile is ascending quickly, resulting in a substantial uptick in the number of applications received each year. Expect admissions standards to rise in accordance. The school considers writing ability a strong indicator of preparedness for college; proceed accordingly.

THE SCHOOL SAYS ". . ."

From the Admissions Office

"Nationally recognized as a Top 20 Business Program and the number one school in entrepreneurship for fifteen years, Babson College defines entrepreneurship education for the world. Our learning concepts provide students with the ability to adapt to ever-changing business environments, the experience to hit the ground running upon graduation, and the know-how to discover opportunities that will create economic and social value everywhere. We believe, as do our graduates and their employers, in the value of an integrated approach combined with experiential education. As a business school where one-half of the classes are in liberal arts, Babson emphasizes creativity, imagination, and risk-taking as essential to learning the foundation of business.

"Babson's close-knit community provides students with the opportunity to form close relationships with faculty and staff. An average class size of twenty-nine and student/faculty ratio of fourteen to one allow faculty to serve as role models and mentors committed to helping our students grow. With about eighty-five percent holding a doctoral degree, these accomplished business executives, authors, entrepreneurs, scholars, researchers, and artists bring an intellectual diversity and real-world experience that adds depth to Babson's programs. Most importantly, faculty members teach 100 percent of the courses.

"At Babson, students receive a world-class education that is innovative and creative, yet practical. They study business, learn about leadership, and undertake a transformative life experience preparing them to create an authentic, powerful brand of success. Our students make friends, find mentors, and develop long-lasting relationships that will thrive long after graduation."

SELECTIVITY	
Admissions Rating	**96**
# of applicants	5,079
% of applicants accepted	34
% of acceptees attending	28
# accepting a place on wait list	981
# admitted from wait list	34
# of early decision applicants	212
# accepted early decision	117
FRESHMAN PROFILE	
Range SAT Critical Reading	580–680
Range SAT Math	640–740
Range SAT Writing	610–700
Range ACT Composite	27–31
Minimum paper TOEFL	600
Minimum web-based TOEFL	100
Average HS GPA	3.56
% graduated top 10% of class	45
% graduated top 25% of class	77
% graduated top 50% of class	99
DEADLINES	
Early decision	
Deadline	11/1
Notification	12/15
Early action	
Deadline	11/1
Notification	1/1
Regular	
Priority	11/1
Deadline	1/1
Notification	4/1
Nonfall registration?	yes
FINANCIAL FACTS	
Financial Aid Rating	**88**
Annual tuition	$40,400
Room and board	$13,330
Books and supplies	$1,020
% needy frosh rec. need-based scholarship or grant aid	94
% needy UG rec. need-based scholarship or grant aid	95
% needy frosh rec. non-need-based scholarship or grant aid	14
% needy UG rec. non-need-based scholarship or grant aid	13
% needy frosh rec. need-based self-help aid	80
% needy UG rec. need-based self-help aid	82
% frosh rec. any financial aid	42
% UG rec. any financial aid	44
% UG borrow to pay for school	49
Average cumulative indebtedness	$34,114
% frosh need fully met	41
% ugrads need fully met	41
Average % of frosh need met	94
Average % of ugrad need met	94

Bard College

Office of Admissions, Annandale-on-Hudson, NY 12504 • Admissions: 845-758-7472 • Fax: 845-758-5208

CAMPUS LIFE

Quality of Life Rating	**74**
Fire Safety Rating	**80**
Green Rating	**86**
Type of school	private
Environment	rural

STUDENTS

Total undergrad enrollment	1,940
% male/female	43/57
% from out of state	70
% from public high school	64
% frosh live on campus	99
% African American	3
% Asian	3
% Caucasian	58
% Hispanic	2
% international	13
# of countries represented	64

SURVEY SAYS . . .

Lots of liberal students
No one cheats
Students aren't religious
Campus feels safe
Frats and sororities are unpopular or nonexistent
Political activism is popular

ACADEMICS

Academic Rating	**97**
% students returning for sophomore year	88
% students graduating within 4 years	64
% students graduating within 6 years	77
Calendar	semester
Student/faculty ratio	9:1
Profs interesting rating	99
Profs accessible rating	97

MOST POPULAR MAJORS

English language and literature; social sciences; visual and performing arts

APPLICANTS ALSO LOOK AT AND OFTEN PREFER

Amherst College, Brown University, Yale University, Harvard College

AND SOMETIMES PREFER

Boston University, Vassar College, Reed College, New York University, Oberlin College

AND RARELY PREFER

Sarah Lawrence College, Skidmore College, Ithaca College, Hampshire College, Macalester College

STUDENTS SAY ". . ."

Academics

Bard College is private, liberal arts institution located in the Hudson Valley that boasts a strong arts focus and a dedication to civic engagement locally, nationally, and worldwide in ways that "are unheard of for an institution of this size." The school's "amazing commitment to the arts" and "the variety of people and opinions and attitudes that are available" truly make Bard "a place to think," and the liberal arts atmosphere encourages students to consider their interests from many perspectives. "Bard is about questioning the fundamental assumptions of your existence in society," says one particularly philosophical student. Professors here are "incredibly intelligent" individuals, who despite being high up in their fields "are very down-to-earth and funny," and they are "extremely interested in their students' academic happiness and welfare." Even in lecture-based classes, discussion is abundant, making for a "really fun classroom environment." "We listen and respond to each other's opinions often, and we are encouraged to speak up in class." In turn, students feel personally committed to what they are learning about, instead of just being in class to get the credit or the grade. "Being here makes me feel as if I am gaining not only knowledge, but also maturity and the capacity for critical thought," says a student. The school has a unique system for declaring your major called "moderation" in which students gradually focus their studies and independent work on one or more areas throughout their four years; this "encourages the student to really think hard about what they choose to major in, and ultimately what they're passionate about." "It made me take a deep breath in the middle of college and figure out what really got me excited, and pursue it because of that passion," says one student.

Life

The "low-key atmosphere" at this thought center is echoed by its serene, idyllic surroundings. "We wake up to look at the mountains. We dance till the cows come home," says a student. There is "an obvious community" at Bard that stretches from the classroom to extracurriculars, and "Students generally don't separate their social lives from their academic interests." "We get into heated debates on thought experiments," says a student. "It's common to talk about academics at a party on the weekends, and that doesn't feel weird at all." Bard students love to plan events, and these are not limited to the school's "famous dinner parties"; on any given weekend, there is "a plethora of student theater productions, garage band shows, dances, dinner parties, dorm activities, club meetings, magazine release parties, cozy gatherings, off-campus ragers, [and] more dinner parties." People also tend to be politically and socially active, and the care for the environment and for getting involved locally is "impressive." "We live for today and for generations ahead," says a student.

Student Body

Bard students are "eccentric intellectuals" who "like pontificating about anything and everything." Most students are "incredibly interested in an area of study outside of their major," and they are "united by a belief that whatever we are studying is personally important to us and makes us into who we are." "Everyone is a walking contradiction and not what you expect when you look at them," says a student. Pretty much each person you will encounter has a specific academic interest, or a special skill, or a unique background. "We are hipsters, hippies, yuppies, nerds, dorks, freaks, dweebs, and socially awkward—the best people you'll ever meet—kind of kids."

FINANCIAL AID: 845-758-7526 • E-MAIL: ADMISSION@BARD.EDU • WEBSITE: WWW.BARD.EDU

THE PRINCETON REVIEW SAYS

Admissions

Very important factors considered include: Application essay, academic GPA, recommendation(s), rigor of secondary school record, character/personal qualities, extracurricular activities, talent/ability. *Important factors considered include:* Volunteer work, work experience. *Other factors considered include:* Class rank, standardized test scores, alumni/ae relation, first generation, geographical residence, interview, level of applicant's interest, racial/ethnic status, religious affiliation/commitment, state residency. ACT with or without writing component accepted. TOEFL required of all international applicants. High school diploma is required and GED is accepted. *Academic units recommended:* 4 English, 4 mathematics, 4 science (3 science labs), 4 foreign language, 4 social studies, 4 history.

Financial Aid

Students should submit: FAFSA, CSS/Financial Aid PROFILE, state aid form, noncustodial PROFILE, business/farm supplement. Regular filing deadline is February 15. The Princeton Review suggests that all financial aid forms be submitted as soon as possible after January 1. *Need-based scholarships/grants offered:* Federal Pell, SEOG, state scholarships/grants, private scholarships, the school's own gift aid. *Loan aid offered:* Direct Subsidized Stafford, Direct Unsubsidized Stafford, Direct PLUS, Federal Perkins, Loans from institutional funds (for international students only). Applicants will be notified of awards on or about April 1. Federal Work-Study Program available. Institutional employment available. Highest amount earned per year from on-campus jobs $1,800. Off-campus job opportunities are good.

The Inside Word

Bard receives more than enough applications from students with the academic credentials to gain admission (ten times more than it can accept each year), so the school has the luxury of focusing on matchmaking. The goal is to find students who can handle the independence allowed here and who will thrive in an intellectually intensive environment. The school requires two application essays; expect both to be very carefully scrutinized by the admissions office.

THE SCHOOL SAYS ". . ."

From the Admissions Office

"An alliance with Rockefeller University, the renowned graduate scientific research institution, gives Bardians access to Rockefeller's professors and laboratories and to places in Rockefeller's Summer Research Fellows Program. Almost all our math and science graduates pursue graduate or professional studies; ninety percent of our applicants to medical and health professional schools are accepted.

"The Globalization and International Affairs (BGIA) Program is a residential program in the heart of New York City that offers undergraduates a unique opportunity to undertake specialized study with leading practitioners and scholars in international affairs and to gain internship experience with international-affairs organizations. Topics in the curriculum include human rights, international economics, global environmental issues, international justice, managing international risk, and writing on international affairs, among others. Internships/tutorials are tailored to students' particular fields of study.

"Civic engagement has become a large and growing part of student life at Bard, with a high percentage of students participating in a wide variety of local, national, and international programs sponsored by the College or initiated by students.

"Beyond the central campus, Bard has created global programs and satellite campuses from Berlin to the West Bank, offering students unique opportunities for study abroad and making Bard's student body strongly international."

SELECTIVITY	
Admissions Rating	**97**
# of applicants	5,670
% of applicants accepted	35
% of acceptees attending	25
# accepting a place on wait list	264
# admitted from wait list	16

FRESHMAN PROFILE	
Range SAT Critical Reading	690–740
Range SAT Math	660–680
Minimum paper TOEFL	600
Average HS GPA	3.5
% graduated top 10% of class	62
% graduated top 25% of class	95
% graduated top 50% of class	100

DEADLINES	
Early action	
Deadline	11/1
Notification	1/1
Regular	
Deadline	1/1
Notification	4/1
Nonfall registration?	no

FINANCIAL FACTS	
Financial Aid Rating	**89**
Annual tuition	$44,176
Room and board	$12,782
Required fees	$830
Books and supplies	$950
% needy frosh rec. need-based scholarship or grant aid	95
% needy UG rec. need-based scholarship or grant aid	94
% needy frosh rec. need-based self-help aid	83
% needy UG rec. need-based self-help aid	81
% frosh rec. any financial aid	70
% UG rec. any financial aid	72
% UG borrow to pay for school	46
Average cumulative indebtedness	$26,879
% frosh need fully met	61
% ugrads need fully met	52
Average % of frosh need met	87
Average % of ugrad need met	87

Bard College at Simon's Rock

84 Alford Road, Great Barrington, MA 01230 • Admissions: 413-528-7312 • Fax: 413-528-7334

CAMPUS LIFE

Quality of Life Rating	**78**
Fire Safety Rating	**76**
Green Rating	**60***
Type of school	private
Environment	village

STUDENTS

Total undergrad enrollment	346
% male/female	34/66
% from out of state	86
% from public high school	66
% frosh live on campus	93
% African American	10
% Asian	7
% Caucasian	54
% Hispanic	5
% international	5
# of countries represented	13

SURVEY SAYS . . .

Class discussions encouraged
No one cheats
Athletic facilities are great
Students aren't religious
Campus feels safe
Frats and sororities are unpopular or nonexistent
Political activism is popular

ACADEMICS

Academic Rating	**98**
% students returning for sophomore year	81
% students graduating within 4 years	23
% students graduating within 6 years	28
Calendar	semester
Student/faculty ratio	7:1
Profs interesting rating	99
Profs accessible rating	97
Most classes have	10–19 students
Most lab/discussion sessions have	10–19 students

MOST POPULAR MAJORS

biology; psychology; literature

STUDENTS SAY ". . ."

Academics

There's no one else doing what Bard College at Simon's Rock is doing. The small, selective "early college" aims "to create a good experience for passionate younger students" through small class sizes, engaging class discussion, and "catering to each student as an individual." All 400 Simon's Rock students come to this "haven for young, bright minds" after tenth or eleventh grade in high school, and while half of the students receive an associate's degree after two years and transfer to other institutions, others moderate into the Simon's Rock B.A. program. The small size of the school "allows for almost unlimited rule-bending, as long as it is beneficial," and the "ability to create your own major" is one of the most lauded academic aspects. "No one has ever told me that a project wasn't my place because I'm an undergrad or that I couldn't do something because there wasn't enough oversight," says a student. "I have been constantly encouraged to pursue my interests by way of independent research, tutorials, internships, etc., and given support at every step of the way."

The school's "idyllic location" in the middle of the Berkshire Mountains provides the perfect level of seclusion for students who mean to get down to business with their studies, and "the professors here make the difficulty and volume of course work worth it." "They are what is amazing about this school." There will be a lot of writing for any class, but "pretty much all the professors are more than happy to help outside of the classroom." "My chemistry professor became upset when she realized that she wouldn't be able to teach a class for week due to break," says one student. Classes are very oriented around discussion, typically are less than twenty students, and "nothing's off the tradition for questioning and examination." Though all who attend here admit that it is "definitely not a walk in the park," they agree that "you will learn an incredible amount and be prepared for the future."

Life

Because it is an early college, the administration "is more strict about normal college past times (partying, etc.)," but most students spend time hanging out with friends on campus, or going into town (though "there is very little to do" there). "We're far from a party school, but we make our own fun," says a student of the dry campus. People's hobbies "tend toward the academic and/or geeky," and "fun is a *Doctor Who* viewing party or rehearsing for *Rocky Horror*." "It's not uncommon to go to the dining hall and discuss the anti-feminism of *Twilight* at one table, Occupy Wall Street at another table, and tell chemistry puns at another table." (Though, the food doesn't have many fans: "Each day I feel as if the dining hall food is progressively getting worse.") Many students here study abroad during their junior years, and student activities are instigated and run by students, "which means that if you want to start a club or activity group, you're given full support." Mainly, Rockers "spend a significant portion of our time studying. We think about work and talk about work."

Student Body

Students come from every end of the spectrum, but they are all here for the same reason: "We were ready to learn, and we weren't going to let a high school diploma stand in our way." The student body is "ninety-nine percent genius"; this is a "liberal, open-minded, bright, precocious" group full of "rigor and self-determination." Most of the incoming students are sixteen or seventeen years of age, but "They can still obtain a bachelor's degree in four years, just like at most other undergraduate schools." This is truly a "ragtag bunch of future political workers and the ragtag misfits from high school mixed in with some cool (albeit tough) professors." "I would say there is relatively little pressure to fit in at all, since a lot of us are high school misfits in the first place," says a student. Unsurprisingly, "You get to know your fellow students very well, as the size of the school is very small."

FINANCIAL AID: 413-528-7297 • E-MAIL: ADMIT@SIMONS-ROCK.EDU • WEBSITE: WWW.SIMONS-ROCK.EDU

THE PRINCETON REVIEW SAYS

Admissions

Very important factors considered include: Application essay, recommendation(s), rigor of secondary school record, character/personal qualities, interview, talent/ability. *Important factors considered include:* Class rank, academic GPA, level of applicant's interest. *Other factors considered include:* Standardized test scores, alumni/ae relation, extracurricular activities, first generation, racial/ethnic status, volunteer work, work experience. ACT with or without writing component accepted. TOEFL required of all international applicants. High school diploma or equivalent is not required. *Academic units recommended:* 2 English, 2 mathematics, 2 science (1 science lab), 2 foreign language, 2 social studies, 2 history.

Financial Aid

Students should submit: FAFSA, CSS/Financial Aid PROFILE, business/farm supplement, parent and student federal taxes/federal verification worksheet. The Princeton Review suggests that all financial aid forms be submitted as soon as possible after January 1. *Need-based scholarships/grants offered:* Federal Pell, SEOG, state scholarships/grants, private scholarships, the school's own gift aid. *Loan aid offered:* Direct Subsidized Stafford, Direct Unsubsidized Stafford, Direct PLUS, Federal Perkins, state loans, alternative educational loans. Applicants will be notified of awards on a rolling basis beginning April 15. Federal Work-Study Program available. Institutional employment available. Highest amount earned per year from on-campus jobs $1,300. Off-campus job opportunities are good.

The Inside Word

Because Simon's Rock boasts healthy application numbers, it's in a position to concentrate on matchmaking. To that end, admissions officers seek students with independent and inquisitive spirits. Applicants who exhibit academic ambition while extending their intellectual curiosity beyond the realm of the classroom are particularly appealing. Successful candidates typically have several honors and advanced placement courses on their transcripts, as well as strong letters of recommendation and well-written personal statements. An interview is required for all applicants.

THE SCHOOL SAYS ". . ."

From the Admissions Office

"Bard College at Simon's Rock is the only four-year college of the liberal arts and sciences specifically designed to provide bright, highly motivated students with the opportunity to begin college in a residential environment immediately after the tenth or eleventh grade.

"Approximately half of our students transfer after the sophomore year and complete their junior and senior years of college elsewhere. The most common transfer destinations are Bard College, Brown University, Cornell University, New York University, Smith College, Stanford University, University of California—Berkeley, and University of Chicago. For those who choose to complete the BA at Simon's Rock, the graduation rate exceeds ninety percent."

SELECTIVITY	
Admissions Rating	**91**
# of applicants	290
% of applicants accepted	87
% of acceptees attending	47

FRESHMAN PROFILE	
Range SAT Critical Reading	670–740
Range SAT Math	590–690
Range SAT Writing	610–730
Range ACT Composite	21–31
Minimum paper TOEFL	600
Minimum web-based TOEFL	100
Average HS GPA	3.4
% graduated top 10% of class	53
% graduated top 25% of class	84
% graduated top 50% of class	93

DEADLINES	
Regular	
Priority	4/15
Deadline	5/31
Nonfall registration?	yes

FINANCIAL FACTS	
Financial Aid Rating	**80**
Annual tuition	$44,075
Room and board	$12,259
Required fees	$840
Books and supplies	$1,000
% needy frosh rec. need-based scholarship or grant aid	86
% needy UG rec. need-based scholarship or grant aid	93
% needy frosh rec. non-need-based scholarship or grant aid	76
% needy UG rec. non-need-based scholarship or grant aid	78
% needy frosh rec. need-based self-help aid	86
% needy UG rec. need-based self-help aid	93
% frosh rec. any financial aid	94
% UG rec. any financial aid	86
% UG borrow to pay for school	68
Average cumulative indebtedness	$30,000
% frosh need fully met	15
% ugrads need fully met	16
Average % of frosh need met	76
Average % of ugrad need met	77

Barnard College

3009 Broadway, New York, NY 10027 • Admissions: 212-854-2014 • Fax: 212-854-6220

CAMPUS LIFE

Quality of Life Rating	**99**
Fire Safety Rating	**67**
Green Rating	**79**
Type of school	private
Environment	metropolis

STUDENTS

Total undergrad enrollment	2,445
% male/female	0/100
% from out of state	69
% from public high school	48
% frosh live on campus	98
% African American	5
% Asian	17
% Caucasian	63
% Hispanic	9
% international	6
# of countries represented	43

SURVEY SAYS . . .

No one cheats
Career services are great
Students love New York, NY
Great off-campus food
Campus feels safe
Political activism is popular

ACADEMICS

Academic Rating	**95**
% students returning for sophomore year	94
% students graduating within 4 years	84
% students graduating within 6 years	92
Calendar	semester
Student/faculty ratio	10:1
Profs interesting rating	97
Profs accessible rating	87
Most classes have	10–19 students
Most lab/discussion sessions have	10–19 students

MOST POPULAR MAJORS

economics, other; English language and literature; psychology

APPLICANTS ALSO LOOK AT AND OFTEN PREFER

Yale University, University of Pennsylvania, Harvard College, Brown University, Columbia University

AND SOMETIMES PREFER

Tufts University, Northwestern University, Princeton University, Wesleyan University, Wellesley College, Stanford University, University of Chicago

AND RARELY PREFER

Boston College, Bryn Mawr College, Fordham University, Vassar College, University of California—Berkeley

STUDENTS SAY ". . ."

Academics

Life is lived in the fast lane at Barnard, an all-women's liberal arts college partnered with Columbia University that incorporates "a small school feel with big school resources and incorporates both campus and city life." Nestled in the Morningside Heights neighborhood of Manhattan on a gated (main) campus, the school maintains an "independent spirit" while providing a "nurturing environment," and its partnership with a larger research university gives it the "best of both worlds" and affords its students the opportunities, course options, and resources that many colleges don't have. The academic experience at Barnard is simply "wonderful," according to the students. Teachers here are "experts in their field" and "value their positions as both teachers and mentors," to the extent "they make you want to stay on Barnard's campus for class and not take classes at Columbia." "I've never been in an environment where there is such a reciprocal relationship between students wanting to learn and be challenged and professors wanting to teach and help," says a junior. Though underclassmen typically aren't able to get into as many of the small classes (the process of which "is a nightmare"), one student claims that "some of the best classes I've had have been in large lecture halls." The administration gets thumbs-up nearly across the board for their accessibility and compassion for students. Deans are always available to students wanting to meet, and the alumni network and career services are singled out for their efficacy. "Every time there is an issue on campus that students care about or an event that has happened, we get e-mails and town-hall style meetings devoted to discussing the issues." "Barnard is New York—busy, exciting, full of opportunity," says one student.

Life

Not much goes on around campus, to the chagrin of a few, but as one freshman puts it, "Why stay on campus when you're in New York?" Students take advantage of the resources available to them in New York City, from Broadway shows and Central Park to museums and restaurants; "The possibilities are endless," and can "make it impossible to stick to a budget." Theater and a capella are also very big here, and many students are involved with clubs and organizations at Columbia, sometimes even dominating them. There are some complaints that facilities and dorms are "crumbling," but the recently opened Diana Center building has fast become a hub of student activities, including studying, learning, socializing, dining, and relaxing. "Life at Barnard is probably sixty to seventy-five percent academic and around twenty-five to forty percent free."

Student Body

Even though it's all women here, Barnard is "the anti-women's college," as "very, very few students are here for the single-sex education"—they're here for the academics and New York. There's a definite liberal slant on campus, and these "usually politically savvy," "very cultured," "energetic and motivated" women are "ambitious and opinionated," with career and leadership goals at the top of their agenda. "Barnard students are not lazy" and have no problems booking their days full of study and activities. Most here learn to "fit into the mad rush" very quickly and take advantage of their four short years. Although quite a few students are from the tristate area and the majority are white, "there is still a sense of diversity" thanks to a variety of different backgrounds, both cultural and geographical; there's also a "tiny gay community" that seems easily accepted.

FINANCIAL AID: 212-854-2154 • E-MAIL: ADMISSIONS@BARNARD.EDU • WEBSITE: WWW.BARNARD.EDU

THE PRINCETON REVIEW SAYS

Admissions

Very important factors considered include: Academic GPA, recommendation(s), rigor of secondary school record, standardized test scores, character/personal qualities, extracurricular activities. *Important factors considered include:* Application essay, talent/ability, volunteer work. *Other factors considered include:* Class rank, alumni/ae relation, first generation, geographical residence, interview, level of applicant's interest, racial/ethnic status, work experience. ACT with writing component required. TOEFL required of all international applicants. High school diploma or equivalent is not required. *Academic units recommended:* 4 English, 3 mathematics, 3 science (2 science labs), 3 foreign language.

Financial Aid

Students should submit: FAFSA, institution's own financial aid form, CSS/Financial Aid PROFILE, state aid form, noncustodial PROFILE, business/farm supplement. federal income tax returns. Regular filing deadline is February 1. The Princeton Review suggests that all financial aid forms be submitted as soon as possible after January 1. *Need-based scholarships/grants offered:* Federal Pell, SEOG, state scholarships/grants, private scholarships, the school's own gift aid. *Loan aid offered:* Direct Subsidized Stafford, Direct Unsubsidized Stafford, Direct PLUS, Federal Perkins, state loans, college/university loans from institutional funds. Applicants will be notified of awards on or about March 31. Federal Work-Study Program available. Institutional employment available. Highest amount earned per year from on-campus jobs $8,325. Off-campus job opportunities are excellent.

The Inside Word

As at many top colleges, early decision applications have increased at Barnard—although the admissions standards are virtually the same as for their regular admissions cycle. The college's admissions staff is suprisingly open and accessible for such a highly selective college with as long and impressive a tradition of excellence. The admissions committee's expectations are high, but their attitude reflects a true interest in who potential students are and what's on their minds. Students have a much better experience throughout the admissions process when treated with sincerity and respect—perhaps this is why Barnard continues to attract and enroll some of the best students in the country.

THE SCHOOL SAYS ". . ."

From the Admissions Office

"Barnard College is a small, distinguished liberal arts college for women that is partnered with Columbia University and located in the heart of New York City. The college enrolls women from all over the United States, Puerto Rico, and the Caribbean. More than thirty countries, including France, England, Hong Kong, and Greece, are also represented in the student body. Students pursue their academic studies in more than forty majors and are able to cross register at Columbia University.

"Applicants for the entering class must submit scores from the SAT Reasoning Test and two SAT Subject Tests of their choice or the ACT with the writing component."

SELECTIVITY	
Admissions Rating	**97**
# of applicants	5,153
% of applicants accepted	25
% of acceptees attending	48
# accepting a place on wait list	896
# admitted from wait list	7
# of early decision applicants	550
# accepted early decision	240

FRESHMAN PROFILE	
Range SAT Critical Reading	630–730
Range SAT Math	620–710
Range SAT Writing	650–750
Range ACT Composite	28–32
Minimum paper TOEFL	600
Average HS GPA	3.8
% graduated top 10% of class	84
% graduated top 25% of class	99
% graduated top 50% of class	99

DEADLINES	
Early decision	
Deadline	11/15
Notification	12/15
Regular	
Deadline	1/1
Notification	4/1
Nonfall registration?	yes

FINANCIAL FACTS	
Financial Aid Rating	**96**
Annual tuition	$41,850
Room and board	$13,810
% needy frosh rec. need-based scholarship or grant aid	96
% needy UG rec. need-based scholarship or grant aid	96
% needy frosh rec. need-based self-help aid	100
% needy UG rec. need-based self-help aid	100
% frosh rec. any financial aid	57
% UG rec. any financial aid	50
Average cumulative indebtedness	$17,360
% frosh need fully met	100
% ugrads need fully met	100
Average % of frosh need met	100
Average % of ugrad need met	100

BATES COLLEGE

23 CAMPUS AVENUE, LEWISTON, ME 04240 • ADMISSIONS: 207-786-6000 • FAX: 207-786-6025

CAMPUS LIFE

Quality of Life Rating	84
Fire Safety Rating	95
Green Rating	93
Type of school	private
Environment	city

STUDENTS

Total undergrad enrollment	1,769
% male/female	47/53
% from out of state	89
% from public high school	58
% frosh live on campus	100
% African American	5
% Asian	5
% Caucasian	74
% Hispanic	5
% international	6
# of countries represented	68

SURVEY SAYS . . .

Students are friendly
Great food on campus
Frats and sororities are unpopular or nonexistent
Student publications are popular
Students are environmentally aware

ACADEMICS

Academic Rating	93
% students returning for sophomore year	93
% students graduating within 4 years	88
% students graduating within 6 years	92
Calendar	4-4-1
Student/faculty ratio	10:1
Profs interesting rating	93
Profs accessible rating	93
Most classes have	10–19 students
Most lab/discussion sessions have	10–19 students

MOST POPULAR MAJORS

economics; political science and government, psychology

APPLICANTS ALSO LOOK AT AND OFTEN PREFER

Dartmouth College, Brown University, Williams College

AND SOMETIMES PREFER

Bowdoin College, Middlebury College, Wesleyan University

AND RARELY PREFER

Bucknell University, Connecticut College, Trinity College (CT)

STUDENTS SAY ". . ."

Academics

A "small liberal arts college," nestled in Maine, Bates College is dedicated to "empowering its students environmentally, academically, and socially." The "picturesque" campus offers the traditional New England atmosphere but "with its own personality." Students are drawn to the "warmth and friendliness of students and teachers, the political awareness of students on campus, and high quality academics!" They describe Bates as "a community of learners who care deeply about doing what [they] love in and outside of the classroom, be it service-learning in the Lewiston schools, adventuring in the outdoors, canvassing for an upcoming election, braving the puddle jump during Winter Carnival, or playing sports with [their] friends." If that isn't enough to draw people there, then consider the "community atmosphere, amazing food, supportive professors, beautiful campus, [the] many activities to be involved in, and grounded students." The athletics program is popular. "Most people play a sport of some kind, whether it's intramural or varsity." One student commends the many options for travel and studying abroad. "I have been to China, Vietnam, and Spain through Bates, and I cherish those opportunities." Professors are "very passionate about helping you succeed and are always willing to meet with you outside of class if you have any questions. Academics are challenging (in a good way!) and help you develop as a writer, thinker, and leader." Another student points out that "Bates focuses on writing skills" and nearly every member of the senior class writes a senior thesis. With all this praise, there are a few complaints about some facilities. "The science labs are a little behind the times," and students tell us that renovations to some of the older buildings would be welcome.

Life

The college's setting, in Lewiston, Maine, near Auburn, is quintessential Maine. Bates is located in a pretty small town, but "The school is amazing at arranging things to go on every week and even on the weekends. Concerts, shows, visiting artists, and movie showings are just a few things that are offered regularly." Students show an interest in the off-campus community. "Bates is extremely involved in Lewiston and Auburn through a myriad of social service and community learning opportunities. Almost every Bates student will volunteer in Lewiston/Auburn before they graduate, and everyone loves it," confirms a student. "Outside of the classroom, there is a strong sense of community that comes from the many events that various groups on campus hold." The atmosphere at Bates lends itself to "a lot of smaller parties," and "there are dances just about every weekend, and hundreds of active clubs." Also, at Bates, "People think a lot about the outdoors." "When it's warmer in the spring and fall everyone goes to a nearby lake or hangs out outside a lot playing Ultimate Frisbee or other active games. In the winter many students go skiing on the weekends or during the week if there is a great snow storm." Definitely not to be overlooked is the food, which, unlike a majority of college campuses, Bates students call "amazing."

Student Body

People who come to Bates are "very engaged and excited to be here." One student describes the majority of students as "upper-middle-class Caucasian with a major in the humanities and a more left-wing political view." But that may be changing. Another student says, "The diversity at Bates has improved dramatically—even having been here just three years. There has been a lot of successful attention put toward expanding diversity on campus." Some may "wish there were more social diversity," but another student does not see a problem. "There are cliques, but they are not exclusive." Whichever group a person may be part of, "the concerns and needs of individual students are never ignored." Together, Bates students are "one strong and open community bonding, growing, and sharing over the course of a four-year education."

FINANCIAL AID: 207-786-6096 • E-MAIL: ADMISSION@BATES.EDU • WEBSITE: WWW.BATES.EDU

THE PRINCETON REVIEW SAYS

Admissions

Very important factors considered include: Class rank, application essay, academic GPA, recommendation(s), rigor of secondary school record, character/personal qualities, extracurricular activities, interview, level of applicant's interest, talent/ability. *Other factors considered include:* Standardized test scores, alumni/ae relation, first generation, geographical residence, racial/ethnic status, state residency, volunteer work, work experience. ACT with or without writing component accepted. TOEFL required of all international applicants. High school diploma is required and GED is not accepted. *Academic units required:* 4 English, 3 mathematics, 3 science (2 science labs), 2 foreign language, 3 social studies. *Academic units recommended:* 4 English, 4 mathematics, 4 science (3 science labs), 4 foreign language, 4 social studies.

Financial Aid

Students should submit: FAFSA, CSS/Financial Aid PROFILE, noncustodial PROFILE, business/farm supplement. Regular filing deadline is February 1. The Princeton Review suggests that all financial aid forms be submitted as soon as possible after January 1. *Need-based scholarships/grants offered:* Federal Pell, SEOG, state scholarships/grants, private scholarships, the school's own gift aid. *Loan aid offered:* Direct Subsidized Stafford, Direct Unsubsidized Stafford, Direct PLUS, Federal Perkins, state loans. Applicants will be notified of awards on or about April 1. Federal Work-Study Program available. Institutional employment available. Off-campus job opportunities are good.

The Inside Word

Bates looks for students who challenge themselves in the classroom and beyond. A student's academic rigor, essays, and recommendations may be even more important than his or her GPA and test scores. Interviews are strongly encouraged, and candidates who opt out of these face-to-face meetings may place themselves at a disadvantage.

THE SCHOOL SAYS ". . ."

From the Admissions Office

"Bates College is widely recognized as one of the finest liberal arts colleges in the nation. The curriculum and faculty challenge students to develop the essential skills of critical assessment, analysis, expression, aesthetic sensibility, and independent thought. Founded by abolitionists in 1855, Bates graduates have always included men and women from diverse ethnic and religious backgrounds. Bates highly values its study abroad programs, unique calendar (4-4-1), and the many opportunities available for one-on-one collaboration with faculty through seminars, research, service-learning, and the capstone experience of senior thesis. Co-curricular life at Bates is rich; most students participate in club or varsity sports; many participate in performing arts; and almost all students participate in one of more than 110 student-run clubs and organizations. More than two-thirds of alumni enroll in graduate study within ten years.

"The Bates College Admissions Staff reads applications very carefully; the high school record and the quality of writing are of particular importance. Applicants are strongly encouraged to have a personal interview, either on campus or with an alumni representative. Students who choose not to interview may place themselves at a disadvantage in the selection process. Bates offers tours, interviews, and information sessions throughout the summer and fall. Drop-ins are welcome for tours and information sessions. Please call ahead to schedule an interview. At Bates, the submission of standardized testing (the SAT, SAT Subject Tests, and the ACT) is not required for admission. After two decades of optional testing, our research shows no differences in academic performance and graduation rates between submitters and nonsubmitters."

SELECTIVITY

Admissions Rating	**96**
# of applicants	5,196
% of applicants accepted	27
% of acceptees attending	36
# accepting a place on wait list	302
# admitted from wait list	12
# of early decision applicants	543
# accepted early decision	232

FRESHMAN PROFILE

Range SAT Critical Reading	630–710
Range SAT Math	630–710
Range SAT Writing	638–720
Range ACT Composite	29–31
% graduated top 10% of class	58
% graduated top 25% of class	88
% graduated top 50% of class	98

DEADLINES

Early decision	
Deadline	11/15
Notification	12/20
Regular	
Deadline	1/1
Notification	3/31
Nonfall registration?	yes

FINANCIAL FACTS

Financial Aid Rating	**95**
Annual tuition	$42,550
Room and board	$12,500
Required fees	$250
Books and supplies	$1,750
% needy frosh rec. need-based scholarship or grant aid	99
% needy UG rec. need-based scholarship or grant aid	97
% needy frosh rec. non-need-based scholarship or grant aid	79
% needy UG rec. non-need-based scholarship or grant aid	92
% needy frosh rec. need-based self-help aid	89
% needy UG rec. need-based self-help aid	93
% frosh rec. any financial aid	47
% UG rec. any financial aid	45
% UG borrow to pay for school	42
Average cumulative indebtedness	$20,706
% frosh need fully met	95
% ugrads need fully met	96
Average % of frosh need met	100
Average % of ugrad need met	100

BAYLOR UNIVERSITY

ONE BEAR PLACE #97056, WACO, TX 76798-7056 • ADMISSIONS: 254-710-3435 • FAX: 254-710-3436

CAMPUS LIFE

Quality of Life Rating	73
Fire Safety Rating	93
Green Rating	86
Type of school	private
Environment	city

STUDENTS

Total undergrad enrollment	12,518
% male/female	42/58
% from out of state	25
% frosh live on campus	98
# of fraternities	22
# of sororities	20
% African American	8
% Asian	6
% Caucasian	65
% Hispanic	13
% international	2
# of countries represented	84

SURVEY SAYS . . .

Lab facilities are great
Great computer facilities
Athletic facilities are great
School is well run
Students are friendly
Students are very religious
Students are happy
Intramural sports are popular
Frats and sororities dominate social scene
Student publications are popular

ACADEMICS

Academic Rating	81
% students returning for sophomore year	85
% students graduating within 4 years	52
% students graduating within 6 years	72
Calendar	semester
Student/faculty ratio	14:1
Profs interesting rating	78
Profs accessible rating	82
Most classes have	10–19 students
Most lab/discussion sessions have	10–19 students

MOST POPULAR MAJORS

biology/biological sciences; marketing/marketing management; psychology

STUDENTS SAY ". . ."

Academics

One typical Baylor student describes her school as "a globally active research university [that] boasts a multitude of intelligent student minds. The spiritual foundations of Baylor attract only the most approachable and helpful student body and faculty." Baylor is praised by undergrads as a place in which to "grow as a student and a person simultaneously." Small class sizes and professors' genuine interest creates "a top-notch, all-encompassing educational experience." Professors are "engaging and passionate about their area of expertise…they infuse the importance of academic and moral integrity into all that they teach." The Honors College, premed, and entrepreneurship program continue to be stand-out features as well as engineering and "strong science programs." "Professors are really accessible and the university provides many tutoring resources and help when needed." Faculty and overall academics are consistently praised, though the prevailing Christian themes are sometimes fuel for criticism: "While the professors are knowledgeable, almost no one at Baylor seems capable of considering possibilities outside of the Christian paradigm," notes a senior. However, a sociology major emphatically states, "If a student wants a good academic education at the university level, with teachers who care about their classes, Baylor is the great choice!" Though there are signs of change on the horizon with the addition of Ken Starr (of White House notoriety) as the new president, "The relationship between the students and administration has started taking a turn for the better."

Life

Undergrads are tired of hearing about the "Baylor Bubble" and point out that it's mainly because some students haven't bothered to explore off-campus destinations. Attractions include the Waco Mammoth Site as well as "the amazing Cameron Park…and various cultural festivals in downtown Waco—such as an annual Greek food festival." "There are so many different intramural sports here, and many people love to get competitive." Academic life is rigorous, so students blow off steam via the numerous biking and running trails circling the well-manicured campus (including the famous Bear Trail.) "Everyone has a great time going to sporting events, whether it's cheering on our highly ranked women's basketball team or our always exciting football team." Make no mistake, "Greek life is big," states one senior. "The social scene is largely off-campus and dominated by the Greek system." Though "there is a good mix of students to provide anyone [with] a group to plug into, but the closer you are to the typical student, the better off you are." Acceptance of other lifestyles and faiths is an underlying theme of the small amount of discontent voiced by students, "This is not a welcoming community if you don't conform." Students living a "fringe lifestyle" tend to feel pressure to keep those differences to themselves.

Student Body

"People here…like to have fun just being with people, so students can always be seen in common areas chilling or even doing homework. Playing some sport is the next most popular activity." Though there's a sense that some undergrads are naïve about the world outside of their "bubble." They're criticized for being "pretty homogeneous" and intolerant of those who "cuss" or don't go to church. Yet Baylor is consistently admired for fostering an embracing student body. "Life at Baylor is great," gushes one student. Overall, most undergrads agree that the community and environment are supportive and welcoming—and studious. "Baylor emphasizes having fun while getting your education. It is well-run, has great facilities, and faculty and staff that care about the students." As one sophomore neatly wraps it up, "Once you're here, you're family."

FINANCIAL AID: 254-710-2611 • E-MAIL: ADMISSIONS@BAYLOR.EDU • WEBSITE: WWW.BAYLOR.EDU

THE PRINCETON REVIEW SAYS

Admissions

Very important factors considered include: Class rank, rigor of secondary school record, standardized test scores. *Important factors considered include:* Academic GPA. *Other factors considered include:* Application essay, recommendation(s), alumni/ae relation, character/personal qualities, extracurricular activities, first generation, interview, level of applicant's interest, religious affiliation/commitment, talent/ability, volunteer work. SAT or ACT required; ACT with writing component required. TOEFL required of all international applicants. High school diploma is required and GED is accepted. *Academic units required:* 4 English, 3 mathematics, 3 science (2 science labs), 2 foreign language, 1 social studies, 1 history.

Financial Aid

Students should submit: FAFSA, state residency affirmation. The Princeton Review suggests that all financial aid forms be submitted as soon as possible after January 1. *Need-based scholarships/grants offered:* Federal Pell, SEOG, state scholarships/grants, the school's own gift aid. *Loan aid offered:* Direct Subsidized Stafford, Direct Unsubsidized Stafford, Direct PLUS, Federal Perkins, Federal Nursing, state loans. Applicants will be notified of awards on a rolling basis beginning March 1. Federal Work-Study Program available. Institutional employment available. Highest amount earned per year from on-campus jobs $9,325. Off-campus job opportunities are good.

The Inside Word

Baylor wants to see applicants who are at the top of their class with strong SAT or ACT scores. Expect to convey your academic commitment and curiosity as well as display your achievements outside of school and within your community. Though not mandatory, you may wish to augment your application by submitting a resume or recommendation letters via your Baylor online account. One advantage to getting your application in early is you'll secure your spot via first-round acceptance and be at the front of the line for your housing application.

THE SCHOOL SAYS "..."

From the Admissions Office

"Baylor University is a Christian university in the Baptist tradition and is affiliated with the Baptist General Convention of Texas. As the oldest institution of higher learning in the state, Baylor's founders sought to establish a college dedicated to Christian principles, superior academics, and a shared sense of community. Students come from all fifty states and some ninety foreign countries. Baylor's nationally recognized academic divisions offer 151 undergraduate degree programs, 76 master's degree programs, and 33 doctoral degree programs. Baylor ranks in the top 100 percent of colleges and universities participating in the National Merit Scholarship program. Baylor is one of the select eleven percent of U.S. colleges and universities with a Phi Beta Kappa chapter. The Templeton Foundation repeatedly names Baylor as one of America's top character-building colleges. Baylor's undergraduate programs emphasize the central importance of vocation (calling) and service in students' lives, helping them explore their value and role in society. Baylor is a charter member of the Independent 529 Tuition Plan, a prepaid college tuition plan. Baylor's tuition is one of the lowest of any major private university in the Southwest and one of the least expensive in the nation. Approximately ninety percent of Baylor students receive student financial assistance. The approximately 1,000-acre main campus adjoins the Brazos River near downtown Waco, a Central Texas city of 110,000 people."

SELECTIVITY	
Admissions Rating	90
# of applicants	38,960
% of applicants accepted	40
% of acceptees attending	20

FRESHMAN PROFILE	
Range SAT Critical Reading	560–660
Range SAT Math	570–680
Range SAT Writing	530–640
Range ACT Composite	24–29
Minimum paper TOEFL	540
Minimum web-based TOEFL	76
% graduated top 10% of class	39
% graduated top 25% of class	74
% graduated top 50% of class	97

DEADLINES	
Early action	
Deadline	11/1
Notification	1/15
Nonfall registration?	yes

FINANCIAL FACTS	
Financial Aid Rating	75
Annual tuition	$30,586
Room and board	$9,422
Required fees	$3,130
Books and supplies	$1,364
% needy frosh rec. need-based scholarship or grant aid	98
% needy UG rec. need-based scholarship or grant aid	95
% needy frosh rec. non-need-based scholarship or grant aid	96
% needy UG rec. non-need-based scholarship or grant aid	89
% needy frosh rec. need-based self-help aid	82
% needy UG rec. need-based self-help aid	80
% frosh rec. any financial aid	97
% UG rec. any financial aid	93
% frosh need fully met	16
% ugrads need fully met	16
Average % of frosh need met	68
Average % of ugrad need met	66

Becker College

61 Sever Street, Worcester, MA 01609 • Admissions: 508-373-9400 • 508-890-1500

CAMPUS LIFE

Quality of Life Rating	**72**
Fire Safety Rating	**60***
Green Rating	**60***
Type of school	private
Environment	urban

STUDENTS

Total undergrad enrollment	1,784
% male/female	42/58
% from out of state	32
% from public high school	86
% frosh live on campus	74
% African American	11
% Asian	1
% Caucasian	74
% Hispanic	11
% Native American	1
# of countries represented	4

SURVEY SAYS . . .

Students are happy
Great lab facilities
Friendly students
Great library

ACADEMICS

Academic Rating	**69**
% students returning for sophomore year	64
% students graduating within 4 years	14
% students graduating within 6 years	27
Calendar	semester
Student/faculty ratio	17:1
Profs interesting rating	77
Profs accessible rating	75

STUDENTS SAY ". . ."

Academics

The mission of Becker College is to deliver a "transformational learning experience—anchored by academic excellence, social responsibility, and creative expression." Becker offers "the ability to pursue unique interests such as veterinary science, animal care, game design, criminal justice, and interior design" in a "calm, friendly environment" that is "flexible with the needs of different students." "I really like how small the campus was and how personal the classes are," says one new student, with another adding how this closeness lets you "be able to know and interact with your professor on a higher level." Professors "do their best to adapt to student's individual learning styles," and the teaching environment lends itself to undergraduates being "able to ask questions and really understand what you are being taught." "If I have anything to add or feel differently about a topic I do not hesitate to bring it up. Never has it been ill received." One student admires how "the teachers show respect for their students which in turn makes me want to produce better work." Undergraduates here are comfortable asking instructors for assistance with things, such as "recommendations, internship assistance, and advice regarding graduate options." Providing a hands-on education is paramount at Becker. For instance, a veterinary clinic and kennel on campus provide "the opportunity for animal care majors to work hands on with live animals." For game design majors, the school sponsors "gamer fairs and competitions," as well as provides "networking opportunities with worker[s] in the video game industry." "The academic experience overall has been…relevant and current." Becker strives diligently to prepare students for the challenges of life in today's global society.

Life

There are two distinctive campuses, located six miles apart. The first is in Worcester, "a great college city," situated amidst New England's second-largest urban center. Students are often in the "Hawk's Nest" which is "a hangout spot" amidst tree-lined streets sporting Victorian-style homes. Leicester is the second campus, in a country town adjacent to an historic village green. This rural setting provides space for athletic team facilities and for the animal sciences programs. With a free shuttle service, students move easily between locations. Becker "offers plenty of student activities to make the campus more of a family and make students feel comfortable." There is a wide range of cultural, social, and recreational options available, being in a metropolitan area. Undergrads "love to go on the Boston and New York City trips," which may include Bruins, Celtics, and Red Sox games. "The Shoppes at Blackstone Valley are only twenty minutes away," and "Spring Carnival is another huge event for our College." For fun closer to campus, students commonly "have house parties. We do not have frats and sororities."

Student Body

Becker undergraduates find the appearance of campus pleasant, "keeping the old world charm but still maintaining a professional look." The environment is "nice, and laid-back;" students are "friendly and accepting" and "treat others with respect." "It's very easy to get around, and it's very easy to fit in." "Typical" students are involved in sports or clubs. "Student-athletes are very popular. Most students interact based on their program, class schedule, interests, and specific sport." "Our school is all about sports, game design, nursing, and vet science." There is a great commitment to diversity; Becker is "a school that teaches everyone how to be a global citizen and how to interact within a community." "Work-study opportunities that pertain to the person's academic major" are also common.

FINANCIAL AID: 508-373-9440 • E-MAIL: ADMISSIONS@BECKER.EDU • WEBSITE: WWW.BECKER.EDU

THE PRINCETON REVIEW SAYS

Admissions

Very important factors considered include: Rigor of secondary school record, academic GPA, standardized test scores. *Important factors considered include:* Class rank, recommendation(s). *Other factors considered include:* Application essay, alumni/ae relation, character/personal qualities, extracurricular activities, interview, level of applicant's interest, volunteer work, work experience. High school diploma is required and GED is accepted. *Academic units recommended:* 4 English, 3 mathematics, 3 science (2 science labs), 2 foreign language, 2 social studies, 2 history.

Financial Aid

Students should submit: FAFSA and state aid form. Regular filing deadline is March 15. The Princeton Review suggests that all financial aid forms be submitted as soon as possible after January 1. *Need-based scholarships/grants offered:* Federal Pell, SEOG, state scholarships/grants, private scholarships, the school's own gift aid. *Loan aid offered:* Direct Subsidized Stafford, Direct Unsubsidized Stafford, Direct PLUS, Federal Perkins. Federal Work-Study Program available. Institutional employment available. Off-campus job opportunities are good.

The Inside Word

The admissions process is personal and unique for each applicant, although Becker College reviews both the SAT and ACT college entrance examinations, as well as advanced placement examination scores if applicable. Recommendations and essays are also taken heavily into consideration. Becker seeks to enroll applicants with not only impressive high school transcripts, but those wanting to contribute to the greater good, both locally and globally.

THE SCHOOL SAYS ". . ."

From the Admissions Office

"Becker College offers forty academic programs, including a choice of twenty-nine bachelor degree programs and extensive adult learning programs. Becker College students are engaged socially, academically, and athletically. The Becker College community promotes core values of excellence, accountability, community and diversity, social responsibility, integrity, and creative expression inside the classroom, on the playing fields, with community service and outreach, and through a number of activities and events.

"Our admissions process reflects the Becker College philosophy that each student is a unique individual. Because of this, our requirements allow you to put your best foot forward and provide as much information as possible about who you are, what you hope to accomplish during your time at Becker College, and what you hope to do upon graduation.

"The admissions process is personal and unique for each applicant. To be considered for admission, applicants must submit a complete application, and should have an earned GPA of 2.0 in a college preparatory curriculum or better (2.5 GPA minimum GPA for consideration for nursing, vet tech, vet science, pre-vet, and equine studies/basic sciences applicants). Applicants whose GPA falls below a 2.0 or whose curriculum was not entirely college preparatory will be reviewed on an individual basis."

SELECTIVITY

Admissions Rating	**69**
# of applicants	2,509
% of applicants accepted	72
% of acceptees attending	23

FRESHMAN PROFILE

Range SAT Critical Reading	400–520
Range SAT Math	410–540
Range SAT Writing	390–500
Range ACT Composite	16–20
Minimum paper TOEFL	550
Minimum web-based TOEFL	79
Average HS GPA	2.8
% graduated top 10% of class	5
% graduated top 25% of class	21
% graduated top 50% of class	50

DEADLINES

Early action	
Deadline	11/15
Notification	12/15
Regular	
Priority	2/15
Notification	rolling

FINANCIAL FACTS

Financial Aid Rating	**70**
Annual tuition	$28,900
Room and board	$11,050
Required fees	$1,440
Books and supplies	$1,100
% needy frosh rec. need-based scholarship or grant aid	92
% needy UG rec. need-based scholarship or grant aid	85
% needy frosh rec. non-need-based scholarship or grant aid	7
% needy UG rec. non-need-based scholarship or grant aid	8
% needy frosh rec. need-based self-help aid	100
% needy UG rec. need-based self-help aid	95
% frosh rec. any financial aid	100
% UG rec. any financial aid	86
% UG borrow to pay for school	84
Average cumulative indebtedness	$34,600
% frosh need fully met	7
% ugrads need fully met	8
Average % of frosh need met	67
Average % of ugrad need met	63

BELLARMINE UNIVERSITY

2001 NEWBURG ROAD, LOUISVILLE, KY 40205 • ADMISSIONS: 502-272-8131 • TOLL-FREE: 800-274-4723 • FAX: 502-272-8002

CAMPUS LIFE

Quality of Life Rating	**90**
Fire Safety Rating	**95**
Green Rating	**72**
Type of school	private
Affiliation	Roman Catholic
Environment	metropolis

STUDENTS

Total undergrad enrollment	2,391
% male/female	36/64
% from out of state	38
% from public high school	69
% frosh live on campus	77
# of fraternities	1
# of sororities	1
% African American	4
% Asian	2
% Caucasian	82
% Hispanic	4
% international	2
# of countries represented	29

SURVEY SAYS . . .

Students get along with local community
Students love Louisville, KY
Great off-campus food
Low cost of living
Very little drug use

ACADEMICS

Academic Rating	**82**
% students returning for sophomore year	77
% students graduating within 4 years	52
% students graduating within 6 years	67
Calendar	semester
Student/faculty ratio	12:1
Profs interesting rating	88
Profs accessible rating	86
Most classes have	10–19 students
Most lab/discussion sessions have	10–19 students

MOST POPULAR MAJORS

business/commerce; nursing/registered nurse (rn, asn, bsn, msn); psychology

STUDENTS SAY ". . ."

Academics

Bellarmine University is a "high-energy school completely focused on academics," with a faculty and staff that are "willing to go beyond the call of duty all in the name of your education." The school has a good amount of prestige in Kentucky (and to some extent, the country) and encourages critical thinking, teaching others, and "building a strong, involved community." Many of its students consider it "a friendly stepping stone to higher education," and the school is on track to improve existing schools and programs (both physical and internal aspects), and to add innovative new ones. As it stands, the "self-directed research opportunities" and sense of community are "absolutely incredible" here. Students admire the school's integrity and dedication to its students' well-being, citing as a main strength its "ability to provide an avenue for every individual to express themselves and to receive the most from their education."

Professors "love their students" and "will do whatever it takes to help them succeed." "Not only are they experts in their field, but they truly care about your learning and whether you are getting the most out of the class possible," says a student. Small class sizes "maximize participation and professor involvement with the student." With so much support from faculty (who are all "readily available for assistance outside of class"), there are "a lot of opportunities for growth," as well as for help on homework, papers, and exams. "I can even wake up for my 8:00 A.M. classes because they are that interesting," says a student.

The administration is similarly "more than helpful." "I've been able to obtain great leadership roles on campus that will help me in the future," says a student. The school's Freshman Orientation process—in which new students go on a retreat before classes start to meet other classmates—also helps to make "anyone and everyone who comes to campus feel welcome." "I've learned many new ways of seeing things, i.e., culturally, critically, etc.," says a student.

Life

Located "in the heart of a beautiful city" (Louisville, Kentucky), Bellarmine "revolves around a community." "I chose Bellarmine because it has the atmosphere of an intimate school, but is in a city-like area," says a student. Also, the campus, located on a giant hill, is "gorgeous," which "makes studying anywhere on campus easy." There are "so many" cute little shops and unique restaurants within walking distance, and "the big city of Louisville offers theaters, baseball, and pretty much everything else you could want!"

A great deal of students are commuters or nontraditional students, but there are many clubs and activities for these students to get involved in so they can find their niche. "There are always events on campus," says a student. School-hosted events around town "are a weekly thing." As for fun, students here are "just like every other college student—working hard on the weekdays and trying to have fun on the weekends!" Since there are no fraternity houses or sorority houses for the one of each at BU, "most evening and weekend shenanigans happen off campus at house parties and bars for those old enough." If there is a complaint, it's that the food in the dining halls "could use some work."

Student Body

This "very friendly" bunch of students has typically "always been in good academic standing," and the students are "full of school spirit and eager to meet new people in classes." A wide variety of personalities exist on campus, and "nobody appears ashamed to be themselves by openly expressing their personality and views." International students in particular are "highly welcomed." The "rigorous" nursing program at Bellarmine is well-regarded, so there are a large number of nursing students on campus. Though the school can be a "little cliquey"—"They don't call it the 'high school on the hill' for nothing"—it's nothing too terrible. "It seems like everyone knows everyone," says a student. "No one feels like a total stranger."

FINANCIAL AID: 502-452-8124 • E-MAIL: ADMISSIONS@BELLARMINE.EDU • WEBSITE: WWW.BELLARMINE.EDU

THE PRINCETON REVIEW SAYS

Admissions

Very important factors considered include: Academic GPA, recommendation(s), rigor of secondary school record, standardized test scores, character/personal qualities, level of applicant's interest. *Important factors considered include:* Class rank, extracurricular activities. *Other factors considered include:* Application essay, alumni/ae relation, first generation, geographical residence, interview, racial/ethnic status, state residency, talent/ability, volunteer work, work experience. SAT or ACT required; ACT with or without writing component accepted. TOEFL required of all international applicants. High school diploma is required and GED is accepted. *Academic units required:* 4 English, 3 mathematics, 3 science (2 science labs), 2 foreign language, 2 social studies, 1 history, 5 academic electives. *Academic units recommended:* 4 English, 4 mathematics, 4 science (2 science labs), 2 foreign language, 3 social studies, 2 history, 7 academic electives.

Financial Aid

Students should submit: FAFSA. The Princeton Review suggests that all financial aid forms be submitted as soon as possible after January 1. *Need-based scholarships/grants offered:* Federal Pell, SEOG, state scholarships/grants, private scholarships, the school's own gift aid. *Loan aid offered:* Direct Subsidized Stafford, Direct Unsubsidized Stafford, Direct PLUS, Federal Perkins, state loans, college/university loans from institutional funds. Applicants will be notified of awards on a rolling basis beginning April 1. Federal Work-Study Program available. Institutional employment available. Highest amount earned per year from on-campus jobs $2,500. Off-campus job opportunities are excellent.

The Inside Word

Admissions at Bellarmine University is competitive. However, much like their mission statement, Bellarmine's admissions committee views applicants' profiles from a composite perspective and is looking for a well-rounded candidate whose qualifications reflect more than the sum total of a GPA and test scores. Recommendations and personal statements—which present a stronger picture of the students' educational goals—volunteer experiences, and extracurricular commitments, hold significant weight. Candidates with strong grades and diverse interests are likely to earn acceptance.

THE SCHOOL SAYS ". . ."

From the Admissions Office

"Bellarmine University prepares its students for success with a broad, liberal arts education combined with training for mastery in a specialized area. We offer over fifty majors in the arts and sciences, humanities, education, communication, business, nursing and health science, plus graduate programs in nursing, education, physical therapy, business and communication. We engage students in state-of-the-art classrooms and expand their horizons through internship and study abroad opportunities. Bellarmine delivers this world-class education just five miles from downtown Louisville, the nation's sixteenth largest city. The 135-acre campus is set in a safe, historic, and eclectic neighborhood and features a fitness center, indoor and outdoor tennis courts, athletics fields, and two beautiful new dining halls. With more than fifty clubs and organizations on campus and twenty NCAA Division II athletic teams, plus Division I men's lacrosse, Bellarmine offers a variety of recreational opportunities for all students. Recent additions to the campus reflect the university's academic emphasis on a liberal arts core curriculum surrounded by competitive graduate and professional schools. Students who reside on campus also find a Bellarmine difference in the living arrangements. From traditional college residence halls to apartment-style and suite living arrangements, plus a new living-learning community, students have many housing options. The university has completed four new residence halls that surround a Tuscan-style piazza. As Bellarmine attracts more residential students, the university has created more spaces for them to hang out, such as the café on the ground floor of the Siena Primo residence hall."

SELECTIVITY

Admissions Rating	**86**
# of applicants	6,955
% of applicants accepted	52
% of acceptees attending	17

FRESHMAN PROFILE

Range SAT Critical Reading	490–580
Range SAT Math	490–600
Range ACT Composite	22–27
Minimum paper TOEFL	550
Minimum web-based TOEFL	80
Average HS GPA	3.5
% graduated top 10% of class	26
% graduated top 25% of class	59
% graduated top 50% of class	87

DEADLINES

Early action	
Deadline	11/1
Notification	12/1
Regular	
Priority	2/1
Deadline	8/15
Nonfall registration?	yes

FINANCIAL FACTS

Financial Aid Rating	**72**
Annual tuition	$30,900
Room and board	$9,560
Required fees	$1,240
Books and supplies	$836
% needy frosh rec. need-based scholarship or grant aid	100
% needy UG rec. need-based scholarship or grant aid	97
% needy frosh rec. non-need-based scholarship or grant aid	30
% needy UG rec. non-need-based scholarship or grant aid	29
% needy frosh rec. need-based self-help aid	67
% needy UG rec. need-based self-help aid	64
% frosh rec. any financial aid	100
% UG rec. any financial aid	98
% UG borrow to pay for school	70
Average cumulative indebtedness	$26,212
% frosh need fully met	18
% ugrads need fully met	11
Average % of frosh need met	76
Average % of ugrad need met	54

BELOIT COLLEGE

700 COLLEGE STREET, BELOIT, WI 53511 • ADMISSIONS: 608-363-2500 • FAX: 608-363-2075

CAMPUS LIFE

Quality of Life Rating	77
Fire Safety Rating	68
Green Rating	65
Type of school	private
Environment	town

STUDENTS

Total undergrad enrollment	1,293
% male/female	42/58
% from out of state	81
% from public high school	79
% frosh live on campus	100
# of fraternities	3
# of sororities	3
% African American	3
% Asian	2
% Caucasian	70
% Hispanic	8
% international	9
# of countries represented	36

SURVEY SAYS . . .

No one cheats
Students are friendly
Different types of students interact
Students aren't religious
Low cost of living
Political activism is popular

ACADEMICS

Academic Rating	92
% students returning for sophomore year	88
% students graduating within 4 years	66
% students graduating within 6 years	76
Calendar	semester
Student/faculty ratio	12:1
Profs interesting rating	96
Profs accessible rating	98
Most classes have	10–19 students

MOST POPULAR MAJORS

anthropology; international relations and affairs; political science and government

APPLICANTS ALSO LOOK AT AND OFTEN PREFER
Carleton College

AND SOMETIMES PREFER
Grinnell College, Macalester College, Oberlin College

AND RARELY PREFER
Ripon College, University of Illinois at Urbana-Champaign, Lewis & Clark College, University of Wisconsin—Madison, Gustavus Adolphus College

STUDENTS SAY ". . ."

Academics

Beloit College is a small, liberal arts institution with "phenomenal academics" where "people are committed to their work out of passion, not out of pressure." As one student notes, "It's more about the community than competitiveness." Another says, "I was most impressed by an emphasis on actual learning as opposed to stiff competition or an exclusive focus on getting grades." A "vibrant, interesting, idiosyncratic place," where "every person is full of little surprises," the school promotes interdisciplinary learning and practical experience. "Education becomes a collaborative and collective experience here." Beloit attempts to "strike an optimal balance between freedom and guidance." Students can create a path that works best for them, as there is "flexibility in everything from class schedules to meal plans. You can customize your experience at Beloit to fit your needs." This creativity also applies to the actual educational process, since "you can learn in whatever way is best for you; teachers mold their lessons to the needs of the students." At the same time, "professors here aren't going to stand up there and feed you information." Interactivity is encouraged, and Beloit's intimate class sizes "usually have a good discussion portion for students to think critically and develop their own ideas." "Professors have lectures, but they really want the students to lead conversations." The ability to work closely with professors is highly prized at Beloit. As one student enthuses, "the personal attention has helped me to "come out of my shell" and become a confident member of our academic community." Beloit provides excellent support services outside of the classroom as well; "Our Liberal Arts in Practice Center and the Office of International Education are great at providing information and support for internships, volunteer opportunities, and study abroad." "My academic experience has been exploratory and invaluable."

Life

"Beloit College graciously takes the stance that its students are adults," and this is evident in their alcohol "philosophy," as well as the setup of residential living. "Many people do look out for each other and tend to be fairly responsible." Students mention that "you are responsible for yourself, and the school is there to help you when you need it," although the alcohol policy at Beloit "has definitely gotten stricter in recent years." Undergrads looking for alternative entertainment need not venture far. Dance parties are prevalent, and "the most popular ones are at Greek houses." "Student Activities hosts shuttles to the movies on Friday nights and to restaurants on Sundays," and "Our Programming Board does an excellent job bringing entertainment to campus." There are frequent lectures from visiting speakers, and two museums. Students enjoy "going to see Voodoo Barbie, our outrageously hilarious improv group," and "events like Folk N' Blues Festival and Apple Day are looked forward to all year." The on-campus bar C-Haus is "always a good place to catch great live music, have a beer, play some pool, or grab some late night snacks." The campus has good proximity to outlying Chicago, Madison, and Milwaukee, and "the parks and forests surrounding Beloit are very nice."

Student Body

According to one undergraduate, "The student body is definitely not homogeneous, save for the liberal bent." Another likes that "at Beloit you are respected for your individuality and your contribution to the community." Beloiters "come in all races, nationalities, social classes, religions, sexual orientations, body types, and hair colors (including pink and blue)." "Our director of spiritual life has made a large impact on incorporating and talking about faith, religion, and spirituality." "The student body has become increasingly more accepting." The social environment is "low-pressure," and being "genuine" is important here. "The best way to fit in is to be yourself; students here do not go for fakes."

FINANCIAL AID: 608-363-2663 • E-MAIL: ADMISS@BELOIT.EDU • WEBSITE: WWW.BELOIT.EDU

THE PRINCETON REVIEW SAYS

Admissions

Very important factors considered include: Application essay, academic GPA, recommendation(s), rigor of secondary school record. *Important factors considered include:* Class rank, standardized test scores, interview. *Other factors considered include:* Alumni/ae relation, character/personal qualities, extracurricular activities, first generation, level of applicant's interest, talent/ability, volunteer work, work experience. SAT or ACT required; ACT with or without writing component accepted. TOEFL required of all international applicants. High school diploma is required and GED is accepted. *Academic units recommended:* 4 English, 4 mathematics, 3 science, 2 foreign language, 4 social studies.

Financial Aid

Students should submit: FAFSA, institution's own financial aid form, state aid form. Regular filing deadline is March 1. The Princeton Review suggests that all financial aid forms be submitted as soon as possible after January 1. *Need-based scholarships/grants offered:* Federal Pell, SEOG, state scholarships/grants, private scholarships, the school's own gift aid. *Loan aid offered:* Direct Subsidized Stafford, Direct Unsubsidized Stafford, Direct PLUS, Federal Perkins, college/university loans from institutional funds. Applicants will be notified of awards on a rolling basis beginning April 1. Federal Work-Study Program available. Institutional employment available. Highest amount earned per year from on-campus jobs $3,000. Off-campus job opportunities are good.

The Inside Word

Beloit seeks to evaluate the entire student when considering potential for admission—from grades and test scores, to essays and recommendations, to personality and strength of character. This holistic approach to assessment leads Beloit to seek students with not only impressive high school transcripts, but those who possess a strong sense of responsibility and show the capacity for leadership.

THE SCHOOL SAYS ". . ."

From the Admissions Office

"Beloiters spend four years challenged to explore their passions, excel in their studies, and apply the lessons of the classroom to the larger world, in their careers, and in service to others. That focus—putting the liberal arts into practice—has long set this college and its graduates apart. Study abroad, internships, research, service, and work opportunities are typical examples of the ways the Beloit experience extends beyond the classroom. Beloit students are more apt to value learning for its own sake and at the same time, understand the connection between college and the rest of their lives as citizens of the world.

"Beloit College uses the Common Application exclusively. Although students must submit test scores from the ACT or SAT, standardized test scores are less important than the strength of the academic program and performance, the essays, and recommendations. Beloit offers two nonbinding early action plans with deadlines of either November 1 or December 1; notification is six weeks hence. Applicants who wish to be considered for merit scholarships are urged to apply under one of the early action plans. The preferred deadline for regular decision applicants in January 15."

SELECTIVITY	
Admissions Rating	88
# of applicants	2,107
% of applicants accepted	75
% of acceptees attending	20
# accepting a place on wait list	76
# admitted from wait list	16
FRESHMAN PROFILE	
Range SAT Critical Reading	560–690
Range SAT Math	550–660
Range ACT Composite	25–32
Minimum paper TOEFL	550
Minimum web-based TOEFL	80
Average HS GPA	3.5
% graduated top 10% of class	36
% graduated top 25% of class	53
% graduated top 50% of class	96
DEADLINES	
Early action	
Deadline	11/1 and 12/1
Notification	12/15 and 1/15
Regular	
Priority	1/15
Notification	4/1
Nonfall registration?	yes
FINANCIAL FACTS	
Financial Aid Rating	91
Annual tuition	$36,444
Room and board	$7,502
Required fees	$230
Books and supplies	$600
% needy frosh rec. need-based scholarship or grant aid	99
% needy UG rec. need-based scholarship or grant aid	99
% needy frosh rec. need-based self-help aid	100
% needy UG rec. need-based self-help aid	99
% frosh rec. any financial aid	94
% UG rec. any financial aid	90
% UG borrow to pay for school	66
Average cumulative indebtedness	$26,771
% frosh need fully met	40
% ugrads need fully met	50
Average % of frosh need met	92
Average % of ugrad need met	93

BENNINGTON COLLEGE

OFFICE OF ADMISSIONS, BENNINGTON, VT 05201-6003 • ADMISSIONS: 802-440-4312 • FAX: 802-440-4320

CAMPUS LIFE

Quality of Life Rating	**84**
Fire Safety Rating	**92**
Green Rating	**84**
Type of school	private
Environment	town

STUDENTS

Total undergrad enrollment	686
% male/female	34/66
% from out of state	97
% from public high school	58
% frosh live on campus	100
% African American	1
% Asian	2
% Caucasian	80
% Hispanic	4
% Native American	1
% international	6
# of countries represented	32

SURVEY SAYS . . .

Lots of liberal students
Class discussions encouraged
Students aren't religious
Dorms are like palaces
Low cost of living
Intercollegiate sports are unpopular or nonexistent
Frats and sororities are unpopular or nonexistent
Theater is popular
Internships are widely available

ACADEMICS

Academic Rating	**98**
% students returning for sophomore year	85
% students graduating within 4 years	58
% students graduating within 6 years	67
Calendar	other
Student/faculty ratio	10:1
Profs interesting rating	98
Profs accessible rating	95
Most classes have	10–19 students
Most lab/discussion sessions have	10–19 students

MOST POPULAR MAJORS

English language and literature; visual and performing arts; social sciences

APPLICANTS ALSO LOOK AT AND OFTEN PREFER

Bard College

AND SOMETIMES PREFER

Lewis & Clark College, Sarah Lawrence College

AND RARELY PREFER

Eugene Lang College The New School for Liberal Arts, Hampshire College, Marlboro College, University of Vermont

STUDENTS SAY ". . ."

Academics

One big draw to Bennington College is its "Field Work Term program, where students intern every year for seven weeks to gain practical experience related to their academic interests." This mandatory program provides a "real-world" opportunity many students appreciate. "It's a huge advantage upon graduation, because with a degree from Bennington, you automatically have four internships or jobs on your resume—and that's only if you do absolutely nothing during summers." An even bigger draw for some students may be Bennington's Plan Process. "Bennington's greatest strength is the opportunity that it gives its students to design our own educations, that we are encouraged to study what we are truly passionate about." This is ideal for students without a clear career focus, as well as those who are "frustrated with the "core requirements" style of education that high school shuttled [them] through" and want to "personally craft your own education tailored to your interests." As one student explains, "I had no idea what I wanted to do or what I wanted to study. I needed to be free to explore however I please." A flexible academic plan and yearly internships mean "students are constantly revisiting and reevaluating the questions of 'What do I want to study and why?'" Students are given "not only the freedom to explore a wide range of disciplines but the ability to discover and study my passions in depth." Bennington's professors received high praise. "The professors here are universally outstanding. Because of Bennington's teacher-practitioner model, which requires professors to be active professionals in their fields of instruction, students at Bennington are privy to professors who not only are immensely knowledgeable in their fields, but are also so excited to teach about them." "Most professors treat you as a future colleague rather than a student, which helps foster the experience of learning a skill or ability to analyze." The school's small size has a lot of benefits: "Classes are mostly discussion-based, small, and seminar style. Lectures are kept to a strict minimum, and classes are rarely more than twenty people." But being small "can occasionally impact the curriculum—for example, few art history classes being offered one term. However, Bennington tries to accommodate this, and thus I took a private art history tutorial with a professor instead."

Life

Life at Bennington "centers around work," which is fine with students since "it's work we really enjoy." Located in an "absolutely, positively stunning" and "very cozy" campus in the small town of Bennington, Vermont, students spend a lot of time on school grounds. The "unique housing" where students "live in houses instead of dorms" builds a "strong community." The arts are very popular on campus. "There's always a concert, or an opening, or a show going on somewhere, and we like to support each other by going to as many events as we can." "Dance, live music, and drama are really well attended here because the work that goes up is just so good." Some students find transportation a challenge; "People do make it to Boston and New York City for performances and weekend getaways, though the surrounding area is much more accessible." "Outside of campus one can walk around the quaint town with lots of shops and restaurants." "We also go out for dinner a lot at local restaurants." "Students love eating and cooking together. The atmosphere is pretty relaxed and conversational."

Student Body

Bennington students are "a body of individuals." They are "hipsters, artists, and the next generation of geniuses having a good time and doing real, amazing things in the world." They are "driven and passionate about their work," and "everyone here is so amazing and artistic." "Students tend to be pretty liberal, open, and tolerant. Most students genuinely care about their studies, and they pride themselves on their intellectual nature and academic successes. Most students are artistically aware, and they enjoy discussing literature, film, music, etc." Although "It's not a super diverse place ethnically or politically, in terms of diversity of interests, it's wonderful." "Everyone truly wants to be here and is engaged in their work."

Financial Aid: 802-440-4325 • E-mail: admissions@bennington.edu • Website: www.bennington.edu

THE PRINCETON REVIEW SAYS

Admissions

Very important factors considered include: Academic GPA, rigor of secondary school record, application essays, recommendations, class rank, character/personal qualities, interview, talents and abilities, extracurricular activities. *Other factors considered include:* Standardized test scores, alumni/ae relation, first generation, geographical residence, level of applicant's interest, racial/ethnic status, volunteer work, work experience. ACT with or without writing component accepted. TOEFL required of all international applicants. High school diploma is required and GED is accepted. *Academic units recommended:* 4 English, 4 mathematics, 3 science, 2 foreign language, 4 social studies, 4 history.

Financial Aid

Students should submit: FAFSA, institution's own financial aid form, CSS/Financial Aid PROFILE, noncustodial PROFILE, student and parent federal tax returns and W-2s. Regular filing deadline is February 15. The Princeton Review suggests that all financial aid forms be submitted as soon as possible after January 1. *Need-based scholarships/grants offered:* Federal Pell, SEOG, state scholarships/grants, private scholarships, the school's own gift aid. *Loan aid offered:* Direct Subsidized Stafford, Direct Unsubsidized Stafford, Direct PLUS, college/university loans from institutional funds. *Note:* College/university loans from institutional funds for international students only. Applicants will be notified of awards on or about April 1. Federal Work-Study Program available. Institutional employment available. Highest amount earned per year from on-campus jobs $2,300. Off-campus job opportunities are good.

The Inside Word

Bennington students need to be academically accomplished, driven, and self-directed to handle the academic freedom granted by the curriculum. The admissions office seeks all these qualities in applicants and, because of the school's prestige, typically finds them in all admitted students. A campus visit isn't required but is strongly recommended as an excellent way to demonstrate your interest in the school and to provide admissions officers with the personal contact they prefer in evaluating candidates.

THE SCHOOL SAYS ". . ."

From the Admissions Office

"At Bennington, your education is unified and fueled by your intellect and imagination, guided by a rigorous and ongoing conversation with your faculty, and shaped by your experience working in the world each year. Bennington is the only college to require that its students spend a term—every year—at work in the world. And its new Center for the Advancement of Public Action provides a unique opportunity for students to explore how the questions that matter to them come together with the questions that matter to the world. Rooted in an abiding faith in the talent, imagination, and responsibility of the individual, Bennington invites students to pursue and shape their own intellectual inquiries and, in doing so, to discover the profound interconnection of things.

"Submission of standardized test scores (the SAT, SAT Subject Tests, or the ACT) is optional."

SELECTIVITY

Admissions Rating	89
# of applicants	1,145
% of applicants accepted	72
% of acceptees attending	26
# accepting a place on wait list	80
# admitted from wait list	3
# of early decision applicants	52
# accepted early decision	40

FRESHMAN PROFILE

Range SAT Critical Reading	620–710
Range SAT Math	550–650
Range SAT Writing	590–690
Range ACT Composite	26–30
Minimum paper TOEFL	577
Average HS GPA	3.5
% graduated top 10% of class	36
% graduated top 25% of class	68
% graduated top 50% of class	94

DEADLINES

Early decision	
Deadline	11/15
Notification	12/20
Early action	
Deadline	12/1
Notification	2/1
Regular	
Deadline	1/3
Notification	4/1
Nonfall registration?	yes

FINANCIAL FACTS

Financial Aid Rating	81
Annual tuition	$41,690
Room and board	$12,160
Required fees	$1,110
Books and supplies	$800
% needy frosh rec. need-based scholarship or grant aid	98
% needy UG rec. need-based scholarship or grant aid	98
% needy frosh rec. non-need-based scholarship or grant aid	8
% needy UG rec. non-need-based scholarship or grant aid	7
% needy frosh rec. need-based self-help aid	87
% needy UG rec. need-based self-help aid	89
% frosh rec. any financial aid	96
% UG rec. any financial aid	88
% UG borrow to pay for school	72
Average cumulative indebtedness	$23,002
% frosh need fully met	12
% ugrads need fully met	10
Average % of frosh need met	81
Average % of ugrad need met	80

BENTLEY UNIVERSITY

175 FOREST STREET, WALTHAM, MA 02452 • ADMISSIONS: 781-891-2244 • FAX: 781-891-3414

CAMPUS LIFE

Quality of Life Rating	**94**
Fire Safety Rating	**99**
Green Rating	**88**
Type of school	private
Environment	town

STUDENTS

Total undergrad enrollment	4,154
% male/female	59/41
% from out of state	59
% from public high school	72
% frosh live on campus	98
# of fraternities	7
# of sororities	5
% African American	3
% Asian	7
% Caucasian	61
% Hispanic	7
% international	12
# of countries represented	96

SURVEY SAYS . . .

Great computer facilities
Great library
Athletic facilities are great
Career services are great
School is well run
Dorms are like palaces
Campus feels safe
Internships are widely available

ACADEMICS

Academic Rating	**80**
% students returning for sophomore year	94
% students graduating within 4 years	82
% students graduating within 6 years	89
Calendar	semester
Student/faculty ratio	14:1
Profs interesting rating	80
Profs accessible rating	84
Most classes have	30–39 students

MOST POPULAR MAJORS

accounting and related services, other; business administration and management; marketing/marketing management

APPLICANTS ALSO LOOK AT AND SOMETIMES PREFER

Babson College, Boston College, Boston University, Bryant University, Northeastern University, University of Massachusetts Amherst, Villanova University

STUDENTS SAY ". . ."

Academics

"If you're looking to work in business in the Boston area, desire a beautiful campus, state-of-the-art trading room, and technologically advanced university, Bentley University is the place for you," one student assures us. Bentley is known for its business program, and many students cite the program's excellent reputation as their reason for choosing to attend college here, as well as strong career services and professional internship opportunities. Students are pleased with Bentley's abilities to create a "career-bound student while instilling the importance of liberal studies," and to "prepare you and help you earn a job with all the technical and educational background you need." They also "love that most of the professors have worked outside of academia and can bring…real-world experience and examples to the classroom." Professors are "great role models and have had a lot of experience in the business world," and "all professors hold office hours, and they are all responsive to e-mail and phone messages." "Class sizes are capped at thirty-five, which gives students a solid relationship with each professor," and "a lot of classes are discussion-based and force you to think about real-world applications." Some students note that classes can be challenging, but that "many of the departments have tutoring labs available for students at all levels." The administration also receives high marks: It's "truly concerned with students' wants," "engaging and open to new ideas," and "very communicative."

Life

Bentley students study hard and are "very business-like" during week, so they use weekends to blow off a little steam. Many seek fun in the local sports teams (Red Sox, Patriots, and Celtics), local bars on Moody Street, and regular shuttles into Cambridge (Boston is also easily accessible via public transportation). "This university really strikes a great balance of fun and work." While students are happy to have a city like Boston nearby, with its "bars, historical sites, theaters, restaurants, clubs, etc.," there's plenty of activity on campus, too, and "entertainment is limitless." "Students are extremely involved at Bentley." "Most students participate in more than one club, and many hold administrative positions in the club. These clubs lead to not only good friends but also networking opportunities." "Many people participate in very competitive intramural sports." Bentley does have a Greek system, though frat houses are located off campus.

Student Body

A typical student at Bentley "is an intelligent, white New Englander." Moreover, they're "very driven and know what they want to do with their life," and they "know how to have ats appear to be the same: serious business students working all the time," good time and balance that with schoolwork." "On the surface, most studenand they're "involved in a few extracurriculars." However, look beneath the surface and you'll notice a significant international population and "a lot of atypical students" who "fit in with the rest of the students perfectly." Some students say they think the majority of their peers come from wealth, but most feel that Bentley is fairly balanced: "While walking through campus, you may see tons of individuals driving expensive cars or walking to class dressed to the nines, [but] you will also encounter people driving inexpensive cars and walking to class dressed in sweats."

FINANCIAL AID: 781-891-3441 • E-MAIL: UGADMISSION@BENTLEY.EDU • WEBSITE: WWW.BENTLEY.EDU

THE PRINCETON REVIEW SAYS

Admissions

Very important factors considered include: Academic GPA, rigor of secondary school record, standardized test scores. *Important factors considered include:* Application essay, recommendation(s), character/personal qualities, extracurricular activities, level of applicant's interest, volunteer work. *Other factors considered include:* Class rank, alumni/ae relation, first generation, geographical residence, interview, racial/ethnic status, state residency, talent/ability, work experience. SAT or ACT required; ACT with writing component required. TOEFL required of all international applicants. High school diploma is required and GED is accepted. *Academic units recommended:* 4 English, 4 mathematics, 3 science (3 science labs), 3 foreign language, 3 social studies, 2 additional English, mathematics, social or lab science, foreign language.

Financial Aid

Students should submit: FAFSA, CSS/Financial Aid PROFILE, noncustodial PROFILE, business/farm supplement. Federal Tax Returns, including all schedules for parents and student. Regular filing deadline is February 1. The Princeton Review suggests that all financial aid forms be submitted as soon as possible after January 1. *Need-based scholarships/grants offered:* Federal Pell, SEOG, state scholarships/grants, private scholarships, the school's own gift aid. *Loan aid offered:* Direct Subsidized Stafford, Direct Unsubsidized Stafford, Direct PLUS, Federal Perkins, state loans. Applicants will be notified of awards on a rolling basis beginning March 25. Federal Work-Study Program available. Institutional employment available. Off-campus job opportunities are good.

The Inside Word

If you have a bunch of electives available to you senior year, you may think that choosing business classes is the best way to impress the Bentley admissions office. Not so; the school would prefer you take a broad range of challenging classes—preferably at the AP level—in English, history/social sciences, math, lab sciences, and foreign language. The school enjoys a sizable applicant pool, so you'll need solid grades and test scores to gain admission.

THE SCHOOL SAYS ". . ."

From the Admissions Office

"Bentley University is a national leader in business education, providing an unparalleled fusion of business and the arts and science. Bentley blends the breadth and technological strength of a university with the values and student focus of a small college.

"Many Bentley students choose both a business major and our nationally acclaimed Liberal Studies major (LSM), gaining a competitive edge in their future careers by building meaningful connections across disciplines. Bentley students also embrace internships, service learning, study abroad, and corporate partnerships. More than eighty percent of Bentley undergraduates complete at least one internship.

"In 2010, Bentley was ranked number six nationally by The Princeton Review for 'Best Career Services.' Also in 2010, ninety-nine percent of Bentley students found employment or enrolled in graduate school within six months of graduation. Their median annual salary was more than $50,000.

"Approximately ninety-eight percent of freshmen live on campus. Students live and learn in a multicultural environment that prepares them to thrive in today's diverse work world. International students representing more than eighty countries are part of the Bentley community. There are more than 100 student organizations, as well as abundant intramurals, recreational sports, and twenty-three varsity teams in NCAA Divisions I and II.

"Bentley's location in Waltham, Massachusetts—just minutes from Boston—puts the city's many resources within easy reach. Bentley's free shuttle makes regular trips to Harvard Square in Cambridge, just a subway ride from the heart of Boston. Boston also offers students many opportunities for internships and jobs after graduation."

SELECTIVITY

Admissions Rating	**92**
# of applicants	6,695
% of applicants accepted	43
% of acceptees attending	31
# accepting a place on wait list	1,400
# admitted from wait list	83
# of early decision applicants	137
# accepted early decision	82

FRESHMAN PROFILE

Range SAT Critical Reading	540–635
Range SAT Math	600–680
Range SAT Writing	550–650
Range ACT Composite	25–29
Minimum paper TOEFL	577
Minimum web-based TOEFL	90
% graduated top 10% of class	45
% graduated top 25% of class	82
% graduated top 50% of class	98

DEADLINES

Early decision	
Deadline	11/1
Notification	Late December (12/15)
Early action	
Deadline	11/1
Notification	Late January (1/15)
Regular	
Deadline	1/7
Notification	3/31
Nonfall registration?	yes

FINANCIAL FACTS

Financial Aid Rating	**84**
Annual tuition	$36,840
Room and board	$12,520
Required fees	$1,488
Books and supplies	$1,100
% needy frosh rec. need-based scholarship or grant aid	87
% needy UG rec. need-based scholarship or grant aid	84
% needy frosh rec. non-need-based scholarship or grant aid	32
% needy UG rec. non-need-based scholarship or grant aid	30
% needy frosh rec. need-based self-help aid	90
% needy UG rec. need-based self-help aid	91
% frosh rec. any financial aid	77
% UG rec. any financial aid	74
% UG borrow to pay for school	64
Average cumulative indebtedness	$33,066
% frosh need fully met	44
% ugrads need fully met	43
Average % of frosh need met	97
Average % of ugrad need met	95

Berea College

CPO 2220, Berea, KY 40404 • Admissions: 859-985-3500 • Fax: 859-985-3512

CAMPUS LIFE

Quality of Life Rating	65
Fire Safety Rating	86
Green Rating	92
Type of school	private
Environment	village

STUDENTS

Total undergrad enrollment	1,613
% male/female	43/57
% from out of state	53
% African American	15
% Asian	1
% Caucasian	65
% Hispanic	3
% international	7
# of countries represented	58

SURVEY SAYS . . .

Great computer facilities
Athletic facilities are great
Diverse student types on campus
Different types of students interact
Low cost of living
Frats and sororities are unpopular or nonexistent
Musical organizations are popular

ACADEMICS

Academic Rating	82
% students returning for sophomore year	79
% students graduating within 4 years	46
% students graduating within 6 years	62
Calendar	semester
Student/faculty ratio	11:1
Profs interesting rating	78
Profs accessible rating	76
Most classes have	10–19 students

MOST POPULAR MAJORS

biology/biological sciences; business/commerce; English; education study

STUDENTS SAY ". . ."

Academics

Berea College in central Kentucky is "about bringing underprivileged high school graduates from the Appalachian region and beyond together for a chance at a higher education, a career, and a better life." Thanks to a labor program that requires all students to work ten to fifteen hours each week and a ton of donated cash, tuition here is "free." "Each student receives a laptop to use while in school" as well. "No tuition does not mean a full ride," though. "Extra costs such as technology fees, insurance, food plans, etc., add up quickly," advises a business major. About two-thirds of the students receive additional financial aid. Berea's administration is efficient, but it "tends to be too parental in nature," and can be overly concerned with image. "Donors hear a story of poor kids who are getting help from a school that sometimes styles itself as a charity," explains a junior. In addition to a decent range of liberal arts and sciences majors, there are several career-oriented programs. The academic atmosphere is "rigorous." Class attendance is mandatory. A few "hardcore" professors "abuse the idea of homework." Others "need refresher courses on how to deal with people." On the whole, though, faculty members are "witty," and they "have a strong passion for what they are teaching." "Everyone who I've had has been completely accessible outside of class," describes a nursing major. "Students are able to get so much more one-on-one time than at larger colleges."

Life

"Buildings, facilities, and technology are not always the newest, nicest, or most expensive" on this "tiny campus." There's no cable television in the dorm rooms, and the "crazy" visitation policy for members of the opposite sex is "borderline nineteenth century." Academics take up a lot of time, and "every student is required to have an on-campus job." Some students make stoneware pottery. Others "feed sheep and goats" on the college farm. However, "janitorial work," computer support, and similarly mundane jobs are more typical. "With work, classes, and studying, there's not much time left for anything else." "There are many clubs" and several religious groups. "Movie marathons" and "dances" are common. "Pick-up games" and intramurals are popular. "Some of us go camping when it's nice out, that kind of thing," says a first-year student. Otherwise, "Life at Berea is generally regarded as boring." "If it weren't for video games, I'd go nuts," speculates a junior. The surrounding town is "very small." "There is not even a movie theater." "Someone from a big city would be in for a shock." With limited space, having a car is a tricky proposition for underclassmen, as permits are distributed according to class quotas. The county is dry, and there are no bars. Berea's alcohol polices are theoretically harsh but more lenient in practice. "If you can hide it, you can drink it." However, alcohol and drug usage is "very low." "We're not a party school," says a junior. "Basically, our weekends consist of walking down to Wal-Mart," explains a sophomore, "and that's if we're really ready for a crazy night."

Student Body

"The typical student at Berea College is broke" but "has big dreams." "Most people are from working-class families." They were "raised in backwoods hollows" around "the Appalachian area." "We are all here because we have no money but are equipped with the hope for a bright future and a desire to learn," declares a senior. Students at Berea are "sleep deprived" and "too busy to really have the time to slack off (though there are some that still manage it)." They're "bright, hardworking," and "studious." "Most of us are nerds," admits a senior. There are "quite a few Bible thumpers." At the same time, Berea is "probably more liberal than conservative," and this is something of "a hippie school." "People are really big about recycling, sustainability, and the environment." Students tell us that Berea has "more diversity than most schools." "There is a very large homeschool population." There are quite a few "young married students." There's also a noticeable contingent of international students and "a large population of African Americans." Most students claim that minorities "blend in well."

FINANCIAL AID: 859-985-3310 • E-MAIL: ADMISSIONS@BEREA.EDU • WEBSITE: WWW.BEREA.EDU

THE PRINCETON REVIEW SAYS

Admissions

Very important factors considered include: Class rank, academic GPA, rigor of secondary school record, standardized test scores, interview. *Important factors considered include:* Character/personal qualities. *Other factors considered include:* Recommendation(s), extracurricular activities, geographical residence, racial/ethnic status, state residency, talent/ability, volunteer work, work experience. SAT or ACT required; ACT with or without writing component accepted. TOEFL required of all international applicants. High school diploma is required and GED is accepted. *Academic units recommended:* 4 English, 3 mathematics, 2 science (2 science labs), 2 foreign language, 1 social studies, 1 history.

Financial Aid

Students should submit: FAFSA. Regular filing deadline is February 1. The Princeton Review suggests that all financial aid forms be submitted as soon as possible after January 1. *Need-based scholarships/grants offered:* Federal Pell, SEOG, state scholarships/grants, private scholarships, the school's own gift aid. *Loan aid offered:* Direct Subsidized Stafford, Direct Unsubsidized Stafford, Direct PLUS, Federal Perkins, college/university loans from institutional funds. Applicants will be notified of awards on a rolling basis beginning April 1. Federal Work-Study Program available.

Inside Word

The full-tuition scholarship that every student receives understandably attracts a lot of applicants. Competition among candidates is intense. To make matters worse, you may be too wealthy to get admitted here. Berea won't admit students whose parents can afford to send them elsewhere. Financially qualified applicants should apply as early as possible.

THE SCHOOL SAYS ". . ."

From the Admissions Office

"Founded in 1855 by ardent abolitionists, Berea College was the first racially integrated coeducational college in the South. Over the past 150 years, Berea has evolved into one of the most distinctive colleges in the United States. Serving students primarily from the Appalachian region, Berea College seeks to serve students who possess great academic promise but have access to limited financial resources. Berea provides an inviting and personal educational experience, evidenced in part by an eleven to one student/faculty ratio and extensive, faculty-led advising and orientation programs.

"In support of students with limited financial resources, every enrolling student receives a full-tuition scholarship, a laptop computer, as well as a paid on-campus job. Students may use earnings from their jobs to assist with their portion of room, board, and fee charges; books and supplies; and other personal expenses. Any remaining housing, meals, and fee charges are covered through scholarships and grant-based aid.

"As a result of this combination of academic reputation and generous financial assistance, Berea attracts many more applicants than are able to be accepted, so admission is competitive. The best means of improving the chances for admission is to complete the application process as early as possible, preferably by October 31 of the senior year."

SELECTIVITY	
Admissions Rating	**96**
# of applicants	1,603
% of applicants accepted	35
FRESHMAN PROFILE	
Range SAT Critical Reading	495–640
Range SAT Math	483–588
Range SAT Writing	513–610
Range ACT Composite	22–27
Minimum paper TOEFL	500
Minimum web-based TOEFL	61
Average HS GPA	3.4
% graduated top 10% of class	31
% graduated top 25% of class	73
% graduated top 50% of class	98
DEADLINES	
Regular	
Priority	10/31
Deadline	4/30
Nonfall registration?	no
FINANCIAL FACTS	
Financial Aid Rating	**88**
Annual tuition	$0
Room and board	$5,792
Required fees	$910
Books and supplies	$700
% needy frosh rec. need-based scholarship or grant aid	100
% needy UG rec. need-based scholarship or grant aid	100
% needy frosh rec. need-based self-help aid	100
% needy UG rec. need-based self-help aid	100
% frosh rec. any financial aid	100
% UG rec. any financial aid	100
% UG borrow to pay for school	77
Average cumulative indebtedness	$7,661
Average % of frosh need met	94
Average % of ugrad need met	92

BIRMINGHAM-SOUTHERN COLLEGE

BOX 549008, BIRMINGHAM, AL 35254 • ADMISSIONS: 205-226-4696 • FAX: 205-226-3074

CAMPUS LIFE

Quality of Life Rating	85
Fire Safety Rating	76
Green Rating	72
Type of school	private
Affiliation	Methodist
Environment	metropolis

STUDENTS

Total undergrad enrollment	1,412
% male/female	49/51
% from out of state	43
% from public high school	65
% frosh live on campus	97
# of fraternities	6
# of sororities	6
% African American	8
% Asian	3
% Caucasian	84
% Hispanic	1
# of countries represented	12

SURVEY SAYS . . .

No one cheats
Lab facilities are great
Great off-campus food
Campus feels safe
Frats and sororities dominate social scene

ACADEMICS

Academic Rating	85
% students returning for sophomore year	75
% students graduating within 4 years	53
% students graduating within 6 years	66
Calendar	4-1-4
Student/faculty ratio	12:1
Profs interesting rating	93
Profs accessible rating	89
Most classes have	10–19 students
Most lab/discussion sessions have	10–19 students

MOST POPULAR MAJORS

business/commerce; English language and literature; psychology

APPLICANTS ALSO LOOK AT AND OFTEN PREFER

Vanderbilt University, Rhodes College

AND SOMETIMES PREFER

University of Alabama—Tuscaloosa, Auburn University, Furman University, Samford University, Sewanee—The University of the South

AND RARELY PREFER

Tulane University, Louisiana State University—Baton Rouge

STUDENTS SAY ". . ."

Academics

Birmingham-Southern College "is an institution that cares for its students and provides them with a high-quality education and opportunities to succeed." A double-major in art and psychology says, "I chose BSC because I wanted a small liberal arts college where I would know my teachers personally and where I would gain a well-rounded education and experience to help me further my career in life." Most students rave about the "academic reputation and the small class sizes that allow for personalized interaction with the professors." The college is known for its strong premed and theater programs, and students say BSC has a "reputation for sending students to some of the most prestigious and reputable graduate and professional schools in the country." Professors get high marks across the board. Students say, "The professors here make BSC what it is" and add, "They're always willing to help you out and meet with you if you need extra help. They make the academic experience here completely fabulous and well worth the hard work you have to put into your studies." Academic standards are considered rigorous, and students say BSC "demands the best from the professors and the best from the students. The faculty is fantastic, and the campus is beautiful."

Life

BSC "is a gated/closed campus, so living on campus is preferred by most students—and many of the activities happen at night for this reason." Students describe the atmosphere on campus as, "welcoming [and] intelligent, where assumptions are challenged, and individuals [are] supported" and say, "In order to 'fit in' one *must* get involved in something." Many students say the small size of the college "allows for a lot of opportunities for students to get involved and become an active part of campus." Clubs and intramurals are popular, and students say, "It definitely never gets boring here on campus." One student adds, "Even if you can't think of anything to do, the school is always having some kind of event that's usually free and pretty fun." The administration earns some grumbles, with students saying, "There is a disconnect with administration and the student population." Better communication around campus "is something students have been looking for in the past few years." A collaborative education major says, "We've recently had some financial troubles, and it has exposed some gaping holes in the way the administration deals with the student body"; however, some are optimistic that "steps have been taken this year to improve that situation." A common complaint is the cafeteria, where students feel frustrated by high prices and a lack of quality.

Student Body

At BSC, typical students are "goal-oriented and focused," but also "hard workers" who "find time for play." One student says, "Simply put, a BSC student is a laid-back workaholic who knows how to have a good time." Another adds, "The model Birmingham-Southern student is over-committed, because at BSC it's cool to be busy." Students say they're "heavily involved in Greek life and student organizations" and that the small student body allows for more leadership roles in extracurricular activities. Despite the popularity of the Greek system and the fact that "most people at BSC drink," drinking is "not required to have friends or fun," and "Students fit in well at BSC regardless of their personal preferences, usually." Most students are "Southern, both in origin and in nature—warm hellos from strangers are a part of life on campus. Overall, it's a pretty likeable" and "smart bunch." Although, "The typical student comes from an upper-middle-class background," one student says, "There are many (like myself) who are here through extensive scholarships and financial aid." Birmingham gets praise as a vibrant community with a local art scene, and a psychology major says, "There is a great coffeehouse scene in Birmingham, and during exams you can often find students studying at various locally owned coffeehouses."

FINANCIAL AID: 205-226-4688 • E-MAIL: ADMISSION@BSC.EDU • WEBSITE: WWW.BSC.EDU

THE PRINCETON REVIEW SAYS

Admissions

Very important factors considered include: Application essay, academic GPA, recommendation(s), rigor of secondary school record, standardized test scores. *Important factors considered include:* Character/personal qualities. *Other factors considered include:* Extracurricular activities, interview, level of applicant's interest, talent/ability, work experience. SAT or ACT required; ACT with writing component recommended. TOEFL required of all international applicants. High school diploma is required and GED is accepted. *Academic units required:* 4 English. *Academic units recommended:* 4 mathematics, 4 science (2 science labs), 2 foreign language, 2 social studies, 2 history, 10 academic electives.

Financial Aid

Students should submit: FAFSA. The Princeton Review suggests that all financial aid forms be submitted as soon as possible after January 1. *Need-based scholarships/grants offered:* Federal Pell, SEOG, state scholarships/grants, private scholarships, the school's own gift aid, United Negro College Fund. *Loan aid offered:* Direct Subsidized Stafford, Direct Unsubsidized Stafford, Direct PLUS, Federal Perkins. Applicants will be notified of awards on a rolling basis beginning March 1. Federal Work-Study Program available. Institutional employment available. Highest amount earned per year from on-campus jobs $1,800. Off-campus job opportunities are excellent.

The Inside Word

BSC is a small college that caters to prospective students during the application process. Admissions counselors routinely "hit the road" traveling to meet students across the country and working with high schools to organize informational sessions about BSC. They put a strong emphasis on the campus visit and offer to help potential applicants plan every aspect of their visit, from transportation to dining.

THE SCHOOL SAYS ". . ."

From the Admissions Office

"Respected publishers continue to recognize Birmingham-Southern College as one of the top-ranked liberal arts colleges in the nation. One guide highlights our small classes and the fact that we still assign each student a 'faculty-mentor,' to assure individualized attention to our students. One notable aspect of our academic calendar is our January interim term, a four-week period in which students can participate in special projects in close collaboration with faculty members, either on or off campus. One dimension of Birmingham-Southern's civic focus is the commitment to volunteerism. The Center for Leadership Studies assists students in realizing their leadership potential by combining the academic study of leadership with significant community service.

"Freshman applicants must present acceptable scores on the SAT or the ACT; they must also submit an original essay and a satisfactory recommendation from the high school."

SELECTIVITY	
Admissions Rating	**83**
# of applicants	2,101
% of applicants accepted	69
% of acceptees attending	31
FRESHMAN PROFILE	
Range SAT Critical Reading	520–540
Range SAT Math	520–630
Range ACT Composite	23–28
Minimum paper TOEFL	500
Minimum web-based TOEFL	61
Average HS GPA	3.4
% graduated top 10% of class	32
% graduated top 25% of class	53
% graduated top 50% of class	82
DEADLINES	
Regular	
Priority	1/1
Nonfall registration?	yes
FINANCIAL FACTS	
Financial Aid Rating	**89**
Annual tuition	$29,600
Room and board	$10,220
Required fees	$1,040
Books and supplies	$1,260
% needy frosh rec. need-based scholarship or grant aid	83
% needy UG rec. need-based scholarship or grant aid	78
% needy frosh rec. non-need-based scholarship or grant aid	99
% needy UG rec. non-need-based scholarship or grant aid	98
% needy frosh rec. need-based self-help aid	77
% needy UG rec. need-based self-help aid	77
% frosh rec. any financial aid	99
% UG rec. any financial aid	98
% UG borrow to pay for school	79
Average cumulative indebtedness	$27,798
% frosh need fully met	61
% ugrads need fully met	52
Average % of frosh need met	99
Average % of ugrad need met	94

BOSTON COLLEGE

140 COMMONWEALTH AVENUE, CHESTNUT HILL, MA 02467-3809 • ADMISSIONS: 617-552-3100 • FAX: 617-552-0798

CAMPUS LIFE

Quality of Life Rating	**88**
Fire Safety Rating	**90**
Green Rating	**87**
Type of school	private
Affiliation	Roman Catholic
Environment	city

STUDENTS

Total undergrad enrollment	9,088
% male/female	47/53
% from out of state	77
% from public high school	53
% frosh live on campus	99
% African American	4
% Asian	9
% Caucasian	62
% Hispanic	10
% international	4
# of countries represented	85

SURVEY SAYS . . .

Students love Chestnut Hill, MA
Campus feels safe
Everyone loves the Eagles
Frats and sororities are unpopular or nonexistent
Student publications are popular
Students are involved in community service

ACADEMICS

Academic Rating	**86**
% students returning for sophomore year	95
Calendar	semester
Student/faculty ratio	14:1
Profs interesting rating	84
Profs accessible rating	83
Most classes have	10–19 students

MOST POPULAR MAJORS

communication and media studies, other; English language and literature; finance

APPLICANTS ALSO LOOK AT AND OFTEN PREFER

Harvard College, Brown University, University of Pennsylvania, Yale University

AND SOMETIMES PREFER

Georgetown University, Cornell University, University of Notre Dame, New York University

AND RARELY PREFER

Boston University, Villanova University, Northeastern University, Fordham University

STUDENTS SAY ". . ."

Academics

Boston College, a small Jesuit school on the outskirts of Boston, "is all about educating the person as a whole." Its strong core curriculum ensures all students receive a "well-rounded" liberal arts education regardless of their chosen major. Boston College's well-respected education and business school attract a lot of students, and there are many other strong programs, including English and communication. Students think Boston College is a "great experience academically" and gush about their "phenomenal professors." A secondary education major student says, "Boston College's professors are truly exceptional and are devoted to undergraduate learning." They're "engaging, challenging, and understanding, [and] are genuinely interested in the student as a whole person." Boston College's "prestigious" academics come with "high expectations," but if students need help professors are "easily accessible outside of classes." Students "feel prepared for whatever is next" and note that their "well-connected" teachers and strong alumni network help with the job search. One student, who was drawn to Boston College because of its stellar reputation, finds it "even better than expected." Another adds, "I have always revered Boston College's academic and athletic reputation, and coming here, I have not been disappointed."

Life

Boston College's "gorgeous campus" and "perfect'" suburban location has created a very rich campus life and given the school a "strong community feel." There's "a superb sense of school spirit, which truly sets it apart." One students raves, "There is just so much school spirit and love for the university!" Boston College's "incredible sports teams" are well-supported by "superfans at every event." "There is also a large service component," to life at Boston College, which allows students "to serve the community in Boston and communities all around the world." Boston College offers a "plethora of extracurricular activities," and students think "there's a club or group for everyone here." The school has "great facilities" and "state-of-the-art resources." Dorms are generally well-reviewed, though students think the housing lottery could be more "fair." Students often go into Boston for all of its entertainment and cultural activities but are happy to return to their "close-knit college" where they "feel very at home."

Student Body

Boston College has gotten some flak for its "preppy," "white," and "homogenous" student body, and a communication student admits, "The school's nickname as 'J. Crew U.' isn't entirely unwarranted." Boston College could definitely use "greater racial diversity," but one student says that each year "the student body becomes more and more diverse." A student double-majoring in economics and German says, "Once you've settled in you'll find that it's not at all difficult to find a group of friends" no matter who you are. "There is a large religious/spiritual community," because of the school's Jesuit affiliation, but "It is only one group of many." Boston College's Division I ranking means there are plenty of athletes and sports fans. Students warn that Boston College is "not the place to go to class in your pajamas." People, particularly women, are "very well-dressed" and "stylish." Students say their peers are "really ambitious" and "hardworking." "The majority of students seem intelligent and academically driven as well as dedicated to and passionate about one or more extracurricular activities." Though people at Boston College are "academically oriented," they're "also into having a good time, and "have a "work hard, play hard mentality." There's a moderate amount of drinking on campus and off, but students say that no matter what, everyone "definitely [has] school as a top priority."

FINANCIAL AID: 617-552-3300 • WEBSITE: WWW.BC.EDU

THE PRINCETON REVIEW SAYS

Admissions

Very important factors considered include: Academic GPA, rigor of secondary school record, standardized test scores. *Important factors considered include:* Class rank, application essay, recommendation(s), alumni/ae relation, character/personal qualities, extracurricular activities, religious affiliation/commitment, talent/ability, volunteer work. *Other factors considered include:* First generation, racial/ethnic status, work experience. ACT with writing component required. TOEFL required of all international applicants. High school diploma is required and GED is accepted. *Academic units recommended:* 4 English, 4 mathematics, 4 science (4 science labs), 4 foreign language, 4 social studies.

Financial Aid

Students should submit: FAFSA, CSS/Financial Aid PROFILE, noncustodial PROFILE, business/farm supplement. The Princeton Review suggests that all financial aid forms be submitted as soon as possible after January 1. *Need-based scholarships/grants offered:* Federal Pell, SEOG, state scholarships/grants, private scholarships, the school's own gift aid. *Loan aid offered:* Direct Subsidized Stafford, Direct Unsubsidized Stafford, Direct PLUS, Federal Perkins, Federal Nursing, state loans. Applicants will be notified of awards on or about April 1. Federal Work-Study Program available. Institutional employment available. Highest amount earned per year from on-campus jobs $2,400. Off-campus job opportunities are good.

The Inside Word

Boston College is one of many selective schools that eschew set admissions formulae. While a challenging high school curriculum and strong test scores are essential for any serious candidate, the college seeks students who are passionate and make connections between academic pursuits and extracurricular activities. The application process should reveal a distinct, mature voice and a student whose interest in education goes beyond the simple desire to earn an A.

THE SCHOOL SAYS "..."

From the Admissions Office

"Boston College students achieve at the highest levels with honors including two Rhodes scholarship winners, nine Fulbrights, and one each for Marshall, Goldwater, Madison, and Truman Postgraduate Fellowship Programs. Junior Year Abroad and Scholar of the College Program offer students flexibility within the curriculum. Facilities opened in the past ten years include the Merkert Chemistry Center, Higgins Hall (housing the Biology and Physics departments), three new residence halls, the Yawkey Athletics Center, the Vanderslice Commons Dining Hall, the Hillside Cafe, and a state-of-the-art library. Students enjoy the vibrant location in Chestnut Hill with easy access to the cultural and historical richness of Boston.

"Boston College requires freshman applicants to take the SAT with writing (or the ACT with the writing exam required). Two SAT Subject Tests are required; students are encouraged to take Subject Tests in fields in which they excel."

SELECTIVITY	
Admissions Rating	**97**
# of applicants	32,974
% of applicants accepted	28
% of acceptees attending	23
# accepting a place on wait list	2,589
# admitted from wait list	367
FRESHMAN PROFILE	
Range SAT Critical Reading	620–710
Range SAT Math	640–730
Range SAT Writing	630–730
Range ACT Composite	29–32
Minimum paper TOEFL	600
Minimum web-based TOEFL	100
% graduated top 10% of class	82
% graduated top 25% of class	95
% graduated top 50% of class	99
DEADLINES	
Early action	
Deadline	11/1
Notification	12/25
Regular	
Deadline	1/1
Notification	4/15
Nonfall registration?	yes
FINANCIAL FACTS	
Financial Aid Rating	**92**
Annual tuition	$43,140
Room and board	$12,608
Required fees	$738
Books and supplies	$1,000
% needy frosh rec. need-based scholarship or grant aid	91
% needy UG rec. need-based scholarship or grant aid	89
% needy frosh rec. non-need-based scholarship or grant aid	2
% needy UG rec. non-need-based scholarship or grant aid	2
% needy frosh rec. need-based self-help aid	95
% needy UG rec. need-based self-help aid	95
% frosh rec. any financial aid	61
% UG rec. any financial aid	66
% UG borrow to pay for school	55
Average cumulative indebtedness	$20,598
% frosh need fully met	100
% ugrads need fully met	100
Average % of frosh need met	100
Average % of ugrad need met	100

Boston University

121 Bay State Road, Boston, MA 02215 • Admissions: 617-353-2300 • Fax: 617-353-9695

CAMPUS LIFE

Quality of Life Rating	93
Fire Safety Rating	77
Green Rating	92
Type of school	private
Environment	metropolis

STUDENTS

Total undergrad enrollment	15,977
% male/female	40/60
% from out of state	80
% from public high school	69
% frosh live on campus	99
# of fraternities	9
# of sororities	9
% African American	3
% Asian	14
% Caucasian	50
% Hispanic	9
% international	12
# of countries represented	133

SURVEY SAYS . . .

Athletic facilities are great
Students love Boston, MA
Great food on campus
Great off-campus food
Student publications are popular

ACADEMICS

Academic Rating	86
% students returning for sophomore year	92
% students graduating within 4 years	80
% students graduating within 6 years	85
Calendar	semester
Student/faculty ratio	13:1
Profs interesting rating	83
Profs accessible rating	83
Most classes have	10–19 students
Most lab/discussion sessions have	20–29 students

MOST POPULAR MAJORS

business/commerce; international relations and affairs; psychology

APPLICANTS ALSO LOOK AT AND OFTEN PREFER

University of Southern California, New York University, The George Washington University

AND SOMETIMES PREFER

Boston College, Cornell University, Syracuse University, Tufts University, Northeastern University

AND RARELY PREFER

University of Massachusetts Amherst, Brown University

STUDENTS SAY ". . ."

Academics

Boston University shrugs off the dichotomy that generally separates public and private institutions, offering both the diversity and choice that only a large school can, while also offering the friendliness, security, and personal attention you would expect from a pricey, private college. The key to BU's success is the varied yet close-knit academic departments: "Boston University is a huge institution full of opportunities to learn and experience the city, but it's also made up of small academic and extracurricular communities that offer students a home away from home." A junior adds, "BU has so many choices when it comes to majors and classes that I find myself struggling to pick just four classes a semester." In addition to coursework, "Internship and study abroad opportunities are easily accessible," and there are "dual-degree and MA/BA opportunities within our many colleges and schools." Despite their prestigious names and careers, "Professors at BU are here to teach, not to research. Students are their primary concern, and that shows through their work." Outside of class, professors "have office hours, but are more than happy to meet if that doesn't match with my schedule," one student shares. When it comes to the nuts and bolts of administering this stellar educational experience, students should be mindful that BU is "a large university with tons of offices" so it can be "difficult to quickly get an answer to a pressing question." At the same time, "The administration does not stay in their offices; they are readily accessible and easy to converse with." Of particular note, the "Dean of Students...is a great resource on campus and is actively working to participate in events with the students."

Life

Academics come first at BU, but social life is a close second. With an urban campus located "in the heart of Boston," students love heading off campus and "exploring places like Chinatown, Quincy Market, the North End, and Boston Common." If you want to mix and mingle with other undergraduates, there's no better atmosphere: "Whether it is on our campus or across the river at Harvard or across town at Northeastern, there is always some kind of social event to attend." On campus, dorms are comfortable, cafeteria food is good, and "There are more than 500 clubs and organizations that are constantly meeting." Of particular note, "There is a great community service center, which offers many different programs that cater to your schedule." While many students spend their free time in the city, campus activities at BU include such sundry offerings as "free concerts at our own mini-club, BU Central, or the laser light show at the BU Beach." In addition, "The different culture clubs at BU will occasionally host themed dances...which are fun and a great opportunity to learn about the culture of your fellow peers." Sports enthusiasts on campus are plentiful—especially when it comes to BU's champion ice hockey team—and "Students with the sports pass, which is normally included in tuition...can even pick up hockey tickets for free and just enjoy the game."

Student Body

Set in one of the world's best college towns, you'll meet kids "from all over America and all over the globe" at BU. At the same time, BU draws "a lot of people from the Northeast coast, and especially from the Boston area," who already know and love the city. Size and diversity make the social experience inclusive and accepting: "There are no real stigmas or cliques on campus because everyone is so diverse." No matter how unique your interests, you're sure to find like minds: "There are an amazing amount of clubs that meet every night of the week—including quidditch, astronomy, camping, religious/ethnic clubs, and many, many more." In fact, many students tell us, "We have such a large student body that there really is someone for everyone here." At the same time, academics are priority number one for most students. A current student explains, "BU is so diverse, but one thing that so many people have in common is a drive to succeed. Grades are competitive and students are driven to succeed, not only in school but also in internships."

FINANCIAL AID: 617-353-4176 • E-MAIL: ADMISSIONS@BU.EDU • WEBSITE: WWW.BU.EDU

THE PRINCETON REVIEW SAYS

Admissions

Very important factors considered include: Rigor of secondary school record. *Important factors considered include:* Class rank, application essay, academic GPA, recommendation(s), standardized test scores. *Other factors considered include:* Alumni/ae relation, character/personal qualities, extracurricular activities, first generation, geographical residence, level of applicant's interest, racial/ ethnic status, state residency, volunteer work, work experience. SAT or ACT required; ACT with writing component required. TOEFL required of all international applicants. High school diploma is required and GED is accepted. *Academic units required:* 4 English, 3 mathematics, 3 science (3 science labs), 2 foreign language, 3 social studies. *Academic units recommended:* 4 English, 4 mathematics, 4 science (4 science labs), 4 foreign language, 4 social studies.

Financial Aid

Students should submit: FAFSA, CSS/Financial Aid PROFILE, state aid form, noncustodial PROFILE, business/farm supplement. Regular filing deadline is February 15. The Princeton Review suggests that all financial aid forms be submitted as soon as possible after January 1. *Need-based scholarships/grants offered:* Federal Pell, SEOG, state scholarships/grants, private scholarships, the school's own gift aid. *Loan aid offered:* Direct Subsidized Stafford, Direct Unsubsidized Stafford, Direct PLUS, Federal Perkins, state loans. Applicants will be notified of awards on a rolling basis beginning March 15. Federal Work-Study Program available. Institutional employment available. Off-campus job opportunities are excellent.

The Inside Word

At BU, your academic performance in high school is the single most important factor in an admission decision. Competitive applicants are those who pursued the most challenging curriculum available at their school. Admissions requirements vary depending on the school or program to which you apply (though students are welcome to apply "undeclared"), so prospective students should check the school's website.

THE SCHOOL SAYS ". . ."

From the Admissions Office

"Boston University is a world-recognized, private teaching and research university committed to excellence in undergraduate education. It is ranked in the top four percent of universities in the nation by U.S. News & World Report. Students study with distinguished faculty that include Fulbright Scholars, Pulitzer Prize winners, MacArthur Fellows, Nobel Prize winners, and a former Poet Laureate. In nine undergraduate schools and colleges, BU offers students more than 250 programs of study, cutting-edge research with faculty mentors, internships in the United States and abroad, and one of the nation's most extensive study abroad programs. Housing is guaranteed for four years in a variety of on-campus residences, including high-rise buildings and historic brownstones. BU students are engaged with their campus community through over 500 student organizations, club and intramural sports, and twenty-three NCAA Division I sports teams. Students experience the city of Boston as an extension of campus for study, internships, employment, and cultural and recreational activities.

"BU requires freshman applicants to take the SAT or the ACT (with Writing). Students applying to the Accelerated Medical or Dental Programs are required to submit Subject Tests in chemistry, math (Level 2), and a foreign language (recommended). Candidates for the College of Fine Arts must present a portfolio or participate in an audition."

SELECTIVITY	
Admissions Rating	**95**
# of applicants	41,802
% of applicants accepted	49
% of acceptees attending	19
# accepting a place on wait list	3,329
# admitted from wait list	329
# of early decision applicants	883
# accepted early decision	368

FRESHMAN PROFILE	
Range SAT Critical Reading	570–670
Range SAT Math	610–700
Range SAT Writing	600–680
Range ACT Composite	26–30
Minimum paper TOEFL	550
Minimum web-based TOEFL	78
Average HS GPA	3.5
% graduated top 10% of class	55
% graduated top 25% of class	86
% graduated top 50% of class	99

DEADLINES	
Early decision	
Deadline	11/1
Notification	12/15
Regular	
Deadline	1/1
Nonfall registration?	yes

FINANCIAL FACTS	
Financial Aid Rating	**93**
Annual tuition	$42,400
Room and board	$13,190
Required fees	$594
Books and supplies	$1,000
% needy frosh rec. need-based scholarship or grant aid	93
% needy UG rec. need-based scholarship or grant aid	95
% needy frosh rec. non-need-based scholarship or grant aid	38
% needy UG rec. non-need-based scholarship or grant aid	29
% needy frosh rec. need-based self-help aid	88
% needy UG rec. need-based self-help aid	90
% frosh rec. any financial aid	60
% UG rec. any financial aid	62
% UG borrow to pay for school	57
Average cumulative indebtedness	$36,488
% frosh need fully met	48
% ugrads need fully met	48
Average % of frosh need met	89
Average % of ugrad need met	89

Bowdoin College

5000 College Station, Brunswick, ME 04011-8441 • Admissions: 207-725-3100 • Fax: 207-725-3101

CAMPUS LIFE

Quality of Life Rating	**99**
Fire Safety Rating	**94**
Green Rating	**96**
Type of school	private
Environment	village

STUDENTS

Total undergrad enrollment	1,772
% male/female	51/49
% from out of state	88
% from public high school	58
% frosh live on campus	100
% African American	5
% Asian	7
% Caucasian	65
% Hispanic	12
% international	4
# of countries represented	35

SURVEY SAYS . . .

School is well run
Great food on campus
Dorms are like palaces
Frats and sororities are unpopular or nonexistent
Students are environmentally aware
Lots of beer drinking

ACADEMICS

Academic Rating	**96**
% students returning for sophomore year	97
% students graduating within 4 years	88
% students graduating within 6 years	92
Calendar	semester
Student/faculty ratio	9:1
Profs interesting rating	96
Profs accessible rating	97
Most classes have	10–19 students
Most lab/discussion sessions have	10–19 students

MOST POPULAR MAJORS

biology/biological sciences; economics; political science and government

APPLICANTS ALSO LOOK AT AND OFTEN PREFER

Harvard College, Princeton University, Yale University

AND SOMETIMES PREFER

Brown University, Dartmouth College, Williams College

AND RARELY PREFER

Middlebury College, Amherst College, Wesleyan University

STUDENTS SAY ". . ."

Academics

Bowdoin students lavish praise on their prestigious small school, celebrating the "range and rigor" of the academic programs, the beautiful Maine setting, and the "vibrant group of faculty and students." They even love the cafeteria food! A classic liberal arts school, the academic curriculum at Bowdoin is "very challenging, discussion-oriented, and [it] demands creativity from the students." Despite the school's small size, you'll find a "varied and interesting course selection" within its more than thirty-five major and minor programs. In addition, students "have the ability to self-design classes and majors" and to participate in "some of the best undergraduate research opportunities liberal arts schools have to offer." According to their adoring students, Bowdoin professors are "extremely intelligent, well-spoken, and effective teachers," who are also "very enthusiastic about their work and welcome students to chat or ask questions one-on-one." At Bowdoin, "Professors put their students first and always make time to meet, whether to talk about a paper, or for coffee, or both." "Academics are highly rigorous," and major programs are typified by "challenging courses with professors who expect a high level of work." Fortunately, the "environment is very laid-back," and students are usually "competitive with themselves but not competitive with others." A current senior adds, "Academically, Bowdoin is very challenging, but I've loved having to put in my best effort to do well. It's good to be challenged!" Throughout the faculty and administration, "student opinions are highly valued and sought out." The school's popular president "invests a significant amount of time in us, the students," and "The first-year deans…make it a point to meet with each first-year student one-on-one, preferably in the first semester."

Life

College life is incredibly comfortable for Bowdoin undergraduates. On this pretty Maine campus, "freshmen dorms are very luxurious," and "facilities are great, including new athletic fields and [a] new fitness center." Cafeteria food gets rave reviews, and the dining services department is "excellent about listening to student opinions and promoting sustainability." A senior admits, "I will probably never eat this well again in my life." While there aren't any fraternities and sororities at Bowdoin, "There are social houses, where many sophomores, juniors, and (some) seniors live. These former Greek houses put on multiple events each week, from themed parties with several kegs, to coffee houses, movies, and discussions with professors." "Work hard, play hard" is a popular mantra on campus, and "There are always multiple parties going on Thursday, Friday, and Saturday nights." Alternately, "Getting outside and exploring Maine is very popular with our outdoorsy student body." In surrounding Brunswick, students enjoy "amazing restaurants and coffee shops on and around Maine Street." In addition, "Portland is thirty minutes away and is a great city with lots of resources." Echoing the sentiments of many happy Bowdoin students, a satisfied sophomore tells us, "I wish I could stay in college forever."

Student Body

You'll meet a lot of "wealthy, athletic, New Englanders" at Bowdoin College. In fact, students joke, "Everyone seems to be from a small town right outside Boston." Those outside the dominant demographic admit that there seems to be "a divide between the typical New England kid and the 'diverse' kids, who come from other states are less well-off, or are racially diverse." However, "Students here work really hard to create a community that is open and accepting," and the majority of students have "no trouble fitting in." On that note, "Bowdoin students truly are nice. We often marvel at how there do not seem to be mean or unfriendly people here." Student athletes are common, and "around seventy percent of the campus is involved in some kind of sport," from intramurals to the outing club. Nonetheless, academics are top priority: "No matter if they are a theater kid or hockey player, everyone can be found in the library during the week." In addition to schoolwork, Bowdoin students are "always passionate about something, be it music, rock-climbing, or volunteer work."

FINANCIAL AID: 207-725-3273 • E-MAIL: ADMISSIONS@BOWDOIN.EDU • WEBSITE: WWW.BOWDOIN.EDU

THE PRINCETON REVIEW SAYS

Admissions

Very important factors considered include: Class rank, application essay, academic GPA, recommendation(s), rigor of secondary school record, character/personal qualities, extracurricular activities, talent/ability. *Important factors considered include:* Standardized test scores, alumni/ae relation, first generation. *Other factors considered include:* Geographical residence, interview, racial/ethnic status, state residency. ACT with or without writing component accepted. TOEFL required of all international applicants. High school diploma is required and GED is not accepted. *Academic units recommended:* 4 English, 4 mathematics, 4 science (3 science labs), 4 foreign language, 4 social studies.

Financial Aid

Students should submit: FAFSA, CSS/Financial Aid PROFILE, noncustodial PROFILE, business/farm supplement. Regular filing deadline is February 15. The Princeton Review suggests that all financial aid forms be submitted as soon as possible after January 1. *Need-based scholarships/grants offered:* Federal Pell, SEOG, state scholarships/grants, private scholarships, the school's own gift aid. *Loan aid offered:* Direct Subsidized Stafford, Direct Unsubsidized Stafford, Direct PLUS, Federal Perkins, state loans. Applicants will be notified of awards on or about April 5. Federal Work-Study Program available. Institutional employment available. Highest amount earned per year from on-campus jobs $2,000. Off-campus job opportunities are good.

The Inside Word

Many students feel instantly at home on the Bowdoin campus. A current freshman reports, "Bowdoin was a great fit for me on paper, and I fell in love with the campus and student body when I visited." A senior agrees, "I had visited over twenty colleges, and they all start to look the same academically, but Bowdoin stood out because of the people." During the admissions process, prospective students can schedule a tour and personal interview with admissions staff or a Bowdoin senior. If it's a fit, the school offers the option to apply early decision.

THE SCHOOL SAYS ". . ."

From the Admissions Office

"A Bowdoin education is best summed up by 'The Offer of the College':"

To be at home in all lands and all ages;
To count Nature a familiar acquaintance,
And Art an intimate friend;
To gain a standard for the appreciation of others' work
And the criticism of your own;
To carry the keys of the world's library in your pocket,
And feel its resources behind you in whatever task you undertake;
To make hosts of friends...
Who are to be leaders in all walks of life;
To lose yourself in generous enthusiasms
And cooperate with others for common ends—
This is the offer of the college for the best four years of your life."

Adapted from the original 'Offer of the College'
by William DeWitt Hyde
President of Bowdoin College 1885–1917"

SELECTIVITY	
Admissions Rating	**98**
# of applicants	6,554
% of applicants accepted	16
% of acceptees attending	46
# of early decision applicants	826
# accepted early decision	225

FRESHMAN PROFILE	
Range SAT Critical Reading	670–750
Range SAT Math	660–740
Range SAT Writing	670–760
Range ACT Composite	30–33
Minimum paper TOEFL	600
Minimum web-based TOEFL	100
Average HS GPA	3.8
% graduated top 10% of class	83
% graduated top 25% of class	97
% graduated top 50% of class	100

DEADLINES	
Early decision	
Deadline	11/15
Notification	12/15
Regular	
Deadline	1/1
Notification	4/5
Nonfall registration?	no

FINANCIAL FACTS	
Financial Aid Rating	**97**
Annual tuition	$42,386
Room and board	$11,654
Required fees	$430
Books and supplies	$820
% needy frosh rec. need-based scholarship or grant aid	100
% needy UG rec. need-based scholarship or grant aid	100
% needy frosh rec. need-based self-help aid	82
% needy UG rec. need-based self-help aid	81
% frosh rec. any financial aid	48
% UG rec. any financial aid	47
% UG borrow to pay for school	35
Average cumulative indebtedness	$17,569
% frosh need fully met	100
% ugrads need fully met	100
Average % of frosh need met	100
Average % of ugrad need met	100

BRADLEY UNIVERSITY

1501 WEST BRADLEY AVENUE, PEORIA, IL 61625 • ADMISSIONS: 309-677-1000 • FAX: 309-677-2797

CAMPUS LIFE

Quality of Life Rating	**70**
Fire Safety Rating	**77**
Green Rating	**60***
Type of school	private
Environment	city

STUDENTS

Total undergrad enrollment	5,061
% male/female	46/54
% from out of state	15
% from public high school	87
# of fraternities	16
# of sororities	11
% African American	7
% Asian	4
% Caucasian	71
% Hispanic	5
% Native American	1
% international	1
# of countries represented	34

SURVEY SAYS . . .

Athletic facilities are great
Students are friendly
Low cost of living
Frats and sororities dominate social scene
Very little drug use

ACADEMICS

Academic Rating	**69**
Calendar	semester
Student/faculty ratio	13:1
Profs interesting rating	77
Profs accessible rating	80
Most classes have	20–29 students

MOST POPULAR MAJORS

mechanical engineering; nursing/registered nurse (rn, asn, bsn, msn); communication

APPLICANTS ALSO LOOK AT AND OFTEN PREFER

Purdue University—West Lafayette, University of Illinois at Urbana-Champaign

AND SOMETIMES PREFER

DePaul University, Marquette University, Loyola University of Chicago, Augustana College (IL), Illinois Wesleyan University, Saint Louis University

AND RARELY PREFER

Illinois State University, University of Missouri, University of Iowa, Iowa State University

STUDENTS SAY ". . ."

Academics

Academically, Bradley provides "the resources of a large university with the familiarity that comes from a small liberal arts school." The goal is to provide students with a hands-on learning environment and to prepare them for the world beyond college. In addition to the traditional liberal arts and sciences, academic programs include business, communication, education, engineering, fine and performing arts, and health sciences. Unique programs include entrepreneurship, health science with a direct entry to the Doctorate of Physical Therapy, interactive media, and sports communication. A recent graduate shares her experience, saying "While Bradley offers the academic choices of a larger university; it also provides students the guidance and mentoring of faculty that only a smaller university can provide." "Ninety-three percent of graduates begin work, graduate school, or other postgraduate experiences of their choice within six months of graduation. I knew I would be prepared and pointed in the right direction." Bradley University provides advantages normally only seen in larger schools with the community and personal attention only a smaller school can deliver.

Life

"It is just the right size. I never imagined myself in a huge university. I like having the ability to meet with my teachers regularly." Another student echoes that sentiment, and adds, "There is always something to do on campus and plenty of activities to become involved in." Located in a residential neighborhood on the west bluff of the Illinois River, the eighty-five-acre campus of Bradley University is just one mile from downtown Peoria, Illinois. The distinctive feel of Bradley comes from a blend of large school opportunities with the quality, personal attention of a small, private college. A current student tells us, "Bradley is a small-scale school with a big personality and something for everyone." What endears the university to most students is that it is able to provide the resources of a large university and the connections to big cities such as Chicago and St. Louis while maintaining the familiarity that comes from a small, liberal arts school. Bradley is all about community, and students tell us that the greatest strength is "the amount of activities and organizations on campus."

Student Body

One of our interviewees provided an interesting insight, saying, "Students here are normal, kind of boring, but beneath all that is a potential for anything, greatness. There are phenomenal opportunities to volunteer and help people here. Bradley is a community of good people who are respectful and awesome." Another student shares, 'Everyone is really involved. I am extremely busy but not overwhelmed. Bradley creates several activities for students to [enjoy]. For fun I mainly hang with friends on campus and go off campus." Another perspective comes from this commuter, "I think life on campus was great, now I live off-campus as an upperclassman. The time that I was on campus I felt that there were various activities to attend on the weekends if we wanted to but a lot of us just hung out together in the dorms." Back on campus, a junior tells us, "Bradley offers a great deal of free and alcohol-free activities that can take the place of partying for those interested. That being said, Bradley is in no way a party school. While there are occasions when the festivities get wild, I would never describe anything as 'out of control.'" Another student explains the Bradley "balance" this way: "Life at school is great…People are still very determined to do well in school, to get their degree, and to get a great job upon graduation.

FINANCIAL AID: 309-677-3089 • E-MAIL: ADMISSIONS@BRADLEY.EDU • WEBSITE: WWW.BRADLEY.EDU

THE PRINCETON REVIEW SAYS

Admissions

Very important factors considered include: Academic GPA, rigor of secondary school record. *Important factors considered include:* Class rank, standardized test scores. *Other factors considered include:* Application essay, recommendation(s), alumni/ae relation, character/personal qualities, extracurricular activities, geographical residence, interview, level of applicant's interest, racial/ethnic status, talent/ability, volunteer work, work experience. SAT or ACT required; ACT with or without writing component accepted. TOEFL required of all international applicants. High school diploma is required and GED is accepted. *Academic units required:* 4 English, 3 mathematics, 2 science (2 science labs), 2 social studies. *Academic units recommended:* 5 English, 4 mathematics, 3 science (3 science labs), 2 foreign language, 3 social studies, 2 history.

Financial Aid

Students should submit: FAFSA. The Princeton Review suggests that all financial aid forms be submitted as soon as possible after January 1. *Need-based scholarships/grants offered:* Federal Pell, SEOG, state scholarships/grants, private scholarships, the school's own gift aid. *Loan aid offered:* Direct Subsidized Stafford, Direct Unsubsidized Stafford, Direct PLUS, Federal Perkins, Federal Nursing. Federal Work-Study Program available. Institutional employment available.

The Inside Word

With much regional appeal, the vast majority of students at Bradley originate from Illinois. With an active eye toward broadening the student body's geographic demographics, the school presents an opportunity for out-of-staters seeking to attend an excellent university without having to endure the grueling admissions process of many private universities. Above-average students should find that gaining admission here is a relatively painless experience.

THE SCHOOL SAYS "..."

From the Admissions Office

"Bradley offers more than 100 undergraduate and 30 graduate programs of study. In addition to the traditional liberal arts and sciences, academic programs include business, communication, education, engineering, fine and performing arts, and health sciences. Unique programs include entrepreneurship, health science with a direct entry to a Doctorate of Physical Therapy, interactive media, game design, and sports communication. While Bradley offers the academic choices of a larger university, the faculty to student ratio of twelve to one allows for mentoring that only smaller universities can provide. All courses are taught by faculty in classes that average just twenty-three students. Beyond a great academic experience, students also choose Bradley for opportunities to join more than 240 student organizations, including more than 60 dedicated to student leadership and community service. Career development begins in a student's freshman year. This career development approach leads to ninety-two percent placement of graduates placed in work, graduate school, or other postgraduate experiences within six months of graduation.

"Bradley's eighty-five-acre campus is located on the west bluff of the Illinois River valley in a residential neighborhood just one mile from downtown Peoria. The river views along the picturesque valley were noted by President Theodore Roosevelt as the world's most beautiful drive when he visited this diverse community of more than 360,000 people. Both Chicago and St. Louis are less than a three-hour drive. Bradley University is recognized for academic excellence, experiential learning and leadership development with an entrepreneurial spirit for a world-class education."

SELECTIVITY

Admissions Rating	**80**
# of applicants	6,343
% of applicants accepted	72
% of acceptees attending	25

FRESHMAN PROFILE

Range SAT Critical Reading	480–630
Range SAT Math	490–640
Range ACT Composite	23–28
Minimum paper TOEFL	550
Average HS GPA	3.6
% graduated top 10% of class	29
% graduated top 25% of class	63
% graduated top 50% of class	92

DEADLINES

Regular	
Priority	3/1
Nonfall registration?	yes

FINANCIAL FACTS

Financial Aid Rating	**75**
Annual tuition	$26,400
Room and board	$8,200
Required fees	$304
Books and supplies	$1,200
% needy frosh rec. need-based scholarship or grant aid	99
% needy UG rec. need-based scholarship or grant aid	95
% needy frosh rec. non-need-based scholarship or grant aid	13
% needy UG rec. non-need-based scholarship or grant aid	10
% needy frosh rec. need-based self-help aid	89
% needy UG rec. need-based self-help aid	76
% frosh rec. any financial aid	96
% UG rec. any financial aid	93
% UG borrow to pay for school	86
Average cumulative indebtedness	$17,859
% frosh need fully met	34
% ugrads need fully met	18
Average % of frosh need met	78
Average % of ugrad need met	67

BRANDEIS UNIVERSITY

415 SOUTH STREET, WALTHAM, MA 02454-9110 • ADMISSIONS: 781-736-3500 • FAX: 781-736-3536

CAMPUS LIFE

Quality of Life Rating	**87**
Fire Safety Rating	**92**
Green Rating	**87**
Type of school	private
Environment	city

STUDENTS

Total undergrad enrollment	3,493
% male/female	43/57
% from out of state	73
% from public high school	72
% frosh live on campus	98
% African American	4
% Asian	13
% Caucasian	49
% Hispanic	6
% international	12
# of countries represented	97

SURVEY SAYS . . .

No one cheats
Students are friendly
Campus feels safe
Musical organizations are popular
Student publications are popular
Political activism is popular
Students are environmentally aware
Students are involved in community service

ACADEMICS

Academic Rating	**88**
% students returning for sophomore year	93
% students graduating within 4 years	88
Calendar	semester
Student/faculty ratio	10:1
Profs interesting rating	89
Profs accessible rating	86
Most classes have	10–19 students

MOST POPULAR MAJORS

biology/biological sciences; economics; psychology

STUDENTS SAY ". . ."

Academics

Located in the Boston area, Brandeis is a private liberal arts university that has "a little bit of everything." The school "gives students the freedom to explore both in and outside of the classroom" It has a (rightful) reputation for tough academics, particularly in the sciences, and this "pays off. Employers, grad schools, and certainly medical schools, know how tough the academics are." The school puts "a great importance on social justice and community," the latter of which "is unmatched" at Brandeis. Academics at Brandeis are "stimulating," and even though a few professors at times can be "inconsistent and unreliable," the faculty on the whole is "extremely dedicated to their subjects" and "truly there for the students." "As a first-year student I was part of a class that was invited to the professor's house for a Thanksgiving pot luck dinner," says one. Getting some sort of outside help is necessary for the sciences, as "classes are often curved, and the competition is tough," but luckily professors are all available, and "all of the introductory classes break down into small groups once a week." People "care about their studies, but the atmosphere isn't competitive." Along with "plenty of scientific research opportunities" for such a small school, many students "find it difficult to choose classes because of all of the awesome course descriptions." Student services have expanded in recent years, and the Hiatt Career Center now offers "Graduate School Thursdays, alumni shadowing, mock interviews, and career fairs specifically themed toward 'green jobs,' government forums, and other student interests." Independence is a huge part of a Brandeis student's life, and the administration is good about "letting students take charge of their own educations." "We create our own experiences: independent study, clubs, and committees. Students own their experiences," says one student. "It is a wonderfully unique college experience with some of the nicest—and occasionally strangest—people you will ever meet."

Life

Because the school is situated in a small city immediately outside of college-rich Boston, it's able to have "sprawling lawns and an atmosphere of community and openness" while still being accessible to an urban cultural center. There is a "massive amount of extracurricular activities," so "there is always something to do," including a "Cheese Club that provides free cheese tasting," "arts outlets," and numerous organizations that place a "strong emphasis on volunteerism and social justice." "This is…a tremendous place to explore your passions—religiously, socially, and academically," says a student. There are "a ton" of theater, a cappella, and improv groups on campus, and if the campus events aren't enough to satiate your appetite for fun, "there are always ways to go and support other extracurricular groups on campus and see what they're all about." Housing and dining services are considered by students to be the most frustrating aspects of the school; students say a few of the dorms are "rundown and need renovation," and one student warns, "If athletics are the center of your universe, then do not go to Brandeis."

Student Body

There are "few social lines that define the student body" at Brandeis, and "a lot of social life revolves around club life." Students are active here, and "it's not unheard of to find a neuroscience major who juggles DJing on WBRS, skydiving, and student government." This "intellectual and exciting" crew includes a "strong Jewish community," and almost everyone is "nerdy in a very, very cool way." People here are "really quirky and different," and most have secondary pursuits or hobbies outside of academics. "Whatever the students' passions and skills might be, everyone is incredibly motivated and driven toward achievement." Everyone is "fairly studious and encourages each other to study and do their best." Students seem to be friendly without fail. "If you stand in one place for too long on campus, you'll immediately find students approaching you asking if you're lost and how they can help," says a student.

FINANCIAL AID: 781-736-3700 • E-MAIL: ADMISSIONS@BRANDEIS.EDU • WEBSITE: WWW.BRANDEIS.EDU

THE PRINCETON REVIEW SAYS

Admissions

Very important factors considered include: Class rank, academic GPA, rigor of secondary school record, standardized test scores, character/personal qualities. *Important factors considered include:* Application essay, recommendation(s), extracurricular activities, level of applicant's interest, talent/ability, volunteer work, work experience. *Other factors considered include:* Alumni/ae relation, first generation, geographical residence, interview, racial/ethnic status. SAT or ACT required; ACT with writing component required. TOEFL required of all international applicants. High school diploma is required and GED is accepted. *Academic units recommended:* 4 English, 4 mathematics, 4 science (2 science labs), 4 foreign language, 4 social studies.

Financial Aid

Students should submit: FAFSA, CSS/Financial Aid PROFILE, noncustodial PROFILE, business/farm supplement. The Princeton Review suggests that all financial aid forms be submitted as soon as possible after January 1. *Need-based scholarships/grants offered:* Federal Pell, SEOG, state scholarships/grants, private scholarships, the school's own gift aid. *Loan aid offered:* Direct Subsidized Stafford, Direct Unsubsidized Stafford, Direct PLUS, Federal Perkins, state loans, college/university loans from institutional funds. Federal Work-Study Program available. Institutional employment available. Off-campus job opportunities are fair.

The Inside Word

Admissions standards have risen at all top schools, and Brandeis is no exception: If you expect to get in here, you've got your work cut out for you. Your application should give evidence of both the ability and enthusiasm to handle demanding academics. A clear demonstration of writing ability will also help a lot.

THE SCHOOL SAYS "..."

From the Admissions Office

"Education at Brandeis is personal, combining the intimacy of a small liberal arts college and the intellectual power of a large research university. Classes are small and are taught by professors, ninety-eight percent of whom hold the highest degree in their fields. They give students personal attention in state-of-the-art resources, giving them the tools to succeed in a variety of postgraduate endeavors.

"This vibrant, free-thinking, intellectual university was founded in 1948. Brandeis University reflects the values of the first Jewish Supreme Court Justice Louis Brandeis, which are passion for learning, commitment to social justice, respect for creativity and diversity, and concern for the world.

"Brandeis has an ideal location on the commuter rail nine miles west of Boston; state-of-the-art sports facilities; and internships that complement interests in law, medicine, government, finance, business, and the arts.

"Brandeis meets 100 percent of demonstrated need for all admitted students."

SELECTIVITY

Admissions Rating	**97**
# of applicants	8,917
% of applicants accepted	40
% of acceptees attending	24
# accepting a place on wait list	1,321
# admitted from wait list	87
# of early decision applicants	483
# accepted early decision	201

FRESHMAN PROFILE

Range SAT Critical Reading	600–710
Range SAT Math	630–740
Range SAT Writing	630–720
Range ACT Composite	28–32
Minimum paper TOEFL	600
Minimum web-based TOEFL	100
Average HS GPA	3.8
% graduated top 10% of class	64
% graduated top 25% of class	94
% graduated top 50% of class	99

DEADLINES

Early decision	
Deadline	11/15
Notification	12/15
Regular	
Deadline	1/15
Notification	4/1
Nonfall registration?	yes

FINANCIAL FACTS

Financial Aid Rating	**79**
Annual tuition	$42,682
Room and board	$12,256
Required fees	$1,612
Books and supplies	$1,000
% needy frosh rec. need-based scholarship or grant aid	93
% needy UG rec. need-based scholarship or grant aid	95
% needy frosh rec. non-need-based scholarship or grant aid	5
% needy UG rec. non-need-based scholarship or grant aid	5
% needy frosh rec. need-based self-help aid	91
% needy UG rec. need-based self-help aid	93
% frosh rec. any financial aid	69
% UG rec. any financial aid	68
% UG borrow to pay for school	59
Average cumulative indebtedness	$28,531
% frosh need fully met	7
% ugrads need fully met	7
Average % of frosh need met	84
Average % of ugrad need met	82

Brigham Young University (UT)

A-153 ASB, Provo, UT 84602-1110 • Admissions: 801-422-2507 • Fax: 801-422-0005

CAMPUS LIFE

Quality of Life Rating	**93**
Fire Safety Rating	**64**
Green Rating	**60***
Type of school	private
Affiliation	Church of Jesus Christ of Latter-day Saints
Environment	city

STUDENTS

Total undergrad enrollment	30,684
% male/female	51/49
% from out of state	67
% frosh live on campus	79
% Asian	1
% Caucasian	66
% Hispanic	4
% international	4
# of countries represented	121

SURVEY SAYS . . .

Students are very religious
Musical organizations are popular
Very little beer drinking
Very little hard liquor
Very little drug use
Students are involved in community service

ACADEMICS

Academic Rating	**88**
% students returning for sophomore year	87
% students graduating within 4 years	35
% students graduating within 6 years	89
Calendar	semester
Student/faculty ratio	21:1
Profs interesting rating	85
Profs accessible rating	77
Most classes have	10–19 students

MOST POPULAR MAJORS

business/commerce; elementary education and teaching; exercise physiology

APPLICANTS ALSO LOOK AT AND SOMETIMES PREFER

University of Utah

STUDENTS SAY ". . ."

Academics

Brigham Young University is a Mormon school that's "all about putting religion and education together" and learning "about secular subjects through spiritual eyes." The school provides a "high-quality" education in a "challenging" academic atmosphere. Students at Brigham Young strive for academic excellence. As one student explains, "Brigham Young pushes us to realize that our 'best' can be a lot better than we ever dreamed, and I love that!" The school offers a wide range of majors, and its education, business, and mathematics programs get great reviews, as does their language program. Classes are generally a "healthy mix of discussion and lecture," and the education classes in particular have "a lot of group work." The school doesn't focus only on classroom learning, however. "Hands-on experience, internships, and study abroad are highly encouraged," and many students take advantage of these opportunities. There are also "tons of undergraduate research opportunities." Professors are "passionate about what they're teaching," and they "really care about their students' success." Another adds, "Professors really do take a genuine interest in their students," and "The vast majority are also very willing to help out students individually." While students at Brigham Young appreciate the academic attention they receive from professors, they also like that it "is committed to spiritual and academic learning for the benefit and betterment of everyone" and that they're being taught to "pursue lifelong learning and service."

Life

Students at Brigham Young love the "atmosphere of spirituality that unites everyone" and "the kindness of those around you." Brigham Young provides a "safe environment," but students "still get to have real-world experiences." Recreationally, "There are multiple clubs across campus to fit the taste of different people," "tons of…performing events," and "fun student body activities, which are cheap." There are also "exceptional weekly devotions and forums." Brigham Young's athletics are well-supported and are a place where "students love to have fun." Students rave about the library and the "Adlab," but more than anything they appreciate that there are "good people everywhere you go."

Student Body

Brigham Young has an extremely conservative "Honor Code" derived from the Mormon Church that requires, among other things, abstinence from drugs, alcohol, tobacco, and caffeine, as well as "inappropriate" "sexual activity, including sex outside of marriage and homosexuality." The Honor Code is a plus for students seeking a like-minded peer group, such as this art education student who "didn't want to have to worry about walking in on my roommate sleeping with someone or have to hold her head up while she was puking her guts out into the toilet." The Honor Code also demands honesty and respect for others, which means the student body is "friendly, outgoing," and "concerned for others." Students are "smart and very confident in their intelligence," as well as "hardworking" and "goal-oriented." Mormon traditions mean that twenty-five percent of students are married, and people appreciate that "the school caters…really well to the average Latter-day Saint student coming in and working with those wanting to get married [or] go on missions." Marriage is definitely on many people's minds. A family studies major notes, "We are constantly encouraged to date." People generally think that "students mesh together well and it is easy to make new friends," though one concedes, "I can see how it could be hard to fit in if you are not used to the Mormon culture or beliefs."

Financial Aid: 801-422-4104 • E-mail: admissions@byu.edu • Website: www.byu.edu

THE PRINCETON REVIEW SAYS

Admissions

Very important factors considered include: Academic GPA, rigor of secondary school record, standardized test scores, character/personal qualities, interview, religious affiliation/commitment. *Important factors considered include:* Application essay, recommendation(s), extracurricular activities, racial/ethnic status, volunteer work. *Other factors considered include:* First generation, talent/ability, work experience. SAT or ACT required; ACT with writing component recommended. TOEFL required of all international applicants. High school diploma is required and GED is accepted. *Academic units required:* 4 English, 3 mathematics, 2 science (2 science labs), 2 foreign language, 2 history, 2 literature or writing. *Academic units recommended:* 4 English, 4 mathematics, 3 science (3 science labs), 4 foreign language.

Financial Aid

Students should submit: FAFSA, institutional application for financial aid. The Princeton Review suggests that all financial aid forms be submitted as soon as possible after January 1. *Need-based scholarships/grants offered:* Federal Pell, state scholarships/grants, private scholarships, the school's own gift aid. *Loan aid offered:* Direct Subsidized Stafford, Direct Unsubsidized Stafford, Direct PLUS. Applicants will be notified of awards on a rolling basis beginning May 1.

The Inside Word

An applicant pool of more than 10,000 necessitates a reliance on numbers, especially during the first round of cuts. Much of the matchmaking done at other schools isn't necessary here, as a highly self-selecting applicant pool typically precludes those who would make a poor fit. Still, admissions officers want to see at least respect (if not reverence) for LDS principles, without which survival here would be difficult indeed.

THE SCHOOL SAYS "..."

From the Admissions Office

"The mission of Brigham Young University—founded, supported, and guided by The Church of Jesus Christ of Latter-day Saints—is to assist individuals in their quest for perfection and eternal life. That assistance should provide a period of intensive learning in a stimulating setting where a commitment to excellence is expected and the full realization of human potential is pursued. All instruction, programs, and services at BYU, including a wide variety of extracurricular experiences, should make their own contribution toward the balanced development of the total person. Such a broadly prepared individual will not only be capable of meeting personal challenge and change but will also bring strength to others in the tasks of home and family life, social relationships, civic duty, and service to mankind.

"Freshman applicants are required to take either the ACT (with the optional writing section) or the SAT. The highest composite score will be used in admissions decisions."

SELECTIVITY	
Admissions Rating	**93**
# of applicants	11,328
% of applicants accepted	63
% of acceptees attending	80

FRESHMAN PROFILE	
Range SAT Critical Reading	570–680
Range SAT Math	580–680
Range SAT Writing	540–650
Range ACT Composite	26–30
Minimum paper TOEFL	500
Average HS GPA	3.8
% graduated top 10% of class	53
% graduated top 25% of class	84
% graduated top 50% of class	98

DEADLINES	
Regular	
Priority	12/1
Deadline	2/1
Notification	2/28
Nonfall registration?	yes

FINANCIAL FACTS	
Financial Aid Rating	**67**
Annual tuition	$4,710
Room and board	$7,228
Books and supplies	$900
% needy frosh rec. need-based scholarship or grant aid	55
% needy UG rec. need-based scholarship or grant aid	79
% needy frosh rec. non-need-based scholarship or grant aid	70
% needy UG rec. non-need-based scholarship or grant aid	46
% needy frosh rec. need-based self-help aid	27
% needy UG rec. need-based self-help aid	33
% frosh rec. any financial aid	53
% UG rec. any financial aid	64
% UG borrow to pay for school	32
Average cumulative indebtedness	$14,320
% frosh need fully met	2
% ugrads need fully met	3
Average % of frosh need met	28
Average % of ugrad need met	38

Brown University

PO Box 1876, Providence, RI 02912 • Admissions: 401-863-2378 • Fax: 401-863-9300

CAMPUS LIFE

Quality of Life Rating	**98**
Fire Safety Rating	**78**
Green Rating	**90**
Type of school	private
Environment	city

STUDENTS

Total undergrad enrollment	6,118
% male/female	49/51
% from out of state	95
% from public high school	59
% frosh live on campus	100
# of fraternities	9
# of sororities	5
% African American	6
% Asian	14
% Caucasian	45
% Hispanic	10
% international	11
# of countries represented	110

SURVEY SAYS . . .

No one cheats
Students are friendly
Great off-campus food
Students are happy
College radio is popular
Student publications are popular
Political activism is popular
Students are environmentally aware

ACADEMICS

Academic Rating	**94**
% students returning for sophomore year	98
% students graduating within 4 years	83
% students graduating within 6 years	95
Calendar	semester
Student/faculty ratio	9:1
Profs interesting rating	87
Profs accessible rating	84
Most classes have	10–19 students

MOST POPULAR MAJORS

biology/biological sciences; economics; international relations and affairs

APPLICANTS ALSO LOOK AT AND OFTEN PREFER

Princeton University, Yale University, Stanford University, Harvard College

AND SOMETIMES PREFER

Columbia University, Dartmouth College, Duke University, Massachusetts Institute of Technology, University of Pennsylvania

AND RARELY PREFER

Bowdoin College, Tufts University, Georgetown University, Oberlin College

STUDENTS SAY ". . ."

Academics

Known for its somewhat unconventional (but still highly regarded) approaches to life and learning, Brown University remains the slightly odd man out of the Ivy League, and the school wouldn't have it any other way. The school's willingness to employ and support different, methods such as the shopping period, the first two weeks of the semester where anyone can drop into any class to "find out if it's something they're interested in enrolling in," or the *Critical Review*, a student publication that produces reviews of courses based on evaluations from students who have completed the course, is designed to treat students "like an adult" through "freedom and choice." This open-minded environment allows them "to practice passion without shame or fear of judgment," the hallmark of a Brown education. Even if students do find themselves exploring the wrong off-the-beaten path, "There are multitudes of built-in support measures to help you succeed despite any odds." Even grades are a non-issue here, "except amongst paranoid premeds."

Professors are mostly hits with a few misses, but there are "amazing professors in every department, and they're not hard to find"; it's just "up to students to find the teaching styles that work for them." "Academics at Brown are what you make of them," and even though students are diligent in their academic pursuits and feel assured they're "getting a wonderful education with the professors," most agree that their education is "really more about the unique student body and learning through active participation in other activities." The administration gets cautiously decent reviews for their accessibility and general running of the school, but it also gets scolded for getting "distracted by the long term." The president, however, is absolutely loved by students for being "an incredible person with a great vision for the school."

Life

Thinking—yes, thinking—and discussing take up a great deal of time at Brown. "People think about life, politics, society at large, global affairs, the state of the economy, developing countries, animals, plants, rocket science, math, poker, each other, sex, sexuality, the human experience, gender studies, what to do with our lives, etc.," says a senior anthropology major. "Most people here don't go home that often," and like any school, "There are people who go out five nights a week and people who go out five nights a semester." "Alcohol and weed are pretty embedded in campus life," and most parties are dorm room events, even though partying "never gets in the way of academics or friendship. If you don't drink/smoke, that's totally cool." There's also plenty of cultural activities, such as indie bands, student performances, jazz, swing dancing, and speakers. Themed housing (art house, tech house, interfaith house) and co-ops are also popular social mediators.

Student Body

It's a pretty unique crowd here, where "athletes, preps, nerds, and everyone in between come together" because they "love learning for the sake of learning, and [they] love Brown equally as much." "The 'mainstream' is full of people who are atypical in sense of fashion, taste in music, and academic interests," says a junior. Unsurprisingly, everyone here's "very smart," as well as "very quirky and often funny," and "a great amount are brilliant and passionate about their interests;" "most have interesting stories to tell." People here are "curious and open about many things," which is perhaps why sexual diversity is a "strong theme" among Brown interactions and events. The overall culture "is pretty laid-back and casual," and "most of the students are friendly and mesh well with everyone."

FINANCIAL AID: 401-863-2721 • E-MAIL: ADMISSION_UNDERGRADUATE@BROWN.EDU • WEBSITE: WWW.BROWN.EDU

THE PRINCETON REVIEW SAYS

Admissions

Very important factors considered include: Rigor of secondary school record, character/personal qualities, level of applicant's interest, talent/ability. *Important factors considered include:* Class rank, application essay, academic GPA, recommendation(s), standardized test scores, extracurricular activities. *Other factors considered include:* Alumni/ae relation, first generation, geographical residence, interview, racial/ethnic status, state residency, volunteer work, work experience. ACT with writing component required. TOEFL required of all international applicants. High school diploma is required and GED is not accepted. *Academic units required:* 4 English, 3 mathematics, 3 science (2 science labs), 3 foreign language, 2 history, 1 academic electives. *Academic units recommended:* 4 English, 4 mathematics, 4 science (3 science labs), 4 foreign language, 2 history, 1 visual/performing arts, 1 academic electives.

Financial Aid

Students should submit: FAFSA, CSS/Financial Aid PROFILE, noncustodial PROFILE. Regular filing deadline is February 1. The Princeton Review suggests that all financial aid forms be submitted as soon as possible after January 1. *Need-based scholarships/grants offered:* Federal Pell, SEOG, state scholarships/grants, private scholarships, the school's own gift aid. *Loan aid offered:* Direct Subsidized Stafford, Direct Unsubsidized Stafford, Direct PLUS, Federal Perkins, college/university loans from institutional funds. Applicants will be notified of awards on or about April 1. Federal Work-Study Program available. Institutional employment available. Off-campus job opportunities are excellent.

The Inside Word

The cream of just about every crop applies to Brown. Gaining admission requires more than just a superior academic profile from high school. Some candidates, such as the sons and daughters of Brown graduates (who are admitted at virtually double the usual acceptance rate), have a better chance for admission than most others. Minority students benefit from some courtship, particularly once admitted. Ivies like to share the wealth and distribute offers of admission across a wide range of constituencies. Candidates from states that are overrepresented in the applicant pool, such as New York, have to be particularly distinguished in order to have the best chance at admission. So do those who attend high schools with many seniors applying to Brown, as it is rare for several students from any one school to be offered admission.

THE SCHOOL SAYS ". . ."

From the Admissions Office

"Brown University is the nation's seventh oldest institution of higher education and the third oldest in New England. Since 1764, Brown has offered the best in liberal arts education, leading-edge scholarship and research, and opportunities for community-based service learning. Its flexible undergraduate curriculum involves more than 6,000 students in the design of their own studies, with nearly eighty concentrations in forty-four different academic areas and the option of independent study. The Warren Alpert Medical School of Brown University, Rhode Island's only medical school, provides more than 400 students with medical instruction and clinical training at seven Brown-affiliated hospitals in and around Providence. Brown is one of eight members of the Ivy League."

SELECTIVITY

Admissions Rating	**99**
# of applicants	30,944
% of applicants accepted	9
% of acceptees attending	55
# of early decision applicants	2,803
# accepted early decision	573

FRESHMAN PROFILE

Range SAT Critical Reading	660–750
Range SAT Math	680–770
Range SAT Writing	670–770
Range ACT Composite	29–33
Minimum paper TOEFL	600
Minimum web-based TOEFL	100
% graduated top 10% of class	91
% graduated top 25% of class	99
% graduated top 50% of class	100

DEADLINES

Early decision	
Deadline	11/1
Notification	12/15
Regular	
Deadline	1/2
Notification	4/1
Nonfall registration?	no

FINANCIAL FACTS

Financial Aid Rating	**93**
Annual tuition	$42,808
Room and board	$11,258
Required fees	$950
Books and supplies	$1,360
% needy frosh rec. need-based scholarship or grant aid	97
% needy UG rec. need-based scholarship or grant aid	95
% needy frosh rec. need-based self-help aid	82
% needy UG rec. need-based self-help aid	90
% frosh rec. any financial aid	61
% UG rec. any financial aid	59
% UG borrow to pay for school	45
Average cumulative indebtedness	$19,463
% frosh need fully met	100
% ugrads need fully met	100
Average % of frosh need met	100
Average % of ugrad need met	100

BRYANT UNIVERSITY

1150 DOUGLAS PIKE, SMITHFIELD, RI 02917-1291 • ADMISSIONS: 401-232-6100 • FAX: 401-232-6731

CAMPUS LIFE

Quality of Life Rating	**76**
Fire Safety Rating	**89**
Green Rating	**72**
Type of school	private
Environment	village

STUDENTS

Total undergrad enrollment	3,312
% male/female	59/41
% from out of state	85
% frosh live on campus	95
# of fraternities	5
# of sororities	3
% African American	4
% Asian	3
% Caucasian	77
% Hispanic	5
% international	6
# of countries represented	58

SURVEY SAYS . . .

Great computer facilities
Great library
Athletic facilities are great
Career services are great
School is well run
Campus feels safe
Lots of beer drinking
Hard liquor is popular

ACADEMICS

Academic Rating	**78**
% students returning for sophomore year	86
% students graduating within 4 years	75
% students graduating within 6 years	77
Calendar	semester
Student/faculty ratio	15:1
Profs interesting rating	75
Profs accessible rating	80
Most classes have	30–39 students
Most lab/discussion sessions have	fewer than 10 students

MOST POPULAR MAJORS

accounting; finance; marketing/marketing management; international business; accounting; actuarial math

APPLICANTS ALSO LOOK AT AND OFTEN PREFER

Babson College, Bentley University, Northeastern University, Boston University

AND SOMETIMES PREFER

University of Massachusetts Amherst, Fairfield University, Stonehill College, University of Connecticut, Providence College

AND RARELY PREFER

Quinnipiac University, University of New Hampshire, University of Rhode Island

STUDENTS SAY "..."

Academics

Rhode Island's Bryant University may offer an attractive "balance between business-focus and liberal arts–focus," but the school's reputation is primarily built on its robust business education. Most professors here "bring a lot of real-world experience in their field to the classroom" and hands-on experience that "provides you with a sense of how business operates." Bryant's "small size" means students will get "personal academic attention"—students consistently brag that "professors are highly accessible outside of the classroom and very passionate about what they teach"—but that does not mean those attending will have an easy time. The school's "rigorous curriculum" can be "a little stringent, especially for majors like accounting and international business," making educators who "clearly love the subject matter and the students" a key to success. Most students praise the faculty, saying "they make learning here interesting rather than a chore." Also appealing for students is the "close-knit community feel." The "engaging and dedicated faculty" lead the way, but that torch is also kept aflame by students who "are so willing to contribute to our 'student community' here."

Life

"Work hard during the week and party hard on the weekends" seems to be a common statement among students, who fill weeks with studying and weekends with themed parties, trips to Providence or Boston, or an array of school clubs and organizations. For those students who enjoy the focus on community service at Bryant—and there are many of them—groups give students "the opportunity to be give back to the community constantly, take on leadership roles, and make a ton of great friends." There is also an active Greek community on campus, as well as varsity sports. In addition, "intramural and club sports are also big on campus for recreational activity." However, the career-oriented student body means that "there are a number of students who don't do much besides go to class." Still, "People at Bryant do like to work hard, but they also do play hard." Overall, "Those who do well are those who can strike that balance easily and recognize when work needs to be done."

Student Body

Students at Bryant tend to be "career-orientated and very focused on succeeding." "The typical Bryant student is from an upper-middle-class New England family, majoring in business," so while the school "does have a growing number of liberal arts majors," as well as "international and multicultural students," the general student population can seem, according to one student's cynical assessment, "rich, spoiled, and white." Most, however, do not have that cynical a view. "Every student feels welcome," others note, and "Groups are pretty open, and it's easy to make friends." Most say it is easy to fit in here. "There are cliques like with any school, but you tend to find your niche group after freshman year." The campus places "less importance on athletes," so the "typical student is very involved and committed to academic work." Those attending Bryant tend to "aspire to go into finance, accounting, and/or work in a large banking/insurance/technology company after graduation." That said, many students say there is a growing diversity in the focus of the student population, including "students who aspire to go into a wider variety of fields after graduation."

FINANCIAL AID: 401-232-6020 • E-MAIL: ADMISSION@BRYANT.EDU • WEBSITE: WWW.BRYANT.EDU

THE PRINCETON REVIEW SAYS

Admissions

Very important factors considered include: Academic GPA, rigor of secondary school record. *Important factors considered include:* Class rank, application essay, recommendation(s), standardized test scores. *Other factors considered include:* Alumni/ae relation, character/personal qualities, extracurricular activities, first generation, geographical residence, interview, level of applicant's interest, racial/ethnic status, state residency, talent/ability, volunteer work, work experience. ACT with or without writing component accepted. TOEFL required of all international applicants. High school diploma is required and GED is accepted. *Academic units required:* 4 English, 4 mathematics, 2 science (2 science labs), 2 foreign language, 2 history. *Academic units recommended:* 4 English, 4 mathematics, 3 science (2 science labs), 3 foreign language, 3 history.

Financial Aid

Students should submit: FAFSA. Regular filing deadline is February 15. The Princeton Review suggests that all financial aid forms be submitted as soon as possible after January 1. *Need-based scholarships/grants offered:* Federal Pell, SEOG, state scholarships/grants, private scholarships, the school's own gift aid. *Loan aid offered:* Direct Subsidized Stafford, Direct Unsubsidized Stafford, Direct PLUS, Federal Perkins, privately funded education loans. Applicants will be notified of awards on or about March 24. Federal Work-Study Program available. Institutional employment available. Highest amount earned per year from on-campus jobs $7,378. Off-campus job opportunities are fair.

The Inside Word

The common wisdom is that liberal arts and business educations are not compatible. Bryant University seeks to change that thinking, and its reputation seems to indicate it is succeeding. Business-focused students who do not want to give up educational opportunities in other areas should have Bryant on their short list—especially considering that Bryant boasts an impressive ninety-six percent job-placement rate.

THE SCHOOL SAYS ". . ."

From the Admissions Office

"Founded in 1863, Bryant University empowers students to realize their personal best in life and their chosen professions. Bryant is the one university that is driving a paradigm shift in undergraduate education by shattering the thinking that liberal arts and business are separate paths. The University's innovative real-world curriculum is made more profound by an unwavering focus on character and ethics. The College of Arts and Sciences offers degrees in applied economics, actuarial mathematics, applied mathematics and statistics, applied psychology, biology, Chinese, communication, environmental science, global studies, history, literary and cultural studies, politics and law, sociology, and Spanish. The College of Business offers a degree in business administration with concentrations in accounting, computer information systems, entrepreneurship, finance, financial services, management, and marketing; a degree in information technology; and an international business degree with concentrations in computer information systems, finance, management, and marketing. Bryant's academic programs are accredited by the New England Association of Schools and Colleges. The College of Business is accredited by AACSB International—The Association to Advance Collegiate Schools of Business, a distinction earned by only five percent of universities. In addition, Bryant's International Business degree program is a member of CUIBE—The Consortium for Undergraduate International Business Education. Bryant has internships and recruiting partnerships with 350 companies; nearly 100 student clubs and organizations; Northeast Conference NCAA Division I, intramural, and club sports; and service learning and leadership development programs. Qualified students can study abroad for a semester, a summer, or an academic year in one of forty-five countries. Bryant is on a beautiful 428-acre campus in Smithfield, Rhode Island, and is fifteen minutes away from the state capital, Providence; forty-five minutes from Boston; and three hours from New York City."

SELECTIVITY	
Admissions Rating	85
# of applicants	5,177
% of applicants accepted	77
% of acceptees attending	20
# accepting a place on wait list	210
# admitted from wait list	19
# of early decision applicants	187
# accepted early decision	114

FRESHMAN PROFILE	
Range SAT Critical Reading	500–590
Range SAT Math	535–630
Range SAT Writing	500–590
Range ACT Composite	22–26
Minimum paper TOEFL	550
Minimum web-based TOEFL	80
Average HS GPA	3.3
% graduated top 10% of class	20
% graduated top 25% of class	52
% graduated top 50% of class	88

DEADLINES	
Early decision	
Deadline	11/15
Notification	12/15
Early action	
Deadline	12/1
Notification	1/15
Regular	
Deadline	2/1
Notification	3/23
Nonfall registration?	yes

FINANCIAL FACTS	
Financial Aid Rating	75
Annual tuition	$35,591
Room and board	$13,240
Required fees	$349
Books and supplies	$1,300
% needy frosh rec. need-based scholarship or grant aid	81
% needy UG rec. need-based scholarship or grant aid	83
% needy frosh rec. non-need-based scholarship or grant aid	46
% needy UG rec. non-need-based scholarship or grant aid	37
% needy frosh rec. need-based self-help aid	87
% needy UG rec. need-based self-help aid	90
% frosh rec. any financial aid	81
% UG rec. any financial aid	81
% UG borrow to pay for school	79
Average cumulative indebtedness	$37,813
% frosh need fully met	50
% ugrads need fully met	50
Average % of frosh need met	54
Average % of ugrad need met	56

BRYN MAWR COLLEGE

101 North Merion Avenue, Bryn Mawr, PA 19010-2859 • Admissions: 610-526-5152 • Fax: 610-526-7471

CAMPUS LIFE

Quality of Life Rating	94
Fire Safety Rating	71
Green Rating	77
Type of school	private
Environment	metropolis

STUDENTS

Total undergrad enrollment	1,302
% male/female	0/100
% from out of state	84
% from public high school	65
% frosh live on campus	100
% African American	4
% Asian	13
% Caucasian	37
% Hispanic	9
% international	16
# of countries represented	61

SURVEY SAYS . . .

Great food on campus
Dorms are like palaces
Low cost of living
Frats and sororities are unpopular or nonexistent
Student government is popular

ACADEMICS

Academic Rating	95
% students returning for sophomore year	90
% students graduating within 4 years	82
Calendar	semester
Student/faculty ratio	8:1
Profs interesting rating	89
Profs accessible rating	92
Most classes have	10–19 students

MOST POPULAR MAJORS

English language and literature; mathematics; psychology

APPLICANTS ALSO LOOK AT AND OFTEN PREFER

University of Pennsylvania, Brown University, Harvard College

AND SOMETIMES PREFER

Smith College, Swarthmore College, Wellesley College, Mount Holyoke College, Scripps College, Haverford College

AND RARELY PREFER

Vassar College, Oberlin College

STUDENTS SAY ". . ."

Academics

Bryn Mawr is all about "empowering women to achieve their dreams." The school has a "reputation for strong academics," and students confirm that work there's "no joke." Bryn Mawr is a small college, which means there's not "a huge variety of classes," but it also means that classes are small. One student reports that most of hers have "around ten people," and another says her largest lecture class had forty students. This leads to "deep discussions [and] meaningful relationships [being] formed with peers and colleagues." Classes are "very interactive," and "great student-teacher relationships [are] established by the way classes are conducted." The faculty is "amazing and no doubt brilliant," and "They go a long way to make sure you don't only feel like students but also like a mini-family." An East Asian studies student says she feels "comfortable talking to faculty members/professors about anything." Students think one of the best parts about Bryn Mawr is the "amazing academic opportunities within the tri-co," and the "Quaker consortium"; agreements that allow students to take classes at Haverford, Swarthmore, and the University of Pennsylvania. All of these great attributes combine to make Bryn Mawr a fantastic college experience. As one student puts it, Bryn Mawr "compels me to be extraordinary in an environment of equally extraordinary students."

Life

Academics are the focus of life at Bryn Mawr, but that doesn't mean students are "a bunch of nuns who sit around studying all day." "We do a lot of studying," a student explains, "but we also enjoy our time here." Not only are there "tons of school-sponsored activities," but there are opportunities to "go to a big party with tons of dancing and tons of people," at Bryn Mawr or at Haverford. "Meals here are really important," adds a student. "Dinner can be the only time we'll see each other, [which] can easily go on for an hour and a half." Bryn Mawr's "amazing food" probably has something to do with that. Bryn Mawr has an "absolutely beautiful campus," with great facilities, including a new gym with an "Olympic-sized swimming pool…TVs, large windows…and state-of-the-art machines that are built for women." Though Bryn Mawr has a suburban location, "The proximity and ease in traveling to Philadelphia, New York, and Washington, D.C., is beyond fantastic." Students love Bryn Mawr's traditions, two of which are the Self-Government Association and the Honor Code. The Self-Government Association, the oldest student government in America, "allows…students to have an input on many aspects of how the college is run." The Honor Code, which every student must sign, emphasizes respect and integrity. The code creates "a strong community" and a safe one. One student says, "I don't lock my door!" Another adds, "You could lose a ring anywhere on campus and just send an e-mail out to the student body and have it back in the next few hours."

Student Body

"There is no typical student," at Bryn Mawr, "aside from women with a passion for learning and a commitment to excellence." A German student reports, "The variety of people here is enormous," and this "creates the…uniqueness that Bryn Mawr prides itself on." People's thoughts on racial diversity, however, "are kind of conflicting." One student explains, "Coming from a big city…Bryn Mawr did not seem very diverse, but my roommate came from a very small town and thought Bryn Mawr was extremely diverse." What students do agree on is that they're "friendly and welcoming," "creative," and "a little quirky." Though the intense workload means students are "very interested in…academics and work hard to get good grades," they "are also social" and "take time to build up strong friendships with other students." Students at Bryn Mawr really respect each other's individuality and love that their peers "have a purposive direction in regards to what they want to do with their future."

FINANCIAL AID: 610-526-5245 • E-MAIL: ADMISSIONS@BRYNMAWR.EDU • WEBSITE: WWW.BRYNMAWR.EDU

THE PRINCETON REVIEW SAYS

Admissions

Very important factors considered include: Recommendation(s), rigor of secondary school record. *Important factors considered include:* Application essay, academic GPA, character/personal qualities, extracurricular activities. *Other factors considered include:* Class rank, standardized test scores, alumni/ae relation, first generation, geographical residence, interview, racial/ethnic status, talent/ability, volunteer work, work experience. ACT with or without writing component accepted. TOEFL required of all international applicants. High school diploma is required and GED is accepted. *Academic units required:* 2 academic electives. *Academic units recommended:* 4 English, 3 mathematics, 2 science (1 science lab), 3 foreign language, 2 social studies, 2 history.

Financial Aid

Students should submit: FAFSA, CSS/Financial Aid PROFILE, business/farm supplement. Statement of earnings from parents' employer. Regular filing deadline is March 1. The Princeton Review suggests that all financial aid forms be submitted as soon as possible after January 1. *Need-based scholarships/grants offered:* Federal Pell, SEOG, state scholarships/grants, the school's own gift aid. *Loan aid offered:* Direct Subsidized Stafford, Direct Unsubsidized Stafford, Direct PLUS, Federal Perkins. Applicants will be notified of awards on or about March 23. Highest amount earned per year from on-campus jobs $2,000.

The Inside Word

Bryn Mawr's student body is among the academically best in the nation. Outstanding preparation for graduate study draws an applicant pool that's well-prepared and intellectually curious. Interviews are strongly recommended but not required. If you're still unsure of how to stand out in the crowd, take advantage of Bryn Mawr's numerous on-campus and online opportunities to connect with current students.

THE SCHOOL SAYS ". . ."

From the Admissions Office

"Bryn Mawr's extraordinary academics, vibrant and diverse community, and focus on global leadership prepare students to challenge convention and take their places in the world. Every year 1,300 women from around the world gather on the college's historic campus to study with leading scholars, conduct advanced research, and expand the boundaries of what is possible. A Bryn Mawr woman is defined by a rare combination of personal characteristics: an intense intellectual commitment; a purposeful vision of her life; and a desire to make a meaningful contribution to the world. Consistently producing outstanding scholars, Bryn Mawr is ranked among the top ten of all colleges and universities in percentage of graduates who go on to earn a PhD, and is considered excellent preparation for the nation's top law, medical and business schools. More than 500 students collaborate with faculty on independent projects every year, and to augment an already strong curriculum, students may choose from more than 5,000 courses offered through nearby Haverford and Swarthmore colleges, as well as the University of Pennsylvania.

"Minutes outside of Philadelphia and only two hours by train from New York City and Washington, D.C., Bryn Mawr is recognized by many as one of the most stunning college campuses in the United States.

"Bryn Mawr has a 'Test Flexible' admissions policy, which allows students the option of using AP exam scores at Bryn Mawr. See the website for full details: www.brynmawr.edu/admissions/apply/tests.html."

SELECTIVITY	
Admissions Rating	**94**
# of applicants	2,335
% of applicants accepted	46
% of acceptees attending	33
# accepting a place on wait list	352
# admitted from wait list	7
# of early decision applicants	151
# accepted early decision	88

FRESHMAN PROFILE	
Range SAT Critical Reading	600–710
Range SAT Math	600–720
Range SAT Writing	630–710
Range ACT Composite	26–31
Minimum paper TOEFL	600
Minimum web-based TOEFL	90
% graduated top 10% of class	60
% graduated top 25% of class	89
% graduated top 50% of class	98

DEADLINES	
Early decision	
Deadline	11/15
Notification	12/15
Regular	
Deadline	1/15
Notification	4/1
Nonfall registration?	no

FINANCIAL FACTS	
Financial Aid Rating	**97**
Annual tuition	$41,260
Room and board	$13,340
Required fees	$986
Books and supplies	$1,000
% needy frosh rec. need-based scholarship or grant aid	100
% needy UG rec. need-based scholarship or grant aid	100
% needy frosh rec. non-need-based scholarship or grant aid	6
% needy UG rec. non-need-based scholarship or grant aid	4
% needy frosh rec. need-based self-help aid	91
% needy UG rec. need-based self-help aid	91
% frosh rec. any financial aid	81
% UG rec. any financial aid	72
% UG borrow to pay for school	58
Average cumulative indebtedness	$22,830
% frosh need fully met	100
% ugrads need fully met	100
Average % of frosh need met	100
Average % of ugrad need met	100

Bucknell University

Freas Hall, Lewisburg, PA 17837 • Admissions: 570-577-1101 • Fax: 570-577-3538

CAMPUS LIFE

Quality of Life Rating	**81**
Fire Safety Rating	**85**
Green Rating	**86**
Type of school	private
Environment	village

STUDENTS

Total undergrad enrollment	3,535
% male/female	48/52
% from out of state	76
% from public high school	61
% frosh live on campus	100
# of fraternities	11
# of sororities	8
% African American	3
% Asian	3
% Caucasian	79
% Hispanic	4
% international	5
# of countries represented	63

SURVEY SAYS . . .

Athletic facilities are great
Low cost of living
Frats and sororities dominate social scene
Lots of beer drinking

ACADEMICS

Academic Rating	**92**
% students returning for sophomore year	94
% students graduating within 4 years	87
% students graduating within 6 years	91
Calendar	semester
Student/faculty ratio	10:1
Profs interesting rating	89
Profs accessible rating	93
Most classes have	10–19 students
Most lab/discussion sessions have	10–19 students

MOST POPULAR MAJORS

business administration and management; economics; English language and literature

APPLICANTS ALSO LOOK AT AND OFTEN PREFER

Cornell University, John Hopkins University, Tufts University, University of Virginia, University of Notre Dame

AND SOMETIMES PREFER

Villanova University, University of Richmond, Colgate University, Carnegie Mellon University, Boston College, Lehigh University

AND RARELY PREFER

University of Maryland, College Park, University of Delaware, Pennsylvania State University—University Park, Lafayette College

STUDENTS SAY ". . ."

Academics

Armed with a great reputation, Bucknell is a small university that still manages to provide a "large amount of resources and opportunities." Surrounded by a "beautiful" campus, undergrads happily become part of a "strong, spirited community." Moreover, students here truly appreciate that the university "places a large emphasis on [both] undergraduate learning and preparation for graduate school." Among the many great disciplines Bucknell offers, students are especially quick to highlight the "extremely strong language, international relations, and science departments, [along with the] engineering and management schools." Undergrads also give their professors high marks, citing them as "extremely engaging," "very knowledgeable," and "deeply involved in their areas of study." One pleased Bucknellian elaborates, "I am extremely lucky in that all of my professors are fantastic! In fact, my organic chemistry professor changed my outlook on organic chemistry as a whole. In high school, chemistry was my least favorite subject. Now, however, I look forward to that class every week!" Professors here are also lauded for being highly "accessible" and always "willing and excited to meet students outside of class." Another content students adds, "Professors devote themselves tirelessly to their students; they are available at a moment's notice and genuinely enjoy interaction with their students both in and outside of the classroom. They seek to become lifelong friends and mentors." Finally, as one student succinctly puts it, "Bucknell provides a student lifestyle that is welcoming, active, and challenging."

Life

Undergrads at Bucknell seem to unanimously agree that most everyone here adopts a "work hard, play hard" mentality. Indeed, "During the week, students are very focused on their work." However, once the weekend rolls around, "Everyone lets loose." Of course, no matter the day of the week, the university is always buzzing with activity. The campus "hosts a lot of events such as BU After Dark and the Spring/Fall Semester Concert." In addition, "The school does a wonderful job of bringing in a lot of diverse and interesting speakers." One pleased undergrad interjects sharing, "There are lots of concerts either for free or for minimal price. The music is [of] all sorts. It can be either Tchaikovsky or Wiz Khalifa. There is a Craft Center that provides with all kinds of art supplies. I go there almost every Friday and either play with clay, do something on potter's wheel, or do a stained glass." Sporting events (intramurals and varsity alike) are also quite popular. As another student reveals, "We have a lot of pride for our teams and love to go to the home games on the weekends." Greek life tends to "dominate the social scene here," and the vast majority of students can be found "partying at the frats" during the weekend. However, for those wary of the Greek lifestyle, rest assured, you'll still enjoy your time at Bucknell. As an undergrad confidently states, "If you don't want to go Greek, no worries. My roommate is not in a sorority, and she loves Bucknell just as much as I do!"

Student Body

At first glance, the typical Bucknell undergrad could be described as "upper-middle-class and white." Further, "preppy" is certainly the look that permeates this campus; as one student sharply notes, "I have never seen so many Sperry's in my life!" However, though some do acknowledge that "there is a lack of diversity," they quickly follow up this assertion by stating, "Everyone is very open-minded and accepting of people with different backgrounds." More importantly, if you push past the exterior, you'll discover a student body that's "smart and eager to learn" as well as "outgoing and friendly to anyone they come in contact with." And perhaps best of all, "The typical student also loves Bucknell and could never see themselves anywhere else."

FINANCIAL AID: 570-577-1331 • E-MAIL: ADMISSIONS@BUCKNELL.EDU • WEBSITE: WWW.BUCKNELL.EDU

THE PRINCETON REVIEW SAYS

Admissions

Very important factors considered include: Class rank, application essay, academic GPA, rigor of secondary school record, standardized test scores, character/personal qualities, talent/ability. *Important factors considered include:* Recommendation(s), extracurricular activities, level of applicant's interest, volunteer work, work experience. *Other factors considered include:* Alumni/ae relation, first generation, geographical residence, racial/ethnic status, religious affiliation/commitment. SAT or ACT required; ACT with writing component required. TOEFL required of all international applicants. High school diploma is required and GED is accepted. *Academic units required:* 4 English, 3 mathematics, 2 science, 2 foreign language, 2 social studies, 2 history, 1 academic elective. *Academic units recommended:* 4 English, 4 mathematics, 3 science, 4 foreign language, 2 social studies, 2 history, 1 academic elective.

Financial Aid

Students should submit: FAFSA, CSS/Financial Aid PROFILE, noncustodial PROFILE. Regular filing deadline is January 15. The Princeton Review suggests that all financial aid forms be submitted as soon as possible after January 1. *Need-based scholarships/grants offered:* Federal Pell, SEOG, state scholarships/grants, private scholarships, the school's own gift aid. *Loan aid offered:* Direct Subsidized Stafford, Direct Unsubsidized Stafford, Direct PLUS, Federal Perkins. Applicants will be notified of awards on or about April 1. Federal Work-Study Program available. Institutional employment available. Highest amount earned per year from on-campus jobs $1,500. Off-campus job opportunities are poor.

The Inside Word

Securing admission to Bucknell is no easy feat. Admissions officers are looking for candidates who excel both inside the classroom and with extracurriculars. The university strives to achieve a complete picture of every candidate so rest assured all application facets will be considered.

THE SCHOOL SAYS ". . ."

From the Admissions Office

"Bucknell combines the personal experience of a small liberal arts college with the breadth and opportunity typically found at larger research universities. With a low student/faculty ratio, students gain exceptional hands-on experience, working closely with faculty in an environment enhanced by first-class academic, residential, and athletic facilities. Together, the College of Arts and Sciences and the College of Engineering offer fifty-six majors and sixty-five minors. Learning opportunities permeate campus life in and out of the classroom and across the disciplines. For example, engineering students participate in music ensembles, theater productions, and poetry readings, while arts and sciences students take engineering courses, conduct scientific research in the field, and produce distinctive creative works. Students also pursue their interests in more than 150 organizations and through athletic competition in the prestigious Division I Patriot League. These activities constitute a comprehensive approach to learning that teaches students how to think critically and develop their leadership skills so that they are prepared to make a difference locally, nationally, and globally."

SELECTIVITY

Admissions Rating	**96**
# of applicants	7,940
% of applicants accepted	28
% of acceptees attending	42
# accepting a place on wait list	2,198
# admitted from wait list	19
# of early decision applicants	761
# accepted early decision	419

FRESHMAN PROFILE

Range SAT Critical Reading	590–680
Range SAT Math	630–720
Range SAT Writing	600–700
Range ACT Composite	27–31
Minimum paper TOEFL	600
Minimum web-based TOEFL	100
Average HS GPA	3.5
% graduated top 10% of class	60
% graduated top 25% of class	91
% graduated top 50% of class	100

DEADLINES

Early decision	
Deadline	11/15
Notification	12/15
Regular	
Deadline	1/15
Notification	4/1
Nonfall registration?	no

FINANCIAL FACTS

Financial Aid Rating	**94**
Annual tuition	$45,132
Room and board	$10,812
Required fees	$246
Books and supplies	$900
% needy frosh rec. need-based scholarship or grant aid	100
% needy UG rec. need-based scholarship or grant aid	95
% needy frosh rec. non-need-based scholarship or grant aid	10
% needy UG rec. non-need-based scholarship or grant aid	13
% needy frosh rec. need-based self-help aid	100
% needy UG rec. need-based self-help aid	100
% frosh rec. any financial aid	61
% UG rec. any financial aid	61
% UG borrow to pay for school	59
Average cumulative indebtedness	$20,149
% frosh need fully met	94
% ugrads need fully met	94
Average % of frosh need met	95
Average % of ugrad need met	95

California Institute of Technology

1200 East California Boulevard, Pasadena, CA 91125 • Admissions: 626-395-6341 • Fax: 626-683-3026

CAMPUS LIFE

Quality of Life Rating	**79**
Fire Safety Rating	**65**
Green Rating	**99**
Type of school	private
Environment	metropolis

STUDENTS

Total undergrad enrollment	978
% male/female	61/39
% from public high school	70
% frosh live on campus	100
% African American	1
% Asian	30
% Caucasian	28
% Hispanic	5
% international	9
# of countries represented	32

SURVEY SAYS . . .

Class discussions are rare
No one cheats
Lab facilities are great
Students are friendly
Campus feels safe
Frats and sororities are unpopular or nonexistent

ACADEMICS

Academic Rating	**90**
% students returning for sophomore year	98
% students graduating within 4 years	76
Calendar	quarter
Student/faculty ratio	3:1
Profs interesting rating	65
Profs accessible rating	74
Most classes have	fewer than 10 students
Most lab/discussion sessions have	20–29 students

MOST POPULAR MAJORS

mathematics; mechanical engineering; physics

APPLICANTS ALSO LOOK AT AND OFTEN PREFER

Massachusetts Institute of Technology

AND SOMETIMES PREFER

Princeton University, Stanford University, Harvard College

AND RARELY PREFER

Rensselaer Polytechnic Institute, Virginia Tech

STUDENTS SAY ". . ."

Academics

According to students at the California Institute of Technology, their tiny school is "the greatest research university out there." "Caltech's math, science, and engineering programs are indisputably first-rate," gloats a senior. "If you like science and know that you want some sort of career in research, engineering, or academia, this is one of the best places to come in the world." The mandatory core curriculum is heavy on math, physics, and chemistry. It also includes a humanities requirement. Beyond that, students can choose from a host of majors and minors. Whatever path you choose, "The resources are incredible," and "lab facilities are top-notch." There are fabulous opportunities "for students to conduct research at every class level," too. Be prepared for "a crippling workload," though. The academic atmosphere here is "probably the most intense you could hope to find." It's "like trying to drink from a fire hose" ("even if this is an overused cliché"). "There is no grade inflation." "Caltech has the ability to crush your own opinion of how smart you are." "If you were the top student all your life, prepare to experience a big dose of humility because you'll have to work hard just to stay in the middle of the pack." "Introductory classes are often taught by Nobel laureates" and world renowned scientists. "The quality of professors as teachers, rather than brilliant researchers, however, is often hit-or-miss," explains an applied physics major. Professors "tend to be very passionate about their subjects," but "only a select few professors teach well."

Life

Life at Caltech "involves doing a lot of homework." "A sizable population of the school does not come out of their rooms much." Clubs and extracurricular activities run the gamut, though, and it's very easy to get involved "no matter your experience." "Computer games, card games, role-playing games," and the like are popular. Otherwise, social life relies heavily on Caltech's unique housing system. First-year students are required to live on campus, in one of eight houses. "The houses combine the feel and purpose of a dorm with the pride and spirit of a fraternity." "Each house plans social events" and "provides the main social community" for students. When Caltech students throw a party, "It's a major operation." "Most parties here involve two weeks of prior planning and construction," and the end result is "usually pretty epic." Off campus, Caltech's location in sunny Pasadena provides ample opportunities for outdoor activities. There are "beaches, mountains, and desert all within a two-hour drive." The proximity of Los Angeles provides a ready escape as well. "Once in a while we'll all pile in a car and go to Los Angeles for a concert or something," notes a senior, "and that's a lot of fun." "Plotting pranks" is another common pastime here. Techers have a notorious reputation for "amusing" and generally harmless mischief. Students once altered the famous Hollywood Sign to read "Caltech." In another instance, they adjusted the scoreboard at the Rose Bowl to show Caltech leading hated MIT by an impressive score of 38 to 9.

Student Body

Caltech is home to "lots of whites and Asians," and the student population is overwhelmingly male. "The ratio sucks," laments a lonely senior. "Your typical student here was the math team/science team/quiz bowl type in high school." "This is nerd heaven." "Everyone's a scientist," and "every student is brilliant." Students also describe themselves as "hardworking," "quirky," and "slightly eccentric." You'll find a wide variety, though, "from cool party types, to scary hardcore nerds, to cool party types who build massive railguns in their spare time." Some students are "terribly creative." Some are "socially inept" and "very strange." Ultimately, it's a hard group to pigeonhole. "You will meet someone who you might think is a total jock if you saw him or her on the street, but [he or she] works late at night on homework and aces exams," promises one student. "If you come here with stereotypes in mind, they will be broken."

FINANCIAL AID: 626-395-6280 • E-MAIL: UGADMISSIONS@CALTECH.EDU • WEBSITE: ADMISSIONS.CALTECH.EDU

THE PRINCETON REVIEW SAYS

Admissions

Very important factors considered include: Rigor of secondary school record. *Important factors considered include:* Class rank, application essay, academic GPA, recommendation(s), standardized test scores, character/personal qualities, extracurricular activities. *Other factors considered include:* Alumni/ae relation, first generation, racial/ethnic status, talent/ability, volunteer work, work experience. SAT or ACT required; ACT with or without writing component accepted. High school diploma or equivalent is not required. *Academic units required:* 3 English, 4 mathematics, 2 science (1 science lab), 1 social studies, 1 history. *Academic units recommended:* 4 English, 4 science, 3 foreign language, 3 social studies, 1 history.

Financial Aid

Students should submit: FAFSA, institution's own financial aid form, CSS/Financial Aid PROFILE, state aid form, noncustodial PROFILE, business/farm supplement. The Princeton Review suggests that all financial aid forms be submitted as soon as possible after January 1. *Need-based scholarships/grants offered:* Federal Pell, SEOG, state scholarships/grants, private scholarships. *Loan aid offered:* Direct Subsidized Stafford, Direct Unsubsidized Stafford, Direct PLUS, Federal Perkins, college/university loans from institutional funds. Applicants will be notified of awards on or about April 15. Federal Work-Study Program available. Institutional employment available.

The Inside Word

Each Caltech application receives three independent reads before it's presented to the admissions committee. This ensures that all candidates receive a thorough evaluation. The school values the unique drive and energy of its current students and desires applicants who display a similar combination of creativity and intellect. Stellar academic credentials are a must, and prospective students must display an aptitude for math and science.

THE SCHOOL SAYS ". . ."

From the Admissions Office

"Admission to the freshman class is based on many factors—some quantifiable, some not. What you say in your application is important! Because we don't interview students for admission, your letters of recommendation are weighed heavily. High school academic performance is very important, as is a demonstrated interest in math, science, and/or engineering. We are also interested in your character, maturity, and motivation. We are very proud of the process we use to select each freshman class. It's very individual, it has great integrity, and we believe it serves all the students who apply. If you have any questions about the process or about Caltech in general, write us a letter or give us a call. We'd like to hear from you!

"Freshman applicants must submit scores from either the SAT or ACT. In addition, students must submit the results of two SAT Subject Tests: mathematics IIC and one of the following—biology (ecological or molecular), chemistry, or physics."

SELECTIVITY	
Admissions Rating	**99**
# of applicants	5,225
% of applicants accepted	13
% of acceptees attending	37
# accepting a place on wait list	556
# admitted from wait list	40
# of early decision applicants	1,395
# accepted early decision	268

FRESHMAN PROFILE	
Range SAT Critical Reading	700–790
Range SAT Math	760–800
Range SAT Writing	700–790
Range ACT Composite	33–35
% graduated top 10% of class	97
% graduated top 25% of class	100
% graduated top 50% of class	100

DEADLINES	
Early action	
Deadline	11/1
Notification	12/15
Regular	
Deadline	1/1
Notification	4/1
Nonfall registration?	no

FINANCIAL FACTS	
Financial Aid Rating	**98**
Annual tuition	$38,050
Room and board	$12,084
Required fees	$1,503
Books and supplies	$1,323
% needy frosh rec. need-based scholarship or grant aid	100
% needy UG rec. need-based scholarship or grant aid	100
% needy frosh rec. non-need-based scholarship or grant aid	3
% needy UG rec. non-need-based scholarship or grant aid	6
% needy frosh rec. need-based self-help aid	61
% needy UG rec. need-based self-help aid	79
% frosh rec. any financial aid	60
% UG rec. any financial aid	60
% UG borrow to pay for school	43
Average cumulative indebtedness	$13,442
% frosh need fully met	100
% ugrads need fully met	100
Average % of frosh need met	100
Average % of ugrad need met	100

California State University Stanislaus

One University Circle, Turlock, CA 95382 • Admissions: 209-667-3070 • Fax: 209-667-3788

CAMPUS LIFE

Quality of Life Rating	91
Fire Safety Rating	94
Green Rating	88
Type of school	public
Environment	town

STUDENTS

Total undergrad enrollment	7,911
% male/female	36/64
% from out of state	1
% from public high school	93
% frosh live on campus	25
# of fraternities	7
# of sororities	9
% African American	3
% Asian	11
% Caucasian	33
% Hispanic	39
% Native American	1
% international	1
# of countries represented	27

SURVEY SAYS . . .

Diverse student types on campus
Low cost of living
Very little drug use

ACADEMICS

Academic Rating	72
% students returning for sophomore year	87
% students graduating within 4 years	22
% students graduating within 6 years	49
Calendar	semester
Student/faculty ratio	24:1
Profs interesting rating	84
Profs accessible rating	70
Most classes have	20–29 students
Most lab/discussion sessions have	20–29 students

MOST POPULAR MAJORS

business/commerce; liberal arts and sciences/liberal studies; criminal justice

STUDENTS SAY ". . ."

Academics

One of the members of California's noted state university system, Stanislaus "provides affordable education" that focuses on helping students prepare for their careers with a "professional, yet laid-back demeanor." This is "a great environment to be a part of," and the school "wants you to succeed, and they give you the info you need to succeed." Many of the students here live nearby, and the in-state tuition offers "rigorous" academics and "a great place to meet mentors and learn different approaches to life." Professors get mixed but mainly positive reviews; "Some are excellent…go above and beyond," and are "wonderful at helping the students as much as they can," but others are just "fair," and "some should not be teaching." Registration could use some rejiggering; students say that the registration priority needs to change each semester, and the more popular departments could use "more of the same classes offered every semester, with multiple sections." Still, for higher-level classes, "small class sizes where you are able to get a lot of help from professors" are a huge boon. Nursing and business are some of "the strongest subjects that come out of here," and it is "very inexpensive for a fully accredited business degree" relative to many other schools. In constructing well-prepared students, Stanislaus personnel are "attentive" on all fronts. "Very rarely are any of your classes taught by a graduate student or someone without a PhD," says a student. The accessibility of departments and staff is "always very easy," and "They are very informative with upcoming changes or events." Job placement is a huge end goal for Stanislaus, and "helping students (especially veterans) during these rough economic times is a priority at CSU Stanislaus."

Life

Though Stanislaus offers "scenery is as beautiful and varied as the students" and "awesome" weather, popular complaints are that "buildings need updating" and "there are too many geese on the grounds." The university's efforts in providing "a ton of organizations on campus" give the commuter students "a college experience like that of any other student living on campus." "It's nice that the school recognizes that we need a break sometimes and promote being a healthy individual, both mind and body," says one student. Events are regularly held in the quad, "student-run shows [such] as dance-offs or karaoke, and "music concerts are regularly held throughout the semesters, usually featuring by guest artists or students." Turlock is "not the biggest town," but there is "easy access to the freeway," and local events and great places "keep everyone occupied." On campus, "There are lounges that you can play pool, darts, video games, etc.," and "Greek life is well-supported." The many commuter students mean that resident community on campus is "small and tightly knit"; there are a fair number of nontraditional students here as well, and they have no problems getting by. "I am an older student, and life on campus is great; everybody accepts me as just another student working toward my degree," says one.

Student Body

Perhaps due to the focus on future careers here, students are "motivated and excited to be at school." "I think we all know that with every class session we are that much closer to graduation," says one. Because the campus is so small, "A big portion of the student life is also Greek." Diversity is "rich" here, and there are "many different ethnicities and culture from all over." Though everyone is friendly and "easygoing," "Typical students keep to themselves but does not hesitant to help another student if he or she asks for it," but even those who want to "can fit in almost anywhere, as most groups found around campus are very accepting."

Financial Aid: 209-667-3336 • E-mail: outreach_help_desk@csustan.edu • Website: www.csustan.edu

THE PRINCETON REVIEW SAYS

Admissions

Very important factors considered include: Academic GPA, rigor of secondary school record, standardized test scores. *Important factors considered include:* Class rank. ACT with or without writing component accepted. TOEFL required of all international applicants. High school diploma is required and GED is accepted. *Academic units required:* 4 English, 3 mathematics, 2 science (2 science labs), 2 foreign language, 1 social studies, 1 history, 1 visual/performing arts, 1 academic elective.

Financial Aid

Students should submit: FAFSA. The Princeton Review suggests that all financial aid forms be submitted as soon as possible after January 1. *Need-based scholarships/grants offered:* Federal Pell, SEOG, state scholarships/grants, private scholarships, the school's own gift aid, Federal Nursing Scholarships. *Loan aid offered:* Direct Subsidized Stafford, Direct Unsubsidized Stafford, Direct PLUS, Federal Perkins, college/university loans from institutional funds. Applicants will be notified of awards on a rolling basis beginning March 15. Federal Work-Study Program available. Institutional employment available. Highest amount earned per year from on-campus jobs $17,680. Off-campus job opportunities are good.

The Inside Word

Like most state schools, CSU Stanislaus admissions practices are fairly straightforward. The university adheres to the eligibility index as defined by the California state system, so applicants who meet GPA and standardized test score minimums are automatically granted admission. Out-of-state candidates face more stringent requirements, as do those applying for highly competitive majors and programs.

THE SCHOOL SAYS ". . ."

From the Admissions Office

"For over fifty years, California State University, Stanislaus, has welcomed students from California's Central Valley and around the world. CSU Stanislaus continues to distinguish itself as an institution that provides top-quality degree programs with a high level of personal attention, offering over 100 undergraduate programs; 25 graduate programs, including a doctorate in educational leadership; 7 credential programs; and 6 certificate programs. With a student-to-faculty ratio of twenty-four to one, CSU Stanislaus demonstrates its commitment to individualized instruction over the more common lecture-hall style of many larger universities. "The university enjoys an ideal location in the Northern San Joaquin Valley, a short distance from the San Francisco Bay Area, Monterey, Big Sur, the Sierra Nevada Mountains and the state capital of Sacramento. The main campus is located in the city of Turlock, a community that prides itself on its small-town atmosphere, clean living space, excellent schools and low crime rate. "Degree programs in these disciplines have earned specialized accreditation: art, business administration, education, genetic counseling, music, nursing, psychology, public administration, social work, and theater. The College of Business Administration and the College of Education have also earned prestigious state and national accreditation. "More than $40 million in merit- and need-based grants and scholarships was awarded for the 2010–2011 school year. Approximately eighty percent of undergraduates receive need-based aid and more than $73 million in total financial assistance is awarded annually. The CSU Stanislaus experience can be summed up as providing a small private school atmosphere at a public school price."

SELECTIVITY	
Admissions Rating	**76**
# of applicants	5,387
% of applicants accepted	77
% of acceptees attending	30

FRESHMAN PROFILE	
Range SAT Critical Reading	400–510
Range SAT Math	410–530
Range SAT Writing	410–510
Range ACT Composite	16–21
Minimum paper TOEFL	500
Minimum web-based TOEFL	61
Average HS GPA	3.3

DEADLINES	
Regular	
Priority	11/30
Deadline	12/15
Nonfall registration?	yes

FINANCIAL FACTS	
Financial Aid Rating	**67**
Annual out-state tuition	$11,160
Room and board	$8,250
Required fees	$5,994
Books and supplies	$1,700
% needy frosh rec. need-based scholarship or grant aid	97
% needy UG rec. need-based scholarship or grant aid	94
% needy frosh rec. non-need-based scholarship or grant aid	9
% needy UG rec. non-need-based scholarship or grant aid	4
% needy frosh rec. need-based self-help aid	52
% needy UG rec. need-based self-help aid	87
% frosh rec. any financial aid	60
% UG rec. any financial aid	76
% UG borrow to pay for school	49
Average cumulative indebtedness	$15,894
% frosh need fully met	23
% ugrads need fully met	5
Average % of frosh need met	68
Average % of ugrad need met	63

Calvin College

3201 Burton Street Southeast, Grand Rapids, MI 49546 • Admissions: 616-526-6106 • Fax: 616-526-6777

CAMPUS LIFE

Quality of Life Rating	**88**
Fire Safety Rating	**68**
Green Rating	**73**
Type of school	private
Affiliation	Christian Reformed
Environment	city

STUDENTS

Total undergrad enrollment	3,797
% male/female	47/53
% from out of state	44
% from public high school	44
% frosh live on campus	97
% African American	3
% Asian	4
% Caucasian	77
% Hispanic	3
% international	9
# of countries represented	54

SURVEY SAYS . . .

Students get along with local community
Great off-campus food
Low cost of living
Frats and sororities are unpopular or nonexistent
Musical organizations are popular
Very little drug use

ACADEMICS

Academic Rating	**81**
% students returning for sophomore year	87
% students graduating within 4 years	60
% students graduating within 6 years	77
Calendar	4-1-4
Student/faculty ratio	11:1
Profs interesting rating	86
Profs accessible rating	89
Most classes have	20–29 students
Most lab/discussion sessions have	10–19 students

MOST POPULAR MAJORS

business/commerce; engineering; nursing/registered nurse (rn, asn, bsn, msn)

APPLICANTS ALSO LOOK AT AND OFTEN PREFER

Wheaton College (IL)

AND SOMETIMES PREFER

University of Michigan—Ann Arbor, Grand Valley State University

AND RARELY PREFER

Western Michigan University, Michigan State University

STUDENTS SAY ". . ."

Academics

Calvin College is a small liberal arts college with "an excellent reputation as a Christian and academic institute." The college is associated with the Christian Reformed Church and has a definite Christian focus. "Calvin prepares people for successful lives of service and building of the Kingdom of God." Calvin takes academics seriously and works to engage "the entire academic world without compromising its Christian worldview." At the same time, "Academic freedom is somewhat limited by the school's religious affiliation." Calvin works hard to make college "affordable for everyone that comes here" and "has a very beautiful campus with amazing people. "I always feel as if I have support and guidance in any of my choices," one student says. Students are very high on the professors, who "make their subjects fascinating" and "genuinely care about the students." "Not only do they know their stuff, but they will go above and beyond to help you." However, students disagree on the rigor of the academics. "Good professors, but [the class work is] very rigorous. Sometimes the standards are unattainably high," one student complains. Another student counters, saying, "Academics aren't always as rigorous as I might hope, but my professors are engaging and enthusiastic." One student sums Calvin up simply: "Small class sizes, good faculty, and good facilities all contribute to make this a strong school."

Life

Campus life at Calvin is influenced by its faith commitments. "If you want to go out and party like the stereotypical college life, you'll have to get off campus" because "if you do drink alcohol or smoke weed, you get kicked out immediately." There are many events on campus and "tons of fun activities to do with people in your dorm—floor dates with crazy Salvation Army outfits, ice skating, weekend retreats, roller skating, and serenading other dorms on campus." Off campus, the streets are "loaded with malls, movie theaters, bowling alleys, restaurants, and stores, so there is never a dull moment." Students look forward to "receiving a good education toward [their] major as well as spiritual growth." The college makes sure that "there are tons of opportunities and organizations for students to get involved [in] outside of the classroom. It builds community very efficiently and rapidly." In general, the small "student body and campus size promote a social atmosphere wherein each student may feel a strong sense of community, friendship and belonging."

Student Body

Most students at Calvin "have grown up in Christian homes" and "are largely from the same mold: religiously steadfast, politically center-right, and Midwestern in values (if not origin)." Although the school is affiliated with the Christian Reformed Church, there's a range of evangelical students and a spectrum of political leanings. "Calvin students are really into social justice issues," one student proudly says. "They want to change the world." Many students appreciate the religious atmosphere. "I feel Christ around me every day, all the time," one student says. However, for others, "The Christian atmosphere can be restricting." Some students lovingly joke, "The stereotypical Calvin student is tall, blond, and Dutch and grew up within a thirty-mile radius of Grand Rapids," but at the same time, "There are plenty of internationals and students from other states, too." The school could still do more to bring "in a more diverse student body. Not only racially, but regionally as well. It seems that most of the students are from Michigan or the surrounding states." However, the small student body creates a close community. "We are learning to live, and living to learn: socially, academically, and spiritually together."

FINANCIAL AID: 800-688-0122 • E-MAIL: ADMISSIONS@CALVIN.EDU • WEBSITE: WWW.CALVIN.EDU

THE PRINCETON REVIEW SAYS

Admissions

Very important factors considered include: Academic GPA, rigor of secondary school record, standardized test scores, religious affiliation/commitment. *Important factors considered include:* Application essay, recommendation(s), character/personal qualities, extracurricular activities. *Other factors considered include:* Class rank, level of applicant's interest, volunteer work, work experience. SAT or ACT required; ACT with or without writing component accepted. TOEFL required of all international applicants. High school diploma is required and GED is accepted. *Academic units required:* 3 English, 3 mathematics, 2 science, 2 social studies, 3 academic electives. *Academic units recommended:* 4 English, 3 mathematics, 2 science (1 science lab), 2 foreign language, 3 social studies, 3 academic electives.

Financial Aid

Students should submit: FAFSA. The Princeton Review suggests that all financial aid forms be submitted as soon as possible after January 1. *Need-based scholarships/grants offered:* Federal Pell, SEOG, state scholarships/grants, private scholarships, the school's own gift aid. *Loan aid offered:* Direct Subsidized Stafford, Direct Unsubsidized Stafford, Direct PLUS, Federal Perkins, state loans, college/university loans from institutional funds, alternative educational loans. Applicants will be notified of awards on a rolling basis beginning March 15. Federal Work-Study Program available. Institutional employment available. Highest amount earned per year from on-campus jobs $5,000. Off-campus job opportunities are excellent.

The Inside Word

Calvin College's website sports the following slogan: "Distinctively Christian, Academically Excellent, Always Reforming." Christian students who seek academic excellence without sacrificing their religious values should find a nurturing environment and a strong education at Calvin.

THE SCHOOL SAYS ". . ."

From the Admissions Office

"Calvin's respected faculty, innovative core curriculum, and well-qualified student body come together in an environment that links intellectual freedom with a heart for service. Calvin's 400-acre campus is home to nearly 4,000 students and 380 professors who chose Calvin because of its international reputation for academic excellence combined with faith-shaped learning.

"Calvin students come from near and far, with a record-setting 2010–2011 class that included ten percent international students and nearly twelve percent racial or ethnic minorities. Calvin encourages students to explore all things and offers nearly 100 majors, minors, and accredited professional programs to choose among.

"Quality teaching and accessibility to students are considered top priorities by faculty members. More than eighty-two percent of Calvin professors hold the highest degree in their field, the student/faculty ratio is eleven to one, and the average class size is twenty-two. In the past four years, Calvin has produced seven Fulbright Scholars. Calvin professors lead thirteen different semester-long study abroad programs and more than thirty January interim courses that take students into other countries and cultures. The Open Doors report of the Institute for International Education consistently ranks Calvin among the top five baccalaureate colleges for the number of students who complete a short-term study abroad.

"Before they graduate, more than eighty percent of Calvin students report having at least one internship, a great way for students to try their individual gifts in the workplace while gaining professional experience. In a survey of recent graduates, nearly 100 percent of responders report that they had either secured a job or begun graduate school within six months of graduation. Calvin is among the top five percent of four-year private colleges in the number of graduates who go on to earn a PhD."

SELECTIVITY	
Admissions Rating	**80**
# of applicants	3,182
% of applicants accepted	75
% of acceptees attending	40

FRESHMAN PROFILE	
Range SAT Critical Reading	500–650
Range SAT Math	530–660
Range ACT Composite	23–29
Minimum paper TOEFL	550
Minimum web-based TOEFL	80
Average HS GPA	3.6
% graduated top 10% of class	28
% graduated top 25% of class	53
% graduated top 50% of class	83

DEADLINES	
Regular Deadline	8/15
Nonfall registration?	yes

FINANCIAL FACTS	
Financial Aid Rating	**79**
Annual tuition	$25,340
Room and board	$8,760
Required fees	$225
Books and supplies	$1,010
% needy frosh rec. need-based scholarship or grant aid	100
% needy UG rec. need-based scholarship or grant aid	99
% needy frosh rec. non-need-based scholarship or grant aid	16
% needy UG rec. non-need-based scholarship or grant aid	16
% needy frosh rec. need-based self-help aid	89
% needy UG rec. need-based self-help aid	92
% frosh rec. any financial aid	96
% UG rec. any financial aid	95
% UG borrow to pay for school	63
Average cumulative indebtedness	$32,957
% frosh need fully met	20
% ugrads need fully met	20
Average % of frosh need met	77
Average % of ugrad need met	74

CARLETON COLLEGE

100 SOUTH COLLEGE STREET, NORTHFIELD, MN 55057 • ADMISSIONS: 507-222-4190 • TOLL FREE: 800-995-2275 • FAX: 507-222-4526

CAMPUS LIFE

Quality of Life Rating	93
Fire Safety Rating	65
Green Rating	93
Type of school	private
Environment	village

STUDENTS

Total undergrad enrollment	2,000
% male/female	48/52
% from out of state	78
% from public high school	60
% frosh live on campus	100
% African American	4
% Asian	7
% Caucasian	68
% Hispanic	6
% international	8
# of countries represented	42

SURVEY SAYS . . .

No one cheats
School is well run
Campus feels safe
Frats and sororities are unpopular or nonexistent

ACADEMICS

Academic Rating	98
% students returning for sophomore year	96
% students graduating within 4 years	88
% students graduating within 6 years	93
Calendar	trimester
Student/faculty ratio	9:1
Profs interesting rating	98
Profs accessible rating	98
Most classes have	10–19 students
Most lab/discussion sessions have	10–19 students

MOST POPULAR MAJORS

biology/biological sciences; economics; political science and government

APPLICANTS ALSO LOOK AT AND OFTEN PREFER

Williams College, Yale University

AND SOMETIMES PREFER

Washington University in St. Louis

AND RARELY PREFER

Oberlin College, Macalester College

STUDENTS SAY ". . ."

Academics

Students seeking a "top-notch" and "cooperative…learning environment that challenges students without leaving them overwhelmed" will find a happy home at Carleton College, an extremely rigorous liberal arts school characterized by what students call "collaborative academia." The "phenomenal" professors, in particular, who "focus on teaching" rather than on research and "seek out…personal relationships with all of their students" are a huge draw. As one undergraduate says, "One of my biology professors got an ovation at the end of the last class of the term." Class sizes have fewer than twenty-five students, with the exception of introductory science classes, and as one student explains, professors "have answered my e-mails past midnight and been available in their offices past 10:00 P.M." Carleton also supports its students with "a plethora of resources" like "a really cool system that gives science, math, and many social science classes student tutors or 'prefects' who have already taken the class and are available for group or one-on-one help" and the Math Skills Center, which "provides tutoring, homework help, and a great space to study." The school could "get better about supporting students in the arts," but "Most professors are very open to pursuing independent studies with students who choose a particular subject that is not offered." Carleton has also opened the new Weitz Center for Creativity as part of an expanding arts program.

Life

While "quaint," Northfield and its "coffee shops, thrift stores, random little bookstores and art shops, [and] restaurants" are "minutes away," Carleton life, or "the famous Carleton Bubble," centers around a balance between "study hard, party hard," and it's "pretty easy to get completely wrapped in what's happening on campus." Weekends bustle with activity since "people go a little bit insane from overwork during the week," and as one student put it, "I often find myself attending a concert at the Cave, the student pub; going to a show one of my friends wrote at the Little Nourse Theater; taking a quick trip to the cities for Mall of America or an uptown excursion; or, most likely, having a surprisingly engaging and deep intellectual discussion with some friends at a party on a Friday night." Intramural sports such as broomball and ultimate Frisbee are "freakishly popular," and "campus traditions are rich and plentiful." Another "huge draw is the Arboretum, an 800-acre forest where students go for runs, go snow-shoeing, or have camp fires;" there is also always the option to "bake cookies at Dacie Moses house." In terms of the party scene, "you can usually find somewhere to do it," and "there's a pretty good gradient—some people live substance free, some people drink heavily every weekend, but most people are somewhere in between." As one student says, "Whichever path you choose, you're bound to make friends."

Student Body

"Quirky," "passionate," and "nerdy" are a few words undergraduates fondly use to describe the community at Carleton. As one student explains, "Due to some sort of unexplainable Carleton magic, a motley crew of odd, but intelligent and disciplined individuals come together at Carleton for an excellent and challenging four years." Another student describes her reasons for choosing Carleton: "Almost everyone is friendly—and I don't mean that only groups of people are friendly, I mean that practically any individual you could come across has this desire in them to learn in a positive environment, which I think is so intense that it translates into sharing that desire with others through encouragement and assistance." The student body reflects geographic diversity but could improve on reflecting more "diversity with political and social backgrounds." Still, "People are very self-aware, but not self-centered," and "The best part about that is that they all keep really open minds."

FINANCIAL AID: 507-222-4138 • E-MAIL: ADMISSIONS@CARLETON.EDU • WEBSITE: WWW.CARLETON.EDU

THE PRINCETON REVIEW SAYS

Admissions

Very important factors considered include: Class rank, academic GPA, rigor of secondary school record. *Important factors considered include:* Application essay, recommendation(s), standardized test scores, alumni/ae relation, character/personal qualities, extracurricular activities, racial/ethnic status, talent/ability, volunteer work, work experience. *Other factors considered include:* First generation, geographical residence, interview, state residency. SAT or ACT required; ACT with writing component required. TOEFL required of all international applicants. High school diploma is required and GED is accepted. *Academic units recommended:* 4 English, 3 mathematics, 3 science (1 science lab), 3 foreign language, 3 social studies and history.

Financial Aid

Students should submit: FAFSA, CSS/Financial Aid PROFILE, noncustodial PROFILE, business/farm supplement. Prior year tax forms. Regular filing deadline is February 15. The Princeton Review suggests that all financial aid forms be submitted as soon as possible after January 1. *Need-based scholarships/grants offered:* Federal Pell, SEOG, state scholarships/grants, private scholarships, the school's own gift aid. *Loan aid offered:* Direct Subsidized Stafford, Direct Unsubsidized Stafford, Direct PLUS, Federal Perkins, state loans, college/university loans from institutional funds, Minnesota SELF Loan program. Applicants will be notified of awards on or about April 1. Federal Work-Study Program available.

The Inside Word

Gaining admission to Carleton is highly competitive. While it is possible to get in without stellar high school grades and test scores if you show tremendous promise or have an exceptional talent, most successful applicants demonstrate all of these qualities. High school records are weighed most heavily here; standardized test scores and your personal essay are also very important. Interviews may not be required, but they are recommended. We encourage you to sit for one, even if you can't schedule a campus visit; local reps are usually available to interview you in or near your hometown.

THE SCHOOL SAYS ". . ."

From the Admissions Office

"In an annual college freshmen survey, Carleton students identify themselves as everything from conservatives to liberals, with a majority of them falling in the moderate to liberal range. Although individualistic and energetic Carls take their academics seriously, they don't take themselves seriously. Participation in athletics, theater or music, religious events, or dining hall discussions marks the Carleton experience. The College recently opened two new LEED-certified, environmentally friendly residence halls and the new Weitz Center for Creativity, 134,000 square feet of performance, rehearsal, exhibition, teaching, and collaboration space. With nearly three-fifths of the student body receiving need-based grant aid, there is a broad socioeconomic representation across the student body. Eight percent of all students are international, and twenty-one percent come from traditionally underrepresented groups, and about eight percent are first-generation students. A look at majors in the past decade shows that graduates cover all areas, with about one-third of them in each of the following: math/science, humanities and arts, and social sciences. More than two-thirds of all students will spend time earning class credits off campus; Carleton participates in programs worldwide from Asia to Africa. You can scuba dive off the Great Barrier Reef or walk the Great Wall of China. Within ten years of graduating, about seventy-five percent of alumni pursue graduate or professional degrees. Carleton ranks third among liberal arts colleges in the number of PhDs earned by its alumni."

SELECTIVITY

Admissions Rating	**97**
# of applicants	$4,988
% of applicants accepted	31
% of acceptees attending	33
# accepting a place on wait list	165
# admitted from wait list	64
# of early decision applicants	416
# accepted early decision	211

FRESHMAN PROFILE

Range SAT Critical Reading	660–750
Range SAT Math	660–760
Range SAT Writing	660–750
Range ACT Composite	29–33
Minimum paper TOEFL	600
Minimum web-based TOEFL	100
% graduated top 10% of class	78
% graduated top 25% of class	98
% graduated top 50% of class	100

DEADLINES

Early decision	
Deadline	11/15 and 1/15
Notification	1/15 and 2/15
Regular	
Deadline	1/15
Notification	4/1
Nonfall registration?	no

FINANCIAL FACTS

Financial Aid Rating	**98**
Annual tuition	$44,184
Room and board	$11,553
Required fees	$261
Books and supplies	$1,502
% needy frosh rec. need-based scholarship or grant aid	100
% needy UG rec. need-based scholarship or grant aid	100
% needy frosh rec. non-need-based scholarship or grant aid	16
% needy UG rec. non-need-based scholarship or grant aid	18
% needy frosh rec. need-based self-help aid	97
% needy UG rec. need-based self-help aid	98
% frosh rec. any financial aid	60
% UG rec. any financial aid	62
% UG borrow to pay for school	45
Average cumulative indebtedness	$19,436
% frosh need fully met	100
% ugrads need fully met	100
Average % of frosh need met	100
Average % of ugrad need met	100

CARNEGIE MELLON UNIVERSITY

5000 FORBES AVENUE, PITTSBURGH, PA 15213 • ADMISSIONS: 412-268-2082 • FAX: 412-268-7838

CAMPUS LIFE

Quality of Life Rating	88
Fire Safety Rating	92
Green Rating	96
Type of school	private
Environment	metropolis

STUDENTS

Total undergrad enrollment	6,178
% male/female	58/42
% from out of state	84
% frosh live on campus	99
# of fraternities	14
# of sororities	8
% African American	5
% Asian	22
% Caucasian	40
% Hispanic	7
% international	17
# of countries represented	118

SURVEY SAYS . . .

Lab facilities are great
Great computer facilities
Diverse student types on campus
Campus feels safe
Theater is popular

ACADEMICS

Academic Rating	87
% students graduating within 4 years	71
% students graduating within 6 years	87
Calendar	semester
Student/faculty ratio	12:1
Profs interesting rating	80
Profs accessible rating	87
Most classes have	fewer than 10 students
Most lab/discussion sessions have	20–29 students

MOST POPULAR MAJORS

computer science

STUDENTS SAY ". . ."

Academics

The dedicated students at Carnegie Mellon range from the hard-core engineers to the artsiest of drama students (making it "a breeding ground for interdisciplinary collaboration"); however, the school's motto—"My heart is in the work"—rings true for all "because of the amount of schoolwork that is required." The school, envisioned by Andrew Carnegie in 1900, gives students the opportunity to become experts in their chosen field while studying a broad range of course work across disciplines. The difficulty of the classes and high expectations from your professors "push you to do your best work. You really do learn in every aspect of academics." "We are in it together to defeat the class rather than ourselves," says a student. The interdisciplinary environment that the school crafts is backed by the tremendous resources afforded students in whatever they choose, particularly engineering, math, science, physics students, and drama, or design majors, at which the school "practically throws opportunities (internships, guidance)." Though the course work is admittedly "stressful," the professors "care immensely about their students," and the "we're all in it together" mantra is a universal refrain. "Academically, you get challenged, but so does everyone else, so the work-heavy culture becomes a social thing," says a student. Though there "have been a few ehh professors," for the most part, they are "extremely vested" in students' learning and "have always been accessible and eager to help with whatever I need." Much as its mission statement promises, CMU "provides excellent preparation for your future, especially the career center." The residence life staff, RAs, and housefellows are also "really committed to improving the social aspects of college." For those who know what they want, there are "unlimited opportunities to pursue your passions." "It is nice to know I will get a good degree, but that it is also unique to me," says a student.

Life

"Most of the students here really push themselves to the max," and most social activity "is based off of academics." "Everyone can find a little niche to fit into and thrive in because there are just so many opportunities to take advantage of." Despite the number of hours spent hitting the books, CMU has a decidedly non-competitive atmosphere: "It's not about being THE best, it's about giving the best performance." Discussions "are just at a higher level," and if students have to work late into a Friday evening, then so be it. "Still, everyone appreciates down time." The mix of student interests and majors provides a curious but totally harmonious balance at every turn: "Carnegie Mellon is the only place where you will see engineers working while an art installation goes in above their heads." Most here "have extremely full plates and are very dedicated to a variety of clubs and interests," but "not everyone is very social." "They say you get to pick two: sleep, good grades, or a social life," goes the mantra. Still, in their spare time, "there is a massive video game 'community,'" and the popular Greek life "is very different here than at a lot of schools, and it is a great way to open up lots of experiences." The Pittsburgh location offers a "safe campus…but it is still within a city that offers many things to do," including free entry into all museums, "great restaurants, and sports teams."

Student Body

There is "no race, religion or special interest [that] takes up more than half" of Carnegie Mellon students; basically, "a few crazy people, a bunch of eccentric people, and a ton of great people rule this place." Everybody is "all quirky in an endearing way," and "there is literally a niche for anything someone could want." "We're all weird in our own way—we're either a scientist or artist so we can seem a strange bunch…eventually the labels artist or scientist fades, and you become friends with people from all over campus," says a student. Basically, all are "closet nerds," "insanely driven," and "all have hidden talents"; however, one common bond abides: "A typical student gets *Monty Python* jokes."

FINANCIAL AID: 412-268-8186 • E-MAIL: UNDERGRADUATE-ADMISSIONS@ANDREW.CMU.EDU • WEBSITE: WWW.CMU.EDU

THE PRINCETON REVIEW SAYS

Admissions

Important factors considered include: Class rank, academic GPA, rigor of secondary school record, standardized test scores, application essay, recommendation(s), alumni/ae relation, character/personal qualities, extracurricular activities, first generation, interview, level of applicant's interest, racial/ethnic status, talent/ability, volunteer work, work experience. SAT or ACT required; ACT with writing component required. TOEFL required of all international applicants. High school diploma is required and GED is accepted. *Academic units required:* 4 English, 4 mathematics, 3 science (3 science labs), 2 foreign language, 3 academic electives. *Academic units recommended:* 4 English, 4 mathematics, 3 science (3 science labs), 2 foreign language, 4 academic electives.

Financial Aid

Students should submit: FAFSA, CSS PROFILE, parent and student federal tax returns, parent W-2 forms. Regular filing deadline is May 1. The Princeton Review suggests that all financial aid forms be submitted as soon as possible after January 1. *Need-based scholarships/grants offered:* Federal Pell, SEOG, state scholarships/grants, private scholarships, the school's own gift aid. *Loan aid offered:* Direct Subsidized Stafford, Direct Unsubsidized Stafford, Direct PLUS, Federal Perkins. Applicants will be notified of awards on or about March 15. Federal Work-Study Program available. Institutional employment available. Off-campus job opportunities are good.

The Inside Word

Don't be misled by Carnegie Mellon's acceptance rate. Although relatively high for a university of this caliber, the applicant pool is fairly self-selecting. If you haven't loaded up on demanding courses in high school, you're not likely to be a serious contender. The admissions office explicitly states that it doesn't use formulas when making decisions. That said, a record of strong academic performance in the area of your intended major is key. Each of the school's seven colleges has varying academic and testing requirements; the various majors in the College of the Fine Arts can also require an essay, portfolio, or audition.

THE SCHOOL SAYS ". . ."

From the Admissions Office

"If you're looking for an intellectual environment that blends academic and artistic richness with classroom innovation, explore Carnegie Mellon. Consistently ranked as a top twenty-five institution, Carnegie Mellon is world-renowned for its unique approach to education and research. Left-brain and right-brain thinking unite within our collaborative culture, and is the foundation of learning at Carnegie Mellon."

"As a student, you will acquire a depth and breadth of knowledge while sharpening your problem-solving, critical thinking, creative and quantitative skills. You will develop sound critical judgment, resourcefulness and professional ethics through a collaborative and hands-on education. As a graduate, you will be one of the innovative leaders and problem-solvers of tomorrow."

"While a Carnegie Mellon education is marked by a strong focus on fundamental and versatile problem-solving skills in a particular discipline, your talents and interests don't remain confined to one area. The university respects academic diversity and provides opportunities for you to explore more than one field of study. Carnegie Mellon consists of seven colleges (six undergraduate): Carnegie Institute of Technology (engineering), College of Fine Arts, Dietrich College of Humanities and Social Sciences (combining liberal arts education with professional specializations), Tepper School of Business, Mellon College of Science, the School of Computer Science, and the Heinz College. Here, music, molecular science, acting, analysis, opera and organic chemistry weave in and out of the lives and minds of Carnegie Mellon students on a daily basis."

"The university's 150-acre main campus is located in the Oakland area of Pittsburgh, five miles from downtown."

SELECTIVITY	
Admissions Rating	**97**
# of applicants	16,527
% of applicants accepted	30
% of acceptees attending	29
# accepting a place on wait list	5,003
# admitted from wait list	6
# of early decision applicants	885
# accepted early decision	308

FRESHMAN PROFILE	
Range SAT Critical Reading	630–730
Range SAT Math	680–780
Range SAT Writing	640–740
Range ACT Composite	29–33
Minimum paper TOEFL	600
Minimum web-based TOEFL	102
Average HS GPA	3.7
% graduated top 10% of class	75
% graduated top 25% of class	92
% graduated top 50% of class	99

DEADLINES	
Early decision	
Deadline	11/1
Notification	12/15
Regular	
Deadline	1/1
Notification	4/15
Nonfall registration?	no

FINANCIAL FACTS	
Financial Aid Rating	**80**
Annual tuition	$44,880
Room and board	$11,550
Required fees	$872
Books and supplies	$2,400
% needy frosh rec. need-based scholarship or grant aid	95
% needy UG rec. need-based scholarship or grant aid	94
% needy frosh rec. non-need-based scholarship or grant aid	37
% needy UG rec. non-need-based scholarship or grant aid	38
% needy frosh rec. need-based self-help aid	96
% needy UG rec. need-based self-help aid	95
% frosh rec. any financial aid	58
% UG rec. any financial aid	48
% UG borrow to pay for school	46
Average cumulative indebtedness	$29,303
% frosh need fully met	29
% ugrads need fully met	30
Average % of frosh need met	83
Average % of ugrad need met	83

CASE WESTERN RESERVE UNIVERSITY

WOLSTEIN HALL, CLEVELAND, OH 44106-7055 • ADMISSIONS: 216-368-4450 • FAX: 216-368-5111

CAMPUS LIFE

Quality of Life Rating	71
Fire Safety Rating	73
Green Rating	92
Type of school	private
Environment	metropolis

STUDENTS

Total undergrad enrollment	3,929
% male/female	57/43
% from out of state	62
% from public high school	70
% frosh live on campus	97
# of fraternities	16
# of sororities	8
% African American	4
% Asian	17
% Caucasian	54
% Hispanic	3
% international	7
# of countries represented	30

SURVEY SAYS . . .

Lab facilities are great
Great computer facilities
Great library
Great off-campus food
Low cost of living
Student publications are popular
Student government is popular

ACADEMICS

Academic Rating	81
% students returning for sophomore year	93
% students graduating within 4 years	60
Calendar	semester
Student/faculty ratio	9:1
Profs interesting rating	70
Profs accessible rating	76
Most classes have	10–19 students
Most lab/discussion sessions have	20–29 students

MOST POPULAR MAJORS

biology/biological sciences; biomedical/medical engineering; psychology

APPLICANTS ALSO LOOK AT AND OFTEN PREFER

Northwestern University, Washington University in St. Louis

AND SOMETIMES PREFER

University of Pittsburgh—Pittsburgh Campus, Boston University, Carnegie Mellon University, The Ohio State University—Columbus

AND RARELY PREFER

Pennsylvania State University—University Park, University of Rochester, Purdue University—West Lafayette

STUDENTS SAY ". . ."

Academics

If you want a school "huge" in research, then CWRU may be the choice for you. This "hidden gem" in Cleveland, Ohio, "deserves at least a second look." At CWRU, you have "the chance to do research [in] a world-class medical school," to take part in one of the "strong engineering programs with numerous undergraduate research opportunities," to participate in an "aerospace program connected to NASA," or to gain "clinical experience in [a] hospital setting" during a nursing program freshman year. "You can study almost anything, get involved in just about any type of research, and you aren't limited by what's available. The only limit you have is what you can imagine." This "midsize school" is for serious, "intellectual individuals looking to pursue a first-class education." CWRU is "a very self-starting campus, so if you are not used to some degree of independence, you might be in over your head." However, "This school has a lot of resources, both materials and people, for students to utilize and grab on to, especially when they're struggling." "Professors are "great," although there may be a "couple of exceptions." Some "aren't quite as entertaining as others, but they are all passionate about what they teach." One fourth-year student comments, "[My] professors have become personal friends and mentors who guide me in cutting-edge research. This provides me with an unbeatable education." Another student says, "The professors I have had are absolutely amazing. They come from various backgrounds. I have had a history professor who is a former chemist for the FDA, a political science professor who is a former employee of the United Nations, and a geology professor who is an Antarctic researcher. The professors are all extremely approachable, very kind, and highly accessible, and they make the students an enormous part of their lives."

Life

Due to the high academic standards, "Life here can be stressful at times, but there is always a support group of close and understanding friends or faculty to help you through it." "There are plenty of service groups and even a service fraternity. There are political activism clubs, musical groups, theater groups, Greek chapters, and so much more." "Greek Life is not at all like the stereotype, but it instead aims for community involvement, better academics, and creating a home away from home." Weekends offer many choices for entertainment. "There are parties, which are fun, but they're not too excessive at Case." "Student affairs groups on campus provide a pretty nice variety of events in which students may participate, ranging from skiing or skydiving, to free Cleveland Orchestra tickets or on campus concerts." Students find there "is a ton to do downtown, as well as in the areas around campus." Explorations include "visiting all the different museums, the aquarium, botanical gardens, an Indians or Browns game, [or] one of the many restaurants." Not all students are comfortable with transportation options to explore Cleveland in the evenings, as it "can get sketchy at night."

Student Body

CWRU "attracts a very diverse group of students" who are "extremely intelligent and know exactly what they want to do with their life and understand that education is the key to their future." Students "come from all different parts of the country, and world, yet still interact very well with one another." They "work hard for good grades," and "most (if not all) are focused on individual improvement and achievement, and not on beating everyone else." So although they are competitive with themselves, they are "helpful to one another." "Most...are overachievers, but it's hard to meet someone who is over-competitive. Most people are friendly and hard workers." Since "most students were the nerd in high school," "dorkiness (e.g., *Lord of the Rings* obsessions) is highly accepted here." With fellow classmates it's "easy to talk about technical things that would have been difficult to discuss with most people off-campus."

FINANCIAL AID: 216-368-4530 • E-MAIL: ADMISSION@CASE.EDU • WEBSITE: WWW.CASE.EDU

THE PRINCETON REVIEW SAYS

Admissions

Very important factors considered include: Class rank, academic GPA, rigor of secondary school record, standardized test scores, extracurricular activities. *Important factors considered include:* Application essay, recommendation(s), character/personal qualities, interview, level of applicant's interest, talent/ability, volunteer work, work experience. *Other factors considered include:* Alumni/ae relation, first generation, racial/ethnic status. SAT or ACT required; ACT with writing component required. TOEFL required of all international applicants. High school diploma is required and GED is accepted. *Academic units required:* 4 English, 3 mathematics, 3 science (2 science labs), 2 foreign language, 3 social studies. *Academic units recommended:* 4 mathematics (3 science labs), 3 foreign language, 4 social studies.

Financial Aid

Students should submit: FAFSA, CSS Finacial Aid PROFILE, institution's own financial aid form, business/farm supplement, parent and student income tax returns and W-2 forms. The Princeton Review suggests that all financial aid forms be submitted as soon as possible after January 1. *Need-based scholarships/grants offered:* Federal Pell, SEOG, state scholarships/grants, private scholarships, the school's own gift aid. *Loan aid offered:* Direct Subsidized Stafford, Direct Unsubsidized Stafford, Direct PLUS, Federal Perkins, Federal Nursing, state loans, college/university loans from institutional funds, alternative loans. Applicants will be notified of awards on a rolling basis beginning March 15. Federal Work-Study Program available. Institutional employment available. Highest amount earned per year from on-campus jobs $3,200. Off-campus job opportunities are excellent.

The Inside Word

CWRU faces tough competition from similar schools and handles it well as both the number of overall applications and out-of-state applications has increased substantially over the past decade, indicating an improving national profile. As a result, CWRU grows ever more selective. CWRU uses a "single-door" admis sions policy, meaning that once you're admitted you can change your intended major without having to reapply, even if it means switching schools (for example, switching from the School of Engineering to the School of Management).

THE SCHOOL SAYS ". . ."

From the Admissions Office

"Challenging and innovative academic programs, next-level technology, experiential learning, real-world environments, and faculty mentors are at the core of the Case Western Reserve University experience. CWRU's faculty challenges and supports motivated students, and its partnerships with world-class cultural, educational, and scientific institutions ensure that your education extends beyond the classroom. CWRU offers more than seventy-five majors and minors and a single-door admission policy; once admitted to CWRU, you can major in any of our programs, or double and even triple major in several of them. Our student/faculty ratio, among the best in the nation, allows students to have close interaction with professors. Co-ops, internships, study abroad, and other opportunities bring theory to life in amazing settings, and sixty-six percent of students participate in research and independent study. SAGES, CWRU's four-year undergraduate core curriculum, connects students with faculty, peers and the community through small seminars that explore effective communication and analytical skills, and culminates in a Senior Capstone project. With eighty-five percent of students living on campus, CWRU has a residential feel unique to urban universities. First-year students live together in one of three themed residential colleges that involve resources from across Northeast Ohio: Cedar (arts), Juniper (world culture), and Mistletoe (leadership through service). Admission Counselors consider all sections of the SAT, taking the best score for each section from multiple dates. The SAT (or ACT with writing) is used for evaluating applications for admission (and not used for course placement purposes)."

SELECTIVITY	
Admissions Rating	**93**
# of applicants	13,545
% of applicants accepted	51
% of acceptees attending	13
# accepting a place on wait list	2,233
# admitted from wait list	419

FRESHMAN PROFILE	
Range SAT Critical Reading	590–700
Range SAT Math	650–740
Range SAT Writing	590–690
Range ACT Composite	28–32
Minimum paper TOEFL	577
Minimum web-based TOEFL	90
% graduated top 10% of class	63
% graduated top 25% of class	92
% graduated top 50% of class	99

DEADLINES	
Early action	
Deadline	11/1
Notification	12/15
Regular	
Deadline	1/15
Notification	3/20
Nonfall registration?	yes

FINANCIAL FACTS	
Financial Aid Rating	**92**
% needy frosh rec. need-based scholarship or grant aid	98
% needy UG rec. need-based scholarship or grant aid	97
% needy frosh rec. non-need-based scholarship or grant aid	96
% needy UG rec. non-need-based scholarship or grant aid	96
% needy frosh rec. need-based self-help aid	80
% needy UG rec. need-based self-help aid	88
% frosh rec. any financial aid	90
% UG rec. any financial aid	84
% UG borrow to pay for school	59
Average cumulative indebtedness	$39,886
% frosh need fully met	76
% ugrads need fully met	85
Average % of frosh need met	92
Average % of ugrad need met	83

Catawba College

2300 West Innes Street, Salisbury, NC 28144 • Admissions: 704-637-4402 • Fax: 704-637-4222

CAMPUS LIFE

Quality of Life Rating	**76**
Fire Safety Rating	**82**
Green Rating	**99**
Type of school	private
Affiliation	United Church of Christ
Environment	town

STUDENTS

Total undergrad enrollment	1,289
% male/female	44/56
% from out of state	22
% from public high school	80
% frosh live on campus	85
# of countries represented	11

SURVEY SAYS . . .

Students are friendly
Students get along with local community
Students are happy
Everyone loves the Catawba Indians
Theater is popular
Student government is popular

ACADEMICS

Academic Rating	**74**
% students graduating within 4 years	43
Calendar	semester
Student/faculty ratio	16:1
Profs interesting rating	85
Profs accessible rating	82
Most classes have	10–19 students
Most lab/discussion sessions have	20–29 students

MOST POPULAR MAJORS

business administration; drama and dramatics/theater arts; elementary education and teaching

APPLICANTS ALSO LOOK AT AND SOMETIMES PREFER

Appalachian State University, The University of North Carolina at Chapel Hill

AND RARELY PREFER

North Carolina State University, The University of North Carolina at Greensboro

STUDENTS SAY ". . ."

Academics

Catawba College sports "a small, close-knit community where you can really get to know your professors and your fellow classmates." The school is known especially for its "high-ranking theater program and the hugely growing music program" as well as its athletics. Don't let its small size fool you, as "big things come in small packages." "Class sizes are small in order for you to receive as much of a personalized education as possible." "Excellent financial aid" attracts many students, although some feel the university isn't doing enough to "increase scholarships to match rising tuition." Catawba is particularly strong for "highly focused programs (theater [and] music in particular)." The honors program also gets high marks among students. "I can get whatever educational experience I make for myself here, especially because of the diversity of the honors program courses." Some students feel that the facilities could be improved. "While our computer labs are good, I feel like that Catawba's computer centers and facilities are not as advanced and developed as [at] other schools." "Most of the professors here really care about the students" and "know your name as well as your interests." As "a melting pot with many opportunities if you reach out for them," Catawba is "a place where you can truly discover who you are through exposure to a variety of thoughts and perspectives."

Life

Life on Catawba campus is driven by the school's strong athletics, theater, and music programs. Students tend to be "busy, busy, busy. Everyone is active. Campus clubs are huge, and there is a school-sponsored event every weekend." There are frequent sporting events, "theater and music performances," and other activities sponsored by the school or clubs. "The students focus a lot on their activities," one student says. "For instance, my life centers around rehearsal for the many performances by the Catawba Singers. The same goes for the theater department as well as athletics." Another student describes life: "My life at school? Class, work in the theater, homework, sleep, rinse, repeat," but also notes that "other students have more free time." "There are usually campus-wide events on the weekends that generally have very high turnouts." When asked what the school could improve on, the chorus responds unanimously: "Food! The food is pretty bad. We pay a lot of money to be here, and our food is sometimes not edible." Consequently, many students leave campus to "go to downtown Salisbury or Charlotte for shopping, restaurants, and clubbing." Note that Catawba does impose an age limit for students to live off campus, although it was recently "lowered to twenty-one."

Student Body

The student body is divided clearly into "three types of students. The athletes are a large make up of the student population. The theater and music students make up the next largest population. Then there is the other category." "We all identify with a category," one student explains, "but that does not mean that we are always divided this way." Others see the campus fairly divided, with the three sections busy in their own work. "Athletes don't go to theater, and theater students don't go to sporting events" although "generally everyone mixes because of our general education classes, so no one really stands out." Students "are either athletes, all about education, or theater/music kids. They all do their own thing, and it works." Most students are from the area, but "thirty-three percent of Catawba students are from out of state." Otherwise, it's "difficult to describe the typical student, because there is such diversity at Catawba College." "Catawba has almost anyone you can imagine, it's a wide array of different cultures of people that go here."

FINANCIAL AID: 704-637-4416 • E-MAIL: ADMISSION@CATAWBA.EDU • WEBSITE: WWW.CATAWBA.EDU

THE PRINCETON REVIEW SAYS

Admissions

Very important factors considered include: Class rank, application essay, academic GPA, recommendation(s), standardized test scores. *Important factors considered include:* Rigor of secondary school record, character/personal qualities, extracurricular activities, interview, level of applicant's interest, talent/ability. *Other factors considered include:* Volunteer work. SAT or ACT required; ACT with writing component recommended. TOEFL or ACT required of all international applicants. High school diploma is required and GED is accepted. *Academic units recommended:* 4 English, 3 mathematics, 3 science (3 science labs), 2 foreign language, 3 social studies.

Financial Aid

Students should submit: FAFSA, state aid form. The Princeton Review suggests that all financial aid forms be submitted as soon as possible after January 1. *Need-based scholarships/grants offered:* Federal Pell, SEOG, state scholarships/grants, private scholarships, the school's own gift aid. *Loan aid offered:* Direct Unsubsidized Stafford, Direct PLUS, Federal Perkins, college/university loans from institutional funds, TERI Loans, Nellie Mae Loans, Advantage Loans, alternative loans. Applicants will be notified of awards on a rolling basis beginning February 15. Federal Work-Study Program available. Institutional employment available. Highest amount earned per year from on-campus jobs $2,000. Off-campus job opportunities are good.

The Inside Word

Since Catawba competes for students with several top regional schools, it's willing to take a chance on students who may not make the cut at Davidson, Chapel Hill, or Duke. Students who may not have been the highest achievers in high school but are ready to excel at the college level should put Catawba on their list. For students of all stripes with an interest in theater or music, Catawba demands consideration.

THE SCHOOL SAYS ". . ."

From the Admissions Office

"Catawba College prepares students for rewarding lives and careers in the liberal arts tradition. This attractive campus is centrally located in Salisbury, North Carolina, a short drive away from the mountains and Atlantic beaches. The community possesses a rich past and commitment to preserving its cultural and historic charm. In contrast, just forty-five minutes away is the much faster pace of Charlotte, North Carolina where shopping, transportation, and entertainment of all kinds are readily available.

"On campus, students study and socialize in a small college setting that offers strong traditions, excellent facilities, and beautiful surroundings. The high standards of quality set by Catawba's academic programs are matched by equally demanding sports and co-curricular programs. Students describe the community as caring and personable. They also exhibit a high rate of involvement in campus activities ranging form the performing arts to homecoming and travel abroad. Faculty and staff are described by students as being important mentors. Whether in a state-of-the-art environmental science facility, attractive music and theatrical performance center, classroom, or one of the college's first-class athletic facilities, students report they feel as if they are among family when on campus.

"Perhaps the most important testimony to the attractiveness of Catawba is found in the words of its graduates who report numerous successful careers and rich memories of their time at school.

"Students applying for admissions to Catawba College are required submit to scores from the SAT, including the writing portion of the test. In lieu of SAT scores, Catawba will accept student scores on the ACT when they include scores on the ACT writing portion of the test. Catawba will use the student's best scores from either test in making admissions decisions."

SELECTIVITY	
Admissions Rating	79
# of applicants	2,710
% of applicants accepted	41
% of acceptees attending	35

FRESHMAN PROFILE	
Range SAT Critical Reading	420–540
Range SAT Math	450–560
Minimum paper TOEFL	525
Average HS GPA	3.4
% graduated top 10% of class	14
% graduated top 25% of class	38
% graduated top 50% of class	67

DEADLINES	
Nonfall registration?	yes

FINANCIAL FACTS	
Financial Aid Rating	77
Annual tuition	$26,040
Room and board	$9,140
Books and supplies	$1,400
% frosh rec. any financial aid	95
% UG rec. any financial aid	95
% UG borrow to pay for school	63
Average cumulative indebtedness	$27,907
Average % of frosh need met	85
Average % of ugrad need met	85

THE CATHOLIC UNIVERSITY OF AMERICA

OFFICE OF UNDERGRADUATE ADMISSIONS, WASHINGTON, D.C. 20064 • ADMISSIONS: 202-319-5305 • FAX: 202-319-6533

CAMPUS LIFE

Quality of Life Rating	**68**
Fire Safety Rating	**84**
Green Rating	**83**
Type of school	private
Affiliation	Roman Catholic
Environment	metropolis

STUDENTS

Total undergrad enrollment	3,544
% male/female	45/55
% from out of state	98
% from public high school	56
% frosh live on campus	90
# of fraternities	1
# of sororities	1
% African American	5
% Asian	3
% Caucasian	62
% Hispanic	8
% international	4
# of countries represented	85

SURVEY SAYS . . .

Students are friendly
Great off-campus food
Frats and sororities are unpopular or nonexistent
Musical organizations are popular
Student government is popular
Political activism is popular
Lots of beer drinking
Hard liquor is popular

ACADEMICS

Academic Rating	**68**
% students returning for sophomore year	80
% students graduating within 4 years	61
% students graduating within 6 years	68
Calendar	semester
Student/faculty ratio	9:1
Profs interesting rating	75
Profs accessible rating	76
Most classes have	10–19 students
Most lab/discussion sessions have	10–19 students

MOST POPULAR MAJORS

architecture (barch, ba/bs, march, ma/ms, phd); engineering (bs, ms, phd); political science and government

APPLICANTS ALSO LOOK AT AND OFTEN PREFER

Boston College, University of Notre Dame

AND SOMETIMES PREFER

University of Virginia

AND RARELY PREFER

Fordham University, American University, The George Washington University

STUDENTS SAY ". . ."

Academics

At The Catholic University of America, strong academic programs are infused with "the values and traditions of conservative Catholicism, including service to the community, family, and Catholic morality." For students seeking a spiritual atmosphere, CUA is a "great learning environment where your faith can grow exponentially." However, "Contrary to popular belief, students do not attend this school based on its religious affiliation." Instead, the "intimate class sizes," generous scholarship packages, and fantastic location lure many top students to this small school. At CUA, academic opportunities (such as overseas studies) are plentiful, and courses are tough but manageable. A current student shares, "I am challenged, and will leave college feeling empowered with the skills needed to succeed in whatever career path I choose." No matter what your major, there are "required religion courses" woven into the curriculum. Students tell us, "The emphasis on classical philosophy for all majors really teaches students how to think in complex ways." While not every professor is unilaterally adored, most "are well-organized and truly knowledgeable about the subject…they teach." Instructors "really care about the individual, and you are definitely not just a number to them." Depending on your perspective, you might describe the school's administration as "an oppressive regime that allows no fun," or you might characterize them as a friendly group of student-oriented individuals who are "strict but fair." Either way, things tend to "run smoothly" on the CUA campus, despite the fact that there are some "communication issues" between administrative departments.

Life

Offering a range of clubs and activities, an active campus ministry, varied social events, and varsity sports, life at CUA is a "good mix of spirituality and fun." "There is a huge spirit [of] community service and giving back" at CUA, and many students are involved in volunteer work with Catholic charities. In fact, "CUA is located in a section of D.C. dubbed 'Little Vatican.' The large number of Catholic organizations in the immediate area provides ample opportunities for spiritual development and self-discovery." In addition to faith-based activities, the surrounding city is a great jumping-off point for culture and recreation. In their spare time, students "go to concerts, museums, parks, [and] political rallies" in surrounding D.C., or they enjoy eating in some of the "amazing restaurants in the area." Given the propitious location, it's not surprising that "a lot of students are interested in politics and become active in political groups." Come the weekend, CUA is a "bit of a party school," and "most people go out to the bars at night on Thursdays, Fridays, and Saturdays for fun." More than sixty percent of undergraduates live on campus, which they describe as a "quiet oasis located amidst a bustling metropolis."

Student Body

With its distinctive personality and cosmopolitan location in Washington, D.C., CUA tends to attract students from a similar background. On this small campus, undergraduates are predominately "white, upper-middle-class, [and] Catholic," and almost "every student is either from New York, Massachusetts, or ROP (right outside Philly)." Most characterize the community as lacking diversity, telling us, "Aside from drama and architecture students, the majority of the undergrads do not stick out." CUA has a "strong Catholic identity" and a good portion of students are "extremely religious." At the same time, "There are a decent number of non-Catholics at the school, as well as kids from other countries and cultures." With academics, as with religion, some students are more committed to their studies than others. A current student elaborates, "Half the students are very religious or academic, while the other half are less interested in academics and more interested in fun activities."

FINANCIAL AID: 202-319-5307 • E-MAIL: CUA-ADMISSIONS@CUA.EDU • WEBSITE: WWW.CUA.EDU

THE PRINCETON REVIEW SAYS

Admissions

Very important factors considered include: Academic GPA, recommendation(s), rigor of secondary school record, standardized test scores, character/personal qualities, level of applicant's interest, volunteer work. *Important factors considered include:* Application essay, extracurricular activities, first generation, interview, talent/ability. *Other factors considered include:* Class rank, alumni/ae relation, racial/ethnic status, work experience. SAT or ACT required; ACT with writing component required. TOEFL required of all international applicants. High school diploma is required and GED is accepted. *Academic units recommended:* 4 English, 3 mathematics, 3 science (1 science lab), 2 foreign language, 4 social studies, 1 fine arts or humanities.

Financial Aid

Students should submit: FAFSA, Alumni and Parish Scholarship Applications if appropriate. Priority filing deadline is February 15. The Princeton Review suggests that all financial aid forms be submitted as soon as possible after January 1. *Need-based scholarships/grants offered:* Federal Pell, SEOG, state scholarships/grants, private scholarships, the school's own gift aid. *Loan aid offered:* Direct Subsidized Stafford, Direct Unsubsidized Stafford, Direct PLUS, Commercial Loans. Applicants will be notified of awards on a rolling basis beginning April 1. Federal Work-Study Program available. Institutional employment available. Off-campus job opportunities are good.

The Inside Word

CUA offers a nonbinding early action program, as well as regular admission. A student's academic record and test scores are important elements in an admissions decision, as is a history of service in his or her school or community. If it sounds like a fit, prospective students can get a feel for life at CUA during an "open house" day, when they're invited to attend mass, meet with the deans, take a tour, and eat lunch on campus.

THE SCHOOL SAYS ". . ."

From the Admissions Office

"The Catholic University of America's friendly atmosphere, rigorous academic programs, and emphasis on time-honored values attract students from all fifty states and more than eighty foreign countries. Its 184-acre, tree-lined campus is only ten minutes from the Capitol building. Distinguished as the national university of the Catholic Church in the United States, CUA is the only institution of higher education established by the U.S. Catholic bishops; however, students from all religious traditions are welcome. CUA offers undergraduate degrees in more than eighty major areas in eight schools of study. Students enroll into the School of Arts and Sciences, Social Work, Architecture, Nursing, Engineering, Music, Philosophy or Professional Studies. Additionally, CUA students can concentrate in areas of preprofessional study including law, dentistry, medicine, or veterinary studies.

"With Capitol Hill, the Smithsonian Institution, NASA, the Kennedy Center, and the National Institutes of Health among the places students obtain internships, firsthand experience is a valuable piece of the experience that CUA offers.

Numerous students also take the opportunity in their junior year to study abroad at one of Catholic's forty-eight different semester programs. Political science majors even have the opportunity to do a Parliamentary Internship in either England or Ireland. With the campus just minutes away from downtown via the Metrorail rapid transit system, students enjoy a residential campus in an exciting city of historical monuments, theaters, festivals, ethnic restaurants, and parks.

"Matriculating students should submit the SAT Subject Test: Foreign Language exam if they plan to continue studying that language at CUA."

SELECTIVITY

Admissions Rating	**75**
# of applicants	6,617
% of applicants accepted	75
% of acceptees attending	18

FRESHMAN PROFILE

Range SAT Critical Reading	510–620
Range SAT Math	500–610
Range ACT Composite	22–27
Minimum paper TOEFL	550
Minimum web-based TOEFL	80
Average HS GPA	3.4

DEADLINES

Early action	
Deadline	11/15
Notification	12/15
Regular	
Deadline	2/15
Nonfall registration?	yes

FINANCIAL FACTS

Financial Aid Rating	**84**
Annual tuition	$35,260
Room and board	$13,824
Required fees	$200
Books and supplies	$1,400
% needy frosh rec. need-based scholarship or grant aid	98
% needy UG rec. need-based scholarship or grant aid	97
% needy frosh rec. need-based self-help aid	90
% needy UG rec. need-based self-help aid	91
% frosh rec. any financial aid	93
% UG rec. any financial aid	90
% frosh need fully met	48
% ugrads need fully met	43
Average % of frosh need met	82
Average % of ugrad need met	79

Centenary College of Louisiana

PO Box 41188, Shreveport, LA 71134-1188 • Admissions: 318-869-5131 • Fax: 318-869-5005

CAMPUS LIFE

Quality of Life Rating	**65**
Fire Safety Rating	**79**
Green Rating	**60***
Type of school	private
Affiliation	Methodist
Environment	metropolis

STUDENTS

Total undergrad enrollment	891
% male/female	41/59
% from out of state	41
% from public high school	70
% frosh live on campus	85
# of fraternities	5
# of sororities	2
% African American	8
% Asian	2
% Caucasian	82
% Hispanic	4
% international	2
# of countries represented	12

SURVEY SAYS . . .

Registration is a breeze
Students are friendly
Students get along with local community
Musical organizations are popular
Student publications are popular
Student government is popular

ACADEMICS

Academic Rating	**86**
% students returning for sophomore year	76
% students graduating within 4 years	43
% students graduating within 6 years	57
Student/faculty ratio	12:1
Profs interesting rating	89
Profs accessible rating	84
Most classes have	10–19 students

MOST POPULAR MAJORS

biology/biological sciences; business/commerce; mass communication/media studies

STUDENTS SAY ". . ."

Academics

With fewer than 1,000 undergraduates, Centenary College of Louisiana certainly qualifies as a small school. In fact, there are only a handful of elite undergraduate institutions smaller. That said, smallness has its virtues. As one student notes, "The small size of the student body gives students the opportunity to receive individual attention in class, be involved in many organizations and hold leadership positions outside of class." It also fosters "a community atmosphere" in which "professors really care about you emotionally and academically," along with providing "a lot of one-on-one help and projects." Premedical sciences are said to be excellent (nearly twenty percent of all students major in life sciences), as are business studies, music, and communications. Academics are "extremely rigorous and thorough," so much so that "no one graduates without expanding their knowledge base." As at many small schools, "the professors are absolutely wonderful. They're engaging, knowledgeable, and really care about what they're teaching and about their students." The school places a premium on such high-caliber teaching skill. "Bad teachers do not last long around here," one undergrad assures us. The downside of a small school, of course, is that certain limitations are an unavoidable fact of life. Some "miss the perks a bigger school [has to offer] like more classes and a better cafeteria."

Life

"Campus life centers around athletics, clubs, and Greek life" at Centenary, where "the real trick is finding that one thing that you love (be it sororities, radio, theater, whatever) and excelling at it. The school has a lot of opportunities for responsible individuals." There's the "awesome" radio station, for one, and lots of lectures, internships, and mentoring opportunities. And while "There are occasional events on weekdays, including sports games," when it comes time for fun "life at Centenary revolves around the weekend" and "includes going to some of the local attractions, to a movie, to dinner, or to either one of the sport teams' house or a fraternity house." Because the campus is officially dry, "those unwilling to hide their contraband alcohol…normally just hang out in residence hall lobbies and watch movies" or they "go down to the fraternity houses (which allow alcohol)." Hometown Shreveport "doesn't offer many options for students, especially students under twenty-one. It's definitely not a 'college town.'" Another student explains, "There is not a lot to do in Shreveport besides shopping, but there are many opportunities to do so in the surrounding area. There are not too many local music shows, but the Shreveport Opera and community theaters are worth the time."

Student Body

For such a small school, Centenary does a good job of drawing a diverse mix of interests and backgrounds. Here "You can find everything from far right-wing ministry majors to highly liberal individuals actively involved in campus organizations promoting gay rights" as well as "a large and diverse number of international students, most notably from Europe and Hong Kong." What you won't find is a lot of minority students; "There are very few minorities on this campus," one student observes. Most students here "are overachievers or hard workers, whether it is in an academic sense or in an extracurricular sense." Though many note that the student body is "generally white, middle-class, and religious," they are also quick to point out that it also accommodates "a lot of gay and lesbian students, and overall, the campus is very accepting and supportive of these students."

FINANCIAL AID: 318-869-5137 • E-MAIL: ADMISSIONS@CENTENARY.EDU • WEBSITE: WWW.CENTENARY.EDU

THE PRINCETON REVIEW SAYS

Admissions

Very important factors considered include: Academic GPA, rigor of secondary school record. *Important factors considered include:* Class rank, application essay, recommendation(s), standardized test scores, alumni/ae relation, character/personal qualities, extracurricular activities, interview, level of applicant's interest, talent/ability, volunteer work, work experience. *Other factors considered include:* First generation, geographical residence, racial/ethnic status, religious affiliation/commitment. SAT or ACT required; ACT with or without writing component accepted. TOEFL required of all international applicants. High school diploma is required and GED is accepted. *Academic units recommended:* 4 English, 3 mathematics, 3 science (2 science labs), 2 foreign language, 3 social studies.

Financial Aid

Students should submit: FAFSA, institution's own financial aid form. The Princeton Review suggests that all financial aid forms be submitted as soon as possible after January 1. *Need-based scholarships/grants offered:* Federal Pell, SEOG, state scholarships/grants, private scholarships, the school's own gift aid. *Loan aid offered:* Direct Subsidized Stafford, Direct Unsubsidized Stafford, Direct PLUS, Federal Perkins. Applicants will be notified of awards on or about March 15. Federal Work-Study Program available. Institutional employment available. Highest amount earned per year from on-campus jobs $4,000. Off-campus job opportunities are good.

The Inside Word

Centenary's applicant pool has grown substantially over the past decade, allowing the school to become more selective in its admissions process. The school's reputation, though regional, is quite solid, and the college does a good job of enrolling those it admits—a sign that the school is tops on more than a few applicants' lists. No doubt a very friendly and efficient admissions office also contributes to this success.

THE SCHOOL SAYS ". . ."

From the Admissions Office

"Just as a student's four-year experience at Centenary will be very personalized, so too is the application process. We pride ourselves on treating each applicant as an individual. We encourage all interested students to visit us—not only so they can see our campus and get a sense of the atmosphere, but also to provide us the opportunity to meet and get to know them.

"Consider Centenary for a life-changing experience. Our professors value your ideas and contributions and are passionate about teaching.We consider the Centenary Experience to be more than just a degree. You will live in a comprehensive learning environment that features connections to your academic, social, personal, and residential lives.

"Our students work and live within a strong community to create personalized, distinctive experiences, and enjoy a vibrant college life and graduate from Centenary prepared for their professional and personal lives.

"First-year applicants must submit either ACT or SAT scores. We recommend, but do not require, the ACT writing component."

SELECTIVITY

Admissions Rating	**79**
# of applicants	1,076
% of applicants accepted	69
% of acceptees attending	33

FRESHMAN PROFILE

Range SAT Critical Reading	520–630
Range SAT Math	520–620
Range ACT Composite	24–28
Minimum paper TOEFL	550
% graduated top 10% of class	33
% graduated top 25% of class	63
% graduated top 50% of class	85

DEADLINES

Early action	
Deadline	12/15
Regular	
Priority	2/15
Deadline	8/1
Nonfall registration?	yes

FINANCIAL FACTS

Financial Aid Rating	**90**
Annual tuition	$29,500
Room and board	$9,320
Required fees	$1,260
Books and supplies	$1,200
% needy frosh rec. need-based scholarship or grant aid	100
% needy UG rec. need-based scholarship or grant aid	99
% needy frosh rec. non-need-based scholarship or grant aid	22
% needy UG rec. non-need-based scholarship or grant aid	28
% needy frosh rec. need-based self-help aid	68
% needy UG rec. need-based self-help aid	60
% frosh rec. any financial aid	98
% UG rec. any financial aid	93
% UG borrow to pay for school	64
Average cumulative indebtedness	$19,206
% frosh need fully met	27
% ugrads need fully met	34
Average % of frosh need met	88
Average % of ugrad need met	84

Centre College

600 West Walnut Street, Danville, KY 40422 • Admissions: 859-238-5350 • Fax: 859-238-5373

CAMPUS LIFE

Quality of Life Rating	**87**
Fire Safety Rating	**60***
Green Rating	**82**
Type of school	private
Affiliation	Presbyterian
Environment	village

STUDENTS

Total undergrad enrollment	1,306
% male/female	47/53
% from out of state	42
% from public high school	79
% frosh live on campus	99
# of fraternities	4
# of sororities	4
% African American	4
% Asian	2
% Caucasian	86
% Hispanic	3
% international	2
# of countries represented	12

SURVEY SAYS . . .

No one cheats
Athletic facilities are great
School is well run
Campus feels safe
Low cost of living
Very little drug use

ACADEMICS

Academic Rating	**94**
% students returning for sophomore year	91
% students graduating within 4 years	81
% students graduating within 6 years	82
Calendar	4-1-4
Student/faculty ratio	11:1
Profs interesting rating	97
Profs accessible rating	98
Most classes have	10–19 students
Most lab/discussion sessions have	10–19 students

MOST POPULAR MAJORS

economics; English language and literature; history

APPLICANTS ALSO LOOK AT AND OFTEN PREFER

Davidson College, Washington and Lee University

AND SOMETIMES PREFER

Kenyon College, Furman University, Rhodes College

AND RARELY PREFER

University of Louisville, University of Kentucky, Transylvania University

STUDENTS SAY ". . ."

Academics

Centre College offers "a genuine, personal, practical education in all areas of life." Its "small classes" are focused and challenging, "and students definitely spend a lot of time studying, reading, and writing papers." An international studies student comments, "I find myself working harder than I ever thought possible…I feel so accomplished at the end of each semester." Students are taught by "extremely passionate and dedicated professors." Teachers are "kind, supportive, caring, and are always available for help outside the classroom," and they make "an effort to work one-on-one with you if necessary." One of Centre's goals is "preparing students to be actively engaged global citizens," and there's "a big movement on getting out of the classroom with the community-based learning." "If a professor doesn't require that kind of learning," a student explains, "then they almost always will still make connections outside the classroom whether to real life or to other classes." Centre has an impressively strong study abroad program, and about eighty-five percent of their students take advantage of it. One student says, "You are guaranteed the chance to have an internship and study abroad." Students love this combination of global, local, and personal learning. One proudly says that Centre "looks toward the future…of our world and the need for students to be prepared for it…Centre has and will continue to prepare me for what comes next in my journey."

Life

Centre College has an active campus life. Fraternities and sororities have a big presence and host a lot of parties. One student says, "There are a lot of students who are involved in Greek life, but there are a fair amount who are not involved in any way." Another adds, "There has been a significant development in alternative organizations, such as the Art House for drama, music, and art majors." There's also the "philanthropic coed fraternity Alpha Phi Omega," which "provides a very different, positive experience for…students who prefer to focus on service and forming strong friendships rather than partying." The Student Activities Council also organizes a lot of events, including "midnight movies." The small, picturesque town of Danville is "very much a college town." "New restaurants and bars have been opening, which is making Danville a little more exciting," but students admit that overall "there isn't much to do off campus." However, "There is so much going on at campus" that students "don't ever want to leave."

Student Body

Centre College's small student body and rural setting lend it a "welcoming atmosphere" and help create a "close-knit community." Students are "kind, respectful, and friendly to peers, professors, and administrators alike." Students are "hyper-involved," either in athletics, Greek life, the many "clubs and organizations," or all three. Students may "work hard all week," but they still find time to "attend club meetings, support their friends in sporting events, relax in the campus center…attend sorority/fraternity activities, and attend events." The stereotype of the Centre student is one who is "white," "Southern," and "middle- or upper-class," but many insist that Centre's student body has "changed dramatically." One student says, "I believe that Centre has lived up to its mission of improving racial diversity on campus." They add, "The number of African American, international, and Hispanic students has increased dramatically." Students admit, "Centre is quite cliquish," but say, "People always find their own place." One student explains, "During the week people tend to stick to their groups," but "barriers break down on weekends."

FINANCIAL AID: 859-238-5365 • E-MAIL: ADMISSION@CENTRE.EDU • WEBSITE: WWW.CENTRE.EDU

THE PRINCETON REVIEW SAYS

Admissions

Very important factors considered include: Academic GPA, rigor of secondary school record. *Important factors considered include:* Class rank, application essay, recommendation(s), standardized test scores. *Other factors considered include:* Alumni/ae relation, character/personal qualities, extracurricular activities, first generation, geographical residence, interview, racial/ethnic status, talent/ability, volunteer work, work experience. SAT or ACT required; ACT with writing component recommended. TOEFL required of all international applicants. High school diploma or equivalent is not required. *Academic units required:* 4 English, 3 mathematics, 2 science (2 science labs), 2 foreign language, 1 social studies, 1 history. *Academic units recommended:* 4 mathematics, 4 science, 4 foreign language, 2 social studies, 2 history, 1 visual/performing arts.

Financial Aid

Students should submit: FAFSA, institution's own financial aid form. The Princeton Review suggests that all financial aid forms be submitted as soon as possible after January 1. *Need-based scholarships/grants offered:* Federal Pell, SEOG, state scholarships/grants, private scholarships, the school's own gift aid, Federal ACG Federal SMART and Federal TEACH. *Loan aid offered:* Direct Subsidized Stafford, Direct Unsubsidized Stafford, Direct PLUS, Federal Perkins, college/university loans from institutional funds. Applicants will be notified of awards on or about April 1. Federal Work-Study Program available. Institutional employment available. Off-campus job opportunities are fair.

The Inside Word

Centre's small but very capable student body reflects solid academic preparation from high school. If you're ranked in the top quarter of your graduating class and have taken challenging courses throughout your high school career, you should have smooth sailing through the admissions process. Those who rank below the top quarter or who have inconsistent academic transcripts will find entrance here more difficult and may benefit from an interview.

THE SCHOOL SAYS ". . ."

From the Admissions Office

"Centre College offers its students a world of opportunities, highlighted by the nation's premier study abroad program. Approximately eighty-five percent of students study abroad at least once. CentreTerm programs explore an ever-increasing number of countries in January; in 2013, they include Barbados, Borneo, China, Ghana, the Holy Land, and Italy, among others. In addition, there are nine permanent, semester-long residential programs: England, Scotland, Northern Ireland, France, Spain, Yucatan, China, and Japan. Centre's personalized approach means that most international study includes at least one Centre professor. Study abroad is so important that it is a component of the Centre Commitment: study abroad, an internship, and graduation in four years—guaranteed, or Centre will provide up to one more year of tuition for free.

"Centre's stellar academic reputation and exceptional commitment to remaining affordable lead to extraordinary success for our students: entrance to top graduate and professional schools, prestigious undergraduate and postgraduate fellowships (Rhodes, Fulbright, Goldwater), and rewarding jobs. (On average, ninety-seven percent are employed or in advanced study within ten months of graduation.)

"Centre is a place where important conversations occur—in and out of the classroom. In 2012, for the second time in a dozen years, Centre's Norton Center for the Arts was the setting for the nation's only vice presidential debate. Even in years without a vice presidential debate, the Norton Center features an amazing array of high-profile arts performances and speakers, including the legendary Vienna Philharmonic, country music icon Dolly Parton, and Nobel prize-winner Elie Wiesel."

SELECTIVITY

Admissions Rating	**90**
# of applicants	2,413
% of applicants accepted	70
% of acceptees attending	22
# accepting a place on wait list	192
# admitted from wait list	9

FRESHMAN PROFILE

Range SAT Critical Reading	560–690
Range SAT Math	560–670
Range SAT Writing	570–670
Range ACT Composite	26–31
Minimum paper TOEFL	580
Average HS GPA	3.7
% graduated top 10% of class	54
% graduated top 25% of class	83
% graduated top 50% of class	98

DEADLINES

Early action	
Deadline	12/1
Notification	1/15
Regular	
Deadline	1/15
Notification	3/15
Nonfall registration?	no

FINANCIAL FACTS

Financial Aid Rating	**82**
Annual tuition	$34,000
Room and board	$8,500
Books and supplies	$1,300

CHAMPLAIN COLLEGE

163 South Willard Street Box 670, Burlington, VT 05402-0670 • Admissions: 802-860-2727 • Fax: 802-860-2767

CAMPUS LIFE

Quality of Life Rating	**95**
Fire Safety Rating	**95**
Green Rating	**89**
Type of school	private
Environment	town

STUDENTS

Total undergrad enrollment	2,067
% male/female	59/41
% from out of state	80
% from public high school	85
% frosh live on campus	90
% African American	2
% Asian	2
% Caucasian	69
% Hispanic	2
% international	2
# of countries represented	42

SURVEY SAYS . . .

Students are happy
Great library
Career services are great
Students are friendly
Different types of students interact
Great off-campus food

ACADEMICS

Academic Rating	**79**
% students returning for sophomore year	78
% students graduating within 4 years	60
% students graduating within 6 years	63
Calendar	semester
Student/faculty ratio	14:1
Profs interesting rating	94
Profs accessible rating	89
Most classes have	10–19 students
Most lab/discussion sessions have	fewer than 10 students

MOST POPULAR MAJORS

marketing; game design; professional writing

APPLICANTS ALSO LOOK AT AND OFTEN PREFER

University of Vermont, University of Massachusetts Amherst, University of New Hampshire

AND SOMETIMES PREFER

Rochester Institute of Technology, Ithaca College, Drexel University, Quinnipiac University, St. Michael's College

STUDENTS SAY ". . ."

Academics

With highly ranked programs in professional majors such as game design and digital forensics, Champlain College "is a hands-on, professionally focused college aimed at creating well-rounded global citizens that excel in critical, interdisciplinary thinking." The school offers "one of the best, most innovative systems around to prepare students for the real-world after college by implementing requirements throughout the program that help shape college students into professional 'job hunters.'" It also has campuses in Montreal and Dublin, and studying abroad is popular. Students love the "Upside-Down Curriculum in which students take major-related classes in their first year." Major classes are complemented by the LEAD program, which helps students develop community-building skills and awareness, and the Core program, which emphasizes interdisciplinary studies and critical thinking. The classes are small—"a class of thirty is rare and considered large"—and this "allows the students and teachers to get to know one another exceptionally well." "The relationship between students and professors is more like a partnership. The professors at Champlain believe the process of learning never stops and that students have just as much to offer as they do." At a school with such strong digital and design programs, it's no surprise that "professors and their class materials [and] structures are constantly updated and mirror many current real-life situations."

Life

Students "absolutely love the Burlington area. It is the perfect college town." "The Champlain College Campus and the city itself are breathtaking," "so many Champlain students spend a good amount of time outside when weather permits." "There is so much to do," and the campus is located in the heart of it all—"only about a five-minute walk from the Church Street Market Place." "It is a great biking and walking town, which makes it easy to get around without a car." In the winter, Champlainers hit one of several nearby mountains to ski and snowboard, and North Beach on the college's namesake lake is a popular destination during warmer months. There are plenty of hiking trails and national forests nearby as well. On campus, Victorian mansions serve as dorms, and student activities abound, "such as rock-climbing... equestrian club, rugby, [and] photography." Campus events include "movie nights, special events in the cafeteria, a semiformal dance in the winter, and stress-relieving activities around exam times (such as massages and henna tattoos)." Downtown Burlington is home to a lot of live music venues and bars, and students partake of the local nightlife, "but it's always a very safe and comfortable environment."

Student Body

Students at Champlain categorize themselves in three groups: gamers, skiers/snowboarders, and everyone else: "There are hippies, photographers, writers, comedians, environmental do-gooders, adventurers, academics, and everything in between." The student body has a strong artsy streak—"hipsters are common" here. But just about everyone is "open-minded, laid-back, tech-savvy, professional," "and serious about their educations." "Many have jobs in addition to school." "The typical student is passionate about their major and is seen with a strong group of friends both in and outside of that major." The small campus and structure of the Core program encourage bonding: "Everyone knows everyone…and it's a very comfortable place to live." "The community feels like a family. We all know each other." As at most small, Northeastern, private colleges, a large portion of the student body is white, middle-class, and from the Northeast; as one student puts it, the school "could be more diverse, but it is in Vermont," and "there are no cookie-cutter students at this school."

FINANCIAL AID: 802-860-2730 • E-MAIL: ADMISSION@CHAMPLAIN.EDU • WEBSITE: WWW.CHAMPLAIN.EDU

THE PRINCETON REVIEW SAYS

Admissions

Very important factors considered include: Application essay, academic GPA, rigor of secondary school record. *Important factors considered include:* Class rank, recommendation(s), standardized test scores, interview. *Other factors considered include:* Alumni/ae relation, character/personal qualities, extracurricular activities, level of applicant's interest, talent/ability, volunteer work, work experience. SAT or ACT required; ACT with or without writing component accepted. TOEFL required of all international applicants. High school diploma is required and GED is accepted. *Academic units required:* 4 English, 3 mathematics, 3 science (2 science labs), 4 history, 3 foreign language. *Academic units recommended:* 4 mathematics, 4 science (3 science labs), 2 social studies.

Financial Aid

Students should submit: FAFSA. The Princeton Review suggests that all financial aid forms be submitted as soon as possible after January 1. *Need-based scholarships/grants offered:* Federal Pell, SEOG, state scholarships/grants, private scholarships, the school's own gift aid. *Loan aid offered:* Direct Lender, Subsidized Stafford, Direct Unsubsidized Stafford, Direct PLUS, Federal Perkins. Applicants will be notified of awards on a rolling basis beginning March 1. Highest amount earned per year from on-campus jobs $2,211.

The Inside Word

Students interested in attending Champlain College should pursue a rigorous secondary school course load and make sure their career goals are a match with Champlain's major offerings. The school's supplement to the Common Application gives students an opportunity to describe their strengths and achievements—applicants should approach this as a chance to emphasize what they can contribute to the Champlain community. Students applying to the Graphic Design (BFA), Game Design, Digital Filmmaking (BFA), Professional Writing, Game Art and Animation (BFA), and Creative Media (BFA) programs will need to submit a portfolio of creative work.

THE SCHOOL SAYS ". . ."

From the Admissions Office

"Preparing students for the opportunities and challenges of an increasingly competitive world is not negotiable for us. When a student graduates from Champlain College, they can be confident that they are not only career-ready, but also life-ready.

"Students at Champlain College are immediately immersed in their prospective major and real-life internships via the Upside-Down Curriculum; they are challenged to think critically and further develop communication and writing abilities from the nationally acclaimed liberal arts core; and they will gain important skills such as financial sophistication, career management, and other life-building knowledge. It is an academic experience that is unparalleled, and our graduates are experiencing the benefits the day after graduation.

"However, in addition to academic preparation, going to college is about experiences, and there is no better college town in the East than Burlington, Vermont. Whether your interests are snowboarding and skiing, art and culture, music and expression, volunteering and community-building, or anything else, Burlington, Vermont, and our amazing campus have it covered. Champlain College students reside in historic Victorian mansions that overlook one of the country's most amazing natural vistas and are only steps from downtown Burlington.

"A Champlain College student is a student that feels optimistic about the future because she is taking control of it. It is a college environment of enrichment, support, and activity, and continually asks the question, what do you need to be successful upon graduation?

"We hope you can visit us soon and get a taste of the Champlain experience."

SELECTIVITY	
Admissions Rating	71
# of applicants	4,453
% of applicants accepted	70
% of acceptees attending	20
# accepting a place on wait list	85
# admitted from wait list	11
# of early decision applicants	303
# accepted early decision	246

FRESHMAN PROFILE	
Range SAT Critical Reading	500–610
Range SAT Math	510–610
Range ACT Composite	21–26
Minimum paper TOEFL	550
Minimum web-based TOEFL	61
% graduated top 10% of class	11
% graduated top 25% of class	35
% graduated top 50% of class	70

DEADLINES	
Early decision	
Deadline	11/15
Notification	12/31
Regular	
Deadline	2/1
Notification	3/15
Nonfall registration?	yes

FINANCIAL FACTS	
Financial Aid Rating	70
Annual tuition	$29,765
Room and board	$13,095
Required fees	$100
Books and supplies	$1,000
% frosh rec. need-based scholarship or grant aid	60
% UG rec. need-based scholarship or grant aid	60
% frosh rec. non-need-based scholarship or grant aid	56
% UG rec. non-need-based scholarship or grant aid	56
% frosh rec. need-based self-help aid	81
% UG rec. need-based self-help aid	88
% frosh rec. any financial aid	91
% UG rec. any financial aid	83
% UG borrow to pay for school	88
% frosh need fully met	17
% ugrads need fully met	12
Average % of frosh need met	72
Average % of ugrad need met	66

CHAPMAN UNIVERSITY

ONE UNIVERSITY DRIVE, ORANGE, CA 92866 • ADMISSIONS: 714-997-6711 • FAX: 714-997-6713

CAMPUS LIFE

Quality of Life Rating	**84**
Fire Safety Rating	**81**
Green Rating	**68**
Type of school	private
Affiliation	Disciples of Christ
Environment	metropolis

STUDENTS

Total undergrad enrollment	5,264
% male/female	43/57
% from out of state	27
% from public high school	70
% frosh live on campus	89
# of fraternities	6
# of sororities	6
% African American	2
% Asian	9
% Caucasian	60
% Hispanic	13
% international	3
# of countries represented	65

SURVEY SAYS . . .

Great computer facilities
Low cost of living
Great off-campus food
Frats and sororities dominate social scene

ACADEMICS

Academic Rating	**79**
% students returning for sophomore year	91
% students graduating within 4 years	53
% students graduating within 6 years	72
Calendar	4-1-4
Student/faculty ratio	14:1
Profs interesting rating	82
Profs accessible rating	83
Most classes have	20–29 students
Most lab/discussion sessions have	10–19 students

MOST POPULAR MAJORS

business administration and management; cinematography and film/video production; public relations/image management

APPLICANTS ALSO LOOK AT AND OFTEN PREFER

Loyola Marymount University, University of San Diego, University of California—Los Angeles, University of Southern California, New York University

AND SOMETIMES PREFER

Pepperdine University

STUDENTS SAY ". . ."

Academics

Orange County's Chapman University boasts "a more personalized education" of a style "you can't find at any other university," according to students, who say the "personal relationship with your professors" and "bigger opportunity to meet one-on-one with my professors" thanks to "small class sizes" sets it apart from other West Coast schools. Sure, the location is a big draw, but so is the "emphasis on personalized education," which aims to "aid students in becoming global citizens, productive workers, and positive impacts to the world." The "amazing and very informative" professors here make classes "engaging" and provide an education "that motivates students to go for their dreams." Indeed, "Professors will go out of their way to get to know students and make sure they are doing well in the class." These educators "bring in real experiences into the classrooms," which give students "real-life case studies" and "assist with networking opportunities." Students agree, "Professors at Chapman are really here to see their students succeed." A few students complain, "Sometimes adjunct faculty are not asked back," which means "it is difficult to keep connections with professors who you never see again." While "there are a few professors who are not as engaging, for the most part all of my teachers have been interesting and have really had a desire to help me learn in whatever way is best for me."

Life

Chapman is in Orange County, California, so Disneyland, Los Angeles, gorgeous West Coast beaches, and more are all seemingly right around the corner. That means it is no surprise that "Chapman students believe in a work hard, play hard mentality." Students here "don't only exceed in the classroom, but they like to have a good time." And it's easy to have a good time here. After all, "with so many entertainment venues nearby, in addition to on-campus events, students can always find something to do." The play hard attitude doesn't necessarily mean your stereotypical, beer-chugging frat party, however. "Because there are a lot of families that live here it can be difficult for "typical college parties" to exist." When it comes to things to do, Disneyland, Disneyland, and Disneyland ends up on a lot of lists. "I go frequently," one student notes, "and quite a few Chapman students are employed there." Some say they get a year pass and go as many as five times a week. But the Mouse is only one of many things to do here. "There is never a boring weekend," students say. "We have so many options available including the beach, Disneyland, or things on campus—from movie nights to open mic nights in the student union to concerts."

Student Body

You had better be ready to socialize if you decide on Chapman, because "the typical student at Chapman is friendly, social, and active." Students are "very busy and pretty involved and committed to their interests" and "are usually very involved in multiple activities and very passionate and excited to be here." In many cases, "Students are leaders on our campus and dedicated to their passions." A willingness to interact is a major factor for those attending this school. "If students are willing to get involved, there is always a place for them to fit in." It's not always easy, but as one student notes, "I would say there is a niche for everyone; it might take a while to find it, though." In addition to sociability, embracing diversity is also a common trait here. The typical person on campus is someone "who is passionate and accepting." Students say, "There is no discrimination here, everyone accepts everyone." The bottom line: "If you are willing to adapt the SoCal lifestyle, Chapman is for you. If you don't like being out and about, constantly in a social situation, Chapman may not feel like home."

FINANCIAL AID: 714-997-6741 • E-MAIL: ADMIT@CHAPMAN.EDU • WEBSITE: WWW.CHAPMAN.EDU

THE PRINCETON REVIEW SAYS

Admissions

Very important factors considered include: Class rank, application essay, academic GPA, rigor of secondary school record, standardized test scores, character/personal qualities. *Important factors considered include:* Extracurricular activities, talent/ability, volunteer work. *Other factors considered include:* Recommendation(s), alumni/ae relation, first generation, geographical residence, racial/ethnic status, state residency, work experience. SAT or ACT required; ACT with writing component required. TOEFL required of all international applicants. High school diploma is required and GED is accepted. *Academic units required:* 2 English, 2 mathematics, 2 science (1 science lab), 2 foreign language, 3 social studies. *Academic units recommended:* 4 English, 3 mathematics, 3 science (1 science lab), 3 foreign language, 4 social studies.

Financial Aid

Students should submit: FAFSA, state aid form. The Princeton Review suggests that all financial aid forms be submitted as soon as possible after January 1. *Need-based scholarships/grants offered:* Federal Pell, SEOG, state scholarships/grants, private scholarships, the school's own gift aid, Academic Competitiveness Grants. *Loan aid offered:* Direct Subsidized Stafford, Direct Unsubsidized Stafford, Direct PLUS, Federal Perkins. Applicants will be notified of awards on a rolling basis beginning March 15. Federal Work-Study Program available. Institutional employment available. Off-campus job opportunities are excellent.

Inside Word

No need to decode arcane admissions formulas or race in your application before everyone else. There is no trick into getting into Chapman other than this: Be as well-rounded a person as possible, with a strong focus on service to your community. This will show that you're a good fit for the school's "global responsibility" program. The approach makes getting accepted tough, but that hasn't slowed down the ceaseless flow of applications, applications that keep coming in despite stiff competition from other California schools.

THE SCHOOL SAYS ". . ."

From the Admissions Office

"During our 150-year history, Chapman has evolved from a small, church-related liberal arts college into a vibrant and comprehensive midsized liberal arts and sciences university distinguished for an eclectic group of nationally recognized programs including athletic training, film and television production, business and economics, dance, music, theater, writing, and teacher education. Our Orange County, California location was recently rated by *Places Rated Almanac* as "the number-one place to live in North America" citing superior climate, cultural, recreational, educational, and career entry opportunities.

"Chapman's environment is involving, and we seek students who are willing to enter an atmosphere of healthy competition where their talents will be nurtured and manifest to the fullest—whether in the classroom, on the stage, or on the athletic field. We challenge prospective students to thoroughly investigate our fine balance of liberal and professional learning so they may make a fully informed decision about 'fit' with regard to their personalities and that of the university.

"Chapman is a member of the Common Application group. Applicants for freshman admission to Chapman University will be required to submit scores from either the SAT or the ACT including the ACT writing section."

SELECTIVITY	
Admissions Rating	**93**
# of applicants	9,616
% of applicants accepted	45
% of acceptees attending	29
# accepting a place on wait list	209
# admitted from wait list	1

FRESHMAN PROFILE	
Range SAT Critical Reading	550–650
Range SAT Math	560–660
Range SAT Writing	570–660
Range ACT Composite	24–29
Minimum paper TOEFL	550
Average HS GPA	3.7
% graduated top 10% of class	49
% graduated top 25% of class	91
% graduated top 50% of class	99

DEADLINES	
Early action	
Deadline	11/15
Notification	1/10
Regular	
Deadline	1/15
Nonfall registration?	yes

FINANCIAL FACTS	
Financial Aid Rating	**96**
Annual tuition	$41,040
Required fees	$1,044
Books and supplies	$1,450
% needy frosh rec. need-based scholarship or grant aid	82
% needy UG rec. need-based scholarship or grant aid	86
% needy frosh rec. non-need-based scholarship or grant aid	69
% needy UG rec. non-need-based scholarship or grant aid	62
% needy frosh rec. need-based self-help aid	87
% needy UG rec. need-based self-help aid	91
% frosh rec. any financial aid	83
% UG rec. any financial aid	81
% UG borrow to pay for school	75
Average cumulative indebtedness	$28,761
% frosh need fully met	16
% ugrads need fully met	14
Average % of frosh need met	49
Average % of ugrad need met	53

CHRISTOPHER NEWPORT UNIVERSITY

1 UNIVERSITY PLACE, NEWPORT NEWS, VA 23606-2998 • ADMISSIONS: 757-594-7015 • FAX: 757-594-7333

CAMPUS LIFE

Quality of Life Rating	81
Fire Safety Rating	84
Green Rating	74
Type of school	public
Environment	city

STUDENTS

Total undergrad enrollment	4,768
% male/female	43/57
% from out of state	7
% frosh live on campus	95
# of fraternities	7
# of sororities	7
% African American	9
% Asian	3
% Caucasian	79
% Hispanic	4
# of countries represented	40

SURVEY SAYS . . .

Students are friendly
Dorms are like palaces
Very little drug use
Great library

ACADEMICS

Academic Rating	76
% students returning for sophomore year	81
% students graduating within 4 years	42
% students graduating within 6 years	60
Calendar	semester
Student/faculty ratio	17:1
Profs interesting rating	85
Profs accessible rating	88
Most classes have	20–29 students

MOST POPULAR MAJORS

biology/biological sciences; business administration and management; communication studies/speech communication and rhetoric

APPLICANTS ALSO LOOK AT AND OFTEN PREFER

James Madison University, Virginia Tech

AND SOMETIMES PREFER

Old Dominion University, University of Mary Washington, University of Virginia

STUDENTS SAY ". . ."

Academics

Named for an English seaman, Christopher Newport University (located in the Hamptons Roads area of Virginia) is a liberal arts college that runs on a "determination for student success." The small school's "modern outlook on education" is matched by its modern facilities (CNU is averaging one new building every year through 2015), and "It does not lack any of the resources of larger schools." Coupled with a well-run honors program, CNU's "growing prestige" means that "the future holds great things for this little school." While teaching methods of the "absolutely fabulous" faculty may vary, quality rarely does, and most professors "make even my least favorite subjects at least interesting." Though there are a few droning bad apples, for the most part, teachers "really [push students] to engage students in the lesson, other than just read to them," and "professors are ready to help any time you need." "The majority of my professors bring both a sense of expertise and uniqueness to their teaching styles...keeping a sense of personality in their teaching to keep students involved," says a student. Many classes are structured like workshops, and even the "few" lecture hall classes are capped at seventy-five students, so "you'll never find yourself drowning in a 500-person classroom here at CNU." Though many students abhor the buggy and complicated registration process, the administration (especially the well-liked president) "cares to listen to students' concerns," and the "free tutoring is amazing here." There's a palpable excitement for this relatively new school among its students, and though "it isn't well known across the nation, perhaps not even in Virginia...this allows those currently associated (students, faculty, administration, etc.) to help put CNU on the map for generations to come."

Life

With a campus right in the heart of the bustling city of Newport News, there are plenty of entertainment options, and "When the weather is warm, we are not too far from Virginia Beach." Almost everyone takes academics pretty seriously, but this "very socially oriented" bunch is still "able to unwind on the weekends." The campus activities board (CAB) provides free activities every weekend, such as ice skating or movie nights, which "are posted every Friday at the front desk of every resident building." The Ferguson Center for the Arts puts on a great deal of shows and events, and anywhere you go "there are people ready to play Frisbee or talk about the deep universal truths and last night's reality show." Much like the academic buildings, the residential halls and campus are "breathtaking." "I feel like I am living in a luxury hotel," says one student. However, this dry campus has a strict alcohol policy that many students wish the administration would "lighten up" on; says one, "As someone who doesn't drink, it even makes me uncomfortable." This doesn't mean that (off-campus) parties aren't a popular pastime, and "Many students think about how to find the next party, which sometimes can be a difficult task." CNU students take their sports very seriously; or, as one student says, "Even though we are a [Division] III school, we have more school spirit than some [Division] I schools." Sundays are notorious for being "homework and housekeeping days."

Student Body

CNU prides itself on its sense of community, and the students within band together to create "a family-like atmosphere." This "incredibly friendly" group is typically the "middle-class, nice," "healthy, all-American sort." Everyone is open-minded and fairly outgoing, and "just a few weeks into classes...you feel like you know half the student body." "We pride ourselves on being a community of 'door holders,'" says a student. There are "very few socially deviant individuals, such as gang members, hardcore punks, goths, skinheads, etc.," but "nobody, regardless of race or background, sticks out like a sore thumb." Though there's a certain devotion to academics, the average student "is able to balance school work and play."

FINANCIAL AID: 757-594-7170 • E-MAIL: ADMIT@CNU.EDU • WEBSITE: WWW.CNU.EDU

THE PRINCETON REVIEW SAYS

Admissions

Very important factors considered include: Academic GPA, rigor of secondary school record. *Important factors considered include:* Recommendation(s), alumni/ae relation, first generation. *Other factors considered include:* Application essay, standardized test scores, character/personal qualities, extracurricular activities, level of applicant's interest, talent/ability, volunteer work, work experience. ACT with or without writing component accepted. TOEFL required of all international applicants. High school diploma is required and GED is accepted. *Academic units required:* 4 English, 4 mathematics, 3 science, 3 foreign language, 3 history. *Academic units recommended:* 4 English, 4 mathematics, 4 science, 4 foreign language, 4 history, 4 academic electives.

Financial Aid

Students should submit: FAFSA. The Princeton Review suggests that all financial aid forms be submitted as soon as possible after January 1. *Need-based scholarships/grants offered:* Federal Pell, SEOG, state scholarships/grants, private scholarships, the school's own gift aid. *Loan aid offered:* Direct Subsidized Stafford, Direct Unsubsidized Stafford, Direct PLUS. Applicants will be notified of awards on a rolling basis beginning February 21. Federal Work-Study Program available. Institutional employment available. Off-campus job opportunities are good.

The Inside Word

As universities go in Virginia, CNU is right up there in selectivity. The admissions people definitely pay close attention to your academic success in high school, especially the strength of the curriculum and any honors or AP courses. The school looks for leaders and students with diverse experiences. Interviews are required for the President's Leadership Program and Honors Program and strongly recommended for all other applicants.

THE SCHOOL SAYS ". . ."

From the Admissions Office

"Christopher Newport University wants you to thrive academically. Even more so, we want you to lead a life of significance. That's why our undergraduate experience—one that combines cutting-edge academics, stellar leadership opportunities, and high-impact service initiatives—inspires great leaders for the twenty-first century.

"Honoring the best of the liberal arts and sciences, our curriculum shapes hearts and minds for a lifetime of service. We seek students of honor who will make the world a better place. Fifty percent of our students score between 1140 and 1200 on the SAT (critical reading and math), and students must live on campus through their junior year. Our contemporary, state-of-the-art residential facilities win rave reviews from students and parents alike.

"Here you will study alongside distinguished professors, and over the last five years, we have added more than 100 tenure-track PhDs to our faculty. Outside the classroom, you will gain hands-on experience through internships with top organizations like NASA and the Thomas Jefferson National Accelerator Facility.

"At CNU, you will enjoy countless opportunities to develop leadership skills. Make an impact through the President's Leadership Program; design a challenging curriculum in the Honors Program; team with faculty on groundbreaking research; take your studies overseas by studying abroad; and share your talents through 200-plus student organizations. We are also home to one of the most successful NCAA Division III programs in the nation with student-athletes who excel both in the classroom and on the field of play.

"Explore our campus further to discover opportunities as rich as your imagination."

SELECTIVITY

Admissions Rating	**85**
# of applicants	7,492
% of applicants accepted	60
% of acceptees attending	25
# accepting a place on wait list	899
# admitted from wait list	88

FRESHMAN PROFILE

Range SAT Critical Reading	560–640
Range SAT Math	560–640
Range ACT Composite	22–27
Minimum paper TOEFL	530
Minimum web-based TOEFL	71
Average HS GPA	3.6
% graduated top 10% of class	19
% graduated top 25% of class	57
% graduated top 50% of class	94

DEADLINES

Early decision	
Deadline	11/15
Notification	12/15
Early action	
Deadline	12/1
Notification	1/15
Regular	
Priority	12/1
Deadline	2/1
Nonfall registration?	yes

FINANCIAL FACTS

Financial Aid Rating	**69**
Annual in-state tuition	$5,914
Annual out-state tuition	$14,776
Room and board	$9,528
Required fees	$4,170
Books and supplies	$1,005
% frosh rec. need-based scholarship or grant aid	72
% UG rec. need-based scholarship or grant aid	69
% frosh rec. non-need-based scholarship or grant aid	45
% UG rec. non-need-based scholarship or grant aid	25
% frosh rec. need-based self-help aid	79
% UG rec. need-based self-help aid	82
% frosh rec. any financial aid	75
% UG rec. any financial aid	70
% UG borrow to pay for school	51
Average cumulative indebtedness	$20,879
% frosh need fully met	15
% ugrads need fully met	16
Average % of frosh need met	72
Average % of ugrad need met	70

City University of New York—Baruch College

Undergraduate Admissions, 151 East 25th Street, New York, NY 10010 • Admissions: 646-312-1400 • Fax: 646-312-1363

CAMPUS LIFE	
Quality of Life Rating	**66**
Fire Safety Rating	**60***
Green Rating	**61**
Type of school	public
Environment	metropolis

STUDENTS	
Total undergrad enrollment	13,938
% male/female	49/51
% from out of state	5
% from public high school	86
% frosh live on campus	8
# of fraternities	9
# of sororities	7
% African American	10
% Asian	34
% Caucasian	30
% Hispanic	14
% international	12
# of countries represented	166

SURVEY SAYS . . .

Great computer facilities
Great library
Diverse student types on campus
Students love New York, NY
Student publications are popular
Very little drug use

ACADEMICS	
Academic Rating	**69**
% students graduating within 4 years	36
% students graduating within 6 years	63
Calendar	semester
Student/faculty ratio	18:1
Profs interesting rating	68
Profs accessible rating	65
Most classes have	20–29 students
Most lab/discussion sessions have	20–29 students

MOST POPULAR MAJORS
accounting; finance

APPLICANTS ALSO LOOK AT AND OFTEN PREFER
Fordham University, New York University

AND SOMETIMES PREFER
State University of New York at Albany, CUNY—Hunter College

AND RARELY PREFER
Pace University

STUDENTS SAY "..."

Academics

Baruch College consists of three schools, and although its School of Arts and Sciences and School of Public Affairs are both fine, it's the Zicklin School of Business that garners nearly all the attention here (as well over three-quarters of the student body). Zicklin offers a "very demanding business-oriented program that provides a great education in an overcrowded environment" where "it's very easy to get lost," but just as easy for go-getters to access "unparalleled internships, career, and networking opportunities to major global companies' headquarters." Because New York City is a worldwide finance capital, Baruch's connections and internships provide "a gateway to the world of finance," and it is for this reason—as well as for the fact that "tuition is about one-fourth what it is at NYU," making it "the best college value in New York City"—that students flock to Baruch. Students warn that you must be willing to "put 110 percent into your studies and take advantage of the NYC network and Starr Career Development Center" to reap all available benefits here. Those who make the effort will discover a career office that "works tirelessly to prepare its students for the working world. Not only do they offer workshops on how to make yourself an attractive candidate, they also offer counseling and even resumé reviews to make sure your resume is perfect, as well as mock interviews that help you analyze your strengths and weaknesses as an interviewer."

Life

Baruch has no campus, just a collection of six buildings scattered over four city blocks. Most of the action centers around the seventeen-story Newman Vertical Campus facility, which is "beautiful" but "does not offer a lot of things to do" between classes. Furthermore, the mostly residential area surrounding the school offers "few places you can hang out at, especially when you have huge breaks between classes." Although the building is fairly new, "the escalators almost never work," and the elevators "are always as packed as the commute on the train." Many here grumpily opt for the stairway. School-related extracurriculars are hampered by the lack of a "real campus" and by the fact that many students are commuters who work part time. Some get involved in community service and/or major-related clubs and organizations, but anyone coming here for a traditional college experience will be sorely disappointed. However access to New York City, for most, more than compensates for this drawback.

Student Body

The "hardworking" student body at Baruch could well be "the most diverse university in the country." It's the sort of place where "You can eat samosas on Tuesday, mooncakes on Wednesday, and falafel on Thursdays for free because of all the cultural events that are held." Students brag that "hundreds of countries are represented in our student body" and note that "The one common thread would be we are mostly business-oriented and have jobs/internships outside of school." While students get along well in class, outside the classroom they can be "very cliquey." One student explains, "If you know people from your high school, you stick with them; if you're a foreign student you stick with others from your home country. Otherwise you get the cold shoulder." Because "the school puts tremendous pressure on grades," most students are "extremely stressed."

FINANCIAL AID: 646-312-1360 • E-MAIL: ADMISSIONS@BARUCH.CUNY.EDU • WEBSITE: WWW.BARUCH.CUNY.EDU

THE PRINCETON REVIEW SAYS

Admissions

Very important factors considered include: Academic GPA, rigor of secondary school record, standardized test scores. *Important factors considered include:* Application essay, recommendation(s). *Other factors considered include:* Class rank, alumni/ae relation, character/personal qualities, extracurricular activities, interview, talent/ability, work experience. SAT or ACT required; ACT with or without writing component accepted. TOEFL required of all international applicants. High school diploma is required and GED is accepted. *Academic units required:* 4 English, 3 mathematics, 2 science (2 science labs), 2 foreign language, 4 social studies. *Academic units recommended:* 4 mathematics, 2 foreign language, 1 academic electives.

Financial Aid

Students should submit: FAFSA, state aid form. Regular filing deadline is April 30. The Princeton Review suggests that all financial aid forms be submitted as soon as possible after January 1. *Need-based scholarships/grants offered:* Federal Pell, SEOG, state scholarships/grants, the school's own gift aid, City merit scholarships. *Loan aid offered:* Direct Subsidized Stafford, Direct Unsubsidized Stafford, Direct PLUS, Federal Perkins. Applicants will be notified of awards on a rolling basis beginning April 1. Federal Work-Study Program available. Institutional employment available. Off-campus job opportunities are excellent.

The Inside Word

Baruch's business school greatly upgrades the school's profile in its hallmark academic field. Admissions have grown steadily more competitive since, especially for students seeking undergraduate business degrees. Today, Baruch receives nearly ten applications for every slot in its freshman class. Your math scores on standardized tests count more heavily here than verbal scores.

THE SCHOOL SAYS "..."

From the Admissions Office

"Baruch College is in the heart of New York City. As an undergraduate, you will join a vibrant learning community of students and scholars in the middle of an exhilarating city full of possibilities. Baruch is a place where theory meets practice. You can network with city leaders; secure business, cultural, and nonprofit internships; access the music, art, and business scene; and meet experts who visit our campus. You will take classes that bridge business, arts, science, and social policy, learning from professors who are among the best in their fields.

"Baruch offers thirty-five majors and sixty-two minors in three schools: the School of Public Affairs, the Weissman School of Arts and Science, and the Zicklin School of Business. Highly qualified undergraduates may apply to the Baruch College Honors program, which offers scholarships, small seminars and honors courses. Students may also study abroad through programs in more than thirty countries.

"Our seventeen-floor Newman Vertical Campus serves as the college's hub. Here you will find the atmosphere and resources of a traditional college campus, but in a lively urban setting. Our classrooms have state-of-the-art technology, and our library was named the top college library in the nation. Baruch also has a simulated trading floor for students who are interested in Wall Street. You can also enjoy a three-level athletics and recreation complex, which features a twenty-five-meter indoor pool as well as a performing arts complex. The College just introduced a residence hall opportunity for undergraduates on Manhattan's vibrant Lower East Side in a newly built building at 101 Ludlow Street. The first residents will move in this August, before classes begin.

"Baruch's selective admission standards, strong academic programs, top national honors, as well as its internship and job-placement opportunities make it an exceptional educational value."

SELECTIVITY	
Admissions Rating	**91**
# of applicants	19,283
% of applicants accepted	22
% of acceptees attending	30

FRESHMAN PROFILE	
Range SAT Critical Reading	500–600
Range SAT Math	580–680
Minimum paper TOEFL	620
Minimum web-based TOEFL	105
Average HS GPA	3.1
% graduated top 10% of class	37
% graduated top 25% of class	63
% graduated top 50% of class	86

DEADLINES	
Regular	
Priority	2/1
Nonfall registration?	yes

FINANCIAL FACTS	
Financial Aid Rating	**65**
Annual in-state tuition	$5,430
Annual out-state tuition	$14,550
Room and board	$8,877
Required fees	$480
Books and supplies	$1,248
% needy frosh rec. need-based scholarship or grant aid	21
% needy UG rec. need-based scholarship or grant aid	10
% needy frosh rec. non-need-based scholarship or grant aid	1
% needy UG rec. non-need-based scholarship or grant aid	1
% needy frosh rec. need-based self-help aid	39
% needy UG rec. need-based self-help aid	36
% frosh rec. any financial aid	51
% UG rec. any financial aid	53
% UG borrow to pay for school	17
Average cumulative indebtedness	$10,924
% frosh need fully met	27
% ugrads need fully met	16
Average % of frosh need met	55
Average % of ugrad need met	59

City University of New York—Brooklyn College

2900 Bedford Avenue, Brooklyn, NY 11210 • Admissions: 718-951-5001 • Fax: 718-951-4506

CAMPUS LIFE

Quality of Life Rating	**68**
Fire Safety Rating	**60***
Green Rating	**90**
Type of school	public
Environment	metropolis

STUDENTS

Total undergrad enrollment	12,162
% male/female	42/58
% from out of state	1
# of fraternities	7
# of sororities	8
% African American	24
% Asian	17
% Caucasian	41
% Hispanic	12
% international	4
# of countries represented	133

SURVEY SAYS . . .

Great computer facilities
Great library
Diverse student types on campus
Very little drug use

ACADEMICS

Academic Rating	**74**
% students returning for sophomore year	82
% students graduating within 4 years	22
% students graduating within 6 years	48
Calendar	semester
Student/faculty ratio	15:1
Profs interesting rating	70
Profs accessible rating	68
Most classes have	20–29 students

MOST POPULAR MAJORS

business management and finance; accounting; psychology

STUDENTS SAY ". . ."

Academics

Brooklyn College "is the perfect representative of Brooklyn as a borough and [of] success in the community," an institution that, like its home borough, "educates its students in an environment that reflects diversity, opportunity (study abroad, research, athletics, employment), and support." "Lauded as one of the best senior colleges in CUNY" and boasting "a beautiful campus," Brooklyn College entices a lot of bright students looking for an affordable, quality, undergraduate experience as well as some attracted by the school's relatively charitable admissions standards. It's easier to get in here than to stay in; Brooklyn College is "an academically challenging and rigorous school" that "feels a lot more competitive than one would anticipate." Professors "are fabulous" and "really passionate about the subjects that they teach and their students' career paths," although there are some "grumpy and nasty professors" that might best be avoided. Students are especially sanguine about special programs here, such as the various honors programs, in which "you will meet tons of highly intelligent people. Honors classes boast very good in-class discussions and highly vibrant, enthusiastic students. Non-honors classes are more run-of-the-mill but still very good academically." The school also works hard to provide "constant and innumerable job opportunities available to students and the Magner Center, which helps students find jobs and internships, and [to] help them prepare for the real world through resume writing workshops [and] job interview workshops." There are also "many financial awards available."

Life

"Apart from all the clubs and athletics on campus, most people come for class and then leave" at Brooklyn College because "we are a commuter school, so it has to be this way. All social activities happen off campus." There are "pretty nice places to hang out around campus for the occasional coffee," and "there are a lot of student organization and a lot of activities done to help enhance student life on campus," but the "immediate surroundings of the Brooklyn College campus are generally not where you would want to stay for hours," and "on weekends the campus usually is dead." That said, "The campus is quite beautiful, and the quad during spring time is usually a nice place to sit and relax." Furthermore, "New York City hotspots are a twenty- to forty-minute [subway] ride away," and Brooklyn itself is "a great place to live" where "there are always fun things happening."

Student Body

"The typical student at Brooklyn College is hardworking, from the NY metro area, and a commuter." Many "hold part-time jobs and pay at least part of their own tuition, so they are usually in a rush because they have a lot more responsibility on their shoulders than the average college student." Like Brooklyn itself, "The student body is very diversified," with everyone from "an aspiring opera singer to quirky film majors to single mothers looking for a better life for their children," and so "no student can be described as being typical. Everyone blends in as normal, and little segregation is noticed (if it exists)." Students here represent more than 100 nations and speak nearly as many languages. There are even students "that come from Long Island to North Carolina, from Connecticut to even Hong Kong."

FINANCIAL AID: 718-951-5051 • E-MAIL: ADMINQRY@BROOKLYN.CUNY.EDU • WEBSITE: WWW.BROOKLYN.CUNY.EDU

THE PRINCETON REVIEW SAYS

Admissions

Very important factors considered include: Academic GPA, rigor of secondary school record, standardized test scores. SAT or ACT required; ACT with or without writing component accepted. TOEFL required of all international applicants. High school diploma is required and GED is accepted. *Academic units recommended:* 4 English, 3 mathematics, 3 science, 3 foreign language, 4 social studies, 4 academic electives.

Financial Aid

Students should submit: FAFSA, state aid form. The Princeton Review suggests that all financial aid forms be submitted as soon as possible after January 1. *Need-based scholarships/grants offered:* Federal Pell, SEOG, state scholarships/grants, private scholarships, the school's own gift aid. *Loan aid offered:* Direct Subsidized Stafford, Direct Unsubsidized Stafford, Direct PLUS, Federal Perkins. Applicants will be notified of awards on a rolling basis beginning May 1. Federal Work-Study Program available. Institutional employment available. Off-campus job opportunities are excellent.

The Inside Word

Brooklyn College doesn't set the bar inordinately high; students with less-than-stellar high school records can receive a chance to prove themselves here. Once they get in, though, they had better be prepared to work; Brooklyn College typically loses about twenty percent of its freshman class each year, and six-year graduation rates rarely exceed fifty percent. Getting into Brooklyn College is one thing; surviving its academic challenges is a whole other thing entirely.

THE SCHOOL SAYS ". . ."

From the Admissions Office

"Brooklyn College is a premier public liberal arts college. For the last five years it has been consistently designated as one of America's Best Value Colleges by The Princeton Review and, in 2009, was cited as one of the top fifty Best Value Public Colleges in the nation.

"Respected nationally for its rigorous academic standards, the college has increased both the size and academic quality of its student body. It takes pride in such innovative programs as its award-winning Freshman Year College; the Honors Academy, which houses six programs for high achievers; and its nationally recognized core curriculum. Its School of Education is ranked among the top twenty in the country for graduates who go on to be considered among the best teachers in New York City. Brooklyn College's strong academic reputation has attracted an outstanding faculty of nationally renowned teachers and scholars. Among the awards they have won are Pulitzers, Guggenheims, Fulbrights, and many National Institutes of Health grants.

"The student body consists of more than 16,000 undergraduate and graduate students who represent the ethnic and cultural diversity of the borough. The college's accessibility by subway or bus allows students to further enrich their educational experience through New York City's many cultural events and institutions. In recent years, student achievements have been acknowledged with Fulbright and Truman Scholarships and an Emmy Award. This year we received our third Rhodes Scholarship in eleven years.

"The Brooklyn College campus, considered to be among the most beautiful in the nation, is in the midst of an ambitious program of expansion and renewal. A new residence hall has opened two blocks from the campus. It includes such amenities as single, as well as shared, rooms, Wi-Fi throughout, community lounges, a fitness center, and kitchenettes in every room. The dazzling library is the most technologically advanced educational and research facility in the CUNY system. Opened in 2009, the West Quad Building has state-of-the-art student services and is home to the physical education department. A separate fitness center, basketball and handball courts, and a competition pool is open for use by students and staff. Ground will be broken soon for a new performing arts center, followed in the coming years with a new science complex."

SELECTIVITY

Admissions Rating	**93**
# of applicants	19,152
% of applicants accepted	28
% of acceptees attending	21

FRESHMAN PROFILE

Range SAT Critical Reading	490–590
Range SAT Math	520–610
Minimum paper TOEFL	500
Average HS GPA	3.3
% graduated top 10% of class	19
% graduated top 25% of class	52
% graduated top 50% of class	81

DEADLINES

Regular	
Priority	2/1
Nonfall registration?	yes

FINANCIAL FACTS

Financial Aid Rating	**93**
Annual in-state tuition	$5,430
Annual out-state tuition	$14,550
Required fees	$454
Books and supplies	$1,179
% needy frosh rec. need-based scholarship or grant aid	83
% needy UG rec. need-based scholarship or grant aid	98
% needy frosh rec. non-need-based scholarship or grant aid	38
% needy UG rec. non-need-based scholarship or grant aid	29
% needy frosh rec. need-based self-help aid	81
% needy UG rec. need-based self-help aid	94
% frosh rec. any financial aid	73
% UG rec. any financial aid	86
% UG borrow to pay for school	56
Average cumulative indebtedness	$9,875
% frosh need fully met	77
% ugrads need fully met	75
Average % of frosh need met	96
Average % of ugrad need met	98

City University of New York—City College

160 Convent Avenue, Wille Administration Building, New York, NY 10031 • Admissions: 212-650-6977 • Fax: 212-650-6417

CAMPUS LIFE

Quality of Life Rating	**70**
Fire Safety Rating	**97**
Green Rating	**84**
Type of school	public
Environment	metropolis

STUDENTS

Total undergrad enrollment	12,938
% male/female	47/53
% from out of state	1
% from public high school	85
# of fraternities	2
# of sororities	1
% African American	22
% Asian	24
% Caucasian	19
% Hispanic	34
% international	8
# of countries represented	100

SURVEY SAYS . . .

Students are happy
Great library
Students are friendly
Diverse student types on campus
Students get along with local community

ACADEMICS

Academic Rating	**70**
% students graduating within 4 years	6
% students graduating within 6 years	39
Calendar	semester
Student/faculty ratio	16:1
Profs interesting rating	70
Profs accessible rating	67
Most classes have	20–29 students

MOST POPULAR MAJORS

communication and media studies, other; electrical, electronics and communications engineering; psychology

STUDENTS SAY ". . ."

Academics

As the first school of the City University of New York system, CCNY "stands for growth, education, and creativity." Many students choose the school due to its "astonishingly low cost" and proximity to home, and its practicality is backed up by "rigorous academic programs." "I fell in love with the school during open house, and it's the exact way I imagined after enrolling," says a student. The university has also made substantial new investments in science and medicine, and it is the only public college in New York City to offer engineering degrees, which is a huge draw for the school (but there is "no coddling here in the engineering school," warns one student). A "multitude" of classes are taught by "awesome professors with experience and wonderful careers" who "are available outside of the class" and "exhibit great love for the materials they teach." Generally, professors "go above and beyond" to ensure that students are able to grasp what they are learning. "My professors devote time and effort to making sure students understand the material being taught," confirms a student. The diversity in the student body, as well as the faculty and administration, "is profound," which "helps many people interact with different people from different cultures and come together to get through each semester in college." No matter their background, all here "take our education and future careers seriously." "There are a lot of talented people in the school overall," says a student, not to mention the "strong ties to research collaborators and institutions." Professors "will make you learn and work for the A," but "It has overall been a very rewarding experience," according to a student.

Life

Since so many students work and live full lives outside of classes, most students commute home each night. "The campus is nice, and there's a lot to do, but there's very little 'campus life,'" according to one student. CCNY has "amazing events," but "Sometimes it's hard to partake due to our employment and fiscal priorities." The clubs "are always having shows, fairs, and other types of events offered to all students." People are "very respectful and helpful," and "A new student will always be able to find help." The library and cafeteria are both popular hangout spots, and "There is a gym, both for workout and for sports." Let's also not forget where the school is located: "It isn't hard to find fun around New York City." Harlem "is very historic," and "There are great places to eat around City College." The radio station WCCR "always has a ton of people having fun, hanging out, and playing music."

Student Body

The diversity at CCNY is not just ethnic—it is also political, economic, academic, age, and every other means of categorization—which means that there is no typical student. This large group of "diverse students seeking excellence" all feel like they fit in because "we each have something to bring to the table." On any average day, "You can walk through the college and see people of all ages and races interacting with each other." Students "live busy lives," and the vast majority "works and goes to school at the same time." Most students are commuters, and many are "immigrant or comes from an immigrant family," but "Most identify first and foremost as New Yorkers." Many subscribe to clubs and other extracurriculars "to fit in and make friends." Most CCNY students are not looking for the "typical college experience," but rather are interested "in the intellectual and emotional growth that comes with higher education."

FINANCIAL AID: 212-650-5819 • E-MAIL: ADMISSIONS@CCNY.CUNY.EDU • WEBSITE: WWW.CCNY.CUNY.EDU

THE PRINCETON REVIEW SAYS

Admissions

Very important factors considered include: Academic GPA, rigor of secondary school record. *Important factors considered include:* Standardized test scores. *Other factors considered include:* Application essay, recommendation(s). SAT or ACT required; TOEFL required of all international applicants. High school diploma is required and GED is accepted. *Academic units recommended:* 4 English, 2 mathematics, 2 science (2 science labs), 2 foreign language, 4 social studies, 1 visual/performing arts.

Financial Aid

Students should submit: FAFSA. The Princeton Review suggests that all financial aid forms be submitted as soon as possible after January 1. *Need-based scholarships/grants offered:* Federal Pell, SEOG, state scholarships/grants, the school's own gift aid. *Loan aid offered:* Direct Subsidized Stafford, Direct Unsubsidized Stafford, Direct PLUS. Applicants will be notified of awards on a rolling basis beginning April 1. Federal Work-Study Program available. Institutional employment available. Highest amount earned per year from on-campus jobs $7,200. Off-campus job opportunities are fair.

The Inside Word

CUNY—City College is one of the toughest CUNY schools get into, with an admissions rate of about thirty-three percent (some schools and programs within can be lower). Selective freshman programs—such as the honors college—may require a supplemental paper application, letters of recommendation, and/or a personal statement. The good news is that students can apply online to as many as six CUNY colleges with one application.

THE SCHOOL SAYS ". . ."

From the Admissions Office

"City is an old school with new ideas. Founded in 1847, we take pride in our tradition, eagerly embrace the present, and ride the cutting edge of the future. CCNY has one of the most diverse student bodies in any college of America, and is a mirror image of New York City. Our mission emphasizes access and excellence in undergraduate and graduate education and research, and opportunities for internships and study abroad abound. Whether you are looking for preparation for an exciting career or graduate and doctoral studies, City College offers the path to your future. We offer over 100 undergraduate and graduate degrees in architecture, education, engineering, the arts and humanities, the social sciences and science, as well as a unique BS/MD program. High achieving students interested in any discipline also may have the opportunity to participate including the Macaulay Honors College and the CCNY Honors Program.

"We are seeking students who will thrive at City both academically and personally, while contributing to the community inside and outside of the classroom. Candidates will be considered on the basis of overall strength of academic preparation (a minimum of 16 academic units must have been completed), grades in individual subjects, overall high school average, and SAT or ACT scores. Applicants who have taken the General Equivalency Diploma (GED) examination must submit test scores and can be eligible provided they have attained a score of at least 3250 or higher. City College admits a small number of academically exceptional high school students upon the completion of their high school junior year. Students enter as matriculated students into the College's Honors program. Applicants generally are from the upper ten percent of their high school class.

"**All** freshmen applying to The Bernard and Anne Spitzer School of Architecture are required to submit a Creative Challenge form; freshmen applying to The Grove School of Engineering are required to submit a supplemental application form; and freshmen applying to the Sophie Davis School of Biomedical Education are required to submit two separate applications."

SELECTIVITY

Admissions Rating	**80**
# of applicants	23,250
% of applicants accepted	32
% of acceptees attending	20

FRESHMAN PROFILE

Range SAT Critical Reading	440–570
Range SAT Math	510–620
Minimum paper TOEFL	500
Minimum web-based TOEFL	61
Average HS GPA	3.0

DEADLINES

Regular	
Priority	2/1
Nonfall registration?	yes

FINANCIAL FACTS

Financial Aid Rating	**91**
Annual in-state tuition	$5,131
Annual out-state tuition	$13,800
Required fees	$329
% needy frosh rec. need-based scholarship or grant aid	95
% needy UG rec. need-based scholarship or grant aid	98
% needy frosh rec. non-need-based scholarship or grant aid	51
% needy UG rec. non-need-based scholarship or grant aid	10
% needy frosh rec. need-based self-help aid	21
% needy UG rec. need-based self-help aid	48
% frosh rec. any financial aid	75
% UG rec. any financial aid	78
% UG borrow to pay for school	20
Average cumulative indebtedness	$15,780
% frosh need fully met	93
% ugrads need fully met	81
Average % of frosh need met	82
Average % of ugrad need met	83

City University of New York—Hunter College

695 Park Avenue, Room N203, New York, NY 10065 • Admissions: 212-772-4490 • Fax: 212-650-3472

CAMPUS LIFE

Quality of Life Rating	**78**
Fire Safety Rating	**89**
Green Rating	**80**
Type of school	public
Environment	metropolis

STUDENTS

Total undergrad enrollment	15,417
% male/female	34/66
% from out of state	4
% from public high school	70
# of fraternities	2
# of sororities	2
% African American	11
% Asian	24
% Caucasian	39
% Hispanic	18
% international	7

SURVEY SAYS . . .

Diverse student types on campus
Different types of students interact
Students get along with local community
Students love New York, NY
Political activism is popular
Very little drug use

ACADEMICS

Academic Rating	**70**
% students graduating within 4 years	20
% students graduating within 6 years	45
Calendar	semester
Student/faculty ratio	15:1
Profs interesting rating	76
Profs accessible rating	79
Most classes have	20–29 students

MOST POPULAR MAJORS

accounting; English literature (British and commonwealth); psychology

STUDENTS SAY ". . ."

Academics

CUNY boasts an "outstanding" reputation based in part on its ability to offer "a solid education at an affordable price" and "exposure to New York City." Students who like to challenge the status quo will find a home here. In CUNY classrooms, "Diversity of thought is not only tolerated, but encouraged." Those classes can be "very tough," forcing students to "work hard to keep good grades." Some students groan that professors here "teach at a fast pace," but students who pay attention will find that their educators generally "know the subjects that they are teaching very well." While there are some "very tedious professors," most students find that professors are "intellectually challenged by brilliant instructors." A few students wish there were more tenured professors on staff and say that part-time educators "would care more if they were paid more." Yet many departments win praise, including the "highly respected" psychology department, which is "affiliated with most of the prestigious hospitals in New York City," as well as challenging English and nursing programs. Maybe most important is that students will get a sense for what their education will mean outside of school. These professors "bring to the table their vast experiences in their field of expertise and have never hesitated to educate on what to expect when we are outside of the classroom, often offering a practical aspect to what in many classrooms are strictly academic discussions."

Life

On one hand, being located in Manhattan means that Hunter has immediate access to almost anything in arts, culture, music, and nightlife that an urban adventurer can imagine. On the other hand, "Hunter is largely a commuter school, so there is not much campus life at night or on the weekends," a situation one student calls "miserable." Students won't get a typical college life here. "Nobody lives on campus at Hunter," and "Most people who attend school at Hunter work part-time or full-time, have apartments, pay bills, and go to school full-time." That is not to say there is no excitement at Hunter. You just "have to make an effort for things to happen and to gather people because they need to make time from their schedules to meet up." Those who put in the effort will find that the city is their oyster. One student notes that whether it is food or music or entertainment, "anything that's not academic-related you can find easily from blocks away," while another notes, "New York is a tourist haven," so there is no shortage of things to do. But again, it won't come to you. Be prepared to make things happen. "The only way to make friends is to dorm (which is nearly impossible) or to hang around campus joining fraternities and clubs." If you're a commuter student or work full-time, as many Hunter students do, "Socializing is nearly impossible."

Student Body

New York City is one of the most diverse metropolitan areas in the world, so it should come as no surprise that "there is no typical student at Hunter." This cultural melting pot of a region means "the diversity here is real and comes in all forms, most especially diversity of thought and opinion." One student notes that "all of my classrooms contain a mix of every ethnicity and nationality, all ages, all types of people." Even with this wide array of cultures, "Somehow, we all manage to fit in and get along with one another." Students here also vary wildly in age, with older attendees common in most classrooms. "Most students work full- or part-time while juggling a full-time schedule," which can make it "extremely difficult to make friends, because it's a commuter school." This also means that "there's little sense of school identity." However, for those who involve themselves with other students, "as long as you are not too shy, it is easy to make friends around here."

FINANCIAL AID: 212-772-4820 • E-MAIL: ADMISSIONS@HUNTER.CUNY.EDU • WEBSITE: WWW.HUNTER.CUNY.EDU

THE PRINCETON REVIEW SAYS

Admissions

Very important factors considered include: Application essay, academic GPA, rigor of secondary school record, standardized test scores. SAT or ACT required; TOEFL required of all international applicants. High school diploma is required and GED is accepted. *Academic units required:* 2 English, 2 mathematics, 1 science (1 science lab). *Academic units recommended:* 4 English, 3 mathematics, 2 science, 2 foreign language, 4 social studies, 1 visual/performing arts, 1 academic electives.

Financial Aid

Students should submit: FAFSA, state aid form. The Princeton Review suggests that all financial aid forms be submitted as soon as possible after January 1. *Need-based scholarships/grants offered:* Federal Pell, state scholarships/grants, the school's own gift aid. *Loan aid offered:* Direct Subsidized Stafford, Direct Unsubsidized Stafford, Direct PLUS, Federal Perkins, state loans, college/university loans from institutional funds, CUNY Student Assistance Program (CUSTA), Aide for Part-Time-Study (APTS), SEEK. Applicants will be notified of awards on a rolling basis beginning May 15. Federal Work-Study Program available. Institutional employment available. Off-campus job opportunities are fair.

The Inside Word

Getting into Hunter is consistently getting harder, with the admissions office getting in excess of 30,000 applications a year. Applicants should be prepared to present strong grades that meet the school's admissions formula. (Hunter officials do not divulge the formula.) Programs fill up fast, so applying early is essential. Wait too long and thousands of students will have gotten in line in front of you.

THE SCHOOL SAYS ". . ."

From the Admissions Office

"Located in the heart of Manhattan, Hunter offers students the stimulating learning environment and career-building opportunities you might expect from a college that's been a part of the world's most exciting city since 1870. The largest college in the City University of New York, Hunter pulses with energy. Hunter's vitality stems from a large, highly diverse faculty and student body. Its schools—Arts and Sciences, Education, Nursing and the CUNY Schoolf of Public Health, and Social Work—provide an affordable first-rate education. Undergraduates have extraordinary opportunities to conduct high-level research under renowned faculty, and many opt for credit-bearing internships in such exciting fields as media, the arts, and government. The college's high standards and special programs ensure a challenging education. The Block Program for first-year students keeps classmates together as they pursue courses in the liberal arts, pre–health science, pre-nursing, premed, or honors. A range of honors programs is available for students with strong academic records, including the highly competitive tuition-free Macaulay Honors College for entering freshmen and the Thomas Hunter Honors Program, which emphasizes small classes with personalized mentoring by outstanding faculty. Qualified students also benefit from Hunter's participation in minority science research and training programs, the prestigious Andrew W. Mellon Minority Undergraduate Program, and many other passports to professional success.

"Applicants for the entering class are required to take either the SAT or the ACT."

SELECTIVITY	
Admissions Rating	**84**
# of applicants	30,529
% of applicants accepted	27
% of acceptees attending	26

FRESHMAN PROFILE	
Range SAT Critical Reading	500–600
Range SAT Math	540–640
Minimum paper TOEFL	500

DEADLINES	
Regular	
Deadline	3/15
Nonfall registration?	yes

FINANCIAL FACTS	
Financial Aid Rating	**82**
Annual in-state tuition	$5,130
Annual out-state tuition	$13,800
Required fees	$399
% needy frosh rec. need-based scholarship or grant aid	97
% needy UG rec. need-based scholarship or grant aid	96
% needy frosh rec. non-need-based scholarship or grant aid	78
% needy UG rec. non-need-based scholarship or grant aid	36
% needy frosh rec. need-based self-help aid	11
% needy UG rec. need-based self-help aid	27
% frosh rec. any financial aid	91
% UG rec. any financial aid	94
% UG borrow to pay for school	58
Average cumulative indebtedness	$9,000
% frosh need fully met	35
% ugrads need fully met	15
Average % of frosh need met	77
Average % of ugrad need met	76

City University of New York—Queens College

6530 Kissena Boulevard, Flushing, NY 11367 • Admissions: 718-997-5600 • Fax: 718-997-5617

CAMPUS LIFE

Quality of Life Rating	**83**
Fire Safety Rating	**96**
Green Rating	**82**
Type of school	public
Environment	metropolis

STUDENTS

Total undergrad enrollment	16,554
% male/female	42/58
% from out of state	1
% frosh live on campus	1
# of fraternities	4
# of sororities	3
% African American	8
% Asian	27
% Caucasian	47
% Hispanic	17
% international	5
# of countries represented	170

SURVEY SAYS . . .

Diverse student types on campus
Students get along with local community
Students love Flushing, NY
Students are happy
Musical organizations are popular
Very little beer drinking
Very little drug use

ACADEMICS

Academic Rating	**69**
% students returning for sophomore year	87
% students graduating within 4 years	25
% students graduating within 6 years	53
Calendar	semester
Student/faculty ratio	16:1
Profs interesting rating	70
Profs accessible rating	68
Most classes have	20–29 students

MOST POPULAR MAJORS

accounting; psychology; economics

STUDENTS SAY ". . ."

Academics

"A great education at an affordable price" could easily be the mantra of Queens College. A stalwart of New York City's university system, Queens offers "an amazingly diverse campus" and a "warm, welcoming" atmosphere. Largely a "commuter" school, undergrads here can choose from "a wide variety of classes," although, as one psych major warns, "They can close out quickly." Despite the fact that "the workload can be quite heavy at times," undergrads speak glowingly of their "understanding" professors who constantly "push you to reach your full economics." They are "extremely intelligent and personable," and they are always "willing to meet with students outside of the classroom to discuss anything and everything." One ecstatic senior goes as far as saying, "I feel like I am around close relatives." However, other students do fret over "the high turnover" among faculty and worry that this can "make it difficult to form meaningful academic connections." Praise also extends to administrators who "always make an effort to connect with students and are always very open and willing to talk." Indeed, even though there's "a lot of bureaucracy," undergrads still find them to be "very down-to-earth" and "approachable." As a media studies major expounds, "Students and administrators host town hall meetings numerous times throughout the semester in order to exchange ideas on how to make the campus a better place."

Life

Some undergrads at Queens College lament that, because of the commuter culture, "There isn't much interaction between the students on campus." They simply "go to class and then go home." However, one content freshman insists, "There are so many activities to attend and clubs to join. You just need to get involved." Indeed, the college offers everything from "literary magazines, newspapers, and radio [to] student government." There are also plenty of opportunities for the altruistically inclined. As a media studies major shares, "I am deeply involved in a growing movement of students that are getting active in the community. We host charity drives, distribute food and clothes to the homeless, and [advocate for] a greener campus." The college also recently opened its first dormitory, which has been a definite boon to campus life. One happy resident tells us, "The Summit is amazing. It's fun to hang around there or sit on the Quad on a nice day and do homework/talk with friends." Fortunately, "There is a nice atmosphere on campus, and it feels safe and comfortable for both commuters and residents." The surrounding area offers plenty of great dining options, especially "Chinese food and Kosher restaurants, depending on which way you walk." And of course, Manhattan is "very close and easily accessible." Students frequently head into the city "to go clubbing, out to eat, or hit the bars and museums."

Student Body

As a finance major shares, "Flushing is one of the most ethnically diverse cities in the United States and the demographics of the school reflect that." Certainly, diversity is a buzzword around the Queens campus, and the college attracts many "Jewish, Asian, and Hispanics students." An impressed sophomore goes further, "There is no typical student at Queens College. If you can name a language, it's spoken here. If you name a country, someone has ethnic ties to it. There are students of all races, sexual orientations, ethnicities, and genders at Queens who live together in harmony." A speech pathology major observes, "Every time I walk through campus, I feel as if I am trekking through the seven continents." Most of these "easygoing," "unassuming," and "liberal" undergrads find common ground in their desire "to get a good education" with an "inexpensive" price tag. As one media studies major sums up, "The school has so many clubs that everyone finds a way to fit in with their own niche groups."

FINANCIAL AID: 718-997-5123 • E-MAIL: VINCENT.ANGRISANI@QC.CUNY.EDU • WEBSITE: WWW.QC.CUNY.EDU

THE PRINCETON REVIEW SAYS

Admissions

Very important factors considered include: Academic GPA, rigor of secondary school record, standardized test scores. SAT or ACT required; ACT with or without writing component accepted. TOEFL required of all international applicants. High school diploma is required and GED is accepted. *Academic units required:* 4 English, 3 mathematics, 2 science (2 science labs), 3 foreign language, 4 social studies. *Academic units recommended:* 3 science (3 science labs).

Financial Aid

Students should submit: FAFSA, institution's own financial aid form, state aid form. The Princeton Review suggests that all financial aid forms be submitted as soon as possible after January 1. *Need-based scholarships/grants offered:* Federal Pell, SEOG, state scholarships/grants, private scholarships, the school's own gift aid. *Loan aid offered:* Direct Subsidized Stafford, Direct Unsubsidized Stafford, Direct PLUS, Federal Perkins. Applicants will be notified of awards on a rolling basis beginning March 1. Federal Work-Study Program available. Institutional employment available. Off-campus job opportunities are good.

The Inside Word

Minority enrollment has declined at CUNY in the past several years, partially as a result of changes to admissions criteria and stiffer competition for minority applicants. The school would love to boost its numbers, meaning that qualified minority students could be able to finagle a pretty nice financial aid package here, making an already economical situation even more affordable.

THE SCHOOL SAYS ". . ."

From the Admissions Office

"At Queens College, you will engage the world of ideas with faculty and students from the world over, prepare for your career, and enjoy the many activities our beautiful, seventy-seven-acre campus has to offer. And with the August 2009 opening of The Summit—our first residence hall—you'll find a place to enjoy everything that comes with a college residential experience.

"Since 1937, we've provided a premier liberal arts education to talented students. From graduate and undergraduate degrees, a variety of honors and pre-professional programs to research and real work internship opportunities, you'll find countless ways to realize your potential under the guidance of our award-winning, dedicated faculty. We offer nationally recognized programs—such as our Aaron Copland School of Music—in many fields. And we're also the ideal choice for aspiring teachers, preparing more future educators than any college in the tristate area.

"Located only minutes from Manhattan, our campus boasts a traditional quad overlooking the skyline. You'll find a stimulating and welcoming environment here, with a bustling student union, an impressive arts center, and opportunities to participate in dozens of clubs and sports. (We're the only City University of New York college to participate in Division II.) Campus-wide Wi-Fi, computer kiosks, and cybercafes keep you informed and in touch. And best of all, as part of CUNY, we can offer all this at an affordable cost. To apply for fall 2013, submit your application online along with your SATs comprising critical reading, writing, and math."

SELECTIVITY	
Admissions Rating	76
# of applicants	21,000
% of applicants accepted	29
% of acceptees attending	24

FRESHMAN PROFILE	
Range SAT Critical Reading	500–590
Range SAT Math	535–630
Range SAT Writing	500–540
Minimum paper TOEFL	500
Minimum web-based TOEFL	62
% graduated top 10% of class	18
% graduated top 25% of class	50
% graduated top 50% of class	89

DEADLINES	
Regular	
Priority	2/1
Deadline	4/30
Nonfall registration?	yes

FINANCIAL FACTS	
Financial Aid Rating	91
Annual in-state tuition	$5,430
Annual out-state tuition	$14,550
Room and board	$9,950
Required fees	$477
Books and supplies	$1,248
% needy frosh rec. need-based scholarship or grant aid	79
% needy UG rec. need-based scholarship or grant aid	82
% needy frosh rec. non-need-based scholarship or grant aid	38
% needy UG rec. non-need-based scholarship or grant aid	16
% needy frosh rec. need-based self-help aid	26
% needy UG rec. need-based self-help aid	36
% frosh rec. any financial aid	71
% UG rec. any financial aid	46
% UG borrow to pay for school	45
Average cumulative indebtedness	$20,100
% frosh need fully met	63
% ugrads need fully met	79
Average % of frosh need met	95
Average % of ugrad need met	95

CLAREMONT MCKENNA COLLEGE

888 COLUMBIA AVENUE, CLAREMONT, CA 91711 • ADMISSIONS: 909-621-8088 • FAX: 909-621-8516

CAMPUS LIFE

Quality of Life Rating	**99**
Fire Safety Rating	**88**
Green Rating	**80**
Type of school	private
Environment	town

STUDENTS

Total undergrad enrollment	1,301
% male/female	53/47
% from out of state	61
% frosh live on campus	100
% African American	3
% Asian	11
% Caucasian	45
% Hispanic	8
% international	9

SURVEY SAYS . . .

School is well run
Great food on campus
Dorms are like palaces
Frats and sororities are unpopular or nonexistent
Student government is popular
Political activism is popular
Internships are widely available

ACADEMICS

Academic Rating	**98**
% students graduating within 4 years	85
Calendar	semester
Student/faculty ratio	9:1
Profs interesting rating	98
Profs accessible rating	99
Most classes have	10–19 students

MOST POPULAR MAJORS

economics; international relations and affairs; political science and government

APPLICANTS ALSO LOOK AT AND OFTEN PREFER

Harvard College, Princeton University, Stanford University, Yale University

AND SOMETIMES PREFER

Amherst College, Darmouth College, Georgetown University, Pomona College, University of Pennsylvania, Williams College

AND RARELY PREFER

Pitzer College, Tufts University, University of Southern California, Washington University in St. Louis, Harvey Mudd College, Scripps College, University of California—Berkeley, University of California—Los Angeles

STUDENTS SAY ". . ."

Academics

Students at Claremont McKenna really love their school. With its "phenomenal academics, "brilliant professors," "amazing career services center," and "perfect weather," it's no wonder CMC students are "the happiest students in America." Claremont McKenna is known for its government and economics majors, but philosophy, international relations, and the joint sciences program also get high marks. Claremont is a part of the College Consortium, so if students are looking for something that Claremont doesn't have, they can probably find it at one of the four affiliated schools. Students rave about Claremont's emphasis on "professionalism" and all of the "great research and internship opportunities." The workload is heavy, and professors set "high expectations," so "students spend their weeks slaving over their papers, books, readings, research projects, problem sets, etc." Despite the intense workload, students love their professors. "Professors are absolute geniuses in their field," one student gushes. They're "helpful and encouraging," "incredibly accessible," and even "willing to Skype on the weekends to answer questions." "This sounds corny," one student admits; "This really is a place where professors become like family." Students spend a "good deal of out-of-classroom time" with their teachers. "Professors and students are so close that it might be considered creepy to outsiders," but students aren't too worried about creeping anyone out because they know how good they've got it. "When you take both academics and quality of life into account," a cognitive neuroscience major says, "I can't believe I almost went to an Ivy over this place."

Life

Life is good at Claremont McKenna. The "constantly beaming California sun and the close vicinity to both mountains and beaches" means students spend their time outdoors when they can. But even when students are lounging in the sun or playing Frisbee, they're not really taking a break. The "conversation doesn't end in the classroom," a student explains, and the "intellectual culture… really allows for twenty-four-hour learning." While Claremont McKenna has the campus and "community-life and identity of a small school" it "still [has] the resources of the other four C's." Even without the other schools students feel "completely pampered" because "the school cares about its students so much." A Spanish major says, "The relationship between the students and the administration is excellent here," and the "student government and Dean of Students Office…subsidize incredible off-campus trips and on-campus parties." One of the best things about Claremont McKenna is the Atheneum, which hosts prestigious guest lecturers three to four nights a week. One student wisely asks, "Where else could you have dinner with Jesse Jackson, Mitt Romney, etc.?" Partying is definitely a part of life here, and a student admits that if you don't drink, it could be "easy to feel left out." However, students agree, "There's a niche for everyone, and the welcoming, accepting atmosphere makes fitting in easy."

Student Body

"Claremont McKenna doesn't accept students who aren't amazing." "Amazing" means a "really smart and very physically fit," person who's "incredibly motivated and career-driven" and "loves drinking and partying." It's "a tight-knit community of driven, competitive, and intelligent people who know how to be successful and have a great time." "A lot of kids are political and well-informed"; most are "active on campus," very into sports, and involved with internships or clubs. But even though the environment is "academically strict, the students… rarely fit the 'nerdy' stereotype." Students are extremely well-rounded; they "know how to lead a discussion…clock hours in the library, play a varsity or club sport, and hold a leadership position in a club or organization," and they also know how to throw "a great party on Saturday night."

FINANCIAL AID: 909-621-8356 • E-MAIL: ADMISSION@CMC.EDU • WEBSITE: WWW.CMC.EDU

THE PRINCETON REVIEW SAYS

Admissions

Very important factors considered include: Rigor of secondary school record, standardized test scores, extracurricular activities. *Important factors considered include:* Application essay, recommendation(s). *Other factors considered include:* Academic GPA, alumni/ae relation, character/personal qualities, first generation, geographical residence, interview, racial/ethnic status, talent/ability, volunteer work, work experience. SAT or ACT required; ACT with writing component required. TOEFL required of all international applicants. High school diploma is required and GED is accepted. *Academic units required:* 4 English, 3 mathematics, 2 science (2 science labs), 3 foreign language, 1 social studies, 1 history. *Academic units recommended:* 4 mathematics, 3 science.

Financial Aid

Students should submit: FAFSA, CSS/Financial Aid PROFILE, noncustodial PROFILE, business/farm supplement. Regular filing deadline is February 1. The Princeton Review suggests that all financial aid forms be submitted as soon as possible after January 1. *Need-based scholarships/grants offered:* Federal Pell, SEOG, state scholarships/grants, private scholarships, the school's own gift aid, United Negro College Fund. *Loan aid offered:* Direct Subsidized Stafford, Direct Unsubsidized Stafford, Direct PLUS, Federal Perkins, college/university loans from institutional funds. Federal Work-Study Program available. Institutional employment available. Off-campus job opportunities are excellent.

The Inside Word

Although applicants have to possess exemplary academic qualifications to gain admission to Claremont McKenna, the importance of making a good match shouldn't be underestimated. Colleges of such small size and selectivity devote much more energy to determining whether the candidate as an individual fits instead of whether a candidate has the appropriate test scores.

THE SCHOOL SAYS ". . ."

From the Admissions Office

"CMC's mission is clear: To educate students for meaningful lives and responsible leadership in business, government, and many other professions. While many other colleges champion either a traditional liberal arts education with emphasis on intellectual breadth or training that stresses acquisition of technical skills, CMC offers a clear alternative. Instead of dividing the liberal arts and working world into separate realms, education at CMC is rooted in the interplay between the world of ideas and the world of events. By combining the intellectual breadth of liberal arts with the more pragmatic concerns of public affairs, CMC students gain the vision, skills, and values necessary for leadership in all sectors of society.

"Applicants must take the SAT Reasoning Test or ACT with writing. We will use the highest scores from the SAT or ACT. SAT Subject Tests are not required."

SELECTIVITY

Admissions Rating	98
# of applicants	4,412
% of applicants accepted	14
% of acceptees attending	49
# accepting a place on wait list	447
# admitted from wait list	3
# of early decision applicants	419
# accepted early decision	139

FRESHMAN PROFILE

Range SAT Critical Reading	630–720
Range SAT Math	670–760
Range SAT Writing	640–730
Range ACT Composite	29–32
Minimum paper TOEFL	600
Minimum web-based TOEFL	100
% graduated top 10% of class	71
% graduated top 25% of class	94
% graduated top 50% of class	100

DEADLINES

Early decision	
Deadline	11/15
Notification	12/15
Regular	
Deadline	1/2
Notification	4/1
Nonfall registration?	no

FINANCIAL FACTS

Financial Aid Rating	99
Annual tuition	$41,995
Room and board	$13,625
Required fees	$245
Books and supplies	$2,000
% needy frosh rec. need-based scholarship or grant aid	100
% needy UG rec. need-based scholarship or grant aid	100
% needy frosh rec. non-need-based scholarship or grant aid	13
% needy UG rec. non-need-based scholarship or grant aid	13
% needy frosh rec. need-based self-help aid	77
% needy UG rec. need-based self-help aid	73
% frosh rec. any financial aid	45
% UG rec. any financial aid	47
% UG borrow to pay for school	34
Average cumulative indebtedness	$9,915
% frosh need fully met	100
% ugrads need fully met	100
Average % of frosh need met	100
Average % of ugrad need met	100

CLARK UNIVERSITY

950 MAIN STREET, WORCESTER, MA 01610-1477 • ADMISSIONS: 508-793-7431 • FAX: 508-793-8821

CAMPUS LIFE

Quality of Life Rating	69
Fire Safety Rating	95
Green Rating	87
Type of school	private
Environment	city

STUDENTS

Total undergrad enrollment	2,252
% male/female	40/60
% from out of state	62
% from public high school	75
% frosh live on campus	98
% African American	3
% Asian	4
% Caucasian	70
% Hispanic	5
% international	7
# of countries represented	73

SURVEY SAYS . . .

Lots of liberal students
No one cheats
Students are friendly
Frats and sororities are unpopular or nonexistent
Political activism is popular

ACADEMICS

Academic Rating	82
% students returning for sophomore year	90
% students graduating within 4 years	73
% students graduating within 6 years	77
Calendar	semester
Student/faculty ratio	10:1
Profs interesting rating	83
Profs accessible rating	81
Most classes have	10–19 students
Most lab/discussion sessions have	10–19 students

MOST POPULAR MAJORS

biology/biological sciences; political science and government; psychology

APPLICANTS ALSO LOOK AT AND OFTEN PREFER

Boston College, Boston University, Tufts University, Vassar College, Brandeis University

AND SOMETIMES PREFER

Skidmore College, Syracuse University, Ithaca College, Connecticut College, University of New Hampshire, Northeastern University

AND RARELY PREFER

University of Vermont, University of Massachusetts Amherst, Wheaton College (MA), University of Connecticut, Goucher College

STUDENTS SAY ". . ."

Academics

Clark University is "an academically rich, research-oriented," small liberal arts school. Despite its size, "The research opportunities here are endless." A psychology major says, "Clark goes out of its way to provide students with as many opportunities as possible to be involved with their field." Additionally, "The professors are always involved in their fields, and they know where to direct the students." A physics student adds, "Professors are always willing to have students from the field come in to help with [their] research and put in some input about it." "Many of them [use] their own research as modern examples, which really helps to explain things." Overall, Clark professors are "extremely impressive." They're "always there for reassurance and support." One student says, "These relationships opened my eyes to all sorts of academic and professional options." Coursework is "hard but manageable," so there's "academic intensity without undue pressure." A student double-majoring in history and theater sums it up by saying that Clark "is a warm environment where the student's education is paramount, and the professors here are devoted to what they research as well as how they teach."

Life

"Community involvement is huge" at Clark. "Clubs provide a common interest point for students to get to know one another and to participate in shared activities," and since "everyone is involved in something on-campus, we all feel immense pride and ownership over the events that take place." One of the more popular campus activities is community service. A global environmental studies student says that community service "gives…students an opportunity to interact with the community," which in turn, "leads to town-gown relations that are better than most other schools in the city." Students are sharply divided on Worcester. Some say it's "depressing and gloomy" and that it's the "poor man's" "microcosm of Boston." Though Worcester does struggle with social and economic problems, it's possible that students are down on it because they "haven't given the city a chance." "Worcester has an incredibly diverse selection of restaurants, live music, and people." Students who don't venture out into the city hang out in their dorms or go to house parties. Currently, "The administration is focused on revamping Clark's image," and "The buildings…are all being renovated, and there is a lot of construction and planning for new things in the upcoming year." Already, some buildings have "undergone dramatic transformations," such as the library, the gym, and two freshman dorms that "have brand new beautiful additions."

Student Body

Clark offers a "great community" full of "friendly, witty, approachable, very conscious, and active" students. Most seem convinced that the student body is made up of "everyone who was a little awkward or uncool in high school," which includes "cool nerds, hipsters, artist/musicians," "hippies," and "jocks." There's also a significant amount of international students. Clark students are "highly optimistic" and "want to save the world." "This is a college that attracts students who want to do things in this world," one student explains, "whether it's change lives or challenge convention." Students are "very open," but the campus leans heavily to the left, and one student says they've "known people to hide their conservative beliefs for fear of being chastised." That said, "Everyone fits in, in their own way," at Clark, and though students do fall into their groups, "The groups are very fluid," and within groups of students "there is a range of ethnic, racial, religious, and academic diversity." "There is," however, "a disconnect between the athletes at Clark and everyone else." One student complains, "While jocks are in the minority, they still seem to think they rule the school." Athletes would like to have more support, which is understandable, because "no one shows up to the games." Though students might not be the strongest sports fans, "Community involvement is huge." "Most of us are involved in some club or community service through the school," and "Clubs turn into small communities themselves."

FINANCIAL AID: 508-793-7478 • E-MAIL: ADMISSIONS@CLARKU.EDU • WEBSITE: WWW.CLARKU.EDU

THE PRINCETON REVIEW SAYS

Admissions

Very important factors considered include: Academic GPA, recommendation(s), rigor of secondary school record, standardized test scores, character/personal qualities. *Important factors considered include:* Application essay, extracurricular activities, talent/ability, volunteer work. *Other factors considered include:* Class rank, alumni/ae relation, first generation, geographical residence, interview, level of applicant's interest, racial/ethnic status, work experience. SAT or ACT required; ACT with or without writing component accepted. TOEFL required of all international applicants. High school diploma is required and GED is accepted. *Academic units recommended:* 4 English, 3 mathematics, 3 science (2 science labs), 2 foreign language, 2 social studies, 2 history.

Financial Aid

Students should submit: FAFSA, CSS/Financial Aid PROFILE, noncustodial PROFILE. Regular filing deadline is February 1. The Princeton Review suggests that all financial aid forms be submitted as soon as possible after January 1. *Need-based scholarships/grants offered:* Federal Pell, SEOG, state scholarships/grants, the school's own gift aid. *Loan aid offered:* Direct Subsidized Stafford, Direct Unsubsidized Stafford, Direct PLUS, Federal Perkins, state loans. Applicants will be notified of awards on or about March 31. Federal Work-Study Program available. Institutional employment available. Highest amount earned per year from on-campus jobs $2,500. Off-campus job opportunities are good.

The Inside Word

Clark is surrounded by formidable competitors, and its selectivity suffers because of it. Most B students will encounter little difficulty gaining admission. Given the university's solid academic environment and access to other member colleges in the Worcester Consortium, it can be a terrific choice for students who aren't up to the ultra-competitive admissions expectations of top-tier universities.

THE SCHOOL SAYS ". . ."

From the Admissions Office

"Founded in 1887 and located in Worcester, Massachusetts, Clark continues to evolve as a small, urban, liberal arts-based research university that transforms students' lives. With a commitment to Liberal Education and Effective Practice (LEEP), Clark is emerging as an innovative force among universities. We connect a traditional liberal arts education with the development of skills and competencies that serve graduates as they develop personal, professional and civic lives.

"We aim to provide an answer to the question, 'What is a college education worth today?' We know you are looking for a university that will provide you with a strong degree and the tools for career and lifelong success. Clark answers questions like, 'How can I use my bachelor's degree to jumpstart my vision?'; 'What are the internship and career opportunities I can take on in my field of study?'; and 'Where are Clark students, faculty and graduates making an impact around the world?'

"If you are particularly ambitious, our nationally recognized Accelerated BA/MA degree program will give you the opportunity—if you meet the program's requirements—to begin graduate-level coursework in your senior year and complete a master's degree in your fifth year tuition-free.

"At Clark, you will not only enjoy a close-knit community of friends and mentors; you'll have access to a dynamic learning environment in a city that will give you the confidence to move beyond the boundaries of traditional academics. You will have the skills and experience to pursue Clark's motto, 'Challenge Convention and Change Our World.'"

SELECTIVITY	
Admissions Rating	87
# of applicants	4,038
% of applicants accepted	69
% of acceptees attending	22
# accepting a place on wait list	0
# admitted from wait list	0

FRESHMAN PROFILE	
Range SAT Critical Reading	540–660
Range SAT Math	530–640
Range SAT Writing	550–650
Range ACT Composite	25–31
Minimum paper TOEFL	550
Average HS GPA	3.5
% graduated top 10% of class	32
% graduated top 25% of class	71
% graduated top 50% of class	95

DEADLINES	
Early action	
Deadline	11/15
Notification	12/23
Regular	
Deadline	1/15
Notification	4/1
Nonfall registration?	yes

FINANCIAL FACTS	
Financial Aid Rating	91
Annual tuition	$38,100
Room and board	$7,320
Required fees	$350
Books and supplies	$800
% needy frosh rec. need-based scholarship or grant aid	99
% needy UG rec. need-based scholarship or grant aid	99
% needy frosh rec. non-need-based scholarship or grant aid	45
% needy UG rec. non-need-based scholarship or grant aid	45
% needy frosh rec. need-based self-help aid	87
% needy UG rec. need-based self-help aid	87
% frosh rec. any financial aid	89
% UG rec. any financial aid	83
% UG borrow to pay for school	92
Average cumulative indebtedness	$24,000
% frosh need fully met	59
% ugrads need fully met	59
Average % of frosh need met	94
Average % of ugrad need met	94

Clarkson University

Holcroft House, Potsdam, NY 13699 • Admissions: 315-268-6480 • Fax: 315-268-7647

CAMPUS LIFE

Quality of Life Rating	**65**
Fire Safety Rating	**83**
Green Rating	**96**
Type of school	private
Environment	village

STUDENTS

Total undergrad enrollment	2,975
% male/female	72/28
% from out of state	26
% from public high school	85
% frosh live on campus	98
# of fraternities	11
# of sororities	3
% African American	3
% Asian	3
% Caucasian	84
% Hispanic	4
% international	4
# of countries represented	47

SURVEY SAYS . . .

Class discussions are rare
Career services are great
Students are friendly
Students aren't religious
Low cost of living
Everyone loves the Golden Knights
Lots of beer drinking
Hard liquor is popular

ACADEMICS

Academic Rating	**67**
% students returning for sophomore year	87
% students graduating within 4 years	63
% students graduating within 6 years	75
Calendar	semester
Student/faculty ratio	15:1
Profs interesting rating	69
Profs accessible rating	74
Most classes have	10–19 students
Most lab/discussion sessions have	10–19 students

MOST POPULAR MAJORS

business/commerce; civil engineering; mechanical engineering

APPLICANTS ALSO LOOK AT AND OFTEN PREFER

Rensselaer Polytechnic Institute, Rochester Institute of Technology

AND SOMETIMES PREFER

University of Rochester, Worcester Polytechnic Institute, Lehigh University

AND RARELY PREFER

Syracuse University

STUDENTS SAY ". . ."

Academics

Clarkson University in upstate New York is a science- and technology-focused school with an "excellent" and "innovative" engineering program. Students say "Clarkson…wants you to succeed and has many resources to help you." It "places a high importance on…preparing [students] to be a professionals" and has a "wonderful job-placement rate." An electrical engineering student says, "The career center has many workshops to help you land a job, from resume help, to appropriate interview dress, to business dining etiquette." "You feel very prepared by the time you are a senior," a student adds, no doubt because of Clarkson's "high academic intensity" and "challenging coursework." Unfortunately, "Professors are all over the place." Most students report, however, "Professors are all interested in helping their students," and "If you need help there is no question that you will receive it." Professors are "passionate and engaging" and "go above and beyond to make sure students can achieve academic excellence." Others find professors care "more about their research than anything else" and are hard to understand because they're non-native English speakers. For students who need academic support, Clarkson offers "free tutoring sessions for those students who are struggling" and a "very professional" writing center. Ultimately, most students find that "Clarkson University is a great environment that helps students develop hands-on experience that is greatly valued in any industry."

Life

Clarkson is working on improving its campus. There's a lot of construction going on, and the school recently completed "a new student center with a huge movie theater, forum, open bar, free pool tables, and a virtual game room." However, "the facilities need to be upgraded." The library is "pitiful," and the "Internet connection is abysmal." Food also gets low marks. The quaint town of Potsdam "may be a small town, but there is always something happening," though it might seem that way only to someone "who is used to living in a small town," because many students think "there isn't much to do at all" in town. "There are so many clubs and activities" at Clarkson, that "no matter what type of person you are, there are multiple places that you will fit in." There's a particularly strong outdoors club. Even though students find aspects of Clarkson life frustrating, a biology major wants you to know that though students complain about "the concrete buildings, food, sex ratio, and weather," they "do it out of love," and that "the campus is a tight-knit community with a 'we're in this together' feel."

Student Body

Clarkson's heavy emphasis on engineering and the sciences has resulted in a student body full of "lots of nerdy kids," particularly "nerdy white males." There are a lot of "socially awkward people" at Clarkson, but a student explains, "If you like to be alone and stay in your room then you will meet other awkward kids who like to hang out in their room." However, "If you attempt to go out and meet people then you will meet a variety of people." Clarkson students "really want to succeed," and many students "study hard during the day and into the night," but on "the weekends they still manage to find time to socialize and have a great time." There are a lot of "frat boys" who appreciate that the "good" Greek life "offers a haven [where] people who aren't socially awkward can congregate." Clarkson's proximity to the beautiful Adirondack Mountains means it attracts students who have "an affinity for the outdoors" and take advantage of the abundant opportunities to go hiking, canoeing, skiing, and ice climbing. Students complain about the male/female ratio even though it's "improving" and is "not as bad as [it] used to be." There's also "plenty of girls at SUNY Potsdam." One student says that one of the best things about Clarkson is that "everyone seems to get along well," and "Most people are more than willing to blur the lines between groups, so sects do not form nearly as often as one might think."

FINANCIAL AID: 315-268-6480 • E-MAIL: ADMISSION@CLARKSON.EDU • WEBSITE: WWW.CLARKSON.EDU

THE PRINCETON REVIEW SAYS

Admissions

Very important factors considered include: Academic GPA, rigor of secondary school record. *Important factors considered include:* Class rank, recommendation(s), standardized test scores, extracurricular activities, volunteer work. *Other factors considered include:* Application essay, alumni/ae relation, character/personal qualities, first generation, level of applicant's interest, talent/ability, work experience. SAT or ACT required; ACT with or without writing component accepted. TOEFL required of all international applicants. High school diploma is required and GED is accepted. *Academic units required:* 4 English, 3 mathematics, 3 science. *Academic units recommended:* 4 mathematics, 4 science.

Financial Aid

Students should submit: FAFSA, state aid form. Regular filing deadline is March 1. The Princeton Review suggests that all financial aid forms be submitted as soon as possible after January 1. *Need-based scholarships/grants offered:* Federal Pell, SEOG, state scholarships/grants, private scholarships, the school's own gift aid, HEOP. *Loan aid offered:* Direct Subsidized Stafford, Direct Unsubsidized Stafford, Direct PLUS, Federal Perkins, college/university loans from institutional funds, private/alternative loans. Applicants will be notified of awards on a rolling basis beginning March 19. Federal Work-Study Program available. Institutional employment available. Off-campus job opportunities are excellent.

The Inside Word

Clarkson wants students with a strong science and math background who also have a curiosity for applying technology and science in the real world. Show them that you're interested in being involved outside the classroom. Clarkson's acceptance rate is too high for solid applicants to lose much sleep about gaining admission. Serious candidates should interview anyway. If you're particularly solid and really want to come here, it could help you get some scholarship money.

THE SCHOOL SAYS ". . ."

From the Admissions Office

"Clarkson University is New York State's highest ranked, small research institution. Clarkson is the institution of choice for 3,000 enterprising students from diverse backgrounds who embrace challenge and thrive in a rigorous, highly collaborative learning environment. Our 640-wooded-acre campus is adjacent to the six-million-acre Adirondack Park, which offers exceptional outdoor recreation and a living laboratory for field research and environmental studies.

"Clarkson's programs in engineering, business, the sciences, liberal arts, and health sciences emphasize team-based learning as well as creative problem solving and leadership skills. Clarkson is also on the leading edge of today's emerging technologies and fields of study offering innovative, boundary-spanning degree programs in engineering and management, digital arts and sciences, and environmental science and policy, among others.

"At Clarkson, students and faculty work closely together in a supportive, friendly environment. Students are encouraged to participate in faculty-mentored research projects from their first year, and to take advantage of co-ops and study abroad programs. Our collaborative approach to education translates into graduates in high demand; our placement rates are among the highest in the country. Alumni experience accelerated career growth. One in seven alumni are already a CEO, president, or vice president of a company.

"Applicants are required to take the ACT with writing section optional or the SAT. We will use the student's best scores from either test. SAT Subject Tests are recommended but not required."

SELECTIVITY

Admissions Rating	**83**
# of applicants	4,686
% of applicants accepted	77
% of acceptees attending	23
# accepting a place on wait list	124
# admitted from wait list	3
# of early decision applicants	155
# accepted early decision	121

FRESHMAN PROFILE

Range SAT Critical Reading	500–610
Range SAT Math	560–650
Range SAT Writing	480–590
Range ACT Composite	23–28
Minimum paper TOEFL	550
Minimum web-based TOEFL	80
Average HS GPA	3.5
% graduated top 10% of class	35
% graduated top 25% of class	69
% graduated top 50% of class	93

DEADLINES

Early decision	
Deadline	12/1
Notification	1/1
Regular	
Deadline	1/15
Nonfall registration?	yes

FINANCIAL FACTS

Financial Aid Rating	**86**
Annual tuition	$37,770
Room and board	$12,534
Required fees	$840
Books and supplies	$1,322
% needy frosh rec. need-based scholarship or grant aid	87
% needy UG rec. need-based scholarship or grant aid	85
% needy frosh rec. non-need-based scholarship or grant aid	13
% needy UG rec. non-need-based scholarship or grant aid	11
% needy frosh rec. need-based self-help aid	86
% needy UG rec. need-based self-help aid	86
% frosh rec. any financial aid	98
% UG rec. any financial aid	96
% UG borrow to pay for school	85
Average cumulative indebtedness	$32,362
% frosh need fully met	19
% ugrads need fully met	19
Average % of frosh need met	90
Average % of ugrad need met	88

CLEMSON UNIVERSITY

105 SIKES HALL, CLEMSON, SC 29634-5124 • ADMISSIONS: 864-656-2287 • FAX: 864-656-2464

CAMPUS LIFE

Quality of Life Rating	97
Fire Safety Rating	92
Green Rating	85
Type of school	public
Environment	village

STUDENTS

Total undergrad enrollment	15,379
% male/female	54/46
% from out of state	35
% from public high school	89
% frosh live on campus	98
# of fraternities	26
# of sororities	17
% African American	7
% Asian	2
% Caucasian	84
% Hispanic	2
% international	1
# of countries represented	84

SURVEY SAYS . . .

Athletic facilities are great
School is well run
Students get along with local community
Low cost of living
Everyone loves the Tigers
Intramural sports are popular

ACADEMICS

Academic Rating	81
% students graduating within 4 years	50
% students graduating within 6 years	76
Calendar	semester
Student/faculty ratio	16:1
Profs interesting rating	82
Profs accessible rating	88
Most classes have	10–19 students
Most lab/discussion sessions have	20–29 students

MOST POPULAR MAJORS

biology/biological sciences; business/commerce; engineering

APPLICANTS ALSO LOOK AT AND SOMETIMES PREFER

Georgia Institute of Technology, University of Virginia, University of Georgia

AND RARELY PREFER

Auburn University, Florida State University, North Carolina State University, University of Maryland, College Park, University of South Carolina—Columbia, College of Charleston

STUDENTS SAY ". . ."

Academics

Located in South Carolina, legendary sports stronghold Clemson University is "all about supporting its academics as well as its athletic teams." This public university is an AACC school that can provide "many opportunities to each student, no matter the major." The "incredible energy" surrounding Clemson academics, sports, and culture yields "a ton of school spirit," and it is apparent from the first step on campus that "the students love Clemson, and professors love Clemson students." The size and Southern charm offer students the best of both worlds: the "friendly atmosphere of a small town college, with the advantages and opportunities of a huge university," including study abroad, myriad research opportunities, and Division I athletics. "No other place makes a student feel so instantly welcomed and at home while making you feel like you are a part of something bigger than yourself." Most of the professors are "very engaging" and "supportive advisers" who relate interesting real-life examples to their lectures. "Professors are willing to delve deep into subjects that they are interested in and love student input and involvement," says a student. They are "lively and make the material interesting to learn" and "put teaching first," and the resulting atmosphere is "enriching and expansive." There is no competitive streak among students, only a desire to succeed, and the whole campus is "full of encouragement, support, and building relationships with those around you." Unsurprisingly, the school is "full of traditions," and it has "a great balance between sports, organizations, and study." The Clemson alumni network is internationally strong. "Clemson is one big family; [you] immediately bond with other Clemson people you meet around the world," says one student. "There is something in these hills that is something special, and you will know it immediately once you become a member of the Clemson Family."

Life

One of the greatest strengths of Clemson University is its heritage, which "resonates with any person who has ever had the privilege to call this campus home." The school is all about uniting 15,500 strangers into "a supportive family grounded in a shared passion for excellence." "Students at Clemson are very interested in Clemson," says a student. "What I mean by that is the students create their own lives and communities within the school." There are "plenty of opportunities" to become involved and active on campus, whether "through sports or academic organizations." Greek life is also "rather popular," but not every student joins. Study abroad is strongly encouraged, and "Almost every student does some sort of study abroad." The school is nestled next to the mountains, and "There are a ton of trails owned by Clemson University" for students to hike and bike. Varsity sports are massively well-attended, and intramural sports are "huge"; "There are always pickup games on Bowman Field." On weekends, many students go downtown to the bars, "where there is a smaller, intimate setting, but still fun and exciting."

Student Body

While the majority of students are Southern and white, students of all backgrounds are bonded "by their sheer love of Clemson." The school spirit bleeds into everyone's demeanor, and this overwhelmingly happy and "very active" bunch "honestly try to include and befriend everyone." They are "very friendly, family oriented, athletic, and well put together." Many are also religious ("mostly Christian") and "go on mission trips and volunteer locally in the community." Most students here are down with Clemson athletics and "are willing to cheer for whatever sport is going on."

Financial Aid: 864-656-2280 • E-mail: cuadmissions@clemson.edu • Website: www.clemson.edu

THE PRINCETON REVIEW SAYS

Admissions

Very important factors considered include: Class rank, academic GPA, rigor of secondary school record, standardized test scores, state residency. *Important factors considered include:* Alumni/ae relation. *Other factors considered include:* Application essay, recommendation(s), extracurricular activities, talent/ability. SAT or ACT required; ACT with writing component required. TOEFL required of all international applicants. High school diploma is required and GED is accepted. *Academic units required:* 4 English, 3 mathematics, 3 science (3 science labs), 3 foreign language, 3 social studies, 1 history, 2 academic electives, 1 PE or ROTC. *Academic units recommended:* 4 mathematics (4 science labs).

Financial Aid

Students should submit: FAFSA. The Princeton Review suggests that all financial aid forms be submitted as soon as possible after January 1. *Need-based scholarships/grants offered:* Federal Pell, SEOG, state scholarships/grants, private scholarships, the school's own gift aid, Federal Nursing Scholarships. *Loan aid offered:* Direct Subsidized Stafford, Direct Unsubsidized Stafford, Direct PLUS, Federal Perkins, state loans, college/university loans from institutional funds. Applicants will be notified of awards on a rolling basis beginning April 1. Federal Work-Study Program available. Institutional employment available. Highest amount earned per year from on-campus jobs $3,500. Off-campus job opportunities are fair.

The Inside Word

With its Southern charm, competitive Division I athletics, and Greek life, Clemson will be an ideal fit for many types of students. But don't think that Clemson doesn't take its academics seriously. Admissions are competitive, and a good GPA and test scores will be needed for all who apply. For the SAT, the middle fifty percent of recently admitted students have test scores ranging from 1160 to 1310 (not including the writing section). For the ACT, the middle fifty percent score range is 26 to 30 for the composite.

THE SCHOOL SAYS ". . ."

From the Admissions Office

"One of the country's most selective public research universities, Clemson University was founded with a mission to be a high seminary of learning dedicated to teaching, research, and service. Nearly 120 years later, these three concepts remain at the heart of this university and provide the framework for an exceptional educational experience for Clemson students.

"At Clemson, professors take the time to get to know students and to explore innovative ways of teaching. Exceptional teaching is one reason Clemson's retention and graduation rates rank among the highest in the country among public universities. Exceptional teaching is also why Clemson continues to attract an increasingly talented student body. The class rank and SAT scores of Clemson's incoming freshman are among the highest of the nation's public research universities.

"Clemson offers over 250 student clubs and organizations; the spirit that students show for this university is unparalleled.

"Midway between Charlotte, North Carolina, and Atlanta, Georgia, Clemson University is located on 1,400 acres of beautiful rolling hills within the foothills of the Blue Ridge Mountains and along the shores of Lake Hartwell.

"Applicants are required to take the SAT or the ACT with the writing section. The best combined scores from SAT test will be used in the admissions process. We do not, however, combine sub scores from the ACT in order to create a new composite score."

SELECTIVITY	
Admissions Rating	90
# accepting a place on wait list	1,200
# admitted from wait list	120
FRESHMAN PROFILE	
Range SAT Critical Reading	550–650
Range SAT Math	580–680
Range SAT Writing	500–600
Range ACT Composite	25–31
Minimum paper TOEFL	550
Average HS GPA	4.1
% graduated top 10% of class	45
% graduated top 25% of class	78
% graduated top 50% of class	97
DEADLINES	
Regular	
Priority	12/1
Deadline	5/1
Nonfall registration?	yes
FINANCIAL FACTS	
Financial Aid Rating	67
Annual in-state tuition	$12,668
Annual out-state tuition	$28,826
Room and board	$7,228
Books and supplies	$1,090
% needy frosh rec. need-based scholarship or grant aid	35
% needy UG rec. need-based scholarship or grant aid	42
% needy frosh rec. non-need-based scholarship or grant aid	86
% needy UG rec. non-need-based scholarship or grant aid	67
% needy frosh rec. need-based self-help aid	61
% needy UG rec. need-based self-help aid	71
% frosh rec. any financial aid	87
% UG rec. any financial aid	71
% UG borrow to pay for school	50
Average cumulative indebtedness	$25,826
% frosh need fully met	27
% ugrads need fully met	21
Average % of frosh need met	64
Average % of ugrad need met	55

Coe College

1220 First Avenue Northeast, Cedar Rapids, IA 52402 • Admissions: 319-399-8500 • Fax: 319-399-8816

CAMPUS LIFE	
Quality of Life Rating	**76**
Fire Safety Rating	**61**
Green Rating	**60***
Type of school	private
Affiliation	Presbyterian
Environment	city

STUDENTS	
Total undergrad enrollment	1,369
% male/female	45/55
% from out of state	50
% from public high school	90
% frosh live on campus	97
# of fraternities	5
# of sororities	3
% African American	2
% Asian	2
% Caucasian	83
% Hispanic	5
% international	3
# of countries represented	15

SURVEY SAYS . . .

Career services are great
Students are friendly
Student government is popular

ACADEMICS	
Academic Rating	**83**
% students returning for sophomore year	80
% students graduating within 4 years	62
% students graduating within 6 years	72
Calendar	semester
Student/faculty ratio	11:1
Profs interesting rating	83
Profs accessible rating	87
Most classes have	10–19 students
Most lab/discussion sessions have	10–19 students

MOST POPULAR MAJORS

biology/biological sciences; business administration and management; psychology

APPLICANTS ALSO LOOK AT AND SOMETIMES PREFER

Knox College, Grinnell College, Beloit College, Cornell College, University of Iowa

STUDENTS SAY "..."

Academics

Located in Cedar Rapids, Iowa, Coe College is a small school with a "tight-knit community feel" that provides "something different for everyone." "Coe has a very warm and friendly atmosphere" that works for "the betterment of each individual Kohawk through experiences, in and out of the classroom, as well as creating a mature adult prepared for the 'real-world.'" Students who need financial help shouldn't worry, because the "financial aid rocks!" Students love "the small class sizes that allow you to have a personable experience with each of your professors." The "small teacher/student ratio" also comes with "excellent, intelligent, helpful, and caring professors" who "all have great abundances of knowledge and all teach in different ways." "I honestly have not had a bad instructor," a chemistry major tells us. "They give you their home phone and cell phone numbers and invite you to call them. No teaching assistants here." A sociology student boasts of "relationships with my professors, and [I] feel that they invest in me and want me to succeed." Although the students rate their professors highly, they didn't feel the same way about the classrooms the professors teach in. "Our academic buildings and dorms are really run down," one student says. Others claimed the college "needs faster Internet." For many, the school is "an ideal size." "Big without being too big." One student lists Coe's strengths up as "the small class sizes, the community atmosphere, the involvement of students, study abroad programs, physics, and athletics." Coe has "the ability [to make] literally anyone feel comfortable."

Life

Although Coe is located in Iowa's second largest city, "people often fall victim to the 'Coe bubble,'" one student warns. "A lot of people are not familiar with the city and refuse to venture out. Most people I know enjoy alcohol on the weekends." While Coe isn't located "in the best neighborhood to go out in, we do have bars that are within blocks from our campus [and that] are attended a lot on the weekends by students." Like many colleges, drinking is a common social activity. "In all honesty, Coe's students typically do drink alcohol—both on campus and off campus at the Cedar Rapids bars." However, other students see a variety of activities available. "There are parties, lots of video games, people playing intramural sports, Friday after class events... something for everyone." "For fun students go to SAC events like free midnight movies, tie-dying, dance socials in the pub, quarter bowling night, ice skating." When asked what the school could improve on, the students were unanimous in their complaint: "The food is something we all wish would improve." To compound matters, "Students are required to have a meal plan," and there aren't many options for "alternative diets such as vegan and vegetarian." The school hosts a regular talent show, Blindspot, which is so named because it's "open for students to perform without judgment."

Student Body

"About one-third of [Coe's] student body is athletes," but "there really isn't a particular social group or type of personality that this school is known for, so it's easy to fit in with one—or any—group on campus." "The average students are exactly that: average," a student explains. "It is a very typical representation of the Midwest. There are very few students (I'd say less than ten people in the entire population on campus) [who] do not truly fit in anywhere." "While Greek organizations maintain a significant presence in numbers," Greek life doesn't dominate the school: "They don't organize for significant events or provide any clear distinction from other students." Students at Coe "are friendly," a trait helped by an "orientation [that] creates a forced interaction [and] gets people mingling." "There is not a typical student at Coe," one student says, "because each student is treated uniquely and takes a unique set of classes."

FINANCIAL AID: 319-399-8540 • E-MAIL: ADMISSION@COE.EDU • WEBSITE: WWW.COE.EDU

THE PRINCETON REVIEW SAYS

Admissions

Very important factors considered include: Academic GPA, standardized test scores. *Important factors considered include:* Class rank, application essay, recommendation(s). *Other factors considered include:* Rigor of secondary school record, alumni/ae relation, character/personal qualities, extracurricular activities, first generation, interview, level of applicant's interest, racial/ethnic status, talent/ability, volunteer work. SAT or ACT required; ACT with or without writing component accepted. TOEFL required of all international applicants. High school diploma is required and GED is accepted. *Academic units recommended:* 4 English, 3 mathematics, 3 science (1 science lab), 2 foreign language, 3 social studies, 2 academic electives.

Financial Aid

Students should submit: FAFSA. The Princeton Review suggests that all financial aid forms be submitted as soon as possible after January 1. *Need-based scholarships/grants offered:* Federal Pell, SEOG, state scholarships/grants, private scholarships, the school's own gift aid. *Loan aid offered:* Direct Subsidized Stafford, Direct Unsubsidized Stafford, Direct PLUS, Federal Perkins, college/university loans from institutional funds. Applicants will be notified of awards on a rolling basis beginning March 15. Federal Work-Study Program available. Institutional employment available. Highest amount earned per year from on-campus jobs $500. Off-campus job opportunities are excellent.

The Inside Word

About 400 new students begin their college journey at Coe College each fall, and classes average a mere sixteen students. Despite its small size, Coe has the largest undergraduate writing center in the country, and many students enjoy its help. If you're seeking an intimate college experience with quality academics—Coe is one of the smallest universities to contain a Phi Beta Kappa chapter—you would do well to consider Coe.

THE SCHOOL SAYS ". . ."

From the Admissions Office

"A Coe education begins to pay off right away. In fact, ninety-eight percent of last year's graduating class was either working or in graduate school within six months of graduation. One reason our graduates do so well is the Coe Plan—a step-by-step sequence of activities designed to prepare our students for life after Coe. This required sequence stretches from the first-year seminar to community service, issue dinners, career planning seminars, and the required hands-on experience. The hands-on component may be satisfied through an internship, research, practicum, or study abroad. One student lived with a Costa Rican family while she studied the effects of selective logging on rain forest organisms. Others have interned at places like Warner Brothers in Los Angeles and the Chicago Board of Trade. Still others combine travel with an internship or student teaching for an unforgettable off-campus experience. Coe College is one of the few liberal arts institutions in the country to require hands-on learning for graduation."

SELECTIVITY	
Admissions Rating	**85**
# of applicants	2,405
% of applicants accepted	64
% of acceptees attending	23
FRESHMAN PROFILE	
Range SAT Critical Reading	490–650
Range SAT Math	520–660
Range SAT Writing	490–600
Range ACT Composite	24–28
Minimum paper TOEFL	500
Average HS GPA	3.6
% graduated top 10% of class	29
% graduated top 25% of class	61
% graduated top 50% of class	90
DEADLINES	
Early action	
Deadline	12/10
Notification	1/20
Regular	
Priority	12/10
Deadline	3/1
Nonfall registration?	yes
FINANCIAL FACTS	
Financial Aid Rating	**85**
Annual tuition	$33,900
Room and board	$7,780
Required fees	$320
% needy frosh rec. need-based scholarship or grant aid	100
% needy UG rec. need-based scholarship or grant aid	100
% needy frosh rec. non-need-based scholarship or grant aid	15
% needy UG rec. non-need-based scholarship or grant aid	16
% needy frosh rec. need-based self-help aid	83
% needy UG rec. need-based self-help aid	81
% frosh rec. any financial aid	99
% UG rec. any financial aid	96
% UG borrow to pay for school	77
Average cumulative indebtedness	$32,614
% frosh need fully met	24
% ugrads need fully met	23
Average % of frosh need met	87
Average % of ugrad need met	81

Colby College

4000 Mayflower Hill, Waterville, ME 04901-8848 • Admissions: 207-859-4800 • Fax: 207-859-4828

CAMPUS LIFE

Quality of Life Rating	**83**
Fire Safety Rating	**93**
Green Rating	**83**
Type of school	private
Environment	village

STUDENTS

Total undergrad enrollment	1,815
% male/female	47/53
% from out of state	86
% from public high school	54
% frosh live on campus	100
% African American	3
% Asian	5
% Caucasian	62
% Hispanic	4
% international	6
# of countries represented	75

SURVEY SAYS . . .

Great food on campus
Dorms are like palaces
Frats and sororities are unpopular or nonexistent
Lots of beer drinking

ACADEMICS

Academic Rating	**96**
% students returning for sophomore year	94
% students graduating within 4 years	86
% students graduating within 6 years	91
Calendar	4-1-4
Student/faculty ratio	10:1
Profs interesting rating	94
Profs accessible rating	97
Most classes have	10–19 students
Most lab/discussion sessions have	10–19 students

MOST POPULAR MAJORS

biology/biological sciences; economics; political science and government

APPLICANTS ALSO LOOK AT AND OFTEN PREFER

Amherst College, Bowdoin College, Dartmouth College, Middlebury College, Williams College, Brown University, Princeton University, Cornell University, Harvard College

AND SOMETIMES PREFER

Bates College, Boston College, Colgate University, Hamilton College, Vassar College

AND RARELY PREFER

Skidmore College, University of Vermont, Franklin & Marshall College, Dickinson College, Union College (NY), Trinity College (CT)

STUDENTS SAY ". . ."

Academics

An absolute gem of Maine's private, liberal arts colleges, Colby College is a "fun and smart community" that places an emphasis on international relations and study abroad. The school's "homey environment" offers "phenomenal academics in a unique setting," and small, discussion-oriented classes encourage teacher-student collaboration outside the classroom. "I love the opportunities that I have been afforded in my major, and I have gotten a lot of great opportunities to do outside research," says a student. With so many chances for students and professors to team up "to create positive relationships and fantastic work," faculty will "do anything they can to help out a student with a project or internship if the student shows initiative." There are a few complaints about the quality of visiting professors, but for the most part, teachers are "experienced, personable, and passionate," and students recognize how professors go out of their way to make sure students "receive individualized academic attention." "It is easy to see what professors are truly interested in and how they apply that interest to the courses they teach," says a student. There is a "varying course selection" for students to round out their education, as Colby is "all about creating people who are great at thinking." "If you want to coast through college, this is not the right school," says one. Students have involvement "in all spheres of the college," and the inclusive community "fosters growth academically, emotionally, and socially by giving its students an ability to play a large role in shaping the college and its direction." There are tons of ways for students to get involved and to have an impact on the campus, simply because "it's small enough to do that." Unfortunately, several students note that the "communication between the administration and the student body is severely lacking."

Life

Everyone at Colby "works very hard," weekdays and weekends alike. It is a "very campus-oriented life style," and students generally stay on campus for activities such as dances and "a lot of partying on the weekends." People "do almost constantly stress about work," but they know that Friday and Saturday is a deserved break. "Most people drink, but there isn't so much drug use"; "Sunday is a big study day," regardless. The campus culture is "dominated" with athletic teams: the "Mule Mob," the student fan section, is always "loud and enthusiastic" at this Division III school's games. People are "fairly to really outdoorsy"; students "love to ski on weekends in the winter" or go to the nearby lake. The spring is "the best for barbeques and hanging outside on the various quads." Meals are a key component of social interaction at Colby; very often "you'll see big groups of friends having leisurely meals together on the weekends." "Gotta love the dining halls and finding all my people there to have deliciously long chats over food," says a student. Plenty of people take advantage of being in Maine, and "without too much effort, you can spend a day on the coast or in the mountains regardless of the season," activities made easier by Colby's popular "outing club." Often, people "take trips down to Freeport, go skiing at Sugarloaf, or go hiking." Additionally, the college organizes "many activities and concerts," and many people "pass through the student union and see people in the 'spa' (cafe on campus)."

Student Body

Everyone at Colby is "really involved," whether in classes, community service, athletics, extracurriculars or clubs, and the typical student is "on some sort of athletic team, is a member of at least two campus clubs, [and] loves the outdoors." These "amiable, enthusiastic," students are most often from a "New England background" (typically "twenty minutes outside of Boston"), though many admit that ethnic diversity is lacking. Students are "genuinely open to learning at Colby," and most everyone here is "friendly and hardworking," though they also "like to go out."

FINANCIAL AID: 207-859-4832 • E-MAIL: ADMISSIONS@COLBY.EDU • WEBSITE: WWW.COLBY.EDU

THE PRINCETON REVIEW SAYS

Admissions

Very important factors considered include: Rigor of secondary school record, character/personal qualities. *Important factors considered include:* Class rank, application essay, academic GPA, recommendation(s), standardized test scores, extracurricular activities, racial/ethnic status, talent/ability. *Other factors considered include:* Alumni/ae relation, first generation, geographical residence, interview, level of applicant's interest, state residency, volunteer work, work experience. ACT with writing component recommended. TOEFL required of all international applicants. High school diploma or equivalent is not required. *Academic units recommended:* 4 English, 3 mathematics, 2 science (2 science labs), 3 foreign language, 2 social studies or history.

Financial Aid

Students should submit: FAFSA, CSS/Financial Aid PROFILE, business/farm supplement, tax returns to finalize aid offers. Regular filing deadline is February 1. The Princeton Review suggests that all financial aid forms be submitted as soon as possible after January 1. *Need-based scholarships/grants offered:* Federal Pell, SEOG, state scholarships/grants, private scholarships, the school's own gift aid. *Loan aid offered:* Direct Subsidized Stafford, Direct Unsubsidized Stafford, Direct PLUS, Federal Perkins, state loans, alternative loans. Applicants will be notified of awards on or about April 1. Federal Work-Study Program available. Institutional employment available. Highest amount earned per year from on-campus jobs $5,600.

The Inside Word

Colby continues to be both very selective and successful in converting admits to enrollees, which makes for a perpetually challenging admissions process. Currently, a little less than thirty percent of applicants are accepted (sixty percent of which graduated in the top five percent of their class), so hit those books and ace those exams to stand a fighting chance. One thing that could set you apart from the pack? An interest in other cultures. Two-thirds of Colby students study abroad—in fact, for some degrees it's required.

THE SCHOOL SAYS ". . ."

From the Admissions Office

"Colby is one of only a handful of liberal arts colleges that offer world-class academic programs, leadership in internationalism, an active community life, and rich opportunities after graduation. Set in Maine on one of the nation's most beautiful campuses, Colby provides students a host of opportunities for active engagement, in Waterville or around the world. The Goldfarb Center for Public Affairs and Civic Engagement connects teaching and research with current political, economic, and social issues at home and abroad. Recently Colby replaced loans in its financial aid packages with grants, which don't have to be repaid, making it possible for students to graduate without college-loan debt. Students' access to Colby's outstanding faculty is extraordinary, and the college is a leader in undergraduate research and project-based learning. The college has won awards for sustainable environmental practices as well as one of the first Senator Paul Simon Awards for Internationalizing the Campus.

"The challenging academic experience at the heart of Colby's programs is complemented by a vibrant community life and campus atmosphere featuring more than 100 student-run organizations, more than fifty athletic and recreational choices, and numerous leadership and volunteer opportunities. Colby graduates succeed. They find their places at the best medical schools and research universities, the finest law and business programs, top financial firms, in the arts, government service, social service, education, and nonprofit organizations, and they are inspired leaders in their communities. Applicants must submit scores from the SAT, ACT, or SAT Subject Tests in three different subject areas. The choice of which test(s) to take is entirely up to each applicant. The optional ACT writing test is recommended."

SELECTIVITY	
Admissions Rating	**96**
# of applicants	5,186
% of applicants accepted	29
% of acceptees attending	31
# accepting a place on wait list	1,198
# admitted from wait list	18
# of early decision applicants	445
# accepted early decision	228

FRESHMAN PROFILE	
Range SAT Critical Reading	620–710
Range SAT Math	630–710
Range SAT Writing	610–710
Range ACT Composite	28–32
Minimum web-based TOEFL	100
% graduated top 10% of class	61
% graduated top 25% of class	90
% graduated top 50% of class	99

DEADLINES	
Early decision	
Deadline	11/15
Notification	12/15
Regular	
Deadline	1/1
Notification	4/1
Nonfall registration?	yes

FINANCIAL FACTS	
Financial Aid Rating	**98**
Fee from tuition	$55,700
Books and supplies	$700
% needy frosh rec. need-based scholarship or grant aid	100
% needy UG rec. need-based scholarship or grant aid	99
% needy frosh rec. non-need-based scholarship or grant aid	2
% needy UG rec. non-need-based scholarship or grant aid	3
% needy frosh rec. need-based self-help aid	76
% needy UG rec. need-based self-help aid	80
% frosh rec. any financial aid	39
% UG rec. any financial aid	41
% UG borrow to pay for school	35
Average cumulative indebtedness	$22,367
% frosh need fully met	100
% ugrads need fully met	100
Average % of frosh need met	100
Average % of ugrad need met	100

COLGATE UNIVERSITY

13 OAK DRIVE, HAMILTON, NY 13346 • ADMISSIONS: 315-228-7401 • FAX: 315-228-7544

CAMPUS LIFE

Quality of Life Rating	79
Fire Safety Rating	84
Green Rating	94
Type of school	private
Environment	rural

STUDENTS

Total undergrad enrollment	2,927
% male/female	47/53
% from out of state	75
% from public high school	62
% frosh live on campus	100
# of fraternities	6
# of sororities	3
% African American	6
% Asian	9
% Caucasian	71
% Hispanic	7
% international	8
# of countries represented	42

SURVEY SAYS . . .

Lab facilities are great
Great computer facilities
Great library
School is well run
Dorms are like palaces
Students are happy
Lots of beer drinking
Hard liquor is popular

ACADEMICS

Academic Rating	93
% students returning for sophomore year	95
% students graduating within 4 years	88
% students graduating within 6 years	92
Calendar	semester
Student/faculty ratio	9:1
Profs interesting rating	87
Profs accessible rating	95
Most classes have	10–19 students
Most lab/discussion sessions have	10–19 students

MOST POPULAR MAJORS

economics; English language and literature; history

APPLICANTS ALSO LOOK AT AND OFTEN PREFER

Cornell University, Middlebury College, Georgetown University, Dartmouth College

AND SOMETIMES PREFER

Boston College, Hamilton College, University of Rochester, New York University

AND RARELY PREFER

Bucknell University, University of Vermont, Villanova University, Lafayette College

STUDENTS SAY ". . ."

Academics

Colgate University is known for its "very rigorous academic curriculum" and "invaluable" professors who "are the glue that hold the university together." Many students say they chose Colgate because of "the opportunity to be a part of a small community where students can genuinely interact with their professors" and "the academic prestige" combined with an alumni network that "makes the Colgate connection a truly valuable resource." All agree that, at Colgate, you're "more than just a number" and say, "The faculty are very interested in helping their students develop as scholars." Although there's the rare "dud," professors get high marks for being "incredibly enthusiastic" and wanting "to support [students] to the fullest." A psychology major says, "I have been to at least one professor's house each semester. Professors sincerely want all of their students to succeed academically," and a junior adds, "One of the wonderful things about Colgate is that these relationships start as early as freshman year. Students do not have to wait until their senior year to build fantastic relationships with the faculty." However, another student grumbles, "Course selection is very stressful, and freshmen often get slighted." Overall, Colgate is "a challenging school, but at the end of the day, the challenge is all about the student's development."

Life

Colgate University "has an amazing campus with people who work hard and have goals but also know how to have a really fun time." Students say the campus is "breathtaking," and they value "its small size and intimate nature." A philosophy major says, "Colgate is great because you can't walk 200 feet without a professor, student, or faculty member acknowledging you by name, yet you're constantly meeting new people and having new experiences. There is never a dull moment at Colgate." Students say, "Colgate strives for the perfect combination of academics and extracurriculars," and they feel the university "does a great job at helping us balance those and gives us opportunities to get involved in all the groups and events around campus." In addition to a plethora of clubs, students are actively involved in Greek life and Division I athletics. A junior says, "I loved how Colgate was located in the middle of nowhere" because "everything revolved around the campus," but in case you're worried about isolation, another student adds, "Colgate brings a lot of interesting speakers to the campus, which helps provide for a more rounded liberal arts experience." Students praise the administration, saying, "It is easy for students to contact the administration and thus have their voices directly heard by the community. The president holds drop-in office hours for students every week and takes notes on what students say during the session."

Student Body

Colgate boasts a "happy and enthusiastic student body" that "follows the motto 'work hard, play hard.'" Many say a typical student is "white, very well-rounded, a hard partier," and "rich and preppy." A sophomore says, "Imagine J. Crew models. Now give them brains, and that is who is walking around Colgate's campus." Fraternities and sororities are popular: "Greek life does have a huge presence in the social life at Colgate," but "it is not exclusive to just those who are members." An English major says, "I wouldn't describe the party scene as being [full of] peer pressure, but there are few alternatives, so if it's not your preferred pastime you may find yourself very bored." There are students who wish the university would be "a little tighter with alcohol control." Some students wish the administration would work harder to "break down huge social barriers that exist between people of different races," and say, "The campus is striving to make the campus more diverse, but unfortunately the diverse groups like to keep…[to] themselves." However, despite the "country club atmosphere," a computer science major says, "When you're stranded in Hamilton, New York, for four years you'll inevitably end up fitting in regardless whether you are the typical student or not."

FINANCIAL AID: 315-228-7431 • E-MAIL: ADMISSION@COLGATE.EDU • WEBSITE: WWW.COLGATE.EDU

THE PRINCETON REVIEW SAYS

Admissions

Very important factors considered include: Class rank, academic GPA, rigor of secondary school record. *Important factors considered include:* Application essay, recommendation(s), standardized test scores, character/personal qualities, extracurricular activities, talent/ability. *Other factors considered include:* Alumni/ae relation, first generation, geographical residence, racial/ethnic status, volunteer work, work experience. SAT or ACT required; ACT with or without writing component accepted. TOEFL required of all international applicants. High school diploma is required and GED is accepted. *Academic units required:* 4 English, 3 mathematics, 3 science (2 science labs), 3 foreign language, 3 social studies. *Academic units recommended:* 4 English, 4 mathematics, 4 science (4 science labs), 4 foreign language, 4 social studies.

Financial Aid

Students should submit: CSS/Financial Aid PROFILE, noncustodial PROFILE. Regular filing deadline is January 15. The Princeton Review suggests that all financial aid forms be submitted as soon as possible after January 1. *Need-based scholarships/grants offered:* Federal Pell, SEOG, state scholarships/grants, private scholarships, the school's own gift aid. *Loan aid offered:* Direct Subsidized Stafford, Direct Unsubsidized Stafford, Direct PLUS, Federal Perkins. Applicants will be notified of awards on or about April 1. Federal Work-Study Program available. Institutional employment available. Off-campus job opportunities are fair.

The Inside Word

Admission to the university is selective, and Colgate places the most value on previous academic achievement, evaluating both the level of courses taken in high school and the success reached in those courses. Applications undergo individual review by the admissions staff, who look for a record of "substantive involvement in extracurricular and community activities." Additionally, the admissions office is committed to the "recruitment and retention" of a diverse student body.

THE SCHOOL SAYS ". . ."

From the Admissions Office

"Colgate provides an environment where students can appreciate, celebrate, and learn about their own cultures as well as those of the people around them. The class of 2015 represents one of Colgate's most diverse class years yet. Of the class of 2015, 25.4 percent self-identified as being from multicultural backgrounds, and 7.9 percent are international students. Colgate's student body also includes students from forty-seven states, the District of Columbia, and forty-two countries. Students and faculty alike are drawn to Colgate by the quality of its academic programs. Faculty initiative has given the university a rich mix of learning opportunities that includes a liberal arts core, fifty-two academic concentrations, and a wealth of Colgate faculty-led, off-campus study programs in the United States and abroad. But there is more to Colgate than academic life, including a full complement of living options set within a campus described as one of the most beautiful in the country. The new Trudy Fitness Center is an integral component of Colgate's Wellness Initiative, which encourages healthy, purposeful, and balanced lifestyles within the community. A center for community service builds upon the tradition of Colgate students interacting with the surrounding community in meaningful ways. Colgate students become extraordinarily devoted alumni, contributing significantly to career networking and exploration programs on and off campus. For students in search of a busy and varied campus life, Colgate is a place to learn and grow."

SELECTIVITY

Admissions Rating	97
# of applicants	7,835
% of applicants accepted	29
% of acceptees attending	33
# accepting a place on wait list	712
# admitted from wait list	1
# of early decision applicants	660
# accepted early decision	348

FRESHMAN PROFILE

Range SAT Critical Reading	620–720
Range SAT Math	640–720
Range ACT Composite	30–32
Average HS GPA	3.6
% graduated top 10% of class	67
% graduated top 25% of class	90
% graduated top 50% of class	98

DEADLINES

Early decision	
Deadline	11/15
Notification	12/15
Regular	
Deadline	1/15
Notification	4/1
Nonfall registration?	no

FINANCIAL FACTS

Financial Aid Rating	99
Annual tuition	$44,330
Room and board	$11,075
Required fees	$310
Books and supplies	$2,030
% needy frosh rec. need-based scholarship or grant aid	100
% needy UG rec. need-based scholarship or grant aid	98
% needy frosh rec. non-need-based scholarship or grant aid	75
% needy UG rec. non-need-based scholarship or grant aid	78
% needy frosh rec. need-based self-help aid	76
% needy UG rec. need-based self-help aid	77
% frosh rec. any financial aid	43
% UG rec. any financial aid	40
% UG borrow to pay for school	27
Average cumulative indebtedness	$13,869
% frosh need fully met	100
% ugrads need fully met	100
Average % of frosh need met	100
Average % of ugrad need met	100

COLLEGE OF THE ATLANTIC

105 EDEN STREET, BAR HARBOR, ME 04609 • ADMISSIONS: 207-288-5015 • FAX: 207-288-4126

CAMPUS LIFE

Quality of Life Rating	**97**
Fire Safety Rating	**97**
Green Rating	**99**
Type of school	private
Environment	rural

STUDENTS

Total undergrad enrollment	340
% male/female	28/72
% from out of state	82
% from public high school	61
% frosh live on campus	100
% African American	1
% Asian	1
% Caucasian	68
% Hispanic	2
% international	17
# of countries represented	36

SURVEY SAYS . . .

No one cheats
Students are friendly
Students aren't religious
Great food on campus
Low cost of living
Intercollegiate sports are unpopular or nonexistent
Frats and sororities are unpopular or nonexistent
Students are environmentally aware
Internships are widely available

ACADEMICS

Academic Rating	**95**
% students returning for sophomore year	86
% students graduating within 4 years	58
% students graduating within 6 years	71
Calendar	trimester
Student/faculty ratio	11:1
Profs interesting rating	98
Profs accessible rating	98
Most classes have	10–19 studens
Most lab/discussion sessions have	10–19 students

MOST POPULAR MAJORS

biology/biological sciences; ecology; education

APPLICANTS ALSO LOOK AT AND OFTEN PREFER

Bowdoin College, Middlebury College

AND SOMETIMES PREFER

Hampshire College, Colby College

AND RARELY PREFER

Green Mountain College, University of Maine, Warren Wilson College, Marlboro College, University of Vermont

STUDENTS SAY ". . ."

Academics

College of the Atlantic is a small liberal arts college in Bar Harbor, on Mount Desert Island, Maine, that its students think of as a "progressive educational experiment that broadens perspective." The college offers the sole major of "human ecology," which allows students to design their own majors around classes they wish to take. Each student can "mix-and-match interests and connect them to one another in a way that works and matters" to them. The population of the school is fairly small, with the student body being less than 400 individuals. The average class size is "around sixteen students," which affords students the kind of one-on-one attention that they love. Some have a little trouble getting in to the classes they want, but most students find that any of their professors "have impressive credentials with diverse backgrounds." Students also find that professors "are extremely passionate" and expect their students to have the same passion. With that kind of attention in class, students agree that it is "rare to graduate without having had dinner at a professor's house at least once." Many find by the time they graduate that they have "several brilliant mentors" in their professors. The motto of the school is "life changing, world changing" and many find that motto pervades the "stimulating academic experience" at College of the Atlantic.

Life

Because each person is taught that "voices and actions count," most students tend to focus on the sustainability efforts within campus and participate in one of the college's many groups. The college allows students to "give faculty reviews" and "even [participate] in the hiring of the staff," making them even more active players in their education. Most students tend to be "outdoorsy," and being on an island just off the coast, there is plenty for students to do. Given that the campus is adjacent to Acadia National park, many cite "hiking, biking, canoeing, kayaking, contradancing, sailboating, and more" as just a few of the many options. There is also "a lot to do on-campus with student art installations," and two of the most recent additions to campus include a student-built "greenhouse at Beech Hill Farm" and "a root cellar." The "very small town" of Bar Harbor attracts many students on the weekends who are looking for a break from campus.

Student Body

One thing is for sure about College of the Atlantic, most students consider themselves "fairly liberal" and "very individualistic." Some are a little put off by the latter saying "at times it seems like an almost requirement," but most seem to love the idea that they have opportunities to express themselves. One student says, "We wear plaid. We play music. We swim in the ocean in the middle of winter," a statement that most students would seem to agree sums up a good deal of the student population. Despite focusing on individualism, most everyone agrees that the entirety of the student body is "respectful, supportive, and passionate" about their fellow students. There is a "friendly" nature that pervades the population, and that sort of friendly nature, "makes up for [its] small size."

FINANCIAL AID: 207-288-5015 • E-MAIL: INQUIRY@COA.EDU • WEBSITE: WWW.COA.EDU

THE PRINCETON REVIEW SAYS

Admissions

Very important factors considered include: Application essay, recommendation(s), rigor of secondary school record. *Important factors considered include:* Class rank, academic GPA, character/personal qualities, extracurricular activities, interview, talent/ability, volunteer work, work experience. *Other factors considered include:* Standardized test scores, alumni/ae relation, first generation, geographical residence, level of applicant's interest, racial/ethnic status, state residency. ACT with or without writing component accepted. TOEFL required of all international applicants. High school diploma is required and GED is accepted. *Academic units required:* 4 English, 3 mathematics, 2 science (2 science labs), 2 social studies. *Academic units recommended:* 4 mathematics, 3 science, 2 foreign language, 2 history, 1 academic elective.

Financial Aid

Students should submit: FAFSA, institution's own financial aid form, noncustodial PROFILE, business/farm supplement. Regular filing deadline is February 15. The Princeton Review suggests that all financial aid forms be submitted as soon as possible after January 1. *Need-based scholarships/grants offered:* Federal Pell, SEOG, state scholarships/grants, private scholarships, the school's own gift aid. *Loan aid offered:* Direct Subsidized Stafford, Direct Unsubsidized Stafford, Direct PLUS, Federal Perkins. Applicants will be notified of awards on or about April 1. Federal Work-Study Program available. Off-campus job opportunities are good.

The Inside Word

College of the Atlantic is looking for a certain type of person. The school really puts emphasis on those individuals who seek learning outside of the classroom and have/want real-world experience. Though submitting standardized test scores (such as the SAT and ACT) is optional, College of the Atlantic says scores do help determine the academic ability of applicants, so a little more than half send in scores with applications. COA offers both merit- and need-based scholarships to qualified students to help them defer costs. The website has a Net Price Calculator, which helps incoming students figure out how financial aid might be of service to them and how much it might help them in the long run.

THE SCHOOL SAYS ". . ."

From the Admissions Office

"College of the Atlantic is a small, intellectually challenging college on Mount Desert Island, Maine. We look for students seeking a rigorous, hands-on, self-directed academic experience. Come for a visit, and you will begin to understand that COA's unique approach to education, governance and community life extends throughout its structure. Resolutely value centered and interdisciplinary—there are no departments and no majors, COA sees its mission as preparing people to become independent thinkers, to challenge conventional wisdom, to deal with pressing global change—both environmental and social—and to be passionately engaged in transforming the world around them into a better place.

"College of the Atlantic does not require standardized testing as part of the application process. Learning and intelligence can be gauged in many ways; standardized test scores are just one of many measures. If an applicant chooses to submit standardized test scores for consideration, the SAT, SAT Subject Tests, or ACT scores are all acceptable."

SELECTIVITY	
Admissions Rating	**90**
# of applicants	400
% of applicants accepted	58
% of acceptees attending	33
# accepting a place on wait list	23
# admitted from wait list	7
# of early decision applicants	38
# accepted early decision	28

FRESHMAN PROFILE	
Range SAT Critical Reading	610–700
Range SAT Math	570–660
Range SAT Writing	570–670
Range ACT Composite	29–30
Minimum paper TOEFL	567
Minimum web-based TOEFL	86
Average HS GPA	3.6
% graduated top 10% of class	24
% graduated top 25% of class	72
% graduated top 50% of class	96

DEADLINES	
Early decision	
Deadline	12/1
Notification	12/15
Regular	
Deadline	2/15
Notification	4/1
Nonfall registration?	yes

FINANCIAL FACTS	
Financial Aid Rating	**89**
Annual tuition	$37,152
Room and board	$9,258
Required fees	$549
Books and supplies	$600
% needy frosh rec. need-based scholarship or grant aid	100
% needy UG rec. need-based scholarship or grant aid	97
% needy frosh rec. non-need-based scholarship or grant aid	12
% needy UG rec. non-need-based scholarship or grant aid	4
% needy frosh rec. need-based self-help aid	97
% needy UG rec. need-based self-help aid	94
% frosh rec. any financial aid	87
% UG rec. any financial aid	85
% UG borrow to pay for school	69
Average cumulative indebtedness	$20,858
% frosh need fully met	26
% ugrads need fully met	26
Average % of frosh need met	96
Average % of ugrad need met	96

COLLEGE OF CHARLESTON

66 GEORGE STREET, CHARLESTON, SC 29424 • ADMISSIONS: 843-953-5670 • FAX: 843-953-6322

CAMPUS LIFE

Quality of Life Rating	90
Fire Safety Rating	95
Green Rating	88
Type of school	public
Environment	city

STUDENTS

Total undergrad enrollment	10,132
% male/female	38/62
% from out of state	46
% from public high school	39
# of fraternities	14
# of sororities	13
% African American	6
% Asian	1
% Caucasian	84
% Hispanic	3
% international	1
# of countries represented	65

SURVEY SAYS . . .

Great library
Students love Charleston, SC
Great off-campus food
Students are happy
Lots of beer drinking
Hard liquor is popular

ACADEMICS

Academic Rating	78
% students graduating within 4 years	52
% students graduating within 6 years	63
Calendar	semester
Student/faculty ratio	16:1
Profs interesting rating	82
Profs accessible rating	85
Most classes have	20–29 students
Most lab/discussion sessions have	20–29 students

MOST POPULAR MAJORS

biology/biological sciences; business administration and management; communication studies/speech communication and rhetoric

APPLICANTS ALSO LOOK AT AND OFTEN PREFER

University of Virginia, The University of North Carolina at Chapel Hill, University of Georgia

AND SOMETIMES PREFER

University of South Carolina—Columbia, James Madison University, Furman University, Clemson University, Tulane University

AND RARELY PREFER

Auburn University, Appalachian State University

STUDENTS SAY ". . ."

Academics

The College of Charleston provides "huge university opportunities with a small college, personalized atmosphere." "It's actually a fairly large school (10,000 students), but it feels much smaller in the historic Charleston setting," explains one student. Even though it's not the smallest university, it "offers great classes in a smaller, one-on-one environment." Located "right in the heart of downtown Charleston," the university is "a Southern secret that welcomes diversity with warm arms." Students can't say enough good things about the location. "The city of Charleston is fun and inviting, the weather is a million times better than the North, and the beach is close by!" Since the "College of Charleston is very old" and was "founded in 1770," many of the facilities "are getting older" and could really "use some work." College of Charleston "exemplifies 'progressive traditionalism'" and "is all about liberal arts; the education is well-rounded and intriguing." The "professors really do care about you." "The professors I've encountered in the history department truly love their field and have greatly shaped my own research," one student testifies. "I'm from Charleston, and I couldn't imagine living anywhere else!" one student boasts. "The weather is great, the city is beautiful, you get a great education for a reasonable price, and of course the people from here are amazing…why not choose College of Charleston?" "I'll use one word [to describe College of Charleston]," a physics student tells us, "underrated."

Life

"It's the city of Charleston that defines the student body and joins them together." Charleston is "one of the most beautiful cities in the South," and students experience "the perfect blend of social life between the university and the city." "Ask any student about Charleston as a city and they'll excitedly tell you about their favorite place to eat or how they went to a wonderful play last week." "Southern hospitality" pervades the campus. Students "love to go the beach, the movies, the park, the theater, the mall, museums, and to the great selections of bars and restaurants." Charleston is known for an active party scene, much of which revolves around Greek life. "Although actual Greek…membership numbers are low, it provides the social life for campus," one student explains. "Most independents spend their time attending [fraternity] parties off campus." Students love "the beach when the weather is nice," which is about a "fifteen- to twenty-minute drive" from campus. "Charleston has become huge in the music scene," and bands such as "Phish, Widespread Panic, StS9, Pat Green, Rebelution, Slightly Stoopid, Yonder Mountain String Band, and Umphrey's fill up the dates." In general, students in Charleston "[live] life to its fullest while preparing for the rest!"

Student Body

The student body is more than sixty percent female—a fact that some love while others wish for "a better girl-to-guy ratio" as well as "more ethnic diversity." "The typical student is Caucasian, female, and wealthy," and "very preppy/Southern. Not too many Northerners." That doesn't mean that the students aren't "friendly" and "accepting." "Students fit in pretty well because there are many groups and clubs on campus where you can meet people." Although an out-of-state student cautions that "it can be difficult for students from out of state to fit in because sixty-four percent of the students are either local or in-state and already know each other." "There are three types of students at this school," one student claims. "(1) Preppy Southerners clad in Vera Bradley and Ralph Lauren. (2) Disaffected hipsters/artists who clearly are not the starving type seeing as their entire wardrobe comes from Urban Outfitters and American Apparel. (3) Everyone else." "Most are the 'prep' or 'hipster' type," another student confirms. "There is a barely a counterculture." However, others see a wider variety in the student body. "There are hippies, sorority girls, fratastic guys, feminists, surfers, preppy Southern gentlemen, people from the Jersey shore, international students, Christians, atheists, pagans, vegans, Republicans, Democrats, Libertarians…it is hard to sum up just one 'typical' student here."

FINANCIAL AID: 843-953-5540 • E-MAIL: ADMISSIONS@COFC.EDU • WEBSITE: WWW.COFC.EDU

THE PRINCETON REVIEW SAYS

Admissions

Very important factors considered include: Academic GPA, rigor of secondary school record, standardized test scores, state residency. *Important factors considered include:* Class rank, character/personal qualities, first generation, talent/ability. *Other factors considered include:* Application essay, recommendation(s), extracurricular activities, racial/ethnic status, volunteer work, work experience. SAT or ACT required; ACT with or without writing component accepted. TOEFL required of all international applicants. High school diploma is required and GED is accepted. *Academic units required:* 4 English, 3 mathematics, 3 science (3 science labs), 3 foreign language, 3 social studies, 4 academic electives. *Academic units recommended:* 4 English, 4 mathematics, 2 history.

Financial Aid

Students should submit: FAFSA. The Princeton Review suggests that all financial aid forms be submitted as soon as possible after January 1. *Need-based scholarships/grants offered:* Federal Pell, SEOG, state scholarships/grants, private scholarships, the school's own gift aid. *Loan aid offered:* Direct Subsidized Stafford, Direct Unsubsidized Stafford, Direct PLUS, Federal Perkins. Applicants will be notified of awards on a rolling basis beginning April 10. Federal Work-Study Program available. Institutional employment available. Highest amount earned per year from on-campus jobs $9,400. Off-campus job opportunities are fair.

The Inside Word

The College of Charleston is the thirteenth oldest university in the country, and its location in historic Charleston provides a truly unique Southern experience with strong liberal arts and sciences academics. Students absolutely rave about the weather, the beaches, the city, and the social life the campus and the city combine to provide.

THE SCHOOL SAYS ". . ."

From the Admissions Office

"To succeed in our increasingly complex world, college graduates must be able to think creatively, explore new ideas, compete, collaborate, and meet the challenges of our global society. At the College of Charleston, students find out about themselves, their lives and the lives of others. They discover how to shape their future, and they prepare to create change and opportunity.

"Founded in 1770, the College of Charleston's mission is to provide students with a first-class education in the arts and sciences, education and business. Students have 118 majors and minors from which to choose—and they often choose to combine several—and complement their academic courses with overseas study, research and internships for a truly customized education.

"Approximately 10,000 undergraduates choose the College for its small-college feel blended with the advantages and diversity of an urban, mid-sized university. The College, home to students from fifty states and sixty-seven countries, provides a creative and intellectually stimulating environment where students are challenged and guided by a committed and caring full-time faculty of 500 distinguished teacher-scholars, all in an incomparable historic setting.

"The city of Charleston serves as a living and learning laboratory for student experiences in business, science, teaching, the humanities, languages and the arts. At the same time, students and faculty are engaged with the community in partnerships to improve education, enhance the business community and enrich the overall quality of life in the region.

"In the great liberal arts tradition, a College of Charleston education focuses on discovery and personal growth, as well as preparation for life, work and service to our society."

SELECTIVITY	
Admissions Rating	85
# of applicants	11,086
% of applicants accepted	74
% of acceptees attending	29
# accepting a place on wait list	391
# admitted from wait list	17

FRESHMAN PROFILE	
Range SAT Critical Reading	560–650
Range SAT Math	550–640
Range ACT Composite	23–27
Minimum paper TOEFL	570
Minimum web-based TOEFL	80
Average HS GPA	3.8
% graduated top 10% of class	28
% graduated top 25% of class	63
% graduated top 50% of class	93

DEADLINES	
Early action	
Deadline	11/1
Regular	
Priority	2/1
Deadline	4/1
Nonfall registration?	yes

FINANCIAL FACTS	
Financial Aid Rating	74
Annual in-state tuition	$9,616
Annual out-state tuition	$24,330
Books and supplies	$1,224
% needy frosh rec. need-based scholarship or grant aid	66
% needy UG rec. need-based scholarship or grant aid	66
% frosh rec. non-need-based scholarship or grant aid	67
% UG rec. non-need-based scholarship or grant aid	41
% needy frosh rec. need-based self-help aid	72
% needy UG rec. need-based self-help aid	79
% frosh rec. any financial aid	47
% UG rec. any financial aid	46
% UG borrow to pay for school	42
Average cumulative indebtedness	$20,541
% frosh need fully met	20
% ugrads need fully met	18
Average % of frosh need met	56
Average % of ugrad need met	58

College of the Holy Cross

Admissions Office, One College Street, Worcester, MA 01610-2395 • Admissions: 508-793-2443 • Fax: 508-793-3888

CAMPUS LIFE

Quality of Life Rating	74
Fire Safety Rating	94
Green Rating	92
Type of school	private
Affiliation	Roman Catholic
Environment	city

STUDENTS

Total undergrad enrollment	2,872
% male/female	47/53
% from out of state	61
% from public high school	52
% frosh live on campus	100
% African American	5
% Asian	5
% Caucasian	66
% Hispanic	10
% international	1
# of countries represented	21

SURVEY SAYS . . .

Frats and sororities are unpopular or nonexistent
Student government is popular
Lots of beer drinking
Hard liquor is popular
Students are involved in community service

ACADEMICS

Academic Rating	95
% students returning for sophomore year	95
% students graduating within 4 years	89
% students graduating within 6 years	91
Calendar	semester
Student/faculty ratio	10:1
Profs interesting rating	94
Profs accessible rating	93
Most classes have	10–19 students
Most lab/discussion sessions have	10–19 students

MOST POPULAR MAJORS

economics; English language and literature; political science and government

APPLICANTS ALSO LOOK AT AND OFTEN PREFER

Boston College, University of Notre Dame, Georgetown University

AND SOMETIMES PREFER

Villanova University, Boston University

STUDENTS SAY ". . ."

Academics

This small, Jesuit liberal arts school in Massachusetts operates under a selfless mission statement of "men and women for others." The school's strong academic tradition marries with "countless opportunities to learn through internships, speaker series," "strong student life," and "small classes" to focus on shaping the student as a whole person. Academics at Holy Cross are "rigorous, and the main priority of students on campus"; a caring faculty and administration foster "an incredible learning environment for students," and through their experiences, students receive "a broad-based foundation to be successful in variety of careers." "From the acceptance letter alone, I knew that my entire application was read thoroughly and that my character was closely examined," says one happy student. At Holy Cross, "You're more than just a number in the classroom and on the field." Professors here are "dedicated to creating an exciting learning environment." They are "always accessible and more than happy to help," and they "get to know you on an individual and personal level." Students are encouraged "to reflect on their experiences and continue to better himself/herself as a whole person." "There are endless opportunities despite the fact that it is a small college," says one student. "It is a place where like in the parable of the mustard seed one can grow." In addition to a "fantastic alumni network" spread across several fields in various industries, there is a strong science program that includes plenty of research opportunities. The college "demands enormous amounts of work from its students, but puts them in a great position to succeed." "Holy Cross equips their students with an intangible set of skills that not only prepares them for a job, but for life," says a student.

Life

Holy Cross has "a multitude" of groups and activities available to its students, as well as a plethora of community service opportunities. Everyone loves "going to sporting events, especially football and basketball." Though the "exceptionally beautiful" campus has a lot of fans, all agree that the college "could update some of the residence halls" and could provide more dining options. The community among freshmen dorms is "outstanding," and "many of the friends you make your first year will stay with you for years to come." During the week and on Sundays, "people take their work very seriously," and the library is generally pretty full, but parties are popular on weekends, and "that nerdy chem major you see working hard all week can turn into the girl riding the mechanical bull at a local bar." For those who choose to abstain from the party circuit, "SGA-sponsored events such as karaoke or dances are a blast." Worcester is a fun little town (and Boston a free weekend shuttle ride away), and the restaurants in the area are "amazing."

Student Body

Many students here are "preppy" and from New England, and most all of this "uncommonly friendly " lot is "studious with an activity or two that defines their interests and what they do during the weekend"; in fact, it is rare "to find someone with no extracurricular responsibilities." Everyone tends to be "very put together" and "generally articulate," and "There is a tremendous sense of community." Surface diversity is lacking, but there is "a diverse set of interests" among the whole student body. In general, "All love being here." "If you want to do well academically, have fun on the weekend...study hard and play hard, then you will fit in at Holy Cross."

FINANCIAL AID: 508-793-2265 • E-MAIL: ADMISSIONS@HOLYCROSS.EDU • WEBSITE: WWW.HOLYCROSS.EDU

THE PRINCETON REVIEW SAYS

Admissions

Very important factors considered include: Class rank, academic GPA, recommendation(s), rigor of secondary school record, interview. *Important factors considered include:* Application essay, character/personal qualities, extracurricular activities, level of applicant's interest. *Other factors considered include:* Standardized test scores, alumni/ae relation, first generation, geographical residence, racial/ethnic status, talent/ability, volunteer work, work experience. ACT with or without writing component accepted. TOEFL required of all international applicants. High school diploma is required and GED is accepted. *Academic units recommended:* 4 English, 4 mathematics, 4 science (2 science labs), 4 foreign language, 2 social studies, 2 history.

Financial Aid

Students should submit: FAFSA, CSS/Financial Aid PROFILE, noncustodial PROFILE, business/farm supplement, parent and student federal tax returns. Regular filing deadline is February 1. The Princeton Review suggests that all financial aid forms be submitted as soon as possible after January 1. *Need-based scholarships/grants offered:* Federal Pell, SEOG, state scholarships/grants, private scholarships, the school's own gift aid. *Loan aid offered:* Direct Subsidized Stafford, Direct Unsubsidized Stafford, Direct PLUS, Federal Perkins, MEFA. Applicants will be notified of awards on or about April 1. Federal Work-Study Program available. Institutional employment available. Highest amount earned per year from on-campus jobs $1,604. Off-campus job opportunities are fair.

The Inside Word

Admission to Holy Cross is competitive; therefore, a demanding high school course load is required to be a viable candidate. The college values effective communication skills—it thoroughly evaluates each applicant's personal statement and short essay responses. Interviews are important, especially for those applying early decision. Students who graduate from a Jesuit high school might find themselves at a slight advantage.

THE SCHOOL SAYS ". . ."

From the Admissions Office

"When applying to Holy Cross, two areas deserve particular attention. First, the essay should be developed thoughtfully, with correct language and syntax in mind. That essay reflects for the Board of Admissions how you think and how you can express yourself. Second, activity beyond the classroom should be clearly defined. Since Holy Cross [has only] 2,800 students, the chance for involvement/participation is exceptional. The board reviews many applications for academically qualified students. A key difference in being accepted is the extent to which a candidate participates in-depth beyond the classroom—don't be modest; define who you are.

"Standardized test scores (i.e., SAT, SAT Subject Tests, and ACT) are optional. Students may submit their scores if they believe the results paint a fuller picture of their achievements and potential, but those students who don't submit scores will not be at a disadvantage in admissions decisions."

SELECTIVITY	
Admissions Rating	**96**
# of applicants	7,353
% of applicants accepted	33
% of acceptees attending	31
# accepting a place on wait list	1,556
# of early decision applicants	512
# accepted early decision	347

FRESHMAN PROFILE	
Range SAT Critical Reading	600–690
Range SAT Math	610–690
Range SAT Writing	600–700
Range ACT Composite	27–31
Minimum paper TOEFL	550
Minimum web-based TOEFL	79
Average HS GPA	3.8
% graduated top 10% of class	61
% graduated top 25% of class	95
% graduated top 50% of class	100

DEADLINES	
Early decision	
Deadline	12/15
Regular	
Deadline	1/15
Nonfall registration?	no

FINANCIAL FACTS	
Financial Aid Rating	**93**
Annual tuition	$42,800
Room and board	$11,730
Required fees	$600
Books and supplies	$700
% needy frosh rec. need-based scholarship or grant aid	81
% needy UG rec. need-based scholarship or grant aid	79
% needy frosh rec. non-need-based scholarship or grant aid	1
% needy UG rec. non-need-based scholarship or grant aid	1
% needy frosh rec. need-based self-help aid	77
% needy UG rec. need-based self-help aid	81
% frosh rec. any financial aid	64
% UG rec. any financial aid	61
% UG borrow to pay for school	63
Average cumulative indebtedness	$26,434
% frosh need fully met	98
% ugrads need fully met	100
Average % of frosh need met	100
Average % of ugrad need met	100

THE COLLEGE OF IDAHO

2112 Cleveland Boulevard, Caldwell, ID 83605-4432 • Admissions: 208-459-5305 • Fax: 208-459-5757

CAMPUS LIFE

Quality of Life Rating	88
Fire Safety Rating	74
Green Rating	76
Type of school	private
Environment	town

STUDENTS

Total undergrad enrollment	1,007
% male/female	42/58
% from out of state	15
# of fraternities	3
# of sororities	4
% African American	1
% Asian	2
% Caucasian	53
% Hispanic	13
% Native American	1
% international	10
# of countries represented	40

SURVEY SAYS . . .

Students are friendly
Different types of students interact
Campus feels safe
Low cost of living

ACADEMICS

Academic Rating	83
% students returning for sophomore year	80
% students graduating within 4 years	51
% students graduating within 6 years	63
Calendar	other
Student/faculty ratio	12:1
Profs interesting rating	95
Profs accessible rating	93
Most classes have	fewer than 10 students

MOST POPULAR MAJORS

biology/biological sciences; business/commerce; psychology

APPLICANTS ALSO LOOK AT AND OFTEN PREFER

Gonzaga University, Brigham Young University (UT), University of Idaho, Idaho State University, Boise State University

STUDENTS SAY ". . ."

Academics

A small liberal arts school, The College of Idaho is "like a diamond in the rough." Students tell us, "You'd be surprised at the very high quality this little school offers!" The small class sizes and low student-to-teacher ratio promote the school's emphasis on "individual learning" and a "personalized education plan." The academic experience at The College of Idaho is "incredibly rigorous but also very rewarding." Though the school has a "well-developed" liberal arts core, students also describe the biology and premed programs as "fantastic." Courses are "challenging," "fascinating," and "great preparation for both graduate school and the professional world." The small school environment provides a "sense of community" and allows students to develop "strong working relationships" with their professors. Students tell us their professors are "attentive," "very accessible," and "passionate about what they teach." One graduating senior described the school as "an academic gold mine of some of the most published and highly regarded professors and researchers in the field." The "personal teaching" approach the professors at The College of Idaho take makes them "consistently recognized nationally and internationally for their contributions to the academic community and to their students." The administration is "involved with the students" and "effective" though "the professors are what make The College of Idaho great." Also great is the fact that the school is "cost competitive" and offers "generous scholarships." As one freshman tells us, "My school is way more than a place for me to learn. My teachers have become more like guardians for my education, and my peers…my second family."

Life

Life in Caldwell can be "pretty quiet" but Boise, the capital, is only about a thirty-minute drive away, and the school regularly hosts trips into the city. However, the campus "strives" and "mostly succeeds" in making up for the town by sponsoring many activities on campus. A student tells us, "On campus there is always something going on…I rarely have a night where there isn't something that I could do for fun." The College of Idaho offers a variety of extracurricular activities. The school's Program Council "puts on great events all year long." Such events as movie and bowling nights are open to all students and are often offered free of charge. Students at The College of Idaho also tend to be very interested in clubs and club-sponsored events. With a multitude of clubs to join, there is a club "for all personality types." One student tells us, "Whether it is attending a theater or band concert, an athletic event, or a club meeting, there are plenty of ways to get involved." Students describe their school life as "great overall," and because the school is so small, "any major campus-sponsored activity brings us all together as one, giant, friendly social club."

Student Body

Students tell us, The College of Idaho has "students from many walks of life" and a "student body full of individuals." While a majority of the student body is "white, middle-class, and right out of high school," students at The College of Idaho promote an "atmosphere of learning from others no matter their background." Many students tell us that there really isn't a "typical student," which isn't so surprising given its large international student population. Each student at The College of Idaho is "an active participant in the campus community." One junior tells us students are, "overly involved" and "extremely busy with clubs, campus activities, athletics, and academics." Students are "hardworking but social," "intelligent," and "well-rounded." According to one sophomore, "though [we are all] different, the commonality of going to C of I brings us together."

FINANCIAL AID: 208-459-5307 • E-MAIL: ADMISSION@COLLEGEOFIDAHO.EDU • WEBSITE: WWW.COLLEGEOFIDAHO.EDU

THE PRINCETON REVIEW SAYS

Admissions

Very important factors considered include: Application essay, academic GPA, recommendation(s), rigor of secondary school record, standardized test scores, character/personal qualities, extracurricular activities, level of applicant's interest. *Important factors considered include:* Class rank, interview. *Other factors considered include:* Alumni/ae relation, first generation, geographical residence, talent/ability, volunteer work. SAT or ACT required; ACT with or without writing component accepted. TOEFL required of all international applicants. High school diploma is required and GED is accepted. *Academic units required:* 3 English, 2 mathematics, 3 social studies, 3 history, 3 academic electives. *Academic units recommended:* 4 English, 4 mathematics, 3 science (3 science labs), 3 foreign language, 3 social studies, 3 history, 3 academic electives.

Financial Aid

Students should submit: FAFSA, institution's own financial aid form. The Princeton Review suggests that all financial aid forms be submitted as soon as possible after January 1. *Need-based scholarships/grants offered:* Federal Pell, SEOG, state scholarships/grants, private scholarships, the school's own gift aid. *Loan aid offered:* Direct Subsidized Stafford, Direct Unsubsidized Stafford, Direct PLUS, Federal Perkins, alternative education loans. Applicants will be notified of awards on a rolling basis beginning February 1. Federal Work-Study Program available. Highest amount earned per year from on-campus jobs $1,536. Off-campus job opportunities are good.

The Inside Word

The admissions committee at The College of Idaho is looking for students who have taken high school seriously. Candidates who demonstrate reasonable academic success and a variety of extracurricular activities will be handed the keys to a quality academic program and a unique college experience, one that stresses self-confidence and social responsibility.

THE SCHOOL SAYS ". . ."

From the Admissions Office

"While the mission of The College of Idaho is traditional in that it remains committed to the teaching of the liberal arts, many of the approaches to accomplishing this goal are unique. Within the campus community is the opportunity to create classroom opportunities for students that span the globe—both technologically and geographically. Here, students are just as apt to attend a biology class on campus as they are to hike in the nearby Owyhee or Sawtooth Mountains to carry out field research. During the college's four-week winter term, more than thirty percent of the students are emailing friends and family from such locales as Australia, Israel, France, Ireland, England, Peru, and or Mexico while taking part in faculty-led, multidisciplinary trips. International students from forty-five different countries comprise nine percent of the student body. Students are invited to visit the campus and the admissions counselors, either in person or online.

"C of I requires all admission candidates (who have not reached sophomore status in college) to submit either the SAT or the ACT with the writing component. The College of Idaho will consider all scores. There is no SAT Subject Test requirement, but scores will be considered as part of a holistic evaluation."

SELECTIVITY	
Admissions Rating	**83**
# of applicants	1,185
% of applicants accepted	66
% of acceptees attending	32

FRESHMAN PROFILE	
Range SAT Critical Reading	445–635
Range SAT Math	480–620
Range SAT Writing	450–595
Range ACT Composite	22–27
Minimum paper TOEFL	550
Minimum web-based TOEFL	79
Average HS GPA	3.7
% graduated top 10% of class	34
% graduated top 25% of class	68
% graduated top 50% of class	90

DEADLINES	
Early action	
Deadline	11/15
Notification	11/15
Regular	
Priority	2/15
Deadline	8/1
Nonfall registration?	yes

FINANCIAL FACTS	
Financial Aid Rating	**80**
Annual tuition	$22,600
Room and board	$8,113
Required fees	$375
Books and supplies	$1,200
% needy frosh rec. need-based scholarship or grant aid	77
% needy UG rec. need-based scholarship or grant aid	72
% needy frosh rec. non-need-based scholarship or grant aid	100
% needy UG rec. non-need-based scholarship or grant aid	97
% needy frosh rec. need-based self-help aid	80
% needy UG rec. need-based self-help aid	78
% frosh rec. any financial aid	99
% UG rec. any financial aid	98
% UG borrow to pay for school	46
Average cumulative indebtedness	$24,939
% frosh need fully met	13
% ugrads need fully met	11
Average % of frosh need met	82
Average % of ugrad need met	77

THE COLLEGE OF NEW JERSEY

PO Box 7718, Ewing, NJ 08628-0718 • Admissions: 609-771-2131 • Fax: 609-637-5174

CAMPUS LIFE

Quality of Life Rating	85
Fire Safety Rating	93
Green Rating	84
Type of school	public
Environment	village

STUDENTS

Total undergrad enrollment	6,445
% male/female	44/56
% from out of state	7
% from public high school	70
% frosh live on campus	91
# of fraternities	13
# of sororities	13
% African American	6
% Asian	7
% Caucasian	66
% Hispanic	10
# of countries represented	30

SURVEY SAYS . . .

Lab facilities are great
Great library
School is well run
Students are friendly
Low cost of living
Students are happy
Student publications are popular

ACADEMICS

Academic Rating	86
% students returning for sophomore year	95
% students graduating within 4 years	73
% students graduating within 6 years	86
Calendar	semester
Student/faculty ratio	13:1
Profs interesting rating	89
Profs accessible rating	85
Most classes have	20–29 students
Most lab/discussion sessions have	10–19 students

MOST POPULAR MAJORS

biology/biological sciences; business administration and management; psychology

APPLICANTS ALSO LOOK AT AND OFTEN PREFER

New York University, Rutgers, The State University of New Jersey—New Brunswick, University of Delaware, Villanova University, Boston College, University of Maryland, College Park

AND SOMETIMES PREFER

Boston University, Pennsylvania State University—University Park, Cornell University, Stevens Institute of Technology, Drexel University, Lehigh University

AND RARELY PREFER

Stevens Institute of Technology, Bucknell University, Loyola University Maryland, Fordham University

STUDENTS SAY ". . ."

Academics

The College of New Jersey is a small public college dedicated to education and to the pursuit of passions, all at an affordable price. Each of TCNJ's "excellent" seven schools offers "an awesome range of classes to choose from" (it is "one of the best schools in the area for future teachers," in particular), and the academic environment "is an open and honest one." On top of all that, "The campus is gorgeous, the students are friendly, and you can't beat the price!" "The College of New Jersey is a community unlike any I have ever been a part of; everyone is proud to be a part of and to contribute to the TCNJ culture," says a satisfied student.

Professors are always available in and out of the "small classes," and they "are truly interested in the progress and well-being of their students." Though the classes for liberal learning requirements are "stressful," teachers want their students to do well and "are eager to help and answer questions." "There has never been a moment where I have felt unsupported in my academic endeavors or felt that I could not reach out for help," says a student. A few students warn that some requirements become hard to fill because "there are only a few options that fit the topic, and everyone is trying to get into those classes."

One of TCNJ's greatest strengths is the Freshman Year Seminar Program. Freshman students choose a class that they are interested in (ranging from "a class on Bruce Springsteen, to one about *Harry Potter,* to one about the meaning of life"), and then live on a floor with all of the students in that class. "This is a wonderful opportunity to build community and to ensure that students are surrounded by people with similar interests and academic goals."

Life

Life at TCNJ is "calm and enjoyable." Students refer to the school as an "island of suburban housing," which works well in terms of building community, but the atmosphere does tend to cut students off from the outside world (especially freshmen, who aren't allowed cars). Students keep busy with their studies, organizations, and "many great events the school hosts," but "They also enjoy spending time with friends and having a good time together." "A lot of people party. A lot of people don't party. Most people love it here," sums up a student simply. While the local origins of the students means that some students do go home on weekends, "Almost every weekend, the school organizes a trip to nearby Princeton, NYC, or Philadelphia" for those who stick around. "The school actually sends out a weekly calendar listing all of the events being held on campus that week," says a student. Students do warn about housing; as selection for upper-class housing is done strictly by a lottery system, "several do not get housing" each year, and some of the freshmen that do get their guaranteed housing find that their dorms are "ancient, dirty, and falling apart."

Student Body

People "are serious about their education here," and students describe themselves as "quite diverse." There is "always a group for somebody": "I don't know anyone that feels like they don't fit in, and if they do feel that way, it's because they aren't putting in the effort to do so," says a student. Everyone is on campus for a reason, whether it's major-/career-specific or "simply to gain leadership or life experiences," and all are "self-motivated, personable, and goal-oriented." While students are accepting of minorities, "The majority is most certainly still white." On the whole, "Students are very happy and friendly and therefore make it much easier to fit in and make friends."

FINANCIAL AID: 609-771-2211 • E-MAIL: TCNJINFO@TCNJ.EDU • WEBSITE: WWW.TCNJ.EDU

THE PRINCETON REVIEW SAYS

Admissions

Very important factors considered include: Class rank, rigor of secondary school record, standardized test scores, extracurricular activities, volunteer work. *Important factors considered include:* Application essay, recommendation(s), character/personal qualities, geographical residence, state residency, talent/ability. *Other factors considered include:* Academic GPA, alumni/ae relation, first generation, level of applicant's interest, racial/ethnic status, work experience. SAT or ACT required; ACT with or without writing component accepted. TOEFL required of all international applicants. High school diploma is required and GED is accepted. *Academic units required:* 4 English, 3 mathematics, 3 science (2 science labs), 2 foreign language, 2 social studies. *Academic units recommended:* 4 English, 3 mathematics, 3 science (3 science labs), 3 foreign language, 3 social studies.

Financial Aid

Students should submit: FAFSA. Regular filing deadline is October 1. The Princeton Review suggests that all financial aid forms be submitted as soon as possible after January 1. *Need-based scholarships/grants offered:* Federal Pell, SEOG, state scholarships/grants, private scholarships, the school's own gift aid. *Loan aid offered:* Direct Subsidized Stafford, Direct Unsubsidized Stafford, Direct PLUS, Federal Perkins, Federal Nursing. Applicants will be notified of awards on a rolling basis beginning June 1. Federal Work-Study Program available. Institutional employment available. Highest amount earned per year from on-campus jobs $9,329. Off-campus job opportunities are excellent.

The Inside Word

TCNJ accepts a high percentage of its 10,000 applicants, but that figure is deceiving; this is a self-selecting applicant pool, and those with no chance of acceptance simply don't bother. Admissions are as competitive as you would expect at a school that offers state residents a small-college experience and a highly respected degree for bargain-basement prices. TCNJ's admissions staff examines every component of a student's application, but none more carefully than the high school transcript. Students should apply a soon as possible once the application becomes available.

THE SCHOOL SAYS ". . ."

From the Admissions Office

"The College of New Jersey is one of the United States' great higher education success stories. With a long history as New Jersey's preeminent teacher of teachers, the college has grown into a new role as educator of the nation's best students in a wide range of fields. The College of New Jersey has created a culture of constant questioning—a place where knowledge is not merely received but reconfigured. In small classes, students and faculty members collaborate in a rewarding process: As they seek to understand fundamental principles, apply key concepts, reveal new problems, and pursue new lines of inquiry, students gain a fluency of thought in their disciplines. The college's 289-acre tree-lined campus is a union of vision, engineering, beauty, and functionality. Neoclassical Georgian Colonial architecture, meticulous landscaping, and thoughtful design merge in a dynamic system, constantly evolving to meet the needs of TCNJ students. About half of TCNJ's entering class will be academic scholars, with large numbers of National Merit finalists and semifinalists. The College of New Jersey is bringing together the best ideas from around the nation and building a new model for public undergraduate education on one campus."

SELECTIVITY	
Admissions Rating	**91**
# of applicants	10,150
% of applicants accepted	46
% of acceptees attending	29
# accepting a place on wait list	1,328
# of early decision applicants	523
# accepted early decision	322

FRESHMAN PROFILE	
Range SAT Critical Reading	550–650
Range SAT Math	580–680
Range SAT Writing	560–660
Minimum paper TOEFL	550
Minimum web-based TOEFL	80
% graduated top 10% of class	56
% graduated top 25% of class	89
% graduated top 50% of class	99

DEADLINES	
Early decision	
Deadline	11/15
Notification	12/15
Regular	
Priority	11/15
Deadline	1/15
Nonfall registration?	yes

FINANCIAL FACTS	
Financial Aid Rating	**65**
Annual in-state tuition	$9,760
Annual out-state tuition	$19,569
Annual comprehensive tuition	$23,907
Room and board	$10,677
Required fees	$4,127
Books and supplies	$1,000
% needy frosh rec. need-based scholarship or grant aid	40
% needy UG rec. need-based scholarship or grant aid	41
% needy frosh rec. non-need-based scholarship or grant aid	46
% needy UG rec. non-need-based scholarship or grant aid	41
% needy frosh rec. need-based self-help aid	61
% needy UG rec. need-based self-help aid	71
% frosh rec. any financial aid	73
% UG rec. any financial aid	68
% UG borrow to pay for school	60
Average cumulative indebtedness	$32,754
% frosh need fully met	12
% ugrads need fully met	14
Average % of frosh need met	44
Average % of ugrad need met	48

College of the Ozarks

Office of Admissions, Point Lookout, MO 65726 • Admissions: 417-690-2636 • Fax: 417-335-2618

CAMPUS LIFE

Quality of Life Rating	85
Fire Safety Rating	76
Green Rating	79
Type of school	private
Environment	rural

STUDENTS

Total undergrad enrollment	1,371
% male/female	43/57
% from out of state	22
% from public high school	76
% frosh live on campus	86
% African American	1
% Asian	1
% Caucasian	92
% Hispanic	2
% Native American	1
% international	1
# of countries represented	14

SURVEY SAYS . . .

Students are very religious
Students get along with local community
Frats and sororities are unpopular or nonexistent
Theater is popular
Very little beer drinking

ACADEMICS

Academic Rating	78
% students returning for sophomore year	86
Calendar	semester
Student/faculty ratio	13:1
Profs interesting rating	79
Profs accessible rating	80
Most classes have	10–19 students
Most lab/discussion sessions have	10–19 students

MOST POPULAR MAJORS

business administration and management; communication studies/speech communication and rhetoric; elementary education and teaching

APPLICANTS ALSO LOOK AT AND OFTEN PREFER
Missouri State University

AND SOMETIMES PREFER
Southwest Baptist University

STUDENTS SAY ". . ."

Academics

Students describe the academic experience at this tuition-free, Christian college as "very challenging and very rewarding." "Time management is very important at C of O," where it's vital to find a balance "between classes, work, and homework." College of the Ozarks places strong emphasis on "high moral value, hard work, and academic integrity," and the school is "dedicated to the growth and maturity of its students." Many students cite "the work-study program and the core values of the school" as "two of the college's greatest strengths." Those values are detailed in the school's mission, which lists its goals in five principle categories: academic, vocational, Christian, patriotic, and cultural. The professors are an integral part of making "character development...a key value of this college," and many "have an open-door policy to all students." Students praise their faculty as "amazing," "second-to-none," and most often as "passionate." One student sums it up by saying, "My professors are amazing. I know that I can go up to any of them and they are more than willing to help me with my academic pursuits and personal issues as well." Though a few students grumble that they "don't always enjoy general education courses," which are "mostly" lectures, the vast majority are very happy with the courses within their chosen areas of study. "Small class sizes provide for easy one-on-one interaction with the professors" and encourage students to "become involved in active classroom learning."

Life

"Life at College of the Ozarks is pretty unique because we support ourselves." All students at C of O participate in a work program in exchange for free tuition, which helps the school live up to its nickname, Hard Work U. "Between the sixteen to eighteen credit hours of classes, fifteen hours of work on campus, and studying, students here are kept pretty dang busy." As on many Christian campuses, "Partying is almost nonexistent," but students don't seem to mind. They're happy "creating lasting friendships while getting not only knowledge in the classroom setting but also working skills for future jobs." "There are groups and organizations for everyone," and "various organizations hold events for the whole campus like Senate Movie Night, and there are plenty of interesting speakers for convocations." "The cafeteria is a cozy place to have a meal with several different selections for all meals," and the campus offers plenty of activities: "swimming, weight lifting, basketball, movies, dances, coffee nights, ballgames, etc." Off campus, "There is always something to do in this area," "whether you hang out with your friends, go to shows in Branson, go to campus-sponsored events, or just go play ping-pong." The college provides a weekly shuttle to Wal-Mart, and nearby Branson is a popular destination, and "many of the attractions give discounts for students," including theme park Silver Dollar City.

Student Body

C of O students describe themselves as "friendly," "hardworking," "down-to-earth," and "very religious, but not pushy." The nature of the school places a strong emphasis on community, and first-year students bond during a week-long orientation called Character Camp. Most students are from Christian backgrounds, and they're "somewhat conservative." Many "are from the local Ozark region." Despite the similarities, students describe their school as "very diverse" and say that everyone is "welcomed into the community" and "always eager to help and support you in any type of situation." "There are the 'aggies,' the 'jocks,' the 'nerds,' and other types of students," like "the prep, the homeschooler...the indie...[and] the geek," but many students happily note the lack of exclusive cliques and say "social barriers are easily crossed."

FINANCIAL AID: 417-690-3292 • E-MAIL: ADMISS4@COFO.EDU • WEBSITE: WWW.COFO.EDU

THE PRINCETON REVIEW SAYS

Admissions

Very important factors considered include: Class rank, rigor of secondary school record, character/personal qualities, interview. *Important factors considered include:* Academic GPA, recommendation(s), standardized test scores, geographical residence, level of applicant's interest, volunteer work, work experience. *Other factors considered include:* Alumni/ae relation, extracurricular activities, first generation, religious affiliation/commitment, state residency, talent/ability. SAT or ACT required; ACT with or without writing component accepted. TOEFL required of all international applicants. High school diploma is required and GED is accepted. *Academic units recommended:* 4 English, 3 mathematics, 2 science (1 science lab), 2 foreign language, 3 social studies, 1 visual/performing arts/public speaking.

Financial Aid

Students should submit: FAFSA. The Princeton Review suggests that all financial aid forms be submitted as soon as possible after January 1. *Need-based scholarships/grants offered:* Federal Pell, SEOG, state scholarships/grants, private scholarships, the school's own gift aid. Applicants will be notified of awards on or about July 1. Federal Work-Study Program available. Off-campus job opportunities are excellent.

The Inside Word

The unusual nature of the C of O translates directly into its admissions process. Because a significant aspect of the school's mission statement is to provide educational opportunities to those in need of financial aid, candidates for admission must demonstrate that need. C of O's free tuition and unique philosophy attract strong interest, and the admissions process is competitive. That said, it's more important to be a good fit with the school philosophically and financially than to have a sky-high GPA. Oh yeah, a serious work ethic is a must!

THE SCHOOL SAYS ". . ."

From the Admissions Office

"College of the Ozarks is unique because of its no-tuition, work-study program, but also because it strives to educate the head, the heart, and the hands. At C of O, there are high expectations of students—the college stresses character development as well as study and work. An education from 'Hard Work U.' offers many opportunities, not the least of which is the chance to graduate debt-free. Life at C of O isn't all hard work and no play, however. There are many opportunities for fun. The nearby resort town of Branson, Missouri, offers ample opportunities for recreation and summer employment, and Table Rock Lake, only a few miles away, is a terrific spot to swim, sun, and relax. Numerous on-campus activities such as Mudfest, Luau Night, dances, and holiday parties give students lots of chances for fun without leaving the college. At 'Hard Work U.,' we work hard, but we know how to have fun, too.

"Applicants are required to submit scores from the ACT or the SAT. We will use the student's best scores from either test. Writing scores are not required."

SELECTIVITY

Admissions Rating	**97**
# of applicants	3,299
% of applicants accepted	9
% of acceptees attending	96
# accepting a place on wait list	734
# admitted from wait list	39

FRESHMAN PROFILE

Range SAT Critical Reading	580–630
Range SAT Math	530–560
Range SAT Writing	540–570
Range ACT Composite	21–24
Minimum paper TOEFL	550
Minimum web-based TOEFL	79
Average HS GPA	3.6
% graduated top 10% of class	17
% graduated top 25% of class	50
% graduated top 50% of class	89

DEADLINES

Regular	
Priority	2/15
Nonfall registration?	no

FINANCIAL FACTS

Financial Aid Rating	**88**
Room and board	$5,900
Required fees	$430
Books and supplies	$800
% needy frosh rec. need-based scholarship or grant aid	100
% needy UG rec. need-based scholarship or grant aid	100
% needy frosh rec. non-need-based scholarship or grant aid	9
% needy UG rec. non-need-based scholarship or grant aid	12
% needy frosh rec. need-based self-help aid	91
% needy UG rec. need-based self-help aid	88
% frosh rec. any financial aid	100
% UG rec. any financial aid	100
% UG borrow to pay for school	12
Average cumulative indebtedness	$7,062
% frosh need fully met	21
% ugrads need fully met	28
Average % of frosh need met	81
Average % of ugrad need met	84

THE COLLEGE OF WILLIAM & MARY

OFFICE OF ADMISSIONS, PO BOX 8795, WILLIAMSBURG, VA 23187-8795 • ADMISSIONS: 757-221-4223 • FAX: 757-221-1242

CAMPUS LIFE

Quality of Life Rating	92
Fire Safety Rating	75
Green Rating	91
Type of school	public
Environment	town

STUDENTS

Total undergrad enrollment	6,020
% male/female	45/55
% from out of state	35
% from public high school	~70
% frosh live on campus	100
# of fraternities	20
# of sororities	11
% African American	7
% Asian	7
% Caucasian	57
% Hispanic	8
% international	3
# of countries represented	64

SURVEY SAYS . . .

No one cheats
Great library
Athletic facilities are great
Students are friendly
Campus feels safe
Students are happy
Student publications are popular
Student government is popular
Students are involved in community service

ACADEMICS

Academic Rating	87
% students returning for sophomore year	95
% students graduating within 4 years	82
% students graduating within 6 years	90
Calendar	semester
Student/faculty ratio	12:1
Profs interesting rating	89
Profs accessible rating	92
Most classes have	10–19 students
Most lab/discussion sessions have	10–19 students

MOST POPULAR MAJORS

English; biology; psychology

APPLICANTS ALSO LOOK AT AND SOMETIMES PREFER

Duke University, Georgetown University, University of Virginia, The University of North Carolina at Chapel Hill, Cornell University, Princeton University, Dartmouth College, Vanderbilt University

STUDENTS SAY ". . ."

Academics

Students at The College of William & Mary are extraordinarily happy with their overall experience and with their academics in particular. One student sums up the school's vibe by saying, "William & Mary achieves a remarkable balance between the dynamic, progressive academics of a liberal arts college and the strong sense of history and tradition one would expect from America's second-oldest school." "There are endless and amazing" opportunities here, with an emphasis on undergraduate research that makes W&M unique among small liberal arts schools. "Professors will engage you outside of the classroom and give you the opportunity to conduct your own research project, even in a non-science curriculum." Many "are often in newspapers and magazines and have relevant and copious work experience in the subjects they're teaching." Across the board, "professors are one of the best things about W&M." They "are always accessible for extra help," and "they also really take the time to get to know their students outside of the classroom." In the classroom, "William & Mary professors truly know how to balance lecture with discussion. Especially in traditionally lecture-based subjects, like history, professors devote a lot of class time to discussion to understand what students think." Slackers take note: "Professors expect a lot of work outside of class," and "classes usually require a good amount of reading, especially for the humanities." All this hard work is very rewarding, though, with many upperclassmen and graduating seniors expressing how well-prepared they feel for the "real-world," and one student says that the professors "have upended the way I thought about their subject, opening completely new veins of inquiry."

Life

When students describe campus life at W&M, the word community comes up—a lot. And this community "is made up of incredibly involved, dedicated, and supportive students who have big dreams and big fun," who say: "We study hard, but we know how to have fun, too." Alma Mater Productions (AMP), the college programming board, "sponsors a lot of different events that are well-attended, including…comedians, music artists, movies, etc." Student organizations are also very strong, from intramural sports, some form of which "almost everyone plays," to arts organizations such as "the William & Mary Symphony Orchestra, three university choirs, the Arabic Music Ensemble, an Early Music Ensemble, an Appalachian string band, a small chamber orchestra, eleven a cappella groups and…two all-student theater companies." "On the weekends, there is always a party to go to" and "the Greek community is very inclusive." Off campus, students enjoy the charms of Colonial Williamsburg, theme park Busch Gardens, Jamestown Beach on the James River, and "great outlet shopping!" Despite a few gripes about parking (which are common on a small campus), students are generally happy with their facilities, with the library and the business school receiving special mention.

Student Body

Students are quick to note that there's a generalization that the "T.W.A.M.P., or Typical William & Mary Person…is the person [who] does all their reading, shows up to class every day, and is a nerd," but most are equally quick to cast this stereotype aside. The real T.W.A.M.P., they tell us, is "open-minded, outgoing, charismatic, driven, dedicated, caring, and unique." The school is full of "well-rounded people who are in touch with their inner nerd," and "intellectual people who care about the world find the zaniest ways to have fun." "Students fit in many social circles," and students credit the close bonding that happens in freshmen dorms for this inclusivity. "You will often see the members of the football team in the library as much as any other student," and "everyone is involved with at least one other thing outside of class, and often…about ten other things." "Students are an eclectic bunch united by our thirst for knowledge and overwhelming Tribe Pride."

FINANCIAL AID: 757-221-2420 • E-MAIL: ADMISSION@WM.EDU • WEBSITE: WWW.WM.EDU

THE PRINCETON REVIEW SAYS

Admissions

Very important factors considered include: Class rank, application essay, academic GPA, recommendation(s), rigor of secondary school record, standardized test scores, character/personal qualities, extracurricular activities, state residency, talent/ability, volunteer work, work experience. *Other factors considered include:* Alumni/ae relation, first generation, geographical residence, interview, racial/ethnic status. SAT or ACT required; ACT with or without writing component accepted. TOEFL recommended of all international applicants. High school diploma or equivalent is not required. *Academic units recommended:* 4 English, 4 mathematics, 4 science (3 science labs), 4 foreign language, 4 social studies.

Financial Aid

Students should submit: FAFSA, CSS PROFILE. Regular filing deadline is March 15. The Princeton Review suggests that all financial aid forms be submitted as soon as possible after January 1. *Need-based scholarships/grants offered:* Federal Pell, SEOG, state scholarships/grants, private scholarships, the school's own gift aid. *Loan aid offered:* Direct Subsidized Stafford, Direct Unsubsidized Stafford, Direct PLUS, Federal Perkins. Applicants will be notified of awards on a rolling basis beginning March 15. Federal Work-Study Program available. Institutional employment available. Highest amount earned per year from on-campus jobs $1,400. Off-campus job opportunities are excellent.

The Inside Word

The volume of applications at W&M is extremely high; thus, admission is ultra-competitive. Only very strong students from out of state should apply. The large applicant pool necessitates a labor-intensive candidate evaluation process; each admissions officer reads roughly 150 application folders per week during the peak review season. But this is one admissions committee that moves fast without sacrificing a thorough holistic review. There probably isn't a tougher public college admissions committee in the country.

THE SCHOOL SAYS ". . ."

From the Admissions Office

"William & Mary is the nation's second-oldest college and preeminent small public university. Yes, we have one of the lowest student/faculty ratio (twelve to one) of any public university. We're also known for having one of the most successful undergraduate business programs in the United States, a model United Nations team that perennially vies for the world championship, and extensive opportunities for undergraduate research. Students at William & Mary follow in the footsteps of alumni ranging from Thomas Jefferson, James Monroe, and John Tyler to Comedy Central's Jon Stewart, Academy Award nominee Glenn Close, Chancellor and former Secretary of Defense Robert Gates, and Super-Bowl-winning Pittsburg Steeler's coach Mike Tomlin. In short, William & Mary offers a top-rated educational experience at a comparatively low cost and in the company of interesting people from a broad variety of backgrounds. If you are an academically strong, involved student looking for a challenge in a great campus community, William & Mary may well be the place for you."

SELECTIVITY

Admissions Rating	97
# of applicants	12,825
% of applicants accepted	35
% of acceptees attending	33
# accepting a place on wait list	1,496
# admitted from wait list	18
# of early decision applicants	1,076
# accepted early decision	535

FRESHMAN PROFILE

Range SAT Critical Reading	620–730
Range SAT Math	620–720
Range SAT Writing	620–720
Range ACT Composite	28–32
Minimum paper TOEFL	600
Minimum web-based TOEFL	100
Average HS GPA	4.0
% graduated top 10% of class	79
% graduated top 25% of class	96
% graduated top 50% of class	99

DEADLINES

Early decision	
Deadline	11/1
Notification	12/1
Regular	
Deadline	1/1
Notification	4/1
Nonfall registration?	no

FINANCIAL FACTS

Financial Aid Rating	73
Annual in-state tuition	$8,270
Annual out-state tuition	$30,547
Room and board	$8,892
Required fees	$4,862
Books and supplies	$1,150
% needy frosh rec. need-based scholarship or grant aid	68
% needy UG rec. need-based scholarship or grant aid	75
% needy frosh rec. non-need-based scholarship or grant aid	44
% needy UG rec. non-need-based scholarship or grant aid	36
% needy frosh rec. need-based self-help aid	60
% needy UG rec. need-based self-help aid	63
% frosh rec. any financial aid	91
% UG rec. any financial aid	95
% UG borrow to pay for school	41
Average cumulative indebtedness	$20,835
% frosh need fully met	32
% ugrads need fully met	27
Average % of frosh need met	77
Average % of ugrad need met	76

THE COLLEGE OF WOOSTER

847 College Avenue, Wooster, OH 44691 • Admissions: 330-263-2322 • Fax: 330-263-2621

CAMPUS LIFE

Quality of Life Rating	**85**
Fire Safety Rating	**69**
Green Rating	**69**
Type of school	private
Environment	town

STUDENTS

Total undergrad enrollment	1,958
% male/female	45/55
% from out of state	58
% from public high school	70
# of fraternities	5
# of sororities	6
% African American	7
% Asian	3
% Caucasian	71
% Hispanic	3
% Native American	1
% international	6
# of countries represented	34

SURVEY SAYS . . .

No one cheats
Lab facilities are great
Great computer facilities
Great library
Students are friendly
Low cost of living
Students are happy
Musical organizations are popular
Lots of beer drinking

ACADEMICS

Academic Rating	**93**
% students returning for sophomore year	89
% students graduating within 4 years	71
% students graduating within 6 years	76
Calendar	semester
Student/faculty ratio	12:1
Profs interesting rating	95
Profs accessible rating	94
Most classes have	10–19 students
Most lab/discussion sessions have	10–19 students

MOST POPULAR MAJORS

English language and literature; history; psychology

STUDENTS SAY ". . ."

Academics

The College of Wooster is "a small liberal arts school" in northeastern Ohio "with strong academics and a great campus community." Students enjoy tons of undergraduate research opportunities, and "small class sizes" are another big plus. "I have never been in a class [where] the professor did not know my name," reflects a physics major. "The biggest strength of this school," according to more than one student, is Wooster's unique Independent Study program. Under the guidance of a faculty adviser, "every senior" "engages in an independent research project that spans the entire senior year." Students love the concept. They say these projects are comparable "to graduate-level work," and they promise that the experience will do wonders for your "writing and research skills." There are some "unnecessary bureaucratic processes" here but the "very responsive" administration "does a good job of running the school and keeping the students up to date with what is going on." "Overall, the professors at Wooster are great," says an international relations major. There are "only a few lousy ones." Students appreciate the fact that faculty members are "always available" and "will do anything—as long as you're trying—to help you pass classes." "The level of interest and caring in students' lives and concerns is pretty outstanding." As far as academic complaints, limited course offerings can be a problem depending on your major. "Some of the departments barely even exist." "The smaller departments obviously have a harder time getting a good variety of classes," explains an art history major, "but the quality of the professors more than makes up for it."

Life

Studying takes up "a lot of time" but students are also "very involved on campus." "Most people who attend Wooster are in many groups and clubs." Students attend intercollegiate sporting events, theatrical and musical productions, and art exhibitions. They also participate in "a variety of other activities that over 100 student-led groups schedule over the course of the semester." Though Greek life definitely doesn't dictate Wooster's social scene, "sorority and fraternity parties are often popular destinations on the weekends." "Many people go out to parties and drink," "but a lot of people also don't." "Some people think that they are huge partiers," pronounces a sophomore, "but compared to bigger schools, they aren't." Wooster "might seem boring if you can't just sit down with your friends and hang out for hours on end," counsels a sophomore. "It's a small school in a small town, and unless you're creative you can run out of things to do. However, the people that you'll meet will make it so easy to just sit around for hours until you go to dinner, or decide to have a snowball fight." Students generally agree that their campus is "beautiful." The residence halls aren't the greatest, though. "Some of them are old and small," warns a junior. "Others are new but they are still small." "The athletic facilities are not in the best shape," either. Off campus, the surrounding town is "in the cornfields" and doesn't offer much in the way of entertainment. There's "nowhere to go shopping" and "local residents can be unfriendly." If you have a car, Cleveland and Columbus are about an hour away.

Student Body

Wooster "is surprisingly diverse given its size." The population here tends to be "studious and usually moderate to left-leaning politically." Beyond that, there's not much of a Wooster type. It's "an awesome mix of people who are jocks, hippies, musicians, preps, artists," and "people with no style at all." Virtually everyone is "eccentric in one way or another." "There is a niche for everybody and those who would commonly be considered atypical seem to find theirs." Students swear that you'll feel welcome here because "anyone feels welcome on campus." "Everyone seems to have a group of friends and every friend group seems to overlap," explains a sophomore. "It may sound empty and too simple but you will really love how people are so close and nice to each other," guarantees a wistful senior. "Emotionally, you will be happy."

FINANCIAL AID: 800-877-3688 • E-MAIL: ADMISSIONS@WOOSTER.EDU • WEBSITE: WWW.WOOSTER.EDU

THE PRINCETON REVIEW SAYS

Admissions

Very important factors considered include: Class rank, academic GPA, rigor of secondary school record. *Important factors considered include:* Application essay, recommendation(s), standardized test scores, character/personal qualities, talent/ability. *Other factors considered include:* Alumni/ae relation, extracurricular activities, geographical residence, interview, racial/ethnic status, state residency, volunteer work, work experience. SAT or ACT required; ACT with writing component required. TOEFL required of all international applicants. High school diploma is required and GED is accepted. *Academic units required:* 4 English, 3 mathematics, 3 science, 2 foreign language, 3 social studies, 2 academic electives. *Academic units recommended:* 4 mathematics, 4 science, 3 foreign language, 4 social studies.

Financial Aid

Students should submit: FAFSA, institution's own financial aid form, CSS/Financial Aid PROFILE. The Princeton Review suggests that all financial aid forms be submitted as soon as possible after January 1. *Need-based scholarships/grants offered:* Federal Pell, SEOG, state scholarships/grants, private scholarships, the school's own gift aid. *Loan aid offered:* Direct Subsidized Stafford, Direct Unsubsidized Stafford, Direct PLUS, Federal Perkins, college/university loans from institutional funds. Applicants will be notified of awards on or about April 1. Federal Work-Study Program available. Institutional employment available. Off-campus job opportunities are good.

The Inside Word

The College of Wooster is a small, selective liberal arts school in a region of the country where there are quite a few small, selective liberal arts schools. For the most part, only solid students get past the gatekeepers here, and you should expect a thorough review of your application. Nevertheless, the admit rate is high. Stiff competition from similar institutions means the school will occasionally admit students who don't have stellar academic records.

THE SCHOOL SAYS ". . ."

From the Admissions Office

"The College of Wooster is America's premier college for mentored undergraduate research. Our mission is to graduate educated, not merely trained, people; to produce responsible, independent thinkers, rather than specialists in any given field. Our commitment to independence is especially evident in IS, the college's distinctive program in which every senior works one-to-one with a faculty mentor to complete a project in the major. IS comes from 'independent study,' but, in reality, it is an intellectual collaboration of the highest order and permits every student the freedom to pursue something in which he or she is passionately interested. IS is the centerpiece of an innovative curriculum. More than just the project itself, the culture that sustains IS—and, in turn, is sustained by IS—is an extraordinary college culture. The same attitudes of student initiative, openness, flexibility, and individual support enrich every aspect of Wooster's vital residential college life."

SELECTIVITY

Admissions Rating	**88**
# of applicants	4,635
% of applicants accepted	67
% of acceptees attending	20
# accepting a place on wait list	333
# admitted from wait list	18
# of early decision applicants	64
# accepted early decision	59

FRESHMAN PROFILE

Range SAT Critical Reading	560–670
Range SAT Math	550–670
Range SAT Writing	550–660
Range ACT Composite	24–29
Minimum paper TOEFL	550
Minimum web-based TOEFL	80
Average HS GPA	3.6
% graduated top 10% of class	39
% graduated top 25% of class	69
% graduated top 50% of class	93

DEADLINES

Early decision	
Deadline	11/15
Notification	12/15
Early action	
Deadline	12/15
Notification	1/15
Regular	
Deadline	2/15
Notification	4/1
Nonfall registration?	yes

FINANCIAL FACTS

Financial Aid Rating	**89**
Annual tuition	$39,810
Room and board	$9,590
Required fees	$290
Books and supplies	$1,000
% needy frosh rec. need-based scholarship or grant aid	99
% needy UG rec. need-based scholarship or grant aid	98
% needy frosh rec. non-need-based scholarship or grant aid	18
% needy UG rec. non-need-based scholarship or grant aid	14
% needy frosh rec. need-based self-help aid	75
% needy UG rec. need-based self-help aid	80
% frosh rec. any financial aid	98
% UG rec. any financial aid	98
% UG borrow to pay for school	58
Average cumulative indebtedness	$25,252
% frosh need fully met	66
% ugrads need fully met	54
Average % of frosh need met	90
Average % of ugrad need met	86

COLORADO COLLEGE

14 EAST CACHE LA POUDRE STREET, COLORADO SPRINGS, CO 80903 • ADMISSIONS: 719-389-6344 • FAX: 719-389-6816

CAMPUS LIFE

Quality of Life Rating	**79**
Fire Safety Rating	**81**
Green Rating	**96**
Type of school	private
Environment	metropolis

STUDENTS

Total undergrad enrollment	2,008
% male/female	46/54
% from out of state	78
% from public high school	49
% frosh live on campus	100
# of fraternities	3
# of sororities	3
% African American	1
% Asian	4
% Caucasian	74
% Hispanic	8
% international	5
# of countries represented	58

SURVEY SAYS . . .

Lab facilities are great
School is well run
Students are friendly
Students are happy
Intramural sports are popular
Lots of beer drinking
Hard liquor is popular

ACADEMICS

Academic Rating	**95**
% students returning for sophomore year	96
% students graduating within 4 years	83
% students graduating within 6 years	88
Calendar	other
Student/faculty ratio	10:1
Profs interesting rating	93
Profs accessible rating	91
Most classes have	10–19 students

MOST POPULAR MAJORS

biology/biological sciences; economics; political science and government

STUDENTS SAY ". . ."

Academics

Colorado College has a unique program that breaks the school year into eight segments, or blocks, of three-and-a-half weeks each. Students take a single course during each block. And unsurprisingly, it's hugely popular. Students "love the block plan," calling it "an incredible way to learn" and a system that will "help you become who you always wanted to be, or someone better." All this is moved along by "incredible" professors who are "extremely smart in their academic area and make it really interesting and fun to learn more about what they do and know." In fact, one student suggests, professors are "the reason to go to CC." They are "absolutely amazing," some of the "most interesting people I have ever met, and they remember their students because classes aren't 700 people large." Classrooms are generally discussion-based, but that doesn't make this "academically rigorous" school easy. "Because you meet for three-plus hours a day, every day, there is no slacking," students note. "Professors hold students to a high standard, and most often, students rise to meet them."

Life

Intellectual activity, outdoor adventures, and learning on a "beautiful campus" are the rule of the day here. But it's with a reward in mind. CC students are "working hard as hell so we can party hard as hell." Make no mistake, however, education is most important to CC students. The school is a "constant sprint of academics, and during whatever free time we have, an intense pursuit of fun of all kinds." When it comes to activities, this college offers what you'd expect from a school in Colorado. Students "do outdoor activities such as skiing, snowboarding, and hiking," and "if it's a sunny day we read, tan, or play Frisbee, maybe slack line." It ranges from the sublime—"student body events" and "the many, many clubs and intramurals on campus"—to the ridiculous, such as "naked hot springs, river rafting, hiking the sand dunes," and "crazy athletic things (like the incline) along with normal athletic things like skiing and snowboarding." You don't even have to go far to find the outdoors. "There are millions of hikes around campus," one student points out, and "at around 3:00 P.M. when sports practices start, you are bound to see at least fifteen CC students run by you on the creek trail next to the fields."

Student Body

The "well-off, white, socially conscious" students of Colorado College tend to be "laid-back, intelligent, and very opinionated." Most of all, students are "really intense about all the things they care about," whether it is the outdoor adventure so popular among students here, environmental awareness, social causes, or just plain having fun. Students disinclined to seek adventure may find themselves in the minority, as most "are very outdoorsy and like to ski, rock climb, and camp." The "generally leftist" student body also enjoys "unique intellectual discussion," often centered around "community service or sustainability efforts," environmental causes, and more. That might lead one to believe pretentiousness is common, but students say this group is "super intelligent" yet "down-to-earth." That's because CC students know life is an adventure. The typical students are "invested in their education but also like to have fun." And when they throw themselves into something, whether for business in pleasure, they go all the way. "One of the big things we have in common is that we are all passionate about something. We exude passion and make sure to include that passion in all that we do at CC."

FINANCIAL AID: 719-389-6651 • E-MAIL: ADMISSION@COLORADOCOLLEGE.EDU • WEBSITE: WWW.COLORADOCOLLEGE.EDU

THE PRINCETON REVIEW SAYS

Admissions

Very important factors considered include: Rigor of secondary school record. *Important factors considered include:* Class rank, application essay, academic GPA, recommendation(s), standardized test scores, extracurricular activities, interview. *Other factors considered include:* Alumni/ae relation, character/personal qualities, first generation, level of applicant's interest, racial/ethnic status, religious affiliation/commitment, talent/ability, volunteer work, work experience. ACT with or without writing component accepted. High school diploma or equivalent is not required. *Academic units required:* 4 English. *Academic units recommended:* 4 English.

Financial Aid

Students should submit: FAFSA, CSS/Financial Aid PROFILE, noncustodial PROFILE, federal 1040 parent and student tax returns and parent W-2 forms. Regular filing deadline is February 15. The Princeton Review suggests that all financial aid forms be submitted as soon as possible after January 1. *Need-based scholarships/grants offered:* Federal Pell, SEOG, state scholarships/grants, private scholarships. *Loan aid offered:* Direct Subsidized Stafford, Direct Unsubsidized Stafford, Direct PLUS, Federal Perkins. Applicants will be notified of awards on or about March 20. Federal Work-Study Program available. Institutional employment available. Off-campus job opportunities are good.

The Inside Word

Colorado College's block program means admissions officers are looking for some very specific traits in applicants, seeking students who are best suited for this nontraditional college structure. Students who have taken demanding course loads in high school will get their attention, especially if supplemented by activities and extracurriculars that go hand-in-hand with their in-class work. And more so than in many other schools, the application essay is genuinely important at CC. Strong writing skills and an interest in guiding the course of your own education are a must.

THE SCHOOL SAYS ". . ."

From the Admissions Office

"Students enter Colorado College for the opportunity to study intensely in small learning communities. Groups of students work closely with one another and faculty in discussion-based classes and hands-on labs. CC encourages a well-rounded education, combining the academic rigor of a traditional liberal arts college, with the focus and flexibility of the block plan. Rich programs in athletics, community service, student government, and the arts balance an engaged student life. The college encourages students to push themselves academically, and many continue their studies at the best graduate and professional schools in the nation. Because eighty-one percent of students study abroad while at CC, the college has been recognized as a national leader in international education. The block plan allows classes to incorporate field study into the curriculum, whether studying winter field ecology at the CC Cabin or Dante and Michelangelo in Italy. Its location at the base of the Rockies makes CC a great choice for students who enjoy backpacking, hiking, climbing, and skiing.

"Colorado College adopted a flexible testing policy, beginning with the 2015 class. We require that applicants submit either the SAT Reasoning Test or ACT or elect a third option, including three exams of the applicant's choice, chosen from a list of acceptable exams."

SELECTIVITY	
Admissions Rating	97
# of applicants	4,916
% of applicants accepted	26
% of acceptees attending	39
# accepting a place on wait list	1,066
# admitted from wait list	14
# of early decision applicants	421
# accepted early decision	173

FRESHMAN PROFILE	
Range SAT Critical Reading	630–720
Range SAT Math	630–700
Range SAT Writing	620–710
Range ACT Composite	29–32
% graduated top 10% of class	70
% graduated top 25% of class	89
% graduated top 50% of class	98

DEADLINES	
Early decision	
Deadline	11/15
Notification	12/15
Early action	
Deadline	11/15
Notification	12/20
Regular	
Priority	1/15
Deadline	1/15
Notification	4/1
Nonfall registration?	yes

FINANCIAL FACTS	
Financial Aid Rating	91
Annual tuition	$41,742
Room and board	$9,728
Books and supplies	$1,214
% needy frosh rec. need-based scholarship or grant aid	97
% needy UG rec. need-based scholarship or grant aid	97
% needy frosh rec. non-need-based scholarship or grant aid	45
% needy UG rec. non-need-based scholarship or grant aid	38
% needy frosh rec. need-based self-help aid	87
% needy UG rec. need-based self-help aid	80
% frosh rec. any financial aid	58
% UG rec. any financial aid	58
% UG borrow to pay for school	32
Average cumulative indebtedness	$19,970
% frosh need fully met	84
% ugrads need fully met	81
Average % of frosh need met	99
Average % of ugrad need met	98

COLORADO STATE UNIVERSITY

1062 CAMPUS DELIVERY, FORT COLLINS, CO 80523-1062 • ADMISSIONS: 970-491-6909 • FAX: 970-491-7799

CAMPUS LIFE

Quality of Life Rating	**89**
Fire Safety Rating	**76**
Green Rating	**98**
Type of school	public
Environment	city

STUDENTS

Total undergrad enrollment	22,300
% male/female	49/51
% from out of state	22
# of fraternities	24
# of sororities	15
% African American	2
% Asian	2
% Caucasian	77
% Hispanic	8
% international	2
# of countries represented	91

SURVEY SAYS . . .

Students love Fort Collins, CO
Great off-campus food
Low cost of living
Student publications are popular

ACADEMICS

Academic Rating	**69**
% students returning for sophomore year	84
% students graduating within 4 years	36
% students graduating within 6 years	64
Calendar	semester
Student/faculty ratio	18:1
Profs interesting rating	75
Profs accessible rating	73
Most classes have	10–19 students
Most lab/discussion sessions have	20–29 students

MOST POPULAR MAJORS

construction management; human development and family studies; psychology

APPLICANTS ALSO LOOK AT AND OFTEN PREFER

Arizona State University, University of Colorado—Boulder, University of Denver, University of Oregon, University of Arizona

STUDENTS SAY ". . ."

Academics

Colorado State University provides its 30,000 students with numerous academic resources that guide them toward academic success. Even in light of its size, there is "open communication" between students and the administration, and "The institution strives to prepare students with hands-on experience while they are students so they can be prepared in the real world." This "hidden gem" offers a "wonderful education, friendly people, and awesome culture," along with "excellent" green efforts, a strong engineering program, and myriad research opportunities. CSU also cares about its students becoming active members in the community ("social responsibility, ethics, and sustainability play a large part in our education at CSU," says one student), and the school is quite connected with its hometown of Fort Collins.

Most professors are "willing to help you however way they can"; their feedback is "honest and beneficial for students." "Our professors genuinely care, and they leave their legacy on campus by helping students network and make an impact in the community," says a student. For those in need of extra assistance, there is free tutoring offered for classes in the College of Natural Sciences and College of Liberal Arts. Even though it is a large campus, the school has "so many ways to meet people and create communities on campus that really help you succeed." Green is god here; no matter what aspect of the university you look at, "everyone is concerned with how their actions affect the environment," and "many majors look toward educating their students about job opportunities in the green job force." As for the working world, "An education at CSU is valued and therefore opens up many career opportunities." The college also "does a great job or bringing resources to campus through speakers, panels, and career fairs."

Life

"People enjoy each other here; they enjoy life here." "Bike-friendly" Fort Collins offers a "big-city, small-town life that is green but not pretentious." When everyone is done with the various meetings they have that evening, they "most likely enjoy some great food in our Old Town then head to the nice nightlife in the area." "Fort Collins is such a fun town with fabulous food and many things to do. There is always something to do around here: go to a concert, go shopping, spend a day in the mountains," says a student. "Living in Colorado encourages us to be better students so we can go outside and enjoy why we live in this beautiful state." People are "definitely more outdoors-oriented"; year-round sports are expected—on the weekends "lots of people will rock-climb, trail-run, bike, ski, snowboard, or ice-climb"—and "the gym is always busy." Once in a while, students go to Denver or Boulder "just to try something new," such as malls, the aquarium, or attending sports games—though CSU football gets some criticism from students due to its performance. Basically, life is "usually hectic, yet productive."

Student Body

CSU is "probably the friendliest campus I visited," according to many student. Rams are "chill and outgoing," "well-rounded, physically fit," and "place an emphasis on grades." They are "laid-back but serious about studies," and they "want to succeed, but also like to have fun outside of class." Most are "generally very involved either in the campus community or the Fort Collins community whether it is with service, jobs, or community events." Everyone here "finds their comfort zone in some way or another, and it seems to work for everyone."

FINANCIAL AID: 970-491-6321 • E-MAIL: ADMISSIONS@COLOSTATE.EDU • WEBSITE: WWW.COLOSTATE.EDU

THE PRINCETON REVIEW SAYS

Admissions

Very important factors considered include: Class rank, academic GPA, rigor of secondary school record. *Important factors considered include:* Application essay, recommendation(s), standardized test scores, character/personal qualities, extracurricular activities, talent/ability, volunteer work. *Other factors considered include:* Alumni/ae relation, first generation, geographical residence, interview, level of applicant's interest, state residency, work experience. SAT or ACT required; ACT with or without writing component accepted. TOEFL required of all international applicants. High school diploma is required and GED is accepted. *Academic units required:* 4 English, 4 mathematics, 3 science (2 science labs), 1 foreign language, 2 social studies, 1 history, 2 academic electives. *Academic units recommended:* 4 English, 4 mathematics, 3 science (2 science labs), 2 foreign language, 2 social studies, 1 history, 2 academic electives.

Financial Aid

Students should submit: FAFSA. The Princeton Review suggests that all financial aid forms be submitted as soon as possible after January 1. *Need-based scholarships/grants offered:* Federal Pell, SEOG, state scholarships/grants, private scholarships, the school's own gift aid. *Loan aid offered:* Direct Subsidized Stafford, Direct Unsubsidized Stafford, Direct PLUS, Federal Perkins, college/university loans from institutional funds, alternative loans. Applicants will be notified of awards on a rolling basis beginning March 1. Federal Work-Study Program available. Institutional employment available. Highest amount earned per year from on-campus jobs $2,500. Off-campus job opportunities are excellent.

The Inside Word

Colorado State University admits about nine out of ten applicants; the primary task of its admissions office is to determine who not to admit. Certain majors and programs are more competitive and impose additional admissions qualifications. Art and design programs, for example, require a portfolio review; programs in art, biomedical sciences, business, computer science, engineering, and technical journalism impose higher GPA and standardized test score floors than the school's other programs.

THE SCHOOL SAYS ". . ."

From the Admissions Office

"As one of the nation's premier research universities, Colorado State offers more than 150 undergraduate programs of study in eight colleges. Students come here from fifty states and eighty-five countries, and they appreciate the quality and breadth of the university's academic offerings. But Colorado State is more than just a place where students can take their scholarship to the highest level. It's also a place where they can gain invaluable experience in the fields of their choice, whether they're immersing themselves in professional internships, studying on the other side of the globe or teaming up with faculty on groundbreaking research projects. In addition to an outstanding experiential learning environment, Colorado State students enjoy a sense of community that's unusual for a large university. They develop meaningful relationships with faculty members who bring out their best work, and they live and learn with diverse peers who value their ideas and expand their perspectives. These types of connections lead to countless opportunities for social networking and professional accomplishments. By the time our students graduate from Colorado State, they have the knowledge, practical experience, and interpersonal skills they need to make a significant contribution to their world.

"Although academic performance is a primary factor in admissions decisions, Colorado State's holistic review process also recognizes personal qualities and experiences that have the potential to enrich the university and the Fort Collins community. To apply, students may submit the Common Application or the Colorado State University application for admission."

SELECTIVITY	
Admissions Rating	78
# of applicants	16,559
% of applicants accepted	76
% of acceptees attending	36

FRESHMAN PROFILE	
Range SAT Critical Reading	510–620
Range SAT Math	520–630
Range ACT Composite	22–27
Minimum paper TOEFL	450
Minimum web-based TOEFL	45
Average HS GPA	3.6
% graduated top 10% of class	22
% graduated top 25% of class	53
% graduated top 50% of class	90

DEADLINES	
Early action	
Deadline	12/1
Notification	2/1
Regular	
Priority	2/1
Deadline	2/1
Nonfall registration?	yes

FINANCIAL FACTS	
Financial Aid Rating	78
Annual in-state tuition	$6,307
Annual out-state tuition	$22,007
Room and board	$9,712
Required fees	$1,735
Books and supplies	$1,126
% needy frosh rec. need-based scholarship or grant aid	72
% needy UG rec. need-based scholarship or grant aid	70
% needy frosh rec. need-based self-help aid	71
% needy UG rec. need-based self-help aid	78
% frosh rec. any financial aid	71
% UG rec. any financial aid	71
% UG borrow to pay for school	57
Average cumulative indebtedness	$19,523
% frosh need fully met	6
% ugrads need fully met	4
Average % of frosh need met	73
Average % of ugrad need met	74

Columbia University

212 Hamilton Hall MC 2807, New York, NY 10027 • Admissions: 212-854-2522 • Fax: 212-894-1209

CAMPUS LIFE

Quality of Life Rating	**95**
Fire Safety Rating	**60***
Green Rating	**99**
Type of school	private
Environment	metropolis

STUDENTS

Total undergrad enrollment	6,027
% male/female	53/47
% from out of state	73
% from public high school	55
% frosh live on campus	99
# of fraternities	17
# of sororities	11
% African American	12
% Asian	18
% Caucasian	34
% Hispanic	14
% Native American	2
% international	11
# of countries represented	94

SURVEY SAYS . . .

Great library
Diverse student types on campus
Great off-campus food
Campus feels safe
Students are happy
Student publications are popular
Political activism is popular

ACADEMICS

Academic Rating	**93**
% students returning for sophomore year	99
% students graduating within 4 years	89
% students graduating within 6 years	96
Calendar	semester
Student/faculty ratio	6:1
Profs interesting rating	76
Profs accessible rating	78
Most classes have	10–19 students

MOST POPULAR MAJORS

engineering; English language and literature; political science and government

APPLICANTS ALSO LOOK AT AND OFTEN PREFER

Massachusetts Institute of Technology, Yale University, Stanford University, Harvard College

AND SOMETIMES PREFER

University of Pennsylvania, Princeton University

AND RARELY PREFER

Brown University, Cornell University, Dartmouth College, New York University

STUDENTS SAY ". . ."

Academics

At Columbia, you are in a "fantastic city" where "everyone loves learning." "Columbia should be considered by students who are willing to develop a breadth of knowledge before specializing, as it actively encourages intellectualism and academic excellence in every form." The fact that this "great" school is located "in the heart of New York City" is a big draw for the majority of Columbia University students. "You can't beat the location." It "offers unlimited resources." "There are many opportunities, and it is such a diverse community of unique individuals." The "highly prestigious name" is also a draw for students to gain "access to great liberal arts academics while still attaining a technical degree." As one student explains, "I get to take everything from art history to music to physics, even though I'm majoring in something completely different." Many students note the strength of the school's teachings, which "value intellectualism over single-minded preprofessionalism, and the core curriculum ensures that students can understand and analyze the foundations of Western thought and contemporary society." For the most part, classes are "thought-provoking," and "Professors are invested in the students and are extremely accessible." One student complains, "I don't like the fact that I have graduate students teaching some of my intro classes." Another student confesses, "Not every class has been a home run, but the ones that have been truly knock it out of the park." Good grades take some hard work. "Although it is difficult to get an A, it is definitely not uncommon." There is room for improvement in dealing with administration. "The red tape is awful, but the individual employees are all wonderful." To stay aligned with today's fast-growing technological needs, Columbia "should probably get better Wi-Fi Internet access in the library and dorms."

Life

Life at Columbia University has "boundless opportunities" both on and off campus. New York City is "vibrant" and "exciting" and "is the best resource ever. There's always something to do, and all you have to do is get on the [subway]." Among other things, students at Columbia can "take advantage of the arts programs in that they get discounted tickets to Broadway shows, operas, and concerts." As much as "people love to take advantage of the activities in the city," they "are also very passionate about events on campus. Performances by student groups are very popular, and it is also very common to just hang out in a suite with a group of friends watching movies and playing board games!" The "huge" campus also offers an "innumerable amount of sports games" as well as a satisfactory amount of parties, "either in dorms or at local bars." It is "by no means a party school, though; most people don't go out on week nights." For many, "It is the perfect balance of a social and academic life."

Student Body

Students describe Columbia as "a school made up of smart, witty, ironic, slightly cynical people." "The average Columbia student also has a wide range of interests. This is not the type of school where science majors are only interested in science or humanities majors are only interested in the humanities." It's a school where "students tend to be globally aware and academically strong; but there are extremes in both directions." "There is no one way to be a Columbian" because "students fit in by being unique and outstanding in something." Here, "being normal is frowned upon." Coming from varying "backgrounds, communities, and cultures," students at Columbia seem united in their "intellectual curiosity and desire to do something positive with their education." The "unparalleled" student body "encompasses multiple political views." "Students fit in by learning to accept that they are different and that others may disagree with them on any number of issues." One student opines, "Because the right-wing portion of the student body is a minority, it is also more outspoken and thus pretty visible on campus." Another comments, "Being religious and/or conservative on this campus is tough." "In terms of socioeconomic status, ethnicity, religion, age, and sexual preference, this school has everything. You will never feel as if you don't belong." A student sums up the general thought by saying, "We fit in because of our diversity."

FINANCIAL AID: 212-854-3711 • WEBSITE: WWW.STUDENTAFFAIRS.COLUMBIA.EDU/ADMISSIONS

THE PRINCETON REVIEW SAYS

Admissions

Very important factors considered include: Class rank, application essay, academic GPA, recommendation(s), rigor of secondary school record, standardized test scores, character/personal qualities. *Important factors considered include:* Extracurricular activities, talent/ability. *Other factors considered include:* Alumni/ae relation, geographical residence, interview, racial/ethnic status, volunteer work, work experience. ACT with writing component required. TOEFL required of all international applicants. High school diploma is required and GED is accepted. *Academic units recommended:* 4 English, 4 mathematics, 4 science (4 science labs), 4 foreign language, 4 history, 4 academic electives.

Financial Aid

Students should submit: FAFSA, CSS/Financial Aid PROFILE, noncustodial PROFILE, parent and student income tax forms. Regular filing deadline is March 1. The Princeton Review suggests that all financial aid forms be submitted as soon as possible after January 1. *Need-based scholarships/grants offered:* Federal Pell, SEOG, state scholarships/grants, private scholarships, the school's own gift aid. *Loan aid offered:* Direct Subsidized Stafford, Direct Unsubsidized Stafford, Direct PLUS, Federal Perkins, alternative loans. Applicants will be notified of awards on or about April 1. Federal Work-Study Program available. Institutional employment available. Off-campus job opportunities are excellent.

The Inside Word

There's no magic formula or pattern to guide students who are seeking admission to Columbia University. Excellent grades in rigorous classes may not be enough, and many great candidates are rejected each year. Admissions officers take a holistic approach to evaluating applications, and they pay extra attention to personal accomplishments in non-academic activities as they look to build a diverse class that will greatly contribute to the university.

THE SCHOOL SAYS ". . ."

From the Admissions Office

"Columbia maintains an intimate college campus within one of the world's most vibrant cities. After a day exploring New York City you come home to a traditional college campus within an intimate neighborhood. Nobel Prize–winning professors will challenge you in class discussions and meet one-on-one afterward. The core curriculum attracts intensely free-minded scholars, and connects all undergraduates. Science and engineering students pursue cutting-edge research in world-class laboratories with faculty members at the forefront of scientific discovery. Classroom discussions are only the beginning of your education. Ideas spill out from the classrooms, electrifying the campus and Morningside Heights. Friendships formed in the residence halls solidify during a game of Frisbee on the South Lawn or over bagels on the steps of Low Library. From your first day on campus, you will be part of our diverse community.

"Columbia offers extensive need-based financial aid and meets the full need of every student admitted as a first-year with grants instead of loans. Parents with calculated incomes below $60,000 are not expected to contribute any income or assets to tuition, room, board and mandatory fees and families with calculated incomes between $60,000 and $100,000 and with typical assets have a significantly reduced contribution. Parents earning over $100,000 can still qualify for significant financial aid. To support students pursuing study abroad, research, internships and community service opportunities, Columbia offers the opportunity to apply for additional funding and exemptions from academic year and summer work expectations. A commitment to diversity—of every kind—is a long-standing Columbia hallmark. We believe cost should not be a barrier to pursuing your educational dreams."

SELECTIVITY	
Admissions Rating	**99**
# of applicants	34,810
% of applicants accepted	7
% of acceptees attending	58
# of early decision applicants	3,274
# accepted early decision	629

FRESHMAN PROFILE	
Range SAT Critical Reading	700–790
Range SAT Math	700–790
Range SAT Writing	700–790
Range ACT Composite	32–35
Minimum paper TOEFL	600

DEADLINES	
Early decision	
Deadline	11/1
Notification	12/15
Regular	
Deadline	1/1
Notification	4/1
Nonfall registration?	no

FINANCIAL FACTS	
Financial Aid Rating	**99**
Annual tuition	$43,088
Room and board	$11,020
Required fees	$2,202
Books and supplies	$1,040
% needy frosh rec. need-based scholarship or grant aid	97
% needy UG rec. need-based scholarship or grant aid	98
% needy frosh rec. non-need-based scholarship or grant aid	3
% needy UG rec. non-need-based scholarship or grant aid	3
% needy frosh rec. need-based self-help aid	75
% needy UG rec. need-based self-help aid	83
% frosh rec. any financial aid	51
% UG rec. any financial aid	52
% frosh need fully met	100
% ugrads need fully met	100
Average % of frosh need met	100
Average % of ugrad need met	100

Connecticut College

270 Mohegan Avenue, New London, CT 06320 • Admissions: 860-439-2200 • Fax: 860-439-4301

CAMPUS LIFE

Quality of Life Rating	81
Fire Safety Rating	76
Green Rating	86
Type of school	private
Environment	town

STUDENTS

Total undergrad enrollment	1,781
% male/female	40/60
% from out of state	87
% from public high school	55
% frosh live on campus	100
% African American	4
% Asian	3
% Caucasian	74
% Hispanic	7
% international	12
# of countries represented	74

SURVEY SAYS . . .

Career services are great
Low cost of living
Frats and sororities are unpopular or nonexistent
Student government is popular
Students are environmentally aware

ACADEMICS

Academic Rating	94
% students returning for sophomore year	90
% students graduating within 4 years	80
% students graduating within 6 years	84
Calendar	semester
Student/faculty ratio	9:1
Profs interesting rating	93
Profs accessible rating	89
Most classes have	10–19 students
Most lab/discussion sessions have	10–19 students

MOST POPULAR MAJORS

economics; political science and government; psychology; biology

APPLICANTS ALSO LOOK AT AND OFTEN PREFER

Bates College, Bowdoin College, Colby College, Hamilton College, Middlebury College, Tufts University, Vassar College, Wesleyan University

AND SOMETIMES PREFER

Trinity College (CT)

AND RARELY PREFER

Skidmore College

STUDENTS SAY "..."

Academics

Located in eastern Connecticut, the picturesque Connecticut College is a classic private New England liberal arts school that shows a "great commitment to being sustainable, to promoting community service, and to learning." The college provides "great academic, extracurricular, and athletic opportunities to all students," and the "beloved" honor code makes for "a close-knit, supportive community." A strong focus on interdisciplinary education, small classes, and self-scheduled exams give students the autonomy to truly tailor their learning around their interests. The academics are "rigorous but continuously relevant, interesting, and enlightening." Most classes are discussion-based, which "allows students to express their own opinions while hearing from their fellow students and professors." Though there are a few bad apples, most professors are always accessible ("especially outside of their office hours") and are "constantly bringing learning outside of the classroom, whether it be within a residence hall, a restaurant, museum, or gallery downtown, or within their own homes." "All of my professors are incredibly engaging and obviously here to excite students about their studies," says a student. Other high points include the "approachability of the staff," excellent career office and internship opportunities, and strong residential programs and academic centers that "help students with a myriad of topics." Connecticut College assures that no student will go through school with "your typical major/minor pairing"; with certificate programs, tons of research opportunities, independent studies and more, every student "has a completely unique and entirely interdisciplinary experience here."

Life

"Life as a student is all about balancing your school work with your extracurricular activities and choosing which events you want to attend," says one. The residential programs lay a great groundwork for student life, and much of the fun on campus "is through social events through the dorms." It helps that "everyone knows one another—between offices, custodial staff, campus safety, and students." There are a wide range of activities to get involved with (everything from athletics, to arts, to activism, to community service, etc.), as well as "numerous faculty-led discussions and speakers every week." Most activities that take place on campus make it "lively and interesting." The campus as a whole is "very friendly, and you are always surrounded by familiar faces," though the relationship with the town of New London is "something that can always be improved upon." For fun, students "attend each others' events, attend social functions in the student center, grab some coffee at one of our coffee shops, and generally hang out with each other." The library is "a very social place during the week," and though students work very hard, they "know how to have a good time on the weekends—every Saturday there is a well-attended dance put on by the Student Activities Council. Day trips to Boston and New York are also common.

Student Body

Many students at Conn are generally "smart, probably upper-class, well-dressed, and white," though the school "embraces diversity." The common theme among all Conn students is "their active involvement both on campus and off and their desire to be challenged is all aspects of their educations." Students fit in by "showing an interest in their studies, but also carrying on an active social life." It is fairly easy to find one's niche within the community, and "While it might take a semester to become adjusted, there are many groups, teams, and other resources…that help freshmen find a place here."

FINANCIAL AID: 860-439-2058 • E-MAIL: ADMISSION@CONNCOLL.EDU • WEBSITE: WWW.CONNCOLL.EDU

THE PRINCETON REVIEW SAYS

Admissions

Very important factors considered include: Class rank, academic GPA, rigor of secondary school record, character/personal qualities. *Important factors considered include:* Application essay, recommendation(s), extracurricular activities, interview, racial/ethnic status, talent/ability, volunteer work, work experience. *Other factors considered include:* Standardized test scores, alumni/ae relation, first generation, geographical residence, level of applicant's interest, religious affiliation/commitment, state residency. ACT with or without writing component accepted. TOEFL required of all international applicants. High school diploma is required and GED is accepted.

Financial Aid

Students should submit: FAFSA, CSS/Financial Aid PROFILE, noncustodial PROFILE, business/farm supplement. Federal tax returns; personal, partnership, and Federal W-2 statements. Regular filing deadline is February 1. The Princeton Review suggests that all financial aid forms be submitted as soon as possible after January 1. *Need-based scholarships/grants offered:* Federal Pell, SEOG, state scholarships/grants, the school's own gift aid. *Loan aid offered:* Direct Subsidized Stafford, Direct Unsubsidized Stafford, Direct PLUS, Federal Perkins. Applicants will be notified of awards on or about April 1. Federal Work-Study Program available. Institutional employment available. Off-campus job opportunities are good.

The Inside Word

Connecticut College is the archetypal selective New England college, and admissions officers are judicious in their decisions. Competitive applicants will have pursued a demanding course load in high school. Admissions officers look for students who are curious and who thrive in challenging academic environments. Since Connecticut College has a close-knit community, personal qualities are also closely evaluated, and interviews are important.

THE SCHOOL SAYS ". . ."

From the Admissions Office

"Chartered in 1911, Connecticut College was founded in the spirit of political and social equality, self-determination, and shared governance. The college seeks students who are not only smart and intellectually curious, but who also bring a wide range of life experiences and perspectives that enable this spirit to endure within the college community. The college's near century-old Honor Code defines campus life and is observed by all students, faculty, and staff. The Honor Code inspires students to challenge themselves and their peers to see the world from diverse perspectives, to remain receptive to new ideas and experiences, and, by instilling a sense of mutual respect, to consider how their actions and education may ultimately better the common good. Ninety-nine percent of students live on campus. There is no Greek system. Dozens of clubs represent the students' numerous activist, volunteer, spiritual, creative, or athletic interests.

"The college offers more than fifty majors and minors and a series of interdisciplinary learning centers. All classes and labs are taught by professors. Students participate in the NCAA Division III New England Small College Athletic Conference (NESCAC). The college is nationally known for pioneering environmental initiatives, including commitments to renewable energy, and career and internship placement. The college has been called a "college with a conscience" by the Princeton Review for fostering social responsibility and public service and is one of the top sending schools for both Teach for America and The Peace Corps. In the past four years, eighteen Connecticut College students have been awarded Fulbright Scholarships and three students have been awarded Goldwater Scholarships."

SELECTIVITY	
Admissions Rating	**96**
# of applicants	5,242
% of applicants accepted	34
% of acceptees attending	28
# accepting a place on wait list	332
# admitted from wait list	61
# of early decision applicants	395
# accepted early decision	227

FRESHMAN PROFILE	
Range SAT Critical Reading	620–710
Range SAT Math	630–700
Range SAT Writing	630–720
Range ACT Composite	28–31
Minimum paper TOEFL	600
Minimum web-based TOEFL	100
% graduated top 10% of class	55
% graduated top 25% of class	91
% graduated top 50% of class	98

DEADLINES	
Early decision	
Deadline	11/15
Notification	12/15
Regular	
Deadline	1/1
Notification	3/31
Nonfall registration?	no

FINANCIAL FACTS	
Financial Aid Rating	**94**
Annual tuition	$44,570
Room and board	$11,900
Required fees	$320
Books and supplies	$1,000
% needy frosh rec. need-based scholarship or grant aid	96
% needy UG rec. need-based scholarship or grant aid	92
% needy frosh rec. non-need-based scholarship or grant aid	49
% needy UG rec. non-need-based scholarship or grant aid	45
% needy frosh rec. need-based self-help aid	46
% needy UG rec. need-based self-help aid	44
% frosh rec. any financial aid	52
% UG rec. any financial aid	49
% UG borrow to pay for school	38
Average cumulative indebtedness	$22,790
% frosh need fully met	100
% ugrads need fully met	100
Average % of frosh need met	100
Average % of ugrad need met	100

The Cooper Union for the Advancement of Science and Art

30 Cooper Square, New York, NY 10003 • Admissions: 212-353-4120 • Fax: 212-353-4342

CAMPUS LIFE

Quality of Life Rating	**69**
Fire Safety Rating	**98**
Green Rating	**80**
Type of school	private
Environment	metropolis

STUDENTS

Total undergrad enrollment	887
% male/female	63/37
% from out of state	46
% from public high school	65
% frosh live on campus	80
# of fraternities	2
# of sororities	1
% African American	6
% Asian	18
% Caucasian	38
% Hispanic	9
% Native American	1
% international	15
# of countries represented	30

SURVEY SAYS . . .

No one cheats
Athletic facilities need improving
Students are friendly
Diverse student types on campus
Students get along with local community
Students love New York, NY
Great off-campus food
Frats and sororities are unpopular or nonexistent

ACADEMICS

Academic Rating	**91**
% students returning for sophomore year	96
% students graduating within 4 years	68
% students graduating within 6 years	86
Calendar	semester
Student/faculty ratio	9:1
Profs interesting rating	74
Profs accessible rating	75
Most classes have	10–19 students
Most lab/discussion sessions have	10–19 students

MOST POPULAR MAJORS

electrical, electronics and communications engineering; fine arts and art studies, other; mechanical engineering

APPLICANTS ALSO LOOK AT AND OFTEN PREFER

Columbia University, Cornell University, Massachusetts Institute of Technology, Princeton University, Harvard College

AND SOMETIMES PREFER

Carnegie Mellon University, Duke University

AND RARELY PREFER

Rochester Institute of Technology

STUDENTS SAY ". . ."

Academics

Believe it or not, "free tuition" isn't the only reason gifted students clamor for a spot at The Cooper Union for the Advancement of Science and Art. Of course, the universal "full-tuition scholarships" are one of the school's major selling points. However, the rigorous and "very reputable" academic programs are the main reason to attend this unique New York City college. "An institution of the highest caliber," Cooper Union has a narrow academic focus, conferring degrees only in fine arts, architecture, and engineering. Cooper Union's "engineering program is considered one of the best in the nation"; there are "plenty of opportunities for independent study in your field," and "lab facilities are incredible." Individual learning is emphasized, and the student-to-teacher ratio is excellent: "The freshman year courses have about twenty to twenty-five students in each, while the courses in later years have as few as five students in a class." When it comes to the teaching staff, adjunct faculty gets mixed reviews, while "full-time professors are really great. They have great experience, like what they do, like the students, [and] are really accessible and happy to help." "Professors vary widely in their teaching methods"; yet most are "very accessible, friendly, [and] expect a high level of quality for work." Unfortunately, if you don't like your instructor, you're out of luck because "there are only a few professors in each department, meaning students have the same professor over and over again." Not surprisingly, academic excellence doesn't come without its share of challenges. In all departments, Cooper Union professors "really make you work hard to earn your grade," and even "extremely intelligent, hardworking students are not necessarily going to do well" in the school's competitive classes.

Life

Located in New York City's East Village, Cooper Union offers "an opportunity to live in one of the most energetic and dynamic cities in the world." Unfortunately, "There isn't time for anything other than your classes" at Cooper Union. To meet the school's high academic demands and "spine-breaking workload," "The typical schedule for any Cooper student who hopes to survive is go to class, study and do homework, sleep for a few hours, and repeat." At Cooper Union, there are few Greek organizations, no dormitories for upperclassmen, and "no recreational facilities or cafeterias on campus." Students are the first to admit that "the social life is rather limited" and "weekends are more often spent in the lab or library than at parties." However, those who make time for a little recreation say, "There are plenty of parties happening in the Village and at NYU that students can attend"—not to mention, plenty of "comedy clubs, movies, bowling, lounges, and bars" throughout New York City. Art students, though also self-professed workaholics, may also make time to "go to art openings of fellow students, professors, and friends, party, [or] play a lot of music." However, most students say that when they "sacrifice a few hours of sleep to do something enjoyable, it usually includes just hanging out with friends."

Student Body

Cooper Union's campus is largely comprised of "three distinct types of students," each delineated by major field: art, architecture, and engineering. Typical art students are "alternative kids" with the "just-rolled-out-of-bed look" while future architects are "very sleek" and fashionable, but "never leave their studio." The more "socially awkward" engineers are also largely like minds. One says, "If you have some obscure technological passion, someone in the engineering school is guaranteed to be as passionate." According to some, "Artists hang out with artists, engineers with engineers, architects with architects." However, most Cooper Union students laugh off stereotypes, telling us the school is filled with "very unique, interesting people," eager to learn and cross-pollinate between departments. A current student reassures us, "Of course, the odds are high that a group of electrical engineers will end up talking about video games, but there seems to be a broad spectrum of personalities present here." Across the board, students in every major are serious about their studies, and most of Cooper's selective admits are "super intelligent, super creative, and/or just super hardworking."

FINANCIAL AID: 212-353-4130 • E-MAIL: ADMISSIONS@COOPER.EDU • WEBSITE: WWW.COOPER.EDU

THE PRINCETON REVIEW SAYS

Admissions

Very important factors considered include: Academic GPA, rigor of secondary school record, standardized test scores, level of applicant's interest, talent/ability. *Important factors considered include:* Application essay, character/personal qualities, extracurricular activities. *Other factors considered include:* Class rank, recommendation(s), first generation, interview, racial/ethnic status, volunteer work, work experience. SAT or ACT required; ACT with writing component recommended. TOEFL required of all international applicants. High school diploma is required and GED is accepted. *Academic units required:* 4 English, 1 mathematics, 1 science, 1 social studies, 1 history, 8 academic electives. *Academic units recommended:* 4 English, 4 mathematics, 4 science (3 science labs), 2 foreign language, 4 social studies.

Financial Aid

Students should submit: FAFSA, CSS/Financial Aid PROFILE. Regular filing deadline is June 1. The Princeton Review suggests that all financial aid forms be submitted as soon as possible after January 1. *Need-based scholarships/grants offered:* Federal Pell, SEOG, state scholarships/grants, private scholarships, the school's own gift aid. *Loan aid offered:* Direct Subsidized Stafford, Direct Unsubsidized Stafford, Direct PLUS, Federal Perkins, college/university loans from institutional funds. Applicants will be notified of awards on or about June 1. Federal Work-Study Program available. Institutional employment available. Off-campus job opportunities are excellent.

The Inside Word

The admission rate to Cooper Union is extremely competitive. In recent years, only about eight percent of applicants have been accepted to the undergraduate program. The fine arts (BFA) program is usually the most competitive of Cooper's three schools, though all admits must be academically accomplished and top of their high school class. Depending on if you plan to pursue engineering, art, or architecture, admissions requirements and applications deadlines vary.

THE SCHOOL SAYS "..."

From the Admissions Office

"Each of Cooper Union's three schools, architecture, art, and engineering, adheres strongly to preparation for its profession and is committed to a problem-solving philosophy of education in a unique, scholarly environment. A rigorous curriculum and group projects reinforce this unique atmosphere in higher education and contribute to a strong sense of community and identity in each school. With McSorley's Ale House and the Joseph Papp Public Theatre nearby, Cooper Union remains at the heart of the city's tradition of free speech, enlightenment, and entertainment. Cooper's Great Hall has hosted national leaders, from Abraham Lincoln to Booker T. Washington, from Mark Twain to Samuel Gompers, from Susan B. Anthony to Betty Friedan, and more recently, President Bill Clinton and President Barack Obama.

"In fall of 2009, we opened the doors of our new academic building. Designed by Pritzker Prize–winning architect, Thom Mayne, the new building was designed to enhance and encourage more interaction between students in all three schools.

"We're seeking students who have a passion to study our professional programs. Cooper Union students are independent thinkers, following the beat of their own drum. Many of our graduates become world-class leaders in the disciplines of architecture, fine arts, design, and engineering.

"For art and architecture applicants, SAT scores are considered after the home test and portfolio work. For engineering applicants, high school grades and the SAT and SAT Subject Test scores are the most important factors considered in admissions decisions. Currently, we do not use the writing section of the SAT to assist in making admissions decisions. We expect to revisit that policy as more data is available in the near future."

SELECTIVITY

Admissions Rating	**99**
# of applicants	3,415
% of applicants accepted	8
% of acceptees attending	75
# accepting a place on wait list	70
# admitted from wait list	10
# of early decision applicants	820
# accepted early decision	70

FRESHMAN PROFILE

Range SAT Critical Reading	610–720
Range SAT Math	650–780
Range SAT Writing	620–730
Range ACT Composite	29–33
Minimum paper TOEFL	600
Minimum web-based TOEFL	100
Average HS GPA	3.6
% graduated top 10% of class	93
% graduated top 25% of class	98
% graduated top 50% of class	99

DEADLINES

Early decision	
Deadline	12/1
Notification	12/23
Regular	
Priority	12/1
Deadline	1/1
Notification	4/1
Nonfall registration?	no

FINANCIAL FACTS

Financial Aid Rating	**92**
Annual tuition	$37,500
Room and board	$13,700
Required fees	$1,650
Books and supplies	$1,800
% needy frosh rec. need-based scholarship or grant aid	100
% needy UG rec. need-based scholarship or grant aid	100
% needy frosh rec. non-need-based scholarship or grant aid	100
% needy UG rec. non-need-based scholarship or grant aid	100
% needy frosh rec. need-based self-help aid	71
% needy UG rec. need-based self-help aid	69
% frosh rec. any financial aid	100
% UG rec. any financial aid	100
% UG borrow to pay for school	30
Average cumulative indebtedness	$13,721
% frosh need fully met	61
% ugrads need fully met	53
Average % of frosh need met	93
Average % of ugrad need met	92

CORNELL COLLEGE

600 FIRST STREET WEST, MOUNT VERNON, IA 52314-1098 • ADMISSIONS: 319-895-4215 • FAX: 319-895-4451

CAMPUS LIFE

Quality of Life Rating	**69**
Fire Safety Rating	**70**
Green Rating	**74**
Type of school	private
Affiliation	Methodist
Environment	rural

STUDENTS

Total undergrad enrollment	1,190
% male/female	46/54
% from out of state	82
% from public high school	79
% frosh live on campus	99
# of fraternities	8
# of sororities	7
% African American	5
% Asian	4
% Caucasian	70
% Hispanic	8
% Native American	1
% international	6
# of countries represented	19

SURVEY SAYS . . .

No one cheats
Students are friendly
Students get along with local community
Low cost of living
Theater is popular

ACADEMICS

Academic Rating	**88**
% students returning for sophomore year	79
% students graduating within 4 years	65
% students graduating within 6 years	70
Calendar	eight 3.5-week terms
Student/faculty ratio	13:1
Profs interesting rating	88
Profs accessible rating	92
Most classes have	10–19 students

MOST POPULAR MAJORS

economics; history; psychology

APPLICANTS ALSO LOOK AT AND SOMETIMES PREFER

Beloit College, Coe College, Colorado College, Knox College, Kalamazoo College

STUDENTS SAY ". . ."

Academics

Cornell College, a small liberal arts school in Iowa, employs a unique one-course-at-a-time program, allowing students to focus on just one course (or "block") each month, providing an "intense, thorough, and complete immersion." Though students agree that this "series of experiences" "doesn't give you any time to think about anything but the class you're in right then," it allows for personalized curricula design, and areas like the humanities "work perfectly with the block plan." Students also "always know when to find people," which makes it easy to get together. Some classes may not be the most challenging, but "upper-level courses are very engaging and fulfilling." "You could have hours and hours of homework one block and practically none the next," says a student. The block plan makes it very easy to gain off-campus field experience or do international study, and it's "easier to try off-campus opportunities." Administration is generally "excellent at taking a personal interest in each student," though some note, "There is not much transparency at the administrative level," which can be "out of touch" at times. The registrar is "the most dreaded office on campus," with residence life a close second. On the classroom side, professors "know how to motivate and encourage their students," and though "you may get a bad apple maybe once a year," they're "not only knowledgeable but dedicated." "The personal attention you can receive from any given professor, given that you seek them out, is especially rewarding," says a student. All in all, students love the block structure and the sense of community it creates, as "no matter what it is you may want to do, you can find someone to do it with you." One student claims he "cannot imagine learning any other way."

Life

Since Cornell is very campus-focused (you "rarely see students venture past the edge of campus"), the school makes sure there's a large variety of campus organizations and "many events going on almost every weekend." Though there's definitely a "small-town quiet," Cedar Rapids and Iowa City are both only a twenty-minute drive away, and "ice climbing, rock-climbing, paddling, and hiking" are popular outdoor pastimes. It's also "fairly easy to start up a new club or group." In addition, the school provides seven "block breaks," which last four and a half days and give students the opportunity to travel, go skiing or camping, and so on. The cold weather can cause problems here, in both a locked-in feel and the possibility for accidents, and students are encouraged to "bring snow boots!" Many here tend to have a love-hate relationship with sports; while athletics are a huge boon, "The athletes and the non-athletes are seldom friends." Much like the curriculum, lunchtimes are pretty unique, and students all eat in a common cafeteria, naturally falling into a somewhat "high school" habit of eating at the same tables every day. The meals themselves are another matter. One student sums up the feelings of all: "Cornell needs to work on the food. There, I said it." Most people stay on campus for entertainment and socializing, "creating a cohesive community." Parties do take place on weekends, and "Drinking is popular on campus but never forced," but in general, "People are more interested in just having a good conversation with their peers."

Student Body

There's "a great diversity of interests" in people who attend Cornell, and the "super busy" students have a hard time defining a more common characteristic than the fact that almost all are driven and involved. Some division into typical groups does occur—"the cafeteria design and Greek life are very conducive to this problem"—but "even group to group there is always mingling because you never know who will be in your next class." Since the classes are so small and "you see the same people four hours a day for three and a half weeks," people are generally accepting, and "You have to be really, really strange here to stick out." As one freshman says, "The only intolerance I've seen is toward the consistently indolent."

FINANCIAL AID: 319-895-4216 • E-MAIL: ADMISSIONS@CORNELLCOLLEGE.EDU • WEBSITE: WWW.CORNELLCOLLEGE.EDU

THE PRINCETON REVIEW SAYS

Admissions

Very important factors considered include: Application essay, academic GPA, recommendation(s), rigor of secondary school record. *Important factors considered include:* Class rank, standardized test scores, character/personal qualities, extracurricular activities, first generation, interview, level of applicant's interest, talent/ability, volunteer work, work experience. *Other factors considered include:* Alumni/ae relation, geographical residence, racial/ethnic status, state residency. SAT or ACT required; ACT with or without writing component accepted. TOEFL required of all international applicants. High school diploma is required and GED is accepted. *Academic units recommended:* 4 English, 3 mathematics, 3 science, 2 foreign language, 3 social studies.

Financial Aid

Students should submit: FAFSA, institution's own financial aid form, noncustodial (divorced/separated) parent's statement. Regular filing deadline is March 1. The Princeton Review suggests that all financial aid forms be submitted as soon as possible after January 1. *Need-based scholarships/grants offered:* Federal Pell, SEOG, state scholarships/grants, private scholarships, the school's own gift aid, AC, SMART, and TEACH Grants. *Loan aid offered:* Direct Subsidized Stafford, Direct Unsubsidized Stafford, Direct PLUS, Sherman Loan, United Methodist Loan. Applicants will be notified of awards on a rolling basis beginning March 1. Federal Work-Study Program available. Institutional employment available. Highest amount earned per year from on-campus jobs $350. Off-campus job opportunities are fair.

The Inside Word

Given Cornell's relatively unique approach to study, it's no surprise that the admissions committee here focuses attention on both academic and personal strengths. Cornell's small, highly self-selected applicant pool is chock-full of students with solid self-awareness, motivation, and discipline.

THE SCHOOL SAYS ". . ."

From the Admissions Office

"Very few colleges are truly distinctive like Cornell College. Founded in 1853, Cornell is recognized as one of the nation's finest colleges of the liberal arts and sciences. It is Cornell's combination of special features, however, that distinguishes it. An attractively diverse, caring residential college, Cornell places special emphasis on service and leadership. Foremost, it is a place where theory and practice are brought together in exciting ways through the college's one-course-at-a-time academic calendar. Here, students enjoy learning as they immerse themselves in a single subject for a 3.5-week term. They and their professor devote all of their efforts to that course in an engagingly interactive learning environment. This academic system also offers wonderful enrichment experiences through field-based-study, travel abroad, student research, and meaningful internship opportunities. Eight terms are offered each year; thirty-two course credits are required for graduation with each course equal to four credit hours. Since all classes are on a standard schedule, students are able to pursue their extracurricular interests, whether in the performing arts, athletics, or interest groups, with the same passion with which they pursue their course work. Typically, each year applicants from all fifty states and more than forty countries apply for admission. Cornell graduates are in demand, with more than two-thirds eventually earning advanced degrees. The college's beautiful hilltop campus is one of only two campuses nationwide listed on the National Register of Historic Places. Located in the charming town of Mount Vernon, Cornell is also within commuting distance of Iowa City (home of the University of Iowa) and Cedar Rapids (the second largest city in the state). Freshman applicants are required to submit their SAT Reasoning or ACT results (the writing component is optional for the ACT, as students are required to submit an essay as part of the application for admission). In addition, for students submitting multiple score reports their best scores from either exam will be used in the application review process. SAT Subject Tests are not required."

SELECTIVITY

Admissions Rating	**92**
# of applicants	3,202
% of applicants accepted	46
% of acceptees attending	23
# accepting a place on wait list	152
# admitted from wait list	33
# of early decision applicants	128
# accepted early decision	32

FRESHMAN PROFILE

Range SAT Critical Reading	540–680
Range SAT Math	540–680
Range SAT Writing	520–660
Range ACT Composite	23–29
Minimum paper TOEFL	550
Average HS GPA	3.5
% graduated top 10% of class	31
% graduated top 25% of class	58
% graduated top 50% of class	86

DEADLINES

Early decision	
Deadline	11/1
Notification	12/15
Early action	
Deadline	12/1
Notification	2/1
Regular	
Priority	12/1
Deadline	2/1
Notification	3/20
Nonfall registration?	yes

FINANCIAL FACTS

Financial Aid Rating	**89**
Annual tuition	$34,480
Room and board	$7,900
Required fees	$225
Books and supplies	$810
% needy frosh rec. need-based scholarship or grant aid	100
% needy UG rec. need-based scholarship or grant aid	100
% needy frosh rec. non-need-based scholarship or grant aid	91
% needy UG rec. non-need-based scholarship or grant aid	86
% needy frosh rec. need-based self-help aid	86
% needy UG rec. need-based self-help aid	84
% frosh rec. any financial aid	76
% UG rec. any financial aid	76
% UG borrow to pay for school	80
Average cumulative indebtedness	$27,805
% frosh need fully met	28
% ugrads need fully met	26
Average % of frosh need met	92
Average % of ugrad need met	87

Cornell University

Undergraduate Admissions, 410 Thurston Avenue, Ithaca, NY 14850 • Admissions: 607-255-5241 • Fax: 607-255-0659

CAMPUS LIFE

Quality of Life Rating	94
Fire Safety Rating	73
Green Rating	97
Type of school	private
Environment	town

STUDENTS

Total undergrad enrollment	14,167
% male/female	50/50
% from out of state	65
% frosh live on campus	100
# of fraternities	46
# of sororities	18
% African American	6
% Asian	16
% Caucasian	46
% Hispanic	9
% international	9
# of countries represented	77

SURVEY SAYS . . .

Great computer facilities
Great library
Great food on campus
Student publications are popular
Lots of beer drinking
Internships are widely available

ACADEMICS

Academic Rating	89
% students returning for sophomore year	97
% students graduating within 4 years	87
% students graduating within 6 years	93
Calendar	semester
Student/faculty ratio	9:1
Profs interesting rating	76
Profs accessible rating	72
Most classes have	10–19 students
Most lab/discussion sessions have	10–19 students

MOST POPULAR MAJORS

biology/biological sciences; hotel/motel administration/management; labor and industrial relations

STUDENTS SAY ". . ."

Academics

"Any person, any study." Thus goes the motto of Cornell University, located in rural, cold upstate New York. The school consists of seven different undergraduate colleges, all of which have "differing focuses and missions that are somehow unified and work together pretty cohesively." These smaller schools, including the well-known Hotel School and College of Agricultural and Life Sciences, allow students to "receive all the benefits of a smaller college with the access, excitement, and opportunity provided by a large university." However, "You have to strongly believe in what you're studying and why you're studying it so as not to be freaked out by others who are in different majors and colleges." Though Cornell "may seem awfully large," students say it makes finding a close-knit community incredibly easy and "constantly challenges you to do better." No matter what major you choose, Cornell offers "rigorous" academics, where "it takes a lot of hard work to succeed, but the resources are there for you to do so." The administration "makes huge attempts to be transparent," often using student panels for advice, though there's still some red tape clinging to a few processes (such as class registration). Class sizes range from small to large, but professors remain "incredible" and attentive across the board, though the size of the school (about 14,000 undergrads) often means you have to be proactive in seeking out help. "If you show genuine interest, [faculty] are more than excited to help you." Many are also focused on their research, which can be distracting, but it also provides students with plenty of opportunities to work with the academic bigwigs themselves. "Just the other day in one of my biology classes, my professor was going over a very important topic and just added in, 'Yeah, I came up with this,'" says a student.

Life

"Cornell is about studying hard, being involved in many activities, and always doing more than the average person can handle, all while still having a social life and partying hard," says a senior. "Work hard, work harder, stress hard, play hard," says another senior about the resounding ethos that makes for a "nice balance" of life. There's also a natural progression for students as they become upperclassmen—living in the dorms and drinking at parties or frat houses is quite popular for freshmen and sophomores, while upperclassmen often find apartments and outside venues for weekend entertainment. There are always "a variety of activities that do not include drinking" on offer, including "a capella concerts, movie nights, special speakers and discussions, and sports games." Hometown Ithaca offers a farmers' market, restaurants, bars, and a movie theater. On campus, extracurricular offerings abound, and "it's not too hard to find something that interests everyone"—there's even an origami club—and the majority of students choose to join multiple organizations. On top of all that Ithaca offers, the school's northeast location also allows for "access to great weekend and break destinations like New York City and Washington, D.C."

Student Body

With such a large student body, "there is always a niche that any individual can fall into." Sure enough, the school's size and Ivy League status make it "a largely diverse and exciting bubble" where there is an abundance of "athletes or frat/sorority people," but at the same time, "you have a large group of students who do other activities." "We have our nerdy engineers, our outgoing hotelies, our hipster art students, [and] our hardcore dairy farmers," brags one proud student. A "strong work ethic" seems to be the unifying thread among Cornell's diverse student body, as all students are "very focused on performing well in the classroom." "Most everyone has a secret nerdiness inside them that actually adds to their 'coolness,'" explains one. The different schools tend to naturally group together more frequently, so that each quad "has its own vibe," but "everyone is very friendly and approachable." Basically, "when you come here, you become the typical Cornellian."

FINANCIAL AID: 607-255-5147 • E-MAIL: ADMISSIONS@CORNELL.EDU • WEBSITE: WWW.CORNELL.EDU

THE PRINCETON REVIEW SAYS

Admissions

Very important factors considered include: Application essay, academic GPA, recommendation(s), rigor of secondary school record, standardized test scores, extracurricular activities, talent/ability. *Important factors considered include:* Class rank. *Other factors considered include:* Alumni/ae relation, character/personal qualities, first generation, geographical residence, interview, racial/ethnic status, state residency, volunteer work, work experience. SAT or ACT required; ACT with writing component required. TOEFL required of all international applicants. High school diploma or equivalent is not required. *Academic units required:* 4 English, 3 mathematics. *Academic units recommended:* 3 science (3 science labs), 3 foreign language, 3 social studies, 3 history.

Financial Aid

Students should submit: FAFSA, CSS/Financial Aid PROFILE, noncustodial PROFILE, business/farm supplement. Prior Year Tax Forms. Regular filing deadline is January 2. The Princeton Review suggests that all financial aid forms be submitted as soon as possible after January 1. *Need-based scholarships/grants offered:* Federal Pell, SEOG, state scholarships/grants, private scholarships, the school's own gift aid. *Loan aid offered:* Direct Subsidized Stafford, Direct Unsubsidized Stafford, Direct PLUS, Federal Perkins, college/university loans from institutional funds. Applicants will be notified of awards on or about April 1. Federal Work-Study Program available. Institutional employment available. Off-campus job opportunities are fair.

The Inside Word

Gaining admission to Cornell is a tough coup regardless of your intended field of study, but some of the university's seven schools are more competitive than others. If you're thinking of trying to "backdoor" your way into one of the most competitive schools—by gaining admission to a less competitive one, then transferring after one year—be aware that you will have to resubmit the entire application and provide a statement outlining your academic plans. It's not impossible to accomplish, but Cornell works hard to discourage this sort of maneuvering.

THE SCHOOL SAYS ". . ."

From the Admissions Office

"Cornell University, an Ivy League school and land-grant college located in the scenic Finger Lakes region of central New York, provides an outstanding education to students in seven small to midsize undergraduate colleges: Agriculture and Life Sciences; Architecture, Art, and Planning; Arts and Sciences; Engineering; Hotel Administration; Human Ecology; and Industrial and Labor Relations. Cornellians come from all fifty states and more than 120 countries, and they pursue their academic goals in more than 100 departments. The College of Arts and Sciences, one of the smallest liberal arts schools in the Ivy League, offers more than forty majors, most of which rank near the top nationwide. Applied programs in the other six colleges also rank among the best in the world. "Other special features of the university include a world-renowned faculty; over 4,000 courses available to all students; an extensive undergraduate research program; superb research, teaching, and library facilities; a large, diverse study abroad program; and more than 800 student organizations and thirty-four varsity sports. Cornell's campus is one of the most beautiful in the country; students pass streams, rocky gorges, and waterfalls on their way to class. First-year students make their home on North Campus, a living-learning community that features a special advising center, faculty-in-residence, a fitness center, and traditional residence halls as well as theme-centered buildings such as Ecology House. Cornell University invites applications from all interested students and uses the Common Application exclusively with a short required Cornell Supplement. Students applying for admissions will submit scores from the SAT or ACT (with writing). We also require SAT Subject Tests. Subject test requirements are college-specific."

SELECTIVITY

Admissions Rating	98
# of applicants	36,387
% of applicants accepted	18
% of acceptees attending	51
# accepting a place on wait list	1,846
# of early decision applicants	3,479
# accepted early decision	1,227

FRESHMAN PROFILE

Range SAT Critical Reading	630–730
Range SAT Math	670–770
Range ACT Composite	29–33
Minimum paper TOEFL	600
Minimum web-based TOEFL	100
% graduated top 10% of class	89
% graduated top 25% of class	98
% graduated top 50% of class	99

DEADLINES

Early decision	
Deadline	11/1
Regular	
Deadline	1/2
Nonfall registration?	no

FINANCIAL FACTS

Financial Aid Rating	95
Annual tuition	$43,185
Room and board	$13,678
Required fees	$229
Books and supplies	$820
% needy frosh rec. need-based scholarship or grant aid	98
% needy UG rec. need-based scholarship or grant aid	98
% needy frosh rec. need-based self-help aid	86
% needy UG rec. need-based self-help aid	92
% frosh rec. any financial aid	52
% UG rec. any financial aid	50
% UG borrow to pay for school	50
Average cumulative indebtedness	$19,180
% frosh need fully met	100
% ugrads need fully met	100
Average % of frosh need met	100
Average % of ugrad need met	100

CREIGHTON UNIVERSITY

2500 CALIFORNIA PLAZA, OMAHA, NE 68178 • ADMISSIONS: 402-280-2703 • FAX: 402-280-2685

CAMPUS LIFE

Quality of Life Rating	**87**
Fire Safety Rating	**84**
Green Rating	**93**
Type of school	private
Affiliation	Roman Catholic
Environment	metropolis

STUDENTS

Total undergrad enrollment	4,153
% male/female	40/60
% from out of state	77
% from public high school	53
% frosh live on campus	95
# of fraternities	6
# of sororities	7
% African American	3
% Asian	10
% Caucasian	74
% Hispanic	6
% Native American	1
% international	2
# of countries represented	38

SURVEY SAYS . . .

Lab facilities are great
Great computer facilities
School is well run
Students are friendly
Students get along with local community
Intramural sports are popular
Students are involved in community service

ACADEMICS

Academic Rating	**84**
% students returning for sophomore year	88
% students graduating within 4 years	66
% students graduating within 6 years	77
Calendar	semester
Student/faculty ratio	12:1
Profs interesting rating	84
Profs accessible rating	85
Most classes have	20–29 students
Most lab/discussion sessions have	10–19 students

MOST POPULAR MAJORS

business/commerce; health/medical preparatory programs, other; psychology

APPLICANTS ALSO LOOK AT AND OFTEN PREFER

University of Notre Dame, University of Missouri

AND SOMETIMES PREFER

University of Kansas, University of Colorado—Boulder, Saint Louis University, Marquette University, Kansas State University, University of Nebraska—Lincoln

AND RARELY PREFER

University of Minnesota—Twin Cities, University of Iowa, Iowa State University

STUDENTS SAY ". . ."

Academics

The voices echoing from this Omaha school are resoundingly pleased with their choice to attend "a great Jesuit university focused on academics and creating well-rounded students." Students are also active outside the classroom, getting "involved" in the campus and local community, and the school makes sure it churns a student out as a complete package: "academically, socially, culturally, faith-filled, and service-oriented." Creighton wants to form students who are driven inside the classroom but "want to find deeper meanings in all that they do to enact change in the world." Though classes are tough, the typical class size is small, which "makes discussion possible in nearly every class." Likewise, professors are extraordinarily helpful and "know how to present material in an interesting manner for the most part." Professors are all "exceptional" and really run the gamut "from quirky nerds to outspoken rebels to hilarious Jesuit priests." Many students come here for medical school, allied health, or business school. There are also a variety of services offered, such as a tutoring program called "The Study," where students get help from other students on a one-on-one basis. "Students at Creighton learn to enjoy the process, rather than just the product," says one. Both the teaching staff and administration are highly accessible; office hours don't seem to stop, and every Wednesday morning the much-loved president has breakfast with a different group of students to listen to their concerns and to talk about how life at Creighton is going. "At Creighton students come first, and it is as simple as that!" chirps a happy junior.

Life

"While academics are a huge part of our schooling, they are not all-encompassing," says a student. Community service happily takes up a lot of students' time, and there are fall break and spring break service trips all over the United States. Sports, both intercollegiate and intramural, are huge on and off campus; Omaha and the Old Market have plenty of music venues, bowling, shopping, and restaurants (a good thing, because the food at Creighton is universally despised and "needs to be improved drastically"). Students would like to see some more options for getting off campus, though; the difficulty and cost of living off campus means on-campus housing is in high demand. The Greek community at Creighton "is not as intense as at state schools," but students in sorority or fraternities hold many leadership positions on campus. Weeknights are mainly for studying, but house parties are available on weekends, and "the bar scene is where many students spend their nights off." The school and student government do an excellent job of providing plenty of activities that are enjoyed by all, such as ice skating, weekly movies, and "mock TV shows like the 'Price is Right,'" and no one has any problem with peer pressure. "It is very easy to be productive and involved but still be able to find time for fun," says a biology and Spanish major.

Student Body

The typical student is white and from the Midwest, and most are "outgoing and friendly," which is probably why atypical students have no problems fitting in. And the "old brick road that runs down the middle of campus (called the mall) provides excellent opportunities to meet new people." "It doesn't matter where you came from or why you're here" as "most students have the same values, which allows the community to feel connected." "Everyone is interconnected through someone; there are very few degrees of separation between individuals," says one student, though others claim that there's no shortage of cliques. Creighton students are incredibly balanced in their work and play and are "over-the-top involved" with activities and community service while maintaining full academic loads. The school is very involved in study abroad programs, so there are a fair number of international students in each class. "I've never been in a place where so many people will hold the door open for me to walk through, if that gives any indication of the type of student here," says a student.

FINANCIAL AID: 402-280-2731 • E-MAIL: ADMISSIONS@CREIGHTON.EDU • WEBSITE: WWW.CREIGHTON.EDU

THE PRINCETON REVIEW SAYS

Admissions

Very important factors considered include: Academic GPA, rigor of secondary school record. *Important factors considered include:* Application essay, standardized test scores. *Other factors considered include:* Class rank, recommendation(s), character/personal qualities, extracurricular activities, first generation, level of applicant's interest, racial/ethnic status, talent/ability, volunteer work. SAT or ACT required; ACT with or without writing component accepted. TOEFL required of all international applicants. High school diploma is required and GED is accepted. *Academic units required:* 4 English, 3 mathematics, 2 science, 2 foreign language, 2 social studies, 3 academic electives. *Academic units recommended:* 4 English, 4 mathematics, 3 science, 3 foreign language, 3 social studies, 1 history, 3 academic electives.

Financial Aid

Students should submit: FAFSA, institution's own financial aid form. The Princeton Review suggests that all financial aid forms be submitted as soon as possible after January 1. *Need-based scholarships/grants offered:* Federal Pell, SEOG, state scholarships/grants, private scholarships, the school's own gift aid. *Loan aid offered:* Direct Subsidized Stafford, Direct Unsubsidized Stafford, Direct PLUS, Federal Perkins, Federal Nursing. Applicants will be notified of awards on a rolling basis beginning March 15. Federal Work-Study Program available. Institutional employment available. Highest amount earned per year from on-campus jobs $1,400. Off-campus job opportunities are excellent.

The Inside Word

Creighton's lack of name recognition and its location can handicap its search for quality students, occasionally forcing the school to lower the bar to fill its incoming classes, so the school's loss could well be your gain. For those comfortable in a Jesuit school, Creighton offers bright, hardworking students a great opportunity at a quality education.

THE SCHOOL SAYS ". . ."

From the Admissions Office

"Creighton is a leading national Jesuit Catholic university, offering sophisticated academic opportunities found normally at schools twice its size. Our reputa tion for diversity and educational excellence draws students from across the nation and around the world. Students find balance in rigorous academics, strong focus on leadership skills, abundant opportunities for internships and undergraduate research, and life-changing community service experiences. Creighton is committed to providing intellectual challenge, promoting critical thinking, and inspiring leader ship and service to others with a faith-filled view of the world.

"With about 7,500 students (4,000 undergraduates); more than fifty undergraduate majors and twenty graduate and professional programs; our small, personal classes; accomplished faculty mentors; a wealth of internship opportunities; and a ninety-four percent job-placement rate within eight months of graduation, Creighton provides a perfect learning environment. With recognition from prestigious organizations such as the Fulbright Fellows and Goldwater Scholars and synergy among undergraduate, graduate, and professional faculty, it's not surprising that Creighton launches about half of its graduates into medical, dental, pharmacy, physical or occupational therapy, graduate, or law school—one of the highest rates in the country.

"Creighton's cutting-edge and highly ranked programs allow students to excel in a wide variety of areas both in and outside the classroom. From our location—within walking distance of five Fortune 500 company headquarters, providing more business internships than we have students to fill them—to our commitment to alternative energy through our Energy Technology major, to our direct entry top-ranked Nursing School, Creighton students succeed personally as well as professionally."

SELECTIVITY	
Admissions Rating	**88**
# of applicants	5,104
% of applicants accepted	78
% of acceptees attending	25
# accepting a place on wait list	12

FRESHMAN PROFILE	
Range SAT Critical Reading	520–640
Range SAT Math	550–660
Range SAT Writing	510–620
Range ACT Composite	24–30
Minimum web-based TOEFL	80
Average HS GPA	3.8
% graduated top 10% of class	44
% graduated top 25% of class	75
% graduated top 50% of class	96

DEADLINES	
Regular	
Priority	12/1
Deadline	2/15
Nonfall registration?	yes

FINANCIAL FACTS	
Financial Aid Rating	**86**
Annual tuition	$31,856
Room and board	$9,446
Required fees	$1,474
Books and supplies	$1,200
% needy frosh rec. need-based scholarship or grant aid	100
% needy UG rec. need-based scholarship or grant aid	98
% needy frosh rec. non-need-based scholarship or grant aid	89
% needy UG rec. non-need-based scholarship or grant aid	74
% needy frosh rec. need-based self-help aid	75
% needy UG rec. need-based self-help aid	75
% frosh rec. any financial aid	96
% UG rec. any financial aid	90
% UG borrow to pay for school	64
Average cumulative indebtedness	$33,901
% frosh need fully met	44
% ugrads need fully met	37
Average % of frosh need met	91
Average % of ugrad need met	88

DARTMOUTH COLLEGE

6016 McNutt Hall, Hanover, NH 03755 • Admissions: 603-646-2875 • Fax: 603-646-1216

CAMPUS LIFE

Quality of Life Rating	**99**
Fire Safety Rating	**87**
Green Rating	**93**
Type of school	private
Environment	village

STUDENTS

Total undergrad enrollment	4,106
% male/female	51/49
% from out of state	97
% from public high school	54
% frosh live on campus	100
# of fraternities	14
# of sororities	6
% African American	8
% Asian	14
% Caucasian	48
% Hispanic	9
% Native American	3
% international	7
# of countries represented	72

SURVEY SAYS . . .

Great computer facilities
School is well run
Campus feels safe
Frats and sororities dominate social scene
Student publications are popular
Lots of beer drinking
Students are environmentally aware
Internships are widely available

ACADEMICS

Academic Rating	**98**
% students returning for sophomore year	98
% students graduating within 4 years	88
% students graduating within 6 years	95
Calendar	quarter
Student/faculty ratio	8:1
Profs interesting rating	96
Profs accessible rating	97
Most classes have	10–19 students

MOST POPULAR MAJORS

economics; political science and government; psychology

STUDENTS SAY ". . ."

Academics

Dartmouth College is an intellectual amusement park, a place where academic and extracurricular life intertwine to create "a tight-knit community dedicated to scholarship, creativity, intellectualism, and the well-rounded individual." While "academic interests vary widely" across campus, the school's "interdisciplinary approach…allows students from all different majors to be able to engage in analytical discussions on issues from the depiction of women and gender roles in science fiction, to the marginalization of the bottom billion in the international political economy, to nostalgia resulting from rural to urban relocation in the age of globalization." Central to this approach is the D-Plan, Dartmouth's quarterly academic calendar "where students take about three classes at a time for ten weeks." Students love it, telling us, "It gives you great flexibility to go abroad and secure fantastic off-term internships and volunteer opportunities." Students typically take advantage of the opportunities; as one explains, "Dartmouth is really big on the 'Dartmouth experience,' which basically means trying to do the most awesome things that you can fit into four years as an undergrad. This means that about two-thirds of undergrads, regardless of major, study abroad at least once. Everyone uses their 'off terms' to either try to save the world by volunteering or doing research if they're not doing some high-profile internship."

Life

Life at Dartmouth "is always busy…after attending classes in the morning, we run from meetings to debates to the library and finally to Frat Row. It is a relentless, fast-paced cycle, but it is so unbelievably fun and rewarding." "Greek life dominates" the Dartmouth campus, where student involvement in the Greek system approaches a whopping fifty percent, although one student notes that "once you get to know the Greek scene, it becomes apparent that it's unique and very welcoming and much more low key than at other schools." For those wondering, "Yes, Dartmouth is the school upon which Animal House was based… we do party a lot, but the mentality is definitely work hard, play hard." Dartmouth has an active drama and dance scene, and "a capella is particularly popular." Students like to stay active: "We throw a Frisbee on the green, hike through the mountains, play hockey on Occom Pond, play tennis, ski at the Skiway," and "sled on cafeteria trays" to burn off extra energy. "A strong sense of school spirit" is fueled by the college's "rich traditions," like "running around a giant bonfire hundreds of times." No matter what they're into, "no one leaves campus on weekends because no one wants to miss a weekend at Dartmouth."

Student Body

The quintessential Dartmouth undergraduate is "athletic, sociable, and very active within the community inside and outside of Dartmouth." "The binding element of the typical Dartmouth student is passion," one student tells us. "Whether it is academics or the environment, students are committed to an area of interest and try to contribute to that field." "There is a ton of diversity," one undergrad reports. "Through my friends I can interact and get a taste of Ghana, Trinidad, and Japan; what it means to be a Sikh, Jew, Buddhist, or Christian; how it feels to be a homosexual or transsexual; what it's like to live below the poverty line or miles above it." Wonder what they all share in common? "Everyone here is exceptional."

FINANCIAL AID: 800-443-3605 • E-MAIL: ADMISSIONS.REPLY@DARTMOUTH.EDU • WEBSITE: WWW.DARTMOUTH.EDU

THE PRINCETON REVIEW SAYS

Admissions

Very important factors considered include: Class rank, application essay, academic GPA, recommendation(s), rigor of secondary school record, standardized test scores, character/personal qualities, extracurricular activities. *Important factors considered include:* Talent/ability, volunteer work. *Other factors considered include:* Alumni/ae relation, first generation, geographical residence, interview, racial/ethnic status. SAT or ACT required; ACT with writing component required. TOEFL required of all international applicants. High school diploma or equivalent is not required. *Academic units recommended:* 4 English, 4 mathematics, 4 science, 3 social studies, 3 history.

Financial Aid

Students should submit: FAFSA, CSS/Financial Aid PROFILE, noncustodial PROFILE, business/farm supplement, current W-2 or federal tax returns. Regular filing deadline is February 1. The Princeton Review suggests that all financial aid forms be submitted as soon as possible after January 1. *Need-based scholarships/grants offered:* Federal Pell, SEOG, state scholarships/grants, private scholarships, the school's own gift aid. *Loan aid offered:* Direct Subsidized Stafford, Direct Unsubsidized Stafford, Direct PLUS, Federal Perkins, college/university loans from institutional funds. Applicants will be notified of awards on or about April 2. Federal Work-Study Program available. Institutional employment available. Off-campus job opportunities are excellent.

The Inside Word

Dartmouth doesn't have any problem attracting qualified applicants. On the contrary, this elite institution receives many, many more applications from fully qualified hopefuls than the school can possibly accommodate. As a result, many students who meet all the qualifications to attend Dartmouth are turned away every year because there simply isn't room for them. Dartmouth reviews applications holistically, meaning your best shot is to compile an application that paints a compelling portrait. Some special talent, life experience, or personal trait may be your ticket in, if Dartmouth thinks it will enhance the education of your classmates.

THE SCHOOL SAYS ". . ."

From the Admissions Office

"With its focus on undergraduate education and a flexible year-round academic calendar that encourages travel and research, Dartmouth is uniquely positioned to help students pursue their interests, prepare for a career and make an impact on the world. All classes are taught by members of the faculty, over 1,000 students per year pursue independent study for credit, and almost two-thirds of students participate in study abroad programs.

"Dartmouth opened the Class of 1978 Life Sciences Center in the fall of 2011, and the Black Family Visual Arts Center is opening in the fall of 2012. These new facilities are designed to expand Dartmouth's commitment to undergraduate research and further the college's collaboration between faculty and students.

"On campus, students participate in nearly 400 student organizations, including thirty-four intercollegiate varsity teams, over forty different community service projects, and more than fifty performing groups. Dartmouth's hometown of Hanover offers an active political scene, a vibrant arts community, and unparalleled outdoors and recreational opportunities (including our own ski mountain!).

"To help all Dartmouth students take advantage of the Dartmouth Experience, the college practices need-blind admission for all applicants, meets the full demonstrated need for all admitted students, and offers free tuition and no loan requirements for all students whose annual family incomes are below $100,000.

"Dartmouth's admissions process is designed to identify students who will thrive in a challenging and flexible academic environment, who value community, and who will take advantage of the college's undergraduate focus."

SELECTIVITY	
Admissions Rating	**99**
# of applicants	22,385
% of applicants accepted	10
% of acceptees attending	49
# accepting a place on wait list	1,047
# admitted from wait list	86
# of early decision applicants	1,754
# accepted early decision	497

FRESHMAN PROFILE	
Range SAT Critical Reading	670–780
Range SAT Math	680–780
Range SAT Writing	680–790
Range ACT Composite	30–34
Minimum paper TOEFL	600
Minimum web-based TOEFL	7
% graduated top 10% of class	90
% graduated top 25% of class	99
% graduated top 50% of class	100

DEADLINES	
Early decision	
Deadline	11/1
Notification	12/15
Regular	
Deadline	1/1
Notification	4/1
Nonfall registration?	no

FINANCIAL FACTS	
Financial Aid Rating	**97**
Annual tuition	$41,736
Room and board	$12,479
Required fees	$1,431
Books and supplies	$1,730
% needy frosh rec. need-based scholarship or grant aid	100
% needy UG rec. need-based scholarship or grant aid	100
% needy frosh rec. need-based self-help aid	88
% needy UG rec. need-based self-help aid	95
% frosh rec. any financial aid	45
% UG rec. any financial aid	57
% UG borrow to pay for school	50
Average cumulative indebtedness	$17,113
% frosh need fully met	100
% ugrads need fully met	100
Average % of frosh need met	100
Average % of ugrad need met	100

DAVIDSON COLLEGE

PO BOX 7156, DAVIDSON, NC 28035-7156 • ADMISSIONS: 704-894-2230 • FAX: 704-894-2016

CAMPUS LIFE

Quality of Life Rating	99
Fire Safety Rating	60*
Green Rating	94
Type of school	private
Affiliation	Presbyterian
Environment	village

STUDENTS

Total undergrad enrollment	1,750
% male/female	51/49
% from out of state	79
% from public high school	52
% frosh live on campus	100
# of fraternities	8
# of sororities	6
% African American	7
% Asian	4
% Caucasian	71
% Hispanic	5
% international	4
# of countries represented	42

SURVEY SAYS . . .

No one cheats
Lab facilities are great
Great computer facilities
School is well run
Students are friendly
Students get along with local community
Campus feels safe
Students are environmentally aware
Students are involved in community service

ACADEMICS

Academic Rating	96
% students returning for sophomore year	96
% students graduating within 4 years	88
% students graduating within 6 years	92
Calendar	semester
Student/faculty ratio	11:1
Profs interesting rating	97
Profs accessible rating	99
Most classes have	10–19 students
Most lab/discussion sessions have	10–19 students

MOST POPULAR MAJORS

biology/biological sciences; English language and literature; history

APPLICANTS ALSO LOOK AT AND OFTEN PREFER

Princeton University, Swarthmore College, Williams College, Stanford University, Duke University, Dartmouth College

AND SOMETIMES PREFER

Vanderbilt University, University of Virginia, The University of North Carolina at Chapel Hill, Washington University in St. Louis

AND RARELY PREFER

Colgate University, Emory University, Furman University, Wake Forest University, University of Richmond

STUDENTS SAY ". . ."

Academics

This small school north of Charlotte, North Carolina, cultivates an environment "that is very open to change and improvement" and empowers students to "be better people and make a difference in the world." The administration works hard to create an on-campus community and constantly makes efforts "to support and improve Davidson," all while keeping students happy and minds full. "I have never witnessed people so eager to come do their job every day. [Professors] are almost too willing to help," says a student. There is also a trickle-down effect because even the student body is supportive and "eager to watch you succeed." The school offers a classic liberal arts education, encouraging students to take classes in all areas, and "all of these people come out smarter than they came in." "If I could spend twenty years being educated by this administration and these professors, I would," says a very happy junior. School is the number one priority for all of the students here, and while academics are all-consuming, time-wise, they are also "fascinating and rewarding." Without a doubt, Davidson is a tough school—"ninety-nine percent of us left our 4.0 GPAs back in high school," claims a student—and professors don't believe in grade inflation or curving grades, but they do readily make themselves available outside of class for help or discussion. There is a lot of work, but it "is accompanied by even more resources with which it can be successfully managed." One student testimonial: "My calculus teacher last semester has office hours in the student union, and he invited the whole class over to his house for chicken dinner—twice!" The dedication of the staff is contagious, and "though the work is rigorous, time spent in school never feels wasted."

Life

Davidson "possesses an intense study culture, and people hit the books regularly; it's cool to be smart." One of the many wonderful things about Davidson "is that academics voluntarily leave the classroom." "It's not uncommon to hear people discussing their current academic topics at lunch or in the gym." Basketball is a huge common ground for the student body at large; "Everyone enjoys being a part of the underdog/Cinderella story." Weeks are devoted to study, as well as extracurricular activities—"you see your friends because you are doing homework together or eating meals together, not because you're vegging out." Of course, even Davidson students need to kick back, and there are always plenty of parties to be found on the weekends. Fraternities and eating houses (the Davidson version of sororities) are popular. Fortunately, "There really is no pressure to drink. You can go out and dance and have a great time or have movie nights with friends," says a student. The combination of the idyllic atmosphere and the workload "can make it hard to stay up-to-date on current events, yet most students remain well-informed."

Student Body

Davidson is "an amalgamation of all types of people, religiously, ethnically, politically, economically, etc.," all "united under the umbrella of intellectual curiosity" and their devotion to the school as a community. The typical Davidson student is "probably white," but in the past few years, admissions has been making progress in racially diversifying the campus, which students agree upon as necessary. Though there are plenty of Southern, preppy, athletic types to fit the brochure examples, there are many niches for every type of "atypical" student. "There are enough people that one can find a similar group to connect with, and there are few enough people that one ends up connecting with dissimilar [people] anyway," says a student. Everyone here is smart and well-rounded; admissions "does a good job...so if you're in you'll probably make the cut all the way through the four years." Most students have several extracurriculars to round out their free time, and they have a healthy desire to enjoy themselves when the books shut. "During the week we work hard. On the weekends we play hard. We don't do anything halfway," says a senior. Though the majority of students lean to the left, there's a strong conservative contingent, and there are no real problems between the two.

FINANCIAL AID: 704-894-2232 • E-MAIL: ADMISSION@DAVIDSON.EDU • WEBSITE: WWW.DAVIDSON.EDU

THE PRINCETON REVIEW SAYS

Admissions

Very important factors considered include: Recommendation(s), rigor of secondary school record, character/personal qualities, volunteer work. *Important factors considered include:* Application essay, standardized test scores, extracurricular activities, interview, talent/ability. *Other factors considered include:* Class rank, alumni/ae relation. SAT or ACT required; ACT with or without writing component accepted. TOEFL required of all international applicants. High school diploma is required and GED is not accepted. *Academic units required:* 4 English, 3 mathematics, 2 science, 2 foreign language, 2 social studies or history. *Academic units recommended:* 4 mathematics, 4 science, 4 foreign language, 4 social studies or history.

Financial Aid

Students should submit: FAFSA, CSS/Financial Aid PROFILE, noncustodial PROFILE, business/farm supplement, noncustodial (divorced/separated) parent's statement, corporate tax return, and/or noncustodial parent tax return (if applicable), parent and student tax returns and W-2 forms. Regular filing deadline is March 15. The Princeton Review suggests that all financial aid forms be submitted as soon as possible after January 1. *Need-based scholarships/grants offered:* Federal Pell, SEOG, state scholarships/grants, private scholarships, the school's own gift aid. *Loan aid offered:* Direct Subsidized Stafford, Direct Unsubsidized Stafford, Direct PLUS, Federal Perkins, alternative loans. Applicants will be notified of awards on or about April 1. Federal Work-Study Program available. Institutional employment available. Off-campus job opportunities are excellent.

The Inside Word

The combination of Davidson's low acceptance rate and high yield really packs a punch. Prospective applicants beware: Securing admission at this prestigious school is no easy feat. Admitted students are typically at the top of their high school classes and have strong standardized test scores. Candidates with leadership experience generally garner the favor of admissions officers. The college takes its honor code seriously and, as a result, seeks out students of demonstrated reputable character.

THE SCHOOL SAYS ". . ."

From the Admissions Office

"Davidson College is one of the nation's premier academic institutions, a college of the liberal arts and sciences respected for its intellectual vigor, the high quality of its faculty and students, and the achievements of its alumni. Davidson is distinguished by its strong honor code, close collaboration between professors and students, an environment that encourages both intellectual growth and community service, and a commitment to international education. Davidson places great value on student participation in extracurricular activities, intercollegiate athletics, and intramural sports. The college has a strong regional identity, grounded in traditions of civility and mutual respect, and has historic ties to the Presbyterian Church. The college has a strong commitment to making a Davidson education affordable. The college doesn't include student loans in its financial aid packages. Through the Davidson Trust, 100 percent of demonstrated financial need will be met with a combination of grants and student employment.

"Applicants are required to complete and submit scores from the SAT and/or the ACT. SAT Subject Tests (mathematics and one of your choice) are recommended. Davidson will utilize the scores that place the student in the greatest possible light."

SELECTIVITY	
Admissions Rating	**98**
# of applicants	4,309
% of applicants accepted	28
% of acceptees attending	40
# of early decision applicants	547
# accepted early decision	238
FRESHMAN PROFILE	
Range SAT Critical Reading	630–730
Range SAT Math	640–720
Range SAT Writing	630–730
Range ACT Composite	29–33
Minimum paper TOEFL	600
Minimum web-based TOEFL	100
Average HS GPA	4.1
% graduated top 10% of class	82
% graduated top 25% of class	98
% graduated top 50% of class	100
DEADLINES	
Early decision	
Deadline	11/15
Notification	12/15
Regular	
Deadline	1/2
Notification	4/1
Nonfall registration?	no
FINANCIAL FACTS	
Financial Aid Rating	**97**
Annual tuition	$40,405
Room and board	$11,346
Required fees	$404
Books and supplies	$1,000
% needy frosh rec. need-based scholarship or grant aid	96
% needy UG rec. need-based scholarship or grant aid	96
% needy frosh rec. non-need-based scholarship or grant aid	17
% needy UG rec. non-need-based scholarship or grant aid	24
% needy frosh rec. need-based self-help aid	69
% needy UG rec. need-based self-help aid	70
% frosh rec. any financial aid	45
% UG rec. any financial aid	45
% UG borrow to pay for school	22
Average cumulative indebtedness	$24,972
% frosh need fully met	100
% ugrads need fully met	100
Average % of frosh need met	100
Average % of ugrad need met	100

DEEP SPRINGS COLLEGE

APPLICATIONS COMMITTEE, DYER, NV 89010 • ADMISSIONS: 760-872-2000 • FAX: 760-872-4466

CAMPUS LIFE

Quality of Life Rating	89
Fire Safety Rating	81
Green Rating	60*
Type of school	private
Environment	rural

STUDENTS

Total undergrad enrollment	28
% male/female	100/0
% from out of state	80
% from public high school	50
% frosh live on campus	100
% international	11
# of countries represented	3

SURVEY SAYS . . .

Lots of liberal students
Class discussions encouraged
Great food on campus
Dorms are like palaces
Low cost of living
Intercollegiate sports are unpopular or nonexistent
Frats and sororities are unpopular or nonexistent
Very little beer drinking
Very little hard liquor
Very little drug use

ACADEMICS

Academic Rating	99
% students returning for sophomore year	92
Student/faculty ratio	4:1
Profs interesting rating	90
Profs accessible rating	99
Most classes have	fewer than 10 students

MOST POPULAR MAJORS

liberal arts and sciences studies and humanities, other

APPLICANTS ALSO LOOK AT AND RARELY PREFER

Swarthmore College, Brown University, Yale University, Stanford University, Cornell University, University of California—Berkeley, University of Chicago, Harvard College

STUDENTS SAY ". . ."

Academics

The "three pillars" of a Deep Springs education—"labor, academics, and self-governance"—combine to produce "unparalleled challenges" that run the gamut "from fixing a hay baler in the middle of the night to puzzling over a particularly difficult passage of Hegel." That's what the twenty-six men who attend Deep Springs tell us. These unique undergraduates basically run their own school, work the ranch where it is located, and complete a rigorous curriculum, an itinerary that "creates an environment of intense growth and responsibility." Class work occurs in a seminar format in which "the distinction between teacher and student becomes fuzzy [because] everyone is equally invested, thoughtful, and engaged." Composition and public speaking are the only required courses; all others are chosen by the student body and taught by a faculty of three long-term professors (one each in the humanities, social sciences, and natural sciences) and three visiting scholars or artists. The system relies on a commitment to self-determination, which means "the smoothness with which many programs run depends largely on the kind of responsibility students take. Sometimes students do a good job taking care of administrative tasks, sometimes a worse job. It's all part of the educational experience." While the size of the school inevitably means that "lab and library facilities are not what they might be," students tell us that the overall Deep Springs experience compensates for any shortcomings. As one student explains, "through intense academics and running the college administratively and practically, we receive an unprecedented education in citizenship of a conscious human being."

Life

Deep Springs is totally unlike other colleges in terms of the everyday life of a student," because "no one drinks, everyone helps run the ranch in some way, and no one can be totally self-absorbed (unless he's out hiking in the desert)." Instead, students immerse themselves in the Deep Springs way. As one student explains, "The Deep Springs program is our whole life. The intellectual questions we're asking and the labor we're doing is all bound up with our identity." Students spend their free time "thinking about intellectual things: moral issues, politics, and the community. 'Fun' is hard to come by, and one has to learn how to enjoy people, work, and engagement." Students do occasionally take a break, however; "On weekends in the rumpus room of the dorm, you can find a group of motley adventurers engaged in a Dungeons & Dragon's quest or a pack of students watching 'Gossip Girl.' You'll find even more people scoffing at such pedantry and watching arty French movies," and "communal soccer is excellent…we even play in the snow." Also, occasionally "We have dance parties called 'boojies,'" and "We do some other strange things for fun, like sledding naked down 800-foot-tall sand dunes in neighboring Eureka Valley." Undergrads concede that Deep Springs "life can be intense. Students usually are utterly exhausted. But most of the time we know that something good is coming out of this," and that keeps undergrads energized and motivated.

Student Body

"Having only twenty-eight students makes it even harder to characterize the 'typical' Deep Springer," students understandably warn, but they add that "we're all very able and driven, but in our own ways, not in the way that most Ivy League students are. Deep Springs isn't a stepping stone to the world of white-collar work but an end in itself that we all pursue with all our hearts. So I guess the typical student has a healthy disgust for the pedagogy of most other universities." Undergrads are also predictably "intelligent, motivated, and responsible," as they "must demonstrate depth of thought to be accepted" to the school. As one student puts it, "The typical student at Deep Springs is committed to the life of the intellect and committed to finding education in our labor program. Most of the students here believe that a life of service, informed by discourse and labor, is a necessary notion to understand in today's world."

FINANCIAL AID: 760-872-2000 • E-MAIL: APCOM@DEEPSPRINGS.EDU • WEBSITE: WWW.DEEPSPRINGS.EDU

THE PRINCETON REVIEW SAYS

Admissions

Very important factors considered include: Application essay, character/personal qualities, interview, level of applicant's interest. *Important factors considered include:* Academic GPA, rigor of secondary school record, extracurricular activities, volunteer work, work experience. *Other factors considered include:* Class rank, recommendation(s), standardized test scores, racial/ethnic status, talent/ability. SAT or ACT required. High school diploma or equivalent is not required.

Financial Aid

The Princeton Review suggests that all financial aid forms be submitted as soon as possible after January 1. All students receive a full scholarship worth more than $50,000. Federal Work-Study Program not available.

The Inside Word

Students will be hard-pressed to find a school with a more personal or thorough application process than Deep Springs. Given the intimate and collegial atmosphere of the school, matchmaking is the top priority. Candidates are evaluated by a body composed of students, faculty, and staff members. The application is writing intensive; finalists are expected to spend several days on campus, during which they will undergo a lengthy interview.

THE SCHOOL SAYS "..."

From the Admissions Office

"Founded in 1917, Deep Springs College lies isolated in a high desert valley of eastern California, thirty miles from the nearest town. Its enrollment is limited to twenty-eight students, each of whom receives a full scholarship that covers tuition and room and board, and is valued at more than $50,000 per year. Students engage in rigorous academics, govern themselves, and participate in the operation of our cattle and alfalfa ranch. After two years, students generally transfer to other schools to complete their studies. Students regularly transfer to Harvard, The University of Chicago, and Brown, but also choose Cornell, Columbia, Stanford, Swarthmore, University of California—Berkeley, and Yale.

In the past five years Deep Springers have won the following national scholarship competitions:

- The Jack Kent Cooke Scholarship (2)
- The Barry M. Goldwater Scholarship (1)
- The Rhodes Scholarship (1)
- The Harry S. Truman Scholarship (5)
- The Morris Udall Scholarship (1)"

SELECTIVITY

Admissions Rating	**99**
# of applicants	170
% of applicants accepted	7
% of acceptees attending	100
# accepting a place on wait list	3

FRESHMAN PROFILE

Range SAT Critical Reading	750–800
Range SAT Math	700–800
% graduated top 10% of class	83
% graduated top 25% of class	93
% graduated top 50% of class	100

DEADLINES

Regular	
Deadline	11/15
Notification	4/15
Nonfall registration?	no

FINANCIAL FACTS

Financial Aid Rating	**60***
Annual comprehensive tuition	$50,000
Books and supplies	$1,200
% frosh rec. any financial aid	100
% UG rec. any financial aid	100
% frosh need fully met	100
% ugrads need fully met	100
Average % of frosh need met	100
Average % of ugrad need met	100

Denison University

Box H, Granville, OH 43023 • Admissions: 740-587-6276 • Fax: 740-587-6306

CAMPUS LIFE	
Quality of Life Rating	**82**
Fire Safety Rating	**87**
Green Rating	**93**
Type of school	private
Environment	village

STUDENTS	
Total undergrad enrollment	2,266
% male/female	43/57
% from out of state	73
% from public high school	72
% frosh live on campus	100
# of fraternities	8
# of sororities	6
% African American	7
% Asian	3
% Caucasian	73
% Hispanic	6
% international	7
# of countries represented	30

SURVEY SAYS . . .

Lab facilities are great
Great computer facilities
School is well run
Campus feels safe
Lots of beer drinking

ACADEMICS	
Academic Rating	**94**
% students returning for sophomore year	90
% students graduating within 4 years	76
% students graduating within 6 years	79
Calendar	semester
Student/faculty ratio	10:1
Profs interesting rating	88
Profs accessible rating	94
Most classes have	10–19 students

MOST POPULAR MAJORS

economics; English language and literature; psychology

APPLICANTS ALSO LOOK AT AND OFTEN PREFER

University of Michigan—Ann Arbor, University of Richmond

AND SOMETIMES PREFER

Kenyon College, Oberlin College, Boston College, Vanderbilt University, Northwestern University, Gettysburg College

AND RARELY PREFER

Case Western Reserve University, Bucknell University, DePauw University, Dickinson College, Miami University, Ohio Wesleyan University, The College of Wooster, The Ohio State University—Columbus, University of Vermont, Allegheny College, Xavier University (OH), Franklin & Marshall College, Wake Forest University

STUDENTS SAY ". . ."

Academics

For those seeking out "a small, liberal arts school with quality academics as well as a penchant for producing students who are well-rounded citizens," Denison University deserves a closer look. The school is "set in a beautiful and very safe town" in rural Ohio and offers "an intelligent and welcoming community ready and willing to help others" as well as "a great support system." Denison offers a campus filled with "continuous construction of new facilities" where "students have diverse opportunities to explore their talents and improve their skills through campus jobs, clubs, internships, and the election of double majors and minors that don't necessarily fit together." "The classes are challenging," and "The academics are competitive and foster interesting class selection." One student also admits, "General education requirements, although somewhat tedious, provide opportunities for students to grow in areas that they normally would not consider investing their time in."

The crown jewels of the school's academic life seem to be the professors who are "tough, but usually fair." One student raves, "At Denison, we have professors that can make a poem out of a picture and a mountain out of a math problem. We are so privileged to be surrounded by scholars who are passionate about teaching and learning what they love." Students get a chance to form close bonds with their professors thanks to the "small student-to-faculty ratio" as well as the high accessibility of the professors outside of the classroom. According to one student, "As far as professor availability goes, I see my professors on campus so often that I'm starting to suspect they sleep in their offices..." Students keep it all in perspective and recognize that "although academics are certainly important here, Denison teaches you how to shape what you know so that you become a more curious, passionate, and interesting individual."

Life

"Life here is a big blur of class, athletics, parties, and down time." That seems to be the general consensus among students at this school. In other words, "Whether you enjoy sports, Greek life, service or quidditch it can all be found at Denison!" Students highlight that "There's a good party scene, largely dominated by fraternities, but there are more and more non-Greek options" and "at least fifty percent of the campus is out partying on any given Friday or Saturday night." Offering another perspective, one student notes, "Parties happen every weekend, but there are plenty of people who prefer to chill with friends in the dorm rooms and just watch movies." For those interested in exploring life off campus, "Granville is small but cute, [and] there's plenty to eat at a good price," and "some cute shops." "Many also choose Columbus for clubbing, the alternative and bucolic Homestead for random parties, or even the Main Street area in Granville for dining in the ten-ish big restaurant options, drinking at Brew's, or just studying in River Road or Village Coffee Co. coffee shops. Whit's Frozen Custard is great too."

Student Body

Denison students generally agree that "We have a reputation as a WASP-y, East-Coast-in-Ohio school, but that is slowly changing." And while many students at Denison can be described as "tall, good-looking, and dressed in Vineyard Vines, J. Crew, or RL," one student explains, "At first, most students will feel like preppy New Englanders, but if you don't conform to this image it's still easy to find friends." This would include the environmentalists who "are a pretty big presence on campus now." At Denison, many seem to agree, "Students are also extremely involved, almost everyone is involved in at least two to three clubs or activities, and many people hold some sort of leadership role." Ultimately, "Denison is a place for real people who love caring about each other and learning, [and] if you don't like having a close-knit group of people there to support you, then don't go to Denison."

DENISON UNIVERSITY

FINANCIAL AID: 800-336-4766 • E-MAIL: ADMISSIONS@DENISON.EDU • WEBSITE: WWW.DENISON.EDU

THE PRINCETON REVIEW SAYS

Admissions

Very important factors considered include: Application essay, academic GPA, recommendation(s), rigor of secondary school record. *Important factors considered include:* Extracurricular activities, interview, level of applicant's interest, talent/ability. *Other factors considered include:* Class rank, standardized test scores, alumni/ae relation, character/personal qualities, first generation, geographical residence, racial/ethnic status, state residency, volunteer work, work experience. ACT with or without writing component accepted. TOEFL required of all international applicants. High school diploma is required and GED is accepted. *Academic units required:* 4 English, 4 mathematics, 4 science, 3 foreign language, 2 social studies, 1 history, 1 academic elective.

Financial Aid

Students should submit: FAFSA. The Princeton Review suggests that all financial aid forms be submitted as soon as possible after January 1. *Need-based scholarships/grants offered:* Federal Pell, SEOG, state scholarships/grants, private scholarships, the school's own gift aid. *Loan aid offered:* Direct Subsidized Stafford, Direct Unsubsidized Stafford, Direct PLUS, Federal Perkins, college/university loans from institutional funds. Applicants will be notified of awards on or about March 28. Federal Work-Study Program available. Institutional employment available. Highest amount earned per year from on-campus jobs $2,530. Off-campus job opportunities are fair.

The Inside Word

Admission to Denison is pretty straightforward. The school "suggests" an interview, meaning you should do one if at all possible. It's a great way to demonstrate your interest in the school, which improves your chances of admission, especially if your grades, test scores, and overall profile put you on the admit/reject borderline.

THE SCHOOL SAYS ". . ."

From the Admissions Office

"Denison is a college that can point with pride to its success in enrolling and retaining intellectually motivated, diverse, and well-balanced students who are being taught to become effective leaders in the twenty-first century. This year, over fifty percent of our first-year students were in the top ten percent of their high school graduating class; their SAT scores average 1300, twenty-five percent of the incoming class is students of color or international; and a large percentage of our student body is receiving some type of financial assistance. Our First-Year Program focuses on helping students make a successful transition from high school to college, and the small classes and accessibility of faculty assure students the opportunity to interact closely with their professors and fellow students. We care about our students, and the success and loyalty of more than 30,000 alumni proves that the Denison experience is one that lasts for a lifetime.

"Denison operates under a 'test optional' and 'need-blind'" admissions policy."

SELECTIVITY	
Admissions Rating	94
# of applicants	4,772
% of applicants accepted	48
% of acceptees attending	26

FRESHMAN PROFILE	
Range SAT Critical Reading	600–690
Range SAT Math	590–670
Range ACT Composite	27–30
Minimum paper TOEFL	599
% graduated top 10% of class	55
% graduated top 25% of class	86
% graduated top 50% of class	100

DEADLINES	
Early decision	
Deadline	11/15
Regular	
Deadline	11/15
Nonfall registration?	no

FINANCIAL FACTS	
Financial Aid Rating	90
Annual tuition	$39,330
Required fees	$880
Books and supplies	$600
% needy frosh rec. need-based scholarship or grant aid	100
% needy UG rec. need-based scholarship or grant aid	100
% needy frosh rec. non-need-based scholarship or grant aid	93
% needy UG rec. non-need-based scholarship or grant aid	89
% needy frosh rec. need-based self-help aid	80
% needy UG rec. need-based self-help aid	79
% frosh rec. any financial aid	97
% UG rec. any financial aid	95
% frosh need fully met	50
% ugrads need fully met	35
Average % of frosh need met	96
Average % of ugrad need met	96

DePaul University

One East Jackson Boulevard, Chicago, IL 60604-2287 • Admissions: 312-362-8300 • Fax: 312-362-5749

CAMPUS LIFE

Quality of Life Rating	**92**
Fire Safety Rating	**98**
Green Rating	**84**
Type of school	private
Affiliation	Roman Catholic
Environment	metropolis

STUDENTS

Total undergrad enrollment	15,801
% male/female	45/55
% from out of state	29
% from public high school	89
% frosh live on campus	70
# of fraternities	9
# of sororities	13
% African American	9
% Asian	8
% Caucasian	55
% Hispanic	15
% international	1
# of countries represented	101

SURVEY SAYS . . .

Athletic facilities are great
Diverse student types on campus
Students love Chicago, IL
Great off-campus food
Low cost of living

ACADEMICS

Academic Rating	**77**
% students graduating within 4 years	48
% students graduating within 6 years	68
Calendar	quarter
Student/faculty ratio	17:1
Profs interesting rating	81
Profs accessible rating	79
Most classes have	20–29 students
Most lab/discussion sessions have	10–19 students

MOST POPULAR MAJORS

accounting; communication studies/speech communication and rhetoric; psychology

STUDENTS SAY ". . ."

Academics

DePaul University's urban setting means this Chicago school is "all about integrating the opportunities of the city into the classroom," offering students "the essentials in order for a student to succeed in the business field." Here, the "dedicated" teaching staff's "extensive experience outside of the classroom… really brings valuable information into the classroom." That experience proves beneficial to career-focused students because it "encourages students to become critical life thinkers so that they are not just prepared for a job, but have the skills to become present in all life decisions." This real-world focus in classroom studies and its "extensive school of commerce curriculum" is part of what has given DePaul a "strong academic reputation." Internship and career-placement opportunities both during school and after graduation result in, according to some graduates, DePaul students being "some of the hardest working and driven college students around." The multiple colleges of DePaul University "stress engaging with other students, working collaboratively, combining previous knowledge with new learning, and being an active participant in one's education." Students praise the easy access provided by the urban setting and its accompanying public transportation, and like the "practical real world experience" brought to the table by the educators here—though some note "there are ones that are tougher graders," so applicants should be prepared to work.

Life

The school's location in downtown Chicago, one of the largest and most vibrant cities in the United States, means that "there is a plethora of choices of things to do" and plenty of transportation to get to them. Students "are always going to the museums, the art institute, Navy pier, shopping on Michigan Ave, the zoo, the beach, etc.," and "in the summer the outdoor concerts and food tasting events take over Grant Park." Throw in "the lakefront, bars and restaurants, sports teams (pro and collegiate)," along with "cultural venues [and] free public events," and it's no wonder students say they "never get bored." Sports fanatics will especially find more than enough to keep themselves busy outside of class. If the wealth of riches that is Chicago professional sports is not enough—the Bulls, Blackhawks, White Sox, Cubs, and Bears all play here—"having DePaul in the Big East conference brings great college basketball to Chicago," too And for those who prefer to stay on campus in this "simply amazing" city, DePaul has a strong Greek scene. The bottom line is, life at DePaul is all about location, location, location, so "the internships, classes, and social life are centered around the city."

Student Body

There is no nailing down the typical DePaul student. "It's like a melting pot of experience and people from all over the world that come to be a part of the DePaul environment," a "unique blend of all kinds of students" who are "like a giant mixed bag of Jelly Bellys...every student is so different you have a little bit of everything." One student goes so far as to suggest it's "possibly the most diverse school in the country." Though attendees "come from all walks of life" and "individuality is promoted strongly," virtually anyone "can fit in easily if they want." "Every student has a place where they feel comfortable," one student says, "and it is hard to find a student that doesn't fit in here." If there is a tie that binds, it is that DePaul students are "kind and friendly," "outgoing and respectful," a group who "study hard to get where they're going but still find time to socialize." Hard work is a common trait. "The majority of students seem to hold outside employment," a student notes, "which brings a strong real world emphasis to the class from staff and students alike." But hard workers aside, the typical DePaul student? "There is no typical anything."

FINANCIAL AID: 312-362-8091 • E-MAIL: ADMISSION@DEPAUL.EDU • WEBSITE: WWW.DEPAUL.EDU

THE PRINCETON REVIEW SAYS

Admissions

Very important factors considered include: Application essay, academic GPA, rigor of secondary school record, standardized test scores. *Important factors considered include:* Class rank, recommendation(s), character/personal qualities, extracurricular activities, level of applicant's interest, talent/ability, volunteer work, work experience. *Other factors considered include:* Alumni/ae relation, first generation, geographical residence, interview, racial/ethnic status, religious affiliation/commitment, state residency. SAT or ACT required; ACT with or without writing component accepted. TOEFL required of all international applicants. High school diploma is required and GED is accepted. *Academic units required:* 4 English, 3 mathematics, 3 science (2 science labs), 2 social science/history. *Academic units recommended:* 2 foreign language.

Financial Aid

Students should submit: FAFSA. The Princeton Review suggests that all financial aid forms be submitted as soon as possible after January 1. *Need-based scholarships/grants offered:* Federal Pell, SEOG, state scholarships/grants, private scholarships, the school's own gift aid, Federal Academic Competitiveness Grant, Federal SMART Grant, and Federal TEACH Grant. *Loan aid offered:* Direct Subsidized Stafford, Direct Unsubsidized Stafford, Direct PLUS, Federal Perkins, private loans. Applicants will be notified of awards on a rolling basis beginning March 15. Federal Work-Study Program available. Institutional employment available. Highest amount earned per year from on-campus jobs $14,000. Off-campus job opportunities are excellent.

The Inside Word

DePaul's reputation as one of the most diverse schools in the country is not mere hyperbole, it's a truth expressed by student after student, and by the actions of the administration itself. The school actively seeks out minority students both as freshmen and transfers, and in an effort to surmount tuition-related obstacles works with local community colleges so students can meet their requirements at a lower cost before transferring to DePaul.

THE SCHOOL SAYS ". . ."

From the Admissions Office

"The nation's largest Catholic university, DePaul University is nationally recognized for its innovative academic programs that embrace a comprehensive learn-by-doing approach. DePaul has two residential campuses and four commuter campuses in the suburbs. The Lincoln Park campus is located in one of Chicago's most exciting neighborhoods, filled with theaters, cafés, clubs, and shops. It is home to DePaul's College of Liberal Arts and Sciences, the School of Education, the Theater School, and the School of Music. New buildings on the thirty-six-acre campus include residence halls, a science building, a student recreational facility, and the student center, which features a café where students can gather with friends. The Loop campus, located in Chicago's downtown—a world-class center for business, government, law, and culture—is home to DePaul's College of Commerce; College of Law; School of Computer Science, Telecommunications, and Information Systems; School for New Learning; and School of Accountancy and Management Information Systems.

"Applicants are required to take either the ACT or the SAT. The writing test on the ACT and the writing section on the SAT are not required for admission consideration."

SELECTIVITY	
Admissions Rating	**81**
# of applicants	12,031
% of applicants accepted	69
% of acceptees attending	27

FRESHMAN PROFILE	
Range SAT Critical Reading	530–650
Range SAT Math	520–620
Range SAT Writing	520–630
Range ACT Composite	22–27
Minimum paper TOEFL	550
Minimum web-based TOEFL	80
Average HS GPA	3.5
% graduated top 10% of class	24
% graduated top 25% of class	55
% graduated top 50% of class	87

DEADLINES	
Early action	
Deadline	11/15
Notification	1/15
Regular	
Priority	11/15
Deadline	2/1
Notification	3/15
Nonfall registration?	yes

FINANCIAL FACTS	
Financial Aid Rating	**68**
Annual tuition	$31,650
Room and board	$11,335
Required fees	$618
Books and supplies	$1,134
% needy frosh rec. need-based scholarship or grant aid	86
% needy UG rec. need-based scholarship or grant aid	81
% needy frosh rec. non-need-based scholarship or grant aid	61
% needy UG rec. non-need-based scholarship or grant aid	38
% needy frosh rec. need-based self-help aid	72
% needy UG rec. need-based self-help aid	77
% frosh rec. any financial aid	90
% UG rec. any financial aid	76
% UG borrow to pay for school	65
Average cumulative indebtedness	$26,190
% frosh need fully met	11
% ugrads need fully met	8
Average % of frosh need met	66
Average % of ugrad need met	62

DePauw University

101 East Seminary, Greencastle, IN 46135 • Admissions: 765-658-4006 • Fax: 765-658-4007

CAMPUS LIFE

Quality of Life Rating	**82**
Fire Safety Rating	**66**
Green Rating	**61**
Type of school	private
Affiliation	Methodist
Environment	village

STUDENTS

Total undergrad enrollment	2,362
% male/female	43/57
% from out of state	59
% from public high school	83
% frosh live on campus	100
# of fraternities	13
# of sororities	11
% African American	7
% Asian	3
% Caucasian	72
% Hispanic	4
% international	10
# of countries represented	34

SURVEY SAYS . . .

Lab facilities are great
Frats and sororities dominate social scene
College radio is popular
Student publications are popular
Lots of beer drinking
Hard liquor is popular

ACADEMICS

Academic Rating	**93**
% students returning for sophomore year	90
% students graduating within 4 years	82
Calendar	4-1-4
Student/faculty ratio	10:1
Profs interesting rating	91
Profs accessible rating	95
Most classes have	10–19 students
Most lab/discussion sessions have	10–19 students

MOST POPULAR MAJORS

communication studies/speech communication and rhetoric; economics; English composition

APPLICANTS ALSO LOOK AT AND OFTEN PREFER

Indiana University—Bloomington, Vanderbilt University, University of Notre Dame, Northwestern University

AND SOMETIMES PREFER

University of Illinois at Urbana-Champaign, Miami University, Denison University, Washington University in St. Louis, Purdue University—West Lafayette

AND RARELY PREFER

Hanover College

STUDENTS SAY ". . ."

Academics

Serious-minded students are drawn to DePauw University for its "small classes," "encouraging" professors, and the "individual academic attention" they can expect to receive. Academically, DePauw is "demanding but rewarding," and "requires a lot of outside studying and discipline" in order to keep up. Professors' "expectations are very high," which means "you can't slack off and get good grades." Be prepared to pull your "fair share of all-nighters." Fortunately, DePauw professors are more than just stern taskmasters. Though they pile on the work, they "are always helpful and available" to students in need. When things get overwhelming, "They are very understanding and will cut you a break if you really deserve" it. As a result, students come to know their professors "on a personal level," making DePauw the kind of school where it is "common [for students] to have dinner at a professor's house." Beyond stellar professors, DePauw's other academic draws include "extraordinary" study abroad opportunities and a "wonderful" alumni network great for "connections and networking opportunities." Alums also "keep our endowment pretty high, making it easy for the school to give out merit scholarships," which undergraduates appreciate. Student opinion regarding the administration ranges from ambivalent to slightly negative. One especially thorny issue is class registration; you "rarely"get into all the classes you want.

Life

Few schools are as Greek as DePauw, but students are quick to point out that "it is by no means *Animal House*." The Greek system here is more holistic than that. It "promotes not only social activities but also philanthropic events." That's not to say there aren't lots of frat parties here. There are. But "the administration has cracked down big time" on the larger frat parties, and "now there are just small parties in apartments and dorms." One recently issued rule is that freshmen "will not be allowed on Greek property until after rush, which is the first week of second semester." In addition to administrative regulation, students exercise their own self-restraint; for the typical undergraduate, "the week is mostly reserved for studying." Beyond the frats and sororities, "there is always a theater production, athletic event, or organization-sponsored event going on," and popular bands occasionally perform on campus. It's a good thing so much is happening at the school because off-campus entertainment options are scarce: "If there is really any fun to be had, it's not in Greencastle." The situation could be greatly improved if there were just a few "more restaurants and stores in the town or a nearby town." As things stand, however, students "have to go to Indianapolis (forty-five miles) to go shopping, watch a good movie, eat at a good restaurant, etc."

Student Body

The typical DePauw student is "upper-middle-class," "a little preppy, a little athletic," and "hardworking;" "parties hard on weekend," and "usually become involved with the Greek system." Students describe their peers as "driven" and wearing "polos and pearls." They "have all had multiple internships, international experience, and [have held] some type of leadership position." Though these folks may seem "overcommitted," they "always get their work done." For those who don't fit this mold, don't fret; most students seem to be "accepting of the different types" of people on campus. Diversity on campus is augmented through the school's partnership with the Posse Foundation, which brings in urban (though not necessarily minority) "students from Chicago and NYC every year." These students are described as "leaders on campus" and "take real initiative to hold their communities together."

FINANCIAL AID: 765-658-4030 • E-MAIL: ADMISSION@DEPAUW.EDU • WEBSITE: WWW.DEPAUW.EDU

THE PRINCETON REVIEW SAYS

Admissions

Very important factors considered include: Academic GPA, rigor of secondary school record, standardized test scores. *Important factors considered include:* Class rank, application essay, recommendation(s). *Other factors considered include:* Alumni/ae relation, character/personal qualities, extracurricular activities, first generation, geographical residence, interview, level of applicant's interest, state residency, talent/ability, volunteer work, work experience. SAT or ACT required; ACT with or without writing component accepted. TOEFL required of all international applicants. High school diploma is required and GED is accepted. *Academic units recommended:* 4 English, 4 mathematics (2 science labs).

Financial Aid

Students should submit: FAFSA, institution's own financial aid form. Regular filing deadline is March 1. The Princeton Review suggests that all financial aid forms be submitted as soon as possible after January 1. *Need-based scholarships/grants offered:* Federal Pell, SEOG, state scholarships/grants, private scholarships, the school's own gift aid, United Negro College Fund. *Loan aid offered:* Direct Subsidized Stafford, Direct Unsubsidized Stafford, Direct PLUS, Federal Perkins, state loans, college/university loans from institutional funds. Applicants will be notified of awards on or about April 1. Federal Work-Study Program available. Institutional employment available. Off-campus job opportunities are fair.

The Inside Word

Prospective applicants should not be deceived by DePauw's high acceptance rate. The students who are accepted and choose to enroll here have the academic goods to justify their admission. Many of them are accepted by more "competitive" schools and still choose DePauw. DePauw's generous merit scholarships have a lot to do with students' choice to enroll.

THE SCHOOL SAYS ". . ."

From the Admissions Office

"DePauw University is nationally recognized for intellectual and experiential challenge that links liberal arts education with life's work, preparing graduates for uncommon professional success, service to others, and personal fulfillment. DePauw graduates count among their ranks a Nobel Laureate, a vice president and United States congressman, Pulitzer Prize winning and Newbery Award winning authors, and a number of CEOs and humanitarian leaders. Our students demonstrate a love for learning, a willingness to serve others, the reason and judgment to lead, an interest in engaging worlds and cultures unknown to them, the courage to question their assumptions, and a strong commitment to community. Pre-professional and career exploration are encouraged through winter term, when more than 700 students pursue their own off-campus internships. This represents more students in experiential learning opportunities than at any other liberal arts college in the nation. Other innovative programs include Honor Scholars, Information Technology Associates Program, Management Fellows, Media Fellows, and Science Research Fellows, affording selected students additional seminar and internship opportunities.

"Freshman applicants are required to submit scores of the writing section of the SAT or the ACT."

SELECTIVITY	
Admissions Rating	**92**
# of applicants	5,206
% of applicants accepted	57
% of acceptees attending	21
# admitted from wait list	6
# of early decision applicants	68
# accepted early decision	56

FRESHMAN PROFILE	
Range SAT Critical Reading	530–640
Range SAT Math	550–670
Range SAT Writing	530–640
Range ACT Composite	24–29
Minimum paper TOEFL	560
Average HS GPA	3.6
% graduated top 10% of class	53
% graduated top 25% of class	83
% graduated top 50% of class	97

DEADLINES	
Early decision	
Deadline	11/1
Notification	1/1
Early action	
Deadline	12/1
Notification	2/15
Regular	
Deadline	2/1
Notification	4/1
Nonfall registration?	yes

FINANCIAL FACTS	
Financial Aid Rating	**88**
Annual tuition	$38,280
Room and board	$10,200
Required fees	$470
Books and supplies	$750
% needy frosh rec. need-based scholarship or grant aid	100
% needy UG rec. need-based scholarship or grant aid	100
% needy frosh rec. non-need-based scholarship or grant aid	22
% needy UG rec. non-need-based scholarship or grant aid	20
% needy frosh rec. need-based self-help aid	68
% needy UG rec. need-based self-help aid	75
% UG borrow to pay for school	53
Average cumulative indebtedness	$23,778
% frosh need fully met	29
% ugrads need fully met	27
Average % of frosh need met	86
Average % of ugrad need met	87

DICKINSON COLLEGE

PO BOX 1773, CARLISLE, PA 17013-2896 • ADMISSIONS: 717-245-1231 • FAX: 717-245-1442

CAMPUS LIFE

Quality of Life Rating	**69**
Fire Safety Rating	**78**
Green Rating	**98**
Type of school	private
Environment	city

STUDENTS

Total undergrad enrollment	2,358
% male/female	44/56
% from out of state	77
% from public high school	53
% frosh live on campus	100
# of fraternities	5
# of sororities	6
% African American	4
% Asian	3
% Caucasian	77
% Hispanic	6
% international	7
# of countries represented	46

SURVEY SAYS . . .

Lab facilities are great
Great computer facilities
Great library
Low cost of living
Lots of beer drinking
Hard liquor is popular

ACADEMICS

Academic Rating	**89**
% students returning for sophomore year	90
% students graduating within 4 years	82
% students graduating within 6 years	84
Calendar	semester
Student/faculty ratio	10:1
Profs interesting rating	88
Profs accessible rating	87
Most classes have	10–19 students

MOST POPULAR MAJORS

international business/trade/commerce; political science and government; economics

APPLICANTS ALSO LOOK AT AND OFTEN PREFER

Middlebury College, Brown University, College of William and Mary

AND SOMETIMES PREFER

Colgate University, Hamilton College, Kenyon College, Connecticut College, Colby College, Lafayette College, Bucknell University, Franklin & Marshall College

AND RARELY PREFER

American University, Skidmore College, Gettysburg College

STUDENTS SAY ". . ."

Academics

Many students cite Dickinson's unique combination of being a small liberal arts institution with a global perspective as their reason for coming here. There's a host of study abroad options, and "it's assumed that most juniors will go abroad." Students who have attended large universities while studying abroad come to appreciate Dickinson's "small class sizes," which "allow professors to get to know their students." "Professors are tremendously accessible" and are "always willing to find a way to help students achieve their goals and meet their potential." "They come with all sorts of life experiences and connections in their respective fields to get students to interact with people in the areas they are studying." Classes are often "discussion-based, and [they] really give you an opportunity to engage and grow into the topic," though a few students wish lab science classes were more accessible to non-majors. "Class materials are very well-chosen, and professors are always passionate about their subjects." While some students gripe about the administration's "superficial changes" and "red tape," many more praise it as accessible and "forward-thinking"—this praise tends to come from students who chose Dickinson in part for its recently adopted emphasis on "promoting sustainable and green lifestyles."

Life

Descriptions of student life at Dickinson vary widely—suggesting a lot of options. While many students subscribe to the "work hard, play hard" philosophy, "the campus has a pretty good social life that does not involve alcohol." "The college's Event Advisory Board makes the plans readily available through e-mail and paper posts for every weekend. These lists are typically pretty extensive as there are many options to do for fun around campus." Sports are very popular, and many students note that participation in a campus group, whether it's a team, club, or Greek organization, is integral to social life. Some feel there's a bit of pressure for men to go Greek, but those who have chosen non-Greek life are generally happy, and for fun they "participate in Dickinson-sponsored dances and events and hang out with friends." Students are satisfied overall with their campus and facilities, and note that the library and cafeteria can be social hotbeds, though many wish for more meal options (one student suggests "the cafeteria should give up cooking fish."). Though small hometown Carlisle "isn't for everyone," "there are quite a few good restaurants within easy walking distance of campus," and the Carlisle Theater "brings in independent films and those sponsored by community groups and offers excellent discounts to students." "There is also a shuttle service that takes students anywhere in the town of Carlisle from 9:00 P.M. to 3:00 A.M."

Student Body

"The typical Dickinson student is outgoing, balanced, and engaged," and "because it's such a small community most people find their niche or group fairly easily." "While some report "most students are pretty preppy," "upper-middle-class," from the Northeast, and "are really fit, go to the gym a lot, [and] play a lot of sports," we also hear that "the beauty of Dickinson is that there is no 'typical' student. Everyone is here to become more globally aware and educated." Dickinson's emphasis on global perspectives and a strong international studies program draw "a lot of international [students], so there is good cultural diversity." "There are different crowds. There is a faction that parties all the time, and there is a faction that is heavily involved in academics, extracurriculars, and community service." "Involved" and "engaged" are two words that come up a lot: "Joining clubs and extracurricular activities is a great way to meet people, and there are plenty of them!"

FINANCIAL AID: 717-245-1308 • E-MAIL: ADMIT@DICKINSON.EDU • WEBSITE: WWW.DICKINSON.EDU

THE PRINCETON REVIEW SAYS

Admissions

Very important factors considered include: Academic GPA, rigor of secondary school record, extracurricular activities, talent/ability, volunteer work. *Important factors considered include:* Class rank, recommendation(s), standardized test scores, alumni/ae relation, work experience. *Other factors considered include:* Application essay, character/personal qualities, first generation, geographical residence, interview, level of applicant's interest, racial/ethnic status, state residency. ACT with or without writing component accepted. SAT or ACT recommended. TOEFL required of all international applicants. High school diploma is required and GED is accepted. *Academic units required:* 4 English, 3 mathematics, 3 science (2 science labs), 2 foreign language, 2 social studies, 2 academic electives. *Academic units recommended:* 3 foreign language.

Financial Aid

Students should submit: FAFSA, CSS/Financial Aid PROFILE, state aid form, noncustodial PROFILE. Regular filing deadline is February 1. The Princeton Review suggests that all financial aid forms be submitted as soon as possible after January 1. *Need-based scholarships/grants offered:* Federal Pell, SEOG, state scholarships/grants, private scholarships, the school's own gift aid. *Loan aid offered:* Direct Subsidized Stafford, Direct Unsubsidized Stafford, Direct PLUS, Federal Perkins, college/university loans from institutional funds. Applicants will be notified of awards on or about March 20. Federal Work-Study Program available. Institutional employment available. Off-campus job opportunities are good.

The Inside Word

The applicant pool for small liberal arts colleges has become increasingly competitive in recent years, and Dickinson is no exception. For admission here, you'll want to be the stereotypical well-rounded student, with a solid GPA in challenging classes, and broad extracurricular involvement.

THE SCHOOL SAYS ". . ."

From the Admissions Office

"Dickinson is a nationally recognized liberal arts college chartered in 1783 in Carlisle, Pennsylvania. Devoted to its revolutionary roots, the college maintains the mission of founder Benjamin Rush—to provide a useful education in the liberal arts and sciences. Dickinson has a robust academic program, offering forty-two majors plus minors, certificates, self-developed majors, independent research, and internships. Our innovative programs range from neuroscience to security studies, and develop intellectual independence by actively engaging in research, fieldwork, lab work in state-of-the-art science programs and other experiential opportunities. Dickinson's global curriculum includes international business and management, international studies, thirteen languages, and many globally oriented courses. Dickinson offers one of the world's most respected study abroad programs, and more than half of Dickinson's students study in more than forty programs in twenty-five countries on six continents. Dickinson is recognized as a leader among educational institutions committed to sustainability and green initiatives. The Center for Sustainability Education integrates sustainability into its academics, facilities, operations, and campus culture. Dickinson has received the highest awards from the Association for the Advancement of Sustainability in Higher Education, Sierra Club, Sustainable Endowments Institute, The Princeton Review, and Second Nature. Dickinson alumni are at the top of their fields as business leaders, professional artists and writers, sports agents and athletes, doctors and researchers. And many of them used their liberal arts foundation to forge their own paths. Our graduate-school partnerships enable our students to enter top programs with greater ease and reflect the high regard in which Dickinson is held."

SELECTIVITY

Admissions Rating	**94**
# of applicants	6,067
% of applicants accepted	42
% of acceptees attending	26
# accepting a place on wait list	469
# admitted from wait list	2
# of early decision applicants	452
# accepted early decision	289

FRESHMAN PROFILE

Range SAT Critical Reading	600–690
Range SAT Math	590–680
Range SAT Writing	600–690
Range ACT Composite	27–30
Minimum web-based TOEFL	89
% graduated top 10% of class	52
% graduated top 25% of class	82
% graduated top 50% of class	95

DEADLINES

Early decision	
Deadline	11/15
Notification	12/15
Early action	
Deadline	12/1
Notification	2/1
Regular	
Deadline	2/1
Notification	3/20
Nonfall registration?	no

FINANCIAL FACTS

Financial Aid Rating	**92**
Annual tuition	$44,101
Room and board	$11,178
Required fees	$475
Books and supplies	$1,000
% needy frosh rec. need-based scholarship or grant aid	93
% needy UG rec. need-based scholarship or grant aid	95
% needy frosh rec. non-need-based scholarship or grant aid	9
% needy UG rec. non-need-based scholarship or grant aid	7
% needy frosh rec. need-based self-help aid	86
% needy UG rec. need-based self-help aid	90
% frosh rec. any financial aid	73
% UG rec. any financial aid	70
% UG borrow to pay for school	52
Average cumulative indebtedness	$26,928
% frosh need fully met	79
% ugrads need fully met	72
Average % of frosh need met	97
Average % of ugrad need met	96

DREW UNIVERSITY

OFFICE OF COLLEGE ADMISSIONS, MADISON, NJ 07940-1493 • ADMISSIONS: 973-408-3739 • FAX: 973-408-3068

CAMPUS LIFE

Quality of Life Rating	70
Fire Safety Rating	95
Green Rating	92
Type of school	private
Affiliation	Methodist
Environment	village

STUDENTS

Total undergrad enrollment	1,676
% male/female	40/60
% from out of state	36
% from public high school	66
% frosh live on campus	86
% African American	9
% Asian	5
% Caucasian	57
% Hispanic	14
% international	2
# of countries represented	24

SURVEY SAYS . . .

Frats and sororities are unpopular or nonexistent
Theater is popular
Student publications are popular
Political activism is popular

ACADEMICS

Academic Rating	81
% students returning for sophomore year	79
% students graduating within 4 years	61
% students graduating within 6 years	68
Calendar	semester
Student/faculty ratio	10:1
Profs interesting rating	82
Profs accessible rating	84
Most classes have	10–19 students
Most lab/discussion sessions have	10–19 students

MOST POPULAR MAJORS

economics; poltical science and government; psychology

STUDENTS SAY ". . ."

Academics

Drew University features three major draws, according to current students: a gorgeous campus, a prime location (an hour from New York City by train), and strong academics. As at many schools, "some majors...are stronger than others," and introductory classes tend to be large lectures, but "class sizes, especially in upper-level courses, are generally small," which allows for "meaningful discussions." Though some say the administration "tends to be aloof," this obviously isn't a problem with the faculty. Students say professors are "very approachable, accommodating, and enthusiastic about what they teach." "They are quite engaging...have PhDs in the field that they teach, and...seem genuinely interested in helping us improve." "They're always there when students want extra help and are very understanding." One happy English major tells us, "My professors have really encouraged me to pursue the most out of my education here. One provided me with the opportunity to read my original poetry in NYC with distinguished poets. Another has influenced my decision to write a senior thesis. Within my major, I feel like part of a family. All of my professors know me, and I think they truly care about my performance." A neuroscience major raves, "Science professors will be acting out the material or showing demos of the material." Study abroad opportunities also abound, and the proximity to New York City gives students amazing internship opportunities.

Life

Life at Drew is typical of life on other small, Northeastern campuses, with a balanced blend of school-sponsored events, student clubs, and "of course, like any other college, students drink and party once the weekend comes, but it's not the only focus here." Students also enjoy heading off campus to nearby Morristown, and "trips to NYC are funded to go to museums, the outlet mall, basketball games, etc." Also on campus is the Shakespeare Theatre of New Jersey, and students are happy to take advantage of work-study opportunities there, as well as performances. On campus, there are a lot of "activities—at least one every night," and "facilities and living councils are constantly making improvements." "Students tend to try and get their money's worth by participating in as many opportunities as they can," and whether it's "environmental film screenings, a lecture by Anderson Cooper, or free food from the Polish Culture Club, there is always something you can become involved in." "There are lots of alcohol-free events planned for the weekends," "for example, sometimes performers like musicians or comedians come and perform, or sometimes there are guests." "The campus coffeehouse, The Other End, holds open mic nights or jazz nights on the weekend. It's a really fun place to hang out or do homework." Club Drew, "a club [night] once a month on campus with a DJ," is well-attended.

Student Body

"A typical student at Drew is smart, driven," and "hardworking, but still parties at least once a week." "Talkative," "outgoing," and "social" also come up a lot when Drew students describe themselves. While some say "the typical Drew student is white, American, [and] from the East Coast," "we have an abundance of students from diverse ethnic backgrounds," and "there's a lot of different types of people, from jocks to hipsters." "There are jocks, theater junkies, musicians, premed students, international students, political science enthusiasts, and everything else." "It's mind-boggling how different the 1,700 undergraduates are," but "with an outstanding number of clubs and other social groups, literally any student can find a group of people to click with," and students suggest "to get the best experience out of Drew...you need to get involved."

FINANCIAL AID: 973-408-3112 • E-MAIL: CADM@DREW.EDU • WEBSITE: WWW.DREW.EDU

THE PRINCETON REVIEW SAYS

Admissions

Very important factors considered include: Academic GPA, rigor of secondary school record, talent/ability. *Important factors considered include:* Application essay, recommendation(s), extracurricular activities, interview, level of applicant's interest. *Other factors considered include:* Class rank, standardized test scores, alumni/ae relation, character/personal qualities, first generation, geographical residence, racial/ethnic status, volunteer work, work experience. ACT with or without writing component accepted. TOEFL required of all international applicants. High school diploma or equivalent is not required. *Academic units recommended:* 4 English, 3 mathematics, 2 science, 2 foreign language, 2 social studies, 2 history, 3 academic electives.

Financial Aid

Students should submit: FAFSA, CSS/Financial Aid PROFILE. Regular filing deadline is February 15. The Princeton Review suggests that all financial aid forms be submitted as soon as possible after January 1. *Need-based scholarships/grants offered:* Federal Pell, SEOG, state scholarships/grants, private scholarships, the school's own gift aid. *Loan aid offered:* Direct Subsidized Stafford, Direct Unsubsidized Stafford, Direct PLUS, Federal Perkins, state loans. Applicants will be notified of awards on or about April 1. Federal Work-Study Program available. Institutional employment available. Highest amount earned per year from on-campus jobs $5,800. Off-campus job opportunities are fair.

The Inside Word

Drew takes a holistic approach to evaluating applications, so you definitely want to showcase more than just your GPA (though that's important, too). In line with this, applicants have the option of submitting a graded analytical writing sample in place of SAT scores. Drew's applicant pool has grown significantly in recent years, so presenting yourself as not only a great student but also a great fit with the school will help you stand out from the pack.

THE SCHOOL SAYS ". . ."

From the Admissions Office

"At Drew, great teachers in small classes are transforming the undergraduate learning experience. With a commitment to civic engagement, nurturing leadership skills and mentoring, Drew professors make educating undergraduates their top priority. With a spirit of innovation, they bring the most distinctive modes of experiential learning into and beyond the Drew classroom. The result is a stimulating and a challenging education that connects the traditional liberal arts and sciences to the community, to the workplace, and to the world. New programs in Business, Public Health, Environmental Science, and new Honors and Civic Scholar Programs complement innovative programs like the Drew International Seminars and NYC semesters focused on Wall Street, the UN, museums, and theaters.

"Drew University is a test optional school; it accepts the SAT, the ACT or, a graded high school research paper. The Selection Committee will consider the highest verbal, math, and writing scores individually in its evaluation of candidates for admission. A student's transcript is considered to be the most important factor during the application process."

SELECTIVITY	
Admissions Rating	**82**
# of applicants	4,195
% of applicants accepted	84
% of acceptees attending	13
# of early decision applicants	88
# accepted early decision	66

FRESHMAN PROFILE	
Range SAT Critical Reading	500–630
Range SAT Math	500–610
Range SAT Writing	500–610
Range ACT Composite	21–28
Minimum paper TOEFL	550
Average HS GPA	3.4
% graduated top 10% of class	38
% graduated top 25% of class	71
% graduated top 50% of class	93

DEADLINES	
Early decision	
Deadline	11/1
Notification	1/15
Early action	
Deadline	1/15
Regular	
Deadline	2/15
Nonfall registration?	yes

FINANCIAL FACTS	
Financial Aid Rating	**79**
Annual tuition	$40,122
Room and board	$11,150
Required fees	$882
Books and supplies	$1,228
% needy frosh rec. need-based scholarship or grant aid	100
% needy UG rec. need-based scholarship or grant aid	99
% needy frosh rec. non-need-based scholarship or grant aid	10
% needy UG rec. non-need-based scholarship or grant aid	11
% needy frosh rec. need-based self-help aid	82
% needy UG rec. need-based self-help aid	84
% frosh rec. any financial aid	98
% UG rec. any financial aid	95
% UG borrow to pay for school	60
Average cumulative indebtedness	$21,303
% frosh need fully met	17
% ugrads need fully met	19
Average % of frosh need met	76
Average % of ugrad need met	76

DREXEL UNIVERSITY

3141 CHESTNUT STREET, PHILADELPHIA, PA 19104 • ADMISSIONS: 215-895-2400 • FAX: 215-895-5939

CAMPUS LIFE

Quality of Life Rating	75
Fire Safety Rating	90
Green Rating	98
Type of school	private
Environment	metropolis

STUDENTS

Total undergrad enrollment	13,652
% male/female	54/46
% from out of state	56
% from public high school	70
% frosh live on campus	89
# of fraternities	12
# of sororities	11
% African American	8
% Asian	12
% Caucasian	61
% Hispanic	4
% Native American	1
% international	8
# of countries represented	104

SURVEY SAYS . . .

Great computer facilities
Career services are great
Diverse student types on campus
Students love Philadelphia, PA
Great off-campus food
Student publications are popular
Lots of beer drinking
Hard liquor is popular

ACADEMICS

Academic Rating	72
% students returning for sophomore year	83
% students graduating within 6 years	68
Calendar	differs by program
Student/faculty ratio	9:1
Profs interesting rating	69
Profs accessible rating	66
Most classes have	10–19 students

MOST POPULAR MAJORS

biology/biological sciences; information science/studies; mechanical engineering

STUDENTS SAY ". . ."

Academics

By far the biggest draw for students seems to be Drexel University's cooperative education program that "gives students the opportunity to gain hands-on experience and develop professionally in their field of study." The co-op program is "an amazing experience" and "really sets [Drexel] apart." The program "offers real-world work experience and contacts at up to three local and/or national companies before graduation—and in this economy, it's all in who you know!" The co-op really helps students get "an excellent job after graduation." "Drexel University has diversified from its roots," and the school is "no longer being about just engineering. [Drexel] has set out to educate students to prepare them for careers in all industries." Students enjoy a "great campus location" in Philadelphia and "prides itself on innovative technologies that value sustainability, progressive learning that encourages constant change, and opportunities for invaluable experience." Although most of the professors "are very knowledgeable in their field" and offer "hands-on learning combined with direct application," many students say that "too many professors speak English as a second language" and "have difficulty communicating to their students." "Some professors need to retake an English language course," one student says bluntly. Students also pinpoint the "red tape" and "bureaucracy" as frustrating, saying that it bogs down the school. "Drexel is unfortunately run too much like a business sometimes," one student explains. "It can be difficult to get through the red tape that ties up departments." Some students also see the tuition as "outrageous." Although "some facilities are old and need work," Drexel is good about "dumping money into improving facilities" and most are "top-quality." One student proudly says, "Drexel is a great school," and it "is only going upward from here."

Life

Drexel University is located "right in the heart" of Philadelphia, one of the country's largest and most vibrant cities. Consequently, much of student life involves exploring this unique city. "It is so easy to learn how to use the subway and go into the heart of the city. It's so much fun to check out new locations, go shopping, and try out some of the best restaurants in town." Students love "the comedy club in center city [and] the bars in Olde City," and they often head to a "Phillies, Flyers, or 76ers game." "The music scene in Philadelphia is great," and "the Philadelphia Museum of Art is just a twenty-minute walk from campus." In addition to having the entire city of Philadelphia at your disposal, the University of Pennsylvania is "right across the street." "If you're into partying, there's always a party going on, if not, head over to UPenn or Temple," one student advises. On campus, "Greek life is a big part of Drexel's community." If there's a downside to Drexel life, it's that there's "very little school spirit." "The basketball team is all the school spirit that exists; there isn't any besides that," a student explains. But as soon as you step off campus, "there are countless other things to do too, like museums, operas, and musicals."

Student Body

"There is no such thing as a typical Drexel student," one student declares. "Our campus is incredibly diverse in every way." "Drexel is a mixing bowl" and "very multicultural." "Everyone is different, and we all interact with each other and fit in [with] all different groups." "There are so many different people from everywhere, and it's amazing. Black, white, gay, straight: it just makes the college life here diverse and exciting." "Most students get involved in one or more student organizations" to fit in. Students are also very hardworking and "busy with classes and studies." "Everyone is focused on careers after college, but people still like to have fun on the weekends." "We're generally pretty mellow people," a chemical engineering student explains. "[We] work hard, but don't get too uptight about grades and classes."

FINANCIAL AID: 215-895-2537 • E-MAIL: ENROLL@DREXEL.EDU • WEBSITE: WWW.DREXEL.EDU

THE PRINCETON REVIEW SAYS

Admissions

Very important factors considered include: Class rank, academic GPA, rigor of secondary school record, standardized test scores. *Important factors considered include:* Application essay, recommendation(s), character/personal qualities. *Other factors considered include:* Alumni/ae relation, extracurricular activities, first generation, interview, level of applicant's interest, talent/ability, volunteer work, work experience. SAT or ACT required; ACT with or without writing component accepted. TOEFL required of all international applicants. High school diploma is required and GED is accepted. *Academic units required:* 3 mathematics, 1 science (1 science lab). *Academic units recommended:* 1 foreign language.

Financial Aid

Students should submit: FAFSA. The Princeton Review suggests that all financial aid forms be submitted as soon as possible after January 1. *Need-based scholarships/grants offered:* Federal Pell, SEOG, state scholarships/grants, private scholarships, the school's own gift aid, United Negro College Fund. *Loan aid offered:* Direct Subsidized Stafford, Direct Unsubsidized Stafford, Direct PLUS, Federal Perkins, Federal Nursing, college/university loans from institutional funds. Applicants will be notified of awards on a rolling basis beginning March 15. Federal Work-Study Program available.

The Inside Word

Drexel University's nationally recognized co-op program provides unique hands-on experience for students with companies in and around Philadelphia to help them in their post-college employment. Given the current state of the economy, that's a huge boost for prospective applicants, especially in the engineering fields that Drexel still specializes in.

THE SCHOOL SAYS ". . ."

From the Admissions Office

"Drexel has gained a reputation for academic excellence since its founding in 1891. In 2006, Drexel became the first top-ranked doctoral university in more than twenty-five years to open a law school. Its main campus is a ten-minute walk from Center City Philadelphia. More than sixty percent of undergraduate students prepare for successful careers through Drexel's prestigious five-year experiential education program—The Drexel Co-op. Alternating periods of full-time, professional employment with periods of classroom study, students can earn an average of $14,000 per six-month co-op. At any one time, about 2,000 full-time undergraduates are on co-op assignments. Drexel integrates science and technology into all seventy undergraduate majors. Students looking for a special challenge can apply to one of fourteen accelerated degree programs including the BS/MBA in business, BA/BS/MD in medicine, BA/BS/TD in law, BS/MS or BS/PhD in engineering, BS/MS in information technology, and BS/DPT in physical therapy.

"Pennoni Honors College offers high achievers unique opportunities. Students Tackling Advanced Research (STAR) allows qualified undergraduates to participate in a paid summer research project, and the Center for Civic Engagement matches students with community service opportunities. Students in any major can take dance, music, and theater classes offered through Drexel's performing arts programs.

"Drexel's study abroad program allows students to spend a term or more earning credits while gaining international experience. Adventurous students can also enjoy co-op abroad. Locations include London, Costa Rica, Prague, Rome, and Paris. The admissions office invites prospective students to schedule a campus visit for a first-hand look at all Drexel offers."

SELECTIVITY	
Admissions Rating	**89**
# of applicants	48,718
% of applicants accepted	55
% of acceptees attending	10

FRESHMAN PROFILE	
Range SAT Critical Reading	540–640
Range SAT Math	570–670
Range SAT Writing	520–630
Range ACT Composite	23–28
Minimum paper TOEFL	550
Average HS GPA	3.4
% graduated top 10% of class	32
% graduated top 25% of class	64
% graduated top 50% of class	89

DEADLINES	
Regular	
Deadline	3/1
Nonfall registration?	yes

FINANCIAL FACTS	
Financial Aid Rating	**73**
Annual tuition	$33,800
Room and board	$14,175
Required fees	$2,300
Books and supplies	$1,950
% needy frosh rec. need-based scholarship or grant aid	99
% needy UG rec. need-based scholarship or grant aid	93
% needy frosh rec. non-need-based scholarship or grant aid	15
% needy UG rec. non-need-based scholarship or grant aid	8
% needy frosh rec. need-based self-help aid	81
% needy UG rec. need-based self-help aid	90
% frosh rec. any financial aid	94
% UG rec. any financial aid	89
% UG borrow to pay for school	73
Average cumulative indebtedness	$35,082
% frosh need fully met	40
% ugrads need fully met	31
Average % of frosh need met	61
Average % of ugrad need met	56

DUKE UNIVERSITY

2138 CAMPUS DRIVE, DURHAM, NC 27708-0586 • ADMISSIONS: 919-684-3214 • FAX: 919-681-8941

CAMPUS LIFE

Quality of Life Rating	**68**
Fire Safety Rating	**60***
Green Rating	**93**
Type of school	private
Affiliation	Methodist
Environment	city

STUDENTS

Total undergrad enrollment	6,066
% male/female	52/48
% from out of state	85
% from public high school	65
% frosh live on campus	100
# of fraternities	21
# of sororities	14
% African American	11
% Asian	15
% Caucasian	58
% Hispanic	7
% international	5
# of countries represented	89

SURVEY SAYS . . .

Lab facilities are great
Great computer facilities
Great library
Athletic facilities are great
Students are happy
Everyone loves the Blue Devils
Student publications are popular
Student government is popular

ACADEMICS

Academic Rating	**92**
% students returning for sophomore year	96
% students graduating within 4 years	86
% students graduating within 6 years	92
Calendar	semester
Student/faculty ratio	11:1
Profs interesting rating	76
Profs accessible rating	77
Most classes have	10–19 students
Most lab/discussion sessions have	10–19 students

MOST POPULAR MAJORS

economics; psychology; public policy analysis

APPLICANTS ALSO LOOK AT AND OFTEN PREFER

Princeton University, Yale University, Stanford University, Harvard College

AND SOMETIMES PREFER

University of Pennsylvania, Brown University, Cornell University, Dartmouth College

AND RARELY PREFER

Georgetown University, University of Virginia, The University of North Carolina at Chapel Hill, Northwestern University

STUDENTS SAY ". . ."

Academics

Duke University is "all about academic excellence complemented by highly competitive Division I sports and an enriching array of extracurricular activities," making the university "an exciting, challenging, and enjoyable place to be." Undergraduates choose Duke because they "are passionate about a wide range of things, including academics, sports, community service, research, and fun." And because the school seems equally committed to accommodating all of those pursuits; as one student puts it, "Duke is for the Ivy League candidate who is a little bit more laid-back about school and overachieving (but just a bit) and a lot more into the party scene." Academics "are very difficult in the quantitative majors (engineering, math, statistics, economics, premed)" and "much easier in the non-quantitative majors," but there's an "across-the-board excellence in all departments from humanities to engineering." In all areas, there's a "supportive environment in which the faculty, staff, and students are willing to look out for the other person and help them succeed." It's the norm to have large study groups, and "The review sessions, peer tutoring system, writing center, and academic support center are always helpful when students are struggling with anything from math homework to creating a resume." Professors' "number-one priority is teaching undergraduates," and their love of discussion means they "would rather that the students lead the class as opposed to them leading the class." "There are a few who make me want to stay at Duke forever," says a student. Because "the school has a lot of confidence in its students," it offers them "seemingly limitless opportunities."

Life

Life at Duke "is very relaxed," and "You can either be a part of nothing, or you can be so over-committed that it's not even funny." Because "the student union and other organizations provide entertainment all the time, from movies to shows to campus-wide parties," there's "a wealth of on-campus opportunities to get involved." Indeed, weekends are for relaxing, and "People usually stay on campus for fun," because hometown Durham "has a few quirky streets and squares with restaurants, shops, clubs, etc., but to really do much you have to go to Raleigh or Chapel Hill," each twenty to thirty minutes away by car. The perception that "Durham is pretty dangerous" further dampens students' enthusiasm for the city. Undergrads' fervor for Blue Devils sports, on the other hand, can be boundless; sports, "especially basketball, are a huge deal here," and undergrads "will paint themselves completely blue and wait in line on the sidewalk in K-ville for three days to jump up and down in Cameron Indoor Stadium." Greek life "plays a big role in the social scene here," but "Almost all the parties are open, so it definitely isn't hard to get into a party." Though it's a "very party-heavy school," a lot of people "just do their own thing—have a movie night, go exploring, go skiing or to the beach for a weekend." Still, the social scene can be "a little too intense" at times.

Student Body

The typical Duke student "is someone who cares a lot about his or her education but at the same time won't sacrifice a social life for it." Life involves "getting a ton of work done first and then finding time to play and have fun." The typical student here is studious but social, athletic but can never be seen in the gym, job hunting but not worrying, and so on and so forth." Everyone is "incredibly focused," but "That includes social success as well." Students tend to be "focused on graduating and obtaining a lucrative and prosperous career," and although they "go out two to three times a week," they're "always looking polished." An "overwhelming number" are athletes, "not just varsity athletes…but athletes in high school or generally active people. Duke's athletic pride attracts this kind of person." The student body "is surprisingly ethnically diverse, with a number of students of Asian, African, and Hispanic descent," and "Every type of person finds a welcoming group where he or she fits in."

FINANCIAL AID: 919-684-6225 • E-MAIL: UNDERGRAD-ADMISSIONS@DUKE.EDU • WEBSITE: WWW.DUKE.EDU

THE PRINCETON REVIEW SAYS

Admissions

Very important factors considered include: Application essay, recommendation(s), rigor of secondary school record, standardized test scores, extracurricular activities, talent/ability. *Important factors considered include:* Character/personal qualities. *Other factors considered include:* Class rank, academic GPA, alumni/ae relation, geographical residence, interview, racial/ethnic status, state residency, volunteer work, work experience. High school diploma is required and GED is not accepted. *Academic units recommended:* 4 English, 4 mathematics, 4 science, 4 foreign language, 4 social studies.

Financial Aid

Students should submit: FAFSA, CSS/Financial Aid PROFILE, noncustodial PROFILE, business/farm supplement, parent and student income tax returns. Regular filing deadline is March 1. The Princeton Review suggests that all financial aid forms be submitted as soon as possible after January 1. *Need-based scholarships/grants offered:* Federal Pell, SEOG, state scholarships/grants, private scholarships, the school's own gift aid, ROTC. *Loan aid offered:* Direct Subsidized Stafford, Direct Unsubsidized Stafford, Direct PLUS, Federal Perkins, college/university loans from institutional funds, private loans. Applicants will be notified of awards on or about April 1. Federal Work-Study Program available. Institutional employment available. Highest amount earned per year from on-campus jobs $1,400. Off-campus job opportunities are good.

The Inside Word

Duke is an extremely selective undergraduate institution, which affords the school the luxury of rejecting many qualified applicants. You'll have to present an exceptional record just to be considered; to make the cut, you'll have to impress the admissions office that you can contribute something unique and valuable to the incoming class. Being one of the best basketball players in the nation (male or female) helps a lot, but even athletes have to show academic excellence to get in the door here.

THE SCHOOL SAYS ". . ."

From the Admissions Office

"Duke University offers an interesting mix of tradition and innovation, undergraduate college and major research university, Southern hospitality and international presence, and athletic prowess and academic excellence. Students come to Duke from all over the United States and the world and from a range of racial, ethnic, and socioeconomic backgrounds. They enjoy contact with a world-class faculty through small classes and independent study. More than forty majors are available in the arts and sciences and engineering; arts and sciences students may also design their own curriculum through Program II. Certificate programs are available in a number of interdisciplinary areas. Special academic opportunities include the Focus Program and seminars for first-year students, study abroad, study at the Duke Marine Laboratory and Duke Primate Center, the Duke in New York and Duke in Los Angeles arts programs, and several international exchange programs. While admission to Duke is highly selective, applications of U.S. citizens and permanent residents are evaluated without regard to financial need and the university pledges to meet 100 percent of the demonstrated need of all admitted U.S. students and permanent residents. A limited amount of financial aid is also available for foreign citizens, and the university will meet the full demonstrated financial need for those admitted students as well.

"Applicants must take either the ACT with the writing exam, or the SAT plus two SAT Subject Tests (mathematics Subject Test required for applicants to the Pratt School of Engineering)."

SELECTIVITY

Admissions Rating	**98**
# of applicants	18,090
% of applicants accepted	22
% of acceptees attending	43
# accepting a place on wait list	1,648
# admitted from wait list	102
# of early decision applicants	1,482
# accepted early decision	470

FRESHMAN PROFILE

Range SAT Critical Reading	690–770
Range SAT Math	690–800
Range ACT Composite	29–34
% graduated top 10% of class	90
% graduated top 25% of class	98
% graduated top 50% of class	100

DEADLINES

Early decision	
Deadline	11/1
Notification	12/15
Regular	
Deadline	1/2
Notification	4/1
Nonfall registration?	no

FINANCIAL FACTS

Financial Aid Rating	**94**
Annual tuition	$44,101
Room and board	$11,830
Books and supplies	$970
% needy frosh rec. need-based scholarship or grant aid	97
% needy UG rec. need-based scholarship or grant aid	94
% needy frosh rec. non-need-based scholarship or grant aid	3
% needy UG rec. non-need-based scholarship or grant aid	2
% needy frosh rec. need-based self-help aid	88
% needy UG rec. need-based self-help aid	91
% UG borrow to pay for school	40
Average cumulative indebtedness	$16,502
% frosh need fully met	92
% ugrads need fully met	90
Average % of frosh need met	100
Average % of ugrad need met	100

DUQUESNE UNIVERSITY

600 FORBES AVENUE, PITTSBURGH, PA 15282 • ADMISSIONS: 412-396-2222 • FAX: 412-396-6223

CAMPUS LIFE

Quality of Life Rating	**79**
Fire Safety Rating	**99**
Green Rating	**85**
Type of school	private
Affiliation	Roman Catholic
Environment	metropolis

STUDENTS

Total undergrad enrollment	5,639
% male/female	43/57
% from out of state	26
% frosh live on campus	92
# of fraternities	11
# of sororities	7
% African American	5
% Asian	2
% Caucasian	83
% Hispanic	3
% international	3
# of countries represented	82

SURVEY SAYS . . .

Students love Pittsburgh, PA
Great off-campus food
Campus feels safe
Lots of beer drinking

ACADEMICS

Academic Rating	**72**
% students returning for sophomore year	87
% students graduating within 4 years	61
Calendar	semester
Student/faculty ratio	14:1
Profs interesting rating	76
Profs accessible rating	80
Most classes have	10–19 students
Most lab/discussion sessions have	fewer than 10 students

MOST POPULAR MAJORS

accounting; nursing/registered nurse (rn, asn, bsn, msn); pharmacy (pharmd [U.S.], pharmd or bs/bpharm [Canada])

APPLICANTS ALSO LOOK AT AND OFTEN PREFER

Pennsylvania State University—University Park, University of Pittsburgh—Pittsburgh Campus, Washington & Jefferson College

AND SOMETIMES PREFER

West Virginia University

STUDENTS SAY ". . ."

Academics

Cosmopolitan yet caring, you get the best of both worlds at Duquesne University. Located in the heart of downtown Pittsburgh, this Catholic school unites "the diversity and opportunities of an urban university with the community and comfort of a small liberal arts college." "Well-respected in the Pittsburgh area," health fields are particularly strong at Duquesne. "The physician assistant program is world-renowned and selective," while pharmacy students say it's unique to find such a "good pharmacy program [at] a smaller university." The music school also receives ample praise and benefits from studio teachers who are "some of the best in the world." Regardless of the specific program, "Professors are eager to really engage with students and are available for extra support whenever you need it." Course work can be challenging, yet "The school wants [its] students to do well, and it offers many different services to aid in this." In fact, "Every department offers free tutors" to help students make the grade. On the flip side, the school's academic advisors often fall short, and many students struggle to schedule classes and meet graduation requirements. A music student admits, "One semester, I was not even a full-time student because my advisor failed to schedule three of my classes!" Fortunately, the majority of the school's staff is accessible, visible, and friendly; "The administrators, the professors, and the school ministers can be seen walking around campus. All of them have been known to stop and talk to groups of students around the school."

Life

Located "on a very pretty, secluded campus in the middle of downtown Pittsburgh," students at Duquesne love their school's location, just steps outside a city with "a rich cultural district and an even better nightlife." During the week, "Life at school consists of going to classes, spending many hours at the library, and going to Starbucks for social interactions." During the weekend, things get more exciting. Thanks to "the free campus buses that shuttle students to the Oakland and South Side areas on Friday and Saturday nights," students enjoy "bars, movie theaters, concerts (big names and locals), and tons of restaurants." While the Duquesne campus is dry, "Many people go out on the weekends, typically to parties on the south side or at the University of Pittsburgh." In addition, "Students also attend a lot of sporting events, including the Pittsburgh Steelers and Penguins, Duquesne games and Pitt games." If you don't feel like straying too far from home, the school manages a campus club called Nite Spot, "where they show movies that haven't come out on DVD yet, have bizarre activities like pillow-making that actually turn out to be really fun, and dance lessons." Another popular hangout is the Power Center—the "nicest facility on campus"—where "the exercise equipment is new and the classes are free."

Student Body

From Greek organizations to the table tennis club, "Many of the students at Duquesne are very involved in campus organizations and service-oriented activities." At the same time, students are "driven to succeed" academically, and "show up to every class with his or her work complete." "Well-mannered and well-dressed," Duquesne students don their best duds to go to lecture, and "The majority of people look like they just walked out a fashion catalog." Students admit the school isn't particularly diverse, and "the typical student at Duquesne is white, from the Pittsburgh area (or at least Pennsylvania), and Catholic." However, "Not all of the student body has Catholic values, and I have found that the student body doesn't push their own values onto anyone else." With 5,800 undergraduates, "The school is big enough that you can meet a lot of different people, but small enough that you have a sense of community by being able to see people you know anywhere you go on campus." Still, most students divide into smaller cliques, and "unless you join a frat or sorority, making a large networked group of friends is difficult."

FINANCIAL AID: 412-396-6607 • E-MAIL: ADMISSIONS@DUQ.EDU • WEBSITE: WWW.DUQ.EDU

THE PRINCETON REVIEW SAYS

Admissions

Very important factors considered include: Application essay, academic GPA, recommendation(s), rigor of secondary school record, standardized test scores. *Important factors considered include:* Class rank, character/personal qualities, extracurricular activities, interview, talent/ability, volunteer work. *Other factors considered include:* Alumni/ae relation, first generation, level of applicant's interest, racial/ethnic status, work experience. SAT or ACT required; ACT with writing component required. High school diploma is required and GED is accepted. *Academic units recommended:* 4 English, 2 mathematics, 2 science, 2 foreign language, 2 social studies, 4 academic electives.

Financial Aid

Students should submit: FAFSA, institution's own financial aid form. Regular filing deadline is May 1. The Princeton Review suggests that all financial aid forms be submitted as soon as possible after January 1. *Need-based scholarships/grants offered:* Federal Pell, SEOG, state scholarships/grants, private scholarships, the school's own gift aid, United Negro College Fund. *Loan aid offered:* Direct Subsidized Stafford, Direct Unsubsidized Stafford, Direct PLUS, Federal Perkins, Federal Nursing, private alternative loans. Applicants will be notified of awards on a rolling basis beginning March 1. Federal Work-Study Program available. Institutional employment available. Off-campus job opportunities are good.

The Inside Word

Duquesne requires all prospective students to complete a college preparatory curriculum in high school; however, there is no minimum GPA required for admission, nor minimum test scores. Nonetheless, a student's academic record and test scores are the only two factors considered in awarding merit scholarships.

THE SCHOOL SAYS ". . ."

From the Admissions Office

"Duquesne University was founded in 1878 by the Holy Ghost Fathers. Although it is a private, Roman Catholic institution, Duquesne is proud of its ecumenical reputation. Duquesne University's attractive and secluded campus is set on a forty-nine-acre hilltop ('the bluff') overlooking the large corporate metropolis of Pittsburgh's Golden Triangle. It offers a wide variety of educational opportunities, from the liberal arts to modern professional training. Duquesne is a medium-sized university striving to offer personal attention to its students in addition to the versatility and opportunities of a true university. A deep sense of tradition is combined with innovation and flexibility to make the Duquesne experience both challenging and rewarding. The Palumbo Convocation/Recreation Complex features a 6,300-seat arena, home court to the university's Division I basketball team; racquetball and handball courts; weight rooms; and saunas. Extracurricular activities are recognized as an essential part of college life, complementing academics in the process of total student development. Students are involved in nearly 100 university-sponsored activities, and Duquesne's location gives students the opportunity to enjoy sports and cultural events both on campus and in the city. There are six residence halls with the capacity to house 3,538 students."

SELECTIVITY	
Admissions Rating	**80**
# of applicants	6,528
% of applicants accepted	70
% of acceptees attending	29
# of early decision applicants	165
# accepted early decision	99

FRESHMAN PROFILE	
Range SAT Critical Reading	520–600
Range SAT Math	520–610
Range SAT Writing	510–600
Range ACT Composite	23–27
Minimum paper TOEFL	575
Minimum web-based TOEFL	90
Average HS GPA	3.6
% graduated top 10% of class	29
% graduated top 25% of class	60
% graduated top 50% of class	89

DEADLINES	
Early decision	
Deadline	11/1
Notification	12/15
Early action	
Deadline	12/1
Notification	1/15
Regular	
Priority	11/1
Deadline	7/1
Nonfall registration?	yes

FINANCIAL FACTS	
Financial Aid Rating	**76**
Annual tuition	$27,668
Room and board	$9,806
Required fees	$2,258
Books and supplies	$1,000
% needy frosh rec. need-based scholarship or grant aid	100
% needy UG rec. need-based scholarship or grant aid	98
% needy frosh rec. non-need-based scholarship or grant aid	98
% needy UG rec. non-need-based scholarship or grant aid	90
% needy frosh rec. need-based self-help aid	88
% needy UG rec. need-based self-help aid	87
% frosh rec. any financial aid	100
% UG rec. any financial aid	97
% frosh need fully met	24
% ugrads need fully met	25
Average % of frosh need met	89
Average % of ugrad need met	79

ECKERD COLLEGE

4200 FIFTY-FOURTH AVENUE SOUTH, ST. PETERSBURG, FL 33711 • ADMISSIONS: 727-864-8331 • FAX: 727-866-2304

CAMPUS LIFE

Quality of Life Rating	75
Fire Safety Rating	74
Green Rating	88
Type of school	private
Affiliation	Presbyterian
Environment	city

STUDENTS

Total undergrad enrollment	1,821
% male/female	41/59
% from out of state	84
% frosh live on campus	98
% African American	3
% Asian	1
% Caucasian	80
% Hispanic	7
% international	3
# of countries represented	33

SURVEY SAYS . . .

Great library
Career services are great
Frats and sororities are unpopular or nonexistent
Lots of beer drinking
Hard liquor is popular

ACADEMICS

Academic Rating	83
% students returning for sophomore year	81
% students graduating within 4 years	55
% students graduating within 6 years	63
Calendar	4-1-4
Student/faculty ratio	13:1
Profs interesting rating	85
Profs accessible rating	88
Most classes have	20–29 students
Most lab/discussion sessions have	10–19 students

MOST POPULAR MAJORS

business administration and management; environmental studies; marine science

STUDENTS SAY ". . ."

Academics

Eckerd College "in sunny Florida" is "a small, personable college with beach bum flare" that offers a "well-rounded," "excellent liberal arts education" and a "beautiful beachfront environment." Standouts include a "great" marine science program—"one of the best in the country" according to scores of students—and "many opportunities for" "freakin' awesome internships." "We also have a really good study abroad program," notes a sophomore. Eckerd really emphasizes international travel and you can study in a host of far-flung locales during your career here. The academic environment is "challenging but not too rough." In addition to your basic two semesters each year, Eckerd has a fairly unique winter term that allows students to focus on one course intensively. You'll find "some horrid teachers" but most classes are "extremely interesting." Professors tend to "encourage discussion," and "you can build very close relationships" with them. "I enjoy that I am not in a room filled with 300 students," relates a human development major. "I get one-on-one help when I need it. The professors seem to love their jobs and love helping students." "Professors are almost always accessible outside of the classroom and love to see you succeed in classes," adds an environmental studies major.

Life

The food on campus is "not so good," and "the older dorms need some work." Also, the campus is "fairly secluded from St. Petersburg, so getting anywhere without a car is difficult." Otherwise, though, life here is grand. "We call it Camp Eckerd," relates a sophomore. Students say the campus is "very easy to get around." The weather is perpetually warm. "You never have to wear shoes." The atmosphere is "laid-back." At the same time, "There is always some type of school- or organization-sponsored event going on." Students are also "very active in the outdoors," not least because the campus is "surrounded by water on three sides." The "really awesome" waterfront program allows students to check out kayaks and boats. You can also take sailing and windsurfing classes. The party scene here is by all accounts outstanding. "Weekends are pretty crazy," explains a senior. "Thursday through Saturday it is not hard to find…some kind of themed party in upper-class dorms." "A lot of beer is consumed on the weekends," observes an awed first-year student. When you feel the urge to get away, two gorgeous beaches are very nearby. Downtown Tampa is only a half-hour from campus, and Busch Gardens and Disney World are within a reasonable drive as well.

Student Body

"Picture what would happen if you combined the school stoner, the class president, the jock, and the funny guy," depicts a first-year student. "Now, subtract the shoes and add a perfect tan." That, in a nutshell, is the typical undergrad at Eckerd. "Students here have a lot of self-confidence" and they are "surprisingly friendly." Most are "pretty physically fit and outdoorsy." It's hard to generalize about this place, though. Many students don't fit that profile at all. "There is a hodgepodge of people." Students "range from complete hippies, to alternative, to party girls," to "pale-skinned gamers," to "artsy marine science people." There's also the jock, the "indie-rocker," and "the math nerd." Cliques happen, especially among athletes, but "everyone can hang out with everyone with 100 percent comfort." "People smile at each other and say hey," describes a senior. "It is a pretty relaxed and friendly atmosphere."

FINANCIAL AID: 727-864-8854 • E-MAIL: ADMISSIONS@ECKERD.EDU • WEBSITE: WWW.ECKERD.EDU

THE PRINCETON REVIEW SAYS

Admissions

Very important factors considered include: Academic GPA, rigor of secondary school record. *Important factors considered include:* Application essay, recommendation(s), standardized test scores, character/personal qualities, extracurricular activities, interview, talent/ability. *Other factors considered include:* Class rank, alumni/ae relation, first generation, level of applicant's interest, volunteer work, work experience. SAT or ACT required; ACT with or without writing component accepted. High school diploma is required and GED is accepted. *Academic units recommended:* 4 English, 3 mathematics, 3 science (2 science labs), 2 foreign language, 2 social studies, 1 history, 3 academic electives.

Financial Aid

Students should submit: FAFSA. The Princeton Review suggests that all financial aid forms be submitted as soon as possible after January 1. *Need-based scholarships/grants offered:* Federal Pell, SEOG, state scholarships/grants, private scholarships, the school's own gift aid. *Loan aid offered:* Direct Subsidized Stafford, Direct Unsubsidized Stafford, Direct PLUS, Federal Perkins, college/university loans from institutional funds. Applicants will be notified of awards on a rolling basis beginning February 15. Federal Work-Study Program available. Institutional employment available. Highest amount earned per year from on-campus jobs $2,500. Off-campus job opportunities are excellent.

The Inside Word

Most of the applicants Eckerd admits come from the top quarter of their high school classes. However, competition from other small liberal arts schools of roughly the same caliber or better is stiff. As a result, Eckerd is a relatively easy admit for B-plus students with decent standardized test scores. The admissions process here is rolling, which means that applying early will help your chances. Eckerd can afford to be more selective later on in the admissions cycle, especially for candidates who profess an interest in its most esteemed programs (for example, marine science). So those with serious interest should consider Eckerd's early admission policy.

THE SCHOOL SAYS ". . ."

From the Admissions Office

"Eckerd, a coeducational college of liberal arts and sciences, has a diverse student body from forty-eight states and thirty-three countries. Located on 188 acres of waterfront property in St. Petersburg, Florida, we take advantage of our spectacular mile of campus waterfront along the Gulf of Mexico for outdoor laboratories in biology, marine science and environmental studies as well as for an array of intramural, club and intercollegiate sports and water recreation. Offerings in the arts and humanities inspire creativity and foster critical thinking and self-awareness.

"A proud signer of the American College and University Presidents' Climate Commitment, Eckerd is dedicated to minimizing its operational footprint and maximizing sustainable practices. Eckerd's Community Garden contributes to our "Eat Local" initiative, and our Yellow Community Bike Program is designed to increase bicycle use on campus and decrease car traffic. In addition to being "green," Eckerd students are service-oriented, volunteering more than 70,000 hours annually in the Tampa Bay community and across the globe.

"Eckerd's innovative 4-1-4 calendar gives students the opportunity to study abroad during the January Winter Term or semester-long programs. Nearly seventy percent of our graduates have spent at least one term overseas, many at Eckerd study centers in London, China and Latin America.

"The Academy of Senior Professionals draws distinguished persons who have retired from the fields our students aspire to enter. Academy members such as Nobel Prize-winner Elie Wiesel enrich classes and offer valuable counsel for career and life planning.

"We venture together in the Eckerd experience to think beyond the conventional questions, methods and solutions. At Eckerd College, we ThinkOUTside."

SELECTIVITY	
Admissions Rating	**85**
# of applicants	3,713
% of applicants accepted	53
% of acceptees attending	25
# accepting a place on wait list	84
# admitted from wait list	4
FRESHMAN PROFILE	
Range SAT Critical Reading	510–620
Range SAT Math	500–610
Range SAT Writing	500–600
Range ACT Composite	22–28
Minimum paper TOEFL	550
Minimum web-based TOEFL	79
Average HS GPA	3.3
DEADLINES	
Early action	
Deadline	11/15
Notification	12/15
Nonfall registration?	yes
FINANCIAL FACTS	
Financial Aid Rating	**82**
Annual tuition	$34,250
Room and board	$9,652
Required fees	$296
Books and supplies	$1,200
% needy frosh rec. need-based scholarship or grant aid	100
% needy UG rec. need-based scholarship or grant aid	99
% needy frosh rec. need-based self-help aid	83
% needy UG rec. need-based self-help aid	84
% frosh rec. any financial aid	96
% UG rec. any financial aid	93
% UG borrow to pay for school	66
Average cumulative indebtedness	$32,245
% frosh need fully met	29
% ugrads need fully met	20
Average % of frosh need met	89
Average % of ugrad need met	87

ELON UNIVERSITY

100 CAMPUS DRIVE, ELON, NC 27244-2010 • ADMISSIONS: 336-278-3566 • FAX: 336-278-7699

CAMPUS LIFE

Quality of Life Rating	**88**
Fire Safety Rating	**81**
Green Rating	**93**
Type of school	private
Environment	town

STUDENTS

Total undergrad enrollment	5,225
% male/female	41/59
% from out of state	80
% from public high school	68
% frosh live on campus	100
# of fraternities	12
# of sororities	14
% African American	6
% Asian	2
% Caucasian	81
% Hispanic	4
% international	1
# of countries represented	57

SURVEY SAYS . . .

Great computer facilities
School is well run
Low cost of living
Frats and sororities dominate social scene
Internships are widely available

ACADEMICS

Academic Rating	**89**
% students returning for sophomore year	90
% students graduating within 4 years	78
% students graduating within 6 years	82
Calendar	4-1-4
Student/faculty ratio	13:1
Profs interesting rating	88
Profs accessible rating	90
Most classes have	10–19 students
Most lab/discussion sessions have	10–19 students

MOST POPULAR MAJORS

business/commerce; communication studies/ speech communication and rhetoric; education

APPLICANTS ALSO LOOK AT AND OFTEN PREFER

The University of North Carolina at Chapel Hill, Wake Forest University

AND SOMETIMES PREFER

North Carolina State University, University of Maryland, College Park, University of Richmond

STUDENTS SAY ". . ."

Academics

If you ask Elon undergrads to capture the essence of their university with one turn of phrase, they'll likely report that it's all about "big-school opportunities with a small-school community." Happily expounding, students are also quick to underscore that "the hard work that Elon puts into giving its students a hands-on, experiential learning environment is recognized from day one." Further, students here appreciate the numerous opportunities for study abroad along with the "small class sizes and individual attention." What's more, Elon's "personable," "engaging" professors are both "enthusiastic about their fields and helping students." They truly "want their students to succeed both in and out of the classroom." Undergrads also value the care and concern the administration shows to students, which extends to even the top brass. As one incredulous student shares, "Our president opens his home to the student body around the holidays, provides us with food on the school's dime, and stands in a holiday hat to take pictures with students that are placed on a holiday card and sent home." It's no wonder this fellow undergrad concludes by simply stating, "I felt an instant comfort when I stepped on campus. At other schools I really felt like a visitor, but at Elon I felt like I belonged there."

Life

Undergrads at Elon certainly know how to "keep themselves busy." Indeed it's difficult to find someone who isn't juggling academics with a myriad of extra-curricular activities. In addition, many students "choose to participate in Greek life, which tends to run the social scene. On the weekends, students go out to the bars in the town or to parties at various off-campus houses." While some claim that those not in the party scene "often feel like [they] are in a minority," others assure us, "There's a lot to do around here, even if you don't drink." As one undergrads explains, "Oftentimes my friends and I will play Frisbee, climb the magnolia trees on campus, have movie nights, play video games, just hang out." Of course, there are also plenty of school-sponsored events to enjoy. Another student adds, "Our Student Union Board holds free events all the time like bingo, movies on the lawn, concerts, midnight meals, and even a hypnotist show. I always have options for something fun to do!" Locally, there are "a lot of great restaurants in the area that range from diner-style places to really authentic Indian and Korean restaurants, so there is a lot of choice. [Certainly,] going out for dinner is a common social activity." Further, students also value Elon's location, which "allows you to get to Raleigh, Chapel Hill, or Greensboro in less than an hour."

Student Body

On the surface, the typical Elon undergrad appears to be "preppy, white, and from a well-off family, [and he or she] probably [attended] a private high school." However, if you're willing to look beyond the "Lily and Southern Tide" exterior, you're sure to discover a student body that's "cordial," "highly motivated," "driven, and engaged." Indeed, on this "hardworking" campus, you'll find students are "passionate about their studies" and "take their schooling very seriously." Leadership is another big attribute that's tossed around as most students are "on the executive board of an organization or more than one organization, and [they are] heavily focused on self-improvement." Perhaps more importantly, undergrads at Elon also report that their peers are "compassionate" and "open and willing to talk and help anybody." Finally, as one content undergrad sums up her campus, "Students fit in by getting involved. Whether it's Greek life, sports, or clubs, I think there is something for everyone."

FINANCIAL AID: 336-278-7640 • E-MAIL: ADMISSIONS@ELON.EDU • WEBSITE: WWW.ELON.EDU

THE PRINCETON REVIEW SAYS

Admissions

Very important factors considered include: Academic GPA, rigor of secondary school record, standardized test scores. *Important factors considered include:* Application essay, recommendation(s), alumni/ae relation, extracurricular activities, talent/ability, volunteer work, work experience. *Other factors considered include:* Class rank, character/personal qualities, first generation, geographical residence, level of applicant's interest, racial/ethnic status, state residency. SAT or ACT required; ACT with writing component required. TOEFL required of all international applicants. High school diploma is required and GED is accepted. *Academic units required:* 4 English, 3 mathematics, 3 science (1 science lab), 2 foreign language, 1 social studies, 2 history. *Academic units recommended:* 4 English, 4 mathematics, 3 science (1 science lab), 3 foreign language, 1 social studies, 2 history.

Financial Aid

Students should submit: FAFSA, institution's own financial aid form, CSS/Financial Aid PROFILE. The Princeton Review suggests that all financial aid forms be submitted as soon as possible after January 1. *Need-based scholarships/grants offered:* PAEE Program, Federal Pell, SEOG, state scholarships/grants, private scholarships, the school's own gift aid. *Loan aid offered:* Direct Subsidized Stafford, Direct Unsubsidized Stafford, Direct PLUS, Federal Perkins, state loans, privately funded alternative loans. Applicants will be notified of awards on a rolling basis beginning March 30. Federal Work-Study Program available. Institutional employment available. Highest amount earned per year from on-campus jobs $4,500. Off-campus job opportunities are good.

The Inside Word

Over the years, securing admittance to Elon has become an increasingly challenging feat. To be successful, it's important to have chosen a rigorous high school curriculum. Indeed, candidates must have gone beyond the basic college prep classes offered. In addition, admissions officers seek out students who have demonstrated leadership savvy. Finally, students looking to transfer should know that the greatest weight will be placed on completed college course work.

THE SCHOOL SAYS ". . ."

From the Admissions Office

"Elon offers the resources of a university in a close-knit community atmosphere. The university's 5,225 undergraduates choose from more than sixty majors. Graduate programs are offered in business administration, law, education, interactive media, physical therapy, and, beginning in 2013, physician assistant studies. The National Survey of Student Engagement recognizes Elon among the nation's most effective universities in promoting hands-on learning. Academic and co-curricular activities are seamlessly blended, especially in the Elon Experiences: study abroad, internships, service, leadership, and undergraduate research. Participation is among the highest in the nation. Seventy-one percent of graduating seniors have studied abroad, seventy-nine percent have internship experiences, and seventy-nine percent have participated in service. Elon's 4-1-4 academic calendar allows students to devote January to international study or to explore innovative on-campus courses. Elon's historic 600-acre campus is recognized as one of the most beautiful in the country. New additions include the Gerald L. Francis Center, home of the School of Health Sciences; residence facilities with living spaces for 624 students, including expanded Greek housing and a junior/senior village; the three-story Elon Town Center, which includes Elon's Barnes & Noble bookstore, a pizzeria and ice cream shop, and offices of *The Pendulum* student newspaper; Colonnades Dining Hall, featuring a full-service restaurant, an organic market and a fire stone oven for pizzas; and Alumni Field House, headquarters of Elon's NCAA Division I Phoenix athletics. The athletics programs compete in the Southern Conference. Freshman applicants are required to take the SAT (or the ACT with the writing section). The best critical reading, math, and writing scores from either test will be used."

SELECTIVITY

Admissions Rating	**92**
# of applicants	9,079
% of applicants accepted	58
% of acceptees attending	27
# accepting a place on wait list	2,334
# admitted from wait list	83
# of early decision applicants	344
# accepted early decision	295

FRESHMAN PROFILE

Range SAT Critical Reading	560–660
Range SAT Math	560–660
Range SAT Writing	560–660
Range ACT Composite	25–29
Minimum paper TOEFL	550
Minimum web-based TOEFL	79
Average HS GPA	4.0
% graduated top 10% of class	32
% graduated top 25% of class	67
% graduated top 50% of class	94

DEADLINES

Early decision	
Deadline	11/1
Notification	12/1
Early action	
Deadline	11/10
Notification	12/20
Regular	
Priority	11/1
Deadline	1/10
Notification	3/15
Nonfall registration?	yes

FINANCIAL FACTS

Financial Aid Rating	**74**
Annual tuition	$27,534
Required fees	$347
Books and supplies	$900
% needy frosh rec. need-based scholarship or grant aid	87
% needy UG rec. need-based scholarship or grant aid	88
% needy frosh rec. non-need-based scholarship or grant aid	34
% needy UG rec. non-need-based scholarship or grant aid	35
% needy frosh rec. need-based self-help aid	82
% needy UG rec. need-based self-help aid	83
% frosh rec. any financial aid	77
% UG rec. any financial aid	72
% UG borrow to pay for school	44
Average cumulative indebtedness	$27,417
Average % of frosh need met	69
Average % of ugrad need met	70

Emerson College

120 Boylston Street, Boston, MA 02116-4624 • Admissions: 617-824-8600 • Fax: 617-824-8609

CAMPUS LIFE

Quality of Life Rating	93
Fire Safety Rating	75
Green Rating	77
Type of school	private
Environment	metropolis

STUDENTS

Total undergrad enrollment	3,454
% male/female	41/59
% from out of state	82
% from public high school	70
% frosh live on campus	99
# of fraternities	4
# of sororities	3
% African American	3
% Asian	5
% Caucasian	62
% Hispanic	8
% international	3
# of countries represented	45

SURVEY SAYS . . .

Great computer facilities
Students aren't religious
Students love Boston, MA
Great off-campus food
College radio is popular
Theater is popular
Student publications are popular

ACADEMICS

Academic Rating	79
% students returning for sophomore year	88
% students graduating within 4 years	74
% students graduating within 6 years	78
Calendar	semester
Student/faculty ratio	13:1
Profs interesting rating	86
Profs accessible rating	82
Most classes have	10–19 students
Most lab/discussion sessions have	10–19 students

MOST POPULAR MAJORS

cinematography and film/video production; creative writing; theater

APPLICANTS ALSO LOOK AT AND OFTEN PREFER

New York University

AND SOMETIMES PREFER

Ithaca College, University of Southern California

AND RARELY PREFER

Syracuse University, Boston University

STUDENTS SAY ". . ."

Academics

Emerson College provides "is a microcosm of professionalism, talent, passion, and skill." "Emerson College is a place where creative individuals can flourish while studying the communication arts and sciences." Among its strengths are "one of the most well-respected theater education programs in the country" and "an *amazing* communications school." Located in Boston, the school is "extremely career-oriented," "provides worthwhile opportunities," and "allows for *lots* of extracurricular involvement." Students who embrace the "environment of motivation" will excel, while those "who are unmotivated or unsure of what they want to do have a hard time." The "faculty and staff are knowledgeable and helpful, and the entire campus is gorgeous, high-tech, modern, and very clean with the most up-to-date resources." Emerson can even be a little too high-tech for some. "Sometimes important notices from the college are tweeted as opposed to e-mailed. It gets very confusing," one student laments. "Ninety percent of the time, professors at Emerson are working professionals who are passionate and extremely knowledgeable in their fields" and "extremely accessible." "Most of [the professors] are part-time," but this can be a benefit because "they're working in their fields while teaching us. That means they're great networking connections and are always learning new things to teach us!" One thing to note: "The school does not have 'typical' college feel, so things like traditions are a lacking." "Anything is possible here, all you need is imagination and motivation," one student explains. "Most importantly, the student body is mainly comprised of driven, independent people who can be mature and professional when working but youthful and adventurous during free time."

Life

Students at Emerson "live and breathe their majors." They are "highly motivated" and know "exactly what they want and come to a school that will guide them in a direction to get exactly that." Much of student life revolves around the artistic fields that students study. "On weekends, most kids are doing projects or film shoots during the day and drinking at night." "Most students participate in clubs or activities that involve what they are studying." Some see Emerson as a "hipster nation where your level of involvement is up to you." "Athletics are not a huge thing except for the people who play them," and Emerson doesn't have much of a Greek presence. "However, during the weekends students often gather around in small, student-owned homes…and have crowded parties." "Emerson is definitely not known for its fabulous social/nightlife," and "Boston isn't as great until you're twenty-one, but there's a lot to do after—bars, clubs, concerts, theaters, etc." "There's just such an amazing energy at Emerson," one happy student says. "Everyone is busy, doing what they love, and there's all this awesome creative, passionate energy that's just bouncing around."

Student Body

"The students at Emerson are the ones who were outcasts at their high schools in some way…but that's a good thing" because "everyone is very creative [and] driven." Students here are busy bees that "just jump onto the speedway of Emerson and press the gas." Everyone "is outspoken, opinionated, passionate, and a little weird—to different degrees." "Yes, we are hipsters," one student admits, "and yes a lot of people like black-and-white movies with cigarettes in hand, but it also means that if you are a little odd, or you were picked on in high school, we're your people." "I just want to point out that Emerson is an extremely accepting school when it comes to gender identity," one student notes. "Almost any type of person can fit in here (except science buffs), because it is a very open and welcoming campus." One student does caution that "because Emerson is such a goal-specific school, you have a lot of students here who are willing to step on others to make it to the top. But you also have a good share of students who work together and build relationships and connections to help each other out." All in all, Emersonians are creative people who work together and have "so much pride in their school" and "the pride continues after graduation. The Emerson mafia is no joke!"

FINANCIAL AID: 617-824-8655 • E-MAIL: ADMISSION@EMERSON.EDU • WEBSITE: WWW.EMERSON.EDU

THE PRINCETON REVIEW SAYS

Admissions

Very important factors considered include: Academic GPA, standardized test scores. *Important factors considered include:* Class rank, application essay, recommendation(s), rigor of secondary school record, character/personal qualities, extracurricular activities, talent/ability. *Other factors considered include:* Alumni/ae relation, first generation, geographical residence, racial/ethnic status, volunteer work, work experience. SAT or ACT required; ACT with writing component required. TOEFL required of all international applicants. High school diploma is required and GED is accepted. *Academic units required:* 4 English, 3 mathematics, 3 science, 3 foreign language, 3 social studies. *Academic units recommended:* 4 English, 3 mathematics, 3 science, 3 foreign language, 3 social studies, 4 academic electives.

Financial Aid

Students should submit: FAFSA, CSS/Financial Aid PROFILE, noncustodial PROFILE, business/farm supplement, tax returns. The Princeton Review suggests that all financial aid forms be submitted as soon as possible after January 1. *Need-based scholarships/grants offered:* Federal Pell, SEOG, state scholarships/grants, private scholarships, the school's own gift aid. *Loan aid offered:* Direct Subsidized Stafford, Direct Unsubsidized Stafford, Direct PLUS, Federal Perkins, state loans. Applicants will be notified of awards on or about April 1. Federal Work-Study Program available. Institutional employment available. Highest amount earned per year from on-campus jobs $2,400. Off-campus job opportunities are excellent.

The Inside Word

Located in the Boston Theatre District, Emerson is one of the premier colleges for students interesting in theater and other artistic fields. That's not to say it's not a high-quality university in other fields as well; Emerson offers hands-on work in creative industries as well as a vibrant and motivated community.

THE SCHOOL SAYS ". . ."

From the Admissions Office

"Founded in 1880, Emerson is one of the premier colleges in the country for communication and the arts. Students may choose from more than two-dozen undergraduate and graduate programs supported by state-of-the-art facilities and a nationally renowned faculty. The campus is home to WERS-FM, the oldest noncommercial radio station in Boston; the historic 1,200-seat Cutler Majestic Theatre; and *Ploughshares*, the award winning literary journal for new writing.

"Located on Boston Common in the heart of the city's Theatre District, the campus is walking distance from the Massachusetts State House, Chinatown, and historic Freedom Trail. More than half the students reside on-campus, some in special learning communities such as the Writers' Block and Digital Culture Floor. There is also a fitness center, athletic field, and new gymnasium and campus center.

"Emerson has nearly eighty student organizations and performance groups as well as fifteen NCAA teams, student publications, and honor societies. The College also sponsors programs in Los Angeles and Washington, D.C.; study abroad in the Netherlands, Taiwan, and Czech Republic; and course cross-registration with the six-member Boston ProArts Consortium.

"Students have access to outstanding facilities, including sound treated television studios, digital editing and audio post-production suites. An eleven-story performance and production center houses a theater design/technology center, makeup lab, and costume shop. There are seven programs to observe speech and hearing therapy, a professional marketing focus group room, and digital newsroom, and new performance development center with a sound stage, scene shop, black box, and film screening room."

SELECTIVITY	
Admissions Rating	**94**
# of applicants	6,943
% of applicants accepted	42
% of acceptees attending	26
# accepting a place on wait list	2,089
# admitted from wait list	104

FRESHMAN PROFILE	
Range SAT Critical Reading	570–670
Range SAT Math	540–640
Range SAT Writing	580–670
Range ACT Composite	24–29
Minimum paper TOEFL	550
Minimum web-based TOEFL	80
Average HS GPA	3.6
% graduated top 10% of class	42
% graduated top 25% of class	77
% graduated top 50% of class	98

DEADLINES	
Early action	
Deadline	11/1
Notification	12/15
Regular	
Deadline	1/15
Notification	4/1
Nonfall registration?	yes

FINANCIAL FACTS	
Financial Aid Rating	**83**
Annual tuition	$33,568
Room and board	$12,958
Required fees	$532
Books and supplies	$800
% needy frosh rec. need-based scholarship or grant aid	84
% needy UG rec. need-based scholarship or grant aid	79
% needy frosh rec. non-need-based scholarship or grant aid	4
% needy UG rec. non-need-based scholarship or grant aid	3
% needy frosh rec. need-based self-help aid	84
% needy UG rec. need-based self-help aid	94
% frosh rec. any financial aid	63
% UG rec. any financial aid	61
% UG borrow to pay for school	59
Average cumulative indebtedness	$15,262
% frosh need fully met	55
% ugrads need fully met	56
Average % of frosh need met	89
Average % of ugrad need met	90

EMORY UNIVERSITY

EMORY UNIVERSITY, BOISEUILLET JONES CENTER, ATLANTA, GA 30322 • ADMISSIONS: 404-727-6036 • FAX: 404-727-4303

CAMPUS LIFE

Quality of Life Rating	**98**
Fire Safety Rating	**70**
Green Rating	**96**
Type of school	private
Affiliation	Methodist
Environment	town

STUDENTS

Total undergrad enrollment	7,337
% male/female	45/55
% from out of state	75
% from public high school	62
% frosh live on campus	70
# of fraternities	14
# of sororities	12
% African American	10
% Asian	24
% Caucasian	42
% Hispanic	5
% international	11
# of countries represented	66

SURVEY SAYS . . .

Lab facilities are great
Great computer facilities
Great library
Students love Atlanta, GA
Great off-campus food
Campus feels safe
Student publications are popular
Students are environmentally aware

ACADEMICS

Academic Rating	**92**
% students returning for sophomore year	96
% students graduating within 4 years	83
% students graduating within 6 years	90
Calendar	semester
Student/faculty ratio	7:1
Profs interesting rating	89
Profs accessible rating	86
Most classes have	10–19 students
Most lab/discussion sessions have	10–19 students

MOST POPULAR MAJORS

business/commerce; economics; political science

APPLICANTS ALSO LOOK AT AND OFTEN PREFER

Washington University in St. Louis, Duke University, The University of North Carolina at Chapel Hill, Georgia Institute of Technology, Vanderbilt University

AND SOMETIMES PREFER

Dartmouth College, Wake Forest University, Amherst College, Boston University, Davidson College

AND RARELY PREFER

Drexel University, DePauw University, Providence College

STUDENTS SAY ". . ."

Academics

As one of the South's premier universities, Emory University provides students with "a rigorous academic environment [where students] are provided with the necessary skills to be successful." Emphasis on a liberal arts education coupled with a "plethora of opportunities including location in Atlanta, proximity to graduate programs, and many ethically engaged programs" make this university a reputed destination for students who are "proactive" and "very involved high achievers." For the many who are interested in "some sort of pre-professional path," Emory has an "excellent science program (for premed or research interests)" and "one of the top undergraduate business programs in the country." Students note, however, that there is no engineering school. "Access to resources such as internships, research, volunteering, [and] alumni relations" is one of Emory's greatest assets, second only to its "excellent and engaged" faculty. Professors are "knowledgeable and relevant to their fields," and as one sophomore put it, "After two years, there has only been one class that I did not feel was worth my time." Emory is seen as "a school where academic inquiry thrives" and where "academically curious students [are encouraged] to go out into the community and serve others." While "it's a hefty price for education," the financial aid department, which sometimes "lacks efficiency," compensates with scholarships and "comprehensive financial aid" packages.

Life

Emory strikes "the perfect balance between social and academic life" where students "work and play hard but are committed to whatever they are part of." "There is a lot of support from upperclassmen and residence life...to guide underclassmen to activities that fit them," and people tend to participate in "activities that are sponsored by university organizations," such as student concerts, movies on campus, and intramurals. Describing university culture as "social but also academically competitive," students are "always in the library" during the week, and on weekends they take advantage of the scarce free time and opportunities for fun. As one student says, "The fraternities are a popular destination for underclassmen, especially freshman…there is definitely a population of non-drinkers and party animals." With the school's "beautiful campus," there are "many great outdoor areas to go relax…The gym, the WoodPec, is…conveniently located right in the center of campus, so people go there often to rock-climb together, play sports such as tennis, badminton or racquetball together." Of course, if you've exhausted activities on campus, students have access to the "so many things to do in Atlanta, which makes it a great city in which to attend college." One student also makes note of "Emory's talent for pulling in famous speakers in such a way that students get to really interact with them…my friend spent his twentieth birthday having dinner with Salman Rushdie at his house."

Student Body

"Community" is the word that undergrads use to describe the student body at Emory University. Due to the fact that the typical student is "very involved," "driven and motivated," and committed to "mutual learning," "you interact with different people in the different organizations you are a part of, [and] there are several students who are a part of a cultural, religious or ethnic clubs different from their own cultural, religious, or ethnic backgrounds." Students cite "diversity in terms of race, religion, and socioeconomic conditions" as a great asset, although some students also feel that Emory attracts "wealthy, white, prep-school kids" from cities "up north like Chicago, Boston, or NYC." Due to an "alternative school spirit" rooted less in sports and more in the fact that "students are very proud to go to Emory," students here are "friendly and engaged," and the "overly competitive and ambitious are few in number."

FINANCIAL AID: 404-727-6039 • E-MAIL: ADMISS@EMORY.EDU • WEBSITE: WWW.EMORY.EDU

THE PRINCETON REVIEW SAYS

Admissions

Very important factors considered include: Application essay, academic GPA, recommendation(s), rigor of secondary school record, standardized test scores, character/personal qualities, extracurricular activities, talent/ability. *Important factors considered include:* Alumni/ae relation, geographical residence, level of applicant's interest, racial/ethnic status, first generation, volunteer work, work experience. *Other factors considered include:* Class rank, interview. SAT or ACT required; ACT with writing component required. TOEFL required of all international applicants. High school diploma is required and GED is not accepted. *Academic units recommended:* 4 English, 3 mathematics, 2 science (2 science labs), 2 foreign language, 2 social studies, 2 history, 1 visual/performing arts, 2 academic electives.

Financial Aid

Students should submit: FAFSA, CSS/Financial Aid PROFILE, noncustodial PROFILE. Regular filing deadline is March 1. The Princeton Review suggests that all financial aid forms be submitted as soon as possible after January 1. *Need-based scholarships/grants offered:* Federal Pell, SEOG, state scholarships/grants, private scholarships, the school's own gift aid. *Loan aid offered:* Direct Subsidized Stafford, Direct Unsubsidized Stafford, Direct PLUS, Federal Perkins, Federal Nursing, state loans, college/university loans from institutional funds. Applicants will be notified of awards on or about April 1.

The Inside Word

Over the past few years, early decision applicants to Emory have risen drastically, creating a quandary for aspiring Emory students: Do they join the growing early applicant crowd, which presumably increases the likelihood of admission, or do they take their chances with regular admission? "The good news?" Emory financial aid has traditionally met 100 percent of applicants' demonstrated need.

THE SCHOOL SAYS ". . ."

From the Admissions Office

"Emory is an inquiry-driven, ethically engaged, and diverse community whose members work collaboratively for positive transformation in the world through courageous leadership in teaching, research scholarship, health care, and social action. The university is internationally recognized for its outstanding liberal arts colleges, superb professional schools, and leading health care system. Emory is noted as one of the most diverse selective universities in the country.

"Emory offers a distinctive undergraduate experience with programs in the humanities, sciences, business, and nursing allowing students to explore their interests and talents in the classroom and in the field. Entering freshman may apply to Emory College, a four-year liberal arts education within the heart of a major research university. Students may also apply to Oxford College where student spend the first two years on Emory's original campus thirty-eight miles east of Atlanta. Emory provides a rich setting for learning from excellent teaching in small classes to lectures from prominent scholars to opportunities for study abroad, research, and internships.

"Emory students balance hard work with having fun. With seventy percent of students living on campus, the community is enhanced by a close-knit living environment. The campus life thrives on constant activity, and students are encouraged to get involved, share opinions, and flourish. Emory is a dynamic place that is constantly in a state of sustainable growth and improvement. Take a look at all Emory has to offer—you'll see why Emory students feel inspired to do more with what they learn here."

SELECTIVITY

Admissions Rating	**98**
# of applicants	17,027
% of applicants accepted	27
% of acceptees attending	30
# accepting a place on wait list	2,960
# admitted from wait list	133
# of early decision applicants	1,404
# accepted early decision	574

FRESHMAN PROFILE

Range SAT Critical Reading	650–740
Range SAT Math	670–770
Range SAT Writing	660–750
Range ACT Composite	30–33
Minimum web-based TOEFL	100
Average HS GPA	3.9
% graduated top 10% of class	87
% graduated top 25% of class	98
% graduated top 50% of class	100

DEADLINES

Early decision	
Deadline	11/1
Notification	12/15
Regular	
Deadline	1/15
Notification	4/1
Nonfall registration?	no

FINANCIAL FACTS

Financial Aid Rating	**94**
Annual tuition	$40,600
Room and board	$11,628
Required fees	$564
Books and supplies	$1,100
% needy frosh rec. need-based scholarship or grant aid	94
% needy UG rec. need-based scholarship or grant aid	96
% needy frosh rec. non-need-based scholarship or grant aid	13
% needy UG rec. non-need-based scholarship or grant aid	14
% needy frosh rec. need-based self-help aid	90
% needy UG rec. need-based self-help aid	91
% frosh rec. any financial aid	52
% UG rec. any financial aid	55
% UG borrow to pay for school	42
Average cumulative indebtedness	$28,076
% frosh need fully met	100
% ugrads need fully met	100
Average % of frosh need met	100
Average % of ugrad need met	100

EUGENE LANG COLLEGE THE NEW SCHOOL FOR LIBERAL ARTS

72 FIFTH AVENUE, NEW YORK, NY 10011 • ADMISSIONS: 212-229-5150 • FAX: 212-229-5355

CAMPUS LIFE

Quality of Life Rating	**65**
Fire Safety Rating	**76**
Green Rating	**91**
Type of school	private
Environment	metropolis

STUDENTS

Total undergrad enrollment	1,472
% male/female	33/67
% from out of state	78
% frosh live on campus	78
% African American	5
% Asian	6
% Caucasian	57
% Hispanic	11
% international	6
# of countries represented	38

SURVEY SAYS . . .

Class discussions encouraged
Athletic facilities need improving
Students aren't religious
Students love New York, NY
Great off-campus food
Intercollegiate sports are unpopular or nonexistent
Intramural sports are unpopular or nonexistent
Frats and sororities are unpopular or nonexistent

ACADEMICS

Academic Rating	**80**
% students returning for sophomore year	73
% students graduating within 4 years	37
Calendar	semester
Student/faculty ratio	15:1
Profs interesting rating	76
Profs accessible rating	73
Most classes have	10–19 students
Most lab/discussion sessions have	10–19 students

APPLICANTS ALSO LOOK AT AND OFTEN PREFER
Sarah Lawrence College, Bard College, New York University

AND SOMETIMES PREFER
Reed College, Hampshire College

AND RARELY PREFER
Bennington College, St. John's College (MD)

STUDENTS SAY ". . ."

Academics

Eugene Lang College is an "unconventional," highly urban school with few academic requirements where courses have "really long poetic titles" and professors "go by their first names." "Lang is about small classes in a big city," summarizes a writing major. There's a "rich intellectual tradition" and, no matter what your major, an "interdisciplinary curriculum." "At Eugene Lang, you have the freedom to pursue your artistic or intellectual direction with absolute freedom," says a philosophy major. However, "students who are uncomfortable in a city and who are not excited about learning for learning's sake should not come to this school." Lang's "clueless," "incredibly bureaucratic" administration is hugely unpopular. The "approachable" and monolithically "radical" faculty is a mixed bag. "Seventy-five percent of the professors are pure gold, but the twenty-five percent who are not really are awful." "Lang's greatest strength (other than location) is its seminar style of teaching," explains a first-year student. "I've yet to be in a class with more then fifteen people." Students say their class discussions are phenomenal. "The students, however, at times can be somewhat draining." "All the teachers are highly susceptible to being led off on long tangents" and some "are too gentle and not comfortable shutting down wandering or irrelevant conversation." Juniors and seniors can take classes at several schools within the larger university (including Parsons The New School for Design and Mannes College The New School for Music). "So if Lang's ultra-liberal, writing-intensive seminars are too much," notes an urban studies major, "you can always take a break." Internships all over Manhattan are common, too.

Life

There are "great talks given on campus every week by a wide variety of academics on almost every social issue imaginable." Otherwise, "Lang is the anti-college experience." "There is very little community" on this speck of a campus on the northern end of Greenwich Village. "Space and facilities are limited." "There is no safe haven in the form of a communal student space" except for "a courtyard of a million cigarette butts." Certainly, "you aren't going to have the traditional college fun" here. On the other hand, few students anywhere else enjoy this glorious level of independence. "Life at Eugene Lang is integrated completely with living in New York City," and "you have the entire city at your fingertips." When you walk out of class, "you walk out into a city of nine million people." There are dorms here, but "most students have apartments," especially after freshman year. For fun, Lang students sometimes "hang around other students' apartments and smoke pot." Many "thoroughly enjoy the club scene." Mostly though, "people band into small groups and then go out adventuring in the city" where "there is always something to do that you've never done, or even heard of, before."

Student Body

"Lang offers the kids with dreadlocks and piercings an alternative place to gather, smoke, and write pretentious essays." It's "overrun with rabid hipsters." "Cool hair" and "avant-garde" attitudes proliferate. So do "tight pants." "Every student at Lang thinks they are an atypical student." "There is a running joke that all Lang students were 'that kid' in high school," says a senior. "Shock is very popular around here," and "everyone fits in as long as they are not too mainstream." "It's the normal ones who have the trouble," suggests a sophomore. "But once they take up smoking and embrace their inner hipster, everything's cool." "There are a lot of queer students, who seem to be comfortable." "We're really not all that ethnically diverse," admits a first-year student. There are "less affluent kids due to great financial aid," and there is a strong contingent of "trust-fund babies" and "over-privileged communists from Connecticut." "Most students are wealthy but won't admit it," says a senior. "To be from a rich family and have it be apparent is a cardinal sin." "Most students are extremely liberal and on the same wavelength politically." "Conservative kids are the freaks at our school. Left is in. But having a Republican in class is so exciting," suggest a senior. "We can finally have a debate."

EUGENE LANG COLLEGE THE NEW SCHOOL FOR LIBERAL ARTS

FINANCIAL AID: 212-229-8930 • E-MAIL: LANG@NEWSCHOOL.EDU • WEBSITE: WWW.LANG.EDU

THE PRINCETON REVIEW SAYS

Admissions

Very important factors considered include: Application essay, academic GPA, recommendation(s), rigor of secondary school record. *Important factors considered include:* Standardized test scores, character/personal qualities, interview, level of applicant's interest, volunteer work. *Other factors considered include:* Class rank, alumni/ae relation, extracurricular activities, first generation, geographical residence, talent/ability, work experience. ACT with or without writing component accepted. TOEFL required of all international applicants. High school diploma is required and GED is accepted. *Academic units required:* 4 English. *Academic units recommended:* 3 mathematics, 3 science, 2 foreign language, 3 social studies, 2 history.

Financial Aid

Students should submit: FAFSA, state aid form. The Princeton Review suggests that all financial aid forms be submitted as soon as possible after January 1. *Need-based scholarships/grants offered:* Federal Pell, SEOG, state scholarships/grants, private scholarships, the school's own gift aid. *Loan aid offered:* Direct Subsidized Stafford, Direct Unsubsidized Stafford, Direct PLUS, Federal Perkins. Applicants will be notified of awards on a rolling basis beginning March 1. Federal Work-Study Program available. Institutional employment available. Off-campus job opportunities are excellent.

The Inside Word

The college draws a very self-selected and intellectually curious pool. Those who demonstrate little self-motivation will find themselves denied.

THE SCHOOL SAYS ". . ."

From the Admissions Office

"Eugene Lang College offers students of diverse backgrounds an innovative and creative approach to a liberal arts education, combining the stimulating classroom activity of a small, intimate college with the rich resources of a dynamic, urban university—The New School. The curriculum at Lang is challenging and flexible. Small classes, limited in size to eighteen students, promote energetic and thoughtful discussions, and writing is an essential component of all classes. Students can earn a bachelor's degree in Liberal Arts by designing their own program of study within one of fourteen interdisciplinary areas in the arts, social sciences, and humanities. Lang also offers bachelor's degrees in the Arts, Culture and Media, Economics, Education Studies, Environmental Studies, Global Studies, History, Interdisciplinary Studies, Literary Studies, Philosophy, Psychology, Politics, and Urban Studies. Students have the opportunity to pursue a five-year BA/BFA or BA/MA with other programs offered at the university. Lang's Greenwich Village location puts many of the city's cultural treasures—museums, libraries, music venues, theaters, and more—at your doorstep."

SELECTIVITY	
Admissions Rating	**82**
# of applicants	1,900
% of applicants accepted	71
% of acceptees attending	28
# accepting a place on wait list	55

FRESHMAN PROFILE	
Range SAT Critical Reading	540–660
Range SAT Math	490–605
Range SAT Writing	540–660
Range ACT Composite	24–28
Minimum paper TOEFL	600
Minimum web-based TOEFL	100
Average HS GPA	3.4
% graduated top 10% of class	29
% graduated top 25% of class	57
% graduated top 50% of class	90

DEADLINES	
Early decision	
Deadline	11/1
Notification	12/1
Regular	
Deadline	1/6
Notification	4/1
Nonfall registration?	yes

FINANCIAL FACTS	
Financial Aid Rating	**67**
Annual tuition	$37,717
Room and board	$15,260
Required fees	$840
Books and supplies	$920
% needy frosh rec. need-based scholarship or grant aid	94
% needy UG rec. need-based scholarship or grant aid	90
% needy frosh rec. non-need-based scholarship or grant aid	13
% needy UG rec. non-need-based scholarship or grant aid	6
% needy frosh rec. need-based self-help aid	80
% needy UG rec. need-based self-help aid	73
% frosh rec. any financial aid	
% UG rec. any financial aid	
% UG borrow to pay for school	65
Average cumulative indebtedness	$28,550
% frosh need fully met	45
% ugrads need fully met	8
Average % of frosh need met	62
Average % of ugrad need met	69

THE EVERGREEN STATE COLLEGE

2700 EVERGREEN PARKWAY, NORTHWEST, OLYMPIA, WA 98505 • ADMISSIONS: 360-867-6170 • FAX: 360-867-5114

CAMPUS LIFE

Quality of Life Rating	**76**
Fire Safety Rating	**81**
Green Rating	**90**
Type of school	public
Environment	city

STUDENTS

Total undergrad enrollment	4,371
% male/female	46/54
% from out of state	47
% frosh live on campus	78
% African American	5
% Asian	2
% Caucasian	68
% Hispanic	6
% Native American	2
% international	1
# of countries represented	21

SURVEY SAYS . . .

Lots of liberal students
Students aren't religious
Low cost of living
Frats and sororities are unpopular or nonexistent
Political activism is popular
Students are environmentally aware

ACADEMICS

Academic Rating	**76**
% students returning for sophomore year	71
% students graduating within 4 years	41
Calendar	quarter
Student/faculty ratio	23:1
Profs interesting rating	90
Profs accessible rating	77
Most classes have	20–29 students

MOST POPULAR MAJORS

environmental studies; liberal arts and sciences/liberal studies; social sciences, other

APPLICANTS ALSO LOOK AT AND OFTEN PREFER

University of Washington, University of Oregon

AND SOMETIMES PREFER

University of California—Santa Cruz, Hampshire College, Seattle University

AND RARELY PREFER

Warren Wilson College, Lewis & Clark College

STUDENTS SAY ". . ."

Academics

"Keeping education in its purest form alive and well in the heart of the Northwest," The Evergreen State College offers "a unique approach" to academics. The school provides an "interactive environment—with a diverse, enriching learning method," which allows students "to focus on your passions and explore them in detail." Everyone creates their own educational paths and directs the pace of their own learning. As a few students say admiringly, "I feel a sense of freedom with the academics at Evergreen." "I have more power as a student." Greatly appreciated is the flexibility found within the curriculum. "I was excited about building my own major." "No self-motivated student will leave Evergreen unsatisfied." Students work collaboratively here and support one another in their endeavors. "It's not about grades or competition; it's about self-improvement and personal fulfillment." Evaluations are used to view student progress, with "interdisciplinary education over declared majors" being the focus. "Your classes are all interconnected, so it's easy to link what you're doing into a defined path." "My transcript says more about me than A's, B's, and C's possibly could." "The philosophy…definitely lowers the stress I experience around academics." Professors assist students in innumerable ways and are "very intimately involved in the educations of their students." "At Evergreen, in order to have a great experience you need to be able to talk to your professors and engage with them." "I have not met a professor yet who was not willing to rework their mode of teaching to better serve the class." The educational atmosphere is highly interactive. Most every student "actively engages the material with field work, undergraduate research, and extended trips." "Class time is spent doing workshops, seminars, or a led discussion where everyone participates." "Even the science programs involve large portions of discussion and peer collaboration." As one undergraduate describes slyly, "My professors have been A++, if Evergreen assigned grades."

Life

Evergreen has a "booming extracurricular life"; students enjoy the "thriving local art and music scene, very hip and fresh," as well as Olympia and Seattle both being nearby. "The Flaming Eggplant, the student-run cafe, is simply the cheapest and most delicious place on the planet," as well as a very popular hangout. The Student Activities office has no shortage of options for undergraduates here, with "more than fifty different clubs and student groups." Physical activity is prevalent, and the recreational center has racquetball, a pool, a rock-climbing wall, and various places to exercise. There is "no shortage of local hiking, backpacking, and biking opportunities." "Hikes in the woods, down to the beach, or up to the bluff are very common as well as late-night stargazing." The physical surroundings are viewed with much admiration at Evergreen. "Our campus is set back in this magical forest with these winding paths down to the beach. There are tree forts, giant sculptures, dream catchers in the trees, hidden drum circles, and music everywhere." As one student describes fondly, "To me, it is reminiscent of Thoreau's solitude in nature."

Student Life

The "kindness and awareness of the community" is frequently said by students to be one of the most valued aspects of their experience here. "Articulate" and "inquisitive" undergraduates are evident in large numbers. "Students tend to be very politically aware and active with very liberal points of view" and are "mostly peaceful relaxed people" amidst an "open-minded social environment." The dorms are divided into different themes, and "The residential staff is professional and keeps the housing community functioning and safe." "The campus police are pretty awesome people," as well. Evergreen is respected by students throughout the college for its "forward-thinking" administration and faculty, with a "dedication to sustainability" being clearly evident around the campus.

FINANCIAL AID: 360-867-6205 • E-MAIL: ADMISSIONS@EVERGREEN.EDU • WEBSITE: WWW.EVERGREEN.EDU

THE PRINCETON REVIEW SAYS

Admissions

Very important factors considered include: Application essay, academic GPA, rigor of secondary school record. *Important factors considered include:* Standardized test scores, first generation, level of applicant's interest. *Other factors considered include:* recommendation(s), extracurricular activities, interview, volunteer work, work experience. SAT or ACT required; ACT with or without writing component accepted. TOEFL required of all international applicants. High school diploma is required and GED is accepted. *Academic units required:* 4 English, 3 mathematics, 2 science (1 science lab), 2 foreign language, 3 social studies, 1 academic electives, 1 fine, visual, or performing arts elective or other college prep elective from the listed areas.

Financial Aid

Students should submit: FAFSA, institution's own financial aid form. Regular filing deadline is March 1. The Princeton Review suggests that all financial aid forms be submitted as soon as possible after January 1. *Need-based scholarships/grants offered:* Federal Pell, SEOG, state scholarships/grants, private scholarships, the school's own gift aid, Federal Academic Competitiveness Grant (ACG); National Science and Mathematics Access to Retain Talent Grant (SMART Grant). *Loan aid offered:* Direct Subsidized Stafford, Direct Unsubsidized Stafford, Direct PLUS, Federal Perkins, private alternative loans. Applicants will be notified of awards on a rolling basis beginning April 1. Federal Work-Study Program available. Institutional employment available. Highest amount earned per year from on-campus jobs $9,975. Off-campus job opportunities are good.

The Inside Word

Students at Evergreen are commonly some of the strongest performers from their high schools, although the admissions department considers a variety of traits from applicants (including strength of character) when considering prospective undergraduates. The school's unique and self-directed academic curriculum favors those students who can adequately handle the responsibility of creating and developing their own educational path.

THE SCHOOL SAYS ". . ."

From the Admissions Office

"Evergreen, a public college of arts and sciences, is a national leader in developing full-time interdisciplinary studies programs. Students work closely with faculty to study an issue or theme from the perspective of several academic disciplines. They apply what's learned to real world issues, complete projects in groups, and discuss concepts in seminars that typically involve a faculty member and twenty-three students. The emphasis on seminars, interdisciplinary problem solving, and collaboration means students are well prepared for graduate school and the world of work. Our students tend to be politically active, environmentally savvy, and more concerned about social justice than competition and personal gain.

"All applicants are encouraged to complete a Free Application for Federal Student Aid (FAFSA). Evergreen's priority financial aid deadline is March 1, though applicants may submit the form later and may be awarded aid if funds are still available.

"Freshman applicants are required to submit test scores from either the SAT or ACT tests. The student's best composite score will be used in the admissions process."

SELECTIVITY

Admissions Rating	**69**
# of applicants	1,725
% of applicants accepted	96
% of acceptees attending	33

FRESHMAN PROFILE

Range SAT Critical Reading	510–640
Range SAT Math	460–580
Range SAT Writing	470–610
Range ACT Composite	21–26
Minimum paper TOEFL	550
Minimum web-based TOEFL	79
Average HS GPA	3.1
% graduated top 10% of class	11
% graduated top 25% of class	28
% graduated top 50% of class	65

DEADLINES

Regular	
Priority	2/1
Nonfall registration?	yes

FINANCIAL FACTS

Financial Aid Rating	**69**
Annual in-state tuition	$6,909
Annual out-state tuition	$18,090
Room and board	$9,000
Required fees	$577
Books and supplies	$972
% needy frosh rec. need-based scholarship or grant aid	67
% needy UG rec. need-based scholarship or grant aid	78
% needy frosh rec. non-need-based scholarship or grant aid	61
% needy UG rec. non-need-based scholarship or grant aid	18
% needy frosh rec. need-based self-help aid	65
% needy UG rec. need-based self-help aid	74
% frosh rec. any financial aid	58
% UG rec. any financial aid	61
% UG borrow to pay for school	48
Average cumulative indebtedness	$17,545
% frosh need fully met	14
% ugrads need fully met	11
Average % of frosh need met	75
Average % of ugrad need met	70

FAIRFIELD UNIVERSITY

1073 North Benson Road, Fairfield, CT 06824-5195 • Admissions: 203-254-4100 • Fax: 203-254-4199

CAMPUS LIFE

Quality of Life Rating	81
Fire Safety Rating	91
Green Rating	79
Type of school	private
Affiliation	Roman Catholic-Jesuit
Environment	town

STUDENTS

Total undergrad enrollment	3,385
% male/female	42/58
% from out of state	70
% from public high school	55
% frosh live on campus	96
% African American	3
% Asian	1
% Caucasian	43
% Hispanic	3
% international	2
# of countries represented	22

SURVEY SAYS . . .

Great library
Diversity lacking on campus
Great off-campus food
Frats and sororities are unpopular or nonexistent
Student publications are popular
Lots of beer drinking
Hard liquor is popular

ACADEMICS

Academic Rating	82
% students returning for sophomore year	88
% students graduating within 4 years	78
Calendar	semester
Student/faculty ratio	13:1
Profs interesting rating	81
Profs accessible rating	84
Most classes have	20–29 students

MOST POPULAR MAJORS

finance; nursing/registered nurse (rn, asn, bsn, msn); psychology

APPLICANTS ALSO LOOK AT AND OFTEN PREFER

Boston College

AND SOMETIMES PREFER

College of the Holy Cross, Villanova University, Boston University

STUDENTS SAY ". . ."

Academics

Fairfield University, founded in 1942, is "a promising young institution short on tradition and diversity, but big on community, cross-disciplinary academics" and "educating the whole person: body, mind, and spirit." This Jesuit institution is based in "an amazing little New England town an hour outside of New York City." "It was everything I wanted in my school," a happy biology student testifies. "Small class size, beautiful campus, approachable professors—it's perfect." The school has a strong "commitment to the Jesuit values," a "friendly atmosphere," and a small size that means you'll "see so many familiar faces every day." Fairfield works hard to prepare "its students for life after college with the tools inherent in a Jesuit education." Students found the professors to be "amazingly engaging and knowledgeable." They're "experienced veterans in their fields of study" who have "actual industry, practical, real-world experience. This gives the students real insight into what a career actually is." Thanks to the small size, professors are "very accessible and tend to truly care about their students." One religious studies student sums up the Fairfield experience as being "about community—between the encouragement to get involved, living and learning communities, and its dedication to service, Fairfield is about forming and improving its own community and the greater community around it."

Life

Although some students can "get stuck in the 'Fairfield bubble,'" New Haven and "New York City [are] not that far away," and "it's easy to get on the train and go to the city if you want real fun." On campus, "students attend parties on the weekends, concerts on campus, or local concerts." The convenient location "enables students to visit other schools as well." "Townhouse parties are the biggest things for the weekend," and going to the "beach is always fun once the weather gets warmer in the spring." "FUSA (Fairfield University Student Association) plans activities for every night of the week (games, speakers, late night food, etc.)." "The extracurricular activities the school provides for its students are really a great diversion from school work when you've had a stressful day!" If there's one downside to campus life, it seems to be "the food in the cafeteria," which was frequently derided, as well as the definite "lack of school spirit." Although one student proclaimed: "We learn and live together; we are Stags!" "Overall, it's a laid-back school with nightlife, and I like it that way, nothing really wild."

Student Body

Fairfield students are typically "white, middle- or upper-class students," who are "usually devoted to studies as well as serving the community and others." However, many students feel the school "should improve in recruiting a more diverse student body." "Perhaps the downfall of Fairfield is that the student population seems pretty homogeneous," one student explains. "White and wealthy would be a fitting description for most. However, diversity is an initiative the university is working on." In particular, "socioeconomic differences are very clearly defined." "Although it is not very diverse, most students are open to people of different backgrounds, and joining clubs or other teams is an easy way to make friends and fit in." One student points out that, while the school isn't racially diverse, that doesn't mean the school isn't accepting: "Being a minority here, I think the openness to minorities is undervalued. Everyone here is accepting, and though there are some things that could be improved upon, it is a very good school to belong." As for fashion, Fairfield "has the 'J. Crew U.' reputation" for a reason. "The typical student owns a Northface, was really good at some sport back in high school, owns some articles of Polo, is moderately attractive, and enjoys a weekend of partying." However, while "everyone always looks put together…no one is going over the top—we do have to go to class."

FINANCIAL AID: 203-254-4125 • E-MAIL: ADMIS@FAIRFIELD.EDU • WEBSITE: WWW.FAIRFIELD.EDU

THE PRINCETON REVIEW SAYS

Admissions

Very important factors considered include: Application essay, academic GPA, recommendation(s), rigor of secondary school record. *Important factors considered include:* Character/personal qualities, extracurricular activities, first generation, interview, talent/ability, volunteer work, work experience. *Other factors considered include:* Class rank, standardized test scores, alumni/ae relation, geographical residence, racial/ethnic status. ACT with or without writing component accepted. TOEFL required of all international applicants. High school diploma is required and GED is not accepted. *Academic units required:* 4 English, 3 mathematics, 2 science (2 science labs), 2 foreign language, 2 social studies, 2 history, 1 academic elective. *Academic units recommended:* 4 English, 4 mathematics, 3 science (2 science labs), 4 foreign language, 2 social studies, 2 history, 1 academic elective.

Financial Aid

Students should submit: FAFSA, CSS/Financial Aid PROFILE, noncustodial PROFILE, business/farm supplement. Regular filing deadline is February 15. The Princeton Review suggests that all financial aid forms be submitted as soon as possible after January 1. *Need-based scholarships/grants offered:* Federal Pell, SEOG, state scholarships/grants, private scholarships, the school's own gift aid, Federal Nursing Scholarships. *Loan aid offered:* Direct Subsidized Stafford, Direct Unsubsidized Stafford, Direct PLUS, Federal Perkins, Federal Nursing, alternative loans. Applicants will be notified of awards on or about April 1. Federal Work-Study Program available. Institutional employment available. Highest amount earned per year from on-campus jobs $1,500. Off-campus job opportunities are good.

The Inside Word

Steady increases in the number of admission applications have nicely increased selectivity in recent years. Fairfield's campus and central location, combined with improvements to the library, campus center, classrooms, athletic facilities, and campus residencies, make this a campus worth seeing.

THE SCHOOL SAYS ". . ."

From the Admissions Office

"Fairfield University welcomes students of unique promise into a learning and living community that will give them a solid intellectual foundation and the confidence they need to reach their individual goals. Students at Fairfield benefit from the deep-rooted Jesuit commitment to education of the whole person—mind, body, and spirit, and our admission policies are consistent with that mission. When considering an applicant, Fairfield looks at measures of academic achievement, students' curricular and extracurricular activities, their life skills and accomplishments, and the degree to which they have an appreciation for Fairfield's mission and outlook. In keeping with its holistic review process, Fairfield is test optional for undergraduate students seeking admission for the fall of 2010 and beyond. Students who decide not to submit SAT or ACT scores will be required to write an additional essay and are encouraged to participate in an admission interview.

"Fairfield University students are challenged to be creative and active members of a community in which diversity is encouraged and honored. With its commitment to education for an inspired life, Fairfield has developed a unique educational model to ensure that students receive the guidance they need to reach their fullest potential. The integration of living and learning is at the heart of a Fairfield education through students' participation in living and learning communities, vocational exploration, civic engagement, and finally, discernment of how they want to put their gifts and education to work in the world. As a result of this holistic model of education, Fairfield graduates are highly successful in gaining admission to selective graduate schools, while others achieve satisfying careers. A signification achievement for the university is that fifty-five Fairfield graduates have been tapped as Fulbright scholars since 1993."

SELECTIVITY	
Admissions Rating	85
# of applicants	8,486
% of applicants accepted	69
% of acceptees attending	15
# accepting a place on wait list	1,434
# admitted from wait list	60

FRESHMAN PROFILE	
Range SAT Critical Reading	530–620
Range SAT Math	540–630
Range SAT Writing	540–630
Range ACT Composite	24–27
Minimum paper TOEFL	550
Minimum web-based TOEFL	86
Average HS GPA	3.4
% graduated top 10% of class	28
% graduated top 25% of class	69
% graduated top 50% of class	94

DEADLINES	
Early decision	
Deadline	1/1
Notification	2/1
Early action	
Deadline	11/1
Notification	1/1
Regular	
Deadline	1/15
Nonfall registration?	no

FINANCIAL FACTS	
Financial Aid Rating	77
Annual tuition	$41,090
Room and board	$12,550
Required fees	$600
Books and supplies	$1,100
% needy frosh rec. need-based scholarship or grant aid	80
% needy UG rec. need-based scholarship or grant aid	83
% needy frosh rec. non-need-based scholarship or grant aid	62
% needy UG rec. non-need-based scholarship or grant aid	41
% needy frosh rec. need-based self-help aid	77
% needy UG rec. need-based self-help aid	83
% frosh rec. any financial aid	91
% UG rec. any financial aid	79
% UG borrow to pay for school	63
Average cumulative indebtedness	$31,099
% frosh need fully met	18
% ugrads need fully met	17
Average % of frosh need met	82
Average % of ugrad need met	82

FLAGLER COLLEGE

74 KING STREET, ST. AUGUSTINE, FL 32085-1027 • ADMISSIONS: 800-304-4208 • FAX: 904-826-0094

CAMPUS LIFE

Quality of Life Rating	**80**
Fire Safety Rating	**83**
Green Rating	**71**
Type of school	private
Environment	town

STUDENTS

Total undergrad enrollment	2,878
% male/female	42/58
% from out of state	39
% from public high school	78
% frosh live on campus	94
% African American	3
% Asian	1
% Caucasian	79
% Hispanic	7
% Native American	1
% international	2
# of countries represented	35

SURVEY SAYS . . .

Students love St. Augustine, FL
Low cost of living
Frats and sororities are unpopular or nonexistent
Very little drug use

ACADEMICS

Academic Rating	**78**
% students returning for sophomore year	77
% students graduating within 4 years	47
% students graduating within 6 years	60
Calendar	semester
Student/faculty ratio	19:1
Profs interesting rating	86
Profs accessible rating	82
Most classes have	20–29 students

MOST POPULAR MAJORS

business/commerce; communication, journalism, and related programs, other; elementary education and teaching; psychology

APPLICANTS ALSO LOOK AT AND RARELY PREFER

Florida Southern College, Eckerd College

STUDENTS SAY ". . ."

Academics

For those seeking "an excellent education in a beautiful location," Flagler College is a small liberal arts school in Florida that offers a "comfortable atmosphere," "tons of history and culture," and "a perfect ratio of professors to student." The school's strong education program is a huge draw here, but there are plenty of other strong programs in Flagler's twenty-five available majors. Hard workers get noticed, and there are plenty of opportunities to excel outside of the classroom, which "has been the most valuable aspect," according to one student.

The faculty here is "extremely enthusiastic about their jobs" and "very knowledgeable in their fields," though "there are a few that I don't think have real direction," says a student. Nevertheless, most are "always willing to meet and discuss work outside of the classroom," and the fact that "it is pretty easy to get to know the professors within your major on a personal basis makes things a lot easier and comfortable." This close-knit community breeds an environment where every person actively wants "to share experiences and knowledge with the faculty and other students." Class time is treated as an "intellectual journey," wherein one main question or discussion topic is introduced, and students explore every aspect of it using the professor as the tour guide. "This system the professors at Flagler College have evokes curiosity from all students, leaving very little room for confusion."

Aside from the "ample help from teachers," the "personable" administration is "good at communicating to all students via school e-mail." The attendance policy can be tough on some students—"you only get a certain number of absences, excused or unexcused, before you get dropped from a course"—but most still know that this tough love is in place to help students be "encouraged in a way that leads to excellent work." The best classes are the ones with eight or so people in them, as "you really lean on each other throughout the semester."

Life

Life is "pretty chill at Flagler," where "homework usually isn't too bad most of the time." As far as making friends, this "relaxed," happy lot has no problems. "Attend a few of the many social activities that Flagler College offers. It's really easy to make friends there!" suggests one student. On the first Friday of the month, all the art galleries "throw their doors wide open and serve treats," and the "casual and quaint" tourist-centric town of St. Augustine "is an awesome place to spend your time, walking around, going out to eat, and doing a little bit of shopping." Campus activities tend to "die around 7:00 P.M.," and many students tend to live nearby off campus (due to Flagler College residential rules, which restrict interdorm visiting, drugs, and alcohol).

Sunny days mean "the pool and West lawn are the places to be," and on weekends, "many times we drive to Jacksonville and go out at night there." Biking, beach volleyball, and walking along the sand dunes are just some of the beachy pastimes here, where "the beach mentality triumphs, including surfer culture." The campus itself "is beautiful, we sometimes even compare it to Hogwarts," says a student.

Student Body

Your typical Flagler student is "easygoing and very laid-back" ("How can you not be with the beach five miles away?" asks a student) as well as "super nice and friendly." It's not difficult to fit in at Flagler College, because "there is a crowd for everybody, despite the small size of the student body," even if this student body as a whole is a bit "homogenous." All students provide different viewpoints and "seem to be very respectful of others' views." There are quite a few surfers and artistic types, and even these groups are "very motivated and ready to broaden their education."

FINANCIAL AID: 904-819-6225 • E-MAIL: ADMISS@FLAGLER.EDU • WEBSITE: WWW.FLAGLER.EDU

THE PRINCETON REVIEW SAYS

Admissions

Very important factors considered include: Rigor of secondary school record. *Important factors considered include:* Application essay, academic GPA, standardized test scores, alumni/ae relation, extracurricular activities. *Other factors considered include:* Class rank, recommendation(s), character/personal qualities, first generation, interview, level of applicant's interest, talent/ability, volunteer work. SAT or ACT required; ACT with writing component recommended. TOEFL required of all international applicants. High school diploma is required and GED is accepted. *Academic units required:* 4 English, 3 mathematics, 2 science (1 science lab), 3 social studies, 1 history, 2 academic electives. *Academic units recommended:* 4 English, 4 mathematics, 3 science (2 science labs), 2 foreign language, 3 social studies, 2 history, 1 visual/performing arts, 1 computer science, 2 academic electives.

Financial Aid

Students should submit: FAFSA, institution's own financial aid form, state aid form. The Princeton Review suggests that all financial aid forms be submitted as soon as possible after January 1. *Need-based scholarships/grants offered:* Federal Pell, SEOG, state scholarships/grants, private scholarships, the school's own gift aid. *Loan aid offered:* Direct Subsidized Stafford, Direct Unsubsidized Stafford, Direct PLUS, Federal Perkins, private alternative loans. Applicants will be notified of awards on a rolling basis beginning April 1. Federal Work-Study Program available. Institutional employment available. Highest amount earned per year from on-campus jobs $1,400. Off-campus job opportunities are excellent.

The Inside Word

Several high-profile programs, a desirable location, and a small, incoming freshman class all conspire to drive down Flagler's admissions rate. Still, Flagler is not top-tier when it comes to selectivity, and strong candidates should meet little resistance from the admissions office. About half of the incoming freshmen graduated in the top quarter of their classes, so make sure you build a strong application with harder courses and strong grades.

THE SCHOOL SAYS ". . ."

From the Admissions Office

"Flagler College is an independent, four-year, coeducational, residential institution located in picturesque St. Augustine. A famous historic tourist center in northeast Florida, it is located to the south of Jacksonville and north of Daytona Beach. Flagler students have ample opportunity to explore the rich cultural heritage and international flavor of St. Augustine, and there's always time for a relaxing day at the beach, about four miles from campus. The annual cost for tuition, room, and board at Flagler is about the same as state universities. The small student body helps to keep one from becoming 'just a number.' Flagler serves a predominately full-time student body and seeks to enroll students who can benefit from the type of educational experience the college offers. Because of the college's unique mission and distinctive characteristics, some students may benefit more from an educational experience at Flagler than others. The college's admission standards and procedures are designed to select from among the applicants those students most likely to succeed academically, to contribute significantly to the student life program at Flagler, and to become graduates of the college. Flagler College provides an exceptional opportunity for a private education at an extremely affordable cost.

"All applicants to Flager College must submit either their SAT or ACT scores."

SELECTIVITY	
Admissions Rating	**90**
# of applicants	3,933
% of applicants accepted	40
% of acceptees attending	42
# accepting a place on wait list	677
# admitted from wait list	33
# of early decision applicants	729
# accepted early decision	393

FRESHMAN PROFILE	
Range SAT Critical Reading	530–600
Range SAT Math	520–580
Range SAT Writing	510–580
Range ACT Composite	22–26
Minimum paper TOEFL	550
Minimum web-based TOEFL	80
Average HS GPA	3.4
% graduated top 10% of class	16
% graduated top 25% of class	46
% graduated top 50% of class	96

DEADLINES	
Early decision	
Deadline	11/1
Notification	12/15
Regular	
Priority	1/15
Deadline	3/1
Notification	3/30
Nonfall registration?	yes

FINANCIAL FACTS	
Financial Aid Rating	**72**
Annual tuition	$15,340
Room and board	$8,350
Books and supplies	$1,000
% needy frosh rec. need-based scholarship or grant aid	98
% needy UG rec. need-based scholarship or grant aid	95
% needy frosh rec. non-need-based scholarship or grant aid	8
% needy UG rec. non-need-based scholarship or grant aid	8
% needy frosh rec. need-based self-help aid	90
% needy UG rec. need-based self-help aid	90
% frosh rec. any financial aid	86
% UG rec. any financial aid	92
% UG borrow to pay for school	61
Average cumulative indebtedness	$23,424
% frosh need fully met	13
% ugrads need fully met	16
Average % of frosh need met	60
Average % of ugrad need met	60

FLORIDA SOUTHERN COLLEGE

111 LAKE HOLLINGSWORTH DRIVE, LAKELAND, FL 33801 • ADMISSIONS: 800-274-4131 • FAX: 863-680-4120

CAMPUS LIFE

Quality of Life Rating	**76**
Fire Safety Rating	**73**
Green Rating	**61**
Type of school	private
Affiliation	Methodist
Environment	city

STUDENTS

Total undergrad enrollment	2,040
% male/female	42/58
% from out of state	34
% from public high school	82
% frosh live on campus	90
# of fraternities	8
# of sororities	7
% African American	6
% Asian	2
% Caucasian	77
% Hispanic	8
% Native American	1
% international	4
# of countries represented	39

SURVEY SAYS . . .

Athletic facilities are great
Students get along with local community
Great off-campus food
Intramural sports are popular
Frats and sororities dominate social scene
Musical organizations are popular
Student government is popular

ACADEMICS

Academic Rating	**75**
% students returning for sophomore year	77
% students graduating within 4 years	48
% students graduating within 6 years	55
Calendar	semester
Student/faculty ratio	13:1
Profs interesting rating	82
Profs accessible rating	78
Most classes have	10–19 students
Most lab/discussion sessions have	10–19 students

MOST POPULAR MAJORS

biology/biological sciences; business administration and management; nursing/registered nurse (rn, asn, bsn, msn)

STUDENTS SAY "..."

Academics

Expect a "personalized education" at Florida Southern College, a small school that's "the perfect size for any student that doesn't want to go unnoticed!" Indeed, students insist, "FSC gives you a great education, both academically and socially, not only because the campus is small…but [also] because the professors want to get to know you as a person, not just a number on their roll call." With "small classes where you can actually ask questions during class and participate in group discussions" and "amazing" professors who "are always available to you if you need anything (every single professor…gives you their cell phone number on their syllabus in case you need anything at all)," students certainly don't lack for attention here. The music program is a definite standout at FSC; nursing, psychology, journalism, advertising, and business all have their enthusiastic adherents among the student body. Administrators "are seen on campus all the time, and [you] can approach them pretty easily," says one student. No wonder students tell us, "FSC is about community. This small school is like a big family where you always have someone to talk to or to help you."

Life

FSC is located "right on a lake so there are all sorts of water activities" for students to enjoy. "Kayaking, canoeing, swimming, biking, jogging, and much more" keep the lakefront hopping throughout daylight hours. The lake is most certainly the main attraction of hometown Lakeland. Students complain that the town is "not too exciting." "There's not really a whole lot to do in Lakeland," one undergrad points out, but fortunately FSC is located "right between Tampa and Orlando, two bigger cities that have more attractions and are only a forty-five-minute drive away." Campus life centers on Greek organizations and events organized by the Association of Campus Entertainment (ACE). The latter is "very creative. They have had casino night, raffle ticket giveaways, comedians, and a variety of other events." Greeks throw the requisite parties but also "go on a lot of service trips, serving food at soup kitchens, gleaning in the fields of local farmers, all sorts of stuff" that "keep members busy, but it's a good busy. It's the perfect balance of work and play." Drinking occurs primarily off campus "since it's not allowed on site," and students warn, "There is little life on campus over the weekend…You are forced to go off campus to find something that's worthwhile to do."

Student Body

The "friendly," "mostly outgoing" student body of FSC is predominantly "white, preppy, and upper-middle-class." Most "are religious, involved in sports, or part of the Greek system," but "There are a few outliers, and enough people are outliers that they hang out together." Students tend to be "involved in a number of clubs and organizations on campus. Our campus is small so it's really easy to get involved." There's a notable subpopulation of "students who did not perform well at their private high school institutions" and so couldn't gain admission to more competitive schools, but most everyone does what he or she has to do to get through. "There are students who are very into their schoolwork, always studying and striving to do their best, and then there are others who are very laid-back but still get their schoolwork done," one student tells us.

FINANCIAL AID: 863-680-4140 • E-MAIL: FSCADM@FLSOUTHERN.EDU • WEBSITE: WWW.FLSOUTHERN.EDU

THE PRINCETON REVIEW SAYS

Admissions

Very important factors considered include: Academic GPA, rigor of secondary school record. *Important factors considered include:* Application essay, recommendation(s), standardized test scores, character/personal qualities, extracurricular activities, level of applicant's interest, talent/ability. *Other factors considered include:* Class rank, alumni/ae relation, first generation, interview, racial/ethnic status, religious affiliation/commitment, volunteer work, work experience. SAT or ACT required; ACT with or without writing component accepted. TOEFL required of all international applicants. High school diploma is required and GED is accepted. *Academic units required:* 4 English, 3 mathematics, 2 science (2 science labs), 3 social studies, 3 history, 2 academic electives. *Academic units recommended:* 2 foreign language.

Financial Aid

Students should submit: FAFSA, institution's own financial aid form. Regular filing deadline is July 1. The Princeton Review suggests that all financial aid forms be submitted as soon as possible after January 1. *Need-based scholarships/grants offered:* Federal Pell, SEOG, state scholarships/grants, private scholarships, the school's own gift aid, Federal Nursing Scholarships. *Loan aid offered:* Direct Subsidized Stafford, Direct Unsubsidized Stafford, Direct PLUS, Federal Perkins. Applicants will be notified of awards on a rolling basis beginning March 1. Federal Work-Study Program available. Institutional employment available. Highest amount earned per year from on-campus jobs $1,500. Off-campus job opportunities are good.

The Inside Word

Individual attention is a cornerstone of the Florida Southern experience, and the experience begins with the admissions process. Admissions officers give each application a careful review, looking for indications of latent capabilities and potential to contribute to campus life and the campus community. Focus is directed not only on grades and test scores, but also on peripherals like personal attributes and unique experiences that speak to extracurricular achievement. Candidates are encouraged to employ creativity throughout their applications and are invited to submit additional academic materials and portfolio samples.

THE SCHOOL SAYS ". . ."

From the Admissions Office

"Florida Southern is a friendly, vibrant, and energetic campus, offering dynamic engaged learning opportunities that include guaranteed internships, student-faculty collaborative research and performance, service learning, and study abroad. An innovative new program—the Junior Journey—guarantees all entering students the opportunity to study domestically or overseas during their junior year at no cost for the trip other than minimal course credit charges. FSC offers more than fifty majors in fields such as art, biology, chemistry, business, communication, education, music and theater performance, nursing, and psychology. Pre-professional programs include premedicine, pre-pharmacy, predentistry, and pre-law. The college is known for its great faculty, small classes (thirteen to one student/faculty), and personalized attention. A new state-of-the-art technology center opened on campus, as well as contemporary residence halls with stunning views of scenic Lake Hollingsworth. New classrooms include a modern language lab, film studies center, and art gallery have recently opened. Our involved student population enjoys rich and varied student life programming that includes championship NCAA Division II events in nineteen sports, intramurals, more than seventy clubs and organizations, an extensive Greek system, and an elaborate and diverse selection of weekend activities. The college's popular lakefront program features free kayaks, canoes, and paddleboats. FSC is home to the world's largest single-site collection of structures designed by Frank Lloyd Wright, which provides a stunning setting for living and academic learning communities. Ninety-six percent of graduates report landing jobs in their fields or continuing their studies at top-tier graduate and professional schools within six months of graduation."

SELECTIVITY

Admissions Rating	**79**
# of applicants	3,159
% of applicants accepted	65
% of acceptees attending	26
# of early decision applicants	75
# accepted early decision	56

FRESHMAN PROFILE

Range SAT Critical Reading	490–590
Range SAT Math	500–590
Range SAT Writing	470–570
Range ACT Composite	22–27
Minimum paper TOEFL	550
Average HS GPA	3.51
% graduated top 10% of class	22
% graduated top 25% of class	51
% graduated top 50% of class	84

DEADLINES

Early decision	
Deadline	12/1
Notification	12/15
Regular	
Deadline	3/1
Nonfall registration?	yes

FINANCIAL FACTS

Financial Aid Rating	**75**
Annual tuition	$26,600
Room and board	$9,100
Required fees	$600
Books and supplies	$1,670
% needy frosh rec. need-based scholarship or grant aid	79
% needy UG rec. need-based scholarship or grant aid	80
% needy frosh rec. non-need-based scholarship or grant aid	100
% needy UG rec. non-need-based scholarship or grant aid	100
% needy frosh rec. need-based self-help aid	8
% needy UG rec. need-based self-help aid	30
% frosh rec. any financial aid	99
% UG rec. any financial aid	97
% UG borrow to pay for school	53
Average cumulative indebtedness	$20,580
% frosh need fully met	28
% ugrads need fully met	30
Average % of frosh need met	73
Average % of ugrad need met	72

FLORIDA STATE UNIVERSITY

PO BOX 3062400, TALLAHASSEE, FL 32306-2400 • ADMISSIONS: 850-644-6200 • FAX: 850-644-0197

CAMPUS LIFE

Quality of Life Rating	**91**
Fire Safety Rating	**78**
Green Rating	**90**
Type of school	public
Environment	city

STUDENTS

Total undergrad enrollment	31,594
% male/female	45/55
% from out of state	11
% from public high school	84
# of fraternities	31
# of sororities	27
% African American	10
% Asian	4
% Caucasian	68
% Hispanic	14
% Native American	1
% international	1
# of countries represented	130

SURVEY SAYS . . .

Athletic facilities are great
Everyone loves the Seminoles
Students are happy
Great library
Lots of beer drinking
Frats and sororities dominate social scene

ACADEMICS

Academic Rating	**74**
% students graduating within 4 years	50
% students graduating within 6 years	74
Calendar	semester
Student/faculty ratio	26:1
Profs interesting rating	80
Profs accessible rating	78
Most classes have	20–29 students

MOST POPULAR MAJORS

English language and literature; finance; political science and government

STUDENTS SAY ". . ."

Academics

Florida State University is "a large, sports-oriented, research-intensive state school that has a niche for everybody, as long as you are willing to search." In addition to its strong academics, students tended to choose FSU for its "sports teams"—the Florida State Seminoles—the "great weather," and the fact that it's "a place with great traditions." "Florida State is a school that is so rooted in tradition it is extremely hard not to proudly call yourself a True Seminole." FSU is also "affordable" for in-state students with "excellent scholarships." "The tight vicinity of the campus [causes] the student body to be a close-unit of individuals." "FSU's reputation as a small-school feel in a big university was what drew me in," says an accounting and finance student. Reviews of the professors are mixed, as is common at many large universities. "About one-fourth of the professors are no good at teaching, about half of them are decent or good, and about one-fourth are great," one student explains. Another attests, "I have had wonderful professors that have eyes, ears, and heart to a world beyond my own, and have shown me that anything is achievable if I try hard enough." Students do wish for "smaller class sizes" and "more discussions in class." If the students have one common complaint, it's *"parking!,"* which is "always a huge hassle." Students also wish for better sustainability, recycling, and green programs. "FSU has traditionally been all about the humanities, and it's great that we're expanding into other areas, but we shouldn't forget our main focus," says one student. An English major sums up FSU: "Florida State University is a school where students are asked to uphold the garnet and gold and to live intentionally in the direction of leadership, academics, and service."

Life

"Sports is basically your whole life here," one student claims. While a university as large as FSU—the population is 40,000 plus—has students of many types, athletics and "school spirit" are what "bring everyone together" at FSU. "Everyone likes to socialize and party, usually off campus, like at bars or houses." Greek life is also "very prominent" FSU has a reputation as a party school, and "many students go out on the weekend or even sometimes during the week. The use of alcohol and marihuana is very common." "The majority of FSU students gets rowdy almost every night of the week," confirms another. However, one student claims that "FSU is a recovering party school." Since its heyday in the mid-nineties, FSU has calmed down a bit, but you can still find thriving parties and clubs any day of the week." "People go to Wakulla Springs to swim or to Bear Paw to go around the river during the weekends." Although "Tallahassee is one of the most boring cities I have ever been to," "the nightlife is…very important in Tallahassee; there are many bars and clubs to attend." "My life at Florida State is busy," one political science student explains. "I am always on the move. From class, to student government, Greek life, internships at the capital, and nightlife. I think people at FSU are constantly thinking about how they can better themselves and the university."

Student Body

Your average FSU student is a "football fan, partier, into academics and community service, [and] passionate." Students tend to be "extremely involved," whether it's in athletics, "Greek life or community service, or one of the other hundreds of groups and clubs here at FSU." "Greek is a huge part of campus, but you are fine if you are not in one."Although "the majority of students are Caucasians," "students of all races and religions work together here to make FSU an enjoyable environment," and "the school continues to become more diverse each year." No matter what their background, every FSU student has "a colossal amount of school spirit and loves to go out and support the team."

FINANCIAL AID: 850-644-5716 • E-MAIL: ADMISSIONS@ADMIN.FSU.EDU • WEBSITE: WWW.FSU.EDU

THE PRINCETON REVIEW SAYS

Admissions

Very important factors considered include: Academic GPA, rigor of secondary school record. *Important factors considered include:* Standardized test scores, state residency, talent/ability. *Other factors considered include:* Class rank, application essay, recommendation(s), alumni/ae relation, character/personal qualities, extracurricular activities, first generation, geographical residence, volunteer work, work experience. SAT or ACT required; ACT with writing component required. TOEFL required of all international applicants. High school diploma is required and GED is accepted. *Academic units required:* 4 English, 4 mathematics, 3 science (2 science labs), 2 foreign language, 1 social studies, 2 history, 3 academic electives. *Academic units recommended:* 4 English, 4 mathematics, 4 science (2 science labs), 4 foreign language, 2 social studies, 2 history, 3 academic electives.

Financial Aid

Students should submit: FAFSA. The Princeton Review suggests that all financial aid forms be submitted as soon as possible after January 1. *Need-based scholarships/grants offered:* Federal Pell, SEOG, state scholarships/grants, private scholarships, the school's own gift aid. *Loan aid offered:* Direct Subsidized Stafford, Direct Unsubsidized Stafford, Direct PLUS, Federal Perkins. Applicants will be notified of awards on a rolling basis beginning March 15. Federal Work-Study Program available. Institutional employment available. Highest amount earned per year from on-campus jobs $10,000. Off-campus job opportunities are good.

The Inside Word

With 25,000 applications to process annually, FSU must rely on a formula-driven approach to triage its applicant pool. With the exception of applicants to special programs, only borderline candidates receive a truly thorough review; all others are either clearly in or clearly out based on grades, curriculum, and test scores. Candidates for programs in fine arts, creative arts, and performing arts must undergo a more rigorous review that includes a portfolio or audition.

THE SCHOOL SAYS ". . ."

From the Admissions Office

"The Florida State University is an internationally recognized teaching and research institution committed to preparing our students for a life that balances knowledge, creativity, leadership, and contribution. Designated as a Carnegie Research University (very high research activity), Florida State offers more than 320 undergraduate, graduate, and professional degree programs, including medicine and law. Our students have the opportunity to conduct research alongside Nobel laureates and Pulitzer Prize winners, Guggenheim Fellows, members of the National Academy of Sciences and American Academy of Arts and Sciences, and other globally recognized teachers and researchers. Through the efforts of our Office of Undergraduate Research, students partner with faculty who share their academic interests, and who encourage them to design and conduct original research projects. Through the Office of National Fellowships, Florida State has become a leader among the state's public universities by setting records in the award of national fellowships and scholarships for our students. We offer state-of-the-art teaching techniques in our technologically enhanced classrooms and wireless networking community. Our innovative student services include a comprehensive campus-wide leadership learning program, a center for community and global-based learning through service, and an award-winning career center. World-class cultural events, championship athletics, extensive recreational facilities, and a friendly, close-knit University community enrich student life and extend learning well beyond the classroom. Our diverse student body hails from all fifty states and more than 130 countries, and our numerous international programs throughout the world include year-round programs in Florence, Italy; London, England; Panama City, Panama; and Valencia, Spain."

SELECTIVITY

Admissions Rating	**89**
# of applicants	28,313
% of applicants accepted	58
% of acceptees attending	37

FRESHMAN PROFILE

Range SAT Critical Reading	550–650
Range SAT Math	560–640
Range SAT Writing	550–630
Range ACT Composite	25–28
Minimum paper TOEFL	550
Minimum web-based TOEFL	80
Average HS GPA	3.8
% graduated top 10% of class	40
% graduated top 25% of class	78
% graduated top 50% of class	97

DEADLINES

Regular	
Deadline	1/14
Nonfall registration?	yes

FINANCIAL FACTS

Financial Aid Rating	**88**
Annual in-state tuition	$3,397
Annual out-state tuition	$18,564
Room and board	$9,412
Required fees	$2,428
Books and supplies	$1,000
% needy frosh rec. need-based scholarship or grant aid	61
% needy UG rec. need-based scholarship or grant aid	59
% needy frosh rec. non-need-based scholarship or grant aid	95
% needy UG rec. non-need-based scholarship or grant aid	80
% needy frosh rec. need-based self-help aid	61
% needy UG rec. need-based self-help aid	67
% frosh rec. any financial aid	96
% UG rec. any financial aid	88
% UG borrow to pay for school	54
Average cumulative indebtedness	$22,139
% frosh need fully met	68
% ugrads need fully met	65
Average % of frosh need met	62
Average % of ugrad need met	64

FORDHAM UNIVERSITY

441 EAST FORDHAM ROAD, NEW YORK, NY 10458 • ADMISSIONS: 718-817-4000 • FAX: 718-367-9404

CAMPUS LIFE

Quality of Life Rating	**78**
Fire Safety Rating	**75**
Green Rating	**60***
Type of school	private
Affiliation	Roman Catholic
Environment	metropolis

STUDENTS

Total undergrad enrollment	8,427
% male/female	47/53
% from out of state	60
% from public high school	40
% frosh live on campus	74
% African American	5
% Asian	8
% Caucasian	60
% Hispanic	14
% international	4
# of countries represented	62

SURVEY SAYS . . .

Great library
Great off-campus food
Campus feels safe
Students are happy
Frats and sororities are unpopular or nonexistent
Student publications are popular
Hard liquor is popular
Internships are widely available

ACADEMICS

Academic Rating	**80**
% students returning for sophomore year	88
% students graduating within 4 years	76
Calendar	semester
Student/faculty ratio	13:1
Profs interesting rating	79
Profs accessible rating	80
Most classes have	10–19 students
Most lab/discussion sessions have	10–19 students

MOST POPULAR MAJORS

business/commerce; communication and media studies, other; social sciences

APPLICANTS ALSO LOOK AT AND OFTEN PREFER

New York University, Boston College, The George Washington University

AND SOMETIMES PREFER

Georgetown University, Loyola University Maryland, College of the Holy Cross

AND RARELY PREFER

Hofstra University, Pace University, Marist College

STUDENTS SAY ". . ."

Academics

Fordham University—"the Jesuit school located in the capital of the world"—"offers a sense of community and a true college experience within the hustle and bustle" of New York City. Noteworthy majors include the performing arts and "an exceptional business program." There's also an "excellent honors program" and "a pretty good library." Students here tell us that they receive "a broad and holistic liberal arts education," thanks in large part to a "strict" and "extensive" core curriculum with a "somewhat large number of degree requirements." Classes are "small," and the "incredibly accessible" professors "love what they do." "Each of my professors has made me interested in their subject, even if I was only taking the class out of requirement," relates a finance major. "I get the impression that they are genuinely interested in what the students think." "I do not think I have ever had a really *bad* professor," adds an English major. Be warned, though: "The grade differentiation between some professors for the same class is absurd." Some students tell us that management is "friendly and approachable." "You can drop anyone an e-mail and expect a response back," proponents say. Critics pan the staff for an "overall lack of collaborative spirit" and gripe that the red tape is "fairly annoying."

Life

Fordham is two schools in one. There's the school's long-established location in Rose Hill, a "beautiful, Gothic, green" college campus complete with a "huge lawn" that is "located in an oasis in the middle of the Bronx," adjacent to "the original Little Italy" and its "amazing Italian food." There's also another, smaller campus at Lincoln Center in the heart of Manhattan. The big complaint here is the on-campus grub, which ranges from "pretty bad" to "prison-grade gruel." "Honestly," asks a mystified first-year student, "what is this stuff?" Otherwise, students are quite happy. Size-wise, Fordham is "just small enough that you'll see people you recognize whenever you walk around, but just large enough that it's always different people." "Life at Fordham is busy," explains a junior. "Obviously, we are all here for the academics, and that is a big focus for everyone but, additionally, almost all students are involved in activities on and off campus." There are "extracurriculars for every taste." "People love to play intramural sports." Fordham is big on community service as well, and "There are so many ways to get involved with volunteering." Students also spend a lot of time just soaking up all the "extensive and vibrant culture" "that New York City has to offer on any given day." "The choices of things to do here are endless." "Students often spend a lot of time in bars," and it's possible to "party four or sometimes five times a week." However, parties are usually "kept under control." Fordham students "know when to put their academic well-being before" a good time.

Student Body

"Students fit into two main groups at Fordham: East Coast prep or NYC hipster." It's generally an "upper-middle-class," "hardworking" crowd. "Dress is stylish." Fashions are especially trendy among the more artsy "urbanites" at Lincoln Center. However, "There is room here for every kind of person imaginable because, after all, this is New York." Students at Fordham "get along very well and tend to dabble in a variety of clubs and programs." Students "tend to socialize in smaller groups," but "stereotypical cliques, like you would classify in high school, don't really apply here." "The Catholic culture contributes to a willingness to suspend typical political labels in exchange for a deeper look at the moral and social issues of our day," reflects a senior. "Everyone finds their niche."

FINANCIAL AID: 718-817-3800 • E-MAIL: ENROLL@FORDHAM.EDU • WEBSITE: WWW.FORDHAM.EDU

THE PRINCETON REVIEW SAYS

Admissions

Very important factors considered include: Class rank, rigor of secondary school record, standardized test scores. *Important factors considered include:* Application essay, recommendation(s), character/personal qualities, extracurricular activities, talent/ability. *Other factors considered include:* Alumni/ae relation, first generation, geographical residence, racial/ethnic status, volunteer work, work experience. SAT or ACT required; ACT with writing component recommended. TOEFL required of all international applicants. High school diploma is required and GED is accepted. *Academic units required:* 4 English, 3 mathematics, 3 science, 2 foreign language, 2 social studies, 2 history, 6 academic electives. *Academic units recommended:* 4 English, 4 mathematics, 4 science, 3 foreign language, 2 social studies, 2 history, 6 academic electives.

Financial Aid

Students should submit: FAFSA, CSS/Financial Aid PROFILE, noncustodial PROFILE, business/farm supplement. Regular filing deadline is February 1. The Princeton Review suggests that all financial aid forms be submitted as soon as possible after January 1. *Need-based scholarships/grants offered:* Federal Pell, SEOG, state scholarships/grants, private scholarships, the school's own gift aid. *Loan aid offered:* Direct Subsidized Stafford, Direct Unsubsidized Stafford, Direct PLUS, Federal Perkins. Applicants will be notified of awards on or about April 1.

The Inside Word

Applicants to Fordham are required to indicate whether they are applying to the Rose Hill campus in the Bronx or the Lincoln Center campus in Manhattan. If you want to enroll in the Gabelli School of Business, you must specify that, too. Admission criteria vary by school, but all are very competitive. Graduation from a Catholic high school—particularly a prestigious one on the East Coast—is always a plus.

THE SCHOOL SAYS ". . ."

From the Admissions Office

"Fordham University offers a distinctive, values-centered educational experience that is rooted in the Jesuit tradition of intellectual rigor and personal attention. Located in New York City, Fordham offers to students the unparalleled educational, cultural and recreational advantages of one of the world's greatest cities. Fordham has two residential campuses in New York—the tree-lined, eighty-five-acre Rose Hill campus in the Bronx, and the cosmopolitan Lincoln Center campus in the heart of Manhattan's performing arts center. The University's state-of-the-art facilities and buildings include one of the most technologically advanced libraries in the country. Fordham offers a variety of majors, concentrations and programs that can be combined with an extensive career planning and placement program. More than 2,600 organizations in the New York metropolitan area offer students internships that provide hands-on experience and valuable networking opportunities in fields such as business, communications, medicine, law and education.

"Applicants are required to take SAT or the ACT with the writing section. SAT Subject Tests are recommended but not required."

SELECTIVITY	
Admissions Rating	**92**
# of applicants	31,792
% of applicants accepted	42
% of acceptees attending	15
# accepting a place on wait list	1,637
# of early decision applicants	607

FRESHMAN PROFILE	
Range SAT Critical Reading	570–670
Range SAT Math	560–670
Range SAT Writing	570–680
Range ACT Composite	26–30
Minimum paper TOEFL	575
Average HS GPA	3.7
% graduated top 10% of class	42
% graduated top 25% of class	78
% graduated top 50% of class	97

DEADLINES	
Early action	
Deadline	11/1
Notification	12/25
Regular	
Priority	1/15
Deadline	1/15
Notification	4/1
Nonfall registration?	yes

FINANCIAL FACTS	
Financial Aid Rating	**75**
Annual tuition	$41,000
Room and board	$15,379
Required fees	$732
Books and supplies	$942
% frosh rec. any financial aid	88
% UG rec. any financial aid	83
% UG borrow to pay for school	65
Average cumulative indebtedness	$33,365
% frosh need fully met	23
% ugrads need fully met	20
Average % of frosh need met	80
Average % of ugrad need met	75

FRANKLIN & MARSHALL COLLEGE

PO Box 3003, Lancaster, PA 17604-3003 • Admissions: 717-291-3953 • Fax: 717-291-4389

CAMPUS LIFE

Quality of Life Rating	**70**
Fire Safety Rating	**90**
Green Rating	**94**
Type of school	private
Environment	town

STUDENTS

Total undergrad enrollment	2,324
% male/female	48/52
% from out of state	74
% from public high school	61
% frosh live on campus	100
# of fraternities	8
# of sororities	4
% African American	4
% Asian	3
% Caucasian	72
% Hispanic	6
% international	9
# of countries represented	41

SURVEY SAYS . . .

No one cheats
Lab facilities are great
Great computer facilities
Great library
School is well run
Lots of beer drinking
Hard liquor is popular

ACADEMICS

Academic Rating	**89**
% students returning for sophomore year	93
% students graduating within 4 years	85
% students graduating within 6 years	85
Calendar	semester
Student/faculty ratio	10:1
Profs interesting rating	84
Profs accessible rating	96
Most classes have	10–19 students
Most lab/discussion sessions have	10–19 students

MOST POPULAR MAJORS

business/commerce; political science and government; psychology

APPLICANTS ALSO LOOK AT AND OFTEN PREFER

University of Pennsylvania, Cornell University, Haverford College, Hamilton College

AND SOMETIMES PREFER

Bucknell University, Colgate University, Lehigh University, Lafayette College, Dickinson College

STUDENTS SAY ". . ."

Academics

Franklin & Marshall College is "a small, focused liberal arts college dedicated to giving every student the opportunity to succeed." Known for its "extremely high academic standards" and "great faculty accessibility," the school is "about furthering academic achievement and providing superior skills and opportunities for success after graduation." Many students say, "F&M is all about good undergrad programs and tight-knit networking," and students laud the opportunity to make connections in their chosen fields. The college has "a slight emphasis on the sciences," which makes an English major grumble, "Some really fantastic humanities programs lack in administrative support whereas science programs get everything and anything they want." Nevertheless, the college's "policy of deferring major declaration until sophomore year...allows undecided students to really find a major that suits their interests." The faculty gets good marks for being available to students outside the classroom, but students acknowledge that, "as with many things, professors vary widely in style and quality." A sophomore notes, "Some are very difficult but interesting; some are very boring, etc. There are enough wonderful professors to go around, though." Many students complain about the course registration process saying it can be "competitive and difficult to get into desired classes."

Life

F&M boasts a "lush and beautiful campus" with "state-of-the-art educational and living facilities" and "a strong community feel." Students say, "Events are constantly being organized, and there's always something interesting going on if you take the time to participate." Students also point out, "If you see that there is a need for a new school group, you can definitely petition for it, and the school will back you up. F&M cares a lot about on-campus diversity." Overall, it's a, "close-knit student body," and students feel that "as an F&M student, you are not a number or a name on a class roster, you are an active contributor on campus." However, students are torn on the issue of school spirit, with some feeling it's strong and others griping that "school spirit is laughable." "There isn't enough student involvement and enthusiasm with clubs and activities." However, all students agree that "the school could stand to improve on campus dining." There are complaints about the mandatory four-year residency requirement, particularly among upperclassmen who feel it "needs to be modified" because it "makes housing far more expensive than it should be." Some feel the administration can be "hard to work with" and think the college should "streamline administrative departments" to "decrease wasteful spending."

Student Body

At F&M, the motto seems to be, "Work hard, play hard." Students say they take their academics seriously, but "because the work is so demanding, on weekends everyone gets pretty crazy." Greek life is a predominant part of the social scene, and some say, "On weekends, it's pretty much the only outlet for socializing." Many say the student body is "preppier and more Greek than you'd expect" and that "the typical student is Caucasian, upper-middle-class, from the tristate area" and looks like "a J. Crew model." However, a neuroscience major says, "While Greek life seems to dominate campus, after one or two years you come to realize that there is a lot more to do for fun," and another student adds, "It's a very laid-back lifestyle so people like to relax and enjoy time with their friends." A junior says, "in reality, everyone has their 'thing' that they're involved in," and in general "students are friendly and pleasant, but they tend to stick to themselves and their small groups of friends." However, many agree that, "For a small school, there is an enormous variety of things to do," and they say, "on any given weekend you can find people all over campus, whether it be at the artsy green room theater, the library...in the college center, in a friend's apartment, or at a frat party."

FINANCIAL AID: 717-291-3991 • E-MAIL: ADMISSION@FANDM.EDU • WEBSITE: WWW.FANDM.EDU

THE PRINCETON REVIEW SAYS

Admissions

Very important factors considered include: Class rank, academic GPA, rigor of secondary school record, character/personal qualities. *Important factors considered include:* Application essay, recommendation(s), standardized test scores, extracurricular activities, interview, talent/ability, volunteer work. *Other factors considered include:* Alumni/ae relation, geographical residence, level of applicant's interest, racial/ethnic status, work experience. ACT with or without writing component accepted. TOEFL required of all international applicants. High school diploma is required and GED is accepted. *Academic units required:* 4 English, 3 mathematics, 2 science (2 science labs), 2 foreign language, 1 social studies, 2 history, 1 visual/performing arts. *Academic units recommended:* 4 mathematics, 3 science (3 science labs), 4 foreign language, 3 social studies, 3 history.

Financial Aid

Students should submit: FAFSA, CSS/Financial Aid PROFILE, noncustodial PROFILE, business/farm supplement. Regular filing deadline is February 15. The Princeton Review suggests that all financial aid forms be submitted as soon as possible after January 1. *Need-based scholarships/grants offered:* Federal Pell, SEOG, state scholarships/grants, private scholarships, the school's own gift aid. *Loan aid offered:* Direct Subsidized Stafford, Direct Unsubsidized Stafford, Direct PLUS, Federal Perkins, college/university loans from institutional funds. Applicants will be notified of awards on or about April 1. Federal Work-Study Program available. Highest amount earned per year from on-campus jobs $2,175.

The Inside Word

While admission at F&M is competitive, the admissions committee does show some flexibility. The college allows students who feel that standardized test scores don't reflect their true academic capacity to submit two graded writing samples to replace the test scores. Applicants are also encouraged to include nontraditional materials, such as art portfolios or recordings of musical performances, in their applications. Finally, F&M offers a "Spring Option," in which students can elect to start classes in the spring semester after spending the fall abroad, or pursuing a "challenging program in consultation with an experienced faculty advisor at F&M."

THE SCHOOL SAYS ". . ."

From the Admissions Office

"The hallmarks of a Franklin & Marshall education are individual attention and a supportive community. Our faculty members challenge you to achieve your personal best and engage you personally on a level you will not find at other institutions. We have one professor for every ten students, and two-thirds of our students collaborate on a research project directly with a faculty member. Here are three more things you should know about F&M: 1) Our professors do not confine learning to classrooms and labs. They take you into the field and the local community to teach you how to *do* what students at other institutions may only read about. 2) We have College Houses, not dorms. Our five College Houses, which group first-year students into smaller cohorts, are student-governed spaces where you socialize, learn, and stretch your intellect. Based in each house are a faculty mentor and an administrative counselor to guide you. 3) No one gets lost. The depth and breadth of student activities and experiences provide everyone with a place to belong. Our students find a strong sense of self, and they find their "homes" in clubs, athletic teams, their College Houses, fraternities and sororities, the performing and musical arts, and the other strong communities they have the freedom to create for themselves."

SELECTIVITY

Admissions Rating	**95**
# of applicants	5,105
% of applicants accepted	38
% of acceptees attending	30
# accepting a place on wait list	647
# admitted from wait list	28
# of early decision applicants	514
# accepted early decision	356

FRESHMAN PROFILE

Range SAT Critical Reading	610–680
Range SAT Math	630–710
Range ACT Composite	28–31
Minimum paper TOEFL	600
Average HS GPA	3.5
% graduated top 10% of class	59
% graduated top 25% of class	87
% graduated top 50% of class	98

DEADLINES

Early decision	
Deadline	11/15
Notification	12/15
Regular	
Deadline	2/1
Notification	4/1
Nonfall registration?	yes

FINANCIAL FACTS

Financial Aid Rating	**93**
Annual tuition	$44,260
Room and board	$11,750
Required fees	$100
Books and supplies	$1,200
% needy frosh rec. need-based scholarship or grant aid	97
% needy UG rec. need-based scholarship or grant aid	96
% needy frosh rec. non-need-based scholarship or grant aid	5
% needy UG rec. non-need-based scholarship or grant aid	6
% needy frosh rec. need-based self-help aid	97
% needy UG rec. need-based self-help aid	96
% frosh rec. any financial aid	50
% UG rec. any financial aid	51
% UG borrow to pay for school	53
Average cumulative indebtedness	$31,617
% frosh need fully met	100
% ugrads need fully met	98
Average % of frosh need met	100
Average % of ugrad need met	98

FRANKLIN W. OLIN COLLEGE OF ENGINEERING

OLIN WAY, NEEDHAM, MA 02492-1245 • ADMISSIONS: 781-292-2222 • FAX: 781-292-2210

CAMPUS LIFE

Quality of Life Rating	**98**
Fire Safety Rating	**91**
Green Rating	**65**
Type of school	private
Environment	town

STUDENTS

Total undergrad enrollment	326
% male/female	52/48
% from out of state	89
% frosh live on campus	99
% African American	1
% Asian	16
% Caucasian	60
% Hispanic	2
% international	6
# of countries represented	17

SURVEY SAYS . . .

No one cheats
Lab facilities are great
Great computer facilities
Students are friendly
Different types of students interact
Students get along with local community
Great food on campus
Dorms are like palaces
Campus feels safe
Students are happy
Student government is popular
Internships are widely available

ACADEMICS

Academic Rating	**99**
% students returning for sophomore year	92
% students graduating within 4 years	94
% students graduating within 6 years	96
Calendar	semester
Student/faculty ratio	9:1
Profs interesting rating	98
Profs accessible rating	94
Most classes have	20–29 students

MOST POPULAR MAJORS

electrical, electronics and communications engineering; engineering; mechanical engineering

APPLICANTS ALSO LOOK AT AND OFTEN PREFER

Massachusetts Institute of Technology, Stanford University, California Institute of Technology, Princeton University, Yale University

AND SOMETIMES PREFER

Carnegie Mellon University, University of California—Berkeley, Harvey Mudd College

AND RARELY PREFER

Rose-Hulman Institute of Technology, Worcester Polytechnic Institute, Rensselaer Polytechnic Institute

STUDENTS SAY ". . ."

Academics

Revered for its "tight-knit community, rigorous academics, project-based learning, and ingenious approach to education," Franklin W. Olin College of Engineering "bridges the gap between a traditional engineering education and [the] real world." On this campus of more than 300 undergraduates where "smart" and "quirky" are the norm, "Students [are] eager to be challenged academically and faculty gladly deliver that challenge." "Learning is doing" at Olin, and students laud the "innovative curriculum" for its "small classes," "hands-on approach," and "group-focused learning." "Olin believes in Renaissance engineers, " and allows "students to pursue passions beyond engineering." Though classes are "wickedly challenging," students say they "bond around the difficulty." The focus on "experiential education" and "entrepreneurial implementation" provides students with "the ability to help design the curriculum and the school culture." Professors are "one of the best—if not the best—part of Olin," and are frequently described as "always available, always knowledgeable, [and] always approachable." Students note that even the higher-ups go by a first name basis: "You can regularly chat with the president at lunch." The kicker? Every enrolled student receives a half-tuition scholarship. Students with additional demonstrated need are awarded grants.

Life

At Olin, the spirit of hands-on collaboration transcends the classroom. This "tight-knit community of eager learners and tinkerers" thrives on a spirit of "innovation and initiative." "Small, quirky, and somewhat in a bubble, but full of amazing adventures and opportunities," Olin is all about "bringing together amazing people to build twenty-first century engineers." "People work hard, but they also know how to play hard, take breaks, and have fun." Though students say that there are "boatloads of work," in general life at Olin is "intense and fun." "There's also a lot going on, like Nerf wars, tyrannosaurus dodge ball, experimental baking, pickup soccer, zombie video games, auditorium movie screenings, midnight dump raids, elevator dance parties, themed hall parties, etc." A typical day includes everything from "watching a movie" to a "midnight bike expedition." Located a stone's throw from Beantown, Olin students "go into Boston" on the weekends. Students here thrive on the spirit of "carpe diem," a phrase that has now become an "e-mail list to which almost all students subscribe." "Students send out these carpes about anything and everything that others might find interesting or fun." The facilities aren't too shabby either. Each room comes with "its own fridge, microwave, freezer, and bathroom/shower."

Student Body

"Olin is a place where intelligent, motivated students can explore their interests both in engineering and in life as a whole." "Take the nation's top engineering students, mix with awesome personalities, add a dash of amazing resources, shake vigorously." When it comes to describing the typical student, there is no status quo. "There are all sorts of people at Olin. Some of us avoid homework by discussing meta-physics and ethics. Others watch old episodes of *Firefly*...Some people read books in their spare time." The commonality? "Students care about their educations," and "everyone takes their own paths." Though students say they "may make geeky jokes," "People don't act like socially stunted nerds." "Passionate, intelligent, witty, [and] exceedingly interesting," "The typical student at Olin is atypical, whether that means having a hidden talent in unicycle fire juggling, a passion for writing musicals, an obsession with velociraptors, or a tendency to make pancakes at three in the morning every Thursday." Students say, "Every student at Olin is interesting enough that you want to sit down and talk to them for hours." "We think about pretty much everything from quantum physics to Obama's health care reform to *Speedracer* to what's for dinner." As innovative and diverse as their curriculum, Olin students "are straight, gay, Jewish, nerdy, partiers, gamers, rich, poor, and encompass all other social groups."

FINANCIAL AID: 781-292-2343 • E-MAIL: INFO@OLIN.EDU • WEBSITE: WWW.OLIN.EDU

THE PRINCETON REVIEW SAYS

Admissions

Very important factors considered include: Academic GPA, rigor of secondary school record, interview, talent/ability. *Important factors considered include:* Standardized test scores, character/personal qualities, extracurricular activities. *Other factors considered include:* Class rank, application essay, recommendation(s), alumni/ae relation, level of applicant's interest, volunteer work, work experience. SAT or ACT required; ACT with or without writing component accepted. High school diploma is required and GED is accepted. *Academic units required:* 4 English, 3 mathematics, 2 science (1 science lab), 2 social studies, 1 history, 4 academic electives, 2 years of algebra recommended. *Academic units recommended:* 4 English, 3 mathematics, 3 science (1 science lab), 2 foreign language, 2 social studies, 1 history, 1 visual/performing arts, 1 computer science, 3 academic electives, 2 years of algebra recommended.

Financial Aid

Students should submit: FAFSA. Filing deadline is February 15. The Princeton Review suggests that all financial aid forms be submitted as soon as possible after January 1. *Need-based scholarships/grants offered:* Federal Pell, SEOG, the school's own gift aid. State scholarships/grants processed for those eligible from their home state. Outside scholarships incorporated into package. *Loan aid offered:* Federal Direct Subsidized and Unsubsidized loans, Federal Direct PLUS loan for parents of dependent students. Applicants will be notified of awards on a rolling basis once accepted. Institutional employment is available—however, it is not considered part of the financial aid package. Highest amount earned per year from on-campus jobs $4,275. Off-campus job opportunities are good.

The Inside Word

Not many colleges can boast that they are filled with students who turned down offers from the likes of MIT, Cal Tech, and Carnegie Mellon, but Olin can. Olin is unique among engineering schools in that the admissions office really looks for more than just brains. Things like social skills and eloquence are taken extremely seriously here. Students who exhibit creativity, passion, and an entrepreneurial spirit are favored over their less adventurous peers. Reclusive geniuses seeking four years of technical monasticism will be at a disadvantage in the application pool.

THE SCHOOL SAYS ". . ."

From the Admissions Office

"Every enrolled student receives a half-tuition scholarship. Students with additional demonstrated need are awarded grants (no loans).

"The selection process at Olin College is unique to college admission. Each year a highly self-selecting pool of approximately 900 applicants is reviewed on traditional selection criteria. Approximately 240 finalists are invited to one of three Candidates' Weekends in February and March. These candidates are grouped in to five-person teams for a weekend of design-and-build exercises, group discussions, and interviews with Olin students, faculty, and alumni. Written evaluations and recommendations for each candidate are prepared by all Olin participants and submitted to the faculty admission committee. The committee admits about 135 candidates to yield a freshman class of eight-five. The result is that the freshman class is ultimately chosen on the strength of personal attributes such as leadership, cooperation, creativity, communication, and their enthusiasm for Olin College.

"A waiting list of approximately twenty to thirty is also established. All wait-list candidates who are not offered a spot in the class may defer enrollment for one year—with the guarantee of the Olin Scholarship. Wait-list students who opt to defer are strongly encouraged to do something unusual, exciting, and productive during their sabbatical year.

"Students applying for admission are required to take the SAT (or the ACT with the writing section). Olin College also requires scores from two SAT Subject Tests: math (Level 1 or 2) and a science of the student's choice."

SELECTIVITY	
Admissions Rating	99
# of applicants	768
% of applicants accepted	16
% of acceptees attending	69
# accepting a place on wait list	25
# admitted from wait list	5

FRESHMAN PROFILE	
Range SAT Critical Reading	660–740
Range SAT Math	700–780
Range SAT Writing	670–750
Range ACT Composite	32–33
Average HS GPA	3.9
% graduated top 10% of class	95
% graduated top 25% of class	99
% graduated top 50% of class	100

DEADLINES	
Regular	
Deadline	1/1
Notification	3/21
Nonfall registration?	no

FINANCIAL FACTS	
Financial Aid Rating	96
Annual tuition	$40,000
Room and board	$14,500
Required fees	$475
Books and supplies	$300
% needy frosh rec. need-based scholarship or grant aid	78
% needy UG rec. need-based scholarship or grant aid	67
% needy frosh rec. non-need-based scholarship or grant aid	100
% needy UG rec. non-need-based scholarship or grant aid	100
% needy frosh rec. need-based self-help aid	100
% needy UG rec. need-based self-help aid	100
% frosh rec. any financial aid	100
% UG rec. any financial aid	100
% UG borrow to pay for school	20
Average cumulative indebtedness	$11,900
% frosh need fully met	100
% ugrads need fully met	100
Average % of frosh need met	100
Average % of ugrad need met	100

FURMAN UNIVERSITY

3300 POINSETT HIGHWAY, GREENVILLE, SC 29613 • ADMISSIONS: 864-294-2034 • FAX: 864-294-2018

CAMPUS LIFE

Quality of Life Rating	**93**
Fire Safety Rating	**80**
Green Rating	**98**
Type of school	private
Environment	city

STUDENTS

Total undergrad enrollment	2,799
% male/female	43/57
% from out of state	72
% from public high school	59
% frosh live on campus	98
# of fraternities	7
# of sororities	7
% African American	5
% Asian	2
% Caucasian	82
% Hispanic	3
% international	2
# of countries represented	49

SURVEY SAYS . . .

Great computer facilities
School is well run
Students are friendly
Musical organizations are popular

ACADEMICS

Academic Rating	**90**
% students returning for sophomore year	89
% students graduating within 4 years	83
% students graduating within 6 years	87
Calendar	semester
Student/faculty ratio	11:1
Profs interesting rating	90
Profs accessible rating	91
Most classes have	10–19 students

MOST POPULAR MAJORS

political science; business administration; health sciences

APPLICANTS ALSO LOOK AT AND OFTEN PREFER

Duke University, Vanderbilt University, Wake Forest University, Washington and Lee University, The University of North Carolina at Chapel Hill

AND SOMETIMES PREFER

Davidson College, Emory University, University of South Carolina—Columbia, Clemson University

STUDENTS SAY ". . ."

Academics

Students can't stop talking about Furman University's "beautiful campus" and "warm, but challenging, academic community." This combination of brains and beauty is what makes Furman "an ideal choice" for four years. "Furman is about academic excellence through engaged learning," says one undergrad. Expect to hear "engaged" used "ad nauseum" on campus, but students claim that such a term "truly describes the kind of personal education available" thanks to "small class sizes," professors "who love to teach and enjoy getting to know their students," and "numerous" academic and extracurricular opportunities. Furman's science programs are "especially" challenging. Professors here are "very qualified (sometimes overqualified), passionate about what they teach, and are not easy graders." That said, they're "very willing to help their students." Despite being described as being "far to the left of the student body politically," the "good" administration is "really accessible." In the words of one undergrad, "They work with students to solve problems and genuinely care about making Furman a better school and not just a higher-ranking institution." However, some students find that the administration can be "very conservative in their thinking about student on-campus social life." Ultimately, while "Furman is not for the academically faint-of-heart," there's pride in knowing that "You're receiving a great education that will help you after you graduate."

Life

With so many students reporting that Furman's campus is "absolutely gorgeous," it's a wonder they ever leave it. However, "The surrounding city of Greenville is great," and its "thriving, small-town feel" brings in plenty of students on the weekends. Life at school is "busy, but so much fun." Students here spend "a lot of time thinking about academics, classes, and their future," but they also "invest a lot of time in their relationships with their friends." The school's "inclusive, close-knit community" is complemented with "lots of interesting things to do on campus, from music concerts to improv shows to sports games." "Weeknights are mostly spent studying," says one undergrad, which makes the library "a popular social spot." However, once the weekend rolls around, students spend their nights "out on the town." "There are tons of bars, restaurants, and clubs for people to go to" in Greenville, while those looking for a "party" can head for "fraternity houses." While the university "is not as crazy party-wise as larger schools," students "can find a party if they want to." Mostly though, students are happy to "meet up with friends for meals, coffee, or just to hang out."

Student Body

Many find that Furman is something of a "country club" when it comes to its student body, not just "because it is private and somewhat expensive," but also because the "typical" student is "wealthy, white, conservative, and preppy." Some find that "The majority of the student body is obsessed with being as 'generic' and 'normal' as possible, so that any student who does not fit the norm, be it due to a difference in religion or clothing style, will find it harder to fit in." However, others have found that there's more to the student body than first meets the eye. As one undergrad says, "The longer I stay at Furman, the more I realize that many students don't fit the stereotype." One thing that everyone seems to agree on is that everyone is "very accepting" and "very committed to their academic pursuits." That said, some wouldn't mind seeing the school "improve by attracting a more diverse student body, as well as lowering the cost of tuition."

FINANCIAL AID: 864-294-2204 • E-MAIL: ADMISSIONS@FURMAN.EDU • WEBSITE: WWW.FURMAN.EDU

THE PRINCETON REVIEW SAYS

Admissions

Very important factors considered include: Rigor of secondary school record. *Important factors considered include:* Class rank, application essay, academic GPA, standardized test scores, character/personal qualities, extracurricular activities. *Other factors considered include:* Recommendation(s), alumni/ae relation, first generation, level of applicant's interest, racial/ethnic status, talent/ability, volunteer work, work experience. ACT with writing component recommended. TOEFL required of all international applicants. High school diploma is required and GED is accepted. *Academic units required:* 4 English, 3 mathematics, 2 science (2 science labs), 2 foreign language, 3 social studies. *Academic units recommended:* 4 English, 4 mathematics, 3 science (2 science labs), 3 foreign language, 4 social studies.

Financial Aid

Students should submit: FAFSA, institution's own financial aid form, CSS/Financial Aid PROFILE, state aid form. South Carolina residents must complete required state forms for South Carolina. Regular filing deadline is January 15. The Princeton Review suggests that all financial aid forms be submitted as soon as possible after January 1. *Need-based scholarships/grants offered:* Federal Pell, SEOG, state scholarships/grants, private scholarships, the school's own gift aid, donor sponsored loans for study abroad. *Loan aid offered:* Direct Subsidized Stafford, Direct Unsubsidized Stafford, Direct PLUS, Federal Perkins, state loans, Federal SMART and ACG grants. Applicants will be notified of awards on or about March 15. Federal Work-Study Program available. Institutional employment available. Highest amount earned per year from on-campus jobs $1,500. Off-campus job opportunities are excellent.

The Inside Word

Chances are, if you're applying to Furman, you already have a good idea if you can get in or not. Furman's applicant pool is highly self-selected, meaning that the university's high acceptance rate doesn't equate to easy admission; in fact, it's the direct opposite, as applicants are typically very strong. Looking for a way to stand out from the crowd? Let the admissions committee know how valuable you are through your extracurriculars—sports, community service, and artistic endeavors will go a long way in making your case.

THE SCHOOL SAYS ". . ."

From the Admissions Office

"Furman University is a private liberal arts university that seeks and cultivates engaged, well-rounded, and passionate students. With 2,700 undergraduates from forty-six states and forty-seven countries, Furman's academic community prepares its students for meaningful lives of service and leadership through engaged learning, a process characterized by small classes, a close-knit community, student-faculty research, internships, and faculty-led study. With emphasis on a collaborative educational experience, Furman challenges students to put into practice the theories and methods learned from a distinguished and active faculty. Furman offers seventeen NCAA Division I men's and women's athletic teams, a nationally competitive music program, and hundreds of organizations and clubs. The stunning campus is located just minutes from vibrant downtown Greenville, noted as one of America's most livable cities, and the foothills of the Blue Ridge Mountains, where hiking and other adventure sports abound. Nearby are also some of the nation's most picturesque beaches and coastal towns. The Admission Committee believes that a student's potential for success is not determined solely by standardized test scores. Rather, it is interested in getting to know the whole student—one who seeks leadership, service, commitment to the community, and civic engagement. Therefore, Furman does not require prospective students to submit test scores unless the student determines the scores best represent academic ability and accomplishment. If a student chooses not to submit standardized test scores, then the university requires the student to participate in a formal interview as part of the application."

SELECTIVITY

Admissions Rating	**91**
# of applicants	4,888
% of applicants accepted	83
% of acceptees attending	19
# accepting a place on wait list	67
# admitted from wait list	4
# of early decision applicants	715
# accepted early decision	621

FRESHMAN PROFILE

Range SAT Critical Reading	560–670
Range SAT Math	570–670
Range SAT Writing	560–670
Range ACT Composite	25–30
Minimum paper TOEFL	570
Average HS GPA	3.5
% graduated top 10% of class	46
% graduated top 25% of class	77
% graduated top 50% of class	94

DEADLINES

Early decision	
Deadline	11/1
Notification	12/1
Early action	
Deadline	12/15
Notification	2/1
Regular	
Deadline	1/15
Notification	4/1
Nonfall registration?	no

FINANCIAL FACTS

Financial Aid Rating	**87**
Annual tuition	$41,152
Room and board	$10,509
Required fees	$380
Books and supplies	$1,110
% needy frosh rec. need-based scholarship or grant aid	98
% needy UG rec. need-based scholarship or grant aid	99
% needy frosh rec. non-need-based scholarship or grant aid	97
% needy UG rec. non-need-based scholarship or grant aid	98
% needy frosh rec. need-based self-help aid	59
% needy UG rec. need-based self-help aid	62
% frosh rec. any financial aid	85
% UG rec. any financial aid	83
% UG borrow to pay for school	43
Average cumulative indebtedness	$26,600
% frosh need fully met	35
% ugrads need fully met	36
Average % of frosh need met	74
Average % of ugrad need met	80

George Mason University

4400 University Drive, Fairfax, VA 22030-4444 • Admissions: 703-993-2400 • Fax: 703-993-4622

CAMPUS LIFE

Quality of Life Rating	**89**
Fire Safety Rating	**87**
Green Rating	**92**
Type of school	public
Environment	city

STUDENTS

Total undergrad enrollment	20,194
% male/female	48/52
% from out of state	23
% from public high school	87
% frosh live on campus	73
# of fraternities	23
# of sororities	15
% African American	9
% Asian	17
% Caucasian	47
% Hispanic	10
% international	3
# of countries represented	129

SURVEY SAYS . . .

Great computer facilities
Athletic facilities are great
Diverse student types on campus

ACADEMICS

Academic Rating	**76**
% students returning for sophomore year	87
% students graduating within 4 years	41
% students graduating within 6 years	64
Calendar	semester
Profs interesting rating	77
Profs accessible rating	80
Most classes have	20–29 students
Most lab/discussion sessions have	20–29 students

MOST POPULAR MAJORS

biology/biological sciences; political science and government; psychology

APPLICANTS ALSO LOOK AT AND SOMETIMES PREFER

The George Washington University, University of Virginia, Virginia Tech, James Madison University

STUDENTS SAY ". . ."

Academics

When describing George Mason University, current students are quick to quote the school motto: This is a place "where innovation is tradition." One student expands on that, saying, "Mason provides a space for students to achieve academic excellence; expand their knowledge of the diverse cultures, practices, and beliefs that surround them; and be prepared to enter the real-world as a global citizen." Diversity of the student body and proximity to Washington, D.C., are major selling points at this large public university, so it's no surprise that government, global affairs, and communication are popular majors. The faculty is "extremely knowledgeable and experienced" here, and "most try to learn your name." The Robinson Professors program brings "distinguished" professors in the liberal arts and sciences to campus, and students highly recommend classes taught by these professors. "They are experts in their fields, know what they are talking about, and have real life experiences they bring into the classroom." As well, "adjunct professors can be a great strength" because many of them are practicing professionals in D.C., and they "bring stories and examples from the real-world into our classroom." "For example, my professor for my Conflict 300 course is one of the main peace facilitators in the Georgian/South Ossetian conflict…when she returned from this conference [between the two countries], she told us everything and we got to see how the material and techniques we were studying are actually applied in our field." Students are equally satisfied with the school's administration: "The school will take action immediately to fix any problems that arise."

Life

Students at GMU never seem to be bored. Campus life is "filled with classes, friends, and work." On campus activities are very popular, and there are many on offer, including the university's ambassador program and intramural sports, such as underwater hockey and even quidditch. Just a few of the regular events on campus include "movies playing in our Johnson Center Cinema that are in between theater and DVD release, there are local bands playing live in the Rathskeller, the HIV/AIDS Awareness Fashion Show, drag competitions, University dances and highlighter parties." Greek life is there for those who want it: "We're not a 'fratty' school by any means, but the Greek community is very active and they do party." The campus is "beautiful," and "there are new housing buildings going up and even new academic buildings" (which is good news, since the two things students want to see improve are parking and housing availability). Students love living close to D.C. without the "hassle of city living," but when they want to head downtown, "it's very easy to get into the city by taking the Mason-to-Metro shuttle to the Vienna Metro Station, hopping on the Orange Line and then taking the Metro into the heart of the city!" Many students have internships in the city, including those "on Capitol Hill." "The music scene and bars are fantastic as well!"

Student Body

"Diversity is off the charts" at GMU, and many students describe their school as "a melting pot." As one student puts it, "There are so many different nationalities represented, so many stories, so many languages spoken. At the same time, it didn't take me long to find a good group of friends that were interested in hanging out and just having a good time together." "The typical GMU student is always busy—between coursework and extracurricular activities we're very involved on campus and are also into other activities, such as having jobs or internships." "Mason students are also politically active and global citizens." While a majority of students come from Virginia, there are also "students from over 130 countries, so everyone adds their own personal flavor to our student body." In spite of all these different backgrounds and cultures, "There are many student organizations that successfully create programs and events to unite students."

FINANCIAL AID: 703-993-2341 • E-MAIL: ADMISSIONS@GMU.EDU • WEBSITE: WWW.GMU.EDU

THE PRINCETON REVIEW SAYS

Admissions

Very important factors considered include: Academic GPA, rigor of secondary school record. *Important factors considered include:* Class rank, application essay, recommendation(s), alumni/ae relation, character/personal qualities, talent/ability. *Other factors considered include:* Standardized test scores, extracurricular activities, first generation, level of applicant's interest, volunteer work, work experience. ACT with or without writing component accepted. TOEFL required of all international applicants. High school diploma is required and GED is accepted. *Academic units required:* 4 English, 3 mathematics, 3 science (3 science labs), 2 foreign language, 3 social studies, 3 academic electives. *Academic units recommended:* 4 English, 4 mathematics, 4 science (4 science labs), 3 foreign language, 4 social studies, 5 academic electives.

Financial Aid

Students should submit: FAFSA. The Princeton Review suggests that all financial aid forms be submitted as soon as possible after January 1. *Need-based scholarships/grants offered:* Federal Pell, SEOG, state scholarships/grants, private scholarships, the school's own gift aid, Federal ACG and SMART Grants. *Loan aid offered:* Direct Subsidized Stafford, Direct Unsubsidized Stafford, Direct PLUS, Federal Perkins, Federal Nursing. Applicants will be notified of awards on a rolling basis beginning April 1. Federal Work-Study Program available. Institutional employment available. Highest amount earned per year from on-campus jobs $7,200. Off-campus job opportunities are excellent.

The Inside Word

GMU is a popular college choice for two key reasons: Its proximity to Washington, D.C., and the fact that its applicant pool isn't as competitive as those of University of Virginia and The College of William & Mary, the two flagships of the Virginia state system. GMU's quality faculty and impressive facilities make it worth consideration, especially if you're looking for a school in the D.C. area and affordability is a factor.

THE SCHOOL SAYS ". . ."

From the Admissions Office

"George Mason University enjoys the best location in the world. Our connections to the D.C. area result in faculty members who are engaged in the top research in their fields. We have professors who are regular contributors on all of the major news networks, and you can hardly listen to a program on National Public Radio without hearing from one of our scholars. This connectivity extends to our students, who take internships and get jobs at some of the best organizations and companies in the world. We have students at AOL/Time Warner, the National Institutes of Health, the Kennedy Center, the World Bank, the White House, and the National Zoo. We have all the advantages of the excitement of our nation's Capital combined with the comfort and security of this beautiful suburban campus. At Mason, we pride ourselves on being among the most innovative universities in the world. Many of our degree programs are the first of their kinds, including the first PhD program in biodefense, the first D.C.-based undergraduate program in conflict resolution, the first integrated school of information technology and engineering based on computer related programs, and one of the most innovative performing arts management programs in the United States. As a result, George Mason University is at the forefront of the emerging field of biotechnology, is a natural leader in the performing arts, and holds a preeminent position in the fields of economics, electronic journalism, and history, just to name a few. George Mason University will accept the ACT and the SAT. Scores from the writing section will not be considered in our admission decisions, as our faculty does not feel the writing section reflects quality or methodology of our award-winning writing across the curriculum program. Mason has the largest score-optional program in the United States."

SELECTIVITY

Admissions Rating	**87**
# of applicants	17,548
% of applicants accepted	53
% of acceptees attending	29
# accepting a place on wait list	1,317
# admitted from wait list	109

FRESHMAN PROFILE

Range SAT Critical Reading	520–620
Range SAT Math	530–630
Range ACT Composite	23–28
Minimum paper TOEFL	570
Minimum web-based TOEFL	88
Average HS GPA	3.7
% graduated top 10% of class	23
% graduated top 25% of class	60
% graduated top 50% of class	93

DEADLINES

Early action	
Deadline	11/1
Notification	12/17
Regular	
Priority	12/1
Deadline	1/15
Notification	4/1
Nonfall registration?	yes

FINANCIAL FACTS

Financial Aid Rating	**71**
Annual in-state tuition	$9,066
Annual out-state tuition	$26,544
Room and board	$8,950
Required fees	$2,514
Books and supplies	$900
% needy frosh rec. need-based scholarship or grant aid	79
% needy UG rec. need-based scholarship or grant aid	74
% needy frosh rec. non-need-based scholarship or grant aid	29
% needy UG rec. non-need-based scholarship or grant aid	15
% needy frosh rec. need-based self-help aid	76
% needy UG rec. need-based self-help aid	77
% frosh rec. any financial aid	68
% UG rec. any financial aid	57
% UG borrow to pay for school	54
Average cumulative indebtedness	$22,219
% frosh need fully met	8
% ugrads need fully met	8
Average % of frosh need met	73
Average % of ugrad need met	67

THE GEORGE WASHINGTON UNIVERSITY

2121 I Street Northwest, Suite 201, Washington, D.C. 20052 • Admissions: 202-994-6040 • Fax: 202-994-0325

CAMPUS LIFE

Quality of Life Rating	**92**
Fire Safety Rating	**60***
Green Rating	**91**
Type of school	private
Environment	metropolis

STUDENTS

Total undergrad enrollment	10,184
% male/female	44/56
% from out of state	99
% from public high school	70
% frosh live on campus	99
# of fraternities	12
# of sororities	9
% African American	7
% Asian	10
% Caucasian	57
% Hispanic	7
% international	7
# of countries represented	134

SURVEY SAYS . . .

Athletic facilities are great
Students love Washington, D.C.
Great off-campus food
Dorms are like palaces
Campus feels safe
Students are happy
Student publications are popular
Student government is popular
Political activism is popular
Internships are widely available

ACADEMICS

Academic Rating	**79**
% students returning for sophomore year	94
% students graduating within 4 years	76
Calendar	semester
Student/faculty ratio	13:1
Profs interesting rating	76
Profs accessible rating	80
Most classes have	10–19 students
Most lab/discussion sessions have	20–29 students

MOST POPULAR MAJORS

business administration and management; international relations and affairs; liberal arts and sciences/liberal studies

APPLICANTS ALSO LOOK AT AND OFTEN PREFER

Boston University, Emory University, Georgetown University, New York University, University of Virginia

AND SOMETIMES PREFER

Tufts University, University of Vermont, American University, The Catholic University of America, University of Maryland, College Park

STUDENTS SAY ". . ."

Academics

Get ready for "hands-on learning in an environment unlike any other" at George Washington University, where a location "four blocks away from the White House, down the street from the State Department, and near nearly all world headquarters" means "connections and opportunity" for undergraduates. Students call it "the perfect place to study international affairs" and praise the "amazing journalism program," the excellent political communications major, the political science program ("What political science major would pass up the chance to go toe-to-toe with protestors every week at the rallies outside the White House and Congress?"), the sciences (benefiting from the region's many research operations), and other departments too numerous to name. As one student puts it, "GW is a place where everyone can find their niche. Whether you are a politically active campaign volunteer, a hip-hop dancer, or a future Broadway actor, there is a place for you at GW." The school places a premium on hiring "professors of practice," teachers who "are either currently working in their field or just retired to teach." The faculty includes "former ambassadors, governors on the Federal Reserve Board, and CNN correspondents." These instructors emphasize "a balance between theory and practice that provides a foundation of knowledge and pragmatism from which students can feel prepared to enter any sector of work after school." The resulting education "gets students prepared for post-college life through an emphasis on internships and career-focused classes," putting "a lot of emphasis on acclimation to the real world."

Life

"Life at GW is about independence," students report. "There are no real cafeterias" on campus, "You have to rely on your own feet for transportation, and there is very little regulation in dorms." As a result, "There is little school spirit, but that fact alone seems to tie everyone together." The campus isn't entirely dead; there are frat parties ("which are hard to attend for non-member males and easy to attend for women"), the "occasional dorm-room party, which is usually small," and "apartment parties off campus" for upperclassmen. Campus organizations offer all sorts of events, and the school hosts a veritable who's who of guest speakers on a regular basis. Students love the school's Midnight Monument Tour, held "during the warmer parts of the year," during which "students walk the five blocks to the National Mall at 2:00 A.M. and tour the monuments. It is an awesome experience." Still, most students prefer to spend free time exploring D.C. on their own. The city provides "so much to do…it's overwhelming: monuments, free museums, fairs, every major sports franchise, and lots of student specials on the above things." D.C.'s upscale Georgetown neighborhood is nearby for "shopping, dining, seeing movies, etc.," while culturally diverse Adams Morgan is great for shopping, ethnic dining, and live music.

Student Body

"GW students are often stereotyped as spoiled and wealthy Northeastern kids," and while quite a few students here concede that there's some basis for the stereotype, most would also add that "white, preppy, fraternity/sorority members" who "like nice labels on their clothing" neither define nor dominate the campus population. "The reality is that there's tremendous diversity here of all stripes—geographic, religious, political, racial, and intellectual," with "students from dozens of countries and all fifty states." "GW is truly a national and even international school," one student writes. "I love walking out of the library and hearing conversations happening in a half-dozen languages." The school has always been a popular destination for Jewish students. There is also "a huge LGBT group on campus, with very little discrimination." Nearly everyone here is "incredibly driven," "combining classes with an internship, maybe a sport, and usually a few extracurriculars."

FINANCIAL AID: 202-994-6620 • E-MAIL: GWADM@GWU.EDU • WEBSITE: WWW.GWU.EDU

THE PRINCETON REVIEW SAYS

Admissions

Very important factors considered include: Academic GPA, rigor of secondary school record. *Important factors considered include:* Class rank, application essay, recommendation(s), standardized test scores, extracurricular activities, interview, talent/ability, volunteer work. *Other factors considered include:* Alumni/ae relation, character/personal qualities, first generation, geographical residence, level of applicant's interest, racial/ethnic status, work experience. SAT or ACT required; ACT with or without writing component accepted. TOEFL required of all international applicants. High school diploma is required and GED is not accepted. *Academic units required:* 4 English, 2 mathematics, 2 science (1 science lab), 2 foreign language, 2 social studies. *Academic units recommended:* 4 English, 4 mathematics, 4 science, 4 foreign language, 4 social studies.

Financial Aid

Students should submit: FAFSA, CSS/Financial Aid PROFILE. Regular filing deadline is February 1. The Princeton Review suggests that all financial aid forms be submitted as soon as possible after January 1. *Need-based scholarships/grants offered:* Federal Pell, SEOG, state scholarships/grants, the school's own gift aid. *Loan aid offered:* Direct Subsidized Stafford, Direct Unsubsidized Stafford, Direct PLUS, Federal Perkins. Applicants will be notified of awards on a rolling basis beginning March 24. Federal Work-Study Program available. Institutional employment available. Highest amount earned per year from on-campus jobs $3,160. Off-campus job opportunities are excellent.

The Inside Word

With more than 21,000 applications to process annually, GW could be forgiven if it gave student essays only a perfunctory glance. The school insists, however, that essays are carefully reviewed. Take note and proceed accordingly. Application rates have surged throughout the past decade. This school is only getting more popular, so applicants should be prepared to bring their A-game.

THE SCHOOL SAYS ". . ."

From the Admissions Office

"GW students are excited about the discovery and application of new knowledge so they can change the world and improve the human experience. At many universities, the edge of campus is the real world, but not at GW, where our campus and Washington, D.C., are seamless. We look for bold, bright students who are ambitious, energetic, and self-motivated. Here, where we are so close to the centers of thought and action in every field we offer, we easily integrate our outstanding academic tradition and faculty connections with the best student research, internship, and job opportunities of Washington, D.C. A generous scholarship and financial assistance program attracts top students from all parts of the country and the world."

SELECTIVITY	
Admissions Rating	**95**
# of applicants	21,591
% of applicants accepted	33
% of acceptees attending	31
# accepting a place on wait list	2,477
# admitted from wait list	112
# of early decision applicants	2,318
# accepted early decision	838
FRESHMAN PROFILE	
Range SAT Critical Reading	600–690
Range SAT Math	610–690
Range SAT Writing	620–710
Range ACT Composite	27–31
Minimum paper TOEFL	550
% graduated top 10% of class	78
% graduated top 25% of class	95
% graduated top 50% of class	100
DEADLINES	
Early decision	
Deadline	11/10
Notification	12/15
Regular	
Priority	12/1
Deadline	1/10
Notification	4/1
Nonfall registration?	yes
FINANCIAL FACTS	
Financial Aid Rating	**91**
Annual tuition	$42,381
Room and board	$12,960
Required fees	$44
Books and supplies	$1,275
% needy frosh rec. need-based scholarship or grant aid	97
% needy UG rec. need-based scholarship or grant aid	95
% needy frosh rec. non-need-based scholarship or grant aid	47
% needy UG rec. non-need-based scholarship or grant aid	27
% needy frosh rec. need-based self-help aid	78
% needy UG rec. need-based self-help aid	81
Average cumulative indebtedness	$32,714
% frosh need fully met	77
% ugrads need fully met	69

GEORGETOWN UNIVERSITY

THIRTY-SEVENTH AND O STREETS, NORTHWEST, WASHINGTON, D.C. 20057 • ADMISSIONS: 202-687-3600 • FAX: 202-687-5084

CAMPUS LIFE

Quality of Life Rating	80
Fire Safety Rating	84
Green Rating	85
Type of school	private
Affiliation	Roman Catholic
Environment	metropolis

STUDENTS

Total undergrad enrollment	7,590
% male/female	45/55
% from out of state	99
% from public high school	46
% frosh live on campus	100
% African American	6
% Asian	9
% Caucasian	61
% Hispanic	7
% international	10
# of countries represented	138

SURVEY SAYS . . .

Students love Washington, D.C.
Great off-campus food
Students are happy
Frats and sororities are unpopular or nonexistent
Student publications are popular
Political activism is popular
Lots of beer drinking

ACADEMICS

Academic Rating	87
% students returning for sophomore year	96
% students graduating within 4 years	85
% students graduating within 6 years	93
Calendar	semester
Student/faculty ratio	10:1
Profs interesting rating	82
Profs accessible rating	76

MOST POPULAR MAJORS

English language and literature; international relations and affairs; political science and government

APPLICANTS ALSO LOOK AT AND OFTEN PREFER

University of Pennsylvania, Duke University

AND SOMETIMES PREFER

Cornell University, University of Virginia, University of Notre Dame, Northwestern University

AND RARELY PREFER

Boston College, Tufts University, New York University, The George Washington University

STUDENTS SAY ". . ."

Academics

This moderately sized elite academic establishment stays true to its Jesuit foundations by educating its students with the idea of "cura personalis," or "care for the whole person." The "well-informed" student body perpetuates upon itself, creating an atmosphere full of vibrant intellectual life, that is "also balanced with extracurricular learning and development." "Georgetown is…a place where people work very, very hard without feeling like they are in direct competition," says an international politics major. Located in Washington, D.C., there's a noted School of Foreign Service here, and the access to internships is a huge perk for those in political or government programs. In addition, the proximity to the nation's capital fetches "high-profile guest speakers," with many of the most powerful people in global politics speaking regularly, as well as a large number of adjunct professors who, either are currently working in government, or have retired from high-level positions.

Georgetown offers a "great selection of very knowledgeable professors, split with a good proportion of those who are experienced in realms outside of academia (such as former government officials) and career academics," though there are a few superstars who might be "somewhat less than totally collegial." Professors tend to be "fantastic scholars and teachers" and are "generally available to students," as well as often being "interested in getting to know you as a person (if you put forth the effort to talk to them and go to office hours)." Though Georgetown has a policy of grade deflation, meaning "A's are hard to come by," there are "a ton of interesting courses available," and TAs are used only for optional discussion sessions and help with grading. The academics "can be challenging or they can be not so much (not that they are ever really easy, just easier);" it all depends on the courses you choose and how much you actually do the work. The school administration is well-meaning and "usually willing to talk and compromise with students," but the process of planning activities can be full of headaches and bureaucracy, and the administration itself "sometimes is overstretched or has trouble transmitting its message." Nevertheless, "a motivated student can get done what he or she wants."

Life

Students are "extremely well aware of the world around them," from government to environment, social to economic, and "Georgetown is the only place where an argument over politics, history, or philosophy is preceded by a keg stand." Hoyas like to have a good time on weekends, and parties at campus and off-campus apartments and townhouses "are generally open to all comers and tend to have a somewhat networking atmosphere; meeting people you don't know is a constant theme." With such a motivated group on such a high-energy campus, "people are always headed somewhere, it seems—to rehearsal, athletic practice, a guest speaker, [or] the gym." Community service and political activism are particularly popular, as is basketball. Everything near Georgetown is in walking distance, including the world of D.C.'s museums, restaurants, and stores, and "grabbing or ordering late night food is a popular option."

Student Body

There are "a lot of wealthy students on campus," and preppy-casual is the fashion de rigueur; this is "definitely not a 'granola' school," but students from diverse backgrounds are typically welcomed by people wanting to learn about different experiences. Indeed, everyone here is well-traveled and well-educated, and there are "a ton of international students." "You better have at least some interest in politics or you will feel out-of-place," says a student. The school can also be "a bit cliquish, with athletes at the top," but there are "plenty of groups for everybody to fit into and find their niche," and "there is much crossover between groups."

FINANCIAL AID: 202-687-4547 • E-MAIL: GUADMISS@GEORGETOWN.EDU • WEBSITE: WWW.GEORGETOWN.EDU

THE PRINCETON REVIEW SAYS

Admissions

Very important factors considered include: Class rank, application essay, academic GPA, recommendation(s), rigor of secondary school record, standardized test scores, character/personal qualities, talent/ability. *Important factors considered include:* Extracurricular activities, interview, volunteer work. *Other factors considered include:* Alumni/ae relation, geographical residence, racial/ethnic status, state residency, work experience. SAT or ACT required; ACT with or without writing component accepted. TOEFL required of all international applicants. High school diploma is required and GED is accepted. *Academic units recommended:* 4 English, 2 mathematics, 1 science, 2 foreign language, 2 social studies, 2 history.

Financial Aid

Students should submit: FAFSA, CSS/Financial Aid PROFILE, noncustodial PROFILE, business/farm supplement, tax returns. Regular filing deadline is February 1. The Princeton Review suggests that all financial aid forms be submitted as soon as possible after January 1. *Need-based scholarships/grants offered:* Federal Pell, SEOG, state scholarships/grants, private scholarships, the school's own gift aid. *Loan aid offered:* Direct Subsidized Stafford, Direct Unsubsidized Stafford, Direct PLUS, Federal Perkins, Federal Nursing, alternative loans. Applicants will be notified of awards on or about April 1. Federal Work-Study Program available. Institutional employment available. Off-campus job opportunities are excellent.

The Inside Word

It was always tough to get admitted to Georgetown, but in the early 1980s Patrick Ewing and the Hoyas created a basketball sensation that catapulted the place into position as one of the most selective universities in the nation. There has been no turning back since. GU gets almost ten applications for every space in the entering class, and the academic strength of the pool is impressive. Virtually fifty percent of the entire student body took AP courses in high school. Candidates who are wait-listed should hold little hope for an offer of admission; over the past several years Georgetown has taken very few off their lists.

THE SCHOOL SAYS ". . ."

From the Admissions Office

"Georgetown was founded in 1789 by John Carroll, who concurred with his contemporaries Benjamin Franklin and Thomas Jefferson in believing that the success of the young democracy depended upon an educated and virtuous citizenry. Carroll founded the school with the dynamic Jesuit tradition of education, characterized by humanism and committed to the assumption of responsibility and action. Georgetown is a national and international university, enrolling students from all fifty states and over 100 foreign countries. Undergraduate students are enrolled in one of four undergraduate schools: the College of Arts and Sciences, School of Foreign Service, Georgetown School of Business, and Georgetown School of Nursing and Health Studies. All students share a common liberal arts core and have access to the entire university curriculum.

"Applicants must submit scores from SAT or the ACT. SAT Subject Tests can also be recommended."

SELECTIVITY	
Admissions Rating	**98**
# of applicants	19,254
% of applicants accepted	18
% of acceptees attending	46
# accepting a place on wait list	1,246
# admitted from wait list	2

FRESHMAN PROFILE	
Range SAT Critical Reading	640–740
Range SAT Math	650–750
Range ACT Composite	29–33
Minimum paper TOEFL	200
% graduated top 10% of class	90
% graduated top 25% of class	97
% graduated top 50% of class	99

DEADLINES	
Early action	
Deadline	11/1
Notification	12/15
Regular	
Deadline	1/10
Notification	4/1
Nonfall registration?	no

FINANCIAL FACTS	
Financial Aid Rating	**95**
Annual tuition	$42,360
Board only	$3,644
Required fees	$570
Books and supplies	$1,200
% needy frosh rec. need-based scholarship or grant aid	99
% needy UG rec. need-based scholarship or grant aid	91
% needy frosh rec. non-need-based scholarship or grant aid	36
% needy UG rec. non-need-based scholarship or grant aid	26
% needy frosh rec. need-based self-help aid	97
% needy UG rec. need-based self-help aid	86
% UG borrow to pay for school	39
Average cumulative indebtedness	$25,315
% frosh need fully met	100
% ugrads need fully met	100
Average % of frosh need met	100
Average % of ugrad need met	100

GEORGIA INSTITUTE OF TECHNOLOGY

OFFICE OF UNDERGRADUATE ADMISSIONS, ATLANTA, GA 30332-0320 • ADMISSIONS: 404-894-4154 • FAX: 404-894-9511

CAMPUS LIFE

Quality of Life Rating	**78**
Fire Safety Rating	**88**
Green Rating	**99**
Type of school	public
Environment	metropolis

STUDENTS

Total undergrad enrollment	13,300
% male/female	68/32
% from out of state	26
% from public high school	86
% frosh live on campus	56
# of fraternities	39
# of sororities	17
% African American	7
% Asian	17
% Caucasian	59
% Hispanic	6
% international	8
# of countries represented	74

SURVEY SAYS . . .

Great computer facilities
Athletic facilities are great
Diverse student types on campus
Students love Atlanta, GA
Great off-campus food
Everyone loves the Yellow Jackets
Student publications are popular

ACADEMICS

Academic Rating	**75**
% students returning for sophomore year	95
% students graduating within 4 years	31
% students graduating within 6 years	80
Calendar	semester
Student/faculty ratio	17:1
Profs interesting rating	67
Profs accessible rating	65
Most classes have	20–29 students
Most lab/discussion sessions have	20–29 students

MOST POPULAR MAJORS

business administration and management; industrial engineering; mechanical engineering

APPLICANTS ALSO LOOK AT AND OFTEN PREFER

Duke University, University of Florida, University of Georgia, University of Michigan—Ann Arbor, Virginia Tech, Massachusetts Institute of Technology

AND SOMETIMES PREFER

University of Virginia, The University of North Carolina at Chapel Hill, University of Illinois at Urbana-Champaign, The University of Texas at Austin, Cornell University, University of California—Berkeley

AND RARELY PREFER

Purdue University—West Lafayette, Rensselaer Polytechnic Institute, Rice University, University of Maryland, College Park

STUDENTS SAY ". . ."

Academics

The Georgia Institute of Technology—Georgia Tech for short—"challenges its students academically while providing a culturally diverse environment, all culminating in preparation for life after college." Students warn that the school "is extremely challenging, academically. If you don't like learning it's probably not for you." They also point out that "since Georgia Tech is a research school, most professors are more concerned about their own research than the quality of their teaching. You're basically teaching yourself the entire subject in order to prepare for an almost impossible exam," although students also add that "while many of the professors at Georgia Tech are focused on their research, there are teachers who truly care about their students and the learning process." As one student advises, "a lot of classes seem to be more about getting the right professor: Some are bad teachers, some are inaccessible, but some are so good that their classes fill up seconds after registration opens." And while "classes are challenging," they're also "interesting" so all of that hard work is "not too bad. If you're organized and get help when you need it, you'll be okay, because we have tons of free tutoring on campus…If you need help with anything, there are countless different places that offer tutoring. The best resource is usually fellow students. Because everyone knows how tough of a school it is, there is a spirit of camaraderie here that you don't find anywhere else." Students also appreciate that Tech "is one of the only schools in the country that offers the BS distinction for liberal arts majors because we [get] such a rigorous grounding in math and science." Finally, students note that "career services are outstanding."

Life

One Georgia Tech engineer sums up the typical student itinerary this way: "Study, study, drink. Repeat." As another student puts it, "there is a saying here that between good grades, a social life, and sleep, you can only have two." That's why "basically people bust their [butts] during the week, and when the weekends arrive they're prepared to let loose a bit." Fortunately, "Georgia Tech has a little something for everyone. Salsa club on weekends, musical groups, intramural sports—even a skydiving club!" Other options include "a 'good enough' NCAA Division I sports program, a good social scene," a welcoming Greek community, "and for everyone else, there's the city of Atlanta right at your doorstep. You're just a short ride away from movies, shopping, the Fox Theatre, the High Museum of Art, Piedmont Park, and one of the best club and bar scenes in the South," centered mainly in the neighborhoods of Buckhead and Midtown. For those without cars in this driving city, transportation comes in the form of "a 'Tech Trolley' that takes a route around midtown, and a 'Stinger Shuttle' that goes to the MARTA [Atlanta's subway] station, giving students access to the airport, downtown (although that is walkable), and Lenox Square Mall." With more than "300 organizations already on campus," students seeking leadership experience can most likely find it, and they can find other students with like-minded interests.

Student Body

"The greatest strength of Georgia Tech is its diversity," undergrads report. "Students, activities, opportunities, teachers—all are diverse." One observes that the school hosts "the full range of stereotypes, from the fraternity boys with their croackies and boat shoes to the socially challenged nerds who stay in their rooms 24/7 programming computers. But no matter what, you know everyone is highly intelligent. Many times it is the students who have the best grades who are the drunkest." One student explains, "Unlike at high school, no one looks down upon you if you know the entire periodic table, if you can do differential equations, or you can speak three languages; rather, you are respected." One sore spot: Men outnumber women here by greater than a two to one ratio. The situation is most pronounced in engineering (three to one) and computer (more than four to one) disciplines. Women actually outnumber men in the liberal arts and science colleges.

FINANCIAL AID: 404-894-4160 • E-MAIL: ADMISSION@GATECH.EDU • WEBSITE: WWW.GATECH.EDU

THE PRINCETON REVIEW SAYS

Admissions

Very important factors considered include: Academic GPA, rigor of secondary school record, extracurricular activities. *Important factors considered include:* Application essay, standardized test scores, character/personal qualities, geographical residence, state residency, talent/ability, volunteer work, work experience. *Other factors considered include:* Alumni/ae relation, racial/ethnic status. SAT or ACT required; ACT with writing component required. High school diploma is required and GED is accepted. *Academic units required:* 4 English, 4 mathematics, 3 science (3 science labs), 2 foreign language, 3 social studies.

Financial Aid

Students should submit: FAFSA, institution's own financial aid form. Regular filing deadline is March 1. The Princeton Review suggests that all financial aid forms be submitted as soon as possible after January 1. *Need-based scholarships/grants offered:* Federal Pell, SEOG, state scholarships/grants, private scholarships, the school's own gift aid. *Loan aid offered:* Direct Subsidized Stafford, Direct Unsubsidized Stafford, Direct PLUS, Federal Perkins, college/university loans from institutional funds. Applicants will be notified of awards on or about April 1. Federal Work-Study Program available. Institutional employment available. Off-campus job opportunities are excellent.

The Inside Word

Students considering Georgia Tech shouldn't be deceived by the relatively high acceptance rate. Georgia Tech is a demanding school, and its applicant pool is largely self-selecting. While admissions counselors have begun to implement a more well-rounded approach to the admissions process, grades and test scores are still where candidates make their mark. Requirements vary depending on the school one applies to at Georgia Tech—applicants are advised to inquire in advance.

THE SCHOOL SAYS ". . ."

From the Admissions Office

"Georgia Tech consistently ranks among the nation's top public universities producing leaders in engineering, computing, management, architecture, and the sciences while remaining one of the best college buys in the country. The 330-acre campus is nestled in the heart of the fun, dynamic and progressive city of Atlanta. During the past decade, over $400 million invested in campus improvements has yielded new state-of-the-art academic and research buildings, apartment-style housing, phenomenal social and recreational facilities, and the most extension fiber-optic cable system on any college campus.

"Georgia Tech has a great academic reputation, and our graduates are well-prepared to meet today's challenges. A unique advantage many students find is Georgia Tech's strong emphasis on undergraduate students. Undergraduates can gain practical work experience through our co-op and internship programs and can begin doing research as early as their freshman year. Students can also gain an international perspective through study abroad, work abroad, or the international plan. In addition, Georgia Tech has added the Clough Undergraduate Center, a state-of-the-art facility that includes forty-one classrooms, two 300-plus seat auditoriums, group study rooms, presentation rehearsal studios, a rooftop garden, and a café.

"With a Division I ACC sports program and access to Atlanta's music, theater, and other cultural venues, Georgia Tech offers its diverse and passionate student body a unique combination of top academics in a thriving and vibrant setting. We encourage you to come visit campus and see why Georgia Tech continues to attract the nation's most motivated, interesting, and creative students."

SELECTIVITY	
Admissions Rating	**96**
# of applicants	14,088
% of applicants accepted	51
% of acceptees attending	37
# accepting a place on wait list	1,219
# admitted from wait list	303
FRESHMAN PROFILE	
Range SAT Critical Reading	600–690
Range SAT Math	660–760
Range SAT Writing	600–700
Range ACT Composite	28–32
Average HS GPA	3.9
% graduated top 10% of class	83
% graduated top 25% of class	98
% graduated top 50% of class	100
DEADLINES	
Early action	
Deadline	10/1
Notification	11/20
Regular	
Deadline	1/10
Notification	3/15
Nonfall registration?	yes
FINANCIAL FACTS	
Financial Aid Rating	**77**
Annual in-state tuition	$7,282
Annual out-state tuition	$25,492
Room and board	$10,924
Required fees	$2,370
Books and supplies	$1,000
% needy frosh rec. need-based scholarship or grant aid	93
% needy UG rec. need-based scholarship or grant aid	84
% needy frosh rec. non-need-based scholarship or grant aid	79
% needy UG rec. non-need-based scholarship or grant aid	63
% needy frosh rec. need-based self-help aid	59
% needy UG rec. need-based self-help aid	53
% frosh rec. any financial aid	82
% UG rec. any financial aid	81
% UG borrow to pay for school	50
Average cumulative indebtedness	$23,427
% frosh need fully met	20
% ugrads need fully met	14
Average % of frosh need met	67
Average % of ugrad need met	58

GETTYSBURG COLLEGE

ADMISSIONS OFFICE, GETTYSBURG, PA 17325-1484 • ADMISSIONS: 717-337-6100 • FAX: 717-337-6145

CAMPUS LIFE

Quality of Life Rating	82
Fire Safety Rating	92
Green Rating	84
Type of school	private
Affiliation	Lutheran
Environment	village

STUDENTS

Total undergrad enrollment	2,500
% male/female	49/51
% from out of state	74
% from public high school	70
% frosh live on campus	100
# of fraternities	12
# of sororities	7
% African American	4
% Asian	2
% Caucasian	81
% Hispanic	4
% international	2
# of countries represented	31

SURVEY SAYS . . .

Lab facilities are great
Great computer facilities
Great food on campus
Dorms are like palaces
Campus feels safe
Students are happy
Frats and sororities dominate social scene
Lots of beer drinking

ACADEMICS

Academic Rating	97
% students returning for sophomore year	92
% students graduating within 4 years	80
% students graduating within 6 years	85
Calendar	semester
Student/faculty ratio	10:1
Profs interesting rating	93
Profs accessible rating	94
Most classes have	10–19 students

MOST POPULAR MAJORS

business/commerce; political science and government; psychology

APPLICANTS ALSO LOOK AT AND OFTEN PREFER

Colgate University

AND SOMETIMES PREFER

Bucknell University

AND RARELY PREFER

Muhlenberg College

STUDENTS SAY ". . ."

Academics

Personal and intellectual growth is at the heart of the Gettysburg College experience. Students eagerly praise the school's "friendly, community-oriented atmosphere," and competent, caring professors. "The faculty takes a developed interest in the students' academics and successes, [and] the campus offers countless opportunities for leadership, self-discovery, and the like." In fact, first-year students are surprised to find that "by the first day, the professor knows each student by name and why they're taking the class." With uniformly small class sizes and an emphasis on discussion in the classroom, "Professors at Gettysburg make sure that students understand why they are learning the things that they are, and there is a lot of emphasis put on putting 'theory into practice' outside of the classroom." "Many professors go above and beyond, making themselves available to aid students." A current student shares, "My Intro to Chemistry professor would be at the Science Center until 11 P.M. before an exam, helping everyone study." Academic opportunities—such as the "amazing study abroad program"—are ample at Gettysburg. Plus, as an exclusively undergraduate institution, Gettysburg "allows for opportunities (i.e., research, publications) that many do not get" at larger universities. In this "nurturing environment," the "administration knows students by name" and even the "registrar, transportation services, off-campus studies, and library staff are lovely and do everything they can to help you." In particular, "President Riggs (a Gettysburg alum and former faculty member) is a phenomenal community leader and makes a sincere effort to connect with students, faculty, and staff."

Life

Enthusiastic and overcommitted, most students at Gettysburg are pursuing "a major and a minor or a double-major, and a majority are involved in at least several college organizations (whether it's a community service group, sports team, or Greek organization)." With so much on their plate, it is no surprise that "the students at Gettysburg buckle down and work hard" during the week. Socially, "Life at Gettysburg is very Greek-oriented," and, come the weekend, "frat hopping" is "popular on this campus." Not your style? No worries: Greek life may be "huge" on campus; "However, that does not mean that that is the only thing to do." For students looking for alternate activities, the school hosts "movie nights, plays, and musical performances." Many students also "love going to our theme parties and Happy Hours at the Attic, our on-campus nightclub," while others "get together with friends and watch movies or go out for coffee." For a relaxing respite, "The surrounding area and town is beautiful, so one of my favorite things to do is just walk around out on the battlefields or through town." In addition, "People also like to get off campus traveling to bigger city areas like Baltimore, Harrisburg, D.C., and even Philly and New York City."

Student Body

Academics come first at Gettysburg, where "The student body is extremely intelligent and motivated and serious about their work." When they're not studying, "Gettysburg's student body is very involved" in the school and local community, and "Volunteering is very popular." "Each student—in one way or another—takes part in community service during their time at Gettysburg." Demographically, "Most of the student body is...middle-class, white, and from the Northeast." And, lest we forget, the Gettysburg student body is also well known for its uniform "tendency to wear preppy clothes." A current student elaborates, "Open up a J. Crew magazine and find the most attractive models in it and you have a typical Gettysburg College student." While some say the student body has a "cookie-cutter" feel to it, others remind us that "While Gettysburg has a reputation for being mostly white, upper-class students, there is diversity all around if you are willing to open up your eyes and see it."

FINANCIAL AID: 717-337-6611 • E-MAIL: ADMISS@GETTYSBURG.EDU • WEBSITE: WWW.GETTYSBURG.EDU

THE PRINCETON REVIEW SAYS

Admissions

Very important factors considered include: Class rank, academic GPA, recommendation(s), rigor of secondary school record. *Important factors considered include:* Application essay, standardized test scores, character/personal qualities, extracurricular activities, interview, talent/ability, volunteer work. *Other factors considered include:* Alumni/ae relation, first generation, geographical residence, level of applicant's interest, racial/ethnic status, work experience. ACT with or without writing component accepted. TOEFL required of all international applicants. High school diploma is required and GED is accepted. *Academic units required:* 4 English, 3 mathematics, 3 science (3 science labs), 3 foreign language, 3 social studies, 3 history. *Academic units recommended:* 4 English, 4 mathematics, 4 science (4 science labs), 4 foreign language, 4 social studies, 4 history.

Financial Aid

Students should submit: FAFSA, CSS/Financial Aid PROFILE, business/farm supplement. Regular filing deadline is February 15. The Princeton Review suggests that all financial aid forms be submitted as soon as possible after January 1. *Need-based scholarships/grants offered:* Federal Pell, SEOG, state scholarships/grants, private scholarships, the school's own gift aid. *Loan aid offered:* Direct Subsidized Stafford, Direct Unsubsidized Stafford, Direct PLUS, Federal Perkins, college/university loans from institutional funds. Applicants will be notified of awards on or about March 26. Federal Work-Study Program available. Institutional employment available. Highest amount earned per year from on-campus jobs $1,500. Off-campus job opportunities are excellent.

The Inside Word

Prospective Gettysburg students can register for an account on the school's website to view Gettysburg events in their area or connect with students on campus. To really get a feel for Gettysburg, however, many students say a campus visit is a must. If you're lucky enough to gain admission to this competitive liberal arts school, a campus visit might be just the thing to seal the deal.

THE SCHOOL SAYS ". . ."

From the Admissions Office

"Four major goals of Gettysburg College to best prepare students to enter the real world, include, first, to accelerate the intellectual development of our first-year students by integrating them more quickly into the intellectual life of the campus; second, to use interdisciplinary courses combining the intellectual approaches of various fields; third, to encourage students to develop an international perspective through course work, study abroad, association with international faculty, and a variety of extracurricular activities; and fourth, to encourage students to develop (1) a capacity for independent study by ensuring that all students work closely with individual faculty members on an extensive project during their undergraduate years and (2) the ability to work with their peers by making the small group a central feature in college life.

"Gettysburg College strongly recommends that freshman applicants submit scores from the SAT. Students may also choose to submit scores from the ACT (with or without the writing component) in lieu of the SAT."

SELECTIVITY	
Admissions Rating	**94**
# of applicants	5,662
% of applicants accepted	40
% of acceptees attending	32
# of early decision applicants	442
# accepted early decision	339

FRESHMAN PROFILE	
Range SAT Critical Reading	610–690
Range SAT Math	610–690
% graduated top 10% of class	71
% graduated top 25% of class	89
% graduated top 50% of class	99

DEADLINES	
Early decision	
Deadline	11/15
Notification	12/15
Regular	
Priority	2/1
Deadline	2/1
Notification	4/1
Nonfall registration?	yes

FINANCIAL FACTS	
Financial Aid Rating	**94**
Annual tuition	$44,210
Room and board	$10,560
Books and supplies	$1,000
% needy frosh rec. need-based scholarship or grant aid	94
% needy UG rec. need-based scholarship or grant aid	93
% needy frosh rec. non-need-based scholarship or grant aid	51
% needy UG rec. non-need-based scholarship or grant aid	47
% needy frosh rec. need-based self-help aid	89
% needy UG rec. need-based self-help aid	88
% frosh rec. any financial aid	56
% UG rec. any financial aid	54
% UG borrow to pay for school	59
Average cumulative indebtedness	$29,067
% frosh need fully met	93
% ugrads need fully met	93
Average % of frosh need met	100
Average % of ugrad need met	100

GONZAGA UNIVERSITY

502 East Boone Avenue, Spokane, WA 99258 • Admissions: 509-313-6572 • Fax: 509-313-5780

CAMPUS LIFE

Quality of Life Rating	**74**
Fire Safety Rating	**87**
Green Rating	**83**
Type of school	private
Affiliation	Roman Catholic
Environment	city

STUDENTS

Total undergrad enrollment	4,796
% male/female	47/53
% from out of state	52
% from public high school	59
% frosh live on campus	98
% African American	1
% Asian	4
% Caucasian	74
% Hispanic	7
% Native American	1
% international	2
# of countries represented	20

SURVEY SAYS . . .

Athletic facilities are great
Students are friendly
Everyone loves the Bulldogs
Intramural sports are popular
Frats and sororities are unpopular or nonexistent

ACADEMICS

Academic Rating	**80**
% students returning for sophomore year	91
% students graduating within 4 years	69
% students graduating within 6 years	83
Calendar	semester
Student/faculty ratio	11:1
Profs interesting rating	82
Profs accessible rating	85
Most classes have	20–29 students
Most lab/discussion sessions have	10–19 students

MOST POPULAR MAJORS

political science and government; psychology

APPLICANTS ALSO LOOK AT AND OFTEN PREFER

University of Notre Dame

AND SOMETIMES PREFER

Santa Clara University, University of Washington

AND RARELY PREFER

Washington State University, University of San Francisco

STUDENTS SAY ". . ."

Academics

Gonzaga University "has a strong Jesuit Catholic tradition and has sustained an environment of academic excellence." By far, the two most commonly cited strengths are the basketball team and the "awesome community!" Gonzaga is a "close-knit community." "At Gonzaga, we are one big family," one student says. "Everyone is incredibly friendly," and there's "a great sense of school spirit and a family-like environment." "Not to mention being able to cheer in of the most intimidating basketball stadiums in the United States." "It is a family here, and you really get to know your professors," one student explains. "Everyone here is interconnected, and basketball is wonderful too! It's a way we all come together." Students also believe "the Jesuit mission of Gonzaga sets it apart from other schools." Gonzaga "is a socially competent, caring institution" where you'll "be constantly challenged to be your best, make lifelong relationships, and develop a critical understanding of the world around you." The professors get mixed reviews: "It is about a fifty percent chance of getting a good professor." "Professors are good in general, but adjunct faculty is typically hired at the last minute and not good," one student explains. "Many of the professors for the core requirements are very religious and not especially open to new ideas." "Gonzaga tries to get students to think about the world in a holistic way—understanding how everything is interrelated—and finding our purpose in that." Students think the "registration processes" and "cafeteria food" could "use some improvement," and "because Gonzaga is a smaller school, it is at times difficult to arrange your schedule due to limited availability of classes and time constraints."

Life

Students at Gonzaga are "devoted equally to…academics and social life." "People generally just want to socialize," one student explains. "Everyone for the most part does do their work, but there is definitely an emphasis on developing relationships." "The party scene is lively" at Gonzaga although students caution "we're not *that* big of a party school." During basketball season, Gonzaga basketball becomes "a way of life," and "basketball games and waiting in line for tickets are the largest social experience on campus." "*Everyone* goes to the basketball games. It's practically required to graduate." This leads some students to wish there was "less focus on men's basketball." Because the school is located in rainy Spokane, Washington, "the worst thing about Gonzaga is the weather, which the school can't really do anything about." Still, many students "stay active through sports" and enjoy the outdoors, "whether that's skiing, hiking, rafting, climbing, wake boarding, or just soaking up some rays." "People often snowboard at Mount Spokane, or if they are feeling adventurous, they drive the hour to Canada or hour to Montana." At Gonzaga, students "Read, Rage, Repent, Repeat. We wake up, work out, eat, and make memories."

Student Body

Although Gonzaga students stress the college's tight-knit community, many feel that while "the university claims to be accepting of all beliefs, opinions, and lifestyles," "in reality that's just not the case." "It is a community for sure, but really only if you're white and upper-middle-class, and the Jesuit Catholic mission can sometimes be troublesome for those of us with liberal and non-mainstream Catholic beliefs," explains one student. "Even feminism is kind of seen as taboo here." Others insist that "everyone here seems to blend well together," and "no matter your background, you are accepted here." Students study "hard through the week" but have "a lot of fun on weekends." Students describe themselves as "friendly, very open," "mostly preppy," "conventionally minded," "well-mannered," "religious," and tending to come "from a good family." Gonzaga has "a mostly Caucasian population," and "diversity is a huge issue, and Gonzaga could definitely improve how it treats students of diverse backgrounds." It should be no shock that "the typical student is a huge basketball fan" with "extreme school spirit."

FINANCIAL AID: 509-313-6582 • E-MAIL: ADMISSIONS@GONZAGA.EDU • WEBSITE: WWW.GONZAGA.EDU

THE PRINCETON REVIEW SAYS

Admissions

Very important factors considered include: Academic GPA, rigor of secondary school record, character/personal qualities, first generation. *Important factors considered include:* Application essay, recommendation(s), standardized test scores, extracurricular activities, talent/ability. *Other factors considered include:* Class rank, alumni/ae relation, interview, level of applicant's interest, racial/ethnic status, volunteer work, work experience. SAT or ACT required; ACT with or without writing component accepted. TOEFL required of all international applicants. High school diploma is required and GED is not accepted. *Academic units required:* 4 English, 3 mathematics, 3 science (3 science labs), 2 foreign language, 2 social studies, 2 history, 2 academic electives. *Academic units recommended:* 4 English, 4 mathematics, 4 science (4 science labs), 4 foreign language, 3 social studies, 3 history, 3 academic electives.

Financial Aid

Students should submit: FAFSA. The Princeton Review suggests that all financial aid forms be submitted as soon as possible after January 1. *Need-based scholarships/grants offered:* Federal Pell, SEOG, state scholarships/grants, private scholarships, the school's own gift aid, United Negro College Fund, Federal Nursing Scholarships. *Loan aid offered:* Direct Subsidized Stafford, Direct Unsubsidized Stafford, Direct PLUS, Federal Perkins, Federal Nursing, state loans, college/university loans from institutional funds. Applicants will be notified of awards on a rolling basis beginning March 1. Federal Work-Study Program available. Institutional employment available. Off-campus job opportunities are excellent.

The Inside Word

Gonzaga is a great example of how a high-profile athletic program can transform a competitive school into a highly competitive one. During the past decade, Gonzaga's admit rate has decreased substantially while class rank, standardized test scores, and high school GPA have all increased measurably. Perhaps the only substandard students admitted here these days are those who can consistently drain three pointers.

THE SCHOOL SAYS ". . ."

From the Admissions Office

"Education at Gonzaga is not comparable to an academic 'assembly line'; rather, it is person-to-person and face-to-face. This personal quality is also true of our admission and financial aid processes. Therefore, allow us to know you beyond the boundaries of your college application. Visit campus, phone us, e-mail us—let us see the person behind the data. Good luck with your college search and your applications. Go Zags!

"All sections of the SAT will be accepted, but the written portion will not receive universal consideration. The written score will be considered in cases where more information specific to writing ability would be helpful in decision making."

SELECTIVITY	
Admissions Rating	**90**
# of applicants	6,851
% of applicants accepted	62
% of acceptees attending	27
# accepting a place on wait list	579
# admitted from wait list	50

FRESHMAN PROFILE	
Range SAT Critical Reading	550–700
Range SAT Math	560–690
Range ACT Composite	24–28
Minimum paper TOEFL	550
Average HS GPA	3.7
% graduated top 10% of class	41
% graduated top 25% of class	72
% graduated top 50% of class	95

DEADLINES	
Early action	
Deadline	11/15
Notification	1/15
Regular	
Priority	2/1
Deadline	2/1
Notification	3/15
Nonfall registration?	yes

FINANCIAL FACTS	
Financial Aid Rating	**85**
Annual tuition	$33,160
Room and board	$8,680
Required fees	$700
Books and supplies	$1,000
% needy frosh rec. need-based scholarship or grant aid	100
% needy UG rec. need-based scholarship or grant aid	100
% needy frosh rec. non-need-based scholarship or grant aid	28
% needy UG rec. non-need-based scholarship or grant aid	19
% needy frosh rec. need-based self-help aid	63
% needy UG rec. need-based self-help aid	70
% frosh rec. any financial aid	100
% UG rec. any financial aid	100
% UG borrow to pay for school	70
Average cumulative indebtedness	$23,522
% frosh need fully met	34
% ugrads need fully met	25
Average % of frosh need met	85
Average % of ugrad need met	79

Goucher College

1021 Dulaney Valley Road, Baltimore, MD 21204-2794 • Admissions: 410-337-6100 • Fax: 410-337-6354

CAMPUS LIFE

Quality of Life Rating	**87**
Fire Safety Rating	**84**
Green Rating	**99**
Type of school	private
Environment	city

STUDENTS

Total undergrad enrollment	1,420
% male/female	33/67
% from out of state	77
% from public high school	64
% frosh live on campus	97
% African American	10
% Asian	4
% Caucasian	64
% Hispanic	6
% Native American	1
% international	2
# of countries represented	28

SURVEY SAYS . . .

Lots of liberal students
No one cheats
Students are friendly
Frats and sororities are unpopular or nonexistent
Political activism is popular

ACADEMICS

Academic Rating	**89**
% students returning for sophomore year	81
% students graduating within 4 years	62
% students graduating within 6 years	70
Calendar	semester
Student/faculty ratio	9:1
Profs interesting rating	89
Profs accessible rating	87
Most classes have	10–19 students

MOST POPULAR MAJORS

biology/biological sciences; business administration and management; elementary education and teaching

STUDENTS SAY ". . ."

Academics

A "small, East Coast, liberal arts school, with a tremendous history," Goucher College provides a "global education" best embodied in the motto "Learn for yourself, learn to be yourself, enjoy yourself, respect everyone else and you will succeed." Located on a "beautiful campus right outside a big city," students say the "intimate size is what is apparent about Goucher through and through." With a "socially informed" student body of self-motivated learners and thinkers, academics at Goucher are about "owning your education." As one student notes, "What you get out of your Goucher experience is directly related to what you put into it." Innovative thinkers flock here for "the openness of the student body, political nature of the institution, and the required study abroad program." Students say Goucher is a "very creative place" where "importance is placed on academics as well as the arts." "Easily accessible and ready to talk about anything and everything, while providing incredible insight and tools for students to investigate their own questions," professors "are what make Goucher great." As one student observes, academics at Goucher are all about "pushing myself beyond my old boundaries and really discovering what I am capable of and who I am." Assignments tend to focus on "challenging you to make your own opinions on a topic and testing them." Though some students feel they "could get rid of the administration for the most part," others note that while "The administration can be a little hands-off, you can access who you need to when it comes down to it." In principle, Goucher is "a place where one feels comfortable to talk to anyone, even the president of the college." "The professors are always available. Many will give you their home phone numbers or eat lunch with you."

Life

"Goucher is about living to learn and having fun in the process." An "eclectic yet tight-knit community," with a focus on "activism and global citizenship," "Goucher strives to represent, explore, and respect all aspects of humanity." Not typically known as a party school, parties on campus "tend to be low key, in people's rooms or apartments." Students say that the absence of fraternities and sororities "really helps to minimize [the] pressure of drinking." As studying abroad is required, it is "a major topic of conversation and a major source of student unity." In addition, there are "lots of school-sponsored events, such as speakers, plays, [and] small-name bands." As one student notes, "We've had everyone from [Karl Rove] to Tuvan Throat Singers to Paul Rusesabagina (the man Hotel Rwanda was based on), to an amazing group of poets called the Elephant Engine High Dive Revival, just this year alone. " On campus, "There's a kind of coffee house/pub/general hang out spot called the Gopher Hole where there are often dance parties, poetry slams, and other…fun activities always happening." Hometown Towson boasts "terrific restaurants, a concert venue, a movie theater, art galleries, quirky shops," [and] a large and modern mall. "When campus starts to feel a little small…there is a free shuttle that runs into Baltimore."

Student Body

A haven for liberal-minded, independent thinkers with a flair for unique hobbies and interests, students jokingly say that Goucher is "a place where students who never 'fit in' in high school come and find each other," "zombies and pirates included." The typical Goucher student is "socially, politically, emotionally, and internationally aware." "Everyone's a little weird, and most of them [are] very intelligent." When asked to give a composite picture, students paint the average Goucher student as "eighteen to twenty years old, female, liberal-minded, and very strong-headed." "We're a group of feminists, hippies, oddballs, geeks, HvZ players, and intellectuals, with the occasional soccer player thrown in." Another notes, "I can walk down Van Meter highway at any given time and see a group of lacrosse boys on the way to the SRC, the Pirate Club selling cupcakes in front of Pearlstone, or kids hanging out in front of the library." "There's a group for everyone at Goucher."

FINANCIAL AID: 410-337-6141 • E-MAIL: ADMISSIONS@GOUCHER.EDU • WEBSITE: WWW.GOUCHER.EDU

THE PRINCETON REVIEW SAYS

Admissions

Very important factors considered include: Academic GPA, rigor of secondary school record. *Important factors considered include:* Application essay, recommendation(s), talent/ability. *Other factors considered include:* Class rank, standardized test scores, alumni/ae relation, character/personal qualities, extracurricular activities, first generation, geographical residence, interview, level of applicant's interest, racial/ethnic status, state residency, volunteer work, work experience. TOEFL required of all international applicants. High school diploma is required and GED is accepted. *Academic units required:* 4 English, 3 mathematics, 2 science, 2 foreign language, 3 social studies, 2 academic electives. *Academic units recommended:* 4 English, 4 mathematics, 3 science, 4 foreign language, 3 social studies, 2 academic electives

Financial Aid

Students should submit: FAFSA, CSS/Financial Aid PROFILE, noncustodial PROFILE, business/farm supplement. Regular filing deadline is February 1. The Princeton Review suggests that all financial aid forms be submitted as soon as possible after January 1. *Need-based scholarships/grants offered:* Federal Pell, SEOG, state scholarships/grants, private scholarships, the school's own gift aid. *Loan aid offered:* Direct Subsidized Stafford, Direct Unsubsidized Stafford, Direct PLUS, Federal Perkins, college/university loans from institutional funds. Applicants will be notified of awards on a rolling basis beginning April 1. Federal Work-Study Program available. Institutional employment available. Highest amount earned per year from on-campus jobs $8,356. Off-campus job opportunities are excellent.

The Inside Word

Although there is a test-optional admissions policy, Goucher accepts the ACT with Writing in lieu of the SAT, and SAT Subject Tests are required for an applicant to be considered for merit funding. Goucher's high admit rate masks a self-selecting applicant pool; you cannot gain acceptance here without a solid high school transcript and test scores.

THE SCHOOL SAYS ". . ."

From the Admissions Office

"Through a broad-based arts and sciences curriculum and a groundbreaking approach to study abroad, Goucher College gives students a sweeping view of the world. Goucher is an independent, coeducational institution dedicated to both the interdisciplinary traditions of the liberal arts and a truly international perspective on education. The first college in the nation to pair required study abroad with a special travel stipend of $1,200 for every undergraduate, Goucher believes in complementing its strong majors and rigorous curriculum with abundant opportunities for hands-on experience. In addition to participating in the college's many study abroad programs (including innovative three-week intensive courses abroad alongside traditional semester and academic year offerings), many students also complete internships and service-learning projects that further enhance their learning.

"The college's almost 1,500 undergraduate students live and learn on a tree-lined campus of 287 acres just north of Baltimore, Maryland. Goucher boasts a student/faculty ratio of just nine to one, and professors routinely collaborate with students on major research projects—often for publication, and sometimes as early as students' first or second years. The curriculum emphasizes international and intercultural awareness throughout, and students are encouraged to explore their academic interests from a variety of perspectives beyond their major disciplines.

"A Goucher College education encompasses a multitude of experiences that ultimately converge into one cohesive academic program that can truly change lives. Students grow in dramatic and surprising ways here. They graduate with a strong sense of direction and self-confidence, ready to engage the world—and succeed—as true global citizens."

SELECTIVITY	
Admissions Rating	**82**
# of applicants	3,763
% of applicants accepted	73
% of acceptees attending	13
# accepting a place on wait list	170
# admitted from wait list	16
# of early decision applicants	70
# accepted early decision	55
FRESHMAN PROFILE	
Range SAT Critical Reading	510–660
Range SAT Math	500–610
Range SAT Writing	510–640
Range ACT Composite	22–28
Minimum paper TOEFL	550
Average HS GPA	3.1
% graduated top 10% of class	28
% graduated top 25% of class	55
% graduated top 50% of class	92
DEADLINES	
Early decision	
Deadline	11/15
Notification	12/15
Early action	
Deadline	12/1
Notification	2/1
Regular	
Deadline	2/1
Notification	4/1
Nonfall registration?	yes
FINANCIAL FACTS	
Financial Aid Rating	**74**
Annual tuition	$36,012
Room and board	$11,482
Required fees	$542
Books and supplies	$800
% needy frosh rec. need-based scholarship or grant aid	97
% needy UG rec. need-based scholarship or grant aid	97
% needy frosh rec. non-need-based scholarship or grant aid	8
% needy UG rec. non-need-based scholarship or grant aid	8
% needy frosh rec. need-based self-help aid	89
% needy UG rec. need-based self-help aid	89
% frosh rec. any financial aid	77
% UG rec. any financial aid	78
% UG borrow to pay for school	55
Average cumulative indebtedness	$28,147
% frosh need fully met	14
% ugrads need fully met	13
Average % of frosh need met	74
Average % of ugrad need met	75

GREEN MOUNTAIN COLLEGE

ONE BRENNAN CIRCLE, POULTNEY, VT 05764-1199 • ADMISSIONS: 802-287-8000 • FAX: 802-287-8099

CAMPUS LIFE

Quality of Life Rating	**75**
Fire Safety Rating	**70**
Green Rating	**99**
Type of school	private
Affiliation	Methodist
Environment	rural

STUDENTS

Total undergrad enrollment	626
% male/female	45/55
% from out of state	89
% from public high school	93
% frosh live on campus	97
% African American	4
% Asian	2
% Caucasian	68
% Hispanic	1
% international	3
# of countries represented	13

SURVEY SAYS . . .

Students are friendly
Low cost of living
Frats and sororities are unpopular or nonexistent
Students are environmentally aware

ACADEMICS

Academic Rating	**85**
% students returning for sophomore year	63
% students graduating within 4 years	31
% students graduating within 6 years	43
Calendar	semester
Student/faculty ratio	14:1
Profs interesting rating	94
Profs accessible rating	88
Most classes have	10–19 students
Most lab/discussion sessions have	10–19 students

MOST POPULAR MAJORS

environmental studies; adventure education; biology; psychology

STUDENTS SAY ". . ."

Academics

Green Mountain College, located in Poultney, Vermont, is a small, private, liberal arts college near the Vermont countryside. One of the goals of Green Mountain is its active focus on sustainability and teaching all of their incoming students to live "responsibly" as global citizens. In fact, the college has a set of thirty-seven credit, core classes known as the Environmental Liberal Arts, which combines a liberal arts education with a strong focus on the environment. With most students saying that their classroom sizes "are usually around fifteen to thirty students," they really feel like they get to know their professors "not only as academic instructors, but as people," and most rave that they really bond with a majority of their teachers, saying they "haven't really met any professor that I can't connect with in some way." Since a lot of professors get to really know their students, most students say they have no problem getting personal letters from professors when they are "ready to apply for a job/internship/graduate school, because they know…you and what you've done with your time here." The students love that the school helps to promote not only the education, but also the individual and how to learn to be themselves "while learning in dynamic and hands-on ways" through the emphasis that an education doesn't come just from a classroom, but from real-world experience as well.

Life

Being located in the Vermont country, Green Mountain College offers its students a great experience for those who love to experience nature. Its location at the foot of the Green Mountains makes it ideal for students who enjoy spending their free time "skiing, snowboarding, camping, [and] hiking." Incoming freshman and transfer students can register for one of the pre-orientation "Wilderness Challenges," where these new people bond together over a five day adventure focused on such activities as rock-climbing, canoeing, and yoga. During the school year, the student run College Programming Board does "a great job with providing concerts and other events on campus" for those wishing to stay nearby. The college isn't located right next to a big city, so many make their own fun on campus. Students also say that there are options to get away such as "a few charming…restaurants on Main Street," but in general, "There is not much to do around town." However, for those students who are willing to take a drive, the ski resort town of Killington is nearby—about forty minutes away—which students call "a huge plus."

Student Body

The student population at Green Mountain College likes to think of itself as a "very tight-knit community," with a "typical" student being "very outgoing [and] friendly." Many students here "want to make a positive impact on the world in some way or another," especially in the area of sustainability. Though many students agree that certainly a certain type of student attends Green Mountain, it's hard to nail down that typical student description. One student clarifies that there are "no [frat] bros, no sorority girls," but explains that the vast majority is happy to live "amongst other weird, happy, wonderful people while learning about sustainability," which is clear in the projects that students take on for the betterment of campus. The students worked together to help build a solar panel on the roof of the student center and a wind turbine to power the campus green house.

FINANCIAL AID: 802-287-8210 • E-MAIL: ADMISS@GREENMTN.EDU • WEBSITE: WWW.GREENMTN.EDU

THE PRINCETON REVIEW SAYS

Admissions

Very important factors considered include: Application essay, academic GPA, rigor of secondary school record, character/personal qualities. *Important factors considered include:* Recommendation(s), extracurricular activities, interview, volunteer work. *Other factors considered include:* Standardized test scores, level of applicant's interest, talent/ability, work experience. ACT with or without writing component accepted. TOEFL required of all international applicants. High school diploma is required and GED is accepted. *Academic units required:* 4 English, 3 mathematics, 3 science (2 science labs), 2 foreign language, 3 social studies, 1 history, 5 academic electives. *Academic units recommended:* 4 mathematics, 4 science, 3 foreign language, 3 social studies, 2 history.

Financial Aid

Students should submit: FAFSA, CSS/Financial Aid PROFILE, noncustodial PROFILE. The Princeton Review suggests that all financial aid forms be submitted as soon as possible after January 1. *Need-based scholarships/grants offered:* Federal Pell, SEOG, state scholarships/grants, private scholarships, the school's own gift aid. *Loan aid offered:* Direct Subsidized Stafford, Direct Unsubsidized Stafford, Direct PLUS, state loans, alternative loans. Applicants will be notified of awards on a rolling basis beginning January 1.

The Inside Word

Green Mountain College has twenty-four majors to choose from. Because the student population sits at about 750 students, it should be known that applications are accepted throughout the year and that Green Mountain has a test-optional policy, so it is not mandatory that applicants supply their ACT or SAT scores, but if students choose not to, they have to fill out the college's Insight Portfolio and provide a graded writing sample that was written within the last two years. For those interested in financial aid, there are numerous programs that the college offers, and ninety-four percent of all GMC students receive financial aid and about ninety percent receive institutional support. Academic-based scholarships are awarded on a rolling basis as well.

THE SCHOOL SAYS ". . ."

From the Admissions Office

"Green Mountain College was named the number one "Coolest School" by Sierra magazine. GMC is a liberal arts college that is on the forefront of sustainability education.

"While we are proud of our national recognition for sustainability, three-quarters of our students do not major in environmental studies, but rather select a liberal arts major that they are passionate about—education, business, art, psychology, biology, etc. The student body is united by a sense of social responsibility and penchant for service. Diversity thrives at Green Mountain College. The academic community is highly engaged and provides a truthful and authentic scholarly environment.

"GMC's working farm is a special attraction for students from all majors. It provides a visible model of sustainability and produces a significant quantity of food for the college community. Students can also major in Sustainable Agriculture and Food Production and/or earn twelve credits over the summer in Farm Life Ecology, a 'field and table' intensive.

"We award scholarships for academic merit, service, leadership, creative arts, and community advancement at the time of admission, so students should submit evidence of these activities with their application for admission. The college is committed to and guarantees graduation in four years for students who meet academic requirements. An entrepreneurial spirit carries throughout the entire community resulting in a one of kind preparation for career and or graduate/professional school upon graduation."

SELECTIVITY	
Admissions Rating	**76**
# of applicants	1,302
% of applicants accepted	67
% of acceptees attending	16

FRESHMAN PROFILE	
Range SAT Critical Reading	478–613
Range SAT Math	460–570
Range SAT Writing	450–583
Range ACT Composite	20–25
Minimum paper TOEFL	500
Average HS GPA	3.0

DEADLINES	
Regular	
Priority	3/1
Nonfall registration?	yes

FINANCIAL FACTS	
Financial Aid Rating	**73**
Annual tuition	$28,238
Room and board	$10,640
Required fees	$1,078
Books and supplies	$1,300
% needy frosh rec. need-based scholarship or grant aid	100
% needy UG rec. need-based scholarship or grant aid	99
% needy frosh rec. non-need-based scholarship or grant aid	9
% needy UG rec. non-need-based scholarship or grant aid	8
% needy frosh rec. need-based self-help aid	84
% needy UG rec. need-based self-help aid	85
% frosh rec. any financial aid	96
% UG rec. any financial aid	95
% UG borrow to pay for school	77
Average cumulative indebtedness	$39,106
% frosh need fully met	10
% ugrads need fully met	12
Average % of frosh need met	69
Average % of ugrad need met	66

GRINNELL COLLEGE

1103 PARK STREET, GRINNELL, IA 50112-1690 • ADMISSIONS: 641-269-3600 • FAX: 641-269-4800

CAMPUS LIFE

Quality of Life Rating	**85**
Fire Safety Rating	**83**
Green Rating	**78**
Type of school	private
Environment	village

STUDENTS

Total undergrad enrollment	1,639
% male/female	45/55
% from out of state	92
% from public high school	70
% frosh live on campus	100
% African American	5
% Asian	6
% Caucasian	59
% Hispanic	8
% international	12
# of countries represented	54

SURVEY SAYS . . .

No one cheats
Frats and sororities are unpopular or nonexistent
Student government is popular
Political activism is popular

ACADEMICS

Academic Rating	**99**
% students returning for sophomore year	93
% students graduating within 4 years	83
% students graduating within 6 years	88
Calendar	semester
Student/faculty ratio	9:1
Profs interesting rating	96
Profs accessible rating	96
Most classes have	10–19 students
Most lab/discussion sessions have	10–19 students

MOST POPULAR MAJORS

economics; political science and government; psychology

STUDENTS SAY ". . ."

Academics

Offering "a great mix of serious academics and a fun community," Grinnell College "is a crazy, unique, busy, caffeinated cornfield of geniuses" whose "hard work, critical thinking, and social consciousness" define the Grinnell experience. The school "is challenging academically," so "you have to work very hard, and it's not always easy. It can be stressful at times, but the pressure all comes from yourself. It's not a competitive atmosphere. And the academics here are extremely effective." An open curriculum ("no requirements other than the freshman tutorial") and a self-governance policy mean that "students feel at home here because we are independent," operating "without stringent rules about how to live our lives and what choices to make." A low teacher-student ratio allows for close relationships, meaning students aren't entirely without guidance. "I have never heard of an inaccessible professor," one student reports. "They are very willing to help and genuinely care about us and our performance in class. In addition, I have never heard of a class with more than thirty people in it: They just don't exist." That commitment to having small classes "ensures group discussion and personal attention: There are no straight lecture classes." Thanks to a "huge endowment," students have tremendous latitude in plotting their studies. One undergrad observes, "Money never really seems to be an issue here. If you can dream it, Grinnell can pay for it." The school is "full of resources! Students needing to do research in museums, archives, and libraries for thesis-level research projects can easily get funding from the college. Also, the arts and science facilities are top-of-the-line."

Life

The academic rigors at Grinnell are substantial. You "won't have to worry about surviving the Midwest winter" here, because "being buried in books and papers and paper revisions and articles and essays and book reviews and to-do lists keeps you surprisingly warm." The environment can be stressful, and many are inclined toward traditional collegiate stress-relieving activities. "That being said, there is no pressure to try things if one is not interested," and there are in fact "many substance-free students, some of whom choose to live in sub-free housing." "The administration, as part of self governance, does not police drinking/drugs," but it does encourage students to act responsibly. "Student security is present at school-sponsored parties." Students agree that "extracurricular activities are highly popular," running the gamut from "artists the college brings in" to "lectures, movies, concerts, even therapy dogs during mid-semester exams" to "just hanging out with some cards or *How I Met Your Mother* DVDs." Hometown Grinnell is "isolated," but not without its charms. One student explains, "I love the town of Grinnell and think Midwest-nice is a great asset, but that's my personal taste. I like recognizing the lady who walks her dog by our house every day and the kid who bags our groceries. And I love going to the farmer's market and things like the 4-H tractor show that took place this summer."

Student Body

Grinnell undergrads describe themselves and their classmates as "students interested in social justice and having a good time." They tend to be "highly intelligent, motivated, and inquisitive" students who constantly challenge one another "to examine topics from different perspectives. This constant thinking outside of the box is a primary aspect of a true liberal arts education." Grinnellians "are frequently left-leaning, but there's not a typical Grinnell student. All the students are different, so there are few issues with fitting in." Intellect and intensity are the most frequent common denominators; as one student explains, "I've heard that every single student is a nerd about something. Perhaps that is what unites us—our passion, whether that be for a sport, academic subject, Joss Whedon, foam-sword fighting, or politics. We all respect that we have different interests but bond because we are interested rather than apathetic, therefore interesting and unique."

FINANCIAL AID: 641-269-3250 • E-MAIL: ASKGRIN@GRINNELL.EDU • WEBSITE: WWW.GRINNELL.EDU

THE PRINCETON REVIEW SAYS

Admissions

Very important factors considered include: Class rank, academic GPA, recommendation(s), rigor of secondary school record, standardized test scores, extracurricular activities, talent/ability. *Important factors considered include:* Application essay, interview, racial/ethnic status. *Other factors considered include:* Alumni/ae relation, character/personal qualities, first generation, geographical residence, level of applicant's interest, state residency, volunteer work, work experience. SAT or ACT required; ACT with or without writing component accepted. TOEFL required of all international applicants. High school diploma is required and GED is accepted. *Academic units recommended:* 4 English, 4 mathematics, 4 science (3 science labs), 4 foreign language, 4 social studies.

Financial Aid

Students should submit: FAFSA, institution's own financial aid form, noncustodial PROFILE. Regular filing deadline is February 1. The Princeton Review suggests that all financial aid forms be submitted as soon as possible after January 1. *Need-based scholarships/grants offered:* Federal Pell, SEOG, state scholarships/grants, private scholarships, the school's own gift aid. *Loan aid offered:* Direct Subsidized Stafford, Direct Unsubsidized Stafford, Direct PLUS, Federal Perkins, college/university loans from institutional funds. Applicants will be notified of awards on or about April 1. Federal Work-Study Program available. Institutional employment available. Highest amount earned per year from on-campus jobs $2,500. Off-campus job opportunities are excellent.

The Inside Word

Grinnell's admissions process is refreshingly straightforward. According to the school's website, the school bases fifty percent of its decision on high school performance, including quality of curriculum, and twenty-five percent depends on standardized test scores. The remaining twenty-five percent is based on the school's assessment of each candidate's potential contributions in the classroom and to the Grinnell campus community. Grinnell is extremely selective, so you'll have to give it your all. An interview isn't required here, but do it anyway.

THE SCHOOL SAYS ". . ."

From the Admissions Office

"Grinnell College is a place where independence of thought and social conscience are instilled. Grinnell is a college with the resources of a school ten times its size, a faculty that reads like a Who's Who of Teaching, and a learning environment where debate does not end in the classroom and often begins in the Campus Center.

"Grinnellians are committed to learning, respect for themselves and others, contributing to global social good, willing collaboration, and the courage to try.

"We look for students who show strong potential, have the courage to try new things, demonstrate a willingness to speak out and share their opinions, and bring different perspectives to our international campus in the middle of Iowa. Grinnell College is filled with students who are serious about learning but are not always serious."

SELECTIVITY	
Admissions Rating	**93**
# of applicants	2,613
% of applicants accepted	51
% of acceptees attending	34
# accepting a place on wait list	541
# admitted from wait list	14
# of early decision applicants	286
# accepted early decision	144

FRESHMAN PROFILE	
Range SAT Critical Reading	600–720
Range SAT Math	610–710
Range ACT Composite	28–32
% graduated top 10% of class	62
% graduated top 25% of class	88
% graduated top 50% of class	99

DEADLINES	
Early decision	
Deadline	11/15
Notification	12/15
Regular	
Deadline	1/15
Notification	4/1
Nonfall registration?	no

FINANCIAL FACTS	
Financial Aid Rating	**99**
Annual tuition	$40,444
Room and board	$9,614
Required fees	$560
Books and supplies	$900
% needy frosh rec. need-based scholarship or grant aid	99
% needy UG rec. need-based scholarship or grant aid	99
% needy frosh rec. non-need-based scholarship or grant aid	7
% needy UG rec. non-need-based scholarship or grant aid	5
% needy frosh rec. need-based self-help aid	91
% needy UG rec. need-based self-help aid	90
% frosh rec. any financial aid	88
% UG rec. any financial aid	86
% UG borrow to pay for school	54
Average cumulative indebtedness	$15,720
% frosh need fully met	100
% ugrads need fully met	100
Average % of frosh need met	100
Average % of ugrad need met	100

Grove City College

100 Campus Drive, Grove City, PA 16127-2104 • Admissions: 724-458-2100 • Fax: 724-458-3395

CAMPUS LIFE

Quality of Life Rating	**71**
Fire Safety Rating	**84**
Green Rating	**60***
Type of school	private
Affiliation	Presbyterian
Environment	rural

STUDENTS

Total undergrad enrollment	2,452
% male/female	50/50
% from out of state	52
% from public high school	65
% frosh live on campus	96
# of fraternities	10
# of sororities	9
% African American	1
% Asian	2
% Caucasian	94
% Hispanic	2
% international	1
# of countries represented	10

SURVEY SAYS . . .

Career services are great
Diversity lacking on campus
Students are very religious
Low cost of living
Intramural sports are popular
Very little drug use

ACADEMICS

Academic Rating	**80**
% students returning for sophomore year	88
% students graduating within 4 years	77
% students graduating within 6 years	82
Calendar	semester
Student/faculty ratio	15:1
Profs interesting rating	81
Profs accessible rating	90
Most classes have	20–29 students
Most lab/discussion sessions have	20–29 students

MOST POPULAR MAJORS

elementary education and teaching; English language and literature; mechanical engineering

APPLICANTS ALSO LOOK AT AND OFTEN PREFER

Wheaton College (IL), Hillsdale College

AND RARELY PREFER

Slippery Rock University of Pennsylvania

STUDENTS SAY ". . ."

Academics

Students avow that Grove City is "a great option for someone who wants to learn from a Christian perspective." Located near Pittsburgh, this "small, conservative, independent" college is renowned for its "great spiritual atmosphere," providing a "very high-quality and competitive education," and having "a high rate of graduate school acceptance and job placement." One student mentions, "Grove City College keeps traditional values and top-of-the-line academics at the heart of everything it does." All courses are taught by professors, seen as "tough but fair and willing to help out their students." "You probably will not do well in most classes if you just do the minimum." Grade competition is almost a pastime for some, but others effectively juggle studies and other activities. "Some people like to over-exaggerate the difficulty of the academics. It is definitely challenging, but very doable." Professors "encourage students to learn and think for themselves, rather than trying to indoctrinate them into a particular ideology." "We are typically religious and conservative in beliefs, but that doesn't mean we're not open-minded." Still, undergraduates believe instructors "are equipping them spiritually and socially to live successful, godly lives." Notes a student, "I am able to learn from people who truly love what they do and do it because they love God." "I've truly grown leaps and bounds in my spiritual life," marvels another thrilled undergraduate.

Life

"Fun outside of class is what you make it" at GCC. Seemingly everyone is involved in multiple organizations and extracurricular activities. Academic groups, social clubs, intramural sports…all are popular, as are opportunities "for spiritual growth through campus ministries, student-initiated small groups, and local churches." "The community is wonderful, and it is a very uplifting place to be," although many students do long for a bit more personal freedom. As one student says, "While the rules at GCC are certainly strict, they are very clearly articulated," although another asserts they "are not as strict as made out to be. Really they are quite lax compared to other conservative Christian colleges." This divide can lead to interaction between the sexes becoming somewhat complex. There are relatively firm "inter-visitation rules" between men and women, and students pine for "more areas to spend time coed." Administratively, registration has reportedly become "quicker and easier" and is "pretty fair as to who gets into classes." The cafeteria does "an excellent job providing a variety of healthy food options," and the food "is amazing compared to most other college campuses." Even though Grove City is a smaller school, "The parking situation for students is very ideal" and "not far from the dorms and academic buildings." Students are effusive in their admiration for the physical surroundings. "Pretty and well-maintained." "Enchanting." "I always feel safe." "Quiet and laid-back." The town itself is small, but has "good churches, a neat old theater, nice restaurants, and a great sense of community."

Student Body

Embraced by some students, rejected by others, the moniker of a "Grover" is said to describe "a studious person, desiring to be involved in as much as possible while striving to still perform excellently in academics." Furthermore, many here describe themselves as "very type-A." "Most students are extremely conscious of their grades." At the same time, others profess to handle everything with more perspective. "Grove City can be stressful, but only if you let it be!" What is universal at Grove City is this: everyone being described as "dedicated, motivated, conscientious, and responsible." Many undergrads "generally have a strong Christian faith and are excited about the opportunities to deepen that faith at college;" however, "People from all walks can further their education, grow relationships, and learn true humility and service." "The unity of the campus body is one of the greatest assets to our school," and Grove City does a "phenomenal job of integrating all freshmen or transfer students."

FINANCIAL AID: 724-458-3300 • E-MAIL: ADMISSIONS@GCC.EDU • WEBSITE: WWW.GCC.EDU

THE PRINCETON REVIEW SAYS

Admissions

Very important factors considered include: Application essay, academic GPA, rigor of secondary school record, standardized test scores, character/personal qualities, interview, level of applicant's interest, religious affiliation/commitment. *Important factors considered include:* Recommendation(s), extracurricular activities, geographical residence. *Other factors considered include:* Class rank, alumni/ae relation, first generation, racial/ethnic status, state residency, talent/ability, volunteer work, work experience. SAT or ACT required; ACT with or without writing component accepted. TOEFL required of all international applicants. High school diploma is required and GED is accepted. *Academic units recommended:* 4 English, 3 mathematics, 3 science (2 science labs), 3 foreign language, 2 social studies, 2 history.

Financial Aid

Students should submit: Institution's own financial aid form. Regular filing deadline is April 15. The Princeton Review suggests that all financial aid forms be submitted as soon as possible after January 1. *Need-based scholarships/grants offered:* State scholarships/grants, private scholarships, the school's own gift aid. *Loan aid offered:* State loans, private loans. Applicants will be notified of awards on or about March 26. Institutional employment available. Highest amount earned per year from on-campus jobs $1,500. Off-campus job opportunities are good.

The Inside Word

Gaining entrance into Grove City College is difficult and highly competitive. Students must have outstanding personal characteristics, and they need to be prepared for a strenuous but workable course load. Christian values are of utmost importance at GCC, and the school values students who seek out surroundings based on those principles. Interviews and recommendations are highly valued as components of the admission process.

THE SCHOOL SAYS ". . ."

From the Admissions Office

"A good college education doesn't have to cost a fortune. For decades, Grove City College has offered a quality education at costs among the lowest nationally. Since the 1990s, increased national academic acclaim has come to Grove City College. Grove City College is a place where professors teach; you will not see graduate assistants or teacher's aides in the classroom. Our professors are also active in the total life of the campus. More than 100 student organizations on campus afford opportunity for a wide variety of cocurricular activities. Outstanding scholars and leaders in education, science, and international affairs visit the campus each year. The environment at GCC is friendly, secure, and dedicated to high standards. Character-building is emphasized and traditional Christian values are supported.

"There is a fresh spiritual vitality on campus that touches every aspect of your college life. In the classroom, we don't shy away from discussing all points of view, however we adhere to Christ's teaching as relevant guidance for living. Come and visit and learn more."

SELECTIVITY	
Admissions Rating	**89**
# of applicants	1,591
% of applicants accepted	76
% of acceptees attending	51
# accepting a place on wait list	302
# admitted from wait list	70
# of early decision applicants	439
# accepted early decision	239

FRESHMAN PROFILE	
Range SAT Critical Reading	559–692
Range SAT Math	560–677
Range ACT Composite	25–30
Minimum paper TOEFL	550
Minimum web-based TOEFL	79
Average HS GPA	3.7
% graduated top 10% of class	48
% graduated top 25% of class	79
% graduated top 50% of class	96

DEADLINES	
Early decision	
Deadline	11/15
Notification	12/15
Regular	
Deadline	2/1
Notification	3/15
Nonfall registration?	yes

FINANCIAL FACTS	
Financial Aid Rating	**67**
Annual tuition	$14,212
Room and board	$7,744
Books and supplies	$1,000
% needy frosh rec. need-based scholarship or grant aid	50
% needy UG rec. need-based scholarship or grant aid	90
% needy frosh rec. non-need-based scholarship or grant aid	3
% needy UG rec. non-need-based scholarship or grant aid	9
% needy frosh rec. need-based self-help aid	26
% needy UG rec. need-based self-help aid	26
% frosh rec. any financial aid	50
% UG rec. any financial aid	41
% UG borrow to pay for school	62
Average cumulative indebtedness	$26,597
% frosh need fully met	4
% ugrads need fully met	9
Average % of frosh need met	53
Average % of ugrad need met	49

Guilford College

5800 West Friendly Avenue, Greensboro, NC 27410 • Admissions: 336-316-2100 • Fax: 336-316-2954

CAMPUS LIFE

Quality of Life Rating	88
Fire Safety Rating	74
Green Rating	91
Type of school	private
Affiliation	Quaker
Environment	city

STUDENTS

Total undergrad enrollment	1,331
% male/female	51/49
% from out of state	56
% from public high school	78
% frosh live on campus	94
% African American	13
% Asian	2
% Caucasian	72
% Hispanic	6
% Native American	1
% international	1
# of countries represented	14

SURVEY SAYS . . .

No one cheats
Students are friendly
Frats and sororities are unpopular or nonexistent
College radio is popular
Political activism is popular

ACADEMICS

Academic Rating	88
% students returning for sophomore year	76
% students graduating within 4 years	49
% students graduating within 6 years	58
Calendar	semester
Student/faculty ratio	16:1
Profs interesting rating	91
Profs accessible rating	90
Most classes have	10–19 students
Most lab/discussion sessions have	10–19 students

MOST POPULAR MAJORS

business/commerce; criminal justice/safety studies; psychology

APPLICANTS ALSO LOOK AT AND OFTEN PREFER

Oberlin College

AND SOMETIMES PREFER

Earlham College, The University of North Carolina at Chapel Hill, Goucher College, Elon University

STUDENTS SAY ". . ."

Academics

Nestled in beautiful Greensboro, North Carolina, Guilford College is a school that places an "emphasis on community." Indeed, as one junior gushes, "When I visited, everyone stopped what they were doing and welcomed me to [the] college. It was such a different atmosphere than anywhere I had ever seen, and I immediately wanted to be a part of it." This convivial environment can likely be attributed to the school's Quaker roots and value system, which continue to permeate the campus. Most importantly, the warmth and openness extends into the classroom. As another junior raves, "The professors here are incredible. We all go on a first-name basis (Quakers love equality), and they go out of their way to make sure everyone is getting the material." Slackers beware! An English major warns, "We are extremely writing intensive; I've done more writing for an intro physics course than I've done for some English courses." Fortunately, the "teachers are available to offer advice and make sure we succeed." Student approval also extends to the college's administration. As one impressed psych major tells us, "The administration works very hard to address all of the school's issues. They even sit and have discussions with students about how they feel things need to be changed and what it is they see as needing to be done for the overall well-being of the school and students."

Life

Though most Guilford undergrads "spend the daytime doing homework," there are plenty of opportunities for students to kick back and take a breather from academics. On this socially conscious campus, many students "join clubs like Pride and Blacks Unifying Society, or participate in politics/community service." One sophomore concurs, adding that "Everywhere you walk you will find some sort of flyer posted about speakers coming to talk and share their beliefs or meetings that students have put together to discuss issues on campus. People love sharing their thoughts about what they want done." Many also praise the efforts of the Campus Activities Board which sponsors a number of "dances, movies, game nights, and biggest of all Serendipity [an annual music festival]." Considering Guilford's "beautiful" setting, it's no wonder that most undergrads also "love to be outside." As one English major shares, "We try to get off campus [during] the weekend with day trips like hiking, apple picking, swimming, etc." The campus is surrounded by a "ton of woods" and "Most people like to be out there when they can." Though there are "no fraternities or sororities," there's a "goofy party scene—lots of bonfires in the woods, lots of themed parties (i.e., '80s Aerobics)" which, as one junior assures us, "*Everyone* is welcome to attend."

Student Body

A number of undergrads are quick to assert that "It's hard to describe the typical Guilford student." As one sophomore brags, "I have met and befriended people from many social classes, sexual orientations, religious and spiritual beliefs, interests and backgrounds." That being said, "Most students have liberal tendencies and the conservatives are definitely in the minority." Indeed, "Guilford seems to breed a second hippie generation." A French major explains, "I think the typical student is very carefree and laid-back and they care a lot about sustainability, local produce, and issues like that." Students do warn that "There is a *great* divide between the athletes and the [rest of the] student body." However, a junior assures us, "There really is a place for any kind of person to fit in." As one English explains, "We are all a little odd [so] we fit in together just fine." "If a kid is sitting alone or is just walking by him/herself someone will talk to them, join them, befriend them. No matter what, Guilford College students take care of one another."

FINANCIAL AID: 336-316-2354 • E-MAIL: ADMISSION@GUILFORD.EDU • WEBSITE: WWW.GUILFORD.EDU

THE PRINCETON REVIEW SAYS

Admissions

Very important factors considered include: Application essay, academic GPA, rigor of secondary school record, character/personal qualities. *Important factors considered include:* Class rank, recommendation(s), standardized test scores, extracurricular activities, interview, level of applicant's interest, talent/ability, volunteer work, work experience. *Other factors considered include:* Alumni/ae relation, first generation, geographical residence, racial/ethnic status, state residency. ACT with or without writing component accepted. TOEFL required of all international applicants. High school diploma is required and GED is accepted. *Academic units recommended:* 4 English, 3 mathematics, 3 science, 2 foreign language, 3 social studies, 3 history.

Financial Aid

Students should submit: FAFSA. The Princeton Review suggests that all financial aid forms be submitted as soon as possible after January 1. *Need-based scholarships/grants offered:* Federal Pell, SEOG, state scholarships/grants, private scholarships, the school's own gift aid. *Loan aid offered:* Direct Subsidized Stafford, Direct Unsubsidized Stafford, Direct PLUS, Federal Perkins, college/university loans from institutional funds. Applicants will be notified of awards on a rolling basis beginning February 15. Federal Work-Study Program available. Institutional employment available. Highest amount earned per year from on-campus jobs $6,911. Off-campus job opportunities are fair.

The Inside Word

Getting into Guilford College goes beyond the numbers. Guilford is looking for students who demonstrate strong drive and personal motivation. Applicants to the school should have a solid high school record and good extracurricular activities (preferably of the tree-hugging and/or varsity sports variety.) While a Quaker connection couldn't hurt, the school is more interested in your character and personal qualities and level of interest in the school. The admissions essay is your chance to make your case.

THE SCHOOL SAYS ". . ."

From the Admissions Office

"Guilford is proud to be included for the twenty-first consecutive year in The Princeton Review's 'Best Colleges' edition. Guilford can best be described by its academic rigor, preparation for graduate school and careers, and its commitment to service in a caring, socially aware and supportive community.

"This is a campus that celebrates all walks of life. Guilford brings together students from many different religious, socioeconomic, geographic, and ethnic backgrounds. You can be yourself here and that's a great feeling. Openmindedness is embraced, especially in the classrooms, living spaces, and social settings on campus where you will challenge others and be challenged yourself.

"There is no stereotypical Guilford student. Our students have many passions including athletics and intramurals, community service, social justice and multiculturalism. However the bond that ties them together is the academic curriculum that prepares them for life and a career. The Guilford experience is truly a transformative one."

SELECTIVITY	
Admissions Rating	79
# of applicants	3,054
% of applicants accepted	64
% of acceptees attending	19
# accepting a place on wait list	127
# admitted from wait list	4

FRESHMAN PROFILE	
Range SAT Critical Reading	470–620
Range SAT Math	480–590
Range SAT Writing	460–600
Range ACT Composite	21–26
Minimum paper TOEFL	550
Average HS GPA	3.1
% graduated top 10% of class	14
% graduated top 25% of class	41
% graduated top 50% of class	81

DEADLINES	
Early action	
Deadline	11/15, 1/15
Notification	12/15, 2/15
Regular	
Deadline	2/15
Notification	4/1
Nonfall registration?	yes

FINANCIAL FACTS	
Financial Aid Rating	77
Annual tuition	$31,000
Room and board	$8,540
Required fees	$390
Books and supplies	$1,350
% frosh rec. any financial aid	79
% UG rec. any financial aid	95
% UG borrow to pay for school	64
Average cumulative indebtedness	$25,495
% frosh need fully met	16
% ugrads need fully met	4
Average % of frosh need met	80
Average % of ugrad need met	81

GUSTAVUS ADOLPHUS COLLEGE

800 COLLEGE AVENUE, SAINT PETER, MN 56082 • ADMISSIONS: 507-933-7676 • FAX: 507-933-7474

CAMPUS LIFE

Quality of Life Rating	**94**
Fire Safety Rating	**91**
Green Rating	**84**
Type of school	private
Affiliation	Lutheran
Environment	village

STUDENTS

Total undergrad enrollment	2,442
% male/female	44/56
% from out of state	19
% from public high school	92
% frosh live on campus	100
# of fraternities	5
# of sororities	5
% African American	3
% Asian	5
% Caucasian	86
% Hispanic	3
% international	2
# of countries represented	15

SURVEY SAYS . . .

Athletic facilities are great
Great food on campus
Musical organizations are popular

ACADEMICS

Academic Rating	**97**
% students returning for sophomore year	93
% students graduating within 4 years	81
Calendar	4-1-4
Student/faculty ratio	11:1
Profs interesting rating	96
Profs accessible rating	94
Most classes have	10–19 students
Most lab/discussion sessions have	10–19 students

MOST POPULAR MAJORS

biology/biological sciences; business/commerce; psychology

APPLICANTS ALSO LOOK AT AND OFTEN PREFER

Carleton College, University of Wisconsin—Madison

STUDENTS SAY ". . ."

Academics

Gustavus Adolphus College, "a school that fosters a close community between the students, staff, and faculty and strives to prepare the students academically and vocationally for the post-college world," gets high marks from undergrads for its "demanding, yet encouraging" professors who are "there to help you learn, not just to give you a grade." As one student explains, "Each year, I become more and more impressed with how devoted members of the faculty and administration are to the students. My professors always bend over backward to meet with students who have questions and work with them on problems related and unrelated to course material." Although professors have "high expectations," the "extra guidance" that is offered helps students achieve "far beyond graduation." Expect to be challenged by classes that are "rigorous and discussion-based." Small class sizes allow for "great interaction with professors" but will leave your "empty chair sticking out like a neon sign" if you are absent. Unique opportunities here include the Curriculum II general-education program, an integrated series of courses that, together, provide a survey of Western civilization, with supplemental study of non-Western cultures for context and comparison. Enrollment is limited to sixty students and typically attracts some of the college's brightest undergrads.

Life

Gustavus boasts "a very academically strong student body" that is also "known for our athletics, specifically tennis, hockey, and soccer." Students "attend a lot of sporting events" as well as "parties and social events on campus and off" over the weekends, when campus is "a great place to be...because very few people go home. We are certainly not a suitcase college." Besides the aforementioned activities, "shows, concerts, and basketball games" are "especially popular," as are the "free movies on Fridays and Saturdays" and the "on-campus student dance club 'The Dive.'" Most students choose to unwind with "a good amount of partying and drinking," but while alcohol and parties are easy to find on campus, abstaining students "never feel any pressure to do either." Being located in a small town is no problem for most; students tell us that "the town is supportive of Gustavus and thankful to have the college in town" and explain that "there are always things going on at school," so the lack of big-city fun isn't that much of a drawback. Students who get cabin fever can head to nearby Mankato and its "excellent mall and restaurants" for entertainment. Although the Minnesotan winter may be long, things heat up during the January "Interim Experience" when a light course load gives students a "chance to take a class outside their major" or just "hang out with friends." When students really want a thrill, they'll "borrow a tray from the cafeteria and sled down the many hills behind the dorms" in a Gustavus tradition called "traying."

Student Body

Gustavus "is known to have a very [close-knit campus] consisting of students who not only achieve academically but are [also] very involved in their community and school. There are more than 140 student organizations on campus. For a student population [of] approximately 2,600, that is a lot." "Virtually everyone here is white and of Scandinavian descent," and "of these, roughly half seem to come from small rural towns in Minnesota or surrounding Midwest states (Iowa, Wisconsin, North and South Dakota, etc.), and the other half from well-off suburbs of Minneapolis–St. Paul...Most tend to have some Christian affiliation, but not necessarily a strong one, and there are a fair amount of non-religious students, which is refreshing." Students are polite in a way that seems unusual on the coasts but less so in the Midwest; it has been said that if students visit the campus, "They don't have to hold any doors because the students are so friendly and welcoming," one student reports.

FINANCIAL AID: 507-933-7527 • E-MAIL: ADMISSION@GUSTAVUS.EDU • WEBSITE: WWW.GUSTAVUS.EDU

THE PRINCETON REVIEW SAYS

Admissions

Very important factors considered include: Rigor of secondary school record. *Important factors considered include:* Application essay, academic GPA, recommendation(s), standardized test scores. *Other factors considered include:* Alumni/ae relation, extracurricular activities, first generation, geographical residence, interview, level of applicant's interest, racial/ethnic status, religious affiliation/commitment, state residency, talent/ability, volunteer work, work experience. ACT with or without writing component accepted. TOEFL required of all international applicants. High school diploma is required and GED is accepted. *Academic units required:* 4 English, 3 mathematics, 2 science (2 science labs), 2 foreign language, 2 social studies, 2 history. *Academic units recommended:* 4 mathematics, 3 science (3 science labs), 3 foreign language, 2 academic electives.

Financial Aid

Students should submit: FAFSA, CSS/Financial Aid PROFILE, CSS Profile required of all students applying for need-based assistance. Regular filing deadline is May 1. The Princeton Review suggests that all financial aid forms be submitted as soon as possible after January 1. *Need-based scholarships/grants offered:* Federal Pell, SEOG, state scholarships/grants, private scholarships, the school's own gift aid. *Loan aid offered:* Direct Subsidized Stafford, Direct Unsubsidized Stafford, Direct PLUS, Federal Perkins, state loans, alternative loans from private lenders. Applicants will be notified of awards on a rolling basis beginning January 20. Federal Work-Study Program available. Institutional employment available. Highest amount earned per year from on-campus jobs $1,800. Off-campus job opportunities are good.

The Inside Word

Gustavus Adolphus considers a variety of factors when making admissions decisions. Students should display motivation for tackling challenging courses and a desire to be active participants in their community. The majority of applicants are from local areas—those who can provide some geographic diversity are welcome. The school has a rolling admissions policy, so interested students should think about sending in their applications early. All available slots are usually filled by early spring.

THE SCHOOL SAYS ". . ."

From the Admissions Office

"Gustavus Adolphus College is all about helping you make your life count-in the classroom, on the field, here in St. Peter, and wherever you go after college. Our college is built on a powerful sense of community and the will to enhance the common good. Everyone is active and involved, doing meaningful things—whether it's service or political action, playing basketball or making music, studying biology or writing a paper. We're part of a great team. We support and respect each other. Ideas are exchanged openly. Everyone's opinion matters. Gustavus students, faculty and alumni lead lives of uncommon passion and purpose, guided by the College's heritage and core values. Founded in 1862 by Swedish Lutheran immigrants, the College is affiliated with the Evangelical Lutheran Church in America and we host the Nobel Conference, which brings the world's greatest minds to campus every October to discuss the most important scientific issues of the day. Gustavus's 340-acre campus sits on a hill overlooking St. Peter, a classic college town of 10,000 residents in the Minnesota River Valley. You should visit. And, we want you to apply. Make the decision to make your life count. Be a Gustie."

SELECTIVITY	
Admissions Rating	**86**
# of applicants	4,818
% of applicants accepted	64
% of acceptees attending	24
# accepting a place on wait list	10

FRESHMAN PROFILE	
Range SAT Critical Reading	580–680
Range SAT Math	570–670
Range SAT Writing	580–680
Range ACT Composite	25–30
Minimum paper TOEFL	55
Minimum web-based TOEFL	80
Average HS GPA	3.6
% graduated top 10% of class	35
% graduated top 25% of class	69
% graduated top 50% of class	96

DEADLINES	
Early action	
Deadline	11/1
Notification	11/20
Regular	
Deadline	4/1
Notification	4/15
Nonfall registration?	yes

FINANCIAL FACTS	
Financial Aid Rating	**86**
Annual tuition	$35,100
Room and board	$8,700
Required fees	$140
Books and supplies	$750
% needy frosh rec. need-based scholarship or grant aid	99
% needy UG rec. need-based scholarship or grant aid	98
% needy frosh rec. non-need-based scholarship or grant aid	14
% needy UG rec. non-need-based scholarship or grant aid	9
% needy frosh rec. need-based self-help aid	99
% needy UG rec. need-based self-help aid	98
% frosh rec. any financial aid	96
% UG rec. any financial aid	95
% UG borrow to pay for school	69
Average cumulative indebtedness	$28,401
% frosh need fully met	48
% ugrads need fully met	24
Average % of frosh need met	93
Average % of ugrad need met	88

Hamilton College

Office of Admission, Clinton, NY 13323 • Admissions: 315-859-4421 • Fax: 315-859-4457

CAMPUS LIFE

Quality of Life Rating	**88**
Fire Safety Rating	**92**
Green Rating	**85**
Type of school	private
Environment	rural

STUDENTS

Total undergrad enrollment	1,843
% male/female	47/53
% from out of state	68
% from public high school	67
% frosh live on campus	100
# of fraternities	9
# of sororities	7
% African American	4
% Asian	6
% Caucasian	65
% Hispanic	6
% international	5
# of countries represented	37

SURVEY SAYS . . .

Lab facilities are great
Great computer facilities
Athletic facilities are great
School is well run
Low cost of living
Lots of beer drinking

ACADEMICS

Academic Rating	**96**
% students returning for sophomore year	94
% students graduating within 4 years	84
% students graduating within 6 years	89
Calendar	semester
Student/faculty ratio	9:1
Profs interesting rating	98
Profs accessible rating	96
Most classes have	10–19 students
Most lab/discussion sessions have	10–19 students

MOST POPULAR MAJORS

economics; political science and government; psychology

APPLICANTS ALSO LOOK AT AND OFTEN PREFER

Middlebury College, Bowdoin College, Dartmouth College, Williams College, Brown University, Amherst College, Princeton University

AND SOMETIMES PREFER

Colgate University, Wesleyan University, Colby College

AND RARELY PREFER

Skidmore College, Union College (NY), Dickinson College

STUDENTS SAY ". . ."

Academics

Upstate New York liberal arts school Hamilton College offers fine academics and an open curriculum that give students "preparation for the future that goes far beyond exam-taking strategies." The focus on writing and speaking, the lack of core requirements, and the small class sizes put a "keen focus on students as unique individuals with different abilities and aspirations." "Hamilton allows you the freedom to be anyone, but gives you the direction to become the best person you can become," says a student. The school's "mix of old-school practices with liberal thinking" allows students to become "true intellectuals beyond the basics of academia." "Hamilton College is all about learning how to think and then conveying those ideas into writing," says a student. The professors at Hamilton are "brilliant but they do not flaunt it and instead defer to class discussions." Professors are also "always available outside of class to discuss anything further." "Their extensive office hours are when you can really connect with them," says one student. In using their "ability to bring classes to life," professors demonstrate their interest in "comprehension of the material beyond grades." The open curriculum allows for classes to be "extremely productive," because "people want to be there learning and talking about what interests them." "I know when I enroll in a class that the people I take that class with are truly interested in the class (just as I am)," says one student. "They aren't there to fulfill a requirement." Though the campus itself is large, the undergraduate population is fewer than 2,000, so class sizes are downright tiny (which is "excellent"), and if you can't get in to a class, "all you have to do is talk to the professors, and they'll usually make room for you." Research opportunities are plentiful, and facilities (such as labs) "are well-equipped." Administration "does what they can to adhere to the needs and wants of the students."

Life

The "beautiful campus" is located in the middle of relatively nowhere, but students are creative in that they "very successfully compensate for our isolated location with themed parties, clubs, and other eclectic activities." Students are "incredibly devoted" to their school work, but they are also devoted to having a good time. "A typical Hamilton student loves to learn on the weekdays, and drink…on the weekends (but gets to bed early enough to study the following afternoon!)" Still, there are plenty of people on campus that prefer to remain sober, though "whether that is a choice or due to lack of confidence in finding parties, I don't know." More often than not, "Hamiltonians aren't strictly about working themselves to death." People who have cars (a huge plus) can go downtown or into New Hartford in their free time, but "Most students spend most of their time on campus." Often, students just catch the van that travels around the area and "go to the movies or the mall and just hang out with friends." Hamilton has "a very intellectually stimulating academic environment," and "It is not at all uncommon to find a whole dorm room debating about an economic theory that only one of them actually learned about in class."

Student Body

The typical student at Hamilton was "a top student at his/her high school," and is "well-rounded and involved." While most students are "white and relatively wealthy," there is "a diversity of personalities." There are "virtually no cliques," but people are often characteristically preppy, athletic "light siders," or artsy "dark siders." Everyone is "exceptionally nice," and "people here aren't afraid to be themselves." "We're all nerds in our own different ways, but that ends up being cool," says a student. Hamilton students are "extremely involved" in extracurriculars, and "everyone is passionate about their academics as well as their activities outside the classroom."

FINANCIAL AID: 800-859-4413 • E-MAIL: ADMISSION@HAMILTON.EDU • WEBSITE: WWW.HAMILTON.EDU

THE PRINCETON REVIEW SAYS

Admissions

Very important factors considered include: Class rank, academic GPA, rigor of secondary school record. *Important factors considered include:* Application essay, recommendation(s), standardized test scores, character/personal qualities, extracurricular activities, interview. *Other factors considered include:* Alumni/ae relation, first generation, geographical residence, level of applicant's interest, racial/ethnic status, talent/ability, volunteer work, work experience. ACT with or without writing component accepted. TOEFL required of all international applicants. High school diploma is required and GED is accepted. *Academic units recommended:* 4 English, 3 mathematics, 3 science, 3 foreign language, 3 social studies.

Financial Aid

Students should submit: FAFSA, institution's own financial aid form, CSS/Financial Aid PROFILE, state aid form, noncustodial PROFILE, business/farm supplement. Regular filing deadline is February 8. The Princeton Review suggests that all financial aid forms be submitted as soon as possible after January 1. *Need-based scholarships/grants offered:* Federal Pell, SEOG, state scholarships/grants, private scholarships, the school's own gift aid. *Loan aid offered:* Direct Subsidized Stafford, Direct Unsubsidized Stafford, Direct PLUS, Federal Perkins, college/university loans from institutional funds. Applicants will be notified of awards on or about April 1. Federal Work-Study Program available. Institutional employment available. Highest amount earned per year from on-campus jobs $1,800.

The Inside Word

Similar to any prestigious liberal arts schools, Hamilton takes a well-rounded, personal approach to admissions. They rely heavily on academic achievement and intellectual promise, but in a mission to create a talented and diverse incoming class, admissions officers also strive to attain a complete, accurate profile of each candidate. The admissions team at Hamilton also strongly recommends interviews either on or off campus with alumni volunteers.

THE SCHOOL SAYS ". . ."

From the Admissions Office

"As a national leader for teaching students to write effectively, learn from one another, and think for themselves, Hamilton produces graduates who have the knowledge, skills, and confidence to make their own voices heard on issues of importance to them and their communities.

"A key component of the Hamilton experience is the college's open, yet rigorous, liberal arts curriculum. In place of distribution requirements that are common at most colleges, Hamilton gives its students freedom to choose the courses that reflect their unique interests and plans. Faculty advisors assist students in planning a coherent and highly individualized academic program. In fact, close student-faculty relationships at Hamilton are a distinguishing characteristic of the college, but ultimately students at Hamilton take responsibility for their own future. Part of that future includes a lifelong relationship with the college. Hamilton alumni are exceptionally loyal and passionate supporters of their alma mater. That support manifests itself through internships, speaking engagements, job-shadowing opportunities, and financial donations.

"The intellectual flexibility that distinguishes a Hamilton education extends to the application process. Students are free to choose which standardized tests to submit, based on a specified set of options, so that those who do not test well on the SAT or ACT may decide to submit the results of their AP or SAT subject tests. The approach allows students the freedom to decide how to present themselves best to the Committee on Admission."

SELECTIVITY

Admissions Rating	**97**
# of applicants	5,265
% of applicants accepted	27
% of acceptees attending	33
# accepting a place on wait list	1,136
# admitted from wait list	34
# of early decision applicants	598
# accepted early decision	249

FRESHMAN PROFILE

Range SAT Critical Reading	650–740
Range SAT Math	660–730
Range SAT Writing	650–730
Range ACT Composite	28–32
% graduated top 10% of class	74
% graduated top 25% of class	93
% graduated top 50% of class	99

DEADLINES

Early decision	
Deadline	11/15
Notification	12/15
Regular	
Deadline	1/1
Notification	4/1
Nonfall registration?	yes

FINANCIAL FACTS

Financial Aid Rating	**97**
Annual tuition	$42,220
Room and board	$10,830
Required fees	$420
Books and supplies	$1,300
% needy frosh rec. need-based scholarship or grant aid	100
% needy UG rec. need-based scholarship or grant aid	100
% needy frosh rec. need-based self-help aid	85
% needy UG rec. need-based self-help aid	87
% frosh rec. any financial aid	58
% UG rec. any financial aid	56
% UG borrow to pay for school	44
Average cumulative indebtedness	$20,262
% frosh need fully met	100
% ugrads need fully met	100
Average % of frosh need met	100
Average % of ugrad need met	100

Hampden-Sydney College

PO Box 667, Hampden-Sydney, VA 23943-0667 • Admissions: 434-223-6120 • Fax: 434-223-6346

CAMPUS LIFE

Quality of Life Rating	**80**
Fire Safety Rating	**75**
Green Rating	**70**
Type of school	private
Affiliation	Presbyterian
Environment	rural

STUDENTS

Total undergrad enrollment	1,057
% male/female	100/0
% from out of state	32
% from public high school	62
% frosh live on campus	100
# of fraternities	11
% African American	8
% Asian	1
% Caucasian	83
% Hispanic	2
% Native American	1
% international	1
# of countries represented	17

SURVEY SAYS . . .

No one cheats
Career services are great
Students are happy
Student government is popular
Lots of beer drinking

ACADEMICS

Academic Rating	**91**
% students graduating within 4 years	63
% students graduating within 6 years	66
Calendar	semester
Student/faculty ratio	10:1
Profs interesting rating	98
Profs accessible rating	98
Most classes have	10–19 students

MOST POPULAR MAJORS

economics; history; political science and government

APPLICANTS ALSO LOOK AT AND OFTEN PREFER

Virginia Tech, University of Virginia

AND SOMETIMES PREFER

James Madison University, Sewanee—The University of the South, University of Georgia, University of South Carolina—Columbia, The University of North Carolina at Chapel Hill

AND RARELY PREFER

Randolph-Macon College

STUDENTS SAY ". . ."

Academics

Hampden-Sydney is "an all-male institution that promotes a community of brotherhood and has a strong liberal arts education." Students enjoy Hampden-Sydney's "rich history and sense of brotherhood," which has been "forming good men and good citizens since 1775." A "Southern tradition in the heart of Virginia," Hampden-Sydney boasts a "small size," good "student/teacher ratio," and a strong "honor code." "Because it's small and is all-male, you don't get the distractions you would at a large college," one student explains. "Hampden-Sydney is all about community" and has "this distinct ability of this place to make you feel at home." There's an "intense" rhetoric program that students are required to complete, and most seem pleased with it. Since the college was founded before the American Revolution, "some facilities are old and historic. This means that some modern-day luxuries are absent." Hampden-Sydney students think of themselves as "gentlemen," and one of the school's primary appeals its old-boy alumni network that "recruits gentlemen upon graduation and helps to guide them on a path of successful endeavors." Students and professors aren't just homogenous in regards to gender, they have a "generally shared perspective on politics" that's strongly conservative. The professors are a strong draw at Hampden-Sydney. "They have a unique way of making you think for yourself," and "many have some very valuable real-world experience that they are able to translate into the classroom." As one student points out, "small classrooms with brilliant professors = outstanding learning opportunity."

Life

Hampden-Sydney students are about "honor and brotherhood. Also beer." Drinking is a huge part of campus life, which is located in the "small town" of Farmville and "about an hour away from anything that could be considered a major city." The "social life [is] anchored in the fraternities." "Our school's social life is based off of Greek life," another student confirms. "We are also an all-guys school, so during the week it's a lot of video games and studying, but during the weekend there are girls all over campus, and we become a huge party school." Even during the weekdays many party, although without women on campus it becomes "mostly just guys hanging out." There's also "high attendance at sporting events, especially football and basketball." If there's one common complaint, it's the "food, food, food," which is "sub-par" even though "for the amount of money we pay it could be loads better."

Student Body

The average Hampden-Sydney student is an "all-American, preppy, white guy from a wealthy middle- or upper-class family." Most students are "very Southern" and "come from usually a high socioeconomic background." "Athletes make up twenty percent of the student population (football about ten percent), and fraternities make up a large portion as well." "Students here are very friendly because we like to promote an environment of gentlemanliness," one student explains, "that is, as a traditional Southern school, we are in touch with the concept that politeness and manners make a better man." However, this politeness seems to extend only to heterosexual and conservative white males. The school needs to "work on discrimination...but the discrimination comes from the other students, not professors," one student says. Another advises: "If you are gay or a liberal don't come here." One student estimates that "ninety-five percent of students are conservative." "There is an informal and unwritten dress code with social consequences if it is not followed; the students are informally expected to dress nicely in an outfit consisting of khaki pants and a button-up shirt or polo shirt." The way to fit in is "by being 'fratty,'" and "students who live alternative lifestyles (nerds, gays, socially awkward people) are hard-pressed to find friends."

FINANCIAL AID: 434-223-6119 • E-MAIL: HSAPP@HSC.EDU • WEBSITE: WWW.HSC.EDU

THE PRINCETON REVIEW SAYS

Admissions

Very important factors considered include: Application essay, academic GPA, recommendation(s), rigor of secondary school record, standardized test scores, character/personal qualities. *Important factors considered include:* Class rank, extracurricular activities. *Other factors considered include:* First generation, interview, level of applicant's interest, talent/ability, volunteer work, work experience. SAT or ACT required; ACT with or without writing component accepted. TOEFL required of all international applicants. High school diploma is required and GED is accepted. *Academic units required:* 4 English, 3 mathematics, 2 science (1 science lab), 2 foreign language, 1 social studies, 1 history, 3 academic electives. *Academic units recommended:* 4 mathematics, 3 science, 3 foreign language.

Financial Aid

Students should submit: FAFSA, CSS/Financial Aid PROFILE, state aid form. Regular filing deadline is March 1. The Princeton Review suggests that all financial aid forms be submitted as soon as possible after January 1. *Need-based scholarships/grants offered:* Federal Pell, SEOG, state scholarships/grants, private scholarships, the school's own gift aid. *Loan aid offered:* Direct Subsidized Stafford, Direct Unsubsidized Stafford, Direct PLUS, Federal Perkins, college/university loans from institutional funds. Applicants will be notified of awards on or about March 15. Federal Work-Study Program available. Institutional employment available. Highest amount earned per year from on-campus jobs $2,884. Off-campus job opportunities are fair.

The Inside Word

Hampden-Sydney is one of the last of its kind. Understandably, the applicant pool is heavily self-selected, and a fairly significant percentage of those who are admitted choose to enroll. This enables the admissions committee to be more selective, which in turn requires candidates to take the process more seriously than might otherwise be necessary. Students with consistently sound academic records should have little to worry about nonetheless.

THE SCHOOL SAYS "..."

From the Admissions Office

"The spirit of Hampden-Sydney is its sense of community. As one of only 1,120 students, you will be in small classes and find it easy to get extra help or inspiration from professors when you want it. Many of our professors live on campus and enjoy being with students in the snack bar as well as in the classroom. They give you the best, most personal education as possible. A big bonus of small-college life is that everybody is invited to go out for everything, and you can be as much of a leader as you want to be. From athletics to debating to publications to fraternity life, this is part of the process that produces a well-rounded Hampden-Sydney graduate.

"Hampden-Sydney College requires either the SAT or ACT standardized test with essay."

SELECTIVITY	
Admissions Rating	84
# of applicants	2,484
% of applicants accepted	55
% of acceptees attending	24
# of early decision applicants	142
# accepted early decision	51

FRESHMAN PROFILE	
Range SAT Critical Reading	490–600
Range SAT Math	510–610
Range SAT Writing	470–580
Range ACT Composite	21–27
Minimum paper TOEFL	600
Minimum web-based TOEFL	100
Average HS GPA	3.4
% graduated top 10% of class	10
% graduated top 25% of class	19
% graduated top 50% of class	73

DEADLINES	
Early decision	
Deadline	11/15
Notification	12/15
Early action	
Deadline	1/15
Notification	2/15
Regular	
Deadline	3/1
Notification	4/15
Nonfall registration?	yes

FINANCIAL FACTS	
Financial Aid Rating	85
Annual tuition	$32,854
Room and board	$10,632
Required fees	$1,020
Books and supplies	$1,236
% needy frosh rec. need-based scholarship or grant aid	100
% needy UG rec. need-based scholarship or grant aid	100
% needy frosh rec. non-need-based scholarship or grant aid	18
% needy UG rec. non-need-based scholarship or grant aid	16
% needy frosh rec. need-based self-help aid	81
% needy UG rec. need-based self-help aid	81
% frosh rec. any financial aid	100
% UG rec. any financial aid	98
% UG borrow to pay for school	50
Average cumulative indebtedness	$27,740
% frosh need fully met	21
% ugrads need fully met	22
Average % of frosh need met	82
Average % of ugrad need met	81

HAMPSHIRE COLLEGE

ADMISSIONS OFFICE, AMHERST, MA 01002 • ADMISSIONS: 413-559-5471 • FAX: 413-559-5631

CAMPUS LIFE

Quality of Life Rating	73
Fire Safety Rating	68
Green Rating	82
Type of school	private
Environment	town

STUDENTS

Total undergrad enrollment	1,475
% male/female	42/58
% from out of state	85
% from public high school	74
% frosh live on campus	100
% African American	3
% Asian	2
% Caucasian	66
% Hispanic	9
% international	5
# of countries represented	31

SURVEY SAYS . . .

Lots of liberal students
Class discussions encouraged
No one cheats
Students aren't religious
Great off-campus food
Frats and sororities are unpopular or nonexistent
Political activism is popular

ACADEMICS

Academic Rating	88
% students returning for sophomore year	78
% students graduating within 4 years	51
% students graduating within 6 years	63
Calendar	4-1-4
Student/faculty ratio	12:1
Profs interesting rating	81
Profs accessible rating	82
Most classes have	10–19 students
Most lab/discussion sessions have	10–19 students

MOST POPULAR MAJORS

creative writing; drama and dramatics/theater arts; film/video and photographic arts, other

APPLICANTS ALSO LOOK AT AND OFTEN PREFER

Bard College, Sarah Lawrence College, New York University

STUDENTS SAY ". . ."

Academics

Undergrads come to Hampshire College "seduced by the prospect of designing [their] own program of study." The school offers students "a self-designed curriculum" facilitated by "close relationships with professors, small classes, and the great combination of communal living and individualism that a true Hampshire student embodies." A "divisional system," with a student's academic career consisting of three divisions, imposes some sense of order. Division I "is first-year requirements and such," while "Divisions II and III constitute the core of your time. That's when you focus down upon the areas that interest you more than the rest of the school." Undergrads explain that "in class, students learn as a group in discussions or hands-on activities (few lectures, no tests), while outside of class one focuses on independent projects (research, reading, writing, art-making)." The experience culminates in a 'Division III,' an all-consuming year-long senior thesis project "that allows students to become excited and completely invested" while "producing a unique product at the end of the year." Students "receive evaluations instead of grades, which we feel is a much more productive system." While Hampshire "is very small," which might limit students' choices, "it belongs to the Five Colleges consortium," a group that includes the massive University of Massachusetts—Amherst. With the course offerings of five colleges available to them, Hampshire students can "take any course we could dream of."

Life

"Life at Hampshire seems extremely spontaneous," so "while one minute we may be complaining of boredom, the next we may start doing something fun and exciting. We are normally very good at entertaining ourselves." "Usually what people do is just hang out with a small group of friends," and "there is partying on the weekends," although "parties here consist generally of fifty people or less, never the roaring, dangerously wild parties that are often found at colleges." Parties often take place in the "mods," apartment-style housing favored by upperclassmen, where students "throw a lot of sweaty dance parties where hippies, scenesters, and geeks all grind up against each other." Also, "live music is very common" on and around campus, "drum circles and random games of Frisbee are unavoidable," and "going to the nearby towns of Amherst or Northampton isn't bad." Students can also choose from "tons of clubs, from Spinsters Unite! to the Red Scare Ultimate Frisbee Team, [or] Students for a Free Tibet to Excalibur, which is the sci-fi and fantasy club. You can even take yoga, karate, or tai chi classes. There are parties all the time for those who like that kind of thing, and movies, video games, clubs, and playing in the forest or on the farm for those who don't." There are also "five colleges in the area to hang out at. Enough said."

Student Body

"Picture all the various groups of misfits in high school" and you'll have a picture of the students at Hampshire, a place where "Nonconformity is so normal it's almost conformist to be nonconformist. You can't say 'the kid with the dreadlocks' because the person would reply with 'Which one?'" Undergrads assure us that "Hampshire is really open to any type of student." Though there many different types of students on campus, all students have "at least one serious and one kitschy academic or extracurricular pursuit. Those who identify as male are usually bearded and wear plaid." The common threads among students: "They are all interesting. They all have talents, stories, and are just plain interesting to be around. They are full of creativity and life and seem to really enjoy where they are." They also tend to be "socially conscious, left-wing, and artistic. We are fond of do-it-yourself philosophies, from [magazines] to music and film production to designing ecologically sustainable communities." One student warns, "this is not a good school for fundamentalist Christians."

FINANCIAL AID: 413-559-5484 • E-MAIL: ADMISSIONS@HAMPSHIRE.EDU • WEBSITE: WWW.HAMPSHIRE.EDU

THE PRINCETON REVIEW SAYS

Admissions

Very important factors considered include: Application essay, character/personal qualities. *Important factors considered include:* Recommendation(s), rigor of secondary school record, extracurricular activities, level of applicant's interest, talent/ability. *Other factors considered include:* Class rank, academic GPA, standardized test scores, alumni/ae relation, interview, racial/ethnic status, volunteer work, work experience. ACT with or without writing component accepted. TOEFL required of all international applicants. High school diploma is required and GED is accepted. *Academic units required:* 4 English, 3 mathematics, 3 science (2 science labs), 3 foreign language, 3 history. *Academic units recommended:* 4 English, 4 mathematics, 4 science (2 science labs), 4 foreign language, 4 history.

Financial Aid

Students should submit: FAFSA, CSS/Financial Aid PROFILE, noncustodial PROFILE. Regular filing deadline is February 1. The Princeton Review suggests that all financial aid forms be submitted as soon as possible after January 1. *Need-based scholarships/grants offered:* Federal Pell, SEOG, state scholarships/grants, private scholarships, the school's own gift aid. *Loan aid offered:* Direct Subsidized Stafford, Direct Unsubsidized Stafford, Direct PLUS, Federal Perkins. Applicants will be notified of awards on or about April 1. Federal Work-Study Program available. Highest amount earned per year from on-campus jobs $2,600.

The Inside Word

Hampshire's admissions policies are the antithesis of formula-based practices. Officers want to know the individual behind the transcript, and personal characteristics hold substantial weight in the admissions decision. Demonstrating discipline and an independent and inquisitive spirit may just carry more weight than a perfect 4.0. Writing is pivotal to a Hampshire education, and applicants must put considerable thought into their personal statements. They will be read carefully.

THE SCHOOL SAYS ". . ."

From the Admissions Office

"The Admissions Committee focuses its selection process on fit over formula. Because all majors at Hampshire are personalized, it is important that you have the passion and ambition requisite to negotiate your education with faculty advisors. Hampshire seeks students who have elected to challenge themselves in high school and demonstrate a genuine passion for learning."

"In addition to the Common Application, Hampshire's supplement asks questions that are meant to reveal more about you as a thinker, learner, and community member. An analytical essay gives the Admissions Committee a sense of your ability to ask complex questions, think critically, synthesize information, and formulate original conclusions. The Admissions Committee welcomes examples of work, whether that be scientific or creative. Personal interviews are valued and strongly encouraged."

"At Hampshire, you will personalize your major. You will gain a strong foundation in the liberal arts and learn the skills to create new knowledge in virtually any chosen field of study. The process of personalizing majors requires a highly personalized, intensive connection with faculty advisors; faculty begin as teachers and mentors and become colleagues and collaborators. As a Hampshire student, you will be able to take courses at four other neighboring colleges for free—and you will have a limitless range of opportunities to engage in outside-the-classroom real-world experiences. Hampshire's program will give you the skills and confidence to create knowledge and accomplish great things as a graduate."

SELECTIVITY	
Admissions Rating	**86**
# of applicants	2,517
% of applicants accepted	71
% of acceptees attending	20
# accepting a place on wait list	214
# admitted from wait list	53
# of early decision applicants	59
# accepted early decision	46

FRESHMAN PROFILE	
Range SAT Critical Reading	590–700
Range SAT Math	540–650
Range SAT Writing	580–670
Range ACT Composite	25–29
Minimum paper TOEFL	577
Minimum web-based TOEFL	91
Average HS GPA	3.3
% graduated top 10% of class	19
% graduated top 25% of class	52
% graduated top 50% of class	85

DEADLINES	
Early decision	
Deadline	11/15
Notification	12/15
Early action	
Deadline	12/1
Notification	2/1
Regular	
Priority	11/15
Deadline	1/1
Notification	4/1
Nonfall registration?	yes

FINANCIAL FACTS	
Financial Aid Rating	**90**
Annual tuition	$43,580
Room and board	$11,620
Books and supplies	$700
% needy frosh rec. need-based scholarship or grant aid	100
% needy UG rec. need-based scholarship or grant aid	100
% needy frosh rec. non-need-based scholarship or grant aid	45
% needy UG rec. non-need-based scholarship or grant aid	54
% needy frosh rec. need-based self-help aid	100
% needy UG rec. need-based self-help aid	100
% frosh rec. any financial aid	70
% UG rec. any financial aid	76
% UG borrow to pay for school	62
Average cumulative indebtedness	$20,430
% frosh need fully met	53
% ugrads need fully met	69
Average % of frosh need met	94
Average % of ugrad need met	97

HAMPTON UNIVERSITY

OFFICE OF ADMISSIONS, HAMPTON, VA 23668 • ADMISSIONS: 757-727-5328 • FAX: 757-727-5095

CAMPUS LIFE

Quality of Life Rating	**65**
Fire Safety Rating	**65**
Green Rating	**60***
Type of school	private
Environment	city

STUDENTS

Total undergrad enrollment	4,265
% male/female	35/65
% from out of state	69
% frosh live on campus	89
# of fraternities	6
# of sororities	3
% African American	84
% Asian	.8
% Caucasian	6
% Hispanic	1
% international	1
# of countries represented	33

SURVEY SAYS . . .

Great library
Campus feels safe
Everyone loves the Pirates
Frats and sororities dominate social scene
Musical organizations are popular
Student publications are popular
Student government is popular

ACADEMICS

Academic Rating	**77**
% students returning for sophomore year	75
% students graduating within 4 years	39
% students graduating within 6 years	65
Calendar	semester
Student/faculty ratio	9:1
Profs interesting rating	74
Profs accessible rating	65
Most classes have	20–29 students

MOST POPULAR MAJORS

business/commerce; journalism; psychology

APPLICANTS ALSO LOOK AT AND OFTEN PREFER

Florida A&M University, Spelman College

AND SOMETIMES PREFER

Howard University, University of Maryland, College Park, Virginia Tech

STUDENTS SAY ". . ."

Academics

Hampton University, "one of the premier Historically Black Colleges and Universities in the country," is "perfect for students who desire to be around other intelligent and focused black students who have a future and are making plans to achieve their goals. Our students are making changes in this world and will always continue to." With popular programs in business and management, psychology, pharmacy, nursing, sociology, the hard sciences, and communication, Hampton "is about producing successful, bright, and talented professionals." The school has made a special commitment to journalism and communication, opening a state-of-the-art facility a few years back that includes a full working studio with editing facilities, a student-run radio station, and five computer labs. Throughout its many departments, Hampton stresses the importance of experiential learning, "presenting a host of opportunities for students to get internships and jobs." One student reports, "I have had three internships and have been on the campus radio station for my entire career at HU." Professors here earn good marks for dedication and teaching skills; "The administration tries," and "overall, they care," and any inconvenience is worth it for "the connections and networking" Hampton provides. As one student notes, "Everyone here is important, related to, or knows someone important, and everyone will become successful and important."

Life

"Hampton is not the typical party school," students agree. One student writes, "Life at Hampton is pretty boring compared to where I'm from." Undergrads report, "Most events take place off campus, so you really have to find your own fun." Fortunately the area provides some diversion, including "malls, fine dining, and parties…Also, Hampton is surrounded by cities that are no more than fifteen to twenty minutes away," including Norfolk, Newport News, and Virginia Beach. "Nearby amusement parks are also great attractions for the spring and summer." On campus, "there is a really nice student center that turns into a virtual party every day from noon to 2:00 P.M. The student center is tri-level and has everything from a theater to [a] bowling ally and a fitness center." Hampton's Greek system is very popular; the most popular ones "are highly competitive and selective, and the whole process is crazy and oh-so-hard to get into." Some here complain that restrictive regulations dampen campus life.

Student Body

Hampton "is a Historically Black [College and] University, but the range of black students here is amazing. There is a niche for everyone, and I mean everyone, and most are universally accepted." Many are "very outgoing and professional," "are well-off, and come from a nice home." Some can be "materialistic and…care a lot about social matters. They all dress well, spend plenty of money on clothes, and drive very nice cars (even better cars than teachers)," but "There are many different types of students." Atypical students here "mesh well with the others," because Hampton students are a part of a family. "We are called Hamptonians, symbolizing our unity. Here we have a bond that is very strong—we all fit in—and it is not to be broken."

FINANCIAL AID: 757-727-5332 • E-MAIL: ADMIT@HAMPTONU.EDU • WEBSITE: WWW.HAMPTONU.EDU

THE PRINCETON REVIEW SAYS

Admissions

Very important factors considered include: Application essay, rigor of secondary school record, standardized test scores, character/personal qualities. *Important factors considered include:* Class rank, recommendation(s). *Other factors considered include:* Alumni/ae relation, extracurricular activities, talent/ability, volunteer work. SAT or ACT required; TOEFL required of all international applicants. High school diploma is required and GED is accepted. *Academic units required:* 4 English, 3 mathematics, 2 science (2 science labs), 2 social studies, 6 academic electives. *Academic units recommended:* 2 foreign language.

Financial Aid

Students should submit: FAFSA. The Princeton Review suggests that all financial aid forms be submitted as soon as possible after January 1. *Need-based scholarships/grants offered:* Federal Pell, SEOG, state scholarships/grants, private scholarships, the school's own gift aid, Federal Nursing Scholarships. *Loan aid offered:* Direct Subsidized Stafford, Direct Unsubsidized Stafford, Direct PLUS, Federal Perkins, alternative loans. Applicants will be notified of awards on a rolling basis beginning April 15. Federal Work-Study Program available. Off-campus job opportunities are excellent.

The Inside Word

Hampton University allows for early action admissions, meaning that students can receive an early decision without having to commit to attending the school. Well more than half of HU's applicant pool pursues this option. You would be wise to follow suit; the school is bound to be more lenient early in the process than later, when it has already admitted many qualified students. Don't be fooled by the fact that the number of applicants to HU has dropped in recent years; that's the result of more stringent admission standards, not a drop in the school's cachet.

THE SCHOOL SAYS ". . ."

From the Admissions Office

"Hampton attempts to provide the environment and structures most conducive to the intellectual, emotional, and aesthetic enlargement of the lives of its members. The university gives priority to effective teaching and scholarly research while placing the student at the center of its planning. Hampton will ask you to look inwardly at your own history and culture and examine your relationship to the aspirations and development of the world."

SELECTIVITY	
Admissions Rating	**90**
# of applicants	10,569
% of applicants accepted	37
% of acceptees attending	24

FRESHMAN PROFILE	
Range SAT Critical Reading	483–603
Range SAT Math	480–592
Range ACT Composite	17–28
Minimum paper TOEFL	550
Average HS GPA	3.2
% graduated top 10% of class	35
% graduated top 25% of class	40
% graduated top 50% of class	67

DEADLINES	
Early action	
Deadline	12/1
Notification	12/15
Regular	
Priority	3/1
Nonfall registration?	yes

FINANCIAL FACTS	
Financial Aid Rating	**66**
Annual tuition	$17,732
Room and board	$8,790
Required fees	$2,006
Books and supplies	$750
% needy frosh rec. need-based scholarship or grant aid	94
% needy UG rec. need-based scholarship or grant aid	95
% needy frosh rec. non-need-based scholarship or grant aid	37
% needy UG rec. non-need-based scholarship or grant aid	26
% needy frosh rec. need-based self-help aid	81
% needy UG rec. need-based self-help aid	83
% UG borrow to pay for school	93
Average cumulative indebtedness	$10,119
% frosh need fully met	56
% ugrads need fully met	52
Average % of frosh need met	58
Average % of ugrad need met	54

HANOVER COLLEGE

PO BOX 108, HANOVER, IN 47243-0108 • ADMISSIONS: 800-213-2178 • FAX: 812-866-7098

CAMPUS LIFE

Quality of Life Rating	**72**
Fire Safety Rating	**74**
Green Rating	**81**
Type of school	private
Affiliation	Presbyterian
Environment	rural

STUDENTS

Total undergrad enrollment	1,064
% male/female	45/55
% from out of state	33
% from public high school	81
% frosh live on campus	98
# of fraternities	5
# of sororities	4
% African American	5
% Asian	1
% Caucasian	83
% Hispanic	2
% international	3
# of countries represented	9

SURVEY SAYS . . .

Lab facilities are great
Athletic facilities are great
Students are friendly
Campus feels safe
Low cost of living
Frats and sororities dominate social scene
Lots of beer drinking
Hard liquor is popular

ACADEMICS

Academic Rating	**92**
% students returning for sophomore year	80
% students graduating within 4 years	69
% students graduating within 6 years	71
Calendar	other
Student/faculty ratio	12:1
Profs interesting rating	95
Profs accessible rating	90
Most classes have	10–19 students

MOST POPULAR MAJORS

communication studies/speech communication and rhetoric; history; psychology

APPLICANTS ALSO LOOK AT AND OFTEN PREFER

DePauw University

AND SOMETIMES PREFER

Indiana University—Bloomington, Miami University, Centre College, Wittenberg University, Wabash College

AND RARELY PREFER

Kenyon College, Earlham College

STUDENTS SAY ". . ."

Academics

A "gem in the Midwest," Hanover College is a rigorous liberal arts school with an impressive focus on the individual learner. Students absolutely love Hanover's "small but engaging classes," led by professors who "show a high level of dedication to the students, and a great affinity for the subjects they teach." Personalized education is the name of the game at Hanover, where professors "take a personal interest in your education and interests, and strive to make every class engaging for every student, even if it means catering to and adapting to a different learning style than the one they're used to." Hanover's "discussion-led classes are great for those who are interested in real-world applications," and the curriculum is successful in building "essential life skills such as problem-solving and organizational skills." Despite the friendliness of the faculty, a Hanover education is no walk in the park: "The academics are rigorous and students are pushed to levels outside of their comfort zone." A current student tells us, "It has been extremely challenging at points, but with the help and understanding of my professors and peers, it has been very enriching." Fortunately, not every moment at Hanover is all stress and study. An oasis of relaxation, the school's unique Spring Term is a "four-week period in May where you only take one class. The rest of the time is devoted to intramurals, parties, and enjoying the weather." On this friendly campus, "The administration is very available" and "very in touch with the students," but students say there's always room for improvement, especially when it comes to "communication."

Life

Large and well-kept, Hanover's "gorgeous campus" provides "the perfect setting for learning." Located in a little town on the Ohio River, students warn us that, "Even if you have a great group of friends, there is not a whole lot to do. So getting involved is a huge key to being happy here." Fortunately, on and around campus, "There are 165 student organizations," including "intramural sports…club-sponsored outings and a massive wooded area to go hiking in." In addition to organized activities, students like to hang out at the "student-run restaurant on campus called the Shoebox, which has great food and entertainment." Parties are another popular way to wile away the weekend hours. A student explains, "although the administration publishes an annual booklet titled '164 Things to Do at Hanover College,' it seems that drinking is still a particularly common pastime, especially on Friday and Saturday nights." However, "Students generally are smart and responsible when drinking," and parties are "fairly safe." In addition to the Greek scene, there are "large groups of people who are happy to simply hang out, talk, watch movies, that kind of thing." In addition, "Most people go off campus at least one day of the weekend, just to break routine a little bit." To enjoy more cosmopolitan environs, "Louisville is about forty minutes away," and nearby Madison is "a great town [in which] to experience community connections and a festive atmosphere."

Student Body

At Hanover College, "The typical student is studious, involved in campus activities, and enjoys spending free time with friends." Among the school's 1,000 undergraduates, "The majority of students are white, but there are many other ethnic groups," as well as "a variety of people of different religious backgrounds, sexualities, political views, and personality types." "Students are split about evenly from large suburban high schools and smaller rural schools," though most come from "Indiana, Kentucky, Illinois, or Ohio." There are "definitely social divisions at Hanover," which tend to form around certain clubs and social groups. If you aren't interested in going Greek, "There is an active 'geek' population that is waiting to be tapped if you search for it (Sci-fi Club, Anime Club)." "Most people are friendly and don't mind crossing-over into a variety of circles of friends."

FINANCIAL AID: 812-866-7029 • E-MAIL: ADMISSION@HANOVER.EDU • WEBSITE: WWW.HANOVER.EDU

THE PRINCETON REVIEW SAYS

Admissions

Very important factors considered include: Class rank, academic GPA, rigor of secondary school record. *Important factors considered include:* Recommendation(s), standardized test scores, talent/ability. *Other factors considered include:* Application essay, alumni/ae relation, character/personal qualities, extracurricular activities, first generation, geographical residence, interview, level of applicant's interest, racial/ethnic status, state residency, volunteer work, work experience. SAT or ACT required; ACT with writing component recommended. TOEFL required of all international applicants. High school diploma is required and GED is not accepted. *Academic units required:* 4 English, 3 mathematics, 3 science (2 science labs), 2 foreign language, 2 social studies, 2 history, 2 academic electives. *Academic units recommended:* 4 English, 4 mathematics, 4 science (3 science labs), 4 foreign language, 3 social studies, 3 history, 3 academic electives.

Financial Aid

Students should submit: FAFSA. Regular filing deadline is March 1. The Princeton Review suggests that all financial aid forms be submitted as soon as possible after January 1. *Need-based scholarships/grants offered:* Federal Pell, SEOG, state scholarships/grants, private scholarships, the school's own gift aid. *Loan aid offered:* Direct Subsidized Stafford, Direct Unsubsidized Stafford, Direct PLUS, college/university loans from institutional funds. Applicants will be notified of awards on a rolling basis beginning March 1. Institutional employment available. Highest amount earned per year from on-campus jobs $3,000. Off-campus job opportunities are fair.

The Inside Word

There are five main criteria that the Hanover admissions committee uses to evaluate applicants: academic record, personal excellence, respect for others, community responsibility, and accountability. If you think you're a good fit, the school will help arrange an overnight visit to campus, which gives you the opportunity to stay in a dorm, attend classes, and interview with the admissions department.

THE SCHOOL SAYS ". . ."

From the Admissions Office

"Since our founding in 1827, we have been committed to providing students with a personal, rigorous, and well-rounded liberal arts education. Part of the college search process is finding that school that proves to be a good match. For those who see the value in an education that demands engagement and who see college as a time for exploration and involvement, they will find that Hanover is all they could hope for and more.

"The admission process serves as an introduction to the personal education that students receive at Hanover College. Every application is considered individually with emphasis being placed on a student's high school curriculum and the student's academic performance in that curriculum. While we realize that not every high school has the same course offerings, we expect students to have selected a college preparatory curriculum as challenging as possible within his or her particular high school or academic setting.

"Hanover College accepts both the SAT and ACT. Students taking the ACT are required to take the optional writing section. For students who have taken one or both of the tests multiple times, we will use the highest sub scores when calculating a student's score on either test for admission and scholarship purposes."

SELECTIVITY	
Admissions Rating	84
# of applicants	3,015
% of applicants accepted	68
% of acceptees attending	16

FRESHMAN PROFILE	
Range SAT Critical Reading	510–620
Range SAT Math	510–610
Range SAT Writing	470–570
Range ACT Composite	22–28
Minimum paper TOEFL	550
Minimum web-based TOEFL	80
Average HS GPA	3.6
% graduated top 10% of class	31
% graduated top 25% of class	66
% graduated top 50% of class	94

DEADLINES	
Early action	
Deadline	12/1
Notification	12/20
Regular	
Deadline	3/1
Nonfall registration?	yes

FINANCIAL FACTS	
Financial Aid Rating	84
Annual tuition	$29,668
Room and board	$9,230
Required fees	$600
Books and supplies	$1,200
% needy frosh rec. need-based scholarship or grant aid	100
% needy UG rec. need-based scholarship or grant aid	100
% needy frosh rec. non-need-based scholarship or grant aid	10
% needy UG rec. non-need-based scholarship or grant aid	11
% needy frosh rec. need-based self-help aid	90
% needy UG rec. need-based self-help aid	88
% frosh rec. any financial aid	100
% UG rec. any financial aid	100
% UG borrow to pay for school	99
Average cumulative indebtedness	$27,325
% frosh need fully met	23
% ugrads need fully met	24
Average % of frosh need met	84
Average % of ugrad need met	85

HARVARD COLLEGE

86 BRATTLE STREET, CAMBRIDGE, MA 02138 • ADMISSIONS: 617-495-1551 • FAX: 617-495-8821

CAMPUS LIFE

Quality of Life Rating	**79**
Fire Safety Rating	**60***
Green Rating	**99**
Type of school	private
Environment	city

STUDENTS

Total undergrad enrollment	6,676
% male/female	50/50
% from out of state	86
% from public high school	68
% frosh live on campus	100
% African American	7
% Asian	18
% Caucasian	45
% Hispanic	9
% international	10
# of countries represented	111

SURVEY SAYS . . .

Lab facilities are great
Great computer facilities
Great library
Diverse student types on campus
Musical organizations are popular
Student publications are popular
Political activism is popular

ACADEMICS

Academic Rating	**96**
% students returning for sophomore year	97
% students graduating within 4 years	87
% students graduating within 6 years	97
Calendar	semester
Student/faculty ratio	7:1
Profs interesting rating	71
Profs accessible rating	65
Most classes have	fewer than 10 students

MOST POPULAR MAJORS

economics; political science and government; sociology

STUDENTS SAY "..."

Academics

Bully to those who get the chance to be a part of the "dynamic universe" that is Harvard College, who find themselves in an "amazing irresistible hell" that pushes them to the extremes of their intellect and ability. Unsurprisingly, the legendarily "very difficult" school attracts some of the country's most promising youth, who rise to the occasion in almost every aspect of their life on campus, not just the classroom. Harvard's recent financial aid enhancements have increased the number of applications by a landslide, but even after getting past the admissions hurdle, "People find ways to make everything (especially clubs and even partying) competitive." Happily, this streak is more of a "latent competition," as there are more than enough opportunity and resources to go around. "It is impossible to 'get the most out of Harvard' because Harvard offers so much," says one student. Much like the students, the professors at this "beautiful, fun, historic, and academically alive place" in Cambridge, Massachusetts, are among "the brightest minds in the world," and "The level of achievement is unbelievable." Some of the larger introductory classes are taught by teaching fellows (TFs), meaning "you do have to go to office hours to get to know your big lecture class professors on a personal level," but once your figurative underclass dues are paid, the access to "incredible" and "every so often, fantastic" professors is perfectly within reach. Top it off with Grade-A internship and employment opportunities, a good old alumni network, and a crimson pedigree for your resume, and you may just end up agreeing with the Harvard student who refers to his experience as "rewarding beyond anything else I've ever done." Though the administration can be "waaaaay out of touch with students" and "reticent to change," it at least "does a good job of watching over its freshmen through extensive advising programs," and students all have faith that their best interests are being kept in mind.

Life

Cambridge and Boston are nothing if not college towns, and students never lack for options if they just want to "go see a play, a concert, hit up a party, go to the movies, or dine out." Students quickly learn when to hit the books and when to hit the streets, so "studying becomes routine." "There is a vibrant social atmosphere on campus and between students and the local community." As one student puts it, "Boredom does not exist here. There are endless opportunities and endless passionate people to do them with." "Basically, if you want to do it, Harvard either has it or has the money to give to you so you can start it." "Partying in a more traditional setting is available at Harvard, but is not a prevalent aspect of the school's social life. While there is a pub on campus that provides an excellent venue to hang out and play a game of pool or have a reasonably priced drink," and parties happen on weekends at Harvard's finals clubs, there's no real pressure for students to partake if they're not interested.

Student Body

Much as you might expect, ambition and achievement are the ties that bind at Harvard, and "Everyone is great for one reason or another," says a student. Most every student can be summed up with the same statement: "Works really hard. Doesn't sleep. Involved in a million extracurriculars." Diversity is found in all aspects of life, from ethnicities to religion to ideology, and "there is a lot of tolerance and acceptance at Harvard for individuals of all races, religions, socioeconomic backgrounds, life styles, etc."

FINANCIAL AID: 617-495-1581 • E-MAIL: COLLEGE@FAS.HARVARD.EDU • WEBSITE: WWW.COLLEGE.HARVARD.EDU

THE PRINCETON REVIEW SAYS

Admissions

Other factors considered include: Application essay, academic GPA, recommendation(s), rigor of secondary school record, standardized test scores, alumni/ae relation, character/personal qualities, extracurricular activities, first generation, geographical residence, interview, racial/ethnic status, talent/ability, volunteer work, work experience. SAT or ACT required; ACT with writing component required. High school diploma or equivalent is not required. *Academic units recommended:* 4 English, 4 mathematics, 4 science, 4 foreign language, 3 social studies, 2 history.

Financial Aid

Students should submit: FAFSA, CSS/Financial Aid PROFILE, tax forms through IDOC. Regular filing deadline is February 1. The Princeton Review suggests that all financial aid forms be submitted as soon as possible after January 1. *Need-based scholarships/grants offered:* Federal Pell, SEOG, state scholarships/grants, private scholarships, the school's own gift aid. *Loan aid offered:* Direct Subsidized Stafford, Direct Unsubsidized Stafford, Direct PLUS, Federal Perkins, college/university loans from institutional funds. Applicants will be notified of awards on or about April 1. Federal Work-Study Program available. Institutional employment available. Highest amount earned per year from on-campus jobs $19,967. Off-campus job opportunities are excellent.

The Inside Word

It just doesn't get any tougher than this. Candidates to Harvard face dual obstacles—an awe-inspiring applicant pool and, as a result, admissions standards that defy explanation in quantifiable terms. Harvard denies admission to the vast majority, and virtually all of them are top students. It all boils down to splitting hairs, which is quite hard to explain and even harder for candidates to understand. Rather than being as detailed and direct as possible about the selection process and criteria, Harvard keeps things close to the vest—before, during, and after. They even refuse to admit that being from lesser populated states like South Dakota is an advantage. Thus the admissions process does more to intimidate candidates than to empower them. Moving to a common application seemed to be a small step in the right direction, but with the current explosion of early decision applicants and a super-high yield of enrollees, things aren't likely to change dramatically.

THE SCHOOL SAYS ". . ."

From the Admissions Office

"The admissions committee looks for energy, ambition, and the capacity to make the most of opportunities. Academic ability and preparation are important, and so is intellectual curiosity—but many of the strongest applicants have significant, non-academic interests and accomplishments, as well. There is no formula for admission, and applicants are considered carefully, with attention to future promise.

"Freshman applicants may submit the SAT. The ACT with writing component is also accepted. All students must also submit three SAT Subject Tests of their choosing."

SELECTIVITY	
Admissions Rating	**99**
# of applicants	34,950
% of applicants accepted	6
% of acceptees attending	76

FRESHMAN PROFILE	
Range SAT Critical Reading	690–790
Range SAT Math	700–800
Range SAT Writing	690–790
Range ACT Composite	31–35
Average HS GPA	4.0
% graduated top 10% of class	95
% graduated top 25% of class	100
% graduated top 50% of class	100

DEADLINES	
Early action	
Deadline	11/1
Notification	12/16
Regular	
Deadline	1/1
Notification	4/1
Nonfall registration?	no

FINANCIAL FACTS	
Financial Aid Rating	**96**
% needy frosh rec. need-based scholarship or grant aid	99
% needy UG rec. need-based scholarship or grant aid	100
% needy frosh rec. need-based self-help aid	62
% needy UG rec. need-based self-help aid	82
% frosh rec. any financial aid	77
% UG rec. any financial aid	69
% UG borrow to pay for school	36
Average cumulative indebtedness	$11,780
% frosh need fully met	100
% ugrads need fully met	100
Average % of frosh need met	100
Average % of ugrad need met	100

HARVEY MUDD COLLEGE

301 PLATT BOULEVARD, CLAREMONT, CA 91711-5990 • ADMISSIONS: 909-621-8011 • FAX: 909-621-8360

CAMPUS LIFE

Quality of Life Rating	**87**
Fire Safety Rating	**73**
Green Rating	**80**
Type of school	private
Environment	town

STUDENTS

Total undergrad enrollment	777
% male/female	58/42
% from out of state	66
% from public high school	69
% frosh live on campus	100
% African American	1
% Asian	21
% Caucasian	59
% Hispanic	6
% Native American	1
% international	7
# of countries represented	23

SURVEY SAYS . . .

No one cheats
Lab facilities are great
Great computer facilities
School is well run
Students are friendly
Dorms are like palaces
Low cost of living
Frats and sororities are unpopular or nonexistent

ACADEMICS

Academic Rating	**94**
Calendar	semester
Student/faculty ratio	8:1
Profs interesting rating	98
Profs accessible rating	98
Most classes have	10–19 students
Most lab/discussion sessions have	10–19 students

MOST POPULAR MAJORS

computer and information sciences; engineering; mathematics

APPLICANTS ALSO LOOK AT AND OFTEN PREFER

California Institute of Technology, Massachusetts Institute of Technology, Stanford University, Harvard College, Princeton University

AND SOMETIMES PREFER

Cornell University, University of California—Berkeley, University of California—Los Angeles

AND RARELY PREFER

University of California—San Diego

STUDENTS SAY ". . ."

Academics

Harvey Mudd College, one of the five Claremont Colleges in Southern California's Inland Empire, "is a small science and math school with a quirky community that is the perfect fit for those who are serious about both their technical studies and having an indefinably strange yet amazing time." With "an excellent program in the sciences and engineering," strong undergraduate research opportunities, and "a very high percentage of students [who] go to graduate school," Harvey Mudd "is unique and offers a personalized education that you can't get at a larger technical university." While the rigorous academics "can be very stressful for some," most students are quick to emphasize the support provided by professors and the student body. "The academic experience is heightened by the students…who act cooperatively rather than competitively to conquer the material rather than each other." This collaborative atmosphere is created in large part by the respected honor code, which students say "defines us and allows us to have take-home finals [and] unproctored tests." "The trust the faculty has for the students gives us a sense of responsibility, and thus everyone lives up to expectations." Students trust the faculty, as well. "I love the professors here," one student says (echoing the sentiments of many). "They are all brilliant and extremely accessible. Most of them know my name and will stop to talk any time." "Lectures and office hours are both amazing! Professors really want you to understand the material." Overall, students say their lives at Harvey Mudd are "tons of work, but really fun."

Life

Because "Harvey Mudd is a highly academic school, a lot of time is spent doing homework and studying." Students manage to find time for fun, though, even at the expense of some shut-eye: "Many people are sleep-deprived but happy in general." "Community is such a big part of Harvey Mudd, people spend a lot of time with each other," and there are many niches within the larger community. "Every dorm has a unique personality, and what people do for fun is different for each person." "Some are devoted to video games and the more classic 'nerd' activities. Some groups are devoted to drinking and partying a ton. There is a wide spectrum of unique dorm communities represented." "One can easily find groups to play sports or video games with, take on carpentry or other independent construction or engineering projects, start an afternoon game of bocce ball or croquet, compete in the fiercely competitive CMS intramural water polo league, and of course, help in the construction of the campus-wide Rube Goldberg Machine, to name a few popular activities." "CAP (Committee for Activities Planning) subsidizes concert tickets, sporting event tickets, ski trips, and other events" if at least eight Mudders plan to attend. "Dorms throw some kick-ass parties," "taking great care to make them fun for people who don't drink as well." Favorites include "Casemas," when "we import five tons of snow to celebrate winter," and "Slippery When Wet" when students "construct decks to support hundreds of dancing people" and then invite the other Claremont Colleges to test their strength over a flooded courtyard.

Student Body

"We are nerds," Mudders tell us, "and we embrace it." They also describe themselves as "outgoing, quirky, and fun but very studious." Students are united by "a brimming passion for science and a love of knowledge for its own sake." "All students are exceptionally intelligent and are able to perform their work in a professional manner." Beyond that, there's "a really diverse group of personalities" at Mudd, who are "not afraid to show their true colors" and who all have "a unique sense of humor." Students say they "are all friendly, smart, and talented, which brings us together. Upperclassmen look out for underclassmen, and students tend to bond together easily over difficult homework." In such a welcoming community, "students primarily fit in by not fitting in—wearing pink pirate hats or skateboarding while playing harmonica or practicing unicycle jousting are all good ways to fit in perfectly."

FINANCIAL AID: 909-621-8055 • E-MAIL: ADMISSION@HMC.EDU • WEBSITE: WWW.HMC.EDU

THE PRINCETON REVIEW SAYS

Admissions

Very important factors considered include: Application essay, academic GPA, recommendation(s), rigor of secondary school record, character/personal qualities, talent/ability. *Important factors considered include:* Class rank, standardized test scores, extracurricular activities. *Other factors considered include:* Alumni/ae relation, first generation, geographical residence, interview, level of applicant's interest, racial/ethnic status, state residency, volunteer work, work experience. SAT or ACT required; ACT with writing component required. TOEFL required of all international applicants. High school diploma is required and GED is accepted. High school diploma or equivalent is not required. *Academic units required:* 4 English, 3 mathematics, 3 science, 1 history. *Academic units recommended:* 4 mathematics, 4 science (2 science labs), 2 foreign language, 2 social studies, 2 history.

Financial Aid

Students should submit: FAFSA, CSS/Financial Aid PROFILE, state aid form, noncustodial PROFILE, business/farm supplement. Regular filing deadline is February 1. The Princeton Review suggests that all financial aid forms be submitted as soon as possible after January 1. *Need-based scholarships/grants offered:* Federal Pell, SEOG, state scholarships/grants, private scholarships, the school's own gift aid Federal ACG and SMART Grants. *Loan aid offered:* Direct Subsidized Stafford, Direct Unsubsidized Stafford, Direct PLUS, Federal Perkins, college/university loans from institutional funds, alternative loans. Applicants will be notified of awards on or about April 1. Federal Work-Study Program available. Institutional employment available. Highest amount earned per year from on-campus jobs $11,776. Off-campus job opportunities are excellent.

The Inside Word

There's little mystery to the admissions process at Harvey Mudd College, but there's a lot of competition. Like most top-tier science, math, and engineering schools, Harvey Mudd considers far more qualified applicants than it can accommodate in its incoming class. Load up on science classes, don't neglect your English courses or extracurriculars, give the application everything you've got, and accept the fact that being perfectly qualified to attend this school is no guarantee of admission.

THE SCHOOL SAYS ". . ."

From the Admissions Office

"HMC is a wonderfully unusual combination of a liberal arts college and research institute. Our students love math and science, want to live and learn deeply in an intimate climate of cooperation and trust, thrive on innovation and discovery, and enjoy rigorous coursework in arts, humanities, and social sciences in addition to a technical curriculum. At least a year of research or our innovative clinic program is required (or guaranteed, if you prefer). The resources at HMC are astounding, and all are accessible to undergraduates: labs, shops, work areas, and most importantly, faculty. You'll find the professors and student body stimulating and supportive—they'll challenge you inside and outside the classroom, and share your love of learning and collaboration. They'll also share your love of fun and sense of humor (math jokes and all). In addition, we benefit from the unique consortium that is the Claremont Colleges.

"While we may not take ourselves too seriously, employers and graduate schools do. We enjoy a powerful reputation for preparing our graduates for all kinds of career paths. A wide range of companies are eager to hire our seniors, and HMC sends the highest proportion of graduates to PhD programs of any undergraduate college in the country."

SELECTIVITY	
Admissions Rating	**98**
# of applicants	2,957
% of applicants accepted	22
% of acceptees attending	29
# accepting a place on wait list	202
# admitted from wait list	46
# of early decision applicants	261
# accepted early decision	56

FRESHMAN PROFILE	
Range SAT Critical Reading	690–770
Range SAT Math	740–800
Range SAT Writing	690–770
Range ACT Composite	32–35
Minimum paper TOEFL	600
Minimum web-based TOEFL	100
% graduated top 10% of class	95
% graduated top 25% of class	100
% graduated top 50% of class	100

DEADLINES	
Early decision	
Deadline	11/15
Notification	12/15
Regular	
Deadline	1/2
Notification	4/1
Nonfall registration?	no

FINANCIAL FACTS	
Financial Aid Rating	**96**
Annual tuition	$42,140
Room and board	$13,858
Required fees	$270
Books and supplies	$800
% needy frosh rec. need-based scholarship or grant aid	99
% needy UG rec. need-based scholarship or grant aid	97
% needy frosh rec. non-need-based scholarship or grant aid	51
% needy UG rec. non-need-based scholarship or grant aid	48
% needy frosh rec. need-based self-help aid	71
% needy UG rec. need-based self-help aid	75
% frosh rec. any financial aid	76
% UG rec. any financial aid	79
% UG borrow to pay for school	56
Average cumulative indebtedness	$25,265
% frosh need fully met	100
% ugrads need fully met	100
Average % of frosh need met	100
Average % of ugrad need met	100

HAVERFORD COLLEGE

370 West Lancaster Avenue, Haverford, PA 19041 • Admissions: 610-896-1350 • Fax: 610-896-1338

CAMPUS LIFE

Quality of Life Rating	94
Fire Safety Rating	75
Green Rating	92
Type of school	private
Environment	town

STUDENTS

Total undergrad enrollment	1,198
% male/female	46/54
% from out of state	86
% from public high school	55
% frosh live on campus	100
% African American	7
% Asian	10
% Caucasian	64
% Hispanic	8
% international	4
# of countries represented	33

SURVEY SAYS . . .

No one cheats
School is well run
Low cost of living
Frats and sororities are unpopular or nonexistent

ACADEMICS

Academic Rating	97
% students returning for sophomore year	96
% students graduating within 4 years	91
% students graduating within 6 years	93
Calendar	semester
Student/faculty ratio	8:1
Profs interesting rating	92
Profs accessible rating	96
Most classes have	fewer than 10 students
Most lab/discussion sessions have	fewer than 10 students

MOST POPULAR MAJORS

biology/biological sciences; economics; English language and literature

STUDENTS SAY "..."

Academics

Founded in 1883, Haverford College in Pennsylvania is "small, but exceptionally vibrant and engaging," offering a "solid academic experience" under one of the country's oldest and most revered honor codes. Though founded by Quakers, the school is nonsectarian, but the community aspect of its founders remains, creating what one student calls "a challenging, interesting environment with the best people I know." The education program is one of the most notable, but there is a strong emphasis on writing and a "breadth of amazing programs" for everyone else. The real love affair is with Haverford's "awesome, invested" professors, who "lead a group of idealistic students to point—but never force—us into a better way of thinking." They want to put in the time to get to know you, and the small size of the school "allows for plenty of opportunities for collaborating with faculty and staff and building a relationship." "You are more than just a face in a classroom of many; you are a unique person that has something to offer," says a student. "My 'big intro lecture course' has forty-one students," says another. "My professor still knows me by name, and we have long conversations when we pass on Founder's Green." The school's learning environment stresses "engaging in hard and honest conversations with your peers," and "students have a lot of power" through their roles in the administration of the college. "I love the amount of independence and autonomy it gives to its students," says a student. Because of the kind of student this attracts, "we wind up with a really conscientious student body invested in the school." The resources available to students here are incredible, as well. You can get "credit for research" (there is plenty of research here in every department), and if you want to go off campus for research, "you can get funding for that as well."

Life

The culture of "trust, concern, and respect" created by the Honor Code carries over into the rest of this "awesome, at times idiosyncratic, place where community thrives and cliques are very loose if existent at all." "The honor code unifies everyone." "Being able to take an exam in your own room, sitting relaxed on your bed because your professor trusts you not to look at your books is one of the luxuries of being here," says a student. People study hard here, but they take a break over the weekend at a party or two "before cracking the books again." Athletics are also "really important" for much of the student body—most here are athletic, even if it's not at a varsity level—and some of the male sports teams" function like fraternities" (which do not exist at HC). Because it's a small place, "sometimes it feels like everyone knows your business," but everyone is so insanely nice that "the social scene is great" and the only thing you'll hear complaints about is the food. Students govern themselves and the happenings at the school through the "Plenaries" that happen twice a year, when the majority of the student body must be present. New York and Philadelphia are both easily accessible by train, and "Suburban Square (the local outdoor shopping center) is a great place to hang out, get coffee, or even go shopping."

Student Body

Everyone is "passionate," "people are always up for intellectual discussion," and "everyone works very hard." Students here were all motivated enough to get in and "want to succeed for themselves and not to appease others." Students describe other students as having "hearts of gold and giant brains that they put to use to change the world for the better." "It's a small school full of nice kids—not naive (well, sometimes naive), just genuinely compassionate and interested in other people, whether or not that's 'cool,'" says a student. Though all are bound by "intellectual passion and interests outside of academics," diversity otherwise on campus "lacks a little." Still, "the great thing about Haverford is that, although we have a variety of students from all different social circles, everyone is a touch awkward." This is a fact that the "nerdy and ridiculously friendly" students embrace. "I feel like I could potentially become friends with anyone on campus," says a student.

FINANCIAL AID: 610-896-1350 • E-MAIL: ADMISSION@HAVERFORD.EDU • WEBSITE: WWW.HAVERFORD.EDU

THE PRINCETON REVIEW SAYS

Admissions

Very important factors considered include: Application essay, academic GPA, recommendation(s), rigor of secondary school record, character/personal qualities, extracurricular activities. *Important factors considered include:* Class rank, standardized test scores, talent/ability, volunteer work, work experience. *Other factors considered include:* Alumni/ae relation, first generation, geographical residence, interview, level of applicant's interest, racial/ethnic status. SAT or ACT required; ACT with writing component recommended. TOEFL required of all international applicants. High school diploma or equivalent is not required.

Financial Aid

Students should submit: FAFSA, CSS/Financial Aid PROFILE, noncustodial PROFILE, business/farm supplement, CSS College Board noncustodial parents' statement is required—not the noncustodial supplement. Regular filing deadline is January 31. The Princeton Review suggests that all financial aid forms be submitted as soon as possible after January 1. *Need-based scholarships/grants offered:* Federal Pell, SEOG, state scholarships/grants, the school's own gift aid. *Loan aid offered:* Direct Subsidized Stafford, Direct Unsubsidized Stafford, Direct PLUS, Federal Perkins. Applicants will be notified of awards on or about April 1. Federal Work-Study Program available. Institutional employment available. Highest amount earned per year from on-campus jobs $2,300. Off-campus job opportunities are good.

The Inside Word

Haverford's applicant pool is an impressive and competitive lot (only about one-quarter of applicants get in). Intellectual curiosity is paramount, and applicants are expected to keep a demanding academic schedule in high school. Additionally, the college places a high value on ethics, as evidenced by its honor code. The admissions office seeks students who will reflect and promote Haverford's ideals.

THE SCHOOL SAYS ". . ."

From the Admissions Office

"Haverford strives to be a college in which integrity, honesty, and concern for others are dominant forces. The college does not have many formal rules; rather, it offers an opportunity for students to govern their affairs and conduct themselves with respect and concern for others. Each student is expected to adhere to the honor code as it is adopted each year by the Students' Association. Haverford's Quaker roots show most clearly in the relationship of faculty and students, in the emphasis on integrity, in the interaction of the individual and the community, and through the college's concern for the uses to which its students put their expanding knowledge. Haverford's 1,100 students represent a wide diversity of interests, backgrounds, and talents. They come from public, parochial, and independent schools across the United States, Puerto Rico, and thirty-eight foreign countries. Students of color are an important part of the Haverford community.

"Haverford College requires that all applicants submit the results of the SAT exam or the ACT with the optional writing test. Two SAT Subject Tests are required."

SELECTIVITY	
Admissions Rating	97
# of applicants	3,470
% of applicants accepted	25
% of acceptees attending	39
# accepting a place on wait list	811
# of early decision applicants	270
# accepted early decision	129

FRESHMAN PROFILE	
Range SAT Critical Reading	650–750
Range SAT Math	650–750
Range SAT Writing	660–760
Minimum paper TOEFL	600
% graduated top 10% of class	94
% graduated top 25% of class	99
% graduated top 50% of class	100

DEADLINES	
Early decision	
Deadline	11/15
Notification	12/15
Regular	
Deadline	1/15
Notification	4/15
Nonfall registration?	no

FINANCIAL FACTS	
Financial Aid Rating	97
Annual tuition	$43,310
Room and board	$13,290
Required fees	$392
Books and supplies	$1,194
% needy frosh rec. need-based scholarship or grant aid	98
% needy UG rec. need-based scholarship or grant aid	95
% needy frosh rec. need-based self-help aid	93
% needy UG rec. need-based self-help aid	91
% frosh rec. any financial aid	51
% UG rec. any financial aid	57
% UG borrow to pay for school	34
Average cumulative indebtedness	$16,238
% frosh need fully met	100
% ugrads need fully met	100
Average % of frosh need met	100
Average % of ugrad need met	100

Hendrix College

1600 Washington Avenue, Conway, AR 72032 • Admissions: 501-450-1362 • Fax: 501-450-3843

CAMPUS LIFE

Quality of Life Rating	**83**
Fire Safety Rating	**69**
Green Rating	**71**
Type of school	private
Affiliation	Methodist
Environment	town

STUDENTS

Total undergrad enrollment	1,413
% male/female	42/58
% from out of state	54
% from public high school	75
% frosh live on campus	99
% African American	3
% Asian	3
% Caucasian	75
% Hispanic	5
% international	4
# of countries represented	11

SURVEY SAYS . . .

Lab facilities are great
Athletic facilities are great
Frats and sororities are unpopular or nonexistent

ACADEMICS

Academic Rating	**89**
% students returning for sophomore year	80
% students graduating within 4 years	64
% students graduating within 6 years	73
Calendar	semester
Student/faculty ratio	12:1
Profs interesting rating	89
Profs accessible rating	89
Most classes have	10–19 students
Most lab/discussion sessions have	20–29 students

MOST POPULAR MAJORS

biochemistry/biophysics and molecular biology; biology/biological sciences; psychology

APPLICANTS ALSO LOOK AT AND OFTEN PREFER

Rhodes College, Trinity University, University of Arkansas—Fayetteville, Tulane University

AND SOMETIMES PREFER

Washington University in St. Louis, Southwestern University, Sewanee—The University of the South, Centenary College of Louisiana

STUDENTS SAY ". . ."

Academics

"Generous" financial aid and "a strong reputation for science" are two hallmarks of Hendrix College, "a progressive liberal arts school filled with Southern hospitality." Another perk is Hendrix's unique Odyssey Program, which allows students to "explore all sorts of things" in a hands-on way. You can learn printmaking, just for example, or maybe jet off to Prague to observe ballroom dancing. Class sizes are "small" here, and the academic atmosphere is "exceptionally rigorous." "There is a *ton* of writing." "A lot of time must be devoted to studying." "Unmotivated students do not last long." "It's sink or swim," contemplates a philosophy major. "If you swim, you're in for a really great experience." Professors are tough, but they're also "unwaveringly genial and helpful." Faculty members "love what they do and are very good at it." "They make the subjects really interesting," swears a religious studies major. They're "passionate about their fields and very accessible in and out of the classroom." Students do have some academic complaints. "The registration process could be better." The level of academic satisfaction is pretty high overall, though, and the fact that about one-third of all newly minted Hendrix grads proceed directly to graduate and professional school is evidence that all the hard work pays off.

Life

Social life here is extremely "campus-centric," and Hendrix is "small enough to evoke a sense of familiarity without feeling boring." "Hendrix is its own little world where you can't help but get caught up in something." "We have everything from sword club, Frisbee team, volunteer committee, to full orchestra," enthuses one student. "There is always something to do." "A lot of kids play intramural sports and stay pretty athletic." "People are very involved in the act of hanging out" as well, and "There are really interesting conversations going on all over campus." "During the week, Hendrix is quiet because everybody is studying or working on something school related." On the weekends, however, "Hendrix definitely has an active party scene." The revelry is "easy to avoid if you want to" but most students embrace it. "The lack of Greek life makes parties much more open and universal." "Super-fun parties" reportedly abound. "Almost every weekend has been predesignated for some sort of ongoing annual event." Off campus, some feel Conway, Arkansas, boasts little to do, but relatively urbane Little Rock is a short drive and "a common destination for Hendrix students wanting to break away from the routine." Students say the campus here is "absolutely gorgeous." However, some note that housing isn't uniformly objectionable, but some of the dorms "have issues." Students have few other gripes about their lives here, though. The food: always "digestible" and occasionally "fantastic."

Student Body

Some students tell us that Hendrix is "a cross between" a hippie school and a nerd school. Others call this place "more preppy than hippie." More often than not, students have left-leaning political views. "Hendrix is the liberal mecca of Arkansas." A fairly high percentage of students smoke—sometimes "heavily." Students describe themselves as "hardworking," "very ambitious," "pretty free-spirited," and "eclectic" "intellectual misfits" who tend to have "lots of interests and hidden abilities." "People with particularly odd or strange quirks fit right in" at Hendrix because "everybody is weird in one way or another." "While I can't say we are ethnically diverse," promises one student, "I can say that everyone is wholeheartedly welcome." In the cafeteria, "you'll see a jock, a gay drama kid, and a hippie all sitting together having a good time together." "People form groups quickly and really just stick to those groups," though.

FINANCIAL AID: 501-450-1368 • E-MAIL: ADM@HENDRIX.EDU • WEBSITE: WWW.HENDRIX.EDU

THE PRINCETON REVIEW SAYS

Admissions

Very important factors considered include: Application essay, academic GPA, rigor of secondary school record, standardized test scores. *Important factors considered include:* Class rank, recommendation(s), extracurricular activities, interview. *Other factors considered include:* Racial/ethnic status, talent/ability, volunteer work. SAT or ACT required; ACT with or without writing component accepted. TOEFL required of all international applicants. High school diploma is required and GED is accepted. *Academic units required:* 4 English, 3 mathematics, 2 science, 2 foreign language, 3 social studies.

Financial Aid

Students should submit: FAFSA, application for admission serves as primary merit-based scholarship application. The Princeton Review suggests that all financial aid forms be submitted as soon as possible after January 1. *Need-based scholarships/grants offered:* Federal Pell, SEOG, state scholarships/grants, private scholarships, the school's own gift aid. *Loan aid offered:* Direct Subsidized Stafford, Direct Unsubsidized Stafford, Direct PLUS, Federal Perkins, private alternative loans as selected by the student. Applicants will be notified of awards on a rolling basis beginning March 1. Federal Work-Study Program available. Institutional employment available. Highest amount earned per year from on-campus jobs $1,500. Off-campus job opportunities are good.

The Inside Word

Don't be fooled by the high acceptance rate; Hendrix is an academically demanding place. The applicant pool here is both very self-selecting and very well-qualified. This school remains a great destination for applicants who have stellar grades but relatively lower standardized test scores.

THE SCHOOL SAYS ". . ."

From the Admissions Office

"Hendrix students are participants, not spectators. They like to be involved, and they like to know that what they do makes a difference. Hendrix students are voting members of almost every campus committee, which gives them an important voice in college governance. They are very hands-on about their education as well. Internships, study abroad, research projects, service projects, expressive arts projects, and leadership development—these are all areas that Hendrix students find attractive. The Hendrix curriculum is demanding, but the environment is one of support and cooperation—not competition. Hendrix students form a close-knit, inclusive community. They build lifetime connections and close friendships, the kind of relationships that grow in a residential college where learning is a 24/7 kind of thing. It doesn't hurt that the campus is beautifully maintained and that Hendrix graduates are admitted to top graduate schools and recruited for good jobs around the world.

"Hendrix believes that you learn best when you can integrate what you learn in your courses with a variety of hands-on learning experiences. In over a century of educating bright, innovative students, Hendrix has perfected the art of seamlessly integrating a traditional liberal arts education with active learning experiences. It's a way of learning that reflects Hendrix's motto: "Unto the whole person." The College recently introduced Your Hendrix Odyssey: Engaging in Active Learning—the ultimate expression of its unique approach to learning. The Odyssey Program guarantees that every Hendrix student will participate in at least three hands-on learning opportunities chosen from six different categories. Students receive transcript credit for their Odyssey experiences. Since the program's inception in 2005, students and faculty have engaged in more than 5,000 Odyssey experiences and been awarded nearly $1.8 million in Odyssey grants for projects that merited special funding."

SELECTIVITY

Admissions Rating	91
# of applicants	1,528
% of applicants accepted	83
% of acceptees attending	30
# accepting a place on wait list	15
# admitted from wait list	5

FRESHMAN PROFILE

Range SAT Critical Reading	570–690
Range SAT Math	550–670
Range ACT Composite	27–32
Minimum paper TOEFL	550
Minimum web-based TOEFL	79
Average HS GPA	3.9
% graduated top 10% of class	59
% graduated top 25% of class	80
% graduated top 50% of class	96

DEADLINES

Early action	
Deadline	11/15
Notification	12/15
Regular	
Priority	2/1
Deadline	6/1
Nonfall registration?	yes

FINANCIAL FACTS

Financial Aid Rating	79
Annual tuition	$35,900
Room and board	$10,408
Required fees	$300
Books and supplies	$1,100
% needy frosh rec. need-based scholarship or grant aid	100
% needy UG rec. need-based scholarship or grant aid	100
% needy frosh rec. non-need-based scholarship or grant aid	38
% needy UG rec. non-need-based scholarship or grant aid	33
% needy frosh rec. need-based self-help aid	61
% needy UG rec. need-based self-help aid	65
% frosh rec. any financial aid	100
% UG rec. any financial aid	100
% UG borrow to pay for school	58
Average cumulative indebtedness	$24,388
% frosh need fully met	30
% ugrads need fully met	25
Average % of frosh need met	87
Average % of ugrad need met	83

HILLSDALE COLLEGE

33 EAST COLLEGE STREET, HILLSDALE, MI 49242 • ADMISSIONS: 517-607-2327 • FAX: 517-607-2223

CAMPUS LIFE

Quality of Life Rating	**87**
Fire Safety Rating	**87**
Green Rating	**60***
Type of school	private
Environment	village

STUDENTS

Total undergrad enrollment	1,326
% male/female	48/52
% from out of state	67
% from public high school	48
% frosh live on campus	99
# of fraternities	3
# of sororities	3
% international	2
# of countries represented	13

SURVEY SAYS . . .

No one cheats
Great computer facilities
Students are friendly
Students are very religious
Campus feels safe
Low cost of living
Students are happy
Musical organizations are popular
Student publications are popular
Political activism is popular
Very little drug use

ACADEMICS

Academic Rating	**92**
% students returning for sophomore year	88
% students graduating within 4 years	67
% students graduating within 6 years	72
Calendar	semester
Student/faculty ratio	10:1
Profs interesting rating	99
Profs accessible rating	99
Most classes have	fewer than 10 students
Most lab/discussion sessions have	20–29 students

MOST POPULAR MAJORS

biology/biological sciences; business administration and management; education

APPLICANTS ALSO LOOK AT AND OFTEN PREFER

Grove City College, University of Michigan—Ann Arbor, University of Notre Dame, Wheaton College (IL), University of Dallas, Northwestern University

AND SOMETIMES PREFER

Purdue University—West Lafayette, Albion College, Pepperdine University, Davidson College, The University of North Carolina at Chapel Hill

AND RARELY PREFER

Kenyon College, Pitzer College, Washington and Lee University, Knox College, University of California—Santa Barbara, Colorado College, Wittenberg University

STUDENTS SAY ". . ."

Academics

Hillsdale College, "a classical liberal arts school," instills "heritage and purpose" through a curriculum that "relies heavily on primary source documents and the classics," "Socratic-style lectures," and "a very strong reputation nationally [for taking] the idea of pursuing truth and liberty seriously." Marked by "academic rigor" and the "Western tradition," "learning isn't a chore here, it's a privilege," and professors are always "accessible and are dedicated to teaching, not researching or publishing." As one student explains, "I loved the idea of going to a school where a class on the U.S. Constitution was part of the core curriculum, where the student/professor ratio was ten to one…it was small enough I would never just be another number." There also is "not any grade inflation" at Hillsdale; thus, "Students spend a lot of time studying." While there has been a trend in recent years "against the economics/business/accounting department and the sciences in favor of less technical education," students find that because Hillsdale notably takes no government funding, it "remains one of two truly free institutions in the nation…uninfluenced by the whims of politicians and biased policymakers." Privately funded scholarships make it possible for "a large segment" of the student body to attend Hillsdale, and the average aid package is more than $12,000.

Life

Hillsdale College's "beautiful campus" offsets any disenchantment with the town of Hillsdale itself, which is "very poor, and the people that live here are referred to as 'townies' by the students." While Hillsdale is "a small campus in a small town," "there are always events to attend or things to do with friends," and "you can find people whose idea of fun is across a wide spectrum." Students spend their weeks "suffering under an endless mountain of homework and papers," but on the weekends, "house parties in which students get together to sing, play games, read together, play music, and have a generally good time together are the norm." As one student states, "There are some disparate groups on campus—the kids who have intellectual discussions in the union and the kids who go out and party on the weekends. There's no animosity between different groups though." "From Greek Life to Bible Study," students "actively engage in student organizations" like intramural sports and embrace "adventures from…attempting to climb the water tower…to driving thirty minutes to an abandoned tourist trap [for] a fake wooly mammoth tusk." Hillsdale also attracts students who want to "compete in Division II athletics" and appreciate "the self-sustaining religious sincerity" on campus. Through enforcement of an honor code, the administration has been according to students "a bit draconian" lately in "cracking down on any party culture."

Student Body

While "there are different types of students at Hillsdale," most would describe the typical student as being "friendly, conservative, [and] religious." Students "come from across the country and from a variety of backgrounds. Each student finds their own niche based on their interests." The admissions process at Hillsdale is blind, therefore making "racial diversity…irrelevant." Even with a "majority [of the student body] as Christian conservatives…Hillsdale is open to any faith or belief system and accepting of anyone who has justifications for why they believe what they believe." "Some strange, narrow-minded fundamentalists still get admitted to the school," but "they choose to remain in their own circles." For the rest, Hillsdale "doesn't have cliques. Greeks, athletes, thespians, homeschoolers, etc., are often one person who falls into multiple categories." Community is shaped at Hillsdale through "a genuine love of learning…a grounding in the ideas that shaped Western society," and students on the whole "are incredibly warm to one another and enjoy the experience of close bonding through intellectual and spiritual pursuit."

FINANCIAL AID: 517-607-2350 • E-MAIL: ADMISSIONS@HILLSDALE.EDU • WEBSITE: WWW.HILLSDALE.EDU

THE PRINCETON REVIEW SAYS

Admissions

Very important factors considered include: Academic GPA, rigor of secondary school record, standardized test scores, character/personal qualities, interview. *Important factors considered include:* Class rank, application essay, recommendation(s), extracurricular activities, level of applicant's interest, volunteer work, work experience. *Other factors considered include:* Alumni/ae relation, talent/ability. SAT or ACT required; ACT with writing component recommended. TOEFL required of all international applicants. High school diploma is required and GED is accepted. *Academic units recommended:* 4 English, 4 mathematics, 3 science (1 science lab), 2 foreign language, 1 social studies, 2 history.

Financial Aid

Students should submit: Institution's own financial aid form, noncustodial PROFILE, business/farm supplement. Regular filing deadline is March 15. The Princeton Review suggests that all financial aid forms be submitted as soon as possible after January 1. *Need-based scholarships/grants offered:* Private scholarships, the school's own gift aid. *Loan aid offered:* College/university loans from institutional funds. Applicants will be notified of awards on a rolling basis beginning February 15. Institutional employment available. Highest amount earned per year from on-campus jobs $1,300. Off-campus job opportunities are good.

Inside Word

Don't let Hillsdale's high acceptance rate fool you. The academic profile of incoming freshmen is tremendous and only serious, solid candidates should bother applying here. Even though you don't have to be politically conservative to get in, a passionate and well-reasoned essay singing the praises of free-market economics or defending traditional values certainly can't hurt you.

THE SCHOOL SAYS ". . ."

From the Admissions Office

"Personal attention is a hallmark at Hillsdale. Small classes are combined with teaching professors who make their students a priority. The academic environment at Hillsdale will actively engage you as a student. Extracurricular activities abound at Hillsdale with the more than 100 clubs and organizations that offer excellent leadership opportunities. From athletics and the fine arts, to Greek life and community volunteer programs, you will find it difficult not to be involved in our thriving campus community. In addition, numerous study abroad programs, a conservation research venture in South Africa, a professional sales internship program with national placements and the Washington-Hillsdale Internship Program (WHIP) are just a few of the unique off-campus opportunities available to you at Hillsdale.

"Our strength as a college is found in our mission and in our curriculum. The core curriculum at Hillsdale contains the essence of the classical liberal arts education. Through it you are introduced to the history, the philosophical and theological ideas, the works of literature, and the scientific discoveries that set Western Civilization apart. As explained in our mission statement, 'the college considers itself a trustee of modern man's intellectual and spiritual inheritance from the Judeo-Christian faith and Greco-Roman culture, a heritage finding its clearest expression in the American experiment of self-government under law.'

"We seek students who are ambitious, intellectually active and who are ready to become leaders worthy of this heritage in their personal as well as professional lives.

"Applicants can meet admissions requirements by submitting the results of the SAT, or the ACT (writing section optional). We will use the student's best composite/combined score in the evaluation process. The SAT Subject Tests in literature and U.S. history are also recommended."

SELECTIVITY	
Admissions Rating	92
# of applicants	1,401
% of applicants accepted	64
% of acceptees attending	42
# accepting a place on wait list	45
# admitted from wait list	5
# of early decision applicants	80
# accepted early decision	68

FRESHMAN PROFILE	
Range SAT Critical Reading	640–720
Range SAT Math	570–660
Range SAT Writing	610–690
Range ACT Composite	25–30
Minimum paper TOEFL	570
Average HS GPA	3.7
% graduated top 10% of class	47
% graduated top 25% of class	75
% graduated top 50% of class	98

DEADLINES	
Early decision	
Deadline	11/15
Notification	12/1
Early action	
Deadline	1/1
Notification	1/20
Regular	
Priority	1/1
Deadline	2/15
Nonfall registration?	yes

FINANCIAL FACTS	
Financial Aid Rating	81
Annual tuition	$21,390
Room and board	$8,640
Required fees	$540
Books and supplies	$850
% needy frosh rec. need-based scholarship or grant aid	57
% needy UG rec. need-based scholarship or grant aid	63
% needy frosh rec. non-need-based scholarship or grant aid	73
% needy UG rec. non-need-based scholarship or grant aid	82
% needy frosh rec. need-based self-help aid	71
% needy UG rec. need-based self-help aid	71
% frosh rec. any financial aid	83
% UG rec. any financial aid	86
% UG borrow to pay for school	61
Average cumulative indebtedness	$17,000
% frosh need fully met	35
% ugrads need fully met	39
Average % of frosh need met	62
Average % of ugrad need met	72

HIRAM COLLEGE

PO BOX 96, HIRAM, OH 44234 • ADMISSIONS: 330-569-5169 • FAX: 330-569-5944

CAMPUS LIFE

Quality of Life Rating	**77**
Fire Safety Rating	**60***
Green Rating	**60***
Type of school	private
Affiliation	Disciples of Christ
Environment	rural

STUDENTS

Total undergrad enrollment	1,313
% male/female	46/54
% from out of state	26
% from public high school	86
% frosh live on campus	94
# of fraternities	3
# of sororities	3
% African American	11
% Asian	1
% Caucasian	66
% Hispanic	2
% Native American	1
% international	5
# of countries represented	17

SURVEY SAYS . . .

Athletic facilities are great
Students are friendly
Different types of students interact
Students get along with local community
Campus feels safe
Low cost of living

ACADEMICS

Academic Rating	**82**
% students returning for sophomore year	80
% students graduating within 4 years	58
% students graduating within 6 years	62
Calendar	other
Student/faculty ratio	12:1
Profs interesting rating	92
Profs accessible rating	89
Most classes have	10–19 students
Most lab/discussion sessions have	10–19 students

MOST POPULAR MAJORS

biology; education

APPLICANTS ALSO LOOK AT AND OFTEN PREFER

Kenyon College, Denison University

AND SOMETIMES PREFER

The College of Wooster

STUDENTS SAY ". . ."

Academics

Students come to Hiram College seeking "a very community-based environment" that provides "not only a feeling of immediate comfort but also the appeal of being in close relationship with my professors," and few leave disappointed. Undergrads here "love how involved all of the professors are into guiding the students through not just classes and majors, but future plans and career paths" and praise the "big-school opportunities in a small-school environment." As one student points out, "Undergrads can work in research with professors here, which is an invaluable skill and great for resumes." Students tell us Hiram boasts "a great biology program that does well getting its students into veterinary and medical school," a "great education program," and strong offerings in environmental science. Throughout the school "small classes of no more than thirty students and the intimate nature of the learning [environment] keep us from feeling lost in a sea of students." A "unique semester system splits terms into a twelve-week main session followed by a three-week intensive class. It gives you fewer classes to have to take all at once, and the three-week is a great opportunity for electives or study abroad trips that I couldn't do for a whole semester for financial reasons or because I can't spare that time away from my major."

Life

Most students concede that Hiram is "in the middle of nowhere," but not all see this as an insurmountable negative. On the contrary, many appreciate how the location "allows for us to meet together and create our own fun, make new friends, and enjoy the simplest pleasures in life. Hiram is especially fun in the winter, as we get tons of snow and have so many hills you [can] sled off. Everyone goes out at night and sleds together." Others "find unique things to do—stargazing, making our own apple cider, going to local square dances…we learn lots of cool things." Furthermore, "The school is excellent for providing the students with gatherings multiple times a week. Each club on campus is required to sponsor a campus-wide event each semester, and the student-run club, KCPB, is devoted to organizing as many on-campus and off-campus events as possible. Examples include movie nights in town, Destressfests before midterms and finals," Bowler First Fridays, talent shows, and game shows. While "drinking is prohibited in rooms where the resident is not twenty-one, and [the rule] is enforced," those looking to party usually can find the opportunity. Undergrads report "for the most part everyone is respectful. The students usually regulate each other and take care of issues when someone gets out of control."

Student Body

Hiram is "a gentle mix of athletes, artists, and scientists, and…Everyone gets along and respects what the others are capable of doing." The school "gets the rap of having 'weird' kids," which most here wear as a badge of honor. As one puts it, "The jocks can be philosophy majors, and the band geeks can be *the* people to hang out with on a Friday night…This place doesn't respect stereotypes." Though proud "each individual brings something unique and interesting to the community here," students are also quick to point out their commonalities. "All students do have a dedication to serving others, in varying degrees and…attempt to include themselves in the community in a variety of different ways (social groups, athletics, community service or social activism groups, student government, etc.)."

FINANCIAL AID: 330-569-5107 • E-MAIL: ADMISSION@HIRAM.EDU • WEBSITE: WWW.HIRAM.EDU

THE PRINCETON REVIEW SAYS

Admissions

TOEFL required of all international applicants.

Financial Aid

Students should submit: FAFSA. The Princeton Review suggests that all financial aid forms be submitted as soon as possible after January 1. Admitted financial aid applicants will be notified of awards on a rolling basis beginning March 1. *Need-based scholarships/grants offered:* Federal Pell, SEOG, state scholarships/grants, private scholarships, the school's own gift aid. *Loan aid offered:* Federal Direct Subsidized Loans, Federal Direct Unsubsidized Loans, Federal Direct PLUS Loan for parents, Federal Perkins Loan, college loans from institutional funds. On-campus employment includes both federal work-study and regular campus employment.

The Inside Word

The typical Hiram admit performed solidly but not spectacularly in a college preparatory high school curriculum and earned above average but not stellar standardized test scores. Applicants seem to know whether they fit the Hiram profile, explaining the school's high admissions rate as few who don't stand a decent chance of getting in bother to apply. A thorough application review process allows hopefuls to make up for academic deficiencies with solid essays and/or strong recommendations. Admissions are rolling, a process that favors early applicants.

THE SCHOOL SAYS ". . ."

From the Admissions Office

"Hiram College offers distinctive programs that set us apart from other small, private liberal arts colleges. About half of Hiram's students study abroad at some point during their four years. In 2010, a group of students led by two faculty members traveled around the world to study climate change, stopping in nine different locations. Common study abroad destinations include France, China, Mexico, Guatemala, Costa Rica, the Galapagos Islands, and several African countries. Because Hiram students receive credits for the courses taught by Hiram faculty on these trips, studying abroad will not impede progress in their majors or delay graduation.

"Another unique aspect of a Hiram education is our academic calendar, known as the Hiram Plan. Our semesters are divided into twelve-week and three-week periods. Students usually enroll in three courses during each twelve-week, and one intensive course during the three-week. Many students spend the three-week on study abroad trips or taking unusual courses not typically offered during the twelve-week. Our small classes encourage interaction between students and their professors. Students can work with professors on original research projects and often participate in musical groups and intramural sports teams alongside faculty members.

"The Hiram College Tuition Guarantee ensures that the annual cost for tuition will not increase between the first year a student is enrolled and the student's senior year."

SELECTIVITY	
Admissions Rating	**74**
# of applicants	1,513
% of applicants accepted	75
% of acceptees attending	29
FRESHMAN PROFILE	
Range SAT Critical Reading	480–610
Range SAT Math	470–590
Range ACT Composite	20–26
Minimum paper TOEFL	550
Average HS GPA	3.3
% graduated top 10% of class	18
% graduated top 25% of class	42
% graduated top 50% of class	79
FINANCIAL FACTS	
Financial Aid Rating	**60***
Annual tuition	$26,435
Room and board	$9,460
Required fees	$950
Books and supplies	$700
% UG borrow to pay for school	78
Average cumulative indebtedness	$21,247

HOBART AND WILLIAM SMITH COLLEGES

629 SOUTH MAIN STREET, GENEVA, NY 14456 • ADMISSIONS: 315-781-3622 • FAX: 315-781-3914

CAMPUS LIFE

Quality of Life Rating	**67**
Fire Safety Rating	**86**
Green Rating	**87**
Type of school	private
Environment	village

STUDENTS

Total undergrad enrollment	2,138
% male/female	45/55
% from out of state	59
% from public high school	60
% frosh live on campus	99
# of fraternities	5
% African American	4
% Asian	2
% Caucasian	63
% Hispanic	4
% international	4
# of countries represented	18

SURVEY SAYS . . .

No one cheats
Great computer facilities
Career services are great
Dorms are like palaces
Students are happy
Everyone loves the Statesmen
Lots of beer drinking
Hard liquor is popular

ACADEMICS

Academic Rating	**84**
% students returning for sophomore year	89
% students graduating within 4 years	70
Calendar	semester
Student/faculty ratio	11:1
Profs interesting rating	86
Profs accessible rating	88
Most classes have	10–19 students

MOST POPULAR MAJORS

biology; economics; psychology

APPLICANTS ALSO LOOK AT AND OFTEN PREFER

Trinity College (CT), Colgate University, Connecticut College

AND SOMETIMES PREFER

St. Lawrence University, Skidmore College, Gettysburg College, Kenyon College, Dickinson College

AND RARELY PREFER

State University of New York at Geneseo, University of Rochester, University of Vermont, Ithaca College

STUDENTS SAY "..."

Academics

Hobart and William Smith Colleges together are "a college that is large enough to provide a wide variety of majors, yet small enough that your professors are able to know you by your name." Students enjoy "small class sizes, [the] feel of community," a "unique liberal arts curriculum, gorgeous campus…[and] one of the country's best study abroad programs." "Everyone knows everyone" at this very small school located right on central New York's Seneca Lake. "Hobart and William Smith College has the most incredible campus community I've ever seen," one student boasts, although beware of the "cold winters!" "There are countless opportunities for involvement [at HWS] such as internships, study abroad, athletics, clubs, and student activities." Because of the small size, the "absolutely fantastic faculty" "knows, remembers, and cares about all their students." "The best thing about the professors here is that they are always accessible outside of class, either with office hours or constant e-mail communication." However, some students caution that while many professors are "amazing," others are "awful and really should not be teaching." Students did feel the school "needs to work on really trying to make environmental sustainability an actual issue on campus." In summary, HWS is "a small, liberal arts college where the professors' first priority is their students," and there's a "*gorgeous lake* outside [your] window!"

Life

"Life at HWS is very comfortable," and "Students fit in by being friendly and spending a lot of money on partying." "People either love HWS or they hate it," one psychology student explains. "Life here is centered almost entirely around the social aspects of the college experience, which is fine, to a point, but it doesn't allow for deeper intellectual rigor." "People think about partying a lot, and on this campus it happens a lot" especially "at frats (there are no sororities) and at on-campus houses." On the weekends, there are "wild woods parties, house parties, frats, a quiet movie night, stargazing, jazz…you can find it all on a Saturday night." Another student laments, "There isn't much to do on weekends. The Campus Activities Board is good at the occasional big event…but there should be more events throughout the year," although the "school-sponsored events are actually enjoyable" when they do occur. Although many students complain about the campus food options, luckily "there are places to [get] good off-campus food and movies in walking distance." Make sure to bring your thickest winter coats, because HWS life slows down during the "endless winter" that "sometimes starts as early as October and can yield snow as late as mid-May."

Student Body

"The males here tend to be 'bros' for the most part, and the women are referred to as 'smithies,'" which means that "they carry expensive bags and wear big sunglasses, and are usually pretty skinny (or at least dress like they think they are)." "'Ho Bros,' the typical Hobart student, will join one of the six frats, own at least one pair of pants in the color 'Nantucket Red,' and probably drive a nicer car than most faculty." However, students caution that "there are always exceptions to the rule" "who don't fit these stereotypes and actually enjoy mocking them." Most students are "WASPs" or "preppy" and "white," and students feel that HWS needs to do more to create a more diverse student body from America and bring in more international students as well. Students in different populations "hardly mingle," and students "tend to stay in separate circles." "North Face and Uggs are far more rampant among the student body now than [the traditional HWS look of] Polo, Lily Pulitzer, and Lacoste."

FINANCIAL AID: 315-781-3315 • E-MAIL: ADMISSIONS@HWS.EDU • WEBSITE: WWW.HWS.EDU

THE PRINCETON REVIEW SAYS

Admissions

Very Important factors considered include: Rigor of secondary school record. *important factors considered include:* Class rank, application essay, academic GPA, recommendation(s), standardized test scores, character/personal qualities, extracurricular activities, volunteer work, work experience. *Other factors considered include:* Alumni/ae relation, first generation, geographical residence, interview, level of applicant's interest, racial/ethnic status, talent/ability. ACT with or without writing component accepted. TOEFL required of all international applicants. High school diploma is required and GED is accepted. *Academic units required:* 4 English, 3 mathematics, 3 science (2 science labs), 2 foreign language, 2 social studies, 2 history, 2 academic electives. *Academic units recommended:* 3 foreign language, 3 social studies, 4 academic electives.

Financial Aid

Students should submit: FAFSA, CSS/Financial Aid PROFILE, state aid form, noncustodial PROFILE, parents' and student's tax return. Regular filing deadline is March 1. The Princeton Review suggests that all financial aid forms be submitted as soon as possible after January 1. *Need-based scholarships/grants offered:* Federal Pell, SEOG, state scholarships/grants, private scholarships, the school's own gift aid. *Loan aid offered:* Direct Subsidized Stafford, Direct Unsubsidized Stafford, Direct PLUS, Federal Perkins. Applicants will be notified of awards on or about April 1. Federal Work-Study Program available. Institutional employment available. Highest amount earned per year from on-campus jobs $600. Off-campus job opportunities are good.

The Inside Word

Applicants to the academic side of Seneca Lake's scene shores should know that HWS likes to see a student who embraces a challenge. They recommend that hopefuls prepare for a rigorous college curriculum by taking at least two years of a foreign language and a couple of AP courses for good measure.

THE SCHOOL SAYS ". . ."

From the Admissions Office

"Hobart and William Smith Colleges seek students with a sense of adventure and a commitment to the life of the mind. Inside the classroom, students find the academic climate to be rigorous, with a faculty that is deeply involved in teaching and working with them. Outside, they discover a supportive community that helps to cultivate a balance and hopes to foster an integration among academics, extracurricular activities, and social life. Hobart and William Smith, as coordinate colleges, have an awareness of gender differences and equality and are committed to respect and a celebration of diversity.

"Hobart and William Smith Colleges are test optional. Students may submit the SAT, ACT, or no standardized tests at all."

SELECTIVITY

Admissions Rating	**85**
# of applicants	4,682
% of applicants accepted	62
% of acceptees attending	21
# accepting a place on wait list	390
# admitted from wait list	4
# of early decision applicants	251
# accepted early decision	213

FRESHMAN PROFILE

Range SAT Critical Reading	560–650
Range SAT Math	560–640
Range ACT Composite	25–28
Minimum paper TOEFL	550
Minimum web-based TOEFL	80
% graduated top 10% of class	43
% graduated top 25% of class	78
% graduated top 50% of class	97

DEADLINES

Early decision	
Deadline	11/15
Notification	12/15
Regular	
Deadline	2/1
Notification	4/1
Nonfall registration?	no

FINANCIAL FACTS

Financial Aid Rating	**92**
Annual tuition	$42,104
Room and board	$10,582
Required fees	$1,206
Books and supplies	$1,300
% needy frosh rec. need-based scholarship or grant aid	99
% needy UG rec. need-based scholarship or grant aid	97
% needy frosh rec. non-need-based scholarship or grant aid	14
% needy UG rec. non-need-based scholarship or grant aid	14
% needy frosh rec. need-based self-help aid	83
% needy UG rec. need-based self-help aid	83
% frosh rec. any financial aid	80
% UG rec. any financial aid	76
% UG borrow to pay for school	82
Average cumulative indebtedness	$29,932
% frosh need fully met	96
% ugrads need fully met	83
Average % of frosh need met	87
Average % of ugrad need met	78

Hofstra University

100 Hofstra University, Hempstead, NY 11549 • Admissions: 516-463-6700 • Fax: 516-463-5100

CAMPUS LIFE

Quality of Life Rating	67
Fire Safety Rating	94
Green Rating	84
Type of school	private
Environment	city

STUDENTS

Total undergrad enrollment	7,059
% male/female	47/53
% from out of state	43
% frosh live on campus	72
# of fraternities	15
# of sororities	10
% African American	9
% Asian	6
% Caucasian	65
% Hispanic	11
% international	2
# of countries represented	67

SURVEY SAYS . . .

Great computer facilities
Great library
Frats and sororities dominate social scene
College radio is popular
Student publications are popular
Lots of beer drinking
Hard liquor is popular

ACADEMICS

Academic Rating	77
% students returning for sophomore year	80
% students graduating within 4 years	43
% students graduating within 6 years	58
Calendar	semester
Student/faculty ratio	14:1
Profs interesting rating	76
Profs accessible rating	75
Most classes have	10–19 students
Most lab/discussion sessions have	10–19 students

MOST POPULAR MAJORS

accounting; biology; psychology

APPLICANTS ALSO LOOK AT AND OFTEN PREFER

New York University, Syracuse University, Boston University

AND SOMETIMES PREFER

State University of New York—Stony Brook University, Pennsylvania State University—University Park, Fordham University, Drexel University, Northeastern University

AND RARELY PREFER

Rutgers, The State University of New Jersey—New Brunswick, St. John's University—Queens, University of Massachusetts Amherst, Quinnipiac University

STUDENTS SAY ". . ."

Academics

Hofstra University, "the most prestigious private university on Long Island," according to students, is "large enough to feel part of something big but small enough to feel a sense of community." Students say the size is just right, providing "admirable" class sizes that "are perfect for nurturing relationships with professors." Hofstra undergraduates are especially bullish on the undergraduate business program and the communications and broadcast journalism programs. The latter are "anchored by [an]…award-winning radio station" and numerous other "opportunities to get hands-on experience in various aspects of broadcast [journalism]." All programs benefit from the school's proximity to New York City, which affords not only "top-notch…guest speakers and lecturers to the university" but also abundant "career-making connections to [your chosen] profession through internships and opportunities." Students also love Hofstra's music and theater programs, but most students look toward more reliably remunerative professions. As one student puts it, "This school is about successfully preparing its students for their professional careers as effectively and efficiently as possible." The rewards here are especially great for go-getters. One student explains, "Hofstra provides all of the opportunities that a college student can ask for," but "Many students don't take advantage of them, so it allows relatively easy access to some amazing programs if you have the drive."

Life

Hofstra "is generally considered a party school," students concede, "but it is easy to avoid that if you want to." Many students "go to the bars and pubs that are around college campus" to blow off steam, or "if not, they make parties at their dorms when their RA is away and invite people over to play beer pong." Greek organizations on campus are "really enjoyable," hosting "fundraisers and activities," not to mention the occasional house party. For those seeking alternatives, "There are several malls and movie theaters nearby, the train station is ten minutes away, and it's only about a half hour ride into NYC, and Nassau Coliseum is also right next door so there are always concerts and events. Jones Beach is also very close and popular when [the weather] is nice." The Student Center Theater shows "popular films that are out of the theaters but not yet released on DVD almost every weekend." College sporting events are less popular—"Our teams aren't great," one student concedes—and the school recently dropped its football program to save money. Hometown Hempstead "is a bit of a bust." Not only is there "nothing to do" in town, but students perceive it as "an area of depression and crime…The campus itself is generally quite safe, but that safety does not extend very far past the limits of the campus." Fortunately, safer destinations are nearby and easily accessible by car or public transportation.

Student Body

You will certainly find examples of the Long Island stereotype here, kids who are into "buying expensive brands that display their logo on their clothing," sport "fake tans, fake hair, and fake personalities," and are "primarily concerned with drinking, getting laid, and finishing their business degrees." But while these may be the most conspicuous students on campus at Hofstra, they hardly make up the entire student body. Opinions differ on whether they are "only a slight majority" or an even smaller percentage, but most here agree that there's plenty of room for everyone. One student explains that "As Hofstra positions itself as a national institution, geographic diversity as well as nontraditional student populations have grown." Another adds, "There is a sizable group of atypical students who hang out with the other atypical students like themselves." Their ranks include "the free-spirited hippies, the metal heads, the guys who just like sports but don't play, and the people who are actually here to study. They fit in because this minority (albeit it's a big one) all acts similarly."

FINANCIAL AID: 516-463-8000 • E-MAIL: ADMISSION@HOFSTRA.EDU • WEBSITE: WWW.HOFSTRA.EDU

THE PRINCETON REVIEW SAYS

Admissions

Very important factors considered include: Class rank, application essay, academic GPA, recommendation(s), rigor of secondary school record, standardized test scores. *Important factors considered include:* Character/personal qualities, extracurricular activities, interview, talent/ability. *Other factors considered include:* Alumni/ae relation, geographical residence, level of applicant's interest, racial/ethnic status, volunteer work, work experience. ACT with writing component required. TOEFL required of all international applicants. High school diploma is required and GED is accepted. *Academic units required:* 4 English, 3 mathematics, 3 science (1 science lab), 2 foreign language, 3 social studies. *Academic units recommended:* 4 mathematics, 4 science (2 science labs), 3 foreign language, 4 social studies.

Financial Aid

Students should submit: FAFSA, state aid form. The Princeton Review suggests that all financial aid forms be submitted as soon as possible after January 1. *Need-based scholarships/grants offered:* Federal Pell, SEOG, state scholarships/grants, private scholarships, the school's own gift aid, ACG & SMART. *Loan aid offered:* Direct Subsidized Stafford, Direct Unsubsidized Stafford, Direct PLUS, Federal Perkins, college/university loans from institutional funds. Applicants will be notified of awards on a rolling basis beginning March 1. Federal Work-Study Program available. Institutional employment available. Highest amount earned per year from on-campus jobs $18,328. Off-campus job opportunities are excellent.

The Inside Word

Hofstra is aggressive about filling its incoming class as quickly as possible, offering two rounds of early action and rolling admissions. This is a process that favors those who apply early, so you'd do well to get your application in here as soon as possible.

THE SCHOOL SAYS ". . ."

From the Admissions Office

"Hofstra is a university on the rise. When you step onto campus you feel the energy and sense the momentum of a university building a global reputation as a center for academic excellence. A new school of engineering and applied science has been established following the new medical school. Political, technology, communications, and business leaders are frequent guests at Hofstra and for the second time the university will serve as the host for a Presidential Debate bringing hundreds of global leaders to the campus.

"At Hofstra, you'll find an outstanding faculty dedicated to teaching, and small classes, averaging just fewer than twenty students. Outside the classroom, you'll find a vibrant campus community, extensive internship and study abroad opportunities, rich cultural experiences in nearby New York City, and a multitude of extracurricular activities.

"The Hofstra campus features new teaching and recreational facilities. At Hofstra, you will share your classrooms, residence halls, and an alumni network with students, faculty, and staff from nearly every state and more than seventy countries."

SELECTIVITY	
Admissions Rating	**86**
# of applicants	21,376
% of applicants accepted	59
% of acceptees attending	13
# accepting a place on wait list	264
# admitted from wait list	55

FRESHMAN PROFILE	
Range SAT Critical Reading	530–620
Range SAT Math	550–630
Range ACT Composite	23–27
Minimum paper TOEFL	550
Minimum web-based TOEFL	80
Average HS GPA	3.5
% graduated top 10% of class	25
% graduated top 25% of class	56
% graduated top 50% of class	87

DEADLINES	
Early action	
Deadline	11/15
Notification	12/15
Nonfall registration?	yes

FINANCIAL FACTS	
Financial Aid Rating	**68**
Annual tuition	$32,500
Room and board	$11,940
Required fees	$1,050
Books and supplies	$1,000
% needy frosh rec. need-based scholarship or grant aid	94
% needy UG rec. need-based scholarship or grant aid	88
% needy frosh rec. non-need-based scholarship or grant aid	9
% needy UG rec. non-need-based scholarship or grant aid	8
% needy frosh rec. need-based self-help aid	83
% needy UG rec. need-based self-help aid	80
% frosh rec. any financial aid	95
% UG rec. any financial aid	87
% UG borrow to pay for school	67
% frosh need fully met	17
% ugrads need fully met	17
Average % of frosh need met	64
Average % of ugrad need met	57

HOLLINS UNIVERSITY

PO BOX 9707, ROANOKE, VA 24020-1707 • ADMISSIONS: 540-362-6401 • FAX: 540-362-6218

CAMPUS LIFE

Quality of Life Rating	**81**
Fire Safety Rating	**76**
Green Rating	**82**
Type of school	private
Environment	city

STUDENTS

Total undergrad enrollment	716
% male/female	0/100
% from out of state	58
% from public high school	75
% frosh live on campus	92
% African American	11
% Asian	2
% Caucasian	72
% Hispanic	5
% international	5
# of countries represented	18

SURVEY SAYS . . .

No one cheats
Great library
Low cost of living
Frats and sororities are unpopular or nonexistent
Student government is popular

ACADEMICS

Academic Rating	**85**
% students returning for sophomore year	67
% students graduating within 4 years	58
Calendar	4-1-4
Student/faculty ratio	10:1
Profs interesting rating	91
Profs accessible rating	84
Most classes have	10–19 students
Most lab/discussion sessions have	10–19 students

MOST POPULAR MAJORS

business/commerce; English language and literature; psychology

STUDENTS SAY "..."

Academics

"Tiny," all-female Hollins University "drips in" "unique traditions" and offers "an intimate atmosphere" that "feels like a community or family, not an institution." Students assure us that "a Hollins education is inspiring and nothing short of life-changing." There are fabulous opportunities to study abroad. Double-majors are mundane. Among the thirty or so majors available here, the "strong English program" is especially notable. The creative writing program in particular is "one of the nation's best." Classes are small and extremely "interactive." "The discussions in class will start slowly," observes an English major, "but they'll suddenly be out of the teacher's control the next minute." "Don't go if you didn't do the readings," adds a physics major. "Professors pour so much time into their students," relates a studio art major. They "want to hear from their students" and "are always more than willing to help." The staff in the financial aid office, on the other hand, can sometimes be "unwilling to help."

Life

Students at Hollins "adore the school." Life on this "gorgeous" and "peaceful" campus is "a unique amalgam of individualistic zaniness and required academic hustle and bustle." "People are very concerned about homework." "Sleepless nights during weekdays" aren't uncommon. At the same time, the student community is "hugely strong." "Hollins really embodies the concept of sisterhood." "Everyone comes together for" a throng of "crazy and not-so-crazy traditions." "It isn't uncommon to put on odd costumes or break into songs or see seniors in decorated robes. It's hard to explain these things other than to say, 'it's a Hollins thing.'" In the fall, the school president cancels morning classes and declares Tinker Day. "Everyone dresses up in wacky costumes, everything from a wetsuit to a prom dress, and hikes Tinker Mountain." Ring Night ("the best weekend of your life") and faculty Christmas caroling are a couple other noteworthy traditions. Hollins is also home to "amazing extracurriculars" including "a great horseback riding program." "There is a high level of student involvement" across the board, and "there is always something happening on campus." Lectures, concerts, and recitals are abundant. The theater program "is excellent, and the shows are always worth going to." "There are several subcultures people can fit into"—everything from intercollegiate athletics to a surprisingly strong anime contingent. "If you want to attend frat parties and keggers, it is very easy with the number of coed universities nearby," but "this isn't the typical 'party school.'" "Life at Hollins is walking down the dorm hall with all the dorm doors open and girls running down the hall to each other's rooms to talk and have fun or do homework together," explains one student. "The friends we make here are still going to be our sisters long after we have gone out into the world to accomplish what our experience at Hollins gave us the courage to do." "The dorms are hospitable but old." "Every now and then, the food is great and wonderful" but, for the gourmand, meals here general have some room for improvement.

Student Body

The women of Hollins describe themselves as "empowered, enthusiastic," "worldly, aware," "strong, and confident." "There are all sorts at Hollins: horse girls, anime girls, art majors, writers, filmmakers, bio students, dancers, feminists, scientists." The gay and transgender population is "large." "The glory of Hollins is that there is seldom a stereotype," agrees another student. "There is no mold that any student must fit, regardless of what activities and groups you are involved in. It is a place to be yourself." "Odd ducks" proliferate. "You name it; you see it (minus males, that is)." "Everyone is so different, and everyone is so amazingly tolerant of everyone's differences." However, some students can be "cliquey and exclusive." "Most people are involved in several clubs and organizations so it's easy to have a very diverse group of friends," describes one student.

FINANCIAL AID: 540-362-6332 • E-MAIL: HUADM@HOLLINS.EDU • WEBSITE: WWW.HOLLINS.EDU

THE PRINCETON REVIEW SAYS

Admissions

Very important factors considered include: Academic GPA, standardized test scores. *Important factors considered include:* Application essay, recommendation(s), talent/ability. *Other factors considered include:* Class rank, rigor of secondary school record, alumni/ae relation, character/personal qualities, extracurricular activities, first generation, interview, level of applicant's interest, volunteer work, work experience. SAT or ACT required; ACT with or without writing component accepted. TOEFL required of all international applicants. High school diploma is required and GED is accepted. *Academic units required:* 4 English, 3 mathematics, 3 science, 3 foreign language, 3 social studies.

Financial Aid

Students should submit: FAFSA, state aid form. The Princeton Review suggests that all financial aid forms be submitted as soon as possible after January 1. *Need-based scholarships/grants offered:* Federal Pell, SEOG, state scholarships/grants, private scholarships, the school's own gift aid. *Loan aid offered:* Direct Subsidized Stafford, Direct Unsubsidized Stafford, Direct PLUS, Federal Perkins, college/university loans from institutional funds, PLATO, CitiAssist, SallieMae, Nelnet, Campus Door. Applicants will be notified of awards on a rolling basis beginning March 1. Federal Work-Study Program available. Institutional employment available. Highest amount earned per year from on-campus jobs $3,067. Off-campus job opportunities are good.

The Inside Word

While the overall stats at Hollins are solid, the admit rate is high, and gaining admission won't be terrifically difficult if you have decent test scores and above-average grades. Keep in mind, though, that the applicants here are a highly self-selecting group and the admissions staff is able to take a long look at everyone who applies. Consequently, your best bet is to demonstrate a sincere desire to be a part of the unique milieu on this campus.

THE SCHOOL SAYS "..."

From the Admissions Office

"Hollins University's slogan, 'Women who are going places start at Hollins,' endures because it captures what this independent liberal arts institution means to its students. Hollins has been a motivating force for women to go places creatively, intellectually, and geographically since it was founded over 165 years ago. As Hollins graduate and Pulitzer Prize–winner Annie Dillard said, Hollins is a place 'where friendships thrive, minds catch fire, careers begin, and hearts open to a world of possibility.'

"Hollins offers majors in twenty-seven fields. While perhaps best known for its creative writing discipline, the university features strong programs in the visual and performing arts (especially dance) and the social and physical sciences. Hollins also has an innovative general education program called Education Through Skills and Perspectives (ESP). In ESP, students acquire knowledge across the curriculum. One of the most sought-after programs at Hollins is the Batten Leadership Institute, a comprehensive curricular program designed to maximize each student's leadership style and potential and teach her skills she will use both now and in the future. It is the only program of its kind in the nation.

"Hollins was among the first colleges in the nation to offer an international study abroad program. Today, almost half of Hollins' students—many times the national average—study abroad. Internship opportunities are another of Hollins' distinctions. Thanks to an active, dedicated network of alumnae and friends of the university, sixty-five percent of Hollins seniors put their education to work with a diverse group of organizations.

"Hollins' slogan underscores the most important question each student is asked from the moment she arrives until the day she leaves, and it is asked by her professors, her peers, and especially by herself: 'Where do you want to go?'"

SELECTIVITY

Admissions Rating	**76**
# of applicants	813
% of applicants accepted	83
% of acceptees attending	27
# of early decision applicants	47
# accepted early decision	43

FRESHMAN PROFILE

Range SAT Critical Reading	460–620
Range SAT Math	450–580
Range SAT Writing	450–610
Range ACT Composite	21–28
Minimum paper TOEFL	550
Minimum web-based TOEFL	79
Average HS GPA	3.5
% graduated top 10% of class	25
% graduated top 25% of class	59
% graduated top 50% of class	87

DEADLINES

Early decision	
Deadline	12/1
Notification	12/15
Regular	
Priority	2/1
Nonfall registration?	yes

FINANCIAL FACTS

Financial Aid Rating	**81**
Annual tuition	$31,490
Room and board	$11,220
Required fees	$585
% needy frosh rec. need-based scholarship or grant aid	100
% needy UG rec. need-based scholarship or grant aid	100
% needy frosh rec. non-need-based scholarship or grant aid	100
% needy UG rec. non-need-based scholarship or grant aid	97
% needy frosh rec. need-based self-help aid	77
% needy UG rec. need-based self-help aid	84
% frosh rec. any financial aid	100
% UG rec. any financial aid	98
% UG borrow to pay for school	71
Average cumulative indebtedness	$30,383
% frosh need fully met	21
% ugrads need fully met	19
Average % of frosh need met	76
Average % of ugrad need met	81

HOWARD UNIVERSITY

2400 Sixth Street Northwest, Washington, D.C. 20059 • Admissions: 202-806-2700 • Fax: 202-806-4467

CAMPUS LIFE

Quality of Life Rating	**65**
Fire Safety Rating	**94**
Green Rating	**60***
Type of school	private
Environment	metropolis

STUDENTS

Total undergrad enrollment	7,086
% male/female	34/66
% from out of state	98
% from public high school	80
% frosh live on campus	92
# of fraternities	10
# of sororities	8
% African American	49
% Hispanic	1
% international	4
# of countries represented	86

SURVEY SAYS . . .

Students are happy
Frats and sororities dominate social scene
Musical organizations are popular
College radio is popular
Student publications are popular
Student government is popular
Political activism is popular

ACADEMICS

Academic Rating	**70**
% students returning for sophomore year	85
% students graduating within 4 years	46
% students graduating within 6 years	65
Calendar	semester
Student/faculty ratio	8:1
Profs interesting rating	65
Profs accessible rating	65
Most classes have	fewer than 10 students
Most lab/discussion sessions have	10–19 students

MOST POPULAR MAJORS

biology/biological sciences; journalism; radio and television

APPLICANTS ALSO LOOK AT AND OFTEN PREFER

Hampton University, Spelman College

AND SOMETIMES PREFER

Florida A&M University, University of Maryland, College Park, The George Washington University

AND RARELY PREFER

Morgan State University

STUDENTS SAY ". . ."

Academics

Noted for "outstanding achievements as an institution as well as the accomplishments of a great majority of its alumni," Howard University takes great pride in preparing students "to compete on a local and global level." With "inspiring faculty and a perspective that cannot be found anywhere else," the school "breeds pride and excellence" and is a "formidable force in producing African American intellectuals." "Howard University is more than a place to get an education, it is a once-in-a-lifetime experience that not only strengthens your mind, but also your spirit and pride in who you are as a person and who you have the potential to become," says an appreciative student. Other undergrads add, "I wanted the experience of attending a Historically Black College," with a rich tradition and history. "Once you become a Bison" you experience "the sense of being a part of such a tremendous legacy." Students here believe that a Howard education is wonderful preparation for life in today's competitive employment environment. "Howard pushes you and teaches patience." Professors are admired for being able to "bridge the gap between the real world and the textbook;" "It is up to you to apply information outside of class through internships and supplementary experiences." They are "supportive and helpful," have "a genuine interest in their subject," and they make sure "course material is appropriate." Discussions are encouraged, which "helps to solidify understanding…I am able to have a voice in the class and share my opinion." Networking opportunities are abundant, and job placement upon graduation is high.

Life

A common theme heard throughout Howard University is how "students are very tight-knit and supportive of one another." "Dormitories are lively," and "life is fast-paced." School events are normally a "major part of the social calendar," and there is great encouragement for students "to be involved in campus organizations and student government." While there are many Greeks on campus, "the main focus of our Greek Life is community service. Any social event or gathering that is hosted by the Greeks normally has most of all of the proceeds going to a charity or community service project." There are also "student-run organizations that work in the community," providing "opportunities to be a part of something bigger than you." Students obviously love taking advantage of all of the opportunities the Washington, D.C., area provides. The Metro is a popular form of transportation, with the station "very easily accessible from the main Howard University campus." Many locations are Metro-accessible, but you must be cognizant of operating hours.

Student Body

At Howard University, there is at least one commonality everyone can agree on: Students are busy. "At any given time a student at Howard can be found taking a full course load, working, and interning." Extracurricular activities and community service are also on the plate of many Howard undergraduates. Students are often described as "friendly, outgoing, stylish, and fashionable." The campus exudes "a culture of achievement and encouragement;" "most students are very goal-oriented and driven." "A Howardite is very career-oriented and knows what he or she wants to do after graduation." Students here are also "very socially conscious." Geographic diversity is prevalent, and "Howard students are educated to think on a global scale." "Students are very accepting of each other and their backgrounds;" "We are an ever-changing, comprehensive, innovative, and supportive community." Meaningful conversation is prevalent, with many "discussions surrounding social and political issues." "Howard represents the best of the educated and progressive African American community."

FINANCIAL AID: 202-806-2840 • E-MAIL: ADMISSION@HOWARD.EDU • WEBSITE: WWW.HOWARD.EDU

THE PRINCETON REVIEW SAYS

Admissions

Very important factors considered include: Class rank, rigor of secondary school record, standardized test scores. *Important factors considered include:* Recommendation(s), character/personal qualities. *Other factors considered include:* Application essay, alumni/ae relation, extracurricular activities, talent/ability, volunteer work, work experience. SAT or ACT required; ACT with writing component required. TOEFL required of all international applicants. High school diploma is required and GED is accepted. *Academic units required:* 4 English, 2 mathematics, 2 science, 2 foreign language, 2 social studies, 2 history. *Academic units recommended:* 4 English, 3 mathematics, 4 science (2 science labs), 2 foreign language, 2 social studies, 2 history, 4 any other academic courses counted toward graduation.

Financial Aid

Students should submit: FAFSA. Regular filing deadline is August 15. The Princeton Review suggests that all financial aid forms be submitted as soon as possible after January 1. *Need-based scholarships/grants offered:* Federal Pell, SEOG, state scholarships/grants, private scholarships, the school's own gift aid, Federal Nursing Scholarships. *Loan aid offered:* Direct Subsidized Stafford, Direct Unsubsidized Stafford, Direct PLUS, Federal Perkins, Federal Nursing. Applicants will be notified of awards on a rolling basis beginning April 1. Federal Work-Study Program available. Institutional employment available. Highest amount earned per year from on-campus jobs $3,500. Off-campus job opportunities are excellent.

The Inside Word

Howard attracts quite a significant number of applicants, and the school maintains a high rate of graduation for those who do gain admittance. While standardized testing is certainly a primary part of evaluating those looking to enroll, this does not preclude other students from seeking entrance; proven ability from high school and the capacity to handle higher learning in a diligent, responsible manner is also highly valued.

THE SCHOOL SAYS ". . ."

From the Admissions Office

"Since its founding, Howard has stood among the few institutions of higher learning where blacks and other minorities have participated freely in a truly comprehensive university experience. Thus, Howard has assumed a special responsibility in preparing its students to exercise leadership wherever their interests and commitments take them. Howard has issued approximately 111,233 degrees, diplomas, and certificates to men and women in the professions, the arts and sciences, and the humanities. The university has produced and continues to produce a high percentage of the nation's African American professionals in the fields of medicine, dentistry, pharmacy, engineering, nursing, architecture, religion, law, music, social work, education, and business. There are more than 10,036 students from across the nation and approximately eighty-five countries and territories attending the university. Their varied customs, cultures, ideas, and interests contribute to Howard's international character and vitality. More than 1,598 faculty members represent the largest concentration of black scholars in any single institution of higher education.

"All applicants who have never been to college are required to submit scores from either the SAT or the ACT (with the writing component)."

SELECTIVITY	
Admissions Rating	**89**
# of applicants	9,750
% of applicants accepted	49
% of acceptees attending	31

FRESHMAN PROFILE	
Range SAT Critical Reading	470–670
Range SAT Math	460–680
Range SAT Writing	430–670
Range ACT Composite	19–29
Minimum paper TOEFL	550
Average HS GPA	3.2
% graduated top 10% of class	26
% graduated top 25% of class	55
% graduated top 50% of class	84

DEADLINES	
Early decision	
Deadline	11/1
Notification	12/24
Early action	
Deadline	11/1
Notification	12/24
Regular	
Priority	11/1
Deadline	2/15
Nonfall registration?	yes

FINANCIAL FACTS	
Financial Aid Rating	**65**
Annual tuition	$19,150
Room and board	$15,341
Required fees	$1,021
Books and supplies	$3,740
% needy frosh rec. need-based scholarship or grant aid	41
% needy UG rec. need-based scholarship or grant aid	54
% needy frosh rec. non-need-based scholarship or grant aid	52
% needy UG rec. non-need-based scholarship or grant aid	22
% needy frosh rec. need-based self-help aid	31
% needy UG rec. need-based self-help aid	30
% frosh rec. any financial aid	96
% UG rec. any financial aid	96
% UG borrow to pay for school	80
Average cumulative indebtedness	$16,473
% frosh need fully met	33
% ugrads need fully met	22
Average % of frosh need met	71
Average % of ugrad need met	36

ILLINOIS INSTITUTE OF TECHNOLOGY

10 WEST THIRTY-THIRD STREET, CHICAGO, IL 60616 • ADMISSIONS: 312-567-3025 • FAX: 312-567-6939

CAMPUS LIFE

Quality of Life Rating	71
Fire Safety Rating	71
Green Rating	92
Type of school	private
Environment	metropolis

STUDENTS

Total undergrad enrollment	2,639
% male/female	69/31
% from out of state	26
% from public high school	79
% frosh live on campus	77
# of fraternities	7
# of sororities	3
% African American	7
% Asian	11
% Caucasian	42
% Hispanic	11
% international	21
# of countries represented	101

SURVEY SAYS . . .

Class discussions are rare
Great computer facilities
Diverse student types on campus
Students love Chicago, IL
Great off-campus food
Very little drug use

ACADEMICS

Academic Rating	76
% students returning for sophomore year	95
% students graduating within 4 years	34
% students graduating within 6 years	64
Calendar	semester
Student/faculty ratio	11:1
Profs interesting rating	69
Profs accessible rating	68
Most classes have	10–19 students
Most lab/discussion sessions have	20–29 students

MOST POPULAR MAJORS

architecture; computer science; electrical engineering

APPLICANTS ALSO LOOK AT AND OFTEN PREFER

Case Western Reserve University, University of Illinois at Urbana-Champaign, University of Michigan—Ann Arbor, Washington University in St. Louis, Northwestern University

AND SOMETIMES PREFER

Purdue University—West Lafayette, University of Minnesota—Twin Cities

AND RARELY PREFER

Loyola University of Chicago, Milwaukee School of Engineering

STUDENTS SAY ". . ."

Academics

Known for its "rigorous academics," "small student-to-teacher ratio," plentiful "research opportunities," and "great financial aid," Illinois Institute of Technology draws students interested in engineering, business, architecture, and the sciences. The curriculum here is focused on "developing technically oriented, yet well-rounded professionals." In addition to its "reputation as a premier engineering school," IIT boasts "one of the best architecture schools in the nation." Designed by Mies Van der Rohe, "The campus has an amazing architectural heritage and continues to foster the growth of cutting-edge, contemporary practice." "Studying architecture in Chicago [is]...a really big incentive," and the program prepares students for the "'real world,' giving not only an aesthetic education in design, but also a technical understanding of structure." The computer engineering program at IIT is also "very good," and "Finding research opportunities is not difficult (even as a freshman)," says one. For the most part, professors are lauded as "very accessible, easy to talk to," and "very knowledgeable"; "My teachers all know me by name, [and] I have the confidence to ask questions in class," one student tells us. "We have recently had many changes in our administration, including a new president, new provost, new chairman of the board of trustees, and three new deans to various colleges/departments. Overall, these changes have been incredibly positive. We have a female Dean of Engineering, and our new president cares passionately about students."

Life

"Life" at IIT "is busy, [and] homework comes first." As one student points out, "The college experience, no matter where you are, is what *you* make of it yourself." Says another, "You can spend all your time not doing anything and being unhappy with life, but with IIT there are so many opportunities to get involved... from programming events such as homecoming, to fundraising for Habitat for Humanity trips to Haiti and even relief efforts in the United States." "There is usually something to do, whether a planned event or random excursion to the city." Students take advantage of nearby Chicago, where they enjoy "the parks, the pier, Michigan Ave., ethnic restaurants, orchestra hall, etc." A serious-minded group of burgeoning engineers, "Occasionally we drink...and go out for parties, but not [so] much." For a more relaxed night of socializing, students congregate at the "BOG, a place inside the school where there are shows and different activities like bowling." In addition, "The Student Activities Center always has discounted movie tickets, and every weekend they try to have some planned event, including group tickets to musicals, plays, and shows." For sports fans, "There are intramural tournaments that are sponsored by the school, programs such as yoga and Pilates also sponsored by the school, a gym with hours that are suitable for a typical student's schedule, and clubs for tennis and other sports." Students' biggest complaint is the food. Though the "large cafeteria has many food options," "they are all always mediocre at best."

Student Body

At IIT the student body is "focused, smart, and quirky." Says one student, IIT is comprised of "geeky tech people who are always crazy busy, never sleep, but still find time to party." "The typical student spends a lot of time in class, and even more time studying." IIT offers "a very diverse population not just ethnically but when it comes to different interests." "There are many international students from various parts of the world, many architect students who are very different from the engineers and computer science majors, plus students from the Vandercook School of Music, making [for an] unbelievably diverse student body." Despite the fact that "students are the most diverse in the entire United States," "Everyone gets along and fits in." One student jokes, "We all share common ground in that we're nerdy."

FINANCIAL AID: 312-567-7219 • E-MAIL: ADMISSION@IIT.EDU • WEBSITE: WWW.IIT.EDU

THE PRINCETON REVIEW SAYS

Admissions

Very Important factors considered include: Academic GPA, rigor of secondary school record. *Important factors considered include:* Class rank, application essay, recommendation(s), standardized test scores. *Other factors considered include:* Alumni/ae relation, character/personal qualities, extracurricular activities, first generation, interview, level of applicant's interest, talent/ability, volunteer work, work experience. ACT with writing component recommended. TOEFL required of all international applicants. High school diploma is required and GED is accepted. *Academic units required:* 4 English, 4 mathematics, 3 science (2 science labs), 2 foreign language, 2 social studies. *Academic units recommended:* 4 English, 4 mathematics, 3 science (2 science labs), 2 foreign language, 2 social studies, 2 history, 1 visual/performing arts, 1 computer science.

Financial Aid

Students should submit: FAFSA. The Princeton Review suggests that all financial aid forms be submitted as soon as possible after January 1. *Need-based scholarships/grants offered:* Federal Pell, SEOG, state scholarships/grants, private scholarships, the school's own gift aid. *Loan aid offered:* Direct Subsidized Stafford, Direct Unsubsidized Stafford, Direct PLUS, Federal Perkins, college/university loans from institutional funds. Applicants will be notified of awards on a rolling basis beginning March 1. Federal Work-Study Program available. Institutional employment available. Off-campus job opportunities are good.

The Inside Word

Students at IIT say it's "easy to get in, tough to get out," but the term "easy" is deceptive in this case. With applicants concurrently looking to MIT and CalTech, IIT remains highly competitive in relation to the vast majority of undergraduate institutions. Few bother applying here unless they suspect they can handle the demanding curriculum. In essence, the admissions pool is somewhat self-selecting. Only the extremely bright and/or extremely ambitious apply. According to the admissions office, "All students are evaluated for significant merit-based scholarships upon admission."

THE SCHOOL SAYS ". . ."

From the Admissions Office

"IIT is committed to providing students a distinctive and relevant education through hands-on learning, dedicated teachers, small class sizes, and undergraduate research opportunities. Classes are taught by senior faculty—not teaching assistants—who foster our culture of innovation with their own firsthand research experience.

"Students are immersed in our interdisciplinary approach to learning through the team-based, creative problem-solving experience of the Interprofessional Projects Program (IPROs). The Office of Undergraduate Research provides mentored collaborative research experiences for undergraduates. Our entrepreneurship program challenges students to develop start-up technology companies. University Technology Park at IIT, a business incubator located on campus, supports this challenge by providing numerous opportunities to work with companies at every stage of growth, from conception to sophistication. The Leadership Academy teaches leadership skills that advance students in their personal and professional development. "IIT's location in the world-class city of Chicago gives students priceless access to the professional world through internships and employment. The university's own diverse student population mirrors the global work environment faced by all graduates.

"First year students applying for admission into the entering class are required to submit an SAT or ACT score. We will use the student's best scores from either test. Subject tests are accepted, but not required. "It is highly recommended that transfer applicants have completed thirty credit hours and have taken calculus and/or physics. Both first-year and transfer students are evaluated for significant merit based scholarships upon admission."

SELECTIVITY	
Admissions Rating	90
# of applicants	2,466
% of applicants accepted	64
% of acceptees attending	29
# of early action applicants	864
# accepted early action	660

FRESHMAN PROFILE	
Range SAT Critical Reading	530–640
Range SAT Math	613–710
Range SAT Writing	523–638
Range ACT Composite	24–31
Minimum paper TOEFL	550
Minimum web-based TOEFL	80
Average HS GPA	4.0
% graduated top 10% of class	46
% graduated top 25% of class	75
% graduated top 50% of class	94

DEADLINES	
Early action	
Deadline	11/15
Notification	12/1
Regular	
Deadline	8/1
Nonfall registration?	yes

FINANCIAL FACTS	
Financial Aid Rating	78
Annual tuition	$33,194
Room and board	$10,464
Required fees	$1,160
Books and supplies	$1,100
% needy frosh rec. need-based scholarship or grant aid	99
% needy UG rec. need-based scholarship or grant aid	99
% needy frosh rec. non-need-based scholarship or grant aid	19
% needy UG rec. non-need-based scholarship or grant aid	10
% needy frosh rec. need-based self-help aid	72
% needy UG rec. need-based self-help aid	79
% frosh rec. any financial aid	98
% UG rec. any financial aid	96
% UG borrow to pay for school	64
Average cumulative indebtedness	$24,004
% frosh need fully met	28
% ugrads need fully met	15
Average % of frosh need met	87
Average % of ugrad need met	77

ILLINOIS WESLEYAN UNIVERSITY

PO BOX 2900, BLOOMINGTON, IL 61702-2900 • ADMISSIONS: 309-556-3031 • FAX: 309-556-3820

CAMPUS LIFE

Quality of Life Rating	**75**
Fire Safety Rating	**76**
Green Rating	**71**
Type of school	private
Environment	city

STUDENTS

Total undergrad enrollment	2,083
% male/female	43/57
% from out of state	11
% from public high school	82
% frosh live on campus	100
# of fraternities	6
# of sororities	5
% African American	4
% Asian	5
% Caucasian	73
% Hispanic	5
% international	4
# of countries represented	23

SURVEY SAYS . . .

Lab facilities are great
Great computer facilities
Great library
Athletic facilities are great
Low cost of living
Musical organizations are popular

ACADEMICS

Academic Rating	**85**
% students returning for sophomore year	90
% students graduating within 4 years	77
Calendar	4-4-1
Student/faculty ratio	11:1
Profs interesting rating	85
Profs accessible rating	86
Most classes have	10–19 students
Most lab/discussion sessions have	10–19 students

MOST POPULAR MAJORS

biology/biological sciences; business/commerce; psychology

APPLICANTS ALSO LOOK AT AND OFTEN PREFER

University of Notre Dame, Northwestern University

AND SOMETIMES PREFER

University of Illinois at Urbana-Champaign, Washington University in St. Louis

AND RARELY PREFER

Augustana College (IL)

STUDENTS SAY ". . ."

Academics

Illinois Wesleyan, a "small school…with the prestige and academic diversity of a larger institution," is "extremely intense academically," students warn. Some—especially those in the sciences—go so far as to bemoan the "unreasonably hard classes," but most "love that at the end of the day you always have dozens of peers to support you and remind you that you'll get through it." Supportive professors "genuinely care about each student's success," which also helps, as do the "almost limitless resources" that allow undergraduates "to do anything and everything that interests them, both in and out of the classroom." Because "there are no graduate students" here, undergraduates are "given many opportunities that wouldn't exist at a larger university." One student reports, "As a sophomore psychology major, I'm gaining valuable lab experience that will prepare me for a career in research. Academic and leadership opportunities are abundant here." The school's relatively small size doesn't hamper its ability to excel in numerous disciplines. Students lavish praise on the "very competitive and very reputable biology program," the "great science program," the "prestigious" accounting program, a "reputable" nursing program, a "stellar music program," and a "highly acclaimed" theater department. Smaller academic departments utilize "adjunct professors from Illinois State" to deliver program requirements. "The anthropology department, for example, has only two full-time professors, but it is still able to tailor classes to specific student requests via ISU adjuncts."

Life

Life at IWU is workload-driven. Students with good time-management skills (or less challenging majors) "involve themselves in extracurricular activities while developing a strong academic background both inside and out[side] of their major's subject area," but others immerse themselves in academics and "only see the light of day when walking between classes. Studying is like breathing to [some] students here, they can't even imagine what it would be like to be able to stop for more than a few minutes." Many here tell us that "Greek life is very strong at this school," as are athletics. "Sports events are big here," one student writes. "This town is literally full of…people that live for Wesleyan athletics, which gives it a good homegrown feel when you are there." Hometown Bloomington, which IWU shares with Illinois State University, "is not exactly a hot spot" but it does have "a lot of bars that are popular with the upperclassmen." On campus, "Music and theater productions are extremely popular…and for a good reason: They're really good!" When all else fails, "Conversation is never lacking, and even on the nights when people can't find entertainment, late night discussions about anything—the Cold War, hypothetical zombie apocalypse, what matters most in life, or simply favorite meals—can be some of the most memorable moments of your college experience."

Student Body

"It's hard to describe a typical Wesleyan student," students tell us, observing "we are all so different. I suppose we are all dedicated to academic success, but you really have everything from bookworms to typical sorority girls to artsy people and athletes. Everyone fits in well together, however, regardless of being so different from one another." If there is a prevailing demographic, it is "an impressive student from…the Chicago suburbs." The number of international students here "is increasing almost exponentially," one undergraduate tells us, "and these students manage to fit in very well, although sometimes [they form a] cohort with fellow international students (which happens everywhere, it seems)."

FINANCIAL AID: 309-556-3096 • E-MAIL: IWUADMIT@IWU.EDU • WEBSITE: WWW.IWU.EDU

THE PRINCETON REVIEW SAYS

Admissions

Very important factors considered include: Academic GPA, rigor of secondary school record, interview. *Important factors considered include:* Class rank, application essay, standardized test scores, character/personal qualities, extracurricular activities, talent/ability. *Other factors considered include:* Recommendation(s), alumni/ae relation, first generation, geographical residence, level of applicant's interest, racial/ethnic status, state residency, volunteer work, work experience. SAT or ACT required; ACT with or without writing component accepted. TOEFL required of all international applicants. High school diploma is required and GED is accepted. *Academic units recommended:* 4 English, 3 mathematics, 3 science (2 science labs), 3 foreign language, 2 social studies.

Financial Aid

Students should submit: FAFSA, institution's own financial aid form, CSS/Financial Aid PROFILE. The Princeton Review suggests that all financial aid forms be submitted as soon as possible after January 1. *Need-based scholarships/grants offered:* Federal Pell, SEOG, state scholarships/grants, private scholarships, the school's own gift aid. *Loan aid offered:* Direct Subsidized Stafford, Direct Unsubsidized Stafford, Direct PLUS, Federal Perkins, Federal Nursing, college/university loans from institutional funds. Applicants will be notified of awards on a rolling basis beginning February 15. Federal Work-Study Program available. Institutional employment available. Off-campus job opportunities are good.

The Inside Word

There's no application fee at IWU, and the school accepts the Common Application (with the IWU Common Application Supplement, which asks for your intended major and includes an essay question about your reasons for wanting to attend IWU), so there are few reasons to not apply to IWU if you're even slightly interested in attending. Don't expect to breeze through, though. You won't get into this highly selective college without a solid academic profile or a compelling story.

THE SCHOOL SAYS ". . ."

From the Admissions Office

"Illinois Wesleyan University attracts a wide variety of students who are interested in pursuing diverse fields such as vocal performance, biology, psychology, German, physics, or business administration. At IWU, students are not forced into either/or choices. Rather, they are encouraged to pursue multiple interests simultaneously—a philosophy that is in keeping with the spirit and value of a liberal arts education. The distinctive 4-4-1 calendar allows students to follow their interests each school year in two semesters followed by an optional month-long class in May. May term opportunities include classes on campus; research collaboration with faculty; travel and study in such places as Australia, China, South Africa, and Europe; as well as local, national, and international internships. Study abroad is very popular, with one out of every two students enjoying a travel experience.

"The IWU mission statement reads in part: 'A liberal education at Illinois Wesleyan fosters creativity, critical thinking, effective communication, strength of character, and a spirit of inquiry; it deepens the specialized knowledge of a discipline with a comprehensive world view. It affords the greatest possibilities for realizing individual potential while preparing students for democratic citizenship and life in a global society...The university, through its policies, programs, and practices, is committed to diversity, social justice, and environmental sustainability. A tightly knit, supportive university community, together with a variety of opportunities for close interaction with excellent faculty, both challenges and supports students in their personal and intellectual development."

SELECTIVITY	
Admissions Rating	91
# of applicants	3,319
% of applicants accepted	61
% of acceptees attending	25
# accepting a place on wait list	290
# admitted from wait list	16

FRESHMAN PROFILE	
Range SAT Critical Reading	540–670
Range SAT Math	590–740
Range ACT Composite	25–30
Minimum paper TOEFL	550
Average HS GPA	3.8
% graduated top 10% of class	45
% graduated top 25% of class	80
% graduated top 50% of class	98

DEADLINES	
Early action	
Deadline	11/15
Notification	1/15
Nonfall registration?	yes

FINANCIAL FACTS	
Financial Aid Rating	88
Annual tuition	$36,392
Room and board	$8,476
Required fees	$180
Books and supplies	$780
% needy frosh rec. need-based scholarship or grant aid	100
% needy UG rec. need-based scholarship or grant aid	100
% needy frosh rec. non-need-based scholarship or grant aid	12
% needy UG rec. non-need-based scholarship or grant aid	11
% needy frosh rec. need-based self-help aid	79
% needy UG rec. need-based self-help aid	84
% frosh rec. any financial aid	99
% UG rec. any financial aid	95
% UG borrow to pay for school	67
Average cumulative indebtedness	$31,091
% frosh need fully met	37
% ugrads need fully met	37
Average % of frosh need met	90
Average % of ugrad need met	95

INDIANA UNIVERSITY—BLOOMINGTON

300 NORTH JORDAN AVENUE, BLOOMINGTON, IN 47405-1106 • ADMISSIONS: 812-855-0661 • FAX: 812-855-5102

CAMPUS LIFE

Quality of Life Rating	**92**
Fire Safety Rating	**79**
Green Rating	**95**
Type of school	public
Environment	city

STUDENTS

Total undergrad enrollment	32,041
% male/female	49/51
% from out of state	32
% African American	4
% Asian	4
% Caucasian	76
% Hispanic	4
% international	9
# of countries represented	139

SURVEY SAYS . . .

Great computer facilities
Great off-campus food
Students are happy
Everyone loves the Hoosiers
Student publications are popular
Hard liquor is popular

ACADEMICS

Academic Rating	**76**
% students returning for sophomore year	89
% students graduating within 4 years	50
% students graduating within 6 years	72
Calendar	semester
Student/faculty ratio	19:1
Profs interesting rating	73
Profs accessible rating	78
Most classes have	20–29 students
Most lab/discussion sessions have	20–29 students

MOST POPULAR MAJORS

business; communication, journalism, and related programs, other; education

STUDENTS SAY ". . ."

Academics

Indiana University—Bloomington focuses on creating well-rounded students who will be successful in and after college. This large state school challenges its students academically, but it "creates a fun collegiate environment, as well." "Academics and school spirit are its specialties!" says one student. The institution offers excellent financial aid and numerous opportunities for graduate and undergraduate students across all departments to conduct research, adding to "the perfect combination of excellent undergraduate teaching, Division I athletic teams backed by a passionate sense of school spirit, and a lively social scene." The "many excellent professors" here "really care about what they do," and they really "know what they're talking about." They "clearly want what's best for their students," and "the learning environment they create is excellent." "I have been very impressed with the individual attention I have received—mostly due to the level of commitment by professors to their students," says one student. The "rigorous and competitive classroom environment" gives students "the knowledge to be successful in our futures through great faculty, facilities, and tradition." Most professors at IU have professional experiences, and therefore "can bring their subjects to life." The "world-renowned business program" and the education and journalism schools are standouts here, but students say that all of the "school systems are great and easy to access," which makes "communicating with students/professors easy." Even with 40,000 people on campus, the administration gives student groups "much freedom of planning," and this warm environment allows students to "collaborate academically and non-academically as one community." This autonomy grants students the chance to explore "anything we want, whenever, but [find] the key thing we'll love through many opportunities and great programs."

Life

This "best-kept secret of the Midwest" is located in "the vibrant city of Bloomington," where "the restaurants off campus are amazing," with "many options to choose from." During the week, people "work really hard," and the campus is very active, with "a good number of students working out or running." There is "always something going on and something to do on campus that will fit the need of any student." Weekends generally start on Thursday night and go through Saturday night, when "house parties are popular," and the Greek system, although it only encompasses roughly twenty percent of the campus, "provides a strong social scene." The legendary IU basketball team is "starting to really rebuild its legacy," and attending games is common enough. There are also "free movies at the Union on weekends," a college mall, and just "a very fun social scene" in general. Looking around the "beautiful" campus, you can see people who go jogging, and if the weather's really nice, you can find people lying outside on the grass and on benches snoozing."

Student Body

With such a large student body, "You are destined to find someone who you 'click' with." "It's unheard of that a student won't be able to fit in somewhere," says one. Typical is hard to nail down with tens of thousands of people, but many here are "very respectful of one another and ready to help out a fellow Hoosier" and "very lively and fun," and each student manages to have "an equal balance of school and social life." International students (often attracted by the business and music schools) are "accepted and encouraged to attend IU." Most students can be called "hard workers who also know how to have fun on the weekends."

FINANCIAL AID: 812-855-0321 • E-MAIL: IUADMIT@INDIANA.EDU • WEBSITE: WWW.IUB.EDU

THE PRINCETON REVIEW SAYS

Admissions

Very Important factors considered include: Class rank, academic GPA, rigor of secondary school record. *Important factors considered include:* Standardized test scores. *Other factors considered include:* Application essay, recommendation(s), alumni/ae relation, character/personal qualities, extracurricular activities, first generation, geographical residence, interview, level of applicant's interest, racial/ethnic status, state residency, talent/ability, volunteer work, work experience. SAT or ACT required; ACT with writing component required. High school diploma is required and GED is accepted. *Academic units required:* 4 English, 3.5 mathematics (specific courses), 3 sciences (2 science labs), 3 social sciences, 2 world languages, 1.5 academic electives. *Academic units recommended:* 1 mathematics, 1 world language.

Financial Aid

Students should submit: FAFSA. The Princeton Review suggests that all financial aid forms be submitted as soon as possible after January 1. *Need-based scholarships/grants offered:* Federal Pell, SEOG, state scholarships/grants, private scholarships, the school's own gift aid. *Loan aid offered:* Direct Subsidized Stafford, Direct Unsubsidized Stafford, Direct PLUS, Federal Perkins, college/university loans from institutional funds. Applicants will be notified of awards on a rolling basis beginning in March. Federal Work-Study Program available. Institutional employment available. Off-campus job opportunities are good.

The Inside Word

Above-average high school performers (defined by both grade point average and test scores) should meet little resistance from the IU admissions office. Preference is given to Indiana residents who are in the top forty percent of their graduating classes and to non-residents who are in the top thirty percent of their graduating classes. Students will have the opportunity to meet admissions representatives at numerous recruiting events held in many locations throughout the country or during a campus visit. Rolling admissions favor those who apply early in the process. IU's music program is highly competitive; admission hinges upon a successful audition.

THE SCHOOL SAYS ". . ."

From the Admissions Office

"Indiana University—Bloomington, one of America's great teaching and research universities, extends learning and teaching beyond the walls of the traditional classroom. When visiting campus, students and parents typically describe IU as 'what a college should look and feel like.' Students bring their diverse experiences, beliefs, and backgrounds from all fifty states and 137 countries, which adds a richness and diversity to life at IU—a campus often cited as one of the most beautiful in the nation. Indiana University—Bloomington truly offers a quintessential college town, campus, and overall experience. Students enjoy all of the advantages, opportunities, and resources that a larger school can offer, while still receiving personal attention and support. Because of the variety of outstanding academic and cultural resources, students at IU have the best of both worlds.

"Indiana offers more than 5,000 courses and 183 undergraduate majors, of which many are known nationally and internationally. IU—Bloomington is known worldwide for outstanding programs in the arts, sciences, humanities, and social sciences as well as for highly rated Schools of Business, Music, Education, Journalism, Optometry; Public and Environmental Affairs; and Health, Physical Education, and Recreation. Students can customize academic programs with double and individualized majors, internships, and research opportunities, while utilizing state-of-the-art technology. Representatives from more than 1,000 businesses, government agencies, and not-for-profit organizations come to campus each year to recruit IU students.

"IUB requires the SAT the ACT with writing component. The university will use the writing sections to determine possible credit, placement, or exemption from writing requirements. All application materials for admission must be submitted online or postmarked by November 1 for Automatic Academic Scholarship consideration."

SELECTIVITY

Admissions Rating	**86**
# of applicants	35,218
% of applicants accepted	72
% of acceptees attending	29

FRESHMAN PROFILE

Range SAT Critical Reading	510–630
Range SAT Math	540–650
Range SAT Writing	510–620
Range ACT Composite	24–29
Minimum paper TOEFL	550
Minimum web-based TOEFL	79
Average HS GPA	3.6
% graduated top 10% of class	37
% graduated top 25% of class	74
% graduated top 50% of class	97

DEADLINES

Regular	
Priority	3/1
Nonfall registration?	yes

FINANCIAL FACTS

Financial Aid Rating	**77**
Annual in-state tuition	$8,433
Annual out-state tuition	$28,449
Room and board	$8,419
Required fees	$1,091
Books and supplies	$824
% needy frosh rec. need-based scholarship or grant aid	77
% needy UG rec. need-based scholarship or grant aid	79
% needy frosh rec. non-need-based scholarship or grant aid	12
% needy UG rec. non-need-based scholarship or grant aid	10
% needy frosh rec. need-based self-help aid	58
% needy UG rec. need-based self-help aid	70
% frosh rec. any financial aid	73
% UG rec. any financial aid	78
% UG borrow to pay for school	53
Average cumulative indebtedness	$28,434
% frosh need fully met	16
% ugrads need fully met	12
Average % of frosh need met	89
Average % of ugrad need met	90

INDIANA UNIVERSITY OF PENNSYLVANIA

1011 South Drive, Indiana, PA 15705 • Admissions: 724-357-2230 • Fax: 724-357-6281

CAMPUS LIFE

Quality of Life Rating	**66**
Fire Safety Rating	**88**
Green Rating	**61**
Type of school	public
Environment	village

STUDENTS

Total undergrad enrollment	12,660
% male/female	43/57
% from out of state	9
% frosh live on campus	85
# of fraternities	14
# of sororities	13
% African American	10
% Asian	1
% Caucasian	81
% Hispanic	3
% international	2
# of countries represented	70

SURVEY SAYS . . .

Great computer facilities
Frats and sororities dominate social scene
Student publications are popular
Lots of beer drinking
Hard liquor is popular

ACADEMICS

Academic Rating	**66**
% students returning for sophomore year	77
Calendar	semester
Student/faculty ratio	19:1
Profs interesting rating	71
Profs accessible rating	70
Most classes have	20–29 students
Most lab/discussion sessions have	10–19 students

MOST POPULAR MAJORS

criminology; management information systems; nursing/registered nurse (rn, asn, bsn, msn)

APPLICANTS ALSO LOOK AT AND OFTEN PREFER

Pennsylvania State University—University Park, Westminster College of Salt Lake City

AND SOMETIMES PREFER

Slippery Rock University of Pennsylvania, West Virginia University, University of Delaware, James Madison University

AND RARELY PREFER

Bloomsburg University of Pennsylvania

STUDENTS SAY

Academics

Nestled in the heart of western Pennsylvania, Indiana University of Pennsylvania provides students with "a quality education at an affordable price." Across the board, undergrads here assert that their university "is the perfect size: not too small [and] not too big." Indeed, "IUP has the size of a large state school, but it has the community feeling seen in smaller, private schools." Academically, the university "prides itself on [offering] a broad range of majors," and undergrads love that there's so much opportunity to study virtually anything. Of course, it's inevitable that some departments will stand out, and students love to highlight the stellar education, nursing, criminology, and geology programs. Overall, professors at IUP get high marks from undergrads. Certainly, students really appreciate that they are pushed "to become better thinkers inside and outside of the classroom." One undergrad explains further, "I feel that my professors are passionate about the subjects that they teach and love it when students participate and/or even challenge them. They are friendly and very willing to help students with class and even with extra interest-related things." Another student quickly concurs stating, "The professors I have had in my business honors track are the best. Many of them have not only had real-world experience, but they are also [at the] top of their department. They are truly interested in what they are teaching their students, and they do all they can to help."

Life

Undergrads at IUP proudly proclaim, "There is always something going on here, and you'll never be bored if you take the time to look around." Certainly, "Living at IUP can be very exciting…depending on [a] student's sense of drive and definition of a 'good time.'" Another undergrad agrees, sharing, "We have a ton of opportunities for campus involvement through programs, events and leadership work…This campus is unique in that if a student is passionate about anything, they can [usually] find other students [it will] resonate with [and] they can form a club/organization if it doesn't exist." In addition, "IUP's party scene exists, but if that's not your style then you don't have to worry about it interfering with your life." And nature lovers will also be delighted to learn that there are plenty of opportunities for outdoor adventure. As one student reveals, "During the winter, people go skiing or ice skating at local places. During the warmer months, we have an awesome school park that has hiking and biking trails and fishing." To the detriment of some and to the delight of others, hometown Indiana is "very rural." Of course, when students do venture into town, they can take advantage of "an old movie theater" and "local restaurants, [which are] very good." Moreover, there's also a "very small mall…[and] a bowling alley." However, when undergrads want a little more excitement, they can head down to Pittsburgh, which provides a myriad of cultural and entertainment options.

Student Body

There seems to be a divide among the student body at IUP. Some undergrads believe you can easily categorize their peers "as the people in fraternities and sororities, and those that are not." Indeed, one student curtly states, "Those that are in the Greek life usually do not hang out with people outside of it, and vice versa." However, there are plenty of students who object to this point of view, insisting that "IUP is not cliquish" and assuring us that undergrads here "fit very nicely with each other." As one satisfied undergrad shares, "A typical student is open-minded and willing to learn." Indeed, many describe their peers as "friendly, outgoing, and eager" and perhaps most important, they "know how to have fun." As one pleased student sums up her experience, "By and large, there seems to be a place for virtually anybody to fit in here at IUP."

FINANCIAL AID: 724-357-2218 • E-MAIL: ADMISSIONS-INQUIRY@IUP.EDU • WEBSITE: WWW.IUP.EDU

THE PRINCETON REVIEW SAYS

Admissions

Very important factors considered include: Academic GPA, standardized test scores. *Important factors considered include:* Rigor of secondary school record. *Other factors considered include:* Class rank, application essay, recommendation(s), extracurricular activities. SAT or ACT required; ACT with or without writing component accepted. TOEFL required of all international applicants. High school diploma is required and GED is accepted. *Academic units recommended:* 3 English, 3 mathematics, 3 science, 2 foreign language, 3 social studies.

Financial Aid

Students should submit: FAFSA. The Princeton Review suggests that all financial aid forms be submitted as soon as possible after January 1. *Need-based scholarships/grants offered:* Federal Pell, SEOG, state scholarships/grants, private scholarships, the school's own gift aid, United Negro College Fund. *Loan aid offered:* Direct Subsidized Stafford, Direct Unsubsidized Stafford, Direct PLUS, Federal Perkins, private alternative loans. Applicants will be notified of awards on a rolling basis beginning March 15. Federal Work-Study Program available. Institutional employment available. Highest amount earned per year from on-campus jobs $8,043. Off-campus job opportunities are good.

The Inside Word

Admissions officers at Indiana University of Pennsylvania follow the typical protocol when making their decisions. That is to say, they look for candidates who have successfully completed a challenging, college-prep curriculum. It should be noted that certain majors such as dietetics, education, speech language pathology and audiology, nursing, and fine arts all maintain specific admissions requirements that applicants must meet.

THE SCHOOL SAYS ". . ."

From the Admissions Office

"At IUP, we look at each applicant as an individual, not as a number. That means we'll review your application materials very carefully. When reviewing applications, the admissions committee's primary focus is on the student's high school record and SAT scores. In addition, the committee often reviews the optional personal essay and letters of recommendations submitted by the student to help aid in the decision-making process. We're always happy to speak with prospective students. Call us toll-free at 800-422-6830 or 724-357-2230, or e-mail us at admissions-inquiry@iup.edu.

"Students applying for admission are required to take the SAT or ACT."

SELECTIVITY	
Admissions Rating	77
# of applicants	12,735
% of applicants accepted	58
% of acceptees attending	39

FRESHMAN PROFILE	
Range SAT Critical Reading	450–540
Range SAT Math	450–540
Range SAT Writing	430–520
Minimum paper TOEFL	500
Minimum web-based TOEFL	61
% graduated top 10% of class	8
% graduated top 25% of class	28
% graduated top 50% of class	61

DEADLINES	
Nonfall registration?	yes

FINANCIAL FACTS	
Financial Aid Rating	66
Annual in-state tuition	$6,240
Annual out-state tuition	$15,600
Room and board	$9,782
Required fees	$2,122
Books and supplies	$1,100
% needy frosh rec. need-based scholarship or grant aid	66
% needy UG rec. need-based scholarship or grant aid	69
% needy frosh rec. non-need-based scholarship or grant aid	30
% needy UG rec. non-need-based scholarship or grant aid	20
% needy frosh rec. need-based self-help aid	92
% needy UG rec. need-based self-help aid	90
% frosh rec. any financial aid	83
% UG rec. any financial aid	83
% UG borrow to pay for school	83
Average cumulative indebtedness	$32,416
% frosh need fully met	5
% ugrads need fully met	6
Average % of frosh need met	63
Average % of ugrad need met	61

Iowa State University

100 Enrollment Services, Ames, IA 50011-2011 • Admissions: 515-294-5836 • Fax: 515-294-2592

CAMPUS LIFE

Quality of Life Rating	93
Fire Safety Rating	80
Green Rating	91
Type of school	public
Environment	town

STUDENTS

Total undergrad enrollment	23,857
% male/female	56/44
% from out of state	36
% from public high school	92
# of fraternities	33
# of sororities	20
% African American	3
% Asian	3
% Caucasian	79
% Hispanic	4
% international	7
# of countries represented	103

SURVEY SAYS . . .

Low cost of living
Student publications are popular
Great library
Athletic facilities are great
Intramural sports are popular

ACADEMICS

Academic Rating	72
% students graduating within 4 years	33
Calendar	semester
Student/faculty ratio	18:1
Profs interesting rating	70
Profs accessible rating	70
Most classes have	20–29 students
Most lab/discussion sessions have	20–29 students

MOST POPULAR MAJORS

finance; marketing/marketing management; mechanical engineering

APPLICANTS ALSO LOOK AT AND OFTEN PREFER

University of Illinois at Urbana-Champaign, University of Minnesota—Twin Cities, University of Wisconsin—Madison, Purdue University—West Lafayette

AND RARELY PREFER

Baylor University, Western Michigan University

STUDENTS SAY ". . ."

Academics

More than 28,000 students come together in Ames to get degrees in more than 100 majors, successfully giving off "a small-school feel with a big-university atmosphere." Science and technology are the main draws at this research university, but this "welcoming and friendly environment" treats all of its students well, regardless of their academic path. Professors, academic advisors, and other staff are all "very willing to help you academically and personally," and the Cyclone Nation is all about "engaging students not only in the classroom, but in the whole college experience." Professors "do what they can" for their students, focusing on experiences outside the classroom. It's also clear to students that the professors "truly love what they teach and bring passion to their lectures," working hard "to make students truly know what they want to spend the rest of their life doing." "Iowa State is all about preparing you for an actual career through hands-on teaching," says a student. Though lecture classes in the early college years can run large, the classroom experience (both in and out) only improves as students specialize. "I've been given the opportunity to work on an independent research project with a faculty mentor, which has been a really rewarding opportunity," says one student. All of the administration, "all the way up to our president and provost," is "dedicated to making student life at Iowa State the main priority." One of the school's greatest strengths is its ability to get students involved in internships, making it "extremely easy to find a job in your area of study"; every year, there are "very large engineering, agriculture, and business/LAS career fairs [that] allow students to find internships and full-time jobs easily." Even if one of your classes isn't the greatest, there "are many computer labs, help sessions, and teacher's assistants to go to for extra help."

Life

Iowa State is all about having "a big college experience (the athletics, the clubs, the shows, the educational opportunities, the school spirit) in a small college town"; indeed, Ames' support of the university "gives it a very at home and smaller feel than it actually is." During the week, students "mostly focus on classes and schoolwork." The weekends provide more of a chance to cut loose, whether that's a free event on campus, hanging out in each others' rooms and playing video games, partying, or playing an intramural sport (basketball, flag football, broomball, and others are "very popular"). "Winning an intramural championship t-shirt is very important and highly coveted on campus," says one student. There are "hundreds of clubs and activities for any of your interests," and the campus "will host bands quite a bit, and also a lot of late-night activities such as bingo, hypnotist shows, speakers, and lots of food." If you can't find what you want on campus, go off campus into downtown Ames, which is "full of fast-food and chain restaurants, bars, movie theaters, a mall, as well as locally owned businesses, restaurants, and novelty shops." Most students live on campus for their first two years, but off campus is "still very close to campus… so it's very comfortable and relatively cheap."

Student Body

Understandably, most students here are "small-town Iowans" or from the Midwest: "corn fed and bred," as they say. There is "some diversity," but "Most of the students are white, and the second largest group is Asian." These "humble," "extremely friendly" students "care about the community and get involved with as many activities as possible." "If someone gets off of the campus and city bus system without thanking the bus driver, it's practically a sin," says a student. Although enrollment is at about 30,000, "students make it feel like a small town where everyone is a member of the Cyclone family."

FINANCIAL AID: 515-294-2223 • E-MAIL: ADMISSIONS@IASTATE.EDU • WEBSITE: WWW.IASTATE.EDU

THE PRINCETON REVIEW SAYS

Admissions

Very important factors considered include: Class rank, academic GPA, rigor of secondary school record, standardized test scores. *Other factors considered include:* Application essay, recommendation(s), character/personal qualities, extracurricular activities, geographical residence, interview, state residency, talent/ability, volunteer work, work experience. SAT or ACT required; ACT with or without writing component accepted. TOEFL required of all international applicants. High school diploma is required and GED is accepted. *Academic units required:* 4 English, 3 mathematics, 3 science (2 science labs), 2 foreign language, 2 social studies. *Academic units recommended:* 4 English, 4 mathematics, 4 science (3 science labs), 3 foreign language, 4 social studies.

Financial Aid

Students should submit: FAFSA. The Princeton Review suggests that all financial aid forms be submitted as soon as possible after January 1. *Need-based scholarships/grants offered:* Federal Pell, SEOG, state scholarships/grants, the school's own gift aid. *Loan aid offered:* Direct Subsidized Stafford, Direct Unsubsidized Stafford, Direct PLUS, Federal Perkins, state loans, college/university loans from institutional funds, private alternative loans. Applicants will be notified of awards on a rolling basis beginning April 1. Federal Work-Study Program available. Institutional employment available. Highest amount earned per year from on-campus jobs $1,877. Off-campus job opportunities are excellent.

The Inside Word

Admission to ISU is formula-driven and based on: ACT composite score; high school GPA; high school percentile rank; and number of high school courses completed in the core subject areas. The formula, known as the Regent Admission Index (RAI), is as follows: RAI = (2 × ACT composite score) + (1 × percentile high school rank) + (20 × high school grade point average) + (5 × number of years of high school courses completed in the core subject areas). Anyone earning an RAI score of at least 245 is automatically admitted; the admissions office reviews applicants scoring below 245 individually to determine which will also be admitted.

THE SCHOOL SAYS ". . ."

From the Admissions Office

"Iowa State University offers all the advantages of a major university along with the friendliness and warmth of a residential campus. There are more than 100 undergraduate programs of study in the Colleges of Agriculture and Life Sciences, Business, Design, Human Sciences, Engineering, Liberal Arts and Sciences, and Veterinary Medicine. Our 1,700 faculty members include Rhodes Scholars, Fulbright Scholars, and National Academy of Sciences and National Academy of Engineering members. Recognized for its high quality of life, Iowa State has taken practical steps to make the university a place where students feel like they belong. Iowa State has been recognized for the high quality of campus life and the exemplary out-of-class experiences offered to its students. Along with a strong academic experience, students also have opportunities for further developing their leadership skills and interpersonal relationships through any of the more than 700 student organizations, sixty intramural sports, and a multitude of arts and recreational activities."

SELECTIVITY	
Admissions Rating	80
# of applicants	14,540
% of applicants accepted	86
% of acceptees attending	40

FRESHMAN PROFILE	
Range SAT Critical Reading	480–630
Range SAT Math	520–660
Range ACT Composite	22–28
Minimum paper TOEFL	530
Minimum web-based TOEFL	71
Average HS GPA	3.5
% graduated top 10% of class	25
% graduated top 25% of class	55
% graduated top 50% of class	90

DEADLINES	
Regular Deadline	7/1
Nonfall registration?	yes

FINANCIAL FACTS	
Financial Aid Rating	84
Annual in-state tuition	$6,648
Annual out-state tuition	$18,760
Room and board	$7,878
Required fees	$1,078
Books and supplies	$1,046
% needy frosh rec. need-based scholarship or grant aid	98
% needy UG rec. need-based scholarship or grant aid	98
% needy frosh rec. non-need-based scholarship or grant aid	46
% needy UG rec. non-need-based scholarship or grant aid	46
% needy frosh rec. need-based self-help aid	71
% needy UG rec. need-based self-help aid	81
% frosh rec. any financial aid	83
% UG rec. any financial aid	78
% UG borrow to pay for school	69
Average cumulative indebtedness	$29,455
% frosh need fully met	42
% ugrads need fully met	40
Average % of frosh need met	83
Average % of ugrad need met	81

Ithaca College

Ithaca College, Office of Admission, Ithaca, NY 14850-7002 • Admissions: 607-274-3124 • Fax: 607-274-1900

CAMPUS LIFE

Quality of Life Rating	78
Fire Safety Rating	82
Green Rating	97
Type of school	private
Environment	town

STUDENTS

Total undergrad enrollment	6,228
% male/female	43/57
% from out of state	57
% from public high school	85
# of fraternities	3
# of sororities	1
% African American	4
% Asian	3
% Caucasian	70
% Hispanic	6
% international	2
# of countries represented	77

SURVEY SAYS . . .

Great off-campus food
Frats and sororities are unpopular or nonexistent
Musical organizations are popular
College radio is popular
Theater is popular
Student publications are popular
Lots of beer drinking
Hard liquor is popular
Students are environmentally aware

ACADEMICS

Academic Rating	72
% students graduating within 4 years	67
Calendar	semester
Student/faculty ratio	12:1
Profs interesting rating	83
Profs accessible rating	86
Most classes have	fewer than 10 students
Most lab/discussion sessions have	10–19 students

MOST POPULAR MAJORS

business/commerce; music; radio and television

APPLICANTS ALSO LOOK AT AND OFTEN PREFER

Boston University, New York University, Northeastern University, Syracuse University

AND SOMETIMES PREFER

Pennsylvania State University—University Park, University of Vermont

AND RARELY PREFER

American University, Fordham University, State University of New York at Albany

STUDENTS SAY "..."

Academics

"Small class sizes" that afford plenty of "personal attention," "outstanding" scholarships, and cross-registration with nearby Cornell University are a few great reasons to choose Ithaca College, a smallish school in central New York that offers many of the resources you would expect to find at a much larger university. "You are able to be a part of a community and get the chance to pursue interests that are not necessarily a part of your chosen course of study," relates an English major. "We have loads of opportunities to do and try a wide variety of things." The vast multitude of academic offerings includes "one of the best communication schools in the country." Also notable are "strong" majors in music, business, and drama; a "highly competitive" six-year doctorate program in physical therapy; and the cinema and photography program. Professors are "really engaging and understand how to present the material so that it is relevant and meaningful." On the whole, faculty members are "really passionate about their fields and have a genuine interest in getting students excited about their passions." By far, the most common academic complaint about academics at Ithaca concerns registration, which can be trying. Some say, "the buildings—inside and out—are a bit outdated." Overall the campus is known for its picturesque beauty. "People aren't kidding when they say 'Ithaca is Gorges (gorgeous),'" promises one student.

Life

The number of extracurricular choices is "considerable" at Ithaca College. At the same time, "the school is small enough for anyone to get involved." There are "speakers and events offered on campus." There's also a pretty much professional-quality college radio station. Many students "are part of an athletic team or participate in intramural athletics." For relaxation, students often "hang out on the quad," throwing Frisbees or "playing music on the lawns on tie-dye sheets." The social situation at Ithaca is "nothing like the party scene you'd find at a larger university," but "there are some good parties" now and then. While the campus is a little "isolated," students also frequently manage to attend frat parties at Cornell and generally "enjoy the social scene" the nearby Ivy offers. "The town of Ithaca is quaint but lively." There's "a good music scene and a lot of cool stores." When the weather is nice, "There's always some festival," or at least it seems that way. "If you're an outdoorsy person," the wooded and rocky surrounding area is a wonderland of activity. "The hiking here is unbelievable," and few other schools offer the opportunity to "go cliff jumping on a hot Saturday." On the negative side, winters are cold as a matter of course, and "the cold and rain do hinder activities." Students joke, be prepared to get your exercise walking between classes, "the hills here will kill you."

Student Body

The typical undergrad here is "genuine," "easygoing," "always busy," "well-dressed," and has a "sunny disposition despite the gray skies." Beyond those qualities, the population is "a wide mix of hipsters, jocks, theater kids, music students," and "crunchy granola hippies." "People of all kinds fit in here." "Everyone finds their niche." Cliques are often based loosely on academics. "Ithaca is not so much one community as a whole," explains one student. "Instead, each school (music, communications, business, etc.) is its own community." Ethnic diversity and other kinds of diversity are "not entirely unheard of." However, people are "usually from the Northeast," and "The population of students that fit into the typical suburban, upper-middle-class family is definitely significant." Politically, "students at Ithaca tend to be liberal." Some students tell us that you'll find "a lot of people are environmentally and socially conscious" here who want "to change the world."

FINANCIAL AID: 607-274-3131 • E-MAIL: ADMISSION@ITHACA.EDU • WEBSITE: WWW.ITHACA.EDU

THE PRINCETON REVIEW SAYS

Admissions

Very important factors considered include: Academic GPA, rigor of secondary school record, standardized test scores. *Important factors considered include:* Class rank, application essay, recommendation(s), character/personal qualities, extracurricular activities, talent/ability. *Other factors considered include:* Alumni/ae relation, first generation, level of applicant's interest, volunteer work, work experience. SAT or ACT required; ACT with writing component required. TOEFL required of all international applicants. High school diploma is required and GED is accepted. *Academic units required:* 4 English, 3 mathematics, 3 science, 2 foreign language, 4 social studies, 1 academic electives.

Financial Aid

Students should submit: FAFSA, CSS/Financial Aid PROFILE. The Princeton Review suggests that all financial aid forms be submitted as soon as possible after January 1. *Need-based scholarships/grants offered:* Federal Pell, SEOG, state scholarships/grants, private scholarships, the school's own gift aid. *Loan aid offered:* Direct Subsidized Stafford, Direct Unsubsidized Stafford, Direct PLUS, Federal Perkins, alternative loans. Applicants will be notified of awards on a rolling basis beginning February 15. Federal Work-Study Program available. Institutional employment available. Highest amount earned per year from on-campus jobs $2,400. Off-campus job opportunities are good.

The Inside Word

Ithaca's admissions profile continues to be on the rise with a good deal of highly competitive applicants. Programs requiring an audition (for example, music) or portfolio review (for example, art) are among Ithaca's most demanding for admission. If you want to pursue the six-year clinical doctorate in physical therapy, focus on completing substantial math and science coursework in high school.

THE SCHOOL SAYS ". . ."

From the Admissions Office

"Ithaca College was founded in 1892 as a music conservatory, and it continues that commitment to performance and excellence. Its modern, residential 750-acre campus, equipped with state-of-the-art facilities, is home to the Schools of Business, Communications, Health Sciences and Human Performance, Humanities and Sciences, and Music. With more than 100 majors—from biochemistry to business administration, journalism to jazz, philosophy to physical therapy, and special programs in Washington, D.C.; Los Angeles; and London—students enjoy the curricular choices of a large campus in a personalized, smaller school environment. And Ithaca's students benefit from an education that emphasizes active learning, small classes, collaborative student-faculty research, and development of the whole student. Located in central New York's spectacular Finger Lakes region in what many consider the classic college town, the college has twenty-five highly competitive varsity teams, more than 130 campus clubs, two radio stations, and a television station, as well as hundreds of concerts, recitals, and theater performances annually.

"Students applying for admission must have official scores from either the SAT or the ACT with the writing section sent to Ithaca College by the testing agency. The college will also consider results of SAT Subject Tests, if submitted."

SELECTIVITY	
Admissions Rating	**80**
# of applicants	13,436
% of applicants accepted	68
% of acceptees attending	18
# accepting a place on wait list	1,633
# admitted from wait list	95
# of early decision applicants	242
# accepted early decision	223

FRESHMAN PROFILE	
Range SAT Critical Reading	520–620
Range SAT Math	520–630
Range SAT Writing	530–630
Minimum paper TOEFL	550
Minimum web-based TOEFL	80
% graduated top 10% of class	31
% graduated top 25% of class	68
% graduated top 50% of class	92

DEADLINES	
Early decision	
Deadline	11/1
Notification	12/15
Regular	
Deadline	2/1
Notification	4/15
Nonfall registration?	yes

FINANCIAL FACTS	
Financial Aid Rating	**87**
Annual tuition	$35,278
Room and board	$12,854
Books and supplies	$1,340
% needy frosh rec. need-based scholarship or grant aid	96
% needy UG rec. need-based scholarship or grant aid	97
% needy frosh rec. non-need-based scholarship or grant aid	25
% needy UG rec. non-need-based scholarship or grant aid	21
% needy frosh rec. need-based self-help aid	93
% needy UG rec. need-based self-help aid	94
% frosh rec. any financial aid	94
% UG rec. any financial aid	92
% frosh need fully met	57
% ugrads need fully met	48
Average % of frosh need met	91
Average % of ugrad need met	87

JAMES MADISON UNIVERSITY

SONNER HALL, MSC 0101, HARRISONBURG, VA 22807 • ADMISSIONS: 540-568-5681 • FAX: 540-568-3332

CAMPUS LIFE

Quality of Life Rating	**91**
Fire Safety Rating	**72**
Green Rating	**90**
Type of school	public
Environment	town

STUDENTS

Total undergrad enrollment	17,575
% male/female	41/59
% from out of state	29
% from public high school	60
% frosh live on campus	99
# of fraternities	15
# of sororities	9
% African American	4
% Asian	5
% Caucasian	80
% Hispanic	4
% international	1
# of countries represented	75

SURVEY SAYS . . .

Athletic facilities are great
School is well run
Students are friendly
Great food on campus
Students are happy
Student publications are popular
Lots of beer drinking

ACADEMICS

Academic Rating	**77**
% students graduating within 4 years	64
Calendar	semester
Student/faculty ratio	16:1
Profs interesting rating	83
Profs accessible rating	81
Most classes have	20–29 students
Most lab/discussion sessions have	20–29 students

MOST POPULAR MAJORS

community health services/liaison/counseling; marketing/marketing management; psychology

APPLICANTS ALSO LOOK AT AND OFTEN PREFER

University of Virginia, Virginia Tech

AND SOMETIMES PREFER

University of Delaware, George Mason University

STUDENTS SAY ". . ."

Academics

James Madison University has a reputation as "a school that values education, respect, and integrity." The university boasts "one of the best BA programs for musical theater on the East Coast," and an "amazing" business school. A communication major says, "James Madison offered a positive, enriching, and supportive learning environment," and most students agree that JMU is an "inspiring environment filled with students striving to be productive members of society." A senior says, "I found the JMU environment to be comfortable and conducive to learning," and it seems clear that "JMU is all about taking your academics seriously." Professors get consistently high marks for being "available to help" and "interested in student achievement." Although they're often described as "challenging," students say professors are "willing to facilitate your education in any way possible" and "are very down to earth, approachable, and huge supporters of discussion based classes." Like any large university, there are "some professors you want to avoid," and students grumble that "registering for classes, if you don't have priority is a pain." It's worth noting, however, that "classrooms and facilities are always well kept and very up-to-date with all the best teaching technology."

Life

Located in Virginia's Shenandoah Valley, JMU is known for its "beautiful" campus, and students rave about the "benefits of walking in the mountains." An English major says, "The moment I walked on campus I was captured by the student spirit and how beautiful it is." School spirit is generally high and students say, "There's a huge sense of JMU pride, everyone loves the Dukes!" A senior adds, "We have so much pride for our school. There is a friendly, collaborative ambiance here that is unparalleled anywhere else." The university is known for its Southern hospitality, and one student describes the student body as "the 'door-holding freaks of America' because even when people are several feet away, we stand there to hold the door for them." There are numerous ways to get involved on campus, and the "sheer number of student activities is stellar." Students rave about the "personal involvement that JMU offer(s)," and say, "They make you feel like a part of the campus, not just another number." Food services and facilities get high marks across the board, and most agree that the "administration and faculty are always willing to talk to students and point them in the right direction," noting that one of "the greatest strengths of the school is the ability to get any sort of assistance when needed." Regardless, there are complaints about traffic on campus, and many feel, "The school could improve on parking, by a long shot."

Student Body

At JMU, "The typical student is friendly, smart, open-minded, and fun." Students describe themselves as "excellent [at] maintaining a round, balanced life," and say, "everyone seems relaxed and knows how to have fun but keep their school work a priority." One student jokes that the typical student is "probably a girl considering our ratio seems like eighty to twenty at times," and another concurs, "more males would be nice." Students tend to be "white from the upper- to middle-class," and an International Affairs major says, "Although we do have all types here, most people consist of your typical prep wearing Uggs and a North Face." Some complain, "There is party atmosphere here that can seem dominating," and "If you do not go out and party you stand out." Others note, however, "Greek life is small," and parties "are usually open to everyone," adding that partying isn't "all students here think about. People will get together and drink for fun, but it isn't a necessity." A sophomore says, "On the weekends, students can go to downtown Harrisonburg to the various restaurants and shops," or enjoy on-campus movies at a reduced rate. Still others take advantage of the "great places to hike and spend time outdoors" and JMU's easy accessibility to nearby ski resorts.

FINANCIAL AID: 540-568-7820 • E-MAIL: ADMISSIONS@JMU.EDU • WEBSITE: WWW.JMU.EDU

THE PRINCETON REVIEW SAYS

Admissions

Very important factors considered include: Academic GPA, rigor of secondary school record. *Important factors considered include:* Standardized test scores. *Other factors considered include:* Class rank, application essay, recommendation(s), alumni/ae relation, character/personal qualities, extracurricular activities, geographical residence, state residency, talent/ability, volunteer work, work experience. SAT or ACT required; ACT with or without writing component accepted. TOEFL required of all international applicants. High school diploma is required and GED is accepted. *Academic units required:* 4 English, 4 mathematics, 3 science (3 science labs), 2 foreign language, 3 social studies. *Academic units recommended:* 4 English, 4 mathematics, 4 science (4 science labs), 3 foreign language, 4 social studies.

Financial Aid

Students should submit: FAFSA. The Princeton Review suggests that all financial aid forms be submitted as soon as possible after January 1. *Need-based scholarships/grants offered:* Federal Pell, SEOG, state scholarships/grants, private scholarships, the school's own gift aid. *Loan aid offered:* Direct Subsidized Stafford, Direct Unsubsidized Stafford, Direct PLUS, Federal Perkins, Federal Nursing. Applicants will be notified of awards on a rolling basis beginning April 1. Federal Work-Study Program available. Institutional employment available. Highest amount earned per year from on-campus jobs $3,640. Off-campus job opportunities are good.

The Inside Word

At JMU admissions are competitive, but the admissions staff insists that they're not searching for a "magic combination" of test scores and GPA. Admissions officers review each application individually and are most interested in the quality of an applicant's secondary school education, followed by performance and test scores. The personal statement is a vehicle for conveying information an applicant deems important but that doesn't appear elsewhere in the application, as such it's optional.

THE SCHOOL SAYS ". . ."

From the Admissions Office

"James Madison University's philosophy of inclusiveness—known as 'all together one'—means that students become a part of a real community that nurtures its own to learn, grow, and succeed. Our professors, many of whom have a wealth of real-world experience, pride themselves on making teaching their top priority. We take seriously the responsibility to maintain an environment that fosters learning and encourages students to excel in and out of the classroom. Our rich variety of educational, social, and extracurricular activities include more than 100 innovative and traditional undergraduate majors and programs, a well-established study abroad program, a cutting-edge information security program, more than 350 student clubs and organizations, and a 147,000-square-foot, state-of-the-art recreation center. The university's picturesque, self-contained campus is located in the heart of the Shenandoah Valley, a four-season area that's easy to call home. Great food, fun times, exciting intercollegiate athletics, and rigorous academics all combine to create the unique James Madison experience. From the library to the residence halls and from our outstanding honors program to our highly successful career placement program, the university is committed to equipping our students with the tools they need to achieve their dreams."

SELECTIVITY	
Admissions Rating	**86**
# of applicants	22,864
% of applicants accepted	60
% of acceptees attending	29

FRESHMAN PROFILE	
Range SAT Critical Reading	520–620
Range SAT Math	530–620
Range SAT Writing	520–610
Range ACT Composite	23–27
Minimum paper TOEFL	550
Average HS GPA	3.8
% graduated top 10% of class	26
% graduated top 25% of class	70
% graduated top 50% of class	98

DEADLINES	
Early action	
Deadline	11/1
Notification	1/1
Regular	
Deadline	1/15
Notification	4/1
Nonfall registration?	no

FINANCIAL FACTS	
Financial Aid Rating	**72**
Annual in-state tuition	$4,642
Annual out-state tuition	$17,932
Room and board	$8,340
Required fees	$3,806
Books and supplies	$876
% needy frosh rec. need-based scholarship or grant aid	47
% needy UG rec. need-based scholarship or grant aid	40
% needy frosh rec. non-need-based scholarship or grant aid	12
% needy UG rec. non-need-based scholarship or grant aid	9
% needy frosh rec. need-based self-help aid	77
% needy UG rec. need-based self-help aid	66
% frosh rec. any financial aid	62
% UG rec. any financial aid	58
% UG borrow to pay for school	52
Average cumulative indebtedness	$22,128
% frosh need fully met	73
% ugrads need fully met	61
Average % of frosh need met	41
Average % of ugrad need met	47

JOHNS HOPKINS UNIVERSITY

3400 NORTH CHARLES STREET, BALTIMORE, MD 21218 • ADMISSIONS: 410-516-8171 • FAX: 410-516-6025

CAMPUS LIFE

Quality of Life Rating	**79**
Fire Safety Rating	**76**
Green Rating	**93**
Type of school	private
Environment	metropolis

STUDENTS

Total undergrad enrollment	4,980
% male/female	52/48
% from out of state	89
% from public high school	69
% frosh live on campus	99
# of fraternities	13
# of sororities	9
% African American	5
% Asian	21
% Caucasian	52
% Hispanic	8
% international	8
# of countries represented	71

SURVEY SAYS . . .

Lab facilities are great
Great computer facilities
Great library
Athletic facilities are great

ACADEMICS

Academic Rating	**85**
% students returning for sophomore year	97
% students graduating within 4 years	84
% students graduating within 6 years	92
Calendar	4-1-4
Student/faculty ratio	12:1
Profs interesting rating	71
Profs accessible rating	74
Most classes have	10–19 students
Most lab/discussion sessions have	20–29 students

MOST POPULAR MAJORS

international relations and affairs; neuroscience; public health, other

APPLICANTS ALSO LOOK AT AND OFTEN PREFER

University of Pennsylvania, Princeton University, Massachusetts Institute of Technology, Yale University, Harvard College

AND SOMETIMES PREFER

Cornell University, Northwestern University

AND RARELY PREFER

Rice University, Washington University in St. Louis

STUDENTS SAY ". . ."

Academics

Johns Hopkins University has a reputation as an academic powerhouse, one that its undergrads wholeheartedly affirm. Although the university offers "a pretty intense environment" with "really rigorous" classes, all of this is made bearable by professors who are "concerned with the individual student" and "extremely approachable, even in [an] organic chemistry class of 300 students." Indeed, "They enjoy being in the classroom and sharing what they know. Each is passionate about their area of study and eager to share it with students who are equally as enthusiastic." A satisfied senior echoes these praises, saying, "All the professors that I've encountered at Hopkins recognize that learning should be fun and thought-provoking. Their lectures or discussions engage students to think about the materials in a different way and pursue further outside study." "Engage" is the operative word here, as undergrads are "treated as though they are participants in their respective academic fields, not just 'students'." However, as one senior cautions, "There's very little grade inflation, and you work hard for the grade you get." Praise also extends to the administration, which students describe as "caring to a fault, willing to help, and generally highly interested in the undergraduate experience." As one junior sums up, "It's clear that our professors and deans genuinely care about the students, as evidenced by their attendance at student fundraisers, fraternity scholarship events, and even plays and a cappella concerts. They want students to learn about anything that interests them, but they want students to grow as people too, and it's astonishing how high their success rate is in that regard."

Life

Life at Hopkins is "certainly based around work." Indeed, most undergrads are diligent students "who put work over everything else." This is a school where "people care about what they study" and it's not uncommon to see fellow students "stay up all night debating philosophy, politics or the theory of evolution." Sound a little intense? No worries: One junior assures us that "there's never a dull moment at Johns Hopkins: You just have to step outside your room and look for five seconds." Another senior confirms, "There's always something cool going on around campus, whether it's from the world of entertainment (like Will Ferrell coming to speak) or academia." There are numerous "free on-campus movies, plays, dance, and a cappella performances" to take in along with "the *best* lacrosse team in America" and "incredibly competitive [Division III] sports like soccer and water polo." And with roughly a quarter of the student body involved in fraternities and sororities, Greek life offers a "tremendous social outlet." Fortunately, when students get bored on campus, they can always explore hometown Baltimore for entertainment options. The city offers "movie theaters, malls, shopping centers, a *ton* of restaurants, a good music scene, and proximity to D.C., clubs, and other colleges. Many undergrads can frequently be found hanging out by the Inner Harbor or the nearby Towson Mall.

Student Body

While it might be difficult to define the typical Hopkins undergrad, the vast majority are "hardworking and care about their GPAs, and will do what they can to get the grades they want." Thankfully, many are also "balance artists; they are able to balance schoolwork, extracurricular activities, jobs, and a social life without getting too bogged down or stressed." Though students "are competitive in the sense that they all want to do well," that competitiveness is never adversarial. One junior declares, "I have found that there is an incredible mutual respect that permeates the student body, one that allows engineers to discuss poetry with English majors, sees historians present at astronomy lectures, and gets linguists to help lacrosse players study for French tests, all while reserving judgment upon each other." A sophomore continues, "I've never been someplace where there are so many diverse interests. As clichéd as it may sound, there truly is a niche for everyone."

FINANCIAL AID: 410-516-8028 • E-MAIL: GOTOJHU@JHU.EDU • WEBSITE: WWW.JHU.EDU

THE PRINCETON REVIEW SAYS

Admissions

Very important factors considered include: Academic GPA, recommendation(s), rigor of secondary school record, character/personal qualities. *Important factors considered include:* Class rank, application essay, standardized test scores, extracurricular activities, talent/ability, volunteer work, work experience. *Other factors considered include:* Alumni/ae relation, first generation, geographical residence, interview, racial/ethnic status, state residency. SAT or ACT required; ACT with writing component required. TOEFL required of all international applicants. High school diploma or equivalent is not required. *Academic units recommended:* 4 English, 4 mathematics, 4 science, 4 foreign language, 2 social studies, 2 history.

Financial Aid

Students should submit: FAFSA, CSS/Financial Aid PROFILE, noncustodial PROFILE, business/farm supplement. current year federal tax returns. Regular filing deadline is March 1. The Princeton Review suggests that all financial aid forms be submitted as soon as possible after January 1. *Need-based scholarships/grants offered:* Federal Pell, SEOG, state scholarships/grants, private scholarships, the school's own gift aid. *Loan aid offered:* Direct Subsidized Stafford, Direct Unsubsidized Stafford, Direct PLUS, Federal Perkins, college/university loans from institutional funds. Applicants will be notified of awards on or about April 1. Federal Work-Study Program available. Institutional employment available. Off-campus job opportunities are good.

The Inside Word

Top schools like Hopkins receive more and more applications every year and, as a result, grow harder and harder to get into. With more than 18,000 applicants, Hopkins has to reject numerous applicants who are thoroughly qualified. Give your application everything you've got, and don't take it personally if you don't get a fat envelope in the mail.

THE SCHOOL SAYS ". . ."

From the Admissions Office

"The Johns Hopkins tradition of preeminent academic excellence naturally attracts the very best students in the nation and from around the world. The admissions committee carefully examines each application for evidence of compelling intellectual interest and academic performance as well as strong personal recommendations and meaningful extracurricular contributions. Every applicant who matriculates to Johns Hopkins University was found qualified by the admissions committee through a 'whole person' assessment, and every applicant accepted for admission is fully expected to graduate. The admissions committee determines whom they believe will take full advantage of the exceptional opportunities offered at Hopkins, contribute the most to the educational process of the institution, and be the most successful in using what they have learned and experienced for the benefit of society."

SELECTIVITY	
Admissions Rating	**99**
# of applicants	18,459
% of applicants accepted	21
% of acceptees attending	33
# admitted from wait list	32
# of early decision applicants	1,097
# accepted early decision	486

FRESHMAN PROFILE	
Range SAT Critical Reading	630–740
Range SAT Math	660–770
Range SAT Writing	640–740
Range ACT Composite	29–33
Minimum paper TOEFL	600
Average HS GPA	3.7
% graduated top 10% of class	87
% graduated top 25% of class	98
% graduated top 50% of class	99

DEADLINES	
Early decision	
Deadline	11/1
Notification	12/15
Regular	
Deadline	1/1
Notification	4/1
Nonfall registration?	no

FINANCIAL FACTS	
Financial Aid Rating	**92**
Annual tuition	$42,280
Room and board	$12,962
Books and supplies	$2,200
% needy frosh rec. need-based scholarship or grant aid	86
% needy UG rec. need-based scholarship or grant aid	87
% needy frosh rec. non-need-based scholarship or grant aid	12
% needy UG rec. non-need-based scholarship or grant aid	11
% needy frosh rec. need-based self-help aid	86
% needy UG rec. need-based self-help aid	89
% frosh rec. any financial aid	59
% UG rec. any financial aid	57
% UG borrow to pay for school	48
Average cumulative indebtedness	$24,307
% frosh need fully met	98
% ugrads need fully met	99
Average % of frosh need met	99
Average % of ugrad need met	100

JUNIATA COLLEGE

1700 MOORE STREET, HUNTINGDON, PA 16652 • ADMISSIONS: 814-641-3420 • FAX: 814-641-3100

CAMPUS LIFE

Quality of Life Rating	77
Fire Safety Rating	77
Green Rating	73
Type of school	private
Environment	village

STUDENTS

Total undergrad enrollment	1,469
% male/female	44/56
% from out of state	33
% from public high school	86
% frosh live on campus	99
% African American	3
% Asian	2
% Caucasian	83
% Hispanic	3
% international	5
# of countries represented	38

SURVEY SAYS . . .

Lab facilities are great
Students are friendly
Campus feels safe
Low cost of living
Frats and sororities are unpopular or nonexistent

ACADEMICS

Academic Rating	84
% students returning for sophomore year	85
% students graduating within 4 years	72
% students graduating within 6 years	76
Calendar	semester
Student/faculty ratio	13:1
Profs interesting rating	88
Profs accessible rating	85
Most classes have	10–19 students
Most lab/discussion sessions have	10–19 students

MOST POPULAR MAJORS

biology/biological sciences; business/commerce; education

APPLICANTS ALSO LOOK AT AND OFTEN PREFER

Franklin & Marshall College

AND SOMETIMES PREFER

Allegheny College, Susquehanna University, Dickinson College

AND RARELY PREFER

Pennsylvania State University—University Park, Ursinus College

STUDENTS SAY ". . ."

Academics

Juniata College is a private liberal arts college located in Huntingdon, Pennsylvania. The college is named after the Juniata River. The school has "excellent science programs," and a few students say that there need to be "more resources [for] non-science programs." However, even students not majoring in science get access to some great facilities with theater students exclaiming, "The theater program is unlike any other in country" and praising their new Halbritter Center for the Performing Arts. At Juniata, students can choose one of the many majors offered, or they can design their own under the Program of Emphasis. Many students do so, about thirty percent, which allows each student to work with two faculty members and choose which classes would best fit their intended area of study. The "outstanding education" is built on a bedrock of strong faculty members who offer "superior education through meaningful personal interaction." Most class sizes tend to be fairly small, and though some classes are "tough to get in to because there is only one professor for a certain subject," many agree that they love the attention that each professor gives and that the teachers "really go out of their way" to help students succeed and "value student success as much as the student does." Success, however, doesn't come without a price at Juniata, with a large amount of the students agreeing that their "good grades do not come without effort," but that the class load is "challenging, but not overwhelming."

Life

Students seem to agree that there "isn't much to do in the town" of Huntington, but Juniata College makes up for it by making sure there is "always something to do" on campus. There are so many activities and groups on campus that some say, "It feels like you're missing out if you go home for the weekend." There are a "lot of traditions such as Storming of the Arch, Mountain Day, and Madrigal" that have been around the campus for decades and help bring students together. For instance, during Mountain Day, classes are canceled, and students and faculty are shuttled to a state park near the school where there are lunches, nature walks, and various games being played, and neither group knows when exactly it is going to be until the morning of the event. While there might be a lot of activities to do on campus, "If you want to party you can find one." If you want to just relax with your fellow students, "Raystown Lake is only twenty minutes away," where many students like to go and relax on the beach. Back on campus, many students seem to think that the "dorms and food" need improvement, but believe that the academic experience they receive outweighs those inconveniences.

Student Body

Students tend to describe themselves as "driven" and "passionately interested in their subjects," though they also take pride in their "laid-back" attitudes, saying they "know how to balance fun and work." During the week students "tend to buckle down and get their work done." A lot of "exchange students from around the world" that come to Juniata College to pursue their education, but for the most part, "almost all the students are Caucasian." Some think "diversity is a bit lacking," but agree that "everyone fits in somewhere" at Juniata College because "people are accepted not despite their differences, but because of them."

FINANCIAL AID: 814-641-3141 • E-MAIL: ADMISSIONS@JUNIATA.EDU • WEBSITE: WWW.JUNIATA.EDU

THE PRINCETON REVIEW SAYS

Admissions

Very important factors considered include: Application essay, academic GPA, recommendation(s), rigor of secondary school record, standardized test scores, character/personal qualities. *Important factors considered include:* Extracurricular activities, first generation, interview, talent/ability, volunteer work. *Other factors considered include:* Alumni/ae relation, geographical residence, level of applicant's interest, racial/ethnic status, state residency. ACT with or without writing component accepted. TOEFL required of all international applicants. High school diploma is required and GED is accepted. *Academic units required:* 4 English, 3 mathematics, 3 science (2 science labs), 2 foreign language, 3 social studies. *Academic units recommended:* 4 English, 4 mathematics, 4 science, 2 foreign language, 3 social studies.

Financial Aid

Students should submit: FAFSA. Regular filing deadline is March 1. The Princeton Review suggests that all financial aid forms be submitted as soon as possible after January 1. *Need-based scholarships/grants offered:* Federal Pell, SEOG, state scholarships/grants, private scholarships, the school's own gift aid. *Loan aid offered:* Direct Subsidized Stafford, Direct Unsubsidized Stafford, Direct PLUS, Federal Perkins, college/university loans from institutional funds. Applicants will be notified of awards on a rolling basis beginning September 1. Federal Work-Study Program available. Institutional employment available. Highest amount earned per year from on-campus jobs $4,596. Off-campus job opportunities are good.

The Inside Word

For those high school seniors looking to apply, they must apply by November 15 for the first early decision and February 1 for those who decide they want to apply after November 15. Interested applicants can submit their SAT or ACT scores, or they can also submit an original, graded document of two to three pages in length and must be from either their junior or senior year in high school. This is in addition to the required essays that are part of the application process. For those looking to save some money, there is no application free for anyone who applies to Juniata via the website. They also provide incoming freshman with Inbound Retreats each August, which allows them to sign up for one of thirty-eight different retreats and get an idea of what college life is like, but without having to go to class.

THE SCHOOL SAYS ". . ."

From the Admissions Office

"Juniata's unique approach to learning has a flexible, student-centered focus. With the help of two advisors, more than half of Juniata's students design their own majors (called the "Program of Emphasis" or "POE"). Those who choose a more traditional academic journey still benefit from the assistance of two faculty advisors and interdisciplinary collaboration between multiple academic departments.

"In addition, all students benefit from the recent, significant investments in academic facilities that help students actively learn by doing. For example, the new Halbritter Center for the Performing Arts houses an innovative theater program where theater professionals work side-by-side with students. The Sill Business Incubator provides $5,000 in seed capital to students with a desire to start their own business. The LEED-certified Raystown Environmental Studies Field Station, located on nearby Raystown Lake, gives unparalleled, hands-on study opportunities to students. And the von Liebig Center for Science provides opportunities for student/faculty research surpassing those available at even large universities.

"As the 2003 Middle States Accreditation Team noted, 'Juniata is truly a student-centered college. There is a remarkable cohesiveness in this commitment—faculty, students, trustees, staff, and alumni, each from their own vantage point, describe a community in which the growth of the student is central.' This cohesiveness creates a dynamic learning environment that enables students to think and grow intellectually, to evolve in their academic careers, and to graduate as active, successful participants in the global community.

"Freshman applicants may submit the SAT (or the ACT with or without the writing component). We will use their best scores from either test. "

SELECTIVITY

Admissions Rating	**86**
# of applicants	2,144
% of applicants accepted	71
% of acceptees attending	24
# accepting a place on wait list	64
# of early decision applicants	72
# accepted early decision	60

FRESHMAN PROFILE

Range SAT Critical Reading	540–640
Range SAT Math	540–640
Minimum paper TOEFL	550
Minimum web-based TOEFL	79
Average HS GPA	3.8
% graduated top 10% of class	40
% graduated top 25% of class	77
% graduated top 50% of class	97

DEADLINES

Early decision	
Deadline	11/15
Notification	12/23
Regular	
Priority	11/15
Deadline	3/15
Nonfall registration?	yes

FINANCIAL FACTS

Financial Aid Rating	**85**
Annual tuition	$35,040
Annual comprehensive tuition	$45,580
Room and board	$9,800
Required fees	$740
Books and supplies	$600
% needy frosh rec. need-based scholarship or grant aid	100
% needy UG rec. need-based scholarship or grant aid	100
% needy frosh rec. non-need-based scholarship or grant aid	18
% needy UG rec. non-need-based scholarship or grant aid	14
% needy frosh rec. need-based self-help aid	83
% needy UG rec. need-based self-help aid	86
% frosh rec. any financial aid	100
% UG rec. any financial aid	100
% UG borrow to pay for school	81
Average cumulative indebtedness	$30,109
% frosh need fully met	24
% ugrads need fully met	21
Average % of frosh need met	86
Average % of ugrad need met	83

KALAMAZOO COLLEGE

1200 ACADEMY STREET, KALAMAZOO, MI 49006 • ADMISSIONS: 269-337-7166 • FAX: 269-337-7390

CAMPUS LIFE

Quality of Life Rating	78
Fire Safety Rating	67
Green Rating	78
Type of school	private
Environment	city

STUDENTS

Total undergrad enrollment	1,374
% male/female	43/57
% from out of state	34
% from public high school	73
% frosh live on campus	100
% African American	4
% Asian	4
% Caucasian	69
% Hispanic	7
% Native American	1
% international	7
# of countries represented	31

SURVEY SAYS . . .

No one cheats
Great library
Frats and sororities are unpopular or nonexistent
Political activism is popular
Students are environmentally aware

ACADEMICS

Academic Rating	91
% students returning for sophomore year	90
% students graduating within 4 years	79
Calendar	quarter
Student/faculty ratio	14:1
Profs interesting rating	95
Profs accessible rating	90
Most classes have	10–19 students
Most lab/discussion sessions have	fewer than 10 students

MOST POPULAR MAJORS

economics; English language and literature; psychology

APPLICANTS ALSO LOOK AT AND OFTEN PREFER

Georgetown University, University of Michigan—Ann Arbor, Dartmouth College, Northwestern University

AND SOMETIMES PREFER

Earlham College, Denison University, The College of Wooster, University of Notre Dame, Oberlin College, Macalester College

AND RARELY PREFER

Albion College, DePauw University

STUDENTS SAY ". . ."

Academics

Study at Kalamazoo College is built around the K-Plan, "a solid liberal arts education combined with study abroad and internships and externships" and "the SIP, a senior individualized project, [which is] a senior thesis with a fun and much-used acronym." Students tell us that all aspects of the K-Plan "emphasize the importance of applying what you've learned in the classroom to other areas of life," allowing students to "see the whole picture and understand what [we] want to do with [our] degrees." A plan like this is only as good as its execution. Fortunately, by nearly all accounts Kalamazoo delivers with well-supported "study abroad, internship, externship, and domestic study-away opportunities" that are "endless" in variety. Students here once complained that demanding general education requirements impeded independent study. The school apparently was listening, as it recently introduced a new curriculum that "gives ultimate flexibility…allowing us to explore new disciplines and classes. We can even double major and still spend a quarter [term] abroad!" Kalamazoo's cozy size creates an "intimate setting [that] fosters community unlike any other school I've ever visited." A faculty that's "out of this world…attentive, engaged, and always available after class, usually for as much help as one needs" further strengthens those bonds. In the end, students leave feeling prepared for the real world. As one explains, "Students graduate completely ready to pursue a career in what they are passionate about or to continue their education on the next level."

Life

"Life goes by fast at K College," where, thanks to the trimester system, "You're in class for just a few weeks, and you already have your first round of exams." While "everyone is busy with classes and their clubs," students "will always somehow find time to help each other out." Most here "tend to take on a lot more classes/activities than they probably should," which "stresses everyone out," but students find creative ways to release the pressure. The Childish Games Commission, for example, which "meets every Friday at midnight to play games like tag, hide and seek, four-square, and Duck Duck Goose" is a popular option for relieving stress. Those seeking the sort of fun more characteristic of big schools can head over to Western Michigan University, where "there are upwards of 20,000 students," which allows K kids to "experience the social aspects of a large school while still enjoying a liberal arts education." Hometown Kalamazoo "is an overgrown artists' commune in a lot of ways," with "a monthly arts festival" and "plenty of shops, museums, and a nice park with concert events." Many here recommend regular trips downtown to escape "the K bubble." As one student explains, "It is sometimes…difficult to get off campus or get away from the people here. Everyone needs that time, and it's difficult to find, especially in winter quarter when there's five feet of snow outside."

Student Body

"Most students are very studious and care a lot about their grades but still know how to have fun," the "book smart, worldly, aware, passionate, argumentative, dedicated, hardworking, opinionated, [and] friendly" undergrads at Kalamazoo assure us. The school "has traditionally drawn a lot of strange students, but this has been changing lately." Across the board, students tend to be "very liberal-minded and idealistic, from a fairly well-off background…There is a lack of ideological diversity, but most students are too busy stressing out about their classes to spend much time focusing on radicalism." Most "are from Michigan or the Midwest, although that percentage decreases every year."

FINANCIAL AID: 269-337-7192 • E-MAIL: ADMISSION@KZOO.EDU • WEBSITE: WWW.KZOO.EDU

THE PRINCETON REVIEW SAYS

Admissions

Very important factors considered include: Academic GPA, rigor of secondary school record, extracurricular activities, volunteer work, work experience. *Important factors considered include:* Application essay, recommendation(s), standardized test scores. *Other factors considered include:* Alumni/ae relation, character/personal qualities, first generation, geographical residence, interview, level of applicant's interest, racial/ethnic status, talent/ability. SAT or ACT required; ACT with writing component required. TOEFL required of all international applicants. High school diploma is required and GED is accepted. *Academic units required:* 4 English, 3 mathematics, 3 science, 3 foreign language, 2 social studies, 2 history. *Academic units recommended:* 4 English, 4 mathematics, 4 science, 4 foreign language, 2 social studies, 2 history.

Financial Aid

Students should submit: FAFSA, CSS/Financial Aid PROFILE. The Princeton Review suggests that all financial aid forms be submitted as soon as possible after January 1. *Need-based scholarships/grants offered:* Federal Pell, SEOG, state scholarships/grants, private scholarships, the school's own gift aid. *Loan aid offered:* Direct Subsidized Stafford, Direct Unsubsidized Stafford, Direct PLUS, Federal Perkins. Applicants will be notified of awards on a rolling basis beginning March 21. Federal Work-Study Program available. Institutional employment available. Off-campus job opportunities are good.

The Inside Word

Kalamazoo admissions officers work hard to find good matches for the school's unique K-Plan. Applicants who demonstrate creativity, the ability to self-motivate, and ambition fit the bill. Solid academics and strong standardized test scores are also pretty much required; admissions are very competitive here. The arts play a central role on the Kalamazoo campus, so if you have special talent in art, theater, music, or writing, by all means submit a portfolio along with your application.

THE SCHOOL SAYS ". . ."

From the Admissions Office

"Anyone can pursue any component of the K-Plan at any college, but it is rare to see the purposeful integration and high participation rate found at Kalamazoo. During the past fifty years, 85 percent of our graduates have formally studied in another country while 80 percent have completed an internship or externship, and 100 percent complete a senior project. Our students often pursue international internships and senior project experiences, in addition to their planned study abroad terms. Also, Kalamazoo is one of the few selective liberal arts colleges to be found in a city—the Kalamazoo metro area has a population of approximately 225,000 with the advantage of being near a university of nearly 30,000 students. It is a diverse and vibrant community with wonderful access to the arts, athletics, service-learning, and community-service opportunities. We are a small and personal college with bigger opportunities.

"An SAT or ACT score is required for admission; SAT Subject Tests are not. Students taking only the ACT must take the writing portion."

SELECTIVITY

Admissions Rating	**90**
# of applicants	2,225
% of applicants accepted	69
% of acceptees attending	24
# accepting a place on wait list	178
# admitted from wait list	11
# of early decision applicants	31
# accepted early decision	30

FRESHMAN PROFILE

Range SAT Critical Reading	560–680
Range SAT Math	550–670
Range SAT Writing	530–660
Range ACT Composite	25–30
Minimum paper TOEFL	550
Minimum web-based TOEFL	80
Average HS GPA	3.6
% graduated top 10% of class	47
% graduated top 25% of class	83
% graduated top 50% of class	99

DEADLINES

Early decision	
Deadline	11/10
Notification	11/20
Early action	
Deadline	11/20
Notification	12/20
Regular	
Priority	11/20
Deadline	2/1
Notification	4/1
Nonfall registration?	no

FINANCIAL FACTS

Financial Aid Rating	**86**
Annual tuition	$35,820
Room and board	$8,079
% needy frosh rec. need-based scholarship or grant aid	96
% needy UG rec. need-based scholarship or grant aid	98
% needy frosh rec. non-need-based scholarship or grant aid	91
% needy UG rec. non-need-based scholarship or grant aid	105
% needy frosh rec. need-based self-help aid	82
% needy UG rec. need-based self-help aid	87
% frosh rec. any financial aid	98
% UG rec. any financial aid	97
% UG borrow to pay for school	49
Average cumulative indebtedness	$24,586
% frosh need fully met	42
% ugrads need fully met	34
Average % of frosh need met	87
Average % of ugrad need met	86

KANSAS STATE UNIVERSITY

119 ANDERSON HALL, MANHATTAN, KS 66506 • ADMISSIONS: 785-532-6250 • FAX: 785-532-6393

CAMPUS LIFE

Quality of Life Rating	**99**
Fire Safety Rating	**64**
Green Rating	**79**
Type of school	public
Environment	town

STUDENTS

Total undergrad enrollment	18,753
% male/female	52/48
% from out of state	17
% from public high school	81
% frosh live on campus	48
# of fraternities	28
# of sororities	16
% African American	4
% Asian	1
% Caucasian	82
% Hispanic	5
% international	5
# of countries represented	102

SURVEY SAYS . . .

Students are friendly
Students get along with local community
Everyone loves the Wildcats

ACADEMICS

Academic Rating	**75**
% students returning for sophomore year	81
% students graduating within 4 years	26
% students graduating within 6 years	60
Calendar	semester
Student/faculty ratio	21:1
Profs interesting rating	78
Profs accessible rating	84
Most classes have	fewer than 10 students

MOST POPULAR MAJORS

animal sciences; business administration and management; elementary education and teaching

STUDENTS SAY ". . ."

Academics

Kansas State University is "all about providing a great education with tons of opportunities at an affordable cost." The low in-state tuition is the major reason many end up here, but the strong academics and plethora of resources are just as a big a draw. "Everyone wants to work together to accomplish as much as possible, which is a wonderful environment to learn in," says a student. Despite its size, K-State "still has a small-town, welcoming feeling" and "a family atmosphere that the whole university buys into," and the institution "shows each student, faculty, or staff just how appreciated and important they are to the university."

Professors are "extremely knowledgeable," "know how to relate the course information well," and make themselves available outside of class. Not only are they "welcoming and willing to help whenever you need it," they are also "doing outstanding research in their fields." "When I visited K-State, I realized as a Wildcat I would have all the opportunities of a large university without feeling like a number," says a student. In providing so many chances for students to get real-life experience, most feel that they "enter the working world well-equipped."

With such a pervasive focus on community, students say that "you'll usually be only a few degrees of separation from any other person." The long history of Kansas State University (students wear purple all the time, since "there's a lot of Wildcat pride across campus") is "something that you can't get anywhere else." Some facilities "could receive a boost," though, as "there are a lot of great buildings on campus, but there are some classrooms that need an update." At the end of the day, K-State "is all about putting students first, and they put you first as soon as you become a freshman."

Life

Manhattan, Kansas, is "the perfect college town—not too big, not too small." There are lots of student discounts, "delicious restaurants, and quirky gift shops," and on the weekends you will find most students in the beloved Aggieville, the restaurant, bar, and shopping district. "Aggieville is the place to go and shop, socialize, and party!" says one student enthusiastically. Manhattan really comes to life during football games, and "the atmosphere is at its peak during these days." "The amount of alumni who come back for the games is incredibly, and the noise that fills the student section is intense," says a student.

Outside of sports, students hit up the local attractions that draw a younger crowd, as well as "the many UPC Events help on campus," such as "one dollar movies on the weekends, dances within the residence halls, and crafts at the union." The school has more than 250 student organizations to get involved in, from religious organizations to athletic clubs; "There is something for everyone here at K-State, and if we don't have it, start it." The Greek system is also "very strong," and "there is never a week when there is not an event happening around campus."

Student Body

The typical student at K-State is first and foremost friendly and "wildly passionate about being a Wildcat." "It is nearly impossible to walk clear across campus without seeing a friendly face," says a student. As most people at this "very Anglo-dominated campus" are Kansans, there is a strong Midwestern vibe amongst these "down-to-earth, family-oriented people," all of whom "consider success in college a very important aspect of their lives." Everyone is "pumped about our sports and traditions"—football is understandably big here—and most people "sport school colors/mascot on a weekly basis.

FINANCIAL AID: 785-532-6420 • E-MAIL: K-STATE@K-STATE.EDU • WEBSITE: WWW.K-STATE.EDU

THE PRINCETON REVIEW SAYS

Admissions

Very important factors considered include: Class rank, academic GPA, rigor of secondary school record, standardized test scores. *Other factors considered include:* Recommendation(s). ACT with or without writing component accepted. High school diploma is required and GED is accepted. *Academic units recommended:* 4 English, 3 mathematics, 3 science (0 science labs), 3 social studies, 1 computer technology.

Financial Aid

Students should submit: FAFSA. The Princeton Review suggests that all financial aid forms be submitted as soon as possible after January 1. *Need-based scholarships/grants offered:* Federal Pell, SEOG, state scholarships/grants, private scholarships, the school's own gift aid. *Loan aid offered:* Direct Subsidized Stafford, Direct Unsubsidized Stafford, Direct PLUS, Federal Perkins, college/university loans from institutional funds, alternative student loans. Applicants will be notified of awards on a rolling basis beginning April 1. Federal Work-Study Program available. Institutional employment available. Off-campus job opportunities are good.

The Inside Word

Though K-State is chock full of strong students, admission is refreshingly straightforward. Basically, get a 21 on the ACT (980 on the CR + M sections of the SAT) or graduate in the top third of your high school class, and you're in. If you're a Kansas resident, a third way to get accepted is to complete a college-bound curriculum with a 2.0 GPA. Non-residents need at least a 2.5.

THE SCHOOL SAYS ". . ."

From the Admissions Office

"Kansas State University offers strong academic programs, a lively intellectual atmosphere, a friendly campus community, and an environment where students achieve: K-State's total of Rhodes, Marshall, Truman, Goldwater, and Udall scholars in the past twenty-five years ranks first in the nation among state universities. In the Goldwater competition, only Princeton, Harvard, and Duke have produced more winners. K-State's Student Governing Association has been recognized several times as one of the nation's top student governments. As part of K-State's shared governance, they allocate $15 million a year for programs and services for K-State students. K-State's Black Student Union was named the Best in the Big 12 by the Big 12 Council on Black Student Government in 2009. Research facilities include the Konza Prairie, the world's largest tall grass prairie preserve, and the Biosecurity Research Institute. K-State is the research hub for the world's top scientists in animal health and food safety.

"Open House, held each spring, is a great way to explore K-State's more than 250 majors and options and 400 student organizations.

"Kansas State University requires ACT or SAT scores to complete a freshman applicant file. The SAT or ACT writing score is not considered for admission to the university. Students may submit scores from any or all test dates. The best score from any one test date is used."

SELECTIVITY	
Admissions Rating	**76**
# of applicants	8,268
% of applicants accepted	99
% of acceptees attending	44

FRESHMAN PROFILE	
Range ACT Composite	21–27
Average HS GPA	3.5
% graduated top 10% of class	20
% graduated top 25% of class	45
% graduated top 50% of class	76

DEADLINES	
Nonfall registration?	yes

FINANCIAL FACTS	
Financial Aid Rating	**76**
Annual in-state tuition	$6,936
Annual out-state tuition	$18,402
Room and board	$7,198
Required fees	$721
Books and supplies	$1,100
% needy frosh rec. need-based scholarship or grant aid	67
% needy UG rec. need-based scholarship or grant aid	61
% needy frosh rec. non-need-based scholarship or grant aid	73
% needy UG rec. non-need-based scholarship or grant aid	46
% needy frosh rec. need-based self-help aid	75
% needy UG rec. need-based self-help aid	82
% UG borrow to pay for school	54
Average cumulative indebtedness	$22,633
% frosh need fully met	25
% ugrads need fully met	20
Average % of frosh need met	86
Average % of ugrad need met	83

KENYON COLLEGE

KENYON COLLEGE, ADMISSION OFFICE, GAMBIER, OH 43022-9623 • ADMISSIONS: 740-427-5776 • FAX: 740-427-5770

CAMPUS LIFE

Quality of Life Rating	**85**
Fire Safety Rating	**65**
Green Rating	**88**
Type of school	private
Environment	rural

STUDENTS

Total undergrad enrollment	1,647
% male/female	46/54
% from out of state	85
% from public high school	53
% frosh live on campus	100
# of fraternities	7
# of sororities	4
% African American	3
% Asian	6
% Caucasian	79
% Hispanic	5
% Native American	1
% international	3
# of countries represented	40

SURVEY SAYS . . .

No one cheats
Lab facilities are great
Athletic facilities are great
Students are friendly
Campus feels safe
Students are happy
Musical organizations are popular
Lots of beer drinking

ACADEMICS

Academic Rating	**95**
% students returning for sophomore year	94
% students graduating within 4 years	83
% students graduating within 6 years	87
Calendar	semester
Student/faculty ratio	10:1
Profs interesting rating	98
Profs accessible rating	96
Most classes have	10–19 students

MOST POPULAR MAJORS

English language and literature; political science and government; psychology

APPLICANTS ALSO LOOK AT AND OFTEN PREFER

Brown University, Wiliams College, Amherst College

AND SOMETIMES PREFER

Bowdoin College, Middlebury College, Carleton College, Swarthmore College, Oberlin College, Grinnell College

STUDENTS SAY ". . ."

Academics

A Kenyon education provides undergraduates with an "opportunity to learn in a creative and caring atmosphere" and encourages students "to think about things in different, innovative, and sometimes daring ways." The college has "an interesting combination of competitive academics and down-to-earth, relaxed students." One of Kenyon's strengths is "interdisciplinary concentration programs, which allow you to create a meaningful synthesis of knowledge across different fields quite effectively." A math major concurs, adding, "Almost every class has challenged me to think about things from a different perspective and has opened my mind to subjects in all aspects of life." Though the workload is "fairly substantial," it's not so "overwhelming so that you can't do anything [aside from] work." Perhaps most importantly, the professors are "intelligent and stimulating, encourage discussion, and constantly [ask] provoking questions." Moreover, they "really go that extra mile" and often "invite [students] over for dinner, bring snacks to class, plan extracurricular departmental events, and are always willing to help with schoolwork." Simply put, "The professors are what make Kenyon so great." And though some undergrads grumble that the administration is "for the most part anti-Greek," most students give them high marks as well. They are "friendly," "visible on campus," and often "seek the opinions of students when making [administrative] decisions."

Life

Since hometown Gambier doesn't provide much "besides corn fields," life at Kenyon really does revolve around the campus. Fortunately, there are always a myriad of events of which to take advantage, from "Kenyon Film Society movie screenings" to "various theater productions, a cappella concerts, and speakers." For those interested in the social scene, "The Greek system facilitates most of the parties on campus, but that doesn't mean that Kenyon has a typical frat culture; you don't ever have to worry about 'getting in' to a party." A psych major agrees, adding, "The social environment is inclusive and fun—most parties have different student bands playing a wide variety of music (from electronic music to Motown) and everyone is invited." Of course, should the typical fare start getting old, Kenyon students are more than happy to find creative ways to have fun. As one pleased junior shares, "We've had midnight sledding parties, swims in the river when it's warm, 'Project Runway' design challenges, movie nights, bike rides through farm country to the local farmers', market [and] fort-building parties." When students do feel the urge to get off campus, they often "go to Wal-Mart," "restaurants in [nearby] Mt. Vernon" or head to Columbus (roughly forty-five minutes away) for "some shopping and culture."

Student Body

On the surface, it appears as though Kenyon students can be divided into two categories: "a North Face, L.L. Bean–wearing, outdoorsy type, or a hipster in skinny jeans, flannel, and boots." "Of course," a classics major assures us, "there are plenty of others who don't fit distinctly into these groups." Indeed, "We have many 'alpha-males' who play rugby by day and are in musicals by night." All of this is indicative of a campus where "everyone finds a comfortable place to fit in." Or, as one English and Spanish double-major bluntly states, "We all get along—we're in the middle of nowhere so we kinda have to." One common trait these "hardworking, intelligent" students do possess is "a love of learning about new things." As a sophomore expounds, "I love classics and Socrates, and I can discuss with my best friend why I think Athens is better than Rome, and she'll argue back." Yes, many undergrads here are self-professed "nerds" and proud of it. As one student sums up, Kenyon manages to attract "all of the quirky, cool smart kids from your high school."

FINANCIAL AID: 740-427-5240 • E-MAIL: ADMISSIONS@KENYON.EDU • WEBSITE: WWW.KENYON.EDU

THE PRINCETON REVIEW SAYS

Admissions

Very important factors considered include: Application essay, academic GPA, recommendation(s), rigor of secondary school record, character/personal qualities. *Important factors considered include:* Class rank, standardized test scores, extracurricular activities, interview, level of applicant's interest, talent/ability. *Other factors considered include:* Alumni/ae relation, first generation, geographical residence, racial/ethnic status, state residency, volunteer work, work experience. SAT or ACT required; ACT with or without writing component accepted. TOEFL required of all international applicants. High school diploma is required and GED is accepted. *Academic units required:* 4 English, 3 mathematics, 3 science (3 science labs), 3 foreign language, 1 social studies, 2 history, 3 academic electives. *Academic units recommended:* 4 English, 4 mathematics, 4 science (3 science labs), 4 foreign language, 1 social studies, 3 history, 3 academic electives.

Financial Aid

Students should submit: FAFSA, CSS/Financial Aid PROFILE, noncustodial PROFILE. Regular filing deadline is February 15. The Princeton Review suggests that all financial aid forms be submitted as soon as possible after January 1. *Need-based scholarships/grants offered:* Federal Pell, SEOG, state scholarships/grants, private scholarships, the school's own gift aid. *Loan aid offered:* Direct Subsidized Stafford, Direct Unsubsidized Stafford, Direct PLUS, Federal Perkins, college/university loans from institutional funds. Applicants will be notified of awards on or about April 1. Federal Work-Study Program available. Institutional employment available. Highest amount earned per year from on-campus jobs $1,255. Off-campus job opportunities are poor.

The Inside Word

In terms of admissions selectivity, Kenyon is of the first order of selective, small, Midwestern, liberal arts schools. Kenyon shares a lot of application and admit overlap with other schools in this niche, and the choice for many students comes down to "best fit." As Kenyon is a writing-intensive institution, applicants should expect that all written material submitted to the school in the admissions process will be scrutinized. Revise and proofread accordingly.

THE SCHOOL SAYS ". . ."

From the Admissions Office

"Students and alumni alike think of Kenyon as a place that fosters 'learning in the company of friends.' While faculty expectations are rigorous and the work challenging, the academic atmosphere is cooperative, not competitive. Indications of intellectual curiosity and passion for learning, more than just high grades and test scores, are what we look for in applications. Important as well are demonstrated interests in non-academic pursuits, whether in athletics, the arts, writing, or another passion. Life in this small college community is fueled by the talents and enthusiasm of our students, so the admission staff seeks students who have a range of talents and interests.

"The high school transcript, recommendations, the personal statement, and answers on the supplement are of primary importance in reviewing preparedness and fit. Standardized tests (SAT or ACT) are of secondary importance."

SELECTIVITY

Admissions Rating	96
# of applicants	4,272
% of applicants accepted	33
% of acceptees attending	33
# accepting a place on wait list	1,152
# admitted from wait list	15
# of early decision applicants	405
# accepted early decision	221

FRESHMAN PROFILE

Range SAT Critical Reading	640–740
Range SAT Math	610–690
Range SAT Writing	640–730
Range ACT Composite	28–32
Minimum paper TOEFL	600
Minimum web-based TOEFL	100
Average HS GPA	3.9
% graduated top 10% of class	59
% graduated top 25% of class	86
% graduated top 50% of class	98

DEADLINES

Early decision	
Deadline	11/15
Notification	12/15
Regular	
Priority	1/15
Deadline	1/15
Notification	4/1
Nonfall registration?	no

FINANCIAL FACTS

Financial Aid Rating	91
Annual tuition	$42,780
Room and board	$10,340
Required fees	$1,480
Books and supplies	$1,800
% needy frosh rec. need-based scholarship or grant aid	99
% needy UG rec. need-based scholarship or grant aid	98
% needy frosh rec. non-need-based scholarship or grant aid	22
% needy UG rec. non-need-based scholarship or grant aid	17
% needy frosh rec. need-based self-help aid	73
% needy UG rec. need-based self-help aid	81
% frosh rec. any financial aid	
% UG rec. any financial aid	
% UG borrow to pay for school	55
Average cumulative indebtedness	$19,480
% frosh need fully met	63
% ugrads need fully met	60
Average % of frosh need met	98
Average % of ugrad need met	98

Knox College

2 East South Street, Campus Box 148, Galesburg, IL 61401 • Admissions: 309-341-7100 • Fax: 309-341-7070

CAMPUS LIFE

Quality of Life Rating	77
Fire Safety Rating	83
Green Rating	72
Type of school	private
Environment	town

STUDENTS

Total undergrad enrollment	1,405
% male/female	42/58
% from out of state	43
% from public high school	72
% frosh live on campus	99
# of fraternities	6
# of sororities	4
% African American	5
% Asian	5
% Caucasian	66
% Hispanic	8
% international	9
# of countries represented	37

SURVEY SAYS . . .

No one cheats
Students are friendly
College radio is popular
Theater is popular
Political activism is popular

ACADEMICS

Academic Rating	93
% students returning for sophomore year	89
% students graduating within 4 years	70
% students graduating within 6 years	78
Calendar	trimester
Student/faculty ratio	12:1
Profs interesting rating	93
Profs accessible rating	92
Most classes have	10–19 students
Most lab/discussion sessions have	10–19 students

MOST POPULAR MAJORS

economics; education; political science and government

APPLICANTS ALSO LOOK AT AND SOMETIMES PREFER

Beloit College, Lawrence University, Grinnell College

AND RARELY PREFER

Loyola University of Chicago, Macalester College, Northwestern University, University of Chicago, Washington University in St. Louis

STUDENTS SAY ". . ."

Academics

Students say that Knox College enjoys a "great academic reputation" for its dedication to providing a "well-rounded liberal arts program" that "values independent initiative," while "staying in tune with its roots as a progressive and accessible institution." The college has a saying about students having "the freedom to flourish." The institution gives everyone "the appropriate space to grow on their own." "I knew that I would be allowed to be myself, choose the classes that I felt would have the most influence on my education and prepare me for the future." Students are highly encouraged to take classes outside of their majors. Undergraduates are "commonly studying two vastly different subjects and allowing them to merge into one interdisciplinary interest." Knox does have "one of the best creative writing programs in the country," as well as the Peace Corps Preparatory Program—offered solely through Knox. The academic trimester system, comprised of three classes each term, provides students with "a semester's worth of course work in a ten-week period." Many in the student body believe that this arrangement "promotes better study habits and more attention focused on each class," which are "tough and require a lot of time studying, reading, writing, and thinking." "You don't come to Knox if you want to shy away from class discussion," and professors "concentrate on the student having good critical thinking skills." Students are pleased to find that "you are academically challenged without fierce competition." "I've never had an easy professor, but I've always had reasonable ones." Projects and presentations are common; if tests are given, there is an honor code, and "They trust you not to cheat." The faculty and administration are spoken of highly, and they "not only encourage the students to take charge and make change, but they listen and act on the student body's opinions."

Life

Popular manners of relaxation and recreation include intramural sports, campus organizations, and "artistic expression, be it poetry, visual art, performance art, music." Students "go to parties, play games, dance, etc., just like any other college campus. The difference is, our fraternity parties are open to the entire campus and do not serve alcohol." Parties here "are places where you generally know everyone there, you have a good time and no one steals your coat or purse." Undergrads here are also very creative. "When we want to do something fun we typically organize it ourselves." A much-anticipated event is "Flunk Day, a day every spring when classes are canceled and the entire campus goes out on the lawn and plays games, eats great food and enjoys free entertainment." Union Board "brings films, entertainers, concerts, and other groups to campus, including Second City," and the Gizmo is "one of the best places to socialize and eat some late night food." Wandering off-campus a bit is also fun. Undergrads say "Galesburg is a charming town...you just have to look a little bit." "McGillacuddy's has amazing burgers, and Knox's music department hosts Jazz Nights there on Thursdays." Students enjoy the town's intimate, relaxing atmosphere. "Good coffee shops, a really nice park with a lake, and many beautiful old historic buildings," and "an annual Chocolate Festival." A twenty-four-hour diner is nearby, and "Students can also drive to Peoria or take the train to Chicago."

Student Body

Knox is praised throughout the campus for its "support for first-generation college students, which really reflects Knox's history and values." "You'll meet a lot of people very fast, and by the end of your first term you'll already be good friends with a pretty big portion of the student body." Many undergrads portray themselves as "weird," with variations on a common theme: "We call it the "Knox awkward." "The smart but sort of socially awkward kids in high school," what they describe as their social "Knoxwardness." "Everyone at Knox is a little eccentric, but we embrace each other's differences." "Students fit in by being themselves, no matter who they are." As one student perceptively notes, there is a "highly diverse combination of creative, intellectual minds here. It's as if every person here is some highly distinctive character from an artsy film." Another puts it a bit more succinctly: "Thank you college admission gods."

FINANCIAL AID: 309-341-7149 • E-MAIL: ADMISSION@KNOX.EDU • WEBSITE: WWW.KNOX.EDU

THE PRINCETON REVIEW SAYS

Admissions

Very important factors considered include: Academic GPA, rigor of secondary school record. *Important factors considered include:* Class rank, application essay, recommendation(s), character/personal qualities. *Other factors considered include:* Standardized test scores, alumni/ae relation, extracurricular activities, first generation, geographical residence, interview, level of applicant's interest, racial/ethnic status, state residency, talent/ability, volunteer work. ACT with or without writing component accepted. TOEFL required of all international applicants. High school diploma is required and GED is accepted. *Academic units recommended:* 4 English, 4 mathematics, 4 science (3 science labs), 3 foreign language, 2 social studies, 2 history.

Financial Aid

Students should submit: FAFSA, institution's own financial aid form. The Princeton Review suggests that all financial aid forms be submitted as soon as possible after January 1. *Need-based scholarships/grants offered:* Federal Pell, SEOG, state scholarships/grants, private scholarships, the school's own gift aid. *Loan aid offered:* Direct Subsidized Stafford, Direct Unsubsidized Stafford, Direct PLUS, Federal Perkins, college/university loans from institutional funds. Applicants will be notified of awards on a rolling basis beginning March 15. Federal Work-Study Program available. Institutional employment available. Highest amount earned per year from on-campus jobs $5,479. Off-campus job opportunities are fair.

The Inside Word

Knox draws students from nearly fifty countries and almost fifty states—with a student body of only 1,400, diversity is hugely important here. Admission standards are high, and prospective students are viewed both qualitatively and quantitatively. Three out of every four freshman were ranked in the top quarter of their high school classes.

THE SCHOOL SAYS ". . ."

From the Admissions Office

"Knox was founded on the idea that education has the power to confer a kind of freedom—what we've come to call 'freedom to flourish.' On the surface, 'freedom to flourish' is a simple and powerful concept—it is the knowledge and skills one needs to live a rewarding personal, professional, and civic life. But 'freedom to flourish' also has more subtle meaning that touches on how education happens at Knox.

"Most schools ask what you want to study and give you a checklist of courses needed for that degree. Knox asks, 'What do you want to know, and what do you want to do with that knowledge?' Within the context of the goals and milestones of one of our many majors, you and your advisor will develop a personalized educational plan of classes, internships, off-campus study, and independent research projects that meet the agenda you set for yourself. In this sense, a Knox education is an act of imagination, an act of entrepreneurship, an act of freedom.'

"That self-direction doesn't end in advising sessions and course selection. You'll be encouraged to bring your own interests and perspective to every class you take, and you'll be challenged to apply what you learn to the world around you. In the end you will learn how to set goals, how to figure out what you need to know to achieve those goals, and how to identify and collaborate with mentors who can help you along the way. That is 'freedom to flourish.'

"At Knox, you'll never be a number. Knox reviews each application holistically, fully considering a student's academic record, course selection, and performance (grades), as well as essays, recommendations, interviews, and other accomplishments. As a result, the submission of SAT or ACT scores is optional for most applicants."

SELECTIVITY	
Admissions Rating	**86**
# of applicants	2,385
% of applicants accepted	72
% of acceptees attending	20
# accepting a place on wait list	41
# admitted from wait list	5

FRESHMAN PROFILE	
Range SAT Critical Reading	580–690
Range SAT Math	570–690
Range SAT Writing	560–670
Range ACT Composite	25–30
Minimum paper TOEFL	550
Minimum web-based TOEFL	80
Average HS GPA	3.4
% graduated top 10% of class	33
% graduated top 25% of class	69
% graduated top 50% of class	96

DEADLINES	
Early action	
Deadline	12/1
Notification	12/31
Regular	
Deadline	2/1
Notification	3/31
Nonfall registration?	no

FINANCIAL FACTS	
Financial Aid Rating	**88**
Annual tuition	$36,138
Room and board	$7,932
Required fees	$354
Books and supplies	$900
% needy frosh rec. need-based scholarship or grant aid	99
% needy UG rec. need-based scholarship or grant aid	99
% needy frosh rec. non-need-based scholarship or grant aid	17
% needy UG rec. non-need-based scholarship or grant aid	13
% needy frosh rec. need-based self-help aid	83
% needy UG rec. need-based self-help aid	85
% frosh rec. any financial aid	99
% UG rec. any financial aid	98
% UG borrow to pay for school	66
Average cumulative indebtedness	$28,169
% frosh need fully met	31
% ugrads need fully met	29
Average % of frosh need met	90
Average % of ugrad need met	88

LAFAYETTE COLLEGE

118 MARKLE HALL, EASTON, PA 18042 • ADMISSIONS: 610-330-5100 • FAX: 610-330-5355

CAMPUS LIFE

Quality of Life Rating	**83**
Fire Safety Rating	**86**
Green Rating	**95**
Type of school	private
Environment	suburban

STUDENTS

Total undergrad enrollment	2,478
% male/female	53/47
% from out of state	79
% from public high school	68
% frosh live on campus	100
# of fraternities	4
# of sororities	6
% African American	5
% Asian	4
% Caucasian	66
% Hispanic	5
% international	6
# of countries represented	40

SURVEY SAYS . . .

Lab facilities are great
Great computer facilities
Athletic facilities are great
Career services are great
School is well run
Campus feels safe

ACADEMICS

Academic Rating	**90**
% students returning for sophomore year	95
% students graduating within 4 years	85
% students graduating within 6 years	88
Calendar	semester
Student/faculty ratio	10:1
Profs interesting rating	86
Profs accessible rating	94
Most classes have	10–19 students
Most lab/discussion sessions have	10–19 students

APPLICANTS ALSO LOOK AT AND OFTEN PREFER

Princeton University, Boston College, Tufts University, Cornell University, Johns Hopkins University

AND SOMETIMES PREFER

Bucknell University, Villanova University, Colgate University, Lehigh University

AND RARELY PREFER

Rensselaer Polytechnic Institute, Pennsylvania State University—University Park, Trinity College (CT), Franklin & Marshall College

STUDENTS SAY ". . ."

Academics

Lafayette College is "a small, prestigious liberal arts school" that offers "a welcoming community that embraces a rigorous and well-respected education." Thanks to the "top-quality engineering education," many students say, "Lafayette is your classic liberal arts college with a twist" and point to the "vast array of research opportunities" available to undergrads. The college "prides itself on student/faculty relationships," and students say, "Each student is provided with the resources he or she needs to really shine and be recognized for his or her achievements and talents." An international affairs major says, "Whether you're an engineer, a premed student, or an art major, there is a great academic program and an embracing group of people waiting for you at Lafayette." Overall the professors get high marks because "their office doors are always open," and they're "the kind of people who learn your name and never forget it." Students say, for the most part, "Professors are interesting and encourage class discussion, which is a staple of Lafayette classes," and add, "It's not very common to hear that someone doesn't like one of their professors at Lafayette." Generally, "Classes are challenging but manageable, if you put in the time," but students gripe, "The class registration system is dicey."

Life

At Lafayette, the "campus is gorgeous," and students say you feel the "close atmosphere of the school" after "immediately walking onto the campus." Overall students feel, "The campus community is very supportive," and a civil engineering major says, "The family atmosphere adds to the education and makes Lafayette feel more like home than school." With "over 200 clubs and organizations on campus," there "is something that will fit everyone's lifestyle and hobbies," and when it comes to their Division I athletics, "Students radiate school pride." Lafayette boasts a "great career center due to the close ties alumni have with the college," and career services are offered to students during all four years of their undergraduate study. A senior says, "Being a small school, students have direct access to administrative offices and deans," and the staff is described as "extremely welcoming." While some say "the facilities are first rate" and improving, others complain, "Certain dorms could use renovation," especially since students are required to live on campus for their first three years. However, many agree that the "cafeteria food could use some improvement."

Student Body

Lafayette students are "passionate and driven" and "tend to be athletic, very preppy, and serious about their education." A sophomore says, "The vast majority of students here are middle- to upper-class Caucasians from the tristate area," but another adds, "Every kind of crowd imaginable is present on campus; whether you're a hipster or a prepster, you'll find a group you're comfortable in." Regardless, some students wish for "better integration of the different cultures represented at school," and say, "More support for the LGBTQ community would be a pleasant change." Many students are "involved with Greek life," and some feel that those "not involved in Greek life or sports can be isolated"; however, an economics major notes, "There are definitely cliques, but nothing even close to the high school scale." On weekends, most students stay on campus, and it's commonly held that "there is quite a bit of drinking," even though "campus safety is very strict and off-campus housing is limited to seniors so the party scene is limited." Many feel there's a "large disconnect between [the] administration and students especially on social issues like the alcohol policy," and say, "instead of trying to keep people safe, they continually try to bust people."

FINANCIAL AID: 610-330-5055 • E-MAIL: ADMISSIONS@LAFAYETTE.EDU • WEBSITE: WWW.LAFAYETTE.EDU

THE PRINCETON REVIEW SAYS

Admissions

Very important factors considered include: Academic GPA, rigor of secondary school record. *Important factors considered include:* Class rank, application essay, recommendation(s), standardized test scores, character/personal qualities, extracurricular activities, talent/ability. *Other factors considered include:* Alumni/ae relation, first generation, geographical residence, interview, level of applicant's interest, racial/ethnic status, volunteer work, work experience. SAT or ACT required; ACT with writing component required. TOEFL required of all international applicants. High school diploma or equivalent is not required. *Academic units recommended:* 4 English, 3 mathematics, 2 science (2 science labs), 2 foreign language, 5 academic electives.

Financial Aid

Students applying for need-based aid must submit: FAFSA, CSS/Financial Aid PROFILE, tax data, and, if applicable, noncustodial PROFILE and related tax data. Regular Decision filing deadline is March 1. The Princeton Review suggests that all financial aid forms be submitted as soon as possible after January 1. *Need-based scholarships/grants offered:* Federal Pell, SEOG, state scholarships/grants, private scholarships, the school's own gift aid. *Loan aid offered:* Direct Subsidized Stafford and Unsubsidized Student Loans, Direct PLUS Loan, Federal Perkins Loan. Regular Decision Applicants will be notified of awards on or about April 1. Federal Work-Study Program available. Institutional employment is available. Off-campus job opportunities may also be available. For information about requirements, deadlines, and more, visit finaid.lafayette.edu.

The Inside Word

Lafayette College takes into account a variety of factors when evaluating prospective students. Emphasis is placed on an applicant's performance in secondary school, the quality of that education, and the class standing. The admissions committee also values a commitment to social awareness and potential for leadership as exhibited through extracurricular activities. The results of standardized tests are recommended but not required for admission.

THE SCHOOL SAYS ". . ."

From the Admissions Office

"Lafayette offers academic choices as broad and diverse as universities many times our size. Students and alumni say our curriculum—with extraordinary breadth and depth for an undergraduate college—is a key strength.

"At Lafayette, education is a dynamic and engaged process—not passive. Students are encouraged to cross traditional academic boundaries to connect and integrate knowledge from different fields in the humanities, social sciences, natural sciences, and engineering and to work together to approach intellectual challenges and wider-world problems from multiple perspectives.

"Our approach is active and global, working in communities locally, nationally, and internationally. Global opportunities range from faculty-led semester programs to concentrated interim session courses to international service projects. Students who experience immersion in international settings or work in student-faculty teams to address global challenges have an advantage in advanced studies and employment after they graduate. These experiences are vital for citizenship and leadership in an increasingly interconnected, globalized world.

"Lafayette is a vibrant environment in which to explore and grow. With more than 250 clubs and activities—including the arts, Division I sports, and community service, to name just a few—students have many ways to balance work and play, develop leadership skills, and have fun. And because of our location, just seventy miles from New York City, Lafayette offers significant opportunities to connect with prominent leaders in many fields who visit campus and to take advantage of the major artistic, cultural, and financial centers of the Eastern United States."

SELECTIVITY

Admissions Rating	95
# of applicants	5,716
% of applicants accepted	40
% of acceptees attending	28
# accepting a place on wait list	1,559
# of early decision applicants	488
# accepted early decision	317

FRESHMAN PROFILE

Range SAT Critical Reading	590–680
Range SAT Math	620–700
Range SAT Writing	580–680
Range ACT Composite	26–31
Minimum paper TOEFL	550
Average HS GPA	3.5
% graduated top 10% of class	65
% graduated top 25% of class	89
% graduated top 50% of class	98

DEADLINES

Early decision	
Deadline	2/1
Regular	
Deadline	1/15
Notification	4/1
Nonfall registration?	yes

FINANCIAL FACTS

Financial Aid Rating	93
Annual tuition	$41,920
Room and board	$12,708
Required fees	$360
Books and supplies	$1,000
% needy frosh rec. need-based scholarship or grant aid	96
% needy UG rec. need-based scholarship or grant aid	96
% needy frosh rec. non-need-based scholarship or grant aid	28
% needy UG rec. non-need-based scholarship or grant aid	25
% needy frosh rec. need-based self-help aid	93
% needy UG rec. need-based self-help aid	90
% frosh rec. any financial aid	53
% UG rec. any financial aid	49
% UG borrow to pay for school	55
Average cumulative indebtedness	$24,441
% frosh need fully met	85
% ugrads need fully met	88
Average % of frosh need met	99
Average % of ugrad need met	99

LAKE FOREST COLLEGE

555 NORTH SHERIDAN ROAD, LAKE FOREST, IL 60045 • ADMISSIONS: 847-735-5000 • FAX: 847-735-6291

CAMPUS LIFE

Quality of Life Rating	**75**
Fire Safety Rating	**68**
Green Rating	**68**
Type of school	private
Environment	village

STUDENTS

Total undergrad enrollment	1,483
% male/female	41/59
% from out of state	43
% from public high school	68
% frosh live on campus	89
# of fraternities	2
# of sororities	4
% African American	6
% Asian	4
% Caucasian	61
% Hispanic	12
% international	12
# of countries represented	78

SURVEY SAYS . . .

Great computer facilities
Great food on campus
Campus feels safe
Lots of beer drinking
Hard liquor is popular

ACADEMICS

Academic Rating	**90**
% students returning for sophomore year	84
% students graduating within 4 years	59
% students graduating within 6 years	68
Calendar	semester
Student/faculty ratio	13:1
Profs interesting rating	88
Profs accessible rating	90
Most classes have	10–19 students
Most lab/discussion sessions have	10–19 students

MOST POPULAR MAJORS

business/commerce; communication studies/speech communication and rhetoric; English language and literature

APPLICANTS ALSO LOOK AT AND OFTEN PREFER

University of Illinois at Urbana-Champaign

STUDENTS SAY ". . ."

Academics

Lake Forest provides a broad-ranging general education curriculum. One student points out, "The teachers really challenge you and generally are really nice and easy to access." The academic breadth at Lake Forest College is both challenging and inspiring. Another student adds, "The small school size means administration can help you, and they actually do. The class sizes and teachers won't let anyone hide or get away with spotty work." The emphasis is giving each student an individual and well-rounded education in the liberal arts, and this cross-disciplinary education is accessible because of the attentive faculty and staff. A current student tells us, "Lake Forest is a solid college with great financial aid." Another facet of the learning experience that Lake Forest students appreciate is that the college provides and promotes numerous opportunities outside of the classroom. Studying abroad, internships, community service, and career development are all encouraged and presented across campus. Overall, the impression is that of "the world is at your fingertips and your campus experience should allow you to sample many options and explore and create in a supportive environment." Lake Forest's professors are by far its strongest asset. A sophomore tells us, "They're accessible, highly knowledgeable in their designated areas of expertise, and have very high expectations for student performance. Additionally, they encourage us as students to learn by doing as opposed to simply lecturing."

Life

When students consider Lake Forest, a word that might come to mind is 'balance.' One student explains, "The town of Lake Forest is not at all a college town, and you'd be hard-pressed to find anything more than a grocery store and a few places to eat. However, almost everything you need is on campus." The beautiful 107-acre campus is located thirty miles north of downtown Chicago, providing access to the city with the respite of a more laid-back town along the shore of Lake Michigan. "Chicago is a huge asset both socially and academically," says one student. "[It] is ever-changing and does not get dull." The school offers transit passes for a discounted price, and students visit the city often. A ten-minute walk will easily get you into the main part of town, and it is an easy train ride to Chicago, but equally attractive is that in the same ten minutes you can walk to the beach and enjoy the shores of Lake Michigan. A freshman describes, "Lake Michigan, and a beautiful beach, is only half a mile from campus, and the campus is beautiful especially in the fall and after the first snowfall." Another student sums it up nicely, saying, "At Lake Forest College, students get a world-class education and the skills they need to succeed in life while immersed in a school-spirit-rich campus lifestyle that doesn't compare to any other school."

Student Body

Student organizations are very strong at Lake Forest, and, therefore, there are always student- run events on campus that are frequented by the student body. "A typical Lake Forest student is usually pretty involved whether it is in a sport, club, theater, or music," says one sophomore. "Everyone usually finds a group that they fit into with friends with similar interests." Another student adds, "Everyone is different, and everyone fits in." Like any college, students say they can get, "Stressed out, but [are] generally upbeat. At this school it is considered normal to be in a thousand different clubs and extracurricular activities and to attend campus events and campus parties." A sophomore explains, "Life at my school can be very challenging because your classes will push you. However, there is still time for fun, and you will see a good number of your peers at social events on campus. One of the most common is the ACPs (All Campus Parties) that are held on Fridays and hosted by various student organizations." In the end, it all comes back to balance—and at Lake Forest students can cultivate the many experiences available into one productive adult life.

FINANCIAL AID: 847-735-5103 • E-MAIL: ADMISSIONS@LAKEFOREST.EDU • WEBSITE: WWW.LAKEFOREST.EDU

THE PRINCETON REVIEW SAYS

Admissions

Very important factors considered include: Academic GPA, recommendation(s), rigor of secondary school record, interview. *Important factors considered include:* Application essay, character/personal qualities, extracurricular activities, level of applicant's interest, talent/ability. *Other factors considered include:* Class rank, standardized test scores, alumni/ae relation, first generation, geographical residence, volunteer work, work experience. ACT with or without writing component accepted. Test optional. TOEFL required of all international applicants. High school diploma is required and GED is accepted. *Academic units required:* 4 English, 3 mathematics, 3 science (3 science labs), 2 foreign language, 2 social studies, 2 history, 3 academic electives. *Academic units recommended:* 4 English, 4 mathematics, 4 science (4 science labs), 4 foreign language, 2 social studies, 2 history, 3 academic electives, 1 honors or AP courses.

Financial Aid

Students should submit: FAFSA, institution's own financial aid form, federal income tax return. Regular filing deadline is May 1. The Princeton Review suggests that all financial aid forms be submitted as soon as possible after January 1. *Need-based scholarships/grants offered:* Federal Pell, SEOG, state scholarships/grants, private scholarships, the school's own gift aid. *Loan aid offered:* Direct Subsidized Stafford, Direct Unsubsidized Stafford, Direct PLUS, Federal Perkins, private loans. Applicants will be notified of awards on a rolling basis beginning February 1. Federal Work-Study Program available. Institutional employment available. Off-campus job opportunities are good.

The Inside Word

Lake Forest is small enough to give each application it receives close and careful consideration. Solid high school performers should have little difficulty gaining admission, but keep in mind that Lake Forest has a prep-school-at-the-college-level feel and likes to assess the whole candidate, not just grades and test scores. In fact, test scores are optional. Students can submit a graded essay instead.

THE SCHOOL SAYS ". . ."

From the Admissions Office

"Lake Forest College's beautiful 107-acre campus is located thirty miles north of downtown Chicago along the shore of Lake Michigan. Lake Forest has a long tradition of academic excellence and is known for its innovative curriculum. In addition to majors in the humanities, social sciences, and natural sciences, the college features programs of study in pre-law, premedicine, communication, business, finance, computer science, and still other practical areas. Abundant internships, research opportunities, personal guidance from professors, and connections to nearby Chicago also set Lake Forest apart. Students learn in a rigorous academic environment in small class settings where professors do all the teaching and also serve as advisors and mentors. Professors are accomplished scholars, published authors, and recipients of prestigious grants.

"Students represent nearly every state and seventy-eight countries around the world and international and ethnic minorities make up more than twenty-five percent of the student body. Together they comprise a learning community that prepares them to succeed in a global society. Just an hour's train ride away, Chicago offers students unique experiential learning opportunities, and professors regularly use the city's resources to complement coursework. The college's Center for Chicago Programs facilitates internships at chicago institutions as well as plans trips to the city's dozens of ethnic neighborhoods. More than sixty student groups provide a host of opportunities that develop leadership skills and enhance students' campus experience and post-college prospects. The college offers recreational music, art, and theater programs, as well as seventeen varsity sports and intramural and club sports."

SELECTIVITY

Admissions Rating	**89**
# of applicants	3,198
% of applicants accepted	54
% of acceptees attending	24
# of early decision applicants	79
# accepted early decision	47

FRESHMAN PROFILE

Range SAT Critical Reading	560–640
Range SAT Math	530–670
Range SAT Writing	550–630
Range ACT Composite	23–28
Minimum paper TOEFL	550
Average HS GPA	3.7
% graduated top 10% of class	33
% graduated top 25% of class	62
% graduated top 50% of class	90

DEADLINES

Early decision	
Deadline	12/1
Early action	
Deadline	12/1
Notification	1/20
Regular	
Priority	2/15
Notification	3/20
Nonfall registration?	yes

FINANCIAL FACTS

Financial Aid Rating	**91**
Annual tuition	$37,660
Room and board	$9,050
Required fees	$640
Books and supplies	$1,000
% needy frosh rec. need-based scholarship or grant aid	100
% needy UG rec. need-based scholarship or grant aid	100
% needy frosh rec. need-based self-help aid	83
% needy UG rec. need-based self-help aid	86
% frosh rec. any financial aid	95
% UG rec. any financial aid	85
% UG borrow to pay for school	71
Average cumulative indebtedness	$30,000
% frosh need fully met	36
% ugrads need fully met	40
Average % of frosh need met	88
Average % of ugrad need met	86

LAWRENCE UNIVERSITY

711 EAST BOLDT WAY SPC 29, APPLETON, WI 54911-5699 • ADMISSIONS: 920-832-6500 • FAX: 920-832-6782

CAMPUS LIFE

Quality of Life Rating	**86**
Fire Safety Rating	**69**
Green Rating	**78**
Type of school	private
Environment	city

STUDENTS

Total undergrad enrollment	1,445
% male/female	46/54
% from out of state	68
% from public high school	71
% frosh live on campus	98
# of fraternities	5
# of sororities	3
% African American	3
% Asian	3
% Caucasian	78
% Hispanic	4
% international	7
# of countries represented	50

SURVEY SAYS . . .

No one cheats
Lab facilities are great
Students are friendly
Campus feels safe
Low cost of living
Students are happy
Musical organizations are popular
Theater is popular

ACADEMICS

Academic Rating	**90**
% students returning for sophomore year	89
% students graduating within 4 years	59
Calendar	trimester
Student/faculty ratio	8:1
Profs interesting rating	91
Profs accessible rating	94
Most classes have	10–19 students

MOST POPULAR MAJORS

biology/biological sciences; psychology; visual and performing arts

APPLICANTS ALSO LOOK AT AND OFTEN PREFER

Beloit College, University of Wisconsin—Madison, St. Olaf College, Macalester College

AND SOMETIMES PREFER

Grinnell College, Knox College, Northwestern University, Oberlin College, Illinois Wesleyan University

STUDENTS SAY ". . ."

Academics

Lawrence University boasts "excellence in both the liberal arts and the fine arts" and "offers small class sizes with top-notch professors" in a "welcoming environment." The university is known for its "prestigious music conservatory" and "individualized and well-rounded approach to learning." Many students take advantage of "interdisciplinary options where departments work together to create specialized majors," and say, "Lawrence is extremely accommodating; they want you to succeed and be happy." Students say, "The people at Lawrence as a whole are very passionate about their studies and seriously want to learn," and the consensus is that there's a general "attitude" of "mutual learning and personal improvement." Professors are "brilliant, passionate about their work and teaching, and…totally engaging in the classroom," and a music education major says, "They really care about their students as people and want to support their education as much as possible and in every way they can!" A senior adds, "If you get the opportunity to have a tutorial with a prof (which is common here), it only gets better." Although "academics at Lawrence are rigorous," students say, "Class size is kept to a minimum" and the "competition between students is not cutthroat but very healthy."

Life

Lawrence University is known for its "student-oriented environment" on an "amazing campus" that's "beautiful yet nicely urban." Students say, "Lawrence is a small, but tight-knit community" and that the university "cares that we are engaged both inside and outside the classroom." Another student adds, "It is unusual to meet students who are not involved in one [or] more extracurricular activities or student groups." The community is one that "promotes open-mindedness and intellectual and individual growth," and a biology major says, "Not only is Lawrence more ethnically diverse than many other liberal arts schools, there is also a lot of diversity in interests." Many students are thankful for having "the Con" on campus because, "there is always great, free music," although the flipside is that "funding for some of the sports teams could be improved." At Lawrence, students are "required to live on campus all four years," which results in "a very strong campus environment," but many students feel the "residence halls are fairly outdated." There are complaints that the "student health center is lacking."

Student Body

At Lawrence, "The typical student has interests and passions all across the map and can usually find ways to express all those interests." A senior says, "A hockey player might be working on an intensive honors thesis in biochemistry." Regardless, some feel, "The conservatory of music students and bachelor of art students are quite segregated" and acknowledge "a friendly rivalry between the two halves of the university, but [say] it's not serious." Most students are "Midwestern, laid-back, open-minded, proud but not pretentious" and "madly in love with music." The student body is "an eclectic blend of musicians, athletes, student government junkies, writers, poets, and wallflowers," and "Students find their niches incredibly easily here." A junior says, "Nerdiness is a bonus," and a theater arts major agrees, "Don't be surprised if a choir or orchestra concert has more attendees than a football game on your average weekend." One student says, "Though there are parties, I think most students are pretty low-key (*not* boring, just not huge partiers)," and another adds, "Various theme houses, frats, and clubs have their own party at least once a term and all parties are open to everyone." Overall, Lawrentians say they're "hardworking and dedicated, but love to chill out and have fun," and that "the school's small size promotes a positive community that isn't difficult to find a place in."

FINANCIAL AID: 920-832-6583 • E-MAIL: EXCEL@LAWRENCE.EDU • WEBSITE: WWW.LAWRENCE.EDU

THE PRINCETON REVIEW SAYS

Admissions

Very important factors considered include: Class rank, academic GPA, rigor of secondary school record. *Important factors considered include:* Application essay, recommendation(s), character/personal qualities, extracurricular activities, talent/ability. *Other factors considered include:* Standardized test scores, alumni/ae relation, first generation, interview, racial/ethnic status, volunteer work, work experience. ACT with or without writing component accepted. TOEFL required of all international applicants. High school diploma is required and GED is not accepted. *Academic units required:* 4 English. *Academic units recommended:* 3 mathematics, 3 science, 2 foreign language, 2 social studies, 2 history.

Financial Aid

Students should submit: FAFSA, institution's own financial aid form, copies of federal tax returns and W-2 forms for parent and student; noncustodial parent form. The Princeton Review suggests that all financial aid forms be submitted as soon as possible after January 1. *Need-based scholarships/grants offered:* Federal Pell, SEOG, state scholarships/grants, private scholarships, the school's own gift aid. *Loan aid offered:* Direct Subsidized Stafford, Direct Unsubsidized Stafford, Direct PLUS, Federal Perkins. Applicants will be notified of awards on a rolling basis beginning March 1. Federal Work-Study Program available. Institutional employment available. Highest amount earned per year from on-campus jobs $4,189. Off-campus job opportunities are good.

The Inside Word

Students interested in applying to Lawrence University's Conservatory are required to schedule an audition and submit a music resume detailing their experiences as a musician, in addition to the traditional application. Furthermore, prospective Conservatory students must submit an additional recommendation from a music teacher qualified to evaluate their musical abilities.

THE SCHOOL SAYS ". . ."

From the Admissions Office

"Lawrence believes college should not be a one-size-fits-all experience, and that you'll learn best when you're educated as a unique individual. Within our college of liberal arts and sciences and our conservatory of music—both devoted exclusively to undergraduate education—you'll have unparalleled opportunities to collaborate closely with your professors in small classes (ninety percent have fewer than twenty students in them; sixty-five percent have total enrollments of one). Our 1,445 students come from nearly every state and about fifty countries to enjoy the distinctive benefits of this engaged—and engaging—community. It's a close-knit, residential, 24/7 campus filled with smart and talented people who are pursuing an astonishing variety of academic and extracurricular interests. Our picturesque, residential campus is nestled on the banks of the Fox River in Appleton, Wisconsin, (metro population: 200,000), one of the fastest growing metropolitan areas in the Midwest. Björklunden, our 425-acre estate on more than one mile of pristine Lake Michigan shoreline (two hours north of campus), provides educational and recreational opportunities for students to enhance their on-campus learning experiences.

"We seek students who are intellectual, imaginative, and innovative: qualities best quantified from a thorough review of your curriculum, academic performance, essay, activities, and recommendations. Accordingly, Lawrence considers—but does not require—the ACT and the SAT in our review of applications for admission and scholarship."

SELECTIVITY

Admissions Rating	**91**
# of applicants	2,666
% of applicants accepted	53
% of acceptees attending	23
# accepting a place on wait list	483
# admitted from wait list	93
# of early decision applicants	47
# accepted early decision	43

FRESHMAN PROFILE

Range SAT Critical Reading	600–710
Range SAT Math	580–690
Range SAT Writing	570–690
Range ACT Composite	27–31
Minimum paper TOEFL	577
Minimum web-based TOEFL	90
Average HS GPA	3.7
% graduated top 10% of class	46
% graduated top 25% of class	81
% graduated top 50% of class	99

DEADLINES

Early decision	
Deadline	11/1
Notification	11/15
Early action	
Deadline	12/1
Notification	1/30
Regular	
Deadline	1/15
Notification	4/1
Nonfall registration?	yes

FINANCIAL FACTS

Financial Aid Rating	**90**
Annual tuition	$39,732
Room and board	$8,247
Required fees	$291
Books and supplies	$1,800
% needy frosh rec. need-based scholarship or grant aid	98
% needy UG rec. need-based scholarship or grant aid	97
% needy frosh rec. non-need-based scholarship or grant aid	2
% needy UG rec. non-need-based scholarship or grant aid	4
% needy frosh rec. need-based self-help aid	85
% needy UG rec. need-based self-help aid	84
% frosh rec. any financial aid	95
% UG rec. any financial aid	94
% UG borrow to pay for school	74
Average cumulative indebtedness	$32,838
% frosh need fully met	55
% ugrads need fully met	52
Average % of frosh need met	89
Average % of ugrad need met	89

LEHIGH UNIVERSITY

27 MEMORIAL DRIVE WEST, BETHLEHEM, PA 18015 • ADMISSIONS: 610-758-3100 • FAX: 610-758-4361

CAMPUS LIFE

Quality of Life Rating	**67**
Fire Safety Rating	**89**
Green Rating	**85**
Type of school	private
Environment	city

STUDENTS

Total undergrad enrollment	4,851
% male/female	57/43
% from out of state	75
% frosh live on campus	99
# of fraternities	21
# of sororities	10
% African American	4
% Asian	6
% Caucasian	70
% Hispanic	8
% international	5
# of countries represented	49

SURVEY SAYS . . .

Great library
Low cost of living
Students are happy
Frats and sororities dominate social scene
Student publications are popular
Lots of beer drinking
Hard liquor is popular

ACADEMICS

Academic Rating	**81**
% students returning for sophomore year	95
% students graduating within 4 years	78
% students graduating within 6 years	87
Calendar	semester
Student/faculty ratio	10:1
Profs interesting rating	75
Profs accessible rating	82
Most classes have	10–19 students
Most lab/discussion sessions have	10–19 students

MOST POPULAR MAJORS

accounting; finance; mechanical engineering

APPLICANTS ALSO LOOK AT AND OFTEN PREFER

Boston College, Carnegie Mellon University, Cornell University, University of Virginia, University of Maryland, College Park

AND SOMETIMES PREFER

Bucknell University, Pennsylvania State University—University Park, Rensselaer Polytechnic Institute, Villanova University, The George Washington University

AND RARELY PREFER

Boston University, Lafayette College, University of Delaware, Rutgers, The State University of New Jersey—New Brunswick, Drexel University

STUDENTS SAY ". . ."

Academics

Lehigh University is a "prestigious," "small- to medium-sized school" that "offers great programs" and the "resources of a large university." It "boasts a strong engineering program," and students say it truly "lives up to its academic reputation." Students "genuinely care about their education" and have "an incredible work ethic." A psychology major says, "People want to learn and want to do well, which creates a really good college environment," and a junior adds, "Students are driven, but not competitive with one another"; instead, "Lehigh expects a lot out of you, which in turn allows you to push and challenge yourself." Students are grateful for the "strong connection with alumni, which is great for prospective employment," and say, "The career opportunities post graduation are excellent for both engineer and business students," and ninety-eight percent of students in all majors find jobs within six months of graduation. Professors get generally high marks, with students saying they're "extremely qualified in their fields" and "do all they can to assure that they succeed." Academics are considered "extremely rigorous and rewarding," leading a freshman to say, "Professors expect a lot from their students, but they do everything they can to help us." It's worth noting, however, that although "professors are extremely qualified in their fields…that does not always qualify them to be effective teachers," and some are "very hard to understand." Students also complain that "registration for courses is a mess."

Life

Lehigh offers "a friendly, community oriented atmosphere" on a hilly campus that is "beyond beautiful." Overall, there's "a vibrant, active student body, and a gorgeous campus, which combines to form a tremendously rich and invigorating experience." Students say, "There's a lot of school spirit," particularly during Lehigh-Laf week when they compete against local rival, Lafayette College, and that's considered "one of the best traditions Lehigh has." At Lehigh, "You always feel like you are part of something," and a junior says, "I've been blown away by the Lehigh community's loyalty to and love for all that is Lehigh." An engineering majors says, "Lehigh's sense of community stretches far past just the years a student spends on campus," noting lasting friendships and successful networking. Students partake in "more than 150 clubs and organizations," and say they "have many opportunities to join groups," adding, "Starting new clubs is also widely supported." Despite this, students wish for "better interaction between the student body and the administration in a way that involves the students in the decisions that the school makes," and say, "The food at the dining halls is often sub-par."

Student Body

Lehigh is "big on Greek life," with roughly one-third of the student body involved in a fraternity and sorority, and students say, "Greek life is huge everyday of the week." Some feel "it's a great way to get involved and meet new people," and say, "Partying on the 'hill' is definitely the most popular activity throughout the year." Yet others feel, "The heavy influence and importance of Greek life" is a "problem," and the university "could work more to integrate Greek life with the rest of the student body." Regardless, students say, "Enough goes on on-campus that if you don't want to go to parties you don't have to to have fun," and say, "It's easy to have fun without alcohol," adding, "There are substance-free halls and dorms as well as school-run activities during weeknights and weekends." Although some gripe, "There isn't much to do locally," the university provides "a free shuttle [that] takes students to the mall and movie theaters on weekends," and a number of new local venues host concerts and other events. Students are typically "from the east coast," "white," "pretty wealthy," and, "children of alumni [who] have [a] legacy." There are complaints that "Lehigh lacks a sense of diversity," and a marketing major says, "While there are numerous programs set up to help increase the racial, socioeconomic diversity here, it still remains a problem." However, minority enrollment has increased in recent classes.

FINANCIAL AID: 610-758-3181 • E-MAIL: ADMISSIONS@LEHIGH.EDU • WEBSITE: WWW.LEHIGH.EDU

THE PRINCETON REVIEW SAYS

Admissions

Very important factors considered include: Recommendation(s), rigor of secondary school record. *Important factors considered include:* Academic GPA, application essay, standardized test scores, character/personal qualities, extracurricular activities, level of applicant's interest, talent/ability, volunteer work. *Other factors considered include:* Class rank, academic GPA, alumni/ae relation, first generation, geographical residence, racial/ethnic status, work experience. SAT or ACT required; the writing component is required for both tests. TOEFL required of all international applicants. High school diploma or equivalent is required. *Academic units required:* 4 English, 3 mathematics, 2 science (2 science labs), 2 foreign language, 2 social studies, 3 academic electives.

Financial Aid

Students should submit: FAFSA, CSS/Financial Aid PROFILE, noncustodial PROFILE, business/farm supplement. Regular filing deadline is February 15. The Princeton Review suggests that all financial aid forms be submitted as soon as possible after January 1. *Need-based scholarships/grants offered:* Federal Pell, SEOG, state scholarships/grants, private scholarships, the school's own gift aid, United Negro College Fund. *Loan aid offered:* Direct Subsidized Stafford, Direct Unsubsidized Stafford, Direct PLUS, Federal Perkins, college/university loans from institutional funds. Applicants will be notified of awards on or about March 30. Federal Work-Study Program available. Institutional employment available. Off-campus job opportunities are good.

The Inside Word

Admission to Lehigh University is competitive and the admissions committee suggests starting process the early and paying careful attention to deadlines and required supplemental materials. For the class of 2016, the university received more than 11,500 applications for a class size that's approximately 1,200. Prospective students are strongly encouraged to visit campus to experience Lehigh firsthand and speak to the admissions staff. Interviews are recommended but not required.

THE SCHOOL SAYS ". . ."

From the Admissions Office

"Lehigh University is located fifty miles north of Philadelphia and seventy-five miles southwest of New York City in Bethlehem, Pennsylvania. We are a premier residential research university, ranked in the top tier of national research universities each year. Lehigh combines the learning opportunities of a large research university with the personal attention of a small, private college. We take an innovative approach to learning, discovery, and teaching by fusing traditionally separate majors to create a richer, fuller, more meaningful experience for you. Learning is connected to real-world applications and reinforced with cutting-edge academic research and hands-on experiences. You can customize your experience by tailoring majors and academic programs across four colleges and dozens of fields of study. Investigation, innovation, and global exposure will drive your educational experience at Lehigh. You'll learn and work alongside faculty who are leaders in their fields and bring the latest knowledge and newest discoveries to the classrooms, laboratories, and workshops to enhance you educational experience and give you real-world exposure. Here, we share a common set of core values: integrity and honesty, equitable community, academic freedom, intellectual curiosity, and leadership. A vibrant campus life offers many social activities from more than 150 clubs and organizations, twenty-five intercollegiate sports, and intramural sports and club programs. Campus Square, a residential and retail complex, integrates the campus with the surrounding community.

"Lehigh requires students to submit scores from the SAT or the ACT. Students submitting either test must also include with the writing portion. SAT Subject Tests are optional."

SELECTIVITY

Admissions Rating	**96**
# of applicants	11,578
% of applicants accepted	33
% of acceptees attending	31
# accepting a place on wait list	1,514
# admitted from wait list	1
# of early decision applicants	878
# accepted early decision	561

FRESHMAN PROFILE

Range SAT Critical Reading	580–680
Range SAT Math	640–720
Range ACT Composite	28–31
Minimum paper TOEFL	570
Minimum web-based TOEFL	90
% graduated top 10% of class	96
% graduated top 25% of class	100
% graduated top 50% of class	100

DEADLINES

Early decision	
Deadline	11/15
Notification	12/15
Regular	
Deadline	1/1
Notification	4/1
Nonfall registration?	yes

FINANCIAL FACTS

Financial Aid Rating	**92**
Annual tuition	$40,660
Room and board	$10,840
Required fees	$300
Books and supplies	$1,000
% needy frosh rec. need-based scholarship or grant aid	97
% needy UG rec. need-based scholarship or grant aid	98
% needy frosh rec. non-need-based scholarship or grant aid	7
% needy UG rec. non-need-based scholarship or grant aid	9
% needy frosh rec. need-based self-help aid	93
% needy UG rec. need-based self-help aid	94
% frosh rec. any financial aid	62
% UG rec. any financial aid	62
% UG borrow to pay for school	52
Average cumulative indebtedness	$29,668
% frosh need fully met	54
% ugrads need fully met	69
Average % of frosh need met	96
Average % of ugrad need met	96

LEWIS & CLARK COLLEGE

0615 SOUTHWEST PALATINE HILL ROAD, PORTLAND, OR 97219-7899 • ADMISSIONS: 503-768-7040 • FAX: 503-768-7055

CAMPUS LIFE

Quality of Life Rating	87
Fire Safety Rating	97
Green Rating	73
Type of school	private
Environment	city

STUDENTS

Total undergrad enrollment	2,031
% male/female	41/59
% from out of state	88
% from public high school	73
% frosh live on campus	98
% African American	2
% Asian	4
% Caucasian	61
% Hispanic	7
% Native American	1
% international	5
# of countries represented	69

SURVEY SAYS . . .

Lots of liberal students
Students aren't religious
Students love Portland, OR
Frats and sororities are unpopular or nonexistent
Political activism is popular

ACADEMICS

Academic Rating	90
% students returning for sophomore year	88
% students graduating within 4 years	66
% students graduating within 6 years	75
Calendar	semester
Student/faculty ratio	12:1
Profs interesting rating	91
Profs accessible rating	88
Most classes have	20–29 students
Most lab/discussion sessions have	20–29 students

MOST POPULAR MAJORS

biology/biological sciences; international relations and affairs; psychology

APPLICANTS ALSO LOOK AT AND OFTEN PREFER

University of California—Santa Cruz

AND SOMETIMES PREFER

University of Puget Sound, Whitman College

AND RARELY PREFER

University of Oregon, Pitzer College, University of Colorado—Boulder

STUDENTS SAY ". . ."

Academics

While living in Portland, Oregon, you may "get rained on a lot," but that doesn't stop many students from extolling about the otherwise "wonderful," "perfect," "ideal," and "exciting" location. This "suburban-hilltop liberal arts college" sits in an "absolutely beautiful" spot "next to a huge forest, [with] downtown only twenty minutes away." Besides the setting, students are lured by the school's "strong outdoors program," "great study abroad opportunities," as well as the promise of "a very green and liberal school." "Lewis & Clark is a utopia for thinkers and outdoors lovers alike. While challenging academically, the emphasis on a holistic education means that students are encouraged to explore all that Portland and the beautiful Northwest has to offer." Professors are noted for their support and "are devoted to their students in a way that wouldn't be possible in a larger school." "Lewis & Clark has professors that care so much, and if you want to put the effort into building relationships with them you will get so much from the education." Students give excellent marks for the "seasoned professors in upper-level classes." However, one student feels that "some of the temporary staff are less excellent."

Life

Life is full, and friends are plentiful at Lewis & Clark. "It's beautiful, small, and an overall friendly place with students who really take education seriously." Community supported agriculture (CSA) is taken seriously here, too. "Many are very concerned about living a healthy and sustainable life style" and are "very active gardeners and composters." The small campus is "beautiful and enjoyable to study and live in." "It feels intimate without feeling claustrophobic." When the weather is nice, "People try to find every excuse to be outside." "They generally enjoy hiking, skiing, camping, and many other activities that bring them closer to nature." Although partying exists, it is not at the forefront here. "Parties are frequent, but hardly out of control." "A lot of students are involved in student-run organizations such as a cappella, theatrical improv, open mic nights, their own bands, and the Co-op (a student-run café). Many people are advocates, and lots of students give significant amounts of their time to assist their communities." With Portland easily accessible using the school's "free shuttle that goes from campus to downtown," escaping campus is "extremely easy." "There are so many fun things to do downtown—concerts, coffee shops, restaurants, and a ton of funky antique shops that are perfect to explore on a nice day. The Pearl District, Hawthorne Street, and of course the Saturday Market are all fun places to go check out." Athletics are popular at Lewis & Clark, and students speak proudly of their teams. Although some students point out of lack of fans cheering them on at games and meets, one classmate puts it into perspective. "L&C was one of the only colleges to really support me being [a part] of the athletic department as a varsity basketball player and the music department as a classical double bass player. I didn't want to go to a college that would force me to choose between my two passions. L&C has allowed me to grow as an athlete, musician, and as a student; not a lot of colleges can do that."

Student Body

To generalize, "Students are usually athletes or hippies." There seems to be some divide between the two groups, but most everyone is "very liberal, engaged in a variety of issues, and smart." One student describes the school as being "full of people that you'd actually want to make friends with." Another says classmates are "genuine" and "really independent." "Most kids are more than willing to try something adventurous, and most take advantage of the fact that our student body has students coming from all over the country and world." Students tend to value "Freedom of expression and thought, and an open environment in which to discuss differences." The fact that many students have traveled or lived in another country enriches the classroom experience. Classmates "constantly have stories about their time abroad," and "It is also very difficult to find someone who has never traveled abroad." The school's downside is that it "is very expensive" and therefore "could benefit from more economic diversity."

FINANCIAL AID: 503-768-7090 • E-MAIL: ADMISSIONS@LCLARK.EDU • WEBSITE: WWW.LCLARK.EDU

THE PRINCETON REVIEW SAYS

Admissions

Very important factors considered include: Academic GPA, rigor of secondary school record, racial/ethnic status. *Important factors considered include:* Class rank, application essay, recommendation(s), standardized test scores, alumni/ae relation, character/personal qualities, extracurricular activities, first generation, talent/ability, volunteer work. *Other factors considered include:* Geographical residence, interview, level of applicant's interest, state residency, work experience. ACT with or without writing component accepted. TOEFL required of all international applicants. High school diploma is required and GED is accepted. *Academic units recommended:* 4 English, 4 mathematics, 3 science (2 science labs), 3 foreign language, 4 social studies, 1 fine arts.

Financial Aid

Students should submit: FAFSA, CSS/Financial Aid PROFILE. The Princeton Review suggests that all financial aid forms be submitted as soon as possible after January 1. *Need-based scholarships/grants offered:* Federal Pell, SEOG, state scholarships/grants, private scholarships, the school's own gift aid. *Loan aid offered:* Direct Subsidized Stafford, Direct Unsubsidized Stafford, Direct PLUS, Federal Perkins. Applicants will be notified of awards on a rolling basis beginning March 1. Federal Work-Study Program available. Institutional employment available. Highest amount earned per year from on-campus jobs $1,800. Off-campus job opportunities are fair.

The Inside Word

If you have your heart set on L&C, make sure you tell that to the admissions committee. While grades and SAT scores are certainly important, L&C is also interested in students who will take advantage of the school's unique philoso phy and educational environment. So make sure your application essay and interview emphasizes why L&C is the right fit for both you and the school.

THE SCHOOL SAYS ". . ."

From the Admissions Office

"The record number of applicants in recent years cited a variety of reasons they were drawn to Lewis & Clark. Many had to do with the multiple environments experienced by our students, including a small arts and sciences college with a twelve to one student/faculty ratio; a location only six miles from downtown Portland (metropolitan population 1.9 million); a setting in the heart of the Pacific Northwest, making more than eighty trips per year possible for our College Outdoors Program; and the rest of the world—almost sixty percent of our graduates included an overseas program in their curriculum. Since 1962, more than 9,600 students and 212 faculty members have participated in 598 programs in sixty-six countries on six continents. Our international curriculum has undergone a total review to better prepare graduates going into the twenty-first century.

"At Lewis & Clark College, SAT Subject Test scores are not required."

SELECTIVITY	
Admissions Rating	92
# of applicants	5,950
% of applicants accepted	66
% of acceptees attending	15
FRESHMAN PROFILE	
Range SAT Critical Reading	610–710
Range SAT Math	580–670
Range SAT Writing	590–680
Range ACT Composite	27–30
Minimum paper TOEFL	550
Average HS GPA	3.7
% graduated top 10% of class	40
% graduated top 25% of class	77
% graduated top 50% of class	99
DEADLINES	
Early action	
Deadline	11/1
Notification	1/15
Regular	
Priority	1/15
Deadline	1/15
Notification	4/1
Nonfall registration?	yes
FINANCIAL FACTS	
Financial Aid Rating	87
Annual tuition	$39,970
Room and board	$10,014
Required fees	$360
Books and supplies	$1,050
% needy frosh rec. need-based scholarship or grant aid	100
% needy UG rec. need-based scholarship or grant aid	100
% needy frosh rec. non-need-based scholarship or grant aid	8
% needy UG rec. non-need-based scholarship or grant aid	7
% needy frosh rec. need-based self-help aid	92
% needy UG rec. need-based self-help aid	90
% frosh rec. any financial aid	69
% UG rec. any financial aid	62
% UG borrow to pay for school	47
Average cumulative indebtedness	$22,956
% frosh need fully met	43
% ugrads need fully met	38
Average % of frosh need met	92
Average % of ugrad need met	89

LOUISIANA STATE UNIVERSITY

1146 PLEASANT HALL, BATON ROUGE, LA 70803 • ADMISSIONS: 225-578-1175 • FAX: 225-575-4433

CAMPUS LIFE

Quality of Life Rating	77
Fire Safety Rating	95
Green Rating	85
Type of school	public
Environment	metropolis

STUDENTS

Total undergrad enrollment	23,977
% male/female	49/51
% from out of state	20
% from public high school	53
% frosh live on campus	24
# of fraternities	23
# of sororities	15
% African American	10
% Asian	3
% Caucasian	78
% Hispanic	4
% international	2
# of countries represented	109

SURVEY SAYS . . .

Athletic facilities are great
Great off-campus food
Everyone loves the Tigers
Frats and sororities dominate social scene
Student publications are popular
Lots of beer drinking
Hard liquor is popular

ACADEMICS

Academic Rating	71
% students returning for sophomore year	84
% students graduating within 4 years	31
% students graduating within 6 years	62
Calendar	semester
Student/faculty ratio	23:1
Profs interesting rating	91
Profs accessible rating	76
Most classes have	20–29 students
Most lab/discussion sessions have	20–29 students

MOST POPULAR MAJORS

biology/biological sciences; mass communication/media studies; physical education teaching and coaching

STUDENTS SAY ". . ."

Academics

At Louisiana State University's flagship campus, you'll find "outstanding academics combined with a great college life." Some students here opt for only the latter as for many, "LSU is about football and partying." "Those who wish to apply themselves," however, "have ample opportunity and resources," and they can learn almost anything, since "the greatest strength of LSU by far is its diversity. [You] can come to LSU for sports, music...science, economics, or nearly any sort of humanities discipline you are interested in." Areas of strength include programs in premedical science, engineering, agriculture, and mass communications. The school is huge, which means "somewhere within that huge number is someone that you can get along with," but also it is easy to "get lost in the crowd," especially in intro-level classes. However, "once you get into classes that are smaller and more geared toward your chosen major, you are able to develop more of a one-on-one relationship with your professors." Fortunately "many administrative tasks" (such as "bills and registration") "can be completed online, and computers are available all across campus for students who don't have personal computers," making the bureaucracy somewhat easier to navigate. The school also offers academic lifelines such as "free tutoring all day long. The tutors are students who have already taken [the] courses."

Life

LSU is a big enough school to offer something for everyone, and undergrads here enjoy countless activities within a variety of subcultures. Most divisions, however, dissolve on game day, when tailgating is raised to the level of "an art form." A freshman reports, "On Saturdays during football season everyone is on campus before the game with friends, beer, and barbeque." Fans "come from all over and stay out all day. It's the one day when it doesn't matter who you are, as long as you're wearing purple and gold." Other entertainment options (for those of age) include Thursday nights at the bars of Tigerland, "a street with three popular college bars right next to each other," and parties wherever and whenever possible. The Greek system here is "highly influential," but students note, "This isn't the kind of school where a student doesn't have a social life if he or she isn't Greek." For the more aesthetically inclined, "LSU has an amazing art center—The Shaw Center—complete with a theater and fancy sushi bar on the top floor, which looks over the Mississippi River." Undergrads report "the beauty of our campus is amazing. The 100-plus-year-old oaks and the Italian Renaissance architecture wow any visitor to LSU's campus."

Student Body

The typical student at LSU "studies moderately—enough to get the grade he or she desires in a class"—and "frequently spends time with friends, possibly going to parties or places that serve alcohol." Mixed in is "a good number of atypical students who study more and do not go partying over the weekends. These students find fulfillment in their own interests regardless of what others think." While "conservative frat boys and sorority girls dominate the campus," the school is home to a diverse population including "many from foreign countries and other ethnic groups." There are even a few who "don't give a damn about LSU football"—hey, at a school this big, anything's possible. The student body also includes a substantial population of legacies.

FINANCIAL AID: 225-578-3103 • E-MAIL: ADMISSIONS@LSU.EDU • WEBSITE: WWW.LSU.EDU

THE PRINCETON REVIEW SAYS

Admissions

There are three factors LSU initially considers in admissions: Incoming freshman must have at least a 3.0 cumulative GPA from academic core courses; they must have completed at least 19 units of new fall 2012 college-preparatory courses; and they must have a minimum SAT score (critical reading and math) of 1030 or a composite ACT score of at least 22. LSU doesn't require the writing section of the SAT or ACT for general admission, though applicants to the honors program must submit writing scores. LSU doesn't offer any remedial courses, so prospective students must have an ACT English sub-score of at least 18 or an SAT critical reading sub-score of 450, and an ACT math sub-score of at least 19 or an SAT math sub-score of 460. Students who don't meet minimum requirements for automatic admission are encouraged to apply, as the admissions committee will take other factors into account, such as rigor of high school curriculum, grade trends, and letters of recommendation. *Academic units required:* 4 English, 4 mathematics, 4 science, 2 foreign language, 4 social studies, and 1 unit of art.

Financial Aid

Students should submit: FAFSA. The Princeton Review suggests that all financial aid forms be submitted as soon as possible after January 1. *Need-based scholarships/grants offered:* Federal Pell, SEOG, state scholarships/grants, private scholarships, the school's own gift aid. *Loan aid offered:* Direct Subsidized Stafford, Direct Unsubsidized Stafford, Direct PLUS, Federal Perkins, alternative/grad PLUS. Applicants will be notified of awards on a rolling basis beginning April 1. Federal Work-Study Program available. Institutional employment available.

The Inside Word

If you've got the right numbers, getting in to LSU is 1-2-3. Guaranteed admission requirements include completion of nineteen core units, 1030 SAT or 22 ACT, and a 3.0 academic GPA. Students who don't meet these requirements should submit supporting documentation and a letter outlining their qualifications for admission with their initial application.

THE SCHOOL SAYS ". . ."

From the Admissions Office

"LSU, one of only twenty-one universities nationwide designated as a land-grant, sea-grant, and space-grant institution, also holds the Carnegie Foundation's 'very high research activity' university designation.

"LSU's instructional programs include 200 undergraduate and graduate or professional degrees. Outside of the classroom, residential colleges, service-learning opportunites, and more than 350 registered student organizations contribute to an exciting and meaningful college experience.

"Louisiana State University offers the Southern hospitality of a small community while providing the benefits of a large, technologically advanced institution.

"Freshman applicants are required to take the SAT or ACT; ACT with writing component required for Honors College applicants. LSU will use the best scores from either SAT or ACT, when making admission decisions."

SELECTIVITY	
Admissions Rating	**80**
# of applicants	14,818
% of applicants accepted	80
% of acceptees attending	45

FRESHMAN PROFILE	
Range SAT Critical Reading	500–610
Range SAT Math	530–630
Range ACT Composite	23–28
Minimum paper TOEFL	550
Minimum web-based TOEFL	79
Average HS GPA	3.5
% graduated top 10% of class	24
% graduated top 25% of class	51
% graduated top 50% of class	81

DEADLINES	
Regular	
Priority	11/15
Deadline	4/15
Nonfall registration?	yes

FINANCIAL FACTS	
Financial Aid Rating	**81**
Annual in-state tuition	$4,558
Annual out-state tuition	$17,566
Room and board	$8,670
Required fees	$1,796
Books and supplies	$1,500
% needy frosh rec. need-based scholarship or grant aid	98
% needy UG rec. need-based scholarship or grant aid	99
% needy frosh rec. non-need-based scholarship or grant aid	6
% needy UG rec. non-need-based scholarship or grant aid	3
% needy frosh rec. need-based self-help aid	62
% needy UG rec. need-based self-help aid	71
% frosh rec. any financial aid	94
% UG rec. any financial aid	82
% UG borrow to pay for school	37
Average cumulative indebtedness	$20,337
% frosh need fully met	16
% ugrads need fully met	11
Average % of frosh need met	79
Average % of ugrad need met	74

LOYOLA MARYMOUNT UNIVERSITY

ONE LMU DRIVE, SUITE 100, LOS ANGELES, CA 90045-8350 • ADMISSIONS: 310-338-2750 • FAX: 310-338-2797

CAMPUS LIFE

Quality of Life Rating	**97**
Fire Safety Rating	**74**
Green Rating	**89**
Type of school	private
Affiliation	Roman Catholic
Environment	metropolis

STUDENTS

Total undergrad enrollment	5,951
% male/female	43/57
% from out of state	23
% from public high school	49
% frosh live on campus	94
# of fraternities	6
# of sororities	10
% African American	6
% Asian	10
% Caucasian	52
% Hispanic	21
% international	4
# of countries represented	86

SURVEY SAYS . . .

Great computer facilities
Athletic facilities are great
Students are friendly
Students love Los Angeles, CA
Great off-campus food
Students are happy
Frats and sororities dominate social scene
Students are involved in community service

ACADEMICS

Academic Rating	**85**
% students returning for sophomore year	92
% students graduating within 4 years	67
% students graduating within 6 years	77
Calendar	semester
Student/faculty ratio	11:1
Profs interesting rating	87
Profs accessible rating	97
Most classes have	10–19 students
Most lab/discussion sessions have	10–19 students

MOST POPULAR MAJORS

business administration and management; communication studies/speech communication and rhetoric; psychology

APPLICANTS ALSO LOOK AT AND OFTEN PREFER

University of California—Los Angeles, University of California—Berkeley, University of Southern California

AND SOMETIMES PREFER

University of California—Santa Barbara, Santa Clara University, University of California—San Diego

AND RARELY PREFER

Chapman University, Pepperdine University, University of San Diego

STUDENTS SAY ". . ."

Academics

Loyola Marymount University is a "fun, beautiful, Jesuit institution," with a top-tier teaching staff and "fabulous location" in sunny Los Angeles, California. The school emphasizes a well-rounded education, which balances academics with spiritual life and community involvement. Every student must complete a core curriculum, which introduces them to the liberal arts within the context of the "Ignation and Marymount traditions of social responsibility and education of the whole person." LMU has more than fifty major fields and almost 6,000 undergraduates; however, individual classes are often "between ten and twelve students and are highly dependent on discussion or the practice of material in the classroom." Within every major, there's a mix of "easy classes and very challenging classes." Fortunately, "professors are approachable and passionate," and always "willing to meet with students outside of class for discussion and help." Beyond academics, "The faculty and staff are concerned about the student's well-being" and "want to create an environment that will successfully facilitate healthy learning." A civil engineering student adds, "I attribute my success at LMU to my professors taking a personal interest in me, which inspired me to work harder for them." Thanks to LMU's "powerful networks of alums" and enviable urban location, many students are able to score "internships at top accounting firms, movie studios, television networks" and other Southern California industries. Through this and other channels, "LMU strives to make this campus a place where students can discover their passion and pursue whatever they want."

Life

"Located on the beautiful Southern California coast," LMU is a "gorgeous place to learn." At this well-polished and well-endowed university, "The facilities, housing, amenities, landscaping, and location are all excellent." Even the "Library is beautiful and functional…and classrooms are large and stocked with all the necessities." Clubs, events, and "community service opportunities" abound on LMU's active campus, and students tend to be joyously juggling a hectic schedule of schoolwork and extracurricular pursuits. The school definitely "brings out the busy bee in students," so "If you want to fit in at LMU, find something you love and join, join, join!" When it's time to relax, "Most of the fun activities revolve around Greek life, such as sorority and fraternity formals and exchanges," although it should be noted that Greek life doesn't include any residential component. However, "Being in Los Angeles also has many perks for off-campus life," like "hanging out with friends at the beach or going out to eat" at restaurants around Hollywood and Santa Monica. Taking advantage of the diverse urban environment, "People go into the city to nightclubs, restaurants, movie theaters, hookah bars, comedy clubs…this is Los Angeles! You can find something that fits your personality in this city." A medium-sized campus, LMU is "not so big that you don't know anyone, but it's not small enough that you see the same people every day."

Student Body

"The typical LMU student is laid-back and friendly, but also hardworking and involved in the many, many aspects of LMU, from service work to Greek life to athletics." "There are a lot of sorority girls and frat guys" on campus, and most students are "socially active," enjoying a good party or a romp around Los Angeles on the weekends. "Students tend to be from California" and, in the true Los Angeles spirit, many are "physically fit," as well as "very fashion-forward and trendy." Most agree, "Everyone is very accepting and chill" at LMU. In fact, "Most people are smart, focused, and engaging young adults," whether or not they don designer duds. Many students also note, "The student body is becoming more and more diverse," and there's a "high degree of tolerance and respect here for people of different cultures, sexual orientations, and religions." On the whole, "students seem to interact quite well together in and outside the classroom."

FINANCIAL AID: 310-338-2753 • E-MAIL: ADMISSIONS@LMU.EDU • WEBSITE: WWW.LMU.EDU

THE PRINCETON REVIEW SAYS

Admissions

Very important factors considered include: Academic GPA, rigor of secondary school record. *Important factors considered include:* Class rank, application essay, standardized test scores, character/personal qualities, talent/ability. *Other factors considered include:* Recommendation(s), alumni/ae relation, extracurricular activities, first generation, geographical residence, interview, volunteer work, work experience. SAT or ACT required; ACT with writing component recommended. TOEFL required of all international applicants. High school diploma is required and GED is accepted. *Academic units recommended:* 4 English, 3 mathematics, 2 science (2 science labs), 3 foreign language, 3 social studies, 1 academic elective.

Financial Aid

Students should submit: FAFSA. The Princeton Review suggests that all financial aid forms be submitted as soon as possible after January 1. *Need-based scholarships/grants offered:* Federal Pell, SEOG, state scholarships/grants, private scholarships, the school's own gift aid. *Loan aid offered:* Direct Subsidized Stafford loans, Direct Unsubsidized Stafford, Direct PLUS, Federal Perkins, college/university loans from institutional funds. Applicants will be notified of awards on a rolling basis beginning March 15. Federal Work-Study Program available. Institutional employment available. Off-campus job opportunities are excellent.

The Inside Word

LMU's admission staff reviews each application individually. There's no minimum GPA or minimum test scores required for admission, and the school strives to consider the student's range of experiences and character. Nonetheless, the academic record is the single most important factor in an admissions decision. For interested students, the school offers an early action program, though students admitted through this program aren't required to attend.

THE SCHOOL SAYS ". . ."

From the Admissions Office

"Loyola Marymount University is a dynamic, student-centered university. We are medium-sized (5,800 undergraduates), and we are the only Jesuit university in the southwestern United States.

"Our campus is located in Westchester, a friendly, residential neighborhood that is removed from the hustle and bustle of Los Angeles, yet offers easy access to all the richnesss of our most cosmopolitan environment. One mile from the ocean, our students enjoy ocean and mountain vistas as well as the moderate climate and crisp breezes characteristic of a coastal location.

"Loyola Marymount is committed to the ideals of Jesuit and Marymount education. We are a student-centered university, dedicated to the education of the whole person and to the preparation of our students for lives of service to their families, communities, and professions. Breadth and rigor are the hallmarks of the curriculum.

"Taken together, our academic program, our Jesuit and Marymount heritage, and our terrific campus environment afford our students unparalleled opportunity to prepare for life and leadership in the twenty-first century."

SELECTIVITY	
Admissions Rating	**90**
# of applicants	11,309
% of applicants accepted	53
% of acceptees attending	21
# accepting a place on wait list	1,280
# admitted from wait list	522

FRESHMAN PROFILE	
Range SAT Critical Reading	540–630
Range SAT Math	560–650
Range SAT Writing	550–650
Range ACT Composite	24–28
Minimum paper TOEFL	550
Minimum web-based TOEFL	80
Average HS GPA	3.7
% graduated top 10% of class	34
% graduated top 25% of class	65
% graduated top 50% of class	93

DEADLINES	
Early action	
Deadline	11/1
Notification	12/21
Regular	
Deadline	1/15
Nonfall registration?	yes

FINANCIAL FACTS	
Financial Aid Rating	**74**
Annual tuition	$38,212
Room and board	$12,722
Required fees	$706
Books and supplies	$1,656
% needy frosh rec. need-based scholarship or grant aid	94
% needy UG rec. need-based scholarship or grant aid	91
% needy frosh rec. non-need-based scholarship or grant aid	21
% needy UG rec. non-need-based scholarship or grant aid	10
% needy frosh rec. need-based self-help aid	76
% needy UG rec. need-based self-help aid	83
% frosh rec. any financial aid	91
% UG rec. any financial aid	83
% UG borrow to pay for school	60
Average cumulative indebtedness	$31,246
% frosh need fully met	25
% ugrads need fully met	16
Average % of frosh need met	72
Average % of ugrad need met	66

LOYOLA UNIVERSITY—CHICAGO

1032 WEST SHERIDAN ROAD, CHICAGO, IL 60660 • ADMISSIONS: 773-508-3075 • FAX: 773-508-8926

CAMPUS LIFE

Quality of Life Rating	70
Fire Safety Rating	71
Green Rating	89
Type of school	private
Affiliation	Roman Catholic-Jesuit
Environment	metropolis

STUDENTS

Total undergrad enrollment	9,483
% male/female	37/63
% from out of state	40
% from public high school	68
# of fraternities	9
# of sororities	12
% African American	4
% Asian	11
% Caucasian	65
% Hispanic	11
% international	1
# of countries represented	105

SURVEY SAYS . . .

Lab facilities are great
Students love Chicago, IL
Great off-campus food

ACADEMICS

Academic Rating	71
% students graduating within 4 years	51
% students graduating within 6 years	70
Calendar	semester
Student/faculty ratio	15:1
Profs interesting rating	71
Profs accessible rating	70
Most classes have	10–19 students
Most lab/discussion sessions have	10–19 students

MOST POPULAR MAJORS

business; communications; education

APPLICANTS ALSO LOOK AT AND OFTEN PREFER

DePaul University, Marquette University, Northwestern University, Saint Louis University, University of Chicago, University of Illinois at Urbana-Champaign, University of Michigan—Ann Arbor, University of Minnesota—Twin Cities, University of Wisconsin—Madison, Indiana University—Bloomington

AND SOMETIMES PREFER

Boston College, Boston University, Bradley University, Fordham University, Illinois State University, Miami University, Michigan State University, Purdue University—West Lafayette, University of Dayton, University of Iowa, University of Notre Dame, Washington University in St. Louis, Xavier University (OH), The Ohio State University—Columbus

AND RARELY PREFER

American University, Augustana College (IL), Creighton University, Northeastern University, Vanderbilt University, Illinois Wesleyan University, University of Missouri, New York University

STUDENTS SAY ". . ."

Academics

Standing tall alongside the shore of Lake Michigan eight miles north of Loyola University—Chicago "provides the best of both worlds: an integrated campus and a taste of the city life." The main campus is located next to Lake Michigan, and the surrounding area is "gorgeous." The academic programs are "rigorous and fascinating," and the school offers "significant financial assistance and plenty of scholarships." The school's location "allows Loyola to attract top-notch faculty while giving students of all disciplines the opportunity to find something that interests them." Built on strong Jesuit values, Loyola cares deeply about social justice ("set the world on fire" is a common credo) and "developing intellectual and socially responsible students." "My school is about preparing students for careers and being aware of problems around us," says a student.

"The majority of the professors [is] excellent." The professors "find a good balance in their teaching methods that allow students to engage the material and engage other students in the classroom." "They are the kind of teachers that one remembers for a long time," says a student. "Many bring in business professionals to relate our classroom material to the real world," and "the work is challenging, but not overbearing." "I've had several professors who I would go out of my way to take again," says a student. "The academics make everyone work hard, regardless of natural ability, but it pays off every time."

The "well-known academic integrity of the school" provides a great reputation in Chicago, and the "connections and opportunities" the school provides to students seeking jobs and internships are numerous. Since the curriculum is centered on being well-rounded, "Students can build an education that will serve them well in the future." "Loyola challenges its students to be the best they can be, no matter what their major or background is."

Life

"What's great about Loyola is that it is very future-focused, but it never forgets about the present either," says a student. People at this school are quite involved, and they "find a good core group of people that they work together with in classes, clubs, organizations, and/or athletics." "Community service opportunities" abound, as do plenty of study abroad opportunities, and people "go on trips that involve doing out of the ordinary activities," including skiing and skydiving.

Many students admit that the "social atmosphere of the campus is very dull," but Chicago is "a gold mine" of clubs, bars, sports venues, shops, and sites. "Basically, the biggest hobby around here is exploring Chicago. We go out every weekend, just looking for things to do and always finding them," says a student. "Many students drink, but not all." The campus itself is "very relaxed, a sort of oasis in a bustling city," and there is even a beach right off campus on Lake Michigan, so "Clearly, it does not feel much like a city most of the time."

Student Body

This group of "witty, hardworking, smart, and outgoing" people are all "studious and fairly involved but able to have fun." The typical student "comes from an upper-middle-class family, has some faith background, and balances school with social life well." Many are from local suburbs of Chicago ("being in the city, many Loyola students are fashionable and like to experiment with clothing") and care about "enjoying the city." "It is very easy to fit in because of how accepting people are," and "There is a real feel of family." Students "normally fit in the best in activities or the freshmen residence halls." Many students comment that there seems to be a lot of premed students here. Most everyone is "involved in some extracurricular or another," and many students have a job, as well.

FINANCIAL AID: 773-508-7704 • E-MAIL: ADMISSION@LUC.EDU • WEBSITE: WWW.LUC.EDU

THE PRINCETON REVIEW SAYS

Admissions

Very important factors considered include: Academic GPA, rigor of secondary school record, standardized test scores. *Important factors considered include:* Application essay, recommendation(s), character/personal qualities, extracurricular activities, level of applicant's interest, volunteer work. *Other factors considered include:* Class rank, alumni/ae relation, first generation, geographical residence, interview, state residency, talent/ability, work experience. SAT or ACT required; ACT with or without writing component accepted. TOEFL or IELTS required of all international applicants. High school diploma is required and GED is accepted. *Academic units required:* 4 English, 3 mathematics, 3 science, 2 foreign language, 2 social studies, 1 history. *Academic units recommended:* 4 English, 4 mathematics, 3 science, 2 foreign language, 2 social studies, 2 history.

Financial Aid

Students should submit: FAFSA. Regular filing deadline is March 1. The Princeton Review suggests that all financial aid forms be submitted as soon as possible after January 1. *Need-based scholarships/grants offered:* Federal Pell, SEOG, state scholarships/grants, private scholarships, the school's own gift aid. *Loan aid offered:* Direct Subsidized Stafford, Direct Unsubsidized Stafford, Direct PLUS, Federal Perkins, Federal Nursing. Applicants will be notified of awards on a rolling basis once all documentation is received. Federal Work-Study Program available. Institutional employment available. Highest amount earned per year from on-campus jobs $12,590. Off-campus job opportunities are good.

The Inside Word

Loyola is fairly conventional when it comes to admissions policies. Successful candidates usually have a combination of strong grades, success in a tough college preparatory curriculum, and solid extracurricular activities. The school adheres to Jesuit teaching, so applicants with significant volunteer work should impress admissions officers.

THE SCHOOL SAYS ". . ."

From the Admissions Office

"Loyola University Chicago continues to open new facilities and renovate existing buildings. Loyola is investing $100 million into reimagine, a campaign to revolutionize the student community at Loyola. This campaign is an ambitious, five-phased building project that will touch every facet of life at the Lake Shore Campus. Expected to be completed in 2015, reimagine will benefit the entire Loyola community. As a result of the campaign, Loyola has already gained a three-story, state-of-the-art athletics facility, a true sports arena, and will gain a new student union, an updated sports center, and a new Centennial Forum, with room for large-scale conferences and a new face for Loyola. In addition, the School of Communication opened a new convergence studio at the Water Tower Campus, which includes television and radio production equipment. Loyola's Information Commons is a high-tech lakefront library featuring large group study spaces, more than 250 computers, wireless Internet connections, and a lakefront café. Loyola frequently enhances its undergraduate academic programs and adds new majors in emerging fields. The Core Curriculum enhances student credentials by emphasizing lifelong skills and values, and giving students the opportunity to easily complete a second major or add a minor. Nationally recognized researchers and scholars continue to teach freshman-level and advanced courses. Loyola's two main campuses enable students to experience both traditional residential campus life, and a vibrant urban environment. With more than 200 campus organizations offering numerous activities and events, as well as cultural, recreational, and internship opportunities throughout the world-class city of Chicago, undergraduate education at Loyola extends well beyond the classroom. For more information about undergraduate academics, housing, student life, financial assistance, and more, please visit www.luc.edu/undergrad. Please note that students whose native language is not English and/or if the primary language of instruction has not been English will be required to take the TOEFL or IELTS."

SELECTIVITY

Admissions Rating	**88**
# of applicants	17,828
% of applicants accepted	55
% of acceptees attending	20

FRESHMAN PROFILE

Range SAT Critical Reading	540–660
Range SAT Math	540–650
Range SAT Writing	530–640
Range ACT Composite	25–29
Minimum paper TOEFL	550
Minimum web-based TOEFL	79
Average HS GPA	3.7
% graduated top 10% of class	32
% graduated top 25% of class	65
% graduated top 50% of class	93

DEADLINES

Regular	
Priority	12/1
Nonfall registration?	yes

FINANCIAL FACTS

Financial Aid Rating	**74**
Annual tuition	$33,450
Room and board	$12,010
Required fees	$1,128
Books and supplies	$1,200
% needy frosh rec. need-based scholarship or grant aid	99
% needy UG rec. need-based scholarship or grant aid	97
% needy frosh rec. non-need-based scholarship or grant aid	9
% needy UG rec. non-need-based scholarship or grant aid	6
% needy frosh rec. need-based self-help aid	87
% needy UG rec. need-based self-help aid	89
% frosh rec. any financial aid	97
% UG rec. any financial aid	92
% UG borrow to pay for school	72
% frosh need fully met	13
% ugrads need fully met	10
Average % of frosh need met	83
Average % of ugrad need met	81

LOYOLA UNIVERSITY MARYLAND

4501 NORTH CHARLES STREET, BALTIMORE, MD 21210 • ADMISSIONS: 410-617-5012 • FAX: 410-617-2176

CAMPUS LIFE

Quality of Life Rating	**91**
Fire Safety Rating	**85**
Green Rating	**92**
Type of school	private
Affiliation	Roman Catholic
Environment	village

STUDENTS

Total undergrad enrollment	3,835
% male/female	39/61
% from out of state	85
% from public high school	52
% frosh live on campus	98
% African American	4
% Asian	3
% Caucasian	82
% Hispanic	7
% international	1
# of countries represented	68

SURVEY SAYS . . .

Athletic facilities are great
School is well run
Dorms are like palaces
Frats and sororities are unpopular or nonexistent
Student government is popular
Students are involved in community service

ACADEMICS

Academic Rating	**91**
% students returning for sophomore year	89
% students graduating within 4 years	79
% students graduating within 6 years	83
Calendar	semester
Student/faculty ratio	13:1
Profs interesting rating	90
Profs accessible rating	90
Most classes have	20–29 students
Most lab/discussion sessions have	10–19 students

MOST POPULAR MAJORS

business/commerce; communications technology/technician; psychology

APPLICANTS ALSO LOOK AT AND OFTEN PREFER

Boston College, Georgetown University, University of Notre Dame

AND SOMETIMES PREFER

Villanova University, College of the Holy Cross, University of Richmond

AND RARELY PREFER

Providence College, Fordham University, Fairfield University

STUDENTS SAY ". . ."

Academics

The Jesuits have a long history of excellence in higher education, and that tradition is richly reflected in the academic programs at Loyola University Maryland. The undergraduate experience is built around Loyola's "fantastic core curriculum," which ensures "a solid foundation in the natural sciences, English, history, philosophy and theology." Through the core, students across disciplines "take some awesome classes that will completely change your perspective on the world." Jesuit values and philosophy are emphasized in the coursework, yet the school strikes the "right balance between religion, spirituality, and the everyday life of college students." No matter what field you choose to study, "The academics are outstanding and the coursework is challenging." A true teaching university, Loyola professors use "different learning techniques to cater to everyone's different learning styles." With small "classes capped at thirty-five," professors "actually know each of their students by name." Serving as both personal and academic mentors, Loyola professors "get to know you personally, take time out of their office hours to have intellectual discussions, show you how to learn and how to teach, and help you out when you are having difficulties." The relationship can even extend off campus, as it's "fairly common for professors to give out their personal cell phone numbers or to even invite the class to their home for dinner." There's extensive "academic support" and tutoring for students in every discipline, and the "Career Center is open for students starting at day one." Though some would like to see a "larger variety of classes" for undergraduates, many praise the "excellent study abroad program," which offers the opportunity to spend a year in one of fourteen countries.

Life

Loyola students juggle school, service, spirituality, and social life with extraordinary flair. Monday through Friday, most undergraduates are "insanely busy doing loads of homework, projects, reading, community service, clubs, lectures, [and] sports." Of particular note, Loyola offers "amazing opportunities to get involved in the Baltimore community through service." In fact, the school uses "Baltimore city as an extension of the classroom," where students learn about real life, rather than living in a college bubble. On the weekends, things slow down around campus, though students can partake of the "numerous speakers, movies, events, or sporting events" hosted by the university. In addition, "A lot of people go out to bars on Fridays and Saturdays," because "there is no Greek life" on campus and Loyola's strict alcohol policies make it difficult to throw parties. Loyola students can be found out and about in Baltimore, "going out to eat, catching an Orioles game, attending a concert at the BSO, [or] walking around the harbor." "Most students live on campus" during the school year, enjoying a surprisingly comfortable lifestyle in Loyola's cushy dormitories. If you score a spot in one of the suites, you and your roommates will "have full kitchens in your dorm by sophomore year."

Student Body

In addition to being predominantly Catholic, "Many of the students are white, from New York or New Jersey, and come from private high schools." You'll see plenty of "Uggs, North Face, pearls, and J. Crew" around campus. Although "the student body may appear homogenous," students insist that, "Everyone can fit in well if you get past the initial stereotypes and immerse yourself in the opportunities Loyola has to offer." On that note, students "try to live out the core values of the university and enjoy being a contributing member of school community." Here, students "care about their academics and do well in school, but they also try to balance that with extracurriculars and their spiritual life." On the whole, the campus "really welcoming and trustworthy," with a "great sense of community." With so many ways to get involved, most students "find their niche at Loyola very quickly."

FINANCIAL AID: 410-617-2576 • WEBSITE: WWW.LOYOLA.EDU

THE PRINCETON REVIEW SAYS

Admissions

Very important factors considered include: Application essay, recommendation(s), rigor of secondary school record, character/personal qualities. *Important factors considered include:* Class rank, alumni/ae relation, extracurricular activities, first generation, talent/ability, volunteer work. *Other factors considered include:* Academic GPA, standardized test scores, geographical residence, interview, level of applicant's interest, racial/ethnic status, work experience. ACT with or without writing component accepted. TOEFL required of all international applicants. High school diploma is required and GED is accepted. *Academic units required:* 4 English, 3 mathematics, 3 science, 3 foreign language, 2 social studies, 2 history. *Academic units recommended:* 4 English, 4 mathematics, 4 science, 4 foreign language, 3 social studies, 3 history, 1 visual/performing arts, 1 computer science.

Financial Aid

Students should submit: FAFSA, CSS/Financial Aid PROFILE, noncustodial PROFILE, business/farm supplement. Regular filing deadline is February 15. The Princeton Review suggests that all financial aid forms be submitted as soon as possible after January 1. *Need-based scholarships/grants offered:* Federal Pell, SEOG, state scholarships/grants, private scholarships, the school's own gift aid. *Loan aid offered:* Direct Subsidized Stafford, Direct Unsubsidized Stafford, Direct PLUS, Federal Perkins, college/university loans from institutional funds. Applicants will be notified of awards on or about April 1. Federal Work-Study Program available. Institutional employment available. Highest amount earned per year from on-campus jobs $2,420. Off-campus job opportunities are good.

The Inside Word

Loyola University Maryland considers a student's academic record to be among the most important factors in an admissions decision. Successful students usually rank in the top quarter of their classes. Although Loyola will consider standardized test scores if you submit them, the SAT or ACT are optional for all first-year applicants. If you decide to apply without taking the SAT, Loyola asks that you submit an additional personal essay or recommendation.

THE SCHOOL SAYS ". . ."

From the Admissions Office

"To make a wise choice about your college plans, you will need to find out more. We extend to you these invitations. Question-and-answer periods with an admissions counselor are helpful to prospective students. An appointment should be made in advance. Admission office hours are 9:00 A.M. to 5:00 P.M., Monday through Friday. College day programs and Saturday information programs are scheduled during the academic year. These programs include a video about Loyola, a general information session, a discussion of various majors, a campus tour, and lunch. Summer information programs can help high school juniors to get a head start on investigating colleges. These programs feature an introductory presentation about the university and a campus tour."

SELECTIVITY

Admissions Rating	**87**
# of applicants	12,066
% of applicants accepted	63
% of acceptees attending	14
# accepting a place on wait list	1,854
# admitted from wait list	143

FRESHMAN PROFILE

Range SAT Critical Reading	540–640
Range SAT Math	560–650
Range ACT Composite	25–28
Minimum paper TOEFL	550
Minimum web-based TOEFL	79
Average HS GPA	3.4
% graduated top 10% of class	34
% graduated top 25% of class	70
% graduated top 50% of class	95

DEADLINES

Early action	
Deadline	11/1
Notification	1/15
Regular	
Priority	11/1
Deadline	1/15
Nonfall registration?	yes

FINANCIAL FACTS

Financial Aid Rating	**94**
Annual tuition	$41,026
Room and board	$12,120
Required fees	$1,400
Books and supplies	$1,210
% needy frosh rec. need-based scholarship or grant aid	89
% needy UG rec. need-based scholarship or grant aid	87
% needy frosh rec. non-need-based scholarship or grant aid	14
% needy UG rec. non-need-based scholarship or grant aid	16
% needy frosh rec. need-based self-help aid	87
% needy UG rec. need-based self-help aid	89
% frosh rec. any financial aid	70
% UG rec. any financial aid	68
% UG borrow to pay for school	64
Average cumulative indebtedness	$31,655
% frosh need fully met	99
% ugrads need fully met	89
Average % of frosh need met	100
Average % of ugrad need met	97

LOYOLA UNIVERSITY—NEW ORLEANS

6363 ST. CHARLES AVENUE, NEW ORLEANS, LA 70118-6195 • ADMISSIONS: 504-865-3240 • FAX: 504-865-3383

CAMPUS LIFE

Quality of Life Rating	**95**
Fire Safety Rating	**98**
Green Rating	**77**
Type of school	private
Affiliation	Roman Catholic
Environment	city

STUDENTS

Total undergrad enrollment	3,095
% male/female	43/57
% from out of state	58
% from public high school	46
# of fraternities	8
# of sororities	7
% African American	15
% Asian	4
% Caucasian	57
% Hispanic	13
% Native American	1
% international	3
# of countries represented	57

SURVEY SAYS . . .

Great computer facilities
Great library
Students get along with local community
Great off-campus food
Musical organizations are popular
Student publications are popular
Hard liquor is popular

ACADEMICS

Academic Rating	**90**
% students returning for sophomore year	77
Calendar	semester
Student/faculty ratio	11:1
Profs interesting rating	89
Profs accessible rating	87
Most classes have	10–19 students
Most lab/discussion sessions have	fewer than 10 students

MOST POPULAR MAJORS

marketing/marketing management; mass communication/media studies; psychology

APPLICANTS ALSO LOOK AT AND OFTEN PREFER

Saint Louis University, University of Miami, Boston University, Fordham University

AND SOMETIMES PREFER

Louisiana State University—Baton Rouge, Tulane University, Xavier University of Louisiana, Loyola University of Chicago

STUDENTS SAY ". . ."

Academics

Loyola University New Orleans provides undergraduates with an education deeply rooted in the Jesuit tradition. The school aims to produce "well-rounded students" who strive "to serve the world around them." Undergraduates are seen "as individuals" and encouraged to "discover their passions." Loyola offers "small classes," which helps to foster strong relationships between students and professors. Indeed, "personal attention" is a hallmark of the academic experience here, and the faculty is eager "to see you succeed." Undergrads are quick to praise their "intelligent, helpful, and kind" professors who "take a genuine interest in every student" and "make a firm decision to learn your name and what type of person you are." By and large, their doors are always open, and most professors make themselves "readily available to answer any and all questions you may have both inside and outside the classroom." The small class size also means that "discussions are frequently encouraged" and, as one political science major divulges, "challenging a professor's ideas [is] completely welcome." Impressively, "Loyola does a great job of encouraging students to apply their knowledge outside of the classroom, through internships as well as service-learning opportunities." The "friendly and very approachable" administration also wins kudos from the undergrads. They are "very open to students and their suggestions," and "you can see them working to make our school a better place."

Life

As one English lit major confidently declares, "Going to school in New Orleans means that you will never be bored. Ever. There is never a shortage of good food, good times, or good music." Yes, these Loyola students bask in the fact that they have New Orleans as their playground. The city offers "great opportunities for theater, music, and art," and many undergrads "go out and listen to live music on the weekends." They also enjoy the "great shopping on Magazine Street" and love to "explore the French Quarter." Students can also frequently be found "riding their bikes through Audubon Park and having a picnic on the Mississippi River." And naturally, "Mardi Gras is definitely the social highlight of the spring semester, closely followed by Jazz Fest." Of course, there's always plenty of activity at the university itself. "Whether [there's] a speaker, movie night, [or] free food, students are up at all hours of the day and night enjoying the campus." A satisfied senior goes further sharing, "Residential life offers some good floor and hall programs [such as] Third Friday quad parties and laser tag." As a music education major succinctly puts it, "There is never a dull day at Loyola."

Student Body

Loyola University undergrads are a "laid-back and friendly" lot who often "greet one another with a smile." Most students view their peers as "creative," "imaginative," and "really down-to-earth." Further, they are a "driven" group, motivated "to do well academically" and "participate in a wide range of activities." Of course, many "also want to let loose and have fun during the weekends." Additionally, "most Loyola students have an interest in music or an interest in service and rebuilding the city." Perhaps most notably, Loyola manages to attract students from a wide variety of backgrounds. As one political science major brags, "We consist of such a diverse group of people that I couldn't put my finger on just one type of person. But then again, that's one of my favorite things about being here. You can be anyone and do anything you want. Everyone fits in here. I have made friends with such a vast variety of people and that is something I never thought possible for me until I came here." Ultimately, as a biology major shares, "we all just mesh well."

FINANCIAL AID: 504-865-3231 • E-MAIL: ADMIT@LOYNO.EDU • WEBSITE: WWW.LOYNO.EDU

THE PRINCETON REVIEW SAYS

Admissions

Very important factors considered include: Academic GPA, rigor of secondary school record, standardized test scores. *Important factors considered include:* Application essay, recommendation(s), extracurricular activities, talent/ability. *Other factors considered include:* Class rank, alumni/ae relation, character/personal qualities, geographical residence, interview, level of applicant's interest, state residency, volunteer work, work experience. SAT or ACT required; ACT with or without writing component accepted. TOEFL required of all international applicants. High school diploma is required and GED is accepted. *Academic units required:* 4 English, 2 mathematics, 2 science, 2 social studies. *Academic units recommended:* 4 English, 3 mathematics, 3 science (1 science lab), 2 foreign language, 2 social studies.

Financial Aid

Students should submit: FAFSA. Regular filing deadline is June 1. The Princeton Review suggests that all financial aid forms be submitted as soon as possible after January 1. *Need-based scholarships/grants offered:* Federal Pell, SEOG, private scholarships, the school's own gift aid. *Loan aid offered:* Direct Subsidized Stafford, Direct Unsubsidized Stafford, Direct PLUS, Federal Perkins. Applicants will be notified of awards on a rolling basis beginning March 1. Federal Work-Study Program available. Institutional employment available. Highest amount earned per year from on-campus jobs $1,920. Off-campus job opportunities are excellent.

The Inside Word

Volunteer work and community service will serve your application to any school well, but they're especially helpful at this Jesuit institution. Post-Katrina New Orleans has spooked some prospective applicants, but the school has made great strides in rebuilding undergraduate enrollment, attracting new faculty members, and keeping alive the spirit of the school.

THE SCHOOL SAYS ". . ."

From the Admissions Office

"Chartered in 1912, Loyola University New Orleans is one of America's twenty-eight Jesuit institutions of higher learning. Its rich history dates back to the early eighteenth century when the Jesuits first arrived in New Orleans. As a Catholic university, Loyola has continued to emphasize the valuable Jesuit tradition of educating the whole person. Our more than 37,000 graduates have excelled in innumerable areas for ninety-seven years; their influence is felt around the world.

"Loyola's growth has increased the diversity of education available, all delivered within the educational values traditionally associated with our Jesuit heritage. This unique, nationally acclaimed institution—the crown jewel for a Jesuit education in the Southern United States—offers a welcoming and festive campus atmosphere and an emphasis on a liberal arts and sciences education, emphasizing self-discovery, exploration of values, while fostering personal initiative and critical thinking. Undergraduates enjoy individual attention in a university that strives to educate not only intellectually, but also spiritually, socially, and athletically. Undergraduate experience is broadened through special programs such as the First-Year Experience, learning communities, research, service learning, study abroad, and internships.

"Students applying for admission are required to take the SAT (or the ACT with the writing section). The highest composite scores will be used in admissions decisions."

SELECTIVITY	
Admissions Rating	**86**
# of applicants	6,386
% of applicants accepted	65
% of acceptees attending	21

FRESHMAN PROFILE	
Range SAT Critical Reading	590–630
Range SAT Math	560–610
Range ACT Composite	23–29
Minimum paper TOEFL	550
Minimum web-based TOEFL	79
Average HS GPA	3.7
% graduated top 10% of class	23
% graduated top 25% of class	50
% graduated top 50% of class	83

DEADLINES	
Regular	
Priority	12/1
Nonfall registration?	yes

FINANCIAL FACTS	
Financial Aid Rating	**82**
Annual tuition	$33,846
Room and board	$11,346
Required fees	$1,416
Books and supplies	$1,200
% needy frosh rec. need-based scholarship or grant aid	95
% needy UG rec. need-based scholarship or grant aid	94
% needy frosh rec. non-need-based scholarship or grant aid	75
% needy UG rec. non-need-based scholarship or grant aid	75
% needy frosh rec. need-based self-help aid	81
% needy UG rec. need-based self-help aid	85
% frosh rec. any financial aid	95
% UG rec. any financial aid	94
% UG borrow to pay for school	77
Average cumulative indebtedness	$12,597
% frosh need fully met	52
% ugrads need fully met	54
Average % of frosh need met	73
Average % of ugrad need met	70

Lynchburg College

1501 Lakeside Drive, Lynchburg, VA 24501 • Admissions: 434-544-8300 • Fax: 434-544-8653

CAMPUS LIFE

Quality of Life Rating	**81**
Fire Safety Rating	**74**
Green Rating	**74**
Type of school	private
Affiliation	Disciples of Christ
Environment	city

STUDENTS

Total undergrad enrollment	2,208
% male/female	41/59
% from out of state	34
% from public high school	85
% frosh live on campus	91
# of fraternities	4
# of sororities	6
% African American	10
% Asian	1
% Caucasian	78
% Hispanic	3
# of countries represented	12

SURVEY SAYS . . .

No one cheats
School is well run
Students are friendly

ACADEMICS

Academic Rating	**77**
% students returning for sophomore year	73
% students graduating within 4 years	44
% students graduating within 6 years	52
Calendar	semester
Student/faculty ratio	12:1
Profs interesting rating	85
Profs accessible rating	87
Most classes have	10–19 students
Most lab/discussion sessions have	10–19 students

MOST POPULAR MAJORS

nursing; elementary education; communication studies; psychology

STUDENTS SAY ". . ."

Academics

This small, "welcoming" school in central Virginia focuses on "preparing students for life's big challenges" through a supportive environment, small class sizes, and ample academic resources. "Classes are small and generally discussion-based." In most Lynchburg classrooms, "Desks are normally arranged in a circular position to allow for easy communication and debating." Lynchburg professors "know how to capture our attention, even during the most boring topics." As at any college, "Some of the professors are better than others," and "Certain teachers do not cater well to certain learning styles." However, almost every professor will "make an effort to connect on a personal level with students, inside and outside the classroom." According to many satisfied undergraduates, "The ability to create personal relationships with classmates and professors" is one of the school's greatest strengths. "People really care about you and your future" at Lynchburg, and the school "provides students with countless resources and tools for success." Students note the "different learning facilities" available on campus, from peer tutoring and the writing center to "breakout study rooms, computer labs, and the library." With so much to offer and a student body of just 2,000, "Lynchburg College is a very nurturing place" that "promotes individual personal growth."

Life

There's strong sense of community on the Lynchburg campus. Right off the bat, first-year programming succeeds at "helping freshmen adjust to college life" and "break the ice" with classmates. Most students agree that it's "really easy to make friends" at Lynchburg, where "Students are not afraid to express their individuality, and no one is criticized for who they are." A current undergrad enthuses, "I enjoy feeling like a part of a family, instead of going through the weeks seeing hundreds or even thousands of new faces." For many, cheering on the school's "excellent athletic teams" is a highlight of the experience. In addition, "Greek life plays a huge role" in the school community, and not just through parties. Here, "Greeks on campus are highly involved in service projects," as are many non-Greek members of the Lynchburg community. On campus, "There is always something going on, from sports, to movies, to game night, to awareness programs." If you feel like getting off campus, "There are a ton of places to eat and hang out at in the vicinity." Though students love to convene for a few drinks on Friday night, "The school cracks down on parties." Therefore, many undergraduates prefer to simply relax or watch movies in the dorms. Living facilities aren't particularly posh, and students admit that academic "facilities are old and could use a facelift." However, the "Campus is beautiful," and many students say it feels like a "home away from home."

Student Body

Lynchburg students are "laid-back but studious," with a shared love of sports. Many undergraduates were "star athletes in high school," and, because of the school's top-ranked athletics, "Most of the kids that go here either do varsity or club sports." The "campus is not that diverse," principally comprised of "nice, middle- to upper-class kids" from Virginia. However, you don't have to fit a mold to be accepted at Lynchburg. No matter their background, "Most students fit in quite well," and "It is not hard to make friends here regardless of sex, age, or anything else." As one student puts it, "The only way someone cannot fit in here at Lynchburg College, is if they blockade themselves in their room and refuse to eat, shower, or attend class." From theater groups to field hockey, "Everyone quickly becomes involved with different organizations" on campus. Although "Students do have their own group of friends," everyone agrees, "There really aren't a lot of cliques" at Lynchburg.

FINANCIAL AID: 434-544-8229 • E-MAIL: ADMISSIONS@LYNCHBURG.EDU • WEBSITE: WWW.LYNCHBURG.EDU

THE PRINCETON REVIEW SAYS

Admissions

Very important factors considered include: Academic GPA, rigor of secondary school record, standardized test scores. *Important factors considered include:* Class rank, interview. *Other factors considered include:* Application essay, recommendation(s), extracurricular activities, level of applicant's interest, talent/ability, volunteer work. SAT or ACT required; ACT with or without writing component accepted. TOEFL required of all international applicants. High school diploma is required and GED is accepted. *Academic units required:* 4 English, 3 mathematics, 3 science (2 science labs), 2 foreign language, 2 social studies, 2 history. *Academic units recommended:* 4 English, 4 mathematics, 4 science (2 science labs), 3 foreign language, 2 social studies, 2 history, 1 academic elective.

Financial Aid

Students should submit: FAFSA, state aid form. Regular preferred filing deadline is March 1. The Princeton Review suggests that all financial aid forms be submitted as soon as possible after January 1. *Need-based scholarships/grants offered:* Federal Pell, SEOG, state scholarships/grants, private scholarships, the school's own gift aid. *Loan aid offered:* Direct Subsidized Stafford, Direct Unsubsidized Stafford, Direct PLUS, Federal Perkins. Applicants will be notified of awards on a rolling basis beginning March 5. Federal Work-Study Program available. Institutional employment available. Off-campus job opportunities are good.

Inside Word

Students seeking admission and scholarship consideration must submit an application, official high school transcripts, and official SAT/ACT test to Lynchburg College. Admission deadlines are made on a rolling basis, but the college also offers both early action and early decision deadlines. Applicants who are admitted to the college are automatically considered for academic scholarships that range from $3,000 to $14,000. Admitted students may also receive an application for the annual invitational scholarship competition to qualify for additional scholarships that range from $1,500 to $5,000. Scholarship application deadlines are typically no later than early February so applying for admission early in the senior year is very important for students who qualify to be a party of the scholarship competition programs.

THE SCHOOL SAYS ". . ."

From the Admissions Office

"Lynchburg College is a nationally recognized private college in Virginia that goes above and beyond to challenge, engage, and inspire students to succeed in a global society. From the moment prospective students step onto this spectacular campus, they can see that LC is committed to student success. Opportunities to excel academically, develop leadership skills, and participate in community service are abundant and prepare students to positively affect their communities throughout their lives.

"The First-Year Experience is a program designed to assist freshmen make a successful transition to college by addressing topics that will enable them to develop and implement strategies to support their academic goals and build a strong sense of community. Designated freshmen residence halls provide a distinctive and enriched living and learning environment; students express tremendous satisfaction.

"The National Survey of Student Engagement (NSSE) measures how colleges and universities engage their students in activities related to learning and personal development. LC ranked high in all five benchmarks: student-faculty interaction, supportive campus environment, level of academic challenge, active and collaborative learning, and enriching education experiences.

"One of only forty colleges included in *Colleges That Change Lives,* LC emphasizes the development of the whole person, with a low student/faculty ratio, service learning, internships, study abroad, faculty-student collaborative research, and a variety of student organizations, athletics, intramurals, and club sports. Visiting is a must! Students and families are invited to attend one of the many visit opportunities throughout the year."

SELECTIVITY

Admissions Rating	74
# of applicants	4,617
% of applicants accepted	68
% of acceptees attending	19
# of early decision applicants	301
# accepted early decision	129

FRESHMAN PROFILE

Range SAT Critical Reading	440–560
Range SAT Math	450–550
Range SAT Writing	440–540
Range ACT Composite	19–24
Minimum paper TOEFL	525
Average HS GPA	3.2
% graduated top 10% of class	16
% graduated top 25% of class	42
% graduated top 50% of class	77

DEADLINES

Early decision	
Deadline	11/15
Notification	12/15
Nonfall registration?	yes

FINANCIAL FACTS

Financial Aid Rating	83
Annual tuition	$31,060
Room and board	$8,680
Required fees	$945
Books and supplies	$1,000
% needy frosh rec. need-based scholarship or grant aid	100
% needy UG rec. need-based scholarship or grant aid	100
% needy frosh rec. non-need-based scholarship or grant aid	14
% needy UG rec. non-need-based scholarship or grant aid	13
% needy frosh rec. need-based self-help aid	83
% needy UG rec. need-based self-help aid	82
% frosh rec. any financial aid	98
% UG rec. any financial aid	95
% UG borrow to pay for school	75
Average cumulative indebtedness	$30,636
% frosh need fully met	19
% ugrads need fully met	20
Average % of frosh need met	82
Average % of ugrad need met	77

MACALESTER COLLEGE

1600 GRAND AVENUE, ST. PAUL, MN 55105 • ADMISSIONS: 651-696-6357 • FAX: 651-696-6724

CAMPUS LIFE

Quality of Life Rating	**95**
Fire Safety Rating	**98**
Green Rating	**85**
Type of school	private
Environment	metropolis

STUDENTS

Total undergrad enrollment	1,988
% male/female	41/59
% from out of state	83
% from public high school	66
% frosh live on campus	100
% African American	3
% Asian	6
% Caucasian	67
% Hispanic	7
% Native American	1
% international	12
# of countries represented	93

SURVEY SAYS . . .

Lots of liberal students
Students aren't religious
Students love St. Paul, MN
Great food on campus
Frats and sororities are unpopular or nonexistent
Political activism is popular
Students are environmentally aware

ACADEMICS

Academic Rating	**97**
% students returning for sophomore year	94
% students graduating within 4 years	84
Calendar	semester
Student/faculty ratio	10:1
Profs interesting rating	95
Profs accessible rating	95
Most classes have	10–19 students
Most lab/discussion sessions have	10–19 students

MOST POPULAR MAJORS

economics; political science; biology

APPLICANTS ALSO LOOK AT AND OFTEN PREFER

Brown University, Swarthmore College

AND SOMETIMES PREFER

University of Chicago, Wesleyan University, Pomona College, Vassar College, Middlebury College

AND RARELY PREFER

Kenyon College, Oberlin College, Colorado College

STUDENTS SAY ". . ."

Academics

Macalester College in Minnesota is fast becoming an academic powerhouse; it "opens myriad doors for students to work incredibly hard at what they love and, through research, explore avenues of interest they may not have previously considered." The school attracts a high quality of "academic-minded" students because of the generous financial aid and places an emphasis on internationalism; the college also strongly encourages students to follow their interests in developing extracurricular student organizations. "Student organizations are provided exceptional guidance and funding from the college," says a student. The atmosphere is "academically challenging without feeling competitive," and Macalester is all about "finding the balance between serious academics, service, and fun." The "genuine, resourceful, accessible, and friendly" professors "are exceptional mentors" who "share the excitement they have about their particular fields." "I have found a lot of variety both in the teaching styles of my instructors and class topics, which is something I really appreciate about my major and Macalester in general," says one student. When professors can, they "change lecture to discussion," "add various different types of course materials," and generally keep students engaged. There is also a lot of interdisciplinary work and collaborations between professors in order to "help develop new courses, research topics, and even academic majors." Personal relationships are incredibly important to the faculty here, and professors "invest their time in the success of each student." Though there's "a definite depth to courses provided," the small size of the school means that "the variety within departments could be sparse." Being in the Twin Cities, there are "a lot of opportunities for volunteering and internships," and non-achievements, whether in sports, arts, or community service, are given "equal recognition." "There is an awareness about the world, our place in it, and how our choices affect it. There is an earnest desire to learn and listen to differing perspectives," says a student.

Life

This "unique international community in the middle of a frozen metropolis" ("I wish I could pick up the entire campus and move it to a warmer climate") has an "ideal" placement in a "beautiful" residential neighborhood dotted with restaurants and shops, with quick access to two major cities. At Mac, "There is so much to do on campus that you're never bored." "So many organizations, so little time!" says a student. With more than 120 organizations, "It's hard to find the time to get involved in everything, but very easy to find something to do." For more casual fun, people "go out into St. Paul and Minneapolis, go to dances on campus, go to house parties off campus, or just hang out and watch movies or have conversations." Parties "only happen on the weekend, and they are nonexistent around midterms or finals"; "Often people end up talking about Marxism or feminist theory at parties anyway." "You know you're at Macalester when the football team had its first winning season in decades, but our poetry slam team is national defending champions." Deep conversations about politics, spirituality, and identity are frequent, and "class and school invade all aspects of life here."

Student Body

Macalester is full of "intelligent," "left-wing," "self-driven students who want to participate in academics, politics, and social issues." There is a "simultaneous lightheartedness and intensity" to Macalester students, and everyone here is "eager to converse and debate with peers who may have a very different background from them." "The socioeconomic range is huge, as is the geographical" diversity with international students composing nineteen percent of the student body." "The experience of sitting in a class of twenty with students from eight different countries discussing the cultural implications of translation is one that can only be found at Macalester," says a student. "It would be easier to define the typical kid who is not at Mac: bro/fraternity-type guys and ditsy, sorority girls," says one student. "Mainstream people without their own opinions don't make it here."

FINANCIAL AID: 651-696-6214 • E-MAIL: ADMISSIONS@MACALESTER.EDU • WEBSITE: WWW.MACALESTER.EDU

THE PRINCETON REVIEW SAYS

Admissions

Very important factors considered include: Academic GPA, rigor of secondary school record. *Important factors considered include:* Application essay, recommendation(s), standardized test scores, character/personal qualities, extracurricular activities. *Other factors considered include:* Class rank, alumni/ae relation, first generation, interview, racial/ethnic status, talent/ability, volunteer work, work experience. SAT or ACT required; ACT with or without writing component accepted. TOEFL required of all international applicants. High school diploma or equivalent is not required. *Academic units recommended:* 4 English, 3 mathematics, 3 science (3 science labs), 3 foreign language, 3 social studies.

Financial Aid

Students should submit: FAFSA, CSS/Financial Aid PROFILE, noncustodial PROFILE. Regular filing deadline is March 1. The Princeton Review suggests that all financial aid forms be submitted as soon as possible after January 1. *Need-based scholarships/grants offered:* Federal Pell, SEOG, state scholarships/grants, private scholarships, the school's own gift aid. *Loan aid offered:* Direct Subsidized Stafford, Direct Unsubsidized Stafford, Direct PLUS, Federal Perkins, state loans. Applicants will be notified of awards on or about April 1. Federal Work-Study Program available. Institutional employment available. Highest amount earned per year from on-campus jobs $2,800. Off-campus job opportunities are excellent.

The Inside Word

To say that Macalester's star is on the rise is to put it very mildly. The number of applicants to the school continues to increase. Accordingly, it has grown substantially more difficult to gain admission here within a very short period of time. Candidates need to put their best foot forward in their applications; two-thirds of the current first year class ranked in the top ten percent of their high school classes.

THE SCHOOL SAYS ". . ."

From the Admissions Office

"Macalester has been preparing students for world citizenship and providing an integrated international education for over six decades. The United Nations flag has flown on campus since 1950 and eighteen percent of the students are citizens of another country, with over ninety countries represented on campus. Over sixty percent of Mac students study abroad, going to nearly fifty countries all over the world each year. Graduates enter the workforce or graduate school with respected scholarship and real experience in a global community, prepared to succeed in their chosen fields. Mac students thrive in a rigorous academic environment, supported by accomplished faculty who love to teach. Located in a friendly residential neighborhood in the heart of a vibrant metropolitan area, Macalester offers unusually broad, easily accessible internship opportunities to add valuable experience, connections and practice at getting things done, often leading to job opportunities after graduation. Two out of three Mac students complete an internship at a Twin Cities business, law firm, hospital, financial institution, museum, theater, state government, research lab, environmental agency, or nonprofit group (and more), all within a few miles of campus. Students rave about the food at Mac, which includes vegetarian fare, food for meat lovers, plenty of variety and entrées from around the world. A new athletic and recreation center opened in the fall of 2009, including a large fitness center, indoor track, gymnasium, natatorium, field house, gathering spaces, juice bar, atrium and more. Athletic teams frequently earn the highest cumulative GPA in the nation. Macalester meets the full demonstrated need for every admitted student, providing broad socioeconomic representation in the student body."

SELECTIVITY

Admissions Rating	**96**
# of applicants	6,111
% of applicants accepted	35
% of acceptees attending	22
# accepting a place on wait list	508
# admitted from wait list	196
# of early decision applicants	227
# accepted early decision	115

FRESHMAN PROFILE

Range SAT Critical Reading	650–740
Range SAT Math	630–710
Range SAT Writing	640–730
Range ACT Composite	28–32
Minimum paper TOEFL	600
Minimum web-based TOEFL	100
% graduated top 10% of class	70
% graduated top 25% of class	94
% graduated top 50% of class	100

DEADLINES

Early decision	
Deadline	11/15
Notification	12/15
Regular	
Deadline	1/15
Notification	3/30
Nonfall registration?	no

FINANCIAL FACTS

Financial Aid Rating	**98**
Annual tuition	$41,800
Room and board	$9,396
Required fees	$221
Books and supplies	$1,010
% needy frosh rec. need-based scholarship or grant aid	99
% needy UG rec. need-based scholarship or grant aid	99
% needy frosh rec. non-need-based scholarship or grant aid	7
% needy UG rec. non-need-based scholarship or grant aid	5
% needy frosh rec. need-based self-help aid	91
% needy UG rec. need-based self-help aid	93
% frosh rec. any financial aid	75
% UG rec. any financial aid	75
% UG borrow to pay for school	63
Average cumulative indebtedness	$21,123
% frosh need fully met	100
% ugrads need fully met	100
Average % of frosh need met	100
Average % of ugrad need met	100

MANHATTANVILLE COLLEGE

2900 PURCHASE STREET, ADMISSIONS OFFICE, PURCHASE, NY 10577 • ADMISSIONS: 914-323-5124 • FAX: 914-694-1732

CAMPUS LIFE

Quality of Life Rating	**84**
Fire Safety Rating	**96**
Green Rating	**82**
Type of school	private
Environment	town

STUDENTS

Total undergrad enrollment	1,733
% male/female	36/64
% from out of state	46
% frosh live on campus	79
% African American	9
% Asian	3
% Caucasian	40
% Hispanic	16
% international	11
# of countries represented	53

SURVEY SAYS . . .

Diverse student types on campus
Different types of students interact
Frats and sororities are unpopular or nonexistent

ACADEMICS

Academic Rating	**70**
% students returning for sophomore year	69
% students graduating within 4 years	51
% students graduating within 6 years	56
Calendar	semester
Student/faculty ratio	11:1
Profs interesting rating	79
Profs accessible rating	81
Most classes have	10–19 students

MOST POPULAR MAJORS

business/commerce; psychology; visual and performing arts, other

APPLICANTS ALSO LOOK AT AND OFTEN PREFER

New York University

AND SOMETIMES PREFER

Fordham University

STUDENTS SAY ". . ."

Academics

Located on a "beautiful, nature-filled campus," the "small, but extremely diverse" Manhattanville College focuses on "building a community among all students." Many students agree that "Manhattanville College is very good at playing to its strengths, which are primarily its international student program and its small class size." Other students praise its "well-known and impressive writing program" and boast that the "music and theater department are very strong." They are also quick to highlight that their school is "committed to raising awareness about various global issues" and that "there is always an opportunity to go abroad for study purposes or volunteering." Students appreciate the "very favorable faculty-to-student ratio" and note that the "small classes allow the professor to create a bond with each and every student." Students also praise the high caliber of the professors who are "knowledgeable and insightful" and "brilliant and fully devoted to their work and passionate about what they're teaching." One discerning student reveals, "My professors are unbelievably versed in their field of expertise, but that does not mean it always translates to their ability to relay that information in a way that is engaging. That is, however, not the norm, but the exception." Students also recognize that their professors have their students' interests at heart and reveal that "if you reach out to a teacher when struggling, almost all will make time to assist you if they see you are putting in the same effort." Students are less enamored with their school administration, which "is in a time of transition and they don't seem to know which direction is the best to take."

Life

According to some students, Manhattanville suffers the fate of many commuter schools in the sense that "no one ever stays on campus, so it's always a ghost town." However, students who do stay on campus find plenty of ways to keep busy. Many students take part in WMVL the "killer radio station," which has "helped to strengthen communication in and around [the] community." They brag, "There are eighty-five DJs, and they broadcast outstanding music." Students report, "Most weekends our school will provide events to keep students around like comedy shows, school dances, and events like that." "When it's nice out, people are always on the quad either tanning or studying or playing Frisbee or skipping class." Students also look forward to Fall Fest and Quad Jam, which are "two huge parties out on the quad, kind of like a carnival." For more adventurous students who seek fun outside the boundaries of Manhattanville, the school offers a "free bus service that goes into White Plains every evening." Many students flock to White Plains for "tons of shops, a few malls, restaurants, and so many things to do." Students also take advantage of free transportation to nearby Manhattan on weekends "to access the museums, shows, exhibits, city life, and the food."

Student Body

As host to a "large number of international students," Manhattanville "is all about student diversity." Students agree, "The diversity is awesome but sometimes people from certain ethnic backgrounds hang out with that group." Creating even more divisions among the student population, "Students seem to clump into cliques based on their socioeconomic backgrounds, sports/interests, etc." At the same time, students also note the "increased efforts at college to break down these barriers and have students from different backgrounds 'mingle' with one another." Students at this school consider themselves "very open and very friendly" and "accepting of people from all backgrounds." They also reveal that they "like to learn but don't go crazy studying." While some students agree, "Spanish-speaking students are probably the most common attendees," others feel, "There is a happy balance between all nationalities." Despite the differences in backgrounds, "Students fit in just by joining clubs and attending school sponsored events." One student insightfully sums it up with the observation that "Manhattanville is a place small enough that people know who you are, but you still have the ability to figure out who you are."

Financial Aid: 914-323-5357 • E-mail: admissions@mville.edu • Website: www.mville.edu

THE PRINCETON REVIEW SAYS

Admissions

Very important factors considered include: Rigor of secondary school record. *Important factors considered include:* Application essay, recommendation(s), extracurricular activities, interview. *Other factors considered include:* Alumni/ae relation, character/personal qualities, geographical residence, talent/ability, volunteer work, work experience. TOEFL required of all international applicants. High school diploma is required and GED is accepted. *Academic units required:* 4 English, 3 mathematics, 2 science, 2 social studies, 5 academic electives.

Financial Aid

Students should submit: FAFSA, state aid form. Regular filing deadline is March 1. The Princeton Review suggests that all financial aid forms be submitted as soon as possible after January 1. *Need-based scholarships/grants offered:* Federal Pell, SEOG, state scholarships/grants, private scholarships, the school's own gift aid. *Loan aid offered:* Direct Subsidized Stafford, Direct Unsubsidized Stafford, Direct PLUS. Applicants will be notified of awards on a rolling basis beginning March 1. Federal Work-Study Program available. Institutional employment available. Off-campus job opportunities are excellent.

The Inside Word

Manhattanville seeks "good fits," however and frequently attempts to assess compatibility with a candidate interview. The college still seeks to achieve greater gender balance, so male candidates enjoy a slightly higher admission rate than female candidates. In addition to meeting regular admissions requirements, students who wish to pursue a degree in fine arts or performing arts must present a portfolio or audition, respectively.

THE SCHOOL SAYS ". . ."

From the Admissions Office

"Manhattanville's mission—to educate ethically and socially responsible leaders for the global community—is evident throughout the college, from academics to athletics to social and extracurricular activities. With almost 1,700 undergraduates from fifty-nine nations and thirty-nine states, our diversity spans geographic, cultural, ethnic, religious, socioeconomic, and academic backgrounds. Students are free to express their views in this tight-knit community, where we value the personal as well as the global. Any six students with similar interest can start a club, and most participate in a variety of campus wide programs. Last year, students engaged in more than 23,380 hours of community service and social justice activity. Study abroad opportunities include the most desirable international locations. In the true liberal arts tradition, students are encouraged to think for themselves and develop new skills—in music, the studio arts, on stage, in the sciences, or on the playing field. With more than fifty areas of study and a popular self-designed major, there is no limit to our academic scope. Our Westchester County location, just thirty-five miles north of New York City, gives students an edge for jobs and internships. Last year, the men's and women's ice hockey teams were ranked number one in the nation for Division III."

SELECTIVITY	
Admissions Rating	**61**
# of applicants	4,772
% of applicants accepted	60
% of acceptees attending	19
FRESHMAN PROFILE	
Minimum paper TOEFL	550
DEADLINES	
Early decision	
Deadline	12/1
Notification	12/31
Regular	
Priority	3/1
Deadline	3/1
Nonfall registration?	yes
FINANCIAL FACTS	
Financial Aid Rating	**77**
Annual tuition	$34,020
Room and board	$14,340
Required fees	$1,350
Books and supplies	$800
% needy frosh rec. need-based scholarship or grant aid	89
% needy UG rec. need-based scholarship or grant aid	92
% needy frosh rec. non-need-based scholarship or grant aid	97
% needy UG rec. non-need-based scholarship or grant aid	84
% needy frosh rec. need-based self-help aid	87
% needy UG rec. need-based self-help aid	87
% frosh rec. any financial aid	75
% UG rec. any financial aid	70
% UG borrow to pay for school	53
Average cumulative indebtedness	$23,138
% frosh need fully met	14
% ugrads need fully met	10
Average % of frosh need met	79
Average % of ugrad need met	83

MARIST COLLEGE

3399 NORTH ROAD, POUGHKEEPSIE, NY 12601-1387 • ADMISSIONS: 845-575-3226 • FAX: 845-575-3215

CAMPUS LIFE

Quality of Life Rating	77
Fire Safety Rating	87
Green Rating	72
Type of school	private
Environment	town

STUDENTS

Total undergrad enrollment	5,019
% male/female	41/59
% from out of state	52
% from public high school	71
% frosh live on campus	92
# of fraternities	3
# of sororities	4
% African American	4
% Asian	2
% Caucasian	79
% Hispanic	8
% international	1
# of countries represented	23

SURVEY SAYS . . .

Great computer facilities
Low cost of living
Great library

ACADEMICS

Academic Rating	84
% students returning for sophomore year	92
% students graduating within 4 years	73
% students graduating within 6 years	80
Calendar	semester
Student/faculty ratio	16:1
Profs interesting rating	80
Profs accessible rating	80
Most classes have	20–29 students
Most lab/discussion sessions have	20–29 students

MOST POPULAR MAJORS

business administration and management; communication; computer science

APPLICANTS ALSO LOOK AT AND OFTEN PREFER

Boston College, Villanova University, New York University

AND SOMETIMES PREFER

Loyola University Maryland, Fordham University

AND RARELY PREFER

Ithaca College, Quinnipiac University

STUDENTS SAY ". . ."

Academics

While students are undoubtedly drawn to Marist College's "beautiful campus on the Hudson" and "magnificent scenery," it is the private school's abundance of academic offerings that really gets students excited. The "well-known business program," "great communications program," "five-year accelerated grad school for psychology," and "unbelievable study abroad programs, offering programs in over twenty countries," all help contribute to "Marist's continually rising prestige and national recognition." A favorite among the study abroad programs is the Freshman Florence Experience. Also of note is the school's "renowned fashion design program" where one student raves that "the job-placement rate coming out of the fashion program is amazing, especially in today's economy." Though comparatively small in size, Marist is able to hold its own against larger schools when it comes to resources. The college boasts a "connection to IBM" that promotes student internships and provides students and faculty access to advanced high performance IBM hardware and software and "an amazing library with very helpful resources and materials for research." However, when it comes to their campus, students do feel that there is one area that could use improvement—student housing. They generally agree, "Marist needs more upperclassmen housing since it is only guaranteed to freshmen and sophomores." When describing the school faculty, students gush about their professors who are "top-notch," "knowledgeable, and lively," and "often accessible and approachable outside of the classroom." One student says, "They are always inclusive in class discussions, and they have a zest and spark for what they're teaching us." A slightly more critical student reports, "Professors in lower-level courses tend to lecture too much, but the teachers in mid- and upper-level courses tend to have a real passion for their subjects and can make even accounting interesting." All in all, students generally agree, "Marist College prepares students to face the real world with knowledge and skills, rather than simply earn impressive grades."

Life

With more than "eighty clubs and organizations," as well as Division I sports at Marist College, it is clear that students aren't exaggerating when they say, "There is always something to do on campus whether it's a lecture from one of the puppeteers from Sesame Street, a hypnotist, a concert, or a live animal demonstration." The school's surrounding environment and entertainment offerings also inspire one student to wax rhapsodic: "Life is simple and beautiful. Who else gets to watch the sunset over the Hudson Highlands of the beautiful Hudson River? The Student Programming Council is on top of their game: Broadway trips, Yankee games, ski/snowboard trips, comedians, pop stars...we had wolves come to our school for a conservation program...what other school gets wolves?" For those students who are less exuberant about having wolves in their proximity, they can always escape off campus. "The Poughkeepsie Galleria is not too far up the road, and that poses as a good break and social outing," and "NYC is an easy train ride away."

Student Body

While it may be easy to buy into the homogenous "Marist Family" sentiment that many students express, the student population and dynamics are more nuanced than that. Some students claim that Marist is "full of bros and preppy girls," while others point out, "The average Marist student is probably white and middle-class, with a Catholic upbringing." One student chimes in, "The school could definitely work to diversify the students who go here. The majority are from New York, New Jersey, and Connecticut." While it seems that "students who are more free-spirited, "hipster," or those who do not like partying will have a much harder time fitting in," some students make the case that "if you give Marist a chance, you will definitely find people that you like to hang out with." In general, students feel warmly about their peers and describe them as "outgoing and goal-oriented" and "nice, kind, caring, and willing to talk to anyone and make them feel like they fit in."

FINANCIAL AID: 845-575-3230 • E-MAIL: ADMISSION@MARIST.EDU • WEBSITE: WWW.MARIST.EDU

THE PRINCETON REVIEW SAYS

Admissions

Very important factors considered include: Rigor of secondary school curriculum, academic GPA, and declared program of study. *Important factors considered include:* Standardized test scores, class rank, essay, recommendation(s), character/personal qualities, extracurricular activities, geographical residence, special talent/ability, volunteer work, work experience. *Other factors considered include:* Alumni/ae relation, level of applicant's interest, racial/ethnic status. TOEFL or IELTS is required of all international applicants. High school diploma is required and GED is accepted. *Academic units required:* 4 English, 3 mathematics, 3 science (2 science labs), 2 foreign language, 2 social studies, 1 history, 2 academic electives. *Academic units recommended:* 4 mathematics, 4 science (3 science labs), 3 foreign language.

Financial Aid

Students should submit: FAFSA. The Princeton Review suggests that all financial aid forms be submitted as soon as possible after January 1. The Marist preferred deadline for incoming freshman is February 15. *Need-based scholarships/grants offered:* Federal Pell, SEOG, state scholarships/grants, private scholarships, institutional grant aid. *Loan aid offered:* Federal Direct Subsidized Stafford, Federal Direct Unsubsidized Stafford, Federal Direct PLUS, Federal Perkins, and private loans. Applicants will be notified of awards on a rolling basis beginning March 15. Federal Work-Study and institutional employment is available. Highest amount earned per year from on-campus jobs is $6,916. Off-campus job opportunities are excellent.

The Inside Word

About one-quarter of its most recent incoming class graduated outside the top twenty-five percent of their high school class. Those lacking academic bona fides will have to make it up in other areas, however; evidence of leadership, ability to contribute to the life of the campus (for example, artistic or athletic skill), an interesting background that will add diversity to classroom discus sion, or a similar distinguishing trait will be needed to make up for a middling academic record.

THE SCHOOL SAYS ". . ."

From the Admissions Office

"Marist is a 'hot school' among prospective students. We are seeing a record number of applications each year. But the number of seats available for the freshman class remains the same, about 1,000. Therefore, becoming an accepted applicant is an increasingly competitive process. Our recommendations: keep your grades up, participate in community service, and exercise leadership in the classroom, in your extracurricular endeavors, and in your community. We encourage a campus visit. When prospective students see Marist—our beautiful location on a scenic stretch of the Hudson River, the quality of our facilities, the interaction between students and faculty, and the fact that everyone really enjoys their time here—they want to become a part of the Marist College community. We'll help you in the transition from high school to college through an innovative first-year program that provides mentors for every student. You'll also learn how to use technology in whatever field you choose. We emphasize three aspects of a true Marist experience: excellence in education, community, and service to others. At Marist, you'll get a premium education, develop your skills, have fun and make lifelong friends, be given the opportunity to gain valuable experience through our great internship and study abroad programs, including our branch campus in Florence, Italy, and be ahead of the competition for graduate school or work."

SELECTIVITY	
Admissions Rating	**94**
# of applicants	11,399
% of applicants accepted	34
% of acceptees attending	31
# accepting a place on wait list	1,051
# of early decision applicants	261
# accepted early decision	199

FRESHMAN PROFILE	
Range SAT Critical Reading	540–630
Range SAT Math	560–640
Range SAT Writing	550–640
Range ACT Composite	24–28
Minimum paper TOEFL	550
Minimum web-based TOEFL	80
Average HS GPA	3.3
% graduated top 10% of class	32
% graduated top 25% of class	70
% graduated top 50% of class	95

DEADLINES	
Early decision	
Deadline	11/1
Notification	12/15
Early action	
Deadline	11/15
Notification	1/30
Regular	
Deadline	2/1
Notification	3/30
Nonfall registration?	yes

FINANCIAL FACTS	
Financial Aid Rating	**70**
Annual tuition	$28,300
Room and board	$12,100
Required fees	$500
Books and supplies	$1,700
% needy frosh rec. need-based scholarship or grant aid	72
% needy UG rec. need-based scholarship or grant aid	67
% needy frosh rec. non-need-based scholarship or grant aid	100
% needy UG rec. non-need-based scholarship or grant aid	84
% needy frosh rec. need-based self-help aid	81
% needy UG rec. need-based self-help aid	83
% frosh rec. any financial aid	66
% UG rec. any financial aid	60
% UG borrow to pay for school	69
Average cumulative indebtedness	$32,507
% frosh need fully met	65
% ugrads need fully met	28

Marlboro College

PO Box A, Marlboro, VT 05344-0300 • Admissions: 802-258-9236 • Fax: 802-451-7555

CAMPUS LIFE

Quality of Life Rating	**84**
Fire Safety Rating	**71**
Green Rating	**69**
Type of school	private
Environment	rural

STUDENTS

Total undergrad enrollment	267
% male/female	49/51
% from out of state	89
% from public high school	70
% frosh live on campus	98
% African American	1
% Asian	3
% Caucasian	63
% Hispanic	2
% international	1
# of countries represented	4

SURVEY SAYS . . .

Lots of liberal students
Class discussions encouraged
No one cheats
Campus feels safe
Frats and sororities are unpopular or nonexistent
Student government is popular

ACADEMICS

Academic Rating	**99**
% students returning for sophomore year	80
% students graduating within 4 years	35
% students graduating within 6 years	45
Calendar	semester
Student/faculty ratio	6:1
Profs interesting rating	99
Profs accessible rating	95
Most classes have	fewer than 10 students
Most lab/discussion sessions have	fewer than 10 students

MOST POPULAR MAJORS

English language and literature; social sciences; visual and performing arts, other

APPLICANTS ALSO LOOK AT AND OFTEN PREFER

Reed College

AND SOMETIMES PREFER

College of the Atlantic, Bard College, The Evergreen State College

AND RARELY PREFER

Bennington College, University of Vermont, Green Mountain College, Hampshire College

STUDENTS SAY ". . ."

Academics

Teeny tiny Marlboro College in Vermont offers a "self-driven, free, and intimate academic climate" with a "rustic feel." With an average class size of just ten students, the school is all about creating a serious academic setting "where students are on equal footing with teachers and decide their own academic paths." "I dictate my own academics at Marlboro; I have the freedom to seriously study most anything," says one student. Marlboro's unique academic system, the Plan, is "incredibly exciting"; through this curriculum, students "can focus right in, very specifically, on the particular books or ideas that interest them most." The "incredibly sharp-witted and compassionate" faculty members at Marlboro "have strong personalities," and relationships with professors are "really intimate (in a good way)." "By the end of a class—provided you participate—they know you well, and you know them well," says a student. There's definitely "a relaxed, humorous atmosphere that manages to coexist with the intense academics, somehow." Discussions can run deep, and "There are few classes here in which the professor talks more than the students do." There are also more than 200 tutorials at Marlboro, which are typically reserved for juniors and seniors; most are one-on-one, and depend on students taking charge of a subject, preparing for and leading a weekly meeting with the faculty member and completing a piece of research or production. In addition, there is a "town-meeting-style community government" in place and "lots of energy from staff going into projects outside the classroom." Though no student lacks for attention or academic assistance, some admit that resources can be spread thin in some areas, including the "limited in number" professors; accessible as they are, some subject areas only have one professor, which means that "if you don't get along with the professor in your department you can either suck it up, or choose a different major." However, all of the "ingenious" professors are "great and really flexible. They just want to help." Grades, "while something that happens," are not considered important—instead the work students produce "is for our own pleasure and pride."

Life

With just a few hundred students enrolled, there aren't a lot of redundancies or waste. The dining hall is a central meeting place, where many students "hang out there for hours talking." People also spend a lot of time in the library, which is open twenty-four hours and "functions as some people's second home." In this "intellectual yet casual atmosphere," everybody "seems to be reading constantly," and students "talk about books a lot, or articles, or things people have read on the internet." "Class materials get inside people's heads, and they seem to want to share it." Parties do occur on weekends, though it's not a huge scene; "It's common to see people talk about epistemology while they're drunk and dance while they're sober." "We party a bit, play lots of video games, watch a lot of movies, and sometimes go into town," says one student. Athletics aren't really very big (other than nearby hiking), and "most of time we like *talking* to each other." People are "constantly philosophizing the state of things."

Student Body

Marlboro is "a place where 'the weird kids' from high schools all across the nation congregate and make beautiful music together (often literally)." "There is no typical student. That's the point," says one. Students here are "functionally eccentrics," "quirky," and "ready to pursue their own passions." There is a "high level of LGBTQ tolerance," and most students here are "usually politically mindful and open to challenging his or her perspectives." "It's kind of crazy, and everyone likes each other," says a student. There are people of all sorts, "from suits to rainbows, dreadlocks to comb-overs, you get the point." Essentially, "There is nothing too weird for Marlboro."

FINANCIAL AID: 802-258-9312 • E-MAIL: ADMISSIONS@MARLBORO.EDU • WEBSITE: WWW.MARLBORO.EDU

THE PRINCETON REVIEW SAYS

Admissions

Very important factors considered include: Application essay, academic GPA, rigor of secondary school record, character/personal qualities. *Important factors considered include:* Extracurricular activities, interview. *Other factors considered include:* Class rank, recommendation(s), standardized test scores, alumni/ae relation, first generation, geographical residence, level of applicant's interest, state residency, talent/ability, volunteer work, work experience. ACT with or without writing component accepted. TOEFL required of all international applicants. High school diploma is required and GED is accepted. *Academic units recommended:* 4 English, 3 mathematics, 3 science (1 science lab), 3 foreign language, 3 social studies, 3 history, 3 academic electives.

Financial Aid

Students should submit: FAFSA. Regular filing deadline is March 1. The Princeton Review suggests that all financial aid forms be submitted as soon as possible after January 1. *Need-based scholarships/grants offered:* Federal Pell, SEOG, state scholarships/grants, private scholarships, the school's own gift aid. *Loan aid offered:* Direct Subsidized Stafford, Direct Unsubsidized Stafford, Direct PLUS. Applicants will be notified of awards on a rolling basis beginning March 15. Federal Work-Study Program available. Institutional employment available. Highest amount earned per year from on-campus jobs $2,050. Off-campus job opportunities are fair.

The Inside Word

Don't be misled by Marlboro's acceptance rate—this isn't the type of school that attracts many applications from students unsure of whether they belong at Marlboro. Most applicants are qualified both in terms of academic achievement and sincere intellectual curiosity. The school seeks candidates "with intellectual promise, a high degree of self-motivation, self-discipline, personal stability, social concern, and the ability and desire to contribute to the college community." These are the qualities you should stress on your application.

THE SCHOOL SAYS ". . ."

From the Admissions Office

"Marlboro College is distinguished by its curriculum, praised in higher education circles as unique; it is known for its self-governing philosophy, in which each student, faculty, and staff has an equal vote on many issues affecting the community; and it is recognized for its sixty-five year history of offering a rigorous, exciting, self-designed course of study taught in very small classes and individualized study with faculty. Marlboro's size also distinguishes it from most other schools. With 300 students and a student/faculty ratio of eight to one, it is one of the nation's smallest liberal arts colleges. Few other schools offer a program where students have such close interaction with faculty, and where community life is inseparable from academic life. The result, the self-designed, self-directed Plan of Concentration, allows students to develop their own unique academic work by defining a problem, setting clear limits on an area of inquiry, and analyzing, evaluating, and reporting on the outcome of a significant project. A Marlboro education teaches you to think for yourself, articulate your thoughts, express your ideas, believe in yourself, and do it all with the clarity, confidence, and self-reliance necessary for later success, no matter what postgraduate path you take."

SELECTIVITY	
Admissions Rating	88
# of applicants	279
% of applicants accepted	75
% of acceptees attending	24
# of early decision applicants	10
# accepted early decision	9

FRESHMAN PROFILE	
Range SAT Critical Reading	610–690
Range SAT Math	510–650
Range SAT Writing	570–680
Range ACT Composite	24–32
Minimum paper TOEFL	550
Minimum web-based TOEFL	80
Average HS GPA	3.2
% graduated top 10% of class	40
% graduated top 25% of class	60
% graduated top 50% of class	80

DEADLINES	
Early decision	
Deadline	12/1
Notification	12/15
Early action	
Deadline	2/1
Notification	2/15
Regular	
Deadline	3/1
Nonfall registration?	yes

FINANCIAL FACTS	
Financial Aid Rating	81
Annual tuition	$36,300
Room and board	$9,930
Required fees	$1,340
Books and supplies	$1,200
% needy frosh rec. need-based scholarship or grant aid	98
% needy UG rec. need-based scholarship or grant aid	96
% needy frosh rec. non-need-based scholarship or grant aid	13
% needy UG rec. non-need-based scholarship or grant aid	11
% needy frosh rec. need-based self-help aid	100
% needy UG rec. need-based self-help aid	94
% frosh rec. any financial aid	75
% UG rec. any financial aid	72
% UG borrow to pay for school	71
Average cumulative indebtedness	$20,886
Average % of frosh need met	75
Average % of ugrad need met	68

MARYWOOD UNIVERSITY

OFFICE OF UNIVERSITY ADMISSIONS, SCRANTON, PA 18509 • ADMISSIONS: 570-348-6234 • FAX: 570-961-4763

CAMPUS LIFE

Quality of Life Rating	**69**
Fire Safety Rating	**94**
Green Rating	**86**
Type of school	private
Affiliation	Roman Catholic
Environment	city

STUDENTS

Total undergrad enrollment	2,190
% male/female	30/70
% from out of state	28
% from public high school	89
% frosh live on campus	73
# of sororities	1
% African American	1
% Asian	2
% Caucasian	85
% Hispanic	4
# of countries represented	20

SURVEY SAYS . . .

Athletic facilities are great
Low cost of living
Musical organizations are popular
Very little drug use

ACADEMICS

Academic Rating	**72**
% students returning for sophomore year	84
% students graduating within 4 years	51
% students graduating within 6 years	63
Calendar	semester
Student/faculty ratio	13:1
Profs interesting rating	75
Profs accessible rating	73
Most classes have	10–19 students

MOST POPULAR MAJORS

elementary education and teaching; nursing/registered nurse (rn, asn, bsn, msn); psychology

STUDENTS SAY ". . ."

Academics

Marywood University is well-known for offering some of the most unique and outstanding pre-professional programs of study in the Pennsylvania area. Students rave about the "really fantastic" education department, and they call the art therapy program "top-notch," while the music program has a "fabulous reputation," and the strength of the speech pathology, nutrition, physician assistant, and interior design programs also draw students from all over the area to the university. In addition to these outstanding programs, this small Catholic university, which consists of four colleges and a School of Architecture, also offers a wide range of traditional undergraduate majors. Students characterize Marywood as "a small community that is serious about its academics." Class sizes are "small, and it is easy to ask for help." "Professors here know your name and are always willing to help you," and according to Marywood students, "Small class sizes and attentive professors tend to favor discussion-based classroom settings." The professors at Marywood "have a good mix of personalities." Some professors "are nuns and priests, but most are not," and "Many of the professors are also currently working in the field," which allows students to have a much richer, interactive learning experience.

Life

Students love "the warm and welcoming feel of the campus. Everyone is so friendly, and there is so much to do. It's more like a home than a school." There is "usually something to do during weeknights"; the student activities club "organizes events like Bingo and Trivia Night a few times each semester as well as organizing other entertainment such as comedians and movie nights. There are clubs for every interest you can imagine." There are also a "large number of recreational sports and classes available to students" on campus. On weekends, however, "Campus usually turns into a ghost town." On-campus rules in regard to alcohol are "overly strict," resulting in weekend activities that often take place off campus, at "house parties and the University of Scranton." "Students also enjoy going to clubs and bars in the downtown Scranton area on weekends," and there are even clubs that allow students ages eighteen and up. First Fridays are a popular "monthly art/music/culture event that occurs downtown, providing the opportunity to meet local artists and musicians." The large population of commuter students at Marywood say, "If you dorm, it is easier to be involved on campus, but commuting life is different for most people…Clubs and events are aimed more toward people who live on campus." As for parking on campus, students say, "Finding a parking spot is as difficult as winning the lottery."

Student Body

Students describe the Marywood University community as "wholesome and welcoming." A typical Marywood student is "well-rounded, friendly, and passionate about [his or her] field of study." There tend to be subtle social divisions between various fields of study: "Students tend to gather in groups based on friendships formed through their majors." Though the campus is not very diverse ethnically or economically, there is a great deal of diversity along the lines of students' interests and personalities. Students "range from the athletic to the very religious to the extremely studious." There are many art students on campus due to the strength of the art department, and there is a "great deal of athletes" as well. There is also a significantly larger percentage of females to males on campus. Many students are local to the area, and in general, the student body is made up of equal parts commuter students and students who dorm. Because of the small size of the university, "you see many of the same faces every day" and "get to know a lot of people" in the small campus community. "Most students interact with each other and get along well."

FINANCIAL AID: 866-279-9663 • E-MAIL: YOURFUTURE@MARYWOOD.EDU • WEBSITE: WWW.MARYWOOD.EDU

THE PRINCETON REVIEW SAYS

Admissions

Very important factors considered include: Class rank, academic GPA, rigor of secondary school record, standardized test scores, character/personal qualities. *Important factors considered include:* Application essay, recommendation(s), interview, talent/ability. *Other factors considered include:* Extracurricular activities, level of applicant's interest, volunteer work. SAT or ACT required; ACT with or without writing component accepted. TOEFL required of all international applicants. High school diploma is required and GED is accepted. *Academic units required:* 4 English, 2 mathematics, 1 science (1 science lab), 3 social studies, 6 academic electives.

Financial Aid

Students should submit: FAFSA. Regular filing deadline is February 15. The Princeton Review suggests that all financial aid forms be submitted as soon as possible after January 1. *Need-based scholarships/grants offered:* Federal Pell, SEOG, state scholarships/grants, private scholarships, the school's own gift aid, Federal Nursing Scholarships. *Loan aid offered:* Direct Subsidized Stafford, Direct Unsubsidized Stafford, Direct PLUS, Federal Perkins, state loans, private alternative loans. Applicants will be notified of awards on a rolling basis beginning February 15. Federal Work-Study Program available.

The Inside Word

Marywood offers applicants a chance to get an inside look at university life through their "College for a Day" program, which gives prospective students the opportunity to observe student life firsthand, from the classroom to the cafeteria. Marywood reviews applications on a rolling basis; therefore, you should apply as early as possible. Once a pro spective student has submitted all of the application materials, the admissions department will usually make a decision within two or three weeks.

THE SCHOOL SAYS ". . ."

From the Admissions Office

"Marywood University is a comprehensive, coeducational, Catholic university of 3,300 full-time, part-time, and adult students, with over ninety undergraduate, graduate, and doctoral degree programs. Established in 1915 by the Sisters, Servants of the Immaculate Heart of Mary, the university houses 1,100 resident students on a national award-winning campus considered one of the most beautiful in the northeast. Marywood University offered the region's first doctoral degree programs in 1996 and is the region's leading provider of graduate education with thirty-four master's degree programs and thirty-three certificate offerings. In recent years, the university made $100 million in improvements to campus, including new athletics, residence hall, and dining facilities, and one of the finest studio arts facilities in the northeast.

"Marywood operates on a rolling admissions basis. High school seniors are encouraged to submit their application for admission before March 1. Students applying for federal and state financial aid should submit the Free Application for Federal Student Aid (FAFSA) by February 15. At Marywood, you will discover that a top-notch private college experience is more affordable than you ever dreamed. In fact, ninety-eight percent of our first-time students receive financial assistance in the form of scholarships, grants, loans, and work-study programs."

SELECTIVITY	
Admissions Rating	77
# of applicants	2,203
% of applicants accepted	70
% of acceptees attending	30
FRESHMAN PROFILE	
Range SAT Critical Reading	470–560
Range SAT Math	480–570
Range SAT Writing	460–560
Range ACT Composite	20–26
Minimum paper TOEFL	530
Minimum web-based TOEFL	71
Average HS GPA	3.2
% graduated top 10% of class	20
% graduated top 25% of class	54
% graduated top 50% of class	83
DEADLINES	
Nonfall registration?	yes
FINANCIAL FACTS	
Financial Aid Rating	78
Annual tuition	$28,080
Room and board	$12,920
Required fees	$1,300
Books and supplies	$1,000
% needy frosh rec. need-based scholarship or grant aid	99
% needy UG rec. need-based scholarship or grant aid	99
% needy frosh rec. non-need-based scholarship or grant aid	12
% needy UG rec. non-need-based scholarship or grant aid	13
% needy frosh rec. need-based self-help aid	83
% needy UG rec. need-based self-help aid	80
% frosh rec. any financial aid	99
% UG rec. any financial aid	97
% UG borrow to pay for school	88
Average cumulative indebtedness	$38,965
% frosh need fully met	15
% ugrads need fully met	18
Average % of frosh need met	79
Average % of ugrad need met	75

MASSACHUSETTS INSTITUTE OF TECHNOLOGY

77 MASSACHUSETTS AVENUE, CAMBRIDGE, MA 02139 • ADMISSIONS: 617-253-3400 • FAX: 617-258-8304

CAMPUS LIFE

Quality of Life Rating	78
Fire Safety Rating	81
Green Rating	93
Type of school	private
Environment	city

STUDENTS

Total undergrad enrollment	4,285
% male/female	55/45
% from out of state	89
% from public high school	65
% frosh live on campus	100
# of fraternities	27
# of sororities	6
% African American	8
% Asian	24
% Caucasian	37
% Hispanic	13
% Native American	1
% international	9
# of countries represented	92

SURVEY SAYS . . .

Registration is a breeze
Lab facilities are great
Great computer facilities
Athletic facilities are great
School is well run
Diverse student types on campus
Students love Cambridge, MA

ACADEMICS

Academic Rating	99
% students returning for sophomore year	97
% students graduating within 4 years	84
% students graduating within 6 years	93
Calendar	4-1-4
Student/faculty ratio	8:1
Profs interesting rating	73
Profs accessible rating	76
Most classes have	fewer than 10 students
Most lab/discussion sessions have	10–19 students

MOST POPULAR MAJORS

business/commerce; computer science; mechanical engineering

APPLICANTS ALSO LOOK AT AND OFTEN PREFER

Harvard College

AND SOMETIMES PREFER

Princeton University, Yale University, Stanford University

AND RARELY PREFER

California Institute of Technology, Cornell University, Duke University, University of Pennsylvania, Columbia University

STUDENTS SAY ". . ."

Academics

Massachusetts Institute of Technology, the East Coast mecca of engineering, science, and mathematics, "is the ultimate place for information overload, endless possibilities, and expanding your horizons." The "amazing collection of creative minds" includes enough Nobel laureates to fill a jury box as well as brilliant students who are given substantial control of their educations; one explains, "The administration's attitude toward students is one of respect. As soon as you come on campus, you are bombarded with choices." Students need to be able to manage a workload that "definitely push[es you] beyond your comfort level." A chemical engineering major elaborates: "MIT is different from many schools in that its goal is not to teach you specific facts in each subject. MIT teaches you how to think, not about opinions but about problem solving. Facts and memorization are useless unless you know how to approach a tough problem." Professors here range from "excellent teachers who make lectures fun and exciting" to "dull and soporific" ones, but most "make a serious effort to make the material they teach interesting by throwing in jokes and cool demonstrations." "Access to an amazing number of resources, both academic and recreational," "research opportunities for undergrads with some of the nation's leading professors," and a rock-solid alumni network complete the picture. If you ask "MIT alumni where they went to college, most will immediately stick out their hand and show you their 'brass rat' (the MIT ring, the second most recognized ring in the world)."

Life

At MIT, "It may seem…like there's no life outside problem sets and studying for exams," but "There's always time for extracurricular activities or just relaxing" for those "with good time-management skills" or the "ability to survive on [a] lack of sleep." Options range from "building rides" (recent projects have included a motorized couch and a human-sized hamster wheel) "to partying at fraternities to enjoying the largest collection of science fiction novels in the United States at the MIT Science Fiction Library." Students occasionally find time to "pull a hack," which is an ethical prank, "like the life-size Wright brothers' plane that appeared on top of the Great Dome for the one-hundredth anniversary of flight." Undergrads tell us, "MIT has great parties—a lot of Wellesley, Harvard, and BU students come to them," but also that "there are tons of things to do other than party" here. "Movies, shopping, museums, and plays are all possible with our location near Boston. There are great restaurants only [blocks] away from campus, too…From what I can tell, MIT students have way more fun on the weekends than their Cambridge counterparts [at] Harvard."

Student Body

"There actually isn't one typical student at MIT," students here assure us, explaining that "hobbies range from building robots and hacking to getting wasted and partying every weekend. The one thing students all have in common is that they are insanely smart and love to learn. Pretty much anyone can find the perfect group of friends to hang out with at MIT." "Most students do have some form of 'nerdiness'" (like telling nerdy jokes, being an avid fan of *Star Wars*, etc.), but "Contrary to MIT's stereotype, most MIT students are not geeks who study all the time and have no social skills. The majority of the students here are actually quite 'normal.'" The "stereotypical student [who] looks techy and unkempt…only represents about twenty-five percent of the school." The rest include "multiple-sport standouts, political activists, fraternity and sorority members, hippies, clean-cut business types, LARPers, hackers, musicians, and artisans. There are people who look like they stepped out of an Abercrombie & Fitch catalog and people who dress in all black and carry flashlights and multi-tools. Not everyone relates to everyone else, but most people get along, and it's almost a guarantee that you'll fit in somewhere."

FINANCIAL AID: 617-258-4917 • E-MAIL: ADMISSIONS@MIT.EDU • WEBSITE: WEB.MIT.EDU

THE PRINCETON REVIEW SAYS

Admissions

Very important factors considered include: Character/personal qualities. *Important factors considered include:* Class rank, academic GPA, recommendation(s), rigor of secondary school record, standardized test scores, extracurricular activities, interview, talent/ability. *Other factors considered include:* Application essay, alumni/ae relation, first generation, geographical residence, racial/ethnic status, volunteer work, work experience. SAT or ACT required; ACT with writing component required. High school diploma or equivalent is not required. *Academic units recommended:* 4 English, 4 mathematics, 4 science, 2 foreign language, 2 social studies.

Financial Aid

Students should submit: FAFSA, CSS/Financial Aid PROFILE, noncustodial PROFILE, business/farm supplement, parent's complete federal income tax returns from prior year and W-2s. Regular filing deadline is February 15. The Princeton Review suggests that all financial aid forms be submitted as soon as possible after January 1. *Need-based scholarships/grants offered:* Federal Pell, SEOG, state scholarships/grants, private scholarships, the school's own gift aid. *Loan aid offered:* Direct Subsidized Stafford, Direct Unsubsidized Stafford, Direct PLUS, Federal Perkins, college/university loans from institutional funds. Applicants will be notified of awards on or about April 1. Federal Work-Study Program available. Institutional employment available. Highest amount earned per year from on-campus jobs $25,990. Off-campus job opportunities are excellent.

The Inside Word

MIT has one of the nation's most competitive admissions processes. The school's applicant pool is so rich it turns away numerous qualified candidates each year. Put your best foot forward and take consolation in the fact that rejection doesn't necessarily mean that you don't belong at MIT, but only that there wasn't enough room for you the year you applied. Your best chance to get an edge: Find ways to stress your creativity, a quality that MIT's admissions director told *USA TODAY* is lacking in many prospective college students.

THE SCHOOL SAYS ". . ."

From the Admissions Office

"The students who come to the Massachusetts Institute of Technology are some of America's—and the world's—best and most creative. As graduates, they leave here to make real contributions—in science, technology, business, education, politics, architecture, and the arts. From any class, many will go on to do work that is historically significant. These young men and women are leaders, achievers, and producers. Helping such students make the most of their talents and dreams would challenge any educational institution. MIT gives them its best advantages: a world-class faculty, unparalleled facilities, and remarkable opportunities. In turn, these students help to make the institute the vital place it is. They bring fresh viewpoints to faculty research: More than three-quarters participate in the Undergraduate Research Opportunities Program, developing solutions for the world's problems in areas such as energy, the environment, cancer, and poverty. They play on MIT's thirty-three intercollegiate teams as well as in its fifty-plus music, theater, and dance groups. To their classes and to their out-of-class activities, they bring enthusiasm, energy, and individual style."

SELECTIVITY	
Admissions Rating	**99**
# of applicants	16,632
% of applicants accepted	10
% of acceptees attending	64
# accepting a place on wait list	723
# admitted from wait list	65

FRESHMAN PROFILE	
Range SAT Critical Reading	670–760
Range SAT Math	740–800
Range SAT Writing	670–770
Range ACT Composite	32–35
Minimum paper TOEFL	577
Minimum web-based TOEFL	90
% graduated top 10% of class	98
% graduated top 25% of class	100
% graduated top 50% of class	100

DEADLINES	
Early action	
Deadline	11/1
Notification	12/20
Regular	
Deadline	1/1
Notification	3/20
Nonfall registration?	no

FINANCIAL FACTS	
Financial Aid Rating	**96**
Annual tuition	$41,770
Room and board	$11,775
Required fees	$272
Books and supplies	$1,050
% needy frosh rec. need-based scholarship or grant aid	98
% needy UG rec. need-based scholarship or grant aid	98
% needy frosh rec. non-need-based scholarship or grant aid	7
% needy UG rec. non-need-based scholarship or grant aid	3
% needy frosh rec. need-based self-help aid	59
% needy UG rec. need-based self-help aid	67
% frosh rec. any financial aid	88
% UG rec. any financial aid	87
% UG borrow to pay for school	44
Average cumulative indebtedness	$15,228
% frosh need fully met	100
% ugrads need fully met	100
Average % of frosh need met	100
Average % of ugrad need met	100

McGill University

845 Sherbrooke Street West, Montreal, QC H3A 064, Canada • Admissions: 514-398-3910 • Fax: 514-398-4193

CAMPUS LIFE	
Quality of Life Rating	74
Fire Safety Rating	66
Green Rating	81
Type of school	public
Environment	metropolis

STUDENTS

Total undergrad enrollment	22,879
% male/female	42/58
% from out of state	41
% frosh live on campus	49
# of fraternities	8
# of sororities	4
% international	18
# of countries represented	136

SURVEY SAYS . . .

Class discussions are rare
Students love Montreal, QC
Great off-campus food
Student publications are popular

ACADEMICS	
Academic Rating	68
% students returning for sophomore year	93
% students graduating within 4 years	67
% students graduating within 6 years	85
Calendar	semester
Student/faculty ratio	16:1
Profs interesting rating	68
Profs accessible rating	65
Most classes have	10–19 students
Most lab/discussion sessions have	20–29 students

MOST POPULAR MAJORS

business/commerce; political science and government; psychology

APPLICANTS ALSO LOOK AT AND OFTEN PREFER

University of Toronto, New York University

AND SOMETIMES PREFER

Columbia University, Harvard College, University of California—Berkeley

STUDENTS SAY ". . ."

Academics

McGill University is "one of Canada's top-rated universities," boasting "prestigious academics" and "high international standing" at a "fraction of the price" of U.S. universities. The university is known for offering an "excellent quality of education in the sciences" and "amazing research opportunities," but students note the lack of humanities funding. Students say, "McGill is a school where you will work hard" and that "McGill is a large university that requires its students take on independence and self-responsibility," adding there's "no hand-holding." It's clear that the university offers "access to a wealth of information," but students say, "Professors at McGill are hit or miss." A biochemistry major says, "My professors are top-notch researchers… but you also have to expect that your questions might be deferred by the prof to the TA," and a junior adds, "Classes definitely get more interesting as they get smaller, but there aren't a lot of small classes because of the size of the university." The consensus seems to be that "the best experiences with profs come in the upper-year courses."

Life

Located in Montreal, McGill University offers "challenging academics in a great urban location," that is, "in the heart of a culturally infused, vibrant city." Students say, "Montreal is a great city. There is anything and everything to do," and a political science adds, "The fact that McGill is one of the best universities in the world merely complements my experience." Most students say they have two lives: "one on campus and one outside"; a sophomore adds, "Once we're done with classes and all, we walk out of campus into the center of an amazing cosmopolitan city." Because of this, some note an absence of campus culture, but students insist, "The school environment is very accepting and peaceful," saying "extracurriculars are abundant." Students grumble about the administration, saying that it's "very bureaucratic," that at times "it's difficult to find the information that you need," and that "all the red tape is kind of like a running joke around campus." It's commonly held that the "registration process, website, [or] anything online really" can be confusing and difficult. Undergrads, particularly freshman, wish for "better support…academically, facilities-wise, and emotionally." Lastly, students say the university "could improve in the areas of offering a better and wider variety of meals throughout the campus," noting "some places are really crowded or really expensive."

Student Body

McGill University has a "large international student body," and students say, "A huge cultural diversity means a pot-luck of students from different backgrounds" and that, "since everyone is different, everyone is accepted." A senior says, "You can just as easily meet someone from the area as someone from outside," and another adds, "Local students tend to be bilingual and will interact with others easily and comfortably." Students are known for being "socially quite liberal," "well-traveled, and culturally aware," and alternative lifestyles find acceptance. A political science major says, "It is a progressive environment where students [from] different backgrounds live and grow together." As a whole, the student body tends to be "focused, hardworking, passionate," and "a typical student is outgoing, likes to party, but also studies a fair amount." An information systems major says, "The reason McGill is popular is also because of Montreal—an incredible city." "Montreal is a party city. Therefore, entertainment at night is great," but students note, "There is a lack of McGill-only events."

FINANCIAL AID: 514-398-6013 • E-MAIL: ADMISSIONS@MCGILL.CA • WEBSITE: WWW.MCGILL.CA

THE PRINCETON REVIEW SAYS

Admissions

Very important factors considered include: Academic GPA, rigor of secondary school record, standardized test scores. *Important factors considered include:* Class rank. *Other factors considered include:* Recommendation(s). ACT with writing component required. TOEFL required of all international applicants. High school diploma is required and GED is not accepted. *Academic units recommended:* 4 English, 4 mathematics, 3 science (3 science labs), 3 foreign language, 2 social studies, 2 history.

Financial Aid

Students should submit: Institution's own financial aid form, Provincial Government Loan Applications. Regular filing deadline is June 30. The Princeton Review suggests that all financial aid forms be submitted as soon as possible after January 1. *Need-based scholarships/grants offered:* Private scholarships, the school's own gift aid, Canadian (federal and provincial) Student Assistance. *Loan aid offered:* Direct Subsidized Stafford, Direct Unsubsidized Stafford, Direct PLUS, college/university loans from institutional funds. Applicants will be notified of awards on a rolling basis beginning March 1. Institutional employment available. Off-campus job opportunities are fair.

The Inside Word

Admission to McGill is highly competitive and decisions are based on an applicant's academic record. Extracurricular activities aren't significant in the admissions decision but may pertain to entrance scholarships. Applicants from the United States are required to submit standardized test scores, and minimum test score requirements are published on the McGill website.

THE SCHOOL SAYS ". . ."

From the Admissions Office

"McGill processes more than 30,000 online applications a year. Very few programs are available to non-Quebec students for January admission; consult the website for details.

"Applicants may submit results from of the SAT (plus at least two appropriate SAT Subject Tests). The ACT is accepted in lieu of the SAT and SAT Subject Test combination. Please note that certain programs can require specific SAT Subject Tests."

SELECTIVITY	
Admissions Rating	93
# of applicants	23,557
% of applicants accepted	54
% of acceptees attending	44

FRESHMAN PROFILE	
Range SAT Critical Reading	640–740
Range SAT Math	650–720
Range SAT Writing	650–730
Range ACT Composite	29–32
Minimum paper TOEFL	577
Minimum web-based TOEFL	90
Average HS GPA	3.5

DEADLINES	
Regular Deadline	1/15
Nonfall registration?	yes

FINANCIAL FACTS	
Financial Aid Rating	65
Annual in-state tuition	$1,968
Annual out-state tuition	$5,500
Room and board	$11,000
Required fees	$1,500
Books and supplies	$1,000
% needy UG rec. need-based scholarship or grant aid	63
% needy UG rec. non-need-based scholarship or grant aid	31
% needy UG rec. need-based self-help aid	89
% UG rec. any financial aid	28
% UG borrow to pay for school	24

MERCER UNIVERSITY—MACON

ADMISSIONS OFFICE, MACON, GA 31207-0001 • ADMISSIONS: 478-301-2650 • FAX: 478-301-2828

CAMPUS LIFE

Quality of Life Rating	72
Fire Safety Rating	77
Green Rating	78
Type of school	private
Affiliation	Baptist
Environment	city

STUDENTS

Total undergrad enrollment	2,284
% male/female	47/53
% from out of state	16
% frosh live on campus	92
# of fraternities	9
# of sororities	7
% African American	19
% Asian	7
% Caucasian	59
% Hispanic	4
% international	4
# of countries represented	35

SURVEY SAYS . . .

Athletic facilities are great
Low cost of living
Frats and sororities dominate social scene
Very little drug use

ACADEMICS

Academic Rating	84
% students returning for sophomore year	84
% students graduating within 4 years	41
% students graduating within 6 years	60
Calendar	semester
Student/faculty ratio	12:1
Profs interesting rating	83
Profs accessible rating	82
Most classes have	10–19 students
Most lab/discussion sessions have	20–29 students

MOST POPULAR MAJORS

biology/biological sciences; business/commerce; engineering

APPLICANTS ALSO LOOK AT AND OFTEN PREFER

University of Georgia, Emory University, Georgia Institute of Technology, Samford University

AND SOMETIMES PREFER

Florida State University, Auburn University, Furman University, Vanderbilt University

AND RARELY PREFER

Clemson University

STUDENTS SAY ". . ."

Academics

Mercer University is a school that students flock to for "its reputation as a rigorous academic institution" where professors "truly want to see students succeed." Variations on that sentiment are offered repeatedly by students who say that at this "unique school" the "professors actually care about your opinion and your well-being." Attendees feel the liberal arts education they get here offers them "intense preparation as an individual and professional for my future career." Small class sizes mean students "have a personal relationship with the professor," and the faculty in general "is so supportive. They don't think your ideas are crazy and naïve; they really listen to you." Some students admit there are some "outliers" who "are a joke," but "for all their quirks they are focused on the students and trying to teach us." The overwhelming majority of students insist, "Professors really care and love to teach" and are educators who "make sure that you understand the material being taught" and who will "devote extra time if needed for those who need it." Despite being a small school, "The number of opportunities available to enhance the student's academic experience is excellent" because "Mercer is a place that respects its students and knows the enormous potential its students have." And that goes over well with the student population, since at Mercer "everyone majors in changing the world."

Life

It's hard to pin down an aspect of college life that isn't represented at Mercer. Unsurprisingly, athletics are popular. "Most people play sports such as football, soccer, and basketball," one student notes. And even those students who don't play sometimes find themselves caught up in sports, since "school spirit is very important" at Mercer. But there are options outside of athletics. There is, of course, Greek life, which "provides a number of parties to attend and good times to be had." However, most would not call Mercer a big party school. "General life at Mercer is quiet and peaceful;" so often "a lot of people end up relaxing in dorms or exploring Macon." "Junior and senior students tend to venture out into Macon more, visiting downtown bars and restaurants and exploring the city." Students can take a trolley to the downtown area, which is "currently being revitalized." Mercer "does try its best to help the poor side of Macon with lots of community service." If not engaging in formal activities, students "watch movies and go out to eat, go to church, and hang out at each other's houses." So, the school is quieter than schools known for frantic social scenes, "but if you know the right people you can do pretty much anything."

Student Body

If there is a buzzword to describe the student body at Mercer University, it is "involved." Students are involved in clubs, sports, and civic groups and "with one another." "Almost everyone aspires to be the president of this or that club and [they] are often actively involved in at least half a dozen others." That may not come as a surprise, since "there are many opportunities for students to interact with one another and become involved on campus." The student body here is "diverse," with the tie that binds being that most "take part in community service through some venue." Mercer students are "bright and intelligent," "extremely involved on campus," "opinionated but respectful," and "well-informed but open-minded." Students say, "It is small enough so I don't feel intimidated" and that the school and upperclassman provide a strong support system. People here are "always willing to help another person with problems." This "intelligent" student body comes together from various areas of study. "English and engineering students converse frequently on all ranges of subjects from synesthesia to Doctor Who." Mercer students are achievers, but even they wouldn't claim to be overachievers. "Most students study well enough to reach their goals, whether high or moderate, but all reserve some time for fun."

FINANCIAL AID: 478-301-2670 • E-MAIL: ADMISSIONS@MERCER.EDU • WEBSITE: WWW.MERCER.EDU

THE PRINCETON REVIEW SAYS

Admissions

Very important factors considered include: Academic GPA, rigor of secondary school record, standardized test scores, level of applicant's interest. *Important factors considered include:* Character/personal qualities, extracurricular activities, talent/ability, volunteer work. *Other factors considered include:* Class rank, recommendation(s), alumni/ae relation, interview, work experience. SAT or ACT required; ACT with or without writing component accepted. TOEFL required of all international applicants. High school diploma is required and GED is accepted. *Academic units required:* 4 English, 4 mathematics, 3 science (2 science labs), 2 foreign language, 1 social studies, 2 history.

Financial Aid

Students should submit: FAFSA, institution's own financial aid form, state aid form. The Princeton Review suggests that all financial aid forms be submitted as soon as possible after January 1. *Need-based scholarships/grants offered:* Federal Pell, SEOG, state scholarships/grants, the school's own gift aid, Federal Nursing Scholarships. *Loan aid offered:* Direct Subsidized Stafford, Direct Unsubsidized Stafford, Direct PLUS, Federal Perkins, Federal Nursing, college/university loans from institutional funds. Applicants will be notified of awards on a rolling basis beginning March 15. Federal Work-Study Program available. Institutional employment available. Off-campus job opportunities are good.

The Inside Word

Being ready to work hard should not be taken lightly for those considering Mercer. Students report that many transfers end up dropping out after a semester, even after coming from a major university. The admissions policy is seen as lenient, yet the work certainly isn't. It may not seem difficult to get into Mercer, but graduating is another matter.

THE SCHOOL SAYS ". . ."

From the Admissions Office

"For many high school seniors, the college search can be a stressful process. As an admissions counseling staff, we are committed to helping each and every student that we meet to identify their best personal 'fit' for a college or university. During this process, many find that Mercer is the right place for their higher education journey. At Mercer, each student is matched with a personal admissions counselor. This counselor remains his or her primary point of contact from application through enrollment. We get to know our applicants through personal contact, high school visits, regional receptions, college fairs, and our numerous campus visitation programs. Our counselors work closely with students and their families through the application, financial aid, housing, orientation, and other enrollment processes to ensure that students make a smooth transition from high school to college. This makes for a truly enjoyable and informed admissions experience for all involved.

"Mercer University begins accepting applications for undergraduate admission on August 1. We encourage high school seniors to submit their completed applications (including official transcripts and test scores) before our priority application deadline of November 15 for top scholarship consideration. Our regular decision deadline is January 15. We evaluate applications on a rolling basis throughout the academic year."

SELECTIVITY	
Admissions Rating	**86**
# of applicants	2,582
% of applicants accepted	83
% of acceptees attending	26
FRESHMAN PROFILE	
Range SAT Critical Reading	520–630
Range SAT Math	540–630
Range ACT Composite	24–29
Minimum paper TOEFL	550
Average HS GPA	3.7
% graduated top 10% of class	44
% graduated top 25% of class	76
% graduated top 50% of class	94
DEADLINES	
Early action	
Deadline	11/1
Notification	11/15
Regular	
Priority	4/1
Deadline	7/1
Nonfall registration?	yes
FINANCIAL FACTS	
Financial Aid Rating	**84**
Annual tuition	$31,248
Room and board	$10,408
Required fees	$300
Books and supplies	$1,200
% needy frosh rec. need-based scholarship or grant aid	100
% needy UG rec. need-based scholarship or grant aid	99
% needy frosh rec. non-need-based scholarship or grant aid	27
% needy UG rec. non-need-based scholarship or grant aid	21
% needy frosh rec. need-based self-help aid	60
% needy UG rec. need-based self-help aid	62
% frosh rec. any financial aid	99
% UG rec. any financial aid	97
% UG borrow to pay for school	70
Average cumulative indebtedness	$30,851
% frosh need fully met	30
% ugrads need fully met	26
Average % of frosh need met	84
Average % of ugrad need met	77

MIAMI UNIVERSITY

301 SOUTH CAMPUS AVENUE, OXFORD, OH 45056 • ADMISSIONS: 513-529-2531 • FAX: 513-529-1550

CAMPUS LIFE

Quality of Life Rating	80
Fire Safety Rating	78
Green Rating	79
Type of school	public
Environment	village

STUDENTS

Total undergrad enrollment	14,831
% male/female	48/52
% from out of state	35
% from public high school	75
% frosh live on campus	98
# of fraternities	33
# of sororities	21
% African American	5
% Asian	2
% Caucasian	82
% Hispanic	3
% international	5
# of countries represented	50

SURVEY SAYS . . .

Athletic facilities are great
Great food on campus
Low cost of living
Frats and sororities dominate social scene
Lots of beer drinking

ACADEMICS

Academic Rating	81
% students returning for sophomore year	89
% students graduating within 4 years	70
% students graduating within 6 years	81
Calendar	semester
Student/faculty ratio	17:1
Profs interesting rating	84
Profs accessible rating	84
Most classes have	20–29 students
Most lab/discussion sessions have	20–29 students

MOST POPULAR MAJORS

finance; marketing/marketing management; psychology

APPLICANTS ALSO LOOK AT AND OFTEN PREFER

Northwestern University, University of Notre Dame, Vanderbilt University, University of Michigan—Ann Arbor

AND SOMETIMES PREFER

Boston College, Indiana University—Bloomington, Purdue University—West Lafayette, The Ohio State University—Columbus, University of Illinois at Urbana-Champaign, University of Wisconsin—Madison, University of Cincinnati, University of Dayton

AND RARELY PREFER

Xavier University (OH)

STUDENTS SAY ". . ."

Academics

Attending school at Miami University may be "the iconic college experience." Located in Oxford, Ohio, "a quaint college town" with a "beautiful red brick campus," which students describe as "gorgeous" and "astoundingly beautiful," the school "has a rich tradition and history" that "is committed to its image as a premier undergraduate institution." The "prestige" of the business school affords many promising opportunities both during school and after graduation. Students agree, "Miami really prepares students for the real world after college." "A degree from Miami is worth a lot to many employers, at least in the business world." "Miami University students are recruited by companies, and that provides great leverage when looking for internships and jobs." The curriculum as a whole offers "a challenging academic workload" that truly tests a student's abilities as well as "prepares students for the workplace after graduation while also giving them the opportunity to thrive while on campus." This "devotion to excellent undergraduate instruction" is backed by "an extremely strong orientation program, a dedicated student affairs department, and an overwhelming amount of student involvement in co-curricular activities." Smaller classrooms that allow for "engaging" discussion are more highly valued than large lectures, which may be "hard to sit through." Professors are a "mixed bag." "If you get the right ones, it makes all the difference." A student in the Honors and Scholars Program calls the experience "phenomenal. It offers the ability to grow as a student and person through in and out of class experiences."

Life

Miami University offers "a vibrant social atmosphere." With 16,000 or so students on campus Miami may be "the perfect size," where you "can see everyone…but still meet many new people." With a "plethora of student activities," "Miami makes it possible to find groups or organizations that can fit any student's interest, and many tend to help in propelling graduates into jobs or programs once they leave the campus." "Greek life is everywhere you look. While roughly a third of the student body is Greek, it often seems as though everyone is because of how visible they are on campus." On the partying front, "If you are looking to drink, you will certainly find it here if you want." "Miami students can find a wealth of great bars and clubs uptown—many of which are eighteen-plus, allowing freshmen and sophomores to enjoy the dance floors and bars that make up almost all of the nightlife." The campus also "offers a lot of alternative programs for students who wish to avoid alcohol." "Late night programming is offered through Miami, as well as athletic events and other cultural events." Among sports, "Hockey is really popular." Students tend to be happy with life at Miami. "There is a ton to do on and off campus. The town is quaint, but it is mainly a college town, so it's like an extension of the school. Nightlife is pretty big here, but so are academics and activities. Students definitely are actively thinking about their futures, and they take academics seriously."

Student Body

The typical student is "very involved on campus, is concerned about his or her academics, and wants to make a good impression on others. We care about how we present ourselves, but in a good way." Another students says, "The typical student is very academically focused, challenge-driven, competitive, extraverted, and demonstrates a preference for dressing well." Several students commented that students tend to "look and dress alike." "It can be very cliquish, especially in the Greek community." Anyone can fit in though, it's "all about finding your niche on campus which is generally done through people in your major, and especially student organizations." Miami tends to attract students who are "white, upper-middle-class, and Christian. The campus lacks diversity socioeconomically, ethnically, and religiously; however, the student body is generally accepting of all students no matter the background." One student relishes the challenge "to find diversity even in people who look similar and [has] grown because of it."

FINANCIAL AID: 513-529-8734 • E-MAIL: ADMISSION@MUOHIO.EDU • WEBSITE: WWW.MIAMI.MUOHIO.EDU

THE PRINCETON REVIEW SAYS

Admissions

Very important factors considered include: Class rank, application essay, academic GPA, recommendation(s), rigor of secondary school record, standardized test scores, character/personal qualities, talent/ability. *Other factors considered include:* Alumni/ae relation, extracurricular activities, first generation, geographical residence, state residency, volunteer work, work experience. SAT or ACT required; ACT with or without writing component accepted. TOEFL required of all international applicants. High school diploma is required and GED is accepted. *Academic units recommended:* 4 English, 3 mathematics, 3 science, 2 foreign language, 2 social studies, 1 history, 1 visual/performing arts.

Financial Aid

Students should submit: FAFSA. The Princeton Review suggests that all financial aid forms be submitted as soon as possible after January 1. *Need-based scholarships/grants offered:* Federal Pell, SEOG, state scholarships/grants, private scholarships, the school's own gift aid. *Loan aid offered:* Direct Subsidized Stafford, Direct Unsubsidized Stafford, Direct PLUS, Federal Perkins, Federal Nursing, college/university loans from institutional funds, Bank Education Loans. Applicants will be notified of awards on a rolling basis beginning March 20. Federal Work-Study Program available. Institutional employment available. Off-campus job opportunities are good.

The Inside Word

Getting into Miami University isn't easy. High grades and SAT scores (math and critical reading) above 1200 are a good start, and there is more you can do to better your odds. Admissions officers favor students who are active in their schools, participate in varsity sports, and volunteer in their community.

THE SCHOOL SAYS ". . ."

From the Admissions Office

"At Miami, you'll find a level of involvement—in your classes, in your research, in your extracurricular activities—that you won't find at other schools. What sets Miami apart is the ability to give students a personalized small-college experience within the excitement and opportunities of a midsize university, all at a public school cost. With more than 100 majors to choose from, and a liberal arts foundation that allows students to explore different areas of interest, finding your true passion—in and out of the classroom—is at the heart of what the MU experience is all about. This deep level of engagement is reflected in the ninety percent freshman to sophomore retention rate and Miami's graduation rate, which is among the top for public universities across the country. Miami's reputation for producing outstanding leaders with real-world experience makes us a target school for top national firms, and our graduates' acceptance rate into law and medical school are far above the national average. Students also benefit from small class sizes—ninety percent of undergraduate classes have fewer than fifty students—and personal attention from faculty members in the classroom, through research opportunities, and through faculty mentoring programs. Outside of the classroom, students can participate in more than 300 student organizations, attend social and cultural events, or get involved with one of the most extensive intramural and club sports program in the country."

SELECTIVITY	
Admissions Rating	**84**
# of applicants	18,482
% of applicants accepted	74
% of acceptees attending	26
# accepting a place on wait list	1,282
# admitted from wait list	32
# of early decision applicants	471
# accepted early decision	378

FRESHMAN PROFILE	
Range SAT Critical Reading	530–620
Range SAT Math	560–660
Range ACT Composite	24–29
Minimum web-based TOEFL	76
Average HS GPA	3.7
% graduated top 10% of class	32
% graduated top 25% of class	68
% graduated top 50% of class	95

DEADLINES	
Early decision	
Deadline	11/1
Notification	12/15
Early action	
Deadline	12/1
Notification	2/1
Regular	
Deadline	2/1
Notification	3/15
Nonfall registration?	yes

FINANCIAL FACTS	
Financial Aid Rating	**66**
Annual in-state tuition	$12,625
Annual out-state tuition	$27,797
Room and board	$10,640
Required fees	$528
Books and supplies	$1,540
% needy frosh rec. need-based scholarship or grant aid	51
% needy UG rec. need-based scholarship or grant aid	53
% needy frosh rec. non-need-based scholarship or grant aid	93
% needy UG rec. non-need-based scholarship or grant aid	56
% needy frosh rec. need-based self-help aid	82
% needy UG rec. need-based self-help aid	80
% UG borrow to pay for school	52
Average cumulative indebtedness	$27,315
% frosh need fully met	16
% ugrads need fully met	12
Average % of frosh need met	58
Average % of ugrad need met	56

Michigan State University

250 Administration Building, East Lansing, MI 48824-1046 • Admissions: 517-355-8332 • Fax: 517-353-1647

CAMPUS LIFE

Quality of Life Rating	**75**
Fire Safety Rating	**60***
Green Rating	**87**
Type of school	public
Environment	town

STUDENTS

Total undergrad enrollment	36,276
% male/female	49/51
% from out of state	9
% frosh live on campus	93
# of fraternities	31
# of sororities	19
% African American	7
% Asian	4
% Caucasian	72
% Hispanic	3
% international	9
# of countries represented	130

SURVEY SAYS . . .

Students are friendly
Everyone loves the Spartans
Student publications are popular

ACADEMICS

Academic Rating	**66**
% students returning for sophomore year	91
% students graduating within 4 years	48
% students graduating within 6 years	77
Calendar	semester
Student/faculty ratio	16:1
Profs interesting rating	66
Profs accessible rating	69
Most classes have	20–29 students
Most lab/discussion sessions have	20–29 students

APPLICANTS ALSO LOOK AT AND OFTEN PREFER

University of Michigan—Ann Arbor, Western Michigan University, Kalamazoo College

AND SOMETIMES PREFER

Indiana University—Bloomington, University of Illinois at Urbana-Champaign, University of Wisconsin—Madison

STUDENTS SAY ". . ."

Academics

The size of Michigan State University "scares some people," students tell us, but for those comfortable in crowds it's "one of the strongest advantages. Where else do you cut through the Cereal Wing of the Human Nutrition Building to get to a Navigating the Universe class (a class on the parallels between art, philosophy, and physics)?" One student sees it this way: "The size of MSU makes it like training wheels for the real world. Every type of person, value, and belief is here, so you learn just as many street smarts as academic smarts, which is what sets it apart from so many other schools." There are more than "200 majors to choose from" here, including "good engineering and science programs," an "amazing communications program," "the best political science program in Michigan," "the only agriculture school in the state," and "an absolutely amazing school of Hospitality Business." Economies of scale also allow MSU to offer "great study abroad programs," "a lot of helpful free tutoring in math and other subjects," and "great Web programs that make it very easy to download class materials and view assignments. You can also e-mail the whole class questions or just your professor, through our Angel system." As far as possible downsides to the school's size, MSU students find you have to "fend for yourself." That means potential peril for students who aren't self-motivated. One undergrad explains, "There are two roads you can follow when at MSU. You can study hard and earn a degree in a reputable, challenging setting; or you can soak your brain cells with alcohol instead of academia."

Life

"It requires a lot of studying to keep up with classes" in most disciplines at MSU, but that doesn't mean students bury their heads in the books 24/7. On the contrary, "Michigan State is great because everyone is there to learn but also to have a good time, which is important for any college to flow smoothly." When the weekend arrives, "everyone likes to go out, usually to frats, and have a good time. We do our share of partying, but we know when and how hard to hit the books. We keep our heads very level," except, perhaps, when attending sporting events. Life on campus "generally revolves around the weekend and the basketball or football game. You get through the week looking forward to one of the two." Indeed, "Sports are huge, and nothing beats football Saturdays or basketball nights. Tailgating is a religion." And if neither sports appeal to you, don't sweat it. "If there's something you want to do, someone else does too. You'll be hard pressed to find an activity that doesn't have its own organization and social network." Hometown East Lansing has its own allures; a student explains, "Walking downtown on Grand River is awesome when it gets warmer out," and there are "decent stores and restaurants. Also, in the warm weather you are bound to see people sitting out on their porches. Many of them are having parties or just hanging out, and a lot of times they'll invite you to come on up!" Or you can just enjoy the "breathtaking beauty of the campus," with its "old buildings and beautiful trees and plants that make every walk to class a great one."

Student Body

MSU's size ensures that "this is a fairly diverse campus, especially considering that it is located in the northern Midwest." One student observes, "You can completely immerse yourself among different people in different situations knowing that you have the comfort of your own dorm, and somewhere there is a group just like you." Because "study abroad is emphasized at MSU," there are "a lot of foreign students, and they seem to fit right into the general population." If anything unites students—besides their love of MSU sports—it is that most "are extremely friendly. Random people in classes ask you if you need a ride home, and, even better, random people offer you a seat on the bus."

FINANCIAL AID: 517-353-5940 • E-MAIL: ADMIS@MSU.EDU • WEBSITE: WWW.MSU.EDU

THE PRINCETON REVIEW SAYS

Admissions

Very important factors considered include: Academic GPA, rigor of secondary school record, standardized test scores. *Important factors considered include:* Application essay, extracurricular activities, first generation, geographical residence. *Other factors considered include:* Class rank, recommendation(s), alumni/ae relation, character/personal qualities, level of applicant's interest, state residency, talent/ability, volunteer work, work experience. SAT or ACT required; ACT with writing component required. TOEFL required of all international applicants. High school diploma is required and GED is accepted. *Academic units required:* 4 English, 3 mathematics, 3 science, 2 foreign language, 3 social studies. *Academic units recommended:* 2 science labs.

Financial Aid

Students should submit: FAFSA. The Princeton Review suggests that all financial aid forms be submitted as soon as possible after January 1. *Need-based scholarships/grants offered:* Federal Pell, SEOG, state scholarships/grants, private scholarships, the school's own gift aid, United Negro College Fund. *Loan aid offered:* Direct Subsidized Stafford, Direct Unsubsidized Stafford, Direct PLUS, Federal Perkins, college/university loans from institutional funds. Applicants will be notified of awards on a rolling basis beginning March 15. Federal Work-Study Program available. Institutional employment available. Off-campus job opportunities are excellent.

The Inside Word

Given the extraordinary volume of applications the admissions office receives, it's no wonder that Michigan State relies primarily on numbers. Decisions typically come down to grades, class rank, and test scores. Applicants who have proven to be capable students in college prep courses are relatively likely to find themselves the proud addressees of fat admissions envelopes. Applications are processed on a rolling basis, a process that typically favors early applicants.

THE SCHOOL SAYS ". . ."

From the Admissions Office

"Although Michigan State University is a graduate and research institution of international stature and acclaim, your undergraduate education is a high priority. More than 2,800 instructional faculty members (ninety percent of whom hold a terminal degree) are dedicated to providing academic instruction, guidance, and assistance to our undergraduate students. Our 36,000 undergraduate students are a select group of academically motivated men and women. The diversity of ethnic, racial, religious, and socioeconomic heritage makes the student body a microcosm of the state, national, and international community.

"Students applying for admission to Michigan State University are required to take the new version of the SAT or the ACT exam with the Writing section. The Writing assessment will be considered in the holistic review of the application for admission. SAT Subject Tests are not required."

SELECTIVITY	
Admissions Rating	82
# of applicants	28,416
% of applicants accepted	73
% of acceptees attending	39
# accepting a place on wait list	600
# admitted from wait list	350

FRESHMAN PROFILE	
Range SAT Critical Reading	440–600
Range SAT Math	540–670
Range SAT Writing	450–600
Range ACT Composite	23–28
Minimum paper TOEFL	550
Minimum web-based TOEFL	79
Average HS GPA	3.6
% graduated top 10% of class	28
% graduated top 25% of class	68
% graduated top 50% of class	96

DEADLINES	
Early action	
Deadline	10/7
Notification	11/11
Regular	
Priority	11/1
Nonfall registration?	yes

FINANCIAL FACTS	
Financial Aid Rating	65
Annual in-state tuition	$12,203
Annual out-state tuition	$31,148
Room and board	$8,154
Books and supplies	$996
% needy frosh rec. need-based scholarship or grant aid	61
% needy UG rec. need-based scholarship or grant aid	64
% needy frosh rec. non-need-based scholarship or grant aid	39
% needy UG rec. non-need-based scholarship or grant aid	26
% needy frosh rec. need-based self-help aid	87
% needy UG rec. need-based self-help aid	88
% frosh rec. any financial aid	49
% UG rec. any financial aid	50
% UG borrow to pay for school	45
Average cumulative indebtedness	$23,725
% frosh need fully met	21
% ugrads need fully met	15
Average % of frosh need met	64
Average % of ugrad need met	62

MICHIGAN TECHNOLOGICAL UNIVERSITY

1400 TOWNSEND DRIVE, HOUGHTON, MI 49931 • ADMISSIONS: 906-487-2335 • FAX: 906-487-2125

CAMPUS LIFE

Quality of Life Rating	**77**
Fire Safety Rating	**99**
Green Rating	**70**
Type of school	public
Environment	village

STUDENTS

Total undergrad enrollment	5,643
% male/female	75/25
% from out of state	22
% from public high school	90
% frosh live on campus	92
# of fraternities	15
# of sororities	8
% African American	1
% Asian	1
% Caucasian	84
% Hispanic	2
% Native American	1
% international	7
# of countries represented	60

SURVEY SAYS . . .

Great computer facilities
Athletic facilities are great
Career services are great
Students get along with local community
Campus feels safe
Lots of beer drinking

ACADEMICS

Academic Rating	**70**
% students returning for sophomore year	83
% students graduating within 4 years	26
% students graduating within 6 years	65
Calendar	semester
Student/faculty ratio	13:1
Profs interesting rating	69
Profs accessible rating	73
Most classes have	10–19 students
Most lab/discussion sessions have	10–19 students

MOST POPULAR MAJORS

business administration and management; civil engineering; mechanical engineering

APPLICANTS ALSO LOOK AT AND SOMETIMES PREFER

Michigan State University, Milwaukee School of Engineering, University of Michigan—Ann Arbor, University of Minnesota—Twin Cities, University of Wisconsin—Madison, Western Michigan University

AND RARELY PREFER

Grand Valley State University

STUDENTS SAY ". . ."

Academics

Michigan Technological University has "very high standards when it comes to education" and offers "serious study in a beautiful (often snowy) environment." It boasts a "really good reputation as an engineering school," and it's no secret that "engineering is a part of everybody's life." All agree, "Michigan Tech provides an atmosphere that nurtures learning" and "puts students first when it comes to their learning experience by providing hands-on experience." The university offers "lots of internship and co-op opportunities" and "pathways for career development and professional advancement." Students say that the courses are "challenging" and that the university "pushes students to excel academically." Professors are "generally interesting and helpful," but some can be "dull." A junior says, "Concentrated courses are great, but Gen Eds are huge, impersonal, and just plain awful," and another student adds, "The experience gets better with more time you put into your program, the professors become more interactive, and the experience becomes more meaningful."

Life

Michigan Tech "is in a small town in the middle of the deep North woods," which makes "the sense of community remarkable." Students say that campus is "incredibly safe," that "the atmosphere is very friendly," and that "there are a lot of opportunities to get involved." A physics major notes, "You start to see people you know everywhere on campus. It is really easy to find a friend and talk to someone." Enhancing the "strong student community" are "over 200 clubs" and a variety of "winter activities to be a part of." Many students take advantage of "free access to Mount Ripley," the university's own ski hill and the oldest one in Michigan. A freshman says, "We have broomball, Winter Carnival, and lots of campus-wide events!" Many students say, "The administration in every department works hard to answer questions and help out as much as possible, which is really great when you're a freshman," but some feel there's a "gap between [the] administration and students," particularly when it comes to spending. There are complaints about dorm food, leading a junior to say, "I would like to see some more selection and variation between dining halls," and students feel there's a need for "more parking spots close to campus." While "the library is a great place to study," some "of the classrooms are dated" and could use technological updating.

Student Body

At Michigan Tech, the typical student "is smart and a little more introspective than average," but still "great at balancing school and hanging out." Most students "are looking to get a good education and are fairly laid-back," and the student body consists of "down-to-earth friendly people," who "work hard during the week and look forward to relaxing and having fun on the weekends." It's no secret that "the ratio is a little guy-heavy" and that, because of this, "girls get doors opened for them across campus." Students tend to be "white and male," and a junior acknowledges, "There's little diversity ethnically, but everyone feels welcome." A chemical engineering major says, "You have to be a little bit of a nerd to fit in," and another student agrees, "I think most people think about classes first, hanging out second." It's common for students to "stay in and play video games," but there's also a large contingent of "outdoorsy people." A sophomore says, "Winters are long and cold up here," and students take advantage of the plentiful snow by "hiking, biking, four-wheeling, skiing, [and] snowmobiling." Students look forward to Winter Carnival, "a long weekend off from classes where students build giant, impressive snow sculptures, play broomball, [and] stay out all night," and for fun they enjoy "house parties and moderate drinking/merrymaking [to] warm up the cold winters."

MICHIGAN TECHNOLOGICAL UNIVERSITY

FINANCIAL AID: 906-487-1742 • E-MAIL: MTU4U@MTU.EDU • WEBSITE: WWW.MTU.EDU

THE PRINCETON REVIEW SAYS

Admissions

Very important factors considered include: Academic GPA, rigor of secondary school record, standardized test scores. *Important factors considered include:* Class rank. *Other factors considered include:* Application essay, recommendation(s), alumni/ae relation, character/personal qualities, extracurricular activities, interview, talent/ability, volunteer work, work experience. SAT or ACT required; ACT with or without writing component accepted. TOEFL required of all international applicants. High school diploma is required and GED is accepted. *Academic units required:* 3 English, 3 mathematics, 2 science. *Academic units recommended:* 4 English, 4 mathematics, 3 science, 2 foreign language, 3 social studies, 1 history, 1 computer science, 2 academic electives.

Financial Aid

Students should submit: FAFSA. The Princeton Review suggests that all financial aid forms be submitted as soon as possible after January 1. *Need-based scholarships/grants offered:* Federal Pell, SEOG, state scholarships/grants, private scholarships, the school's own gift aid. *Loan aid offered:* Direct Subsidized Stafford, Direct Unsubsidized Stafford, Direct PLUS, Federal Perkins, college/university loans from institutional funds, external private loans. Federal Work-Study Program available. Institutional employment available. Highest amount earned per year from on-campus jobs $4,500. Off-campus job opportunities are excellent.

The Inside Word

Michigan Tech strives to enroll bright, adventurous students. Students aren't required to submit recommendations from teachers, although they may submit a "High School Counselor Information Page" if they would like their counselor to share information regarding their high school performance. Applicants to the Visual and Performing Arts Department degree programs are required to submit supplemental materials, including an essay.

THE SCHOOL SAYS ". . ."

From the Admissions Office

"At Michigan Tech, our students create the future. Our unique Enterprise Program lets students work on real industry problems such as bicycle design, alternative fuels, groundwater analysis, and video production. Through student groups like Engineers without Borders and the campus-wide Make a Difference Day, our students impact lives in our community and around the world. Students can choose from 130 degree programs in engineering; forest resources; computing; technology; business; economics; natural, physical and environmental sciences; arts; humanities; and social sciences. We offer exciting degree programs in growing fields including biomedical engineering, applied ecology and environmental science, and pre-health studies.

"Outside of the classrooms and labs, students enjoy our golf course, ski hill, trails and recreational forest, and friendly, small-town atmosphere in beautiful Upper Michigan. Located on Portage Waterway, the campus is only minutes from Lake Superior. During Winter Carnival, students build huge snow statues and play broomball, the biggest game on campus, among many other activities.

"We recommend that students applying for admission take the SAT (or the ACT with the writing section)."

SELECTIVITY	
Admissions Rating	83
# of applicants	4,573
% of applicants accepted	75
% of acceptees attending	34

FRESHMAN PROFILE	
Range SAT Critical Reading	550–680
Range SAT Math	580–690
Range SAT Writing	520–620
Range ACT Composite	24–29
Minimum paper TOEFL	550
Minimum web-based TOEFL	79
Average HS GPA	3.6
% graduated top 10% of class	30
% graduated top 25% of class	61
% graduated top 50% of class	89

DEADLINES	
Regular	
Priority	1/15
Nonfall registration?	yes

FINANCIAL FACTS	
Financial Aid Rating	71
Annual in-state tuition	$12,615
Annual out-state tuition	$25,710
Room and board	$8,648
Required fees	$238
Books and supplies	$1,200
% needy frosh rec. need-based scholarship or grant aid	83
% needy UG rec. need-based scholarship or grant aid	79
% needy frosh rec. non-need-based scholarship or grant aid	81
% needy UG rec. non-need-based scholarship or grant aid	66
% needy frosh rec. need-based self-help aid	85
% needy UG rec. need-based self-help aid	88
% frosh rec. any financial aid	91
% UG rec. any financial aid	87
% UG borrow to pay for school	71
Average cumulative indebtedness	$33,141
% frosh need fully met	19
% ugrads need fully met	16
Average % of frosh need met	79
Average % of ugrad need met	70

MIDDLEBURY COLLEGE

THE EMMA WILLARD HOUSE, MIDDLEBURY, VT 05753-6002 • ADMISSIONS: 802-443-3000 • FAX: 802-443-2056

CAMPUS LIFE

Quality of Life Rating	97
Fire Safety Rating	89
Green Rating	98
Type of school	private
Environment	village

STUDENTS

Total undergrad enrollment	2,474
% male/female	49/51
% from out of state	96
% from public high school	52
% frosh live on campus	100
% African American	2
% Asian	6
% Caucasian	67
% Hispanic	6
% international	10
# of countries represented	64

SURVEY SAYS . . .

Lab facilities are great
Athletic facilities are great
School is well run
Great food on campus
Campus feels safe
Students are environmentally aware

ACADEMICS

Academic Rating	98
% students returning for sophomore year	95
% students graduating within 4 years	84
% students graduating within 6 years	90
Calendar	4-1-4
Student/faculty ratio	9:1
Profs interesting rating	99
Profs accessible rating	95
Most classes have	10–19 students

MOST POPULAR MAJORS

economics; English language and literature; psychology

APPLICANTS ALSO LOOK AT AND OFTEN PREFER

Amherst College, Williams College, Dartmouth College, Harvard College

AND SOMETIMES PREFER

Brown University, Yale University, Stanford University, Duke University, Pomona College

AND RARELY PREFER

Bowdoin College, Colby College, Colgate University, Hamilton College

STUDENTS SAY ". . ."

Academics

One of the most highly regarded liberal arts colleges in the United States, Middlebury College in Vermont is about "creating a person both socially and intellectually prepared for the world." The school has "a high level of global thinking and language acquisition in such a rural place," and there is an "emerging focus on creativity and entrepreneurship." When teaching students to develop communication, writing, creativity, and critical thinking skills, the school "allows you to develop these skills in whatever subject or subjects that one is most passionate about." Students' needs and choices are "of very high priority" to the administration, and there is "institutional support for whatever absurd idea might strike you." Professors are, on the whole, "truly top-notch"; not only are they "brilliant academics, but they are also adept teachers and classroom leaders." They come here because they want to teach undergraduates and research; "Middlebury expects both; most professors deliver." "Several of my professors have given out their cell phone numbers after particularly difficult lectures to make sure that students can figure things out," says one. "It's almost impossible to actually be 'invisible.'" The overall academic experience is "very intense" ("If you haven't done the reading, prepare to be called out for it"), but "students reliably enjoy their classes."

Life

Empty hours at Middlebury are in short supply; "If you've got free time in your day at Middlebury, you're doing something wrong," says a student. However, after all that reading, "at the end of the day, we all just like to get together and hit up the Snow Bowl to go skiing." "Vermont does make a difference," says one student of Middlebury's location near mountains, lakes, and ski trails, and its focus on "how important the outdoor experience is for the school." Drinking is "fairly prevalent" on Fridays and Saturdays, but "not during the week." It's a healthy culture, and "public safety does a good job of keeping things safe while not being overly intrusive." The dorms are "gorgeous," and there is even one called the Chateau, modeled after the largest chateau in Fontainebleau, France. The number of activities available are admirable, and "most people actually choose not to go into cities on weekends because they would hate to miss what's going on on-campus that weekend."

Student Body

The pervasive atmosphere at Middlebury is "super friendly and caring," and there is not only the pressure to work hard, but "also the encouragement to make sure students succeed." Students "compete with themselves, not their classmates." With a happy population, beautiful environs, and not a single student going unchallenged, the school encompasses "a perfect blend of intellectual curiosity, responsible living, and fun." As one student eloquently puts it, it's a bunch of "bright kids doing too many things—all of them good, none related to sleep." This "engaged, active," "preppy" student body "doesn't take themselves too seriously but do take serious initiative." A typical go-getter student "pursues at least one major, a minor, and is the star of at least one sports team or special interest group, but usually more." Social life can be "very centered around athletic teams," but these "well-read, outgoing," and "well-rounded students from stable backgrounds" always end up connecting with people they can relate with easily. "You will struggle to find time to spend with all the different friends you will make," says a student. Social ease is a common trait among MiddKids, and most students "know how to hold a conversation and [are] open to new experiences."

FINANCIAL AID: 802-443-5158 • E-MAIL: ADMISSIONS@MIDDLEBURY.EDU • WEBSITE: WWW.MIDDLEBURY.EDU

THE PRINCETON REVIEW SAYS

Admissions

Very important factors considered include: Class rank, academic GPA, rigor of secondary school record, character/personal qualities, extracurricular activities, talent/ability. *Important factors considered include:* Application essay, recommendation(s), standardized test scores, racial/ethnic status. *Other factors considered include:* Alumni/ae relation, first generation, geographical residence, interview, level of applicant's interest, volunteer work, work experience. ACT with or without writing component accepted. High school diploma or equivalent is not required. *Academic units recommended:* 4 English, 4 mathematics, 3 science (3 science labs), 4 foreign language, 3 social studies, 2 history, 1 academic electives, 1 fine arts, music, or drama courses recommended.

Financial Aid

Students should submit: FAFSA, CSS/Financial Aid PROFILE, noncustodial PROFILE. Regular filing deadline is February 1. The Princeton Review suggests that all financial aid forms be submitted as soon as possible after January 1. *Need-based scholarships/grants offered:* Federal Pell, SEOG, state scholarships/grants, private scholarships, the school's own gift aid. *Loan aid offered:* Direct Subsidized Stafford, Direct Unsubsidized Stafford, Direct PLUS, Federal Perkins, college/university loans from institutional funds. Applicants will be notified of awards on or about April 1.

The Inside Word

Middlebury gives you options in standardized testing. The school will accept either the ACT or the SAT or three SAT subject tests (the tests must be in three different subject areas, however). Middlebury is extremely competitive; improve your chances of admission by crafting a standardized test profile that shows you in the best possible light.

THE SCHOOL SAYS ". . ."

From the Admissions Office

"The successful Middlebury candidate excels in a variety of areas including academics, athletics, the arts, leadership, and service to others. These strengths and interests permit students to grow beyond their traditional 'comfort zones' and conventional limits. Our classrooms are as varied as the Green Mountains, the Metropolitan Museum of Art, or the great cities of Russia and Japan. Outside the classroom, students informally interact with professors in activities such as intramural basketball games and community service. At Middlebury, students develop critical-thinking skills, enduring bonds of friendship, and the ability to challenge themselves.

"Middlebury offers majors and programs in forty-five different fields, with particular strengths in languages, international studies, environmental studies, literature and creative writing, and the sciences. Opportunities for engaging in individual research with faculty abound at Middlebury."

SELECTIVITY

Admissions Rating	**98**
# of applicants	8,533
% of applicants accepted	18
% of acceptees attending	39
# accepting a place on wait list	2,114
# admitted from wait list	20
# of early decision applicants	988
# accepted early decision	282

FRESHMAN PROFILE

Range SAT Critical Reading	640–740
Range SAT Math	650–740
Range SAT Writing	650–760
Range ACT Composite	30–33
% graduated top 50% of class	100

DEADLINES

Early decision	
Deadline	11/15
Notification	12/15
Regular	
Deadline	1/1
Notification	4/1
Nonfall registration?	yes

FINANCIAL FACTS

Financial Aid Rating	**98**
Annual tuition	$53,420
Books and supplies	$1,000
% needy frosh rec. need-based scholarship or grant aid	100
% needy UG rec. need-based scholarship or grant aid	100
% needy frosh rec. need-based self-help aid	86
% needy UG rec. need-based self-help aid	88
% frosh rec. any financial aid	37
% UG rec. any financial aid	42
% UG borrow to pay for school	46
Average cumulative indebtedness	$20,514
% frosh need fully met	100
% ugrads need fully met	100
Average % of frosh need met	100
Average % of ugrad need met	100

MILLS COLLEGE

5000 MACARTHUR BOULEVARD, OAKLAND, CA 94613 • ADMISSIONS: 510-430-2135 • FAX: 510-430-3314

CAMPUS LIFE

Quality of Life Rating	**79**
Fire Safety Rating	**67**
Green Rating	**97**
Type of school	private
Environment	metropolis

STUDENTS

Total undergrad enrollment	924
% male/female	0/100
% from out of state	23
% from public high school	80
% frosh live on campus	91
% African American	8
% Asian	10
% Caucasian	43
% Hispanic	18
% Native American	1
% international	2
# of countries represented	7

SURVEY SAYS . . .

Lots of liberal students
Great computer facilities
Low cost of living
Frats and sororities are unpopular or nonexistent
Political activism is popular
Very little drug use

ACADEMICS

Academic Rating	**87**
% students returning for sophomore year	78
% students graduating within 4 years	51
Calendar	semester
Student/faculty ratio	11:1
Profs interesting rating	91
Profs accessible rating	85
Most classes have	10–19 students
Most lab/discussion sessions have	10–19 students

MOST POPULAR MAJORS

English language and literature; political science and government; psychology

APPLICANTS ALSO LOOK AT AND OFTEN PREFER

Santa Clara University, University of California—Santa Barbara, University of California—Berkeley, University of California—Davis, University of California—Los Angeles, University of California—San Diego, University of California—Santa Cruz, University of the Pacific, Saint Mary's College (CA), University of San Francisco, Smith College

AND SOMETIMES PREFER

University of Puget Sound, Occidental College, New York University, Mount Holyoke College, Chapman University, Bryn Mawr College, University of Redlands, Whitman College, Willamette University

AND RARELY PREFER

Pepperdine University, Scripps College, University of Southern California, Hampshire College, Colby College

STUDENTS SAY "..."

Academics

Mills College in Oakland, California, is a small women's institution with a "rigorous academic program" defined as "the epitome of a liberal arts education." "I was drawn to the small class sizes, the beauty of the campus, and the wonderfully articulate and confident women that I came in contact with." With fewer than 1,000 undergraduates and fairly small class sizes, it is no wonder that professors "know almost all of [their students] individually." As one student attests, "Even in introductory lecture classes, you can get to know your professors." Another student concurs, "Not only am I on a first-name basis with all of my professors, I have their personal phone numbers and e-mail addresses! I feel that I matter here!" Students have high praise for the faculty. "The professors are amazing. They are extremely smart and totally accessible." "Professors are interesting and insightful and promote lively discussions in class. Standards are high and challenging. Topics are very relevant to today's issues." "Mills College is all about empowering its students and creating an environment that encourages hard work and social and political awareness." "There is great support for students with disabilities or special needs." "The library and several computer labs make it easy to find a place to get things done."

Life

"School life is pretty academically focused. Little time is spent off campus if you live on campus because social interaction usually involves study groups. There is little to no real partying on campus, though you can find it off campus if you are looking for it." "The beauty of the campus" is a significant plus for many students. Situated on 135 acres, the school has plenty of natural areas, and the atmosphere is relaxing and peaceful, which means it is very conducive to studying. "Mills exceeds expectations in creating an intimate and welcoming environment as well as in promoting student activism." Students agree that Mills is a special place. "The atmosphere at Mills is incredible! It is academic, empowering, creative, and always intellectually stimulating." Students here seem to know how to balance their schedules and how to appreciate the education they are receiving. Mills "offers a very rigorous education that is stimulating yet fun." But this enthusiasm for their school does not carry over to campus life on the weekends when "it sort of turns into a ghost town." Students also warn, "If you're looking for a party school, look elsewhere." You do not have to go very far for entertainment. "Many students love the Berkeley and San Francisco nightlife."

Student Body

Here's how some Mills students describe themselves and their peers: "The typical student is female, academically inclined, and individualistic (possesses few stereotypically mainstream qualities)." "Students are typically politically active in some way, and many have one or two causes they know really well. Students are inquisitive and very intent on doing well academically. We don't party very much. We're also very welcoming." At Mills College, "The students are really diverse; pretty much everyone is different. In order to fit in, all you have to do is be yourself." This diversity is what seems to set it apart from most other schools. "It's a unique group of people, and the school is not everyone's cup of tea." One student clarifies, "Mills is full of "nontraditional" students from all over the world. I didn't want to be in a place where everyone was on the same track, with the same agenda. I wanted to be in a place where every other person would have their own cause, their own independent ideas." This "very open-minded environment" sets itself from most other colleges in how students "embrace diversity and gender equality in hopes of creating a better world." With a wide range of ages and backgrounds, the traditional student is anything but traditional. "It's a unique group of people, and the school not everyone's cup of tea."

FINANCIAL AID: 510-430-2000 • E-MAIL: ADMISSION@MILLS.EDU • WEBSITE: WWW.MILLS.EDU

THE PRINCETON REVIEW SAYS

Admissions

Very important factors considered include: Rigor of secondary school record. *Important factors considered include:* Class rank, application essay, academic GPA, recommendation(s), standardized test scores, character/personal qualities, extracurricular activities. *Other factors considered include:* Alumni/ae relation, first generation, interview, level of applicant's interest, talent/ability, volunteer work, work experience. SAT or ACT required; ACT with or without writing component accepted. TOEFL required of all international applicants. High school diploma is required and GED is accepted. *Academic units required:* 4 English, 3 mathematics, 2 science (2 science labs), 2 foreign language, 2 social studies, 2 history. *Academic units recommended:* 4 English, 4 mathematics, 4 science (2 science labs), 4 foreign language, 4 social studies, 4 history, 2 visual/performing arts, 2 academic electives.

Financial Aid

Students should submit: FAFSA and institution's own financial aid form. The Princeton Review suggests that all financial aid forms be submitted as soon as possible after January 1. *Need-based scholarships/grants offered:* Federal Pell, SEOG, state scholarships/grants, private scholarships, the school's own gift aid. *Loan aid offered:* Direct Subsidized Stafford, Direct Unsubsidized Stafford, Direct PLUS, Federal Perkins, college/university loans from institutional funds. Applicants will be notified of awards on a rolling basis beginning March 1. Federal Work-Study Program available. Institutional employment available. Highest amount earned per year from on-campus jobs $2,700. Off-campus job opportunities are excellent.

Inside Word

Mills strives to create a diverse community of students and welcomes older, nontraditional undergraduates. In fact, sixteen percent of the Mills undergraduate population is older than twenty-three. In addition to the application, test scores, and transcripts, Mills requests that all first-year applicants submit a graded writing sample. Admissions interviews, though not required, are highly encouraged.

THE SCHOOL SAYS ". . ."

From the Admissions Office

"For more than 150 years, Mills College has shaped women's lives. Offering a progressive liberal arts and sciences curriculum taught by nationally renowned faculty, Mills gives students the personal attention that leads to extraordinary learning. Through intensive, collaborative study in a community of forward-thinking individuals, students gain the ability to make their voices heard, the strength to risk bold visions, an eagerness to experiment, and a desire to change the world.

"Nestled on 135 lush acres in the heart of the San Francisco Bay Area, Mills draws energy from the college's dynamic location. Mills students connect with centers of learning, business, and technology; pursue research and internship opportunities; and explore the Bay Area's many sources of cultural, social, and recreational enrichment.

"Ranked fourth among top colleges in the West, Mills offers a renowned education for students who are seeking an intimate, collaborative college experience. You'll learn from distinguished professors who are truly dedicated to teaching. You'll interact with dynamic women of different backgrounds, ethnicities, cultures, ages, and mindsets, making your learning rich and inspiring.

"With more than forty different majors to choose from at Mills, you'll have a wide variety of education options. Mills also offers six unique programs that enable undergraduates with clear career goals in certain fields to streamline their college and graduate school programs. At Mills, the classroom debate will be your intellectual catalyst, but you'll find plenty of opportunities to express yourself, both inside and outside of the classroom."

SELECTIVITY

Admissions Rating	**88**
# of applicants	2,251
% of applicants accepted	57
% of acceptees attending	13

FRESHMAN PROFILE

Range SAT Critical Reading	530–660
Range SAT Math	520–620
Range SAT Writing	520–630
Range ACT Composite	24–29
Minimum paper TOEFL	550
Minimum web-based TOEFL	80
Average HS GPA	3.7
% graduated top 10% of class	40
% graduated top 25% of class	79
% graduated top 50% of class	93

DEADLINES

Early action	
Deadline	11/15
Notification	12/1
Regular	
Priority	2/1
Deadline	8/1
Nonfall registration?	yes

FINANCIAL FACTS

Financial Aid Rating	**85**
Annual tuition	$38,066
Room and board	$11,306
Required fees	$1,198
Books and supplies	$1,430
% needy frosh rec. need-based scholarship or grant aid	95
% needy UG rec. need-based scholarship or grant aid	94
% needy frosh rec. non-need-based scholarship or grant aid	10
% needy UG rec. non-need-based scholarship or grant aid	5
% needy frosh rec. need-based self-help aid	89
% needy UG rec. need-based self-help aid	89
% frosh rec. any financial aid	98
% UG rec. any financial aid	97
% UG borrow to pay for school	70
Average cumulative indebtedness	$27,342
% frosh need fully met	26
% ugrads need fully met	16
Average % of frosh need met	85
Average % of ugrad need met	79

MILLSAPS COLLEGE

1701 NORTH STATE STREET, JACKSON, MS 39210 • ADMISSIONS: 601-974-1050 • FAX: 601-974-1059

CAMPUS LIFE

Quality of Life Rating	**81**
Fire Safety Rating	**83**
Green Rating	**61**
Type of school	private
Affiliation	Methodist
Environment	metropolis

STUDENTS

Total undergrad enrollment	893
% male/female	51/49
% from out of state	58
% from public high school	54
% frosh live on campus	98
# of fraternities	6
# of sororities	6
% African American	9
% Asian	5
% Caucasian	76
% Hispanic	3
% Native American	1
% international	3
# of countries represented	23

SURVEY SAYS . . .

No one cheats
Low cost of living
Frats and sororities dominate social scene
Student publications are popular
Students are involved in community service

ACADEMICS

Academic Rating	**87**
% students returning for sophomore year	88
% students graduating within 4 years	61
% students graduating within 6 years	66
Calendar	semester
Student/faculty ratio	9:1
Profs interesting rating	96
Profs accessible rating	93
Most classes have	10–19 students
Most lab/discussion sessions have	10–19 students

MOST POPULAR MAJORS

biology/biological sciences; business administration and management; English language and literature

APPLICANTS ALSO LOOK AT AND OFTEN PREFER
Birmingham-Southern College

AND SOMETIMES PREFER
Rhodes College

AND RARELY PREFER
Texas Christian University, Furman University, Samford University

STUDENTS SAY ". . ."

Academics

Millsaps is a small college, so students "get a lot of personal attention." It is a "school where everybody knows your name," as well as "a place where every student has to work hard to stay above water; excellence is the norm, not the exception." What makes Millsaps unique is how it "breaks the mold by providing superb education as well as fun, combining the two in ways so subtle that a student may not even realize they're learning!" The school "offers great courses taught by charismatic professors" who "bring the material to life...through their innovative teaching methods." "Classes are not easy but the quality of learning is top notch." "Professors always encourage students to discuss class material and voice their opinions and questions about it. They encourage you to form your own ideas." These "friendly and approachable" professors "continue to teach outside of the classroom." "They welcome one-on-one time…to further develop understanding." Students have praise for the education they are receiving saying, "coming out of Millsaps I will be fully prepared for grad school. My professors not only lecture, but they turn the material into hands-on learning opportunities," and "I seriously respect my school's standard of excellence in hiring people who are wonderful at their jobs." Besides "great professors," the school offers "a prestigious business school," "abundant study abroad programs," and "strong Southern hospitality and heritage." The school's small size provides opportunities to receive "a top-notch education, while also getting to play sports and be in clubs." Although Millsaps may not be affordable for everyone, it "strives to be generous with scholarships." One student was pleased to report, "They offered the most financial assistance by far." Although student surveys were mostly positive, like this one: "Millsaps College provides the ideal learning atmosphere for liberal arts studies where they teach us how to think and not what to think," there were complaints about "the internet and networking capabilities," and "The cafeteria is an area where great improvement is needed."

Life

"Students at Millsaps think about their classwork first and foremost. After that, we think about hanging out with friends and having fun." The campus is "so beautiful and filled with cozy spots that many students spend a lot of their time outside." "While most schools have 'the quad' where students hang out between classes, Millsaps has 'The Bowl.' It is a beautiful area of grass and trees in the center of campus." But one student notes that there is still room for improvement. "The campus is beautiful, but the insides of the buildings need a serious upgrade. Every time I walk into a building, I feel like I've been transported back to the seventies." Although "most of the upperclassmen dorms are amazing," the "freshman dorms are a little sketchy." On campus "There are concerts and fun days all throughout the semester." "There are parties at the fraternity houses, and…some really cool things to do from concerts to oxygen bars to laser tag." "I would definitely call it a 'party school,' despite the tough academics." "There is a lot of partying on the weekends but almost everyone still manages to get studying finished." Students also point out, "We don't have to drink to have fun at Millsaps, though. You can always find a friend to hang out with, go to the movies, shop, or find a new great place to eat. The Millsaps curriculum even makes study groups fun (for the most part), believe it or not." Off campus, students venture into Jackson where "there are great restaurants."

Student Body

Is there a typical Millsaps student? Some students think so: "The typical student at Millsaps was an over-involved, cool nerd in high school. We throw ourselves into sports, clubs, Greek life, and community service like it's our job. It's how we thrive." "Students fit in by being involved in Greek life and other organizations." "A typical student is involved in many activities from sports to community service clubs. Student interests are diverse, and the student body in general is very friendly and interactive." Another student disagrees, "There is no 'typical student' really—the most common thread is a desire to change the world (usually, with a stop at graduate school)."

FINANCIAL AID: 800-352-1050 • E-MAIL: ADMISSIONS@MILLSAPS.EDU • WEBSITE: WWW.MILLSAPS.EDU

THE PRINCETON REVIEW SAYS

Admissions

Very important factors considered include: Academic GPA, rigor of secondary school record, standardized test scores, character/personal qualities. *Important factors considered include:* Class rank, application essay, recommendation(s), extracurricular activities, interview, talent/ability, volunteer work. *Other factors considered include:* Work experience. SAT or ACT required; ACT with or without writing component accepted. TOEFL required of all international applicants. High school diploma is required and GED is accepted. *Academic units required:* 4 English, 3 mathematics, 3 science (1 science lab), 2 social studies, 2 history. *Academic units recommended:* 4 English, 4 mathematics, 4 science (1 science lab), 2 foreign language, 2 social studies, 2 history, 2 academic electives.

Financial Aid

Students should submit: FAFSA. The Princeton Review suggests that all financial aid forms be submitted as soon as possible after January 1. *Need-based scholarships/grants offered:* Federal Pell, SEOG, state scholarships/grants, private scholarships, the school's own gift aid. *Loan aid offered:* Direct Subsidized Stafford, Direct Unsubsidized Stafford, Direct PLUS, Federal Perkins, college/university loans from institutional funds. Applicants will be notified of awards on a rolling basis beginning March 15. Federal Work-Study Program available. Institutional employment available. Highest amount earned per year from on-campus jobs $8,429. Off-campus job opportunities are good.

The Inside Word

Millsaps' trademark friendliness begins during the admissions process. The school encourages prospective students to get in touch with an admissions counselor to ask questions, arrange a visit, or connect you with a current student. For early action admission or scholarships, students need to apply in January. After that, the school admits students on a rolling basis.

THE SCHOOL SAYS ". . ."

From the Admissions Office

"Millsaps offers outstanding value in nationally ranked liberal arts education. Your academic journey begins with Critical Thinking and Academic Literacy, a comprehensive freshman experience that develops reasoning, communication, quantitative thinking, historical consciousness, aesthetic judgment, global, and multicultural awareness, and valuing and decision making. Throughout your Millsaps years you'll be encouraged to think differently; learn critical, analytical skills; embrace independence of thought; and prepare for study in your chosen major. We offer unique opportunities such as study abroad and in the field at our Yucatán Program; an exploration of your personal and professional future in relation to issues of ethics, values, faith, and the common good through our Faith and Work Initiative; highly respected pre-professional programs in law, medicine, and social work; and a five-year business track leading to an MBA or master's in accountancy with a liberal arts perspective that is accredited by the Association to Advance Collegiate Schools of Business. Our student body included Mississippi's 2003–2004 Rhodes scholar, a 2008–2009 Fulbright Scholar, and the faculty included the Carnegie Foundation's 2006, 2007, 2008, and 2009 Mississippi Professor of the Year. Our courses are taught without graduate assistants and our intimate student-faculty-community relationship is a hallmark of a Millsaps education. The emerging cultural climate in Jackson, Mississippi's capital city, provides unique artistic, athletic, and social opportunities in the modern south. We encourage you to look at Millsaps College. You'll appreciate the quality of our educational experience in comparison to the costs you'll discover at other national liberal arts institutions."

SELECTIVITY	
Admissions Rating	**85**
# of applicants	1,779
% of applicants accepted	61
% of acceptees attending	21
# of early decision applicants	1
# accepted early decision	1

FRESHMAN PROFILE	
Range SAT Critical Reading	510–650
Range SAT Math	545–650
Range ACT Composite	23–29
Minimum paper TOEFL	550
Minimum web-based TOEFL	80
Average HS GPA	3.5
% graduated top 10% of class	33
% graduated top 25% of class	62
% graduated top 50% of class	86

DEADLINES	
Early decision	
Deadline	11/15
Notification	12/1
Early action	
Deadline	12/1
Nonfall registration?	yes

FINANCIAL FACTS	
Financial Aid Rating	**86**
Annual tuition	$27,650
Room and board	$10,312
Required fees	$1,832
Books and supplies	$1,100
% needy frosh rec. need-based scholarship or grant aid	100
% needy UG rec. need-based scholarship or grant aid	99
% needy frosh rec. non-need-based scholarship or grant aid	16
% needy UG rec. non-need-based scholarship or grant aid	20
% needy frosh rec. need-based self-help aid	79
% needy UG rec. need-based self-help aid	72
% frosh rec. any financial aid	100
% UG rec. any financial aid	96
% UG borrow to pay for school	53
Average cumulative indebtedness	$25,902
% frosh need fully met	27
% ugrads need fully met	32
Average % of frosh need met	83
Average % of ugrad need met	81

Missouri University of Science and Technology

300 West 13th Street; 106 Parker Hall, Rolla, MO 65409-1060 • Admissions: 573-341-4165 • Fax: 573-341-4082

CAMPUS LIFE

Quality of Life Rating	**69**
Fire Safety Rating	**76**
Green Rating	**68**
Type of school	public
Environment	village

STUDENTS

Total undergrad enrollment	5,672
% male/female	77/23
% from out of state	21
% from public high school	85
% frosh live on campus	96
# of fraternities	23
# of sororities	5
% African American	5
% Asian	2
% Caucasian	80
% Hispanic	2
% Native American	1
% international	5
# of countries represented	61

SURVEY SAYS . . .

Class discussions are rare
Career services are great
Low cost of living
Very little drug use
Internships are widely available

ACADEMICS

Academic Rating	**72**
% students returning for sophomore year	83
% students graduating within 4 years	24
% students graduating within 6 years	67
Calendar	semester
Student/faculty ratio	17:1
Profs interesting rating	71
Profs accessible rating	74
Most classes have	10–19 students
Most lab/discussion sessions have	20–29 students

MOST POPULAR MAJORS

civil engineering; electrical, electronics and communications engineering; mechanical engineering

APPLICANTS ALSO LOOK AT AND OFTEN PREFER

Massachusetts Institute of Technology, University of Illinois at Urbana-Champaign, University of Wisconsin—Madison, Washington University in St. Louis, University of Missouri, Truman State University, Saint Louis University

AND SOMETIMES PREFER

Georgia Institute of Technology, Purdue University—West Lafayette, University of Iowa, Iowa State University

STUDENTS SAY ". . ."

Academics

Formerly known as University of Missouri—Rolla, Missouri University of Science and Technology has undergone a name change, but its "reputation for academic excellence" has remained the same. Its focus on "challenging" academics ensures "the classes are tough," so "don't expect to walk right on through, but be glad that you aren't able to." Luckily, the school offers a "large number of assets" to students, including "lots of opportunities for students to lead" and professors who "really want the students to understand the material." Most students describe the professors as "very knowledgeable" and "willing to help students whenever they are in need of assistance." Some find them "varied," noting that "you have a good chance of getting an excellent professor, but then again some have thick accents, some have thick heads, and some just make you wonder if they really know and believe in what they're talking about." One thing nearly all students agree on is that the "extensive and very strong engineering and science programs" are the school's "biggest strength." "Missouri S&T does a lot of research and funds a lot of experiments and expeditions that give it an edge over other colleges," says one undergrad. They also appreciate Missouri S&T's "cheaper cost" than comparable colleges, as well as the fact their "tuition goes toward academics, not athletics." Opinions on the administration are mixed. Some find they "do a very good job at keeping the students informed about what is going on throughout the school" and "listen heavily to the students." Others would like to have more interaction with the school's administrators.

Life

"Classes, studying, and homework dominate the weeks" at Missouri S&T, "so the weekends are when the campus comes alive." But "alive" can be a relative term. Some find life on campus is "great." "Most people get together in large groups and play outside sports for fun, work out together, or play video games in large groups," says one undergrad. "There is a great sense of community." On the other hand, when students are working so hard during the week, sometimes all they want to do with their free time is rest. "What I do for fun is sleep," explains one student, "because I'm always losing it." Either way the wind blows, "there's an organization for everyone" at Missouri S&T, with "fraternities and sororities being a very prominent part of residential life." There are also "a lot of social events that Residential Life puts on." Most agree the town of Rolla "doesn't offer a lot of entertainment." As one student puts it, "It's Rolla. Quarter Bowling night is the most fun thing to do." Many students "leave on the weekends," but most agree "part of that is that there are many different places to go within a three-hour drive." For those who stay, most "have fun with what they learn." While "pranking isn't as prevalent as it was in the past, it still happens." So expect the "normal college pastimes" of "potato cannons" and "siege machines" to take on a "more competitive level when students design equations or create programs to improve their designs."

Student Body

The typical student here is described as "a Midwestern white boy" or, as one student puts it, "a white male, nerdy, who never sees the sun." Either way, one thing is clear, women are "in the minority" here. This is reflected on both sides of the gender coin, with guys noting "there aren't many girls here, which stinks," and girls sometimes feeling that they're being "treated differently" by their peers. That said, some say "what once was a huge gap in gender population is now becoming a more respectable margin" and "the ethnic makeup of the student population is quite diverse." Fundamentally, students here are "smart," "welcoming," and "open-minded." They "make their own fun," and a good deal of bonding is done with video games: Rock Band, Guitar Hero, and World of Warcraft are "hugely popular" here.

FINANCIAL AID: 573-341-4282 • E-MAIL: ADMISSIONS@MST.EDU • WEBSITE: WWW.MST.EDU

THE PRINCETON REVIEW SAYS

Admissions

Very important factors considered include: Class rank, academic GPA, rigor of secondary school record, standardized test scores. *Important factors considered include:* Recommendation(s). *Other factors considered include:* Application essay, character/personal qualities, extracurricular activities, interview, talent/ability, volunteer work, work experience. SAT or ACT required; ACT with or without writing component accepted. TOEFL required of all international applicants. High school diploma is required and GED is accepted. *Academic units required:* 4 English, 4 mathematics, 3 science (1 science lab), 2 foreign language, 3 social studies, 1 visual/performing arts.

Financial Aid

Students should submit: FAFSA. The Princeton Review suggests that all financial aid forms be submitted as soon as possible after January 1. *Need-based scholarships/grants offered:* Federal Pell, state scholarships/grants, private scholarships, the school's own gift aid. *Loan aid offered:* Direct Subsidized Stafford, Direct Unsubsidized Stafford, Direct PLUS, Federal Perkins. Federal Work-Study Program available. Institutional employment available. Off-campus job opportunities are good.

The Inside Word

In line with other leading public universities, gaining entrance to Missouri S&T is largely a numbers game. Applicants who meet class rank and standardized test cut-offs, as well as distribution requirements, will be granted admission. But don't rest on your laurels if you have them—the university draws a competitive, self-selecting pool of applicants, meaning the earlier you apply, the better the advantage you'll have.

THE SCHOOL SAYS ". . ."

From the Admissions Office

"Missouri S&T is one of the nation's top technological research universities. Our students go beyond books and lectures to apply knowledge in bold new ways. With more than 7,600 students, our campus exudes a passion and energy few universities can foster. S&T students collaborate with great researchers and other talented students to meet the global challenges of our times—in areas like energy, infrastructure, e-commerce, materials, education, and environmental sustainability.

"We're ranked among the top five public universities for highest starting salaries for graduates—averaging nearly $60,000. It's easy to see how investing in an S&T education pays off. Nearly ninety percent of grads have firm career plans (career, grad school, law/medical school, or military) even before they graduate. As a top ten "Best Value" public university, S&T is committed to small classes, quality academic advising, and personal attention. Nearly half of graduates complete a research program or study abroad. With more than 200 student organizations, you'll never run out of things to do. Enjoy the outdoors? We've got skydiving, spelunking, and more. Feeling creative? Join the student radio station, theater, orchestra, debate team, or student newspaper. Like to stay active? Join an intramural or club sports team. Want more? Start your own organization.

"Widely recognized as one of the nation's best universities for science, engineering, computing, math, and social sciences, Missouri S&T provides students an outstanding education at a price they can afford. Admissions decisions are based primarily on each applicant's academic achievement."

SELECTIVITY	
Admissions Rating	**83**
# of applicants	2,779
% of applicants accepted	90
% of acceptees attending	39

FRESHMAN PROFILE	
Range SAT Critical Reading	590–690
Range SAT Math	590–710
Range ACT Composite	25–31
Minimum paper TOEFL	550
Minimum web-based TOEFL	79
Average HS GPA	3.53
% graduated top 10% of class	35
% graduated top 25% of class	70
% graduated top 50% of class	92

DEADLINES	
Regular	
Priority	12/1
Deadline	7/1
Nonfall registration?	yes

FINANCIAL FACTS	
Financial Aid Rating	**86**
Annual in-state tuition	$7,848
Annual out-state tuition	$20,643
Room and board	$8,520
Required fees	$1,236
Books and supplies	$952
% needy frosh rec. need-based scholarship or grant aid	100
% needy UG rec. need-based scholarship or grant aid	100
% needy frosh rec. non-need-based scholarship or grant aid	86
% needy UG rec. non-need-based scholarship or grant aid	87
% needy frosh rec. need-based self-help aid	57
% needy UG rec. need-based self-help aid	88
% UG borrow to pay for school	64
Average cumulative indebtedness	$21,700
% frosh need fully met	62
% ugrads need fully met	62
Average % of frosh need met	61
Average % of ugrad need met	61

MONMOUTH UNIVERSITY (NJ)

ADMISSION, MONMOUTH UNIVERSITY, WEST LONG BRANCH, NJ 07764-1898 • ADMISSIONS: 732-571-3456 • FAX: 732-263-5166

CAMPUS LIFE

Quality of Life Rating	76
Fire Safety Rating	98
Green Rating	83
Type of school	private
Environment	village

STUDENTS

Total undergrad enrollment	4,652
% male/female	42/58
% from out of state	12
% from public high school	86
% frosh live on campus	88
# of fraternities	5
# of sororities	6
% African American	4
% Asian	2
% Caucasian	80
% Hispanic	7
% international	1
# of countries represented	20

SURVEY SAYS . . .

Great computer facilities
Great library
Students love West Long Branch, NJ
Great off-campus food
Campus feels safe
Hard liquor is popular

ACADEMICS

Academic Rating	73
% students graduating within 4 years	46
% students graduating within 6 years	66
Calendar	semester
Student/faculty ratio	15:1
Profs interesting rating	78
Profs accessible rating	80
Most classes have	10–19 students

MOST POPULAR MAJORS

business administration and management; communication studies/speech communication and rhetoric; education

STUDENTS SAY ". . ."

Academics

Monmouth University "is a small school that...provides an excellent community-like atmosphere," where you "can really get to know your instructors" "because of the small class size," which is twenty-two students on average. Professors are "very accomplished and have impressive backgrounds," and students feel that they're learning from "professionals in their fields [who] know exactly what they are talking about" and are willing to "share their career experiences." Monmouth offers thirty-three undergraduate majors: business administration, general communication studies/speech communication, education, music, criminal justice, premedical sciences, and psychology are among the most popular and have a "good reputation." One confident English major says that the university is interested in "creating leaders and looking toward the future." Monmouth also has a "very good" honors school with "excellent teachers," though professors throughout the school "seem to love their jobs" and "truly care about helping their students succeed." One student speaks for many when he says, "I know many Monmouth University alumni, and all have loved their experience. They say MU prepared them for their careers."

Life

At Monmouth University, "everyone is able to find something fun to do." While "academics are the top priority" for many, the school "is dedicated to ensuring that students have fun when class isn't in session." Students enjoy the "free weekend movies" or intramural sports such as "flag football, dodgeball, and volleyball" and report that "clubs are always planning and executing charity events [and] drives." Of course, Monmouth's "beautiful campus" and close proximity to the ocean mean students spend a lot of time outdoors, and it's a given that students "love to relax at the beach." Greek life is "very popular on campus," so "there are always frat parties," though students complain they "usually get busted extremely early" because local police are "very strict." This means that "people don't usually party in the dorms," either, and instead hit local bars, leading some to complain that if you're "under twenty-one, it is extremely difficult to find activities to do in the community." A political science major notes that "You can't get around without a car, and many kids go home for the weekend." Those who don't often have cars take advantage of the school's location and take day trips to "New York City and Philadelphia." Those who do have cars may have an advantage, but they also must contend with one big problem: "limited parking."

Student Body

At Monmouth, "the typical student...is an outgoing, friendly, easygoing individual who is ready to experience everything Monmouth has to offer," and many students seem to find that "making friends is quite easy." Students tend to be from "affluent" or "upper-middle-class" families, and drive "BMWs [and] Mercedes" and carry "Louis Vuitton bags," which leads some to say the student body can be "snobby." Many students are in fraternities or sororities, and athletes have a big presence on campus. While "there is little diversity," "the school is becoming more diverse" and "there have been no conflicts with diversity." The majority of students are "homegrown," from New Jersey or New York, and some students feel that local and commuter students "don't bother making new friends." At Monmouth, there are plenty of "laid-back" beach kids, but most students agree that Monmouth students "know when to hit the books hard."

FINANCIAL AID: 732-571-3463 • E-MAIL: ADMISSION@MONMOUTH.EDU • WEBSITE: WWW.MONMOUTH.EDU

THE PRINCETON REVIEW SAYS

Admissions

Very important factors considered include: Academic GPA, rigor of secondary school record, standardized test scores. *Important factors considered include:* Extracurricular activities, volunteer work, work experience. *Other factors considered include:* Application essay, recommendation(s), alumni/ae relation, character/personal qualities. SAT or ACT required; ACT with writing component required. TOEFL required of all international applicants. High school diploma is required and GED is accepted. *Academic units required:* 4 English, 3 mathematics, 2 science (1 science lab), 2 history, 5 academic electives. *Academic units recommended:* 2 foreign language, 2 social studies.

Financial Aid

Students should submit: FAFSA. Regular filing deadline is June 30. The Princeton Review suggests that all financial aid forms be submitted as soon as possible after January 1. *Need-based scholarships/grants offered:* Federal Pell, SEOG, state scholarships/grants, private scholarships, the school's own gift aid, Federal Nursing Scholarships. *Loan aid offered:* Direct Subsidized Stafford, Direct Unsubsidized Stafford, Direct PLUS, Direct PLUS, Federal Perkins, state loans, college/university loans from institutional funds, alternative loans. Applicants will be notified of awards on a rolling basis beginning February 15. Federal Work-Study Program available. Institutional employment available. Highest amount earned per year from on-campus jobs $5,000. Off-campus job opportunities are good.

Inside Word

B students with slightly above-average SAT or ACT scores should find little impediment to gaining admission to Monmouth. The school's national stature is on the rise, resulting in more competitive applicant base, but Monmouth must still compete with a lot of heavy hitters for top regional students.

THE SCHOOL SAYS ". . ."

From the Admissions Office

"Monmouth University, a first-tier, dynamic private university, empowers students to reach their full potential as leaders who make significant contributions to their community and society. Small classes, allowing for individual attention and student-faculty dialogue, are hallmarks of a Monmouth education. A ratio of fifteen students to each professor ensures active and engaged learning. At Monmouth, students and faculty connect. In and out of the classroom, ideas are nurtured and then become real, hands-on experiences.

"Experiential education, which includes study abroad, select service learning projects, dedicated experiential coursework, internships, or cooperative learning experiences, is a required part of the curriculum. Before graduation, more than seventy percent of Monmouth students have completed a 'real-world' experience; only fifty percent of graduating students at comparable institutions have done this according to the 2011 National Survey of Student Engagement.

"Monmouth University is located in the New York metropolitan area, home to many prominent firms that are leaders in the technology, media, and financial industries. This allows students access to exceptional hands-on learning opportunities.

"Monmouth's student life, including cultural events, festivals, and active student clubs and organizations, reflects the school's spirit. Monmouth's twenty NCAA Division I athletic teams attract lively support from students and other members of the Monmouth and local community.

"Monmouth's President, Paul G. Gaffney II, believes the reputation of the university starts with the achievements and successes of its students. Monmouth provides students with a value-added education, personalized experience, and the support and guidance needed to move forward and make their mark."

SELECTIVITY	
Admissions Rating	**79**
# of applicants	6,491
% of applicants accepted	63
% of acceptees attending	23
FRESHMAN PROFILE	
Range SAT Critical Reading	480–560
Range SAT Math	500–580
Range SAT Writing	500–580
Range ACT Composite	22–25
Minimum paper TOEFL	550
Minimum web-based TOEFL	79
Average HS GPA	3.4
% graduated top 10% of class	20
% graduated top 25% of class	55
% graduated top 50% of class	87
DEADLINES	
Early action	
Deadline	12/1
Notification	1/15
Regular	
Priority	12/1
Deadline	3/1
Nonfall registration?	yes
FINANCIAL FACTS	
Financial Aid Rating	**68**
Annual tuition	$27,372
Room and board	$10,459
Required fees	$628
Books and supplies	$1,200
% needy frosh rec. need-based scholarship or grant aid	47
% needy UG rec. need-based scholarship or grant aid	47
% needy frosh rec. non-need-based scholarship or grant aid	94
% needy UG rec. non-need-based scholarship or grant aid	94
% needy frosh rec. need-based self-help aid	83
% needy UG rec. need-based self-help aid	84
% frosh rec. any financial aid	99
% UG rec. any financial aid	95
% UG borrow to pay for school	77
Average cumulative indebtedness	$34,859
% frosh need fully met	5
% ugrads need fully met	6
Average % of frosh need met	69
Average % of ugrad need met	67

MONTANA TECH OF THE UNIVERSITY OF MONTANA

1300 West Park Street, Butte, MT 59701 • Admissions: 406-496-4256 • Fax: 406-496-4710

CAMPUS LIFE

Quality of Life Rating	**69**
Fire Safety Rating	**98**
Green Rating	**60***
Type of school	public
Environment	town

STUDENTS

Total undergrad enrollment	2,406
% male/female	62/38
% from out of state	15
% frosh live on campus	41
% African American	1
% Asian	1
% Caucasian	81
% Hispanic	2
% Native American	2
% international	8
# of countries represented	14

SURVEY SAYS . . .

Great computer facilities
Career services are great
Students get along with local community
Frats and sororities are unpopular or nonexistent

ACADEMICS

Academic Rating	**68**
% students returning for sophomore year	68
% students graduating within 4 years	19
% students graduating within 6 years	41
Calendar	semester
Student/faculty ratio	15:1
Profs interesting rating	72
Profs accessible rating	75
Most classes have	fewer than 10 students
Most lab/discussion sessions have	10–19 students

MOST POPULAR MAJORS

petroleum engineering; general engineering; nursing; business; information technology

APPLICANTS ALSO LOOK AT AND OFTEN PREFER

Michigan Technological University, Montana State University, The University of Montana

AND SOMETIMES PREFER

University of Washington

STUDENTS SAY "..."

Academics

Montana Tech is a small state school that's "all about giving students a high-quality education and getting students successful careers in the work force." Though the school emphasizes the sciences, and has particularly strong engineering, science, and technology majors, Montana Tech also offers degrees in nursing and liberal studies. Classes at Montana Tech are small, "which gives opportunity for one-on-one learning," and students really get "to know their professors on a personal level." Course loads are very "challenging" and students are aware of the "high level" at which they have to perform. However, they find their professors "are well-trained and offer good guidance," and "bring real life experience into the classroom," which "makes understanding the applicability of theory interesting." Additionally, professors "go above and beyond" to help students "reach [their] educational and professional goals." A mechanical engineering student says professors "are very willing to help and will meet with you even if it isn't their office hours." Getting a job after graduation is huge priority here, and with a job-placement rate of ninety-seven percent, students rightfully feel that "the majors here deliver when it comes to work after graduation." Professional placement is helped by the "hands-on practical lab experience and the number of internships a student can complete by the time they graduate." The ultimate combination of class size and support makes one student feel that Montana Tech is a "college built entirely for students."

Life

Students at Montana Tech say "there is always lots of school work to be done," and that most students "are very dedicated to their school work and have to be." However, though they work hard, they "play hard as well." An engineering student explains that the rigorous curriculum means "students are...very good at time management," and that they "try to get all of their work done in a way that leaves them time to do other things." With its enviable location halfway between Yellowstone and Glacier National Parks, those other things often include "fishing, snowboarding, skiing, hiking, [and] mountain biking." One student brags that "you can literally take a five-minute drive off campus into the countryside," which is great, because "being outdoors helps ease stress." In addition to blowing off steam outdoors, the school has "many activities to get people involved, especially when you live in the dorms, such as movie nights or intramural sports." Students "get e-mails from the school all the time about different stuff going on," such as "trips to concerts, trips to swimming hot springs, different contests, games, dances, parties," and more. Drinking can be part of life at Montana Tech for those students who seek it out. As one student notes, parties can get "a little rowdy." In addition, Butte is small but has "lots of bars to socialize in." However, though "most love a good time," "when it's time to study/hit the books, there is an extreme amount of dedication."

Student Body

Students at Montana Tech are "driven" but "nice" and "very friendly." While the school has "tons of little niches," such as "groups of cowboys, goths, athletes," and so on, everyone is generally united by their desire to succeed. As one student says, "It is hard to find students here that aren't nerds." Though students are devoted to their work, they don't mention a competitive atmosphere. In fact, many believe they "get along great together because they depend on each other" and they'll "help each other out" anytime. The school is predominantly male, and most are from Montana. It attracts a sizable portion of older, "nontraditional" students, so there's "a greater diversity of learning styles and experiences." There are also lots of international students, particularly from the Middle East, and though "there is a wide variety of cultures and beliefs," most people feel that "everybody gets along with everybody."

FINANCIAL AID: 406-496-4213 • E-MAIL: ENROLLMENT@MTECH.EDU • WEBSITE: WWW.MTECH.EDU

THE PRINCETON REVIEW SAYS

Admissions

Other factors considered include: Class rank, academic GPA, standardized test scores. SAT or ACT required; ACT with writing component recommended. TOEFL required of all international applicants. High school diploma is required and GED is accepted. *Academic units required:* 4 English, 3 mathematics, 2 science (2 science labs), 3 social studies, 2 combined years of foreign language, visual and performing arts, computer science, or vocational education. *Academic units recommended:* 4 English, 4 mathematics, 2 science (2 science labs), 2 foreign language.

Financial Aid

Students should submit: FAFSA, institution's own financial aid form. The Princeton Review suggests that all financial aid forms be submitted as soon as possible after January 1. *Need-based scholarships/grants offered:* Federal Pell, SEOG, state scholarships/grants, private scholarships, the school's own gift aid. *Loan aid offered:* Direct Subsidized Stafford, Direct Unsubsidized Stafford, Direct PLUS, Federal Perkins, college/university loans from institutional funds. Applicants will be notified of awards on a rolling basis beginning March 15. Federal Work-Study Program available. Institutional employment available. Highest amount earned per year from on-campus jobs $4,200. Off-campus job opportunities are good.

The Inside Word

Montana Tech is a godsend for students who are strong academically but not likely to be offered admission to nationally renowned technical institutes. In fact, because of its small size and relatively remote location, Montana Tech is a good choice for anyone leaning toward a technical career. You would be hard-pressed to find many other places as low-key and personal in the realm of academia.

THE SCHOOL SAYS ". . ."

From the Admissions Office

"Characterize Montana Tech by listening to what employers say. They tell us Tech graduates stand out with an incredible work ethic and top-notch technical skills. Last year, 189 companies held on-campus interviews and attended Montana Tech's career fairs competing for our students and graduates. The beneficiaries: the students! Montana Tech has had a ten-year annual average placement rate of ninety-six percent with exceptional starting salaries. Learning takes place in a personalized environment, in first-class academic facilities, and in the heart of the Rocky Mountains. Students at Tech work hard and play hard. Outdoor recreation provides a great balance to the rigors of the course work at Montana Tech. It's not a large, multifaceted university with lots of frills, but our students get a terrific education, and in the end, great jobs! The SAT (or the ACT with the writing section) is recommended for all students applying for admission. Students who do not take the tests with the writing component may be required to take an additional English placement test from the college before they enroll."

SELECTIVITY	
Admissions Rating	71
# of applicants	858
% of applicants accepted	89
% of acceptees attending	62

FRESHMAN PROFILE	
Range SAT Critical Reading	480–590
Range SAT Math	500–630
Range SAT Writing	450–580
Range ACT Composite	22–27
Minimum paper TOEFL	525
Minimum web-based TOEFL	71
Average HS GPA	3.4
% graduated top 10% of class	22
% graduated top 25% of class	47
% graduated top 50% of class	79

DEADLINES	
Nonfall registration?	yes

FINANCIAL FACTS	
Financial Aid Rating	82
Annual in-state tuition	$6,420
Annual out-state tuition	$17,598
Room and board	$7,266
Books and supplies	$900
% needy frosh rec. need-based scholarship or grant aid	93
% needy UG rec. need-based scholarship or grant aid	88
% needy frosh rec. non-need-based scholarship or grant aid	14
% needy UG rec. non-need-based scholarship or grant aid	6
% needy frosh rec. need-based self-help aid	69
% needy UG rec. need-based self-help aid	79
% frosh rec. any financial aid	78
% UG rec. any financial aid	69
% UG borrow to pay for school	70
Average cumulative indebtedness	$23,000
% frosh need fully met	47
% ugrads need fully met	40
Average % of frosh need met	82
Average % of ugrad need met	81

Moravian College

1200 Main Street, Bethlehem, PA 18018 • Admissions: 610-861-1320 • Fax: 610-625-7930

CAMPUS LIFE

Quality of Life Rating	74
Fire Safety Rating	82
Green Rating	71
Type of school	private
Affiliation	Moravian
Environment	city

STUDENTS

Total undergrad enrollment	1,551
% male/female	41/59
% from out of state	44
% from public high school	53
% frosh live on campus	87
# of fraternities	3
# of sororities	4
% African American	4
% Asian	2
% Caucasian	82
% Hispanic	9
# of countries represented	12

SURVEY SAYS . . .

Great computer facilities
Low cost of living
Students are happy
Musical organizations are popular

ACADEMICS

Academic Rating	82
% students graduating within 4 years	73
% students graduating within 6 years	76
Calendar	semester
Student/faculty ratio	11:1
Profs interesting rating	83
Profs accessible rating	87
Most classes have	20–29 students
Most lab/discussion sessions have	10–19 students

MOST POPULAR MAJORS

business/commerce; psychology; sociology

APPLICANTS ALSO LOOK AT AND OFTEN PREFER

Bucknell University, Muhlenberg College, Lafayette College

AND SOMETIMES PREFER

Susquehanna University, Ursinus College, Gettysburg College

STUDENTS SAY ". . ."

Academics

Moravian College "challenges students academically" in a "small environment," where "professors know their students on a personal level." The college is known for its "strong faculty and academic programs," and students say, "Moravian College bends over backward to accommodate its students." Students are exposed to "a good education" through "Learning in Common, which is a set of courses in multidisciplinary categories that interconnect different fields of study." Students boast about "personal attention and genuine enthusiasm from professors," and say, "Moravian College is dedicated to the education of its students as well as building a community between students and faculty." Professors are "accessible, approachable, helpful, and always willing to spend that extra time making sure you understand the material," and students attribute this to "the small student population" and the "mentoring relationship" that develops as a result. A chemistry major says, "The student-professor interactions improve the speed with which students understand course materials." However, a freshman says, "Like any school, there are the great professors and there are the not so great," adding, "You take the bad with the excellent, and it makes you a better student."

Life

Moravian College is known for being a "small school with a friendly atmosphere" that fosters a "supportive environment" for "students to learn and grow." A sophomore says, "I love the atmosphere of the campus," and another student adds, "I love the kindness and genuine concern that people have for others." Students say, "The campus itself is beautiful," and "you always run into someone you know," which creates a "sense of community and pride." A psychology major says, "Even though it's a relatively small school, there are so many things to do," and another student concurs that Moravian is "all about engaging students in real life experiences outside of the classroom using campus speakers, internships, and field study experiences." Students participate in "clubs, organizations, Greek life, and sports teams," and say, "Moravian College provides many opportunities to exceed above and beyond," noting being small allows "opportunities to get involved in different organizations and take leadership roles." Students speak highly of the staff, saying it's "a very personal experience overall" and that the "maintenance of facilities is outstanding." However, some gripe, "Communication between administration and students" could be improved in regards to "decisions [about the] use of funds." There are complaints about the requirement that students live on campus all four years, particularly because many feel "housing could be greatly improved upon."

Student Body

The typical Moravian student is "fun and hardworking," "very laid-back and sociable," and "dedicated to their education during the weekday, but able to relax and have fun on the weekends." A sophomore says, "The greatest quality is the school's diversity and acceptance of all backgrounds, religions, lifestyles," and another student adds, "You not only meet students who are like you, but students who are different in a positive way." However, others feel there's still much to be desired in terms of diversity and say most students are "middle-class [and] white," although they note, "There are [more] students of color, especially in recent years" and say generally "these individuals are not at all excluded from any aspects of campus life." When "the weekend comes, students tend to let loose and enjoy themselves while they spend time with friends," and "Much of the campus population attends some sort of party over the weekend." However, because "off campus housing was taken away…it makes it easier for campus safety to bust the parties on campus during the weekends." A music education major says, "There is also a large part of the school that does not party and participates in many school events," and another student adds, "Moravian always has something to do. On weekends they offer alternatives to drinking such as movies and bingo." The small town of Bethlehem also "offers many places to eat, take a stroll, shop, or hang out."

FINANCIAL AID: 610-861-1330 • E-MAIL: ADMISSIONS@MORAVIAN.EDU • WEBSITE: WWW.MORAVIAN.EDU

THE PRINCETON REVIEW SAYS

Admissions

Very important factors considered include: Class rank, academic GPA, rigor of secondary school record, alumni/ae relation, character/personal qualities. *Important factors considered include:* Application essay, recommendation(s), standardized test scores, extracurricular activities, first generation, level of applicant's interest, racial/ethnic status, talent/ability, volunteer work. *Other factors considered include:* Geographical residence, interview, work experience. ACT with writing component required. TOEFL required of all international applicants. High school diploma is required and GED is accepted. *Academic units required:* 4 English, 3 mathematics, 3 science (2 science labs), 2 foreign language, 4 social studies. *Academic units recommended:* 4 mathematics, 3 foreign language.

Financial Aid

Students should submit: FAFSA, CSS/Financial Aid PROFILE, noncustodial PROFILE, business/farm supplement. Copies of parent and student W-2s and 1040s. The Princeton Review suggests that all financial aid forms be submitted as soon as possible after January 1. *Need-based scholarships/grants offered:* Federal Pell, SEOG, state scholarships/grants, the school's own gift aid. *Loan aid offered:* Direct Subsidized Stafford, Direct Unsubsidized Stafford, Direct PLUS, Federal Perkins. Applicants will be notified of awards on or about April 1. Highest amount earned per year from on-campus jobs $3,000

The Inside Word

Admissions officers at Moravian College base admissions decisions primarily on an applicant's secondary school career. Course selection and performance are crucial elements and outweigh standardized test scores. Recommendations and community activism are also weighed heavily. The admissions staff strongly encourages a campus visit and although interviews aren't required they're recommended.

THE SCHOOL SAYS ". . ."

From the Admissions Office

"Moravian partners with students to build a foundation for their future. In today's challenging and highly competitive work environment, college graduates need more than a college degree to succeed in the world. Students today require in-depth knowledge of their subject, real-world experience, and leadership and social skills. Moravian College puts students first. We're committed to providing students with the well-rounded, strong foundation they need to succeed.

"With more than 250 years of experience in providing equal access to education for all, Moravian promises to partner with students to build a strong foundation for their personal and professional future. Moravian College students are challenged to reach their full potential as individuals while they benefit from our supportive learning community.

"Moravian challenges students with a strong, personalized academic major. Students grow intellectually from programs that develop from our faculty's innovative teaching, from the intellectual relationships between faculty and students, and from the broad range of opportunities for personalized learning.

"At Moravian, students also experience hands-on learning. They participate in collaborative research and scholarship such as the SOAR and honors programs, internships, study abroad, leadership, work study, and community service opportunities.

"Students live and learn in an environment that promotes the development of a deeper enjoyment of life. They develop personally through co-curricular activities such as athletics and recreation, music and the arts, and opportunities for an active social life.

"Students leave Moravian with the skills, knowledge, and support necessary to more deeply enjoy life, work, and their role in the world."

SELECTIVITY	
Admissions Rating	75
# of applicants	1,940
% of applicants accepted	80
% of acceptees attending	24
# accepting a place on wait list	81
# admitted from wait list	14
# of early decision applicants	125
# accepted early decision	105

FRESHMAN PROFILE	
Range SAT Critical Reading	470–580
Range SAT Math	480–590
Range SAT Writing	470–580
Range ACT Composite	20–22
Minimum paper TOEFL	550
Average HS GPA	3.3
% graduated top 10% of class	19
% graduated top 25% of class	49
% graduated top 50% of class	83

DEADLINES	
Early decision	
Deadline	2/1
Notification	12/15
Early action	
Deadline	12/1
Notification	12/15
Regular	
Priority	3/1
Deadline	3/1
Notification	3/15
Nonfall registration?	yes

FINANCIAL FACTS	
Financial Aid Rating	79
Annual tuition	$33,919
Required fees	$705
% needy frosh rec. need-based scholarship or grant aid	100
% needy UG rec. need-based scholarship or grant aid	99
% needy frosh rec. non-need-based scholarship or grant aid	9
% needy UG rec. non-need-based scholarship or grant aid	8
% needy frosh rec. need-based self-help aid	91
% needy UG rec. need-based self-help aid	92
% frosh rec. any financial aid	96
% UG rec. any financial aid	91
% UG borrow to pay for school	83
Average cumulative indebtedness	$40,912
% frosh need fully met	11
% ugrads need fully met	12
Average % of frosh need met	77
Average % of ugrad need met	75

MOUNT HOLYOKE COLLEGE

NEWHALL CENTER, SOUTH HADLEY, MA 01075 • ADMISSIONS: 413-538-2023 • FAX: 413-538-2409

CAMPUS LIFE

Quality of Life Rating	**93**
Fire Safety Rating	**80**
Green Rating	**72**
Type of school	private
Environment	town

STUDENTS

Total undergrad enrollment	2,317
% male/female	0/100
% from out of state	76
% from public high school	62
% frosh live on campus	100
% African American	6
% Asian	7
% Caucasian	47
% Hispanic	9
% international	23
# of countries represented	79

SURVEY SAYS . . .

Lab facilities are great
Great computer facilities
Diverse student types on campus
Dorms are like palaces
Campus feels safe
Frats and sororities are unpopular or nonexistent
Musical organizations are popular
Political activism is popular

ACADEMICS

Academic Rating	**98**
% students returning for sophomore year	92
% students graduating within 4 years	80
% students graduating within 6 years	85
Calendar	semester
Student/faculty ratio	9:1
Profs interesting rating	97
Profs accessible rating	96
Most classes have	10–19 students
Most lab/discussion sessions have	10–19 students

MOST POPULAR MAJORS

biology/biological sciences; English language and literature; psychology

APPLICANTS ALSO LOOK AT AND OFTEN PREFER

Brown University, Harvard College, Wellesley College, Yale University, Amherst College, Vassar College, Barnard College, Dartmouth College, Williams College

AND SOMETIMES PREFER

Smith College, Middlebury College, Bryn Mawr College, Columbia University, Tufts University

AND RARELY PREFER

Skidmore College, University of Massachusetts Amherst, Boston University

STUDENTS SAY ". . ."

Academics

Mount Holyoke is a "small student-focused liberal arts college," "specializing in the higher education of women." Students say it's "an amazing school with a strong history of producing remarkable and intelligent young women who go on to achieve great things" and rave about the "supportive all-women environment and the excellent academics." A freshman says, "It's a traditional yet modern school with brilliant alumnae and top-notch academics." Mount Holyoke is known for its "academic rigor" and "consortium opportunities," with the other schools in the Five College consortium. The school "provides a fantastic learning environment where students value their education" and offers a "balance between the sciences and a liberal arts education." A history major says, "Mount Holyoke College provides an incredible academic experience with outstanding faculty [and] engaged classmates," and professors are deemed "incredibly motivated and interesting." Students say, "Mount Holyoke professors are brilliant, but human and accessible," and "From your first year to senior year, you feel very supported by the faculty" who are "interested in getting to know students on a personal level."

Life

Mount Holyoke is known for its "beautiful campus" that provides a "plethora of opportunities beyond the classroom in terms of extracurricular activities." Students say, "It's a wonderful, inviting and challenging environment," where "smart, passionate, diverse women come together…in a beautiful campus setting"…"to form a strong community and to pursue their educational goals." A freshman says the college "makes sure its students are involved, proactive, and learning the rest of the time that they're on campus," and another student adds, "I'm consistently impressed with the involvement of the students here." Students say, "The support system here is great," and "I feel like I can really count on my peers," adding "the Alumnae Association does a wonderful job at helping current students connect in terms of careers, internships, or just common interest." Most feel, "The administration listens to the students and does its best to provide for us," although some disagree saying, "Communication between the administration and the student body is not always prompt or clear." There are complaints about being "forced to live on campus," with students saying, "Residential life could use some work," and "some of the dorms need more maintenance." Despite the "warm, loving, and open," community, a psychology major says, "The school-sponsored events are poorly attended, and there isn't much of a social life on campus for heterosexual students."

Student Body

At Mount Holyoke, "The students are happy, intelligent women dedicated to making a real difference in the world." Typical students are "poised, eloquent, passionate, and doing interesting things both inside and outside the classroom" and "down-to-earth and laid-back but also willing to have complex conversations over breakfast." It's clear most are "very into being left-wing and excited about political awareness," and a sophomore says, "Mt. Holyoke is full of geeky feminists," who are "at least socially engaged if not activists." There is "a very strong gay community and much of the party scene is queer-based social networks," and students say, "Sexual orientation is often flexible." However, there are also those who complain, "There aren't any men around, which is less than ideal," and say, "Despite the percentages touting great racial/ethnic diversity, much improvement is needed." Most agree, "The typical student is incredibly smart, a tad quirky, and above all passionate," and say "There's definitely a niche for everyone, regardless of sexual orientation or gender expression." Students are "studious, ambitious, and determined," and "able to laugh and enjoy camaraderie."

FINANCIAL AID: 413-538-2291 • E-MAIL: ADMISSION@MTHOLYOKE.EDU • WEBSITE: WWW.MTHOLYOKE.EDU

THE PRINCETON REVIEW SAYS

Admissions

Very important factors considered include: Class rank, application essay, academic GPA, recommendation(s), rigor of secondary school record. *Important factors considered include:* Character/personal qualities, extracurricular activities, first generation, interview, talent/ability, volunteer work, work experience. *Other factors considered include:* Standardized test scores, alumni/ae relation, geographical residence, level of applicant's interest, racial/ethnic status. ACT with or without writing component accepted. TOEFL required of all international applicants. High school diploma is required and GED is accepted. *Academic units recommended:* 4 English (3 science labs), 3 history, 1 academic electives.

Financial Aid

Students should submit: FAFSA, CSS/Financial Aid PROFILE, noncustodial PROFILE, business/farm supplement. Regular filing deadline is March 1. The Princeton Review suggests that all financial aid forms be submitted as soon as possible after January 1. *Need-based scholarships/grants offered:* Federal Pell, SEOG, state scholarships/grants, private scholarships, the school's own gift aid. *Loan aid offered:* Direct Subsidized Stafford, Direct Unsubsidized Stafford, Direct PLUS, Federal Perkins, state loans, college/university loans from institutional funds. Applicants will be notified of awards on or about April 1. Federal Work-Study Program available. Institutional employment available. Highest amount earned per year from on-campus jobs $2,100. Off-campus job opportunities are fair.

The Inside Word

Mount Holyoke follows traditional admissions requirements, but encourages applicants to submit supplemental materials exhibiting artistic or athletic talents. The admission committee is happy to receive portfolios, slides, and so on, that showcase an applicant's talents. In addition, interviews are strongly encouraged as way for the admission staff to learn more about a prospective student's academic goals and personal experiences.

THE SCHOOL SAYS ". . ."

From the Admissions Office

"The majority of students who choose Mount Holyoke do so simply because it is an outstanding liberal arts college. After a semester or two, they start to appreciate the fact that Mount Holyoke is a women's college, even though most Mount Holyoke students never thought they'd go to a women's college when they started their college search. They appreciate the remarkable array of opportunities—for academic achievement, career exploration, internships, study abroad, and leadership—and the impressive, creative accomplishments of their peers. If you're looking for a college that will challenge you to be your best, most powerful self and to fulfill your potential, Mount Holyoke should be at the top of your list.

"Submission of standardized test scores is optional for most applicants to Mount Holyoke College. However, the TOEFL is required of students for whom English is not their primary language, and the SAT Subject Tests are required for homeschooled students."

SELECTIVITY	
Admissions Rating	**95**
# of applicants	3,416
% of applicants accepted	51
% of acceptees attending	34
# accepting a place on wait list	503
# of early decision applicants	292
# accepted early decision	161

FRESHMAN PROFILE	
Range SAT Critical Reading	610–720
Range SAT Math	590–700
Range SAT Writing	620–710
Range ACT Composite	27–31
Minimum web-based TOEFL	100
Average HS GPA	3.7
% graduated top 10% of class	57
% graduated top 25% of class	88
% graduated top 50% of class	99

DEADLINES	
Early decision	
Deadline	11/15
Notification	1/1
Regular	
Deadline	1/15
Notification	4/1
Nonfall registration?	yes

FINANCIAL FACTS	
Financial Aid Rating	**96**
Annual tuition	$41,270
Room and board	$12,140
Required fees	$186
Books and supplies	$950
% needy frosh rec. need-based scholarship or grant aid	68
% needy UG rec. need-based scholarship or grant aid	69
% needy frosh rec. non-need-based scholarship or grant aid	14
% needy UG rec. non-need-based scholarship or grant aid	11
% needy frosh rec. need-based self-help aid	58
% needy UG rec. need-based self-help aid	66
% frosh rec. any financial aid	82
% UG rec. any financial aid	81
% UG borrow to pay for school	69
Average cumulative indebtedness	$23,254
% frosh need fully met	100
% ugrads need fully met	100
Average % of frosh need met	100
Average % of ugrad need met	100

MUHLENBERG COLLEGE

2400 WEST CHEW STREET, ALLENTOWN, PA 18104-5596 • ADMISSIONS: 484-664-3200 • FAX: 484-664-3234

CAMPUS LIFE

Quality of Life Rating	**75**
Fire Safety Rating	**88**
Green Rating	**78**
Type of school	private
Affiliation	Lutheran
Environment	city

STUDENTS

Total undergrad enrollment	2,384
% male/female	42/58
% from out of state	78
% from public high school	72
% frosh live on campus	99
# of fraternities	4
# of sororities	5
% African American	3
% Asian	3
% Caucasian	76
% Hispanic	4
# of countries represented	7

SURVEY SAYS . . .

Athletic facilities are great
Students are friendly
Low cost of living
Theater is popular

ACADEMICS

Academic Rating	**88**
% students returning for sophomore year	90
% students graduating within 4 years	79
% students graduating within 6 years	86
Calendar	semester
Student/faculty ratio	12:1
Profs interesting rating	88
Profs accessible rating	90
Most classes have	10–19 students
Most lab/discussion sessions have	10–19 students

MOST POPULAR MAJORS

business/commerce; communication studies/ speech communication and rhetoric; psychology

APPLICANTS ALSO LOOK AT AND OFTEN PREFER

Bucknell University, Villanova University, Lehigh University, Lafayette College

AND SOMETIMES PREFER

Dickinson College, Franklin & Marshall College, Gettysburg College, University of Delaware, Ursinus College, Skidmore College, The College of New Jersey

AND RARELY PREFER

Susquehanna University, Pennsylvania State University—University Park, Drew University, Ithaca College, Goucher College

STUDENTS SAY ". . ."

Academics

Muhlenberg College, a small "caring college" located in Allentown, Pennsylvania, is "all about a sense of community," both within the school's borders and outside of them. Add to that a rigorous academic curriculum (with a particularly good theater department) and an "extremely high" overall involvement of both the professors and students in both academic and extracurricular pursuits, and you've got a community of students, faculty, and staff committed to "delivering and receiving a quality, liberal arts education that will craft the next generation into responsible, intelligent leaders of this quickly changing world." "The brochures are not a joke; the people here really are friendly and open," says a student. Students are incredibly thankful for the school's balance of resources throughout all of the majors. "I wanted a liberal arts experience, and I appreciate how much focus Muhlenberg puts on both the arts and the sciences," says a student. The "very responsive" professors are "engaging and accommodating to students' needs," which helps to "[develop] relationships that will help you grow through your educational journey and eventually into the work force." Almost all are "easily approachable" and open to direct arguments against the topics and theories discussed in class, which "provides for an engaging classroom environment that lets students push past the direct facts of the material and learn more about what the material means for the world." The college is "very flexible" and allows students to create their own majors to reflect their interests; established majors on campus are always changing to reflect progress in the field. Students agree that the school "definitely offers a rich amount of courses that will prepare you for your future and open your mind to possibilities," and it has "many resources to help you with a variety of situations that may arise."

Life

This "friendly, tight-knit community" is "about being able to be unique yet finding a common ground with others." There are "a fair amount of clubs" on campus, and "The school works hard to make sure that there are always fun events going on so students have fun activity options." A cappella groups are popular and can be seen performing at an event almost every weekend. Come Thursday it's the weekend, as "most students don't have class Fridays." For some, this means "tame parties," as "things don't change all that often unfortunately, and you may wind up going to the same three parties each weekend." However, "There is no pressure to drink. If someone does not drink, they do not have to worry about being judged." When the weather is nice, everyone is outside, whether "playing pickup Frisbee, lacrosse, football, or just relaxing on a blanket in the sun." Generally, "People don't have an awful lot of free time between class, studying, and clubs." For those who want to get off campus, shuttles run on the weekends to the movie theater, the Lehigh Valley Mall, Target, and other local places of interest.

Student Body

The typical Muhlenberg student is "from a middle- to upper-middle-class family on the East Coast" and "driven but not type-A," with a large percentage hailing from New Jersey. There are also sizable Jewish, premed, and theater contingents. Many students "have one weird quirky talent that everyone mocked them for in high school, but here, there's a club for that." Every student here "cares about the whole community, even members of it they have not met," most "would give away a swipe meal into the dining area to a total stranger." Students come from diverse backgrounds, although not from diverse ethnic/race backgrounds ("While ethnic diversity is pretty low, our social diversity is high."), which means that "students fit in very well with all types of groups since our school is so accepting."

FINANCIAL AID: 484-664-3175 • E-MAIL: ADMISSION@MUHLENBERG.EDU • WEBSITE: WWW.MUHLENBERG.EDU

THE PRINCETON REVIEW SAYS

Admissions

Very important factors considered include: Academic GPA, rigor of secondary school record. *Important factors considered include:* Application essay, recommendation(s), standardized test scores, character/personal qualities, extracurricular activities, interview, talent/ability. *Other factors considered include:* Class rank, alumni/ae relation, first generation, level of applicant's interest, racial/ethnic status, volunteer work, work experience. ACT with writing component recommended. TOEFL required of all international applicants. High school diploma is required and GED is accepted. *Academic units required:* 4 English, 3 mathematics, 2 science, 2 foreign language, 2 history. *Academic units recommended:* 4 English, 4 mathematics, 3 science, 4 foreign language, 2 social studies, 3 history.

Financial Aid

Students should submit: FAFSA, institution's own financial aid form, CSS/Financial Aid PROFILE, noncustodial PROFILE. Regular filing deadline is February 15. The Princeton Review suggests that all financial aid forms be submitted as soon as possible after January 1. *Need-based scholarships/grants offered:* Federal Pell, SEOG, state scholarships/grants, private scholarships, the school's own gift aid. *Loan aid offered:* Direct Subsidized Stafford, Direct Unsubsidized Stafford, Direct PLUS, Federal Perkins, private. Applicants will be notified of awards on or about April 1. Federal Work-Study Program available. Institutional employment available. Highest amount earned per year from on-campus jobs $1,800. Off-campus job opportunities are excellent.

The Inside Word

Muhlenberg College accepts only the Common Application and doesn't require any supplemental essays, unless you're applying early decision. Your high school GPA and course selection are of primary importance. Muhlenberg is also part of a growing group of colleges that don't require SAT scores or other standardized tests for admission. Students who don't submit test scores are required to appear for an admissions interview and to submit an SAT-optional statement.

THE SCHOOL SAYS ". . ."

From the Admissions Office

"Listening to our own students, we've learned that most picked Muhlenberg mainly because it has a long-standing reputation for being academically demanding on one hand but personally supportive on the other. We expect a lot from our students, but we also expect a lot from ourselves in providing the challenge and support they need to stretch, grow, and succeed. It's not unusual for professors to put their home phone numbers on the course syllabus and encourage students to call them at home with questions. Upperclassmen are helpful to underclassmen. 'We really know about collegiality here,' says an alumna who now works at Muhlenberg. 'It's that kind of place.' The supportive atmosphere and strong work ethic produce lots of successes. The premed and pre-law programs are very strong, as are programs in theater arts, English, psychology, the sciences, business, and accounting. 'When I was a student here,' recalls Dr. Walter Loy, now a professor emeritus of physics, 'we were encouraged to live life to its fullest, to do our best, to be honest, to deal openly with others, and to treat everyone as an individual. Those are important things, and they haven't changed at Muhlenberg.'

"Students have the option of submitting SAT or ACT scores (including the writing sections) or submitting a graded paper with teacher's comments and grade on it from junior or senior year and interviewing with a member of the admissions staff."

SELECTIVITY

Admissions Rating	92
# of applicants	4,876
% of applicants accepted	43
% of acceptees attending	28
# accepting a place on wait list	1,670
# admitted from wait list	21
# of early decision applicants	413
# accepted early decision	310

FRESHMAN PROFILE

Range SAT Critical Reading	560–670
Range SAT Math	560–670
Range SAT Writing	560–670
Range ACT Composite	25–31
Minimum paper TOEFL	550
Average HS GPA	3.3
% graduated top 10% of class	51
% graduated top 25% of class	78
% graduated top 50% of class	96

DEADLINES

Early decision	
Deadline	2/15
Notification	12/1
Regular	
Priority	2/15
Deadline	2/15
Notification	4/1
Nonfall registration?	yes

FINANCIAL FACTS

Financial Aid Rating	94
Annual tuition	$39,915
Room and board	$9,610
Required fees	$285
Books and supplies	$1,400
% needy frosh rec. need-based scholarship or grant aid	95
% needy UG rec. need-based scholarship or grant aid	93
% needy frosh rec. non-need-based scholarship or grant aid	26
% needy UG rec. non-need-based scholarship or grant aid	20
% needy frosh rec. need-based self-help aid	67
% needy UG rec. need-based self-help aid	72
% frosh rec. any financial aid	83
% UG rec. any financial aid	81
% UG borrow to pay for school	64
Average cumulative indebtedness	$26,270
% frosh need fully met	92
% ugrads need fully met	91
Average % of frosh need met	94
Average % of ugrad need met	94

National University of Ireland Maynooth

International Office, Maynooth, Co. Kildare, Ireland • Admissions: +353-1-7083868 • Fax: +353-1-7086113

CAMPUS LIFE

Quality of Life Rating	**90**
Fire Safety Rating	**86**
Green Rating	**82**
Type of school	international
Environment	town

STUDENTS

Total undergrad enrollment	8,400
% male/female	45/55
% frosh live on campus	40
% international	12
# of countries represented	93

SURVEY SAYS . . .

Students are happy
Lab facilities are great
Great library
Students are friendly
Great off-campus food
Campus feels safe
Athletic facilities are great
Lots of beer drinking

ACADEMICS

Academic Rating	**65**
Calendar	semester
Student/faculty ratio	11:1
Profs interesting rating	82
Profs accessible rating	78

STUDENTS SAY ". . ."

Academics

In emerald Ireland, just outside of Dublin, there lies the country's second-oldest and fastest growing university, the National University of Ireland Maynooth. The school's town location and its relatively small size give off a "community atmosphere," and "modern and up-to-date" facilities and a "beautiful campus" make it "a nice environment to study in" with a "great history" to back it up. "The academic standard at Maynooth is impeccable, with lecturers, lecture halls, tutors, and labs of the finest stature," says a science major. There's a wide selection of classes available at Maynooth, and course content "is generally well-explained, with tutorials and support centers available." Professors "are without exception experts in their field" and "continually encouraging us to engage in discussions, to ask questions, and to develop not only a well-informed but independent way of thinking." "Almost all my lecturers are great orators that bring their subjects to life, creating a genuine interest among their students," says a Spanish major. Add to that the fact that they're "very, very, very approachable outside of class" ("There is always someone that you can approach for help and guidance"), and students are happy to receive "the best learning experience possible." Administration is responsive to student concerns, and there's a "friendliness of everyone on campus, from the president right down to the cleaners." The services the school provides are all "brilliant," from the library to the residence services. People also all love the "great" online class system, Moodle, which allows you to upload assignments and download class notes. "You are given every little or big piece of help you require or request to ensure you can achieve your highest grades," says a student. "In my six months here, I have yet to hear a disgruntled word aimed at the campus or the staff."

Life

Maynooth is a "very vibrant town" that "has all facilities needed by third-level students (including clubs, pubs, and pizzerias)." The student body "isn't too big," and the majority "keep on top of college work, participate in a club or society or two, and enjoy a night in the pub with their friends." There's a "vast amount" of clubs and societies, which means "there's always somewhere for you to go, whether it's the Play-Doh society or the Harry Potter appreciation society—we got it all!" The student union also "hosts concerts and social events regularly," and everyone enjoys the "good mood" of their compatriots. "For fun, the nightlife is key," and "every Wednesday and Thursday [are] party nights," when people go to the nightclubs or bars, play card games, drink beers, and "hang out with…mates." The school consists of two connected campuses, which "combine the old with the new." "South campus covered in snow is like a scene from Hogwarts in Harry Potter, [and] then "the north campus is modern." For those who live on campus, "Everything is just at your fingertips," including a free gym. Though there are "few facilities in the university for simply sitting and studying," there are plenty of computers for students, and a new cafeteria is under construction.

Student Body

Look around Maynooth, and for the most part you'll just see a whole bunch of "your normal average twenty-year-old Irish girl [or] boy," though there's "a great mix of both city students and those from a rural background," as well as international, traditional, and "mature" students. "Individuality is very much encouraged" here, and in the midst of this "bubbly," "friendly" group is "a good place to make new friends." "Being Irish, we all like to have the 'craic' with people, meaning have fun," says a student. This group is also very "trustworthy," and "You can leave your laptop in the library for hours, and no one would ever take it."

National University of Ireland Maynooth

E-mail: international.applications@nuim.ie • Website: www.nuim.ie/international

THE PRINCETON REVIEW SAYS

Admissions

Very important factors considered include: Academic GPA, rigor of secondary school record, standardized test scores, character/personal qualities, talent/ ability. *Important factors considered include:* Extracurricular activities, volunteer work, work experience. *Other factors considered include:* Level of applicant's interest, recommendation(s). High school diploma is required, and GED is accepted. SAT or ACT results are required from all U.S. applicants. Evidence of classes/tests taken in subject area relevant to chosen major is recommended. *Academic units required:* Depends on the student's chosen degree program. Academic requirements for each course can be found at www.nuim.ie/ courses/. The deadline for application is August 1 of the year of entry. Early action students can apply up to one year in advance of entry. Notification of acceptance is on a rolling basis beginning November 1 of the year before entry.

Financial Aid

Students should submit: FAFSA. Regular filing deadline is June 1. The Princeton Review suggests that all financial aid forms be submitted as soon as possible after January 1. *Need-based scholarships/grants offered:* Private scholarships, school scholarship or grant aid from institutional funds. *Loan aid offered:* Direct Subsidized Stafford, Direct Unsubsidized Stafford, Direct PLUS. Applicants will be notified of awards on a rolling basis beginning March 1, with the condition that the student has received an offer of a place at the university.

THE SCHOOL SAYS ". . ."

From the Admissions Office

"National University of Ireland Maynooth is pleased to be one of the few international universities to be included in The Princeton Review Best Colleges series. You do not require a visa to study in Ireland if you are a U.S. citizen, and the fees for National University of Ireland Maynooth are comparable to most in-state tuition fees in the United States. So, for the price of your flights, you could get an international university experience for nearly the same price as staying at home!

"Degrees awarded by Irish Universities are internationally recognized as being of high quality. Irish universities do not have a general education requirement, which means that students begin studying their chosen major immediately. Due to this, degrees in the Arts and Humanities will be completed in three years, while Science and Engineering degrees will be completed in four years. Students registered on undergraduate degrees at NUIM can also apply to study abroad in their third year, in Europe, Asia, South America, or Australia. This extends your degree by one year, and you will earn a Bachelor (International) degree.

"The International Office offers full support to all international students during the application process and once you arrive on campus. National University of Ireland Maynooth is very popular with U.S. students studying in Ireland and the campus is known as one of the friendliest in Ireland, so you will receive a warm welcome. If you have questions about studying at NUIM, contact the International Office at any time."

SELECTIVITY

Admissions Rating	**61**
# of applicants	4,620
% of applicants accepted	54
% of acceptees attending	89

FRESHMAN PROFILE

Minimum SAT Composite	1500
Minimum ACT	22
Minimum IELTS	6
Minimum computer TOEFL	220
Minimum web-based TOEFL	80
Average HS GPA	3.4
Minimum HS GPA	3.0

DEADLINES

Regular	
Deadline	7/1
Notification	rolling
Nonfall registration?	yes

FINANCIAL FACTS

Financial Aid Rating	**60***
Annual tuition	
Arts and Humanities	€11,500/ $16,300*
Social Sciences	€12,500/ $17,700
Science and Engineering	€14,500/ $20,600*
Room	€3,500–€4,200/ $5,000–$6,000*
Average cumulative indebtedness	$12,297

* Fees and room rates are guidelines. Dollar amounts are subject to currency exchange rate fluctuation. To obtain an accurate quote for specific course fees, visit www.nuim.ie/international. Room rates don't include any meal plans. All on-campus accommodation is in the format of apartments. Each apartment contains four to five private/twin bedrooms with shared kitchen facilities and living space.

NAZARETH COLLEGE

4245 EAST AVENUE, ROCHESTER, NY 14618-3790 • ADMISSIONS: 585-389-2860 • FAX: 585-389-2826

CAMPUS LIFE

Quality of Life Rating	**91**
Fire Safety Rating	**61**
Green Rating	**60***
Type of school	private
Environment	suburban

STUDENTS

Total undergrad enrollment	2,144
% male/female	24/76
% from out of state	8
% from public high school	90
% frosh live on campus	90
% African American	5
% Asian	2
% Caucasian	83
% Hispanic	3
% international	1
# of countries represented	13

SURVEY SAYS . . .

Students are friendly
Students get along with local community
Students love Rochester, NY
Great off-campus food
Frats and sororities are unpopular or nonexistent
Musical organizations are popular
Theater is popular

ACADEMICS

Academic Rating	**81**
% students returning for sophomore year	83
% students graduating within 4 years	60
% students graduating within 6 years	72
Calendar	semester
Student/faculty ratio	12:1
Profs interesting rating	87
Profs accessible rating	85
Most classes have	10–19 students
Most lab/discussion sessions have	10–19 students

MOST POPULAR MAJORS

business administration, music; education; physical therapy/therapist

STUDENTS SAY ". . ."

Academics

Nazareth College "is a small liberal arts school located in a great suburb of Rochester" that offers "a great atmosphere to learn and grow as an individual and as a professional." The college has "a high focus on education," is known for an "outstanding" music program, and is made up of "a community full of ambitious and serious learners." Students say, "Nazareth is a close community of students and faculty working together to pursue positive educational experiences," and "Class sizes are small, which helps students to get the attention [they] need." Professors get high marks for being "very flexible and understanding," and students say they "The professors know their material, and they all want you to succeed so they give you all the tools necessary to do so." A social work major says, "The professors at Naz are great. They take the time to help you in and outside of class," and another student adds, "The professors here are passionate, interested, funny, and accessible. The lack of pretension is palpable." However, a sophomore notes, "Professors are people too, and they are allowed to be as varied and diverse as we students are," and another concurs: "My professors, just like professors from any other college, vary drastically in my book."

Life

Nazareth College offers "a small close-knit community" on an "intimate campus," where "there is a general tone of friendliness and politeness amongst students, faculty, and staff." Students say, "Nazareth is a beautiful school with many opportunities," and "The greatest strength is the sense of community. Everyone looks out for everyone else." There are "many activities on campus and a wide range of clubs," and students say, "There is always something happening on campus whether it's a program by an RA or an event in the Arts Center open to the community." Nazareth is good at "reaching out to the student population," and students say, "The students are full of school spirit and the campus is a very safe environment to be living in." A junior says, "The school provides a ton of extracurricular activities to participate in," and another student adds, "Student life is wonderful and service opportunities are always available." Students are grateful for the "underground tunnels" during the cold winter months, and "Security is great." Some complain, "Technology programs could be improved to work more efficiently and reliably," and "The residential facilities and faculties could improve on the efficiency and quality of services provided." Almost everyone gripes that the "food could use some improvement," but raves that "free laundry" is great.

Student Body

At Nazareth, "The student body is friendly and spirited" and "dedicated to balancing work and play." Students say they "care about their education, but are not overly studious—they want to have fun as well." Most students are "middle-class white women," and a sophomore says, "I think I speak for the majority of the girls on campus when I say: men. We need more men on campus." There's an active community of gay men, and a sophomore says, "Everyone has their groups: There are jocks, music majors, etc., but people mingle between groups a lot." Students say they know "when it's time to study and when it's time to relax or have fun," and "people like to go to mixers and hang out." A music education major says, "There are two types of people on campus: partiers and non-partiers," but another adds, "I like how at Nazareth if you are into partying/drinking or if you are not there is always someone to hang out with or something to do on the weekend." Students say, "Weekends at Nazareth are always the same, but with Rochester being so close it is easy to find something to do," and "There are also many activities such as mixers and movie nights on weekends for people who are not into partying."

FINANCIAL AID: 585-389-2310 • E-MAIL: ADMISSIONS@NAZ.EDU • WEBSITE: WWW.NAZ.EDU

THE PRINCETON REVIEW SAYS

Admissions

Very important factors considered include: Rigor of secondary school record, academic GPA, class rank, recommendation(s), application essay. *Important factors considered include:* Character/personal qualities, extracurricular activities, geographical residence, interview, level of applicant's interest, racial/ethnic status, state residency, talent/ability, volunteer work, work experience. *Other factors considered include:* Standardized test scores, alumni/ae relation, first generation, ACT with or without writing component accepted. TOEFL required of all international applicants. High school diploma is required and GED is accepted. *Academic units required:* 4 English, 3 mathematics, 3 science (2 science labs), 3 foreign language, 3 social studies. *Academic units recommended:* 4 English, 4 mathematics, 4 science, 4 foreign language, 4 social studies.

Financial Aid

Students should submit: FAFSA. Regular filing deadline is May 1. The Princeton Review suggests that all financial aid forms be submitted as soon as possible after January 1. *Need-based scholarships/grants offered:* Federal Pell, SEOG, state scholarships/grants, private scholarships, the school's own gift aid. *Loan aid offered:* Direct Subsidized Stafford, Direct Unsubsidized Stafford, Direct PLUS, Federal Perkins. Applicants will be notified of awards on a rolling basis beginning February 20. Federal Work-Study Program available. Institutional employment available. Off-campus job opportunities are excellent.

The Inside Word

The admissions staff at Nazareth College gives primary consideration to secondary school academic achievement but also sees talent in the arts and co-curricular activities as enhancements to an application. Applicants to the art, theater, and music programs are required to schedule and an audition or portfolio review. Prospective students aren't required to submit standardized test scores.

THE SCHOOL SAYS ". . ."

From the Admissions Office

"Growing interest in Nazareth—applications have grown forty-one percent in five years—is a result of many factors. New facilities have increased and improved academic, performing arts, residential, and athletic spaces. Major offerings now include music/business, toxicology, occupational therapy, and music theater. Nazareth has worked diligently to keep tuition at $5,000 less than the New York State average for private colleges. Our track record is strong—retention and graduation rates exceed national averages; seventy-five percent of our students participate in a career-related internship with ninety-three percent of them citing this a very worthwhile experience; and ninety-three percent of our students are employed or in graduate school within one year of graduation. The College has produced ten Fulbright scholars in the past two years alone, along with two Thomas R. Pickering Graduate Foreign Affairs Fellowships. The Center for International Education has developed more opportunities for our students to study abroad and for international students to study at Nazareth. With civic engagement and service learning as hallmarks of the Nazareth experience, ninety-one percent of undergrads participate in community service while at Nazareth. A proactive approach to campus security and state-of-the-art emergency notification system places Nazareth ahead of the curve regarding student safety. Student athletes, veterans of conference and national championships, have one of the highest graduation rates among NCAA Division III institutions. The Nazareth College Arts Center brings an international roster of performing art companies to campus, and provides high-quality facilities for student productions."

SELECTIVITY	
Admissions Rating	**81**
# of applicants	3,000
% of applicants accepted	69
% of acceptees attending	22
# accepting a place on wait list	83
# admitted from wait list	23
# of early decision applicants	60
# accepted early decision	49

FRESHMAN PROFILE	
Range SAT Critical Reading	530–630
Range SAT Math	530–630
Range SAT Writing	510–610
Range ACT Composite	23–27
Minimum paper TOEFL	550
Minimum web-based TOEFL	79
Average HS GPA	3.4
% graduated top 10% of class	30
% graduated top 25% of class	67
% graduated top 50% of class	91

DEADLINES	
Early decision	
Deadline	11/1
Notification	12/1
Early action	
Deadline	12/1
Notification	1/15
Regular	
Priority	12/15
Deadline	2/1
Notification	2/15
Nonfall registration?	yes

FINANCIAL FACTS	
Financial Aid Rating	**80**
Annual tuition	$26,048
Room and board	$11,144
Required fees	$1,174
Books and supplies	$1,100
% needy frosh rec. need-based scholarship or grant aid	80
% needy UG rec. need-based scholarship or grant aid	73
% needy frosh rec. non-need-based scholarship or grant aid	89
% needy UG rec. non-need-based scholarship or grant aid	81
% needy frosh rec. need-based self-help aid	81
% needy UG rec. need-based self-help aid	83
% frosh rec. any financial aid	100
% UG rec. any financial aid	98
% UG borrow to pay for school	89
Average cumulative indebtedness	$32,957
% frosh need fully met	21
% ugrads need fully met	18
Average % of frosh need met	75
Average % of ugrad need met	71

New College of Florida

5800 Bay Shore Road, Sarasota, FL 34243-2109 • Admissions: 941-487-5000 • Fax: 941-487-5001

CAMPUS LIFE

Quality of Life Rating	**78**
Fire Safety Rating	**80**
Green Rating	**69**
Type of school	public
Environment	town

STUDENTS

Total undergrad enrollment	845
% male/female	39/61
% from out of state	19
% from public high school	84
% frosh live on campus	98
% African American	1
% Asian	3
% Caucasian	75
% Hispanic	13
% Native American	1
# of countries represented	16

SURVEY SAYS . . .

Lots of liberal students
No one cheats
Students are friendly
Students aren't religious
Dorms are like palaces
Campus feels safe
Intercollegiate sports are unpopular or nonexistent
Frats and sororities are unpopular or nonexistent
Student government is popular
Political activism is popular

ACADEMICS

Academic Rating	**96**
% students returning for sophomore year	86
% students graduating within 4 years	50
% students graduating within 6 years	68
Calendar	4-1-4
Student/faculty ratio	10:1
Profs interesting rating	96
Profs accessible rating	89
Most classes have	10–19 students
Most lab/discussion sessions have	10–19 students

MOST POPULAR MAJORS

biology; psychology; political science; art; anthropology; sociology

APPLICANTS ALSO LOOK AT AND OFTEN PREFER

University of Florida, Florida State University, University of Central Florida, University of Miami, University of South Florida, Florida Atlantic University

AND SOMETIMES PREFER

Oberlin College, Pitzer College, Reed College, The University of North Carolina at Chapel Hill, New York University, American University, Eckerd College, Rollins College

STUDENTS SAY ". . ."

Academics

New College of Florida, a uniquely small and unconventional public institution, "provides challenging courses for highly self-motivated students who want a large amount of control over their academic choices." It's all about "self-directed learning" here (working closely with faculty advisers, "the student decides what she is going to learn and how she is going to learn it") that leaves undergrads "free to do what they please—with their bodies, their studies, their behavior—but while also being held to high academic standards." Those who can balance the intellectual freedom NCF offers with the academic accountability it demands, wind up with "a rounded education that enables them to critically and pragmatically examine and understand the world in which we live…and weird parties." The academics "are undeniably awesome" at NCF, while the small-school setting and the student body "encourage a love of learning, whether it be academic, political, or hobby-related." It's the sort of school where "it is very popular for groups of students to get together to talk about class readings outside of the classroom, usually at the college coffee shop, as a means of socializing." NCF undergrads receive "narrative evaluations instead of grades. These evaluations give advice and help us to become better students." Many here "love having written evaluations in which our process and progress are documented, not only the final outcome. The evaluations force students to fully participate and the professors to pay close attention." All students must write a senior thesis to graduate; reports one undergrad, "recently we had a survey…on which one of the sections dealt with the possibility of making the senior thesis optional. There was an overwhelming response that this was unacceptable. I think that says a lot about how proud we are of our academic standards."

Life

Having fun "in a glorified retirement community requires ingenuity of the New College student population," but "thankfully, most grew up in suburban Florida" and so are used to a slower pace. It helps that the campus is near Lido and Siesta Beaches, "where [students] enjoy unlimited swimming, sunning, and Frisbee playing," and that "downtown Sarasota isn't that bad either," since it's home to a number of "ethnic eateries. Thai food, in particular, seems to have a strange cult following on campus—with constant debate as to which restaurant is the best or most authentic and student events that advertise Thai food are bound to pull in dozens of followers." On campus, students enjoy everything "from club meetings to public speakers to 'hip' bands playing shows. There's usually something to do and usually free food to be found!" There are also "school-wide parties every Friday and Saturday night in a courtyard outside of the dorms. Different students get to decide the theme of each dance party and the music to be played. Most on-campus students never leave campus during the weekend because of these dance parties."

Student Body

New College students share "a few things in common: Most…are friendly, passionate about the things they believe in, very hard workers, liberal, and most of all, try to be open to new experiences." There is "largely middle-class, white, and liberal. There are of course exceptions, but the school is rather small,'" there is "a fairly strong queer community here, and many transgendered people who have decided to make New College their coming-out grounds. The student body is generally aware of gender issues and respectful of queer people of all types." There are even "some Republicans on campus. Maybe four. I'm not sure. We're not the type of school that generally attracts heavy right-wingers."

FINANCIAL AID: 941-487-5000 • E-MAIL: ADMISSIONS@NCF.EDU • WEBSITE: WWW.NCF.EDU

THE PRINCETON REVIEW SAYS

Admissions

Very important factors considered include: Application essay, academic GPA, rigor of secondary school record. *Important factors considered include:* Recommendation(s), standardized test scores, character/personal qualities. *Other factors considered include:* Class rank, alumni/ae relation, extracurricular activities, first generation, geographical residence, level of applicant's interest, state residency, talent/ability, volunteer work, work experience. SAT or ACT required; ACT with writing component required. TOEFL required of all international applicants. High school diploma is required and GED is accepted. *Academic units required:* 4 English, 4 mathematics, 3 science (2 science labs), 2 foreign language, 3 social studies, 2 academic electives. *Academic units recommended:* 4 English, 4 mathematics, 4 science (2 science labs), 4 foreign language, 4 social studies, 5 academic electives.

Financial Aid

Students should submit: FAFSA. Priority filing deadline is February 15, though applications are processed on a rolling basis. The Princeton Review suggests that all financial aid forms be submitted as soon as possible after January 1. *Need-based scholarships/grants offered:* Federal Pell, SEOG, state scholarships/grants, private scholarships, the school's own gift aid, Federal Academic Competitiveness Grant. *Loan aid offered:* Direct Subsidized Stafford, Direct Unsubsidized Stafford, Direct PLUS, alternative loans. Applicants will be notified of awards on a rolling basis beginning October 1. Federal Work-Study Program available. Institutional employment available. Highest amount earned per year from on-campus jobs $5,328. Off-campus job opportunities are good.

The Inside Word

New College isn't your typical public school. The tiny student body allows admissions officers here to review each application carefully; expect a thorough going over of your essays, recommendations, and extracurricular activities. Iconoclastic students tend to thrive here, and the admissions staff knows that. Don't be afraid to let your freak flag fly; it won't get you in here if your academics aren't top flight, but it certainly won't hurt you either.

THE SCHOOL SAYS ". . ."

From the Admissions Office

"Inspired individualism, with a dash of quirkiness, best describes New College of Florida and its students. At New College, you participate directly in your education by collaborating with faculty to develop an individualized program of classes, seminars, independent research projects, and off-campus experiences designed to meet your personal academic interests and needs. As a result, you receive the high-quality, personalized education of a top-tier private college yet at the affordable cost of a public university. If you are independent, open-minded, and welcome the challenge of a rigorous academic program matched with a relaxed social environment, then New College may be the perfect fit for you.

"Students applying must submit scores from the SAT (or ACT) with the writing section). We will use the student's best scores from either test."

SELECTIVITY	
Admissions Rating	**94**
# of applicants	1,272
% of applicants accepted	56
% of acceptees attending	33
# accepting a place on wait list	47
# admitted from wait list	26

FRESHMAN PROFILE	
Range SAT Critical Reading	630–740
Range SAT Math	570–680
Range SAT Writing	600–680
Range ACT Composite	27–31
Minimum paper TOEFL	560
Minimum web-based TOEFL	83
Average HS GPA	3.98
% graduated top 10% of class	43
% graduated top 25% of class	82
% graduated top 50% of class	98

DEADLINES	
Regular	
Priority	11/1
Deadline	4/15
Nonfall registration?	yes

FINANCIAL FACTS	
Financial Aid Rating	**90**
Annual in-state tuition	$6,060
Annual out-state tuition	$29,089
Room and board	$8,598
Books and supplies	$800
% needy frosh rec. need-based scholarship or grant aid	100
% needy UG rec. need-based scholarship or grant aid	98
% needy frosh rec. non-need-based scholarship or grant aid	15
% needy UG rec. non-need-based scholarship or grant aid	8
% needy frosh rec. need-based self-help aid	84
% needy UG rec. need-based self-help aid	86
% frosh rec. any financial aid	100
% UG rec. any financial aid	99
% UG borrow to pay for school	32
Average cumulative indebtedness	$13,977
% frosh need fully met	100
% ugrads need fully met	99
Average % of frosh need met	100
Average % of ugrad need met	100

NEW JERSEY INSTITUTE OF TECHNOLOGY

OFFICE OF UNIVERSITY ADMISSIONS, NEWARK, NJ 07102 • ADMISSIONS: 973-596-3300 • FAX: 973-596-3461

CAMPUS LIFE

Quality of Life Rating	**65**
Fire Safety Rating	**95**
Green Rating	**77**
Type of school	public
Environment	metropolis

STUDENTS

Total undergrad enrollment	5,996
% male/female	79/21
% from out of state	7
% from public high school	85
% frosh live on campus	47
# of fraternities	15
# of sororities	7
% African American	10
% Asian	21
% Caucasian	36
% Hispanic	21
% Native American	1
% international	4
# of countries represented	83

SURVEY SAYS . . .

Diverse student types on campus
Low cost of living
Very little drug use

ACADEMICS

Academic Rating	**67**
% students returning for sophomore year	82
% students graduating within 4 years	17
% students graduating within 6 years	54
Calendar	semester
Student/faculty ratio	16:1
Profs interesting rating	68
Profs accessible rating	65
Most classes have	20–29 students

MOST POPULAR MAJORS

architecture (barch, ba/bs, march, ma/ms, phd); civil engineering; mechanical engineering

APPLICANTS ALSO LOOK AT AND OFTEN PREFER

Drexel University, Rensselaer Polytechnic Institute, The College of New Jersey

AND SOMETIMES PREFER

Pennsylvania State University—University Park, Virginia Tech, Worcester Polytechnic Institute, Stevens Institute of Technology

STUDENTS SAY ". . ."

Academics

NJIT is certainly a crown jewel within New Jersey's public university system. Indeed, armed with a great reputation, NJIT offers undergrads "quality academic programs" at an "affordable" price. Students here truly appreciate that they are surrounded by a "challenging, intellectual environment" that provides "plenty of advancement for high-achieving students." Fully embracing its name, NJIT is definitely a "technology-centered school," and students are quick to praise the strong engineering, math, and architecture programs. Undergrads do warn, "You must be dedicated and serious about learning, because a lot of the courses here are demanding." Moreover, students here are decidedly mixed when it comes to opinions about their professors. Some undergrads complain, "Classes are very monotonous, as they are straight lectures [with] professors adhering very strongly to the textbook." However, other students counter, "The professors hold their degrees because of their knowledge of the subject, not because of their teaching skills. Most of the learning comes from your own hard work, and the professors can be a great resource." Many also appreciate that they are able to "bring real-world experience to class projects." Further, a handful of undergrads assert, "Most professors are always willing to make time outside of classroom to talk or to explain things further"—and that's certainly the hallmark of teachers who "are very helpful and want their students to succeed."

Life

Undergrads at NJIT spend a good deal of their time hitting the books. As one student reveals (perhaps facetiously), "Fun on campus usually consists of group projects, homework, lab reports, and studying." A fellow undergrad concurs simply stating, "Most people, including myself, eat, breathe, and live for their classes because of the time commitment to the material." Of course, even these conscientious students need to kick back every now and again. Unfortunately, some undergrads grumble about the lack of options on campus: "Social events are actually nonexistent." However, another group of students assure us, "There is always some sort of activity going on every day. [For example] we have countless comedy nights and cultural nights." Additionally, while some question the safety of the surrounding area, others extol the virtues of NJIT's location. As one content student shares, "The food in the Ironbound district of Newark is fantastic. Anyone who is anyone goes there either for the food or the lounges." Moreover, "There are many bars close to the school, so they are generally a secondary option for most [students]." And, of course, NJIT undergrads love to take advantage of the school's proximity to New York City "which is only [a fifteen-minute] Path ride away!"

Student Body

Undergrads at NJIT proudly self-identify as "nerds" and assert that the main attribute unifying the student body is "a determination to learn." Perhaps even more important, undergrads are quick to call their peers "friendly" and suggest "students interact easily due to the closeness of majors and interests." For example, "Video games are a popular bonding activity here." Of course, regardless of whether you are into tennis or Magic the Gathering, you can rest assured that "it's not hard to fit in." Indeed, as one pleased undergrad happily reveals, "You will find any type and every type of student here on this campus. Diversity is our forte."

FINANCIAL AID: 973-596-3479 • E-MAIL: ADMISSIONS@NJIT.EDU • WEBSITE: WWW.NJIT.EDU

THE PRINCETON REVIEW SAYS

Admissions

Very important factors considered include: Class rank, rigor of secondary school record, standardized test scores. *Important factors considered include:* Academic GPA. *Other factors considered include:* Application essay, recommendation(s), alumni/ae relation, character/personal qualities, extracurricular activities, geographical residence, interview, level of applicant's interest, racial/ethnic status, religious affiliation/commitment, state residency, talent/ability, volunteer work, work experience. SAT or ACT required; TOEFL required of all international applicants. High school diploma is required and GED is accepted. *Academic units required:* 4 English, 4 mathematics, 2 science (2 science labs). *Academic units recommended:* 2 foreign language, 1 social studies, 1 history, 2 academic electives.

Financial Aid

Students should submit: FAFSA. The Princeton Review suggests that all financial aid forms be submitted as soon as possible after January 1. *Need-based scholarships/grants offered:* Federal Pell, SEOG, state scholarships/grants, private scholarships, the school's own gift aid. *Loan aid offered:* Direct Subsidized Stafford, Direct Unsubsidized Stafford, Direct PLUS, Federal Perkins, state loans, college/university loans from institutional funds. Applicants will be notified of awards on a rolling basis beginning December 20. Federal Work-Study Program available. Institutional employment available. Highest amount earned per year from on-campus jobs $5,500. Off-campus job opportunities are good.

The Inside Word

The academics at NJIT are certainly rigorous. Therefore, admissions officers at the college are on the lookout for students whom they believe can handle the challenging workload. Successful candidates are usually in the top thirty percent of their classes with especially strong math, science, and English grades. Applicants should take heart (or heed); the committee will take note of performance trends.

THE SCHOOL SAYS ". . ."

From the Admissions Office

"Talented high school graduates from across the nation come to NJIT to prepare for leadership roles in architecture, business, engineering, medical, legal, science, and technological fields. Students experience a public research university conducting nearly $90 million in research that maintains a small-college atmosphere at a modest cost. Our attractive forty-five-acre campus is just minutes from New York City and less than an hour from the Jersey shore. Students find an outstanding faculty and a safe, diverse, and caring learning and residential community. NJIT's academic environment challenges and prepares students for rewarding careers and full-time advanced study after graduation. The campus is computing-intensive. NJIT is a *Top 50 Best Value College,* according to The Princeton Review

"Students applying for admission to NJIT may provide scores from either the SAT or the ACT. writing sample scores will not be used for admission purposes, but are used for placement in first-year courses. SAT Subject Test scores are not required for any major."

SELECTIVITY	
Admissions Rating	**78**
# of applicants	4,068
% of applicants accepted	69
% of acceptees attending	36

FRESHMAN PROFILE	
Range SAT Critical Reading	470–580
Range SAT Math	540–650
Range SAT Writing	460–580
Minimum paper TOEFL	550
Minimum web-based TOEFL	79
% graduated top 10% of class	29
% graduated top 25% of class	55
% graduated top 50% of class	86

DEADLINES	
Regular	
Deadline	3/1
Nonfall registration?	yes

FINANCIAL FACTS	
Financial Aid Rating	**70**
Annual in-state tuition	$11,756
Annual out-state tuition	$23,116
Room and board	$11,000
Required fees	$2,218
Books and supplies	$1,900
% needy frosh rec. need-based scholarship or grant aid	86
% needy UG rec. need-based scholarship or grant aid	82
% needy frosh rec. non-need-based scholarship or grant aid	46
% needy UG rec. non-need-based scholarship or grant aid	36
% needy frosh rec. need-based self-help aid	70
% needy UG rec. need-based self-help aid	89
% frosh rec. any financial aid	60
% UG rec. any financial aid	51
% UG borrow to pay for school	49
Average cumulative indebtedness	$26,045
% frosh need fully met	14
% ugrads need fully met	9
Average % of frosh need met	66
Average % of ugrad need met	68

NEW YORK UNIVERSITY

665 BROADWAY, NEW YORK, NY 10012 • ADMISSIONS: 212-998-4500 • FAX: 212-995-4902

CAMPUS LIFE

Quality of Life Rating	**88**
Fire Safety Rating	**89**
Green Rating	**93**
Type of school	private
Environment	metropolis

STUDENTS

Total undergrad enrollment	21,820
% male/female	40/60
% from out of state	73
% from public high school	62
% frosh live on campus	88
# of fraternities	16
# of sororities	12
% African American	4
% Asian	20
% Caucasian	42
% Hispanic	9
% international	10
# of countries represented	129

SURVEY SAYS . . .

Lots of liberal students
Students love New York, NY
Great off-campus food
Intercollegiate sports are unpopular or nonexistent
Frats and sororities are unpopular or nonexistent
Internships are widely available

ACADEMICS

Academic Rating	**85**
% students returning for sophomore year	92
% students graduating within 4 years	79
% students graduating within 6 years	86
Calendar	semester
Profs interesting rating	84
Profs accessible rating	72
Most classes have	10–19 students
Most lab/discussion sessions have	10–19 students

MOST POPULAR MAJORS

drama and dramatics/theater arts; finance; liberal arts and sciences/liberal studies

STUDENTS SAY ". . ."

Academics

"Location, location, location" in "the most amazing city on earth," along with "great facilities" and "top-notch faculty," makes New York University an excellent choice for those seeking "an untraditional college experience" in "a paradise for the independent and motivated." With more than 20,000 students and eleven distinct schools offering more than 230 areas of study, NYU "is about diversity. Students are from all over the world; they come from different cultures, and they have different talents and interests. Similarly, NYU offers endless opportunities for students, no matter what their interests or ambitions are." The school offers voluminous opportunities to participate in research, pursue an internship, or begin a career in the arts (although "you have to be active and willing to find these opportunities"). Given the school's size, many students are "actually quite surprised by the accessibility of both the faculty and administration." Although "this is not the kind of school where students really get to know all of their teachers, as it is unlikely that a student will have a professor more than once," those who make the effort report that "It is so easy to meet with [professors] outside of class, and I still get e-mails from professors about internships, jobs, and scholarship recommendations." Many here also tout the "great study abroad programs."

Life

"Living in New York City is the biggest part of going to school at New York University," NYU students agree. The school's New York City campus is located in the heart of Greenwich Village, one of the city's major nightlife destinations, so "there is always something to do at any hour of the day," usually within walking distance of the school. One student reports, "Every weekend there are tons of things to do, both at NYU and in New York City. NYU really takes advantage of its location, so a lot of the programming provided by residence life or the student resource center is engaging you in the city that has become your new home." Living in the Big Apple means that "on any given day you can go to a museum, concert, sporting event, or theater performance…and a lot of the times, NYU will foot the bill if you go to an event in the city with your RA or with a club." The location also provides plenty of internship opportunities, which is good because "The vast majority of students at NYU are interested in interning and finding jobs through that gateway." The school has no campus per se; it surrounds Washington Square Park, a busy public square where students love to relax when the weather is accommodating.

Student Body

"There is no typical student at NYU," where an undergraduate student body of more than 20,000 and a broad range of academic interests ensure a broad demographic. "Each school at NYU attracts a different group," students tell us. "The Tisch School of the Arts attracts a very out-there group of actors and the like," while the Stern Business School "has a massive population of Asians and Indians." "Hipsters are pretty pervasive throghout all schools except Stern," although "every school has people who break those stereotypes. [Even so,] few students can find ways to not fit in because of the huge number of students" at the university. Throughout NYU, "Students tend to be incredibly motivated and ambitious." Students insist that "it is also important to note that NYU students are very accepting of each other's differences," an important factor at a school that brings together "students of all different backgrounds, ethnicities, and gender identities and makes them coexist within the university."

FINANCIAL AID: 212-998-4444 • E-MAIL: ADMISSIONS@NYU.EDU • WEBSITE: WWW.NYU.EDU

THE PRINCETON REVIEW SAYS

Admissions

Very important factors considered include: Application essay, academic GPA, recommendation(s), rigor of secondary school record, standardized test scores, extracurricular activities, talent/ability. *Important factors considered include:* Class rank, alumni/ae relation, character/personal qualities, first generation, geographical residence. *Other factors considered include:* Racial/ethnic status, volunteer work, work experience. SAT or ACT required; ACT with writing component required. TOEFL required of all international applicants. High school diploma is required and GED is accepted. *Academic units required:* 4 English, 3 mathematics, 3 science, 2 foreign language, 4 history. *Academic units recommended:* 4 English, 4 mathematics, 4 science, 3 foreign language, 4 history.

Financial Aid

Students should submit: FAFSA, state aid form, early decision applicants may submit an institutional form for an estimated award. Regular filing deadline is February 15. The Princeton Review suggests that all financial aid forms be submitted as soon as possible after January 1. *Need-based scholarships/grants offered:* Federal Pell, SEOG, state scholarships/grants, private scholarships, the school's own gift aid. *Loan aid offered:* Direct Subsidized Stafford, Direct Unsubsidized Stafford, Direct PLUS, Federal Perkins, Federal Nursing. Applicants will be notified of awards on a rolling basis beginning April 1. Federal Work-Study Program available. Institutional employment available. Highest amount earned per year from on-campus jobs $24,026. Off-campus job opportunities are excellent.

The Inside Word

Undergraduates must apply to one of NYU's undergraduate schools and colleges: the College of Arts and Science; the Liberal Studies Program; the Stern School of Business; the College of Nursing; the Gallatin School of Individualized Study; the Silver School of Social Work; the Steinhardt School of Culture, Education, and Human Development; the Tisch School of the Arts; or the Preston Robert Tisch Center for Hospitality, Tourism, and Sports. This is different from the application process at some universities and obviously requires some forethought. Remember that this is a highly competitive university; if your application doesn't reflect a serious interest in your intended area of study, your chances of gaining admission will be diminished.

THE SCHOOL SAYS ". . ."

From the Admissions Office

"NYU is unlike any other institution of higher edu cation in the world. It is a university of micro-communities within a larger global network university with three portals of entry. The energy and resources of New York City serve as an exten sion of our Washington Square campus in the heart of Greenwich Village. NYU welcomed students to its new honors college in Abu Dhabi in fall 2010 and will open a new portal campus in Shanghai in 2012. With a staggering 4,300 course offerings and over 230 areas of study from which to choose, you can explore and develop your academic and professional interests from your first semester. NYU's intellectual climate is fostered by a faculty of world-famous scholars, researchers, and artists who teach both undergradu ate and graduate courses. To fuel its reputation as the world's first truly global network university, NYU offers ten global academic centers for study abroad—Berlin, Buenos Aires, Florence, Ghana, London, Madrid, Paris, Prague, Shanghai, and Tel Aviv, with plans for two more—in Washington, D.C., and Sydney. As a result, NYU sends more students abroad than any other American college or university."

SELECTIVITY

Admissions Rating	**96**
# of applicants	41,243
% of applicants accepted	33
% of acceptees attending	36
# accepting a place on wait list	2,966
# of early decision applicants	5,333
# accepted early decision	1,414

FRESHMAN PROFILE

Range SAT Critical Reading	630–720
Range SAT Math	630–740
Range SAT Writing	640–730
Range ACT Composite	29–32
Minimum paper TOEFL	600
Minimum web-based TOEFL	100
Average HS GPA	3.6
% graduated top 10% of class	62
% graduated top 25% of class	91
% graduated top 50% of class	99

DEADLINES

Early decision	
Deadline	11/1
Notification	12/15
Regular	
Deadline	1/1
Notification	4/1
Nonfall registration?	no

FINANCIAL FACTS

Financial Aid Rating	**73**
Annual tuition	$39,344
Required fees	$1,131
% needy frosh rec. need-based scholarship or grant aid	94
% needy UG rec. need-based scholarship or grant aid	94
% needy frosh rec. non-need-based scholarship or grant aid	2
% needy UG rec. non-need-based scholarship or grant aid	3
% needy frosh rec. need-based self-help aid	92
% needy UG rec. need-based self-help aid	90
% frosh rec. any financial aid	55
% UG rec. any financial aid	58
% UG borrow to pay for school	54
Average cumulative indebtedness	$36,351
% frosh need fully met	4
% ugrads need fully met	6
Average % of frosh need met	61
Average % of ugrad need met	59

North Carolina State University

Box 7103, Raleigh, NC 27695 • Admissions: 919-515-2434 • Fax: 919-515-5039

CAMPUS LIFE

Quality of Life Rating	95
Fire Safety Rating	98
Green Rating	95
Type of school	public
Environment	metropolis

STUDENTS

Total undergrad enrollment	25,176
% male/female	57/43
% from out of state	11
% from public high school	80
% frosh live on campus	76
# of fraternities	33
# of sororities	18
% African American	8
% Asian	5
% Caucasian	76
% Hispanic	4
% international	1
# of countries represented	117

SURVEY SAYS . . .

Lab facilities are great
Great computer facilities
Everyone loves the Wolfpack
Student publications are popular

ACADEMICS

Academic Rating	81
% students returning for sophomore year	91
Calendar	semester
Student/faculty ratio	18:1
Profs interesting rating	83
Profs accessible rating	82
Most classes have	20–29 students
Most lab/discussion sessions have	20–29 students

MOST POPULAR MAJORS

biology/biological sciences; business administration and management; mechanical engineering

APPLICANTS ALSO LOOK AT AND OFTEN PREFER

The University of North Carolina at Chapel Hill

AND SOMETIMES PREFER

Wake Forest University

AND RARELY PREFER

Auburn University, Clemson University, Georgia Institute of Technology, Virginia Tech, University of South Carolina—Columbia

STUDENTS SAY "..."

Academics

Blending a close-knit community with a prestigious name, North Carolina State University offers "big-school opportunity with a small-school feel." The sheer number of academic options is impressive—the engineering department alone offers eighteen different majors. With "plenty of opportunities to study abroad or get an internship," as well extensive opportunities to conduct research as an undergraduate, students say "NCSU is all about developing skills in school that will help you throughout your professional career." A biochemistry student adds, "Professors are often active in research, and there are tons of opportunities for students to get involved in the exciting research that is going on here." Resources are plentiful: "If you need a computer, they've got them everywhere. If you need a camera, you can rent one." Despite the sizable student population, "The way the school is split up into colleges makes it seem less intimidating." Within the colleges, "each department is pretty tight." As one student explains, "With the 33,000-plus students who attend [the school], you wonder where they all are." NCSU professors "are smart, they are funny, and they are accessible. Above all, they love what they teach, and it shows." While "there are lots of students in most freshman lectures," students say that "Even in the larger classes, [professors] strive to engage students and keep classes interesting." More importantly, "most of the professors genuinely care about their students," and "Even the professors whose teaching abilities [are] questionable are still very approachable, friendly, and readily available to the students." Despite recent shake-ups in the administration, "Everything at North Carolina State seems to run pretty efficiently."

Life

On NCSU's outgoing and lively campus, students balance academic work with an active social calendar. While they may suffer some sleepless nights, "Everyone has their own way of making academic and social life work." From Greek life to honor societies to "tons of intramural sports," "There are multitudes of organizations and activities to participate in on campus." Boredom is not an issue: "Between theater, music, cultural events, and athletics, there's no point when the campus feels 'dead' or inactive." "Students at NCSU are really into sports," and the whole campus comes out to tailgate before football games. Students also love the "great recreational facilities and gyms on campus," which boast multiple racquetball courts and pools, among other amenities. Socially, "NCSU is a very friendly, social campus," and on the weekends "going to nightclubs is popular, as are parties," while other students like to "just hang out with friends." A cosmopolitan, medium-sized city, "Downtown Raleigh has a lot to offer, from local bands, to Broadway musicals, to art nights, and amazing food." "There are a few independent movie theaters in town, like the Rialto, which plays independent movies or local documentaries." Many students also mention the local music scene, pointing out that "Raleigh is a hoppin' and boppin' place, and there [are] always shows and concerts of every kind in the area."

Student Body

NCSU "students have a reputation for being very practical," and most are "very driven" academically. "The students [on campus] vary from Southern-born-and-raised crop science majors, to devout Muslims, to 4.0 Columbia-bound premeds, to partying fraternity boys...and sometimes all of these are combined into one." "The city student is typically a Democrat, not particularly religious, [and] very friendly. The smaller-town student is typically a religious Republican and is also very friendly." Fortunately, "people of all ethnicities and backgrounds interact seamlessly," though on the whole, "The student body is somewhat conservative compared to other schools in the area." If there's any uniting factor on campus, it's that "Everyone loves the Wolfpack...everyone is very loyal and very passionate about the school's athletic program, no matter how successful or unsuccessful it might be that year."

FINANCIAL AID: 919-515-2421 • E-MAIL: UNDERGRAD_ADMISSIONS@NCSU.EDU • WEBSITE: WWW.NCSU.EDU

THE PRINCETON REVIEW SAYS

Admissions

Very important factors considered include: Class rank, academic GPA, rigor of secondary school record, standardized test scores. *Other factors considered include:* Application essay, recommendation(s), alumni/ae relation, character/personal qualities, extracurricular activities, first generation, geographical residence, racial/ethnic status, state residency, talent/ability, volunteer work, work experience. SAT or ACT required; ACT with writing component required. TOEFL required of all international applicants. High school diploma is required and GED is not accepted. *Academic units required:* 4 English, 4 mathematics, 3 science (1 science lab), 2 foreign language, 1 social studies, 1 history, 1 academic electives. *Academic units recommended:* 4 English, 4 mathematics, 4 science (2 science labs), 2 foreign language, 1 social studies, 1 history, 4 academic electives.

Financial Aid

Students should submit: FAFSA, institution's own financial aid form. The Princeton Review suggests that all financial aid forms be submitted as soon as possible after January 1. *Need-based scholarships/grants offered:* Federal Pell, SEOG, state scholarships/grants, private scholarships, the school's own gift aid, United Negro College Fund. *Loan aid offered:* Direct Subsidized Stafford, Direct Unsubsidized Stafford, Direct PLUS, Federal Perkins, state loans, college/university loans from institutional funds. Applicants will be notified of awards on a rolling basis beginning April 1. Federal Work-Study Program available. Institutional employment available. Highest amount earned per year from on-campus jobs $7,300. Off-campus job opportunities are excellent.

The Inside Word

At North Carolina State University, the most important factor in the admissions decision is a student's high school record. Competitive applicants will have at least a B-plus average in a college preparatory curriculum. SAT or ACT scores are also considered, though the school puts more emphasis on a student's coursework, grade point average, and class rank than on test scores.

THE SCHOOL SAYS ". . ."

From the Admissions Office

"NC State is arguably the most popular university in the state, with more NC students seeking admission than at any other college or university. More than 20,000 students from across the nation seek one of the 4,250 available freshman spaces. Students choose NC State for its strong and varied academic programs, national reputation for excellence, low cost, location in Raleigh and the Research Triangle Park area, and very friendly atmosphere. Our students like the excitement of a large campus and the many opportunities it offers, such as Cooperative Education, Study Abroad, extensive honors programming, and theme residence halls. Each year, hundreds of NC State graduates are accepted into medical or law schools or other areas of advanced professional study. More corporate and government entities recruit graduates from NC State than from any other university in the United States.

"Freshman applicants must take either the SAT or the ACT with the writing component."

SELECTIVITY	
Admissions Rating	**91**
# of applicants	20,489
% of applicants accepted	48
% of acceptees attending	44

FRESHMAN PROFILE	
Range SAT Critical Reading	530–620
Range SAT Math	560–660
Range SAT Writing	510–610
Range ACT Composite	23–28
Minimum paper TOEFL	550
Minimum web-based TOEFL	80
Average HS GPA	4.3
% graduated top 10% of class	43
% graduated top 25% of class	83
% graduated top 50% of class	99

DEADLINES	
Early action	
Deadline	11/1
Notification	1/30
Regular	
Priority	11/1
Deadline	2/1
Nonfall registration?	yes

FINANCIAL FACTS	
Financial Aid Rating	**84**
Annual in-state tuition	$5,153
Annual out-state tuition	$17,988
Room and board	$8,536
Required fees	$1,865
Books and supplies	$1,000
% needy frosh rec. need-based scholarship or grant aid	94
% needy UG rec. need-based scholarship or grant aid	90
% needy frosh rec. non-need-based scholarship or grant aid	23
% needy UG rec. non-need-based scholarship or grant aid	13
% needy frosh rec. need-based self-help aid	77
% needy UG rec. need-based self-help aid	79
% frosh rec. any financial aid	75
% UG rec. any financial aid	69
% UG borrow to pay for school	55
Average cumulative indebtedness	$17,317
% frosh need fully met	36
% ugrads need fully met	35
Average % of frosh need met	88
Average % of ugrad need met	83

NORTHEASTERN UNIVERSITY

360 HUNTINGTON AVENUE, BOSTON, MA 02115 • ADMISSIONS: 617-373-2200 • FAX: 617-373-8780

CAMPUS LIFE

Quality of Life Rating	**94**
Fire Safety Rating	**81**
Green Rating	**99**
Type of school	private
Environment	metropolis

STUDENTS

Total undergrad enrollment	16,385
% male/female	50/50
% from out of state	64
% frosh live on campus	53
# of fraternities	13
# of sororities	13
% African American	3
% Asian	9
% Caucasian	52
% Hispanic	5
% international	13
# of countries represented	122

SURVEY SAYS . . .

Athletic facilities are great
Career services are great
Students love Boston, MA
Great off-campus food
Students are happy
Student publications are popular
Hard liquor is popular
Internships are widely available

ACADEMICS

Academic Rating	**79**
% students returning for sophomore year	95
% students graduating within 6 years	77
Calendar	semester
Student/faculty ratio	13:1
Profs interesting rating	71
Profs accessible rating	74
Most classes have	10–19 students

MOST POPULAR MAJORS

business/commerce; engineering; health services/allied health/health sciences

STUDENTS SAY ". . ."

Academics

Northeastern University is renowned for its "unique cooperative programming," which "integrates real-world experience and academics to form experiential learning." Students say Northeastern is an "institution that is dedicated to real-world experiences coupled with classroom guidance," and many students list "cooperative learning" opportunities as main reason for choosing the school. Additionally, the students boast about the school's "stellar academic reputation," and a junior says, "Northeastern is about equipping students with the academic prowess to have successful careers and dynamic, multifaceted lives." A political science major says, "Professors come from a wide array of fields and bring their expertise from the outside world to the classroom and then challenge us to do the same." Professors are generally "educated, engaging, [and] enthusiastic," but students say, "There's a range"—some "aren't as exciting," and a sophomore says, "I've had a good mix of mediocre and fantastic professors." Regardless, "They all expect a high level of dedication and hard work on [the] student's part to their classes," and they're "always looking to help us connect and apply our learning to our lives outside of the classroom."

Life

Northeastern University offers "the campus feel in an urban setting," "providing [an] outstanding campus life in the great city of Boston." A sophomore says, "It's a city school, but our campus has so much green space," and another student adds, "It's a closed-in campus in the middle of a city filled with opportunities." Students say, "We've got awesome facilities, and we're always building and improving them," and "The student population is very passionate about a wide variety of things, and that's manifested through student life and activities." Students say, "Getting involved in campus clubs and organizations is the best way to meet people and make lasting friendships," and "A good amount of students are involved in leadership activities and student organizations." A communication studies major adds, "If students want to get involved and fit in, just join any of the more than 280 clubs/organizations on campus." Despite the high level of student involvement, there are complaints that "school spirit and athletics are not as strong as at other colleges." Students also lament the notorious "NU shuffle," which means, "You'll get tossed from one office to another just to get a single question answered." A sophomore says, "We're a big school, but the bureaucracy is the number one complaint of students."

Student Body

At Northeastern, "The typical student is driven, ambitious, extremely practical," and "career-oriented." Northeastern students are "more mature than most college students earlier in their careers because of the city environment and the co-op program." "The majority [of students] are from the East Coast," and students say, "Boston is just one giant college town—anything you want, it has." The typical student "works hard in school, but definitely knows how to fit a raucous hockey game or obscenely crowded off-campus party," and "People do work hard and study hard, but there is somewhat of a relaxing and partying culture." A criminal justice majors says, "There is always a party (or ten) off campus and never far, but it is easy to avoid them if you choose." However, a sophomore describes other weekend activities: "It could mean shopping in the Prudential Center…or participating in one of Boston's many college-friendly events." In general, students feel, "There's a ton to do on and off campus, and it's really easy to get around town on the weekends." When it comes to diversity, some complain that the campus is "not a very diverse place even though they make it sound like it is." Although others contradict that, saying, "Students come from every corner of the world, and you can't walk through a quad without hearing at least three languages being spoken."

FINANCIAL AID: 617-373-3190 • E-MAIL: ADMISSIONS@NEU.EDU • WEBSITE: WWW.NORTHEASTERN.EDU

THE PRINCETON REVIEW SAYS

Admissions

Very important factors considered include: Academic GPA, rigor of secondary school record. *Important factors considered include:* Application essay, recommendation(s), standardized test scores, character/personal qualities, extracurricular activities, first generation, talent/ability, volunteer work. *Other factors considered include:* Class rank, alumni/ae relation, geographical residence, interview, racial/ethnic status, state residency, work experience. SAT or ACT required; ACT with writing component required. TOEFL required of all international applicants. High school diploma is required and GED is accepted. *Academic units required:* 4 English, 3 mathematics, 3 science (2 science labs), 2 foreign language, 3 social studies, 2 history. *Academic units recommended:* 4 mathematics, 4 science (4 science labs), 4 foreign language.

Financial Aid

Students should submit: FAFSA, CSS/Financial Aid PROFILE. The Princeton Review suggests that all financial aid forms be submitted as soon as possible after January 1. *Need-based scholarships/grants offered:* Federal Pell, SEOG, state scholarships/grants, private scholarships, the school's own gift aid. *Loan aid offered:* Direct Subsidized Stafford, Direct Unsubsidized Stafford, Direct PLUS, Federal Perkins, Federal Nursing, state loans. Applicants will be notified of awards on a rolling basis beginning March 15. Federal Work-Study Program available. Institutional employment available. Off-campus job opportunities are excellent.

The Inside Word

Applicants to Northeastern are evaluated based on their secondary school performance, with the difficulty of courses given emphasis, and you should go beyond minimum graduation requirements for high school to show broad intellectual curiosity. The committee recommends having strong standardized test scores and does consider the writing section of the SAT in its decision.

THE SCHOOL SAYS ". . ."

From the Admissions Office

"Northeastern students take charge of their education in a way you'll find nowhere else, because a Northeastern education is like no other. Our students don't just take class: They take class further, integrating their course work with real-world experiences—professional co-op placements, research, study abroad, and community service. Northeastern's dynamic of academic excellence and experience means that our students are better prepared to succeed in the lives they choose. On top of that, they experience all of this on a beautifully landscaped, seventy-three-acre campus in the heart of Boston, where culture, commerce, civic pride, and college students from around the globe are all a part of the mix."

SELECTIVITY	
Admissions Rating	**96**
# of applicants	43,255
% of applicants accepted	35
% of acceptees attending	21

FRESHMAN PROFILE	
Range SAT Critical Reading	610–700
Range SAT Math	640–730
Range SAT Writing	600–700
Range ACT Composite	28–32
Minimum paper TOEFL	563
Minimum web-based TOEFL	84
% graduated top 10% of class	56
% graduated top 25% of class	83
% graduated top 50% of class	96

DEADLINES	
Early action	
Deadline	11/1
Notification	12/31
Regular	
Deadline	1/15
Notification	4/1
Nonfall registration?	no

FINANCIAL FACTS	
Financial Aid Rating	**76**
Annual tuition	$39,320
Room and board	$13,620
Required fees	$416
Books and supplies	$1,000
% needy frosh rec. need-based scholarship or grant aid	42
% needy UG rec. need-based scholarship or grant aid	44
% needy frosh rec. non-need-based scholarship or grant aid	16
% needy UG rec. non-need-based scholarship or grant aid	12
% needy frosh rec. need-based self-help aid	38
% needy UG rec. need-based self-help aid	41

Northwestern University

PO Box 3060, Evanston, IL 60208-3060 • Admissions: 847-491-7271

CAMPUS LIFE

Quality of Life Rating	72
Fire Safety Rating	71
Green Rating	85
Type of school	private
Environment	town

STUDENTS

Total undergrad enrollment	8,485
% male/female	48/52
% from out of state	78
% from public high school	65
% frosh live on campus	99
# of fraternities	17
# of sororities	19
% African American	6
% Asian	19
% Caucasian	56
% Hispanic	7
% international	6
# of countries represented	42

SURVEY SAYS . . .

Athletic facilities are great
Great off-campus food
Frats and sororities dominate social scene
Musical organizations are popular
Student publications are popular

ACADEMICS

Academic Rating	86
% students returning for sophomore year	97
% students graduating within 4 years	86
% students graduating within 6 years	93
Calendar	quarter
Student/faculty ratio	7:1
Profs interesting rating	78
Profs accessible rating	71
Most classes have	fewer than 10 students
Most lab/discussion sessions have	10–19 students

MOST POPULAR MAJORS

economics; engineering; journalism

APPLICANTS ALSO LOOK AT AND OFTEN PREFER

Yale University, Harvard College

AND SOMETIMES PREFER

Princeton University, Stanford University, University of Chicago

AND RARELY PREFER

DePaul University, Purdue University—West Lafayette, Marquette University

STUDENTS SAY ". . ."

Academics

"The strength of the school is its range." Northwestern students agree, vowing their school "has everything": "Intelligent but laid-back students, excel[lence] in academic fields," "great extracurriculars and good parties," "strong [Big Ten] sports spirit," and "so many connections and opportunities during and after graduation." Undergrads here brag of "nationally acclaimed programs for almost anything anyone could be interested in, from engineering to theater to journalism to music," and report "everything is given fairly equal weight. Northwestern students and faculty do not show a considerable bias" toward specific fields. The school accomplishes all this while maintaining a manageable scale. While its relatively small size allows for good student-professor interaction, it has "all the perks" of a big school, including "many opportunities" for research and internships. Be aware, however, "Northwestern is not an easy school. It takes hard work to be average here." If you "learn from your failures quickly and love to learn for the sake of learning rather than the grade," students say it is quite possible to stay afloat and even to excel. Helping matters are numerous resources established by administrators and professors, including tutoring programs such as Northwestern's Gateway Science Workshop. Those who take advantage of these opportunities find the going much easier than those who don't.

Life

There are two distinct sections of the Northwestern campus. The North Campus is where "you can find a party every night of the week" and "the Greek scene is strong." The South Campus, about a one-mile trek from the action to the north, is "more artsy and has minimal partying on weeknights," but is closer to town so "it is easy" to "buy dinner, see a show at the movies, and go shopping. People who live on North Campus have a harder time getting motivated to go into Evanston and tap into all that is offered." As one South Campus resident puts it, "South Campus is nice and quiet in its own way. I enjoy reading and watching movies here, and the quietude is appreciated when study time rolls around. But for more exciting fun, a trip north is a must." Regardless of where students live, extracurriculars are "incredible here. There is a group for every interest, and the groups are amazingly well-managed by students alone. This goes hand-in-hand with how passionate students at Northwestern are about what they love." Many students "are involved in plays, a cappella groups, comedy troupes, and other organizations geared toward the performing arts. Activism is also very popular, with many involved in political groups, human-rights activism, and volunteering." In addition, Northwestern's membership in the Big Ten means students "attend some of the best sporting events in the country." Chicago, of course, "is a wonderful resource. People go into the city for a wide variety of things—daily excursions, jobs, internships, nights out, parties, etc."

Student Body

The typical Northwestern student "was high school class president with a 4.0, swim team captain, and on the chess team." So it makes sense everyone here "is an excellent student who works hard" and "has a leadership position in at least two clubs, plus an on-campus job." Students also tell us "there's [a] great separation between North Campus (think: fraternities, engineering, state school mentality) and South Campus (think: closer to Chicago and its culture, arts and letters, liberal arts school mentality). Students segregate themselves depending on background and interests, and it's rare for these two groups to interact beyond a superficial level." The student body here includes sizeable Jewish, Indian, and East-Asian populations.

FINANCIAL AID: 847-491-7400 • E-MAIL: UG-ADMISSION@NORTHWESTERN.EDU • WEBSITE: WWW.NORTHWESTERN.EDU

THE PRINCETON REVIEW SAYS

Admissions

Very important factors considered include: Class rank, application essay, academic GPA, rigor of secondary school record, standardized test scores. *Important factors considered include:* Recommendation(s), character/personal qualities, extracurricular activities, talent/ability. *Other factors considered include:* Alumni/ae relation, first generation, interview, level of applicant's interest, racial/ethnic status, volunteer work, work experience. SAT or ACT required; ACT with writing component required. TOEFL required of all international applicants. High school diploma or equivalent is not required. *Academic units recommended:* 4 English, 3 mathematics, 2 science (2 science labs), 2 foreign language, 2 social studies, 1 academic electives.

Financial Aid

Students should submit: FAFSA, CSS/Financial Aid PROFILE, noncustodial PROFILE, business/farm supplement, parent and student federal tax returns. Regular filing deadline is February 15. The Princeton Review suggests that all financial aid forms be submitted as soon as possible after January 1. *Need-based scholarships/grants offered:* Federal Pell, SEOG, state scholarships/grants, private scholarships, the school's own gift aid, United Negro College Fund. *Loan aid offered:* Direct Subsidized Stafford, Direct Unsubsidized Stafford, Direct PLUS, Federal Perkins, college/university loans from institutional funds. Applicants will be notified of awards on or about April 15. Federal Work-Study Program available. Institutional employment available. Off-campus job opportunities are excellent.

The Inside Word

Northwestern is among the nation's most expensive undergraduate institutions, a fact that dissuades some qualified students from applying. The school is working to attract more low-income applicants by increasing the number of full scholarships available for students whose family income is less than $45,000. Low-income students who score well on the ACT may receive a letter from the school encouraging them to apply. Even if you don't receive this letter, you should consider applying if you've got the goods—you may be pleasantly surprised by the offer you receive from the financial aid office.

THE SCHOOL SAYS ". . ."

From the Admissions Office

"Consistent with its dedication to excellence, Northwestern provides both an educational and an extracurricular environment that enables its undergraduate students to become accomplished individuals and informed and responsible citizens. To the students in all its undergraduate schools, Northwestern offers liberal learning and professional education to help them gain the depth of knowledge that will empower them to become leaders in their professions and communities. Furthermore, Northwestern fosters in its students a broad understanding of the world in which we live as well as excellence in the competencies that transcend any particular field of study: writing and oral communication, analytical and creative thinking and expression, and quantitative and qualitative methods of thinking.

"Applicants are required to take the SAT or the ACT with the writing section."

SELECTIVITY	
Admissions Rating	**98**
# of applicants	25,369
% of applicants accepted	27
% of acceptees attending	31
# accepting a place on wait list	2,850
# admitted from wait list	45
# of early decision applicants	1,498
# accepted early decision	590

FRESHMAN PROFILE	
Range SAT Critical Reading	670–750
Range SAT Math	690–780
Range SAT Writing	670–760
Range ACT Composite	31–33
Minimum paper TOEFL	600
% graduated top 10% of class	90
% graduated top 25% of class	99
% graduated top 50% of class	100

DEADLINES	
Early decision	
Deadline	11/1
Notification	12/15
Regular	
Deadline	1/1
Notification	4/15
Nonfall registration?	yes

FINANCIAL FACTS	
Financial Aid Rating	**93**
Annual tuition	$43,380
Room and board	$13,329
Required fees	$399
Books and supplies	$1,737
% needy frosh rec. need-based scholarship or grant aid	94
% needy UG rec. need-based scholarship or grant aid	94
% needy frosh rec. need-based self-help aid	86
% needy UG rec. need-based self-help aid	87
% frosh rec. any financial aid	60
% UG rec. any financial aid	60
% UG borrow to pay for school	48
Average cumulative indebtedness	$20,802
% frosh need fully met	100
% ugrads need fully met	100
Average % of frosh need met	100
Average % of ugrad need met	100

OBERLIN COLLEGE

101 NORTH PROFESSOR STREET, OBERLIN, OH 44074 • ADMISSIONS: 440-775-8411 • FAX: 440-775-6905

CAMPUS LIFE

Quality of Life Rating	**72**
Fire Safety Rating	**69**
Green Rating	**90**
Type of school	private
Environment	rural

STUDENTS

Total undergrad enrollment	2,839
% male/female	45/55
% from out of state	91
% from public high school	60
% frosh live on campus	100
% African American	6
% Asian	7
% Caucasian	75
% Hispanic	5
% Native American	1
% international	6

SURVEY SAYS . . .

Lots of liberal students
No one cheats
Low cost of living
Frats and sororities are unpopular or nonexistent
Musical organizations are popular
Political activism is popular

ACADEMICS

Academic Rating	**93**
% students returning for sophomore year	94
% students graduating within 4 years	69
% students graduating within 6 years	83
Calendar	4-1-4
Student/faculty ratio	9:1
Profs interesting rating	89
Profs accessible rating	91
Most classes have	10–19 students
Most lab/discussion sessions have	fewer than 10 students

MOST POPULAR MAJORS

biology; English language and literature; history

APPLICANTS ALSO LOOK AT AND OFTEN PREFER

Swarthmore College, Brown University, Wesleyan University, Yale University, Stanford University

AND SOMETIMES PREFER

Vassar College, Williams College, Grinnell College, Carleton College, Macalester College, Northwestern University

AND RARELY PREFER

Connecticut College

STUDENTS SAY ". . ."

Academics

Oberlin College, a school "for laid-back people who enjoy learning and expanding social norms, allows each and every student to have the undergrad experience for which he or she is looking, all the while challenging the students to change themselves and the world for the better." Oberlin is a place where students "focus on learning for learning's sake rather than making money in a career." As one student explains, "I didn't plan on becoming a scholar when I entered Oberlin....As fate would have it, I ended up loving my college classes and professors. Now I hope to be a professor of religion." At Oberlin, "academics are very highly valued, but balanced with a strong interest in the arts and a commitment to society." Some might suggest Oberlin puts the "liberal" in "liberal arts," and the school's staunchest supporters agree, stressing the school's emphasis on open-mindedness and the belief that "one person can change the world." Among the school's offerings, "the sciences, English, politics, religion, music, environmental studies, and East-Asian studies are particularly noteworthy." The presence of a prestigious music school imbues the entire campus community. One undergrad writes, "Oberlin's greatest strength is the combination of the college and the conservatory. They are not separated, so students mix with each other all the time." Professors here—the "heart and soul of the school"—are dedicated teachers who "treat you more like collaborators and realize that even with their PhDs, they can learn and grow from you, as well as you from them." They are "excellent instructors and fantastic people" who are "focused on learning instead of deadlines." Undergrads also appreciate "a cooperative learning environment" in which "Students bond over studying together for difficult exams."

Life

Life during the week at Oberlin can be "pretty bland," as "almost everyone has to crack the books and study it up." It's not always bland, though. Some here manage to find time for the many "events [going on] each weekend—operas, plays, organ pumps, etc.," or "rally to stage to help the oppressed." Thursday afternoons at Oberlin means "Classical Thursdays," an event during which "you get free beer from the college if you bring a professor to the on-campus pub." Another feature of campus life is "the musical scene, which has its heart in the conservatory. All of the other arts—performing, studio, whatever—are intertwined with the talent in the conservatory." On weekends, "people let loose and drink beer. Not everyone does this every weekend. Some don't do it at all," and "there is absolutely no pressure on those who don't." There are also "tons of student-produced social events like parties, fundraisers, concerts, dances, etc.," keeping students "very connected to each other and to what's going on in the community." Hometown Oberlin "is a small town, and about all there is to do there is go out for pizza or Chinese, see a movie for two or three dollars at the Apollo, or go to the Feve, the bar in town."

Student Body

"If you're a liberal, artsy, indie loner who likes to throw around the phrase 'heteronormative white privilege,'" then Oberlin might be the place for you. "We're like the Island of Misfit Toys, but together we make a great toy chest." "We're all different and unusual, which creates a common bond between students." "Musicians, jocks, science geeks, creative writing majors, straight, bi, questioning, queer, and trans [students]," all have their place here, alongside "straight-edge, international, local, and joker students." Oberlin has a reputation for a left-leaning and active student body. One undergrad observes, "They are less active politically than they would like to think, but still more active than most people elsewhere." Another adds, "Most students are very liberal, but the moderates and (few) Republicans have a fine time of it. Every student has different interests and isn't afraid to talk about them." Some here worry "Oberlin's student body is becoming more and more mainstream each year."

FINANCIAL AID: 440-775-8142 • E-MAIL: COLLEGE.ADMISSIONS@OBERLIN.EDU • WEBSITE: WWW.OBERLIN.EDU

THE PRINCETON REVIEW SAYS

Admissions

Very important factors considered include: Class rank, academic GPA, rigor of secondary school record, standardized test scores. *Important factors considered include:* Application essay, recommendation(s), character/personal qualities, extracurricular activities, first generation, talent/ability. *Other factors considered include:* Alumni/ae relation, interview, level of applicant's interest, racial/ethnic status, volunteer work, work experience. SAT or ACT required; ACT with writing component required. TOEFL required of all international applicants. High school diploma is required and GED is accepted. *Academic units required:* 4 English, 4 mathematics, 3 science, 3 foreign language, 3 social studies.

Financial Aid

Students should submit: FAFSA, institution's own financial aid form, CSS/Financial Aid PROFILE, state aid form, noncustodial PROFILE, business/farm supplement. Regular filing deadline is February 1. The Princeton Review suggests that all financial aid forms be submitted as soon as possible after January 1. *Need-based scholarships/grants offered:* Federal Pell, SEOG, state scholarships/grants, private scholarships, the school's own gift aid. *Loan aid offered:* Direct Subsidized Stafford, Direct Unsubsidized Stafford, Direct PLUS, Federal Perkins, college/university loans from institutional funds. Applicants will be notified of awards on or about April 1. Highest amount earned per year from on-campus jobs $1,750.

The Inside Word

Oberlin's music conservatory is one of the most elite programs in the nation. Aspiring music students should expect stiff competition for one of the 600 available slots. Other applicants won't have a much easier time of it. Oberlin is a highly selective institution that attracts a highly competitive applicant pool. Your personal statement could be the make-or-break factor here.

THE SCHOOL SAYS ". . ."

From the Admissions Office

"Oberlin College is an independent, coeducational, liberal arts college. It comprises two divisions, the College of Arts and Sciences, with roughly 2,800 students enrolled, and the Conservatory of Music, with about 600 students. Students in both divisions share one campus; they also share residence and dining halls as part of one academic community. Many students take courses in both divisions. Oberlin awards the Bachelor of Arts and the Bachelor of Music degrees; a five-year program leads to both degrees. Selected master's degrees are offered in the conservatory. Oberlin is located thirty-five miles southwest of Cleveland. Founded in 1833, Oberlin College is highly selective and dedicated to recruiting students from diverse backgrounds. Oberlin was the first coeducational college in the United States, as well as a historic leader in educating African Americans. Oberlin's 440-acre campus provides outstanding facilities, modern scientific laboratories, a large computing center, a library unexcelled by other college libraries for the depth and range of its resources, and one of the top-five college- or university-based art museums in the country.

"Freshman applicants must take the SAT the ACT with writing component."

SELECTIVITY	
Admissions Rating	**98**
# of applicants	7,006
% of applicants accepted	33
% of acceptees attending	34
# accepting a place on wait list	934
# admitted from wait list	8
# of early decision applicants	341
# accepted early decision	225

FRESHMAN PROFILE	
Range SAT Critical Reading	640–740
Range SAT Math	620–710
Range SAT Writing	640–730
Range ACT Composite	27–32
Minimum paper TOEFL	600
Average HS GPA	3.6
% graduated top 10% of class	69
% graduated top 25% of class	91
% graduated top 50% of class	99

DEADLINES	
Early decision	
Deadline	11/15
Notification	12/20
Regular	
Deadline	1/15
Notification	4/1
Nonfall registration?	no

FINANCIAL FACTS	
Financial Aid Rating	**92**
Annual tuition	$44,512
Room and board	$12,120
Required fees	$393
Books and supplies	$1,956
% needy frosh rec. need-based scholarship or grant aid	100
% needy UG rec. need-based scholarship or grant aid	74
% needy frosh rec. non-need-based scholarship or grant aid	0
% needy UG rec. non-need-based scholarship or grant aid	0
% needy frosh rec. need-based self-help aid	78
% needy UG rec. need-based self-help aid	62
% frosh rec. any financial aid	61
% UG rec. any financial aid	60
% frosh need fully met	100
% ugrads need fully met	100
Average % of frosh need met	100
Average % of ugrad need met	100

OCCIDENTAL COLLEGE

1600 CAMPUS ROAD, LOS ANGELES, CA 90041-3314 • ADMISSIONS: 323-259-2700 • FAX: 323-341-4875

CAMPUS LIFE

Quality of Life Rating	**85**
Fire Safety Rating	**68**
Green Rating	**79**
Type of school	private
Environment	metropolis

STUDENTS

Total undergrad enrollment	2,107
% male/female	43/57
% from out of state	51
% from public high school	60
% frosh live on campus	100
# of fraternities	3
# of sororities	4
% African American	4
% Asian	14
% Caucasian	56
% Hispanic	14
% Native American	1
% international	3
# of countries represented	25

SURVEY SAYS . . .

No one cheats
Students are friendly
Diverse student types on campus
Great food on campus

ACADEMICS

Academic Rating	**95**
% students returning for sophomore year	94
% students graduating within 4 years	81
% students graduating within 6 years	84
Calendar	semester
Student/faculty ratio	10:1
Profs interesting rating	93
Profs accessible rating	84
Most classes have	10–19 students
Most lab/discussion sessions have	10–19 students

MOST POPULAR MAJORS

economics; art history and visual arts; international relations and affairs

APPLICANTS ALSO LOOK AT AND OFTEN PREFER

Stanford University, University of California—Berkeley, University of California—Los Angeles, University of Southern California, Pomona College

AND SOMETIMES PREFER

Claremont McKenna College, Macalester College

STUDENTS SAY ". . ."

Academics

"Combine sunny weather with big-city opportunities, amazing professors, a gorgeous campus, and an emphasis on diversity, and you get Oxy!" That's how Occidental College is affectionately known by its "happy, outgoing, and bright" students. Located "just over the hill from bustling Los Angeles," Oxy is "a small school that provides the opportunity to develop one's intellect in a safe, friendly, and mentally challenging environment." This "very prestigious school" is "tough academically. The work is hard, and there's a high level of work expected of all students. But the benefits of getting an education here are worth all the work." Strong instruction is a big part of the equation; Oxy profs "are the absolute best because they are extremely personable toward and available for the students. They have a great desire for all their students to succeed, especially those who are on the premedicine track." Profs here don't exist to "publish or perish"; "they actually are at Oxy to teach—and not to teach so they can research." That said, Oxy is no slacker when it comes to research either. Students say it is "really easy" to get "independent study, internships, and grants" that would "not be offered anywhere else to undergraduates." Students love "class sizes [that] are small for the most part" and the school's Center for Academic Excellence, "which provides free tutoring for many academic subjects."

Life

Los Angeles "is an amazing town to learn in," and Oxy exploits this asset. "Every week the school offers trips around Southern California." Extracurricular diversions are copious, but most require access to an automobile. "Everyone who doesn't have a car wishes they did and hangs out with people who do," undergrads warn. For those with wheels, "there's so much to do" in Los Angeles "that you can always find something to do on weekends. Old Town Pasadena is only ten minutes away, and it's a great place to spend a Saturday night." Students also sojourn "to Chinatown, Disneyland, the beach, the movies, plays, museums, the Glendale Galleria, [and] the Santa Monica Promenade. The location definitely has advantages," and so does the Oxy campus, where "there is always something fun going on," such as "a thematic party or just a cool social gathering," more than one "speaker series hosted by departments, movies projected on the dining hall wall, and many other things." Students "stay connected to what's going through our very effective 'daily digest e-mail.'" While most students are "fairly social," Oxy is "not what I would call a party school." Most of the parties "are all just off campus," and "drinks are easy to obtain but also easy to refuse."

Student Body

The typical Oxy undergrad "is politically and globally aware, is passionate about more than one interest, and loves to speak up about any and every issue (both related to the school and outside of it)." Most are "very liberal, studious, hardworking, and playful." Atypical students "are usually conservative or party animals. The conservative students have a bit of a hard time since the college and its students are typically very left-winged, yet they manage. The party animals fit in very well, although [they are] not necessarily liked in all situations, such as group projects, since they are a bit less hardworking." In terms of personality types, "we range from kids who are proud of being hicks to the artsy hipsters to some Goth kids to just your average run-of-the-mill sandwich-eating college kid." Common threads are "intelligence and desire to discuss issues, whatever they may be" and "the laid-back groove of California," which most here embody.

FINANCIAL AID: 323-259-2548 • E-MAIL: ADMISSION@OXY.EDU • WEBSITE: WWW.OXY.EDU

THE PRINCETON REVIEW SAYS

Admissions

Very important factors considered include: Rigor of secondary school record, extracurricular activities, volunteer work, work experience. *Important factors considered include:* Class rank, academic GPA, character/personal qualities, application essay, recommendation(s), standardized test scores. *Other factors considered include:* Alumni/ae relation, first generation, geographical residence, interview, level of applicant's interest, racial/ethnic status, talent/ability. SAT or ACT required; ACT with writing component required. TOEFL required of all international applicants. High school diploma is required and GED is accepted. *Academic units recommended:* 4 English, 4 mathematics, 3 science (2 science labs), 3 foreign language, 2 social studies, 2 history, 2 academic electives.

Financial Aid

Students should submit: FAFSA, CSS/Financial Aid PROFILE, state aid form, noncustodial PROFILE. Regular filing deadline is February 1. The Princeton Review suggests that all financial aid forms be submitted as soon as possible after January 1. *Need-based scholarships/grants offered:* Federal Pell, SEOG, state scholarships/grants, private scholarships, the school's own gift aid. *Loan aid offered:* Direct Subsidized Stafford, Direct Unsubsidized Stafford, Direct PLUS, Federal Perkins, college/university loans from institutional funds. Applicants will be notified of awards on a rolling basis beginning April 1. Federal Work-Study Program available. Institutional employment available. Off-campus job opportunities are good.

The Inside Word

The admissions team at Occidental is adamant about not adhering to formulas. They rely heavily on essays and recommendations in their mission to create a talented and diverse incoming class. The college attracts some excellent students, so a demanding course load in high school is essential for the most competitive candidates. Successful applicants tend to be creative and academically motivated.

THE SCHOOL SAYS ". . ."

From the Admissions Office

"Here's what our students tell us:

'The professors have all been just amazing. They're all very willing to coordinate times to meet and discuss how you feel about a class and what you want to get out of it.'

'I realize the caliber of discussion that occurs at Oxy is not easily matched. I've developed very strong relationships with many professors, and that's something I believe is unique to Oxy.'

'The program has been awesome. Whether you want to go to med school or grad school, it's a great experience. The professors really want you to succeed.'

'I've been working with postdoctoral researchers as an undergraduate. It's very rewarding. Oxy challenges me both inside and outside the classroom.'

'Occidental opened my eyes to different beliefs, values, and ideas. Discussions in class are much more interesting, because you consider things you might not have thought about before.'

'Oxy's close-knit community and its size make me feel this is a place I can call home.'

'Oxy instills curiosity and makes students want to go out and learn a subject on their own. I've gotten a broader sense of self and have been able to fulfill my learning goals.'

Occidental requires all applicants (including international students) to take either the SAT or ACT with the writing component. SAT subject tests are recommended but not required."

SELECTIVITY	
Admissions Rating	**95**
# of applicants	6,107
% of applicants accepted	39
% of acceptees attending	23
# accepting a place on wait list	1,019
# admitted from wait list	40
# of early decision applicants	233
# accepted early decision	106

FRESHMAN PROFILE	
Range SAT Critical Reading	600–690
Range SAT Math	600–690
Range SAT Writing	600–700
Range ACT Composite	27–31
Minimum paper TOEFL	600
Average HS GPA	3.6
% graduated top 10% of class	61
% graduated top 25% of class	91
% graduated top 50% of class	100

DEADLINES	
Early decision	
Deadline	11/15
Notification	12/15
Regular	
Deadline	1/10
Notification	4/1
Nonfall registration?	no

FINANCIAL FACTS	
Financial Aid Rating	**96**
Annual tuition	$43,490
Annual comprehensive tuition	$55,948
Room and board	$12,458
Required fees	$1,050
Books and supplies	$1,213
% needy frosh rec. need-based scholarship or grant aid	100
% needy UG rec. need-based scholarship or grant aid	99
% needy frosh rec. non-need-based scholarship or grant aid	10
% needy UG rec. non-need-based scholarship or grant aid	9
% needy frosh rec. need-based self-help aid	88
% needy UG rec. need-based self-help aid	90
% frosh rec. any financial aid	68
% UG rec. any financial aid	77
% UG borrow to pay for school	50
Average cumulative indebtedness	$25,480
% frosh need fully met	100
% ugrads need fully met	100
Average % of frosh need met	100
Average % of ugrad need met	100

OHIO NORTHERN UNIVERSITY

525 SOUTH MAIN STREET, ADA, OH 45810 • ADMISSIONS: 419-772-2260 • FAX: 419-772-2821

CAMPUS LIFE

Quality of Life Rating	**70**
Fire Safety Rating	**60***
Green Rating	**60***
Type of school	private
Affiliation	Methodist
Environment	village

STUDENTS

Total undergrad enrollment	2,313
% male/female	53/47
% from out of state	20
# of fraternities	6
# of sororities	4
% African American	3
% Asian	1
% Caucasian	89
% Hispanic	1
% international	2
# of countries represented	17

SURVEY SAYS . . .

Students are friendly
Campus feels safe
Low cost of living

ACADEMICS

Academic Rating	**75**
% students returning for sophomore year	84
% students graduating within 4 years	47
% students graduating within 6 years	66
Calendar	quarter
Student/faculty ratio	12:1
Profs interesting rating	77
Profs accessible rating	88
Most classes have	20–29 students

MOST POPULAR MAJORS

biological and biomedical sciences, other; business, management, marketing, and related support services, other; engineering

APPLICANTS ALSO LOOK AT AND SOMETIMES PREFER

Miami University, Wittenberg University, The Ohio State University—Columbus

STUDENTS SAY ". . ."

Academics

The fairly remote location of Ohio Northern University has done little to prevent the school from developing "a great academic reputation, especially in the Midwest." This "great all-around school…really places an emphasis on life after college," especially in "teaching students to think critically and out of the box." Students admit the academics are "tough," and that toughness "challenges us to do our best," but they say the small class sizes and "personal attention from teachers" make the challenge one that "allows students the opportunity to be successful." The cozy school size means "it is much easier to get to know your professors on a more personal level." This benefits students since educators at Ohio Northern "are so willing to help you succeed in whatever way they can." Indeed, the "extraordinarily friendly" staff "are always willing to help," and "Every professor has office hours and encourages you to utilize them." The goal of the teaching staff, students say, is "preparing their students to be contributing members of society" and giving them "the knowledge, skills, and abilities to be successful throughout life." The result is that the typical ONU student is "a hardworking individual who strives to do well in the classroom and gives back to the community."

Life

The "cozy village" of Ada, Ohio, "provides all the essentials, from groceries to a movie theater to bowling lanes to bars." However, it doesn't provide the kind of vibrant nightlife of an urban setting, so students often have to make their own entertainment. And they do. "There are tons of on-campus activities provided by the student planning committee," such as open music nights, music, "a ghost hunt around Halloween, a comedy show, or a foam party." Relaxing and studying consumes plenty of free time. "Education comes first," one student notes, while another says, "School is my number one priority, and I spend quite a bit of time in the library." Many students take to leaving town for things to do. Nearby Lima, for instance, has "a shopping mall, movie theater, and tons of restaurants and grocery stores." Ada itself provides "a small bowling alley, movie theater that plays one movie a week at discounted prices, a ferocious pizza parlor, and a Mexican restaurant." And, of course, there are parties. "If students are looking to find parties," students note, "they will." That said, "People who never drink have plenty of options for having fun, and ONU often brings entertainment to campus, too." Dorm luxuries increase as students climb through the grades, and Ada's small town feel means that "the campus is also very safe."

Student Body

Ohio Northern is not a campus teeming with diversity. Its students are "typically middle- to upper-class white students," though students are noticing efforts to address this in recent years. ONU students share other common traits. They are "intelligent and outgoing," a "very friendly and easy to talk to" group who tend to have "strong leadership skills and is outgoing, compassionate, intelligent, and very involved on campus." Though it is true that "students often tend to hang out with other students similar to them," this is not a sign of divisions on campus. "There is definitely no tension between any groups of people." The school's size means "you don't go anywhere without seeing someone you know," a direct result of the "close-knit feel of the campus." Those attending recognize that "being a student at Northern requires dedication to academics," but they also acknowledge, "It helps to have a balanced social life on campus." Overall, "Students interact well with one another and work well together."

FINANCIAL AID: 419-772-2272 • E-MAIL: ADMISSIONS-UG@ONU.EDU • WEBSITE: WWW.ONU.EDU

THE PRINCETON REVIEW SAYS

Admissions

Very important factors considered include: Academic GPA, rigor of secondary school record, standardized test scores. *Important factors considered include:* Class rank, extracurricular activities, interview. *Other factors considered include:* Application essay, recommendation(s), alumni/ae relation, character/personal qualities, first generation, level of applicant's interest, talent/ability, volunteer work. SAT or ACT required; ACT with or without writing component accepted. TOEFL required of all international applicants. High school diploma is required and GED is accepted. *Academic units required:* 4 English, 2 mathematics, 2 science (2 science labs), 2 social studies, 2 history, 4 academic electives. *Academic units recommended:* 4 English, 4 mathematics, 3 science (2 science labs), 2 foreign language, 3 social studies, 2 history, 1 visual/performing arts, 1 computer science, 4 academic electives.

Financial Aid

Students should submit: FAFSA. The Princeton Review suggests that all financial aid forms be submitted as soon as possible after January 1. *Need-based scholarships/grants offered:* Federal Pell, SEOG, state scholarships/grants, private scholarships, the school's own gift aid, External Scholarships. *Loan aid offered:* Direct Subsidized Stafford, Direct Unsubsidized Stafford, Direct PLUS, Federal Perkins, college/university loans from institutional funds, alternative loans, Federal Health Professions Loan. Applicants will be notified of awards on a rolling basis beginning March 1. Federal Work-Study Program available. Institutional employment available. Off-campus job opportunities are good.

The Inside Word

Ohio Northern is a school focused on high academic achievement, so the best way to get your foot in the door is with good high school grades and strong standardized test scores. Those test scores and high school grades could help applicants qualify for generous merit-based scholarships. The school's website provides details. Take note that the highly acclaimed pharmacy school demands much higher standards.

THE SCHOOL SAYS "..."

From the Admissions Office

"The purpose of Ohio Northern is to help students develop into self-reliant, mature men and women capable of clear and logical thinking and sensitive to the higher values of truth, beauty, and goodness. ONU selects its student body from among those students possessing characteristics congruent with the institution's objectives. Generally, a student must be prepared to use the resources of the institution to achieve personal and educational goals.

"Students applying for admission are urged to submit scores for the SAT or the ACT with the writing section. The student's best composite scores will be used for scholarship purposes.

"The Office of Admissions highly encourages a campus visit. To schedule a visit, please visit www.onu.edu/admissions/visit_us or call 888-408-4668."

SELECTIVITY	
Admissions Rating	85
# of applicants	3,147
% of applicants accepted	81
% of acceptees attending	24

FRESHMAN PROFILE	
Range SAT Critical Reading	520–630
Range SAT Math	560–670
Range SAT Writing	510–620
Range ACT Composite	24–29
Minimum paper TOEFL	480
Minimum web-based TOEFL	54
Average HS GPA	3.7
% graduated top 10% of class	50
% graduated top 25% of class	74
% graduated top 50% of class	91

DEADLINES	
Regular	
Priority	12/1
Deadline	8/1
Nonfall registration?	yes

FINANCIAL FACTS	
Financial Aid Rating	76
Annual tuition	$34,380
Room and board	$9,844
Required fees	$240
Books and supplies	$1,800
% needy frosh rec. need-based scholarship or grant aid	100
% needy UG rec. need-based scholarship or grant aid	100
% needy frosh rec. non-need-based scholarship or grant aid	15
% needy UG rec. non-need-based scholarship or grant aid	7
% needy frosh rec. need-based self-help aid	81
% needy UG rec. need-based self-help aid	86
% UG borrow to pay for school	85
Average cumulative indebtedness	$48,886
% frosh need fully met	18
% ugrads need fully met	14
Average % of frosh need met	80
Average % of ugrad need met	76

THE OHIO STATE UNIVERSITY—COLUMBUS

UNDERGRADUATE ADMISSIONS 110 ENARSON HALL, COLUMBUS, OH 43210 • ADMISSIONS: 614-292-3980 • FAX: 614-292-4818

CAMPUS LIFE

Quality of Life Rating	86
Fire Safety Rating	77
Green Rating	93
Type of school	public
Environment	metropolis

STUDENTS

Total undergrad enrollment	41,709
% male/female	53/47
% from out of state	18
% from public high school	84
% frosh live on campus	92
# of fraternities	42
# of sororities	25
% African American	6
% Asian	5
% Caucasian	76
% Hispanic	3
% international	6
# of countries represented	112

SURVEY SAYS . . .

Athletic facilities are great
Great off-campus food
Everyone loves the Buckeyes
Student publications are popular

ACADEMICS

Academic Rating	76
% students graduating within 4 years	44
% students graduating within 6 years	80
Calendar	semester
Student/faculty ratio	19:1
Profs interesting rating	70
Profs accessible rating	72
Most classes have	20–29 students
Most lab/discussion sessions have	20–29 students

MOST POPULAR MAJORS

biology/biological sciences; finance; political science and government

APPLICANTS ALSO LOOK AT AND SOMETIMES PREFER

University of Cincinnati, Purdue University—West Lafayette, Case Western Reserve University

STUDENTS SAY ". . ."

Academics

Opportunities abound at Ohio State University in Columbus, Ohio. Located "in a growing city," OSU has the distinction of being one of the largest schools in the United States. The "amazing opportunities" that come from such a large campus extend beyond the classrooms, "both academically and socially." "Everywhere you turn, there are always new and exciting things to be doing and learning." But the school's above-average size should not intimidate students. "OSU has a great way of breaking down the large school into much smaller communities." Established in 1870, "Ohio State has traditions like [nowhere] else. The feeling you get by being a Buckeye is truly one of a kind." What makes OSU special is how it "combines the love of tradition with the excellence of modern facilities and technology." "Ohio State really wants to offer students the most it can, including providing some state-of-the-art facilities and unique opportunities on campus to engage in the community. The school is very committed to bringing Ohio State students into the world as educated individuals." Students have many decisions to make when choosing from all the "very prestigious majors and classes" available. Student opinions about professors vary. One student says, "Some are better than others." Another is more enthusiastic about the faculty: "My academic experience has been great! I have admired and become very close to many professors, and I feel as though I have taken something away from every class I have taken." Overall, most students feel they "can learn a great deal here and take away an abundance of knowledge." Although "some of the big lectures are hard to keep up with…there is always free tutoring to help students get caught up."

Life

"Ohio State is a sports fan's paradise. [The] campus is bursting with Buckeye spirit, and it's infectious." "There may not be another school in the country that is as excited, spirited, and proud of literally everything they do like Ohio State is." "Not only do students love attending games, but we also have so many intramural sports that students get involved in for fun. You really never need to leave campus because there is always something fun happening." Plus, "There is a large city to explore as well. People who love sports, theater, and the arts will never run out of activities." Taking advantage of these options is easy because "students ride the city bus for free." Still, students feel the need to be careful and are concerned about "on and off campus safety." For some, the sheer number of choices can be overwhelming. "There are so many opportunities that it is easy to get lost in everything you feel you should be doing." Another student wonders if the school is doing its best to get messages out to everyone. "There have been occasions where things are not communicated to the entire student body as a whole, most likely due to the large student population. Sometimes I feel like I miss out on interesting and exciting things because I just wasn't made aware it was available." One student strongly recommends a visit to the school before you apply: "You will know as soon as you step on campus if it's the perfect fit for you!"

Student Body

Many students had good things to say about how the large amount of diversity positively affects life on campus. "Students here are open to different types of people—there is little or no discrimination. Diversity is valued here." "We have people from all different backgrounds, all different ethnicities. Students embrace the diversity and learn about new cultures and meet new people!" Somehow, Ohio State manages to bring everyone together. "The one common thing that seems to unite [us] is the love for our institution. Not everyone is a sports fan, but everyone bleeds scarlet about something on this campus, whether it be sports, their research, or their classes." While at Ohio State, many students take advantage of the vast opportunity to travel to further broaden their world knowledge. "Studying abroad is something a lot of students do to learn more about other types of people, but there are also students here from so many places that a student can learn a lot by just making friends from different geographical areas."

FINANCIAL AID: 614-292-0300 • E-MAIL: ASKABUCKEYE@OSU.EDU • WEBSITE: WWW.OSU.EDU

THE PRINCETON REVIEW SAYS

Admissions

Very important factors considered include: Class rank, academic GPA, rigor of secondary school record, standardized test scores. *Important factors considered include:* Application essay, recommendation(s), extracurricular activities, first generation, talent/ability, volunteer work, work experience. *Other factors considered include:* Character/personal qualities, geographical residence, racial/ethnic status, state residency. SAT or ACT required; ACT with writing component required. TOEFL required of all international applicants. High school diploma is required and GED is accepted. *Academic units required:* 4 English, 3 mathematics, 2 science (2 science labs), 2 foreign language, 2 social studies, 1 visual/performing arts, 1 academic electives. *Academic units recommended:* 4 English, 4 mathematics, 3 science (3 science labs), 3 foreign language, 3 social studies, 1 visual/performing arts, 1 academic electives.

Financial Aid

Students should submit: FAFSA. Regular filing deadline is February 1. The Princeton Review suggests that all financial aid forms be submitted as soon as possible after January 1. *Need-based scholarships/grants offered:* Federal Pell, SEOG, state scholarships/grants, private scholarships, the school's own gift aid. *Loan aid offered:* Direct Subsidized Stafford, Direct Unsubsidized Stafford, Direct PLUS, Federal Perkins, Federal Nursing, college/university loans from institutional funds. Applicants will be notified of awards on or about April 5. Federal Work-Study Program available. Institutional employment available. Off-campus job opportunities are good.

The Inside Word

Standards are high at OSU, which attracts a huge number of applicants. But OSU is still worth a shot for the average student. Applications are reviewed with an eye for more than just grades and class rank, and the university's great reputation and affordable cost make it a good choice for anyone looking at large schools.

THE SCHOOL SAYS ". . ."

From the Admissions Office

"The Ohio State University has changed dramatically in the last decade, and, as a result, has seen its academic reputation thrive. A strong focus on helping first-year students make a successful transition to the university, competitive admissions, and a physical transformation (amazing new and renovated facilities across campus) are changes that have increased Ohio State's ability to draw students and faculty of exceptional scholarly talent."

"Once you're on campus, "big school" translates to depth, diversity, and opportunity. Ohio State prides itself on offering about any academic or extracurricular opportunity a student could dream of: 175-plus majors; 1,000-plus student organizations; 100 study abroad programs; internship, research, and service-learning opportunities in every college; multiple Honors and Scholars programs; and nearly forty learning communities. Professional and faculty advisors assigned to each student help identify the opportunities that meet the student's interests and goals.

"Ohio State consistently boasts an impressive first-year retention rate over ninety percent. Ohio State's focus on the first year is campus-wide, including strong orientation and first-year programs."

SELECTIVITY	
Admissions Rating	86
# of applicants	26,100
% of applicants accepted	63
% of acceptees attending	43
# accepting a place on wait list	814
# admitted from wait list	4

FRESHMAN PROFILE	
Range SAT Critical Reading	540–660
Range SAT Math	600–700
Range SAT Writing	550–650
Range ACT Composite	26–30
Minimum paper TOEFL	550
Minimum web-based TOEFL	79
% graduated top 10% of class	55
% graduated top 25% of class	89
% graduated top 50% of class	99

DEADLINES	
Regular Deadline	2/1
Nonfall registration?	yes

FINANCIAL FACTS	
Financial Aid Rating	67
Annual in-state tuition	$8,994
Annual out-state tuition	$23,178
Room and board	$9,180
Required fees	$426
Books and supplies	$1,554
% needy frosh rec. need-based scholarship or grant aid	84
% needy UG rec. need-based scholarship or grant aid	72
% needy frosh rec. non-need-based scholarship or grant aid	5
% needy UG rec. non-need-based scholarship or grant aid	2
% needy frosh rec. need-based self-help aid	82
% needy UG rec. need-based self-help aid	88
% frosh rec. any financial aid	98
% UG rec. any financial aid	89
% UG borrow to pay for school	58
Average cumulative indebtedness	$24,840
% frosh need fully met	19
% ugrads need fully met	13
Average % of frosh need met	59
Average % of ugrad need met	55

OHIO UNIVERSITY—ATHENS

120 CHUBB HALL, ATHENS, OH 45701 • ADMISSIONS: 740-593-4100 • FAX: 740-593-0560

CAMPUS LIFE

Quality of Life Rating	**76**
Fire Safety Rating	**69**
Green Rating	**87**
Type of school	public
Environment	village

STUDENTS

Total undergrad enrollment	21,503
% male/female	42/58
% from out of state	11
% from public high school	85
% frosh live on campus	95
# of fraternities	17
# of sororities	13
% African American	5
% Asian	1
% Caucasian	85
% Hispanic	2
% international	4
# of countries represented	104

SURVEY SAYS . . .

Great computer facilities
Athletic facilities are great
Students are friendly
Students are happy
Student publications are popular
Lots of beer drinking
Hard liquor is popular

ACADEMICS

Academic Rating	**73**
% students returning for sophomore year	80
% students graduating within 4 years	44
% students graduating within 6 years	65
Calendar	quarter
Student/faculty ratio	20:1
Profs interesting rating	75
Profs accessible rating	74
Most classes have	10–19 students
Most lab/discussion sessions have	10–19 students

MOST POPULAR MAJORS

biology/biological sciences; journalism; psychology

APPLICANTS ALSO LOOK AT AND OFTEN PREFER

Miami University, The Ohio State University—Columbus, Bowling Green State University, Kent State University

STUDENTS SAY ". . ."

Academics

"Academically, Ohio University has something for everyone, from astrophysics to the history of rock and roll," students at this large state-run university boast. And students have an equally wide range of choices when it comes to committing themselves to academics; "You can take advantage of the vast amount of knowledge and resources directly available, or you can forget studies and party," students tell us. Those seeking a challenge will have no trouble finding it here, however; OU boasts "a strong engineering faculty," a noteworthy aviation program offered within the university's demanding school of engineering and technology, an "excellent and very selective early childhood education program," and "one of the best journalism schools in the country"—the E.W. Scripps School of Journalism—which offers "frequent opportunities to learn and grow outside the classroom with guest speakers and special events." Scripps houses "a great communications school" offering great hands-on experience; one student informs us that "Southeast Ohio depends on our college television and radio station for their news, weather, and high school sports." As at any large university, unassertive students are in danger of getting lost in the crowd, but those who make the effort to seek out faculty and administrators assure us that "The school is very supportive of the students. I have close relationships with multiple professors, and I think that they generally take a strong interest in the students."

Life

"Ohio University has a beautiful campus with lots of character, both in academia and nightlife," students here report. Greek organizations play a major role in the life of the campus, providing service to the community and serving as a social catalyst. Undergraduates assure us that the school "truly lives up to its reputation as a party school. It is never hard to find a party on any given night, whether in the dorms or off campus." One undergrad writes "a nationwide reputation as a party school is not something I'm proud of," but most accept things as they are, noting that "Ohio University is a school where everyone can find a group of people doing whatever they're particularly interested in," which is to say that partying is hardly the only option here. College athletics are a big draw (especially football, men's basketball, and women's volleyball), as are such annual events as Homecoming and Halloween celebrations, and the school is host to literally hundreds of student clubs and organizations serving interests of every variety. Hometown Athens is a typical small college town with access to a wide variety of outdoor activities. The closest cities of note—Columbus; Ohio and Charleston, West Virginia—are each about a ninety-minute drive from the OU campus.

Student Body

The OU student body "is pretty homogenous," with a large contingent of undergrads who are "white, middle- to upper-class, and from Ohio." "We have a small minority population, especially in the undergraduate programs," one student concedes, "but it's easy to interact with other cultures if you seek them out." Students here "try to get involved in community service, especially those involved in Greek life," and they are "generally friendly." Most work hard enough to get by but rarely harder; one student observes that "students totally devoted to their schoolwork are atypical here."

FINANCIAL AID: 740-593-4141 • E-MAIL: ADMISSIONS@OHIO.EDU • WEBSITE: WWW.OHIO.EDU

THE PRINCETON REVIEW SAYS

Admissions

Very important factors considered include: Academic GPA, rigor of secondary school record. *Important factors considered include:* Class rank, standardized test scores. *Other factors considered include:* Application essay, recommendation(s), alumni/ae relation, character/personal qualities, extracurricular activities, talent/ability, volunteer work, work experience. SAT or ACT required; ACT with writing component recommended. High school diploma is required and GED is accepted. *Academic units required:* 4 English, 3 mathematics, 3 science, 2 foreign language, 3 social studies, 1 visual or performing arts.

Financial Aid

Students should submit: FAFSA. Regular filing deadline is March 15. The Princeton Review suggests that all financial aid forms be submitted as soon as possible after January 1. *Need-based scholarships/grants offered:* Federal Pell, SEOG, state scholarships/grants, private scholarships, the school's own gift aid. *Loan aid offered:* Direct Subsidized Stafford, Direct Unsubsidized Stafford, Direct PLUS, Federal Perkins, Institutional short term loans are repaid in thirty to sixty days. Applicants will be notified of awards on or about April 1. Federal Work-Study Program available. Institutional employment available. Highest amount earned per year from on-campus jobs $1,784.

The Inside Word

Admissions requirements vary from school to school at Ohio University. The Honors Tutorial is most selective (you should be in the top ten percent of your graduating class and earn at least a 30/1300 on your ACT/SAT), followed by the journalism school (top fifteen percent, 25/1140), the business school (top twenty percent, 24/1100), media arts and visual studies, engineering, and visual communication. Admissions decisions are numbers-driven; those on the cusp should get in if they've demonstrated academic improvement during their junior and senior years.

THE SCHOOL SAYS ". . ."

From the Admissions Office

"Ohio University offers limitless opportunities for students to fulfill their promise and effect positive change. We do this through an accessible, engaging, and transforming student experience; through the breadth and excellence of our degree programs and facilities; and through the documented academic success and career accomplishments of our students, faculty, and alumni.

"Education at Ohio University extends beyond the classroom. Students study abroad, participate in research and internship programs, and get involved in community service as well as in 323 student organizations. Ohio is an incubator for research, exploration, creativity, innovation, and collaboration, enabling students to develop leadership skills, form new ideas, and reach potential they did not know they had. Our high graduation rate, welcoming residential living campus—rated as one of the country's most beautiful—and successful learning communities make Ohio a unique place to live and learn. Ohio values the importance of citizenship and educating students for success in their careers and their lives. Our nationally ranked colleges and degree programs, such as the Scripps College of Communication, Centers of Excellence in energy/environment and biomedicine/health care, and our unique Honors Tutorial College, make a degree from Ohio an instant advantage.

"Students, faculty, and alumni are consistently recognized for their contributions across campus and around the globe. Our students' success in winning many of the nation's most prestigious and competitive academic awards remains at a record high. Our total number of Fulbright winners, for example, consistently ranks us first in Ohio and has placed us in elite company nationally with schools such as Boston College, Princeton, and UCLA. Faculty members are engaged in renowned, world-class research in energy, biological sciences, health care, avionics, and more. For over 200 years, more than 200,000 alumni have enjoyed leadership positions in all walks of life through the path to promise they followed as proud Ohio students."

SELECTIVITY

Admissions Rating	73
# of applicants	13,251
% of applicants accepted	86
% of acceptees attending	34
# accepting a place on wait list	233
# admitted from wait list	96

FRESHMAN PROFILE

Range SAT Critical Reading	480–600
Range SAT Math	480–590
Range SAT Writing	470–570
Range ACT Composite	21–26
Average HS GPA	3.3
% graduated top 10% of class	15
% graduated top 25% of class	39
% graduated top 50% of class	77

DEADLINES

Regular Deadline	2/1
Nonfall registration?	yes

FINANCIAL FACTS

Financial Aid Rating	65
Annual in-state tuition	$9,936
Annual out-state tuition	$18,900
Room and board	$9,753
Books and supplies	$885
% needy frosh rec. need-based scholarship or grant aid	45
% needy UG rec. need-based scholarship or grant aid	46
% needy frosh rec. non-need-based scholarship or grant aid	56
% needy UG rec. non-need-based scholarship or grant aid	41
% needy frosh rec. need-based self-help aid	83
% needy UG rec. need-based self-help aid	89
% frosh rec. any financial aid	62
% UG rec. any financial aid	45
% UG borrow to pay for school	69
Average cumulative indebtedness	$26,909

OHIO WESLEYAN UNIVERSITY

61 SOUTH SANDUSKY STREET, DELAWARE, OH 43015 • ADMISSIONS: 740-368-3020 • FAX: 740-368-3314

CAMPUS LIFE

Quality of Life Rating	**79**
Fire Safety Rating	**70**
Green Rating	**86**
Type of school	private
Affiliation	Methodist
Environment	town

STUDENTS

Total undergrad enrollment	1,819
% male/female	44/56
% from out of state	48
% from public high school	77
% frosh live on campus	97
# of fraternities	8
# of sororities	5
% African American	4
% Asian	2
% Caucasian	78
% Hispanic	2
% international	8
# of countries represented	41

SURVEY SAYS . . .

Lab facilities are great
Students are friendly
Diverse student types on campus
Frats and sororities dominate social scene
Lots of beer drinking

ACADEMICS

Academic Rating	**86**
% students returning for sophomore year	82
% students graduating within 4 years	52
% students graduating within 6 years	61
Calendar	semester
Student/faculty ratio	11:1
Profs interesting rating	90
Profs accessible rating	88
Most classes have	10–19 students
Most lab/discussion sessions have	10–19 students

MOST POPULAR MAJORS

economics; premedicine/premedical studies; psychology

APPLICANTS ALSO LOOK AT AND OFTEN PREFER

Denison University, Miami University, The College of Wooster, The Ohio State University—Columbus, Wittenberg University

AND SOMETIMES PREFER

Kenyon College, University of Dayton

AND RARELY PREFER

Oberlin College

STUDENTS SAY ". . ."

Academics

Ohio Wesleyan University is "an outstanding, small, liberal arts college" that manages to cultivate a "welcoming and diverse" community. With "fantastic scholarships," a "beautiful" campus, and academic "flexibility" that allows undergrads to pursue multiple passions, it's no wonder students love it here. Undergrads truly appreciate the school's "emphasis on having an international experience," which is fostered "through our large percentage of international students, OWU's travel learning courses, and studying abroad." And while the university is bursting with academic options and opportunities, students especially like to tout the premed, zoology and English programs. Of course, no matter the major, OWU undergrads value that their "educational experience is marked by close relationships with professors." Indeed, these "incredibly supportive [and] knowledgeable" teachers manage to create a "wonderful" classroom environment. Moreover, as one pleased student adds, "Professors are enthusiastic and genuinely enjoy teaching the material. They are eager to help you outside of the classroom and strive to form personal bonds with their students." And a fellow student supports this sentiment, sharing, "Professors have amazing dedication to their students. They have office hours daily, respond to e-mails frequently, answer questions whenever available, and are active in all aspects of their students' lives." All in all, "OWU is a place where students can experience the opportunities of a larger school with the personality and personal attention of a smaller school."

Life

Ohio Wesleyan students are typically always on the go, as most undergrads are "active in politics, school government, sports, and other special interest clubs." What's more, undergrads excitedly tell us that "there [is] almost always some sort of event going on [be it] performing arts [shows], parties…or free food on the JAYwalk." Additionally, fraternities and sororities are popular hangouts on the weekend for "relaxing, drinking, dancing, and having fun. But if you're not into that, there are constantly fun nonalcoholic parties thrown by the school. There are plenty of mixers so that everyone gets to know each other." When students are itching to get off campus for a bit, they'll head into downtown Delaware, which is "easily in walking distance" and offers "cute little shops and restaurants." Indeed, "It's pretty common to find people studying in the [local] bookstore or coffee shop." And should students be feeling slightly more adventurous, Columbus is only about a thirty-minute ride away. In short, "If you are bored at this school, it's because you are trying to be."

Student Body

While undergrads at OWU admit, "There are several groups of typical students (sorority girls, lax bros, athletes, fraternity boys, eccentric kids, etc.)," they assert just as fervently that "no single stereotype is predominant on campus; there's pretty much an equal distribution among the groups." In turn, this makes for an "outgoing [and] involved" student body that's "willing to try new things and meet new people." Of course, if pressed to find additional common ground, undergrads would also likely say their fellow students are also "fairly politically aware, passionate about something, tolerant of diversity, involved on campus, like to learn inside and outside of the classroom, and care about academics." Moreover, they "are very driven and motivated to do well and succeed." Most important, we're told that "any kind of person can feel pretty comfortable at Ohio Wesleyan, as long as they can be friendly and accepting in a small, tight-knit community." Perhaps this happy student sums up his peers best, "Everyone has their own unique style, and they're not afraid to be who they are. It's interesting to watch students walk up and down the JAYwalk. There's this buzz on campus that just keeps the community going."

FINANCIAL AID: 740-368-3050 • E-MAIL: OWUADMIT@OWU.EDU • WEBSITE: WWW.OWU.EDU

THE PRINCETON REVIEW SAYS

Admissions

Very important factors considered include: Application essay, academic GPA, recommendation(s), rigor of secondary school record, character/personal qualities, interview. *Important factors considered include:* Class rank, standardized test scores, extracurricular activities, talent/ability. *Other factors considered include:* Alumni/ae relation, first generation, geographical residence, level of applicant's interest, racial/ethnic status, volunteer work, work experience. SAT or ACT required; ACT with or without writing component accepted. TOEFL required of all international applicants. High school diploma is required and GED is accepted. *Academic units required:* 4 English, 3 mathematics, 3 science, 2 foreign language, 3 social studies. *Academic units recommended:* 4 mathematics, 4 science, 3 foreign language, 4 social studies.

Financial Aid

Students should submit: FAFSA, institution's own financial aid form. The Princeton Review suggests that all financial aid forms be submitted as soon as possible after January 1. *Need-based scholarships/grants offered:* Federal Pell, SEOG, state scholarships/grants, private scholarships, the school's own gift aid. *Loan aid offered:* Direct Subsidized Stafford, Direct Unsubsidized Stafford, Direct PLUS, Federal Perkins, college/university loans from institutional funds. Applicants will be notified of awards on a rolling basis beginning February 15. Federal Work-Study Program available. Institutional employment available. Highest amount earned per year from on-campus jobs $2,400. Off-campus job opportunities are excellent.

The Inside Word

Ohio Wesleyan takes a well-rounded approach to the admissions game. The school is looking for students who will actively contribute to and thrive within OWU. To that end, all application components, from transcript to teacher evaluations, matter. Make sure you don't slack on any facet.

THE SCHOOL SAYS ". . ."

From the Admissions Office

"Ohio Wesleyan University, a national liberal arts university with a major international presence, is remarkable for the depth of its academic and pre-professional programs, the international dimensions of its curriculum, an emphasis on community through leadership and service, and an unwavering commitment to linking theory and practice in every field of study. The university is located in Delaware, Ohio, just north of Columbus, the capital city.

"OWU's theory-to-practice initiative includes competitive university-funded grants that allow students to propose and conduct original research, serve meaningful internships, and participate in service opportunities and cultural immersion throughout the world. Travel-learning courses augment classroom theory with international travel and practical experience in a variety of cultures. The university offers ninety-three majors, sequences, and courses of study, far more than most institutions of its size.

"For the past four years, the university has been on the President's Honor Roll for Community Service, with Distinction; in 2010, OWU was one of three colleges nationwide to win the 2009 Presidential Award for Excellence in General Community Service.

"Ohio Wesleyan has twenty-three varsity athletic teams: eleven men's and twelve women's. OWU boasts more team championships and Academic All-America scholar-athletes than any other school in the North Coast Athletic Conference and has won Division III national championships in men's soccer (two), women's soccer (two), and men's basketball, with individual national titles in several other sports.

"Applicants may submit the SAT or the ACT. Best scores from either test will considered in the application review."

SELECTIVITY	
Admissions Rating	**84**
# of applicants	4,226
% of applicants accepted	70
% of acceptees attending	16
# accepting a place on wait list	37
# admitted from wait list	7

FRESHMAN PROFILE	
Range SAT Critical Reading	520–650
Range SAT Math	510–650
Range ACT Composite	22–29
Minimum paper TOEFL	550
Average HS GPA	3.4
% graduated top 10% of class	29
% graduated top 25% of class	61
% graduated top 50% of class	89

DEADLINES	
Early action	
Deadline	12/15
Notification	1/15
Regular	
Priority	3/1
Notification	3/1
Nonfall registration?	yes

FINANCIAL FACTS	
Financial Aid Rating	**86**
Annual tuition	$38,890
Room and board	$10,310
Required fees	$260
Books and supplies	$2,100
% needy frosh rec. need-based scholarship or grant aid	100
% needy UG rec. need-based scholarship or grant aid	100
% needy frosh rec. non-need-based scholarship or grant aid	27
% needy UG rec. non-need-based scholarship or grant aid	82
% needy frosh rec. need-based self-help aid	78
% needy UG rec. need-based self-help aid	99
% frosh rec. any financial aid	97
% UG rec. any financial aid	97
% UG borrow to pay for school	76
Average cumulative indebtedness	$30,900
% frosh need fully met	31
% ugrads need fully met	24
Average % of frosh need met	91
Average % of ugrad need met	83

PENNSYLVANIA STATE UNIVERSITY—UNIVERSITY PARK

201 SHIELDS BUILDING, BOX 3000, UNIVERSITY PARK, PA 16802-3000 • ADMISSIONS: 814-865-5471 • FAX: 814-863-7590

CAMPUS LIFE

Quality of Life Rating	97
Fire Safety Rating	95
Green Rating	94
Type of school	public
Environment	town

STUDENTS

Total undergrad enrollment	37,855
% male/female	55/45
% from out of state	34
# of fraternities	53
# of sororities	31
% African American	4
% Asian	5
% Caucasian	78
% Hispanic	4
# of countries represented	119

SURVEY SAYS . . .

Athletic facilities are great
Everyone loves the Nittany Lions
Student publications are popular
Hard liquor is popular
Lots of beer drinking

ACADEMICS

Academic Rating	78
% students graduating within 4 years	62
% students graduating within 6 years	85
Calendar	semester
Student/faculty ratio	17:1
Profs interesting rating	75
Profs accessible rating	82
Most classes have	20–29 students
Most lab/discussion sessions have	20–29 students

MOST POPULAR MAJORS

business administration and management; engineering

APPLICANTS ALSO LOOK AT AND OFTEN PREFER

Carnegie Mellon University, Cornell University, Lehigh University, University of Michigan—Ann Arbor, University of Maryland, College Park

AND SOMETIMES PREFER

Emory University, Georgetown University, Harvard College, Johns Hopkins University, University of Virginia

STUDENTS SAY ". . ."

Academics

Pennsylvania State University "offers an amazing education [and] a sense of community, family, and pride," its students tell us, and while students appreciate the "hundreds of classes to choose from (you can literally take any class you could ever dream of)" and the "endless opportunities for academic and personal growth," it's the "amazing sense of pride and tradition" that truly captivates most. As one student explains, "It's about…the feeling you get even when you come back to visit twenty years later. Once you're a Penn Stater, you're always a Penn Stater. You don't get the same feeling anywhere else. Believe me, I've looked." With "strong academics in the sciences, engineering, and business," PSU has the means to educate the go-getters of tomorrow, then help them find jobs through "a very strong alumni base" that students tell us is "the largest dues-paying alumni association in the world." Academics are "incredible," with "innumerable opportunities to connect with administrators and professors, although it is up to the student to take advantage of them." Online course management services "make keeping up to date in your classes really easy." All these options and opportunities have students bragging that PSU is "a Public Ivy." One with way better football.

Life

"Once the weekend arrives it's either party time or rest-up time" at Penn State, and students tell us that "it's usually party time." "Fraternities are very popular at Penn State for first-year students, and apartments and house parties go well with the upperclassmen." Students also tout University Park's "many places to go out to dinner" ("people go out to eat a lot!"), and close proximity to "Target, Wal-Mart, and movie theaters that can all be accessed by cheap buses that run on campus." In addition, students can attend "a ton of concerts that come through State College because the Bryce Jordan Center is the biggest arena between Pittsburgh and Philadelphia" and "free events sponsored by the Student Programming Association." "Almost every weekend there is a student group performing on campus, whether it be comedy, singing, or acting," one student reports. And then there's Nittany Lion football. As one student puts it, "Football is a way of life here." Many students are also active in philanthropy; THON, the school's annual dance marathon, is "the largest student-run philanthropy in the world, raising money for pediatric cancer research."

Student Body

PSU is a big school with lots of different types of students, but there is definitely a predominant look on campus, which is "sweatpants and t-shirts. We like to be comfortable, relaxed, but always school spirited." Indeed, your typical PSU undergrad is "a diehard football fan" with "a plethora of pride for the school and lion." About one-quarter of the student body originates from outside Pennsylvania ("there's a large number of students from New Jersey"), with the majority of Keystone State natives coming "usually from either the Philadelphia or Pittsburgh area" as well as representing "middle-class white kids from central Pennsylvania." Whatever their geographical roots, the typical PSU undergrad "is someone who works hard during the week [and] is involved in activities on campus, but definitely wants to have a good time once the weekend comes." As one student puts it, "The libraries and study areas on campus are always packed but so are the streets downtown on weekends."

FINANCIAL AID: 814-865-6301 • E-MAIL: ADMISSIONS@PSU.EDU • WEBSITE: WWW.PSU.EDU

THE PRINCETON REVIEW SAYS

Admissions

Very important factors considered include: Academic GPA, standardized test scores, *Important factors considered include:* rigor of secondary school record. *Other factors considered include:* Class rank, application essay, recommendation(s), alumni/ae relation, character/personal qualities, extracurricular activities, talent/ability, volunteer work, work experience. SAT or ACT required; ACT with writing component required. TOEFL required of all international applicants. High school diploma is required and GED is accepted. *Academic units required:* 4 English, 3 mathematics, 3 science, 2 foreign language, 3 social studies.

Financial Aid

Students should submit: FAFSA. The Princeton Review suggests that all financial aid forms be submitted as soon as possible after January 1. *Need-based scholarships/grants offered:* Federal Pell, SEOG, state scholarships/grants, private scholarships, the school's own gift aid. *Loan aid offered:* Direct Subsidized Stafford, Direct Unsubsidized Stafford, Direct PLUS, Federal Perkins, college/university loans from institutional funds, private loans. Applicants will be notified of awards on a rolling basis beginning March 1. Federal Work-Study Program available. Institutional employment available. Off-campus job opportunities are good.

The Inside Word

High school GPA is by far the most important factor in PSU admissions. According to the school's website, high school grades account for two-thirds of the final admissions decision. Standardized test scores, class rank, extracurricular activities, and other factors make up the remaining one-third. PSU admits on a rolling basis. Given this school's popularity with Pennsylvania residents, applicants would do well to get their applications in as early as possible.

THE SCHOOL SAYS ". . ."

From the Admissions Office

"Unique among large public universities, Penn State combines the almost 38,000-student setting of its University Park campus with twenty academically and administratively integrated undergraduate locations—small-college settings ranging in size from 600 to 3,400 students. Each year, more than sixty percent of incoming freshmen begin their studies at these residential and commuter campuses, while nearly forty percent begin at the University Park campus. The smaller locations focus on the needs of new students by offering the first two years of most Penn State baccalaureate degrees in settings that stress close interaction with faculty. Depending on the major selected, students may choose to complete their degree at University Park or one of the smaller locations. Your application to Penn State qualifies you for review for any of our campuses. Your two choices of location are reviewed in the order given. Entrance difficulty is based, in part, on the demand. Due to its popularity, the University Park campus is the most competitive for admission.

"Freshman applicants may submit the results from the SAT or the ACT with the writing component. The writing portions of these tests will not necessarily be factored into admission decisions."

SELECTIVITY	
Admissions Rating	92
# of applicants	40,714
% of applicants accepted	52
% of acceptees attending	31
# accepting a place on wait list	14,949
# admitted from wait list	1,455

FRESHMAN PROFILE	
Range SAT Critical Reading	530–630
Range SAT Math	560–670
Range SAT Writing	540–640
Minimum paper TOEFL	550
Minimum web-based TOEFL	80
Average HS GPA	3.6
% graduated top 10% of class	50
% graduated top 25% of class	86
% graduated top 50% of class	98

DEADLINES	
Regular	
Priority	11/30
Nonfall registration?	yes

FINANCIAL FACTS	
Financial Aid Rating	65
Annual in-state tuition	$15,124
Annual out-state tuition	$27,206
Room and board	$9,420
Required fees	$860
% needy frosh rec. need-based scholarship or grant aid	47
% needy UG rec. need-based scholarship or grant aid	54
% needy frosh rec. non-need-based scholarship or grant aid	47
% needy UG rec. non-need-based scholarship or grant aid	32
% needy frosh rec. need-based self-help aid	74
% needy UG rec. need-based self-help aid	84
% frosh rec. any financial aid	69
% UG rec. any financial aid	71
% UG borrow to pay for school	67
Average cumulative indebtedness	$31,135
% frosh need fully met	8
% ugrads need fully met	8
Average % of frosh need met	56
Average % of ugrad need met	58

PEPPERDINE UNIVERSITY

24255 PACIFIC COAST HIGHWAY, MALIBU, CA 90263 • ADMISSIONS: 310-456-4392 • FAX: 310-506-4861

CAMPUS LIFE

Quality of Life Rating	**91**
Fire Safety Rating	**63**
Green Rating	**85**
Type of school	private
Affiliation	Church of Christ
Environment	suburban

STUDENTS

Total undergrad enrollment	3,461
% male/female	44/56
% from out of state	47
% frosh live on campus	55
# of fraternities	5
# of sororities	7
% African American	7
% Asian	11
% Caucasian	49
% Hispanic	14
% Native American	1
% international	7
# of countries represented	50

SURVEY SAYS . . .

Lab facilities are great
Great computer facilities
School is well run
Students are friendly
Dorms are like palaces
Campus feels safe
Students are happy
Students are involved in community service

ACADEMICS

Academic Rating	**84**
% students returning for sophomore year	93
% students graduating within 4 years	70
Calendar	semester
Student/faculty ratio	13:1
Profs interesting rating	85
Profs accessible rating	88
Most classes have	10–19 students
Most lab/discussion sessions have	10–19 students

MOST POPULAR MAJORS

business administration; economics; political science; psychology; sports medicine

APPLICANTS ALSO LOOK AT AND OFTEN PREFER

University of Southern California, University of California—Los Angeles, University of San Diego, University of California—San Diego, Loyola Marymount University

AND SOMETIMES PREFER

Vanderbilt University, New York University

AND RARELY PREFER

Occidental College

STUDENTS SAY ". . ."

Academics

A small private college overlooking the Pacific Ocean, Pepperdine is an "amazingly beautiful" place to get an education. With about 3,000 undergraduates and an excellent teacher/student ratio, Pepperdine and its "smaller class sizes make it beyond easy to form personal yet academic relationships with your professors." Although "academics are quite challenging," professors "take their role as a mentor seriously. They invite classes over for meals, meet students for coffee, and are eager to help you move in the direction of your dreams." While universally supportive, professors get mixed reviews regarding the ability to keep your attention: Some professors "are very lively and exciting, while some are boring and you would rather take a nap." Career and internship opportunities naturally grow out of the school's prime location, strong alumni network, and regional ties. "Professors are well-connected with both corporations and the surrounding community," and there are "endless internship and volunteer opportunities" in the region. Plus, "Pepperdine's International Program is consistently ranked as one of the best," offering "programs in Florence, London, Shanghai, Buenos Aires…the list goes on! Anyone who is looking forward to studying abroad should definitely look into our programs." Pepperdine is affiliated with the Church of Christ, and Christian values are "prevalent but not overwhelming" in academic curriculum; all students, regardless of their background, are required to attend the "mandatory Convocation program"—a series of chapels, Bible studies, and speakers, designed to promote spirituality. While there's a conservative slant among the higher-ups, Pepperdine's administration is "much more moderate than what you would find at other small, Christian schools."

Life

Pepperdine students gloat about their school's perfect location in Malibu, California, where "there is a 360-degree view of the Pacific Ocean, and students can walk to the beach." The "campus is surrounded by national parks and beach," so nature lovers enjoy "countless opportunities for hiking, swimming, running, waterfall jumping, camping, [and] rock-climbing." "The close proximity to LA, Santa Monica, Hollywood, and the Pacific Coast Highway make it easy for students to find things to do." Students say that a car is a necessity. Fortunately, "There are enough students with cars to hitch a ride," if you don't have your own set of wheels. Alcohol is prohibited at Pepperdine, and "the dry campus policy is strictly enforced." Therefore, "People have to go off campus to drink and party." "The people who party can do so without it affecting the people who don't at all." While the campus is undeniably dreamy, students would like to see the school "improve is the student health facilities and workout facilities"—as well as provide more student parking.

Student Body

"Academics, service, athletics, and social events are all a big part of the life of a typical student." During college, "The typical Pepperdine student is involved in two service projects, spends their spring break building homes in Central America, has huge career goals, is involved in a performing arts group, looks forward to new student orientation all year, and studies abroad as a sophomore." Pepperdine students are also good about "being healthy and eating well and exercising right." It can feel "as if all the popular kids across all the different high schools across America convened in Malibu." However, students tell us "there is a lot more diversity" at Pepperdine today. You get a nice mix of "art majors to the science kids to the surfers to the hardcore studiers to the philosophy majors." Most students come from "a Christian background whether or not they are religious now," and some students are strongly religious and conservative. "Finding alternative viewpoints may be tough," but most students are "fairly open-minded" and "extremely nice."

FINANCIAL AID: 310-506-4301 • E-MAIL: ADMISSION-SEAVER@PEPPERDINE.EDU • WEBSITE: WWW.PEPPERDINE.EDU

THE PRINCETON REVIEW SAYS

Admissions

Very important factors considered include: Application essay, academic GPA, recommendation(s), rigor of secondary school record, standardized test scores, character/personal qualities, extracurricular activities, talent/ability. *Important factors considered include:* Religious affiliation/commitment, volunteer work. *Other factors considered include:* Alumni/ae relation, first generation, racial/ethnic status, work experience. SAT or ACT required; ACT with writing component recommended. TOEFL required of all international applicants. High school diploma is required and GED is accepted. *Academic units recommended:* 4 English, 4 mathematics, 4 science (3 science labs), 3 foreign language, 3 social studies, 3 history, 3 academic electives, 1 speech.

Financial Aid

Students should submit: FAFSA. Regular filing deadline is February 15. The Princeton Review suggests that all financial aid forms be submitted as soon as possible after January 1. *Need-based scholarships/grants offered:* Federal Pell, SEOG, state scholarships/grants, private scholarships, the school's own gift aid, United Negro College Fund, ACG, SMART. *Loan aid offered:* Direct Subsidized Stafford, Direct Unsubsidized Stafford, Direct PLUS, Federal Perkins, college/university loans from institutional funds. Applicants will be notified of awards on or about April 15. Federal Work-Study Program available. Institutional employment available. Off-campus job opportunities are good.

The Inside Word

Admission to Pepperdine is highly selective. The school generally receives almost 8,000 applications for the incoming class of fewer than 1,000 students. Decisions are made based on a student's academic record, standardized test scores, and two letters of recommendation—one personal and the other academic. Students affiliated with the Church of Christ are eligible for special Church of Christ scholarships; to be considered, applicants must submit a letter of recommendation from a church leader.

THE SCHOOL SAYS ". . ."

From the Admissions Office

"As a selective university, Pepperdine seeks students who show promise of academic achievement at the collegiate level. However, we also seek students who are committed to serving the university community, as well as others with whom they come into contact. We look for community-service activities, volunteer efforts, and strong leadership qualities, as well as a demonstrated commitment to academic studies and an interest in the liberal arts.

"Seaver College of Pepperdine University requires freshman applicants to submit scores from either the SAT Reasoning Test (including the writing portion) or the ACT (including the writing test). The scores are evaluated in conjunction with the grade point average in specific courses completed."

SELECTIVITY

Admissions Rating	**94**
# of applicants	9,384
% of applicants accepted	32
% of acceptees attending	23
# accepting a place on wait list	1,734
# admitted from wait list	113

FRESHMAN PROFILE

Range SAT Critical Reading	540–650
Range SAT Math	560–680
Range SAT Writing	560–660
Range ACT Composite	25–31
Minimum paper TOEFL	550
Minimum web-based TOEFL	80
Average HS GPA	3.7
% graduated top 10% of class	39
% graduated top 25% of class	77
% graduated top 50% of class	95

DEADLINES

Regular	
Deadline	1/15
Notification	4/1
Nonfall registration?	yes

FINANCIAL FACTS

Financial Aid Rating	**80**
Annual tuition	$42,520
Room and board	$12,600
Required fees	$252
Books and supplies	$1,200
% needy frosh rec. need-based scholarship or grant aid	44
% needy UG rec. need-based scholarship or grant aid	45
% needy frosh rec. non-need-based scholarship or grant aid	89
% needy UG rec. non-need-based scholarship or grant aid	92
% needy frosh rec. need-based self-help aid	78
% needy UG rec. need-based self-help aid	76
% UG borrow to pay for school	50
Average cumulative indebtedness	$30,175
% frosh need fully met	26
% ugrads need fully met	28
Average % of frosh need met	78
Average % of ugrad need met	80

PITZER COLLEGE

1050 NORTH MILLS AVENUE, CLAREMONT, CA 91711-6101 • ADMISSIONS: 909-621-8129 • FAX: 909-621-8770

CAMPUS LIFE

Quality of Life Rating	**92**
Fire Safety Rating	**77**
Green Rating	**95**
Type of school	private
Environment	town

STUDENTS

Total undergrad enrollment	1,099
% male/female	38/62
% from out of state	58
% frosh live on campus	100
% African American	6
% Asian	8
% Caucasian	46
% Hispanic	16
% Native American	1
% international	3
# of countries represented	15

SURVEY SAYS . . .

Lots of liberal students
Students are friendly
Different types of students interact
Students aren't religious
Frats and sororities are unpopular or nonexistent
Student government is popular
Political activism is popular
Students are environmentally aware
Students are involved in community service

ACADEMICS

Academic Rating	**96**
% students graduating within 4 years	75
% students graduating within 6 years	81
Calendar	semester
Student/faculty ratio	12:1
Profs interesting rating	91
Profs accessible rating	93
Most classes have	10–19 students

MOST POPULAR MAJORS

film/cinema studies; psychology; sociology

APPLICANTS ALSO LOOK AT AND OFTEN PREFER

Claremont McKenna College, Scripps College, University of California—Berkeley, University of California—Los Angeles, Occidental College, University of Southern California, Pomona College

AND SOMETIMES PREFER

Boston University, Colorado College, Whitman College, Lewis & Clark College, New York University

STUDENTS SAY ". . ."

Academics

Pitzer College is "small, personal, and unique," but because students have access to the classes and "excellent resources" at four other local colleges through the Claremont Consortium, "you can choose to make your college experience as large or as small as you want!" Pitzer doesn't have a lot of requirements, so there's a high degree of academic freedom and flexibility, including the opportunity to create your own major. Students gush about the level of "student autonomy," calling Pitzer "a challenging school that allows students to become effective leaders." Emphasis is on "social responsibility" and "intercultural understanding," and classes "are constantly being connected to present society and how you can pursue social issues through your field of study." "Professors are as zesty and zany as they are brilliant and intriguing" and they "encourage respectful dialogue inside and outside the classroom." Generally, "emphasis [is] on discussion; besides intro courses you won't find many lecture classes." "Pitzer is all about analytical thinking and learning to think beyond the material in front of you. Professors won't settle for summary; be prepared to form and argue your own opinions." Students are very positive about their professors, calling them "life changing" and "dedicated and enthusiastic." A history major says professors "demand a lot from their students," and a political science major adds that "they want to know each of their students individually and help them out as much as they can."

Life

Pitzer's location means great weather, which means "year-round outdoor activities." "Everyday walking through campus you'll see classes being held outside on the grass, students lying in hammocks reading, students studying while laying out by the pool, or students fixing old bikes at the Green Bike Program (a student-run club, promoting green transportation by providing bikes for the community)." Pitzer students love the "very laid-back and easy-going environment," but find the school is still able to enforce "a serious education." The College Consortium means there's always something going on, whether it's a "speaker series, dances, parties, or concerts," and there's "no shortage of things to do." Students report an "average" amount of drinking and drug use, and a few noted that though there's "a lot of pot smoking" they "never felt pressured" to take part. The five colleges "sponsor parties...with kegs, deejays, etc.," though the big parties usually take place at the other colleges, or off campus. Pitzer is "close enough to Los Angeles to head in for concerts, museums, shopping, etc., [and] many students do camping trips in Southern California [or] head to the beach." There's also a campus organization, Pitzer Outdoor Adventures (POA), that "funds students each week to basically go out on epic adventures. Want gas money for surfing? Okay! Want some funds for a back packing trip? Done!" A leader of POA admits with the school funding adventures, it "doesn't get much better."

Student Body

"The one thing all Pitzer students do have in common is awareness and community involvement. Every student on this campus has a strong voice." Pitzer students are hard workers and "passionate thinkers," "intelligent, chill, accepting, and friendly." Though Pitzer is small, "there is such a wide variety of people [that] you'll find a place where you fit in," and a sociology student adds that, "You only really don't fit in if you're unfriendly and mean." "At Pitzer, there are countless ways to meet people...and if you can't find something at Pitzer you can definitely find it at one of the other Claremont Colleges." Pitzer has a reputation as a "hippie" (and sometimes "hipster") school, but students say the "diversity among personalities is growing rapidly." One student says that Pitzer students "are a collection of creative people who, in their different ways, like to think outside of the box."

FINANCIAL AID: 909-621-8208 • E-MAIL: ADMISSION@PITZER.EDU • WEBSITE: WWW.PITZER.EDU

THE PRINCETON REVIEW SAYS

Admissions

Very important factors considered include: Class rank, application essay, academic GPA, recommendation(s), rigor of secondary school record, character/personal qualities, extracurricular activities, racial/ethnic status. *Important factors considered include:* First generation, geographical residence, interview, level of applicant's interest, talent/ability, volunteer work. *Other factors considered include:* Standardized test scores, alumni/ae relation, work experience. ACT with writing component recommended. TOEFL required of all international applicants. High school diploma is required and GED is accepted. *Academic units required:* 4 English, 3 mathematics, 3 science (3 science labs), 3 foreign language, 3 social studies, 1 history, 1 visual/performing arts.

Financial Aid

Students should submit: FAFSA, CSS/Financial Aid PROFILE, state aid form, noncustodial PROFILE, business/farm supplement. Regular filing deadline is February 1. The Princeton Review suggests that all financial aid forms be submitted as soon as possible after January 1. *Need-based scholarships/grants offered:* Federal Pell, SEOG, state scholarships/grants, private scholarships, the school's own gift aid, Federal ACG and National SMART. *Loan aid offered:* Direct Subsidized Stafford, Direct Unsubsidized Stafford, Direct PLUS, Federal Perkins, college/university loans from institutional funds. Applicants will be notified of awards on or about April 1. Federal Work-Study Program available. Institutional employment available. Off-campus job opportunities are good.

The Inside Word

This is a place where applicants can feel confident in letting their thoughts flow freely on admissions essays. Not only does the committee read them (a circumstance more rare in college admissions that one is led to believe), but they've also set up the process to emphasize them! Thus, what you have to say for yourself will go much further than numbers in determining your suitability for Pitzer.

THE SCHOOL SAYS ". . ."

From the Admissions Office

"Pitzer is about opportunities. It's about possibilities. The students who come here are looking for something different from the usual 'take two courses from column A, two courses from column B, and two courses from column C.' That kind of arbitrary selection doesn't make a satisfying education at Pitzer. So we look for students who want to have an impact on their own education, who want the chief responsibility—with help from their faculty advisors—in designing their own futures.

"Pitzer's admission policy uses a test-optional policy. Students in the top ten percent of their class or those who have an unweighted academic GPA of 3.5 or higher are not required to submit test scores. Others are allowed to choose from a variety of choices, including standardized tests (i.e., the SAT and ACT with the writing component)."

SELECTIVITY	
Admissions Rating	**97**
# of applicants	3,743
% of applicants accepted	24
% of acceptees attending	30

FRESHMAN PROFILE	
Range SAT Critical Reading	605–710
Range SAT Math	590–690
Minimum paper TOEFL	520
Minimum web-based TOEFL	70
Average HS GPA	3.9
% graduated top 10% of class	55
% graduated top 25% of class	89
% graduated top 50% of class	100

DEADLINES	
Early decision	
Deadline	11/15
Notification	1/1
Regular	
Deadline	1/1
Notification	4/1
Nonfall registration?	no

FINANCIAL FACTS	
Financial Aid Rating	**98**
Annual tuition	$38,832
Room and board	$12,438
Required fees	$3,718
Books and supplies	$1,000
% needy frosh rec. need-based scholarship or grant aid	95
% needy UG rec. need-based scholarship or grant aid	98
% needy frosh rec. non-need-based scholarship or grant aid	0
% needy UG rec. non-need-based scholarship or grant aid	0
% needy frosh rec. need-based self-help aid	89
% needy UG rec. need-based self-help aid	95
% frosh rec. any financial aid	34
% UG rec. any financial aid	40
% UG borrow to pay for school	35
Average cumulative indebtedness	$22,568
% frosh need fully met	100
% ugrads need fully met	98
Average % of frosh need met	100
Average % of ugrad need met	100

POMONA COLLEGE

333 NORTH COLLEGE WAY, CLAREMONT, CA 91711-6312 • ADMISSIONS: 909-621-8134 • FAX: 909-621-8952

CAMPUS LIFE

Quality of Life Rating	98
Fire Safety Rating	98
Green Rating	93
Type of school	private
Environment	town

STUDENTS

Total undergrad enrollment	1,567
% male/female	49/51
% from out of state	66
% from public high school	70
% frosh live on campus	100
# of fraternities	3
% African American	6
% Asian	10
% Caucasian	46
% Hispanic	13
% international	5
# of countries represented	21

SURVEY SAYS . . .

No one cheats
School is well run
Students are friendly
Students aren't religious
Dorms are like palaces
Low cost of living
Students are happy
Musical organizations are popular
Students are environmentally aware

ACADEMICS

Academic Rating	96
% students returning for sophomore year	99
% students graduating within 4 years	91
% students graduating within 6 years	95
Calendar	semester
Student/faculty ratio	8:1
Profs interesting rating	93
Profs accessible rating	97
Most classes have	10–19 students
Most lab/discussion sessions have	10–19 students

MOST POPULAR MAJORS

biology/biological sciences; economics; English language and literature

APPLICANTS ALSO LOOK AT AND OFTEN PREFER

Princeton University, Yale University, Stanford University, University of California—Berkeley, Harvard College

AND SOMETIMES PREFER

Williams College, Brown University, University of California—Los Angeles

STUDENTS SAY ". . ."

Academics

At Pomona College in Claremont, you can get "an academically rigorous education" in a "low-stress California atmosphere." At this prestigious liberal arts school, "The professors are, for the most part, fantastic—engaging, creative, and sharp," and "All classes are taught by professors, not grad students or TAs." With small class sizes in every department, "There is an emphasis on collaborative learning," and "Many professors are great discussion leaders and really motivate students to get involved in class." Students have the advantage of "getting to know professors outside the classroom, in any setting, from office hours, to Thanksgiving dinner at their homes." Illustrating how personal the experience can be, a student tells us, "Today, I had a class with seven people in it, then lunch with a physics professor, and then a personal tutorial with a philosophy professor." Another student adds, "Between department barbecues, parties, and weekend retreats, by the time you're an upperclassman, you will know most of the professors in your major department quite well." In complement to the intimate academic atmosphere, Pomona "offers the resources of a large university" through the Claremont Consortium, which offers joint events and cross-registration with four adjoining colleges. Among other programs, "Pomona pays for students to take otherwise unpaid internship positions." Students praise Pomona's "efficiency in taking care of administrative tasks such as financial aid and registration," adding that the administration "is very good at responding to what students want."

Life

Pomona students are "ridiculously happy" about their lot in life, and why shouldn't they be? They're living in a "perfect world full of intelligent, engaging, and open individuals, amazing academics, brilliant opportunities to get involved in, and enough sunshine to make anyone happy to be alive." The weather is a key aspect of the experience, and "On a nice day, everyone heads outside in shorts and t-shirts to do their class work." On any given day, "You'll see people setting up telescopes outside the dorms at night to try to get a glimpse of the stars, you'll find people practicing ukulele on our quad, you'll see students filming for a project in the dining halls, [or] you'll see someone riding around campus on a bamboo bike." "Many people are involved in intramural sports," and students love "hiking, skiing, and going to the beach year round." There are many beautiful beaches in the area, and "Joshua Tree is only an hour and a half away, so there are camping trips there just about every weekend." Though the school is small, there are four other colleges in the Claremont Consortium, and Pomona students can "take their classes, eat at their dining halls, go to their parties, swim in their pools, and generally share in a great experience." When its time to blow off steam, "There are large 5C-sponsored parties that people go to and enjoy."

Student Body

At Pomona, "Only a third or so of students are from California," yet the California attitude reigns supreme. Here, you'll find a number of "tree-hugging, rock-climbing, Tom's shoes–wearing" undergraduates, with most students generally falling within the "liberal, upper-middle-class, hipster-athlete" continuum. Students report a "decent level of diversity and a strong international community." Studious and talented, Pomona undergraduates "excel in the classroom and usually have some sort of passion that they pursue outside of the classroom." "Underneath our sundresses and rainbow flip-flops, we're all closet nerds—everybody is really passionate about something or other." At Pomona, "You will meet the football player who got a perfect score on his SAT or the dreadlocked hippie who took multivariable calculus when he was sixteen." Dress code is uniformly casual, and "flip-flops, polo, or tank tops and shorts" are the unofficial uniform.

FINANCIAL AID: 909-621-8205 • E-MAIL: ADMISSIONS@POMONA.EDU • WEBSITE: WWW.POMONA.EDU

THE PRINCETON REVIEW SAYS

Admissions

Very important factors considered include: Class rank, application essay, academic GPA, recommendation(s), rigor of secondary school record, standardized test scores, character/personal qualities, extracurricular activities, talent/ability. *Important factors considered include:* Interview. *Other factors considered include:* Alumni/ae relation, first generation, geographical residence, racial/ethnic status, volunteer work, work experience. ACT with writing component recommended. TOEFL required of all international applicants. High school diploma or equivalent is not required. *Academic units required:* 4 English, 3 mathematics, 3 science (2 science labs), 2 foreign language, 2 social studies, 3 history. *Academic units recommended:* 4 mathematics, 4 science (3 science labs), 3 foreign language, 2 social studies, 3 history.

Financial Aid

Students should submit: FAFSA, CSS/Financial Aid PROFILE, noncustodial PROFILE, business/farm supplement. Tax returns for both the student and parents. Regular filing deadline is February 1. The Princeton Review suggests that all financial aid forms be submitted as soon as possible after January 1. *Need-based scholarships/grants offered:* Federal Pell, SEOG, state scholarships/grants, private scholarships, the school's own gift aid. *Loan aid offered:* Direct Subsidized Stafford, Direct Unsubsidized Stafford, Direct PLUS, Federal Perkins, college/university loans from institutional funds. Applicants will be notified of awards on or about April 1. Federal Work-Study Program available. Institutional employment available. Off-campus job opportunities are good.

The Inside Word

For first-year applicants, Pomona College offers regular decision admissions, as well as a binding early decision program. Admissions officials evaluate a student's academic record carefully, examining the rigor of high school coursework, class rank, and grade point average. Ninety percent of Pomona admits rank in the top ten percent of their class. If you live in Southern California, Pomona expects you to interview on campus; students in other regions are strongly encouraged to visit campus and meet with admissions staff, though it's not required.

THE SCHOOL SAYS ". . ."

From the Admissions Office

"Perhaps the most important thing to know about Pomona College is that we are what we say we are. There is enormous integrity between the statements of mission and philosophy governing the college and the reality that students, faculty, and administrators experience. The balance in the curriculum is unusual. Sciences, social sciences, humanities, and the arts receive equal attention, support, and emphasis. Most importantly, the commitment to undergraduate education is absolute. Teaching awards remain the highest honor the trustees can bestow upon faculty. The typical method of instruction is the seminar and the average class size of fifteen offers students the opportunity to become full partners in the learning process. Our location in the Los Angeles basin and in Claremont, with four other colleges, provides a remarkable community.

"Pomona College requires the SAT plus two SAT Subject Tests (in different fields) or the ACT with the writing component."

SELECTIVITY	
Admissions Rating	**99**
# of applicants	7,207
% of applicants accepted	14
% of acceptees attending	39
# accepting a place on wait list	899
# admitted from wait list	31
# of early decision applicants	643
# accepted early decision	132

FRESHMAN PROFILE	
Range SAT Critical Reading	680–780
Range SAT Math	690–770
Range SAT Writing	680–780
Range ACT Composite	31–34
Minimum paper TOEFL	600
Minimum web-based TOEFL	100
% graduated top 10% of class	90
% graduated top 25% of class	100
% graduated top 50% of class	100

DEADLINES	
Early decision	
Deadline	11/1
Notification	12/15
Regular	
Deadline	1/2
Notification	4/1
Nonfall registration?	no

FINANCIAL FACTS	
Financial Aid Rating	**99**
Annual tuition	$39,572
Room and board	$13,227
Required fees	$311
Books and supplies	$900
% needy frosh rec. need-based scholarship or grant aid	100
% needy UG rec. need-based scholarship or grant aid	100
% needy frosh rec. need-based self-help aid	100
% needy UG rec. need-based self-help aid	99
% frosh rec. any financial aid	55
% UG rec. any financial aid	52
% UG borrow to pay for school	53
Average cumulative indebtedness	$10,580
% frosh need fully met	100
% ugrads need fully met	100
Average % of frosh need met	100
Average % of ugrad need met	100

PORTLAND STATE UNIVERSITY

OFFICE OF ADMISSIONS AND RECORDS, PORTLAND, OR 97207-0751 • ADMISSIONS: 503-725-3511 • FAX: 503-725-5525

CAMPUS LIFE

Quality of Life Rating	**73**
Fire Safety Rating	**66**
Green Rating	**86**
Type of school	public
Environment	metropolis

STUDENTS

Total undergrad enrollment	19,752
% male/female	47/53
% from out of state	20
% from public high school	85
% frosh live on campus	40
# of fraternities	3
# of sororities	3
% African American	3
% Asian	9
% Caucasian	66
% Hispanic	6
% Native American	1
% international	5
# of countries represented	94

SURVEY SAYS . . .

Athletic facilities are great
Students love Portland, OR
Great off-campus food
Great library

ACADEMICS

Academic Rating	**68**
% students returning for sophomore year	70
% students graduating within 4 years	11
% students graduating within 6 years	34
Calendar	quarter
Student/faculty ratio	18:1
Profs interesting rating	74
Profs accessible rating	65
Most classes have	20–29 students
Most lab/discussion sessions have	20–29 students

MOST POPULAR MAJORS

business/commerce; fine/studio arts; psychology

STUDENTS SAY "..."

Academics

Portland State University's motto is "let knowledge serve the city," and students echo this philosophy, saying their school "has a strong focus on civic engagement and sustainability." "PSU is a great learning environment in the heart of the city" and a "good value" for your tuition dollars. It's also "a green-minded urban school" that's "training students to be good community members." "There is a wealth of courses" on offer here, with degrees in social work, a range of business majors, and the hard sciences all receiving praise. "Classes are usually pretty small," and professors "promote lots of in-class discussion and are readily available to meet outside of class as well." "They really care about the student's success, and they really help broaden our scope of learning [and] thinking critically." Adjunct professors are "very connected to the community and their particular areas of expertise." Overall, students are happy with their instructors, saying, "Most professors are engaging and truly want to challenge you and help you succeed." They "are well-educated [and] well-versed in current issues and research." There's "the occasional dud thrown into the mix," though. Generally, "They are prepared and are passionate about the classes they teach. They have a wealth of experiences to bring to classroom," and they're "easily accessible for questions or further assistance," "students just need to reach out."

Life

The city of Portland is a big draw for PSU students. "The campus is extraordinarily beautiful and ideally located." Outdoor activities are big here: "There's skiing, hiking, camping, [and] fishing." "The downtown area has plenty of microbrew pubs, nightlife, eateries, and theaters." "The people are friendly, and the city is gorgeous and easy to navigate. You can go to the beach or to the mountain in about two hours, and there are many things to do outdoors. There are great parks throughout the city." "The public transportation is outstanding." It's bike- and vegan-friendly. "There are lots of activist and awareness-raising events going on all the time, and lots of students are involved in volunteering (on and off campus)." Because PSU has a large nontraditional undergraduate population and the majority of students live off campus, the sense of community extends beyond the school and into the city. "There are a lot of things to do on campus, and there are different groups on campus that promote going out into the community at large and helping out." "Because the student body is so big and really diverse, PSU has tons of programs/clubs/groups that help make you feel more involved with your school. PSU is also committed to sustainability: Any new buildings are made with the latest green technology, and recycling is a big deal."

Student Body

"It is difficult to define the typical PSU student, because there are so many of us from so many different backgrounds," one student says, and diversity does indeed seem to be the name of the game at PSU. Students describe themselves as "environmentally aware, hip," and "very liberal." Overall, people at PSU are "invested in their education and are friendly." There's a large population of nontraditional undergraduates, so students are "either typical college-age…or people in their thirties and forties with kids and full-time job trying to juggle everything." Even within this large, diverse student body, "everyone finds a niche pretty quickly." "It's easy to find people you get along with, but it's also easy to find people who are completely different from you, which makes school a lot more interesting."

FINANCIAL AID: 800-547-8887 • E-MAIL: ADMISSIONS@PDX.EDU • WEBSITE: WWW.PDX.EDU

THE PRINCETON REVIEW SAYS

Admissions

Very important factors considered include: Academic GPA, rigor of secondary school record. *Other factors considered include:* Standardized test scores. SAT or ACT required; ACT with writing component required. TOEFL required of all international applicants. High school diploma is required and GED is accepted. *Academic units required:* 4 English, 3 mathematics, 2 science, 2 foreign language, 2 social studies, 1 history. *Academic units recommended:* 1 science lab.

Financial Aid

Students should submit: FAFSA. The Princeton Review suggests that all financial aid forms be submitted as soon as possible after January 1. *Need-based scholarships/grants offered:* Federal Pell, SEOG, state scholarships / grants, private scholarships, the school's own gift aid, United Negro College Fund. *Loan aid offered:* Direct Subsidized Stafford, Direct Unsubsidized Stafford, Direct PLUS, Federal Perkins, state loans. Federal Work-Study Program available. Institutional employment available. Off-campus job opportunities are excellent.

The Inside Word

PSU offers a range of admission options for new freshmen, transfers, students enrolled at local community colleges, continuing students, and those with nontraditional high school backgrounds. Regardless of an applicant's status, admissions officers look for a secondary school GPA of at least 3.0, though high test scores can make up for a lower average.

THE SCHOOL SAYS ". . ."

From the Admissions Office

"Portland State University is Oregon's largest and most diverse public university located in the heart of one of America's most progressive cities. It offers more than sixty undergraduate and forty graduate programs in fine and performing arts, liberal arts and sciences, business administration, education, urban and public affairs, social work, engineering, and computer science. PSU offers more than 120 bachelor's, master's, and doctoral degrees.

"The forty-nine-acre downtown campus—whose motto is "Let Knowledge Serve the City"—places students in a vibrant center of culture, business, and technology. Portland State's urban mission offers opportunities for every student to participate in internships and community-based projects in business, education, social services, government, technology, and the arts and sciences.

"The award-winning University Studies curriculum provides small class sizes and mentoring for undergraduates and culminates in Senior Capstone, which takes students out of the classroom and into the field, where they utilize their knowledge and skills to develop community projects.

"Portland State has taken aggressive steps to enhance the student experience and campus life, with new student housing and a comprehensive recreation complex and remodeled science and performing arts facilities. The university also has hired more academic and career advisers and created new programs to support students. Sustainability—initiatives that balance environmental, economic, and social concerns—is incorporated throughout the curriculum and across the campus."

SELECTIVITY	
Admissions Rating	73
# of applicants	4,924
% of applicants accepted	71
% of acceptees attending	41

FRESHMAN PROFILE	
Range SAT Critical Reading	460–590
Range SAT Math	460–570
Range SAT Writing	430–560
Range ACT Composite	19–25
Minimum paper TOEFL	527
Minimum web-based TOEFL	71
Average HS GPA	3.3

DEADLINES	
Nonfall registration?	yes

FINANCIAL FACTS	
Financial Aid Rating	74
Annual in-state tuition	$6,156
Annual out-state tuition	$22,983
Room and board	$9,801
Required fees	$1,608
Books and supplies	$1,968
% needy frosh rec. need-based scholarship or grant aid	72
% needy UG rec. need-based scholarship or grant aid	74
% needy frosh rec. non-need-based scholarship or grant aid	2
% needy frosh rec. need-based self-help aid	85
% needy UG rec. need-based self-help aid	92
% frosh rec. any financial aid	75
% UG rec. any financial aid	56
% UG borrow to pay for school	64
Average cumulative indebtedness	$26,287
% frosh need fully met	13
% ugrads need fully met	6
Average % of frosh need met	76
Average % of ugrad need met	80

PRESCOTT COLLEGE

220 GROVE AVENUE, PRESCOTT, AZ 86301 • ADMISSIONS: 877-350-2100 • FAX: 928-776-5242

CAMPUS LIFE

Quality of Life Rating	**86**
Fire Safety Rating	**69**
Green Rating	**83**
Type of school	private
Environment	town

STUDENTS

Total undergrad enrollment	769
% male/female	41/59
% from out of state	86
% from public high school	78
% frosh live on campus	36
% African American	2
% Asian	1
% Caucasian	82
% Hispanic	6
% Native American	2
% international	1
# of countries represented	12

SURVEY SAYS . . .

Lots of liberal students
Class discussions encouraged
No one cheats
Students are friendly
Different types of students interact
Students aren't religious
Great food on campus
Students are happy
Intercollegiate sports are unpopular or nonexistent
Frats and sororities are unpopular or nonexistent
Political activism is popular
Students are environmentally aware

ACADEMICS

Academic Rating	**84**
% students returning for sophomore year	64
% students graduating within 4 years	20
% students graduating within 6 years	40
Calendar	semester
Student/faculty ratio	7:1
Profs interesting rating	95
Profs accessible rating	95
Most classes have	10–19 students

MOST POPULAR MAJORS

education, other; elementary education and teaching; environmental studies

APPLICANTS ALSO LOOK AT AND OFTEN PREFER

College of the Atlantic, Mills College

AND SOMETIMES PREFER

Whitman College

AND RARELY PREFER

Sarah Lawrence College, The Evergreen State College, University of Arizona, Reed College, Hendrix College

STUDENTS SAY ". . ."

Academics

Prescott College, a small, progressive school, "encourages critical and forward thinking around issues of social justice and sustainability." The school shines in interdisciplinary fields, such as environmental studies, human development and psychology, outdoor adventure education, and arts-based fields such as photography and creative writing. Prescott "is about taking learning out of the classroom," and true to its word, classes, according to the university, "take place in field sites throughout the Southwest, in art galleries, wilderness areas, along the U.S./Mexico border and in local schools, to name a few." Students see their education as "experiential, hands-on, real-world, and self-directed," and consider it to be a "journey, not a destination." Prescott's academic calendar is a unique "block and quarter system," which is "very effective at immersing students in their studies." Students take only one course for three four-week blocks before entering a ten-week semester. The quality of teaching "really varies. Some teachers are excellent and experienced and work well with the majority of the student body," and are "engaging and committed to their students." However, many students feel that "visiting" and "adjunct" professors "tend to be not so good." All the freedom at Prescott means that "academics are what you make them," and while some students find Prescott to be "academically stimulating but not very challenging," others think "there are plenty of opportunities for a rigorous academic experience."

Life

Prescott's emphasis on outdoor education and its ideal location near 1.4 million acres of National Forest mean that most students "live and play outside." One student says, "The majority of students rock climb, mountain bike, ski, snowboard, surf, raft, kayak, skydive, or ice climb." "If you want to go on an adventure, have no fear, you'll have an accomplice in less than an hour." The laid-back, artsy town of Prescott has a few bars that host "some good live music," which lots of students see whenever possible, though "sometimes you have to go to a larger city for that." Most students at Prescott are community-minded individuals, so it makes sense that one of the most popular social activities is to go to, or host, a potluck. As one student enthuses, "students also love potlucks; cooking is huge here." Others confirm that "potlucks are a huge part of student life," and that "much revolves around food." These gatherings can be "really fun and sometimes is crazy and sometimes really low-key." At potlucks and other gatherings, students "really enjoy each other's company." Generally, students do "not drink to get drunk, but drink as a part of a great evening out with friends," and most students seem to think people at Prescott "have good heads on their shoulders" and don't indulge in out-of-control partying.

Student Body

Prescott's emphasis on individual education, the environment, and sustainability means students are "environmentally and politically conscious" and "committed to their learning and creating a better community." Students are there because "they want to better themselves and have a positive impact on the world at large," and they're "motivated, empowered, and feisty." Additionally, students are very invested in social activism. Prescott's location means it attracts "athletic nerds" and "typical students love spending time outdoors." Yes, you'll probably see a lot of "hippies, hippies, hippies," but many students "wouldn't identify themselves that way." Though the school is predominantly white, students feel the community is "from a wide variety of cultural backgrounds" and that there's "a colorful array of people." As one student put it, the school "is made up of hundreds of different individuals who all bring their unique aspects to classes and social settings." Though students at Prescott tend to lean left, they say "any student fits in here. Everyone talks to everyone."

FINANCIAL AID: 928-350-1112 • E-MAIL: ADMISSIONS@PRESCOTT.EDU • WEBSITE: WWW.PRESCOTT.EDU

THE PRINCETON REVIEW SAYS

Admissions

Very important factors considered include: Application essay, recommendation(s), rigor of secondary school record. *Important factors considered include:* Academic GPA, standardized test scores, character/personal qualities, extracurricular activities, interview, level of applicant's interest, talent/ability, volunteer work, work experience. *Other factors considered include:* First generation. SAT or ACT required; ACT with or without writing component accepted. TOEFL required of all international applicants. High school diploma is required and GED is accepted. *Academic units recommended:* 4 English, 3 mathematics, 2 science, 1 foreign language, 3 social studies, 2 history, 1 visual/performing arts.

Financial Aid

Students should submit: FAFSA. The Princeton Review suggests that all financial aid forms be submitted as soon as possible after January 1. *Need-based scholarships/grants offered:* Federal Pell, SEOG, state scholarships/grants, private scholarships, the school's own gift aid, ACT and SMART. *Loan aid offered:* Direct Subsidized Stafford, Direct Unsubsidized Stafford, Direct PLUS. Applicants will be notified of awards on a rolling basis beginning March 15. Federal Work-Study Program available. Institutional employment available. Highest amount earned per year from on-campus jobs $2,744. Off-campus job opportunities are good.

The Inside Word

The acceptance rate at Prescott is high, but the applicant pool is very self-selecting, and Prescott is the kind of place where you have to want to be. For example, while many colleges have fun-filled, low-pressure orientation programs for incoming students, Prescott students spend their first four weeks engaged in an immersion orientation experience in the Arizona wilderness that builds student's experiential education skills and integrates them into the Prescott academic community.

THE SCHOOL SAYS ". . ."

From the Admissions Office

"Prescott College highlights the dramatic educational return on investment when experience is at the center of learning. Tucked into a corner of the town in central Arizona of the same name, Prescott College is an evolving experiment in rejecting hierarchical thinking for collaboration and teamwork as the cornerstone of learning. This is an educational institution that puts students at the center in everything it does and is. Optional Grades. Narrative Evaluations. No barriers. Limited bureaucracy. No summa or magna or 'best in show' ribbons. Just a peripatetic community of lively intellects and fearless explorers whose connecting threads are a passion for social responsibility and the environment, and a keen sense of adventure.

"At Prescott College, our goal is to fuel your passion and give you a deeper understanding of the world around you through collaborative learning and personal experience. We don't settle for the mundane college experience. Instead, we take learning outside the classroom and into the real world through experiential and field-based learning. From field studies, internships, and independent studies to community service and study abroad opportunities, our students are challenged to think critically, explore the world up close, and form solutions through collaborative efforts.

"If you're looking for a college experience unlike any other—the kind that enables you to take control of your education and truly make a positive impact in your community and in the world—then Prescott College is the ideal college for you."

SELECTIVITY	
Admissions Rating	71
# of applicants	363
% of applicants accepted	99
% of acceptees attending	21
# of early decision applicants	6
# accepted early decision	4

FRESHMAN PROFILE	
Range SAT Critical Reading	510–670
Range SAT Math	480–570
Range SAT Writing	500–620
Range ACT Composite	20–28
Minimum paper TOEFL	550
Minimum web-based TOEFL	61
Average HS GPA	2.9
% graduated top 10% of class	17
% graduated top 25% of class	17
% graduated top 50% of class	66

DEADLINES	
Early decision	
Deadline	12/1
Notification	12/15
Regular	
Priority	3/1
Deadline	8/15
Nonfall registration?	yes

FINANCIAL FACTS	
Financial Aid Rating	70
Annual tuition	$27,408
Room and board	$5,600
Required fees	$611
Books and supplies	$720
% needy frosh rec. need-based scholarship or grant aid	100
% needy UG rec. need-based scholarship or grant aid	98
% needy frosh rec. non-need-based scholarship or grant aid	8
% needy UG rec. non-need-based scholarship or grant aid	3
% needy frosh rec. need-based self-help aid	94
% needy UG rec. need-based self-help aid	97
% frosh rec. any financial aid	93
% UG rec. any financial aid	88
% UG borrow to pay for school	67
Average cumulative indebtedness	$15,182
% frosh need fully met	6
% ugrads need fully met	4
Average % of frosh need met	63
Average % of ugrad need met	54

PRINCETON UNIVERSITY

PO Box 430, Admission Office, Princeton, NJ 08542-0430 • Admissions: 609-258-3060 • Fax: 609-258-6743

CAMPUS LIFE

Quality of Life Rating	**92**
Fire Safety Rating	**96**
Green Rating	**95**
Type of school	private
Environment	town

STUDENTS

Total undergrad enrollment	5,173
% male/female	51/49
% from out of state	83
% from public high school	58
% frosh live on campus	100
% African American	7
% Asian	18
% Caucasian	49
% Hispanic	8
% international	11
# of countries represented	95

SURVEY SAYS . . .

No one cheats
Great computer facilities
Great library
School is well run
Campus feels safe
Low cost of living

ACADEMICS

Academic Rating	**92**
% students returning for sophomore year	96
% students graduating within 4 years	87
Calendar	semester
Student/faculty ratio	6:1
Profs interesting rating	83
Profs accessible rating	79
Most classes have	10–19 students
Most lab/discussion sessions have	10–19 students

MOST POPULAR MAJORS

economics; history; political science and government

APPLICANTS ALSO LOOK AT AND SOMETIMES PREFER

Massachusetts Institute of Technology, Yale University, Stanford University, Harvard College

AND RARELY PREFER

University of Pennsylvania, Brown University

STUDENTS SAY ". . ."

Academics

As a member of the grand old Ivy League, Princeton University has long maintained a "sterling reputation" for quality academics; however, students say Princeton's "unique focus on the undergraduate experience" is what makes their school stand out among institutions. It attracts "really experienced and big-name professors, who actually want to teach undergraduate." Introductory lecture classes can be rather large, but "Once you take upper-level courses, you'll have a lot of chances to work closely with professors and study what you are most interested in." A current undergrad enthuses, "The discussions I have in seminar are the reason I get out of bed in the morning; after a great class, I feel incredibly invigorated." Though all Princeton professors are "leading scholars in their field," students admit that some classes can be "dry." Fortunately, "The overwhelming majority of professors are wonderful, captivating lecturers" who are "dedicated to their students." While you may be taking a class from a Nobel laureate, "The humility and accessibility of world-famous researchers and public figures is always remarkable." At Princeton, "There are so many chances to meet writers, performers, and professionals you admire." A student details, "The two years I've been here, I've been in discussions with Frank Gehry, David Sedaris, Peter Hessler, John McPhee, Jeff Koons, Chang-Rae Lee, Joyce Carol Oates, W.S. Merwin, and on and on." No matter what you study, Princeton is an "intellectually challenging place," and the student experience is "intense in almost every way." Hard work pays off, though "the academic caliber of the school is unparalleled," and a Princeton education is "magnificently rewarding."

Life

Princeton students "tend to participate in a lot of different activities, from varsity sports (recruits), intramural sports (high school athletes), and more academically restricted activities like autonomous vehicle design club, Engineers Without Borders, and the literary magazine." In and out of the classroom, there are a "billion opportunities to do what you know you love" on the Princeton campus, from performance to sports to research. "Princeton offers a lot of different opportunities to relax and de-stress," including "sporting events, concerts, recreational facilities," "a movie theater that frequently screens current films for free," and "arts and crafts at the student center." For some, social life is centered along Prospect Avenue, where "Princeton's eating clubs are lined up like ten booze-soaked ducklings in a row." These eating clubs—private houses that serve as social clubs and cafeterias for upperclassmen—"play a large role in the social scene at the university." On the weekends, "The eating clubs are extremely popular for partying, chatting, drinking, and dancing"—not to mention, "free beer." "The campus is gorgeous year-round;" however, when students need a break from the college atmosphere, "There's NJ Transit if you want to go to New York, Philly, or even just the local mall."

Student Body

It's not surprising that most undergraduates are "driven, competitive, and obsessed with perfection." "Academics come first," and Princeton students are typified by dedication to their studies and "a tendency to overwork." "Almost everyone at Princeton is involved with something other than school about which they are extremely passionate," and most have "at least one distinct, remarkable talent." "It's fairly easy for most people to find a good group of friends with whom they have something in common," and many students get involved in one of the "infinite number of clubs" on campus. Superficially, "The preppy Ivy League stereotype" is reflected in the student population, and many students are "well-spoken," "dress nicely," and stay in shape. A student jokes, "Going to Princeton is like being in a contest to see who can be the biggest nerd while simultaneously appearing least nerdy."

FINANCIAL AID: 609-258-3330 • E-MAIL: UAOFFICE@PRINCETON.EDU • WEBSITE: WWW.PRINCETON.EDU

THE PRINCETON REVIEW SAYS

Admissions

Very important factors considered include: Class rank, application essay, academic GPA, recommendation(s), rigor of secondary school record, standardized test scores, character/personal qualities, talent/ability. *Important factors considered include:* Extracurricular activities. *Other factors considered include:* Alumni/ae relation, first generation, geographical residence, interview, racial/ethnic status, volunteer work, work experience. SAT or ACT required; ACT with writing component required. TOEFL required of all international applicants. High school diploma or equivalent is not required. *Academic units recommended:* 4 English, 4 mathematics, 4 science (2 science labs), 4 foreign language, 2 social studies, 2 history, 1 visual/performing arts.

Financial Aid

Students should submit: FAFSA, institution's own financial aid form. The Princeton Review suggests that all financial aid forms be submitted as soon as possible after January 1. *Need-based scholarships/grants offered:* Federal Pell, SEOG, state scholarships/grants, private scholarships, the school's own gift aid. *Loan aid offered:* Direct Subsidized Stafford, Direct Unsubsidized Stafford, Direct PLUS, Federal Perkins, college/university loans from institutional funds. Applicants will be notified of awards on or about April 1. Federal Work-Study Program available. Institutional employment available. Highest amount earned per year from on-campus jobs $3,500. Off-campus job opportunities are good.

The Inside Word

Not surprisingly, admission to Princeton is highly selective. Only about nine percent of applicants are accepted, and these students usually rank at the top of their high school class. Prospective students should prepare for Princeton by excelling in honors, AP, and upper-level coursework during high school. The application materials and personal essays are carefully read and evaluated, so students should also allocate time to prepare their applications. Admission to Princeton comes with a great deal of prestige, and to make the deal even sweeter, Princeton's remarkable no-loan financial aid program means that every student has 100 percent of their financial need met, without student loans.

THE SCHOOL SAYS ". . ."

From the Admissions Office

"Methods of instruction [at Princeton] vary widely, but common to all areas is a strong emphasis on individual responsibility and the free interchange of ideas. This is displayed most notably in the wide use of preceptorials and seminars, in the provision of independent study for all upperclass students and qualified underclass students, and in the availability of a series of special programs to meet a range of individual interests. The undergraduate college encourages the student to be an independent seeker of information and to assume responsibility for gaining both knowledge and judgment that will strengthen later contributions to society. Two hallmarks of the academic experience are the junior paper and senior thesis, which allow students the opportunity to pursue original research and scholarship in a field of their choosing.

"Princeton offers a distinctive financial aid program that provides grants, which do not have to be repaid, rather than loans. Princeton meets the full demonstrated financial need of all students—domestic and international—offered admission. About sixty percent of Princeton's undergraduates receive financial aid.

"All applicants must submit results for both the SAT as well as SAT Subject Tests in two different subject areas."

SELECTIVITY	
Admissions Rating	99
# of applicants	27,189
% of applicants accepted	9
% of acceptees attending	57
# accepting a place on wait list	869
# admitted from wait list	19

FRESHMAN PROFILE	
Range SAT Critical Reading	700–790
Range SAT Math	710–800
Range SAT Writing	700–790
Range ACT Composite	31–34
Average HS GPA	3.9
% graduated top 10% of class	93
% graduated top 25% of class	99
% graduated top 50% of class	100

DEADLINES	
Early action	
Deadline	11/1
Notification	12/15
Regular	
Priority	12/15
Deadline	1/1
Notification	3/31
Nonfall registration?	no

FINANCIAL FACTS	
Financial Aid Rating	99
Annual tuition	$38,650
Room and board	$12,630
Books and supplies	$1,200
% needy frosh rec. need-based scholarship or grant aid	100
% needy UG rec. need-based scholarship or grant aid	100
% needy frosh rec. need-based self-help aid	100
% needy UG rec. need-based self-help aid	100
% frosh rec. any financial aid	59
% UG rec. any financial aid	59
% UG borrow to pay for school	24
Average cumulative indebtedness	$5,330
% frosh need fully met	100
% ugrads need fully met	100
Average % of frosh need met	100
Average % of ugrad need met	100

PROVIDENCE COLLEGE

HARKINS 222, PROVIDENCE, RI 02918 • ADMISSIONS: 401-865-2535 • FAX: 401-865-2826

CAMPUS LIFE

Quality of Life Rating	**69**
Fire Safety Rating	**98**
Green Rating	**69**
Type of school	private
Affiliation	Roman Catholic
Environment	city

STUDENTS

Total undergrad enrollment	3,840
% male/female	42/58
% from out of state	87
% from public high school	57
% frosh live on campus	97
% African American	4
% Asian	1
% Caucasian	76
% Hispanic	4
% international	2
# of countries represented	28

SURVEY SAYS . . .

Diversity lacking on campus
Everyone loves the Friars
Intramural sports are popular
Frats and sororities are unpopular or nonexistent
Student government is popular
Lots of beer drinking
Hard liquor is popular

ACADEMICS

Academic Rating	**78**
% students returning for sophomore year	90
% students graduating within 4 years	81
% students graduating within 6 years	85
Calendar	semester
Student/faculty ratio	12:1
Profs interesting rating	74
Profs accessible rating	75
Most classes have	20–29 students
Most lab/discussion sessions have	20–29 students

MOST POPULAR MAJORS

biology/biological sciences; business administration and management; marketing/marketing management

APPLICANTS ALSO LOOK AT AND OFTEN PREFER

Boston College, Tufts University, College of the Holy Cross, Georgetown University, University of Richmond, University of Notre Dame

AND SOMETIMES PREFER

Boston University, Villanova University, Loyola University Maryland, Northeastern University

AND RARELY PREFER

St. Anselm College, University of Scranton, Stonehill College, University of Massachusetts Amherst, Fordham University, University of Connecticut, Fairfield University

STUDENTS SAY ". . ."

Academics

"Governed by the thought of St. Thomas Aquinas," Providence College is "a tight-knit community of well-rounded, charismatic, and intelligent kids" benefiting from "a definite emphasis on a Catholic intellectual approach to the world." Nowhere is that approach more evident then in PC's "well-rounded core curriculum," one student writes. The cornerstone of the curriculum is the Development of Western Civilization course sequence, "a great asset to the school" that "produces students who have an awareness of the West's cultural heritage." Outside of the core, students flock to business and marketing, premedical studies, and education programs; a "great political science program" is also popular among students. Students report that "PC is full of wonderful professors, very genuine people who want to share their knowledge…and help their students to become thoughtful and conscientious adults." Likewise, their classmates "are caring individuals who are…willing to go the extra-mile for their peers." The result is a "sense of community—the smaller campus and student body mean that you see familiar faces every day, definitely something that comforts new students" and encourages them to participate in the life of the campus. As one student sums up, "PC in a nutshell is thinking about Kant, Hegel, or Dostoevsky, listening to Taylor Swift, making lifelong relationships and getting involved in student-run clubs."

Life

Life at PC can get a bit "monotonous during the week" when students "are engrossed in their work," but campus life "changes dramatically when the weekend arrives." "Most everyone likes to party Thursday, Friday, and Saturday night (and some even during the week)," with a typical night starting at a bar. Seniors usually "go to McPhail's, the on-campus bar") and ending at a party in off-campus houses "after the bars close." Basketball and hockey games "are big school events," and many students are "very involved in clubs, some of the most popular being Student Congress, Friars Club, Board of Programmers, and Board of Multicultural Student Affairs." Intramurals are also "very popular at PC." Students love venturing out into hometown Providence, "a great city with so many options." "There is a great mall about ten minutes from campus with a movie theater and an Imax," as well as "great restaurants" and "a lot of other colleges in the area." Getting to these places is "easy," "as PC students can take the RIPTA bus for free with their student ID card." While most here like to have fun, most also know when to stop. "Whenever I visit the library it is full, and I hardly find a place to sit, and this is not because the library is too small," one student warns.

Student Body

The Providence College population is largely "white and Catholic from New England, New York, or New Jersey." There is "not a great amount of diversity" in this "preppy," "sheltered" crowd of kids. "Everyone is the same," one student cautions. "Girls all have Vera Bradley bags, [and] every student has a North Face jacket." Students tend to be "very focused on their academics while remaining highly involved in extracurricular activities and volunteerism" and very career-minded; most "will probably work in the business world upon graduation." The number of international students here "is quite small," but they "fit in perfectly with the rest of the American students," according to one international student.

FINANCIAL AID: 401-865-2286 • E-MAIL: PCADMISS@PROVIDENCE.EDU • WEBSITE: WWW.PROVIDENCE.EDU

THE PRINCETON REVIEW SAYS

Admissions

Very important factors considered include: Academic GPA, recommendation(s), rigor of secondary school record. *Important factors considered include:* Application essay, character/personal qualities, extracurricular activities. *Other factors considered include:* Class rank, standardized test scores, alumni/ae relation, first generation, geographical residence, level of applicant's interest, racial/ethnic status, state residency, talent/ability, volunteer work, work experience. ACT with or without writing component accepted. TOEFL required of all international applicants. High school diploma is required and GED is not accepted. *Academic units required:* 4 English, 4 mathematics, 3 science (2 science labs), 3 foreign language, 2 social studies, 2 history. *Academic units recommended:* 4 English, 4 mathematics, 4 science (2 science labs), 3 foreign language, 2 social studies, 2 history.

Financial Aid

Students should submit: FAFSA, CSS/Financial Aid PROFILE, business/farm supplement. Regular filing deadline is February 1. The Princeton Review suggests that all financial aid forms be submitted as soon as possible after January 1. *Need-based scholarships/grants offered:* Federal Pell, SEOG, state scholarships/grants, private scholarships, the school's own gift aid, Federal Academic Competitive Grant/Smart Grant. *Loan aid offered:* Direct Subsidized Stafford, Direct Unsubsidized Stafford, Direct PLUS, Federal Perkins. Applicants will be notified of awards on or about April 1. Federal Work-Study Program available. Institutional employment available. Highest amount earned per year from on-campus jobs $6,500. Off-campus job opportunities are good.

The Inside Word

Few schools can claim a more transparent admissions process than Providence College. The admissions section of the school's website includes a voluminous blog authored by the assistant dean of admissions. Surf on over to http://providence-admission.ning.com/profiles/blog/list?user=14a913c5rthjg and learn everything you could possibly want to know about the how, what, when, and why of Providence admissions. Providence has a test-optional policy, meaning applicants aren't required to submit standardized test scores.

THE SCHOOL SAYS ". . ."

From the Admissions Office

"Infused with the history, tradition, and learning of a 700-year-old Catholic teaching order, the Dominican Friars, Providence College offers a value-affirming environment where students are challenged on every level—body, mind, heart, and soul. Providence College offers forty-nine majors leading to baccalaureate degrees in business, education, the sciences, arts, and humanities. Our faculty is noted for a strong commitment to teaching. A close student/faculty relationship allows for in-depth classwork, independent research projects, and detailed career exploration. While noted for the physical facilities and academic opportunities associated with larger universities, Providence also fosters personal growth through a small, spirited, family-like atmosphere that encourages involvement in student activities and athletics.

"Submission of standardized test scores is optional for students applying for admission. This policy change allows each student to decide whether they wish to have their standardized test results considered as part of their application for admission. Students who choose not to submit SAT or ACT test scores will not be penalized in the review for admission. Additional details about the test-optional policy can be found on our website at www.providence.edu/admission/Pages/test-optional-policy.aspx."

SELECTIVITY

Admissions Rating	87
# of applicants	8,398
% of applicants accepted	67
% of acceptees attending	20
# accepting a place on wait list	1,865
# admitted from wait list	429

FRESHMAN PROFILE

Range SAT Critical Reading	520–630
Range SAT Math	530–640
Range SAT Writing	540–640
Range ACT Composite	23–28
Minimum paper TOEFL	550
Minimum web-based TOEFL	80
Average HS GPA	3.4
% graduated top 10% of class	37
% graduated top 25% of class	66
% graduated top 50% of class	95

DEADLINES

Early action	
Deadline	11/1
Notification	1/1
Regular	
Deadline	1/15
Notification	4/1
Nonfall registration?	yes

FINANCIAL FACTS

Financial Aid Rating	83
Annual tuition	$40,150
Room and board	$12,140
Required fees	$825
Books and supplies	$900
% needy frosh rec. need-based scholarship or grant aid	95
% needy UG rec. need-based scholarship or grant aid	99
% needy frosh rec. non-need-based scholarship or grant aid	9
% needy UG rec. non-need-based scholarship or grant aid	9
% needy frosh rec. need-based self-help aid	92
% needy UG rec. need-based self-help aid	88
% frosh rec. any financial aid	81
% UG rec. any financial aid	85
% UG borrow to pay for school	74
Average cumulative indebtedness	$32,850
% frosh need fully met	44
% ugrads need fully met	40
Average % of frosh need met	87
Average % of ugrad need met	83

PURDUE UNIVERSITY—WEST LAFAYETTE

1080 SCHLEMAN HALL, WEST LAFAYETTE, IN 47907-2050 • ADMISSIONS: 765-494-1776 • FAX: 765-494-0544

CAMPUS LIFE

Quality of Life Rating	**85**
Fire Safety Rating	**83**
Green Rating	**90**
Type of school	public
Environment	town

STUDENTS

Total undergrad enrollment	30,766
% male/female	57/43
% from out of state	30
% frosh live on campus	29
# of fraternities	50
# of sororities	31
% African American	4
% Asian	5
% Caucasian	70
% Hispanic	3
% international	15
# of countries represented	124

SURVEY SAYS . . .

Great computer facilities
Great food on campus
Students are happy
Everyone loves the Boilermakers
Student publications are popular

ACADEMICS

Academic Rating	**74**
% students returning for sophomore year	91
% students graduating within 4 years	42
% students graduating within 6 years	69
Calendar	semester
Student/faculty ratio	14:1
Profs interesting rating	71
Profs accessible rating	76
Most classes have	20–29 students
Most lab/discussion sessions have	20–29 students

MOST POPULAR MAJORS

biology/biological sciences; family and consumer sciences/human sciences; mechanical engineering

APPLICANTS ALSO LOOK AT AND SOMETIMES PREFER

Indiana University—Bloomington, Rose-Hulman Institute of Technology, University of Illinois at Urbana-Champaign, Valparaiso University

STUDENTS SAY ". . ."

Academics

When people think of Purdue University, what usually comes to mind is its "outstanding" engineering and agricultural programs, but students pursuing other degrees want you to know there are "many other prestigious majors." There are "an abundance of professors and programs…in areas other than engineering that are top-notch," such as liberal arts, education, nursing, business, and hotel management. Regardless of your major, "Purdue prepares students to be leaders by helping them grow personally and professionally during their collegiate years through a combination of strong academic programs, leadership opportunities, and social activities." It provides "one-of-a-kind experiences in research, professors, and organizations." The registration process has improved recently, but many students still voice frustration about some of the professors, calling them "hit or miss." A computer graphics technology major says, "There are enough foreign professors who are hard to understand that it sometimes makes things harder, but most professors are knowledgeable, passionate, fun, and easy to work with." One student says that while "the first year, the professors are a little harder to contact," in the upper years, "the professors are surprisingly engaged with the students and encourage them to succeed not only academically but in obtaining experiences (lab and intern) as well." Ultimately, many students think Purdue prepares them "to be leaders by helping them grow personally and professionally…through a combination of strong academic programs, leadership opportunities, and social activities."

Life

With its large student body, life at Purdue is "whatever you want to make it… There are art galleries, concerts, plays, community service, sports, etc." More than a few students say that though people "study during the week, once Thursday comes people are pretty into partying." There's "a large Greek population on campus, and it is a huge school, so parties are fairly prevalent on weekends and sometimes even during the week. A lot of people drink, but certainly not everyone. There are plenty of organized nonalcoholic events on campus as well as off." "Boilermaker pride" runs deep, and "Big Ten sports are huge…but not so huge that those who are uninterested in sports feel left out." Tailgating parties are popular, as well as "breakfast club where students dress up in costumes before a home football game and go out to the bars around 7:00 A.M.!" An agricultural economics student says she participates in "a wide variety of activities from concerts to international food festivals," and another notes that "a lot of musical performances and Broadway shows," come to the area. Lafayette, "has plenty of restaurants, movie theaters, bowling, and shopping," but those who find it "kind of boring" appreciate that "Chicago and Indianapolis are also near enough for day trips!"

Student Body

Students are "very relaxed and friendly," despite always being "aware of their obligations, be it for school or one of the student organizations that they may be involved with." The majority of students come from Indiana, and are "conservative, but not radically conservative. They are what you expect from twenty-somethings in the Midwest." Happily, students think Purdue's size means "that no matter who you are or where your interests may lie, you will be able to find another group of students that share similar interests." "The Greek System is pretty big here, but by no means is that necessary for someone to fit in," and the same goes for sports. Some say that "it is true that science and engineering majors sometimes look down on other students," a growing number of others say "The technical majors do not think that other majors are less intelligent. Campus life affords a mutual respect, and though there is joking around, everyone understands that having a Purdue degree is prestigious, no matter what their major is titled."

FINANCIAL AID: 765-494-0998 • E-MAIL: ADMISSIONS@PURDUE.EDU • WEBSITE: WWW.PURDUE.EDU

THE PRINCETON REVIEW SAYS

Admissions

Very important factors considered include: Application essay, rigor of secondary school record, standardized test scores. *Important factors considered include:* Class rank, academic GPA. *Other factors considered include:* Recommendation(s), alumni/ae relation, character/personal qualities, extracurricular activities, first generation, state residency, volunteer work, work experience. SAT or ACT required; ACT with writing component required. TOEFL required of all international applicants. High school diploma is required and GED is accepted. *Academic units required:* 4 English, 4 mathematics, 3 science (3 science labs), 2 foreign language, 3 social studies.

Financial Aid

Students should submit: FAFSA. Regular filing deadline is March 1. The Princeton Review suggests that all financial aid forms be submitted as soon as possible after January 1. *Need-based scholarships/grants offered:* Federal Pell, SEOG, state scholarships/grants, private scholarships, the school's own gift aid, Federal Academic Competitiveness Grant (ACG) and National SMART Grant Program. *Loan aid offered:* Direct Subsidized Stafford, Direct Unsubsidized Stafford, Direct PLUS, Federal Perkins, college/university loans from institutional funds. Applicants will be notified of awards on or about April 15. Federal Work-Study Program available. Institutional employment available. Off-campus job opportunities are good.

The Inside Word

Purdue will consider your class rank when reviewing your application (along with your grades, test scores, and application essay, of course). Don't panic if you're not valedictorian—admissions officers look at your rank in the context of your class choices as well as your high school's size and rigor.

THE SCHOOL SAYS ". . ."

From the Admissions Office

"Although it is one of America's largest universities, Purdue does not 'feel' big to its students. The campus is very compact when compared to universities with similar enrollment. Purdue is a comprehensive university with an international reputation in a wide range of academic fields. A strong work ethic prevails at Purdue. As a member of the Big Ten, Purdue has a strong and diverse athletic program. Purdue offers more than 900 clubs and organizations. The residence halls and Greek community offer many participatory activities for students. Numerous convocations and lectures are presented each year. Purdue is all about people, and allowing students to grow academically as well as socially, preparing them for the real world.

"Applicants seeking admission are required to have their SAT or ACT test score sent from the testing agency. Purdue accepts either test, will use the best score, and requires a writing score.

"To be considered for the full range of merit-based scholarships, students must apply by November 15."

SELECTIVITY	
Admissions Rating	**86**
# of applicants	29,513
% of applicants accepted	68
% of acceptees attending	33
# accepting a place on wait list	190

FRESHMAN PROFILE	
Range SAT Critical Reading	490–610
Range SAT Math	550–690
Range SAT Writing	500–610
Range ACT Composite	24–30
Minimum paper TOEFL	550
Minimum web-based TOEFL	79
Average HS GPA	3.6
% graduated top 10% of class	39
% graduated top 25% of class	74
% graduated top 50% of class	97

DEADLINES	
Regular	
Priority	3/1
Notification	12/7
Nonfall registration?	yes

FINANCIAL FACTS	
Financial Aid Rating	**83**
Annual in-state tuition	$8,893
Annual out-state tuition	$27,061
Room and board	$9,510
Required fees	$585
Books and supplies	$1,330
% needy frosh rec. need-based scholarship or grant aid	60
% needy UG rec. need-based scholarship or grant aid	62
% needy frosh rec. non-need-based scholarship or grant aid	45
% needy UG rec. non-need-based scholarship or grant aid	37
% needy frosh rec. need-based self-help aid	82
% needy UG rec. need-based self-help aid	89
% UG borrow to pay for school	54
Average cumulative indebtedness	$27,286
% frosh need fully met	45
% ugrads need fully met	40
Average % of frosh need met	94
Average % of ugrad need met	95

Quinnipiac University

275 Mount Carmel Avenue, Hamden, CT 06518 • Admissions: 203-582-8600 • Fax: 203-582-8906

CAMPUS LIFE

Quality of Life Rating	69
Fire Safety Rating	97
Green Rating	77
Type of school	private
Environment	town

STUDENTS

Total undergrad enrollment	6,155
% male/female	38/62
% from out of state	80
% from public high school	70
% frosh live on campus	96
# of fraternities	4
# of sororities	6
% African American	4
% Asian	3
% Caucasian	79
% Hispanic	7
% international	1
# of countries represented	23

SURVEY SAYS . . .

Great computer facilities
Diversity lacking on campus
Low cost of living
Hard liquor is popular

ACADEMICS

Academic Rating	78
% students graduating within 4 years	70
% students graduating within 6 years	77
Calendar	semester
Student/faculty ratio	12:1
Profs interesting rating	78
Profs accessible rating	77
Most classes have	10–19 students
Most lab/discussion sessions have	10–19 students

MOST POPULAR MAJORS

business/commerce; physical therapy/therapist; psychology

APPLICANTS ALSO LOOK AT AND OFTEN PREFER

Boston University, Villanova University, University of Connecticut

AND SOMETIMES PREFER

Fairfield University, Northeastern University, University of Delaware, University of Massachusetts Amherst, Marist College

AND RARELY PREFER

Sacred Heart University, Ithaca College

STUDENTS SAY ". . ."

Academics

Located on a "beautiful" campus near New Haven, Connecticut, Quinnipiac University is a liberal arts school that "wants every student to graduate with a well-rounded education." The school "is about educating students in both their major and in general knowledge so they are prepared for life after college." Though health science and communications are the school's most notable programs, the entire university "takes pride in its academics" and is "invested in preparing students for their potential career in the best way possible." No matter your major, the school stresses that "the most important aspect is the student's undergraduate experience on the journey of finding themselves."

Since class sizes are so small, teachers "are able to engage with each student individually." The professors at Quinnipiac "really look out for the students and want them to achieve." Like any college, "There are amazing professors and terrible professors," but "looking up the reviews and trusting students' opinions" will help you know which ones to pick. Professors all "encourage discussion and bring in real-life stories," and "They are always enthusiastic to share their knowledge. They implement hands-on learning, too." Students cite "the accessibility to meet with professors during their office hours" as a huge plus. "It is very easy to get in contact with them when needed," says a student. "I have close bonds with several, and my academic experience has been nothing but enjoyable," says another. As one student sums up, "Quinnipiac University is extremely dedicated to helping students make their college experience not only beneficial, but enjoyable as well."

Life

Students at the school "value the closeness of our community and bringing everyone together," according to a student. The campus is "just plain gorgeous" ("When I came to this school I got the 'wedding dress feeling,'" says a student.), and there's a lot going on there, too. "Campus life is awesome!" There are "so many ways" of getting involved: "numerous clubs and activities, supporting the athletic teams, intramural sports, and much more." The student body is "heavily devoted" to the subjects they are involved in, and everywhere you look "friendly faces" are taking advantage of the "very programmed schedule" of events. A "good majority of the students here like to party hard Thursday through Saturday night," but if you don't like to drink or go out, the programming board "does an excellent job providing events on campus such as casino night, drive-in movies, stand-up comics, games, etc."

Despite the Quinnipiac love, there are some gripes. The living facilities "could stand to be updated," "more onsite parking" is definitely needed, and everyone pretty much universally agrees that the "food could always be better." However, people do love the duality of a "college-town feel with a city nearby," and the shuttles that run into nearby New Haven are extremely popular. The "great sports teams" also help bring together the student body, and "On Friday nights, hockey and basketball are big."

Student Body

The typical student here is a "middle- to upper-class Caucasian from the tristate area" and "a little preppy, but casual at the same time." "Students are easy to make friends with," so "It's easy to find a niche here." "Students all seem to have a place, there are so many different groups that it's hard not to find someplace for everyone," says one. "I feel like it's a good place to go if you want a balance between social life and school work," says a student. This "studious" and "well-motivated" group is usually "involved in at least one program outside of academics," but also "likes to enjoy themselves on weekends." Though Quinnipiac "is not very diverse" (unsurprising for "a school that looks like a country club"), it "is becoming more diverse." Many students are "very interested in fashion and culture."

FINANCIAL AID: 203-582-8750 • E-MAIL: ADMISSIONS@QUINNIPIAC.EDU • WEBSITE: WWW.QUINNIPIAC.EDU

THE PRINCETON REVIEW SAYS

Admissions

Very important factors considered include: Academic GPA, rigor of secondary school record. *Important factors considered include:* Class rank, application essay, standardized test scores. *Other factors considered include:* Recommendation(s), alumni/ae relation, character/personal qualities, extracurricular activities, interview, level of applicant's interest, racial/ethnic status, talent/ability, volunteer work, work experience. SAT or ACT required; ACT with writing component recommended. TOEFL required of all international applicants. High school diploma is required and GED is accepted. *Academic units required:* 4 English, 3 mathematics, 3 science (2 science labs), 2 foreign language, 2 social studies, 4 years of science and math required in PT, OT, Nursing, and PA. *Academic units recommended:* 4 English, 4 mathematics, 4 science (3 science labs), 2 foreign language, 3 social studies.

Financial Aid

Students should submit: FAFSA, CSS/Financial Aid PROFILE. Regular filing deadline is March 1. The Princeton Review suggests that all financial aid forms be submitted as soon as possible after January 1. *Need-based scholarships/grants offered:* Federal Pell, SEOG, state scholarships/grants, private scholarships, the school's own gift aid, Federal Nursing Scholarships. *Loan aid offered:* Direct Subsidized Stafford, Direct Unsubsidized Stafford, Direct PLUS, Federal Perkins, Federal Nursing, state loans. Applicants will be notified of awards on a rolling basis beginning February 15. Federal Work-Study Program available. Institutional employment available. Highest amount earned per year from on-campus jobs $2,100. Off-campus job opportunities are excellent.

The Inside Word

Quinnipiac offers early decision (deadline November 1) and also admits students on a rolling basis, a process that favors those who get their applications in early. Programs in physical therapy, nursing, and physician assistant are quite competitive. The school strongly recommends that those seeking spots in these programs apply no later than November 15.

THE SCHOOL SAYS ". . ."

From the Admissions Office

"Quinnipiac today is 'three settings, one university,' with an undergraduate population growing to 6,500, many of whom remain at QU for the ever expanding graduate programs, and a continuing focus on our core values: academic excellence, a student oriented environment and a strong sense of community.

"The Mount Carmel campus, the academic home to all undergraduates with traditional, suite and apartment housing for freshmen and sophomores, is 250 acres in a stunning setting adjacent to Sleeping Giant state park. The nearby 250 acre York Hill campus is home to juniors and seniors in apartments with breathtaking views, a lodge style student center, covered parking, and the TD Bank sports center with twin arenas for hockey and basketball. The 100 acre North Haven campus, just four miles distant, is the home to graduate programs in Health Sciences, and Education, and a soon to open Medical School (est. opening 2013/2014).

"Academic initiatives such as the honors program, 'writing across the curriculum', QU seminar series, extensive internship experiences, study abroad opportunities and a highly regarded emerging leaders student-life program form the foundation for excellence in business, communication, health sciences, nursing, engineering, education, liberal arts, and law.

"State of the art facilities include the Financial Technology Center, HD fully digital production studio, extensive health science labs, recreation and sports fields and arenas. More than 100 student organizations, twenty-one Division I teams, community service, student publications, and a strong student government offer a variety of outside-of-class experiences."

SELECTIVITY	
Admissions Rating	85
# of applicants	18,642
% of applicants accepted	63
% of acceptees attending	13
# accepting a place on wait list	1,640
# admitted from wait list	180

FRESHMAN PROFILE	
Range SAT Critical Reading	520–590
Range SAT Math	530–610
Range SAT Writing	540–610
Range ACT Composite	23–27
Minimum paper TOEFL	550
Minimum web-based TOEFL	77
Average HS GPA	3.4
% graduated top 10% of class	25
% graduated top 25% of class	66
% graduated top 50% of class	92

DEADLINES	
Early decision	
Deadline	11/1
Notification	12/1
Regular	
Priority	2/1
Nonfall registration?	yes

FINANCIAL FACTS	
Financial Aid Rating	69
Annual tuition	$36,510
Room and board	$13,610
Required fees	$1,490
Books and supplies	$800
% needy frosh rec. need-based scholarship or grant aid	94
% needy UG rec. need-based scholarship or grant aid	97
% needy frosh rec. non-need-based scholarship or grant aid	48
% needy UG rec. non-need-based scholarship or grant aid	44
% needy frosh rec. need-based self-help aid	82
% needy UG rec. need-based self-help aid	85
% frosh rec. any financial aid	72
% UG rec. any financial aid	70
% UG borrow to pay for school	69
Average cumulative indebtedness	$39,500
% frosh need fully met	15
% ugrads need fully met	13
Average % of frosh need met	62
Average % of ugrad need met	64

Randolph College

2500 Rivermont Avenue, Lynchburg, VA 24503-1555 • Admissions: 434-947-8100 • Fax: 434-947-8996

CAMPUS LIFE

Quality of Life Rating	**84**
Fire Safety Rating	**89**
Green Rating	**75**
Type of school	private
Affiliation	Methodist
Environment	city

STUDENTS

Total undergrad enrollment	571
% male/female	34/66
% from out of state	48
% from public high school	81
% frosh live on campus	97
% African American	9
% Asian	2
% Caucasian	69
% Hispanic	6
% international	12
# of countries represented	33

SURVEY SAYS . . .

No one cheats
Great computer facilities
Diverse student types on campus
Different types of students interact
Dorms are like palaces
Campus feels safe
Frats and sororities are unpopular or nonexistent
Student government is popular

ACADEMICS

Academic Rating	**89**
% students returning for sophomore year	75
% students graduating within 4 years	63
% students graduating within 6 years	64
Calendar	semester
Student/faculty ratio	8:1
Profs interesting rating	97
Profs accessible rating	96
Most classes have	fewer than 10 students
Most lab/discussion sessions have	fewer than 10 students

MOST POPULAR MAJORS

biology/biological sciences; political science and government; psychology

APPLICANTS ALSO LOOK AT AND OFTEN PREFER

University of Virginia, James Madison University

AND SOMETIMES PREFER

Sweet Briar College, College of William and Mary

AND RARELY PREFER

Virginia Tech, Hollins University, Randolph-Macon College

STUDENTS SAY "..."

Academics

Rest assured, at Randolph College, "You're not just a number; you matter as an individual." Indeed, this "small, tight-knit community" instantly "makes you feel welcome." Additionally, students at Randolph are grateful they attend a college that "promotes self discovery, personal growth, and individuality." Further, "Small class sizes" allow for an "emphasis on student-professor relationships," a hallmark of a Randolph education. One undergrad happily confirms, "My academic experience has been challenging, there's no doubt, but the professor support has made that challenge enjoyable and exciting." A fellow student agrees, sharing, "My professors are excellent. Everyone I have had here has been supremely knowledgeable, understanding and helpful to students. The number one goal is always to make students better thinkers." Finally, as this student gushes, "My professors are amazing! Their passion for the subject matter and course content is infectious. I look forward to each class each day and feel confident in my education. Learning is interesting and fun here, and professors are eager to answer questions and provide resources to supplement lectures and experiments. Often professors list their home phone numbers on syllabi to allow students to contact them outside of office hours. Every professor replies to e-mail quickly, and professors are all very easy to communicate with in the classroom and one-on-one."

Life

According to many undergrads, "Life at Randolph is always busy and exciting." As one ecstatic student quickly asserts, "I don't think I have [been] bored [since] the day I stepped foot on this campus." And why would you be? Indeed, there are "a wide variety of clubs and organizations [in which] to become involved." Moreover, there are "many sports teams and exciting competitions to watch" as well as intramurals, which "offer a chance for non-athletes to" participate." In addition, there are a myriad of "parties and dances...sponsored by various organizations." These events are typically well-attended by students, as "they never disappoint." And for those undergrads looking for an activity a little more out of the box, there's "even a game called HumansvsZombies where students dress up and try to 'turn people into zombies' with Nerf guns. It's a lot of fun." Randolph is also home to many proud traditions and students love to partake. An insider reveals, "The even-odd class rivalry is definitely one popular school tradition. Skeller Sings are one of the events where the even spirit society (ETAs) and odd spirit society (Gammas) will sing (read: shout) songs at each other and try to create distractions while the other group sings." Finally, when students want to look beyond the campus for fun, they can "go hiking, swimming, and boating at all the lakes, rivers, and trails. [Indeed] there is a lot of nature and history surrounding the Lynchburg area."

Student Body

Undergrads at Randolph emphatically state that there's no typical student to be found wandering around campus. As one knowing undergrad shares, "Students vary widely in background and personality, preferences, [and] habits." Additionally, a "considerable percentage of the student body is comprised of international students," which certainly adds to the diversity of the school. Of course, if pressed to throw out some adjectives, Randolph undergrads will likely say that their peers are "hardworking, artistic, and caring." They are also "intelligent," "unafraid to speak their minds," and "committed to doing excellent work." Fortunately, "Being such a small campus, it is hard not [to] develop lots of friends from several different social groups," and certainly, "Campus traditions help form a very strong sense of community here." Or, as one content undergrad simply states, "Everyone gets along fairly well and it's not too hard to fit in when there aren't really any labels for people."

FINANCIAL AID: 434-947-8128 • E-MAIL: ADMISSIONS@RANDOLPHCOLLEGE.EDU • WEBSITE: WWW.RANDOLPHCOLLEGE.EDU

THE PRINCETON REVIEW SAYS

Admissions

Very important factors considered include: Academic GPA, rigor of secondary school record, character/personal qualities. *Important factors considered include:* Class rank, application essay, recommendation(s), standardized test scores, extracurricular activities. *Other factors considered include:* Alumni/ae relation, first generation, interview, level of applicant's interest, talent/ability, volunteer work, work experience. SAT or ACT required; ACT with or without writing component accepted. TOEFL required of all international applicants. High school diploma is required and GED is accepted. *Academic units required:* 4 English, 3 mathematics, 2 science (2 science labs), 3 foreign language, 2 history, 2 academic electives.

Financial Aid

Students should submit: FAFSA, state aid form. The Princeton Review suggests that all financial aid forms be submitted as soon as possible after January 1. *Need-based scholarships/grants offered:* Federal Pell, SEOG, state scholarships/grants, private scholarships, the school's own gift aid. *Loan aid offered:* Direct Subsidized Stafford, Direct Unsubsidized Stafford, Direct PLUS, Federal Perkins, college/university loans from institutional funds, private. Applicants will be notified of awards on a rolling basis beginning March 1. Federal Work-Study Program available. Institutional employment available. Off-campus job opportunities are good.

The Inside Word

Officers at Randolph College take a fairly traditional approach to their admissions decisions. Certainly your transcript and test scores hold the most weight. However, recommendations, personal essays, and extracurricular activities are also taken into consideration, so it's best not to slack off any facet of your application.

THE SCHOOL SAYS ". . ."

From the Admissions Office

"Students who thrive in a close-knit community that values original thinking and research will enjoy the educational and cultural environment at Randolph College where they may earn a BA, BS, or BFA degree.

"Nationally ranked for both its academic programs and affordability, Randolph College offers students the best features of an honors education with a wide range of majors and an emphasis on developing intercultural competence. Embedded within the strong, liberal arts foundation are ample opportunities for study abroad, leadership roles, working closely with faculty on research, and real-world experience through internships and service learning. All students are encouraged to pursue and achieve goals with personal meaning.

"A graduate of Randolph College understands the intellectual foundations of the arts, sciences, and humanities and has developed critical skills to learn, adapt, and succeed in a rapidly changing global environment. The college's strong emphasis on writing enables students to communicate clearly and persuasively, and the diverse student population and study abroad programs enable students to see and live through the eyes of another culture. The long-standing and distinctive honor system is a central part of daily life at Randolph and adds to the already close-knit community feel.

"A member of the Old Dominion Athletic Conference and IHSA (Randolph has a 100-acre riding center), Randolph enables scholar-athletes to excel and participate in a variety of sports while focusing on academics. Located in the heart of Virginia near the Blue Ridge Mountains, Randolph College's campus is part of the growing college town of Lynchburg with its abundant cultural, entertainment, and recreational opportunities."

SELECTIVITY	
Admissions Rating	**78**
# of applicants	979
% of applicants accepted	71
% of acceptees attending	25
FRESHMAN PROFILE	
Range SAT Critical Reading	490–620
Range SAT Math	480–620
Range SAT Writing	470–610
Range ACT Composite	20–25
Minimum paper TOEFL	550
Minimum web-based TOEFL	79
Average HS GPA	3.5
% graduated top 10% of class	27
% graduated top 25% of class	55
% graduated top 50% of class	96
DEADLINES	
Early action	
Deadline	12/1
Notification	1/1
Regular	
Priority	12/1
Deadline	3/1
Nonfall registration?	yes
FINANCIAL FACTS	
Financial Aid Rating	**82**
Annual tuition	$29,866
Room and board	$10,386
Required fees	$570
Books and supplies	$1,000
% needy frosh rec. need-based scholarship or grant aid	100
% needy UG rec. need-based scholarship or grant aid	99
% needy frosh rec. non-need-based scholarship or grant aid	17
% needy UG rec. non-need-based scholarship or grant aid	14
% needy frosh rec. need-based self-help aid	83
% needy UG rec. need-based self-help aid	85
% frosh rec. any financial aid	99
% UG rec. any financial aid	96
% UG borrow to pay for school	67
Average cumulative indebtedness	$29,842
% frosh need fully met	23
% ugrads need fully met	20
Average % of frosh need met	79
Average % of ugrad need met	77

REED COLLEGE

3203 SOUTHEAST WOODSTOCK BOULEVARD, PORTLAND, OR 97202-8199 • ADMISSIONS: 503-777-7511 • FAX: 503-777-7553

CAMPUS LIFE

Quality of Life Rating	**95**
Fire Safety Rating	**90**
Green Rating	**79**
Type of school	private
Environment	metropolis

STUDENTS

Total undergrad enrollment	1,418
% male/female	44/56
% from out of state	93
% from public high school	59
% frosh live on campus	98
% African American	2
% Asian	6
% Caucasian	56
% Hispanic	4
% international	5
# of countries represented	46

SURVEY SAYS . . .

Great computer facilities
Students aren't religious
Dorms are like palaces
Campus feels safe
Frats and sororities are unpopular or nonexistent

ACADEMICS

Academic Rating	**99**
% students returning for sophomore year	90
% students graduating within 4 years	59
% students graduating within 6 years	79
Calendar	semester
Student/faculty ratio	10:1
Profs interesting rating	99
Profs accessible rating	99
Most classes have	10–19 students
Most lab/discussion sessions have	10–19 students

MOST POPULAR MAJORS

biology/biological sciences; English language and literature; psychology

APPLICANTS ALSO LOOK AT AND OFTEN PREFER

University of California—Berkeley, University of Chicago

AND SOMETIMES PREFER

Oberlin College, Swarthmore College

AND RARELY PREFER

Lewis & Clark College

STUDENTS SAY "..."

Academics

Reed College, "offers a serious liberal-arts education in a small, creative, community" where "intellectualism is highly respected" and students pursue "learning for learning's sake" in "a challenging academic atmosphere." "We are a collection of those weird kids in high school who had a passionate interest in learning about something and made that interest academic, even if it wasn't beforehand," one student explains. They're the sort of students who seek out an "academic rigor that definitely prepares us for graduate school and scholarly work." "Small, discussion based classes, frequent interaction with professors, and general intellectual curiosity override all other aspects of the life at Reed," where "studying and going to classes is not somehow the price to pay for staying here (with the ultimate goal being the weekend and, eventually, a diploma); rather, it is the core joy of being at Reed." Unsurprisingly, "students work incredibly hard," but "the school is there for us every step of the way. As freshmen, students meet with their humanities professors after every paper one-on-one for paper conferences." Seniors must complete a thesis project; "When writing one's senior thesis, students meet with professors one-on-one for an hour every week." It's exactly the right sort of place for students who "want to be excited about school again," says one student. "I wanted to be around other people who were both excited about academics and excited about being at a place where academics excited them. I wanted to be in a place where people didn't take themselves too seriously but took their work seriously." Welcome to Reed.

Life

Reed is an academically intense school, so "a great amount of time is spent on academics, even on the weekends" here. "Late at night, it is not uncommon to see Reedies debating the merits of Thucydides and Herodotus or discussing the financial bailout package in the library lobby, dorm common rooms, and at the hotcake house (a nearby twenty-four-hour pancake joint)," one student reports. But although "people are very involved in their studies, especially seniors and their individual theses...everyone keeps his or her own passions alive with student government, various hobbies (baking, knitting, singing, dancing), sports (rugby, ultimate Frisbee, and basketball), and often trips around the multiple neighborhoods of Portland." The city justly is celebrated for its coffee shops, restaurants, and bookstores. Annual campus traditions include Renn Fayre, "a three-day party at the end of the year at which students celebrate the completion of senior theses. Renn Fayre begins with Thesis Parade, in which seniors burn their thesis drafts in a bonfire in front of the library and then march in costume, covered in champagne and confetti through the library across the lawn to the registrar's office to turn in their [completed] theses."

Student Body

Reed students tend to be "smart, intellectually curious, and a little quirky." Politics tilt strongly to the left. One student reports, "There is virtually no political dialogue. The student body is so liberal the only dialogue is really between socialists and communists. For students who regard themselves as liberal and, consequentially, open-minded, there is very little acceptance of people who don't identify themselves as liberal or who simply like political dialogue." The student body is also "overwhelmingly Caucasian" and affluent, although students note there is "a growing population of minority students (minority in various senses) and they are making efforts constantly to establish themselves as a social presence on campus. Student groups like the Latino, Asian, and Black and African Student Unions and places like the Multicultural Resource Center offer places for support."

FINANCIAL AID: 503-777-7223 • E-MAIL: ADMISSION@REED.EDU • WEBSITE: WWW.REED.EDU

THE PRINCETON REVIEW SAYS

Admissions

Very important factors considered include: Application essay, academic GPA, rigor of secondary school record. *Important factors considered include:* Class rank, recommendation(s), standardized test scores, interview, level of applicant's interest. *Other factors considered include:* Alumni/ae relation, character/personal qualities, extracurricular activities, first generation, geographical residence, racial/ethnic status, talent/ability, volunteer work, work experience. SAT or ACT required; ACT with or without writing component accepted. TOEFL required of all international applicants. High school diploma is required and GED is accepted. *Academic units recommended:* 4 English, 4 mathematics, 3 science, 3 foreign language, 1 social studies, 3 history.

Financial Aid

Students should submit: FAFSA, institution's own financial aid form, CSS/Financial Aid PROFILE, noncustodial PROFILE. Regular filing deadline is February 1. The Princeton Review suggests that all financial aid forms be submitted as soon as possible after January 1. *Need-based scholarships/grants offered:* Federal Pell, SEOG, state scholarships/grants, private scholarships, the school's own gift aid. *Loan aid offered:* Direct Subsidized Stafford, Direct Unsubsidized Stafford, Direct PLUS, Federal Perkins. Applicants will be notified of awards on or about April 1. Federal Work-Study Program available. Institutional employment available. Highest amount earned per year from on-campus jobs $12,006.

The Inside Word

Reed admissions officers know exactly what type of student will thrive here, and that's who they seek. Being smart isn't enough to get in here. Reedies are fiercely intellectual and more concerned with academic pursuits for their own sake than for any financial rewards their educations will produce. Successful applicants demonstrate genuine intellectual curiosity as well as the aptitude to handle a demanding curriculum.

THE SCHOOL SAYS ". . ."

From the Admissions Office

"Reed is animated and energized by its seemingly paradoxical features. Reed has, for example: (1) a traditional, classical, highly structured curriculum—yet, at the same time, a progressive, free-thinking, decidedly unstructured community culture; (2) a powerful emphasis on intellectuality, serious study, and the very highest standards of academic achievement—yet, at the same time, a rich and rewarding program of recreational and extracurricular activity, including a physical education requirement; (3) a refusal to overemphasize grades—yet, third in the nation in the production of future PhDs; (4) a faculty culture absolutely dedicated to superb undergraduate teaching—yet, at the same time, a faculty culture that supports and celebrates high-level research and scholarship at the cutting edge of each academic discipline.

"Reed is not a simple place. It's a complex amalgam of diverse elements. But those elements have been chosen and developed over the years with great care. The result is an intricate—even ornate—but utterly coherent and clearly articulated architecture that has been called by at least one outside observer 'exquisite' and by another 'the most intellectual college in the country.' Reed is not for everyone. But for students who are interested both in exploring great ideas and in developing personal autonomy, it makes very good sense indeed.

"Reed accepts either the ACT or SAT and does not require SAT Subject Tests or the ACT writing exam."

SELECTIVITY

Admissions Rating	**98**
# of applicants	3,075
% of applicants accepted	43
% of acceptees attending	28
# accepting a place on wait list	620
# admitted from wait list	9
# of early decision applicants	179
# accepted early decision	94

FRESHMAN PROFILE

Range SAT Critical Reading	670–750
Range SAT Math	640–710
Range SAT Writing	660–730
Range ACT Composite	30–33
Minimum paper TOEFL	600
Minimum web-based TOEFL	100
Average HS GPA	3.9
% graduated top 10% of class	63
% graduated top 25% of class	90
% graduated top 50% of class	99

DEADLINES

Early decision	
Deadline	11/15
Notification	12/15
Regular	
Deadline	1/15
Notification	4/1
Nonfall registration?	no

FINANCIAL FACTS

Financial Aid Rating	**95**
Annual tuition	$42,540
Room and board	$11,430
Required fees	$260
Books and supplies	$950
% needy frosh rec. need-based scholarship or grant aid	87
% needy UG rec. need-based scholarship or grant aid	89
% needy frosh rec. need-based self-help aid	92
% needy UG rec. need-based self-help aid	93
% frosh rec. any financial aid	53
% UG rec. any financial aid	54
% UG borrow to pay for school	53
Average cumulative indebtedness	$16,910
% frosh need fully met	100
% ugrads need fully met	99
Average % of frosh need met	100
Average % of ugrad need met	100

Rensselaer Polytechnic Institute

110 Eighth Street, Troy, NY 12180-3590 • Admissions: 518-276-6216 • Fax: 518-276-4072

CAMPUS LIFE

Quality of Life Rating	**76**
Fire Safety Rating	**77**
Green Rating	**79**
Type of school	private
Environment	city

STUDENTS

Total undergrad enrollment	5,240
% male/female	71/29
% from out of state	69
% from public high school	73
% frosh live on campus	100
# of fraternities	32
# of sororities	5
% African American	2
% Asian	10
% Caucasian	71
% Hispanic	6
% international	5
# of countries represented	64

SURVEY SAYS . . .

Lab facilities are great
Great computer facilities
Students are happy
Frats and sororities dominate social scene
Student publications are popular

ACADEMICS

Academic Rating	**83**
% students returning for sophomore year	93
% students graduating within 4 years	60
% students graduating within 6 years	84
Calendar	semester
Student/faculty ratio	15:1
Profs interesting rating	71
Profs accessible rating	86
Most classes have	10–19 students
Most lab/discussion sessions have	10–19 students

MOST POPULAR MAJORS

business/commerce; computer engineering; electrical, electronics and communications engineering

APPLICANTS ALSO LOOK AT AND OFTEN PREFER

Massachusetts Institute of Technology, Cornell University

AND SOMETIMES PREFER

University of Rochester, Boston University, Carnegie Mellon University

AND RARELY PREFER

State University of New York at Binghamton, Rochester Institute of Technology, Syracuse University, Clarkson University, Worcester Polytechnic Institute

STUDENTS SAY ". . ."

Academics

As the nation's oldest technological university, Rensselaer Polytechnic Institute in upstate New York has a rightfully deserved reputation in the science and engineering world, having led tens of thousands of bright minds to look at "innovation and the future." "Research opportunities" and facilities are everywhere, and students are encouraged to work in interdisciplinary programs that allow them to combine scholarly work from several departments or schools. When their four years are complete, students are encouraged to take what they learn and use it for the greater good. "Why not change the world?" asks a student.

The professors at RPI are "passionate about teaching," "very accessible, and really there for the students." Though there are certainly some "dull" professors ("I've seen the good, the bad, and the ugly!" says one student), most find that the faculty is praiseworthy and "serve as great mentors for students." "My professors in my direct major are extremely hands-on and discussion-based," says a student. Thanks to the "focus on problem-solving," professors are always looking to get students involved in projects, and one of "the greatest strengths of [the] school is the resources that they offer." On top of that, the "welcoming overall community" fosters success, as "students are not extremely competitive and everyone tends to help each other out."

The school is "rigorous," but the students "do find time to enjoy the downtime when we get it." RPI is "is a place where nerds can get both an excellent education and an enjoyable four years," according to one student. The student union is entirely student-run, giving students "a lot of freedom to control our educational experience." Many of the student clubs both "suit your interests and work toward your professional career after college." All in all, "Community and knowledge drive this school to push students to excel in school and after graduation."

Life

Everyone agrees that RPI is just the right size: "The kind of size where you don't know everybody but you see ten people you know as you walk across campus (and it only takes ten minutes to walk across campus)." People at RPI "don't care how weird or different you are, they let you be." "You can be anyone you want—the kid sword-fighting with his friends in quad or an avid musician who has a 4.0," says a student. Most students do have a "nerdy" side to them, and they inherently love math/science—"Even the humanities at RPI are laced with the sweet smell of science," and "Physics equation graffiti" can be found on some walls.

Academics are definitely an important priority here, but "extracurricular activities are balanced alongside the classes, labs, homework, and studying." There are hundreds of clubs on campus (such as Engineers for a Sustainable World and the Model Railroad Society, which does model railroading of upstate New York and Vermont all circa the early- to mid-1950s), and "most people are involved in several." There are always campus events that students can attend, which range from "athletic events and cultural programs to student ensemble concerts and open mic shows." Downtown Troy has some "quaint cafes and places to explore," Albany has shopping malls, parks, and movie theaters, and a ski trip to Lake Placid is easily accomplished. "There is so much to do around here—you'll never be bored if you take the time to explore." Men's hockey games are a large part of student life here, and "Greek life accounts for about one-fourth of the undergraduate student body and is a great leadership experience and a large contributor to the social scene."

Student Body

Everyone here is pretty much without a doubt "a little bit nerdy, but friendly and helpful." This tinge of nerdiness in everyone "brings the students together and makes it a fun environment with little to no discrimination." "The typical student at my school is studious, but also social in their own way," explains a student. There is a whole spectrum of social students, which ranges "from socializing with a select few to the person that is a social butterfly," but no matter which path you choose, "People don't judge at RPI."

FINANCIAL AID: 518-276-6813 • E-MAIL: ADMISSIONS@RPI.EDU • WEBSITE: WWW.RPI.EDU

THE PRINCETON REVIEW SAYS

Admissions

Very important factors considered include: Class rank, academic GPA, rigor of secondary school record, standardized test scores. *Important factors considered include:* Application essay, recommendation(s), character/personal qualities, extracurricular activities, level of applicant's interest. *Other factors considered include:* Alumni/ae relation, geographical residence, racial/ethnic status, talent/ability, volunteer work, work experience. SAT or ACT required; ACT with writing component required. TOEFL required of all international applicants. High school diploma is required and GED is accepted. *Academic units required:* 4 English, 4 mathematics, 3 science, 2 social studies. *Academic units recommended:* 4 science, 3 social studies.

Financial Aid

Students should submit: FAFSA, CSS/Financial Aid PROFILE. The Princeton Review suggests that all financial aid forms be submitted as soon as possible after January 1. *Need-based scholarships/grants offered:* Federal Pell, SEOG, state scholarships/grants, private scholarships, the school's own gift aid, Gates Millennium Scholarship, ACG, Smart Grants. *Loan aid offered:* Direct Subsidized Stafford, Direct Unsubsidized Stafford, Direct PLUS, Federal Perkins, state loans, college/university loans from institutional funds. Applicants will be notified of awards on or about March 25. Federal Work-Study Program available. Institutional employment available. Highest amount earned per year from on-campus jobs $2,000. Off-campus job opportunities are good.

The Inside Word

Outstanding test scores and grades are pretty much a must for any applicant hopeful of impressing the RPI admissions committee. Underrepresented minorities and women—two demographics the school would like to augment—will get a little more leeway than others, but in all cases, the school is unlikely to admit anyone who lacks the skills and background to survive here.

THE SCHOOL SAYS ". . ."

From the Admissions Office

"The oldest degree-granting technological research university in North America, RPI or Rensselaer was founded in 1824 to instruct students to apply 'science to the common purposes of life.' Rensselaer offers more than 100 programs and 1,000 courses leading to bachelor's, master's, and doctoral degrees. Undergraduates pursue studies in architecture, engineering, humanities, arts, and social sciences, business and management, science, and information technology (IT). A pioneer in interactive learning, Rensselaer provides real-world, hands-on educational opportunities that cut across academic disciplines. Students have ready access to laboratories and attend classes involving lively discussion, problem solving, and faculty mentoring. The Office of First-Year Experience provides programs for students and their primary support persons that begin even before students arrive on campus. Students are able to take full advantage of Rensselaer's three unique research platforms: the $80 million state-of-the-art Center for Biotechnology and Interdisciplinary Studies (CBIS); one of the world's most powerful academic supercomputers, the Computational Center for Nanotechnology Innovations (CCNI); and the Experimental Media and Performing Arts Center (EMPAC), which encourages students to explore the intersection of science, technology, and the arts. Newly renovated residence halls, wireless computing network, and studio classrooms create a fertile environment for study and learning. Rensselaer offers recreational and fitness facilities plus numerous student-run organizations and activities, including fraternities and sororities, a newspaper, a radio station, drama and musical groups, and more than 200 clubs. In addition to intramural sports, NCAA varsity sports include Division I men's and women's ice hockey teams and twenty-one Division III men's and women's teams in thirteen sports. The East Campus Athletic Village, opened in 2009, raises the bar for student athletic facilities for varsity and non-varsity athletes alike, and includes a new football arena, basketball stadium, and sports medicine complex."

SELECTIVITY

Admissions Rating	**96**
# of applicants	14,584
% of applicants accepted	40
% of acceptees attending	21
# accepting a place on wait list	3,584
# admitted from wait list	82
# of early decision applicants	1,141
# accepted early decision	364

FRESHMAN PROFILE

Range SAT Critical Reading	620–710
Range SAT Math	670–760
Range SAT Writing	590–700
Range ACT Composite	26–30
Minimum paper TOEFL	570
Minimum web-based TOEFL	88
% graduated top 10% of class	65
% graduated top 25% of class	94
% graduated top 50% of class	99

DEADLINES

Early decision	
Deadline	11/1
Notification	12/10
Regular	
Deadline	1/15
Notification	3/12
Nonfall registration?	yes

FINANCIAL FACTS

Financial Aid Rating	**83**
Annual tuition	$41,600
Room and board	$11,975
Required fees	$1,104
Books and supplies	$2,500
% needy frosh rec. need-based scholarship or grant aid	100
% needy UG rec. need-based scholarship or grant aid	100
% needy frosh rec. non-need-based scholarship or grant aid	19
% needy UG rec. non-need-based scholarship or grant aid	11
% needy frosh rec. need-based self-help aid	99
% needy UG rec. need-based self-help aid	96
% frosh rec. any financial aid	94
% UG rec. any financial aid	95
% UG borrow to pay for school	70
Average cumulative indebtedness	$29,625
% frosh need fully met	35
% ugrads need fully met	26
Average % of frosh need met	88
Average % of ugrad need met	80

RHODES COLLEGE

2000 NORTH PARKWAY, MEMPHIS, TN 38112 • ADMISSIONS: 901-843-3700 • FAX: 901-843-3631

CAMPUS LIFE

Quality of Life Rating	**84**
Fire Safety Rating	**79**
Green Rating	**78**
Type of school	private
Affiliation	Presbyterian
Environment	metropolis

STUDENTS

Total undergrad enrollment	1,801
% male/female	40/60
% from out of state	73
% from public high school	50
% frosh live on campus	97
# of fraternities	7
# of sororities	6
% African American	7
% Asian	5
% Caucasian	75
% Hispanic	2
% Native American	1
% international	3
# of countries represented	13

SURVEY SAYS . . .

No one cheats
Great computer facilities
School is well run
Great off-campus food
Low cost of living

ACADEMICS

Academic Rating	**97**
% students returning for sophomore year	90
% students graduating within 4 years	73
Calendar	semester
Student/faculty ratio	10:1
Profs interesting rating	96
Profs accessible rating	95
Most classes have	10–19 students
Most lab/discussion sessions have	10–19 students

MOST POPULAR MAJORS

biology/biological sciences; business/commerce; English language and literature

APPLICANTS ALSO LOOK AT AND OFTEN PREFER

The University of Texas at Austin, Davidson College, Washington and Lee University, Washington University in St. Louis

AND SOMETIMES PREFER

Trinity University, Furman University, Vanderbilt University, University of Richmond, Sewanee—The University of the South

AND RARELY PREFER

Birmingham-Southern College, Millsaps College

STUDENTS SAY ". . ."

Academics

A "beautiful" campus located in the heart of Memphis, Tennessee, the "tight-knit community" of Rhodes College offers "individual study in a liberal arts mold," which involves exposing students to "as many different disciplines as possible in order to gain a broader understanding of the world." Academics here are extremely challenging, "but nothing that hard work and study time can't handle." "I have been pushed (in a good way) to the outer limits of my academic capabilities," says a sophomore. Professors are undoubtedly "one of Rhodes' best assets"—invitations to faculty members' houses for dinner are par for the course—and "truly care about our achievement, grasping the right concepts, and progressing in our education." "Professors don't just care about passing the tests, they want students to be able to take what they have learned and apply it to real life," beams a student. The "small classes" and "comprehensive honor code" only help to further students' love of the Rhodes' classroom experience. The concerned individuals making up the Rhodes administration are "not just doing a job," they are "dedicated to the mission of this college and committed to the students they serve." Though some students have had some bad experiences with administrators, most are content, and it doesn't hurt that the school just "took all of the different offices that were spread throughout campus and consolidated them into one newly-renovated building that makes any form or process/meeting much simpler."

Life

With "gothic architecture [that] will make you feel like you live in a fantasy world," the Rhodes campus is "easy on the eyes," while the food is tough on the gut ("mediocre at best" says one of the less harsh critics, of which there are many). There is a huge Greek contingent here—"frat parties on campus are always fun and wild"—and all students are sure to find their fratastic niche since "each fraternity is different." Generally speaking, the typical student schedule breaks down like this: "weekdays and nights in the library (which is beautiful, so it's not as bad as it could be), and starting Thursdays, partying." Don't be fooled, though: "Most people here work hard and see it academically pay off." "Students focus on getting their school work done before going out and hold their friends accountable so not many get behind," says another student. The school itself offers tons of service activities, cultural events, speakers, and intramurals, and people like to get off campus and have fun in Memphis, which is "surrounded by fun sports teams" to which the school provides cheap tickets. The library can also be a social place, especially during exams, "because so many people spend their time there."

Student Body

Rhodes has its fair share of "white, upper-middle-class" students, but "no one is elitist," and the overall student body itself is diverse on many fronts. Many students here are from the South and "preppy," and you can spot many "polos and khakis around campus." "Everyone is well accepted regardless of socio-economic status," and the few atypical student groups "mix freely" and "interact with few problems." The school is full of hard workers ("academic but not full of nerds") and the school's honor code is taken very seriously. "People rarely ever cheat or steal"—most students live on campus and "a large percentage don't ever lock their doom rooms." One thing is for certain, though—students here are "busy" in all areas of their life: studying, taking advantage of the "countless service opportunities," arts/athletics, and Greek life. The typical student is generally an "overachiever" while still "[liking] to have fun and enjoy him or herself." "Rhodes is filled with the types of students that are any high school counselor's…dream," sums up a student.

FINANCIAL AID: 901-843-3810 • E-MAIL: ADMINFO@RHODES.EDU • WEBSITE: WWW.RHODES.EDU

THE PRINCETON REVIEW SAYS

Admissions

Very important factors considered include: Class rank, academic GPA, rigor of secondary school record. *Important factors considered include:* Application essay, recommendation(s), standardized test scores, alumni/ae relation, character/personal qualities, racial/ethnic status. *Other factors considered include:* Extracurricular activities, first generation, geographical residence, interview, level of applicant's interest, state residency, talent/ability, volunteer work, work experience. SAT or ACT required; ACT with or without writing component accepted. TOEFL required of all international applicants. High school diploma is required and GED is accepted. *Academic units required:* 4 English, 3 mathematics, 2 science (2 science labs), 2 foreign language, 2 social studies, 3 academic electives.

Financial Aid

Students should submit: FAFSA, CSS/Financial Aid PROFILE, noncustodial PROFILE. Regular filing deadline is March 1. The Princeton Review suggests that all financial aid forms be submitted as soon as possible after January 1. *Need-based scholarships/grants offered:* Federal Pell, SEOG, state scholarships/grants, private scholarships, the school's own gift aid. *Loan aid offered:* Direct Subsidized Stafford, Direct Unsubsidized Stafford, Direct PLUS, Federal Perkins. Federal Work-Study Program available. Institutional employment available. Highest amount earned per year from on-campus jobs $5,140. Off-campus job opportunities are good.

The Inside Word

Rhodes' national profile is growing. Even though the majority of students come from Tennessee and nearby states, students from farther-flung points of origin will enjoy a leg up because they add to the geographic diversity. As with all small, selective schools, applicants are advised to schedule a campus visit and to interview to demonstrate their interest in attending.

THE SCHOOL SAYS ". . ."

From the Admissions Office

"Rhodes is a residential college committed to liberal arts and sciences. Our highest priorities are intellectual engagement, service to others, and honor among ourselves. We live this life on one of the country's most beautiful campuses in the heart of Memphis, Tennessee, an economic, political, and cultural center, making Rhodes one of a handful of top-tier, liberal arts colleges in a major metropolitan area.

"Rhodes has the soul of a liberal arts college coupled with a real-world mindset. Our students put their liberal arts knowledge to work in the world starting their first year. You'll be encouraged to engage in research, leadership and service opportunities—and to take responsibility for shaping your educational experience to meet your personal interests and goals. Memphis is a thriving city right on Rhodes' doorstep, with spectacular resources for students, and the college has pioneered the establishment of programs with world-class institutions and companies, including St. Jude Children's Research Hospital, FedEx and the Memphis Zoo, which take advantage of the college's metropolitan location and provide students with real-world opportunities for academic and personal growth."

SELECTIVITY

Admissions Rating	**95**
# of applicants	5,211
% of applicants accepted	50
% of acceptees attending	21
# accepting a place on wait list	561
# admitted from wait list	6
# of early decision applicants	99
# accepted early decision	30

FRESHMAN PROFILE

Range SAT Critical Reading	590–690
Range SAT Math	600–690
Range ACT Composite	26–31
Minimum paper TOEFL	550
Average HS GPA	3.8
% graduated top 10% of class	51
% graduated top 25% of class	83
% graduated top 50% of class	99

DEADLINES

Early decision	
Deadline	11/1
Notification	12/1
Early action	
Deadline	11/15
Notification	1/15
Regular	
Priority	1/15
Notification	4/1
Nonfall registration?	yes

FINANCIAL FACTS

Financial Aid Rating	**89**
Annual tuition	$37,782
Room and board	$9,504
Required fees	$310
Books and supplies	$1,071
% needy frosh rec. need-based scholarship or grant aid	99
% needy UG rec. need-based scholarship or grant aid	98
% needy frosh rec. non-need-based scholarship or grant aid	38
% needy UG rec. non-need-based scholarship or grant aid	30
% needy frosh rec. need-based self-help aid	68
% needy UG rec. need-based self-help aid	68
% frosh rec. any financial aid	96
% UG rec. any financial aid	92
% UG borrow to pay for school	44
Average cumulative indebtedness	$26,147
% frosh need fully met	54
% ugrads need fully met	52
Average % of frosh need met	94
Average % of ugrad need met	92

RICE UNIVERSITY

MS 17, PO BOX 1892, HOUSTON, TX 77251-1892 • ADMISSIONS: 713-348-7423 • FAX: 713-348-5952

CAMPUS LIFE

Quality of Life Rating	**99**
Fire Safety Rating	**88**
Green Rating	**76**
Type of school	private
Environment	metropolis

STUDENTS

Total undergrad enrollment	3,708
% male/female	52/48
% from out of state	49
% African American	7
% Asian	20
% Caucasian	42
% Hispanic	14
% international	10
# of countries represented	47

SURVEY SAYS . . .

Students are friendly
Great off-campus food
Dorms are like palaces
Students are happy
Frats and sororities are unpopular or nonexistent

ACADEMICS

Academic Rating	**92**
% students graduating within 4 years	79
% students graduating within 6 years	92
Calendar	semester
Student/faculty ratio	6:1
Profs interesting rating	87
Profs accessible rating	90
Most classes have	10–19 students

MOST POPULAR MAJORS

biology/biological sciences; economics; psychology

APPLICANTS ALSO LOOK AT AND OFTEN PREFER

Yale University, Stanford University, Harvard College

AND SOMETIMES PREFER

University of Pennsylvania, Cornell University, Duke University

AND RARELY PREFER

The University of Texas at Austin, Vanderbilt University, Washington University in St. Louis

STUDENTS SAY ". . ."

Academics

A sunny and social place to get a prestigious degree, Rice University is Houston's answer to the Ivy League. Consistently ranked as "one of the top universities of the nation," Rice maintains a stellar faculty, a "vibrant research program," and a "diverse selection of courses and departments." "Professors of big intro classes don't do a lot of discussion." Fortunately, "Classes are more interactive and small as you progress to the upper level," and students often develop a strong rapport with their instructors. A student details, "Most Rice professors love what they're doing, and you can tell that they are truly passionate about the material. They may show this by literally dancing around in the front of the classroom or by simply being available at any time to help students." Another student adds affectionately, "I want to adopt my bio-chem professor as my surrogate grandpa." Beyond traditional academics, Rice excels at offering "strong research opportunities for undergraduate students," including mentored lab work, independent projects, and "internships in the social sciences." There is also a "great engineering program" at Rice, and future doctors point out that the campus is located "next to the largest medical center in the world." Maybe it's all that Texan sunshine, but students say Rice is "not cutthroat academically, in spite of its very good academic reputation." Instead, "Academics are very challenging, but working hard will take you a long way." "Academic advising is amazing," and professors are an important source of support, "inviting students to join them for coffee in the student center or visit them in office hours to discuss class material, research, papers, or even what's going on in our lives!"

Life

Rice University offers "the most amazing balance of serious education and an unbelievably rewarding personal life." According to most undergraduates, "The college system is the key to life at Rice University," through which students are assigned to residential communities for all four years of study. The cornerstone of the Rice community, "The 'Hogwarts style' housing system creates an intimate place to create lasting friendships, as well as friendly competition between different dorms." "From the minute you walk onto Rice campus, you have upperclassmen advisors, peer academic advisors, Rice health advisors, the masters, resident associates, the counseling center, the wellness center, and many more campus groups that help you navigate your way through freshman year." "Most Friday and Saturday nights, there are parties open to the entire university, sponsored by a residential college," and everyone comes out for the annual campus-wide shindig, Beer Bike. Surrounding Houston is a big city and great college town, and students "love exploring new restaurants, going to Chinatown, volunteering, spending a lot of time at the swimming pool, shopping at thrift stores, [and] going on trips to Austin and Dallas." "The weather is fantastic."

Student Body

While they look like a bunch of "outgoing, down-to-earth kids," students reveal, "Everyone at Rice is, in some way, a nerd." At this "geek chic" school, "Regardless of your interest and no matter how nerdy it might be now, you'll definitely find someone else who shares your passion." "There is something unique about every Rice student," and career goals and intellectual interests run the gamut. A current undergraduate details, "Among my best friends, I have one who is working for Google next year, one who will be training for the Olympic trials over summer, and one who is currently working at a station in Antarctica." "Rice genuinely has a diverse community that accepts people of all backgrounds." Nonetheless, Rice students do share some common traits, generally described as "liberal for Texas," low-key, and "good natured." While most undergraduates are "studious," they're not overly serious. The typical student "rolls out of bed in a t-shirt" and is "willing to help you out in times of need."

FINANCIAL AID: 713-348-4958 • E-MAIL: ADMI@RICE.EDU • WEBSITE: WWW.RICE.EDU

THE PRINCETON REVIEW SAYS

Admissions

Very important factors considered include: Class rank, application essay, academic GPA, recommendation(s), rigor of secondary school record, standardized test scores, character/personal qualities, extracurricular activities, talent/ability. *Other factors considered include:* Alumni/ae relation, first generation, geographical residence, interview, level of applicant's interest, racial/ethnic status, state residency, volunteer work, work experience. SAT or ACT required; ACT with writing component required. TOEFL required of all international applicants. High school diploma or equivalent is not required. *Academic units required:* 4 English, 3 mathematics, 2 science (2 science labs), 2 foreign language, 2 social studies, 3 academic electives, Natural Science and Engineering Division requires trigonometry or advance math courses and both chemistry and physics. May substitute a second year of chemistry or biology for physics. *Academic units recommended:* 4 English, 4 mathematics, 4 science (3 science labs), 4 foreign language, 2 social studies, 2 academic electives.

Financial Aid

Students should submit: FAFSA, CSS/Financial Aid PROFILE, noncustodial PROFILE, business/farm supplement, tax returns and W-2s. The Princeton Review suggests that all financial aid forms be submitted as soon as possible after January 1. *Need-based scholarships/grants offered:* Federal Pell, SEOG, state scholarships/grants, private scholarships, the school's own gift aid. *Loan aid offered:* Direct Subsidized Stafford, Direct Unsubsidized Stafford, Direct PLUS, Federal Perkins. Applicants will be notified of awards on a rolling basis beginning April 1. Federal Work-Study Program available. Institutional employment available. Off-campus job opportunities are excellent.

The Inside Word

Rice is a competitive university and admission is granted only to top students. In recent years, less than eighteen percent of regular decision applicants were offered a spot in the incoming class. (For a variety of reasons, early decision applicants are accepted at a slightly higher rate.) Though not required, students are encouraged to interview with an admissions counselor on the Rice campus or arrange to meet with alumni in their area. Students applying to the school of architecture must accompany their application with a portfolio of creative work, while music students must audition on the Rice campus.

THE SCHOOL SAYS ". . ."

From the Admissions Office

"We seek students of keen intellect and diverse backgrounds who show potential to succeed at Rice and will also contribute to the educational environment of those around them.

"Student applications are reviewed within the context of the division to which they apply. Admission committee decisions are based not only on high school grades and test scores but also on such qualities as leadership, participation in extracurricular activities, and personal creativity. Admission is extremely competitive. Rice attempts to seek out and identify those students who have demonstrated exceptional ability and the potential for personal and intellectual growth.

"Our individualized, holistic evaluation process employs many different means to identify these qualities in applicants.

"Required admission testing includes the SAT and two Subject tests, or ACT with writing. All test scores must be sent to Rice directly from the official testing agency."

SELECTIVITY	
Admissions Rating	**98**
# of applicants	13,816
% of applicants accepted	19
% of acceptees attending	38
# accepting a place on wait list	2,342
# admitted from wait list	1
# of early decision applicants	1,036
# accepted early decision	310

FRESHMAN PROFILE	
Range SAT Critical Reading	650–750
Range SAT Math	680–780
Range SAT Writing	650–760
Range ACT Composite	30–34
Minimum paper TOEFL	600
Minimum web-based TOEFL	100
% graduated top 10% of class	89
% graduated top 25% of class	96
% graduated top 50% of class	100

DEADLINES	
Early decision	
Deadline	11/1
Notification	12/15
Regular	
Deadline	1/1
Notification	4/1
Nonfall registration?	no

FINANCIAL FACTS	
Financial Aid Rating	**98**
Annual tuition	$36,610
Room and board	$12,600
Required fees	$682
Books and supplies	$800
% needy frosh rec. need-based scholarship or grant aid	100
% needy UG rec. need-based scholarship or grant aid	100
% needy frosh rec. non-need-based scholarship or grant aid	34
% needy UG rec. non-need-based scholarship or grant aid	21
% needy frosh rec. need-based self-help aid	67
% needy UG rec. need-based self-help aid	71
% frosh rec. any financial aid	61
% UG rec. any financial aid	62
% UG borrow to pay for school	24
Average cumulative indebtedness	$16,528
% frosh need fully met	100
% ugrads need fully met	100
Average % of frosh need met	100
Average % of ugrad need met	100

RIDER UNIVERSITY

2083 LAWRENCEVILLE ROAD, LAWRENCEVILLE, NJ 08648-3099 • ADMISSIONS: 609-896-5042 • FAX: 609-895-6645

CAMPUS LIFE

Quality of Life Rating	**67**
Fire Safety Rating	**76**
Green Rating	**90**
Type of school	private
Environment	village

STUDENTS

Total undergrad enrollment	4,504
% male/female	41/59
% from out of state	24
% frosh live on campus	88
# of fraternities	4
# of sororities	8
% African American	10
% Asian	4
% Caucasian	65
% Hispanic	9
% international	2
# of countries represented	65

SURVEY SAYS . . .

Athletic facilities are great
Student publications are popular
Lots of beer drinking

ACADEMICS

Academic Rating	**70**
% students returning for sophomore year	83
% students graduating within 4 years	52
% students graduating within 6 years	64
Calendar	semester
Student/faculty ratio	13:1
Profs interesting rating	72
Profs accessible rating	71
Most classes have	10–19 students
Most lab/discussion sessions have	10–19 students

MOST POPULAR MAJORS

accounting; business/commerce; elementary education and teaching

STUDENTS SAY ". . ."

Academics

A private coed institution in Lawrenceville, New Jersey, Rider University offers a friendly and intimate college experience to a largely local crowd. In addition to dozens of majors in the liberal arts and sciences, Rider operates a "highly respected business school" and an accounting program that's "the best in the state of New Jersey." Rider "prepares you for all facets of life after college," fostering "interpersonal relationships between successful alumni and undergraduates" and offering great services like "tutoring for every class, writing labs, career services, internships, and co-ops." A current student attests, "The science professors have been really helpful with helping me achieve my goals by introducing me to opportunities for grants, internships, and other experiential learning." While coursework can be challenging, "The professors present the material in a way in which you can do well if you work hard." Teaching is emphasized, and there are "some phenomenal professors at Rider University who go out of their way to give their students a great education." At the same time, students admit, "While many professors are highly accessible, there are surely a few—mostly adjunct-professors—who are inadequate," both as mentors and as teachers. On the whole, Rider is "very student-oriented," and the administration "goes the extra mile in making sure all students are treated equally." Even so, things don't always run smoothly, and "Dealing with financial aid, administrative offices such as residence life, and career services is the hardest part about going to Rider University." While Rider is a private college, it helps students finance their education through "generous financial aid package," loans, and "lots of opportunities for work study."

Life

Whether they live on campus or commute to school, students enjoy a friendly and social atmosphere at Rider. On campus, "Basketball games are always a big draw," and the university hosts "major comedians, musicians, [and] film nights" in the evenings. Even though the university's alcohol rules are rather strict, "Most students drink for fun, either on campus or off." For mellower times, the "residence advisors set up a lot events in their respective dorm," or students get together to "play video games, go to Zumba classes, hold hallway-parties (no alcohol), or movie nights." In addition, the "Student Rec Center is a great place to hang out because it's got basketball courts, a pool table, ping pong table, all the video game systems, a gym, a track, and a pool." When they want to pop off campus, "There are coffee shops, frozen yogurt places, [and] a house of cupcakes" in the nearby town of Princeton, and "New York City and Philly are only a train ride away." "On the weekends, the school empties out pretty quickly," as most students go home. While some complain that Rider is a "suitcase school," others insist, "The lifestyle on campus is what people make of it." For those who want a more traditional college experience, "Greek life is a great way to meet new people and get involved in campus."

Student Body

Many Rider students come from a "middle-class background," and most are East Coasters "from the Lawrenceville area" or greater New Jersey. However, "The student body is very diverse politically, socially, and academically," reflecting the "vastly varied demographics of the state of New Jersey: all races, all religions, and all levels of mental and physical abilities." "There is a good mix of jocks, brainy people who are committed to studying, and artsy hipster types," so most "students can usually find at least one group to fit in with." While some students "love to party," others "really care about how well they do in school and are involved in so many different organizations on campus." Rider also operates an evening program, which attracts "older, working, returning students," who are often very serious about their studies.

FINANCIAL AID: 609-896-5360 • E-MAIL: ADMISSIONS@RIDER.EDU • WEBSITE: WWW.RIDER.EDU

THE PRINCETON REVIEW SAYS

Admissions

Very important factors considered include: Application essay, academic GPA, recommendation(s), rigor of secondary school record, standardized test scores. *Important factors considered include:* Level of applicant's interest. *Other factors considered include:* Class rank, alumni/ae relation, character/personal qualities, extracurricular activities, geographical residence, interview, state residency, talent/ability, volunteer work, work experience. SAT or ACT required; ACT with writing component required. TOEFL required of all international applicants. High school diploma is required and GED is accepted. *Academic units required:* 4 English, 3 mathematics. *Academic units recommended:* 4 mathematics, 4 science (2 science labs), 2 foreign language, 2 social studies, 2 history.

Financial Aid

Students should submit: FAFSA. Regular filing deadline is March 1. The Princeton Review suggests that all financial aid forms be submitted as soon as possible after January 1. *Need-based scholarships/grants offered:* Federal Pell, SEOG, state scholarships/grants, private scholarships, the school's own gift aid. *Loan aid offered:* Direct Subsidized Stafford, Direct Unsubsidized Stafford, Direct PLUS, Federal Perkins, state loans, college/university loans from institutional funds. Applicants will be notified of awards on a rolling basis beginning February 20. Federal Work-Study Program available. Institutional employment available. Highest amount earned per year from on-campus jobs $6,195. Off-campus job opportunities are good.

The Inside Word

To prepare for college, Rider University suggests that high school students follow a rigorous curriculum of college prep courses, including AP and honors classes. Students need at least four years of high school English and three years of math to be considered for admission to Rider. The most recent incoming class had an average high school GPA of 3.35 and a SAT score of 1610. Although most students major in the liberal arts and sciences, more than a quarter of undergraduates are enrolled in the business school.

THE SCHOOL SAYS ". . ."

From the Admissions Office

"Rider students are driven by their dreams of a fulfilling career and a desire to have an impact on the world around them. Rider is a place to apply your imagination, talents and aspirations in ways that will make a difference. A Rider education will prepare you as a leader and as a member of a team. When you graduate from Rider, you'll be a different person, confidently ready for your life's challenges and opportunities.

"We invite you to visit and experience Rider firsthand. Open houses are offered in the fall. Tours are available daily and Information Sessions are offered most weekends throughout the academic year and weekdays in the summer.

"Freshmen applicants are required to submit the results of either the SAT or ACT exam. The highest scores from either test will be considered for admission."

SELECTIVITY	
Admissions Rating	**76**
# of applicants	7,947
% of applicants accepted	73
% of acceptees attending	16
# accepting a place on wait list	44
# admitted from wait list	13

FRESHMAN PROFILE	
Range SAT Critical Reading	460–570
Range SAT Math	480–580
Range SAT Writing	460–570
Range ACT Composite	19–24
Minimum paper TOEFL	550
Minimum web-based TOEFL	80
Average HS GPA	3.3
% graduated top 10% of class	15
% graduated top 25% of class	43
% graduated top 50% of class	81

DEADLINES	
Early action	
Deadline	11/15
Notification	12/15
Regular	
Priority	1/15
Nonfall registration?	yes

FINANCIAL FACTS	
Financial Aid Rating	**88**
Annual tuition	$31,330
Room and board	$11,810
Required fees	$600
Books and supplies	$1,500
% needy frosh rec. need-based scholarship or grant aid	100
% needy UG rec. need-based scholarship or grant aid	97
% needy frosh rec. non-need-based scholarship or grant aid	15
% needy UG rec. non-need-based scholarship or grant aid	14
% needy frosh rec. need-based self-help aid	82
% needy UG rec. need-based self-help aid	79
% frosh rec. any financial aid	78
% UG rec. any financial aid	73
% UG borrow to pay for school	72
Average cumulative indebtedness	$35,449
% frosh need fully met	17
% ugrads need fully met	17
Average % of frosh need met	71
Average % of ugrad need met	69

RIPON COLLEGE

PO BOX 248, RIPON, WI 54971 • ADMISSIONS: 920-748-8337 • FAX: 920-748-8335

CAMPUS LIFE

Quality of Life Rating	**89**
Fire Safety Rating	**64**
Green Rating	**68**
Type of school	private
Environment	village

STUDENTS

Total undergrad enrollment	968
% male/female	49/51
% from out of state	29
% from public high school	75
% frosh live on campus	98
# of fraternities	5
# of sororities	3
% African American	2
% Asian	1
% Caucasian	87
% Hispanic	4
% Native American	1
% international	3
# of countries represented	11

SURVEY SAYS . . .

Students are friendly
Students get along with local community
Low cost of living
Students are friendly

ACADEMICS

Academic Rating	**86**
% students returning for sophomore year	81
% students graduating within 6 years	70
Calendar	semester
Student/faculty ratio	13:1
Profs interesting rating	92
Profs accessible rating	93
Most classes have	10–19 students
Most lab/discussion sessions have	10–19 students

MOST POPULAR MAJORS
business/commerce; history; psychology

APPLICANTS ALSO LOOK AT AND OFTEN PREFER
St. Norbert College, Carroll College (WI)

AND SOMETIMES PREFER
University of Wisconsin—Madison

AND RARELY PREFER
Lawrence University, Beloit College

STUDENTS SAY ". . ."

Academics

Described as a "close-knit community," "Ripon is a place where a student's best interest matters; all other agendas are secondary." One student chose Ripon because, " I was looking for a liberal arts school that allowed me to do the things I like, namely, be involved in multiple student groups, study abroad, and take classes in different fields, all of which I have been able to do at Ripon." The "quiet beauty," "welcoming nature of the campus," along with "small class sizes and a lot of personal attention from professors" create a "friendly, home-away-from-home atmosphere." Students appreciate the education they are receiving and how it prepares them for a productive life after college. The school's motto, "more together" "is exactly what our school is all about; becoming something more with the help of those here to guide us." "Ripon College prepares students to be productive, service-minded leaders who are ready and willing to influence the direction of our nation's future." "Ripon College is not all about sitting in a classroom listening to lectures and taking notes; it's about teaching us to become more educated in the world around us and helping us to develop the skills needed to succeed." "The hands-on, experiential, service-learning projects have been particularly valuable for my own personal growth and for preparing me for life after college." Another student agrees, saying, "Ripon is a prime example of a college with a positive and supportive living and learning community." "Ripon professors provide an interesting and intellectually challenging environment for students to discuss and to learn." Students say, Ripon is an "amazing community of learners and educators who support one another" and a "unique institution that helps ordinary people uncover their extraordinary potential to do great things." Professors "are not just teachers, but mentors!" Scholarships make a Ripon College education possible for some that otherwise could not attend. One student says, "They offered me a great scholarship and were really willing to work with me to make my college education affordable."

Life

With its "tight-knit and welcoming community," Ripon conveys "a friendly environment conducive to learning, fun, and overall personal growth." It is "not uncommon to sit down to lunch with a professor, or even go over to their house for tea." Life at Ripon has proven blissful for one student who now says, "I cannot remember a time when I wanted to be anywhere else." Besides a "strong academic core," Ripon College has "many successful sports teams," and Greek life "is abundant." Greeks host events and are a big part of many students' life. Partying "is evident but not huge by any respect." "Since Ripon College is in a small town, the college sets up a lot of events on weekends for us to take part in!" "The small-town feel of Ripon forces you sometimes to create your own fun, which usually makes for the best memories." "Being close to several metropolitan areas (Chicago, Milwaukee, Madison, and the Twin Cities), there is rarely a weekend when people are not getting off campus to go explore." But if you are looking for snow days to figure into your schedule, then Ripon may not be for you "because most professors will keep classes going even in negative temperatures with two feet of snow."

Student Body

A typical Ripon student is described as "laid-back and friendly." One student cautions, "You have to plan extra time in between classes because you're guaranteed to be stopped by someone you know along the way to talk for a few minutes." Students are "outgoing, personable, and motivated," "involved in multiple clubs," and may "hold more than one internship at a time. From Student Senate to Ultimate Frisbee to volunteering in the community, there is never a lack of activities in which one can participate." Students are "always looking for something new and exciting to do, and [are] ready to volunteer their time and energy to someone in need."

FINANCIAL AID: 920-748-8301 • E-MAIL: ADMINFO@RIPON.EDU • WEBSITE: WWW.RIPON.EDU

THE PRINCETON REVIEW SAYS

Admissions

Very important factors considered include: Rigor of secondary school record, interview. *Important factors considered include:* Class rank, academic GPA, recommendation(s), standardized test scores, character/personal qualities, extracurricular activities. *Other factors considered include:* Application essay, talent/ability, volunteer work. SAT or ACT required; ACT with or without writing component accepted. TOEFL required of all international applicants. High school diploma is required and GED is accepted. *Academic units required:* 4 English, 2 mathematics, 2 science, 2 social studies. *Academic units recommended:* 4 mathematics, 4 science, 2 foreign language, 4 social studies.

Financial Aid

Students should submit: FAFSA. The Princeton Review suggests that all financial aid forms be submitted as soon as possible after January 1. *Need-based scholarships/grants offered:* Federal Pell, SEOG, state scholarships/grants, private scholarships, the school's own gift aid. *Loan aid offered:* Direct Subsidized Stafford, Direct Unsubsidized Stafford, Direct PLUS, Federal Perkins. Applicants will be notified of awards on a rolling basis beginning March 1. Federal Work-Study Program available. Institutional employment available. Highest amount earned per year from on-campus jobs $1,200. Off-campus job opportunities are good.

The Inside Word

Ripon seeks accomplished high school students who have challenged themselves in and out of the classroom. Solid performers—those earning a B-plus average in a college-prep curriculum and exceeding 1100 SAT/22 ACT—should find a clear path awaiting them, although the school does also consider such peripherals as potential contribution to extracurricular life and the likelihood a candidate will flourish in a small-school environment.

THE SCHOOL SAYS "..."

From the Admissions Office

"Since its founding in 1851, Ripon College has adhered to the philosophy that the liberal arts offer the richest foundation for intellectual, cultural, social, and spiritual growth. Academic strength is a 150-year tradition at Ripon. We attract excellent professors who are dedicated to their disciplines; they in turn attract bright, committed students. Together with the other members of our tightly knit learning community, students at Ripon learn more deeply, live more fully, and achieve more success. Students are surprised to discover that here there are more opportunities—to be involved, to lead, to speak out, to make a difference, to explore new interests—than at a college ten times our size. Through collaborative learning, group living, teamwork, and networking, students tap into the power of a community where we all work together to ensure success—at Ripon and beyond.

"All of the best residential liberal arts colleges strive to be true learning communities like Ripon. We succeed better than most because our enrollment of about 1,000 students is perfect for fostering connections inside and outside the classroom. Our students flourish in this environment of mutual respect, where shared values are elevated and diverse ideas are valued. If you are seeking academic challenge and want to benefit from an environment of personal attention and support—then you should take a closer look at Ripon.

"Applicants to Ripon College must submit scores from either the ACT (writing section not required) or the SAT."

SELECTIVITY	
Admissions Rating	83
# of applicants	1,115
% of applicants accepted	75
% of acceptees attending	27

FRESHMAN PROFILE	
Range SAT Critical Reading	500–650
Range SAT Math	490–580
Range ACT Composite	22–27
Minimum paper TOEFL	550
Minimum web-based TOEFL	79
Average HS GPA	3.4
% graduated top 10% of class	23
% graduated top 25% of class	54
% graduated top 50% of class	90

DEADLINES	
Early action	
Deadline	11/1
Notification	11/15
Regular	
Priority	3/15
Nonfall registration?	yes

FINANCIAL FACTS	
Financial Aid Rating	85
Annual tuition	$29,835
Room and board	$8,545
Required fees	$275
Books and supplies	$1,000
% needy frosh rec. need-based scholarship or grant aid	100
% needy UG rec. need-based scholarship or grant aid	100
% needy frosh rec. non-need-based scholarship or grant aid	11
% needy UG rec. non-need-based scholarship or grant aid	11
% needy frosh rec. need-based self-help aid	89
% needy UG rec. need-based self-help aid	88
% frosh rec. any financial aid	87
% UG rec. any financial aid	89
% UG borrow to pay for school	81
Average cumulative indebtedness	$32,056
% frosh need fully met	16
% ugrads need fully met	19
Average % of frosh need met	87
Average % of ugrad need met	86

ROANOKE COLLEGE

221 COLLEGE LANE, SALEM, VA 24153-3794 • ADMISSIONS: 540-375-2270 • FAX: 540-375-2267

CAMPUS LIFE

Quality of Life Rating	**81**
Fire Safety Rating	**76**
Green Rating	**77**
Type of school	private
Affiliation	Lutheran
Environment	city

STUDENTS

Total undergrad enrollment	1,997
% male/female	44/56
% from out of state	51
% from public high school	83
% frosh live on campus	90
# of fraternities	4
# of sororities	5
% African American	4
% Asian	1
% Caucasian	88
% Hispanic	3
% international	1
# of countries represented	23

SURVEY SAYS . . .

Students are happy
Great library
Career services are great
Students are friendly
Great off-campus food
Campus feels safe
Lots of beer drinking

ACADEMICS

Academic Rating	**80**
% students returning for sophomore year	77
% students graduating within 4 years	59
% students graduating within 6 years	69
Calendar	semester
Student/faculty ratio	11:1
Profs interesting rating	86
Profs accessible rating	86
Most classes have	10–19 students
Most lab/discussion sessions have	10–19 students

MOST POPULAR MAJORS

business/commerce; history; psychology

APPLICANTS ALSO LOOK AT AND OFTEN PREFER

University of Virginia, James Madison University

AND SOMETIMES PREFER

Christopher Newport University, Lynchburg College, University of Mary Washington, Virginia Tech, Elon University

STUDENTS SAY ". . ."

Academics

Lutheran-affiliated Roanoke College "is a small school [that] allows you to stand out." With an emphasis on contemporary applications of a classic education, and a campus of green quads, red bricks, and white columns, Roanoke gives students a liberal arts curriculum in a palatial setting in the shadow of the Blue Ridge Mountains. As one student puts it, "Roanoke College is an amazing school that has given me the opportunity to challenge myself and to experience things in school and in the community that I would not have gotten anywhere else." It "provides students with an education that is challenging but at the same time rewarding for the effort you put in." As at many schools that emphasize the liberal arts and feature a low student/teacher ratio, the professors really make this place. "They are all eager to help students as much as possible, and they treat students like individuals." "They encourage students to come ask questions outside of class or just stop by for a chat." "The professors are very lively and passionate about the subjects they teach. They frequently choose interesting reading material." "They push our thinking to a new level." The English and economics departments receive high praise, as do the sciences: "I was able to do graduate level research synthesizing carbon nanotubes the very first week of school," brags one health sciences major.

Life

Life at Roanoke is, to put it simply, pretty sweet. "Because of the location in southwestern Virginia, there are many hiking and other outdoor activities available. Downtown Roanoke is only a short drive away, where there is plenty of shopping, movies, etc. Additionally, Blacksburg/Virginia Tech, James Madison University, and Natural Bridge are all close enough for a day or weekend trip." "Students go outside, hike in the mountains that surround the campus, there are water sports, [and] skiing in the winter." "There are always Outdoor Adventures activities that go on during the weekends." On campus, Roanoke features a healthy Greek scene and "a great Campus Activities Board" that "has special events every weekend that are free to students, which provides a safe and fun environment." "RC After Dark [events] are always fun, like bingo and karaoke." Concerts and theater performances are regularly held in Olin Hall, and current students note, "We just held the Virginia Gubernatorial debates and also had Sandra Day O'Connor visit our campus."

Student Body

The typical Roanoke student comes from either New England or the mid-Atlantic, and "comes from an upper-middle-class upbringing, and it shows." "They look like they can fit in at the country club." But "Roanoke has a lot more variety to it than just WASPs. There is a niche for just about everyone," and "The stereotypes of 'preppy plaid' Roanoke still lurk in Greek houses, but the majority seem to be pink- and green-free." Greek life is pervasive here, which is something to keep in mind if you don't plan on pledging, but most "students are generally happy, outgoing, fun, and well-dressed." "Students tend to find their own niche and fit into it, whether it be a club or a Greek organization." "There is not a whole lot of diversity, but the typical student is very nice and welcoming" and "very dedicated to getting the most out of their education as well as have a fun and enjoyable time at college." Athletes take note: "The school lacks a football team, making lacrosse the marquee sport here."

FINANCIAL AID: 540-375-2235 • E-MAIL: ADMISSIONS@ROANOKE.EDU • WEBSITE: WWW.ROANOKE.EDU

THE PRINCETON REVIEW SAYS

Admissions

Very important factors considered include: Class rank, academic GPA, rigor of secondary school record, standardized test scores, character/personal qualities. *Important factors considered include:* Recommendation(s), extracurricular activities, interview. *Other factors considered include:* Application essay, alumni/ae relation, level of applicant's interest, racial/ethnic status, talent/ability, volunteer work, work experience. SAT or ACT required; ACT with or without writing component accepted. TOEFL required of all international applicants. High school diploma is required and GED is accepted. *Academic units required:* 4 English, 3 mathematics, 2 science (2 science labs), 2 social studies, 5 academic electives. *Academic units recommended:* 4 foreign language.

Financial Aid

Students should submit: FAFSA, state aid form. The Princeton Review suggests that all financial aid forms be submitted as soon as possible after January 1. *Need-based scholarships/grants offered:* Federal Pell, SEOG, state scholarships/grants, private scholarships, the school's own gift aid. *Loan aid offered:* Direct Subsidized Stafford, Direct Unsubsidized Stafford, Direct PLUS, Federal Perkins, college/university loans from institutional funds, alternative loans. Applicants will be notified of awards on a rolling basis beginning November 1. Federal Work-Study Program available. Institutional employment available. Highest amount earned per year from on-campus jobs $2,000. Off-campus job opportunities are good.

The Inside Word

Roanoke takes a holistic approach to the admissions process, so the story your whole application tells is important. While the average grades and test scores of accepted students are high, there are no formulas here, and applicants should show they're well-rounded, emphasizing their passions and extracurriculars. The optional personal statement is highly recommended; use it as an opportunity to both show off your achievements and speak to the specific reasons Roanoke appeals to you.

THE SCHOOL SAYS ". . ."

From the Admissions Office

"Roanoke College prepares students for their futures by providing a classic undergraduate liberal arts experience that is applied to modern issues. Roanoke is one of only ten percent of colleges in the U.S. that qualify academically to house a chapter of the prestigious Phi Beta Kappa honor society. Over ninety-five percent of Roanoke seniors receive job offers or continue on to graduate school within six months of graduation, and approximately forty-nine percent of Roanoke graduates attend or complete graduate school within six years.

"Roanoke is nationally recognized for its core curriculum. Unlike most colleges that require a series of introductory courses in various disciplines, all of Roanoke's core courses are topic based, and students see firsthand how fundamental concepts are applied to important issues. For example, instead of taking a generic Introduction to Chemistry course, students might choose Chemistry and Crime, where they use forensic chemistry to solve crimes. Or, instead of Statistics 101, students might choose Statistics and the Weather and discover how statistical analysis is used in weather forecasting.

"Experiential learning is a cornerstone of academics at Roanoke. While every student experiences firsthand learning, over seventy percent of Roanoke students study abroad, conduct internships, or participate in research. Ask students to describe what makes Roanoke special and they'll invariably talk about the close relationships with their professors and peers. However, there's no reason not to have fun along the way—with more than 100 clubs, it's easy for students to meet others with common interests."

SELECTIVITY	
Admissions Rating	**79**
# of applicants	4,184
% of applicants accepted	70
% of acceptees attending	18
# accepting a place on wait list	283
% admitted from wait list	36
# of early decision applicants	81
% accepted early decision	44

FRESHMAN PROFILE	
Range SAT Critical Reading	500–590
Range SAT Math	490–590
Range SAT Writing	488–590
Range ACT Composite	21–25.8
Minimum paper TOEFL	520
Minimum web-based TOEFL	68
Average HS GPA	3.4
% graduated top 10% of class	22
% graduated top 25% of class	55
% graduated top 50% of class	82

DEADLINES	
Early decision	
Deadline	11/1
Notification	12/1
Early action	
Notification	10/1
Regular	
Deadline	3/15
Nonfall registration?	yes

FINANCIAL FACTS	
Financial Aid Rating	**83**
Annual tuition	$33,516
Room and board	$11,142
Required fees	$980
Books and supplies	$1,000
% needy frosh rec. need-based scholarship or grant aid	100
% needy UG rec. need-based scholarship or grant aid	100
% needy frosh rec. non-need-based scholarship or grant aid	97
% needy UG rec. non-need-based scholarship or grant aid	97
% needy frosh rec. need-based self-help aid	84
% needy UG rec. need-based self-help aid	83
% frosh rec. any financial aid	98
% UG rec. any financial aid	97
% UG borrow to pay for school	70
Average cumulative indebtedness	$34,645
% frosh need fully met	20
% ugrads need fully met	21
Average % of frosh need met	77
Average % of ugrad need met	77

Rochester Institute of Technology

60 Lomb Memorial Drive, Rochester, NY 14623-5604 • Admissions: 585-475-5502 • Fax: 585-475-7424

CAMPUS LIFE

Quality of Life Rating	74
Fire Safety Rating	86
Green Rating	94
Type of school	private
Environment	city

STUDENTS

Total undergrad enrollment	13,048
% male/female	68/32
% from out of state	48
% from public high school	85
% frosh live on campus	95
# of fraternities	19
# of sororities	10
% African American	6
% Asian	5
% Caucasian	63
% Hispanic	5
% international	5
# of countries represented	107

SURVEY SAYS . . .

Lab facilities are great
Great computer facilities
Great library
Athletic facilities are great
Career services are great
Diverse student types on campus
Internships are widely available

ACADEMICS

Academic Rating	74
% students graduating within 4 years	30
% students graduating within 6 years	66
Calendar	quarter
Student/faculty ratio	12:1
Profs interesting rating	73
Profs accessible rating	76
Most classes have	10–19 students
Most lab/discussion sessions have	10–19 students

MOST POPULAR MAJORS

business/commerce; information technology; photography

APPLICANTS ALSO LOOK AT AND OFTEN PREFER

Cornell University, Carnegie Mellon University

AND SOMETIMES PREFER

Worcester Polytechnic Institute, University of Rochester, Rensselaer Polytechnic Institute

AND RARELY PREFER

State University of New York—University at Buffalo, Drexel University

STUDENTS SAY ". . ."

Academics

Uniting creativity, innovation, and applied knowledge, Rochester Institute of Technology is the place "where the technical left and artistic right brains collide." RIT offers a range of majors in technical fields—from game design to bioinformatics—as well as programs in design, engineering, and business. Across the board, there's an "emphasis on hands-on learning," and most majors require students to complete a cooperative work experience (basically, a paid internship), designed to "give you the opportunity to make connections in [an] industry within your field." On campus, undergraduates are encouraged to pursue research. Fortunately, "Funding is everywhere if a student takes the initiative to apply." The academic calendar at RIT is built around a "rigorous and fast-paced quarter system" that allows students to take more classes annually—but also keeps them burning the midnight oil. Not everyone is up to the challenge, and "The academic rigors of the school often force people to transfer or drop out." For those willing to put in the work, RIT offers all the tools for success: "All of the teachers I have had for problem-based classes (such as calculus and computer science) set up weekly office hours," and "Free tutoring is also widely available and excellent." In the classroom, "Professors are generally good, with the occasional whack-job or stellar teacher thrown in for good measure." Thanks to the "relatively small class sizes," teachers and students often develop personal relationships, and "Even in the large lecture halls, [professors] try to get to know each student." Administrators get mixed reviews, but most students agree, "President Destler definitely shakes things up a bit (in a good way). He's all about the students and makes that very obvious."

Life

Thanks to RIT's demanding course work, "a lot of school life revolves around homework," and students are accustomed to "spending many nights in [the] lab working on an assignment." For fun, there are "huge campus events that happen once a year," and "[Division I] hockey is very popular" during the winter term. But, "For the most part, students don't really care about the clubs and organizations and simply do their own thing in their free time." In particular, students at RIT like to "play video games and drink"—though not necessarily in that order. RIT students also "go sledding in the winter, go to the movies," or make "late night diner runs." If you feel like taking a break from campus life, "There are many things to do on and off campus in the Rochester area. Museums and theaters are abundant, along with local festivals." However, not much lies within walking distance, so "a car is a necessity."

Student Body

With an unusual assortment of undergraduate majors on offer, RIT attracts a "wide variety" of people and personalities, including "art students, engineers, computer geeks, ROTC guys, deaf students, GLBTQ students, [and] foreign students." A unique addition to the student population, "There are also many deaf/hard-of-hearing students, since RIT is home to the National Technical Institute for the Deaf (NTID)." Socially, students are divided into two major categories: "Half of the students play video games all the time and the other half socialize, go to the gym, and party." No matter what camp they fall into, "There's 15,000 undergrads, so everyone has a nook somewhere" and most students "find people like them and make friends easily." Given the school's technical focus, it's no surprise that "most students are self-proclaimed computer nerds," and "even the 'cool kids' have secret passions for *Star Trek*." A fortunate perk of attending school here is that "At any time, someone within 100 feet of you can fix your computer for you." Unfortunately, to the chagrin of many students, "Women are still underrepresented on campus," ringing in at about thirty-three percent of the undergraduate population.

FINANCIAL AID: 585-475-5502 • E-MAIL: ADMISSIONS@RIT.EDU • WEBSITE: WWW.RIT.EDU

THE PRINCETON REVIEW SAYS

Admissions

Very important factors considered include: Academic GPA, rigor of secondary school record. *Important factors considered include:* Class rank, standardized test scores. *Other factors considered include:* Application essay, recommendation(s), alumni/ae relation, character/personal qualities, extracurricular activities, first generation, geographical residence, interview, level of applicant's interest, racial/ethnic status, talent/ability, volunteer work, work experience. SAT or ACT required; ACT with or without writing component accepted. TOEFL required of all international applicants. High school diploma is required and GED is accepted. *Academic units required:* 4 English, 2 mathematics, 2 science (1 science lab), 4 social studies, 10 academic electives. *Academic units recommended:* 4 English, 3 mathematics, 3 science (2 science labs), 3 foreign language, 4 social studies, 5 academic electives.

Financial Aid

Students should submit: FAFSA, institution's own financial aid form, state aid form. Regular filing deadline is March 1. The Princeton Review suggests that all financial aid forms be submitted as soon as possible after January 1. *Need-based scholarships/grants offered:* Federal Pell, SEOG, state scholarships/grants, private scholarships, the school's own gift aid, NACME. *Loan aid offered:* Direct Subsidized Stafford, Direct Unsubsidized Stafford, Direct PLUS, Federal Perkins, RIT Loan program; alternative loans. Applicants will be notified of awards on a rolling basis beginning March 15. Federal Work-Study Program available. Institutional employment available. Highest amount earned per year from on-campus jobs $2,500. Off-campus job opportunities are excellent.

The Inside Word

The RIT admissions department is wired. Through their website, you can live chat with admissions or other students, follow their Twitter feed, join their Facebook community, or read blogs written by current students. When applying to RIT, prospective students must indicate their intended major (as well as a second and third choice) on their applications. Admissions requirements vary based on a student's desired field of study, though a student's academic record, test scores, personal essay, and recommendations are usually the most important factors in an admissions decision.

THE SCHOOL SAYS ". . ."

From the Admissions Office

"RIT is a place where brilliant minds pool together their individual talents across disciplines in service of big projects and big ideas. It is a vibrant community of students collaborating with experts and specialists: a hub of innovation and creativity. As one of the world's leading technological universities, RIT offers undergraduate and graduate programs in areas such as engineering, computing, engineering technology, business, hospitality, science, visual arts, biomedical sciences, game design and development, psychology, advertising, public relations, and public policy. Students may choose from more than ninety different minors to develop personal and professional interests. Ambitious, creative, and diverse students from every state and more than 100 foreign countries find a home at RIT. As home of the National Technical Institute for the Deaf (NTID), RIT is a leader in providing educational opportunities and access services for deaf and hard-of-hearing students. Experiential learning has been a hallmark of an RIT education since 1912. Every academic program offers some form of experiential education opportunity, which may include cooperative education, internships, study abroad, and undergraduate research. Students work hard, but learning is complemented with plenty of organized and spontaneous events and activities. RIT is a unique blend of rigor and fun, creativity and specialization, intellect and practice. It is a launching pad for a brilliant career, and a highly unique state of mind. It is a perfect environment in which to pursue your passion."

SELECTIVITY	
Admissions Rating	**87**
# of applicants	15,806
% of applicants accepted	59
% of acceptees attending	29
# accepting a place on wait list	376
# admitted from wait list	80
# of early decision applicants	1,461
# accepted early decision	970

FRESHMAN PROFILE	
Range SAT Critical Reading	530–650
Range SAT Math	570–680
Range SAT Writing	520–630
Range ACT Composite	25–30
Minimum paper TOEFL	550
Minimum web-based TOEFL	79
Average HS GPA	3.6
% graduated top 10% of class	37
% graduated top 25% of class	68
% graduated top 50% of class	93

DEADLINES	
Early decision	
Deadline	12/1
Notification	1/15
Regular	
Priority	2/1
Deadline	2/1
Nonfall registration?	yes

FINANCIAL FACTS	
Financial Aid Rating	**91**
Annual tuition	$31,584
Room and board	$10,413
Required fees	$453
Books and supplies	$1,050
% needy frosh rec. need-based scholarship or grant aid	94
% needy UG rec. need-based scholarship or grant aid	93
% needy frosh rec. non-need-based scholarship or grant aid	26
% needy UG rec. non-need-based scholarship or grant aid	29
% needy frosh rec. need-based self-help aid	90
% needy UG rec. need-based self-help aid	89
% frosh rec. any financial aid	88
% UG rec. any financial aid	77
Average cumulative indebtedness	$24,200
% frosh need fully met	82
% ugrads need fully met	83
Average % of frosh need met	88
Average % of ugrad need met	88

Rollins College

1000 Holt Avenue, Winter Park, FL 32789-4499 • Admissions: 407-646-2161 • Fax: 407-646-1502

CAMPUS LIFE

Quality of Life Rating	**79**
Fire Safety Rating	**91**
Green Rating	**75**
Type of school	private
Environment	town

STUDENTS

Total undergrad enrollment	1,818
% male/female	41/59
% from out of state	50
% from public high school	53
% frosh live on campus	88
# of fraternities	5
# of sororities	7
% African American	4
% Asian	2
% Caucasian	66
% Hispanic	10
% international	6
# of countries represented	54

SURVEY SAYS . . .

Great computer facilities
Athletic facilities are great
Students love Winter Park, FL
Great off-campus food
Frats and sororities dominate social scene
Lots of beer drinking
Hard liquor is popular

ACADEMICS

Academic Rating	**91**
% students returning for sophomore year	81
% students graduating within 4 years	65
% students graduating within 6 years	70
Calendar	semester
Student/faculty ratio	10:1
Profs interesting rating	91
Profs accessible rating	89
Most classes have	10–19 students

MOST POPULAR MAJORS

economics; international business/trade/commerce; psychology

APPLICANTS ALSO LOOK AT AND OFTEN PREFER

Florida State University, University of Florida

AND SOMETIMES PREFER

University of Miami, College of Charleston, Furman University, Southern Methodist University

AND RARELY PREFER

University of Tampa, University of Central Florida, Elon University, Eckerd College

STUDENTS SAY ". . ."

Academics

Located in sunny central Florida, Rollins College is "small enough to help the individual but is fortunate enough to have a large endowment capable of providing each student with necessary academic means." The generous academic merit scholarships bring in a smart crowd, and the small class sizes, dedicated faculty, and numerous "student leadership opportunities, internships, academic presentations, [and] conference opportunities" sweeten the pot.

Rollins is "all about individual growth personally and educationally," but it also stresses "responsible community leadership both on and off campus." Students have a great deal of freedom to study what they choose, and many large projects are individualized toward the student, meaning a student "can tailor my topic to my interests." In addition to the autonomy this approach grants students, it "reinforces the idea of a holistic education," which helps to "make [students] competitive in an ever-changing job market." Working at this speed, students are able to "discover purpose and identify goals." Many services are also available to students, such as free tutoring and counseling.

Professors "perform very well" and create an "open and invigorating classroom environment" that is "open to diverse ideas and perspectives." Teachers "know every student's name, and they will remember you throughout your college experience." "My first year, one called my cell phone when I missed class," says a student. "The interactions that I have with the professors are second to none," says another. The small class sizes (even introductory courses are tiny) make it "very easy to learn and share your opinion," and since professors are "very engaging and willing to hear all points of view," "no one is left feeling like they don't matter."

Life

The "very beautiful and relaxing" campus can often feel sort of like a "country club" in both appearance and attitude. With "so many attractions in the Orlando area, the accessibility of the lake and the beach it is hard not to bring your books outside." Some people like "to go out to nearby downtown Orlando" (which is fifteen minutes away from school), some "live for Disney World," and some just stay in and hang out. A favorite activity among students is "walking up Park Avenue and exploring the delicious culinary endeavors there," and Lake Virginia is a great spot for perching, wakeboarding, or sailing. Students here tend "to travel a lot and explore other towns in Florida during the school year."

There are "always events on campus that are fun," like "a student who is a DJ [who] had a concert on the lawn one night," and almost one-third of the school is involved in Greek life. Community service is also "a pretty big part of the campus," and there is "always something service-related going on either from student groups or from the community engagement office."

Student Body

Rollins is such a small school that "everyone knows everyone." It's a true split at Rollins between in-staters and out-of-staters (and the international contingent) and among socioeconomic classes. "There are extremely wealthy spoiled kids driving Mercedes and smoking, [and] then there are true nerds who busted their butts to get in," says a student. Since the two groups mix constantly, "It is often hard to differentiate between the students who are set to inherit their parent's company after they graduate and those here on scholarship." Luckily, the "family environment and the closeness of all of the campus bring all the students together as scholars." Everyone may have small groups to which they belong, but "There is intermingling going on all the time."

FINANCIAL AID: 407-646-2395 • E-MAIL: ADMISSION@ROLLINS.EDU • WEBSITE: WWW.ROLLINS.EDU

THE PRINCETON REVIEW SAYS

Admissions

Very important factors considered include: Academic GPA, rigor of secondary school record. *Important factors considered include:* Application essay, recommendation(s), standardized test scores, extracurricular activities, talent/ability. *Other factors considered include:* Class rank, alumni/ae relation, character/personal qualities, first generation, interview, level of applicant's interest, volunteer work, work experience. ACT with writing component recommended. TOEFL required of all international applicants. High school diploma is required and GED is accepted. *Academic units required:* 4 English, 3 mathematics, 2 science, 2 foreign language, 2 social studies, 2 history, 2 academic electives. *Academic units recommended:* 4 English, 4 mathematics, 4 science, 3 foreign language, 3 social studies, 3 history, 3 academic electives.

Financial Aid

Students should submit: FAFSA. The Princeton Review suggests that all financial aid forms be submitted as soon as possible after January 1. *Need-based scholarships/grants offered:* Federal Pell, SEOG, state scholarships/grants, private scholarships, the school's own gift aid. *Loan aid offered:* Direct Subsidized Stafford, Direct Unsubsidized Stafford, Direct PLUS, Federal Perkins. Applicants will be notified of awards on a rolling basis beginning March 1. Federal Work-Study Program available. Institutional employment available.

The Inside Word

Applicants to Rollins who don't seek academic merit scholarships have the option of submitting a teacher recommendation and personal representation of their strengths, talents, or interests (such as a YouTube video, poem, slideshow, or scrapbook) in place of SAT or ACT scores. It's the school's way of creating another opportunity for students who test poorly but otherwise excel in academics, and it's characteristic of the individualized approach taken here (about ten percent of applicants opt for this method). Each applicant is assigned an admissions officer who acts as his or her liaison, ensuring a personalized admissions experience. Early decision applicants are given priority in admissions as well as in considerations for merit-based scholarships and need-based financial aid.

THE SCHOOL SAYS ". . ."

From the Admissions Office

"As you begin the college selection process, remember that you are in control of your destiny. Your academic record—course load, grades earned, test scores—are the most important part of your application credentials. But Rollins also pays close attention to your personal dimension—interests, strengths, values, and potential to contribute to college life. Don't sell yourself short in the application process. Be proud of what you've accomplished and who you are, and be honest when you describe yourself. Finally, the admission committee always likes to see candidates who express interest in the college. If we're your first choice, apply early decision. Each year we admit approximately one-third of the entering class through the early decision process. Are you unsure about your choice? If you can, schedule some visits, meet with an admission counselor, tour campus, and spend time in a class so you can see for yourself what Rollins and other colleges are all about. Take control of your destiny, and enjoy the process along the way.

"First-year applicants may submit either SAT or ACT scores for admission consideration. Candidates are strongly encouraged to complete the writing components, but results without Writing will be considered. Each candidate's best score combination will be used in the selection process; we strongly recommend that candidates consider taking both the SAT and the ACT."

SELECTIVITY	
Admissions Rating	**89**
# of applicants	4,416
% of applicants accepted	54
% of acceptees attending	23
# accepting a place on wait list	210
# of early decision applicants	327
# accepted early decision	206

FRESHMAN PROFILE	
Range SAT Critical Reading	550–640
Range SAT Math	545–640
Range ACT Composite	24–28
Minimum paper TOEFL	550
Minimum web-based TOEFL	80
Average HS GPA	3.3
% graduated top 10% of class	44
% graduated top 25% of class	77
% graduated top 50% of class	95

DEADLINES	
Early decision	
Deadline	11/15
Notification	12/15
Regular	
Deadline	2/15
Notification	4/1
Nonfall registration?	yes

FINANCIAL FACTS	
Financial Aid Rating	**86**
Annual tuition	$39,900
Room and board	$12,000
Books and supplies	$780
% needy frosh rec. need-based scholarship or grant aid	99
% needy UG rec. need-based scholarship or grant aid	98
% needy frosh rec. non-need-based scholarship or grant aid	19
% needy UG rec. non-need-based scholarship or grant aid	13
% needy frosh rec. need-based self-help aid	66
% needy UG rec. need-based self-help aid	73
% frosh rec. any financial aid	83
% UG rec. any financial aid	79
% UG borrow to pay for school	46
Average cumulative indebtedness	$22,719
% frosh need fully met	26
% ugrads need fully met	20
Average % of frosh need met	80
Average % of ugrad need met	80

ROSE-HULMAN INSTITUTE OF TECHNOLOGY

5500 WABASH AVENUE-CM 1, TERRE HAUTE, IN 47803-3999 • ADMISSIONS: 812-877-8213 • FAX: 812-877-8941

CAMPUS LIFE

Quality of Life Rating	**87**
Fire Safety Rating	**95**
Green Rating	**76**
Type of school	private
Environment	town

STUDENTS

Total undergrad enrollment	1,893
% male/female	79/21
% from out of state	60
# of fraternities	8
# of sororities	3
% African American	2
% Asian	3
% Caucasian	81
% Hispanic	3
% international	6
# of countries represented	15

SURVEY SAYS . . .

Lab facilities are great
Great computer facilities
Athletic facilities are great
Career services are great
School is well run
Campus feels safe

ACADEMICS

Academic Rating	**90**
% students graduating within 4 years	67
% students graduating within 6 years	77
Calendar	quarter
Student/faculty ratio	12:1
Profs interesting rating	90
Profs accessible rating	96
Most classes have	20–29 students
Most lab/discussion sessions have	20–29 students

MOST POPULAR MAJORS

chemical engineering; electrical, electronics and communications engineering; mechanical engineering

STUDENTS SAY ". . ."

Academics

Rose-Hulman earns its "reputation as an excellent undergraduate engineering school" with a combination of strong academics and "personal attention, small class sizes, and a family atmosphere" a rarity among tech schools. Sure, "The workload is fairly heavy, especially sophomore year with the engineering curriculum." Sometimes students feel "Rose is about beating you up and putting you through hell so when you graduate you'll be the only engineer who knows what it's like to be on a project that completely sucks, but you've been taught that all projects are like that so you're the only engineer who will see it all the way through." However, students enjoy an unusually strong support system, and that mitigates the strain. "The transition is made as smooth as possible from high school to college for freshmen" with "on-campus tutoring in the learning center (an excellent resource for students to get homework help)" and "professors who are always available outside of class." One student elaborates, "Our professors are personal and focus on undergraduate education. They will know your name, ask if you are okay if you miss a class or two, and even pull up a chair next to your table at the bar." Those who make it through four years here enjoy the added benefit of "a great alumni base. With almost ninety-nine percent job placement, if you get a decent GPA you're almost guaranteed a job in the field of your choice."

Life

"Life at Rose is academically demanding," but "the community here is so supportive and safe that you get through it," and while "students do a lot of homework and study a lot," they do occasionally find time to close the books and relax. "It's all work and little play Sunday through Thursday," but come Friday "we play hard.'" Students inform us "there's always something to do on campus, whether it's going to a fraternity party or attending a concert or going to a dance or just watching a movie with friends." Greek life is big, "but it's not your typical *Animal House*," and both intramural and Division III intercollegiate athletics have their supporters. There are also "tons of different groups to get involved in" on campus. Hometown Terre Haute, on the other hand, isn't so lively. "There isn't much to do" in town other than "go to the shadiest bars and check out the locals." As one student points out, "We are located in the middle of nowhere…not much they can do about it, but it is not so great."

Student Body

"The kids who attend Rose-Hulman are smart, dedicated, and consequently, nerds," but "this is not a negative thing. Within the students here, there are no outcasts, and even our athletes are most likely also math-letes." "Everyone definitely marches to the beat of his own drum," students assure us. Personality types run the gamut from "geniuses, average students, student-athletes, outspoken, quiet, etc." Demographically, undergrads are "mostly white male engineers from the Midwest" (partly a function of Rose-Hulman's location), but "we are slowly expanding the Rose-Hulman name and getting people from all over the United States and globe." The population "is mostly boys, although the females are catching up," albeit slowly. About half of the incoming freshman class played varsity sports in high school, which is about as many had been involved in the performing arts.

FINANCIAL AID: 812-877-8259 • E-MAIL: ADMISSIONS@ROSE-HULMAN.EDU • WEBSITE: WWW.ROSE-HULMAN.EDU

THE PRINCETON REVIEW SAYS

Admissions

Very important factors considered include: Class rank, rigor of secondary school record. *Important factors considered include:* Academic GPA, recommendation(s), standardized test scores, character/personal qualities. *Other factors considered include:* Application essay, alumni/ae relation, extracurricular activities, interview, talent/ability, volunteer work, work experience. SAT or ACT required; ACT with or without writing component accepted. TOEFL required of all international applicants. High school diploma is required and GED is not accepted. *Academic units required:* 4 English, 4 mathematics, 2 science (2 science labs), 2 social studies, 4 academic electives. *Academic units recommended:* 5 mathematics, 3 science.

Financial Aid

Students should submit: FAFSA. The Princeton Review suggests that all financial aid forms be submitted as soon as possible after January 1. *Need-based scholarships/grants offered:* Federal Pell, SEOG, state scholarships/grants, the school's own gift aid. *Loan aid offered:* Direct Subsidized Stafford, Direct Unsubsidized Stafford, Direct PLUS. Applicants will be notified of awards on or about March 10. Federal Work-Study Program available. Institutional employment available. Highest amount earned per year from on-campus jobs $1,500.

The Inside Word

Rose-Hulman attracts an accomplished applicant pool and counselors believe only its less-than-optimally-desirable location prevents it from attracting an even more competitive group. Grades and test scores are paramount in the review process, but the school invites applicants to submit any supporting materials they think will help their case; such as an essay explaining why you want to be an engineer. Qualified women applicants should receive an especially favorable review, as Rose-Hulman—like most engineering schools—would love to reduce its gender imbalance.

THE SCHOOL SAYS ". . ."

From the Admissions Office

"Rose-Hulman Institute of Technology is nationally recognized as the premier undergraduate college of engineering, science and mathematics in the country. Our emphasis on teaching is the core element to our success. At Rose-Hulman, we educate the next generation of technological leaders. The rich extracurricular life gives students the opportunity to hone their leadership and teaming skills while also making college more fun. With ninety clubs and student organizations, every student has the chance to grow as a human being as well as grow in their profession. World-class undergraduate laboratories complement the instruction."

SELECTIVITY

Admissions Rating	**94**
# of applicants	4,298
% of applicants accepted	62
% of acceptees attending	19
# accepting a place on wait list	163
# admitted from wait list	16

FRESHMAN PROFILE

Range SAT Critical Reading	550–670
Range SAT Math	630–720
Range SAT Writing	530–640
Range ACT Composite	27–32
Minimum paper TOEFL	550
Minimum web-based TOEFL	80
Average HS GPA	3.9
% graduated top 10% of class	62
% graduated top 25% of class	93
% graduated top 50% of class	99

DEADLINES

Regular	
Priority	12/1
Deadline	3/1
Nonfall registration?	no

FINANCIAL FACTS

Financial Aid Rating	**80**
Annual tuition	$37,197
Room and board	$10,445
Required fees	$750
Books and supplies	$1,500
% needy frosh rec. need-based scholarship or grant aid	100
% needy UG rec. need-based scholarship or grant aid	100
% needy frosh rec. non-need-based scholarship or grant aid	13
% needy UG rec. non-need-based scholarship or grant aid	4
% needy frosh rec. need-based self-help aid	96
% needy UG rec. need-based self-help aid	92
% frosh rec. any financial aid	98
% UG rec. any financial aid	98
% UG borrow to pay for school	70
Average cumulative indebtedness	$42,689
% frosh need fully met	14
% ugrads need fully met	19
Average % of frosh need met	86
Average % of ugrad need met	82

Rutgers, The State University of New Jersey—New Brunswick

65 Davidson Road, Piscataway, NJ 08854-8097 • Admissions: 732-932-4636 • Fax: 732-445-0237

CAMPUS LIFE

Quality of Life Rating	**68**
Fire Safety Rating	**78**
Green Rating	**60***
Type of school	public
Environment	town

STUDENTS

Total undergrad enrollment	30,926
% male/female	52/48
% from out of state	11
# of fraternities	29
# of sororities	15
% African American	8
% Asian	25
% Caucasian	49
% Hispanic	11
% international	2
# of countries represented	117

SURVEY SAYS . . .

Class discussions are rare
Great computer facilities
Athletic facilities are great
Diverse student types on campus
Everyone loves the Scarlet Knights
Student publications are popular
Lots of beer drinking
Hard liquor is popular

ACADEMICS

Academic Rating	**69**
% students returning for sophomore year	91
% students graduating within 4 years	52
% students graduating within 6 years	77
Calendar	semester
Student/faculty ratio	15:1
Profs interesting rating	66
Profs accessible rating	70

MOST POPULAR MAJORS

biology/biological sciences; engineering

APPLICANTS ALSO LOOK AT AND OFTEN PREFER

University of Pennsylvania, Cornell University, University of Virginia

AND SOMETIMES PREFER

Pennsylvania State University—University Park, Boston College

AND RARELY PREFER

The George Washington University

STUDENTS SAY ". . ."

Academics

Rutgers is "a big school with many different types of people," a "diverse university in all aspects of the word—academically, culturally, politically, ethnically, linguistically, and socially," which offers "opportunities around every corner." No matter what students seek from their educations, they're likely to find it here, from engineering to business to pharmacy programs and more. That kind of all-encompassing diversity means the school "offers everyone the opportunity to pursue anything they're interested in." It also means, however, that your instructors will run the gamut "from vivacious to narcoleptic"; students will have their "fair share of great professors, average professors, and bad professors." However, for every professor who is "rude when dealing with students," there are ten who are "intelligent people who have a lot of information to share and a lot of experience that allows them to elaborate on many topics." The best of these professors are "experienced, intelligent, and helpful," as well as "diverse, accessible, proactive, involved in research, and interested in students who take initiative." These educators know how to make learning "enjoyable and informative." Most classes employ a traditional lecture format, but many elective classes "are much smaller and thus much more open to discussion and student presentation." Even more attractive for many, Rutgers' status as a research university means there are ample opportunities for undergraduates "to conduct research and work with professors in any number of fields."

Life

A big campus, "awesome" public transportation, and activities of every type mean staying active at Rutgers is easy. There is certainly no lack of things to do. "There is always something going on," students boast, with sports, "movie screenings, arcade games at the RutgersZone, performing arts, local theaters, university-sponsored concert, free food events, community service days, Greek life," and more filling whatever down time students might have. Local restaurants abound. School clubs and organizations exist by the dozen, including those dedicated to theater, music, dance, and community service. "The party scene is definitely present, more so in the warmer months," and there are plenty of bars popular with students. The on-campus party scene tends to be safe, since the school "sends out (campus) police to patrol around the campus twenty-four hours to ensure student safety." Maybe most popular of all is rooting for the scarlet. "During football season…everyone can be found cheering in the student section at the games." For those who need to get off campus, New York City and Philadelphia are both a modest bus drive away. With so many opportunities, "Rutgers allows students to do well in school, be a part of an organization, have relationships with friends, and even have a job." Here, "There's rarely a dull moment."

Student Body

Typical student? Not here. The universal refrain from Rutgers students is there is no such thing. "The one common thread most students have is that they are from New Jersey, since it is a state school." Other than that, "Rutgers is truly a melting pot of people from all over the world of all different backgrounds with different interests." Rather than making it more difficult to fit in, students say this melting pot makes it easier because "no matter what you're interested in, there is a group of students here who share the same exact interests. It's really easy to find your own niche." Most students are "dedicated to academics and community service and also to having fun," students who, no matter which group they fall in with, are "very friendly, funny, and nice." Notice the combination of strong academics and a dedication to fun? That, too, is a frequently cited trait common at Rutgers. Even though "there is not one typical student," at the very least most are "serious about their work and studying but know how to party and have fun." With a large, diverse campus of 30,000, it doesn't matter the kind of person you are. "It is not uncommon to meet someone new weekly… With so many students here, everyone is able to find someone to befriend and interact with."

RUTGERS, THE STATE UNIVERSITY OF NEW JERSEY—NEW BRUNSWICK

FINANCIAL AID: 732-932-7305 • E-MAIL: ADMISSIONS@UGADM.RUTGERS.EDU • WEBSITE: WWW.RUTGERS.EDU

THE PRINCETON REVIEW SAYS

Admissions

Very important factors considered include: Class rank, academic GPA, rigor of secondary school record, standardized test scores. *Other factors considered include:* Application essay, recommendation(s), extracurricular activities, first generation, geographical residence, interview, racial/ethnic status, state residency, talent/ability, volunteer work, work experience. SAT or ACT required; TOEFL required of all international applicants. High school diploma is required and GED is accepted. *Academic units required:* 4 English, 3 mathematics, 2 science, 2 foreign language, 5 academic electives. *Academic units recommended:* 4 mathematics, 2 foreign language.

Financial Aid

Students should submit: FAFSA. The Princeton Review suggests that all financial aid forms be submitted as soon as possible after January 1. *Need-based scholarships/grants offered:* Federal Pell, SEOG, state scholarships/grants, private scholarships, the school's own gift aid, Outside Scholarships. *Loan aid offered:* Direct Subsidized Stafford, Direct Unsubsidized Stafford, Direct PLUS, Federal Perkins, state loans, college/university loans from institutional funds, Other Educational Loans. Applicants will be notified of awards on a rolling basis beginning February 1. Highest amount earned per year from on-campus jobs $1,374.

The Inside Word

One does not need to jump through hoops to get into Rutgers. Because of the vast number of applications the university gets each year, applicants will be reviewed based on the standard criteria—grades, the quality of your high school curriculum, standardized test scores, and your student essay—without much beyond that. Solid students should find acceptance into Rutgers a relatively painless process.

THE SCHOOL SAYS ". . ."

From the Admissions Office

"Rutgers, The State University of New Jersey, one of only sixty-two members of the Association of American Universities, is a research university that attracts students from across the nation and around the world. What does it take to be accepted for admission to Rutgers University? Our primary emphasis is on your past academic performance as indicated by your high school grades (particularly in required academic subjects), your class rank or cumulative average, the strength of your academic program, your standardized test scores on the SAT or ACT, any special talents you may have, and your participation in school and community activities. We seek students with a broad diversity of talents, interests, and backgrounds. Above all else, we're looking for students who will get the most out of a Rutgers education—students with the intellect, initiative, and motivation to make full use of the opportunities we have to offer.

"First-year applicants should take the SAT or the ACT (with writing component). Test scores are not required for students who graduated high school more than two years ago or have completed more than twelve college credits since graduating."

SELECTIVITY	
Admissions Rating	**85**
# of applicants	28,602
% of applicants accepted	61
% of acceptees attending	35

FRESHMAN PROFILE	
Range SAT Critical Reading	520–630
Range SAT Math	560–680
Range SAT Writing	530–640
Minimum paper TOEFL	550

DEADLINES	
Regular	
Priority	12/1
Notification	3/1
Nonfall registration?	yes

FINANCIAL FACTS	
Financial Aid Rating	**70**
Annual in-state tuition	$10,104
Annual out-state tuition	$22,766
Room and board	$11,262
Required fees	$2,651
Books and supplies	$1,474
% needy frosh rec. need-based scholarship or grant aid	68
% needy UG rec. need-based scholarship or grant aid	67
% needy frosh rec. non-need-based scholarship or grant aid	19
% needy UG rec. non-need-based scholarship or grant aid	19
% needy frosh rec. need-based self-help aid	87
% needy UG rec. need-based self-help aid	85
% frosh rec. any financial aid	67
% UG rec. any financial aid	69
% UG borrow to pay for school	68
Average cumulative indebtedness	$16,766
% frosh need fully met	2
Average % of frosh need met	34
Average % of ugrad need met	73

SACRED HEART UNIVERSITY

5151 PARK AVENUE, FAIRFIELD, CT 06825 • ADMISSIONS: 203-371-7880 • FAX: 203-365-7607

CAMPUS LIFE

Quality of Life Rating	**73**
Fire Safety Rating	**80**
Green Rating	**69**
Type of school	private
Affiliation	Roman Catholic
Environment	town

STUDENTS

Total undergrad enrollment	4,173
% male/female	39/61
% from out of state	72
% from public high school	65
% frosh live on campus	92
# of fraternities	3
# of sororities	6
% African American	5
% Asian	2
% Caucasian	67
% Hispanic	6
% international	2
# of countries represented	28

SURVEY SAYS . . .

Great computer facilities
Athletic facilities are great
Career services are great
Dorms are like palaces
Campus feels safe
Everyone loves the Pioneers
Student government is popular

ACADEMICS

Academic Rating	**76**
% students returning for sophomore year	75
% students graduating within 4 years	57
% students graduating within 6 years	66
Calendar	semester
Student/faculty ratio	14:1
Profs interesting rating	81
Profs accessible rating	80
Most classes have	20–29 students

MOST POPULAR MAJORS

business/commerce; nursing/registered nurse (rn, asn, bsn, msn); psychology

APPLICANTS ALSO LOOK AT AND OFTEN PREFER

University of Connecticut, Villanova University

AND SOMETIMES PREFER

Fordham University, Providence College, Loyola University Maryland, Fairfield University

AND RARELY PREFER

Hofstra University, St. John's University—Queens

STUDENTS SAY ". . ."

Academics

Business is big business at Sacred Heart University, where one-third of a recent class graduated with an undergraduate business degree. The "up-and-coming" Welch College of Business (named for former General Electric CEO Jack Welch) uses the school's proximity to New York City to "enable students majoring in business, finance, media studies, etc., with tremendous opportunities" for internships. Nursing, physical therapy, and athletic training are among the school's other strong programs. "The surrounding towns provide amazing sites for...clinical experiences," so many members of SHU's career-minded student body leave here with solid experience under their belts to go along with course knowledge. However, pre-professional preparation is only part of the picture at this "small, Catholic university that prides itself [on] religion and faith." To ensure that students gain general knowledge along with expertise in their specialization (and to reinforce the school's commitment to the liberal arts–driven Catholic Intellectual Tradition), SHU recently introduced a Common Core Curriculum focusing on such lofty topics as justice and humanity's place in the cosmos. A number of students complain about the added requirements and deem the program "a waste of time," but most prefer to focus on the positives, telling us that SHU is "full of spirit along with great academics in a well-balanced manner that allows for the best and fullest college experience one could ask for."

Life

"People are heavily involved in community service, [with] Habitat for Humanity being the largest [service organization] on campus." "If you're into community service and volunteering"—and most students here are—"you'll be in your glory with the opportunities that are available for students." SHU undergrads take the school's mission of service seriously, although that doesn't mean they don't also know how to have a good time. "During the week the school is pretty laid-back," but on weekends, "A good portion of the student population goes out to clubs to drink." One student explains, "Sacred Heart isn't a party school so much as a bar school." Weekends are spent "frivolously" by many, although those who shun the alcohol scene say, "The school does supply fun activities on campus" for them, including movie nights and concerts. Intercollegiate football, basketball, and hockey are all popular as well. Hometown Fairfield "offers shopping, good food, and the beach during warmer months" in addition to the clubs, and "The train is very close [to campus] so you can ride to New Haven or New York City for the day."

Student Body

The typical SHU undergrad "is pretty well-rounded [and is] involved in sports, community service, and clubs." She (two out of three students are female) is "preppy, friendly, and likes to have fun." The small size of the student body means that "everyone is involved in many different groups on campus" and that many "are student athletes. If they are not on one of the Division I sports teams then they are doing some type of club team." There are "a lot of people from Long Island" and an overall "strong Northeast presence (New York, New Jersey, Massachusetts in addition to Connecticut natives)." Many students (though hardly all) come from affluent families. As one student observes, "The parking lot says a lot. Lots of BMWs, Mercedes, and Audis." Other than their charitable undertakings, which are considerable, students tend not to look far beyond their daily lives and obligations. "The majority of students are not very active thinkers on world and political issues outside of their own lives," one student observes.

FINANCIAL AID: 203-371-7980 • E-MAIL: ENROLL@SACREDHEART.EDU • WEBSITE: WWW.SACREDHEART.EDU

THE PRINCETON REVIEW SAYS

Admissions

Very important factors considered include: Academic GPA, rigor of secondary school record. *Important factors considered include:* Class rank, application essay, recommendation(s), character/personal qualities, extracurricular activities, talent/ability, volunteer work, work experience. *Other factors considered include:* Standardized test scores, interview, alumni/ae relation, first generation, geographical residence, level of applicant's interest, racial/ethnic status, religious affiliation/commitment, state residency. ACT with or without writing component accepted. TOEFL required of all international applicants. High school diploma is required and GED is accepted. *Academic units required:* 4 English, 3 mathematics, 3 science (1 science lab), 2 foreign language, 3 social studies, 3 history, 3 academic electives. *Academic units recommended:* 4 English, 4 mathematics, 4 science (2 science labs), 4 foreign language, 4 social studies, 4 history, 4 academic electives.

Financial Aid

Students should submit: FAFSA, CSS/Financial Aid PROFILE, noncustodial PROFILE. The Princeton Review suggests that all financial aid forms be submitted as soon as possible after January 1. *Need-based scholarships/grants offered:* Federal Pell, SEOG, state scholarships/grants, private scholarships, the school's own gift aid. *Loan aid offered:* Direct Subsidized Stafford, Direct Unsubsidized Stafford, Direct PLUS, Federal Perkins, state loans, alternative loans. Applicants will be notified of awards on a rolling basis beginning March 1. Federal Work-Study Program available. Institutional employment available. Off-campus job opportunities are excellent

The Inside Word

Admissions officers at Sacred Heart take the time to consider each applicant on his or her own merits. There's no formula-crunching here; applicants have ample opportunity to make the case why they belong here on their applications. A campus visit is strongly recommended as a way of expressing your interest in the school and setting yourself apart from the crowd. SHU accepts the Common Application.

THE SCHOOL SAYS ". . ."

From the Admissions Office

"Sacred Heart University, distinguished by the personal attention it provides its students, is a thriving, dynamic university known for its commitment to academic excellence, cutting-edge technology, and community service. The second-largest Catholic university in New England, Sacred Heart continues to be innovative in its offerings to students; recently launched programs include Connecticut's first doctoral program in physical therapy, an MBA program for liberal arts undergraduates at the newly AACSB-accredited John F. Welch College of Business, and a campus in County Kerry, Ireland. The university's commitment to experiential learning incorporates concrete, real-life study for students in all majors. Drawing on the robust resources in New England and New York City, students are connected with research and internship opportunities ranging from co-ops at international advertising agencies to research with faculty on marine life in the Long Island Sound. These experiential learning opportunities are complemented by a rich student life program offering more than eighty student organizations including strong music programs, media clubs, and academic honor societies. Sacred Heart University is test-optional; SAT/ACT scores are not required but will be considered is submitted. For students taking the SAT more than once, the highest math score and the highest critical reading score will be evaluated by the admissions committee. No current policy exists for the use of the SAT writing component."

SELECTIVITY	
Admissions Rating	**79**
# of applicants	8,722
% of applicants accepted	55
% of acceptees attending	20
# of early decision applicants	222
# accepted early decision	167

FRESHMAN PROFILE	
Range SAT Critical Reading	480–560
Range SAT Math	490–580
Minimum paper TOEFL	570
Minimum web-based TOEFL	92
Average HS GPA	3.3
% graduated top 10% of class	6
% graduated top 25% of class	32
% graduated top 50% of class	36

DEADLINES	
Early decision	
Deadline	11/15
Notification	12/17
Regular	
Priority	2/15
Nonfall registration?	yes

FINANCIAL FACTS	
Financial Aid Rating	**69**
Annual tuition	$34,030
Room and board	$13,230
Required fees	$250
Books and supplies	$1,200
% needy frosh rec. need-based scholarship or grant aid	72
% needy UG rec. need-based scholarship or grant aid	72
% needy frosh rec. non-need-based scholarship or grant aid	6
% needy UG rec. non-need-based scholarship or grant aid	6
% needy frosh rec. need-based self-help aid	63
% needy UG rec. need-based self-help aid	63
% frosh rec. any financial aid	92
% UG rec. any financial aid	91
% UG borrow to pay for school	77
Average cumulative indebtedness	$45,402
% frosh need fully met	8
% ugrads need fully met	9
Average % of frosh need met	55
Average % of ugrad need met	58

SAINT ANSELM COLLEGE

100 SAINT ANSELM DRIVE, MANCHESTER, NH 03102-1310 • ADMISSIONS: 603-641-7500 • FAX: 603-641-7550

CAMPUS LIFE

Quality of Life Rating	**80**
Fire Safety Rating	**80**
Green Rating	**60***
Type of school	private
Affiliation	Roman Catholic
Environment	city

STUDENTS

Total undergrad enrollment	1,866
% male/female	44/56
% from out of state	78
% from public high school	65
% frosh live on campus	95
% African American	1
% Asian	1
% Caucasian	88
% Hispanic	2
# of countries represented	20

SURVEY SAYS . . .

Great food on campus
Student government is popular
Students get along with local community
Students are friendly

ACADEMICS

Academic Rating	**81**
% students returning for sophomore year	84
% students graduating within 4 years	72
% students graduating within 6 years	74
Calendar	semester
Student/faculty ratio	12:1
Profs interesting rating	84
Profs accessible rating	83
Most classes have	10–19 students
Most lab/discussion sessions have	10–19 students

APPLICANTS ALSO LOOK AT AND OFTEN PREFER

Stonehill College, Providence College, Boston College, College of the Holy Cross, Fairfield University

AND SOMETIMES PREFER

University of Massachusetts Amherst, University of New Hampshire

STUDENTS SAY ". . ."

Academics

Tiny Saint Anselm College offers a well-rounded, high-standard curriculum, as well as a close-knit community, all while upholding a liberal arts education with an emphasis on the Benedictine values of hospitality and service. In addition to having a well-regarded nursing program, the school gives students "a solid foundation academically, politically, socially, and in sports," which means students emerge, "in one word, well-rounded." "Saint Anselm works very hard to produce intellectual students with good morals," says a student. Saint Anselm also has a legendarily strict attendance policy, which has its detractors, but its fans as well: "I love the attendance policy. You will not hear many students say that, but the extra motivation gets you out of bed at eight!" says a student. The professors in this "intimate college community" are "enthusiastic about what they do," and that's what makes the classes more motivating and interesting." Depending on the major and classes the student has enrolled in, "class discussion and participation are crucial." In the liberal arts majors, such as philosophy and great books, "There is much more discussion than in most nursing and science courses. " However, "the amount of discussion and participation is proper and proportional to its importance in one's major." Regardless, the faculty is "always there to answer questions," and the small classroom setting "makes the learning environment a lot easier." In accordance with the school's Benedictine Catholic tradition, there are plenty of "opportunities for service involvement," and there is a monastic community to help students keep the faith. The school is also "one of the centers of politics in New England," and students are all required to take three courses in theology or philosophy. "Saint Anselm College is all about creating an educational, fun, respectful, and peaceful environment that is open to all faculty and students."

Life

The scenic campus in New Hampshire has plenty going for it (though certainly not "internet speed"), but one particular affirmation isn't heard all that often on college campuses: "The food rules!" Many who go here speak of the feeling of acceptance from before they matriculated: "When I first toured the campus, it instantly felt like home. Everyone was very welcoming, and the beauty of the campus really lured me in." "Saint A's always has some sort of event going on, and the gym, Carr Center, coffee shop, and pub are always great places to hang out and have some fun," says a student. Since the school is right in the Manchester area, off campus is also fruitful in its options; "You can always get to restaurants, the mall, clubs, and stores pretty easily." Many students party over the weekend, "but it's not crazy at all," and "if you don't want to drink you don't have to." Service in general is also a popular extracurricular, and "a good portion of the students are involved in one way or another through course-based experiences, service societies, or Campus Ministry or participation in volunteering through the Meelia Center for Community Engagement." There are also "a lot of club sports and intramurals that are fun and easy to join," including the popular flag football and club hockey teams. If you aren't into athletics, you can "definitely find people who like video games and board games as well." The overwhelming majority of students do live on campus, so a lot of people "hang out in the common rooms on each floor and interact with their floor mates."

Student Body

"Academics are the number one priority for all the students here," so it shouldn't be surprising that "people work hard for the most part and are smart about their studies" Many students describe the typical student as white, Catholic ("mass is always crowded with students"), and from the Boston area (or New England at least), and there is a "large percentage of preppy, Red Sox–loving students." All students are quick to point out that the student body as a whole is "very friendly" and "extremely polite to anyone they meet or just pass by." Students "create a very comfortable and friendly environment for everyone on campus," says a student. It "can be sort of cliquey, but if you find the right group of people you will meet some of your greatest friends." By following your interests, "You will meet a lot of people who share your interest and find a lot of new friends that way."

FINANCIAL AID: 603-641-7110 • E-MAIL: ADMISSION@ANSELM.EDU • WEBSITE: WWW.ANSELM.EDU

THE PRINCETON REVIEW SAYS

Admissions

Very important factors considered include: Application essay, academic GPA, recommendation(s), rigor of secondary school record, standardized test scores. *Other factors considered include:* Class rank, alumni/ae relation, character/personal qualities, extracurricular activities, geographical residence, racial/ethnic status, state residency, talent/ability, volunteer work, work experience. ACT with or without writing component accepted. TOEFL required of all international applicants. High school diploma is required and GED is accepted. *Academic units required:* 4 English, 3 mathematics, 3 science (2 science labs), 2 foreign language, 2 social studies. *Academic units recommended:* 4 mathematics, 4 science, 4 foreign language.

Financial Aid

Students should submit: FAFSA, CSS/Financial Aid PROFILE, noncustodial PROFILE, business/farm supplement. Regular filing deadline is March 15. The Princeton Review suggests that all financial aid forms be submitted as soon as possible after January 1. *Need-based scholarships/grants offered:* Federal Pell, SEOG, state scholarships/grants, private scholarships, the school's own gift aid. *Loan aid offered:* Direct Subsidized Stafford, Direct Unsubsidized Stafford, Direct PLUS, Federal Perkins. Applicants will be notified of awards on a rolling basis beginning March 1. Federal Work-Study Program available. Institutional employment available. Off-campus job opportunities are excellent.

The Inside Word

Admission to St. Anselm isn't too hard to come by if you have strong grades and some service-based extracurriculars. The school exclusively uses the Common Application, and SAT and ACT scores are optional (except for those applying to the nursing school). Still, as with most schools that provide this as an option, most students (about seventy percent) do provide scores.

THE SCHOOL SAYS ". . ."

From the Admissions Office

"Saint Anselm is New England's only Benedictine College, a place where a 1,500 year tradition that values a love of learning and a balanced life is coupled with a very contemporary liberal arts education with strong professional preparation on a beautiful 400 acre campus. The college offers over sixty academic programs, but is particularly well-known for nursing, criminal justice, business, politics and psychology. Located in the first in the nation primary state, Saint Anselm is the home of the New Hampshire Institute of Politics which hosts national debates and provides countless opportunities for students of any major to engage with candidates, journalists, elected officials and scholars. A student who wants to meet the next President of the United States has a reasonably good chance of doing so here. Saint Anselm has been named a 'college with a conscience' by the Princeton Review, hailed by the Carnegie Foundation with Classification in both Curricular Engagement and Outreach and Partnerships, and has won federal grants to support its work in public advocacy and engagement with social problems. The college's Humanities Program, now in its third decade, has been hailed as a model of interdisciplinary study in philosophy, theology, science, and art. Faculty from many departments teach in the seminar-based program where students contemplate the fundamental question of what it means to be great. The college's Dana Center for the Arts and Humanities, used by both students and the public, hosts a broad and eclectic range of theater programming including contemporary dance and music. Saint Anselm's Chapel Arts Center provides an extraordinary array of art exhibitions from classic to contemporary with recent acquisitions focused on the human form in art. Eighty-five percent of the college's students participates in athletics, intramurals and club sports. New academic majors have been added over the past two years. Saint Anselm College offers more than eighty academic programs."

SELECTIVITY	
Admissions Rating	74
# of applicants	3,646
% of applicants accepted	77
% of acceptees attending	19
# accepting a place on wait list	442
FRESHMAN PROFILE	
Range SAT Critical Reading	490–590
Range SAT Math	490–590
Range SAT Writing	490–590
Range ACT Composite	21–26
Minimum paper TOEFL	550
Minimum web-based TOEFL	80
Average HS GPA	3.1
DEADLINES	
Early action	
Deadline	11/15
Notification	1/15
Regular	
Deadline	2/15
Nonfall registration?	yes
FINANCIAL FACTS	
Financial Aid Rating	81
Annual tuition	$31,530
Room and board	$11,930
Required fees	$835
Books and supplies	$1,000
% needy frosh rec. need-based scholarship or grant aid	100
% needy UG rec. need-based scholarship or grant aid	99
% needy frosh rec. non-need-based scholarship or grant aid	11
% needy UG rec. non-need-based scholarship or grant aid	9
% needy frosh rec. need-based self-help aid	86
% needy UG rec. need-based self-help aid	89
% UG borrow to pay for school	82
Average cumulative indebtedness	$38,858
% frosh need fully met	16
% ugrads need fully met	16
Average % of frosh need met	80
Average % of ugrad need met	81

SAINT LOUIS UNIVERSITY

221 NORTH GRAND BOULEVARD, SAINT LOUIS, MO 63103 • ADMISSIONS: 314-977-2500 • FAX: 314-977-7136

CAMPUS LIFE

Quality of Life Rating	70
Fire Safety Rating	83
Green Rating	77
Type of school	private
Affiliation	Roman Catholic
Environment	metropolis

STUDENTS

Total undergrad enrollment	8,447
% male/female	41/59
% from out of state	67
% frosh live on campus	91
# of fraternities	9
# of sororities	6
% African American	7
% Asian	7
% Caucasian	65
% Hispanic	4
% international	8
# of countries represented	71

SURVEY SAYS . . .

Students are friendly
Student government is popular
Lots of beer drinking
Hard liquor is popular
Very little drug use

ACADEMICS

Academic Rating	73
% students returning for sophomore year	86
% students graduating within 4 years	61
Calendar	semester
Student/faculty ratio	12:1
Profs interesting rating	68
Profs accessible rating	70
Most classes have	10–19 students
Most lab/discussion sessions have	10–19 students

MOST POPULAR MAJORS

biology/biological sciences; business administration and management; nursing/registered nurse (rn, asn, bsn, msn)

APPLICANTS ALSO LOOK AT AND OFTEN PREFER

Marquette University, University of Illinois at Urbana-Champaign, University of Missouri

AND SOMETIMES PREFER

Creighton University, Truman State University, University of Dayton, Loyola University of Chicago

AND RARELY PREFER

Xavier University (OH)

STUDENTS SAY ". . ."

Academics

"The Jesuit tradition really resonates in everything that happens at SLU," a place where "service, social justice, and political awareness are stressed at every level of your education." This "medium-sized Jesuit school with solid academic programs and a campus that feels close-knit" is best known for its "great premedical programs," which include "a great direct-entry physical therapy program" and "a well-respected accelerated nursing program" as well as the school's premed tracks. Students also speak highly of SLU's offerings in business and pre-law, as well as its unique programs in aviation and "the one-of-a-kind nutrition program with a culinary emphasis." Students praise the way this curriculum "forces you to examine your worldview from the moment you step on campus and helps you discover what your beliefs really are." Academics, especially in the high-profile departments, can be rigorous. In this regard, SLU is "perfect for high achievers and scholars who strive for the best. The professors are nice and professional but are very stern about assignments being turned in on time." One student says, "When it comes to natural sciences, particularly chemistry, biology, etc., I think SLU can be very hard. I guess it works, though. A nursing degree or physical therapy degree from SLU is very highly respected in the health care profession."

Life

"SLU manages to provide everything your parents wish for your college experience and still everything you wouldn't want them to know about," undergrads here confide. Campus life includes "a lot of fun activities the student government puts on…such as outdoor movies, balls, and dances." "Dorm life is very strict and not much fun." The party scene "is decent," because "there are a lot of off-campus living opportunities that are close by and great places to live. The Lofts and Coronado are two great off-campus apartments that are extremely close by." College sports are in the mix. "With the new arena, basketball games are becoming the thing to do." Greek life "is great at SLU." The fraternities and sororities "provide many parties and events for the students and activities such as laser tag and barbecue" to help the students "become involved" and "get to know each other." Being in St. Louis means "great city life around, but most of it is for students that are twenty-one and above," and "off-campus eateries that are close by and range from Drunken Fish Sushi to Rally's Burgers." Students tell us "safety is a huge importance in SLU since we are so close to the city, [and fortunately] there is usually a DPS officer that is always close by to help students in need." "SLU's Jesuit influence encourages the student body to become active in the community. SLU's efforts to encourage community service give many students their first taste of the real world and better prepare them to venture out into it after graduation."

Student Body

SLU "has a pretty homogeneous student population of white, upper-middle-class students coming from a private high school (usually Jesuit, and single-sex) or from the suburbs of bigger Midwestern cities. The girls wear Uggs and North Face fleeces and dye their hair, while the boys live in their…American Eagle jeans." Many "have been in the Catholic school system their entire lives," although there are also "quite a few kids who went to public school and kids who are lower-middle-class." Students are generally committed to the concept of service, and they "put forth a lot of community service hours into the surrounding area, from Habitat for Humanity to the Big Brothers/Big Sisters programs. There are plenty of clubs students use to help raise money for their organizations."

FINANCIAL AID: 314-977-2350 • E-MAIL: ADMITME@SLU.EDU • WEBSITE: WWW.SLU.EDU

THE PRINCETON REVIEW SAYS

Admissions

Very important factors considered include: Academic GPA, standardized test scores. *Important factors considered include:* Application essay, rigor of secondary school record, character/personal qualities, extracurricular activities, talent/ability. *Other factors considered include:* Recommendation(s), alumni/ae relation, first generation, interview, level of applicant's interest, volunteer work. SAT or ACT required; ACT with or without writing component accepted. TOEFL required of all international applicants. High school diploma is required and GED is accepted. *Academic units required:* 4 English, 4 mathematics, 3 science, 3 foreign language, 3 social studies, 3 academic electives. *Academic units recommended:* 4 English, 4 mathematics, 3 science, 3 foreign language, 3 social studies, 3 academic electives.

Financial Aid

Students should submit: FAFSA. The Princeton Review suggests that all financial aid forms be submitted as soon as possible after January 1. *Need-based scholarships/grants offered:* Federal Pell, SEOG, state scholarships/grants, private scholarships, the school's own gift aid, Federal Nursing Scholarships. *Loan aid offered:* Direct Subsidized Stafford, Direct Unsubsidized Stafford, Direct PLUS, Federal Perkins, Federal Nursing, college/university loans from institutional funds. Applicants will be notified of awards on a rolling basis beginning March 1. Federal Work-Study Program available. Institutional employment available. Highest amount earned per year from on-campus jobs $14,068. Off-campus job opportunities are good.

The Inside Word

Saint Louis University's student body is primarily regional, but it continually expands its draw so that today nearly fifty-eight percent of all undergrads arrive from out of state. This increase in geographic diversity has brought with it elevated admissions standards. The grades and test scores that got your older brother or sister in here may not be good enough for you (although family ties to the school are a plus). Admissions officers look for students who display a commitment to both scholarship and Jesuit principles. Applicants must demonstrate success in college preparatory classes and a desire to be active participants in the community.

THE SCHOOL SAYS ". . ."

From the Admissions Office

"A hot Midwestern university with a growing national and international reputation, Saint Louis University gives students the knowledge, skills, and values to build a successful career and make a difference in the lives of those around them. Students live and learn in a safe and attractive campus environment. The beautiful urban, residential campus offers loads of internship, outreach, and recreational opportunities. Ranked as one of the best educational values in the country, the university welcomes students from all fifty states and seventy-five foreign countries who pursue rigorous majors that invite individualization. Accessible faculty, study abroad opportunities, and many small, interactive classes make SLU a great place to learn.

"A leading Jesuit, Catholic university, SLU's goal is to graduate men and women of competence and conscience—individuals who are not only capable of making wise decisions but who also understand why they made them. Since 1818, Saint Louis University has been dedicated to academic excellence, service to others, and preparing students to be leaders in society. Saint Louis University truly is the place where knowledge touches lives.

"For admission, Saint Louis University will accept either the SAT or the ACT with or without the writing component."

SELECTIVITY	
Admissions Rating	**90**
# of applicants	13,389
% of applicants accepted	61
% of acceptees attending	21
# accepting a place on wait list	160
# admitted from wait list	111

FRESHMAN PROFILE	
Range SAT Critical Reading	530–660
Range SAT Math	550–670
Range ACT Composite	25–30
Minimum paper TOEFL	550
Minimum web-based TOEFL	80
Average HS GPA	3.8
% graduated top 10% of class	40
% graduated top 25% of class	70
% graduated top 50% of class	92

DEADLINES	
Regular	
Priority	12/1
Deadline	8/1
Notification	8/1
Nonfall registration?	yes

FINANCIAL FACTS	
Financial Aid Rating	**69**
Annual tuition	$34,740
Room and board	$9,432
Required fees	$506
Books and supplies	$1,660
% needy frosh rec. need-based scholarship or grant aid	98
% needy UG rec. need-based scholarship or grant aid	94
% needy frosh rec. non-need-based scholarship or grant aid	10
% needy UG rec. non-need-based scholarship or grant aid	8
% needy frosh rec. need-based self-help aid	75
% needy UG rec. need-based self-help aid	80
% frosh rec. any financial aid	95
% UG rec. any financial aid	87
% UG borrow to pay for school	63
Average cumulative indebtedness	$36,601
% frosh need fully met	17
% ugrads need fully met	14
Average % of frosh need met	70
Average % of ugrad need met	65

SAINT MARY'S COLLEGE OF CALIFORNIA

PO BOX 4800, MORAGA, CA 94575-4800 • ADMISSIONS: 925-631-4224 • FAX: 925-376-7193

CAMPUS LIFE

Quality of Life Rating	81
Fire Safety Rating	79
Green Rating	82
Type of school	private
Affiliation	Roman Catholic
Environment	village

STUDENTS

Total undergrad enrollment	2,823
% male/female	38/62
% from out of state	15
% from public high school	57
% frosh live on campus	99
% African American	5
% Asian	20
% Caucasian	46
% Hispanic	26
% Native American	3
% international	2
# of countries represented	19

SURVEY SAYS . . .

Lab facilities are great
Campus feels safe
Frats and sororities are unpopular or nonexistent
Lots of beer drinking
Hard liquor is popular

ACADEMICS

Academic Rating	82
% students graduating within 4 years	48
% students graduating within 6 years	62
Calendar	4-1-4
Student/faculty ratio	12:1
Profs interesting rating	90
Profs accessible rating	87
Most classes have	10–19 students

MOST POPULAR MAJORS

business administration, management and operations, other; communication and media studies, other; psychology

APPLICANTS ALSO LOOK AT AND OFTEN PREFER

Santa Clara University, University of California—Davis, Gonzaga University, Loyola Marymount University

AND SOMETIMES PREFER

University of San Francisco

AND RARELY PREFER

Sonoma State University, University of the Pacific, University of California—Santa Cruz

STUDENTS SAY ". . ."

Academics

A "small, Catholic college with a beautiful campus," Saint Mary's College "believes in the importance of education along with the idea that a student can gain faith, friendship, and their identity on their journey." The school's legendary Integrated Liberal Arts great books program combines a "unique liberal arts education" with a focus on "inspiring community, diversity, and intellectual thought," "as well as service work." As one student says, "Saint Mary's transforms students into modern-day philosophers. [It's] a college where questioning the truth is just as important as finding it." Adds another, "I am in a program where every single one of my classes encourages me to make opinions, form arguments, and listen. I read the roots of modern-day philosophy, science, mathematics and politics. I'm expected to grapple with the most difficult texts in Western civilization." Students universally sing the praises of the school's tight-knit community, an asset which "is truly reflected throughout the campus, from interactive class sizes to student-professor relationships." At Saint Mary's, "you are not simply a number, but a face with a story," one student assures us. Many are drawn to the school for its "personal attention to students, large scholarships, easy access to study abroad, and a large amount of student resources." In essence, "Saint Mary's is about teaching students of various backgrounds, how to effect change in the world." Many say that life here offers the perfect fusion of independent thought and guided mentorship; "SMC fosters a support network of faculty, advisors, and students that very few schools can compete with." Professors are "always there to lend a helping hand. They are the perfect mix between forcing you to grow but also being available at any moment for a question."

Life

"There was a sense of 'home' when I came on to campus for the first time," on student says. Beyond the "amazing campus," "A quick ride on BART leaves all of San Francisco at your fingertips." In addition, Oakland is "twenty minutes way" and "Berkeley is even closer!" The town itself is "small but nice." There are "infinite opportunities for outdoor activities," and "many restaurants and a big shopping center ten minutes away." Saint Mary's "is a community waiting to welcome anyone and everyone who enters." "Walking from class to class, [students] will pass many people they know. People are never hesitant to say hello." Students enjoy "the sunny weather," and "Sports games (mainly men's basketball and rugby) are one of the main highlights…bringing all students together." "Our school is a total basketball school where school spirit remains supreme." Students "take their academics seriously, while maintaining a social life." Beyond the ever-popular sporting events, the school promotes unity through "guest speakers, Poetry Slams, open mic night, etc." During the week, when they're not contemplating the complexities of western civilization, students "watch TV, go out to eat, go to the club in the city, go to parties, go bowling, [or] are involved in the intramural sports." Despite the lure of the campus's natural beauty, students say that some of the "facilities need improvement, especially [the] sports facilities."

Student Body

The typical Saint Mary's student is "active and open-minded," and "easy to get along with." In general, most are "dedicated to academics and involved in at least one club or sports team." Though many say that the "typical student is wealthy and Caucasian," and lament the fact that "most of the different ethnic groups stay together," the overall spirit of the student body "is not discriminatory towards race, religion, or gender." Saint Mary's students are "usually pretty involved, if not in community service or school senate, then in athletics." In the way of the Lasallian tradition, "They wouldn't hesitate to lend a helping hand and generally get along well with everyone."

FINANCIAL AID: 925-631-4522 • E-MAIL: SMCADMIT@STMARYS-CA.EDU • WEBSITE: WWW.STMARYS-CA.EDU

THE PRINCETON REVIEW SAYS

Admissions

Very important factors considered include: Academic GPA, rigor of secondary school record, standardized test scores. *Important factors considered include:* Application essay, recommendation(s), first generation. *Other factors considered include:* Class rank, alumni/ae relation, character/personal qualities, extracurricular activities, geographical residence, interview, level of applicant's interest, racial/ethnic status, religious affiliation/commitment, talent/ability, volunteer work, work experience. SAT or ACT required; ACT with or without writing component accepted. TOEFL required of all international applicants. High school diploma is required and GED is accepted. *Academic units required:* 4 English, 3 mathematics, 2 science (1 science lab), 2 foreign language, 1 social studies, 1 history, 2 academic electives. *Academic units recommended:* 4 English, 4 mathematics, 3 science (1 science lab), 3 foreign language, 1 social studies, 1 history, 2 academic electives.

Financial Aid

Students should submit: FAFSA, state aid form. The Princeton Review suggests that all financial aid forms be submitted as soon as possible after January 1. *Need-based scholarships/grants offered:* Federal Pell, SEOG, state scholarships/grants, private scholarships, the school's own gift aid. *Loan aid offered:* Direct Subsidized Stafford, Direct Unsubsidized Stafford, Direct PLUS, Federal Perkins. Applicants will be notified of awards on a rolling basis beginning March 15. Federal Work-Study Program available. Institutional employment available. Highest amount earned per year from on-campus jobs $12,744. Off-campus job opportunities are good.

The Inside Word

Saint Mary's adheres to its Lasallian awareness of social and economic injustice. In line with this, it reserves one quarter of its undergraduate population for students from the lowest economic status. The school will continue to boost it own funding of financial aid in order to help such students attend the school. Here the commitment to serving the underprivileged provides a great opportunity for low-income students with strong academic potential.

THE SCHOOL SAYS ". . ."

From the Admissions Office

"Today, Saint Mary's College continues to offer a value-oriented education by providing a classical liberal arts background second to none. The emphasis is on teaching an individual how to think independently and responsibly, how to analyze information in all situations, and how to make choices based on logical thinking and rational examination. Such a program develops students' ability to ask the right questions and to formulate meaningful answers, not only within their professional careers but also for the rest of their lives. Saint Mary's College is committed to preparing young men and women for the challenge of an ever-changing world, while remaining faithful to an enduring academic and spiritual heritage. We believe the purpose of a college experience is to prepare men and women for an unlimited number of opportunities, and that this is best accomplished by educating the whole person, both intellectually and ethically. We strive to recruit, admit, enroll, and graduate students who are generous, faith-filled, and human, and we believe this is reaffirmed in our community of brothers, in our faculty, and in our personal concern for each student.

"For freshman applicants, we will accept the SAT, and the ACT is also accepted. The ACT writing assessment is optional. The highest critical reading and the highest math scores attained on the SAT will be used. SAT Subject Tests are not required."

SELECTIVITY

Admissions Rating	**72**
# of applicants	4,874
% of applicants accepted	69
% of acceptees attending	19
# accepting a place on wait list	219
# admitted from wait list	38
# of early decision applicants	1,307
# accepted early decision	1,151

FRESHMAN PROFILE

Range SAT Critical Reading	500–600
Range SAT Math	500–610
Range ACT Composite	22–26
Minimum paper TOEFL	550
Minimum web-based TOEFL	79
Average HS GPA	3.56
% graduated top 10% of class	28
% graduated top 25% of class	62
% graduated top 50% of class	89

DEADLINES

Early action	
Deadline	11/15
Notification	1/15
Regular	
Priority	11/15
Deadline	2/1
Notification	3/15
Nonfall registration?	yes

FINANCIAL FACTS

Financial Aid Rating	**70**
Annual tuition	$38,300
Room and board	$13,270
Required fees	$150
Books and supplies	$1,665
% needy frosh rec. need-based scholarship or grant aid	84
% needy UG rec. need-based scholarship or grant aid	83
% needy frosh rec. non-need-based scholarship or grant aid	42
% needy UG rec. non-need-based scholarship or grant aid	27
% needy frosh rec. need-based self-help aid	85
% needy UG rec. need-based self-help aid	87
% frosh rec. any financial aid	94
% UG rec. any financial aid	84
% UG borrow to pay for school	52
Average cumulative indebtedness	$36,745
% frosh need fully met	7
% ugrads need fully met	9
Average % of frosh need met	81
Average % of ugrad need met	72

SAINT MICHAEL'S COLLEGE

ONE WINOOSKI PARK, BOX 7, COLCHESTER, VT 05439 • ADMISSIONS: 802-654-3000 • FAX: 802-654-2906

CAMPUS LIFE

Quality of Life Rating	**96**
Fire Safety Rating	**71**
Green Rating	**83**
Type of school	private
Affiliation	Roman Catholic
Environment	city

STUDENTS

Total undergrad enrollment	1,948
% male/female	48/52
% from out of state	81
% from public high school	69
% frosh live on campus	99
% African American	1
% Asian	1
% Caucasian	90
% Hispanic	3
% international	2
# of countries represented	47

SURVEY SAYS . . .

Students are friendly
Students get along with local community
Students love Colchester, VT
Great off-campus food
Students are happy
Frats and sororities are unpopular or nonexistent
Student publications are popular
Students are involved in community service

ACADEMICS

Academic Rating	**83**
% students returning for sophomore year	87
% students graduating within 4 years	77
% students graduating within 6 years	82
Calendar	semester
Student/faculty ratio	12:1
Profs interesting rating	86
Profs accessible rating	95
Most classes have	10–19 students
Most lab/discussion sessions have	20–29 students

MOST POPULAR MAJORS

biology/biological sciences; business/commerce; psychology

APPLICANTS ALSO LOOK AT AND OFTEN PREFER

Boston College, College of the Holy Cross

AND SOMETIMES PREFER

Stonehill College, University of Vermont, Fairfield University

AND RARELY PREFER

St. Anselm College

STUDENTS SAY ". . ."

Academics

Tucked away in "the heart of Vermont ski country," Saint Michael's College offers a "close-knit and familial atmosphere" where everyone "will always value and support you." "Small classes" help to ensure that "you are not just another number in a lecture hall." Indeed, the college "really wants to help its students realize their full potential." Many tout the "strong academics" and highlight the education, biology, and religion departments in particular. Classes are often "discussion-based" and "require a conscientious student who will actively participate in discussion." Moreover, undergrads here speak effusively about their professors. As one English and theater double-major shares, "the professors strongly encourage you to visit them during office hours and are always working hard to engage students and keep them interested in learning. It is clear that the majority of the professors at St. Mike's care about what they are teaching and seem genuinely interested in the subject matter." A history major succinctly adds, "Whether you like it or not, your professor will know your name." And another satisfied undergrad concludes that the professors "bring real life experience to the material, apply it to current events and to our lives, and are always available to talk about a paper, grade, or class in general. I've been able to push the limits of my mind and branch out during classes, exploring [in ways] that traditional textbook approaches don't [afford]."

Life

Though undergrads at St. Mike's take their academics seriously, they also love to take advantage of life beyond the library. While "partying is popular at Saint Mike's" it's certainly "not a requirement." Fortunately, "the college is great at providing alternative activities on weekends for those who choose to abstain." Indeed, "whether it's a benefit concert, a dance, or a pie-eating contest organized by residential life," one content student promises us that "there is always something to do on campus." A psych major adds to the list, exclaiming, "There are always socials to [attend], bowling, athletic events, concerts, plays, [and] guest speakers." Volunteering is also extremely popular. When students are itching to get off campus, they frequently head to nearby Burlington. "Church Street is crowded with unique shops, fantastic restaurants, and interesting people." Many also love to take advantage of Vermont's outdoor recreational options and the school counts many avid skiers, snowboarders, and hikers among it ranks. In fact, "Saint Michael's provides amazing ski pass deals and transportation to amazing ski resorts in the area." All these options help ensure that life at St. Mike's is "never boring."

Student Body

At first glance, the typical St. Mike's student appears to be a "white, middle-class New Englander" who quickly dons "North Faces and UGGs during the cold Vermont winters." However, once you look past the surface you'll find a vibrant undergrad community where "everyone is unique and different" and even "a little quirky." And though the college is Catholic, undergrads assure us that "there are students of other [faiths and students] who do not practice [a] religion and they are not treated any differently." Undergrads define their peers as "intelligent, outgoing, and active" and quickly assert that "they're friendly and open to new perspectives and new types of people." Indeed, it's even commonplace to "hold doors open for people who are ridiculously far away." Many students are active in "social justice movements, green movements, [and] community service" and also frequently participate in "the school's wilderness program." And don't be fooled: While the average St. Mike's undergrad is "laid-back," students here are "committed to their studies" and "focused on getting all they can out of their college experience." As this math and econ double-major sums up, "Every student here is passionate about something, and it shows in their education and in their actions."

FINANCIAL AID: 802-654-3243 • E-MAIL: ADMISSION@SMCVT.EDU • WEBSITE: WWW.SMCVT.EDU

THE PRINCETON REVIEW SAYS

Admissions

Very important factors considered include: Class rank, academic GPA, rigor of secondary school record. *Important factors considered include:* Application essay, recommendation(s), standardized test scores, character/personal qualities, extracurricular activities, talent/ability. *Other factors considered include:* Alumni/ae relation, first generation, geographical residence, level of applicant's interest, racial/ethnic status, state residency, volunteer work, work experience. ACT with writing component required. TOEFL required of all international applicants. High school diploma is required and GED is accepted. *Academic units required:* 4 English, 3 mathematics, 3 science (2 science labs), 3 foreign language, 3 social studies. *Academic units recommended:* 4 English, 4 mathematics, 4 science (3 science labs), 4 foreign language, 4 social studies.

Financial Aid

Students should submit: FAFSA, signed copies of parent's federal tax return, parent's federal W-2 forms, signed copies of student's federal tax return, student's federal W-2 forms, dependent verification worksheet (Please check the Student Financial Services forms library for the latest version.). Regular filing deadline is February 15. The Princeton Review suggests that all financial aid forms be submitted as soon as possible after January 1. *Need-based scholarships/grants offered:* Federal Pell, SEOG, state scholarships/grants, private scholarships, the school's own gift aid. *Loan aid offered:* Direct Subsidized Stafford, Direct Unsubsidized Stafford, Direct PLUS, Federal Perkins. Applicants will be notified of awards on a rolling basis beginning January 15. Federal Work-Study Program available. Institutional employment available. Highest amount earned per year from on-campus jobs $15,649. Off-campus job opportunities are excellent.

Inside Word

Applicants to St. Mike's are more than just a number, and admissions officers do their utmost to consider candidates in their entirety. Officers consider everything from essays to extracurricular activities, though most weight is given to academic record. The college has recently made standardized tests optional, and applicants won't be penalized if they choose not to submit their scores.

THE SCHOOL SAYS ". . ."

From the Admissions Office

"Saint Michael's is a residential, Catholic, liberal arts college for students who want to 'Learn What Matters.'

A Saint Michael's education will prepare you for life, as each of our thirty majors is grounded in our liberal studies core. Our superb faculty is committed first and foremost to teaching and is known for really caring about students while simultaneously challenging them to reach higher than they ever thought possible. Because of our holistic approach, Saint Michael's graduates are prepared for their entire careers, not just their first jobs out of college.

"With nearly 100 percent of students living on campus, our '24/7' learning environment means exceptional teaching goes beyond the classroom and into the living areas, which include three new suite-style residences, townhouse apartments, and traditional residence halls. The remarkable sense of community encourages students to get involved, take risks, and think differently. A unique passion for social justice issues on campus reflects the heritage of the Edmundite priests who founded Saint Michael's in 1904.

"Saint Michael's is situated three minutes from Burlington, Vermont, one of America's top ten college towns. A unique Cultural Pass program allows students to see an array of music, dance, theater, and Broadway productions at the Flynn Center downtown. Students also take advantage of some of the best skiing in the East through an agreement with Smugglers' Notch ski resort—an all-access season pass is provided to any Saint Michael's student in good academic standing."

SELECTIVITY	
Admissions Rating	82
# of applicants	4,474
% of applicants accepted	78
% of acceptees attending	16
# accepting a place on wait list	235
# admitted from wait list	17
FRESHMAN PROFILE	
Range SAT Critical Reading	530–630
Range SAT Math	530–610
Range SAT Writing	530–620
Range ACT Composite	23–27
Minimum paper TOEFL	550
Average HS GPA	3.5
% graduated top 10% of class	27
% graduated top 25% of class	59
% graduated top 50% of class	86
DEADLINES	
Regular	
Priority	11/1
Deadline	2/1
Notification	4/1
Nonfall registration?	yes
FINANCIAL FACTS	
Financial Aid Rating	83
Annual tuition	$37,200
Room and board	$9,350
Required fees	$310
Books and supplies	$1,200
% needy frosh rec. need-based scholarship or grant aid	100
% needy UG rec. need-based scholarship or grant aid	99
% needy frosh rec. non-need-based scholarship or grant aid	23
% needy UG rec. non-need-based scholarship or grant aid	19
% needy frosh rec. need-based self-help aid	76
% needy UG rec. need-based self-help aid	79
% frosh rec. any financial aid	99
% UG rec. any financial aid	95
% UG borrow to pay for school	69
Average cumulative indebtedness	$31,736
% frosh need fully met	23
% ugrads need fully met	27
Average % of frosh need met	78
Average % of ugrad need met	76

SALISBURY UNIVERSITY

ADMISSIONS OFFICE, SALISBURY, MD 21801 • ADMISSIONS: 410-543-6161 • FAX: 410-546-6016

CAMPUS LIFE

Quality of Life Rating	69
Fire Safety Rating	73
Green Rating	92
Type of school	public
Environment	town

STUDENTS

Total undergrad enrollment	7,758
% male/female	43/57
% from out of state	14
% from public high school	80
% frosh live on campus	88
# of fraternities	7
# of sororities	4
% African American	11
% Asian	2
% Caucasian	78
% Hispanic	4
% international	1
# of countries represented	68

SURVEY SAYS . . .

Lab facilities are great
Great computer facilities
Great food on campus
Intramural sports are popular
Lots of beer drinking
Hard liquor is popular

ACADEMICS

Academic Rating	73
% students returning for sophomore year	83
% students graduating within 4 years	47
% students graduating within 6 years	67
Calendar	4-1-4
Student/faculty ratio	17:1
Profs interesting rating	80
Profs accessible rating	81
Most classes have	20–29 students
Most lab/discussion sessions have	20–29 students

MOST POPULAR MAJORS

biology/biological sciences; communication studies/speech communication and rhetoric; nursing

APPLICANTS ALSO LOOK AT AND SOMETIMES PREFER

St. Mary's College of Maryland, University of Maryland, Baltimore County, University of Maryland, College Park

STUDENTS SAY ". . ."

Academics

A member of Maryland's university system, Salisbury provides undergraduates with stellar academic programs coupled with the benefit of a state school price tag. A "moderately sized" college, Salisbury is "big enough where [you] can meet new people all the time" and yet "small enough where [you are] treated as a student rather than a number." The school really works to foster a "comfortable and personalized environment in which students focus on learning and achievement." Additionally, "Salisbury strives to not only challenge students academically, but also to make them well-rounded as people." The university is an especially good option for those students interested in pursuing a major in education, exercise science, nursing, or environmental studies. For the most part, undergrads at Salisbury speak very highly of their professors. As one elementary education major shares, "The professors here are down-to-earth, friendly, and just passionate about what they are teaching." Fortunately, because most classes are relatively small, "it is easy to form close relationships with [them]." And an environmental studies and biology dual major sums up, "I have met so many amazing captivating professors while at Salisbury. They make the classes interesting and real. They are always willing to answer questions and share experiences with you. The wonderful professors are what I attribute much of my success in college to."

Life

Undergrads at Salisbury are experts at balancing work and play. Though plenty of students "party every weekend," one biology major says that "there [are] definitely other options." Indeed, "it's not uncommon for friends to just hang out on weekends, play board games, watch movies, or have a bonfire." And while some people grumble that "there's not much going on," others maintain that "Salisbury has lots of different clubs and organizations for people who want to join one." Students also get creative and make their own fun, as this happy undergrad shares: "One time we put bubble wrap down in the hall while no one was watching and then a bunch of us jumped on it and danced around." A handful of undergrads are less than enamored with hometown Salisbury and proclaim some neighborhoods a little "rough." Others enjoy taking advantage of the "movie theater, mall, bowling alleys, great restaurants, and...job opportunities" that the surrounding area offers. However, students are nearly unanimous in agreeing that "when the weather is warm, everyone tries to find time to go to Ocean City (only thirty minutes away!)" to escape academic stress and relax on the beach.

Student Body

Salisbury University appears to attract "all types of people," and most undergrads describe their peers as generally "welcoming and friendly." One student expands further, exclaiming, "Finding a group of people you agree with or get along with is rather easy and the diversity of people and things to do seem limitless at times. We each fit into the campus in our own way." A significant portion of students hail "from Maryland, New Jersey, or New York." Salisbury students are also highly active individuals and many are "involved outside of the classroom with a sports team, a club, or a student organization." A number of undergrads also keep "part-time jobs to help pay for tuition." Despite all the activity, we're told that the typical student is "fairly laid-back." Of course, he or she "will put a lot of effort into their field of study." Perhaps the one thing that truly unites these kids is the pride they feel in their school. As an earth science major coyly reveals, "The typical student...never passes up the opportunity to squawk proudly when told [to] by the president as a Salisbury Sea Gull."

FINANCIAL AID: 410-543-6165 • E-MAIL: ADMISSIONS@SALISBURY.EDU • WEBSITE: WWW.SALISBURY.EDU

THE PRINCETON REVIEW SAYS

Admissions

Very important factors considered include: Academic GPA, rigor of secondary school record, extracurricular activities, talent/ability. *Important factors considered include:* Class rank, standardized test scores, alumni/ae relation, volunteer work. *Other factors considered include:* Application essay, recommendation(s), character/personal qualities, racial/ethnic status, geographical residence, work experience. ACT with or without writing component accepted. TOEFL required of all international applicants. High school diploma is required and GED is accepted. *Academic units required:* 4 English, 3 mathematics, 3 science (2 science labs), 2 foreign language, 3 social studies. *Academic units recommended:* 4 English, 4 mathematics, 4 science (3 science labs), 3 foreign language, 3 social studies, 3 academic electives.

Financial Aid

Students should submit: FAFSA. Regular filing deadline is December 31. The Princeton Review suggests that all financial aid forms be submitted as soon as possible after January 1. *Need-based scholarships/grants offered:* Federal Pell, SEOG, state scholarships/grants, private scholarships, the school's own gift aid. *Loan aid offered:* Direct Subsidized Stafford, Direct Unsubsidized Stafford, Federal Perkins. Applicants will be notified of awards on a rolling basis beginning March 15. Federal Work-Study Program available. Institutional employment available. Off-campus job opportunities are fair.

The Inside Word

Admission to Salisbury is competitive, and admissions officers want to admit students who will not only succeed but also thrive. While each applicant's academic record is given the most weight, officers also consider personal traits such as leadership qualities, artistic and athletic talent, and diversity. Standardized tests are optional for those candidates who have earned a cumulative weighted GPA of 3.5 or higher (on a 4.0 scale). However, all applicants should submit test scores for scholarship consideration.

THE SCHOOL SAYS ". . ."

From the Admissions Office

"Friendly, convenient, safe, and beautiful are just a few of the words used to describe the campus of Salisbury University. The campus is a compact, self-contained community that offers the full range of student services. Beautiful, traditional-style architecture and impeccably landscaped grounds combine to create an atmosphere that inspires learning and fosters student pride. Located just thirty minutes from the beaches of Ocean City, Maryland, SU students enjoy a year-round resort social life as well as an inside track on summer jobs. Situated less than two hours from the urban excitement of Baltimore and Washington, D.C., greater Salisbury makes up for its lack of size—its population is about 80,000—by being strategically located. Within easy driving distance of a number of other major cities, including New York City, Philadelphia, and Norfolk, Salisbury is the hub of the Delmarva Peninsula, a mostly rural region flavored by the salty air of the Chesapeake Bay and Atlantic Ocean.

"Submission of SAT and/or ACT scores when applying would be optional to freshman applicants who present a weighted high school grade point average (GPA) of 3.5 or higher on a 4.0 scale. Any student applying with less than a 3.5 would still need to submit a standardized test score to supplement the official high school transcript. Additionally, an applicant may wish to submit a standardized test score subsequent to admission for full scholarship consideration as the majority of the university's scholarships include test scores as a requirement."

SELECTIVITY	
Admissions Rating	86
# of applicants	8,021
% of applicants accepted	53
% of acceptees attending	29

FRESHMAN PROFILE	
Range SAT Critical Reading	530–600
Range SAT Math	540–620
Range SAT Writing	530–600
Range ACT Composite	22–26
Minimum paper TOEFL	550
Average HS GPA	3.7
% graduated top 10% of class	25
% graduated top 25% of class	59
% graduated top 50% of class	91

DEADLINES	
Early action	
Deadline	12/1
Notification	1/15
Regular	
Priority	1/15
Deadline	1/15
Notification	3/15
Nonfall registration?	yes

FINANCIAL FACTS	
Financial Aid Rating	69
Annual in-state tuition	$5,260
Annual out-state tuition	$13,606
Room and board	$8,686
Required fees	$2,072
Books and supplies	$1,300
% needy frosh rec. need-based scholarship or grant aid	90
% needy UG rec. need-based scholarship or grant aid	86
% needy frosh rec. need-based self-help aid	76
% needy UG rec. need-based self-help aid	80
% frosh rec. any financial aid	88
% UG rec. any financial aid	79
% UG borrow to pay for school	58
Average cumulative indebtedness	$20,693
% frosh need fully met	15
% ugrads need fully met	12
Average % of frosh need met	57
Average % of ugrad need met	53

Santa Clara University

500 El Camino Real, Santa Clara, CA 95053 • Admissions: 408-554-4700 • Fax: 408-554-5255

CAMPUS LIFE

Quality of Life Rating	**90**
Fire Safety Rating	**79**
Green Rating	**97**
Type of school	private
Affiliation	Roman Catholic
Environment	city

STUDENTS

Total undergrad enrollment	5,182
% male/female	49/51
% from out of state	39
% from public high school	50
% frosh live on campus	94
% African American	3
% Asian	14
% Caucasian	44
% Hispanic	18
% international	3
# of countries represented	40

SURVEY SAYS . . .

Great computer facilities
Athletic facilities are great
Career services are great
School is well run
Students are happy
Lots of beer drinking
Hard liquor is popular

ACADEMICS

Academic Rating	**86**
% students returning for sophomore year	94
% students graduating within 4 years	77
% students graduating within 6 years	85
Calendar	4-1-4
Student/faculty ratio	13:1
Profs interesting rating	85
Profs accessible rating	89
Most classes have	20–29 students
Most lab/discussion sessions have	10–19 students

MOST POPULAR MAJORS

accounting; marketing; finance

APPLICANTS ALSO LOOK AT AND OFTEN PREFER

Stanford University, University of Southern California

AND SOMETIMES PREFER

Loyola Marymount University, University of San Diego, University of California—Davis

AND RARELY PREFER

University of San Francisco

STUDENTS SAY ". . ."

Academics

Santa Clara University is a small Jesuit school, distinctly influenced by its unique location in California's Silicon Valley. SCU is known for its strong programs in the liberal arts; however, the school also operates a "nationally ranked business school" and "fabulous engineering degree." No matter what your field, SCU is "exceptionally good at preparing students for the real world," and, within all academic programs, the "focus of the coursework is very application-based." In the Jesuit tradition, the school "encourages us to apply our education to our surrounding communities." As such, many "courses are based on social justice, so they think about the global application. Even math classes." Serious students recommend the university honors program, with "its small seminar styled classes led by the school's top professors." While there are "a handful of teachers that just don't make the cut," most SCU professors are "highly qualified" and "very enthusiastic about the material they teach." With a teacher to student ratio of thirteen to one, "Classes are discussion-based, with an emphasis on learning from each other instead of only from the professor." Professors consistently "take the time necessary to ensure that students understand the material discussed in class," and outside of class, "They are always available for office hours for extra help." For anyone looking to get into the software or Internet industry, you can't beat SCU's "great location in the heart of the Silicon Valley." "Santa Clara has a fantastic career center that provides numerous resources to students in their internship and job searches," and participating in a local internship can "enrich what we've learned through classroom curriculum with on-the-job experience." Though some students feel the campus could be even greener, they're happy to report that "the school is huge on sustainability and having a green mindset."

Life

For campus residents, life at SCU is largely defined by the school's system of Residential Learning Communities (RLCs), which group students in housing according to their interests. From your first day on campus, "RLC is a place where you meet most of your friends and are able to hang out and have a great time." With more than 100 student groups on campus, "Most people are involved in numerous clubs, whether that is community service or athletics." There's also a prevailing interest in current events, social responsibility, and service: "Volunteering and community service is a cool thing to do at SCU." In their free time, "Students work out together, volunteer together, get involved with clubs, go shopping, go clubbing, go out to dinner, hang out in San Francisco, hang out in Santa Cruz, and party." With "only two or three bars conveniently close by" and strict campus policies against alcohol, "SCU is mainly a house party school." In student residences near campus, "Parties are big on the weekends, and students get to let loose and have fun." Things get particularly upbeat when the sun comes out, and "You will never see more people outside boozing and partying in the sun than spring quarter at Santa Clara." Though surrounding town of SCU can be rather quiet, the campus is located "across the street from the Caltrain and bus stop, making it easy to get to Santa Cruz or San Francisco for the weekend."

Student Body

Embodying the laid-back California lifestyle, SCU "students are the flip-flop and tank-top-wearing type" and are generally "social and sun loving." "Students are concerned with sustainability, politics, and improving our nation," and "Many students spend time volunteering in support of the local community." "The typical student is middle-class," yet, "There are students of all races, shapes, and sizes." Philosophically, "The Jesuits encourage acceptance of all races, religions, and sexual orientations," and there's "a lot of support for minority groups and cultural awareness on campus." "Most students come from a Catholic background," and the prevailing personality is "amiable, culturally understanding, and welcoming of all people." "A lot of the campus population is committed to remaining fit, so you'll see a lot of people at the gym."

FINANCIAL AID: 408-554-4505 • E-MAIL: ADMISSION@SCU.EDU • WEBSITE: WWW.SCU.EDU

THE PRINCETON REVIEW SAYS

Admissions

Very important factors considered include: Application essay, academic GPA, rigor of secondary school record. *Important factors considered include:* Recommendation(s), standardized test scores, character/personal qualities, extracurricular activities, racial/ethnic status, talent/ability, volunteer work, class rank, alumni/ae relation. *Other factors considered include:* First generation, geographical residence, level of applicant's interest, religious affiliation/commitment, state residency, work experience. SAT or ACT required; ACT with or without writing component accepted. TOEFL required of all international applicants. High school diploma is required and GED is accepted. *Academic units required:* 4 English, 3 mathematics, 2 science, 2 foreign language, 3 social studies, 1 academic electives. *Academic units recommended:* 4 English, 4 mathematics, 3 science, 3 foreign language, 3 social studies, 1 visual/performing arts, 1 academic electives.

Financial Aid

Students should submit: FAFSA, CSS/Financial Aid PROFILE. The Princeton Review suggests that all financial aid forms be submitted as soon as possible after January 1. *Need-based scholarships/grants offered:* Federal Pell, SEOG, state scholarships/grants, private scholarships, the school's own gift aid. *Loan aid offered:* Direct Subsidized Stafford, Direct Unsubsidized Stafford, Direct PLUS, Federal Perkins, private alternative loans. Applicants will be notified of awards on or about April 1. Federal Work-Study Program available. Institutional employment available. Off-campus job opportunities are good.

The Inside Word

SCU carefully evaluates each applicant's file, considering a student's academic record and test scores in addition to his or her personal qualities and family background. Extracurricular activities, letters of recommendation, and personal statements are all carefully reviewed. Accepted students had an average GPA of 3.4 to 3.8 on a 4.0 scale. Students can apply regular decision or through the nonbinding early action program. For the 2012–2013 school year, binding early decision will be available.

THE SCHOOL SAYS ". . ."

From the Admissions Office

"Santa Clara University, located one hour south of San Francisco, offers its undergraduates an opportunity to be educated within a challenging, dynamic, and caring community. The university blends a sense of tradition and history (as the oldest college in California) with a vision that values innovation and a deep commitment to social justice. Santa Clara's faculty members are talented scholars who are demanding, supportive, and accessible. The students are serious about academics, are ethnically diverse, and enjoy a full range of athletic, social, community service, religious, and cultural activities—both on campus and through the many options presented by our northern California location. The undergraduate program includes three divisions: the College of Arts and Sciences, the School of Business, and the School of Engineering.

"Santa Clara University will accept either the SAT or the ACT. The ACT writing component is optional. The highest verbal and the highest math scores attained on the SAT will be used."

SELECTIVITY	
Admissions Rating	90
# of applicants	13,342
% of applicants accepted	54
% of acceptees attending	18
# accepting a place on wait list	2,532
# admitted from wait list	218

FRESHMAN PROFILE	
Range SAT Critical Reading	570–680
Range SAT Math	600–690
Range ACT Composite	27–31
Minimum paper TOEFL	575
Minimum web-based TOEFL	90
Average HS GPA	3.6
% graduated top 10% of class	42
% graduated top 25% of class	75
% graduated top 50% of class	93

DEADLINES	
Early decision	
Deadline	11/1
Early action	
Deadline	11/1
Notification	12/23
Regular	
Deadline	1/7
Notification	4/1
Nonfall registration?	no

FINANCIAL FACTS	
Financial Aid Rating	72
Annual tuition	$39,048
Room and board	$11,997
Books and supplies	$1,656
% needy frosh rec. need-based scholarship or grant aid	72
% needy UG rec. need-based scholarship or grant aid	69
% needy frosh rec. non-need-based scholarship or grant aid	47
% needy UG rec. non-need-based scholarship or grant aid	33
% needy frosh rec. need-based self-help aid	59
% needy UG rec. need-based self-help aid	59
% frosh rec. any financial aid	82
% UG rec. any financial aid	84
% UG borrow to pay for school	41
Average cumulative indebtedness	$27,121
% frosh need fully met	37
% ugrads need fully met	33
Average % of frosh need met	69
Average % of ugrad need met	67

Sarah Lawrence College

One Mead Way, Bronxville, NY 10708-5999 • Admissions: 914-395-2510 • Fax: 914-395-2515

CAMPUS LIFE

Quality of Life Rating	**67**
Fire Safety Rating	**91**
Green Rating	**79**
Type of school	private
Environment	metropolis

STUDENTS

Total undergrad enrollment	1,387
% male/female	28/72
% from out of state	75
% from public high school	51
% frosh live on campus	95
% African American	4
% Asian	8
% Caucasian	70
% Hispanic	9
% international	5
# of countries represented	32

SURVEY SAYS . . .

Lots of liberal students
Class discussions encouraged
No one cheats
Students aren't religious
Frats and sororities are unpopular or nonexistent

ACADEMICS

Academic Rating	**96**
% students returning for sophomore year	89
% students graduating within 4 years	63
% students graduating within 6 years	70
Calendar	semester
Student/faculty ratio	9:1
Profs interesting rating	98
Profs accessible rating	97
Most classes have	10–19 students

STUDENTS SAY ". . ."

Academics

Nestled in a picturesque suburb of New York City, Sarah Lawrence College is a breath of fresh air for intellectually curious students who would chafe within the confines of a more traditional academic setting. The college prides itself on offering "a personal education" that's "tailored to [each] student's interests and needs." Indeed, "self-directed" is the key phrase here, and students really value "the flexibility and openness" that SLC provides. There are no majors or grades at SLC, only concentrations and evaluations (grades are given by professors and recorded by the Registrar). Undergrads are unanimous in their praise for the "conference system," which allows students to conduct "one-on-one" research with professors in topics of their choosing. Students also greatly appreciate "the strong focus on truly learning versus simply preparing…for [a] career." Importantly, "small" class sizes allow for lots of "discussion" and "close teacher relations." And when it comes to describing their professors, undergrads are full of superlatives. One content student describes them as "passionate, engaging, and extremely intelligent." She goes on to explain, "They take an interest in you personally to understand your goals, and then they cater their teaching to that." Further, they "are also readily available for any questions outside of class." Another student simply concludes, "I couldn't ask for more."

Life

While undergrads at SLC are very academically oriented, they also fortunately "engage in a wide variety of social activities." The arts are huge here, and attendance is always high for "theatrical productions, burlesque shows, [and] the annual *Rocky Horror Picture Show* shadowcast on Halloween." Additionally, "concerts by local and campus bands are pretty popular, as are dances." Moreover, "student art shows, film screenings, political lectures, guest speakers, and workshops take place on campus throughout the year." Though a "party scene exists and thrives," it's more common to attend smaller get-togethers or gather with close friends. A "typical Friday night involves an overcrowded room, several bottles of wine, a variety of poets and musicians jamming, and often home-cooked food." Students also love to take advantage of SLC's proximity to New York City (roughly twenty minutes away by train). Many people "go into the city on the weekends" and take in "a Broadway show, check out the farmers market in Union Square, or have a picnic in Central Park."

Student Body

Though undergrads at SLC would debate vociferously as to whether a typical student exists, many define their peers as "artistically and musically inclined, intelligent, voraciously well-read, [and] outspoken with a biting wit." While some might assert you could roam the campus playing a game of spot the "hipster," others insist that "you can find any type of person at Sarah Lawrence." One student goes further, saying, "We're all different, and we all love that. We fit in by not fitting in." Although undergrads are "friendly," some caution that they can also be "aloof" and "reclusive." Fortunately, everyone "can find their niche" and make a "close-knit" group of friends. Additionally, "lots of students here are also in the process of figuring out their sexual orientation and/or gender identity, so most people (even those who aren't figuring that out) are pretty open-minded." Indeed, students at SLC "take risks with style and identity." Perhaps this satisfied undergrad sums his fellow students up best: "Everyone is passionate about something and often several things, be they academic subjects, creative outlets, sports, or political causes, but you will never find two of us who are exactly alike in our interests. I think that makes us the most interesting student body there is, and there's no better place to find an engaging conversation about something completely unexpected."

FINANCIAL AID: 914-395-2570 • E-MAIL: SLCADMIT@SLC.EDU • WEBSITE: WWW.SARAHLAWRENCE.EDU

THE PRINCETON REVIEW SAYS

Admissions

Very important factors considered include: Application essay, recommendation(s), rigor of secondary school record. *Important factors considered include:* Academic GPA, extracurricular activities, talent/ability. *Other factors considered include:* Class rank, alumni/ae relation, character/personal qualities, first generation, geographical residence, interview, level of applicant's interest, racial/ethnic status, volunteer work, work experience. TOEFL required of all international applicants. High school diploma is required and GED is accepted. *Academic units required:* 4 English, 2 mathematics, 2 science, 2 foreign language, 2 history. *Academic units recommended:* 4 mathematics, 4 science, 4 foreign language, 4 social studies, 4 history.

Financial Aid

Students should submit: FAFSA, CSS/Financial Aid PROFILE, state aid form, noncustodial PROFILE. Regular filing deadline is February 1. The Princeton Review suggests that all financial aid forms be submitted as soon as possible after January 1. *Need-based scholarships/grants offered:* Federal Pell, SEOG, state scholarships/grants, private scholarships, the school's own gift aid. *Loan aid offered:* Direct Subsidized Stafford, Direct Unsubsidized Stafford, Direct PLUS, Federal Perkins. Applicants will be notified of awards on or about April 1. Federal Work-Study Program available. Institutional employment available. Highest amount earned per year from on-campus jobs $1,500. Off-campus job opportunities are good.

The Inside Word

Admissions officers at SLC really take the time to try and understand who each applicant is, not only as a student but also as an individual. Candidates should display an inquisitive nature, a passion for learning, and the ability to be an independent thinker. Writing skills are considered critical at SLC and heavy consideration is given to each applicant's essays and short-answer questions. To the relief of some, standardized tests are optional.

THE SCHOOL SAYS ". . ."

From the Admissions Office

"Students who come to Sarah Lawrence are curious about the world, and they have an ardent desire to satisfy that curiosity. Sarah Lawrence offers such students two innovative academic structures: the seminar/conference system and the arts components. Courses in the humanities, social sciences, natural sciences, and mathematics are taught in the seminar/conference style. The seminars enroll an average of eleven students and consist of lecture, discussion, readings, and assigned papers. For each seminar, students also meet one-on-one in biweekly conferences, for which they conceive of individualized projects and shape them under the direction of professors. Arts components let students combine history and theory with practice. Painters, printmakers, photographers, sculptors, filmmakers, composers, musicians, choreographers, dancers, actors, and directors work in readily available studios, editing facilities, and darkrooms, guided by accomplished professionals. The secure, wooded campus is thirty minutes from midtown Manhattan, and the diversity of people and ideas at Sarah Lawrence make it an extraordinary educational environment.

"Sarah Lawrence College no longer uses standardized test scores in the admission process. This decision reflects our conviction that overemphasis on test preparation can distort results and make the application process inordinately stressful, and that academic success is better predicted by the student's course rigor, their grades, recommendations, and writing ability."

SELECTIVITY	
Admissions Rating	85
# of applicants	2,012
% of applicants accepted	61
% of acceptees attending	31
# of early decision applicants	149
# accepted early decision	90

FRESHMAN PROFILE	
Minimum paper TOEFL	600
Average HS GPA	3.6
% graduated top 10% of class	37
% graduated top 25% of class	59
% graduated top 50% of class	91

DEADLINES	
Early decision	
Deadline	11/1
Notification	12/15
Regular	
Deadline	1/1
Notification	4/1
Nonfall registration?	no

FINANCIAL FACTS	
Financial Aid Rating	90
Annual tuition	$45,900
Room and board	$13,504
Required fees	$1,024
Books and supplies	$600
% needy frosh rec. need-based scholarship or grant aid	62
% needy UG rec. need-based scholarship or grant aid	59
% needy frosh rec. need-based self-help aid	59
% needy UG rec. need-based self-help aid	59
% frosh rec. any financial aid	66
% UG rec. any financial aid	59
% UG borrow to pay for school	59
Average cumulative indebtedness	$18,360
% frosh need fully met	27
% ugrads need fully met	22
Average % of frosh need met	90
Average % of ugrad need met	89

Scripps College

1030 Columbia Avenue, Claremont, CA 91711 • Admissions: 909-621-8149 • Fax: 909-607-7508

CAMPUS LIFE

Quality of Life Rating	95
Fire Safety Rating	72
Green Rating	81
Type of school	private
Environment	town

STUDENTS

Total undergrad enrollment	956
% male/female	0/100
% from out of state	48
% from public high school	60
% frosh live on campus	100
% African American	5
% Asian	17
% Caucasian	48
% Hispanic	8
% Native American	1
% international	4
# of countries represented	20

SURVEY SAYS . . .

No one cheats
Great food on campus
Dorms are like palaces
Frats and sororities are unpopular or nonexistent
Political activism is popular

ACADEMICS

Academic Rating	97
% students returning for sophomore year	91
% students graduating within 4 years	83
% students graduating within 6 years	88
Calendar	semester
Student/faculty ratio	11:1
Profs interesting rating	95
Profs accessible rating	96
Most classes have	10–19 students
Most lab/discussion sessions have	10–19 students

MOST POPULAR MAJORS

English language and literature; international relations and affairs; psychology

APPLICANTS ALSO LOOK AT AND OFTEN PREFER

Barnard College, Pitzer College, Pomona College, University of California—Berkeley, University of California—Los Angeles, University of Southern California, Wellesley College, Claremont McKenna College, Princeton University, Whitman College

STUDENTS SAY ". . ."

Academics

Academically focused women seeking "a more personalized education" will find it at Claremont, California's Scripps College. Small class sizes, "extremely approachable, personable" professors who are "ready to sit down to help you one on one," and strong academics are the rule of the day here. And because the school is part of the five-school Claremont College Consortium, students can have their cake and eat it, too, enjoying the benefits of a small- to mid-sized school while also having access to the resources of a large university. The school's focus on "challenging the whole person" means women attending Scripps will engage with educators who work toward "fostering and strengthening the voice of its students by piquing our curiosity, honing our critical thinking skills, and developing our confidence." The workload can be "challenging…rigorous, and sometimes daunting," but professors are "always willing to meet with you and help you" because they "want you to succeed more than anything else." Students find that the "beautiful campus" and "fun living environment" help reduce the stress of the workload. Others feel that going to an all-female school provides "an educational environment where I could be free to be myself, something I didn't feel I could do in classes that were male-dominated." Those seeking "the personal attention and relationships with professors of a liberal arts college with the resources of a mid-size university" will find it at Scripps.

Life

"The most common group activity is studying in groups." Most students find they are "completely absorbed in class time and homework during the week" because "Scripps students are here to be in school and are very engaged in their school work." These "very smart" students "know the difference between study time and party time." The lack of males on campus does not mean there is a lack of partying at Scripps. "If you wanted to, you could go to a big party any day of the week." Those inclined toward big get-togethers will find that "the party scene is mostly off campus, at the other Claremont colleges." Movies, dancing, and other activities help provide distractions during the down time students get from their studies, as well as "participating in volunteer clubs and working with the local community." Indeed, "Scripps has a ton of extracurricular options," including options available via the Consortium. One student summed it up like this: "I'm on the mock trial team, my best friend is on the track team, and my co-RA is in the Latina students group. There really is a hobby for everyone."

Student Body

As an acclaimed women's college, it should come as no surprise that Scripps boasts "assertive women who do not fear taking on the world." These "friendly yet strong women…welcome all types of people with open arms." Demographically, Scripps skews white and upper-middle class, but when it comes to personality "students range from girly daddy's girls to LGBT to work-oriented introverts." Unsurprisingly, many students at Scripps are politically minded, women who are "very critical of the world around them and love to use the knowledge they gain in class to examine society in new ways. " Even those students who don't enter Scripps with strong political views sometimes find it "impossible to go through Core without learning to see social constructs in everything." Most say that despite the eclectic student body "everyone treats each other kindly and respectfully, and there's a lot of crossing over between social groups," though some complain that "students can be very cliquey," making it "difficult to survive socially and to make friends if you are not a clique person." By and large, however, there is usually somewhere for students to fit in. The women of Scripps "pride themselves on being unique and independent, so there is not really a culture to fit in to, but there is any number of subcultures."

FINANCIAL AID: 909-621-8275 • E-MAIL: ADMISSION@SCRIPPSCOLLEGE.EDU • WEBSITE: WWW.SCRIPPSCOLLEGE.EDU

THE PRINCETON REVIEW SAYS

Admissions

Very important factors considered include: Class rank, application essay, academic GPA, recommendation(s), rigor of secondary school record, standardized test scores, alumni/ae relation, character/personal qualities, extracurricular activities, first generation, interview, racial/ethnic status, talent/ability, volunteer work, work experience. *Important factors considered include:* Geographical residence. SAT or ACT required; ACT with writing component required. TOEFL required of all international applicants. High school diploma is required and GED is accepted. *Academic units required:* 4 English, 3 mathematics, 3 science, 3 foreign language, 3 social studies.

Financial Aid

Students should submit: FAFSA, CSS/Financial Aid PROFILE, state aid form, noncustodial PROFILE, business/farm supplement, verification worksheet, signed copies of parent institution verification form, parent and student federal tax returns. Regular filing deadline is February 1. The Princeton Review suggests that all financial aid forms be submitted as soon as possible after January 1. *Need-based scholarships/grants offered:* Federal Pell, SEOG, state scholarships/grants, private scholarships, the school's own gift aid. *Loan aid offered:* Direct Subsidized Stafford, Direct Unsubsidized Stafford, Direct PLUS, Federal Perkins, college/university loans from institutional funds. Applicants will be notified of awards on or about April 1. Federal Work-Study Program available. Institutional employment available. Off-campus job opportunities are good.

The Inside Word

Strong academics are important, yes, but women hoping to be accepted to Scripps should be ready to showcase more than academic excellence. A strong and unique personal statement, powerful writing skills, and intellectual curiosity are all vital to being accepted here. Successful applicants will show strengths in all aspects of their application, with a focus on what sets them apart from the average college student.

THE SCHOOL SAYS ". . ."

From the Admissions Office

"What distinguishes Scripps College from other liberal arts colleges is our interdisciplinary Core Curriculum, which emphasizes critical thinking and intellectual innovation. We believe that learning involves much more than amassing information. A truly educated person can think analytically, communicate effectively, question confidently, and create change in the world. Our curriculum balances breadth requirements in all areas of the liberal arts; a multicultural and a gender studies requirement; and major coursework in sixty different fields. With an average class size of fifteen, students are comfortable participating, challenging old assumptions, and testing new ideas. More than a quarter of all Scripps College students dual or double major, and all complete a senior thesis or performance/project. Almost half study abroad, and, on campus, they can choose from a vast range of clubs, organizations, and activities to participate in through the Claremont Colleges Consortium."

SELECTIVITY

Admissions Rating	**96**
# of applicants	2,163
% of applicants accepted	36
% of acceptees attending	33
# accepting a place on wait list	366
# of early decision applicants	123
# accepted early decision	70

FRESHMAN PROFILE

Range SAT Critical Reading	640–740
Range SAT Math	640–710
Range SAT Writing	660–740
Range ACT Composite	29–32
Minimum paper TOEFL	600
Minimum web-based TOEFL	100
Average HS GPA	4.1
% graduated top 10% of class	79
% graduated top 25% of class	93
% graduated top 50% of class	100

DEADLINES

Early decision	
Deadline	11/15
Notification	12/15
Regular	
Deadline	1/2
Notification	4/1
Nonfall registration?	yes

FINANCIAL FACTS

Financial Aid Rating	**96**
Annual tuition	$43,406
Room and board	$13,468
Required fees	$214
Books and supplies	$800
% needy frosh rec. need-based scholarship or grant aid	96
% needy UG rec. need-based scholarship or grant aid	96
% needy frosh rec. non-need-based scholarship or grant aid	5
% needy UG rec. non-need-based scholarship or grant aid	15
% needy frosh rec. need-based self-help aid	86
% needy UG rec. need-based self-help aid	83
% frosh rec. any financial aid	54
% UG rec. any financial aid	58
% UG borrow to pay for school	41
Average cumulative indebtedness	$13,121
% frosh need fully met	100
% ugrads need fully met	100
Average % of frosh need met	100
Average % of ugrad need met	100

SEATTLE UNIVERSITY

ADMISSIONS OFFICE, SEATTLE, WA 98122-1090 • ADMISSIONS: 206-296-2000 • FAX: 206-296-5656

CAMPUS LIFE

Quality of Life Rating	**91**
Fire Safety Rating	**81**
Green Rating	**95**
Type of school	private
Affiliation	Roman Catholic-Jesuit
Environment	metropolis

STUDENTS

Total undergrad enrollment	4,593
% male/female	40/60
% from out of state	59
% from public high school	63
% frosh live on campus	94
% African American	4
% Asian	16
% Caucasian	50
% Hispanic	8
% Native American	1
% international	9
# of countries represented	90

SURVEY SAYS . . .

No one cheats
Great computer facilities
School is well run
Diverse student types on campus
Students get along with local community
Students love Seattle, WA
Great off-campus food
Frats and sororities are unpopular or nonexistent

ACADEMICS

Academic Rating	**87**
% students returning for sophomore year	86
% students graduating within 4 years	57
% students graduating within 6 years	71
Calendar	quarter
Student/faculty ratio	13:1
Profs interesting rating	86
Profs accessible rating	87
Most classes have	10–19 students
Most lab/discussion sessions have	10–19 students

MOST POPULAR MAJORS

biology; nursing; political science

APPLICANTS ALSO LOOK AT AND OFTEN PREFER

University of Washington, Gonzaga University

AND SOMETIMES PREFER

Santa Clara University, Washington State University

STUDENTS SAY ". . ."

Academics

Though Seattle University is renowned for its excellent academics, particularly a "sensational" nursing program, it is its Jesuit philosophy of holistic education that is its main claim to fame. The university requires students to take a collection of core classes that are more than "just a random collection of math, writing, and social science classes. There's a lot more philosophy, theology, psychology, ethics, and actual service-learning" involved, and students say that "often times the core classes that I was required to take ended up being the most memorable classes." The university's commitment to social justice issues is "more than just rhetoric—there are classes structured *around* specific kinds of service learning." Professors "encourage discussion and active participation" by students, and in turn, students receive a lot of "personal attention from faculty" in "intimate and inviting classroom environments." They can also be counted on to be "helpful in finding internships and networking." It is significant to note, that while Seattle University is steeped in a strong Jesuit tradition, it is "not an extremely religious school." Overall, students here are very happy with the "wonderful academic atmosphere."

Life

Students love Seattle University because it "provides a small campus experience in the middle of an exciting big city." "Seattle is our playground," say the students of the university. "As soon as you step off campus, you are in the hustle and bustle of Capitol Hill, a booming, youthful neighborhood that is LGBT friendly. There are coffee shops…concert venues, and parks within a two-block radius." Getting to downtown Seattle is "easy by bus or foot." It's even easier when "the university loans out bus passes free of charge. It's a quick bus ride to downtown and Pike's Place Market or a nice half-hour walk. Chinatown is nearby, too." On weekends, "Being in the heart of Seattle…means that you can never run out of fun things to do: walk to Pike's Place Market, shop at the stores downtown, see plays, go to the Seattle Arts museum, eat all sorts of different types of food, hang out in the international district, attend film festivals; you name it, Seattle has it!" Live music is a popular attraction here too and is "at the top of most people's lists for a good time." The party scene is "present but not crazy." As for life on campus, students couldn't be happier in this "small, homey, and very welcoming" environment. The campus is "super green," providing students with "composting and recycling options in every location possible." The food is not only "delicious," but is also "locally grown, organic, [and] well-prepared." The recent switch to Division I athletics has added a new emphasis on athletics on campus, much to the chagrin of some students, who think that more money "should be more directed to class resources and the arts" rather than sports.

Student Body

As "one of the most liberal Catholic schools," Seattle University is a place where "all faiths are not only accepted, but they are welcomed and encouraged." The "majority of students are liberal," and "everyone is aware of social issues." Because people are so "politically and socially aware, you can always find a good debate if you're looking for it." The "typical student is committed to academics, involved on campus outside of school, friendly, loves the city of Seattle, and [is] environmentally conscious." There is a "very large LGBTQ community" on campus, as well as "lots of international students" and "hipsters galore." In short, "There are many different types of people here, and they all try to be inclusive." "Every student who graduates from Seattle University will have become a well-rounded individual, recognizing the importance of diversity, sustainability, justice, academic excellence, and leadership on creating a better world for the future."

FINANCIAL AID: 206-296-2000 • E-MAIL: ADMISSIONS@SEATTLEU.EDU • WEBSITE: WWW.SEATTLEU.EDU

THE PRINCETON REVIEW SAYS

Admissions

Very important factors considered include: Academic GPA, rigor of secondary school record, standardized test scores, character/personal qualities. *Important factors considered include:* Application essay, recommendation(s), extracurricular activities, level of applicant's interest. *Other factors considered include:* Class rank, alumni/ae relation, first generation, geographical residence, interview, racial/ethnic status, religious affiliation/commitment, state residency, talent/ability, volunteer work, work experience. SAT or ACT required; ACT with or without writing component accepted. TOEFL required of all international applicants. High school diploma is required and GED is accepted. *Academic units required:* 4 English, 3 mathematics, 2 science (2 science labs), 2 foreign language, 3 social studies, 2 academic electives. *Academic units recommended:* 4 English, 4 mathematics, 2 science (2 science labs), 3 foreign language, 3 social studies, 2 academic electives.

Financial Aid

Students should submit: FAFSA. Regular filing deadline is February 1. The Princeton Review suggests that all financial aid forms be submitted as soon as possible after January 1. *Need-based scholarships/grants offered:* Federal Pell, SEOG, state scholarships/grants, private scholarships, the school's own gift aid, Federal Nursing Scholarships. *Loan aid offered:* Direct Subsidized Stafford, Direct Unsubsidized Stafford, Direct PLUS, Federal Perkins, Federal Nursing. Applicants will be notified of awards on a rolling basis beginning March 21.

The Inside Word

Because this is a Jesuit school, admissions officers tend to value community service. Those who demonstrate a significant commitment to volunteering will find themselves at an advantage, as will those who convey a clear sense of their academic and career goals. Applicants should keep in mind that Seattle University has more stringent test score and course work requirements for certain majors.

THE SCHOOL SAYS ". . ."

From the Admissions Office

"Seattle University provides an ideal environment for motivated students interested in self-reliance, awareness of different cultures, social justice, and the fulfillment that comes from making a difference. Our urban setting promotes the development of leadership skills and independence as well as providing a variety of opportunities for students to apply what they learn through internships, clinical experiences, and volunteer work. It is an environment that allows us to empower leaders for a just and humane world.

"Our academic offerings are designed to provide leadership opportunities as well as to develop global awareness and enable graduates to serve society through a demanding liberal arts and sciences foundation. In the Jesuit tradition, we teach our students how to think, not what to think. Professional undergraduate offerings include highly respected schools of business, nursing, and science and engineering, as well as career-oriented liberal arts programs such as creative writing, journalism, communications, and criminal justice.

"While located in the center of the city, Seattle University is a true residential campus, including students from forty-eight states and territories and ninety-five different nations. Washington State has designated the campus as an 'official backyard sanctuary' for its striking landscaping and environmentally conscious practices—several buildings enjoy official 'green' designations, and the student-run recycling program continually receives national recognition. Additionally, Seattle University is proud of its distinction as the most ethnically diverse institution in the Northwest—all students are valued and respected for their individual strengths, experiences, and worth."

SELECTIVITY

Admissions Rating	**84**
# of applicants	6,317
% of applicants accepted	71
% of acceptees attending	20
# accepting a place on wait list	1,385
# admitted from wait list	341

FRESHMAN PROFILE

Range SAT Critical Reading	520–630
Range SAT Math	530–630
Range SAT Writing	530–630
Range ACT Composite	24–28
Minimum paper TOEFL	520
Minimum web-based TOEFL	68
Average HS GPA	3.6
% graduated top 10% of class	29
% graduated top 25% of class	60
% graduated top 50% of class	88

DEADLINES

Early action	
Deadline	11/15
Notification	12/23
Regular	
Priority	1/15
Deadline	3/1
Nonfall registration?	yes

FINANCIAL FACTS

Financial Aid Rating	**78**
Annual tuition	$34,200
Room and board	$10,296
Required fees	$600
Books and supplies	$1,485
% needy frosh rec. need-based scholarship or grant aid	90
% needy UG rec. need-based scholarship or grant aid	89
% needy frosh rec. non-need-based scholarship or grant aid	60
% needy UG rec. non-need-based scholarship or grant aid	43
% needy frosh rec. need-based self-help aid	75
% needy UG rec. need-based self-help aid	80
% frosh rec. any financial aid	88
% UG rec. any financial aid	76
% UG borrow to pay for school	74
Average cumulative indebtedness	$27,741
% frosh need fully met	9
% ugrads need fully met	9
Average % of frosh need met	65
Average % of ugrad need met	65

SETON HALL UNIVERSITY

ENROLLMENT SERVICES, SOUTH ORANGE, NJ 07079 • ADMISSIONS: 973-761-9332 • FAX: 973-275-2040

CAMPUS LIFE

Quality of Life Rating	73
Fire Safety Rating	81
Green Rating	60*
Type of school	private
Affiliation	Roman Catholic
Environment	village

STUDENTS

Total undergrad enrollment	4,972
% male/female	42/58
% from out of state	29
% from public high school	70
% frosh live on campus	72
% African American	14
% Asian	7
% Caucasian	53
% Hispanic	12
% international	2
# of countries represented	71

SURVEY SAYS . . .

Great computer facilities
Diverse student types on campus
College radio is popular
Student publications are popular

ACADEMICS

Academic Rating	73
% students returning for sophomore year	82
% students graduating within 4 years	50
% students graduating within 6 years	63
Calendar	quarter
Student/faculty ratio	14:1
Profs interesting rating	71
Profs accessible rating	77
Most classes have	10–19 students
Most lab/discussion sessions have	10–19 students

MOST POPULAR MAJORS

communication studies/speech communication and rhetoric; criminal justice/safety studies; nursing/registered nurse (rn, asn, bsn, msn)

APPLICANTS ALSO LOOK AT AND OFTEN PREFER

Pennsylvania State University—University Park, New York Universit

AND SOMETIMES PREFER

Rider University, Fordham University, University of Connecticut, Fairfield University

AND RARELY PREFER

St. Bonaventure University, Monmouth University (NJ), Hofstra University

STUDENTS SAY ". . ."

Academics

"All the colleges within the university are well regarded" at Seton Hall, a prominent Catholic university just down the road from New York City, but the Stillman School of Business and the Whitehead School of Diplomacy and International Relations "are considered the best schools on campus" and thus typically garner the most attention, and understandably so. The former features "a great sports management program" and an attractive, five-year BA/Masters in accounting. Students benefit from proximity to New York, which creates the opportunity for valuable internships, especially in finance. The latter "is directly affiliated with the United Nations," a relationship that "provides students with professors who have had experience with international relations, whether it be ambassadors or foreign correspondents." SHU also excels in nursing, and the university's commitment to keeping pace with technology gives all students a leg up in the modern job market. Indeed, the school works hard "to link the academic world with the real world" through "study abroad, internships, international speakers and events." "The core curriculum gives all students a great foundation beyond their majors so that students are well-rounded individuals with a variety of experiences upon graduation," undergrads report. Students warn, "There is a lot of red tape at Seton Hall."

Life

The school is located in South Orange, "a boring town for college-age students." A much more appealing town, New York City, is "a twenty-minute train ride [from campus], so a lot of people go to the city for fun." Add to that the fact that "most of the student body lives in North Jersey, so it's easy for them to go home for the weekend," and many do just that. Greek life "is very popular," and the school's "big-time men's basketball program" is a huge draw. "Students are always attending basketball games" and "praying that the team does not suck." Intramurals "can be very competitive," "the athletic facilities are state-of-the-art."

Student Body

Seton Hall "is sort of a mishmash of different types. There are a lot of jocks who are definitely treated like stars by the administration, although not so much by the average professor," and "there are some very academic students who mostly try to ignore the actual school and focus on internships and study abroad opportunities." And then there's "the average student, who is from New Jersey, has a major in the School of Arts and Sciences or Business, parties on Thursdays, goes home on weekends, and coasts through college on loans their parents have taken out." "While Seton Hall is a Catholic university, "it is not difficult to find students of other religions," and "the school is accepting of all religious beliefs." Indeed, SHU is big enough that "there are a lot of different kinds of people," and "everyone finds his place by sophomore year."

FINANCIAL AID: 973-761-9332 • E-MAIL: THEHALL@SHU.EDU • WEBSITE: WWW.SHU.EDU

THE PRINCETON REVIEW SAYS

Admissions

SAT or ACT required; ACT with writing component required. TOEFL required of all international applicants.

Financial Aid

The Princeton Review suggests that all financial aid forms be submitted as soon as possible after January 1.

The Inside Word

Students seeking a good school with solid, Catholic roots should consider Seton Hall, whose proximity to New York City helps the school draw prestigious faculty and affords students excellent access to educational, internship, and entertainment opportunities. Applicants who show decent grades in a college preparatory curriculum coupled with strong recommendations should have little trouble gaining admission here. Top students may be pleasantly surprised by the school's financial aid offers.

THE SCHOOL SAYS ". . ."

From the Admissions Office

"For more than 150 years, Seton Hall University has been a catalyst for leadership, developing the whole student—mind, heart and spirit. As a Catholic university that embraces students of all races and religions, Seton Hall combines the resources of a large university with the personal attention of a small liberal arts college. The university's attractive suburban campus is only fourteen miles by train, bus or car to New York City, with the wealth of employment, internship, cultural, and entertainment opportunities the city offers. Outstanding faculty, a technologically advanced campus, and a values-centered curriculum challenge Seton Hall students. Students are exposed to a world of ideas from great scholars, opening their minds to the perspectives, history and achievements of many cultures. Our new core curriculum focuses on the need for our students to have common experiences and encourages them to become thinking, caring, communicative and ethically responsible leaders while emphasizing practical proficiencies and intellectual development. Our commitment to our students goes beyond textbooks and homework assignments, though. At Seton Hall, developing servant leaders who will make a difference in the world is a priority. That's why all students take classes in ethics and learn in a community informed by Catholic ideals and universal values. While Seton Hall certainly enjoys a big reputation, our campus community is close-knit and inclusive. Students, faculty and staff come from around the world, bringing with them a kaleidoscope of experiences and perspectives to create a diverse yet unified campus environment."

SELECTIVITY	
Admissions Rating	78
# of applicants	10,851
% of applicants accepted	79
% of acceptees attending	13

FRESHMAN PROFILE	
Range SAT Critical Reading	470–570
Range SAT Math	470–580
Range SAT Writing	480–580
Range ACT Composite	20–25
Minimum paper TOEFL	550
Average HS GPA	3.1
% graduated top 10% of class	22
% graduated top 25% of class	50
% graduated top 50% of class	83

DEADLINES	
Early action	
Deadline	11/15
Notification	12/31
Regular	
Priority	3/1
Nonfall registration?	yes

FINANCIAL FACTS	
Financial Aid Rating	67
Annual tuition	$32,700
Room and board	$12,906
Required fees	$2,050
Books and supplies	$1,300
% needy frosh rec. need-based scholarship or grant aid	79
% needy UG rec. need-based scholarship or grant aid	62
% needy frosh rec. non-need-based scholarship or grant aid	67
% needy UG rec. non-need-based scholarship or grant aid	54
% needy frosh rec. need-based self-help aid	66
% needy UG rec. need-based self-help aid	74
% frosh rec. any financial aid	91
% UG rec. any financial aid	86
% UG borrow to pay for school	6
Average cumulative indebtedness	$16,160
% frosh need fully met	17
% ugrads need fully met	22
Average % of frosh need met	71
Average % of ugrad need met	66

SEWANEE—THE UNIVERSITY OF THE SOUTH

735 UNIVERSITY AVENUE, SEWANEE, TN 37383-1000 • ADMISSIONS: 931-598-1238 • FAX: 931-538-3248

CAMPUS LIFE

Quality of Life Rating	**78**
Fire Safety Rating	**93**
Green Rating	**91**
Type of school	private
Affiliation	Episcopal
Environment	rural

STUDENTS

Total undergrad enrollment	1,454
% male/female	49/51
% from out of state	71
% from public high school	50
% frosh live on campus	100
# of fraternities	12
# of sororities	9
% African American	4
% Asian	2
% Caucasian	83
% Hispanic	4
% international	2
# of countries represented	23

SURVEY SAYS . . .

No one cheats
Students are friendly
Campus feels safe
Students are happy
Frats and sororities dominate social scene
Lots of beer drinking
Hard liquor is popular

ACADEMICS

Academic Rating	**92**
% students returning for sophomore year	90
% students graduating within 4 years	80
Calendar	semester
Student/faculty ratio	10:1
Profs interesting rating	92
Profs accessible rating	94
Most classes have	10–19 students
Most lab/discussion sessions have	20–29 students

MOST POPULAR MAJORS

economics; English language and literature; history

APPLICANTS ALSO LOOK AT AND OFTEN PREFER

University of Georgia, Washington and Lee University, Rhodes College, University of Tennessee, University of Virginia, Furman University, Vanderbilt University, University of Alabama—Tuscaloosa, Auburn University, Centre College

STUDENTS SAY ". . ."

Academics

The University of the South is a small, "very demanding" school "in the middle of rural Tennessee." Students describe it as "an oasis of perfection" "dripping with both Southern and academic tradition." "Sewanee embodies what a liberal arts education should," beams a history major. Classes are "small" and there's a "well-rounded curriculum." "The volume of work can make you want to pull your hair out," warns an economics major. "Sewanee does not inflate grades," either. "You must work hard to earn an A." "Occasionally a professor or two takes the absent-minded professor stereotype to a ridiculous level," but "it is hard to find a truly bad teacher among the whole lot." Professors here "care about their students." "Their passion for their fields and students is unparalleled." Profs are also very approachable. "We have incredible access to the faculty," gushes a religion major. "Many professors invite students to their homes for social and educational activities somewhat regularly," adds a music major. Students also love the "extremely reachable" administration. The only complaint we hear about academic life concerns the lack of course availability.

Life

Some dorms at Sewanee "really need some work." "Give me air conditioning," demands a sweaty sophomore. The school is generally "behind technologically" as well. The "secluded" town that surrounds the school is "void of any good restaurants, bars, and general distractions a city provides." The campus is "absolutely gorgeous," though. It's a "serene haven" in "an idyllic setting" atop a mountain. Also, the school owns an "incredible amount of land." "Hiking the beautiful perimeter trail" is a favorite pastime, and students can bike, kayak, and "play in the woods" to their hearts' content. Socially, "Sewanee is unique in its quirks." There's a revered honor code. Faculty members wear academic gowns when they teach, and "most Sewanee students follow the tradition of dressing up for class." You'll see men in bow ties and seersucker suits and women in "pointy heels and pearls." There's also an "ever-present" sense of community. "You can't compartmentalize your life here," and for good or ill, "everyone knows what everyone else did last night." During the week, studying is paramount. "We spend a lot of time in the library," notes a sophomore. However, alcohol policies here are "lenient" and "Sewanee is a pretty big party school." Booze is "by no means forced upon you," but "students here drink often and heavily." The frat scene is absolutely massive. "Almost everyone becomes involved in a fraternity or a sorority." "The administration requires all Greek events to be open to the entire campus," but "There is no other social network except the Greek organizations."

Student Body

Even though the administration here is "pushing the diversity card to the nth degree," Sewanee is "strikingly homogenous." "A lot more students here are liberal than you would guess," and Yankees are "not viewed as aliens," but "Sewanee is a Southern and conservative school in every sense of the word." Students are typically "laid-back," "rich, conservative, and fun" "children of the Southern aristocracy" who like to "get drunk on the weekends." Some are "heavily spoiled and coddled." "We have lots of cookie-cutter, preppy, extreme social drinkers, but then again you can also find people who wear only organic hemp, sleep outside, and have dreadlocks," explains a junior. "There are a lot of outdoorsy styles mixed in as well." While "social arrangements are very cliquish," students tell us they are "relatively peacefully coexisting." "It really is one of the friendliest communities that I have ever seen," declares a sophomore.

FINANCIAL AID: 800-522-2234 • E-MAIL: ADMISS@SEWANEE.EDU • WEBSITE: WWW.SEWANEE.EDU

THE PRINCETON REVIEW SAYS

Admissions

Very important factors considered include: Academic GPA, recommendation(s), rigor of secondary school record. *Important factors considered include:* Application essay, standardized test scores, character/personal qualities, extracurricular activities, volunteer work, work experience. *Other factors considered include:* Class rank, alumni/ae relation, first generation, geographical residence, interview, level of applicant's interest, racial/ethnic status, talent/ability. ACT with writing component required. TOEFL required of all international applicants. High school diploma is required and GED is not accepted. *Academic units required:* 4 English, 3 mathematics, 2 science (2 science labs), 2 foreign language, 1 social studies, 1 history. *Academic units recommended:* 4 English, 4 mathematics, 4 science (3 science labs), 4 foreign language, 2 social studies, 2 history.

Financial Aid

Students should submit: FAFSA, institution's own financial aid form. The Princeton Review suggests that all financial aid forms be submitted as soon as possible after January 1. *Need-based scholarships/grants offered:* Federal Pell, SEOG, state scholarships/grants, private scholarships, the school's own gift aid. *Loan aid offered:* Direct Subsidized Stafford, Direct Unsubsidized Stafford, Direct PLUS, Federal Perkins, state loans, college/university loans from institutional funds, private alternative loans. Applicants will be notified of awards on or about April 1. Federal Work-Study Program available. Institutional employment available. Highest amount earned per year from on-campus jobs $1,500. Off-campus job opportunities are fair.

The Inside Word

The admissions office at Sewanee is very personable and accessible to students. Its staff includes some of the most well-respected admissions professionals in the South, and it shows in the way they work with students. Despite a fairly high acceptance rate, candidates who take the admissions process here lightly may find themselves disappointed. Applicant evaluation is too personal for a lackadaisical approach to succeed.

THE SCHOOL SAYS ". . ."

From the Admissions Office

"Sewanee is consistently ranked among the top tier of national liberal arts universities. Sewanee is committed to a rigorous academic curriculum that focuses on the liberal arts as the most enlightening and valuable form of undergraduate education. It offers thirty-six majors, thirty-two minors, and pre-professional programs including business, medicine, and education. Founded by leaders of the Episcopal Church in 1857, Sewanee continues to be owned by twenty-eight Episcopal dioceses in twelve states. The university is located on a 13,000-acre campus atop Tennessee's Cumberland Plateau between Chattanooga and Nashville. Largely forested, rich in biodiversity, this land is a distinctive asset offering an unparalleled outdoor laboratory and boundless recreational opportunities.

"The university has an impressive record of academic achievement—twenty-five Rhodes Scholars and twenty-seven NCAA postgraduate scholarship recipients have graduated from Sewanee. Four of the last eight Tennessee Professors of the Year have been members of Sewanee's faculty. Professors are leading scholars and researchers with a commitment to teaching, and in Sewanee's close community they develop rich and enduring relationships with their students.

"Beginning in 2009, prospective students may choose not to submit standardized test scores. Those who make that choice must instead submit a graded academic paper and complete an evaluative interview with a Sewanee representative. Other critical factors long considered in the Sewanee admission process remain, including strength of the high school curriculum, high school academic performance, extracurricular activities, and evidence of character and talent."

SELECTIVITY

Admissions Rating	**92**
# of applicants	2,920
% of applicants accepted	61
% of acceptees attending	24
# accepting a place on wait list	426
# admitted from wait list	43
# of early decision applicants	105
# accepted early decision	80

FRESHMAN PROFILE

Range SAT Critical Reading	580–680
Range SAT Math	560–650
Range SAT Writing	560–670
Range ACT Composite	26–30
Minimum paper TOEFL	550
Minimum web-based TOEFL	80
Average HS GPA	3.6
% graduated top 10% of class	44
% graduated top 25% of class	77
% graduated top 50% of class	91

DEADLINES

Early decision	
Deadline	11/15
Notification	12/17
Early action	
Deadline	12/1
Notification	1/25
Regular	
Deadline	2/1
Notification	3/17
Nonfall registration?	no

FINANCIAL FACTS

Financial Aid Rating	**91**
Annual tuition	$34,442
Room and board	$9,916
Required fees	$272
Books and supplies	$800
% needy frosh rec. need-based scholarship or grant aid	100
% needy UG rec. need-based scholarship or grant aid	96
% needy frosh rec. non-need-based scholarship or grant aid	0
% needy UG rec. non-need-based scholarship or grant aid	0
% needy frosh rec. need-based self-help aid	81
% needy UG rec. need-based self-help aid	75
% frosh rec. any financial aid	79
% UG rec. any financial aid	74
% UG borrow to pay for school	41
Average cumulative indebtedness	$22,480
% frosh need fully met	76
% ugrads need fully met	81
Average % of frosh need met	96
Average % of ugrad need met	97

Simmons College

300 The Fenway, Boston, MA 02115 • Admissions: 617-521-2051 • Fax: 617-521-3190

CAMPUS LIFE

Quality of Life Rating	**83**
Fire Safety Rating	**90**
Green Rating	**81**
Type of school	private
Environment	city

STUDENTS

Total undergrad enrollment	1,785
% male/female	0/100
% from out of state	38
% frosh live on campus	99
% African American	7
% Asian	8
% Caucasian	66
% Hispanic	5
% Native American	1
% international	3
# of countries represented	46

SURVEY SAYS . . .

Great computer facilities
Great library
Students get along with local community
Students love Boston, MA
Great off-campus food
Frats and sororities are unpopular or nonexistent
Student government is popular

ACADEMICS

Academic Rating	**86**
% students returning for sophomore year	85
% students graduating within 4 years	63
% students graduating within 6 years	69
Calendar	semester
Student/faculty ratio	13:1
Profs interesting rating	89
Profs accessible rating	82
Most classes have	10–19 students

MOST POPULAR MAJORS

nursing (bsn); communications; psychology

APPLICANTS ALSO LOOK AT AND OFTEN PREFER

Massachusetts College of Pharmacy and Health Sciences, Boston University, University of Massachusetts Amherst, Mount Holyoke, Emmanuel College

AND SOMETIMES PREFER

Northeastern University, University of Massachusetts Boston, Bridgewater State University, Smith College, University of Massachusetts Dartmouth

AND RARELY PREFER

University of Massachusetts Lowell, University of Rhode Island, George Washington University, Goucher College, Providence College

STUDENTS SAY ". . ."

Academics

A women's college "rich in history and achievement," Simmons College equips its undergraduates with the tools and confidence they need to succeed in the real-world. With a small student population of about 2,000, Simmons offers a surprisingly wide range of undergraduate majors, while also running one of the "top nursing schools in the state." Across academic programs, there's a "particular focus on experiential learning and leadership," and the curriculum excels at "educating women for positions of powerful and principled leadership." Simmons professors "do everything in their power to help us get an internship, to learn, to interact with the material, and to prepare us for life after college" and students get valuable hands-on experience through research, "community engagement," and "leadership opportunities" in campus groups. A chemistry major remembers, "My college has many research opportunities and connections. I have been able to do scientific research every semester since my first year at Simmons." Small discussion-based classes "really challenge you to do your best and to actually put some thought into your work," and Simmons professors are "interested in every student succeeding in the classroom, as well as in their future endeavors." Within administrative offices, there's "very little red tape," and the school succeeds at "giving students power to make decisions in the school, including policy, academics, administration, [and] events." "Resources are wonderful, from the career education center to the writing center to the technology center," and the college "takes advantage of its Boston location through class trips, job placement, and internship opportunities." However, when it comes to the all-important problem of paying for school, students admit that the "financial aid counselors could be more helpful."

Life

America's most college-friendly city, Boston makes a great backdrop for life at Simmons. Packed with culture and entertainment, "The city offers many great places to hang out like bowling places, karaoke bars, college parties at other colleges, and great scenery." In addition, Simmons is part of the Colleges of the Fenway association, so "Students get discounts at art museums and cultural events around the city such as plays or dances." "Simmons is not a party school," so those who want to carouse "venture out in the city" or head to nearby colleges. Other students prefer mellower activities, like "sitting in the common room and talking or watching a show together." Since so much social life takes place off campus, "The dorms are quiet and a great place to concentrate on school work." The peacefulness of campus is a plus for many students, who "spend a lot of time studying and preparing for labs and lecture." To blow off steam, "A lot of students here use the gym on a regular basis," and the campus athletic center offers "Zumba, kick-boxing, spinning, and boot camps." "Simmons College is also very big on community service," and many students volunteer at organizations around Boston.

Student Body

Besides the fact that they're all female, Simmons students say there's a lot of diversity on their small campus. "Diversity is strongly valued," and "The community here is very accepting, regardless of race, ethnicity, economic status, religion, sexual orientation, gender expression, or disability." Politically, you'll meet students who are "very conservative to very liberal," though "most students are very supportive of the LGBTA community and women's rights in general." When it come to academics, "Students are very dedicated and take their school work seriously," though they also make time for fun. Socially, "Birds of a feather flock together," and students admit, "There are different cliques within the student body." However, "Everyone is generally accepted" on this friendly and community-oriented campus. In fact, some students say Simmons feels "like a big sorority."

FINANCIAL AID: 617-521-2001 • E-MAIL: UGADM@SIMMONS.EDU • WEBSITE: WWW.SIMMONS.EDU

THE PRINCETON REVIEW SAYS

Admissions

Very important factors considered include: Academic GPA, rigor of secondary school record. *Important factors considered include:* Class rank, application essay, recommendation(s), standardized test scores. *Other factors considered include:* Extracurricular activities, interview, talent/ability, volunteer work, work experience. SAT or ACT required; ACT with or without writing component accepted. TOEFL required of all international applicants. High school diploma is required and GED is accepted. *Academic units required:* 4 English, 3 mathematics, 3 science, 3 foreign language, 3 social studies, 3 history. *Academic units recommended:* 4 English, 4 mathematics, 3 science, 4 foreign language, 4 social studies, 3 history.

Financial Aid

Students should submit: FAFSA, institution's own financial aid form. Regular filing deadline is March 1. The Princeton Review suggests that all financial aid forms be submitted as soon as possible after January 1. *Need-based scholarships/grants offered:* Federal Pell, SEOG, state scholarships/grants, private scholarships, the school's own gift aid. *Loan aid offered:* Direct Subsidized Stafford, Direct Unsubsidized Stafford, Direct PLUS, state loans, college/university loans from institutional funds. Applicants will be notified of awards on a rolling basis beginning March 15. Federal Work-Study Program available. Institutional employment available. Highest amount earned per year from on-campus jobs $2,000. Off-campus job opportunities are excellent.

The Inside Word

Simmons evaluates prospective students for both academic strength and personal qualities, like community involvement or leadership. Applicants to Simmons should use their personal essays, letters of recommendation, and applications to show the admissions committee who they are as a person. Although a personal interview isn't required, it can be a great way to augment your application, as well as a chance to experience Simmons unique environment. A current student tells us, "I stepped onto campus, and instantly it felt like the right fit."

THE SCHOOL SAYS ". . ."

From the Admissions Office

"Founded in 1899, Simmons was the first college in the nation to offer women a liberal arts education integrated with professional preparation. Today, Simmons is known for providing transformative learning that links passion with lifelong purpose. The college is committed to preparing students for their careers, while also helping them discover who they are and what they can contribute to society over the course of their lifetimes.

"As a student-focused institution, Simmons offers a learning experience that is highly collaborative and much more personal than that of large universities. Simmons professors include distinguished researchers, published authors, Fulbright scholars, health professionals, and community leaders. More than fifty percent are women, and approximately 100 percent hold doctorate degrees in their field. They advise numerous government, nonprofit, and corporate organizations in the United States and around the world—yet passionately uphold their primary obligation to teach.

"To help students succeed, career support starts as soon as students step on campus and continues as an ongoing, lifelong service. Ninety-seven percent of the class of 2010 were employed or in graduate school within one year of graduation (either full or part time). And, of this population, more than eighty-nine percent are employed at jobs in a field related, or closely related, to their major while at Simmons. At Simmons, we are committed to preparing women to be well-informed, open-minded, intellectually curious, and lifelong learners."

SELECTIVITY	
Admissions Rating	**84**
# of applicants	4,528
% of applicants accepted	47
% of acceptees attending	16
# accepting a place on wait list	31
# admitted from wait list	16

FRESHMAN PROFILE	
Range SAT Critical Reading	510–620
Range SAT Math	510–610
Range SAT Writing	520–620
Range ACT Composite	22–27
Minimum paper TOEFL	560
Minimum web-based TOEFL	83
Average HS GPA	3.3
% graduated top 10% of class	22
% graduated top 25% of class	56
% graduated top 50% of class	86

DEADLINES	
Early action	
Deadline	12/1
Notification	1/15
Regular	
Deadline	2/1
Notification	3/15
Nonfall registration?	yes

FINANCIAL FACTS	
Financial Aid Rating	**70**
Annual tuition	$33,500
Room and board	$13,140
Required fees	$1,000
Books and supplies	$1,280
% needy frosh rec. need-based scholarship or grant aid	81
% needy UG rec. need-based scholarship or grant aid	73
% needy frosh rec. non-need-based scholarship or grant aid	15
% needy UG rec. non-need-based scholarship or grant aid	14
% needy frosh rec. need-based self-help aid	73
% needy UG rec. need-based self-help aid	69
% frosh rec. any financial aid	96
% UG rec. any financial aid	88
% UG borrow to pay for school	78
% frosh need fully met	10
% ugrads need fully met	7
Average % of frosh need met	69
Average % of ugrad need met	64

SKIDMORE COLLEGE

815 North Broadway, Saratoga Springs, NY 12866-1632 • Admissions: 518-580-5570 • Fax: 518-580-5584

CAMPUS LIFE

Quality of Life Rating	**95**
Fire Safety Rating	**60***
Green Rating	**60***
Type of school	private
Environment	town

STUDENTS

Total undergrad enrollment	2,655
% male/female	39/61
% from out of state	65
% from public high school	59
% frosh live on campus	100
% African American	3
% Asian	5
% Caucasian	69
% Hispanic	7
% international	4
# of countries represented	51

SURVEY SAYS . . .

Students aren't religious
Students love Saratoga Springs, NY
Great off-campus food
Dorms are like palaces
Frats and sororities are unpopular or nonexistent

ACADEMICS

Academic Rating	**94**
% students returning for sophomore year	95
% students graduating within 4 years	82
% students graduating within 6 years	84
Calendar	semester
Student/faculty ratio	9:1
Profs interesting rating	92
Profs accessible rating	96
Most classes have	10–19 students
Most lab/discussion sessions have	10–19 students

MOST POPULAR MAJORS

business/commerce; English language and literature; psychology

APPLICANTS ALSO LOOK AT AND OFTEN PREFER

Boston College, Wesleyan University, Colby College

AND SOMETIMES PREFER

Syracuse University, Connecticut College, New York University

AND RARELY PREFER

University of Vermont, Wheaton College (MA), Ithaca College

STUDENTS SAY ". . ."

Academics

Skidmore College is a "school that values independence, creativity, and passion." At this unique, small college, "Creative approaches to learning and education are infused into the curriculum and daily life." Skidmore's strong majors in the liberal arts and sciences are complemented by top-rated programs in art, theater, music, and dance. A senior tells us, "I couldn't decide between Ivy League academics or an arts conservatory, so this seemed to be the compromise." Skidmore "allows students with a variety of interests to take classes that they are interested in," and "interdisciplinary courses and work are common" here. Professors are "extremely enthusiastic about their subjects," and "All classes are really personal. You get to know everyone in the class, and the professors urge [you] to meet with them at least a few times one-on-one so that they can get to know you." A current student affirms, "I've been given many wonderful academic opportunities—I even started doing research as a first-semester freshman." Administrators are receptive to students, and "Every month or so the president will have fireside chats where students are open to discuss their issues with him."

Life

Fun, fulfilling, and a bit rowdy, life at Skidmore is "like summer camp for college students." On this busy campus, "Your typical student is a part of at least one club or extracurricular [activity], sometimes two or three or four." Thanks to the school's artistic inclinations, "Art openings, theater performances, student bands, a capella shows, and comedy shows are all really popular." In fact, a typical weekend night out would include "a performance and then the after-party." Here, "strong friendships and a great sense of community keep things interesting on campus," and students really like the fact that, "We don't have frats or sororities so there is no pressure to join or conform to anything." Students convene in the campus's central cafeteria, and "When the weather is nice out, students love to spend time outside talking, reading, playing tennis, or playing chess." You will also find "a network of hiking trails called 'Northwoods' that is a very popular place to exercise, talk, or have a bonfire on a Friday night." Described as "the perfect college town," Saratoga Springs is "extremely fun and accepting of college students" with "amazing restaurants" and tons of shops. In addition to recreational activities, "Skidmore students are very involved in the Saratoga community through everything from sustainability efforts to mentoring local children." You'll find "a mix of smaller parties on campus and larger ones in off-campus houses" on Friday and Saturday nights. "The dining hall offers freshly made food which is delicious and gives students a variety, from vegetarian to full-out carnivor[ous]."

Student Body

With strong arts and athletics programs, "Skidmore's enduring stereotype is that there are two groups of students: the jocks and the hipsters." In reality, things aren't so black and white. "Most students are white, upper-middle-class" and hail from New England; however, "there is a wide range of racial and geographic backgrounds" within the student body. Whether it's music, dance, theater, or visual arts, "Most people are artistically inclined or at least interested in art." In fact, "The typical student here seems to be the atypical student elsewhere: super-liberal and socially conscious, 'creative' or artsy, weirdly dressed." Some undergraduates even claim, "You can't be a Skid kid unless you are a little weird." "If you can carry on an intelligent or quirky conversation you will have no trouble-making friends." A student adds, "My group of friends in particular is always having discussions about what we are learning in classes, theoretical physics, political, and environmental issues."

FINANCIAL AID: 518-580-5750 • E-MAIL: ADMISSIONS@SKIDMORE.EDU • WEBSITE: WWW.SKIDMORE.EDU

THE PRINCETON REVIEW SAYS

Admissions

Very important factors considered include: Rigor of secondary school record. *Important factors considered include:* Class rank, application essay, academic GPA, recommendation(s), character/personal qualities, extracurricular activities, talent/ability, volunteer work, work experience. *Other factors considered include:* Standardized test scores, alumni/ae relation, first generation, geographical residence, interview, level of applicant's interest, racial/ethnic status. SAT or ACT required; ACT with writing component required. TOEFL required of all international applicants. High school diploma is required and GED is accepted. *Academic units recommended:* 4 English, 4 mathematics, 4 science (3 science labs), 4 foreign language, 4 social studies.

Financial Aid

Students should submit: FAFSA, CSS/Financial Aid PROFILE. Regular filing deadline is February 1. The Princeton Review suggests that all financial aid forms be submitted as soon as possible after January 1. *Need-based scholarships/grants offered:* Federal Pell, SEOG, state scholarships/grants, the school's own gift aid. *Loan aid offered:* Direct Subsidized Stafford, Direct Unsubsidized Stafford, Direct PLUS, Federal Perkins. Applicants will be notified of awards on or about April 1. Federal Work-Study Program available. Institutional employment available. Highest amount earned per year from on-campus jobs $2,300. Off-campus job opportunities are fair.

The Inside Word

Admission to Skidmore is highly competitive, and the admissions staff carefully considers each applicant's academic background and standardized test scores. However, consistent with their motto—"creative thought matters"—Skidmore carefully reviews a student's extracurricular talents, achievements, and passions when making an admissions decision. While admissions interviews aren't a requirement for a Skidmore applicant, students may request a personal interview on campus or with an alumnus in their area.

THE SCHOOL SAYS ". . ."

From the Admissions Office

"At Skidmore, we believe a great education is about putting academic theory and creative expression into practice; hence, our belief that creative thought matters. It's a place where faculty and students work together, then figure out how to use what they've learned to make a difference. This often leads to multidisciplinary approaches, where students carry more than one major, student-faculty research is common, most students study abroad, and internships and community service are standard. Skidmore students develop into independent, creative problem-solvers who aren't restricted to looking at things in traditional ways.

This personal journey starts with the First-Year Experience—fifty seminars from which to choose, faculty and peer mentors, and living in close proximity to seminar classmates in residence halls. It's meant to ensure that first-year students hit the ground running on day one, connected and involved. When it comes to your major, you can choose from sixty-five offerings in the sciences, social sciences, and humanities, as well as pre-professional fields like management and business.

"Since we have no fraternities or sororities, student life centers on the nearly 100 student clubs and organizations, which range from the Environmental Action Club to a capella groups to snowboarding. Add to this the prominence of the arts, which has long set Skidmore apart. Science classes collaborate on exhibits at the Tang Museum. Hundreds of students perform, often in the new Zankel Music Center. Enroll in dance courses. Do theater performances. Most not even arts majors. At Skidmore, the arts don't dominate, they permeate.

"As for location, who wouldn't want to go to college in Saratoga Springs? A downtown brimming with shops, galleries, coffeehouses, and great restaurants. Boston, New York City, and Montreal are a three-hour car ride from campus. And the Adirondacks, Berkshires, and Green Mountains provide opportunities for skiing, mountain biking, hiking, rock-climbing, and kayaking."

SELECTIVITY

Admissions Rating	93
# of applicants	5,780
% of applicants accepted	42
% of acceptees attending	27
# accepting a place on wait list	966
# admitted from wait list	2
# of early decision applicants	398
# accepted early decision	287

FRESHMAN PROFILE

Range SAT Critical Reading	570–680
Range SAT Math	580–670
Range SAT Writing	580–680
Range ACT Composite	26–30
Minimum paper TOEFL	590
% graduated top 10% of class	42
% graduated top 25% of class	75
% graduated top 50% of class	97

DEADLINES

Early decision	
Deadline	11/15
Notification	12/15
Regular	
Deadline	1/15
Notification	4/1
Nonfall registration?	no

FINANCIAL FACTS

Financial Aid Rating	94
Annual tuition	$41,520
Room and board	$11,304
Required fees	$860
Books and supplies	$1,300
% needy frosh rec. need-based scholarship or grant aid	99
% needy UG rec. need-based scholarship or grant aid	95
% needy frosh rec. non-need-based scholarship or grant aid	9
% needy UG rec. non-need-based scholarship or grant aid	8
% needy frosh rec. need-based self-help aid	84
% needy UG rec. need-based self-help aid	77
% frosh rec. any financial aid	54
% UG rec. any financial aid	51
% UG borrow to pay for school	48
Average cumulative indebtedness	$21,000
% frosh need fully met	99
% ugrads need fully met	89
Average % of frosh need met	100
Average % of ugrad need met	93

SMITH COLLEGE

SEVEN COLLEGE LANE, NORTHAMPTON, MA 01063 • ADMISSIONS: 413-585-2500 • FAX: 413-585-2527

CAMPUS LIFE

Quality of Life Rating	98
Fire Safety Rating	72
Green Rating	95
Type of school	private
Environment	town

STUDENTS

Total undergrad enrollment	2,627
% male/female	0/100
% from out of state	77
% from public high school	61
% frosh live on campus	100
% African American	5
% Asian	12
% Caucasian	44
% Hispanic	8
% international	11
# of countries represented	65

SURVEY SAYS . . .

Great off-campus food
Dorms are like palaces
Frats and sororities are unpopular or nonexistent
Student government is popular
Political activism is popular

ACADEMICS

Academic Rating	97
% students returning for sophomore year	94
% students graduating within 4 years	80
% students graduating within 6 years	85
Calendar	semester
Student/faculty ratio	9:1
Profs interesting rating	93
Profs accessible rating	91
Most classes have	10–19 students

MOST POPULAR MAJORS

economics; political science and government; psychology

APPLICANTS ALSO LOOK AT AND OFTEN PREFER

Brown University

AND SOMETIMES PREFER

Wellesley College

AND RARELY PREFER

Mount Holyoke College

STUDENTS SAY ". . ."

Academics

Smith College is "an incredibly prestigious, diverse, academically rigorous, socially liberal, and well-respected institution," located in the consummate college town of Northampton, Massachusetts. A Smith education is all about "finding and pursuing your passions." Offering "academic freedom," "Smith doesn't have course requirements" beyond the major, and "self-scheduled finals" allow students to take exam week at their own pace. "One of the most prominent women's colleges in the country," Smith "builds the self-confidence of smart women," and "Most classes, even in math and sciences, are very interdisciplinary and often have a feminist bias." Classes are "engaging and promote critical thought," and professors are "inspiring, dynamic, accessible, and brilliant." Smith professors "care deeply about students" and "take the time to get to know you on a first-name basis." Smith also offers fabulous academic facilities and "countless resources" to augment your education, including a "wonderful study abroad department" and ample opportunities for research. There's "a large number of undergrads doing serious scientific research" in addition to coursework. If they can't find what they need amid Smith's ample course selection, students "can take classes at the other four schools nearby (UMass Amherst, Amherst College, Hampshire College, and Mount Holyoke College)" through the Northampton Five College Consortium. When graduation approaches, Smith students benefit from the school's "excellent alumni network." "The Career Development Office will do everything in its power to help you get a job."

Life

Smith attracts hardworking and idealistic students, who are "striving to succeed in our classes, as well as make a difference in the Smith College community and the outside community." There's a decided "focus on academics" at Smith, and most students "study, write papers, rehearse, or practice the majority of the time." Students augment coursework with "lectures and symposium on campus," as well as "involvement in community service and activism for global issues, women's rights, LGBTQ rights, the environment, and pretty much anything that fights oppression." When they want to relax, Smithies can attend "free movies and concerts, plays, speakers, sports events, and dances," as well as "school-sponsored house parties almost every weekend." When they want to branch out or rub elbows with the opposite sex, students "go to other college parties at surrounding campuses," or head out in Northampton, which is "always bustling" with "concerts, restaurants, and cute shops." The "quality of life is outstanding" on campus, where "The dorms are not dorms but beautiful houses," and cafeteria food is a cut above the average.

Student Body

"Smithies are passionate about everything they do," especially academics. Throughout the semester, undergraduates are known to "study hard" and get "ridiculously stressed" about course work. "It's the nature of Smithies to be driven, but we all want to see our friends and housemates succeed at well." Smith's unique environment attracts "a great mix of nerdy, edgy, [and] traditional" students, including "hipsters, WASPs, crazy partiers, international students, and the average New Englander." Fortunately, there's a "strong sense of community," and "Students fit in easily, even if they have different interests." Despite diversity, "One thing all students have in common here is the will for women's empowerment and acceptance of any gender or sexual preference." On that note, many students "love the queer life on campus," where many students are either gay or have "a fluid perception of sexuality." Though there's some political diversity on campus, most Smithies hold "very liberal views," and many are "very conscious and aware, not only of their community but the world in general."

FINANCIAL AID: 413-585-2530 • E-MAIL: ADMISSION@SMITH.EDU • WEBSITE: WWW.SMITH.EDU

THE PRINCETON REVIEW SAYS

Admissions

Very important factors considered include: Academic GPA, recommendation(s), rigor of secondary school record, character/personal qualities. *Important factors considered include:* Class rank, application essay, extracurricular activities, interview, talent/ability. *Other factors considered include:* Standardized test scores, alumni/ae relation, first generation, racial/ethnic status, volunteer work, work experience. ACT with or without writing component accepted (test optional). TOEFL required of all international applicants. High school diploma or equivalent is not required. *Academic units recommended:* 4 English, 3 mathematics, 3 science (3 science labs), 3 foreign language, 2 history, 1 academic elective.

Financial Aid

Students should submit: FAFSA, CSS/Financial Aid PROFILE, noncustodial PROFILE, business/farm supplement. Regular filing deadline is February 15. The Princeton Review suggests that all financial aid forms be submitted as soon as possible after January 1. *Need-based scholarships/grants offered:* Federal Pell, SEOG, state scholarships/grants, the school's own gift aid. *Loan aid offered:* Direct Subsidized Stafford, Direct Unsubsidized Stafford, Direct PLUS, Federal Perkins, state loans, college/university loans from institutional funds. Applicants will be notified of awards on or about April 1. Federal Work-Study Program available. Institutional employment available. Highest amount earned per year from on-campus jobs $2,650. Off-campus job opportunities are excellent.

The Inside Word

Every prospective Smithie is carefully evaluated by at least two members of the admissions staff. No hard numbers guarantee admission: Smith is looking for students who will succeed academically and socially in college, evaluating each applicant for both personal and intellectual qualities. To best prepare for admission, Smith recommends that students follow a rigorous college prep curriculum in high school. If you're feeling particularly enthused about your future at Smith, you can become a fan of the admissions department on Facebook, take the online tour, or read student blogs on the admission page.

THE SCHOOL SAYS ". . ."

From the Admissions Office

"Smith students choose from 1,000 courses in more than fifty areas of study. There are no specific course requirements outside the major; students meet individually with faculty advisers to plan a balanced curriculum. Smith programs offer unique opportunities, including the chance to study abroad, or at another college in the United States, and a semester in Washington, D.C. The Ada Comstock Scholars Program encourages women beyond the traditional age to return to college and complete their undergraduate studies. Smith is located in the scenic Connecticut River valley of western Massachusetts near a number of other outstanding educational institutions. Through the Five College Consortium, Smith, Amherst, Hampshire, and Mount Holyoke colleges, and the University of Massachusetts enrich their academic, social, and cultural offerings by means of joint faculty appointments, joint courses, student and faculty exchanges, shared facilities, and other cooperative arrangements. Smith is the only women's college to offer an accredited major in engineering; it's also the only college in the country that offers a guaranteed paid internship program ('Praxis')."

SELECTIVITY	
Admissions Rating	97
# of applicants	4,128
% of applicants accepted	45
% of acceptees attending	37
# accepting a place on wait list	475
# of early decision applicants	330
# accepted early decision	177

FRESHMAN PROFILE	
Range SAT Critical Reading	600–730
Range SAT Math	600–710
Range SAT Writing	620–720
Range ACT Composite	27–31
Minimum paper TOEFL	600
Minimum web-based TOEFL	90
Average HS GPA	3.9
% graduated top 10% of class	60
% graduated top 25% of class	89
% graduated top 50% of class	99

DEADLINES	
Early decision	
Deadline	11/15
Notification	12/15
Regular	
Deadline	1/15
Nonfall registration?	no

FINANCIAL FACTS	
Financial Aid Rating	95
Annual tuition	$41,190
Room and board	$13,860
Required fees	$270
Books and supplies	$800
% needy frosh rec. need-based scholarship or grant aid	97
% needy UG rec. need-based scholarship or grant aid	94
% needy UG rec. non-need-based scholarship or grant aid	1
% needy frosh rec. need-based self-help aid	94
% needy UG rec. need-based self-help aid	96
% frosh rec. any financial aid	61
% UG rec. any financial aid	63
% UG borrow to pay for school	65
Average cumulative indebtedness	$22,531
% frosh need fully met	100
% ugrads need fully met	100
Average % of frosh need met	100
Average % of ugrad need met	100

SONOMA STATE UNIVERSITY

1801 EAST COTATI AVENUE, ROHNERT PARK, CA 94928 • ADMISSIONS: 707-664-2778 • FAX: 707-664-2060

CAMPUS LIFE

Quality of Life Rating	70
Fire Safety Rating	79
Green Rating	72
Type of school	public
Environment	town

STUDENTS

Total undergrad enrollment	7,704
% male/female	40/60
% from out of state	1
% from public high school	71
% frosh live on campus	90
# of fraternities	8
# of sororities	10
% African American	2
% Asian	4
% Caucasian	66
% Hispanic	15
% Native American	1
% international	1
# of countries represented	19

SURVEY SAYS . . .

Great computer facilities
Great library
Athletic facilities are great
Low cost of living
Very little drug use

ACADEMICS

Academic Rating	67
% students returning for sophomore year	78
% students graduating within 4 years	26
Calendar	semester
Student/faculty ratio	25:1
Profs interesting rating	77
Profs accessible rating	70
Most classes have	20–29 students

MOST POPULAR MAJORS

business/commerce; liberal arts and sciences studies and humanities, other; psychology

STUDENTS SAY ". . ."

Academics

For a state school, SSU's student body is on the smaller side, and the environment is friendly and casual. Major coursework takes a "one-on-one" approach, and, in most departments, "professors make it easy to build a relationship with them outside of the classroom." While SSU professors "enjoy teaching," students admit that class quality is "hit-or-miss," especially in lectures and general education courses. Fortunately, professors "want to see their students succeed and therefore, are willing to go above and beyond in assisting them." A student says, "Not only do my professors know my name, but they actually know my character as well, and whenever I need letters of recommendation, I can always ask actual professors instead of TAs." Students warn, "Classes can be hard to get, especially with budget cuts," making it more difficult to graduate in four years. For example, "All art classes are only available for art majors, and only drama majors are allowed to audition for plays."

Life

The school's dorms and suites are "beautiful," the gym and recreational center are state-of-the-art, and there are an "abundance of extracurricular activities that make the university setting more than just academics." In the evenings, "the Residential Student Association at SSU puts on many fantastic activities for students to attend, such as weekly movie nights, karaoke, crafts, pizza feeds, comedians, open mic nights, guest speakers, and so on." "A lot of people go to the cafe or just hang around campus" during their spare time. Although fraternities and sororities do not have housing, "the nightlife around Sonoma State University focuses on Greek events," and for many (though not all) students, "partying is a staple." For those looking for an alternative to the Greek system, "Sonoma State has great leadership opportunities for students on campus." Sonoma's stellar location makes the school a perfect home base for day trips in Northern California. From SSU, "The beach is less than an hour's drive from campus, as is San Francisco."

Student Body

Nestled amidst Northern California redwoods, Sonoma State attracts students from across the state. In addition to locals, "there are a significant amount of southern California students," who may initially stand out from their Bay Area counterparts. Eventually, however, everyone is "socialized to the laid-back atmosphere." "Most students are politically aware, care about the environment, and are accepting to those who are different." Students acknowledge that "there is personality diversity but not ethnic diversity." In any case, "you are bound to have an interesting conversation at least once a day," and everyone is "respectful of others with different opinions." No matter what you like to do, you'll find a niche; "People looking for a social realm can experience that, and those looking for a quiet, academic realm can experience that as well." "The typical students at Sonoma are dedicated to their studies but not afraid to go out and have some fun."

FINANCIAL AID: 707-664-2389 • E-MAIL: STUDENT.OUTREACH@SONOMA.EDU • WEBSITE: WWW.SONOMA.EDU

THE PRINCETON REVIEW SAYS

Admissions

Very important factors considered include: Academic GPA, rigor of secondary school record, standardized test scores. *Other factors considered include:* First generation, geographical residence, state residency. SAT or ACT required; ACT with or without writing component accepted. TOEFL required of all international applicants. High school diploma is required and GED is accepted. *Academic units required:* 4 English, 3 mathematics, 2 science (1 science lab), 2 foreign language, 2 history, 1 visual/performing arts, 1 academic electives, 1 visual/performing arts, U.S. government.

Financial Aid

Students should submit: FAFSA. The Princeton Review suggests that all financial aid forms be submitted as soon as possible after January 1. *Need-based scholarships/grants offered:* Federal Pell, SEOG, state scholarships/grants, private scholarships, ACG, SMART. *Loan aid offered:* Direct Subsidized Stafford, Direct Unsubsidized Stafford, Direct PLUS, Federal Perkins. Applicants will be notified of awards on a rolling basis beginning March 25. Federal Work-Study Program available. Institutional employment available. Highest amount earned per year from on-campus jobs $9,000. Off-campus job opportunities are good.

The Inside Word

To determine an applicant's eligibility for admission, SSU calculates an admissions index number based on his or her standardized test scores and GPA. Due to the school's budget problems, students applying for admission to impacted majors must submit higher GPAs and test scores than applicants to non-impacted programs. Currently, impacted majors include communication studies, human development, liberal studies, pre-nursing and nursing, and psychology.

THE SCHOOL SAYS ". . ."

From the Admissions Office

"Sonoma State University occupies 275 acres in the beautiful wine country of Sonoma county, in northern California. Located at the foot of the Sonoma hills, the campus is an hour's drive north of San Francisco and centrally located between the Pacific Ocean to the west and the wine country to the north and east. SSU is deeply committed to the teaching of the liberal arts and sciences. The campus has earned a national reputation as a leader in integrating the use of technology into its curriculum. Within its thirty-two academic departments, SSU awards bachelor's degrees in forty-one areas of specialization and master's degrees in fourteen areas. In addition, the university offers a joint master's degree in mathematics with San Francisco State University. The campus ushered in the twenty-first century with the opening of a new library and technology center, the Jean and Charles Schulz Information Center.

"All freshmen applicants are required to provide SAT or ACT scores."

SELECTIVITY

Admissions Rating	68
# of applicants	12,151
% of applicants accepted	85
% of acceptees attending	18

FRESHMAN PROFILE

Range SAT Critical Reading	450–560
Range SAT Math	450–560
Range ACT Composite	18–24
Minimum paper TOEFL	500
Minimum web-based TOEFL	61
Average HS GPA	3.4

DEADLINES

Regular	
Priority	11/30
Deadline	11/30
Notification	3/1
Nonfall registration?	yes

FINANCIAL FACTS

Financial Aid Rating	69
Annual out-state tuition	$17,334
Room and board	$10,961
Required fees	$6,174
Books and supplies	$1,746
% needy frosh rec. need-based scholarship or grant aid	63
% needy UG rec. need-based scholarship or grant aid	67
% needy frosh rec. non-need-based scholarship or grant aid	10
% needy UG rec. non-need-based scholarship or grant aid	15
% needy frosh rec. need-based self-help aid	85
% needy UG rec. need-based self-help aid	71
% frosh rec. any financial aid	47
% UG rec. any financial aid	65
% UG borrow to pay for school	58
Average cumulative indebtedness	$18,608
% frosh need fully met	10
% ugrads need fully met	16
Average % of frosh need met	87
Average % of ugrad need met	86

SOUTHERN METHODIST UNIVERSITY

PO BOX 750181, DALLAS, TX 75275-0181 • ADMISSIONS: 214-768-3147 • FAX: 214-768-1083

CAMPUS LIFE

Quality of Life Rating	**85**
Fire Safety Rating	**93**
Green Rating	**82**
Type of school	private
Affiliation	Methodist
Environment	metropolis

STUDENTS

Total undergrad enrollment	6,150
% male/female	48/52
% from out of state	47
% from public high school	61
% frosh live on campus	97
# of fraternities	15
# of sororities	13
% African American	6
% Asian	6
% Caucasian	67
% Hispanic	11
% international	7
# of countries represented	93

SURVEY SAYS . . .

Athletic facilities are great
School is well run
Students love Dallas, TX
Great off-campus food
Frats and sororities dominate social scene
Lots of beer drinking
Hard liquor is popular

ACADEMICS

Academic Rating	**80**
% students returning for sophomore year	89
% students graduating within 4 years	60
% students graduating within 6 years	75
Calendar	semester
Student/faculty ratio	11:1
Profs interesting rating	80
Profs accessible rating	92
Most classes have	10–19 students
Most lab/discussion sessions have	20–29 students

MOST POPULAR MAJORS

business administration and management; social sciences; communication; journalism

APPLICANTS ALSO LOOK AT AND OFTEN PREFER

University of Southern California, Vanderbilt University

AND SOMETIMES PREFER

Trinity University, The University of Texas at Austin, University of Miami, Tulane University

AND RARELY PREFER

Texas Christian University, University of Arizona, Baylor University, University of Colorado—Boulder

STUDENTS SAY ". . ."

Academics

Located on a tree-lined, "beautiful campus" in the heart of Dallas, Southern Methodist University is a mid-size private university with a lot going on. The school has a "unique culture" that relies on "top academics" and a "long-standing history of strong traditions" to build "incredible alumni support," which in turn brings students excellent internship and job opportunities. SMU offers everything "from a great social life and extracurricular activities to fun and interesting classes," including a "phenomenal business school" and "amazing" facilities. The school prides itself on being "a close-knit community of the intellectually elite," and this translates into "a wealth of academic resources [with which] to be successful, a flood of opportunities for those who want them, and thus a community of intellectuals who happen to genuinely care about each other." Professors are "incredibly gifted in their fields and exceptional communicators." They "love interacting with students" and "are willing to put in extra time to convey the material accurately to students." "If their office hours don't match yours, they will change their schedule to accommodate people," says a student. Most have worked in the industry that they teach in, and therefore they "can offer real-life connections to the material we learn." The syllabus is also modeled "to what you'll face in the real world." The legion of SMU alumni provides excellent connections into the business world (among others), and a "dedicated career services center" only sweetens the employment pot. Since many attend SMU for the Cox School of Business, it helps that the school is in the ideal location "to secure great jobs with Fortune 500 companies right here in Dallas." The school's administration also "understands that studying abroad, internships, extracurriculars, etc., also play a crucial role in developing students into the adults and professionals they want to become." "SMU puts the 'classy' back in classical education," says a student.

Life

Despite the fact it is located in the heart of Dallas, "the atmosphere is very calm and relaxing." SMU students frequently head to uptown Dallas "for fine dining and dancing" and often see movies, shop, and attend concerts and sports games. Everyone is always on campus for the football games for "boulevarding" ("basically tailgating but on steroids"), and "we love to have alums come visit us for the tailgate," says a student. Students generally fit in with this "a vibrant social life" best once they have found an extracurricular organization that is right for them, and oftentimes "sororities and fraternities tend to be this venue." However, some wish there was "less emphasis on Greek Life," since "if you're not Greek, you can sometimes feel left out or looked down on." Students devote a large portion of their time to their studies, but "there is always a social event every weekend night to blow off steam." This heavy concentration on future careers means that most here are "definitely wanting to become leaders in their field or profession," so "fraternity parties and formals are popular, but at the same time so are speeches from prominent members of the community and theatrical performances."

Student Body

This student body is "happy and leads a balanced life" at a school that it loves. Most students at SMU "tend to be a bit preppy," "polite," and tend to come from "influential backgrounds." Many "work a lot for pay or do internships," take a lot of class hours, "are involved…and have fun a lot." "They are very busy people, and they prefer it that way," says one student. All of these "motivated, outgoing," people "thrive on leadership" and are "dedicated to academics and involvement, both at SMU and in the greater community." Fashion "is a big part of SMU culture." This group is "very social" and frequently interacts with the Dallas community and "amazing arts and restaurant scene around campus."

FINANCIAL AID: 214-768-3147 • E-MAIL: UGADMISSION@SMU.EDU • WEBSITE: WWW.SMU.EDU

THE PRINCETON REVIEW SAYS

Admissions

Very important factors considered include: Class rank, application essay, academic GPA, recommendation(s), rigor of secondary school record, standardized test scores. *Important factors considered include:* Character/personal qualities, extracurricular activities, talent/ability, volunteer work, work experience. *Other factors considered include:* Alumni/ae relation, first generation, level of applicant's interest. SAT or ACT required; ACT with or without writing component accepted. TOEFL required of all international applicants. High school diploma is required and GED is not accepted. *Academic units required:* 4 English, 3 mathematics, 3 science (2 science labs), 2 foreign language, 1 social studies, 2 history. *Academic units recommended:* 4 English, 4 mathematics, 4 science (3 science labs), 3 foreign language, 2 social studies, 3 history.

Financial Aid

Students should submit: FAFSA, CSS/Financial Aid PROFILE, noncustodial PROFILE, business/farm supplement. Regular filing deadline is February 15. The Princeton Review suggests that all financial aid forms be submitted as soon as possible after January 1. *Need-based scholarships/grants offered:* Federal Pell, SEOG, state scholarships/grants, private scholarships, the school's own gift aid. *Loan aid offered:* Direct Subsidized Stafford, Direct Unsubsidized Stafford, Direct PLUS, Federal Perkins, state loans, college/university loans from institutional funds. Applicants will be notified of awards on a rolling basis beginning March 15. Off-campus job opportunities are good.

The Inside Word

SMU boasts a potent combination: high-caliber academics, a desirable location, and a beautiful campus. No surprise then that gaining admission is challenging, and growing more so all the time. Solid high school grades and a compelling list of extracurricular activities will usually do the trick. "Special talent" students—aesthetes and athletes in particular—can make up for academic deficiencies; those in the arts must undergo an audition/portfolio review, while promising athletes are scouted. Except for those in the performing arts, all admitted students enter as "pre-majors" in the Dedman College of Humanities and Sciences.

THE SCHOOL SAYS ". . ."

From the Admissions Office

"SMU students balance challenging academic programs with a vibrant campus experience in a vibrant city. Students receive personal attention in small classes led by professors dedicated to teaching while also pursuing research. Reflecting its student-centered focus, SMU is one of the few universities to have a voting student member on its Board of Trustees. Internships, community service, student research opportunities, and study abroad programs abound. SMU offers a thriving honors community and generous merit scholarship programs. More than 400 arts and cultural events each year add vitality to campus life. About 180 student organizations provide opportunities for leadership. Through the George W. Bush Presidential Center and the renowned Tate Lecture Series, students have access to dignitaries ranging from former presidents to Nobel laureates. Another unique resource is a mountain campus near Taos, New Mexico. SMU welcomes a diverse student body representing every state, over ninety countries and a wide array of backgrounds. More than seventy percent of SMU undergraduates receive some form of financial aid. Graduates attend some of the best graduate and professional schools in the nation and find career opportunities through SMU's close ties with the global city of Dallas.

"SMU requires either the ACT or SAT. Assessment of written communication skills remains an important component of the SMU application review process. To that end, it is recommended that applicants use every opportunity, including the ACT or SAT, to display their writing skills in the application process."

SELECTIVITY	
Admissions Rating	92
# of applicants	10,338
% of applicants accepted	55
% of acceptees attending	24
# accepting a place on wait list	504
# admitted from wait list	42

FRESHMAN PROFILE	
Range SAT Critical Reading	580–680
Range SAT Math	600–690
Range SAT Writing	570–670
Range ACT Composite	26.25–31
Minimum paper TOEFL	550
Minimum web-based TOEFL	80
Average HS GPA	3.6
% graduated top 10% of class	49
% graduated top 25% of class	78
% graduated top 50% of class	94

DEADLINES	
Early action	
Deadline	11/1
Notification	12/31
Regular	
Priority	1/15
Deadline	3/15
Nonfall registration?	yes

FINANCIAL FACTS	
Financial Aid Rating	80
Annual tuition	$37,050
Room and board	$13,539
Required fees	$4,700
Books and supplies	$800
% needy frosh rec. need-based scholarship or grant aid	76
% needy UG rec. need-based scholarship or grant aid	80
% needy frosh rec. non-need-based scholarship or grant aid	74
% needy UG rec. non-need-based scholarship or grant aid	64
% needy frosh rec. need-based self-help aid	87
% needy UG rec. need-based self-help aid	90
% frosh rec. any financial aid	77
% UG rec. any financial aid	73
% UG borrow to pay for school	38
Average cumulative indebtedness	$26,297
% frosh need fully met	33
% ugrads need fully met	31
Average % of frosh need met	85
Average % of ugrad need met	85

SOUTHWESTERN UNIVERSITY

ADMISSIONS OFFICE, GEORGETOWN, TX 78627-0770 • ADMISSIONS: 512-863-1200 • FAX: 512-863-9601

CAMPUS LIFE

Quality of Life Rating	**89**
Fire Safety Rating	**89**
Green Rating	**68**
Type of school	private
Affiliation	Methodist
Environment	town

STUDENTS

Total undergrad enrollment	1,347
% male/female	40/60
% from out of state	12
% frosh live on campus	100
# of fraternities	4
# of sororities	4
% African American	3
% Asian	4
% Caucasian	73
% Hispanic	17
% Native American	1
# of countries represented	9

SURVEY SAYS . . .

No one cheats
Great computer facilities
Career services are great
School is well run
Students are friendly
Dorms are like palaces
Campus feels safe
Students are happy

ACADEMICS

Academic Rating	**88**
% students returning for sophomore year	85
% students graduating within 4 years	57
% students graduating within 6 years	72
Calendar	semester
Student/faculty ratio	10:1
Profs interesting rating	94
Profs accessible rating	93
Most classes have	10–19 students
Most lab/discussion sessions have	10–19 students

MOST POPULAR MAJORS

business/commerce; communication studies/speech communication and rhetoric; political science and government

APPLICANTS ALSO LOOK AT AND OFTEN PREFER

Rice University, Trinity University

AND SOMETIMES PREFER

Texas A&M University—College Station, The University of Texas at Austin, Tulane University, Vanderbilt University, Rhodes College

AND RARELY PREFER

Austin College, Texas Christian University, Baylor University, Southern Methodist University

STUDENTS SAY ". . ."

Academics

One of Texas' top-ranked universities, Southwestern offers students a "welcoming environment" and invites them to become part of a "close community" of scholars. "Small and rigorous," undergrads here truly appreciate that Southwestern "focuses heavily on student development and improvement." Though at times they might complain about the "huge work load," many value the fact that they're really learning "to think critically" and gaining "leadership skills." Impressively, a number of students feels that the university really imbues them with "the love for knowledge." Undergrads are quick to praise their professors, noting that they "sincerely care about their students' education" and are always "willing to help students in any way they can." For the most part, they encourage "participation, whether it is a class discussion or in the middle of a lecture, which allows you to get a feel for the real core of whatever topic you're studying." One history major does caution, "Don't expect to just show up and succeed—you're going to have to work." Fortunately, though the academics might be "challenging," professors are always ready to "meet with you whenever you need guidance or clarification on an assignment." Overall, the university provides a "very engaging learning experience" and allows undergrads to reach their "full potential." And as this supremely satisfied student shares, Southwestern is "the best liberal arts school you've never heard of."

Life

Though students at Southwestern are "very focused on their studies," many also try and take advantage of the myriad activities happening around campus. Fraternities and sororities are fairly popular here, and "Greek life provides the main entertainment for students if they're into the partying scene." However, don't fret if you fear that frat life isn't for you; they're not the only game in town. As one math and music double-major tells us, "There are plenty of opportunities to see shows put on by the theater department, concerts of all types, or recitals. The school also brings in music groups like Cake or Spoon or comedians like Eric O'Shea for Friday Night Live every week." Additionally, campus sponsored events like "movie nights" and "casino nights" are usually well-attended. Undergrads also appreciate leisure time outdoors and students can frequently be found "lounging on the academic mall or riding their bikes to the local park." Though some students find that the surrounding Georgetown area offers "little to do," others enjoy taking advantage of the local "movie theater or bowling alley." And when undergrads are anxious for a little more action, they often head to nearby Austin.

Student Body

Southwestern attracts "intelligent," academically inclined students who fortunately don't "obsess over their grades." They manage to be both "studious" and "fun-loving" and are typically "swamped with a million activities." Though it's a small school, undergrads assure us that "everybody finds their niche somewhere." Indeed, people at Southwestern are "warm," friendly," and "pretty approachable." And an English major adds, "Students are willing to make friends with just about anyone." While the majority are "white, middle- or upper-middle-class, [and] Christian" there are students "from every race, religion, and background," and many people are "open-minded." A large number of students are "in sororities/fraternities," and "liberals outnumber conservatives." Further, most "people dress fairly conservatively, but it is not unheard of to see colored hair, Disturbed t-shirts, or a random guy in a skirt." Perhaps this English and business double-major says it best: "It doesn't take long to find some people you fit in with at school, because you find so many types of people here that it is hard to feel like an outcast."

FINANCIAL AID: 512-863-1259 • E-MAIL: ADMISSION@SOUTHWESTERN.EDU • WEBSITE: WWW.SOUTHWESTERN.EDU

THE PRINCETON REVIEW SAYS

Admissions

Very important factors considered include: Class rank, application essay, academic GPA, recommendation(s), rigor of secondary school record, standardized test scores. *Important factors considered include:* Alumni/ae relation, character/personal qualities, extracurricular activities, first generation, geographical residence, interview, level of applicant's interest, racial/ethnic status, talent/ability, volunteer work, work experience. SAT or ACT required; ACT with writing component required. TOEFL required of all international applicants. High school diploma is required and GED is accepted. *Academic units required:* 4 English, 4 mathematics, 3 science (2 science labs), 2 foreign language, 2 social studies, 1 history, 1 academic electives. *Academic units recommended:* 4 English, 4 mathematics, 4 science (3 science labs), 3 foreign language, 3 social studies, 2 history.

Financial Aid

Students should submit: FAFSA. Regular filing deadline is March 1. The Princeton Review suggests that all financial aid forms be submitted as soon as possible after January 1. *Need-based scholarships/grants offered:* Federal Pell, SEOG, state scholarships/grants, private scholarships, the school's own gift aid. *Loan aid offered:* Direct Subsidized Stafford, Direct Unsubsidized Stafford, Direct PLUS, Federal Perkins, state loans, college/university loans from institutional funds. Applicants will be notified of awards on a rolling basis beginning March 1. Federal Work-Study Program available. Institutional employment available. Off-campus job opportunities are good.

The Inside Word

Successful applicants to Southwestern demonstrate intellectual curiosity and a strong desire to participate in an active collegiate community. Students need to be well-rounded and highly motivated. The vast majority of those who receive that coveted thick envelope are in the top quarter of their class and have above-average SAT scores.

THE SCHOOL SAYS ". . ."

From the Admissions Office

"Southwestern University, the state's first institution of higher learning. On the outskirts of Texas's vibrant capital city of Austin. Southwestern is committed to helping students achieve personal and professional success as well as a passion for lifelong learning. The Paideia Program, funded in 2002 by an $8.5 million grant, is a distinctive new option for select students beginning their sophomore year that provides opportunities to compare, contrast, and integrate knowledge and skills gained in various areas of study. In addition to their regular studies, students work with the same Paideia professor over a three-year period in seminar groups of ten. They work to discover the powerful connections between Southwestern's rigorous academic experience and the dynamic programs available outside the classroom—through leadership, service, intercultural learning, and collaborative research or creative works. All Southwestern students discover that a premier liberal arts education leads to high acceptance rates into prestigious graduate and professional programs and careers right out of college. Southwestern is today what it has always been: a highly personal liberal arts experience that equips students with the strengths they need to develop fulfilling lives.

"Southwestern University will accept SAT scores. The writing component will be considered in a comprehensive manner, along with overall academic record, application essay, extracurricular activities, recommendations, and a personal interview."

SELECTIVITY	
Admissions Rating	**85**
# of applicants	2,613
% of applicants accepted	65
% of acceptees attending	20
# accepting a place on wait list	28

FRESHMAN PROFILE	
Range SAT Critical Reading	560–680
Range SAT Math	560–650
Range ACT Composite	25–30
Minimum paper TOEFL	570
% graduated top 10% of class	45
% graduated top 25% of class	82
% graduated top 50% of class	96

DEADLINES	
Early decision	
Deadline	11/1
Notification	12/15
Early action	
Deadline	12/1
Notification	2/1
Regular	
Priority	2/1
Notification	4/1
Nonfall registration?	yes

FINANCIAL FACTS	
Financial Aid Rating	**88**
Annual tuition	$33,440
Room and board	$9,680
Books and supplies	$1,000
% needy frosh rec. need-based scholarship or grant aid	100
% needy UG rec. need-based scholarship or grant aid	99
% needy frosh rec. non-need-based scholarship or grant aid	84
% needy UG rec. non-need-based scholarship or grant aid	83
% needy frosh rec. need-based self-help aid	79
% needy UG rec. need-based self-help aid	84
% UG borrow to pay for school	61
Average cumulative indebtedness	$31,848
% frosh need fully met	31
% ugrads need fully met	30
Average % of frosh need met	88
Average % of ugrad need met	86

SPELMAN COLLEGE

350 SPELMAN LANE, SOUTHWEST, ATLANTA, GA 30314-4399 • ADMISSIONS: 404-270-5193 • FAX: 404-270-5201

CAMPUS LIFE

Quality of Life Rating	**75**
Fire Safety Rating	**93**
Green Rating	**75**
Type of school	private
Environment	metropolis

STUDENTS

Total undergrad enrollment	2,170
% male/female	0/100
% from out of state	70
% from public high school	84
% frosh live on campus	96
# of sororities	4
% African American	81
% international	1
# of countries represented	18

SURVEY SAYS . . .

Lab facilities are great
Career services are great
Campus feels safe
Students are happy
Frats and sororities dominate social scene
Musical organizations are popular
Student government is popular
Very little drug use

ACADEMICS

Academic Rating	**81**
% students returning for sophomore year	89
% students graduating within 4 years	70
% students graduating within 6 years	77
Calendar	semester
Student/faculty ratio	11:1
Profs interesting rating	79
Profs accessible rating	74
Most classes have	10–19 students
Most lab/discussion sessions have	20–29 students

MOST POPULAR MAJORS

political science and government; psychology

APPLICANTS ALSO LOOK AT AND OFTEN PREFER

Georgia Institute of Technology

AND SOMETIMES PREFER

Howard University, Hampton University, Florida A&M University, Tuskegee University

AND RARELY PREFER

University of Georgia, Emory University, University of Maryland, College Park

STUDENTS SAY ". . ."

Academics

A historically black women's institution, Spelman College has built a strong reputation for "molding intelligent, goal-oriented young ladies into determined, successful, free-thinking women." Many prospective students are attracted to the school's "powerful history," including the "long list of successful, educated, strong, black women who have attended Spelman College" during the century since its founding. Once on campus, students are happy to report that Spelman's "professors are committed to the mission of the school," and they really "bring out the best" in their students. In the classroom, students are "encouraged to state our opinions," and professors "allow room for us to challenge and discuss what they present." You'll definitely work hard to stay afloat in this "challenging academic environment," because professors "do not allow for even a minute amount of slacking when it comes to completing assignments and being on time for class." Fortunately, there are "many academic resources available to help us, such as tutoring services and a writing center." Plus, the majority of Spelman professors "take additional time outside of instructional time to assist their students" with coursework. Of particular note, Spelman is "very focused on the sciences and improving the number of African American women in this field, and they offer many facilities, faculty, and opportunities" for advanced study. As graduation approaches, the "Career Counseling Center is extremely strong and has helped numerous students find employment and graduate school placements." While the future looks bright for Spelman grads, many say this private institution could better serve its students by freeing up "more money for scholarships and financial aid."

Life

There's a "strong sense of tradition and loyalty" on the Spelman campus, and most students are deeply involved in the community. From service groups to sororities, "There are so many organizations and clubs that you're bound to find one that fits you." There are tons of "opportunities to obtain leadership positions" outside the classroom, and many students are "very involved in campus life." A first-year student details, "In my freshman year already, I've walked in a fashion show, I was crowned Miss Glee Club, I write for the campus newspaper, and I play on the softball team." There's a constant buzz of activity on campus, and "Informational forums, career fairs, college fairs, performances, and sporting events are at the forefront of everyone's campus life." Socially, "Greek Life is quite important at Spelman College, but isn't a must." Even if you don't join a sorority, "There are a lot of social events on campus," and two other historically black colleges, Clark Atlanta and Morehouse, "are only inches away." Spelman undergrads say, "The camaraderie between the schools is great," and "Joint homecoming with Morehouse is the highlight of the entire year." Off campus, students "go skating, bowling, and to Six Flags Over Georgia, as well as to Atlanta Falcons, Hawks, Braves, and Thrasher games." Nearby, Atlantic Station is home to "a major movie theater, shopping, restaurants, and a bowling alley."

Student Body

Spelman College is "full of warm, welcoming, sisterly, and highly educated African American women." A unique environment, "Spelman College offers a chance for African American women to be the majority," and students appreciate being "surrounded and empowered by other young, intelligent, and goal-oriented women like myself." At the same time, "The institution promotes diversity within the student body," and Spelman women "come in all shapes and sizes and from all walks of life, though linked by our African descent. Anyone can find their place here." Confidence and individuality are prized at Spelman, and the typical undergraduate "speaks her mind, wears what she wants, [and] is comfortable in her own skin, yet she has empathy and a strong sense of social justice." Many students "love to do service for the community" and are involved in philanthropic projects around Atlanta. Spelman women are "hardworking and focused on academics." However, most are "excellent at balancing a full course load and an active social life."

FINANCIAL AID: 404-270-5212 • E-MAIL: ADMISS@SPELMAN.EDU • WEBSITE: WWW.SPELMAN.EDU

THE PRINCETON REVIEW SAYS

Admissions

Very important factors considered include: Application essay, academic GPA, rigor of secondary school record, standardized test scores, character/personal qualities. *Important factors considered include:* Recommendation(s), extracurricular activities. *Other factors considered include:* Class rank, alumni/ae relation, first generation, geographical residence, level of applicant's interest, volunteer work, work experience. SAT or ACT required; ACT with or without writing component accepted. TOEFL required of all international applicants. High school diploma is required and GED is accepted. *Academic units required:* 4 English, 3 mathematics, 3 science (2 science labs), 2 foreign language, 3 social studies, 2 history, 2 academic electives. *Academic units recommended:* 4 English, 4 mathematics, 4 science (3 science labs), 4 foreign language, 4 social studies, 3 history, 2 academic electives.

Financial Aid

Students should submit: institution's own financial aid form, CSS/Financial Aid PROFILE. The Princeton Review suggests that all financial aid forms be submitted as soon as possible after January 1. *Need-based scholarships/grants offered:* Federal Pell, SEOG, state scholarships/grants, private scholarships, the school's own gift aid, United Negro College Fund. *Loan aid offered:* Direct Subsidized Stafford, Direct Unsubsidized Stafford, Direct PLUS. Federal Work-Study Program available. Institutional employment available. Off-campus job opportunities are good.

The Inside Word

The best way to prepare for admission to Spelman is to pursue a strong, precollege academic curriculum during high school. In 2010, admitted students had an average GPA of 3.65. Students who are particularly interested in Spelman have two early application options: early decision, which is binding, and early notification, which is nonbinding, but allows students to receive a response more quickly.

THE SCHOOL SAYS ". . ."

From the Admissions Office

"As an outstanding Historically Black College for women, Spelman strives for academic excellence in liberal arts education. This predominantly residential private college provides students with an academic climate conducive to the full development of their intellectual and leadership potential. The college is a member of the Atlanta University Center consortium, and Spelman students enjoy the benefits of a small college while having access to the resources of the other three participating institutions. The purpose extends beyond intellectual development and professional career preparation of students. It seeks to develop the total person. The college provides an academic and social environment that strengthens those qualities that enable women to be self-confident as well as culturally and spiritually enriched. This environment attempts to instill in students both an appreciation for the multicultural communities of the world and a sense of responsibility for bringing about positive change in those communities.

"Applicants for are required to submit standardized test scores from an appropriate venue (i.e., ACT, TOEFL, SAT). The highest composite score will be used in admissions decisions. Writing scores from either the SAT or ACT will not be taken into consideration in the admission process."

SELECTIVITY	
Admissions Rating	**92**
# of applicants	5,864
% of applicants accepted	38
% of acceptees attending	24
# accepting a place on wait list	82
# admitted from wait list	31
# of early decision applicants	337
# accepted early decision	116

FRESHMAN PROFILE	
Range SAT Critical Reading	480–570
Range SAT Math	465–560
Range ACT Composite	20–24
Minimum paper TOEFL	500
Average HS GPA	3.6
% graduated top 10% of class	33
% graduated top 25% of class	70
% graduated top 50% of class	97

DEADLINES	
Early decision	
Deadline	11/1
Notification	12/15
Early action	
Deadline	11/15
Notification	12/31
Regular	
Deadline	2/1
Notification	4/1
Nonfall registration?	no

FINANCIAL FACTS	
Financial Aid Rating	**67**
Annual tuition	$19,684
Room and board	$10,987
Required fees	$3,570
Books and supplies	$2,000
% needy frosh rec. need-based scholarship or grant aid	90
% needy UG rec. need-based scholarship or grant aid	85
% needy frosh rec. need-based self-help aid	80
% needy UG rec. need-based self-help aid	82
% frosh rec. any financial aid	82
% UG rec. any financial aid	75
% UG borrow to pay for school	79
Average cumulative indebtedness	$35,138
% frosh need fully met	6
% ugrads need fully met	6
Average % of frosh need met	40
Average % of ugrad need met	43

St. Bonaventure University

3261 West State Road, Bonaventure, NY 14778 • Admissions: 716-375-2400 • Fax: 716-375-4005

CAMPUS LIFE

Quality of Life Rating	**69**
Fire Safety Rating	**61**
Green Rating	**67**
Type of school	private
Affiliation	Roman Catholic
Environment	village

STUDENTS

Total undergrad enrollment	1,894
% male/female	48/52
% from out of state	74
% frosh live on campus	99
% African American	5
% Asian	2
% Caucasian	70
% Hispanic	4
% Native American	1
% international	2
# of countries represented	24

SURVEY SAYS . . .

Athletic facilities are great
Students are friendly
Frats and sororities are unpopular or nonexistent
College radio is popular
Student publications are popular
Lots of beer drinking
Hard liquor is popular

ACADEMICS

Academic Rating	**69**
% students returning for sophomore year	80
% students graduating within 4 years	48
% students graduating within 6 years	63
Calendar	semester
Student/faculty ratio	13:1
Profs interesting rating	81
Profs accessible rating	84
Most classes have	10–19 students
Most lab/discussion sessions have	10–19 students

MOST POPULAR MAJORS

business/commerce; elementary education and teaching; journalism

APPLICANTS ALSO LOOK AT AND RARELY PREFER

Syracuse University

STUDENTS SAY ". . ."

Academics

Uniting a liberal arts education with "Franciscan values," St. Bonaventure University is a small Catholic school that succeeds in "shaping its students into well-rounded, intelligent, and good people." Many students choose St. Bonaventure for its "nationally recognized journalism program" or for one of several prestigious "dual-admissions programs with medical, dental, physical therapy, and pharmacy schools" in the region. No matter what their major, undergrads must complete the Clare College curriculum, which provides an "overall liberal arts education" mixed with religion and philosophy. While students are encouraged to "become extraordinary" and ethics are woven into the curriculum, "Religion is by no means forced on you," despite the college's Catholic heritage. Within major departments, "Classes are no larger than thirty students per classroom" and "professors are always available if you need help." Talented instructors "make class both fun and informative," and most "do a good job at engaging the class and promoting discussion" between students. "The school is very focused on making successful graduates, and not just in the classroom;" therefore, the curriculum "puts a huge emphasis on real-world experience in a student's field, whether it is journalism, business, or education." Students are further benefited by the school's "amazing alumni network" in and around New York State. While engaging and worthwhile, "Academics are serious, no matter your major." However, "a steady effort will get you good grades" in most Bonaventure classes, and students appreciate the fact that "the school isn't super-competitive like the Ivy League schools. Students are willing to help each other out, and there's no cutthroat competition for internships or job interviews."

Life

Outgoing and social, students enjoy a classic college lifestyle in the "Bona bubble." "November to March is Bonnie's basketball season," and attending games is a universally popular pastime. There's also an active intramural sports program, and many students "love going to the fitness center on campus" to work out or take classes. "Student involvement in the radio station is huge," and many claim, "WSBU is the best college radio station in the country." Because the school is located in upstate New York, "It is ridiculously snowy about six months of the year" and there's little to do in surrounding Olean, a "very, very small town." "People drink, snowboard, or leave for Buffalo." On campus, "Nearly everyone parties every Friday and Saturday." A student elaborates, "Occasionally people will go to the movies or order in and have a quiet night in the dorm, but parties are definitely the big plans on the weekend." At the same time, "There are options for people who do not want to party and drink." In particular, "The Campus Activities Board always has something going on." By the time they graduate, most Bonas share "a lifetime bond forged over beer, basketball, and the worst weather ever."

Student Body

St. Bonaventure students describe their classmates as "hardworking, religious, fun-loving, outgoing, involved in many activities, friendly, and accepting." "Everyone loves sports, as evidenced by the huge intramural program," and "nearly all students love to party." Demographically similar, most undergraduates are "white and from the tristate area." However, the "student body is becoming increasingly diverse" and currently includes students "from all different age groups and backgrounds." Despite the school's religious affiliation, "not everyone is Catholic," and politically speaking, "There are some diehard conservatives, but most people are pretty open-minded." When it comes to social groups, you'll meet plenty of East Coast preppies, but also "edgy kids who work at the campus radio station and listen to underground music." With extracurricular activities catering to a wide range of interests, "It's easy to make friends and find a good fit" at St. Bonaventure. There are some cliques; however, most "people tend to branch out of their comfort zone" to make friends.

FINANCIAL AID: 800-462-5050 • E-MAIL: ADMISSIONS@SBU.EDU • WEBSITE: WWW.SBU.EDU

THE PRINCETON REVIEW SAYS

Admissions

Very important factors considered include: Academic GPA, recommendation(s), rigor of secondary school record, character/personal qualities, interview. *Important factors considered include:* Application essay, standardized test scores, extracurricular activities, level of applicant's interest, talent/ability, volunteer work. *Other factors considered include:* Class rank, alumni/ae relation, first generation, work experience. SAT or ACT required; ACT with or without writing component accepted. TOEFL required of all international applicants. High school diploma is required and GED is accepted. *Academic units required:* 4 English, 3 mathematics, 3 science, 2 foreign language, 4 social studies. *Academic units recommended:* 4 English, 3 mathematics, 3 science (3 science labs), 2 foreign language, 4 social studies.

Financial Aid

Students should submit: FAFSA, institution's own financial aid form, state aid form. The Princeton Review suggests that all financial aid forms be submitted as soon as possible after January 1. *Need-based scholarships/grants offered:* Federal Pell, SEOG, state scholarships/grants, private scholarships, the school's own gift aid. *Loan aid offered:* Direct Subsidized Stafford, Direct Unsubsidized Stafford, Direct PLUS, Federal Perkins, college/university loans from institutional funds. Applicants will be notified of awards on a rolling basis beginning April 1. Highest amount earned per year from on-campus jobs $815.

The Inside Word

There's no admissions formula at St. Bonaventure. Here, prospective students are evaluated individually and accepted based on their capacity for success in college. Though St. Bonaventure recommends that applicants submit academic transcripts, standardized test scores, recommendations, and a personal essay, the admissions committee will consider any other supporting materials that prove a student's overall eligibility for admission. St. Bonaventure has a rolling admissions program, so applications are reviewed as soon as they arrive at the admissions office.

THE SCHOOL SAYS ". . ."

From the Admissions Office

"The St. Bonaventure University family has been imparting an extraordinary Franciscan tradition to men and women of a rich diversity of backgrounds for more than 150 years. This tradition encourages all who become a part of it to face the world confidently, respect the earthly environment, and work for productive change in the world. The charm of our campus and the inspirational beauty of the surrounding hills provide a special place where growth in learning and living is abundantly realized. The Richter Student Fitness Center, which opened in 2004, provides all students with state-of-the-art facilities for athletics and wellness. Academics at St. Bonaventure are challenging. Small classes and personalized attention encourage individual growth and development. St. Bonaventure's nationally known Schools of Arts and Sciences, Business Administration, Journalism/Mass Communication, and Education offers more than forty majors. The School of Graduate Studies also offers several programs leading to the master's degree.

"Applicants can submit scores from either the SAT or the ACT. The biology Subject Test is required only for students applying to one of our dual-admission medical programs."

SELECTIVITY	
Admissions Rating	72
# of applicants	2,545
% of applicants accepted	80
% of acceptees attending	24

FRESHMAN PROFILE	
Range SAT Critical Reading	470–585
Range SAT Math	475–590
Range SAT Writing	450–570
Range ACT Composite	20–26
Minimum paper TOEFL	550
Average HS GPA	3.2
% graduated top 10% of class	20
% graduated top 25% of class	45
% graduated top 50% of class	74

DEADLINES	
Regular	
Priority	2/15
Deadline	7/1
Nonfall registration?	yes

FINANCIAL FACTS	
Financial Aid Rating	84
Annual tuition	$26,925
Room and board	$10,342
Required fees	$965
Books and supplies	$800
% needy frosh rec. need-based scholarship or grant aid	100
% needy UG rec. need-based scholarship or grant aid	100
% needy frosh rec. non-need-based scholarship or grant aid	93
% needy UG rec. non-need-based scholarship or grant aid	93
% needy frosh rec. need-based self-help aid	90
% needy UG rec. need-based self-help aid	83
% UG borrow to pay for school	82
Average cumulative indebtedness	$34,622
% frosh need fully met	21
% ugrads need fully met	25
Average % of frosh need met	79
Average % of ugrad need met	77

St. John's College (MD)

PO Box 2800, Annapolis, MD 21404 • Admissions: 410-626-2522 • Fax: 410-269-7916

CAMPUS LIFE

Quality of Life Rating	**91**
Fire Safety Rating	**94**
Green Rating	**70**
Type of school	private
Environment	town

STUDENTS

Total undergrad enrollment	463
% male/female	54/46
% from out of state	74
% from public high school	60
% frosh live on campus	100
% Asian	1
% Caucasian	79
% Hispanic	4
% Native American	1
% international	7
# of countries represented	14

SURVEY SAYS . . .

Class discussions encouraged
No one cheats
Registration is a breeze
Frats and sororities are unpopular or nonexistent

ACADEMICS

Academic Rating	**98**
% students returning for sophomore year	82
% students graduating within 4 years	60
Calendar	semester
Student/faculty ratio	8:1
Profs interesting rating	99
Profs accessible rating	99
Most classes have	10–19 students

MOST POPULAR MAJORS

liberal arts and sciences studies and humanities, other

APPLICANTS ALSO LOOK AT AND OFTEN PREFER

Swarthmore College, University of Chicago, University of Virginia

AND SOMETIMES PREFER

Smith College, Reed College, Kenyon College, Oberlin College

AND RARELY PREFER

Bard College

STUDENTS SAY ". . ."

Academics

St. John's College is a "one of a kind" institution, which "teaches its students how to think for themselves" through a series of rigorous, discussion-based seminars. Here, every student follows the same academic curriculum, which consists entirely of "reading and discussing the great books of Western civilization." Students study "math, science, philosophy, language, history, and literature," and then, through in-class debate, are "encouraged to question everything, develop their own logical conclusions, and understand Western thought starting at the basics." The school's "brilliant" professors (known as tutors in St. John's parlance) gently oversee class discussions, though they're "more like moderators" in that they "do not lecture or 'teach' in the traditional sense." Tutors always "treat the students as equals," and "outside of class, they are available and friendly." A current undergrad relates, "The fact that tutors are always available (for lunch, coffee, or just to chat with a student) is wonderful. I have had many delightful discussions with tutors outside of class on topics ranging from Baudelaire to quantum mechanics." With tons of assigned reading and provoking in-class debates, the curriculum is "difficult and taxing, yet supremely rewarding." Tutors "don't cut you slack if you don't deserve it," and most "have high expectations" for their students throughout the semester. "Grades are sometimes based on a tutor's subjective opinion of the student's personality," which can be frustrating for those accustomed to receiving top marks. "Work is sometimes stressful, and the material is often difficult," but students reassure us that "there is always someone to work through it with you, and you can always ask for help."

Life

There's no strict division between study and social life at St. John's. "Discussions from in class spill out into the quad." While most Johnnies say their school is sublime, they also warn that, "If you don't like endlessly talking about books, you'll feel oppressed by the social scene at St. John's." While "school is intense and exhausting," students "rarely differentiate between schoolwork and lives outside of class." On this quirky campus, "Fun can be translating Greek or it can be taking a nap; it can be playing intramurals or drinking a beer and watching les sportifs run around; it can be making music or researching Appalachian folk songs." For a lighter evening, students attend "school-run dance parties" or get together for "hard liquor, film noir, classical books, cigarettes, and being off on an adventure." "Impromptu trips off campus are frequent," and students head to Annapolis for "sailing, watching tourists, bowling, [or] ice skating." In addition, "Many students participate in the excellent intramural sports program," which includes "soccer, football, Ultimate Frisbee, basketball, croquet, crew, fencing, aikido, boxing, and more." Social dance is also remarkably popular, and there are "swing dancing parties on a regular basis."

Student Body

The unusual St. John's curriculum tends to attract students who are "intellectual, very thoughtful, and inclined to discuss Aristotle, Hobbes, or Tolstoy at the dinner table." Talkative and analytical, St. John's students are "always down for a good conversation, whether one-on-one or in a group, whether the topic is personal or impersonal." "Students come from across the country and around the world, from all religious, political, and economic backgrounds," though there's a noticeable "proliferation of East Coast preppies and hipsters." "The diversity of personalities is astounding," and, exclusivity is minimized on this "friendly" campus. "Because the school is so small, and because of the universal curriculum, by your senior year you have a pretty strong bond with your entire class." Activists and pop culture junkies take note: "If you're interested in current events, or pretty much anything that happened after, say, 1925, it can sometimes be hard to find people who know what you're talking about."

FINANCIAL AID: 410-295-6932 • E-MAIL: ADMISSIONS@SJCA.EDU • WEBSITE: WWW.SJCA.EDU

THE PRINCETON REVIEW SAYS

Admissions

Very important factors considered include: Application essay. *Important factors considered include:* Recommendation(s), rigor of secondary school record, character/personal qualities. *Other factors considered include:* Class rank, academic GPA, standardized test scores, alumni/ae relation, extracurricular activities, first generation, interview, racial/ethnic status, talent/ability. ACT with or without writing component accepted. TOEFL required of all international applicants. High school diploma is required and GED is accepted. *Academic units required:* 3 mathematics, 2 foreign language. *Academic units recommended:* 4 English, 4 mathematics, 3 science (3 science labs), 4 foreign language, 2 social studies, 2 history.

Financial Aid

Students should submit: FAFSA, CSS/Financial Aid PROFILE, state aid form, noncustodial PROFILE, business/farm supplement. The Princeton Review suggests that all financial aid forms be submitted as soon as possible after January 1. *Need-based scholarships/grants offered:* Federal Pell, SEOG, state scholarships/grants, private scholarships, the school's own gift aid. *Loan aid offered:* Direct Subsidized Stafford, Direct Unsubsidized Stafford, Direct PLUS, Federal Perkins, college/university loans from institutional funds. Applicants will be notified of awards on a rolling basis beginning December 1. Federal Work-Study Program available. Institutional employment available. Highest amount earned per year from on-campus jobs $2,999. Off-campus job opportunities are good.

The Inside Word

St. John's is a unique environment, best suited to students of a quirky yet serious intellectual predilection. To test the waters before you jump in, consider taking a campus tour or even sitting in on an active tutorial session with students. You can also send your questions about the school to a current student through the St. John's website. Each applicant is evaluated individually for potential success in the program. Among application materials, SAT scores are an optional component, though the school generally recommends that you submit them.

THE SCHOOL SAYS ". . ."

From the Admissions Office

"The purpose of the admission process is to determine whether an applicant has the necessary preparation and ability to complete the St. John's program satisfactorily. The essays are designed to enable applicants to give a full account of themselves. They can tell the committee much more than statistical records reveal. Previous academic records show whether an applicant has the habits of study necessary at St. John's. Letters of reference, particularly those of teachers, are carefully read for indications that the applicant has the maturity, self-discipline, ability, energy, and initiative to succeed in the St. John's program. St. John's attaches little importance to 'objective' test scores, and no applicant is accepted or rejected because of such scores.

"St. John's College does not require the results of standardized tests, except in the case of international students, homeschooled students, and those who will not receive a high school diploma. Results of the ACT or SAT are sufficient for these students."

SELECTIVITY	
Admissions Rating	82
# of applicants	357
% of applicants accepted	81
% of acceptees attending	47

FRESHMAN PROFILE	
Range SAT Critical Reading	640–740
Range SAT Math	590–680
Range ACT Composite	27–30
Minimum paper TOEFL	600
Minimum web-based TOEFL	100
% graduated top 10% of class	29
% graduated top 25% of class	54
% graduated top 50% of class	80

DEADLINES	
Regular	
Priority	3/1
Nonfall registration?	yes

FINANCIAL FACTS	
Financial Aid Rating	83
Annual tuition	$43,256
Room and board	$10,334
Required fees	$400
Books and supplies	$630
% needy frosh rec. need-based scholarship or grant aid	90
% needy UG rec. need-based scholarship or grant aid	93
% needy frosh rec. non-need-based scholarship or grant aid	8
% needy UG rec. non-need-based scholarship or grant aid	7
% needy frosh rec. need-based self-help aid	92
% needy UG rec. need-based self-help aid	97
% frosh rec. any financial aid	76
% UG rec. any financial aid	73
% UG borrow to pay for school	64
Average cumulative indebtedness	$29,869
% frosh need fully met	93
% ugrads need fully met	99

St. John's College (NM)

1160 Camino Cruz Blanca, Santa Fe, NM 87505 • Admissions: 505-984-6060 • Fax: 505-984-6162

CAMPUS LIFE

Quality of Life Rating	85
Fire Safety Rating	60*
Green Rating	78
Type of school	private
Environment	city

STUDENTS

Total undergrad enrollment	365
% male/female	59/41
% from out of state	91
% from public high school	68
% frosh live on campus	96
% Asian	1
% Caucasian	75
% Hispanic	6
% international	9
# of countries represented	24

SURVEY SAYS . . .

Class discussions encouraged
No one cheats
Registration is a breeze
Students are happy
Intercollegiate sports are unpopular or nonexistent
Frats and sororities are unpopular or nonexistent

ACADEMICS

Academic Rating	98
% students returning for sophomore year	77
% students graduating within 4 years	49
Calendar	semester
Student/faculty ratio	8:1
Profs interesting rating	92
Profs accessible rating	98
Most classes have	10–19 students

APPLICANTS ALSO LOOK AT AND OFTEN PREFER
Stanford University, Deep Springs College

AND SOMETIMES PREFER
Bard College, Rice University, University of Chicago, Reed College

AND RARELY PREFER
Whitman College, Grinnell College, Oberlin College

STUDENTS SAY ". . ."

Academics

St. John's College in Santa Fe operates on a similar program as the Annapolis campus: Students read and explore a common body of "great books"—including many of the most important books in history—in close partnership with their classmates and teachers. Every professor "must teach (learn) Euclid, Plato, and Darwin, whether he or she has a PhD in mathematics, classics, or biology." This common curriculum and dedication to the liberal arts means that "students are respected for what they can bring, and need never feel self-conscious about whether they're 'smart enough.'" Everywhere you look, there is a "commitment, sincerity, and passion for learning of the community and the faculty." This truly is an academic community that sincerely loves "the journey in its pursuit of knowledge, not simply the destination." The "liberation of the mind" at SJC comes primarily by means of the Socratic Method. SJC does not have professors, but tutors, who are there not to lecture, but to "help lead the class through the curriculum." The tutors are "very different in personality," but also "very knowledgeable and excitable about what we do." As experienced academics, they are "skillful when it comes to managing the classroom discussions and helping students articulate their thoughts" and are "truly open-minded and give everyone a chance to give participate." "They really care about their students and treat us as peers in the classroom since they consider themselves also to be constantly learning." "Everyone shares fundamental values of how to treat others in the classroom," says a student. The greatest asset of SJC is the community; with everyone on board this nontraditional learning train, it's hard not to be at your best. "You're thinking nonstop at SJC," says a student. Though the self-selecting student body pretty much ensures success, students can choose how connected they wish to be to the rest of the school. "You can go four years without having an interaction with the president of the college, or you can see him every Tuesday at the Foreign Relations study group," says a student.

Life

At St. John's, "you have to work intensely and relax intensely. Life is more distilled, here." "Is it hard work?" asks a student. "Yes and no. Does staying up until 1:00 A.M. reading Shakespeare or Darwin sound like work?" Santa Fe is "stunning," and the proximity of the mountains (for hiking and skiing) is more than welcome. Though each week is "epic" in its schoolwork, there are dozens of clubs and activities to take part in, from "dance (beginners always welcome) to search and rescue to astronomy to rock-climbing." If you're artsy, there are many galleries in Santa Fe, or "You can stay on campus, join a study group or sports team, or go to the gym." The student government is also responsible for dispersing several thousand dollars to support student clubs annually, so "if you can get signatures to show support, you can probably get funding for snacks or supplies." Many say that food services could have better hours and prices. There are "frequent" field trips to some of the extraordinary places in New Mexico.

Student Body

Most of the 450 undergrads at St. John's are "friendly," "big readers," and "interested in discussions." It's easy to find commonalities, since "you're always able to discuss the program as long as they're the same year or lower." All are here "because we have a genuine interest in the larger questions that are posed in life through academia," and "That's enough for most of us to feel like we're 'fitting in,' however that may be defined." Johnnies are "fascinated with learning in a way different from most schools" and "thrive on epiphanies through the 'great books,' especially ones shared with others."

FINANCIAL AID: 505-984-6058 • E-MAIL: ADMISSIONS@MAIL.SJCSF.EDU • WEBSITE: WWW.SJCSF.EDU

THE PRINCETON REVIEW SAYS

Admissions

Very important factors considered include: Application essay. *Important factors considered include:* Recommendation(s), rigor of secondary school record, character/personal qualities, level of applicant's interest. *Other factors considered include:* Class rank, academic GPA, standardized test scores, alumni/ae relation, extracurricular activities, first generation, interview, racial/ethnic status, talent/ability, volunteer work, work experience. ACT with or without writing component accepted. TOEFL required of all international applicants. High school diploma is required and GED is accepted. *Academic units required:* 3 mathematics, 2 foreign language. *Academic units recommended:* 4 English, 1 mathematics, 3 science (3 science labs), 4 foreign language, 2 history.

Financial Aid

Students should submit: FAFSA, CSS/Financial Aid PROFILE, noncustodial PROFILE, business/farm supplement. The Princeton Review suggests that all financial aid forms be submitted as soon as possible after January 1. *Need-based scholarships/grants offered:* Federal Pell, SEOG, state scholarships/grants, private scholarships, the school's own gift aid, Academic Competitiveness Grant/SMART Grants. *Loan aid offered:* Direct Subsidized Stafford, Direct Unsubsidized Stafford, Direct PLUS, Federal Perkins, college/university loans from institutional funds. Applicants will be notified of awards on a rolling basis beginning December 10. Federal Work-Study Program available. Institutional employment available. Highest amount earned per year from on-campus jobs $2,800. Off-campus job opportunities are excellent.

The Inside Word

Self-selection drives this admissions process—more than one-half of the entire applicant pool each year indicates that St. John's is their first choice, and half of those admitted send in tuition deposits. Even so, no one in admissions takes things for granted, and neither should any student considering an application. The admissions process is highly personal on both sides of the coin. Only the intellectually curious and highly motivated need apply.

THE SCHOOL SAYS ". . ."

From the Admissions Office

"St. John's appeals to students who value good books, love to read, and are passionate about discourse and debate. There are no lectures and virtually no tests or electives. Instead, classes of sixteen to twenty students occur around conference tables where professors are as likely to be asked to defend their points of view as are students. Great books provide the direction, context, and stimulus for conversation. The entire student body adheres to the same, all-required arts and science curriculum. Someone once said, 'A classic is a house we still live in,' and at St. John's, students and professors alike approach each reading on the list as if the ideas it holds were being expressed for the first time—questioning the logic behind a geometrical proof, challenging the premise of a scientific development, or dissecting the progression of modern political theory as it unfolds."

SELECTIVITY	
Admissions Rating	80
# of applicants	269
% of applicants accepted	86
% of acceptees attending	52
# accepting a place on wait list	2

FRESHMAN PROFILE	
Range SAT Critical Reading	610–740
Range SAT Math	570–660
Range ACT Composite	25–32
Minimum paper TOEFL	550
% graduated top 10% of class	33
% graduated top 25% of class	52
% graduated top 50% of class	81

DEADLINES	
Regular	
Priority	3/1
Nonfall registration?	yes

FINANCIAL FACTS	
Financial Aid Rating	95
Annual tuition	$41,792
Room and board	$9,984
Required fees	$400
Books and supplies	$630
% frosh rec. any financial aid	81
% UG rec. any financial aid	75
% UG borrow to pay for school	68
Average cumulative indebtedness	$27,650
% frosh need fully met	91
% ugrads need fully met	95
Average % of frosh need met	96
Average % of ugrad need met	94

ST. JOHN'S UNIVERSITY

8000 UTOPIA PARKWAY, QUEENS, NY 11439 • ADMISSIONS: 718-990-2000 • FAX: 718-990-2096

CAMPUS LIFE

Quality of Life Rating	**74**
Fire Safety Rating	**93**
Green Rating	**87**
Type of school	private
Affiliation	Roman Catholic
Environment	metropolis

STUDENTS

Total undergrad enrollment	11,764
% male/female	47/53
% from out of state	28
% from public high school	67
% frosh live on campus	59
# of fraternities	22
# of sororities	17
% African American	19
% Asian	18
% Caucasian	36
% Hispanic	16
% international	5
# of countries represented	112

SURVEY SAYS . . .

Great computer facilities
Athletic facilities are great
Diverse student types on campus
Students get along with local community
Students love Queens, NY
Everyone loves the Red Storm

ACADEMICS

Academic Rating	**69**
% students returning for sophomore year	79
% students graduating within 4 years	37
% students graduating within 6 years	58
Calendar	semester
Student/faculty ratio	18:1
Profs interesting rating	70
Profs accessible rating	67
Most classes have	20–29 students
Most lab/discussion sessions have	20–29 students

MOST POPULAR MAJORS

liberal arts and sciences/liberal studies; pharmacy (pharmd [U.S.], pharmd or bs/bpharm [Canada]); psychology

APPLICANTS ALSO LOOK AT AND OFTEN PREFER

State University of New York—Stony Brook University, Rutgers, The State University of New Jersey—New Brunswick, Fordham University

AND SOMETIMES PREFER

New York University, Syracuse University, Temple University, University of Connecticut

STUDENTS SAY ". . ."

Academics

Like its hometown of Queens, New York, St. John's moves inexorably forward without forgetting its history and traditions. The school's administration is committed to constantly "updating the university's facilities." Recent improvements include "a state-of-the-art athletic training facility and revamped cafeterias," as well as an upgrade to science facilities, added townhouse residences for students, and a new 127,000 square foot University Center. In addition, the school distributes "brand-new laptops to all incoming students" and has "done a tremendous job of implementing technology throughout the campus," which "is completely wireless except for a few athletic fields and parking lots." On the traditions side of the balance, the school maintains "a lot of policies and politics opposed by typical college students [such as] the visitor policies in the dorms." Many praise St. John's' study abroad programs and Institute for Writing Studies, which provides writing support to all students. When it comes to classroom experience, "professors are professors. Like [at] any school, some are better than others." Students report that "the experience you have at St. John's really depends on what you do with it. Don't take a professor just because he/she is easy—chances are that means they suck! If you are self-motivated...you will find challenging professors." Big-picture people will see that St. John's offers "a quality private education" and, in many instances, a "generous" financial aid package that translates to an overall "low cost."

Life

Students say "There are a lot of opportunities to get involved on campus," at St. John's. "Our student government works very hard on student engagement, creating popular events to foster the University community." Still, "Life for most St. John's students is not centered around the campus. We have NYC as our playground, so time not spent in classes is often [spent] off campus." For those who prefer off-campus activities in their spare time, the school helps to make that possible. There are "shuttles that can take us into the city [aka Manhattan, to those outside New York City] and on weekends...to the mall." In addition, the "school runs programs to see Broadway shows for free." Even without the school's help, however, New York is at students' fingertips; almost everything the city has to offer "is just a subway ride away." "Clubs, sports events, parties, restaurants"—you name it, NYC's got it, and St. John's students sample it. The faithful will be happy to know that "St. John's makes it easy to incorporate a spiritual life with an academic one." For the altruistic, there are "community-service initiatives galore."

Student Body

Because it is "located in Queens, the most diverse place on Earth," it's no surprise that St. John's itself is "very, very diverse." Though "everyone gets along exceptionally well," getting along well doesn't equal total integration. Each "ethnic group tends [to] hang around with itself. Yet students' external differences belie less visible similarities. Many are the first in their family to attend college, so a strong work ethic is pervasive. Everyone "wants to achieve something greater than their parents." The second major similarity stems from the first: "Students here generally have many responsibilities outside of their schoolwork."

FINANCIAL AID: 718-990-2000 • E-MAIL: ADMHELP@STJOHNS.EDU • WEBSITE: WWW.STJOHNS.EDU

THE PRINCETON REVIEW SAYS

Admissions

Very important factors considered include: Academic GPA, standardized test scores. *Important factors considered include:* Rigor of secondary school record. *Other factors considered include:* Class rank, application essay, recommendation(s), alumni/ae relation, character/personal qualities, extracurricular activities, geographical residence, interview, level of applicant's interest, volunteer work, work experience. SAT or ACT required; ACT with or without writing component accepted. TOEFL required of all international applicants. High school diploma is required and GED is accepted. *Academic units required:* 4 English. *Academic units recommended:* 3 mathematics, 2 science (2 science labs), 2 foreign language, 2 history, 1 social studies/history units.

Financial Aid

Students should submit: FAFSA. The Princeton Review suggests that all financial aid forms be submitted as soon as possible after January 1. *Need-based scholarships/grants offered:* Federal Pell, SEOG, state scholarships/grants, private scholarships, the school's own gift aid. *Loan aid offered:* Direct Subsidized Stafford, Direct Unsubsidized Stafford, Direct PLUS, Federal Perkins. Applicants will be notified of awards on a rolling basis beginning March 15. Federal Work-Study Program available. Institutional employment available. Highest amount earned per year from on-campus jobs $5,000. Off-campus job opportunities are good.

The Inside Word

The admissions process at St. John's doesn't include many surprises. High school grades and standardized test scores are undoubtedly the most important factors though volunteer work and extracurricular activities are also highly regarded. What is surprising is that this Catholic university doesn't consider religious affiliation at all when making admissions decisions; there are students of every religious stripe here.

THE SCHOOL SAYS ". . ."

From the Admissions Office

"Founded by the Vincentian Fathers in 1870, St. John's is a major Catholic university that prepares students for ethical leadership in today's global society. St. John's offers quality academics, high-tech resources and confidence-building service activities enlivened by the vast opportunities available only in exciting New York City. Representing forty-six states and 112 foreign countries, students pursue more than 100 programs and concentrations in the arts, sciences, business, education, pharmacy, and allied health. Internationally respected scholars, more than ninety percent of St. John's professors hold a PhD or comparable degree. The eighteen to one student/faculty ratio ensures personal attention in class.

"St. John's also offers these advantages:

- The freshman Passport Program lets students study abroad in their very first year at St. John's, with two weeks at our Rome campus.
- Unique core courses like Discover New York use the city as a 'living classroom.'
- All entering students receive wireless laptop computers with access to our award-winning network.
- Reflecting our Vincentian heritage, course-related academic service-learning activities provide real-world experience while serving those in need.
- Global studies programs like Discover the World allow students to earn fifteen credits while studying in three foreign cities in a single semester.

"St. John's has three residential New York City campuses—our flagship campus in Queens; the wooded Staten Island campus; and a 'vertical' campus in lower Manhattan. St. John's also has a campus in Rome, Italy, and locations in Oakdale, NY, and Paris, France."

SELECTIVITY	
Admissions Rating	82
# of applicants	52,972
% of applicants accepted	49
% of acceptees attending	11
FRESHMAN PROFILE	
Range SAT Critical Reading	480–580
Range SAT Math	490–610
Range ACT Composite	21–27
Minimum paper TOEFL	600
Minimum web-based TOEFL	100
Average HS GPA	3.2
% graduated top 10% of class	11
% graduated top 25% of class	30
% graduated top 50% of class	60
DEADLINES	
Regular	
Priority	2/1
Nonfall registration?	yes
FINANCIAL FACTS	
Financial Aid Rating	72
Annual tuition	$33,125
Room and board	$14,600
Required fees	$750
Books and supplies	$1,015
% needy frosh rec. need-based scholarship or grant aid	100
% needy UG rec. need-based scholarship or grant aid	100
% needy frosh rec. non-need-based scholarship or grant aid	85
% needy UG rec. non-need-based scholarship or grant aid	76
% needy frosh rec. need-based self-help aid	88
% needy UG rec. need-based self-help aid	89
% frosh rec. any financial aid	97
% UG rec. any financial aid	96
% UG borrow to pay for school	73
Average cumulative indebtedness	$35,451
% frosh need fully met	11
% ugrads need fully met	9
Average % of frosh need met	83
Average % of ugrad need met	62

ST. LAWRENCE UNIVERSITY

PAYSON HALL, CANTON, NY 13617 • ADMISSIONS: 315-229-5261 • FAX: 315-229-5818

CAMPUS LIFE

Quality of Life Rating	**80**
Fire Safety Rating	**77**
Green Rating	**78**
Type of school	private
Environment	village

STUDENTS

Total undergrad enrollment	2,295
% male/female	46/54
% from out of state	57
% from public high school	68
% frosh live on campus	100
# of fraternities	2
# of sororities	4
% African American	3
% Asian	1
% Caucasian	82
% Hispanic	4
% international	6
# of countries represented	50

SURVEY SAYS . . .

Lab facilities are great
Athletic facilities are great
Low cost of living
Great library
Lots of beer drinking

ACADEMICS

Academic Rating	**93**
% students graduating within 4 years	78
% students graduating within 6 years	83
Calendar	semester
Student/faculty ratio	12:1
Profs interesting rating	88
Profs accessible rating	87
Most classes have	10–19 students
Most lab/discussion sessions have	10–19 students

MOST POPULAR MAJORS

economics; political science and government; psychology

APPLICANTS ALSO LOOK AT AND OFTEN PREFER

Middlebury College, Williams College, Dartmouth College

AND SOMETIMES PREFER

Bowdoin College, Colby College, Colgate University

AND RARELY PREFER

Ithaca College

STUDENTS SAY ". . ."

Academics

"The best-kept secret in the Northeast," St. Lawrence University provides an "excellent well-rounded liberal arts education" that is "intellectually stimulating, personally enriching, and culturally engaging." "The high quality of professors and facilities" attract "individuals who are serious about their education" and build "an oasis of learning, separated from distractions, but preparing you for the real world." Boasting a science program that "is one of the strongest" among liberal arts schools, "well-developed study abroad programs," and "admissions and financial aid offices [that] seek to offer many scholarship opportunities," St. Lawrence offers a wide array of academic prospects. Although some students feel that the university may be "understaffed," small class sizes and a "faculty who desire achievement" play a critical role in the St. Lawrence experience. Professors are "approachable, funny, and extremely able" and they "have flexible hours." As one student says, "The professors here are truly exceptional…they put so much time into ensuring you grow as a scholar and as a person." "Very rarely will a professor lecture for the full amount of class time," which encourages discussion and "experiential learning." Students are encouraged to "make a sustainable and meaningful impact in communities on both local and global scales" and cite that "alumni are extremely successful."

Life

Canton is "a quaint town that has a lot of farms" located "in the beautiful Adirondacks." Perhaps this is why much of campus life is centered on the outdoors. Aside from the typical Canton "haunts" like Hoot Owl and Tick Tock, students at St. Lawrence go "canoeing on campus, rock-climbing, hiking, and even cross-country skiing" or participate in the school's "excellent outdoor program" and outing club. Every year, Peak Weekend takes place and assigns adventurers to "every high peak in the Adirondacks." "A large portion of the student body are varsity athletes" who were drawn to the school for its "strong athletic tradition," while others are "passionate, active students who work hard and play hard." One student proudly described her weekly routine: "Monday [through] Thursday school, homework, and campus involvement in clubs and organization. Thursday: pre-game and ticker. Friday: Chill out in the dorms, casual drinking. Saturday: pre-game and ticker. Sunday: Dana Brunch and library all day." "Theme houses" provide an "alternative party-hangout spot for the students not involved with the 'Greek life' system," and while drinking is prevalent, it is "not forced" on campus life. In terms of the "huge" music scene, "people like to go to Java, the music venue on campus, which books small bands every weekend," and students "also go to Ottawa or Montreal and Burlington fairly often for concerts." Life here may be nature-focused, but students do criticize the administration for not "following through with the green initiatives they pride themselves on" and providing more public transportation resources. Still, the "unique environment" of St. Lawrence leaves students here "genuinely happy."

Student Body

Though "Bean boots, Patagonia, and J. Crew" describe the "homogeneous" dominant atmosphere at St. Lawrence, the school "seamlessly fuses the three major social categories of preps, jocks, and hippies" and "blends future activists, executives, and business professionals…to foster a mixed culture of preppiness and crunchiness." Extracurricular activities are vehicles for fitting in on campus, and students characterize the student body as "made up of overachievers" who are "easy to get along with and a lot of fun." Students are "motivated to be successful and are genuinely interested in their classes" while also being "engaging and thoughtful, seeking to take advantage of campus activities and to make a difference." Despite the fact that "many members of the student body are definitely rich, there is a lot of economic diversity that goes unnoticed." More than anything, it's the "strong sense of community" and the feeling that "everybody loves everybody" that make this "a wonderful place for just about anyone who can stand the cold."

FINANCIAL AID: 315-229-5265 • E-MAIL: ADMISSIONS@STLAWU.EDU • WEBSITE: WWW.STLAWU.EDU

THE PRINCETON REVIEW SAYS

Admissions

Very important factors considered include: Application essay, academic GPA, recommendation(s), character/personal qualities. *Important factors considered include:* Class rank, rigor of secondary school record, extracurricular activities, interview, racial/ethnic status. *Other factors considered include:* Standardized test scores, alumni/ae relation, first generation, geographical residence, level of applicant's interest, talent/ability, volunteer work, work experience. ACT with or without writing component accepted. TOEFL required of all international applicants. High school diploma is required and GED is accepted. *Academic units recommended:* 4 English, 4 mathematics, 4 science (0 science labs), 4 foreign language, 2 social studies, 2 history.

Financial Aid

Students should submit: FAFSA, noncustodial PROFILE, business/farm supplement, institution's own financial aid form or CSS/Financial Aid PROFILE. Regular filing deadline is February 1. The Princeton Review suggests that all financial aid forms be submitted as soon as possible after January 1. *Need-based scholarships/grants offered:* Federal Pell, SEOG, state scholarships/grants, private scholarships, the school's own gift aid. *Loan aid offered:* Direct Subsidized Stafford, Direct Unsubsidized Stafford, Direct PLUS, Federal Perkins, college/university loans from institutional funds. Applicants will be notified of awards on or about March 30. Federal Work-Study Program available. Institutional employment available. Highest amount earned per year from on-campus jobs $2,000. Off-campus job opportunities are poor.

The Inside Word

At St. Lawrence, you're not required to submit scores from the SAT or the ACT—it is "test-optional"— but that means your high school transcript and teacher recommendations better be stellar. If you're a homeschooled student or an international student seeking financial aid, it's probably a good idea to submit some standardized test scores. Good scores help since scholarship selection is based on overall academic profile.

THE SCHOOL SAYS ". . ."

From the Admissions Office

"In an ideal location, St. Lawrence is a diverse liberal arts learning community of inspiring faculty and talented students guided by tradition and focused on the future. The students who live and learn at St. Lawrence are interesting and interested; they enroll with myriad accomplishments and talents, as well as desire to explore new challenges. Our faculty has chosen St. Lawrence intentionally because they know that there is institutional commitment to support great teaching. They are dedicated to making each student's experience challenging and rewarding. Our graduates make up one of the strongest networks of support among any alumni body and are ready, willing, and able to connect with students and help them succeed.

"Which students are happiest at St. Lawrence? Students who like to be actively involved. Students who are open-minded and interested in meeting people with backgrounds different from their own. Students who value having a voice in decisions that affect them. Students who appreciate all that is available to them and cannot wait to take advantage of both the curriculum and the co-curricular options. Students who want to enjoy their college experience and are able to find joy in working hard.

"You can learn the facts about us from this guidebook: We have about 2,200 students; we offer more than thirty majors; the average class size is sixteen students; a great new science center; close to fifty percent of our students study abroad; and we have an environmental consciousness that fits our natural setting between the Adirondack Mountains and St. Lawrence River. You must visit, meet students and faculty, and sense the energy on campus to begin to understand just how special St. Lawrence University is.

"The submission of standardized test scores (SAT or ACT) is optional. Students must indicate on the St. Lawrence Common Application supplement which scores, if any, they wish to have considered in the application process."

SELECTIVITY	
Admissions Rating	**94**
# of applicants	4,900
% of applicants accepted	39
% of acceptees attending	32
# accepting a place on wait list	464
# admitted from wait list	39
# of early decision applicants	230
# accepted early decision	201

FRESHMAN PROFILE	
Range SAT Critical Reading	560–660
Range SAT Math	570–660
Range SAT Writing	550–660
Range ACT Composite	25–29
Minimum paper TOEFL	600
Minimum web-based TOEFL	82
Average HS GPA	3.6
% graduated top 10% of class	44
% graduated top 25% of class	78
% graduated top 50% of class	95

DEADLINES	
Early decision	
Deadline	11/1
Regular	
Deadline	2/1
Nonfall registration?	yes

FINANCIAL FACTS	
Financial Aid Rating	**87**
Annual tuition	$42,420
Room and board	$11,005
Required fees	$315
% needy frosh rec. need-based scholarship or grant aid	100
% needy UG rec. need-based scholarship or grant aid	99
% needy frosh rec. non-need-based scholarship or grant aid	20
% needy UG rec. non-need-based scholarship or grant aid	14
% needy frosh rec. need-based self-help aid	74
% needy UG rec. need-based self-help aid	78
% frosh rec. any financial aid	89
% UG rec. any financial aid	85
% UG borrow to pay for school	66
Average cumulative indebtedness	$29,489
% frosh need fully met	39
% ugrads need fully met	36
Average % of frosh need met	91
Average % of ugrad need met	89

St. Mary's College of Maryland

Admissions Office, 18952 East Fisher Road, St. Mary's City, MD 20686-3001 • Admissions: 240-895-5000 • Fax: 240-895-5001

CAMPUS LIFE

Quality of Life Rating	**90**
Fire Safety Rating	**77**
Green Rating	**96**
Type of school	public
Environment	rural

STUDENTS

Total undergrad enrollment	1,908
% male/female	41/59
% from out of state	13
% from public high school	70
% frosh live on campus	97
% African American	8
% Asian	3
% Caucasian	77
% Hispanic	4
% international	2
# of countries represented	33

SURVEY SAYS . . .

Athletic facilities are great
Students are friendly
Different types of students interact
Great food on campus
Campus feels safe
Students are happy
Frats and sororities are unpopular or nonexistent
Students are environmentally aware

ACADEMICS

Academic Rating	**89**
% students graduating within 4 years	72
% students graduating within 6 years	79
Calendar	semester
Student/faculty ratio	12:1
Profs interesting rating	92
Profs accessible rating	92
Most classes have	10–19 students
Most lab/discussion sessions have	10–19 students

MOST POPULAR MAJORS

biology/biological sciences; English language and literature; psychology

STUDENTS SAY "..."

Academics

Undergrads at St. Mary's College of Maryland proudly boast, from the moment you step onto campus your freshman year, "You are instantly part of a family." Indeed there's an "immense sense of community" here, and it's no surprise that a "friendly atmosphere" reverberates throughout the school. Importantly, as "a public honors college," St. Mary's is able to provide "a rigorous academic curriculum" at an affordable price. It also offers a "small and intimate learning environment" with "classes where the professors actually care about teaching and your success." Classes tend to have "a great combination of lecture, discussion, and experiential learning," which translates into "a stimulating, challenging and altogether high-quality academic experience." Additionally, students are quick to brag about their "passionate" and "approachable" professors who are "always available for discussion and clarification." As one public policy major further explains, "Most [teachers] are willing to meet outside their office hours for as long as needed to help a student and many professors are known to give out their cell phone numbers…in case a student needs to reach them at night." They truly want "students to succeed" and work hard to ensure you'll "enjoy even the hardest of classes." A content senior sums up, "At St. Mary's, you are not just a number in the classroom, but an essential part of the classroom experience."

Life

Similar to many college kids, undergrads at St. Mary's have a "work hard, play hard mentality." While they're "definitely focused on their studies," students here also make the most of their time outside of the library. One psych major shares, "There are many opportunities to get involved on campus whether by participating in club activities or taking a student position in campus affairs, or just becoming a student tutor." The school also sponsors a number of events. For example, "Every Thursday we have coffeehouse where artists perform at our local coffee shop, we have comedians Friday nights, and we also have movies showing Fridays, Saturdays, and Sundays." Further, "There are intramural events that take place every semester for almost every sport." Though St. Mary's is a "non-Greek" campus, "themed and house parties are always a hit." Fortunately, "Nobody's looked down upon if they choose not to drink." St. Mary's students also love to take advantage of their location on the water. An anthropology majors explains, "When it's nice out, *everyone* is outside, and on the weekends, the docks are crowded by 11:00 A.M. People throw Frisbees [and] footballs, run around barefoot, grill, and chill." As an added bonus, "Students can take out sail boats or kayaks whenever they want for free." With all these options, it's no wonder why one bio student exclaims that undergrads here "will never be bored."

Student Body

"Friendliness" is the hallmark of the typical St. Mary's undergrad, and many are quick to assert that there's "a very welcoming student body." Indeed, as this junior gushes, "You could sit down and have dinner with someone you have never seen before, and be completely comfortable." The average "Seahawk" is also "focused on their studies" and "involved in all sorts of activities." Students here tend to be "politically aware and left-leaning, and very concerned with the environment." While many St. Mary's undergrads do often share these attributes, another junior assures us, "There are many different types of students [here]: some preppy kids, jocks, the artsy kids, bookworms, hippies, country kids, city kids. Everyone finds their niche, but then mixes up with other people." An excited sophomore interjects, "Quirkiness is more than tolerated here; it is often the norm." And a knowledgeable senior concludes, "With every new class there is an opportunity to make new friends, which makes every semester here exciting."

FINANCIAL AID: 240-895-3000 • E-MAIL: ADMISSIONS@SMCM.EDU • WEBSITE: WWW.SMCM.EDU

THE PRINCETON REVIEW SAYS

Admissions

Very important factors considered include: Academic GPA, rigor of secondary school record. *Important factors considered include:* Application essay, recommendation(s), standardized test scores, extracurricular activities, first generation, talent/ability, volunteer work. *Other factors considered include:* Alumni/ae relation, geographical residence, interview, racial/ethnic status, state residency, work experience. SAT or ACT required; ACT with or without writing component accepted. TOEFL required of all international applicants. High school diploma is required and GED is accepted. *Academic units required:* 4 English, 3 mathematics, 3 science (2 science labs), 2 foreign language, 2 social studies, 1 history, 3. *Academic units recommended:* 4 mathematics, 4 foreign language, 2 history.

Financial Aid

Students should submit: FAFSA. Regular filing deadline is March 1. The Princeton Review suggests that all financial aid forms be submitted as soon as possible after January 1. *Need-based scholarships/grants offered:* Federal Pell, SEOG, state scholarships/grants, private scholarships, the school's own gift aid. *Loan aid offered:* Direct Subsidized Stafford, Direct Unsubsidized Stafford, Direct PLUS, Federal Perkins. Applicants will be notified of awards on or about April 1. Federal Work-Study Program available. Institutional employment available. Highest amount earned per year from on-campus jobs $1,100. Off-campus job opportunities are good.

The Inside Word

As Maryland's public honors college, gaining admissions to St. Mary's is competitive. Admissions officers here really strive to get to know the applicant as an individual, not just a set of numbers on a paper. While academic rigor definitely holds the most weight, admissions officers thoroughly evaluate your essays, recommendations, and extracurricular activities as well.

THE SCHOOL SAYS ". . ."

From the Admissions Office

"St. Mary's College of Maryland occupies a distinctive niche and represents a real value in American higher education. It is a public college, dedicated to the ideal of affordable, accessible education and committed to quality teaching and excellent programs for undergraduate students. St. Mary's is designated by law the state of Maryland's 'public honors college,' one of only two public colleges in the nation to hold that distinction. It is this mix of honors and affordability that makes St. Mary's an education for the twenty-first century."

SELECTIVITY	
Admissions Rating	**88**
# of applicants	2,398
% of applicants accepted	61
% of acceptees attending	30
# accepting a place on wait list	254
# admitted from wait list	40
# of early decision applicants	282
# accepted early decision	150

FRESHMAN PROFILE	
Range SAT Critical Reading	560–680
Range SAT Math	540–650
Range SAT Writing	550–670
Range ACT Composite	25–29
Minimum paper TOEFL	550
Minimum web-based TOEFL	90
Average HS GPA	3.3

DEADLINES	
Early decision	
Deadline	11/1
Notification	12/20
Regular	
Deadline	1/1
Notification	4/1
Nonfall registration?	yes

FINANCIAL FACTS	
Financial Aid Rating	**78**
Annual in-state tuition	$11,325
Annual out-state tuition	$22,718
Room and board	$10,250
Required fees	$2,305
Books and supplies	$1,000
% needy frosh rec. need-based scholarship or grant aid	73
% needy UG rec. need-based scholarship or grant aid	72
% needy frosh rec. non-need-based scholarship or grant aid	54
% needy UG rec. non-need-based scholarship or grant aid	51
% needy frosh rec. need-based self-help aid	73
% needy UG rec. need-based self-help aid	74
% frosh rec. any financial aid	81
% UG rec. any financial aid	75
% UG borrow to pay for school	53
Average cumulative indebtedness	$17,505
% frosh need fully met	4
% ugrads need fully met	2
Average % of frosh need met	62
Average % of ugrad need met	63

St. Olaf College

1520 St. Olaf Avenue, Northfield, MN 55057 • Admissions: 507-786-3025 • Fax: 507-786-3832

CAMPUS LIFE

Quality of Life Rating	**89**
Fire Safety Rating	**66**
Green Rating	**82**
Type of school	private
Affiliation	Lutheran
Environment	village

STUDENTS

Total undergrad enrollment	3,128
% male/female	44/56
% from out of state	51
% from public high school	82
% frosh live on campus	99
% African American	2
% Asian	5
% Caucasian	82
% Hispanic	3
% international	4
# of countries represented	44

SURVEY SAYS . . .

Athletic facilities are great
Students get along with local community
Great food on campus
Frats and sororities are unpopular or nonexistent
Musical organizations are popular
Students are environmentally aware

ACADEMICS

Academic Rating	**93**
% students graduating within 4 years	81
% students graduating within 6 years	85
Calendar	4-1-4
Student/faculty ratio	12:1
Profs interesting rating	88
Profs accessible rating	94
Most classes have	10–19 students
Most lab/discussion sessions have	20–29 students

MOST POPULAR MAJORS

biology/biological sciences; economics; English language and literature

APPLICANTS ALSO LOOK AT AND SOMETIMES PREFER

Carleton College, Gustavus Adolphus College, University of Minnesota—Twin Cities, University of Wisconsin—Madison, Grinnell College, Lawrence University, Macalester College, Northwestern University

STUDENTS SAY ". . ."

Academics

St. Olaf, a small Lutheran liberal arts school located forty-five miles south of downtown Minneapolis, provides a "great liberal arts education rich with musical, academic, and social opportunities in a tight-knit, caring community." The school is renowned for its "amazing and extensive" music department (with which "most students are involved somehow"), but that's hardly the school's only asset. On the contrary, St. Olaf offers "excellent vocational training programs in nursing, social work, and education" (supplemented by "great…hands-on learning in addition to classroom learning through internships") as well as "an amazing science and math program. The 200,000 square foot Regents Hall of Natural and Mathematical Sciences opened in 2008. One of the best things about this school is the broad range of academics and academic experiences you can have." For most here, those experiences include study abroad; the school's numerous study abroad programs mean that "almost everyone goes abroad for at least a month." Writes one student, "St. Olaf has an amazing study abroad program. I've ridden camels in Egypt, climbed the Great Wall in China, seen the ruins of the Acropolis, and gone drinking in Switzerland all in the same semester!" Many students here complete a five-course sequence called "the Great Conversation Program, which provides a rigorous introduction to college, exploring the many 'Great Books' of western culture. The liberal arts requirements make everyone somewhat knowledgeable on every field."

Life

"There isn't much to do in Northfield," so life at St. Olaf "is very centered on campus." The school and student organizations make sure that "there is always something to do on campus, despite the small size of the student body. Bands are brought in to the student nightclub; there are more than 100 concerts a year. The theater and dance programs put on frequent shows, and sports events are happening constantly. Students have the ability to participate in most of these activities, usually without too much prior experience, either." Also, undergraduates are "very focused on clubs and special interest groups. For about 3,000 students there are more than 200 clubs on campus, serving everything from religious beliefs to environmental concerns to just having fun." Undergraduates "are very progressive…Their passion for creating progressive social and political change often springs from their religious convictions." Intramural sports "are huge, so if varsity sports aren't your thing there are outside options," and because students "walk absolutely everywhere…the freshman fifteen is more like the freshman five, if that. We're very healthy." When students need some big-city diversion, the Twin Cities are only about forty-five minutes away. "Many students go up there to eat, see a play, sporting event, concert, or just to shop on weekends."

Student Body

"The stereotype that St. Olaf is completely made up of blond-haired, blue-eyed, Scandinavian Lutherans is not true," students insist, although they quickly admit that "We do have a large number of them!" As one student explains, "We joke about how it seems like every girl is five-foot-four, blond, and fair-skinned, but that isn't totally true. There is a place for more diverse students. It seems like the typical St. Olaf student's mindset is open enough to embrace different religions, races, ideas, and beliefs." The true common ground here is that most St. Olaf undergraduates are "highly motivated toward success, whether academic or vocational," and are "also likely…type-A personalities" who are "involved in many extracurricular events yet maintain good grades under a full academic load." While St. Olaf is a college of the Evangelical Lutheran Church in America, its student body is quite diverse when it comes to religious orientation. One student notes, "The population is not particularly conservative or evangelical. They are more liberal politically and ideologically."

FINANCIAL AID: 507-786-3019 • E-MAIL: ADMISSIONS@STOLAF.EDU • WEBSITE: WWW.STOLAF.EDU

THE PRINCETON REVIEW SAYS

Admissions

Very important factors considered include: Application essay, academic GPA, rigor of secondary school record. *Important factors considered include:* Class rank, recommendation(s), standardized test scores, character/personal qualities, extracurricular activities. *Other factors considered include:* Alumni/ae relation, first generation, geographical residence, interview, level of applicant's interest, racial/ethnic status, religious affiliation/commitment, state residency, talent/ability, volunteer work, work experience. SAT or ACT required; ACT with or without writing component accepted. TOEFL required of all international applicants. High school diploma is required and GED is accepted. *Academic units recommended:* 4 English, 4 mathematics, 4 science (2 science labs), 4 foreign language, 4 social studies.

Financial Aid

Students should submit: FAFSA, CSS/Financial Aid PROFILE, noncustodial PROFILE, business/farm supplement. Regular filing deadline is March 1. The Princeton Review suggests that all financial aid forms be submitted as soon as possible after January 1. *Need-based scholarships/grants offered:* Federal Pell, SEOG, state scholarships/grants, private scholarships, the school's own gift aid. *Loan aid offered:* Direct Subsidized Stafford, Direct Unsubsidized Stafford, Direct PLUS, Federal Perkins, Federal Nursing, state loans, college/university loans from institutional funds. Applicants will be notified of awards on a rolling basis beginning March 1. Federal Work-Study Program available. Off-campus job opportunities are fair.

The Inside Word

St. Olaf's national reputation is sharply on the rise. This elevated prominence means St. Olaf must compete for candidates with more prestigious schools; hence, the acceptance rate hasn't dropped as dramatically as one might expect, as these days the school loses more of its admits to the Harvards and Northwesterns of the world than it did in the past. The artificially high acceptance rate masks a highly selective, highly competitive admissions process. Bring your A game.

THE SCHOOL SAYS ". . ."

From the Admissions Office

"One of the nation's leading liberal arts colleges, St. Olaf College offers an academically rigorous education with a vibrant faith tradition as a college of the Evangelical Lutheran Church in America. St. Olaf prepares students to become responsible citizens by fostering the development of mind, body, and spirit. Widely known for its programs in mathematics, the natural sciences, and music, St. Olaf also provides dynamic opportunities for interdisciplinary study. Committed to global education, more than two-thirds of St. Olaf students study abroad before graduating. St. Olaf College is a leader among undergraduate colleges in Rhodes Scholars, Fulbright Fellows, and Peace Corps volunteers."

SELECTIVITY	
Admissions Rating	94
# of applicants	4,181
% of applicants accepted	53
% of acceptees attending	33
# accepting a place on wait list	212
# admitted from wait list	53
# of early decision applicants	317
# accepted early decision	252

FRESHMAN PROFILE	
Range SAT Critical Reading	590–720
Range SAT Math	600–710
Range SAT Writing	580–710
Range ACT Composite	27–32
Minimum web-based TOEFL	90
Average HS GPA	3.6
% graduated top 10% of class	60
% graduated top 25% of class	86
% graduated top 50% of class	99

DEADLINES	
Early decision	
Deadline	11/15
Notification	12/15
Regular	
Deadline	1/15
Notification	3/15
Nonfall registration?	yes

FINANCIAL FACTS	
Financial Aid Rating	95
Annual tuition	$39,590
Room and board	$9,090
Books and supplies	$1,000
% needy frosh rec. need-based scholarship or grant aid	100
% needy UG rec. need-based scholarship or grant aid	100
% needy frosh rec. non-need-based scholarship or grant aid	58
% needy UG rec. non-need-based scholarship or grant aid	51
% needy frosh rec. need-based self-help aid	95
% needy UG rec. need-based self-help aid	97
% frosh rec. any financial aid	86
% UG rec. any financial aid	86
% UG borrow to pay for school	64
Average cumulative indebtedness	$25,440
% frosh need fully met	100
% ugrads need fully met	100
Average % of frosh need met	100
Average % of ugrad need met	100

STANFORD UNIVERSITY

UNDERGRADUATE ADMISSION, STANFORD, CA 94305-6106 • ADMISSIONS: 650-723-2091 • FAX: 650-725-2846

CAMPUS LIFE

Quality of Life Rating	97
Fire Safety Rating	80
Green Rating	96
Type of school	private
Environment	city

STUDENTS

Total undergrad enrollment	6,988
% male/female	52/48
% from out of state	55
% from public high school	58
% frosh live on campus	100
# of fraternities	17
# of sororities	13
% African American	10
% Asian	21
% Caucasian	38
% Hispanic	14
% Native American	3
% international	8
# of countries represented	89

SURVEY SAYS . . .

School is well run
Students are friendly
Dorms are like palaces
Campus feels safe

ACADEMICS

Academic Rating	96
% students returning for sophomore year	98
% students graduating within 4 years	79
% students graduating within 6 years	96
Calendar	quarter
Student/faculty ratio	5:1
Profs interesting rating	87
Profs accessible rating	84
Most classes have	10–19 students
Most lab/discussion sessions have	10–19 students

MOST POPULAR MAJORS

biology/biological sciences; economics; international relations and affairs

APPLICANTS ALSO LOOK AT AND OFTEN PREFER

Harvard College

AND SOMETIMES PREFER

Massachusetts Institute of Technology, Yale University, Princeton University

STUDENTS SAY ". . ."

Academics

The "passionate" undergrads at this academic powerhouse are enamored with the "amazing and unique" opportunities that Stanford has to offer. As a delighted sophomore explains, "Stanford has incredible resources, incredible people...and an unrivaled atmosphere of openness and collaboration." An "entrepreneurial spirit" and "intellectual curiosity" permeate the campus along with a general "irreverent and laid-back" attitude. Students boast that their professors are "some of the most well-respected experts in their field," and students truly appreciate the "opportunity to engage with them on a regular basis." "Flexible and enthusiastic," teachers here are "wonderful resources for guidance and tutoring." "They have regular office hours and focus on the needs of freshmen just as much as the needs of graduate students." Moreover, they "actively try and get students...to [conduct] research with them." And perhaps most impressive, as one junior highlights, "They make learning so interesting that I can't wait to go home and tell all my friends about whatever we're talking about in class." As one happy senior concludes, "To me, Stanford is a surreal utopia of Nobel Prize faculty, stellar academics, groundbreaking research, top-ranking athletics, passionate and distinguished classmates, and a beautiful campus where the sun is always shining."

Life

Fear not prospective students! Though Stanford's academics are rigorous and demanding, undergrads have been known to back away from the books every now and again. As a relieved political science major assures us, "Before I came to Stanford I thought I would be one of the few people who didn't want to spend my weekend nights in the library...I was wrong." Indeed, undergrads here are an active lot, and most are "involved in student organizations, particularly social justice, ethnic, Greek, or volunteer orgs, as well as student government and positions on University policy boards." When the weekend rolls around, "There are always frat parties or smaller house parties, student plays, musical performances, friends hiking up to the Stanford Dish, people floating around in one of our many fountains, [and] free new movies shown at Flicks." Students also appreciate Stanford's phenomenal athletics program. "Saturdays are dedicated to football (and other sports)," or "You can drive forty-five minutes west to the coast for some of the best surfing in the world, take the train forty-five minutes north to San Francisco for a Giants game, or you can even drive a few hours east to Lake Tahoe and find some of the best skiing in the world. Only at Stanford can you go from snowy mountains, to sunny beaches, to bustling city life all in one day."

Student Body

"It's easy to find your own niche" here. "There isn't a typical student." The university offers "immense diversity of race, religion, and sexual orientation," and most find their peers "incredibly accepting." While students are "driven," they're fortunately "not that competitive or intense." Indeed, the "preppy button-down [types]...are replaced with chilled-out" students in "shorts and flip-flops." Undergrads are "smart yet unassuming" and typically "committed to a million different things." Additionally, they're "generally pretty social and athletic," as well as "service-minded and focused on their future careers." One junior adds, "The jock is doing better than you in chemistry, [and] the cute party animal is double-majoring and president of an activist group." He concludes by saying, "I guess the thing that unites us is that we're all nerds, even if it's not the first thing you see."

FINANCIAL AID: 650-723-3058 • E-MAIL: ADMISSION@STANFORD.EDU • WEBSITE: WWW.STANFORD.EDU

THE PRINCETON REVIEW SAYS

Admissions

Very important factors considered include: Academic GPA, application essay, recommendation(s), rigor of secondary school record, standardized test scores, character/personal qualities, extracurricular activities, talent/ability. *Other factors considered include:* Alumni/ae relation, first generation, geographical residence, racial/ethnic status, volunteer work, work experience. SAT or ACT with writing component required. High school diploma is required and GED is accepted. *Academic units recommended:* 4 English, 4 mathematics, 3 science (3 science labs), 3 foreign language, 3 history/social studies.

Financial Aid

Students should submit: FAFSA, CSS/Financial Aid PROFILE. Regular filing deadline is February 15. The Princeton Review suggests that all financial aid forms be submitted as soon as possible after January 1. *Need-based scholarships/grants offered:* Federal Pell, SEOG, state scholarships/grants, private scholarships, school scholarship or grant aid from institutional funds. *Loan aid offered:* Direct Subsidized Stafford, Direct Unsubsidized Stafford, Direct PLUS, Federal Perkins. Applicants will be notified of awards with the admissions packet. Federal Work-Study Program available. Off-campus job opportunities are good.

The Inside Word

Stanford is one of the nation's top universities, and landing that coveted acceptance is no easy feat. With record application numbers, open spots in this renowned institution are incredibly tight. Impressive grades in demanding courses and high standardized test scores will be given strong consideration. Admissions officers also want well-rounded individuals who will contribute to Stanford's storied campus. It will be important to demonstrate creativity, leadership, and intellectual curiosity.

THE SCHOOL SAYS ". . ."

From the Admissions Office

"Stanford looks for distinctive students who exhibit energy, personality, a sense of intellectual vitality and extraordinary impact outside the classroom. While there is no minimum grade point average, class rank, or test score one needs to be admitted to Stanford, the vast majority of successful applicants will be among the strongest students (academically) in their secondary schools. The most compelling applicants for admission will be those who have thus far achieved state, regional, national, and international recognition in their academic and extracurricular areas of interest.

"Stanford accepts the Common Application as its exclusive application for admission. In addition to the online version of the Common Application, all applicants must submit an online Stanford-specific supplement to be considered for admission. The online supplement allows candidates to detail information about an experience they find intellectually engaging; write a note to their freshman year roommate sharing a personal experience they have had; and explain what matters to them.

"While the SAT or ACT is required for admission, SAT subject tests are not required (and only recommended). AP scores are also not required but may be influential in admission decision and can be used for placement/credit purposes if an applicant decides to enroll."

SELECTIVITY	
Admissions Rating	**99**
# of applicants	34,348
% of applicants accepted	7
% of acceptees attending	70
# accepting a place on wait list	1,078
# admitted from wait list	13

FRESHMAN PROFILE	
Range SAT Critical Reading	670–770
Range SAT Math	690–780
Range SAT Writing	680–780
Range ACT Composite	30–34
% graduated top 10% of class	92
% graduated top 25% of class	98
% graduated top 50% of class	100

DEADLINES	
Early action	
Deadline	11/1
Notification	12/15
Regular	
Deadline	1/1
Notification	4/1
Nonfall registration?	no

FINANCIAL FACTS	
Financial Aid Rating	**96**
Annual tuition	$40,050
Room and board	$12,291
Required fees	$519
Books and supplies	$1,500
% needy frosh rec. need-based scholarship or grant aid	97
% needy UG rec. need-based scholarship or grant aid	97
% needy frosh rec. non-need-based scholarship or grant aid	11
% needy UG rec. non-need-based scholarship or grant aid	17
% needy frosh rec. need-based self-help aid	56
% needy UG rec. need-based self-help aid	63
% UG rec. any financial aid	80
% UG borrow to pay for school	28
Average cumulative indebtedness	$16,458
% frosh need fully met	89
% ugrads need fully met	84
Average % of frosh need met	100
Average % of ugrad need met	100

STATE UNIVERSITY OF NEW YORK AT BINGHAMTON

PO BOX 6001, BINGHAMTON, NY 13902-6001 • ADMISSIONS: 607-777-2171 • FAX: 607-777-4445

CAMPUS LIFE

Quality of Life Rating	**66**
Fire Safety Rating	**80**
Green Rating	**96**
Type of school	public
Environment	city

STUDENTS

Total undergrad enrollment	11,861
% male/female	53/47
% from out of state	13
% from public high school	89
% frosh live on campus	98
# of fraternities	28
# of sororities	18
% African American	5
% Asian	13
% Caucasian	51
% Hispanic	9
% international	10
# of countries represented	116

SURVEY SAYS . . .

Diverse student types on campus
Campus feels safe
Student publications are popular
Lots of beer drinking

ACADEMICS

Academic Rating	**81**
% students returning for sophomore year	91
% students graduating within 4 years	67
% students graduating within 6 years	78
Calendar	semester
Student/faculty ratio	20:1
Profs interesting rating	69
Profs accessible rating	67
Most classes have	10–19 students
Most lab/discussion sessions have	20–29 students

MOST POPULAR MAJORS

biology/biological sciences; business administration and management; engineering

APPLICANTS ALSO LOOK AT AND OFTEN PREFER

Cornell University

AND SOMETIMES PREFER

Boston University, New York University, Pennsylvania State University—University Park

AND RARELY PREFER

State University of New York—Stony Brook University

STUDENTS SAY ". . ."

Academics

Known to students as being "one of the top public universities of the region," SUNY Binghamton provides a "high-quality education at a low financial cost." Indeed, it's tough to beat Binghamton's combination of "top-tier academics" and palatable sticker price. The university strives to help students become "well-rounded individuals" who are "globally aware and environmentally conscious." Importantly, Binghamton offers an excellent "variety of majors," and students have the opportunity to study nearly any subject that piques their interest. Undergrads are especially quick to highlight the "great business program" as well as the biology, psychology, and anthropology departments. And though classes are "tough," a psych major assures that "with enough effort, you can do well." By and large, students find their professors "interesting and engaging" and "very friendly and accommodating." As one impressed freshman notes, "They really try to make the students involved even when there are 400 [undergrads in the class]." However, some grumble that a handful of professors "couldn't care less about teaching" and are there simply "to get funded for their own research projects." And others feel that some professors "rely too much on the TAs." Overall though, they genuinely "want students to succeed" and "show true enthusiasm for their subjects."

Life

While students at Binghamton definitely hit the books hard, they also manage to find plenty of time for socializing. According to one ecstatic engineering major, "There are always about a million things going on at one time or another." The only downfall is "it's impossible to do it all." The university sponsors a number of "fun events like hot dog eating competitions [and] Battle of the Bands." Further, "There are always charity events going on, like date auctions" or benefit concerts for "donating food to the needy." Entertainment can also be found very close to home. As one happy freshman shares, "My dorm…does cooking nights, where they invite us down for free pancakes at midnight or even crepes." Like most typical college kids, when the weekend rolls around, "Students often go to parties and the bars downtown." However, "If you're not someone who likes to drink or party every weekend, there is always the option of going to the Union for some Late Nite Binghamton where you can shoot pool, go bowling, sing karaoke, etc." Though the surrounding area is "pretty quiet," when undergrads do want to get off campus, they often take advantage of the "great" skiing and snowboarding that can be found "within decent driving [distance]."

Student Body

It might seem that the typical SUNY Binghamton student "looks as if they walked out of the Hollister catalogue." However, if you scratch the surface, you'll quickly find "many different types of students," and most undergrads find the campus "very diverse in terms of interests, cultures, religions, etc." Of course, geographically speaking, it often feels like "a large percentage of the school is from Long Island and Westchester." Fortunately, "Everyone here just goes out of their way to be friendly and to make you feel like part of the community." Most people "usually find their niche within their residential communities, or based on similar interests and student organizations." Many undergrads define their peers as "intelligent," and nearly everyone "takes their classes very seriously, which provides an intellectually stimulating environment." Further, Binghamton students are "always on the move. If not in class or studying, they will be off to some sort of club or team meeting, volunteer project, athletic training, or even heading out to a party whether it is a small dorm party or a bar bash." As this junior sums up, "From poor to rich, Canadian to Indian, stuck-up to completely relaxed, everyone fits in."

FINANCIAL AID: 607-777-2428 • E-MAIL: ADMIT@BINGHAMTON.EDU • WEBSITE: WWW.BINGHAMTON.EDU

THE PRINCETON REVIEW SAYS

Admissions

Very important factors considered include: Academic GPA, rigor of secondary school record, standardized test scores. *Important factors considered include:* Class rank, application essay, recommendation(s), extracurricular activities, first generation. *Other factors considered include:* Alumni/ae relation, character/personal qualities, geographical residence, level of applicant's interest, racial/ethnic status, state residency, talent/ability, volunteer work, work experience. SAT or ACT required; ACT with writing component required. TOEFL required of all international applicants. High school diploma is required and GED is accepted. *Academic units required:* 4 English, 3 mathematics, 2 science, 3 foreign language, 2 social studies. *Academic units recommended:* 4 mathematics, 4 science, 3 foreign language, 4 social studies, 4 history.

Financial Aid

Students should submit: FAFSA, state aid form. The Princeton Review suggests that all financial aid forms be submitted as soon as possible after January 1. *Need-based scholarships/grants offered:* Federal Pell, SEOG, state scholarships/grants, private scholarships, the school's own gift aid. *Loan aid offered:* Direct Subsidized Stafford, Direct Unsubsidized Stafford, Direct PLUS, Federal Perkins, Federal Nursing, college/university loans from institutional funds. Applicants will be notified of awards on a rolling basis beginning April 1. Federal Work-Study Program available. Institutional employment available. Highest amount earned per year from on-campus jobs $5,700. Off-campus job opportunities are excellent.

The Inside Word

SUNY Binghamton is one of the premiere public institutions on the East Coast. There's no magic formula for gaining entrance here. You'll need to have taken a rigorous course load in high school and demonstrated academic success within advanced placement or honors courses. Application essay, SAT scores, and activities will all be analyzed and considered. If you're hoping to secure a coveted spot, don't slack in any area.

THE SCHOOL SAYS ". . ."

From the Admissions Office

"Binghamton has established itself as the premier public university in the Northeast, because of our outstanding undergraduate programs, vibrant campus culture, and committed faculty. Students are academically motivated, but there is a great deal of mutual help as they compete against the standard of a class rather than each other. Faculty and students work side by side in research labs or on artistic pursuits. Achievement, exploration, and leadership are hallmarks of a Binghamton education. Add to that a campus wide commitment to internationalization that includes a robust study abroad program, cultural offerings, languages and international studies, and you have a place where graduates leave prepared for success. Binghamton University graduates lead the nation in top starting salaries among public universities, demonstrating that our students are recognized by employers and recruiters for having strong abilities to be leaders, critical thinkers, decision makers, analysts, and researchers in many fields and industries."

SELECTIVITY	
Admissions Rating	**94**
# of applicants	28,101
% of applicants accepted	41
% of acceptees attending	22
# accepting a place on wait list	519
# admitted from wait list	20

FRESHMAN PROFILE	
Range SAT Critical Reading	600–680
Range SAT Math	620–710
Range SAT Writing	580–670
Range ACT Composite	27–31
Minimum paper TOEFL	550
Minimum web-based TOEFL	82
Average HS GPA	3.6
% graduated top 10% of class	57
% graduated top 25% of class	87
% graduated top 50% of class	98

DEADLINES	
Early action	
Deadline	11/15
Notification	1/15
Regular	
Priority	1/15
Nonfall registration?	yes

FINANCIAL FACTS	
Financial Aid Rating	**73**
Annual in-state tuition	$5,270
Annual out-state tuition	$13,380
Room and board	$11,810
Required fees	$1,946
Books and supplies	$1,000
% needy frosh rec. need-based scholarship or grant aid	78
% needy UG rec. need-based scholarship or grant aid	82
% needy frosh rec. non-need-based scholarship or grant aid	16
% needy UG rec. non-need-based scholarship or grant aid	10
% needy frosh rec. need-based self-help aid	97
% needy UG rec. need-based self-help aid	97
% frosh rec. any financial aid	80
% UG rec. any financial aid	70
% UG borrow to pay for school	52
Average cumulative indebtedness	$22,634
% frosh need fully met	15
% ugrads need fully met	12
Average % of frosh need met	72
Average % of ugrad need met	72

STATE UNIVERSITY OF NEW YORK AT GENESEO

ONE COLLEGE CIRCLE, GENESEO, NY 14454-1401 • ADMISSIONS: 585-245-5571 • FAX: 585-245-5550

CAMPUS LIFE

Quality of Life Rating	**79**
Fire Safety Rating	**89**
Green Rating	**89**
Type of school	public
Environment	village

STUDENTS

Total undergrad enrollment	5,454
% male/female	43/57
% from out of state	2
% from public high school	81
% frosh live on campus	99
# of fraternities	8
# of sororities	11
% African American	2
% Asian	7
% Caucasian	76
% Hispanic	5
% Native American	<1
% international	3
# of countries represented	39

SURVEY SAYS . . .

Lab facilities are great
Great computer facilities
Students are friendly
Campus feels safe
Low cost of living
Students are happy
Student publications are popular
Lots of beer drinking
Hard liquor is popular

ACADEMICS

Academic Rating	**78**
% students returning for sophomore year	91
% students graduating within 4 years	69
% students graduating within 6 years	81
Calendar	semester
Student/faculty ratio	20:1
Profs interesting rating	80
Profs accessible rating	84
Most classes have	20–29 students
Most lab/discussion sessions have	10–19 students

MOST POPULAR MAJORS

biology/biological sciences; business administration and management; psychology

APPLICANTS ALSO LOOK AT AND OFTEN PREFER

Colgate University, Cornell University, Hamilton College, New York University

AND SOMETIMES PREFER

Skidmore College, State University of New York at Binghamton, University of Rochester, Vassar College, Boston College

AND RARELY PREFER

State University of New York—Stony Brook University, Syracuse University, Nazareth College

STUDENTS SAY "..."

Academics

Undergrads at SUNY Geneseo laud their university for offering "an outstanding education [at] an affordable price." And with the combined "top-notch" academics and "small-town feel," it's no wonder so many students "feel at home" the minute they set foot on the campus. Indeed, Geneseo provides a "close-knit community," which in turn creates "a family environment." While the university has a number of great programs, students are especially quick to highlight the stellar education, business, and science departments. Importantly, "small classes" translates into highly "accessible" professors. Moreover, they're "truly dedicated to helping students succeed" and "are always open to talk… even during non-office hours." Undergrads do caution that you can't slack off here. Professors "seek to challenge" their students, and the "course load is tough" especially given that Geneseo is "doing a lot to combat grade inflation." Luckily, for the most part, students find their teachers "very engaging" and appreciate that they're able "to make classes very interesting" in large part through "personal stories that are relevant to the material." Perhaps this knowing senior says it best: "Geneseo has a great atmosphere, challenging classes, a wonderful student population, and the best price!"

Life

By and large, undergrads proclaim that "life is great" at SUNY Geneseo. Students "study hard and play hard" and are quite adept at striking a balance between the two. Fortunately, "Weekends are very lively, both on campus and off." An active lot, undergrads like to take advantage of Geneseo's "good" athletic facilities, which include "an ice rink, a swimming pool, a cardio room, and a weight room, as well as lots of intramural and club sports." Additionally, "Varsity sports competitions are extremely popular, especially hockey." There are also "many on-campus activities for students to get involved in throughout the week and especially late at night on the weekends." Indeed, there's "everything from laser tag to crafts to midnight bowling." Of course, "There are also outstanding clubs that [offer] a variety of services and activities such as Colleges Against Cancer, Figure Skating Club, Sports Medicine Club, Outing Club, Ski and Snowboard Club, and so many more." Though "many people do party on the weekend," students assure us, "You don't have to go to parties or join a Greek organization to have a good time." And for those with an itch to explore, a content sophomore shares, "The surrounding country is beautiful and provides lots of fun outdoorsy activities. Rochester and Buffalo are within reach, and Livingston County provides bus service to Rochester."

Student Body

What is one thing that unites Geneseo undergrads? Students here agree that their peers are "very good at time management." Indeed, "They know how to study, but they also know how to have a good time." Having multitasking down to an art form, "They are able to get their work done and excel in classes while still participating in social events and hanging out with their friends." Fortunately, Geneseo is "not a pressure cooker school," and most students are "pretty relaxed." While some assert that the school is "very diverse," others say that the "typical student is a white, middle-class, well-rounded, high school overachiever." Regardless of stereotype, students are very "open to meeting new people," and "making friends [is] really easy here." As one content freshman elaborates, "The students are very accepting. They come together frequently and support each other, causes, and the community." And a fellow classmate adds, "It's really hard to find anyone who doesn't fit in with at least one group on campus because there are so many with so many different interests."

FINANCIAL AID: 716-245-5731 • E-MAIL: ADMISSIONS@GENESEO.EDU • WEBSITE: WWW.GENESEO.EDU

THE PRINCETON REVIEW SAYS

Admissions

Very important factors considered include: Rigor of secondary school record, standardized test scores. *Important factors considered include:* Class rank, application essay, academic GPA, recommendation(s), extracurricular activities, racial/ethnic status, talent/ability. *Other factors considered include:* Alumni/ae relation, character/personal qualities, first generation, level of applicant's interest, volunteer work, work experience. SAT or ACT required; ACT with or without writing component accepted. TOEFL required of all international applicants. High school diploma is required and GED is accepted. *Academic units recommended:* 4 English, 4 mathematics, 4 science, 4 foreign language, 4 social studies.

Financial Aid

Students should submit: FAFSA, state aid form. Regular filing deadline is February 15. The Princeton Review suggests that all financial aid forms be submitted as soon as possible after January 1. *Need-based scholarships/grants offered:* Federal Pell, SEOG, state scholarships/grants. *Loan aid offered:* Direct Subsidized Stafford, Direct Unsubsidized Stafford, Direct PLUS, Federal Perkins. Applicants will be notified of awards on a rolling basis beginning March 15. Federal Work-Study Program available. Institutional employment available. Highest amount earned per year from on-campus jobs $3,500. Off-campus job opportunities are poor.

The Inside Word

SUNY Geneseo increasingly receives applications from a strong candidate pool, and gaining admission is no easy feat. First and foremost, the admissions committee reviews your high school transcript and college entrance exam scores. Applicants who have excelled in honors, IB, or advanced placement courses will have a leg up. Additionally, those reviewing prospective students attempt to take a holistic approach so be sure to submit a well-crafted essay and to demonstrate extracurricular commitment.

THE SCHOOL SAYS ". . ."

From the Admissions Office

"Geneseo has carved a distinctive niche among the nation's premier public liberal arts colleges. Geneseo is the only undergraduate college in the state of New York system to be granted a chapter of Phi Beta Kappa. The college now competes for students with some of the nation's most selective private colleges, including Colgate, Vassar, Hamilton, and Boston College. Founded in 1871, the college occupies a 220-acre hillside campus in the historic Village of Geneseo, overlooking the scenic Genesee Valley. As a residential campus—with nearly two-thirds of the students living in college residence halls—it provides a rich and varied program of social, cultural, recreational, and scholarly activities as well as numerous volunteer service opportunities. Geneseo is noted for its distinctive core curriculum and the extraordinary opportunities it offers undergraduates to pursue independent study and research with faculty who value close working relationships with talented students. Equally impressive is the remarkable success of its graduates, forty-nine percent of whom study at leading graduate and professional schools immediately following graduation. Geneseo is in the top 10 among all the country's primarily undergraduate institutions in the number of alumni who earn doctorate in STEM fields and in the top 25 in the number who earn doctorates in all disciplines.

"SUNY Geneseo will use either SAT or ACT test results in the admission selection process. The SAT writing test result will not be used. SAT Subject Test results are not required but will be considered if the applicant submits the test results."

SELECTIVITY

Admissions Rating	95
# of applicants	9,569
% of applicants accepted	43
% of acceptees attending	24
# accepting a place on wait list	342
# of early decision applicants	300
# accepted early decision	138

FRESHMAN PROFILE

Range SAT Critical Reading	590–690
Range SAT Math	600–690
Range ACT Composite	27–30
Minimum paper TOEFL	525
Minimum web-based TOEFL	71
Average HS GPA	3.7
% graduated top 10% of class	47
% graduated top 25% of class	85
% graduated top 50% of class	99

DEADLINES

Early decision	
Deadline	11/15
Notification	12/15
Regular	
Deadline	1/1
Notification	3/1
Nonfall registration?	yes

FINANCIAL FACTS

Financial Aid Rating	89
Annual in-state tuition	$5,270
Annual out-state tuition	$14,320
Room and board	$10,476
Required fees	$1,488
Books and supplies	$1,000
% needy frosh rec. need-based scholarship or grant aid	94
% needy UG rec. need-based scholarship or grant aid	100
% needy frosh rec. non-need-based scholarship or grant aid	19
% needy UG rec. non-need-based scholarship or grant aid	41
% needy frosh rec. need-based self-help aid	83
% needy UG rec. need-based self-help aid	95
% frosh rec. any financial aid	60
% UG rec. any financial aid	70
% UG borrow to pay for school	67
Average cumulative indebtedness	$21,000
% frosh need fully met	62
% ugrads need fully met	68
Average % of frosh need met	62
Average % of ugrad need met	68

STATE UNIVERSITY OF NEW YORK—PURCHASE COLLEGE

735 ANDERSON HILL ROAD, PURCHASE, NY 10577 • ADMISSIONS: 914-251-6300 • FAX: 914-251-6314

CAMPUS LIFE

Quality of Life Rating	71
Fire Safety Rating	60*
Green Rating	82
Type of school	public
Environment	town

STUDENTS

Total undergrad enrollment	3,884
% male/female	44/56
% from out of state	21
% frosh live on campus	90
% African American	6
% Asian	2
% Caucasian	50
% Hispanic	14
% international	2
# of countries represented	21

SURVEY SAYS . . .

Diverse student types on campus
Students aren't religious
Frats and sororities are unpopular or nonexistent
Musical organizations are popular
Student publications are popular
Student government is popular
Political activism is popular
Hard liquor is popular
Students are environmentally aware

ACADEMICS

Academic Rating	77
% students returning for sophomore year	81
% students graduating within 4 years	44
Calendar	semester
Student/faculty ratio	16:1
Profs interesting rating	90
Profs accessible rating	79
Most classes have	10–19 students
Most lab/discussion sessions have	fewer than 10 students

MOST POPULAR MAJORS

liberal arts and sciences/liberal studies; visual and performing arts

APPLICANTS ALSO LOOK AT AND OFTEN PREFER

The Juilliard School, New York University

STUDENTS SAY ". . ."

Academics

"Think Wide Open" is the motto at Purchase College, where "an eccentric environment...helps to fuel people's creativity and open-mindedness." "Purchase is about unapologetically being yourself," a place that "teaches real-world lessons with an 'against the grain' sort of approach." This unusual environment is due primarily to a large performing and creative arts program, in which just over one-third of all undergraduates are enrolled. These programs, which include dance, theater, music, film, and creative writing, benefit greatly from the school's proximity to New York City, an international leader in the arts. But while "the conservatories are the best known part of Purchase College," they are hardly the school's only assets. Students tell us "we do in fact have an almost equally strong liberal arts program," with excellent offerings in psychology, media studies, journalism, and premedical sciences, leading undergrads to praise "an artistic atmosphere with loads of academic opportunities." As a smaller school, Purchase can provide "the attention you need from caring professors" and can accommodate more student input; undergraduates tell us that "There is always the possibility of discussion in class, and teachers are tolerant of most thought." Professors "are very engaged, enthusiastic, and simply love learning and teaching."

Life

"Purchase is located in an area that is by no means a college town," meaning students need to rely on campus life for extracurricular fun. Fortunately, "each night there are opportunities to find something to do" without leaving the campus confines. The high concentration of creative and performing artists at Purchase means that "there's always something going on," including "concerts, plays, recitals" and "art exhibits." There are "fewer 'let's drink to drink' parties here" than at most state campuses, students believe. Instead, "Parties are organized around diversity and themes. Dance parties are common, celebrating African American or Latino culture (there are two very active groups on campus: SOCA and a chapter of Latinos Unidos). Club activities such as Cheese Club or Hillel are [also] popular." In quieter moments, "Fun can range from hiking in the woods to playing video games, [to] playing music." Or just shooting the breeze, as Purchase is home to "more philosophical people than you would expect at a state school. Not pretentiously, though. Even athletes are influenced by the community and begin to think in different ways." When all else fails, "New York City is a quick half-hour express train away on the Metro North, which has anything you could imagine available."

Student Body

"As one of the few public arts colleges that also integrates...reputable science and humanities departments," Purchase provides a home to a remarkably diverse student body. "We have athletes, cheerleaders, musicians, singers, dancers, and actors; this is just some of the diversity that is present at Purchase College," one undergrad reports. One thing many here share in common: They're likely to be a bit nerdy. As one student explains, "Imagine if you will, that you're back in grade school. Remember the last four students to be chosen [for teams in gym]? Those are Purchase College students, and the four of them are majoring in music composition, dance, biology, and literature. Or sociology, or printmaking, or gender studies." It's hardly wall-to-wall nerds, though; it's just that "The anime community is just as large as the athletic community or the premed students." As on many artsy campuses, "we have a lot of drag queens, hipsters, hippies...etc." but because "It is still a state school, students wanting to study science or language or anything...else also come here, and still fit in."

FINANCIAL AID: 914-251-6350 • E-MAIL: ADMISSIONS@PURCHASE.EDU • WEBSITE: WWW.PURCHASE.EDU

THE PRINCETON REVIEW SAYS

Admissions

Very important factors considered include: Application essay, academic GPA, talent/ability. *Important factors considered include:* Standardized test scores. *Other factors considered include:* Class rank, recommendation(s), rigor of secondary school record, character/personal qualities, extracurricular activities, interview. SAT or ACT required; ACT with or without writing component accepted. TOEFL required of all international applicants. High school diploma is required and GED is accepted.

Financial Aid

Students should submit: FAFSA, state aid form. The Princeton Review suggests that all financial aid forms be submitted as soon as possible after January 1. *Need-based scholarships/grants offered:* Federal Pell, SEOG, state scholarships/grants, private scholarships, the school's own gift aid. *Loan aid offered:* Direct Subsidized Stafford, Direct Unsubsidized Stafford, Direct PLUS, Federal Perkins. Applicants will be notified of awards on a rolling basis beginning March 1. Federal Work-Study Program available. Institutional employment available. Off-campus job opportunities are excellent.

The Inside Word

Just more than one-third of Purchase College undergraduates enroll in the School of the Arts. All must undergo either an audition or portfolio review as part of the application process; for such students, this is the most important part of the application. Traditional application components—such as high school transcript, test scores, and personal essay—are also considered, but figure less prominently. Applicants to the School of Liberal Arts and Sciences undergo a more conventional application review.

THE SCHOOL SAYS ". . ."

From the Admissions Office

"At Purchase College, you're encouraged to 'Think Wide Open.' The campus combines the energy and excitement of professional training in the performing and the visual arts with the intellectual traditions and spirit of discovery of the humanities and sciences. A Purchase College education emphasizes creativity, individual accomplishment, openness, and exploration. It culminates in a senior research or creative project that may focus on civic engagement or interdisciplinary work to become an excellent springboard to a career or to graduate or professional school. The Conservatories of Art and Design, Dance, Music, and Theatre Arts and Film that make up the School of the Arts deliver a cohort-based education with apprenticeships and other professional opportunities in nearby New York City.

"You'll find a unique and engaging atmosphere at Purchase, whether you are a student in the arts, humanities, natural sciences, or social sciences. You choose among a wide variety of programs, including arts management, journalism, creative writing, environmental science, new media, dramatic writing, premed, pre-law, and education. You'll attend performances by your friends, see world-renowned artists on stage at the Performing Arts Center, and experience the artworks on display in the Neuberger Museum of Art (one of the largest campus art museums in the country)—all without leaving campus. The new student services building, along with an enhanced student services website, is making Purchase a lot more user-friendly for its students.

"Admissions requirements vary with each program in the college and can include auditions, portfolio reviews, essays, writing samples, and interviews.

"In addition to individual program requirements, Purchase College requires SAT or ACT scores to complete your application."

SELECTIVITY	
Admissions Rating	**91**
# of applicants	8,949
% of applicants accepted	34
% of acceptees attending	26

FRESHMAN PROFILE	
Range SAT Critical Reading	500–620
Range SAT Math	480–580
Range SAT Writing	500–600
Range ACT Composite	21–26
Minimum paper TOEFL	550
Average HS GPA	3.2
% graduated top 10% of class	11
% graduated top 25% of class	36
% graduated top 50% of class	78

DEADLINES	
Early action	
Deadline	11/15
Notification	12/15
Regular	
Priority	3/1
Deadline	7/15
Nonfall registration?	yes

FINANCIAL FACTS	
Financial Aid Rating	**66**
Annual in-state tuition	$5,270
Annual out-state tuition	$14,320
Room and board	$11,058
Required fees	$1,559
Books and supplies	$1,138
% needy frosh rec. need-based scholarship or grant aid	82
% needy UG rec. need-based scholarship or grant aid	84
% needy frosh rec. non-need-based scholarship or grant aid	1
% needy UG rec. non-need-based scholarship or grant aid	1
% needy frosh rec. need-based self-help aid	99
% needy UG rec. need-based self-help aid	97
% UG borrow to pay for school	63
Average cumulative indebtedness	$32,440
% frosh need fully met	3
% ugrads need fully met	3
Average % of frosh need met	50
Average % of ugrad need met	56

State University of New York—Stony Brook University

Office of Admissions, Stony Brook, NY 11794-1901 • Admissions: 631-632-6868 • Fax: 631-632-9898

CAMPUS LIFE

Quality of Life Rating	**69**
Fire Safety Rating	**73**
Green Rating	**90**
Type of school	public
Environment	town

STUDENTS

Total undergrad enrollment	15,968
% male/female	53/47
% from out of state	17
% from public high school	90
% frosh live on campus	83
# of fraternities	15
# of sororities	14
% African American	6
% Asian	24
% Caucasian	37
% Hispanic	10
% international	9
# of countries represented	111

SURVEY SAYS . . .

Class discussions are rare
Great computer facilities
Great library
Diverse student types on campus
Low cost of living
Lots of beer drinking

ACADEMICS

Academic Rating	**68**
% students returning for sophomore year	92
% students graduating within 4 years	47
% students graduating within 6 years	67
Calendar	semester
Student/faculty ratio	19:1
Profs interesting rating	68
Profs accessible rating	65
Most classes have	20–29 students
Most lab/discussion sessions have	20–29 students

MOST POPULAR MAJORS

biology/biological sciences; business/commerce; psychology

APPLICANTS ALSO LOOK AT AND OFTEN PREFER

State University of New York at Binghamton, New York University, Rensselaer Polytechnic Institute, Cornell University

AND SOMETIMES PREFER

Pennsylvania State University—University Park, Rutgers, The State University of New Jersey—New Brunswick, State University of New York at Geneseo, University of Connecticut

AND RARELY PREFER

Pace University, Hofstra University

STUDENTS SAY ". . ."

Academics

Stony Brook University combines affordability and excellence with academic prestige, offering a "great academic reputation," ample research opportunities, and the chance to learn from "world-renowned professors for a great price." Don't let Stony Brook's "best value" reputation fool you; known as a "science powerhouse," the school is also a leader in premedical preparation. With over 150 academic programs on offer, "the breadth of the school's curriculum" is impressive, including "a wide variety of classes that you can take, ranging from [topics] such as theory of dance to nuclear physics." Academics are challenging and "Everyone lives in the library." In particular, "The science courses are no joke. They are large and hard, and you will most likely learn most of the material yourself." Fortunately, students paint a generally positive picture of the faculty, describing professors as "approachable and interested in their subject, making them good educators." Stony Brook is a research university, so while "it is relatively easy to find internships and research opportunities" as an undergraduate, you should also be aware that "Many professors feel their lab work is more important than their students." With almost 16,000 undergraduates, you'll end up in plenty of big lecture courses, making it more difficult to get to know your instructors personally. However, faculty maintains "reasonable office hours," and most are "very accessible" if you seek them out. In fact, Stony Brook students tell us that their "school is about taking initiative and taking advantage of opportunities that are available," rather than having your hand held—a happy condition for those who feel they are "too old to be spoon-fed." A current student explains, "Professors and staff are more than willing to help, but you have to ask for it…I feel that the balance between independence and assistance has prepared me well for entering a profession."

Life

Nothing at Stony Brook University will be handed to you on a silver platter, yet students reassure us that, "If you are willing to seek out activities and events, you will never be bored." On campus, there are almost 300 clubs and organizations, including sports teams, environmental groups, several student-run newspaper, and fraternities and sororities. In their downtime, students "hang out with friends," play video games or intramural sports, "head over to the University Café, or watch movies in their rooms." For additional distraction, "Each dorm building has its own ping-pong table and pool table in the basement." If you want to take a break from college life, "campus buses go to places like the mall and Walmart every weekend," and the surrounding community offers "movie theaters, bowling, Dave and Buster's, [and] countless restaurants." In addition, New York City is "fairly close," while nearby Southampton boasts "one of the top beaches in the United States." While people get together socially, SUNY Stony Brook is not a major party school, and "The campus is very quiet on weekends because many students live nearby and go home."

Student Body

Drawing a large crowd from the state of New York and a smattering of international students, Stony Brook University "combines the diversity of New York City with academic excellence to create a truly unique experience." At this large school, "Every personality type is represented…and it is easy to find a group to fit in with." Politically, "there are both strong right-wing and left-wing school newspapers," though "many more people support the liberal side." No matter what your persuasion, the community is generally open and accepting of different backgrounds, opinions, and interests. A current student elaborates, "I've never seen such a heterogeneous mixture of individuals in my life. And yet, despite the vast differences amongst students, everyone seems to get along." Across the board, academics are a priority, but most students strike a balance between work and play. At Stony Brook, "A typical student will go to class, spend a lot of their time studying, and try to have some fun on Thursday nights and the weekends."

FINANCIAL AID: 631-632-6840 • E-MAIL: ENROLL@STONYBROOK.EDU • WEBSITE: WWW.STONYBROOK.EDU

THE PRINCETON REVIEW SAYS

Admissions

Very important factors considered include: Academic GPA, rigor of secondary school record, standardized test scores. *Important factors considered include:* Class rank. *Other factors considered include:* Application essay, recommendation(s), alumni/ae relation, character/personal qualities, extracurricular activities, first generation, interview, level of applicant's interest, state residency, talent/ability, volunteer work, work experience. SAT or ACT required; ACT with writing component required. TOEFL required of all international applicants. High school diploma is required and GED is accepted. *Academic units required:* 4 English, 3 mathematics, 3 science, 2 foreign language, 4 social studies. *Academic units recommended:* 4 mathematics, 4 science, 3 foreign language.

Financial Aid

Students should submit: FAFSA, program specific forms. The Princeton Review suggests that all financial aid forms be submitted as soon as possible after January 1. *Need-based scholarships/grants offered:* Federal Pell, SEOG, state scholarships/grants, the school's own gift aid. *Loan aid offered:* Direct Subsidized Stafford, Direct Unsubsidized Stafford, Direct PLUS, Federal Perkins. Applicants will be notified of awards on a rolling basis beginning March 1. Federal Work-Study Program available. Institutional employment available. Highest amount earned per year from on-campus jobs $12,638. Off-campus job opportunities are excellent.

The Inside Word

Admission to Stony Brook University is competitive. Students with a particularly strong academic record may be considered for the university's special programs, including the Honors Program, the University Scholars program, and the Scholars in Medicine program. Admits to the Scholars in Medicine program can earn a bachelor's degree and MD through an integrated, eight-year curriculum; but applicants must meet high minimum GPA and test score requirements to be considered.

THE SCHOOL SAYS ". . ."

From the Admissions Office

"Our graduates include Carolyn Porco, the leader of the Imaging Team for the Cassini mission to Saturn; John Hennessy, the president of Stanford University; and Scott Higham, a Pulitzer Prize–winning investigative journalist for the Washington Post who has come to speak to students at our new School of Journalism. Situated on 1,000 wooded acres on the North Shore of Long Island, Stony Brook offers more than 150 majors, minors, and combined-degree programs for undergraduates, including our Fast Track MBA program, a thriving research environment, and a dynamic first-year experience in one of six small undergraduate communities. Faculty include four members of our School of Marine and Atmospheric Sciences who are recent co-winners of the Nobel Peace Prize. Students enjoy comfortable campus housing, outstanding recreational facilities that include an 8,300 seat stadium, modern student activities center, indoor sports complex, and 85,000-square foot campus recreation center due to open in 2012. In addition, the Staller Center for the Arts offers spectacular theatrical and musical performances throughout the year. We invite students who possess both intellectual curiosity and academic ability to explore the countless exciting opportunities available at Stony Brook. Freshmen applying for admission to the university are required to take the SAT (or the ACT with the writing section). SAT Subject Test scores are recommended, but not required."

SELECTIVITY

Admissions Rating	**92**
# of applicants	26,911
% of applicants accepted	39
% of acceptees attending	24
# accepting a place on wait list	1,096
# admitted from wait list	25

FRESHMAN PROFILE

Range SAT Critical Reading	540–640
Range SAT Math	590–690
Range SAT Writing	530–640
Range ACT Composite	25–29
Minimum paper TOEFL	550
Minimum web-based TOEFL	80
Average HS GPA	3.6
% graduated top 10% of class	40
% graduated top 25% of class	73
% graduated top 50% of class	94

DEADLINES

Regular	
Priority	1/15
Notification	4/1
Nonfall registration?	yes

FINANCIAL FACTS

Financial Aid Rating	**70**
Annual in-state tuition	$5,570
Annual out-state tuition	$16,190
Room and board	$10,998
Required fees	$1,944
Books and supplies	$900
% needy frosh rec. need-based scholarship or grant aid	93
% needy UG rec. need-based scholarship or grant aid	89
% needy frosh rec. non-need-based scholarship or grant aid	12
% needy UG rec. non-need-based scholarship or grant aid	7
% needy frosh rec. need-based self-help aid	96
% needy UG rec. need-based self-help aid	97
% frosh rec. any financial aid	78
% UG rec. any financial aid	70
% UG borrow to pay for school	58
Average cumulative indebtedness	$20,370
% frosh need fully met	20
% ugrads need fully met	26
Average % of frosh need met	72
Average % of ugrad need met	74

STATE UNIVERSITY OF NEW YORK—UNIVERSITY AT ALBANY

OFFICE OF UNDERGRADUATE ADMISSIONS, ALBANY, NY 12222 • ADMISSIONS: 518-442-5435 • FAX: 518-442-5383

CAMPUS LIFE

Quality of Life Rating	**65**
Fire Safety Rating	**77**
Green Rating	**90**
Type of school	public
Environment	city

STUDENTS

Total undergrad enrollment	12,425
% male/female	52/48
% from out of state	7
% frosh live on campus	95
# of fraternities	19
# of sororities	19
% African American	11
% Asian	7
% Caucasian	58
% Hispanic	11
% international	4
# of countries represented	84

SURVEY SAYS . . .

Class discussions are rare
Diverse student types on campus
Lousy food on campus
Lots of beer drinking
Hard liquor is popular

ACADEMICS

Academic Rating	**66**
% students returning for sophomore year	86
% students graduating within 4 years	53
% students graduating within 6 years	65
Calendar	semester
Student/faculty ratio	19:1
Profs interesting rating	65
Profs accessible rating	65
Most classes have	20–29 students
Most lab/discussion sessions have	10–19 students

MOST POPULAR MAJORS

business administration and management; English language and literature; psychology

STUDENTS SAY ". . ."

Academics

Is SUNY Albany (UAlbany to those in the know) the perfect-sized school? Many here think so. Students describe it as "a big school numbers-wise that feels small." Notes one student, "It has a very broad range of quality academic programs, which is very important for an undecided senior in high school." Another adds, "If you know what you want and are motivated, the sky is the limit." The school exploits its location in the state capital to bolster programs in political science, criminal justice, and business, and it "offers internship opportunities to college students that very few schools can." Other standout departments include psychology, Japanese studies, mathematics, and many of the hard sciences. Professors here vary widely in quality, but a surprising number "are receptive, active, and engaging"—in other words, "a lot more accessible than I would have thought for a school this big." Teachers are especially willing to "go out of their way to help students who are interested in learning, come to class regularly, and care about their academic work." The administration, as at most state-run schools, "is basically an over-bloated bureaucracy. Students are sent from department to department in each of their endeavors. It is advisable to avoid [the] administration if at all possible."

Life

There are three distinct social orbits on the Albany campus. Some students take the initiative "by joining one of the many clubs or groups or getting involved with the student government." Others "party for a good time," telling us that "any night of the week you can find people to go out to the bars and clubs with you" and that "the average night ends between 2:30 and 4:00 A.M." Both of these groups are likely to tell you that "there is a lot to do in Albany and the surrounding area," including "a great arts district, tons of awesome restaurants, museums, [and] a state park." A third, sizable group primarily complains about the cold weather and asserts that "there's nothing to do in Albany." The school works to excite these students with "fun programs and entertainers who come to the campus. We have had a series of comedians, rappers/singers, guests from MTV and VH1, authors, political figures, musical performances, sporting events, spirit events, and many other things around campus." School spirit is on the rise among all groups, we're told. The reason? "A few years ago, basketball team began winning, and everyone came out of the woodwork to support them—it was really a great thing to see."

Student Body

Undergrads here believe that the student body is very diverse in terms of ethnicity and also in terms of personality type; one student observes, "You have your motivated students [who] get good grades, are involved, and get amazing jobs in NYC after college. Then you have your unmotivated kids [who] complain, don't go to class, and blame a bad grade on the professor (when really it is because they crammed the night before and didn't go to class)." Geographically, the school is less diverse. Nearly everyone is a New York State resident, with many coming from "downstate New York"—Long Island, New York City, and Westchester County. There's a fair amount of upstate kids as well, and "a lot of people have certain stereotypes in their heads when they first come to Albany. The Long Islander has his idea about the upstater and vice versa. After a few weeks, though, people see that these aren't always true. I think people from anywhere get along pretty well." The international students, who form a small but noticeable contingent, "tend to keep to themselves," perhaps "due to a culture or language barrier." About one-quarter of the campus population is Jewish.

State University of New York—University at Albany

Financial Aid: 518-442-3202 • E-mail: ugadmissions@albany.edu • Website: www.albany.edu

THE PRINCETON REVIEW SAYS

Admissions

Very important factors considered include: Class rank, academic GPA, recommendation(s), rigor of secondary school record, standardized test scores, character/personal qualities. *Important factors considered include:* Application essay. *Other factors considered include:* Alumni/ae relation, extracurricular activities, first generation, geographical residence, talent/ability, volunteer work, work experience. SAT or ACT required; ACT with writing component required. TOEFL required of all international applicants. High school diploma is required and GED is accepted. *Academic units required:* 4 English, 2 mathematics, 2 science (2 science labs), 1 foreign language, 3 social studies, 2 history, 4 academic electives. *Academic units recommended:* 4 mathematics, 3 science (3 science labs), 3 foreign language.

Financial Aid

Students should submit: FAFSA. NY State residents should apply for TAP online at www.tapweb.org. The Princeton Review suggests that all financial aid forms be submitted as soon as possible after January 1. *Need-based scholarships/grants offered:* Federal Pell, SEOG, state scholarships/grants, private scholarships, the school's own gift aid. *Loan aid offered:* Direct Subsidized Stafford, Direct Unsubsidized Stafford, Direct PLUS, Federal Perkins. Applicants will be notified of awards on a rolling basis beginning March 20. Federal Work-Study Program available. Institutional employment available. Highest amount earned per year from on-campus jobs $6,840. Off-campus job opportunities are good.

The Inside Word

The Wall Street Journal has noted a growing trend among students who, in the past, had limited their postsecondary options to high-end private schools: More such students, the paper reported, have broadened their vision to include prestigious state schools such as SUNY Albany. The driving force, unsurprisingly, is economic. In the event of an unlikely decline in the cost of private education, expect admissions at schools like UAlbany to grow more competitive in coming years.

THE SCHOOL SAYS ". . ."

From the Admissions Office

"Increasing numbers of well-prepared students are discovering the benefits of study in UAlbany's nationally ranked programs and are taking advantage of outstanding internship and employment opportunities in upstate New York's 'Tech Valley.' The already strong undergraduate program is further enhanced by the Honors College, a university-wide program for ambitious students. The Honors College offers enhanced honors courses and co-curricular options including honors housing.

"Nine schools and colleges, including the nation's first College of Nanoscale Science and Engineering, offer bachelor's, master's, and doctoral programs to more than nearly 13,000 undergraduates and 5,000 graduate students. An award-winning advisement program helps students take advantage of all these options by customizing the undergraduate experiences. More than two-thirds of Albany graduates go on for advanced degrees, and acceptance to law and medical school is above the national average.

"Student life on campus includes 200 clubs, honor societies, and other groups, and nineteen Division I varsity teams. With twenty other colleges in the region, Albany is a great college town, adjacent to the spectacular natural and recreational centers of New York and New England.

"Freshmen are awarded more than $800,000 in merit scholarships each year and nearly three-quarters of our students receive financial aid."

SELECTIVITY	
Admissions Rating	89
# of applicants	22,188
% of applicants accepted	47
% of acceptees attending	22

FRESHMAN PROFILE	
Range SAT Critical Reading	500–590
Range SAT Math	530–620
Minimum paper TOEFL	550
Minimum web-based TOEFL	79
Average HS GPA	3.4
% graduated top 10% of class	21
% graduated top 25% of class	60
% graduated top 50% of class	94

DEADLINES	
Early action	
Deadline	11/15
Notification	1/15
Regular	
Priority	3/1
Deadline	3/1
Nonfall registration?	yes

FINANCIAL FACTS	
Financial Aid Rating	67
Annual tuition	$5,570
Annual out-state tuition	$16,190
Room and board	$11,276
Required fees	$1,902
Books and supplies	$1,200
% needy frosh rec. need-based scholarship or grant aid	82
% needy UG rec. need-based scholarship or grant aid	85
% needy frosh rec. non-need-based scholarship or grant aid	2
% needy UG rec. non-need-based scholarship or grant aid	2
% needy frosh rec. need-based self-help aid	80
% needy UG rec. need-based self-help aid	80
% frosh rec. any financial aid	64
% UG rec. any financial aid	62
% UG borrow to pay for school	70
Average cumulative indebtedness	$24,146
% frosh need fully met	7
% ugrads need fully met	8
Average % of frosh need met	63
Average % of ugrad need met	64

State University of New York—University at Buffalo

12 Capen Hall, Buffalo, NY 14260-1660 • Admissions: 716-645-6900 • Fax: 716-645-6411

CAMPUS LIFE

Quality of Life Rating	**69**
Fire Safety Rating	**60***
Green Rating	**61**
Type of school	public
Environment	city

STUDENTS

Total undergrad enrollment	19,058
% male/female	54/46
% from out of state	5
% frosh live on campus	74
# of fraternities	22
# of sororities	17
% African American	7
% Asian	11
% Caucasian	53
% Hispanic	7
% Native American	1
% international	16
# of countries represented	108

SURVEY SAYS . . .

Diverse student types on campus
Student publications are popular
Lots of beer drinking
Hard liquor is popular

ACADEMICS

Academic Rating	**69**
% students returning for sophomore year	88
% students graduating within 4 years	44
% students graduating within 6 years	68
Calendar	semester
Profs interesting rating	70
Profs accessible rating	66
Most classes have	20–29 students
Most lab/discussion sessions have	20–29 students

MOST POPULAR MAJORS

business/commerce; engineering; social sciences

STUDENTS SAY ". . ."

Academics

Offering "more academic programs per dollar than any other university in the state," SUNY Buffalo (UB for short) "is about choices. You can choose many different…combinations of academics and social activities with the support in place." Students brag that UB's "programs are all of the highest quality, translating [into] a best-value education for students." The School of Engineering and Applied Sciences in particular "is well respected" and "works with corporate partners in a variety of ways that range from joint-research ventures to continuing education to co-op work arrangements for our students." Other stand-out offerings include pharmacy, physical therapy, a popular business and management school "that is ranked highly," "a solid undergrad and grad architecture program," and "one of the top nursing programs in the state." Of course, a school with this much to offer is bound to be large, making it "easy not to attend class and fall through the cracks, so one must be self-motivated to do well." Administrative tasks are occasionally Kafkaesque, with "a lot of red tape to go through to get anything done. I feel like a pebble being kicked around when trying to get support or services," notes one student. Many students point out that support services and contact with professors improves during junior and senior years when students are pursuing their majors and forging stronger relationships within their departments.

Life

UB is divided into three campuses. Traditionally, South Campus in Northeast Buffalo has been where "the parties are," though students say that "it's much less safe than North Campus," which is located in the suburban enclave of Amherst. The school also has a downtown campus but with no residence halls. The recent closing of several bars near South Campus has made it less of a party destination than it was in years past; these days many students report going to downtown Buffalo "to go clubbing." Students living on North Campus describe it as "its own little city. We have food services, our own bus system, a highway, even our own zip codes. If you know how to play, North Campus is just as much fun as Main Street [which runs by South Campus]; you just need to know where to go." The North Campus, which features "a lake and a nice bike path for when you want to escape from the hectic [atmosphere]" of academic life, is the more populous of the two; the intercampus bus system is "convenient," although a car is preferred. Students tell us that "between all of the clubs and organizations, the Office of Student Life, athletics, and the Student Association, there is always something to do" on campus. The school's Division I sports teams "are a big hit around here. Even if we are the worst in the division, we still cheer hard and go crazy for our guys and girls." Those who explore Buffalo extol its "amazing art and music scene."

Student Body

Because of UB's size, "You can find just about every kind of person there is here. Everyone has a place in this large and diverse student population." As one student notes, "Although the typical student is of traditional college age, there really isn't a 'typical' student—the student body is very diverse in terms of religion, ethnicity, nationality, age, gender, and orientation. 'Atypical' students fit in well because of the diversity of the student population." Another student adds, "There are a lot of foreign and minority students, to the point that the actual 'majority' is the minority here at UB." Geographically, UB draws "from urban areas, rural areas, NYC, Long Island, and most every country in the world." Because UB is a state school, "a lot of the students are from New York State, but with differing areas of the state, there are many different types of students."

FINANCIAL AID: 716-645-2450 • E-MAIL: UB-ADMISSIONS@BUFFALO.EDU • WEBSITE: WWW.BUFFALO.EDU

THE PRINCETON REVIEW SAYS

Admissions

Very important factors considered include: Academic GPA, rigor of secondary school program, standardized test scores. *Important factors considered include:* Class rank, recommendation(s), interview. *Other factors considered include:* Application essay, character/personal qualities, extracurricular activities, first generation, geographical residence, racial/ethnic status, talent/ability, volunteer work, work experience. SAT or ACT required; ACT with writing component required. TOEFL required of all international applicants. High school diploma is required and GED is accepted. *Academic units recommended:* 4 English, 3 mathematics, 3 science, 3 foreign language, 4 social studies.

Financial Aid

Students should submit: FAFSA. Priority due date is March 1. The Princeton Review suggests that all financial aid forms be submitted as soon as possible after January 1. *Need-based scholarships/grants offered:* Federal Pell, SEOG, state scholarships/grants, private scholarships, the school's own gift aid, Federal Nursing Scholarships. *Loan aid offered:* Direct Subsidized Stafford, Direct Unsubsidized Stafford, Direct PLUS, Federal Perkins, Federal Nursing, college/university loans from institutional funds. Applicants will be notified of awards on a rolling basis beginning February 1. Federal Work-Study Program available. Institutional employment available. Off-campus job opportunities are good.

The Inside Word

As students point out, UB "is famous for its architecture, nursing, and pharmacy schools," making those majors harder to get into. In fact, admissions standards at UB have grown more demanding across all programs in recent years. Despite the school's large applicant pool, it takes a close look at applications, searching for evidence of special talents and experiences that will enrich campus life.

THE SCHOOL SAYS ". . ."

From the Admissions Office

"The University at Buffalo (UB) is among the nation's finest public research universities—a learning community where you'll work side by side with world-renowned faculty, who have included Nobel, Pulitzer, National Medal of Science, and other award winners. As the largest, most comprehensive university center in the State University of New York (SUNY) system, UB offers more undergraduate majors than any public university in New York or New England. Through innovative resources like our Center for Undergraduate Research and Creative Activities, Discovery Seminars, and Undergraduate Academies, you'll be free to chart an academic course that meets your individual goals. At UB you can even design your own major. Our University Honors College and University Scholars Program offer an enhanced academic experience, including opportunities for independent study, advanced research, and specialized advisement. We're so committed to your success that we now offer Finish in 4, a program to keep qualified students on track for their four-year degree. If you meet your requirements and still aren't able to graduate in four years, you can complete the UB courses required for your degree free of any tuition or comprehensive fee charges. UB also places a high priority on offering an exciting campus environment. With nonstop festivals, Division I sporting events, concerts, and celebrity speakers, you'll have plenty to do outside of the classroom. We encourage you and your family to visit campus to see UB up close and in person. Our Visit UB campus tours and presentations are offered year-round."

SELECTIVITY	
Admissions Rating	87
# of applicants	21,357
% of applicants accepted	53
% of acceptees attending	29
# accepting a place on wait list	639
# admitted from wait list	155
# of early decision applicants	444
# accepted early decision	282

FRESHMAN PROFILE	
Range SAT Critical Reading	500–600
Range SAT Math	550–650
Range ACT Composite	23–28
Minimum paper TOEFL	550
Minimum web-based TOEFL	79
Average HS GPA	3.3
% graduated top 10% of class	26
% graduated top 25% of class	63
% graduated top 50% of class	93

DEADLINES	
Early decision	
Deadline	11/1
Notification	12/15
Regular	
Priority	11/1
Nonfall registration?	yes

FINANCIAL FACTS	
Financial Aid Rating	87
Annual in-state tuition	$5,270
Annual out-state tuition	$14,720
Room and board	$11,162
Required fees	$2,212
Books and supplies	$1,034
% needy frosh rec. need-based scholarship or grant aid	85
% needy UG rec. need-based scholarship or grant aid	86
% needy frosh rec. non-need-based scholarship or grant aid	20
% needy UG rec. non-need-based scholarship or grant aid	20
% needy frosh rec. need-based self-help aid	91
% needy UG rec. need-based self-help aid	90
% UG borrow to pay for school	45
Average cumulative indebtedness	$16,010
% frosh need fully met	97
% ugrads need fully met	97
Average % of frosh need met	65
Average % of ugrad need met	66

Stevens Institute of Technology

Castle Point on Hudson, Hoboken, NJ 07030 • Admissions: 201-216-5194 • Fax: 201-216-8348

CAMPUS LIFE

Quality of Life Rating	**92**
Fire Safety Rating	**95**
Green Rating	**63**
Type of school	private
Environment	town

STUDENTS

Total undergrad enrollment	2,927
% male/female	75/25
% from out of state	44
% from public high school	72
% frosh live on campus	92
# of fraternities	10
# of sororities	3
% African American	3
% Asian	10
% Caucasian	58
% Hispanic	9
% international	4
# of countries represented	34

SURVEY SAYS . . .

Class discussions are rare
Career services are great
Students love Hoboken, NJ
Great off-campus food
Campus feels safe
Frats and sororities dominate social scene
Lots of beer drinking
Internships are widely available

ACADEMICS

Academic Rating	**75**
% students returning for sophomore year	92
% students graduating within 4 years	34
% students graduating within 6 years	79
Calendar	semester
Student/faculty ratio	8:1
Profs interesting rating	65
Profs accessible rating	66

MOST POPULAR MAJORS

business administration and management; computer science; chemical engineering; mechanical engineering

APPLICANTS ALSO LOOK AT AND OFTEN PREFER

Princeton University, Massachusetts Institute of Technology, Carnegie Mellon University, Cornell University

AND SOMETIMES PREFER

Lehigh University, New York University, Johns Hopkins University

AND RARELY PREFER

Rensselaer Polytechnic Institute, Worcester Polytechnic Institute, Drexel University

STUDENTS SAY ". . ."

Academics

Stevens Institute of Technology "is all about preparing scientists and engineers for a real work experience through research, co-op, and hands-on classes." "Engineering dominates" the curriculum here—"almost every major is engineering, and those that aren't, they throw 'and engineering' on the end to make it sound like it is"—and "The course load is demanding in its math, physics and engineering classes." Just less than half of Stevens' undergraduates participate in the school's cooperative education program (co-op), which students brag is "one of the best in the country." The program places students in real-world work environments that "allow [them] to learn more outside the classroom than inside it." As one undergrad sees it, "Stevens prepares students to actually work in these advanced technical fields as opposed to other colleges that focus solely on book smarts." As a "smaller school," Stevens can address student needs and concerns with "a lot less bureaucracy, a lot less red tape, and more direct communication" than other schools. Professors, similarly, tend to be more accessible than at larger schools, making the educational experience "a lot less stressful than it could be." It's not all rosy, though; as at many tech schools, "Some professors and lab assistants speak English poorly, and are consequently difficult to understand." When students graduate, the school "really does try hard to increase job placement," and its "career fairs and workshops…are worth every minute."

Life

"Academics are the main focus here at Stevens," but "there are also lots of activities available both on and off campus," and most students manage to find at least some time for them. The student-run entertainment committee "does a great job [of] bringing in a variety of shows," including "two big campus festivals offered in the fall and spring, known as Techfest and Boken respectively. There are lots of games, prizes, comedians, bands and much more…offered during this [event]." Many students "are very active in the ninety-plus RSOs (Registered Student Organizations) on campus," and "many play sports" as well ("The sports teams are very good overall in our conference and NCAA play"). "On Thursday, Friday, and Saturday nights, there are usually parties in dorm rooms and at the frats," but "if drinking and partying isn't your thing, there is still a lot for you to do," off campus as well as on. Hometown Hoboken "is a great place to walk around, go shopping, and hang out." It also has "a great social life and is filled with many bars to go to." And, "The train station is only a couple blocks away, making traveling into New York City easy and convenient." New York, of course, offers "endless possibilities for activities, no matter who the person is."

Student Body

Sure, there are "way too many people who are into anime" at Stevens, the kinds of kids who make jokes like "Stevens has 10 types of students: Those who know binary, and those who are hung over and forgot it." But students here insist that Stevens isn't all nerd, all the time. Most agree that "half of the students are obsessed with video games and are pretty nerdy," while the other half, "who are probably business and technology majors," "are so involved on campus it almost seems like they are running the entire school. Many of them have Blackberries and daily organizers to show just how busy they are." The student body includes "a huge proportion of athletes" as well as "great artists, great writers, great actors, and great singers." "There's absolutely a place for everyone to fit in. If you can't find a place, you must be doing something wrong," one student says.

FINANCIAL AID: 201-216-5555 • E-MAIL: ADMISSIONS@STEVENS.EDU • WEBSITE: WWW.STEVENS.EDU

THE PRINCETON REVIEW SAYS

Admissions

Very important factors considered include: Application essay, academic GPA, recommendation(s), rigor of secondary school record, standardized test scores, character/personal qualities, extracurricular activities, interview, volunteer work, work experience. *Important factors considered include:* Class rank, talent/ability. *Other factors considered include:* Alumni/ae relation. SAT or ACT required; ACT with or without writing component accepted. TOEFL required of all international applicants. High school diploma is required and GED is not accepted. *Academic units required:* 4 English, 4 mathematics, 3 science (3 science labs). *Academic units recommended:* 4 science (4 science labs), 2 foreign language, 2 social studies, 2 history, 1 computer science, 4 academic electives.

Financial Aid

Students should submit: FAFSA. Regular filing deadline is February 1. The Princeton Review suggests that all financial aid forms be submitted as soon as possible after January 1. *Need-based scholarships/grants offered:* Federal Pell, SEOG, state scholarships/grants, private scholarships, the school's own gift aid. *Loan aid offered:* Direct PLUS, Federal Perkins, state loans, Signature Loans, NJ CLASS, CitiAssist. Federal Work-Study Program available. Institutional employment available. Highest amount earned per year from on-campus jobs $1,300. Off-campus job opportunities are excellent.

The Inside Word

Stevens remains among the most desirable "second tier" engineering/science/math schools; its location and cachet with employers guarantee it will always rank fairly high. If you can handle the grueling curriculum of a top tech school but can't make the cut at MIT or Caltech—in other words, if you're merely mortal—Stevens is a solid alternative. The school waives its application fee for those who apply online.

THE SCHOOL SAYS ". . ."

From the Admissions Office

"Founded in 1870 as the first college of mechanical engineering in the U.S., Stevens Institute of Technology stands today as one of the nation's premier research institutions and consistently ranks in the top ten percent of all U.S. universities in terms of the value of its educational, research, and placement outcomes. Noted for its unique academic approach, Stevens inexorably links its students to real-world innovation and entrepreneurship, distinct and exceptionally regarded research programs, and well-established partnerships in business, industry, and government. Stevens was recently ranked in the top twenty-five schools in the nation for annualized return on investment (ROI) for students by Bloomberg Business Week in a study of more than 850 colleges and universities.

"Stevens' broad-based education leads to prestigious degrees in business, science, computer science, engineering, or humanities and provides diverse and interdisciplinary programs within four schools: the Schaefer School of Engineering and Science, the Howe School of Technology Management, the School of Systems and Enterprises, and the College of Arts and Letters. Research activities are vital to the university's educational mission, thus Stevens attracts world-renowned faculty to complement its exceptional on-campus facilities. In addition, Stevens maintains an honor system that has been in existence since 1908. Stevens' 2,427 undergraduate students come from more than forty states and thirty-four countries, creating a diverse, dynamic environment. Stevens also boasts an outstanding campus life—students will find more than 150 student clubs and organizations and twenty-six NCAA Division III athletics teams.

SELECTIVITY	
Admissions Rating	**95**
# of applicants	3,600
% of applicants accepted	42
% of acceptees attending	37
# accepting a place on wait list	742
# admitted from wait list	6
# of early decision applicants	554
# accepted early decision	317

FRESHMAN PROFILE	
Range SAT Critical Reading	560–670
Range SAT Math	630–720
Range SAT Writing	560–660
Range ACT Composite	26–30
Minimum paper TOEFL	550
Minimum web-based TOEFL	82
Average HS GPA	3.8
% graduated top 10% of class	56
% graduated top 25% of class	88
% graduated top 50% of class	99

DEADLINES	
Early decision	
Deadline	11/15
Notification	12/15
Regular	
Deadline	2/1
Notification	3/15
Nonfall registration?	yes

FINANCIAL FACTS	
Financial Aid Rating	**69**
Annual tuition	$40,300
Room and board	$13,340
Required fees	$1,500
Books and supplies	$900
% needy frosh rec. need-based scholarship or grant aid	83
% needy UG rec. need-based scholarship or grant aid	69
% needy frosh rec. non-need-based scholarship or grant aid	79
% needy UG rec. non-need-based scholarship or grant aid	68
% needy frosh rec. need-based self-help aid	83
% needy UG rec. need-based self-help aid	71
% frosh rec. any financial aid	83
% UG rec. any financial aid	77
% UG borrow to pay for school	66
Average cumulative indebtedness	$37,819
% frosh need fully met	20
% ugrads need fully met	16
Average % of frosh need met	83
Average % of ugrad need met	76

STONEHILL COLLEGE

320 WASHINGTON STREET, EASTON, MA 02357-5610 • ADMISSIONS: 508-565-1373 • FAX: 508-565-1545

CAMPUS LIFE

Quality of Life Rating	**89**
Fire Safety Rating	**90**
Green Rating	**73**
Type of school	private
Affiliation	Roman Catholic
Environment	village

STUDENTS

Total undergrad enrollment	2,464
% male/female	39/61
% from out of state	42
% from public high school	66
% frosh live on campus	97
% African American	3
% Asian	1
% Caucasian	88
% Hispanic	3
% international	1
# of countries represented	9

SURVEY SAYS . . .

Students are friendly
Students get along with local community
Dorms are like palaces
Students are happy
Frats and sororities are unpopular or nonexistent
Student government is popular

ACADEMICS

Academic Rating	**95**
% students returning for sophomore year	88
% students graduating within 4 years	78
Calendar	semester
Student/faculty ratio	13:1
Profs interesting rating	92
Profs accessible rating	95
Most classes have	20–29 students
Most lab/discussion sessions have	10–19 students

MOST POPULAR MAJORS

biology/biological sciences; English language and literature; psychology

APPLICANTS ALSO LOOK AT AND OFTEN PREFER

Providence College, Northeastern University, College of the Holy Cross, Boston College, Bentley University

AND SOMETIMES PREFER

University of Massachusetts Amherst, University of Connecticut, University of New Hampshire

STUDENTS SAY ". . ."

Academics

"Stonehill is a small liberal arts college" "focused on educating the mind and soul" in the Roman Catholic tradition. "With a great small, interactive classroom experience" and "amazing" professors who "will help you no matter what," the academic experience here is distinctly "personal." "You won't be lost in the crowd at Stonehill. Professors know who you are and want to help you succeed." (Dare we say they will also notice when you are absent and may call you to find out why?) But that does not mean professors don't expect students to work hard. To the contrary, they "challenge you to question: question your readings, your professors, yourself." The whole point is to teach "how to be a critical thinker, and to look more in depth on ideas and topics." Faculty and administrators are extremely accessible."Many [faculty members] give students not only their school e-mail addresses, but their cell phone or home phone numbers as well as their AIM screen names if they have them!" Students also appreciate the learning opportunities off campus. "Stonehill has an amazing focus on internships and studying abroad and is known for having connections in the working world. The internships and opportunities given to students are pretty unique."

Life

"Being in the middle of Boston and Providence as well as having more than seventy clubs and organizations on campus that host two events a semester, there is always something to do" at Stonehill. "During the week, most people are considerate and allow you to get work done." "We have quiet hours at 10:00 P.M. on the weekdays and 1:00 A.M. on the weekends." But on the weekends, students cut loose. "For fun, people head into Boston a lot; the school has a shuttle to take us to the metro T station so it's very accessible if you don't have a car." On campus, "each night of the week there are different events sponsored by different groups on campus or by the Student Activities building. Some of the more widely attended events include our mixers (dances), which are held at various points throughout the year." "If you're looking for the frat/sorority party school, this isn't the place for you. It's much more laid-back, with drinking in the dorm rooms or in the twenty-one-plus common rooms." And it should be noted that alcohol is taken seriously here; many call the school's alcohol policy "way too strict," though it's possible to "learn the ways around it." The dorms here "are beautiful, and you get to choose your housing based on a point system. You get points for being active in the school (sports, clubs, attending lectures, etc.), so the more you participate the better housing you get. You can lose points for misbehavior, so the best housing goes to the best students, which is a huge plus!"

Student Body

"Stonehill is a pretty homogeneous place." Most students are "Caucasian and from middle-class families in New England." They tend to be "preppy" and "love to party on the weekends." However, they "also know how to crack down during the week and excel in class." "The typical student at Stonehill is kind, considerate, friendly, and smart. At Stonehill we hold doors, sometimes for an akwardly long time."

FINANCIAL AID: 508-565-1088 • E-MAIL: ADMISSIONS@STONEHILL.EDU • WEBSITE: WWW.STONEHILL.EDU

THE PRINCETON REVIEW SAYS

Admissions

Very important factors considered include: Class rank, academic GPA, rigor of secondary school record, character/personal qualities, talent/ability. *Important factors considered include:* Application essay, recommendation(s), extracurricular activities, level of applicant's interest, volunteer work, work experience. *Other factors considered include:* Standardized test scores, alumni/ae relation, first generation, geographical residence, interview, racial/ethnic status, religious affiliation/commitment. ACT with writing component recommended. TOEFL required of all international applicants. High school diploma is required and GED is accepted. *Academic units required:* 4 English, 3 mathematics, 1 science (1 science lab), 2 foreign language, 3 history, 3 academic electives. *Academic units recommended:* 4 English, 4 mathematics, 3 science (2 science labs), 3 foreign language, 3 history, 3 academic electives.

Financial Aid

Students should submit: FAFSA, CSS/Financial Aid PROFILE, noncustodial PROFILE, business/farm supplement. Regular filing deadline is February 1. The Princeton Review suggests that all financial aid forms be submitted as soon as possible after January 1. *Need-based scholarships/grants offered:* Federal Pell, SEOG, state scholarships/grants, private scholarships, the school's own gift aid. *Loan aid offered:* Direct Subsidized Stafford, Direct Unsubsidized Stafford, Direct PLUS, Federal Perkins, state loans. Applicants will be notified of awards on or about April 1. Federal Work-Study Program available. Institutional employment available. Highest amount earned per year from on-campus jobs $2,505. Off-campus job opportunities are good.

The Inside Word

Though not nearly as selective as some of its fellow Boston-area colleges, Stonehill students are no dummies. Half of them graduated in the top ten percent of their high school classes. Members of ethnic minorities may feel a bit isolated here.

THE SCHOOL SAYS ". . ."

From the Admissions Office

"Located twenty-two miles south of Boston, Stonehill is a selective Catholic college with an academically challenging, welcoming community on a beautiful, active campus. With an average class size of twenty, Stonehill's dedicated and supportive faculty make personal connections with each of our 2,400 students and mentor them throughout all four years and beyond. Stonehill offers more than seventy diverse majors and minors in the liberal arts, sciences, and business. Nearly ninety percent of our students participate in enriching opportunities such as competitive international and U.S. internships; nationally ranked study abroad programs; and top-notch undergraduate research, practicum, and field work experiences. Our proximity to America's premier college town allows you to join a network of 250,000 students and offers easy access to theaters, museums, professional sports games, restaurants, and more. But most importantly, Stonehill is a vibrant community where many minds come together for one purpose: to educate students for lives that make a difference."

SELECTIVITY

Admissions Rating	88
# of applicants	7,200
% of applicants accepted	65
% of acceptees attending	12
# accepting a place on wait list	713
# admitted from wait list	265
# of early decision applicants	30
# accepted early decision	28

FRESHMAN PROFILE

Range SAT Critical Reading	550–630
Range SAT Math	560–640
Range ACT Composite	25–29
Minimum paper TOEFL	550
Minimum web-based TOEFL	79
Average HS GPA	3.4
% graduated top 10% of class	43
% graduated top 25% of class	78
% graduated top 50% of class	96

DEADLINES

Early decision	
Deadline	11/1
Notification	12/25
Early action	
Deadline	11/1
Notification	1/15
Regular	
Deadline	1/15
Notification	3/15
Nonfall registration?	yes

FINANCIAL FACTS

Financial Aid Rating	77
Annual tuition	$33,920
Room and board	$12,860
Books and supplies	$586
% needy frosh rec. need-based scholarship or grant aid	74
% needy UG rec. need-based scholarship or grant aid	79
% needy frosh rec. non-need-based scholarship or grant aid	24
% needy UG rec. non-need-based scholarship or grant aid	20
% needy frosh rec. need-based self-help aid	55
% needy UG rec. need-based self-help aid	66
% frosh rec. any financial aid	93
% UG rec. any financial aid	93
% UG borrow to pay for school	75
Average cumulative indebtedness	$29,659
% frosh need fully met	54
% ugrads need fully met	51
Average % of frosh need met	89
Average % of ugrad need met	91

SUFFOLK UNIVERSITY

EIGHT ASHBURTON PLACE, BOSTON, MA 02108 • ADMISSIONS: 617-573-8460 • FAX: 617-573-1574

CAMPUS LIFE

Quality of Life Rating	**82**
Fire Safety Rating	**99**
Green Rating	**85**
Type of school	private
Environment	metropolis

STUDENTS

Total undergrad enrollment	5,682
% male/female	44/56
% from out of state	38
% from public high school	63
# of fraternities	1
# of sororities	1
% African American	5
% Asian	7
% Caucasian	47
% Hispanic	9
% international	15
# of countries represented	107

SURVEY SAYS . . .

Great library
Diverse student types on campus
Students love Boston, MA
Great off-campus food
Dorms are like palaces
Student government is popular

ACADEMICS

Academic Rating	**71**
% students returning for sophomore year	75
% students graduating within 4 years	35
% students graduating within 6 years	56
Calendar	semester
Student/faculty ratio	11:1
Profs interesting rating	79
Profs accessible rating	73
Most classes have	10–19 students
Most lab/discussion sessions have	10–19 students

MOST POPULAR MAJORS

business/corporate communications; interior design; sociology

STUDENTS SAY ". . ."

Academics

Located in "the heart of downtown Boston," Suffolk University offers a "happy environment" for "anyone who wants to be at a school and still be directly in the city." The university offers "a wide selection of interesting majors" and small class sizes throughout its College of Arts and Sciences and business school, giving this "united, diverse mass of students" a "global perspective in a real-world, urban setting." Students observe that depending on "[which] professor you have…you will like the class or not." Across the board, the teachers come across as being "very friendly" and genuine, and they "speak to you like an adult with respect." Some professors are "a bit dry;" however, "when you find [a great professor], they will be there for you through anything." Many here "wish the classes were more challenging," saying that coursework is "not as challenging as the school implies, but it is not easy." The school "offers students the resources they need should they want to put more effort into classes, job searching, and anything else, really;" students simply need to be self-motivated to take advantage of it. "Class participation comes naturally because class size is so small and the professor knows your name," says a freshman. "The administration is a little ridiculous sometimes with [its] rules," but overall it has "good relationships with the students."

Life

With the city as its "campus and playground," there is an "endless array of things to do" at Suffolk University, including shopping, museums, restaurants, and culture. "The students become part of the city," says a sophomore. "Suffolk doesn't really have a campus," though no one really seems to mind, as most students knew what they had signed on for when they enrolled. Due to space constraints, not all upperclassmen can live on campus, and many happily choose to live in Boston apartments. "My classes require me to walk through the Common everyday," says one student. For those who do live on campus, the university offers freshman orientation activities that "students can participate [in] to ease the tensions of moving into a dorm and being on your own." Most students take their social lives off campus, choosing to hang out at other colleges and in the city itself. Suffolk's campus is dry, so "students have to find other places in which to party" on the weekends (weeknights are typically dedicated to homework). As for the commuters, most "don't interact directly with [resident] students as much." Unsurprisingly, "there's a lot of Boston pride among Suffolk students." "Everyone loves the Red Sox, the Celtics, and the Bruins."

Student Body

Most of the kids here come out of "a medium to high income family" and are from "some town in Massachusetts," though Suffolk has a lot of international students. "It is very easy for a student to blend in due to Suffolk being a very diverse campus." Cultures and beliefs do indeed vary greatly—"that is definitely a part of what makes Suffolk so unique"—but "most students are friendly and interact with one another regardless of where they are from." However, there is a slight—though not tense—divide between two other classifications of Suffolk students: the large commuter populations and those who live in on-campus housing. "Suffolk is not very successful at integrating the two, but everyone seems to get along okay," says a student. Luckily, classes also require several group projects, "forcing students to work together." Preppy seems to be what the Suffolk student body preaches, and button downs, polo shirts, and Uggs abound—"most would *never* wear pajamas or sweatpants to class."

FINANCIAL AID: 617-573-8470 • E-MAIL: ADMISSION@SUFFOLK.EDU • WEBSITE: WWW.SUFFOLK.EDU

THE PRINCETON REVIEW SAYS

Admissions

Very important factors considered include: Rigor of secondary school record. *Important factors considered include:* Class rank, application essay, academic GPA, standardized test scores, character/personal qualities. *Other factors considered include:* Recommendation(s), alumni/ae relation, extracurricular activities, first generation, geographical residence, interview, level of applicant's interest, talent/ability, volunteer work, work experience. SAT or ACT required; ACT with writing component required. TOEFL required of all international applicants. High school diploma is required and GED is accepted. *Academic units required:* 4 English, 3 mathematics, 2 science (1 science lab), 2 foreign language, 1 history, 4 academic electives. *Academic units recommended:* 4 English, 4 mathematics, 4 science (1 science lab), 3 foreign language, 4 history, 4 academic electives.

Financial Aid

Students should submit: FAFSA, institution's own financial aid form. Regular filing deadline is February 15. The Princeton Review suggests that all financial aid forms be submitted as soon as possible after January 1. *Need-based scholarships/grants offered:* Federal Pell, SEOG, state scholarships/grants, private scholarships, the school's own gift aid. *Loan aid offered:* Direct Subsidized Stafford, Direct Unsubsidized Stafford, Direct PLUS, Federal Perkins, state loans, college/university loans from institutional funds. Applicants will be notified of awards on a rolling basis beginning February 5. Federal Work-Study Program available. Institutional employment available. Highest amount earned per year from on-campus jobs $8,217. Off-campus job opportunities are excellent.

The Inside Word

Suffolk is unapologetic about its mission to provide access and opportunity to college-bound students. That said, test scores and high school GPA requirements are average. Applicants whose numbers are above-average have a good chance of gaining admission.

THE SCHOOL SAYS ". . ."

From the Admissions Office

"Ask any student, and they'll tell you: The best thing about Suffolk is the professors. They go the extra mile to help students to succeed. Suffolk faculty members are noted scholars and experienced professionals, but first and foremost, they are teachers and mentors. Suffolk's faculty is of the highest caliber. Ninety-four percent of the faculty hold PhDs. Suffolk maintains a thirteen to one student/faculty ratio with an average class size of nineteen.

"Career preparation is a high priority at Suffolk. Many students work during the school year in paid internships, co-op jobs, or work-study positions. Suffolk has an excellent job placement record. More than ninety-four percent of recent graduates are either employed or enrolled in graduate school at the time of graduation.

"The university's academic programs emphasize quality teaching, small class size, real-world career applications, and an international experience. There are more than fifty study abroad sites available to students. The undergraduate academic program offers more than seventy majors and 1,000 courses.

"We require applicants to submit the SAT with the essay score or the ACT taken with the writing component. Standardized tests are used for both placement and assessment. International students may submit any of the following tests for admission: the TOEFL or ELPT, IELTS, CPE, CAE, and FCE. The role of standardized testing is still a secondary role when considering admission to the university. The candidate's grades and the overall strength of curriculum are primary factors in the admission decision.

"Independent, eclectic, self-starters do best at Suffolk as do students who thrive in small classes and make the most of living in the city of Boston."

SELECTIVITY	
Admissions Rating	71
# of applicants	9,137
% of applicants accepted	79
% of acceptees attending	17
# accepting a place on wait list	468
# admitted from wait list	85

FRESHMAN PROFILE	
Range SAT Critical Reading	450–570
Range SAT Math	460–570
Range SAT Writing	460–570
Range ACT Composite	21–25
Minimum paper TOEFL	525
Minimum web-based TOEFL	71
Average HS GPA	3.0
% graduated top 10% of class	13
% graduated top 25% of class	36
% graduated top 50% of class	74

DEADLINES	
Early action	
Deadline	11/15
Notification	12/20
Regular	
Deadline	2/15
Nonfall registration?	yes

FINANCIAL FACTS	
Financial Aid Rating	69
Annual tuition	$30,672
Room and board	$12,124
% needy frosh rec. need-based scholarship or grant aid	94
% needy UG rec. need-based scholarship or grant aid	93
% needy frosh rec. non-need-based scholarship or grant aid	32
% needy UG rec. non-need-based scholarship or grant aid	36
% needy frosh rec. need-based self-help aid	93
% needy UG rec. need-based self-help aid	93
% frosh rec. any financial aid	77
% UG rec. any financial aid	74
% UG borrow to pay for school	74
Average cumulative indebtedness	$31,364
% frosh need fully met	8
% ugrads need fully met	11
Average % of frosh need met	66
Average % of ugrad need met	67

Susquehanna University

514 University Avenue, Selinsgrove, PA 17870 • Admissions: 570-372-4260 • Fax: 570-372-2722

CAMPUS LIFE

Quality of Life Rating	**77**
Fire Safety Rating	**97**
Green Rating	**69**
Type of school	private
Affiliation	Lutheran
Environment	town

STUDENTS

Total undergrad enrollment	2,190
% male/female	46/54
% from out of state	51
% from public high school	79
% frosh live on campus	97
# of fraternities	6
# of sororities	5
% African American	3
% Asian	1
% Caucasian	88
% Hispanic	4
% international	1
# of countries represented	15

SURVEY SAYS . . .

Great computer facilities
Athletic facilities are great
Dorms are like palaces
Campus feels safe
Musical organizations are popular

ACADEMICS

Academic Rating	**77**
% students returning for sophomore year	84
% students graduating within 4 years	75
% students graduating within 6 years	79
Calendar	semester
Student/faculty ratio	12:1
Profs interesting rating	77
Profs accessible rating	81
Most classes have	10–19 students
Most lab/discussion sessions have	10–19 students

MOST POPULAR MAJORS

business administration and management; communication studies/speech communication and rhetoric; creative writing

APPLICANTS ALSO LOOK AT AND OFTEN PREFER

Bucknell University, Villanova University, Gettysburg College, Muhlenberg College, Franklin & Marshall College, Dickinson College, Lafayette College

AND SOMETIMES PREFER

Quinnipiac University, Ithaca College, University of Delaware, Lehigh University, Skidmore College

AND RARELY PREFER

Ursinus College, Juniata College

STUDENTS SAY ". . ."

Academics

With its "beautiful" campus and "home-y" atmosphere, it's no surprise that Susquehanna University "is a school that really cares about its students." As one ecstatic freshman quips, "When I saw that even the squirrels were friendly, I knew this was the place!" Indeed, the college provides a "strong, inclusive community" where it seems as if everyone "knows your name." Academically, "SU offers so many different majors and minors and an amazing professor-to-student ratio." While there are a number of fantastic departments, undergrads give special praise to the "outstanding creative writing program," "great business school," and the "excellent" music education department. Though there might be the occasional "dud," the "majority of professors are excellent." As this biochemistry major shares, "They are passionate about what they teach, they want their students to succeed, and [they] are always willing to help." Additionally, "The class size is excellent, and you really get to know your teachers." Though one psych major does caution that there's "no sitting in the back where you think you won't be called on, because it will happen!" And one pleased senior sums up her professors and academic experience stating, "The passion they so clearly feel for their subject areas is inspiring and refreshing, the interest they take in their students is genuine and heartwarming, and the ease with which they can be contacted is impressive. For the most part, I have felt appropriately challenged by all of my classes and have taken valuable lessons away from each one."

Life

In a word, life at Susquehanna is "busy." Students here do an admirable job of juggling their academic demands with the myriad of activities available to them. Many undergrads appreciate that the "Student Activities Committee (SAC) tries really hard to keep us entertained, and usually does so quite successfully." A creative writing major chimes in, "Every weekend there is one event at the club on campus with free drinks and food, and there are often student recitals and performances. The coffee shop on campus has movie nights every week, as well as open mics and special events." Sadly, others sometimes grumble, "There's not much to do if you don't have a car." Fortunately, students are able to get creative and "learn to make [their] own fun by going sledding or playing board games [or with] impromptu dance parties or late-night word-association games." Additionally, "Most people are involved in sports or fraternities and sororities." One freshman assures us that while "partying is big on campus," you're "in no way pressured to drink or take part in it." Though some students find the surrounding area "quiet" and "small," others love to take advantage of the "cute little shops and cafes" that are "within walking distance."

Student Body

Undergrads at Susquehanna are "focused on their education" and very "involved with different clubs and organizations on campus." There's a friendliness that pervades the student body, and people are "not afraid to leave their doors open." Indeed, most "fit in quite easily," especially given the fact that there's "a spectrum of students with wide ranging interests." That being said, it often can feel as though the vast majority of undergrads either "join a sports team" or participate in Greek life. While students define their peers as "easy-going and fun to be with," nearly everyone also "has a very serious side when it comes to academics, their classes, and their commitments." On the surface, "Students tend to be well-off [and] very preppy." However, "Despite the general cookie-cutter facade, most students are really involved in diverse activities and are really curious and accepting of the world around them."

FINANCIAL AID: 570-372-4450 • E-MAIL: SUADMISS@SUSQU.EDU • WEBSITE: WWW.SUSQU.EDU

THE PRINCETON REVIEW SAYS

Admissions

Very important factors considered include: Academic GPA, rigor of secondary school record. *Important factors considered include:* Class rank, application essay, recommendation(s), standardized test scores, alumni/ae relation, character/personal qualities, extracurricular activities, interview, level of applicant's interest, racial/ethnic status, talent/ability, volunteer work, work experience. *Other factors considered include:* First generation, geographical residence, religious affiliation/commitment, state residency. ACT with or without writing component accepted. TOEFL required of all international applicants. High school diploma is required and GED is accepted. *Academic units required:* 4 English, 3 mathematics, 3 science (2 science labs), 2 foreign language, 2 social studies, 2 history, 2 academic electives. *Academic units recommended:* 4 English, 4 mathematics, 4 science (3 science labs), 4 foreign language, 4 social studies, 2 history, 3 academic electives.

Financial Aid

Students should submit: FAFSA, CSS/Financial Aid PROFILE, business/farm supplement. Prior year Federal tax return. Regular filing deadline is May 1. The Princeton Review suggests that all financial aid forms be submitted as soon as possible after January 1. *Need-based scholarships/grants offered:* Federal Pell, SEOG, state scholarships/grants, private scholarships, the school's own gift aid. *Loan aid offered:* Direct Subsidized Stafford, Direct Unsubsidized Stafford, Direct PLUS, Federal Perkins, college/university loans from institutional funds. Applicants will be notified of awards on or about March 1. Federal Work-Study Program available. Institutional employment available. Highest amount earned per year from on-campus jobs $8,337. Off-campus job opportunities are good.

The Inside Word

Susquehanna is a selective university, and it's somewhat competitive to gain entry. Admissions officers are looking for bright, motivated candidates who greatly contribute to the Susquehanna community. They go to great lengths to consider the whole applicant and know that a candidate is more than their test results. To that end, they allow applicants to submit academic writing samples as opposed to SAT or ACT scores.

THE SCHOOL SAYS ". . ."

From the Admissions Office

"Susquehanna University prepares its graduates to achieve, lead, and serve in a diverse and interconnected world. Graduates consistently say their Susquehanna experiences give them a competitive edge over other recent graduates entering the workplace. Susquehanna's central curriculum features the GO (Global Opportunities) program, the only one of its kind in the nation. GO requires every student to prepare, complete, and reflect on an immersion experience in a culture different from one's own, either in the United States or abroad. A cross-cultural experience is designed to take students out of their everyday environment. It might be a traditional semester study abroad program (GO Long), a short-term faculty/staff-led program (GO Short), a self-designed experience proposed and accepted in advance, or service in a cross-cultural setting.

With more than fifty majors and minors, students find a fine balance of liberal arts and professional studies, and state-of-the-art facilities to support intellectual and personal growth. The Sigmund Weis School of Business is accredited by the prestigious Association to Advance Collegiate Schools of Business (AACSB). A new 'green' science facility opened in 2010. As the largest academic building on campus, it includes nineteen teaching and research labs, thirty prep and support spaces, and a rooftop greenhouse.

"Susquehanna's success is demonstrated by its placement rate. Typically ninety-four percent of Susquehanna's graduates have a job or are attending graduate school within six months of graduation. About ninety-four percent of our graduates report they would likely choose Susquehanna again, and ninety-seven percent would recommend Susquehanna University to a high school senior."

SELECTIVITY	
Admissions Rating	**80**
# of applicants	3,610
% of applicants accepted	73
% of acceptees attending	23
# accepting a place on wait list	243
# admitted from wait list	19
# of early decision applicants	118
# accepted early decision	84
FRESHMAN PROFILE	
Range SAT Critical Reading	510–610
Range SAT Math	510–610
Range SAT Writing	490–600
Range ACT Composite	23–28
Minimum paper TOEFL	550
Minimum web-based TOEFL	81
Average HS GPA	3.3
% graduated top 10% of class	25
% graduated top 25% of class	52
% graduated top 50% of class	82
DEADLINES	
Early decision	
Deadline	12/1
Notification	12/15
Regular	
Priority	1/1
Deadline	3/1
Nonfall registration?	yes

FINANCIAL FACTS	
Financial Aid Rating	**82**
Annual tuition	$35,400
Room and board	$9,600
Required fees	$460
Books and supplies	$850
% needy frosh rec. need-based scholarship or grant aid	100
% needy UG rec. need-based scholarship or grant aid	99
% needy frosh rec. non-need-based scholarship or grant aid	15
% needy UG rec. non-need-based scholarship or grant aid	13
% needy frosh rec. need-based self-help aid	84
% needy UG rec. need-based self-help aid	86
% frosh rec. any financial aid	94
% UG rec. any financial aid	94
% UG borrow to pay for school	76
Average cumulative indebtedness	$29,356
% frosh need fully met	22
% ugrads need fully met	19
Average % of frosh need met	83
Average % of ugrad need met	80

SWARTHMORE COLLEGE

500 COLLEGE AVENUE, SWARTHMORE, PA 19081 • ADMISSIONS: 610-328-8300 • FAX: 610-328-8580

CAMPUS LIFE

Quality of Life Rating	**80**
Fire Safety Rating	**87**
Green Rating	**86**
Type of school	private
Environment	village

STUDENTS

Total undergrad enrollment	1,545
% male/female	49/51
% from out of state	87
% from public high school	58
% frosh live on campus	100
# of fraternities	2
% African American	7
% Asian	14
% Caucasian	43
% Hispanic	13
% international	8
# of countries represented	57

SURVEY SAYS . . .

No one cheats
Lab facilities are great
School is well run
Low cost of living
Musical organizations are popular
Political activism is popular

ACADEMICS

Academic Rating	**99**
% students returning for sophomore year	97
% students graduating within 4 years	91
% students graduating within 6 years	95
Calendar	semester
Student/faculty ratio	8:1
Profs interesting rating	99
Profs accessible rating	96
Most classes have	10–19 students
Most lab/discussion sessions have	fewer than 10 students

MOST POPULAR MAJORS

biology/biological sciences; economics; political science and government

STUDENTS SAY ". . ."

Academics

Swarthmore College "has a lovely campus, the people are almost unbelievably friendly, it's a safe environment, and it's really, really challenging academically," and "although it's not one of the most well-known schools, those who do know of it also know of its wonderful reputation. It's where to go for a real education—for learning for the sake of truly learning, rather than just for grades." Students warn that "academics here are definitely stressful, especially when you sign up for extracurricular activities that take up some more time—and almost everyone here is involved in something outside of classes, because you don't want to just go to class, study, and sleep every day." As a result, "Swarthmore is truly challenging. It teaches its students tough lessons not only about classes but about life, and though it may be extremely, almost unbearably difficult sometimes, it's totally worth it." Undergrads also note that "there are tons of resources to help you—professors, academic mentors, writing associates (who are really helpful to talk to when you have major papers), residential assistants, psychological counseling, multicultural support groups, queer/trans support groups—basically, whenever you need help with something, there's someone you can talk to." Swatties also love how "Swarthmore is amazingly flexible. The requirements are very limited, allowing you to explore whatever you are interested in and change your mind millions of times about your major and career path. If they don't offer a major you want, you can design your own with ease."

Life

The Swarthmore community is "a family of students who are engaged in academics, learning, politics, activism, and civic responsibility, with a work hard, play hard, intense mentality, who don't get enough sleep because they're too busy doing all they want to do in their time here, and who (this is kind of cheesy, but true) when you really think about it are really just smart students who care about the world and want to make it better." There "is a misconception that Swarthmore students do nothing but study, [but] while we certainly do a lot of it, we still find many ways to have fun." Not so much in hometown Swarthmore—"there isn't a lot to do right in the area"—but "with a train station on campus, Philly is very accessible." Additionally, "There are so many organizations and clubs on campus that you'd be pressed to find none of the activities interesting. Even then, you can start your own club, so that takes care of it." The small size of the school means that "opportunities to participate in many different programs" are usually available. On-campus activities "are varied, and there is almost always something to do on the weekend. There are student musical performances, drama performances, movies, speakers, and comedy shows," as well as "several parties every weekend, with and without alcohol, and a lot of pre-partying with friends." One student sums up, "While it is tough to generalize on the life of a Swarthmore student, one word definitely applies to us all: busy. All of us are either working on extracurriculars, studying, or fighting sleep to do more work."

Student Body

Students are "not sure if there is a typical Swattie" but suspect that "the defining feature among us is that each person is brilliant at something: maybe dance, maybe quantum physics, maybe philosophy. Each person here has at least one thing that [he or she does] extraordinarily well." A Swattie "is [typically] liberal, involved in some kind of activism group or multicultural group, talks about classes all the time, was labeled a nerd by people in high school, and is really smart—one of those people where you just have to wonder, how do they get all their homework done and manage their extracurriculars and still have time for parties?" The campus "is very diverse racially but not in terms of thought—in other words, pretty much everyone's liberal, you don't get many different points of view. Multicultural and queer issues are big here, but you don't have to be involved in that to enjoy Swarthmore. You just have to accept it."

FINANCIAL AID: 610-328-8358 • E-MAIL: ADMISSIONS@SWARTHMORE.EDU • WEBSITE: WWW.SWARTHMORE.EDU

THE PRINCETON REVIEW SAYS

Admissions

Very important factors considered include: Rigor of secondary school record, GPA, character/personal qualities, application essay, recommendation(s), class rank. *Important factors considered include:* Standardized test scores, extracurricular activities. *Other factors considered include:* Alumni/ae relation, first generation, geographical residence, interview, level of applicant's interest, racial/ethnic status, talent/ability, volunteer work, work experience. High school diploma or equivalent is not required. *Academic units recommended:* 4 English, 3 mathematics, 3 science.

Financial Aid

Students should submit: FAFSA, institution's own financial aid form, CSS/Financial Aid PROFILE, state aid form, noncustodial PROFILE, business/farm supplement. Federal tax return, W-2 statements, year-end paycheck stub. Regular filing deadline is February 15. The Princeton Review suggests that all financial aid forms be submitted as soon as possible after January 1. *Need-based scholarships/grants offered:* Federal Pell, SEOG, state scholarships/grants, private scholarships, the school's own gift aid. *Loan aid offered:* Direct Subsidized Stafford, Direct Unsubsidized Stafford, Direct PLUS, and Federal Perkins loans. Applicants will be notified of awards on or about April 1. Federal Work-Study Program available. Institutional employment available. Off-campus job opportunities are good.

The Inside Word

Competition for admission to Swarthmore remains fierce, as the school consistently receives applications from top students across the country. Applicants should understand that Swarthmore receives more than enough applications from well-qualified students to fill its classrooms. At some point, perfectly good candidates get rejected simply because there's no more room. Admissions officers comb applications carefully for evidence of intellectually curious, highly motivated, and creative-minded candidates.

THE SCHOOL SAYS ". . ."

From the Admissions Office

"Swarthmore College, a highly selective college of liberal arts and engineering, celebrates the life of the mind. Since its founding in 1864, Swarthmore has given students the knowledge, insight, skills, and experience to become leaders for the common good. The college is private, yet open to all regardless of financial need, and decidedly global in outlook, drawing students from around the world and all fifty states. So much of what Swarthmore stands for, from its commitment to curricular breadth and rigor to its demonstrated interest in facilitating discovery and fostering social responsibility, lies in the quality and passion of its faculty. A student/faculty ratio of eight to one ensures that students have close, meaningful engagement with their professors, preparing them to translate the skills and understanding gained at Swarthmore into the mark they want to make on the world. The college's honors program features small groups of dedicated and accomplished students working closely with faculty; an emphasis on independent learning; students entering into a dialogue with peers, teachers, and examiners; and an examination at the end of two years study by outside scholars. Swarthmore's idyllic, 425-acre arboretum campus features rolling lawns, a creek, wooded hills, and hiking trails and is located just eleven miles from Philadelphia.

"Swarthmore maintains a need-blind admissions policy for U.S. citizens and permanent residents, wherein admission and financial aid decisions are made independently. Financial aid is also available for international students. All Swarthmore aid awards are loan-free and meet the full demonstrated need for admitted students."

SELECTIVITY	
Admissions Rating	99
# of applicants	6,547
% of applicants accepted	15
% of acceptees attending	39
# admitted from wait list	10
# of early decision applicants	533
# accepted early decision	156

FRESHMAN PROFILE	
Range SAT Critical Reading	680–770
Range SAT Math	670–760
Range SAT Writing	680–770
Range ACT Composite	30–34
% graduated top 10% of class	84
% graduated top 25% of class	98
% graduated top 50% of class	100

DEADLINES	
Early decision	
Deadline	11/15
Notification	12/15
Regular	
Deadline	1/1
Notification	4/1
Nonfall registration?	no

FINANCIAL FACTS	
Financial Aid Rating	99
Annual tuition	$40,816
Required fees	$334
Books and supplies	$1,150
% needy frosh rec. need-based scholarship or grant aid	100
% needy UG rec. need-based scholarship or grant aid	100
% needy frosh rec. need-based self-help aid	97
% needy UG rec. need-based self-help aid	97
% frosh rec. any financial aid	57
% UG rec. any financial aid	54
% UG borrow to pay for school	38
Average cumulative indebtedness	$16,975
% frosh need fully met	100
% ugrads need fully met	100
Average % of frosh need met	100
Average % of ugrad need met	100

SWEET BRIAR COLLEGE

PO BOX 1052, SWEET BRIAR, VA 24595 • ADMISSIONS: 434-381-6142 • FAX: 434-381-6152

CAMPUS LIFE

Quality of Life Rating	**82**
Fire Safety Rating	**98**
Green Rating	**80**
Type of school	private
Environment	rural

STUDENTS

Total undergrad enrollment	610
% male/female	0/100
% from out of state	47
% from public high school	75
% frosh live on campus	95
% African American	7
% Asian	2
% Caucasian	81
% Hispanic	6
% Native American	1
% international	2
# of countries represented	16

SURVEY SAYS . . .

No one cheats
Great computer facilities
Career services are great
School is well run
Students are friendly
Students get along with local community
Dorms are like palaces
Campus feels safe
Students are happy
Student government is popular

ACADEMICS

Academic Rating	**93**
% students returning for sophomore year	78
% students graduating within 4 years	64
% students graduating within 6 years	70
Calendar	semester
Student/faculty ratio	8:1
Profs interesting rating	96
Profs accessible rating	98
Most classes have	10–19 students
Most lab/discussion sessions have	fewer than 10 students

MOST POPULAR MAJORS

biology/biological sciences; business/commerce; psychology

STUDENTS SAY ". . ."

Academics

"A place where students want to be a part of something bigger than themselves," Sweet Briar College is a small, all-female, liberal arts college set in rural Virginia. Known as "a sisterhood" that fosters "leadership in and out of the classroom," this college attracts women interested in a personalized academic environment where "my professors know me by name, and [the] administration has immense respect for me." "Small class sizes" and "professors [that] become like family" are the school's biggest draws. The professors provide "so many opportunities for students to do undergraduate research, hands-on projects…fieldtrips, networking, jobs, and internships," but they are engaged enough with the student body that "they will join you for lunch in the cafeteria or joke around with you in class." This type of care and attention, so characteristic of Sweet Briar, begins even before students are admitted to the school through "truly special" hand-written recruitment letters sent from the admissions office. As one student explains, "Sweet Briar creates a whole person, one capable of taking on the world's problems with creativity, enthusiasm, and class." In addition to "an incredible study abroad program" and career services center, Sweet Briar boasts "100 percent job-placement rate post-graduation" in particular programs like education and a dedicated network of alumna that "have time to sit down and talk with you, let you stay with them if you are visiting the area, or even help you find a job, and take you to happy hour."

Life

Set in the foothills of the beautiful Blue Ridge Mountains of the rural South, the school offers access to the outdoors, and that is a big draw for many here. With more than "3,000 acres to explore," students at Sweet Briar are involved in many outdoors activities "like hiking, camping, and rock-climbing, with kayaking thrown in as well" in an environment that makes this campus "one of the most beautiful in the country." In addition to its "wonderful horse riding program," athletics like lacrosse and Division III field hockey are also popular. Sweet Briar strikes a balance between being "a suitcase school" where the campus "becomes a ghost town" on weekends and being a bustling campus full of student involvement. The weeks are spent "focusing on school work Monday through Friday," while on the weekends, students "jet off to Hampden-Sydney, VMI, W&L, or UVA" for a more "raging nightlife." Nightlife at Sweet Briar itself—marked by "boathouse" parties held on campus every Thursday—is more of a "'girls' night' with a box of wine and good girlfriends" rather than debaucherous partying. In addition, students have a wide range of activities to choose from, such as movie nights, laser tag, "clubs, Campus Christian Fellowship, music, [and] theater." A campus cooking club that "has breakfast at the president's and dean's houses" and traditions such as "freshmen versus sophomore paint wards, junior week, secret sophomores and seniors" continue to foster "an extremely close and tightly knit community."

Student Body

"Students come to Sweet Briar to discover who they are [and] to learn to challenge themselves." It is overwhelmingly felt that their "goals of achieving in life" is what bonds the student body together. While there's still a want of diversity and marketing, for the school seems "to aim for a certain demographic" of the "preppy, white girl who…comes from a middle- to upper-middle-class family," the typical Sweet Briar woman "isn't always in pearls and talking about the latest stuff from Lilly Pulitzer…[She] is clever, independent, and adaptable." Sweet Briar women also "tend to fill their plates completely," and it "is not unusual for a student to be involved in four or more clubs or leadership opportunities on campus." The most important facet of the student body, however, is the friendship developed between its students. "Every student is able to find a niche," and through shared values and the many available campus activities, women here create "lasting memories" and "friends that will last a lifetime."

FINANCIAL AID: 434-381-6156 • E-MAIL: ADMISSIONS@SBC.EDU • WEBSITE: WWW.SBC.EDU

THE PRINCETON REVIEW SAYS

Admissions

Very important factors considered include: Academic GPA, rigor of secondary school record. *Important factors considered include:* Application essay, recommendation(s), standardized test scores, interview. *Other factors considered include:* Class rank, alumni/ae relation, character/personal qualities, extracurricular activities, first generation, racial/ethnic status, talent/ability, volunteer work, work experience. SAT or ACT required; ACT with or without writing component accepted. TOEFL required of all international applicants. High school diploma is required and GED is accepted. *Academic units required:* 4 English, 3 mathematics, 3 science (2 science labs), 2 foreign language, 3 social studies. *Academic units recommended:* 4 English, 4 mathematics, 4 science (3 science labs), 4 foreign language, 4 social studies.

Financial Aid

Students should submit: FAFSA, noncustodial PROFILE. Regular filing deadline is February 15. The Princeton Review suggests that all financial aid forms be submitted as soon as possible after January 1. *Need-based scholarships/grants offered:* Federal Pell, SEOG, state scholarships/grants, private scholarships, the school's own gift aid. *Loan aid offered:* Direct Subsidized Stafford, Direct Unsubsidized Stafford, Direct PLUS, Federal Perkins, college/university loans from institutional funds. Applicants will be notified of awards on or about March 1. Federal Work-Study Program available. Institutional employment available. Highest amount earned per year from on-campus jobs $1,000. Off-campus job opportunities are fair.

The Inside Word

Due to its fairly self-selecting applicant pool, Sweet Briar is able to consider each application closely. The school looks for "fit" with the school as much as it looks for evidence of academic achievement and ability. The question then is, how well will you meld with the Sweet Briar community? Can the school deliver quality academics in your areas of interest? (After all, a school this small can't provide in-depth instruction in every discipline.) Especially if your test scores and/or high school grades are less than stellar, these are the questions that will determine your admission to Sweet Briar.

THE SCHOOL SAYS ". . ."

From the Admissions Office

"The woman who applies to Sweet Briar is mature and far-sighted enough to know what she wants from her college experience. She is intellectually adventuresome, more willing to explore new fields, and more open to challenging her boundaries. Sweet Briar attracts the ambitious, confident woman who enjoys being immersed not only in a first-rate academic program, but in a variety of meaningful activities outside the classroom. Our students take charge and revel in their accomplishments. This attitude follows graduates, enabling them to compete confidently in the corporate world and in graduate school.

"The faculty and staff do not simply give students individual attention; rather they pay attention to individuals. As an institution, we commit to every student, and our mission is to provide a learning community that prepares her to be successful in whatever she chooses to do after college."

SELECTIVITY

Admissions Rating	78
# of applicants	688
% of applicants accepted	80
% of acceptees attending	35

FRESHMAN PROFILE

Range SAT Critical Reading	480–610
Range SAT Math	433–580
Range SAT Writing	473–600
Range ACT Composite	22–27
Minimum paper TOEFL	550
Minimum web-based TOEFL	79
Average HS GPA	3.4
% graduated top 10% of class	20
% graduated top 25% of class	50
% graduated top 50% of class	82

DEADLINES

Regular	
Priority	2/1
Deadline	2/1
Nonfall registration?	yes

FINANCIAL FACTS

Financial Aid Rating	88
Annual tuition	$31,850
Room and board	$11,440
Required fees	$475
Books and supplies	$1,168
% needy frosh rec. need-based scholarship or grant aid	100
% needy UG rec. need-based scholarship or grant aid	97
% needy frosh rec. non-need-based scholarship or grant aid	99
% needy UG rec. non-need-based scholarship or grant aid	69
% needy frosh rec. need-based self-help aid	70
% needy UG rec. need-based self-help aid	67
% frosh rec. any financial aid	100
% UG rec. any financial aid	99
% UG borrow to pay for school	53
Average cumulative indebtedness	$24,689
% frosh need fully met	35
% ugrads need fully met	34
Average % of frosh need met	76
Average % of ugrad need met	72

SYRACUSE UNIVERSITY

100 CROUSE-HINDS HALL, SYRACUSE, NY 13244-2130 • ADMISSIONS: 315-443-3611 • FAX: 315-443-4226

CAMPUS LIFE

Quality of Life Rating	69
Fire Safety Rating	85
Green Rating	94
Type of school	private
Environment	metropolis

STUDENTS

Total undergrad enrollment	14,220
% male/female	44/56
% from out of state	59
% from public high school	67
% frosh live on campus	99
# of fraternities	29
# of sororities	20
% African American	8
% Asian	9
% Caucasian	56
% Hispanic	9
% Native American	1
% international	8
# of countries represented	77

SURVEY SAYS . . .

Everyone loves the Orange
Frats and sororities dominate social scene
Student publications are popular
Lots of beer drinking
Hard liquor is popular

ACADEMICS

Academic Rating	76
Calendar	semester
Student/faculty ratio	16:1
Profs interesting rating	75
Profs accessible rating	74
Most classes have	10–19 students
Most lab/discussion sessions have	20–29 students

MOST POPULAR MAJORS

commercial and advertising art; psychology; radio and television

STUDENTS SAY ". . ."

Academics

Syracuse University "is cold weather, good academics, and amazing sports," one student sums up, and that about captures the prevailing sentiment among SU undergrads. Sure, Syracuse students recognize and appreciate the "top-quality education" they receive, but they typically frame it in the totality of Syracuse living, which includes not only "an excellent academic experience" but also athletics and extracurriculars that together create "the perfect balance of a great education and an amazing social atmosphere, [making] for an excellent college experience." The result is a student body fiercely proud of its school. "Syracuse bleeds Orange," students inform us. On the basis of academics alone, they would have just cause. Opportunities abound: "If you take advantage of all the great resources available to all students, it's impossible not to have a great college experience," one student observes. Most do. Syracuse students "are, for the most part, very serious about their work and know what they want to do in life after college." The school provides lots of choices. Its Newhouse School of Public Communications is "as good as it gets for journalism schools," students tell us. They're nearly as bullish on the school's separate colleges for citizenship and public affairs, architecture, engineering and computer science, and management. No wonder one student brags, "I'm a magazine journalism major with a specialization in fashion and a minor in theater. The best part about Syracuse is that it offers hundreds of specific programs that allow you to learn by doing."

Life

"People are very committed to their work Monday through Thursday" at SU, but "as soon as Thursday classes are over, people will start to party." Greek life attracts nearly one-fifth of the student body. The frats throw "a lot of parties, which are crowded, hot, noisy, and run out of alcohol frequently," but they are hardly the only game in town. "Social life is very well-rounded and consists of bars, fraternities/sororities, house parties, and apartment parties," students report. The perception that "there's not much to do off campus in Syracuse" amplifies the importance of the party scene. Students note, however, "There are many other options for students who don't drink." "During the winter, basketball season is huge, and we have one of the best student sections in the country. The school also provides free shuttles on the weekend to Carousel Mall, the country's fourth-largest mall." There are "easily accessible gyms" located "nearby both ends of the campus," and the school is home to "amazing musical groups" ranging from a cappella ensembles to jazz bands, an orchestra, and rock bands. In addition, "The university provides ways of having fun on the weekends as well, such as free movie screenings in lecture halls or activities such as water rafting (with a fee, of course)."

Student Body

Your standard issue Syracuse male "wears khakis, Polo, and Patagonias," while his female counterpart "wears American Apparel zip-ups, solid-colored v-neck tees, skinny jeans and leggings, Uggs, a North Face jacket, and a brand-name handbag" and "is glued to her Blackberry." Syracuse is a big university, though, with plenty of room for diversity, so pretty much everyone finds a comfortable niche here. There's "a huge population of hipsters…woodsy folk, city kids, and pretty average everyday people all over. It depends on what social scene you spend your time in." Dig deep enough and you'll find "students of every race, religion, and political background you can think of. There is a strong Asian and international student population as well as a noticeable percentage of gay, lesbian, and bisexual [students]." While groups "have their own cliques," there "is no animosity or unspoken status quo between different sorts of people."

FINANCIAL AID: 315-443-1513 • E-MAIL: ORANGE@SYR.EDU • WEBSITE: WWW.SYR.EDU

THE PRINCETON REVIEW SAYS

Admissions

Very important factors considered include: Application essay, academic GPA, recommendation(s), rigor of secondary school record, standardized test scores, character/personal qualities, extracurricular activities, interview, level of applicant's interest, talent/ability. *Important factors considered include:* Alumni/ae relation, first generation, geographical residence, state residency, volunteer work, work experience. *Other factors considered include:* Racial/ethnic status. SAT or ACT required; ACT with writing component required. TOEFL required of all international applicants. High school diploma is required and GED is accepted. *Academic units required:* 4 English, 4 mathematics, 4 science (4 science labs), 3 foreign language, 4 social studies.

Financial Aid

Students should submit: FAFSA, CSS/Financial Aid PROFILE, noncustodial PROFILE. Regular filing deadline is February 1. The Princeton Review suggests that all financial aid forms be submitted as soon as possible after January 1. *Need-based scholarships/grants offered:* Federal Pell, SEOG, state scholarships/grants, private scholarships, the school's own gift aid. *Loan aid offered:* Direct Subsidized Stafford, Direct Unsubsidized Stafford, Direct PLUS, Federal Perkins. Applicants will be notified of awards on or about March 21. Federal Work-Study Program available. Institutional employment available. Off-campus job opportunities are good.

The Inside Word

Syracuse University is divided into nine colleges, and applicants apply to the college in which they are interested. Some colleges make specific requirements of applicants (for example, a portfolio, or an audition in addition to SU's general admission requirements. Applicants are allowed to indicate a second or third choice program, so you may still gain admission even if you don't get into your first-choice program.

THE SCHOOL SAYS ". . ."

From the Admissions Office

"Syracuse University students prepare FOR the world IN the world. You'll customize your education through interdisciplinary study across a collection of prominent schools and colleges; and connect classroom learning and hands-on experience through internships, research, start-up ventures, and professional immersion experiences in the City of Syracuse and via University centers in New York City, Washington D.C., and Los Angeles. SU experiential learning also spans the globe, and nearly half of undergraduates study abroad. The University operates centers in Beijing, Florence, Hong Kong, Istanbul, London, Madrid, Santiago, and Strasbourg, and offers short-term, summer, and semester options in these and many other cities.

"An SU education is also defined by breadth of opportunity combined with individualized attention. You'll choose from more than 200 majors and 90 minors, and work closely with top scholars who are professionals in their fields that share their research/writing to further the classroom experience. You can pursue multiple majors and/or minors, and round out your experience with participation in one or more of 300 extracurricular groups. Upon graduation, you'll join one of the proudest, most supportive alumni networks in the world with alum that include founding principal of Fox & Fowle Architects Bruce Fowle 1960, space shuttle commander Eileen Collins 1978, screenwriter Aaron Sorkin 1983, actor Taye Diggs 1993, and Foursquare cofounder Dennis Crowley 1998."

SELECTIVITY	
Admissions Rating	**89**
# of applicants	25,884
% of applicants accepted	49
% of acceptees attending	27
# accepting a place on wait list	1,983
# admitted from wait list	521
# of early decision applicants	1,107
# accepted early decision	853

FRESHMAN PROFILE	
Range SAT Critical Reading	510–620
Range SAT Math	540–650
Range SAT Writing	520–630
Range ACT Composite	23–28
Minimum paper TOEFL	550
Minimum web-based TOEFL	80
Average HS GPA	3.6
% graduated top 10% of class	40
% graduated top 25% of class	73
% graduated top 50% of class	95

DEADLINES	
Early decision	
Deadline	11/15
Notification	12/16
Regular	
Deadline	1/1
Nonfall registration?	yes

FINANCIAL FACTS	
Financial Aid Rating	**89**
Annual tuition	$37,610
Room and board	$13,692
Required fees	$1,394
Books and supplies	$1,342
% needy frosh rec. need-based scholarship or grant aid	92
% needy UG rec. need-based scholarship or grant aid	90
% needy frosh rec. non-need-based scholarship or grant aid	6
% needy UG rec. non-need-based scholarship or grant aid	5
% needy frosh rec. need-based self-help aid	99
% needy UG rec. need-based self-help aid	99
% frosh rec. any financial aid	80
% UG rec. any financial aid	80
% UG borrow to pay for school	65
Average cumulative indebtedness	$32,663
% frosh need fully met	80
% ugrads need fully met	65
Average % of frosh need met	96
Average % of ugrad need met	92

TEMPLE UNIVERSITY

1801 North Broad Street (041-09), Philadelphia, PA 19122-6096 • Admissions: 215-204-7200 • Fax: 215-204-5694

CAMPUS LIFE

Quality of Life Rating	75
Fire Safety Rating	93
Green Rating	86
Type of school	public
Environment	metropolis

STUDENTS

Total undergrad enrollment	27,702
% male/female	49/51
% from out of state	19
% from public high school	73
% frosh live on campus	77
# of fraternities	11
# of sororities	15
% African American	14
% Asian	10
% Caucasian	61
% Hispanic	4
% international	1
# of countries represented	47

SURVEY SAYS . . .

Great computer facilities
Diverse student types on campus
Low cost of living
Very little drug use

ACADEMICS

Academic Rating	71
% students returning for sophomore year	87
% students graduating within 4 years	36
% students graduating within 6 years	67
Calendar	semester
Student/faculty ratio	15:1
Profs interesting rating	70
Profs accessible rating	69
Most classes have	20–29 students
Most lab/discussion sessions have	20–29 students

MOST POPULAR MAJORS

biology; psychology

APPLICANTS ALSO LOOK AT AND OFTEN PREFER

Pennsylvania State University—University Park, Drexel University, Rutgers, The State University of New Jersey—New Brunswick, University of Pittsburgh—Pittsburgh Campus

AND SOMETIMES PREFER

University of Maryland, College Park, Syracuse University, University of Massachusetts Amherst

STUDENTS SAY ". . ."

Academics

Temple University is "a large school" that "makes you feel at home in the city of Philadelphia" and offers "rigorous academic classes and many outside activities." This "wonderful" school is "located right in the city," and students praise the campus as being "one of the most diverse in the country." "Temple University is a place where everyone fits in and walks away with a little more knowledge than they had the day before," says one undergrad. This diversity also extends to classes. There's a "wide variety of classes" and "lots of awesome majors," all of which are supported by a "helpful and passionate set of professors who learn right along with students." There's also the "top-notch" honors program, which is a "favorite part of Temple by far," explains one student. "It's an outstanding program, and I feel very fortunate to be a part of it." Most here agree their academic experience has been "amazing." In the words of one undergrad, "Temple's standard of access and excellence is evident in its students' success." The "knowledgeable" professors "really want to see students succeed." While some feel that the administration "doesn't always run so smoothly," noting that "Temple is pretty much a small city, and it often runs like a bureaucracy," overall, students agree that administrators are "accessible at any time" and are "helpful when you need them."

Life

As you'd expect from a big school in a big city, "Temple has something for everyone." Whether you're looking for "city life," "friendly people," or "a million and one clubs or groups to join," you'll find it here at Temple. "There are tons of things to do," says one student. "If students get bored on campus, they were probably boring to begin with." Life on campus is "very interconnected," and "there's usually always something going on" thanks to "student organizations that appeal to every interest and social group." Most students keep busy during by "studying," "going to the gym," and "playing intramural sports," but even if nothing is happening on campus, "there's much to do in the city." Not surprisingly, Philadelphia plays a substantial part in students' social lives. "There are amazing bars in the city," says one undergrad. "The only nights that students do not go out for drinks are Sunday and Monday." That said, if imbibing isn't your cup of tea, not to worry—there's plenty more on offer than watering holes. "You can have tons of fun on campus without drinking," explains a student. "There are lots of fun things to do because of our close proximity to Center City Philadelphia." Some examples are "great clubs, shopping, hookah bars, and restaurants." Also, if you get tired of Temple's campus you can always check out another—"Drexel, LaSalle, and UPenn's campuses are close by."

Student Body

Diversity isn't just a word at Temple; it's a fact. "At Temple, the atypical students are the typical students," explains an undergrad. "The majority population is made up of ethnic minorities." The student body here is made up of "many different kinds of ethnicities, sexual orientations, and economic and political stances," all of whom "contribute to the overall sense of school spirit and pride." Students agree that everyone here is "unique," and that makes for a place where "everyone becomes comfortable with each other's differences." "Every student brings their own light to Temple, which is what makes the school shine so bright," says one student. Despite this "huge mixture of types," students here do share similarities, particularly in their "motivation" to do well. Students here fill their time with "studying" and "extracurricular activities," all while also "experiencing life in the city of Philadelphia." One thing that all students agree on is that "The typical student at Temple University is approachable and greatly accepts diversity." As one undergrad says, "Everyone just kind of fits in, which is why the students like Temple so much."

FINANCIAL AID: 215-204-8760 • E-MAIL: TUADM@TEMPLE.EDU • WEBSITE: WWW.TEMPLE.EDU

THE PRINCETON REVIEW SAYS

Admissions

Very important factors considered include: Academic GPA, rigor of secondary school record. *Important factors considered include:* Class rank, standardized test scores. *Other factors considered include:* Application essay, recommendation(s), alumni/ae relation, character/personal qualities, extracurricular activities, talent/ability, volunteer work, work experience. SAT or ACT required; ACT with writing component required. TOEFL required of all international applicants. High school diploma is required and GED is accepted. *Academic units required:* 4 English, 3 mathematics, 2 science (1 science lab), 2 foreign language, 2 social studies, 1 history, 1 academic elective. *Academic units recommended:* 4 English, 4 mathematics, 3 science (2 science labs), 2 foreign language, 2 social studies, 2 history, 3 academic electives.

Financial Aid

Students should submit: FAFSA. The Princeton Review suggests that all financial aid forms be submitted as soon as possible after January 1. *Need-based scholarships/grants offered:* Federal Pell, SEOG, state scholarships/grants, private scholarships, the school's own gift aid, Federal Nursing Scholarships. *Loan aid offered:* Direct Subsidized Stafford, Direct Unsubsidized Stafford, Direct PLUS, Federal Perkins, Federal Nursing, state loans, college/university loans from institutional funds. Applicants will be notified of awards on a rolling basis beginning February 15. Federal Work-Study Program available. Institutional employment available. Off-campus job opportunities are excellent.

The Inside Word

Temple is a well-recognized name in higher education, and its location is one of the nation's most popular cities. Competition can be steep when it comes to admissions, particularly if you aren't a resident of Pennsylvania. Admissions officers are fairly objective about their approach to application assessment in that they focus primarily on the solid numbers: class rank, GPA, and standardized test scores. That said, keep in mind that there are no minimum requirements, so if you have skills and talents that can't be mathematically calculated, it would behoove you to point them out in your application.

THE SCHOOL SAYS ". . ."

From the Admissions Office

"Temple combines the academic resources and intellectual stimulation of a large research university with the intimacy of a small college. The university experienced record growth in attracting new students from all fifty states and more than 125 countries. Students choose from 141 undergraduate majors. Special academic programs include honors, learning communities for first-year undergraduates, co-op education, and study abroad. Temple has seven regional campuses, including Main Campus and the Health Sciences Center in historic Philadelphia, suburban Temple University, Ambler, and overseas campuses in Tokyo and Rome. Main Campus is home to Alter Hall for the Fox School of Business, and the Tyler School of Art, both state-of-the-art facilities that opened in 2009. Our TECH Center has more than 600 computer workstations, 100 laptops, and a Starbucks. The Liacouras Center is a modern entertainment, recreation, and sports complex that hosts concerts, plays, trade shows, and college and professional athletics. It also includes the Independence Blue Cross Student Recreation Center, a major fitness facility for students now and in the future. Students can also take advantage of our Student Fieldhouse. The university is currently constructing a new residence hall, built to meet an unprecedented demand for main campus housing.

"Applicants are required to take the SAT (or the ACT with writing). The best critical reading, math and writing scores from either test will be considered."

SELECTIVITY

Admissions Rating	82
# of applicants	18,977
% of applicants accepted	63
% of acceptees attending	36
# accepting a place on wait list	1,421
# admitted from wait list	264

FRESHMAN PROFILE

Range SAT Critical Reading	500–600
Range SAT Math	510–610
Range SAT Writing	500–600
Range ACT Composite	21–26
Minimum paper TOEFL	550
Minimum web-based TOEFL	79
Average HS GPA	3.4
% graduated top 10% of class	18
% graduated top 25% of class	53
% graduated top 50% of class	91

DEADLINES

Regular	
Deadline	3/1
Nonfall registration?	yes

FINANCIAL FACTS

Financial Aid Rating	80
Annual in-state tuition	$13,006
Annual out-state tuition	$22,832
Room and board	$9,886
Required fees	$590
Books and supplies	$1,000
% needy frosh rec. need-based scholarship or grant aid	98
% needy UG rec. need-based scholarship or grant aid	92
% needy frosh rec. non-need-based scholarship or grant aid	55
% needy UG rec. non-need-based scholarship or grant aid	36
% needy frosh rec. need-based self-help aid	83
% needy UG rec. need-based self-help aid	80
% frosh rec. any financial aid	69
% UG rec. any financial aid	63
% UG borrow to pay for school	75
Average cumulative indebtedness	$ 32,766
% frosh need fully met	32
% ugrads need fully met	24
Average % of frosh need met	84
Average % of ugrad need met	83

Texas A&M University—College Station

PO Box 30014, College Station, TX 77843-3014 • Admissions: 979-845-3741 • Fax: 979-847-8737

CAMPUS LIFE

Quality of Life Rating	86
Fire Safety Rating	83
Green Rating	79
Type of school	public
Environment	city

STUDENTS

Total undergrad enrollment	39,867
% male/female	52/48
% from out of state	4
# of fraternities	33
# of sororities	23
% African American	3
% Asian	5
% Caucasian	71
% Hispanic	17
% international	1
# of countries represented	127

SURVEY SAYS . . .

Great computer facilities
Athletic facilities are great
Students are friendly
Everyone loves the Aggies
Student publications are popular
Students are involved in community service

ACADEMICS

Academic Rating	74
% students returning for sophomore year	92
% students graduating within 4 years	50
% students graduating within 6 years	80
Calendar	semester
Student/faculty ratio	21:1
Profs interesting rating	76
Profs accessible rating	72
Most classes have	20–29 students
Most lab/discussion sessions have	20–29 students

MOST POPULAR MAJORS

biological and physical sciences; multi-/interdisciplinary studies, other; operations management and supervision

APPLICANTS ALSO LOOK AT AND OFTEN PREFER

Rice University

AND SOMETIMES PREFER

The University of Texas at Austin, Baylor University, Louisiana State University—Baton Rouge

AND RARELY PREFER

Southern Methodist University

STUDENTS SAY ". . ."

Academics

The "untold spirit at Texas A&M" lies in its tradition, which is "the underlying pulse of Aggieland." This large research school has "deep-rooted values" and "runs as a tight-knit family despite the numerous population." This strong family dynamic makes the school an "open, friendly place to learn and grow," and the incredibly strong engineering and life science programs certainly don't hurt. The academics can be "difficult," but "The goal is to set us apart from the rest, so we can excel." The "wonderful" professors "do their best to bring the topics from pages to the real world." They "all have life experiences working with the topics that they teach making them the perfect resource for information." These "top-notch" professors (well, aside from a very few who are "extremely dry") come back to A&M after working in powerful industry positions "because they love the atmosphere and the students." "I have never skipped a class because I thoroughly enjoy going," says one student. Particularly with the sciences, professors offer students the opportunity to participate in "world-changing research," and all such experiences "have had something useful to add to the material," which helps students when they go out into the real world. The "Aggie network" is something to behold; it reaches far across the nation ("Aggie alumni are loyal to their school forever") and "is good for getting jobs after graduation." The sense of pride here motivates students to do well "because they're part of something bigger than themselves." There is "great support" from both the faculty and staff together. "The mindset they have is to effectively prepare students for world-class challenges," says one student. "At Texas A&M, you learn to be a well-rounded, moral, and ethical person."

Life

Student organizations positively abound at Texas A&M (there are more than 800), and they are a huge social outlet for students looking to find those with similar interests. "Get involved in something you're passionate about; there is a club for just about *everything*," says a student. Off-campus, there are "four-dollar movies, many dancehalls, endless restaurants to eat at, and a large mall," as well as "an ice-skating rink, bowling alley, and miniature golf place." Students at Texas A&M are "loyal to one another and are always willing to support their fellow Aggies." "Tradition and chivalry run the school," and students all "work hard during the week so we can party hard on the weekends," usually at Northgate, the "bar street." "Texas A&M is kind of like a cult—a really happy cult," explains a student. The "immense school spirit" is derived from the many "time-honored traditions," including the Big Event, which is the largest one-day, student-run service project in the nation. That's not even to mention the football: "Saturdays in the fall are owned by football." "Although the school is very large, whenever the…Aggies at Kyle Field are belting the war hymn and linking arms, I feel like I am part of a huge family." As one student cryptically sums up his school's mythology, "From the outside looking in, you can't understand it. From the inside looking out you can't explain it."

Student Body

A typical student is "white," "conservative," "involved in at least one club, spends a fair amount of time studying, and learns to two-step for Thursday nights." This being Texas, "some wear cowboy boots, a flannel shirt, a cowboy hat/baseball cap, and jeans." There is also a strong faction of members of the Corps of Cadets, as well as religious folk (the school has "the largest Bible study in the world"). Though lacking cultural diversity, interests and hobbies run the gamut, and "Students from other races and classes fit in just fine and are able to make friends just like anybody else." While it's a big school, "a lot of classes are pretty small, so it's easy to make friends in class." There are "no pretenses" among Aggies, and "Everyone shows who they are." "Most of the people I have met here are truly genuine individuals," says a student.

FINANCIAL AID: 979-845-3236 • E-MAIL: ADMISSIONS@TAMU.EDU • WEBSITE: WWW.TAMU.EDU

THE PRINCETON REVIEW SAYS

Admissions

Very important factors considered include: Class rank, academic GPA, rigor of secondary school record, standardized test scores, extracurricular activities, talent/ability. *Important factors considered include:* Application essay, first generation, geographical residence, state residency, volunteer work, work experience. *Other factors considered include:* recommendation(s), character/personal qualities. SAT or ACT required; ACT with writing component required. TOEFL required of all international applicants. High school diploma is required and GED is accepted. *Academic units required:* 4 English, 3 mathematics, 3 science (2 science labs), 2 foreign language, 2 social studies, 1 history. *Academic units recommended:* 4 English, 3 mathematics, 3 science (2 science labs), 2 foreign language, 2 social studies, 1 history, 1 computer science.

Financial Aid

Students should submit: FAFSA, institution's own financial aid form, Financial Aid Transcripts (for transfer students). The Princeton Review suggests that all financial aid forms be submitted as soon as possible after January 1. *Need-based scholarships/grants offered:* Federal Pell, SEOG, state scholarships/grants, private scholarships, the school's own gift aid. *Loan aid offered:* Direct Subsidized Stafford, Direct Unsubsidized Stafford, Direct PLUS, Federal Perkins, state loans, college/university loans from institutional funds. Applicants will be notified of awards on a rolling basis beginning April 1. Federal Work-Study Program available. Institutional employment available. Highest amount earned per year from on-campus jobs $2,639. Off-campus job opportunities are excellent.

The Inside Word

Texas A&M uses some cut-and-dried admissions criteria: Students graduating in the top ten percent of a recognized public or private high school in the state of Texas are automatically in; all they have to do is get their applications in on time. Applicants in the top quarter of their graduating class who have a combined SAT Math/Critical Reading score of 1300 (minimum score of 600 in each component) are also automatically in, as are such students who earn a composite ACT score of 30 (minimum 27 on the math and English sections). Students must also take the writing component of the SAT and/or ACT for the test score to be considered. All other applications are deemed "Review Admits" to be sorted through by the admissions committee.

THE SCHOOL SAYS ". . ."

From the Admissions Office

"Established in 1876 as the first public college in the state, Texas A&M University has become a world leader in teaching, research, and public service. Located in College Station in the heart of Texas, it is centrally situated among three of the country's ten largest cities: Dallas, Houston, and San Antonio. Texas A&M is ranked nationally in these four areas: enrollment, enrollment of top students, value of research, and endowment.

"Freshman applicants are required to take the SAT or the ACT. We will use the applicant's best single testing date score in decision making."

SELECTIVITY	
Admissions Rating	84
# of applicants	25,949
% of applicants accepted	64
% of acceptees attending	50
# accepting a place on wait list	8,044
# admitted from wait list	995
FRESHMAN PROFILE	
Range SAT Critical Reading	530–650
Range SAT Math	570–670
Range SAT Writing	510–620
Range ACT Composite	23–30
Minimum paper TOEFL	550
% graduated top 10% of class	55
% graduated top 25% of class	90
% graduated top 50% of class	99
DEADLINES	
Regular	
Priority	12/1
Deadline	1/15
Nonfall registration?	yes
FINANCIAL FACTS	
Financial Aid Rating	83
Annual in-state tuition	$5,297
Annual out-state tuition	$20,687
Room and board	$8,200
Required fees	$3,122
Books and supplies	$1,340
% needy frosh rec. need-based scholarship or grant aid	96
% needy UG rec. need-based scholarship or grant aid	87
% needy frosh rec. non-need-based scholarship or grant aid	17
% needy UG rec. non-need-based scholarship or grant aid	9
% needy frosh rec. need-based self-help aid	49
% needy UG rec. need-based self-help aid	63
% frosh rec. any financial aid	75
% UG rec. any financial aid	65
% UG borrow to pay for school	47
Average cumulative indebtedness	$22,243
% frosh need fully met	60
% ugrads need fully met	45
Average % of frosh need met	79
Average % of ugrad need met	71

TEXAS CHRISTIAN UNIVERSITY

OFFICE OF ADMISSIONS, FORT WORTH, TX 76129 • ADMISSIONS: 817-257-7490 • FAX: 817-257-7268

CAMPUS LIFE

Quality of Life Rating	**86**
Fire Safety Rating	**87**
Green Rating	**76**
Type of school	private
Affiliation	Disciples of Christ
Environment	metropolis

STUDENTS

Total undergrad enrollment	8,229
% male/female	41/59
% from out of state	33
% from public high school	64
% frosh live on campus	97
# of fraternities	15
# of sororities	18
% African American	5
% Asian	3
% Caucasian	74
% Hispanic	10
% Native American	1
% international	5
# of countries represented	83

SURVEY SAYS . . .

Great computer facilities
Athletic facilities are great
Students love Fort Worth, TX
Frats and sororities dominate social scene

ACADEMICS

Academic Rating	**79**
% students returning for sophomore year	87
% students graduating within 4 years	59
% students graduating within 6 years	74
Calendar	semester
Student/faculty ratio	14:1
Profs interesting rating	87
Profs accessible rating	86
Most classes have	10–19 students
Most lab/discussion sessions have	20–29 students

MOST POPULAR MAJORS

business administration and management; nursing/registered nurse (rn, asn, bsn, msn); public relations, advertising, and applied communication, other any instructional program in organizational communication, public relations, and advertising not listed

STUDENTS SAY ". . ."

Academics

The popular conception of Texas is that everything there is big, big, big, but Texas Christian University is one Lone Star institution that bucks this trend, insisting on "smaller classroom sizes" that allows professors to be "very interested in [students] personally." One undergrad explains: "If I have a problem and need to talk with the profs, they go out of their way to meet with me, especially when it comes to career options and what my best options are in terms of what I want to do. They are very helpful." While "there are some programs with more students than others, overall the academic experience at TCU is very personal and rewarding. Many students are easily able to latch onto a professor's lab research…Getting involved in the academic programs at TCU will really pay off." Students enjoy a strong support network; the school "offers many resources such as the library, writing center, career center, student support services, and other educational and personal resources," and alumni "are really involved and give a lot back to the school." Business, education, and physical therapy are among the standout offerings here. Access to the Fort Worth–Dallas business community means plenty of good internship and networking opportunities.

Life

"Greek life is one of the most popular activities" at TCU; some say "the Greeks rule the social scene at the school," while others see slightly more diverse options. The school "puts a lot of its money to good use, such as new residence halls, a nice recreational facility, funding for numerous clubs and organizations, and great activities to bring the campus community together," creating "a focus on the student community" that extends beyond the Greek houses. TCU football is another pillar of campus life, and students "have a lot of pride" in both the program and the school itself. Beyond these choices, life at TCU "is what you make it. If you want to make grades your top priority, it's very easy to do so. If you want to go out and party a lot, it's very easy to do [that] as well. Lots of people drink on campus, but not everyone makes that their life. It's all about what your priorities are because it is easy to go either way." Off-campus opportunities are plentiful thanks to access to Fort Worth–Dallas, a major metropolis.

Student Body

Undergrads tend to be "middle- to upper-class…in good physical shape, and like to have a good time." Many, "but not all, dress extremely well…First impressions mean a lot here, so do not mess up." "The student body is very Greek" at TCU. Students differ on how this impacts social dynamics; some insist that "if you aren't in a fraternity or sorority, it is very hard to fit in," while others point out that "there are other types of people on campus", and "if you are open-minded and have a good personality overall you won't find it hard to make friends inside and outside of Greek life and find yourself belonging at TCU." While "the student population is mostly made up of Caucasian students," there is "a growing minority student population," the largest segment of which is Latina. Some complain about the pervasive materialism, but others think the issue is overblown; one tells us, "Some may find the money an issue, but that's only because they make it an issue. I've never been ashamed that I can't buy the latest Prada handbag, and no one has ever looked down on me because of that. If you don't bring it up, nobody cares. A lack of character may make these people feel left out."

FINANCIAL AID: 817-257-7858 • E-MAIL: FROGMAIL@TCU.EDU • WEBSITE: WWW.TCU.EDU

THE PRINCETON REVIEW SAYS

Admissions

Very important factors considered include: Class rank, application essay, academic GPA, recommendation(s), rigor of secondary school record, standardized test scores, character/personal qualities. *Important factors considered include:* Extracurricular activities, first generation, geographical residence, level of applicant's interest, racial/ethnic status, religious affiliation/commitment, talent/ability, volunteer work, work experience. *Other factors considered include:* Alumni/ae relation, interview. SAT or ACT required; ACT with or without writing component accepted. TOEFL required of all international applicants. High school diploma is required and GED is not accepted. *Academic units required:* 4 English, 3 mathematics, 3 science, 2 foreign language, 3 social studies, 2 academic electives. *Academic units recommended:* 4 English, 4 mathematics, 4 science, 4 foreign language, 4 social studies, 4 academic electives.

Financial Aid

Students should submit: FAFSA. Regular filing deadline is May 1. The Princeton Review suggests that all financial aid forms be submitted as soon as possible after January 1. *Need-based scholarships/grants offered:* Federal Pell, SEOG, state scholarships/grants, private scholarships, the school's own gift aid. *Loan aid offered:* Direct Subsidized Stafford, Direct Unsubsidized Stafford, Direct PLUS, Federal Perkins, Federal Nursing, state loans. TCU's scholarship deadline is December 15. Applicants will be notified of awards on a rolling basis beginning March 15. Federal Work-Study Program available. Institutional employment available. Highest amount earned per year from on-campus jobs $12,750. Off-campus job opportunities are excellent.

The Inside Word

The sheer volume of applications sent to TCU—the school receives more than 19,000 each year—requires the school to apply some baseline criteria for winnowing out unlikely candidates. That said, the school works hard to consider applications holistically and to find mitigating evidence to offset sub-par performance in any one category (for example, standardized test scores).

THE SCHOOL SAYS ". . ."

From the Admissions Office

"TCU is a major teaching and research university with the feel of a small college. The TCU academic experience includes small classes with top faculty; cutting-edge technology; a liberal arts and sciences core curriculum; and real-life application though faculty-directed research, group projects, and internships. While TCU faculty members are recognized for research, their main focus is on teaching and mentoring students. The friendly campus community welcomes new students at Frog Camp before classes begin, where students find three days of fun meeting new friends, learning campus traditions, and serving the community. Campus life includes 200 clubs and organizations, a spirited NCAA Division I athletics program in the Big 12 Conference, and numerous productions from professional schools of the arts. More than half of the students participate in a wide array of intramural sports, and about forty percent are involved in Greek organizations, including ones emphasizing ethnic diversity as well as the Christian faith. The historic relationship to the Christian Church (Disciples of Christ) means that instead of teaching a particular viewpoint, TCU encourages students to consider and follow their own beliefs. The university's mission—to educate individuals to think and act as ethical leaders and responsible citizens in a global community—influences everything from course work to study abroad to the way Horned Frogs act and interact. From National Merit Scholars to those just now realizing their academic potential, TCU attracts and serves students who are learning to change the world.

"TCU will accept either the SAT or the ACT (with or without the writing component) in admission and scholarship processes. The writing sections will be considered alongside the TCU application essay."

SELECTIVITY

Admissions Rating	**89**
# of applicants	19,166
% of applicants accepted	38
% of acceptees attending	26
# accepting a place on wait list	2,986
# admitted from wait list	201

FRESHMAN PROFILE

Range SAT Critical Reading	520–630
Range SAT Math	540–650
Range SAT Writing	540–640
Range ACT Composite	24–29
Minimum paper TOEFL	550
Minimum web-based TOEFL	80
% graduated top 10% of class	38
% graduated top 25% of class	73
% graduated top 50% of class	95

DEADLINES

Early action	
Deadline	11/1
Notification	1/1
Regular	
Priority	2/15
Deadline	2/15
Notification	4/1
Nonfall registration?	yes

FINANCIAL FACTS

Financial Aid Rating	**73**
Annual tuition	$34,500
Room and board	$10,410
Required fees	$90
Books and supplies	$1,050
% needy frosh rec. need-based scholarship or grant aid	98
% needy UG rec. need-based scholarship or grant aid	92
% needy frosh rec. non-need-based scholarship or grant aid	65
% needy UG rec. non-need-based scholarship or grant aid	57
% needy frosh rec. need-based self-help aid	72
% needy UG rec. need-based self-help aid	75
% frosh rec. any financial aid	78
% UG rec. any financial aid	75
% UG borrow to pay for school	41
Average cumulative indebtedness	$36,468
% frosh need fully met	29
% ugrads need fully met	25
Average % of frosh need met	68
Average % of ugrad need met	61

THOMAS AQUINAS COLLEGE

10000 OJAI ROAD, SANTA PAULA, CA 93060 • ADMISSION: 805-525-4417 • FAX: 805-421-5905

CAMPUS LIFE

Quality of Life Rating	**97**
Fire Safety Rating	**87**
Green Rating	**60***
Type of school	private
Affiliation	Roman Catholic
Environment	rural

STUDENTS

Total undergrad enrollment	358
% male/female	49/51
% from out of state	69
% from public high school	12
% frosh live on campus	100
% Asian	1
% Caucasian	73
% Hispanic	13
% international	6
# of countries represented	6

SURVEY SAYS . . .

Lots of conservative students
Class discussions encouraged
No one cheats
Students are very religious
Dorms are like palaces
Low cost of living
Intercollegiate sports are unpopular or nonexistent
Frats and sororities are unpopular or nonexistent
Very little drug use

ACADEMICS

Academic Rating	**99**
% students returning for sophomore year	90
% students graduating within 4 years	64
% students graduating within 6 years	68
Calendar	semester
Student/faculty ratio	11:1
Profs interesting rating	97
Profs accessible rating	91
Most classes have	10–19 students

APPLICANTS ALSO LOOK AT AND OFTEN PREFER
University of Notre Dame

AND SOMETIMES PREFER
The Catholic University of America, University of Dallas

STUDENTS SAY ". . ."

Academics

Students at Thomas Aquinas College relish attending a school that "takes learning seriously for its own sake, not just as preparation for a job." With a "strong Catholic identity" and "rigorous curriculum," TAC offers a "holistic education" that's "demanding on every level." The college promotes a "Great Books education," which really forces its undergrads to "read and think critically." All classes are seminar-based, a method many students here feel "better facilitates learning." Importantly, the "Catholic/small-college setting creates an atmosphere of trust and faith that makes it easier to study, to live, and to grow at school." Unlike other colleges, "There aren't any majors at Thomas Aquinas." Students simply graduate with a bachelor's degree in liberal arts. Class time is solely "devoted to discussion of the [reading] material assigned" with professors (or tutors as they are known) facilitating said discussion. Undergrads happily report that professors are "more than happy to continue the discussion outside class and are always ready to help their students." Moreover, they're "welcoming" and "easy to talk to," and all seem to "have a passion for intellectual formation." As one content senior succinctly states, "The professors are great and lead you to truth without forcing it on you."

Life

TAC inspires and encourages a contemplative life, and students spend a large portion of their time in "an intellectual discussion." That being said, even TAC undergrads need to kick back every now and again. On this active campus, intramural sports are quite popular, and "running, hiking, basketball, soccer, and football are major pastimes on campus." Further, "Four times a year there is a formal dance hosted by one of the classes." As one enthusiastic sophomore explains, "I waltz, swing, lindy hop, tango, salsa, rumba, contra dance, polka, Virginia reel, and do other dances. People on this campus actually learn and know how to dance well." Students here also know how to make their own fun. As one freshman shares, there are "spontaneous student pranks, such as the day the freshmen men all wore blue while the freshmen women wore pink (officially titled 'Trip Out the Tudors Tuesday')." Additionally, "Once or twice a semester, the school arranges field trips to the Getty Center, Villa, operas, art galleries, science museums, and other points of interest in the wider LA area." It's also quite common for students to "leave campus for the weekend for fun activities either to Ventura Beach (thirty minutes), Santa Barbara (one hour), or Ojai (twenty minutes)."

Student Body

Undergrads at TAC might, in some respects, appear "homogenous." Indeed, the vast majority of students "are Catholic," "devoted to learning and their faith," and politically "conservative." That being said, a senior assures us, "Any student with any interest can usually find a group that shares his or her passion." Importantly, many agree that their peers are "very kind and inclusive" as well as "joyful and inviting." One junior elaborates saying, "You walk down the hallways and sidewalks and are personally greeted by freshmen and seniors alike." An overwhelming number of undergrads here declare their fellow students "intellectually curious" and "somewhat obsessed with philosophy." Indeed, the typical student "is a thinker [who] will never hesitate to get in[to] a philosophical argument." Naturally, people here are "committed to the academic life," and most students study "very hard." They're "focused [and] mature" and make a point of "coming prepared to class." As one honest and insightful senior admits, "Most [students] would probably be considered a bit geeky elsewhere." But perhaps this student sums up his TAC peers the best, "You get all different kinds of people here—but one thing they have in common is a desire to search for the truth."

FINANCIAL AID: 800-634-9797 • E-MAIL: ADMISSIONS@THOMASAQUINAS.EDU • WEBSITE: WWW.THOMASAQUINAS.EDU

THE PRINCETON REVIEW SAYS

Admissions

Very important factors considered include: Application essay, recommendation(s), rigor of secondary school record, standardized test scores, character/personal qualities, level of applicant's interest. *Important factors considered include:* Academic GPA. *Other factors considered include:* Class rank, extracurricular activities, interview, religious affiliation/commitment, talent/ability, volunteer work, work experience. SAT or ACT required; ACT with or without writing component accepted. TOEFL required of all international applicants. High school diploma is required and GED is accepted. *Academic units required:* 4 English, 3 mathematics, 2 science, 2 foreign language, 2 history. *Academic units recommended:* 4 English, 4 mathematics, 3 science (2 science labs), 2 history, 3 academic electives.

Financial Aid

Students should submit: FAFSA, institution's own financial aid form, state aid form, business/farm supplement, tax return, noncustodial parent statement. Regular filing deadline is March 2. The Princeton Review suggests that all financial aid forms be submitted as soon as possible after January 1. *Need-based scholarships/grants offered:* Federal Pell, state scholarships/grants, private scholarships, the school's own gift aid. *Loan aid offered:* Direct Subsidized Stafford, Direct Unsubsidized Stafford, Direct PLUS, college/university loans from institutional funds, Canadian student loans. Applicants will be notified of awards on a rolling basis beginning January 1. Off-campus job opportunities are fair.

The Inside Word

A unique academic institution, TAC thoroughly analyzes their applicants to ensure their accepted students will be a good fit. Academic prowess is a must, and candidates should also demonstrate intellectual curiosity. Because of their holistic approach, admissions officers pay close attention to the application essays. The college operates on a rolling admissions schedule and, if interested, you should apply as early as possible.

THE SCHOOL SAYS ". . ."

From the Admissions Office

"Thomas Aquinas College holds with confidence that the human mind is capable of knowing the truth about reality, that living according to the truth is necessary for human happiness, and that truth is best comprehended through the harmonious work of faith and reason. The intellectual virtues are understood to be essential, and the college considers the cultivation of those virtues the primary work of Catholic liberal education.

"The academic program designed to achieve this goal is comprehensive and unified—and it includes no textbooks or lecture classes. In every subject—from philosophy, theology, mathematics, and science to language, music, literature, and history—students read the greatest written works in those disciplines, both ancient and modern: Homer, Plato, Aristotle, Augustine, Aquinas, Newton, Maxwell, Einstein, the Founding Fathers of the American Republic, Shakespeare, and T. S. Eliot, to name just a few. Instead of attending lecture classes, students gather in small tutorials, seminars, and laboratories for Socratic-style discussions.

"One mark of the program's success is the variety of professions and careers that graduates enter. Many attend graduate and professional schools in a wide array of disciplines; among them, philosophy, theology, law, literature, and the sciences are most often chosen.

"SAT or ACT scores are required, and the writing component on each test is encouraged. However, scores in critical reading and math (SAT), or English and mathematics (ACT) are more central in the consideration of that aspect of a student's application."

SELECTIVITY	
Admissions Rating	**88**
# of applicants	171
% of applicants accepted	79
% of acceptees attending	67
# accepting a place on wait list	35
# admitted from wait list	13

FRESHMAN PROFILE	
Range SAT Critical Reading	610–710
Range SAT Math	550–660
Range SAT Writing	580–690
Range ACT Composite	25–29
Minimum paper TOEFL	570
Average HS GPA	3.7
% graduated top 10% of class	40
% graduated top 25% of class	40
% graduated top 50% of class	80

DEADLINES	
Nonfall registration?	no

FINANCIAL FACTS	
Financial Aid Rating	**99**
Annual tuition	$23,600
Room and board	$7,800
Books and supplies	$450
% needy frosh rec. need-based scholarship or grant aid	91
% needy UG rec. need-based scholarship or grant aid	91
% needy frosh rec. need-based self-help aid	100
% needy UG rec. need-based self-help aid	100
% frosh rec. any financial aid	81
% UG rec. any financial aid	79
% UG borrow to pay for school	88
Average cumulative indebtedness	$16,582
% frosh need fully met	100
% ugrads need fully met	100
Average % of frosh need met	100
Average % of ugrad need met	100

TRANSYLVANIA UNIVERSITY

300 NORTH BROADWAY, LEXINGTON, KY 40508-1797 • ADMISSIONS: 859-233-8242 • FAX: 859-281-3649

CAMPUS LIFE

Quality of Life Rating	**84**
Fire Safety Rating	**82**
Green Rating	**68**
Type of school	private
Affiliation	Disciples of Christ
Environment	city

STUDENTS

Total undergrad enrollment	1,025
% male/female	40/60
% from out of state	20
% from public high school	78
% frosh live on campus	96
# of fraternities	4
# of sororities	4
% African American	4
% Asian	1
% Caucasian	87
% Hispanic	1
% international	1
# of countries represented	7

SURVEY SAYS . . .

No one cheats
Athletic facilities are great
Students love Lexington, KY
Great off-campus food
Frats and sororities dominate social scene

ACADEMICS

Academic Rating	**85**
% students returning for sophomore year	87
% students graduating within 4 years	66
% students graduating within 6 years	70
Calendar	semester
Student/faculty ratio	11:1
Profs interesting rating	92
Profs accessible rating	91
Most classes have	10–19 students
Most lab/discussion sessions have	10–19 students

MOST POPULAR MAJORS

biology/biological sciences; business/commerce; psychology

APPLICANTS ALSO LOOK AT AND SOMETIMES PREFER

Centre College, University of Kentucky

STUDENTS SAY ". . ."

Academics

Tucked away in the heart of Lexington, Kentucky, Transylvania University is able to marry a "small-school atmosphere" with "big-city" living. An "extremely close-knit campus," one truly feels a "strong sense of community" while strolling around the grounds. Undergrads here greatly appreciate that the school "values community, education for the sake of education, and producing students with the skills to tackle any career the job market has to offer." Moreover, Transy strives to provide "a holistic educational experience where one can grow intellectually and academically while participating in a vibrant social community." Students are quick to heap praise on their professors who "are both very knowledgeable and fun to be around." They're all "accomplished within their fields" and seem to "love teaching here at Transylvania." As one pleased Spanish and English double-major confidently declares, "It doesn't matter whether a class is lecture- or discussion-based, because either way you're guaranteed to learn something." One junior does warn that most professors "require students [to] participate in classroom discussion," which can be "intimidating" for some. Perhaps most important, their accessibility is "amazing," and they "are almost always willing to let you stop by during their office hours and discuss just about anything." And, as this anthropology major simply and smartly quips, "I am never bored."

Life

During the week, life at Transylvania University can be fairly harried and "stressful," and most students have their noses "to the grindstone." In turn, because of working "ridiculously hard," students are pumped to "have some fun when [the week] is over." The vast majority of undergrads "are involved in Greek life," and "parties in the fraternity dorms are very popular." Fortunately, we have been assured that neither the fraternities nor sororities are "exclusive." Moreover, "every social event is practically open invitation." Of course, there's plenty to do aside from simply attending frat parties. For example, the "Student Activities Board [sponsors] a lot of activities that are pretty fun and have a relatively good turn out." There's always something to do as one freshman indicates, "This weekend I'll be going to a huge musical/talent show, then tomorrow I'll be volunteering to raise money for a local church, then after that I'll be going ice skating with some friends." Athletics are also fairly big, and "Transylvania has several perennially successful sports programs, some of which include men's and women's basketball, men's and women's soccer, and softball." Undergrads also love to take advantage of hometown Lexington, and you'll often find students "walking downtown to theaters, art exhibits, or other downtown events" as well as "the shopping district."

Student Body

Transylvania manages to attract students who "seem to be genuinely concerned with their education." Indeed, undergrads are quick to define their peers as "studious," "intellectually motivated," and full of "ambitious goals." As a result, "The average Transylvania student is extremely adept at balancing his or her academics with the many extracurricular activities available." Additionally, "Greek life is very prominent on campus." However, one student insists that overall, the "Transy campus has very diverse individuals." Of course, a handful of students begrudge the "lack of…geographic diversity," asserting that "most students come from the region around Lexington" and are "upper-middle-class." Others take issue with this sentiment, quickly stating, "We also have a huge population of individuals from different backgrounds including differences in sexual orientation, class, religion, region, and political orientation." Fortunately, undergrads do find their fellow students "approachable and friendly," and "most students will find themselves right at home on campus."

FINANCIAL AID: 859-233-8239 • E-MAIL: ADMISSIONS@TRANSY.EDU • WEBSITE: WWW.TRANSY.EDU

THE PRINCETON REVIEW SAYS

Admissions

Very important factors considered include: Academic GPA, rigor of secondary school record, standardized test scores. *Important factors considered include:* Application essay, recommendation(s), extracurricular activities. *Other factors considered include:* Class rank, alumni/ae relation, character/personal qualities, first generation, geographical residence, interview, talent/ability, volunteer work, work experience. SAT or ACT required; ACT with or without writing component accepted. TOEFL required of all international applicants. High school diploma is required and GED is accepted. *Academic units required:* 4 English, 3 mathematics, 3 science, 2 social studies. *Academic units recommended:* 4 English, 4 mathematics, 4 science (2 science labs), 2 foreign language, 2 social studies, 1 history, 1 academic elective.

Financial Aid

Students should submit: FAFSA. The Princeton Review suggests that all financial aid forms be submitted as soon as possible after January 1. *Need-based scholarships/grants offered:* Federal Pell, SEOG, state scholarships/grants, private scholarships, the school's own gift aid. *Loan aid offered:* Direct Subsidized Stafford, Direct Unsubsidized Stafford, Direct PLUS, Federal Perkins, college/university loans from institutional funds. Applicants will be notified of awards on a rolling basis beginning March 15. Federal Work-Study Program available. Institutional employment available. Off-campus job opportunities are excellent.

Inside Word

The admissions committee at Transylvania University is tasked with finding a freshman class that will mesh well with the existing Transy community. That being the case, they do their utmost to consider the entire applicant. Of course, academic rigor is the most important factor. However, don't shirk on your essays, recommendations, or extracurricular involvement.

THE SCHOOL SAYS ". . ."

From the Admissions Office

"Bright, highly motivated students choose Transylvania for our personal approach to learning and our record of success in preparing them for rewarding careers and fulfilling lives. They attend small classes (many have fewer than ten students) with highly qualified professors (no teaching assistants) and tackle faculty-directed student research projects in intriguing subjects like neurotransmitters and receptors, computer animation, and local Hispanic culture. Transylvania graduates have won prestigious scholarships and distinguished themselves at highly selective graduate and professional schools.

"Transylvania students consider the world their classroom. They enjoy May term travel courses studying the ancient polis in Greece, language and culture in France, and tropical ecology in Hawaii. Study abroad takes them to Germany, England, Japan, Mexico, and other destinations for a summer, a semester, or a year.

"You'll find Transylvania, a small college, nestled in a big city. Transylvania students soak up the advantages of Lexington, Kentucky, with its population of 300,000, numerous internships and job opportunities, and lots of entertainment. On campus, we have more than fifty co-curricular activities, and twenty-three varsity teams competing in NCAA Division III.

"While Transylvania is the nation's sixteenth oldest college and proud of its rich history, its commitments to the exploration of a variety of disciplines, to intellectual inquiry, and to critical thinking have never been more relevant than in today's rapidly changing twenty-first-century world.

"Applicants are not required to submit writing scores from the ACT or the SAT."

SELECTIVITY	
Admissions Rating	**84**
# of applicants	1,267
% of applicants accepted	85
% of acceptees attending	23
FRESHMAN PROFILE	
Range SAT Critical Reading	570–680
Range SAT Math	540–660
Range ACT Composite	24–30
Minimum paper TOEFL	550
Minimum web-based TOEFL	80
Average HS GPA	3.8
% graduated top 10% of class	43
% graduated top 25% of class	73
% graduated top 50% of class	96
DEADLINES	
Early action	
Deadline	12/1
Notification	1/15
Regular	
Priority	12/1
Deadline	2/1
Notification	3/15
Nonfall registration?	yes
FINANCIAL FACTS	
Financial Aid Rating	**84**
Annual tuition	$28,645
Room and board	$8,750
Required fees	$1,220
Books and supplies	$1,000
% needy frosh rec. need-based scholarship or grant aid	100
% needy UG rec. need-based scholarship or grant aid	100
% needy frosh rec. non-need-based scholarship or grant aid	19
% needy UG rec. non-need-based scholarship or grant aid	14
% needy frosh rec. need-based self-help aid	76
% needy UG rec. need-based self-help aid	80
% frosh rec. any financial aid	99
% UG rec. any financial aid	98
% UG borrow to pay for school	67
Average cumulative indebtedness	$24,679
% frosh need fully met	26
% ugrads need fully met	22
Average % of frosh need met	83
Average % of ugrad need met	80

TRINITY COLLEGE (CT)

300 SUMMIT STREET, HARTFORD, CT 06016 • ADMISSIONS: 860-297-2180 • FAX: 860-297-2287

CAMPUS LIFE

Quality of Life Rating	**66**
Fire Safety Rating	**90**
Green Rating	**61**
Type of school	private
Environment	metropolis

STUDENTS

Total undergrad enrollment	2,254
% male/female	51/49
% from out of state	84
% from public high school	40
% frosh live on campus	99
# of fraternities	7
# of sororities	3
% African American	6
% Asian	5
% Caucasian	65
% Hispanic	8
% international	7
# of countries represented	48

SURVEY SAYS . . .

Great computer facilities
Great library
Students aren't religious
Everyone loves the Bantams
Frats and sororities dominate social scene
Student publications are popular
Lots of beer drinking
Hard liquor is popular

ACADEMICS

Academic Rating	**95**
% students returning for sophomore year	92
% students graduating within 4 years	82
% students graduating within 6 years	86
Calendar	4-1-4
Student/faculty ratio	10:1
Profs interesting rating	86
Profs accessible rating	85
Most classes have	10–19 students
Most lab/discussion sessions have	10–19 students

MOST POPULAR MAJORS

economics; English language and literature; political science and government

APPLICANTS ALSO LOOK AT AND SOMETIMES PREFER

Middlebury College, Wesleyan University, Boston College

AND RARELY PREFER

Boston University

STUDENTS SAY ". . ."

Academics

"[It's all] about getting a top-notch education in small classes with professors who know you and being able to also have a good time outside of class" at Trinity College, a small and prestigious liberal arts school located in Connecticut's state capital. A "great political science department" exploits TC's location "about two blocks away from the state capitol, which is great for internships." Other social sciences, including economics and history, earn students' praises, as do offerings in engineering and education. Strength across the liberal arts bolsters the school's Guided Studies Program, in which students undertake a fixed curriculum of interdisciplinary study to survey the entirety of Western civilization from the classical age to the present. In all disciplines, "small classes, very involved professors, and a very conscious student body" combine to provide "an excellent liberal arts education that will provide [students] with the skills to be thoughtful, independent adults." Professors "are always available to talk and offer help to students. They often invite students out to lunch." Likewise, administrators are easy to access. "Even the president of the school, James F. Jones, is accessible. He goes on the Quest Orientation hiking trip for first-year students and regularly attends various student events on campus." Students also appreciate that "the career services office is amazing" here.

Life

"The fraternity scene is the draw for the majority of campus" at Trinity College, where "On a typical weekend night, people go out to dinner, go back to their room and nap, get ready for the evening, and go meet up with a friend or two where they chill out and then go to someone's room for pregaming...Then when it's about 1:00 A.M. they go out and do some frat hopping. It's great for people who like their life to be predictable." The frats are hardly the only option, though; in fact, "There are a ton of underappreciated options on or near campus. Hartford has amazing restaurants, there are movie theaters and bowling alleys nearby, the Cinestudio is a ninety-second walk from the main dining hall, and there are two dorms on campus devoted specifically to alcohol-free activities. Plus, plenty of student groups hold events" in such places as "the arts and cultural houses." Trinity's theater and dance department offer regular performances. Hometown Hartford "may be [an economically] depressed city, but it is still a city, and it affords benefits that tiny college towns just can't match."

Student Body

The stereotype about Trinity undergrads is that "most...are from the tri-state area and appear to have just stepped off a yacht or out of a country club," and students confirm that while "there are a lot of students who are not" in this crowd, the preppy contingent is "the main group" and "socially dominant" here. "There are definitely some very preppy girls and boys—blond hair, sunglasses, Chanel flats, a polo," one student concedes before adding that "sometimes people identify these students as typical Trinity students; however there are many students who are not like that at all." All students tend to be "well-rounded" and "very passionate," "intelligent but also social," with "good verbal skills." They "care deeply about their work and really like to have fun when they can," and while many gravitate to the Greek community for their fun, "There are [also] communities here for those who do not enjoy the frat scene, for people who are passionate about music and acting, and [for] those who want to spend their weekends giving back to the community."

FINANCIAL AID: 860-297-2047 • E-MAIL: ADMISSIONS.OFFICE@TRINCOLL.EDU • WEBSITE: WWW.TRINCOLL.EDU

THE PRINCETON REVIEW SAYS

Admissions

Very important factors considered include: Rigor of secondary school record. *Important factors considered include:* Class rank, application essay, academic GPA, recommendation(s), standardized test scores, character/personal qualities, extracurricular activities, interview, racial/ethnic status, talent/ability. *Other factors considered include:* Alumni/ae relation, first generation, geographical residence, level of applicant's interest, volunteer work, work experience. SAT or ACT required; ACT with writing component recommended. High school diploma is required and GED is accepted. *Academic units required:* 4 English, 3 mathematics, 2 science (2 science labs), 3 foreign language, 2 history.

Financial Aid

Students should submit: FAFSA, CSS/Financial Aid PROFILE, noncustodial PROFILE, business/farm supplement, federal income tax returns. Regular filing deadline is March 1. The Princeton Review suggests that all financial aid forms be submitted as soon as possible after January 1. *Need-based scholarships/grants offered:* Federal Pell, SEOG, state scholarships/grants, private scholarships, the school's own gift aid. *Loan aid offered:* Direct Subsidized Stafford, Direct Unsubsidized Stafford, Direct PLUS, Federal Perkins, college/university loans from institutional funds. Applicants will be notified of awards on or about April 1. Federal Work-Study Program available. Institutional employment available. Highest amount earned per year from on-campus jobs $6,000. Off-campus job opportunities are good.

The Inside Word

Students describe Trinity as "the home of Yale rejects," an appraisal that accurately, if somewhat hyperbolically, characterizes the school's reputation as an Ivy safety. The hefty tuition and fees here ensure that a large percentage of the student body is made up of wealthy, preppy types, but the school does offer generous financial aid packages to top candidates who can't afford the considerable price of attending. The school would love to broaden its demographic, so competitive minority students should receive a very welcome reception here.

THE SCHOOL SAYS ". . ."

From the Admissions Office

"An array of distinctive curricular options—including an interdisciplinary neuroscience major and a professionally accredited engineering degree program, a unique Human Rights Program, a Health Fellows Program, and interdisciplinary programs such as the Cities Program, Interdisciplinary Science Program, and InterArts—is one reason record numbers of students are applying to Trinity. In fact, applications are up eighty percent over the past five years. In addition, the college has been recognized for its commitment to diversity; students of color have represented approximately twenty percent of the freshman class for the past four years, setting Trinity apart from many of its peers. Trinity's capital city location offers students unparalleled 'real-world' learning experiences to complement classroom learning. Students take advantage of extensive opportunities for internships for academic credit and community service, and these opportunities extend to Trinity's global learning sites in cities around the world. Trinity's faculty is a devoted and accomplished group of exceptional teacher-scholars; our 100-acre campus is beautiful; Hartford is an educational asset that differentiates Trinity from other liberal arts colleges; our global connections and foreign study opportunities prepare students to be good citizens of the world; and our graduates go on to excel in virtually every field. We invite you to learn more about why Trinity might be the best choice for you.

"Students applying for admission may submit the following testing options: SAT or ACT with writing."

SELECTIVITY

Admissions Rating	**95**
# of applicants	6,967
% of applicants accepted	30
% of acceptees attending	28
# accepting a place on wait list	2,449
# admitted from wait list	255
# of early decision applicants	493
# accepted early decision	335

FRESHMAN PROFILE

Range SAT Critical Reading	580–678
Range SAT Math	600–690
Range SAT Writing	610–698
Range ACT Composite	26–29
% graduated top 10% of class	55
% graduated top 25% of class	77
% graduated top 50% of class	98

DEADLINES

Early decision	
Deadline	11/15
Notification	12/15
Regular	
Deadline	1/1
Notification	4/1
Nonfall registration?	no

FINANCIAL FACTS

Financial Aid Rating	**98**
Annual tuition	$41,980
Room and board	$11,380
Required fees	$2,090
Books and supplies	$1,000
% needy frosh rec. need-based scholarship or grant aid	93
% needy UG rec. need-based scholarship or grant aid	94
% needy frosh rec. non-need-based scholarship or grant aid	2
% needy UG rec. non-need-based scholarship or grant aid	2
% needy frosh rec. need-based self-help aid	80
% needy UG rec. need-based self-help aid	82
% frosh rec. any financial aid	38
% UG rec. any financial aid	43
% UG borrow to pay for school	39
Average cumulative indebtedness	$13,453
% frosh need fully met	100
% ugrads need fully met	100
Average % of frosh need met	100
Average % of ugrad need met	100

TRINITY UNIVERSITY (TX)

ONE TRINITY PLACE, SAN ANTONIO, TX 78212-7200 • ADMISSIONS: 210-999-7207 • FAX: 210-999-8164

CAMPUS LIFE

Quality of Life Rating	**90**
Fire Safety Rating	**89**
Green Rating	**74**
Type of school	private
Affiliation	Presbyterian
Environment	metropolis

STUDENTS

Total undergrad enrollment	2,404
% male/female	46/54
% from out of state	32
% from public high school	64
% frosh live on campus	100
# of fraternities	7
# of sororities	6
% African American	3
% Asian	7
% Caucasian	63
% Hispanic	13
% international	7
# of countries represented	69

SURVEY SAYS . . .

Great computer facilities
Great library
School is well run
Great off-campus food
Dorms are like palaces
Campus feels safe

ACADEMICS

Academic Rating	**87**
% students returning for sophomore year	89
% students graduating within 4 years	69
Calendar	semester
Student/faculty ratio	9:1
Profs interesting rating	88
Profs accessible rating	92
Most classes have	10–19 students
Most lab/discussion sessions have	10–19 students

MOST POPULAR MAJORS

business administration, management and operations, other; English language and literature

APPLICANTS ALSO LOOK AT AND OFTEN PREFER

Rice University, The University of Texas at Austin

AND SOMETIMES PREFER

Texas Christian University, Texas A&M University—College Station, Emory University, Tulane University, Vanderbilt University

AND RARELY PREFER

Rhodes College

STUDENTS SAY ". . ."

Academics

"Trinity University is a place where one can be focused and diligent with studies—while also being in a great place to have fun on the side." In other words, this school is ideal for those seeking a well-rounded college experience and an "outstanding liberal arts education." Premed, accounting, and education are all popular majors, and the school offers "excellent science departments," and "the arts are amazing." Students praise the small class sizes and say they have access to "Ivy League smarts without the attitude." "The lectures are interesting, and class activities are unique and engaging." "The professors here, on the whole, are brilliant and helpful and are willing to work with you." "Professors are *always* accessible (some even give out home/cell phone numbers). They generally seem to enjoy students who stop by [during] office hours for help [or] just to chat." Slackers beware: While "the professors are usually very dedicated and excited to teach their subjects…that also means they expect each of their classes to be the most important class at Trinity." "Trinity professors assign a ridiculous amount of course work, but most will go to any length to help the students understand and complete the assignments." There are some complaints about the challenges of the current registration process, but overall, Trinity students are very happy with their classes, their extracurriculars, and their "gorgeous" campus.

Life

"Just about everybody at Trinity is involved in extracurricular activities," making the campus "fairly lively on its own, and it's easy to almost never leave it," though hometown San Antonio "is a great location: lots to do, lots to see, and it's right in the middle of everything exciting. Austin is only an hour away, and Padre Island is only a two-hour drive." Students have free admission to local art museums, too. But back to campus (students are required to live there for three years, after all): "There are plenty of clubs and organizations to get involved with, and Greek life at Trinity is great." Greek life and athletics are popular activities, but Trinity offers "something for everyone." Students tell us they're "always blown away by the stage productions on campus," and they enjoy working at the radio station, "which is an enormously respected jazz station by day and [broadcasts] quirky college indie radio by night." A typical week includes "a lecture one night, a cultural taste test the night after, and a concert over the weekend. There is always something to do." "There is always a party going on" at Trinity, "but they hardly dominate the social landscape." Plenty of students "watch movies or bake" for fun, and "it's not unusual to spend an afternoon with friends talking about a lecture from earlier in the day."

Student Body

"The typical student is pretty easygoing but hardworking. They want to embrace the college experience while still getting an education." Pretty much what you would expect at a university that offers such a well-balanced experience. Most students come from an "upper-middle-class upbringing…and likely came to Trinity to be a 'big fish in a small pond.'" Students do say "the school can be a bit cliquey at times," and "because [it] is so small, there is certainly a high school–like feel," but "there are many organizations and groups that anyone can join," and most students make friends easily in the dorms or via extracurricular activities. "The student body is very active in different organizations and athletics," and students note that "people who are happy at Trinity generally don't take advantage of all the different activities it has to offer." Lastly, "even though it's in Texas, it's a fairly liberal and tolerant school."

FINANCIAL AID: 210-999-8315 • E-MAIL: ADMISSIONS@TRINITY.EDU • WEBSITE: WWW.TRINITY.EDU

THE PRINCETON REVIEW SAYS

Admissions

Very important factors considered include: Class rank, academic GPA, rigor of secondary school record. *Important factors considered include:* Application essay, recommendation(s), standardized test scores, character/personal qualities, extracurricular activities, interview, talent/ability. *Other factors considered include:* Alumni/ae relation, first generation, geographical residence, level of applicant's interest, racial/ethnic status, volunteer work, work experience. SAT or ACT required; ACT with or without writing component accepted. TOEFL required of all international applicants. High school diploma is required and GED is accepted. *Academic units required:* 4 English, 3 mathematics, 3 science (2 science labs), 2 foreign language, 3 social studies. *Academic units recommended:* 4 English, 3 mathematics, 3 science (3 science labs), 3 foreign language, 3 social studies, 3 academic electives.

Financial Aid

Students should submit: FAFSA. Regular filing deadline is April 1. The Princeton Review suggests that all financial aid forms be submitted as soon as possible after January 1. *Need-based scholarships/grants offered:* Federal Pell, SEOG, state scholarships/grants, private scholarships, the school's own gift aid. *Loan aid offered:* Direct Subsidized Stafford, Direct Unsubsidized Stafford, Direct PLUS, Federal Perkins, state loans, college/university loans from institutional funds. Applicants will be notified of awards on or about April 1. Federal Work-Study Program available. Institutional employment available. Off-campus job opportunities are good.

The Inside Word

As Trinity embraces a small, close-knit community of students, admissions officers are looking for the complete package: bright, capable, motivated students who are ready to take advantage of all the school has to offer. While academic performance is the factor considered most heavily on each application, recommendations, extracurricular activities, and standardized test scores should all be very strong as well.

THE SCHOOL SAYS ". . ."

From the Admissions Office

"Three qualities separate Trinity University from other selective, academically challenging institutions around the country. First, Trinity is unusual in the quality and quantity of resources devoted almost exclusively to its undergraduate students. Those resources give rise to a second distinctive aspect of Trinity—its emphasis on undergraduate research. Our students prefer being involved over observing. With superior laboratory facilities and strong, dedicated faculty, our undergraduates fill many of the roles formerly reserved for graduate students, and our professors often go to their undergraduates for help with their research. Other hands-on learning experiences including internships, study abroad, and service projects are also available to students. Finally, Trinity stands apart for the attitude of its students. In an atmosphere of academic camaraderie and fellowship, our students work together to stretch their minds and broaden their horizons across academic disciplines. For quality of resources, for dedication to undergraduate research, and for the disposition of its student body, Trinity University holds a unique position in American higher education.

"Students applying for admission must submit either the SAT or the ACT. The highest composite test scores from one or multiple dates are evaluated. The SAT writing section and ACT writing component are not required."

SELECTIVITY	
Admissions Rating	**91**
# of applicants	4,507
% of applicants accepted	61
% of acceptees attending	23
# accepting a place on wait list	363
# admitted from wait list	24
# of early decision applicants	70
# accepted early decision	54

FRESHMAN PROFILE	
Range SAT Critical Reading	570–680
Range SAT Math	590–680
Range ACT Composite	26–31
Minimum paper TOEFL	600
Average HS GPA	3.5
% graduated top 10% of class	50
% graduated top 25% of class	79
% graduated top 50% of class	96

DEADLINES	
Early decision	
Deadline	11/1
Notification	12/1
Early action	
Deadline	12/1
Notification	2/1
Regular	
Deadline	2/1
Notification	4/1
Nonfall registration?	no

FINANCIAL FACTS	
Financial Aid Rating	**88**
Annual tuition	$33,678
Room and board	$10,496
Required fees	$180
Books and supplies	$1,000
% needy frosh rec. need-based scholarship or grant aid	100
% needy UG rec. need-based scholarship or grant aid	98
% needy frosh rec. non-need-based scholarship or grant aid	14
% needy UG rec. non-need-based scholarship or grant aid	13
% needy frosh rec. need-based self-help aid	83
% needy UG rec. need-based self-help aid	80
% frosh rec. any financial aid	94
% UG rec. any financial aid	87
% frosh need fully met	37
% ugrads need fully met	40
Average % of frosh need met	90
Average % of ugrad need met	88

TRUMAN STATE UNIVERSITY

100 EAST NORMAL AVENUE, KIRKSVILLE, MO 63501 • ADMISSIONS: 660-785-4114 • FAX: 660-785-7456

CAMPUS LIFE

Quality of Life Rating	**78**
Fire Safety Rating	**82**
Green Rating	**69**
Type of school	public
Environment	village

STUDENTS

Total undergrad enrollment	5,550
% male/female	41/59
% from out of state	17
% from public high school	81
% frosh live on campus	98
# of fraternities	21
# of sororities	16
% African American	4
% Asian	2
% Caucasian	81
% Hispanic	3
% Native American	1
% international	5
# of countries represented	44

SURVEY SAYS . . .

Students are friendly
Campus feels safe
Low cost of living
Students are happy
Very little drug use

ACADEMICS

Academic Rating	**85**
% students returning for sophomore year	86
% students graduating within 4 years	43
% students graduating within 6 years	69
Calendar	semester
Student/faculty ratio	17:1
Profs interesting rating	84
Profs accessible rating	88
Most classes have	20–29 students
Most lab/discussion sessions have	20–29 students

MOST POPULAR MAJORS

biology/biological sciences; business administration and management; English language and literature

APPLICANTS ALSO LOOK AT AND OFTEN PREFER

University of Missouri, Saint Louis University, Missouri State University

AND SOMETIMES PREFER

Washington University in St. Louis

AND RARELY PREFER

Illinois State University, Illinois Wesleyan University, University of Iowa

STUDENTS SAY ". . ."

Academics

If you are looking for "value," check out Truman State University. "Few schools can provide a similar undergraduate experience at a comparable price." Most current students were hard-pressed to find a better deal than they got at this "highly regarded," "very affordable" school located in Kirksville, Missouri. A high percentage of students receive financial aid and/or scholarships making Truman State "far more affordable than other institutions." One out-of-state student who experienced this firsthand says, "It was far cheaper for me to go to Truman than to any of the schools in my own state or to any private school to which I applied. Between Truman scholarships and private scholarships, I'm basically being paid to go here. My friends from high school are already panicking about how they're going to pay off their loans, and knowing I'm graduating debt-free is the best feeling in the world." Students do not appear to be sacrificing quality for a cheaper education. They say professors "really push you to work hard." They are all "very qualified," and students say, "Grades actually reflect the student's qualifications." Small class sizes enable "fantastic one-on-one experience between professors and students." "The faculty care way more about teaching than about their own research or interests." Classes are "small and engaging," and "Nearly all [professors] are available beyond their scheduled office hours and do their best to make sure we understand material." Students did also mention that there seems to be a lack of funding recently and that "some majors seem short-staffed." "Truman could improve by offering more classes and hiring more professors in order to decrease the congestion in classrooms for the more popular courses." One student sums up why this school was a good choice: "I wanted a college where I could be academically challenged as well as actively involved in [extracurricular] activities. I wanted to be surrounded by intellectually stimulating peers and professors in order to gain a comprehensive liberal arts education. I found all of this at Truman and saved a significant amount of money in the process." Another student is concerned that "Truman is a small school and is not easily recognized on a national scale. In the post-graduation job search, this fact could become very frustrating."

Life

"College life is hectic and amazing all at the same time." "Truman is an academically challenging school, so separating your school time and social life is an important task that we need to learn." The school's "very pretty" campus might be "in the middle of nowhere," but Truman brings "tons of really great activities, shows, bands, etc., to campus to keep us entertained." "Kirksville is not a big town," and homework consumes much of a student's day. Still, "There is always time to have a social life though. Hanging out with friends and just watching a movie or going out to [see] a comedian or performance on campus are viable options on any given weekend. A social life is just something that you have to plan for rather than something that is just given to you." "On the weekends, students usually go out to parties. The students who do not party will go to events on campus or hang out with friends in the dorms." Students are pleased with facilities, including "newly renovated" dorms, and the "library is excellent." "Also, the atmosphere on campus is very safe and welcoming." However, administrative services sometimes make life difficult. "A lot of the offices (financial aid, study abroad, registrar, etc.) are extremely disorganized."

Student Body

Students coined the "term T.T.S. (Typical Truman Student)…to describe academically focused, very studious students." This is reflected in classrooms where "teachers barely ever take attendance because people go to class." That term seems to fit most, but definitely not everyone on campus. Students point out, "People definitely party, somewhat during the week, and a lot on the weekends, especially if they're involved in a sorority/fraternity." Truman is not an overly diverse campus, but classmates are "accepting of others." A student says, "It is not hard to fit in at this school. Every single person I have met brings something unique to this institution."

FINANCIAL AID: 660-785-4130 • E-MAIL: ADMISSIONS@TRUMAN.EDU • WEBSITE: WWW.TRUMAN.EDU

THE PRINCETON REVIEW SAYS

Admissions

Very important factors considered include: Class rank, academic GPA, rigor of secondary school record, standardized test scores. *Important factors considered include:* application essay. *Other factors considered include:* Recommendation(s), alumni/ae relation, character/personal qualities, extracurricular activities, first generation, geographical residence, racial/ethnic status, state residency, talent/ability, volunteer work, work experience. SAT or ACT required; ACT with or without writing component accepted. TOEFL required of all international applicants. High school diploma is required and GED is accepted. *Academic units required:* 4 English, 3 mathematics, 3 science (1 science lab), 2 foreign language, 2 social studies, 1 history, 1 visual/performing arts. *Academic units recommended:* 4 mathematics (2 science labs).

Financial Aid

Students should submit: FAFSA, institution's own financial aid form. The Princeton Review suggests that all financial aid forms be submitted as soon as possible after January 1. *Need-based scholarships/grants offered:* Federal Pell, SEOG, state scholarships/grants, private scholarships, the school's own gift aid, Federal ACG, SMART and TEACH Grants. *Loan aid offered:* Direct Subsidized Stafford, Direct Unsubsidized Stafford, Direct PLUS, Federal Perkins, Federal Nursing, college/university loans from institutional funds, alternative loans. Applicants will be notified of awards on a rolling basis beginning March 1. Federal Work-Study Program available. Institutional employment available. Highest amount earned per year from on-campus jobs $4,208. Off-campus job opportunities are good.

The Inside Word

Those interested in studying at Truman State had better get to work; the school places a large emphasis on GPA, class rank, and academic rigor. The selectivity and quality of education numbers are high, but annual tuition is low for all students. Although early application has no bearing on admission, greatest scholarship consideration is given to those who apply early.

THE SCHOOL SAYS ". . ."

From the Admissions Office

"Truman's talented student body enjoys small classes where undergraduate research and personal interaction with professors are the norm. Truman's commitment to providing an exemplary liberal arts and sciences education with outstanding internship and study abroad opportunities allows students to attend top graduate schools and have great job prospects.

"Truman is recognized consistently as one of the nation's "Best Values" in higher education. The University offers a variety of competitive scholarships, and there is no separate scholarship application. Students wishing to be considered for all scholarship programs are strongly encouraged to apply for admission by December 1.

"Students applying to Truman State University can submit scores from both the ACT and the SAT. The best composite score from either test will be considered in admission and scholarship selection. The writing section is not currently required for admission to Truman. Admission requirements are selective and there is no application fee."

"At Truman, we believe a quality college experience does not stop at the classroom door. It should permeate the entire campus, offering opportunities that entertain, pique students' interest, and invite them to fully embrace this extraordinary journey. It is about making great friends, getting involved in one of over 250 student organizations, exploring the amazing world that surrounds them and creating memories that will last a lifetime. This is a university that transforms lives. Truman's success as one of the nation's premier public liberal arts and sciences institutions can be traced to one guiding principle: an unwavering commitment to the undergraduate student."

SELECTIVITY	
Admissions Rating	**88**
# of applicants	4,569
% of applicants accepted	75
% of acceptees attending	40
FRESHMAN PROFILE	
Range SAT Critical Reading	553–628
Range SAT Math	563–648
Range ACT Composite	25–30
Minimum paper TOEFL	550
Minimum web-based TOEFL	79
Average HS GPA	3.76
% graduated top 10% of class	49
% graduated top 25% of class	82
% graduated top 50% of class	98
DEADLINES	
Regular	
Priority	12/1
Nonfall registration?	yes
FINANCIAL FACTS	
Financial Aid Rating	**87**
Annual in-state tuition	$6,772
Annual out-state tuition	$12,316
Room and board	$7,254
Required fees	$240
Books and supplies	$1,000
% needy frosh rec. need-based scholarship or grant aid	98
% needy UG rec. need-based scholarship or grant aid	89
% needy frosh rec. non-need-based scholarship or grant aid	93
% needy UG rec. non-need-based scholarship or grant aid	78
% needy frosh rec. need-based self-help aid	70
% needy UG rec. need-based self-help aid	79
% frosh rec. any financial aid	98
% UG rec. any financial aid	91
% UG borrow to pay for school	54
Average cumulative indebtedness	$20,777
% frosh need fully met	43
% ugrads need fully met	36
Average % of frosh need met	87
Average % of ugrad need met	85

TUFTS UNIVERSITY

BENDETSON HALL, MEDFORD, MA 02155 • ADMISSIONS: 617-627-3170 • FAX: 617-627-3860

CAMPUS LIFE

Quality of Life Rating	**95**
Fire Safety Rating	**91**
Green Rating	**84**
Type of school	private
Environment	town

STUDENTS

Total undergrad enrollment	5,187
% male/female	49/51
% from out of state	79
% from public high school	59
# of fraternities	11
# of sororities	3
% African American	5
% Asian	11
% Caucasian	57
% Hispanic	6
% international	6
# of countries represented	93

SURVEY SAYS . . .

Great computer facilities
Great food on campus
Great off-campus food
Campus feels safe
Student publications are popular
Political activism is popular
Students are environmentally aware

ACADEMICS

Academic Rating	**91**
% students returning for sophomore year	97
% students graduating within 4 years	86
% students graduating within 6 years	91
Calendar	semester
Student/faculty ratio	9:1
Profs interesting rating	87
Profs accessible rating	86
Most classes have	10–19 students
Most lab/discussion sessions have	10–19 students

MOST POPULAR MAJORS

economics; English language and literature; international relations and affairs

STUDENTS SAY ". . ."

Academics

"Mid-sized" and "very internationally focused," Tufts University boasts "an incredible blend of academics, extracurriculars, and athletics, and really emphasizes the impact an individual can have on his or her community." Tufts is probably best known for its world-class science programs (especially pre-med) and its prestigious international relations programs. Full-year and semester-long study abroad options in places such as Chile, Ghana, and Oxford are so amazing that almost half the students here participate before heading off into the real-world. Back on campus, students have a lot of latitude in their studies: "They do internships; they devise their own research projects; they assist professors on their work." Most faculty members are "brilliant," "dedicated to students," and "extremely accessible and friendly." A few, however, are "out of touch with reality." Classes, especially at the lower levels, can be "bigger than you think they'll be." The academic atmosphere is tough overall but it really varies by department. "Some classes are disproportionately easy, while others are disproportionately hard." "If you're premed, life is going to be miserable," warns a biomedical engineering major. "If you're an English or psych major, there are great professors in those departments and the majors are cake." "[In] some classes, you're forced to learn a lot," adds a computer science major. "[In others] you need to do a lot of the learning yourself." The administration at Tufts is "always there when you want them," but is otherwise "neither awful nor particularly noteworthy." "Some things could be smoother, but that is true almost everywhere."

Life

This "beautiful" campus offers a "great view of Boston" but some of the facilities "are not outstanding." Dorms in particular "can be a little gross." "Rooms are on the small side and the common areas are really subpar." Social life at Tufts can be "as big or small" as you want it to be. "Everyone loves to meet up in the dining halls and socialize," and "There is always so much going on around campus." "Fantastic extracurricular opportunities" proliferate. "Everyone is involved in something." "I ride on the equestrian team and I'm a member of the classics and archaeology club," declares a sophomore. Tufts also "holds a few social events each semester that most of the student body attends, which is a lot of fun." Students tend to "work hard" and stay "very focused on studying" during the week. They also "love to be ridiculous" on weekends. While "non-drinkers and moderate drinkers will be comfortable here," "alcoholic partygoers" will be happy, too. "There's kind of an expectation during freshman year that you go to fraternities on the weekend and get drunk." Older students "tend to be a little choosier and will have more exclusive off-campus gatherings or go to the bars." "Going into Boston is always really fun" as well. Beantown is "a city full of opportunity and entertainment." Tufts runs a shuttle to public transportation in Somerville.

Student Body

Students say this campus is a paradise of "cosmopolitanism and ethnic tolerance." Students at Tufts range from "preppy North Face and Ugg wearers, to hipsters," to "self-aware dorky" types. "There are a lot of nerdy kids but it's great for them because they come here and find each other." "There are also a lot of international kids, which is great." Tufts students describe themselves as "generally very hardworking," "intellectually stimulating people." They're also "very real and unpretentious" and "very eclectic." "To be eccentrically passionate about something is absolutely necessary" here. "Some people are a little strange, but Tufts is known for that." "I have never met an unquirky person associated with Tufts," swears a senior.

FINANCIAL AID: 617-627-2000 • E-MAIL: ADMISSIONS.INQUIRY@ASE.TUFTS.EDU • WEBSITE: WWW.TUFTS.EDU

THE PRINCETON REVIEW SAYS

Admissions

Very important factors considered include: Application essay, academic GPA, rigor of secondary school record, character/personal qualities. *Important factors considered include:* Class rank, recommendation(s), standardized test scores, extracurricular activities, talent/ability, volunteer work, work experience. *Other factors considered include:* Alumni/ae relation, first generation, geographical residence, interview, racial/ethnic status. ACT with writing component required. TOEFL required of all international applicants. High school diploma is required and GED is accepted. *Academic units recommended:* 4 English, 4 mathematics, 4 science, 4 foreign language, 4 social studies, 4 history.

Financial Aid

Students should submit: FAFSA, CSS/Financial Aid PROFILE, noncustodial PROFILE, parent and student federal income tax returns. Regular filing deadline is February 15. The Princeton Review suggests that all financial aid forms be submitted as soon as possible after January 1. *Need-based scholarships/grants offered:* Federal Pell, SEOG, state scholarships/grants, the school's own gift aid. *Loan aid offered:* Direct Subsidized Stafford, Direct Unsubsidized Stafford, Federal Perkins, college/university loans from institutional funds. Applicants will be notified of awards on or about April 1. Federal Work-Study Program available. Institutional employment available. Off-campus job opportunities are good.

The Inside Word

The admissions process is rigorous. Tufts rejects more than seventy-five percent of its applicants. You'll need to demonstrate fairly exceptional academic accomplishments and submit a thorough and well-prepared application to get admitted. On the bright side, Tufts is still a little bit of a safety school for aspiring Ivy Leaguers. Since many applicants will also get into an Ivy League school and will likely pass on Tufts, it has spots for "mere mortals" at the end of the day.

THE SCHOOL SAYS ". . ."

From the Admissions Office

"Tufts University, on the boundary between Medford and Somerville, sits on a hill overlooking Boston, five miles northwest of the city. The campus is a tranquil New England setting within easy access by subway and bus to the cultural, social, and entertainment resources of Boston and Somerville. Since its founding in 1852 by members of the Universalist church, Tufts has grown from a small liberal arts college into a nonsectarian university of more than 10,000 students with undergraduate programs in arts and sciences and engineering. By 1900 the college had added a medical school, a dental school, and graduate studies. The university now also includes the Fletcher School of Law and Diplomacy, the Graduate School of Arts & Sciences, the Cummings School of Veterinary Medicine, the Friedman School of Nutrition Science and Policy, the Sackler School of Graduate Biomedical Sciences, and the Gordon Institute of Engineering Management.

"Applicants are required to submit scores (including the writing assessment) from either the SAT or ACT. If an applicant submits the SAT, SAT Subject Tests are also required (candidates for the School of Engineering are encouraged to submit math and either chemistry or physics)."

SELECTIVITY	
Admissions Rating	**98**
# of applicants	12,130
% of applicants accepted	22
% of acceptees attending	35
FRESHMAN PROFILE	
Range SAT Critical Reading	680–740
Range SAT Math	680–760
Range SAT Writing	680–760
Range ACT Composite	30–33
Minimum paper TOEFL	600
% graduated top 10% of class	89
% graduated top 25% of class	99
% graduated top 50% of class	100
DEADLINES	
Early decision	
Deadline	11/1
Notification	12/15
Regular	
Deadline	1/1
Notification	4/1
Nonfall registration?	no
FINANCIAL FACTS	
Financial Aid Rating	**94**
Annual tuition	$41,998
Room and board	$11,512
Required fees	$964
Books and supplies	$800
% needy frosh rec. need-based scholarship or grant aid	93
% needy UG rec. need-based scholarship or grant aid	91
% needy frosh rec. non-need-based scholarship or grant aid	3
% needy UG rec. non-need-based scholarship or grant aid	2
% needy frosh rec. need-based self-help aid	90
% needy UG rec. need-based self-help aid	92
% frosh rec. any financial aid	43
% UG rec. any financial aid	40
% UG borrow to pay for school	41
Average cumulative indebtedness	$24,468
% frosh need fully met	100
% ugrads need fully met	98
Average % of frosh need met	100
Average % of ugrad need met	100

TULANE UNIVERSITY

6823 St. Charles Avenue, New Orleans, LA 70118 • Admissions: 504-865-5260 • Fax: 504-862-8715

CAMPUS LIFE

Quality of Life Rating	**97**
Fire Safety Rating	**84**
Green Rating	**89**
Type of school	private
Environment	city

STUDENTS

Total undergrad enrollment	8,271
% male/female	42/58
% from out of state	86
% frosh live on campus	98
# of fraternities	15
# of sororities	11
% African American	8
% Asian	4
% Caucasian	67
% Hispanic	4
% international	3
# of countries represented	37

SURVEY SAYS . . .

Athletic facilities are great
Students love New Orleans, LA
Great off-campus food
Students are happy
Lots of beer drinking
Hard liquor is popular
Students are involved in community service

ACADEMICS

Academic Rating	**91**
% students returning for sophomore year	90
Calendar	semester
Student/faculty ratio	11:1
Profs interesting rating	86
Profs accessible rating	91
Most classes have	10–19 students

MOST POPULAR MAJORS

business/commerce; health services/allied health/health sciences; psychology

APPLICANTS ALSO LOOK AT AND RARELY PREFER

Skidmore College, Southern Methodist University, University of Richmond

STUDENTS SAY "..."

Academics

"Medium-sized" Tulane University is "small enough for individual attention but big enough that you don't know everybody." Students call Tulane "the perfect mix between top-fifty private college and party school." Its business school is nationally renowned, and a wealth of international programs provide opportunities to study abroad in more than forty countries. "Academics are rigorous but rewarding." "By no means is it a school for slackers," cautions a marketing major. "It's a challenging school," agrees an art major, "but not challenging to the point of mental insanity." Professors here are "really smart and even pretty funny." They "care a ton" and they're "extremely personable and easy to talk to." "Due to our small class sizes, individual attention is incredibly realistic," adds a neuroscience major. "Most professors know your name and who you are. Even intro classes have, at most, like eighty kids, and even then, there are smaller labs." The general sentiment is that Tulane's "visible" and "very accessible" administration "works hard to treat each student as an individual rather than a number."

Life

"Club and intramural sports are very popular" on this "absolutely beautiful campus." "Greek life is here, but it's not a huge deal." The administration works hard to provide alcohol-free events. Students say these events are "actually very fun," but that drinking, or at least being around drinking, is "inevitable" at Tulane. "Going out is part of the social culture," relates a senior. "Students embrace it." They "take full advantage of the party scene in New Orleans, a city where bars don't close and where Mardi Gras is a huge party in the spring semester." At the same time, you won't last long if you don't hit the books. "Tulane is about balance." Success "necessitates a large amount of self-control and willpower." "While the school has a reputation as a party school, it's more of a school in a party city," explains a sophomore. "Most people think we spend all our time on Bourbon Street, but [it's]...usually only reserved for twenty-first birthdays and a quick visit when friends from other colleges visit." "Laid-back, fun-loving," "thrilling," and "practically lawless," New Orleans is "the most incredible city in the world," though, and a fabulous asset. "There is always an amazing concert or festival going on." "New Orleans is abundant in culture and [offers] a surprise at every turn," and it's "very much an outdoors city because of the weather." You can explore "great historical restaurants and antique stores" or just "listen to a jazz band while eating a beignet, looking out onto the Mississippi River."

Student Body

Students describe themselves as "independent and confident," "happy kids" who "are academics-focused and want to get a good education while having a good time." "Everyone is very smart but a kind of cool smart," claims a junior. "The typical Tulane student is what I call a closet nerd," adds a sophomore. "Basically, you see them having fun and it looks like they never do work. But the truth is that they study way more than you think." While "Tulane could use a little more racial diversity," the population is very "geographically diverse." "There are large Jewish and Catholic populations. Many students are from the Northeast, Florida, Texas, and California." "There are a lot of wealthy kids here but there are also a lot of hardworking kids on scholarship." "People do dress well," notes a senior. "Sorority girls with their leggings" and guys with "gelled hair" certainly aren't uncommon. "You can wear whatever you want," but you'll fit in best if your attire is "kind of preppy." "We don't have so many artsy kids or crazy, pink-haired nonconformists," says a sophomore.

FINANCIAL AID: 504-865-5723 • E-MAIL: UNDERGRAD.ADMISSION@TULANE.EDU • WEBSITE: WWW.TULANE.EDU

THE PRINCETON REVIEW SAYS

Admissions

Very important factors considered include: Class rank, academic GPA, rigor of secondary school record, standardized test scores. *Important factors considered include:* Application essay, recommendation(s), character/personal qualities. *Other factors considered include:* Alumni/ae relation, extracurricular activities, first generation, interview, talent/ability, volunteer work, work experience. SAT or ACT required; ACT with writing component recommended. TOEFL required of all international applicants. High school diploma is required and GED is accepted. *Academic units recommended:* 4 English, 4 mathematics, 4 science (4 science labs), 3 foreign language, 3 social studies, 3 academic electives.

Financial Aid

Students should submit: FAFSA, CSS/Financial Aid PROFILE, noncustodial PROFILE, business/farm supplement. Regular filing deadline is February 15. The Princeton Review suggests that all financial aid forms be submitted as soon as possible after January 1. *Need-based scholarships/grants offered:* Federal Pell, SEOG, state scholarships/grants, private scholarships, the school's own gift aid, Academic Competitiveness Grant, SMART Grant. *Loan aid offered:* Direct Subsidized Stafford, Direct Unsubsidized Stafford, Direct PLUS, Federal Perkins. Applicants will be notified of awards on a rolling basis beginning March 15. Federal Work-Study Program available. Institutional employment available. Highest amount earned per year from on-campus jobs $2,500. Off-campus job opportunities are good.

The Inside Word

Students come to Tulane from all over the country, and admission is very competitive. Serious candidates need an excellent record of academic achievement. On the plus side, Tulane is perpetually on the cusp of truly elite college and universities, and it has to fight to get its share of ultra-accomplished students. If you're one of them, your financial aid package will likely be extremely generous.

THE SCHOOL SAYS ". . ."

From the Admissions Office

"More than 6,700 full-time undergraduate students in five schools, Tulane University offers the personal attention and teaching excellence traditionally associated with small colleges together with the facilities and interdisciplinary resources found only at major research universities. Following Hurricane Katrina, the university underwent a spectacular renewal: renovating facilities and restructuring academic programs. The opportunities for students to be involved in the rebirth of New Orleans offer an experience unavailable at any other place, at any other time.

"Tulane is committed to undergraduate education. Senior faculty members teach most introductory and lower-level courses, and most classes have twenty-five or fewer students. The close student-teacher relationship pays off. Tulane graduates are among the most likely to be selected for several prestigious fellowships that support graduate study abroad. Founded in 1834 and reorganized as Tulane University in 1884, Tulane is one of the major private research universities in the South.

"The Tulane campus offers a traditional collegiate setting in an attractive residential neighborhood, which is now thriving after Hurricane Katrina."

SELECTIVITY	
Admissions Rating	**97**
# of applicants	37,767
% of applicants accepted	25
% of acceptees attending	17
# accepting a place on wait list	3,745
# admitted from wait list	15

FRESHMAN PROFILE	
Range SAT Critical Reading	620–710
Range SAT Math	620–700
Range SAT Writing	640–720
Range ACT Composite	29–32
Minimum paper TOEFL	550
Average HS GPA	3.6
% graduated top 10% of class	59
% graduated top 25% of class	86
% graduated top 50% of class	98

DEADLINES	
Early action	
Deadline	11/15
Notification	12/15
Regular	
Deadline	1/15
Notification	4/1
Nonfall registration?	yes

FINANCIAL FACTS	
Financial Aid Rating	**90**
Annual tuition	$39,850
Room and board	$10,850
Required fees	$3,584
Books and supplies	$1,200
% needy frosh rec. need-based scholarship or grant aid	99
% needy UG rec. need-based scholarship or grant aid	98
% needy frosh rec. non-need-based scholarship or grant aid	34
% needy UG rec. non-need-based scholarship or grant aid	29
% needy frosh rec. need-based self-help aid	61
% needy UG rec. need-based self-help aid	64
% UG borrow to pay for school	48
Average cumulative indebtedness	$31,172
% frosh need fully met	61
% ugrads need fully met	53
Average % of frosh need met	92
Average % of ugrad need met	89

TUSKEGEE UNIVERSITY

OLD ADMINISTRATION BUILDING, TUSKEGEE, AL 36088 • ADMISSIONS: 334-727-8500 • FAX: 334-727-5750

CAMPUS LIFE

Quality of Life Rating	65
Fire Safety Rating	80
Green Rating	77
Type of school	private
Environment	rural

STUDENTS

Total undergrad enrollment	2,684
% male/female	43/57
% from out of state	67
% frosh live on campus	98
# of fraternities	5
# of sororities	6
% African American	87
% international	1
# of countries represented	19

SURVEY SAYS . . .

Registration is a pain
Students are friendly
Students don't like Tuskegee, AL
Low cost of living
Everyone loves the Golden Tigers
Frats and sororities dominate social scene
Musical organizations are popular
Student government is popular
Hard liquor is popular

ACADEMICS

Academic Rating	66
% students returning for sophomore year	74
% students graduating within 4 years	17
Calendar	semester
Student/faculty ratio	12:1
Profs interesting rating	66
Profs accessible rating	67
Most classes have	10–19 students

MOST POPULAR MAJORS

electrical, electronics and communications engineering; veterinary medicine (dvm)

APPLICANTS ALSO LOOK AT AND RARELY PREFER

University of Alabama—Tuscaloosa, Auburn University

STUDENTS SAY ". . ."

Academics

For the past 131 years, Tuskegee University has strived to continue the legacy of higher learning created by Booker T. Washington and upheld by its other notable presidents and benefactors. The "rich history" of the school has always been about "achieving the…highest level of performance" in all areas of service, leadership, and academics, and everyone in the community works to ensure that "the Tuskegee Experience is like none other." The veterinary and engineering schools are standouts here, but the school can transform any individual into a leader. "Tuskegee, figuratively speaking, is often given coal, and it *always* produces diamonds," says one student. Academics are "a top priority" for Tuskegee, and the classes and structure are designed to "effectively nurture students' academic, social, and professional potentials and produce great leaders in society." "School is about gaining independence and responsibility so that you will be able to grow and compete in the real world." Small classes and personal interaction with professors help further this process along, and the school aims for "excellence within every aspect of education offered at the institution." "My professors don't teach because it's their job, they do it because they care and want you to learn and succeed. It's very obvious," says one student. Though the alumni network is positively rock solid, and fundraising isn't a problem, some students question the allocation of funds. Many agree that "the development of new facilities/buildings around the campus" is a sore spot, and though the administration is in the process of updating some, "there is a lot of work to be done," particularly in the student housing arena.

Life

The heritage of Tuskegee is felt in every step; "We literally walk on historic grounds," says a student of going to school on the only college or university campus in the nation to be designated a National Historic Site by Congress. The traditional festivities the school usually hosts are "quite enjoyable," and the school is in a "very quaint" town, which "allows for constant interaction among students on campus to occur." When there is nothing to do in Tuskegee, students usually go to Auburn, Montgomery, or even Atlanta. TU is for "academically inclined individuals," but when the books do shut, most people "go to the local clubs (The Soul Inn or Club Extreme)," or hangout at houses off campus. "Home football and basketball games are usually really fun," as well. "Even though people are serious about their work and classes, we all know how to have fun," says one student. "We're a school of weekend warriors." "It can be raining cats and dogs…and you will still see people going to class, or if it's the weekend you will see students going to a party."

Student Body

At this go-getter university, the typical student here is "someone who is driven to becoming successful in the future through studious methods." Though this HBCU is naturally predominantly black, there is much diversity in that "people from all across the country come to school in this small city in Alabama." Most students here are "very outspoken and easy to work with" and "open to meeting and interacting with new people"; with students from all over the world, "The diverse environment helps keep the campus from getting too dull."

FINANCIAL AID: 334-727-8500 • E-MAIL: ADMISSIONS@TUSKEGEE.EDU • WEBSITE: WWW.TUSKEGEE.EDU

THE PRINCETON REVIEW SAYS

Admissions

Very important factors considered include: Class rank, academic GPA, recommendation(s), rigor of secondary school record, standardized test scores, talent/ability. *Important factors considered include:* Alumni/ae relation, character/personal qualities. *Other factors considered include:* Application essay, extracurricular activities, first generation, geographical residence, interview, state residency, volunteer work, work experience. SAT or ACT required; TOEFL required of all international applicants. High school diploma is required and GED is accepted. *Academic units required:* 4 English, 3 mathematics, 2 science, 3 social studies, 4 academic electives.

Financial Aid

Students should submit: FAFSA, institution's own financial aid form, CSS/ Financial Aid PROFILE. The Princeton Review suggests that all financial aid forms be submitted as soon as possible after January 1. *Need-based scholarships/ grants offered:* Federal Pell, SEOG, state scholarships/grants, private scholarships, the school's own gift aid, United Negro College Fund, Federal Nursing Scholarships. *Loan aid offered:* Direct Subsidized Stafford, Direct Unsubsidized Stafford, Direct PLUS, Federal Perkins, Federal Nursing, state loans, college/ university loans from institutional funds. Federal Work-Study Program available. Institutional employment available. Highest amount earned per year from on-campus jobs $1,540. Off-campus job opportunities are good.

The Inside Word

Tuskegee presents its students with a myriad of opportunities for discovery and research. Therefore, Tuskegee seeks applicants who have proven themselves successful in the classroom. Admissions counselors consider each application holistically and individually. What they really like to see, though, is a GPA of at least 3.0 and a composite ACT score of 21 or better. Note also that requirements for the nursing and engineering programs are more stringent. For example, you'll probably need four years of high school math if you want to major in engineering here. Prospective students interested in either field should investigate the specific criteria.

THE SCHOOL SAYS ". . ."

From the Admissions Office

"Tuskegee University, located in south central Alabama, was founded in 1881 under the dynamic and creative leadership of Booker T. Washington. As a state-related, independent institution, Tuskegee offers undergraduate and graduate degrees through five colleges and two schools: the College of Agriculture, Environment and Nutrition Sciences; the Brimmer College of Business and Information Sciences; the College of Engineering; the College of Veterinary Medicine, Nursing and Allied Health; the Taylor School of Architecture and Construction Science; and the School of Education. Substantial research and service programs make Tuskegee University an effective comprehensive institution geared toward preparing tomorrow's leaders today."

"First-year applicants must take the SAT or ACT; the SAT is preferred. International applicants must complete the TOEFL. Nursing applicants must complete the National Nursing exam."

SELECTIVITY	
Admissions Rating	**78**
# of applicants	2,471
% of applicants accepted	64
% of acceptees attending	44

FRESHMAN PROFILE	
Range SAT Critical Reading	400–500
Range SAT Math	398–490
Range ACT Composite	17–22
Minimum paper TOEFL	500
Average HS GPA	3.1
% graduated top 10% of class	20
% graduated top 25% of class	59
% graduated top 50% of class	100

DEADLINES	
Regular	
Priority	3/31
Deadline	7/15
Notification	3/15
Nonfall registration?	yes

FINANCIAL FACTS	
Financial Aid Rating	**80**
Annual tuition	$17,070
Room and board	$7,950
Required fees	$800
Books and supplies	$1,109
% needy frosh rec. need-based scholarship or grant aid	84
% needy UG rec. need-based scholarship or grant aid	86
% needy frosh rec. non-need-based scholarship or grant aid	47
% needy UG rec. non-need-based scholarship or grant aid	41
% needy frosh rec. need-based self-help aid	49
% needy UG rec. need-based self-help aid	53
% frosh rec. any financial aid	80
% UG rec. any financial aid	92
% UG borrow to pay for school	91
Average cumulative indebtedness	$23,000
% frosh need fully met	48
% ugrads need fully met	61
Average % of frosh need met	75
Average % of ugrad need met	75

UNION COLLEGE (NY)

GRANT HALL, SCHENECTADY, NY 12308 • ADMISSIONS: 518-388-6112 • FAX: 518-388-6986

CAMPUS LIFE

Quality of Life Rating	72
Fire Safety Rating	85
Green Rating	89
Type of school	private
Environment	town

STUDENTS

Total undergrad enrollment	2,174
% male/female	53/47
% from out of state	58
% from public high school	63
% frosh live on campus	100
# of fraternities	12
# of sororities	6
% African American	5
% Asian	6
% Caucasian	77
% Hispanic	6
% international	5
# of countries represented	39

SURVEY SAYS . . .

Athletic facilities are great
Frats and sororities dominate social scene
Lots of beer drinking
Hard liquor is popular

ACADEMICS

Academic Rating	92
% students returning for sophomore year	94
% students graduating within 4 years	78
% students graduating within 6 years	86
Calendar	semester
Student/faculty ratio	10:1
Profs interesting rating	92
Profs accessible rating	93
Most classes have	10–19 students
Most lab/discussion sessions have	10–19 students

MOST POPULAR MAJORS

economics; English language and literature; political science and government

APPLICANTS ALSO LOOK AT AND OFTEN PREFER

Colgate University, Cornell University, Tufts University

AND SOMETIMES PREFER

Hamilton College, Skidmore College, Lehigh University

AND RARELY PREFER

University of Rochester, Syracuse University, Hobart and William Smith Colleges

STUDENTS SAY ". . ."

Academics

At Union College, challenging academic programs, friendly faculty, and diverse co-curricular experiences are all rolled up into one pretty little campus in upstate New York. Union "is small in size, yet prestigious in nearly every major it offers," making it a good choice for students interested in anything from the arts to engineering—or both! Here, "Students are encouraged to follow their passions and pursue all areas of interest." A current student chimes in, "As an engineering major, I am able to take courses that I would not normally take at a technical school, making the 'gen eds' [general education requirements] and electives enjoyable." In addition to diverse courses, "Union has fantastic research opportunities for undergraduate students (especially in the sciences)," and more than half the campus pursues studies or volunteer work overseas. Internships are also popular, and "Union has an awesome career center that is always reaching out to students to help them with life after college." Across disciplines, "Professors are wonderful, extremely qualified, compassionate, and interested in their students." Teaching is taken seriously, and "All of the professors do everything possible to engage their students and get discussions going." Relationships between students and faculty often extend beyond the classroom, and "Professors can often be seen sitting with students at lunch, literally bringing the classroom discussion into the lunchroom." You must be prepared to work at Union, as academic standards are high. Fortunately, most students feel "the workload is very manageable as long as you don't fall behind," not to mention "the rewards that come of those challenges make all the effort completely worthwhile." As a small private school, all of this doesn't come cheap, but "Union College is very generous with its financial aid and scholarship money" for qualified students.

Life

There are just 2,000 undergraduates at Union College, yet "There are always a million things to do" on the Union campus. During the week, "The homework load is pretty heavy," but come the weekend, Union students "like to go to a few off-campus bars on Wednesday nights and Thursday nights," while "Friday and Saturday are dominated by Greek life." For an alternative to parties, "Student activities and Minerva houses provide many nonalcohol[ic] events," including concerts and speakers. Union students can also be found going to "campus movie [screenings], going to [hear] a speaker, [attending] a hockey game, running around campus…going downtown for a bite to eat." School spirit is healthy, and "In the winter, our [Division I] hockey team's home games are the place to be." Hometown Schenectady draws few praises, and students would like to see the school promote "more involvement in the local community." For a break from campus life, "Some of the clubs on campus also organize ski trips or trips out of town such as to Montreal and New York City."

Student Body

On Union's small campus, "Students are always moving, always involved, always engaged," and most participate in "at least three organizations or clubs" on campus. Bright and motivated, students "are able to easily manage personal and professional time," and the typical student manages to "get great grades while volunteering and balancing a busy schedule." Located in upstate New York, this school draws a lot of students from the Northeast, and "the typical student is Caucasian, middle to upper-class, [and] from a private school or highly regarded public school." However, the student population is evolving, and "The college is clearly becoming more diverse, with more international and underrepresented student populations increasing by the year." Socially, "everyone seems to find their niche." In addition to the visible preppy contingent, "There is also a pretty strong indie scene that tends to be more involved in environmental awareness, community service, and the arts." In addition, "There are a lot of athletes."

FINANCIAL AID: 518-388-6123 • E-MAIL: ADMISSIONS@UNION.EDU • WEBSITE: WWW.UNION.EDU

THE PRINCETON REVIEW SAYS

Admissions

Very important factors considered include: Class rank, academic GPA, rigor of secondary school record, *Important factors considered include:* Recommendation(s), standardized test scores, character/personal qualities, extracurricular activities, talent/ability. *Other factors considered include:* Application essay, alumni/ae relation, first generation, geographical residence, interview, level of applicant's interest, racial/ethnic status, state residency, volunteer work, work experience. ACT with or without writing component accepted. TOEFL required of all international applicants. High school diploma is required and GED is not accepted. *Academic units required:* 4 English, 3 mathematics, 2 science (2 science labs), 2 foreign language, 1 social studies, 1 history. *Academic units recommended:* 4 English, 4 mathematics, 4 science (4 science labs), 4 foreign language, 2 social studies, 2 history.

Financial Aid

Students should submit: FAFSA, CSS/Financial Aid PROFILE, state aid form, noncustodial PROFILE, business/farm supplement. Regular filing deadline is February 1. The Princeton Review suggests that all financial aid forms be submitted as soon as possible after January 1. *Need-based scholarships/grants offered:* Federal Pell, SEOG, state scholarships/grants, private scholarships, the school's own gift aid. *Loan aid offered:* Direct Subsidized Stafford, Direct Unsubsidized Stafford, Direct PLUS, Federal Perkins, college/university loans from institutional funds. Federal Work-Study Program available. Institutional employment available. Highest amount earned per year from on-campus jobs $3,800. Off-campus job opportunities are good.

The Inside Word

Union College is an SAT-optional college. Students may simply indicate on their application if they would like the admissions committee to consider their test scores or not. However, applicants to the Leadership in Medicine Program (an eight-year MD/MBA program with Albany Medical College) and to the Law and Public Policy program (a combined BA and JD) must submit test scores for consideration. For students who know that Union is their first choice, the school offers two early decision deadlines.

THE SCHOOL SAYS ". . ."

From the Admissions Office

"The Union academic program is characterized by breadth and flexibility across a range of disciplines and interdisciplinary programs in the liberal arts and engineering. With nearly 1,000 courses to choose from, Union students may major in a single field, combine work in two or more departments or create their own organizing-theme major. Opportunities for undergraduate research are robust and give students a chance to work closely with professors year-round, take part in professional-level conferences and use sophisticated scientific equipment. More than half of Union's students take advantage of the college's extensive international study program, with new opportunities created regularly. A rich array of service learning programs and strong athletic, cultural, and social activities also enhance the overall Union experience. Union's seven student-run Minerva Houses are lively hubs for intellectual and social activities. They bring together students, faculty and staff for hundreds of events, from dinners with invited speakers, lectures, and live bands, to trips to local attractions.

"The Union community welcomes talented and diverse students, and we work closely with each one to help identify and cultivate their passions. Admission to the college is based on excellent academic credentials as reflected in the high school transcript, quality of courses selected, teacher and counselor recommendations, personal essays, and writing samples. Personal interviews are strongly recommended. All candidates who apply to Union receive a thorough and thoughtful review of their application. Submission of SAT and ACT scores is optional except for the law and medicine programs."

SELECTIVITY	
Admissions Rating	**95**
# of applicants	5,151
% of applicants accepted	43
% of acceptees attending	27
# accepting a place on wait list	908
# admitted from wait list	11
# of early decision applicants	318
# accepted early decision	242

FRESHMAN PROFILE	
Range SAT Critical Reading	590–680
Range SAT Math	610–700
Range SAT Writing	600–680
Range ACT Composite	28–31
Minimum paper TOEFL	600
Minimum web-based TOEFL	90
Average HS GPA	3.5
% graduated top 10% of class	57
% graduated top 25% of class	85
% graduated top 50% of class	98

DEADLINES	
Early decision	
Deadline	11/15
Notification	12/15
Regular	
Deadline	1/15
Notification	4/1
Nonfall registration?	yes

FINANCIAL FACTS	
Financial Aid Rating	**95**
Annual tuition	$44,478
Room and board	$11,070
Required fees	$471
Books and supplies	$542
% needy frosh rec. need-based scholarship or grant aid	94
% needy UG rec. need-based scholarship or grant aid	95
% needy frosh rec. non-need-based scholarship or grant aid	4
% needy UG rec. non-need-based scholarship or grant aid	2
% needy frosh rec. need-based self-help aid	89
% needy UG rec. need-based self-help aid	94
% frosh rec. any financial aid	76
% UG rec. any financial aid	71
% UG borrow to pay for school	66
Average cumulative indebtedness	$26,252
% frosh need fully met	99
% ugrads need fully met	97
Average % of frosh need met	100
Average % of ugrad need met	97

UNITED STATES AIR FORCE ACADEMY

HQ USAFA/RRS, USAF ACADEMY, CO 80840-5025 • ADMISSIONS: 719-333-2520 • FAX: 719-333-3012

CAMPUS LIFE

Quality of Life Rating	**78**
Fire Safety Rating	**80**
Green Rating	**80**
Type of school	public
Environment	metropolis

STUDENTS

Total undergrad enrollment	4,413
% male/female	78/22
% from out of state	93
% frosh live on campus	100
% African American	7
% Asian	7
% Caucasian	71
% Hispanic	9
% Native American	1
% international	1
# of countries represented	36

SURVEY SAYS . . .

No one cheats
Lab facilities are great
Great computer facilities
Athletic facilities are great
Career services are great
Campus feels safe
Frats and sororities are unpopular or nonexistent
Very little drug use

ACADEMICS

Academic Rating	**98**
% students returning for sophomore year	89
% students graduating within 4 years	76
% students graduating within 6 years	76
Calendar	trimester
Student/faculty ratio	8:1
Profs interesting rating	88
Profs accessible rating	96
Most classes have	10–19 students
Most lab/discussion sessions have	10–19 students

MOST POPULAR MAJORS

aerospace, aeronautical and astronautical engineering; business/commerce; social sciences

APPLICANTS ALSO LOOK AT AND SOMETIMES PREFER

United States Military Academy, United States Naval Academy, United States Coast Guard Academy, United States Merchant Marine Academy

STUDENTS SAY ". . ."

Academics

The United States Air Force Academy is "a leadership laboratory" and "an incredibly prestigious institution" that provides "rigorous academic and military training" for future Air Force officers. Students here have "the opportunity to travel the world, making a difference in lives and in history." There's military free-fall parachute training, combat survival, skydiving, internships at national labs, and, of course, the best flying programs in the solar system. Everyone leaves here with a really cool skill set. There's "free tuition," too (and a nominal monthly stipend). "Very tough" professors bring "a lot of real-world experience" and "rival those of any of the top schools in the country." "Class sizes are very small," and extra help is copious. "The teachers are always there," promises a physics major. "The professors and officers who teach classes go the extra mile to make themselves available." "If you can get in, the tools are here to help you stay." You'll "owe at least five years of service" as an active-duty officer upon graduation, though, and nothing about this place is easy. The "very broad" core curriculum is "hard and tedious" and heavy on science and engineering. "Courses and course loads are very demanding." "You have to be on top of your game 24/7," cautions a first-year cadet. "Slacking is not tolerated, and constant professionalism is the minimum standard."

Life

"The Air Force Academy will break you down mentally and physically and then build you into something greater than you ever could have imagined." Like the other military academies, though, Air Force is "better to be from than to go to." "The campus has a pretty cold, sterile feel to it." "The dining facility and food quality are not the greatest." The "stressful, time-crunched environment" "challenges each cadet academically, militarily, and athletically." In addition to tons of homework, "There is military training almost every day." Rules are "strict." There are "room inspections." There are "random urine tests." "It's really easy to get in trouble." The "grueling" first year is especially difficult. You can leave the confines of the campus only rarely. "Your life is miserable, and the upperclassmen treat you with contempt." "Every action and word is under scrutiny." Life becomes a little easier, and free time becomes somewhat more abundant, as you rise through the ranks. "Weekends offer a good time to relax or get away, provided the weekend does not include military training." "Snowboarding and skiing are very popular in the winter." Drinking simply doesn't happen on campus, but "The cadets that are of age go out drinking a lot" when they can. Some students just catch up on sleep during their free time. "USAFA has made me appreciate and enjoy doing nothing," one cadet says.

Student Body

"We are all a bunch of college kids in a very different environment," explains one cadet. "This school forces you to grow up and obtain a more mature outlook on life, yet, at the same time, the kids are normal kids who know when and how to have fun." The population at Air Force is overwhelmingly male. It's a "tight-knit community," and people tend to be "similar in beliefs and backgrounds." The military aspect limits how "atypical" anyone can really be. "You probably will not do well here" if you don't fit the mold. Cadets describe themselves as "hardworking and motivated," "fairly conservative," and "very patriotic." "The sense of pride and duty that comes from serving your country is something that you cannot explain to a civilian," one student says. They're "inventive," "studious," "physically fit," and "smart as a whip." "The typical cadet is tired of being here and wants to go home on break" as well.

E-MAIL: RR_WEBMAIL@USAFA.EDU • WEBSITE: WWW.ACADEMYADMISSIONS.COM

THE PRINCETON REVIEW SAYS

Admissions

Very important factors considered include: Class rank, application essay, academic GPA, recommendation(s), rigor of secondary school record, standardized test scores, character/personal qualities, interview. *Important factors considered include:* Extracurricular activities, talent/ability, volunteer work, work experience. *Other factors considered include:* Alumni/ae relation, first generation, geographical residence, racial/ethnic status, state residency. SAT or ACT required; ACT with writing component recommended. High school diploma is required and GED is accepted. *Academic units recommended:* 4 English, 4 mathematics, 4 science (4 science labs), 2 foreign language, 3 social studies, 3 history, 1 computer science.

Financial Aid

The Princeton Review suggests that all financial aid forms be submitted as soon as possible after January 1.

The Inside Word

The Air Force Academy promises a demanding four years, and the faint-hearted need not apply. Due to the arduous nature of the school, it's no wonder that applicants face stringent requirements right at the outset. Aside from an excellent academic record, successful candidates need to be physically fit. They also must win a nomination from their congressperson. Honor is a valued quality at the academy, and admissions officers will accept only those with the strength of character and determination necessary to succeed at one of the country's most elite institutions.

THE SCHOOL SAYS ". . ."

From the Admissions Office

"The Air Force Academy offers one of the most prestigious and respected undergraduate programs available. Each cadet completes a balanced sequence of core curriculum, which includes courses in basic sciences, engineering, humanities and social sciences. Air Force Academy graduates earn a Bachelor of Science degree from one of thirty-two majors and two minors. The academy education is tailored to develop future Air Force officers with innovative, analytical and resourceful minds. Upon graduation from the academy, one receives a commission as a second lieutenant in the United States Air Force.

"The academy's extensive athletic program includes intercollegiate or intramural sports, physical education courses, and physical fitness tests. These programs are tailored to help prepare you for Air Force leadership by building confidence, emotional control, physical courage, and the ability to perform under pressure. The twenty-seven men's and ten women's intercollegiate teams compete in the NCAA Division I and are members of the Mountain West Conference.

"The academy experience requires cadets to become active participants in leadership roles and opportunities that give a sense of honor and duty. The academy is a leadership laboratory, and our mission is to educate, train and inspire men and women to become officers of character motivated to lead the United States Air Force in service to our nation. If you choose to accept the challenges, you will be rewarded with unique experiences and opportunities incomparable to any other college experience."

SELECTIVITY	
Admissions Rating	**98**
# of applicants	12,732
% of applicants accepted	11
% of acceptees attending	82
FRESHMAN PROFILE	
Range SAT Critical Reading	590–680
Range SAT Math	630–710
Range ACT Composite	28–32
% graduated top 10% of class	55
% graduated top 25% of class	80
% graduated top 50% of class	97
DEADLINES	
Regular	
Deadline	12/31
Nonfall registration?	no
FINANCIAL FACTS	
Financial Aid Rating	**60***
Annual in-state tuition	$0
Annual out-state tuition	$0
Room and board	$0
Required fees	$0
Books and supplies	$0

UNITED STATES COAST GUARD ACADEMY

31 Mohegan Avenue, New London, CT 06320-8103 • Admissions: 860-444-8503 • Fax: 860-701-6700

CAMPUS LIFE

Quality of Life Rating	**70**
Fire Safety Rating	**77**
Green Rating	**78**
Type of school	public
Environment	city

STUDENTS

Total undergrad enrollment	1,045
% male/female	70/30
% from out of state	96
% from public high school	81
% frosh live on campus	100
% African American	3
% Asian	4
% Caucasian	75
% Hispanic	10
% Native American	1
% international	2
# of countries represented	12

SURVEY SAYS . . .

No one cheats
Career services are great
Campus feels safe
Everyone loves the Bears
Intramural sports are popular
Frats and sororities are unpopular or nonexistent
Political activism is unpopular or nonexistent
Very little drug use
Students are involved in community service

ACADEMICS

Academic Rating	**87**
% students returning for sophomore year	89
% students graduating within 4 years	82
% students graduating within 6 years	83
Calendar	semester
Student/faculty ratio	8:1
Profs interesting rating	79
Profs accessible rating	98
Most classes have	10–19 students
Most lab/discussion sessions have	fewer than 10 students

MOST POPULAR MAJORS

business administration and management; civil engineering; political science and government

STUDENTS SAY ". . ."

Academics

Students at the United States Coast Guard Academy applaud their school for providing "an outstanding education" while affording undergrads the "opportunity to [become] America's leaders of tomorrow." Many appreciate the "regimented environment," which, according to one management major, "gives me a standard to live up to and hold myself to, even when I am away from here." Cadets are "pushed to [the] limits" "academically, emotionally, and physically," and they wouldn't have it any other way. Importantly, "The Academy fosters camaraderie amongst the Corps of Cadets that can't be found anywhere else. With a student body numbering a little over 1,000, the Coast Guard Academy is truly unique in its ability to provide an environment where classmates become shipmates, friends, and eventually family." Though there are a number of excellent programs, cadets call the most attention to the strong engineering department. The academics are "challenging but rewarding." Professors are "extremely dedicated and expect the same from students." A third-year cadet elaborates about how professors are "willing to give up their time and stay after hours to help students succeed." As one impressed freshman proudly states, "You become a better person for going there."

Life

Day-to-day life at the Coast Guard Academy is "orderly and predictable." During the week, it's difficult for people to do anything "outside of their military, athletic, and academic obligations." As one honest marine and environmental science major reveals, "Every moment of every day is planned out." A government major chimes in that even "the times in which we are allowed to sleep are regulated (can't sleep between 6:20 A.M. and 4:00 P.M. without special permission)." Of course, life at the Academy isn't 100 percent work and stress. Many people "pass [the] time and unwind by playing computer/video games, surfing the Internet, working out, going to movies on weekends, etc." A senior shares, "Golf and outdoor activities are popular in the spring, and trips to Boston or NYC are often planned." While "students aren't allowed off campus during the week," unless participating in an academy sanctioned activity, "most try and get away for the weekend." Another senior elaborates, "Underage students tend to go to the movies or the local mall. Of-age students usually spend their time off drinking at the BYO pizza place down the street or at the bars downtown." Additionally, "You can go out and have some fun at beaches or other local attractions in the summer, and snowboarding/skiing is a favorite in the winter." Though life can be "difficult" as one sage senior divulges, "The idea that gets most people through is the fact that they are serving their country and are part of something bigger than themselves."

Student Body

Coast Guard cadets admit, "Despite the academy's best efforts," the campus can appear fairly homogenous. Indeed, "The typical student is still an upper-middle-class, white, Christian from a coastal state, most likely the Northeast." Luckily, a civil engineering major assures us, "Those students of different backgrounds easily fit in with everyone else." Not surprisingly, the academy seems to attract "highly motivated [people] with a strong desire to serve in the Coast Guard." Certainly, another hallmark of Coast Guard cadets is that they're "smart, hardworking, and eager to work with each other." A naval architecture and marine engineering major adds, "Type-A personalities are most common among the Corps." A first-year cadet is quick to say that "everyone is very welcoming." He goes on to attribute this to the "lasting bonds and friendship" we all form "because of going through boot camp together." And this sophomore cheekily sums up his peers, "A typical student here is just like a typical student anywhere else but works harder, follows stricter rules, is in better shape, and is owned by the federal government."

FINANCIAL AID: 860-444-8309 • E-MAIL: ADMISSIONS@USCGA.EDU • WEBSITE: WWW.USCGA.EDU

THE PRINCETON REVIEW SAYS

Admissions

Very important factors considered include: Class rank, academic GPA, rigor of secondary school record, standardized test scores, character/personal qualities, extracurricular activities. *Important factors considered include:* Application essay, recommendation(s), talent/ability. *Other factors considered include:* Alumni/ae relation, interview, level of applicant's interest, volunteer work, work experience. SAT or ACT required; ACT with writing component required. TOEFL required of all international applicants. High school diploma is required and GED is accepted. *Academic units required:* 4 English, 4 mathematics, 3 science (3 science labs).

Financial Aid

The Princeton Review suggests that all financial aid forms be submitted as soon as possible after January 1.

The Inside Word

Gaining acceptance into the Coast Guard Academy is a highly competitive process. The admissions committee is looking not only for outstanding academic achievement but also for applicants who demonstrate leadership ability and strong moral character. In addition, unlike other colleges, you'll also need a physical fitness examination and evaluation.

THE SCHOOL SAYS ". . ."

From the Admissions Office

"Founded in 1876, the United States Coast Guard Academy enjoys a proud tradition of graduating leaders of character. The academy experience melds academic rigor, leadership development, and athletic participation to prepare you to graduate as a commissioned officer. Character development of cadets is founded on the core values of honor, respect, and devotion to duty. You build friendships that last a lifetime, study with inspiring professors in small classes, and train during the summer aboard America's tall ship Eagle, as well as the service's ships and aircraft. Top performers spend their senior summer traveling on exciting internships around the nation and overseas. Graduates serve for five years and have unmatched opportunities to attend flight school and graduate school, all funded by the Coast Guard.

"Appointments to the academy are based on a selective admissions process; Congressional nominations are not required. Your leadership potential and desire to serve your country are what counts. Our student body reflects the best America has to offer—with all its potential and diversity!

"Applicants are required to take the SAT (or the ACT with the writing section).

"The Coast Guard Academy boasts a prolific honor's program that has produces three consecutive Truman Scholars and several Fulbright Scholars over the last three years. The academy is ranked nationally among the top ten for women in STEM fields. The academy embraces a diversity of race and gender. Women comprise approximately thirty percent of the student body and approximately twenty percent of the student body are underrepresented minorities."

SELECTIVITY	
Admissions Rating	97
# of applicants	2,374
% of applicants accepted	16
% of acceptees attending	78
# accepting a place on wait list	400
# admitted from wait list	54

FRESHMAN PROFILE	
Range SAT Critical Reading	550–640
Range SAT Math	590–670
Range SAT Writing	540–630
Range ACT Composite	25–29
Minimum paper TOEFL	560
Average HS GPA	3.8
% graduated top 10% of class	52
% graduated top 25% of class	85
% graduated top 50% of class	99

DEADLINES	
Early action	
Deadline	11/1
Notification	1/20
Regular	
Priority	11/1
Deadline	2/1
Notification	4/15
Nonfall registration?	no

FINANCIAL FACTS	
Financial Aid Rating	60*
Annual in-state tuition	$0
Annual out-of-state tuition	$0
Room and board	$0
Required fees	$0
Books and supplies	$0

United States Merchant Marine Academy

Office of Admissions, Kings Point, NY 11024-1699 • Admissions: 516-773-5391 • Fax: 516-773-5390

CAMPUS LIFE

Quality of Life Rating	**65**
Fire Safety Rating	**60***
Green Rating	**60***
Type of school	public
Environment	village

STUDENTS

Total undergrad enrollment	1,034
% male/female	87/13
% from out of state	88
% from public high school	75
% frosh live on campus	100
% African American	2
% Asian	4
% Caucasian	84
% Hispanic	5
% Native American	1
% international	2
# of countries represented	4

SURVEY SAYS . . .

Class discussions are rare
Career services are great
Lousy food on campus
Low cost of living
Frats and sororities are unpopular or nonexistent
Political activism is unpopular or nonexistent
Very little drug use

ACADEMICS

Academic Rating	**65**
% students returning for sophomore year	84
% students graduating within 4 years	65
% students graduating within 6 years	74
Calendar	trimester
Student/faculty ratio	13:1
Profs interesting rating	65
Profs accessible rating	65
Most classes have	10–19 students
Most lab/discussion sessions have	10–19 students

MOST POPULAR MAJORS

marine transportation; marine engineering

APPLICANTS ALSO LOOK AT AND OFTEN PREFER

United States Naval Academy

AND SOMETIMES PREFER

United States Military Academy, United States Coast Guard Academy, United States Air Force Academy

STUDENTS SAY ". . ."

Academics

Tucked away on Long Island, the United States Merchant Marine Academy offers students the chance to pursue a prestigious though rigorous and regimented education. Further, it allows undergrads to join "a group of elite students who work hard and [are] honest and patriotic." Students here caution that the academics are "extremely difficult," especially given the "fast-paced classroom environment." Additionally, when asked about their professors, students dole out mixed reviews. Though most assert that their teachers are "very intelligent," some bemoan a "lack of enthusiasm." And while some professors are described as "fair, approachable, and extremely helpful," other professors come across as "heartless and condescending." Regardless of which classes you enroll in, the Merchant Marine Academy is "a school that requires plenty of effort on behalf of the student." As one midshipman proudly sums up, "The opportunities afforded by this Academy are unparalleled by any other college I have come across. Despite the immense sacrifices and hardships of this school, it is completely worth it for the right person."

Life

Undergrads at the Merchant Marine Academy don't mince words about life at their school. Indeed, the majority seem to be in agreement that because "it is a military academy, fun is generally limited." As one straightforward student explains, "We are restricted to the campus grounds during the week until senior year. Life is pretty drab, dull, and boring [with] most time spent either in class, studying, or working out." Moreover, undergrads are "restricted by the regiment and disciplinary system." Of course, even these hardworking midshipmen get to kick back every now and again. Another undergrad cheerfully shares, "When the spring comes, everyone gets out to play rec sports (Ultimate Frisbee, tag football, soccer, swim, or bike ride) and goes to the park to BBQ." And a fellow student chimes in, "We have a good time, and usually, it is the little things that make us happy. We enjoy hanging out on weekends and doing things that normal college students would do. Recently a few friends and I had a Nerf gun battle, which was pretty fun." And when they are allowed, midshipmen rush to get off campus. Indeed, students here love to take advantage of the fact that they are "only twenty minutes from downtown NYC." As this wise midshipman concludes, "New York City in uniform boils down to cheap food, movies, plays, concerts, easy way to meet girls, you name it...we work hard all week, but when it comes time, we get to play hard as well."

Student Body

At first glance, the average Merchant Marine Academy midshipman could be described as "a white, conservative male." Of course, there's definitely more to these students than race, gender, and political views. Certainly, undergrads can also be depicted as "respectful," "athletic," and "outgoing." They can also be categorized as "those that want to work in the maritime industry and those that want to join the military." Moreover, many are "hardworking and serious." As one undergrad explains, "If you aren't willing to work, you won't be here long." Another student continues, "The typical student has tons on his plate, whether it's regimental duties or academic ones. [However], no matter what, if you need help with something, somebody will be there for you." A fellow midshipman concurs, summing up, "The students here are all a family. Each one of us here at the Merchant Marine Academy [has] experienced the same rigorous training and tough treatment plebe year. We all work together in everything we do, and without one another it is almost impossible to succeed at the Academy." Actually, the U.S. Merchant Marine Academy is increasing the diversity of its student body. The number of women in the current graduating class was twelve percent, while the class of 2015 is at fourteen percent. Ethnic minorities are now at more than sixteen percent.

FINANCIAL AID: 516-773-5295 • E-MAIL: ADMISSIONS@USMMA.EDU • WEBSITE: WWW.USMMA.EDU

THE PRINCETON REVIEW SAYS

Admissions

Very important factors considered include: Rigor of secondary school record, standardized test scores, character/personal qualities. *Important factors considered include:* Class rank, application essay, academic GPA, recommendation(s), extracurricular activities, level of applicant's interest, talent/ability. *Other factors considered include:* Geographical residence, interview, racial/ethnic status, state residency, volunteer work, work experience. SAT or ACT required; ACT with or without writing component accepted. TOEFL required of all international applicants. High school diploma is required and GED is accepted. *Academic units required:* 4 English, 3 mathematics, 3 science (1 science lab), 8 academic electives. *Academic units recommended:* 4 English, 4 mathematics, 4 science (2 science labs), 2 foreign language, 4 social studies.

Financial Aid

Students should submit: FAFSA, institution's own financial aid form. Regular filing deadline is May 1. The Princeton Review suggests that all financial aid forms be submitted as soon as possible after January 1. *Need-based scholarships/grants offered:* Federal Pell, private scholarships, Federal SMART Grants & Federal Academic Competitiveness Grants. *Loan aid offered:* Direct Subsidized Stafford, Direct Unsubsidized Stafford, Direct PLUS. Applicants will be notified of awards on a rolling basis beginning January 31. Off-campus job opportunities are poor.

The Inside Word

Securing admittance to the Merchant Marine Academy is no easy feat. The admissions committee is looking for stellar candidates who have the intelligence, fortitude, and leadership capabilities to survive (and thrive) at this institution. In addition to your transcripts and test scores, the admissions crew will closely assess your letters of recommendation. Moreover, unlike traditional colleges, you'll also have to pass a fitness requirement and secure a nomination from a U.S. representative or senator.

THE SCHOOL SAYS ". . ."

From the Admissions Office

"What makes the U.S. Merchant Marine Academy different from the other federal service academies? The difference can be summarized in two phrases that appear in our publications. The first: 'The World Is Your Campus.' You will spend a year at sea—a third of your sophomore year and two-thirds of your junior year—teamed with a classmate aboard a U.S. merchant ship. You will visit an average of eighteen foreign nations while you work and learn in a mariner's true environment. You will graduate with seafaring experience and as a citizen of the world. The second phrase is 'Options and Opportunities.' Unlike students at the other federal academies, who are required to enter the service connected to their academy, you have the option of working in the seagoing merchant marine and transportation industry or applying for active duty in the Navy, Coast Guard, Marine Corps, Air Force, or Army. Nearly twenty-five percent of our most recent graduating class entered various branches of the armed forces with an officer rank. As a graduate of the U.S. Merchant Marine Academy, you will receive a Bachelor of Science degree, a government-issued merchant marine officer's license, and a Naval Reserve commission (unless you have been accepted for active military duty). No other service academy offers so attractive a package. The Academy is currently embarking on a $50 million capital improvement plan, which will include the renovation and redesign of the school's dining hall, its dorms, its piers, and other projects in support of its new strategic plan initiative.

"Applicants must take the SAT or the ACT with the writing component. For homeschooled students, we recommend they also submit scores from SAT Subject Tests in chemistry and/or physics."

SELECTIVITY

Admissions Rating	**96**
# of applicants	2,076
% of applicants accepted	20
% of acceptees attending	69

FRESHMAN PROFILE

Range SAT Critical Reading	555–635
Range SAT Math	600–680
Range ACT Composite	25–29
Minimum paper TOEFL	533
Minimum web-based TOEFL	73
Average HS GPA	3.6
% graduated top 10% of class	24
% graduated top 25% of class	62
% graduated top 50% of class	92

DEADLINES

Regular Deadline	3/1
Nonfall registration?	no

FINANCIAL FACTS

Financial Aid Rating	**60***
Annual in-state tuition	$0
Annual out-state tuition	$0
Room and board	$0
Required fees	$1,000
Average % of frosh need met	100
Average % of ugrad need met	100

United States Military Academy

646 Swift Road, West Point, NY 10996-1905 • Admissions: 845-938-4041 • Fax: 845-938-3021

CAMPUS LIFE

Quality of Life Rating	**80**
Fire Safety Rating	**83**
Green Rating	**74**
Type of school	public
Environment	village

STUDENTS

Total undergrad enrollment	4,624
% male/female	84/16
% from out of state	93
% from public high school	73
% frosh live on campus	100
% African American	7
% Asian	5
% Caucasian	72
% Hispanic	9
% Native American	1
% international	1
# of countries represented	29

SURVEY SAYS . . .

No one cheats
Great computer facilities
Athletic facilities are great
Career services are great
School is well run
Campus feels safe
Frats and sororities are unpopular or nonexistent
Very little drug use
Students are involved in community service

ACADEMICS

Academic Rating	**99**
% students returning for sophomore year	94
% students graduating within 4 years	80
Calendar	semester
Student/faculty ratio	8:1
Profs interesting rating	97
Profs accessible rating	99
Most classes have	10–19 students
Most lab/discussion sessions have	10–19 students

MOST POPULAR MAJORS

business administration and management; economics; engineering/industrial management

APPLICANTS ALSO LOOK AT AND SOMETIMES PREFER

United States Naval Academy, United States Air Force Academy

STUDENTS SAY ". . ."

Academics

West Point "is all about transforming a regular citizen into an intellectual soldier with unparalleled skills of leadership, fit to lead America's sons and daughters," a grueling process to be sure. The West Point experience entails "an intensive academic, physical, and military curriculum" in which students undergo "four years of breaking down to build up, unlearning to learn again, and narrowing purpose to open vast opportunities" in a highly regimented program in which "you need to be willing to put up with things you won't deal with anywhere else." Academics start with "a very large core curriculum" that some grouse about but most accept as "helping us become problem solvers…and critical thinkers" with "a broad base of knowledge to understand the world around us." The school employs the Thayer Method of instruction, "which means students prepare for class ahead of time and then discuss the material in class as opposed to the other way around." Cadets warn that it's "very difficult in some of the courses, particularly math and sciences," and also that there is often "not sufficient time to prepare for class" due to their busy academic and training schedules. Fortunately, professors are there to help cadets survive the challenging experience. They "are absolutely excellent" instructors who "put an incredible amount of effort and work into making sure the students succeed." "One-on-one tutoring from instructors is available on a daily basis," one grateful cadet reports.

Life

Asked to describe life at West Point, one cadet quoted Winston Churchill: "If you're going through hell, keep on going!" Campus life "is very structured. Everything is planned out and executed," with most time consumed by "a heavy course load, military duties and physical fitness," Cadets "are able to have fun, but not in the ways typical college students have fun. [Even] weekends can be busy with mandatory sporting events or other obligations." The demands of the West Point experience can doubtless seem overwhelming at times, but "there are bright moments…For fun, we have lots of athletic activities available and a surprisingly wide range of student clubs (ranging from a Korean American relations seminar to the fly-fishing club) compared to the size of the student body." Alcohol and drugs are strictly forbidden on campus, and "penalties for breaking [the rules] are harsh." Once students are of age, they can drink "at designated locations on campus, which many take advantage of on Thursdays, as they often leave on Fridays." New York City is the most frequently mentioned getaway for those procuring precious leaves. In sum, life can be monotonous at West Point, "but it's worth it" because "more is accomplished at this school in one day than anywhere else. No other school has such great commitment to [developing] a well-rounded student."

Student Body

"Physically fit," "type-A" "workaholics" fill the ranks at West Point, where "due to Army regulations, many people look the same in regards to facial hair and hair cuts. The uniform does not help either." There are a lot of "high school hero," "Captain America–type people" here. Not too many students stray from that prototype. One student warns, "Most people that do not eventually mold into the typical student do not make it through all four years. Cooperate and graduate." Although all students are "very competitive," there is a "great sense of duty to help out your classmates. Most students are very intelligent, polite, and professional." Other descriptors that pop up frequently include "patriotic," "religious," and "conservative." "While statistically the student body is probably mostly white and male," one student observes, "there is a good representation of all ethnic groups and both genders, and there are no discrimination issues that I have observed."

FINANCIAL AID: 845-938-4041 • E-MAIL: ADMISSIONS@USMA.EDU • WEBSITE: WWW.WESTPOINT.EDU

THE PRINCETON REVIEW SAYS

Admissions

Very important factors considered include: Class rank, academic GPA, standardized test scores, extracurricular activities, character/personal qualities, and rigor of secondary school record. *Important factors considered include:* Application essay, recommendations, talent/ability, and level of applicant's interest. *Other factors considered include:* Interview, first generation, racial/ethnic status, volunteer work, and work experience.

Financial Aid

The Princeton Review suggests that all financial aid forms be submitted as soon as possible after January 1. *Need-based scholarships/grants offered:* All students receive an annual salary of approximately $10,148. Room and board, medical, and dental care is provided by the Army. A one-time deposit of $2,000 is required upon admission to pay for the initial issue of uniforms, books, supplies, equipment and fees. If needed, loans for the deposit are available for $100 to $2,400.

The Inside Word

The fact that you must be nominated by your Congressional representative in order to apply to West Point tells you all you need to know about the school's selectivity. Contact your district's Congressional representative to learn the deadline for nomination requests; typically these are made in the spring of your junior year. Successful candidates must demonstrate excellence in academics, physical conditioning, extracurricular involvement, and leadership. They must also be willing to commit to five years of active duty and three years of reserve duty upon graduation. The rigorous requirements and demanding commitments of a West Point education hardly dissuade applicants. Almost 15,000 applied for the 1,150 available slots.

THE SCHOOL SAYS ". . ."

From the Admissions Office

"West Point is searching for applicants who possess the leadership skills, cultural sensibilities, and the moral fiber to handle the volatile, uncertain, complex, and ambiguous contemporary operating environment of today's world as a future U.S. Army Officer. As a crucible for leadership, we are looking for critical thinkers that have who have the judgment and experience to become a leader of character upon graduation.

"To assess your ability and preparation, admissions looks at more than your GPA or standardized test scores. The applications of almost 15,000 students are evaluated based on academic, physical, and leadership potential to find approximately 1,150 candidates who are ready to be offered the challenge of admission into the Corps of Cadets. With an amazingly high offer-acceptance rate, only the most dedicated, enthusiastic applicants make it to the finish line for the report date each June.

"If you accept the challenge, you will be immersed in a military training program that ranges from marksmanship to orienteering, an academic program that offers over forty majors ranging from electrical engineering to philosophy, and a physical program that finds every cadet participating in an intercollegiate, club, or intramural-level sport. The fully funded, four-year college education includes tuition, room, board, and full medical and dental care. In return, you will graduate with a Bachelor of Science degree and be commissioned as a U.S. Army Officer with an active duty service obligation of five years active and three years reserve. Complete admissions guidance found online."

SELECTIVITY	
Admissions Rating	**98**
# of applicants	13,954
% of applicants accepted	11
% of acceptees attending	84
# accepting a place on wait list	149
# admitted from wait list	15

FRESHMAN PROFILE	
Range SAT Critical Reading	560–680
Range SAT Math	590–690
Range SAT Writing	550–660
Range ACT Composite	25–31
Minimum paper TOEFL	500
Minimum web-based TOEFL	75
% graduated top 10% of class	48
% graduated top 25% of class	75
% graduated top 50% of class	96

DEADLINES	
Regular	
Deadline	2/28
Notification	4/15
Nonfall registration?	no

FINANCIAL FACTS	
Financial Aid Rating	**60***
Annual comprehensive tuition	$0
Books and supplies	$0

UNITED STATES NAVAL ACADEMY

117 DECATUR ROAD, ANNAPOLIS, MD 21402 • ADMISSIONS: 410-293-4361 • FAX: 410-295-1815

CAMPUS LIFE

Quality of Life Rating	75
Fire Safety Rating	67
Green Rating	60*
Type of school	public
Environment	town

STUDENTS

Total undergrad enrollment	4,576
% male/female	80/20
% from out of state	93
% from public high school	60
% frosh live on campus	100
% African American	6
% Asian	5
% Caucasian	66
% Hispanic	12
% international	1
# of countries represented	30

SURVEY SAYS . . .

Lab facilities are great
Great computer facilities
Athletic facilities are great
Career services are great
Campus feels safe
Everyone loves the Navy
Frats and sororities are unpopular or nonexistent
Very little drug use

ACADEMICS

Academic Rating	90
% students returning for sophomore year	95
% students graduating within 4 years	89
% students graduating within 6 years	90
Calendar	semester
Student/faculty ratio	10:1
Profs interesting rating	79
Profs accessible rating	97
Most classes have	10–19 students

MOST POPULAR MAJORS

economics; political science and government; systems engineering

APPLICANTS ALSO LOOK AT AND OFTEN PREFER

Duke University, Harvard College, University of Virginia, United States Air Force Academy

AND SOMETIMES PREFER

Pennsylvania State University—University Park, Massachusetts Institute of Technology, Georgia Institute of Technology, United States Military Academy

AND RARELY PREFER

Boston University, St. John's College (MD), Purdue University—West Lafayette

STUDENTS SAY ". . ."

Academics

Students at the United State Naval Academy, known as midshipmen, are overjoyed about the amount of discipline involved, both academically and militarily. Students feel "the structure is unparalleled, and the fact that PhDs routinely teach in class even for freshman core classes is amazing." Midshipmen here appreciate personalized attention saying, "You get more face time with your professors and actually get to know them better than you would at any other college." There's an intense focus not only on discipline, but also on the shaping of students moral character. Additionally, students note, "with such a wide selection of professors and an extra instruction system [that's] second-to-none, it is difficult to blame unsatisfactory academic performance on poor professors." There's a great deal of emphasis on personal and professional responsibility and on grooming the best possible naval officers while offering the best possible undergraduate education, free of charge. There's about a 50/50 split between civilian and military personnel, with students noting that "all civilian professors have PhDs, and all military professors have, at least, a master's." The course load is "very difficult," but the vast majority of the professors are "experts in their fields of study," and they "devote a lot of personal time to making sure we succeed."

Life

Students feel that the thing that makes USNA unique is "the combination of academic and military life. Our overall rank is determined not only by our grade. We are also being graded in our physical fitness, military knowledge, professionalism, and leadership abilities. World conflicts are always being discussed because in a few short years that is where we are possibly going to be. Monday to Friday midshipmen put every hour of their lives into their development. Sometimes training evolutions are on the weekends, and we have to sacrifice some fun time. Midshipmen life is very difficult, but the rewards are so great in four short years." Students note that their day-to-day "is very routine," with "classes from 0800 to 1545, then an athletic reserve period." There's "time to exercise every day," and "evenings are dedicated to studying and seeking out help in academics as well as extra curricular activities." "People tend to think about their jobs and tasks assigned, the people here are very locked on." Although classes at the academy follow a strict routine, life here is "enjoyable." But when given the chance and time to have fun, midshipmen have fun, "whether it's going out in town and socializing with friends and family or just staying back in the hall and having fun." Student privileges increase as midshipmen advance from freshmen to upperclassmen. As one student notes, "first year you get nothing; no media, no naps, must greet all upper-class by name, and you are only allowed to leave campus on Saturday from noon to midnight." As can be expected, USNA has a strict code when it comes to drugs and alcohol, which aren't permitted; the "punishment for drug abuse is very strict, and as it is a military school, random urinalysis and breathalyzer tests are taken." However, as the same student notes, "I love it here. Standards are enforced, people are safe, and we are learning."

Student Body

At USNA, the average student is a "type-A personality that works hard to uphold the standards of the academy and to ultimately receive the service selection of their choice." There's an intense camaraderie among the midshipmen here; "the initial summer training really brings students together into a good group that works well together for the remainder of their four years." The typical student is "a pretty well-rounded blend of academic, athletic, and cultural values."

E-MAIL: WEBMAIL@USNA.EDU • WEBSITE: WWW.USNA.EDU

THE PRINCETON REVIEW SAYS

Admissions

Very important factors considered include: Class rank, application essay, academic GPA, recommendation(s), rigor of secondary school record, character/personal qualities, extracurricular activities, interview, Congressional or other nominations, and physical fitness. *Important factors considered include:* Standardized test scores, talent/ability. *Other factors considered include:* Geographical residence, state residency, volunteer work, work experience. SAT or ACT required; ACT with or without writing component accepted. TOEFL required of all international applicants. High school diploma or equivalent is not required. *Academic units recommended:* 4 English, 4 mathematics, 2 science (1 science lab), 2 foreign language, 2 history, 1 introductory computer course.

Financial Aid

The Navy pays for the tuition, room and board, medical and dental care of Naval Academy Midshipmen. Midshipmen also earns a monthly salary while at the academy.

The Inside Word

USNA is an intensely rigorous and demanding program that requires and expects and receives the best possible candidates. The most important non-academic criteria are the personal interview, the applicant's character, and the desire of the applicant to attend the academy. It's the perfect program for anyone wanting to both serve in the U.S. Navy or Marines and receive a first-class education.

THE SCHOOL SAYS ". . ."

From the Admissions Office

"The finest young men and women in the country come to the Naval Academy to develop into leaders to serve the nation; USNA is the school of admirals, presidents, Nobel Prize winners, astronauts, jet pilots and CEOs. At USNA, you will have the opportunity to pursue a four-year degree program that develops you mentally, morally, and physically as no civilian college can. As you might expect, this program is demanding, but the opportunities are limitless and more than worth the effort.

"Upon throwing the iconic Midshipmen hat into the air at graduation, you will serve your country in one of dozens of professional fields—primarily aviation, submarines, ships, or the Marine Corps, but with additional limited options for the SEALs, medical, and other communities."

SELECTIVITY	
Admissions Rating	**98**
# of applicants	19,145
% of applicants accepted	7
% of acceptees attending	86
# accepting a place on wait list	125
# admitted from wait list	15

FRESHMAN PROFILE	
Range SAT Critical Reading	560–680
Range SAT Math	600–700
% graduated top 10% of class	52
% graduated top 25% of class	79
% graduated top 50% of class	94

DEADLINES	
Regular	
Deadline	1/31
Notification	4/15
Nonfall registration?	no

FINANCIAL FACTS	
Financial Aid Rating	**60***
Annual in-state tuition	$0
Annual out-of-state tuition	$0
Room and board	$0
Required fees	$0
Books and supplies	$0

THE UNIVERSITY OF ALABAMA AT BIRMINGHAM

OFFICE OF UNDERGRADUATE ADMISSIONS, BIRMINGHAM, AL 35294-1150 • ADMISSIONS: 205-934-8221 • FAX: 205-975-7114

CAMPUS LIFE

Quality of Life Rating	**91**
Fire Safety Rating	**94**
Green Rating	**66**
Type of school	public
Environment	metropolis

STUDENTS

Total undergrad enrollment	10,854
% male/female	42/58
% from out of state	10
% frosh live on campus	67
# of fraternities	10
# of sororities	10
% African American	27
% Asian	4
% Caucasian	60
% Hispanic	2
% international	2
# of countries represented	78

SURVEY SAYS . . .

Registration is a breeze
Lab facilities are great
Athletic facilities are great
School is well run
Diverse student types on campus
Different types of students interact
Students get along with local community
Dorms are like palaces
Students are happy

ACADEMICS

Academic Rating	**72**
% students graduating within 4 years	19
Calendar	semester
Student/faculty ratio	18:1
Profs interesting rating	82
Profs accessible rating	81
Most classes have	10–19 students
Most lab/discussion sessions have	20–29 students

MOST POPULAR MAJORS

accounting; biology/biological sciences; psychology

APPLICANTS ALSO LOOK AT AND OFTEN PREFER

Florida State University, University of Georgia, Duke University, University of Tennessee, Vanderbilt University

AND SOMETIMES PREFER

Auburn University, Tulane University, Samford University, Louisiana State University—Baton Rouge

STUDENTS SAY ". . ."

Academics

At the University of Alabama at Birmingham, professors and administrators "care about you." "For many of the professors, it's not just about a grade in a class that you are taking. Rather it's an experience and preparation for any of our further endeavors." The professors here are "experts in their fields," they're "accessible and exciting," and "they're down-to-earth enough to give students a real view of what it's like to enter the world of academia." Despite the fact that this is a large university, there are "small class sizes in even the 100-level classes," and "many professors are available for help outside the classroom and care about teaching their subjects to the students." Of particular note, students say professors in the science departments "are great. They do a great job with interactive learning, and they really put forth every effort to make sure that those who want help get it." Academically, students feel that the workload is rigorous, but "certainly worth the challenge." As one student notes, a graduate tends to feel like "a better person for having experienced the challenge of UAB as well as the diversity." With an annual student forum, "The faculty and administration are very close with students and actively look to pursuing perfection and improving the collegiate experience."

Life

"Campus life is vibrant and exciting," boasts the student body. With UAB being "in the city of Birmingham, right outside of the school is something for everyone. There are malls, many restaurants, museums, and live music." UAB "strongly encourages their students to get involved on campus in some shape or form," presenting the student body with such opportunities as "the widely used Campus Recreation Center where students can take free U-Fit Classes (kickboxing, krunk/hip-hop class, yoga, spin, etc.), swim in the wave pool, climb the rock wall, or play intramurals (flag football, dodgeball, soccer, volleyball, slow pitch softball, etc.)." In addition, the surrounding city of Birmingham offers many venues for arts and entertainment; "students can dine or shop at the many malls located throughout the city. There are also many museums, art shows, concerts, dance clubs, [and] movie theaters to choose from." Students say that the list of attractions in Birmingham "goes on and on." "Students have the problem of having to narrow down their opportunities, rather than having to find something to do." Students "love the size of the school," finding it "like a small town in a big city." The impression is that "the campus is large enough that [you] meet and see new faces daily, but small enough to where [you] have personal relationships with teachers and the administration." Additionally, "there is a genuine interest among students in learning about the other cultures and religions represented on campus and in other cultures around the world."

Student Body

"Everyone is so diverse that there is literally something for everyone to get involved in." With more than 150 campus organizations, students say "you literally have to choose to not become involved." Many students love "how no one looks down on anyone," and how "everyone is so down-to-earth!" Most feel that they all come "from modest households." Regarding potential changes that could be made, "The meal plan situation could use some serious help." At UAB students feel, "It is easy to find a place where you fit in." Although the student body will insist that "there is no typical student!" In general, students are "hardworking and serious," while doing their best to always "enjoy weekend fun with friends."

FINANCIAL AID: 205-934-8223 • E-MAIL: UNDERGRADADMIT@UAB.EDU • WEBSITE: WWW.UAB.EDU

THE PRINCETON REVIEW SAYS

Admissions

Very important factors considered include: Academic GPA, rigor of secondary school record, standardized test scores. SAT or ACT required; ACT with writing component required. TOEFL required of all international applicants. High school diploma is required and GED is accepted. *Academic units required:* 4 English, 3 mathematics, 3 science (2 science labs), 1 foreign language, 3 social studies, 3 academic electives.

Financial Aid

Students should submit: FAFSA. The Princeton Review suggests that all financial aid forms be submitted as soon as possible after January 1. *Need-based scholarships/grants offered:* Federal Pell, SEOG, state scholarships/grants, private scholarships, the school's own gift aid, United Negro College Fund. *Loan aid offered:* Direct Subsidized Stafford, Direct Unsubsidized Stafford, Direct PLUS, Federal Perkins, state loans, college/university loans from institutional funds. Applicants will be notified of awards on a rolling basis beginning April 1. Federal Work-Study Program available. Institutional employment available. Off-campus job opportunities are excellent.

The Inside Word

UAB's incoming class tends to have an average GPA of 3.5. The most important factors for admission are GPA and test scores. At the minimum, students need a GPA of 2.25 and a 950 SAT score. Administrators here are looking to admit a student body that's friendly, diverse, and intelligent with students who strive to be active in the community.

THE SCHOOL SAYS ". . ."

From the Admissions Office

"*Breakthrough*...it's a great word to describe UAB. From undergraduate research and interest-specific honors programs to a cutting-edge medical center known internationally for discovery, UAB is a place where great minds come together to make a difference. We are an energetic, exciting place; one of the state's largest universities with eight undergraduate schools, a large graduate school, four medical professional schools, and a renowned medical center.

"UAB is the place for students who seek a world-class research university in the heart of a fun and diverse city and for students who want to take what they learn in the classroom directly to the best companies, career options, and graduate schools available. UAB is also for students who seek diversity in culture and thought, and who are creative, inquisitive, and motivated to get involved and to make a difference.

"On campus you'll discover more than 150 active student organizations and countless activities. And off campus, Alabama's largest city—recently named one of the most livable in America by a national organization—offers must-see attractions and can't-miss events just down the street or mere minutes away. So it's easy to explore your interests, try new experiences, create memories, enjoy old friends and make new ones.

"UAB...for students who expect more from college—students who take achievement seriously—students who want to make a *breakthrough*."

SELECTIVITY	
Admissions Rating	75
# of applicants	5,575
% of applicants accepted	72
% of acceptees attending	40
FRESHMAN PROFILE	
Range ACT Composite	21–27
Minimum paper TOEFL	500
Minimum web-based TOEFL	61
Average HS GPA	3.5
% graduated top 10% of class	24
% graduated top 25% of class	50
% graduated top 50% of class	77
DEADLINES	
Regular Deadline	5/1
Nonfall registration?	yes
FINANCIAL FACTS	
Financial Aid Rating	68
Annual in-state tuition	$7,740
Annual out-state tuition	$17,730
Books and supplies	$1,000
% needy frosh rec. need-based scholarship or grant aid	65
% needy UG rec. need-based scholarship or grant aid	66
% needy frosh rec. non-need-based scholarship or grant aid	56
% needy UG rec. non-need-based scholarship or grant aid	30
% needy frosh rec. need-based self-help aid	75
% needy UG rec. need-based self-help aid	80
% UG borrow to pay for school	60
Average cumulative indebtedness	$24,936
% frosh need fully met	11
% ugrads need fully met	14
Average % of frosh need met	48
Average % of ugrad need met	46

THE UNIVERSITY OF ALABAMA—TUSCALOOSA

BOX 870132, TUSCALOOSA, AL 35487-0132 • ADMISSIONS: 205-348-5666 • FAX: 205-348-9046

CAMPUS LIFE

Quality of Life Rating	**74**
Fire Safety Rating	**64**
Green Rating	**86**
Type of school	public
Environment	city

STUDENTS

Total undergrad enrollment	25,613
% male/female	47/53
% from out of state	35
# of fraternities	32
# of sororities	23
% African American	13
% Asian	1
% Caucasian	80
% Hispanic	2
% Native American	1
% international	2
# of countries represented	73

SURVEY SAYS . . .

Athletic facilities are great
Everyone loves the Crimson Tide
Frats and sororities dominate social scene
Student publications are popular

ACADEMICS

Academic Rating	**71**
% students graduating within 4 years	38
% students graduating within 6 years	66
Calendar	semester
Student/faculty ratio	19:1
Profs interesting rating	76
Profs accessible rating	81
Most classes have	10–19 students
Most lab/discussion sessions have	10–19 students

MOST POPULAR MAJORS

elementary education and teaching; general business; nursing/registered nurse (rn, asn, bsn, msn)

APPLICANTS ALSO LOOK AT AND OFTEN PREFER

Florida State University, University of Georgia, Duke University, University of Tennessee, Vanderbilt University

AND SOMETIMES PREFER

Auburn University, Tulane University, Samford University, Louisiana State University—Baton Rouge

STUDENTS SAY ". . ."

Academics

The University of Alabama is a ridiculously affordable, "technologically advanced," "student-centered" institution that enjoys an outrageous degree of alumni support. "Course offerings are pretty diverse," and there are "tons of majors." Highlights include a "great" engineering college and three honors programs. Other standout programs include business, communication studies, and nursing. Some students say that the "bold and visionary" top brass runs the school "fairly well." Others gripe that the administration is "very bogged down in red tape." "Working with the administration is really terrible sometimes," undergrads say. Professors here are "top researchers or writers in their fields," and some are "very enthusiastic about having undergraduate students helping them with research." The faculty as a whole is also "approachable" and "generally very easy to get in touch with for outside assistance." Teaching ability is "hit-or-miss," though. While many professors are "very animated and interesting to listen to," "Others do not have the same talent." "Being a great researcher does not necessarily make a person a good teacher," notes one student.

Life

"An atmosphere of almost antebellum charm" permeates this "pretty" campus. "On sunny days in the fall and spring, students enjoy studying and playing on the quad." Recreational facilities are "excellent." "Life during football season revolves around football." So does morale. Win or lose, though, UA boasts "one of the best college football atmospheres in the country. On Saturdays when the Crimson Tide plays at home, the campus is "a sea of tents for tailgating," "and Alabama fans are singing the fight song." Otherwise, "the Greek organizations rule this campus." They wield "an inordinate amount of power" in student government as well. Whether you pledge or not, though, students promise "an outstanding social atmosphere." "While not everyone participates in the party scene on campus, it is very popular." In addition to the house parties and the festivities at the frat houses, "people enjoying going to the bars on the strip." "Comfort" abounds in surrounding Tuscaloosa, and it is "definitely a college town." People are "very open and courteous" to the students, and virtually everything you need is within "walking distance." When students at UA hanker for more urban environs, "Birmingham is only an hour away, and there is plenty to do there."

Student Body

Students here are "extremely friendly" and "usually well-dressed and well-mannered." "People tend to be a bit conservative," and "a lot are religious." "The typical student is active in a few organizations, makes decent grades, and finds time to relax, too." African American students are the largest minority group. They represent more than ten percent of the student body. Some students maintain that UA is "not diverse socially, ideologically, and culturally." "The different ethnic groups stick together," they say. They look around campus and see "frat boys or sorority girls for the most part"—"same hair, same sunglasses with a string on the back, and stupid visors." Other students vigorously disagree. "We truly aren't a university filled with cookie-cutter people," asserts one student. "There are many diverse groups of students who all have their own roles on campus." "It is easy for someone to come from up north and say this campus is full of close-minded Southern Baptist Republicans, just like it is easy for someone to come from a small town…and think this campus is full of liberal heathens," points out another student. "Few people are really atypical, because no matter where you fall in any category, there are people around you who you can connect with."

FINANCIAL AID: 205-348-6756 • E-MAIL: ADMISSIONS@UA.EDU • WEBSITE: WWW.UA.EDU

THE PRINCETON REVIEW SAYS

Admissions

Very important factors considered include: Academic GPA, rigor of secondary school record, standardized test scores. *Important factors considered include:* Class rank. *Other factors considered include:* Application essay, recommendation(s), alumni/ae relation, character/personal qualities, extracurricular activities, first generation, interview, talent/ability, volunteer work, work experience. ACT with or without writing component accepted. TOEFL required of all international applicants. High school diploma is required and GED is accepted. *Academic units required:* 4 English, 3 mathematics, 3 science (2 science labs), 1 foreign language, 4 social studies, 1 history, 5 academic electives. *Academic units recommended:* 4 English, 3 mathematics, 3 science (2 science labs), 1 foreign language, 4 social studies, 1 history, 5 academic electives.

Financial Aid

Students should submit: FAFSA. The Princeton Review suggests that all financial aid forms be submitted as soon as possible after January 1. *Need-based scholarships/grants offered:* Federal Pell, SEOG, state scholarships/grants, private scholarships, the school's own gift aid, Federal Nursing Scholarships. *Loan aid offered:* Direct Subsidized Stafford, Direct Unsubsidized Stafford, Direct PLUS, Federal Perkins, college/university loans from institutional funds. Applicants will be notified of awards on a rolling basis beginning April 1. Federal Work-Study Program available. Institutional employment available. Highest amount earned per year from on-campus jobs $2,466. Off-campus job opportunities are good.

The Inside Word

The University of Alabama relies heavily on objective data in the application process. Admission is not highly competitive, and applicants with satisfactory grades and modest test scores are likely to be accepted.

THE SCHOOL SAYS ". . ."

From the Admissions Office

"Since its founding in 1831 as the first public university in the state, the University of Alabama has been committed to providing the best, most complete education possible for its students. Our commitment to that goal means that as times change, we sharpen our focus and methods to keep our graduates competitive in their fields. By offering outstanding teaching in a solid core curriculum enhanced by multimedia classrooms and campus-wide computer labs, the University of Alabama keeps its focus on the future while maintaining a traditional college atmosphere. Extensive international study opportunities, internship programs, and cooperative education placements help our students prepare for successful futures. Consisting of eleven colleges and schools offering 220 degrees in more than 100 fields of study, the university gives its students a wide range of choices and offers courses of study at the bachelor's, master's, specialist, and doctoral levels. The university emphasizes quality and breadth of academic opportunities and challenging programs for well-prepared students through its Honors College, including the University Honors Program, International Honors Program, and Computer-Based Honors Programs and Blount Undergraduate Initiative (liberal arts program). Thirty-one percent of undergraduates are from out of state, providing an enriching social and cultural environment.

"Applicants may submit either the SAT or the ACT. The writing component is required for admission."

SELECTIVITY	
Admissions Rating	**90**
# of applicants	22,136
% of applicants accepted	44
% of acceptees attending	59

FRESHMAN PROFILE	
Range SAT Critical Reading	500–620
Range SAT Math	495–640
Range SAT Writing	490–610
Range ACT Composite	22–29
Minimum paper TOEFL	500
Minimum web-based TOEFL	71
Average HS GPA	3.5
% graduated top 10% of class	43
% graduated top 25% of class	63
% graduated top 50% of class	83

DEADLINES	
Regular	
Deadline	3/1
Nonfall registration?	yes

FINANCIAL FACTS	
Financial Aid Rating	**69**
Annual in-state tuition	$8,600
Annual out-state tuition	$21,900
Room and board	$8,564
Books and supplies	$1,100
% needy frosh rec. need-based scholarship or grant aid	80
% needy UG rec. need-based scholarship or grant aid	75
% needy frosh rec. non-need-based scholarship or grant aid	55
% needy UG rec. non-need-based scholarship or grant aid	40
% needy frosh rec. need-based self-help aid	78
% needy UG rec. need-based self-help aid	85
% frosh rec. any financial aid	65
% UG rec. any financial aid	62
% UG borrow to pay for school	47
Average cumulative indebtedness	$26,718
% frosh need fully met	21
% ugrads need fully met	15
Average % of frosh need met	57
Average % of ugrad need met	55

UNIVERSITY OF ARIZONA

PO BOX 210073, TUCSON, AZ 85721-0073 • ADMISSIONS: 520-621-3237 • FAX: 520-621-9799

CAMPUS LIFE

Quality of Life Rating	**83**
Fire Safety Rating	**86**
Green Rating	**96**
Type of school	public
Environment	metropolis

STUDENTS

Total undergrad enrollment	30,665
% male/female	48/52
% from out of state	29
% from public high school	93
% frosh live on campus	89
# of fraternities	26
# of sororities	24
% African American	3
% Asian	5
% Caucasian	59
% Hispanic	22
% Native American	1
% international	4
# of countries represented	111

SURVEY SAYS . . .

Great computer facilities
School is well run
Everyone loves the Wildcats
Student publications are popular

ACADEMICS

Academic Rating	**70**
% students graduating within 4 years	36
Calendar	semester
Student/faculty ratio	20:1
Profs interesting rating	72
Profs accessible rating	72
Most classes have	20–29 students
Most lab/discussion sessions have	20–29 students

MOST POPULAR MAJORS

cell/cellular and molecular biology; political science and government; psychology

APPLICANTS ALSO LOOK AT AND OFTEN PREFER
University of Washington

AND RARELY PREFER
Baylor University, Arizona State University

STUDENTS SAY ". . ."

Academics

In the simplest terms, University of Arizona is all about providing its students with "endless opportunities." Located on a "gorgeous" campus in vibrant Tucson, U of A offers a "great education" in a "relaxed community." Students here truly appreciate the university's "strong commitment to undergraduate research." Moreover, Arizona really "helps make the cost of education manageable," even "offering many scholarships to out-of-state students who qualify." While undergrads are impressed by a myriad of disciplines, they call special attention to the "excellent" agriculture department and the "great" engineering program. Students also highlight the physiology program and note that U of A is "the only university that offers an undergraduate major through its medical school." Undergrads do admit that professors can range from "very boring" to "extremely fun and interesting." One sophomore does assure us, by and large, "Professors are enthusiastic and genuinely care about students." And a knowledgeable junior adds, "As I get into the higher level classes or the classes that are more focused on my major, I find that the teachers are more enthusiastic and dedicated to their students to see that they succeed." Fortunately, "One thing that is consistent about all of them (and the TAs as well) is their availability through office hours for one-on-one instruction." As this public health major concludes, "The University of Arizona is an institution that provides a well-rounded education and numerous opportunities that prepare students for their future ambitions, whatever they may be."

Life

Students at the U of A are "motivated academically" and devote a decent percentage of their weekdays to hitting the books. Of course, undergrads here are also "very social," and as a sophomore enthusiastically shares, "There is always something to do on campus, and there are a variety of clubs to get involved in." Indeed, there are a number of activities available, ranging "from swing dance to intramural volleyball," which "help alleviate stress." Additionally, "people are really into the athletics. It builds school spirit for everyone involved, [and] tailgates are common on the weekends." Greek life is also extremely popular, and "on the weekends, frats have huge [theme] parties including ZBTahiti, AEPirates, Heaven and Hell, Swampwater, Pajama Jam, and many more." Undergrads also enjoy hometown Tucson, which has "great live music, art, and cinema." The city also "generally has a lot of community activities like Day of the Dead, which is extremely popular." Lastly, students also like to take advantage of the numerous outdoor recreation options available, and many often go "hiking or biking at the nearby mountain ranges."

Student Body

Undergrads at U of A report that the "relaxed" nature of their peers contributes to a "laid-back" atmosphere, which permeates the campus. While some students are most assuredly "in school to learn," others seem "to party their way through." However, an optical engineering major confidently states, "There is a place for you to fit in no matter what you want to get out of your college education." And a fellow engineering student adds, "Most students are very friendly and will greet each other around campus." U of A is quite "diverse," and you can easily find students of/from all different "socioeconomic statuses, states, countries, races, ethnicities, ages, etc." A junior tells us that people often make friends by simply getting "involved with something they are interested in and meeting like-minded individuals." One thing that unites these undergrads? Nearly all these "Wildcats" are "full of pride for their school." Perhaps this content freshman says it best, "In a school of 30,000, there is really no typical student, but with such a great number of students, people find their niche."

FINANCIAL AID: 520-621-1858 • E-MAIL: ADMISSIONS@ARIZONA.EDU • WEBSITE: WWW.ARIZONA.EDU

THE PRINCETON REVIEW SAYS

Admissions

Very important factors considered include: Academic GPA, rigor of secondary school record. *Other factors considered include:* Class rank, application essay, recommendation(s), standardized test scores, character/personal qualities, extracurricular activities, first generation, geographical residence, interview, racial/ethnic status, state residency, talent/ability, volunteer work, work experience. SAT or ACT required; ACT with or without writing component accepted. TOEFL required of all international applicants. High school diploma is required and GED is accepted. *Academic units required:* 4 English, 4 mathematics, 3 science (3 science labs), 2 foreign language, 1 social studies, 1 history, 1 fine art. *Academic units recommended:* 4 English, 3 science (3 science labs), 2 foreign language, 2 social studies, 1 history, 1 fine art.

Financial Aid

Students should submit: FAFSA. The Princeton Review suggests that all financial aid forms be submitted as soon as possible after January 1. *Need-based scholarships/grants offered:* Federal Pell, SEOG, state scholarships/grants, private scholarships, the school's own gift aid, Federal Nursing Scholarships. *Loan aid offered:* Direct Subsidized Stafford, Direct Unsubsidized Stafford, Direct PLUS, Federal Perkins, Federal Nursing, college/university loans from institutional funds. Federal Work-Study Program available. Institutional employment available. Off-campus job opportunities are good.

The Inside Word

Admission to the U of A is competitive, and you'll need to demonstrate achievement in college prep courses. Arizona resident should take note: Candidates applying from within the state who graduate in the top twenty-five percent of their class and meet all course requirements gain automatic acceptance through the assured admission program. Applicants should also recognize that some programs, such as the College of Engineering and College of Fine Arts, mandate additional materials and requirements.

THE SCHOOL SAYS ". . ."

From the Admissions Office

"Surrounded by the scenic beauty of desert mountain ranges and basking in 350 days of sunshine per year, the University of Arizona offers a top-notch education in a resort-like setting. From day one students are part of Arizona's 100 percent engagement mission, which holds that every undergrad will gain real-world experience in the form of internships, research or community service by the time they graduate. The clear Arizona skies provide an ideal setting for one of the country's best astronomy programs and nationally rated programs including business (entrepreneurship), nursing, management information systems, computer and aerospace engineering, anthropology, sociology, and creative writing. The UA balances its world-class research curriculum with a faculty that incluces Nobel and Pulitzer Prize winners. A wealth of academic choices and support—114 majors, with numerous concentration options—is supplemented by an active, cheerful, and inviting campus atmosphere that includes more than 500 student clubs and organizations, conference-winning and national title–winning basketball, baseball, swimming, softball, and football teams; and countless recreational opportunities."

SELECTIVITY	
Admissions Rating	**81**
# of applicants	32,227
% of applicants accepted	69
% of acceptees attending	33

FRESHMAN PROFILE	
Range SAT Critical Reading	480–600
Range SAT Math	490–620
Range SAT Writing	480–600
Range ACT Composite	21–27
Minimum paper TOEFL	550
Minimum web-based TOEFL	79
Average HS GPA	3.4

DEADLINES	
Early action	
Notification	12/15
Regular	
Deadline	5/1
Nonfall registration?	yes

FINANCIAL FACTS	
Financial Aid Rating	**75**
Annual in-state tuition	$9,114
Annual out-state tuition	$25,310
Room and board	$8,540
Required fees	$921
Books and supplies	$1,000
% needy frosh rec. need-based scholarship or grant aid	92
% needy UG rec. need-based scholarship or grant aid	90
% needy frosh rec. non-need-based scholarship or grant aid	11
% needy UG rec. non-need-based scholarship or grant aid	8
% needy frosh rec. need-based self-help aid	57
% needy UG rec. need-based self-help aid	65
% UG borrow to pay for school	46
Average cumulative indebtedness	$21,247
% frosh need fully met	13
% ugrads need fully met	11
Average % of frosh need met	66
Average % of ugrad need met	63

UNIVERSITY OF ARKANSAS—FAYETTEVILLE

232 SILAS HUNT HALL, FAYETTEVILLE, AR 72701 • ADMISSIONS: 479-575-5346 • FAX: 479-575-7515

CAMPUS LIFE

Quality of Life Rating	**89**
Fire Safety Rating	**82**
Green Rating	**93**
Type of school	public
Environment	town

STUDENTS

Total undergrad enrollment	16,794
% male/female	52/48
% from out of state	39
% from public high school	84
% frosh live on campus	89
# of fraternities	16
# of sororities	11
% African American	5
% Asian	3
% Caucasian	81
% Hispanic	5
% Native American	2
% international	3
# of countries represented	106

SURVEY SAYS . . .

Athletic facilities are great
Students love Fayetteville, AR
Everyone loves the Razorbacks
Frats and sororities dominate social scene

ACADEMICS

Academic Rating	**73**
% students returning for sophomore year	83
% students graduating within 4 years	35
% students graduating within 6 years	58
Calendar	semester
Student/faculty ratio	18:1
Profs interesting rating	71
Profs accessible rating	73
Most classes have	20–29 students
Most lab/discussion sessions have	20–29 students

MOST POPULAR MAJORS

finance; journalism; marketing/marketing management

APPLICANTS ALSO LOOK AT AND OFTEN PREFER

Stanford University

AND SOMETIMES PREFER

University of California—Los Angeles

AND RARELY PREFER

University of California—Santa Barbara, University of California—Davis, University of California—Santa Cruz, University of California—San Diego

STUDENTS SAY "..."

Academics

The University of Arkansas is affordable, "student-centered," and large but not gargantuan. Though you'll see some sizeable lectures during your first year, most classes are "relatively small." "The facilities are exceptional" and otherwise "state-of-the-art." More than 100 undergraduate majors and programs are available. The Sam Walton College of Business is awash in cash and "one of the strongest assets." Engineering majors can participate in cutting-edge research. Agricultural programs are strong and diverse. The honors college is "wonderful." Also, some twenty-five percent of all Arkansas students study abroad. There are summer programs available in China and Egypt, just to a name two examples. Programs during the academic year take place in every nook and cranny of the globe. Student opinion is split with regard to the administration. Some students call the management "very friendly." "Things run pretty smoothly," they say. Others contend that UA is "overly bureaucratic." "The odds of being sent to three different buildings, none of which is right, are pretty much even," wagers one malcontent. Despite "a few really atrocious instructors," students generally praise Arkansas's "dynamic faculty." "The professors are almost always good teachers," and they "know their material." Outside of class, professors tend to be "accessible" and "willing to do anything it takes for the success of their students."

Life

"Parking is horrible," but UA boasts a "beautiful," "well-defined campus with lots of green space." The rolling hills provide plenty of "great exercise," too. Students here reportedly enjoy a "vibrant extracurricular and social scene." "There are lots of things to do that don't involve booze." With more than 300 clubs and groups to choose from "the vast majority of students participate in at least a few campus organizations." "Greek life is prevalent," according to some students. "Intramural sports are popular." Razorback football "is the big highlight of the fall," and the campus has "a lot of spirit" for the beloved Hogs. There are ample activities that do involve booze as well. "Parties are everywhere." "A lot of people will go to the fraternity houses" for revelry. There's also "great nightlife" and "a very enthusiastic bar scene" off campus. "Funky," "charming," and "not-too-expensive," Fayetteville is, by all accounts, a "pretty neat town." Eclectic restaurants and live music venues are ample. "The always-enticing Dickson Street," "located a couple blocks away," is the hub of it all. "On the weekends, it borders on insanity." For outdoorsy types, wilderness activities abound throughout northwestern Arkansas. "The nearby mountains" provide numerous opportunities for climbing, biking, and hiking.

Student Body

They typical student here is "overly friendly," "fun-loving," "at least somewhat religious, and has a southern accent." Most students come "from either Arkansas or Texas." There are "a lot of international students," but "there is little ethnic diversity." Like at virtually every other flagship state university, you'll find "all kinds of students" on this campus. Fayetteville is called "the melting pot of Arkansas." Politics range from "conservative" to "incredibly liberal." "Students come from all walks of life and have many different experiences to share with others." "Party-frat kids abound," as do "southern sorority girls who walk to class in pearls and heels." However, you'll also find "hicks," "artists, musicians, nerds," and "NPR listening, sandal-wearing, health-food-shopping people," as well as the occasional "middle-aged boomer returning to school to start a whole new career." "There is always someone just as weird as you to run with," and students generally "mesh well" even if "groups don't often commingle."

FINANCIAL AID: 479-575-3806 • E-MAIL: UOFA@UARK.EDU • WEBSITE: WWW.UARK.EDU

THE PRINCETON REVIEW SAYS

Admissions

Very important factors considered include: Class rank, academic GPA, rigor of secondary school record, standardized test scores. *Other factors considered include:* Application essay, recommendation(s), alumni/ae relation, character/personal qualities, extracurricular activities, first generation, geographical residence, racial/ethnic status, state residency, talent/ability, volunteer work, work experience. SAT or ACT required; ACT with writing component required. TOEFL required of all international applicants. High school diploma is required and GED is accepted. *Academic units required:* 4 English, 4 mathematics, 3 science (2 science labs), 3 social studies, 2 academic electives. *Academic units recommended:* 2 foreign language.

Financial Aid

Students should submit: FAFSA. Regular filing deadline is March 2. The Princeton Review suggests that all financial aid forms be submitted as soon as possible after January 1. *Need-based scholarships/grants offered:* Federal Pell, SEOG, state scholarships/grants, private scholarships, the school's own gift aid. *Loan aid offered:* Direct Subsidized Stafford, Direct Unsubsidized Stafford, Direct PLUS, Federal Perkins, state loans, college/university loans from institutional funds, alternative loans. Applicants will be notified of awards on a rolling basis beginning April 1. Federal Work-Study Program available. Institutional employment available. Highest amount earned per year from on-campus jobs $3,000.

The Inside Word

The admissions policy at the University of Arkansas is very straightforward. You need a 3.0 grade-point average (on a 4.0 scale) in your serious academic coursework and at least a 20 on the ACT. The SAT is fine, too, as long as get a comparable minimum score. If you fail to meet these requirements, you still may gain admission based on a case-by-case review process. Also, UA has a rolling admissions policy. As such, candidates will find it in their best interest to apply early.

THE SCHOOL SAYS ". . ."

From the Admissions Office

"The University of Arkansas, the flagship campus of the University of Arkansas System, is located in Fayetteville and overlooks the beautiful Ozark Mountains. The university is both the major land-grant university for Arkansas and the state university, encompassing more than 130 buildings on 345 acres and providing more than 200 graduate and undergraduate academic programs—more than some universities twice its size.

"At the same time, the University of Arkansas maintains a low student-to-faculty ratio—currently eighteen to one—that makes personal attention possible. The university aggressively promotes undergraduate research in virtually every discipline and makes higher education affordable with competitively priced tuition and generous financial aid. In the last decade, university undergraduates have earned many honors: thirty-four received Goldwater Scholarships; twelve have been recognized by the USA Today All-USA College Academic Team. There have been thirty-eight National Science Foundation graduate fellows; thirty-two Fulbright scholars; three British Marshall scholars and six Truman scholars. Four undergraduates have received Udall scholarships; four earned Madison scholarships; three have received Tylenol scholarships; and one was named a Rhodes scholar. Quality programs, affordable tuition and the level of student achievement all contribute to the University of Arkansas consistently being ranked in the top tier of national universities.

"The city of Fayetteville is home to more than 73,000 people and is growing every day. Northwest Arkansas is the headquarters to several major international corporations that have close ties to the university: Tyson Foods, the world's largest protein producer; J.B. Hunt Transport Services Inc., a major transportation and logistics company; and Wal-Mart Stores Inc., the world's largest corporation. Fayetteville has been named "One of America's Most Livable Cities," "One of America's 'Hottest' Cities," one of the nation's "least stressful" metro areas, and among the "Best Places to Live in America" by publications such as Forbes, Frommer's Guide, and Money magazine."

SELECTIVITY	
Admissions Rating	85
# of applicants	14,019
% of applicants accepted	60
% of acceptees attending	45
# admitted from wait list	139

FRESHMAN PROFILE	
Range SAT Critical Reading	500–610
Range SAT Math	520–640
Range ACT Composite	23–28
Minimum paper TOEFL	550
Minimum web-based TOEFL	79
Average HS GPA	3.6
% graduated top 10% of class	27
% graduated top 25% of class	56
% graduated top 50% of class	87

DEADLINES	
Early action	
Deadline	11/15
Notification	12/15
Regular	
Priority	11/15
Deadline	8/1
Nonfall registration?	yes

FINANCIAL FACTS	
Financial Aid Rating	74
Annual in-state tuition	$5,888
Annual out-state tuition	$16,320
Room and board	$8,330
Required fees	$1,286
Books and supplies	$1,214
% needy frosh rec. need-based scholarship or grant aid	87
% needy UG rec. need-based scholarship or grant aid	81
% needy frosh rec. non-need-based scholarship or grant aid	21
% needy UG rec. non-need-based scholarship or grant aid	14
% needy frosh rec. need-based self-help aid	55
% needy UG rec. need-based self-help aid	66
% UG borrow to pay for school	45
Average cumulative indebtedness	$21,562
% frosh need fully met	29
% ugrads need fully met	22
Average % of frosh need met	68
Average % of ugrad need met	64

University of California—Berkeley

110 Sproul Hall, Berkeley, CA 94720-5800 • Admissions: 510-642-3175 • Fax: 510-642-7333

CAMPUS LIFE

Quality of Life Rating	**67**
Fire Safety Rating	**78**
Green Rating	**97**
Type of school	public
Environment	city

STUDENTS

Total undergrad enrollment	25,885
% male/female	47/53
% from out of state	10
# of fraternities	38
# of sororities	19
% African American	9
% Asian	37
% Caucasian	30
% Hispanic	12
% Native American	1
% international	9

SURVEY SAYS . . .

Great library
Great off-campus food
Everyone loves the Golden Bears
Student publications are popular
Political activism is popular

ACADEMICS

Academic Rating	**83**
% students returning for sophomore year	97
% students graduating within 4 years	71
% students graduating within 6 years	90
Calendar	semester
Student/faculty ratio	17:1
Profs interesting rating	73
Profs accessible rating	66

MOST POPULAR MAJORS

computer engineering; English language and literature; political science and government

APPLICANTS ALSO LOOK AT AND OFTEN PREFER

Stanford University

AND SOMETIMES PREFER

University of California—Los Angeles

AND RARELY PREFER

University of California—Santa Barbara, University of California—Davis, University of California—Santa Cruz, University of California—San Diego

STUDENTS SAY ". . ."

Academics

The University of California—Berkeley is a large public university where students feel that their "professors [are] all warm, open, and inviting." In fact, many students choose UC Berkeley because they feel "it's the best public university in the world." Students are quick to point out, "There are some amazing and inspiring minds at Berkeley." With an "all-star faculty and resources," professors here are "intelligent, accessible," with many departments boasting "the best [academics] in their field." Academics here are "on par with the best in the nation." For those students seeking a first-class education, UC Berkeley is "a place of incredible academic opportunity." Students here are a self-motivated lot. As some students note, "you don't get the coddling that the private universities show. You don't have a billion counselors catering to your every need." In addition, "there is no grade inflation." Though students note that survey classes here can sometimes be "enormous," professors "make themselves very accessible via e-mail and office hours." In addition, students find individual attention within "upper-division classes." These classes tend to have "smaller class sizes," while "lower-division classes" are pretty large and, in some cases, the quality "really depends on" the graduate student instructor. In general, UC Berkeley features the opportunity to work with "amazing professors from every department. Challenging, yet stimulating." However, students offer the occasional cautious caveat that, much like every public university in the country, "some professors obviously are more into research than teaching, but others make learning so enjoyable. I would say that the latter occurs way more than the former."

Life

Full of their signature optimism, students here say that "life at Berkeley has no limits;" we "study and hear obscure languages, meet famous scientists, engage with brilliant students, eat delicious food, and just relax with friends daily." Students also note, "The plus about Berkeley is that because of its location in the San Francisco Bay Area, there is a wealth of activities." For those who enjoy off-campus, outdoor recreation, there are "museums, parks, fairs, cultural events, plus gorgeous hiking trails and some of the best views in the bay." San Francisco is simply a short Bay Area Rapid Transit ride away. Though academics take up a large amount of students' free time, with a diversity of majors and interests, students note life here is "anything you want it to be." The general consensus is that "everyone here is not afraid to express themselves, and the opportunity to make a fresh start in college is amazingly liberating." Furthermore, "The friends you make here are closer than you have ever had and probably ever will have." Others note, "The amount of fun you'll have depends on your course load, though there are always events on campus, whether they are concerts, circus performances, club-sponsored activities or events in the dorms." Even "the busiest college student" finds time to attend campus events and his or her niche in the campus community. At UC Berkeley, "You simply won't have the chance to be bored."

Student Body

To simply label this school as "diverse" seems like a simplification. Here, people "think about everything." It's a place where "it's not uncommon to hear conversations vary from the wicked party last night…turn into debates about the roles of women in Hindu mythology to the specifics behind DNA replication." Students here "are ambitious, but fun to be around." For the most part, "Students fit in just fine, but the experience they have is what they make of it."

FINANCIAL AID: 510-642-6442 • WEBSITE: WWW.BERKELEY.EDU

THE PRINCETON REVIEW SAYS

Admissions

Very important factors considered include: Application essay, academic GPA, rigor of secondary school record, state residency. *Important factors considered include:* Standardized test scores, character/personal qualities, extracurricular activities, talent/ability, volunteer work, work experience. *Other factors considered include:* First generation, geographical residence. SAT or ACT required; ACT with writing component required. TOEFL required of all international applicants. High school diploma is required and GED is accepted. *Academic units required:* 4 English, 3 mathematics, 2 science (2 science labs), 2 foreign language, 2 history, 1 visual/performing arts, 1 academic elective. *Academic units recommended:* 4 English, 4 mathematics, 3 science (3 science labs), 3 foreign language, 2 history, 1 visual/performing arts, 1 academic elective.

Financial Aid

Students should submit: FAFSA, state aid form. The Princeton Review suggests that all financial aid forms be submitted as soon as possible after January 1. *Need-based scholarships/grants offered:* Federal Pell, SEOG, state scholarships/grants, private scholarships, the school's own gift aid. *Loan aid offered:* Direct Subsidized Stafford, Direct Unsubsidized Stafford, Direct PLUS, Federal Perkins. Applicants will be notified of awards on or about April 15. Federal Work-Study Program available. Institutional employment available. Off-campus job opportunities are excellent.

The Inside Word

UC Berkeley is a top-notch public university with a well-regarded English and Literature department. Importance is placed on the totality of a student's application with a joint focus on the personal essay and academic excellence as noted by a student's GPA. Class rank isn't considered. The school is home to an incredible amount of students with as wide a range of interests. Successful applicants here are generally stellar both academically and personally. Applications, especially the essay, should create a picture of a unique candidate with a diversity of skills to offer this active community.

THE SCHOOL SAYS ". . ."

From the Admissions Office

"One of the top public universities in the nation and the world, the University of California—Berkeley offers a vast range of courses and a full menu of extracurricular activities. Berkeley's academic programs are internationally recognized for their excellence. Undergraduates can choose one of 100 majors. Thirty-five departments are top ranked, more than any other college or university in the country. Access to one of the foremost university libraries enriches studies. There are twenty-three specialized libraries on campus and distinguished museums of anthropology, paleontology, and science.

"All applicants must take the ACT plus writing or the SAT Reasoning Test. UC admissions requirements are found at http://www.universityofcalifornia.edu/admissions/freshman/requirements/index.html."

SELECTIVITY	
Admissions Rating	98
# of applicants	52,966
% of applicants accepted	22
% of acceptees attending	39
# admitted from wait list	129

FRESHMAN PROFILE	
Range SAT Critical Reading	600–720
Range SAT Math	650–770
Range SAT Writing	620–740
Range ACT Composite	28–33
Minimum paper TOEFL	550
Minimum web-based TOEFL	80
Average HS GPA	3.8
% graduated top 10% of class	98
% graduated top 25% of class	100
% graduated top 50% of class	100

DEADLINES	
Regular	
Deadline	11/30
Notification	3/31
Nonfall registration?	yes

FINANCIAL FACTS	
Financial Aid Rating	75
Annual in-state tuition	$11,220
Annual out-state tuition	$34,098
Room and board	$14,990
Required fees	$1,615
Books and supplies	$1,202
% needy frosh rec. need-based scholarship or grant aid	91
% needy UG rec. need-based scholarship or grant aid	95
% needy frosh rec. non-need-based scholarship or grant aid	33
% needy UG rec. non-need-based scholarship or grant aid	10
% needy frosh rec. need-based self-help aid	87
% needy UG rec. need-based self-help aid	87
% UG borrow to pay for school	42
Average cumulative indebtedness	$17,116
% frosh need fully met	17
% ugrads need fully met	19
Average % of frosh need met	82
Average % of ugrad need met	83

UNIVERSITY OF CALIFORNIA—DAVIS

178 MRAK HALL, ONE SHIELDS AVENUE, DAVIS, CA 95616 • ADMISSIONS: 530-752-2971 • FAX: 530-752-1280

CAMPUS LIFE

Quality of Life Rating	**90**
Fire Safety Rating	**72**
Green Rating	**94**
Type of school	public
Environment	town

STUDENTS

Total undergrad enrollment	24,913
% male/female	44/55
% from out of state	5
% from public high school	84
% frosh live on campus	92
# of fraternities	28
# of sororities	21
% African American	2
% Asian	37
% Caucasian	34
% Hispanic	16
% international	3
# of countries represented	121

SURVEY SAYS . . .

Athletic facilities are great
Student publications are popular
Great library
Low cost of living

ACADEMICS

Academic Rating	**72**
% students returning for sophomore year	93
% students graduating within 4 years	51
% students graduating within 6 years	82
Calendar	quarter
Student/faculty ratio	16:1
Profs interesting rating	68
Profs accessible rating	68
Most classes have	20–29 students
Most lab/discussion sessions have	20–29 students

MOST POPULAR MAJORS

biology/biological sciences; economics; psychology

APPLICANTS ALSO LOOK AT AND OFTEN PREFER

University of California—Berkeley, University of California—San Diego, University of California—Los Angeles

AND SOMETIMES PREFER

University of California—Santa Barbara

AND RARELY PREFER

University of California—Riverside

STUDENTS SAY ". . ."

Academics

It's not every university where you can "touch a pig, pet a baby goat, and milk a cow if you'd like." But what else would you expect from "one of the top agriculture and animal science schools in the United States?" Backed by "strong science programs," "cutting-edge research," and "the incredible amount of internships available," UC Davis is many students' idea of great academia. For those who don't handle stress all that well, "UC Davis is the perfect combination of a top-rated institution and a calm and non-competitive student body." This "prestigious" school is located in northern California and is well-known for its "agricultural sustainability and awareness." "The campus is very green and embraces biking to the maximum." "If you can't bike, you probably shouldn't go here." Opinions on professors vary but most students agree that they "are all experts in their field." Some students report that UC Davis professors "are driven by their research" and "tend to take teaching as a secondary position to [it]. However, when they integrate their research and knowledge of the subject in their classes, it can make for a very interesting and enlightening education." Students also point out that UC Davis offers "a lot of majors to choose from and a variety of interesting classes that most schools don't offer." Not everyone is comfortable with classes divided by the quarter system because "learning material and exams go by kind of fast." For some, "The quarter system is a drastic change from the pace, but not necessarily the demands, of the semester system. In what most schools cover in about fifteen weeks, UCD covers in ten weeks."

Life

Known for its "good weather," UC Davis is located about "an hour out of the Bay Area [where] every outdoor option [is] possible." Davis is "a quaint little college town "with a great personality," and "the campus is beautiful." It is a "beautiful farmland university" that is "very safe and clean." One student comments, "I love how there are places where you can take a break and a nap without worrying about your safety." Although there are your typical "parties at frat houses," there are tons of other forms of entertainment to be had. "There's more than just partying. The clubs open you up to anything from rock climbing and water skiing to badminton and pool." There is also a bowling alley on campus. The school is proactive in promoting both "sustainable living" and a "healthy lifestyle." There is a "good variety of healthy meals/food to choose from (and local products)," and students are encouraged to exercise and make use of the numerous bike paths (albeit "bumpy" ones). According to one student, "The gym is the best of any campus I have seen." There is also a "giant library" that gets rave reviews from many students. When venturing off campus, "The Davis Farmer's Market is legendary and a requirement at least once while you're here. And there are also a great many small businesses and fantastic restaurants downtown that offer students great experiences at fairly reasonable prices." The "small" town of Davis has a "community feel" as well as a "college town atmosphere." As one student eloquently explains, "Although it smells like cows, you'll miss it after you graduate."

Student Body

"The student body here is very diverse." They range from "athletes to engineers. But they all have one thing in common. They are here to have a serious college education." The vibe from students at UC Davis is "liberal, challenging, and accepting," while also "very friendly, easygoing," and "environmentally aware." Although students are "very studious," they "know how to manage their priorities and still find ways to enjoy themselves." Even though, "Everyone is so different; you have the agriculture people, the political science people, and the premed people all mixed together," problems are minimal. "Everyone is so accepting of everyone else and fitting in just comes naturally because everyone gets along very well." "There is such a huge variety of clubs, fraternities/sororities, societies and groups on campus, it is almost impossible to not have friends."

FINANCIAL AID: 530-752-2396 • E-MAIL: UNDERGRADUATEADMISSIONS@UCDAVIS.EDU • WEBSITE: WWW.UCDAVIS.EDU

THE PRINCETON REVIEW SAYS

Admissions

Very important factors considered include: Academic GPA, rigor of secondary school record, standardized test scores. *Important factors considered include:* Application essay, character/personal qualities, extracurricular activities, first generation, talent/ability. *Other factors considered include:* State residency, volunteer work, work experience. SAT or ACT required; ACT with writing component required. TOEFL required of all international applicants. High school diploma is required and GED is accepted. *Academic units required:* 4 English, 3 mathematics, 2 science (2 science labs), 2 foreign language, 2 social studies, 1 visual/performing arts, 1 academic electives. *Academic units recommended:* 4 English, 4 mathematics, 3 science (3 science labs), 3 foreign language, 2 social studies, 1 visual/performing arts, 1 academic electives.

Financial Aid

Students should submit: FAFSA. The Princeton Review suggests that all financial aid forms be submitted as soon as possible after January 1. *Need-based scholarships/grants offered:* Federal Pell, SEOG, state scholarships/grants, private scholarships, the school's own gift aid, specify):Academic Competitiveness Grant (ACG) and National Science and Mathematics Access to Retain Talent Grant (SMART). *Loan aid offered:* Direct Subsidized Stafford, Direct Unsubsidized Stafford, Direct PLUS, Federal Perkins, college/university loans from institutional funds. Applicants will be notified of awards on a rolling basis beginning March 12. Highest amount earned per year from on-campus jobs $7,280.

The Inside Word

Admission to UC Davis is considerably easier than, say, admission to Berkeley. Nevertheless, every school in the UC system is world-class, and the UC system in general is geared toward the best and brightest of California's high school students.

THE SCHOOL SAYS "..."

From the Admissions Office

"UC Davis is characterized by a distinguished faculty of scholars, scientists, and artists; a treasured sense of community; and a dedication to innovative teaching, research, and public service. Student involvement in academics, leadership, and honors programs, as well as internships, education abroad, and research, typify the undergraduate experience. These experiences serve as vehicles for enhancing the quality of faculty-student interactions at a premier research university that addresses the critical issues facing our world today. Students can earn degrees in more than 100 majors, work alongside professional researchers, and receive pre-graduate advising in nearly any field imaginable.

"The friendly, supportive nature of the campus and Davis community also defines the undergraduate experience. More than 500 student-run clubs and organizations, themed residence hall programs, and cultural celebrations provide opportunities for students to learn about themselves and other cultures. UC Davis offers its active student body NCAA Division I athletics and stunning cultural, academic, and recreational facilities such as the Mondavi Center for the Performing Arts, the Robert Mondavi Institute for Wine and Food Science, and the Activities and Recreation Center. UC Davis also provides many resources to help undergraduates build social and career networks before they graduate, so that students are well-connected by the time they don their cap and gown.

"Freshman applicants are required to take the ACT assessment plus writing or the SAT Reasoning Test no later than December, the month following application to UC Davis. SAT Subject Tests are not required."

SELECTIVITY

Admissions Rating	**96**
# of applicants	45,806
% of applicants accepted	46
% of acceptees attending	22
# accepting a place on wait list	2,220
# admitted from wait list	871

FRESHMAN PROFILE

Range SAT Critical Reading	520–650
Range SAT Math	570–690
Range SAT Writing	540–670
Range ACT Composite	24–30
Minimum paper TOEFL	550
Minimum web-based TOEFL	60
Average HS GPA	3.9
% graduated top 10% of class	100
% graduated top 25% of class	100
% graduated top 50% of class	100

DEADLINES

Regular	
Deadline	11/30
Notification	3/31
Nonfall registration?	no

FINANCIAL FACTS

Financial Aid Rating	**79**
Annual in-state tuition	$11,220
Annual out-state tuition	$34,098
Room and board	$12,697
Required fees	$2,640
Books and supplies	$1,589
% needy frosh rec. need-based scholarship or grant aid	95
% needy UG rec. need-based scholarship or grant aid	95
% needy frosh rec. non-need-based scholarship or grant aid	1
% needy UG rec. non-need-based scholarship or grant aid	1
% needy frosh rec. need-based self-help aid	68
% needy UG rec. need-based self-help aid	67
% UG rec. any financial aid	54
Average cumulative indebtedness	$16,659
% frosh need fully met	14
% ugrads need fully met	20
Average % of frosh need met	82
Average % of ugrad need met	81

UNIVERSITY OF CALIFORNIA—LOS ANGELES

1147 Murphy Hall, Los Angeles, CA 90095-1436 • Admissions: 310-825-3101 • Fax: 310-206-1206

CAMPUS LIFE

Quality of Life Rating	85
Fire Safety Rating	95
Green Rating	95
Type of school	public
Environment	metropolis

STUDENTS

Total undergrad enrollment	26,162
% male/female	45/55
% from out of state	9
% from public high school	76
% frosh live on campus	94
# of fraternities	36
# of sororities	28
% African American	4
% Asian	36
% Caucasian	32
% Hispanic	16
% international	6
# of countries represented	104

SURVEY SAYS . . .

Athletic facilities are great
Students love Los Angeles, CA
Great food on campus
Great off-campus food
Everyone loves the Bruins
Student publications are popular

ACADEMICS

Academic Rating	79
% students returning for sophomore year	97
% students graduating within 4 years	68
% students graduating within 6 years	90
Calendar	quarter
Student/faculty ratio	17:1
Profs interesting rating	69
Profs accessible rating	65
Most classes have	10–19 students
Most lab/discussion sessions have	20–29 students

MOST POPULAR MAJORS

business/managerial economics; political science and government; psychology

STUDENTS SAY ". . ."

Academics

Undergrads at this esteemed university don't mince words when boasting about all that UCLA has to offer. As a geography and environmental science double-major proudly declares, "There's nothing that can't be accomplished at UCLA. The possibilities are endless, and the resources are unparalleled." Moreover, students appreciate the "ideal" location as well as the "pride of going to a Division I school with more NCAA championships than any other college/university." Perhaps more notable, "UCLA is the kind of school that pushes you to work hard academically but reminds you that interaction with people outside of the classroom is just as important." Students are continually impressed by their professors who are "leaders in their field." Indeed, most consider it "a privilege to study under them." While some undergrads caution that you might encounter some teachers simply "in it for the research," others insist, "Most professors care about their students." A political science major interjects, saying that professors "are willing to work extra hours with students and help us with anything we need." And an English major concurs, sharing, "I have never had a professor that I did not feel comfortable approaching, which has made my academic experience incredibly more beneficial." As this grateful junior succinctly explains, "UCLA is the campus. The people, the weather, the academics, the sports; it has absolutely everything I could ever want."

Life

There's so much "hustle and bustle" at UCLA that it would be virtually "impossible to [be] bored." While nearly everyone's "main focus is on school," most students also know how to "play hard." Indeed, "whether it be in Greek life, a club or organization, everybody has somewhere they can go to relax and have some fun. The apartments are close to campus, so nearly everybody lives in a small area with close proximity." Sports "are extremely popular here, and conversations about the Bruins are common." There are also "tons of movie showings on campus, recreation centers, pools, activities, [and] events." Additionally, students love being located in Los Angeles. A happy senior reveals, "You can take a five-minute drive and you'll be soaking in the Pacific Ocean, or take an hour drive where you can be hitting the slopes in Big Bear. You can walk down to the theater and run into Jennifer Lopez or head to the UCLA gym and watch…Kobe Bryant practicing. The possibilities are endless here, with or without money."

Student Body

UCLA "is the mold that fits you." Indeed, "26,000 students and more than 950 student groups," virtually assures that "there is no 'typical' student" to be found at UCLA. This wide range of individuals and activities guarantees that "everyone has their niche." Certainly, the Bruin community is a "vibrant" one, and "the unmatched diversity broadens students' horizons culturally and socially." Of course, undergrads here do tread some common ground. Many define their peers as "very hardworking and ambitious," and they typically "strive for success and to do their absolute best." They "know how to have a good time, but they also know when it is time to study." Further, it's an active student body, and it often "seems like everyone is in at least one club or organization." Friendliness is another trademark of UCLA undergrads as a physiology major assures us, "It is very easy to talk to and meet new people and make new friends." Fortunately, most people are "laid-back" and while "academically invested…[they're] not outright competitive with other students." This bio major sums up his peers easily by saying, "Everyone comes from different backgrounds with varied interests. The only common denominator is truly an appetite for excellence."

Financial Aid: 310-206-0400 • E-mail: ugadm@saonet.ucla.edu • Website: www.ucla.edu

THE PRINCETON REVIEW SAYS

Admissions

Very important factors considered include: Application essay, academic GPA, rigor of secondary school record, standardized test scores. *Important factors considered include:* Character/personal qualities, extracurricular activities, talent/ability, volunteer work, work experience. *Other factors considered include:* First generation, geographical residence. SAT or ACT required; ACT with writing component required. TOEFL required of all international applicants. High school diploma is required and GED is accepted. *Academic units required:* 4 English, 3 mathematics, 2 science (2 science labs), 2 foreign language, 2 history, 1 academic electives, 1 visual and performing arts. *Academic units recommended:* 4 English, 4 mathematics, 3 science (3 science labs), 3 foreign language, 2 history, 1 academic electives, 1 visual and performing arts.

Financial Aid

Students should submit: FAFSA. Regular filing deadline is March 2. The Princeton Review suggests that all financial aid forms be submitted as soon as possible after January 1. *Need-based scholarships/grants offered:* Federal Pell, SEOG, state scholarships/grants, private scholarships, the school's own gift aid, United Negro College Fund, Federal Nursing Scholarships. *Loan aid offered:* Direct Subsidized Stafford, Direct Unsubsidized Stafford, Direct PLUS, Federal Perkins, Federal Nursing, state loans, college/university loans from institutional funds. Applicants will be notified of awards on a rolling basis beginning March 15. Federal Work-Study Program available. Institutional employment available. Off-campus job opportunities are good.

The Inside Word

Competition is fierce to secure admittance to one of the nation's top public universities. Academic success is paramount, and your GPA and standardized test scores factor heavily into admissions decisions. You'll want to load up on challenging courses in high school. Indeed, taking advancement placement, IB, or honors classes is a must. Of course, UCLA also wants students who will actively contribute to their community, and it's also important to demonstrate commitment to extracurricular activities.

THE SCHOOL SAYS ". . ."

From the Admissions Office

"Undergraduates arrive at UCLA from throughout California and around the world with exceptional levels of academic preparation. They are attracted by our acclaimed degree programs, distinguished faculty, and the beauty of a park-like campus set amid the dynamism of the nation's second-largest city. UCLA's highly ranked undergraduate programs incorporate cutting-edge technology and teaching techniques that hone the critical-thinking skills and the global perspectives necessary for success in our rapidly changing world. The diversity of these programs draws strength from a student body that mirrors the cultural and ethnic vibrancy of Los Angeles. Generally ranked among the nation's top half-dozen universities, UCLA is at once distinguished and dynamic, academically rigorous and responsive.

"All applicants must take the ACT plus writing or the SAT Reasoning Test. Be sure to complete these tests by December. Engineering applicants are strongly urged to take the SAT Subject Test in Mathematics, Level 2, to demonstrate the proficiency in mathematics needed for success in Engineering courses."

SELECTIVITY	
Admissions Rating	**98**
# of applicants	61,564
% of applicants accepted	26
% of acceptees attending	37
FRESHMAN PROFILE	
Range SAT Critical Reading	570–680
Range SAT Math	600–740
Range SAT Writing	580–710
Range ACT Composite	25–31
Minimum paper TOEFL	550
Minimum web-based TOEFL	83
Average HS GPA	4.3
% graduated top 10% of class	97
% graduated top 25% of class	100
% graduated top 50% of class	100
DEADLINES	
Regular	
Deadline	11/30
Nonfall registration?	no
FINANCIAL FACTS	
Financial Aid Rating	**82**
Annual in-state tuition	$12,686
Annual out-state tuition	$35,564
Room and board	$14,208
Books and supplies	$1,521
% needy frosh rec. need-based scholarship or grant aid	96
% needy UG rec. need-based scholarship or grant aid	95
% needy frosh rec. non-need-based scholarship or grant aid	2
% needy UG rec. non-need-based scholarship or grant aid	1
% needy frosh rec. need-based self-help aid	66
% needy UG rec. need-based self-help aid	59
% frosh rec. any financial aid	54
% UG rec. any financial aid	56
% UG borrow to pay for school	44
Average cumulative indebtedness	$18,814
% frosh need fully met	15
% ugrads need fully met	15
Average % of frosh need met	85
Average % of ugrad need met	84

UNIVERSITY OF CALIFORNIA—RIVERSIDE

3106 STUDENT SERVICES BUILDING, RIVERSIDE, CA 92521 • ADMISSIONS: 951-827-3411 • FAX: 951-827-6344

CAMPUS LIFE

Quality of Life Rating	**85**
Fire Safety Rating	**85**
Green Rating	**93**
Type of school	public
Environment	city

STUDENTS

Total undergrad enrollment	18,532
% male/female	48/52
% from out of state	1
% from public high school	91
% frosh live on campus	77
# of fraternities	20
# of sororities	20
% African American	6
% Asian	37
% Caucasian	16
% Hispanic	33
% international	2
# of countries represented	62

SURVEY SAYS . . .

Great library
Athletic facilities are great
Diverse student types on campus
Different types of students interact
Frats and sororities dominate social scene
Student publications are popular

ACADEMICS

Academic Rating	**67**
% students returning for sophomore year	87
% students graduating within 4 years	42
% students graduating within 6 years	70
Calendar	quarter
Student/faculty ratio	18:1
Profs interesting rating	65
Profs accessible rating	70
Most classes have	20–29 students
Most lab/discussion sessions have	20–29 students

MOST POPULAR MAJORS

biology/biological sciences; business administration and management; psychology

APPLICANTS ALSO LOOK AT AND OFTEN PREFER

University of California—Los Angeles, University of California—Berkeley, University of California—San Diego

AND SOMETIMES PREFER

University of California—Santa Barbara, University of California—Davis

AND RARELY PREFER

University of California—Santa Cruz

STUDENTS SAY ". . ."

Academics

Students at the University of California—Riverside are in love with many things—the "small class size" and "beautiful campus" come up often—but the educators here receive the lion's share of the praise. Professors here are "very skilled in teaching" and "have passion to teach and help their students." Teachers "don't just read from a book and teach you the stuff, they also bring the material to life and make class really enjoyable." This is because they "really know the material they are teaching and are very passionate about it," resulting in "lively discussions" and an "open and diverse campus." This is a school that is devoted to "helping students achieve their academic goals while at the same time connecting them to their community." Some students admit their "overall academic experience has had its ups and downs," saying, "Some classes were interesting and structured well, while others were not," but by and large, educators are "willing to dedicate an enormous amount of time to interact with and help students in order for us to succeed." Career-minded students will find that counselors here are "more than willing to help you with your career path," and the school also "has great connections and support, which is vital for creating a network that helps with internships and future jobs in your major." Graduates of UCR "have integrity, accountability, excellence, and respect."

Life

It's not hard to make friends at UCR, "but I know it would've been easier if I tried joining a club or organization," one student comments, which comes as no surprise, since "many students are involved in campus clubs and organizations." It's easy to find activities for the student who looks, since "there is always an event going on such as athletic games, plays, and musical shows." Students here "aren't under extreme pressure," so they manage to "find the time to explore our own interests and ideas with others." School-based clubs and organizations may be the option of choice, however, since "Riverside city isn't the prettiest, and it gets ridiculously hot during the summer." That said, some students think that "downtown Riverside is beautiful," and UCR students like going there to "go ice skating or shopping at the various malls." Outdoorsy types will be glad to know that the "weather is awesome," and "The beaches are an hour away, and so are the mountains and desert in opposite directions." Active students say, "It's always nice to travel, hike, camp, and just have fun with friends."

Student Body

The active, community-focused students of UCR are "usually part of at least one extracurricular group," the result of "a diverse student body anxious to learn about the world and what they can do to make the world a better place." Though UCR's campus can't be called cozy, it is small enough that "everyone knows everyone through at least one connection." The typical student is "friendly, engaging, outgoing, and eager to learn." Those attending almost universally report that making friends here is easy "because the acceptance level at UCR [among students] is 100 percent." The school "is like a giant melting pot; every student is different but we all fit together perfectly." Getting involved in social causes is not unusual among the student body, though "a typical student is always more worried about their outfits than politics and social issues," which isn't to say many aren't driven by such causes. One student reports, "I like to organize forums and participate in social justice rallies on and off campus." Overall, though, laid-back and inviting is the rule of the day. "Students fit in by being who they are because everyone is friendly," and they "always attend classes, go to org meetings, and campus events, and make it home in time to do four to five hours of studying."

FINANCIAL AID: 951-827-3878 • E-MAIL: ADMIT@UCR.EDU • WEBSITE: WWW.UCR.EDU

THE PRINCETON REVIEW SAYS

Admissions

Very important factors considered include: Academic GPA, rigor of secondary school record, standardized test scores, state residency. *Important factors considered include:* Application essay. *Other factors considered include:* First generation. SAT or ACT required; ACT with writing component required. TOEFL required of all international applicants. High school diploma is required and GED is accepted. *Academic units required:* 4 English, 3 mathematics, 2 science (2 science labs), 2 foreign language, 2 history, 1 visual/performing arts, 1 academic electives. *Academic units recommended:* 4 mathematics, 3 science (3 science labs), 3 foreign language.

Financial Aid

Students should submit: FAFSA, state aid form. The Princeton Review suggests that all financial aid forms be submitted as soon as possible after January 1. *Need-based scholarships/grants offered:* Federal Pell, SEOG, state scholarships/grants, private scholarships, the school's own gift aid. *Loan aid offered:* Direct Subsidized Stafford, Direct Unsubsidized Stafford, Direct PLUS, Federal Perkins, college/university loans from institutional funds. Applicants will be notified of awards on a rolling basis beginning March 1. Federal Work-Study Program available. Institutional employment available. Off-campus job opportunities are excellent.

The Inside Word

The UC—Riverside admissions process is based heavily on quantitative fac tors. Applicants who have strong GPAs and standardized test scores should have no problem gaining acceptance. There is a priority filing period, so stu dents should apply as early as possible.

THE SCHOOL SAYS ". . ."

From the Admissions Office

"The University of California—Riverside offers the quality, rigor, and facilities of a major research institution, while assuring its undergraduates personal attention and a sense of community. Academic programs, teaching, advising, and student services all reflect the supportive attitudes that characterize the campus. Among the exceptional opportunities are the Thomas Haider Program in Biomedical Sciences, which provides an exclusive path to medical school: the University Honors Program, an extensive undergraduate research program, UC's largest undergraduate program is psychology, and UC's only bachelor's degree in creative writing. Additionally, the opening of UCR's School of Medicine is anticipated for August 2013. More than 300 student clubs and organizations and a variety of athletic and arts events give students a myriad of ways to get involved and have fun.

"Effective fall 2012, all applicants must take the ACT plus writing or the SAT Reasoning Test. The SAT Subject Tests will no longer be required for admission; however, students interested in admission to any major in the College of Natural and Agricultural Sciences or the Bourns College of Engineering are strongly recommended to take the SAT Subject Test math Level 2 and the SAT Subject Test in chemistry or physics."

SELECTIVITY	
Admissions Rating	92
# of applicants	28,101
% of applicants accepted	69
% of acceptees attending	13
# accepting a place on wait list	1,580
# admitted from wait list	1,014

FRESHMAN PROFILE	
Range SAT Critical Reading	460–580
Range SAT Math	490–630
Range SAT Writing	470–580
Range ACT Composite	19–25
Minimum paper TOEFL	550
Minimum web-based TOEFL	80
Average HS GPA	3.6
% graduated top 10% of class	94
% graduated top 25% of class	100
% graduated top 50% of class	100

DEADLINES	
Regular	
Deadline	11/30
Notification	3/31
Nonfall registration?	no

FINANCIAL FACTS	
Financial Aid Rating	81
Annual in-state tuition	$13,607
Annual out-state tuition	$36,485
Room and board	$12,100
Required fees	$1,703
Books and supplies	$1,800
% needy frosh rec. need-based scholarship or grant aid	97
% needy UG rec. need-based scholarship or grant aid	95
% needy frosh rec. non-need-based scholarship or grant aid	1
% needy UG rec. non-need-based scholarship or grant aid	2
% needy frosh rec. need-based self-help aid	85
% needy UG rec. need-based self-help aid	76
% frosh rec. any financial aid	79
% UG rec. any financial aid	77
% UG borrow to pay for school	68
Average cumulative indebtedness	$21,828
% frosh need fully met	39
% ugrads need fully met	31
Average % of frosh need met	91
Average % of ugrad need met	85

UNIVERSITY OF CALIFORNIA—SAN DIEGO

9500 GILMAN DRIVE, LA JOLLA, CA 92093-0021 • ADMISSIONS: 858-534-4831 • FAX: 858-534-5723

CAMPUS LIFE

Quality of Life Rating	**73**
Fire Safety Rating	**80**
Green Rating	**98**
Type of school	public
Environment	metropolis

STUDENTS

Total undergrad enrollment	23,046
% male/female	49/51
% from out of state	5
% frosh live on campus	93
# of fraternities	21
# of sororities	18
% African American	2
% Asian	41
% Caucasian	23
% Hispanic	15
% international	9
# of countries represented	83

SURVEY SAYS . . .

Class discussions are rare
Great computer facilities
Great library
Athletic facilities are great
Low cost of living
Very little drug use

ACADEMICS

Academic Rating	**77**
% students returning for sophomore year	96
% students graduating within 4 years	56
% students graduating within 6 years	85
Calendar	quarter
Student/faculty ratio	19:1
Profs interesting rating	69
Profs accessible rating	67
Most classes have	10–19 students
Most lab/discussion sessions have	20–29 students

MOST POPULAR MAJORS

biology/biological sciences; economics; psychology

APPLICANTS ALSO LOOK AT AND OFTEN PREFER

University of Southern California, University of California—Los Angeles, University of California—Davis, University of California—Berkeley, Stanford University

AND SOMETIMES PREFER

Stanford University, University of California—Davis, University of California—Santa Barbara

STUDENTS SAY ". . ."

Academics

UCSD is widely regarded by students as "one of the top science universities in the United States." As a result, the school attracts bright students who benefit from "access to cutting edge technology and theories" and "great opportunities for undergraduates to do research." Professors "are incredibly knowledgeable about their material, and many of them are actively doing research in their field." Research opportunities are widely available to undergraduate science majors. However, sciences are not the only attraction at UCSD. The university is home to six separate colleges, a system that students say is "a great way to not feel like a small fish in a huge ocean." Whereas it might seem like some science professors "are more interested in research than teaching," students say, "Humanities professors tend to be more accessible and more interested in their students as well as what they are teaching." Overall, however, "Professors are very helpful and willing to take extra time to help students understand material." Given the fact that UCSD is a large public university, students say, "Professors are extremely willing to help and mentor students if you seek them out." Another major benefit to attending a large university is that "there are a lot of resources, and there is always a faculty member or organization that will help you achieve what you want." Students say they are excited about "where UCSD is going; this university will undoubtedly set the new standard of what it means to be an elite public university in the years to come."

Life

Students love to take advantage of UCSD's "unbeatable location," ten minutes from the beach and a quick ride away from downtown San Diego. It is easy to enjoy "all the nature around the campus by hiking, biking, [and] camping," or taking surf lessons, which "are offered on campus for a modest fee." It is also "super easy to get to San Diego proper for a fun night out." There is a perception that social life is somewhat lacking on the campus itself, which may be the result of UCSD being such a large, academically intensive school. While some students have trouble fitting a social life into their busy study schedules, others say that, in fact, there are "tons of resources and ways to get involved" on campus; students "just have to actively seek them." Plenty of people "play sports or participate in clubs." "Lots of people enjoy kickbacks and small parties but the party scene isn't too big here." In the spring, the Sun God Festival is "always a popular event" that brings the entire campus together. There "is not really a huge emphasis on the athletics department," much to the annoyance of some students. However, students who make the most of their experience here maintain, "There is always an event going on and so many clubs to be involved in. From the Greek life, to the intramural sports, to the variety of clubs, there is literally a place for everyone."

Student Body

The typical student at UCSD "is a little nerdy and studies a lot." "Doing well academically at UCSD is an extreme priority, even to students who are not good students. Most of the students are geared toward extended education or professional school." However, "There are plenty of students who balance academics with other things, like sports or clubs." The student body "has such a diverse range of personalities" that most anyone "can fit in here because it's such a big school, and there are so many different organizations and places where you can find people that enjoy the same things as you." Students say that the population of students in the humanities has been growing "rapidly" in recent years, but some still see room for improvement among the diversity of the student body. There are those who would love "to see more students become socially conscious" to enhance the overall student body experience on campus.

FINANCIAL AID: 858-534-4480 • E-MAIL: ADMISSIONSINFO@UCSD.EDU • WEBSITE: WWW.UCSD.EDU

THE PRINCETON REVIEW SAYS

Admissions

Very important factors considered include: Application essay, academic GPA, rigor of secondary school record, standardized test scores, character/personal qualities, state residency, talent/ability. *Important factors considered include:* Extracurricular activities, volunteer work. *Other factors considered include:* First generation, work experience. SAT or ACT required; ACT with writing component required. TOEFL required of all international applicants. High school diploma is required and GED is accepted. *Academic units required:* 4 English, 3 mathematics, 2 science (2 science labs), 2 foreign language, 2 history, 1 visual/performing arts, 1 academic elective. *Academic units recommended:* 4 English, 4 mathematics, 3 science (3 science labs), 3 foreign language, 2 history, 1 academic elective.

Financial Aid

Students should submit: FAFSA, state aid form. Regular filing deadline is May 31. The Princeton Review suggests that all financial aid forms be submitted as soon as possible after January 1. *Need-based scholarships/grants offered:* Federal Pell, state scholarships/grants, private scholarships, the school's own gift aid. *Loan aid offered:* Direct Subsidized Stafford, Direct Unsubsidized Stafford, Direct PLUS, Federal Perkins, college/university loans from institutional funds, alternative loans. Applicants will be notified of awards on a rolling basis beginning March 15. Federal Work-Study Program available. Institutional employment available. Highest amount earned per year from on-campus jobs $15,840. Off-campus job opportunities are good.

The Inside Word

While not as lauded as Berkeley or UCLA, UCSD is rapidly earning its place as one of the gems of the UC system. It distinguishes itself in a num ber of ways, including its individualized approach to admissions. Although admissions officers do implement a formula, they factor in extracurricular pursuits and personal experiences. Applicants will need to be strong in all areas if they hope to attend UCSD.

THE SCHOOL SAYS ". . ."

From the Admissions Office

"UCSD is recognized for the exceptional quality of its academic programs. UCSD ranks fifth in the nation and first in the University of California system for the amount of federal research dollars spent on research and development; and the university ranks tenth in the nation in the excellence of its graduate programs and the quality of its faculty, according to the most recent National Research Council college rankings."

"About forty percent of UCSD's undergraduates participate in research, developing critical thinking and effective communication skills as well as greater cultural understanding. Their faculty mentors are in the divisions and schools of arts and humanities, biology, engineering, medicine, pharmacy, physical sciences, social sciences, and UCSD's Scripps Institution of Oceanography, California Institute for Telecommunications and Information Technology and the San Diego Supercomputer Center. Undergraduates also participate in research at the Salk Institute for Biological Studies and other nearby research institutes and biotechnology companies."

"All applicants must take the ACT plus writing or the SAT Reasoning Test. In addition, all applicants must take two SAT Subject Tests in two different subject areas. (If a math SAT Subject Test is chosen by the applicant, he/she must take the math Level II exam.)"

SELECTIVITY	
Admissions Rating	96
# of applicants	53,448
% of applicants accepted	36
% of acceptees attending	18
# accepting a place on wait list	3,384

FRESHMAN PROFILE	
Range SAT Critical Reading	520–650
Range SAT Math	590–710
Range SAT Writing	550–670
Range ACT Composite	24–30
Minimum paper TOEFL	550
Average HS GPA	4.0
% graduated top 10% of class	100
% graduated top 25% of class	100
% graduated top 50% of class	100

DEADLINES	
Regular	
Deadline	11/30
Notification	3/1
Nonfall registration?	yes

FINANCIAL FACTS	
Financial Aid Rating	78
Annual in-state tuition	$13,234
Annual out-state tuition	$22,878
Room and board	$11,571
Required fees	$930
Books and supplies	$1,427
% needy frosh rec. need-based scholarship or grant aid	94
% needy UG rec. need-based scholarship or grant aid	93
% needy frosh rec. non-need-based scholarship or grant aid	1
% needy frosh rec. need-based self-help aid	83
% needy UG rec. need-based self-help aid	80
% frosh rec. any financial aid	77
% UG rec. any financial aid	63
% UG borrow to pay for school	48
Average cumulative indebtedness	$18,757
% frosh need fully met	18
% ugrads need fully met	20
Average % of frosh need met	88
Average % of ugrad need met	86

University of California—Santa Barbara

Office of Admissions, Santa Barbara, CA 93106-2014 • Admissions: 805-893-2881 • Fax: 805-893-2676

CAMPUS LIFE

Quality of Life Rating	96
Fire Safety Rating	89
Green Rating	98
Type of school	public
Environment	city

STUDENTS

Total undergrad enrollment	18,617
% male/female	48/52
% from out of state	5
% from public high school	87
% frosh live on campus	33
# of fraternities	11
# of sororities	13
% African American	4
% Asian	20
% Caucasian	45
% Hispanic	24
% Native American	1
% international	2
# of countries represented	72

SURVEY SAYS . . .

Athletic facilities are great
Students are friendly
Student publications are popular
Lots of beer drinking
Hard liquor is popular
Students are environmentally aware

ACADEMICS

Academic Rating	82
% students returning for sophomore year	92
% students graduating within 4 years	66
% students graduating within 6 years	80
Calendar	quarter
Student/faculty ratio	17:1
Profs interesting rating	81
Profs accessible rating	85
Most classes have	fewer than 10 students
Most lab/discussion sessions have	20–29 students

MOST POPULAR MAJORS

biology/biological sciences; economics; psychology

APPLICANTS ALSO LOOK AT AND OFTEN PREFER

University of California—Davis, University of California—Berkeley

AND SOMETIMES PREFER

University of California—Los Angeles

AND RARELY PREFER

University of California—Santa Cruz

STUDENTS SAY ". . ."

Academics

University of California—Santa Barbara is "a beautiful, laid-back learning institute on the beach," yet students say it's much more than a great place to get a tan. This prestigious public school is "one of the best research universities in the country," which "attracts many excellent professors" as well as a cadre of dedicated students. Maybe it's the sunny weather, but "professors here are more accessible than [at] other universities," and they are "genuinely interested in helping the students learn." To offset anonymity at this large school, high-achieving students can apply to the school's College of Creative Studies (CCS), "a selective and prestigious small college within the university," which allows students to pursue advanced coursework in their declared major from day one. Within the CCS, "The class sizes are very small, the teachers are experienced and knowledgeable, [and] the program is really great for learning without pressure." Throughout the university, undergraduates have the opportunity to participate in faculty projects or to "do original research," and "The library is enormous and is connected to the libraries of each UC campus, giving students access to the second largest library system in the world." Despite a myriad of resources, prospective students should be aware that, "The UC budget crisis is causing calamity when it comes to registering for the classes you want—especially if you are a lowly freshman."

Life

"Bordered by the mountains to the north, the ocean to the south, and the college town to the west," UCSB is a veritable paradise. Here, students have the luxury of deciding, "whether they want to go surf or spend the day playing volleyball in the park." "Greek life is not as large at UC Santa Barbara as it is at other universities"; however, the school is "widely known for its massive parties" in the Isla Vista neighborhood near campus. Expressive rather than exclusive, "The parties are as varied as the students, with an emphasis on having fun and not on drugs, violence, or risky behavior. Every person, no matter who they are, can find a party that they will enjoy." In addition to nightlife, students love "exploring downtown Santa Barbara—which is so much more than just State Street—hiking around campus, kayaking in the ocean, or simply spending quality time with friends." On campus, "a cappella groups, orchestras and bands, and theater groups provide outlets for artsy students," and many students "love playing sports with other students, both in intramural games and independently organized [games]." When describing the campus environment, the word "idyllic" comes to mind. A resident student details, "I step out of my door and am only a few steps away from Carrillo, one of the three on-campus dining halls. Directly next to Carrillo is a swimming pool, and right across the way there is a community center with a piano, televisions, a pool and ping-pong table, and comfortable chairs."

Student Body

At this beautiful, beachfront school, the typical undergraduate is a "white kid from California that likes to have fun, go out on the weekends, but knows when to take his or her studies seriously." UCSB has a reputation as a party school, and you'll certainly meet a student or two who "enjoys 'ragers' and [is] failing calculus because they were too busy surfing." But, on the opposite side of the spectrum, many students (especially those in the College of Creative Studies) "are highly driven toward the field that they choose for their major." UCSB does not have the diversity you might find at University of California's urban campuses. Nonetheless, "there are people from all sorts of backgrounds, levels of income, and religions," and "Almost everybody here at UCSB is extremely friendly. Nobody is judgmental or discriminatory." Given the school's spectacular surroundings, it's not surprising that "a general commonality among many people seems to be a love of the beach or at least an appreciation for the beautiful surroundings."

FINANCIAL AID: 805-893-2118 • E-MAIL: ADMISSIONS@SA.UCSB.EDU • WEBSITE: WWW.UCSB.EDU

THE PRINCETON REVIEW SAYS

Admissions

Very important factors considered include: Application essay, academic GPA, rigor of secondary school record, standardized test scores. *Other factors considered include:* Class rank, character/personal qualities, extracurricular activities, first generation, state residency, talent/ability, volunteer work, work experience. SAT or ACT required; ACT with writing component required. TOEFL required of all international applicants. High school diploma is required and GED is accepted. *Academic units required:* 4 English, 3 mathematics (2 science labs), 2 foreign language, 2 history, 1 visual/performing arts, 1 academic elective. *Academic units recommended:* 4 mathematics (3 science labs), 3 foreign language.

Financial Aid

Students should submit: FAFSA. Regular filing deadline is March 2. The Princeton Review suggests that all financial aid forms be submitted as soon as possible after January 1. *Need-based scholarships/grants offered:* Federal Pell, SEOG, state scholarships/grants, private scholarships, the school's own gift aid, Work Study is also available as need-based aid. *Loan aid offered:* Direct Subsidized Stafford, Direct Unsubsidized Stafford, Direct PLUS, Federal Perkins. Applicants will be notified of awards on a rolling basis beginning March 15. Federal Work-Study Program available. Institutional employment available. Off-campus job opportunities are good.

The Inside Word

To be considered for admission to UC—Santa Barbara, students must meet the minimum "eligibility index"—a formula based on your GPA and standardized test scores. In some cases, a lower GPA may be balanced out by higher test scores, or vice versa. Nonetheless, the minimum GPA for prospective students is 3.0 for California residents and 3.4 for non-residents. Applicants to the College of Creative Studies must submit a supplemental application.

The School Says ". . ."
From the Admissions Office

"The University of California—Santa Barbara is a major research institution offering undergraduate and graduate education in the arts, humanities, sciences and technology, and social sciences. Large enough to have excellent facilities for study, research, and other creative activities, the campus is also small enough to foster close relationships among faculty and students. The faculty numbers more than 1,000. A member of the most distinguished system of public higher education in the nation, UC—Santa Barbara is committed equally to excellence in scholarship and instruction. Through the general education program, students acquire good grounding in the skills, perceptions, and methods of a variety of disciplines. In addition, because they study with a research faculty, they not only acquire basic skills and broad knowledge but also are exposed to the imagination, inventiveness, and intense concentration that scholars bring to their work. UCSB is one of sixty-one members of the prestigous Association of American Universities.

"All applicants must take the ACT plus writing or the SAT Reasoning Test. SAT subject tests are no longer required by the University of California. Students applying to engineering majors are encouraged to take SAT subject exams in math (level 2) and a science exam of their choice."

SELECTIVITY	
Admissions Rating	90
# of applicants	49,008
% of applicants accepted	46
% of acceptees attending	18
# accepting a place on wait list	2,200

FRESHMAN PROFILE	
Range SAT Critical Reading	550–670
Range SAT Math	570–690
Range SAT Writing	550–670
Range ACT Composite	24–30
Minimum paper TOEFL	550
Minimum web-based TOEFL	80
Average HS GPA	3.9
% graduated top 10% of class	96
% graduated top 25% of class	98
% graduated top 50% of class	100

DEADLINES	
Regular	
Deadline	11/30
Notification	3/31
Nonfall registration?	yes

FINANCIAL FACTS	
Financial Aid Rating	74
Annual in-state tuition	$11,220
Annual out-state tuition	$33,030
Room and board	$13,110
Required fees	$2,356
Books and supplies	$1,414
% frosh rec. any financial aid	62
% UG rec. any financial aid	59
% UG borrow to pay for school	59
Average cumulative indebtedness	$17,387

UNIVERSITY OF CALIFORNIA—SANTA CRUZ

OFFICE OF ADMISSIONS, COOK HOUSE, SANTA CRUZ, CA 95064 • ADMISSIONS: 831-459-4008 • FAX: 831-459-4452

CAMPUS LIFE

Quality of Life Rating	79
Fire Safety Rating	72
Green Rating	99
Type of school	public
Environment	city

STUDENTS

Total undergrad enrollment	15,945
% male/female	48/52
% from out of state	2
% from public high school	87
% frosh live on campus	99
# of fraternities	6
# of sororities	11
% African American	2
% Asian	20
% Caucasian	43
% Hispanic	23
% Native American	1
# of countries represented	87

SURVEY SAYS . . .

Great computer facilities
Students are friendly
Students are happy
Political activism is popular
Students are environmentally aware

ACADEMICS

Academic Rating	82
% students graduating within 4 years	50
% students graduating within 6 years	74
Calendar	quarter
Student/faculty ratio	19:1
Profs interesting rating	69
Profs accessible rating	73
Most classes have	10–19 students
Most lab/discussion sessions have	10–19 students

MOST POPULAR MAJORS

art/art studies; business/commerce; psychology

APPLICANTS ALSO LOOK AT AND OFTEN PREFER

Stanford University, University of California—Berkeley, University of California—Los Angeles

AND SOMETIMES PREFER

Universityof California—Santa Barbara, University of California—Davis, University of California—San Diego

AND RARELY PREFER

University of California—Riverside

STUDENTS SAY ". . ."

Academics

The University of California—Santa Cruz offers one of the nation's best combinations of "focus on scholastic endeavors in a beautiful forest setting" and is, by all accounts "a great place to live and study!" Students attribute their enthusiasm to "intelligent, eloquent, and easily accessible professors," academics that are "impressive and challenging," and fellow students who are "happy, open-minded, and a little bit crazy." This school is best suited to those who can motivate themselves in a "chill" environment and the sort of student whose motto might be, "There's no point in learning if you're too stressed to enjoy it." The sciences are "world-class" at UCSC, and the school also boasts "one of the finest engineering programs in the UCs" as well as "a great marine biology program." While the "professors all do research," what sets them apart from those at the typical research-driven university is that "they are very passionate about their subject even when teaching undergrads," and they "also tend to be quite approachable despite having large class sizes and allow students to attend their office hours for extra help." The school also offers undergrads "a lot of opportunities in terms of internships, research opportunities, job opportunities, and networking." "There's a focus on undergraduate study" here, one student contentedly reports.

Life

Undergrads rave about the "take-your-breath-away beauty" of the heavily wooded UCSC campus; one says it's like "taking paths through the forest that resemble Endor only to find a lecture hall at the end." Another adds, "Almost every time my friends and I walk around outside, someone comments on how lucky we are to be surrounded by such beauty. Whether the silvery ocean, the fog in the trees, the wind in the fields of green, the wildlife such as deer, raccoons, squirrels, newts, etc., it all comes together like a painting." The school's setting means "there is much to do recreationally, such as hiking, biking, swimming, trail running, tree climbing, or rock-climbing. You can walk in any direction and find some hiking trail that leads to some other part of the forest." Students note that, "It is also nice to get off campus from time to time and enjoy the city of Santa Cruz. Downtown is lively and usually has something fun going on such as local farmer's markets and cultural festivals." Ambitious students "may head to San Jose or San Francisco on the weekend for a more rowdy bar or club scene." Both cities are "readily accessible via public transportation." The party scene on and off campus consists of "mostly decentralized, smaller parties, due to the near-absence of fraternities and sororities." It also includes "a lot of drug use" that is limited to "specific locations" and "easy to avoid" for abstaining students.

Student Body

"The 'stereotypical' Santa Cruz student is a hippie," and the school certainly has its fair share of those "The typical student is very hardworking until about 9:00 P.M., when hikes to the forest are common practice and returning to your room smelling like reefer is acceptable," one undergrad explains—but "there are many different types who attend UCSC." "It seems that almost every student here has a personal passion, whether it be an activism or cause of some sort, etc.," one student writes. "Everyone is so...alive." "Most are liberal," and there's a definite propensity for earnestness; it's the sort of place where students declare without irony that they "not only possess a great respect for one another but the world and life in general. The world to an average UCSC student is a sacred and beautiful place to be shared and enjoyed by all its inhabitants."

FINANCIAL AID: 831-459-2963 • E-MAIL: ADMISSIONS@UCSC.EDU • WEBSITE: WWW.UCSC.EDU

THE PRINCETON REVIEW SAYS

Admissions

Very important factors considered include: Application essay, academic GPA, rigor of secondary school record, standardized test scores, state residency. *Important factors considered include:* Class rank, character/personal qualities, extracurricular activities, first generation, geographical residence, talent/ability. *Other factors considered include:* Volunteer work, work experience. SAT or ACT required; ACT with writing component required. TOEFL required of all international applicants. High school diploma is required and GED is accepted. *Academic units required:* 4 English, 3 mathematics, 2 science (2 science labs), 2 foreign language, 1 social studies, 1 history, 1 visual/performing arts, 1 academic electives, 1. *Academic units recommended:* 4 English, 4 mathematics, 3 science (3 science labs), 3 foreign language.

Financial Aid

Students should submit: FAFSA, state aid form, CA Student Adi Commission, GPA verification form for CA residents. Regular filing deadline is June 30. The Princeton Review suggests that all financial aid forms be submitted as soon as possible after January 1. *Need-based scholarships/grants offered:* Federal Pell, SEOG, state scholarships/grants, private scholarships, the school's own gift aid. *Loan aid offered:* Direct Subsidized Stafford, Direct Unsubsidized Stafford, Direct PLUS, Federal Perkins. Applicants will be notified of awards on a rolling basis beginning April 1. Federal Work-Study Program available. Institutional employment available. Off-campus job opportunities are excellent.

The Inside Word

UC—Santa Cruz scores all applicants on a 9,200-point scale encompassing fourteen criteria. High school GPA accounts for 4,400 of those points; standardized test scores, 2,400 points; up to 700 points for academic accomplishment within life experiences; and lower point amounts in such areas as special talents, achievement, awards, geographic location, and outstanding performance in a particular academic discipline. UCSC's acceptance rate belies the high caliber of applicants it regularly receives.

THE SCHOOL SAYS ". . ."

From the Admissions Office

"UC—Santa Cruz students, faculty, and researchers are working together to make a world of difference. Within our extraordinary educational community, students participate in the creation of new knowledge, new technologies, and new forms of expressing and understanding cultures. From helping teachers improve their skills to building more efficient solar cells and working to save endangered sea turtles, our focus is on improving our planet and the lives of all its inhabitants. The academic programs at UCSC are challenging and rigorous, and many of them are in newer fields that focus on interdisciplinary thinking. At UCSC, undergraduates conduct and publish research, working closely with faculty on leading-edge projects. Taking advantage of the campus' proximity to centers of industry and innovation such as the Monterey Bay National Marine Sanctuary and Silicon Valley, many students at UC—Santa Cruz take part in fieldwork and internships that complement their studies and provide practical experience in their fields."

"All frosh applicants must take the ACT assessment plus the ACT writing test or the new SAT Reasoning Test."

SELECTIVITY

Admissions Rating	**94**
# of applicants	28,236
% of applicants accepted	68
% of acceptees attending	19

FRESHMAN PROFILE

Range SAT Critical Reading	500–630
Range SAT Math	520–640
Range SAT Writing	510–630
Range ACT Composite	22–29
Minimum paper TOEFL	550
Minimum web-based TOEFL	83
Average HS GPA	3.6
% graduated top 10% of class	96
% graduated top 25% of class	100
% graduated top 50% of class	100

DEADLINES

Regular	
Deadline	11/30
Notification	3/31
Nonfall registration?	yes

FINANCIAL FACTS

Financial Aid Rating	**77**
Annual in-state tuition	$13,417
Annual out-state tuition	$22,878
Room and board	$14,871
Required fees	$13,538
Books and supplies	$1,407
% needy frosh rec. need-based scholarship or grant aid	87
% needy UG rec. need-based scholarship or grant aid	88
% needy frosh rec. non-need-based scholarship or grant aid	1
% needy UG rec. non-need-based scholarship or grant aid	1
% needy frosh rec. need-based self-help aid	86
% needy UG rec. need-based self-help aid	86
% frosh rec. any financial aid	59
% UG rec. any financial aid	56
% UG borrow to pay for school	53
Average cumulative indebtedness	$16,024
% frosh need fully met	48
% ugrads need fully met	47
Average % of frosh need met	89
Average % of ugrad need met	89

UNIVERSITY OF CENTRAL FLORIDA

PO BOX 160111, ORLANDO, FL 32816-0111 • ADMISSIONS: 407-823-3000 • FAX: 407-823-5625

CAMPUS LIFE

Quality of Life Rating	88
Fire Safety Rating	84
Green Rating	94
Type of school	public
Environment	city

STUDENTS

Total undergrad enrollment	49,634
% male/female	46/54
% from out of state	7
% frosh live on campus	68
# of fraternities	25
# of sororities	22
% African American	10
% Asian	6
% Caucasian	61
% Hispanic	19
% international	1
# of countries represented	146

SURVEY SAYS . . .

Great computer facilities
Athletic facilities are great
Great off-campus food
Student publications are popular
Student government is popular

ACADEMICS

Academic Rating	72
% students graduating within 4 years	33
% students graduating within 6 years	63
Calendar	semester
Student/faculty ratio	32:1
Profs interesting rating	70
Profs accessible rating	68
Most classes have	20–29 students
Most lab/discussion sessions have	30–39 students

MOST POPULAR MAJORS

health services/allied health/health sciences; marketing/marketing management; psychology

STUDENTS SAY ". . ."

Academics

One of Florida's premiere institutions, University of Central Florida is rapidly gaining a strong national reputation. Impressively, despite being one of the largest universities in the country, UCF manages to feel "like one big family." Indeed, undergrads here stress that the administration truly "cares about the success of each student." While UCF offers many great academic options, students are quick to emphasize the phenomenal nursing, engineering, sports medicine, psychology, speech disorder, and communication programs. Though some undergrads gripe that professors can be "hit and miss," most students are full of praise for their teachers. As one appreciative undergrad relays, "My professors always [make] sure we [are] involved and engaged [with] material and that the material covered in class [is] relevant to the degree we [are] earning." A fellow student agrees, stating, "Professors are very creative when it comes to teaching and make learning fun and interesting." Moreover, they are "always willing to help and available for contact outside of classroom hours." And they truly "want to make sure we make the most of our educational opportunities." As this truly satisfied undergrad gratefully sums up his experience, "UCF is an amazing college, and deciding to attend is one of the best decisions I have ever made in my life."

Life

University of Central Florida is always abuzz with activity. Indeed, "Between classes, sporting events, our top of the line two-story gym, canoeing Lake Claire, concerts and shows, or even Light Up UCF (a holiday carnival on campus for the general public as well as students), one never has a reason to be bored." Further, there are "so many different clubs [for students to join] from recreational [and] religious [groups to] food [organizations and] volunteering." Moreover, "UCF is big on school spirit, especially when it comes to football." And tailgating is definitely a popular pastime during the season. Students also love to take advantage of hometown Orlando, which offers a myriad of cultural and entertainment options. Shares one undergrad, "People around here love going clubbing and bar-hopping. It's totally normal for the typical student to have a Disney pass or Universal pass and carloads of students can be seen at either of these parks." Additionally, "there are some fun college bars right across from campus that are very popular, and Orlando has an amazing downtown that is great for once students turn twenty-one and want something new." And when undergrads are itching to get a little farther away, it's common to "go to either coast to visit the awesome beaches."

Student Body

Though undergrads assert that with a population this large, this is "no typical student" at UCF, they're still able to make a few generalizations regarding their peers. If pressed to define their fellow students, undergrads are likely to suggest that they're "generally laid-back," and "fit into the Florida [stereotype]: flip-flops, very down-to-earth, not uptight, [and] likes to have fun." They are also "very kind, intelligent, and hardworking." Most students "are welcoming [and] if you want to find people with like-[minded] interests, there are tons of clubs and organizations." Impressively, many undergrads here confidently declare that students just seem to "fit in." "Whether its clubs or study groups or coming into class late and having to take the seat furthest in the row and closest to the wall, conversations brew naturally." One student concurs succinctly, stating, "I feel like you'd have to go out of your way to not make friends." Simply put, "There's a little bit of everything [and everyone] at UCF."

FINANCIAL AID: 407-823-2827 • E-MAIL: ADMISSION@UCF.EDU • WEBSITE: WWW.UCF.EDU

THE PRINCETON REVIEW SAYS

Admissions

Very important factors considered include: Academic GPA, rigor of secondary school record, standardized test scores. *Important factors considered include:* application essay, recommendation(s). *Other factors considered include:* Class rank, alumni/ae relation, character/personal qualities, extracurricular activities, first generation, geographical residence, interview, level of applicant's interest, state residency, talent/ability, volunteer work, work experience. SAT or ACT required; ACT with or without writing component accepted. TOEFL required of all international applicants. High school diploma is required and GED is accepted. *Academic units required:* 4 English, 4 mathematics, 3 science (2 science labs), 2 foreign language, 3 social studies, 2 academic electives.

Financial Aid

Students should submit: FAFSA. Regular filing deadline is August 15. The Princeton Review suggests that all financial aid forms be submitted as soon as possible after January 1. *Need-based scholarships/grants offered:* Federal Pell, SEOG, state scholarships/grants, private scholarships, the school's own gift aid, University scholarships and grants. *Loan aid offered:* Direct Subsidized Stafford, Direct Unsubsidized Stafford, Direct PLUS, Federal Perkins. Applicants will be notified of awards on a rolling basis beginning March 15. Federal Work-Study Program available. Institutional employment available.

Inside Word

Not surprising for a school of its size, University of Central Florida takes a quantitative approach to its admissions game. Therefore, your cumulative high school GPA and standardized test scores will likely hold the most weight when it comes to deciding factors.

THE SCHOOL SAYS ". . ."

From the Admissions Office

"The University of Central Florida offers competitive advantages to its student body. We're committed to teaching, providing advisement, and academic support services for all students. Our undergraduates have access to state-of-the-art wireless buildings, high-tech classrooms, research labs, web-based classes, and an undergraduate research and mentoring program.

"Our Career Services professionals help students gain practical experiences at NASA, schools, hospitals, high-tech companies, local municipalities, and the entertainment industry. With an international focus to our curricula and research programs, we enroll international students from 126 nations. Our study abroad programs and other study and research opportunities include agreements with ninety-eight institutions and thirty-six countries.

"UCF's 1,415-acre campus provides a safe and serene setting for learning, with natural lakes and woodlands. The bustle of Orlando lies a short distance away: the pro sport teams, the Kennedy Space Center, film studios, Walt Disney World, Universal Orlando, Sea World, and sandy beaches are all nearby.

"Applicants are required to take the SAT (or the ACT with the writing section). We will use a student's best scores from either test."

SELECTIVITY	
Admissions Rating	**91**
# of applicants	33,968
% of applicants accepted	45
% of acceptees attending	41
# accepting a place on wait list	1,168
# admitted from wait list	90
FRESHMAN PROFILE	
Range SAT Critical Reading	530–630
Range SAT Math	560–650
Range SAT Writing	510–610
Range ACT Composite	24–28
Minimum paper TOEFL	550
Minimum web-based TOEFL	80
Average HS GPA	3.8
% graduated top 10% of class	34
% graduated top 25% of class	72
% graduated top 50% of class	96
DEADLINES	
Regular	
Priority	1/1
Deadline	5/1
Nonfall registration?	yes
FINANCIAL FACTS	
Financial Aid Rating	**67**
Annual in-state tuition	$5,806
Annual out-state tuition	$21,732
Room and board	$9,300
Books and supplies	$1,146
% needy frosh rec. need-based scholarship or grant aid	54
% needy UG rec. need-based scholarship or grant aid	61
% needy frosh rec. non-need-based scholarship or grant aid	95
% needy UG rec. non-need-based scholarship or grant aid	63
% needy frosh rec. need-based self-help aid	39
% needy UG rec. need-based self-help aid	51
% frosh rec. any financial aid	96
% UG rec. any financial aid	84
% UG borrow to pay for school	42
Average cumulative indebtedness	$20,624
% frosh need fully met	16
% ugrads need fully met	10
Average % of frosh need met	63
Average % of ugrad need met	60

THE UNIVERSITY OF CHICAGO

1101 EAST FIFTY-EIGHTH STREET, CHICAGO, IL 60637 • ADMISSIONS: 773-702-8650 • FAX: 773-702-4199

CAMPUS LIFE

Quality of Life Rating	82
Fire Safety Rating	78
Green Rating	81
Type of school	private
Environment	metropolis

STUDENTS

Total undergrad enrollment	5,377
% male/female	53/47
% from out of state	81
% from public high school	62
% frosh live on campus	77
# of sororities	3
% African American	7
% Asian	19
% Caucasian	43
% Hispanic	11
% international	11
# of countries represented	109

SURVEY SAYS . . .

No one cheats
Lab facilities are great
Great computer facilities
Great library
Athletic facilities are great
School is well run
Students love Chicago, IL
Dorms are like palaces

ACADEMICS

Academic Rating	98
% students returning for sophomore year	99
% students graduating within 4 years	86
% students graduating within 6 years	92
Calendar	quarter
Student/faculty ratio	7:1
Profs interesting rating	85
Profs accessible rating	82
Most classes have	fewer than 10 students
Most lab/discussion sessions have	10–19 students

MOST POPULAR MAJORS

biological sciences; economics; political science and government

STUDENTS SAY ". . ."

Academics

Described as "an academic paradise near an awesome city," the University of Chicago is a place where students "aren't embarrassed by the fact that they're smart." Students say, "It is extremely competitive," and they celebrate the fact that "you can't just stick up your hand and not expect to be challenged by your professors and your peers." Classrooms are small and foster a "collaborative learning environment." "It's a place that pushes smart people to make new discoveries, challenge their limits, and find new ways of understanding the world." The "wide array of strong academic programs" offered at UChicago are set on the quarter system, which can be "a bit intensive." "The sheer amount of material one covers in any given quarter is simply massive." If you are up for it, you can "learn a ton" in this fast-paced system. The "rigorous" core curriculum "forces you to learn about things that you never thought you would enjoy." "The school is at the forefront of research in most subjects, and the core really helps develop students into thinkers." There is "lots of focus on discussion, analyzing original texts, and critical thinking." Professors are a main reason students love this school. "Professors are celebrities in their field—it's extremely common to begin doing research on a topic and realize that the world's expert is two buildings down." Remarkably, even "first-year students are often exposed to the best professors the school has to offer." "This school is challenging, but it's not anything you can't handle. Everyone gets to pick the classes they take and how many they take at any time. You can make it as easy or hard as you want."

Life

The housing system is a very important aspect of student life and gets rave reviews for being a "supportive, fun, community environment" with a "family atmosphere." "Your house becomes your family and the center of your social life on campus. You go to parties with your house, your best friends come from the house, and you will likely move off campus with members of your house. The house system is truly one of the great aspects of the University of Chicago." Although the "harsh Chicago winter" may not appeal to everyone, the city of Chicago clearly does. "Chicago offers anything that you want," from "the great nightlife," to "concerts, restaurants, movies, [and] plays," to "operas at the Lyric." "The most difficult part of finding fun is deciding which of your many options you want to pursue that day!" Staying on school grounds is also a popular option. "There's a healthy party scene on campus during the weekends, with frats and apartments throwing events." There are other happenings, "like cultural shows, food festivals, and movie screenings that you can enjoy on a day-to-day basis." The library is a popular place "when it comes to crunch-time studying."

Student Body

Students at UChicago are an "engaged" lot, "attracted to living and learning among really smart, interesting people." Students find it difficult to describe a typical student except as someone "you wouldn't expect. Football players are computer programmers, sorority girls are poets, [and] nerds are hip-hop dance prodigies." "It runs the gamut from complete nerd to complete jock. It even includes people who are both!" What students do "have in common is a genuine interest in ideas and a profound investment in the life of the mind." They take pride in "a commitment to a certain kind of excellence here, one that values intellectualism both inside and outside the classroom, [and one] that places a premium on the ability to think critically, and integrate and apply these skills in ways not traditionally used." One student advises that UChicago is "an incredibly intense place, academically speaking, and students should be prepared to live what they learn because studies surround every aspect of campus life here. This doesn't mean that people are constantly in the library, though. It means that people bring with them wherever they go a certain spirit of adventurous inquiry that makes every conversation an interesting one."

FINANCIAL AID: 773-702-8655 • E-MAIL: COLLEGEADMISSIONS@UCHICAGO.EDU • WEBSITE: WWW.UCHICAGO.EDU

THE PRINCETON REVIEW SAYS

Admissions

Very important factors considered include: Application essay, recommendation(s), rigor of secondary school record, character/personal qualities, talent/ability. *Important factors considered include:* Class rank, academic GPA, extracurricular activities, volunteer work. *Other factors considered include:* Standardized test scores, alumni/ae relation, first generation, interview, level of applicant's interest, racial/ethnic status, work experience. SAT or ACT required. TOEFL required of all international applicants. High school diploma or equivalent is required. *Academic units recommended:* 4 English, 4 mathematics, 4 science, 3 foreign language, 2 social studies, 2 history.

Financial Aid

Students should submit: FAFSA, CSS/Financial Aid PROFILE, noncustodial PROFILE. The Princeton Review suggests that all financial aid forms be submitted as soon as possible after January 1. *Need-based scholarships/grants offered:* Federal Pell, SEOG, state scholarships/grants, private scholarships, the school's own gift aid. *Loan aid offered:* Direct Subsidized Stafford, Direct Unsubsidized Stafford, Direct PLUS, Federal Perkins. Applicants will be notified of awards on or about April 15.

The Inside Word

People at the University of Chicago dwell on deep thoughts and big ideas. In your application, you'll need to demonstrate outstanding grades in the tough courses and that you will fit in with a bunch of thinkers. Although the University of Chicago uses the common application, essay topics remain "uncommon" and thought-provoking. Interviews are recommended but not required.

THE SCHOOL SAYS ". . ."

From the Admissions Office

"The University of Chicago is universally recognized for its devotion to open and rigorous inquiry. The strength of our intellectual traditions—intense critical analysis, lively debate, and creative solutions to complex problems—rests on the scholars who continue to engage them. Our college graduates have made discoveries in every field of academic study; they are ambitious thinkers who are unafraid to take on the most pressing questions of our time. Their accomplishments have helped establish the University's legacy as one of the world's finest academic institutions. The University of Chicago has been home to over eighty-five Nobel Prize winners, thirty Macarthur "genius" fellows, and twenty Pulitzer Prize winners. With over 140 research centers and institutes, numerous cultural opportunities, and three of the nation's top professional schools in law, business, and medicine—all within blocks of one another on our campus—UChicago is known for the unparalleled resources it provides its undergraduate students.

"UChicago maintains a student-faculty ratio of seven to one, ensuring that every classroom experience exemplifies our commitment to a student's ability to interact closely with our faculty. Our core curriculum provides students with a common vocabulary and a well-balanced academic experience, while allowing the flexibility to explore their own particular interests in small discussion-style seminars. Students also enjoy a successful Division III sports program, small but active Greek life, forty student theatrical productions a year, a rich music scene, celebrations of culture and community—and the extraordinary opportunities in politics, music, theater, commerce, architecture, and neighborhood life in the city of Chicago."

SELECTIVITY	
Admissions Rating	99
# of applicants	21,762
% of applicants accepted	16
% of acceptees attending	40

FRESHMAN PROFILE	
Range SAT Critical Reading	700–790
Range SAT Math	700–780
Range SAT Writing	700–780
Range ACT Composite	31–34
Minimum paper TOEFL	600
Minimum web-based TOEFL	104
% graduated top 10% of class	95
% graduated top 25% of class	99
% graduated top 50% of class	100

DEADLINES	
Regular	
Priority	12/1
Deadline	1/1
Nonfall registration?	no

FINANCIAL FACTS	
Financial Aid Rating	96
Annual tuition	$43,581
Room and board	$13,137
Required fees	$993
Books and supplies	$3,679
% needy frosh rec. need-based scholarship or grant aid	98
% needy UG rec. need-based scholarship or grant aid	98
% needy frosh rec. need-based self-help aid	72
% needy UG rec. need-based self-help aid	82
% frosh rec. any financial aid	60
% UG rec. any financial aid	59
% UG borrow to pay for school	34
Average cumulative indebtedness	$22,663
% frosh need fully met	26
% ugrads need fully met	21
Average % of frosh need met	71
Average % of ugrad need met	67

UNIVERSITY OF CINCINNATI

PO Box 210091, Cincinnati, OH 45221-0091 • Admissions: 513-556-1100 • Fax: 513-556-1105

CAMPUS LIFE

Quality of Life Rating	**72**
Fire Safety Rating	**91**
Green Rating	**95**
Type of school	public
Environment	metropolis

STUDENTS

Total undergrad enrollment	22,543
% male/female	49/51
% from out of state	14
% frosh live on campus	76
# of fraternities	23
# of sororities	10
% African American	8
% Asian	3
% Caucasian	78
% Hispanic	2
% international	3
# of countries represented	111

SURVEY SAYS . . .

Great computer facilities
Athletic facilities are great
Diverse student types on campus
Registration is a breeze
Great library
Great off-campus food

ACADEMICS

Academic Rating	**72**
% students returning for sophomore year	85
% students graduating within 4 years	22
% students graduating within 6 years	59
Calendar	quarter
Student/faculty ratio	18:1
Profs interesting rating	71
Profs accessible rating	71
Most classes have	20–29 students

MOST POPULAR MAJORS

communication studies/speech communication and rhetoric; marketing/marketing management; psychology

STUDENTS SAY ". . ."

Academics

The University of Cincinnati "offers students a balance of educational excellence and real-world experience" on an expansive campus comprised of twelve separate colleges. Students agree it's "a large school with many great programs and infinite opportunities that still retains the feeling of a small university." Many have praise for the "cooperative education program that gives students a real edge in the job market" by allowing them the opportunity to pursue competitive internships while enrolled. Students also feel confident that "UC provides excellent opportunities outside of the classroom to make me successful post-graduation." As one student puts it, "The University of Cincinnati is not only known for its great academics, but for all of the incredible opportunities students have including cooperative education, on-campus activities and clubs, along with athletics and one of the most beautiful campuses in the world." The university's size assures that there are "a wide variety of majors to choose from," and students name the Conservatory of Music, the School of Architecture and Design, and the engineering programs as stand outs. Nevertheless, many carp, "The school could be a little bit better at communicating" and say the "registration process is terrible." Overall, students feel that "the professors here have so much life experience in what they are teaching. It makes me trust and respect them more," and "Advisors have been helpful." However, they note, "The professors are as diverse as the classes offered here," which means that, "like anything else, there is variation. Some are horrible, and some are fantastic."

Life

It's common for students to remark on the "ample green spaces, [and] innovative architectural designs" that make up the "beautiful campus" at UC. One student explains, "The University of Cincinnati has rewarding educational programs and a beautiful urban campus with many opportunities to stay involved. What more can I ask for?" Although most feel that "campus is very safe," some note, "As soon as you step off of campus, it's a different story." However, many acknowledge, "The school does work hard on maintaining a safe environment for us to live and work in." The majority of students describe campus as having a "fun atmosphere" that makes "UC great" but are divided on the topic of university-sponsored activities. Some think the administration should provide "more afterschool activities," while others believe "UC offers a million and one activities for students to partake in during school and on the weekend. Friday Night Live is an extremely popular program offering awesome activities that don't involve alcohol or drugs." A significant portion of undergraduates are from Cincinnati and point out that UC "is a huge commuter school, so many of the students do things all over the city." However, all agree, "People are very passionate about sports here and have great school spirit." A common campus exclamation is "go Bearcats!!"

Student Body

The most common sentiment from UC students is that "there really isn't a typical student." Although "many students are from Cincinnati," most agree, "UC has students from all walks of life, which makes it extremely diverse and very interesting." While many say, "Students can find their niche, be it in LGBTQ groups, ethnic groups, or academic intercollegiate groups," some reveal that although "students fit in well…racial cliques are obvious around campus." However, all concur that the student body is "outgoing and expressive" and proclaim that "students come together to work on issues they care about such as sustainability." Most UC students can be found in a "sweatshirt, [and] jeans…[with a] coffee in hand," and students like to point out that "many students work as well so they seem to be more 'grounded' and well-rounded." Speaking about the student body, one UC student declares, "The majority are young sports fans that like to party, but being a research school there are some academic heavyweights as well." The consensus seems to be that "students at UC are open-minded, and everyone can find a place to fit in."

FINANCIAL AID: 513-556-6982 • E-MAIL: ADMISSIONS@UC.EDU • WEBSITE: WWW.UC.EDU

THE PRINCETON REVIEW SAYS

Admissions

Very important factors considered include: Academic GPA, class rank, rigor of secondary school record, standardized test scores. *Other factors considered include:* Application essay, extracurricular activities. SAT or ACT required; ACT with writing component required. TOEFL required of all international applicants. High school diploma is required, and GED is accepted. *Academic units required:* 4 English, 3 mathematics, 2 science, 2 foreign language, 2 social studies, 2 academic electives. *Academic units recommended:* 4 mathematics, 3 science, 1 history.

Financial Aid

Students should submit: FAFSA. The Princeton Review suggests that all financial aid forms be submitted as soon as possible after January 1. *Need-based scholarships/grants offered:* Federal Pell, SEOG, state scholarships/grants, private scholarships, school scholarship or grant aid from institutional funds, United Negro College Fund, Federal Nursing Scholarships. *Loan aid offered:* Direct Subsidized Stafford, Direct Unsubsidized Stafford, Direct PLUS, Federal Perkins, Federal Nursing loans, state loans, university loans from institutional funds. Applicants will be notified of awards on a rolling basis beginning March 26. Federal Work-Study Program available. Off-campus job opportunities are excellent.

The Inside Word

The UC offers hundreds of undergraduate majors and stresses the importance of exploring the specific admission criteria for your program of choice. Prospective students are reminded to work hard while still in high school, with admissions representative saying to hone your GPA from ninth grade on because "it counts!" UC seeks a student who shows evidence of self-reflection. Ideal candidates will exhibit this self-awareness through participation in extracurricular activities that speak to who they are, not to what they think an admissions board wants. Campus visits are strongly suggested.

THE SCHOOL SAYS ". . ."

From the Admissions Office

"Remarkable architecture, park-like open spaces, engaging student tour guides, and a welcoming admissions staff make the University of Cincinnati a must-visit destination. UC campus has been transformed over the past ten years and is drawing national and international attention for blending student life, learning, research, and recreation in a unique urban environment.

"Freshman application materials include high school transcripts, test scores, a personal statement, and a list of co-curricular activities. Some academic programs require additional materials.

"Sign up for a visit, become a Bearcat VIP, and apply online. Information about all UC majors is linked from the website. We also have Tuesday-night online chat sessions for students and parents. Nothing beats a visit, however, for assessing how well you'll fit in here.

"Either the SAT or ACT is required for students applying to bachelor's degree programs; the ACT writing component is required. SAT Subject Tests are not required."

SELECTIVITY	
Admissions Rating	**82**
# of applicants	17,020
% of applicants accepted	65
% of acceptees attending	39

FRESHMAN PROFILE	
Range SAT Critical Reading	500–620
Range SAT Math	520–640
Range SAT Writing	480–590
Range ACT Composite	22–27
Minimum paper TOEFL	515
Average HS GPA	3.4
% graduated top 10% of class	22
% graduated top 25% of class	50
% graduated top 50% of class	83

DEADLINES	
Early action	
Deadline	12/1
Notification	1/15
Regular	
Priority	12/1
Deadline	2/1
Nonfall registration?	yes

FINANCIAL FACTS	
Financial Aid Rating	**66**
Annual in-state tuition	$8,805
Annual out-state tuition	$23,328
Room and board	$9,780
Required fees	$1,614
Books and supplies	$1,275
% needy frosh rec. need-based scholarship or grant aid	43
% needy UG rec. need-based scholarship or grant aid	47
% needy frosh rec. non-need-based scholarship or grant aid	47
% needy UG rec. non-need-based scholarship or grant aid	34
% needy frosh rec. need-based self-help aid	18
% needy UG rec. need-based self-help aid	15
% frosh rec. any financial aid	80
% UG rec. any financial aid	75
% UG borrow to pay for school	67
Average cumulative indebtedness	$27,593
% frosh need fully met	5
% ugrads need fully met	5
Average % of frosh need met	68
Average % of ugrad need met	66

UNIVERSITY OF COLORADO—BOULDER

552 UCB, BOULDER, CO 80309-0552 • ADMISSIONS: 303-492-6301 • FAX: 303-492-6301

CAMPUS LIFE

Quality of Life Rating	83
Fire Safety Rating	82
Green Rating	91
Type of school	public
Environment	city

STUDENTS

Total undergrad enrollment	25,774
% male/female	53/47
% from out of state	43
% frosh live on campus	95
# of fraternities	20
# of sororities	15
% African American	2
% Asian	6
% Caucasian	76
% Hispanic	8
% Native American	1
% international	2
# of countries represented	97

SURVEY SAYS . . .

Great computer facilities
Athletic facilities are great
Students love Boulder, CO
Great off-campus food
Everyone loves the The Colorado Buffaloes
Lots of beer drinking
Hard liquor is popular
Students are environmentally aware

ACADEMICS

Academic Rating	74
% students returning for sophomore year	84
% students graduating within 4 years	40
% students graduating within 6 years	68
Calendar	semester
Student/faculty ratio	20:1
Profs interesting rating	76
Profs accessible rating	70
Most classes have	10–19 students
Most lab/discussion sessions have	20–29 students

MOST POPULAR MAJORS

international/global studies; physiology; psychology

APPLICANTS ALSO LOOK AT AND RARELY PREFER

University of Utah, University of Wyoming

STUDENTS SAY ". . ."

Academics

Strong academics paired with many opportunities to get involved with research and obtain work experience make UC—Boulder appealing. One sophomore tells us, "UC does a fantastic job of keeping students up-to-date on the goings-on and important news around school, town, and the world." Another current student sums it up perfectly, explaining that UC—Boulder has "a sense of vitality and curiosity that fills the campus, and yet it's comfortable and relaxed." Students repeatedly tell us, "UC is an amazing place because you can find an array of challenges and opportunities whether your drive is research, the arts, sports, a job, or tough class work. However, at the same time, you can find a great social life outside of school in an amazing place like Boulder." Another student shares, "I am being taught not only about class material, but also about finding who I am as a student, individual, and community member, [as well as] how to efficiently apply that to today's world."

UC—Boulder offers an excellent liberal arts education, and the social life is diverse enough so that everyone is able to find a niche that suits their interests. Students point out, "UC has some of the best research facilities in the world." When asked about staff, students say, "Most professors are here for research but that isn't necessarily a bad thing because many incorporate and relate their fascinating work experience with lecture." Another student tells us, "My professors represent a wide range of ages, nationalities, and genders. Professors are helpful and entertaining, and they have real-world experience." Students seem satisfied with the academics overall. A member of the junior class tells us, "I have very involved professors who have helped me better my overall academic experience by providing me the possibilities to learn beyond the classroom." Another junior adds, "Professors are usually knowledgeable, and a few are exceptional. Academic experience has transferred very well to internships that I found while attending a university sponsored career fair."

Life

The city of Boulder is a place of beauty and academic prominence at the foot of the Rocky Mountains. It is full of coffee shops and quaint shopping areas, in addition to being the home to UC—Boulder. Students say, "The campus at UC—Boulder is gorgeous, and there is always something to do, much of it outdoors." Another student adds, "People are very active in Boulder. Hiking, kayaking, mountain biking, skiing, and snowboarding are all popular weekend (or weekday) activities." One student reflects, "People think about having fun and making the most of their time while at the same time figuring out what their purposes and life goals are." A junior observes, "There are many smart conversations going on around campus; walking from class to class you hear people debating anything from the newest engineering or physics discovery, to philosophy, to politics, to the state of contemporary education." Learning is not an experience isolated to the classroom, as this student points out, "You can learn so much—it's great talking to students studying different things."

Student Body

Students choose UC—Boulder because of the many opportunities available academically, socially, and financially. We hear, "My school is all about progress, inclusion, and sustainability." In-state tuition benefits are a large draw, as well as the prolific research facilities. One student tells us, "I received a full-ride scholarship, and I felt comfortable going to a school with a diversity of majors and opportunities." In addition, one in four graduates has studied abroad. One student shares her experience, saying, "The students and staff are friendly and open-minded, and the academics are excellent." "I wanted a large public university that would allow me access to a diverse selection of student groups, research labs, fellow peers, faculty, and life experiences, and I found it here at UC—Boulder." Another student sums it up, "I think there are many different types of students, but they all interact smoothly and efficiently. Most students enjoy the outdoors and being outside." "UC—Boulder offers an excellent liberal arts education, and the social life is diverse enough so that everyone is able to find a niche that suits his or her interests."

FINANCIAL AID: 303-492-5091 • E-MAIL: APPLY@COLORADO.EDU • WEBSITE: WWW.COLORADO.EDU

THE PRINCETON REVIEW SAYS

Admissions

Very important factors considered include: Class rank, application essay, academic GPA, recommendation(s), rigor of secondary school record. *Important factors considered include:* Standardized test scores, character/personal qualities, first generation, state residency. *Other factors considered include:* Alumni/ae relation, extracurricular activities, geographical residence, level of applicant's interest, talent/ability, volunteer work, work experience. SAT or ACT required; ACT with writing component required. TOEFL required of all international applicants. High school diploma is required and GED is accepted. *Academic units required:* 4 English, 4 mathematics, 3 science (2 science labs), 3 foreign language, 3 social studies, 1 history, 1 geography.

Financial Aid

Students should submit: FAFSA, tax return required. The Princeton Review suggests that all financial aid forms be submitted as soon as possible after January 1. *Need-based scholarships/grants offered:* Federal Pell, SEOG, state scholarships/grants, private scholarships, the school's own gift aid. *Loan aid offered:* Direct Subsidized Stafford, Direct Unsubsidized Stafford, Direct PLUS, Federal Perkins, college/university loans from institutional funds, private lenders. Applicants will be notified of awards on a rolling basis beginning March 1. Federal Work-Study Program available. Institutional employment available. Highest amount earned per year from on-campus jobs $12,050. Off-campus job opportunities are excellent.

The Inside Word

Applicants must indicate the school within CU to which they wish to be admitted. Engineering and Applied Science is most competitive, followed by the College of Music, the Leeds School of Business, and the College of Architecture and Planning. The College of Arts and Sciences is the least competitive; those applying to and not selected by the more competitive schools are automatically entered into consideration for admission to the College of Arts and Sciences. With nearly one-third of the student body from out of state, CU boasts far more geographic diversity than most state schools.

THE SCHOOL SAYS ". . ."

From the Admissions Office

"The University of Colorado—Boulder is a place of beauty and academic prominence at the foot of the Rocky Mountains. A sense of vitality and curiosity fills the campus, and yet it's comfortable and relaxed. It's a place you can be yourself and let your imagination soar. We have programs for you if you seek leadership training, research experience, academic honors, international experience (one in four graduates has studied abroad), community involvement, and more. There are a number of enrichment programs that give exceptionally talented and intellectually committed students the opportunity to expand their education outside the classroom, build a sense of community, and help prepare for post-graduate opportunities. Residential Academic Programs (RAPs) and Living and Learning Communities (LLCs) in several residence halls provide undergraduates with shared learning and living experiences.

"Getting involved is easy at CU—Boulder. If you are interested in student government, clubs, athletics, recreation, Greek life, volunteer work, theater, dance, film, exhibits, planetarium shows, or concerts, you will find them here.

"To find out if CU—Boulder is the place for you, we encourage you to visit. Contact the office of admissions, or take a virtual tour online. The University of Colorado at Boulder requires either SAT or ACT scores for admissions; the writing tests are currently not used in making decisions. SAT Subject Test scores are not required."

SELECTIVITY	
Admissions Rating	**80**
# of applicants	20,506
% of applicants accepted	87
% of acceptees attending	32
# accepting a place on wait list	155

FRESHMAN PROFILE	
Range SAT Critical Reading	520–630
Range SAT Math	540–650
Range ACT Composite	24–28
Minimum paper TOEFL	537
Minimum web-based TOEFL	75
Average HS GPA	3.6
% graduated top 10% of class	24
% graduated top 25% of class	54
% graduated top 50% of class	89

DEADLINES	
Early action	
Deadline	12/1
Notification	1/15
Regular	
Priority	12/1
Deadline	1/15
Notification	4/1
Nonfall registration?	yes

FINANCIAL FACTS	
Financial Aid Rating	**85**
Annual in-state tuition	$7,672
Annual out-state tuition	$28,000
Room and board	$11,278
Required fees	$1,480
Books and supplies	$1,992
% needy frosh rec. need-based scholarship or grant aid	71
% needy UG rec. need-based scholarship or grant aid	72
% needy frosh rec. non-need-based scholarship or grant aid	2
% needy UG rec. non-need-based scholarship or grant aid	1
% needy frosh rec. need-based self-help aid	90
% needy UG rec. need-based self-help aid	92
% frosh rec. any financial aid	69
% UG rec. any financial aid	61
% UG borrow to pay for school	46
Average cumulative indebtedness	$22,683
% frosh need fully met	61
% ugrads need fully met	56
Average % of frosh need met	87
Average % of ugrad need met	88

University of Connecticut

2131 Hillside Road, Storrs, CT 06268-3088 • Admissions: 860-486-3137 • Fax: 860-486-1476

CAMPUS LIFE

Quality of Life Rating	**72**
Fire Safety Rating	**80**
Green Rating	**94**
Type of school	public
Environment	town

STUDENTS

Total undergrad enrollment	17,450
% male/female	51/49
% from out of state	23
% from public high school	86
% frosh live on campus	97
# of fraternities	18
# of sororities	15
% African American	6
% Asian	8
% Caucasian	64
% Hispanic	7
% international	2
# of countries represented	104

SURVEY SAYS . . .

Low cost of living
Everyone loves the Huskies
Student publications are popular
Great library
Intercollegiate sports are popular

ACADEMICS

Academic Rating	**72**
% students returning for sophomore year	92
% students graduating within 4 years	68
% students graduating within 6 years	83
Calendar	semester
Student/faculty ratio	18:1
Profs interesting rating	70
Profs accessible rating	71
Most classes have	10–19 students
Most lab/discussion sessions have	10–19 students

MOST POPULAR MAJORS

business/commerce; political science and government; psychology

APPLICANTS ALSO LOOK AT AND OFTEN PREFER

University of Maryland, College Park, University of Delaware, Boston College

AND SOMETIMES PREFER

Boston University, Northeastern University, Pennsylvania State University—University Park

AND RARELY PREFER

University of Massachusetts-Amherst, University of New Hampshire, University of Rhode Island, Rutgers-The State University of New Jersey—New Brunswick, University of Vermont

STUDENTS SAY ". . ."

Academics

The flagship school University of Connecticut "has everything you need—sports, academics, clubs," and a sense of school pride that has people proclaiming "Students Today, Huskies Forever" all across the world. Such a large institution has plenty of resources for its students, as well as the opportunity for "internships, research, and jobs." Between the "great education for a fantastic price" and the athletics, UConn "fosters an environment that makes someone genuinely proud to go here." "UConn is inexpensive, but that does not compromise for the quality of its education," says a student.

The "broad array of course opportunities" provides "a challenging curriculum supplemented by in-class discussions and individual research." While some students state that they were nervous about large classes, most say, "The professors were all so kind and really wanted to get to know each student individually" (especially in upper-level classes). Though there are a few duds, faculty on the whole are "very into what they're teaching and often take the material farther than necessary." They also "use all of the research that they do and incorporate that into their classes," which helps to keep classes interesting. "Every staff member here loves it, and that comes across in the work that they do," says a student.

The biggest complaint among the student body by far is parking, as "it's impossible to find a parking space after 10 A.M.!" Though some dorms are a bit rundown, "New buildings are being built constantly, which is keeping the school up-to-date." One thing that students cite in the positive is the diversity, which "encourages us to be well-rounded and to think critically and actively participate in the world around us."

Life

With more than 500 clubs to join, there's "always something to do." Every semester, there is an "involvement fair," and students can sign up for groups of interest. Also, "Have you watched the basketball team?!" asks a student. "They're incredible!" As the school is in the rural town of Storrs, there "is not much to do off of campus," but UConn is currently developing a downtown area that students are looking forward to. Students are appropriately autonomous; everyone is an "independent individual on campus." "I feel totally in control of my own agenda, course work, eating habits, and social activities," says one student.

Weekends are generally reserved "for partying and sleeping in, but the majority of students drink responsibly and take care of their bodies." There are "many diligent students," as well. "The library is seldom empty at any hour," says a student. Although there is Greek life, students don't feel pressured to join a sorority or fraternity because "there are many other ways to make friends and have a successful social life." The state provides the school money to offer events to discourage students from drinking, and "Attending concerts, shows, and movies at hugely discounted prices [is] an easy way to keep yourself busy." There are also Friday late nights at the Student Union, where students "can meet new people and get free stuff."

Student Body

Most students here are "your typical Connecticut young adult," but there is also "a fairly substantial amount of out-of-state students." There are students of all gender and sexual orientations, races, athletic, and academic ability. "It's like taking a slice of Connecticut," says a student. Everyone is "friendly and active, whether it be partying, school spirit, or community service." "As long as you look for the things that interest you, you'll find people you fit in with," says a student. "We all have our quirks, so no one is shunned or discriminated against for them."

FINANCIAL AID: 860-486-2819 • E-MAIL: BEAHUSKY@UCONN.EDU • WEBSITE: WWW.UCONN.EDU

THE PRINCETON REVIEW SAYS

Admissions

Very important factors considered include: Class rank, academic GPA, rigor of secondary school record, standardized test scores. *Important factors considered include:* Application essay, recommendation(s), character/personal qualities, extracurricular activities, first generation, racial/ethnic status, talent/ability, volunteer work. *Other factors considered include:* Alumni/ae relation, geographical residence, level of applicant's interest, state residency, work experience. SAT or ACT required; ACT with writing component required. TOEFL required of all international applicants. High school diploma is required and GED is accepted. *Academic units required:* 4 English, 3 mathematics, 2 science (2 science labs), 2 foreign language, 2 social studies, 3 academic electives. *Academic units recommended:* 3 foreign language.

Financial Aid

Students should submit: FAFSA. Regular filing deadline is March 1. The Princeton Review suggests that all financial aid forms be submitted as soon as possible after January 1. *Need-based scholarships/grants offered:* Federal Pell, SEOG, state scholarships/grants, private scholarships, the school's own gift aid. *Loan aid offered:* Direct Subsidized Stafford, Direct Unsubsidized Stafford, Direct PLUS, Federal Perkins. Applicants will be notified of awards on a rolling basis beginning March 1. Federal Work-Study Program available. Institutional employment available. Highest amount earned per year from on-campus jobs $3,500. Off-campus job opportunities are good.

The Inside Word

When reviewing applications, the UConn admissions committee evaluates students based on a wide range of factors, including standardized test scores, rigor of high school curriculum, classroom performance, extracurricular activities, and community involvement. Honors and AP classes aren't required, but they're viewed favorably by the admissions committee. Competitive applicants have a cumulative grade point average of 3.3 on a 4.0 scale and usually rank in the top quarter of their high school class.

THE SCHOOL SAYS ". . ."

From the Admissions Office

"Thanks to a $2.8 billion construction program that is impacting every area of university life, the University of Connecticut provides students a high-quality and personalized education on one of the most attractive and technologically advanced college campuses in the United States. Applications are soaring nationally as an increasing number of high-achieving students from diverse backgrounds are making UConn their school of choice. From award-winning actors to governmental leaders, students enjoy an assortment of fascinating speakers each year, while performances by premier dance, jazz, and rock musicians enliven student life. Our beautiful New England campus is convenient and safe, and most students walk to class or ride university shuttle buses. State-of-the-art residential facilities include interest-based learning communities and honors housing as well as on-campus suite-style and apartment living. Championship Division I athletics have created fervor known as Huskymania among UConn students.

"Freshman applicants seeking admittance are required to submit official score reports from the SAT or ACT with writing component."

SELECTIVITY	
Admissions Rating	**91**
# of applicants	27,247
% of applicants accepted	47
% of acceptees attending	26
# accepting a place on wait list	5,768
# admitted from wait list	2,067

FRESHMAN PROFILE	
Range SAT Critical Reading	550–640
Range SAT Math	580–670
Range SAT Writing	550–650
Range ACT Composite	25–29
Minimum paper TOEFL	550
Minimum web-based TOEFL	79
% graduated top 10% of class	43
% graduated top 25% of class	82
% graduated top 50% of class	98

DEADLINES	
Early action	
Deadline	12/1
Notification	2/1
Regular	
Deadline	2/1
Notification	rolling
Nonfall registration?	yes

FINANCIAL FACTS	
Financial Aid Rating	**69**
Annual in-state tuition	$8,712
Annual out-state tuition	$26,544
Room and board	$11,380
Required fees	$2,530
Books and supplies	$850
% needy frosh rec. need-based scholarship or grant aid	81
% needy UG rec. need-based scholarship or grant aid	77
% needy frosh rec. non-need-based scholarship or grant aid	70
% needy UG rec. non-need-based scholarship or grant aid	51
% needy frosh rec. need-based self-help aid	73
% needy UG rec. need-based self-help aid	77
% frosh rec. any financial aid	59
% UG rec. any financial aid	56
% UG borrow to pay for school	63
Average cumulative indebtedness	$23,822
% frosh need fully met	15
% ugrads need fully met	15
Average % of frosh need met	67
Average % of ugrad need met	65

UNIVERSITY OF DALLAS

1845 EAST NORTHGATE DRIVE, IRVING, TX 75062 • ADMISSIONS: 972-721-5266 • FAX: 972-721-5017

CAMPUS LIFE

Quality of Life Rating	**73**
Fire Safety Rating	**82**
Green Rating	**61**
Type of school	private
Affiliation	Roman Catholic
Environment	city

STUDENTS

Total undergrad enrollment	1,333
% male/female	49/51
% from out of state	56
% from public high school	43
% frosh live on campus	91
% African American	1
% Asian	4
% Caucasian	69
% Hispanic	16
% international	2
# of countries represented	53

SURVEY SAYS . . .

Students are friendly
Students are very religious
Low cost of living
Frats and sororities are unpopular or nonexistent
Very little drug use

ACADEMICS

Academic Rating	**83**
% students returning for sophomore year	82
% students graduating within 4 years	63
% students graduating within 6 years	74
Calendar	semester
Student/faculty ratio	10:1
Profs interesting rating	94
Profs accessible rating	91
Most classes have	20–29 students
Most lab/discussion sessions have	10–19 students

MOST POPULAR MAJORS

biology/biological sciences; business administration and management; English language and literature

APPLICANTS ALSO LOOK AT AND OFTEN PREFER

Southern Methodist University, University of Notre Dame

AND SOMETIMES PREFER

Austin College, Texas Christian University, Trinity University

AND RARELY PREFER

Texas A&M University—College Station, The University of Texas at Austin, Loyola University New Orleans, Saint Louis University

STUDENTS SAY ". . ."

Academics

This "Catholic University for Independent Thinkers" prides itself on its Core curriculum, in which students undertake "a deep and penetrating study of the Western tradition, from Ancient Greece to today" by reading "the greatest works of literature in all subjects." Students love the focus on primary sources throughout their four years. "The idea of learning politics from the writings of the democratic world's greatest minds is much more appealing to me than learning from a textbook," says one freshman. UD students are encouraged to approach everything—including their own faith—from a critical perspective. "The spirit of truth-seeking that pervades everything and everyone, both in and out of the classroom," can make for an "intense" environment. "I had one professor freshman year who said he was up until 3 A.M. doing the reading, so we better have done it, too," says a sophomore politics major. But it's easy to get motivated "when your professors care so much about what the students gain from the class discussions and the texts themselves." The small size of the school also adds to the academic intensity and makes students "feel like part of a big family." The administration gets poor marks: "They seem to be more concerned with keeping us from drinking and having sex than providing basic services all other college students take for granted." But any grumbling is overshadowed by enthusiasm for the school's unique character, including a study abroad program that sends most sophomores to Rome. The semester in Italy "brings our studies to life and helps us to connect what we learn in the classrooms with real, on-site visits to places like ancient Greece and Pompeii."

Life

At UD, "you're either studying, praying, or going to parties." The administration can be "very strict," and underage students are often written up for drinking. But that doesn't mean life here is boring. There are boisterous and popular celebrations for Groundhog Day and other holidays, weeknights bring "many, many on-campus activities organized by clubs, academic departments, or residence hall associations," and many students attend parties at off-campus apartments on weekends. Although Dallas is accessible by car, "undergraduate students (especially freshmen and sophomores) spend most of their time hanging out on campus." Students complain that the campus is in need of an overhaul: "A lot of the buildings are pretty ugly," and the school "needs to provide better facilities, [such as] library, computer lab, and study areas." But students find ways to have fun despite the barren surroundings. "We love to play intramurals, especially flag football and ultimate Frisbee. We like dancing, as evidenced by our very popular swing dancing club." And then there's that semester in Rome: "If you haven't gone yet, you're thinking about it, and if you have gone, you're talking about it and posting your photos."

Student Body

The typical UD student "studies one of the humanities (preferably English, history, or philosophy), is very, very studious and strongly committed to the Catholic faith but also knows how to have a good time." "It is not uncommon to encounter deep theological or philosophical discussions in diverse extracurricular settings—such as cross-country meets or weekend parties!" Students here take their studies seriously, and "few who are not enthusiastic about this intellectual pursuit come to the school." UD students are also serious about their faith: "Those who aren't very Catholic become more so." Campus nightlife is fun but not wild; most students "drink moderately or not at all," and there is no Greek scene. The student body is conservative politically, but everyone is "welcoming toward the liberal minority and dignifies alternative stances with respect and with very philosophical and very friendly discussions." Despite any differences, the core program unites the student body: "No matter what year you are, you have the same academic background as every student when it comes to discussing literary traditions, such as Dante or Homer, philosophy, politics, and more."

FINANCIAL AID: 972-721-5266 • E-MAIL: UGADMIS@UDALLAS.EDU • WEBSITE: WWW.UDALLAS.EDU

THE PRINCETON REVIEW SAYS

Admissions

Very important factors considered include: Application essay, academic GPA, recommendation(s), rigor of secondary school record, standardized test scores, character/personal qualities. *Important factors considered include:* Class rank, talent/ability. *Other factors considered include:* Alumni/ae relation, extracurricular activities, first generation, interview, level of applicant's interest, volunteer work, work experience. SAT or ACT required; ACT with or without writing component accepted. TOEFL required of all international applicants. High school diploma is required and GED is accepted. *Academic units required:* 4 English, 3 mathematics, 3 science, 2 foreign language, 3 social studies, 3 history, 2 visual/performing arts, 4 academic electives. *Academic units recommended:* 4 English, 4 mathematics, 3 science (3 science labs), 3 foreign language, 4 social studies, 4 history, 2 visual/performing arts, 4 academic electives.

Financial Aid

Students should submit: FAFSA. The Princeton Review suggests that all financial aid forms be submitted as soon as possible after January 1. *Need-based scholarships/grants offered:* Federal Pell, state scholarships/grants, the school's own gift aid. *Loan aid offered:* Direct Subsidized Stafford, Direct Unsubsidized Stafford, Direct PLUS, state loans. Applicants will be notified of awards on a rolling basis beginning March 30. Federal Work-Study Program available. Institutional employment available. Highest amount earned per year from on-campus jobs $1,500. Off-campus job opportunities are fair.

The Inside Word

The university's conservative nature means that UD admissions officers place significant emphasis on the "fit" part of the admissions process. Having a solid academic background counts for a lot, but a dedication to the classics or just serious academic inquiry can be even more important.

THE SCHOOL SAYS ". . ."

From the Admissions Office

"Quite unabashedly, the curriculum at the University of Dallas is based on the supposition that truth and virtue exist and are the proper objects of search in an education. The curriculum further supposes that this search is best pursued through an acquisition of philosophical and theological principles on the part of a student and has for its analogical field a vast body of great literature—perhaps more extensive than is likely to be encountered elsewhere—supplemented by a survey of the sweep of history and an introduction to the political and economic principles of society. An understanding of these subjects, along with an introduction to the quantitative and scientific worldview and a mastery of a language, is expected to form a comprehensive and coherent experience, which, in effect, governs the intellect of a student in a manner that develops independence of thought in its most effective mode.

"Students applying for admission are required to take the SAT Reasoning Test or the ACT with writing assessment."

SELECTIVITY	
Admissions Rating	**84**
# of applicants	1,041
% of applicants accepted	91
% of acceptees attending	40

FRESHMAN PROFILE	
Range SAT Critical Reading	550–700
Range SAT Math	530–650
Range SAT Writing	540–680
Range ACT Composite	24–30
Minimum paper TOEFL	550
Minimum web-based TOEFL	79
Average HS GPA	3.8
% graduated top 10% of class	47
% graduated top 25% of class	64
% graduated top 50% of class	84

DEADLINES	
Early action	
Deadline	12/1
Notification	1/15
Regular	
Priority	12/1
Deadline	3/1
Nonfall registration?	no

FINANCIAL FACTS	
Financial Aid Rating	**79**
Annual tuition	$27,500
Room and board	$9,326
Required fees	$1,825
Books and supplies	$1,700
% needy frosh rec. need-based scholarship or grant aid	100
% needy UG rec. need-based scholarship or grant aid	98
% needy frosh rec. non-need-based scholarship or grant aid	3
% needy UG rec. non-need-based scholarship or grant aid	4
% needy frosh rec. need-based self-help aid	71
% needy UG rec. need-based self-help aid	81
% frosh rec. any financial aid	96
% UG rec. any financial aid	93
% UG borrow to pay for school	55
Average cumulative indebtedness	$28,020
% frosh need fully met	21
% ugrads need fully met	22
Average % of frosh need met	76
Average % of ugrad need met	73

UNIVERSITY OF DAYTON

300 COLLEGE PARK, DAYTON, OH 45469-1300 • ADMISSIONS: 937-229-4411 • FAX: 937-229-4729

CAMPUS LIFE

Quality of Life Rating	91
Fire Safety Rating	73
Green Rating	78
Type of school	private
Affiliation	Roman Catholic
Environment	city

STUDENTS

Total undergrad enrollment	7,843
% male/female	51/49
% from out of state	41
% from public high school	52
% frosh live on campus	96
# of fraternities	11
# of sororities	7
% African American	4
% Asian	1
% Caucasian	85
% Hispanic	3
% international	4
# of countries represented	55

SURVEY SAYS . . .

School is well run
Students are friendly
Students get along with local community
Students are happy
Intramural sports are popular
Lots of beer drinking
Students are involved in community service

ACADEMICS

Academic Rating	77
% students returning for sophomore year	86
% students graduating within 4 years	58
% students graduating within 6 years	76
Calendar	semester
Student/faculty ratio	15:1
Profs interesting rating	81
Profs accessible rating	89
Most classes have	20–29 students
Most lab/discussion sessions have	10–19 students

MOST POPULAR MAJORS

business, management, marketing, and related support services, other; mechanical engineering; psychology

APPLICANTS ALSO LOOK AT AND OFTEN PREFER

The Ohio State University—Columbus,, Miami University

AND SOMETIMES PREFER

Indiana University—Bloomington, Xavier University (OH), University of Cincinnati, Saint Louis University, Purdue University—West Lafayette

AND RARELY PREFER

Marquette University, Loyola University of Chicago

STUDENTS SAY ". . ."

Academics

The University of Dayton not only prepares students for the real world, but it also "challenges them to better that world." This institution takes the Marianist values of "intense education, strong community, and deep faithfulness, and wraps it into a place that is a fun place to be"; there is also a palpable connection among all levels of the university. The school is "large enough to have all of the necessary resources and opportunities, but it is small enough to have a feeling of intimacy," and students have the "opportunity to meet with the president and administration and bring ideas up to them" on a regular basis. "No one likes UD—everyone loves it," says one of many happy students. Professors at UD are "always willing to help their students and do their part to make our course work academically challenging." "My professors are extremely intelligent; they provide optimal learning experiences," says a student. They bring their real-life experiences to the classroom, and the courses have "taught me not only to think on a more global scale, but they have armed me to make more conscious decisions in my day-to-day life," according to one student. "I have never had a professor here that I did not enjoy, and I have had many that I sincerely admire," says another. Under the university's requirements, fieldwork abounds, and students are "not just sitting in a classroom for four years, we actually go out and see our learning in action." Students also note that the university "has a promising vision for the future of the school." There is always change occurring on campus, whether it's "new residential halls, cafeterias, or new student programs and clubs," and "Faculty and administration respect and listen to the advice of students." The focus on giving back means that numerous resources are devoted to making it easy "for students to get involved here in Dayton or in another country."

Life

"Open doors in dorms and an inviting campus" make UD an inviting and friendly place to be. With so many organizations, clubs, and (extremely popular) intramural sports "there are always new things to do and new people to meet." The vast majority of students live on campus all four years, which "helps keep a very strong community." "The focus on community cannot be described in words; I instantly felt something different when I stepped on the campus," says one student. Service orientation is prevalent in UD life: "UD has opened up so many doors for me to explore service, while having fun and connecting with fellow UD students," says a student. Weekdays, there are "all kinds of club meetings and practices that keep people busy into the evening," but on weekends, most people venture out to the "ghetto," (the jokingly named student neighborhood), where "upperclassman open up their houses for other students." This neighborhood rests next to campus and consists of more than 400 homes, which "provides a student with a quintessential college experience." Campus clubs and organizations also plan bigger events on campus and off campus on weekends, including "art programs and performances," "Cincinnati Reds Baseball games, shopping trips to Columbus, and white-water rafting trips to West Virginia."

Student Body

Though many admit that diversity is lacking (but growing) at UD, it is generally agreed that every single student here is "friendly, outgoing, involved, and service-oriented." "[Students are] the most welcoming people I have ever known," says one. Most here are from the Midwest, and sweat/yoga pants and UD gear are the standard uniform. Students are so friendly at this close-knit campus of around 7,500 or so that there are "two to three degrees of separation" between everyone. Most people "love UD basketball," participate in "multiple intramural sports, do a lot of service in the community," and "go out both Friday and Saturday night (and most Thursdays)."

FINANCIAL AID: 800-427-5029 • E-MAIL: ADMISSION@UDAYTON.EDU • WEBSITE: WWW.UDAYTON.EDU

THE PRINCETON REVIEW SAYS

Admissions

Very important factors considered include: Academic GPA. *Important factors considered include:* Class rank, talent/ability. *Other factors considered include:* Application essay, recommendation(s), alumni/ae relation, character/personal qualities, extracurricular activities, first generation, interview, racial/ethnic status, volunteer work, work experience. SAT or ACT required. TOEFL required of all international applicants. High school diploma is required and GED is accepted. *Academic units required:* 2 units of foreign language are required for admission to the College of Arts and Sciences. *Academic units recommended:* 4 English, 4 mathematics, 4 science (1 science lab), 4 social studies, 4 academic electives.

Financial Aid

Students should submit: FAFSA. Regular filing deadline is March 1. The Princeton Review suggests that all financial aid forms be submitted as soon as possible after January 1. *Need-based scholarships/grants offered:* Federal Pell, SEOG, state scholarships/grants, private scholarships, the school's own gift aid, ACG, SMART. *Loan aid offered:* Direct Subsidized Stafford, Direct Unsubsidized Stafford, Direct PLUS, Federal Perkins. Applicants will be notified of awards on a rolling basis beginning March 15. Federal Work-Study Program available. Institutional employment available. Off-campus job opportunities are good.

The Inside Word

University of Dayton is an excellent option for students who want to attend a Catholic university but don't meet the stringent criteria of Georgetown or Notre Dame. UD gives "balanced consideration" to all academic factors—for example, class rank, GPA—on the application. Candidates who demonstrate a modicum of success in the classroom and intellectual promise will most likely be accepted. Applicants must apply to one of the university's four divisions; admissions criteria vary slightly among the different divisions.

THE SCHOOL SAYS ". . ."

From the Admissions Office

"The University of Dayton founded in 1850 by the Society of Mary, is a top ten Catholic research university. The university seeks outstanding diverse faculty, staff, and students who value its mission and share its commitment to academic excellence in teaching, study, research and creativity, the development of the whole person, and leadership and service in the local and global community. More than seventy challenging academic programs are offered in the College of Arts and Sciences and the Schools of Business Administration, Education and Allied Professions, Engineering, and Law. Classes are small—twenty-six students on average. Our more than 1,000 full-time and part-time faculty are committed to teaching undergraduate students and involving them in their research projects. The University of Dayton Research Institute ranks second in the nation in the amount of materials research performed annually. Technology-enhanced learning ensures students gain expertise in the tools that will prepare them for the future. All areas of campus and surrounding neighborhoods have access to our high speed wireless network. Recent campus construction provides a modern home for the university's cutting-edge academic programs. A new fitness and recreation complex, the RecPlex, provides 130,000 square feet of space for classrooms, courts, a natatorium, offices, and other recreational facilities. A strong sense of community is a hallmark feature of the university; a dual emphasis on leadership and service contributes to students' participation in more than 180 clubs and organizations. Division I intercollegiate athletics and club and intramural sports are also popular.

"Students applying for admission may provide scores from either the SAT or the ACT. The highest composite scores from either test will be used in admission and merit-based aid decisions."

SELECTIVITY	
Admissions Rating	**81**
# of applicants	12,041
% of applicants accepted	76
% of acceptees attending	22

FRESHMAN PROFILE	
Range SAT Critical Reading	510–610
Range SAT Math	520–640
Range SAT Writing	510–610
Range ACT Composite	24–29
Minimum paper TOEFL	523
Minimum web-based TOEFL	70
Average HS GPA	3.6
% graduated top 10% of class	26
% graduated top 25% of class	56
% graduated top 50% of class	88

DEADLINES	
Early action	
Deadline	12/15
Notification	2/1
Regular	
Priority	12/15
Deadline	3/1
Notification	3/15
Nonfall registration?	yes

FINANCIAL FACTS	
Financial Aid Rating	**87**
Annual tuition	$30,340
Required fees	$1,300
Books and supplies	$1,000
% needy frosh rec. need-based scholarship or grant aid	100
% needy UG rec. need-based scholarship or grant aid	98
% needy frosh rec. non-need-based scholarship or grant aid	23
% needy UG rec. non-need-based scholarship or grant aid	19
% needy frosh rec. need-based self-help aid	100
% needy UG rec. need-based self-help aid	99
% frosh rec. any financial aid	94
% UG rec. any financial aid	89
% UG borrow to pay for school	67
Average cumulative indebtedness	$36,331
% frosh need fully met	43
% ugrads need fully met	47
Average % of frosh need met	79
Average % of ugrad need met	79

UNIVERSITY OF DELAWARE

210 SOUTH COLLEGE AVENUE, NEWARK, DE 19716-6210 • ADMISSIONS: 302-831-8123 • FAX: 302-831-6905

CAMPUS LIFE

Quality of Life Rating	82
Fire Safety Rating	94
Green Rating	87
Type of school	public
Environment	town

STUDENTS

Total undergrad enrollment	15,887
% male/female	43/57
% from out of state	65
% from public high school	80
% frosh live on campus	92
# of fraternities	22
# of sororities	15
% African American	5
% Asian	4
% Caucasian	78
% Hispanic	6
% international	3
# of countries represented	91

SURVEY SAYS . . .

Great computer facilities
Great library
Great off-campus food
Students are happy
Student publications are popular
Lots of beer drinking
Hard liquor is popular

ACADEMICS

Academic Rating	75
% students returning for sophomore year	82
% students graduating within 4 years	62
% students graduating within 6 years	77
Calendar	4-1-4
Student/faculty ratio	15:1
Profs interesting rating	72
Profs accessible rating	81
Most classes have	20–29 students
Most lab/discussion sessions have	10–19 students

MOST POPULAR MAJORS

biology/biological sciences; nursing/registered nurse (rn, asn, bsn, msn); psychology

APPLICANTS ALSO LOOK AT AND OFTEN PREFER

University of Pennsylvania, Princeton University, College of William and Mary

AND SOMETIMES PREFER

Cornell University, University of Virginia, New York University, Brandeis University, University of Michigan—Ann Arbor, Washington University in St. Louis, Georgetown University, Syracuse University, Virginia Tech, The George Washington University

AND RARELY PREFER

Northeastern University, Rutgers-The State University of New Jersey—New Brunswick, State University of New York at Binghamton, University of Maryland, College Park, University of Massachusetts-Amherst, University of Vermont, Villanova University

STUDENTS SAY ". . ."

Academics

If you're looking for a "well-rounded" college experience, University of Delaware delivers on every front. According to the school's satisfied undergraduates, "the University of Delaware is everything college should be," from its "gorgeous campus" and "amazing school spirit," to "top notch" academics and "vibrant campus life." At UD, as at many public schools, "College is what you make it: If you take easy classes, college is a breeze; if you challenge yourself, classes will be more difficult." First-year courses are often large and impersonal; fortunately, major classes are usually smaller and "electives are interesting and engaging." Highly qualified students may also apply to the school's "excellent" honors program, which provides access to "challenging, interesting classes taught by distinguished yet friendly professors." Through the touted undergraduate research program, students have access to "diverse research opportunities," and the school's extensive study abroad program is "one of the best in the nation." Overall, faculty get good reviews, though students warn it's a mixed bag: "Some professors shouldn't be allowed within ten miles of a classroom; others will change your life. It's up to you to weed out the bad ones." While you won't have your hand held, professors are responsive to student needs: "If you ever need any help, a quick e-mail or a phone call usually solves your problem." On a similar note, "The administration is extremely approachable and talks to students on the same level."

Life

Work and play come together at the University of Delaware, an institution that offers "the perfect balance of academic intensity and excellent social life." Come the weekend (or even during the week), "UD kids like to have their share of fun," and "There is always a party happening." For an alternative to the party scene, students go to "movies in the student center or to ice skating on Fridays," and "There are a lot of great guest speakers, bands, and cultural events on campus." In addition, "There are social groups for almost anything you can think of from the adventure club to organic cooking to ultimate Frisbee." While fraternities and sororities do exist, they do not dominate the social scene; still Greeks are "very spirited, have a ton of fun, and are widely supported by our campus community." Intramural and varsity sports are wildly popular, both for athletes and their raucous fans. In fact, "Homecoming is a university holiday where people wake up as early as 5:00 A.M. to start tailgating." What's more, the campus location can't be beat. Main Street, which runs right through campus, "is packed with great restaurants and shopping." For a fun day trip, "Philly is cheap and easy to get to by Septa train," and "the Chinatown bus costs thirty-five dollars round trip into NYC."

Student Body

It's a largely East Coast crowd at University of Delaware, drawing the vast majority of its undergraduates from "around NYC, Philly, or Baltimore." Within that demographic, "Preppy sorority kids are probably the most common, but no matter who you are or what your into, the school population is big enough [that] you're bound to find a group that shares your interest." At UD, "You'll have your jocks and frat boys, but you'll also find skaters, rockers, artsy types, and everything else in between." However, most UD students share an incredible enthusiasm for their school community, and "A typical student is engaged in coursework and a multitude of various extracurricular [activities]." Despite its long-standing repute as a party school, "students here have become more focused on academics. Most students here really do have a passion for learning and study really hard in order to get those grades and graduate." Even so, UD's reputation for revelry isn't lost on undergraduates: "The typical UD student cares about their school work but loves to have fun on the weekends."

FINANCIAL AID: 302-831-8761 • E-MAIL: ADMISSIONS@UDEL.EDU • WEBSITE: WWW.UDEL.EDU

THE PRINCETON REVIEW SAYS

Admissions

Very important factors considered include: Academic GPA, rigor of secondary school record, state residency. *Important factors considered include:* Application essay, recommendation(s), standardized test scores, character/personal qualities, extracurricular activities, talent/ability, volunteer work, work experience. *Other factors considered include:* Class rank, alumni/ae relation, first generation, geographical residence, interview, level of applicant's interest, racial/ethnic status. SAT or ACT required; ACT with or without writing component accepted. TOEFL required of all international applicants. High school diploma is required and GED is accepted. *Academic units required:* 4 English, 3 mathematics, 3 science (2 science labs), 2 foreign language, 2 social studies, 2 history, 2 academic electives. *Academic units recommended:* 4 English, 4 mathematics, 4 science (3 science labs), 4 foreign language, 2 social studies, 2 history.

Financial Aid

Students should submit: FAFSA. Regular filing deadline is May 1. The Princeton Review suggests that all financial aid forms be submitted as soon as possible after January 1. *Need-based scholarships/grants offered:* Federal Pell, SEOG, state scholarships/grants, private scholarships, the school's own gift aid. *Loan aid offered:* Direct Subsidized Stafford, Direct Unsubsidized Stafford, Direct PLUS, Federal Perkins, Federal Nursing, college/university loans from institutional funds. Applicants will be notified of awards on a rolling basis beginning March 15. Federal Work-Study Program available. Institutional employment available. Highest amount earned per year from on-campus jobs $2,000. Off-campus job opportunities are excellent.

Inside Word

Although UD is run by the state of Delaware, out-of-state students also benefit from the school's excellent academic and social offerings at a reasonable tuition. Even so, the school is expressly committed to supporting Delawarean students, who comprise about forty percent of the student body. More details and samples of qualifying high school curricula are available on the admissions department website. In all admissions decisions, UD considers the entirety of a student's application; there are no minimum test scores or grades.

THE SCHOOL SAYS ". . ."

From the Admissions Office

"An East Coast classic, the University of Delaware is a rich, historic campus in Newark, Delaware, midway between New York City and Washington, D.C. UD is known for its problem-based, hands-on learning in every college and a relatively small enrollment that engages students with interested, accessible faculty. Over ninety percent of our students land jobs within six months of graduation and continue their educations at the top graduate and professional schools in the world. Three signers of the Declaration of Independence were among our first class and recent alumni include the vice president of the United States, the governor of New Jersey, and the top campaign strategist for the president of the U.S. UD is also a talent magnet, attracting top scholars and innovators, including a recent Nobel Prize winner and a Rhodes Scholar. The University of Delaware is working on the most compelling social, civic, artistic, and scientific challenges of our age. As the flagship university in the first state of the union, we dare to be first in ways that matter—first in new energy technologies, first in global study, first in political leadership, first in interdisciplinary engineering, first in educating teachers, first in design innovation, first in championship athletics, first in translational medicine. We challenge our students to be first in what matters most to them."

SELECTIVITY

Admissions Rating	**91**
# of applicants	23,510
% of applicants accepted	54
% of acceptees attending	27
# accepting a place on wait list	767
# admitted from wait list	591

FRESHMAN PROFILE

Range SAT Critical Reading	540–640
Range SAT Math	550–660
Range SAT Writing	540–650
Range ACT Composite	27–29
Minimum paper TOEFL	550
Minimum web-based TOEFL	80
Average HS GPA	3.6
% graduated top 10% of class	39
% graduated top 25% of class	76
% graduated top 50% of class	97

DEADLINES

Regular	
Priority	12/1
Deadline	1/15
Notification	3/15
Nonfall registration?	yes

FINANCIAL FACTS

Financial Aid Rating	**77**
Annual in-state tuition	$9,670
Annual out-state tuition	$25,940
Room and board	$10,196
Required fees	$1,522
Books and supplies	$800
% needy frosh rec. need-based scholarship or grant aid	77
% needy UG rec. need-based scholarship or grant aid	67
% needy frosh rec. non-need-based scholarship or grant aid	41
% needy UG rec. non-need-based scholarship or grant aid	23
% needy frosh rec. need-based self-help aid	77
% needy UG rec. need-based self-help aid	83
% frosh rec. any financial aid	57
% UG rec. any financial aid	55
% UG borrow to pay for school	44
Average cumulative indebtedness	$17,200
% frosh need fully met	48
% ugrads need fully met	46
Average % of frosh need met	76
Average % of ugrad need met	74

UNIVERSITY OF DENVER

OFFICE OF ADMISSION, DENVER, CO 80208 • ADMISSIONS: 303-871-2036 • FAX: 303-871-3301

CAMPUS LIFE

Quality of Life Rating	**85**
Fire Safety Rating	**74**
Green Rating	**88**
Type of school	private
Environment	metropolis

STUDENTS

Total undergrad enrollment	5,453
% male/female	44/56
% from out of state	59
% frosh live on campus	95
# of fraternities	9
# of sororities	7
% African American	3
% Asian	4
% Caucasian	68
% Hispanic	8
% Native American	1
% international	9
# of countries represented	91

SURVEY SAYS . . .

Athletic facilities are great
Students love Denver, CO
Low cost of living
Registration is a breeze

ACADEMICS

Academic Rating	**80**
% students returning for sophomore year	89
% students graduating within 4 years	61
% students graduating within 6 years	79
Calendar	quarter
Student/faculty ratio	8:1
Profs interesting rating	85
Profs accessible rating	81
Most classes have	10–19 students
Most lab/discussion sessions have	10–19 students

MOST POPULAR MAJORS

biology/biological sciences; business, management, marketing, and related support services, other; business/commerce

APPLICANTS ALSO LOOK AT AND OFTEN PREFER

Colorado College, Colorado State University, University of Colorado—Boulder

AND SOMETIMES PREFER

Boston University, University of Vermont, University of Puget Sound

STUDENTS SAY ". . ."

Academics

From the moment you set foot on campus, it's evident that the University of Denver is truly "committed to its students." Undoubtedly, the school offers "academic rigor," a "beautiful campus" and an unbeatable location. Moreover, with a student population hovering at nearly 5,500, DU is "big enough to meet new people constantly" yet small enough to maintain an "intimate" feel. Undergrads here also value that the university operates on a quarter system, providing "a great alternative to the [traditional] semester." Academically, Denver has "a wide array of very unique majors" and especially strong programs in international studies, music, and business. And students really appreciate their experiences in the classroom. One content undergrad shares, "The professors engage the students; the students engage with the material. We dig deeply into each subject. It's the most amazing learning environment I've ever experienced." Further, professors are "very knowledgeable and passionate. The majority are very willing to help and are accessible out of class. They treat students as unique individuals, not just a 'number.'" As this wholly satisfied student encapsulates her school, "DU is about providing opportunities both socially and academically that go above and beyond students' wildest dreams!"

Life

Undergrads at DU are "very dedicated to school" but also "like to kick back and have a good time on weekends." And fortunately, there's no shortage of opportunity for fun and amusement around campus. To begin with, "like all schools, there is partying going on, but the pressure to go out and party is nonexistent." Additionally, the "majority of the student body goes to many [weekly] sporting events, and if you are a Pioneer you try to attend as many hockey games as possible." Further, the "DU programs board hosts a free movie every Thursday night, and it's a great way to relax after a long day of classes." Of course, "There are [also] endless events, seminars, and other opportunities [for] student [participation]." Outdoor activities are also all the rage here. Indeed, "Skiing and spending time in the mountains is huge—hiking, biking, and climbing as well." After all, "Some of the world's best alpine areas [are] just an hour or two away." Music is also pretty popular, and "Lots of people go to concerts downtown or at Red Rocks in the fall and spring." Just as important, "Downtown Denver is easily accessible by light rail, [with] a stop located right next to the campus." Students love to take advantage of everything from the great restaurant scene to a Rockies baseball game. Simply put, "If you can't find something to do, you're doing something wrong."

Student Body

On the surface, University of Denver's student population tends to skew "white" and "affluent." Thankfully, while acknowledging this truth, undergrads quickly stress that "most students fit in quite well, regardless of background or ethnicity." They are also quick to point out, "We have every type of person from the foreign exchange students to the engineers to the bank geeks and theater majors to the athletes." Indeed, "If you look for it, you will meet interesting people from all around the country and the world." Undergrads at DU generally find their peers to be "outgoing and welcoming" and confidently assert, "Everyone seems to have a group that they can easily belong in." Moreover, the vast majority are "very athletic or like to participate in outdoor activities." And perhaps more important, "Most students care about their education and are motivated to complete their degree and even more." Of course, regardless of adjectives or categorizations, DU is "a great community no matter what your interests are, [and] you will find some way to fit in."

FINANCIAL AID: 303-871-4020 • E-MAIL: ADMISSION@DU.EDU • WEBSITE: WWW.DU.EDU

THE PRINCETON REVIEW SAYS

Admissions

Very important factors considered include: Academic GPA, rigor of secondary school record, standardized test scores, character/personal qualities. *Important factors considered include:* Application essay, recommendation(s), extracurricular activities, interview, level of applicant's interest, talent/ability, volunteer work, work experience. SAT or ACT required. High school diploma is required and GED is accepted. *Academic units recommended:* 4 English, 4 mathematics, 4 science (2 science labs), 4 foreign language, 2 social studies, 2 history.

Financial Aid

Students should submit: FAFSA, CSS/Financial Aid PROFILE, noncustodial PROFILE. Regular filing deadline is February 15. The Princeton Review suggests that all financial aid forms be submitted as soon as possible after January 1. *Need-based scholarships/grants offered:* Federal Pell, SEOG, state scholarships/grants, private scholarships, the school's own gift aid. *Loan aid offered:* Direct Subsidized Stafford, Direct Unsubsidized Stafford, Direct PLUS, Federal Perkins, college/university loans from institutional funds. Applicants will be notified of awards on or about April 1. Off-campus job opportunities are excellent.

The Inside Word

Admissions officers at University of Denver take a holistic approach to the application process. Therefore, they strive to look beyond quantitative factors and will heavily review your essay, recommendations, and extracurricular activities. It's also highly recommended that you sit for an interview.

THE SCHOOL SAYS ". . ."

From the Admissions Office

"When you start from a higher place at the University of Denver—in our setting of great natural beauty, cultural richness, and intellectual energy—you'll experience meaningful interaction with professors who set you on paths toward personal discovery, paths that can change the course of your future. Our diverse student body, engaged faculty, and prime location provide a culture of opportunity that is unique and unrivaled. DU is continually developing educational initiatives that help students prepare for an ever-changing world. Our Living and Learning Communities provide extracurricular and co-curricular programming in specialized areas; the Partners in Scholarship (PinS) program funds undergraduate research for students wishing to pursue a topic of personal interest in greater depth; and sixty-five to seventy percent of our students are taking advantage of invaluable internship opportunities in laboratories, corporate offices, government agencies, and cultural settings. One of the university's signature offerings is the Cherrington Global Scholars program, which allows students to study abroad at the same cost of a quarter at DU. Nearly seventy-five percent of our students study abroad, which ranks DU third in the nation among doctoral and research institutions for percentage of students participating. Outside the classroom, DU students put ideas and ideals into action. They are active members of our community and they take advantage of the numerous recreational opportunities available to them, including club, intramural, and seventeen Division I sports. Whatever their majors and interests, DU students are groomed to excel in their life's work and to confront the great issues of the day."

SELECTIVITY

Admissions Rating	**90**
# of applicants	10,504
% of applicants accepted	68
% of acceptees attending	17
# accepting a place on wait list	445
# admitted from wait list	47

FRESHMAN PROFILE

Range SAT Critical Reading	550–660
Range SAT Math	560–670
Range SAT Writing	540–640
Range ACT Composite	25–30
Minimum paper TOEFL	550
Minimum web-based TOEFL	80
Average HS GPA	3.7
% graduated top 10% of class	44
% graduated top 25% of class	81
% graduated top 50% of class	97

DEADLINES

Early action	
Deadline	11/1
Notification	1/15
Regular	
Deadline	1/15
Notification	3/15
Nonfall registration?	yes

FINANCIAL FACTS

Financial Aid Rating	**83**
Annual tuition	$38,232
Room and board	$10,818
Required fees	$945
Books and supplies	$1,800
% needy frosh rec. need-based scholarship or grant aid	98
% needy UG rec. need-based scholarship or grant aid	97
% needy frosh rec. non-need-based scholarship or grant aid	21
% needy UG rec. non-need-based scholarship or grant aid	17
% needy frosh rec. need-based self-help aid	78
% needy UG rec. need-based self-help aid	79
% frosh rec. any financial aid	85
% UG rec. any financial aid	77
% UG borrow to pay for school	44
Average cumulative indebtedness	$26,628
% frosh need fully met	32
% ugrads need fully met	30
Average % of frosh need met	82
Average % of ugrad need met	82

University of Florida

201 Criser Hall, Gainesville, FL 32611-4000 • Admissions: 352-392-1365 • Fax: 352-392-3987

CAMPUS LIFE

Quality of Life Rating	**88**
Fire Safety Rating	**60***
Green Rating	**91**
Type of school	public
Environment	city

STUDENTS

Total undergrad enrollment	31,988
% male/female	45/55
% from out of state	3
% from public high school	81
# of fraternities	38
# of sororities	26
% African American	9
% Asian	8
% Caucasian	59
% Hispanic	18
% international	1
# of countries represented	157

SURVEY SAYS . . .

Athletic facilities are great
Everyone loves the Gators
Intramural sports are popular
Frats and sororities dominate social scene
Student publications are popular
Student government is popular
Lots of beer drinking
Hard liquor is popular

ACADEMICS

Academic Rating	**71**
% students returning for sophomore year	95
% students graduating within 4 years	65
% students graduating within 6 years	84
Calendar	semester
Student/faculty ratio	21:1
Profs interesting rating	72
Profs accessible rating	69
Most classes have	10–19 students
Most lab/discussion sessions have	10–19 students

MOST POPULAR MAJORS

biology; political science and government; psychology

STUDENTS SAY ". . ."

Academics

"A top-tier research institute" that "is full of bright students who still know how to have fun," the University of Florida offers "an environment unparalleled by an other university in the world with its first-class amenities, athletics, academics, campus, and students," enthusiastic students insist. The school "has excellent academic programs all across the board: You're not limited to just a great engineering program or journalism program" here; the sciences (including premedical studies, which piggyback on "a strong teaching hospital on campus"), business, education, communications, and engineering are among the many standout offerings. In short, "UF is a great school" that's "not expensive, even for out-of-state students. Plus, there is a great sense of family here: You really are a part of the Gator Nation!" It is, of course, a very large university that at times "runs more [like] a machine than a place that fosters learning and growth." As one student reports, "The school never even knew I had a name. The first thing anyone ever asks you is 'What's your UF-ID?'" Also, students must be prepared for "the annoyance of the size of the more generalized prerequisite courses, e.g., lower-level courses required by two or three majors." Still, "the professors are almost always wonderful: They are helpful and definitely know their stuff."

Life

"The greatest strength [of this school] is UF's spirit," students agree, telling us that "there's just something about being a Gator. It doesn't matter where you are in the world, UF students and alumni are everywhere and ready to greet you with open arms and a hearty 'Go Gators!' You belong there." While here, you can party to your heart's content. "Every day is a weekend in Gainesville, and you will always find something going on Sunday through Saturday. There's midtown, a strip right across from the stadium that has the infamous Swamp restaurant, clubs, bars, and plenty of food to satiate hunger in between classes. There's also 'downtown' Gainesville, which houses more bars, clubs, and restaurants and shopping to keep you busy throughout the entire semester." And "if you're not into the party scene, there's the Hippodrome Theatre, Lake Wauberg, and the local mall and movie theaters to keep you occupied. Gainesville is definitely a college town, and it is perfect for anyone looking for the true college experience." College sports are huge, "and there are hardly any people that aren't proud of Gator athletes and always ready to sport the orange and blue." UF's Greek community "is very prominent, and a large number of students belong [to] a fraternity/sorority or associate with students who do."

Student Body

The typical UF student "has a popular major like engineering or business," "is witty, loves Gator football, and likes to party. An atypical student may be someone who doesn't party or may deviate from mainstream beliefs, practices, or political parties, but for the most part, any student is accepted as a member of the Gator nation," and most "seem to maintain a well-balanced life of studying and socializing." While "the sorority/fraternity people are the most dominant group on campus," there's also "a really strong indie scene (the two never interact)." In fact, "There are people all over the spectrum," although the place is so big that "half of them you may never meet." "We are one of the most diverse campuses in the nation," one student explains, "and we are all Gators at heart, first and foremost."

FINANCIAL AID: 352-392-6684 • WEBSITE: WWW.UFL.EDU

THE PRINCETON REVIEW SAYS

Admissions

Very important factors considered include: Academic GPA, rigor of secondary school record. *Important factors considered include:* Application essay, character/personal qualities, extracurricular activities, first generation, talent/ability. *Other factors considered include:* Class rank, standardized test scores, alumni/ae relation, geographical residence, level of applicant's interest, state residency, volunteer work, work experience. SAT or ACT required; ACT with writing component required. TOEFL required of all international applicants. High school diploma is required and GED is accepted. *Academic units required:* 4 English, 3 mathematics, 3 science (2 science labs), 2 foreign language, 3 social studies, 0 history, 3 academic electives.

Financial Aid

Students should submit: FAFSA. The Princeton Review suggests that all financial aid forms be submitted as soon as possible after January 1. *Need-based scholarships/grants offered:* Federal Pell, SEOG, state scholarships/grants, private scholarships, the school's own gift aid, state, academic, creative arts/performance, special achievements/activities, special characteristics, athletic and ROTC. *Loan aid offered:* Direct Subsidized Stafford, Direct Unsubsidized Stafford, Direct PLUS, Federal Perkins, college/university loans from institutional funds. Applicants will be notified of awards on a rolling basis beginning April 1. Federal Work-Study Program available. Institutional employment available. Highest amount earned per year from on-campus jobs $19,744. Off-campus job opportunities are fair.

The Inside Word

First-generation college students from disadvantaged backgrounds qualify for the Florida Opportunity Scholars program, which fully covers four years of educational costs. The program is not limited to minority students, the average family income of recipients is just less than $25,000 per year.

THE SCHOOL SAYS ". . ."

From the Admissions Office

"University of Florida students come from more than 100 countries, all fifty states, and every one of the sixty-seven counties in Florida. Twenty-three percent of the student body is comprised of graduate students. Approximately 4,300 African American students, 6,600 Hispanic students, and 4,100 Asian American students attend UF. Ninety percent of the entering freshmen rank above the national mean of scores on standard entrance exams. UF consistently ranks near the top among public universities in the number of new National Merit and Achievement scholars in attendance.

"Students must submit the SAT or ACT with the writing section. UF considers your highest section scores across all SAT test dates."

SELECTIVITY	
Admissions Rating	93
# of applicants	27,295
% of applicants accepted	43
% of acceptees attending	55

FRESHMAN PROFILE	
Range SAT Critical Reading	570–670
Range SAT Math	290–690
Range ACT Composite	24–30
Average HS GPA	4.2
% graduated top 10% of class	74
% graduated top 25% of class	93
% graduated top 50% of class	99

DEADLINES	
Regular Deadline	11/1
Nonfall registration?	yes

FINANCIAL FACTS	
Financial Aid Rating	82
Annual in-state tuition	$5,656
Annual out-state tuition	$27,933
Room and board	$8,800
Books and supplies	$1,070
% needy frosh rec. need-based scholarship or grant aid	64
% needy UG rec. need-based scholarship or grant aid	69
% needy frosh rec. non-need-based scholarship or grant aid	98
% needy UG rec. non-need-based scholarship or grant aid	80
% needy frosh rec. need-based self-help aid	37
% needy UG rec. need-based self-help aid	50
% frosh rec. any financial aid	98
% UG rec. any financial aid	90
% UG borrow to pay for school	40
Average cumulative indebtedness	$16,013
% frosh need fully met	29
% ugrads need fully met	31
Average % of frosh need met	83
Average % of ugrad need met	83

UNIVERSITY OF GEORGIA

TERRELL HALL, ATHENS, GA 30602 • ADMISSIONS: 706-542-8776 • FAX: 706-542-1466

CAMPUS LIFE

Quality of Life Rating	93
Fire Safety Rating	77
Green Rating	97
Type of school	public
Environment	city

STUDENTS

Total undergrad enrollment	26,177
% male/female	42/58
% from out of state	11
% from public high school	79
% frosh live on campus	98
# of fraternities	33
# of sororities	26
% African American	7
% Asian	8
% Caucasian	76
% Hispanic	4
% international	1
# of countries represented	121

SURVEY SAYS . . .

Athletic facilities are great
Great food on campus
Great off-campus food
Low cost of living
Everyone loves the Bulldogs

ACADEMICS

Academic Rating	74
% students returning for sophomore year	94
% students graduating within 4 years	55
% students graduating within 6 years	83
Calendar	semester
Student/faculty ratio	18:1
Profs interesting rating	78
Profs accessible rating	71
Most classes have	20–29 students

MOST POPULAR MAJORS

biology/biological sciences; English language and literature; psychology

STUDENTS SAY ". . ."

Academics

As at many large universities, UGA has a "mixed bag of professors," but there are "more good teachers" than bad. Though students don't love the core curriculum classes due to their large size and the prevalence of TAs, "once [you're] in your particular program, the teachers are outstanding and easy to reach." "The professors really do want to see you at office hours if you have questions," and they "want to share their love of learning with you." "My major-related classes are very small, and each student receives individual attention." The honors program also receives raves: "Many of my best classes and favorite teachers have come from the honors program, but non-honors classes are generally good as well." "The study spaces are well-equipped and quiet," but "the school of social work is still housed in an old dorm." "Administration is a pain (not the people, only the requirements), but I think that describes academia in general." In general students "feel that the administration can be very accommodating at times, but at other times it can seem like it is full of red tape." Registration technology "needs to be brought out of the 1980s and into the twenty-first century." "The administration [can] seem like a bunch of penny-pinchers, but they must be to run a major research facility."

Life

Life at UGA seems to be a good mix of the two different worlds of sports and arts: football, frats, and tailgating on campus come together nicely with the coffee shops and music scene in downtown Athens. "On Saturday afternoons in the fall, nearly everyone on campus is at the football game. It's a way of life here." "Everybody really gets behind the team, and Saturdays in Athens feel like mini vacations." Fraternities and sororities dominate the party scene, but "there is definitely plenty to do, even if you don't go Greek." Students love to brag about the high number of bars per capita in Athens, but there's plenty more to boast about. "The Athens music and art scene is very inspiring, and there are tons of opportunities for creativity here." "Downtown Athens is fabulous! Whether you drink or don't drink, all are welcome and all congregate there." Campus life offers plenty of activity, too. "Fun is a part of daily life...with a dozen intramural sports each semester...and many community activities (multiple movie theaters, bowling allies, golf course)." "Ultimate Frisbee, walks around the multiple parks, days lounging on North Campus, and spending *lots* of time downtown are a couple ways I like to have fun at school." "There are so many organizations that everyone can find a place that will feel like home or find a place to meet new people." "It's no secret that UGA knows how to party. However, most of the students know how to manage social and academic time."

Student Body

"Students are generally white, upper-middle-class, smart, [and] involved, and [they] have a good time," "seem to be predominantly conservative," and "are usually involved in at least one organization whether it be Greek, a club, or sports." "The typical student at UGA is one who knows how and when to study but allows himself or herself to have a very active social life." The majority are Southerners, with many students from within Georgia. "The stereotype is Southern, Republican, football-loving, and beer-drinking. While many, many of UGA's students do not fit this description, there is no lack of the above," and "there is a social scene for everyone in Athens." "There are a great number of atypical students in the liberal arts," which "creates a unique and exciting student body with greatly contrasting opinions."

FINANCIAL AID: 706-542-6147 • E-MAIL: ADMPROC@UGA.EDU • WEBSITE: WWW.UGA.EDU

THE PRINCETON REVIEW SAYS

Admissions

Very important factors considered include: Academic GPA, rigor of secondary school record. *Important factors considered include:* Standardized test scores. *Other factors considered include:* Application essay, recommendation(s), character/personal qualities, extracurricular activities, first generation, talent/ability, volunteer work, work experience. SAT or ACT required; ACT with writing component required. TOEFL required of all international applicants. High school diploma is required and GED is accepted. *Academic units required:* 4 English, 4 mathematics, 3 science (2 science labs), 2 foreign language, 3 social studies. *Academic units recommended:* 4 English, 4 mathematics, 3 science (2 science labs), 3 foreign language, 1 social studies, 2 history, 1 academic electives.

Financial Aid

Students should submit: FAFSA. The Princeton Review suggests that all financial aid forms be submitted as soon as possible after January 1. *Need-based scholarships/grants offered:* Federal Pell, SEOG, state scholarships/grants, private scholarships, the school's own gift aid. *Loan aid offered:* Direct Subsidized Stafford, Direct Unsubsidized Stafford, Direct PLUS, Federal Perkins, state loans, college/university loans from institutional funds. Applicants will be notified of awards on a rolling basis beginning May 15.

The Inside Word

A school as large as UGA must start winnowing applicants by the numbers. If you fail to meet certain baseline curricular, GPA, and standardized-test-score floors, only exceptional talent elsewhere (a gift for the arts or, better still, throwing a football) will get you past the first cut. Some students here are Georgia residents reaping the benefits of the state's HOPE scholarship program, which pays tuition and most school-related fees for state residents who earn at least a 3.7 GPA in high school, a 1200 SAT or 26 ACT score, and maintain a 3.3 in college. George state residents who earn at least a 3.0 in high school will also have a large portion of their tuition paid.

THE SCHOOL SAYS ". . ."

From the Admissions Office

"The University of Georgia offers students the advantages and resources of a top public research university, including a wide range of majors and exceptional academic facilities such as the 200,000-square-foot Miller Learning Center. At the same time, UGA provides opportunities more common to smaller, private schools, such as first-year seminars led by distinguished faculty and learning communities that connect students with similar academic interests. The university is committed to challenging its academically superior students in the classroom and beyond, with increased emphasis on undergraduate research, service-learning, and study abroad. UGA students taking advantage of such offerings find themselves well positioned to compete with the best undergraduates in the country, as evidenced by their recent string of successes in winning Rhodes, Marshall, Truman, and other major scholarships.

"The UGA campus, considered one of the most beautiful in the nation, adjoins vibrant downtown Athens. While Athens is renowned for its local music scene, UGA also houses the Performing Arts Center, the Hugh Hodgson School of Music, the Lamar Dodd School of Art, and the Georgia Museum of Art. Sports—from football to gymnastics—are also a major attraction, with UGA teams perennially ranked among the best in the country. "To experience the excitement of UGA, most prospective students visit campus, a ninety-minute drive northeast of the Atlanta airport. See the admissions website to sign up for a tour with the Visitors Center, view the weekday schedule of admissions information sessions, and find application details.

"Applicants for first-year admission will be required to submit either the SAT or ACT. Students submitting only the ACT must also submit the optional ACT writing test."

SELECTIVITY

Admissions Rating	**91**
# of applicants	17,569
% of applicants accepted	63
% of acceptees attending	50
# accepting a place on wait list	615
# admitted from wait list	11

FRESHMAN PROFILE

Range SAT Critical Reading	560–650
Range SAT Math	560–660
Range SAT Writing	560–650
Range ACT Composite	25–30
Minimum paper TOEFL	550
Minimum web-based TOEFL	80
Average HS GPA	3.6
% graduated top 10% of class	47
% graduated top 25% of class	89
% graduated top 50% of class	98

DEADLINES

Early action	
Deadline	10/15
Notification	12/1
Regular	
Priority	10/15
Deadline	1/15
Notification	4/1
Nonfall registration?	yes

FINANCIAL FACTS

Financial Aid Rating	**76**
Annual in-state tuition	$9,472
Annual out-state tuition	$27,682
Room and board	$8,708
Books and supplies	$1,078
% needy frosh rec. need-based scholarship or grant aid	98
% needy UG rec. need-based scholarship or grant aid	91
% needy frosh rec. non-need-based scholarship or grant aid	16
% needy UG rec. non-need-based scholarship or grant aid	10
% needy frosh rec. need-based self-help aid	67
% needy UG rec. need-based self-help aid	72
% frosh rec. any financial aid	49
% UG rec. any financial aid	45
% UG borrow to pay for school	46
Average cumulative indebtedness	$18,569
% frosh need fully met	23
% ugrads need fully met	19
Average % of frosh need met	73
Average % of ugrad need met	67

UNIVERSITY OF HAWAII—MANOA

2600 CAMPUS ROAD, HONOLULU, HI 96822 • ADMISSIONS: 808-956-8975 • FAX: 808-956-4148

CAMPUS LIFE

Quality of Life Rating	**66**
Fire Safety Rating	**84**
Green Rating	**90**
Type of school	public
Environment	metropolis

STUDENTS

Total undergrad enrollment	14,054
% male/female	47/53
% from out of state	23
% from public high school	66
% frosh live on campus	55
# of fraternities	3
# of sororities	2
% African American	1
% Asian	59
% Caucasian	21
% Hispanic	2
% Native American	1
% international	3
# of countries represented	98

SURVEY SAYS . . .

Students are happy
Students are friendly
Diverse student types on campus
Different types of students interact
Students get along with local community

ACADEMICS

Academic Rating	**66**
% students returning for sophomore year	79
% students graduating within 4 years	24
% students graduating within 6 years	50
Calendar	semester
Student/faculty ratio	14:1
Profs interesting rating	65
Profs accessible rating	65
Most classes have	10–19 students
Most lab/discussion sessions have	10–19 students

MOST POPULAR MAJORS

art/art studies; biology/biological sciences; hospitality administration/management, other

STUDENTS SAY ". . ."

Academics

The University of Hawaii—Manoa, the flagship school of the University of Hawaii system, offers a solid education and university experience at a competitive price. Students appreciate the diversity of the school—"not only of the students and staff, but of what is offered"—and the "great feeling of collaboration and integration across all levels—amongst colleges, students, faculty, and the community." Even those who are not from Hawaii are treated with "the aloha spirit" in which the school goes out of its way to "include those who are not from Hawaii into the UH Ohana" (a Hawaiian term that refers to a family).

Professors are "knowledgeable in their field, share their knowledge easily, and seem to be enthusiastic in making sure that I understand the subject matter." The majority of the faculty gets top marks, and most "care more about the actual education of the students…others are just there to teach." "My professors are incredibly helpful and always willing to lend an ear if I need it," says a student. "A lot of them are laid-back, reflecting the Hawaiian lifestyle." While some admit that "the absolute academic standards are not high," the school is "always encouraging interested students to push themselves and think outside the box. There is just enough competition between students to maintain quality." Notably, the Hawaiian program is strong here. "We have a lo'i, which is a taro patch where students plant and learn sustainability through the old Hawaiian irrigation system," says a student. As a large state school, UH "has a lot of research going on," but students admit, "The administrative organization leaves much to be desired." The school "is big on improvements for students," and it does "a very good job when it comes to presenting students with all types of internship and job opportunities."

Life

As expected, the campus is located in a "paradise with an urban center," though some of the buildings are "rundown." Almost everyone, from students to staff, lead a "laid-back lifestyle," including—of course—surfing. For the most part, "Students think about going to the beach, surfing, and many of the activities you can do here in Hawaii." There are many other student organizations and extracurricular activities to choose from, and "The different clubs are always hosting events that everyone is invited to enjoy, which makes a great way to wind down for the weekend." The commuting students do tend to empty out the campus and school spirit a little, but the beach certainly helps to fill that void. Many of the out-of-state students "feel great living in an environment with so much beauty and cultural influences."

Student Body

This large school represents an "amalgamation of many different cultures," and students fit in "by doing the usual college biz—joining clubs, mingling with classmates, and not being a wallflower." Everyone gets along just fine, as "there are too many students to form any sort of social hierarchy." There are a decent number of nontraditional aged students, and many students are from one of the islands of Hawaii, "so most go home on holidays or even for weekends." Though a lot of students like to go to the beach and have fun on their days off, "A lot of people here work really hard and have jobs in addition to being full-time students, because the cost of living out here is pretty high." All in all, "It's a very easygoing place. You can stop and talk to any random student and they will chat with you."

FINANCIAL AID: 808-956-7251 • E-MAIL: UHMANOA.ADMISSIONS@HAWAII.EDU • WEBSITE: MANOA.HAWAII.EDU

THE PRINCETON REVIEW SAYS

Admissions

Very important factors considered include: Academic GPA, rigor of secondary school record, standardized test scores. *Important factors considered include:* Class rank, state residency. *Other factors considered include:* Application essay, recommendation(s), extracurricular activities, geographical residence, interview, talent/ability. SAT or ACT required; ACT with writing component accepted. TOEFL required of all international applicants. High school diploma is required and GED is accepted. *Academic units required:* 4 English, 3 mathematics, 3 science, 3 social studies, 5 academic electives, 4 college prep courses.

Financial Aid

Students should submit: FAFSA. Priority filing deadline is March 1. The Princeton Review suggests that all financial aid forms be submitted as soon as possible after January 1. *Need-based scholarships/grants offered:* Federal Pell, SEOG, state scholarships/grants, private scholarships, the school's own gift aid. *Loan aid offered:* Direct Subsidized Stafford, Direct Unsubsidized Stafford, Direct PLUS, Federal Perkins, Federal Nursing, state loans. Applicants will be notified of awards on a rolling basis beginning April 1. Federal Work-Study Program available. Institutional employment available. Highest amount earned per year from on-campus jobs $5,897. Off-campus job opportunities are good.

The Inside Word

All students must have a minimum GPA of 2.8 and must take either the SAT or the ACT. All applicants are encouraged to apply by the priority consideration deadline of January 5, as this deadline increases your chance of receiving financial aid and student housing. Certain programs (nursing, social work, education, and others) may have earlier admission deadlines.

THE SCHOOL SAYS ". . ."

From the Admissions Office

"Aloha and welcome to UH Manoa, the largest campus in the University of Hawaii System. We are located on the island of O'ahu, in Honolulu's lush Manoa valley. With almost 90 undergraduate majors, over 200 student organizations, and a variety of Division I and intramural sports to choose from, we think you'll agree that UH Manoa is a great place for you to realize your academic, professional, and personal dreams.

"UH Manoa is one of only thirteen institutions to hold the distinction of being a land-, sea-, and space-grant research institution. Classified by the Carnegie Foundation as having 'very high research activity,' UH Manoa is known for its pioneering research in such fields as oceanography, astronomy, Pacific Islands and Asian area studies, linguistics, cancer research, and genetics.

"Applicants to UH Manoa are expected to have a minimum score of 510 on all three sections of the SAT (or a 22 on all four sections of the ACT), and have completed a college preparatory high school curriculum. All applicants are encouraged to apply for priority consideration. Applying by this deadline (January 5 for fall admission, September 1 for spring) increases your chance of receiving financial aid and student housing."

SELECTIVITY	
Admissions Rating	**81**
# of applicants	6,541
% of applicants accepted	78
% of acceptees attending	39
FRESHMAN PROFILE	
Range SAT Critical Reading	480–580
Range SAT Math	500–610
Range SAT Writing	470–560
Minimum paper TOEFL	500
Minimum web-based TOEFL	61
Average HS GPA	3.4
% graduated top 10% of class	28
% graduated top 25% of class	63
% graduated top 50% of class	94
DEADLINES	
Regular	
Priority	1/5
Deadline	5/1
Nonfall registration?	yes
FINANCIAL FACTS	
Financial Aid Rating	**67**
Annual in-state tuition	$8,400
Annual out-state tuition	$23,232
Room and board	$10,279
Required fees	$700
Books and supplies	$1,170
% needy frosh rec. need-based scholarship or grant aid	92
% needy UG rec. need-based scholarship or grant aid	85
% needy frosh rec. non-need-based scholarship or grant aid	44
% needy UG rec. non-need-based scholarship or grant aid	29
% needy frosh rec. need-based self-help aid	58
% needy UG rec. need-based self-help aid	64
% frosh rec. any financial aid	62
% UG rec. any financial aid	59
% UG borrow to pay for school	38
Average cumulative indebtedness	$17,447
% frosh need fully met	45
% ugrads need fully met	32
Average % of frosh need met	81
Average % of ugrad need met	73

University of Houston

Office of Admissions, Houston, TX 77204-2023 • Admissions: 713-743-1010

CAMPUS LIFE

Quality of Life Rating	**73**
Fire Safety Rating	**88**
Green Rating	**86**
Type of school	public
Environment	metropolis

STUDENTS

Total undergrad enrollment	31,764
% male/female	50/50
% from out of state	1
% from public high school	92
% frosh live on campus	43
# of fraternities	26
# of sororities	20
% African American	13
% Asian	21
% Caucasian	31
% Hispanic	27
% international	4
# of countries represented	125

SURVEY SAYS . . .

Great library
Career services are great
Students are friendly
Diverse student types on campus
Great off-campus food
Athletic facilities are great

ACADEMICS

Academic Rating	**71**
% students returning for sophomore year	81
% students graduating within 4 years	15
% students graduating within 6 years	46
Calendar	semester
Student/faculty ratio	23:1
Profs interesting rating	73
Profs accessible rating	69
Most classes have	20–29 students
Most lab/discussion sessions have	20–29 students

MOST POPULAR MAJORS

business administration and management; engineering; psychology

STUDENTS SAY ". . ."

Academics

With more than 100 undergraduate majors and minors, a 594-acre campus, and 39,000 students, the University of Houston is a world-class research institution and fixture in Texas education. The school "provides some of the greatest opportunities in the world" at an affordable price and urges its students to achieve as much as they can "while living in a real-world environment." The school has been on the rise in recent years and "is attracting many more bright students to the university" as it begins to toughen up admission standards.

Professors here are "always prepared and make lecture interesting" through "effective teaching strategies" that "provide eye opening real-life information" to what can be "a motley group of students coming together to pursue higher education." Though there are a few who receive low marks, most "take into consideration the needs of students and many post lectures and notes online." Even in the larger classes, professors make and keep their office hours, so "if you are willing to work hard, you do have the tools available to learn the material." TAs are especially helpful, and "the tutoring services are very accessible and widely used."

Careers are a main focus of Cougars, and there is a wide range of majors and many interdisciplinary systems for students looking to specify their education, and there are also "many ties to local business and industry," including the chemical and space industries, and the medical center. "The flexibility of my degree plan cannot be found in any other school," says a student. Red tape is the main grumble for UH students, with the financial aid office drawing the most ire, and many students also "have difficulty fixing problems regarding registration and enrollment for classes."

Life

A very large percentage of the student body lives at home, so "the campus grows much more quiet in the evenings and on weekends," and stores and restaurants close earlier than normal. However, UH "is in the middle of a transition from being a commuter campus to a residential campus" and has announced plans to build two more dorms in the next few years and to require freshmen to live on campus. Even for those who travel home at night, "the recreational facility and other organizations are a way to meet friendly people." Flyers for events "can be found everywhere on campus," which is "great for networking purposes or if you just need a break from studying."

Football is understandably huge, but be warned: "If you don't come early enough to the football game, forget about it." Basically, "Unless you are supremely shy, there are countless opportunities to make friends and fit in." "We also can't leave out the tiny fact that we are in Houston," says a proud local. There are plenty of fun places "to eat, party, hang out, and exercise, and it's all within a fifteen-minute radius." As one student sums up, "If you feel there's nothing you could do here…you, my friend, are wrong."

Student Body

University of Houston "is the epitome of the grand melting pot." This remarkably "ethnically and culturally diverse" student body loves the variety that the university offers and the ensuing "acceptance on all levels." "One can come and grow socially, politically, and intellectually," says a student. One commonality is the "dedicated spirit" of all Cougars, helped in part of their devotion to UH sports, and "A typical student supports our athletic teams by wearing our red." Many take part in some sort of extracurricular club, but mostly, "Everyone is trying to pass their classes and set themselves on the best track to get a job after school."

Financial Aid: 713-743-1010 • E-mail: admissions@uh.edu • Website: www.uh.edu

THE PRINCETON REVIEW SAYS

Admissions

Very important factors considered include: Class rank, rigor of secondary school record. *Important factors considered include:* Academic GPA, standardized test scores. *Other factors considered include:* Recommendation(s), extracurricular activities, first generation, talent/ability, volunteer work, work experience. SAT or ACT required; ACT with or without writing component accepted. TOEFL required of all international applicants. High school diploma is required and GED is accepted. *Academic units required:* 4 English, 4 mathematics, 4 science, 4 social studies. *Academic units recommended:* 1 computer science, 2 foreign language, 1 visual performance art.

Financial Aid

Students should submit: FAFSA. The Princeton Review suggests that all financial aid forms be submitted as soon as possible after January 1. *Need-based scholarships/grants offered:* Federal Pell, SEOG, state scholarships/grants, private scholarships, the school's own gift aid. *Loan aid offered:* Direct Subsidized Stafford, Direct Unsubsidized Stafford, Direct PLUS, Federal Perkins, state loans. Applicants will be notified of awards on a rolling basis beginning May 1. Federal Work-Study Program available. Institutional employment available. Off-campus job opportunities are good.

Inside Word

The school's large size means that acceptance is easier to achieve than at some smaller schools. Students who meet the State of Texas Uniform Admissions Policy and satisfy a certain scale of requirements for class ranking and/or SAT or ACT scores are assured admission. But even if your grades aren't seemingly up to par, the admissions committee will consider students individually based on a holistic review of certain aspects, such as first-generation, socioeconomic background, rigor of high school curriculum, family responsibilities, special talents, public service, and strong letters of recommendation or a persuasive statement explaining your special circumstances.

THE SCHOOL SAYS ". . ."

From the Admissions Office

"The University of Houston is a Carnegie-designated Tier-One public research university that is recognized throughout the world as a leader in energy research, which is centered in a visionary Energy Research Park, law, business, and environmental education. Located in America's fourth-largest city, the University of Houston is the most ethnically diverse metropolitan research university in the United States. Its 39,820 students hail from 125 countries.

"In addition to preparing its students to succeed in today's global economy, the University of Houston also is a catalyst within its own community—changing lives through health, education, and outreach projects that help build a future for children in Houston, in Texas, and in the world.

"Other distinctive merits of the University of Houston include a strong student experience, a historic Division I athletic programs, top-level arts programs, and an internationally recognized faculty including a Nobel Laureate; winners of the National Medal of Science, Pulitzer, and Tony awards; and members of prestigious National Academies. The Princeton Review has chosen the University of Houston for inclusion in its guidebook of the nation's best colleges.

"Discover the greatness of the University of Houston's dynamic tree-lined campus of more than 650 acres—nestled just minutes from Houston's bustling theater and museum districts—where world-class teaching, revolutionary research, and nationally recognized students work together to create a globally competitive educational environment."

SELECTIVITY

Admissions Rating	**81**
# of applicants	14,725
% of applicants accepted	64
% of acceptees attending	40

FRESHMAN PROFILE

Range SAT Critical Reading	480–590
Range SAT Math	520–630
Range ACT Composite	21–26
Minimum paper TOEFL	550
Minimum web-based TOEFL	79
% graduated top 10% of class	31
% graduated top 25% of class	63
% graduated top 50% of class	89

DEADLINES

Regular	
Priority	12/1
Deadline	4/1
Nonfall registration?	yes

FINANCIAL FACTS

Financial Aid Rating	**76**
Annual in-state tuition	$6,466
Annual out-state tuition	$15,856
Room and board	$8,318
Required fees	$2,745
Books and supplies	$1,200
% needy frosh rec. need-based scholarship or grant aid	93
% needy UG rec. need-based scholarship or grant aid	88
% needy frosh rec. non-need-based scholarship or grant aid	5
% needy UG rec. non-need-based scholarship or grant aid	2
% needy frosh rec. need-based self-help aid	76
% needy UG rec. need-based self-help aid	86
% frosh rec. any financial aid	87
% UG rec. any financial aid	75
% UG borrow to pay for school	49
Average cumulative indebtedness	$15,613
% frosh need fully met	24
% ugrads need fully met	17
Average % of frosh need met	77
Average % of ugrade need met	71

UNIVERSITY OF IDAHO

UI ADMISSIONS OFFICE, MOSCOW, ID 83844-4264 • ADMISSIONS: 208-885-6326 • FAX: 208-885-9119

CAMPUS LIFE

Quality of Life Rating	71
Fire Safety Rating	79
Green Rating	87
Type of school	public
Environment	town

STUDENTS

Total undergrad enrollment	9,221
% male/female	53/47
% from out of state	29
% from public high school	90
% frosh live on campus	84
# of fraternities	17
# of sororities	15
% African American	1
% Asian	2
% Caucasian	82
% Hispanic	7
% Native American	1
% international	2
# of countries represented	39

SURVEY SAYS . . .

Great computer facilities
Athletic facilities are great
Frats and sororities dominate social scene
Lots of beer drinking
Hard liquor is popular

ACADEMICS

Academic Rating	70
% students returning for sophomore year	80
% students graduating within 4 years	25
% students graduating within 6 years	51
Calendar	semester
Student/faculty ratio	18:1
Profs interesting rating	69
Profs accessible rating	66
Most classes have	20–29 students
Most lab/discussion sessions have	10–19 students

MOST POPULAR MAJORS

elementary education and teaching; mechanical engineering; business

APPLICANTS ALSO LOOK AT AND OFTEN PREFER

Boise State University, Washington State University

AND SOMETIMES PREFER

Eastern Washington University, Idaho State University, College of Southern Idaho

STUDENTS SAY ". . ."

Academics

While huge lectures and inaccessible administrators beleaguer many other state schools, the University of Idaho comes with a friendly and intimate academic environment. Even better, this school comes with a tremendously affordable price tag. Idaho residents attend UI for a pittance. "We don't cost a lot," dryly notes a senior. All students must complete a straightforward core curriculum. Beyond that, you can choose from more than 150 majors. The engineering programs here are nationally recognized. The College of Natural Resources boasts excellent forestry and ecology programs as well as one of the biggest genetics laboratories in the country. Students describe the academic atmosphere here as "relaxed," and they report a high level of satisfaction with their academic experiences. "The administration is active and visible." Many facilities are world-class. Classes are usually small, particularly once you get past the introductory courses. "With a few exceptions," the faculty is "very knowledgeable" and generally "incredible." Professors are "pretty easy to get a hold of after class and are always willing to help you." Also, many are "constantly involved in doing research," in a good way. As a result, undergraduate research opportunities are ample.

Life

The University of Idaho's "beautiful" campus is chock full of trees, expansive lawns, and traditionally collegiate buildings. Students laud the fact that UI "isn't too big or too small." Students portray a lively campus atmosphere and a thriving party scene. Cultural events include the Lionel Hampton Jazz Festival, which attracts big name musicians each year. Intramural sports are popular. The student recreation center boasts saunas, professional massage therapy, and a massive fifty-five-foot climbing wall. There are "many student organizations"—more than 200, in fact. When it comes to social life, though, "Greek life rules the school." While that may be a bit of an exaggeration (only twenty percent of the student body is actually part of the Greek system), students here take full advantage and "party a lot." Some are thrilled about this situation. Still others find the focus on frats and sororities to be a bit much. Off campus, "podunk" Moscow "is not and will never be a big city," but students assure us that it is "the perfect college town." Restaurants and bars are plentiful. Coffee shops are "numerous." "Good music" abounds. You can't really beat Moscow for organic food. Also, the social amenities at Washington State University are "right next door" (about 10 miles west). Another big draw here is the great outdoors. The plethora of nearby rivers, lakes, and mountains provides opportunities galore for adrenaline sports and wilderness recreation.

Student Body

The student population at UI has a "laid-back" vibe. "It is really easy to meet people." If you are having any trouble, just head over to the famed Hello Walk, a sidewalk on campus where it's customary for students and everyone else to greet "one another with a friendly hello." "A lot of UI students are Greek," but there are also plenty of rugged, "earthy-hippie, outdoorsy types." You'll find every personality type, though, "from cowboys to cosmopolitan city residents." That said, pretty much everyone is "white, middle-class," and "from the Northwest." There are few minorities. Some students lament the lack of ethnic diversity. Others call our attention to the school's geographic limitations in this regard. "It's Idaho," says a senior. "Idaho just isn't diverse."

FINANCIAL AID: 208-885-6312 • E-MAIL: ADMISSIONS@UIDAHO.EDU • WEBSITE: WWW.UIDAHO.EDU

THE PRINCETON REVIEW SAYS

Admissions

Very important factors considered include: Academic GPA, standardized test scores. *Other factors considered include:* Recommendation(s). SAT or ACT required; ACT with writing component required. TOEFL required of all international applicants. High school diploma is required and GED is accepted. *Academic units required:* 4 English, 3 mathematics, 3 science (1 science lab), 1 foreign language.

Financial Aid

Students should submit: FAFSA. The Princeton Review suggests that all financial aid forms be submitted as soon as possible after January 1. *Need-based scholarships/grants offered:* Federal Pell, SEOG, state scholarships/grants, private scholarships, the school's own gift aid. *Loan aid offered:* Direct Subsidized Stafford, Direct Unsubsidized Stafford, Direct PLUS, Federal Perkins, college/university loans from institutional funds. Applicants will be notified of awards on a rolling basis beginning March 30. Federal Work-Study Program available. Institutional employment available. Off-campus job opportunities are good.

The Inside Word

The University of Idaho's straightforward approach to admissions is a welcome change for students completing more involved applications. In a way that's typical of large, public universities; admissions officers arrive at decisions based on high school GPA and test scores. Most applicants are admitted and welcome the opportunity to attend a strong school at an affordable price.

THE SCHOOL SAYS ". . ."

From the Admissions Office

"A leading public research university in the West, the University of Idaho offers a traditional residential campus experience in a spectacular natural setting. It provides more than 130 undergraduate degree options and graduate degrees in forty-seven discipline areas, which helps provide unprecedented undergraduate research opportunities. Idaho has become known for its academic excellence, student-centered, experiential learning, and an exceptional stu dent living environment that coupled with dedicated faculty, world-class facilities, and renowned research has produced a proven track record of high-achieving graduates. The student population of 12,000 includes first-generation college students and ethnically diverse scholars, who select from hands-on learning experiences in the colleges of Agricultural and Life Sciences; Art and Architecture; Business and Economics; Education; Engineering; Law; Letters, Arts, and Social Sciences; Natural Resources; and Science. The university also provides medical education for the state through the WWAMI program. Increasingly its interdisciplinary teams involved in environmental, sustainability, engagement, and resource management have gained national recognition. Idaho combines the strength of a large, land grant university with the intimacy of a small learning community to help students succeed and become leaders. It is home to the Vandals and competes in the Western Athletic Conference.

"Students applying for admission are required to take either the SAT or the ACT. The writing component is not required from the ACT. SAT Subject Test scores are not used for admission purposes."

SELECTIVITY	
Admissions Rating	**81**
# of applicants	8,248
% of applicants accepted	61
% of acceptees attending	32

FRESHMAN PROFILE	
Range SAT Critical Reading	480–600
Range SAT Math	490–610
Range SAT Writing	460–570
Range ACT Composite	20–26
Minimum paper TOEFL	550
Minimum web-based TOEFL	70
Average HS GPA	3.3
% graduated top 10% of class	18
% graduated top 25% of class	44
% graduated top 50% of class	74

DEADLINES	
Regular	
Priority	2/15
Deadline	8/1
Notification	rolling
Nonfall registration?	yes

FINANCIAL FACTS	
Financial Aid Rating	**67**
Annual in-state tuition	$3,874
Annual out-state tuition	$16,394
Room and board	$7,304
Required fees	$1,982
Books and supplies	$1,474
% needy frosh rec. need-based scholarship or grant aid	63
% needy UG rec. need-based scholarship or grant aid	71
% needy frosh rec. non-need-based scholarship or grant aid	90
% needy UG rec. non-need-based scholarship or grant aid	86
% needy frosh rec. need-based self-help aid	74
% needy UG rec. need-based self-help aid	82
% frosh rec. any financial aid	87
% UG rec. any financial aid	84
% UG borrow to pay for school	66
Average cumulative indebtedness	$24,396
% frosh need fully met	38
% ugrads need fully met	27
Average % of frosh need met	79
Average % of ugrad need met	75

UNIVERSITY OF ILLINOIS AT URBANA-CHAMPAIGN

901 WEST ILLINOIS STREET, URBANA, IL 61801 • ADMISSIONS: 217-333-0302 • FAX: 217-244-0903

CAMPUS LIFE

Quality of Life Rating	**79**
Fire Safety Rating	**65**
Green Rating	**94**
Type of school	public
Environment	city

STUDENTS

Total undergrad enrollment	30,721
% male/female	54/46
% from public high school	75
% frosh live on campus	100
# of fraternities	60
# of sororities	36
% African American	6
% Asian	13
% Caucasian	61
% Hispanic	7
% international	10
# of countries represented	123

SURVEY SAYS . . .

Great computer facilities
Athletic facilities are great
Everyone loves the Fighting Illini
Frats and sororities dominate social scene
Student publications are popular
Lots of beer drinking
Hard liquor is popular

ACADEMICS

Academic Rating	**74**
% students returning for sophomore year	94
% students graduating within 4 years	67
% students graduating within 6 years	84
Calendar	semester
Student/faculty ratio	16:1
Profs interesting rating	68
Profs accessible rating	65
Most classes have	20–29 students
Most lab/discussion sessions have	20–29 students

MOST POPULAR MAJORS

cell/cellular and molecular biology; political science and government; psychology

APPLICANTS ALSO LOOK AT AND OFTEN PREFER

University of Michigan—Ann Arbor, Northwestern University

AND SOMETIMES PREFER

Indiana University—Bloomington, University of Wisconsin-Madison, Washington University in St. Louis, University of Iowa

AND RARELY PREFER

Illinois State University, Purdue University—West Lafayette

STUDENTS SAY ". . ."

Academics

The epically large flagship campus of the University of Illinois "is very challenging and gives you freedom to do anything." Students here enjoy "all the benefits of a great public university." There are more than 150 undergraduate programs. The colleges of engineering and business are of the "most prestigious and hardest to get into," but there are dozens of other "very strong and reputable" departments as well. "The research resources are amazing," raves a Russian literature major. "The library has almost any resource an undergraduate or even an advanced researcher would ever need." However, the drawbacks that come with such an expansive campus are present as well. Lower-level class sizes "are horrendously large." "My largest class had 800 students," says a biochemistry major. "The massive bureaucracy" is a constant source of irritation. "Simple things like adding or dropping a class a few weeks into a semester can require five or six trips to different buildings to talk to different people, each time requiring you to explain your situation." "Professors are more impersonal to freshmen but seem to warm up to upperclassmen," explains one student. "There are some professors that should not be teaching anywhere," though. "A lot of times, it's a toss-up with bad/good professors," counsels a geology major. "You can learn a lot and have a great teacher, but you need to ask around and find out who that good teacher is." "There are professors and classes that you come across that certainly leave something to be desired," agrees a women's studies major. "But overall, I am very pleased with my academic experience at UIUC, and I have met some astoundingly intelligent, influential professors."

Life

At the University of Illinois, there is "never a dull moment, despite the surrounding cornfields." More than a thousand clubs and organizations provide students with a wide array of options. "Anything that you are interested in, you can do," gloats an engineering major. "It's a huge campus, but it's not too spread out," says a Spanish major. "You can get around anywhere by bike or bus, and you don't need a car." "The campus is very Greek-oriented," and the students who pledge the myriad of frats and sororities "love the Greek life." Some students notice serious animosity between the independent students and students involved in the frat scene. "It seems at times to take over our campus," says one independent. Other students just don't see the problem. "I think plenty of non-Greeks associate with Greeks," asserts a finance major. "Drinking is a big thing at U of I," and there is an "outstanding bar culture." "If you don't want to party all the time, there are plenty of other options." "Intramural sports and playing sports on the quad and in frat park are popular." The campus is "alive with the Big Ten spirit," and students are very supportive of their beloved Illini. "Awesome concerts" proliferate, and "there is a really good artsy theater, which runs foreign and indie films."

Student Body

The U of I has a decidedly Midwestern feel, and "Midwestern hospitality" is abundant. "Kids from out-of-state and small-town farm students" definitely have a presence, but, sometimes, it seems like "practically everyone is from the northwest suburbs of Chicago." There's a lot of ethnic diversity "visible on campus." On the whole, the majority of students are "very smart kids who like to party." "The typical student is involved and really good at balancing schoolwork, clubs and organizations, and a social life." "They really study fairly hard, and when you ask, it turns out that they're majoring in something like rocket science." "There is a niche for everyone."

FINANCIAL AID: 217-333-0100 • E-MAIL: UGRADADMISSIONS@ILLINOIS.EDU • WEBSITE: WWW.ILLINOIS.EDU

THE PRINCETON REVIEW SAYS

Admissions

Very important factors considered include: Class rank, application essay, academic GPA, rigor of secondary school record, standardized test scores. *Important factors considered include:* Character/personal qualities, extracurricular activities, first generation, talent/ability, volunteer work, work experience. *Other factors considered include:* Geographical residence, racial/ethnic status, state residency. SAT or ACT required; ACT with writing component recommended. TOEFL required of all international applicants. High school diploma is required and GED is accepted. *Academic units required:* 4 English, 3 mathematics, 2 science (2 science labs), 2 foreign language, 2 social studies, 0 history, 2 academic electives, 3.5 years of mathematics including trigonometry are required in the agricultural program.

Financial Aid

Students should submit: FAFSA. The Princeton Review suggests that all financial aid forms be submitted as soon as possible after January 1. *Need-based scholarships/grants offered:* Federal Pell, SEOG, state scholarships/grants, private scholarships, the school's own gift aid, United Negro College Fund. *Loan aid offered:* Direct Subsidized Stafford, Direct Unsubsidized Stafford, Direct PLUS, Federal Perkins, college/university loans from institutional funds. Federal Work-Study Program available. Institutional employment available. Highest amount earned per year from on-campus jobs $13,377. Off-campus job opportunities are excellent.

The Inside Word

Few candidates are deceived by Illinois's relatively high acceptance rate; the university has a well-deserved reputation for expecting applicants to be strong students, and those who aren't usually don't bother to apply. Despite a jumbo applicant pool, the admissions office reports that every candidate is individually reviewed, which deserves mention as rare in universities of this size.

THE SCHOOL SAYS ". . ."

From the Admissions Office

"The campus has been aptly described as a collection of neighborhoods constituting a diverse and vibrant city. The neighborhoods are of many types: students and faculty within a department; people sharing a room or house; the members of a professional organization, a service club, or an intramural team; or simply people who, starting out as strangers sharing a class or a study lounge or a fondness for a weekly film series, have become friends. And the city of this description is the university itself—a rich cosmopolitan environment constructed by students and faculty to meet their educational and personal goals. The quality of intellectual life parallels that of other great universities, and many faculty and students who have their choice of top institutions select Illinois over its peers. While such choices are based often on the quality of individual programs of study, another crucial factor is the 'tone' of the campus life that is linked with the virtues of Midwestern culture. There is an informality and a near-absence of pretension, which, coupled with a tradition of commitment to excellence, creates an atmosphere that is unique among the finest institutions.

"Applicants are required to take the SAT or the ACT with the writing section."

SELECTIVITY

Admissions Rating	87
# of applicants	27,291
% of applicants accepted	67
% of acceptees attending	38
# accepting a place on wait list	142
# admitted from wait list	126

FRESHMAN PROFILE

Range SAT Critical Reading	530–660
Range SAT Math	680–770
Range SAT Writing	570–670
Range ACT Composite	26–31
Minimum paper TOEFL	550
Minimum web-based TOEFL	79
% graduated top 10% of class	56
% graduated top 25% of class	93
% graduated top 50% of class	99

DEADLINES

Regular	
Priority	11/1
Deadline	1/2
Notification	2/18
Nonfall registration?	yes

FINANCIAL FACTS

Financial Aid Rating	78
Annual in-state tuition	$9,484
Annual out-state tuition	$23,626
Room and board	$10,080
Required fees	$3,310
Books and supplies	$1,200
% needy frosh rec. need-based scholarship or grant aid	77
% needy UG rec. need-based scholarship or grant aid	75
% needy frosh rec. non-need-based scholarship or grant aid	18
% needy UG rec. non-need-based scholarship or grant aid	11
% needy frosh rec. need-based self-help aid	81
% needy UG rec. need-based self-help aid	85
% frosh rec. any financial aid	69
% UG rec. any financial aid	72
% UG borrow to pay for school	51
Average cumulative indebtedness	$21,543
% frosh need fully met	35
% ugrads need fully met	29
Average % of frosh need met	70
Average % of ugrad need met	68

UNIVERSITY OF IOWA

107 Calvin Hall, Iowa City, IA 52242 • Admissions: 319-335-3847 • Fax: 319-333-1535

CAMPUS LIFE

Quality of Life Rating	**80**
Fire Safety Rating	**77**
Green Rating	**91**
Type of school	public
Environment	city

STUDENTS

Total undergrad enrollment	20,954
% male/female	48/52
% from out of state	49
% from public high school	90
% frosh live on campus	92
# of fraternities	21
# of sororities	19
% African American	3
% Asian	3
% Caucasian	76
% Hispanic	5
% international	8
# of countries represented	102

SURVEY SAYS . . .

Low cost of living
Everyone loves the Hawkeyes
Lots of beer drinking
Hard liquor is popular

ACADEMICS

Academic Rating	**71**
% students returning for sophomore year	86
% students graduating within 4 years	46
% students graduating within 6 years	71
Calendar	semester
Student/faculty ratio	16:1
Profs interesting rating	70
Profs accessible rating	74
Most classes have	10–19 students
Most lab/discussion sessions have	20–29 students

MOST POPULAR MAJORS

business/commerce; engineering; psychology

APPLICANTS ALSO LOOK AT AND OFTEN PREFER

University of Illinois at Urbana-Champaign, Northwestern University

AND SOMETIMES PREFER

Indiana University—Bloomington, Iowa State University

AND RARELY PREFER

Illinois State University, Missouri University of Science and Technology (formerly University of Missouri—Rolla), Cornell College

STUDENTS SAY ". . ."

Academics

University of Iowa manages to pull off an amazing feat: It's a "Big Ten university full of exciting opportunities," yet it's still able to maintain "a small-college feel." Moreover, as the state's flagship school, Iowa provides a "great education" at a "reasonable price." Additionally, students here welcome the fact that "requirements are minimal." In turn, this truly encourages undergrads to "make [their] education [their] own." While there are certainly a "[wide] range of degree programs" from which to choose, students here are especially impressed with Iowa's journalism, premed, writing, nursing, and engineering departments. Though professors certainly run the gamut from "amazing" to "boring," the majority of them is "very engaged with students and are always helpful to any student looking to push their learning beyond the classroom." A fellow student concurs adding that her professors are "passionate, encouraging, and invested in the success of their students both inside and outside of academia." Undergrads at Iowa also appreciate that their teachers really "do a nice job of balancing lectures with real-world applications of the material." Finally, as this pleased undergrad summarizes her school, "The University of Iowa is a platform to launch yourself to the top of your field at an affordable price."

Life

If there's one thing that undergrads tend to agree on, it's that "life is pretty fun at the University of Iowa." To begin with, sports culture is definitely big here. As one student relays, "During football season, Saturdays get crazy. There is just a sea of black and gold swarming toward the stadium. Nothing can really compare to 70,000 Hawkeye fans in one place." Additionally, students love the new rec center, which frequently runs trips "to go rock-climbing, camping, hiking, or kayaking." Of course, the university also sponsors a number of other events outside of athletics. For example, "There are always concerts and comedians on campus, [and] many [of these shows] are even free to students. There are also free movies shown at the Iowa Memorial Union." Students also stress that the university has a lively drinking scene. Indeed, "There is always a party going on here at Iowa." Lastly, undergrads also love hometown Iowa City, which offers a "vibrant downtown" that's "literally across the street from campus." Students happily take advantage of the city's "unique places to eat, shop, or go out." As this undergrad poetically concludes, "When a man is tired of Iowa City, he is tired of life."

Student Body

With such a large student body, undergrads here all posit that there is no "typical" student. One pleased undergrad elaborates, "Everyone is unique and has a different story, but that's one thing that makes life here so great. You have the ability to meet people from around the country and around the world, and we all get to share the experience of college together." Indeed, students feel very fortunate to be surrounded by such diversity. "We have a strong LGBTQA presence on campus, [along with] different religious places near campus. [In addition,] there are many different organizations for minorities, religions, and everything else here on campus. I couldn't imagine someone coming here and not being able to find a student organization that is for them." Of course, if pressed to generalize, students will describe their fellow Hawkeyes as "friendly, hardworking, and studious" but also "laid-back" and "very social." However, what ultimately unites this student body is the fact that most undergrads have "their season football tickets by June."

FINANCIAL AID: 319-335-1450 • E-MAIL: ADMISSIONS@UIOWA.EDU • WEBSITE: WWW.UIOWA.EDU

THE PRINCETON REVIEW SAYS

Admissions

Very important factors considered include: Class rank, academic GPA, rigor of secondary school record, standardized test scores. *Other factors considered include:* Recommendation(s), character/personal qualities, state residency, talent/ability. SAT or ACT required; ACT with or without writing component accepted. TOEFL required of all international applicants. High school diploma is required and GED is accepted. *Academic units required:* 4 English, 3 mathematics, 3 science, 2 foreign language, 3 social studies. *Academic units recommended:* 4 mathematics, 4 foreign language.

Financial Aid

Students should submit: FAFSA, institution's own financial aid form. The Princeton Review suggests that all financial aid forms be submitted as soon as possible after January 1. *Need-based scholarships/grants offered:* Federal Pell, SEOG, state scholarships/grants, private scholarships, the school's own gift aid. *Loan aid offered:* Direct Subsidized Stafford, Direct Unsubsidized Stafford, Direct PLUS, Federal Perkins, Federal Nursing, college/university loans from institutional funds, Short term. Applicants will be notified of awards on a rolling basis beginning March 15. Federal Work-Study Program available. Institutional employment available. Highest amount earned per year from on-campus jobs $7,200. Off-campus job opportunities are good.

The Inside Word

Like many large public universities, admissions officers at the University of Iowa rely heavily on quantitative factors when determining an applicant's status. Therefore, GPA and standardized test scores will likely hold the most weight. It should also be noted that the majority of applicants are admitted to the College of Liberal Arts & Sciences or the College of Engineering. Students interested in other programs (say within the College of Business or Nursing) often apply after they have enrolled in the university.

THE SCHOOL SAYS ". . ."

From the Admissions Office

"The University of Iowa has outstanding programs in the creative arts, notably the Iowa Writers' Workshop and the world-renowned International Writing Program. It also has strong programs in business, communication studies, journalism, English, engineering, political science, and psychology, and was the birthplace of the discipline of speech pathology and audiology. It offers excellent programs in the basic health sciences and health care programs, led by the top ranked College of Medicine and the closely associated University Hospitals and Clinics.

"The University of Iowa will accept either the SAT or the ACT. The ACT writing test is not required but we recommend you take it."

SELECTIVITY	
Admissions Rating	**79**
# of applicants	18,939
% of applicants accepted	80
% of acceptees attending	30

FRESHMAN PROFILE	
Range SAT Critical Reading	450–630
Range SAT Math	540–690
Range ACT Composite	23–28
Minimum paper TOEFL	530
Minimum web-based TOEFL	80
Average HS GPA	3.6
% graduated top 10% of class	24
% graduated top 25% of class	56
% graduated top 50% of class	92

DEADLINES	
Regular Deadline	4/1
Nonfall registration?	yes

FINANCIAL FACTS	
Financial Aid Rating	**79**
Annual in-state tuition	$6,678
Annual out-state tuition	$24,900
Room and board	$9,170
Required fees	$1,379
Books and supplies	$1,090
% needy frosh rec. need-based scholarship or grant aid	67
% needy UG rec. need-based scholarship or grant aid	65
% needy frosh rec. non-need-based scholarship or grant aid	57
% needy UG rec. non-need-based scholarship or grant aid	39
% needy frosh rec. need-based self-help aid	75
% needy UG rec. need-based self-help aid	82
% frosh rec. any financial aid	79
% UG rec. any financial aid	72
% UG borrow to pay for school	56
Average cumulative indebtedness	$27,480
% frosh need fully met	29
% ugrads need fully met	29
Average % of frosh need met	64
Average % of ugrad need met	65

UNIVERSITY OF KANSAS

OFFICE OF ADMISSIONS, LAWRENCE, KS 66045-7576 • ADMISSIONS: 785-864-3911 • FAX: 785-864-5017

CAMPUS LIFE

Quality of Life Rating	**96**
Fire Safety Rating	**81**
Green Rating	**80**
Type of school	public
Environment	city

STUDENTS

Total undergrad enrollment	19,372
% male/female	50/50
% from out of state	21
% frosh live on campus	58
# of fraternities	26
# of sororities	15
% African American	4
% Asian	4
% Caucasian	78
% Hispanic	5
% Native American	1
% international	5
# of countries represented	105

SURVEY SAYS . . .

Athletic facilities are great
Great off-campus food
Everyone loves the Jayhawks
Student publications are popular

ACADEMICS

Academic Rating	**76**
% students returning for sophomore year	80
% students graduating within 4 years	32
% students graduating within 6 years	61
Calendar	semester
Student/faculty ratio	19:1
Profs interesting rating	80
Profs accessible rating	81
Most classes have	20–29 students
Most lab/discussion sessions have	10–19 students

MOST POPULAR MAJORS

biology/biological sciences; business/commerce; psychology

STUDENTS SAY ". . ."

Academics

The University of Kansas—KU for short—"can offer an unbelievable education but can also provide the quintessential college sports and party scene if the student so chooses. It is a school where the student chooses [his or] her own experience." For those seeking them, the school "provides numerous, wonderful opportunities to every student" through "the integration of tradition and new media…to form a new level of excellence." University resources allow KU to excel in a broad range of disciplines, from business to biology to social welfare to art to engineering to architecture, and, thanks to state sponsorship, can do so "at an affordable price." Universities mean research, of course, and "KU has great undergrad research opportunities. Since it is such a big school, there are some great facilities and a lot of funding. Also, the professors are very interested in helping undergrads, and not just graduate students, start working on research." For those up to the challenge, the Honors Program "is an unbelievable resource" that "offers fabulous classes…[and] plenty of opportunities for students to connect with each other and faculty."

Life

"Life at KU is extraordinary," undergraduates gloat. "From going downtown to Mass Street to attending basketball and football games, there is always something to do in Lawrence." Division I athletics "are fantastic" here; "a certain awe seems to radiate throughout Allen Fieldhouse as an energetic student section cheers for their team," according to one diehard Jayhawks fan. Greek life attracts a substantial number of KU undergraduates, and the Greek houses serve as a center of weekend fun. Students "work hard to get through classes and activities and work during the week so that they can party hard on the weekends. It's pretty easy to find several frat parties or keggers and go party-hopping." KU's first-rate recreation center is also "a popular place, offering a huge climbing wall, basketball courts, equipment, and other programs," and the campus is home to "every club imaginable…If you like something, someone else does too. If the club does not already exist, you can start it." Hometown Lawrence "has a pretty nice bar scene, and there are enough bands that come through and local concerts to keep things entertaining. One thing that is great about Lawrence is the city really supports local business[es], so there are several local restaurants, coffee shops, etc. It has a unique feel to it." Lawrence is "halfway between Kansas City and Topeka as well as Omaha and Wichita, [so] even if you can't find something to do in Lawrence, you can head to another city and catch a concert or show or just go on a road trip."

Student Body

The typical KU student "would be from one of the big suburbs in Kansas such as Overland Park, Topeka, or Wichita," but "because the university is so big with many different colleges, there is a place for everyone." On this campus you'll find everything "from international students from across the globe to white Republicans to gays and lesbians." The student body divides into "two distinct categories: the Greeks and everyone else. There is no animosity between the two groups but they don't intermingle very much." They are also divided by their devotion to academics. As one student explains, "There are those who come to KU, take large lecture classes (which they sleep through), party on the weekend, and catch every basketball game. Then there are those who have three separate majors, two internships, four jobs, and no sleep. The rest of us fall somewhere between those two extremes." "Lawrence is very liberal," at least by Kansas standards, and many students follow suit, although "there are some very conservative students here" who "are generally accepted and their views respected." Wondering what the uniting factor is among this diverse student body? Most everyone "is a loyal Jayhawk," passionate about KU sports.

Financial Aid: 785-864-4700 • E-mail: adm@ku.edu • Website: www.ku.edu

THE PRINCETON REVIEW SAYS

Admissions

Very important factors considered include: Class rank, academic GPA, standardized test scores. SAT or ACT required; ACT with or without writing component accepted. TOEFL required of all international applicants. High school diploma is required and GED is accepted. *Academic units required:* 4 English, 3 mathematics, 3 science, 3 social studies. *Academic units recommended:* 4 English, 4 mathematics, 3 science, 2 foreign language, 3 social studies.

Financial Aid

Students should submit: FAFSA. Priority filing deadline is March 1. The Princeton Review suggests that all financial aid forms be submitted as soon as possible after January 1. *Need-based scholarships/grants offered:* Federal Pell, SEOG, state scholarships/grants, private scholarships, the school's own gift aid. *Loan aid offered:* Direct Subsidized Stafford, Direct Unsubsidized Stafford, Direct PLUS, Federal Perkins, college/university loans from institutional funds. Applicants will be notified of awards on a rolling basis beginning April 1. Federal Work-Study Program available. Institutional employment available. Highest amount earned per year from on-campus jobs $4,800. Off-campus job opportunities are excellent.

The Inside Word

You want instant gratification? KU will process your application in forty-eight hours if you apply to the College of Liberal Arts and Sciences (CLAS) or the School of Engineering (with the exception of the architectural engineering program). Formulas drive admissions at this large state school, and the right combination of test scores and high school grades can get you in without too much sweat. In-state applicants with average test scores and at least a 2.0 GPA in the Kansas Board of Regents high school curriculum are shoo-ins; out-of-state applicants need slightly better test scores and at least a 2.5 GPA. Any applicant who ranks in the top third of his high school class is admitted regardless of test scores or GPA. Requirements at the School of Engineering are considerably more rigorous (at least 3.0 GPA just to be considered).

THE SCHOOL SAYS ". . ."

From the Admissions Office

"The University of Kansas has a long and distinguished tradition for academic excellence. Outstanding students from across the nation are attracted to KU's top-ranked academics, four-year-renewable scholarships and four-year fixed tuition for first-time freshmen, beautiful campus, and contagious school spirit. KU provides students extraordinary opportunities in honors programs, service learning, undergraduate research, internships, and study abroad. The university is located in Lawrence (forty minutes from Kansas City), a vibrant community of 90,000 consistently recognized as one of the nation's top 10 college towns.

"Students applying for admissions may submit an ACT or SAT score, and KU will only look at math and critical reading (verbal) section of SAT for admissions purposes."

SELECTIVITY	
Admissions Rating	76
# of applicants	10,035
% of applicants accepted	93
% of acceptees attending	38

FRESHMAN PROFILE	
Range ACT Composite	22–28
Minimum paper TOEFL	530
Minimum web-based TOEFL	70
Average HS GPA	3.5
% graduated top 10% of class	27
% graduated top 25% of class	53
% graduated top 50% of class	83

DEADLINES	
Regular	
Priority	11/1
Deadline	4/1
Nonfall registration?	yes

FINANCIAL FACTS	
Financial Aid Rating	72
Annual in-state tuition	$7,611
Annual out-state tuition	$19,500
Room and board	$7,080
Required fees	$858
Books and supplies	$850
% needy frosh rec. need-based scholarship or grant aid	67
% needy UG rec. need-based scholarship or grant aid	68
% needy frosh rec. non-need-based scholarship or grant aid	45
% needy UG rec. non-need-based scholarship or grant aid	29
% needy frosh rec. need-based self-help aid	72
% needy UG rec. need-based self-help aid	79
% frosh rec. any financial aid	63
% UG rec. any financial aid	55
% UG borrow to pay for school	53
Average cumulative indebtedness	$22,114
% frosh need fully met	16
% ugrads need fully met	14
Average % of frosh need met	60
Average % of ugrad need met	61

University of Kentucky

100 Funkhouser Building, Lexington, KY 40506 • Admissions: 859-257-2000 • Fax: 859-257-3823

CAMPUS LIFE

Quality of Life Rating	**77**
Fire Safety Rating	**87**
Green Rating	**60***
Type of school	public
Environment	city

STUDENTS

Total undergrad enrollment	20,099
% male/female	51/49
% from out of state	24
% frosh live on campus	91
# of fraternities	24
# of sororities	20
% African American	7
% Asian	2
% Caucasian	81
% Hispanic	2
% international	2
# of countries represented	117

SURVEY SAYS . . .

Great computer facilities
Great library
Athletic facilities are great
Everyone loves the Wildcats
Student publications are popular

ACADEMICS

Academic Rating	**67**
% students graduating within 4 years	34
% students graduating within 6 years	59
Calendar	semester
Student/faculty ratio	18:1
Profs interesting rating	65
Profs accessible rating	63
Most classes have	20–29 students
Most lab/discussion sessions have	20–29 students

APPLICANTS ALSO LOOK AT AND OFTEN PREFER

Indiana University—Bloomington, Miami University, Centre College, Transylvania University

AND SOMETIMES PREFER

University of Louisville, Bellarmine University, University of Tennessee

AND RARELY PREFER

Florida State University, University of Florida, University of Illinois at Urbana-Champaign, Purdue University—West Lafayette, The Ohio State University—Columbus

STUDENTS SAY ". . ."

Academics

The University of Kentucky in Lexington is "all about making a name for yourself by preparing for and getting involved in future career goals while having fun and enjoying what college is all about." "Making a name for yourself" here requires distinguishing yourself in a crowd of almost 19,000 undergraduates; daunting as that sounds, students tell us it can be done. "Getting involved in future career goals" is easy enough, given the "great selection of courses and majors" available. Kentucky offers undergraduate degrees in twelve of its nineteen divisions. Choices include the College of Agriculture (with popular majors in animal science, agricultural economics, and hospitality management), the College of Business and Management, the College of Education, the College of Engineering, the College of Communications and Information Studies (advertising, journalism, and library science), and the College of Arts and Sciences (biology, history, and political science). Students here laud the "impressive teaching staff, dedicated to enhancing student knowledge and teaching students about the future." UK's brand-new library "is also quite amazing. It is the perfect place to go study because usually the dorms can be a bit too distracting." All told, go-getters willing to take initiative will find UK offers "a safe and fun atmosphere where you have unlimited opportunities to get involved at a reasonable price."

Life

"Everyone is a Wildcat" at UK, because "UK has tremendous sports programs and big fans all around the United States." Men's basketball fans "are among the craziest in the nation," and students "would be football fanatics if our team would win a game every now and then." "Because UK is dry, most parties are held off campus." Social life for many revolves around the off-campus Greek houses where "There is always a party going on, but you have to be a part of a fraternity or sorority to really know about it and attend." Some students report, "There are a lot of nonalcoholic parties in the dorms that might be crazier than the alcoholic parties," although others advise, "It's better to live off campus because the residence halls are pretty bad (except for the new ones), the meal plan is awful, and everything off campus is a lot cheaper." Hometown Lexington "is a great city with much to do and lots of opportunities. It offers many different clubs, bars, and restaurants that college students can go to as well as horse racing. All of these venues have a 'College Day' where students get discounts." One sophomore warns, however, "Small-town students can become distracted by the lights of the city."

Student Body

"The typical UK student has a Southern accent, likes to party, and often shops at J. Crew," but, "as the undergraduate population is about 19,000, there are a lot of people who do not fit that description." True, one of the most common "types"—or at least the most conspicuous one—are the "beautiful people, the hot girls and guys who roam the campus and dress up to go to class." But for every "collar-popping, stuck-up frat boy" there's also "your typical country Kentucky boy, boots and all." What you won't find many of at UK are "liberals—they are few and far between—and the type of atypical student with wild hair colors or other style extremes." Most "lean right politically, but generally the student body is apathetic." School spirit is rampant, so much so that "on an average day, one in three students will have some sort of UK clothing on."

FINANCIAL AID: 859-257-3172 • E-MAIL: ADMISSION@UKY.EDU • WEBSITE: WWW.UKY.EDU

THE PRINCETON REVIEW SAYS

Admissions

Very important factors considered include: Academic GPA, rigor of secondary school record, standardized test scores. *Other factors considered include:* Class rank, application essay, recommendation(s), alumni/ae relation, character/personal qualities, extracurricular activities, first generation, geographical residence, interview, racial/ethnic status, talent/ability, volunteer work. SAT or ACT required; ACT with or without writing component accepted. TOEFL required of all international applicants. High school diploma is required and GED is accepted. *Academic units required:* 4 English, 3 mathematics, 3 science, 2 foreign language, 3 social studies, 5 academic electives, 2 fine or performing arts, 0.5 health, and 0.5 physical education. *Academic units recommended:* 4 English, 4 mathematics, 4 science, 2 foreign language, 3 social studies, 3 academic electives, 2 fine or performing arts, 0.5 health, and 0.5 physical education.

Financial Aid

Students should submit: FAFSA. The Princeton Review suggests that all financial aid forms be submitted as soon as possible after January 1. *Need-based scholarships/grants offered:* Federal Pell, SEOG, state scholarships/grants, private scholarships, the school's own gift aid. *Loan aid offered:* Direct Subsidized Stafford, Direct Unsubsidized Stafford, Direct PLUS, Federal Perkins, state loans, college/university loans from institutional funds. Applicants will be notified of awards on a rolling basis beginning April 1. Federal Work-Study Program available.

The Inside Word

The University of Kentucky's admissions team is about as objective as they come. If you have the GPA, class rank, and test scores, you'll in all likelihood be welcomed into the Wildcat community. The university is continually looking to improve its selectivity, so hitting the books is a must if you want to be a serious contender.

THE SCHOOL SAYS ". . ."

From the Admissions Office

"The University of Kentucky offers you an outstanding learning environment and quality instruction through its excellent faculty. Of the 1,892 full-time faculty, ninety-eight percent hold the doctorate degree or the highest degree in their field of study. Many are nationally and internationally known for their research, distinguished teaching, and scholarly service to Kentucky, the nation, and the world. UK's scholars (students, faculty, and alumni) have been honored by Nobel, Pulitzer, Rhodes, Fulbright, Guggenheim, and Grammy awards, and most recently the Metropolitan Opera and the Marshall Foundation. Yet, with a student to teacher ratio of only seventeen to one, UK faculty are accessible and willing to answer your questions and discuss your interests.

"UK will accept the SAT. The writing sections of the ACT and SAT will not be used in the admission process."

SELECTIVITY	
Admissions Rating	80
# of applicants	15,153
% of applicants accepted	68
% of acceptees attending	40

FRESHMAN PROFILE	
Range SAT Critical Reading	490–610
Range SAT Math	500–630
Range SAT Writing	470–600
Range ACT Composite	23–28
Minimum paper TOEFL	527
Average HS GPA	3.5
% graduated top 10% of class	33
% graduated top 25% of class	62
% graduated top 50% of class	88

DEADLINES	
Regular	
Priority	2/15
Deadline	2/15
Nonfall registration?	yes

FINANCIAL FACTS	
Financial Aid Rating	78
Annual in-state tuition	$8,122
Annual out-state tuition	$17,734
Room and board	$9,974
Required fees	$1,006
Books and supplies	$800
% needy frosh rec. need-based scholarship or grant aid	39
% needy UG rec. need-based scholarship or grant aid	41
% needy frosh rec. non-need-based scholarship or grant aid	90
% needy UG rec. non-need-based scholarship or grant aid	69
% needy frosh rec. need-based self-help aid	62
% needy UG rec. need-based self-help aid	69
% frosh rec. any financial aid	40
% UG rec. any financial aid	38
% UG borrow to pay for school	33
Average cumulative indebtedness	$22,943
% frosh need fully met	20
% ugrads need fully met	16
Average % of frosh need met	79
Average % of ugrad need met	79

UNIVERSITY OF LOUISIANA AT LAFAYETTE

PO DRAWER 41210, LAFAYETTE, LA 70504 • ADMISSIONS: 337-482-6553 • FAX: 337-482-1112

CAMPUS LIFE

Quality of Life Rating	**89**
Fire Safety Rating	**85**
Green Rating	**60***
Type of school	public
Environment	city

STUDENTS

Total undergrad enrollment	14,796
% male/female	44/56
% from out of state	3
% frosh live on campus	36
# of fraternities	11
# of sororities	9
% African American	21
% Asian	2
% Caucasian	70
% Hispanic	3
% international	2
# of countries represented	101

SURVEY SAYS . . .

Students are friendly
Diverse student types on campus
Students get along with local community
Students love Lafayette, LA
Great off-campus food
Student publications are popular
Student government is popular

ACADEMICS

Academic Rating	**65**
% students returning for sophomore year	74
% students graduating within 4 years	12
% students graduating within 6 years	42
Calendar	semester
Student/faculty ratio	23:1
Profs interesting rating	70
Profs accessible rating	70
Most classes have	20–29 students

MOST POPULAR MAJORS

biology/biological sciences; business administration and management; nursing/registered nurse (rn, asn, bsn, msn)

STUDENTS SAY "..."

Academics

At the "medium-sized" University of Louisiana at Lafayette—in "the heart of Cajun country"—many students feel "under the shadow" of their mammoth cousin, LSU. We really don't know why. UL Lafayette offers "serious bang for your buck;" tremendously generous grant and scholarship programs and out-of-state fee waivers make UL Lafayette one of the best bargains in the country. Programs in "education, computer science, and engineering" are "ranked as some of the best in the nation." The nursing program is the "third largest" in the country and "one of the best" anywhere. "Seasoned" and "overwhelmingly helpful" professors are "friendly, fun," and "honestly interested in having you learn." "The experience has been absolutely wonderful academically," gushes a senior. "In more than 120 hours of course study, I cannot remember having one bad professor." Other students disagree; they remember a "couple of bad apples." A perennial complaint among students at UL Lafayette is that many professors from other countries "cannot be understood by the students." The administration is generally unpopular. "The bureaucracy is ridiculous," reports a general studies major. "The university is run like an out-of-date chicken farm," adds a finance major. "No one knows the answer to anything" and "Getting financial aid in a timely manner is a real problem." Students are generally very satisfied, though. "My overall college experience at University of Louisiana at Lafayette has been terrific," asserts a junior. "I would recommend this college to anyone."

Life

UL Lafayette's "beautiful campus" is "full of big trees and handsome Southern architecture." Unfortunately, "It always floods when it rains," some "lousy buildings" "need updating," and the parking situation is just "painful." Nevertheless, "school spirit is really high." "Football games are huge events," and Lafayette is, by all accounts, a "great" college town. "Believe me," swears a wide-eyed first-year student, "it is an experience." The Strip "is right by campus" and "lined with numerous bars and clubs." "Most people," however, "congregate downtown," where it's "almost like Bourbon Street in New Orleans." The local music scene is hopping, and festivals are frequent, including a very large International Music Festival and a gigantic Mardi Gras celebration. If partying isn't your bag, or if you get sick of it, Lafayette also offers an "abundance of coffee shops" and "numerous art venues." "There is so much history and culture in Louisiana" that, frankly, it's hard to "ever be bored or without something fun to do on any day of the week," and you can find "great food anywhere." "If you're looking for a good, inexpensive college education that is packed with good food, cold beer, and excitement, look no further than UL Lafayette."

Student Body

Students at UL Lafayette are "friendly and fun" and "always seem to be in a good mood." They have "Southern flair with a little bit of our Cajun cayenne," a marketing major quips. They're also "very strongly rooted in their religions;" in that regard, "Catholic conservatives" seem to dominate. Many "are from the surrounding area of Acadiana," are "lower- to upper-middle-class," and "receive some financial support from [their] parents." Many also "have part-time job[s]." Beyond that, "there are many different types of people," and "everyone seems to get along together." One undergrad reports, "Our campus includes a very diverse group of students from various religious and racial backgrounds." There are also "a few oddballs" who "try to get themselves noticed by the way they dress and their eccentric hair." For the most part, however, "everyone blends in." "No one really points out or harasses other students here at UL Lafayette, unless that student happens to be wearing LSU paraphernalia."

FINANCIAL AID: 337-482-6506 • E-MAIL: ENROLL@LOUISIANA.EDU • WEBSITE: WWW.LOUISIANA.EDU

THE PRINCETON REVIEW SAYS

Admissions

Very important factors considered include: Class rank, academic GPA, rigor of secondary school record, standardized test scores. *Other factors considered include:* State residency. SAT or ACT required; ACT with or without writing component accepted. TOEFL required of all international applicants. High school diploma is required and GED is accepted. *Academic units required:* 4 English, 4 mathematics, 3 science (0 science labs), 2 foreign language, 1 social studies, 2 history, 1 visual/performing arts, 1 computer science/literacy.

Financial Aid

Students should submit: FAFSA. Regular filing deadline is May 1. The Princeton Review suggests that all financial aid forms be submitted as soon as possible after January 1. *Need-based scholarships/grants offered:* Federal Pell, SEOG, state scholarships/grants, private scholarships, the school's own gift aid, Federal Nursing Scholarships. *Loan aid offered:* Direct Subsidized Stafford, Direct Unsubsidized Stafford, Direct PLUS, Federal Perkins, Federal Nursing. Applicants will be notified of awards on a rolling basis beginning April 1. Federal Work-Study Program available. Institutional employment available. Off-campus job opportunities are good.

The Inside Word

UL Lafayette is still a fallback school for many applicants. You are pretty much guaranteed admission if you carry an ACT score of at least 18 and complete a basic college-prep high school curriculum with a GPA of 2.5 or better. If your numbers are a little lower, you can submit an essay and some other credentials for possible admission through UL Lafayette's admission by committee. It should be noted, however, that admission by committee is limited to seven percent of each incoming class.

THE SCHOOL SAYS ". . ."

From the Admissions Office

"The University of Louisiana at Lafayette offers students from throughout the United States and more than ninety countries strong academic training and personal enrichment opportunities in a friendly, comfortable, student-centered environment. UL Lafayette students are taught, mentored, and advised by some of the brightest and most accomplished faculty members in the United States. Although UL Lafayette offers more than 100 programs of study and the research opportunities, internship possibilities, and facilities of a major research-intensive university, average class size is approximately the same as that at many high schools and smaller higher education institutions. "UL students receive a good deal of individual attention and support—both personal and academic—from faculty and staff.

"A wide range of cultural, recreational, and social activities are available on and off campus, including more than 150 campus organizations and clubs, NCAA Division I and intramural athletics, a state-of-the-art aquatic center, a thriving arts scene, a wide range of live music venues, shopping, a great variety of excellent restaurants, theaters, the second largest Mardi Gras in the nation, and an international music festival. In fact, Utne Reader magazine selected the city of Lafayette as Louisiana's 'Most Enlightened Town.'

"Our relatively low tuition and generous financial aid and scholarship programs, including an out-of-state tuition waiver for qualified students, make UL Lafayette one of the most affordable universities in the nation. "Students who have completed the required college preparatory core curriculum in high school may qualify for admission on the basis of a combination of their high school cumulative grade point average and ACT or SAT scores. Writing scores are not required."

SELECTIVITY	
Admissions Rating	73
# of applicants	9,062
% of applicants accepted	66
% of acceptees attending	50

FRESHMAN PROFILE	
Range ACT Composite	20–24
Minimum paper TOEFL	525
Average HS GPA	3.2
% graduated top 10% of class	17
% graduated top 25% of class	42
% graduated top 50% of class	73

DEADLINES	
Regular	
Priority	7/20
Nonfall registration?	yes

FINANCIAL FACTS	
Financial Aid Rating	67
Annual in-state tuition	$3,440
Annual out-state tuition	$12,062
Room and board	$8,236
Required fees	$1,417
Books and supplies	$1,200
% needy frosh rec. need-based scholarship or grant aid	94
% needy UG rec. need-based scholarship or grant aid	88
% needy frosh rec. non-need-based scholarship or grant aid	14
% needy UG rec. non-need-based scholarship or grant aid	9
% needy frosh rec. need-based self-help aid	42
% needy UG rec. need-based self-help aid	56
% frosh rec. any financial aid	87
% UG rec. any financial aid	72
% frosh need fully met	15
% ugrads need fully met	10
Average % of frosh need met	65
Average % of ugrad need met	56

UNIVERSITY OF MAINE

5713 Chadbourne Hall, Orono, ME 04469-5713 • Admissions: 207-581-1561 • Fax: 207-581-1213

CAMPUS LIFE

Quality of Life Rating	**68**
Fire Safety Rating	**86**
Green Rating	**97**
Type of school	public
Environment	village

STUDENTS

Total undergrad enrollment	8,911
% male/female	51/49
% from out of state	23
% frosh live on campus	93
# of fraternities	18
# of sororities	7
% African American	2
% Asian	1
% Caucasian	77
% Hispanic	1
% Native American	1
% international	2
# of countries represented	84

SURVEY SAYS . . .

Athletic facilities are great
Everyone loves the Black Bears
Student publications are popular
Lots of beer drinking
Hard liquor is popular

ACADEMICS

Academic Rating	**67**
% students returning for sophomore year	78
% students graduating within 4 years	36
% students graduating within 6 years	60
Calendar	semester
Student/faculty ratio	15:1
Profs interesting rating	70
Profs accessible rating	67
Most classes have	10–19 students
Most lab/discussion sessions have	10–19 students

MOST POPULAR MAJORS

business administration; education; engineering

APPLICANTS ALSO LOOK AT AND OFTEN PREFER

University of Vermont, University of New Hampshire

AND SOMETIMES PREFER

University of Rhode Island, University of Masschusetts Amherst, University of Connecticut

STUDENTS SAY ". . ."

Academics

The University of Maine is proud to have "one of the top engineering schools in the Northeast!" Students describe the atmosphere as "engineering with a dash of liberal art," and also praise the forestry and business programs. However, some point out, "As with many schools focused on funding their science departments, the arts programs tend to suffer and feel like the neglected, malnourished stepchildren." Yet, the overall consensus is that "UMaine has challenging courses that push students to reach their potential." Many students say they chose UMaine for its balance of "the friendly, small feeling while still at a state university," and Maine residents cite the "financially feasible" in-state tuition combined with the fact that "it's close to home but far enough away and large enough to feel different and exciting" as big selling points. Most agree, "The faculty and administrators take an active interest in the students" and say, "Education is top priority." Professor reviews offer a mixed bag, with some students saying, "The professors here are open-minded and teach with enthusiasm," and others finding, "There is the occasional dud professor." One zoology major sums up the disparity this way: "Professors in the lower-level courses tend to be more focused on lecturing than anything else. As you move up in the course levels, and classes get smaller, the professors tend to pay more attention to class discussion and the opinions of individual students."

Life

Despite the fact that "it can get rather gloomy with the long winters" and "winters are pretty harsh," UMaine students agree, "The administration, in conjunction with the student government, does whatever they can to make it better." One business administration major says, "We have a saying: If you're bored, you're doing something wrong. There is stuff going on six nights a week, and there is lots to do in the Bangor area. Hiking, dining, arts, sports, anything you need, really." Most students point to the overall "outdoorsyness" of campus life, saying, "The only thing more plentiful than the friendly people are the deer and the squirrels." UMaine students "love to use the recreation facilities and explore the great outdoors," and they're proud to add, "Our school has a really strong campus culture." A common sentiment is that "UMaine is a great place to work and play." One sophomore says, "Hockey is life; the rest is just classes." The Division I hockey team at UMaine has many shouting, "Go Black Bears!" and all agree that "UMaine Hockey is a huge event for any Maine student." While some rave about the recently upgraded gym complex, others grumble that some "facilities are old and falling apart," and some students believe the university should focus on "upgrading outdated classroom buildings in some majors." The most common complaint about the administration: "They could start by backing off with the parking tickets…It's crazy."

Student Body

The majority of students here hail from Maine and the Northeast. However, despite a lack of external diversity, students say, "There is a wide range of diversity in thought and belief," and students say that although "diversity is rare because of the school's location…it is encouraged and accepted." One thing's for sure, in the "winter, we all look like Eskimos." In fact, most students agree, "One of the best aspects of UMaine is the camaraderie that everyone has for each other," and agree, "Students have many opportunities to meet people in and out of class." In fact, one theater major proclaims, "The majority of the students who attend the University of Maine are either athletes or soon-to-be scientists…however, both groups tend to mix fairly well with each other." Another student concurs, "I've seen former high school jocks socializing with brilliant engineers." UMaine has a reputation for its lively social life; "There is no denying that most everybody drinks for fun," but students are careful to point out, "The campus is huge, so if partying isn't your scene it's easy to find another one."

FINANCIAL AID: 207-581-1324 • E-MAIL: UM-ADMIT@MAINE.EDU • WEBSITE: WWW.UMAINE.EDU

THE PRINCETON REVIEW SAYS

Admissions

Very important factors considered include: Class rank, academic GPA, rigor of secondary school record, standardized test scores. *Important factors considered include:* Application essay, recommendation(s). *Other factors considered include:* Character/personal qualities, extracurricular activities, geographical residence, interview, talent/ability, volunteer work, work experience. SAT or ACT required; ACT with or without writing component accepted. TOEFL required of all international applicants. High school diploma is required and GED is accepted. *Academic units required:* 4 English, 3 mathematics, 2 science (2 science labs), 2 foreign language, 2 social studies, 4 academic electives, 1 physical education for education majors. *Academic units recommended:* 4 English, 4 mathematics, 4 science (3 science labs), 2 foreign language, 2 social studies, 1 history, 4 academic electives.

Financial Aid

Students should submit: FAFSA. Regular filing deadline is March 1. The Princeton Review suggests that all financial aid forms be submitted as soon as possible after January 1. *Need-based scholarships/grants offered:* Federal Pell, SEOG, state scholarships/grants, private scholarships, school scholarship or grant aid from institutional funds. *Loan aid offered:* Direct Subsidized Stafford, Direct Unsubsidized Stafford, Direct PLUS, Federal Perkins, state loans. Applicants will be notified of awards on a rolling basis beginning March 15. Federal Work-Study Program available. Off-campus job opportunities are good.

The Inside Word

UMaine has rolling admissions but cautions that deadlines are still important, particularly for early action students who want to be considered for merit scholarships. The university recommends campus visits; tours are available at the Buchanan Alumni House. While interviews aren't required, they're considered mutually beneficial and informative for prospective students and admissions representatives.

THE SCHOOL SAYS ". . ."

From the Admissions Office

"The University of Maine offers the extensive academic opportunities you'd expect from a major research university with the close-knit feel of a small college. As Maine's flagship university, UMaine offers the state's most comprehensive academic experience, with more than ninety undergraduate majors and academic programs, seventy-five master's programs and thirty doctoral programs. All majors benefit from a firm foundation in the liberal arts. Top students are invited to join UMaine's Honors College, one of the country's oldest honors programs.

"The University of Maine is one of the National Science Foundation's top 100 research universities, and our facilities and faculty have an international reputation for excellence. Among the highlights are the Climate Change Institute, which has been featured on "60 Minutes," the Laboratory for Surface Science and Technology, which is a hub for cutting-edge sensor and nanotechnology research, and the Advanced Structures & Composites Center, which is leading the nation in deepwater offshore wind energy development.

"At UMaine, the majority of undergraduate classes are taught by professors—and many of those faculty members go on to become friends and mentors to their students. Here, professors are known for having an open-door policy. Our students can work alongside some of the most renowned scholars and scientists in the world—whether they're talking Civil Engineering over dinner at Pat's Pizza or traversing an Antarctic ice sheet with climate researchers.

"UMaine students have extraordinary opportunities to gain real-world experience. For example, SPIFFY, our student investment club, manages a $1.6 million real-money portfolio. Wildlife ecology majors learn about bear behavior by going out and tagging cubs. Engineering majors take advantage of co-ops and internships that often lead to employment after graduation."

SELECTIVITY

Admissions Rating	74
# of applicants	8,093
% of applicants accepted	78
% of acceptees attending	28
# accepting a place on wait list	378
# admitted from wait list	120

FRESHMAN PROFILE

Range SAT Critical Reading	480–590
Range SAT Math	490–600
Range SAT Writing	470–580
Range ACT Composite	21–26
Minimum paper TOEFL	530
Minimum web-based TOEFL	71
Average HS GPA	3.3
% graduated top 10% of class	21
% graduated top 25% of class	51
% graduated top 50% of class	86

DEADLINES

Early action	
Deadline	12/15
Notification	1/31
Regular	
Priority	12/15
Deadline	2/1
Notification	4/1
Nonfall registration?	yes

FINANCIAL FACTS

Financial Aid Rating	79
Annual in-state tuition	$8,370
Annual out-state tuition	$24,090
Room and board	$8,644
Required fees	$2,218
Books and supplies	$1,000
% needy frosh rec. need-based scholarship or grant aid	86
% needy UG rec. need-based scholarship or grant aid	82
% needy frosh rec. non-need-based scholarship or grant aid	7
% needy UG rec. non-need-based scholarship or grant aid	4
% needy frosh rec. need-based self-help aid	87
% needy UG rec. need-based self-help aid	88
% frosh rec. any financial aid	82
% UG rec. any financial aid	83
% UG borrow to pay for school	75
Average cumulative indebtedness	$29,753
% frosh need fully met	17
% ugrads need fully met	15
Average % of frosh need met	83
Average % of ugrad need met	81

UNIVERSITY OF MARY WASHINGTON

1301 COLLEGE AVENUE, FREDERICKSBURG, VA 22401 • ADMISSIONS: 540-654-2000 • FAX: 540-654-1857

CAMPUS LIFE

Quality of Life Rating	**73**
Fire Safety Rating	**83**
Green Rating	**69**
Type of school	public
Environment	city

STUDENTS

Total undergrad enrollment	4,312
% male/female	36/64
% from out of state	16
% from public high school	78
% frosh live on campus	93
% African American	6
% Asian	5
% Caucasian	62
% Hispanic	6
# of countries represented	20

SURVEY SAYS . . .

No one cheats
Athletic facilities are great
Students are friendly
Great off-campus food
Students are happy
Frats and sororities are unpopular or nonexistent
Student publications are popular
Student government is popular
Political activism is popular

ACADEMICS

Academic Rating	**71**
% students returning for sophomore year	84
% students graduating within 4 years	62
Calendar	differs by program
Student/faculty ratio	15:1
Profs interesting rating	85
Profs accessible rating	83
Most classes have	20–29 students
Most lab/discussion sessions have	20–29 students

MOST POPULAR MAJORS

business administration and management; English language and literature; psychology

APPLICANTS ALSO LOOK AT AND OFTEN PREFER

College of William and Mary, University of Virginia

AND SOMETIMES PREFER

James Madison University, University of Richmond, Virginia Tech

AND RARELY PREFER

Christopher Newport University, George Mason University

STUDENTS SAY ". . ."

Academics

The University of Mary Washington is known as a "lovely state university that gives you a private school education." A political science major raves, "Even though it's a public university it feels like a small liberal arts school." In fact, students laud the "small student body and class sizes" for facilitating "individual interactions with professors." Most students agree, "The professors really make UMW shine." Although they admit that "the professors vary, just like at any other university," they say, "The professors are always available outside of class." The overall sentiment is that "Mary Washington is a solid academic school that could use a little growth," but students believe UMW is "a hidden jewel that delivers on a historical campus" and say courses are "engaging and intellectually stimulating." Students are particularly enthusiastic about the historic preservation and education programs, and many take pride in the university's honor code, which they believe "provides a good environment for students to build a community" and "encourages people to try hard in an honest way." Overall, students agree, "Mary Washington is all about getting a well-rounded education while becoming a part of a great community" and point out that "professors are included in that as well."

Life

Students say, "The population size and the layout of the campus make it impossible to not bump into someone you know," and admit that the "beautiful campus" and "Jeffersonian architecture" are a large part of UMW's draw. A large proportion feels that "the atmosphere is incredibly friendly," and say, "Community and campus participation is paramount." However, some students complain that UMW "could use improvement in school spirit," and point out that "the student activities and clubs aren't as abundant here as they are at other schools." Still, there's a consensus that the clubs in existence are "welcoming" and that it's "easy to get involved." Most students agree, "The administration needs to do a better job of communicating with students," especially in relation to "the upcoming campus remodel." An English major clarifies, saying, "Our school needs to understand how important the integrity of our current campus is to us." Students grumble, "The registration process is a mess," and say, "Although having smaller classes is nice, sometimes it is hard…to get into a desired class because of this." Despite these grievances, students agree that UMW is "a small school with a big heart," and "It is a tight-knit community with an atmosphere that pushes you to your potential."

Student Body

UMW students describe their fellow classmates as "typically bright, fairly hardworking but easygoing for the most part," and say, "Most students fit in very well." An anthropology major says, "There are prepsters with pearls and Ralph Lauren, athletes sporting sweats, punks with gauges and flannel, and everyone in between." However, one student notes, "We have lots of diversity in terms of religious background, sexual orientation, and the gender ratio, but the school needs to work on becoming more racially balanced." "As with anywhere, groups tend to form," but students say, "There isn't a feeling of exclusivity," and they assert that "students have a lot of opportunity to connect… through the mandatory two years they need to live on campus." A common freshman complaint is that "there is nothing to do on the weekends," but upperclassmen insist that "below the surface, Mary Wash is a hotspot of activity" and rave about programs like "Cheap Seats," which sponsors dollar movies on campus. Either way, it's commonly held that "there are not many raging parties, usually just low key house parties." However, many students praise UMW's location, exclaiming that "Fredericksburg is a fantastic town" and pointing out that the school is "within an hour's distance to Richmond or D.C., so there are frequent trips for class or for fun."

FINANCIAL AID: 800-468-5614 • E-MAIL: ADMIT@UMW.EDU • WEBSITE: WWW.UMW.EDU

THE PRINCETON REVIEW SAYS

Admissions

Very important factors considered include: Academic GPA, rigor of secondary school record. *Important factors considered include:* Class rank, application essay, recommendation(s), standardized test scores, extracurricular activities. *Other factors considered include:* Alumni/ae relation, character/personal qualities, first generation, geographical residence, racial/ethnic status, state residency, talent/ability, volunteer work, work experience. SAT or ACT required; ACT with or without writing component accepted. TOEFL required of all international applicants. High school diploma is required and GED is accepted. *Academic units required:* 4 English, 3 mathematics, 3 science (3 science labs), 2 foreign language, 2 social studies, 1 history. *Academic units recommended:* 4 English, 4 mathematics, 4 science (4 science labs), 4 foreign language, 2 social studies, 2 history.

Financial Aid

Students should submit: FAFSA, institution's own financial aid form. The Princeton Review suggests that all financial aid forms be submitted as soon as possible after January 1. *Need-based scholarships/grants offered:* Federal Pell, SEOG, state scholarships/grants, private scholarships, the school's own gift aid, unendowed gifts. *Loan aid offered:* Direct Subsidized Stafford, Direct Unsubsidized Stafford, Direct PLUS, Federal Perkins. Applicants will be notified of awards on or about April 15. Federal Work-Study Program available. Institutional employment available. Highest amount earned per year from on-campus jobs $5,200. Off-campus job opportunities are good.

The Inside Word

UMW seeks to enroll a well-rounded student body and doesn't follow a particular blueprint when evaluating applicants. The admissions team gives each application a focused review, looking for students with a strong secondary school curriculum that has prepared them for successful study at the university level. Honors level and AP work is highly encouraged as evidence of this.

THE SCHOOL SAYS ". . ."

From the Admissions Office

"The University of Mary Washington is one of the nation's premier public, liberal arts and sciences institutions. Highly respected for its commitment to academic excellence, the University boasts three colleges—business, education and arts and sciences and three campuses, conveniently located between Richmond, Va., and Washington, D.C. These two capitals provide a rich resource for undergraduate student internships, as well as a promising job market for graduates. Mary Washington's talented and intellectually curious students work collaboratively in small, interactive classes with innovative and accessible master teachers, including a Pulitzer Prize-winning poet and Fulbright scholars, who motivate them to think critically, engage meaningfully and communicate effectively.

"In addition to rigorous academics, the UMW experience is based on a culture of honor as well as community and global service, exemplified in the 2011 Peace Corps ranking of Mary Washington as the nation's top volunteer producer among small colleges. With multiple opportunities for student research and service learning, UMW graduates thrive in our fast-changing society.

"Distinctive to UMW is one of the nation's leading historic preservation programs, as well as strong creative writing and debate programs. Other top majors include political science and international affairs, English, biology, psychology, earth and environmental science, history, visual and performing arts, economics and business. With its classic Jeffersonian architecture, and beautifully manicured grounds, UMW offers an unparalleled American college experience.. More than 100 student organizations and clubs provide opportunities for leadership. UMW Eagles varsity teams compete at the championship level in NCAA Division III."

SELECTIVITY	
Admissions Rating	**76**
# of applicants	4,807
% of applicants accepted	76
% of acceptees attending	27
# accepting a place on wait list	143
# admitted from wait list	120

FRESHMAN PROFILE	
Range SAT Critical Reading	530–640
Range SAT Math	500–610
Range SAT Writing	520–620
Range ACT Composite	22–27
Minimum paper TOEFL	57
Minimum web-based TOEFL	88
Average HS GPA	3.6

DEADLINES	
Early action	
Deadline	11/15
Notification	1/31
Regular	
Priority	11/15
Deadline	2/1
Notification	4/1
Nonfall registration?	yes

FINANCIAL FACTS	
Financial Aid Rating	**66**
Annual in-state tuition	$4,462
Annual out-state tuition	$16,190
Room and board	$8,900
Required fees	$4,344
Books and supplies	$1,000
% needy frosh rec. need-based scholarship or grant aid	47
% needy UG rec. need-based scholarship or grant aid	50
% needy frosh rec. non-need-based scholarship or grant aid	50
% needy UG rec. non-need-based scholarship or grant aid	28
% needy frosh rec. need-based self-help aid	70
% needy UG rec. need-based self-help aid	55
% frosh rec. any financial aid	58
% UG rec. any financial aid	61
% UG borrow to pay for school	46
Average cumulative indebtedness	$23,800
% frosh need fully met	11
% ugrads need fully met	13
Average % of frosh need met	52
Average % of ugrad need met	53

University of Maryland—Baltimore County

1000 Hilltop Circle, Baltimore, MD 21250 • Admissions: 410-455-2291 • Fax: 410-455-1094

CAMPUS LIFE

Quality of Life Rating	**76**
Fire Safety Rating	**96**
Green Rating	**89**
Type of school	public
Environment	metropolis

STUDENTS

Total undergrad enrollment	10,573
% male/female	55/45
% from out of state	9
% frosh live on campus	72
# of fraternities	11
# of sororities	12
% African American	12
% Asian	24
% Caucasian	60
% Hispanic	4
% international	4
# of countries represented	96

SURVEY SAYS . . .

Great computer facilities
Great library
Diverse student types on campus
Campus feels safe

ACADEMICS

Academic Rating	**76**
Calendar	4-1-4
Student/faculty ratio	20:1
Profs interesting rating	80
Profs accessible rating	73
Most classes have	20–29 students
Most lab/discussion sessions have	10–19 students

MOST POPULAR MAJORS

biology/biological sciences; computer and information sciences; psychology

APPLICANTS ALSO LOOK AT AND OFTEN PREFER

John Hopkins University, Virginia Tech

AND SOMETIMES PREFER

Pennsylvania State University—University Park, University of Maryland, College Park

AND RARELY PREFER

Salisbury University, St. Mary's College of Maryland

STUDENTS SAY ". . ."

Academics

The University of Maryland, Baltimore County has a "great regional reputation" as a "quiet academic school" where "students take education seriously." Undergraduates are enthusiastic about the "academic opportunities and scholarship programs available," and say, "UMBC wants to see every student succeed—they provide you with the tools, people, and resources to make sure you get where you want to go in life." The university is particularly known for its "strong" science and mathematics programs and a commitment to the performing arts. Some students grumble, "The school needs to serve those with different majors apart from the sciences," but others are quick to point out that "UMBC is changing a bit to offer more to the fine arts students," including construction of a new technologically advanced fine arts building. Most agree the university has "extremely intelligent professors that have a knack for inspiring the students," and say, "UMBC is a place where professors aren't just talking heads." Although some complain about dull lectures, a common consensus is that "this is a university where teaching comes first, followed by research, and it shows," and say, "Most of the professors are so helpful, you can find most of them sitting in their office and they don't mind if you come and ask them questions."

Life

UMBC has a large contingent of commuters and one ancient studies major says, "There are a lot of activities held by student organizations on campus during the week and on the weekends, but many students live close to campus and choose to go home for the weekend." While some may see this as a downside others say, "The location of UMBC is true brilliance—so close to Baltimore. We hop over there on the weekdays even to go shopping or go out to eat." Most lament the absence of a football team and say, "The only real issue with UMBC is the lack of visible school spirit…People have made efforts to try and pump up the school, but nothing's come to fruition yet." In fact, students give the administration poor marks, saying, "Students are not given adequate attention on the matters of housing, financial aid, and advising," and there are complaints about the parking facilities, as well as a desire for "better buildings and food options." Despite these criticisms, a sociology major says, "Everyone on campus is nice and helpful to other students. People will always hold a door for you, help you pick up a dropped folder, or offer to share their notes with a student who missed class."

Student Body

More than one student says, "UMBC is a place where it is cool to be smart, and everything about the campus, including the students, exudes 'nerd-chic.'" In fact, an English major says that even "our president likes to say that it's cool to be smart at UMBC." This mentality is captured by a student who remarks, "Life at UMBC, aside from special events, revolves around classes and learning," and most undergrads agree, "The typical student at UMBC is interested in doing well academically and not just here to party until graduation." However, despite their dedication to hard work, UMBC students call themselves "enthusiastic and bright" and say "that almost every student at UMBC is involved with at least a couple of extracurricular activities, which connect them to the campus." The school has a strong reputation for diversity and students feel "it enriches our school and everyone gets to know everyone despite culture or ethnicity." A mechanical engineering student says, "This is even reflected in the high number of interracial couples I see on campus." Overall, it seems, "People fit in by being intellectually creative and finding a community with which to discuss important issues."

FINANCIAL AID: 410-455-2387 • E-MAIL: ADMISSIONS@UMBC.EDU • WEBSITE: WWW.UMBC.EDU

THE PRINCETON REVIEW SAYS

Admissions

Very important factors considered include: Academic GPA, rigor of secondary school record, standardized test scores. *Important factors considered include:* Class rank, application essay, recommendation(s), talent/ability. *Other factors considered include:* Character/personal qualities, extracurricular activities. SAT or ACT required; ACT with writing component required. TOEFL required of all international applicants. High school diploma is required and GED is accepted. *Academic units required:* 4 English, 3 mathematics, 3 science, 2 foreign language, 3 social studies, 3 social studies and history. *Academic units recommended:* 4 mathematics.

Financial Aid

Students should submit: FAFSA. The Princeton Review suggests that all financial aid forms be submitted as soon as possible after January 1. *Need-based scholarships/grants offered:* Federal Pell, SEOG, state scholarships/grants, private scholarships, the school's own gift aid. *Loan aid offered:* Direct Subsidized Stafford, Direct Unsubsidized Stafford, Direct PLUS, Federal Perkins. Applicants will be notified of awards on a rolling basis beginning March 15. Federal Work-Study Program available. Institutional employment available. Off-campus job opportunities are excellent.

The Inside Word

UMBC maintains an Admissions Counselor Blog where prospective students can connect with current members of the admissions team to questions during the application process. The admissions committee considers the strength of your secondary school curriculum and class rank in combination with traditional factors, such as GPA, test scores, and essay when making an acceptance decision. Additionally, it's suggested that at least one letter of recommendation be written by a teacher.

THE SCHOOL SAYS ". . ."

From the Admissions Office

"When it comes to universities, a mid-sized school can be just right. Some students want the resources of a large community. Others are looking for the attention found at a smaller one. With an undergraduate population of over 9,000, UMBC can offer the best of both. There are always new people to meet and things to do—from Division I sports to more than 170 student clubs. As a research university, we offer an abundance of programs, technology, and opportunities for hands-on experiences. Yet we are small enough that students don't get lost in the shuffle. More than eighty percent of our classes have fewer than forty students. Among public research universities, UMBC is recognized for its success in placing students in the most competitive graduate programs and careers. Of course, much of the success of UMBC has to do with the students themselves—highly motivated students who get involved in their education."

"Freshman applicants are required to take the SAT or ACT."

SELECTIVITY	
Admissions Rating	**86**
# of applicants	8,099
% of applicants accepted	61
% of acceptees attending	29
# accepting a place on wait list	530
# admitted from wait list	487

FRESHMAN PROFILE	
Range SAT Critical Reading	540–640
Range SAT Math	570–670
Range SAT Writing	530–630
Range ACT Composite	24–29
Minimum paper TOEFL	460
Minimum web-based TOEFL	48
Average HS GPA	3.5
% graduated top 10% of class	25
% graduated top 25% of class	52
% graduated top 50% of class	85

DEADLINES	
Early action	
Deadline	11/1
Notification	12/1
Regular	
Priority	11/1
Deadline	2/1
Nonfall registration?	yes

FINANCIAL FACTS	
Financial Aid Rating	**75**
Annual in-state tuition	$9,467
Annual out-state tuition	$19,870
Room and board	$10,021
Books and supplies	$1,200
% needy frosh rec. need-based scholarship or grant aid	70
% needy UG rec. need-based scholarship or grant aid	75
% needy frosh rec. non-need-based scholarship or grant aid	22
% needy UG rec. non-need-based scholarship or grant aid	9
% needy frosh rec. need-based self-help aid	55
% needy UG rec. need-based self-help aid	67
% frosh rec. any financial aid	70
% UG rec. any financial aid	64
% UG borrow to pay for school	50
Average cumulative indebtedness	$21,098
% frosh need fully met	17
% ugrads need fully met	14
Average % of frosh need met	61
Average % of ugrad need met	60

UNIVERSITY OF MARYLAND—COLLEGE PARK

MITCHELL BUILDING, COLLEGE PARK, MD 20742-5235 • ADMISSIONS: 301-314-8385 • FAX: 301-314-9693

CAMPUS LIFE

Quality of Life Rating	**69**
Fire Safety Rating	**74**
Green Rating	**96**
Type of school	public
Environment	metropolis

STUDENTS

Total undergrad enrollment	26,826
% male/female	53/47
% from out of state	23
% frosh live on campus	93
# of fraternities	36
# of sororities	27
% African American	12
% Asian	15
% Caucasian	56
% Hispanic	8
% international	3
# of countries represented	103

SURVEY SAYS . . .

Athletic facilities are great
Diverse student types on campus
Everyone loves the Terrapins
Student publications are popular
Lots of beer drinking

ACADEMICS

Academic Rating	**78**
% students returning for sophomore year	95
% students graduating within 4 years	66
% students graduating within 6 years	82
Calendar	semester
Student/faculty ratio	18:1
Profs interesting rating	76
Profs accessible rating	70
Most classes have	20–29 students
Most lab/discussion sessions have	20–29 students

MOST POPULAR MAJORS

criminology; economics; political science and government

APPLICANTS ALSO LOOK AT AND SOMETIMES PREFER

Pennsylvania State University, University of Delaware, University of Maryland, Baltimore County, University of Michigan—Ann Arbor, Virginia Tech

STUDENTS SAY ". . ."

Academics

The University of Maryland—College Park is a grand mix of "twenty-minute walks to class across one of the country's most beautiful campuses, [an introduction] to high-level courses taught by the nation's top researchers, [and] a motivated 'green' campus" as well as "crowded, smelly frat parties, [and] living-learning communities that can make the gigantic campus much smaller." Students are quick to boast about sports, too, especially the school's titles as "the 2008 national champions in men's soccer and women's field hockey." In short: It's a quintessential large university, offering "a great experience with a variety of opportunities that are what you make of them." Students crow about Maryland's "nationally recognized business program," a "top-ranked criminology program," a solid engineering school, a great political science department that capitalizes on the school's proximity to Washington, D.C., and the "top-notch honors program." Most of all, they love the "great price. This school gives you a great education for a really cheap price." Low cost doesn't translate to budget accommodations. On the contrary, "the administration shows a desire to always upgrade facilities, as can be witnessed by the tremendous business school and the brand new engineering building." In conclusion, students applaud "the widely diverse opportunities available at UMD. You can never get bored because there is always something to do."

Life

"Life at UMD is awesome," with "a good mix of fun activities" including "school-sponsored parties, games," a "campus recreation center that has virtually everything you could wish for, including pools, an extensive gym, a rock wall, squash courts, an indoor track," and a student union "loaded with fun places like the arcade area, bowling alley," and "tons of places to eat as well." In addition, "there are always open games of soccer, football, or ultimate Frisbee being played on the mall and elsewhere." There are bars close to campus, and "students are always having parties," especially along College Park's raucous Frat Row. Terrapin sports are a passion for many. And if all that isn't enough, "the proximity to D.C. makes clubbing, nights out on the town, and general visits to D.C. frequent." With all this going on, no wonder students say that "the social life at UMD is unsurpassed." Some warn the surrounding area is dicey; "It's pretty annoying and scary to get crime alerts from the police informing us of incidents close to campus," one student explains. Undergrads also warn that parking regulations are brutal. "Bus transportation around campus provided by the university is great, but for students and visitors with cars, it's a huge hassle. Permits are expensive, and free parking for visitors is impossible to find. School officials are strict with violations, and tickets are seventy-five dollars. They are hard to refute and very costly."

Student Body

"The University of Maryland is a very large school," so "there is no 'typical' student here. Everyone will find that they can fit in somewhere." Better still, "different groups are very accepting of other groups. Students in Greek life are just as accepting of students in non-Greek life. Athletes blend in with non-athletes. UMD provides a great environment for students to meet people they would normally not know and helps to provide great connections with these people." UMD is "an especially diverse school," and this makes people "more tolerant and accepting of people from different backgrounds and cultures." A student from New Jersey explains it this way: "Coming from a very diverse area, I thought it was going to be hard to find a school that had that same representation of minority and atypical students until I found Maryland. I don't think I have ever learned so much about different religions, cultures, orientations, or lifestyles. All of them are accepted and even celebrated" at UMD.

FINANCIAL AID: 301-314-9000 • E-MAIL: UM-ADMIT@UGA.UMD.EDU • WEBSITE: WWW.MARYLAND.EDU

THE PRINCETON REVIEW SAYS

Admissions

Very important factors considered include: Academic GPA, rigor of secondary school record, standardized test scores. *Important factors considered include:* Class rank, application essay, recommendation(s), first generation, state residency, talent/ability. *Other factors considered include:* Alumni/ae relation, character/personal qualities, extracurricular activities, geographical residence, racial/ethnic status, volunteer work, work experience. SAT or ACT required; ACT with writing component recommended. TOEFL required of all international applicants. High school diploma is required and GED is accepted. *Academic units required:* 4 English, 3 mathematics, 3 science (2 science labs), 2 foreign language, 3 social studies. *Academic units recommended:* 4 mathematics.

Financial Aid

Students should submit: FAFSA. The Princeton Review suggests that all financial aid forms be submitted as soon as possible after January 1. *Need-based scholarships/grants offered:* Federal Pell, SEOG, state scholarships/grants, private scholarships, the school's own gift aid. *Loan aid offered:* Direct Subsidized Stafford, Direct Unsubsidized Stafford, Direct PLUS, Federal Perkins. Applicants will be notified of awards on a rolling basis beginning April 1. Federal Work-Study Program available. Institutional employment available. Off-campus job opportunities are good.

The Inside Word

Maryland admissions officers don't simply crunch numbers and apply a formula. The school considers no fewer than twenty-five factors when determining who's in and who's out. Essays, recommendations, extracurricular activities, talents and skills, and demographic factors all figure into the mix along with high school transcript and standardized test scores. Give all aspects of your application your utmost attention; admissions are very competitive.

THE SCHOOL SAYS ". . ."

From the Admissions Office

"The University of Maryland is one of the nation's top-ranked universities, offering students unique opportunities to learn, explore and discover in the D.C. region and around the world. It attracts outstanding faculty—including Nobel, Pulitzer, Emmy and Tony winners—and some of the most accomplished students in the nation. The beautiful 1,250-acre campus is located just outside Washington, D.C., making it easy for students to extend their education beyond the classroom, whether in the College Park community or through internships in federal agencies, labs and think tanks; the media; or some of the country's most successful companies. The university strongly encourages innovation, entrepreneurship and creativity, whether helping students and state residents launch startups or serving as a model of cultural excellence through its arts programming. The campus also thrives on diversity and engagement, celebrating similarities and differences and preparing graduates to become leaders in their communities and careers."

SELECTIVITY	
Admissions Rating	95
# of applicants	26,310
% of applicants accepted	45
% of acceptees attending	34
# accepting a place on wait list	969

FRESHMAN PROFILE	
Range SAT Critical Reading	580–680
Range SAT Math	610–720
Minimum paper TOEFL	575
Average HS GPA	4.0
% graduated top 10% of class	70
% graduated top 25% of class	89
% graduated top 50% of class	98

DEADLINES	
Early action	
Deadline	11/1
Notification	1/31
Regular	
Priority	11/1
Deadline	1/20
Notification	4/1
Nonfall registration?	yes

FINANCIAL FACTS	
Financial Aid Rating	66
Annual in-state tuition	$6,966
Annual out-state tuition	$24,337
Room and board	$9,678
Required fees	$1,689
Books and supplies	$1,076
% needy frosh rec. need-based scholarship or grant aid	51
% needy UG rec. need-based scholarship or grant aid	61
% needy frosh rec. non-need-based scholarship or grant aid	56
% needy UG rec. non-need-based scholarship or grant aid	39
% needy frosh rec. need-based self-help aid	57
% needy UG rec. need-based self-help aid	64
% frosh rec. any financial aid	75
% UG rec. any financial aid	64
% UG borrow to pay for school	43
Average cumulative indebtedness	$22,696
% frosh need fully met	14
% ugrads need fully met	7
Average % of frosh need met	64
Average % of ugrad need met	58

University of Massachusetts Amherst

University Admissions Center, Amherst, MA 01003-9291 • Admissions: 413-545-0222 • Fax: 413-545-4312

CAMPUS LIFE

Quality of Life Rating	**92**
Fire Safety Rating	**79**
Green Rating	**85**
Type of school	public
Environment	town

STUDENTS

Total undergrad enrollment	21,265
% male/female	51/49
% from out of state	26
% frosh live on campus	100
# of fraternities	21
# of sororities	15
% African American	4
% Asian	7
% Caucasian	69
% Hispanic	5
% international	1
# of countries represented	50

SURVEY SAYS . . .

Lots of liberal students
Class discussions are rare
Great computer facilities
Great library
Students aren't religious
Great off-campus food
Low cost of living
Student publications are popular

ACADEMICS

Academic Rating	**75**
% students graduating within 4 years	51
Calendar	semester
Student/faculty ratio	18:1
Profs interesting rating	71
Profs accessible rating	71
Most classes have	20–29 students
Most lab/discussion sessions have	20–29 students

MOST POPULAR MAJORS

biology/biological sciences; business administration and management; psychology

APPLICANTS ALSO LOOK AT AND OFTEN PREFER

Boston University, Boston College, Syracuse University, University of Delaware, Tufts University

AND SOMETIMES PREFER

University of Connecticut, Northeastern University

AND RARELY PREFER

University of New Hampshire, University of Vermont, University of Rhode Island

STUDENTS SAY ". . ."

Academics

It's all about "finding out where you fit in" at the University of Massachusetts Amherst, where students say the experience is "all what you make of it. If you want to party, there is one available to you almost every night," but a pre-law student warns that "academics are challenging," and other students agree, especially in the engineering program, the hard sciences, the sports management program ("one of the oldest and best in the country"), and at the Isenberg School of Management. As at many big schools, "It is easy to not go to class because they are so large, although many teachers now use the PRS [a handheld wireless interactive remote unit], which quizzes you and is a method of [taking] attendance during each class." You will also have the opportunity to get a degree with an "individual concentration" that allows you to design your own interdisciplinary majors. Students can also enroll—at no extra charge—in courses at Amherst, Hampshire, Mount Holyoke, and Smith colleges through the Five College Consortium. The consortium includes open library borrowing, a meal exchange, and a free bus system connecting the campuses. Unlike many major research institutions, UMass Amherst has a surprising number of professors who "show a passion for teaching. I have yet to see a professor who just teaches for money," a sports management major reports. By all accounts, "More than half of the professors are awesome." Students agree that "UMass Amherst has countless opportunities for one to get involved and improve his or her leadership and responsibilities."

Life

"There is so much to do on campus here that you rarely have to leave the school to find something," students report, pointing out that, in addition to attending one of the school's ubiquitous sporting events, "You can go ice skating on campus, go to a play, see bands play, see a movie, etc." Are you sitting down? "Most of these things are also free of charge, or available for a reduced fee." When the weather permits, "Numerous people are outside doing some sort of activity, whether it's playing catch, playing a sport with a bunch of people, or just laying out in the sun. In the Southwest Residential area, there is a horseshoe that people call Southwest Beach because on nice days it is packed with hundreds of people." If you're into socializing, "There is something going on every night of the week somewhere." One student says, "Drinking is big here but not totally out of control like some say." And another student assures us that, "It is more than possible to stay in on a Friday night, do your laundry, and watch a movie with friends. Parties are available, but not required." More students seem to want to live on campus now, lured perhaps by the new apartment style residence halls and dining services. Hometown Amherst provides "great restaurants and shows." Northampton and Holyoke, both close by, are "good places to go shopping."

Student Body

"There is no such thing as a typical student at UMass Amherst." An undergraduate population of more than 20,000 makes that impossible; however, students do seem to fall into a few readily identified groups. There are "plenty of students who are here strictly for academics," people who are here for the party scene," and a "lot of people who came here for academics but fell into the party scene." Most learn to balance fun and work; those who don't exit long before graduation. Students also "tend to fit the mold of their residence," undergrads tell us. one student writes, "Southwest houses students of mainstream culture. Students there can be seen wearing everything from UMass Amherst sweats to couture. Students in Central (especially Upper Central) tend to be the 'hippie' or scene type kids. Northeast houses…the more reserved types. Orchard Hill typically houses the more quiet types as well."

FINANCIAL AID: 413-545-0801 • E-MAIL: MAIL@ADMISSIONS.UMASS.EDU • WEBSITE: WWW.UMASS.EDU

THE PRINCETON REVIEW SAYS

Admissions

Very important factors considered include: Academic GPA, rigor of secondary school record. *Important factors considered include:* Class rank, standardized test scores. *Other factors considered include:* Application essay, recommendation(s), character/personal qualities, extracurricular activities, first generation, geographical residence, level of applicant's interest, racial/ethnic status, state residency, talent/ability, volunteer work, work experience. SAT or ACT required; ACT with or without writing component accepted. TOEFL required of all international applicants. High school diploma is required and GED is accepted. *Academic units required:* 4 English, 3 mathematics, 3 science (2 science labs), 2 foreign language, 2 social studies, 2 academic electives.

Financial Aid

Students should submit: FAFSA. The Princeton Review suggests that all financial aid forms be submitted as soon as possible after January 1. *Need-based scholarships/grants offered:* Federal Pell, SEOG, state scholarships/grants, private scholarships, the school's own gift aid. *Loan aid offered:* Direct Subsidized Stafford, Direct Unsubsidized Stafford, Direct PLUS, Federal Perkins, state loans. Applicants will be notified of awards on a rolling basis beginning March 1. Federal Work-Study Program available. Institutional employment available. Off-campus job opportunities are good.

The Inside Word

University of Massachusetts Amherst requires applicants to identify a first-choice and a second-choice major; admissions standards are tougher in the school's most prestigious programs (such as engineering, business, communications and journalism, economics, computer science, and sports management). It is possible to be admitted for your second-choice major but not your first; it is also possible to be admitted as an "undeclared" student if you fail to gain admission via your chosen majors. You can transfer into either major later, although doing so will require you to excel in your freshman and sophomore classes.

THE SCHOOL SAYS ". . ."

From the Admissions Office

"The University of Massachusetts Amherst is the largest public university in New England, offering its students an almost limitless variety of academic programs and activities. Over eighty-five majors are offered, including a unique program called Bachelor's Degree with Individual Concentration (BDIC) in which students create their own program of study. The outstanding full-time faculty of over 1,100 is the best in their fields and they take teaching seriously. Students can take courses through the honors program and sample classes at nearby Amherst, Hampshire, Mount Holyoke, and Smith Colleges at no extra charge. First-year students participate in the Residential First-Year Year Experience with opportunities to explore every possible interest through residential life. The extensive library system is the largest at any public institution in the Northeast. The Center for Student Development brings together more than 200 clubs and organizations, fraternities and sororities, multicultural and religious centers. The campus completes in NCAA Division I sports for men and women, with teams winning national recognition. Award-winning student-operated businesses, the largest college daily newspaper in the region, and an active student government provide hands-on experience. About 5,000 students a year participate in the intramural sports program. The picturesque New England Town of Amherst offers shopping and dining, and the ski slopes of western Massachusetts and southern Vermont are close by. SAT or ACT scores are required for admission to the university. The school takes a holistic view of the student's application package and considers these scores as only part of the evaluation criteria. Additionally, any Advanced Placement, Honors, and SAT Subject Test scores are considered when reviewing each applicant. Increased applications in recent years have made admission more selective."

SELECTIVITY	
Admissions Rating	**85**
# of applicants	32,564
% of applicants accepted	66
% of acceptees attending	22
# accepting a place on wait list	1,261
# admitted from wait list	125
FRESHMAN PROFILE	
Range SAT Critical Reading	530–630
Range SAT Math	560–650
Range ACT Composite	24–28
Minimum paper TOEFL	550
Average HS GPA	3.6
% graduated top 10% of class	26
% graduated top 25% of class	67
% graduated top 50% of class	97
DEADLINES	
Early action	
Deadline	11/1
Regular	
Deadline	1/15
Nonfall registration?	yes
FINANCIAL FACTS	
Financial Aid Rating	**79**
Annual in-state tuition	$12,612
Annual out-state tuition	$25,400
Room and board	$10,310
Books and supplies	$1,000
% needy frosh rec. need-based scholarship or grant aid	89
% needy UG rec. need-based scholarship or grant aid	82
% needy frosh rec. non-need-based scholarship or grant aid	7
% needy UG rec. non-need-based scholarship or grant aid	8
% needy frosh rec. need-based self-help aid	83
% needy UG rec. need-based self-help aid	85
% frosh rec. any financial aid	85
% UG rec. any financial aid	90
% UG borrow to pay for school	69
Average cumulative indebtedness	$26,893
% frosh need fully met	16
% ugrads need fully met	21
Average % of frosh need met	82
Average % of ugrad need met	84

UNIVERSITY OF MIAMI

PO BOX 248025, CORAL GABLES, FL 33124-4616 • ADMISSIONS: 305-284-4323 • FAX: 305-284-6605

CAMPUS LIFE

Quality of Life Rating	**96**
Fire Safety Rating	**81**
Green Rating	**87**
Type of school	private
Environment	town

STUDENTS

Total undergrad enrollment	10,144
% male/female	49/51
% from out of state	51
% from public high school	58
% frosh live on campus	84
# of fraternities	20
# of sororities	14
% African American	7
% Asian	6
% Caucasian	44
% Hispanic	24
% international	11
# of countries represented	110

SURVEY SAYS . . .

Athletic facilities are great
Diverse student types on campus
Students are happy
Great library
Students love Miami, FL
Great off-campus food
Intercollegiate sports are popular

ACADEMICS

Academic Rating	**83**
% students returning for sophomore year	91
% students graduating within 6 years	78
Calendar	semester
Student/faculty ratio	11:1
Profs interesting rating	77
Profs accessible rating	81
Most classes have	10–19 students
Most lab/discussion sessions have	10–19 students

MOST POPULAR MAJORS

business/marketing; biological/life sciences; communication/journalism

APPLICANTS ALSO LOOK AT AND OFTEN PREFER

Michigan State University, Northwestern University, University of Illinois at Urbana-Champaign, Purdue University—West Lafayette

AND SOMETIMES PREFER

University of Chicago, University of Wisconsin—Madison, Indiana University—Bloomington, The Ohio State University—Columbus

AND RARELY PREFER

University of California—Berkeley

STUDENTS SAY ". . ."

Academics

"A force, much like a real hurricane, to be reckoned with academically and in athletics," the "heavily sports-oriented" University of Miami offers "academic excellence along with cultural diversity." The reputation is a result of the efforts of the university's president, Donna Shalala, whose "forward thinking" has "transformed this university into an academic leader." In addition to its "top-notch" nursing program, the school's other notable programs include business and communications. "Coursework is often challenging, even for those students who got straight A's in high school." Class size ranges from "200-plus person classes" to "small interactive classes," and students are generally pleased with their professors who "are always available and very willing to talk to students." One student says, "The majority of the teachers were good, and those that weren't made up for it with sheer enthusiasm." The school's administration is both "very visible and approachable" and "is working hard to improve the quality of the university through facility improvements and additions, as well as program restructuring and evaluation." "It is not uncommon to see multiple administrators showing their support at school events and club meetings." During final exams, "faculty, trustees, and student government executives served free breakfast to students from 9:00 P.M. [to] past midnight" and also "strung up thirty-some hammocks between the palm trees behind the library for [students] to study or sleep."

Life

Depending on which student you talk to, the University of Miami "can be the hottest party spot" or "the ideal place to gain experience in almost any field of work or research while living in a beautiful place with a culture mix that is truly unique." One international student raves that "the school's rich culture and proud spirit acted like a sponge and soaked me into the Canes culture." Students compare their "very mellow" campus to "a country club" that is "secluded from the poverty and sham politics of Miami, where students live in a party-life bubble, protected from the real world." The "vibrant student life" includes "going out clubbing" as well as "following the football team" and "tailgating." Students also agree that "sorority/fraternity life is also a major part of life." "Every day, there are dozens of programs (cultural, social, physical, or academic) to participate in," and students can get involved in "theater productions, musical performances, cultural events, student shows and showcases, on-campus movie showings, service events, leadership opportunities, and seminars." For off-campus fun, "the beach is a popular weekend destination," and "people either go to Coconut Grove or South Beach."

Student Body

At first glance, "it can appear that the University of Miami admits only super-thin or super-buff students looking for the perfect spot for a tan while cruising in their Mercedes down the ritzy streets of Coral Gables." University of Miami students "all love warm weather and not wearing an excess amount of clothing" and "develop an urge to wear shades at one point or another." However, "the students at Miami are not all about tanning and partying; [they] are a competitive bunch." "The typical Miami student is probably from either Miami-Dade/Broward Counties or the Northeast" and is "into athletics." Students seem to fall into three categories: "those who go to South Beach, those who just have fun and party, and those who choose to remain for the most part academic." "While "students are not politically active," "most students perform community service." The student body "is very diverse," and "international students have formed various cultural organizations that reach out to their respective cultures." Although "it can seem that people are a little 'cliquey' when it comes to their culture," University of Miami students seem "widely accepting of many cultural groups" and manage to "all live together symbiotically."

FINANCIAL AID: 305-284-5212 • E-MAIL: ADMISSION@MIAMI.EDU • WEBSITE: WWW.MIAMI.EDU

THE PRINCETON REVIEW SAYS

Admissions

Very important factors considered include: Class rank, application essay, academic GPA, recommendation(s), rigor of secondary school record, standardized test scores, extracurricular activities, volunteer work, character/personal qualities, work experience. *Other factors considered include:* Alumni/ae relation, first generation, geographical residence, racial/ethnic status, talent/ability, applicant's interest level. SAT or ACT required. TOEFL required of all international applicants. High school diploma is required and GED is accepted. *Academic units recommended:* 4 English, 4 mathematics, 3 science (2 science labs), 2 foreign language, 3 social studies, 2 history, 1 visual/performing arts, 1 computer science.

Financial Aid

Students should submit: FAFSA. Priority filing deadline is February 1. The Princeton Review suggests that all financial aid forms be submitted as soon as possible after January 1. *Need-based scholarships/grants offered:* Federal Pell, SEOG, state scholarships/grants, private scholarships, the school's own gift aid. *Loan aid offered:* Direct Subsidized Stafford, Direct Unsubsidized Stafford, Direct PLUS, Federal Perkins, Federal Nursing, college/university loans from institutional funds, private alternative education loans. Applicants will be notified of awards on a rolling basis beginning March 1. Federal Work-Study Program available. Institutional employment available. Off-campus job opportunities are excellent.

The Inside Word

The University of Miami's campaign to overcome its reputation as a "football school" is an unqualified success. Each recent academic year has seen an increase in applications, and UM's selectivity is on the rise. The school partially attributes this accomplishment to its alumni and gladly repays them by giving legacies a boost during the admissions process. Of course, having a Cane for a parent isn't enough; students must demonstrate achievement in arduous classes, intellectual promise, and strong moral character.

THE SCHOOL SAYS ". . ."

From the Admissions Office

"The University of Miami in Coral Gables, is an innovative private research university in a location unlike any other in the country. Located ten miles from the vibrant international city of Miami, UM's more than 9,000 undergraduates come from every state and 110 nations, allowing people of many cultures to challenge and champion each other. Faculty work closely with students, and internships and research experiences are integral to academic life. Students work hard as community volunteers and exert leadership in a range of lively clubs and organizations, including the student-managed TV station, radio station, and newspaper.

"The University of Miami will accept the critical reading and math scores from the SAT, as well as the ACT with or without the writing component."

SELECTIVITY	
Admissions Rating	**96**
# of applicants	27,745
% of applicants accepted	38
% of acceptees attending	20
# of early decision applicants	693
# accepted early decision	225

FRESHMAN PROFILE	
Range SAT Critical Reading	600–690
Range SAT Math	630–710
Range SAT Writing	600–690
Range ACT Composite	28–32
Minimum paper TOEFL	550
Minimum web-based TOEFL	80
Average HS GPA	4.2
% graduated top 10% of class	72
% graduated top 25% of class	92
% graduated top 50% of class	98

DEADLINES	
Early decision	
Deadline	11/1
Notification	12/15
Early action	
Deadline	11/1
Notification	2/1
Regular	
Deadline	1/1
Notification	4/15
Nonfall registration?	yes

FINANCIAL FACTS	
Financial Aid Rating	**84**
Annual tuition	$39,980
Room and board	$11,882
Required fees	$1,240
Books and supplies	$900
% needy frosh rec. need-based scholarship or grant aid	99
% needy UG rec. need-based scholarship or grant aid	97
% needy frosh rec. non-need-based scholarship or grant aid	42
% needy UG rec. non-need-based scholarship or grant aid	30
% needy frosh rec. need-based self-help aid	76
% needy UG rec. need-based self-help aid	85
% frosh rec. any financial aid	65
% UG rec. any financial aid	76
% UG borrow to pay for school	53
Average cumulative indebtedness	$26,297
% frosh need fully met	45
% ugrads need fully met	35
Average % of frosh need met	82
Average % of ugrad need met	79

UNIVERSITY OF MICHIGAN—ANN ARBOR

1220 STUDENT ACTIVITIES BUILDING, ANN ARBOR, MI 48109-1316 • ADMISSIONS: 734-764-7433 • FAX: 734-936-0740

CAMPUS LIFE

Quality of Life Rating	**93**
Fire Safety Rating	**91**
Green Rating	**89**
Type of school	public
Environment	city

STUDENTS

Total undergrad enrollment	27,226
% male/female	51/49
% from out of state	41
% frosh live on campus	98
# of fraternities	40
# of sororities	27
% African American	4
% Asian	12
% Caucasian	66
% Hispanic	4
% international	6
# of countries represented	122

SURVEY SAYS . . .

Students love Ann Arbor, MI
Great off-campus food
Everyone loves the Wolverines
Student publications are popular
Political activism is popular

ACADEMICS

Academic Rating	**90**
% students returning for sophomore year	96
Calendar	trimester
Student/faculty ratio	16:1
Profs interesting rating	75
Profs accessible rating	74
Most classes have	10–19 students
Most lab/discussion sessions have	20–29 students

MOST POPULAR MAJORS

business administration and management; mechanical engineering; psychology

APPLICANTS ALSO LOOK AT AND OFTEN PREFER

Michigan State University, Northwestern University, University of Illinois at Urbana-Champaign, Purdue University—West Lafayette

AND SOMETIMES PREFER

University of Chicago, University of Wisconsin-Madison, Indiana University—Bloomington, The Ohio State University—Columbus

AND RARELY PREFER

University of California—Berkeley

STUDENTS SAY ". . ."

Academics

Among the many allures of the University of Michigan—Ann Arbor is that the school offers "a great environment both academically and socially." One student explains, "It has the social, fun atmosphere of any Big Ten university, but most people are still incredibly focused on their studies. It's great to be at a place where there is always something to do, but your friends completely understand when you have to stay in and get work done." With "an amazing honors program," a "wide range of travel-abroad opportunities," and "research strength" all available "at a low cost," it's no wonder students tell us that UM "provides every kind of opportunity at all times to all people." Academically, Michigan "is very competitive, and the professors have high academic standards for all the students." In fact, some here insist that "Michigan is as good as Ivy League schools in many disciplines." Standout offerings include business ("We have access to some of the brightest leaders" in the business world, students report), a "great engineering program," and "a good undergraduate program for medical school preparation." Those seeking add-on academic experiences here will find "a vast amount of resources. Internships, career opportunities, tutoring, community service projects, a plethora of student organizations, and a wealth of other resources" are all available, but "you need to make the first move" because no one "will seek you out."

Life

Michigan is a huge university, meaning that students have endless extracurricular options here. One explains: "If you seek it out, you can find organizations for *any* interest. There are always people out there who share your interests. That's part of the benefit of 40,000-plus students!" There is a robust party scene. Students tell us that "most students go to house parties [or] hit the bars." There's also a vigorous social scene for the non-drinking crowd, with "great programs like UMix…phenomenal cultural opportunities in Ann Arbor especially music and movies," and "the hugely popular football Saturdays. The sense of school spirit here is impressive." Michigan students tend to be both academically serious and socially outgoing, which "is great because you can have a stimulating conversation with someone one day, and, the next day, be watching a silly movie or playing video games with this person."

Student Body

The Michigan student body "is hugely diverse," which "is one of the things Michigan prides itself on." "If you participate in extracurricular activities and make an effort to get to know other students in class and elsewhere, you'll definitely end up with a pretty diverse group of friends," undergrads assure us. Although varied, students tend to be similar in that they "are social but very academically driven." A number of students "are on the cutting edge of both research and progressive thinking," and there is a decided liberal tilt to campus politics. Even so, there's a place for everyone here, because "there are hundreds of mini-communities within the campus, made of everything from service fraternities to political organizations to dance groups. If you have an interest, you can find a group of people who enjoy the same thing."

FINANCIAL AID: 734-763-6600 • WEBSITE: WWW.UMICH.EDU

THE PRINCETON REVIEW SAYS

Admissions

Very important factors considered include: Rigor of secondary school record. *Important factors considered include:* Application essay, academic GPA, recommendation(s), standardized test scores, character/personal qualities, first generation. *Other factors considered include:* Class rank, alumni/ae relation, extracurricular activities, geographical residence, level of applicant's interest, state residency, talent/ability, volunteer work, work experience. SAT or ACT required; ACT with writing component required. TOEFL required of all international applicants. High school diploma is required and GED is accepted. *Academic units required:* 4 English (1 science lab), 3 social studies, 3 history, 1 academic electives. *Academic units recommended:* 4 English, 4 mathematics, 4 science (1 science lab), 4 foreign language, 3 social studies, 3 history, 2 visual/performing arts, 1 computer science, 1 academic electives.

Financial Aid

Students should submit: FAFSA, CSS/Financial Aid PROFILE. The Princeton Review suggests that all financial aid forms be submitted as soon as possible after January 1. *Need-based scholarships/grants offered:* Federal Pell, SEOG, state scholarships/grants, private scholarships, the school's own gift aid, Academic Competitive Grant (ACG); National SMART; D.C. Tag Program; Byrd; Teach Grant. *Loan aid offered:* Direct Subsidized Stafford, Direct Unsubsidized Stafford, Direct PLUS, Federal Perkins, Federal Nursing, college/university loans from institutional funds, Direct Loan Grad Plus; Health Professional Student Loans. Applicants will be notified of awards on a rolling basis beginning March 15. Federal Work-Study Program available. Institutional employment available. Off-campus job opportunities are excellent.

The Inside Word

Michigan admissions are extremely competitive. Generally, about a quarter of the incoming freshman class graduates in the top one percent of their high school class. The volume of applications—Michigan receives nearly 30,000 applications—means the admissions office must rely heavily on numbers to make its decision, so do what you can to get those test scores and GPA as high as you can. Michigan admits on a rolling basis, a process that favors those who apply early.

THE SCHOOL SAYS ". . ."

From the Admissions Office

"Michigan is a place of incredible possibility. Students shape that possibility according to their diverse interests, goals, energy, and initiative. Undergraduate education is in the academic spotlight at Michigan, offering more than 220 fields of study in twelve schools and colleges; more than 150 first-year seminars with twenty or fewer students taught by senior faculty; composition classes of twenty or fewer students; more than 1,200 first- and second-year students in undergraduate research partnerships with faculty; and numerous service learning programs linking academics with volunteerism. Some introductory courses have large lectures, but these are combined with labs or small group discussions where students get plenty of individualized attention. A Michigan degree is one of distinction and promise; graduates are successful in medical, law, and graduate schools all over the nation and world. A year after graduation, more than ninety-five percent of UM alumni report that they are in the "next step" of their career—whether that is graduate or professional school, working, or volunteering."

SELECTIVITY	
Admissions Rating	**96**
# of applicants	39,584
% of applicants accepted	41
% of acceptees attending	39
# accepting a place on wait list	4,498
# admitted from wait list	42

FRESHMAN PROFILE	
Range SAT Critical Reading	600–700
Range SAT Math	650–750
Range SAT Writing	620–720
Range ACT Composite	28–32
Minimum paper TOEFL	570
Minimum web-based TOEFL	88
Average HS GPA	3.8

DEADLINES	
Early action	
Deadline	11/1
Notification	12/22
Regular	
Priority	11/1
Deadline	2/1
Nonfall registration?	yes

FINANCIAL FACTS	
Financial Aid Rating	**89**
Annual in-state tuition	$13,243
Annual out-state tuition	$38,915
Room and board	$9,468
Required fees	$194
Books and supplies	$1,048
% needy frosh rec. need-based scholarship or grant aid	67
% needy UG rec. need-based scholarship or grant aid	68
% needy frosh rec. non-need-based scholarship or grant aid	68
% needy UG rec. non-need-based scholarship or grant aid	52
% needy frosh rec. need-based self-help aid	100
% needy UG rec. need-based self-help aid	100
% UG borrow to pay for school	44
Average cumulative indebtedness	$27,644
% frosh need fully met	90
% ugrads need fully met	90
Average % of frosh need met	90
Average % of ugrad need met	90

University of Minnesota—Twin Cities

240 Williamson Hall, Minneapolis, MN 55455-0213 • Admissions: 612-625-2008

CAMPUS LIFE

Quality of Life Rating	**84**
Fire Safety Rating	**84**
Green Rating	**95**
Type of school	public
Environment	metropolis

STUDENTS

Total undergrad enrollment	30,519
% male/female	48/52
% from out of state	32
% frosh live on campus	86
# of fraternities	22
# of sororities	12
% African American	5
% Asian	9
% Caucasian	74
% Hispanic	3
% Native American	1
% international	6
# of countries represented	135

SURVEY SAYS . . .

Students love Minneapolis, MN
Great off-campus food
Student publications are popular
Great library
Political activism is popular

ACADEMICS

Academic Rating	**76**
% students returning for sophomore year	89
% students graduating within 4 years	46
% students graduating within 6 years	70
Calendar	semester
Student/faculty ratio	21:1
Profs interesting rating	69
Profs accessible rating	66
Most classes have	20–29 students
Most lab/discussion sessions have	10–19 students

MOST POPULAR MAJORS

biology/biological sciences; journalism; psychology

APPLICANTS ALSO LOOK AT AND OFTEN PREFER

University of Michigan—Ann Arbor, Northwestern University

STUDENTS SAY "..."

Academics

The University of Minnesota is a massive, well-run, public research university located in the Twin Cities. The science departments here are "across the board...superb," and the prestigious Carlson School of Management is "one of the best business schools in the Midwest, with a reasonable tuition" to boot. Students say that the university boasts "just about every major you can think of," and students appreciate the "never-ending resources available to them" within the university and the city. Research is of paramount importance at the university, which means that "There are incredible opportunities [for undergraduates] to work in ANY field of research." Given the size of the university, students have to contend with "introductory level classes with 300-plus students, but as you get into the higher level classes, there are fewer students and the professors make lots of effort to connect personally." Many professors are "professionals working in the field; therefore, they have practical working knowledge of the subject material," which improves students' academic experience. Additionally, "The school does a good job of connecting with the outside community to set up internships and service learning opportunities" for students. The fact that the university is so "close to the city [makes] it easy to make connections with professionals" and provides ample "opportunities to intern in your field of study." Students of the University of Minnesota's Honors Program give it rave reviews and add that it is a "very valuable part of the university, and it sets Minnesota apart."

Life

Life on the University of Minnesota's "beautiful" and "environmentally friendly" campus is filled with "unlimited opportunities" for fun and recreation. Students say they "love how easy it is to get involved" on campus, whether it is in the popular Greek life on campus or the multitudes of clubs and sports readily available to them. On the weekends, "Drinking is very wide-spread but is by no means the only source of fun." Many students say that their "favorite part of living at the U of M is that there is plenty to do on and near campus, but you are also in the heart of a vibrant, exciting city." Due to its location in an "incredible city" with a flourishing music and arts scene, students often "venture into the heart of Minneapolis to clubs, music shows, sporting events, and more." Outdoor activities are also "popular year-round—we have famous biking and walking trails, parks, and wide open spaces for students to take advantage of...to ski, skate, run, unicycle, and leapfrog around to their hearts' content." The campus in general is "pretty active, which has led to our recreation center being expanded. It's nice to live in an encouraging, athletic environment like that because it makes it easier to make healthy choices." Though the University of Minnesota is a huge school, students say they feel a sense of pride in their community: "I love the atmosphere, I love the city, and I love the size. It isn't a school incredibly focused on a high octane 'school spirit,' but I do feel incredibly united with the rest of the student body."

Student Body

The university is filled with a diverse body of students that runs the gamut from "typical Midwesterners" to "pockets of people from all over the world, most notably from China and India," as well as a good deal of hipsters and a large LGBT community. Students "respect the differences in each other," and students are, overall, "very welcoming and friendly." "It's not difficult to find friends or people to talk to in any class. The students are one of the university's high points." Though the campus "tends to lean liberal," students say that "political activeness/awareness is lacking." "Students have strong affiliation with their individual colleges and student groups that they are involved in." Students find their different niches "by joining different clubs and activities outside of the classroom." The general consensus is that the typical University of Minnesota student "has no trouble fitting in here. We have such a large, diverse community that it is almost impossible not to find people you get along with and share the same values with."

FAX: 612-626-1693 • FINANCIAL AID: 612-624-1111 • WEBSITE: WWW.UMN.EDU

THE PRINCETON REVIEW SAYS

Admissions

Very important factors considered include: Class rank, academic GPA, rigor of secondary school record, standardized test scores. *Other factors considered include:* Alumni/ae relation, character/personal qualities, extracurricular activities, first generation, geographical residence, racial/ethnic status, talent/ability, volunteer work, work experience. TOEFL required of all international applicants. High school diploma is required and GED is accepted. *Academic units required:* 4 English, 3 mathematics, 3 science, 2 foreign language, 3 social studies, 1 history.

Financial Aid

Students should submit: FAFSA, institution's own financial aid form. The Princeton Review suggests that all financial aid forms be submitted as soon as possible after January 1. *Need-based scholarships/grants offered:* Federal Pell, SEOG, state scholarships/grants, private scholarships, the school's own gift aid, Federal Nursing Scholarships. *Loan aid offered:* Direct Subsidized Stafford, Direct Unsubsidized Stafford, Direct PLUS, Federal Perkins, Federal Nursing, state loans, college/university loans from institutional funds. Applicants will be notified of awards on a rolling basis beginning February 15. Federal Work-Study Program available. Institutional employment available.

The Inside Word

The University of Minnesota receives an enormous volume of applications every year, creating what looks like a fairly selective admissions rate. Make sure your grades, extracurriculars, and test scores are competitive.

THE SCHOOL SAYS ". . ."

From the Admissions Office

"The University of Minnesota is one of the nation's top public research universities. That means your college experience will be enhanced by world-renowned faculty, state-of-the-art learning facilities, and an unprecedented variety of options (such as 135 majors). Eighty-three percent of our classes have fewer than fifty students, and our caring advisers will help you find opportunities that are right for you.

"Hands-on courses, volunteer opportunities, internships, study abroad, and undergraduate research are part of the U of M experience. Students benefit from programs and traditions designed to support their success, like Welcome Week, where freshmen explore campus, meet their classmates, and connect with faculty and staff before the school year begins. Our classic Big Ten campus is located in the heart of the vibrant Twin Cities. Just minutes away, intern at a Fortune 500 company, volunteer at a major hospital, or relax at the beautiful Chain of Lakes. With a wealth of cultural, career, and recreational opportunities, there's no better place to earn your degree.

"The University of Minnesota offers a fantastic education and prestigious degree at a great value. Residents of Minnesota benefit from in-state tuition. Minnesota residents may also qualify for the University of Minnesota Promise Scholarship, which guarantees tuition aid to eligible students with a family income up to $100,000."

"Residents of North Dakota, South Dakota, Wisconsin, or Manitoba qualify for special reciprocity tuition rates. Out-of-state students benefit from the most affordable non-resident tuition in the Big Ten. Last year, we awarded over $12 million in four-year scholarship packages."

SELECTIVITY	
Admissions Rating	92
# of applicants	36,853
% of applicants accepted	48
% of acceptees attending	30

FRESHMAN PROFILE	
Range SAT Critical Reading	530–690
Range SAT Math	600–720
Range SAT Writing	550–670
Range ACT Composite	25–30
Minimum paper TOEFL	550
% graduated top 10% of class	43
% graduated top 25% of class	83
% graduated top 50% of class	99

DEADLINES	
Regular	
Priority	12/15
Nonfall registration?	yes

FINANCIAL FACTS	
Financial Aid Rating	80
Annual in-state tuition	$11,650
Annual out-state tuition	$16,650
Room and board	$7,834
Required fees	$1,348
Books and supplies	$1,000
% needy frosh rec. need-based scholarship or grant aid	98
% needy UG rec. need-based scholarship or grant aid	96
% needy frosh rec. non-need-based scholarship or grant aid	15
% needy UG rec. non-need-based scholarship or grant aid	12
% needy frosh rec. need-based self-help aid	88
% needy UG rec. need-based self-help aid	85
% UG borrow to pay for school	63
Average cumulative indebtedness	$27,578
% frosh need fully met	35
% ugrads need fully met	30
Average % of frosh need met	79
Average % of ugrad need met	74

UNIVERSITY OF MISSISSIPPI

145 MARTINDALE, UNIVERSITY, MS 38677 • ADMISSIONS: 662-915-7226 • FAX: 662-915-5869

CAMPUS LIFE

Quality of Life Rating	**96**
Fire Safety Rating	**60***
Green Rating	**86**
Type of school	public
Environment	village

STUDENTS

Total undergrad enrollment	15,111
% male/female	45/55
% from out of state	48
# of fraternities	18
# of sororities	13
% African American	17
% Asian	1
% Caucasian	76
% Hispanic	2
% international	1

SURVEY SAYS . . .

Great off-campus food
Everyone loves the Ole Miss Rebels
Frats and sororities dominate social scene
Student publications are popular
Lots of beer drinking
Hard liquor is popular

ACADEMICS

Academic Rating	**73**
% students graduating within 4 years	38
% students graduating within 6 years	60
Calendar	semester
Student/faculty ratio	19:1
Profs interesting rating	80
Profs accessible rating	83
Most classes have	10–19 students
Most lab/discussion sessions have	20–29 students

MOST POPULAR MAJORS

accounting; elementary education and teaching; marketing/marketing management

STUDENTS SAY "..."

Academics

Ole Miss is a prime example of Southern hospitality combined with the opportunity for greatness. Founded in 1844, the legendary university offers "'big-time' SEC athletics in the safe, quaint, and picturesque town of Oxford." Many of the school's services "are cheap if not free," and the school "puts on many programs that bring together lots of different people of different backgrounds." "It has a togetherness about it…there is something for a person with any interest here," says a student. There is also "a highly academic side to Ole Miss that many outsiders do not see." Business and international studies are programs of note, and the Honors College is a particular standout here, as it provides "unparalleled academic opportunities, such as beginning research as a freshman."

Most of the professors "hit the ball out of the park" when it comes to teaching, being available, and helping students acquire internships. Professors constantly organize discussion groups, dinner events, and other gatherings in order to "develop our ability to speak academically in a non-academic setting." Going to class is "critical"; professors "add much more than the textbook has to offer." Classes are designed to be "informative but also engaging and dynamic," and there is a deep understanding that individuals have an effect on the whole. "The teachers care, the university cares, [and] the students all care about the school and what it stands for."

It can be said again and again, but even beyond the "world-class programs and faculty," the thing that students at Ole Miss value the most is the traditions and legacy of this school. People "are proud to have graduated from Ole Miss," and the tremendous amount of alumni support "gives Ole Miss a lot of confidence."

Life

An Ole Miss existence is "always super busy." There is "a lot of work to be done" as "school and grades are a very important aspect of life," but there are also "a lot of opportunities for fun." "During football season, the Grove consumes our weekends. It's an amazing experience!" says a student. As a school that most admit is "known for its Greek life, beautiful women, and great parties," it's a common misconception that "most people's minds revolve around drinking, college football, and church on Sunday." If you take a closer look, you'll find that there is a huge literary scene "with Thacker Mountain Radio on Thursdays and poetry readings monthly at Proud Larry's," and students here also "really want to be active in making changes in the world."

The closeness of the community makes it easy to feel part of the University. "You'll hear the term the 'Ole Miss family,' and it won't seem forced or strange," explains a student. Oxford is also very appealing due to its "small, hometown feel," and the rich history you see everywhere you go (the Square is the center of town life, and most students can be found there at some point in a week). Basically, "there is never a dull moment, especially on the weekends."

Student Body

Ole Miss is a fairly diverse campus, with most students possessing "decent grades and an extravagant social life." The most common student "belongs to either a fraternity or sorority, fancying the appropriate attire of a Polo shirt and loafers or baggy t-shirts and Nike shorts." The divide between Greek and non-Greek is stark here, though the two groups are not necessarily always adverse towards each other; this is a group of "open minds" in "a small-town" setting, with "a blend of Southern charm and laid-back manners" thrown in, after all. "Studying for your next exam over a glass of sweet tea is a common practice." As there are a lot of different groups on campus, "You can find a group of friends without much effort."

FINANCIAL AID: 800-891-4596 • E-MAIL: ADMISSIONS@OLEMISS.EDU • WEBSITE: WWW.OLEMISS.EDU

THE PRINCETON REVIEW SAYS

Admissions

Very important factors considered include: Academic GPA, rigor of secondary school record. *Important factors considered include:* Class rank, standardized test scores. *Other factors considered include:* Alumni/ae relation, state residency, talent/ability. SAT or ACT required; ACT with or without writing component accepted. TOEFL required of all international applicants. High school diploma is required and GED is accepted. *Academic units required:* 4 English, 3 mathematics, 3 science (2 science labs), 1 foreign language, 1 social studies, 2 history, 1 academic electives. *Academic units recommended:* 4 mathematics, 4 science, 2 foreign language, 2 social studies.

Financial Aid

Students should submit: FAFSA. The Princeton Review suggests that all financial aid forms be submitted as soon as possible after January 1. *Need-based scholarships/grants offered:* Federal Pell, SEOG, state scholarships/grants, private scholarships, the school's own gift aid. *Loan aid offered:* Direct Subsidized Stafford, Direct Unsubsidized Stafford, Direct PLUS, Federal Perkins, college/university loans from institutional funds. Applicants will be notified of awards on a rolling basis beginning April 1. Federal Work-Study Program available. Institutional employment available. Off-campus job opportunities are fair.

The Inside Word

While Ole Miss offers students tremendous educational opportunities, the university's admissions policies are less than strenuous. Applicants who demonstrate moderate success (a 3.2 GPA or greater, or a 2.5 GPA and a 16 on the ACT) in college prep curricula will secure admittance.

THE SCHOOL SAYS ". . ."

From the Admissions Office

"The flagship university of the state, The University of Mississippi, widely known as Ole Miss, offers extraordinary opportunities through more than 100 areas of study, including programs such as the Sally McDonnell Barksdale Honors College and the Croft Institute for International Studies. UM students are the only public university students in the state who have the opportunity to be tapped by the nation's oldest and most prestigious honor society, Phi Beta Kappa. Strong academic programs and a rich and varied campus life have helped Ole Miss graduate twenty-four Rhodes Scholars, and eleven Truman Scholars. Since 1998 alone, UM has produced five Goldwater Scholars, a Marshall Scholar, and four Fulbright Scholars.

"The campus is diverse; thirty-two percent come from other states and countries and thirteen percent are black Americans. Recent significant campus improvements include the $25 million Gertrude Ford Performing Arts Center and the privately funded Paris-Yates Chapel and Peddle Bell Tower. UM ranks thirty-third in the nation among public universities for endowment per student. Ole Miss is home to twenty research centers, including the National Center for Justice and the Rule of Law, which provides training on investigating and prosecuting cybercrime; the William Winter Institute for Racial Reconciliation; and the National Center for Natural Products Research.

"The university is located in Oxford, consistently recognized as a great college town and as a center for writers and other artists. Like Ole Miss, Oxford is modest in size and large in the opportunities it provides residents, offering many of the advantages of a larger place in a friendly and open environment.

"Students applying will be allowed to take the SAT or the ACT but are not required to take the ACT writing section. The university will not consider the writing section of either exam when evaluating students for admission, but certain specialty programs may request these scores."

SELECTIVITY

Admissions Rating	75
# of applicants	13,321
% of applicants accepted	79
% of acceptees attending	34

FRESHMAN PROFILE

Range SAT Critical Reading	460–590
Range SAT Math	470–590
Range ACT Composite	20–27
Minimum paper TOEFL	550
Average HS GPA	3.4
% graduated top 10% of class	25
% graduated top 25% of class	47
% graduated top 50% of class	76

DEADLINES

Regular	
Priority	6/15
Deadline	7/20
Nonfall registration?	yes

FINANCIAL FACTS

Financial Aid Rating	77
% needy frosh rec. need-based scholarship or grant aid	89
% needy UG rec. need-based scholarship or grant aid	87
% needy frosh rec. non-need-based scholarship or grant aid	14
% needy UG rec. non-need-based scholarship or grant aid	8
% needy frosh rec. need-based self-help aid	69
% needy UG rec. need-based self-help aid	74
% frosh rec. any financial aid	81
% UG rec. any financial aid	83
% UG borrow to pay for school	43
Average cumulative indebtedness	$21,393
% frosh need fully met	12
% ugrads need fully met	11
Average % of frosh need met	77
Average % of ugrad need met	74

UNIVERSITY OF MISSOURI

230 JESSE HALL, COLUMBIA, MO 65211 • ADMISSIONS: 573-882-7786 • FAX: 573-882-7887

CAMPUS LIFE

Quality of Life Rating	**88**
Fire Safety Rating	**87**
Green Rating	**89**
Type of school	public
Environment	city

STUDENTS

Total undergrad enrollment	26,024
% male/female	48/52
% from out of state	27
% frosh live on campus	87
# of fraternities	33
# of sororities	16
% African American	8
% Asian	2
% Caucasian	81
% Hispanic	3
% international	2
# of countries represented	121

SURVEY SAYS . . .

Students are happy
Great library
Students love Columbia, MO
Great off-campus food
Athletic facilities are great
Lots of beer drinking
Everyone loves the Tigers
Frats and sororities dominate social scene

ACADEMICS

Academic Rating	**68**
% students returning for sophomore year	85
% students graduating within 6 years	69
Calendar	semester
Student/faculty ratio	20:1
Profs interesting rating	70
Profs accessible rating	72
Most classes have	10–19 students
Most lab/discussion sessions have	20–29 students

MOST POPULAR MAJORS

business/marketing, communications/journalism, health professions

STUDENTS SAY ". . ."

Academics

The "gorgeous campus" at the University of Missouri is filled with "a diverse group of students who are eager to learn and a staff that is eager to teach them." The school is all about "learning while networking," and the administration always has an ear to the students. "When we say there is a problem, it gets fixed," one student says. Mizzou takes pride in tradition, which is to be found "in all aspects that involve the University name," which makes for "a campus full of pride and spirit." There is a "constant focus on beautification, which makes for a great campus," and "top-of-the-line facilities" are available to all. One of the university's greatest strengths is its dependability: "From mass e-mails to mass texts, if there is an issue anywhere on campus you will know about it."

Professors teach "comprehensive courses" and "are always available to answer a question"; "Even with large classes they are very attentive to individuals." "I've always had professors who have had a million ways to explain any given theory, problem, or question," says a student. The school boasts one of the country's best and most "intense" journalism schools (nursing is also a strong suit), and there are tons of "participation opportunities" for whatever area you choose to study. Classes may be hard, but "good grades are attainable." In addition to the "quality" academics, the advising system is "great," and Mizzou sets itself as a real model for its students: "It is always striving to achieve better, and not in just one specific category or area, but all around." "I came into college undecided and wanted to have plenty of options and opportunities to decide on a major," says a student of her reasoning for choosing Mizzou.

Life

"There is never a dull moment to be had" at the University of Missouri. All athletic events are "heavily attended," especially football and basketball. Everyone walks or bikes everywhere in Columbia "because it's such a pedestrian friendly place," and "there are plenty of opportunities to chill out downtown." It is "the perfect mixture of small town and big city," and local attractions include a mall, small shops, micro-breweries, and tons of parks and hiking trails. If you're used to bigger cities, then it also happens to be located between Kansas City and St. Louis. "Best of both worlds!" says a student. The school has "a huge Greek Life," and "it's a pretty close community." "Students enjoy going to off-campus parties or the bars downtown." "A lot of students spend their time in class, but every night of the week there is a party to go to," explains a student. Many agree that both the residential life system and the dorms "could use some work," and "having a car is the key to living off campus."

Student Body

The school has a giant spectrum of diversity, meaning "Everyone is different. Anyone could fit in and find a group here." If a typical student has to be defined, most here are "friendly, outgoing, social, [and] very involved." Most of all, they are "proud to be a Tiger." "We all fit in because we have this in common," says a student. "It's pretty, great company." "Classes have always felt like big families," and the majority of students find friends "by joining one of our million organizations," which is a common pastime among this "on-the-go" group. As everyone is "pretty easygoing and easy to get along with," "fitting in is easy; you just act like yourself!"

FINANCIAL AID: 573-882-7506 • E-MAIL: MU4U@MISSOURI.EDU • WEBSITE: WWW.MISSOURI.EDU

THE PRINCETON REVIEW SAYS

Admissions

Very important factors considered include: Class rank, academic GPA, standardized test scores. *Important factors considered include:* Rigor of secondary school record. *Other factors considered include:* Recommendation(s), first generation, level of applicant's interest, racial/ethnic status, talent/ability, volunteer work, work experience. SAT or ACT required; ACT with or without writing component accepted. TOEFL required of all international applicants. High school diploma is required and GED is accepted. *Academic units required:* 4 English, 4 mathematics, 3 science (1 science lab), 2 foreign language, 3 social studies, 1 fine arts.

Financial Aid

Students should submit: FAFSA. The Princeton Review suggests that all financial aid forms be submitted as soon as possible after January 1. *Need-based scholarships/grants offered:* Federal Pell, SEOG, state scholarships/grants, private scholarships, the school's own gift aid, outside. *Loan aid offered:* Direct Subsidized Stafford, Direct Unsubsidized Stafford, Direct PLUS, Federal Perkins, Federal Nursing, state loans, college/university loans from institutional funds, outside or third party. Applicants will be notified of awards on a rolling basis beginning April 1. Federal Work-Study Program available. Institutional employment available. Off-campus job opportunities are excellent.

The Inside Word

If your application suggests that you can handle the workload here, the school will find a place for you. Average test scores in conjunction with a college-prep high school curriculum should be all it takes. Even those who don't meet these criteria have a chance; admissions officers consider essays, recommendations, and special talents in the cases of borderline candidates.

THE SCHOOL SAYS ". . ."

From the Admissions Office

"Founded in 1839 as the first public university west of the Mississippi River, MU is a member of the nation's most prestigious group of sixty-one public and private teaching/research institutions: the Association of American Universities. The National Science Foundation has recognized MU as one of the top ten universities in the country for integrating research into undergraduate education; Mizzou offers undergraduate research to some students as early as their freshman year.

"Service learning is important at Mizzou. The Service Learning Center at MU integrates service to others into students' academic experiences through collaborative partnerships on campus and throughout the community.

"More than thirty percent of the fall 2011 freshman class came from another state or another country, and a strong international community thrives in Columbia. At the same time, Mizzou also has a growing Study Abroad program, with nearly 400 programs in more than sixty countries.

"Mizzou offers many strong, unique programs. Some in the sciences are taught in collaboration with MU's medical school, and humanities classes include such areas as music composition and creative writing where students frequently win national awards.

"Students can find admissions requirements at missouri.edu. As students apply online, it is clear whether they are admissible or not. That may partially explain Missouri's high acceptance rate."

SELECTIVITY	
Admissions Rating	73
# of applicants	18,125
% of applicants accepted	82
% of acceptees attending	41
FRESHMAN PROFILE	
Range SAT Critical Reading	530–650
Range SAT Math	520–650
Range ACT Composite	23–28
Minimum paper TOEFL	500
Minimum web-based TOEFL	61
% graduated top 10% of class	25
% graduated top 25% of class	56
% graduated top 50% of class	86
DEADLINES	
Regular	
Priority	1/15
Deadline	5/1
Nonfall registration?	yes
FINANCIAL FACTS	
Financial Aid Rating	74
Annual in-state tuition	$7,848
Annual out-state tuition	$20,643
Room and board	$8,643
Required fees	$1,141
Books and supplies	$1,086
% needy frosh rec. need-based scholarship or grant aid	85
% needy UG rec. need-based scholarship or grant aid	81
% needy frosh rec. non-need-based scholarship or grant aid	6
% needy UG rec. non-need-based scholarship or grant aid	4
% needy frosh rec. need-based self-help aid	74
% needy UG rec. need-based self-help aid	78
% UG borrow to pay for school	56
Average cumulative indebtedness	$22,145
% frosh need fully met	15
% ugrads need fully met	15
Average % of frosh need met	84
Average % of ugrad need met	81

THE UNIVERSITY OF MONTANA—MISSOULA

LOMMASSON CENTER 103, MISSOULA, MT 59812 • ADMISSIONS: 406-243-6266 • FAX: 406-243-5711

CAMPUS LIFE

Quality of Life Rating	86
Fire Safety Rating	86
Green Rating	94
Type of school	public
Environment	city

STUDENTS

Total undergrad enrollment	13,370
% male/female	47/53
% from out of state	28
% frosh live on campus	86
# of fraternities	5
# of sororities	4
% African American	1
% Asian	1
% Caucasian	86
% Hispanic	3
% Native American	3
% international	2
# of countries represented	66

SURVEY SAYS . . .

Athletic facilities are great
Students love Missoula, MT
Low cost of living
Student publications are popular

ACADEMICS

Academic Rating	67
% students returning for sophomore year	74
% students graduating within 4 years	23
% students graduating within 6 years	48
Calendar	semester
Student/faculty ratio	21:1
Profs interesting rating	84
Profs accessible rating	70
Most classes have	10–19 students
Most lab/discussion sessions have	20–29 students

MOST POPULAR MAJORS

business administration and management; education; psychology

STUDENTS SAY ". . ."

Academics

Nestled in beautiful Missoula, The University of Montana is "a great place to live, work, and study." Indeed, Montana's awesome location and solid reputation coupled with low in-state tuition make it "hard to beat." Moreover, while it has a substantial number of students, we're assured that you're never "just a number" here. Undergrads also appreciate the university's focus on "environmental sustainability…and social justice" along with the fact that the University of Montana strives to develop "creative thinkers and engaged citizens." While the university maintains a fantastic liberal arts program, students especially laud the wildlife biology, forestry, physical therapy, and forensic anthropology departments. Moreover, undergrads at Montana are highly complementary of their teachers who are generally "helpful, engaging, and accessible." One thrilled student claims that the professors are "amazing!! Math and science has never come easy for me, and my professors have taught in a way I completely understand the material." And another enthusiastic student summarizes her experience by stating, "The professors here are very knowledgeable and passionate about what they are teaching, because of this, the learning experience is always interesting and inviting. I truly appreciate all the effort that is put forward to help students succeed and prepare for the next steps in their life."

Life

Undergrads seem to truly enjoy life at U of M. Indeed, the campus is often buzzing with activity. As one student happily shares, "When it's not snowing in the fall or spring you can find people playing Frisbee, walking their dogs, catching footballs, and even playing with lightsabers." Additionally, there are "many music concerts and dance parties" one can attend. "Football is [also] really big here," and games are often packed with students. Beyond the campus, Montana offers a myriad of options for the outdoor enthusiast. As one ecstatic undergrad tells us, "Western Montana is a divine place for hiking, hunting, fishing, camping, snowshoeing, swimming, huckleberry picking, going to hot springs, mushroom picking, antler collecting, and just being immersed in nature. Near where I live there is access to the Rattlesnake Wilderness, mountains surround the valley, and the Clark Fork River runs right through town." And those with a more adventurous spirit can delight in "skiing and skydiving, hand gliding and parasailing, mountain climbing and repelling, caving and biking." As this pleased undergrad summarizes, "There is always something to do no matter what your interest are and great people to do them with."

Student Body

The University of Montana attracts a student body that's "pretty laid-back and easygoing." Many are "outdoorsy" and self-described as "hippies." Indeed, there are "quite a few granola kids" and "Carhartt-sporting, plaid-proud, future biologists" types. Though many students hail from within the state, one undergrad assures us that "increasing diversity efforts have begun to show in the past three years." Fortunately, for the most part, everyone is "accepting, friendly, and very involved in college and community life." Another student expands on this idea, stating, "People here do not seem to judge others or hold stereotypes against each other. If you're lost or need to ask a question you can ask anyone, and they're willing to give you the best answer they know in order to help you out even if they don't know you." A fellow undergrad agrees softly, sharing, "I feel like I've stepped into a melting pot of all beliefs and ideals. You can be yourself, and never be looked down on for that at this school."

FINANCIAL AID: 406-243-5373 • E-MAIL: ADMISS@UMONTANA.EDU • WEBSITE: WWW.UMONTANA.EDU

THE PRINCETON REVIEW SAYS

Admissions

Very important factors considered include: Class rank, academic GPA, rigor of secondary school record, standardized test scores. *Important factors considered include:* Extracurricular activities, talent/ability. SAT or ACT required; ACT with writing component recommended. TOEFL required of all international applicants. High school diploma is required and GED is accepted. *Academic units required:* 4 English, 3 mathematics, 2 science (2 science labs), 3 social studies, 2 history. *Academic units recommended:* 2 foreign language, 2 visual/performing arts, 2 computer science, 2 foreign language or vocational education.

Financial Aid

Students should submit: FAFSA, UM supplemental information sheet. The Princeton Review suggests that all financial aid forms be submitted as soon as possible after January 1. *Need-based scholarships/grants offered:* Federal Pell, SEOG, state scholarships/grants, private scholarships, the school's own gift aid. *Loan aid offered:* Direct Subsidized Stafford, Direct Unsubsidized Stafford, Direct PLUS, Federal Perkins. Applicants will be notified of awards on a rolling basis beginning April 1. Federal Work-Study Program available. Institutional employment available. Off-campus job opportunities are good.

The Inside Word

The admissions game at the University of Montana is fairly straightforward. Officers here rely heavily on quantitative data. Applicants who meet standardized test and GPA minimums and are in the top half of their graduating class generally receive an acceptance letter. Those who did not meet the minimum requirements can often enroll on a conditional basis.

THE SCHOOL SAYS ". . ."

From the Admissions Office

"There's something special about this place. It's something different for each person. For some, it's the blend of academic quality and outdoor recreation. The University of Montana ranks fifth in the nation among public institutions for producing Rhodes scholars, and Outside Magazine lists Missoula in its 'Top Ten Amazing Places for Outdoor Recreation.'" For others, it's size—not too big, not too small. The University of Montana is a midsized university in the heart of the Rocky Mountains—accessible in both admission and tuition bills—that produces graduates considered among the best and brightest in the world. It is located in a community that could pass for a cozy college town or a bustling big city, depending on your point of view. There's a lot happening, but you won't get lost. People are friendly and diverse. They come from all over the world to study and learn and to live a good life. They come to a place to be inspired, a place where they feel comfortable yet challenged. Some never leave. Most never want to."

SELECTIVITY	
Admissions Rating	71
# of applicants	5,609
% of applicants accepted	94
% of acceptees attending	41

FRESHMAN PROFILE	
Range SAT Critical Reading	490–610
Range SAT Math	490–590
Range SAT Writing	470–580
Range ACT Composite	21–26
Minimum paper TOEFL	500
Minimum web-based TOEFL	61
Average HS GPA	3.3
% graduated top 10% of class	18
% graduated top 25% of class	42
% graduated top 50% of class	74

DEADLINES	
Regular	
Priority	3/1
Nonfall registration?	yes

FINANCIAL FACTS	
Financial Aid Rating	66
Annual in-state tuition	$4,384
Annual out-state tuition	$19,164
Room and board	$7,060
Required fees	$1,558
Books and supplies	$950
% needy frosh rec. need-based scholarship or grant aid	63
% needy UG rec. need-based scholarship or grant aid	69
% needy frosh rec. non-need-based scholarship or grant aid	43
% needy UG rec. non-need-based scholarship or grant aid	29
% needy frosh rec. need-based self-help aid	82
% needy UG rec. need-based self-help aid	97
% frosh rec. any financial aid	82
% UG rec. any financial aid	76
% UG borrow to pay for school	47
Average cumulative indebtedness	$22,829
% frosh need fully met	9
% ugrads need fully met	2
Average % of frosh need met	55
Average % of ugrad need met	58

UNIVERSITY OF NEBRASKA—LINCOLN

1410 Q STREET, LINCOLN, NE 68588-0417 • ADMISSIONS: 402-472-2023

CAMPUS LIFE

Quality of Life Rating	**94**
Fire Safety Rating	**72**
Green Rating	**76**
Type of school	public
Environment	city

STUDENTS

Total undergrad enrollment	19,345
% male/female	53/47
% from out of state	20
% frosh live on campus	92
# of fraternities	20
# of sororities	15
% African American	2
% Asian	2
% Caucasian	80
% Hispanic	4
% international	8
# of countries represented	92

SURVEY SAYS . . .

Athletic facilities are great
Everyone loves the Cornhuskers
Intramural sports are popular
Student publications are popular

ACADEMICS

Academic Rating	**75**
% students returning for sophomore year	84
% students graduating within 4 years	32
Calendar	semester
Student/faculty ratio	21:1
Profs interesting rating	72
Profs accessible rating	79
Most classes have	20–29 students
Most lab/discussion sessions have	20–29 students

MOST POPULAR MAJORS

business administration and management; finance; psychology

STUDENTS SAY ". . ."

Academics

Students love the University of Nebraska—Lincoln for its "great community atmosphere" within what is actually a large, "major research institution." The school offers a "wide range of majors" and "opportunities to be involved in research" for those who seek them. Students say that "Although UNL is a large college, most professors here are very approachable and willing to help students, as long as they are willing to ask for it." According to one student, "If I ever have an issue come up, most professors are willing to work with me to get things resolved; however, some departments (usually the larger ones) are not as "student-friendly" as others." Another student says that "UNL professors have pushed me to be a better, well-rounded student who looks at situations from every angle." Academic resources abound at UNL. "With many of our professors performing research, there is such a great opportunity to get experience." Also, "We have so many resources such as the Career Center, Student Involvement, Writing Resource Center, etc." Students are "particularly pleased with the honors program at the University of Nebraska—Lincoln…The opportunities for unique academic projects are endless and strongly supported by the faculty." Because of the university's location "right next to downtown Lincoln… there are infinite opportunities for socializing or jobs and internships within walking distance." Students are very happy with "the endless opportunities available" at UNL, which "extends to majors, extracurricular activities, research, internships, study abroad, volunteering, jobs, and so on."

Life

"The sense of community on our campus is second to none," according to students. They are proud to be members of the University of Nebraska—Lincoln and think that the sense of "tradition here is amazing, and the support from the alumni and the community is awesome." "There is a real sense of unity around the athletics here," as students rally around Husker football games with "so much school spirit and pride." Life around campus is "lively," and it is "really easy to get involved on campus." "UNL offers many activities throughout the week. Whether it is the performing arts with the dance, choir, or theater performances, or the athletics with collegiate, club, or intramural sports, UNL has something going on for everyone." Lincoln is a beautiful, small-sized city and "a good college town, so there are lots of things to go do—concert halls, restaurants, sports teams, theaters, bars, coffee shops, shops and boutiques, two malls, etc." UNL helps students access to all that Lincoln has to offer by "offering a program called Arts-For-All, which allows students to go to shows at the Lied Performing Arts Center for free." These cultural activities are supplemented by "great nightlife" off campus and in downtown Lincoln. Some students think that the school "could certainly improve on our sustainability efforts and awareness," but "This issue is beginning to be addressed," with the help of some passionate students and a progressive administration.

Student Body

Students say that some of UNL's greatest strengths are "the unity among the student body and the acceptance of everyone." Though they admit that their university does "lack the multiculturalism…of other schools," they say, "There is no typical student here." "There are so many different types of people with different interests. Everyone can find a place to fit in." One thing most students have in common is that they are "friendly, fun, and laid-back," as well as "hardworking and involved." It is "easy to make friends in classes or the residence halls because everyone wants to meet people." Students love to get involved in extracurricular activities and campus-wide events, which is usually how "everyone can find a niche that suits them." "Even though it's a big school," says one student, "I never feel lost in the crowd."

FAX: 402-472-0670 • FINANCIAL AID: 402-472-2030 • E-MAIL: ADMISSIONS@UNL.EDU • WEBSITE: WWW.UNL.EDU

THE PRINCETON REVIEW SAYS

Admissions

Very important factors considered include: Class rank, standardized test scores. *Important factors considered include:* Rigor of secondary school record. *Other factors considered include:* Academic GPA, recommendation(s), first generation, talent/ability. SAT or ACT required; ACT with writing component required. TOEFL required of all international applicants. High school diploma is required and GED is accepted. *Academic units required:* 4 English, 4 mathematics, 3 science (1 science lab), 2 foreign language, 3 social studies. *Academic units recommended:* 1 history.

Financial Aid

Students should submit: FAFSA. Regular filing deadline is March 1. The Princeton Review suggests that all financial aid forms be submitted as soon as possible after January 1. *Need-based scholarships/grants offered:* Federal Pell, SEOG, state scholarships/grants, private scholarships, the school's own gift aid. *Loan aid offered:* Direct Subsidized Stafford, Direct Unsubsidized Stafford, Direct PLUS, Federal Perkins, college/university loans from institutional funds. Applicants will be notified of awards on a rolling basis beginning April 1. Federal Work-Study Program available. Institutional employment available. Off-campus job opportunities are excellent.

The Inside Word

UNL offers 150 majors and 285 programs of study. All applications will be weighed on the combined strength of course work, GPAs, and test scores. Applicants interested in applying to a specific school at UNL should take into account those school's specialized requirements as they may include additional high school course work than what is required by UNL's general studies program.

THE SCHOOL SAYS ". . ."

From the Admissions Office

"The University of Nebraska—Lincoln offers one of today's most dynamic college experiences. The university has developed a national reputation for its substantial out-of-state scholarship program, and now for its participation in the Big Ten Conference. As a result, more students nationwide are finding that the university, with all its strength in undergraduate research and education, its tradition of student engagement, its lively campus atmosphere, and its connection to downtown Lincoln, is uniquely suited to provide an enriching student experience. It is an exciting time on the University of Nebraska—Lincoln campus. As a Big Ten institution, students are able to take advantage of all the Big Ten Conference has to offer including more academic opportunities, collaboration, student discovery and value.

"Established in 1869, the University of Nebraska—Lincoln has a rich tradition of excellence. Students join more than 200,000 alumni who have made their mark as industry leaders in business, engineering, the arts, journalism, education, and the sciences. Employers and grad schools have always held UNL degrees in high regard, and the added value of Big Ten affiliation gives UNL alumni an even bigger advantage in the U.S. and around the world.

"Freshman students seeking admission should either be ranked in the upper one-half of their high school class, or have received an ACT composite score of 20 or higher or an SAT total score of 950 or higher (critical reading and math only; writing portion not considered)."

SELECTIVITY	
Admissions Rating	85
# of applicants	13,607
% of applicants accepted	96
% of acceptees attending	51

FRESHMAN PROFILE	
Range SAT Critical Reading	510–660
Range SAT Math	520–670
Range ACT Composite	22–28
Minimum paper TOEFL	523
Minimum web-based TOEFL	70
% graduated top 10% of class	26
% graduated top 25% of class	53
% graduated top 50% of class	84

DEADLINES	
Regular	
Priority	1/15
Deadline	5/1
Nonfall registration?	yes

FINANCIAL FACTS	
Financial Aid Rating	78
Annual in-state tuition	$7,648
Annual out-state tuition	$19,932
Room and board	$8,648
Books and supplies	$1,040
% needy frosh rec. need-based scholarship or grant aid	82
% needy UG rec. need-based scholarship or grant aid	78
% needy frosh rec. non-need-based scholarship or grant aid	10
% needy UG rec. non-need-based scholarship or grant aid	7
% needy frosh rec. need-based self-help aid	66
% needy UG rec. need-based self-help aid	74
% frosh rec. any financial aid	75
% UG rec. any financial aid	64
% UG borrow to pay for school	62
Average cumulative indebtedness	$21,604
% frosh need fully met	17
% ugrads need fully met	14
Average % of frosh need met	82
Average % of ugrad need met	78

University of New Hampshire

UNH Office of Admissions, Durham, NH 03824 • Admissions: 603-862-1360 • Fax: 603-862-0077

CAMPUS LIFE

Quality of Life Rating	72
Fire Safety Rating	93
Green Rating	96
Type of school	public
Environment	village

STUDENTS

Total undergrad enrollment	12,339
% male/female	45/55
% from out of state	44
% from public high school	79
% frosh live on campus	94
# of fraternities	10
# of sororities	7
% African American	1
% Asian	2
% Caucasian	87
% Hispanic	2
% international	1
# of countries represented	56

SURVEY SAYS . . .

Great library
Athletic facilities are great
Diversity lacking on campus
Frats and sororities dominate social scene
Lots of beer drinking
Hard liquor is popular

ACADEMICS

Academic Rating	74
% students returning for sophomore year	87
% students graduating within 4 years	64
Calendar	semester
Student/faculty ratio	18:1
Profs interesting rating	72
Profs accessible rating	69
Most classes have	20–29 students
Most lab/discussion sessions have	20–29 students

MOST POPULAR MAJORS

business administration and management; English language and literature; psychology

APPLICANTS ALSO LOOK AT AND OFTEN PREFER

University of Vermont, University of Massachusetts-Amherst, University of Connecticut

AND SOMETIMES PREFER

University of Rhode Island, Providence College, Boston University, Northeastern University

AND RARELY PREFER

University of Maine, Syracuse University, Boston College

STUDENTS SAY ". . ."

Academics

The benefits of going to a large, well-established state school, such as the University of New Hampshire, are exactly what one expects—its low in-state tuition, firmly established reputation, and place in the system allow it to offer "many resources to help students out in life." Located in tiny, beautiful Durham, the school "emphasizes research in every field, including non-science fields," and a lot of importance is placed "on the outdoors and the environment." The small town really fosters "lots of school spirit," and the laid-back denizens of UNH make it known that "having a good time" is a priority in their lives: "Weekends are for the Warriors." Most professors "truly care" about the students' learning so that "you never feel like a number at the school but rather a respected student," and professors "will get down and dirty when it comes to experiencing what they're teaching firsthand." Though there are definitely complaints that some can be "sub-par," a student "just needs to posses the initiative to go to their office hours" and they will get all the help they need. Some of the general education classes "are *huge*," and TAs can be difficult to understand, but for the most part, students report that they've had a "good experience" and that their academic careers has been "very successful." The Honors program is particularly challenging (in a very positive way) and offers "great seminar/inquiry classes that have about fifteen students." Students universally pan the administration, claiming it "is a massive bureaucracy that gets little done," partially due to poor communication, or one student puts it that "the left hand has no idea what the right hand is doing." "The school is way more challenging than I thought it would be because the administration makes things harder than they need to be," says a sophomore.

Life

The school is just "fifteen minutes to the beach, one hour to the mountains, and one hour to Boston," making the world a Wildcat's oyster. Partying is big here, and the weekends are crazy; "Everyone goes out pretty much every Thursday, Friday, and Saturday night." The small number of bars in town "makes the age limit pretty well enforced." After a hard night out, "there are many late night convenience stores and food places to go to." In fact, it can be "difficult to find activities to do on the weekend that don't involve drinking," though UNH does a good job of bringing in "popular comedians, musicians, bands, political figures, etc.," and the school has tons of "amazing" a capella groups, so there is "almost always something to go see." Sports are also big here: "We love our hockey and football," says a student. Though there's a pretty big housing crunch, the oft-used athletic and recreational facilities here are both convenient and excellent, and since everything on this "beautiful" campus is only about ten minutes away, "you walk pretty much everywhere," though public transportation and school-provided buses run often. Students do a lot of socializing over meals at the "eight cafés or in any of the three dining halls."

Student Body

This being New Hampshire, people are "very politically and socially aware." Students here are mostly middle-class and hail from New England (especially from New Hampshire, naturally), and a main point of contention among students is that there "is not a lot of ethnic/racial diversity," though the school is working on it. The size of UNH means that "even the most unique individual will find a group of friends," and even the most atypical students "fit in perfectly well." Most of these "laid-back" and "easy-to-get-along-with" Wildcats party, and it can be "hard to find one that doesn't." "*Everyone* skis or snowboards," and in the cold weather "Uggs and North Face fleece jackets abound."

FINANCIAL AID: 603-862-3600 • E-MAIL: ADMISSIONS@UNH.EDU • WEBSITE: WWW.UNH.EDU

THE PRINCETON REVIEW SAYS

Admissions

Very important factors considered include: Class rank, rigor of secondary school record. *Important factors considered include:* Academic GPA, recommendation(s). *Other factors considered include:* Application essay, standardized test scores, alumni/ae relation, character/personal qualities, extracurricular activities, first generation, geographical residence, racial/ethnic status, state residency, talent/ability, volunteer work, work experience. SAT or ACT required; ACT with or without writing component accepted. TOEFL required of all international applicants. High school diploma is required and GED is accepted. *Academic units required:* 4 English, 3 mathematics, 3 science (2 science labs), 2 foreign language, 3 social studies. *Academic units recommended:* 4 English, 4 mathematics, 4 science (3 science labs), 3 foreign language, 3 social studies, 1 academic electives.

Financial Aid

Students should submit: FAFSA. The Princeton Review suggests that all financial aid forms be submitted as soon as possible after January 1. *Need-based scholarships/grants offered:* Federal Pell, SEOG, state scholarships/grants, private scholarships, the school's own gift aid, Veterans Educational Benefits. *Loan aid offered:* Direct Subsidized Stafford, Direct Unsubsidized Stafford, Direct PLUS, Federal Perkins, college/university loans from institutional funds. Applicants will be notified of awards on a rolling basis beginning March 1. Federal Work-Study Program available. Institutional employment available. Highest amount earned per year from on-campus jobs $25,487. Off-campus job opportunities are excellent.

The Inside Word

New Hampshire's emphasis on academic accomplishment in the admissions process makes it clear that the admissions committee is looking for students who have taken high school seriously. Standardized tests take as much of a backseat here as is possible at a large, public university.

THE SCHOOL SAYS ". . ."

From the Admissions Office

"The University of New Hampshire is an institution best defined by the students who take advantage of its opportunities. Enrolled students who are willing to engage in a high-quality academic community in some meaningful way, who have a genuine interest in discovering or developing new ideas, and who believe in each person's obligation to improve the community they live in typify the most successful students at UNH. Undergraduate students practice these three basic values in a variety of ways: by undertaking their own, independent research projects; by collaborating in faculty research; and by participating in study abroad, residential communities, community service, and other cultural programs.

"University of New Hampshire will require all high school graduates to submit results from the new SAT or the ACT (with the writing component). The Writing portions will not be used for admissions decisions during the first two to three admissions cycles. Students graduating from high school prior to 2006 can submit results from the old SAT or ACT. The UNH admissions process does not require SAT Subject tests."

SELECTIVITY	
Admissions Rating	75
# of applicants	17,344
% of applicants accepted	74
% of acceptees attending	23

FRESHMAN PROFILE	
Range SAT Critical Reading	500–590
Range SAT Math	510–620
Range SAT Writing	500–600
Range ACT Composite	23–27
Minimum paper TOEFL	550
Minimum web-based TOEFL	80
% graduated top 10% of class	20
% graduated top 25% of class	58
% graduated top 50% of class	93

DEADLINES	
Early action	
Deadline	11/15
Notification	1/15
Regular	
Priority	2/1
Nonfall registration?	yes

FINANCIAL FACTS	
Financial Aid Rating	72
Annual in-state tuition	$13,670
Annual out-state tuition	$26,130
Room and board	$9,764
Required fees	$2,752
Books and supplies	$1,200
% needy frosh rec. need-based scholarship or grant aid	70
% needy UG rec. need-based scholarship or grant aid	65
% needy frosh rec. non-need-based scholarship or grant aid	6
% needy UG rec. non-need-based scholarship or grant aid	5
% needy frosh rec. need-based self-help aid	94
% needy UG rec. need-based self-help aid	95
% frosh rec. any financial aid	86
% UG rec. any financial aid	81
% UG borrow to pay for school	77
Average cumulative indebtedness	$34,194
% frosh need fully met	14
% ugrads need fully met	17
Average % of frosh need met	78
Average % of ugrad need met	82

UNIVERSITY OF NEW MEXICO

OFFICE OF ADMISSIONS, ALBUQUERQUE, NM 87196-4895 • ADMISSIONS: 505-277-2446 • FAX: 505-277-6686

CAMPUS LIFE

Quality of Life Rating	78
Fire Safety Rating	69
Green Rating	89
Type of school	public
Environment	metropolis

STUDENTS

Total undergrad enrollment	20,935
% male/female	45/55
% from out of state	12
% frosh live on campus	42
# of fraternities	10
# of sororities	10
% African American	3
% Asian	3
% Caucasian	40
% Hispanic	42
% international	1
# of countries represented	63

SURVEY SAYS . . .

Great computer facilities
Diverse student types on campus
Different types of students interact
Students get along with local community
Great off-campus food
Low cost of living
Students are happy
Student publications are popular

ACADEMICS

Academic Rating	68
% students returning for sophomore year	74
% students graduating within 4 years	23
% students graduating within 6 years	45
Calendar	semester
Student/faculty ratio	23:1
Profs interesting rating	72
Profs accessible rating	66
Most classes have	20–29 students
Most lab/discussion sessions have	20–29 students

MOST POPULAR MAJORS

biology/biological sciences; business administration and management; psychology

STUDENTS SAY ". . ."

Academics

Offering a "solid education" in a beautiful setting, the University of New Mexico offers "academic excellence...through some of the best teachers and tough classes." Students also cited affordability and excellent scholarships awarded to both in-state and out-of-state applicants as a decisive factor in attending UNM. The affordability also extends to "amazing opportunities to travel abroad." At UNM, "there is something here for everyone." The education program and variety of science programs—including Earth and planetary sciences, biology, and the premed and nursing programs—also attract students. Some students express frustration with it at times being "difficult to work your way around the student services system," but the "very knowledgeable" teaching faculty are roundly praised as "teachers who care." UNM students also agree that "professors are helpful [and] genuinely interested in your personal success." Professors are approachable both in class and out and "talk to and with you and not just at you." "It's very easy to come to instructors outside of class with questions," and "most professors are willing to meet with you at your convenience." As for UNM's greatest strengths, students cite both the "research-oriented staff" and "the research opportunities available. Oftentimes the research can be done with top-of-the-line equipment" nearby at Sandia National Labs, Los Alamos National Labs, and other well-known research institutes. In UNM's collaborative environment, students also often work together and "are eager to form study groups." Also, students who need additional help can rely on academic support with "tutoring, study groups and, supplemental instruction for most courses."

Life

With "ways for everyone to get involved," UNM offers "hundreds of great student organizations" providing "opportunities for fun events." There is a student group "that will fit everyone," and at UNM, "everyone seems to find their niche." Offering another opportunity to become more involved on campus, the Greek community "makes up a lot of the senate and other extracurricular activities" and "with them, any activity has fun attached." UNM students are divided in their support of the school's athletics program. With some thinking "this school should concentrate less on sports and more on academics," other students feel "attending games is a must." Students enjoy spending time at the Student Union Building (SUB), because "there is always something going on." Even with a dry campus, "a lot of people drink, just like at any college." Students often leave campus for Albuquerque and its "excellent nightlife." UNM students also mentioned attending concerts and art shows for fun. Students also go to the weekly free movies at The Cellar, and to stay active, students frequent the Johnson Gym. Students say that "hanging out at the duck pond is a great way to pass time between classes in warmer months" and, "during the winter season, there are numerous ski resorts and places to go snowboarding that are not far away."

Student Body

Time and time again, students select UNM's "diversity" as its greatest strength, and one student even stated "no one will ever feel ethnically alone since there are so many different kinds of people." This also means at UNM, "people never get boring," and "you meet someone different every day." In addition to the diversity, the prevailing atmosphere is a friendly one where "people get along regardless of origin," but "like any school there are cliques...but that does not mean they do not interact with each other." One student reserved special praise for the university, "UNM is sensitive and very engaged with its diverse population of students...concerned with facilitating in-depth inquiry and learning," and more than one student observed that at UNM, "everyone brings something to the table."

FINANCIAL AID: 505-277-8900 • E-MAIL: APPLY@UNM.EDU • WEBSITE: WWW.UNM.EDU

THE PRINCETON REVIEW SAYS

Admissions

Very important factors considered include: Academic GPA, rigor of secondary school record. *Important factors considered include:* Class rank, standardized test scores. *Other factors considered include:* Application essay, recommendation(s), character/personal qualities, extracurricular activities, first generation, volunteer work, work experience. SAT or ACT required; ACT with or without writing component accepted. TOEFL required of all international applicants. High school diploma is required and GED is accepted. *Academic units required:* 4 English, 3 mathematics, 2 science (1 science lab), 2 foreign language, 1 social studies, 1 history.

Financial Aid

Students should submit: FAFSA. The Princeton Review suggests that all financial aid forms be submitted as soon as possible after January 1. *Need-based scholarships/grants offered:* Federal Pell, SEOG, state scholarships/grants, private scholarships, the school's own gift aid, United Negro College Fund, Federal Nursing Scholarships. *Loan aid offered:* Direct Subsidized Stafford, Direct Unsubsidized Stafford, Direct PLUS, Federal Perkins, Federal Nursing, state loans, college/university loans from institutional funds. Applicants will be notified of awards on a rolling basis beginning April 15. Federal Work-Study Program available.

The Inside Word

UNM offers online applications through its website, and you will also find specific scholastic standards for traditional and nontraditional students interested in applying to UNM. Traditional applicants should have completed core coursework, taken the ACT or SAT exam and have an average or above-average GPA if they would like to be considered for admission at UNM.

THE SCHOOL SAYS ". . ."

From the Admissions Office

"The University of New Mexico is a major research institution nestled in the heart of multicultural Albuquerque on one of the nation's most beautiful and unique campuses. Students learn in an environment graced by distinctive Southwestern architecture, beautiful plazas and fountains, spectacular art and a national arboretum…all within view of the 10,000-foot Sandia Mountains. At UNM, diversity is a way of learning with education enriched by a lively mix of students being taught by a world-class research faculty that includes a Nobel laureate, a MacArthur Fellow, and members of several national academies. UNM offers more than 200 degree programs and majors and has earned national recognition in dozens of disciplines, ranging from primary care medicine and clinical law to engineering, photography, Latin American history, and intercultural communications. Research and the quest for new knowledge fuels the university's commitment to an undergraduate education where students work side-by-side with many of the finest scholars in their fields.

"The university will continue to accept SAT or ACT scores, but the University of New Mexico does not require the writing component at this time. The SAT critical reading portion will be used with the SAT Math to be considered in any admission decision based on formula. The use of ACT composite remains unchanged. These requirements are subject to change."

SELECTIVITY

Admissions Rating	**79**
# of applicants	11,410
% of applicants accepted	64
% of acceptees attending	46

FRESHMAN PROFILE

Range SAT Critical Reading	470–600
Range SAT Math	470–590
Range ACT Composite	19–25
Minimum paper TOEFL	520
Minimum web-based TOEFL	68
Average HS GPA	3.2

DEADLINES

Regular	
Priority	6/15
Nonfall registration?	yes

FINANCIAL FACTS

Financial Aid Rating	**60***
Annual in-state tuition	$6,049
Annual out-state tuition	$20,688
Room and board	$8,292
Required fees	$692
Books and supplies	$958

UNIVERSITY OF NEW ORLEANS

UNIVERSITY OF NEW ORLEANS ADMISSIONS, NEW ORLEANS, LA 70148 • ADMISSIONS: 504-280-6595 • FAX: 504-280-5522

CAMPUS LIFE

Quality of Life Rating	71
Fire Safety Rating	65
Green Rating	61
Type of school	public
Environment	metropolis

STUDENTS

Total undergrad enrollment	8,028
% male/female	51/49
% from out of state	4
% from public high school	64
% frosh live on campus	21
# of fraternities	7
# of sororities	7
% African American	16
% Asian	7
% Caucasian	55
% Hispanic	8
% Native American	1
% international	4
# of countries represented	84

SURVEY SAYS . . .

Great computer facilities
Athletic facilities are great
Diverse student types on campus
Students get along with local community

ACADEMICS

Academic Rating	67
% students returning for sophomore year	67
% students graduating within 4 years	17
Calendar	semester
Student/faculty ratio	20:1
Profs interesting rating	73
Profs accessible rating	73
Most classes have	20–29 students

MOST POPULAR MAJORS

business administration and management; general studies; psychology

STUDENTS SAY ". . ."

Academics

The University of New Orleans is a public research university in one of the world's most fascinating and unique cities. This "not too big, not too small" school is a "diverse environment that makes it a welcoming area to be" and provides "lots of opportunities to develop our personality, leadership skills, and career skills." The diversity is a huge draw to students from all over the world (international students can even receive financial aid), and UNO "opens doors to students who come from different social and economic backgrounds," giving them "the opportunity to get an education that helps students to get a better future."

Professors at this "inclusive" school "push students to do excellence." You "can always find them in their office during office hours," and they "really connect with students." The engineering, film, and accounting programs are all "programs of distinction" at UNO (accounting is one of the few accredited by AACSB International), and classes stress real-world applicability. "There has never been a moment at UNO that I wasn't able to leave the classroom and go apply what I learned to my job immediately," says one part-time student. "My professors are generous with their time and knowledge," says another. Class sizes are small, and many classes focus on discussion, which "allows for increased learning and understanding." The school is "blessed" with having a large traditional student body matched with an equal percentage of nontraditional students (adult education), which "allows great mentorship between students and also pushed both sides to be aware of how they can positively affect the other generation's education."

Life

Obviously, the fact that the school is located in New Orleans "is a big plus," and "There is never a dull moment." "Eating and nightlife in New Orleans is a big part of our lives," says a student. "There is so much to do on campus and around the city, students often have to make efforts to keep their social calendars in check so that they have time to study," says a student. The campus is large enough to offer "many diverse academic, extracurricular, and social activities," yet small enough to easily access all classes. However, "upgrading facilities" (and cleaning them) is on the wish list of pretty much everyone here.

UNO offers "plenty of on campus activities" for students "to meet and work with other students of all backgrounds," including sports, movies, and "a lot of free entertainment." There are also "always political discussions happening on campus, as well as debates." "You can feel at home here but not get bored," says a student. The older students feel similarly comfortable in their environment. "I am unusual in that I am a much older student living on campus. Yet, the younger students have accepted me warmly and I have many friends," says one.

Student Body

More so than most schools, there really is no typical at this "very eclectic university," other than "determined, hardworking, and considerate." The school's large number of international students, adult learners, commuters, and locals "tend to get along rather well," with "those who live right on or near campus probably being more close-knit." Many students live off campus and work full time, which "creates in an environment where the people in your classes are there for a purpose." People here are "very colorful and outgoing" and "have no problem expressing themselves whether it's through clothing, lifestyles, or speech." "It is very easy to make friends here," says a student.

FINANCIAL AID: 504-280-6603 • E-MAIL: ADMISSIONS@UNO.EDU • WEBSITE: WWW.UNO.EDU

THE PRINCETON REVIEW SAYS

Admissions

Very important factors considered include: Class rank, academic GPA, rigor of secondary school record, standardized test scores. *Other factors considered include:* Recommendation(s), geographical residence, state residency. SAT or ACT required; ACT with or without writing component accepted. TOEFL required of all international applicants. High school diploma is required and GED is accepted. *Academic units required:* 4 English, 3 mathematics, 3 science, 2 foreign language, 1 social studies, 2 history, 1 visual/performing arts.

Financial Aid

Students should submit: FAFSA. The Princeton Review suggests that all financial aid forms be submitted as soon as possible after January 1. *Need-based scholarships/grants offered:* Federal Pell, SEOG, state scholarships/grants, private scholarships, the school's own gift aid. *Loan aid offered:* Direct Subsidized Stafford, Direct Unsubsidized Stafford, Direct PLUS, Federal Perkins, college/university loans from institutional funds. Applicants will be notified of awards on a rolling basis beginning April 20. Federal Work-Study Program available. Institutional employment available. Highest amount earned per year from on-campus jobs $23,920.

The Inside Word

Admission is straightforward here. Complete a basic college-bound high school curriculum with a GPA of at least 2.5 (with no remedial course work) and get at least an 23 on your ACT (SAT 1060), including a minimum score at or above 19 Math (460 SAT), 18 English (450 SAT). Nontraditional students who don't want to pay the exorbitant prices of the more well-known private universities in New Orleans can find their niche at UNO; if you're twenty-five or older, the only requirement for admission is a legitimate high school diploma or a GED.

THE SCHOOL SAYS ". . ."

From the Admissions Office

"The University of New Orleans has a wide array of academic programs. Quality student life programs include a campus bar, first-run movies, and a host of exciting student activities."

"UNO embraces its mission by providing the best educational opportunities for undergraduate and graduate students, conducting world-class research, and serving a diverse and cultured community in critical areas. UNO's most outstanding offerings include a doctoral program in conservation biology, providing training in the most advanced molecular biological techniques; the largest U.S. undergraduate program in Naval Architecture and Marine Engineering; a leading jazz studies program; one of the top five film programs in the country; and the only graduate arts administration program in the Gulf South.

"UNO will use the total score from the critical reading/verbal and math sub sections of the SAT or the composite score for the ACT. The writing components of the ACT and SAT will be used for placement purposes, but not for admission purposes, at the time."

SELECTIVITY	
Admissions Rating	82
# of applicants	3,353
% of applicants accepted	56
% of acceptees attending	59
FRESHMAN PROFILE	
Range SAT Critical Reading	480–590
Range SAT Math	460–590
Range ACT Composite	19–24
Minimum paper TOEFL	525
Minimum web-based TOEFL	71
Average HS GPA	3.0
% graduated top 10% of class	12
% graduated top 25% of class	30
% graduated top 50% of class	61
DEADLINES	
Regular	
Priority	7/1
Nonfall registration?	yes
FINANCIAL FACTS	
Financial Aid Rating	66
Annual in-state tuition	$4,644
Annual out-state tuition	$16,168
Room and board	$8,310
Required fees	$613
Books and supplies	$1,300
% needy frosh rec. need-based scholarship or grant aid	76
% needy UG rec. need-based scholarship or grant aid	63
% needy frosh rec. non-need-based scholarship or grant aid	55
% needy UG rec. non-need-based scholarship or grant aid	34
% needy frosh rec. need-based self-help aid	43
% needy UG rec. need-based self-help aid	45
% frosh rec. any financial aid	75
% UG rec. any financial aid	63
% UG borrow to pay for school	19
Average cumulative indebtedness	$18,106
% frosh need fully met	6
% ugrads need fully met	9
Average % of frosh need met	50
Average % of ugrad need met	57

THE UNIVERSITY OF NORTH CAROLINA AT ASHEVILLE

CPO #1320, ASHEVILLE, NC 28804-8502 • ADMISSIONS: 828-251-6481 • FAX: 828-251-6482

CAMPUS LIFE

Quality of Life Rating	93
Fire Safety Rating	92
Green Rating	80
Type of school	public
Environment	town

STUDENTS

Total undergrad enrollment	3,334
% male/female	43/57
% from out of state	14
% from public high school	87
% frosh live on campus	93
# of fraternities	1
# of sororities	2
% African American	3
% Asian	1
% Caucasian	86
% Hispanic	4
% international	1
# of countries represented	24

SURVEY SAYS . . .

No one cheats
Students are friendly
Students get along with local community
Students love Asheville, NC
Great off-campus food
Dorms are like palaces
Students are happy
Political activism is popular
Students are environmentally aware

ACADEMICS

Academic Rating	84
% students returning for sophomore year	81
% students graduating within 4 years	33
% students graduating within 6 years	61
Calendar	semester
Student/faculty ratio	14:1
Profs interesting rating	96
Profs accessible rating	90
Most classes have	10–19 students
Most lab/discussion sessions have	20–29 students

MOST POPULAR MAJORS

English language and literature; psychology; sociology

STUDENTS SAY ". . ."

Academics

Undergrads at UNC—Asheville rave about their top-notch academic experience. Professors are "devoted and passionate [about] their fields of study, and it shows in the classroom." Importantly, "even though you may not be totally fascinated by the subject initially, the professors' enthusiasm for each course is contagious." Students also appreciate Asheville's "liberal arts ideology." As one senior English lit major says, "It's wonderful when every semester, at least two seemingly unrelated classes end up teaching the same lessons through different means and subjects." Though "course material is challenging," students take solace in knowing that "an A is totally achievable." This is due in part to the fact that "professors are available and more than willing to assist students outside of class." One environmental studies major adds, "The classes are small enough that the professors know you by name and seem to care if you do well." Furthermore, "tutoring sessions…are free and plentiful" for those undergrads who feel that they require more assistance. There are some undergrads who feel that the administration is "relatively detached from school life" and "out of touch with the students," others taut the deans as being "unusually accessible."

Life

With roughly "two-thirds of [the] student [body] living off-campus," some undergrads warn that life "can be slow on the weekends." Fortunately, one senior confidently declares that campus life "has started to pick up in the last few years." Freshman are required to live on campus their first year. Indeed, "students enjoy a wide range of activities" from playing "Frisbee golf on the quad" to attending one of many "lectures" or "basketball games" held on campus. While there is a Greek system, "partying does not define the school." Many students are "environmentally conscious" and spend a lot of energy helping shape "campus policies, including [instituting] new, reusable take-out boxes from the school cafeteria." Undergrads love the fact that they are nestled "in the Blue Ridge Mountains." The university offers a fantastic "outdoors program that [hosts] popular rock-climbing, caving, hiking, and kayaking [trips]." Students also give hometown Asheville high marks. One student says, "You can't take three steps downtown without tripping over some kind of festival or street performance." A favorite Asheville activity for many students is "the drum circle" where "people gather every Friday evening (in warm weather), circulating, dancing, thrumming, and drumming. Drummers, amateur to experienced, bring their own instruments to bang upon. People without personal beat abilities twist through the crowds to dance or simply watch from the sidelines."

Student Body

UNC—Asheville seems to hold appeal for self-described "hippies." One sophomore says, "This school attracts the sort of people who get excited about local, organic, dairy-free muffins and sandals made from recycled flax." Indeed many undergrads "care about the environment, [are] liberal-leaning, enjoy the outdoors, [and are] pretty sociable." Happily, the university "fosters the idea that individuality is essential," and students assure us that everyone "is easily accepted here" regardless of political affiliation. Perhaps this acceptance stems from the fact that the campus welcomes students from a variety of "economic backgrounds, religious backgrounds and sexual orientations." Asheville does manage to attract both a large number of "commuter students" as well as "a lot of nontraditional students."

FINANCIAL AID: 828-251-6535 • E-MAIL: ADMISSIONS@UNCA.EDU • WEBSITE: WWW.UNCA.EDU

THE PRINCETON REVIEW SAYS

Admissions

Very important factors considered include: Class rank, academic GPA, rigor of secondary school record. *Important factors considered include:* Application essay, recommendation(s), standardized test scores. *Other factors considered include:* Alumni/ae relation, extracurricular activities, first generation, geographical residence, interview, level of applicant's interest, racial/ethnic status, state residency, talent/ability, volunteer work, work experience. SAT or ACT required; ACT with writing component required. TOEFL required of all international applicants. High school diploma is required and GED is not accepted. *Academic units required:* 4 English, 4 mathematics, 3 science (1 science lab), 2 foreign language, 1 social studies, 1 history. *Academic units recommended:* 4 academic electives.

Financial Aid

Students should submit: FAFSA. The Princeton Review suggests that all financial aid forms be submitted as soon as possible after January 1. *Need-based scholarships/grants offered:* Federal Pell, SEOG, state scholarships/grants, private scholarships, the school's own gift aid. *Loan aid offered:* Direct Subsidized Stafford, Direct Unsubsidized Stafford, Direct PLUS, Federal Perkins, state loans, college/university loans from institutional funds. Applicants will be notified of awards on a rolling basis beginning March 15. Federal Work-Study Program available. Institutional employment available. Off-campus job opportunities are good.

The Inside Word

UNC—Asheville provides a sound public education in a small campus atmosphere, and an increasing number of students are setting their sights on it each year. In kind, the school works diligently to create a diverse student body and thoroughly analyzes each application it receives. Although selectivity is rising, candidates who demonstrate reasonable academic success and involvement in a variety of extracurricular activities should be able to secure admittance.

THE SCHOOL SAYS ". . ."

From the Admissions Office

"If you want to learn how to think, how to analyze and solve problems on your own, and how to become your own best teacher then, a broad-based liberal arts education is the key. UNC Asheville focuses on undergraduates, with a core curriculum covering natural science, math, social sciences, humanities, language and culture, arts and ideas, and health and fitness. Students thrive in small classes, with a faculty dedicated first of all to teaching. The liberal arts emphasis develops discriminating thinkers, expert and creative communicators with a passion for learning. These are qualities you need for today's challenges and the changes of tomorrow.

"The University of North Carolina at Asheville requires the SAT or for students submitting an ACT score, the ACT with the writing component."

SELECTIVITY	
Admissions Rating	83
# of applicants	2,947
% of applicants accepted	68
% of acceptees attending	27

FRESHMAN PROFILE	
Range SAT Critical Reading	540–640
Range SAT Math	530–620
Range SAT Writing	510–630
Range ACT Composite	24–28
Minimum paper TOEFL	550
Minimum web-based TOEFL	79
Average HS GPA	3.9
% graduated top 10% of class	20
% graduated top 25% of class	55
% graduated top 50% of class	95

DEADLINES	
Early action	
Deadline	11/15
Notification	12/15
Regular	
Priority	11/15
Deadline	2/15
Notification	3/15
Nonfall registration?	yes

FINANCIAL FACTS	
Financial Aid Rating	86
Annual in-state tuition	$3,166
Annual out-state tuition	$16,798
Room and board	$7,302
Required fees	$2,227
Books and supplies	$950
% needy frosh rec. need-based scholarship or grant aid	97
% needy UG rec. need-based scholarship or grant aid	95
% needy frosh rec. non-need-based scholarship or grant aid	10
% needy UG rec. non-need-based scholarship or grant aid	13
% needy frosh rec. need-based self-help aid	66
% needy UG rec. need-based self-help aid	70
% frosh rec. any financial aid	72
% UG rec. any financial aid	68
% UG borrow to pay for school	53
Average cumulative indebtedness	$16,252
% frosh need fully met	41
% ugrads need fully met	44
Average % of frosh need met	83
Average % of ugrad need met	84

THE UNIVERSITY OF NORTH CAROLINA AT CHAPEL HILL

CAMPUS BOX #2200, CHAPEL HILL, NC 27599-2200 • ADMISSIONS: 919-966-3621 • FAX: 919-962-3045

CAMPUS LIFE

Quality of Life Rating	**96**
Fire Safety Rating	**86**
Green Rating	**95**
Type of school	public
Environment	town

STUDENTS

Total undergrad enrollment	17,791
% male/female	42/58
% from out of state	17
% from public high school	79
# of fraternities	32
# of sororities	23
% African American	9
% Asian	7
% Caucasian	66
% Hispanic	9
% Native American	1
% international	3
# of countries represented	97

SURVEY SAYS . . .

Low cost of living
Everyone loves the Tar Heels
Student publications are popular
Students are happy
Great library
Students love Chapel Hill, NC
Great off-campus food
Athletic facilities are great
Intramural sports are popular

ACADEMICS

Academic Rating	**82**
% students graduating within 4 years	77
Calendar	semester
Student/faculty ratio	14:1
Profs interesting rating	79
Profs accessible rating	77
Most classes have	10–19 students
Most lab/discussion sessions have	10–19 students

MOST POPULAR MAJORS

biology/biological sciences; business administration and management; psychology

APPLICANTS ALSO LOOK AT AND SOMETIMES PREFER

Duke University, University of Virginia

AND RARELY PREFER

Wake Forest University, North Carolina State University

STUDENTS SAY ". . ."

Academics

It's quite an understatement to say students at UNC—Chapel Hill are proud of their school. One calls it his "dream school," while another calls it the "perfect mixture of academics, sports, and social life." Although its relative low cost makes UNC a great bargain in higher education, academic rigor doesn't take a back seat, and the vast majority of students say it's one of the main reasons they chose the school. The journalism, business, and nursing programs are ranked among the best in the country, but the students hail the overall liberal arts curriculum because it creates well-rounded adults who "can handle any intellectual obstacle." In describing the instructors, students use words like "world-class," "brilliant," and "incredible," while also noting that they're "warm," "welcoming," and "passionate" about their work and their students. "Most of my professors have been great, and some have been phenomenal." Faculty members are generous with their time outside of class, patiently explaining "even the most difficult material" and using e-mail to announce changes. Some complain about large classes and warn incoming students that they will have to take the initiative and "speak up," because they won't be "coddled." The school's academic-advising system still comes in for sharp criticism. "Students are on their own there," one student says.

Life

With more than 17,000 undergrads, UNC is large enough that students rarely are lacking for something to do. Tar Heel men's basketball probably is at the top of the list; indeed, for many rabid fans, the Dean Smith Center is the center of the universe, especially when Duke is the opponent. One student sums up the school's essence this way: "It's the feeling of running through the beautiful old quad by Davie Poplar on the way to Franklin Street after a big win." The consensus is maintaining grades requires such an effort, letting off steam on weekends is a reward. "Life at UNC is full throttle. People work hard and play hard." Many flock to the bars, restaurants and coffee shops of Franklin Street, but others prefer the music scene in nearby Carrboro or staying on campus to participate in a function sponsored by one of the hundreds of student groups. The campus itself is gorgeous and filled with history. Although only seventeen percent of students belong to a fraternity or sorority, the Greek organizations are a big part of the social scene. "When you're writing thirty-page papers on twentieth-century German philosophy and working two jobs, a night where you get to dress up as a biker chick and listen to AC/DC all night at the bar is a welcome reprieve," one sorority member says.

Student Body

One student after another comments about the feeling of generosity that pervades UNC—"the epitome of Southern hospitality"—and how it extends beyond mere school spirit and the wearing of Carolina blue and white on game days. "Carolina is family," one student says. "Most of us here are crazy about sports, but most will do anything at all to help a fellow UNC student." "Although the student body is very diverse, a commonality among students is the desire to serve others and work for humanitarian efforts." One reason for the closeness is that the vast majority of students hail from the Tar Heel state. So there are "lots of down-home, North Carolina types who excelled in their rural high schools." Students and faculty are viewed as leaning liberal politically, which makes for some interesting exchanges. "Political activism is huge here," a student says. But even though it's a vast school, "it has a place for everyone." "There are really only two common denominators: commitment to some kind of excellence (academic, extracurricular, etc.) and rooting against Duke."

THE UNIVERSITY OF NORTH CAROLINA AT CHAPEL HILL

FINANCIAL AID: 919-962-8396 • E-MAIL: UNCHELP@ADMISSIONS.UNC.EDU • WEBSITE: WWW.UNC.EDU

THE PRINCETON REVIEW SAYS

Admissions

Very important factors considered include: Class rank, application essay, academic GPA, recommendation(s), rigor of secondary school record, standardized test scores, character/personal qualities, extracurricular activities, state residency, talent/ability. *Important factors considered include:* Alumni/ae relation, first generation, racial/ethnic status, volunteer work, work experience. SAT or ACT required; ACT with writing component required. TOEFL required of all international applicants. High school diploma is required and GED is not accepted. *Academic units required:* 4 English, 4 mathematics, 3 science (1 science lab), 2 foreign language, 1 social studies, 1 history.

Financial Aid

Students should submit: FAFSA, CSS/Financial Aid PROFILE. The Princeton Review suggests that all financial aid forms be submitted as soon as possible after January 1. *Need-based scholarships/grants offered:* Federal Pell, SEOG, state scholarships/grants, private scholarships, the school's own gift aid, State Grants. *Loan aid offered:* Direct Subsidized Stafford, Direct Unsubsidized Stafford, Direct PLUS, Federal Perkins, state loans, college/university loans from institutional funds, alternative loans. Applicants will be notified of awards on a rolling basis beginning March 15. Federal Work-Study Program available. Institutional employment available. Off-campus job opportunities are good.

The Inside Word

UNC's admissions process is highly selective. North Carolina students compete against other students from across the state for eighty-two percent of all spaces available in the freshman class; out-of-state students compete for the remaining eighteen percent of the spaces. State residents will find the admissions standards high, and out-of-state applicants will find that it's one of the hardest offers of admission to come by in the country.

THE SCHOOL SAYS ". . ."

From the Admissions Office

"One of the leading research and teaching institutions in the world, UNC Chapel Hill offers first-rate faculty, innovative academic programs, and students who are smart, friendly, and committed to public service. Students take full advantage of extensive undergraduate research opportunities, a study abroad program with programs on every continent except Antarctica, and 600-plus clubs and organizations. We offer all this in Chapel Hill, one of the greatest and most welcoming college towns anywhere.

"Carolina's commitment to excellence, access, and affordability is reflected in premier scholarships, such as the prestigious Morehead and Robertson Scholarships, as well the Carolina Covenant, a national model that enables students from low-income families to graduate from Carolina debt-free. We invite you to visit—talk with our professors, attend a class, spend time with our students, and stroll across our beautiful residential campus, where friendly people and exciting events are within easy walking distance.

"All first-year applicants are required to submit an SAT or an ACT writing component score. While test scores are important, our holistic review process includes other important factors such course work, grades, and extracurricular activities."

SELECTIVITY	
Admissions Rating	98
# of applicants	22,652
% of applicants accepted	33
% of acceptees attending	54
# accepting a place on wait list	2,015
# admitted from wait list	192
FRESHMAN PROFILE	
Range SAT Critical Reading	590–70
Range SAT Math	610–700
Range SAT Writing	590–690
Range ACT Composite	27–32
Minimum paper TOEFL	600
Minimum web-based TOEFL	100
Average HS GPA	4.5
% graduated top 10% of class	80
% graduated top 25% of class	97
% graduated top 50% of class	99
DEADLINES	
Early action	
Deadline	10/15
Notification	1/31
Regular	
Deadline	1/5
Nonfall registration?	no
FINANCIAL FACTS	
Financial Aid Rating	92
Annual in-state tuition	$7,008
Annual out-state tuition	$26,834
Room and board	$9,470
Required fees	$1,880
Books and supplies	$1,150
% needy frosh rec. need-based scholarship or grant aid	98
% needy UG rec. need-based scholarship or grant aid	98
% needy frosh rec. non-need-based scholarship or grant aid	10
% needy UG rec. non-need-based scholarship or grant aid	7
% needy frosh rec. need-based self-help aid	54
% needy UG rec. need-based self-help aid	65
% frosh rec. any financial aid	71
% UG rec. any financial aid	64
% UG borrow to pay for school	37
Average cumulative indebtedness	$17,525
% frosh need fully met	88
% ugrads need fully met	87
Average % of frosh need met	100
Average % of ugrad need met	100

THE UNIVERSITY OF NORTH CAROLINA AT GREENSBORO

1400 Spring Garden Street, Greensboro, NC 27402-6170 • Admissions: 336-334-5243 • Fax: 336-334-4180

CAMPUS LIFE

Quality of Life Rating	73
Fire Safety Rating	71
Green Rating	73
Type of school	public
Environment	city

STUDENTS

Total undergrad enrollment	14,545
% male/female	33/67
% from out of state	8
% from public high school	95
% frosh live on campus	81
# of fraternities	11
# of sororities	11
% African American	24
% Asian	4
% Caucasian	65
% Hispanic	5
% international	1
# of countries represented	82

SURVEY SAYS . . .

Great computer facilities
Diverse student types on campus
Different types of students interact
Students get along with local community
Students are happy

ACADEMICS

Academic Rating	70
% students returning for sophomore year	77
% students graduating within 4 years	29
% students graduating within 6 years	53
Calendar	semester
Student/faculty ratio	17:1
Profs interesting rating	72
Profs accessible rating	69
Most classes have	20–29 students
Most lab/discussion sessions have	20–29 students

MOST POPULAR MAJORS

biology/biological sciences; business administration and management; nursing/registered nurse (rn, asn, bsn, msn)

STUDENTS SAY ". . ."

Academics

Students describe the University of North Carolina at Greensboro as "about a half-and-half commuter school with great specialized programs and schools such as nursing, education, dance, and music." Undergrads here praise the "high quality of education at a significantly reduced rate, while having the smaller classes allowing closer bonds between faculty and students" than one could reasonably expect for the tuition charged. The key here is the faculty, because according to one student, "UNCG places a big emphasis on having great teachers. There are some duds, but overall, more of them are fantastic than anything else." The school excels in some off-the-beaten-path areas like programs in kinesiology, deaf education, human development, and family studies, which all receive enthusiastic praise from students. Undergrads also love the "opportunities that are given to network with businesses and people outside of campus" and the "great internships" the school helps them find. Nontraditional students appreciate the "great support system for adult students." As the school's reputation continues to improve, some worry this "historically moderate-sized university where student well-being was the first priority...will change into a large research university where the focus is raising more and more money." One undeniable upside of the school's increased stature is that "you feel like you are respected in the community when you tell someone that you are a student at UNCG."

Life

UNCG is conveniently located "a mile from downtown and close to surrounding schools: Guilford College, NC A&T, Greensboro College, Elon, UNC, NC State." One student observes, "With six colleges around UNCG, a metropolis of 250,000-plus (1.1 million in the metro area), and access within a three-hour drive to both beaches and mountains, there is always something to do." On campus "UNCG makes it easy for anyone and everyone to fit in and feel included. Through clubs, students have the ability to offer ideas and have them implemented. There's also intramural sports and free events." The high-profile arts programs on campus yield some wonderful cultural opportunities. "The Weatherspoon Museum of Art is amazing at showcasing the most modern American art and keeps this provincial little town on its toes," writes one artist. A performing arts student adds, "There are wonderful concerts and plays and lectures here. It's a great cultural center and you can always have something to do as long as you look for it." Intercollegiate athletics, students tell us, "are not as popular as they could be, even though they are often ranked nationally, or at least ranked in the conference." Many here feel the addition of a football team (the school has none) would change that. "It would really bring the school spirit up," opines one undergrad. The school's many commuters warn that "parking is horrendous."

Student Body

UNCG is a big school with "many people from all walks of life, social/cultural backgrounds, etc. The university promotes cultural diversity and acceptance and tolerance of people of different backgrounds." One student reports, "One minute you see a bunch of music majors talking about how much Bach has affected their life, and the next minute, you see a bunch of sorority girls discussing the Gap. Mainly, I have observed that sorority girls stick together, jocks stick together, etc." As at many state schools, "about half of the students at UNCG came here to party. The other half consists of hard-working students who are generally frustrated with the slacker mentality in a lot of our classes. This is less of a problem once you get past the intro-level lectures."

FINANCIAL AID: 336-334-5702 • E-MAIL: ADMISSIONS@UNCG.EDU • WEBSITE: WWW.UNCG.EDU

THE PRINCETON REVIEW SAYS

Admissions

Very important factors considered include: Academic GPA, rigor of secondary school record, essay. *Other factors considered include:* Recommendation(s). SAT or ACT required; ACT with writing component required. TOEFL required of all international applicants. High school diploma is required and GED is not accepted. *Academic units required:* 4 English, 4 mathematics, 3 science (1 science lab), 2 foreign language, 2 social studies.

Financial Aid

Students should submit: FAFSA. The Princeton Review suggests that all financial aid forms be submitted as soon as possible after January 1. *Need-based scholarships/grants offered:* Federal Pell, SEOG, state scholarships/grants, private scholarships, the school's own gift aid. *Loan aid offered:* Direct Subsidized Stafford, Direct Unsubsidized Stafford, Direct PLUS, Federal Perkins, college/university loans from institutional funds. Applicants will be notified of awards on a rolling basis beginning March 15. Federal Work-Study Program available. Institutional employment available. Off-campus job opportunities are good.

The Inside Word

UNCG has yet to gain much attention outside of regional circles so, at least for the moment, gaining admission is not particularly difficult. The usual public university considerations apply; expect the admissions office to focus on grades and test scores, and not much else. Out-of-staters will find a much smoother path to admission here than at Chapel Hill and will still be within reasonable reach of internship and career possibilities in the Research Triangle.

THE SCHOOL SAYS ". . ."

From the Admissions Office

"UNCG is committed to student success. Challenging academic programs and exceptional teaching provide a solid learning foundation in a supportive environment. Hands-on experiences in internships, undergraduate research, and service-learning programs bring learning to life. An ambitious expansion of on-campus housing and learning communities (now open to more than half of our freshman class) creates a close-knit campus atmosphere and an engaged community.

"In addition to excellence in our academic programs, we are looking for students with outstanding records who will benefit from these challenging programs. As admission to UNCG becomes more competitive, our goal is to assess students' entire academic record, beginning with a combination of their overall cumulative grade point average (GPA) and SAT or ACT scores. Freshmen applicants must submit at least one SAT or ACT score (including the writing component). We also will review other factors such as students' entire high school record, course selection, senior class schedule, and a short essay.

"UNCG students can broaden their experience by taking advantage of one of the most extensive and affordable study abroad programs in the country. The Lloyd International Honors College offers a unique opportunity for talented students in any major to benefit from a rich intellectual life with a global perspective. UNCG's ideal size enables students to excel as individuals and get connected through more than 180 student organizations, intramural, club and intercollegiate sports, Greeks, outdoor adventures, a vibrant arts community, and a friendly Southern city that quickly starts to feel like home."

SELECTIVITY	
Admissions Rating	**79**
# of applicants	10,936
% of applicants accepted	58
% of acceptees attending	38

FRESHMAN PROFILE	
Range SAT Critical Reading	470–570
Range SAT Math	490–580
Range SAT Writing	460–560
Minimum paper TOEFL	550
Minimum web-based TOEFL	79
Average HS GPA	3.6
% graduated top 10% of class	19
% graduated top 25% of class	44
% graduated top 50% of class	80

DEADLINES	
Regular	
Priority	11/1
Deadline	3/1
Nonfall registration?	yes

FINANCIAL FACTS	
Financial Aid Rating	**72**
Annual in-state tuition	$3,779
Annual out-state tuition	$17,577
Room and board	$6,564
Required fees	$2,357
Books and supplies	$1,300
% needy frosh rec. need-based scholarship or grant aid	58
% needy UG rec. need-based scholarship or grant aid	59
% needy frosh rec. non-need-based scholarship or grant aid	75
% needy UG rec. non-need-based scholarship or grant aid	72
% needy frosh rec. need-based self-help aid	60
% needy UG rec. need-based self-help aid	64
% frosh rec. any financial aid	77
% UG rec. any financial aid	71
% UG borrow to pay for school	67
Average cumulative indebtedness	$23,772
% frosh need fully met	25
% ugrads need fully met	23
Average % of frosh need met	58
Average % of ugrad need met	58

UNIVERSITY OF NORTH DAKOTA

205 TWAMLEY HALL, 264 CENTENNIAL DRIVE STREET, GRAND FORKS, ND 58202-8357 • ADMISSIONS: 800-225-5863 • FAX: 701-777-3367

CAMPUS LIFE

Quality of Life Rating	**68**
Fire Safety Rating	**74**
Green Rating	**85**
Type of school	public
Environment	town

STUDENTS

Total undergrad enrollment	11,522
% male/female	55/45
% from out of state	56
% from public high school	92
% frosh live on campus	88
# of fraternities	12
# of sororities	6
% African American	2
% Asian	1
% Caucasian	83
% Hispanic	2
% Native American	2
% international	6
# of countries represented	60

SURVEY SAYS . . .

Great computer facilities
Athletic facilities are great
Students are friendly
Everyone loves the Fighting Sioux
Student publications are popular
Lots of beer drinking
Hard liquor is popular

ACADEMICS

Academic Rating	**66**
% students returning for sophomore year	77
% students graduating within 4 years	24
% students graduating within 6 years	51
Calendar	semester
Student/faculty ratio	21.1:1
Profs interesting rating	67
Profs accessible rating	66
Most classes have	20–29 students
Most lab/discussion sessions have	20–29 students

MOST POPULAR MAJORS

airline/commercial/professional pilot and flight crew; nursing/registered nurse (rn, asn, bsn, msn); psychology

APPLICANTS ALSO LOOK AT AND OFTEN PREFER

Saint Cloud State University, University of Minnesota-Duluth

AND RARELY PREFER

Concordia College-Moorehead, Minot State University, University of Minnesota-Crookston

STUDENTS SAY ". . ."

Academics

The University of North Dakota, located in the town of Grand Forks, is a public university that is "incredibly proud of its aviation department," and many students agree that the pride shows through. While the professors early in a student's career may be a little some of "a mixed bag," everyone agrees that almost every professor is "willing to help…outside of class at any time." And once students get beyond the general education classes and into their majors, most professors are "absolutely great and inspiring," "specifically in [the] College of Aerospace Sciences." Many of the professors in the College of Aerospace Sciences, and a few other colleges in the university, such as the College of Nursing, have "worked in [their respective] industry," before coming to UND to teach. It's a sincere desire of the professors that each student learns the material and real-world applications and doesn't just "pass the class," that probably leads to the school's "high employment rate after graduation." The school also offers a "distance education program" that allows students to attend "completely online" and to participate in "intensive labs" and lectures via the Internet for those who want to pursue their educations without giving up their full-time jobs. Whichever path students choose, everyone praises the "low cost" and says, "You will not find a better education for the same amount of money." Students also understand that with those reasonable tuitions come some compromises. While there are quite a few nice buildings, such as the previously mentioned aviation department, students remark that the general education buildings are "a tad outdated."

Life

Opinions range on the size and options for scenic hang outs in the city of Grand Forks, with some calling it a "pretty decent-sized town," and others saying, "The town offers little to do." Most people tend to make their own fun, and "partying" seems to be fairly prevalent. Most students tend to stay inside as the weather can get "freezing cold" during the winter months. A program called Nightlife, put together by various student organizations, holds events every Friday and Saturday night, and most students try "to attend every UND Nightlife [event]." Hockey games are another event that everyone raves about, saying they are "a blast to go to, whether you like hockey or not." There is also a new "state-of-the-art" gym that is "extremely popular," and it offers a lot of free classes for students. While many students choose to live off-campus, a decent amount of students complain about the "lack of parking" for those who commute.

Student Body

A "typical" student at University of North Dakota is "someone who goes to class, but also balances their time being involved in organizations." Most are usually involved in numerous student groups, but they always make sure to have the time to "work out and hang with friends." Students seem to mostly come from one of two places: either "rural North Dakota or from the Twin Cities." Many notice "a divide along those lines." Most are Caucasian, leading some students to cite the University's need to draw in a slightly "more diverse" crowd.

FINANCIAL AID: 701-777-3121 • E-MAIL: ENROLLMENTSERVICES@UND.EDU • WEBSITE: WWW.UND.EDU

THE PRINCETON REVIEW SAYS

Admissions

Very important factors considered include: Academic GPA, standardized test scores. *Other factors considered include:* Class rank, rigor of secondary school record. SAT or ACT required; ACT with or without writing component accepted. TOEFL required of all international applicants. High school diploma is required and GED is accepted. *Academic units required:* 4 English, 3 mathematics, 3 science (3 science labs), 3 social studies. *Academic units recommended:* 1 foreign language.

Financial Aid

Students should submit: FAFSA. Regular filing deadline is February 15. The Princeton Review suggests that all financial aid forms be submitted as soon as possible after January 1. *Need-based scholarships/grants offered:* Federal Pell, SEOG, state scholarships/grants, private scholarships, the school's own gift aid, Federal Nursing Scholarships. *Loan aid offered:* Direct Subsidized Stafford, Direct Unsubsidized Stafford, Direct PLUS, Federal Perkins, Federal Nursing, alternative commercial loans. Applicants will be notified of awards on a rolling basis beginning May 15. Federal Work-Study Program available. Institutional employment available. Highest amount earned per year from on-campus jobs $2,071. Off-campus job opportunities are excellent.

The Inside Word

As a potential incoming undergraduate or transfer student, the University of North Dakota is ready and willing to help you apply; the website has applications broken down by section, and for those unable to schedule a visit in person, there is also a virtual tour of campus. You'll also find an admission chart to help you see if you would be acceptable for admission: The higher your GPA, the lower your SAT and ACT scores can be and vice-versa. However, the school says that everyone should apply for admission, even if you don't meet these standards, since your application will be reviewed by a committee that may make the decision based on other factors.

THE SCHOOL SAYS ". . ."

From the Admissions Office

"More than 11,000 undergraduate students come to the University of North Dakota each year, from every state in the nation and more than sixty countries. They're impressed by our academic excellence, more than 200 programs, our dedication to the liberal arts mission, and alumni success record. Nearly all of the university's new students rank in the top half of their high school classes, with about half in the top quarter. As the oldest and most diversified institution of higher education in the Dakotas, Montana, Wyoming, and western Minnesota, UND is a comprehensive teaching and research university. Yet the university provides individual attention that may be missing at very large universities. UND graduates are highly regarded among prospective employers. Representatives from more than 200 regional and national companies recruit UND students every year. Our campus is approximately ninety-eight percent accessible.

"Students applying for admission to UND are required to take either the ACT or SAT unless they are older than twenty-five. The ACT writing component is not a requirement for admission, and SAT results considered include only the math and critical reading sections."

SELECTIVITY	
Admissions Rating	**74**
# of applicants	4,857
% of applicants accepted	71
% of acceptees attending	61
FRESHMAN PROFILE	
Range ACT Composite	21–26
Minimum paper TOEFL	525
Minimum web-based TOEFL	195
Average HS GPA	3.4
% graduated top 10% of class	14
% graduated top 25% of class	42
% graduated top 50% of class	73
DEADLINES	
Nonfall registration?	yes
FINANCIAL FACTS	
Financial Aid Rating	**85**
Annual in-state tuition	$5,793
Annual out-state tuition	$15,468
Room and board	$6,100
Required fees	$1,298
Books and supplies	$800
% needy frosh rec. need-based scholarship or grant aid	79
% needy UG rec. need-based scholarship or grant aid	73
% needy frosh rec. non-need-based scholarship or grant aid	2
% needy UG rec. non-need-based scholarship or grant aid	1
% needy frosh rec. need-based self-help aid	90
% needy UG rec. need-based self-help aid	90
% frosh rec. any financial aid	84
% UG rec. any financial aid	65
% UG borrow to pay for school	85
Average cumulative indebtedness	$31,959
% frosh need fully met	97
% ugrads need fully met	98
Average % of frosh need met	47
Average % of ugrad need met	54

University of Notre Dame

220 Main Building, Notre Dame, IN 46556 • Admissions: 574-631-7505 • Fax: 574-631-8865

CAMPUS LIFE

Quality of Life Rating	76
Fire Safety Rating	85
Green Rating	85
Type of school	private
Affiliation	Roman Catholic
Environment	city

STUDENTS

Total undergrad enrollment	8,433
% male/female	54/46
% from out of state	89
% from public high school	50
% frosh live on campus	100
% African American	3
% Asian	6
% Caucasian	74
% Hispanic	10
% international	3
# of countries represented	89

SURVEY SAYS . . .

School is well run
Great food on campus
Everyone loves the Fighting Irish
Frats and sororities are unpopular or nonexistent
Student publications are popular

ACADEMICS

Academic Rating	84
% students returning for sophomore year	98
% students graduating within 4 years	90
Calendar	semester
Profs interesting rating	83
Profs accessible rating	91
Most classes have	10–19 students
Most lab/discussion sessions have	10–19 students

MOST POPULAR MAJORS

finance; political science and government; psychology

APPLICANTS ALSO LOOK AT AND OFTEN PREFER

Princeton University, Stanford University

AND SOMETIMES PREFER

Cornell University, Duke University, Georgetown University, Northwestern University

AND RARELY PREFER

Boston College, University of Illinois at Urbana-Champaign, University of Michigan—Ann Arbor

STUDENTS SAY "..."

Academics

Notre Dame has many traditions, including a "devotion to undergraduate education" you might not expect from a school with such an athletic reputation. Professors here are, by all accounts, "wonderful": "Not only are they invested in their students," they're "genuinely passionate about their fields of study," "enthusiastic and animated in lectures," and "always willing to meet outside of class to give extra help." Wary that distance might breed academic disengagement, professors ensure "large lectures are broken down into smaller discussion groups once a week to help with class material and...give the class a personal touch." For its part, "the administration tries its best to stay on top of the students' wants and needs." They make it "extremely easy to get in touch with anyone." Like the professors, administrators try to make personal connections with students. For example, "our president (a priest), as well as both of our presidents emeritus, make it a point to interact with the students in a variety of ways—teaching a class, saying mass in the dorms, etc." Overall, "while classes are difficult," "students are competitive against one another," and "it's necessary to study hard and often, [but] there's also time to do other things."

Life

Life at Notre Dame is centered around two things—"residential life" and "sports." The "dorms on campus provide the social structure" and supply undergrads with tons of opportunities to get involved and have fun." "During the school week" students "study a lot, but on the weekends everyone seems to make up for the lack of partying during the week." The school "does not have any fraternities or sororities, but campus is not dry, and drinking/partying is permitted within the residence halls." The administration reportedly tries "to keep the parties on campus due to the fact that campus is such a safe place and they truly do care about our safety." In addition to parties the dorms are really competitive in the Interhall Sport System, and "virtually every student plays some kind of sport [in] his/her residence hall." Intercollegiate sports, to put it mildly, "are huge." "If someone is not interested in sports upon arrival, he or she will be by the time he or she leaves." "Everybody goes to the football games, and it's common to see 1,000 students at a home soccer game." Beyond residential life and sports, "religious activities," volunteering, "campus publications, student government, and academic clubs round out the rest of ND life."

Student Body

Undergrads at Notre Dame report "the vast majority" of their peers are "very smart" "white kids from upper- to middle-class backgrounds from all over the country, especially the Midwest and Northeast." The typical student "is a type-A personality that studies a lot, yet is athletic and involved in the community. They are usually the outstanding seniors in their high schools," the "sort of people who can talk about the BCS rankings and Derrida in the same breath." Additionally, something like "eighty-five percent of Notre Dame students earned a varsity letter in high school." "Not all are Catholic" here, though most are, and it seems that most undergrads "have some sort of spirituality present in their daily lives." "ND is slowly improving in diversity concerning economic backgrounds, with the university's policy to meet all demonstrated financial need." As things stand now, those who "don't tend to fit in with everyone else hang out in their own groups made up by others like them (based on ethnicity, sexual orientation, etc.)."

FINANCIAL AID: 574-631-6436 • E-MAIL: ADMISSIONS@ND.EDU • WEBSITE: WWW.ND.EDU

THE PRINCETON REVIEW SAYS

Admissions

Very important factors considered include: Rigor of secondary school record. *Important factors considered include:* Class rank, application essay, academic GPA, recommendation(s), standardized test scores, alumni/ae relation, character/personal qualities, extracurricular activities, talent/ability, volunteer work. *Other factors considered include:* First generation, level of applicant's interest, racial/ethnic status, religious affiliation/commitment, work experience. SAT or ACT required; ACT with or without writing component accepted. TOEFL required of all international applicants. High school diploma is required and GED is not accepted. *Academic units required:* 4 English, 3 mathematics, 2 science (2 science labs), 2 foreign language, 2 history, 3 academic electives. *Academic units recommended:* 4 English, 4 mathematics, 4 science (2 science labs), 4 foreign language, 4 history.

Financial Aid

Students should submit: FAFSA, CSS/Financial Aid PROFILE, business/farm supplement. The Princeton Review suggests that all financial aid forms be submitted as soon as possible after January 1. *Need-based scholarships/grants offered:* Federal Pell, SEOG, state scholarships/grants, private scholarships, the school's own gift aid, Federal ACG and SMART Grants. *Loan aid offered:* Direct Subsidized Stafford, Direct Unsubsidized Stafford, Direct PLUS, Federal Perkins, private student loans. Applicants will be notified of awards on or about April 1. Highest amount earned per year from on-campus jobs $6,300. Off-campus job opportunities are fair.

The Inside Word

Notre Dame is one of the most selective colleges in the country. Almost everyone who enrolls is in the top ten percent of their graduating class and possesses test scores in the highest percentiles. But, as the student respondents suggest, strong academic ability isn't enough to get you in here. The school looks for students with other talents, and seems to have a predilection for athletic achievement. Legacy students get a leg up but are by no means assured of admission.

THE SCHOOL SAYS ". . ."

From the Admissions Office

"Notre Dame is a Catholic university, which means it offers unique opportunities for academic, ethical, spiritual, and social service development. The First Year of Studies program provides special assistance to our students as they make the adjustment from high school to college. The first-year curriculum includes many core requirements, while allowing students to explore several areas of possible future study. Each residence hall is home to students from all classes; most will live in the same hall for all their years on campus. An average of ninety-three percent of entering students will graduate within five years.

"The highest critical reading score and the highest math score from either test will be accepted; the writing component score is not required. The ACT is also accepted (with or without writing component) in lieu of the SAT."

SELECTIVITY

Admissions Rating	97
# of applicants	14,521
% of applicants accepted	29
% of acceptees attending	50
# accepting a place on wait list	1,021
# admitted from wait list	136

FRESHMAN PROFILE

Range SAT Critical Reading	650–740
Range SAT Math	670–770
Range SAT Writing	650–740
Range ACT Composite	31–34
Minimum paper TOEFL	560
Minimum web-based TOEFL	100
% graduated top 10% of class	87
% graduated top 25% of class	96
% graduated top 50% of class	100

DEADLINES

Early action	
Deadline	11/1
Notification	12/21
Regular	
Deadline	12/31
Notification	4/10
Nonfall registration?	yes

FINANCIAL FACTS

Financial Aid Rating	92
Annual tuition	$42,464
Room and board	$11,934
Required fees	$507
Books and supplies	$950
% needy frosh rec. need-based scholarship or grant aid	97
% needy UG rec. need-based scholarship or grant aid	96
% needy frosh rec. non-need-based scholarship or grant aid	66
% needy UG rec. non-need-based scholarship or grant aid	59
% needy frosh rec. need-based self-help aid	80
% needy UG rec. need-based self-help aid	85
% UG borrow to pay for school	56
Average cumulative indebtedness	$30,341
% frosh need fully met	98
% ugrads need fully met	98
Average % of frosh need met	99
Average % of ugrad need met	99

UNIVERSITY OF OKLAHOMA

1000 Asp Avenue, Norman, OK 73019-4076 • Admissions: 405-325-2252 • Fax: 405-325-7124

CAMPUS LIFE

Quality of Life Rating	**90**
Fire Safety Rating	**98**
Green Rating	**88**
Type of school	public
Environment	city

STUDENTS

Total undergrad enrollment	21,413
% male/female	48/52
% from out of state	31
% frosh live on campus	82
# of fraternities	31
# of sororities	20
% African American	5
% Asian	5
% Caucasian	64
% Hispanic	6
% Native American	5
% international	4
# of countries represented	125

SURVEY SAYS . . .

Athletic facilities are great
Low cost of living
Everyone loves the Sooners
Great library
Great off-campus food
Intercollegiate sports are popular
Frats and sororities dominate social scene

ACADEMICS

Academic Rating	**71**
Calendar	semester
Student/faculty ratio	18:1
Profs interesting rating	75
Profs accessible rating	72
Most classes have	10–19 students
Most lab/discussion sessions have	20–29 students

MOST POPULAR MAJORS

nursing; multidisciplinary studies; psychology

STUDENTS SAY ". . ."

Academics

Students "just swell with school pride" when they talk about the University of Oklahoma. They note, for example, that this "dynamic," "affordable," and "very research-oriented" institution reels in a slew of national merit scholars. They extol the "extensive" study abroad program. The meteorology program is "outstanding." "The engineering facilities are fantastic," and the campus as a whole is "gorgeous" and "well-kept." "The library is beautiful," reports a journalism major. "I could live in there." Like at any similar "big-time university," "The education here is what you make of it." "Anyone who truly wants to learn and achieve can find all sorts of opportunities." Then again, "If you just want to get by," you can "take easy blow-off classes." The faculty runs the gamut as well. "Most professors are great," relates an industrial engineering major. They "know what they are talking about," and they're "approachable." Professors "usually lecture more than they promote discussions." "The best can keep you riveted until the very end of the class period," promises an economics major. Others are "dry" and "overeager" teaching assistants "could use some work." Also, lower-level courses are often "huge," and they tend occur in "ancient coliseum-type" spaces.

Life

"There are tons of organizations" on OU's campus, and "There's no way you could possibly be bored." "From the Indonesian Student Association to the Bocce Ball League of Excellence, there's a group for" you. "The programming board here brings in a lot of great acts and keeps us very entertained in the middle of Oklahoma," adds one student. "School spirit is rampant," and intercollegiate athletics are insanely popular—particularly football. "Not everyone likes Sooner football," but it sure seems that way. Students at OU "live and breathe football" "to the point of near-frightening cultism." Game days in the fall are "an unforgettable experience," because "the campus goes into a frenzy." Fraternities and sororities are also "a large part of social life." Some students insist that the Greek system isn't a dominant feature of the OU landscape. "You hardly notice their presence" if you're not involved, they say, and "The majority of students aren't involved." Other students disagree. "Greek life is really big, unfortunately," they tell us. "It feels as though everyone here is Greek," and "There is a division" between the students who pledge and the students who don't. The "friendly and cute little town" of Norman is reportedly an ideal place to spend a day when not in class. Right next to campus is an area "full of" boutique shops and "a fine selection of bars and restaurants." "Norman is such a great town," gushes one student. "It's not too little to be boring but not too big to be impersonal."

Student Body

The typical student here is "pretty laid-back," "very good at prioritizing," "in some sort of organization or club," and "from Oklahoma or Texas." That student also "loves football," has "a penchant for fun," and has "no outrageous features." OU is home to "a wide variety of students with different political, religious, and economic backgrounds" though, and "There are plenty of options for every major and lifestyle." A lot of students come from a "suburban background" while "many come from small towns." There's also a "quite impressive" contingent of international students. Many students are "vaguely to devoutly Christian." Politically, "The atmosphere on campus tends to be conservative," but the left is well-represented. "We have a ton of liberals," relates one student, "and they are very much liberal." "There are the fraternity dudes and sorority girls" dressed in "North Face apparel and Nike shorts." "You have your partiers, hardcore studiers, and those in between who may lean one way or the other."

FINANCIAL AID: 405-325-5505 • E-MAIL: ADMREC@OU.EDU • WEBSITE: WWW.OU.EDU

THE PRINCETON REVIEW SAYS

Admissions

Very important factors considered include: Class rank, academic GPA, rigor of secondary school record, standardized test scores. *Other factors considered include:* Application essay, recommendation(s), state residency. SAT or ACT required. TOEFL required of all international applicants. High school diploma is required and GED is accepted. *Academic units required:* 4 English, 3 mathematics, 3 science (3 science labs), 2 social studies, 1 history, 2 academic electives. *Academic units recommended:* 2 foreign language, 1 mathematics, 1 computer science.

Financial Aid

Students should submit: FAFSA. The Princeton Review suggests that all financial aid forms be submitted as soon as possible after January 1. *Need-based scholarships/grants offered:* Federal Pell, SEOG, state scholarships/grants, private scholarships, the school's own gift aid, United Negro College Fund. *Loan aid offered:* Federal Perkins, Federal Nursing, college/university loans from institutional funds. Applicants will be notified of awards on a rolling basis beginning March 15. Federal Work-Study Program available. Institutional employment available. Highest amount earned per year from on-campus jobs $3,108. Off-campus job opportunities are excellent.

The Inside Word

Like at a lot of large public schools, the admissions process at the University of Oklahoma is a fairly standardized affair that favors state residents. Students who graduate in the top half of their high school class and have decent grades in college prep courses and solid standardized test scores, stand a good chance at admission. Also worth noting: national merit scholars get a lot of perks here including a sweet scholarship package.

THE SCHOOL SAYS ". . ."

From the Admissions Office

"Ask yourself some significant questions. What are your ambitions, goals, and dreams? Do you desire opportunity, and are you ready to accept challenge? What do you hope to gain from your educational experience? Are you looking for a university that will provide you with the tools, resources, and motivation to convert ambitions, opportunities, and challenges into meaningful achievement? To effectively answer these questions you must carefully seek out your options, look for direction, and make the right choice. The University of Oklahoma combines a unique mixture of academic excellence, varied social cultures, and a variety of campus activities to make your educational experience complete. At OU, comprehensive learning is our goal for your life. Not only do you receive a valuable classroom learning experience, but OU is also one of the finest research institutions in the United States. This allows OU students the opportunity to be a part of technology in progress. It's not just learning, it's discovery, invention, and dynamic creativity, a hands-on experience that allows you to be on the cutting edge of knowledge. Make the right choice and consider the University of Oklahoma!

"The SAT (or ACT) will be used when considering freshman applicants for admission. The writing component of either test is not required of students and is not used in determining admission to the university. The student's best composite score from any one test will be used."

SELECTIVITY	
Admissions Rating	82
# of applicants	11,456
% of applicants accepted	82
% of acceptees attending	43
# accepting a place on wait list	2,607
# admitted from wait list	1,719

FRESHMAN PROFILE	
Range SAT Critical Reading	510–650
Range SAT Math	540–660
Range ACT Composite	23–29
Minimum paper TOEFL	550
Minimum web-based TOEFL	79
Average HS GPA	3.6
% graduated top 10% of class	36
% graduated top 25% of class	70
% graduated top 50% of class	95

DEADLINES	
Regular	
Deadline	4/1
Notification	roling
Nonfall registration?	yes

FINANCIAL FACTS	
Financial Aid Rating	84
Annual in-state tuition	$3,849
Annual out-state tuition	$14,802
Room and board	$8,060
Required fees	$3,276
Books and supplies	$1,043
% needy frosh rec. need-based scholarship or grant aid	57
% needy UG rec. need-based scholarship or grant aid	59
% needy frosh rec. non-need-based scholarship or grant aid	53
% needy UG rec. non-need-based scholarship or grant aid	39
% needy frosh rec. need-based self-help aid	69
% needy UG rec. need-based self-help aid	74
% frosh rec. any financial aid	80
% UG rec. any financial aid	79
% UG borrow to pay for school	52
Average cumulative indebtedness	$26,198
% frosh need fully met	80
% ugrads need fully met	78
Average % of frosh need met	82
Average % of ugrad need met	81

UNIVERSITY OF OREGON

1217 UNIVERSITY OF OREGON, EUGENE, OR 97403-1217 • ADMISSIONS: 541-346-3201 • FAX: 541-346-5815

CAMPUS LIFE

Quality of Life Rating	78
Fire Safety Rating	69
Green Rating	95
Type of school	public
Environment	city

STUDENTS

Total undergrad enrollment	20,248
% male/female	48/52
% from out of state	37
% frosh live on campus	80
# of fraternities	15
# of sororities	13
% African American	2
% Asian	5
% Caucasian	70
% Hispanic	6
% Native American	1
% international	8
# of countries represented	86

SURVEY SAYS . . .

Athletic facilities are great
Everyone loves the Ducks
Student publications are popular
Great library
Intercollegiate sports are popular

ACADEMICS

Academic Rating	71
% students returning for sophomore year	86
% students graduating within 4 years	41
% students graduating within 6 years	67
Calendar	quarter
Student/faculty ratio	20:1
Profs interesting rating	75
Profs accessible rating	73
Most classes have	20–29 students
Most lab/discussion sessions have	20–29 students

MOST POPULAR MAJORS

business/commerce; journalism; psychology

APPLICANTS ALSO LOOK AT

AND OFTEN PREFER

University of California—Santa Barbara, University of California—Berkeley, University of Colorado—Boulder

AND SOMETIMES PREFER

Oregon State University, University of Arizona

AND RARELY PREFER

University of California—Davis, University of California—Los Angeles, University of Washington

STUDENTS SAY ". . ."

Academics

If the University of Oregon excels at anything, it is in providing students with a wealth of academic opportunities. Indeed, students feel it is "a perfect place for someone seeking a well-rounded liberal arts secondary education," a school that has "all of the creative perks of a small learning environment with all of the excitement of a big school." Sports are a big deal here, "but there is also an emphasis on rigorous academics." Business, architecture, ecology, international studies, and political science all win accolades, but journalism is "pretty much the crown jewel of our academic programs." If there is a chink in UO's armor, it is the "inability for some students to get the classes they need." With such a wide array of fields of study available, some students find that essential classes are only available at difficult hours. Students also give mixed grades to the professors, who range from "remarkable" and "really passionate" educators who "are invested in their students" to a few "quite terrible" teachers who "are not dedicated to the students." Those attending UO should be self-motivating, since "the weight falls on the students to create relationships with professors." It is worth the effort, though, as "doing so can open many doors." When it all clicks—and many students report that once that once they were focused on their major things began to fall into place—students have enjoyed an education that "deeply altered the way I see things."

Life

Eugene, Oregon, is not going to give the nation's big cities a run for their money, but students here like it that way. When the weather is nice, students can be found outside "playing Frisbee, football, soccer, or just lounging in the grass," and when the rainy weather of the Pacific Northwest forces people indoors, "You find students in coffee shops on campus and off, studying, visiting, or relaxing." Music, hiking, and other outdoor activities are also popular pastimes. Indeed, the scenery proves a draw for many. "The coast is an hour away, hiking trails and mountains are everywhere, and you can even drive or take a bus up to Portland to get some city life." Greek life is growing on campus but does not dominate the school, and despite prohibitions on drinking in the dorms, students manage it anyway. "We are a dry campus," one attendee notes, "but that doesn't stop students." With the gorgeous scenery and wealth of things to do, it's no wonder students think that "life at school is pretty great."

Student Body

What kind of student attends the University of Oregon? The typical answer is that there is no typical answer. "You have your hipsters, hippies, jocks, athletes, drunks, nerds, and every other cliché you can think of"—students from "dreadlocked hippies to straight-laced conservatives, and everything else in between." That diversity in the student body means, "If you're willing to put forth any sort of effort into meeting people, you'll find a group" who will click with you. "No matter who you are," another student agrees, "there are programs and clubs on campus to take part in." Greek or non-Greek does make a difference. Students say there is a "huge divide between Greek-life and the rest of the student body." But overall, University of Oregon students are "friendly, open-minded, and generally environmentally/socially conscious." In other words, "There are all sorts of students at Oregon, and it is pretty diverse."

FINANCIAL AID: 800-760-6953 • E-MAIL: UOADMIT@UOREGON.EDU • WEBSITE: WWW.UOREGON.EDU

THE PRINCETON REVIEW SAYS

Admissions

Very important factors considered include: Academic GPA, rigor of secondary school record. *Important factors considered include:* Standardized test scores. *Other factors considered include:* Class rank, application essay, recommendation(s), extracurricular activities, first generation, geographical residence, racial/ethnic status, state residency, talent/ability, volunteer work, work experience. SAT or ACT required. ACT with writing component required. TOEFL required of all international applicants. High school diploma is required and GED is accepted. *Academic units required:* 4 English, 3 mathematics, 3 science, 2 foreign language, 3 social studies. *Academic units recommended:* 1 science lab.

Financial Aid

Students should submit: FAFSA. The Princeton Review suggests that all financial aid forms be submitted as soon as possible after January 1. *Need-based scholarships/grants offered:* Federal Pell, SEOG, state scholarships/grants, private scholarships, the school's own gift aid. *Loan aid offered:* Direct Subsidized Stafford, Direct Unsubsidized Stafford, Direct PLUS, Federal Perkins, college/university loans from institutional funds. Applicants will be notified of awards on a rolling basis beginning April 15. Federal Work-Study Program available. Institutional employment available. Off-campus job opportunities are good.

The Inside Word

No need to worry about elaborate written statements and mile-long academic resumes. Maintain a 3.0 or better GPA in a college prep curriculum and your ticket to UO is all but written. Even substandard test scores can be overlooked for applicants who meet that requirement. There is further leniency for less than stellar grades if personal circumstances got in the way of academic achievement; applicants for whom this applies should make the school aware when applying.

THE SCHOOL SAYS ". . ."

From the Admissions Office

"At the UO, you'll be part of a community dedicated to making a difference in the world. Whether you want to change a community, a law, or one person's mind, the UO will provide you with the inspiration and resources you'll need to succeed. You'll attend classes alongside students from all fifty states, three U.S. territories, and eighty-six other countries, learn from people with diverse cultural, ethnic, and spiritual heritages, and have opportunities to participate in cutting-edge research and engage in intellectual dialog with renowned faculty. You'll graduate from the UO with the knowledge, experience, and research, writing, and critical thinking skills necessary to succeed in an increasingly global and diverse community. Set in a 295-acre arboretum, the UO is literally green. Both academic and outdoor programs will bring you into contact with forests, mountains, rivers, and lakes. The first facilities of their kind in the nation, the Green Chemistry Laboratory uses only nontoxic materials and the Tyler Instrumentation Center provides the full range of instruments needed in green chemistry. The Lillis Business Complex is the country's most environmentally friendly business school facility, and nationally recognized programs in sustainable business, architecture, and technology demonstrate the UO's ongoing commitment to the environment. With a student/teacher ratio of twenty to one, average class size of twenty-two students, 273 academic programs, and more than 250 student organizations, you'll find that the UO is uniquely able to provide the advantages of a smaller liberal arts university in addition to all the resources of a major research institution. To be eligible for freshman admission, you must have a high school GPA of at least 3.0, be a graduate of a standard or accredited high school, and submit SAT or ACT scores."

SELECTIVITY

Admissions Rating	**81**
# of applicants	23,012
% of applicants accepted	73
% of acceptees attending	25
# accepting a place on wait list	1,087
# admitted from wait list	947

FRESHMAN PROFILE

Range SAT Critical Reading	492–610
Range SAT Math	501–613
Minimum paper TOEFL	500
Minimum web-based TOEFL	61
Average HS GPA	3.6
% graduated top 10% of class	28
% graduated top 25% of class	63
% graduated top 50% of class	93

DEADLINES

Early action	
Deadline	11/1
Notification	12/15
Regular	
Priority	11/1
Deadline	1/15
Notification	12/15
Nonfall registration?	yes

FINANCIAL FACTS

Financial Aid Rating	**66**
Annual in-state tuition	$7,551
Annual out-state tuition	$26,415
Room and board	$9,801
Required fees	$1,238
Books and supplies	$1,050
% needy frosh rec. need-based scholarship or grant aid	49
% needy UG rec. need-based scholarship or grant aid	57
% needy frosh rec. non-need-based scholarship or grant aid	45
% needy UG rec. non-need-based scholarship or grant aid	33
% needy frosh rec. need-based self-help aid	81
% needy UG rec. need-based self-help aid	83
% frosh rec. any financial aid	72
% UG rec. any financial aid	68
% UG borrow to pay for school	53
Average cumulative indebtedness	$22,736
% frosh need fully met	10
% ugrads need fully met	9
Average % of frosh need met	44
Average % of ugrad need met	50

UNIVERSITY OF THE PACIFIC

3601 PACIFIC AVENUE, STOCKTON, CA 95211 • ADMISSIONS: 209-946-2211 • FAX: 209-946-2413

CAMPUS LIFE

Quality of Life Rating	**70**
Fire Safety Rating	**86**
Green Rating	**80**
Type of school	private
Environment	city

STUDENTS

Total undergrad enrollment	3,872
% male/female	45/55
% from out of state	9
% from public high school	82
% frosh live on campus	51
# of fraternities	5
# of sororities	6
% African American	4
% Asian	33
% Caucasian	36
% Hispanic	14
% Native American	2
% international	4
# of countries represented	66

SURVEY SAYS . . .

Low cost of living
Very little drug use
Registration is a breeze

ACADEMICS

Academic Rating	**82**
% students returning for sophomore year	87
% students graduating within 4 years	46
% students graduating within 6 years	69
Calendar	semester
Student/faculty ratio	13:1
Profs interesting rating	82
Profs accessible rating	83
Most classes have	fewer than 10 students
Most lab/discussion sessions have	10–19 students

MOST POPULAR MAJORS

biology/biological sciences; business/commerce; engineering

APPLICANTS ALSO LOOK AT AND OFTEN PREFER

University of California—Davis, University of California—Berkeley

AND SOMETIMES PREFER

University of California—Davis, University of California—Berkeley, University of California—Los Angeles, University of Southern California

STUDENTS SAY ". . ."

Academics

Educational diversity and strong academic programs bring many students to the University of the Pacific in Stockton, California. The school "provides an array of opportunities to suit anyone." "The accelerated programs in dentistry, law, and pharmacy" are a big hit, as well as the "amazing co-op program for engineers" and the "prestigious speech and language pathology program." The "four year guarantee" for some majors and the time and money saved by finishing earlier than other schools' programs is the deciding factor for many. "The Elementary Education program appealed to me because I would get my teaching credential and degree in four years, rather than five or six." Another reason people choose Pacific is the appeal of "very small" and "intimate" classes. One student says this allows for "the proper and necessary attention that I need in order to succeed academically." "Professors know you by name, and they are very involved and helpful." This "emphasis on close relationships between staff and students" shows that Pacific is "a school that truly cares about each student's education." A good deal of students describe professors as "extremely challenging," but also "extremely motivating." "They encourage me and push me to put 110 percent effort in everything inside and outside the classroom." Another student confirms that each class is "manageable but requires effort." If needed, assistance is readily available. "There is always someone around who can help you and plenty of tutors." "There are so many resources in place to help students succeed, that it's practically impossible not to do well." Although the cost may seem high, several students did benefit from "a lot of financial aid."

Life

Students love the "gorgeous and well-maintained" campus, but the surrounding city of Stockton does not get rave reviews. One student describes the University of the Pacific as a "nice school in an unlikely neighborhood." One student does not recommend "walking around certain parts of campus late at night," but adds, "We have great campus police and a STRIPE program that can transport you wherever you want on golf carts if you call them and let you know where you are." Students say the campus is fairly self-contained, with "a movie theater that shows free movies on the weekends for all Pacific students. We also have an on-campus grocery store and a cafeteria that is open until 1:00 A.M." Since there is no strong pull to leave campus, "Students tend to resort to joining fraternities to give them something to do. It isn't always partying though. Pacific is not usually considered a party school since the campus "drug and alcohol policy is extremely strict." A lot of frats on campus are professional ones (i.e. pharmacy fraternities) that are committed to giving back to the community and hosting health fairs." Students say, "Student life varies widely by major." "Some majors are a lot more difficult than others, so not everyone studies." Keeping active and fit are also popular. "Our gym is very nice and hygienic. We also have a swimming pool with open hours and several soccer fields for recreational use."

Student Body

Some students agree that there is "a wide gap between the 'serious' students and the 'not serious' students." This may explain the seemingly contradictory observations that "people seem to party a lot" and that there is "not much time for anything but studying." Student comments suggest that the typical student "is involved in multiple organizations on campus, gets good grades, finds time for fun on the weekends, [and] stays late in the library even if they are just socializing." Pacific's size lends itself to a "friendly atmosphere." The "small campus contributes to a small town ambiance where you know everyone." One downside to this is that "student life becomes very cliquey, almost like high school."

FINANCIAL AID: 209-946-2421 • E-MAIL: ADMISSIONS@PACIFIC.EDU • WEBSITE: WWW.PACIFIC.EDU

THE PRINCETON REVIEW SAYS

Admissions

Very important factors considered include: Rigor of secondary school record. *Important factors considered include:* Application essay, academic GPA, recommendation(s), standardized test scores, extracurricular activities, first generation. *Other factors considered include:* Class rank, alumni/ae relation, character/personal qualities, geographical residence, level of applicant's interest, talent/ability, volunteer work, work experience. SAT or ACT required; ACT with writing component required. TOEFL required of all international applicants. High school diploma is required and GED is accepted. *Academic units recommended:* 4 English, 2 foreign language, 2 social studies, 1 history, 1 visual/performing arts, 1 academic electives.

Financial Aid

Students should submit: FAFSA. The Princeton Review suggests that all financial aid forms be submitted as soon as possible after January 1. *Need-based scholarships/grants offered:* Federal Pell, SEOG, state scholarships/grants, private scholarships, the school's own gift aid, ACG, SMART. *Loan aid offered:* Direct Subsidized Stafford, Direct Unsubsidized Stafford, Direct PLUS, Federal Perkins, Direct Graduate/Professional PLUS Loans. Applicants will be notified of awards on a rolling basis beginning March 15.

The Inside Word

While many factors are considered on applications, competition throughout California is intense. Exceptional performance in honors and advanced placement courses will help you stand out in the crowd.

THE SCHOOL SAYS ". . ."

From the Admissions Office

"One of the most concise ways of describing the University of the Pacific is that it is 'a major university in a small college package.' Our 3,740 undergraduates get the personal attention that you would expect at a small, residential college. But they also have the kinds of opportunities offered at much larger institutions, including more than ninety majors and programs; hundreds of student organizations; drama, dance, and musical productions; sixteen NCAA Division I athletic teams; and two dozen club and intramural sports. We offer undergraduate major programs in the arts, sciences and humanities, business, education, engineering, international studies, music, pharmacy, and health sciences. Some of the unique aspects of our academic programs include the following: We have the only independent, coed, nonsectarian liberal arts and sciences college located between Los Angeles and central Oregon; we have the only undergraduate professional school of international studies in California—and it's the only one in the nation that actually requires you to study abroad; we have the only engineering program in the West that requires students to complete a year's worth of paid work experience as part of their degree; our Conservatory of Music focuses on performance but also offers majors in music management, music therapy, and music education; and we offer several accelerated programs in business, dentistry, dental hygiene, education, law, engineering, and pharmacy. Our beautiful New England–style main campus is located in Stockton (population: 287,245) and is within two hours or less of San Francisco, Santa Cruz, Yosemite National Park, and Lake Tahoe. SAT Subject Tests recommended: mathematics, chemistry (natural science majors only)."

SELECTIVITY	
Admissions Rating	93
# of applicants	21,230
% of applicants accepted	36
% of acceptees attending	12

FRESHMAN PROFILE	
Range SAT Critical Reading	510–630
Range SAT Math	540–688
Range SAT Writing	500–630
Range ACT Composite	23–29
Minimum paper TOEFL	475
Minimum web-based TOEFL	52
Average HS GPA	3.5
% graduated top 10% of class	38
% graduated top 25% of class	69
% graduated top 50% of class	92

DEADLINES	
Early action	
Deadline	11/15
Notification	11/15
Regular	
Priority	11/15
Deadline	1/15
Nonfall registration?	yes

FINANCIAL FACTS	
Financial Aid Rating	67
Annual tuition	$37,800
Room and board	$12,038
Required fees	$620
Books and supplies	$1,656
% needy frosh rec. need-based scholarship or grant aid	97
% needy UG rec. need-based scholarship or grant aid	96
% needy frosh rec. need-based self-help aid	90
% needy UG rec. need-based self-help aid	93
% frosh rec. any financial aid	91
% UG rec. any financial aid	83
% frosh need fully met	10
% ugrads need fully met	10

UNIVERSITY OF PENNSYLVANIA

ONE COLLEGE HALL, PHILADELPHIA, PA 19104 • ADMISSIONS: 215-898-7507 • FAX: 215-898-9670

CAMPUS LIFE

Quality of Life Rating	90
Fire Safety Rating	70
Green Rating	87
Type of school	private
Environment	metropolis

STUDENTS

Total undergrad enrollment	9,779
% male/female	49/51
% from out of state	81
% from public high school	60
% frosh live on campus	100
# of fraternities	36
# of sororities	13
% African American	7
% Asian	19
% Caucasian	46
% Hispanic	8
% international	11
# of countries represented	126

SURVEY SAYS . . .

Athletic facilities are great
Diverse student types on campus
Great off-campus food
Students are happy
Student publications are popular
Student government is popular
Hard liquor is popular

ACADEMICS

Academic Rating	94
% students graduating within 4 years	87
% students graduating within 6 years	96
Calendar	semester
Student/faculty ratio	6:1
Profs interesting rating	80
Profs accessible rating	83
Most classes have	10–19 students

MOST POPULAR MAJORS

business administration and management; finance; nursing/registered nurse (rn, asn, bsn, msn)

APPLICANTS ALSO LOOK AT AND OFTEN PREFER

Harvard College, Princeton University, Yale University

AND SOMETIMES PREFER

Stanford University, Columbia University, Massachusetts Institute of Technology, Brown University

AND RARELY PREFER

Cornell University, Georgetown University, Duke University, University of Chicago

STUDENTS SAY "..."

Academics

At the University of Pennsylvania, everyone shares an intellectual curiosity and top-notch resources but doesn't "buy into the stigma of being an Ivy League school." Students here are "very passionate about what they do outside the classroom" and the "flexible core requirements." The university is composed of four undergraduate schools (and "a library for pretty much any topic"). "You can take courses in any of the schools, including graduate-level courses." Luckily, there's a vast variety of disciplines available to students: "I can take a course in old Icelandic and even another one about the politics of food," says a student. Wharton, Penn's highly regarded, "highly competitive undergraduate business school" attracts "career-oriented" students who don't mind a "strenuous course load." There are "more than enough" resources, funding, and opportunity here for any student to take advantage of, and "Penn encourages students to truly take advantage of it all!" Professors can "sometimes seem to be caught up more in their research than their classes," but all "are incredibly well-versed in their subject (as well as their audience)." If you're willing to put in the time and effort, your professors "will be happy to reciprocate." In general, the instructors here are "very challenging academically" and are "always willing to offer their more than relevant life experience in class discussion."

Life

Penn students don't mind getting into intellectual conversations during dinner—"Politics and religion come up often, but so does baseball, types of wine, and restaurants"—but some "partying is a much higher priority here than it is at other Ivy League schools." "Campus is split between the downtown club scene and the frat/bar scene, depending on your preference." However, when it comes down to midterms and finals, "People get really serious and...buckle down and study." There's easy access to downtown Philadelphia, yet "still the comfortable feeling of having our own campus," giving students plenty of access to restaurants (BYO restaurants in Philly are "a huge hit"), shopping, concerts, and sports games, as well as plain old "hanging out with hallmates playing Mario Kart." "It's the perfect mix between an urban setting a traditional college campus." The school provides plenty of guest speakers, cultural events, clubs, and organizations for students to channel their energies (all of which "makes the campus feel smaller"), and seniors can even attend "Feb Club" in the month of February, which is essentially an event every night. The weekend buses to/from New York and D.C. "are always packed." It's a busy life at Penn, and "People are constantly trying to think about how they can balance getting good grades academically and their weekend plans."

Student Body

This "determined" bunch "is either focused on one specific interest, or very well-rounded." Pretty much everyone "was an overachiever ('that kid') in high school," and some students "are off-the-charts brilliant," making everyone here "sort of fascinated by everyone else." Everyone has "a strong sense of personal style and his or her own credo," but no group deviates too far from the more mainstream stereotypes. There's a definite lack of "emos" and hippies. There's "the career-driven Wharton kid who will stab you in the back to get your interview slot" and "the nursing kid who's practically nonexistent," but on the whole, there's tremendous school diversity, with "people from all over the world of all kinds of experiences of all perspectives."

FINANCIAL AID: 215-898-1988 • E-MAIL: INFO@ADMISSIONS.UGAO.UPENN.EDU • WEBSITE: WWW.UPENN.EDU

THE PRINCETON REVIEW SAYS

Admissions

Very important factors considered include: Recommendation(s), rigor of secondary school record, character/personal qualities. *Important factors considered include:* Class rank, application essay, academic GPA, standardized test scores, extracurricular activities, work experience. *Other factors considered include:* Alumni/ae relation, first generation, geographical residence, interview, racial/ethnic status, talent/ability, volunteer work. SAT or ACT required; ACT with writing component required. TOEFL required of all international applicants. High school diploma or equivalent is not required. *Academic units required:* 4 English, 4 mathematics, 3 science (3 science labs), 4 foreign language, 3 history.

Financial Aid

Students should submit: FAFSA, institution's own financial aid form, CSS/Financial Aid PROFILE, noncustodial PROFILE, business/farm supplement, parents' and student's most recently completed income tax. The Princeton Review suggests that all financial aid forms be submitted as soon as possible after January 1. *Need-based scholarships/grants offered:* Federal Pell, state scholarships/grants, private scholarships, the school's own gift aid. *Loan aid offered:* Direct Subsidized Stafford, Direct Unsubsidized Stafford, Direct PLUS, Federal Perkins, Federal Nursing, college/university loans from institutional funds, supplemental third party loans guaranteed by institution. Applicants will be notified of awards on or about April 1. Federal Work-Study Program available. Institutional employment available. Off-campus job opportunities are excellent.

The Inside Word

After a small decline four cycles ago, applications are once again climbing at Penn—the fifth increase in six years. The competition in the applicant pool is formidable. Applicants can safely assume that they need to be one of the strongest students in their graduating class in order to be successful.

THE SCHOOL SAYS ". . ."

From the Admissions Office

"Founded by Benjamin Franklin in 1740 to push the frontiers of knowledge, teaching, and problem solving to benefit society, Penn combines opportunities for practical training with foundations in the liberal arts and sciences all in one institution. A community that reflects the diversity of our world, with one of the largest international undergraduate student population in the Ivy League, our students and faculty work toward the shared goal of enacting change by questioning, thinking, and doing—often across traditional academic disciplines. The integration of knowledge and learning is created through access to four undergraduate schools: the College of Arts & Sciences, the School of Engineering & Applied Science, the Wharton School of Business, and the School of Nursing. Penn offers more than ninety majors, eighty minors, and the ability to earn more than one degree in four years.

"Penn believes that learning is only realized when put to use. The Penn community thrives on the open exchange of ideas and shared learning experiences, engaging students to access courses in twelve graduate schools, collaborate with faculty on research, and actively participate in over 450 clubs and organizations. Education through engagement is made possible by Penn's extensive partnerships for transformative civic outreach—around the world and close to our Philadelphia campus. More than 150 Academically Based Community-Service courses link Penn students to work in the community.

"Penn understands that the best minds should have access to the finest education, regardless of their families' ability to pay. To achieve this, Penn practices need-blind admissions, meets 100 percent of demonstrated financial need, and provides a no-loan aid package for all undergraduates receiving financial aid. Our goal is to allow students to pursue their aspirations without assuming a burden of debt, which is why we provide students the opportunity to graduate debt-free."

SELECTIVITY

Admissions Rating	**99**
# of applicants	31,663
% of applicants accepted	12
% of acceptees attending	63
# accepting a place on wait list	1,385
# admitted from wait list	56
# of early decision applicants	4,571
# accepted early decision	1,188

FRESHMAN PROFILE

Range SAT Critical Reading	660–750
Range SAT Math	690–780
Range SAT Writing	670–770
Range ACT Composite	30–34
Average HS GPA	3.9

DEADLINES

Early decision	
Deadline	11/1
Notification	12/15
Regular	
Deadline	1/1
Notification	4/1
Nonfall registration?	yes

FINANCIAL FACTS

Financial Aid Rating	**97**
Annual tuition	$39,088
Room and board	$12,368
Required fees	$4,650
Books and supplies	$1,210
% needy frosh rec. need-based scholarship or grant aid	97
% needy UG rec. need-based scholarship or grant aid	97
% needy frosh rec. need-based self-help aid	100
% needy UG rec. need-based self-help aid	100
% frosh rec. any financial aid	47
% UG rec. any financial aid	45
% UG borrow to pay for school	43
Average cumulative indebtedness	$17,013
% frosh need fully met	100
% ugrads need fully met	100
Average % of frosh need met	100
Average % of ugrad need met	100

UNIVERSITY OF PITTSBURGH—PITTSBURGH CAMPUS

4227 FIFTH AVENUE, PITTSBURGH, PA 15260 • ADMISSIONS: 412-624-7488 • FAX: 412-648-8815

CAMPUS LIFE

Quality of Life Rating	96
Fire Safety Rating	77
Green Rating	97
Type of school	public
Environment	metropolis

STUDENTS

Total undergrad enrollment	18,092
% male/female	50/50
% from out of state	32
% frosh live on campus	97
# of fraternities	22
# of sororities	16
% African American	7
% Asian	6
% Caucasian	78
% Hispanic	2
% international	3
# of countries represented	46

SURVEY SAYS . . .

Athletic facilities are great
Low cost of living
Student publications are popular
Students are happy
Registration is a breeze
Great library

ACADEMICS

Academic Rating	80
% students returning for sophomore year	90
% students graduating within 4 years	61
% students graduating within 6 years	79
Calendar	semester
Student/faculty ratio	14:1
Profs interesting rating	77
Profs accessible rating	79
Most classes have	10–19 students
Most lab/discussion sessions have	20–29 students

MOST POPULAR MAJORS

psychology, business/commerce, rhetoric and composition

APPLICANTS ALSO LOOK AT AND OFTEN PREFER

Boston University, Carnegie Mellon University, University of Pennsylvania, New York University

AND SOMETIMES PREFER

Pennsylvania State University—University Park, University of Delaware, University of Maryland, College Park, University of Michigan—Ann Arbor

AND RARELY PREFER

Slippery Rock University, University of Pennsylvania, Temple University, Indiana University of Pennsylvania, Duquesne University

STUDENTS SAY ". . ."

Academics

Known for its "wide variety of quality academic programs," the University of Pittsburgh is a moderately sized school in a moderately sized city. One of the school's key programs, however, is the Swanson School of Engineering. Engineering students love the program, calling it "great" and "affordable." They also say that the program is "about finding out what you truly want to do in life." Students love that the program "prepares its students for research, internship, and co-op opportunities from day one." Outside of the program, some of the students complain that the professors are "an extremely diverse group" as far as quality goes, calling them "hit-or-miss." The vast majority are "really passionate about the material" and "will do anything to assure [the students] know and understand the material." A few students say that other professors seem to "only care about promoting their research" or "simply read off PowerPoint slides," but those professors appear to be in the minority. Students agree that each person "just needs to figure out which ones [those] are early" and try to grab classes with the professors who they want to work with.

Life

Students seem to love the fact that University of Pittsburgh (affectionately referred to by its students as "Pitt"), is a school that's "not too big, not too small." Though there are about 18,000 undergraduates, many feel that the school "does everything in its power to make each student feel like more than just a number." There are more than "400 student organizations" that many students use to not only pass the time, but to enrich their lives as well. From the college radio station, to rock-climbing, to any number of activities, there is "an extreme range of fun things to do." The campus is located in the Oakland section of Pittsburgh, and students really enjoy the fact that they have such close proximity to the downtown area, but "It's nice to be [near] the city without actually being in the city." For those looking to get off campus, they can "always find something to do" in the city including going to a number of "unique restaurants," "tourist attractions," and "a rich art heritage." Many students complain about the food served in the cafeterias, but they laud the "great restaurants to eat [at] on, and off, campus."

Student Body

Incoming freshman will find students at the University of Pittsburgh "really welcoming and helpful." Individuals seem to hold their fellow students in great esteem saying not only that they're "friendly," but also that they "know how to work hard" and "know how to have fun." A "typical" student seems to be from Pennsylvania or a neighboring state. However, with 18,000 students, there is still a fairly "large and diverse student population," and having such a large number of people, and groups, to choose from can really help people find their niche. Greek life "is small at Pitt, but it definitely has a strong presence." Those people looking for a party can find one, but "not everyone parties all weekend," and most people just "like to hang out."

UNIVERSITY OF PITTSBURGH—PITTSBURGH CAMPUS

FINANCIAL AID: 412-624-7488 • E-MAIL: OAFA@PITT.EDU • WEBSITE: WWW.PITT.EDU

THE PRINCETON REVIEW SAYS

Admissions

Very important factors considered include: Academic GPA, rigor of secondary school record. *Important factors considered include:* Standardized test scores. *Other factors considered include:* Class rank, application essay, recommendation(s), character/personal qualities, extracurricular activities, first generation, geographical residence, interview, level of applicant's interest, racial/ethnic status, talent/ability, volunteer work, work experience. SAT or ACT required; ACT with writing component recommended. TOEFL required of all international applicants. High school diploma is required and GED is not accepted. *Academic units required:* 4 English, 3 mathematics, 3 science (3 science labs), 2 foreign language, 2 social studies, 3 academic electives. *Academic units recommended:* 4 English, 4 mathematics, 4 science (4 science labs), 3 foreign language, 3 social studies, 5 academic electives.

Financial Aid

Students should submit: FAFSA. The Princeton Review suggests that all financial aid forms be submitted as soon as possible after January 1. *Need-based scholarships/grants offered:* Federal Pell, SEOG, state scholarships/grants, private scholarships, the school's own gift aid, Federal Nursing Scholarships. *Loan aid offered:* Direct Subsidized Stafford, Direct Unsubsidized Stafford, Direct PLUS, Federal Perkins, Federal Nursing, college/university loans from institutional funds. Applicants will be notified of awards on a rolling basis beginning March 15. Federal Work-Study Program available. Institutional employment available. Off-campus job opportunities are excellent.

The Inside Word

University of Pittsburgh operates on a rolling admission policy, which means the school offers admission to any student applying at any time until the admissions office is notified by the dean that admission is closed, so the earlier you apply, the more likely you are to get in. Applicants can also visit the school's website or call the school to schedule a visit to campus. For those looking for financial aid, six out of ten incoming freshman who apply for need-based aid receive it. However the school also offers a range of other types of financial aid, including the University Academic scholarship, which is a merit-based aid that offers students anything from $2,000 per year to full tuition and room and board. To be eligible, interested students need to have the application for the scholarship completed by January 15.

THE SCHOOL SAYS ". . ."

From the Admissions Office

"The University of Pittsburgh is one of sixty-one members of the Association of American Universities, a prestigious group whose members include the major research uni versities of North America. There are over 440 degree programs available at the sixteen Pittsburgh campus schools (one offering only undergraduate degree programs, six offering graduate degree programs, and eight offering both) and four regional campuses, allowing students a wide latitude of choices, both academically and in setting and style, size, and pace of campus. Programs ranked nationally include philosophy, history and philosophy of science, chemistry, economics, English, his tory, physics, political science, and psychology. Some of the company the University of Pittsburgh keeps: In four of the past five years, Pitt has ranked in the very top cluster of U.S. public research universities according to the Top American Research Universities annual report, issued by the Center for Measuring University Performance. Over that five-year period, only eight universities have ranked in that top cluster: along with Berkeley, Illinois, Michigan, UCLA, UNC, Florida, Pitt, and Wisconsin. It has a notable record of high achieving graduates—since 1995 Pitt undergraduates have won four Rhodes, six Marshall, five Truman, five Udall, one Churchill, one Gate Cambridge, and thirty-five Goldwater scholarships. In research, Pitt ranks fifth among all U.S. universities in terms of competitive grants awarded to faculty by the National Institutes of Health. In inter national education, Pitt's University Center for International Studies offers seven area studies centers, three of which are designated National Resource Centers by the U.S. Department of Education."

SELECTIVITY	
Admissions Rating	93
# of applicants	23,409
% of applicants accepted	58
% of acceptees attending	28
# accepting a place on wait list	315
# admitted from wait list	15

FRESHMAN PROFILE	
Range SAT Critical Reading	570–690
Range SAT Math	600–690
Range SAT Writing	560–660
Range ACT Composite	25–30
Minimum paper TOEFL	550
Minimum web-based TOEFL	80
Average HS GPA	3.9
% graduated top 10% of class	54
% graduated top 25% of class	86
% graduated top 50% of class	99

DEADLINES	
Early decision	
Deadline	11/15
Notification	12/15
Regular	
Priority	1/15
Deadline	1/15
Notification	4/1
Nonfall registration?	yes

FINANCIAL FACTS	
Financial Aid Rating	78
Annual in-state tuition	$15,272
Annual out-state tuition	$24,680
Room and board	$9,430
Required fees	$860
Books and supplies	$1,110
% needy frosh rec. need-based scholarship or grant aid	72
% needy UG rec. need-based scholarship or grant aid	69
% needy frosh rec. non-need-based scholarship or grant aid	9
% needy UG rec. non-need-based scholarship or grant aid	5
% needy frosh rec. need-based self-help aid	81
% needy UG rec. need-based self-help aid	85
% frosh rec. any financial aid	61
% UG rec. any financial aid	58
% UG borrow to pay for school	63
Average cumulative indebtedness	$26,612
% frosh need fully met	12
% ugrads need fully met	9
Average % of frosh need met	59
Average % of ugrad need met	56

UNIVERSITY OF PUGET SOUND

1500 NORTH WARNER STREET CMB 1062, TACOMA, WA 98416-1062 • ADMISSIONS: 253-879-3211 • FAX: 253-879-3993

CAMPUS LIFE

Quality of Life Rating	**85**
Fire Safety Rating	**73**
Green Rating	**97**
Type of school	private
Environment	city

STUDENTS

Total undergrad enrollment	2,645
% male/female	43/57
% from out of state	81
% from public high school	72
% frosh live on campus	98
# of fraternities	3
# of sororities	4
% African American	2
% Asian	7
% Caucasian	75
% Hispanic	5
% Native American	1
% international	1
# of countries represented	13

SURVEY SAYS . . .

Lab facilities are great
School is well run
Musical organizations are popular

ACADEMICS

Academic Rating	**93**
% students returning for sophomore year	88
% students graduating within 4 years	67
Calendar	semester
Student/faculty ratio	12:1
Profs interesting rating	94
Profs accessible rating	99
Most classes have	10–19 students
Most lab/discussion sessions have	10–19 students

MOST POPULAR MAJORS

business/commerce; English language and literature; psychology

APPLICANTS ALSO LOOK AT AND RARELY PREFER

The College of Idaho, Gonzaga University

STUDENTS SAY ". . ."

Academics

University of Puget Sound "is all about creating an intimate learning environment in order to encourage a well-rounded educational experience." Indeed, one of the most common reasons students give for choosing to attend Puget Sound is the "close-knit community," with strong financial aid and the beautiful campus running close behind. Puget Sound is a small liberal arts school that offers a business major—a rare combination with big appeal. Other popular majors include the sciences, psychology, and music programs, and "Most classes in all majors emphasize writing and communicating ideas effectively." Professors are almost universally praised, and students are very happy with the "personal attention to undergraduates" here. "It's small, so students have greater access to professors, and many professors are willing to work outside of class with students." "All are genuinely passionate about their subjects, and accessible for extra help or attention." "Professors care a lot about your understanding of the material and if you can't make the [three or four] hours that they have scheduled as office hours, every professor will find a time that works for your schedule." In the classroom, "They bring enthusiasm and a lively approach," "they make class very interesting and are good at articulating the material in a way that makes learning easy," and "they also expect a high quality of work from all the students." Overall, Puget Sound "provides the 360 [degree] education; not only do students get a rich and rigorous academic experience, but they are also strongly encouraged to explore the urban and natural world around them" (though "the administration could do better to find new innovative ways to implement more green strategies such as composting [food waste]").

Life

While Puget Sound offers an active campus life, the surrounding area holds many attractions: The Puget Sound, the Cascades, and the Olympic National Park are all nearby and "people love being outdoors, walking down to the waterfront… taking bike rides, going to Mount Rainier." Camping, hiking, and whitewater rafting are all popular outdoor activities, and "There are usually people playing Frisbee-golf or Ultimate Frisbee out on the quad." Seattle is forty-five minutes away by car, and it "has an awesome live music scene (that definitely spills over into Tacoma), and being able to go to live shows all the time is a big draw." On campus, "There [is] a considerable amount of leadership opportunities" and "so much to do! There are clubs for everything, and if there isn't one for what you want, you can create it. There's dancing, movie nights, boat cruises." "There's a lot to do and a lot to think about. [Students have] conversations ranging from the latest video game to the presidential election, from the best joke a professor has told to how to get away with swimming naked in the fountain. People do all sorts of things for fun. There is drinking, of course, but it's definitely not a 'requirement'—there is plenty else to do." Greek life is popular but not dominant, as there are a lot of extracurricular offerings here, and "The theme houses are something completely unique and absolutely wonderful for meeting people and being introduced to new interests." All around, students say, "We know how to have an amazing time on the weekend, but during the week and during finals, the library is full to the gills with students working hard."

Student Body

On one hand, students in this "easygoing and friendly" community are loathe to generalize about themselves—"Everybody here is a very unique and exciting person and we are all passionate about our diverse areas of study!"—and on the other, some will admit, "Generally, the students are left wing, outdoorsy, committed to sustainability efforts," and suggest, "If you don't own flannel, get the hell out!" Overall, though, "There are people from all walks of life" on this campus, and "You're bound to find somewhere you fit in whether it is through BGLAD [the gay/straight alliance group], sports, classes, events, or the Greek system," and one student sums up the environment, saying, "I haven't ever been in a place that is more accepting of all backgrounds."

FINANCIAL AID: 253-879-3214 • E-MAIL: ADMISSION@PUGETSOUND.EDU • WEBSITE: WWW.PUGETSOUND.EDU

THE PRINCETON REVIEW SAYS

Admissions

Very important factors considered include: Academic GPA, rigor of secondary school record, standardized test scores. *Important factors considered include:* Application essay, recommendation(s), alumni/ae relation, character/personal qualities, extracurricular activities, racial/ethnic status, talent/ability. *Other factors considered include:* Class rank, first generation, interview, level of applicant's interest, volunteer work, work experience. SAT or ACT required; ACT with writing component recommended. TOEFL required of all international applicants. High school diploma is required and GED is accepted. *Academic units recommended:* 4 English, 4 mathematics, 4 science (4 science labs), 3 foreign language, 3 social studies, 3 history, 1 fine/visual/performing arts.

Financial Aid

Students should submit: FAFSA. The Princeton Review suggests that all financial aid forms be submitted as soon as possible after January 1. *Need-based scholarships/grants offered:* Federal Pell, SEOG, state scholarships/grants, private scholarships, the school's own gift aid. *Loan aid offered:* Direct Subsidized Stafford, Direct Unsubsidized Stafford, Direct PLUS, Federal Perkins. Applicants will be notified of awards on a rolling basis beginning March 15. Federal Work-Study Program available. Institutional employment available. Highest amount earned per year from on-campus jobs $2,650. Off-campus job opportunities are excellent.

The Inside Word

Puget Sound supplies students with detailed information about the selection process, which can help alleviate some of that college application angst. While academic background is the primary consideration of every admissions committee (and that includes both grades and the rigor of the classes in which those grades were obtained), Puget Sound considers the whole candidate, and demonstrated interest in a particular issue or extracurricular activity will strengthen any application. Applicants can count on a considerate and caring attitude before, during, and after the review process.

THE SCHOOL SAYS ". . ."

From the Admissions Office

"For over more than 100 years, students from many locations and backgrounds have chosen to join our community. It is a community committed to excellence in the classroom and in student organizations and activities. Puget Sound students are serious about rowing and writing, management and music, skiing and sciences, leadership and languages. At Puget Sound you'll be challenged—and helped—to perform at the peak of your ability."

SELECTIVITY	
Admissions Rating	**90**
# of applicants	7,194
% of applicants accepted	52
% of acceptees attending	18

FRESHMAN PROFILE	
Range SAT Critical Reading	570–680
Range SAT Math	560–660
Range SAT Writing	570–670
Range ACT Composite	26–30
Minimum paper TOEFL	550
Minimum web-based TOEFL	79
Average HS GPA	3.5
% graduated top 10% of class	32
% graduated top 25% of class	69
% graduated top 50% of class	94

DEADLINES	
Early decision	
Deadline	11/15 and 1/2
Notification	12/15 and 2/15
Regular	
Priority	1/15
Deadline	1/15
Notification	4/1
Nonfall registration?	yes

FINANCIAL FACTS	
Financial Aid Rating	**83**
Annual tuition	$40,040
Room and board	$10,390
Required fees	$210
Books and supplies	$1,000
% needy frosh rec. need-based scholarship or grant aid	100
% needy UG rec. need-based scholarship or grant aid	100
% needy frosh rec. non-need-based scholarship or grant aid	15
% needy UG rec. non-need-based scholarship or grant aid	8
% needy frosh rec. need-based self-help aid	75
% needy UG rec. need-based self-help aid	78
% frosh rec. any financial aid	89
% UG rec. any financial aid	90
% UG borrow to pay for school	60
Average cumulative indebtedness	$28,524
% frosh need fully met	16
% ugrads need fully met	18
Average % of frosh need met	73
Average % of ugrad need met	77

University of Redlands

1200 East Colton Avenue, Redlands, CA 92373 • Admissions: 909-335-4074 • Fax: 909-335-4089

CAMPUS LIFE

Quality of Life Rating	91
Fire Safety Rating	76
Green Rating	78
Type of school	private
Environment	town

STUDENTS

Total undergrad enrollment	3,175
% male/female	44/56
% from out of state	31
% frosh live on campus	92
# of fraternities	5
# of sororities	5
% African American	4
% Asian	4
% Caucasian	50
% Hispanic	19
% Native American	1
# of countries represented	17

SURVEY SAYS . . .

Lab facilities are great
Great computer facilities
Athletic facilities are great
Students are friendly
Students are happy
Musical organizations are popular

ACADEMICS

Academic Rating	90
% students returning for sophomore year	87
% students graduating within 4 years	56
% students graduating within 6 years	63
Calendar	4-4-1
Student/faculty ratio	12:1
Profs interesting rating	90
Profs accessible rating	91
Most classes have	10–19 students

MOST POPULAR MAJORS

business/commerce; liberal arts and sciences/liberal studies; psychology

APPLICANTS ALSO LOOK AT AND OFTEN PREFER

Loyola Marymount University, University of San Diego, Chapman University

AND SOMETIMES PREFER

University of Puget Sound, Santa Clara University, Occidental University

AND RARELY PREFER

Whittier Collge, Mills College

STUDENTS SAY ". . ."

Academics

The University of Redlands is a smallish liberal arts college in Southern California that offers "great financial aid" and "emphasizes a balanced, broad education." "Small class sizes provide a more hands-on learning experience" and "personal attention." Class discussions are "often spicy and provoking." Professors are "friendly," "always prepared," and "willing to help you with anything." Some students call the coursework here "demanding." Whatever the case, there are "endless academic opportunities," and Redlands has the "resources for just about anything" you can conjure up to study. Through the College of Arts and Sciences (CAS), the majority of students follow a conventional undergraduate curriculum, declaring majors and minors. About 200 students choose the innovative approach of the Johnston Center for Integrative Studies. They design their own majors, work with professors to create contracts for their courses, and receive narrative evaluations of their work (instead of letter grades). Other academic highlights at Redlands include an impressive school of music, an uncommon major in communicative disorders, and excellence across the hard sciences. The study abroad program is also awesome. Some forty percent of these undergrads take coursework in places far-flung, either for a traditional semester or during the fairly unique May Term, an intensive four-week period when students focus on one class. As far as complaints, red tape is pretty annoying—especially for a school this size. "Any bureaucratic task takes a million years to accomplish." Also, "A lot of courses aren't offered every year," and the ones that are available tend to "fill up fast."

Life

No one could deny that the Redlands campus "has incredible aesthetic appeal" and eye-popping scenery. It's also "bustling with fun people and tons of activities." "The whole campus is full of creativity." "There are programs and things to do every night, usually so much that you end up overbooking yourself and having to run from one thing to another in order to be everywhere you want to be." Though some note, "Some of the facilities are really old and outdated." This doesn't flag students' enthusiasm. "There is a lot of school spirit," and intercollegiate sports are popular. The Greek system, which consists of a handful of sororities and fraternities that are "not nationally affiliated," is pretty popular. However, "The party scene is only one part of life on campus and does not take over social life by any means." "There's a real spectrum of hard partiers and stone-cold sober people." The town of Redlands is "quirky" but "a bit isolated." Critics gripe that "there is not a lot to do" off campus. Devotees of the surrounding area tell us that there's "an excellent downtown" "with coffee shops, restaurants, and bars." "If you give the town half a chance," they maintain, "it actually has some cool features." In addition, the school sponsors a wealth of outdoor adventures and "rents out equipment such as snowboards, backpacks, sleeping bags, and anything else you would need in the wilderness." Students also take "trips up to Joshua Tree and Big Bear" or, for more urban fare, trek to Los Angeles.

Student Body

Students at Redlands are "passionate." They have a "sense of wonder and enthusiasm" and "a huge variety of interests." As a whole, students are "quite liberal" politically. Most students are "fairly involved in many aspects of school," and they promise that "everyone can find a niche somewhere on campus." The undergraduate population melds pretty well. There's "no separation of athletes, geeks, Greeks, etc." To the extent that there's any division, it's between Johnston students and students in the CAS. Johnston students—the ones who make their own majors and get evaluations instead of grades—definitely "pride themselves on their uniqueness," and they can be "eccentric." "There are colorful characters on both sides of the spectrum," though, and students assure us that any segregation is self-imposed. "I really don't see a line between the CAS and Johnston," observes one student. "It is only there for those who want it to be."

FINANCIAL AID: 909-748-8047 • E-MAIL: ADMISSIONS@REDLANDS.EDU • WEBSITE: WWW.REDLANDS.EDU

THE PRINCETON REVIEW SAYS

Admissions

Very important factors considered include: Academic GPA, recommendation(s), rigor of secondary school record, character/personal qualities, talent/ability. *Important factors considered include:* Application essay, standardized test scores. *Other factors considered include:* Alumni/ae relation, extracurricular activities, first generation, geographical residence, interview, volunteer work, work experience. SAT or ACT required; ACT with writing component recommended. TOEFL required of all international applicants. High school diploma is required and GED is accepted. *Academic units required:* 4 English, 3 mathematics, 2 science (1 science lab), 2 foreign language, 2 social studies. *Academic units recommended:* 4 English, 4 mathematics (including Algebra II), 3 science (1 science lab), 3 foreign language, 2 social studies, 1 history.

Financial Aid

Students should submit: FAFSA. The Princeton Review suggests that all financial aid forms be submitted as soon as possible after January 1. *Need-based scholarships/grants offered:* Federal Pell, SEOG, state scholarships/grants, private scholarships, school scholarship or grant aid from institutional funds. *Loan aid offered:* Federal Perkins, university loans from institutional funds. Applicants will be notified of awards on a rolling basis beginning February 28. Federal Work-Study Program available. Highest amount earned per year from on-campus jobs $2,400. Off-campus job opportunities are fair.

The Inside Word

The admit rate here is reasonably high and students with above-average high school records and respectable standardized test scores should could the school as a target. Candidates who are interested in pursuing the self-designed programs available through the Johnston Center will find the admissions process to be distinctly more personal. Note, though, that you have to be admitted as a regular student in the CAS first.

THE SCHOOL SAYS ". . ."

From the Admissions Office

"We've created an unusually blended curriculum of the liberal arts and pre-professional study because we think education is about learning how to think and learning how to do. For example, our environmental studies students have synthesized their study of sociology, biology, and economics to develop an actual resource management plan for the local mountain communities. Our creative writing program encourages internships with publishing or television production companies. We educate managers, poets, environmental scientists, teachers, musicians, and speech therapists to be reflective about culture and society so that they can better understand and improve the world they'll enter upon graduation.

"First-year students applying for admission are required to submit the results of either the SAT or the ACT. We do not require the writing section of either test."

SELECTIVITY	
Admissions Rating	87
# of applicants	4,125
% of applicants accepted	65
% of acceptees attending	24

FRESHMAN PROFILE	
Range SAT Critical Reading	520–620
Range SAT Math	520–620
Range SAT Writing	500–610
Range ACT Composite	22–27
Minimum paper TOEFL	550
Average HS GPA	3.6
% graduated top 10% of class	35
% graduated top 25% of class	37
% graduated top 50% of class	91

DEADLINES	
Early action	
Deadline	11/15
Notification	rolling
Regular	
Deadline	1/15
Notification	rolling
Nonfall registration?	yes

FINANCIAL FACTS	
Financial Aid Rating	89
Annual tuition	$39,038
Room and board	$11,924
Required fees	$300
Books and supplies	$1,650
% needy frosh rec. need-based scholarship or grant aid	90
% needy UG rec. need-based scholarship or grant aid	85
% needy frosh rec. non-need-based scholarship or grant aid	21
% needy UG rec. non-need-based scholarship or grant aid	10
% needy frosh rec. need-based self-help aid	83
% needy UG rec. need-based self-help aid	91
% frosh rec. any financial aid	90
% UG rec. any financial aid	88
% UG borrow to pay for school	67
% frosh need fully met	37
% ugrads need fully met	34
Average % of frosh need met	90
Average % of ugrad need met	88

UNIVERSITY OF RHODE ISLAND

NEWMAN HALL, KINGSTON, RI 02881 • ADMISSIONS: 401-874-7100 • FAX: 401-874-5523

CAMPUS LIFE

Quality of Life Rating	**66**
Fire Safety Rating	**88**
Green Rating	**92**
Type of school	public
Environment	village

STUDENTS

Total undergrad enrollment	12,943
% male/female	45/55
% from out of state	54
% frosh live on campus	90
# of fraternities	13
# of sororities	10
% African American	5
% Asian	3
% Caucasian	71
% Hispanic	7
# of countries represented	45

SURVEY SAYS . . .

Great library
Frats and sororities dominate social scene
Student publications are popular
Lots of beer drinking
Hard liquor is popular

ACADEMICS

Academic Rating	**66**
% students returning for sophomore year	82
% students graduating within 4 years	41
% students graduating within 6 years	63
Calendar	semester
Student/faculty ratio	16:1
Profs interesting rating	69
Profs accessible rating	68
Most classes have	20–29 students
Most lab/discussion sessions have	10–19 students

MOST POPULAR MAJORS

communication studies/speech communication and rhetoric; nursing/registered nurse (rn, asn, bsn, msn); psychology

APPLICANTS ALSO LOOK AT AND RARELY PREFER

Carnegie Mellon University, Occidental College, University of Maryland, Baltimore County

STUDENTS SAY ". . ."

Academics

The University of Rhode Island "is a school that challenges me to think big and outside the box," says one student. URI is known for having "excellent science programs," including a "marine biology program [that] is one of the best in the Northeast." Other stand-out majors include "nursing, pharmacy, and engineering." Praise for teachers and staff garners varied reactions, as this student notes, "You have bad mixed in with good, but I will say that the good professors are top-notch." As far as transitioning to the workplace, a sophomore says, "URI has impressive programs that help get your career started as soon as possible and also act as a bridge to graduate school." Another student observes that the staff is also "great at helping freshmen transferring from home to college, and there are lots of different programs offered to help students excel academically." Overall, URI is known to have a solid liberal ideology with "openness to creative and critical exploration." This engineering major finds the environment to be rather "forward-thinking [with an] emphasis on today's global workforce." URI is described as providing a "great sense of community" with a philosophical message that students should be connected to the world around them.

Life

The school's proximity to the beach and to other major cities like Providence and Boston make it appealing to students from all over the Northeast. "I think its beauty is definitely a strength, and the location near the beach is great," says a communication major. If fine dining is meaningful to your quality of life, it's worth noting that URI's dining hall has "won a national award the past two years in a row." There are complaints about the dry campus. One senior says, "Because we have a dry campus, people usually live in the surrounding neighborhoods, so you can travel to your friends' houses and party." Others say that students who live nearby still choose to stay on campus during weekends, since this is where their social life is centered. Life isn't all about "getting wasted," chides one sophomore. "Sometimes we get together [to] make dinner and just have a movie night inside our apartment." Students are said to have a "two brain track" in terms of serious attention to study followed by equal attention to "relaxing and having a good time." One student says, "Basketball games are really fun to watch," and "Newport cliff walks are popular during the nice weather." Greek life is a big part of URI's campus yet many students don't feel obliged to pledge; still they enjoy the Greek life's social offerings, "which accounts for the majority of on-campus activities."

Student Body

URI, as an affordable state school, naturally attracts a large percentage of Rhode Islanders. Rumor has it that this group "sticks to their friends from high school," yet one undergrad observes, "Rhody-borns are so afraid of college turning into another four years of high school that we go searching for new people to meet." As far as categorizing a "typical student," undergrads are reluctant to stereotype. "URI is diverse, and the students cannot be generalized into a certain type." Campus diversity is strong, and most groups intermingle without issue. One junior sums it up: "Just like any other college, some come to party and some come to learn, but in the end they are all good people."

FINANCIAL AID: 401-874-7530 • E-MAIL: ADMISSION@URI.EDU • WEBSITE: WWW.URI.EDU

THE PRINCETON REVIEW SAYS

Admissions

Very important factors considered include: Rigor of secondary school record. *Important factors considered include:* Class rank, application essay, academic GPA, standardized test scores. *Other factors considered include:* Recommendation(s), alumni/ae relation, character/personal qualities, extracurricular activities, first generation, geographical residence, level of applicant's interest, racial/ethnic status, state residency, talent/ability, volunteer work, work experience. SAT or ACT required; ACT with or without writing component accepted. TOEFL required of all international applicants. High school diploma is required and GED is accepted. *Academic units required:* 4 English, 3 mathematics, 2 science (1 science lab), 2 foreign language, 2 social studies, 5 academic electives.

Financial Aid

Students should submit: FAFSA. Regular filing deadline is February 15. The Princeton Review suggests that all financial aid forms be submitted as soon as possible after January 1. *Need-based scholarships/grants offered:* Federal Pell, SEOG, state scholarships/grants, private scholarships, the school's own gift aid. *Loan aid offered:* Direct Subsidized Stafford, Direct Unsubsidized Stafford, Direct PLUS, Federal Perkins, Federal Nursing, state loans, college/university loans from institutional funds. Applicants will be notified of awards on a rolling basis beginning March 31. Federal Work-Study Program available. Institutional employment available. Highest amount earned per year from on-campus jobs $2,000. Off-campus job opportunities are good.

The Inside Word

Early decision deadline is December 1. Don't forget to apply to URI's merit-based scholarships, which are open to international students as well. Remember if you're a resident of another New England state (besides Rhode Island) you may be eligible, depending on your major, for discounted tuition.

THE SCHOOL SAYS ". . ."

From the Admissions Office

"Outstanding freshman candidates admission with a minimum SAT score of 1200 (combined Critical Reading and Math) or ACT composite score of 25 who rank in the top quarter of their high school class are eligible to be considered for a Centennial Scholarship. These merit-based scholarships range up to full tuition and are renewable each semester if the student maintains full-time continuous enrollment and a 3.0 average or better. In order to be eligible for consideration, all application materials must be received in the Admission Office by the December 1, early action deadline. Applications are not considered complete until the application fee, completed application, official high school transcript, list of senior courses, personal essay, and SAT or ACT scores (sent directly from the testing agency) are received.

"If a student is awarded a Centennial Scholarship, and his or her residency status changes from out-of-state to regional or in-state, the amount of the award will be reduced to reflect the reduced tuition rate.

"The SAT math and critical reading scores are used for admission evaluation and Centennial Scholarship consideration. The writing score is not currently used for admission evaluation or Centennial Scholarship consideration."

SELECTIVITY

Admissions Rating	75
# of applicants	20,012
% of applicants accepted	76
% of acceptees attending	21
# accepting a place on wait list	526
# admitted from wait list	28

FRESHMAN PROFILE

Range SAT Critical Reading	490–590
Range SAT Math	500–610
Range SAT Writing	490–590
Range ACT Composite	21–26
Minimum paper TOEFL	550
Minimum web-based TOEFL	79
Average HS GPA	3.4
% graduated top 10% of class	18
% graduated top 25% of class	49
% graduated top 50% of class	87

DEADLINES

Early action	
Deadline	12/1
Notification	2/3
Regular	
Deadline	2/1
Notification	3/31
Nonfall registration?	yes

FINANCIAL FACTS

Financial Aid Rating	81
Annual in-state tuition	$9,824
Annual out-state tuition	$25,912
Room and board	$10,767
Required fees	$1,542
Books and supplies	$1,200
% needy frosh rec. need-based scholarship or grant aid	91
% needy UG rec. need-based scholarship or grant aid	82
% needy frosh rec. non-need-based scholarship or grant aid	11
% needy UG rec. non-need-based scholarship or grant aid	7
% needy frosh rec. need-based self-help aid	84
% needy UG rec. need-based self-help aid	77
% frosh rec. any financial aid	79
% UG rec. any financial aid	72
% UG borrow to pay for school	73
Average cumulative indebtedness	$25,973
% frosh need fully met	65
% ugrads need fully met	69
Average % of frosh need met	63
Average % of ugrad need met	69

UNIVERSITY OF RICHMOND

BRUNET SARAH HALL, 28 WESTHAMPTON WAY, RICHMOND, VA 23173 • ADMISSIONS: 804-289-8640 • FAX: 804-287-6003

CAMPUS LIFE

Quality of Life Rating	90
Fire Safety Rating	77
Green Rating	94
Type of school	private
Environment	metropolis

STUDENTS

Total undergrad enrollment	2,886
% male/female	46/54
% from out of state	78
% from public high school	57
% frosh live on campus	100
# of fraternities	8
# of sororities	7
% African American	7
% Asian	5
% Caucasian	61
% Hispanic	6
% international	7
# of countries represented	68

SURVEY SAYS . . .

Great computer facilities
Athletic facilities are great
Great food on campus
Campus feels safe
Low cost of living

ACADEMICS

Academic Rating	94
% students returning for sophomore year	94
% students graduating within 4 years	77
% students graduating within 6 years	83
Calendar	semester
Student/faculty ratio	8:1
Profs interesting rating	90
Profs accessible rating	91
Most classes have	10–19 students
Most lab/discussion sessions have	10–19 students

MOST POPULAR MAJORS

business administration and management; English language and literature; accounting

APPLICANTS ALSO LOOK AT AND OFTEN PREFER

College of William and Mary, Boston College, Georgetown University, Princeton University, The University of North Carolina at Chapel Hill, University of Notre Dame

AND SOMETIMES PREFER

University of Virginia, Villanova University, Wake Forest University

AND RARELY PREFER

Loyola University Maryland, Elon University, University of Pennsylvania

STUDENTS SAY ". . ."

Academics

The University of Richmond provides "the resources of a large university with the personal attention of a small college" and just "a hint of Southern charm." Financial aid is "generous." Facilities are "outstanding." "Students have access to state-of-the-art technologies and research labs that normally only graduate students would be able to work with." Among the sixty or so undergraduate majors, students call our attention to the "great business program" and the "excellent premed program." "Another of Richmond's strengths is its study abroad programs." Every year, a few hundred Richmond students take classes in more than thirty countries or complete a summer internship in one of six countries. The "core liberal arts program" here is reasonably broad and pretty much all coursework is "rigorous." "There are no easy classes," "and there is a significant amount of homework." The degree of difficulty notwithstanding, though, faculty members are overwhelmingly "brilliant," "insightful, accommodating," and "extremely accessible." "They genuinely care about their students and they make themselves totally available," gushes a political science major. "We're a school where professors know all of their students' names," expounds an English major, "and where the president of the university stops and talks to you on the way to your next class."

Life

This "gorgeous," "peaceful," "isolated" suburban campus comes complete with "glistening lake in the center of it." During the week, "Students get down to business" academically. "Everybody is in the library." However, "Every single student is involved with an extracurricular activity or two" as well, "and since there aren't 20,000 students here, everyone has a chance to make a difference." A solid contingent of students plays intercollegiate or intramural sports or is "extremely invested" in a club sport. Fraternities and sororities also play a "very big" social role. However, some students "really dislike Greek life," and they insist that the Greek system "does not dominate the social scene." Other students flatly assert, "Greek life rules the Richmond campus." Parties are popular at the "frat lodges" (essentially an edifice containing a large dance floor with an area to serve beer, a deck, and a backyard). For those looking for a more intimate scene, apartment parties are also popular. "There are concerts, sporting events, movies, and just groups of friends doing a wide variety of things" as well. Off campus, "Richmond contains so many options for things to do and meaningful place to volunteer. The city itself contains so much history." Though some believe the university should be "more involved in the greater Richmond community."

Student Body

Nearly eighty percent of the students at Richmond come from out of state. "A large percentage of the students here are attending on scholarship or with a very generous financial aid package," and "more and more, the school is starting to diversify from its stereotype as just rich white kids" "who seem to have unlimited spending budgets." There's also a "growing number of" international students. Nevertheless, "Richmond is pretty homogenous." The typical student is "from 'outside Philly' or 'outside Boston'" or is a "Mid-Atlantic prep school kid" "who probably owns several pairs of Sperrys." Many students "dress well" and "obviously care about their physical appearance." There are "lots of Polos, button-downs, and sundresses." Otherwise, these "clean cut," and (if they don't mind saying so themselves) "good looking" students are "ambitious," "friendly," "outgoing," "overcommitted, and usually a little stressed." There's also "a great mixture of nerds and athletes," and "Everyone brings their own sense of individuality."

FINANCIAL AID: 804-289-8438 • E-MAIL: ADMISSION@RICHMOND.EDU • WEBSITE: WWW.RICHMOND.EDU

THE PRINCETON REVIEW SAYS

Admissions

Very important factors considered include: Academic GPA, rigor of secondary school record. *Important factors considered include:* Application essay, class rank, standardized test scores, character/personal qualities, talent/ability. *Other factors considered include:* First generation, recommendation(s), alumni/ae relation, extracurricular activities, geographical residence, interview, racial/ethnic status, state residency, volunteer work, work experience. SAT or ACT required; ACT with or without writing component accepted. TOEFL required of all international applicants. High school diploma is required and GED is accepted. *Academic units required:* 4 English, 3 mathematics, 2 science (2 science labs), 2 foreign language, 2 social studies. *Academic units recommended:* 4 English, 4 mathematics, 4 science (4 science labs), 4 foreign language, 4 social studies.

Financial Aid

Students should submit: FAFSA, CSS PROFILE, copies of federal tax returns. Regular filing deadline is February 15. The Princeton Review suggests that all financial aid forms be submitted as soon as possible after January 1. *Need-based scholarships/grants offered:* Federal Pell, SEOG, state scholarships/grants, private scholarships, school scholarships or grant aid from institutional funds. *Loan aid offered:* Direct Subsidized Stafford, Direct Unsubsidized Stafford, Direct PLUS, Federal Perkins. Applicants will be notified of awards beginning in April. Federal Work-Study Program available and institutional work program available. Off-campus job opportunities are excellent.

The Inside Word

While the University of Richmond remains a little bit of a safety school for students with loftier goals, the standardized test scores and grades of incoming students at Richmond are tremendous and most undergraduates here finished in the top quarter of their high school classes. Note also the pile of financial aid that's available here to students with exceptional credentials.

THE SCHOOL SAYS ". . ."

From the Admissions Office

"The University of Richmond combines the characteristics of a small college with the dynamics of a large university. The unique size, beautiful suburban campus, and world-class facilities offer students an extraordinary mix of opportunities for personal growth and intellectual achievement. At Richmond, students are encouraged to engage themselves in their environment. Discussion and dialogue are at the forefront of the academic experience, while research, internships, and international experiences are important components of students' co-curricular lives. The university is committed to providing undergraduate students with a rigorous academic experience, while integrating these studies with opportunities for experiential learning and promoting total individual development. The university also places a high value on diversity and believes in taking full advantage of the rich benefits of learning in a community of individuals from varied backgrounds.

"The University of Richmond requires either the SAT or the ACT. We do not prefer either test. We evaluate all three sections of the SAT (critical reading, math, and writing); the writing section of the ACT is optional. If multiple tests are submitted, the admission committee considers those results that are most favorable to the applicant. We do not require or recommend SAT Subject Tests."

SELECTIVITY

Admissions Rating	**95**
# of applicants	9,431
% of applicants accepted	33
% of acceptees attending	25
# accepting a place on wait list	1,192
# admitted from wait list	83
# of early decision applicants	758
# accepted early decision	292

FRESHMAN PROFILE

Range SAT Critical Reading	580–690
Range SAT Math	610–700
Range SAT Writing	580–690
Range ACT Composite	28–31
Minimum paper TOEFL	550
Minimum web-based TOEFL	80
% graduated top 10% of class	59
% graduated top 25% of class	85
% graduated top 50% of class	98

DEADLINES

Early decision	
Deadline	11/15
Notification	12/15
Regular	
Deadline	1/15
Notification	4/1
Nonfall registration?	no

FINANCIAL FACTS

Financial Aid Rating	**97**
Annual tuition	$44,210
Room and board	$9,760
Books and supplies	$1,050
% needy frosh rec. need-based scholarship or grant aid	99
% needy UG rec. need-based scholarship or grant aid	99
% needy frosh rec. non-need-based scholarship or grant aid	17
% needy UG rec. non-need-based scholarship or grant aid	10
% needy frosh rec. need-based self-help aid	81
% needy UG rec. need-based self-help aid	86
% frosh rec. any financial aid	61
% UG rec. any financial aid	69
% UG borrow to pay for school	46
Average cumulative indebtedness	$22,915
% frosh need fully met	94
% ugrads need fully met	93
Average % of frosh need met	100
Average % of ugrad need met	100

UNIVERSITY OF ROCHESTER

300 WILSON BOULEVARD, ROCHESTER, NY 14627 • ADMISSIONS: 585-275-3221 • FAX: 585-461-4595

CAMPUS LIFE

Quality of Life Rating	**77**
Fire Safety Rating	**80**
Green Rating	**86**
Type of school	private
Environment	metropolis

STUDENTS

Total undergrad enrollment	5,643
% male/female	49/51
% from out of state	58
% from public high school	74
% frosh live on campus	96
# of fraternities	17
# of sororities	13
% African American	4
% Asian	11
% Caucasian	59
% Hispanic	5
% international	11
# of countries represented	92

SURVEY SAYS . . .

Great library
Low cost of living
Musical organizations are popular
Very little drug use

ACADEMICS

Academic Rating	**84**
% students returning for sophomore year	95
% students graduating within 4 years	74
% students graduating within 6 years	84
Calendar	semester
Student/faculty ratio	9:1
Profs interesting rating	77
Profs accessible rating	78
Most classes have	10–19 students

MOST POPULAR MAJORS

biology/biological sciences; economics; psychology

STUDENTS SAY ". . ."

Academics

The University of Rochester's "innovative core curriculum, where there are essentially no required classes," is a strong draw for many students. This flexibility "is extremely rare and truly encourages personal exploration rather than conventional general education." "Instead of the college telling us what we have to study...students must chart out their own academic paths." Students agree this key difference ensures "Everyone is passionate about what they study because they get to choose every single class." The classes students have to choose from are described as "top-notch." As one student points out, "I definitely perceive the academics at University of Rochester as Ivy League caliber." U of R is highly regarded as a "cutting-edge research university." "There's a spirit of intellectual curiosity and student camaraderie at the U of R." Although the professors are highly praised for their "uniform brilliance," among other qualities, some students feel that "their intellectual know-how does not always translate into strong teaching skills." But most students focus on the strengths of their professors saying they "care about the subjects they teach and are constantly in the process of expanding knowledge in their fields. It is an honor to be influenced by and to influence such incredible minds." Students are also quick to mention the strong musical influence at the school. This "awesome music scene" is due to the Eastman School of Music, which "brings many interesting and world-famous performers to our little city." Of the many clubs on campus, the a cappella groups are "immensely popular" at U of R, with four different groups on campus that "easily sell out our biggest auditorium."

Life

Although the University of Rochester has several hot selling points for undergraduates, the weather is not high on the list. One student described the typical student as "nerdy and normally freezing!" Locals don't seem to complain though. They know that "being in western New York, we can get a lot of snow," and so they just add an extra layer of clothes. For others, there is simply too much else going on to notice. The more than 200 clubs available on campus are very popular. Students are "extremely involved" and are "a part of at least two or three clubs. And [a part means] they are actively involved and may even be on the executive board." Music, athletics, and studying in the library (which "is both a social and study place") are popular ways to spend time. Many students enjoy "getting off campus to bowl, ice skate, or go to the mall." Some students feel the school is "overly strict on fraternity parties as well as off-campus bar nights." Other students appreciate that vigilance, "Because our campus is not situated in the safest area of the city, it is necessary that security is strict."

Student Body

Students at U of R strive to "be the best that you can be." The school's motto, "Meliora," is a Latin word meaning "ever better" and may "sum up what U of R is all about." As one student expounds, "Everyone on campus is doing something to change the world. This means that students are super involved in their own thing, but it also means that the school is supportive of you and how you wish to change the world." This "genuine and extremely passionate" view of their school and themselves creates a strong bond and sense of "community" among students. "Everyone here really loves learning; it's wonderful being at a place where everyone is a self-proclaimed nerd." "A typical student here is someone who took honors classes in high school and lots of AP classes and did amazing." "Most people here are also quirky, but in a friendly, cool way." Students tend to put academics first, which may explain why although many students participate in sports, athletics do not rule the school. The plus side to being a Division III school is that "it is not impossible to join a sports team and actually get playing time."

FINANCIAL AID: 585-275-3226 • E-MAIL: ADMIT@ADMISSIONS.ROCHESTER.EDU • WEBSITE: WWW.ROCHESTER.EDU

THE PRINCETON REVIEW SAYS

Admissions

Very important factors considered include: Recommendation(s), rigor of secondary school record, character/personal qualities. *Important factors considered include:* Application essay, academic GPA, standardized test scores, extracurricular activities, interview, talent/ability. *Other factors considered include:* Class rank, alumni/ae relation, first generation, geographical residence, level of applicant's interest, racial/ethnic status, volunteer work, work experience. SAT or ACT required; ACT with writing component required. TOEFL required of all international applicants. High school diploma is required and GED is accepted.

Financial Aid

Students should submit: FAFSA, CSS/Financial Aid PROFILE, state aid form, noncustodial PROFILE, business/farm supplement. Regular filing deadline is February 1. The Princeton Review suggests that all financial aid forms be submitted as soon as possible after January 1. *Need-based scholarships/grants offered:* Federal Pell, SEOG, state scholarships/grants, the school's own gift aid. *Loan aid offered:* Direct Subsidized Stafford, Direct Unsubsidized Stafford, Direct PLUS, Federal Perkins, Federal Nursing, college/university loans from institutional funds. Applicants will be notified of awards on or about April 1. Federal Work-Study Program available. Institutional employment available. Off-campus job opportunities are excellent.

The Inside Word

With nearly 5,300 undergrads, applicants to Rochester can expect a highly individualized academic experience—something that makes this school not only a great place to learn, but also an increasingly competitive institution when it comes to admissions. The most important consideration for admission is grades and standardized test scores, followed closely by the rigor of class work and recommendations. Keep in mind that Rochester is looking for students who will fit well within the school's academic environment and dem onstrate a true interest in attending—that is, scheduling an interview could go a long way in increasing your odds.

THE SCHOOL SAYS ". . ."

From the Admissions Office

"Rochester believes that excellence requires freedom. In the Rochester Curriculum, students are free to select the courses that appeal to them most. There are no required subjects; students' interests drive their education. Students major in either sciences and engineering, humanities, or social sciences and complete a "cluster" of at least three related courses in each of the other two areas. Because Rochester is among America's smallest research universities, its students can pursue advanced studies and research in graduate courses, in arts and science or in any one of Rochester's nationally ranked schools of engineering, medicine, nursing, music, education, and business.

"Learning here takes place on a personal scale. Rochester remains one of the most collegiate among top research universities, with smaller classes and a nine to one student-faculty ratio—all within a university setting that attracts more than $400 million in research funding each year. Rochester faculty publish articles across the globe, win awards for their work, and collaborate with undergraduate students on a level that is rare in higher education.

"The expectation is that each student will live up to Rochester's motto, "Meliora" (ever better), recognizing that they are future leaders in industry, education, and culture. Navigating through world-renowned facilities and resources, a day in the life of two Rochester students—or any two days in the life of a single student—is never the same."

SELECTIVITY	
Admissions Rating	**96**
# of applicants	13,678
% of applicants accepted	37
% of acceptees attending	23
# accepting a place on wait list	577
# admitted from wait list	47
# of early decision applicants	705
# accepted early decision	263
FRESHMAN PROFILE	
Range SAT Critical Reading	600–700
Range SAT Math	650–740
Range SAT Writing	610–700
Range ACT Composite	28–32
Minimum paper TOEFL	600
Minimum web-based TOEFL	100
Average HS GPA	3.8
% graduated top 10% of class	74
% graduated top 25% of class	92
% graduated top 50% of class	100
DEADLINES	
Early decision	
Deadline	11/1
Notification	12/15
Regular	
Priority	12/1
Deadline	1/1
Notification	4/1
Nonfall registration?	yes
FINANCIAL FACTS	
Financial Aid Rating	**89**
Annual tuition	$41,040
Room and board	$12,120
Required fees	$786
Books and supplies	$1,250
% needy frosh rec. need-based scholarship or grant aid	99
% needy UG rec. need-based scholarship or grant aid	98
% needy frosh rec. non-need-based scholarship or grant aid	12
% needy UG rec. non-need-based scholarship or grant aid	8
% needy frosh rec. need-based self-help aid	87
% needy UG rec. need-based self-help aid	90
% frosh rec. any financial aid	85
% UG rec. any financial aid	85
% UG borrow to pay for school	64
Average cumulative indebtedness	$28,100
% frosh need fully met	100
% ugrads need fully met	97
Average % of frosh need met	100
Average % of ugrad need met	97

UNIVERSITY OF SAN DIEGO

5998 Alcala Park, San Diego, CA 92110-2492 • Admissions: 619-260-4506 • Fax: 619-260-6836

CAMPUS LIFE

Quality of Life Rating	**90**
Fire Safety Rating	**73**
Green Rating	**96**
Type of school	private
Affiliation	Roman Catholic
Environment	metropolis

STUDENTS

Total undergrad enrollment	5,409
% male/female	45/55
% from out of state	46
% from public high school	57
% frosh live on campus	96
# of fraternities	5
# of sororities	7
% African American	2
% Asian	6
% Caucasian	58
% Hispanic	17
% international	5
# of countries represented	70

SURVEY SAYS . . .

Lab facilities are great
Great computer facilities
Students get along with local community
Students love San Diego, CA
Great off-campus food
Dorms are like palaces
Campus feels safe
Students are happy

ACADEMICS

Academic Rating	**82**
% students returning for sophomore year	87
% students graduating within 4 years	64
Calendar	4-1-4
Student/faculty ratio	16:1
Profs interesting rating	80
Profs accessible rating	85
Most classes have	30–39 students
Most lab/discussion sessions have	10–19 students

MOST POPULAR MAJORS

business administration and management; communication studies/speech communication and rhetoric; finance

APPLICANTS ALSO LOOK AT AND OFTEN PREFER

University of Southern California

AND SOMETIMES PREFER

Loyola Marymount University

AND RARELY PREFER

University of California—San Diego

STUDENTS SAY ". . ."

Academics

This "academically challenging, Roman Catholic" institution couples "amazing academics" and "wonderful teachers and programs" with "great weather and a beautiful campus." As one liberal studies major notes, "I just felt an overwhelming sense of belonging the very first time I stepped on campus. I fell in love right away." USD "strives and puts into action ways to create a well-rounded student who is able to succeed out in the real world." Major draws to the curriculum here include "small class sizes, potential relationships with professors, and the caring nature of the faculty." The professors "are there for you and want you to do your best…I love that the classes are taught by instructors with PhDs rather than TAs. It is great having your professor know you personally." Beyond the picturesque coastal campus—"It is in San Diego"—"undergraduate research opportunities are great!" In addition, USD has a strong undergraduate business program. USD is all about "discovering one's passions in the classroom in order to fulfill them in the real world." Besides the high caliber academics, "It is vacation weather year round. I went to the beach and tanned in January; very few other college students can say that."

Life

Life at USD boasts "beauty and brains!" USD is a "laid-back school overlooking the ocean, so people are happy to be at school and in class every day." Many tout a picture of the campus as a "country club escape from the city with outstanding professors, a friendly student body, and a five-minute drive to the beach." It's a "beach town, so surfing, laying out, bathing suits, sunglasses, and flip-flops are very prevalent." Going to the beach "is easy, you can see the ocean from campus." A car "is not totally necessary, the campus is equipped with everything you need and we have Zipcar on campus!" "It's a very active and fit" community. Some note that they "would love to see more diversity on campus." "There is a big difference between students with scholarships and those who don't need scholarships to attend." Yet others note that there are "tremendous opportunities to get involved at USD, local community and abroad!" "San Diego is about working hard for what you want, but it has everything you need to enjoy your undergraduate years." At USD, "There is always something to do for fun." There "is a party scene, but it is not overbearing to the point where it is necessary to drink." A typical day in the life of a USD student "is to go to class, get a delicious breakfast burrito at La Paloma (served all day) and hit the beach for parties on the weekend." Those adventurers looking to relax "can go to the pool, beach, parties at the beach, downtown's Gaslamp District, and Sea World on the weekends." Plus, "You are only 1.5 hours away from Disneyland and Los Angeles and four hours from Las Vegas!" Surrounding San Diego is "an amazing city."

Student Body

USD "produces students who have a desire to pursue their dreams with philanthropy." In general, all students at USD are "motivated" and "looking to better themselves and achieve personal success." As one student says, "The students here are like the protagonists in a TV series." However, "Don't let the students' good looks, high fashion, or athletic prowess and wealth fool you, these students had 4.0s in high school, have intense internships, compete for graduate and professional school spots, and are constantly serving the community." Others concede, the typical student "comes from substantial wealth, [is] white, has a strong work ethic, [and is] laid-back, athletic, outgoing, and friendly." Though, others note, "There are exceptions to the USD stereotype." Many students "receive financial aid" and thus join the leagues of those who "are very motivated to get good grades." Since USD is a Catholic school, "There are quite a few of us who are religious." Others note, "It feels a lot like high school…all the groups keep to themselves." Yet others say with the wealth of campus clubs, sporting events, internship, and community service opportunities, "There seems to be a niche for everyone."

FINANCIAL AID: 619-260-4514 • E-MAIL: ADMISSIONS@SANDIEGO.EDU • WEBSITE: WWW.SANDIEGO.EDU

THE PRINCETON REVIEW SAYS

Admissions

Very important factors considered include: Academic GPA, rigor of secondary school record, standardized test scores, religious affiliation/commitment. *Important factors considered include:* Class rank, application essay, recommendation(s), character/personal qualities, extracurricular activities, talent/ability, volunteer work. *Other factors considered include:* Alumni/ae relation, first generation, geographical residence, level of applicant's interest, racial/ethnic status, work experience. SAT or ACT required; ACT with writing component required. TOEFL required of all international applicants. High school diploma is required and GED is accepted. *Academic units required:* 4 English, 3 mathematics, 3 science (2 science labs), 2 foreign language, 3 social studies. *Academic units recommended:* 4 English, 4 mathematics, 4 science (3 science labs), 3 foreign language, 4 social studies.

Financial Aid

Students should submit: FAFSA. The Princeton Review suggests that all financial aid forms be submitted as soon as possible after January 1. *Need-based scholarships/grants offered:* Federal Pell, SEOG, state scholarships/grants, private scholarships, the school's own gift aid, Federal Nursing Scholarships. *Loan aid offered:* Direct Subsidized Stafford, Direct Unsubsidized Stafford, Direct PLUS, Federal Perkins, college/university loans from institutional funds. Applicants will be notified of awards on a rolling basis beginning March 1. Federal Work-Study Program available. Institutional employment available. Off-campus job opportunities are good.

The Inside Word

USD offers a broad liberal arts core, small classes, and close interaction between students and professors. The dazzling campus and an unbeatable location are just gravy. As such, admission here is competitive. Solid test scores and outstanding grades should be a given for applicants.

THE SCHOOL SAYS ". . ."

From the Admissions Office

"The University of San Diego has received many local, regional, and national honors in its short, sixty-year history. We are known around the world for our beautiful campus, our outstanding faculty, our sustainability efforts, study abroad programs and the community service work done by our students. Recently, USD was selected as a "change maker" campus, one of only fourteen schools in the world so designated by the Ashoka Foundation. It is this honor that captures the spirit of USD and ties together all the others.

"We believe that the world's problems can be solved. We believe that the solution to these problems will not be found through a single discipline or focus. Instead, we know that the world's problems will be solved through innovation, collaboration, and compassion. USD was founded six decades ago with the principles of Catholic social teaching, a living tradition to work for socially just and peaceful societies and a mission to prepare generations of people changing the world for the better.

"We seek students who also believe in social innovation and change. Students at USD are bright, as our rapidly-growing student profile attests. But they also bring a passion for learning and making a difference. Through our strong liberal arts curriculum, international experiences, faculty and programs, we take that passion and turn it into a lifetime of making the world a better place."

SELECTIVITY	
Admissions Rating	93
# of applicants	13,867
% of applicants accepted	48
% of acceptees attending	17
# accepting a place on wait list	628
# admitted from wait list	28

FRESHMAN PROFILE	
Range SAT Critical Reading	560–650
Range SAT Math	570–670
Range SAT Writing	570–660
Range ACT Composite	26–30
Minimum paper TOEFL	550
Minimum web-based TOEFL	80
Average HS GPA	3.9
% graduated top 10% of class	44
% graduated top 25% of class	81
% graduated top 50% of class	98

DEADLINES	
Early action	
Deadline	11/15
Notification	1/31
Regular	
Deadline	1/15
Notification	4/15
Nonfall registration?	yes

FINANCIAL FACTS	
Financial Aid Rating	75
% needy frosh rec. need-based scholarship or grant aid	95
% needy UG rec. need-based scholarship or grant aid	93
% needy frosh rec. non-need-based scholarship or grant aid	55
% needy UG rec. non-need-based scholarship or grant aid	43
% needy frosh rec. need-based self-help aid	78
% needy UG rec. need-based self-help aid	81
% frosh rec. any financial aid	77
% UG rec. any financial aid	70
% UG borrow to pay for school	49
Average cumulative indebtedness	$31,937
% frosh need fully met	14
% ugrads need fully met	14
Average % of frosh need met	72
Average % of ugrad need met	69

UNIVERSITY OF SAN FRANCISCO

2130 FULTON STREET, SAN FRANCISCO, CA 94117 • ADMISSIONS: 415-422-6563 • FAX: 415-422-2217

CAMPUS LIFE

Quality of Life Rating	**78**
Fire Safety Rating	**60***
Green Rating	**78**
Type of school	private
Affiliation	Roman Catholic
Environment	metropolis

STUDENTS

Total undergrad enrollment	5,329
% male/female	36/64
% from out of state	33
% from public high school	52
% frosh live on campus	86
# of fraternities	4
# of sororities	4
% African American	3
% Asian	19
% Caucasian	38
% Hispanic	17
% international	11
# of countries represented	78

SURVEY SAYS . . .

Great library
Athletic facilities are great
Diverse student types on campus
Students get along with local community
Students love San Francisco, CA
Great off-campus food

ACADEMICS

Academic Rating	**77**
% students graduating within 4 years	53
% students graduating within 6 years	70
Calendar	4-1-4
Student/faculty ratio	13:1
Profs interesting rating	80
Profs accessible rating	77
Most classes have	10–19 students
Most lab/discussion sessions have	10–19 students

MOST POPULAR MAJORS

business/commerce; nursing/registered nurse (rn, asn, bsn, msn); psychology

APPLICANTS ALSO LOOK AT AND OFTEN PREFER

Santa Clara University, University of California—Berkeley, University of Southern California, Stanford University, University of California—Davis

AND SOMETIMES PREFER

Loyola Marymount University, University of San Diego, University of California—Santa Cruz, University of California—Santa Barbara, Seattle University

AND RARELY PREFER

Fordham University, Boston College

STUDENTS SAY ". . ."

Academics

With its "Jesuit morals" and "close-knit" community, this "academically rigorous school" focuses on "promoting social justice, tolerance, and community spirit." USF "teaches its students about the importance of helping others and making a difference in today's society." The curriculum here not only focuses "a lot on education but on making students aware of issues in the world and, on a smaller scale, the local community." Classes here are about "educating minds and hearts to change the world." As one student notes, "I wanted to go to a small school in a big city that promotes important issues like social justice and community service." Many tout the school's "diversity" and "remarkable education." "Because the school is small, classes are too." "One-on-one attention from professors is common." "Professors are sincerely passionate about their subject and try to engage students and share their passion while ensuring learning and comprehension." "Most of the professors are really enthusiastic about their classes because most of them have already worked in the areas they're teaching and can enlighten us on their past failures and successes." "During my junior and senior semesters at USF, I began to really appreciate my professors of upper-division courses that are really devoted to their teachings."

Life

"People here love to go out and have a good time." Living in San Francisco, "There is always something to do." People "go out into the city to enjoy the beach, parks, downtown, city landmarks, club events, social justice groups, protests, and rallies for causes." When looking for a place to spend an idle-while afternoon, students "go to Golden Gate Park [or] take MUNI downtown." "There are too many places to eat!" Chinatown "is always fun; Fisherman's wharf and Pier 39 are always fun too." On campus, students are "very involved." This typical motto reverberates, "I have two on campus jobs, and I'm active in three clubs!" When it comes to socializing, "People think and discuss a lot of things; topics like religion, politics, international issues, [and] the environment." Using the gym "is also something to do since you get free membership to Koret Gym if you are a student at USF." On the weekend, for fun, students go to "the free festivals that are going on in the city…go shopping in downtown, hang out at the park, or check out a neighborhood or area I've never been to before with my friends." Those with an outdoors bent "enjoy going on bike rides through Golden Gate Park or to China Beach and watching the sunset." In general, life here is all about "managing my time in a way that I can get all my work done and still have time to hang out with friends." Dorms are generally well accommodated, but "like any other campus," students note, "The facilities in some of the building could be updated and the computer labs could be updated."

Student Body

A typical student at USF "cannot clearly be defined" as "the students at the University of San Francisco are from all walks of life"; "Students easily fit in to the school," which is "extremely diverse." Students "are very accepting of all cultures." True to their Jesuit values and passion for community service, students here call out the following attributes like roll call. Students are "outgoing, cheerful, fashionable, and active socially, politically, [and] environmentally." "Everyone is very friendly and tolerant," and "There are always new people to meet." While "there is no 'typical student'" at USF, "Many students here are definitely involved in a green movement, sustainability, community service or international affairs." Those who are quick to affix a label cast the following stereotype, "Guys [at USF] are more of the grungy or hipster types. For girls, the school is a show…you find out quickly that many intend to see and be seen. Athletes [tend to] stick together." Whatever cues their fashion code may call for, the average student here "studies a lot [and is] always on the move helping out someone in need." "Ambitious goals" pervade student thinking, and everyone is "kind toward others." In essence, "San Francisco is home to a wide variety of people and, as such, so is USF."

UNIVERSITY OF SAN FRANCISCO

FINANCIAL AID: 415-422-6303 • E-MAIL: ADMISSION@USFCA.EDU • WEBSITE: WWW.USFCA.EDU

THE PRINCETON REVIEW SAYS

Admissions

Very important factors considered include: Academic GPA, recommendation(s), rigor of secondary school record, standardized test scores. *Important factors considered include:* Class rank, application essay. *Other factors considered include:* Alumni/ae relation, character/personal qualities, extracurricular activities, interview, talent/ability, volunteer work. SAT or ACT required; ACT with or without writing component accepted. TOEFL required of all international applicants. High school diploma is required and GED is accepted. *Academic units recommended:* 4 English, 3 mathematics, 2 science (2 science labs), 2 foreign language, 3 social studies, 6 academic electives, 1 chemistry and 1 biology or physics is required of nursing and science applicants.

Financial Aid

Students should submit: FAFSA. The Princeton Review suggests that all financial aid forms be submitted as soon as possible after January 1. *Need-based scholarships/grants offered:* Federal Pell, SEOG, state scholarships/grants, private scholarships, the school's own gift aid, Federal Nursing Scholarships. *Loan aid offered:* Direct Subsidized Stafford, Direct Unsubsidized Stafford, Direct PLUS, Federal Perkins, Federal Nursing, college/university loans from institutional funds. Note: Direct loans are for graduate students only. Applicants will be notified of awards on a rolling basis beginning April 1. Federal Work-Study Program available. Institutional employment available. Highest amount earned per year from on-campus jobs $2,000. Off-campus job opportunities are excellent.

The Inside Word

The admissions committee at USF isn't purely numbers-focused. They'll evaluate your full picture here, using your academic strengths and weaknesses along with your personal character strengths, essays, and recommendations to assess your suitability for admission. It's matchmaking. If you fit well in the USF community, you'll be welcome.

THE SCHOOL SAYS ". . ."

From the Admissions Office

"The University of San Francisco has experienced a significant increase in applications for admission over the past five years. We select applicants with strong academic credentials who will make the most of the university's academic opportunities, location in San Francisco, and its mission to educate minds and hearts to challenge the world. Community outreach and service to others, along with academic excellence, are characteristics that help distinguish those offered admission.

"The University has just completed a major upgrade to all administrative computer systems, including software that will help with student compatibility matching in residence halls.

"Applicants are required to take the SAT reasoning test (or the ACT with the writing section). The writing sections will be used for advising and placement purposes. SAT subject test scores will also be accepted."

SELECTIVITY	
Admissions Rating	84
# of applicants	8,485
% of applicants accepted	64
% of acceptees attending	19
FRESHMAN PROFILE	
Range SAT Critical Reading	510–620
Range SAT Math	520–620
Range SAT Writing	510–620
Range ACT Composite	22–27
Minimum paper TOEFL	550
Minimum web-based TOEFL	79
Average HS GPA	3.5
% graduated top 10% of class	26
% graduated top 25% of class	61
% graduated top 50% of class	91
DEADLINES	
Early action	
Deadline	11/15
Notification	1/16
Regular	
Priority	1/15
Deadline	4/1
Nonfall registration?	yes
FINANCIAL FACTS	
Financial Aid Rating	69
Annual tuition	$36,000
Room and board	$11,540
Required fees	$380
Books and supplies	$1,500
% needy frosh rec. need-based scholarship or grant aid	87
% needy UG rec. need-based scholarship or grant aid	87
% needy frosh rec. non-need-based scholarship or grant aid	9
% needy UG rec. non-need-based scholarship or grant aid	7
% needy frosh rec. need-based self-help aid	90
% needy UG rec. need-based self-help aid	89
% UG borrow to pay for school	64
Average cumulative indebtedness	$26,886
% frosh need fully met	7
% ugrads need fully met	6
Average % of frosh need met	67
Average % of ugrad need met	65

UNIVERSITY OF SCRANTON

800 LINDEN STREET, SCRANTON, PA 18510-4699 • ADMISSIONS: 570-941-7540 FAX: 570-941-5928

CAMPUS LIFE

Quality of Life Rating	**84**
Fire Safety Rating	**88**
Green Rating	**67**
Type of school	private
Affiliation	Roman Catholic-Jesuit
Environment	city

STUDENTS

Total undergrad enrollment	4,069
% male/female	45/55
% from out of state	58
% frosh live on campus	61
% African American	2
% Asian	2
% Caucasian	82
% Hispanic	7
% international	1
# of countries represented	21

SURVEY SAYS . . .

School is well run
Students are friendly
Frats and sororities are unpopular or nonexistent
Lots of beer drinking
Hard liquor is popular

ACADEMICS

Academic Rating	**79**
% students returning for sophomore year	88
% students graduating within 4 years	65
% students graduating within 6 years	77
Calendar	semester
Student/faculty ratio	11:1
Profs interesting rating	84
Profs accessible rating	85
Most classes have	10–19 students
Most lab/discussion sessions have	10–19 students

MOST POPULAR MAJORS

biology/biological sciences; nursing; exercise science

APPLICANTS ALSO LOOK AT AND OFTEN PREFER

St. Joseph's University, Loyola College (MD), Quinnipiac University, University of Delaware

AND SOMETIMES PREFER

Drexel University, Sacred Heart University, James Madison University

STUDENTS SAY ". . ."

Academics

With "an outstanding record for admission to graduate programs, not only in law and medicine but also in several other fields," The University of Scranton is a good fit for ambitious students seeking "a Jesuit school in every sense of the word. If you come here, expect to be challenged to become a better person, to develop a strong concern for the poor and marginalized, and to grow spiritually and intellectually." The school manages to accomplish this without "forcing religion upon you, which is nice." Undergraduates also approve of the mandatory liberal-arts-based curriculum that "forces you to learn about broader things than your own major." Strong majors here include "an amazing occupational therapy program. "This is a great place for premeds and other sciences," students agree. While the workload can be difficult, "a tutoring center provides free tutoring for any students who may need it, and also provides work-study positions for students who qualify to tutor." Need more help? Professors "are extremely accessible. They will go to any lengths to help you understand material and do well," while administrators "are here for the students, and show that every day inside and outside of the classroom." Community ties here are strong; as one student points out, "the Jesuits live in our dorms, creating an even greater sense of community, because we don't view them as just priests, we view them as real people who can relate on our level."

Life

"There is a whole range of activities to do on the weekends" at The University of Scranton, including "frequent trips, dances, and movies that are screened for free." Students tell us "the school and student organizations provide plenty of options, such as retreats, talent shows, and other various activities." There are also "many intramurals to become involved in, and the varsity sports (specifically the women's) are very successful." Furthermore, "being a Jesuit school, social justice issues are huge. They are taught in the classroom, and students spend a lot of time volunteering." Hometown Scranton is big enough to provide "movie theaters, two malls, parks, a bowling alley, and a skiing/snowboarding mountain." In short, there are plenty of choices for the non-partier at Scranton. Many we heard from in our survey reported busy extracurricular schedules. But those seeking a party won't be disappointed here, either. Scranton undergrads "party a lot, but they balance it with studying. Parties are chances to go out, see people, dance, and drink if you want." You "can find a party any time of day, seven days a week" here, usually with a keg tapped and pouring. Few here feel the party scene is out of hand, however a typical student writes, "It's very different than at schools with Greek systems. It is a lot more laid-back, and all about everyone having a good time."

Student Body

While "the typical Scranton student is white, Catholic, and from the suburbs," students hasten to point out "within this sameness, there is much diversity. There are people who couldn't care at all about religion, and there are people who are deeply religious. Even in the Catholic atmosphere of the school, the school only requires that you learn about Catholicism as it stands. Theology classes…are prefaced with the idea that 'You do not have to believe this!'" Undergrads here are generally "friendly and welcoming. Cliques are pretty much nonexistent, and anyone who would be classified as 'popular' is only considered so because they are extremely friendly, outgoing, and seek out friendships with as many people as possible." Students tend to be on the Abercrombie-preppy side, with lots of undergrads of Italian, Irish, and Polish descent.

FINANCIAL AID: 570-941-7700 • E-MAIL: ADMISSIONS@SCRANTON.EDU • WEBSITE: WWW.SCRANTON.EDU

THE PRINCETON REVIEW SAYS

Admissions

Very important factors considered include: Class rank, academic GPA, rigor of secondary school record, standardized test scores. *Important factors considered include:* Extracurricular activities. *Other factors considered include:* Application essay, recommendation(s), alumni/ae relation, character/personal qualities, interview, level of applicant's interest, talent/ability, volunteer work, work experience. SAT or ACT required; ACT with writing component required. TOEFL required of all international applicants. High school diploma is required and GED is accepted. *Academic units required:* 4 English, 3 mathematics, 3 science (1 science lab), 2 foreign language, 2 social studies, 2 history, 4 academic electives. *Academic units recommended:* 4 English, 4 mathematics, 3 science (1 science lab), 2 foreign language, 3 social studies, 3 history, 4 academic electives.

Financial Aid

Students should submit: FAFSA. The Princeton Review suggests that all financial aid forms be submitted as soon as possible after January 1. *Need-based scholarships/grants offered:* Federal Pell, SEOG, state scholarships/grants, private scholarships, the school's own gift aid. *Loan aid offered:* Direct Subsidized Stafford, Direct Unsubsidized Stafford, Direct PLUS, Federal Perkins, Federal Nursing. Applicants will be notified of awards on a rolling basis beginning March 15. Federal Work-Study Program available. Institutional employment available. Off-campus job opportunities are good.

The Inside Word

Admission to Scranton gets harder each year. A steady stream of smart kids from the tristate area keeps classes full and the admit rate low. Successful applicants will need solid grades and test scores. As with many religiously affiliated schools, students should be a good match philosophically as well.

THE SCHOOL SAYS ". . ."

From the Admissions Office

"The University of Scranton is a Catholic and Jesuit university that is known for outstanding academic quality, a beautiful and technology-rich campus and a sense of community that helps students feel right at home. Our fifty-eight-acre hillside campus in northeastern Pennsylvania is just two hours from New York City and Philadelphia. Since 2003, we've invested more than $237 million in campus improvements, either completed or under way. The first phase of the Loyola Science Center, as well as the new apartment/fitness complex on Mulberry Street, were completed in fall 2011. Our location offers the best of both worlds—the city and the mountains. From campus, you can walk downtown to shop, watch a movie, visit a museum or see a show. The area also features minor league ice hockey and baseball, concerts, skiing, hiking, malls and shopping outlets.

"The University offers more than sixty majors, eighty clubs and activities, and eighteen Division III athletic teams to the 4,069 undergraduate students in attendance. Scranton develops leaders in every sense through rigorous preparation in students' chosen fields coupled with a commitment to educating the whole person in the liberal arts tradition. Students extend their academic experience through participation in honors programs, internships, faculty-student research and study abroad, and the University provides excellent preparation for medical and other health professions doctoral programs, law school, graduate school, and post-graduate fellowships and scholarships.

"Students can apply online for free at scranton.edu/apply, or schedule a visit online at scranton.edu/visit, or by calling us at 1-888-SCRANTON."

SELECTIVITY

Admissions Rating	82
# of applicants	9,046
% of applicants accepted	72
% of acceptees attending	16
# accepting a place on wait list	323
# admitted from wait list	29

FRESHMAN PROFILE

Range SAT Critical Reading	510–600
Range SAT Math	520–610
Range ACT Composite	22–26
Minimum paper TOEFL	500
Minimum web-based TOEFL	61
Average HS GPA	3.4
% graduated top 10% of class	26
% graduated top 25% of class	59
% graduated top 50% of class	88

DEADLINES

Early action	
Deadline	11/15
Notification	12/15
Regular	
Deadline	3/1
Notification	rolling
Nonfall registration?	yes

FINANCIAL FACTS

Financial Aid Rating	76
Annual tuition	$37,106
Room and board	$13,804
Required fees	$350
Books and supplies	$1,200
% needy frosh rec. need-based scholarship or grant aid	97
% needy UG rec. need-based scholarship or grant aid	96
% needy frosh rec. non-need-based scholarship or grant aid	6
% needy UG rec. non-need-based scholarship or grant aid	6
% needy frosh rec. need-based self-help aid	86
% needy UG rec. need-based self-help aid	87
% frosh rec. any financial aid	72
% UG rec. any financial aid	71
% UG borrow to pay for school	74
Average cumulative indebtedness	$32,582
% frosh need fully met	11
% ugrads need fully met	11
Average % of frosh need met	72
Average % of ugrad need met	74

UNIVERSITY OF SOUTH CAROLINA—COLUMBIA

OFFICE OF UNDERGRADUATE ADMISSIONS, COLUMBIA, SC 29208 • ADMISSIONS: 803-777-7700 • FAX: 803-777-0101

CAMPUS LIFE

Quality of Life Rating	**88**
Fire Safety Rating	**88**
Green Rating	**99**
Type of school	public
Environment	city

STUDENTS

Total undergrad enrollment	22,556
% male/female	46/54
% from out of state	35
% frosh live on campus	94
# of fraternities	24
# of sororities	15
% African American	11
% Asian	3
% Caucasian	78
% Hispanic	4
% international	1
# of countries represented	112

SURVEY SAYS . . .

Athletic facilities are great
Everyone loves the Fighting Gamecocks
Frats and sororities dominate social scene
Student publications are popular
Lots of beer drinking
Hard liquor is popular

ACADEMICS

Academic Rating	**71**
% students returning for sophomore year	87
% students graduating within 4 years	54
% students graduating within 6 years	70
Calendar	semester
Student/faculty ratio	17:1
Profs interesting rating	75
Profs accessible rating	79
Most classes have	20–29 students
Most lab/discussion sessions have	20–29 students

MOST POPULAR MAJORS

experimental psychology; nursing/registered nurse (rn, asn, bsn, msn); sport and fitness administration/management

APPLICANTS ALSO LOOK AT AND OFTEN PREFER

Clemson University, University of Georgia

AND SOMETIMES PREFER

University of North Carolina—Chapel Hill, College of Charleston, North Carolina State University, Virginia Tech

AND RARELY PREFER

Florida State University

STUDENTS SAY ". . ."

Academics

At the University of South Carolina's flagship campus, you'll find "a mixture of deep South tradition and an increasingly progressive education." You can get "a good degree in just about any field" here. The nationally recognized business school is "definitely a strength." There's a "great nursing program" as well. USC also excels in journalism, chemistry, and hospitality management. In most majors, the academic atmosphere is "not impossible, but a good amount of time goes into studying outside of class." "It is just the right amount of work to still have a good social life," opines a broadcast journalism major. Students in the "fantastic" honors college enjoy "small, discussion-based classes and a lot of personal attention." Meanwhile, for the run of USC-ers, classes are much bigger, teaching assistants are common, and the professors "vary vastly." A lot of professors are "very well-prepared," "very approachable," and "passionate about their subjects." "Most of the teachers I have had here have been outstanding," reports a business major. Other faculty members "just read through slides." Still others are "generally unhelpful, unapproachable, and more concerned with their research." USC's administration is "very friendly" and "student-oriented." Getting things done "can be slow" and advising can be "completely unorganized," but "the bureaucracy is easy to navigate," which definitely isn't the norm at your average state school.

Life

Students here enjoy "awesome" weather and a "pretty," "historical campus." "A lot of the buildings are very old" and could use a serious makeover, though. "Parking is a problem," too. For many students, "Attending college sporting events is the most fun thing to do at USC." "The school spirit is crazy," reports a senior. "In the fall, student life revolves strongly around football." Home games "are an all-day event." "The tailgating is epic." However, you can have "good fun year-round." "It's a big school, so there's a little of everything." "There are tons of resources for the students to use," including "a world-class gym." "Intramural sports are very popular." Guest speakers and big-name performers are numerous. Greek life is "huge" and Columbia is a "fun college town." "People party hard here at USC." It's easy to "get trashed on the weekends" because "the campus is surrounded by nightlife." Five Points is a bar district within "walking distance" "that is super fun." The Vista, which is similar to Five Points but a bit more upscale, is another bar-filled area of town that "students love to visit." When the hankering for road trips arises, students appreciate that the campus is "close to Charleston and Charlotte, and not too far from Atlanta."

Student Body

Archetypal students at USC are "politically conservative, openly religious (mostly Christian), and traditionally Southern." The atmosphere "can be intimidating to non-Southerners at times." "If you are from a different part of the country," counsels a first-year student, "it's a culture shock." Students here are also "very involved on campus" and exceedingly proud of their school. "We all have Gamecock pride," explains a sophomore. Otherwise, this place is "a huge melting pot," with "a wide range" of students and organizations. Students who pledge fraternities and sororities constitute the most visible bloc. "A lot of the girls are the classic blond Southern girl and many of the guys are preppy" types sporting "boat shoes," "sunglasses around their necks," and a "frat-boy swoop" hairdo. "There is a different group for everyone down here," though. "Good old boys and some more progressive types," "artsy" kids, "gothic" kids, "theater kids, ROTC kids," and "self-proclaimed honors college nerds" all have their respective niches. "Every type of person goes to this school," says a sophomore.

FINANCIAL AID: 803-777-8134 • E-MAIL: ADMISSIONS-UGRAD@SC.EDU • WEBSITE: WWW.SC.EDU

THE PRINCETON REVIEW SAYS

Admissions

Very important factors considered include: Academic GPA, rigor of secondary school record, standardized test scores. *Important factors considered include:* Class rank. *Other factors considered include:* Application essay, recommendation(s), alumni/ae relation, character/personal qualities, extracurricular activities, first generation, racial/ethnic status, state residency, talent/ability, volunteer work, work experience. SAT or ACT required; ACT with writing component required. TOEFL required of all international applicants. High school diploma is required and GED is accepted. *Academic units required:* 4 English, 4 mathematics, 3 science (3 science labs), 2 foreign language, 2 social studies, 1 history, 1 academic electives, 2 PE or ROTC and fine arts.

Financial Aid

Students should submit: FAFSA. The Princeton Review suggests that all financial aid forms be submitted as soon as possible after January 1. *Need-based scholarships/grants offered:* Federal Pell, SEOG, state scholarships/grants, private scholarships, the school's own gift aid, United Negro College Fund, Federal Nursing Scholarships, USC Opportunity Grant—Institutional Gamecock Guarantee. *Loan aid offered:* Direct Subsidized Stafford, Direct Unsubsidized Stafford, Direct PLUS, Federal Perkins, Federal Nursing. Applicants will be notified of awards on a rolling basis beginning January 4. Federal Work-Study Program available. Institutional employment available. Off-campus job opportunities are good.

The Inside Word

Provided that you've completed a strong and serious college preparatory curriculum, it's not tremendously difficult to get admitted here. Like at most large schools, the process is largely based on grades and test scores. Applicants with a B-plus average and SAT section scores in the mid 500s (or an ACT composite in the low 20s) often get in. With higher standardized scores, you can sneak in with spottier grades. Likewise, if your grades are really good, your test scores can be lower.

THE SCHOOL SAYS ". . ."

From the Admissions Office

"In just six years, the number of annual undergraduate applicants to USC has doubled, making it more critical than ever for students to meet the university's priority application deadline. The University of South Carolina's national prominence in academics and research activities also has increased. USC is one of only thirty-five public research institutions to earn a designated status of 'very high research activity' by the Carnegie Foundation. As early as their freshman year, undergraduates are encouraged to compete for research grants. As South Carolina's flagship institution, USC offers more than 350 degree programs. More than 30,000 students seek baccalaureate, masters, or doctoral degrees. USC is known for its top-ranked academic programs, including its international business and exercise science programs—both rated number one nationally. Other notable programs include chemical and nuclear engineering; health education; hotel, restaurant, and tourism; marine science; law; medicine; nursing; and psychology, among others. USC is recognized for its pioneering efforts in freshman outreach, and the South Carolina Honors College is ranked number one in the country compared to all other honors colleges in public university settings. USC offers student support in such areas as career development, disability services, preprofessional planning, and study abroad. On campus, students enjoy a state-of-the-art fitness center, an 18,000-seat arena, an 80,000-seat stadium, and nearly 300 student organizations. Off campus, South Carolina's world-famous beaches and the Blue Ridge Mountains are each less than a three-hour drive away. The University of South Carolina is located in the state's capital city, making it a great place for internships and job opportunities."

SELECTIVITY	
Admissions Rating	85
# of applicants	21,311
% of applicants accepted	63
% of acceptees attending	34

FRESHMAN PROFILE	
Range SAT Critical Reading	540–640
Range SAT Math	560–650
Range ACT Composite	24–29
Minimum paper TOEFL	550
Minimum web-based TOEFL	77
Average HS GPA	3.9
% graduated top 10% of class	28
% graduated top 25% of class	62
% graduated top 50% of class	91

DEADLINES	
Early action	
Deadline	10/15
Notification	12/21
Regular	
Deadline	12/1
Notification	3/22
Nonfall registration?	yes

FINANCIAL FACTS	
Financial Aid Rating	76
Annual in-state tuition	$9,768
Annual out-state tuition	$25,952
Room and board	$8,026
Required fees	$400
Books and supplies	$950
% needy frosh rec. need-based scholarship or grant aid	47
% needy UG rec. need-based scholarship or grant aid	53
% needy frosh rec. non-need-based scholarship or grant aid	86
% needy UG rec. non-need-based scholarship or grant aid	61
% needy frosh rec. need-based self-help aid	91
% needy UG rec. need-based self-help aid	91
% frosh rec. any financial aid	91
% UG rec. any financial aid	85
% UG borrow to pay for school	47
Average cumulative indebtedness	$24,837
% frosh need fully met	31
% ugrads need fully met	29
Average % of frosh need met	76
Average % of ugrad need met	76

The University of South Dakota

414 East Clark, Vermillion, SD 57069 • Admissions: 605-677-5434 • Fax: 605-677-6323

CAMPUS LIFE

Quality of Life Rating	**67**
Fire Safety Rating	**91**
Green Rating	**76**
Type of school	public
Environment	village

STUDENTS

Total undergrad enrollment	6,220
% male/female	38/62
% from out of state	36
% frosh live on campus	84
# of fraternities	8
# of sororities	3
% African American	2
% Asian	1
% Caucasian	89
% Hispanic	3
% Native American	2
% international	1
# of countries represented	41

SURVEY SAYS . . .

Low cost of living
Student publications are popular
Lots of beer drinking
Very little drug use

ACADEMICS

Academic Rating	**67**
% students returning for sophomore year	76
% students graduating within 4 years	25
% students graduating within 6 years	49
Calendar	semester
Student/faculty ratio	18:1
Profs interesting rating	73
Profs accessible rating	69
Most classes have	10–19 students
Most lab/discussion sessions have	20–29 students

MOST POPULAR MAJORS

business/commerce; education; psychology

APPLICANTS ALSO LOOK AT AND OFTEN PREFER

University of Nebraska—Lincoln

STUDENTS SAY ". . ."

Academics

With an honors program that is "the best-kept secret in the country" and professors who are "nearly always willing to go the extra mile for students," the University of South Dakota offers a "great student to faculty communicative experience at a reasonable price." Numerous departments garner praise from students, and the University boasts winners "almost every year for big scholarships like the Goldwater and Truman, competing with big, Ivy League, private colleges that charge quadruple the amount for the same education." While the nursing school is the most frequently praised, the "business, biology, premed, law, and psychology classes are very solid," and the "dental hygiene, music, and journalism schools" also stand out, with the most copious laurels heaped on the music department's professors who are "some of the best." All told, the wide selection of quality academics "gives students many options as far as majors go," and for students willing to throw themselves into their studies "the odds of getting into a professional or graduate program are good."

Life

"We work hard, so we can play hard," sums up the undergraduate philosophy at USD. "Although there is a lot of partying that happens, the students keep themselves occupied with school work, intramural sports, and hanging out with their friends." Vermillion's small size seems to be a double-edged sword; some insist that "the size of the town means no one is more than a 10-minute walk/bike ride away!" and that "since it is a smaller campus students have more opportunities to be involved in internships and various other activities." But the fact remains that "Many of the upperclassmen live in the larger cities to the north and south." In general, "students have to make their own fun, which often involves partying or taking small road trips to other cities in the area." For those planning to roam further afield, "Vermillion is located very close to Yankton, Sioux City (IA), and Sioux Falls (all within an hour). They are bigger cities and offer everything a person would want to do (shopping, movies, entertainment)."

Student Body

A typical USD student "would be a conservative Midwesterner. He or she would be Caucasian" and would most likely have originated in "small towns in South Dakota, Iowa, and Nebraska." "Many people join a Greek system or are athletes or musicians. Those who do not fit into these three main groups seem to focus on their academics" and "[fit] in fine with the majority because of the open mindedness of most students." For example, "Gay students are able to get along with the rest of student population." There's no denying that "partying is a definite part of the culture, though many of the 'smart' kids both party and work hard." Student organizations call out to many, and "it seems like every person on campus is part of at least one of them. It is a great way to meet new people and [to participate in] activities."

FINANCIAL AID: 605-677-5446 • E-MAIL: ADMISSIONS@USD.EDU • WEBSITE: WWW.USD.EDU

THE PRINCETON REVIEW SAYS

Admissions

Very important factors considered include: Class rank, academic GPA, rigor of secondary school record, standardized test scores. *Important factors considered include:* Alumni/ae relation. *Other factors considered include:* Application essay, recommendation(s), character/personal qualities, extracurricular activities, geographical residence, racial/ethnic status, state residency, talent/ability, volunteer work, work experience. SAT or ACT required; ACT with or without writing component accepted. TOEFL required of all international applicants. High school diploma is required and GED is accepted. *Academic units required:* 4 English, 3 mathematics, 3 science (3 science labs), 3 social studies, 1 fine arts. *Academic units recommended:* 4 English, 4 mathematics, 4 science (3 science labs), 2 foreign language, 3 social studies, 1 fine arts.

Financial Aid

Students should submit: FAFSA. The Princeton Review suggests that all financial aid forms be submitted as soon as possible after January 1. *Need-based scholarships/grants offered:* Federal Pell, SEOG, private scholarships, the school's own gift aid, Federal Nursing Scholarships. *Loan aid offered:* Direct Subsidized Stafford, Direct Unsubsidized Stafford, Direct PLUS, Federal Perkins, Federal Nursing, college/university loans from institutional funds. Applicants will be notified of awards on a rolling basis beginning March 1. Federal Work-Study Program available. Institutional employment available. Highest amount earned per year from on-campus jobs $3,300. Off-campus job opportunities are good.

The Inside Word

To be a candidate for general admission to USD, you must meet one of three general requirements: rank in the top fifty percent of your graduating class or obtain an ACT/SAT composite score of 21/990 or higher or have a minimum grade point average of at least 2.6 on a 4.0 scale in all high school courses. An applicant's high school curricula must also meet certain minimum requirements.

THE SCHOOL SAYS ". . ."

From the Admissions Office

"The University of South Dakota is the perfect fit for students looking for a smart educational investment. USD is South Dakota's only designated liberal arts university and is consistently rated among the top doctoral institutions in the country. Annually, USD awards scholarships to more than 800 first-year students, and more than eighty percent of USD students receive some form of finan cial aid through grants, loans, and work-study jobs.

"USD students earn the nation's most prestigious scholarships. Our quality of teaching and research prepares students to pursue their passions all over the world, at institutions such as Columbia, Johns Hopkins, The University of Chicago, and beyond. Fifty-nine students have been awarded prestigious Fulbright, Rhodes, National Science Foundation, Boren, Truman, Udall, Gilman, and Goldwater scholarships and grants for graduate study. Personal attention from our award-winning faculty and our welcoming environment makes students feel right at home.

"As the flagship liberal arts institution in South Dakota, USD—founded in 1862—has long been regarded as a leader in the state and the region. Notable undergraduate and postgraduate alumni include journalist Ken Bode, author and former news anchor Tom Brokaw, writer and Emmy Award–winner Dorothy Cooper Foote, U.S. Senator Tim Johnson, USA Today founder Al Neuharth, and U.S. Senator John Thune.

"Applicants are not required to take the writing test for either SAT or ACT. USD recommends taking the ACT over the SAT. Students who wish to send their SAT scores will have their scores converted to ACT scores for placement and scholarship consideration."

SELECTIVITY

Admissions Rating	71
# of applicants	3,287
% of applicants accepted	89
% of acceptees attending	43

FRESHMAN PROFILE

Range SAT Critical Reading	460–550
Range SAT Math	460–580
Range ACT Composite	20–26
Minimum paper TOEFL	550
Minimum web-based TOEFL	81
Average HS GPA	3.3
% graduated top 10% of class	13
% graduated top 25% of class	37
% graduated top 50% of class	73

DEADLINES

Nonfall registration?	yes

FINANCIAL FACTS

Financial Aid Rating	85
Annual in-state tuition	$3,897
Annual out-state tuition	$5,843
Annual comprehensive tuition	$14,352
Room and board	$6,648
Required fees	$3,807
Books and supplies	$1,200
% needy frosh rec. need-based scholarship or grant aid	51
% needy UG rec. need-based scholarship or grant aid	54
% needy frosh rec. non-need-based scholarship or grant aid	72
% needy UG rec. non-need-based scholarship or grant aid	52
% needy frosh rec. need-based self-help aid	83
% needy UG rec. need-based self-help aid	88
% frosh rec. any financial aid	92
% UG rec. any financial aid	67
% UG borrow to pay for school	77
Average cumulative indebtedness	$23,338
% frosh need fully met	53
% ugrads need fully met	53
Average % of frosh need met	77
Average % of ugrad need met	74

UNIVERSITY OF SOUTH FLORIDA

4202 EAST FOWLER AVENUE, TAMPA, FL 33620-9951 • ADMISSIONS: 813-974-3350 • FAX: 813-974-9689

CAMPUS LIFE

Quality of Life Rating	**71**
Fire Safety Rating	**81**
Green Rating	**85**
Type of school	public
Environment	metropolis

STUDENTS

Total undergrad enrollment	29,310
% male/female	44/56
% from out of state	8
% from public high school	95
% frosh live on campus	76
# of fraternities	23
# of sororities	12
% African American	12
% Asian	6
% Caucasian	61
% Hispanic	17
% international	4
# of countries represented	157

SURVEY SAYS . . .

Diverse student types on campus
Different types of students interact
Students get along with local community
Great off-campus food
Everyone loves the Bulls
Student publications are popular
Student government is popular

ACADEMICS

Academic Rating	**72**
% students returning for sophomore year	89
% students graduating within 4 years	51
% students graduating within 6 years	53
Calendar	semester
Student/faculty ratio	28:1
Profs interesting rating	71
Profs accessible rating	68
Most classes have	20–29 students
Most lab/discussion sessions have	20–29 students

MOST POPULAR MAJORS

biomedical sciences; business/commerce; psychology

APPLICANTS ALSO LOOK AT AND OFTEN PREFER

University of Florida

AND SOMETIMES PREFER

Florida State University, University of Central Florida

STUDENTS SAY ". . ."

Academics

Conveniently located in Tampa, Florida, this top-tier state university attracts students for whom "price, diversity, and opportunities" are as important as a location that's "close to home." The University of South Florida "is all about community." One student says, "It was close to home, offered the degree that I wanted, offered me the most financial aid, and had many ties to the community and surrounding areas culturally and academically." USF may be huge, but this "does not affect the level of personal attention that students receive." Many here laud the honors program: "Classes are almost always discussion-based." In general, professors here "really want you to succeed." Students universally cheer, "The campus is beautiful!" Most of the professors "have worked twenty plus years in the field and are not strictly academia experienced, which results in more content-related discussions." Another adds, "Most professors, especially the business and philosophy related people, know their material and provide an open forum for learning." The College of Education has a sterling reputation for building "a caring community that expects excellence." With a large commuter population, there's a great diversity in the student body, "not just ethnically or culturally, but older students that bring experience and students from all socioeconomic levels." In addition, USF "is a top school for medical-related studies." USF offers the total package; "Fair tuition prices, a great city/location, excellent professors and [an excellent] learning atmosphere." USF is "doing everything within its capacity to provide the best education it can to every student, regardless of major, background, or ethnicity." This is an institution "dedicated to enriching their students and communities lives through eclectic methods."

Life

Life at USF "strongly promotes building a cohesive, comfortable community." The university enjoys "a diverse student population on a beautiful urban campus surrounded by a bustling city." Tampa "has a lot to offer for students. USF has so many clubs that each have various events, there is always something going on." Popular recreations include the "flea markets, poster sales, Patio Tuesdays (social event in the student center), clubs and organizations, free speech areas, residence hall parties, coffee houses, performances put on by the orchestras, bands, and theater, sports (Go Bulls!), guest speakers, etc." Many students enjoy the bustling club scene in Ybor City, a historic-district-turned-night-clubbing-district in Tampa's Latin Quarter where "there are a plethora of local bars and clubs to hang out at for fun."

Student Body

The USF student body is "a diverse mix socioeconomically, culturally, religiously, and racially." As one returning student testifies, "I am a non-traditional student in my fifties, and [I] feel completely comfortable in classes with students half my age. It's a very friendly school. All walks of life. I could not describe a typical student." USF "is a huge university." Every student "is completely different, so it's impossible to describe a 'typical' one." This makes for a welcome mix of professional and extracurricular interests; "So far, in every class it's been incredibly easy to get along with other classmates and everyone is really accepting of each other, no matter your background." As is often noted at many large universities with an active nightlife, "Most people here have two personalities. One is extremely studious persona and the other is a party animal. Basically when it's time to let loose we let loose." On-campus students "are involved in campus and community activities, friendly, busy, and often have active social lives." There's "a strong sense of community fostered by club and organization involvement." USF "offers plenty of places to gather on campus." Despite the size of the school, social life is filled by "all sorts of activities and organizations that make it very easy to interact with people who share your views and interests."

FINANCIAL AID: 813-974-4700 • E-MAIL: ADMISSIONS@ADMIN.USF.EDU • WEBSITE: WWW.USF.EDU

THE PRINCETON REVIEW SAYS

Admissions

Very important factors considered include: Academic GPA, rigor of secondary school record. *Important factors considered include:* Standardized test scores, first generation. *Other factors considered include:* Class rank, application essay, recommendation(s), character/personal qualities, extracurricular activities, geographical residence, state residency, talent/ability, volunteer work, work experience. SAT or ACT required; ACT with writing component required. High school diploma is required and GED is accepted. *Academic units required:* 4 English, 4 mathematics, 3 science (2 science labs), 2 foreign language, 3 social studies, 3 academic electives. *Academic units recommended:* 4 science (3 science labs), 4 foreign language.

Financial Aid

Students should submit: FAFSA. The Princeton Review suggests that all financial aid forms be submitted as soon as possible after January 1. *Need-based scholarships/grants offered:* Federal Pell, SEOG, state scholarships/grants, private scholarships, the school's own gift aid. *Loan aid offered:* Direct Subsidized Stafford, Direct Unsubsidized Stafford, Direct PLUS, Federal Perkins, college/university loans from institutional funds. Applicants will be notified of awards on a rolling basis beginning March 15. Federal Work-Study Program available. Institutional employment available. Off-campus job opportunities are good.

The Inside Word

A traditional college-prep high school course load is required for admission to USF. Beyond making sure that you complete all prerequisite classes, however, keep two other things in mind when applying to USF. First, admissions decisions are made on a rolling basis, so the earlier one applies, the better his or her chance of acceptance since there are more unfilled seats early in the admissions cycle. Second, AP and international baccalaureate classes are looked on favorably in the admissions office, so if your school offers them, load up on them and do well.

THE SCHOOL SAYS ". . ."

From the Admissions Office

"Located in the Tampa Bay metropolitan area, USF is recognized as one of the nation's top 27 public research universities. USF takes great pride in its faculty. Professors in all academic areas are responsible for discovering new solutions to existing and emerging problems. As an undergraduate at USF, you can participate actively in the creation of the knowledge that will be taught on other college campuses for decades to come. And, the faculty at USF is diverse as well.

"As students begin the application process, they should become familiar with USF's admission requirements. USF used extensive institutional research to validate that the high school GPA coupled with grade trends and the rigor of student's curriculum in high school are the most critical factors in student academic success at USF. Preference in admission, therefore, is given to students who complete at least three AP or IB courses, at least two college-level courses through dual enrollment, and additional coursework in math, science or foreign language beyond minimum requirements. "SAT and ACT scores, while important, are less critical in USF's admission decisions when the high school GPA and rigor of curriculum are both strong. USF does use the SAT writing and the ACT English/writing components to make decisions, as scores of 550 and 24 respectively are additional indicators of potential for academic success. USF also takes into account special talents in and outside of the classroom as well as whether a student would be in the first generation of the family to attend college.

"With some of the best weather in the country, it's always a great time to visit USF. Campus tours, information sessions and tours of the residence halls are offered on weekdays throughout the year and on most Saturday mornings from September through April. Reservations are strongly encouraged."

SELECTIVITY

Admissions Rating	**91**
# of applicants	30,921
% of applicants accepted	37
% of acceptees attending	32

FRESHMAN PROFILE

Range SAT Critical Reading	520–620
Range SAT Math	540–630
Range SAT Writing	500–600
Range ACT Composite	23–27
Minimum paper TOEFL	550
Average HS GPA	3.9
% graduated top 10% of class	32
% graduated top 25% of class	60
% graduated top 50% of class	73

DEADLINES

Regular	
Priority	1/2
Deadline	3/1
Notification	rolling
Nonfall registration?	yes

FINANCIAL FACTS

Financial Aid Rating	**65**
Annual in-state tuition	$4,060
Annual out-state tuition	$14,919
Room and board	$9,190
Required fees	$1,746
Books and supplies	$1,500
% needy frosh rec. need-based scholarship or grant aid	65
% needy UG rec. need-based scholarship or grant aid	13
% needy frosh rec. non-need-based scholarship or grant aid	94
% needy UG rec. non-need-based scholarship or grant aid	5
% needy frosh rec. need-based self-help aid	56
% needy UG rec. need-based self-help aid	63
% frosh rec. any financial aid	80
% UG rec. any financial aid	86
% UG borrow to pay for school	53
Average cumulative indebtedness	$21,784
% frosh need fully met	6
% ugrads need fully met	6
Average % of frosh need met	51
Average % of ugrad need met	47

University of Southern California

Office of Admission/John Hubbard Hall, Los Angeles, CA 90089-0911 • Admissions: 213-740-1111 • Fax: 213-821-0200

CAMPUS LIFE

Quality of Life Rating	**82**
Fire Safety Rating	**93**
Green Rating	**94**
Type of school	private
Environment	metropolis

STUDENTS

Total undergrad enrollment	17,090
% male/female	49/51
% from out of state	43
% from public high school	58
% frosh live on campus	98
# of fraternities	36
# of sororities	25
% African American	5
% Asian	23
% Caucasian	42
% Hispanic	14
% international	12
# of countries represented	115

SURVEY SAYS . . .

Great computer facilities
Everyone loves the Trojans
Frats and sororities dominate social scene
Musical organizations are popular
Student publications are popular

ACADEMICS

Academic Rating	**87**
% students returning for sophomore year	97
% students graduating within 4 years	73
% students graduating within 6 years	90
Calendar	semester
Student/faculty ratio	9:1
Profs interesting rating	81
Profs accessible rating	75
Most classes have	10–19 students
Most lab/discussion sessions have	20–29 students

MOST POPULAR MAJORS

business administration and management; communication studies/speech communication and rhetoric; psychology

APPLICANTS ALSO LOOK AT AND OFTEN PREFER

California Institute of Technology, Duke University, Harvard College, Massachusetts Institute of Technology, Stanford University, University of Pennsylvania, Yale University, Brown University

AND SOMETIMES PREFER

University of California—Berkeley, Northwestern University, Princeton University, Cornell University, Georgetown University, Washington University in St. Louis, John Hopkins University, Rice University, University of Virginia

AND RARELY PREFER

University of California—Los Angeles, University of California—San Diego, University of Michigan—Ann Arbor, Vanderbilt University

STUDENTS SAY ". . ."

Academics

The University of Southern California boasts "a dynamic and culturally diverse campus located in a world-class city which is equally dynamic and culturally diverse." Everything related to cinema is "top notch." Among the other 150 or so majors here, programs in journalism, business, engineering, and architecture are particularly notable. The honors programs are "very good," too. One of the best perks about USC is its "large and enthusiastic alumni network." Becoming "part of the Trojan Family" is a great way to jump-start your career because USC graduates love to hire other USC graduates. "Almost everyone talks about getting job offers based solely on going to USC." "The school seems to run very smoothly, with few administrative issues ever being problematic enough to reach the awareness of the USC student community," says an international relations major. The top brass "is a bit mysterious and heavy handed," though. Also, "they milk every dime they can get from you." Academically, some students call the general education courses "a complete waste of time." There are a few "real narcissists" on the faculty as well as some professors "who seem to just be there because they want to do research." Overall, though, students report professors "make the subject matter come alive" and make themselves "very available" outside the classroom. "My academic experience at USC is fabulous," gushes an aerospace engineering major. "I would not choose any other school."

Life

On campus, life is "vibrant." There are more than 600 student organizations. Theatrical and musical productions are "excellent." School spirit is "extreme" and "infectious." "Football games are huge." "There is absolutely nothing that can top watching our unbelievable football team throttle the competition," says a merciless sophomore. "Drinking is a big part of the social scene" as well. "We definitely have some of the sickest parties ever," claims an impressed freshman. "Greek life is very big" and, on the weekends, a strong contingent of students "religiously" visits "The Row, the street lined with all the fraternity and sorority houses." Students also have "the sprawling city of Los Angeles as their playground." It's an "eclectic place with both high and low culture and some of the best shopping in the world." "Hollywood clubs and downtown bars" are popular destinations. Art exhibits, concerts, and "hip restaurants" are everywhere. However, "you need a car." Los Angeles traffic may be "a buzz kill" but students report that it's considerably preferable to the "absolutely terrible" public transportation system.

Student Body

The one thing that unites everyone here is "tons of Trojan pride." USC students are also "intensely ambitious" and, while there are some "complete slackers," many students hit the books "harder than they let on." Otherwise, students insist that, "contrary to popular belief, USC has immense diversity." "The stereotypical USC student is a surfer fraternity bro or a tan, trendy sorority girl from the O.C." You'll find plenty of those. Many students are also "extremely good looking." "No one cares what your orientation is," says a first-year student. There are "prissy Los Angeles types" and "spoiled" kids. In some circles, "family income and the brands of clothes you wear definitely matter." However, "though there are quite a few who come from mega wealth, there are also many who are here on a great deal of financial aid." There are "lots of nerds," too, and a smattering of "band geeks and film freaks."

FINANCIAL AID: 213-740-1111 • E-MAIL: ADMITUSC@USC.EDU • WEBSITE: WWW.USC.EDU

THE PRINCETON REVIEW SAYS

Admissions

Very important factors considered include: Application essay, academic GPA, recommendation(s), rigor of secondary school record, standardized test scores. *Important factors considered include:* Extracurricular activities, talent/ability. *Other factors considered include:* Class rank, alumni/ae relation, character/personal qualities, first generation, interview, racial/ethnic status, volunteer work, work experience. SAT or ACT required; ACT with writing component recommended. TOEFL required of all international applicants. High school diploma is required and GED is not accepted. *Academic units required:* 4 English, 3 mathematics, 2 science (2 science labs), 2 foreign language, 2 social studies, 3 academic electives. *Academic units recommended:* 4 English, 4 mathematics, 3 science (3 science labs), 3 foreign language, 3 social studies, 3 academic electives.

Financial Aid

Students should submit: FAFSA, CSS/Financial Aid PROFILE, parent and student federal income tax form with all schedules and W-2s, USC nonfiling forms for those not required to file. The Princeton Review suggests that all financial aid forms be submitted as soon as possible after January 1. *Need-based scholarships/grants offered:* Federal Pell, SEOG, state scholarships/grants, private scholarships, the school's own gift aid. *Loan aid offered:* Direct Subsidized Stafford, Direct Unsubsidized Stafford, Direct PLUS, Federal Perkins, "Credit Ready" and credit-based loans. Applicants will be notified of awards on a rolling basis beginning March 15. Federal Work-Study Program available. Institutional employment available. Off-campus job opportunities are excellent.

The Inside Word

USC doesn't have the toughest admissions standards in California but it's up there. Your grades and test scores need to be outstanding to compete. Even if you are a borderline candidate, though, USC is certainly worth a shot. Few schools on the planet have a better alumni network and the "Trojan Family" really does create all kinds of opportunities for its members upon graduation.

THE SCHOOL SAYS ". . ."

From the Admissions Office

"One of the best ways to discover if USC is right for you is to walk around campus, talk to students, and get a feel for the area both as a place to study and a place to live. If you can't visit, we hold admission information programs around the country. Watch your mailbox for an invitation, or send us an e-mail if you're interested.

"Freshman applicants are required to submit a standardized writing exam. We will accept either the SAT or the ACT with its optional writing section."

SELECTIVITY

Admissions Rating	**98**
# of applicants	37,210
% of applicants accepted	23
% of acceptees attending	34

FRESHMAN PROFILE

Range SAT Critical Reading	610–720
Range SAT Math	670–770
Range SAT Writing	650–740
Range ACT Composite	29–33
Average HS GPA	3.7
% graduated top 10% of class	88
% graduated top 25% of class	97
% graduated top 50% of class	100

DEADLINES

Regular	
Priority	12/1
Deadline	1/10
Notification	4/1
Nonfall registration?	yes

FINANCIAL FACTS

Financial Aid Rating	**93**
Annual tuition	$42,162
Room and board	$12,078
Required fees	$656
Books and supplies	$1,500
% needy frosh rec. need-based scholarship or grant aid	87
% needy UG rec. need-based scholarship or grant aid	90
% needy frosh rec. non-need-based scholarship or grant aid	58
% needy UG rec. non-need-based scholarship or grant aid	44
% needy frosh rec. need-based self-help aid	91
% needy UG rec. need-based self-help aid	94
% frosh rec. any financial aid	74
% UG rec. any financial aid	66
% UG borrow to pay for school	46
Average cumulative indebtedness	$30,217
% frosh need fully met	98
% ugrads need fully met	95
Average % of frosh need met	100
Average % of ugrad need met	100

UNIVERSITY OF TAMPA

401 West Kennedy Boulevard, Tampa, FL 33606-1490 • Admissions: 813-253-6211 • Fax: 813-258-7398

CAMPUS LIFE

Quality of Life Rating	**86**
Fire Safety Rating	**94**
Green Rating	**60***
Type of school	private
Environment	metropolis

STUDENTS

Total undergrad enrollment	6,025
% male/female	43/57
% from out of state	73
% from public high school	73
# of fraternities	10
# of sororities	10
% African American	6
% Asian	1
% Caucasian	60
% Hispanic	12
% international	9
# of countries represented	114

SURVEY SAYS . . .

Students are friendly
Student love Tampa
Students get along with local community
Great off-campus food

ACADEMICS

Academic Rating	**70**
% students returning for sophomore year	74
% students graduating within 4 years	45
% students graduating within 6 years	57
Calendar	semester
Student/faculty ratio	16:1
Profs interesting rating	78
Profs accessible rating	78
Most classes have	20–29 students
Most lab/discussion sessions have	10–19 students

MOST POPULAR MAJORS

business administration and management; communication studies/speech communication and rhetoric; psychology

STUDENTS SAY ". . ."

Academics

The riverfront campus in Tampa, Florida, may be a big draw for the University of Tampa, but the school boasts more than an appealing location. It is a "great university in general with an exceptional business school," and students say that the academics "are hands-on and actually fun." The goal here is "preparing students to function as global citizens in specified career fields." Leading the way to help students achieve this goal are "very thorough" professors who "make themselves available for office hours so that students are able to do their best." Students here like the small class sizes, working with "professors that love what they teach," and the fact that "the student/teacher ratio is very good." Some complain that the professors "go too fast," making classes "hard to follow," but most students praise these educators as "very insightful and understanding when I had trouble in class." The university's business, nursing, communication, and education programs have all won acclaim, especially in preparing students for post-college careers. "I learn a lot about the subject and how it applies to the real-world," one student notes. "I never feel scared to ask questions and to comment about something we are discussing." All in all, one student summarizes, "The University of Tampa is a school that brings individuals from all around the world together with excellent classes, professors, athletics, clubs, and other extracurriculars."

Life

Pointing out that a university in Tampa, Florida, offers boundless opportunities when it comes to things to do is like pointing out the sky is blue. Boredom will never be an issue here. The Gulf of Mexico and its beaches are a short drive away. "Movies, malls, restaurants, and a lot of activities" provide entertainment when students are out of class. "Parties are great. Exploring the city and going to the beach are also great." Greek life thrives. So do sports, whether collegiate or professional (in addition to the native pro sports teams, dozens of major league baseball teams train here). Since most students "are very sociable," it's easy to make friend and meet new people. Students say, "Most of the time people are thinking about the weekend and the parties they will go to," but "no one pressures you." Overall, "Whether it's clubbing, the beach, scuba-diving, skydiving, we have it all here in paradise!"

Student Body

Friendly. Hardworking. The University of Tampa is home to "students from all over the world," a "very diverse" bunch "with different backgrounds [who] still mesh together fairly well." A friendly focus on fun ensures that "even though some cliques form, everyone fits in with each other." Students at Tampa should be prepared to embrace diversity, since there are "probably more international kids than in-state kids." Indeed, "Our school is too diverse to even consider describing a typical student." For those who embrace the diversity—and most of the "smart, courteous" students here do—they will find that it "creates a really interesting and fun atmosphere to learn in and meet friends from all around the world." It is not difficult to find a place to fit in, nor is it difficult to be embraced by others. Though there are a few comments about some students being "spoiled and parent privileged," not everyone agrees. Other students say UT attendees support one another without reservation. "A fellow student will usually gladly help you out if need be." No matter how varied the student body, the tie that binds is a willingness to embrace fun.

FINANCIAL AID: 813-253-6219 • E-MAIL: ADMISSIONS@UT.EDU • WEBSITE: WWW.UT.EDU

THE PRINCETON REVIEW SAYS

Admissions

Very important factors considered include: Academic GPA, rigor of secondary school record, standardized test scores. *Important factors considered include:* Application essay, recommendation(s), talent/ability. *Other factors considered include:* Class rank, alumni/ae relation, character/personal qualities, extracurricular activities, first generation, interview, level of applicant's interest, volunteer work, work experience. SAT or ACT required; ACT with or without writing component accepted. TOEFL required of all international applicants. High school diploma is required and GED is accepted. *Academic units required:* 4 English, 3 mathematics, 3 science (2 science labs), 2 foreign language, 3 social studies, 3 academic electives.

Financial Aid

Students should submit: FAFSA, state aid form. The Princeton Review suggests that all financial aid forms be submitted as soon as possible after January 1. *Need-based scholarships/grants offered:* Federal Pell, SEOG, state scholarships/grants, private scholarships, the school's own gift aid. *Loan aid offered:* Direct Subsidized Stafford, Direct Unsubsidized Stafford, Direct PLUS, Federal Perkins, college/university loans from institutional funds. Applicants will be notified of awards on a rolling basis beginning February 1. Federal Work-Study Program available. Institutional employment available. Off-campus job opportunities are fair.

The Inside Word

Strong academic credentials are just the start for those seeking acceptance to UT. Applicants should be prepared to show that they've embraced active, hands-on learning. Participation in sports, internships, and other extracurriculars, as well as an educational background that embraces diversity, are all seen as big positives.

THE SCHOOL SAYS ". . ."

From the Admissions Office

"High school students may apply for admission at the end of their junior year. Applicants are evaluated on many criteria; guidance counselor or teacher recommendations and an essay are not required if you have graduated high school and completed some college credits. A college preparatory curriculum is required; including a minimum of eighteen academic units (four English, three science—two must be laboratory sciences, three mathematics, three social studies, two foreign language, and three academic electives). The incoming 2011–2012 class had an average (unweighted) GPA of 3.3, 1100 SAT (math and critical reading sections only), or a score of 24 on the ACT. Certain majors require separate departmental applications and/or requirements.

"The interdisciplinary Honors Program allows students to go beyond the classroom and regular course work to study one-on-one with faculty through enrichment tutorials, Honors Abroad, internships, research and classroom-to-community outreach. Students are automatically considered for the Honors Program when they apply to the University."

SELECTIVITY	
Admissions Rating	**83**
# of applicants	13,690
% of applicants accepted	53
% of acceptees attending	22

FRESHMAN PROFILE	
Range SAT Critical Reading	480–570
Range SAT Math	490–580
Range SAT Writing	480–570
Range ACT Composite	21–25
Minimum paper TOEFL	550
Minimum web-based TOEFL	79
Average HS GPA	3.3
% graduated top 10% of class	16
% graduated top 25% of class	44
% graduated top 50% of class	83

DEADLINES	
Early action	
Deadline	11/15
Notification	12/15
Regular	
Priority	1/15
Deadline	3/15
Notification	rolling
Nonfall registration?	yes

FINANCIAL FACTS	
Financial Aid Rating	**67**
Annual tuition	$22,834
Room and board	$8,830
Required fees	$1,142
Books and supplies	$1,050
% needy frosh rec. need-based scholarship or grant aid	76
% needy UG rec. need-based scholarship or grant aid	69
% needy frosh rec. non-need-based scholarship or grant aid	92
% needy UG rec. non-need-based scholarship or grant aid	91
% needy frosh rec. need-based self-help aid	76
% needy UG rec. need-based self-help aid	75
% frosh rec. any financial aid	95
% UG rec. any financial aid	86
% UG borrow to pay for school	57
Average cumulative indebtedness	$30,285
% frosh need fully met	14
% ugrads need fully met	12
Average % of frosh need met	52
Average % of ugrade need met	50

THE UNIVERSITY OF TENNESSEE AT KNOXVILLE

320 STUDENT SERVICE BUILDING, KNOXVILLE, TN 37996-0230 • ADMISSIONS: 865-974-2184

CAMPUS LIFE

Quality of Life Rating	**73**
Fire Safety Rating	**87**
Green Rating	**83**
Type of school	public
Environment	city

STUDENTS

Total undergrad enrollment	20,963
% male/female	51/49
% from out of state	9
% frosh live on campus	90
# of fraternities	23
# of sororities	18
% African American	7
% Asian	3
% Caucasian	82
% Hispanic	3
% international	1
# of countries represented	56

SURVEY SAYS . . .

Great library
Athletic facilities are great
Students are happy
Everyone loves the Volunteers
Student publications are popular

ACADEMICS

Academic Rating	**70**
% students graduating within 4 years	34
% students graduating within 6 years	63
Calendar	semester
Student/faculty ratio	15:1
Profs interesting rating	70
Profs accessible rating	71
Most classes have	20–29 students
Most lab/discussion sessions have	20–29 students

MOST POPULAR MAJORS

psychology; logistics and transportation; biological science

APPLICANTS ALSO LOOK AT AND SOMETIMES PREFER

Clemson University, Vanderbilt University, University of South Carolina—Columbia

AND RARELY PREFER

University of Alabama—Tuscaloosa, University of Mississippi, Virginia Tech

STUDENTS SAY ". . ."

Academics

The University of Tennessee "provides a family-like atmosphere full of opportunity and support!" Life at UT is all about "atmosphere, affordability, and school spirit." Many here tout "the school spirit and sense of community." In addition, the "in-state tuition and scholarship money" make "Tennessee a good deal for the amount you pay. I have fabulous teachers, great friends, fun activities to participate in, nice housing, a decent meal plan, and I pay $2,000 for all of it." "Although [UT is] a large school, you're not just a number; you're a face, a person, and a name." In general, "Professors greatly appreciate an appetite to learn, and they welcome challenges that help us learn and grow as students." Most are "very intelligent, open to debate, well-versed on their topics, and willing to meet with students outside of class for any reason." One student says, "The majority of my experience with academia and professors has been diverse and excellent." UT embraces a classic liberal arts core dedicated to "helping students find their passions by providing a friendly and intellectually enriching environment to learn, lead, and grow." UT offers "many opportunities for involvement" and "sets a high standard for success." Attending the UT "is about pursuing excellence in all areas of your life and using the knowledge you gain to prepare you for your future." It also "has a well-known medical program" and—for many—is "close to home."

Life

The typical UT student "loves all aspects of the university's life from its sports to its long-standing traditions." Students flock here for "family history, athletics, and to sing 'Rocky Top.'" "We love football just about as much as academics." However, academics here are just as intense as athletics, "Being a larger university, I have had many more opportunities than people I know at smaller schools in education as well as extracurriculars." "The University of Tennessee combines the best of all worlds: great education for a great price, sports, social life, and a ton of extracurriculars to choose from." In fact, many say, "There are so many clubs and groups that on a social level UT doesn't feel large at all." "There's also a great selection of food and a wonderful gym." Life at UT is all "about education, community, and becoming a true Tennessee volunteer." "There's a great sense of unity." The university "tries extremely hard to encourage acceptance of several kinds of diversity." A "LGBTQ Resource Center [recently] opened on campus." "There is also a large 'Stop Bias' program that is promoted." In general, there are "tons of clubs and organizations to get involved with if you are passionate about something." If pressed to note a campus flaw, students say UT is "stuck between a river and downtown Knoxville, so it now has no room to expand and way too many hills. So they've crammed all these buildings into too small of a space."

Student Body

"There is not one 'popular' group of students. We have athletes, artists, musicians, dancers, religious students, scientists, Greeks, volunteers, etc." In general a live-and-let-live atmosphere pervades this "friendly" "energetic," "personable" campus; "All students fit in extremely well." The Greek community here "is especially prevalent." Some wonder "how non-Greeks fit in." "The conservative, upper-class attitude is definitely the one with the strongest voice." However, others counter this stalwart image. "The best thing about being an average student here? If you don't want to conform, you don't have to." "Once you go beyond the surface and away from the jocks and sorority girls, there are all types of students at UT." Others enthusiastically concede, "The literary snob crowd is small, but it's here, they do cool stuff, and they welcome new folks all the time with open arms." A typical student "studies hard, but parties even harder at the appropriate times." Classical entrees to social life include "to become part of the Greek system here or be an athlete." Most students exhibit the hallmark "Southern hospitality" and are "industrious, honest, charitable, and compassionate."

FINANCIAL AID: 865-974-3131 • E-MAIL: ADMISSIONS@UTK.EDU • WEBSITE: WWW.UTK.EDU

THE PRINCETON REVIEW SAYS

Admissions

Very important factors considered include: Academic GPA, rigor of secondary school record, standardized test scores. *Other factors considered include:* Class rank, application essay, recommendation(s), alumni/ae relation, character/personal qualities, extracurricular activities, first generation, geographical residence, level of applicant's interest, racial/ethnic status, state residency, talent/ability, volunteer work, work experience. SAT or ACT required; ACT with or without writing component accepted. TOEFL required of all international applicants. High school diploma is required and GED is accepted. *Academic units required:* 4 English, 4 mathematics, 3 science (3 science labs), 2 foreign language, 2 social studies, 1 history, 1 visual/performing arts.

Financial Aid

Students should submit: FAFSA. The Princeton Review suggests that all financial aid forms be submitted as soon as possible after February 15. *Need-based scholarships/grants offered:* Federal Pell, SEOG, state scholarships/grants, private scholarships, the school's own gift aid, Federal Nursing Scholarships. *Loan aid offered:* Direct Subsidized Stafford, Direct Unsubsidized Stafford, Direct PLUS, Federal Perkins, college/university loans from institutional funds. Applicants will be notified of awards on a rolling basis beginning March 15. Federal Work-Study Program available. Off-campus job opportunities are fair.

The Inside Word

UT must winnow through more than 13,000 freshman applications each year. That sort of volume doesn't allow for nuance. Students with above-average high school GPAs (achieved in a reasonable college prep curriculum) and above-average standardized test scores pretty much all make the cut. The school will consider additional evidence of an applicant's potential (school and community involvement, awards, essays, special talents, and recommendations) in making admissions decisions, particularly for marginal candidates.

THE SCHOOL SAYS ". . ."

From the Admissions Office

"The University of Tennessee, Knoxville, offers students the great program diversity of a major university, opportunities for research or original creative work in every degree program, and a welcoming campus environment. Nine colleges offer more than 170 undergraduate majors and concentrations to students from all fifty states and 100 foreign countries, and UT students can make the world their campus through study abroad programs. More than 400 clubs and organizations on campus allow students to further individualize their college experience in service, recreation, academics, and professional development. UT blends more than 200 years of history, tradition, and 'Volunteer Spirit' with the latest technology and innovation."

SELECTIVITY	
Admissions Rating	85
# of applicants	13,768
% of applicants accepted	70
% of acceptees attending	44

FRESHMAN PROFILE	
Range SAT Critical Reading	520–640
Range SAT Math	530–640
Range ACT Composite	24–29
Minimum paper TOEFL	523
Minimum web-based TOEFL	70
Average HS GPA	3.9

DEADLINES	
Regular	
Priority	11/1
Deadline	12/1
Notification	3/31
Nonfall registration?	yes

FINANCIAL FACTS	
Financial Aid Rating	77
Annual in-state tuition	$7,224
Annual out-state tuition	$24,066
Room and board	$8,480
Required fees	$1,172
Books and supplies	$1,448
% needy frosh rec. need-based scholarship or grant aid	98
% needy UG rec. need-based scholarship or grant aid	90
% needy frosh rec. need-based self-help aid	55
% needy UG rec. need-based self-help aid	63
% frosh rec. any financial aid	61
% UG rec. any financial aid	58
% UG borrow to pay for school	50
Average cumulative indebtedness	$20,926
% frosh need fully met	24
% ugrads need fully met	21
Average % of frosh need met	76
Average % of ugrad need met	69

THE UNIVERSITY OF TEXAS AT AUSTIN

PO BOX 8058, AUSTIN, TX 78713-8058 • ADMISSIONS: 512-475-7440 • FAX: 512-475-7478

CAMPUS LIFE

Quality of Life Rating	**95**
Fire Safety Rating	**79**
Green Rating	**96**
Type of school	public
Environment	metropolis

STUDENTS

Total undergrad enrollment	38,437
% male/female	49/51
% from out of state	5
% frosh live on campus	19
# of fraternities	37
# of sororities	28
% African American	5
% Asian	18
% Caucasian	50
% Hispanic	20
% international	5
# of countries represented	121

SURVEY SAYS . . .

Athletic facilities are great
Students love Austin, TX
Everyone loves the Longhorns
Student publications are popular
Political activism is popular

ACADEMICS

Academic Rating	**76**
% students returning for sophomore year	92
% students graduating within 4 years	53
% students graduating within 6 years	81
Calendar	semester
Student/faculty ratio	18:1
Profs interesting rating	78
Profs accessible rating	75
Most classes have	10–19 students
Most lab/discussion sessions have	10–19 students

MOST POPULAR MAJORS

biology/biological sciences; business/commerce; liberal arts and sciences/liberal studies

STUDENTS SAY ". . ."

Academics

Students insist that the University of Texas at Austin has "everything you want in a college: academics, athletics, social life, location," and it's hard to argue with them. UT is "a huge school and has a lot to offer," meaning students have "an infinite number of possibilities open to them and can use them in their own way to figure out what they want for their lives." As one student tells us about arriving on campus, "I did not realize how much was available to me just as an enrolled student. There is free tutoring, gym membership, professional counseling, doctors visits, legal help, career advising, and many distinguished outside speakers. The campus is crawling with experts in every field you can imagine." Standout academic departments are numerous: from the sciences to the humanities to creative arts, UT makes a strong bid for the much-sought-after mantle of "Harvard of the south." Also, the school does a surprisingly good job of avoiding the factory-like feel of many large schools. One student observes: "Coming to a large university, there was a prejudgment that the huge classes will make it impossible to know your professor and vice versa. The university has dispelled that myth with professors who want to know you and [who] provide opportunities to get to know them." And while professors "can vary greatly across a spectrum from 'I'm smarter than him' to 'I want to follow in his footsteps,'" "the class offerings at UT are generally vast and diverse, and students can often avoid taking the less-qualified professors with a little research."

Life

Life at UT—Austin is "very relaxed…Students usually wear shorts and a t-shirt to class. When the weather gets cold, you might find students wearing the same shorts and t-shirt with a sweatshirt. Students and faculty frequently picnic all over campus. There are plenty of outdoor tables and grassy areas to sit." Undergrads "are often found throwing a Frisbee outside the tower or taking a nap under a tree. It's truly what you see in one of those cheesy brochures with everyone studying and smiling. Of course, the smiles aren't so bright during finals. We switch to an over-caffeinated, glazed-eye look instead." Hometown Austin "provides a social education that a college student newly out on his own would not find anywhere else," with "festivals or fairs of some kind going on downtown all the time" and "the infamous 6th Street with nightlife that dies down only after the bars close." Campus and the surrounding area offer "many hike-and-bike trails and fitness organizations. It's possible for students to train for marathons, half marathons, and triathlons while in school. Barton Springs pool is a natural spring that is very popular year-round. On any given Saturday you will find students throwing a football, going for a run, biking through the hills, kayaking in the river, having a late lunch at one of Austin's great restaurants, or just sleeping in."

Student Body

"Because of the huge Greek life at UT, a 'typical student' would be a sorority girl or fraternity boy," but—and it's a big but—such students "are hardly the majority, since UT is actually made of more 'atypical' people than most other schools. Everyone here has his own niche, and I could not think of any type of individual who would not be able to find one of his own." Indeed, "Everyone at Texas is different! When you walk across campus, you see every type of ethnicity. There are a lot of minorities at Texas. Also, I see many disabled people, whom the school accommodates well. Everyone seems to get along. The different types of students just blend in together." Especially by Texas standards, "Austin is known for being 'weird.' If you see someone dressed in a way you've never seen before, you just shrug it off and say 'That's Austin!'"

FINANCIAL AID: 512-475-6203 • WEBSITE: WWW.UTEXAS.EDU

THE PRINCETON REVIEW SAYS

Admissions

Very important factors considered include: Class rank, rigor of secondary school record. *Important factors considered include:* Application essay, standardized test scores, extracurricular activities, talent/ability, volunteer work, work experience. *Other factors considered include:* Recommendation(s), character/personal qualities, first generation, level of applicant's interest, racial/ethnic status, state residency. SAT or ACT required; ACT with writing component required. TOEFL required of all international applicants. High school diploma is required and GED is accepted. *Academic units required:* 4 language arts, 4 mathematics, 4 science, 3.5 social studies, 0.5 economics, 1 physical education, 1 fine arts, 2 foreign language, 0.5 speech, 6 electives.

Financial Aid

Students should submit: FAFSA. Priority filing deadline is March 15. The Princeton Review suggests that all financial aid forms be submitted as soon as possible after January 1. *Need-based scholarships/grants offered:* Federal Pell, SEOG, state scholarships/grants, private scholarships, the school's own gift aid. *Loan aid offered:* Direct Subsidized Stafford, Direct Unsubsidized Stafford, Direct PLUS, Federal Perkins, state loans. Applicants will be notified of awards on a rolling basis beginning March 15. Federal Work-Study Program available. Off-campus job opportunities are fair.

The Inside Word

The university is required to automatically admit enough Texas applicants to fill seventy-five percent of available spaces set aside for students from Texas. The university will admit applicants from Texas who are in the top eight percent of their high school class for the summer/fall 2013 and the spring 2014 entering freshman class. The rank needed for automatic admission for future classes will be announced each September. All students, including those eligible for automatic admission, should submit the strongest possible application to increase the likelihood of admission to the university and to their requested major. Admissions are quite competitive. Space for out-of-state students is limited, meaning they'll have even higher hurdles to clear.

THE SCHOOL SAYS ". . ."

From the Admissions Office

"For more than 125 years, students from all over the world have come to The University of Texas at Austin to obtain a first-class education. Recognized for research, teaching, and public service, the university boasts more than 130 undergraduate academic programs, more than 350 study abroad programs, outstanding student services, cultural centers, and volunteer and leadership opportunities designed to prepare students to make a difference in the world. Along with its nationally ranked athletic programs, the university's spirit is enhanced by cultural, artistic, and scientific opportunities that help to make Austin one of the most inviting destinations in the country. The Performing Arts Center hosts plays, Austin's opera and symphony, and visiting musical and dance groups. Students access more than eight million volumes in the university's seventeen libraries and study prehistoric fossils at the Texas Memorial Museum, Renaissance and Baroque paintings in the Blanton Museum, original manuscripts at the Ransom Center, and life in the 1960s at the Lyndon B. Johnson Library and Museum. Each year the university enrolls about 50,000 students from richly varied ethnic and geographic backgrounds. Every day graduates contribute to the world community as volunteers, teachers, journalists, artists, engineers, business leaders, scientists, and lawyers. With world-renowned faculty, top-rated academic programs, successful alumni, and such an enticing location, it's no surprise that The University of Texas at Austin ranks among the best universities in the world."

SELECTIVITY	
Admissions Rating	92
# of applicants	32,589
% of applicants accepted	47
% of acceptees attending	47
# accepting a place on wait list	456
# admitted from wait list	92

FRESHMAN PROFILE	
Range SAT Critical Reading	540–670
Range SAT Math	580–710
Range SAT Writing	540–680
Range ACT Composite	25–31
Minimum paper TOEFL	550
Minimum web-based TOEFL	79
% graduated top 10% of class	73
% graduated top 25% of class	91
% graduated top 50% of class	98

DEADLINES	
Regular Deadline	12/1
Nonfall registration?	yes

FINANCIAL FACTS	
Financial Aid Rating	87
Annual in-state tuition	$9,792
Annual out-state tuition	$32,379
Room and board	$10,422
Books and supplies	$874
% needy frosh rec. need-based scholarship or grant aid	92
% needy UG rec. need-based scholarship or grant aid	80
% needy frosh rec. non-need-based scholarship or grant aid	47
% needy UG rec. non-need-based scholarship or grant aid	26
% needy frosh rec. need-based self-help aid	66
% needy UG rec. need-based self-help aid	77
% frosh rec. any financial aid	48
% UG rec. any financial aid	46
% UG borrow to pay for school	49
Average cumulative indebtedness	$25,227
% frosh need fully met	27
% ugrads need fully met	18
Average % of frosh need met	75
Average % of ugrad need met	67

UNIVERSITY OF TORONTO

172 ST. GEORGE STREET, TORONTO, ON M5R 0A3 • ADMISSIONS: 416-978-2190 • FAX: 416-978-7022

CAMPUS LIFE

Quality of Life Rating	**79**
Fire Safety Rating	**71**
Green Rating	**70**
Type of school	public
Environment	metropolis

STUDENTS

Total undergrad enrollment	63,808
% male/female	44/56
% from out of state	17
% international	13
# of countries represented	166

SURVEY SAYS . . .

Class discussions are rare
Great computer facilities
Great library
Diverse student types on campus
Students love Toronto, ON
Great off-campus food
Student publications are popular

ACADEMICS

Academic Rating	**65**
% students graduating within 6 years	82
Calendar	2 terms (fall and winter); 2 summer
Student/faculty ratio	10:1
Profs interesting rating	72
Profs accessible rating	65

MOST POPULAR MAJORS

social sciences; humanities; education

STUDENTS SAY ". . ."

Academics

With "an excellent reputation and a huge selection of courses" as well as "a world-class city" to call home, the University of Toronto "provides expert knowledge in every field" to its 50,000-plus undergraduates and nearly 11,000 graduate students. True, it can be "hard to relate to the instructors given that the class sizes are so huge," and those looking for an intimate and supportive academic environment might not find a good fit at U of T. "The general attitude is one of professionalism and very little mercy [here]." Still, self-starters will find the limitless opportunities outweigh the drawbacks. As one puts it, "Most of the professors are premier representatives of their respective industries." Another adds, "The fact that you are learning from Nobel Prize winners in a city full of adventures is unbeatable." "Excellent research facilities" are among the other assets here. The school also capitalizes on its location in the center of Toronto: "The city and the university draw on each other in a variety of ways—clinical opportunities and research flow in both directions." On top of that, industrious undergrads tell us, "The libraries and other research facilities here are excellent and contribute much to the overall academic experience."

Life

When they aren't hitting the books, University of Toronto students enjoy life in "one of the coolest cities in North America" where "there's always something new happening: the Toronto International Film Festival, skating in Nathan Phillips Square, etc." Students benefit from the fact that "the Royal Ontario Museum is on campus, a ton of pubs and art galleries are within walking distance, and a nightlife to suit just about any type of person" can be found in Toronto. When it comes to campus life, many students feel the school's spirit and unity is negatively affected by the large number of commuter students. "Off-campus students, of whom there are many, rarely participate in extracurricular activities," one student complains adds that "Interest in varsity sports is just pathetic" among all undergraduates. Others focus on the positives, pointing out the social and recreational opportunities available to those willing to look. A junior says, "Getting involved here takes some research in terms of navigating the 300 clubs and endless academic/research opportunities, but once I did some searching, I found several places where I fit in well and have fun." For those who live on campus, sororities and fraternities help nurture social bonds, and "most of the residential colleges have tons of events, from campus-wide capture the flag [games] to movie nights" or "intramural sports."

Student Body

At this large public school, the demographics on campus reflect those of surrounding Toronto, "one of the most diverse cities around." As one junior puts it, "It can be said that all students here have in common an excellent academic record prior to university. Beyond that, anything goes: There are huge variances in race, religion, sexual orientation, academic focus, postgraduate aspirations, socioeconomic background, disability, nationality, athleticism, and community involvement." A freshman chimes in, "On my floor alone there are kids from at least ten different countries and, even with the different cultures, we have blended together to make a big family." Most students say it's relatively easy to find a social group among like-minded individuals, despite the school's impressive size and diversity. According to one senior, "Most students will find a niche where they feel comfortable; there's a place for everyone."

FINANCIAL AID: 416-978-2190 • E-MAIL: ADMISSIONS.HELP@UTORONTO.CA • WEBSITE: WWW.UTORONTO.CA

THE PRINCETON REVIEW SAYS

Admissions

Very important factors considered include: Academic GPA, standardized test scores. SAT or ACT required; ACT with or without writing component accepted. TOEFL required of all international applicants. High school diploma is required and GED is accepted.

Financial Aid

Students should submit: OSAP. The Princeton Review suggests that all financial aid forms be submitted as soon as possible after January 1.

The Inside Word

University of Toronto takes a numbers-based approach to admissions. American students must submit not only high school transcripts and SAT/ACT scores but also results for three SAT subject tests/APs/IBs. Only those who perform well by all these metrics are likely to gain admission. Candidates should be aware that qualifications vary from program to program, and as an international student you'll have more paperwork to file. The University of Toronto is a recognized postsecondary institution for Federal Stafford Loans. All applicants are automatically considered for admission scholarships.

THE SCHOOL SAYS ". . ."

From the Admissions Office

"The University of Toronto is committed to being an internationally significant research university with undergraduate, graduate, and professional programs of study.

"For arts, science, commerce/management, concurrent teacher education, music, physical education & health/kinesiology, U.S. Grade 12 in an accredited high school with a high grade point average and high scores on SAT Reasoning/ACT exams and a minimum of two appropriate SAT Subject Tests/APs/IBs (or a combination of SAT Subject Tests/APs/IBs covering different subjects). English Grade 12/AP is required for all programs. Those seeking admission to science or commerce programs are strongly advised to complete AP Calculus.

"The minimum admission requirements are an excellent CGPA and Grade 12 GPA; scores of at least 1800 on SAT Reasoning and 26 on the ACT; no score below 500 on SAT Subject Tests. SAT scores below 500 in any part of the SAT Reasoning or Subject Tests are not acceptable.

"For engineering, applicants must present AP/IB Calculus, as well as AP/IB or SAT Subject Tests in both chemistry and physics. English Grade 12/AP is required for all programs. Applicants seeking admission to engineering after one year of university in the United States are required to present a GPA of at least 3.5 with two semesters of math, physics and chemistry. Refer to www.engineering.utoronto.ca for complete information."

SELECTIVITY	
Admissions Rating	61
# of applicants	67,955
% of applicants accepted	69
% of acceptees attending	18
FRESHMAN PROFILE	
Minimum paper TOEFL	600
DEADLINES	
Regular Deadline	3/1
Nonfall registration?	yes
FINANCIAL FACTS	
Financial Aid Rating	60*
Annual in-state tuition	$5,695
Annual out-state tuition	$28,409
Room and board	$8,165–$14,149
Books and supplies	$1,500

THE UNIVERSITY OF TULSA

800 SOUTH TUCKER DRIVE, TULSA, OK 74104 • ADMISSIONS: 918-631-2307 • FAX: 918-631-5003

CAMPUS LIFE

Quality of Life Rating	**85**
Fire Safety Rating	**85**
Green Rating	**74**
Type of school	private
Affiliation	Presbyterian
Environment	metropolis

STUDENTS

Total undergrad enrollment	2,948
% male/female	55/45
% from out of state	48
% from public high school	72
% frosh live on campus	85
# of fraternities	7
# of sororities	9
% African American	6
% Asian	3
% Caucasian	61
% Hispanic	4
% Native American	4
% international	18
# of countries represented	68

SURVEY SAYS . . .

Great computer facilities
Athletic facilities are great
Students are friendly
Students get along with local community
Students are happy

ACADEMICS

Academic Rating	**82**
% students returning for sophomore year	86
% students graduating within 4 years	51
% students graduating within 6 years	68
Calendar	semester
Student/faculty ratio	11:1
Profs interesting rating	80
Profs accessible rating	84
Most classes have	10–19 students
Most lab/discussion sessions have	10–19 students

MOST POPULAR MAJORS

marketing/marketing management; petroleum engineering; psychology

APPLICANTS ALSO LOOK AT AND OFTEN PREFER

Texas Christian University, University of Oklahoma, Southern Methodist University, Saint Louis University

AND SOMETIMES PREFER

Trinity University, Baylor University, Tulane University, Washington University in St. Louis

AND RARELY PREFER

Texas A&M University—College Station, University of Kansas, University of Missouri

STUDENTS SAY ". . ."

Academics

The University of Tulsa is a mid-size, private school that provides a superior learning environment and a myriad of academic opportunities to its 3,000 undergraduate students. Across disciplines, the academic experience is high quality and stimulating, incorporating "rigorous and invigorating lectures and well instructed lab periods." In addition to coursework, undergraduates benefit from unmatched "academic and professional opportunities reserved only for graduate students at other schools." A current student attests, "I had no trouble getting undergraduate research experience in biochemistry as early as sophomore year." Students rave about TU's outgoing professors, saying that "the faculty and staff at TU seem to take a personal interest in the students here. They are accessible and love to help students in any way possible, not only academically, but professionally and personally as well." How's this for involved? "I have even received a text message from a professor when I forgot to turn in a homework assignment," reports a sophomore. While course selection is occasionally limited by the school's size, "professors will frequently tailor independent study projects with students." When it comes to the administration, some students worry that they are too preoccupied with improving the college's rankings. Others insist that the administrative offices are just as student-friendly as the teaching staff. A sophomore shares, "I became involved in student government my third semester here, and I am so impressed by how accessible the administration is. The deans and president of the university really care about students."

Life

Student life at TU reflects the school's unequivocal emphasis on academics. Studious undergraduates agree that the University of Tulsa "is definitely not a big party school. Most of the students here are focused on studies." Nonetheless, there are plenty of opportunities for extracurricular involvement, and campus clubs range "from honor societies to multicultural groups to religious gatherings." The campus isn't too big, so students looking for leadership experience will be pleased to learn that "anyone can be involved and 'be someone' on campus." In addition to student clubs, "collegiate, intramural, and pick-up sports are really popular." About twenty percent of the campus is involved in a Greek organization, and "a lot of student life revolves strongly around sororities and fraternities." However, students reassure us that "even non-Greek students can visit the houses and hang out on a Friday night." If you don't feel like partying at fraternities, there's plenty more to do, on and off campus. A sophomore shares, "For fun my friends and I go bowling, explore the parks of Tulsa, watch movies, do arts and crafts, and go to the occasional party." While students readily admit that Tulsa isn't New York City, they appreciate the myriad of pleasures of their manageable mid-size city, which boasts "some really great restaurants and coffee shops around TU and in historic Tulsa."

Student Body

Defined in broad strokes, most TU undergraduates hail from affluent, Christian families in the Midwest. However, TU students insist that, while there are some similarities within the campus community, they cannot be summed up so easily. In addition to the array of "jocks, computer geeks, fashionistas, 'good' students, loners, and partygoers," The University of Tulsa has a "strong international community. Programs such as the petroleum engineering department attract a diverse international populace. One can hear five different languages simply walking to class!" Thanks, in part, to the international students, there is "a diverse religious life on campus, several activist groups that meet on campus, and countless student organizations." No matter what your background, "The majority of students I know at TU are very open and accepting of everyone else, regardless of religion, race, sexual orientation, athletic ability, major, and Greek affiliation." In fact, it's easy to feel at home on the TU campus. A junior explains, "Because the campus is small, even if you don't know somebody's name, you normally recognize their face from somewhere; this leads to a great sense of community."

FINANCIAL AID: 918-631-2526 • E-MAIL: ADMISSION@UTULSA.EDU • WEBSITE: WWW.UTULSA.EDU

THE PRINCETON REVIEW SAYS

Admissions

Very important factors considered include: Academic GPA, rigor of secondary school record, standardized test scores, interview. *Important factors considered include:* Application essay, recommendation(s), character/personal qualities, extracurricular activities, talent/ability. *Other factors considered include:* Alumni/ae relation, first generation, level of applicant's interest, racial/ethnic status, volunteer work, work experience. SAT or ACT required; ACT without writing component accepted. TOEFL required of all international applicants. High school diploma is required and GED is accepted. *Academic units recommended:* 4 English, 3 mathematics, 3 science (2 science labs), 2 foreign language, 1 social studies, 2 history, 1 academic elective.

Financial Aid

Students should submit: FAFSA. The Princeton Review suggests that all financial aid forms be submitted as soon as possible after January 1. *Need-based scholarships/grants offered:* Federal Pell, SEOG, state scholarships/grants, private scholarships, the school's own gift aid. *Loan aid offered:* Direct Subsidized Stafford, Direct Unsubsidized Stafford, Direct PLUS, Federal Perkins. Applicants will be notified of awards on a rolling basis beginning March 1. Federal Work-Study Program available. Institutional employment available. Highest amount earned per year from on-campus jobs $2,600. Off-campus job opportunities are good.

The Inside Word

TU is a university with solid academic offerings, a strong sense of community, lots of student-faculty interaction, and attainable admission standards. The school's commitment to undergrads is clear. One of TU's most impressive programs, The Tulsa Undergraduate Research Challenge (TURC), allows undergrads to complete original research along with faculty.

THE SCHOOL SAYS ". . ."

From the Admissions Office

"The University of Tulsa is a private university with a comprehensive scope. Students choose from more than eighty majors offered through three undergraduate colleges—Arts and Sciences, Business Administration, and Engineering and Natural Sciences. Curricula can be customized with collaborative research, joint undergraduate and graduate programs, and an honors program, among others. Professors are equally committed to teaching undergraduates and to scholarly research. This results in extraordinary individual achievement, resulting in the nationally competitive scholarships students have won since 1995: fifty-one Goldwaters, forty-one National Science Foundation scholars, nine Trumans, seven Department of Defense scholars, nine Fulbrights, nine Phi Kappa Phi, nine Udalls, and five British Marshalls. Over the past decade over 1,000,000 square feet of facilities have been added costing over $250 million. These include athletic venues, 400 additional apartments, fitness center, Legal Information Center, literacy expansion and renovation, and a new performing arts center. Over 160 registered clubs, and interest groups, including intramural and recreational sports teams exist along with six fraternities and nine sororities. The 8,300 seat Reynolds Center is home to the standout Golden Hurricane NCAA Division I men's basketball team, campus events, and concerts. A forty-acre sports complex includes the fitness center and indoor tennis center that hosted the 2008 NCAA Division I Men's and Women's tennis finals. An outdoor freshman orientation program launches an entire first-year experience dedicated to developing students' full potential.

"Applicants are required to submit the SAT or ACT. The writing component is not required. For admission and scholarship review, the best composite score of submitted tests will be used."

SELECTIVITY	
Admissions Rating	95
# of applicants	6,257
% of applicants accepted	41
% of acceptees attending	24
# accepting a place on wait list	318
# admitted from wait list	71

FRESHMAN PROFILE	
Range SAT Critical Reading	550–690
Range SAT Math	570–690
Range ACT Composite	24–31
Minimum paper TOEFL	500
Minimum web-based TOEFL	61
Average HS GPA	3.8
% graduated top 10% of class	74
% graduated top 25% of class	86
% graduated top 50% of class	97

DEADLINES	
Early action	
Deadline	11/1
Notification	11/22
Regular	
Priority	2/1
Nonfall registration?	yes

FINANCIAL FACTS	
Financial Aid Rating	86
Annual tuition	$29,464
Room and board	$9,464
Required fees	$260
Books and supplies	$1,200
% needy frosh rec. need-based scholarship or grant aid	45
% needy UG rec. need-based scholarship or grant aid	49
% needy frosh rec. non-need-based scholarship or grant aid	98
% needy UG rec. non-need-based scholarship or grant aid	94
% needy frosh rec. need-based self-help aid	79
% needy UG rec. need-based self-help aid	82
% frosh rec. any financial aid	94
% UG rec. any financial aid	88
% UG borrow to pay for school	42
Average cumulative indebtedness	$36,470
% frosh need fully met	49
% ugrads need fully met	49
Average % of frosh need met	85
Average % of ugrad need met	84

UNIVERSITY OF UTAH

201 SOUTH 1460 EAST, ROOM 250 S, SALT LAKE CITY, UT 84112 • ADMISSIONS: 801-581-7281 • FAX: 801-585-7864

CAMPUS LIFE

Quality of Life Rating	73
Fire Safety Rating	86
Green Rating	88
Type of school	public
Environment	metropolis

STUDENTS

Total undergrad enrollment	23,275
% male/female	56/44
% from out of state	20
% from public high school	94
% frosh live on campus	34
# of fraternities	8
# of sororities	6
% African American	1
% Asian	5
% Caucasian	75
% Hispanic	8
% Native American	1
% international	5
# of countries represented	118

SURVEY SAYS . . .

Registration is a breeze
Great computer facilities
Great library
Students get along with local community
Students love Salt Lake City, UT
Great off-campus food
Campus feels safe
Students are happy
Everyone loves the Utes
Student publications are popular

ACADEMICS

Academic Rating	72
% students returning for sophomore year	87
% students graduating within 4 years	21
Calendar	semester
Student/faculty ratio	14:1
Profs interesting rating	73
Profs accessible rating	66
Most classes have	20–29 students
Most lab/discussion sessions have	10–19 students

MOST POPULAR MAJORS

biology/biological sciences; business/commerce; economics

STUDENTS SAY ". . ."

Academics

Nestled amid Salt Lake City's snowcapped mountains, the University of Utah is a large public school that offers extensive academic programs, ample research opportunities, and a surprisingly student-friendly atmosphere. No matter what your interests, you'll find like minds at U of U. "I have studied everything from Tai Chi/Yoga movement and stage combat to differential equations and linear algebra," says a junior. "The one thing that has remained consistent throughout is the appreciation and dedication the people have for the topic they are involved in." U of U is a research university that actually takes teaching seriously, and "every teacher that I've had shows incredible knowledge in their area, as well as personality and wit." "Classes are informative, challenging, and genuinely enjoyable." As is the case in many larger universities, "most general education courses are taught by grad students," whose teaching abilities can range from great to below average. "Ninety percent of my professors are fantastic; the ones that aren't are usually grad students," explains a junior. On this large campus, students have little contact with the school's administration and "there's definitely no hand-holding at the U of U. If you're unsure of your major or career plans, it's easy to slip through the cracks." However, students assure us. "The administration puts student interests first whenever possible with a focus on keeping tuition low, creating a diverse environment, and providing opportunities and experience in order to prepare students to be productive citizens."

Life

While a large percentage of the undergraduate community at the University of Utah commutes to campus, there are still plenty of activities for the school's 4,000 resident students. There are many people "active in politics, environmental issues, and international issues," and, after hours, "the school holds different events throughout the year, such as Crimson Nights that feature activities such as bowling, crafts, games, food, and music." Socially, "Greek life is not as large as at other schools but is definitely a lot of fun and the best way to get to know more people your age." In addition, "during football season there are great tailgate parties with friends, drinks, and food." Right off campus, there are a range of great restaurants, and "the nightlife is hard to keep up with." There's always something good going on—whether it's at the bars and clubs downtown, or at small music venues." For outdoorsy types, U of U is a paradise. "We have all four seasons and some of the best outdoors in the nation," explains one student. "Killer snow, amazing hills, mountains, lakes, and streams." In this natural wonderland, "hiking, biking, boating, snow-skiing, and snowboarding are just a few of the hundreds of activities available to students."

Student Body

Located in Salt Lake City, hometown to the Church of Latter Day Saints, "a majority of students at the U of U are Mormon, but not a vast majority. There are plenty of social niches to fall into, and none of them are rigidly exclusive." A current student adds, "About half the student body is the typical Utah Mormon, and the other half is a mix of everything. The two halves usually stay separate but they get along." U of U students agree that "there is more diversity here than in any other part of the state." However, out-of-state students are uncommon, and "those of us not from Utah are definitely in the minority." While there are a number of residential students, a very large percentage of students also chose to commute to school while living with their parents or family. In addition, "there are a lot of older students and a lot of married students." Academically, however, U of U undergraduates are "independent, smart, and come to class ready to discuss ideas."

FINANCIAL AID: 801-581-6211 • E-MAIL: ADMISSIONS@SA.UTAH.EDU • WEBSITE: WWW.UTAH.EDU

THE PRINCETON REVIEW SAYS

Admissions

Very important factors considered include: Academic GPA, rigor of secondary school record, standardized test scores. *Important factors considered include:* Talent/ability. *Other factors considered include:* Class rank, recommendation(s), extracurricular activities, interview, racial/ethnic status. SAT or ACT required; ACT with writing component required. TOEFL required of all international applicants. High school diploma is required and GED is accepted. *Academic units required:* 4 English, 2 mathematics, 3 science (1 science lab), 2 foreign language, 1 history, 4 academic electives.

Financial Aid

Students should submit: FAFSA, institution's own financial aid form. The Princeton Review suggests that all financial aid forms be submitted as soon as possible after January 1. *Need-based scholarships/grants offered:* Federal Pell, SEOG, state scholarships/grants, private scholarships, the school's own gift aid, Federal Nursing Scholarships, ACG, National SMART Grant, and TEACH Grant. *Loan aid offered:* Direct Subsidized Stafford, Direct Unsubsidized Stafford, Direct PLUS, Federal Perkins, Federal Nursing, college/university loans from institutional funds, private alternative loans. Applicants will be notified of awards on a rolling basis beginning April 15. Federal Work-Study Program available. Institutional employment available. Highest amount earned per year from on-campus jobs $8,800. Off-campus job opportunities are excellent.

The Inside Word

Utah is another state in which low numbers of high school grads keep selectivity down at its public flagship university. Admission is based primarily on the big three: Course selection, grades, and test scores. If you have a 3.0 GPA or better and average test scores, you're close to a sure bet for admission.

THE SCHOOL SAYS ". . ."

From the Admissions Office

"The University of Utah is a distinctive community of learning in the American West. Today's 30,819 students are from every state and 129 foreign countries. The university has research ties worldwide, with national standing among the top comprehensive research institutions. The university offers 100 undergraduate and more than ninety graduate degree programs. Nationally recognized honors and undergraduate research programs stimulate intellectual inquiry. Undergraduates collaborate with faculty on important investigations. In 2011–2012, the university's intercollegiate athletes will begin competing in the NCAA PAC-12 Conference. The football team has been nationally ranked for several years, as have our women's gymnastics and skiing teams. The university's location in Salt Lake City provides easy access to the arts, theater, Utah Jazz basketball, and hockey. Utah's great outdoors—skiing, hiking, and five national parks—are nearby. The university was the site for the opening and closing ceremonies and the Athletes Village for the 2002 Winter Olympic Games.

"Housing and residential education has greatly expanded the opportunity for students to live on campus with a new and wide variety of housing. Heritage Commons, constructed during the 2002 Olympics, is located in historic Fort Douglas on campus, and consists of twenty-one buildings, which accommodate more than 2,500 students. The university also has apartment housing available for students located minutes from campus in downtown Salt Lake City. In addition, construction is underway for a 'living/learning community' that will house approximately 300 honors students.

"Applicants are required to submit ACT scores. SAT scores are also accepted, although ACT scores are preferred. Students are urged to take the ACT near the end of their junior year or early in the senior year of high school."

SELECTIVITY

Admissions Rating	**77**
# of applicants	9,545
% of applicants accepted	83
% of acceptees attending	41

FRESHMAN PROFILE

Range SAT Critical Reading	490–630
Range SAT Math	513–650
Range SAT Writing	490–610
Range ACT Composite	21–27
Minimum paper TOEFL	500
Minimum web-based TOEFL	61
Average HS GPA	3.5
% graduated top 10% of class	21
% graduated top 25% of class	48
% graduated top 50% of class	80

DEADLINES

Regular	
Priority	12/15
Deadline	4/1
Nonfall registration?	yes

FINANCIAL FACTS

Financial Aid Rating	**69**
Annual in-state tuition	$5,850
Annual out-state tuition	$20,476
Room and board	$6,699
Required fees	$913
Books and supplies	$1,090
% needy frosh rec. need-based scholarship or grant aid	79
% needy UG rec. need-based scholarship or grant aid	78
% needy frosh rec. non-need-based scholarship or grant aid	7
% needy UG rec. non-need-based scholarship or grant aid	2
% needy frosh rec. need-based self-help aid	84
% needy UG rec. need-based self-help aid	92
% frosh rec. any financial aid	44
% UG rec. any financial aid	47
% UG borrow to pay for school	42
Average cumulative indebtedness	$18,991
% frosh need fully met	16
% ugrads need fully met	10
Average % of frosh need met	61
Average % of ugrad need met	62

UNIVERSITY OF VERMONT

UNIVERSITY OF VERMONT ADMISSIONS, BURLINGTON, VT 05401-3596 • ADMISSIONS: 802-656-3370 • FAX: 802-656-8611

CAMPUS LIFE

Quality of Life Rating	**76**
Fire Safety Rating	**89**
Green Rating	**96**
Type of school	public
Environment	town

STUDENTS

Total undergrad enrollment	10,459
% male/female	44/56
% from out of state	73
% from public high school	70
% frosh live on campus	97
# of fraternities	9
# of sororities	6
% African American	1
% Asian	2
% Caucasian	85
% Hispanic	4
% international	1
# of countries represented	53

SURVEY SAYS . . .

Students are friendly
Students love Burlington, VT
Great off-campus food
Political activism is popular
Lots of beer drinking
Hard liquor is popular
Students are environmentally aware

ACADEMICS

Academic Rating	**68**
% students returning for sophomore year	85
% students graduating within 4 years	57
Calendar	semester
Student/faculty ratio	17:1
Profs interesting rating	75
Profs accessible rating	72
Most classes have	fewer than 10 students
Most lab/discussion sessions have	20–29 students

MOST POPULAR MAJORS

biology/biological sciences; business administration and management; psychology

STUDENTS SAY ". . ."

Academics

Quality of life issues are important to most University of Vermont undergrads; when discussing their reasons for choosing UVM, they're as likely to cite the "laid-back environment," the "proximity to skiing facilities," the "great parties," and their "amazing" hometown of Burlington as they are to mention the academics. But, students remind us, "That doesn't mean that there are not strong academics [at UVM]." On the contrary, UVM is made up of several well-established colleges and offers "a wide variety of majors." "You can jump around between majors, and then leave with a recognized diploma in hand for something you love to do." Students single out the business school, the "top-notch" education program, the psychology department, premedical sciences, and "the amazing animal science program" for praise, and are especially proud of The Rubenstein School of Natural Resources. It's home to UVM's environmental science majors; students tell us it "is a great college that feels like it's much smaller, [more] separate, and just cozier than the rest of the school." No matter which discipline, "You get out what you put in." "Teachers are readily available and are willing to help you do well in your classes. They encourage you to get help if you need it and are enthusiastic about what they teach. It's all there; you just have to take advantage of it." The size of the university, we're told, is just right. UVM is "a moderately large school," and it allows undergrads "to feel at home while still offering just about any activity possible."

Life

"UVM is known to be a party school," "even though the university has cracked down on drinking." Indeed, students tell us that one can find "a good balance of having fun and academics" at UVM, "but it's tough, because there's always a party going on somewhere." Students who want to dodge the party scene will find "there is always something" happening in Burlington. The town has "lots of wonderful restaurants, a few movie theaters, a rockin' music scene, several bars, some dancing, and various environmental and social activities downtown." "On campus, there is typically at least one university-sponsored event each night, including interesting lectures, movies, games, or social events." Students love outdoor activities. "When it snows, it's very popular to go to the ski resorts around here and ski or snowboard for the day. When it's still warm out, going to the waterfront and swimming in Lake Champlain is popular too." UVM is an intercollegiate hockey powerhouse, and "in the fall and winter, hockey games are huge social events." They're so popular "that you have to get tickets to them the Monday before the game, or they will be sold out!"

Student Body

There's a "great variety of students" at UVM "because it's a big university," undergrads report, but they also note that "students at UVM are mostly white" and there's "a lot of money at this school." While the most prevalent UVM archetype is "the guitar-loving, earth-saving, relaxed hippie" who "care[s] strongly about the environment" and "social justice," the student body also includes "your athletic types, your artsy people, and a number of other groups" including "vocal LGBTQ and ALANA populations" who, "usually hang out in their own groups," but "are also active in all sorts of clubs across campus." Not surprisingly, there are many "New England types," "potheads," and "snow bums." Students report they "pretty much get along well with everyone." They either come here loving the outdoors or learn to love the outdoors by the time they leave.

FINANCIAL AID: 802-656-5700 • E-MAIL: ADMISSIONS@UVM.EDU • WEBSITE: WWW.UVM.EDU

THE PRINCETON REVIEW SAYS

Admissions

Very important factors considered include: Rigor of secondary school record. *Important factors considered include:* Class rank, application essay, academic GPA, standardized test scores, character/personal qualities, state residency. *Other factors considered include:* Recommendation(s), alumni/ae relation, extracurricular activities, first generation, geographical residence, interview, level of applicant's interest, racial/ethnic status, talent/ability, volunteer work, work experience. SAT or ACT required; ACT with writing component required. TOEFL required of all international applicants. High school diploma is required and GED is accepted. *Academic units required:* 4 English, 3 mathematics, 2 science (1 science lab), 2 foreign language, 3 social studies.

Financial Aid

Students should submit: FAFSA. The Princeton Review suggests that all financial aid forms be submitted as soon as possible after January 1. *Need-based scholarships/grants offered:* Federal Pell, SEOG, state scholarships/grants, private scholarships, the school's own gift aid, Federal Nursing Scholarships. *Loan aid offered:* Direct Subsidized Stafford, Direct Unsubsidized Stafford, Direct PLUS, Federal Perkins, Federal Nursing, college/university loans from institutional funds. Applicants will be notified of awards on a rolling basis beginning March 15. Federal Work-Study Program available. Institutional employment available. Off-campus job opportunities are good.

The Inside Word

UVM is a very popular choice among out-of-state students, whom the school welcomes; more than half the student body originates from outside of Vermont. While admissions standards are significantly more rigorous for out-of-staters, solid candidates (B-plus/A-minus average, about a 600 on each section of the SAT) should do fine here. The school assesses applications holistically, meaning students who are weak in one area may be able to make up for it with strengths or distinguishing skills and characteristics in other areas.

THE SCHOOL SAYS ". . ."

From the Admissions Office

"Founded in 1791, the University of Vermont is among the oldest universities in the United States and one of the nation's premier small research universities. During much of its first century, the university was a private liberal college dedicated to undergraduate teaching. In 1868, it became Vermont's public land grant university and expanded its mission to include research and service.

"Today, UVM combines both elements of its heritage. Undergraduates work in small classes with faculty who are both mentors and world-class researchers. UVM's location in Vermont, known for its civic-mindedness, commitment to the environment, and essential values, strengthens the overall spirit of the university as a tolerant, enlightened, and unusually welcoming community. Yet UVM students hail from 48 states (a third come from Vermont) and 20 countries.

"Academics at UVM are supplemented and deepened by a world of hands-on learning opportunities, from travel-study to service learning, and a wide array of internships in locations ranging from Vermont to China. Many students also assist faculty with their groundbreaking research in research facilities across campus, including UVM's highly-ranked medical school. The university is widely recognized for its environmental conscience, commitment to social justice, and global perspective. In recognition of this achievement outside the classroom, more than 70 UVM students have been selected as winners or finalists in the country's most competitive scholarships, such as the Truman, Fulbright, Udall and Goldwater.

"The University of Vermont is located in Burlington, one of America's liveliest small cities surrounded by idyllic countryside, the Green Mountains, and Lake Champlain. As the state's educational, medical, financial and cultural epicenter, Burlington is ranked one of the most desirable place to live and a top college town. In addition, Vermont's "human scale" is often cited as offering UVM students unique opportunities to get involved and gain essential experience."

SELECTIVITY

Admissions Rating	79
# of applicants	22,341
% of applicants accepted	75
% of acceptees attending	14
# accepting a place on wait list	1,027
# admitted from wait list	572

FRESHMAN PROFILE

Range SAT Critical Reading	540–640
Range SAT Math	550–640
Range SAT Writing	540–640
Range ACT Composite	24–29
Minimum paper TOEFL	550
% graduated top 10% of class	28
% graduated top 25% of class	68
% graduated top 50% of class	96

DEADLINES

Early action	
Deadline	11/1
Notification	12/5
Regular	
Deadline	1/15
Notification	3/31
Nonfall registration?	yes

FINANCIAL FACTS

Financial Aid Rating	72
Annual in-state tuition	$12,888
Annual out-state tuition	$32,528
Room and board	$9,708
Required fees	$1,896
Books and supplies	$1,200
% needy frosh rec. need-based scholarship or grant aid	98
% needy UG rec. need-based scholarship or grant aid	97
% needy frosh rec. non-need-based scholarship or grant aid	6
% needy UG rec. non-need-based scholarship or grant aid	4
% needy frosh rec. need-based self-help aid	77
% needy UG rec. need-based self-help aid	77
% frosh rec. any financial aid	90
% UG rec. any financial aid	84
% UG borrow to pay for school	61
Average cumulative indebtedness	$26,941
% frosh need fully met	13
% ugrads need fully met	13
Average % of frosh need met	72
Average % of ugrad need met	68

University of Virginia

Office of Admission, Charlottesville, VA 22906 • Admissions: 434-982-3200 • Fax: 434-924-3587

CAMPUS LIFE

Quality of Life Rating	**91**
Fire Safety Rating	**69**
Green Rating	**93**
Type of school	public
Environment	city

STUDENTS

Total undergrad enrollment	14,591
% male/female	45/55
% from out of state	31
% from public high school	74
% frosh live on campus	100
# of fraternities	34
# of sororities	24
% African American	7
% Asian	12
% Caucasian	60
% Hispanic	5
% international	6
# of countries represented	119

SURVEY SAYS . . .

Athletic facilities are great
Low cost of living
Great library
Great off-campus food
Students are happy
Lots of beer drinking
No one cheats

ACADEMICS

Academic Rating	**83**
% students returning for sophomore year	97
% students graduating within 4 years	87
% students graduating within 6 years	94
Calendar	semester
Student/faculty ratio	16:1
Profs interesting rating	84
Profs accessible rating	77
Most classes have	10–19 students
Most lab/discussion sessions have	20–29 students

MOST POPULAR MAJORS

business/commerce; economics; psychology

APPLICANTS ALSO LOOK AT AND OFTEN PREFER

College of William and Mary, Virginia Tech, Princeton University

AND SOMETIMES PREFER

Duke University, The University of North Carolina at Chapel Hill, Cornell University

AND RARELY PREFER

James Madison University

STUDENTS SAY ". . ."

Academics

There is much to love about the University of Virginia, one of the country's top public universities. Just to name a few: "Tradition, student self-governance, the honor system, the access to world renowned professors, [and] the beauty of the architecture." The school's affordable in-state tuition guarantees students access to "the perfect balance of world-class academics, a tradition of school spirit, and a great party scene." While there are a lot of opportunities at UVa, "No one is going to hold your hand and help you find what you're interested in." However, those who proactively seek out their own answers "find the UVa community is fully supportive of [their] passions, and there are tons of resources to pursue whatever interest you might have." The academic program is "definitely our greatest strength—no matter what you choose to major in, you will encounter great professors and stimulating courses," according to one student. Many of the school's most accomplished professors teach introductory and lower-level courses "to make themselves accessible to every student at UVa." Professors "want to get to know you as a person and are always helpful if you approach them with questions on content or other academic problems." Courses are "very flexible," and the faculty are "always coming up with new course options," though the class registration system is notoriously frustrating. The school has a "very strong honor system" that is run entirely by students (as are all extracurricular groups), so "it's rare to hear about someone's stuff being stolen or cheating on assignments." This autonomy is a huge boon to students' feelings toward their school, as is the universal "respect for tradition."

Life

Living on campus "is definitely a huge part of your first-year experience," and students all greatly appreciate "the unique history" and "hilarious and fun traditions" of the school (especially those upheld by the popular Greek system), "which help to foster a sense of community." The school offers a ton of resources, including "free counseling and psychological services, plenty of places to grab a bite to eat, a twenty-four-hour library, a movie theater, free transportation on both University and local transport services, a fabulous career services center, four gyms, and constant sporting events." "Whether I'm in the mood to go for a hike in the Blue Ridge Mountains or go shopping in the downtown mall, there is never a dull moment," says a student.

Most students instantly fall in love with the "accessible and charming" Charlottesville, with its "awesome, local, and iconic" food, "local quirky shops," "a thriving music scene, multicultural festivals," and "three great coffee places." On campus, the lawn or gardens "always sport students lounging and reading, people walking their dogs, townies with their kids, and professors and students having coffee." As for more traditionally collegiate forms of kicking back, UVa kids do enjoy "lots of drinking/partying," but "you can find people who don't like to if you try." "We put an incredible amount of effort into our academic lives, and then when the weekend comes we let loose like there's no tomorrow," says one student.

Student Body

The tough admissions standards mean that most all who attend here are "highly motivated, resourceful, [and] passionate about learning," and the student body does have a reputation as "a bunch of hard partying, politically aware, go-getters." There really is "a pervasive can-do attitude around UVa," and the "self-starter and very smart" students reflect that "with all the things we do only with support from other." Almost seventy percent of students come from Virginia and are "typical preppy Southerners," and there are terrific town-gown relations; students here are also "really environmentally friendly and socially conscious." "We like to be activists and get involved in the community," says a student. You're also "practically an outcast if you don't join a student group…once you see the vast number of student groups around grounds, you'll find it hard not to join one—or maybe seventeen."

FINANCIAL AID: 434-982-6000 • E-MAIL: UNDERGRADADMISSION@VIRGINIA.EDU • WEBSITE: WWW.VIRGINIA.EDU

THE PRINCETON REVIEW SAYS

Admissions

Very important factors considered include: Class rank, academic GPA, recommendation(s), rigor of secondary school record, alumni/ae relation, first generation, racial/ethnic status, state residency. *Important factors considered include:* Application essay, standardized test scores, character/personal qualities, extracurricular activities, talent/ability. *Other factors considered include:* Geographical residence, volunteer work, work experience. SAT or ACT required; ACT with writing component required. TOEFL required of all international applicants. High school diploma is required and GED is accepted. *Academic units required:* 4 English, 4 mathematics, 2 science, 2 foreign language, 1 social studies. *Academic units recommended:* 5 mathematics, 4 science, 5 foreign language, 4 social studies.

Financial Aid

Students should submit: FAFSA, CSS PROFILE. The priority filing date for FAFSA and the CSS Profile for entering and transfer students is March 1—if students want to receive information about awards by the time admission decisions are made. The deadline for applying for state and institutional need-based aid is April 30. *Need-based scholarships/grants offered:* Federal Pell, SEOG, state scholarships/grants, private scholarships, the school's own gift aid, Federal Nursing Scholarships. *Loan aid offered:* Direct Subsidized Stafford, Direct Unsubsidized Stafford, Direct PLUS, Federal Perkins, Federal Nursing, college/university loans from institutional funds, alternative/private loans. Federal Work-Study Program available. Institutional employment available.

The Inside Word

As one of the premier public universities in the country, UVA holds its applicants to high standards. While admissions officers don't set minimum requirements, all viable candidates have stellar academic records. Intellectual ability is imperative, and prospective students are expected to have taken a rigorous course load in high school. Applicants should be aware that geographical location holds significant weight, as Virginia residents are given preference.

THE SCHOOL SAYS ". . ."

From the Admissions Office

"Admission to competitive schools requires strong academic credentials. Students who stretch themselves and take rigorous courses (honors-level, AP, IB and DE courses, when offered) are significantly more competitive than those who do not. Experienced admissions officers know that most students are capable of presenting superb academic credentials, and the reality is that a very high percentage of those applying do so. Other considerations, then, come into play in important ways for academically strong candidates, as they must be seen as 'selective' as well as academically competitive.

"SAT or ACT is required. Neither is preferred. It is strongly recommended that applicants take two SAT Subject Tests of the applicant's choice."

SELECTIVITY	
Admissions Rating	**98**
# of applicants	23,587
% of applicants accepted	33
% of acceptees attending	44
# accepting a place on wait list	2,371
# admitted from wait list	117

FRESHMAN PROFILE	
Range SAT Critical Reading	610–720
Range SAT Math	630–740
Range SAT Writing	620–720
Range ACT Composite	28–32
Average HS GPA	4.2
% graduated top 10% of class	91
% graduated top 25% of class	98
% graduated top 50% of class	100

DEADLINES	
Early action	
Deadline	11/1
Notification	1/31
Regular	
Deadline	1/1
Notification	4/1
Nonfall registration?	yes

FINANCIAL FACTS	
Financial Aid Rating	**93**
Annual in-state tuition	$9,622
Annual out-state tuition	$34,952
Room and board	$9,419
Required fees	$2,384
Books and supplies	$1,200
% needy frosh rec. need-based scholarship or grant aid	85
% needy UG rec. need-based scholarship or grant aid	86
% needy frosh rec. non-need-based scholarship or grant aid	12
% needy UG rec. non-need-based scholarship or grant aid	9
% needy frosh rec. need-based self-help aid	56
% needy UG rec. need-based self-help aid	59
% frosh rec. any financial aid	58
% UG rec. any financial aid	53
% UG borrow to pay for school	35
Average cumulative indebtedness	$20,951
% frosh need fully met	100
% ugrads need fully met	100
Average % of frosh need met	100
Average % of ugrad need met	100

UNIVERSITY OF WASHINGTON

1410 NORTHEAST CAMPUS PARKWAY, SEATTLE, WA 98195-5852 • ADMISSIONS: 206-543-9686

CAMPUS LIFE

Quality of Life Rating	**82**
Fire Safety Rating	**91**
Green Rating	**99**
Type of school	public
Environment	metropolis

STUDENTS

Total undergrad enrollment	27,867
% male/female	48/52
% from out of state	20
% frosh live on campus	65
# of fraternities	32
# of sororities	16
% African American	2
% Asian	14
% Caucasian	28
% Hispanic	3
% Native American	1
% international	4
# of countries represented	107

SURVEY SAYS . . .

Great computer facilities
Great library
Athletic facilities are great
Students love Seattle, WA
Great off-campus food
Everyone loves the Huskies
Student publications are popular
Students are environmentally aware

ACADEMICS

Academic Rating	**77**
% students returning for sophomore year	93
% students graduating within 6 years	80
Calendar	quarter
Student/faculty ratio	13:1
Profs interesting rating	70
Profs accessible rating	69
Most classes have	20–29 students
Most lab/discussion sessions have	20–29 students

MOST POPULAR MAJORS

economics; political science and government; psychology

APPLICANTS ALSO LOOK AT AND OFTEN PREFER

University of Southern California

AND SOMETIMES PREFER

Gonzaga University

AND RARELY PREFER

Washington State University, University of Puget Sound, University of Colorado—Boulder

STUDENTS SAY ". . ."

Academics

Students find "a great combination of high-powered academics, an excellent social life, and a wide variety of courses, all in the midst of the exciting Seattle life" at the University of Washington, the state's flagship institution of higher learning. UW offers "a lot of really stellar programs and the best bang for the buck, especially for in-state students or those in the sciences." Indeed, science programs "are incredible. The research going on here is cutting-edge and the leaders of biomedical sciences, stem cell research, etc. are accessible to students." Undergrads warn, however, that science programs are extremely competitive, "high pressure," and "challenging," with "core classes taught in lectures that seat more than 500 people," creating the sense that "professors don't seem to care too much whether you succeed." Pre-professional programs in business, law, nursing, medicine and engineering all earn high marks, although again with the caveat that the workload is tough and the hand-holding nominal. As one student puts it, "The University of Washington provides every resource and opportunity for its students to succeed. You just have to take advantage of them. No one will do it for you." For those fortunate enough to get in, the Honors Program "creates a smaller community of highly motivated students…It puts this school on top."

Life

UW students typically "have a good balance in their lives of education and fun." They "generally study hard and work in the libraries, but once the nighttime hits, they look forward to enjoying the night with their friends." Between the large university community and the surrounding city of Seattle, undergrads have a near-limitless selection of extracurricular choices. As one student explains, "There are tons of options for fun in Seattle. Going down to Pike's Market on a Saturday and eating your way through is always popular. There are tons of places to eat on 'The Ave,'" the shopping district that abuts campus, "and the UVillage shopping mall is a five minute walk from campus with chain-store comfort available. Intramural sports are big for activities, and going to undergraduate theater productions is never a disappointing experience. And during autumn or spring renting a canoe and paddling around lake Washington down by the stadium is fun." Husky football games "are amazing," and the Greek community "is very big" without dominating campus social life. In short, "the UW has anything you could want to do in your free time."

Student Body

"At such a large university, there is no 'typical' student," undergrads tell us, observing "one can find just about any demographic here and there is a huge variety in personalities." There "are quite a lot of yuppies, but then again, it's Seattle," and by and large "the campus is ultraliberal. Most students care about the environment, are not religious, and are generally accepting of other diverse individuals." Otherwise, "You've got your stereotypes: the Greeks, the street fashion pioneers, the various ethnic communities, the Oxford-looking grad students, etc." In terms of demographics, "The typical student at UW is white, middle-class, and is from the Seattle area," but "There are a lot of African American students and a very large number of Asian students." All groups "seem to socialize with each other."

FAX: 206-685-3655 • FINANCIAL AID: 206-543-6101 • WEBSITE: WWW.WASHINGTON.EDU

THE PRINCETON REVIEW SAYS

Admissions

Very important factors considered include: Application essay, academic GPA, rigor of secondary school record. *Important factors considered include:* Standardized test scores, character/personal qualities, extracurricular activities, first generation, talent/ability, volunteer work, work experience. *Other factors considered include:* State residency. SAT or ACT required; ACT with writing component required. TOEFL required of all international applicants. High school diploma or equivalent is not required. *Academic units required:* 4 English, 3 mathematics, 2 science (1 science lab), 2 foreign language, 3 social studies. *Academic units recommended:* 4 English, 4 mathematics, 3 science (3 science labs), 3 foreign language, 4 social studies, 1 history, 1 visual/performing arts, 1 computer science.

Financial Aid

Students should submit: FAFSA. The Princeton Review suggests that all financial aid forms be submitted as soon as possible after January 1. *Need-based scholarships/grants offered:* Federal Pell, SEOG, state scholarships/grants, private scholarships, the school's own gift aid. *Loan aid offered:* Direct Subsidized Stafford, Direct Unsubsidized Stafford, Direct PLUS, Federal Perkins, Federal Nursing, college/university loans from institutional funds. Applicants will be notified of awards on or about March 31. Federal Work-Study Program available. Institutional employment available. Off-campus job opportunities are excellent.

The Inside Word

In recent years, UW committed to a thorough review of all freshman applications, abandoning the previous process by which a formula was used to rank applicants according to high school GPA and standardized test scores. The new, holistic approach allows admissions officers to take into account a student's background, the degree to which he or she has overcome personal adversity, and such intangibles as leadership quality and special skills. The move has so far resulted in increased racial and socioeconomic diversity, a result praised by some and criticized by others, who regard the new system as a poorly disguised affirmative action program.

THE SCHOOL SAYS ". . ."

From the Admissions Office

"Are you curious about everything, from comet dust to computer game design, salmon to Salman Rushdie, ancient Rome to the atmospherics of Mars? Do you seek the freedom to chart your own course—and work on breakthrough research? Are you ready to cheer on the Division I Huskies and spend your weekends sea kayaking? Would you like to walk to class on a 700-acre stunning, ivy-covered campus, yet be only fifteen minutes from downtown Seattle? If the answers are yes, then the University of Washington may be the place for you. Offering more than 140 majors and 450 student organizations, the UW is looking for students who are both excited about the vast academic and social possibilities available to them and eager to contribute to the campus' cultural and intellectual life.

"We encourage you to take advantage of every opportunity in the application, especially the personal statement and activities summary, to tell us why Washington would be good fit for you and how you will contribute to the freshman class.

"Freshman applicants to the University of Washington are required to submit scores from either the SAT or ACT (with the writing component)."

SELECTIVITY

Admissions Rating	**91**
# of applicants	24,540
% of applicants accepted	58
% of acceptees attending	40
# accepting a place on wait list	1,412
# admitted from wait list	284

FRESHMAN PROFILE

Range SAT Critical Reading	510–650
Range SAT Math	570–700
Range SAT Writing	520–640
Range ACT Composite	24–30
Minimum paper TOEFL	540
Minimum web-based TOEFL	76
Average HS GPA	3.8
% graduated top 10% of class	92
% graduated top 25% of class	98
% graduated top 50% of class	100

DEADLINES

Regular	
Deadline	12/1
Notification	3/31
Nonfall registration?	yes

FINANCIAL FACTS

Financial Aid Rating	**71**
Annual in-state tuition	$9,746
Annual out-state tuition	$27,230
Room and board	$9,771
Required fees	$828
Books and supplies	$1,035
% needy frosh rec. need-based scholarship or grant aid	73
% needy UG rec. need-based scholarship or grant aid	73
% needy frosh rec. non-need-based scholarship or grant aid	17
% needy UG rec. non-need-based scholarship or grant aid	10
% needy frosh rec. need-based self-help aid	52
% needy UG rec. need-based self-help aid	61
% frosh rec. any financial aid	50
% UG rec. any financial aid	50
% UG borrow to pay for school	50
Average cumulative indebtedness	$16,800
% frosh need fully met	36
% ugrads need fully met	33
Average % of frosh need met	80
Average % of ugrad need met	79

UNIVERSITY OF WISCONSIN—MADISON

702 WEST JOHNSON STREET, SUITE 101, MADISON, WI 53715-1007 • ADMISSIONS: 608-262-3961 • FAX: 608-262-7706

CAMPUS LIFE

Quality of Life Rating	**89**
Fire Safety Rating	**67**
Green Rating	**84**
Type of school	public
Environment	city

STUDENTS

Total undergrad enrollment	28,737
% male/female	48/52
% from out of state	38
% frosh live on campus	90
# of fraternities	26
# of sororities	11
% African American	2
% Asian	5
% Caucasian	78
% Hispanic	4
% international	6
# of countries represented	144

SURVEY SAYS . . .

Students love Madison, WI
Great off-campus food
Everyone loves the Badgers
Student publications are popular
Political activism is popular
Lots of beer drinking
Hard liquor is popular
Students are environmentally aware

ACADEMICS

Academic Rating	**83**
% students returning for sophomore year	94
% students graduating within 4 years	53
% students graduating within 6 years	83
Calendar	semester
Student/faculty ratio	17:1
Profs interesting rating	81
Profs accessible rating	82
Most classes have	10–19 students
Most lab/discussion sessions have	20–29 students

MOST POPULAR MAJORS

biology/biological sciences; economics; political science and government

APPLICANTS ALSO LOOK AT AND OFTEN PREFER

University of Illinois at Urbana-Champaign, University of Minnesota—Twin Cities, University of Michigan—Ann Arbor, Marquette University

AND SOMETIMES PREFER

Northwestern University, University of Colorado—Boulder

STUDENTS SAY ". . ."

Academics

"The resources are phenomenal" at University of Wisconsin—Madison. "If you are proactive, you basically have the means and resources to pursue any academic or creative feat," promises a journalism major. "The liberal arts majors are fantastic." However, Madison is mostly known as "an amazing research institution," and the hard sciences and engineering programs get most of the pub. They iodized salt here, after all, and cultivated the first lab-based embryonic stem cells. The school of business is "excellent" as well and boasts "some of the best facilities on campus." Overall the school runs surprisingly smoothly" despite some "red tape." Many lecture courses are large and "impersonal." But class sizes often "plummet" after the intro courses, and the academic atmosphere is "challenging." Madison "definitely makes you earn your grades." "Some professors are amazing, and some suck." Also, "a lot of the classes for the undergrads are taught by teaching assistants who are not so good." "It becomes clear within the first few weeks which of your professors actually have lectures that are worthwhile for you to attend, which is probably about half," suggests a first-year student.

Life

UW—Madison's "reputation as a party school" is legendary. Halloween and the Mifflin Street Block Party are epic. "The weekend pretty much starts on Thursday night" as the streets of Madison "fill to the brim with drunk co-eds." There are house parties and frat parties galore. "Getting up at 9:00 a.m." to "bong a few beers for breakfast" before football games in the fall is common, and "nothing—absolutely nothing—can beat being in the student section at a Badger home football game." "The stadium is usually full" for hockey games, too. However, "no one looks at you differently if you choose not to drink" or attend sporting events. And, for everyone, "if you don't have a strong dedication to your education, you will slip up." Beyond the party and sports scene, UW is "energetic" and mammoth. "No one's going to hold your hand and point you to what it is you want." At the same time, whoever you are, "there is a group for you and a ton of activities for you." Two daily student newspapers "serve as the penultimate example of free speech in action." UW's lakefront campus provides "gorgeous" scenery. Many of the buildings "aren't that appealing," though, and some dorms are "absolutely horrible." Off-campus, "having the streets crawling with the homeless isn't so great," but Madison is teeming with culture, "live music," "late-night coffee shops," and "exceptional" chow from around the globe.

Student Body

Ethnic diversity at Madison is in the eye of the beholder. "If you're from a big city, it's pretty white," proposes a sophomore. "But, then again, I've met people here who had one black person in their high school and had never met a Jewish person." Without question, socioeconomic diversity flourishes. "There is a prevalent rivalry between [Wisconsin] students (sconnies) and the coasties who are generally wealthier and from the East or West Coast." Beyond that, it's impossible to generalize. "All types of people make up the student body here, ranging from the peace-preaching grass-root activist, to the protein-shake-a-day jock, to the overly privileged coastie, to the studious bookworm, to the computer geek," explains a first-year student. "There is a niche for everyone." "There are a lot of atypical students, but that is what makes UW—Madison so special," adds a senior. "Normal doesn't exist on this campus." Politically, "Madison is a hotbed for political and social debate." "Many people are passionate about many things, and it provides a great opportunity to see things from others' points of view."

FINANCIAL AID: 608-262-3060 • E-MAIL: ONWISCONSIN@ADMISSIONS.WISC.EDU • WEBSITE: WWW.WISC.EDU

THE PRINCETON REVIEW SAYS

Admissions

Very important factors considered include: Class rank, academic GPA, rigor of secondary school record. *Important factors considered include:* Application essay, standardized test scores, state residency. *Other factors considered include:* Recommendation(s), alumni/ae relation, character/personal qualities, extracurricular activities, first generation, level of applicant's interest, racial/ethnic status, talent/ability, volunteer work, work experience. SAT or ACT required; ACT with writing component required. TOEFL required of all international applicants. High school diploma is required and GED is accepted. *Academic units required:* 4 English, 3 mathematics, 3 science, 2 foreign language, 3 social studies, 2 academic electives. *Academic units recommended:* 4 English, 4 mathematics, 4 science, 4 foreign language, 4 social studies, 2 academic electives.

Financial Aid

Students should submit: FAFSA, institution's own financial aid form. The Princeton Review suggests that all financial aid forms be submitted as soon as possible after January 1. *Need-based scholarships/grants offered:* Federal Pell, SEOG, state scholarships/grants, private scholarships, the school's own gift aid. *Loan aid offered:* Direct Subsidized Stafford, Direct Unsubsidized Stafford, Direct PLUS, Federal Perkins, Federal Nursing, state loans. Applicants will be notified of awards on a rolling basis beginning April 1. Federal Work-Study Program available. Institutional employment available. Off-campus job opportunities are excellent.

The Inside Word

Though it's not at the top tier of selectivity, Wisconsin has high expectations of its candidates. Admissions officers are most concerned with the high school transcript (course selection and grades), although test scores are also important. And they won't ignore compelling essays, recommendations, or extracurricular achievements.

THE SCHOOL SAYS ". . ."

From the Admissions Office

"UW—Madison is the university of choice for some of the best and brightest students. Our freshman class has an average ACT score of 28 and an average SAT of 1276. Almost sixty percent are from the top ten percent of their high school class, and nearly all are from the top quarter.

"These factors combine to make admission to UW—Madison both competitive and selective. We consider academic record, course selection, strength of curriculum (honors, AP, IB, etc.), grade trend, class rank, results of the ACT/SAT, and non-academic factors. There is no prescribed minimum test score, GPA, or class rank criteria. Rather, we admit the best and most well-prepared students—students who have challenged themselves and who will contribute to Wisconsin's strength and diversity—for the limited space available.

"Each application is personally reviewed by our admission counselors. All domestic freshman applications completed by February 1 receive full and equal consideration. We offer two notification periods for domestic freshman applicants. To receive a decision during the First Notification Period, you must complete the application and submit all required materials (application fee, official high school transcript, official test scores, personal statements, and recommendations) postmarked by November 1. Admission decisions for these students will be made by the end of January. All students who complete their applications during the Second Notification Period (after November 1 but before the February 1 deadline) will have decision made on or by the end of March. All students receive equal consideration for admission whether they apply during the First or Second Notification Periods."

SELECTIVITY

Admissions Rating	93
# of applicants	28,983
% of applicants accepted	50
% of acceptees attending	40

FRESHMAN PROFILE

Range SAT Critical Reading	550–670
Range SAT Math	620–740
Range SAT Writing	590–680
Range ACT Composite	26–30
Minimum paper TOEFL	550
Minimum web-based TOEFL	80
Average HS GPA	3.7
% graduated top 10% of class	58
% graduated top 25% of class	94
% graduated top 50% of class	100

DEADLINES

Regular	
Priority	2/1
Deadline	2/1
Nonfall registration?	yes

FINANCIAL FACTS

Financial Aid Rating	71
Annual in-state tuition	$8,592
Annual out-state tuition	$24,342
Room and board	$7,780
Required fees	$1,079
Books and supplies	$1,140
% needy frosh rec. need-based scholarship or grant aid	55
% needy UG rec. need-based scholarship or grant aid	63
% needy frosh rec. non-need-based scholarship or grant aid	75
% needy UG rec. non-need-based scholarship or grant aid	72
% needy frosh rec. need-based self-help aid	81
% needy UG rec. need-based self-help aid	84
% frosh rec. any financial aid	51
% UG rec. any financial aid	48
% UG borrow to pay for school	48
Average cumulative indebtedness	$24,140
% frosh need fully met	26
% ugrads need fully met	24
Average % of frosh need met	71
Average % of ugrad need met	73

UNIVERSITY OF WYOMING

DEPARTMENT 3435, LARAMIE, WY 82071 • ADMISSIONS: 307-766-5160 • FAX: 307-766-4042

CAMPUS LIFE

Quality of Life Rating	**70**
Fire Safety Rating	**78**
Green Rating	**81**
Type of school	public
Environment	town

STUDENTS

Total undergrad enrollment	9,993
% male/female	48/52
% from out of state	46
% frosh live on campus	88
# of fraternities	9
# of sororities	6
% African American	1
% Asian	1
% Caucasian	81
% Hispanic	5
% Native American	1
% international	3
# of countries represented	91

SURVEY SAYS . . .

Great computer facilities
Athletic facilities are great
Students are friendly
Students get along with local community
Everyone loves the Cowboys
Lots of beer drinking
Hard liquor is popular

ACADEMICS

Academic Rating	**70**
% students returning for sophomore year	73
Calendar	semester
Student/faculty ratio	14:1
Profs interesting rating	73
Profs accessible rating	75
Most classes have	20–29 students
Most lab/discussion sessions have	20–29 students

MOST POPULAR MAJORS

elementary education and teaching; nursing/registered nurse (rn, asn, bsn, msn); psychology

STUDENTS SAY "..."

Academics

Why choose University of Wyoming? "Wyoming scholarships rock!" Hathaway Scholarships allow state residents to graduate virtually debt free, and financial aid for out-of-state students isn't too shabby, either. This allows students to get "an outstanding education for pennies on the dollar." This is a large university, though, which means "you have to make the commitment to do well." In other words, those grades aren't going to earn themselves! The business school, engineering school, and English departments all receive high marks from students, and the school's agricultural programs also have an excellent reputation. "They are on top of developing degree programs and courses focused on sustainability, green design, and climate change." There's "a 50/50 [split between] professors who love what they do and those who are just going with the flow," but "Nine times out of ten they will go well out of their way to help you." Many faculty members "have real-world job experience that helps bring their lectures to life." Many students complain about the registration process, which favors athletes and members of the honors program, but others suggest that kicking up a fuss will get you into the classes you want, or they suggest applying for the honors program: "They pull in the best professors across campus, and the requirements are a piece of cake. Plus, you get free printing," semester-long book checkout at the library, and priority registration. (Conservatives take note: Some students describe the honors classes as "very biased and liberal.") "The new library is great and full of awesome resources," and study abroad resources are "absolutely amazing" as well.

Life

"Cowboy football is a blast! We may not have the best team or biggest crowd, but we make up for it in dedicated fans!" Supporting UW's Division I football team is a bit pastime in the fall. Winter in Laramie, Wyoming, may be freezing (student wish lists include reopening underground tunnels for travel between buildings, and/or "fire pits for staying warm on your way to your next class!"), but it's "a great town if you enjoy the outdoors," and "Skiing, mountain biking, hiking, camping, fishing, mountain climbing, hunting are all popular activities." "People often say that there is nothing to do in Laramie but drink," and UW has its fair share of partying, though members of the large religious and nontraditional student populations are quick to point out that not everyone is searching for a house party every weekend. "The school offers a wide breadth of other activities from free ice skating to free movies, fly-fishing classes to a capella concerts, and many of these are run by students and are widely attended." Fort Collins and Denver, Colorado, are both about two and a half hours away by car, though if you're bringing a vehicle to campus, four-wheel drive is strongly recommended.

Student Body

"The majority of the students are Wyoming residents with a large portion of the rest coming from Colorado." Students tend to be "good-natured kids [who have] grown up on ranches or farms where a strong work ethic has been established," "usually nice with strong family values and a conservative upbringing." Politically, there seems to be a bit of a divide among students, which reflects the geography of the university: Laramie is considered a more liberal enclave in a traditionally conservative state. "The school creates an open-minded atmosphere within one of the most conservative states in the union," but on the other hand, "Many of the Christian campus ministries are very outspoken." Students say, "We are not incredibly diverse ethnically, but we are diverse in so many other ways," and "Every semester brings more and more minority and foreign students." There's "a huge amount of nontrad students as well."

FINANCIAL AID: 307-766-2116 • E-MAIL: ADMISSIONS@UWYO.EDU • WEBSITE: WWW.UWYO.EDU

THE PRINCETON REVIEW SAYS

Admissions

Very important factors considered include: Academic GPA, rigor of secondary school record, standardized test scores. *Important factors considered include:* Level of applicant's interest. *Other factors considered include:* Application essay, recommendation(s), character/personal qualities, extracurricular activities, interview, state residency, talent/ability. ACT with or without writing component accepted. TOEFL required of all international applicants. High school diploma is required and GED is accepted. *Academic units required:* 4 English, 3 mathematics, 3 science (3 science labs), 3 cultural context. *Academic units recommended:* 4 English, 4 mathematics, 4 science (3 science labs), 2 foreign language, 3 cultural context electives, 3 behavioral or social sciences, 3 visual or performing arts, 3 humanities or earth/space sciences.

Financial Aid

Students should submit: FAFSA. Regular filing deadline is February 15. The Princeton Review suggests that all financial aid forms be submitted as soon as possible after January 1. *Need-based scholarships/grants offered:* Federal Pell, SEOG, state scholarships/grants, private scholarships, the school's own gift aid. *Loan aid offered:* Direct Subsidized Stafford, Direct Unsubsidized Stafford, Direct PLUS, Federal Perkins. Applicants will be notified of awards on a rolling basis beginning March 15. Federal Work-Study Program available. Institutional employment available. Off-campus job opportunities are good.

The Inside Word

The admissions process at UW is formula-driven. State residents need a minimum high school GPA of 2.75 to gain admission, and non-residents need a 3.0 GPA. That combined with some solid test scores will open the door to this university.

THE SCHOOL SAYS ". . ."

From the Admissions Office

"The University of Wyoming and the town of Laramie are relatively small, affording students the opportunity to get the personal attention and develop a close rapport with their professors. They can easily make friends and find peers with similar interests and values. More than 200 student organizations offer students a great way to get involved and encourage growth and learning. Couple the small size with a great location, and you have a winning combination. Laramie sits between the Laramie and Snowy Range Mountains. There are numerous outdoor activities in which one can participate. Furthermore, the university works hard to attract other great cultural events. Major-label recording artists come to UW as well as some of today's great minds. In all, the University of Wyoming is a great place to be because of its wonderful blend of small-town atmosphere with 'big city' activities.

"The University of Wyoming requires first-time, incoming freshmen to submit scores from either the ACT or SAT. The writing component of the ACT and SAT is not required."

SELECTIVITY	
Admissions Rating	73
# of applicants	3,883
% of applicants accepted	96
% of acceptees attending	41

FRESHMAN PROFILE	
Range SAT Critical Reading	490–600
Range SAT Math	490–630
Range ACT Composite	22–27
Minimum paper TOEFL	540
Minimum web-based TOEFL	76
Average HS GPA	3.5
% graduated top 10% of class	21
% graduated top 25% of class	51
% graduated top 50% of class	79

DEADLINES	
Early decision	
Deadline	1/15
Notification	2/15
Early action	
Deadline	12/1
Regular	
Priority	3/1
Deadline	8/10
Nonfall registration?	yes

FINANCIAL FACTS	
Financial Aid Rating	68
Annual in-state tuition	$3,120
Annual out-state tuition	$11,850
Room and board	$8,759
Required fees	$1,005
Books and supplies	$1,200
% needy frosh rec. need-based scholarship or grant aid	53
% needy UG rec. need-based scholarship or grant aid	61
% needy frosh rec. non-need-based scholarship or grant aid	86
% needy UG rec. non-need-based scholarship or grant aid	66
% needy frosh rec. need-based self-help aid	55
% needy UG rec. need-based self-help aid	64
% frosh rec. any financial aid	95
% UG rec. any financial aid	84
% UG borrow to pay for school	56
Average cumulative indebtedness	$20,759
% frosh need fully met	28
% ugrads need fully met	16
Average % of frosh need met	32
Average % of ugrad need met	44

Ursinus College

Ursinus College, Collegeville, PA 19426 • Admissions: 610-409-3200 • Fax: 610-409-3662

CAMPUS LIFE

Quality of Life Rating	81
Fire Safety Rating	88
Green Rating	87
Type of school	private
Environment	city

STUDENTS

Total undergrad enrollment	1,741
% male/female	47/53
% from out of state	50
% from public high school	61
% frosh live on campus	99
# of fraternities	8
# of sororities	5
% African American	6
% Asian	4
% Caucasian	76
% Hispanic	4
% international	1
# of countries represented	13

SURVEY SAYS . . .

Athletic facilities are great
Lots of beer drinking
Students are friendly

ACADEMICS

Academic Rating	89
% students returning for sophomore year	89
% students graduating within 4 years	75
Calendar	semester
Student/faculty ratio	11:1
Profs interesting rating	87
Profs accessible rating	91
Most classes have	fewer than 10 students
Most lab/discussion sessions have	10–19 students

MOST POPULAR MAJORS

biology/biological sciences; economics; psychology

STUDENTS SAY ". . ."

Academics

Set in Collegeville, Pennsylvania, this "small, close-knit college community" offers "an exceptional academic record" and "small-school atmosphere," which "provides accessibility to professors and successful students, enabling a better learning experience." This is "a campus filled with motivated students and professors who worked toward every student's success." "Academic integrity" is "high," "yet fostering leadership, community and personal growth [is] also extremely prided." The "greatest strengths" of Ursinus's program "are probably the focus on community service, the strength of the academic programs, and programs such as CIE (common intellectual experience, an entire class [where the focus is on] the whole campus reading and discussing the same books or movies." Ursinus is also known for its "strong biology and science program," which "allow students to maintain strong connections in other fields, from art to education." Classes "are small," and professors "are accessible and have extensive knowledge in their fields." The academic bar here is high. Professors expect "students to be engaged." They "tend to be very attentive to your performance in class and are available to help if you need it." While "[professors] expect a lot from you, and it is challenging," the workload is "very doable because of the relationships with professors and students." Overall, this small, rigorous program is "about creating free-thinking, intelligent, [and] contributing members of society" and "letting people be who they are without fear and while accomplishing learning beyond the classroom."

Life

During the week, "Mostly everyone goes to class and then to the library or another study room to finish homework and study." "There is always something happening on campus, which is contrary to the big misconception about smaller schools." "Because the student population is low, everyone receives e-mails about everything going on." In addition, there "is a large athletic population, and games are highly attended." "Almost every night there is some party going on, and on weekends it can get crazy, but the drinking scene is easily avoidable." Others agree, "The school offers a lot of weekend activities for those of us who do not partake in drinking. They have movie nights, casino nights, game show nights, special dinners, [and] a lot of off campus events." While "the town [of Collegeville] is small, they are expanding and building upon it. Philadelphia is close as is King of Prussia, Phoenixville, Skippack, and Limerick so students have places to go off campus and have fun." "Most students stay on weekends and either attend a campus event or hang out with friends." "Partying does happen; it happens only Thursday through Saturday because most students are extremely serious about their academics."

Student Body

Ursinus students are "well-rounded, mature, and friendly." Everyone at Ursinus "has an interest in their academics as well as their social life." "Because of various requirements, students interact with all sorts of students with different majors, especially our CIE class, which requires a lot of introspection." Most students "can find a group of students they fit in with easily." The typical student "has a core group of friends, friends that they have classes with, many are involved with some kind of sport (intramural or collegiate), and many are involved with community service." While some tout the stereotypical badge of being "upper-middle- or middle-class, involved in a sport in some way"; however, by in large the student body here is "very open to other beliefs and opinions" and "willing to branch out into different areas other than their specified major." Overall, a "supportive and friendly" atmosphere pervades. Ursinus students "are all hard-working and must go above and beyond to compete academically." Students at Ursinus tend to balance their "very studious" academic aspirations "with an active and healthy extracurricular lifestyle." They're "outgoing to others [and] involved in campus and in the society." "Many students are athletes," and "About twenty percent of the campus is affiliated with a Greek organization." In a sentence, "Ursinus students are overachievers."

FINANCIAL AID: 610-409-3600 • E-MAIL: ADMISSIONS@URSINUS.EDU • WEBSITE: WWW.URSINUS.EDU

THE PRINCETON REVIEW SAYS

Admissions

Very important factors considered include: Class rank, rigor of secondary school record, extracurricular activities. *Important factors considered include:* Application essay, academic GPA, recommendation(s), standardized test scores, alumni/ae relation, racial/ethnic status, talent/ability, volunteer work, work experience. *Other factors considered include:* Character/personal qualities, first generation, geographical residence, interview, level of applicant's interest. SAT or ACT required; ACT with writing component recommended. TOEFL required of all international applicants. High school diploma is required and GED is accepted. *Academic units required:* 4 English, 3 mathematics, 1 science (1 science lab), 2 foreign language, 1 social studies. *Academic units recommended:* 4 English, 4 mathematics, 4 science (2 science labs), 4 foreign language, 4 social studies.

Financial Aid

Students should submit: FAFSA, institution's own financial aid form, CSS/Financial Aid PROFILE. The Princeton Review suggests that all financial aid forms be submitted as soon as possible after January 1. *Need-based scholarships/grants offered:* Federal Pell, SEOG, state scholarships/grants, private scholarships, the school's own gift aid. *Loan aid offered:* Direct Subsidized Stafford, Direct Unsubsidized Stafford, Direct PLUS, Federal Perkins. Applicants will be notified of awards on or about April 1. Federal Work-Study Program available. Institutional employment available. Highest amount earned per year from on-campus jobs $1,200. Off-campus job opportunities are excellent.

The Inside Word

Grades, test scores, and class rank count for more than anything else, and unless you're academically inconsistent, you'll likely get good news. If you're hoping to snag a scholarship, it's essential that you visit campus for an interview, and interviews are strongly encouraged anyway. Students in the top ten percent of their graduating classes rank out of having to submit SAT scores.

THE SCHOOL SAYS ". . ."

From the Admissions Office

"Located in suburban Philadelphia, the college boasts a beautiful 168-acre campus that includes the Residential Village (renovated Victorian-style homes that decorate the Main Street and house our students) and the nationally recognized Berman Museum of Art. Ursinus is a member of the Centennial Conference, competing both in academics and in intercollegiate athletics with institutions such as Dickinson, Franklin & Marshall, Gettysburg, and Muhlenberg. The academic environment is enhanced with such fine programs as a chapter of Phi Beta Kappa, an early assurance program to medical school with the Drexel University College of Medicine, and myriad student exchanges both at home and abroad. A heavy emphasis is placed on student research—an emphasis that can only be carried out with the one-on-one attention Ursinus students receive from their professors.

"Ursinus will continue to ask applicants for writing samples—both a series of application essays and a graded high school paper."

SELECTIVITY

Admissions Rating	**90**
# of applicants	3,851
% of applicants accepted	70
% of acceptees attending	16
# accepting a place on wait list	68
# admitted from wait list	38
# of early decision applicants	197
# accepted early decision	122

FRESHMAN PROFILE

Range SAT Critical Reading	550–650
Range SAT Math	560–670
Range SAT Writing	540–640
Range ACT Composite	25–30
Minimum paper TOEFL	500
% graduated top 10% of class	33
% graduated top 25% of class	70
% graduated top 50% of class	94

DEADLINES

Early decision	
Deadline	1/15
Notification	12/15
Early action	
Deadline	12/1
Regular	
Deadline	2/15
Notification	4/1
Nonfall registration?	yes

FINANCIAL FACTS

Financial Aid Rating	**84**
Annual tuition	$43,100
Room and board	$10,750
Required fees	$170
% needy frosh rec. need-based scholarship or grant aid	100
% needy UG rec. need-based scholarship or grant aid	100
% needy frosh rec. non-need-based scholarship or grant aid	27
% needy UG rec. non-need-based scholarship or grant aid	24
% needy frosh rec. need-based self-help aid	77
% needy UG rec. need-based self-help aid	82
% frosh rec. any financial aid	92
% UG rec. any financial aid	91
% UG borrow to pay for school	75
Average cumulative indebtedness	$21,171
% frosh need fully met	27
% ugrads need fully met	24
Average % of frosh need met	84
Average % of ugrad need met	80

Valparaiso University

Office of Admissions, Kretzmann Hall, Valparaiso, IN 46383 • Admissions: 219-464-5011 • Fax: 219-464-6898

CAMPUS LIFE

Quality of Life Rating	**71**
Fire Safety Rating	**68**
Green Rating	**78**
Type of school	private
Affiliation	Lutheran
Environment	town

STUDENTS

Total undergrad enrollment	2,785
% male/female	45/55
% from out of state	63
% frosh live on campus	90
# of fraternities	8
# of sororities	7
% African American	5
% Asian	2
% Caucasian	80
% Hispanic	6
% international	4
# of countries represented	59

SURVEY SAYS . . .

Great library
Students are friendly
Campus feels safe
Students are happy
Musical organizations are popular
Very little drug use

ACADEMICS

Academic Rating	**79**
% students returning for sophomore year	81
% students graduating within 4 years	63
% students graduating within 6 years	71
Calendar	semester
Student/faculty ratio	12:1
Profs interesting rating	82
Profs accessible rating	83
Most classes have	10–19 students
Most lab/discussion sessions have	10–19 students

MOST POPULAR MAJORS

nursing/registered nurse (rn, asn, bsn, msn); political science and government; psychology

APPLICANTS ALSO LOOK AT AND OFTEN PREFER

Indiana University—Bloomington, Purdue University—West Lafayette

AND SOMETIMES PREFER

Bradley University, University of Illinois at Urbana-Champaign

AND RARELY PREFER

Marquette University, Illinois State University

STUDENTS SAY ". . ."

Academics

Valparaiso University, a small Lutheran university, "is a serious academic community with strong, but not forceful, religious background" that "prepares, motivates, and challenges tomorrow's leaders, engineers, nurses, and teachers while giving the opportunity for religious growth." Business, education, and engineering are the most popular general areas of study, and are among Valpo's most celebrated departments. Other standout disciplines include nursing, music, theater ("the department involves touring professional directors a couple times a year, which speaks for itself" and "puts on great plays"), and one of the nation's largest meteorology programs (which "just erected a state-of-the-art Doppler radar, putting Valpo at the forefront for undergrad meteorology"). Undergrads here appreciate the breadth of excellent offerings as well as "the school's ability to integrate the liberal arts with a variety of majors…As a student, I have been able to study engineering as well as hermeneutics, child development, and read classic texts ranging from Aristotle and Plato to Chuang Tzu and Derrida." Valpo operates under an honor code students say, "creates an environment of trust and high moral responsibility." "People follow the honor code, especially because the punishments are strict, such as failing the class for a first offense," one student tells us. A few dissenters feel "the honor code may reduce some cheating, but I don't think it comes near to eliminating it." Outstanding students may enroll in Christ College, an honors college, which they describe as "very intense but very rewarding."

Life

"There are several activities to choose from on Valparaiso's campus on a typical weekend, ranging from philanthropic dance parties at fraternity houses to music recitals to special guests speakers (to name just a few)," students tell us. Religious groups are active, and not just the Lutherans. The Catholic Church "is very active" here, offering "a student mass Sunday nights with a meal afterward, which is very nice" and "at least three events each week." Athletics are also popular. "We have Division I athletics, so it's fun to watch if you don't play, but Valpo also offers club sports (like Ultimate Frisbee) and intramurals for all student to participate in." The VU campus is officially dry, but that doesn't mean students don't drink. An aggressive campus police force means "there is lots of fear of getting arrested when drinking, but people do it anyway." Fraternities "have parties every Friday night," which helps to offset the perception that "the city of Valpo is horrible" because "there's not much to do" there. "If you can't entertain yourself, this is not the place for you," students warn. When they need big-city diversion, students will "hop on the train to go over to Chicago, an hour ride, for about six dollars, and get a CTA day pass for four dollars (to ride Chicago's transit all day)."

Student Body

One student estimates that "conservative, churchgoing studiers" make up about two-thirds of the Valpo student body. Most "come from somewhere in the Midwest," with many "from the Chicagoland area." The typical student is "here to learn. There are some who are just here for the party, but there are not many." Because "meteorology and engineering are large areas of study, there are some students who are 'nerdy,' but no one is left out of university activities." Valpo has "few minority students," and "it would be nice to have a little bit more diversity."

FINANCIAL AID: 219-464-5015 • E-MAIL: UNDERGRAD.ADMISSION@VALPO.EDU • WEBSITE: WWW.VALPO.EDU

THE PRINCETON REVIEW SAYS

Admissions

Very important factors considered include: Academic GPA, rigor of secondary school record. *Important factors considered include:* Class rank, standardized test scores, alumni/ae relation, character/personal qualities, extracurricular activities, talent/ability. *Other factors considered include:* Application essay, recommendation(s), first generation, interview, level of applicant's interest, racial/ethnic status, religious affiliation/commitment, volunteer work. SAT or ACT required; ACT with writing component required. TOEFL required of all international applicants. High school diploma is required and GED is accepted. *Academic units required:* 4 English, 3 mathematics, 2 science (2 science labs), 2 foreign language, 2 history, 3 academic electives. *Academic units recommended:* 4 English, 4 mathematics, 3 science (3 science labs), 2 foreign language, 1 social studies, 2 history, 3 academic electives.

Financial Aid

Students should submit: FAFSA. The Princeton Review suggests that all financial aid forms be submitted as soon as possible after January 1. *Need-based scholarships/grants offered:* Federal Pell, SEOG, state scholarships/grants, private scholarships, the school's own gift aid. *Loan aid offered:* Direct Subsidized Stafford, Direct Unsubsidized Stafford, Direct PLUS, Federal Perkins, college/university loans from institutional funds, private/alternative education loans if credit standards are met. Applicants will be notified of awards on a rolling basis beginning March 1. Federal Work-Study Program available. Institutional employment available. Highest amount earned per year from on-campus jobs $5,481. Off-campus job opportunities are good.

The Inside Word

Valparaiso's ninety percent admit rate suggests a pretty generous admissions office. The figure is somewhat misleading; Valpo's applicant pool consists largely of students familiar enough with the school to know whether it's worth their while to apply here. In other words, the school doesn't receive a lot of 'reach' applications. Applicants indicating an interest in meteorology should expect a more rigorous review, as space in the program is limited.

THE SCHOOL SAYS ". . ."

From the Admissions Office

"Valpo provides students a blend of academic excellence, social experience, and spiritual exploration. The concern demonstrated by faculty and administration for the total well-being of students reflects a long history as a Lutheran-affiliated university."

SELECTIVITY

Admissions Rating	82
# of applicants	5,418
% of applicants accepted	74
% of acceptees attending	17

FRESHMAN PROFILE

Range SAT Critical Reading	490–610
Range SAT Math	490–610
Range SAT Writing	470–590
Range ACT Composite	23–29
Minimum paper TOEFL	550
Minimum web-based TOEFL	80
Average HS GPA	3.6
% graduated top 10% of class	34
% graduated top 25% of class	64
% graduated top 50% of class	90

DEADLINES

Nonfall registration?	yes

FINANCIAL FACTS

Financial Aid Rating	78
Annual tuition	$31,170
Room and board	$9,164
Required fees	$1,080
Books and supplies	$1,200
% needy frosh rec. need-based scholarship or grant aid	100
% needy UG rec. need-based scholarship or grant aid	99
% needy frosh rec. non-need-based scholarship or grant aid	18
% needy UG rec. non-need-based scholarship or grant aid	18
% needy frosh rec. need-based self-help aid	75
% needy UG rec. need-based self-help aid	77
% frosh rec. any financial aid	98
% UG rec. any financial aid	97
% UG borrow to pay for school	72
Average cumulative indebtedness	$33,104
% frosh need fully met	25
% ugrads need fully met	23
Average % of frosh need met	81
Average % of ugrad need met	78

VANDERBILT UNIVERSITY

2305 WEST END AVENUE, NASHVILLE, TN 37203 • ADMISSIONS: 615-322-2561 • FAX: 615-343-7765

CAMPUS LIFE

Quality of Life Rating	**98**
Fire Safety Rating	**91**
Green Rating	**99**
Type of school	private
Environment	metropolis

STUDENTS

Total undergrad enrollment	6,817
% male/female	50/50
% from out of state	86
% from public high school	58
% frosh live on campus	100
# of fraternities	19
# of sororities	16
% African American	8
% Asian	8
% Caucasian	73
% Hispanic	8
% Native American	1
% international	5
# of countries represented	101

SURVEY SAYS . . .

Lab facilities are great
School is well run
Students love Nashville, TN
Great off-campus food
Frats and sororities dominate social scene
Student publications are popular
Student government is popular

ACADEMICS

Academic Rating	**93**
% students returning for sophomore year	96
% students graduating within 4 years	86
% students graduating within 6 years	92
Calendar	semester
Student/faculty ratio	8:1
Profs interesting rating	91
Profs accessible rating	89
Most classes have	10–19 students
Most lab/discussion sessions have	10–19 students

MOST POPULAR MAJORS

engineering science; psychology; social sciences

APPLICANTS ALSO LOOK AT AND OFTEN PREFER

Harvard College, Massachusetts Institute of Technology, Princeton University, Stanford University, Yale University

AND SOMETIMES PREFER

Brown University, Cornell University, Duke University, Georgetown University, Northwestern University, Rice University, University of Chicago

AND RARELY PREFER

Emory University, Tulane University, University of Georgia, University of Michigan--Ann Arbor , Washington University in St. Louis, The University of North Carolina at Chapel Hill

STUDENTS SAY ". . ."

Academics

The word "balance" is much used by students in describing Vanderbilt University, whether it is the "campus mixed with city, academics mixed with social life, small population mixed with big athletics," or the "unique balance [that] exists between social life and schoolwork." Students say this "balance" "makes [Vanderbilt] the best place to get a well-rounded college experience." As one student explains, "Everyone takes academics seriously, but everyone has other interests, too. No one is just a student. Everyone is involved in something." Another student says, "At Vanderbilt, I could [pursue] my interest in music while majoring in engineering, which was not the case in most other schools." The school is heavily influenced by the "incredible city" of Nashville. The "idyllic campus" is "only minutes away from being in the heart of the city," where people "are very social" and "like being involved." This correlates well with Vandy students who "are very passionate about their extracurricular interests" and stay very "involved with organizations on campus and within the Nashville community. Within the more than 300 student organizations on campus, a student is hard-pressed not to find a few organizations that they can relate to." "The professors are engaging and love their jobs, which makes the students excited and eager to learn." Professors are "dedicated to the undergraduates" and "are always willing to meet with you outside of the classroom to discuss material from class or anything you want to. They make it clear that you are their first priority." "And in the event that the class is too big, there are TAs who are more than willing to help." Besides the "truly enriching academic environment," there are many "opportunities that challenge me beyond the books," says a student. When asked about what improvements might be made to their school, many agreed, "Dining and parking are mediocre at best." "The lines at lunch can be really long, and not as many options are open on the weekends." Although vehicles do not seem essential to partake in Nashville and campus life, an improvement in "parking around campus" would be appreciated by students.

Life

"While courses are challenging and demanding, the environment is also fun." Students profess, "School comes first, but having a good time is a close second." "The social life is extremely fun and inclusive." "Greek life is large" here. For many freshman and sophomores, social life "revolves around frat parties." "Older students will go to parties at their friend's place and then go downtown to continue the night." One student explains, "There is [a] Greek scene at the school that offers one kind of Vanderbilt experience, then there are a whole lot of independents who have a different experience. Both groups seem to really enjoy their time here and interact frequently, but the experiences are different." "The campus is beautiful" and "the people—staff, students, professors—are warm and welcoming." "There are always free events going on around campus including everything from casino night, to free movies, to parties, to philanthropy events. There is never a lack of opportunities for fun on campus. On the weekends, people like to use our meal plan to eat off campus and ride our bus downtown to experience Nashville life." "There are so many unique local bars within walking distance!" On the whole, "People here are happy. I feel like I am either partying or doing homework, but it's a good mix."

Student Body

At Vanderbilt, "Students hail from all over America and the world, but they all embrace the Southern spirit." A typical student is described as "extremely social," as well as "naturally very bright and motivated." Students stress the "atmosphere of individual achievement instead of competition. The students are academic…but at the same time they are not 'showy' about it." While the main stereotype of a Vanderbilt student still is "preppy, wealthy, upper-class," and "involved in Greek life." "Geographic diversity has certainly expanded in the past ten years." "Students come from all over and the freshman experience does a good job making us a united class."

FINANCIAL AID: 800-288-0204 • E-MAIL: ADMISSIONS@VANDERBILT.EDU • WEBSITE: WWW.VANDERBILT.EDU

THE PRINCETON REVIEW SAYS

Admissions

Very important factors considered include: Class rank, application essay, academic GPA, rigor of secondary school record, standardized test scores, character/personal qualities, extracurricular activities. *Important factors considered include:* Recommendation(s), talent/ability. *Other factors considered include:* Alumni/ae relation, first generation, geographical residence, interview, racial/ethnic status, state residency, volunteer work, work experience. ACT with writing component required. TOEFL required of all international applicants. High school diploma is required and GED is accepted. *Academic units required:* 4 English, 3 mathematics, 3 science (2 science labs), 2 foreign language, 2 social studies, 1 history, 3 academic electives. *Academic units recommended:* 4 English, 4 mathematics, 4 science (3 science labs), 2 foreign language, 3 social studies, 1 history, 3 academic electives.

Financial Aid

Students should submit: FAFSA, CSS/Financial Aid PROFILE. Regular filing deadline is February 5. The Princeton Review suggests that all financial aid forms be submitted as soon as possible after January 1. *Need-based scholarships/grants offered:* Federal Pell, SEOG, state scholarships/grants, private scholarships, the school's own gift aid. *Loan aid offered:* Direct Subsidized Stafford, Direct Unsubsidized Stafford, Direct PLUS, Federal Perkins, Federal Nursing, college/university loans from institutional funds, undergrad education loan. Applicants will be notified of awards on or about April 1. Federal Work-Study Program available. Institutional employment available. Highest amount earned per year from on-campus jobs $2,300. Off-campus job opportunities are excellent.

The Inside Word

With a first year class of 1,600 and applications numbering nearly 25,000, competition for admission can be intense at this elite Nashville institution. Early decision is a popular route with about 40% of the class of 2015 being admitted in this fashion. But before you pull the trigger, take full advantage of Vandy's excellent admissions website featuring an extensive virtual tour and student blogs.

THE SCHOOL SAYS ". . ."

From the Admissions Office

"The Vanderbilt undergraduate experience is often described as uniquely balanced. Within the context of an outstanding academic landscape, students are encouraged to participate in a broad spectrum of campus organizations (more than 350) among a highly diverse population. Many students take classes in all four undergraduate schools, stretching their intellectual experience far beyond that of their declared major. Students live on campus all four years beginning with a year at The Commons, Vanderbilt's living and learning residential community. Students take full advantage of Nashville, Tennessee, by participating in government-related internships, getting involved in area secondary schools, working in any one of many Nashville-based industries, and enjoying the cultural offerings of a major metropolitan area.

"Vanderbilt makes a three-pronged commitment regarding financial aid:

1. Applications are considered without regard for financial need (need-blind).
2. Vanderbilt meets 100 percent of a family's demonstrated financial need for all admitted U.S. citizens and eligible non-citizens.
3. Financial aid awards do not include loans. Instead of offering need-based loans, Vanderbilt offers additional grant assistance.

"Early decision applicants who submit the CSS Profile at the time of application will be provided with a provisional award of need-based financial aid. The admissions process is holistic—the student's complete academic and non-academic record is reviewed in conjunction with recommendations and personal essays. The audition is of primary importance for students applying to the Blair School of Music. Students admitted to Vanderbilt typically show exceptional academic accomplishment within the context of their high school, and are highly engaged in their communities, often serving in leadership roles."

SELECTIVITY	
Admissions Rating	**99**
# of applicants	24,837
% of applicants accepted	16
% of acceptees attending	39
# accepting a place on wait list	1,831
# admitted from wait list	212
# of early decision applicants	2,561
# accepted early decision	664

FRESHMAN PROFILE	
Range SAT Critical Reading	680–770
Range SAT Math	700–780
Range SAT Writing	670–760
Range ACT Composite	31–34
Minimum paper TOEFL	570
Average HS GPA	3.7
% graduated top 10% of class	89
% graduated top 25% of class	97
% graduated top 50% of class	99

DEADLINES	
Early decision	
Deadline	11/1
Notification	12/15
Regular	
Deadline	1/3
Notification	4/1
Nonfall registration?	no

FINANCIAL FACTS	
Financial Aid Rating	**97**
Annual tuition	$41,086
Room and board	$14,100
Required fees	$1,042
Books and supplies	$1,344
% needy frosh rec. need-based scholarship or grant aid	87
% needy UG rec. need-based scholarship or grant aid	92
% needy frosh rec. non-need-based scholarship or grant aid	59
% needy UG rec. non-need-based scholarship or grant aid	46
% needy frosh rec. need-based self-help aid	38
% needy UG rec. need-based self-help aid	47
% frosh rec. any financial aid	66
% UG rec. any financial aid	63
% UG borrow to pay for school	38
Average cumulative indebtedness	$18,543
% frosh need fully met	100
% ugrads need fully met	100
Average % of frosh need met	100
Average % of ugrad need met	100

VASSAR COLLEGE

124 RAYMOND AVENUE, POUGHKEEPSIE, NY 12604 • ADMISSIONS: 845-437-7300 • FAX: 845-437-7063

CAMPUS LIFE

Quality of Life Rating	**69**
Fire Safety Rating	**89**
Green Rating	**87**
Type of school	private
Environment	town

STUDENTS

Total undergrad enrollment	2,408
% male/female	42/58
% from out of state	75
% from public high school	63
% frosh live on campus	99
% African American	5
% Asian	9
% Caucasian	67
% Hispanic	9
% international	6
# of countries represented	43

SURVEY SAYS . . .

No one cheats
Students aren't religious
Frats and sororities are unpopular or nonexistent
Theater is popular
Political activism is popular

ACADEMICS

Academic Rating	**97**
% students returning for sophomore year	96
% students graduating within 4 years	90
% students graduating within 6 years	93
Calendar	semester
Student/faculty ratio	8:1
Profs interesting rating	88
Profs accessible rating	84
Most classes have	10–19 students
Most lab/discussion sessions have	10–19 students

MOST POPULAR MAJORS

English language and literature; political science and government; psychology

APPLICANTS ALSO LOOK AT AND OFTEN PREFER

Williams College, Harvard College, Amherst College, Yale University, Brown University

AND SOMETIMES PREFER

Wesleyan University, Columbia University, Tufts University

AND RARELY PREFER

New York University, Skidmore College

STUDENTS SAY ". . ."

Academics

Vassar College gives students "the chance to experiment with [their] life in an encouraging and stimulating environment," providing an unusual amount of academic freedom because "there's no real core curriculum. All you need in the way of requirements are one quantitative class and one foreign language credit. Plus, one-quarter of your credits must be outside of your major." This approach, students agree, "really encourages students to think creatively and pursue whatever they're passionate about, whether medieval tapestries, neuroscience, or unicycles. Not having a core curriculum is great because it gives students the opportunity to delve into many different interests." Of course, a system like this only works if students are motivated and teachers are dedicated. Fortunately, that's exactly how it shakes out at Vassar. The school boasts "world-class professors, small classes, and a faculty that really is interested in us as students. Every teacher and member of the faculty goes the extra mile to [be] available outside of class and [to] meet students for lunch or dinner." Vassar places "a real focus on the undergraduate students. There is big-time research just like at major universities, but there are no graduate students to fill all the spots. All assisting positions go to undergraduates." The school excels in the visual and performing arts—the "drama department is huge"—as well as in English, psychology, history, life sciences, and natural sciences.

Life

"Life is very campus-centered" at Vassar; the farthest off campus people regularly go is the twenty-four-hour diner two blocks north of campus. This is partly because hometown Poughkeepsie "does not offer much in the way of entertainment." For whatever reason, insularity is a defining characteristic of life at Vassar, so much so that students speak of "The Vassar Bubble. This is a term any student will immediately become familiar with. Essentially, Vassar is an island closed off from the rest of the town and community. It would be entirely possible (and not even rare) for a student to not leave campus once in an entire semester. While this is good for some, others will likely go a little crazy stuck on campus." Some escape to New York City whenever possible, but unfortunately the trip to the city is a relatively "expensive endeavor for weekly entertainment; it's about thirty-five dollars round-trip, and that doesn't include doing stuff once you get there." Fortunately, "there is a huge array of things to do every night on campus. Comedy shows, improv, an incredibly wide array of theater productions"—including "several shows a year and three student groups devoted to drama"—"four comedy groups, five a cappella groups," and "interesting lectures create numerous opportunities to get out of the dorms at night." Weekends are for parties; there's "no Greek life, so lots of parties are awesome, school-sponsored, theme events." There's also "lots of socializing at senior housing," and "Halloween is huge. People really go all out."

Student Body

There are "lots of hipsters" at Vassar including kids who are "very left-wing politically" and "very into the music scene." The school is "not entirely dominated by hipsters," however; there are "lots of different groups" on campus. "Walking around you'll see students who walked out of a thrift store next to students who walked out of a *J. Crew* catalog," one student tells us. Another adds that Vassar is a comfortable respite for "indie-chic students who revel in obscurity, some socially awkward archetypes, and some prep school pin-ups with their collars popped. But the majority of kids on campus are a mix of these people, which is why we mesh pretty well despite the cliques that inevitably form." What students share is having "an amazing talent or something they passionately believe in" that makes them distinctive. "Vassar admissions works tremendously hard to ensure every student at Vassar is unique and mold-breaking," students brag.

FINANCIAL AID: 845-437-5230 • E-MAIL: ADMISSIONS@VASSAR.EDU • WEBSITE: WWW.VASSAR.EDU

THE PRINCETON REVIEW SAYS

Admissions

Very important factors considered include: Rigor of secondary school record. *Important factors considered include:* Class rank, application essay, academic GPA, recommendation(s), standardized test scores, extracurricular activities, talent/ability. *Other factors considered include:* Alumni/ae relation, character/personal qualities, first generation, geographical residence, interview, level of applicant's interest, racial/ethnic status, volunteer work, work experience. SAT or ACT required; ACT with writing component required. TOEFL required of all international applicants. High school diploma is required and GED is accepted. *Academic units required:* 4 English, 4 mathematics, 4 science (3 science labs), 3 foreign language, 2 social studies, 2 history, 4 academic electives. *Academic units recommended:* 4 English, 4 mathematics, 4 science (3 science labs), 4 foreign language, 4 social studies, 2 history.

Financial Aid

Students should submit: FAFSA, CSS/Financial Aid PROFILE, noncustodial PROFILE, business/farm supplement. The Princeton Review suggests that all financial aid forms be submitted as soon as possible after January 1. *Need-based scholarships/grants offered:* Federal Pell, SEOG, state scholarships/grants, private scholarships, the school's own gift aid. *Loan aid offered:* Direct Subsidized Stafford, Direct Unsubsidized Stafford, Direct PLUS, Federal Perkins, loans for noncitizens with need. Applicants will be notified of awards on or about March 30. Federal Work-Study Program available. Institutional employment available. Highest amount earned per year from on-campus jobs $4,350. Off-campus job opportunities are fair.

The Inside Word

With acceptance rates hitting record lows, stellar academic credentials are a must for any serious Vassar candidate. Importantly, the college prides itself on selecting students who will add to the vitality of the campus. Once admissions officers see you meet their rigorous scholastic standards, they'll closely assess your personal essay, recommendations, and extracurricular activities. Demonstrating an intellectual curiosity that extends outside the classroom is as important as success within it.

THE SCHOOL SAYS ". . ."

From the Admissions Office

"Vassar presents a rich variety of social and cultural activities, clubs, sports, living arrangements, and regional attractions. Vassar is a vital, residential college community recognized for its respect for the rights and individuality of others.

"Candidates must submit either the SAT Reasoning Test and two SAT Subject Tests taken in different subject fields, or the ACT exam (the optional ACT writing component is required)."

SELECTIVITY	
Admissions Rating	**98**
# of applicants	7,822
% of applicants accepted	24
% of acceptees attending	36
# accepting a place on wait list	568
# of early decision applicants	693
# accepted early decision	265

FRESHMAN PROFILE	
Range SAT Critical Reading	670–740
Range SAT Math	640–720
Range SAT Writing	660–750
Range ACT Composite	29–32
Minimum paper TOEFL	600
Minimum web-based TOEFL	100
Average HS GPA	3.8
% graduated top 10% of class	65
% graduated top 25% of class	96
% graduated top 50% of class	100

DEADLINES	
Early decision	
Deadline	11/15
Regular	
Deadline	1/1
Notification	4/1
Nonfall registration?	no

FINANCIAL FACTS	
Financial Aid Rating	**99**
Annual tuition	$45,580
Room and board	$10,800
Required fees	$690
Books and supplies	$860
% needy frosh rec. need-based scholarship or grant aid	100
% needy UG rec. need-based scholarship or grant aid	99
% needy frosh rec. need-based self-help aid	100
% needy UG rec. need-based self-help aid	100
% frosh rec. any financial aid	64
% UG rec. any financial aid	63
% UG borrow to pay for school	49
Average cumulative indebtedness	$18,153
% frosh need fully met	100
% ugrads need fully met	100
Average % of frosh need met	100
Average % of ugrad need met	100

Villanova University

Austin Hall, 800 Lancaster Avenue, Villanova, PA 19085 • Admissions: 610-519-4000 • Fax: 610-519-6450

CAMPUS LIFE

Quality of Life Rating	**90**
Fire Safety Rating	**87**
Green Rating	**86**
Type of school	private
Affiliation	Roman Catholic
Environment	village

STUDENTS

Total undergrad enrollment	6,898
% male/female	49/51
% from out of state	82
% from public high school	51
% frosh live on campus	98
# of fraternities	10
# of sororities	10
% African American	5
% Asian	6
% Caucasian	76
% Hispanic	7
% international	3
# of countries represented	50

SURVEY SAYS . . .

School is well run
Low cost of living
Everyone loves the Wildcats
Students are involved in community service
Internships are widely available

ACADEMICS

Academic Rating	**88**
% students returning for sophomore year	94
% students graduating within 4 years	88
Calendar	semester
Student/faculty ratio	11:1
Profs interesting rating	88
Profs accessible rating	88
Most classes have	10–19 students
Most lab/discussion sessions have	10–19 students

MOST POPULAR MAJORS

communication studies/speech communication and rhetoric; finance; nursing/registered nurse (rn, asn, bsn, msn)

APPLICANTS ALSO LOOK AT AND OFTEN PREFER

University of Notre Dame, Cornell University, Duke University, Georgetown University, Princeton University, University of Pennsylvania, University of Virginia

AND SOMETIMES PREFER

Boston College, Bucknell University, University of Richmond, Vanderbilt University

AND RARELY PREFER

University of Delaware, Boston University, Drexel University, Fordham University, Lehigh University, Loyola University Maryland, Northeastern University, Pennsylvania State University—University Park

STUDENTS SAY "..."

Academics

Though long ago it was known for being a basketball powerhouse, Villanova University (located in Pennsylvania) has developed an equally impressive reputation for academics. The school's admissions standards have continued to rise, and there is a "great support system" in place to help students achieve, between professors, advisors, tutors, research librarians, as well as a writing, math, and language learning center. Nova's career center and internship offices focus on getting students into jobs after college, and "the opportunities outside of the classroom really complement your education." "Villanova is full of resources for my success now, as a student, and will continue to be after I graduate as an alum," says a student. There is a real sense of community here, "stemming from service, school spirit around the basketball team, and everyone actively pursuing their own area of academic interest." The "passionate" professors are "true teachers and scholars," and they "go above and beyond their office hours." They are "easily accessible," and though some will seek you out, "It is mostly up to you to take advantage of them as a resource." "If you want to succeed, the community will do everything in its power to make sure you can do so," says a student. In addition to superior classroom quality (the faculty gets "fired up about what they teach"), there are "a lot of projects across majors that have real-world applications and are designed to help students in the long run." Classes are often a mixture of "lecture, discussion, individual/group projects, [and] fieldtrips." Villanova's "emphasis on service" is a positive sticking point for the student body, and everyone here embraces a sense of duty to make the world a better place. "We are the Nova Nation, built upon an unbreakable foundation of community," says a student.

Life

Many buildings are new or have been recently renovated, and "Most residence halls are really impressive and kept up very well." Most of campus "has a focused atmosphere during the week," but come Thursday afternoon, "You can feel campus relax and people are more likely to go out," mainly off campus. During basketball season, "People get their work done early to flock to the stadium for games." Almost everyone is involved in at least one (but probably more) extracurricular activities and clubs, and "A ton of students get involved with intramurals or club sports teams, as well." The Campus Activity Team puts on different events over the weekend, including "a cinema that is always showing a movie," and the school also offers great service experiences, whether " week-long service break experiences all over the world, cheering on the athletes at Special Olympics Fall Festival, or driving into Philly to play with kids and help them with their studies." Formals are also "a big deal" on campus. For those who want to take a break from college life, the massive King of Prussia Mall is found nearby (with a free weekend shuttle), and it is "an easy short train ride to go to Philadelphia."

Student Body

This "outstanding community" is built on "a lot of mutual respect." People are "well-rounded," "very friendly," and "proud of Villanova," and most everyone here "dresses well and comes from a good family" and is "extremely affable, professional, and an achiever." "Sometimes I think of Villanova as a school full of all the high school superstars," says one student. Balance is a skill that all Villanovans possess, and most are involved in some sort of volunteer activity; many also "party on the weekends, and show up ready to all of their classes." One can find a "very attractive student body" here, as well.

FINANCIAL AID: 610-519-4010 • E-MAIL: GOTOVU@VILLANOVA.EDU • WEBSITE: WWW.VILLANOVA.EDU

THE PRINCETON REVIEW SAYS

Admissions

Very important factors considered include: Class rank, academic GPA, rigor of secondary school record, standardized test scores. *Important factors considered include:* Application essay, recommendation(s), character/personal qualities, extracurricular activities, talent/ability, volunteer work, work experience. *Other factors considered include:* Alumni/ae relation, first generation, geographical residence, level of applicant's interest, racial/ethnic status, state residency. SAT or ACT required; ACT with writing component required. TOEFL required of all international applicants. High school diploma is required and GED is accepted. *Academic units required:* 4 English, 4 mathematics, 4 science (2 science labs), 2 foreign language, 2 academic electives. *Academic units recommended:* 4 English, 4 mathematics, 4 science (3 science labs), 4 foreign language, 2 academic electives.

Financial Aid

Students should submit: FAFSA, institution's own financial aid form. The Princeton Review suggests that all financial aid forms be submitted as soon as possible after January 1. *Need-based scholarships/grants offered:* Federal Pell, SEOG, state scholarships/grants, private scholarships, the school's own gift aid. *Loan aid offered:* Direct Subsidized Stafford, Direct Unsubsidized Stafford, Direct PLUS, Federal Perkins, Federal Nursing. Applicants will be notified of awards on or about April 1. Federal Work-Study Program available. Institutional employment available. Off-campus job opportunities are excellent.

The Inside Word

Villanova's growing academic reputation means its application process is growing more competitive as well: ninety-nine percent of the most recent admitted freshman class ranked in the top twenty percent of their high school graduating class. But while academic achievement is important, the university looks at the whole package when considering applicants and expects candidates to do the same. As a private university, Villanova is not exactly cheap, but the school offers a wide variety of scholarships and aid to qualifying students.

THE SCHOOL SAYS ". . ."

From the Admissions Office

"Villanova is the oldest and largest Catholic university in Pennsylvania, founded in 1842 by the Order of Saint Augustine. Students of all faiths are welcome. The university tends to attract students who are interested in volunteerism. Villanovans provide more than 200,000 hours of service annually and host the largest student-run Special Olympics in the nation. Villanova's scenic campus is located twelve miles west of Philadelphia. The university offers programs through four undergraduate colleges: Liberal Arts and Sciences, Engineering, Nursing, and the Villanova School of Business. There are 250 student organizations and thirty-six National Honor Societies at Villanova. Incoming freshmen can opt to be part of a Learning Community, through which student groups live together in specially-designated residence halls and learn together in courses and co-curricular programs. The university offers Naval and Marine Reserve Officers Training Corps (ROTC) programs and hundreds of options for studying abroad. 'Nova's alumni body is comprised of 108,000 people. Some prominent grads include: Maria Bello, Golden Globe-Nominated Actress; Rear Admiral Christine Bruzek-Kohler, Executive Director of Healthcare Operations, Joint Task Force—National Capital Region; Sean McDermott, CEO of Winward IT Solutions; Robert Moran, President and COO of PetSmart; James O'Donnell, CEO of American Eagle Outfitters; and Dianna Sugg, Pulitzer Prize Recipient for Journalism.

"If you're looking to join 'Nova Nation, be prepared: The competition for admission is getting tougher every year."

SELECTIVITY	
Admissions Rating	**95**
# of applicants	15,394
% of applicants accepted	44
% of acceptees attending	24
# accepting a place on wait list	2,272
# admitted from wait list	152

FRESHMAN PROFILE	
Range SAT Critical Reading	590–680
Range SAT Math	620–710
Range SAT Writing	590–690
Range ACT Composite	28–31
Minimum paper TOEFL	550
Average HS GPA	3.9
% graduated top 10% of class	64
% graduated top 25% of class	89
% graduated top 50% of class	97

DEADLINES	
Early action	
Deadline	11/1
Notification	12/20
Regular	
Priority	12/15
Deadline	1/7
Notification	4/1
Nonfall registration?	no

FINANCIAL FACTS	
Financial Aid Rating	**72**
Annual tuition	$42,150
Room and board	$11,393
Required fees	$590
Books and supplies	$950
% needy frosh rec. need-based scholarship or grant aid	89
% needy UG rec. need-based scholarship or grant aid	89
% needy frosh rec. non-need-based scholarship or grant aid	31
% needy UG rec. non-need-based scholarship or grant aid	29
% needy frosh rec. need-based self-help aid	89
% needy UG rec. need-based self-help aid	89
% frosh rec. any financial aid	47
% UG rec. any financial aid	49
% UG borrow to pay for school	55
Average cumulative indebtedness	$38,055
% frosh need fully met	19
% ugrads need fully met	15
Average % of frosh need met	82
Average % of ugrad need met	81

Virginia Polytechnic Institute and State University (Virginia Tech)

Undergraduate Admissions, Blacksburg, VA 24061 • Admissions: 540-231-6267 • Fax: 540-231-3242

CAMPUS LIFE

Quality of Life Rating	**99**
Fire Safety Rating	**76**
Green Rating	**98**
Type of school	public
Environment	town

STUDENTS

Total undergrad enrollment	23,589
% male/female	58/42
% from out of state	29
% frosh live on campus	99
# of fraternities	31
# of sororities	12
% African American	4
% Asian	8
% Caucasian	75
% Hispanic	4
% international	3
# of countries represented	113

SURVEY SAYS . . .

Athletic facilities are great
Great food on campus
Everyone loves the Hokies
Student publications are popular
Students are involved in community service

ACADEMICS

Academic Rating	**78**
% students graduating within 6 years	82
Calendar	semester
Student/faculty ratio	16:1
Profs interesting rating	78
Profs accessible rating	83
Most classes have	20–29 students
Most lab/discussion sessions have	20–29 students

MOST POPULAR MAJORS

biology/biological sciences; engineering

APPLICANTS ALSO LOOK AT AND OFTEN PREFER

University of Virginia, College of William and Mary

AND RARELY PREFER

College of William and Mary, The University of North Carolina at Chapel Hill

STUDENTS SAY ". . ."

Academics

Virginia Tech is a school with a reputation as big as its campus. Known for its "beautiful campus, amazing community feel, top-notch engineering field," and as a "good value"—not to mention its renowned athletics—Virginia Tech offers "a perfect blend of challenging and fun, encompassed in an unparalleled community feel." That community feel is a big part of the attraction to this top-ranked school, with students saying they feel "more comfortable here than anywhere in the world." Students are here, of course, for an education at a well-respected research university. At Virginia Tech, that education is provided by "passionate professors who bring real-life examples and cases into their teachings." The school's size and correspondingly large teaching staff mean that at times "professors are hit-or-miss," with "a few who just see it as another job." Most, however, "are really there to help you know as much as you can," a group who are "are extremely helpful and devoted to their students." The best of this school's professors "really make students eager to learn." One student enthuses, "My professors here have changed the way I look at the world and have become some of my biggest heroes." But maybe another student sums it up best: "I would definitely say that my academic experience has been outstanding and that it has opened my eyes to even more possibilities.

Life

Living "in the middle of nowhere" may seem like a recipe for boredom, but members of VT's Hokie Nation make the most of this "perfect college town." After all, when "there are 30,000 people around you that are the same age as you, you find stuff to do." When not consumed with Virginia Tech football—you'll see more maroon and orange in a single day here than most people will see in a lifetime—students here do, well, a little bit of everything. "School-related and Greek-life functions are the main sources of weekend activities," students say, but deceptively quiet Blacksburg and the surrounding area offer plenty of other options. On weekends, students "go out to parties or downtown with friends, we go out to eat, we play tennis, lay out on the 'drillfield,' play in the snow when we have some, go on hikes, and go to the river." And that's just a start. Students find "there is always something fun going on to do with your friends," including "bowling, movies, club sports, video games," and more. If you can't find it in Blacksburg, it's ten minutes away in Christiansburg. Students enjoy relaxing, getting into discussions, or having outdoor adventures in a pastoral setting. When autumn arrives, "Football games dominate the social scene."

Student Body

Better be ready to be part of the Hokie Nation, because the "typical student is someone who has a love for all things Virginia Tech." Those who attend VT "are proud of our school," and "A typical student here wears Virginia Tech clothes practically every day." Indeed, "You will find them at every VT football game." But the student body is about more than cheering for the maroon and orange. These "middle-class, decent-looking" students study hard "but play harder." Education matters here, but maybe not as much as living life. "The typical student is serious about schoolwork," students say, "but also knows how to have a good time." Most of the student body are "white and from Virginia or North Carolina," a group who are "smart, approachable, and kind." "While we may be lacking in racial diversity," one student notes, "we have every personality type and quirk you could ever imagine." If you are "well-rounded, involved, and [have] lots of school spirit," you are likely to fit in at VT.

Virginia Polytechnic Institute and State University (Virginia Tech)

Financial Aid: 540-231-5179 • E-mail: vtadmiss@vt.edu • Website: www.vt.edu

THE PRINCETON REVIEW SAYS

Admissions

Very important factors considered include: Academic GPA, rigor of secondary school record, standardized test scores. *Other factors considered include:* Recommendation(s), alumni/ae relation, character/personal qualities, extracurricular activities, first generation, geographical residence, racial/ethnic status, state residency, talent/ability, volunteer work, work experience. SAT or ACT required; ACT with writing component required. TOEFL required of all international applicants. High school diploma is required and GED is accepted. *Academic units required:* 4 English, 3 mathematics, 2 science (2 science labs), 1 social studies, 1 history, 4 academic electives. *Academic units recommended:* 4 mathematics, 3 science, 3 foreign language.

Financial Aid

Students should submit: FAFSA, general scholarship application. Regular filing deadline is March 1. The Princeton Review suggests that all financial aid forms be submitted as soon as possible after January 1. *Need-based scholarships/grants offered:* Federal Pell, SEOG, state scholarships/grants, private scholarships, the school's own gift aid, cadet scholarships/grants. *Loan aid offered:* Direct Subsidized Stafford, Direct Unsubsidized Stafford, Direct PLUS, Federal Perkins, college/university loans from institutional funds. Applicants will be notified of awards on a rolling basis beginning March 30. Federal Work-Study Program available. Off-campus job opportunities are excellent.

The Inside Word

With some 20,000 applications pouring into the admissions office each year, it's no wonder that the game here is all about numbers, numbers, numbers. Your high school grades will be top priority, so maintain strong grades. Standardized tests also play a big role. Most solid performers will find that acceptance comes with few problems, though the schools competitive disciplines—engineering and architecture, for example—will demand a higher caliber of student.

THE SCHOOL SAYS ". . ."

From the Admissions Office

"Virginia Tech offers the opportunities of a large research university in a small-town setting. Undergraduates choose from more than seventy majors in seven colleges, including nationally ranked architecture, business, forestry, and engineering schools, as well as excellent computer science, biology, and communication studies, and architecture programs. Technology is a key focus, both in classes and in general. All first-year students are required to own a personal computer, each residence hall room has Ethernet connections, and every student is provided e-mail and Internet access. Faculty incorporate a wide variety of technology into class, utilizing chat rooms, online lecture notes, and multimedia presentations. The university offers cutting-edge facilities for classes and research, abundant opportunities for advanced study in the honors program, undergraduate research opportunities, study abroad, internships, and cooperative education. Students enjoy nearly 700 organizations which offer something for everyone. Tech offers the best of both worlds—everything a large university can provide and a small-town atmosphere.

"Freshman applicants must take the SAT or ACT with writing section. We will use the highest scores from any SAT or ACT test scores submitted."

SELECTIVITY	
Admissions Rating	**90**
# of applicants	20,993
% of applicants accepted	64
% of acceptees attending	38
# accepting a place on wait list	2,399
# admitted from wait list	241
# of early decision applicants	2,024
# accepted early decision	1,031
FRESHMAN PROFILE	
Range SAT Critical Reading	540–640
Range SAT Math	570–670
Minimum paper TOEFL	550
Average HS GPA	4.0
% graduated top 10% of class	43
% graduated top 25% of class	85
% graduated top 50% of class	99
DEADLINES	
Early decision	
Deadline	11/1
Notification	12/15
Regular	
Deadline	1/15
Notification	4/1
Nonfall registration?	yes
FINANCIAL FACTS	
Financial Aid Rating	**70**
Annual in-state tuition	$10,509
Annual out-state tuition	$24,480
Room and board	$6,856
Required fees	$1,657
Books and supplies	$1,080
% needy frosh rec. need-based scholarship or grant aid	64
% needy UG rec. need-based scholarship or grant aid	69
% needy frosh rec. non-need-based scholarship or grant aid	75
% needy UG rec. non-need-based scholarship or grant aid	83
% needy frosh rec. need-based self-help aid	63
% needy UG rec. need-based self-help aid	75
% frosh rec. any financial aid	62
% UG rec. any financial aid	69
% UG borrow to pay for school	52
Average cumulative indebtedness	$24,320
% frosh need fully met	12
% ugrads need fully met	17
Average % of frosh need met	62
Average % of ugrad need met	66

Virginia Wesleyan College

1584 Wesleyan Drive, Norfolk/Virginia Beach, VA 23502-5599 • Admissions: 757-455-3208 • Fax: 757-461-5238

CAMPUS LIFE

Quality of Life Rating	**77**
Fire Safety Rating	**71**
Green Rating	**81**
Type of school	private
Affiliation	Methodist
Environment	metropolis

STUDENTS

Total undergrad enrollment	1,367
% male/female	37/63
% from out of state	33
% frosh live on campus	85
# of fraternities	4
# of sororities	4
% African American	23
% Asian	1
% Caucasian	62
% Hispanic	6
# of countries represented	6

SURVEY SAYS . . .

Great off-campus food
Intercollegiate sports are popular
Frats and sororities dominate social scene
Students get along with local community

ACADEMICS

Academic Rating	**75**
% students graduating within 4 years	42
% students graduating within 6 years	48
Calendar	4-1-4
Student/faculty ratio	12:1
Profs interesting rating	86
Profs accessible rating	83
Most classes have	10–19 students

MOST POPULAR MAJORS

business administration and management; communication studies/speech communication and rhetoric; criminal justice/safety studies

APPLICANTS ALSO LOOK AT AND SOMETIMES PREFER

Christopher Newport University, James Madison University, Old Dominion University

AND RARELY PREFER

Ferrum College, George Mason University, Lynchburg College

STUDENTS SAY ". . ."

Academics

The strength of tiny Virginia Wesleyan College, located across 300 "beautiful" wooded acres in Norfolk, lies in its capability "to create a community feel and successfully bring new students into the fold seamlessly." Students love the college's compact size, which is "small enough that you can walk into a room and name at least five people whom you know and like, but big enough that it is not full of clones." In trying to give each student a devoted personal experience, the school makes students "feel welcome and proud to be a Marlin." "It is easy to get help in classes," due to the small student/faculty ratio and the fact that professors here "truly care about each student as individuals." The "very intelligent, innovative student tutors" also provide support for those who need it. These "scholarly relationships between educators and students" create a sort of academic "home away from home" for everyone who sets foot on campus, and most class sizes are so small that "professors can focus more on helping the students than just spitting out information." "Every professor I've had so far has been a character who loves what they teach and whose enthusiasm is catching," says one student. Lesson plans at VWC are "very well structured, but also allow for some variation," which "allows for students to think more in depth about every subject." The professors "welcome questions during the lecture" and "are focused on ensuring each student understands the material." "They never want to move on if their students do not understand," says a student.

Life

"Life at VWC is pleasant." The small size of the "quaint" campus means that "you can get anywhere you need in the matter of minutes, and anyone is willing to help you if you need any assistance." At this "very free-spirited" school, having fun "is simply a matter of how creatively you want to waste time and/or be productive," though be warned that campus security is "strict." People definitely "get involved" here (particularly with volunteering), and there are "plenty of school- and club-sponsored events that are very well-planned." A lot of people also go to "THE BEACH!!!" (both the Chesapeake Bay and the ocean are close) or head to the shopping malls, bars, and concert venues of Virginia Beach and Norfolk about ten minutes away; however, "Unless you have a car, it can be difficult to get to things." On campus, many agree, "The cafeteria food is awful," and the Wi-Fi is shoddy, if existent at all in the "run-down" student housing. The school also could use more "entertainment areas for students, like a lounge for movies or games," particularly for commuters, who often feel "left out back." However, at night, the school is "very supportive of its adult students."

Student Body

Most students here "seem to care about their success here, and many of them care deeply about the community." There are "many student athletes," and most at VWC are "involved in several activities," including "some form of community service." The majority of students also lives on campus, and "Everyone hangs out with everyone during the weekend." Though everyone here is undoubtedly "friendly," a few admit, "If you don't play a sport or aren't in a Greek organization, then it's harder to find friends."

FINANCIAL AID: 757-455-3345 • E-MAIL: ADMISSIONS@VWC.EDU • WEBSITE: WWW.VWC.EDU

THE PRINCETON REVIEW SAYS

Admissions

Very important factors considered include: Academic GPA, rigor of secondary school record, level of applicant's interest. *Important factors considered include:* Application essay, recommendation(s), standardized test scores, extracurricular activities. *Other factors considered include:* Alumni/ae relation, character/personal qualities, first generation, interview, talent/ability, volunteer work, work experience. SAT or ACT required; ACT with or without writing component accepted. TOEFL required of all international applicants. High school diploma is required and GED is accepted. *Academic units required:* 4 English, 3 mathematics, 2 science (2 science labs), 2 foreign language, 1 history, 1 computer science. *Academic units recommended:* 4 English, 3 mathematics, 2 science (2 science labs), 2 foreign language, 1 history, 1 computer science, 4 academic electives.

Financial Aid

Students should submit: FAFSA, state aid form. Regular filing deadline is March 1. The Princeton Review suggests that all financial aid forms be submitted as soon as possible after January 1. *Need-based scholarships/grants offered:* Federal Pell, SEOG, state scholarships/grants, private scholarships, the school's own gift aid, Virginia Coalition for Independent Colleges; United Methodist Greater Higher Education Board. *Loan aid offered:* Direct Subsidized Stafford, Direct Unsubsidized Stafford, Direct PLUS, Federal Perkins, state loans, private alternative loan program. Applicants will be notified of awards on a rolling basis beginning February 1. Federal Work-Study Program available. Institutional employment available. Highest amount earned per year from on-campus jobs $1,200. Off-campus job opportunities are good.

The Inside Word

Getting in isn't too difficult at Virginia Wesleyan. Prospective freshmen who present a 3.5 GPA on a 4.0 scale and who have taken a strong, college preparatory curriculum in high school can apply for test-optional admission. Admission is rolling, and decisions are usually released within two weeks of application submission.

THE SCHOOL SAYS ". . ."

From the Admissions Office

"Virginia Wesleyan College seeks to enroll qualified students from diverse social, religious, racial, economic, and geographic backgrounds. Admission is based solely on the applicant's academic and personal qualifications. Factors considered include the application essay, recommendations, standardized test scores, and extracurricular activities. Virginia Wesleyan requires either the SAT 1 or ACT scores. Although we do not require more than one SAT or ACT score, we do take the highest individual Verbal and Math scores from all of the tests taken. The College offers test optional admission to prospective freshmen who present a 3.5 GPA on a 4.0 scale and who have taken a strong, college preparatory curriculum in high school. A high school diploma is required (GED accepted) and TOEFL is required for all international applicants. Recommended academic units include four English, three mathematics, two science, two foreign language, one history, one computer science, and four academic electives. Virginia Wesleyan considers applications on a rolling admissions basis. Applicants can typically expect notification within two to three weeks after we receive your completed application and supporting documents. While there is no specific deadline for admission, we encourage students to submit applications for Early Action by December 10 and for Wesleyan Scholarship consideration by January 1. Priority decisions for spring freshman applications is January 1; for fall freshman applications, March 1. Prospective students are encouraged to visit our beautiful 300-acre wooded campus for a tour and to meet with an admissions counselor. Learn more about admissions at www.vwc.edu."

SELECTIVITY

Admissions Rating	**70**
# of applicants	3,174
% of applicants accepted	86
% of acceptees attending	16

FRESHMAN PROFILE

Range SAT Critical Reading	440–540
Range SAT Math	430–540
Range SAT Writing	430–520
Range ACT Composite	19–23
Minimum paper TOEFL	550
Average HS GPA	3.2
% graduated top 10% of class	14
% graduated top 25% of class	40
% graduated top 50% of class	74

DEADLINES

Regular	
Priority	3/1
Notification	9/15
Nonfall registration?	yes

FINANCIAL FACTS

Financial Aid Rating	**79**
Annual tuition	$30,348
Room and board	$8,188
Required fees	$650
Books and supplies	$1,000
% needy frosh rec. need-based scholarship or grant aid	99
% needy UG rec. need-based scholarship or grant aid	97
% needy frosh rec. non-need-based scholarship or grant aid	13
% needy UG rec. non-need-based scholarship or grant aid	16
% needy frosh rec. need-based self-help aid	82
% needy UG rec. need-based self-help aid	83
% frosh rec. any financial aid	97
% UG rec. any financial aid	94
% UG borrow to pay for school	76
Average cumulative indebtedness	$23,424
% frosh need fully met	9
% ugrads need fully met	11
Average % of frosh need met	63
Average % of ugrade need met	65

WABASH COLLEGE

PO Box 352, Crawfordsville, IN 47933 • Admissions: 765-361-6225 • Fax: 765-361-6437

CAMPUS LIFE

Quality of Life Rating	**82**
Fire Safety Rating	**84**
Green Rating	**73**
Type of school	private
Environment	village

STUDENTS

Total undergrad enrollment	903
% male/female	100/0
% from out of state	30
% from public high school	91
% frosh live on campus	100
# of fraternities	9
% African American	5
% Asian	2
% Caucasian	76
% Hispanic	5
% Native American	1
% international	7
# of countries represented	12

SURVEY SAYS . . .

Lab facilities are great
Athletic facilities are great
Career services are great
School is well run
Everyone loves the Little Giants
Intramural sports are popular
Frats and sororities dominate social scene

ACADEMICS

Academic Rating	**96**
% students returning for sophomore year	83
% students graduating within 4 years	68
% students graduating within 6 years	75
Calendar	semester
Student/faculty ratio	11:1
Profs interesting rating	97
Profs accessible rating	98
Most classes have	10–19 students
Most lab/discussion sessions have	fewer than 10 students

MOST POPULAR MAJORS

history; psychology; religion/religious studies

APPLICANTS ALSO LOOK AT AND OFTEN PREFER

Indiana University—Bloomington, Purdue University—West Lafayette

AND SOMETIMES PREFER

DePauw University

AND RARELY PREFER

Miami University

STUDENTS SAY ". . ."

Academics

A "small, personalized, rigorous, elite institution" with an all-male student body, "Wabash College is a powerful small school that changes lives." In a word, Wabash is all about "tradition." The men here "live by a Wabash motto: 'Think Critically, Act Responsibly, Live Humanely, and Lead Effectively.'" With a "ninety-five percent acceptance rate into law school and a ninety percent acceptance rate into medical school," academics here are nothing to shake a stick at. Wabash is "a very challenging academic environment," "but you are provided with every opportunity needed to succeed and excel." Students flock here for the "devoted alumni network, strong, academically focused Greek system, small classes, personal professors, [and] emphasis on reading and writing." "One of the best things about Wabash is the opportunities it provides." The campus boasts "a state-of-the-art athletic center, an incredibly supportive faculty and staff, and an extensive alumni network." "Whether you strive for academic, athletic, community, or professional success, Wabash provides the means to achieve your goals." Professors here "are, generally speaking, the biggest selling point for Wabash." "They are world-class teachers [and] researchers." When not teaching, "Professors are nearly always available, and most departments have a tutoring center led by upperclassmen open every night of the week if you need assistance." "Many of the professors are also active in the social life of the school and can be seen tailgating with students before games or participating in different student-run clubs." All members of this unique community tout the understanding that Wabash College "is a school where boys come to become men, and men come to become gentlemen."

Life

The campus as a whole "is incredibly intimate." "The depth of the relationships between students and faculty is incredible." Furthermore, "The type of scholastic discourse that takes place both within and outside of the classroom is unparalleled." The school has a strict "honesty policy, which most, if not everybody, take seriously." Must hold fast to the credo that "what makes this place special [is] the life blood of our school: exceptional men who wish to learn and lead." "We work hard at classes five days a week, but the upperclassmen often make time to go to the Neon Cactus at Purdue on Thursday." "Friday and Saturday are devoted to releasing the stress from the week with a lot of cold beer." "In the warm months, we grill outside and have drinks with professors. In the cold months, we hang out in the fraternity house talking about movies, or world events, or what the pledges did last week." The academic buildings are built around a grassy field, called the "mall," and "There are frequently pickup games of soccer or ultimate Frisbee." Some say that "the absence of women is hard to bear." "After a while, you begin to embrace the lifestyle." "When you are done with class you might go to ESH (Employment Self-Help), an on-campus job, or you might go relax with your friends at your fraternity."

Student Body

A typical Wabash student "is an athlete who is willing to work long hours to get good grades." "Studious, eager to learn and to get work done, [and] serious about school," students here are "almost treated like peers by professors." "Everyone at Wabash works very hard and benefits from the rigorous academic requirements." "Lower-class to upper-class backgrounds allow for a variety of perspectives and previous educations." Regardless of where they hail from, "Students embrace the backgrounds of their classmates and work together to learn." Others say, "It's an all-male college, but that's where the universal attributes end." "There could stand to be some more ethnic diversity"; however, others say, "I think that's got more to with self-selection than anything else." "The library is packed Sunday through Thursday evening"; on the weekends, everyone "cuts loose and hangs out with friends." The most dominant social factor "is fraternity, followed by sports." The typical student is "from the Midwest, plays a sport, and will be going into business or grad school after graduation."

FINANCIAL AID: 765-361-6370 • E-MAIL: ADMISSIONS@WABASH.EDU • WEBSITE: WWW.WABASH.EDU

THE PRINCETON REVIEW SAYS

Admissions

Very important factors considered include: Class rank, academic GPA, rigor of secondary school record. *Important factors considered include:* Recommendation(s), standardized test scores, extracurricular activities, interview, level of applicant's interest, talent/ability. *Other factors considered include:* Application essay, alumni/ae relation, character/personal qualities, first generation, geographical residence, racial/ethnic status, volunteer work, work experience. ACT with or without writing component accepted. TOEFL required of all international applicants. High school diploma is required and GED is accepted. *Academic units recommended:* 4 English, 4 mathematics, 2 science (2 science labs), 2 foreign language, 2 social studies, 2 history, 3 academic electives.

Financial Aid

Students should submit: FAFSA, CSS/Financial Aid PROFILE, noncustodial PROFILE, federal tax returns and W-2 statements. The Princeton Review suggests that all financial aid forms be submitted as soon as possible after January 1. *Need-based scholarships/grants offered:* Federal Pell, state scholarships/grants, private scholarships, the school's own gift aid. *Loan aid offered:* Direct Subsidized Stafford, Direct Unsubsidized Stafford, Direct PLUS, college/university loans from institutional funds. Applicants will be notified of awards on or about March 31. Institutional employment available. Highest amount earned per year from on-campus jobs $3,000. Off-campus job opportunities are good.

The Inside Word

Wabash is one of the few remaining all-male colleges in the country, and like the rest of the brotherhood, it has a small applicant pool. The pool is highly self-selected, and the academic standards for admission, while selective, aren't especially demanding. Graduating is a whole other matter. Don't consider applying if you're not ready to do the grueling work required for success here.

THE SCHOOL SAYS ". . ."

From the Admissions Office

"Wabash College is different—and distinctive—from other liberal arts colleges. Different in that Wabash is an outstanding college for men only. Distinctive in the quality and character of the faculty, in the demanding nature of the academic program, in the farsightedness and maturity of the men who enroll, and in the richness of the traditions that have evolved throughout its 180-year history. Wabash is preeminently a teaching institution, and fundamental to the learning experience is the way faculty and students talk to each other—with mutual respect for the expression of informed opinion. For example, students who collaborate with faculty on research projects are considered their peers in the research—an esteem not usually extended to undergraduates. The college takes pride in the sense of community that such a learning environment fosters. But perhaps the single most striking aspect of student life at Wabash is personal freedom. The college has only one rule: 'The student is expected to conduct himself at all times, both on and off the campus, as a gentleman and a responsible citizen.' Wabash College treats students as adults, and such treatment attracts responsible freshmen and fosters their independence and maturity.

"For students seeking admission, Wabash will accept the SAT or the ACT. Wabash will use the student's best scores from either examination and will accept the SAT or ACT writing portions in place of an essay. Wabash does not require SAT Subject Tests."

SELECTIVITY

Admissions Rating	87
# of applicants	1,456
% of applicants accepted	63
% of acceptees attending	31
# accepting a place on wait list	53
# admitted from wait list	2
# of early decision applicants	69
# accepted early decision	60

FRESHMAN PROFILE

Range SAT Critical Reading	508–610
Range SAT Math	540–650
Range SAT Writing	490–590
Range ACT Composite	22–27
Minimum paper TOEFL	550
Average HS GPA	3.6
% graduated top 10% of class	37
% graduated top 25% of class	70
% graduated top 50% of class	97

DEADLINES

Early decision	
Deadline	11/15
Notification	12/15
Early action	
Deadline	12/1
Notification	12/21
Regular	
Priority	12/1
Nonfall registration?	yes

FINANCIAL FACTS

Financial Aid Rating	95
Annual tuition	$33,300
Room and board	$8,700
Required fees	$550
Books and supplies	$800
% needy frosh rec. need-based scholarship or grant aid	95
% needy UG rec. need-based scholarship or grant aid	98
% needy frosh rec. non-need-based scholarship or grant aid	14
% needy UG rec. non-need-based scholarship or grant aid	13
% needy frosh rec. need-based self-help aid	88
% needy UG rec. need-based self-help aid	86
% frosh rec. any financial aid	85
% UG rec. any financial aid	81
% UG borrow to pay for school	68
Average cumulative indebtedness	$28,311
% frosh need fully met	100
% ugrads need fully met	85
Average % of frosh need met	99
Average % of ugrad need met	98

WAGNER COLLEGE

PAPE ADMISSIONS BUILDING, STATEN ISLAND, NY 10301-4495 • ADMISSIONS: 718-390-3411 • FAX: 718-390-3105

CAMPUS LIFE

Quality of Life Rating	**82**
Fire Safety Rating	**96**
Green Rating	**70**
Type of school	private
Environment	metropolis

STUDENTS

Total undergrad enrollment	1,860
% male/female	38/62
% from out of state	60
% frosh live on campus	82
# of fraternities	10
# of sororities	7
% African American	6
% Asian	2
% Caucasian	70
% Hispanic	8
% international	3
# of countries represented	31

SURVEY SAYS . . .

Athletic facilities are great
Students are friendly
Campus feels safe
Musical organizations are popular
Theater is popular
Student publications are popular
Student government is popular
Lots of beer drinking
Hard liquor is popular

ACADEMICS

Academic Rating	**78**
% students returning for sophomore year	81
% students graduating within 4 years	67
% students graduating within 6 years	68
Calendar	semester
Student/faculty ratio	14:1
Profs interesting rating	82
Profs accessible rating	84
Most classes have	10–19 students
Most lab/discussion sessions have	10–19 students

MOST POPULAR MAJORS

biology/biological sciences; business/commerce; psychology

APPLICANTS ALSO LOOK AT AND OFTEN PREFER

New York University, Fairfield University

AND SOMETIMES PREFER

Muhlenberg College, Ithaca College, Northeastern University

AND RARELY PREFER

Quinnipiac University, Marist College, Drew University

STUDENTS SAY ". . ."

Academics

Wagner College, located on Staten Island, is a "tight-knit and fun, yet academically challenging," liberal arts school that operates under the Wagner Plan, combining a solid foundation in the liberal arts with practical and applied experiences like internships, with a commitment to service learning and community. The school is "in the perfect location with a surplus of unique resources" and is composed of "an excellent and vibrant community that supports its students every step of the way." The "commitment of the faculty and staff have for the student body is outstanding." Thanks to the plan, students are encouraged "to explore and reflect upon a myriad of subjects and issues." "Even though I am a biology major, I have the wonderful opportunity to explore interdisciplinary topics in the humanities and social sciences throughout my undergraduate career," says one student. The college's unique first-year program consists of a set of three classes with the same twenty-eight students, which "helps transition us from high school to college by progressively learning how to write college-level pieces as well as by engaging in a mandatory thirty-hour community service requirement." This "small, beautiful learning community" is guided by an "extremely attentive and competent" faculty. The professors "ask you to do your best and to push your limitations away" and are "extremely accessible outside of class." "The first time I was nervous about registration, my advisor sat down had lunch, and we registered together," says a student. "It is comforting that I can go to my professors whenever I need assistance with work." The school's science and physician's assistant programs are notably strong, as are the "fantastic" theater and musical programs. Students all universally agree that Wagner "lets you experience all different types of subjects by following the concept: learning by doing."

Life

At Wagner, students are "mostly concerned about their careers, whether they want to make it on Broadway or find the cure for cancer." There's plenty of school-run activities "through co-curricular programs and various clubs," so there are "countless things to do." Beyond all doubt, "The best thing to do…is to take advantage of New York City." The campus is just "a ferry ride away from Manhattan," and the majority of people takes the Wagner shuttle to the S.I. ferry ("all for free!") and goes to the city, whether to shop, eat, or go to a Broadway show. On weekends, there are "parties run by organizations from time to time" or in dorm rooms, since "there is no off-campus housing." Every year, the school has an event called Wagner Stock, where a famous musician or group comes to play. Food is a huge pain point here: Students want "more access to the dining hall in the late hours of the night," "more food options," and just better food in general.

Student Body

The student body here celebrates its "diverse" makeup but Division I athletics and the "great theater program" are very visible in this "small close community." But a student not in either of these programs can find their group through clubs and the major that they are in." Many students have "one major and a minor," and "half of them might study abroad for a semester and or have one or two internships before they graduate." Everyone basically goes about their own business, but "is very approachable." No one seems to have any trouble finding their own crowd, but even once that occurs, "Different crowds frequently mingle and almost everyone gets along." "People just talk to everyone," says a student.

FINANCIAL AID: 718-390-3183 • E-MAIL: ADM@WAGNER.EDU • WEBSITE: WWW.WAGNER.EDU

THE PRINCETON REVIEW SAYS

Admissions

Very important factors considered include: Class rank, academic GPA, rigor of secondary school record. *Important factors considered include:* Application essay, recommendation(s), standardized test scores, extracurricular activities, interview. *Other factors considered include:* Character/personal qualities, geographical residence, level of applicant's interest, talent/ability, volunteer work, work experience. TOEFL required of all international applicants. High school diploma is required and GED is accepted. *Academic units required:* 4 English, 3 mathematics, 2 science (1 science lab), 2 foreign language, 1 social studies, 3 history, 6 academic electives.

Financial Aid

Students should submit: FAFSA, institution's own financial aid form, state aid form. Regular filing deadline is March 1. The Princeton Review suggests that all financial aid forms be submitted as soon as possible after January 1. *Need-based scholarships/grants offered:* Federal Pell, SEOG, state scholarships/grants, private scholarships. *Loan aid offered:* Direct Subsidized Stafford, Direct Unsubsidized Stafford, Direct PLUS, Federal Perkins, Federal Nursing, alternative loans. Applicants will be notified of awards on a rolling basis beginning March 1. Federal Work-Study Program available. Institutional employment available. Highest amount earned per year from on-campus jobs $1,000. Off-campus job opportunities are good.

The Inside Word

As far as grades and test scores, the profile of the average freshman class at Wagner is solid. Standardized tests are optional, and there is more value placed on the strength of your course work and your grades in those classes. The admissions staff here is dedicated to finding the right students for their school. Wagner is looking for students who like to be involved in community events, so make sure your application reflects your extracurriculars. An interview bodes well for serious applicants.

THE SCHOOL SAYS ". . ."

From the Admissions Office

"At Wagner College, we attract and develop active learners and future leaders. Wagner College has received national acclaim (Time magazine, American Association of Colleges and Universities) for its innovative curriculum, The Wagner Plan for the Practical Liberal Arts. At Wagner, we capitalize on our unique geography; we are a traditional, scenic, residential campus, which happens to sit atop a hill on an island overlooking lower Manhattan. Our location allows us to offer a program that couples required off-campus experiences (experiential learning), with 'learning community' clusters of courses. This program begins in the first semester and continues through the senior capstone experience in the major. Fieldwork and internships, writing-intensive reflective tutorials, connected learning, 'reading, writing, and doing': At Wagner College our students truly discover 'the practical liberal arts in New York City.'"

SELECTIVITY

Admissions Rating	**82**
# of applicants	3,001
% of applicants accepted	67
% of acceptees attending	24
# of early decision applicants	110
# accepted early decision	59

FRESHMAN PROFILE

Range SAT Critical Reading	530–640
Range SAT Math	520–640
Range SAT Writing	520–630
Range ACT Composite	22–28
Minimum paper TOEFL	550
Minimum web-based TOEFL	17
% graduated top 10% of class	14
% graduated top 25% of class	71
% graduated top 50% of class	91

DEADLINES

Early decision	
Deadline	12/15
Notification	1/15
Regular	
Deadline	2/15
Notification	2/15
Nonfall registration?	no

FINANCIAL FACTS

Financial Aid Rating	**80**
Annual tuition	$37,240
Room and board	$11,160
Required fees	$300
Books and supplies	$757
% needy frosh rec. need-based scholarship or grant aid	100
% needy UG rec. need-based scholarship or grant aid	99
% needy frosh rec. need-based self-help aid	82
% needy UG rec. need-based self-help aid	83
% frosh rec. any financial aid	95
% UG rec. any financial aid	90
% UG borrow to pay for school	56
Average cumulative indebtedness	$40,110
% frosh need fully met	20
% ugrads need fully met	22
Average % of frosh need met	74
Average % of ugrad need met	73

WAKE FOREST UNIVERSITY

PO BOX 7305, WINSTON SALEM, NC 27109 • ADMISSIONS: 336-758-5201 • FAX: 336-758-4324

CAMPUS LIFE

Quality of Life Rating	77
Fire Safety Rating	87
Green Rating	78
Type of school	private
Environment	city

STUDENTS

Total undergrad enrollment	4,775
% male/female	48/52
% from out of state	76
% from public high school	65
% frosh live on campus	99
# of fraternities	15
# of sororities	9
% African American	8
% Asian	5
% Caucasian	78
% Hispanic	5
% international	2
# of countries represented	27

SURVEY SAYS . . .

Great computer facilities
Great library
Students are happy
Everyone loves the Demon Deacons
Intramural sports are popular
Frats and sororities dominate social scene
Lots of beer drinking
Hard liquor is popular

ACADEMICS

Academic Rating	92
% students returning for sophomore year	93
% students graduating within 4 years	83
% students graduating within 6 years	88
Calendar	semester
Student/faculty ratio	11:1
Profs interesting rating	94
Profs accessible rating	97
Most classes have	10–19 students
Most lab/discussion sessions have	10–19 students

MOST POPULAR MAJORS

business/commerce; political science and government; psychology

APPLICANTS ALSO LOOK AT AND SOMETIMES PREFER

Duke University, Vanderbilt University, University of Virginia, The University of North Carolina at Chapel Hill

STUDENTS SAY ". . ."

Academics

This classic Southern school in North Carolina "has everything a college should have; great academic reputation, small class size, fun athletics, and a bangin' social scene." This is a campus of "extremely driven students" with "a worldwide awareness, particularly in the areas of service and study abroad." The school's motto is Pro Humanitate ("for humanity"), which matches neatly with its emphasis on humanitarian work and volunteering. Relationships with professors are "an integral part of the Wake Forest experience," and the professors here, for the most part, "will do anything to see you succeed." They "make great efforts to meet with anyone who is struggling and make class time as enjoyable as possible." They "effortlessly ignite passion within the students," demonstrate an "unprecedented" level "of personal commitment to the academic success of each and every student," and "are often invested in building relationships that extend beyond a single semester, developing mentorships that continue throughout your time at Wake." This small campus (with a "perfect blend of intellect and Southern charm") has a "plethora of opportunities available and endless amounts of people who want to connect you with those opportunities," including many leadership roles. The fully student-centric administration "really listens to student input and takes immediate action to improve, based on our suggestions," a setup that "allows [for] great working relationships." "The best thing about Wake is how community-minded it is," says one student. "From freshman orientation to even the fact that the Greek organizations are all in dorms on campus, it really is a whole community effort." Students also cite Wake Forest's encouragement in study abroad "to broad horizon of students" as a huge benefit. Also, the strength of a degree from Wake Forest is "incredible when applying for a job."

Life

Students are used to living in "the bubble," which is "the shell that figuratively covers campus from news of the outside world." Students do enjoy getting off campus whenever possible (such as going into Winston "for food or shopping or a movie"), but "People are incredibly immersed in life on campus." There is no shortage of things that can be done around campus; the Mag Quad is where most of the academic buildings are located, and "You will always see someone you know during the day in that location," often throwing a Frisbee or a baseball. Additionally, "Attending football games in 'Southern attire' and tailgating always make for a fun weekend in the fall!" During the week, it's "very popular to be seen at the library at all hours of the night, and all-nighters are a common occurrence." However, on the weekends, "The party scene is pretty big." Greek life "dominates the campus, but everyone is encouraged to participate"; there are "many fraternity parties each weekend, and many mixers between Greek organizations." Extracurricular activities, club sports, and intramurals also "thrive for fun activities." Beach weekends are also very popular come spring, along with events like the Carolina Cup (a horse race in South Carolina).

Student Body

Students admit that Wake "definitely could use more diversity, since most students are wealthy, white Christians," but "respect exists among everyone, [as well as] appreciation for our differences and similarities." Everyone here is involved in many different areas across campus, from extracurriculars to academics, "so it's very inclusive." Everyone is "incredibly bright and works very hard," and there seems to be an insatiable "thirst for knowledge." Most students are also involved in Greek life, and "That's where people typically find their best friends." Professors and faculty stress the importance of presentation, and therefore, "Students pay close attention to looking their best every day and putting their best foot forward."

FINANCIAL AID: 336-758-5154 • E-MAIL: ADMISSIONS@WFU.EDU • WEBSITE: WWW.WFU.EDU

THE PRINCETON REVIEW SAYS

Admissions

Very important factors considered include: Class rank, application essay, academic GPA, rigor of secondary school record, character/personal qualities. *Important factors considered include:* Recommendation(s), extracurricular activities, interview, talent/ability. *Other factors considered include:* Standardized test scores, alumni/ae relation, first generation, geographical residence, level of applicant's interest, racial/ethnic status, religious affiliation/commitment, state residency, volunteer work. SAT or ACT required; ACT with or without writing component accepted. TOEFL required of all international applicants. High school diploma is required and GED is accepted. *Academic units required:* 4 English, 3 mathematics, 1 science, 2 foreign language, 2 social studies. *Academic units recommended:* 4 English, 4 mathematics, 4 science, 4 foreign language, 4 social studies.

Financial Aid

Students should submit: FAFSA, CSS/Financial Aid PROFILE, state aid form, noncustodial PROFILE. The Princeton Review suggests that all financial aid forms be submitted as soon as possible after January 1. *Need-based scholarships/grants offered:* Federal Pell, SEOG, state scholarships/grants, private scholarships, the school's own gift aid. *Loan aid offered:* Direct Subsidized Stafford, Direct Unsubsidized Stafford, Direct PLUS, Federal Perkins, state loans, college/university loans from institutional funds. Applicants will be notified of awards on a rolling basis beginning April 1. Federal Work-Study Program available. Institutional employment available. Highest amount earned per year from on-campus jobs $2,495. Off-campus job opportunities are excellent.

The Inside Word

Wake Forest's considerable application numbers afford admissions officers the opportunity to be rather selective. In particular, admissions officers remain diligent in their matchmaking efforts—finding students who are good fits for the school—and their hard work is rewarded by a high graduation rate. Candidates will need to be impressive in all areas to gain admission, since all areas of their applications are considered carefully. A relatively large number of qualified students find themselves on Wake Forest's wait list.

THE SCHOOL SAYS ". . ."

From the Admissions Office

"Wake Forest University has been dedicated to the liberal arts for over a century and a half; this means education in the fundamental fields of human knowledge and achievement. It seeks to encourage habits of mind that ask why, that evaluate evidence, that are open to new ideas, that attempt to understand and appreciate the perspective of others, that accept complexity and grapple with it, that admit error, and that pursue truth.

"Wake Forest is among a small, elite group of American colleges and universities recognized for their outstanding academic quality. It offers small classes taught by full-time faculty—not graduate assistants—and a commitment to student interaction with those professors. Students are provided ThinkPad computers. Classroom and residence halls are fully networked. Students are admitted based on the unique qualities they bring to our community. Wake Forest's generous financial aid program allows deserving students to enroll regardless of their financial circumstances.

"Wake Forest is the first top thirty national university in the United States to make standardized tests such as the SAT and ACT with writing optional in the admissions process. If applicants feel that their SAT or ACT with writing scores are a good indicator of their abilities, they may submit them and they will be considered in the admissions decision. If, however, a prospective student does not feel that their scores accurately represent their academic abilities, they do not need to submit them until after they have been accepted and choose to enroll. Wake Forest takes a holistic look at each applicant."

SELECTIVITY	
Admissions Rating	**94**
# of applicants	9,869
% of applicants accepted	40
% of acceptees attending	32
# of early decision applicants	762
# accepted early decision	323

FRESHMAN PROFILE	
Range SAT Critical Reading	610–700
Range SAT Math	620–700
Range ACT Composite	28–32
Minimum paper TOEFL	600
% graduated top 10% of class	83
% graduated top 25% of class	96
% graduated top 50% of class	98

DEADLINES	
Early decision	
Deadline	11/15
Notification	1/1
Regular	
Deadline	1/1
Nonfall registration?	yes

FINANCIAL FACTS	
Financial Aid Rating	**90**
Annual tuition	$42,700
Room and board	$11,660
Required fees	$500
Books and supplies	$1,100
% needy frosh rec. need-based scholarship or grant aid	97
% needy UG rec. need-based scholarship or grant aid	95
% needy frosh rec. non-need-based scholarship or grant aid	49
% needy UG rec. non-need-based scholarship or grant aid	70
% needy frosh rec. need-based self-help aid	80
% needy UG rec. need-based self-help aid	88
% frosh rec. any financial aid	39
% UG rec. any financial aid	34
% UG borrow to pay for school	39
Average cumulative indebtedness	$35,070
% frosh need fully met	89
% ugrads need fully met	65
Average % of frosh need met	99
Average % of ugrad need met	99

WARREN WILSON COLLEGE

PO BOX 9000, ASHEVILLE, NC 28815-9000 • ADMISSIONS: 800-934-3536 • FAX: 828-298-1440

CAMPUS LIFE

Quality of Life Rating	**89**
Fire Safety Rating	**63**
Green Rating	**99**
Type of school	private
Affiliation	Presbyterian
Environment	village

STUDENTS

Total undergrad enrollment	903
% male/female	38/62
% from out of state	82
% from public high school	71
% frosh live on campus	98
% African American	2
% Asian	2
% Caucasian	85
% Hispanic	3
% international	3
# of countries represented	12

SURVEY SAYS . . .

Lots of liberal students
Students are friendly
Low cost of living
Frats and sororities are unpopular or nonexistent
Political activism is popular
Students are environmentally aware
Students are involved in community service

ACADEMICS

Academic Rating	**76**
% students returning for sophomore year	64
% students graduating within 4 years	30
% students graduating within 6 years	45
Calendar	semester
Student/faculty ratio	13:1
Profs interesting rating	84
Profs accessible rating	84
Most classes have	10–19 students
Most lab/discussion sessions have	10–19 students

MOST POPULAR MAJORS

parks, recreation, leisure, and fitness studies, other; psychology

APPLICANTS ALSO LOOK AT AND OFTEN PREFER

Earlham College

AND SOMETIMES PREFER

The Evergreen State College

AND RARELY PREFER

Guilford College, Arizona State University

STUDENTS SAY ". . ."

Academics

Warren Wilson's unique approach to education is encapsulated in its "Triad program." This distinctive curriculum combines academics with "work and service." And though this program might demand more of your time, undergrads here speak quite highly of it. As one psych major shares, Triad "allows students to deepen their understanding of the world's needs and prepares them for a lifestyle of service beyond college." Additionally, it's an "active style of learning" that "really pushes students…to become well-rounded individuals." Undergrads are especially enthusiastic about the college's "environmental focus and strong science programs." There's "a working farm on campus that students run, and it [lends] excellent opportunity for hands-on experience." Undergrads also laud the "good creative writing department." Importantly, "the majority of the faculty are genuinely interested in the well-being of each and every student." Professors are "easy to talk to and highly available." This accessibility extends to the administration as well. As one impressed junior tells us, "We know our administration by first name, and if we want to talk to them, it's no problem to schedule an appointment or have the admin attend a student government meeting."

Life

Undergrads at Warren Wilson tend to lead hectic lives. Many concur that "students are really busy during the week" and therefore view the weekend as "a time for release." However, the intellectual debates don't just stop because it's leisure time. As one freshman shares, life often "revolves around political arguments and philosophical discussions held over cans of Pabst Blue Ribbon." Of course, activities extend beyond delightful and thought-provoking conversation. Students "greatly enjoy" the outdoors, and many can often be found "exploring trails, visiting the animals on the farm, swimming, kayaking, and canoeing on the Swannanoa River." Additionally, "fall soccer games, Friday night themed dance parties…and Thursday night contra dances" are all well attended. And one senior adds that "poetry slams, talent shows, theatrical productions, and parties that are held in the common areas of the dorms" are all great fun. Students are also "very politically and environmentally active, and community service" is extremely popular. Venturing into downtown Asheville is common as well. The town center is only "a fifteen-minute ride from campus, and there is a bus that goes back and forth during specific hours." The "funky" area has "a great arts and music scene," and "there are lots of concerts, performances, restaurants and local stores to visit."

Student Body

Warren Wilson is a college that "is very open to the idea of individuality" and thus manages to attract "a wide range of students." Many undergrads proclaim their peers to be "dynamic people" who are all "atypical." As a sophomore proudly boasts, "The great thing about this school is that a person, in all their weirdness, is loved and embraced by the community." Of course, for all this diversity, some commonalities do seep through. The "vast majority of people who go here are liberal" and are concerned "with social justice issues." Indeed, the mantle "hippie" is frequently bandied about. While some might object to this stereotype, many undergrads are "committed to environmental awareness." And a freshman notes that his fellow students "care about the outdoors, recycle, unplug appliances not in use, and would rather eat an organic salad than a steak." Additionally, most undergrads are hardworking and very industrious, constantly thinking of new projects to do and coming up with interesting ideas." But perhaps this math major sums up his peers best, "If you like people with weird haircuts, people with a different gender identity, vegans, feminists, and future organic farmers—or are one of these people—you will probably fit right in."

FINANCIAL AID: 828-771-2082 • E-MAIL: ADMIT@WARREN-WILSON.EDU • WEBSITE: WWW.WARREN-WILSON.EDU

THE PRINCETON REVIEW SAYS

Admissions

Very important factors considered include: Application essay, rigor of secondary school record, standardized test scores, character/personal qualities, interview, volunteer work, work experience. *Important factors considered include:* Class rank, recommendation(s). *Other factors considered include:* Alumni/ae relation, extracurricular activities, state residency, talent/ability. ACT with or without writing component accepted. TOEFL required of all international applicants. High school diploma is required and GED is accepted. *Academic units required:* 4 English, 3 mathematics, 2 science (2 science labs), 3 history. *Academic units recommended:* 2 foreign language.

Financial Aid

Students should submit: FAFSA, institution's own financial aid form, state aid form. The Princeton Review suggests that all financial aid forms be submitted as soon as possible after January 1. *Need-based scholarships/grants offered:* Federal Pell, SEOG, state scholarships/grants, the school's own gift aid. *Loan aid offered:* Direct Subsidized Stafford, Direct Unsubsidized Stafford, Direct PLUS, Federal Perkins, college/university loans from institutional funds. Applicants will be notified of awards on a rolling basis beginning March 2. Highest amount earned per year from on-campus jobs $3,144. Off-campus job opportunities are good.

The Inside Word

At Warren Wilson College, one's sense of social commitment is as vital to the admissions process as one's high school transcript—the college desires students who are actively engaged in their communities. Admissions officers are interested in applicants who seek to make connections and who understand how to apply what they learn in the classroom to outside projects and activities.

THE SCHOOL SAYS ". . ."

From the Admissions Office

"This book is *The Best 377 Colleges,* but Warren Wilson College may not be the best college for many students. There are 3,500 colleges in the U.S., and there is a best place for everyone. The 'best college' is one that has the right size, location, programs, and above all, the right feel for you, even if it is not listed here. Warren Wilson College may be the best choice if you think and act independently, actively participate in your education, and want a college that provides a sense of community. Your hands will get dirty here, your mind will be stretched, and you'll not be anonymous. If you are looking for the traditional college experience with football and frats and a campus on a quad, this probably is not the right place. However, if you want to be a part of an academic community that works and serves together, this might be exactly what you are looking for.

"Students applying for fall admission should provide results of the SAT or ACT."

SELECTIVITY

Admissions Rating	**78**
# of applicants	986
% of applicants accepted	93
% of acceptees attending	25

FRESHMAN PROFILE

Range SAT Critical Reading	540–660
Range SAT Math	490–590
Range SAT Writing	510–630
Range ACT Composite	22–28
Minimum paper TOEFL	550
Average HS GPA	3.2
% graduated top 10% of class	14
% graduated top 25% of class	42
% graduated top 50% of class	78

DEADLINES

Early decision	
Deadline	11/15
Early action	
Deadline	1/15
Notification	2/15
Regular	
Deadline	2/15
Nonfall registration?	yes

FINANCIAL FACTS

Financial Aid Rating	**74**
Annual tuition	$27,740
Room and board	$8,566
Required fees	$300
Books and supplies	$870
% needy frosh rec. need-based scholarship or grant aid	91
% needy UG rec. need-based scholarship or grant aid	91
% needy frosh rec. non-need-based scholarship or grant aid	24
% needy UG rec. non-need-based scholarship or grant aid	17
% needy frosh rec. need-based self-help aid	100
% needy UG rec. need-based self-help aid	100
% frosh rec. any financial aid	90
% UG rec. any financial aid	90
% UG borrow to pay for school	44
Average cumulative indebtedness	$17,533
% frosh need fully met	11
% ugrads need fully met	14
Average % of frosh need met	73
Average % of ugrad need met	72

WASHINGTON COLLEGE

300 Washington Avenue, Chestertown, MD 21620 • Admissions: 410-778-7700 • Fax: 410-778-7287

CAMPUS LIFE

Quality of Life Rating	72
Fire Safety Rating	97
Green Rating	67
Type of school	private
Environment	rural

STUDENTS

Total undergrad enrollment	1,453
% male/female	42/58
% from out of state	52
% from public high school	67
% frosh live on campus	98
# of fraternities	4
# of sororities	3
% African American	4
% Asian	2
% Caucasian	84
% Hispanic	3
% international	1
# of countries represented	25

SURVEY SAYS . . .

Lab facilities are great
Great computer facilities
Students are friendly
Student government is popular
Lots of beer drinking
Hard liquor is popular

ACADEMICS

Academic Rating	82
% students returning for sophomore year	82
% students graduating within 4 years	72
% students graduating within 6 years	76
Calendar	semester
Student/faculty ratio	12:1
Profs interesting rating	92
Profs accessible rating	88
Most classes have	10–19 students
Most lab/discussion sessions have	fewer than 10 students

MOST POPULAR MAJORS

business administration and management; English language and literature; psychology

APPLICANTS ALSO LOOK AT AND OFTEN PREFER

University of Maryland College Park

AND SOMETIMES PREFER

University of Delaware

AND RARELY PREFER

McDaniel College

STUDENTS SAY ". . ."

Academics

Washington College is all about "gaining a distinctive and strong education in the liberal arts through personalized programs and hands-on experience." Located in small-town Chestertown, Maryland, this "small, tight-knit" community fosters a "high level of education" and an "intimate and personalized education experience." Washington College is a place where "students learn to think outside of the box while becoming better people and having the time of their lives." Centrally located between "three major employment markets: Washington, D.C., Philadelphia, and Baltimore," this "beautiful campus" "provides the perfect setting for a learning environment." "There are not as many distractions, but there is enough to keep you busy." Professors here are "highly educated, very personal, and willing to bend over backwards to ensure your education." Unlike at large research universities, faculty at Washington College are "here to teach, and they love to teach." The "attention given to the students by faculty is undeniable." The English and creative writing programs are among "the best in the country," earning Washington College a reputation "as a writing school," with the famous "Rose O'Neill Literary House, and the Sophie Kerr Prize." Students say all in one breath, "The professors are world-class, and the campus is beautiful. Also the Eastern Shore of Maryland is an incredible place to be."

Life

Living at Washington College "is as good as a college experience can get." "No matter what your interests are there is plenty to do." Some note that because of "the small-town environment, we have to make our own fun on weekends, but there's usually something on-campus to make it less of a challenge." "I personally love the environment and being outdoors. I spend a lot of time kayaking at our boat house on the Chester River, fishing on the Eastern Shore of Maryland, and supporting our athletic teams." "The school's rather small, so we know almost all of the athletes, so we're not only supporting a program, we're supporting our best friends." On campus, "There are plenty of student-run activities." When it comes to facilities, "The athletic department is great, and the dining hall is new and wonderful." For fun, students "often go to plays hosted by the drama department, attend interesting guest lectures, play Wii in the dorm rooms, play Frisbee on the campus green, play pool in the student center, go to movies, or stroll around Chestertown and the waterfront." We drink in the dorms and suites because almost everyone lives on campus." Washington College "is located within a rural town; however, we are not completely isolated. We are about forty minutes away from Annapolis." Students do warn, "Being in a rural town was hard at first."

Student Body

A typical Washington College student "is preppy—from the way they dress to the way that they interact with each other and their professors." It's "an athletic campus, as even non-athletes are generally fit and participate in intramural sports." Most students "come from a somewhat affluent background, and the majority study and work very hard, but they also party very hard on the weekends." Though some note "there is very little diversity on campus," others say while the campus "might lack in racial diversity, people have diverse morals, values, and political views." There seem to be "two major, distinct campus cultures: the athletic/Greek life people and the English/drama people. People generally gravitate to one or the other." "It isn't hard to find your 'place,' though." Most students are "involved in several different types of activities." Students "usually fit in by playing a sport or joining Greek life, but there is always a club for everyone." Others concur, Washington College is a "melting pot of individuals from different backgrounds, but the typical student is open-minded, ambitious, and extremely innovative." Athletes and burgeoning writers alike "have strong pride and love for our school."

FINANCIAL AID: 410-778-7214 • E-MAIL: ADM.OFF@WASHCOLL.EDU • WEBSITE: WWW.WASHCOLL.EDU

THE PRINCETON REVIEW SAYS

Admissions

Very important factors considered include: Academic GPA, rigor of secondary school record, interview. *Important factors considered include:* Class rank, standardized test scores, level of applicant's interest, work experience. *Other factors considered include:* Application essay, recommendation(s), alumni/ae relation, character/personal qualities, extracurricular activities, first generation, geographical residence, racial/ethnic status, state residency, talent/ability, volunteer work. SAT or ACT required; ACT with or without writing component accepted. TOEFL required of all international applicants. High school diploma is required and GED is accepted. *Academic units required:* 4 English, 3 mathematics, 3 science (2 science labs), 2 foreign language, 2 social studies, 2 history. *Academic units recommended:* 4 English, 4 mathematics, 4 science (3 science labs), 4 foreign language, 4 social studies.

Financial Aid

Students should submit: FAFSA, institution's own financial aid form. The Princeton Review suggests that all financial aid forms be submitted as soon as possible after January 1. *Need-based scholarships/grants offered:* Federal Pell, SEOG, state scholarships/grants, private scholarships, the school's own gift aid. *Loan aid offered:* Direct Subsidized Stafford, Direct Unsubsidized Stafford, Direct PLUS, Federal Perkins. Applicants will be notified of awards on a rolling basis beginning February 15. Federal Work-Study Program available. Institutional employment available. Highest amount earned per year from on-campus jobs $2,000. Off-campus job opportunities are good.

The Inside Word

The profile of a typical successful applicant at Washington College is that of the solid but not exceptional high school student. Above-average standardized test scores and respectable grades in a college-prep high school curriculum should be enough to get you past the gatekeepers here. Students who rank in the top ten percent of their high school class or have a GPA above 3.5 can request a "score optional" admissions review. Washington College is up front about its preference for students who visit campus and/or complete an interview; the school says that such applicants "are processed and admitted before qualified non-visitors." Proceed accordingly.

THE SCHOOL SAYS ". . ."

From the Admissions Office

"We tell our students, 'Your revolution starts here,' because the person who graduates from Washington College is not the same one who matriculated four years earlier; and because through your experiences here, you can be empowered and emboldened to change the world. Your education reflects the maxims of our founder, George Washington: The strength of America's democracy depends on critical and independent thinkers who persevere in the face of challenge and assume the responsibilities and privileges of informed citizenship. We provide a truly personalized education that tests—and stretches—each student's talents and potentials. We create challenges and opportunities that expand your brainpower and creativity through collaborative research with faculty and through independent study."

"All this happens on a campus that has been through its own physical revolution in the past several years: some $70 million in improvements that include a brand new Commons with a food court, coffee shop, student center and game room; a totally renovated and expanded Arts Center; two new residence halls with geothermal heating, and dramatic landscape improvements. Beyond campus, a wonderfully distinct setting—historic Chestertown, on the Chester River, amid the ecological bounty of Maryland's Chesapeake Bay—helps define us and enriches our programs in history, literature and ecology."

"Admission to Washington College is selective; decisions are based primarily on a student's record of academic achievement. SAT/ACT scores are optional for students who rank in the top ten percent of their class. Interviews are strongly recommended."

SELECTIVITY	
Admissions Rating	87
# of applicants	4,799
% of applicants accepted	57
% of acceptees attending	15
# accepting a place on wait list	123
# admitted from wait list	56
# of early decision applicants	50
# accepted early decision	34

FRESHMAN PROFILE	
Range SAT Critical Reading	550–630
Range SAT Math	540–610
Range SAT Writing	520–620
Range ACT Composite	21–27
Average HS GPA	3.6
% graduated top 10% of class	32
% graduated top 25% of class	66
% graduated top 50% of class	95

DEADLINES	
Early decision	
Deadline	11/1
Notification	12/1
Early action	
Deadline	12/1
Notification	1/15
Regular	
Priority	2/15
Deadline	rolling
Notification	rolling
Nonfall registration?	yes

FINANCIAL FACTS	
Financial Aid Rating	82
Annual tuition	$37,882
Room and board	$8,228
Required fees	$660
Books and supplies	$1,250
% needy frosh rec. need-based scholarship or grant aid	100
% needy UG rec. need-based scholarship or grant aid	98
% needy frosh rec. non-need-based scholarship or grant aid	27
% needy UG rec. non-need-based scholarship or grant aid	25
% needy frosh rec. need-based self-help aid	97
% needy UG rec. need-based self-help aid	97
% frosh rec. any financial aid	94
% UG rec. any financial aid	88
% UG borrow to pay for school	61
Average cumulative indebtedness	$37,303
% frosh need fully met	46
% ugrads need fully met	29
Average % of frosh need met	92
Average % of ugrad need met	75

WASHINGTON & JEFFERSON COLLEGE

60 SOUTH LINCOLN STREET, WASHINGTON, PA 15301 • ADMISSIONS: 724-223-6025

CAMPUS LIFE

Quality of Life Rating	68
Fire Safety Rating	84
Green Rating	82
Type of school	private
Environment	village

STUDENTS

Total undergrad enrollment	1,418
% male/female	50/50
% from out of state	31
% from public high school	83
% frosh live on campus	94
# of fraternities	6
# of sororities	4
% African American	3
% Asian	2
% Caucasian	81
% Hispanic	2
% Native American	1
# of countries represented	16

SURVEY SAYS . . .

Low cost of living
Frats and sororities dominate social scene
Very little drug use
Lots of beer drinking

ACADEMICS

Academic Rating	82
% students returning for sophomore year	88
% students graduating within 4 years	68
% students graduating within 6 years	74
Calendar	4-1-4
Student/faculty ratio	11:1
Profs interesting rating	91
Profs accessible rating	90
Most classes have	10–19 students
Most lab/discussion sessions have	10–19 students

MOST POPULAR MAJORS

English; business/commerce; psychology

STUDENTS SAY ". . ."

Academics

Washington & Jefferson College is a small, elite school known for its "academic rigor" and "prestigious reputation." In addition to two conventional semesters, the college also features a unique intercession period in January, "which allows for a month of focused learning on a topic that is often much different than something…offered during a semester, including travel and topics of specific interest to professors." Professors bring their passion to the classroom on a regular basis; students say that they are "very interactive and enjoy the small class sizes and getting to know each student's personality." "Professors are there because they love to teach and will go the extra mile for students." "They are very knowledgeable and are very accessible outside of class," and personal connections with professors "oftentimes leads to internships or research projects" for undergraduate students. In general, the college is excellent at providing students with ample opportunities to prepare for their futures. It boasts "a great reputation for graduate school preparation" and has an "impeccable record at placing students in medical, graduate, and law schools." Additionally, there are "so many opportunities with alumni relations." The study abroad office is also excellent, and there are many opportunities for students to develop their own research projects overseas or at home with funding from the Magellan Project. In short, students think that "a degree from Washington & Jefferson College is valuable." The academics here are "very demanding, but the opportunities that you will get both during and after your time there are unmatched."

Life

Student life at Washington & Jefferson College is a "good balance of schoolwork, athletics, and fun." The "beautiful, small campus" is home to a "friendly, warm," "family-like environment," where the emphasis is placed on the well-being of the students. It is "easy to get involved and be active in campus organizations." Greek life is extremely popular on campus, as are sports and club activities. Students "study hard during the week, but party hard on the weekends." "Parties are regular on weekends," but alternatively, the school also "provides multiple activities over the weekends—especially for students who do not drink." "There are always music, art, speakers, and events" on campus. "A lot of students…will attend these, but most are more likely to party for fun." Some students complain, "There needs to be more to do on campus on the weekends," and the school is trying to respond to this demand by "working hard to produce more student activities, such as bringing in great bands for concerts" to campus. Washington & Jefferson's home city of Washington "isn't ideal" for college students, but student services provides a shuttle to and from nearby Pittsburgh on the weekends, which can be "a great escape from the close-knit campus community."

Student Body

Students at Washington & Jefferson College tend to have "similar backgrounds, beliefs, and morals." A typical student" works hard in the classroom and is serious about getting good grades but likes to go out and have fun on weekends with friends." Students tend to be "athletic, sporty, smart," "well-off financially," and "relatively preppy." However, students are also noted for being very social, as well as "extremely friendly and helpful." Many students are a part of Greek life, and many are "student athletes who seem to balance sports and academics with much success." Some say, "It would be nicer to have more of a range of ethnic and social backgrounds" at the college, and the administration is making small but sure strides to increase diversity on campus. The typical student at W&J is focused on his or her course work; he or she is "also involved outside of the classroom in clubs, athletics, Greek Life, or one of a variety of other things the school has to offer." The students here "have a common goal to be successful in life," and with this goal in mind, everyone works together to form a tight-knit community and "gets along pretty well."

FAX : 724-223-6534 • FINANCIAL AID: 724-223-6019 • E-MAIL: ADMISSION@WASHJEFF.EDU • WEBSITE: WWW.WASHJEFF.EDU

THE PRINCETON REVIEW SAYS

Admissions

Very important factors considered include: Class rank, application essay, academic GPA, recommendation(s), rigor of secondary school record, character/personal qualities, interview. *Important factors considered include:* Standardized test scores, extracurricular activities. *Other factors considered include:* Alumni/ae relation, geographical residence, level of applicant's interest, racial/ethnic status, state residency, talent/ability, volunteer work, work experience. SAT or ACT required; ACT with or without writing component accepted. High school diploma is required and GED is accepted. *Academic units required:* 3 English, 3 mathematics, 2 foreign language, 1 history, 6 or more academic courses from English, mathematics, foreign language, history (social or natural).

Financial Aid

Students should submit: FAFSA. The Princeton Review suggests that all financial aid forms be submitted as soon as possible after January 1. *Need-based scholarships/grants offered:* Federal Pell, SEOG, state scholarships/grants, private scholarships, the school's own gift aid. *Loan aid offered:* Direct Subsidized Stafford, Direct Unsubsidized Stafford, Direct PLUS, Federal Perkins, college/university loans from institutional funds. Applicants will be notified of awards on a rolling basis beginning March 1. Federal Work-Study Program available. Institutional employment available. Highest amount earned per year from on-campus jobs $3,440. Off-campus job opportunities are good.

The Inside Word

Washington & Jefferson College takes a well-rounded approach to admissions, reflecting the type of student the school aims to admit. Academic record, class rank, personal statement, and extracurricular activities are all thoroughly evaluated. Most prospective students are high work diligently to secure a spot at this prestigious institution. The lucky applicants who receive a fat letter in the mail are wel comed into a distinctive community that promises to broaden their horizons and to prepare them for a successful future.

THE SCHOOL SAYS ". . ."

From the Admissions Office

"At Washington & Jefferson College, the entire community is devoted to ensuring student success. In the last three years, 100 percent of W&J graduates taking the Pennsylvania bar exam passed, and we regularly see admission rates of 90 percent for graduates headed to medical and law school. The College has added $100 million in new facilities since 2002, including residence halls, athletic facilities, a state-of-the-art technology center, the Burnett Center (housing accounting, business, economics, education, entrepreneurial studies, and modern languages), and the new Swanson Science Center (dedicated to the physical sciences, including physics, chemistry, biochemistry, and bioinformatics). Unique to W&J is the Magellan Project, providing stipends for innovative internships, research fellowships, and independent study-travel programs, domestic or international. Alumni mentors help students attain valuable internships and, upon graduation, assist with career placement. You dream it; we help make it happen. Our students are balanced, goal oriented, active, engaged, and involved, and we look for applicants who demonstrate these qualities in every stage of the admissions process. If you are a student who thrives on academic rigor, wants a close personal relationship with top-notch faculty, and values being a member of a true college community, we encourage you to consider W&J. Finally, W&J recommends but does not require scores from the SAT (or ACT). We will use the best scores from either test. The new version of the SAT (or the ACT with Writing section) is not required. And be sure to check out our new four-year Graduation Guarantee at washjeff.edu."

SELECTIVITY

Admissions Rating	**90**
# of applicants	6,643
% of applicants accepted	43
% of acceptees attending	14
# accepting a place on wait list	17
# admitted from wait list	2
# of early decision applicants	20
# accepted early decision	15

FRESHMAN PROFILE

Range SAT Critical Reading	510–610
Range SAT Math	530–615
Range ACT Composite	23–28
Minimum paper TOEFL	580
Minimum web-based TOEFL	85
Average HS GPA	3.3
% graduated top 10% of class	34
% graduated top 25% of class	65
% graduated top 50% of class	93

DEADLINES

Early decision	
Deadline	12/1
Notification	12/15
Early action	
Deadline	1/15
Notification	2/15
Regular	
Priority	1/15
Deadline	3/1
Nonfall registration?	yes

FINANCIAL FACTS

Financial Aid Rating	**72**
Annual tuition	$37,850
Room and board	$9,960
Required fees	$460
Books and supplies	$800
% needy frosh rec. need-based scholarship or grant aid	82
% needy UG rec. need-based scholarship or grant aid	83
% needy frosh rec. non-need-based scholarship or grant aid	94
% needy UG rec. non-need-based scholarship or grant aid	85
% needy frosh rec. need-based self-help aid	86
% needy UG rec. need-based self-help aid	88
% frosh rec. any financial aid	99
% UG rec. any financial aid	98
% UG borrow to pay for school	81
% frosh need fully met	19
% ugrads need fully met	18
Average % of frosh need met	78
Average % of ugrad need met	75

WASHINGTON STATE UNIVERSITY

PO BOX 641067, PULLMAN, WA 99164-1067 • ADMISSIONS: 509-335-5586 • FAX: 509-335-4902

CAMPUS LIFE

Quality of Life Rating	**80**
Fire Safety Rating	**76**
Green Rating	**88**
Type of school	public
Environment	town

STUDENTS

Total undergrad enrollment	22,421
% male/female	49/51
% from out of state	12
% from public high school	99
% frosh live on campus	94
# of fraternities	25
# of sororities	14
% African American	3
% Asian	5
% Caucasian	70
% Hispanic	8
% Native American	1
% international	4
# of countries represented	98

SURVEY SAYS . . .

Athletic facilities are great
Everyone loves the Cougars
Frats and sororities dominate social scene
Student publications are popular
Lots of beer drinking
Hard liquor is popular

ACADEMICS

Academic Rating	**68**
% students returning for sophomore year	84
% students graduating within 4 years	38
% students graduating within 6 years	67
Calendar	semester
Student/faculty ratio	16:1
Profs interesting rating	73
Profs accessible rating	81
Most classes have	20–29 students

MOST POPULAR MAJORS

business administration and management; communication, journalism, and related programs, other; social sciences

APPLICANTS ALSO LOOK AT AND OFTEN PREFER

Central Washington University, Eastern Washington University, University of Washington, Western Washington University

AND SOMETIMES PREFER

Gonzaga University, Oregon State University, Seattle University, University of Idaho, University of Oregon, University of Portland

AND RARELY PREFER

Pacific Lutheran University, Seattle Pacific University, Whitworth College

STUDENTS SAY ". . ."

Academics

From the moment you arrive on the campus of Washington State, you sense that the university is a "tight-knit community." In turn, this helps to foster a "friendly atmosphere" and "great spirit," both of which permeate the school. As one happy undergrad shares, "Washington State University became part of my family once I [set] foot on this campus. Every staff member is so nice and very welcoming. It is home away from home." Another student quickly adds, "I felt like WSU wanted me to attend their school. They called, they encouraged, they gave information, and checked frequently about any questions I had." Academically, Washington State excels in the sciences, especially with their pre-veterinary and animal sciences programs. Undergrads also like to highlight the fantastic communications department. When it comes to professors, WSU students think theirs are top-notch. Indeed, many find their teachers to be "passionate about their material and eager to pass on their knowledge to students." Moreover, they "treat students respectfully, avoid condescension, and create an environment where students are able to learn not just 'what' but 'how.'" Another aspect undergrads appreciate is that their professors really "try [and] make you think outside the box." Perhaps most important, they are "incredibly friendly and accessible." As one relieved student shares, "There was never a point when I felt I could not go to a professor for additional help." And a fellow undergrad succinctly states, "WSU is a place where you can live, laugh, and learn alongside some the best faculty and students in the world."

Life

Life at Washington State moves at a frenzied pace. Indeed, "Every weekend there is a free movie at our Student Union building. On campus there [are] always advertisements for fun events put on by various clubs. The Student Entertainment Board brings in comedians and musicians for low costs. There are also often educational and interesting lectures by accomplished professors or outside people. Many resident halls have board games for the residents to use as well as at least one TV lounge and often a pool table." Moreover, Cougar spirit is alive and well in this student body, and many undergrads love to go out and root for various WSU sports teams. "Football Saturdays are a campus wide event. There is nothing quite like freezing your butt off watching your team, good or not. There is also Beasly Coliseum to watch basketball and Bohler to watch volleyball." Certainly, it's an active campus in general. As one undergrad shares, "The Student Recreation center or rec is superb and many people can be seen there on a daily basis not only to work out but also to attend fitness classes." In addition, "There are [plenty of] intramural and club sports...that students can be a part of." Further, "When the weather is nice, outdoor activities are really popular: Eco-Adventure trips with the Outdoor Recreation Center...the Pullman-Moscow bike trail, a trip to the dunes or the cliffs, or just lying in the grass outside Thompson Hall!"

Student Body

When asked to describe their peers, undoubtedly the first word that comes to mind for most WSU students is "friendly." Indeed, these "easygoing" undergrads strive to cultivate a campus where "everyone is welcome." Perhaps it's easy to do that given that "there's no 'typical' student" here. One undergrad expounds, "The thing about WSU is that there is a niche for everyone—seriously. I was [pleasantly] surprised by how many international students [are here.] [What's more,] there are people from all different sexual orientations, backgrounds, and ethnicities." A fellow student continues, "You are bound to find groups of people that you fit in with, whether its long boarding, going to church, academic clubs, charity groups, Greek community, and the list goes on. WSU facilitates a greatly diverse community and provides excellent support to anyone who seeks it."

FINANCIAL AID: 509-335-9711 • E-MAIL: ADMISSIONS@WSU.EDU • WEBSITE: WWW.WSU.EDU

THE PRINCETON REVIEW SAYS

Admissions

Very important factors considered include: Academic GPA, standardized test scores. *Important factors considered include:* Application essay, rigor of secondary school record, grade trends. *Other factors considered include:* Recommendation(s), extracurricular activities, talent/ability, volunteer work, work experience. SAT or ACT required; ACT with or without writing compo nent accepted. English language proficiency required of all international applicants. High school diploma is required and GED is accepted. *Academic credits required (1 credit = 1 year):* 4 English, 3 mathematics (math in the senior year required), 2 world language, 3 social sciences, 2 lab sciences (1 algebra-based), 1 fine, visual, or performing arts, or 1 additional credit of academic elective. *Academic credits recommended (1 credit = 1 year):* 4 English, 4 mathematics (math in the senior year required), 2 world language, 3 social sciences, 2 lab sciences (1 algebra-based), 1 fine, visual, or performing arts, or 1 additional credit of academic elective.

Financial Aid

Students should submit: FAFSA. Priority filing deadline is February 15. The Princeton Review suggests that all financial aid forms be submitted as soon as possible after January 1. The scholarship application deadline is January 31 *Need-based scholarships/grants offered:* Federal Pell, SEOG, state scholarships/grants, private scholarships, the school's own gift aid, Federal Nursing Scholarships. *Loan aid offered:* Direct Subsidized Stafford, Direct Unsubsidized Stafford, Direct PLUS, Federal Perkins, Federal Nursing. Applicants will be notified of awards on a rolling basis begin ning April 15. Federal and state Work-Study Program available. Institutional employment available. Highest amount earned per year from on-campus jobs $18,199.25. Off-campus job opportunities are good.

The Inside Word

Admission to Washington State University requires successful completion of a college prep curriculum. In addition, the committee will consider standardized test scores and a personal statement. Applicants who are either in the top ten percent of their class or have a mini mum GPA of 3.5 are guaranteed admission. If you're a borderline candidate, use your personal statement (essay) to sell your self as someone who can contribute substantially to the campus community.

THE SCHOOL SAYS ". . ."

From the Admissions Office

"At Washington State University, you work side-by-side with nationally renowned faculty who help you succeed. Many academic programs rank among the nation's best. Programs are designed to give you real-world experience through internships, community service, in-depth labs, and study abroad experiences. Plus, many disciplines encourage you to participate in faculty research or conduct your own. If you have top grades and a passion for learning, the highly acclaimed Honors College challenges you with interdisciplinary studies, rich classroom discussions, and research opportunities.

"The campus forms the heart of a friendly college town where faculty and fellow students help you achieve your greatest potential. More than 300 campus organizations connect you with others who share your interests. Each year employers return to campus seeking WSU graduates. The university stands among the top twenty-five in the nation that best prepare students for workforce success (2010 Wall Street Journal survey). The main Pullman campus was named the safest among peers nationwide. WSU also has three non-residential urban campuses in Spokane, the Tri-Cities (Richland), and Vancouver.

"The priority date to apply for admission and the deadline to apply for scholarships is January 31. For your candidacy to be considered, you must complete the high school core curriculum and provide official scores from the SAT or ACT. We urge you to deliver a strong personal statement (essay). If you apply by January 31 and are among the top ten percent of your high school class or have at least a 3.5 GPA, you're assured admission."

SELECTIVITY

Admissions Rating	79
# of applicants	14,071
% of applicants accepted	82
% of acceptees attending	39

FRESHMAN PROFILE

Range SAT Critical Reading	470–580
Range SAT Math	480–600
Range SAT Writing	460–560
Range ACT Composite	20–26
Minimum paper TOEFL	550
Minimum web-based TOEFL	79
Average HS GPA	3.4
% graduated top 10% of class	26
% graduated top 25% of class	46
% graduated top 50% of class	78

DEADLINES

Regular	
Priority	1/31
Notification	11/1
Nonfall registration?	no

FINANCIAL FACTS

Financial Aid Rating	88
Annual in-state tuition	$11,386
Annual out-state tuition	$22,816
Room and board	$10,524
Required fees	$914
Books and supplies	$934
% needy frosh rec. need-based scholarship or grant aid	65
% needy UG rec. need-based scholarship or grant aid	68
% needy frosh rec. non-need-based scholarship or grant aid	59
% needy UG rec. non-need-based scholarship or grant aid	37
% needy frosh rec. need-based self-help aid	69
% needy UG rec. need-based self-help aid	79
% frosh rec. any financial aid	79
% UG rec. any financial aid	72
% UG borrow to pay for school	59
Average cumulative indebtedness	$22,686
% frosh need fully met	72
% ugrads need fully met	71
Average % of frosh need met	94
Average % of ugrad need met	93

WASHINGTON UNIVERSITY IN ST. LOUIS

CAMPUS BOX 1089, ST. LOUIS, MO 63130-4899 • ADMISSIONS: 314-935-6000 • FAX: 314-935-4290

CAMPUS LIFE

Quality of Life Rating	**99**
Fire Safety Rating	**86**
Green Rating	**94**
Type of school	private
Environment	city

STUDENTS

Total undergrad enrollment	6,658
% male/female	50/50
% from out of state	93
% from public high school	58
% frosh live on campus	99
# of fraternities	11
# of sororities	7
% African American	6
% Asian	15
% Caucasian	57
% Hispanic	5
% international	7
# of countries represented	84

SURVEY SAYS . . .

Lab facilities are great
School is well run
Students are friendly
Great food on campus
Great off-campus food
Dorms are like palaces

ACADEMICS

Academic Rating	**93**
% students returning for sophomore year	97
% students graduating within 4 years	86
% students graduating within 6 years	93
Calendar	semester
Student/faculty ratio	7:1
Profs interesting rating	86
Profs accessible rating	92
Most classes have	10–19 students
Most lab/discussion sessions have	10–19 students

MOST POPULAR MAJORS

biology/biological sciences; finance; psychology

APPLICANTS ALSO LOOK AT AND OFTEN PREFER

Harvard College, Stanford University, University of Pennsylvania, Yale University, Princeton University

AND SOMETIMES PREFER

Duke University, Northwestern University, University of Chicago, Cornell University, Rice University

AND RARELY PREFER

Tulane University, Tufts University, University of Michigan—Ann Arbor, Emory University

STUDENTS SAY ". . ."

Academics

Washington University "is a top-tier university" that "offers students an opportunity to explore interests in a number of areas both academically and extracurricularly" and, "manages to maintain core Midwestern values." As one student notes, "While it may not be as well known on the East Coast, it is a hidden gem in the Midwest, rich with great people, amazing extracurricular opportunities, an underrated city just down the street, and an education that will challenge you." "I was impressed by students' abilities to pursue academically rigorous classes, balance numerous activities, and still find time to spend at various campus events with friends." "Collaboration" over competition here "is key." Washington University "provides the education of an Ivy League university with the atmosphere and warmth of home." The co-curricular programs "are flexible enough to allow students to pursue academic interests in business, arts and sciences, art and architecture, and engineering all at once." Undergraduates "truly have the flexibility to study what you want: You can take any class offered in any college, double major or minor across colleges, or even get dual degrees." Professors "are engaged and lively." Their "passion for the subject is contagious for the student body." "Community is probably [Wash U's] greatest asset." "It's a very positive, vibrant environment."

Life

Wash U boasts "a beautiful campus" and "an active and friendly student body." Students are also "genuinely concerned about the city of St. Louis and actively participate in social justice measures." The food "is delicious," the dorms "are beautiful," and students "are happy." Be it "an intramural sport, organizing a charity event, Greek life, the radio station, or the new live sketch comedy show, every student takes part in non-academic activities that build friendships and make college life far more colorful." During their downtime, students "go to concerts, movies, the local mall, etc., for fun." The popular Delmar Loop is "just a ten-minute walk from main campus." Loaded with restaurants and small storefronts, "It's an extremely popular place for students to walk around, shop at small boutiques, and grab a bite to eat." Whether it's "seeing a show," "eating out on the Loop," "chilling with friends," or "watching a movie," "There is always something to do." "Thursdays, Fridays, and Saturdays are party night." Though some confess, "A lot of people drink on the weekends…the fraternities' parties are primarily open to all grades and are not exclusive," others say, "There is very little pressure for people to drink, even for students involved in Greek Life." Beyond campus parties and Greek life, there are "a ton of options for social events." Headline-grabbing events include "W.I.L.D.," "a huge all-day concert held in the quad with great musical performers." Other "big draws" include the "performances held on campus, such as Diwali, Carnival, Mr. WU, and Black Anthology, which are always sold out." Recently, "There has been a lot of programming in our student center, where we recently broke the world record for the largest nerf gun fight with more than 470 students participating."

Student Body

Students here quickly fall captive to the "positive atmosphere." "Everyone here is happy! Seriously, you'll always see smiles everywhere you go on campus." Students say there's not "a 'typical' student at Wash U…I guess the best way to describe students here is that they defy the typical stereotypes. You'll have a fraternity brother who's a dancer [or] a premed student who's minoring in architecture, etc." Students "embrace that their fellow classmates have their own interests, even picking up new hobbies from their friends." Wash U provides the backdrop for "a diverse set of social circles." "There are the suburban East-coasters, the liberal Texans, the local kids from St. Louis, the California jocks, etc." "The typical Wash U student graduated in the top two percent of her high school class, participated in at least four different clubs with an office in at least one (but probably two), was homecoming queen, and volunteered at an animal shelter on the weekends." Students here are "very involved and take both academics and extracurriculars (particularly community service) very seriously."

FINANCIAL AID: 888-547-6670 • E-MAIL: ADMISSIONS@WUSTL.EDU • WEBSITE: WUSTL.EDU

THE PRINCETON REVIEW SAYS

Admissions

Very important factors considered include: Academic GPA, application essay, class rank, recommendation(s), rigor of secondary school record, standardized test scores, character/personal qualities, extracurricular activities, talent/ability, vol unteer work, work experience. *Other factors considered include:* Alumni/ae relation, first generation, interview, level of applicant's interest, racial/ethnic status. SAT or ACT required; ACT with or without writing component accepted. TOEFL required of all international applicants. High school diploma is required, and GED is accepted. *Academic units recommended:* 4 English, 4 mathe matics, 4 science (4 science labs), 2 foreign language, 4 social studies, 4 history.

Financial Aid

Students should submit: FAFSA, CSS/Financial Aid PROFILE, non-custodial pro file, student and parent 1040 tax return or signed waiver, if there's no tax return. Regular filing deadline is February 1. The Princeton Review suggests that all financial aid forms be submitted as soon as possible after January 1. *Need-based scholarships/grants offered:* Federal Pell, SEOG, state scholarships/grants, private scholarships, school scholarship or grant aid from institutional funds. *Loan aid offered:* Direct Subsidized Stafford, Direct Unsubsidized Stafford, Direct PLUS, Federal Perkins, state loans, university loans from institutional funds. Applicants will be notified of awards on or about April 1. Federal Work-Study Program available. Institutional employment available. Off-campus job opportunities are excellent.

The Inside Word

The fact that Wash U doesn't have much play as a nationally respected car-window decal is about all that prevents it from being among the most selective universities. In every other respect—that is, in any way that really matters—this place is hard to beat and easily ranks as one of the best. No other university with as impressive a record of excellence across the board has a more accommodating admissions process. Not that it's easy to get in here, but lack of instant name recognition does affect Wash U's admission rate. Students with above-average academic records who aren't quite Ivy material are the big winners. Marginal candidates with high financial need may find difficulty; the admissions process at Wash U isn't need-blind and may take into account candidates' ability to pay if they're not strong applicants.

THE SCHOOL SAYS ". . ."

From the Admissions Office

"Washington University in St. Louis is a research university that offers a unique environment for undergraduate students to learn and grow. Unparalleled curriculum flexibility and learning opportunities in a friendly and supportive community inspire undergraduates to explore their interests and to develop new ones. Working with their advisors, undergraduates may choose a traditional single major, as many do. Others combine majors with minors, second majors, and pre-professional programs—all within their four-year undergraduate experience. We encourage our students to participate in internships, study abroad programs, research and scholarship, and more than 300 clubs and organizations, rounding out Washington University's commitment to help each student identify and pursue his or her passion. Our students pursue their passions every day. Visit campus and ask them about their experiences. As part of this commitment to help our students, Washington University is working to eliminate need-based loans as part of its undergraduate financial aid awards to students from low-income families. This new initiative and its goal of helping families with the most need will not lessen our desire, responsibility, or ability to work with all families to ensure they have the financial resources they need. We remain committed to a flexible and independent approach to delivering financial aid to those who need it most. Applicants are required to submit scores from either the SAT or ACT test. Applicants who submit scores from the ACT test may submit with or without the writing component."

SELECTIVITY	
Admissions Rating	**99**
# of applicants	28,823
% of applicants accepted	17
% of acceptees attending	31

FRESHMAN PROFILE	
Range SAT Critical Reading	690–760
Range SAT Math	710–780
Range ACT Composite	32–34
% graduated top 10% of class	96
% graduated top 25% of class	100
% graduated top 50% of class	100

DEADLINES	
Early decision	
Deadline	11/15
Notification	12/15
Regular	
Deadline	1/15
Notification	4/1
Nonfall registration?	no

FINANCIAL FACTS	
Financial Aid Rating	**97**
Annual tuition	$42,500
Room and board	$13,580
Required fees	$1,205
Books and supplies	$1,110
% needy frosh rec. need-based scholarship or grant aid	91
% needy UG rec. need-based scholarship or grant aid	95
% needy frosh rec. non-need-based scholarship or grant aid	10
% needy UG rec. non-need-based scholarship or grant aid	6
% needy frosh rec. need-based self-help aid	74
% needy UG rec. need-based self-help aid	69
% frosh rec. any financial aid	38
% UG rec. any financial aid	39
% UG borrow to pay for school	36
% frosh need fully met	97
% ugrads need fully met	99
Average % of frosh need met	100
Average % of ugrad need met	100

WEBB INSTITUTE

298 Crescent Beach Road, Glen Cove, NY 11542 • Admissions: 516-671-2213, ext. 107 • Fax: 516-674-9838

CAMPUS LIFE

Quality of Life Rating	**88**
Fire Safety Rating	**67**
Green Rating	**60***
Type of school	private
Environment	village

STUDENTS

Total undergrad enrollment	81
% male/female	84/16
% from out of state	68
% from public high school	91
% frosh live on campus	100
% Asian	9
% Caucasian	36
% Hispanic	3

SURVEY SAYS . . .

Registration is a breeze
Career services are great
Different types of students interact
Dorms are like palaces
Frats and sororities are unpopular or nonexistent
Student government is popular
Political activism is unpopular or nonexistent
Very little drug use

ACADEMICS

Academic Rating	**92**
% students returning for sophomore year	83
% students graduating within 4 years	80
% students graduating within 6 years	80
Calendar	semester
Student/faculty ratio	7:1
Profs interesting rating	84
Profs accessible rating	94
Most classes have	20–29 students

APPLICANTS ALSO LOOK AT AND OFTEN PREFER

United States Coast Guard Academy, United States Naval Academy, University of Michigan—Ann Arbor

AND SOMETIMES PREFER

The Cooper Union for the Advancement of Science and Art, Virginia Tech

STUDENTS SAY ". . ."

Academics

Webb Institute on Long Island is a very small school that focuses on the complex field of ship design engineering. If you feel destined to become one of "America's future ship designers and engineers," enroll here. Every student receives a four-year, full-tuition scholarship. The only costs are books and supplies, Room and board, and personal expenses. Everyone majors in naval architecture and marine engineering, although non-engineering electives are available to juniors and seniors. Webbies are exposed to a smattering of the liberal arts and a ton of advanced math and physics. Virtually every other course involves ship design. There's also a senior thesis and a "required internship program." In January and February, all students get real, paying jobs in the marine industry. Job prospects are phenomenal. Newly minted Webb graduates enjoy "a 100 percent placement rate in grad schools and careers." Coursework is "rigorous," but the academic atmosphere is very intimate. "A huge plus of Webb's small size is that everyone knows everyone," relates a junior. "You're not just another number." "The administration, professors, and students all work in the same building every day, every week." "The [President] can get carried away when he perceives a problem," but the faculty is "approachable," "always accessible," and "very dedicated to the school and students." "Professors have a great deal of respect for the students and work closely with us to accomplish our goals," says a sophomore. "If you're passionate about architecture and engineering, you cannot hope for a better learning environment."

Life

Webb has a "family-like atmosphere." It's "a tiny student body living, eating, sleeping, and learning ship design in a mansion" "in a residential area overlooking the beautiful Long Island Sound." There's an honor code "that is strictly adhered to by all students." Cheating and stealing just don't happen here. "You can leave your wallet lying in the reception room, and if someone doesn't return it to you just because they know what your wallet looks like compared to the other 90 wallets in the school, it will still be there the next day and even the next week." Life at Webb "revolves around course load and the attempts to find distractions from it." "We average about five to seven hours of homework per night," advises a freshman. At the end of the semesters, life [can get crazy] due to a ton of projects." "People generally think about homework and spend most of their time discussing class assignments." When students find some down time, movies and unorganized sports are common. Not surprisingly, "many people turn to the water" for amusement as well. "Sailing is popular." "The school has a skiff and sailboats, which are frequently used during the warm months," says a sophomore. Annual whitewater rafting and ski trips are well attended. New York City is a little less than an hour away, and "a bunch of people venture into" Manhattan on the weekends. "A lot of spontaneous and off-the-wall things occur" too, and "a fair amount of partying goes on at least once a week."

Student Body

The average Webbie is a "middle-class, white male who enjoys engineering and sciences." "Everyone is motivated and works hard." Basically, you have your bookworms who "don't socialize as much" and your more social students who get their work done but also play sports and "have a good time." Camaraderie is reportedly easy due to the academic stress and Webb's small size. Everyone interacts with everyone else, regardless of background. With fewer than 100 students, it's "impossible to completely isolate yourself." "There are no social cliques, and everyone is included in anything they'd like to be included in." As at most engineering schools, the ratio between males and females is pretty severely lopsided here. "We want more women!" plead many students.

FINANCIAL AID: 516-671-2213 • E-MAIL: ADMISSIONS@WEBB-INSTITUTE.EDU • WEBSITE: WWW.WEBB-INSTITUTE.EDU

THE PRINCETON REVIEW SAYS

Admissions

Very important factors considered include: Class rank, academic GPA, rigor of secondary school record, standardized test scores, character/personal qualities, interview, level of applicant's interest. *Important factors considered include:* Recommendation(s), extracurricular activities. *Other factors considered include:* Talent/ability, volunteer work, work experience. ACT with writing component required. High school diploma is required and GED is not accepted. *Academic units required:* 4 English, 4 mathematics, 2 science (2 science labs), 2 social studies, 4 academic electives.

Financial Aid

Students should submit: FAFSA. The Princeton Review suggests that all financial aid forms be submitted as soon as possible after January 1. *Need-based scholarships/grants offered:* Federal Pell, state scholarships/grants, private scholarships, the school's own gift aid. *Loan aid offered:* Direct Subsidized Stafford, Direct Unsubsidized Stafford, Direct PLUS. Applicants will be notified of awards on or about August 1. Off-campus job opportunities are fair.

The Inside Word

Let's not mince words; admission to Webb is mega-tough. Webb's Admissions Counselors are out to find the right kid for their curriculum—one that can survive the school's rigorous academics. The applicant pool is highly self-selected because of the focused program of study: naval architecture and marine engineering.

THE SCHOOL SAYS ". . ."

From the Admissions Office

"Webb, the only college in the country that specializes in the engineering field of naval architecture and marine engineering, seeks young men and women of all races from all over the country who are interested in receiving an excellent engineering education with a full-tuition scholarship. Students don't have to know anything about ships, they just have to be motivated to study how mechanical, civil, structural, and electrical engineering come together with the design elements that make up a ship and all its systems. Being small and private has its major advantages. Every applicant is special and the President will interview all entering students personally. The student/faculty ratio is eight to one, and since there are no teaching assistants, interaction with the faculty occurs daily in class and labs at a level not found at most other colleges. The entire campus operates under the Student Organization's honor system that allows unsupervised exams and twenty-four-hour access to the library, every classroom and laboratory, and the shop and gymnasium. Despite a total enrollment of between eighty-five and ninety students and a demanding workload, Webb manages to field five intercollegiate teams. Currently more than sixty percent of the members of the student body play on one or more intercollegiate teams. Work hard, play hard and the payoff is a job for every student upon graduation. The placement record of the college is 100 percent every year.

"Freshman applicants must take the SAT. We also require scores from two SAT Subject Tests: Math Level I or II and either physics or chemistry."

SELECTIVITY	
Admissions Rating	**97**
# of applicants	73
% of applicants accepted	34
% of acceptees attending	81
# of early decision applicants	6
# accepted early decision	6

FRESHMAN PROFILE	
Range SAT Critical Reading	630–740
Range SAT Math	700–770
Range SAT Writing	620–730
Average HS GPA	4.0
% graduated top 10% of class	64
% graduated top 25% of class	100
% graduated top 50% of class	100

DEADLINES	
Early decision	
Deadline	10/15
Notification	12/15
Regular	
Deadline	2/15
Notification	4/15
Nonfall registration?	no

FINANCIAL FACTS	
Financial Aid Rating	**80**
Annual tuition	$0
Room and board	$12,480
Books and supplies	$950
% needy frosh rec. need-based scholarship or grant aid	100
% needy UG rec. need-based scholarship or grant aid	100
% frosh rec. any financial aid	17
% UG rec. any financial aid	25
% UG borrow to pay for school	15
Average cumulative indebtedness	$3,500
% frosh need fully met	67
% ugrads need fully met	35
Average % of frosh need met	75
Average % of ugrad need met	75

WELLESLEY COLLEGE

BOARD OF ADMISSION, WELLESLEY, MA 02481-8203 • ADMISSIONS: 781-283-2270 • FAX: 781-283-3678

CAMPUS LIFE

Quality of Life Rating	**92**
Fire Safety Rating	**80**
Green Rating	**84**
Type of school	private
Environment	town

STUDENTS

Total undergrad enrollment	2,367
% male/female	0/100
% from out of state	86
% from public high school	59
% frosh live on campus	100
% African American	7
% Asian	22
% Caucasian	43
% Hispanic	7
% international	11
# of countries represented	83

SURVEY SAYS . . .

No one cheats
Lab facilities are great
Great computer facilities
School is well run
Diverse student types on campus
Dorms are like palaces
Campus feels safe
Frats and sororities are unpopular or nonexistent
Student government is popular
Political activism is popular

ACADEMICS

Academic Rating	**97**
% students returning for sophomore year	95
% students graduating within 4 years	86
% students graduating within 6 years	92
Calendar	semester
Student/faculty ratio	8:1
Profs interesting rating	99
Profs accessible rating	98
Most classes have	10–19 students
Most lab/discussion sessions have	10–19 students

MOST POPULAR MAJORS

economics; political science and government; psychology

APPLICANTS ALSO LOOK AT AND OFTEN PREFER

Brown University, Princeton University, Harvard College

AND SOMETIMES PREFER

Cornell University, Duke University, Georgetown University, New York University, Washington University in St. Louis, Middlebury College, University of Chicago, Wesleyan University

AND RARELY PREFER

University of California—Berkeley, University of California—Los Angeles, Mount Holyoke College

STUDENTS SAY ". . ."

Academics

This "rigorous" all-womens' school in Massachusetts is one of the most selective liberal arts schools in the country, boasting notable alumnae such as Madeline Albright, Nora Ephron, and Hillary Rodham Clinton. Since Wellesley is all about "supporting women who will run the world," students are "very well taken care of here," finding themselves part of "a great community that encourages and frees women to find their inner strength." Coupled with "amazing financial aid" and study abroad opportunities, the college "is a supportive, engaging, and downright fun community." The "vibrant," "worldly, interesting" professors here are "top-of-the-line," and "They know so much about their fields [that] an A paper is hard to come by." Students embrace the fact that "they expect a lot from us"; such an atmosphere may not allow for slack classes, but "It does allow for an impressive amount of growth." These "masters of their fields" offer "an immense amount of resources and time" to their students, and "Class lectures combine the perfect balance of lecture and discussion to keep them engaging." "If I am not in class, my professors will notice and care to make sure I am doing all right," says one student. Faculty members are also very open to having students help with their research. "My name will be published alongside the professor for whom I worked in her next book!" says one. Alumnae stick together, and Wellesley's support system and alumnae network "guarantee you a top spot in places you are interested in, or at least some guidance on how to get in there." There is plenty of help and resources available to students from the administration (such as "tons of grants, academic/health advising"), as well as the ability to cross register with MIT, Babson, and Olin, giving students access to a "rich array of courses" and classmates.

Life

The town of Wellesley is "cute, but there's nothing to do after 6:00 P.M." No matter what kind of scene you're into, most students "like to get off the Wellesley campus on the weekend, if not for partying then just for sanity." Many Wellesley women "enjoy going to parties at local coed schools like MIT, Harvard, Babson, and Olin"; going into Boston to "escape the intensity of the campus" (there is a bus that runs, though not as frequently as some would like) is also a great way to relax, see a movie, or grab a bite. If students decide to stay on campus, "Organizations are really great about throwing engaging events, bringing off-campus speakers, and creating a fun environment close to home." Wellesley women love to "meet over food and discuss everything under the sun." A typical activity/discussion cycle runs as such: "class work, homework, midterms, politics, the future of the country, the environment, going to MIT to party, going to Harvard to party, music, social construction of gender, you name it." People "actually do a lot of academic things" for fun here, mostly involving extracurricular clubs that explore their interests.

Student Body

Students are "very intense and motivated" at Wellesley, but at the same time remain "passionate, active, and intelligent women." The term used on campus is "Wendy Wellesley," which is someone "who is on top of all their class work plus some extra material, is concerned with the world, has extreme (almost impossible) ambition, and can interact with people in an extremely thoughtful and confident manner." It can be "competitive" here, but "There is a strong belief in women's rights, which comes with women's college territory." "Students are stressed constantly, but mainly because they stress themselves out," says one woman of her "type-A, very hardworking, perfectionist" fellow students. Still, "Students here really accept each other for all their quirks." The common denominator among all Wellesley students is that "we all strive to do our best and have a greater vision for the world beyond Wellesley."

FINANCIAL AID: 781-283-2360 • E-MAIL: ADMISSION@WELLESLEY.EDU • WEBSITE: WWW.WELLESLEY.EDU

THE PRINCETON REVIEW SAYS

Admissions

Very important factors considered include: Application essay, academic GPA, recommendation(s), rigor of secondary school record, standardized test scores, character/personal qualities. *Important factors considered include:* Class rank, extracurricular activities. *Other factors considered include:* Alumni/ae relation, first generation, geographical residence, interview, level of applicant's interest, racial/ethnic status, state residency, talent/ability, volunteer work, work experience. SAT or ACT required. High school diploma is not required. *Academic units recommended:* 4 English, 4 mathematics, 3 science (2 science labs), 4 foreign language, 4 social studies, 4 history.

Financial Aid

Students should submit: FAFSA, CSS/Financial Aid PROFILE, noncustodial PROFILE, business/farm supplement, business taxes, if applicable. Regular filing deadline is January 15. The Princeton Review suggests that all financial aid forms be submitted as soon as possible after January 1. *Need-based scholarships/grants offered:* Federal Pell, SEOG, state scholarships/grants, private scholarships, the school's own gift aid, ACG Grant and SMART Grant. *Loan aid offered:* Direct Subsidized Stafford, Direct Unsubsidized Stafford, Direct PLUS, Federal Perkins, state loans, college/university loans from institutional funds. Applicants will be notified of awards on or about April 1. Federal Work-Study Program available. Institutional employment available. Off-campus job opportunities are excellent.

The Inside Word

When making an admissions decision, Wellesley considers a broad range of factors, including a student's academic record, the difficulty of her high school curriculum, participation in extracurricular activities, class rank, recommendations, personal essay, standardized test scores, leadership, and special talents (students may submit art, music, or theater supplements along with their applications). Personal interviews are highly recommended, but not required, though they can be a useful way to help you stand out in Wellesley's extraordinary applicant pool.

THE SCHOOL SAYS ". . ."

From the Admissions Office

"Widely acknowledged as the nation's best women's college, Wellesley College provides students with numerous opportunities on campus and beyond. With a long-standing commitment to and established reputation for academic excellence, Wellesley offers more than 1,000 courses in fifty-four established majors and supports 180 clubs, organizations, and activities for its students. The college is easily accessible to Boston, a great city in which to meet other college students and to experience theater, art, sports, and entertainment. Considered one of the most diverse colleges in the nation, Wellesley students hail from seventy countries and all fifty states.

"As a community, we are looking for students who possess intellectual curiosity: the ability to think independently, ask challenging questions, and grapple with answers. Strong candidates demonstrate both academic achievement and an excitement for learning. They also display leadership, an appreciation for diverse perspectives, and an understanding of the college's mission to educate women who will make a difference in the world.

"The SAT and two SAT Subject Tests or ACT with writing component are required. We strongly recommend that students planning to apply early decision complete the tests before the end of their junior year and no later than October of their senior year."

SELECTIVITY	
Admissions Rating	97
# of applicants	4,400
% of applicants accepted	31
% of acceptees attending	42
# accepting a place on wait list	551
# admitted from wait list	87
# of early decision applicants	275
# accepted early decision	124

FRESHMAN PROFILE	
Range SAT Critical Reading	650–740
Range SAT Math	640–750
Range SAT Writing	660–750
Range ACT Composite	29–32
% graduated top 10% of class	78
% graduated top 25% of class	93
% graduated top 50% of class	100

DEADLINES	
Early decision	
Deadline	11/1
Notification	12/15
Regular	
Deadline	1/15
Notification	4/1
Nonfall registration?	yes

FINANCIAL FACTS	
Financial Aid Rating	98
Annual tuition	$39,420
Room and board	$12,284
Required fees	$246
Books and supplies	$800
% needy frosh rec. need-based scholarship or grant aid	96
% needy UG rec. need-based scholarship or grant aid	97
% needy frosh rec. need-based self-help aid	90
% needy UG rec. need-based self-help aid	92
% frosh rec. any financial aid	56
% UG rec. any financial aid	59
% UG borrow to pay for school	52
Average cumulative indebtedness	$13,579
% frosh need fully met	100
% ugrads need fully met	100
Average % of frosh need met	100
Average % of ugrad need met	100

WELLS COLLEGE

ROUTE 90, AURORA, NY 13026 • ADMISSIONS: 315-364-3264 • FAX: 315-364-3227

CAMPUS LIFE

Quality of Life Rating	67
Fire Safety Rating	79
Green Rating	71
Type of school	private
Environment	rural

STUDENTS

Total undergrad enrollment	552
% male/female	29/71
% from out of state	36
% from public high school	88
% frosh live on campus	98
% African American	6
% Asian	2
% Caucasian	67
% Hispanic	4
% Native American	1
% international	2
# of countries represented	13

SURVEY SAYS . . .

No one cheats
Lousy food on campus
Low cost of living
Frats and sororities are unpopular or nonexistent
Musical organizations are popular
Very little drug use
Internships are widely available

ACADEMICS

Academic Rating	84
% students graduating within 4 years	53
% students graduating within 6 years	51
Calendar	semester
Student/faculty ratio	10:1
Profs interesting rating	90
Profs accessible rating	79
Most classes have	10–19 students

MOST POPULAR MAJORS

English language and literature; molecular biology; psychology

APPLICANTS ALSO LOOK AT AND OFTEN PREFER

Smith College, Mount Holyoke College, Hobart and William Smith Colleges

AND SOMETIMES PREFER

Alfred University, State University of New York at Binghamton, State University of New York at Geneseo, Syracuse University, Bryn Mawr College, Colgate University, Ithaca College, Hamilton College

STUDENTS SAY ". . ."

Academics

Located in a beautiful area close to Ithaca, New York, Wells College has the availability of a larger college town without being directly in a largely populated area. The emphasis is on community, offering an outstanding classroom experience and innovative liberal arts curriculum that prepares students for leadership in a variety of fields. One student shares, "Even professors who are very busy with other academic work make time for students. Classroom discussion is always encouraged, and most professors seem to genuinely value students' opinions, concerns, and experiences." "I love my professors, and I love my classes. They can be challenging, but it's the best sort of challenge." Another student adds, "The professors here know you by name, and they know your strengths and weaknesses well enough to push you in all the right ways. They care about making your educational experience truly be your educational experience, not their own, and they care more about your personal growth than about the grade you get on their exam." A current student adds, "The campus community is great. It's a very safe, comfortable atmosphere, and the small size means no student is going to slip through the cracks." Most students appreciate the small-school environment, as this junior affirms; "I can get to know my professors one on and one and don't have to be just another number to them." Another student agrees, "Professors are great; they're approachable, engaging, and truly do care about the students' education. I am encouraged to explore and learn and expand my horizons."

Life

Aurora is a small town on Lake Cayuga in New York State. "When it's hot, we go swimming in the lake, and that's always fun. We sometimes go sailing, or we go for a drive to any of the hundreds of tiny museums, antique stores, and small wineries in the area. In the winter, we go sledding down the big hill that leads to the athletic center. It's a picturesque existence." Transportation can sometimes be an issue, but students know they don't have to get off campus to have fun, as this student tells us: "Occasionally, we get off campus to bigger towns for fun. Our school is definitely more education-based, but we know how to have fun in our own way." At Wells, students will find a community rich with traditions. One junior reveals, "The traditions on campus are superior and amazing!" In turn, they foster "a great sense of community." Another student shares, "We participate in silly contests and traditions and love every second of it! I participated in the May Day Dance in my freshman year, and I get dressed up and sing my heart out for Odd/Even every year!" Overall when asked why Wells is a good choice, one student tells us, "I received a good scholarship, I found the traditions fascinating, and I loved the level of academic engagement that I saw from sitting in on classes as a prospective student."

Student Body

Wells transitioned to a coed college in 2005, but the school has overcome any growing pains." This can partly be attributed to the fact the college "has a strong emphasis on community." Students say, "Everyone is important and has a place here." Another student adds, "Wells seems to attract friendly, eccentric people who are socially and politically conscious, academic-minded, and tolerant. It doesn't matter if you're a student, professor, or a member of the cleaning crew—we're all learning together, and not matter what happens, we've got each other's backs." In essence, Wells provides a community of learning with "great student diversity, everyone has their own unique traits, but above all, everyone is accepted." One sophomore sums it up nicely, stating, "The typical student is a focused, engaged student who enjoys learning and works hard. Students at Wells find themselves bonding over their similar interests, and they treat each other like family."

FINANCIAL AID: 315-364-3289 • E-MAIL: ADMISSIONS@WELLS.EDU • WEBSITE: WWW.WELLS.EDU

THE PRINCETON REVIEW SAYS

Admissions

Very important factors considered include: Academic GPA, recommendation(s), rigor of secondary school record, standardized test scores, extracurricular activities. *Important factors considered include:* Application essay, interview. *Other factors considered include:* Class rank, alumnae relation, character/personal qualities, level of applicant's interest, talent/ability, volunteer work, work experience. SAT or ACT required; ACT with or without writing component accepted. TOEFL required of all international applicants. High school diploma is required and GED is accepted. *Academic units required:* 4 English, 3 mathematics, 2 science (2 science labs), 1 social studies, 3 history, 2 academic electives. *Academic units recommended:* 4 mathematics, 3 science (3 science labs), 2 foreign language, 2 social studies, 2 history, 3 academic electives, 2 music, art, computer science.

Financial Aid

Students should submit: FAFSA, CSS/Financial Aid Profile for early decision applicants only. Regular filing deadline is June 3. The Princeton Review suggests that all financial aid forms be submitted as soon as possible after January 1. *Need-based scholarships/grants offered:* Federal Pell, SEOG, state scholarships/grants, private scholarships, the school's own gift aid. *Loan aid offered:* Direct Subsidized Stafford, Direct Unsubsidized Stafford, Direct PLUS, Federal Perkins. Applicants will be notified of awards on a rolling basis beginning March 1. Federal Work-Study Program available. Institutional employment available. Highest amount earned per year from on-campus jobs $1,600. Off-campus job opportunities are poor.

The Inside Word

Wells is engaged in that age-old admissions game called matchmaking. There are no minimums or cutoffs in the admissions process here. But don't be fooled by the high admit rate. The admissions committee will look closely at your academic accomplishments. However, they will also give attention to your essay, recommendations, and extracurricular pursuits. The committee also recommends an interview; we suggest taking them up on it.

THE SCHOOL SAYS ". . ."

From the Admissions Office

"Wells College believes the twenty-first century needs well-educated individuals with the ability, self-confidence, and vision to contribute to an ever-changing world. Wells offers an outstanding classroom experience and innovative liberal arts curriculum that prepares students for leadership in a variety of fields, including business, government, the arts, sciences, medicine, and education. By directly connecting the liberal arts curriculum to experience and career development through internships, off-campus study, study abroad, research with professors, and community service, each student has an ideal preparation for graduate and professional school as well as for the twenty-first century."

SELECTIVITY

Admissions Rating	82
# of applicants	1,673
% of applicants accepted	71
% of acceptees attending	12
# accepting a place on wait list	56
# admitted from wait list	57
# of early decision applicants	15
# accepted early decision	4

FRESHMAN PROFILE

Range SAT Critical Reading	500–630
Range SAT Math	480–600
Range SAT Writing	480–590
Range ACT Composite	22–27
Minimum paper TOEFL	550
Average HS GPA	3.5
% graduated top 10% of class	31
% graduated top 25% of class	65
% graduated top 50% of class	91

DEADLINES

Early decision	
Deadline	12/15
Notification	1/15
Early action	
Deadline	12/15
Notification	2/1
Regular	
Priority	12/15
Deadline	3/1
Notification	4/1
Nonfall registration?	yes

FINANCIAL FACTS

Financial Aid Rating	75
Annual tuition	$33,200
Room and board	$11,900
Required fees	$1,500
Books and supplies	$800
% needy frosh rec. need-based scholarship or grant aid	93
% needy UG rec. need-based scholarship or grant aid	93
% needy frosh rec. non-need-based scholarship or grant aid	13
% needy UG rec. non-need-based scholarship or grant aid	15
% needy frosh rec. need-based self-help aid	75
% needy UG rec. need-based self-help aid	69
% frosh rec. any financial aid	96
% UG rec. any financial aid	95
% UG borrow to pay for school	90
Average cumulative indebtedness	$26,207
% frosh need fully met	13
% ugrads need fully met	15
Average % of frosh need met	75
Average % of ugrad need met	78

Wesleyan College

4760 Forsyth Road, Macon, GA 31210-4462 • Admissions: 478-477-1110 • Fax: 478-757-4030

CAMPUS LIFE

Quality of Life Rating	80
Fire Safety Rating	79
Green Rating	82
Type of school	private
Affiliation	Methodist
Environment	city

STUDENTS

Total undergrad enrollment	630
% male/female	0/100
% from out of state	9
% from public high school	81
% frosh live on campus	90
% African American	15
% Asian	1
% Caucasian	24
% Hispanic	2
% international	10
# of countries represented	21

SURVEY SAYS . . .

Lab facilities are great
Diverse student types on campus
Low cost of living
Very little drug use

ACADEMICS

Academic Rating	91
% students returning for sophomore year	78
% students graduating within 4 years	51
% students graduating within 6 years	1
Calendar	semester
Student/faculty ratio	8:1
Profs interesting rating	90
Profs accessible rating	80
Most classes have	10–19 students

MOST POPULAR MAJORS

business administration, management and operations, other; international business/trade/commerce; psychology

APPLICANTS ALSO LOOK AT AND OFTEN PREFER

Mercer University

AND SOMETIMES PREFER

University of Georgia, Emory University, Mercer University, Agnes Scott College

AND RARELY PREFER

Florida State University, University of Florida, Rhodes College

STUDENTS SAY ". . ."

Academics

To many of its students, the words "sisterhood" and "tradition" are synonymous with Wesleyan College. Founded in 1836, Wesleyan "was the first college to offer degrees to women." This private women's college located in Macon, Georgia, is "all about community, academics, and faith." Students say, "Everyone develops into a big family." Although this "diverse college full of brilliant women [is] devoted to sisterhood and tradition," it still manages to "[balance] more modern ideas and practices." Students compliment the "academic rigor, supportive atmosphere, diverse student body, nice facilities, and excellent classroom environment." Professors and academics receive the most praise. "Professors are definitely the best part of Wesleyan. [They are] totally dedicated and engaging." With hardly a negative word against them on student surveys, these "excellent," "open-minded" professors teach "challenging" material, and although they tend to be "strict," they are also "nice" and "encourage critical thinking and looking at things from different perspectives." "The professors here actually care about you, so don't be surprised when you receive an e-mail asking why you were not in class the previous day!" Classes may be "challenging" but "The academic experience is worth the cost of tuition." "The atmosphere is very uplifting and supportive," and students ensure, "There is no failing unless you absolutely, positively strive to fail."

Life

Life at Wesleyan College is not one big party. Students are "very studious and competitive in the classroom." "Everyone came here to get a good education, and that's what drives most of us here." The campus is dry. If you stay on campus, "You have to make your own fun. Alcohol is not permitted whether you're twenty-one or not." Although some may complain, "There's nothing to do on campus," others like that "it is small and quiet, a good place to study without all the distractions." "Students are usually very busy with classes and most are involved with some kind of school club/organization, so people don't typically spend a lot of time off campus." "If on-campus facilities are closed—the gym, athletic building, barn, science or music building, academic center, etc.—then there are plenty of off-campus facilities, usually within walking distance." "The Macon area has many clubs in it so a lot of girls gather up large groups and hit the town on the weekends. There is a movie theatre five minutes up the road that plays all the latest movies." Although the campus "has lots of trees and good places to take walks," some students would like to see a few improvements. "Upgrades to buildings need to be done," and "The food (has improved drastically) but we need more [vegetarian and health] options."

Student Body

Students at Wesleyan "are all very different from places all over the world." "The great international population leads to diverse religious, ethnic, and cultural backgrounds." They are different "in terms of political views, religious affiliation, and sexual orientation," and they are "opinionated." Some are "young and vibrant ready to tackle the world, while some are older ladies with children and jobs but [all] take pride in their education." What ties these students together is academics, sisterhood, and honor code. "The sisterhood program is an amazing tool that helps those who need a support system." "By being assigned a big sister, we have an easier way of adjusting and meeting new people." "There are sisterhood pep rallies every two months, which unite the school as a whole." Unity is important at an all-women school. As noted by one student, "We are all female, so we bump heads occasionally." Due to all the positive comments on student surveys, most would probably echo this comment of a fellow student: "I have had an amazing four years here, and I don't want to leave!"

FINANCIAL AID: 478-757-5205 • E-MAIL: ADMISSION@WESLEYANCOLLEGE.EDU • WEBSITE: WWW.WESLEYANCOLLEGE.EDU

THE PRINCETON REVIEW SAYS

Admissions

Very important factors considered include: Rigor of secondary school record. *Important factors considered include:* Academic GPA, class rank, recommendation(s), standardized test scores, extracurricular activities, interview, talent/ability. *Other factors considered include:* Application essay, alumni/ae relation, level of applicant's interest, volunteer work, work experience. SAT or ACT required; ACT with or without writing component accepted. TOEFL required of all international applicants. High school diploma is required and GED is accepted. *Academic units required:* 4 English, 3 mathematics, 3 science (2 science labs), 2 foreign language, 3 social studies. *Academic units recommended:* 4 English, 4 mathematics, 4 science (3 science labs), 4 foreign language, 4 social studies, 2 academic electives.

Financial Aid

Students should submit: FAFSA, institution's own financial aid form. Regular filing deadline is June 3. The Princeton Review suggests that all financial aid forms be submitted as soon as possible after January 1. *Need-based scholarships/grants offered:* Federal Pell, SEOG, state scholarships/grants, private scholarships, school scholarship or grant aid from institutional funds. *Loan aid offered:* Direct Subsidized Stafford, Direct Unsubsidized Stafford, Direct PLUS, Federal Perkins, state loans, university loans from institutional funds. Applicants will be notified of awards on a rolling basis beginning March 1. Off-campus job opportunities are good.

The Inside Word

Wesleyan College values diversity. At this small college, you'll find students from more than twenty countries and twenty-one states, with a wide range of interests. To evaluate a student's qualitative characteristics, Wesleyan recom mends that applicants submit a teacher recommendation and have a personal interview with the admissions staff (though neither is required). Students are also encouraged to submit samples of their creative work, such as poetry, music, or research projects.

THE SCHOOL SAYS ". . ."

From the Admissions Office

"Mention the term 'women's college' and most people envision ivy-covered towers in the Northeastern U.S. However, Wesleyan College in Macon, Georgia was founded in 1836 as the first college in the world chartered to grant degrees to women. Today it is recognized as one of the nation's most diverse and affordable selective four-year liberal arts colleges. Students value the college's tradition of service and rigorous academic program renowned for its quality. An exceptional faculty teaches classes in seminar style. A student/faculty ratio of ten to one ensures that students are known by more than just a grade or a number. The acceptance rate of Wesleyan students into medical, law, business, and other graduate programs is exemplary. Undergraduate degrees are offered in thirty-two majors and twenty-nine minors including self-designed majors and interdisciplinary programs, plus eight pre-professional programs that include seminary, engineering, medicine, pharmacy, veterinary medicine, health sciences, dental, and law. A $12.5 million science center added to the college's offerings for 2007. Master of Education and an accelerated Executive Master of Business Administration program enroll both men and women.

"Beyond the academic, Wesleyan offers a thriving residence life program, NCAA Division III athletics, championship IHSA equestrian program, and meaningful opportunities for community involvement and leadership. The college's beautiful 200-acre wooded campus, along with thirty historically significant buildings, is listed in the National Register of Historic Places as the Wesleyan College Historic District. Wesleyan is nestled in a northern suburb of Macon, the third largest city in the state. First-year applicants must take either the SAT or ACT."

SELECTIVITY	
Admissions Rating	**89**
# of applicants	516
% of applicants accepted	40
% of acceptees attending	50

FRESHMAN PROFILE	
Range SAT Critical Reading	420–660
Range SAT Math	400–610
Range ACT Composite	18–25
Minimum paper TOEFL	550
Minimum web-based TOEFL	80

DEADLINES	
Early decision	
Deadline	11/15
Notification	12/15
Early action	
Deadline	2/15
Notification	3/15
Regular	
Priority	3/1
Deadline	6/1
Nonfall registration?	yes

FINANCIAL FACTS	
Financial Aid Rating	**83**
Annual tuition	$19,000
Room and board	$8,200
Books and supplies	$1,500
% needy frosh rec. need-based scholarship or grant aid	100
% needy UG rec. need-based scholarship or grant aid	99
% needy frosh rec. non-need-based scholarship or grant aid	21
% needy UG rec. non-need-based scholarship or grant aid	19
% needy frosh rec. need-based self-help aid	77
% needy UG rec. need-based self-help aid	81
% frosh rec. any financial aid	100
% UG rec. any financial aid	99
% UG borrow to pay for school	72
Average cumulative indebtedness	$29,480
% frosh need fully met	22
% ugrads need fully met	19
Average % of frosh need met	80
Average % of ugrad need met	74

WESLEYAN UNIVERSITY

70 WYLLYS AVENUE, MIDDLETOWN, CT 06459-0265 • ADMISSIONS: 860-685-3000 • FAX: 860-685-3001

CAMPUS LIFE

Quality of Life Rating	**89**
Fire Safety Rating	**82**
Green Rating	**90**
Type of school	private
Environment	town

STUDENTS

Total undergrad enrollment	2,854
% male/female	49/51
% from out of state	91
% from public high school	54
% frosh live on campus	99
# of fraternities	9
# of sororities	4
% African American	7
% Asian	8
% Caucasian	53
% Hispanic	10
% international	8
# of countries represented	46

SURVEY SAYS . . .

Lots of liberal students
No one cheats
Great computer facilities
Great library
Athletic facilities are great
Students are friendly
Students aren't religious
Students are happy
Political activism is popular

ACADEMICS

Academic Rating	**96**
% students returning for sophomore year	94
% students graduating within 4 years	87
% students graduating within 6 years	92
Calendar	semester
Student/faculty ratio	9:1
Profs interesting rating	89
Profs accessible rating	94
Most classes have	10–19 students
Most lab/discussion sessions have	20–29 students

MOST POPULAR MAJORS

English language and literature; political science and government; psychology

APPLICANTS ALSO LOOK AT AND OFTEN PREFER

Brown University, Yale University, Stanford University, Harvard College

AND SOMETIMES PREFER

Amherst College, Princeton University, Swarthmore College, Bowdoin College, Williams College

AND RARELY PREFER

Tufts University, Vassar College, Middlebury College, Brandeis University, Oberlin College

STUDENTS SAY ". . ."

Academics

Tucked away in Middletown, Connecticut, Wesleyan University is a dynamic institution "committed [to] catering to its undergraduates." The school certainly attracts those with a high level of "intellectual interest and curiosity" and students "really engage their education in a meaningful way." Fortunately, there's a "lack of…competitive cutthroat [behavior which] really promotes a community of learning." Undergrads at Wesleyan also appreciate "the lack of core curriculum," which gives students the flexibility to really "explore new areas" and "obtain a broad education." Academics here are "very challenging" but students find their classes immensely "rewarding." This is wholly due to professors that are "always available and eager to speak with students, and have a terrific passion for their work." Many of them maintain "intimate relationships with students" and a junior tells us that "having a meal with a professor at their home is not a rare occurrence." While a few students find that "the administration is full of red tape," others insist that they are "generally very responsive to student needs" and "very invested in the happiness of the students." As one senior concludes, "I feel that the administration as well as faculty work hard to make Wesleyan a strong community where everyone's voice matters."

Life

Wesleyan students have eclectic interests and passions and the social scene really reflects that. An intellectual group, undergrads can frequently be found deep in conversation with their peers, discussing anything from "the ethics of grading [or] the rendering of astrophysics into tangible graphics [to] the analysis of the feminist meanings of a Spanish worksheet." Of course, you shouldn't let this deceive you. These students also know how to kick back and have fun. "From the traditional frat party, to a gathering at a program house, [to] a performance or movie with friends in somebody's living room, Wesleyan offers a variety of social scenes for students to get involved in." Activities certainly run the gamut. An African American studies major shares, "For fun, people go to performances, sporting events, lectures, protests, restaurants, open mics, parties, campus events, etc." On any given day these lucky students might enjoy "anything from an Indian dance festival to an open forum on the economic recession to a frat party that's also a charity event for a school in Kenya." Of course, Wesleyan students are also quite adept at making their own fun and they can be found "sledding on the snow, rolling down the hill, playing Duck Duck Goose, [and] having awesome corny dance parties."

Student Body

Undergrads at Wesleyan are fairly adamant about the fact that they cannot "be pigeon-holed." While many insist "there are no typical students," others concede that there "are a few traits that often connect [everyone]." Most people "are interested in engaging with the world around them, often in hopes of improving it." Indeed this is a "passionate" group who are very "socially-conscious, politically aware, and [into] activism." Moreover, Wesleyan students are "driven," "intellectually curious" and "eager to learn and experience new things." These are kids who are "serious about academics" but also know how to "relax and have fun." They are also "very proud to be part of a diverse community" and are always excited to "meet new people." Another commonality is that undergrads here tend to "have a variety of interests." As a Spanish and film studies double-major illustrates, "Your best friend might be captain of the football team and double-majoring in chemistry and art studio." Perhaps most importantly, students at Wesleyan "aren't afraid to associate with many different kinds of people." A content senior sums up, "Students here are committed to creating a strong and close-knit community made up of open-minded people."

FINANCIAL AID: 860-685-2800 • E-MAIL: ADMISSIONS@WESLEYAN.EDU • WEBSITE: WWW.WESLEYAN.EDU

THE PRINCETON REVIEW SAYS

Admissions

Very important factors considered include: Rigor of secondary school record. *Important factors considered include:* Academic GPA, application essay, class rank, recommendation(s), standardized test scores, character/personal qualities, first generation, racial/ethnic status, talent/ability. *Other factors considered include:* Alumni/ae relation, extracurricular activities, geographical residence, interview, volunteer work, work experience. ACT with writing component recommended. TOEFL required of all international applicants. High school diploma is required and GED is accepted. *Academic units recommended:* 4 English, 4 mathematics, 4 science (3 science labs), 4 foreign language, 4 social studies, 4 history.

Financial Aid

Students should submit: FAFSA, CSS/Financial Aid PROFILE. Regular filing deadline is February 15. The Princeton Review suggests that all financial aid forms be submitted as soon as possible after January 1. *Need-based scholarships/grants offered:* Federal Pell, SEOG, state scholarships/grants, private scholarships, school scholarship or grant aid from institutional funds. *Loan aid offered:* Direct Subsidized Stafford, Direct Unsubsidized Stafford, Direct PLUS, Federal Perkins, university loans from institutional funds. Federal Work-Study Program available. Off-campus job opportunities are good.

The Inside Word

You want the inside word on Wesleyan admissions? Read The Gatekeepers: Inside the Admissions Process at a Premier College, by Jacques Steinberg. The author spent an entire admissions season at the Wesleyan admissions office. His book is a wonderfully detailed description of the Wesleyan admissions process (which is quite similar to processes at other private, highly selective colleges and universities).

THE SCHOOL SAYS ". . ."

From the Admissions Office

"Wesleyan faculty believe in an education that is flexible and affords individual freedom and that a strong liberal arts education is the best foundation for success in any endeavor. The broad curriculum focuses on essential communication skills and analytical abilities through course content and teaching methodology, allowing students to pursue their intellectual interests with passion while honing those capabilities. As a result, Wesleyan students achieve a very personalized but broad education. Wesleyan's Dean of Admission and Financial Aid, Nancy Hargrave Meislahn, describes the qualities Wesleyan seeks in its students: 'Our very holistic process seeks to identify academically accomplished and intellectually curious students who can thrive in Wesleyan's rigorous and vibrant academic environment; we look for personal strengths, accomplishments, and potential for real contribution to our diverse community.'

"Applicants will meet standardized testing requirements one of two ways: by taking the SAT plus two SAT Subject Tests of the student's choice or by taking the ACT (writing component recommended)."

SELECTIVITY

Admissions Rating	98
# of applicants	9,658
% of applicants accepted	24
% of acceptees attending	35
# accepting a place on wait list	843
# of early decision applicants	918
# accepted early decision	380

FRESHMAN PROFILE

Range SAT Critical Reading	640–740
Range SAT Math	660–740
Range SAT Writing	660–750
Range ACT Composite	29–33
Minimum paper TOEFL	600
Minimum web-based TOEFL	100
Average HS GPA	3.8
% graduated top 10% of class	66
% graduated top 25% of class	88
% graduated top 50% of class	99

DEADLINES

Early decision	
Deadline	11/15
Notification	12/15
Regular	
Deadline	1/1
Notification	4/1
Nonfall registration?	no

FINANCIAL FACTS

Financial Aid Rating	95
Annual tuition	$45,358
Room and board	$12,574
Required fees	$270
% needy frosh rec. need-based scholarship or grant aid	93
% needy UG rec. need-based scholarship or grant aid	93
% needy frosh rec. need-based self-help aid	97
% needy UG rec. need-based self-help aid	97
% frosh rec. any financial aid	51
% UG rec. any financial aid	49
% UG borrow to pay for school	46
Average cumulative indebtedness	$25,864
% frosh need fully met	100
% ugrads need fully met	100
Average % of frosh need met	100
Average % of ugrad need met	100

West Virginia University

Admissions Office, Morgantown, WV 26506-6009 • Admissions: 304-293-2121 • Fax: 304-293-3080

CAMPUS LIFE

Quality of Life Rating	76
Fire Safety Rating	93
Green Rating	95
Type of school	public
Environment	town

STUDENTS

Total undergrad enrollment	22,189
% male/female	55/45
% from out of state	55
% frosh live on campus	84
# of fraternities	16
# of sororities	9
% African American	4
% Asian	2
% Caucasian	86
% Hispanic	3
% international	3

SURVEY SAYS . . .

Great computer facilities
Athletic facilities are great
Students are friendly
Everyone loves the WV Mountaineers
Student publications are popular
Lots of beer drinking
Hard liquor is popular

ACADEMICS

Academic Rating	67
Calendar	semester
Student/faculty ratio	23:1
Profs interesting rating	73
Profs accessible rating	75
Most classes have	20–29 students
Most lab/discussion sessions have	20–29 students

MOST POPULAR MAJORS

business/commerce; engineering; health professions and related clinical sciences, other

APPLICANTS ALSO LOOK AT AND OFTEN PREFER

Virginia Tech, Pennsylvania State University—University Park, University of Maryland, College Park

AND SOMETIMES PREFER

James Madison University, University of Pittsburgh—Pittsburgh Campus

STUDENTS SAY ". . ."

Academics

"One student reports that West Virginia University boasts "a relaxed, social, and extremely school-spirited environment," and that WVU's academics "challenge students in the classroom" and prepare them "to be successful in the next step of life after college." Another student praises the engineering program, which offers "many opportunities for seniors looking for jobs. I also like the fact that it is a big university, but being in Morgantown gives it a homey feel." Students find a happy medium that combines studying and socializing. "The school is all about connecting academics and leadership with incredible enthusiasm for school activities." "A wonderful experience with a good balance of academics and fun opportunities." "Great academic experience wrapped up in a fun college atmosphere." For in-state undergraduates, affordability is the key to choosing WVU. Many students are drawn to the "diversity of programs" offered at West Virginia University. With this variety of programs comes a "diversified faculty who bring a wide range of knowledge and experiences." Some students would prefer smaller classes because, as one student put it, "The large classes make it difficult to form solid teacher-student relationships." But another student offers a different perspective, "If you put forth any type of effort, you'll get to know your professors at WVU. Of course, with some of the bigger classes, you can sit in the back and go unnoticed, but that's a personal choice."

Life

There is no escaping the "pride" West Virginia University students feel for their school, many of whom say they were "born to be a Mountaineer." Whether it's describing their majors, the marching band, alumni, or the football and basketball teams, it seems unanimous that the "spirit of the university is outstanding." As one student states, "West Virginia University is all about combining such high academic standards with the atmosphere of Mountaineer pride, only something you can feel at a football game singing 'Country Roads' with 50,000 of your closest friends." "Fun" seems to best describe student life at WVU. Whether on campus at the "amazing student recreational center," which is "complete with weight room, indoor swimming pool, hot tubs, indoor track, indoor basketball and racquetball courts, ping-pong tables, and boxing equipment," at the Mountainlair student union watching free movies, or off campus exploring Morgantown, everyone seems to be having a good time. "One of the best things about Morgantown is downtown High Street. People always ask, 'you goin downtown tonight?'" This is referring to the very wide selection of bars, clubs, lounges, and restaurants that are located downtown, most concentrated along High Street. High Street starts at the south end of downtown and travels all the way up through the downtown campus. Some students would like to see an improvement in both parking and transportation, but the beauty of the area and the level of student assistance "outside the classroom with learning centers, free tutors, [and] group work areas" all get high marks.

Student Body

Students describe themselves as "outgoing" as well as "relaxed and social." School spirit is evident. "The typical student always has some piece of WVU apparel on, and that's usually sweatpants." "Students are very involved on campus with academics and various clubs and organizations. It is a very lively campus and there is always something going on. Although one student reports, "A lot of people here drink quite often," students also say that there is plenty to do on campus that doesn't include alcohol.

FINANCIAL AID: 304-293-5242 • E-MAIL: GO2WVU@MAIL.WVU.EDU • WEBSITE: WWW.WVU.EDU

THE PRINCETON REVIEW SAYS

Admissions

Very important factors considered include: Academic GPA, standardized test scores. *Important factors considered include:* Rigor of secondary school record, level of applicant's interest, state residency. *Other factors considered include:* Recommendation(s), extracurricular activities, talent/ability, volunteer work. SAT or ACT required; ACT with or without writing component accepted. TOEFL required of all international applicants. High school diploma is required and GED is accepted. *Academic units required:* 4 English, 4 mathematics, 3 science (3 science labs), 2 foreign language, 3 social studies, 1 visual/performing arts.

Financial Aid

Students should submit: FAFSA, state aid form. Regular filing deadline is March 1. The Princeton Review suggests that all financial aid forms be submitted as soon as possible after January 1. *Need-based scholarships/grants offered:* Federal Pell, SEOG, state scholarships/grants, private scholarships, the school's own gift aid. *Loan aid offered:* Direct Subsidized Stafford, Direct Unsubsidized Stafford, Direct PLUS, Federal Perkins, college/university loans from institutional funds. Applicants will be notified of awards on a rolling basis beginning March 15. Federal Work-Study Program available. Institutional employment available. Highest amount earned per year from on-campus jobs $2,500. Off-campus job opportunities are good.

The Inside Word

While standards for general admission to WVU aren't especially rigorous, you'll find admission to its premier programs to be quite competitive. Admission to the College of Business and Economics, for example, requires a high school GPA of at least 3.75 and an SAT math score of at least 610. Programs in computer science, education, engineering, fine arts, forensics, journalism, medicine, and nursing all require fairly impressive credentials. If you're not admitted to the program of your choice, you may be able to transfer to it later if your grades are good enough, but it won't be easy.

THE SCHOOL SAYS ". . ."

From the Admissions Office

"From quality academic programs and outstanding, caring faculty, to incredible new facilities and a campus environment that focuses on students' needs, WVU is a place where dreams can come true. Our tradition of academic excellence attracts some of the region's best high school seniors. WVU has produced twenty-four Rhodes Scholars, thirty-five Goldwater Scholars, twenty-two Truman Scholars, six members of the USA Today's All-USA College Academic First Team, and two Udall Scholarship winners. Whether your goal is to be an aerospace engineer, reporter, physicist, athletic trainer, opera singer, forensic investigator, pharmacist, or CEO, WVU's 191 degree choices can make it happen. Unique student-centered initiatives help students experience true education beyond the classroom. The Mountaineer parents club connects more than 20,000 families, and a parents' helpline (800-WVU-0096) leads to a full-time parent advocate. A Student Recreation Center includes athletic courts, pools, weight/fitness equipment, and a fifty-foot indoor climbing wall. A major building program is creating new classrooms, labs, health-care facilities, an art museum, and a student wellness center. With programs for studying abroad, a Center from Black Culture and Research, and Office of Disability Services, and a student body that comes from every WV county, fifty states, and 100 different countries, WVU encourages diversity. WVU research funding has topped $174 million for the second consecutive year, making WVU a major research institution where undergraduates can participate. All applicants are required to take the ACT writing assessment as part of the ACT exam, or take the SAT to be considered for admission."

SELECTIVITY	
Admissions Rating	74
# of applicants	15,815
% of applicants accepted	85
% of acceptees attending	37
FRESHMAN PROFILE	
Range SAT Critical Reading	470–570
Range SAT Math	480–590
Range ACT Composite	21–26
Minimum paper TOEFL	550
Minimum web-based TOEFL	61
Average HS GPA	3.4
% graduated top 10% of class	20
% graduated top 25% of class	45
% graduated top 50% of class	78
DEADLINES	
Regular	
Priority	3/1
Deadline	8/1
Nonfall registration?	yes
FINANCIAL FACTS	
Financial Aid Rating	70
Annual in-state tuition	$5,674
Annual out-state tuition	$17,844
Room and board	$8,404
Books and supplies	$1,140
% needy frosh rec. need-based scholarship or grant aid	50
% needy UG rec. need-based scholarship or grant aid	55
% needy frosh rec. non-need-based scholarship or grant aid	81
% needy UG rec. non-need-based scholarship or grant aid	57
% needy frosh rec. need-based self-help aid	54
% needy UG rec. need-based self-help aid	62
% frosh rec. any financial aid	72
% UG rec. any financial aid	75
% UG borrow to pay for school	59
Average cumulative indebtedness	$27,003
% frosh need fully met	29
% ugrads need fully met	29
Average % of frosh need met	72
Average % of ugrad need met	75

WESTMINSTER COLLEGE (PA)

319 SOUTH MARKET STREET, NEW WILMINGTON, PA 16172 • ADMISSIONS: 724-946-7100 • FAX: 724-946-7171

CAMPUS LIFE

Quality of Life Rating	**86**
Fire Safety Rating	**94**
Green Rating	**60***
Type of school	private
Affiliation	Presbyterian
Environment	village

STUDENTS

Total undergrad enrollment	1,537
% male/female	41/59
% from out of state	25
% from public high school	90
% frosh live on campus	95
# of fraternities	5
# of sororities	5
% African American	3
% Asian	1
% Caucasian	80
% Hispanic	1
% Native American	1
% international	1
# of countries represented	3

SURVEY SAYS . . .

Career services are great
Students are friendly
Students get along with local community
Campus feels safe
Students are happy
Frats and sororities dominate social scene
Student government is popular

ACADEMICS

Academic Rating	**78**
% students returning for sophomore year	87
% students graduating within 4 years	60
% students graduating within 6 years	79
Calendar	semester
Student/faculty ratio	12:1
Profs interesting rating	80
Profs accessible rating	86
Most classes have	10–19 students
Most lab/discussion sessions have	10–19 students

MOST POPULAR MAJORS

biology/biological sciences; business/commerce; education

APPLICANTS ALSO LOOK AT AND OFTEN PREFER

Pennsylvania State University, University of Pittsburgh

AND SOMETIMES PREFER

Grove City College, Duquesne University

AND RARELY PREFER

Allegheny College, Washington & Jefferson College

STUDENTS SAY ". . ."

Academics

Since 1852, Westminster College has remained intent crafting a personalized learning process for students, with the aim of turning out well-rounded individuals who "can live and affect the world around us in a positive way." The "challenging" liberal arts curriculum provides a broad foundation for academic study, and the school heavily stresses the application of what's learned by pushing students "to prepare themselves for the future using real life simulations." At this "very happy place," the administration always "keeps the interests of the students in mind," the classes are small, and "Students get the attention they need." Westminster runs on personal relationships between faculty and students, and "Even the janitor knows your name." The low student/teacher ratio means the "extremely accessible and helpful" professors are devoted to ensuring that every last student understands the material, and "Office doors are always open." This care extends far beyond the classroom, as professors love to see students involved in interesting activities outside of classes, and they "pretty much beg you to study abroad because they know it will be so beneficial for you as a person." "If you see some slacking there is always someone there, whether a classmate or professor, to bring you up," says one student. A few students do remark on the school's rather slow adoption of modern technology ("We just got wireless Internet this year"), but this is more than made up for by the "variety of courses," "student-teacher bonds," and "opportunities to get involved." "Contrary to popular belief, Westminster College, not Disneyland, is the happiest place on earth," says a student.

Life

"This school has so much going on that it is almost impossible to not be involved," says one student of the busy hive that is Westminster. There are more than 100 clubs and a wide range of activities offered, including "concerts, competitions, Humans versus Zombies, a Frisbee team, philosophy club, jazz band, flute choir, an equestrian team, an ice skating class, [and] karate class." The administration plan events all throughout the week ("Most people stay on campus on the weekends"), such as "movies on weekends, concerts on Friday or Saturday nights, sports events at least once a week, [and] special cuisine nights at the [cafeteria]." Located in the heart of Amish country, the dry town and campus "creates a great place to focus and learn" with "small-town appeal and charm that's irresistible." Greek life "is especially important for socialization," and many join it in some form or another (whether a social sorority or fraternity, or an honors society). Some students do choose to party off campus, but "It's far enough off of campus that you don't feel pressured to join in if you don't want to." Off-campus malls, restaurants, and cities "are not too far away," but "So much is happening on campus during the week and weekends that I do not see much need to go off-campus often."

Student Body

The typical Titan is "extremely friendly" and academically driven; students "know how to have fun but also know when to study and hit the books." Though the majority of Westminster students are white and Christian, "No one at Westminster is discriminatory towards other races, genders, religions, or sexual orientations." The student body is small enough that it can be called "tight-knit," and there's a lot of frequent interaction among students, because almost all who go to school here "get involved with a number of extracurricular activities" or "community service and philanthropic events." This easygoing crowd "gets along very well," and "Just about everyone fits in to the mix somewhere." Many students say, "Westminster is your family," and "It is a quick and easy process to make friends and find a niche."

FINANCIAL AID: 724-946-7102 • E-MAIL: ADMIS@WESTMINSTER.EDU • WEBSITE: WWW.WESTMINSTER.EDU

THE PRINCETON REVIEW SAYS

Admissions

Very important factors considered include: Rigor of secondary school record, standardized test scores, interview. *Important factors considered include:* Class rank, application essay, recommendation(s), character/personal qualities. *Other factors considered include:* Alumni/ae relation, extracurricular activities, racial/ethnic status, talent/ability, volunteer work, work experience. SAT or ACT required; ACT with or without writing component accepted. TOEFL required of all international applicants. High school diploma is required and GED is accepted. *Academic units required:* 4 English, 3 mathematics, 2 science (2 science labs), 2 foreign language, 2 social studies, 1 history, 3 academic electives.

Financial Aid

Students should submit: FAFSA, institution's own financial aid form. The Princeton Review suggests that all financial aid forms be submitted as soon as possible after January 1. *Need-based scholarships/grants offered:* Federal Pell, SEOG, state scholarships/grants, private scholarships, the school's own gift aid. *Loan aid offered:* Direct Subsidized Stafford, Direct Unsubsidized Stafford, Direct PLUS, Federal Perkins, resource loans. Applicants will be notified of awards on a rolling basis beginning November 1. Highest amount earned per year from on-campus jobs $1,300.

The Inside Word

Westminster offers both early action and rolling admissions (following the December 15 deadline). The school will accept either the SAT or ACT test scores and also has an organization of student volunteers dedicated to assisting the Office of Admissions in the recruitment of qualified students. Most of your competition will be from Pennsylvania, with the rest mostly coming from Ohio.

THE SCHOOL SAYS ". . ."

From the Admissions Office

"Founded in 1852 and related to the Presbyterian Church (U.S.A.), Westminster College ranks first in the nation as "Best College for Women in Science, Technology, Engineering and Math," according to Forbes.com. Westminster, a top-tier liberal arts college, ranks third in graduation rate performance, according to *U.S. News Best Colleges* guide. Westminster ranked 6th among liberal arts colleges in social mobility, according to the *Washington Monthly College Guide,* and is one of the most affordable national liberal arts colleges in Pennsylvania. Westminster is also honored as one of "The Best 376 Colleges" by *The Princeton Review,* and is named to the President's Honor Roll for excellence in service learning.

"Nearly 1,600 undergraduate and graduate students benefit from individualized attention from dedicated faculty while choosing from 42 majors and nearly 100 organizations on the New Wilmington, Pa., campus. Visit Westminster.edu for more information."

SELECTIVITY	
Admissions Rating	77
# of applicants	3,839
% of applicants accepted	60
% of acceptees attending	16

FRESHMAN PROFILE	
Range SAT Critical Reading	470–580
Range SAT Math	480–590
Range ACT Composite	21–26
Minimum paper TOEFL	550
Average HS GPA	3.5
% graduated top 10% of class	27
% graduated top 25% of class	59
% graduated top 50% of class	91

DEADLINES	
Early action	
Deadline	11/15
Notification	12/1
Regular	
Deadline	4/15
Nonfall registration?	no

FINANCIAL FACTS	
Financial Aid Rating	82
Annual tuition	$30,320
Room and board	$9,570
Required fees	$1,190
Books and supplies	$1,000
% needy frosh rec. need-based scholarship or grant aid	91
% needy UG rec. need-based scholarship or grant aid	92
% needy frosh rec. non-need-based scholarship or grant aid	90
% needy UG rec. non-need-based scholarship or grant aid	90
% needy frosh rec. need-based self-help aid	71
% needy UG rec. need-based self-help aid	75
% frosh rec. any financial aid	91
% UG rec. any financial aid	93
% UG borrow to pay for school	84
Average cumulative indebtedness	$28,262
% frosh need fully met	15
% ugrads need fully met	16
Average % of frosh need met	80
Average % of ugrad need met	80

Westminster College (UT)

1840 South 1300 East, Salt Lake City, UT 84105 • Admissions: 801-832-2200 • Fax: 801-832-3101

CAMPUS LIFE

Quality of Life Rating	94
Fire Safety Rating	96
Green Rating	86
Type of school	private
Environment	metropolis

STUDENTS

Total undergrad enrollment	2,376
% male/female	45/55
% from out of state	36
% from public high school	81
% frosh live on campus	71
% African American	1
% Asian	2
% Caucasian	50
% Hispanic	6
% international	3
# of countries represented	40

SURVEY SAYS . . .

Registration is a breeze
Great computer facilities
Athletic facilities are great
School is well run
Students get along with local community
Campus feels safe
Students are happy
Frats and sororities are unpopular or nonexistent

ACADEMICS

Academic Rating	87
% students returning for sophomore year	80
% students graduating within 4 years	46
% students graduating within 6 years	66
Calendar	4-1-4
Student/faculty ratio	10:1
Profs interesting rating	96
Profs accessible rating	87
Most classes have	10–19 students
Most lab/discussion sessions have	10–19 students

MOST POPULAR MAJORS

business/commerce; nursing/registered nurse (rn, asn, bsn, msn); social sciences

APPLICANTS ALSO LOOK AT AND OFTEN PREFER

Brigham Young University (UT)

AND SOMETIMES PREFER

University of Utah, University of Idaho, Utah State University

STUDENTS SAY ". . ."

Academics

Westminster College "has the perfect balance of everything: it focuses on being academically challenging but [that] is also equally weighted by all the fun events." The opportunity "to ski, climb, work, attend classes, hang out with friends, and be active on campus every day" makes the Westminster experience "the absolute best package of any college available," according to the many boosters among its student body. Academics are by no means neglected here; they are "challenging but manageable," students report. About one in three undergrads pursue a business major in a program that "prepares you for a global career [and] being able to work in many different cultures." The nursing program is also "highly respected," and the education program is "very good." In all fields, small class sizes "give all students the opportunity to be seen and heard by their professors and also give classes a chance to turn from strict lecturing to a more discussion-based learning that allows everyone to say something if they desire." "The small class sizes are amazing," one student writes. "You don't feel as though you are just a number and no one cares about you like at some big universities." Many also appreciate Westminster's reputation as "a liberal oasis" in the "sea of conservatism" known as Utah.

Life

"There are a lot of physically active students" at Westminster, "so it's not hard to find someone to work out with. In fact, it's not hard to find someone to do anything with: walk to a local restaurant, study with, party with, etc." That's both because "everyone is friendly and helpful" and because the school "has somehow made it very easy to meet people as well as do many different things in the local area." The student-run Associated Students of Westminster College organization "provides many opportunities for students to have fun and meet other students, from Casino Night to Pizza Tasting to bringing in popular comedians from around the state." Students also enjoy "lots of…skiing and other outdoor activities" such as hiking, camping, kayaking, and snowboarding. The school is especially hospitable to rock climbers, with "an indoor gym and outdoor bouldering wall, outdoor locations nearby, and several gyms in the city" for their use. On weekends, some here "like to unwind and enjoy the weekend with some partying" that includes "drinking games" and "beer runs," but (this being Utah) there is also a considerable population that will have none of that. Sugar House, the college-friendly neighborhood surrounding the school, accommodates both types of students well.

Student Body

"There is a large concentration of skiers and snowboarders" at Westminster, as one might expect from its location, but "there are also other types of students… that don't do snow sports." Likewise, the student body "is primarily Caucasian, much like Utah as a whole," but "the ethnic variety on campus is improving." An influx of Asian students "due to an exchange program within China and increased international recruiting efforts by the administration" contributes substantially to the diversity. There's a distinct Western vibe here, as students tend to be "liberal, environmentally friendly, laid-back, achieving, and accepting." Their ranks include the requisite kids who "don't really care," and many more who are "very studious" and "engaged in many opportunities on campus."

FINANCIAL AID: 801-832-2502 • E-MAIL: ADMISSION@WESTMINSTERCOLLEGE.EDU • WEBSITE: WWW.WESTMINSTERCOLLEGE.EDU

THE PRINCETON REVIEW SAYS

Admissions

Very important factors considered include: Academic GPA, rigor of secondary school record. *Important factors considered include:* Class rank, application essay, standardized test scores, interview. *Other factors considered include:* Recommendation(s), alumni/ae relation, character/personal qualities, extracurricular activities, geographical residence, talent/ability. SAT or ACT required; ACT with writing component recommended. TOEFL required of all international applicants. High school diploma is required and GED is accepted. *Academic units required:* 4 English, 2 mathematics, 3 science, 2 foreign language, 2 social studies, 1 history, 2 academic electives. *Academic units recommended:* 4 English, 3 mathematics, 3 science, 3 foreign language, 2 social studies, 1 history, 3 academic electives.

Financial Aid

Students should submit: FAFSA. The Princeton Review suggests that all financial aid forms be submitted as soon as possible after January 1. *Need-based scholarships/grants offered:* Federal Pell, SEOG, state scholarships/grants, private scholarships, the school's own gift aid. *Loan aid offered:* Direct Subsidized Stafford, Direct Unsubsidized Stafford, Direct PLUS, Federal Perkins. Applicants will be notified of awards on a rolling basis beginning March 1. Federal Work-Study Program available. Institutional employment available. Highest amount earned per year from on-campus jobs $6,934. Off-campus job opportunities are excellent.

The Inside Word

You don't need to clear lofty hurdles to gain admission to Westminster. Solid grades in a college-prep curriculum—we're not talking straight A's here, just mostly A's and B's—should make the grade. Test scores need to be decent (at or above the national average) but needn't be astronomical. If your record shows you can handle the workload at Westminster, you're likely to gain admission. The school reviews applications closely, allowing applicants who fall somewhat short in the GPA or test score department to impress through essays, extracurricular achievement, and demonstration of special skills or talent.

THE SCHOOL SAYS ". . ."

From the Admissions Office

"Founded in 1875, Westminster College is a private, comprehensive, liberal arts college dedicated to students and their learning, and offers one of the most unique learning environments in the country. Located where the Rocky Mountains meet the vibrant city of Salt Lake, Westminster blends classroom learning with experiences derived from its unique location to help students develop skills and attributes critical for success in a rapidly changing world. Impassioned teaching and active learning are the hallmarks of the Westminster experience.

"Each application is read and reviewed individually by an admissions committee who takes into account both level of challenge in course work and grades received. Either the SAT or ACT exam is accepted. Writing ability will be assessed through the writing sections of the SAT, ACT, application essays, and in some cases, other writing samples such as graded papers.

"Westminster College has a rolling application deadline and will accept applications until the class is filled. To be eligible for the widest array of financial aid—and more than ninety-seven percent of freshmen receive some financial aid—April 15 is the priority consideration deadline for fall semester, and May 15 is the deadline for on-campus housing applications."

SELECTIVITY	
Admissions Rating	**80**
# of applicants	3,414
% of applicants accepted	68
% of acceptees attending	22
FRESHMAN PROFILE	
Range SAT Critical Reading	487.5–620
Range SAT Math	500–620
Range ACT Composite	22–27
Minimum paper TOEFL	550
Minimum web-based TOEFL	79
Average HS GPA	3.5
% graduated top 10% of class	23
% graduated top 25% of class	56
% graduated top 50% of class	85
DEADLINES	
Regular	
Priority	3/1
Deadline	8/27
Nonfall registration?	yes
FINANCIAL FACTS	
Financial Aid Rating	**81**
Annual tuition	$26,712
Room and board	$7,584
Required fees	$470
Books and supplies	$1,000
% needy frosh rec. need-based scholarship or grant aid	100
% needy UG rec. need-based scholarship or grant aid	94
% needy frosh rec. non-need-based scholarship or grant aid	10
% needy UG rec. non-need-based scholarship or grant aid	11
% needy frosh rec. need-based self-help aid	88
% needy UG rec. need-based self-help aid	90
% frosh rec. any financial aid	97
% UG rec. any financial aid	95
% UG borrow to pay for school	62
Average cumulative indebtedness	$22,557
% frosh need fully met	23
% ugrads need fully met	20
Average % of frosh need met	84
Average % of ugrad need met	76

WHEATON COLLEGE (IL)

501 COLLEGE AVENUE, WHEATON, IL 60187 • ADMISSIONS: 630-752-5005 • FAX: 630-752-5285

CAMPUS LIFE

Quality of Life Rating	97
Fire Safety Rating	85
Green Rating	74
Type of school	private
Environment	town

STUDENTS

Total undergrad enrollment	2,410
% male/female	50/50
% from out of state	76
% from public high school	52
% frosh live on campus	100
% African American	3
% Asian	8
% Caucasian	82
% Hispanic	4
% international	1
# of countries represented	40

SURVEY SAYS . . .

Students are very religious
Students get along with local community
Great food on campus
Frats and sororities are unpopular or nonexistent
Very little beer drinking
Very little drug use
Students are involved in community service

ACADEMICS

Academic Rating	87
% students graduating within 4 years	79
Calendar	semester
Student/faculty ratio	12:1
Profs interesting rating	94
Profs accessible rating	93
Most classes have	10–19 students
Most lab/discussion sessions have	10–19 students

MOST POPULAR MAJORS

business/managerial economics; English language and literature; health services/allied health/health sciences

APPLICANTS ALSO LOOK AT AND SOMETIMES PREFER

Grove City College

AND RARELY PREFER

Baylor University, Calvin College, College of William and Mary, Davidson College

STUDENTS SAY ". . ."

Academics

Wheaton College strives to cultivate students' knowledge and to "prepare them to enter the world as strong and capable individuals who serve Christ and His Kingdom." This "academically rigorous" and deeply religious liberal arts school is equally as interested in the character of each student, with a focus on "developing yourself in ways [that] will affect you long after you've left the school campus." Professors here are "the heart and soul of this campus," and they're "exceptional teachers who genuinely care for the academic and spiritual well-being of their students." They "attempt to connect with students in ways other than the material they are told to teach," and it's "not unusual to meet professors outside of class, whether that be for a meal, coffee, or fun activities." That's not to say that there aren't a few bad apples or that the grading isn't tough; professors "rarely curve," but they do provide "many mentoring and tutoring sessions" to those in need. There's a "serious integration of faith and learning" that "places a high emphasis on opening up our eyes to serious issues going on around the world." "When you see other people using their gifts for God and hear them encouraging you to do the same, it's inspiring," says one student. Class sizes at Wheaton are pleasantly small, and one-on-one interaction is very common through "internships, teaching assistants, research opportunities, and the 'Dine with a Mind' program." This student body that's truly "sincere about learning" goes on to form a "very close-knit network of graduates" that's easily accessible after graduation. Other than that, students laud the "successful career placement, top-notch music conservatory, [and] excellent science facilities."

Life

All Wheaton students adhere to a community covenant, which is a set of rules and regulations governing students that forbids things, such as drinking, smoking, and "spontaneous" dancing. While several students wish that the school was "more lenient in their punishment system," most are happy to comply and even claim that it "forces us to come up with super-creative ways to have fun." "Everyone has at least one costume—bring one if you come here because you will need it," says a mysterious student. Drink-wise, "Wheaton students don't need alcohol to have an awesome time," and food-wise, the school has what some students call the "greatest college food in the country." The train station is a few minutes' walk from campus, which can bring you to nearby Chicago, but most students "just find fun activities to do on campus… like bond with [students who live on their housing] floor or play campus-wide Sardines." The college offers lots of activities during the weekend and has tons of "random traditions," such as a "student 'Iron Chef' competition in the dining hall." Students here are very passionate about social justice issues and "just as likely to be found discussing theology or philosophy as the latest sports game." ESL tutoring, mentoring, and serving on spring break service trips are also popular extracurricular activities for Wheaties.

Student Body

Pretty much the entirety of Wheaton is composed of "academically strong, driven, and Christian students," and the phrase "type-A personality" is oft-used. The school draws students from all over the country (including "quite a lot of homeschooled and international students"), and the diversity isn't as strong as some students would like, though "they are making a lot of efforts to change that in the admissions office." Students at Wheaton "take their studies extremely seriously and work very hard to keep high grades," but most still get involved with student activities, ministries, and sports, and enjoy the groups of friends that form when people share a "common identity." In their downtime, people "have a respectful and creative sense of fun and do not waste their time." All in all, "Most students find some way to fit in."

FINANCIAL AID: 630-752-5021 • E-MAIL: ADMISSIONS@WHEATON.EDU • WEBSITE: WWW.WHEATON.EDU

THE PRINCETON REVIEW SAYS

Admissions

Very important factors considered include: Application essay, academic GPA, recommendation(s), rigor of secondary school record, standardized test scores, character/personal qualities, interview, religious affiliation/commitment. *Important factors considered include:* Extracurricular activities, talent/ability, volunteer work, work experience. *Other factors considered include:* Class rank, alumni/ae relation, first generation, geographical residence, level of applicant's interest, racial/ethnic status, state residency. SAT or ACT required; ACT with writing component required. TOEFL required of all international applicants. High school diploma is required and GED is accepted. *Academic units recommended:* 4 English.

Financial Aid

Students should submit: FAFSA, institution's own financial aid form. The Princeton Review suggests that all financial aid forms be submitted as soon as possible after January 1. *Need-based scholarships/grants offered:* Federal Pell, SEOG, state scholarships/grants, the school's own gift aid. *Loan aid offered:* Direct Subsidized Stafford, Direct Unsubsidized Stafford, Direct PLUS, Federal Perkins. Applicants will be notified of awards on a rolling basis beginning March 1. Federal Work-Study Program available. Institutional employment available. Off-campus job opportunities are excellent.

The Inside Word

Although Wheaton College looks for students who are strong academically, the college doesn't have any minimum requirements for GPA, class rank, or standardized test scores. The school does look for evidence of Christian faith when making its decision, and proof of Christian commitment is necessary for admission, but you'll also have to prove the quality of your high school courses.

THE SCHOOL SAYS ". . ."

From the Admissions Office

"At Wheaton, we're commited to being a community that fearlessly pursues truth, upholds an academically rigorous curriculum, and promotes virtue. The college takes seriously its impact on society. The influence of Wheaton is seen in fields ranging from government (the former speaker of the house) to sports (two NBA coaches) to business (the CEO of John Deere) to music (Metropolitan Opera National Competition winners) to education (over forty college presidents) to global ministry (Billy Graham). Wheaton seeks students who want to make a difference and are passionate about their Christian faith and rigorous academic pursuit.

"Applicants are required to submit results from the SAT or the ACT with writing section. Wheaton will use the highest of these scores from either test in evaluating a student's application."

SELECTIVITY

Admissions Rating	**93**
# of applicants	2,050
% of applicants accepted	65
% of acceptees attending	45
# accepting a place on wait list	389
# admitted from wait list	23

FRESHMAN PROFILE

Range SAT Critical Reading	610–710
Range SAT Math	610–690
Range SAT Writing	600–700
Range ACT Composite	27–32
Minimum paper TOEF600L	587
Minimum web-based TOEFL	95
Average HS GPA	3.7
% graduated top 10% of class	50
% graduated top 25% of class	81
% graduated top 50% of class	96

DEADLINES

Early action	
Deadline	11/1
Notification	12/31
Regular	
Deadline	1/10
Notification	4/1
Nonfall registration?	no

FINANCIAL FACTS

Financial Aid Rating	**85**
Annual tuition	$28,960
Room and board	$8,220
Books and supplies	$816
% needy frosh rec. need-based scholarship or grant aid	97
% needy UG rec. need-based scholarship or grant aid	97
% needy frosh rec. non-need-based scholarship or grant aid	37
% needy UG rec. non-need-based scholarship or grant aid	33
% needy frosh rec. need-based self-help aid	95
% needy UG rec. need-based self-help aid	95
% frosh rec. any financial aid	74
% UG rec. any financial aid	70
% UG borrow to pay for school	54
Average cumulative indebtedness	$23,022
% frosh need fully met	14
% ugrads need fully met	27
Average % of frosh need met	87
Average % of ugrad need met	89

WHEATON COLLEGE (MA)

OFFICE OF ADMISSION, NORTON, MA 02766 • ADMISSIONS: 508-286-8251 • FAX: 508-286-8271

CAMPUS LIFE

Quality of Life Rating	**68**
Fire Safety Rating	**77**
Green Rating	**81**
Type of school	private
Environment	village

STUDENTS

Total undergrad enrollment	1,622
% male/female	36/64
% from out of state	68
% from public high school	61
% frosh live on campus	100
% African American	5
% Asian	2
% Caucasian	74
% Hispanic	7
% international	8
# of countries represented	41

SURVEY SAYS . . .

Frats and sororities are unpopular or nonexistent
Student government is popular
Lots of beer drinking
Hard liquor is popular

ACADEMICS

Academic Rating	**90**
% students returning for sophomore year	86
% students graduating within 4 years	73
% students graduating within 6 years	77
Calendar	semester
Student/faculty ratio	11:1
Profs interesting rating	88
Profs accessible rating	86
Most classes have	10–19 students
Most lab/discussion sessions have	10–19 students

MOST POPULAR MAJORS

economics; English language and literature; psychology; biology

APPLICANTS ALSO LOOK AT AND OFTEN PREFER

Bates College, Connecticut College

AND SOMETIMES PREFER

Skidmore College, University of Vermont, Hamilton College

AND RARELY PREFER

Boston University, Clark University, Brandeis University

STUDENTS SAY ". . ."

Academics

Wheaton College is a historic private liberal arts college located in Southeastern Massachusetts, where an intimate campus and small student body create a tight-knit community and much-appreciated "small class sizes." There's certainly a "rigor of the academics" here, but "Work in class is very reasonable," and there are "resources available to help students…everywhere." Administration "is very good with letting us know what is going on," and "The school's honor code is taken very seriously," creating "a strong bond between students and staff all over campus." Faculty are "easily the strong point of Wheaton," as "tenured, associate, and visiting professors are all extremely well-educated and aren't pretentious in their teaching style." No TAs teach classes, and the "well-informed" professors encourage dialogue in all classrooms, are "super accessible" to students that need extra help or counsel, and "make an honest effort to know and understand you as a person, not just a student." The professors don't talk at us, they discuss with us," says a student of Wheaton's classes, many of which have a participation grade. Each student also has the unique option to take classes at surrounding schools (Brown, Wellesley, the Boston Aquarium, etc.). Many people at Wheaton go on to postgraduate studies, and the close relationships between professors and students open doors for numerous research opportunities and useful connections; there are also "many funds available for individual projects and studies." Study abroad programs are a popular, robust option here. Really, "Wheaton provides every individual with the opportunities to try anything and everything that you are interested in."

Life

Classes demand that a student works hard during the week, but that means "they can relax and have a little fun on the weekend." Sundays are "sort of a transition day for students to get ready for the week ahead." The vast majority of students live on campus and stick around for Friday and Saturday, but the school's restrictive drug and alcohol policies (which many students believe "could be changed") relegate most partying to off-campus locales, creating some tension with the local community. Wheaton doesn't have fraternities or sororities, but "There is still a pretty big party scene at Wheaton." The small town location "is not the most ideal" ("Norton is not a college town," says one student emphatically), but there's a bus that runs from the school to the nearest train station, which is "very, very, very convenient to go to Boston or Providence." "Having a car makes you a god for getting off campus." Students are active in all sorts of clubs and community service activities, and individuals "usually manage to fit it once they find a club, organization, or group of some kind that they enjoy being a part of." Luckily, there are many at Wheaton, and "There are always events going on around the school." Dance and music shows are "well-attended," and popular movies are shown every weekend. "If students cannot find something to do, it's because they aren't trying," says one. The historic upper campus, designed by Ralph Adams Cram, is "a beautiful addition to life," but the food is "a big issue" here, even though "it's improving."

Student Body

There's a wide range of students at Wheaton, but the standard issue is "studious but not obsessive" and "involved in a variety of activities." "Any student could fit in this community pretty easily," and most "acclimate to the 'New England' style by the end of freshman year." On this "fairly liberal" campus, "artists, activists, and average Joes are as common as athletes"; or, as one student puts it, "There are bros and activists and party animals and computer science people…You have to seek out 'your people.'" Everyone is "very open to multicultural students," and the school is "surprisingly diverse." There's "a moderate level of political discussion" that abounds.

FINANCIAL AID: 508-286-8232 • E-MAIL: ADMISSION@WHEATONCOLLEGE.EDU • WEBSITE: WWW.WHEATONCOLLEGE.EDU

THE PRINCETON REVIEW SAYS

Admissions

Very important factors considered include: Application essay, academic GPA, rigor of secondary school record, character/personal qualities, extracurricular activities, first generation, talent/ability. *Important factors considered include:* Class rank, recommendation(s), alumni/ae relation, interview, volunteer work, work experience. *Other factors considered include:* Geographical residence, level of applicant's interest, racial/ethnic status, state residency. ACT with or without writing component accepted. TOEFL required of all international applicants. High school diploma is required and GED is accepted. *Academic units recommended:* 4 English, 4 mathematics, 3 science (2 science labs), 4 foreign language, 3 social studies, 2 history.

Financial Aid

Students should submit: FAFSA, CSS/Financial Aid PROFILE, noncustodial PROFILE, business/farm supplement, parent and student federal tax returns and W-2s. Regular filing deadline is February 1. The Princeton Review suggests that all financial aid forms be submitted as soon as possible after January 1. *Need-based scholarships/grants offered:* Federal Pell, SEOG, state scholarships/grants, private scholarships, the school's own gift aid. *Loan aid offered:* Direct Subsidized Stafford, Direct Unsubsidized Stafford, Direct PLUS, Federal Perkins. Applicants will be notified of awards on or about April 1. Federal Work-Study Program available. Institutional employment available. Highest amount earned per year from on-campus jobs $4,622. Off-campus job opportunities are good.

The Inside Word

Wheaton gives applicants the option of not submitting standardized test scores. The school also invites applicants to submit optional personal academic portfolios, collections of completed schoolwork that demonstrates talents the applicant wants to highlight. All applicants should seriously consider this option; for those who do not submit test scores, an academic portfolio is practically imperative, both as an indicator of the applicant's seriousness about Wheaton and as evidence of academic excellence (evidence that standardized test scores might otherwise provide).

THE SCHOOL SAYS ". . ."

From the Admissions Office

"What makes for a 'best college'? Is it rankings or is it outcomes? We think what makes college 'best' (and best for you) is a school that will help you become a first-rate thinker and writer, a pragmatic professional in your work, and an ethical practitioner in your life. To get you to all these places, Wheaton offers several great combinations: a beautiful, classic New England campus with easy access to Boston and Providence; a strong liberal arts and sciences curriculum combined with award-winning internship, job, and community-service programs; and a supportive environment that respects your individuality within the context of the larger community. What's the 'best' outcome of a Wheaton education? It is a start on life that combines meaningful work, significant relationships, and a commitment to your local and global community. Over the past decade, more than 150 Wheaton students have won both national and international scholarship competitions including Rhodes, Marshall, Fulbright, Truman and Watson awards. We are proud of what our graduates study and the careers they pursue as well as who they become.

"Wheaton does not require students to submit the results of any standardized testing. The only exception is the TOEFL for students for whom English is a second language. Students who choose to submit standardized testing may use results from the SAT or the ACT."

SELECTIVITY	
Admissions Rating	**88**
# of applicants	3,448
% of applicants accepted	60
% of acceptees attending	21
# accepting a place on wait list	198
# admitted from wait list	38
# of early decision applicants	128
# accepted early decision	108

FRESHMAN PROFILE	
Range SAT Critical Reading	580–680
Range SAT Math	580–660
Range ACT Composite	26–30
Minimum paper TOEFL	580
Minimum web-based TOEFL	90
Average HS GPA	3.5
% graduated top 10% of class	42
% graduated top 25% of class	29
% graduated top 50% of class	98

DEADLINES	
Early decision	
Deadline	11/15
Notification	12/15
Early action	
Deadline	11/15
Notification	1/15
Regular	
Deadline	1/15
Notification	4/1
Nonfall registration?	yes

FINANCIAL FACTS	
Financial Aid Rating	**90**
Annual tuition	$43,480
Room and board	$11,180
Required fees	$294
Books and supplies	$940
% needy frosh rec. need-based scholarship or grant aid	95
% needy UG rec. need-based scholarship or grant aid	95
% needy frosh rec. non-need-based scholarship or grant aid	2
% needy UG rec. non-need-based scholarship or grant aid	2
% needy frosh rec. need-based self-help aid	96
% needy UG rec. need-based self-help aid	97
% frosh rec. any financial aid	83
% UG rec. any financial aid	76
% UG borrow to pay for school	59
Average cumulative indebtedness	$25,778
% frosh need fully met	44
% ugrads need fully met	50
Average % of frosh need met	95
Average % of ugrad need met	96

WHITMAN COLLEGE

345 BOYER AVENUE, WALLA WALLA, WA 99362 • ADMISSIONS: 509-527-5176 • FAX: 509-527-4967

CAMPUS LIFE

Quality of Life Rating	**98**
Fire Safety Rating	**83**
Green Rating	**80**
Type of school	private
Environment	town

STUDENTS

Total undergrad enrollment	1,580
% male/female	42/58
% from out of state	67
% from public high school	75
% frosh live on campus	100
# of fraternities	4
# of sororities	3
% African American	2
% Asian	8
% Caucasian	70
% Hispanic	6
% Native American	1
% international	2
# of countries represented	30

SURVEY SAYS . . .

Great computer facilities
Athletic facilities are great
School is well run
Students are friendly
Dorms are like palaces
Intramural sports are popular
Musical organizations are popular
Students are environmentally aware

ACADEMICS

Academic Rating	**97**
% students returning for sophomore year	96
% students graduating within 4 years	82
% students graduating within 6 years	88
Calendar	semester
Student/faculty ratio	10:1
Profs interesting rating	99
Profs accessible rating	99
Most classes have	10–19 students
Most lab/discussion sessions have	20–29 students

MOST POPULAR MAJORS

biology/biological sciences; history; political science and government; environmental studies

APPLICANTS ALSO LOOK AT AND OFTEN PREFER

Pomona College, Stanford University, Middlebury College, Carleton College

AND SOMETIMES PREFER

Colorado College, Macalester College

AND RARELY PREFER

University of Washington, University of Puget Sound, Willamette University, Lewis & Clark College

STUDENTS SAY ". . ."

Academics

If learning can be both rigorous and laid-back at the same time, it happens at Whitman College in Walla Walla, WA. The "challenging" academics here are coupled with a "relaxed attitude" in order to give students "the best education possible without sacrificing all the fun one expects of college." Populated mainly by "intelligent, ambitious liberals with far-reaching goals," this somewhat idealistic school seeks to build critical thinking skills through "an earnest discourse about 'life, the universe, and everything.'" So no one starts off with a blank slate, all first-year students are required to take a course referred to as "Encounters" which offers a survey of Western thought, starting with The Odyssey, working through Socrates, Plato, Augustine, up through Marx, Voltaire, and other thinkers who shaped modern thought. Distribution requirements ensure that all students get a breadth of courses, and a lack of TAs ensures that they get all the attention they need. Although there's always a dud or two in the mix, professors are "genuinely brilliant and interesting people" and "love to spend time with students outside of class," whether it be for academic help or just conversation. "It is not uncommon to have potlucks, classes, or movie night over at your professor's house with your class," says one student.

On the administrative side of things, bureaucracy and red tape are kept to a minimum in this chill environment through "effortless use of the 'system'" and the administration gets raves all around for its devotion to "maintaining quality student life," which is something of a rarity. "I have never heard of *any* college being as supportive as this place has been to me in just the past two years," says a student. "Whitman's president gave me a ride to campus one semester after I met him at the airport," says another. As one can imagine, all these things come together to form a student body that's "happy, well-balanced, and well-cared-for."

Life

Most people stay on campus for their fun, "especially first-years," and throughout this "bubble" the "sense of closeness and comradeship is very evident through attendance at student-run concerts, art shows, etc." Everything is within ten minutes' walking distance. Academics take precedence for almost everyone, but "most students find time to party on the weekends," due to a "lenient and fair" alcohol policy. Thanks to the campus activities board, "there's almost always something fun going on, whether or not a person chooses to drink," such as Drive-In Movie Night and Casino Night. With "four beautiful seasons," outdoor activities are also very popular, thanks to "a great gear rental program that gets people outside hiking, biking, kayaking, and rock-climbing," and "Frisbees are everywhere when it's warm." In fact, there's so much going on "if someone says they are bored, students laugh and wish they could relate."

Student Body

It's a sociable bunch at Whitman, where most students "are interested in trying new things and meeting new people" and "everyone seems to have a weird interest or talent or passion." The quirky Whitties "usually have a strong opinion about *something*," and one freshman refers to her classmates as ""cool nerds." Diversity has risen steadily over the past several years, as the school has made an effort to recruit beyond the typical "mid- to upper-class and white" contingent. Everyone here is pretty outdoorsy and environmentally aware ("to the point where you almost feel guilty for printing an assignment"), and a significant number of students have won fellowships and scholarships such as the Fulbright, Watson, Truman, and Udall."

FINANCIAL AID: 509-527-5178 • E-MAIL: ADMISSION@WHITMAN.EDU • WEBSITE: WWW.WHITMAN.EDU

THE PRINCETON REVIEW SAYS

Admissions

Very important factors considered include: Application essay, academic GPA, rigor of secondary school record, character/personal qualities. *Important factors considered include:* Recommendation(s), standardized test scores, extracurricular activities, racial/ethnic status, talent/ability. *Other factors considered include:* Class rank, alumni/ae relation, first generation, geographical residence, interview, level of applicant's interest, state residency, volunteer work, work experience. SAT or ACT required; ACT with writing component required. TOEFL required of all international applicants. High school diploma is required and GED is accepted. *Academic units recommended:* 4 English, 4 mathematics, 3 science (2 science labs), 2 foreign language, 2 social studies, 2 history, 1 arts.

Financial Aid

Students should submit: FAFSA, CSS/Financial Aid PROFILE. Regular filing deadline is February 1. The Princeton Review suggests that all financial aid forms be submitted as soon as possible after January 1. *Need-based scholarships/grants offered:* Federal Pell, SEOG, state scholarships/grants, private scholarships, the school's own gift aid. *Loan aid offered:* Direct Subsidized Stafford, Direct Unsubsidized Stafford, Direct PLUS, Federal Perkins, state loans, alternative student loans. Applicants will be notified of awards on a rolling basis beginning December 20. Federal Work-Study Program available. Institutional employment available. Highest amount earned per year from on-campus jobs $2,463. Off-campus job opportunities are good.

The Inside Word

Whitman's admissions committee emphasizes essays and extracurriculars more than SAT scores. The college cares much more about who you are and what you have to offer if you enroll than it does about what your numbers will do for the freshman academic profile. Whitman is a mega-sleeper. Educators all over the country know it as an excellent institution, and the college's alums support it at one of the highest rates of giving at any college in the nation. Students seeking a top-quality liberal arts college owe it to themselves to take a look.

THE SCHOOL SAYS ". . ."

From the Admissions Office

"Located in historic Walla Walla in a valley at the foot of the Blue Mountains in sunny Southeastern Washington State, Whitman College offers a combination of a rigorous academic environment that is collaborative; a down-to-earth Northwest culture; and a vibrant, engaging campus life. Whitman is also distinguished by the following:

- Capstone written and oral assessments in one's major field of study
- Numerous winners of Ford Foundation, Fulbright, Goldwater, National Science Foundation, Rhodes, Truman, Beinecke, Udall, and Watson fellowships and scholarships
- Science departments that have been recognized by the National Science Foundation as among the top fifty colleges per capita producing graduates who earn PhD's in science and engineering
- State of the art facilities including a library, computer labs and a health center open 24/7
- An undergraduate research conference in which over 200 students present their original research to the Whitman community
- Recent national championships in Debate, Ultimate Frisbee, and Road Cycling
- A nationally renowned Outdoor Program
- Semester in the West, an experiential, on-the-road study of economic, cultural and environmental issues
- An eighty-eight percent graduation rate, a sixty-five percent graduate school rate, and a fifty percent study abroad rate
- An award winning Main Street in a tourist destination town known for its four seasons, wine, and arts culture"

SELECTIVITY

Admissions Rating	**96**
# of applicants	2,956
% of applicants accepted	48
% of acceptees attending	24
# accepting a place on wait list	520
# of early decision applicants	158
# accepted early decision	126

FRESHMAN PROFILE

Range SAT Critical Reading	620–730
Range SAT Math	610–700
Range SAT Writing	630–710
Range ACT Composite	28–32
Minimum paper TOEFL	560
Minimum web-based TOEFL	85
Average HS GPA	3.8
% graduated top 10% of class	68
% graduated top 25% of class	92
% graduated top 50% of class	99

DEADLINES

Early decision	
Deadline	11/15 and 1/1
Notification	12/19 and 1/20
Regular	
Deadline	1/15
Notification	4/1
Nonfall registration?	yes

FINANCIAL FACTS

Financial Aid Rating	**91**
Annual tuition	$41,790
Room and board	$10,560
Required fees	$336
Books and supplies	$1,400
% needy frosh rec. need-based scholarship or grant aid	100
% needy UG rec. need-based scholarship or grant aid	99
% needy frosh rec. non-need-based scholarship or grant aid	39
% needy UG rec. non-need-based scholarship or grant aid	26
% needy frosh rec. need-based self-help aid	79
% needy UG rec. need-based self-help aid	83
% frosh rec. any financial aid	76
% UG rec. any financial aid	78
% UG borrow to pay for school	45
Average cumulative indebtedness	$16,700
% frosh need fully met	50
% ugrads need fully met	56
Average % of frosh need met	91
Average % of ugrad need met	97

WHITTIER COLLEGE

13406 PHILADELPHIA STREET, WHITTIER, CA 90608 • ADMISSIONS: 562-907-4238 • FAX: 562-907-4870

CAMPUS LIFE

Quality of Life Rating	**67**
Fire Safety Rating	**84**
Green Rating	**72**
Type of school	private
Environment	city

STUDENTS

Total undergrad enrollment	1,643
% male/female	46/54
% from out of state	31
% frosh live on campus	80
# of fraternities	4
# of sororities	5
% African American	5
% Asian	10
% Caucasian	37
% Hispanic	33
% international	3
# of countries represented	23

SURVEY SAYS . . .

Great computer facilities
Great library
Diverse student types on campus
Different types of students interact
Great off-campus food
Student publications are popular
Lots of beer drinking
Hard liquor is popular

ACADEMICS

Academic Rating	**75**
% students graduating within 4 years	55
% students graduating within 6 years	61
Calendar	4-1-4
Student/faculty ratio	13:1
Profs interesting rating	81
Profs accessible rating	80
Most classes have	10–19 students
Most lab/discussion sessions have	20–29 students

MOST POPULAR MAJORS

biology/biological sciences; business administration and management; psychology

APPLICANTS ALSO LOOK AT AND OFTEN PREFER

University of Redlands, Occidental College

AND SOMETIMES PREFER

Loyola Marymount University, Pitzer College

AND RARELY PREFER

Chapman University, Claremont McKenna College

STUDENTS SAY ". . ."

Academics

At tiny Whittier College in California, there's a proud emphasis placed on the interconnectedness of all of the liberal arts disciplines. Students are challenged to learn things relevant to their field and "encouraged to take courses in seemingly unrelated fields and then make connections to see how they actually all relate." In being allowed "to pursue their educations in a comfortable and friendly environment," students enjoy how the school allows for a "strengthening of student integrity" by providing a tight-knit community. Professors are "all passionate about their subject material," and their understanding and flexibility are spoken of highly; although "a course [may be] geared to a particular subject, the professors make it a point to relate the discipline to others we may be interested in, too." "All of your professors will know you by name, and not by number, because you matter to them." Aside from being knowledgeable and sincere, faculty also help students to "pursue larger goals in life," and encourage students "to take their own initiative in developing their goals and future." Small class sizes (and an "amazing" range of classes) at Whittier provide students with the opportunity to ask questions and to receive personalized attention, and teachers "make you feel welcome and always informed." Academics are "challenging, but not…difficult to where it is impossible." Whittier also offers a January term to help students graduate on time [or] early, and there's free tutoring to help with homework and studies. Internships, work study, and leadership are all available starting as a freshman, and it's "easy to travel abroad." Basically, "If you utilize the resources available on campus, you can truly make your own experience."

Life

When schoolwork is done, busy Whittier students "do their best to promote their own strengths in extracurricular activities." This is a true California school at heart, and "You can always find students laying out on the quad soaking up the beautiful Southern California sun." "On sunny days (which is basically everyday), I have seen slip-n-slides on the quad." The whole town "is supportive of Whittier College," and "There are several unique mom-and-pop shops and eateries throughout Uptown, along with a movie theater," all within walking distance. Still, a lot of students get out of Whittier by driving to Los Angeles or the nearby beach, and "getting a Disneyland annual pass is very popular." In recent years, housing has been overcrowded, resulting in some busy cafeterias and creative living arrangements. On weekends, some "like to party at the houses off campus that certain students rent out," but for those who don't, there are a "lot of on-campus activities are offered in the evening." "The school does not revolve around the 'party scene' like other campuses, although one does exist if it's desired," says a student. Societies, intramurals, and clubs on campus "are constantly organizing events" though some commuter students who aren't able to participate in these events speak of feeling disconnected from the Whittier community.

Student Body

Predictably, there are a number of California natives at Whittier, but those from out-of-state find themselves happily adopted. Students here are extremely friendly and "mostly fit in with their types," but there's a fair amount of cross-pollination among the groups because "everyone sort of meets each other in all the different classes." Everyone at Whittier "has a niche," and for the most part, "Everyone respects, as well as embraces, each others' uniqueness." The Division III school is athletically inclined, and a fair number of people play sports, though "it's not 'that' athletic of a student body."

FINANCIAL AID: 562-907-4285 • E-MAIL: ADMISSION@WHITTIER.EDU • WEBSITE: WWW.WHITTIER.EDU

THE PRINCETON REVIEW SAYS

Admissions

Very important factors considered include: Application essay, rigor of secondary school record. *Important factors considered include:* Academic GPA, recommendation(s), standardized test scores, character/personal qualities, extracurricular activities, interview, talent/ability, volunteer work. *Other factors considered include:* Class rank, alumni/ae relation, first generation, geographical residence, racial/ethnic status, state residency, work experience. SAT or ACT required; ACT with writing component required. TOEFL required of all international applicants. High school diploma is required and GED is accepted. *Academic units required:* 3 English, 2 mathematics, 1 science (1 science lab), 2 foreign language, 1 social studies. *Academic units recommended:* 4 English, 3 mathematics, 2 science, 3 foreign language, 2 social studies.

Financial Aid

Students should submit: FAFSA. Regular filing deadline is March 2. The Princeton Review suggests that all financial aid forms be submitted as soon as possible after January 1. *Need-based scholarships/grants offered:* Federal Pell, SEOG, state scholarships/grants, private scholarships, the school's own gift aid. *Loan aid offered:* Direct Subsidized Stafford, Direct Unsubsidized Stafford, Direct PLUS, Federal Perkins, alternative financing loans. Applicants will be notified of awards on a rolling basis beginning February 15. Federal Work-Study Program available. Highest amount earned per year from on-campus jobs $1,250. Off-campus job opportunities are good.

The Inside Word

Whittier is looking for well-rounded students, and so activities and recommendations are just as important as scores and grades—the admissions office hates to focus just on numbers. Though sixty-five percent of students hail from California, no preference is given to state of origin. Through the Whittier Scholars program, students may construct a personalized major that fits academic and career goals.

THE SCHOOL SAYS ". . ."

From the Admissions Office

"Faculty and students at Whittier share a love of learning and delight in the life of the mind. They join in understanding the value of the intellectual quest, the use of reason, and a respect for values. They seek knowledge of their own culture and the informed appreciation of other traditions, and they explore the interrelatedness of knowledge and the connections among disciplines. An extraordinary community emerges from teachers and students representing a variety of academic pursuits, individuals who have come together at Whittier in the belief that study within the liberal arts forms the best foundation for rewarding endeavor throughout a lifetime.

"Whittier College is a vibrant, residential, four-year liberal arts institution where intellectual inquiry and experiential learning are fostered in a community that promotes respect for diversity of thought and culture. A Whittier College education produces enthusiastic, independent thinkers who flourish in graduate studies, the evolving global workplace, and life."

SELECTIVITY	
Admissions Rating	76
# of applicants	2,989
% of applicants accepted	71
% of acceptees attending	20
FRESHMAN PROFILE	
Range SAT Critical Reading	480–580
Range SAT Math	480–590
Range SAT Writing	480–570
Range ACT Composite	20.25–26
Minimum paper TOEFL	550
Minimum web-based TOEFL	80
Average HS GPA	3.5
% graduated top 10% of class	24
% graduated top 25% of class	34
% graduated top 50% of class	88
DEADLINES	
Early action	
Deadline	12/1
Notification	12/30
Regular	
Priority	2/1
Nonfall registration?	yes
FINANCIAL FACTS	
Financial Aid Rating	82
Annual tuition	$38,280
Room and board	$10,948
Required fees	$360
Books and supplies	$1,110
% needy frosh rec. need-based scholarship or grant aid	89
% needy UG rec. need-based scholarship or grant aid	92
% needy frosh rec. non-need-based scholarship or grant aid	10
% needy UG rec. non-need-based scholarship or grant aid	8
% needy frosh rec. need-based self-help aid	89
% needy UG rec. need-based self-help aid	88
% frosh rec. any financial aid	90
% UG rec. any financial aid	91
% UG borrow to pay for school	68
Average cumulative indebtedness	$24,687
% frosh need fully met	13
% ugrads need fully met	12
Average % of frosh need met	78
Average % of ugrad need met	74

WILLAMETTE UNIVERSITY

900 STATE STREET, SALEM, OR 97301 • ADMISSIONS: 503-370-6303 • FAX: 503-375-5363

CAMPUS LIFE

Quality of Life Rating	**85**
Fire Safety Rating	**76**
Green Rating	**80**
Type of school	private
Affiliation	Methodist
Environment	city

STUDENTS

Total undergrad enrollment	1,967
% male/female	44/56
% from out of state	73
% from public high school	80
% frosh live on campus	97
# of fraternities	4
# of sororities	3
% African American	2
% Asian	6
% Caucasian	64
% Hispanic	6
% Native American	1
% international	1
# of countries represented	42

SURVEY SAYS . . .

No one cheats
Lab facilities are great
Great computer facilities
Great library
Students are friendly
Musical organizations are popular
Students are environmentally aware

ACADEMICS

Academic Rating	**93**
% students returning for sophomore year	88
% students graduating within 4 years	70
Calendar	semester
Student/faculty ratio	10:1
Profs interesting rating	94
Profs accessible rating	91
Most classes have	10–19 students

MOST POPULAR MAJORS

biology/biological sciences; economics; psychology

APPLICANTS ALSO LOOK AT AND OFTEN PREFER

Whitman College

AND SOMETIMES PREFER

University of Puget Sound, Lewis & Clark College, University of Washington, Colorado College, Santa Clara University, Occidental College

AND RARELY PREFER

University of Oregon

STUDENTS SAY ". . ."

Academics

Willamette University offers "serious academics without the snobbery." In both its educational and extracurricular offerings, "Willamette is very focused on learning in a team environment," and the school "cultivates a strong feeling of community" throughout its academic programs. Students are encouraged to work together, and there is a "designated 'hearth' (common area) for every department where students can go for tutoring, group project collaboration, or just to do homework with classmates." Willamette's "knowledgeable" professors are "dedicated to what they teach and genuinely interested in helping students learn." Students warn, however, that, "Classes are demanding and instructors expect you to come to class prepared to discuss, not just listen." A sophomore agrees, "Professors expect the most out of us as true adults instead of as 'students,' thus I do my best to live up to that high expectation." Beyond academics, Willamette promotes a well-rounded lifestyle, and professors are "always checking to make sure that everything is going well both in the class and outside." In fact, "many professors socialize with students outside of class," and "It's not unusual to be asked to dinner at a professor's house." Located in the capital city of Salem, Oregon, co-curricular opportunities are abundant. Through the school, there are many "community service options, internship options, [and] on-campus job options," and students praise the "ease of getting state government internships" at the Oregon State capitol—just across the street!

Life

"The library on Sunday nights is a great merging of social and academic worlds—[you're] practically guaranteed to find a table of people working on assignments for your class or in your department." In addition to schoolwork, "There is a huge population that is involved in clubs on campus, anything from soccer club to juggling club or knitting club." In particular, "Lots of people are involved in sports," whether varsity or intramural, and many socially minded students "do a lot of community volunteering." Laid-back and casual, at Willamette "parties do happen but they're low-key compared to larger schools." There are also "two substance-free dorms" for those who don't like to indulge. For fun, students hit "the local bars on the weekends, or stick around campus and go to an a cappella night, a movie being shown on campus, or a Greek event, such as a dance." Surrounding Salem is a sleepy town, and "most everything off campus closes early"; however, there are "tons of coffee shops" in the local area, as well as "a mall easily within walking distance." "Students take trips to Portland and the ocean, and also head out to the mountains for skiing as well as hiking along paths decorated with waterfalls (weather permitting)."

Student Body

Willamette students are "smart, politically focused, interested, social, outgoing, [and] athletic or outdoorsy in some way," as well as "environmentally conscious." The community is varied, "open-minded," and mature: "Though there are many communities on campus (i.e., community service groups, Greek houses, clubs, sports teams, etc.), nearly every student is involved in more than one community and thus floats freely between groups, eliminating cliquishness." A student adds, "Regardless of if you're a football player, or environmentalist, or bio-chem double major, everyone fits in because we are all very open and inclusive people." Willamette students are "involved in many campus activities, including classes, clubs, and on-campus jobs." Outside the classroom, they are "active in leadership, eager to volunteer, [and] interested in a well-rounded education instead of primarily a 'book' education." Almost seventy percent of Willamette's undergraduates are from the West Coast, and some students say, "Our campus is not very culturally diverse." However, through a partner program with Tokyo International University, about 100 Japanese students come to Willamette each year to study English and liberal arts.

FINANCIAL AID: 503-370-6273 • E-MAIL: LIBARTS@WILLAMETTE.EDU • WEBSITE: WWW.WILLAMETTE.EDU

THE PRINCETON REVIEW SAYS

Admissions

Very important factors considered include: Class rank, application essay, academic GPA, rigor of secondary school record, standardized test scores. *Important factors considered include:* Recommendation(s), interview. *Other factors considered include:* Alumni/ae relation, character/personal qualities, extracurricular activities, first generation, geographical residence, racial/ethnic status, talent/ability. SAT or ACT required; ACT with writing component required. TOEFL required of all international applicants. *Academic units required:* 4 English, 4 mathematics, 3 science (3 science labs), 1 foreign language, 2 social studies. *Academic units recommended:* 4 English, 4 mathematics, 3 science (4 science labs), 1 foreign language, 2 social studies, 2 history.

Financial Aid

Students should submit: FAFSA. The Princeton Review suggests that all financial aid forms be submitted as soon as possible after January 1. *Need-based scholarships/grants offered:* Federal Pell, SEOG, state scholarships/grants, private scholarships, the school's own gift aid. *Loan aid offered:* Direct Subsidized Stafford, Direct Unsubsidized Stafford, Direct PLUS, Federal Perkins. Applicants will be notified of awards on a rolling basis beginning April 1. Federal Work-Study Program available. Institutional employment available. Highest amount earned per year from on-campus jobs $2,000. Off-campus job opportunities are excellent.

The Inside Word

When evaluating prospective students, Willamette places the most emphasis on academic record, including rigor of high school coursework, grades, and grade trends. Drastic variations in academic performance during high school will not be viewed favorably by Willamette's admissions officers. As a residential campus, Willamette is also interested in accepting students who will contribute something to the campus community. Evidence of community service and extracurricular involvement reflect a habit of participation that will only enhance your application in the eyes of Willamette's discerning admissions officers.

THE SCHOOL SAYS ". . ."

From the Admissions Office

"As one of the nation's premier liberal arts universities, Willamette has superb academic programs and noted professors who work with students one-on-one. Ten of the past twenty-two Oregon Professors of the Year come from Willamette, illustrating our faculty's teaching excellence.

"Our faculty help you develop the skills necessary to succeed in our global workforce: critical reading, writing, thinking, and verbal communication. Willamette also helps you hone your creativity, critical thinking, and global perspective outside of class. Half of our students study abroad, twenty-five percent perform joint research with faculty members, and seventy percent complete one or more internships. You'll learn how to analyze issues from a variety of perspectives preparing you to creatively address the challenges of the world.

"College is more than preparation for the future; it's about friends and fun. Willamette has 100-plus student organizations, twenty varsity sports, many club and intramural teams, and countless social activities on campus to bring students together. You can also get involved in Willamette's nationally recognized sustainability efforts. You'll build lifelong friendships in addition to building your intellect.

"Our graduates credit their Willamette education with developing the expertise they needed for successful careers at businesses, government agencies and nonprofits. They frequently find careers at companies such as Nike, Intel, and Microsoft, and many enter top-notch graduate programs across the country. Our students and graduates often earn competitive, national awards that provide money for research or graduate school."

SELECTIVITY	
Admissions Rating	92
# of applicants	8,175
% of applicants accepted	57
% of acceptees attending	13
# accepting a place on wait list	54

FRESHMAN PROFILE	
Range SAT Critical Reading	560–670
Range SAT Math	540–650
Range SAT Writing	540–650
Range ACT Composite	26–30
Minimum paper TOEFL	550
Average HS GPA	3.5
% graduated top 10% of class	41
% graduated top 25% of class	74
% graduated top 50% of class	100

DEADLINES	
Regular	
Priority	2/1
Nonfall registration?	yes

FINANCIAL FACTS	
Financial Aid Rating	88
Annual tuition	$40,560
Room and board	$9,820
Required fees	$214
Books and supplies	$948
% needy frosh rec. need-based scholarship or grant aid	99
% needy UG rec. need-based scholarship or grant aid	99
% needy frosh rec. non-need-based scholarship or grant aid	37
% needy UG rec. non-need-based scholarship or grant aid	22
% needy frosh rec. need-based self-help aid	73
% needy UG rec. need-based self-help aid	81
% frosh rec. any financial aid	98
% UG rec. any financial aid	96
% UG borrow to pay for school	67
Average cumulative indebtedness	$25,932
% frosh need fully met	44
% ugrads need fully met	39
Average % of frosh need met	87
Average % of ugrad need met	87

William Jewell College

500 College Hill, Liberty, MO 64068 • Admissions: 816-781-7700 • Fax: 816-415-5040

CAMPUS LIFE

Quality of Life Rating	**87**
Fire Safety Rating	**80**
Green Rating	**64**
Type of school	private
Environment	town

STUDENTS

Total undergrad enrollment	1,060
% male/female	41/59
% from out of state	36
% from public high school	90
% frosh live on campus	91
# of fraternities	3
# of sororities	4
% African American	4
% Asian	2
% Caucasian	82
% Hispanic	4
% Native American	1
% international	3
# of countries represented	12

SURVEY SAYS . . .

No one cheats
Career services are great
Students are friendly
Students get along with local community
Students love Liberty, MO
Great off-campus food
Students are happy
Frats and sororities dominate social scene
Musical organizations are popular
Student publications are popular
Very little drug use

ACADEMICS

Academic Rating	**85**
% students returning for sophomore year	75
% students graduating within 4 years	58
% students graduating within 6 years	63
Calendar	semester
Student/faculty ratio	11:1
Profs interesting rating	92
Profs accessible rating	89
Most classes have	fewer than 10 students
Most lab/discussion sessions have	30–39 students

MOST POPULAR MAJORS

business/commerce; nursing/registered nurse (rn, asn, bsn, msn); psychology

APPLICANTS ALSO LOOK AT AND OFTEN PREFER

Truman State University, University of Missouri

AND RARELY PREFER

Northwest Missouri State University

STUDENTS SAY ". . ."

Academics

Often called "the Harvard of the Midwest," William Jewell College is a prestigious small school with a strong sense of community. In both philosophy and practice, "Jewell is the quintessential liberal arts college, thoroughly engaging students in critical study of both the self and the world as a whole." Undergraduate programs are "extremely academically challenging" and the workload is heavy. However, students assure us that Jewell offers "an incredible learning opportunity, available to all who are willing to put in the work." Jewell students have the opportunity to shape their education in a way they couldn't do at larger schools; "If you want something to be changed in the cafe they'll do it; if you want to design your own major they'll do it." More importantly, the school's "incredibly brilliant" professors are accessible and supportive; "Most teachers will work with you personally should you have a problem with the class, or even on a personal level." Through internships and service projects, "Jewell is big on getting [its] students into real-world situations as soon as possible," and the career counseling office excels at "getting students a job in their field of study directly after graduating." While most are highly satisfied with the Jewell experience, students admit that, "there have been rough patches for the administration," who aren't always responsive to student concerns. Fortunately, the winds of change are in the air, as "President Sallee is a very competent and popular administrator."

Life

At Jewell, life never slows down. In addition to keeping up with academic demands, "The typical student is involved in a bazillion activities, from sports to Greek life and clubs." "Participation in school functions is pretty high" and there is always something going on, "whether it's bowling, or Sundae night on Sunday, or free movie night, worship jams, pool, study groups, or just hanging out with your friends." Friendships blossom in this unique environment, and students say "It's amazing how well we all get to know each other in such a short amount of time." Chats in the cafeteria "range from very deep, philosophical inquiries to lighthearted bantering." Socially, "Lots of students are involved in Greek life and enjoy Greek-related activities." On the weekends, "it is easy to find a party"; however, "If you like to stay in and have fun, there are always people to hang out with." Under any circumstance, academics come first: "When Monday hits, we know how to stop partying and start studying." All students are required to live on campus, yet "the weekends are pretty dead" because most students go home or travel to a nearby city. A student explains, "After spending five days stuck in what we call the 'bubble,' we want to get away and do something different."

Student Body

At this competitive, small college, students are "incredibly bright," and most "were in the top twenty-five percent of the class" in high school. Ambitious by nature, academics are first priority for most of Jewell's "hardworking" students, who are "here to succeed." You'll meet a largely "Midwestern, middle-class" crowd at this college, yet one that encompasses "various personalities, interests, [and] communication skills." Recently, the school community has become even more open: "Since our split with the Baptist church, Jewell has been making efforts to attract students of other ethnicities and sexual orientations, and such students seem to feel welcome." In fact, "We have a strong group that supports the GLBT community and a group called Unity that promotes understanding of people from other cultures and colors." Most students are "extremely busy and involved" with campus activities, and the school community is often described as "close-knit." At Jewell, "everyone says hi, even if you don't know them," and "even the freshmen feel that they can just go sit down at an all-senior table and fit in just fine."

FINANCIAL AID: 816-415-5975 • E-MAIL: ADMISSION@WILLIAM.JEWELL.EDU • WEBSITE: WWW.JEWELL.EDU

THE PRINCETON REVIEW SAYS

Admissions

Very important factors considered include: Rigor of secondary school record. *Important factors considered include:* Class rank, academic GPA, recommendation(s), standardized test scores. *Other factors considered include:* Application essay, alumni/ae relation, character/personal qualities, extracurricular activities, first generation, interview, talent/ability, volunteer work, work experience. SAT or ACT required; ACT with writing component recommended. TOEFL required of all international applicants. High school diploma is required and GED is accepted. *Academic units required:* 4 English, 3 mathematics, 3 science (1 science lab), 2 foreign language, 3 social studies. *Academic units recommended:* 4 English, 4 mathematics, 3 science (1 science lab), 3 foreign language, 3 social studies, 2 academic electives.

Financial Aid

Students should submit: FAFSA. The Princeton Review suggests that all financial aid forms be submitted as soon as possible after January 1. *Need-based scholarships/grants offered:* Federal Pell, SEOG, state scholarships/grants, the school's own gift aid. *Loan aid offered:* Direct Subsidized Stafford, Direct Unsubsidized Stafford, Direct PLUS, Federal Perkins, Federal Nursing, nonfederal private loans. Applicants will be notified of awards on a rolling basis beginning February 15. Federal Work-Study Program available. Institutional employment available. Highest amount earned per year from on-campus jobs $1,300. Off-campus job opportunities are excellent.

The Inside Word

Jewell brings a personal touch to the admissions process. Prospective students can make arrangements for a personal visit—or "individual experience"—at Jewell, through which they can meet with their admissions counselor, as well as current students. If you've already submitted an application, you can even stay overnight in the dorms. All students who apply by the priority deadline will be considered for admission and merit-based scholarships, and will be notified of the decision before winter break.

THE SCHOOL SAYS ". . ."

From the Admissions Office

"William Jewell College is committed to bringing together talented students and gifted faculty mentors within a vibrant community sparked by a rigorous and intentional liberal arts curriculum. A full range of personal and professional development experiences are presented by the selective national liberal arts college's location within the Kansas City metroplex of more than two million. The William Jewell College experience focuses on enhancing the student's ability to apply learning to complex ethical, scientific and cultural problems. The College places a high value on experiential learning and gives students the opportunity to "live what they learn." By completing the College's thirty-eight-hour liberal arts core plus three applied learning experiences, Jewell students can receive a second major in Applied Critical Thought and Inquiry. This means that all students can graduate with double majors and some with triple majors. The internationally recognized Oxbridge Honors Program combines British tutorial methods of instruction with opportunities for a year of study in Oxford or Cambridge. It is the only program of its kind in the nation. Jewell's undergraduate Nonprofit Leadership major is one of only thirteen nationwide and ranks among the top three in academic rigor. The Pryor Leadership Studies Program includes course work, community service projects and internships that help students enhance their leadership skills in a variety of settings. William Jewell students graduate equipped with deep content knowledge in their major(s), a host of social and real-world experiences, personal maturity and the intellectual habits of mind for success in a world of change and challenge."

SELECTIVITY

Admissions Rating	87
# of applicants	3,333
% of applicants accepted	54
% of acceptees attending	15

FRESHMAN PROFILE

Range SAT Critical Reading	490–640
Range SAT Math	520–620
Range ACT Composite	23–28
Minimum paper TOEFL	550
Minimum web-based TOEFL	80
Average HS GPA	3.7
% graduated top 10% of class	25
% graduated top 25% of class	59
% graduated top 50% of class	91

DEADLINES

Regular	
Priority	12/1
Deadline	8/15
Nonfall registration?	yes

FINANCIAL FACTS

Financial Aid Rating	72
Annual tuition	$30,200
Room and board	$7,790
Books and supplies	$1,100
% needy frosh rec. need-based scholarship or grant aid	100
% needy UG rec. need-based scholarship or grant aid	98
% needy frosh rec. non-need-based scholarship or grant aid	96
% needy UG rec. non-need-based scholarship or grant aid	91
% needy frosh rec. need-based self-help aid	83
% needy UG rec. need-based self-help aid	81
% frosh rec. any financial aid	99
% UG rec. any financial aid	96
% UG borrow to pay for school	77
Average cumulative indebtedness	$23,210
% frosh need fully met	12
% ugrads need fully met	14
Average % of frosh need met	68
Average % of ugrad need met	63

WILLIAMS COLLEGE

PO Box 487, Williamstown, MA 01267 • Admissions: 413-597-2211 • Fax: 413-597-4052

CAMPUS LIFE

Quality of Life Rating	**80**
Fire Safety Rating	**93**
Green Rating	**88**
Type of school	private
Environment	village

STUDENTS

Total undergrad enrollment	2,010
% male/female	49/51
% from out of state	89
% from public high school	58
% frosh live on campus	100
% African American	8
% Asian	11
% Caucasian	59
% Hispanic	11
% international	7
# of countries represented	75

SURVEY SAYS . . .

Lab facilities are great
School is well run
Dorms are like palaces
Campus feels safe
Everyone loves the Ephs
Frats and sororities are unpopular or nonexistent

ACADEMICS

Academic Rating	**99**
% students returning for sophomore year	97
% students graduating within 4 years	89
% students graduating within 6 years	95
Calendar	4-1-4
Student/faculty ratio	7:1
Profs interesting rating	91
Profs accessible rating	96
Most classes have	fewer than 10 students
Most lab/discussion sessions have	10–19 students

MOST POPULAR MAJORS

economics; English language and literature/letters, other; visual and performing arts

APPLICANTS ALSO LOOK AT AND OFTEN PREFER

Harvard College, Yale University, Princeton University

AND SOMETIMES PREFER

Amherst College

AND RARELY PREFER

University of Chicago, Middlebury College

STUDENTS SAY ". . ."

Academics

Williams College is a small bastion of the liberal arts "with a fantastic academic reputation." "Williams students tend to spend a lot of time complaining about how much work they have" but they say the academic experience is "absolutely incomparable." Classes are "small" and "intense." "The facilities are absolutely top-notch in almost everything." Research opportunities are plentiful. A one-month January term offers study abroad programs and a host of short pass/fail courses that are "a college student's dream come true." "The hard science departments are incredible." Economics, art history, and English are equally outstanding. Despite the occasional professor "who should not even be teaching at the high school level," the faculty at Williams is one of the best. Most professors "jump at every opportunity to help you love their subject." "They're here because they want to interact with undergrads." "If you complain about a Williams education then you would complain about education anywhere," wagers an economics major.

Life

Students at Williams enjoy a "stunning campus." "The Berkshire mountains are in the background every day as you walk to class" and opportunities for outdoor activity are numerous. The location is in "the boonies," though, and the surrounding "one-horse college town" is "quaint" at best. "There is no nearby place to buy necessities that is not ridiculously overpriced." Student life happens almost exclusively on campus. Dorm rooms are "large" and "well above par" but the housing system is "very weird." While some students like it, there is a general consensus that its creators "should be slapped and sent back to Amherst." Entertainment options include "lots of" performances, plays, and lectures. Some students are "obsessed with a capella groups." Intramurals are popular, especially broomball ("a sacred tradition involving a hockey rink, sneakers, a rubber ball, and paddles"). Intercollegiate sports are "a huge part of the social scene." For many students, the various varsity teams "are the basic social blocks at Williams." "Everyone for the most part gets along, but the sports teams seem to band together," explains a sophomore. Booze-laden parties" "and general disorder on weekends" are common. "A lot of people spend their lives between homework and practice and then just get completely smashed on weekends." Nothing gets out of hand, though. "We know how to unwind without being stupid," says a sophomore.

Student Body

The student population at Williams is not the most humble. They describe their peers as "interesting and beautiful" "geniuses of varying interests." They're "quirky, passionate, zany, and fun." They're "athletically awesome." They're "freakishly unique" and at the same time "cookie-cutter amazing." Ethnic diversity is stellar and you'll find all kinds of students including "the goth students," "nerdier students," "a ladle of environmentally conscious pseudo-vegetarians," and a few "west coast hippies." However, "a typical student looks like a rich white kid" who grew up "playing field hockey just outside Boston" and spends summers "vacationing on the Cape." Sporty students abound. "There definitely is segregation between the artsy kids and the athlete types but there is also a significant amount of crossover." "Williams is a place where normal social labels tend not to apply," reports a junior. "Everyone here got in for a reason. So that football player in your theater class has amazing insight on Chekhov and that outspoken environmental activist also specializes in improv comedy."

FINANCIAL AID: 413-597-4181 • E-MAIL: ADMISSION@WILLIAMS.EDU • WEBSITE: WWW.WILLIAMS.EDU

THE PRINCETON REVIEW SAYS

Admissions

Very important factors considered include: Application essay, academic GPA, recommendation(s), rigor of secondary school record, standardized test scores. *Important factors considered include:* Class rank, extracurricular activities, talent/ability. *Other factors considered include:* Alumni/ae relation, character/personal qualities, first generation, geographical residence, racial/ethnic status, volunteer work, work experience. SAT or ACT required; ACT with writing component required. High school diploma or equivalent is not required. *Academic units recommended:* 4 English, 4 mathematics, 3 science (3 science labs), 4 foreign language, 3 social studies.

Financial Aid

Students should submit: FAFSA, CSS/Financial Aid PROFILE, noncustodial PROFILE, business/farm supplement, parent and student federal taxes and W-2s. Regular filing deadline is February 1. The Princeton Review suggests that all financial aid forms be submitted as soon as possible after January 1. *Need-based scholarships/grants offered:* Federal Pell, SEOG, state scholarships/grants, private scholarships, the school's own gift aid. *Loan aid offered:* Direct Subsidized Stafford, Direct Unsubsidized Stafford, Direct PLUS, Federal Perkins, college/university loans from institutional funds. Applicants will be notified of awards on or about April 1. Federal Work-Study Program available. Institutional employment available.

The Inside Word

As is typical of highly selective colleges, at Williams high grades and test scores work more as qualifiers than to determine admissibility. Beyond a strong record of achievement, evidence of intellectual curiosity, noteworthy non-academic talents, and a non-college family background are some aspects of a candidate's application that might make for an offer of admission. But there are no guarantees—the evaluation process here is rigorous. The admissions committee (the entire admissions staff) discusses each candidate in comparison to the entire applicant pool. The pool is divided alphabetically for individual reading; after weak candidates are eliminated, those who remain undergo additional evaluations by different members of the staff. Admission decisions must be confirmed by the agreement of a plurality of the committee. Such close scrutiny demands a well-prepared candidate and application.

THE SCHOOL SAYS ". . ."

From the Admissions Office

"Special course offerings at Williams include Oxford-style tutorials, where students (in teams of two) research and defend ideas, engaging in weekly debate with a faculty tutor. Half of Williams' students pursue study abroad at some point, with about thirty students annually spending at year at Oxford. Four weeks of winter study each January provide time for individualized projects, research, and novel fields of study. Students compete in thirty-two Division III athletic teams, perform in twenty-five musical groups, stage ten theatrical productions, and volunteer in thirty service organizations. The college receives several million dollars annually for undergraduate science research and equipment. The town offers two distinguished art museums, the Williams College Museum of Art and the Clark Art Institute, and 2.200 forest acres—complete with a treetop canopy walkway—for environmental research and recreation.

"Students are required to submit either the SAT or the ACT including the optional writing section. Applicants should also submit scores from any two SAT Subject Tests. To limit the debt obligations of its graduates, Williams maintains one of the lowest loan expectations of any college or university in the country. Often the aid packages of students whose families demonstrate high financial need are made up entirely of grants and a campus job—and do not include any loans."

SELECTIVITY

Admissions Rating	**99**
# of applicants	7,030
% of applicants accepted	17
% of acceptees attending	45
# accepting a place on wait list	1,352
# admitted from wait list	14
# of early decision applicants	574
# accepted early decision	216

FRESHMAN PROFILE

Range SAT Critical Reading	660–770
Range SAT Math	650–760
Range ACT Composite	30–34
% graduated top 10% of class	91
% graduated top 25% of class	98
% graduated top 50% of class	100

DEADLINES

Early decision	
Deadline	11/10
Notification	12/15
Regular	
Deadline	1/1
Notification	4/1
Nonfall registration?	no

FINANCIAL FACTS

Financial Aid Rating	**93**
Annual tuition	$42,938
Room and board	$11,370
Required fees	$252
Books and supplies	$800
% needy frosh rec. need-based scholarship or grant aid	100
% needy UG rec. need-based scholarship or grant aid	100
% needy frosh rec. need-based self-help aid	100
% needy UG rec. need-based self-help aid	100
% frosh rec. any financial aid	53
% UG rec. any financial aid	53
% UG borrow to pay for school	44
Average cumulative indebtedness	$8,801
% frosh need fully met	100
% ugrads need fully met	100
Average % of frosh need met	100
Average % of ugrad need met	100

WITTENBERG UNIVERSITY

PO Box 720, Springfield, OH 45501 • Admissions: 937-327-6314 • Fax: 937-327-6379

CAMPUS LIFE

Quality of Life Rating	74
Fire Safety Rating	96
Green Rating	83
Type of school	private
Affiliation	Lutheran
Environment	town

STUDENTS

Total undergrad enrollment	1,735
% male/female	44/56
% from out of state	34
% from public high school	79
% frosh live on campus	95
# of fraternities	6
# of sororities	5
% African American	6
% Asian	1
% Caucasian	88
% Hispanic	3
% international	2
# of countries represented	25

SURVEY SAYS . . .

Students are friendly
Students are happy
Everyone loves the Tigers
Intramural sports are popular
Frats and sororities dominate social scene
Student government is popular

ACADEMICS

Academic Rating	87
% students returning for sophomore year	79
% students graduating within 4 years	66
% students graduating within 6 years	71
Calendar	semester
Student/faculty ratio	11:1
Profs interesting rating	95
Profs accessible rating	99
Most classes have	10–19 students
Most lab/discussion sessions have	10–19 students

MOST POPULAR MAJORS

biology/biological sciences; business/commerce; education

APPLICANTS ALSO LOOK AT AND OFTEN PREFER

Miami University, Ohio Wesleyan University, The Ohio State University—Columbus, The College of Wooster Denison University

AND SOMETIMES PREFER

Ohio Northern University

STUDENTS SAY ". . ."

Academics

At Wittenberg University, a Lutheran-affiliated liberal arts college, the motto, "Having light, we pass it on to others," rings throughout the minds of every student. This small community of students and faculty in Springfield, Ohio, emphasizes personal attention and development of the person as a whole, and the administration "encourages students to try new things" both inside and outside of the classroom to "broaden student horizons." In doing so, students become "committed to their own success and the success of the greater school community." Almost every Wittenberg student speaks glowingly of their professors, for both their teaching abilities and their caring nature. ("They treat us more like peers instead of people younger than they are," says one.) Most classes are in lecture format, and all are taught by professors who "do a great job of creating a dialogue in the classroom with students and between students that extends beyond the classroom." And professors "are always willing to meet up and discuss anything that is on our minds." "We work extra hard, because we know we can't get away with slacking (for better or for worse)." "Even in my largest class of seventy-five people (which is one of the largest at the university), my professor still knew who I was," says one student. The faculty also makes teaching their current students and advisees as "a top priority over their own research interests." While Wittenberg is "intellectually challenging," there are many great resources that students can avail themselves of, such as the Math Workshop, Writing Center, Oral Communication Center, and Foreign Language Learning Center. The administration "[wants] you to do well, but also love what you are doing."

Life

It's a friendly and "home-y" environment at Wittenberg, where "you know most people, but there's always new faces as well." The school has a strong freshman acclimation program called "The First-Year Experience," which allows for incoming students to meet each other and make friends at school-sponsored events, but "new friendships develop through clubs, sports, and other activities." Many friends come from the multitude of living options offered (dorms, off-campus housing, etc.). Everyone agrees, "The food is not the best," and the meal plans can be restrictive. Springfield is big enough that there are movie theaters and bowling alleys that students can go to off campus, but "Most students end up staying on campus for the weekends." Though the campus itself is "gorgeous," there are "some safety concerns with Springfield residents" when you leave it at night. Greek life here is "pretty epic," with more than a third of all students participating; students typically work "very hard at times that call for hard work, but weekends are time for play." Though a fair amount of drinking takes place, there are plenty of alternatives offered, such as "Witt Wednesday" events, and there are also games "for just about every sport on almost every day of the week."

Student Body

Tigers are a "relaxed, friendly" group who are "more than happy to make new friends all the time." While there's a "tolerant community" at Wittenberg where "everyone is accepted," students admit, "We are rather…homogeneous." However, similarities end at appearance, because "interests are as variant as Lady Gaga's dress collection." Everyone agrees that as long as you make an effort, there's "always a group or club and friends with the same interests." Wittenberg has a fair number of athletes and Ohioans, in no particular order, and no one has any trouble learning "how to balance play with studies."

FINANCIAL AID: 937-327-7321 • E-MAIL: ADMISSION@WITTENBERG.EDU • WEBSITE: WWW.WITTENBERG.EDU

THE PRINCETON REVIEW SAYS

Admissions

Very important factors considered include: Class rank, academic GPA, rigor of secondary school record. *Important factors considered include:* Application essay, recommendation(s), character/personal qualities, extracurricular activities, talent/ability, volunteer work. *Other factors considered include:* Standardized test scores, alumni/ae relation, first generation, interview, work experience. ACT with or without writing component accepted. TOEFL required of all international applicants. High school diploma is required and GED is accepted. *Academic units required:* 4 English, 3 mathematics, 3 science (2 science labs), 2 foreign language, 2 history. *Academic units recommended:* 4 English, 4 mathematics, 5 science (2 science labs), 3 foreign language, 3 history.

Financial Aid

Students should submit: FAFSA. The Princeton Review suggests that all financial aid forms be submitted as soon as possible after January 1. *Need-based scholarships/grants offered:* Federal Pell, SEOG, state scholarships/grants, private scholarships, the school's own gift aid. *Loan aid offered:* Direct Subsidized Stafford, Direct Unsubsidized Stafford, Direct PLUS, Federal Perkins, college/university loans from institutional funds, private alternative loans. Applicants will be notified of awards on a rolling basis beginning March 1. Federal Work-Study Program available. Institutional employment available. Off-campus job opportunities are excellent.

The Inside Word

Wittenberg's applicant pool is small but quite solid coming off of a couple of strong years. Students who haven't successfully reached an above-average academic level in high school will meet with little success in the admissions process. Candidate evaluation is thorough and personal; applicants should devote serious attention to all aspects of their candidacy.

THE SCHOOL SAYS ". . ."

From the Admissions Office

"At Wittenberg, you will experience an active and engaged learning environment, a setting where you can refine your definition of self yet gain exposure to the varied kinds of knowledge, people, views, activities, options, and ideas that add richness to our lives. Wittenberg is a university where students are able to thrive in a small campus environment with many opportunities for intellectual and personal growth in and out of the classroom. Campus life is as diverse as the interests of our students. Wittenberg attracts students from all over the United States and from many other countries. Historically, the university has been committed to geographical, educational, cultural, and religious diversity. With their varied backgrounds and interests, Wittenberg students have helped initiate many of the more than 125 student organizations that are active on campus. The students will be the first to tell you there's never a lack of things to do on or near the campus any day of the week, if you're willing to get involved.

"Wittenberg University is test score optional. Freshman applicants can choose to submit either ACT (with or without writing component) or SAT scores."

SELECTIVITY

Admissions Rating	**80**
# of applicants	4,412
% of applicants accepted	85
% of acceptees attending	14
# of early decision applicants	33
# accepted early decision	24

FRESHMAN PROFILE

Range SAT Critical Reading	510–630
Range SAT Math	510–630
Range ACT Composite	22–30
Minimum paper TOEFL	550
Average HS GPA	3.5
% graduated top 10% of class	27
% graduated top 25% of class	54
% graduated top 50% of class	86

DEADLINES

Early decision	
Deadline	11/15
Notification	12/15
Early action	
Deadline	12/1
Notification	1/1
Regular	
Priority	3/15
Nonfall registration?	yes

FINANCIAL FACTS

Financial Aid Rating	**86**
Annual tuition	$37,230
Room and board	$9,736
Required fees	$800
Books and supplies	$1,000
% needy frosh rec. need-based scholarship or grant aid	98
% needy UG rec. need-based scholarship or grant aid	99
% needy frosh rec. need-based self-help aid	97
% needy UG rec. need-based self-help aid	96
% UG borrow to pay for school	68
Average cumulative indebtedness	$30,919
% frosh need fully met	35
% ugrads need fully met	29
Average % of frosh need met	88
Average % of ugrad need met	83

WOFFORD COLLEGE

429 NORTH CHURCH STREET, SPARTANBURG, SC 29303-3663 • ADMISSIONS: 864-597-4130 • FAX: 864-597-4147

CAMPUS LIFE

Quality of Life Rating	**87**
Fire Safety Rating	**77**
Green Rating	**78**
Type of school	private
Affiliation	Methodist
Environment	city

STUDENTS

Total undergrad enrollment	1,515
% male/female	51/49
% from out of state	44
% from public high school	68
% frosh live on campus	95
# of fraternities	8
# of sororities	4
% African American	8
% Asian	2
% Caucasian	83
% Hispanic	2
% international	2
# of countries represented	15

SURVEY SAYS . . .

Lab facilities are great
Great computer facilities
School is well run
Low cost of living
Frats and sororities dominate social scene

ACADEMICS

Academic Rating	**91**
% students returning for sophomore year	88
% students graduating within 4 years	75
% students graduating within 6 years	79
Calendar	4-1-4
Student/faculty ratio	11:1
Profs interesting rating	95
Profs accessible rating	95
Most classes have	10–19 students
Most lab/discussion sessions have	20–29 students

MOST POPULAR MAJORS

biology/biological sciences; business/managerial economics; finance

APPLICANTS ALSO LOOK AT AND SOMETIMES PREFER

Furman University

AND RARELY PREFER

Clemson University, University of South Carolina—Columbia

STUDENTS SAY ". . ."

Academics

Wofford's "excellent reputation with graduate programs" and "challenging" classes have established this South Carolina school as "a liberal arts college that provides an excellent education and opportunities to expand your horizon." Wofford is known as "a great and successful academic school," a "community of learning where individuality, curiosity, and success are fostered every day" in large part thanks to a staff of educators that "challenges students to think and discuss their ideas in every class." Teachers here "expect a lot," but students don't have to go it alone. The "extremely knowledgeable, engaging, and helpful" professors are "willing to assist in any way they can," educators who "go over and beyond to help you achieve even the hardest goal." Even in popular-but-difficult courses like premed and government, Wofford's small campus means "it's easy to have interaction between teachers and students." "Many even give home or cell phone numbers," another student comments. "It is challenging," students say, "but the professors make it fun!" That same passion for learning extends to the student body. This is a campus "where all of the students look out for each other and help one another succeed."

Life

Greek life is a big deal at Wofford. Even those not directly involved in fraternities and sororities find that "the most popular destination on Friday and Saturday nights" is Fraternity Row, where there are "live bands, music, dancing, and much more that the students enjoy." "Greeks and non-Greeks are generally out, and there are often bands performing at the houses," though on Saturdays, "It closes at midnight, so then we go to the seniors' apartments." Though there is "a beautiful downtown area that students like to walk around and shop," staying close to school is not unusual since "the campus is very much its own small community." Indeed, "There is barely any need to get off campus." For those who want to escape the "Wofford Bubble," there is Spartanburg, which may be "lacking in interesting thing to do," but "does have a good variety of restaurants." Even better, "A lot of the restaurants, bars, and shops will give you a discount if you are a Wofford student." For those disinclined to party or travel, "Almost every day there is a school-sponsored event on campus. From painting on the lawn to an oyster roast, there is always something to do." But Wofford students are also hardworking students, so before and after all that, they "go to the library and the science center a lot."

Student Body

It should come as no surprise that "the frat scene is high" at Wofford, since "the typical Wofford student is very similar to the 'stereotypical' Southerner: polite, tied to tradition, friendly, welcoming, living life at a slower pace, and very passionate about their beliefs." Many students say they are "not involved in Greek life," but are "just as happy as the people who are." Students here are "preppy, studious, from South Carolina, and conservative." If that sounds limiting, students say it is not. Wofford students say, "While groups generally stick together, tolerance and acceptance is the norm." That is because, on campus, "it doesn't matter what club or group you are involved in, you will be included no matter what. I have been here for almost two years and have failed to meet an unkind student." Though the campus is predominantly white, "There is some diversity on campus," including significant populations of Asian American and African American students. Perhaps one student sums it up best when they say this school offers "a unique culture: diverse in background, ethnicity, and views, but united by the communal notion that at our essence, we are all Wofford."

FINANCIAL AID: 864-597-4160 • E-MAIL: ADMISSION@WOFFORD.EDU • WEBSITE: WWW.WOFFORD.EDU

THE PRINCETON REVIEW SAYS

Admissions

Very important factors considered include: Academic GPA, rigor of secondary school record. *Important factors considered include:* Class rank, application essay, standardized test scores, character/personal qualities, extracurricular activities, talent/ability, volunteer work. *Other factors considered include:* Recommendation(s), alumni/ae relation, first generation, geographical residence, interview, racial/ethnic status, work experience. SAT or ACT required; ACT with writing component required. TOEFL required of all international applicants. High school diploma is required and GED is accepted. *Academic units recommended:* 4 English, 4 mathematics, 3 science (3 science labs), 3 foreign language, 2 social studies, 1 history, 1 visual/performing arts, 1 computer science, 1 academic electives.

Financial Aid

Students should submit: FAFSA. The Princeton Review suggests that all financial aid forms be submitted as soon as possible after January 1. *Need-based scholarships/grants offered:* Federal Pell, SEOG, state scholarships/grants, the school's own gift aid. *Loan aid offered:* Direct Subsidized Stafford, Direct Unsubsidized Stafford, Direct PLUS, Federal Perkins. Applicants will be notified of awards on or about March 31. Federal Work-Study Program available. Institutional employment available. Highest amount earned per year from on-campus jobs $1,940. Off-campus job opportunities are good.

The Inside Word

Wofford College distinguishes itself by providing its students with an extremely supportive environment. This concern extends to the applications it receives, each of which is given careful consideration. Students who have earned decent grades in challenging courses should find themselves with an opportunity to attend a school that is gaining a reputation as one of the South's premier liberal arts colleges.

THE SCHOOL SAYS ". . ."

From the Admissions Office

"A century ago, Wofford athletics team chose the Boston Terrier as their mascot. These beloved dogs are small, but they are full of intelligence and energy. Similarly, with an enrollment of about 1600 students, Wofford is small, but campus life is ideal for learning and fun. In fact, the college's scores on the National Survey of Student Engagement (NSSE) have ranked with the best in the country for several years. According to the 2011 'Open Doors' study of participation in international programs, Wofford stands second among all the nation's liberal arts colleges. Our "new Urban" Village Housing for seniors and our environmental studies center have won architectural awards, and our entire historic campus is a national arboretum. Our athletics teams have won recent Southern Conference championships in football and basketball, and our quarterback and point guard in 2012 were members of Phi Beta Kappa. Wofford thus remains committed to its historic mission— turning out graduates who can make international connections and become difference makers in a variety of vocations and professions."

SELECTIVITY	
Admissions Rating	92
# of applicants	2,871
% of applicants accepted	65
% of acceptees attending	24
# accepting a place on wait list	77
# admitted from wait list	5
# of early decision applicants	872
# accepted early decision	635

FRESHMAN PROFILE	
Range SAT Critical Reading	570–680
Range SAT Math	580–690
Range SAT Writing	570–670
Range ACT Composite	23–28
Minimum paper TOEFL	550
Minimum web-based TOEFL	80
Average HS GPA	3.6
% graduated top 10% of class	56
% graduated top 25% of class	85
% graduated top 50% of class	99

DEADLINES	
Early decision	
Deadline	11/15
Notification	12/5
Regular	
Deadline	2/1
Notification	3/15
Nonfall registration?	yes

FINANCIAL FACTS	
Financial Aid Rating	88
Annual tuition	$33,190
Room and board	$9,375
Books and supplies	$1,200
% needy frosh rec. need-based scholarship or grant aid	90
% needy UG rec. need-based scholarship or grant aid	92
% needy frosh rec. non-need-based scholarship or grant aid	31
% needy UG rec. non-need-based scholarship or grant aid	31
% needy frosh rec. need-based self-help aid	50
% needy UG rec. need-based self-help aid	53
% frosh rec. any financial aid	95
% UG rec. any financial aid	93
% UG borrow to pay for school	43
Average cumulative indebtedness	$24,355
% frosh need fully met	41
% ugrads need fully met	44
Average % of frosh need met	82
Average % of ugrad need met	84

WORCESTER POLYTECHNIC INSTITUTE

ADMISSIONS OFFICE, BARTLETT CENTER, WORCESTER, MA 01609 • ADMISSIONS: 508-831-5286 • FAX: 508-831-5875

CAMPUS LIFE

Quality of Life Rating	**84**
Fire Safety Rating	**79**
Green Rating	**83**
Type of school	private
Environment	city

STUDENTS

Total undergrad enrollment	3,746
% male/female	69/31
% from out of state	58
% from public high school	66
% frosh live on campus	90
# of fraternities	13
# of sororities	5
% African American	3
% Asian	5
% Caucasian	69
% Hispanic	8
% international	11
# of countries represented	80

SURVEY SAYS . . .

Lab facilities are great
Great computer facilities
Career services are great
School is well run
Dorms are like palaces
Students are happy
Frats and sororities dominate social scene
Student government is popular

ACADEMICS

Academic Rating	**84**
% students returning for sophomore year	95
% students graduating within 4 years	64
% students graduating within 6 years	76
Calendar	quarter
Student/faculty ratio	14:1
Profs interesting rating	72
Profs accessible rating	83
Most classes have	fewer than 10 students
Most lab/discussion sessions have	20–29 students

MOST POPULAR MAJORS

computer science; electrical, electronics and communications engineering; mechanical engineering

APPLICANTS ALSO LOOK AT AND OFTEN PREFER

Massachusetts Institute of Technology, Cornell University, Carnegie Mellon University, Brown University

AND SOMETIMES PREFER

Tufts University, Rensselaer Polytechnic Institute, Boston University, University of Rochester

AND RARELY PREFER

University of Massachusetts Amherst, University of Connecticut, Rochester Institute of Technology, Northeastern University

STUDENTS SAY ". . ."

Academics

Learning "is project-based and very hands on" at Worcester Polytechnic Institute, a prestigious engineering, mathematics, and science university located in central Massachusetts. Here, "students are encouraged to do some hands-on work in almost every class" through a "project-based curriculum," in which "students are given the opportunity to work on projects with minimal guidance from their advisors." Students describe this approach as "a good and realistic experience that is helpful for future career plans." The project-based system "emphasizes the understanding of technical concepts, the practical implementation of these concepts, and also an appreciation for how technological advances can benefit mankind." WPI's unique grading system of A/B/C/NR—"fail a class and it won't show up on your transcript," one student explains—means "there is a lot of freedom to take riskier classes" and the school "promotes a culture of cooperation over competition." "Even though the curriculum is hard, [and] even though we have homework due every day, we are all happy because we know that failing is just another chance to try again. It's a good philosophy." A quarterly academic calendar "allows students to take a more diverse array of classes, and forces them to learn quickly or fall behind," but also means "if you're sick for two weeks, you have lots of make-up work to do." "Incredible technological resources" are the cherry on the sundae here.

Life

"Students are very involved with schoolwork, studying, and homework" during the week at WPI, where a heavy workload and rapid-paced academic calendar keep kids busy ("With classes that last only seven weeks, midterms hit fast, and then by the time they're over, it's already time to start up on finals," one student warns). Thank goodness "the social life is unbeatable." The campus hosts "a very large amount of active clubs and organizations," including a student-run social committee that "is always holding really outrageous and fun events," including "concerts with really good and popular bands." WPI also has a well supported "sports scene—football and basketball are pretty popular," and intramurals draw plenty of participants as well. WPI's "awesome," "strong and very popular" Parties "are really fun," drawing "people from all the neighboring schools," and students insist that the parties "are always fun-themed and not sketchy. You can have a fun time and not have to be concerned about your safety" due to "a driving service with a no-questions-asked policy" and "a detail cop so nothing goes wrong."

Student Body

"We have a very nice mix of students here who do not fit the typical engineering student [profile]," which "stands us apart from other engineering schools," one student writes. Even so, most here concede that "the typical student is nerdy." "We're all nerdy in our own way, whether it be a love of calculus or getting excited over video games," one undergrad relates. Another student breaks down the population this way: "There are four groups of students at WPI. One group consists of the kids who are involved on campus, one consists of kids who never leave their rooms because they are playing video games, one consists of kids who spend all their time studying, and the final group consists of kids who go to class but just want to go to parties the rest of the time." Nearly everyone here is "very driven and self-motivated," because you can't survive WPI long without those qualities. The population includes "a lot of stereotypical Massachusetts or general New England people" and "lots of international students," with China and India especially well represented.

FINANCIAL AID: 508-831-5469 • E-MAIL: ADMISSIONS@WPI.EDU • WEBSITE: WWW.WPI.EDU

THE PRINCETON REVIEW SAYS

Admissions

Very important factors considered include: Academic GPA, rigor of secondary school record. *Important factors considered include:* Class rank, application essay, recommendation(s), standardized test scores, character/personal qualities, extracurricular activities. *Other factors considered include:* Alumni/ae relation, first generation, geographical residence, interview, level of applicant's interest, talent/ability, volunteer work, work experience. ACT with or without writing component accepted. TOEFL required of all international applicants. High school diploma is required and GED is accepted. *Academic units required:* 4 English, 4 mathematics, 2 science (2 science labs). *Academic units recommended:* 4 science, 2 foreign language, 2 social studies, 1 history, 1 computer science.

Financial Aid

Students should submit: FAFSA, CSS/Financial Aid PROFILE, noncustodial PROFILE. Regular filing deadline is February 1. The Princeton Review suggests that all financial aid forms be submitted as soon as possible after January 1. *Need-based scholarships/grants offered:* Federal Pell, SEOG, state scholarships/grants, private scholarships, the school's own gift aid. *Loan aid offered:* Direct Subsidized Stafford, Direct Unsubsidized Stafford, Direct PLUS, Federal Perkins, state loans, college/university loans from institutional funds. Applicants will be notified of awards on or about April 1. Federal Work-Study Program available. Institutional employment available. Off-campus job opportunities are good.

The Inside Word

WPI's high admission rate is the result of a self-selecting applicant pool; those who don't have a decent chance of getting in here rarely bother to apply. The relatively low rate of conversion of accepted students to enrollees is due to the fact that WPI is a 'safety' school for many applicants. Those who get in here and at MIT, CalTech, Cornell, or Carnegie Mellon usually wind up elsewhere.

THE SCHOOL SAYS ". . ."

From the Admissions Office

"Projects and research enrich WPI's academic program. WPI believes that in these times simply passing courses and accumulating theoretical knowledge is not enough to truly educate tomorrow's leaders. Tomorrow's professionals ought to be involved in project work that prepares them today for future challenges. Projects at WPI come as close to professional experience as a college program can possibly achieve. In fact, WPI works with more than 200 companies, government agencies, and private organizations each year. These groups provide opportunities where students get a chance to work in real, professional settings. Students gain invaluable experience in planning, coordinating team efforts, meeting deadlines, writing proposals and reports, making oral presentations, doing cost analyses, and making decisions.

Applicants are required to submit SAT or ACT scores, or in lieu of test scores may submit supplemental materials through WPI's Flex Path program. Students who choose the Flex Path are encouraged to submit examples of academic work or extracurricular projects that reflect a high level of organization, motivation, creativity and problem-solving ability."

SELECTIVITY

Admissions Rating	94
# of applicants	7,049
% of applicants accepted	57
% of acceptees attending	25
# accepting a place on wait list	1,571

FRESHMAN PROFILE

Range SAT Critical Reading	560–670
Range SAT Math	640–730
Range SAT Writing	560–660
Range ACT Composite	27–31
Minimum paper TOEFL	550
Minimum web-based TOEFL	79
Average HS GPA	3.8
% graduated top 10% of class	65
% graduated top 25% of class	93
% graduated top 50% of class	100

DEADLINES

Early action	
Deadline	11/10
Notification	12/20
Regular	
Deadline	2/1
Notification	4/1
Nonfall registration?	yes

FINANCIAL FACTS

Financial Aid Rating	82
Annual tuition	$40,790
Room and board	$12,340
Required fees	$590
Books and supplies	$1,000
% needy frosh rec. need-based scholarship or grant aid	99
% needy UG rec. need-based scholarship or grant aid	94
% needy frosh rec. non-need-based scholarship or grant aid	36
% needy UG rec. non-need-based scholarship or grant aid	27
% needy frosh rec. need-based self-help aid	59
% needy UG rec. need-based self-help aid	61
% frosh rec. any financial aid	99
% UG rec. any financial aid	95
% frosh need fully met	48
% ugrads need fully met	39
Average % of frosh need met	71
Average % of ugrad need met	74

XAVIER UNIVERSITY OF LOUISIANA

ONE DREXEL DRIVE, NEW ORLEANS, LA 70125 • ADMISSIONS: 504-520-7388 • FAX: 504-520-7941

CAMPUS LIFE

Quality of Life Rating	**66**
Fire Safety Rating	**87**
Green Rating	**60***
Type of school	private
Affiliation	Roman Catholic
Environment	metropolis

STUDENTS

Total undergrad enrollment	2,725
% male/female	29/71
% from out of state	51
% from public high school	81
% frosh live on campus	69
# of fraternities	4
# of sororities	4
% African American	79
% Asian	9
% Caucasian	4
% Hispanic	2
% international	2
# of countries represented	8

SURVEY SAYS . . .

Lab facilities are great
Great computer facilities
Students get along with local community
Great off-campus food
Frats and sororities dominate social scene
Student government is popular
Very little drug use

ACADEMICS

Academic Rating	**77**
% students returning for sophomore year	69
% students graduating within 4 years	35
Calendar	semester
Student/faculty ratio	13:1
Profs interesting rating	81
Profs accessible rating	83
Most classes have	10–19 students
Most lab/discussion sessions have	20–29 students

MOST POPULAR MAJORS

premedicine/premedical studies; pre-pharmacy studies; psychology

STUDENTS SAY ". . ."

Academics

One of the top Historically Black Colleges/Universities (HBCU), Xavier University of Louisiana prides itself on educating students in a range of subjects, to provide a "thriving underlying foundation, upon which students can achieve the very best for themselves." Though perhaps best known for its science departments, the New Orleans-based school has both a College of Arts and Sciences and a College of Pharmacy and requires "high academic standards" for all of majors across the board. Between its academic reputation and the emphasis placed on community leadership, no matter the reason that you go to XU, you leave "fully educated." "I was challenged academically, but not broken. The workload was not overwhelming," says a student. Small class sizes means great interaction with professors, and the ensuing "close-knit relationships" are cited by many as a major part of their satisfaction with the school. Also on that list? "The education you receive at XU, considering the extremely low tuition cost and financial aid opportunities for a private university, is unparalleled." Professors at XU are dedicated to ensuring that all students "are proficient, if not masters, in the materials taught," and they provide "an excellent foundation for further academic and career success." XU produces a tremendous number of graduates who go on to medical school and other professional schools in "the pursuit of success." Most faculty members are "almost always available in some form or fashion to help you with any questions you may have," and the school itself provides "multiple resources for any problems that need reinforcement." One exception, however, is the financial aid and fiscal services departments, which "have very little time to discuss things with students."

Life

Despite its location, XU "is by no means a party school." Because the student body is mostly composed of science majors, people "are always studying," and "Study groups are a common thing." Students "will take occasional breaks," but for the most part, grades are the important thing at XU. "We are not a school that places as much emphasis on 'fun' as we do making sure we are productive and contributing citizens by the time we graduate," says a student. Though the school offers "lots of opportunities to volunteer," many students complain that there aren't enough social activities to keep students occupied, and school spirit suffers as a result. "We have a strong academic standing, but our campus life is pretty limited," says one student. The dry campus also enforces a curfew ("Sometimes it feels like a boarding school"), so the typical college experience and hair-letting-loose happens off-campus: "Campus is a place to work." Not everyone is familiar with the city (there's no off-campus housing associated with XU), so going out to movies, clubs, and shopping on weekends usually happens in groups. There's also a fair amount of interaction with neighboring schools like Tulane, Loyola, and Dillard. "There are so many things to do right around the corner from Xavier; I can see musicals, watch the Saints, see the Hornets play, salsa dance, get amazing Southern cuisine, listen to 'bounce' music, and learn how to dance, see parades and second lines," sums up a Big Easy lover.

Student Body

Studious, studious, studious. Most students are "very focused, driven, and destined for success," and unsurprisingly, you run into a lot of "aspiring" doctors and pharmacists. The majority of students are African American or Asian, and the female-to-male ratio is quite high. The student body as a whole has a "conservative mentality." It's "very easy" to make friends here, particularly through study groups, and the small campus means that "everyone recognizes everyone" and "gets along with each other."

FINANCIAL AID: 504-520-7835 • E-MAIL: APPLY@XULA.EDU • WEBSITE: WWW.XULA.EDU

THE PRINCETON REVIEW SAYS

Admissions

Very important factors considered include: Academic GPA, recommendation(s), rigor of secondary school record, standardized test scores. *Important factors considered include:* Class rank, application essay. *Other factors considered include:* Alumni/ae relation, character/personal qualities, extracurricular activities, interview, talent/ability, volunteer work, work experience. SAT or ACT required; ACT with writing component recommended. TOEFL required of all international applicants. High school diploma is required and GED is accepted. *Academic units required:* 4 English, 2 mathematics, 1 science, 1 social studies, 8 academic electives. *Academic units recommended:* 4 mathematics, 3 science, 1 foreign language, 1 history.

Financial Aid

Students should submit: FAFSA. The Princeton Review suggests that all financial aid forms be submitted as soon as possible after January 1. *Need-based scholarships/grants offered:* Federal Pell, SEOG, state scholarships/grants, private scholarships, the school's own gift aid, United Negro College Fund. *Loan aid offered:* Direct Subsidized Stafford, Direct Unsubsidized Stafford, Direct PLUS, Federal Perkins. Applicants will be notified of awards on a rolling basis beginning April 1. Federal Work-Study Program available. Institutional employment available. Highest amount earned per year from on-campus jobs $1,000. Off-campus job opportunities are good.

Inside Word

This HBCU has a rolling admissions process, and applicants typically receive notification of the school's decision within one month of completed application submission. Campus visits are encouraged. If you want to be considered for scholarships, you'll need to include a strong personal statement that reflects evidence of leadership. Admission to the school's College of Pharmacy is separate from that of the College of Arts and Sciences and is subject to a different set of requirements.

THE SCHOOL SAYS ". . ."

From the Admissions Office

A Message from the SGA president:

"It is my pleasure to invite you to a college experience that will change and enhance your life. Xavier alumni are known for being exceptional doctors, lawyers, educators, business leaders, journalists, and the like.

"As a graduating biology major, I know Xavier has prepared me for my career in medicine while nurturing me academically and socially.

"With hardship often comes an opportunity to rise to greater heights. In its own way, Hurricane Katrina in 2005 may have added to the character of our people and enhanced the very principles upon which this university was founded.

"St. Katharine Drexel clearly understood when she founded Xavier, the necessity to provide minority students with a quality education and the skills needed to become leaders in their communities. Her vision was to help build a more just and humane society. What better time than now to become a part of the rebuilding of one of America's most unique cities, New Orleans.

"Higher education is not only about gaining intellectual knowledge, but acquiring social and community skills as well. At Xavier we offer a wide array of clubs, organizations and teams to suit the needs and interests of the student body."

SELECTIVITY

Admissions Rating	77
# of applicants	4,463
% of applicants accepted	64
% of acceptees attending	27
# accepting a place on wait list	91
# admitted from wait list	13

FRESHMAN PROFILE

Range SAT Critical Reading	430–540
Range SAT Math	430–540
Range SAT Writing	410–520
Range ACT Composite	19–24
Minimum paper TOEFL	550
Average HS GPA	3.3
% graduated top 10% of class	29
% graduated top 25% of class	55
% graduated top 50% of class	82

DEADLINES

Regular	
Priority	3/1
Deadline	7/1
Notification	10/15
Nonfall registration?	yes

FINANCIAL FACTS

Financial Aid Rating	65
Annual tuition	$17,700
Room and board	$7,600
Required fees	$1,000
Books and supplies	$1,200
% needy frosh rec. need-based scholarship or grant aid	74
% needy UG rec. need-based scholarship or grant aid	73
% needy frosh rec. non-need-based scholarship or grant aid	88
% needy UG rec. non-need-based scholarship or grant aid	75
% needy frosh rec. need-based self-help aid	97
% needy UG rec. need-based self-help aid	97
% frosh rec. any financial aid	94
% UG rec. any financial aid	24
% UG borrow to pay for school	83
Average cumulative indebtedness	$26,106
% ugrads need fully met	1
Average % of frosh need met	11
Average % of ugrade need met	13

XAVIER UNIVERSITY (OH)

3800 VICTORY PARKWAY, CINCINNATI, OH 45207-5311 • ADMISSIONS: 513-745-3301 • FAX: 513-745-4319

CAMPUS LIFE

Quality of Life Rating	**83**
Fire Safety Rating	**76**
Green Rating	**89**
Type of school	private
Affiliation	Roman Catholic-Jesuit
Environment	metropolis

STUDENTS

Total undergrad enrollment	4,355
% male/female	47/53
% from out of state	40
% from public high school	51
% frosh live on campus	87
% African American	10
% Asian	2
% Caucasian	77
% Hispanic	4
% international	1
# of countries represented	42

SURVEY SAYS . . .

School is well run
Students are friendly
Dorms are like palaces
Everyone loves the Musketeers
Frats and sororities are unpopular or nonexistent
Student government is popular

ACADEMICS

Academic Rating	**81**
% students returning for sophomore year	84
% students graduating within 4 years	70
% students graduating within 6 years	79
Calendar	semester
Student/faculty ratio	12:1
Profs interesting rating	84
Profs accessible rating	85
Most classes have	20–29 students
Most lab/discussion sessions have	10–19 students

MOST POPULAR MAJORS

business/commerce; liberal arts and sciences/liberal studies; nursing/registered nurse (rn, asn, bsn, msn)

APPLICANTS ALSO LOOK AT AND OFTEN PREFER

University of Notre Dame

AND SOMETIMES PREFER

Indiana University—Bloomington, Loyola University of Chicago, Marquette University, Miami University, The Ohio State University—Columbus, University of Dayton, University of Cincinnati

AND RARELY PREFER

University of Kentucky, Saint Louis University, Purdue University—West Lafayette

STUDENTS SAY ". . ."

Academics

Xavier University, a medium-sized Jesuit institution "in the heart of Cincinnati," instills "a real sense of community and social conscience" while still "giving students the needed skills to succeed in all of their life endeavors." Xavier even tosses in a broad liberal arts education for good measure, courtesy of a core curriculum and distribution requirements that include lots of theology, philosophy, English, history, and foreign language. But it's business that many students—one in four, to be more precise—major in here. Undergrads tout the "great entrepreneurship program" and XU's "great record" for placing accounting students in graduate schools. XU's nursing program is also "very strong," with "an excellent" "pass rate on the NCLEX," and the education program earns similar plaudits. In all areas, XU offers "relatively small" classes, "which can make it hard when it's time for registration, but when you're in class it's great." Academics are "challenging, but the teachers and administration help make the transition [from high school] smooth and are there whenever you need their help." "Academically, it is nearly impossible to fail," a freshman adds. "There are always tutoring centers and help [is] available for any subject, whenever you need it." The school also "excels at real-world placement. If you want an internship, just ask. There's even a team of people here whose only job is to find internships and co-ops for students." Undergrads also appreciate their classmates' low-key approach; they "care but are very laid-back in classes."

Life

"Xavier University has a little bit of everything—service projects, strong academics, social events, religious events, weekend trips, and lots of other activities to get involved in." A good number of the aforementioned activities "are put on by [the] Student Activities Council and by student government." Many Xavier students "go to the sporting events," with a heavy focus on the men's basketball team, which "is obviously a huge deal here" (the team has made the NCAA Sweet 16 four times in the last five years). Students say XU parties "usually don't get too out of control. I've never really heard or experienced any…of the typical bad college party experiences," a sophomore reports. They also tell us "there are few bars around (mainly only one, for upper classmen) so people generally party at houses." Big-city living lures some students off campus. Cincinnati "is a great city to go out in—there are areas such as Mt. Adams and Newport that provide entertainment and dining for both college-aged students and young professionals."

Student Body

"I'd say ninety-five percent of the students at this school are friendly and always willing to meet new people or help you if you have a problem," writes one student, expressing a commonly held perception of Xavier undergrads. Students "spend a lot of time with varieties of people—not just a 'clique' or single group of people—[so] it is fairly easy to get to know a large percentage of your classmates, especially the peers in your graduating class." In terms of demographics, "Lots of kids come from suburban areas and went to Catholic schools, so there is a large population of wealthy, religious students." Adding some ethnic diversity are "significant populations of minority students (black, Asian, international, etc.) who each have [a] strong voice on campus." Alternative culture is hardly found here, one student notes; "It's rare to find a kid with a mohawk unless the rugby team shaved his head. Most kids are clean-cut." An accounting and finance major adds, "There are no real emo/goth kids at this school (thank God)." However, a weekend degree program and night classes draw a substantial, nontraditional population to the school.

FINANCIAL AID: 513-745-3142 • E-MAIL: XUADMIT@XAVIER.EDU • WEBSITE: WWW.XAVIER.EDU

THE PRINCETON REVIEW SAYS

Admissions

Very important factors considered include: Rigor of secondary school record. *Important factors considered include:* Class rank, application essay, academic GPA, recommendation(s), standardized test scores, character/personal qualities. *Other factors considered include:* Alumni/ae relation, extracurricular activities, first generation, level of applicant's interest, talent/ability, volunteer work, work experience. SAT or ACT required; ACT with or without writing component accepted. TOEFL required of all international applicants. High school diploma is required and GED is accepted. *Academic units recommended:* 4 English, 3 mathematics, 3 science, 2 foreign language, 3 social studies, 5 academic electives, 1 health/physical education.

Financial Aid

Students should submit: FAFSA. The Princeton Review suggests that all financial aid forms be submitted as soon as possible after January 1. *Need-based scholarships/grants offered:* Federal Pell, SEOG, state scholarships/grants, private scholarships, the school's own gift aid. *Loan aid offered:* Direct Subsidized Stafford, Direct Unsubsidized Stafford, Direct PLUS, Federal Perkins. Applicants will be notified of awards on a rolling basis beginning February 15. Federal Work-Study Program available. Institutional employment available. Highest amount earned per year from on-campus jobs $4,900. Off-campus job opportunities are excellent.

The Inside Word

Above-average students should encounter little difficulty in gaining admission to Xavier. Others may be able to finagle their way in with some elbow grease, credible demonstrations of commitment to academics and Jesuit ideals of service, and a Catholic approach to academics.

THE SCHOOL SAYS ". . ."

From the Admissions Office

"Founded in 1831, Xavier University is the fourth oldest of the twenty-eight Jesuit colleges and universities in the United States. The Jesuit tradition is evident in the university's core curriculum, degree programs, and involvement opportunities. Xavier is home to approximately 7,000 total students; 4,300 degree-seeking undergraduates. The student population represents more than forty-five states and forty-three foreign countries. Xavier offers more than eighty undergraduate academic majors and more than fifty minors in the College of Arts and Sciences; the Williams College of Business; and the College of Social Sciences, Health, and Education. Most popular majors include business, natural sciences, communication arts, education, psychology, biology, sport management/marketing, and pre-professional study. Other programs of note include University Scholars; Honors AB; Philosophy, Politics, and the Public; Army ROTC, study abroad, academic service-learning, and community engagement fellowship. There are more than 100 academic clubs, social and service organizations, and recreational sports activities on campus. Students participate in groups such as student government, campus ministry, performing arts, and intramural sports as well as one of the largest service-oriented Alternative Break clubs in the country. Xavier is a member of the Division I Atlantic 10 Conference and fields teams in men's and women's basketball, cross-country, track, golf, soccer, swimming, and tennis, as well as men's baseball and women's volleyball.

"Xavier is situated on more than 148 acres in a residential area of Cincinnati, Ohio. The face of Xavier continues to change with the addition of the technology-based Conaton Learning Commons and Smith Hall, a new building for the Williams College of Business, both which opened in fall 2010, and Fenwick Place which includes a 535 bed residence hall, a dining hall and offices that opened in fall 2011.

"Applicants must submit results from the SAT or ACT. The student's best score(s) from either test will be used. The writing portion of the SAT/ACT is not required and will not be used in admission and scholarship decisions."

SELECTIVITY

Admissions Rating	81
# of applicants	9,783
% of applicants accepted	70
% of acceptees attending	16
# accepting a place on wait list	139
# admitted from wait list	13

FRESHMAN PROFILE

Range SAT Critical Reading	480–600
Range SAT Math	500–610
Range SAT Writing	470–600
Range ACT Composite	22–27
Minimum web-based TOEFL	71
% graduated top 10% of class	22
% graduated top 25% of class	54
% graduated top 50% of class	85

DEADLINES

Regular Deadline	2/1
Nonfall registration?	yes

FINANCIAL FACTS

Financial Aid Rating	76
Annual tuition	$30,230
Room and board	$11,730
Required fees	$930
Books and supplies	$1,000
% needy frosh rec. need-based scholarship or grant aid	98
% needy UG rec. need-based scholarship or grant aid	95
% needy frosh rec. non-need-based scholarship or grant aid	16
% needy UG rec. non-need-based scholarship or grant aid	13
% needy frosh rec. need-based self-help aid	79
% needy UG rec. need-based self-help aid	79
% frosh rec. any financial aid	100
% UG rec. any financial aid	95
% UG borrow to pay for school	71
Average cumulative indebtedness	$29,575
% frosh need fully met	21
% ugrads need fully met	21
Average % of frosh need met	74
Average % of ugrade need met	72

Yale University

PO Box 208234, New Haven, CT 06520-8234 • Admissions: 203-432-9300 • Fax: 203-432-9392

CAMPUS LIFE

Quality of Life Rating	**96**
Fire Safety Rating	**60***
Green Rating	**93**
Type of school	private
Environment	city

STUDENTS

Total undergrad enrollment	5,296
% male/female	50/50
% from out of state	93
% from public high school	55
% frosh live on campus	100
% African American	6
% Asian	14
% Caucasian	47
% Hispanic	9
% international	10
# of countries represented	108

SURVEY SAYS . . .

School is well run
Musical organizations are popular
Theater is popular
Student publications are popular
Political activism is popular

ACADEMICS

Academic Rating	**96**
% students returning for sophomore year	99
% students graduating within 4 years	89
% students graduating within 6 years	96
Calendar	semester
Student/faculty ratio	6:1
Profs interesting rating	87
Profs accessible rating	86
Most classes have	10–19 students

MOST POPULAR MAJORS

economics; history; political science and government

STUDENTS SAY "..."

Academics

Listening to Yale students wax rhapsodic about their school, one can be forgiven for wondering whether they aren't actually describing the platonic form of the university. By their own account, students here benefit not only from "amazing academics and extensive resources" that provide "phenomenal in- and out-of-class education," but also from participation in "a student body that is committed to learning and to each other." Unlike some other prestigious, prominent research universities, Yale "places unparalleled focus on undergraduate education," requiring all professors to teach at least one undergraduate course each year. "[You know] the professors actually love teaching, because if they just wanted to do their research, they could have easily gone elsewhere." A residential college system further personalizes the experience. Each residential college "has a Dean and a Master, each of which is only responsible for 300 to 500 students, so administrative attention is highly specialized and widely available." Students further enjoy access to "a seemingly never-ending supply of resources (they really just love throwing money at us)" that includes "the twelve million volumes in our libraries." In short, "The opportunities are truly endless." "The experiences you have here and the people that you meet will change your life and strengthen your dreams," says ones student. Looking for the flip side to all this? "If the weather were a bit nicer, that would be excellent," one student offers. Guess that will have to do.

Life

Yale is, of course, extremely challenging academically, but students assure us that "Aside from the stress of midterms and finals, life at Yale is relatively carefree." Work doesn't keep undergrads from participating in "a huge variety of activities for fun. There are more than 300 student groups, including singing, dancing, juggling fire, theater...the list goes on. Because of all of these groups, there are shows on-campus all the time, which are a lot of fun and usually free or less than five dollars. On top of that, there are parties and events on campus and off campus, as well as many subsidized trips to New York City and Boston." Many here "are politically active (or at least politically aware)" and "a very large number of students either volunteer or try to get involved in some sort of organization to make a difference in the world." When the weekend comes around, "there are always parties to go to, whether at the frats or in rooms, but there's definitely no pressure to drink if you don't want to. A good friend of mine pledged a frat without drinking and that's definitely not unheard of (but still not common)." The relationship between Yale and the city of New Haven "sometimes leaves a little to be desired, but overall it's a great place to be for four years."

Student Body

A typical Yalie is "tough to define because so much of what makes Yale special is the unique convergence of different students to form one cohesive entity. Nonetheless, the one common characteristic of Yale students is passion—each Yalie is driven and dedicated to what he or she loves most, and it creates a palpable atmosphere of enthusiasm on campus." True enough, the student body represents a wide variety of ethnic, religious, economic, and academic backgrounds, but they all "thrive on learning, whether in a class, from a book, or from a conversation with a new friend." Students here also "tend to do a lot." "Everyone has many activities that they are a part of, which in turn fosters the closely connected feel of the campus." Undergrads tend to lean to the left politically, but for "those whose political views aren't as liberal as the rest of the campus...there are several campus organizations that cater to them."

FINANCIAL AID: 203-432-2700 • E-MAIL: STUDENT.QUESTIONS@YALE.EDU • WEBSITE: WWW.YALE.EDU

THE PRINCETON REVIEW SAYS

Admissions

Very important factors considered include: Class rank, application essay, academic GPA, recommendation(s), rigor of secondary school record, standardized test scores, character/personal qualities, extracurricular activities, talent/ability. *Other factors considered include:* Alumni/ae relation, first generation, geographical residence, interview, level of applicant's interest, racial/ethnic status, state residency, volunteer work, work experience. ACT with writing component required. TOEFL required of all international applicants. High school diploma or equivalent is not required.

Financial Aid

Students should submit: FAFSA, CSS/Financial Aid PROFILE, noncustodial PROFILE, business/farm supplement, parent tax returns. Regular filing deadline is March 1. The Princeton Review suggests that all financial aid forms be submitted as soon as possible after January 1. *Need-based scholarships/grants offered:* Federal Pell, SEOG, state scholarships/grants, private scholarships, the school's own gift aid, United Negro College Fund. *Loan aid offered:* Direct Subsidized Stafford, Direct Unsubsidized Stafford, Direct PLUS, Federal Perkins, state loans, college/university loans from institutional funds. Applicants will be notified of awards on or about April 1. Institutional employment available.

The Inside Word

Yale estimates that over three-quarters of all its applicants are qualified to attend the university, but less than ten percent get in. That adds up to a lot of broken hearts among kids who, if admitted, could probably handle the academic program. With so many qualified applicants to choose from, Yale can winnow to build an incoming class that is balanced in terms of income level, racial/ethnic background, geographic origin, and academic interest. For all but the most qualified, getting in typically hinges on offering just what an admissions officer is looking for to fill a specific slot. Legacies (descendents of Yale grads) gain some advantage—although they still need exceptionally strong credentials.

THE SCHOOL SAYS ". . ."

From the Admissions Office

"The most important questions the admissions committee must resolve are 'Who is likely to make the most of Yale's resources?' and 'Who will contribute significantly to the Yale community?' These questions suggest an approach to evaluating applicants that is more complex than whether Yale would rather admit well-rounded people or those with specialized talents. In selecting a class of 1,300 from more than 22,000 applicants, the admissions committee looks for academic ability and achievement combined with such personal characteristics as motivation, curiosity, energy, and leadership ability. The nature of these qualities is such that there is no simple profile of grades, scores, interests, and activities that will assure admission. Diversity within the student population is important, and the admissions committee selects a class of able and contributing individuals from a variety of backgrounds and with a broad range of interests and skills.

"Applicants for the entering class will be required to take the two SAT Subject Tests of their choice. Applicants may take the ACT, with the writing component, as an alternative to the SAT and SAT Subject Tests."

SELECTIVITY	
Admissions Rating	99
# of applicants	25,869
% of applicants accepted	8
% of acceptees attending	66
# admitted from wait list	98

FRESHMAN PROFILE	
Range SAT Critical Reading	700–800
Range SAT Math	710–790
Range SAT Writing	710–800
Range ACT Composite	32–35
Minimum paper TOEFL	600
Minimum web-based TOEFL	100
% graduated top 10% of class	97
% graduated top 25% of class	100
% graduated top 50% of class	100

DEADLINES	
Early action	
Deadline	11/1
Notification	12/15
Regular	
Deadline	12/31
Notification	4/1
Nonfall registration?	no

FINANCIAL FACTS	
Financial Aid Rating	99
Annual tuition	$40,500
Room and board	$12,200
Books and supplies	$1,000
% needy frosh rec. need-based scholarship or grant aid	100
% needy UG rec. need-based scholarship or grant aid	100
% needy frosh rec. need-based self-help aid	70
% needy UG rec. need-based self-help aid	83
% frosh rec. any financial aid	58
% UG rec. any financial aid	52
% UG borrow to pay for school	31
Average cumulative indebtedness	$10,717
% frosh need fully met	100
% ugrads need fully met	100
Average % of frosh need met	100
Average % of ugrade need met	100

PART 4

INDEXES

INDEPENDENT COUNSELING

There are currently two professional organizations for independent counselors that require professional credential review: Independent Educational Consultants Association (IECA) and National Association for College Admission Counseling (NACAC). Counselors affiliated with both groups provide varied and detailed services to students and families exploring future educational opportunities. Should you consider seeking the services of an independent counselor, I encourage you to visit both the IECA and NACAC websites for up-to-date information and listings.

Sincerely,

Robert Franek

Lead Author, *The Best 377 Colleges*

SVP—Publisher

The Princeton Review

IECA—The Independent Educational Consultants Association is a national nonprofit professional association of independent consultants.

www.iecaonline.com

NACAC—The National Association for College Admission Counseling is an organization of 9,000 global professionals dedicated to serving students as they make choices in pursuing postsecondary education.

www.nacacnet.org

ABOUT THE AUTHORS

Robert Franek is a graduate of Drew University and vice president and publisher for The Princeton Review. He has proudly been a part of the company since 1999. Robert comes to The Princeton Review with an extensive admissions background. In addition, he owns a walking tour business, leading historically driven, yet not boring, walking tours of his favorite town, New York City!

Christopher Maier is a graduate of Dickinson College. During the past five years, he's lived variously in New York City, coastal Maine, western Oregon, central Pennsylvania, and eastern England. Now he's at an oasis somewhere in the Midwestern cornfields—the University of Illinois—where he's earning his MFA in fiction. Aside from writing for magazines, newspapers, and The Princeton Review, he's worked as a radio disc jockey, a helping hand in a bakery, and a laborer on a highway construction crew. He's trying to avoid highway construction these days.

Carson Brown graduated from Stanford University in 1998, and after getting paid too much for working for various Internet companies for several years, sold her BMW and moved to Mexico. She has now overstayed her welcome south of the border and is returning to San Francisco to be responsible and further her career working as a writer and editor.

Julie Doherty is a freelance writer, web designer, and preschool teacher. She lives in Mexico City.

Andrew Friedman graduated in 2003 from Stanford University, where he was a President's Scholar. He lives in New York City.

INDEX OF SCHOOLS

INDEX OF SCHOOLS BY LOCATION

INDEX OF SCHOOLS BY TUITION

Price categories are based on figures the schools reported to us in early spring 2012 for tuition (out-of-state tuition for public schools) and do not include fees, room, board, transportation, or other expenses.

LESS THAN $15,000

$15,000–$30,000

MORE THAN $30,000

THE PRINCETON REVIEW NATIONAL COLLEGE COUNSELOR ADVISORY BOARD, 2012–2013

We thank the members of this board for their careful and considered input on our products and services.

Michael A. Acquilano, Director of College Guidance, Staten Island Academy, Staten Island, NY

Roland M. Allen, Director of College Counseling, St. Margaret's Episcopal School, San Juan Capistrano, CA

Carol I. Bernstein, Director of College Guidance, Chadwick School, Palos Verdes Peninsula, CA

Lee Bierer, Weekly Countdown to College Syndicated Columnist and Independent College Counselor, College Admission Strategies, Charlotte, NC

Marianne M. Borgmann, Director of Guidance, Cincinnati Hills Christian Academy, Cincinnati, OH

Vicki Brunnick, MA, LPC, Counselor/Scholarship Chair, Myers Park High School Charlotte, NC

Mark T. Davis, College Counselor, Upper Arlington High School, Upper Arlington, OH

Mary Ann Doll, College Advisor, Palisades Charter High School, Pacific Palisades, CA

J.T. Duck, Director of College Counseling, Boston University Academy, Boston, MA

Judy S. Fairfull, Head Guidance Counselor, Doherty Memorial High School and Guidance Liaison, Worcester Public School District, MA

Ann R. Harris, PhD, Director of College Guidance, Parish Episcopal School, TX

Meghan Farley, Co-Director of College Counseling, Pingree School, South Hamilton, MA

Maureen Ferrell, Director of College Counseling, The Summit Country Day School, Cincinnati, OH

Nancy Grisemer, MPA, Columnist for Examiner.com and Independent College Consultant, College Explorations, Oakton, VA

Chuck Gutman, College Counselor, Waukegan High School, Waukegan, IL

Troy B. Hammond, Director of University Counseling, Bayview Glen School, Toronto, Ontario, Canada

Ann Herbener, College Counselor, Papillion-La Vista High School, Papillion, NE

William Hirt, College Counselor, Professional Children's School, New York, NY

Tricia Georgi Howard, Director of College Counseling, St. Ursula Academy, Toledo, OH

Marilyn J. Kaufman, Certified College Counselor, President of College Admission Consultants, Dallas, TX

Geri Kellogg, Counselor, LPC, J.J. Pearce High School, Richardson, TX

Joanne Levy-Previtt, College Admissions Advisor, Morana CA

Moira McKinnon, Director of College Counseling, Berwick Academy, South Berwick, ME

Dr. Marianna P. Marchese, President of the New Jersey Association for College Admissions Counseling, Director of Pupil Personnel Servicew, West Morris Mendham High School, Mendham, NJ

Susan S. Marrs, Director, College Counseling, Seven Hills School, Cincinnati OH

Bruce Richardson, Director of Guidance, Plano Senior High School, Plano, TX

Kimberly R. Simpson, Educational Consultant, Collegiate Admissions Consulting Services, LLC, Covington, LA

Chris Teare, Director of College Counseling, Antilles School, Saint Thomas, VI

Theresa Urist, Director of College Counseling, Prospect Hill Academy Charter School, Cambridge, MA

Michael Wilner, Educational Consultant and Founder, Wilner Education, Putney, VT

“COW TIPPING IS
DEFINITELY
PASSÉ HERE.”

Our survey has seven questions that allow students to answer in narrative form. We tell students that we don't care what they write: If it is "witty, informative, or accurate," we try to get it into this book. We use all the informative and accurate essays to write the "Students Speak Out" sections; below are excerpts from the wittiest, pithiest, and most outrageous narrative responses to our open-ended questions.

FOOD...

"When students first arrive, they call the Observatory Hill Dining Facility 'O-Hill.' They soon learn to call it 'O-Hell,' because the food here is beyond revolting."

—Greg F.,
University of Virginia

"If I had known that I'd be rooming with roaches and poisoned by the cafeteria staff I would have gone to Wayne State. I really can't complain, though, because I have met my husband here, like my mom did 20 years before."

—M.L.P., Fisk University

HOMETOWN...

"In my experience New York is a place that allows people to be anyone they want to be. You can wear a zebra-striped bikini in the middle of winter on a snow-covered street here, and people would hardly look twice."

—Sophomore, Barnard College

"Connecticut is a cute state. It's a great place to go to school, but I wouldn't want to live here."

—Claire S., NJ native,
Fairfield University

"Socially, the surrounding area is so dead that the Denny's closes at night."

—Thomas R., UC—Riverside

"The local liquor stores and towing companies make a lot of money."

—Katherine R.,
University of Rhode Island

"It is definitely important to have a car, as the population of Canton frequently matches our winter temperature. 'Canton gray,' our perennial sky color, is one Crayola missed."

—Daniel R., St. Lawrence University

"Montreal is the sh@!"*

—Elizabeth R., McGill University

SECURITY...

"Campus security is made up of a bunch of midget high school dropouts with Napoleonic complexes who can spot a beer can from a mile away."

—Anonymous, UC—San Diego

"Public safety here is a joke. The public safety officers are like the Keystone Kops on Thorazine."

—Anonymous, Bryn Mawr College

CLASSMATES...

"If you're thinking of applying to MIT, go ahead. Because, believe it or not, most people here are at least as stupid as you are."

—Patrick L., MIT

"The typical student is mostly an easygoing, skirt-wearing, intelligent, procrastinating kid. Although, there [are] of course, many many many variations on this. Not all kids wear skirts. Not all the boys in skirts are straight. Not all the girls in skirts are straight. 'Everybody here looks like Jesus!' was a pretty accurate description from an outsider."

—Amy P., New College of Florida

"Students here mostly get along, and since it is a business school we all have a common goal of being rich."

—Female Sophomore, Babson College

"People who go to school here are all pretty good looking, especially the women. It should be renamed UKB, the University of Ken and Barbie."

—Tony H., Arizona State University

"Mt. Holyoke students are friendly and respectful with the exception of the occasions when the entire campus gets PMS."

—Abigail K., Mount Holyoke College

"A school can be defined by its graffiti and its level of cleverness. Three-quarters of our school graffiti is pro- or anti- a specific fraternity, with the other one-quarter devoted to homophobic or misogynist theories."

—Matthew E., College of William & Mary

"This is a great university if you're not studying sciences involving animal research, politics, teacher education (certification), or anything that offends any long-haired leftist who's a vegetarian."

—Brock M., University of Oregon

"Everyone here is too smart for their own good. As one upper-level executive in the Houston area put it, 'The students at Rice know how to make it rain, but they don't know to come in out of it.'"

—John B., Rice University

"Bates is so diverse! Yesterday I met somebody from Connecticut!"

—Ellen H., Bates College

"We have this typical student stereotype we call 'Wendy Wellesley.' Wendy takes copious notes, is a devoted member of 10 organizations, always has an internship, goes over the page limit on every assignment, takes six classes, goes to all the office hours, triple majors, and is basically diligent, overcommitted, extroverted, overachieving, and energetic (but without a sense of humor or ability to relax)."

—R.D., Wellesley College

"I am constantly impressed with the creativity of hell-raisers on campus. One day I walked past the Manor House to find a dozen plastic babies climbing all over the roof! Right before Parents' Weekend, some people hung up signs saying 'Princeton Review reports: "LC students ignore herpes on a regular basis." Please visit the health clinic!'"

—Anonymous, Lewis & Clark College

"Diversity in the female population means different shades of hair color . . . we often joke that Burberry is SMU Sorority Camouflage."

—Male Senior,
Southern Methodist University

ADMINISTRATION...

"Despite the best efforts of the administration to provide TCNJ students with an inefficient, cold-hearted, red-tape-infested, snafu-riddled Soviet-style administrative bureaucracy, The College of New Jersey is a pretty decent place to go for a fairly reasonable amount of money."

—Anonymous,
The College of New Jersey

"Administration is like the stock market, you invest time and money, sometimes you get a return, other times you don't."

—J.W.R., Albertson College of Idaho

"Columbia is like a fruit truck. It picks up varied and exotic fruits and deposits them rotten at their destination."

—Paul L., Columbia University

"The University of Minnesota is a huge black hole of knowledge. It sucks things into it from far and wide, compressing to the essence. Unfortunately, it is very hard to get anything out of a black hole. What I have managed to eke out has been both rewarding and depressing."

—James McDonald,
University of Minnesota

"The strangest incident I've ever had in class was when one of my journalism profs burnt our tests in the microwave. But he decided to give everyone in the class an A, instead of retesting."

—Ashlea K., Ohio University

"Going to Northwestern is like having a beautiful girlfriend who treats you like crap."

—Jonathan J. G., Northwestern University

"Getting an education from MIT is like getting a drink from a firehose."

—Juan G., MIT

"Intro classes have the consistency of Cheez Whiz: They go down easy, they taste horrible, and they are not good for you."

—Pat T., University of Vermont

SEX, DRUGS, ROCK & ROLL...

"Beam, Bud, beer, babes—the four essential B's."

—"Jim Beam," Wittenberg University

"Yeah, there aren't any guys, but who doesn't like doing homework on a Saturday night?"

—Nicole C., Wellesley College

"The dances here are a riot because I love watching nerds and intellectuals dance."

—Male Senior, Columbia University

"Any campus attempt to provide drug-free entertainment shuts down at 10:20 P.M. to allow plenty of time to be drunk. The general campus motto is 'If you weren't wasted, the night was.'"

—Junior, Lehigh University

"Drug use here is extremely prevalent. People smoke pot everywhere, even outdoors."

—Freshman, New College of Florida

SCHOOL SAYS . . .

In this section you'll find advertisements directly from colleges with information they'd like you to consider about their schools. The editorial in these pages is entirely the responsibility of the colleges. It does not reflect any opinion of The Princeton Review about the schools, and The Princeton Review did not create the advertisements. The Princeton Review charges the schools a fee to offset the cost of printing their advertisements in this section which has been added to the book.

The Princeton Review does not charge schools a fee to be profiled in this book, or in any of our books. The company has never required colleges, universities, or any institutions to pay a fee for their profiles or inclusions in our books.

For information about how we selected the 377 outstanding schools in this book, see page 20, "How and Why We Produce This Book."

ANGELO STATE UNIVERSITY
• 1928 •
FIAT LUX
1928
TRUE BLUE

BECKER COLLEGE

Be the change. Be the future. Be at Becker.

Becker College has been recognized as one of the nation's best institutions for undergraduate education.

Excellence | The Princeton Review has recognized Becker College as one of the nation's best institutions for undergraduate education, and ranked our game design program in the top 10 for the past three years. We are one of only two private colleges in New England to offer AVMA-accredited undergraduate programs in veterinary technology and operate a working animal clinic on campus, treating over 1,000 patients annually. Our nursing program is ranked among the best in Massachusetts, with a 2011 NCLEX pass rate of 99%. Our Division III student-athletes excel in athletics and academics.

Accountability | Our mission is to deliver to each student a transformational learning experience—anchored by academic excellence, social responsibility, and creative expression—that prepares graduates to thrive, contribute to, and lead in a global society.

Community and Diversity | We promote an open and diverse community, close personalized attention, a collaborative atmosphere, and a strong focus on preparing our students to become responsible citizens who can lead in a global society.

Social Responsibility | In our neighborhoods, across the country, and around the world, Becker College students believe that by helping others, they enhance their own lives and the lives of others. Our students assist those in need in schools, communities, and a wide range of organizations, including the Be Like Brit Foundation in Haiti and the Mázunte Turtle Project in Mexico.

Integrity | Our community upholds the highest ethical standards, promotes respect for one another, and values an open and welcoming environment.

Creative Expression | We believe that learning is rooted and grows in creative thought, inquiry, and self-discovery. Our students are encouraged to explore possibilities, ask questions, and express themselves.

BECKER COLLEGE

61 Sever Street • Worcester, MA 01609

www.becker.edu

THE PRINCETON REVIEW
377
BEST
COLLEGES
2013 EDITION
Experience Champlain College
A Smarter Way to Learn
CHAMPLAIN

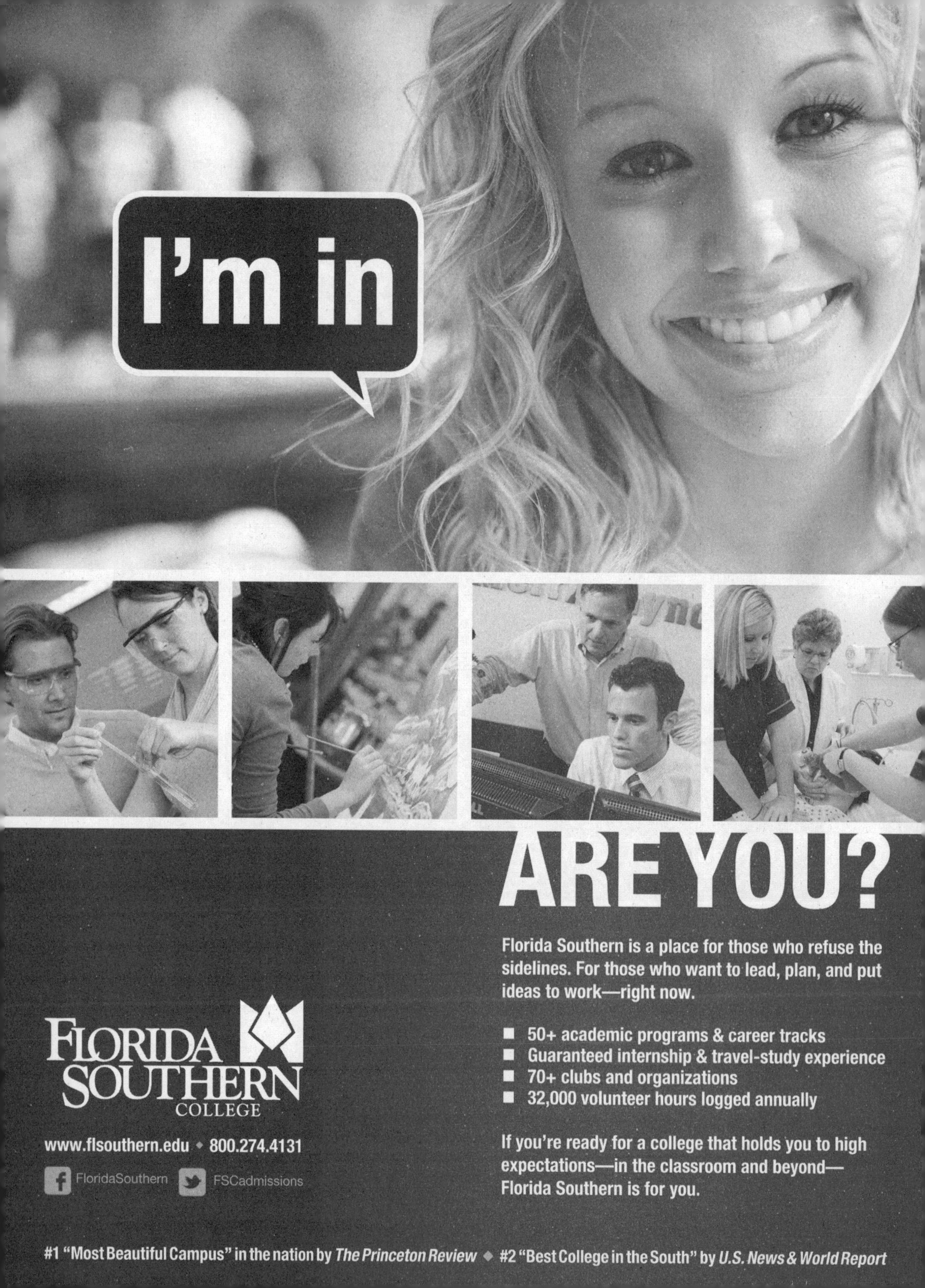
I'm in
ARE YOU?
Florida Southern is a place for those who refuse the sidelines. For those who want to lead, plan, and put ideas to work—right now.
■ 50+ academic programs & career tracks
■ Guaranteed internship & travel-study experience
■ 70+ clubs and organizations
■ 32,000 volunteer hours logged annually
If you're ready for a college that holds you to high expectations—in the classroom and beyond—Florida Southern is for you.
FLORIDA SOUTHERN COLLEGE
www.flsouthern.edu • 800.274.4131
FloridaSouthern
FSCadmissions
#1 "Most Beautiful Campus" in the nation by The Princeton Review • #2 "Best College in the South" by U.S. News & World Report

Because faith and
freedom matter.

SAINT ANSELM COLLEGE
1889
Manchester, New Hampshire
www.anselm.edu
A comprehensive liberal arts education where you'll gain true insight into how the world works—and how you can make it work better.
The basics
95
Percent of students are awarded financial aid
18
Our average class size
198
Professors, zero Teaching Assistants
11:1
Our student/faculty ratio
60
Minutes to skiing, beaches, and Boston
THE PRINCETON REVIEW 377 BEST COLLEGES 2013 EDITION
Fall Open House Programs
September 22, 2012
November 10, 2012

NOTES

NOTES

NOTES

College Hopes & Worries Survey 2013

Mail to The Princeton Review, 2013 College Hopes & Worries Survey, c/o Robert Franek, 317 Madison Ave., 4th Fl., New York, NY 10017 (mailed entries must be received by February 21, 2013) or fill out online (online entries can be submitted between February 1 and February 28, 2013) at www.PrincetonReview.com/go/survey.

Name ______________________

Address (optional) ______________________

City / State / ZIP ______________________

Daytime phone ______________________

E-mail address ______________________

I am ____ a parent of a student ____ a student applying to attend college beginning in

____ Spring or Fall 2013 ____ Spring or Fall 2014 ____ Later (indicate year: ________).

1 What would be your "dream" college? What college would you most like to attend (or see your child attend) if chance of being accepted or cost were not an issue? (Please write full name of school, not initials such as "OU".)

____

2 How many colleges will you (your child) apply to?

____ 1 to 4

____ 5 to 8

____ 9 to 12

____ 13 or more

3 What is (or will be) the toughest part of your (your child's) college application experience? (Choose one.)

____ Researching colleges schools to apply to

____ Taking the SAT, ACT, or AP exams

____ Completing applications for admission and financial aid

____ Waiting for the decision letters and deciding which college to attend

4 What do you estimate your (or your child's) college degree will cost, including four years of tuition, room and board, fees, books and other expenses? (Choose one.)

____ More than $100,000

____ $75,000 to $100,000

____ $50,000 to 75,000

____ $25,000 to $50,000

____ Up to $25,000

5 How necessary will financial aid (education loans, scholarships, or grants) be to pay for your (your child's) college education? (Choose one.)

___ Extremely

___ Very

___ Somewhat

___ Not at all

6 What's your biggest concern about applying to or attending college? (Choose one.)

___ Won't get into first-choice college

___ Will get into first-choice college, but won't be able to attend due to high cost and/or insufficient financial aid

___ Level of debt I (my child) will take on to pay for the degree

___ Will attend a college I (my child) may regret

7 How would you gauge your stress level about the college application process? (Choose one.)

___ Very High

___ High

___ Average

___ Low

___ Very Low

8 Ideally, how far from home would you like the college you (your child) attend(s) to be? (Choose one.)

___ 0 to 250 miles

___ 250 to 500 miles

___ 500 to 1,000

___ 1,000 miles or more

9 When it comes to choosing the college you (your child) will attend, which of the following do you think it is most likely to be? (Choose one.)

___ College with best academic reputation

___ College with best program for my (my child's) career interests

___ College that will be the most affordable

___ College that will be the best overall fit

10 If you (your child) had a way to compare colleges based on their commitment to environmental issues (from academic offerings to practices concerning energy use, recycling, etc.), how much would this contribute to your (your child's) decision to apply to or attend a school?

___ Strongly

___ Very much

___ Somewhat

___ Not much

___ Not at all

11 Has the state of the economy affected your (your child's) decisions about applying to or attending college? (Choose one.)

___ Yes: Extremely

___ Yes: Very much

___ Yes: Somewhat

___ No: Not at all

12 If your answer to the previous question was one of the three "Yes" choices, how would you describe the *major way* the economy has affected your (your child's) college application decisions. (Choose one.)

___ Am applying to colleges with lower "sticker" prices.

___ Am applying to more 'financial aid safety' schools.

___ Am applying to colleges closer to home to save on travel costs.

13 What will be the biggest benefit of your (your child) getting a college degree?

___ The education overall

___ The experience: exposure to new ideas, places, and people

___ The potentially better job and higher income

14 On the whole, do you believe college will be "worth it" for you (your child)?

___ Yes

___ No

Optional: What advice would you give to college applicants or parents of applicants going through this experience next year?

____

____

____

____

____

____

____

____

____

____

____

____

____

____

____

____

____

____

____

____

Navigate the admissions process with more guidance from the experts.

Ace the APs:

Cracking the AP Biology Exam, 2013 Edition
978-0-307-94508-2 • $18.99/$21.99 Can.
Ebook: 978-0-307-94580-8

Cracking the AP Calculus AB & BC Exams, 2013 Edition
978-0-307-94486-3 • $19.99/$23.99 Can.
Ebook: 978-0-307-94451-1

Cracking the AP Chemistry Exam, 2013 Edition
978-0-307-94488-7 • $18.99/$21.99 Can.
Ebook: 978-0-307-94452-8

Cracking the AP Economics Macro & Micro Exams, 2013 Edition
978-0-307-94509-9 • $18.00/$21.00 Can.
Ebook: 978-0-307-94581-5

Cracking the AP English Language & Composition Exam, 2013 Edition
978-0-307-94511-2 • $18.00/$21.00 Can.
Ebook: 978-0-307-94582-2

Cracking the AP English Literature & Composition Exam, 2013 Edition
978-0-307-94512-9 • $18.00/$21.00 Can.
Ebook: 978-0-307-94583-9

Cracking the AP Environmental Science Exam, 2013 Edition
978-0-307-94513-6 • $18.99/$21.99 Can.
Ebook: 978-0-307-94584-6

Cracking the AP European History Exam, 2013 Edition
978-0-307-94489-4 • $18.99/$21.99 Can.
Ebook: 978-0-307-94453-5

Cracking the AP Human Geography Exam, 2013 Edition
978-0-307-94514-3 • $18.00/$21.00 Can.

Cracking the AP Physics B Exam, 2013 Edition
978-0-307-94515-0 • $18.99/$21.99 Can.
Ebook: 978-0-307-94585-3

Cracking the AP Physics C Exam, 2013 Edition
978-0-307-94516-7 • $18.99/$21.99 Can.

Cracking the AP Psychology Exam, 2013 Edition
978-0-307-94517-4 • $18.00/$21.00 Can.
Ebook: 978-0-307-94586-0

Cracking the AP Spanish Exam with Audio CD, 2013 Edition
978-0-307-94518-1 • $24.99/$28.99 Can.

Cracking the AP Statistics Exam, 2013 Edition
978-0-307-94519-8 • $19.99/$23.99 Can.

Cracking the AP U.S. Government & Politics Exam, 2013 Edition
978-0-307-94520-4 • $18.99/$21.99 Can.
Ebook: 978-0-307-94587-7

Cracking the AP U.S. History Exam, 2013 Edition
978-0-307-94490-7 • $18.99/$21.99 Can.
Ebook: 978-0-307-94447-4

Cracking the AP World History Exam, 2013 Edition
978-0-307-94491-7 • $18.99/$21.99 Can.
Ebook: 978-0-307-94445-0

Essential AP Biology (flashcards)
978-0-375-42803-6 • $18.99/$20.99 Can.

Essential AP Psychology (flashcards)
978-0-375-42801-2 • $18.99/$20.99 Can.

Essential AP U.S. Government & Politics (flashcards)
978-0-375-42804-3 • $18.99/$20.99 Can.

Essential AP U.S. History (flashcards)
978-0-375-42800-5 • $18.99/$20.99 Can.

Essential AP World History (flashcards)
978-0-375-42802-9 • $18.99/$20.99 Can.

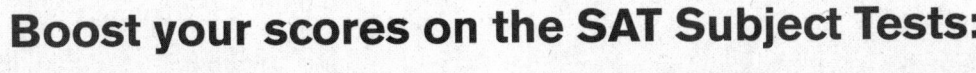